CollegeBoard

2015
Book of
Majors

CollegeBoard

2015
Book of Majors

Ninth Edition
The College Board, New York

About the College Board

The College Board is a mission-driven not-for-profit organization that connects students to college success and opportunity. Founded in 1900, the College Board was created to expand access to higher education. Today, the membership association is made up of over 6,000 of the world's leading educational institutions and is dedicated to promoting excellence and equity in education. Each year, the College Board helps more than seven million students prepare for a successful transition to college through programs and services in college readiness and college success — including the SAT® and the Advanced Placement Program®. The organization also serves the education community through research and advocacy on behalf of students, educators, and schools.

For further information, visit www.collegeboard.org.

Copies of this book may be ordered from College Board Publications, P.O. Box 4699, Mount Vernon, IL 62864, or online at www.collegeboard.org. The price is $28.99.

Editorial inquiries concerning this book should be directed to Guidance Publications, The College Board, 45 Columbus Avenue, New York, NY 10023-6992.

ISBN: 978-1-4573-0317-3

Printed in the United States of America

Distributed by Macmillan. For information on bulk purchases please contact Macmillan Corporate and Premium Sales Department at (800) 221-7945 x5442.

Contents

Preface

The *College Board Book of Majors* is the only book of its kind that provides a complete, all-in-one source for what students exploring majors need to know: what the majors are about, *and* where they can be studied.

The 201 majors profiled in Part I of this book are primarily undergraduate programs, taught at the associate or bachelor's degree level. These majors represent not only those that are most widely offered, but also those that students most often express interest in.

Each profile of a major is compiled from detailed questionnaires submitted by college professors teaching in the field. Where appropriate, information was also compiled from secondary sources—including professional and academic associations, national newspapers, and the federal Department of Labor's *Occupational Outlook Handbook*. Additional insights are included from college students enrolled in these majors.

In Part II of this book are brief descriptions of more than 1,200 majors contained in the current version of the *Classification of Instructional Programs* (*CIP* for short), developed by the National Center for Educational Statistics for the U.S. Department of Education.

In Part III, those 1,200 majors are listed alphabetically, with the colleges and graduate schools that offer them presented state by state. Each college listing also indicates at which degree level or levels the major can be studied (certificate, associate, bachelor's, master's, doctorate, or first-professional). Following these are 31 special academic programs, similarly arranged alphabetically, with state-by-state listings of the colleges offering them.

What's New

For this edition we've added a new major, Health Information Management, which is of particular interest and increased importance due to recent health care reforms that are driving doctors and hospitals to rapidly shift to electronic records, and the need to keep those records both private and secure.

In addition, each profile in Part I has been reviewed by the editors, with special emphasis on the latest career trends reported by the Bureau of Labor Statistics in the *Occupational Outlook Handbook (2014-2015)*. The contact information that appears in the "For more info" section of each profile has also been verified and updated.

About the College Data

The data in the college listings were provided by the schools themselves in the College Board's Annual Survey of Colleges, conducted in the spring of 2014. Colleges reported their programs of majors according to the *CIP* (even though the names they give majors may differ slightly from the *CIP* titles).

The information provided by the colleges was verified by a staff of editors to ensure that the data are as complete and accurate as possible. However, program changes occur, and readers are urged to contact colleges directly to confirm facts related to their major of choice.

To be eligible for inclusion, a college must be accredited by a national or regional accrediting association recognized by the U.S. Department of Education, and offer at least an associate degree. Graduate programs are listed only for those schools that also have undergraduate programs. An alphabetical index of every major profiled in Part I and/or listed in Part III appears at the end of this book.

Acknowledgments

Many people helped with the creation and publication of this book, and it is a pleasure to acknowledge them here:

First of all, thanks are due to Renee Gernand, whose efforts, assistance, and guidance were essential to the successful launch of the first edition. "What to know about majors" and the introductions to the major categories in Part I were written by Barbara Kram. Regina Sampogna provided editorial assistance for this edition. The enormous task of collecting and verifying the college information in Part III of this book was directed by Suzette Stone-Busa and Andy Costello, with the assistance of Doris Chow. Susan Bailey, May Cooper, Marci Harman, Randy Peery, Leah Swaggerty, and Jenny Xie compiled, edited and verified the data. Additional support was provided by Stan Bernstein, Matt Sutor, Elizabeth Skepnek, and Eileen Thompson. Technical support was provided by Assar Tarazi, Satish Atmuri, Amalnath Sirigireddy, Wayne Lau and Elizabeth Shroyer. Thanks also to the staff at DataStream Content Solutions, Inc., who provide the technological savvy that helps us turn our data into books.

The professors, who made gifts of their knowledge, insights, and enthusiasm for their subjects, are individually acknowledged in the list of contributors beginning on the following page. It is a privilege to forward those gifts along to the students who, we all hope, will find guidance in this book.

Tom Vanderberg
Senior Editor, Guidance Publications
The College Board

List of Contributors

Agriculture

Arthur Cameron
Professor of Horticulture
Michigan State University

Stephanie Doores
Associate Professor of Food Science
Penn State University Park

Lee A. Edgerton
Director of Undergraduate Studies, Department of
    Animal Sciences
University of Kentucky

Karen S. Kubena
Professor, Department of Nutrition & Food Science
Texas A&M University

Donald W. Larson
Professor, Department of Agricultural, Environmental,
    and Development Economics
Ohio State University

Kenneth L. Larson
Professor Emeritus, Department of Agronomy
Iowa State University

Murray H. Milford
Professor Emeritus, Department of Soil and Crop
    Sciences
Texas A&M University

M. Edward Rister
Professor of Agricultural Economics
Texas A&M University

Marianne Sarrantonio
Associate Professor of Sustainable Agriculture
University of Maine

H. Jerry Schurink
Director of Equine Studies and IHSA Team Coach
University of Massachusetts Amherst

Douglas L. Young
Professor, College of Agricultural, Human and Natural
    Resource Sciences
Washington State University

Architecture

Michael Bednar
Professor of Architecture
University of Virginia

Philip N. Pregill
Professor and Chair, Landscape Architecture
California State University: Pomona

Alfred D. Price
Associate Professor, Department of Urban and Regional
    Planning
State University of New York at Buffalo

John B. Wright
Professor of Geography and Planning
New Mexico State University

Area, ethnic, and gender studies

Lynne S. Abel
Associate Dean for Undergraduate Education, College
    of Arts and Sciences
Cornell University

Sandra Lipsitz Bem
Professor of Psychology
Cornell University

Bernard Haykel
Associate Professor of Middle Eastern and Islamic
    Studies
New York University

Eleuteria Hernández
Student Affairs Officer, Department of Chicana/o
    Studies
University of California: Los Angeles

Daniel Horowitz
Professor of American Studies
Smith College

Theresa Chang-whei Jen
Professor and Director, East Asian Studies
Lauder Institute, Wharton School, University of
    Pennsylvania

Reynaldo F. Macías
Professor of Chicana/o Studies, Education & Applied
    Linguistics
University of California: Los Angeles

R. Baxter Miller
Professor of English and Director, Institute for African
    American Studies
University of Georgia

Peter W. Rees
Associate Professor of Geography and Former Director,
    Latin American Studies Program
University of Delaware

Kathryn W. Shanley
Associate Professor, Native American Studies
University of Montana

Biological sciences

Austin E. Brooks
Treves Professor of Biology
Wabash College

William H. Coleman
Professor of Biology
University of Hartford

Carter Denniston
Professor, Genetics and Medical Genetics
University of Wisconsin–Madison

Robert S. Greene
Professor of Biology
Niagara University

Eileen Gregory
Professor of Biology
Rollins College

Kenneth F. Haynes
Professor, Department of Entomology
University of Kentucky

Donald L. Lovett
Associate Professor, Department of Biology
The College of New Jersey

Douglas Meikle
Professor and Chair, Department of Zoology
Miami University

Amanda Norvell
Assistant Professor, Department of Biology
The College of New Jersey

C.O. Patterson
Associate Professor, Department of Biology and
    Molecular and Environmental Plant Sciences
Texas A&M University

Gregory M. Raner
Associate Professor, Chemistry and Biochemistry
University of North Carolina at Greensboro

Dean E. Wendt
Assistant Professor, Biological Sciences Department and
    Center for Coastal Marine Science
California Polytechnic State University

Business

Gedas Adomavicius
Assistant Professor, Carlson School of Management
University of Minnesota

Stephen J. Brown
David S. Loeb Professor of Finance
Stern School of Business, New York University

Peter Bycio
Professor, Department of Management and
    Entrepreneurship
Williams College of Business, Xavier University

Wayne F. Cascio
U.S. Bank Term Professor of Management
University of Colorado at Denver

Diane Kaufman Fredette
Chair and Professor, Construction Management
    Program, School of Architecture
Pratt Institute

Lorin M. Hitt
Alberto Vitale Term Associate Professor of Operations
    and Information Management
The Wharton School, University of Pennsylvania

Susan Ivancevich
Associate Professor of Accounting
University of North Carolina at Wilmington

Carol A.B. Jordan
Eminent Scholar of Risk Management and Insurance
Troy State University

Ann-Mary Kapusta
Associate Dean, McDonough School of Business
Georgetown University

Mark Lee Levine
Professor, Burns School of Real Estate and Construction
    Management
University of Denver

Charles J. Metelka
Professor, Department of Hospitality and Tourism
University of Wisconsin–Stout

Patricia Rigia
Professor and Director, Fashion Merchandising
    Division, School of Business
University of Bridgeport

Stephen Spinelli, Jr.
Vice Provost for Entrepreneurship and Global
    Management
Babson College

Debbie M. Thorne
Associate Vice President for Academic Affairs and
    Professor of Marketing
Texas State University: San Marcos

Communications

Thomas A. Bowers
James L. Knight Professor and Interim Dean, School of
    Journalism and Mass Communication
University of North Carolina at Chapel Hill

John Doolittle
Associate Director, Center for Teaching Excellence, and
    Associate Professor
American University

Seth Gitner
Assistant Professor of Newspaper and Online
    Journalism
Syracuse University

Bruce E. Gronbeck
A. Craig Baird Distinguished Professor of Public Address
University of Iowa

Peter Johanns
Associate Professor and Program Director, Television-Radio Degree
Ithaca College

Kathleen S. Kelly
Professor of Public Relations
University of Florida

Joel A. Kline
Assistant Professor of Business and Economics and Director, Digital Communications Program
Lebanon Valley College

Janet H. Murray
Ivan Allen College Dean's Professor, Graduate Program in Digital Media
Georgia Institute of Technology

Diana Owen
Associate Professor, Communication, Culture, and Technology Program
Georgetown University

Keith Strudler
Department Chair and Assistant Professor of Communication
Marist College

Patsy G. Watkins
Associate Professor and Chair, Lemke Department of Journalism
University of Arkansas

Computer and information sciences

Cristian Balan
Program Director and Assistant Professor of Computer and Digital Forensics
Champlain College

Tom Dowd
Assistant Professor, Department of Interactive Arts and Media
Columbia College Chicago

Sampath Kannan
Associate Dean of Engineering
University of Pennsylvania

Anne Marchant
Associate Professor, Applied Information Department
George Mason University

Kathryn M. Stewart
Chair, Computer Technology
Tallahassee Community College

Murray Turoff
Professor Emeritus, Information Systems Department
New Jersey Institute of Technology

Education

Mary C. Clement
Associate Professor of Teacher Education
Berry College

Jeanneine P. Jones
Professor of Middle Grades Education
University of North Carolina at Charlotte

Dawn Eddy Molloy
Faculty Research Associate
University of Maryland

Lynda M. Nilges
Associate Professor, Department of Physical Education
University of South Carolina

Susan J. Olson
Professor and Chair, Department of Educational Foundations and Leadership
The University of Akron

Engineering

Stanley M. Barnett
Professor of Chemical Engineering and Pharmaceutics
University of Rhode Island

Roger H. Compton
Dean and Professor of Naval Architecture
Webb Institute

Roger D. Doherty
A.W. Grosvenor Professor of Materials Engineering Emeritus
Drexel University

Lyle. D. Feisel
Dean Emeritus, Watson School of Engineering and Applied Science
State University of New York at Binghamton

Audeen W. Fentiman
Chair, Nuclear Engineering Program
Ohio State University

Stephan Grilli
Chair and Professor of Ocean Engineering
University of Rhode Island

Edward A. Hiler
Dean of Agriculture and Life Sciences Emeritus
Texas A&M University

Keith D. Hjelmstad
Professor of Civil Engineering
University of Illinois at Urbana–Champaign

Charles A. Kliche
Professor, Mining Engineering and Management Department
South Dakota School of Mines and Technology

C. Patrick Koelling
Associate Professor, Grado Department of Industrial and Systems Engineering
Virginia Polytechnic Institute and State University

Brian A. Rock
Associate Professor of Architectural Engineering
University of Kansas

Malcolm L. Spaulding
Professor of Ocean Engineering
University of Rhode Island

Alfred G. Striz
Professor and L.A. Comp Chair in Engineering
University of Oklahoma

Calvin L. White
Professor of Materials Science and Engineering
Michigan Technological University

Frank H. Young
Professor Emeritus of Computer Science and Software
    Engineering
Rose-Hulman Institute of Technology

Engineering technology

Harold L. Broberg
Associate Dean of Engineering, Technology, and
    Computer Science
Indiana University–Purdue University Fort Wayne

Pierre Catala
Senior Lecturer Emeritus
Texas A&M University

Paul Clarke
Lead Instructor, Drafting and Engineering Technology
MiraCosta College

Thomas M. Hall, Jr.
Professor and Head, Department of Engineering
    Technology
Northwestern State University

James Kamm
Professor of Mechanical Engineering Technology
University of Toledo

Mark R. Steinle
Professor, Department of Trades and Technology
Casper College

Indrajith Wijayratne
Associate Professor of Surveying
Michigan Technological University

English language and literature

Jonathan Fink
Creative Writing Fellow in Poetry
Emory University

David A. McMurrey
Program Chair, Technical Communications
Austin Community College

Brett C. Millier
Reginald L. Cook Professor of American Literature
Middlebury College

James G. Taaffe
Emeritus Professor of English
University of Alabama

Family and consumer sciences

Eva L. Essa
Foundation Professor and Chair, Human Development
    and Family Studies
University of Nevada: Reno

Sally L. Fortenberry
Associate Professor and Internship Coordinator,
    Department of Design, Merchandising and Textiles
Texas Christian University

Bonita A. Glatz
Professor of Food Science and Human Nutrition
Iowa State University

Penny A. Ralston
Professor and Dean Emeritus, College of Human
    Sciences
Florida State University, Tallahassee

Paul Sorgule
Dean of Culinary Arts and Hospitality
Paul Smith's College

Anne L. Sweaney
Professor and Head, Housing and Consumer
    Economics, College of Family and Consumer
    Sciences
University of Georgia

Health

Debra L. Agard
Assistant Dean, Office of Student Affairs
University of Illinois at Chicago College of Pharmacy

Marcia A. Armstrong
Director, Medical/Laboratory Technology and
    Phlebotomy Programs
University of Hawaii: Kapiolani Community College

Paula Owens Ashby
Assistant Director of Academic Services and Chief
    Health Professions Advisor
University of Maryland: Baltimore County

Jean E. Bartels
Chair and Professor of Nursing
Georgia Southern University

Georgine W. Bills
Program Director, Respiratory Therapy
Weber State University

Stan S. Cooke
Professor and Head of Department of Communication
    Disorders
Western Kentucky University

Susan S. Deusinger
Director, Program in Physical Therapy
Washington University School of Medicine

Anne E. Dickerson
Professor and Chair, Department of Occupational
    Therapy
East Carolina University

Leonard H. Friedman
Associate Professor of Public Health
Oregon State University

Paul N. Gonzales
Director, Radiologic Technology Program
Fresno City College

Rosann M. Ippolito
Associate Director, Physician Assistant Program
Northeastern University

Mary Anne Marsh
Chair, Department of Nursing
Dickinson University

Connie L. Peterson
Assistant Professor
James Madison University

Professor Nicholas G. Popovich
Head, Department of Pharmacy Administration
University of Illinois at Chicago College of Pharmacy

Susan H. Stadler
Director, Veterinary Technician Program
Lehigh Carbon and Northampton Community College

Annmary E. Thomas
Assistant Professor, Emergency Medical Services
    Program
Drexel University

Valerie J.M. Watzlaf
Associate Professor, Department of Health Information
    Management
University of Pittsburgh

Olivia Bennett Wood
Associate Professor and Director, Didactic Program in
    Dietetics
Purdue University

Pamela R. Yokubaitis
Fellow of the American Health Information
    Management Association

Nancy C. Zinser
Professor and Chair, Dental Health Services
Palm Beach Community College

Humanities

D. Terence Langendoen
Professor Emeritus, Department of Linguistics
University of Arizona

Richard T. Lee
Brownell Professor of Philosophy
Trinity College

Michael D. Richards
Samford Professor of History
Sweet Briar College

Kenneth S. Rothwell, Jr.
Associate Professor and Chair, Department of Classics
University of Massachusetts Boston

Tobin Siebers
Professor and Chair, Department of Comparative
    Literature
University of Michigan

Joseph Ugoretz
Professor of English and Director of Teaching and
    Learning with Technology
Borough of Manhattan Community College

Languages

Theresa A. Antes
Associate Professor of French and Linguistics
University of Florida

Scott Cook
Associate Professor of Chinese
Grinnell College

Michael Fishbein
Lecturer in Arabic
University of California: Los Angeles

Melissa Frazier
Professor of Russian Language and Literature
Sarah Lawrence College

H. Mack Horton
Professor of Japanese Literature
University of California, Berkeley

Mike Kemp
Professor, Department of ASL and Deaf Studies
Gallaudet University

María Negroni
Assistant Professor
Sarah Lawrence College

Robert E. Proctor
Joanne Toor Cummings '50 Professor of Italian
Connecticut College

Heidi Thomann Tewarson
Professor and Chair, Department of German Language
    and Literature
Oberlin College

Legal studies

Diane Curtis
Prelaw Advisor
University of Massachusetts Amherst

Jeffrey J. Davis
Assistant Professor of Political Science
University of Maryland, Baltimore County

Lenore M. Molee
Associate Professor and Coordinator of Paralegal
    Studies Program, Department of Legal Studies
Montclair State University

Mathematics

James Alexander
Chair, Department of Mathematics
Case Western Reserve University

David M. Bressoud
DeWitt Wallace Professor of Mathematics
Macalester College

Michele Marini
Undergraduate Administrator, Department of Statistics
Virginia Polytechnic Institute and State University

Multi/interdisciplinary studies

Stephen M. Buhler
Professor of English
University of Nebraska–Lincoln

Joseph F. Cimini
Associate Professor, Department of Sociology &
    Criminal Justice
University of Scranton

Caroline Higgins
Professor of History and Convener, Peace and Global
    Studies
Earlham College

Richard S. Lewis
Associate Professor of Psychology and Neuroscience
Pomona College

Ann Milkovich McKee
Assistant Professor and Director, Undergraduate
    Historic Preservation
Goucher College

Eve Walsh Stoddard
Professor of English and Chair, Global Studies
    Department
St. Lawrence University

Natural resources and conservation

Eric M. Hallerman
Professor and Head, Department of Fisheries and
    Wildlife Sciences
Virginia Polytechnic Institute and State University

David H. Hirth
Associate Professor and Chair, Wildlife and Fisheries
    Biology Program
University of Vermont

Steven E. Jungst
Professor, Department of Forestry
Iowa State University

David K. Loomis
Associate Professor, Human Dimensions Research Unit,
    Department of Natural Resources Conservation
University of Massachusetts Amherst

Michael Maniates
Professor of Environmental Science and Political
    Science
Allegheny College

David E. Smith
Professor, Department of Environmental Sciences
University of Virginia

Parks and recreation

Lowell Caneday
Professor of Leisure Studies
Oklahoma State University

Stephen W. Jefferson
Chief Undergraduate Adviser and Undergraduate
    Program Director, Sport Management Program
University of Massachusetts Amherst

Physical sciences

Neta A. Bahcall
Eugene Higgins Professor of Astrophysics
Princeton University

Dave Esser
Professor and Program Coordinator, Department of
    Aeronautical Science
Embry-Riddle Aeronautical University

Richard G. French
Professor and Chair, Astronomy Department, and
    Director, Whitin Observatory
Wellesley College

Ronald E. Johnson
University Professor and Associate Professor of
    Oceanography
Old Dominion University

Stanley T. Jones
Professor and Chair, Department of Physics &
    Astronomy
University of Alabama

James P. Koermer
Professor of Meteorology
Plymouth State University

Jonathan W. Peterson
Associate Professor of Geology and Environmental
    Science
Hope College

Bahram Roughani
Professor and Department Head of Physics
Kettering University

James N. Spencer
Emeritus William G. and Elizabeth R. Simeral Professor
    of Chemistry
Franklin & Marshall College

Protective services

Daniel Klenow
Professor and Chair, Department of Sociology,
    Anthropology, and Emergency Management
North Dakota State University

Dennis R. Longmire
Professor, College of Criminal Justice
Sam Houston State University

Frank Vozzo
Associate Professor of Forensic Science
Russell Sage College for Women

Thomas J. Woodford
Associate Professor and Department Head, Fire
    Protection and Safety Technology
Oklahoma State University

Public administration

Danny L. Balfour
Professor and Director, School of Public and Nonprofit
    Administration
Grand Valley State University

Tuesday L. Cooper
Dean, Long Island Center
Empire State College

Irene Queiro-Tajalli
Professor and Executive Director of Undergraduate
    Education, School of Social Work
Indiana University–Purdue University Indianapolis

Religion and theology

Kamran S. Aghaie
Assistant Professor of Islamic Studies
University of Texas at Austin

Sandra Billy
Director, Center for Sacred Music
Virginia Wesleyan College

Shmuel Bolozky
Professor of Hebrew
University of Massachusetts Amherst

John A. Grim
Professor of Religion
Bucknell University

Andrew E. Hill
Professor of Old Testament
Wheaton College (IL)

Richard B. Pilgrim
Professor Emeritus, Department of Religion
Syracuse University

Shelley Shepherd
Preministerial studies advisor
Southern Methodist University

David G. Truemper
Professor and Chair of Theology
Valparaiso University

Social sciences

David L. Browman
Chairman, Interdisciplinary Program in Archaeology
Washington University in St. Louis

Gregory A. Elmes
Professor of Geography, Department of Geology and
    Geography
West Virginia University

Jacqueline Johnson
Assistant Professor, Sociology
Fordham University

Andrew A. Latham
Associate Professor of Political Science and Associate
    Director, Center for Scholarship and Teaching
Macalester College

Robert Mandel
Professor and Chair, International Affairs Department
Lewis and Clark College

Lee McCann
Professor of Psychology
University of Wisconsin–Oshkosh

Baron Perlman
Professor of Psychology
University of Wisconsin–Oshkosh

John J. Siegfried
Professor of Economics
Vanderbilt University

Visual and performing arts

Sven Anderson
Assistant Professor, Computer Art and Printmaking
State University of New York College at Oneonta

Chrystelle Trump Bond
Professor of Dance and Founding Chair, Dance
    Department
Goucher College

Lilly Ann Boruszkowski
Associate Professor
Southern Illinois University Carbondale

David B. Brownlee
Professor of the History of Art
University of Pennsylvania

Jo Anne Caputo
Professor
Cleveland Institute of Music

Meredith Davis
Professor of Graphic Design
North Carolina State University College of Design

Bevin Engman
Associate Professor of Art
Colby College

David B. Greene
Professor of Arts Studies Emeritus
North Carolina State University

Janine King
Associate Professor and Chair, Department of Interior
    Design
University of Florida

Anthony J. LaMagra
Professor and Director of Music Emeritus
Manhattanville College

Judy Lochhead
Professor of Music and Graduate Program Director
State University of New York at Stony Brook

Ronald Naversen
Professor of Scenic Design
Southern Illinois University Carbondale

Fred Niles
Professor and Chair, Department of Visual Arts
University of Dayton

Donald Poynter
Animation Instructor
School of Visual Arts

Mary Stephens
Director of Fashion Design, Advanced Study Programs
Fashion Institute of Design and Merchandising

Diane Timmerman
Professor of Theatre
Butler University

Allen Winold
Professor Emeritus of Music
Indiana University Bloomington

How to use this book

Find a major, find a college

If you are thinking about college majors, this book offers a lot of help.

If you have no idea what you want to study in college, it can help you discover majors that might appeal to you.

If there are several majors that interest you, it can help you make an informed choice.

If you already know what you want to major in, it can help you prepare for the program by letting you know what to expect. (Or it might present a completely different but more attractive option you never knew existed—which just might be the best help of all.)

But choosing a major is only half the job— you also have to find a college that offers it, at the degree level that is right for you, and in a place where you want, or need, to be. This book helps you do that, too. (The description of Part II below will tell you how.)

Part I: Full Descriptions of Majors

According to the U.S. Department of Education's *Classification of Instructional Programs* (*CIP*), there are over 1,200 fields of study— majors, that is. Part I describes 200 of these in full detail; all are briefly described in Part II.

Major categories

The 201 profiled majors are grouped into 26 broad categories, arranged alphabetically. Each category begins with a short write-up about the field of study as a whole, to guide your exploration of the majors and the colleges that offer them. You'll get a feel for the different ways colleges approach the majors, insights from professors, and guidance on questions to ask as you explore the majors in the group.

The category introductions are just a starting point. You'll want to read all the details in the individual profiles of the majors that interest you.

The profiles

Each profile is based on information gathered from college professors teaching in the field. The major is described as it is generally taught at colleges across the United States, not just at a particular school. Throughout, the term *college* refers to any institution of higher education— two-year college, four-year college, university, technical school, professional school, and so on.

How did we pick the majors to profile? First, we looked at the majors that high school students (almost 2 million of them) said they were most interested in when they completed a brief questionnaire on their SAT registration forms. Then we examined which majors are most widely offered at colleges across the country, to be sure a broad spectrum was represented. And we added a few that we believe are noteworthy or up-and-coming (like Game design and Emergency management/homeland security), even if they are not among the most popular or the most available.

Almost all the profiled majors are for undergraduate study, either at the two-year associate degree level or in a four-year bachelor's degree program. For the few majors that are available only as graduate programs (physical therapy, for instance), we've described the undergraduate course of study that will prepare you for grad school. We also describe preprofessional programs (such as prelaw and pre-medicine) that are technically not majors.

The following headings correspond to what you will find in the profiles.

Name of major: This is the generic name of the major that is most often used and most widely recognized. You are likely to see variations in individual college catalogs, but they should be similar to the name shown here.

Also known as: Colleges don't always agree on what to call a major; alternative names that you might come across are listed here.

What it's about: This paragraph gives you a quick idea of the subject area the major covers and the careers it prepares you for.

Is this for you? This section should help you select a major according to what you like to do or to study, what you are good at, and what your personal qualities are. We've listed some characteristics common to students who have succeeded in the major. They are not requirements, and you certainly don't have to match them all, or even any of them; your interest in a particular field may be based on something totally different and be just as valid.

Recommended high school prep: The course units recommended here refer to years of study in a four-year high school. "Math 3" refers to Algebra I, geometry, and Algebra II; "lab science 3" includes earth science, biology, and either chemistry or physics, each with a lab component. "Social studies 3" includes U.S. history, world history, and either geography or government/economics.

The recommended courses tend to be similar for all majors, because a well-rounded high school curriculum, with courses in English, math, science, social studies, and a foreign language, is generally required for admission to most colleges, regardless of major. The recommendations will differ with respect to additional units or elective courses that can help you prepare for a particular major. But these are suggestions only; your high school may not teach some of the courses mentioned here.

What if you don't know what you want to major in? Preserve your options by taking the most rigorous courses you can. The College Board recommends four years of English, four years of math (including Algebra I, Algebra II, Geometry, and pre-Calculus or Calculus), a minimum of two years of lab science (some colleges require more), three years of social science and history, and at least two years of the same foreign language. Your school counselor will have the best advice as to whether your choice of high school courses will support your college goals.

Did you know...? Included here are important aspects or interesting facts about the major, or the careers it may lead to, that many students entering the major are not aware of.

Typical courses in the major: This list is a sampling of courses commonly offered in the major, in roughly the order of sequence they are taken. Some colleges offer fewer courses than these and some more, and course titles may vary.

Concentrations: You can sometimes concentrate your studies, or specialize, in a certain area within your major. The concentrations listed here are not available at all colleges. Concentrations that are generally not available until grad school are listed separately.

What the study of this major is like: This section tells you what you'll actually study in a major, and how the major is generally taught and learned. We've described differences in emphasis, requirements, and philosophies among colleges that offer the major, to help you evaluate the program at the colleges you are considering. You will also get a sense of what your academic lifestyle will be like, and what challenges to expect.

Other majors you might like: This section lists majors that are related by subject matter, approach, or the interests and characteristics of the students who study them. Some of the related fields are obvious, but some may surprise you; they are included to help you cover all the bases, or perhaps to suggest an option you may not have known about. Majors in **bold type** are fully profiled in this book. Those in regular type are briefly described in Part II.

Questions to ask colleges: These questions are designed to help you find colleges that have strong programs for your major, or that approach the subject area in a way that is compatible with your goals and interests. Good for college visits, interviews, or an email to the websites of the colleges you are considering.

Career options and trends: This section lists job titles in careers the major may lead to—an asterisk indicates a type of job that graduates most often pursue. Also described are any additional education, certification, or licensure requirements for the careers listed, plus trends occurring or likely to occur in careers related to the major.

Insider's viewpoint: We asked professors to tell something about what appeals to them about the major. We also asked college students actually enrolled in the major to give some pointers or insights, or to describe their experiences as a major in class, internships, or field studies.

For more info: Contact information is provided here for associations (educational and business) that you should investigate to explore further the major and/or related careers. Most of these associations have robust sections for students, although sometimes you have to drill down to find them.

Part II: Brief Descriptions of Majors

Adapted from the latest version of the U.S. Department of Education's *Classification of Instructional Programs* (*CIP*), these descriptions cover the whole spectrum of majors offered by colleges throughout the United States, and are included to supplement the college listings in Part III. Each description indicates the scope of the major and, where appropriate, the jobs for which you are prepared. Some of these majors are only available at the graduate degree level.

Part III: College Listings

Colleges Listed by Major and State

Here you will find the colleges that offer the major (or majors) you are interested in. The majors are presented alphabetically, and under each major is a state-by-state list of the colleges that teach it. Some colleges listed here do not offer majors in the traditional sense but provide in-depth specialization that is very similar to the course work usually required for a degree.

A lot more majors are listed here than are profiled in Part I. There are over 1,200, in fact—all the undergraduate majors and graduate programs offered by the schools responding to the College Board's Annual Survey of Colleges. The names of the majors conform to the *CIP*, but individual colleges may use different names in their course catalogs.

Levels of study

Are you looking for a two-year program or a four-year program? Going on to graduate school? Thinking about beefing up your credentials with a certificate in your career area? Then you need to know that the colleges offering the major you want also offer it at the right level of study for you.

In the list of colleges by major, the different degree levels offered for each major are designated by the following letters found after the college name:

C Certificate or diploma
A Associate degree
B Bachelor's degree
T Teacher certification
M Master's degree
D Doctorate
P Professional degree (e.g., J.D., M.D.)

Certificate or diploma. Certificates are awarded to students who complete nondegree programs, which usually take one year or less and are most frequently offered in technical and vocational fields of study. Entry requirements for the programs may vary; for some you might need only a high school diploma or equivalent, while for others (accounting, for example) you might have to have some college under your belt.

Associate degree. The degrees most frequently earned at this level are the associate of arts (A.A.) (in the context of academic degrees, arts refers to the humanities, not to painting and drawing) and the associate of science (A.S.). The associate in applied science (A.A.S.) is also used for technological or vocational fields. Usually two years in length, associate degree programs are most often found at community colleges and technical schools, but they are also offered at many four-year colleges. Associate degrees in transfer programs are designed to provide the first two years of a four-year bachelor's degree at most colleges.

Bachelor's degree. Programs in which you earn a bachelor's (sometimes called a baccalaureate) degree usually take four years, but some programs can be completed in three years and some take five. The bachelor of arts (B.A.) and the bachelor of science (B.S.) are the most common; both include general education courses, a major, and electives. Some programs offer specialized degrees, such as the bachelor of fine arts (B.F.A.) or bachelor of architecture (B.Arch.). There are no absolute, or universally accepted, differences between the degrees, and colleges may vary in whether they give an arts or a science degree to graduates in a particular program.

Teacher certification. Each state sets its own certification standards, and all colleges that prepare teachers are accredited by the state in which they are located. Students must meet both bachelor's degree requirements and state certification requirements. Most states require candidates to pass an examination in the field they plan to teach.

Master's degree. Master of arts (M.A.) and master of science (M.S.) programs are graduate degrees in the liberal arts and sciences, intended for students with B.A. or B.S. degrees, and usually take one or two years to complete. Among other master's degree programs are the master of business administration (MBA), the master of library science (M.L.S.), and the master of social work (M.S.W.) In some fields, such as law and medicine, the master's degree follows the professional degree (J.D., M.D.).

Doctorate. The most common type of doctorate is the doctor of philosophy (Ph.D.), awarded in most of the humanities, the arts, and the sciences. Examples of other programs are the doctor of education (Ed.D.) and the doctor of public health (D.P.H.). Doctoral programs usually consist of course work and independent research culminating in a dissertation or other formal presentation of the results of independent study. Length of study varies widely, and is usually self-determined.

Professional degree. These programs provide the academic prerequisites to become licensed in a recognized profession, such as medicine, law, or veterinary medicine. At least two years of prior college-level study are required for entrance into the program, and the total registered time of study must equal six academic years. Professional degrees are awarded in the following fields:

Chiropractic	D.C., D.C.M.
Dentistry	D.D.S., D.M.D.
Divinity/Ministry	D.D., M.Div.
Law	L.L.B., J.D.
Medicine	M.D.
Optometry	O.D.
Osteopathic medicine	D.O.
Pharmacy	Pharm.D.
Podiatry	D.P.M.
Rabbinical/Talmudic studies	M.H.L., Rav.
Veterinary medicine	D.V.M.

Special academic programs

In addition to majors, minors, and concentrations, many colleges offer other ways to enhance, focus, or further shape your undergraduate education. For each of the following programs, there is a state-by-state listing of colleges that offer them.

Combined bachelor's graduate program. In this program, you study at both the undergraduate and the graduate levels. Usually, you can earn a bachelor's degree and a master's or a professional degree in less time than if you pursued the two degrees separately.

Double major. Colleges listed here allow you to complete the requirements of two majors at the same time.

External degree. If you want or need to earn a college degree with minimal or no classroom attendance, an external degree program allows you to do so through independent study, distance learning, proficiency exams, and demonstrated personal experience.

Semester at sea. You spend a semester on a research vessel, doing field work in the marine sciences and taking academic course work.

Student-designed major. This program allows you to create for yourself a major that is not formally offered by the college. You develop your major, which is likely to be nontraditional and interdisciplinary, with the approval of a college officer or a committee.

Teacher certification. Colleges that have certification programs can prepare you to meet state requirements for teaching in elementary and secondary schools. [See a more detailed explanation of teacher certification in "Levels of Study" above.]

United Nations semester. The colleges listed here let you take courses at a college in the New York City area while you participate in an internship program at the United Nations.

Urban semester. You spend a semester in a major city, such as New York, Chicago, Los Angeles, or Houston, experiencing life in an urban center while pursuing course work, seminars, and/or internships related to your major.

Washington semester. You take an internship program with a government agency or department in the Washington, D.C., metro area. You can earn field service credit for your work and may also take courses at area colleges.

Alphabetical index of majors

A page reference in bold indicates a full profile of the major begins on that page. Otherwise, the page references are to the "Colleges listed by major" in Part III.

What to know about majors

What is a major?

Your college major is the subject that you will take the most courses in and learn most about. It's the area of study that your degree will be in, after you complete the required courses.

As an undergraduate, you will most likely work toward a two-year Associate of Arts (A.A.) or Associate of Science (A.S.) degree, or a four-year Bachelor of Arts (B.A.), Bachelor of Science (B.S.), or Bachelor of Fine Arts (B.F.A.) degree.

Whatever your major, you'll probably take up to half your courses in the liberal arts, to fulfill what's known as "general education" or "core" requirements. This group of subjects includes the humanities, such as literature, the fine arts (such as music and art), philosophy, and history; foreign languages; the social sciences (like anthropology, psychology, economics, political science, and sociology); math; and the biological sciences (such as zoology) and the physical sciences (for example, astronomy, chemistry, geology, and physics). Most students take these general education requirements in the first two years of a four-year program. Many two-year colleges also have liberal arts requirements.

Why so much work outside your major? Colleges want to make sure that you have a well-rounded education—that you become familiar with a wide variety of subjects. If you're an English major, for example, you're likely to benefit more from your literature courses if you also explore, say, psychology and history. If you're a math major, you'll need to be able to communicate your ideas. Think of general education as a foundation of knowledge to support your major studies. The liberal arts expose you to new ideas, and open your mind to many ways of thinking and understanding the world.

How to choose a major

You may have no idea, at the moment, what you want to study in college. A good way to zero in on a major is to think of what interests you and what you are good at. Examine your academic strengths and the subjects that inspire you to learn. Which are your favorite classes in high school? Where did you get the best grades?

What activities do you enjoy, either in or outside school? Are you a whiz at creating cartoons on the computer? Does teaching a younger sibling to cook give you pleasure? Do you love working with your hands or being outdoors? Maybe you're a political junkie who can't get enough current events. Or do you make sense of the world by learning about the past? Any of these skills and interests might suggest a major (for instance, animation, chef training, forestry, journalism, archaeology).

For many students, hobbies and extracurricular activities are as important as class work. If that's you, then maybe your major will relate to your experience in community or volunteer work, religious activities, camping or Scouting, sports or the arts.

What are your values and your vision of the future? What do you see yourself doing for a living? Do you plan to go on to graduate or professional school? Do you want to make sure that you are financially comfortable above all else? Maybe you see yourself as a leader and a motivator of others. Can you picture yourself doing scientific research or working in health care? Does technology excite you? Are you an artist? Have you always wanted to be a teacher? Think about what matters to you and how your priorities may affect your choice of a major.

Then, look around and ask yourself how the world affects you. Are there careers, like nursing, that have a shortage of professionals, so that a degree in the subject should be a passport to a good job? Are you worried that, in a global economy, many jobs may be shipped overseas? If so, you may want to choose a major based on the likely needs of the job market. (You can go to www.bls.gov/oco for more information.)

Look inside yourself and look outside at other forces in your life. Before you know it, you'll start to make some choices about what to study.

When to decide on your major

Many first-year college students are undecided about their majors, and there's nothing wrong with needing more time to make a decision. Most four-year colleges expect you to declare (choose) your major at the end of your second year or at the beginning of your third year. That gives you time to take courses, including the liberal arts requirements, in a number of fields before you settle on a major.

During your first two years as an undergraduate, you can usually take some electives—nonrequired courses that interest you. If you have not yet decided on a major, you can use your electives to sample several areas of study—for instance, you might take introductory courses in two or three fields that you are considering as a major. Whether you choose electives as a way to test-drive a major or simply to learn more about a subject that appeals to you, electives will give you the opportunity to explore new ideas.

For some degrees, however, you will want to declare a major as soon as possible. That's because some majors have requirements that you'll have to meet in your first year or two of college. An example is nursing: you may have to qualify for the major by achieving a certain grade-point average in prerequisite courses before being admitted to the college's nursing program. Another example is an education major: you may need certain grades in liberal arts courses in order to qualify for a teaching program. Being accepted by a college doesn't guarantee that you'll get into the program you want at the college. Before you begin your first year, find out what's required, so you can work out your education plan.

Applied and academic majors

You can divide majors into two big groups. One group consists of the *applied majors*. These programs prepare you for a specific career by giving you the knowledge and skills you'll need in a particular line of work. When you go to work in that field, you'll put into action the information and skills you learned in college. Some examples are food science, landscape architecture, finance, graphic design, forestry, special education, electrical engineering technology, nursing, veterinary technology, and forensic science. Applied majors also prepare you for the special licensing or certifications you'll need in jobs like accounting, teaching, occupational therapy, and social work.

The other big group covers the *academic majors*. Many of these majors are in the arts and sciences and include the humanities, science, and math. The academic majors don't necessarily lead to specific careers, though. They prepare you for graduate studies or for professions in which a wide range of skills and creative talents are valued—the ability to communicate, to understanding people, to read, to think about the world, or to work with numbers. Some examples of academic majors are African-American studies and Latin American studies, English, history, mathematics, chemistry, economics, and communications. (Colleges don't always agree on which majors fall into the liberal arts category. You'll find both applied and academic majors in this book.)

Applied and academic majors each have advantages and disadvantages. For the academic majors, the downside is that you will enter the job market without specific job training; you might have to settle for a lower starting salary. On the plus side, your academic training enables you to understand texts, express yourself verbally, and analyze and solve problems. Employers value these skills because they help you adapt to change. Academic majors also prepare you for graduate school in many fields. In graduate school, you can continue your education as you work toward a master's degree (M.A. or M.S.) or, maybe a doctorate degree (Ph.D.) or professional degree (law degree, medical degree).

The applied majors are popular choices because students can target their college work to launch a career. But by committing to a particular field, you will probably have fewer options, and you'll have to worry about job cycles and economic slumps in your field, or the possibility that your education and training will become out of date.

The right major at the right college

Which comes first, your choice of a major or your choice of a college? You should have some idea of what you want to study as you search for colleges because you'll want a school with a strong program in that area. Look for colleges that offer the majors you like and the related majors, too (they are listed with the majors profiled in this book). If you choose a college that teaches several majors that appeal to you, you'll be less likely to have to transfer to another college if, for any reason, you change your major.

Is a two-year or a four-year college right for you? Many two-year colleges, usually called community colleges, offer excellent training for a variety of careers, such as engineering technology, business administration, and support services in health care.

Another option is to earn a two-year associate degree in a transfer program. You'll study the equivalent of the first two years of a bachelor's degree program, and then transfer the credits when you apply to and are accepted by a four-year college. But be sure to find out which courses will be accepted for credit at the four-year college you would apply to.

As you start thinking about majors, it's good to know how colleges work. For instance, many small, private colleges are known for their liberal arts offerings. Larger universities often emphasize graduate programs. Most big-name schools, including state universities, are made up of several colleges. Sometimes it's clear what an undergraduate college or school in a university system, such as the college of agriculture or the school of nursing, has to offer. But sometimes the name of a college doesn't provide many clues. For instance, the college of arts and sciences and the school of business administration, in the same university system, might both offer a major in economics. But the course requirements might differ, and so might the admission requirements. As you look for a major, do some research on colleges. You can find more information on official college websites (their Internet addresses usually end in .edu).

When you scout about for the right college, you'll probably read magazines and websites that rank the most competitive schools—that is, label one college as the best, another as the next best, and so on. Keep in mind, though, that rankings can't convey many of the features of a college, and that a listing may be based on factors that are not very important to you. So before examining a ranking, try to find out what the ratings were based on.

Your choice of college depends on what's right for you, and only you can come up with the college list that really matters. To help find colleges with good programs in the majors of interest to you, check out "Questions to ask colleges" in the major profiles in this book.

Concentrations, minors, double majors, and special programs

When you get to college, you may have even more options besides the choice of major. For example, you might select a concentration that allows you to specialize in a topic within your major, by taking a cluster of courses in the subject area. If you major in history, for instance, you might concentrate on Europe during the Middle Ages; or as a studio arts major, you might concentrate on painting. The availability of a concentration will vary from major to major and from college to college. Occasionally, a concentration may be required. In music performance, for example, you may have to choose a particular instrument that you'll concentrate on. Concentrations are less common in smaller colleges, and some programs offer concentrations only in graduate school.

Another option is to add a minor to your major. A minor is course work in which you explore another field, but not as widely or as deeply as for your major. You might minor in a subject that complements, or adds strength to, your major, such as a minor in business administration with a major in public relations, or an Arabic-language minor with a major in international relations. Then again, you could minor in a subject that's not related to your major, to give your brain a break from the type of work you do in your major courses. For example, computer science majors might enjoy studying creative writing, too.

Some colleges let you take a double major in related or even unrelated fields. In a double major, you complete two majors at the same time. For example, you could major in art history and in fine/studio arts, or in anthropology and Native American studies. You can even combine an academic and an applied major—for example, majoring in linguistics and in computer science. Double majors aren't for everyone, because college is tough enough without taking required courses for two majors. But it's something to think about if you can handle the workload and want to boost your academic résumé.

Another option to consider is a combined bachelor's and graduate degree. For many of these joint degrees, you are accepted into both programs when you apply to college. That way, you won't have to apply to grad school after you finish your undergraduate degree. These special programs (listed in Part III of this book) often include three years of study for a bachelor's degree, and then you begin the graduate program in your fourth year. The advantage is that you can complete both degrees in less time than it would take to earn the two degrees in the traditional way (often saving a year). As an example, you could earn a bachelor's degree in biology plus a master's in physical therapy in six years. Some schools of education offer five-year programs combining a bachelor's in education and a Master of Teaching degree.

Even if you know what major you want, adding concentrations, minors, or double majors, or entering combined programs, expands your choices of what to study in college. And here's another option: at some colleges you can create your own major or work with a professor on an independent project.

Preprofessional programs

Sometimes college is a stepping stone to… more college. That's not a bad thing. The more education people have, the lower their unemployment and the higher their earnings. Also, lawyers, doctors, and other health care professionals, including pharmacists, dentists, and physical therapists, must have professional degrees. Many members of the clergy and business executives also earn advanced degrees.

To prepare you for advanced studies, some colleges offer preprofessional programs. These are advisory programs, or "tracks," that lead you through a group of requirements that you can fulfill in almost any major.

Take law school, for example. More students earn law degrees than any other professional degree. In law school, the emphasis is on the writing, reading, and understanding of documents and texts. These skills are needed in nearly every undergraduate college course. So if you intend to apply to law school, you have a wide choice of undergrad majors, including history, political science, English, philosophy, criminal justice, the sciences, math, engineering, and a foreign language.

Medical schools do not insist that applicants have specific undergraduate majors, either. However, it's no surprise that most med school applicants major in the biological sciences. Others study the physical or social sciences, or one of the liberal arts. Med school applicants are typically required to have taken five year-long courses in math and science, as well as some general education courses. The requirements, and the number of credits and labs they include, are spelled out by the college in its premed program.

The best thing you can do, if you plan to go to law school or medical school or to graduate programs, is to get excellent grades in your undergraduate work. You'll also need to prepare for the appropriate professional school or grad school entrance exam.

Switching majors

Many students switch majors in college. This can be risky depending upon how far along you are in your college career, because you may have to spend more time than you'd planned, and more money, to finish your degree. But your original major might not be right for you, or an elective course might spark within you a passion for another field of study. Many options are open to you, even after you enroll in college.

If you find yourself in a major that you want to change, be sure to check with your college academic adviser. Like a high school counselor who can give you guidance, a college academic adviser can help you sort through electives, choose a major, change your major, and steer you toward completion of your degree.

Planning for now and for later

You don't have to feel overwhelmed by the choice of a major and of a college. Having a lot of choices can only benefit you. Think about your interests and talents while you read about the majors. Once you narrow the selection to a few majors you like, do some research on college programs in those majors (you might also ask about the credentials, or qualifications, of faculty members, and about the availability of libraries, computers, and labs).

You can also visit the websites of professional associations for specific careers and of leading employers of graduates in a particular major (employers may include corporations, small businesses, nonprofit organizations, and various levels of government). A look at the job descriptions and career opportunities will give you an idea of the educational requirements that employers expect. Websites for professional associations are included in the descriptions of majors in this book.

Thinking about a career as you are deciding on a major and a college is understandable, but try to remain flexible. The world is changing so rapidly that the jobs in demand when you declare a major may be different after you graduate.That's just one good reason to choose a major that fits the person you are. Do that, and success will follow.

Glossary

Academic adviser. A professor assigned to help students choose appropriate courses each semester. Many students consult their adviser for help in selecting a major. At some schools, when a student declares a major, he or she is assigned an adviser who teaches in the student's chosen field of study.

Academic year. A measure of the academic work that a student is expected to accomplish. Each college defines its own academic year, but federal regulations set minimum standards. Every program must have a defined academic year that contains a minimum of 30 weeks of instructional time. For undergraduate programs, a full-time enrolled student is expected to complete at least 24 semester or trimester hours, 36 quarter hours, or 900 clock hours over the 30-week period.

Accelerated study. A college program of study completed in less time than is usually required, most often by attending classes in summer or by taking extra courses during the regular academic term. Completion of a bachelor's degree program in three years is an example of acceleration.

Accreditation. Recognition by an accrediting organization or agency that a college meets acceptable standards in its programs, facilities, and services. National or regional accreditation applies to a college as a whole. Some programs or majors within colleges, such as engineering or nursing, may be accredited by professional organizations. The descriptions of majors in Part 1 of this book discuss program accreditation if it is significant in the field.

Adjunct professor. A member of the faculty who is not on the track for tenure and may teach part-time or full-time. Some colleges may refer to adjuncts as "lecturers" or "visiting professors." See also *professor and teaching assistant*.

Advanced placement. Admission or assignment of a first-year student to an advanced course in a subject, on the basis of evidence that the student has completed the equivalent of the college's first-year course in that subject.

Advanced Placement Program® (AP®). An academic program of the College Board that provides high school students with the opportunity to study and learn at the college level. AP offers courses in 36 subjects, each culminating in a rigorous exam. High schools offer the courses and administer the exams to interested students. Most colleges accept qualifying AP Exam scores for credit, advanced placement, or both.

Adviser. See *academic adviser*.

Applied study. The practice of putting theoretical knowledge to practical use, as in the use of engineering principles to design machinery.

Area studies. A program of study that focuses on the history, geography, economics, politics, and culture of a region of the world—for example, Latin America, Eastern Europe.

Articulation agreement. An agreement between two colleges to facilitate the transfer of students from one college to the other without duplication of course work.

Associate degree. A degree granted by a college or university after the satisfactory completion of a two-year, full-time program of study. In general, the Associate of Arts (A.A.) or Associate of Science (A.S.) degree is granted after students complete a program similar to the first two years of a four-year college curriculum. The Associate in Applied Science (A.A.S.) is awarded by many colleges on completion of technological or vocational programs of study.

Bachelor's, or baccalaureate, degree. A degree received after the satisfactory completion of a four-or five-year, full-time program of study (or its part-time equivalent) at a college or university. The bachelor of arts (B.A.), bachelor of science (B.S.), and bachelor of fine arts

(B.F.A.) are the most common bachelor's degrees. Policies concerning their award vary from college to college.

Calendar. The system by which a college divides its year into shorter periods for providing instruction and for awarding credit. The most common systems are those based on the semester, the trimester, the quarter, and the 4-1-4 calendar.

Capstone course. A senior-year course in which students use information and skills learned in previous course work to address a topic, issue, or set of problems.

Carnegie unit. A unit of credit given for successful completion of one year's study of a college preparatory or academic subject in high school. Some colleges refer to Carnegie units as academic units. The name comes from the Carnegie Foundation for the Advancement of Teaching.

Case study. A means of learning by studying a specific example. For instance, students of hotel management might observe the work of an actual hotel to learn how to conduct a marketing survey, hire and train staff, and advertise.

Certificate. An award for completing a particular program or course of study, usually given by two-year colleges or vocational or technical schools for non-degree programs of a year or less.

College. The generic term for an institution of higher learning; also a term used to designate divisions within a university. A university may consist of various colleges: of arts and sciences, of engineering, of music, of agriculture, of architecture, and more. When a university is divided into colleges, students usually have to apply for admission to a specific college. Colleges in a university usually have their own requirements. For example, the college of arts and science may require two units of a foreign language, and the college of music may require an audition.

College calendar. See *calendar*.

College-Level Examination Program® (CLEP®). A program in which students receive college credit by earning a qualifying score in

any of 33 examinations in business, composition and literature, world languages, history and social sciences, and science and mathematics. Sponsored by the College Board, exams are administered at over 1800 test centers. Over 2900 colleges and universities grant credit for passing a CLEP exam.

College preparatory subjects. Areas of study required for admission to, or recommended as preparation for, college. College prep subjects usually include English, history and social studies, foreign languages, mathematics, science, and the arts.

Combined bachelor's/graduate degree. A program in which students complete a bachelor's degree and a master's degree or first-professional degree in less than the usual amount of time. In most programs, students apply to undergraduate study and begin the graduate program in their fourth year of college. Graduates of the program are awarded both bachelor's and graduate degrees. At some colleges, this option is called a joint degree program.

Combined liberal arts/career program. A program in which a student typically completes three years of study in a liberal arts field and then two years of professional or technical study (for example, engineering). Graduates of the program are awarded a Bachelor of Arts degree and a Bachelor of Science degree. The combination is also referred to as a 3+2 program.

Community/junior college. A college offering two-year programs leading to an associate degree. Community colleges are public institutions, while junior colleges are privately operated on a not-for-profit basis. Most two-year colleges offer both vocational programs (also called "career" or "terminal" programs), as well as the first two years of a four-year program ("academic" or "transfer" programs). Students in the vocational program usually go directly into a vocation after graduation, while students in the academic program usually intend to transfer to a four-year institution or an upper-division college.

Concentration. A specialized branch of study within a major. For example, students majoring in psychology might choose a concentration in personality and social psychology; in fulfilling the requirements of the major, they would select courses focusing on personality and social psychology. In some programs, a concentration consists of a few courses in the area of specialty; in others, students may take 30 to 40 credits in their chosen area. A concentration may help students prepare for graduate study.

Cooperative education (co-op). A career-oriented program in which students divide their time between traditional academic study and employment in business, industry, or government. Students are typically paid for their work. Under a cooperative plan, students normally need five years to earn a bachelor's degree, but graduates have the advantage of about a year's work experience in addition to their studies.

Core curriculum. A group of courses, in varied areas of the arts and sciences, designated by a college as one of the requirements for a degree. See also *general education requirements*.

Course load. The number of class hours the student is permitted to schedule, in a given semester or quarter. It is usually 16–18 hours on a semester calendar, and 15–16 hours on a quarter calendar.

Credit hour. A standard unit of measurement for a college course. Each credit hour represents one classroom hour per week. Credit hours are used to determine the total number of hours needed to complete the requirements of a degree, diploma, certificate, or other formal award.

Curriculum. A set or program of courses. Students complete a certain curriculum, often consisting of liberal arts courses, electives, and courses in their major, to earn their degree.

Degree. An award given by a college or university certifying that a student has completed a course of study. See *bachelor's degree, associate degree, graduate degree*. See also *certificate*.

Department. A group of related programs of study within a college. The Romance languages department, for example, may include programs in French, Italian, and Spanish. Some colleges have only a few departments, and some have a wide variety. Most departments offer several majors. A biology department might offer majors in marine biology, in microbiology, and in botany, for example.

Discipline. An academic area of study. Literature, history, social science, natural science, mathematics, the arts, and foreign language are disciplines; each takes a certain approach to knowledge

Discussion section. A supplement to a large lecture course in which students meet with either the professor or a teaching assistant, usually once a week, to discuss the lectures and assigned reading.

Distance learning. An option for earning course credit off campus, via cable television, Internet, satellite classes, DVD or videotape, correspondence courses, or other means.

Doctoral degree. See *graduate degree*.

Double major. Any program in which a student completes the requirements of two majors at the same time.

Dual enrollment. The practice of allowing students to enroll in college courses while still in high school.

Elective. A course that is not required for one's chosen major or the college's core curriculum, and can be used to fulfill the credit hour requirement for graduation.

Ethnic studies. A group of courses that focus on the culture, society, literature, and history of an ethnic group such as African Americans or Hispanic Americans.

Exchange student program. Any arrangement that permits a student to study for a semester or more at another college in the United States without extending the amount of time required for a degree.

External degree program. A system of study in which a student earns credit toward a degree through independent study, college courses, proficiency examinations, and personal experience. External degree colleges generally have no campus or classroom facilities.

Field of study. See *major*.

Fieldwork. Study that takes place outside the classroom and provides students with hands-on experience in their major. Geology majors may spend time in a ravine studying rock formations; major in food science may spend time in a hospital kitchen.

4-1-4 calendar. A variation of the semester calendar system that consists of two terms of about 16 weeks each, separated by a one-month intersession used for intensive short courses, independent study, off-campus work, or other types of instruction.

Full-time student. An enrolled student who is carrying a full-time academic workload (other than correspondence courses). What makes up a full-time workload is determined by the institution and is applicable to all students enrolled in a program.

General education requirements. Courses that give undergraduates background in the primary academic disciplines: natural sciences, social sciences, mathematics, literature and language, and fine arts. Most colleges require students to take general education courses in their first and second years, as a way to sample a wide range of courses before choosing a major. At some colleges, general education courses are referred to as the core curriculum; at others, a few courses within the general education requirements are core courses that all students must take.

Grade point average (GPA). A system used by many schools for evaluating the overall scholastic performance of students. Grade points are usually determined by first multiplying the number of hours given for a course by the numerical value of the grade, and then dividing the sum of all grade points by the total number of hours carried. The most common system of numerical values for grades is: A = 4, B = 3, C = 2, D = 1, and E or F = 0.

Graduate degree. A degree (sometimes called a postgraduate degree) pursued after a student has earned a bachelor's degree. The master's degree, which requires one to three years of study, is usually the degree earned after the bachelor's. The doctoral degree requires further study. First-professional degrees are also graduate degrees.

Honors program. Any special program for very able students that offers the opportunity for educational enrichment, independent study, acceleration, or some combination of these.

Humanities. The branches of learning that usually include art, the classics, dramatic art, English, general and comparative literature, journalism, music, philosophy, and religion. Many colleges divide their offerings into three divisions: humanities, social sciences, and natural sciences.

Independent study. Academic work chosen or designed by the student, with the approval of the department concerned, and pursued under an instructor's supervision. The work is usually undertaken outside the regular classroom structure.

Interdisciplinary major. See *multidisciplinary major*.

International Baccalaureate (IB). A high school curriculum offered by some schools in the United States and other countries. Some colleges award credit for completion of this curriculum. Please visit the organization's website for further information.

Internship. A short-term, supervised work experience, usually related to a student's major field, for which the student earns academic credit. The work can be full- or part-time, on or off campus, paid or unpaid. Student teaching and apprenticeships are examples.

Junior college. See *community college*.

Laboratory course. A course, usually supplemented by lectures, in which students perform scientific experiments under the supervision of a professor or a teaching assistant.

Land-grant university. One of the universities established by the federal government in 1862. The institutions were intended to educate the agricultural workforce the country needed. Many are now large universities teaching a wide range of subjects, but they still offer numerous agriculture-related majors.

Lecture course. A midsize or large course, in which the instructor speaks from prepared notes on a topic relating to the assigned reading or laboratory work. Lectures are usually supplemented by discussion sections or laboratories.

Liberal arts. The study of the humanities (literature, the arts, and philosophy), history, foreign languages, social sciences, mathematics, and natural sciences. The liberal arts and humanities stress the development of general knowledge and reasoning ability rather than specific skills.

Liberal arts/career combination. See *combined liberal arts/career program*.

Licensure. The procedure in which graduates pass one or several examinations and are awarded a license to practice a profession. For example, an accounting major must take a licensing exam after graduation to become a certified public accountant (CPA). Some of the majors described in this book prepare students to take licensing examinations after earning their bachelor's degree.

Lower-division courses. Courses that students are expected to take in their first two years of college. These courses lay the foundation for further study in the subject area.

Major. The field of study in which students concentrate, or specialize, during their undergraduate study. At most colleges, students take a third to a half of their course work in the major; the rest is devoted to liberal arts requirements and electives. In academic majors, students generally take a third of their courses in their academic field, which they usually must choose by the beginning of their junior year. In career-related, or applied, programs, such as nursing and engineering, students may take up to half their courses in their major. See concentration and minor.

Master's degree. See *graduate degree*.

Matriculation. The process in which a student is accepted, pays fees, and enrolls in classes, officially becoming a student at the college. This term is applied only to first-year students or to transfer students' first enrollment.

Minor. Course work that is not as extensive as that in a major but gives students some specialized knowledge of a second field. Students may choose a minor in the department of their major (for example, a major in comparative literature with a minor in German literature), or in a different department (for example, a biology major with a minor in philosophy). College catalogs describe the requirements for minors.

Multidisciplinary major. A major that uses the perspectives of many disciplines, or academic subjects, simultaneously, to explore problems, events, or situations. For example, women's studies uses anthropology, history, sociology, literature, and psychology to examine women in various times and cultures.

Pass/fail course. A course in which a student's achievement is noted only as either passing or failing. In some cases, the course may be offered only as a pass/fail course. In others, a student, with the instructor's permission, may take a regular course on a pass/fail basis.

Placement test. A battery of tests designed to assess a student's aptitude and level of achievement in various academic areas so that he or she can select the most appropriate courses.

Portfolio. A physical collection of examples of a student's work assembled to provide a representation of the student's achievements and skill level.

Postgraduate degree. See *graduate degree*.

Practicum. A course, usually taken in the third or fourth year of college, in which classroom learning is put into practice in a clinic (for students in medical fields) or in a classroom (for education majors). Students are supervised by a working professional during this phase of their education.

Preprofessional program. An advising program and recommended course of study for undergraduate students intending to pursue a professional degree after college. Although there is no prescribed major for entrance to professional school, students planning for a career in law, ministry, or a medical profession need to take an undergraduate program that lays the groundwork for their training. Premed students, for example, must complete certain science courses. Preprofessional advisors help students plan their undergraduate studies and to prepare for admission to professional school.

Prerequisite. A course that must be taken as preparation for more advanced course work in a particular field. For example, introductory calculus would be a prerequisite for differential mathematics. College catalogs usually indicate whether a course has a prerequisite.

Professional degree. A degree granted on completion of academic requirements to become licensed in a recognized profession. The programs of study require at least two years of college work for entrance, and at least six years of college work for completion.

Professor. A member of the faculty at a college or university who either has tenure or is on the "track" for tenure. See also *adjunct professor and teaching assistant*.

Program. See *major*; see also *honors program*.

PSAT/NMSQT® (Preliminary SAT/National Merit Scholarship Qualifying Test). A comprehensive program that helps schools put students on the path to college. The PSAT/NMSQT is administered by high schools to sophomores and juniors each year in October and serves as the qualifying test for scholarships awarded by the National Merit Scholarship Corporation.

Quarter. An academic calendar period of about 12 weeks. Four quarters make up an academic year, but at colleges using the quarter system, students make normal progress by attending three quarters each year. In some colleges, students can accelerate their progress by attending all four quarters in one or more years.

Reserve Officers' Training Corps (ROTC). Programs conducted by some colleges in cooperation with the U.S. Air Force, Army, and Navy. Naval ROTC includes the Marine Corps (the Coast Guard and the Merchant Marine do not sponsor ROTC programs). Local recruiting offices of the military services themselves can supply detailed information about these programs, as can participating colleges.

SAT®. A college entrance exam that tests critical reading, writing and mathematics skills, given on specified dates through the year at test centers in the United States and other countries. The SAT is used by most colleges and sponsors of financial aid programs.

SAT Subject Tests™. Admissions tests in specific subjects given at test centers in the United States and other countries on specified dates throughout the year. The tests are used by colleges for help in both evaluating applicants for admission and determining course placement, and exemption of enrolled first-year students.

School. One name for a subdivision of a university. For example, the administrative unit that offers nursing courses may be called the "college of nursing" at one institution, and the "school of nursing" at another.

Semester. On a college's calendar, a period of about 16 weeks. Colleges on a semester system offer two periods of instruction, fall and spring, a year; there may also be a summer session (usually a shorter, more concentrated period of time).

Semester at sea. A program for credit, usually for students majoring in oceanography, marine biology, or related fields, in which students live for part of a semester on a ship, usually a research vessel. Academic courses are generally taken in conjunction with the sea experience or at other times during the semester.

Seminar. A course, with a small enrollment, that focuses on a specific topic. Class discussions, student presentations, and student writing are usually emphasized over lectures and exams.

Short course. A course, generally a seminar, offered during the middle term at colleges on a 4-1-4 calendar, or sometimes offered as a one-credit class during a regular term. Students often take short courses, which usually focus on limited topics of general interest, on a pass/fail basis.

Specialization. See *concentration*.

Student-designed major. An academic program that allows a student to construct a major that the college does not formally offer. Often nontraditional and multidisciplinary, the major is developed with the approval of a college officer or committee.

Student teaching. A program in which education majors, in their fourth year, teach in a local school, under the supervision of a licensed teacher.

Studio course. A course in which students create works of art and/or design, under the guidance of an instructor, rather than receive information through lectures.

Study abroad. An arrangement by which a student completes part of the college program—typically the third year but sometimes only a semester or a summer—studying in another country. A college may operate a campus abroad, or it may have a cooperative agreement with another U.S. college or with an institution in the host country.

Teacher certification. A college program designed to prepare students to meet the requirements for certification as teachers in elementary and secondary schools.

Teaching assistant. A graduate student who aids a professor by grading papers, leading discussion sections, and/or supervising labs.

Tenure. Permanent appointment to the faculty of a college. Professors who have tenure cannot be dismissed from the faculty except for gross misconduct.

Term. The shorter period into which colleges divide the school year. Some colleges are on the semester system, in which students complete two semesters, or terms, each year. Others are on the quarter system, in which they attend three quarters each year. Many colleges offer a summer term, so that students can attend college year-round and thus receive their degree more quickly, or can finish incomplete credits. See also *calendar*.

Terminal degree. The highest degree that can be earned in a particular field. For most faculty members, it is the doctoral degree. In certain fields, however, a master's degree is the highest level.

Terminal program. An education program designed to prepare students for immediate employment. These programs usually can be completed in less than four years beyond high school and are available in most community colleges, career colleges, and vocational-technical institutes.

Thesis. A long research paper written as a requirement for a degree. At some colleges, departments may require an undergraduate thesis for a bachelor's degree. At others, an undergraduate thesis may be required of students only in certain programs. Theses are usually written under the supervision of a faculty adviser over a semester or an entire academic year.

3+2 program. See *combined liberal arts/career program*.

Transcript. A copy of a student's official academic record, listing all courses taken and grades achieved.

Transfer program. An education program in a two-year college (or four-year college that offers associate degrees), designed primarily for students who plan to continue their studies in a four-year college. See also *community/junior college*.

Transfer student. A student who attends a college—typically for a period ranging from a single term up to three years—and then is accepted by and enrolls in another college. A transfer student may receive credit for all or some of the courses successfully completed before the transfer.

Trimester. An academic calendar period of about 15 weeks. Three trimesters make up one year. Students normally progress by attending two of the trimesters each year and in some colleges can accelerate their progress by attending all three trimesters in one or more years.

Two-year upper-division college. A college offering bachelor's degree programs that begin with the third year. An entering student must have completed the first and second years at another college.

Undergraduate. A student in the first, second, third, or fourth year of an academic program leading to an associate or bachelor's degree, as opposed to a graduate student, who has earned a bachelor's degree and is pursuing a master's, doctoral, or professional degree.

United Nations semester. A program for credit in which students generally take courses at a college in the New York City metropolitan area while participating in an internship program at the United Nations.

University. An institution of higher learning that incorporates together several colleges and graduate schools. When a university is divided into colleges, students usually have to apply for admission to a specific college. Colleges within a university will have different requirements.

For example, a college of arts and science may require two units of a foreign language, and the college of music may require an audition.

Upper division. The third and fourth years of study. See also *two-year upper-division college*

Upper-division courses. Courses taken during the third and fourth years of study. Often numbered 300, 400, or 500, these courses build on the foundation of knowledge gained during the first two years and provide an in-depth exploration of the topic.

Urban semester. A program for credit in which students of diverse majors spend a semester in a major city, such as New York, Philadelphia, Chicago, Denver, or San Francisco, experiencing the complexities of an urban center through course work, seminars, and/or internship related to their major.

Virtual university. A degree-granting, accredited institution in which all courses are delivered by distance learning, with no physical campus.

Washington semester. A program in which students participate in an internship program with a government agency or department in the Washington, D.C., metropolitan area. Students earn field service credit for their work and frequently take courses at area colleges.

Weekend college. A program that allows students to take a complete academic course by attending classes only on weekends. The program, generally restricted to a few areas of study at a college, requires more than the traditional number of years to complete.

Part I: Full Descriptions of Majors

About Part I

Here you will find in-depth descriptions of 196 undergraduate majors, plus 5 preprofessional programs. These profiles are grouped into 26 broad categories. See the Table of Contents for a complete listing.

The headings below correspond to what you will find in the profiles. For more on how to interpret the profiles, read "How to Use This Book" on pages 11 to 15.

Name of major: This is the generic name of the major that is most often used by colleges.

Also known as: Alternative names that you might come across are listed here.

What it's about: This gives you a quick idea of the subject area the major covers and the careers it prepares you for.

Is this for you? This section should help you select a major according to what you like to do or to study, what you are good at, and what your personal qualities are.

Recommended high school prep: The course units recommended here refer to years of study in a four-year high school.

Did you know ...? Included here are important aspects or interesting facts about the major that many students entering the major are not aware of.

Typical courses in the major: This list is a sampling of courses commonly offered in the major, in roughly the order of sequence they are taken.

Concentrations: You can sometimes concentrate your studies in a certain area within your major. The concentrations listed here are not available at all colleges.

What the study of this major is like: This section tells you what you'll actually study in a major, and how the major is generally taught and learned.

Other majors you might like: Some of these will be obvious, but some may surprise you. We encourage you to consider them with an open mind. Majors in bold type are fully profiled in this book. Those in regular type are briefly described in Part II.

Questions to ask colleges: Good for college visits, interviews, or an email to the websites of the colleges you are considering.

Career options and trends: This section lists job titles in careers the major may lead to—an asterisk indicates a type of job that graduates most often pursue. Also described are any additional education, certification, or licensure requirements for the careers listed, plus trends occurring or likely to occur in careers related to the major.

Insider's viewpoint: We asked professors and students to give some insight or describe what appeals to them about the major.

For more info: Contact information is provided here for associations (educational and business) that you should investigate to explore further the major and/or related careers.

Agriculture

Agriculture is an ancient practice that has become a cutting-edge science and industry. It's all about the production of crops, livestock, feed, and fiber. People need agriculture for the basics like food and clothing.

"The things that we do have a major impact on everyone—everyone must eat," says Bonita A. Glatz, a food science professor at Iowa State University.

Farmers and ranchers have gotten pretty good at growing and raising crops and food. The big push in agriculture now is to increase the quality and quantity of plant and animal products, while preserving the ecology of our systems. Things are really getting technical. In many majors, agricultural study is a type of applied biology or applied chemistry. It's a science. So if you study agriculture in a four-year program, you're likely to get a solid science background followed by an in-depth exploration of chemistry, biochemistry, genetics, pathology (study of diseases), meteorology (weather), economics, or education.

Is agriculture for you? People who study and work in farming represent a wide variety of skills and interests. If you care about people, animals, or planet Earth, you might consider an agricultural major. Do you have a passion for vegetable gardening or horseback riding? Maybe you love nature, plants, or the outdoors. Perhaps you want to protect the environment or help developing countries that are struggling with poverty and malnutrition. Many students bring experience in farming and ranching with them to college. During college, they gain an interest in economics and business or a particular branch of agriscience. You don't have to come from a farming background or plan to work on a farm to be an ag major. But you will need quantitative skills—math and statistics—to study this field.

What about job prospects? We all need agricultural products, but the industry is so efficient that we don't need as many farms and traditional farm jobs as we did in the past. Farms are merging so that we have fewer and larger farms now. Agriculture is big business. That means a smaller number of jobs for farmers and ranchers. On the other hand, the business of farming and the global scale of food distribution expand the role of other things like agribusiness and agricultural economics. In fact, students in these two majors will take many of the same classes. The difference is that agribusiness students will probably have a career path toward management in a food company. Agricultural economics is more analytical and good preparation for either research or business. Your choice of major and level of degree affect your job prospects.

What's hot in the field

If you're thinking that agriculture is just plants and soil, no way. Computers, telecommunications, and other high-tech tools play a huge role. "Precision agriculture guided by geographic information systems, satellite guidance, and computer-equipped tractors increases production and conserves natural resources," explains Professor Douglas L. Young of Washington State University.

What else is happening? You've probably seen news stories about environmental regulations or about real estate development in what were once rural areas. These trends may require agriculture students to learn more about the environment and resource economics. "The sustainability of the way we produce food is becoming more important as fuel, transportation and food safety issues are intensifying," says Professor Marianne Sarrantonio, who coordinates the sustainable agriculture program at the University of Maine. She sees increasing demand for graduates in that field.

Another new area of study is the economics of biotechnology. The job picture is also bright for students in food science, partly because people's tastes change and consumers are learning more about nutrition, health, and wellness. And don't forget food safety and biosecurity. They couldn't be more important. Other hot jobs are in plant breeding and genetics, financial management, information systems, and teaching.

From field to table, from the plant to the planet, agriculture requires more knowledge and education than ever before. Today's agricultural professionals have business, economic, scientific, and technical skills and expertise.

It's no surprise that during graduate-level studies, students focus on a very specific area. For example, in agronomy, grad students zoom in on things like crop production and physiology; or soil sciences including soil chemistry, microbiology, and biochemistry. If you're interested in a business track, keep in mind that nearly all agribusiness professions require advanced degrees; grad studies veer toward agricultural marketing or agricultural trade.

But not all colleges and universities define majors in the same way. Colleges vary in the areas of study they emphasize. The differences could stem from the regional climate and its specific crop or soil suitability, or even a college's size and priorities. In college catalogs and on the Internet, look under agricultural sciences, biological sciences, environmental sciences, and natural resources. And be sure to go to the websites of the land-grant universities and the big state schools, which dominate agricultural education. Another section in this book related to agriculture is Natural resources and conservation. There you'll find majors in forestry, fisheries, and environmental studies.

Here are some websites to get you started thinking about your future in agriculture: the U.S. Department of Agriculture (www.usda.gov), the U.S. Food and Drug Administration (www.fda.gov), the National FFA Organization (www.ffa.org), and the American Farm Bureau (www.fb.org).

Agricultural business

Also known as:
Agribusiness

What it's about:
Agricultural business deals with the management, marketing, and financing of food and fiber, "from the field to the table." You study principles from agricultural sciences, economics, business, and statistics in preparation for a career in agribusiness, farming, natural resources, government, and related areas.

Is this for you?
You might like this major if you also like: 4-H projects and competitions; debating; organizing or leading a club or other group activity; solving problems; sports. A concern for the problems of developing countries that are struggling with poverty and malnutrition might also lead you to this major.

Consider this major if you are good at: attention to detail; critical reading/thinking; leadership; organizing; persuading/influencing; quantitative analysis; teamwork *...or have...* initiative; verbal skills; writing skills.

Recommended high school prep:
English 4, math 3 (including precalculus), lab science 3 (including biology and chemistry), social studies 3, and a foreign language 2–3. If available, take a computer course covering basic office applications and spreadsheets.

Did you know...
...that to be successful in agricultural business, you must know math and statistics? Many students are surprised by the idea, as well as by the need for excellent writing and speaking skills.

Typical courses in this major:
Introduction to agribusiness
Managerial accounting
Economics (micro and macro)
Statistics
Farming technologies
Production management
Farm and ranch management
Human resources management
Agricultural marketing
International trade
Agricultural finance
Farm management laboratory
Agricultural history and law
Agricultural policy
Business/environmental law
Management information systems

Concentrations:
In college: agricultural economics; agricultural marketing; farm and ranch management; agricultural finance; environmental economics; crop or animal production; international agriculture and trade.

If you go on to grad school: econometrics; agricultural policy; rural and community economic development.

What the study of this major is like:
The agricultural business major prepares you to apply business and economic principles to the production and marketing of food and other agricultural products and to the management of natural resources. In order to make economically and environmentally sound decisions in this field, you need to understand accounting, economics, finance, labor, marketing, management, and public policy, as you analyze and deal with business and environmental risk; identify and respond to changes in the demand for food products and services; and improve profitability.

You learn principles associated with best practices for product development, profit maximization, and investment planning. You become familiar with accounting tools like balance sheets, income statements, and cash flow statements. You are taught to use quantitative tools such as statistics, accounting methods, computer programs, and investment analysis to solve management and planning problems.

You also learn the importance of risk management in an industry in which prices can zigzag (because of the uncertainties of worldwide markets) and production is at the mercy of weather, pests, and natural disasters. To thrive despite the risks, you must make smart use of futures markets, insurance, contracting, machinery maintenance, emerging technologies, and labor management. You also take supporting courses in data analysis, international studies, biological sciences, social sciences, and written and oral communication. A number of agribusinesses offer internships that give you a chance to get some real business experience.

Many majors are challenged by such requirements as calculus and courses in the humanities and social sciences. Third- and fourth-year team and individual projects—which can sometimes conflict with off-campus employment or other activities—require long hours of work. But problem-centered assignments help you build a solid foundation for future employment.

Leading agricultural colleges may emphasize agribusiness, marketing, farm/ranch management, technology, natural resource economics, or statistics/econometrics, but most colleges offer courses in all these areas. If you are interested in other areas, such as international agricultural development or rural development, explore the catalogs or websites of various programs to see what they offer. If you want to combine an agribusiness degree with another field (for instance, wine grape production), examine course offerings and prerequisites in departments such as crop and soil sciences. The agricultural business major is also offered at the two-year associate degree level; the program is generally geared for transfer into a four-year agribusiness program.

Other majors you might like:
Economics
Business administration and management
Accounting
Agronomy and crop science
Animal sciences
Forest resources production
Range science
Agricultural and biological engineering
Geography
Farm and ranch management
International business
Aquaculture

Questions to ask colleges:
Does the program feature the latest technologies being applied to agricultural production?

What ties do the faculty members have to the industry? Are undergrads given assistance in finding internships?

Where have recent graduates gone to work?

Career options and trends:
Agribusiness manager or marketer*; farmer or rancher*; loan officer*; government agency employee; production supervisor; financial analyst; commodity merchandiser.

The long-term trend toward consolidation into fewer and larger farms is projected to continue, further reducing the number of jobs for farmers and ranchers but increasing employment opportunities for agricultural managers since owners of these farms rarely live on their land. Most graduates obtain jobs in business and industry. There is demand for managers and specialists trained in accounting, credit analysis, marketing, and international trade. Job prospects are generally good, especially if you are willing to relocate.

For more info:
United Agribusiness League
54 Corporate Park
Irvine, CA 92606-5105
(800) 223-4590
www.ual.org

Agricultural economics

What it's about:
The agricultural economics major teaches you to understand agriculture from both the national and the international perspective. You apply economic principles to the study of agricultural trends, productivity, investment, and the use and conservation of natural resources.

Is this for you?
You might like this major if you also like: social studies; math; business; government; working with numbers; looking at the big picture; environmental issues.

Consider this major if you are good at: critical reading/thinking; leadership; math; persuading/influencing; quantitative analysis; teamwork ...*or have...* initiative; verbal skills; writing skills.

Recommended high school prep:
English 4, math 4 (including precalculus), lab science 3, social studies 3, and a foreign language 3. If possible, take courses in computer science, economics, and statistics. A foreign language is especially helpful because agricultural markets are increasingly global.

Did you know...
...that most graduates in this major, contrary to popular belief, do not farm? While nearly 20 percent of all jobs in the United States are in the food and fiber industries, fewer than 3 percent of the employees in those industries actually work on a farm.

Typical courses in this major:
Accounting
Economics (micro and macro)
Statistics
Quantative methods in agricultural economics
Agricultural marketing and sales
Agricultural price analysis
Agribusiness management
Agricultural cooperatives
Agricultural finance
Agricultural policy
Commodity futures markets
International trade and finance
Agricultural and business law
Environmental resources development
Rural economic development
Professional career development

Concentrations:
Farm and ranch management; marketing; finance; environmental economics; rural development; international economic development.

What the study of this major is like:
Economics is the study of the way societies use available resources to meet people's needs. Since farming is the largest user of the earth's resources, agricultural economics is a wide-ranging field. You are most likely to benefit from the major if you have a broad educational background. Your general education courses may include English, speech, data analysis, chemistry, physics, economics, the natural and social sciences, history, literature, and the arts.

Many of the courses offered in this major are the same as in the agricultural business major, and sometimes it's hard to distinguish the two. Both majors cover economic principles, technical agricultural sciences, and business management tools. Whereas the agricultural business major provides management, operational, and production skills for business careers in the industry, agricultural economics focuses analytically on a broader range of issues to prepare you for graduate study or for careers in research and public policy as well as in business. You explore the relationship between agriculture and other sectors of the economy; you evaluate responses to economic problems created by the changing agricultural environment. You learn quantitative problem solving and qualitative reasoning, as well as how to make ethical judgments.

You also take upper-level electives in your chosen concentration, which may focus on public policy and regional development issues; natural resource allocation and environmental issues; management and production; or international trade. In many programs, a capstone project teaches you to debate concepts and integrate them into a wider perspective. Some colleges require you to do an internship or declare a minor. You may be able to earn college credit by participating in a study-abroad program.

You need good preparation in math and science to succeed in this major (students are often surprised by how much math is used in economics). Joining a student chapter of a national agricultural association will help you to learn more about the field, make valuable career contacts, and find internships and job opportunities.

This major is typically found in colleges of agriculture at land-grant universities; but similar programs are offered by other four-year private and public colleges, particularly in regions where agriculture is a significant industry. Admission and course requirements differ slightly among colleges. Some colleges combine agricultural business and agricultural economics into one program. There may also be differences in the areas of concentration offered.

Other majors you might like:
Agricultural business
Farm and ranch management
Agricultural education services
Environmental studies
Finance
Development economics
Mathematics
Statistics
Management information systems
Global studies
Public policy analysis
International business

Questions to ask colleges:
How much emphasis is placed on math and quantitative analysis?

How does the agricultural economics program differ from the agribusiness major? Are courses in the agricultural technical sciences included?

Is a senior capstone project required? What sort of projects have recent graduates submitted?

Career options and trends:
Agricultural statistician; agricultural consultant; government agency employee (e.g., USDA); financial analyst; bank manager or loan officer; sales representative; natural resources manager; public policy analyst; commodities broker, trader, or merchandiser.

The food and fiber industries are changing rapidly, because of corporate mergers and consolidations, the increasing reliance on telecommunications, and the growth of global trade and competition. As a result, companies want educated, productive, and flexible employees who can adapt in a rapidly shifting world market.

Demand for economists in general remains fairly constant, in good times and bad. Opportunities for agricultural economists in particular are increasing, as is the diversity, globalization, and high-tech nature of the profession.

Insider's viewpoint:
"I have enjoyed almost all the classes that are offered through this major, especially those dealing with commodities, farm planning, and managerial and decision-making economics. All of these classes deal with real-world situations; they are not all just about theories and concepts."

—Christopher, senior, University of Wisconsin

For more info:
Agricultural & Applied Economics Association
555 East Wells St., Suite 1100
Milwaukee, WI 53202
(414) 918-3190
www.aaea.org

Agronomy and crop science

What it's about:

This major provides the theoretical and practical knowledge needed for the efficient and sustainable production of food, fuel, feed, and fiber. You will gain a broad understanding of the diversity of, and relationships among, plants, soils, and climates. You will also explore the ethical, cultural, and environmental issues facing professionals in agriculture and natural resources.

Is this for you?

You might like this major if you also like: 4-H or FFA (Future Farmers of America) projects and competitions; Boy/Girl Scouts; science and math; the Weather Channel; gardening; outdoor activities; collecting or observing insects; seed collecting; issues relating to world hunger and the environment.

Consider this major if you are good at: attention to detail; critical reading/thinking; leadership; organizing; quantitative analysis; research; teamwork ...*or have...* initiative; manual dexterity; verbal skills.

Recommended high school prep:

English 4, math 3 (including precalculus), lab science 4 (including biology, physics, and chemistry), social studies 3, and a foreign language 2–3. Take as much math and science as you can, and a computer science course if available. Courses that help you develop good writing and oral communication skills are also important.

Did you know...

...that a farm background is not essential for a major in agronomy?

Typical courses in this major:

Plant pathology
Entomology
Pest management
Soil fertility
Weed science
Ecology
World food issues
Sustainable agriculture
Genetics
Weather and climate
Seed science and technology
Global climate change
Plant breeding
Crop management and production
Soil science
Statistics

Concentrations:

In college: agroecology; crop and soil management; plant breeding; pest management; seed production and technology; soil conservation; turfgrass management; climatology; biotechnology.

If you go on to grad school: agricultural meteorology; crop production and physiology, with specializations in seed science and weed science; plant breeding; and soil science, with specializations in soil chemistry, physics, morphology, genesis, biology, fertility, and management.

What the study of this major is like:

Agronomists work to provide consumers with a sufficient supply of food; to help producers increase profitability and efficiency; and to protect the environment. As an agronomy and crop science major, you learn how the plant and soil sciences are used in the production of abundant, high-quality food, fuel, feed, and fiber. Crop and plant sciences relate primarily to the genetics, breeding, physiology, and management of crops. Soil science covers the physics, chemistry, origin, microbiology, fertility, and management of soil. Majors also study weather and climate.

You generally begin with courses in soil science, crop production, botany or biology, geology, chemistry, English, and statistics. In addition, you study the physical and social sciences, communications, economics, and math. You'll be encouraged to take at least one course in plant pathology, entomology, weed science, and soil fertility/plant nutrition. As you learn more about the discipline, you may develop specific interests in crop science, soil science, or climatology. You can generally double-major (or minor) in agronomy/crop science and agribusiness, agricultural journalism, animal science, environmental sciences, or extension education.

Core courses (natural sciences, math, English, and social sciences) are usually taught in a lecture/lab format. Upper-level agronomy and crop science courses focus on problem solving, real-life situations, and professional competency. Integrated into the instruction is an emphasis on teamwork, leadership, communication, critical analysis, and management skills, as well as sustainability principles and ethical values.

Your course work is often supplemented by field trips, industrial tours, or seminars on agronomy issues. Majors can participate in regional and national contests with crop and soil judging teams. You are also encouraged to seek internships and summer/part-time employment in government agencies, agricultural businesses (seed, fertilizer, agricultural chemicals), conservation centers, pest control companies, or other areas relating to food, fuel, feed, and fiber production. You can generally earn academic credit for such work.

Colleges may vary in their emphasis on the role of science in response to world hunger and pollution. If you plan to go on to grad school, you generally need to complete an undergraduate program that stresses agronomic, biological, mathematical, and physical sciences.

Other majors you might like:
Forestry
Sustainable agriculture
Plant sciences
Atmospheric science
Plant protection/pest management
Range science
Soil science
Biochemistry
Agricultural and biological engineering
Genetics
Turf management
Agricultural education services

Questions to ask colleges:
Are internships and summer work opportunities available? When you evaluate a curriculum, you should take into account the availability of internships and exchange programs that provide work in the profession and study-abroad experiences.

Does the program provide learning experiences at a working farm or in a campus greenhouse?

Does the program include courses covering leadership qualities and skills, especially in communications, ethics, and decision-making?

Career options and trends:
Agricultural business manager*; plant breeder; seed production specialist*; environmental and natural resources manager; farm manager; government agency employee*; range management specialist; crop and soil management specialist; soil conservationist and surveyor*.

Demand for Agronomists is expected to be good. The need to provide sustainable sources of food, energy, and raw materials will grow as our global population grows, and this need will become even more pressing if the trend towards loss of arable land continues.

Agronomy is increasingly international— you should expect to travel during your career. The "green revolution" occurring in developing countries calls for expertise in seed physiology, soil science, and plant breeding, to counter the effects of pests, disease, and drought. The role of genetic engineering will increase in importance as well, and you should expect a greater emphasis on biorenewables and food management and safety practices.

For more info:
American Society of Agronomy
5585 Guilford Rd.
Madison, WI 53711-5801
(608) 273-8080
www.agronomy.org

Animal sciences

What it's about:
The animal sciences major deals with the breeding, raising, and management of livestock and poultry, and the foods and products obtained from them. The care and welfare of companion or captive animals may also be covered.

Is this for you?
You might like this major if you also like: working with large animals; biology; Animal Planet; working outdoors; physical challenges; 4H groups; farmwork.

Consider this major if you are good at: attention to detail; caring/nurturing; critical reading/thinking; math; organizing; quantitative analysis ...*or have...* initiative; patience; physical stamina; writing skills.

Recommended high school prep:
English 4, math 4 (including precalculus or calculus), lab science 4, social studies 3, and a foreign language 2–3. If available, take an advanced biology course.

Did you know...
...that this major is not for the squeamish? You have to be willing to get up close and personal with the animals, and not mind the aroma—or maybe even like it.

Typical courses in this major:
Animal behavior
Animal biology
Animal evaluation
Nutrition
Livestock management
Poultry science
Dairy science
Endocrinology
Genetics
Growth and development
Lactation
Livestock marketing
Reproductive physiology
Artificial insemination practices
Companion animal management
Meat science and processing

Concentrations:
In college: reproductive physiology; genetics and breeding; endocrinology; animal nutrition; animal behavior.

If you go on to grad school: reproductive physiology; genetics and breeding; endocrinology; animal behavior.

What the study of this major is like:
Like most science majors, you will spend at least 40 percent of your time in courses in the humanities, social sciences, natural sciences, and math—typically during your first two years. A solid foundation in the biological and physical sciences will help you get the most from the animal science courses you will take in your third and fourth years.

Biological concepts and animal science terminology are usually presented in lectures; you then get hands-on experience in class demonstrations and labs. You will also be encouraged (in some programs, required) to gain practice outside the classroom, by participating in an internship, research project, livestock judging competition, or extension work.

Because animal agriculture is a process that depends on cooperation among professionals and technicians, your courses will probably include teamwork activities. In fact, communication skills are essential in this discipline. You will also benefit from sharpening your understanding of math and chemistry. Most students who transfer out of animal sciences do so because they are having difficulty with one or both of these subjects.

Most colleges offer several options in the major: a production track, business/management track, science track, or preveterinary track. Colleges in regions with a livestock industry may focus on production systems and offer plenty of hands-on training. Colleges with strong research programs may emphasize the biology of animal growth and reproduction, biotechnology, and genetics. Some programs stress compatibility with the preprofessional requirements of veterinary medicine and human medicine, as well as with grad school requirements. A business option will emphasize agricultural economics.

If a species is prominent in the area around a college, its presence will likely be reflected in the expertise of the faculty and the courses offered. You can strengthen your ability to observe similarities and differences if you study not only the commonly found species but others as well.

Other majors you might like:
Zoology
Livestock management
Wildlife and wilderness management
Veterinary technology
Biochemistry
Aquaculture
Dairy science
Entomology
Food science
Microbiology
Poultry science
Agricultural and biological engineering

Questions to ask colleges:
Does the program have adequate resources, including labs and animal facilities, to provide practice in the animal handling skills you will need professionally? Access to facilities in which you can study meat, dairy, and other food processing and testing is also desirable.

Are there opportunities to participate with faculty members in their research programs? Such experiences are essential if you wish to go on to a graduate or professional program.

Career options and trends:
Livestock production manager*; artificial breeding technician; research technician; vocational agriculture teacher; sales representative for agricultural supplier*; extension agent; farm or ranch manager; veterinarian*.

According to the Bureau of Labor Statistics, employment in this field is projected to be strong, growing faster than average through 2022.

For certain positions, such as consulting work, it may be desirable or necessary to be certified by ARPAS (American Registry of Professional Animal

Scientists). To become a veterinarian, you must obtain a doctorate of veterinarian medicine (D.V.M.) and pass a licensing exam.

An understanding of environmental issues associated with animal production; concerns about animal welfare; and a sense of the ethical issues associated with animal product development are increasingly important to animal scientists. Global issues, such as growing populations, decreasing arable land, and climate change, will create opportunities for innovative professionals.

Insider's viewpoint:
"I liked being able to apply to real life the knowledge I gained through my classes. It's enjoyable to consult with a farmer on the best way to manage his dairy cattle, or to help a horse owner formulate a diet for her dressage horse."

—Kristen, senior, University of Maryland

For more info:
American Society of Animal Science (ASAS)
PO Box 7410
Champaign, IL 61826-7410
(217) 356-9050
www.asas.org

Equestrian studies

Also known as:
Equine studies

What it's about:
This major deals with horses and horsemanship (in Latin, *equus* means "horse"). You learn the scientific principles needed for the care, breeding, and conditioning of horses; the business principles needed for managing horse-related enterprises and facilities; and the equitation and training skills needed for teaching horseback riding and for training horses.

Is this for you?
You might like this major if you also like: horses and horseback riding; working outdoors; sports and competition; tutoring; business activities; taking care of animals.

Consider this major if you are good at: attention to detail; caring/nurturing; coaching; counseling; memorizing; organizing ...*or have...* a sense of responsibility to your work; initiative; patience; physical stamina.

Recommended high school prep:
English 4, math 3, lab science 3, social studies 3, and a foreign language 2–3. If available, take anatomy and physiology.

Typical courses in this major:
Equine anatomy and physiology
Equine nutrition
Equine breed types and selection
Stable management
Equine lameness and disease
Stud farm management
Equine breeding lab
Equine business management
Equine health management
Management of equine events
Equine breaking and training
Equitation (riding) classes
Care and prevention of athletic injuries
Teaching horsemanship
Entrepreneurship

Concentrations:
Equine business management.

What the study of this major is like:
As an equestrian studies major, you learn to understand the horse and its role in society today. If you have little familiarity with horses, you take handling and riding courses and gain practice in caring for horses and horse tackle. If you are more experienced, you are taught how to break and train horses, instruct riders, and ride at an advanced level (such as dressage and jumping). To learn how to live and work responsibly with horses, all majors study the animal's history and its health and safety needs. Most likely, you will also explore various horse-related enterprises, such as feed sales, racing, breeding, and equine publications.

In general, programs allow students at all levels to be stimulated by their course work. You typically begin with general science courses (for example, biology and chemistry) and then specialize, taking courses in anatomy and physiology, equine breeds, and types and selection. In higher-level courses, such as a breeding lab, you apply what you learn. Equitation courses (involving actual horseback riding) are also taught at beginning, intermediate, and advanced levels.

Many programs offer a two-year associate of science or applied science degree. You can usually choose one of three tracks—equestrian, equine science, or equine business management. In the equestrian track, you concentrate on horsemanship, teaching, and training skills, as you prepare to enter the field of horse training and riding instruction. The science and business tracks generally prepare you to transfer to a four-year program.

In a four-year program, a concentration in science and preveterinary courses focuses on biology, chemistry, math, and equine health and breeding and usually leads to a Bachelor of Science degree. An equine management track includes business subjects and stresses industry-oriented courses, such as stable or stud farm management, equine economics, and equine marketing. At some colleges, equestrian studies (or equine science) is offered only as a concentration in an animal sciences program.

Other majors you might like:
Animal sciences
Physical education
Horse husbandry/equine science
Veterinary technology
Wildlife and wilderness management
Sports and fitness administration
Athletic training
Biology
Zoology
Entrepreneurial studies

Questions to ask colleges:
What are the graduates of the equine degree program doing in the industry now? The answer should indicate whether the program is a strong one.

Career options and trends:
Horse care technician; assistant manager/trainer; farrier (individual who shoes horses); riding instructor; equine massage therapist; veterinarian; biomedical technician; nutritional consultant; pharmaceutical representative.

Jobs as a professional horse trainer are very hard to come by; graduates might find positions as assistant trainers at best, or, more probably, as managers, assistant managers, and grooms. Graduates with a solid science background can investigate alternative career opportunities in the biomedical field and in the pharmaceutical and nutritional industries.

Today, horses represent a larger financial commitment than in years past. As a result, employers in the industry look for better-educated, more qualified personnel than previously.

Insider's viewpoint:
"I look at every student and every horse similarly. Each is an individual that needs support and the freedom of self-expression in order to grow and realize his or her full potential."

—H. Jerry Schurink, Director of Equine Studies, University of Massachusetts Amherst

For more info:
United States Pony Clubs, Inc.
4041 Iron Works Parkway
Lexington, KY 40511
(859) 254-7669
www.ponyclub.org

Farm and ranch management

What it's about:
By combining courses in economics, business, and agriculture, this major prepares students to manage a farm, a ranch, and other rural businesses and to do commercial and professional work related to agriculture.

Is this for you?
You might like this major if you also like: working outdoors; using equipment; rural communities; team sports; animals.

Consider this major if you are good at: attention to detail; critical reading/thinking; organizing; quantitative analysis; research; teamwork *...or have...* initiative; manual dexterity; physical stamina.

Recommended high school prep:
English 4, math 3, lab science 3, social studies 3, and a foreign language 2–3. Three years of vocational agriculture is recommended, if available; as well as two years of computers and speech, and an accounting course.

Typical courses in this major:
Introduction to agricultural economics
Microeconomic theory
Marketing agricultural products
Principles of farm and ranch management
Equipment operation and maintenance
Financial management in agriculture
Accounting principles
Animal health and nutrition
Feedlot management
Livestock production
Advanced farm and ranch management
Agricultural price analysis
Agricultural commodity futures
Agricultural policy
Macroeconomics of agriculture
Rural entrepreneurship

Concentrations:
Crop production; animal husbandry; agricultural mechanization; agricultural marketing.

What the study of this major is like:
Your course work in this major provides a foundation in accounting, finance, marketing, management, economics, and technical production and/or processing. You use computer applications to integrate what you learn into a comprehensive set of entrepreneurial skills. Although you will be expected to study subjects in a number of academic and technical disciplines, you will have flexibility when it comes to identifying your specialty field.

At some colleges, the program emphasizes accounting and a traditional farm and ranch management–oriented curriculum. At others, more attention is placed on technical applications; some colleges may relax their focus and teach general rural entrepreneurship. And while some cover a variety of business, economic, and technical subjects, others stress the application of those subjects to a comprehensive business plan. Programs may also vary in the extent to which they explore risk management.

This major provides opportunities for you to learn and apply business and economic principles, concepts, and tools to a broad spectrum of rural management areas. Career opportunities include the operation of your own farm, ranch, or other rural business; professional farm and ranch management; and agricultural real estate appraisal. During college, you can benefit from interning with a rural lending institution or business.

Other majors you might like:
Range science
Agronomy and crop science
Veterinary technology
Animal breeding
Dairy science
Sustainable agriculture
Mining and mineral engineering
Entomology
Heavy equipment maintenance
Operations management
Turf management
Entrepreneurial studies

Questions to ask colleges:

What are the experiences and interests of faculty members who teach the core courses?

What computer resources are available, and how are they used in the curriculum?

How are "real-world" professionals involved in the program? People employed in rural management can help prepare you for challenges you may face in your career.

Career options and trends:

Farmer*; rancher*; business owner or manager*; farm/ranch appraiser; rural loan officer*; consultant; farm machinery company representative.

The number of self-employed farmers and ranchers continues to decline; farm/ranch consolidation, increased agricultural productivity, and the high cost of running a farm or ranch are all contributing factors.

However, many small-scale farmers have developed niche markets in horticulture and organic food production, which is among the fastest growing segments of agriculture.

If you are good at integrating business, economics, and technical expertise, you may be able to take advantage of other types of rural entrepreneurial opportunities that are increasing. A growing number of small-scale farmers have found success in "niche" (closely targeted) markets, organic farming, farmers' markets, and agricultural and marketing cooperatives. In fact, organic farming, while still a small part of the overall U.S. food supply, is one of the fastest-growing sectors in agriculture.

For more info:

National FFA Organization (formerly Future
   Farmers of America)
P.O. Box 68960
6060 FFA Drive
Indianapolis, IN 46268-0960
(317) 802-6060
www.ffa.org

Food science

What it's about:

In the food science major, you integrate and apply your knowledge of chemistry, biology, nutrition, and engineering as you learn to preserve, process, package, and distribute foods that are wholesome, affordable, and safe to eat.

Is this for you?

You might like this major if you also like: science and math; cooking; hands-on learning; working individually or in teams; applying scientific principles to real-world problems.

Consider this major if you are good at: attention to detail; critical reading/thinking; quantitative analysis; research; teamwork *...or have...* initiative; lab skills; manual dexterity; verbal skills.

Recommended high school prep:

English 4, math 4 (including precalculus), lab science 4 (including chemistry, biology, and physics), social studies 3, and a foreign language 2–3. Chemistry is essential; courses in health and nutrition are helpful if available.

Typical courses in this major:

Introduction to food science
Agricultural economics
Food chemistry
Food microbiology
Food engineering
Packaging and distribution
Nutrition
Dairy foods processing
Plant foods processing
Meat processing
Food laws and regulations
Sensory analysis
Food quality control and management
Unit operations

Concentrations:

Food chemistry; food-processing technology; packaging; safety and quality assurance; sensory evaluation; food microbiology; food engineering; nutrition.

What the study of this major is like:

Food science is an interdisciplinary program. It brings together principles from the natural sciences, the social sciences, engineering, and business to shed light on the nature and characteristics of food and the nutritional needs of people of various ages, cultures, and lifestyles.

The first two years of a typical food science program consist of required core courses in general chemistry, organic chemistry, and biochemistry; biology; general microbiology; physics; calculus; statistics; human nutrition; communications; and humanities. Most courses have a practical, hands-on laboratory work or project assignment in which you put into practice the facts and concepts you've learned in the classroom.

The course of study is rigorous, but it lays a solid foundation for the food science courses you take in the third and fourth years. Because scientists, technicians, producers, and business people work together in the food industry, you need to develop good communication skills and to understand the differing perspectives these individuals represent.

In upper-level courses, you learn and apply technology to the sanitary processing, preservation, storage, and marketing of foods. You become skilled at using food science instruments and processing equipment. You also receive extensive training in laboratory techniques. Internships with industry or government agencies provide valuable experience.

Special emphasis may vary among colleges, depending on the particular strengths of the faculty members or the needs of local industry. Programs that stress basic science, as it applies to food and food ingredients, focus on food microbiology, food chemistry, or food engineering. Other programs are more commodity-oriented; they focus on dairy processing, meat processing, or plant processing. You may be encouraged to take a minor concentration in food marketing, consumer education, nutrition, business, or economics.

Other majors you might like:

Food and nutrition studies
Dietetics
Agricultural and biological engineering
Animal sciences
Dairy science
Plant sciences
Agricultural business
Microbiology
Chemical engineering
Biotechnology
Restaurant/food services management
Culinary arts and chef training

Career options and trends:

Food technologist; research and development scientist; quality assurance manager; food inspector; process engineer; packaging technologist.

A graduate degree (master's or doctorate) is required for a position as a research scientist or extension food technologist.

Employment can be found with manufacturers of retail food products, as well as with companies that supply food ingredients, processing equipment, and packaging materials, or are involved in institutional food service. Positions are also available in various government agencies and in independent testing laboratories.

Prospects are generally good in this field, even during economic downturns. According to the Bureau of Labor Statistics, employment in this field is projected to be strong through 2022. Job growth will be driven in part by the demand for new food safety measures, and heightened public awareness of diet, health, food safety, and biosecurity issues.

For more info:
Institute of Food Technologists (IFT)
525 West Van Buren, Suite 1000
Chicago, IL 60607
(800) 438-3663
www.ift.org

Horticulture

What it's about:

Horticulture is a diverse field that includes plant biology, physical sciences, systems management, and the arts. Horticulturists study fruits, vegetables, herbs, trees, shrubs, flowers, and ornamental perennials and annuals, as well as the operation and management of field and greenhouse production, and the design and construction of gardens and landscapes.

Is this for you?

You might like this major if you also like: being outdoors; working with your hands; the arts; science; gardening clubs; arboretums; the environment.

Consider this major if you are good at: attention to detail; caring/nurturing; creativity; critical reading/thinking; math; memorizing; organizing; spacial thinking/analysis; teamwork ...*or have...* manual dexterity.

Recommended high school prep:

English 4, math 3, lab science 3 (including biology, chemistry, and physics), social studies 3, visual arts 1, and a foreign language 2–3.

Typical courses in this major:

Plant biology
Plant propagation
Plant taxonomy and identification
Soil science and plant nutrition
Plant genetics
Greenhouse management
Floriculture production
Vegetable production
Nursery management
Organic and sustainable plant production
Fruit production
Viticulture (grapes and wine making)
Plant physiology
Landscape design
Plant pathology
Entomology

Concentrations:

In college: floriculture; environmental horticulture; ornamental horticulture; field crops; nursery management; greenhouse operations; landscape design; fruit crops.

If you go on to grad school: plant breeding and genetics; plant pathology; environmental plant physiology; horticulture management.

What the study of this major is like:

As a horticulture major, you study the biological and physical sciences as they relate to plants and plant growth (the effects of temperature, light, moisture, and nutrition) and to the environment. You will probably be required to take general and organic chemistry, and math at least through trigonometry. You should also expect to take a computer systems course.

Because many graduates eventually take on managerial positions, curricula often include horticultural business management and economics. You are encouraged to develop problem-solving and quantitative reasoning skills. To help you learn the techniques of sustaining production systems, your course work combines principles of biological sciences, ecology, and horticultural technology. You usually concentrate in one of the following:

General horticulture is the study of crops, including fruits, vegetables, and herbs.

Landscape design and construction trains you in plant materials, irrigation control, and other aspects of landscape maintenance.

Floriculture examines the production, marketing, and use of cut flowers and potted plants. You learn about plant breeding, nutrition, disease, and insect pests; effects of the environment on plant growth; floral design; and interior plantscaping.

Olericulture/vegetable science covers the production and marketing of vegetables and herbs. You explore greenhouse, field, organic, and inorganic production techniques; plant breeding, nutrition, disease, and insect pests; and related human health issues.

Environmental horticulture teaches you about urban and natural landscapes. You learn how native plants are selected, produced, and installed to restore disturbed habitats. Environmental ethics and issues relating to sustainability are also covered.

Ornamental horticulture studies landscape and greenhouse crops, including trees, shrubs, potted plants, and foliage plants.

Greenhouse operations is the study of the construction and operations of greenhouses, with an emphasis on producing ornamental and vegetable crops.

Nursery operations focuses on the outdoor or protected production of ornamentals, perennials, fruit trees, and other crops.

Turfgrass management explores the production, marketing, installation, and maintenance of grasses used in golf courses, athletic fields, parks, and commercial and residential landscapes.

Although you learn horticultural basics in the classroom, your training involves plenty of hands-on work, such as greenhouse production or landscape design. In most programs, you get to know your professors and interact with students of diverse interests and ages. Horticulture clubs are often an important part of your academic (and perhaps social) life.

Generally, research horticulture is conducted at land-grant universities, which usually have good facilities and strong programs. The most significant differences among programs relate to the fact that horticulture generally focuses on crops specific to a state or a region. For example, you would not go to Minnesota to study banana production!

Other majors you might like:
Botany
Plant sciences
Forestry
Entomology
Natural resource conservation
Sustainable agriculture
Landscaping/groundskeeping
Turf management
Agricultural and biological engineering

Landscape architecture
Fine/studio arts

Questions to ask colleges:
Does the program utilize teaching greenhouses and field plots?

Which areas of specialization are available? If, like most entering students, you don't know which area of horticulture to pursue, you should look for a strong program that offers a range of possibilities.

Career options and trends:
Plant production manager; manager of garden center or retail florist; golf course or resort landscape manager; fruit or vegetable grower; greenhouse grower; nursery manager; landscape designer; organic producer; viticulturalist (wine grower); research technician.

According to the Bureau of Labor Statistics, horticulture is one of the fastest growing segments of agriculture and a great place to get started in the field. Opportunities exist in landscaping, ornamentals, organic production, health aspects of plants, and greenhouse operations. More efficient production often means more sophisticated techniques, so there is a market for well-trained, motivated, creative professionals. In an exciting trend, horticulture and education join forces to set up "children's gardens" as an imaginative method of teaching and learning.

For more info:
American Society for Horticultural Science (ASHS)
1018 Duke St.
Alexandria, VA 22314
(703) 836-4606
www.ashs.org

Soil science

What it's about:

Soil science applies principles of biology, chemistry, mathematics, geology, and physics to one of the most important and dynamic natural resources—often abused, sometimes reclaimable, and only slowly renewable. Soil science majors examine the nature and properties of soils and gain the skills needed for wise use, conservation, and management of this resource.

Is this for you?

You might like this major if you also like: nature and the outdoors; working with your hands; science and math; solving complex and multi-faceted problems; farming; gardening; environmental issues.

Consider this major if you are good at: attention to detail; critical reading/thinking; organizing; quantitative analysis; spacial thinking/analysis ...*or have...* initiative; manual dexterity; verbal skills.

Recommended high school prep:

English 4, math 4 (including precalculus), lab science 4 (including earth science, biology, physics, and chemistry), social studies 3, and a foreign language 2–3. If they are available, take a computer science course and an environmental science course.

Did you know...

...that soil is not just dirt, but a complex, varied ecosystem that makes up as much as one third of our environment? Critical for life, this natural resource is often taken for granted; but after years of being studied and put to a variety of uses, soils still hold many secrets for scientists to unlock.

Typical courses in this major:

General and organic chemistry
Quantitative soil analysis
Meteorology
Geology
Soil chemistry
Soil morphology, genesis, and taxonomy
Soils and land use
Soil fertility
Environmental soil management
Soil microbiology
Agronomic crop science
Soil contaminants
Plant and soil water relations
Soil physics
Introductory plant pathology
Hydrogeology

Concentrations:

Generally, none in college; but if you go on to grad school: soil microbiology; soil chemistry; soil mineralogy; soil physics; soil conservation; soil management; soil fertility; forest soils; land reclamation.

What the study of this major is like:

Soil scientists have prime responsibility for determining the distribution of soils on the landscape, assessing their characteristics, and predicting their suitability for different purposes. Professionals also help promote practices that will conserve or reclaim soils. Majors learn to describe soils in the field, recognize their uses and limitations, and make recommendations for erosion control, reclamation practices, water movement, and soil improvement.

Soil science is sometimes a concentration within agronomy and crop science; geology and earth science; environmental science; or natural resources and conservation majors. Whether you major or concentrate in soil science, you need a solid foundation in chemistry, biology, physics, and mathematics, along with courses in the humanities and the social sciences. Courses in geology, geography, economics, plant sciences, statistics, nutrition, and genetics are often recommended or required.

In your first and second years, you may be discouraged by the emphasis on university core and basic science courses—soils are hardly mentioned. But if you master the basics, you will likely be rewarded later: in upper-level, soil-oriented courses, you will be expected to apply what you've learned earlier.

Because many courses are in lecture-laboratory format, you will spend more hours a week in class/lab than students who take only lecture classes. On the other hand, you generally learn more through hands-on experimentation and probably have to spend less out-of-class time reading and writing.

You are usually encouraged (if not required) to do summer internships and/or part-time work with field soil scientists. Many organizations that employ graduates—such as contractors, mining companies, government agencies, power companies, and landscaping firms—also offer summer internship opportunities.

Relatively few colleges, other than the land-grant state universities, offer the number of credit hours in soil science needed for certification or licensure as a soil scientist. Among those that do, some may emphasize agronomic applications, and others may focus on environmental aspects; but generally there are few differences. Look for a program that is strong not only in soil science but also in the basic sciences.

Other majors you might like:
Horticulture
Environmental science
Natural resources and conservation
Agronomy and crop science
Landscape architecture
Microbiology
Range science
Agricultural and biological engineering
Botany
Farm and ranch management
Geology/earth science
Biochemistry

Questions to ask colleges:
Does the program have a soil judging team? This competitive activity helps you solidify your understanding of soil morphology, classification, interpretations, and landscape distribution, and provides a way to meet other people in the field.

Are the teaching labs well equipped for soil analysis? Are agricultural research stations, as well as farm, forest, and/or range lands, close by and accessible?

Career options and trends:
Soil surveyor*; researcher; field soil scientist with federal or state agricultural or environmental agency, or with private industry*; environmental consultant; soil chemistry consultant; hazardous waste specialist.

Several states require certification or licensing in order to practice as a professional soil scientist. Requirements vary but usually involve taking a certification exam and three to five years of experience.

Soil scientists find more jobs in nonagricultural areas than agricultural. Traditionally, most jobs were in government agencies, but opportunities have been growing in the private sector, especially in environmentally related fields. Overall, the number of job opportunities is much greater than the number of graduates in this field.

Insider's viewpoint:
"I interned with a field soil scientist to run soil transects and update the soil surveys in Delaware. I worked outside almost every day in the summer, investigating the different soils in the lower part of Delaware, and scientifically classifying these soils so that they can be mapped and correlated."

—Kristin, sophomore, University of Delaware

For more info:
The Soil Science Society of America (SSSA)
5585 Guilford Rd.
Madison, WI 53711
(608) 273-8085
www.soils.org

Soil science education home page:
http://soil.gsfc.nasa.gov

Sustainable agriculture

Also known as:
Agroecology
Environmental agriculture

What it's about:
Sustainable agriculture is an ecological approach to farming that conserves and protects natural resources while profitably providing healthy food to local communities.

Is this for you?
You might like this major if you also like: science; working outdoors; community service; involvement with social justice or environmental issues. Most students in this major actually don't have much farming experience, but they usually enjoy working with others on socially meaningful projects, such as hunger awareness activities or farmland preservation workshops.

Consider this major if you are good at... synthesizing ideas; organizing; critical reading/thinking; advocating and persuading; doing research; writing...*or have...* initiative, creativity, a love of nature and a desire to help bring positive change in society.

Recommended high school prep:
English 4, math 3, lab science 3 (including biology and chemistry), social studies 3, and a foreign language 2–3. If available, take a course in environmental studies or ecology.

Did you know...
...that sustainable agriculture does not mean farming "the old-fashioned way" or rejecting modern technology? Rather, it combines the best practices of the past with current science and cutting-edge "green" technologies.

Typical courses in this major:
Principles and practices of sustainable agriculture
Agroecology
Cropping systems
Weed ecology and management
Integrated pest management
Soil science
Organic soil management
Organic vegetable and fruit production
Crop ecology
Watershed ecosystem analysis
Human nutrition
Land use history and planning
Resource and environmental economics
Environmental policy and law
Rural sociology
Agriculture and environmental ethics

Concentrations:
Entomology; plant pathology; agricultural economics; rural sociology

What the study of this major is like:
Since sustainable agriculture is as much a way of life as a system of farming, it is taught as an interdisciplinary major, blending agricultural, physical, environmental, and social sciences.

The program typically starts with a combination of basic science courses (biology, chemistry and plant science) and courses that will introduce you to the methods and concepts of sustainable agriculture, such as how to boost crops without chemical fertilizers, or how to protect against pests using natural, rather than synthetic, controls. You are also introduced to the social dimensions of agriculture, such as how to maintain family farms and how to establish and support local food supply chains.

Upper division courses go into more detail in these areas, and you will begin to work on projects that pull together what you have learned. Most colleges have a student farm, or provide hands-on internships, where you will have ample opportunities to put theory to practice.

Students participate in all levels of planning and operations on the student farm. They determine how much land will be planted with a variety of vegetable and herbs, based on the markets they are likely to have. They order seed, prepare the soil, and start transplants in the greenhouse. As classes wind down in the spring, they begin planting their vegetable seeds and transplants, then manage them throughout the summer (weeding, fertilizing, controlling pests). Harvesting begins when the earliest crops are ready, usually in mid-summer.

Some student farms operate a farm stand at their site, or participate in local farmers' markets. Others supply the college cafeteria with produce or sell to local restaurants. Many operate a Community Supported Agriculture (CSA) program, in which community members purchase a "share" of the farm's produce.

How this all works can vary at different colleges. Students may work under the supervision of an experienced farm manager on many student farms, or they may manage the farm themselves, with faculty and farm staff available for help and advice as needed.

Back in the classroom, you will be taught in a variety of styles, including traditional lectures and class discussion. There may also be a service-learning project, where you work in a group to help the local farming community

The main difference between colleges offering this major is whether their primary focus is on classroom science and theory, or on hands-on practical training. Many try to blend both approaches. Some offer training opportunities in such areas as tractor safety and repair, farm equipment maintenance and operation, or pesticide application certification.

Other majors you might like:
Agronomy and crop science
Farm and ranch management
Agricultural education services
Global studies
Plant protection/pest management
Urban, community, and regional planning
Agricultural and biological engineering
Botany
Food and nutrition studies
Solar energy technology
Environmental studies
Natural resources and conservation

Questions to ask colleges:
Is this major housed in a school of agriculture with special admission requirements?

How much contact will students have with working farms and farmers?

What opportunities exist for summer on-farm jobs?

What are recent grads doing now?

Career options and trends:
Farmer or farm manager*; organic farm certifier; agricultural educator*; Natural Resources & Conservation Service (NRCS) agent; crop consultant; community farm manager*; community food bank manager; agribusiness employee.

The U.S Department of Agriculture foresees strong growth in the sustainable agriculture industry, fueled by rising consumer demand for organic food and the growing trend to "buy local" produce. And because everyone must eat, employment of agricultural and food scientists is projected to be fairly stable even during difficult economic times.

For more info:
Sustainable Agriculture Research and Education
1122 Patapsco Building
University of Maryland
College Park, MD 20742-6715
(202) 720-5384
www.sare.org

National Sustainable Agriculture Information
    Service (ATTRA)
P.O. Box 3838
Butte, MT 59702
(800) 346-9140
http://attra.ncat.org

Architecture

A professor once gave his architecture class an assignment: to enter a national design competition for a memorial honoring those who had served in the Vietnam War. You may already know the rest. One student's vision was chosen unanimously by the experts and was built on the National Mall in Washington, D.C. The Vietnam Veterans Memorial was designed by a Yale University undergraduate, Maya Lin.

Of course, very few people start their careers so successfully. Lin created an inspiring physical environment in an urban park by integrating architectural and landscape design. What was once an ordinary space became a national treasure.

"Students who want to understand the connections between people and the environment and want to do something to improve the world" should consider majoring in architecture, suggests Professor John B. Wright of New Mexico State University.

"It is thrilling to recognize that the physical shape of our destiny is in our own hands," says Alfred D. Price, School of Architecture and Planning, State University of New York at Buffalo. "Good environmental design, sound planning, engaging architecture, responsible landscape design can, do, and will make a difference."

To learn architecture, you study many things: humanities, math, natural sciences, architectural history, graphics, design, photography, economic development, environmental planning, geography, and more.

You don't have to be a great artist to be an architect, but design is a big part of the program. Some schools are based more in studio art and creative expression, while other colleges take the engineering angle to solve problems through analysis. In between are colleges that do both.

"The median approach is one that integrates creative artistic responses with methodical analysis, the art and science of design, the poetic and the practical," notes Professor Michael Bednar of the University of Virginia. "The best way to assess the design philosophy is by speaking with faculty and students. Viewing student work is another useful means of assessing a school's design direction."

Still another helpful guide is the college's list of required courses for majors in architecture, planning, landscape, or environmental design.

That list will tell you what's covered in the degree program. Keep in mind that some bachelor's degree programs take five years. On the graduate level, concentrations include ecological planning, urban design, land use, building conservation, transportation, universal design, and community development. Among the emerging fields of study are environmental and sustainable architecture.

Your model campus

Okay, let's get real. You probably won't be designing a national memorial anytime soon. But you can plan your studies and prepare for work in the highly professional field of architecture. Some architects work for government or nonprofit organizations; some are employees of contractors, real estate developers, or engineering firms; many are independent professionals who are hired as consultants. Specific jobs include architect, landscape architect, neighborhood and community planner, industrial designer, conservator, graphic designer, and other careers. Employment prospects will be favorable for those with backgrounds in environmentally friendly and energy efficient design, as more and more buildings today are being built to "green" standards.

Look for architecture and related majors in schools of architecture, colleges of environmental design, colleges of arts and sciences or natural resource management; and departments of geography, landscape architecture, and public administration. You might even look at schools of engineering for some city planning studies.

And while you're comparing colleges, ask about the design studios. After all, you'll be spending plenty of time there working on projects.

"Students spend long hours individually designing their projects and making drawings and models to express their design intentions," explains Bednar. "Drawings are in all media from informal sketches to formal presentations."

Ask how often the design studios meet and if you can get into the studio after class. Are the studios equipped with state-of-the-art computer hardware and specialized software? What are the other facilities and libraries like?

The faculty's credentials may be an attraction at a particular college. Are professors accomplished, practicing architects? If so, what do their designs look like? Has the work of students in the department been recognized nationally in recent years as outstanding?

Do you have particular interests such as the environment, urban planning, historical preservation, or high-tech design? If so, look for colleges with those priorities. And see if the program is accredited. One accreditation to look for is by the National Architectural Accrediting Board.

And don't forget to think about your degree options. What is the first degree you'll earn? Is it an accredited professional degree or a preprofessional degree that will qualify you to apply to grad school? Will your undergrad program take four or five years? For each type of degree, you'll want to find out about the requirements and the career options.

Important sources of information include the American Institute of Architects at www.aia.org; the Association of Collegiate Schools of Architecture at www.acsa-arch.org; the American Planning Association at www.planning.org; and the American Society of Landscape Architects at www.asla.org.

One last thing: be ready for a pretty competitive field if you choose to study an architectural major. Maya Lin only got a B in that class!

Architecture

What it's about:
Architecture majors prepare for the professional practice of architecture by learning how to design buildings and other aspects of the built environment.

Is this for you?
You might like this major if you also like: drawing; photography; making models; crafts of all kinds; science; art; history; cities; landscapes.

Consider this major if you are good at: creativity; critical reading/thinking; organizing; persuading/influencing; quantitative analysis; sketching ideas; spacial thinking/analysis *...or have...* initiative; manual dexterity; visual sensitivity.

Recommended high school prep:
English 4, math 4 (including precalculus), lab science 4 (including physics), social studies 4, visual arts 1, and a foreign language 3–4. If they are available, courses in environmental science, drafting/technical drawing, and computer science are also recommended.

Did you know...
...that artistic talent is not essential to be successful in this major?

Typical courses in this major:
Architectural history
Architectural graphics
Design fundamentals
Architectural design
Architectural theory
Construction materials and methods
Structural design
Environmental controls
Site design
Engineering mechanics
Computer-aided design (CAD)
Construction economics

Concentrations:
Generally, none in college; but if you go on to grad school: historic preservation; urban design; environmental design; architectural engineering.

What the study of this major is like:
The architecture major combines courses in the liberal arts and sciences with architecture. Along with technical and design skills, architects must understand the culture they work in (humanities), the physical world (physical sciences), and human relations (social sciences). They must also be familiar with the history of art and architecture.

After two years of liberal arts, you begin studying architecture by taking courses in visual and graphic skills. Courses in history and theory of architecture teach you how the built environment was formed, and the role of related disciplines.

The most important courses in every architecture program are the design studio courses. In beginning studios, you learn to design objects, furniture, and rooms. Intermediate studios stress the design of small buildings, such as museums, libraries, and schools. In your final year, you design larger buildings for urban areas.

In the studio, you work on a series of projects. Your instructor assigns a project, outlines expectations, and provides resources. As you develop your design, you benefit from group feedback from fellow students. The project itself, which includes drawings and models you've created in various media, will be evaluated by faculty members for its strengths and weaknesses. Studio work can also include field trips, documentation, photography, interviews, research, model making, and graphic analysis. Your work is supported by classes in construction technology, computer graphics, and design theory.

Be ready to spend long hours on your projects. The studio is both a supportive and a competitive environment—design work is stimulating, spontaneous, and often difficult. To be successful, you need to be resourceful and to have good critical-thinking and time management skills. You will also need to become technically savvy with 3D modeling tools and other design software.

Programs can take different approaches to architectural design. In one approach, based in studio art, you are encouraged to express yourself creatively. In an opposite, engineering-oriented approach, you analyze the needs of a project and evaluate various solutions. Balanced programs, which emphasize both the art and the science of design, combine artistic responses and methodical analysis. But even balanced programs can vary: some may use historical models; others may draw on cultural philosophies; still others may favor social or environmental ethics. You may have difficulty telling how a college approaches architectural design if the focus is not clearly stated in the catalog. The best way to find out is to speak with faculty members and students and to view student work.

In order to work as a professional architect, you need to be licensed by the state where you will practice. Requirements vary from state to state, but generally you must satisfy both an educational and internship requirement, and pass an examination. A professional degree from a school with a program accredited by the National Architectural Accrediting Board (NAAB) will satisfy any state's educational requirements.

Other majors you might like:
Civil engineering
Architectural history /criticism
Historic preservation
Real estate
Environmental design
Industrial design
Drafting and design technology
Housing and human environments
Physics
Interior design
Construction management
Marine engineering /naval architecture

Questions to ask colleges:
How are the design studios set up?

How often do they meet and how many students are in each section?

Is the studio space you are assigned available to you exclusively, 24/7?

What role do computers play in the studio process?

Do the faculty members practice architecture?

What kind of buildings have they designed?

Career options and trends:
Architect; urban planner; landscape architect; architectural historian; graphic designer; industrial designer; construction manager.

Recently, more architects are working for contractors or real estate developers as employees than as independent professionals that are hired as consultants. Many also work for public agencies or for corporations as in-house architects.

Employment opportunities for architects are expected to grow faster than average through 2022, in order to meet the needs of a growing population. Architects with knowledge of sustainable design will be in particular demand because of environmental concerns and rising energy costs.

Insider's viewpoint:
"The combination of the poetic and the practical, the art and the science, is what has always attracted me to this field. An architect needs to use both sides of the brain simultaneously to produce good architectural design."

—Professor Michael Bednar, University of Virginia

For more info:
Association of Collegiate Schools of Architecture
1735 New York Ave., N.W.
Washington, DC 20006-5292
(202) 785-2324
www.acsa-arch.org

Environmental design

What it's about:

This major will prepare you to design public and private spaces, indoor and outdoor, in a way that shapes, restores, preserves, and sustains both the built and the natural environments. It can also ready you for professional practice as an environmental designer or architect.

Is this for you?

You might like this major if you also like: drawing; nature study; natural and physical sciences; joining volunteer activities; model-building; computers; crafts; photography; cities; landscapes. Most students in this major share a passionate concern both for the environment and for people.

Consider this major if you are good at: attention to detail; creativity; critical reading/thinking; math; organizing; spacial thinking/analysis; teamwork *...or have...* manual dexterity; patience; writing skills.

Recommended high school prep:

English 4, math 4 (including precalculus), lab science 4 (including biology, chemistry, and physics), social studies 4, visual arts 1, and a foreign language 3–4. Drawing (freehand) is important. A course in computer-aided drafting is helpful, since much of your college course work will use that technique, but it's not required.

Typical courses in this major:

Architectural and landscape drawing
Behavior and environment
Materials and methods
Construction technology
Environmental control systems
Urban history
Computer-aided design
Landscape design
Community planning
Architectural history
Landscape ecology
Law and urban land use
Site systems and engineering
Geographical information systems (GIS)
Restoration and reclamation ecology
Facilities planning and design

Concentrations:

Landscape and horticultural design; urban planning and design; facilities planning; designing for universal access; designing for special populations (elderly, physically-challenged, etc.).

What the study of this major is like:

In this major, you study the various aspects of the environment from a design point of view. You learn to consider the built, natural, and human components of space and place holistically. Your goal will be to create designs for structures and spaces that harmonize these components, while meeting the requirements of function, environmental safety, and ecological sustainability.

For this reason environmental design is an interdisciplinary major that combines creative concepts in architecture, landscape, interiors, and environmental graphics (signs and information boards) with courses covering social science, health science, environmental science, and physical science.

These topics are taught through a combination of lecture courses, research seminars, field assignments, and studio workshops. In your first two years of study, you'll fulfill your college's general education requirements in the liberal arts and sciences, along with required introductory and foundation courses in environmental design. In your third and fourth years you will spend almost all your time on upper-level elective courses within a concentration of your choice, such as urban and regional planning or landscape design.

What's most distinctive about this major are the studio or workshop courses. They require a far greater time commitment than usual—for both class work and projects outside class. Especially in your third and fourth years, you'll understand why design students are known for burning the midnight oil.

Workshops and internships introduce you to real-world exercises in planning and design. You might work with a local public, private, or nonprofit organization to analyze the economic, social, political, and design issues involved in a community planning or development project. Or you might work hands-on in a machine and assembly shop, learning about construction methods and materials.

In the studio, you'll learn that for any given problem, there is no single solution, as there is in math or chemistry. Designers continually revise their concepts, each time seeking to refine and improve their ideas. Critical-thinking skills, good judgment, and the capacity for reflection and healthy self-criticism are key to success.

An environmental design program can usually be distinguished from ones taught at other colleges by its primary focus. Some programs emphasize traditional physical design; others feature research-based design for special-needs populations; still others stress community-based approaches to planning.

Programs that highlight physical design are usually found in schools of architecture, interior design, landscape design, or possibly engineering (for industrial or product design). Programs at colleges that are more research-oriented will have formal research centers that are doing important new work, and that work should be described on their websites. Programs that are geared toward planning and policy (which are most common) are closely allied with departments of city/urban/regional planning.

Other majors you might like:
Landscape architecture
Interior design
Urban studies
Parks, recreation, and leisure studies
Environmental studies
Historic preservation
Industrial design
Geology/earth science
Construction management
Land use planning
Housing and human environments
Drafting and design technology

Questions to ask colleges:
Are there specialized, dedicated computing facilities for environmental design majors, or is access shared with all other students at the campus computing center?

Are the program's design studios equipped with state-of-the-art hardware and software?

Does the program use faculty members or administrative staff as academic advisers for undergraduates?

Has any student work received national recognition in recent years?

Career options and trends:
City or community planner*; neighborhood housing specialist; architect; interior designer; landscape architect; construction manager*; facilities planner/manager*; real estate developer.

All architects must be licensed, as must most landscape architects and interior designers, depending on the state in which they intend to practice.

Because there are relatively few graduates in this field, employment prospects are good. However, demand for designers and planners is greatest where populations are growing, so it might be necessary to relocate in order to find a job. In recent years, the employment opportunities have been most notable in the South, the West, and the Southwest, particularly in environmentally-conscious development and sustainable areas.

For more info:
Environmental Design Research Association
  (EDRA)
1760 Old Meadow Rd.
Suite 500
McLean, VA 22102
(703) 506-2895
www.edra.org

Landscape architecture

What it's about:

Landscape architecture explores contemporary issues related to the design, planning, and management of the constructed landscape. You learn fundamental techniques of site design and planning and receive studio training in advanced areas such as urban and regional landscape design and planning.

Is this for you?

You might like this major if you also like: tackling environmental concerns; environmental art; gardening; arboretums; outdoor activities; drawing and graphic expression.

Consider this major if you are good at: active listening; attention to detail; creativity; critical reading/thinking; organizing; quantitative analysis; spacial thinking/analysis; teamwork ...*or have...* initiative; verbal skills.

Recommended high school prep:

English 4, math 3, lab science 4 (including physics), social studies 3, and a foreign language 2. If possible, take a year of computer drafting, one to two years of art, and a business course.

Did you know...

...that landscape architecture can range from designing a skateboard park to an entire wilderness area? It's not just about the trees and shrubs around buildings.

Typical courses in this major:

Fundamentals of design
Computer-aided drafting (CAD)
Landscape planning
Landscape design
Landscape technology
Graphic communications
Applied ecology
Landscape construction
Plant materials
Plant identification
Plane surveying
Landscape architectural history
Landscape architectural theory

Concentrations:

Landscape restoration; landscape technology; ecological planning.

What the study of this major is like:

Landscape architects plan, design, and manage outdoor settings, such as parks and areas around buildings, to make these displays useful, beautiful, and in harmony with nature. As a landscape architecture major, you work with the land: drawing, painting, and mapping it; describing it; examining and analyzing it; and imagining what it might become in the future. You learn about the complex ecology of natural landscapes and the even more complex human ecology of urban landscapes.

Landscape architecture is a studio-based program that requires you to become thoroughly familiar with the ways in which natural vistas can be created or changed. First you learn traditional techniques of site planning and design, including drawing and computer graphics, and the principles and vocabulary of design. In addition to the studio curriculum, you take courses in graphic communications, history and theory, materials, and professional practice. You study ecological systems, learn to identify and work with a broad range of locally grown plants, and analyze the relationships between social and political institutions, on the one hand, and the land, on the other.

Later you study advanced techniques that include urban design, landscape technology, and regional planning and analysis. Building on your foundations, you shape increasingly complex landscapes and develop detailed drawings, specifications, and other means of bringing your plans to life. In a typical studio course in your third or fourth year, you might design a park, a public garden, or a plaza; plan a site for an apartment house or a sports arena; or develop a management program for a natural reserve. In construction courses, you learn how to produce the detailed drawings for projects like these.

As a major, you might join college organizations devoted to environmental issues, urban design, and regional landscape awareness. You can often find volunteer opportunities that include mentoring high school students about landscape architecture. Some students participate in community planning groups. At the conclusion of a four- or five-year program, you should be qualified to enter the profession, with a private firm or a public agency.

Landscape architecture departments differ a great deal in the approach they take to the major. Some programs focus on physical design, while others concentrate on sustainability and regeneration (to protect natural settings and to ensure their survival). Still other programs stress both physical design and ecological issues. Geographic and social distinctions may also influence the focus of a particular program. Programs at colleges in cities are more likely to devote themselves to urban landscape design than programs in suburban or rural areas. Another reason for differences in programs is that some colleges encourage faculty members to conduct research, whereas in other programs, instructors spend more time in professional practice. Finally, some programs are based on a four-year curriculum and award a Bachelor of Science in Landscape Architecture (B.S.L.A.), while others offer a five-year degree, the Bachelor of Landscape Architecture (B.L.A.), which requires you to complete additional studio and lecture courses.

Other majors you might like:
Environmental design
Environmental studies
Landscaping/groundskeeping
Horticulture
Land use planning
Mining and mineral engineering
Urban forestry
Graphic design
Parks/recreational/leisure facilities management
Environmental engineering
Botany
Turf management

Questions to ask colleges:
Does the program offer a degree in four years or in five years? What is the academic focus of the program? What are the professional and academic activities of the faculty members?

Career options and trends:
Landscape architect; landscape construction manager; political advocate; urban planner; environmental agency manager; natural resource manager.

Most states require landscape architects to be licensed or registered, based on the Landscape Architect Registration Examination (LARE) and one to four years work experience. Some states also require an additional state-specific exam focusing on local laws and environments.

Most graduates of landscape architecture programs work in private consulting firms as designers, planners, or managers. Landscape architects can also work in city planning, recreation, and parks departments at the local level and in land management agencies such as the National Park Service, National Forest Service, and Bureau of Land Management at the federal level. In addition, the training you receive in landscape architecture provides a foundation for other careers related to shaping the environment, such as landscape restoration.

Employment prospects are projected to be strong especially in planning and development of new construction and reconstruction. However, new graduates may face strong competition for entry-level jobs. Demand for landscape architects will be driven by growth in development, the need to comply with environmental regulations and security requirements, and continued efforts to restore and preserve lands, wetlands, and ecosystems.

For more info:
American Society of Landscape Architects (ASLA)
636 Eye Street, N.W.
Washington, DC 20001-3736
1-888-999-2752
www.asla.org

Urban, community, and regional planning

What it's about:

The urban, community, and regional planning major focuses on creating livable, responsibly financed, and environmentally healthy communities. You learn about transportation, economic development, housing, land-use regulations, infrastructure management, and preservation of parks and other open spaces. Planners shape surroundings that are appropriate to the needs of urban, suburban, or rural residents.

Is this for you?

You might like this major if you also like: the outdoors; maps; architecture; history; working with people; exploring cities and small towns; environmental and social causes; community service activities.

Consider this major if you are good at: attention to detail; creativity; organizing; persuading/influencing; spacial thinking/analysis; teamwork *...or have...* initiative; patience; verbal skills; writing skills.

Recommended high school prep:

English 4, math 3, lab science 3, social studies 3, and a foreign language 3–4. If possible, also take classes in geography, environmental issues, statistics, and computer applications.

Typical courses in this major:

Planning theories
Planning practice
Regional studies
Technology of urban life
History of cities
Urban and landscape design
Social issues
Land use regulation and law
Transportation planning
Economic development
Community development
Housing
Environmental planning
Geographic information systems (GIS)
Cartography
Field/design project

Concentrations:

Generally, none in college; but if you go on to grad school: land use regulation; transportation planning; urban design; community development (including housing, economic development, and social issues).

What the study of this major is like:

To create a livable community, planners must reduce conflicts between competing interests (real estate developers and residents, for example) and ensure that the development is fiscally, structurally, and environmentally sound. As an urban, community, and regional planning major, you explore such topics as physical and environmental geography, urban studies, transportation, land use and real estate law, community development and economic development, mapping, statistics, economics, history, political science, and human geography.

In this major, courses are mostly in lecture format, although there are some design classes. Your course work will cover a range of tools and techniques—from computer modeling to group decision-making; from statistical programming to brainstorming and values clarification. You will often work in groups, addressing difficult questions as a team: Can a community learn to recycle, conserve resources, and protect wildlife? Are a community's transportation systems appropriate for conditions anticipated in the next hundred years? How can a city upgrade the standard of living of its low-income residents? How can conflicts be resolved between developers and architectural preservation groups? How can volunteer groups, corporations, and governments work together to solve problems? Together with your team, you may visit project sites and tour development areas.

Generally, majors do internships with public planning agencies, nonprofit groups, or private businesses. Independent projects (usually research papers) are also common. Students often have the most trouble with "spatial thinking"—understanding how the landscape is structured and how communities function. After a few required courses, though, most students catch on. Group projects and small classes tend to create a friendly, supportive environment.

Planning programs may be housed in departments of geography, landscape architecture, or public administration, or in their own department. Planning programs tend to break down into three areas of concentration: urban, rural/regional, and environmental. Although all programs focus on land use regulations, the first two approaches emphasize distinct types of communities, and environmental planning deals with issues like pollution, environmental impact statements, cleanup of toxic waste sites, and natural hazards such as flooding and earthquakes. Because planning overlaps with many other fields, you may double-major in planning and another subject, or minor in a related field.

Planning is a hands-on major—you learn to analyze a situation, to imagine a better one, and to determine how to bridge the gap. Planning offers you a career in which you can conserve nature and help build a better world.

Other majors you might like:
Civil engineering
Urban forestry
Emergency management/homeland security
Landscape architecture
Land use planning
Historic preservation
Housing and human environments
Environmental design
Public administration
Urban studies
Political science
Sociology

Career options and trends:
Land use planner; geographic information systems director; transportation planner; grant writer; housing coordinator; parks/open space planner; architect; cartographer.

Planners also find work in local government agencies dealing with zoning and community/economic development; fish and game agencies; and parks, transportation, and environment departments; in federal agencies such as the Forest Service, Environmental Protection Agency, Defense Mapping Agency, Housing and Urban Development, and Natural Resources Conservation Service; in environmental consulting companies, engineering firms, real estate companies, land development companies, and surveyors' offices; and in nonprofit groups such as the Nature Conservancy, Trust for Public Lands, and American Farmland Trust.

With cities and rural areas growing in all regions of the country, there is a high demand for planners in the United States. Employment prospects will be best for those with a masters degree as well as those with strong technical skills, and also for planners who can help communities prepare for both natural and man-made disasters.

Insider's viewpoint:
"All-time famous misperception about the major: planning equals architecture. Planning is a very political field, and the program recognizes this in its courses. If you don't like politics, you might not like planning."

—Kacey, senior, Cornell University

For more info:
American Planning Association (APA)
1030 15th St., NW, Suite 750 West
Washington, DC 20005-1503
(202) 872-0611
www.planning.org

Area, ethnic, and gender studies

At first glance, these majors seem to be devoted to the interests of a minority of people. Not so. These studies embrace the vast majority of the world's population.

"The primary objective of the curriculum, regardless of race or color, is education for positive and productive citizenship," says R. Baxter Miller of the University of Georgia's Institute for African American Studies. "One would see oneself as a thoughtful and creative agent of cultural transformation and change—a guardian of the true implementation of American democracy."

From the studies of indigenous peoples to those from faraway lands, these majors help students understand other cultures and their own.

"Most students don't realize the inextricable connections between the Middle East with our own Western history and traditions—we are in fact part of the same civilizational unit," says Professor Bernard Haykel of New York University. "By engaging in Middle Eastern studies, one acquires an entirely novel way of looking at one's own identity and develops a much broader understanding of the world we live in."

In some majors, such as Latin American studies, language is central. "To me the most important aspect of this field is the opportunity to learn about and communicate with a variety of peoples and cultures," says Professor César G. López of Scripps College.

The women's studies major cuts across many cultures. Women hold up half the sky, as the Chinese proverb goes. The major explores gender, sexuality, power, inequality, racism, class issues, oppression, and the connection between these topics.

The area, ethnic, and gender studies majors cover everything imaginable—history, culture, language, literature, anthropology, political science, religion, the arts—you name it. If these subjects appeal to you, you might check other sections in this book: Humanities, Languages, Multi/interdisciplinary studies, Religion and theology, Social sciences, and Visual and performing arts.

"The American studies major enables students to understand the world around them from a variety of perspectives," says Daniel Horowitz of Smith College. "It enables students to understand how the nation's history, literature, arts, politics, and society illuminate their nation's experiences."

The culture of work

Okay, let's look at these studies from the shameless, self-serving, capitalistic perspective of what they can do for you. Fortunately, many of the subjects taught in area and ethnic majors translate to valuable job skills. For example, "area studies" means just what it sounds like, the study of a particular region of the world. Such majors are great preparation for jobs with companies that do business in the region being studied. It's a big plus in today's multicultural workplaces and in the expanding global markets, especially Asia.

If you speak an Asian language, Arabic, or Spanish, you automatically have a marketable skill. "Spanish is today the second language in the United States after English," says López. "There is a big demand for teachers at all levels. In some states, the knowledge of Spanish is necessary for medical personnel (especially pediatricians), lawyers, and social workers."

Clearly, Middle Eastern experts are also in demand. "In the post-9/11 world, and because of the political and economic turbulence in the Middle East, the United States, at the level of the public and private sectors, will be intensely engaged in the region for years if not decades to come," says Haykel. "Persons with language and other skills pertaining to the Middle East will easily find gainful and rewarding employment."

In addition to language, critical thinking and human understanding are aspects of these majors that are essential in professions including communications, law, teaching, public service, social services, labor relations, business, counseling, Foreign Service/diplomacy, and humanitarian work.

When choosing a school, look for colleges of arts and sciences or liberal arts, and divisions of humanities or social sciences. While you're at it, see how the college balances the humanities and the social sciences. Is the curriculum mostly language-based or does it focus more on history and political science? If the emphasis is on history, the courses may concentrate on a time period, such as the Middle Ages or the present. If the focus is on language, look into the quality of the school's language labs. Also, what are the library holdings to support your studies and research? Will you be studying abroad as a requirement or as an elective?

Ethnic and gender majors are so broad that no one college can cover them all. Check the core requirements to get a feel for the program. Do the courses build on one another? Is the major supported with its own department? How many full-time faculty members are in the department? Are they prominent, published scholars? Do the professors teach undergraduates?

Oddly, no matter which of these diverse majors you may choose, your studies will be influenced by a dead white guy, Socrates. The Greek philosopher's method of teaching was to ask the class questions. Students learned through participation and conversation, and that's how these majors are often taught. The technique makes the quality of the faculty even more important.

African-American studies

Also known as:
Black studies

What it's about:
The major in African-American studies includes the history, politics, traditions, literature, art, and lives of North American peoples of African descent. Traditional assumptions about race are tested and examined to help students make enlightened choices for themselves and their society. The primary objective of this major is to prepare all students, regardless of race or color, for positive, productive citizenship.

Is this for you?
You might like this major if you also like: community involvement; reading; debating; travel; foreign languages; sports; music; dance; theater; politics.

Consider this major if you are good at: caring/nurturing; creativity; critical reading/thinking; leadership; persuading/influencing...*or have...* initiative; verbal skills; writing skills.

Recommended high school prep:
English 4, math 3, lab science 3, social studies 4, and a foreign language 2–3. Courses in government, economics, music, and art are also recommended.

Did you know...
...that in business and government, there is an increasing demand for graduates trained in multiculturalism? In a society in which power is distributed unequally, multiculturalists can mediate disputes between individuals or communities of different ethnic or racial backgrounds.

Typical courses in this major:
American history to 1865
African-American politics
History and cultures of Africa
Multiculturalism in modern America
Modern African-American experience
Caribbean history and society
Christianity and colonialism in Africa
African-American religions
African-American society
African-American folklore
African-American poetry
Modern African literature
African-American music
Women in African-American cinema
Seminar in race and ethnicity

Concentrations:
In college: African-American history; African-American language, literature, and art; social and political inquiry.

If you go on to grad school: African-American literature; African-Hispanic literature; African-American drama; African-American psychology, African-American sociology, African-American religions.

What the study of this major is like:
African-American studies is an interdisciplinary major in the liberal arts and social sciences. You learn through a Socratic method that takes place within a human laboratory of constant challenges. Learning reveals a discrepancy between tradition and dissent in American life; a vitality of diversity in redefining the ideal of freedom. Majors develop the ability to communicate highly charged cultural and emotional issues into well-reasoned proposals subject to logical debate and resolution.

Your introductory courses examine the history of African-Americans, prepare you for interdisciplinary work, and place black history in the context of world history. You examine the works of anthropologists, economists, political scientists, psychologists, theologians, and sociologists. In most introductory courses, you also study music, dance, and the arts of African-Americans.

Throughout the program, the emphasis is on how people of color see themselves and how others see them. You examine the heritage of slavery from the perspectives of both the slaveholder and the slave: you are asked to reconcile opposing viewpoints, sort out the emotions and motivations of whites and blacks alike, explore your own feelings about race, and reach a balanced conclusion about the effects of slavery on whites and blacks today.

Advanced courses, which build on this introduction, provide in-depth analysis and allow you to develop a concentration reflecting your interests.

Courses in art and literature cover such topics as slave and folk songs of the mid-nineteenth century; the Harlem Renaissance of the 1920s; contemporary rap; the poetry of Langston Hughes, Margaret Walker, Gwendolyn Brooks, Sonia Sanchez, and Amiri Baraka; and the stories, novels, and other works of Frances Harper, Richard Wright, Jean Toomer, Ralph Ellison, James Baldwin, Alice Walker, and Toni Morrison.

Courses taught from a historical, sociological, and political viewpoint explore the impact of social class, status, and power relations on African-Americans, as members of the current social structure and as descendants of the African diaspora (forced migration). After studying such issues as the civil rights movement, affirmative action, the role of African-American women, and urban families, you examine ways of turning theory into public policy. Most programs require you to take one or two courses in the history and cultures of the African continent.

Programs can usually be distinguished by the emphasis they give to politics, humanities, and the social sciences. One program may stress the formulation of public policy, whereas another focuses on theory. One may take a somewhat radical approach; another, a more traditional one. Some may emphasize arts, literature, and drama; others may focus on social and multicultural issues; still others may be stronger in history. You can probably learn about a program's orientation by speaking with graduates and faculty members.

Other majors you might like:
African studies
Latin American studies
Chicano studies
Jazz studies
American literature
Intercultural /diversity studies
Islamic studies
Caribbean studies
Women's studies

Urban studies
Anthropology
Sociology

Questions to ask colleges:
How do faculty members and majors interact in and out of class? Which events and activities help majors bond as a unified group?

Which outstanding graduates in the discipline have come out of the program in the last decade or so?

Career options and trends:
African-American studies prepares students for careers in education, social service, public administration, business, and a range of other areas. It is also excellent preparation for graduate or professional study in law, business, religion, medicine, or social work.

As the population becomes more diverse, multiculturalists, who can explain reasons behind conflicts, help create bonds among employees, and strengthen the body politic by promoting education and equality, will be of increasing value to society.

Insider's viewpoint:
"It's only in my ethnic studies classes that I've learned about the Civil Rights movement, the brown power movement, the women's rights movement, and gay liberation. This is all stuff that the departments called history don't teach."

—Ronald, senior, University of California: Berkeley

For more info:
National Council for Black Studies
University of Cincinnati, Africana Studies
   Department
P.O. Box 210370
Cincinnati, OH 45221-0370
(513) 556-0785
www.ncbsonline.org

Association for the Study of African American Life
   and History
Howard Center
2225 Georgia Ave., NW, Suite 311
Washington, DC 20059
(202) 238-5910
www.asalh.org

American studies

What it's about:

The American studies major uses a wide variety of materials and approaches to give you a comprehensive understanding of American society and values. As an interdisciplinary program, it integrates courses in American history, literature, popular culture, and contemporary social concerns.

Is this for you?

You might like this major if you also like: the History Channel; movies; talk radio; studying media and popular culture; biographies; debating; antiquing; traveling and sight-seeing; learning about people who are different from you.

Consider this major if you are good at: creativity; critical reading/thinking; research *...or have...* curiosity; initiative; self-motivation; sense of adventure; verbal skills; writing skills.

Recommended high school prep:

English 4, math 3, lab science 3, social studies 4, and a foreign language 3.

Did you know...

...that, in this major, you often analyze forms of cultural expression, such as songs, novels, magazines, and movies?

Typical courses in this major:

American civilization
Women in American society
American literature
American film
The American wilderness
American art and architecture
American folklore
Ethnicity in America
American regional cultures
Religion in America
American music
American popular culture
American eras
Contemporary America
American political culture
Native American cultures

Concentrations:

In college: ethnic studies (including a focus on specific groups); media studies; popular culture studies; gender and/or gay and lesbian studies.

If you go on to grad school: American literature; American history; cultural theory.

What the study of this major is like:

American studies is an interdisciplinary major that relies on a number of approaches to study the United States. Although history and literature were once the focus of the field, the major now also draws on such disciplines as sociology, anthropology, political science, African-American studies, film studies, women's studies, theater criticism, and music. By analyzing the United States in terms of, for example, region, ethnicity, gender, and class, you learn to understand the world around you from a variety of perspectives, including that of trans-nationalism, the ways in which people and ideas cross national borders. While programs vary according to faculty strengths and college requirements, all have a common aim: to explore American society and values, past and present.

Among the typical core courses are those focusing on a chronological period (the 1890s; the 1960s), a topic (the West; individualism and community), or a scholarly approach (literary criticism; cultural analysis). In your first and second years, you usually take survey courses that trace American society from colonization to the present. Topics in the first semester may include immigration (history), the rise of American architecture (art), and the evolution of colonial politics (political science), all as part of the study of pre-Revolutionary society. In the next semester, you may focus on family life and urbanization (sociology), the rise of advertising (history), and the origins of American realism in the 1880s and 1890s (art and literature).

During your third and fourth years, you are likely to concentrate on a few subjects. You consult with

74

a faculty adviser and develop an area of interest. In history and literature (a popular concentration), for instance, your course work might include political history, modern literature, and film. To explore American pluralism (the nation's diverse population), you can enroll in courses on ethnic studies, sociology, religion, and history. Majors are usually stimulated by this interdisciplinary approach—you may gain a greater appreciation of literature, art, and film by studying the country's political and economic development.

American studies programs usually include fourth-year seminars (or capstone courses), which build on your previous work. Although these seminars vary from one program to the next, most use in-depth readings to examine the development of American society and culture. In some programs, you can also pursue a special research project.

The interdisciplinary focus of American studies encourages you to spend a good deal of time with other undergrads and with faculty members. Instructors are usually easy to talk to, and classes tend to be relatively small. Thus, the strong bond with other students you are likely to develop should make the program as enjoyable as it is useful.

Other majors you might like:
American literature
Political science
Sociology
Art history
Anthropology
African-American studies
Women's studies
Latin American studies
Geography
Native American studies
Chicano studies

Questions to ask colleges:
What are the core requirements in the program? Most strong programs have core courses that bring together the diverse fields the major draws from. Also, it is good to have some flexibility when choosing your courses.

Are the primary loyalties of the faculty members (as teachers, advisers, and program developers) to American studies rather than to other fields?

How extensive are offerings in American history, American literature, fine arts, film studies, African-American studies, Hispanic-American studies, sociology, women's studies, and American government?

Career options and trends:
High school teacher; writer; journalist; literary or media critic; political consultant.

Many graduates with American studies degrees are employed in helping professions (such as social service), museums, historical societies, and communications. Communications fields such as the media, Internet, advertising, television, and film attract graduates who can interpret American culture from a variety of perspectives. With graduate or professional training, majors can pursue careers in higher education (college teaching), museum administration, law, medicine, public policy, and business.

Insider's viewpoint:
"I don't know how many times I've heard people say, 'Oh, what's American studies? The study of America?' A lot of people think it's a basket-weaving discipline, but I've gotten a lot of calls from potential employers who didn't care what I studied, they just cared that I studied it well."

—Michael, senior, University of Colorado

For more info:
American Studies Association (ASA)
1120 19th St., N.W.
Suite 301
Washington, DC 20036
(202) 467-4783
www.theasa.net

Asian studies

What it's about:

The major in Asian studies is designed to provide a background in Asian languages and cultures. Programs may concentrate on one area of Asia (Japan, China, Korea, Southeast Asia, or South Asia) or focus on a comparative study of the entire region. Students usually study an Asian language and take a range of social science and humanities courses to gain insight into Asian societies, history, politics, and economics.

Is this for you?

You might like this major if you also like: exploring other cultures and societies; travel; new experiences; learning a foreign language; art; literature; mythology; learning about philosophies and religions.

Consider this major if you are good at: attention to detail; memorizing; research ...*or have*... curiosity; verbal skills; writing skills.

Recommended high school prep:

English 4, math 3, lab science 3, social studies 4, and a foreign language 4.

Typical courses in this major:

Asian language (I, II)
Religions of India
Buddhist thought and values
Introduction to Asian art
Classical Asian civilizations: China and Japan
Asian politics and economic development
Masterpieces of Asian literature
Political philosophy in Southeast Asia
Japanese art and culture
Chinese calligraphy
Modern Japan
The Chinese-American experience
Political power in contemporary China
Premodern Japanese literature
Music of Asia
Tibetan civilization

Concentrations:

An Asian language; East Asian literature; South Asian literature; politics and history; anthropology; geography; art history.

What the study of this major is like:

In the major in Asian studies, you study the languages, cultures, religions, societies, politics, and economic characteristics of all of Asia or one of its primary subdivisions: Japan, China, Southeast Asia, or South Asia. The program usually includes interdisciplinary courses that survey a wide range of topics in the social sciences and humanities, providing you with an historical and contemporary overview of the region. With this background, you choose additional courses in fields such as history, anthropology, political science, art history, literature, and religion.

Programs may cover traditional aspects of Asian culture, the impact of the prominent religions (Hinduism, Buddhism, Islam, Taoism, and Shinto), the history of art (architecture, music, literature, and film), the role of women, and interaction with the West.

Central to any program is the study of an Asian language (for example, Chinese, Japanese, Korean, Thai, Hindi). All programs require at least two semesters (most require four) of language study. Learning the language will enrich your appreciation of the cultures of Asia. Intensive summer programs in the United States and Asia, together with one-year programs in Asia, enable you to obtain additional language training and practice. Many Asian studies programs encourage students to spend a summer or a year in Asia. The experience can be very rewarding.

In general, work in Asian studies builds a feeling of solidarity among fellow majors. In addition, faculty members, who share a commitment to increasing your knowledge about and contacts with Asia, tend to be accessible and supportive. With more than half the world's population and the fastest-growing economies, Asia will be a dominant force in the twenty-first century. Asian studies majors are likely to find opportunities to help foster understanding and to enhance communications between Asian and Western societies.

Other majors you might like:

Asian-American studies
Chinese

Linguistics
Anthropology
Archaeology
Geography
Global studies
Religious studies
Islamic studies
International business
International relations
Art history

Career options and trends:
International trade consultant; importer/exporter; journalist; Foreign Service officer; ESL teacher.

Graduates in Asian studies often pursue careers in education, government, journalism, communications, international business, the travel industry, and international law. Teachers with special knowledge of Asia are needed at graduate, undergraduate, and secondary levels. There are positions in government agencies (State Department, development agencies, CIA) and in private foundations and international agencies. Businesses, particularly banks, seek Asia specialists to work overseas; international law firms also provide opportunities for Asia generalists and specialists. As is usually the case, the more language training you have, the more job opportunities will be available to you.

Insider's viewpoint:
"I like interesting stories, so Asian history, culture, and politics really fascinate me. There is so much that has happened in Asia in the past fifty years, not to mention the wealth of history that dates back as far or farther than some of the more widely recognized cultures."

—Min, senior, University of California: Berkeley

For more info:
Association for Asian Studies
825 Victors Way, Suite 310
Ann Arbor, MI 48108
(734) 665-2490
http://www.asian-studies.org

Chicano studies

Also known as:
Mexican American studies

What it's about:
This major is an interdisciplinary, comparative exploration of the history, sociology, politics, culture, and economics of Mexican-origin communities in the United States, studied within a regional, national, and global context. The field also examines other Latino and indigenous populations of the Americas, and the ways they influence Chicano communities.

Is this for you?
You might like this major if you also like: community involvement; reading; talking about social justice issues; music, dance, theater, and art; Chicano/Latino culture; languages. Students who see themselves heading for the "helping professions" or wish to give back to their communities are often attracted to this major.

Consider this major if you are good at: attention to detail; creativity; critical reading/thinking; leadership; organizing; research *...or have...* initiative; patience; verbal skills; writing skills.

Recommended high school prep:
English 4, math 3, lab science 3, social studies 4 (including history and geography), and a foreign language 3–4. If available, economics and sociology are also recommended.

Did you know...
...that Chicano studies is not an "identity, feel-good" major for Chicanos only? While it may be particularly advantageous for Mexican-American and other *raza* students to learn about their history and cultures, non-Latinos can also benefit from exploring one of the fastest-growing populations in the United States.

Typical courses in this major:
History of Chicano Los Angeles
Recent Chicano literature
Farmworker movements, social justice
Chicano folklore and oral tradition
Contemporary Chicano theater
Music of Latin America
Chicana feminism
Barrio popular culture
Immigration and Latino identity
Border consciousness
The Mexican mural
Health in Chicano/Latino populations
Mexican Americans and U.S. education
U.S.–Mexico relations
Bilingual writing workshop
Interracial dynamics in American society

Concentrations:
Generally, none in college; but if you go on to grad school: Barrio, community and urban studies; Chicano languages and literature; political, economic, and social issues; Chicano/Latino history and culture; Chicano/Latino music, art, theater

What the study of this major is like:
Topics in this major cover a wide range of issues. You'll study both the history of Mexican-origin peoples and the conditions in which they are living today—primarily in the United States but also across North America and around the world.

You'll explore this group from within, by looking at its literature, art, music, theater, oral history, and folklore. And you'll also explore the group from an external focus, by looking at the way the U.S. society and government has treated Chicanos over time. During this exploration you'll compare how the experience of Chicanos is similar to or different from the experiences of other groups in the United States and elsewhere in the world.

In Chicano studies, majors analyze the world with an eye toward social justice, and the scholarship emphasizes social change, social ethics, and equity. The program focuses on the real world; a service learning component, included in many of your courses, involves interaction with the Chicano community. Even as an undergraduate, you'll have an opportunity to engage in research training.

Some students are challenged by the breadth of the field and its interdisciplinary nature—they may have difficulty synthesizing the various perspectives. And this major does not shirk the hard issues—the focus on inequality, stereotypes, and discrimination can be unsettling at first.

Most programs encourage students to be scholar-activists (in the sense of being civically engaged); as a result, extracurricular activities, volunteerism, and commitment to the community are emphasized. Many programs also expect students to participate in academic advising and governance, as part of their responsibility for their own education and development, by taking part in departmental committees and student senates, or by designing student-initiated courses.

Where this major is housed within a college (under social sciences, humanities, or the arts) can affect the content and curriculum of the program. The geographic location of the college itself is also important to consider—having access to large concentrations of Chicanos in Los Angeles, for example, as opposed to smaller communities elsewhere, can make a difference in the service learning and civic engagement aspects of the program. At some colleges, courses might be taught in English, Spanish, or bilingually, and some programs require a Spanish (or Mexican-indigenous) language competency.

Other majors you might like:
Anthropology
Sociology
Urban, community, and regional planning
Intercultural/diversity studies
ESL teacher education
Latino studies
Journalism
Caribbean studies
Latin American studies
Native American studies
Labor studies
Geography

Questions to ask colleges:
How many students take this major?

How often are required courses offered?

Will I meet with a faculty adviser or a counselor? How often is this person available?

Are classes normally large or small?

Career options and trends:
Chicano studies (like most liberal arts majors) is not "vocational" preparation for an occupation. It is as useful in the job market as most other liberal arts majors (history, English, etc.). Since most Chicano studies majors are bilingual and biliterate, however, they are attractive job candidates in many fields, especially business, education, and government. Majors often go on to graduate or professional school to prepare for careers in law, health and medicine, teaching, and social work.

Insider's viewpoint:
"I love this major because for the first time in my life I feel empowered. I love learning about my own history, but at the same time learning about others who have also been marginalized and the struggles they face."

—Robert, senior, University of California: Los Angeles

For more info:
National Association for Chicana and Chicano Studies (NACCS)
P.O. Box 720052
San Jose, CA 95172-0052
www.naccs.org

Mujeres Activas en Letras y Cambio Social
www.malcs.org

European studies

What it's about:

European studies is an interdisciplinary major for students who want to increase their understanding of the languages, cultures, societies, history, and economics of the peoples of Europe and European civilization, from antiquity to the present.

Is this for you?

You might like this major if you also like: learning a foreign language; reading; travel; exploring different cultures; history; politics; current events; art; music; philosophical discussions.

Consider this major if you are good at: critical reading/thinking; languages; research ...*or have...* initiative; verbal skills; writing skills.

Recommended high school prep:

English 4, math 3, lab science 3, social studies 4, and a foreign language 4. Courses in music, art, government, and economics are also recommended.

Typical courses in this major:

Greece and Rome
Cities of Europe
Medieval Europe
United States and the European Economic Union
Post-Communist Russia
Baroque art
Indo-European comparative mythology
European cinema
Folk music of Eastern Europe
Irish nationalism
Modern Britain
Women in Italian culture
The Mediterranean world, past and present
Don Quixote
Dante's *Divine Comedy*
The Third Reich and the Holocaust

Concentrations:

Comparative literature; international relations; government and politics; history and culture of a particular country (for instance, Italian studies, Russian studies), region (Mediterranean, Scandinavian), or historical period (the Renaissance, Europe since 1945).

What the study of this major is like:

The study of European civilization—past and present—is a vast interdisciplinary undertaking. It covers several millennia of political, social, and economic history; the development of art, music, religions, philosophy, and literatures in more than a dozen languages; monumental contributions to science, mathematics, and technology; and the study, often comparative, of politics, religion, philosophy, and the arts in present-day Europe. If you find a wide variety of topics and disciplines to choose from liberating rather than overwhelming, then this major might be a good choice.

Usually you are introduced to this wealth of material in one of two ways: in a survey course in European civilization, or in a course that deals with a particular era of European history (the Renaissance, the Age of Reason, the Romantic period) or with the culture of a single country in modern Europe (France, Germany, Spain). Occasionally, both approaches are used. You also begin to fulfill the language requirement—most programs expect you to take a language (other than English) through the intermediate level.

Within a framework that ensures that you acquire both a historical and a contemporary perspective, you are given wide latitude to work out the rest of your studies. In other words, you will mostly design the major yourself, to fit your own interests, talents, and background.

For example, if you have studied Latin and have an interest in the medieval period, you might take further work in Latin and courses in the history, philosophy, theology, and literature of the Middle Ages. Or if you know some German and enjoy reading about Germany today, you can, after basic work in economics and comparative politics, focus on the challenges of reunification. Perhaps you have learned Polish at home; after preparation in history and comparative politics, you might concentrate on Poland's transition from a socialist country under the former Soviet Union to a democracy. As another example, if examining the relationships between music, painting, and literature in early-twentieth-century Europe appeals to you, why not obtain the needed background in music and art history and complete the major with appropriate courses in the humanities?

European studies programs may recommend, or even require, that you spend a semester or a year (usually the third year) in Europe. Living and studying in Europe and using a language other than English (except in the United Kingdom and Ireland) can be an extraordinary experience. Colleges that do not have a study-abroad program usually honor work taken under the auspices of another institution. Or you can enroll at a European university whose credits will transfer to your college at home.

You may be required, in your final year, to complete a capstone project related to your area of concentration. Most likely, you will do a research paper or thesis, based on independent study or on participation in a seminar.

Other majors you might like:
International business
Linguistics
Anthropology
History
Geography
Global studies
Tourism/travel management
Journalism
Architectural history/criticism
Classics
Medieval and Renaissance studies
Art history

Questions to ask colleges:
Does the program include a study-abroad semester or year with an affiliated European university? Are the costs comparable to those for your college at home? Do students remain registered while abroad, and do all credits earned overseas count toward the major and general degree requirements?

Is there an adviser to help students design their areas of concentration?

Can students "test out" of the language requirement? Can the language requirement be fulfilled by study abroad in a university in which the instruction is not in English?

Career options and trends:
The European studies major is not designed to lead to any particular profession, but rather to prepare you for a wide variety of careers. Government service, international business and finance, travel and tourism, journalism, law, management, public relations, teaching—are all possible career paths. Many of these careers require graduate or professional study, for which the major is a strong foundation.

For more info:
Council for European Studies
420 West 118th St., MC 3307
New York, NY 10027
(212) 854-4172
www.councilforeuropeanstudies.org

Latin American studies

What it's about:

Latin American studies is an interdisciplinary major that provides you with comprehensive training in the Spanish and Portuguese languages, as well as Latin American literature, history, politics, geography, anthropology, art and music, and economics.

Is this for you?

You might like this major if you also like: traveling; Hispanic culture; history; learning about international politics and trade; discovering connections across subject areas; languages.

Consider this major if you are good at: attention to detail; creativity; critical reading/thinking; leadership; learning languages; organizing; spacial thinking/analysis; teamwork *...or have...* initiative; verbal skills; writing skills.

Recommended high school prep:

English 4, math 3, lab science 3, social studies 4 (including history and geography), and a foreign language 3–4. If they are available, economics and sociology are also recommended.

Did you know...

...that the most widely spoken indigenous language in the Americas is Kechwa (also spelled Quechua), the language of the Incas? About a quarter of the population of Peru still speaks Kechwa, and for many it is the only language they speak.

Typical courses in this major:

Introduction to Latin American studies
Latin American history
Latin American economics
Latin American geography
Latin American art
Latin American anthropology
Latin American literature
Current Latin American politics
High civilizations of the Americas
Peoples and cultures of modern Latin America
Latin American environmental issues
Colonial rule in Latin America
Revolutionary change in Latin America
The United States and Latin America

Concentrations:

Economics; history; political science; Spanish literature; Portuguese literature; geography; sociology; anthropology; international business; particular geographic areas.

What the study of this major is like:

As a Latin American studies major, you examine the diverse area in the Western Hemisphere that stretches from Mexico to the southern tip of Chile and Argentina. Some programs also include the islands of the Caribbean. You focus on the region's evolution and its relationship to other parts of the world, particularly the United States. Because the major is interdisciplinary, it makes use of courses and faculty members from a number of departments. For example, by taking courses offered by the departments of art history, political science, and ecology, you look at Latin America from artistic, political, and environmental perspectives.

All Latin American studies majors begin with a core of social sciences, natural sciences, and humanities requirements (such as math and English composition), along with courses specific to Latin America. After getting an overview of the region, you choose a concentration—usually from such disciplines as anthropology, political science, sociology, history, geography, business, agriculture, journalism, art history, government, ecology, Portuguese, or Spanish.

Some programs require you to take your concentration in one department (for example, Mexican history within the history department). At other colleges, concentrations may cut across departments (such as a Latin American business and economics concentration that draws from business and economics departments).

Most likely, you will be required to take at least two years of either Spanish or Portuguese—the chief languages of Latin America (Portuguese is the language of the continent's largest nation, Brazil). Languages such as Kechwa, Kaqchikel Maya (still spoken in Guatemala), and Haitian Creole (a mixture of European and Native languages) may also be available. You are encouraged to study for a summer, semester, or year in Latin America, in a program sponsored by your own or another college. Some students double-major—in Latin American studies and, for example, geography, economics, history, or political science.

Your courses vary in size, and language courses are generally small. The major typically attracts U.S. and foreign students, from both Hispanic and Anglo cultures, and you can expect to interact with a diverse group of people. In many programs, Portuguese is not stressed as much as Spanish. Also, some programs have a strong emphasis on literature and culture, while others focus on politics and international economics.

Other majors you might like:
Chicano studies
Spanish
Portuguese
International economics
Women's studies
History
Geography
International business
Anthropology
Caribbean studies
International relations
Sociology

Questions to ask colleges:
Is the program balanced across all subject areas, from the arts to social studies? Is the program geographically balanced, or is more emphasis given to certain countries or regions?

Does the program offer opportunities for students to study in Latin America?

Career options and trends:
International business manager/consultant; export-import manager; translator/interpreter; journalist; Foreign Service officer.

Careers in the Foreign Service are usually open only to U.S. citizens.

Graduates also pursue careers in government (CIA, State Department, or developmental agencies), non-governmental organizations (NGOs), teaching (such as teaching English in Latin America), international business (especially marketing and banking), social work (especially with agencies that work in Latin America), the travel industry, or law. Diplomatic service may require additional specialized training; translators and teachers usually need certification. Some graduates participate in the Peace Corps before beginning a career.

The presence of substantial numbers of recent immigrants from Latin America in many parts of the United States is likely to generate additional jobs—particularly in education, health care, social services, translation, journalism, and government—for those with a Latin American studies background.

Insider's viewpoint:
"I find myself easily bored by routine things. I can't imagine sitting through class after class of one discipline, like you have to do in English or business. In Latin American studies, your classes come from all different majors: language, government, history, economics, anthropology."

—Jennie, senior, University of Texas at Austin

For more info:
Latin American Studies Association (LASA)
416 Bellefield Hall
University of Pittsburgh
Pittsburgh, PA 15260
(412) 648-7929
www.lasa.international.pitt.edu

Native American studies

What it's about:

The Native American studies major provides an overview of tribes that are indigenous to the United States (including Alaska) and a history of cross-cultural relations from first contact with Europeans up to the present. You study tribal literatures, art, dance, song, religious traditions, philosophies, educational institutions, political and economic structures, and ecological perspectives.

Is this for you?

You might like this major if you also like: tackling social justice and/or environmental issues; Native American culture; non-traditional religions; mythology; other cultures.

Consider this major if you are good at: creativity; critical reading/thinking; persuading/influencing; research; teamwork ...*or have...* initiative; verbal skills; writing skills.

Recommended high school prep:

English 4, math 3, lab science 3, social studies 4, and a foreign language 3–4.

Typical courses in this major:

Cultures of Native North America and Alaska
Tribal governments
Contemporary issues in Native American studies
Oral and written traditions of Native Americans
Native American health and healing
Native American religion and philosophy
Native American arts
Contemporary indigenous issues and literatures
Native American history until 1865
Ecological perspectives of Native Americans
Sociology of Native Americans
Native Americans and film
Research and methods in Native American studies
Gender issues in Native American studies
Indigenous worldview perspectives
Native language study/linguistics

Concentrations:

Concentrations can be based on discipline, e.g., anthropology, political science, sociology, literature, or history; or on a particular region, e.g., North America, Mexico, Central America, or South America.

What the study of this major is like:

As a major in Native American studies, you must first catch up on any significant history you may not have covered in high school—in particular, the treatment of Native American tribal cultures by Europeans settling the Americas. Because your studies will include information not often presented in mainstream education and media, your first courses in the major may leave you feeling both dismayed and inspired. You will learn Native perspectives on a range of subjects, including the treaty-making process through which European Americans obtained access to and/or ownership of land and resources. In upper-level courses, you delve more deeply into art, literature, government, and religion; regions such as Alaska and the Southwest; and historical development, such as U.S.–Native contact before 1865.

Most faculty members who teach Native American studies have degrees in a subject such as history, anthropology, or English, but they draw from a variety of disciplines to develop their courses. For example, a course on present-day issues might incorporate writing by Native Americans (literary studies), as-told-to autobiographies (anthropology or literature), tribal arts and crafts (contemporary or historical art), sociological information (sociology), tribal newspapers (journalism), historical documents (history), court cases (law), or archaeological study (archaeology). Thus, because of the variety of academic approaches and cultural perspectives, the Native American studies classroom experience can be varied and exciting.

You may have a few large historical-overview courses, but most classes will be small groups that foster discussion and encourage you to sharpen your researching and writing abilities. Your two biggest challenges will be to deepen your cross-cultural understanding and to enhance your communication skills. Although much of your course work will consist of research and writing, you might also do projects, field studies, or interviews that take you off campus. And Native American elders, community activists, artists, scholars, and other visiting speakers may give on-campus talks that enrich your studies.

Native American studies programs tend to focus on the regions in which the college resides; for example, colleges in the Southwest are likely to have specialized courses on the Native American cultures and languages of Arizona and New Mexico, and on the connections between these tribal groups and those of Mexico and Latin America. Programs often have a disciplinary emphasis or strong link to another academic department, such as anthropology, social work, or history. These bonds exist because many Native American studies programs have grown out of traditional academic departments. Some programs are known for a particular strength; one college, for example, might support a project on Native voices and the media, while another offers a joint master's degree in Native American studies and law.

Native American studies can offer fresh perspectives that may give you a sense of purpose. Majors often strive to make a difference; they learn all they can about indigenous thought, traditions, values, and contributions to the global community. Their goal is to help Native Americans retain land and resources and revitalize cultural practices and beliefs.

Other majors you might like:
American history (U.S.)
Anthropology
Environmental studies
Linguistics
Latin American studies
Chicano studies
Musicology/ethnomusicology
Archaeology
Historic preservation
Sociology
Social work
Community health services

Questions to ask colleges:
Does the program cover Latin America, Alaska, or Canada, or does it focus on the United States, particularly on the lower 48 states? Although each type of program has merits, you should consider whether your interests fit a program's emphases.

Career options and trends:
Teacher*; park ranger; government officer (e.g., Indian Health Service, Bureau of Indian Affairs)*; lawyer (American Indian law); social worker*.

A state certificate or license is required for teaching in public schools. A law degree and license are required for practicing American Indian law off-reservation. Civil service exams are needed for most government employment.

Native American studies majors also pursue careers in environmental monitoring, business, Native American cultural preservation, tourism, tribal and nontribal criminal justice, health professions, and Native language preservation.

States are increasing their requirements for certification in Native American studies. Businesses are demanding an understanding of cultural diversity from employees, and social service and law enforcement agencies are looking for culturally appropriate ways to approach the populations they serve. These developments should increase employment opportunities for graduates with in-depth knowledge of Native American issues and traditions.

For more info:
American Indian Higher Education Consortium
121 Oronoco St.
Alexandria, VA 22314
(703) 838-0400
www.aihec.org

Near and Middle Eastern studies

What it's about:

Near and Middle Eastern studies focuses on a vast, culturally diverse geographic area that extends from North Africa to Central Asia. Using interdisciplinary and comparative approaches, you study the cultures and languages of the region. In addition, you examine the area's history, from antiquity to the present day, with particular focus on the period after the emergence of Islam.

Is this for you?

You might like this major if you also like: the History Channel; travel; adventure; languages; politics; reading about international events and military affairs; learning about other religions and cultures; languages written in unfamiliar alphabets.

Consider this major if you are good at: attention to detail; critical reading/thinking; memorizing; research...*or have...* curiosity; patience; verbal skills; writing skills.

Recommended high school prep:

English 4, math 3, lab science 3, social studies 3, and a foreign language 2–3. You are not expected to have studied the region in high school, but it is helpful if you can study a Near and Middle Eastern language. Other useful languages (especially if you intend to go to grad school in the field) are German and French.

Did you know...

...that some of the languages of the Middle East— Persian for instance—are among the easiest to learn? Arabic, on the other hand, is among the more difficult.

Typical courses in this major:

Arabic
Arabic literature in translation
Modern Near and Middle Eastern history
Near and Middle Eastern politics
Turkish
Islamic history and civilization
Islamic religion
People of the Near and Middle East
Hebrew
Persian
Islam and politics
Christianity, Judaism, and Islam
The United States and the Near and Middle East
Colonialism, imperialism, and nationalism
Palestine, Zionism, and Israel
Art in the Islamic world

Concentrations:

Geographic areas; area languages (Arabic, Turkish, Persian, Hebrew, etc.); area literature; disciplines with Near and Middle Eastern focus (such as Turkish history).

What the study of this major is like:

In a typical program, you take an introductory survey course covering the geography, history, and religious traditions of Asia Minor, Southwestern Asia, the Arabian Peninsula, and North Africa. In your second year, you take one or two specialized courses in history, political science, anthropology, religion, or literature translation. You should begin language study early enough to complete at least three years of Arabic and two years of Turkish, Persian (also known as Farsi, the language of Iran), or Hebrew. (At some colleges, you can take other languages, such as Armenian, Kurdish, or Berber.) If Middle Eastern language courses are not offered, try to take them at a neighboring college or as independent study, particularly if you plan to apply to grad school in the field.

You'll study languages in small classes, with professors who are generally native speakers. Learning a language will probably take at least four semesters of intensive daily study. Once you learn to decipher an unfamiliar alphabet and master the grammar, you may feel exhilarated to be able to read the works of contemporary as well as medieval authors from the Near and Middle East.

While studying a language, you attend lecture courses and seminars (in English) that address history, literature, politics, and other aspects of the region. Seminars usually have only about 10 to 20 students, and all of them are expected to take part in class discussion. In general, majors passionately debate current events; they readily observe links between the past and the present. Many majors spend a semester or a year abroad at a university (for example, the American University of Beirut, American University of Cairo, and Hebrew University of Jerusalem).

Near and Middle Eastern studies programs are differentiated mainly in two ways. First, programs concentrate either on the classical and medieval periods or on the modern period. Second, programs have either a language-and-literature approach or a discipline-based approach (historical, anthropological, political, philosophical, for example). Programs that stress the classical and medieval tend also to emphasize languages and literatures; the modern-oriented programs tend to take the discipline-based (or even multidisciplinary) approach. Some programs have a good mix of the medieval and the modern, and they include, as well, languages, literature and discipline-based studies.

Other majors you might like:
Arabic
History
Journalism
Linguistics
Archaeology
Art history
Islamic studies
Peace and conflict studies
Religious studies
Judaic studies
Ancient Near Eastern/Biblical languages
International relations

Questions to ask colleges:
What is the program's definition of Near and Middle Eastern studies? For example, a major may not fit the needs of students interested in contemporary issues and politics. Such students may be better served by majoring in history or political science and taking a Near and Middle Eastern language on the side.

Career options and trends:
Foreign Service Officer; international business or trade consultant; teacher; college professor; transla-

tor/interpreter; intelligence analyst; journalist; social worker.

Careers in the Foreign Service are usually open only to U.S. citizens.

Because of the political and economic turbulence in the Near and Middle East, the United States (including both the public and the private sector) will be intensely engaged in the region for years to come. People with language and other skills pertaining to the region should have a relatively easy time finding rewarding jobs.

Insider's viewpoint:
"Not only are there many areas of Middle Eastern history yet to be discovered (e.g., unknown and unedited medieval manuscripts), but what I teach and write about the Middle East has real contemporary relevance."

—Professor Bernard Haykel, New York University

For more info:
Middle East Studies Association (MESA)
University of Arizona
1219 North Santa Rita Ave.
Tucson, AZ 85721
(520) 621-5850
http://www.mesa.arizona.edu

Women's studies

Also known as:
Feminist, gender, and sexuality studies

What it's about:
Women's studies is an interdisciplinary major that examines the connections between gender, sexuality, power, and inequality. You study such issues as oppression of women and sexual minorities; class exploitation; racism; and women's cultural and historical roles, both in the U.S. and around the world.

Is this for you?
You might like this major if you also like: thinking about the differences between men and women; seeing connections between ideas, people, and systems; thinking about issues in a comprehensive way.

Consider this major if you are good at: critical reading/thinking; organizing; persuading/influencing; research; teamwork *...or have...* tolerance for ambiguity; writing skills.

Recommended high school prep:
English 4, math 4, lab science 3, social studies 4, and a foreign language 3. If it is available, take statistics.

Typical courses in this major:
Women's history
Women in the economy
Women and literature
Gender, race, and class
Biological basis of sex differences
Feminism, state, and public policy
Feminist theories
Gender and colonization
Gender and language
Gender and sexuality in cross-cultural perspective
Gender inequality
Global perspectives on gender
Gender, sexuality, and law
History of sexuality
Women in cinema
Sociology of marriage

Concentrations:
Race, class, and ethnicity in the United States; lesbian, bisexual, gay, and transgender studies; global perspectives; feminist theory; women's history; movements, institutions, and social policy; gender, science, and health; women's art and literature.

What the study of this major is like:
If you are curious about gender and sexuality issues, women's studies is a good major to choose. It seeks to understand what it means now, and has meant in the past, to be a woman. You examine differences among women themselves, as well as the concept and uses of gender—that is, the changing definitions that societies attach to being women and men. Because gender can reflect and determine differences in power and opportunity, majors learn to analyze economic and social systems, ask searching questions about equality, and discuss ways in which society can be transformed. In addition, you explore the political and cultural effects of race, class, age, nationality, sexual identity, and ethnicity.

Women's studies began in the late 1960s as an attempt to make up for the lack of information, in most college courses, about women. What started as an effort to fill in the gaps has become a comprehensive analysis of the role of women in all areas of life. Besides supplying research about women, the major questions accepted beliefs and unexamined norms. Almost every discipline in the arts, humanities, and social sciences contributes to women's studies. For many majors in the field, women's studies becomes a window on the rest of the world.

A typical program includes courses offered within women's studies as well as courses offered by other departments. You will probably take an introductory women's studies course; a series of electives in the humanities, social sciences, and, where possible, natural sciences. A capstone experience is usually required in the form of a fourth-year seminar, fieldwork or internship project, or independent study. Many programs also require courses in feminist theory as well as in race, ethnicity, or non-Western culture.

Over the years, the major has concerned itself not only with *what* is taught but also *how* the material is taught. Classes seek to foster dialogue and to create a safe arena in which to debate. Course work often includes various methods of presentation, group activities, self-defined papers and projects, and invitations to tie theory to your own experience. Most programs offer the flexibility to tailor your program to meet your needs and interests. Many students double-major in a traditional liberal arts discipline and in women's studies.

Colleges may vary in their name for the major— the most common are gender and sexuality studies, feminist studies, and women's studies—and the differences in the name may signal variations in emphases. Because the field is wide-ranging, most programs cannot cover everything. Therefore, you should read course catalogs to find out which aspects individual programs emphasize.

Other majors you might like:
African-American studies
European studies
Native American studies
Latin American studies
American literature
Anthropology
Comparative literature
Psychology
Sociology
Human development and family studies
History
Gay/lesbian studies

Questions to ask colleges:
Are the faculty members permanent, full-time professors? What are some faculty research projects?

Do the courses build on and connect to one another? Are they offered regularly?

What research opportunities are available to undergraduates?

You should make sure that the college supports women's studies as a serious field of inquiry.

Career options and trends:
Some women's studies graduates go on to activist careers in social and political issues or social services. Others find jobs in education (all levels), business, public policy and administration, health services, communications, and film, and (with appro-

priate graduate degrees) in college teaching, research, law, and medicine.

Insider's viewpoint:
"The way I understand women's studies, it's a critique of traditional disciplines and so it was a way of looking at things I'd seen my entire life from a different viewpoint."

—Paulette, senior, Oberlin College

For more info:
National Women's Studies Association (NWSA)
11 E Mount Royal Ave., Suite 100
Baltimore, Maryland 21202
(410) 528-0355
www.nwsa.org

Biological sciences

The biological sciences are no less than the study of life itself. Biologists often see the big picture by looking through a microscope.

Studies focus on animals, plants, and microbes, all on the levels of molecules and cells; organs, such as the heart; organisms (individuals of a species); populations (such as migrating birds); and environments, such as rain forests. Some biologists research particular life forms. Botanists study plants, marine biologists investigate sea life, and entomologists look into the world of insects.

Professors talk about the many fields of biology as explorations into the frontiers of biochemistry, biotechnology, and the rapidly growing areas of genetics and molecular and cellular biology.

"The complexity of living organisms represents an ideal outlet for satisfying the need to discover," says biochemist Gregory M. Raner of the University of North Carolina at Greensboro.

"Molecular biology is for people who are constantly asking why," notes Eileen Gregory of Rollins College. And according to the botanist C. O. Patterson of Texas A&M University, "New discoveries and invention of new techniques have generated an explosion of understanding and interest in this field."

Many scientific journeys in biological and medical research are aimed at improving health through vaccines, medicines, and cures for cancer, heart disease, AIDS, Alzheimer's, and other diseases. Some researchers venture into realms of genetic engineering, immune system therapies, and stem cell research. These emerging fields are reflected in new majors, which include bioengineering, genomics, biostatistics, and molecular modeling.

The life sciences prepare you to work in any number of professions—as a clinician, research assistant or technician, or scientist. Biotech labs, pharmaceutical companies, hospitals, and medical testing firms all hire biologists, as does the government, which has increased funding for research.

Employment growth in the life sciences varies by specialty. Growth will be best in fields that can put new discoveries to use, such as fighting disease with gene therapies. Naturally, the more education, training, and experience you have, the better the job you're likely to get. For instance, a four-year Bachelor of Science degree is a must for most nonresearch jobs in the life sciences. Researchers usually need even more education. A master's degree is okay for some researchers but a doctorate (Ph.D.) is required in the competition for other research jobs. No matter what level you study, professors say, you'll need to know chemistry as well as biology from the get-go.

Colleges great and small

When you compare biology programs, keep in mind the size of the colleges. While smaller colleges provide a solid foundation in the biological sciences, many of the newer majors are offered only at large universities. Also, larger universities have more funding for research. On the other hand, small colleges often pride themselves on the quality of their teaching. Find out if the college's faculty members are active in research and have published their work. Ask, too, whether undergrads can do research, in the college or on an internship. It's valuable experience, especially if you plan to go for a graduate degree and need an edge by getting hands-on experience.

"One of the most important things a graduate admission committee looks for is a good letter of recommendation from a respected researcher in whose laboratory you have participated," suggests Carter Denniston, professor of genetics at the University of Wisconsin, Madison.

You can study practically any area in biology in graduate school, including hot topics like microbial, plant, and animal genetics. Genetics is now central to biology, providing "general concepts and techniques for the study of inheritance, development, disease, and evolution in all living organisms and viruses," Denniston says.

You may find that molecular biology, virology, or another course you want is offered only at the graduate level—it all depends on the college. Some examples of graduate programs are bacterial physiology, pharmacogenetics, community and evolutionary ecology, environmental or conservation biology, toxicology, immunology, and neurobiology.

When you study biology, expect to do class work, fieldwork, and especially laboratory work. You'll spend a lot of quality time in the lab. So, if possible, compare the labs and equipment, as well as courses and faculty members, in the colleges you may apply to. Find out if your studies will cover a range of biology topics or zero in on one aspect of the life sciences, such as molecular or cellular biology or biochemistry. The course list will give you an idea of what the college stresses. And remember, some colleges are geared for premed students—those who plan to become doctors.

When searching for colleges with bio programs, look for colleges or divisions of arts and sciences, biological sciences, colleges of medicine, natural science and mathematics, health sciences, or applied science and technology.

Your career as a researcher begins now. Start your college search by reading about the majors in this section and visiting the American Institute of Biological Sciences's website (www.aibs.org). For information about other majors related to the life sciences, go to the sections on Agriculture, Health, and Natural resources and conservation.

Biochemistry

What it's about:

Biochemistry majors study the principles that enable living things to function as they do. Combining knowledge of chemical structure and of the behavior of molecules with a "big picture" view of biological processes helps you understand how "life" occurs at its most basic level.

Is this for you?

You might like this major if you also like: all areas of science; all varieties of living things; new technologies; mysteries (novels, movies, computer games) and puzzles; finding out how things work; seeking answers to fundamental questions about nature and living things.

Consider this major if you are good at: attention to detail; creativity; critical reading/thinking; math; memorizing; quantitative analysis; research; spacial thinking/analysis; teamwork *...or have...* initiative; manual dexterity.

Recommended high school prep:

English 4, math 4 (including precalculus or trigonometry), lab science 4 (biology, chemistry, physics, earth science), social studies 3, and a foreign language 2–3. Take as many advanced or honors-level science courses as you can. Any computer courses would also be useful.

Did you know...

...that many students in this major find biochemistry easier to learn than the more traditional branches of science? This is because you study the basic principles in a familiar context: the world of living organisms. In fact, many students do better with chemistry and physics when the material is linked to principles of biology.

Typical courses in this major:

Analytic chemistry
Organic chemistry
Calculus
Physics
Microbiology
Physical chemistry
Biochemistry
Quantitative analysis
Cell biology
Genetics
Inorganic chemistry
Physiology
Immunology
Physical biochemistry

Concentrations:

Biotechnology; toxicology; pharmacology; cell biology; immunology; neurochemistry; genetics; hematology; bacteriology.

What the study of this major is like:

Biochemists, who study the chemistry of organisms, relate the principles of chemistry to the functions of living systems. Biochemistry majors learn how to recognize the chemical nature of biological molecules by taking many of the core courses needed for a chemistry degree. You will also take courses that introduce you to human metabolism; DNA replication (how cells reproduce themselves) and the conversion of genetic information into functional cell components; human and mammalian physiology; and real-world applications of biotechnology.

Many people define biochemistry too narrowly; they think that it is simply a fifth division of chemistry, along with physical, inorganic, organic, and analytical. In reality, biochemistry includes all of the traditional divisions of chemistry and extends beyond the physical sciences into the life sciences and medicine as well.

Most courses in biochemistry are in lecture format and may include laboratory work. In many courses, you'll have plenty of homework, especially problem sets to complete and daily reading assignments. Most programs strongly encourage you to do some type of research. You may also be required to give oral presentations. Usually the biggest challenges students face is scheduling their courses and managing their time. Students sometimes take light course loads early on, not realizing that they are simply shifting the weight of their work to their third or fourth year, when courses become more challenging and time-consuming. You can help balance your workload by developing and sticking to a study plan.

There are many different approaches to the study of biochemistry. At some colleges the program emphasizes the chemical nature of biological systems. These programs are usually in departments of chemistry or physical science. Biochemistry programs in life science or medical departments may focus on physiology or molecular and cellular biology. Probably the best way to determine the emphasis of a program is to examine the required courses for the major. A program that does not require physical or inorganic chemistry would be likely to emphasize the biological aspects of biochemistry, with less attention to the chemistry of biomolecules. In contrast, a stress on chemistry might indicate a commitment to the fundamental aspects of biological interactions.

Other majors you might like:
Cell biology and histology
Microbiology
Molecular biology
Clinical nutrition
Neuroscience
Pharmacy
Chemistry
Biotechnology
Clinical/medical laboratory technology
Biomedical engineering
Chemical engineering
Forensic science

Career options and trends:
College professor*; physician*; research technician; research scientist*; science teacher.

Graduate or professional school after college is required for careers in medicine and scientific research. To teach in college you will need at least a master's degree and preferably a Ph.D. Additional credits in education and certification are usually needed for teaching in high school as well.

A major in biochemistry is a logical choice to prepare for medical, dental, or veterinary school, or for health and agricultural careers in such areas as toxicology, biomedical engineering, clinical chemistry, plant pathology, and animal sciences. Industries that may employ biochemistry majors include biotechnology, pharmaceutical, and medical testing and diagnostic firms. Biochemistry majors who also obtain a certificate in specialized lab training (DNA sequencing, in vitro cell biology, genetic engineering, for example) will improve their prospects.

For more info:
American Society of Biochemistry and Molecular Biology
9650 Rockville Pike
Bethesda, MD 20814-3996
(301) 634-7145
www.asbmb.org

Biology

Also known as:
Life science

What it's about:
Biology is the study of the structure, function, heredity, and evolution of all living things—microorganisms, fungi, plants, and animals. These life forms are studied at the levels of molecule, cell, organism, and population. Through lab work and fieldwork, you acquire a basic understanding of organisms, their habitats, and the processes that govern their life activities.

Is this for you?
You might like this major if you also like: pets; wildlife; gardening; wellness/fitness activities; environmental issues; outdoor activities (hiking, canoeing, rock climbing, etc.); zoos; insects.

Consider this major if you are good at: attention to detail; creativity; critical reading/thinking; memorizing; organizing; quantitative analysis; research; teamwork *...or have...* critical observation; manual dexterity; patience.

Recommended high school prep:
English 4; math 4 (including trigonometry and precalculus); lab science 4 (including earth science, biology, chemistry, and physics); social studies 2; a foreign language 2–3; and a computer applications course. Because biology is increasingly quantitative, a strong foundation in the physical sciences and math is essential.

Did you know...
...that mathematics is becoming increasingly important in biological research and innovation? If you are strong in both areas you will be in a good position for 21st century jobs.

Typical courses in this major:
Genetics
Cell biology
Microbiology
Molecular biology
Developmental biology
Immunology
Animal or plant physiology
Comparative anatomy and embryology
Animal behavior
Plant biology
Invertebrate biology
Parasitology
Aquatic biology
Environmental biology
Ecology
Evolution

Concentrations:
In college: biochemistry; botany; environmental science; microbiology; molecular biology; neuroscience; zoology.

If you go on to grad school: anatomy; behavioral biology; bioinformatics, cell biology; developmental biology; evolutionary biology; genetics; immunology; limnology; mycology; ornithology; paleontology; parasitology; pharmacology; physiology (animal and plant); systematics (animal and plant).

What the study of this major is like:
As a biology major, you'll focus on the way organisms solve the problems they face in their environments. In addition, you'll seek answers to the question most biology programs ask: How have ecological and hereditary factors contributed to the evolution of plants, animals, and microbes?

Generally, biology courses are taught through a combination of lectures and coordinated labs. Some professors provide opportunities for collaborative activities and online assignments as well. In the lab, hands-on experiences include observational exercises and open-ended experiments; for both types of work, you analyze data and then write reports.

After the intro courses, which stress the primary concepts, processes, and vocabulary of biology, you'll examine many of the subjects in greater depth. In cell biology and physiology, for instance, you analyze the link between the structure and function of cells—how they divide and then differentiate (take on new forms and new tasks). You'll observe cells through the microscope and do data-gathering experiments on different kinds of cells.

In genetics, you identify the molecular and cellular aspects of heredity in animals and in plants. You may also cover topics such as human hereditary disorders and DNA technology. Labs usually require you to work independently on fruit flies, molds, bacteria, and viruses. In ecology, you study the relation of plants and animals to their environment. Most likely, you'll follow up fieldwork with data analysis based on varied computational and statistical methods.

Courses beyond the intro level may include botany and more-specialized courses in seed plants, algae, fungi; invertebrate zoology and more-specialized classes in entomology (insects), protozoology (amoebas and other one-celled forms); and vertebrate zoology and more-specialized courses in ornithology (birds), ichthyology (fish), and so on.

Again, as you observe the relationship between function and structure, you'll consider how evolution has led to the diversity of the animal and plant kingdoms. In labs, you dissect fresh and preserved material, and sometimes apply culture techniques. Microbiology concentrates on the structure, function, genetics, and ecology of bacteria and viruses. Molecular biology and biochemistry are concerned with the substances that help regulate living systems. In these and other advanced courses, you read, analyze, and discuss current biology literature and often conduct independent research. Some advanced courses offer extended fieldwork.

The greatest challenge for biology majors is to deal with the large amount of information you must learn. Also, in most semesters you have to take two or even three lab courses. The most successful majors keep up-to-date with their assignments and learn to manage their time effectively. An upside of the workload, though, is that you often do lab projects with a partner or a small team of students, so you have the benefit of a support group and a chance to develop friendships with other majors.

Although most biology programs cover all aspects of the field, programs may emphasize different areas of biology. For example, one department might focus on cellular and molecular biology, while another emphasizes the organism or environmental studies. Some programs feature extended field trips to unique habitats, such as rain forests, mountains, or deserts. Another difference among programs is the amount of emphasis placed on undergrad research. Requirements for the major may also vary from college to college, particularly in the number of chemistry, physics, and math courses you must complete before you graduate.

Other majors you might like:
Agronomy and crop science
Environmental science
Wildlife and wilderness management
Forestry
Horticulture
Veterinary technology
Marine biology
Anthropology
Biomedical engineering
Entomology
Zoology
Biotechnology

Questions to ask colleges:
Are there opportunities for independent study and research?

Are the lab facilities up-to-date and sufficient for the number of students in the program?

Is this primarily a premed program, or do many of the graduates go on to pursue the science of biology in grad school and industry?

Career options and trends:
Teacher*; naturalist; industrial or university researcher*; lab technician; state or federal government biologist; health care professional (physician, dentist, vet, nurse)*; health care administrator; sales/marketing representative (pharmaceutical/biotech).

You will need to go on to graduate or professional school for a career in research or medicine, or to teach at the college level. Additional education credits and certification is usually needed to teach in high school as well.

Most biologists work for federal, state, and local government agencies (environmental, agricultural, health), and in the pharmaceutical and biotech industries. Job growth in the biotechnology industry continues to be strong but at a slower pace after rapid expansion in that field. Biologists with diverse knowledge and training, particularly in math and computer science, will enjoy the best prospects and demand.

Insider's viewpoint:

"I'm not premed, but a lot of people in my classes are. They're really, really competitive. For me, I'm taking the class because it's interesting to me, but for them, they have to get 100 percent on everything, so the curve is really high."

—Romi, sophomore, University of California: Los Angeles

For more info:

American Institute of Biological Sciences (AIBS)
1900 Campus Commons Dr., Suite 200
Reston, VA 20191
(703) 674-2500
www.aibs.org

Biotechnology

What it's about:

The biotechnology major combines the molecular life sciences and engineering. You learn how to use living cells, cellular and molecular processes, and genetic information to solve problems and to create new products.

Is this for you?

You might like this major if you also like: science and technology (a lot); science fairs; putting theory to practical use; building things; running your own business; working with people.

Consider this major if you are good at: attention to detail; creativity; critical reading/thinking; organizing; quantitative analysis; research; teamwork ...*or have...* initiative; patience; verbal skills.

Recommended high school prep:

English 4, math 4 (including precalculus), lab science 4, social studies 3, and a foreign language 2–3. Take computer science if offered. If possible, participate in a summer research program for high school students, available at many research institutes (such as Roswell Park Cancer Institute Summer High School Research Program).

Did you know...

...that biotechnology involves nanotechnology—working with materials (genes and DNA) that are invisible without powerful microscopes?

...that biotechnology is one of the oldest technologies? Humankind has been using the biological processes of microorganisms—such as yeast—for over 6,000 years. On the other hand, 70 percent of all biotechnologically produced medicines now on the market were approved since the early 1990s.

Typical courses in this major:

General biology I & II
Cell biology
Cell physiology
Microbiology
Developmental biology
Organic chemistry
Biochemistry
Immunology
Virology
Tissue culture methods
Bioanalytical techniques
Plant biotechnology
Genetic engineering
Genomics (gene function)
Bioinformatics
Proteinomics

Concentrations:

Bioinformatics; genomics; protenomics; toxicogenomics; pharmacogenomics; bioprocess; molecular modeling; computational chemistry.

What the study of this major is like:

In biotechnology, which combines molecular life sciences and engineering, you use living matter to develop products and services in agriculture (plant growth hormones, food additives), health care (vaccines, improved medicines and vitamins), the environment (detoxification of chemicals), and other areas. The study of biotechnology has greatly expanded with the sequencing of the human genome, as well as many other genomes. In fact, all of life's processes are now open to study—from the human to the bacterial.

As a biotechnology major, you learn to use several technologies to explore organisms: genetic engineering (changing gene characteristics for a specific purpose); bioprocessing (using separating and purifying techniques); immunobiochemistry; protein engineering; and biocatalysis (using enzymes to produce a biochemical reaction). In fact, biotechnologists need all the tools of the biochemist, the molecular biologist, the immunologist, and even the engineer, to prepare a product or an application on a large scale for the marketplace.

Because biotechnology course work covers all the life sciences (including areas such as exobiology and nuclear transfer cell therapy), you are likely to find subjects that interest you. The major is taught in both lecture and lecture/lab formats. In some classes, you may work on research projects with faculty members—an experience worth seeking out. You might also be required to complete independent research. An individual research project in biotechnology at the undergraduate level is a big undertaking. But producing an original contribution will give you a taste of what science has to offer—a chance to do something unique.

You can find biotechnology offered at the four-year bachelor's degree level, the two-year associate degree level, and even as a ten-week certificate program. Community colleges across the country have been increasing their offerings in this field in order to match growth in the industry, particularly in the areas of medical, pharmaceutical, and agricultural manufacturing.

Differences among biotechnology programs occur because of differences in the size of the institutions and the funding available for the undergraduate program. At well-funded institutions, the program may be good, but teaching may be less valued than research. At small institutions, teaching is often the primary concern, but funding may be nonexistent. If there's a balance between size and funding, faculty members can be active in research but still have the time and interest to help undergraduates.

Other majors you might like:
Agricultural and biological engineering
Microbiology
Biochemistry
Applied physics
Biological/physical sciences
Forest technology
Chemical engineering
Biomedical technology
Biomedical engineering
Clinical/medical laboratory technology
Environmental engineering
Bioinformatics

Career options and trends:
Biomedical researcher*; biochemical development engineer; environmental health and safety specialist; pharmaceutical product development researcher or engineer*; forensic scientist; medical diagnostician; biotechnology industry researcher, engineer or man-

ager*; quality control analyst or engineer; regulatory affairs specialist.

The biotechnology field is large and growing, so job opportunities will be strong in the foreseeable future. The fastest employment growth is projected to occur in the pharmaceutical and medical manufacturing industry and in firms providing research for agriculture, alternative energy, and "green" technology.

Insider's viewpoint:
"I'm doing independent research with a professor in the med school, and I'm working directly under the president of a biotech company, helping him with scientific literature research. These experiences help me tremendously; I learned how to network and overcame the fear of talking to professors. In addition, there's the research experience itself. It's very hard-core and takes a lot of endurance, patience, and stamina. Being single-minded is key."

—Clare, senior, University of California: Davis

For more info:
Biotechnology Industry Organization (BIO)
1201 Maryland Avenue, S.W.
Suite 900
Washington, DC 20024
(202) 962-9200
www.bio.org

National Center for Biotechnology Information
National Library of Medicine
Building 38A
Bethesda, MD 20894
(301) 496-2475
www.ncbi.nlm.nih.gov

Botany

Also known as:
Plant biology

What it's about:
Majors in botany study all aspects of plant life, which ranges from the smallest to the largest organisms on earth. Courses teach both microscopic and field investigation techniques.

Is this for you?
You might like this major if you also like: discovering new things, observing nature, gardening, hiking, working and playing outdoors, natural history.

Consider this major if you are good at: attention to detail; creativity; logical reasoning; quantitative analysis; research; teamwork…*or have…* manual dexterity; observation skills; patience.

Recommended high school prep:
English 4, math 4 (including precalculus and statistics), lab science 4 (including biology, chemistry and physics), social studies 3, and a foreign language 2–3.

Typical courses in this major:
General biology
Biochemistry
Microbiology
Genetics
Plant anatomy and physiology
Field ecology
Plant evolution
Photosynthesis
Plant taxonomy and systematics
Mycology (fungi)
Pteridophytes (ferns)
Phycology (algae)
Lichens and bryophytes
Vascular plant morphology
Paleobotany

Concentrations:
In college: plant physiology; plant ecology; plant genetics.

If you go on to grad school: paleobotany; plant genomics; plant development and hormonal regulation; plant cell biology; plant systematics; community and evolutionary ecology.

What the study of this major is like:
Although people have been studying plants for thousands of years, discoveries made and techniques developed in the last few decades have generated an explosion of interest in botany. This is indeed an exciting time in the plant sciences.

Introductory courses in botany (first- and second-year courses) usually have both lecture and lab components. In courses that include fieldwork, you study organisms in their natural habitats, where you may observe interesting examples of anatomical and physiological adaptations to features of the environment. While even a handheld lens can provide vital information about many species, most botanical studies rely on sophisticated tools. That's why it's useful to take as many courses as possible that offer hands-on experience with a range of equipment and techniques.

In cell biology courses, you will study the biochemical pathways that maintain and promote life through each of the cell's parts. In plant anatomy and plant physiology, you will explore the unique nature of plants: how cells are organized; how organs are formed and function; and how growth, development, and reproduction processes are coordinated. Plant ecology focuses on the way individual plants integrate into communities of organisms and the way plants respond to their environment—for example, how plants coexist with animals that eat them or how plants use animals to help them pollinate and reproduce.

The diversity of plants is so great that you may, at first, feel overwhelmed by the amount of information available. But as you examine plants more closely, you will see that most of the basic features of plants are the same for nearly all species. Rather than try to learn every detail about every kind of plant, you can begin to focus on one plant group.

Some colleges stress ecology and the evolution of plants, while others emphasize molecular and ultrastructural studies. At many colleges, you must complete a set of core courses in biology before beginning specialized botany courses; on other campuses, you may take botany courses in your first year.

Because botanists spend a lot of time in the lab or in the field, they tend to dress comfortably and informally. Likewise, they often have laid-back attitudes. Nevertheless, they work hard, both physically and intellectually. Some botanists visit unexplored regions looking for new species, even putting themselves in danger in the search. Others rarely stray outside their lab, although they may put in 16-hour days carrying out complex experiments. Because plants function on their own schedules, without regard for human convenience, botanists usually plan their days (and nights) to meet the needs of their research organisms. So a botanist may be in the lab at 3:00 a.m. to observe the unfurling of a flower bud, the division of a growing cell, the opening and closing of stomata—but the thrill of discovery makes any loss of sleep worth while.

Other majors you might like:
Horticulture
Genetics
Ecology
Plant pathology
Agricultural and biological engineering
Wood science/paper/pulp technology
Agronomy and crop science
Range science
Landscape architecture
Herbalism
Floriculture
Forestry

Questions to ask colleges:
Is there access to a nearby nature reserve or other protected, undisturbed area? For plant ecology studies, this would be very valuable.

Is there a well-equipped herbarium on campus? It would be useful for taxonomic and systematics work. For most areas of research in botany, modern, fully equipped labs are essential.

Career options and trends:
Laboratory technician; manager of a nature conservancy or environmentally protected area; technical artist, illustrator, or photographer; curator of a museum, herbarium, or arboretum; pharmaceutical researcher or investigator; plant breeder.

Employment opportunities are generally good, with higher salaries closely linked to advanced education and training and/or experience. The two areas showing most rapid expansion are the molecular biology of plants, and field studies of protected or endangered plant species.

Insider's viewpoint:
"Think about botany in relation to horticulture and decide if the science of plants sounds interesting or if the growing of plants is more interesting to you. I, myself, love both but I really wanted to learn the science."

—Deborah, senior, University of Wisconsin

For more info:
American Society of Plant Biologists (ASPB)
15501 Monona Drive
Rockville, MD 20855-2768
(301) 251-0560
www.aspb.org

Botanical Society of America (BSA)
P.O. Box 299
St. Louis, MO 63166-0299
(314) 577-9566
www.botany.org

Cell biology and histology

What it's about:

Cell biology emphasizes the cell as the basic unit for examining characteristics common to all living organisms. Histology is the study of how cells are organized into functional units called tissues, and how tissues are organized into organs.

Is this for you?

You might like this major if you also like: microscopes and lab work; math and science, especially biology and chemistry.

Consider this major if you are good at: attention to detail; creativity; critical reading/thinking; math; organizing; quantitative analysis; research *...or have...* initiative; manual dexterity; patience.

Recommended high school prep:

English 4, math 3, lab science 4 (including biology, chemistry and physics), social studies 3, and a foreign language 2–3. Take as many advanced or honors science courses as possible.

Typical courses in this major:

Physics
Calculus
Organic chemistry
Cell biology
Molecular biology
Genetics
Biochemistry
Cell physiology
Immunology
Developmental biology
Neurobiology
Structural biology
Virology
Histology/microanatomy
Microscopy/microtechnique
Electron microscopy

Concentrations:

Generally, none available.

What the study of this major is like:

Cell biology is often offered as a concentration within the broad-based major in biology; in some cases it is offered as a major in cellular and molecular biology. Histology, also called microscopic anatomy, may be included under histotechnology, cytotechnology, microtechnique, or even microscopy. Histology is usually taught as a course within a major or as a separate associate's degree or certification program.

In cell biology, the focus is on the cell as the basic unit of life. You will explore the fundamental processes that are common to all living cells, and investigate the unique characteristics and processes of more specialized cell types such as lymphocytes and neurons. Additionally, you should acquire a broad, general foundation in biology, chemistry, and physics.

Most of your classes will involve lectures. However, as is usual for science classes, most of your learning will take place in the lab. In cell biology laboratory sections, you will take part in various aspects of research. You may also have the opportunity to participate in research on your own, either on an independent-study project mentored by faculty members or on an internship.

Since cellular biology and molecular biology are two rapidly growing areas in biology, the amount of information you will have to deal with can be overwhelming. You'll find that the work requires both attention to detail and the ability to appreciate and comprehend broad concepts. As a biologist, you should be ready to take initiative and to work cooperatively with others. Although you will often study alone, you will sometimes work in pairs or in small groups in the lab. Because of the emphasis on real-life learning, many laboratory experiments cannot be completed within a typical laboratory period (3 hours). Therefore, you can expect to work outside of class, either alone or in small groups. Keep in mind, too, that much of the laboratory learning may at first seem repetitious; but this valuable experience will help you master the hands-on research skills you'll need.

In some colleges, the biology degree offers a broad exposure to the hierarchy of living things, spanning molecules, cells, organisms, ecologies, and ecosystems. In other colleges, the biology major focuses on molecular, cellular, or biochemical processes. If you select a broad-based program, it is possible that you may discover a field that interests you more than the one you initially selected. In a narrower program, you might have fewer options if you decide to make a change. With a strong background in basic biology, however, you can take supplemental courses in graduate school to keep yourself competitive with students coming from more specialized undergraduate programs.

Other majors you might like:
Molecular biology
Microbiology
Biochemistry
Chemistry
Zoology
Botany
Genetics
Biomedical engineering
Chemical engineering
Biomedical technology
Biotechnology
Clinical/medical laboratory technology

Questions to ask colleges:
What is the laboratory enrollment size? Do full-time faculty members, teaching assistants, or adjunct instructors teach laboratory courses? What type of access do undergraduates have to laboratory equipment?

Career options and trends:
Research scientist; physician or health care professional; research assistant or technician; regulatory compliance officer; college professor.

For work as a research technician, certain laboratories require certification in areas such as histotechnology.

Most growth will likely be in the private industry, mainly with pharmaceutical companies. But cell biology is a fast-moving field, so it is hard to predict trends. Today's discoveries may become tomorrow's ordinary tools and techniques.

For more info:
American Society for Cell Biology (ASCB)
8120 Woodmont Ave.
Suite 750
Bethesda, MD 20814-2762
(301) 347-9300
www.ascb.org

Entomology

Also known as:
Insect biology

What it's about:
Entomology deals with the biology and economic importance of insects and their relatives. If you are interested in understanding the diversity of insects in all their habitats, or their impact on human health and resources, you may find this major a better match than the broader life sciences majors.

Is this for you?
You might like this major if you also like: bugs, of course; nature and the environment; farming and agriculture; lab sciences.

Consider this major if you are good at: attention to detail; critical reading/thinking; organizing; quantitative analysis; research; teamwork ...*or have...* curiousity; initiative; verbal skills.

Recommended high school prep:
English 4, math 4, lab science 4, social studies 3, and a foreign language 2–3. Take a course in computer science or computer applications if one is available.

Did you know...
...that not many students major in this subject? Those who do, therefore, have more opportunity for one-on-one interactions with their advisers and professors.

...that over a million different species of insects have been identified so far? Some experts believe that there may be another 30 million species yet to be discovered.

Typical courses in this major:
General biology
Microbiology
Chemistry
General entomology
Insect physiology
Insect taxonomy and systematics
Field crop insects

Horticultural entomology
Livestock entomology
Insect behavior
Aquatic entomology
Beekeeping
Agricultural entomology (pest management)
Medical entomology
Forest entomology
Urban entomology

Concentrations:
Generally, none in college; but if you go on to grad school: evolution and behavior; molecular entomology; pest management

What the study of this major is like:
Entomology evolved into a field of its own because of the enormous impact insects have on humans. Some entomologists teach farmers how to use efficient, environmentally safe methods of pest control. Others work in forest management or in ornamental plant industries to protect trees from destructive bugs. Still others, employed by public health agencies, help ranchers deal with insects that plague livestock. Entomologists also conduct basic research in ecology, physiology, toxicology, genetics, and biotechnology, since insects can serve as test organisms for the examination of principles common to all animal life.

Before you begin study in entomology, you take introductory courses in plant and animal biology and in chemistry (including organic chemistry). Because entomology is a biological science, you will be taking biology courses throughout your undergraduate studies. From a general entomology course you progress to advanced classes in the morphology, taxonomy, physiology, ecology, and behavior of insects. Other advanced courses may deal with the importance of insects to human health and welfare (for example, pest management or medical entomology). Elective courses include plant physiology, plant pathology, nematology (nematodes or roundworms), microbiology, parasitology, agricultural engineering, agronomy, sociology, and economics.

Laboratories are an important part of many entomology courses. In some courses, you may even be required to collect insects. You will probably be encouraged to conduct an independent research project under the supervision of a professor. The electives you choose should reflect your educational and career objectives. If, after college, you plan to go directly into pest management, you should take courses in other agricultural sciences, such as weed science or plant pathology. If, on the other hand, you would like to go to graduate school, take advanced courses in biology and entomology that relate to your interests.

Entomology is not generally offered as an undergraduate major except in large public research universities and land grant colleges. Some programs may focus more on pest management (usually those in agricultural departments); others emphasize basic science.

Other majors you might like:
Plant protection/pest management
Environmental science
Ecology
Sustainable agriculture
Zoology
Agricultural and biological engineering
Agronomy and crop science
Wildlife biology
Animal sciences
Aquatic biology/limnology

Questions to ask colleges:
What are the opportunities for independent research?

How flexible is the major in meeting my career objectives (for example, pest management or basic science)?

Do graduates get jobs that relate to their major in entomology?

Career options and trends:
Urban or agricultural pest management specialist*; government research technician or scientist; university research technician*; industry researcher; industry technical or sales representative; university extension agent.

Entry-level positions in industry and government may be obtained with a bachelor's degree, but a graduate degree is required for most research and upper-level jobs.

For more info:
Entomological Society of America
10001 Derekwood Lane
Suite 100
Lanham, MD 20706-4876
(301) 731-4535
www.entsoc.org

Genetics

What it's about:

Genetics began when an Austrian monk examined the heredity of simple traits in peas. It now serves as the framework for the biological sciences, by providing concepts and techniques for studying inheritance, development, disease, and evolution in all living organisms and viruses. As a major in genetics, you gain a solid background from which you can specialize in most areas of biology.

Is this for you?

You might like this major if you also like: science and technology; finding out how things work; solving puzzles; natural and human history; research; learning about medicine and evolution.

Consider this major if you are good at: attention to detail; creativity; critical reading/thinking; math; quantitative analysis; research ...*or have...* manual dexterity; patience; writing skills.

Recommended high school prep:

English 4, math 4 (including calculus), lab science 4 (including biology, physics, and chemistry), social studies 3, and a foreign language 2–3. Be sure to take all available computer science courses.

Typical courses in this major:

Calculus
Organic chemistry
Inorganic chemistry
Biochemistry
Statistics
Physics
General biology
Principles of genetics
Advanced genetics
Human genetics
Molecular genetics
Quantitative genetics and breeding
Evolutionary genetics
Population genetics
Developmental genetics
Genetic data analysis

Concentrations:

Generally, none in college; but if you go on to grad school: human genetics; plant genetics; animal genetics; microbial genetics; viral genetics; developmental genetics; population genetics; cytology; quantitative genetics; behavioral genetics.

What the study of this major is like:

Genetics majors usually begin with a solid grounding in chemistry, biochemistry, and general biology. Math and statistics requirements vary from college to college. Within the major, your work can be diverse, including courses in classical genetics, molecular biology, plant and animal genetics, population genetics, cytology, human genetics, microbial genetics (bacteria and viruses), behavioral genetics, and specialized courses related to model organisms (such as maize, roundworms, or mice) or to laboratory skills such as molecular genetics techniques.

Some colleges do not have the undergraduate major "genetics," but they offer similar courses under "molecular biology." Most programs contain a mix of lecture, laboratory, and independent research opportunities; in addition, some programs have a capstone course in which you read original research papers and discuss them. To be a successful major, you should be committed to genetics and have good study habits. Some students find genetics challenging because it is a research-oriented major. If you don't like research (many people don't), then genetics is probably not for you. But if you love working in the lab at all hours, you should do well.

If you plan on going for a Ph.D. in genetics or another biological science, pick a college that offers quality undergraduate research opportunities. A graduate admissions committee will probably expect you to supply a letter of recommendation from a respected researcher in whose laboratory you worked.

Genetics is a good undergraduate major for students heading for medical school, veterinary school, and most other graduate programs in biology. On the other hand, you don't have to major in genetics to get into a graduate program in the field. Graduate programs accept majors in biochemistry, bacteriology, biology, zoology, botany, and other biological sciences.

Other majors you might like:
Biomedical engineering
Agricultural and biological engineering
Botany
Zoology
Genetic counseling
Biotechnology
Forensic science
Animal breeding
Biomedical technology
Biochemistry
Molecular biology

Career options and trends:
Genetics counselor*; medical or veterinary doctor*; genetics researcher or investigator*; lab bench scientist or technician, or lab manager; science writer; executive, manager, or sales rep in the biotechnology industry; clinical and medical geneticist.

A degree from a professional school and licensing are required for those wishing to become physicians or veterinarians, and most jobs in genetic research require a Ph.D.

The biotechnology industry has a number of career opportunities for students with just a baccalaureate. The aggressive growth that occurred in that industry in the past has slowed somewhat but is still going strong, and is expected to remain strong for the foreseeable future, especially for genetic counselors. There is also an increasing need for people with a solid background in both genetics and communications.

For more info:
Genetics Society of America (GSA)
9650 Rockville Pike
Bethesda, MD 20814-3998
(301) 634-7300
www.genetics-gsa.org

Marine biology

What it's about:

Students in marine biology explore the diversity of sea life, the functioning of marine ecosystems, and the chemical and physical nature of the oceans. As a marine biology major, you will gain a broad understanding of the processes that control life in underwater environments.

Is this for you?

You might like this major if you also like: the sea and shore; boats and boating; water sports; aquariums; the outdoors; nature; travel; science and technology.

Consider this major if you are good at: attention to detail; creativity; critical reading/thinking; leadership; math; quantitative analysis; research; spacial thinking/analysis; teamwork *...or have...* communication skills; initiative.

Recommended high school prep:

English 4, math 4 (including precalculus), lab science 4 (including earth science, chemistry and physics, and field biology if available), social studies 3, and a foreign language 2–3. You will need calculus and computer skills in college. The ability to communicate well, in writing and in speaking, is important in this field, so don't neglect your English courses. If possible, participate in a summer internship program at an aquarium or a research center.

Did you know...

...that marine biology covers more than fish and sea mammals? You study everything from the microscopic, single-cell plants that float in the oceans, to ecosystems like coral reefs, kelp forests, and the intertidal zone (at the edge of the sea where tides ebb and flow) and widely differing environments, such as hydrothermal vents miles below the ocean's surface and the frigid waters of the Antarctic Ocean.

...that this major requires a sound training in chemistry? Chemistry is important in understanding the building blocks of life, such as DNA and proteins, and the way the biological world affects and is affected by the physical world undersea.

Typical courses in this major:

Chemical oceanography
Physical oceanography
Ichthyology
Invertebrate biology
Marine botany
Deep-sea biology
Fisheries biology
Limnology (freshwater environments)
Marine ecology
Marine mammals
Aquaculture
Coastal ornithology
Marine policy
Plankton biology
Phycology (algae)
Computer modeling

Concentrations:

Generally, none in college; but if you go on to grad school: vertebrates; invertebrates; coastal ecology; coral reef ecology; fisheries biology; marine mammals

What the study of this major is like:

Marine biologists study the ocean as a system—how underwater species relate to one another as food and prey and how various species depend on the ocean's physics and chemistry. As a major, you will have in-depth exposure to this complex ecosystem and will gain insight into environmental problems, such as the consequences of global climate changes and ocean pollution. And you will examine the consequences of humankind's reliance on the seas.

Courses cover the form, structure, development, evolution, physiology, biochemistry, and genetics of marine systems, including fisheries. Emphasis is placed on the spatial and regional distributions of species—for example, whether they inhabit coastal or open ocean, cold or warm water, deep or shallow water. You may study why certain species are endangered and how they can be protected, or you can pursue special interests, such as the economics of harvesting marine organisms for food and energy.

During the first two years, majors take basic courses including math, chemistry, physics, and biology. You may also take a first-year survey, with field trips, of marine environments. In your second year, you might conduct laboratory examinations of the ecology, physiology, and behavior of marine organisms. Upper-level work focuses on the chemical and physical characteristics of the ocean. In addition, you will probably take courses in conservation, marine resources, and policy (coastal law, pollution, economic resources of the ocean).

The coursework is generally a mix of lectures, laboratory activities, and, especially in the third and fourth years, fieldwork. Many students do summer internships or research outside college, and a senior thesis—an independent research project, conducted under faculty supervision and summarized in a written report—is often required.

A frequent challenge for majors is to develop a coordinated path through the field. Marine biology is not a distinct area of study; rather, it draws heavily on other disciplines such as biology, chemistry, and physics. Avoid taking just a collection of survey courses from various areas of science. Instead, try to explore one field of marine biology in depth. Also, majors often spend a lot of time on fieldwork. But although they work hard, they generally enjoy what they do.

Because marine biology is such a broad area, different programs have different emphases. For example, professors at some colleges may concentrate on open-ocean rather than near-shore species; at other colleges, faculty members may have expertise in marine mammals and know little about fisheries. Some colleges offer a biological concentration within a broader oceanography major. Take a look at course catalogs, which should reflect colleges' emphases.

Other majors you might like:
Oceanography
Aquaculture
Ecology
Environmental biology
Ocean engineering
Environmental science
Aquatic biology/limnology
Zoology

Marine engineering/naval architecture
Water, wetlands, and marine management
Fishing and fisheries

Questions to ask colleges:
In which area of marine biology do faculty members have the most expertise?

Which types of marine field research or internships are available to undergraduates?

Career options and trends:
Government resource manager*; science teacher; fisheries biologist; laboratory research technician*; environmental consultant*; staff member at a museum or aquarium.

The job market is tight in this field. A strong math background and computer skills will give you a competitive edge, especially in the fisheries industry. Most research and academic positions will require a graduate degree.

Insider's viewpoint:
"A misconception is that fieldwork, such as scuba diving and cruises, is all fun and games. Taking a midnight dive—and my fifth dive of the day—in the pouring rain or being seasick is not fun."

—Amy, senior, University of San Diego

For more info:
American Fisheries Society (AFS)
5410 Grosvenor Lane
Bethesda, MD 20814
(301) 897-8616
www.fisheries.org

Sea Grant Marine Careers
Kingman Farm/UNH
Durham, NH 03824
www.marinecareers.net

Microbiology

What it's about:

The microbiology major focuses on the biology of microscopic organisms, such as bacteria, algae, and fungi. Your goal is to understand the function of microbes in agriculture, medicine, ecology, and biotechnology. You will also receive training in sterile procedures; the identification, enumeration, and growth of microorganisms; the evaluation of antimicrobials and antibiotics; and the practice of microbial genetics.

Is this for you?

You might like this major if you also like: science projects; gardening; environmental causes; microscopes; caring for people; keeping things organized.

Consider this major if you are good at: attention to detail; creativity; critical reading/thinking; organizing; quantitative analysis; research; spacial thinking/analysis; teamwork ...*or have...* manual dexterity.

Recommended high school prep:

English 4 (a writing course would be helpful), math 4 (including precalculus or calculus), lab science 4 (including chemistry and physics), social studies 3, and a foreign language 2–3. If possible, take a course in statistics and in computer science.

Did you know...

...that the study of microorganisms is not just about germs and disease? Oil prospecting, soil use and management, agriculture, development of nanosystems, genetic engineering, uses and misuses of microbes in military activities, and monitoring for microbes are just some of the many applications.

Typical courses in this major:

General biology I, II
Organic chemistry
Inorganic chemistry
Cell biology
Genetics
Bacteriology
Biochemistry

Microbial ecology
Bioinformatics/computational biology
Advanced microbiology
Bacterial physiology
Medical bacteriology
Immunology
Virology
Recombinant DNA techniques
Mycology and parasitology

Concentrations:

Generally, none in college; but if you go on to grad school: bacteriology; virology; mycology (fungi); phycology (algae); microbial physiology; genetics; biotechnology.

What the study of this major is like:

As a microbiology major, you will probably begin by familiarizing yourself with microscopes. You'll get an overview of the diversity, structure, function, growth, reproduction, genetics, physiology, preservation, and control of microorganisms. You'll then learn to grow and catalog a wide variety of microorganisms, including bacteria, algae, fungi, protozoa, and viruses. When you progress to biochemistry and molecular genetics, the work becomes more abstract. In labs and lectures, you use critical-thinking skills to prepare and conduct experiments. As you advance, your work focuses on bacterial mutants, the documentation of agents (including viruses, which are not usually seen directly), and measurements with biochemical tools.

Microbiology majors develop laboratory procedures that enable them to study a type or a group of microorganisms. Students sometimes have trouble attending to the many important details and thoroughly applying sterile procedures and techniques. You must work well in a group, even if you are doing an individual research project. Majors have to cooperate in order to maintain and use shared equipment and materials safely, often under sterile conditions. Sometimes you need to develop new skills for a particular project, such as the ability to search gene databases. For most investigations, you'll need to understand the molecular biology and biochemistry of both hosts and parasites. To be successful in this field, you should be willing to learn unfamiliar methodologies and adapt to unexpected situations.

Some colleges emphasize a premedical curriculum in biology, and give less attention to other biological sciences. In such programs you may be limited to broader applications in microbiology. Other colleges emphasize environmental science or molecular biology rather than a more integrated approach to the diverse areas within microbiology. Most small colleges offer solid foundations in the biological sciences, teaching concepts (such as the theories behind evolution, genetics, respiration, photosynthesis, and biochemistry) as well as technical skills. Conceptual skills are useful because the field of microbiology is changing rapidly, and certain technologies and methods might one day be out-of-date.

Other majors you might like:
Clinical/medical laboratory technology
Biotechnology
Biomedical engineering
Cell biology and histology
Zoology
Genetics
Biochemistry
Entomology
Chemistry
Soil science
Ecology
Agricultural and biological engineering

Questions to ask colleges:
Do undergraduates learn lab techniques and practical skills that would qualify them for entry into the job market? Where do most majors go after graduation—medical school, graduate school, or employment?

Career options and trends:
Physician*; veterinarian; high school and college teacher; research technician*; environmental scientist; hospital administrator; biotechnologist*; health care professional (respiratory therapist, phlebotomist, etc.); government agency microbiologist.

Graduates with a degree in microbiology find positions in health care and in the biotechnology, agricultural, food, and pharmaceutical industries. Job opportunities are projected to grow faster in this field than in the biological field as a whole. Job growth remains strong in the biotechnology industry, especially in the areas of pharmaceutical and medical manufacturing. Health care is a particularly strong field even in tight job markets.

Insider's viewpoint:
"I had a misconception of what people do in labs. I thought you just go there and do your experiments. In fact it's far more involved. You think about the experiments, you talk to your instructor, you talk to other students who work with you, and you go to conferences. It's a very different culture. You're not completely isolated."

—Julio, senior, San Francisco State University

For more info:
American Society for Microbiology (ASM)
1752 N St., N.W.
Washington, DC 20036-2904
(202) 737-3600
www.asm.org

Molecular biology

Also known as:

Cell and molecular biology

What it's about:

As a major in molecular biology, you investigate the basic mechanisms of life by studying the macromolecules—proteins, for example—essential to living organisms. Using chemical analysis, you explore metabolism, gene function and regulation, cell differentiation, and development. Special emphasis is placed on the role of proteins and nucleic acids in cellular processes.

Is this for you?

You might like this major if you also like: science clubs and projects; new technology; thinking creatively and abstractly; exploring the inner workings of things. Molecular biology is for people who are constantly asking "Why?" and are not satisfied until something is completely explained.

Consider this major if you are good at: attention to detail; critical reading/thinking; math; quantitative analysis; research; spacial thinking/analysis; teamwork *...or have...* initiative; manual dexterity; perseverance.

Recommended high school prep:

English 4, math 4 (including calculus and statistics), lab science 4 (including biology, chemistry, and physics), social studies 3, and a foreign language 2–3. Take as many advanced science courses as possible, and a course in computer science if available.

Did you know...

...that you must have an understanding of chemistry when you study living organisms? The ability to apply chemical principles to the function and structure of cells is the basis of molecular biology.

Typical courses in this major:

General biology (I, II)
General chemistry (I, II)
Organic chemistry (I, II)
General physics (I, II)
Cellular biology
General molecular biology
General microbiology
Biochemistry
Plant molecular biology
Molecular genetics
Biostatistics
Endocrinology
Nucleic acid chemistry
Developmental biology
Protein isolation and characterization (lab)
Writing in molecular biology

Concentrations:

Generally, none in college; but if you go on to grad school: bioinformatics; structural biology; computational biology; molecular medicine; functional genomics; molecular genetics; pharmacogenetics.

What the study of this major is like:

As a molecular biology major, you focus on subcellular components. You'll investigate cellular mechanisms (including cell metabolism and genetics) and learn to apply principles of chemistry to biological systems.

Most likely, you'll begin with an introduction to the essential macromolecules, especially the structure and function of proteins and nucleic acids. Then you'll conduct an in-depth study of DNA replication and function. You also focus on protein biosynthesis and enzyme regulation. In the required biochemistry courses, you cover metabolic pathways for energy and precursor production.

Cellular biology courses combine molecular and biochemical information to describe the production of cellular material. Because successful molecular biologists need well-developed analytical skills, most majors enroll in biostatistics and quantitative analysis courses. You are also expected to have strong computer skills. If you don't have experience with database searches, spreadsheets, and presentation software, you should take technology courses in your early college years.

Advanced courses focus on the interaction of specific proteins and the role of DNA in the regulation of cellular processes. In biotechnology courses, you begin to apply these principles to real-world problems. In bioinformatics and computational biology, you'll learn to use information obtained from genome sequencing. Besides lectures and seminars, most courses have labs in which you practice basic research techniques, including DNA and protein isolation, purification, and manipulation. Advanced courses generally require you to do an independent research project.

Majors spend a considerable amount of time working independently in the lab. The field of molecular biology depends on experimentation, so you must develop excellent laboratory skills and good hand-eye coordination. You spend additional out-of-class time reading journals and writing scientific reports. Although you need to be creative, you also have to develop an organized approach to problem solving, be able to memorize technical terms, and do complex data analysis and application. Most students in molecular biology study and work in groups; teamwork is essential to success. In addition to lightening individual workloads, study groups provide a strong support system.

Other majors you might like:
Biochemistry
Cell biology and histology
Agricultural and biological engineering
Biomedical engineering
Neuroscience
Microbiology
Genetics
Clinical/medical laboratory technology
Biomedical technology
Physics
Chemistry
Forensic science

Questions to ask colleges:
What is the primary focus of the program? At some colleges, the program may emphasize one aspect of biology (such as genetics) or a particular group of organisms; while other colleges may focus on the chemistry/biochemistry aspects. You may also have to choose between a biotech track and a preprofessional (premed) track.

Which lab equipment is available for undergraduates? Because the field of molecular biology is highly dependent on experimentation, undergrads must develop excellent lab skills.

Career options and trends:
University researcher/professor; medical or pharmaceutical researcher*; forensic scientist; health professional (such as physician, nurse)*; genetic counselor; high school teacher; agricultural researcher; laboratory technician*; public health officer.

Research positions may require a graduate degree.

Technological developments such as genome sequencing and DNA arrays have significantly increased the role of molecular biology research in the field.

For more info:
American Society for Biochemistry and Molecular Biology (ASBMB)
11200 Rockville Pike, Suite 302
Rockville, MD 20852-3110
(240) 283-6600
www.asbmb.org

Zoology

Also known as:
Animal biology

What it's about:
Zoology majors study animals—their origin, cell structure, genetics, physiology, behavior, ecology, and life processes. They also receive training in molecular biology techniques, quantitative field sampling, and statistical analysis.

Is this for you?
You might like this major if you also like: all creatures great and small; natural history museums; the outdoors; lab work and fieldwork; identifying animals; bird watching; anatomy; environmental issues.

Consider this major if you are good at: attention to detail; critical reading/thinking; memorizing; organizing; quantitative analysis ...*or have...* communication skills; initiative; manual dexterity; patience.

Recommended high school prep:
English 4, math 4 (including precalculus or calculus), lab science 4, social studies 3, and a foreign language 2–3. If they are available, take additional science courses in anatomy, physiology, or genetics.

Did you know...
...that the proper pronunciation of this major is "zo" (like "no") -ology, not "zoo" –ology? The word "zoo" is actually a mispronounced abbreviation for "zoological park."

Typical courses in this major:
Animal behavior
Animal physiology
Comparative anatomy
Ecology
Endocrinology
Genetics
Entomology (insects)
Evolutionary biology
Herpetology (reptiles and amphibians)
Invertebrate biology
Limnology (ponds and lakes)
Mammalogy
Ornithology
Parasitology
Primatology
Vertebrate zoology

Concentrations:
In college: Conservation or environmental biology; ecology and evolution; entomology; marine biology; neurobiology; physiology.

If you go on to grad school: anatomy and histology; ornithology (the study of birds); herpetology; developmental zoology; endocrinology; invertebrate zoology; parasitology; population biology.

What the study of this major is like:
As a zoology major, you explore how animals function. You study the way an organism acquires energy and material for growth and reproduction, and examine animals' interaction with their own kind as well as with other living and nonliving things. You also consider how animals have evolved.

In your first year, you will probably enroll in introductory courses in both biology and chemistry. Biology courses cover the significant concepts, from molecular biology to ecosystem ecology. In your second and third years, you take focused core courses, such as anatomy, cell biology, ecology, evolution, genetics, and physiology. Zoology majors usually study at least two years of chemistry, a year of physics, and some advanced math such as calculus. In your third and fourth years, you select upper-level electives specific to zoology.

In most zoology courses, you study the basic concepts in lectures; then, in a lab or field setting, you are introduced to data collection and techniques of analysis. Zoology majors usually spend about the same amount of time in lectures and in labs. After the first year, many majors do independent research projects with faculty members or sometimes with graduate students. Most first-year majors face serious challenges, especially in the first semester. Introductory biology and chemistry are generally taught in greater depth and more rigorously than in high school. If you do not complete the assignments on time, you may find it difficult to keep up with the work as the semester progresses. You need to call on your self-discipline in lectures, the laboratory or fieldwork, and no-nonsense studying.

Course offerings tend to mirror the research activities of the faculty. Different zoology departments may emphasize one area of biology or zoology over others. For example, some departments focus on molecular and cell biology and feature courses that explore how the parts of organisms (such as molecules and tissues) function. Other departments may stress whole organisms and populations and offer courses in ecology, environmental biology, and taxonomic groups (entomology, invertebrate zoology, ornithology, for example). Because most high school biology classes take only a brief look at the diversity of the animal kingdom, your interests may change in college as you encounter new areas of study. A department with a well-balanced curriculum that offers a wide variety of courses may give you the most options.

Other majors you might like:
Anthropology
Biology teacher education
Ecology
Evolutionary biology
Microbiology
Wildlife and wilderness management
Animal sciences
Livestock management
Marine biology
Veterinary technology
Entomology
Aquatic biology/limnology

Questions to ask colleges:
Is the major broad-based or does it concentrate on one particular area of zoological study?

What percentage of zoology majors are admitted into medical and other professional schools?

Which facilities are unique to the zoology program (such as a breeding facility), and which facilities are shared with other biological programs (electron microscope, computers)?

Career options and trends:
Health care professional; park ranger or guide; research assistant; teacher or college professor; environmental consultant; staff member at an aquarium, zoo, or animal park; veterinarian or veterinarian technician.

There will continue to be demand for those looking to enter the field of zoology, although opportunities will be limited because of the small size of this field. The best prospects are in the health care, biomedical, and environmental industries. A graduate or professional degree is necessary for most research, academic, and medical positions. A graduate degree is generally required for work as a zoologist. Summer employment in a medical, environmental, or other career area is increasingly expected of job applicants.

For more info:
American Institute of Biological Sciences (AIBS)
1900 Campus Commons Dr., Suite 200
Reston, VA 20191
(703) 674-2500
www.aibs.org

Business

Business has been tough lately, as we all know. But according to the National Association of Colleges and Employers (www. naceweb.org), prospects for students graduating later in this decade remain strong, mostly because of a rapidly aging workforce. Even if the economy rebuilds slowly, there will be a need for managers in all sectors of business to get things done.

Do you have what it takes to succeed in business? Business abilities cover a wide range of talent—"people skills" and communication, technical expertise, math and analytical skills, leadership, teamwork, and creativity— as well as commitment to integrity.

The main subject areas in business are topics that everyone should know something about.

"Knowledge of finance is an essential life skill," says Stephen J. Brown of the Stern School of Business, New York University.

"The same management concepts that ensure that the resources of a business organization are used effectively and efficiently can and should be applied to the choices one makes in life generally," observes Peter Bycio, Williams College of Business, Xavier University.

No matter what you're interested in, a knowledge of business can enhance your career.

"Entrepreneurship is applicable to any number of other careers," says Stephen Spinelli, Jr. of Babson College. "If someone has a passion for theater, studying business can help that person create, grow, and manage a theater company. Engineers, doctors, and lawyers need entrepreneurial skills to grow and succeed. The list goes on and on."

One way to think about business studies is to group them into functions, like finance, accounting, and marketing. Some majors cut across these functions. For instance, if you study business management or management information systems, you'll need to know about all aspects of operations and administration. Still other business majors, such as real estate, insurance, fashion merchandising, hospitality, and construction management, take you into specific industries or professions.

If you study business, you'll learn more than how to use a spreadsheet. Understanding human behavior is so important that many business programs contain courses in sociology, psychology, and the humanities.

Trends in business may also affect what you'll study. Current economic forces include globalization of companies and markets, a shift from manufacturing to service industries, corporate mergers, rapid developments in technology, changes in government regulations, price pressures, and shifting demographics. These trends have resulted in the creation of such business majors and courses as risk management, information management, e-commerce, supply chain management, and entrepreneurship. "We live in a world in which *change* may be the only constant," says Professor Diane Kaufman Fredette of Pratt Institute. "Given this trend, *managing change* has become an increasingly critical skill for managers."

On the undergraduate level, colleges have different philosophies of teaching business. Some colleges focus on quantitative, analytical, and technological aspects of business, while others emphasize strategy and management. Some programs get you ready to apply to grad school by teaching all about business theory. Other schools, taking a more practical, hands-on approach, prepare you for a business career with your bachelor's degree. Sometimes bachelor's and master's degrees are combined in a five-year program. A two-year degree is what you need for some jobs in hospitality and fashion merchandising.

Is grad school for you?

Each year, more than 150,000 students get master's degrees in business administration. That's a lot of competition for top jobs. Is the MBA a one-way ticket to a corner office? Not necessarily, but a recent survey of MBA students by the Graduate Management Admission Council shows that 91 percent of the students polled felt that their degree was of outstanding value, even as the economy remained weak. Wall Street, however, is not the immediate goal it once was. MBA's need to think of alternative routes to success, according to Diane Riemer, assistant director for graduate career services at Boston University's School of Management. She advises students to think of a "bridge strategy" where jobs can be stepping stones toward an ultimate career.

What do grad students in business actually study? It all depends on the major. Graduate tracks might include quality management; franchise, distributorship, and license ownership; corporate or international finance; investment banking; compensation and labor relations; information technology and systems; marketing research; and accounting information systems.

In the meantime, think about where you might go as an undergrad. Often, the location of the college dictates its business offerings. If the school is in an urban area and you're studying finance, for example, the program may prep you to work in financial services, which have offices in the city, rather than in financial management in suburban businesses.

Here are a few things to ask at all business-degree levels when comparing colleges: How long has the major been offered? Who are the faculty members? Are they full-time professors, or adjunct (part-time) professors (who are business professionals), or a combination? It's good to learn from the experts, but if they're on campus only a few hours a week, can you contact them easily? Are courses lecture-oriented, project-oriented, or action-oriented, and do you have a preference? How is technology used in class?

What kinds of resources do students have? Seed funding? Business-plan competitions? Internships? Access to industry experts? Do student organizations have chapters on campus? What kind of job placement assistance and career counseling will you get after you graduate? What career paths do most graduates follow? Which employers interview business majors on campus?

Make it your business to find out about colleges that offer these majors. They include schools of business, management, commerce, business administration, and arts and sciences.

Accounting

What it's about:

Accounting is known as the language of business. The major prepares you to gather, record, analyze, interpret, and communicate financial information about an individual's or an organization's performance and risks. You study such topics as financial statement preparation and analysis, risk assessment and control, management decision-making, tax preparation and planning, management of accounting information systems, auditing, and fraud.

Is this for you?

You might like this major if you also like: computers; leadership roles; working with numbers; interacting and working with people; seeing both the details and the "big picture" when analyzing situations.

Consider this major if you are good at: attention to detail; critical reading/thinking; leadership; organizing; quantitative analysis; teamwork ...*or have...* people skills; verbal skills; writing skills.

Recommended high school prep:

English 4 (including writing), math 3 (including trigonometry), lab science 3, social studies 3, and a foreign language 2–3. If possible, also take communications, speech, and computer courses.

Did you know...

...that accounting is not just about crunching numbers? Communication and critical-thinking skills are essential for success in the profession, because accountants spend most of their time advising, analyzing, communicating, and managing. The profession is often viewed as the fast track to upper-level management positions like controller, chief financial officer (CFO), or chief executive officer (CEO).

Typical courses in this major:

Introductory accounting
Intermediate accounting
Advanced accounting
Auditing
Cost accounting
Taxation
International accounting
Accounting information systems
Government and not-for-profit accounting
Financial statement analysis

Concentrations:

Generally, none in college; but if you go on to grad school: financial accounting; accounting information systems; cost accounting; managerial accounting; forensic accounting.

What the study of this major is like:

Accounting is a popular major available at most colleges, often housed in a school of business or management. Otherwise, accounting may be offered as part of a program in the liberal arts or sciences, usually in the economics or social sciences department. The accounting major includes both technical and application-based course work. The technical nature of some courses makes them well suited to the lecture format, which is often supplemented with interactive learning tools such as case analyses, computer simulations, and research projects. Many courses are taught as seminars, with plenty of student participation; some courses include hands-on, real-world experience.

Undergraduate concentrations are rare. You take courses in economics and finance, business law, business organization and management, marketing, and computer information sciences. You learn to measure costs, compile data, and determine how the data affect efficiency and profitability. After your introductory accounting courses, you study financial statements and how they are used to make business decisions. You also study such topics as risk assurance, e-commerce accounting and control, fraud investigation, internal auditing, and ethics.

One of the more challenging areas you may face as a major is financial accounting. Many students find it difficult at first—comprehending it can be like solving a complex puzzle. But once you master the subject, its framework and logic become second nature.

In addition to your accounting curriculum, you are usually required to take a range of liberal arts and science courses. Especially important are those in history and foreign languages (finance has become global). Because good communication is vital to the profession, you will also benefit from classes that sharpen your writing, speaking, and problem-solving skills.

In some accounting programs, you focus on theory. Other programs take an applied approach that stresses the skills you will need as an accountant. Some programs also have a niche emphasis, such as internal auditing or accounting information systems. Although some programs still have separate undergraduate and master's degrees, others offer a five-year program—a bachelor's and a master's are awarded jointly at graduation. These programs have become more popular with the phasing in of the rule requiring students who want to become a certified public accountant (CPA) to complete 150 credit hours of course work.

The accounting major prepares you for careers in public or managerial accounting. Public accountants work with auditing firms to produce credible financial reports; managerial accountants work with management to monitor an organization's financial health. Managerial accountants often need special knowledge about taxes, budgeting, and investing. While often helpful, a CPA designation is not essential for internal auditing, corporate accounting, and government accounting.

Other majors you might like:
Finance
Management information systems
Accounting technology/bookkeeping
Information systems
Statistics
Economics
Insurance
Public administration
Real estate
International business
Marketing
Theater arts management

Questions to ask colleges:
Does the program encourage internships?

Is course work primarily applied (analysis-based) or conceptual (theory-based)?

Are bachelor's and master's degrees offered in separate programs or in a unified, five-year program?

Career options and trends:
Auditor*; tax accountant/adviser*; risk assurance/ information technology consultant*; corporate accountant*; financial planner; fraud examiner; government investigator (IRS, FBI).

The job outlook for accountants is very good. The best prospects will be for those with CPA certification or an MBA in accounting. To become a CPA, you must pass the national CPA exam, and also meet the certification requirements of the state where you want to practice; most states require a period of professional work experience and the equivalent of five years of college (150 credit hours).

Large-scale business scandals and the financial crises have put accounting, auditing, and fraud investigations in the spotlight. CFOs and auditors have greater responsibilities and tighter rules governing their behavior. Thus the demand for well-qualified accounting professionals should remain high. The growth of global business will also lead to more demand for those with knowledge of international accounting rules.

For more info:
American Accounting Association (AAA)
5717 Bessie Drive
Sarasota, FL 34233-2399
(941) 921-7747
www.aaahq.org

American Institute of Certified Public Accountants
1211 Avenue of the Americas
New York, NY 10036-8775
(212) 596-6200
www.aicpa.org

Business administration and management

What it's about:

This major teaches you how to plan, organize, lead, and control the human, financial, and physical resources of an organization to achieve business goals. As a manager, you will be expected to meet the many demands of your employer, your organization's internal and external customers, and society in general.

Is this for you?

You might like this major if you also like: working with people; starting and running a business; the *Wall Street Journal*; debating; organizing or leading a club or group activity; solving problems; taking risks; competing; sports; helping others to succeed.

Consider this major if you are good at: attention to detail; critical reading/thinking; leadership; organizing; persuading/influencing; quantitative analysis; teamwork ...*or have...* initiative; verbal skills.

Recommended high school prep:

English 4, math 4 (including precalculus), lab science 3, social studies 3, and a foreign language 2–3. If available, take calculus and a computer course covering basic office applications and spreadsheets.

Did you know...

...that this is by far the most popular major? That means you'll have lots of company—and a wide choice of colleges that offer this major.

...that math skills are important for a business degree? Quantitative analysis is required for several areas of business, such as accounting, finance, and business statistics.

Typical courses in this major:

Accounting I, II
Business law
Economics
International trade and business
Business finance
Human resources
Managing information technology
Managerial communication
Principles of marketing
Business statistics
Production management
Operations management
Organizational design and development
Leadership
Quality planning and improvement
Strategic formulation and implementation

Concentrations:

Accounting; entrepreneurship; finance; international business; leadership; marketing; organizational behavior; production operations management

What the study of this major is like:

Few people can avoid management. One day, you will probably either be a manager or work for one. The business management and administration major prepares you to serve as an effective, responsible manager in business, government, or nonprofit sectors. Managers have both the opportunity and the duty to make a difference: receiving good service can reflect good management; an employee's unethical behavior can reflect poor management; and good managers make sure that organizations generate value for their stakeholders on a sustained basis.

In the major, you typically learn how to achieve goals by planning (defining goals and deciding how to achieve them), organizing (deciding what resources need to go where to best support the plan), leading (influencing people to work toward accomplishing goals), and controlling (monitoring progress toward achieving goals and adjusting initial plans as needed). You study how managers respond to the complex, ever-changing expectations of employees, bosses, customers, governments, the legal community, and society as a whole. Majors begin with basic courses in accounting, marketing, and finance. You then take specialized courses, such as organizational behavior, human resources management, supervisory skills, and international management. In your fourth year, you usually take a capstone course in business strategy or business policy; applying what you have learned, you explore the way an organization interacts with the outside world and operates internally.

Most management programs offer internships, usually for a semester, to help you gain experience, learn about possible careers, and relate classroom learning to the workplace. Most internships award academic credit and require you to submit material to be graded. Some internships can lead to future job opportunities. Many colleges offer a semester-abroad program that lets you practice your management skills in another country. Because the policies and practices of employees, customers, organizations, and their competitors can reflect—positively or negatively—on the society in which they are located, managers must understand the cultural expectations of their host country.

Nevertheless, the objective of the major is to prepare you to lead others in an organization. Most management courses stimulate your persuasive and creative abilities—memorizing facts is generally not top priority. Courses are typically taught through lectures, videos, case studies, and, perhaps, role-playing. Professors use case studies to develop your problem-solving and analytical skills, to teach you to defend ideas logically, and to push you to challenge the ideas of others. You analyze actual business problems, develop realistic responses, and present your recommendations to professors and classmates. Working managers are often brought in to share their experiences. You use computers for spreadsheet programs, databases, and other programs that help you conduct statistical analysis, prepare financial projections, and do marketing research. If you choose this major, you should be ready to work hard.

Although most agree on a definition of general management, different colleges may have different emphases. Some programs take a quantitative approach and focus on decision-making techniques. Other programs may emphasize a management function such as leadership or an area of general management—for example, human resource management or organizational behavior. Differences among programs are also reflected in their readiness to adapt to changes in the field. For example, supply chain management, project management, and entrepreneurship are emerging topics. Some programs will be relatively conservative in their approach to such topics, offering only a course or two at first, while others may develop new concentrations or even new majors.

Other majors you might like:
Agribusiness operations
Entrepreneurial studies
Marketing
International business
Construction management
Emergency management/homeland security
Music management
Parks/recreational/leisure facilities management
E-commerce
Public administration
Economics
Nonprofit/public organization management

Questions to ask colleges:
Is the program accredited by the Association to Advance Collegiate Schools of Business? If so, the program has been examined for quality from a number of perspectives.

Are there internships or co-op programs available in this major?

Do companies recruit on campus?

Career options and trends:
Management trainee or assistant manager*; sales or account representative*; corporate executive; management consultant; franchise or small business owner; human resources specialist; systems analyst; financial analyst; venture capitalist.

The job outlook mirrors the economic times, but organizations are always looking for good managers. As the world of business grows more complex, risky, and global in scope, the need for professional managers increases. Job growth is projected to be steady through 2022, particularly in smaller companies specializing in specific industries or types of business functions.

An MBA is usually essential if you want to climb the corporate ladder; but many well-known companies will help you obtain this advanced degree while you're working.

Insider's viewpoint:
"Some classes, like accounting or information systems, are a much bigger time commitment. But I

would estimate that on average, I spend about four hours per class per week on homework. However, that doesn't include the group projects, which take much more time. Business-school classes have many more group projects than any other classes I've taken."

—Dan, junior, University of Washington

For more info:
Association to Advance Collegiate Schools of
    Business (AACSB)
777 South Harbor Island Blvd.
Suite 750
Tampa, FL 33602-5730
(813) 769-6500
www.aacsb.edu

American Management Association (AMA)
1601 Broadway
New York, NY 10019
(877) 566-9441
www.amanet.org

Construction management

What it's about:
Construction management is the art of orchestrating all the components necessary to complete a building project within budget and on time. This major combines courses in business management, technology, and the liberal arts to provide the practical knowledge and critical thinking skills that a leadership role in construction requires.

Is this for you?
You might like this major if you also like: the outdoors; running a group project; working in teams; taking responsibility; working with your hands; achieving goals and results; watching construction sites.

Consider this major if you are good at: attention to detail; leadership; multi-tasking; organizing; persuading/influencing; quantitative analysis; spacial thinking/analysis; teamwork *...or have...* verbal skills.

Recommended high school prep:
English 4, math 3 (including trigonometry), lab science 3, social studies 3, industrial arts 2, and a foreign language 2. Spanish is recommended because it is spoken by many workers in the construction industry. If available, courses in business, accounting, and computer-aided drafting (CAD) are also helpful.

Did you know...
...that the ability to think in three dimensions is essential in this field? Before giving instructions or solving problems, construction managers often have to visualize how a structure should take shape.

Typical courses in this major:
Principles of management
Principles of accounting
Labor relations
Business law and ethics
Project scheduling
Construction estimating
Blueprint reading
Specifications
Construction materials
Structural methods
Mechanical and electrical systems
Environmental compliance
Project budgeting and cost management
Construction law, codes, and regulations
Site logistics
Safety management

Concentrations:
Construction technology; safety management; planning and logistics

What the study of this major is like:
Construction management is both an on-site job (making sure that the project is going smoothly and according to plan) and a desk job (dealing with bids, contracts, insurance, and other paperwork). A successful manager has expertise in three areas: construction, management, and people skills.

This major helps you develop this expertise by blending business management training with technical know-how. Course work covers creative problem solving, emerging technologies, best practices, and ethical principles. The goal is to prepare you to become a professional manager who can combine business acumen with an awareness of the diverse interests of the developer, contractor, owner, architect, and engineer.

Beginning with basic studies of blueprints and drawings, construction materials and techniques, you progress to an understanding of more complex components such as site logistics, specifications, cost estimating, and design, mechanical, structural, electrical, and legal issues. You learn to consider construction drawings as a picture not only of the planned structure but also of the complex process involving five dimensions—which include time and money, referred to as "schedule" and "budget."

Crunching numbers may not sound much like construction work, but nothing gets built before a budget is in place. That's why courses in estimating and accounting are usually required. You'll learn, step by step, how to figure the costs for everything from building materials to labor. You'll practice looking for clues in floor plans, and you'll get a handle on competitive bidding.

Many students enjoy the technical and graphic aspects of the major but find that writing skills do not come as easily. To help bring these skills together, most programs require a capstone project in the final year. For that you research a topic of your own interest and present a professional quality report to be reviewed by faculty or invited professionals.

Most programs include practical exposure to the profession. Lectures and lab courses are supplemented by opportunities for internships in which you do hands-on work under the guidance of a mentor. Actual construction experience is as essential as a degree when it comes to finding a job after graduation.

While construction management can be considered a business major, it is usually housed in a school or department of technology, engineering, or architecture. The emphasis on business management skills may vary depending on the overall strength of the college's business program. Architecturally based programs usually focus on design and on a team approach to problem solving.

This major is offered at both the associate degree and the bachelor's degree level. Four-year programs include more business management skills and liberal arts requirements. Two-year programs usually concentrate on construction technology.

Other majors you might like:
Civil engineering
Construction technology
Architectural engineering
Land use planning
Operations management
Real estate
Surveying technology
Geology/earth science
Mining and mineral engineering
Historic preservation
Heavy/earthmoving equipment operation
Architecture

Questions to ask colleges:
Is the program accredited by the American Council for Construction Education (ACCE)?

Do the professors incorporate their field experience into their classroom instruction?

What kinds of hands-on experiences are provided? Is there an internship program?

Career options and trends:
Construction manager; general contractor; site inspector; cost estimator; specifications writer; contract administrator.

Even though the construction industry has been hard hit lately, the Bureau of Labor Statistics is bullish on the construction industry, projecting faster than average growth through 2022, and projects good job prospects for construction managers in particular because there are not enough graduates in this field to meet expected demand. As the economy recovers that demand will become more acute. Employment in this field will always be subject, however, to cyclical fluctuations in the industry.

Prospects will be best for those with a bachelor's degree and construction work experience gained through internships and summer jobs.

For more info:
American Council for Construction Education
1717 N. Loop 1604 East, Suite 320
San Antonio, TX 78232-1570
(210) 495-6161
www.acce-hq.org

Construction Management Association of America
7926 Jones Branch Drive, Suite 800
McLean, VA 22102-3303
(703) 356-2622
www.cmaanet.org

E-commerce

Also known as:
Digital business strategy

What it's about:
This major focuses on how to use marketing concepts, business strategies, economics, and computer science to develop new businesses, or to transform an existing business, through the use of the Internet and related information technology.

Is this for you?
You might like this major if you also like: computers; e-Bay; social networking; starting or running a business venture; new technology; taking risks; science fiction; advertisements; buying and selling.

Consider this major if you are good at: attention to detail; creativity; leadership; math; organizing; persuading/influencing; quantitative analysis; research ...*or have*... computer skills; initiative.

Recommended high school prep:
English 4, math 3, lab science 3, social studies 3, and a foreign language 2–3. If available, take a computer science course and an economics course that covers microeconomics.

Did you know...
...that e-commerce is not solely about technology, but rather the linking of technology and new business approaches? So you don't have to be a computer geek to do well in this major.

...that most of the interesting applications of e-commerce are likely to be in established businesses rather than in start-up ventures? This makes the long-term prospects of an e-commerce-related career more stable and broadens the types of job opportunities available.

Typical courses in this major:
Management information systems
Introduction to e-business
E-commerce marketing
E-commerce strategy
Law of electronic commerce
Strategic management
Entrepreneurial management
Venture capital
New venture initiation
Business application development (programming)
Internet technology
Computer networking and communications
Systems analysis and design
World Wide Web design
Business transformation/reengineering

Concentrations:
Business to consumer (B2C) e-commerce; business to business (B2B) e-commerce; electronic marketing; business strategies; computer technology.

What the study of this major is like:
While you might think e-commerce has been around your whole life, e-commerce as a discipline, or academic subject, is still in its infancy. New technologies and creative individuals are continually remaking e-commerce and keeping it interesting. How many other disciplines transform themselves so extensively every few years? Another factor that makes e-commerce exciting is that you can apply your ideas quickly; you may have the satisfaction of producing immediate results.

The e-commerce major usually begins with a combination of general courses in technology and management fundamentals. Next, you take courses focusing on how e-commerce can be used in creating businesses or improving the performance of existing businesses. In many of your courses, you'll examine recent developments in electronics, such as smart phones, and then identify opportunities to apply the new tools. You may also focus on finding technological solutions to classic business problems—for instance, figuring out how computers can help deliver customized products more efficiently. Because much of your work involves exploring ways to apply technology, you will probably spend considerable time brainstorming with others on team projects.

The biggest difference among programs is whether they emphasize technology or business. Almost all programs have a mix of the two areas, but the number of technology or business offerings can vary dramatically. Some programs focus almost entirely on technology. In these programs, courses usually deal with computer programming, network technology, and the development of Web content. Other programs focus on management issues, such as marketing, business case analyses, business plan development, or business strategies made possible by the Internet. In still other programs, you cannot take e-commerce as a stand-alone major; you must combine it with a major in computer science, management, marketing, or information technology. Ask yourself if you are more business or technology oriented to figure out which programs are a better fit for you.

Other majors you might like:
Marketing
Business administration and management
Information technology
Electrical and communications engineering
Economics
Digital media
Entrepreneurial studies
Management information systems
Web/multimedia management
Advertising
Computer engineering
Consumer merchandising

Questions to ask colleges:
Does the program focus primarily on the technological aspects or the business aspects of e-commerce?

Are the courses staffed with regular faculty members or with outside professionals and visiting professors? Are the faculty members engaged in the field? How do they keep current with fast-changing developments?

Career options and trends:
Web developer*; Internet business developer (analyst or manager); network engineer; product manager/marketing manager; business alliance manager; technology analyst*; venture capitalist/fund manager; investment banking analyst; market analyst*; Internet applications designer.

The long-term employment prospects for e-commerce and related professions are very strong. The Bureau of Labor Statistics describes the growth of e-commerce as "explosive" and notes that the expansion of mobile technology will spur the need for managers with both business savvy and technical proficiency. Technology constantly improves, and each advance presents new business opportunities.

Insider's viewpoint:
"It's exciting to be in a field where things thought to be impossible only a decade before become commonplace."

—Professor Lorin Hitt, Wharton School of Business

For more info:
Association for Computing Machinery (ACM)
2 Penn Plaza
Suite 701
New York, NY 10121-0701
(800) 342-6626
www.acm.org

Entrepreneurial studies

Also known as:
Enterprise management

What it's about:
The entrepreneurial studies major teaches you how to recognize, evaluate, and respond to new business opportunities. You learn to use management skills to set up and run your own business or franchise, or to apply your creativity and energy to increase the productivity of an existing business.

Is this for you?
You might like this major if you also like: thinking of better ways to do things; learning new ideas, exploring new places, and meeting new people; starting or running a business; puzzles; sports; competition; taking charge of a group activity; taking risks.

Consider this major if you are good at: creativity; critical reading/thinking; leadership; organizing; persuading/influencing; teamwork ...*or have...* initiative; perseverance; self-confidence; verbal skills.

Recommended high school prep:
English 4, math 3, lab science 3, social studies 3, and a foreign language 2–3. If available, take a business course, an economics course, and statistics.

Did you know...
...that entrepreneurship is about more than creating a new business? There are opportunities to apply entrepreneurial thinking to the corporate world, socially focused projects, venture capital financing, and a host of other possibilities.

...that in this major, risk and failure are rewarded? Because many businesses disappear within the first five years of operation, most entrepreneurship professors expect students to explore risky ideas that have a greater than 50 percent chance of failing. If an opportunity is worth taking, most likely it will be risky (otherwise, someone would have already taken it).

Typical courses in this major:
Foundations of entrepreneurship
Living the entrepreneurial experience
New ventures and the business plan
Entrepreneurial finance
Managing a growing business
Family business
Social enterprise management
Investor relations and funding
Business and tax planning
Entrepreneurial marketing
New product design and development

Concentrations:
New-venture creation; entrepreneurial finance; corporate entrepreneurship; family-controlled enterprise management; franchise, distributorship, and license ownership; entrepreneurial economics.

What the study of this major is like:
Entrepreneurial studies is the liberal arts major of business school. To be successful as an entrepreneurial major, you need to be able to see the "big picture" and still remain focused enough to take action. You can apply entrepreneurial thinking to almost any field of study—from liberal arts and social sciences to mathematics and physics—and to a variety of careers. If you have a passion for, say, theater, you can use what you learn in entrepreneurial studies to help you create, grow, and manage a drama company. An engineer with an entrepreneurial studies degree can develop innovations that are not just new, but that people will want and buy. Doctors and lawyers who work on their own can use entrepreneurial skills to make their private practices develop and thrive. Business executives can use their entrepreneurial skills to capitalize on opportunities from within their companies. This major prepares you not only for a career but also for life.

Almost all entrepreneurship programs require you to complete a core of business courses. Most programs also offer courses in developing a business plan and in entrepreneurial finance. Good programs blend academic exercises such as case studies and class discussion with hands-on experience creating an enterprise or working with an existing organization.

They also provide a variety of specialty paths that may include social entrepreneurship, management of a growing business, and family-controlled enterprises.

The challenges you will face depend on the rigor of the program you attend. Students in strong programs often have to deal with real-world experiences that are outside the bounds of traditional academic activities—for instance, handling professional vendors or actual customers. In general, entrepreneurship can be emotionally demanding because you must make a personal commitment, to your stakeholders (investors, employees, your family, society), that you will create value or improve social conditions. And you don't commit to try—you commit to *do*.

The most obvious difference among programs is how much the sponsoring school or college focuses on entrepreneurship. The programs generally evolve as follows: first, a handful of entrepreneurs and management professors teach a course or two on new-venture creation; then a division of professors teach a number of concentrations in the discipline (such as new ventures or financing) with little interaction with other departments; finally, the college (or school of business) reshapes it curriculum, teaching business in the context of entrepreneurship.

Other majors you might like:
E-commerce
Business administration and management
Franchise operations
Marketing
Consumer economics
Farm and ranch management
Real estate
Small business administration/management
Arts management
Economics
Development economics
Finance

Questions to ask colleges:
How many full-time faculty members teach and research entrepreneurship as their principal endeavor? Do any of the professors have real-world experience or background as entrepreneurs?

How long has the major been offered at this college?

Which career path do graduates from the college generally follow: start-up? industry? finance?

Which kinds of resources are available for students (such as incubator space, seed funding, business plan competitions, access to industry experts and sources of funding)?

Career options and trends:
Business owner/new-venture creator*; investment banker; consultant*; sales and marketing professional*; venture capitalist; operations manager.

Entrepreneurship remains strong in both good and bad economic periods. When the economy is strong, entrepreneurs find an abundance of opportunity, and companies and consumers have more money to spend on the emerging products and services that entrepreneurs provide. When the economy is weak and jobs are scarce, entrepreneurs will spend their time creating a job rather than looking for one.

For more info:
Junior Achievement Inc.
One Education Way
Colorado Springs, CO 80906
(719) 540-8000
www.ja.org

National Foundation for Teaching
   Entrepreneurship (NFTE)
120 Wall St.
18th Fl.
New York, NY 10005
(212) 232-3333
www.nfte.com

Fashion merchandising

What it's about:

The major in fashion merchandising introduces you to all areas of the industry, including design, product development, textiles, buying, marketing, advertising, importing and exporting, sales, and retail management. You learn how to identify and acquire the fashions that customers want, and to sell those fashions.

Is this for you?

You might like this major if you also like: shopping at secondhand stores, consignment shops, and tag sales; fashion magazines; art and photography; travel; interesting people; learning about different cultures; clothes, fabrics, and fashion accessories; cosmetics; keeping up with trends; thinking creatively.

Consider this major if you are good at: attention to detail; creativity; critical reading/thinking; leadership; organizing; stress management; teamwork ...*or have...* an eye for color and design; initiative; verbal skills; writing skills.

Recommended high school prep:

English 4, math 3, lab science 3, social studies 3, and a foreign language 3–4. Courses in art, art history, and business are also recommended. Because the fashion industry operates in the global marketplace, a foreign language is highly desirable.

Typical courses in this major:

History of fashion
Textiles
Sales
Advertising
Marketing
Fashion buying
Merchandising accounting
Fashion show
Consumer behavior
Retail management
International fashion marketing
Mass marketing
Product pevelopment
Computer-aided design (CAD)

Concentrations:

In college: fashion buying; textiles; marketing and advertising; visual merchandising; retail management; apparel production.

If you go on to grad school: production; supply chain management.

What the study of this major is like:

The fashion merchandising major prepares you for a wide variety of career opportunities in the business of marketing and distributing fashion products. Fashion merchandising is an exciting field, reflecting a fast-paced global industry that shapes worldwide trends. The glitz of fashion shows and fashion magazines is the result of creative and analytical thinking, market research, and hard work.

You can learn to manage a retail firm, buy goods for a firm, or work with designers in planning an apparel manufacturer's fashion message. To acquire the communication, analytic, and computer skills necessary to succeed in this competitive industry, you will probably begin with courses in writing, speech, mathematics, history, social science, and natural science. During your first and second years, you take courses such as fashion analysis and textiles, which provide an introduction to the field. In advanced courses, you learn to organize and operate a retail clothing business; to plan, promote, and manage merchandise inventories; and to calculate retail figures for a profitable business. You may also study historical and multicultural costumes—you can later draw on this interesting subject to develop special promotions or store events.

Fashion merchandising programs can lead to either two-year (associate) or four-year (bachelor's) degrees. Associate degree programs generally include courses on the fashion industry, textiles, buying, advertising, sales, and retail management. Sometimes students who have earned a bachelor's degree in another field obtain an associate degree in fashion merchandising. Bachelor's programs in fashion merchandising include traditional liberal arts courses and professional courses in product development, importing and exporting, marketing textiles, product design, retail management, and business law. At some colleges, you can minor in marketing, textiles, and design. Many programs offer field experiences for college credit. Associate degree programs generally offer one opportunity for an industry internship. In bachelor's programs, you may be able to take more than one internship, as well as to study abroad for a semester.

The program is a combination of traditional academic courses and less traditional fashion merchandising courses. The academic courses, which are generally lectures and discussions or laboratory sessions, usually require tests and papers. The fashion merchandising classes generally include lots of hands-on work. Most faculty members and academic advisers have extensive industry experience and do not teach only from textbooks. Fashion merchandising courses are often enriched by field trips and guest speakers. Some programs offer study tours of major U.S. fashion markets (such as New York, Dallas, and Los Angeles) or of European fashion centers. In advanced courses, you are assigned group projects to help you become an effective team player. Many fashion merchandising majors hold jobs while carrying a full-time class load.

Some colleges offer only associate degree programs; some offer only bachelor's degree programs; and some offer both. Certain colleges allow you to move from an associate degree directly into the bachelor's program with no loss of credit. Other associate degree programs provide credit transfer arrangements with four-year colleges.

Other majors you might like:
Marketing
Retailing
Hospitality administration and management
Fiber/textile arts
Fashion and apparel design
Commercial/advertising art
Photography
Anthropology
Psychology
Clothing, apparel and textile studies

Family and consumer sciences
Cosmetic services

Questions to ask colleges:
Do faculty members keep current in their field by continuing to work in the industry? Do they maintain contacts in the field?

Is help available for students looking for internships? Is there a cooperative education program? Students who make contacts in the industry and do networking are likely to receive job offers before graduation.

Career options and trends:
Fashion designer; buyer*; fashion marketing executive*; showroom account executive*; fashion editor; textile designer*; import/export specialist; fashion advertising director; visual merchandiser*; merchandise manager.

Competition for jobs is strong. A BA or BFA in fashion design, an excellent portfolio, and internship experience will provide the best job prospects. Many majors think that the only careers open to them are fashion design and retail buying. However, a survey has identified 31 additional fashion careers, including computer-assisted apparel design; color forecasting; storyboard design; catalog production; mall management; private label development; Web-based retailing; online direct marketing; and fashion consulting. Experience on the job and good networking skills should lead to promotions and future job offers.

For more info:
International Textile and Apparel Association (ITAA)
PO Box 70687
Knoxville, TN 37938-0687
(865) 992-1535
www.itaaonline.org

Finance

What it's about:

The finance major provides you with a general understanding of financial decision-making and an insight into the way financial markets perform. Emphasis is on the financial management function in firms and not-for-profit organizations, the valuation of financial securities, and the appropriate management of financial risk.

Is this for you?

You might like this major if you also like: family business discussions; the *Wall Street Journal*; doing research; following the stock market; investment clubs.

Consider this major if you are good at: attention to detail; creativity; critical reading/thinking; math; quantitative analysis; research; teamwork...*or have...* mental stamina; writing skills.

Recommended high school prep:

English 4, math 4 (including precalculus), lab science 3, social studies 3, and a foreign language 2–3. If possible, take computer science, economics, and statistics courses. Calculus is also helpful, although not required.

Did you know...

...that even though this major deals with money, you should not count on getting rich quick? Most entry-level positions open to undergraduate finance majors involve hard work and long hours. Students who have become successful have usually exerted considerable effort early on in their career.

...that even bright, well-motivated students often think that finance is a difficult major and that the language of finance is incomprehensible? Most majors quickly learn, however, that the subject matter is made up of simple, straightforward concepts.

Typical courses in this major:

Financial management
Financial institutions and markets
Corporate finance
Futures and options
Portfolio analysis
International finance
Investment banking
Real estate finance
Risk and insurance
Working capital management
Bank management
Investments
Accounting
Economics

Concentrations:

Corporate finance; real estate finance; investment banking.

What the study of this major is like:

In many business schools, finance classes are offered only to students in their second year or higher; because of the technical nature of the material, you'll need to have mastered a number of foundation courses. During your first two years, your general education requirements usually include mathematics, humanities, natural sciences, and social sciences courses. Most programs also require three to six credits each of economics, statistics, and accounting.

After completing the prerequisites, majors take introductory courses in finance and other functional areas of business, such as accounting, management, marketing, and management of information systems (MIS). Usually you must also take one or more courses in financial management/corporate finance and in financial institutions and markets, most of them taught in a large lecture format.

Your first finance course will probably focus on corporate financial analysis, as well as on valuation principles for financial assets such as stocks and bonds. Emphasis is on the tools of analysis, including the evaluation of financial statements and the time value of money calculations. Subsequent classes cover investments and portfolio managements, corporate finance, banking and financial institutions, and international finance. Then you're likely to take smaller classes or seminars on a variety of finance subspecialties that interest you. Because of the critical relation of economics and accounting to finance, most finance programs require at least 12 to 15 semester hours of course work in both economics and accounting.

Many finance courses require the use of computers for problem solving, to improve your facility with spreadsheet programs, statistical and financial analysis, financial forecasting, and the preparation of financial reports. Electives may be in statistics, economics, accounting, computer applications, and communications.

Most of your classes will demand a level of familiarity and comfort with quantitative analysis. This subject area may well be your biggest challenge. The style of teaching varies according to subspecialty. Most advanced corporate finance and financial management courses are taught by means of case analysis; you are presented with a situation and, either individually or as a group, you prepare a presentation. Some areas (particularly derivative securities and futures and options classes) are math-oriented; if you have not covered precalculus or other advanced math in high school, you may have to play catch-up.

Programs typically differ on whether they emphasize financial markets, investment and financial management, or corporate finance. The split will often reflect the college's evaluation of job opportunities in the locality. For example, colleges close to financial centers may stress financial markets and investments, on the assumption that many graduates will head for the financial services sector. Colleges in other regions may emphasize financial management, on the assumption that most graduates will seek employment in the finance departments of nearby corporations.

Other majors you might like:
Accounting
Actuarial science
Banking/financial services
Business administration and management
Economics
Financial planning
International finance
Investments/securities
Insurance

Management science
Real estate
Credit management

Questions to ask colleges:
What is the emphasis of the program? If you want to work in a corporate setting, a program that focuses on financial management would seem appropriate. If you'd rather work in the financial services sector, then you might prefer a program featuring the financial markets and investments.

Career options and trends:
Stockbroker; security sales representative; financial analyst; investment banker; commercial banker; portfolio or mutual fund manager; financial planner; government regulator.

To be a stockbroker or to engage in securities sales and trading, you must pass the general securities registered representative examination (Series 7), administered by the National Association of Security Dealers (NASD). Portfolio managers and other investment management professionals typically acquire the postgraduate chartered financial analysts (CFA) certification, administered by the Association for Investment Management and Research (AIMR). Certification requirements for other positions vary on a state-by-state basis.

Employment in the financial services sector will always be affected by the state of the economy on Wall Street. Demand for personal financial advisors, however, is projected to be quite strong through 2022, according to the Bureau of Labor Statistics, because of the needs of the "baby boomer" generation approaching retirement. Job growth for financial managers, on the other hand, will be modest. Increased government oversight of the securities industry should create job opportunities in regulatory agencies.

A sound training in finance is considered useful for any general management position. Banks often employ finance majors in a variety of areas, from corporate lending to trust operations. Corporations hire graduates as financial managers, as financial controllers, or in international financial operations. Brokerage and investment banking firms offer opportunities as account executives or financial consultants for clients. Insurance companies and real estate developers also offer entry-level opportunities. Competition can be tough in this field, and those with an MBA or other certifications will have the best employment prospects.

Insider's viewpoint:
"I like to think of this field as 'advanced common sense.' "

—Professor Stephen J. Brown, Stern School of Business, New York University

For more info:
Financial Management Association International
University of South Florida College of Business
    Administration
4202 East Fowler Ave., BSN 3331
Tampa, FL 33620-5500
(813) 974-2084
www.fma.org

Hospitality administration and management

Also known as:
Hotel, restaurant, and tourism management

What it's about:
Hospitality management is a career-oriented program focusing on anticipating and satisfying the needs of the traveling visitor/guest. It prepares you for professions in the travel, lodging, food service, and recreation industries.

Is this for you?
You might like this major if you also like: travel; meeting new people; cooking; giving parties; working with people; sports; learning about different cultures; socializing in large groups; leadership roles.

Consider this major if you are good at: attention to detail; creativity; critical reading/thinking; leadership; math; teamwork *...or have...* initiative; verbal skills; writing skills.

Recommended high school prep:
English 4, math 3, lab science 3, social studies 3, and a foreign language 3–4. Courses covering accounting and geography would also be helpful. The Hospitality Business Alliance (www.nraef.org) has spearheaded the School to Career Partnership of hotels, restaurants, high schools, and colleges. High school students can earn credits that are transferable to two- and four-year colleges.

Did you know...
...that the hospitality and tourism industry is one of the top three employers in the U.S., and is estimated to be the largest industry in the world? Whether for a business conference, a rock concert, or a family wedding, the industry can provide the transportation, accommodations, meals, sound systems, security—whatever is needed to make the event happen.

Typical courses in this major:
Introduction to tourism
Management principles
Marketing
Employee labor relations
Facilities design
Lodging administration
Resort operations
Hospitality law
Hospitality finance/accounting
Geography of tourism
Festival and event management
Food service operations

Concentrations:
Casino management; community economic development; time-share management; hotel/motel management; club management; restaurant management; tourism and service management.

What the study of this major is like:
Hospitality is serious business, a fact that is often overshadowed by media images of a carefree vacation destination. The major requires a wide variety of business courses. In addition, you can expect hands-on experiences, including restaurant operation, front-office management, and housekeeping supervision. The program usually requires co-op service or an internship (which may be paid); study abroad opportunities are especially valuable in this major.

Often the faculty members have industry experience in addition to academic credentials. Moreover, there are generally several active student associations that arrange industry speakers, on-site facility visits, and fund-raisers to finance these activities.

When comparing programs, remember that there is no one best format. Colleges may take advantage of their closeness to large hotels, casinos, small resorts, or other establishments that attract business travelers and international visitors. Majors housed in a college of business tend to offer modified versions of traditional business courses. An emphasis on food and beverage operations is also a feature at some colleges. Customer/guest contact is the cornerstone of any variation of the major.

The hospitality industry thrives on outgoing, creative people. There is no routine day. The industry strives to produce satisfied guests by customizing their experience, and in a well-managed facility, employees know how to to meet the challenge. The ability to pay attention to detail is also required. A hospitality property rarely has a second chance to make a good impression. It is also a well-recognized reality that students in this major will have to adjust to the fact that they will be working while almost everyone else around them is playing! Finally, expect to travel.

Other majors you might like:
Geography
Tourism/travel management
Hotel/motel administration/management
Resort management
Interior design
Restaurant/catering management
Landscape architecture
Culinary arts and chef training
Security services management
Sports and fitness administration
Parks, recreation, and leisure studies
International business

Questions to ask colleges:
Do the faculty members have industry experience?

To what extent has the college invested in the excellence of the major by providing course-linked restaurant laboratories, design labs, computer simulations, and, in some cases, hotel facilities operated by students?

Career options and trends:
Restaurant manager; hotel/resort manager; club manager; convention and visitor's bureau director; supplier salesperson; convention and meeting planner; festival and event organizer; caterer; state tourism department employee.

This industry is sensitive to the business cycle, but opportunities always exist if you are willing to travel or relocate. Technological advancements in the form of "virtual meetings" and "virtual vacations" are having an impact on the industry (a simulation of a vacation destination may serve as an ideal preparation for an actual visit), and people who can manage that technology will be in demand. Security is a major concern and represents a rapidly growing career opportunity. While travel agents have been

hit hard in recent years by the popularity of self-service, Web-based travel planning, those who specialize in specific destinations or particular types of travelers will have the best prospects.

Insider's viewpoint:
"We're doing a design-your-own-resort project, and you have to go into what type of people you want to come, what type of buildings you want to have, and where you're going to put everything. Our teacher wants us to get a realistic view of how difficult and expensive it is to develop a resort."

—Jennifer, senior, San Francisco State University

For more info:
American Hotel & Lodging Association (AHLA)
1201 New York Ave., N.W.
Suite 600
Washington, DC 20005-3931
(202) 289-3100
www.ahla.com

National Restaurant Association
2055 L St., N.W., Suite 700
Washington, DC 20036
(202) 331-5900
www.restaurant.org

Human resources management

Also known as:
Personnel management

What it's about:
Majors in human resources (HR) management study employment-related issues that affect men and women at work. You study topics such as recruitment, staffing, training, performance management, compensation, labor relations, and health and safety, in order to support the goals and strategies of business organizations.

Is this for you?
You might like this major if you also like: working with people; working with numbers; serving people; helping people reach their goals; team sports; clubs; tutoring; camp counseling.

Consider this major if you are good at: counseling; listening; negotiating; organizing; quantitative analysis; teamwork *...or have...* patience; verbal skills.

Recommended high school prep:
English 4, math 3, lab science 3, social studies 3, and a foreign language 2–3. If available, the following courses would also be helpful: statistics, psychology, geography, speech, computer applications, accounting, and business.

Typical courses in this major:
Organizational behavior
Managing individuals and teams
Recruitment and staffing
Occupational safety and health
Employment law
Statistics
Compensation and benefits
Training and development
Performance management
Employee and labor relations
International human resources management

Concentrations:
Generally, none in college; but if you go on to grad school: compensation; labor relations.

What the study of this major is like:
This major prepares you to work with employees in business and nonprofit organizations. The field of human resources management is exciting because it is continually evolving. Frequent developments in the law, in judicial rulings, in technology (for example, the Internet), and in research in many specialty areas of the field require that HR professionals constantly "reinvent" themselves.

As a major, you begin with a sound foundation in the humanities, fine arts, mathematics, and social sciences, including philosophy, psychology, and sociology. In your third and fourth years, you mix business administration and HR management course work. Business administration courses include marketing, finance, accounting, statistics, information systems, and organizational behavior. Human resources management courses include the following:

Employment law. Your study of laws dealing with civil rights, pay, benefits, and health and safety, as well as important court rulings on employment relationships, will help you advise employees of their rights and obligations at work.

Recruitment and staffing. You learn how to attract potential employees and how to decide which ones to hire. Tools in decision-making include interviews, psychological and performance tests, reference checking, and screening devices to identify the most-qualified candidates.

Training and development. You learn how to create and evaluate programs designed to enhance the skills and productivity of individuals and teams.

Compensation and benefits. You focus on designing and putting in place improved systems of pay, benefits, and incentives. Key topics include social security, unemployment and workers' compensation programs, pensions, and life and health insurance.

Employee and labor relations. You examine the history and legal framework of labor-management relations, including collective bargaining, strikes, and dispute-resolution mechanisms (such as arbitration) in union and nonunion companies.

International human resources management. You examine the role of HR management in international business.

The chief difference among programs is in their emphasis on quantitative (numbers-oriented) study. For example, engineering colleges that offer the HR management major tend to require a background in mathematics. A familiarity with statistics can be a big help in courses like compensation and benefits. Staffing can also be highly quantitative, especially if professors assign readings in the research literature. Liberal arts colleges generally require fewer math courses.

Other majors you might like:
Human services
Occupational therapy
Occupational health/industrial hygiene
Industrial engineering
Psychology
Sociology
Labor/industrial relations
Counselor education
Family/community services
Hospitality administration and management
Medical records administration
Human resources development

Questions to ask colleges:
Is there an active student association chapter for HR majors on campus? Is there a professional association chapter nearby? If so, students can work as administrative aides and attend the meetings, make connections with people who have similar interests, and hear invited speakers discuss cutting-edge issues in the field.

Career options and trends:
Human resources manager; management consultant; compensation consultant; labor lawyer; office manager; pension manager; recruiter.

Employment in this field is projected to grow at an average rate through 2022 subject to fluctuations in the economy and the growth and performance of individual companies. Many HR responsibilities are outsourced (the work is contracted to be done outside the organization), especially such tasks as benefits administration and claims processing. Some other responsibilities may be handled by computerized human resources information systems. There will also be some job growth due to increased demand for specialists with experience in international human resources management and information systems.

To remain relevant and in demand, professionals in the field need to build HR systems that "fit" the business strategy of their organization. Doing so will demonstrate the value of their services in quantifiable terms. An MBA will also improve job prospects.

For more info:
Society for Human Resource Management (SHRM)
1800 Duke St.
Alexandria, VA 22314
(800) 283-7476
www.shrm.org

American Society for Training and Development
  (ASTD)
1640 King St., Box 1443
Alexandria, VA 22313-2043
(800) 628-2783
www.astd.org

Insurance

Also known as:
Risk management

What it's about:
As an insurance major, you learn how to help people and businesses manage risk, recover from losses, and plan for the future. You study the legal principles underlying insurance; the types of insurance (including liability, life, property); employee benefits and pension plans; the role of insurance in financial planning; risk assessment and loss evaluation; the preparation of insurance contracts (underwriting); and the way insurance companies operate.

Is this for you?
You might like this major if you also like:

Consider this major if you are good at: attention to detail; building relationships; communicating; leadership; math; quantitative analysis; teamwork *...or have...* initiative; writing skills.

Recommended high school prep:
English 4, math 3–4, lab science 3, social studies 3, and a foreign language 3. If possible, take courses in statistics and computer applications. Courses in accounting and economics, if available, are also recommended.

Did you know...
...that insurance is an important part of business planning and creation? Many people think a career in insurance involves only selling policies and adjusting claims. But in a global economy, risk management is vital to the economies of all nations.

Typical courses in this major:
Principles of insurance
Property and liability insurance
Personal insurance
Insurance operations
Corporate risk management
Insurance accounting
Surplus lines and reinsurance
Life and health insurance
Employee benefits
Estate planning
Financial planning
Ethics of insurance

Concentrations:
Risk management; property and casualty insurance; employee benefit planning; estate planning; financial planning.

What the study of this major is like:
Individuals, families, and businesses invest in insurance to protect and provide for themselves if, one day, their situation changes or disaster strikes. Because people and businesses are increasingly looking to shield themselves from liability lawsuits (in which they may be held responsible, or liable, for harm to another) and losses resulting from serious illness, theft, or death in the family, job prospects in the insurance field continue to grow.

As an insurance professional, you will need to be a "people person" and, in particular, be successful at relationship building. You should enjoy challenges, problem solving, and multitasking. And because every insurance contract represents an act of "utmost good faith," you must also have a sense of integrity and responsibility.

In your first two years of study, you typically concentrate on the liberal arts (English, history, and sociology, for example). A core of business courses (such as accounting, economics, and management information systems) either overlaps with or follows your liberal arts courses. You usually take specialized insurance courses in your third and fourth years. These courses may focus on property loss and legal liability, as well as on employee-related plans dealing with health, disability, and retirement. In many courses, you'll explore methods of minimizing the impact of such problems (risk management); then you'll analyze how well these methods work.

Because insurance providers are regulated by the government, you need to become thoroughly familiar with the laws and rules that apply. You learn how to assess the risks taken by profit-seeking and nonprofit organizations—and how to respond to disaster. In classes on contracts, there is a lot of required reading. You also need to develop critical-thinking skills—the skills insurance underwriters and risk managers use in assessing potential losses to which organizations may be exposed.

Courses in the major build on and relate to each other, so as you progress through your studies, you'll be applying what you learned in previous courses. Many programs encourage or require you to do internships that make use of the material you've studied in class. Internships are a good way to interact with industry professionals before you graduate.

Some programs, especially those preparing you for graduate school, are highly theoretical in their approach to insurance. Other programs take a more practical approach, teaching you the knowledge and skills you need if you plan to enter the workplace with a bachelor's degree. Some colleges incorporate the insurance major into their finance programs.

Other majors you might like:
Actuarial science
Fire protection and safety technology
Finance
Real estate
Accounting
Financial planning
Statistics
Economics
Human resources management
Security services management
Entrepreneurial studies
Medical insurance specialist

Career options and trends:
Commercial lines underwriter*; property risk analyst*; liability risk analyst*; claims adjuster*; risk manager; broker/agent; financial planner; actuarial trainee; reinsurance intermediary or reinsurance underwriter.

Insurance executives report that one of their most critical problems is to find enough entry-level candidates educated in the professional areas discussed here.

The Bureau of Labor Statistics projects strong job growth through 2022 for sales agents, despite the ability of consumers to find and purchase insurance products online. For underwriters, the best prospects will be in the health insurance industry.

For more info:
American Institute for CPCU/Insurance Institute
   of America
720 Providence Rd.
Suite 100
Malvern, PA 19355-3433
(800) 644-2101
www.theinstitutes.org

American Risk and Insurance Association
716 Providence Rd.
Malvern, PA 19355-3402
(610) 640-1997
www.aria.org

International business

What it's about:

This major prepares you to think globally and manage complexity in an international environment and in cultures other than your own. While learning basic business management techniques and practices, you study how business is conducted in and between nations and how it is affected by the financial systems, government policies, cultural differences, management styles, and other factors that apply.

Is this for you?

You might like this major if you also like: travel; new ideas, people, and places; adventure; unusual challenges; leadership roles.

Consider this major if you are good at: creativity; critical reading/thinking; leadership; teamwork ...*or have...* cross-cultural sensitivity; initiative; patience; self-confidence; verbal skills; writing skills.

Recommended high school prep:

English 4, math 4 (including precalculus), lab science 3, social studies 3, and a foreign language 4. If possible, take calculus.

Did you know...

...that your first position will likely be a domestic, not an overseas, assignment? Within two years after graduation, you probably will not be overlooking the Eiffel Tower but will be employed stateside, working for either a domestic or a foreign multinational corporation, a bank with international operations, or perhaps an international organization such as the United Nations or the World Bank.

Typical courses in this major:

International finance
Derivatives and financial markets
International marketing
Intercultural communication
Global logistics
International operations
Advanced seminar in international business
Economics
Accounting
Management
Business in specific regions

Concentrations:

In college: international economics and trade; marketing; finance.

If you go on to grad school: developing nations; public policy; banking and finance in different regions of the world; business–government relations; international security.

What the study of this major is like:

The international business major provides you with a solid foundation in accounting, marketing, finance, and management. It includes courses that train you to analyze information about overseas businesses and that encourage you to think globally when making work-related decisions. Business environments vary from country to country, and it is increasingly important for managers to understand the causes and consequences of the differences.

As a major, you begin with basic business courses and then advance to ones with an international focus. These courses may examine how money and capital (equipment and other goods) move within and between countries; how technology is transferred between nations; and what management skills are practiced abroad. You analyze the international economic scene, study competition and interdependence, and assess cultural distinctions among nations. You may learn how to market goods and services from the United States and to evaluate the strength of overseas investments. Because an understanding of politics and government is essential to the practice of international business, you should take electives in these areas.

Most programs require you to master a foreign language. Many international business majors gain experience by studying abroad for a semester, a summer, or even a year. Sometimes there are opportunities to visit foreign companies and meet with managers working in U.S. companies.

Although some students think that the international business major is less difficult than other business majors, they soon discover it's not the case. In this major, you are expected to take a variety of demanding courses, such as international marketing, international finance, international management, and international operations. The combination of international business and another major, such as finance or marketing, can be especially challenging.

When comparing programs at different colleges, you'll find that some take an interdisciplinary approach, stressing a wide range of knowledge, with extensive offerings in the liberal arts as well as business; while others may emphasize specific areas of business, such as the ethical dilemmas you may encounter as you do international work.

Other majors you might like:
Accounting
Finance
International relations
Marketing
Tourism/travel management
Global studies
Comparative literature
International marketing
Foreign languages/literatures
Latin American studies
Asian studies
Development economics

Questions to ask colleges:
Do most of the students select international business as a solo major or as a double major?

What is the career track of the most recent graduates?

Is there a study-abroad requirement? How is it financed?

Is there a language requirement?

Are there internship opportunities with an international focus?

Career options and trends:
Derivatives trader; investment banker*; management consultant*; real estate developer; government employee; financial analyst*; brand manager; import/export manager.

Because almost all business has become global, qualified managers with an international perspective are increasingly in demand. In many quarters, in fact, graduates are assumed to have a global view of the world. Now more than ever, with the world a less certain place and with the growing volatility of the economy, business leaders who can operate effectively in a variety of cultural environments are needed.

Insider's viewpoint:
"It is exciting to see a student from Kansas form a worldview, or a student from New Jersey who had never traveled beyond the East Coast corridor discover that, contrary to her prior beliefs, the United States is not the center of the universe."

—Professor Ann-Mary Kapusta, Georgetown University

For more info:
AIESEC United States
11 Hanover Square,
Suite 1700
New York, NY 10005
(212) 757 3774
www.aiesecus.org

Washington International Trade Association
 (WITA)
1300 Pennsylvania Ave., N.W.
Suite 350
Washington, DC 20004
(202) 312-1600
www.wita.org

Management information systems

Also known as:
Information technology

What it's about:
In this major, you learn how to apply information technology to solve business problems. MIS prepares you to understand the function of information technologies and systems in business organizations, and it provides the knowledge and skills you will need when you analyze, design, develop, and manage information systems.

Is this for you?
You might like this major if you also like: team sports; computers and electronics; solving problems; working with people; reading; tutoring.

Consider this major if you are good at: attention to detail; creativity; critical reading/thinking; leadership; math; organizing; research; teamwork ...*or have...* communication skills; initiative.

Recommended high school prep:
English 4, math 4 (including precalculus), lab science 3, social studies 3, and a foreign language 2–3. If available, take calculus, a writing course, a business or economics course, and an introductory computer science course.

Did you know...
...that computers and technology are not the sole focus of this major? The functional areas of business (operations, finance, accounting, marketing, etc.) and the information itself, as well as the people who will use the information, are primary concerns you must deal with.

Typical courses in this major:
Programming for systems development
Systems analysis and design
Database design
Database management and administration
Networks and telecommunication
Financial information systems
E-commerce
Information services management
Emerging technologies
Advanced software development
Data warehousing
Decision support technologies
Project management and practice

Concentrations:
Information systems design and development; information technology infrastructure; information services management; e-commerce; software development; information technology (IT) strategy.

What the study of this major is like:
As a management information systems major, you must be comfortable with all types of computers, software, and communications (such as wireless phone systems). You study the design, development, and maintenance of information support systems; the ways in which they support business processes and managerial decision making; managerial approaches to effective systems development; and emerging technologies used by information systems. You learn critical-thinking and problem-solving skills so you can handle changing situations and apply the right technology to problems as they arise.

Because you'll be working in organizations and businesses, you must also learn how they operate, by studying finance, human resources, marketing, and accounting. In addition, you are often encouraged to take courses in sociology and psychology and to sharpen your communication skills (writing, speaking, and listening). By understanding human behavior and perfecting your "people skills," you learn how to be a successful link between technology and the people who use it.

Management information systems courses are taught in a variety of ways, including lectures. In labs you can use various software packages to help you with your course work· readings, quizzes, homework assignments, midterm and final examinations, individual and group projects, and term papers. Students interested in research may have opportunities to work on an independent project under the supervision of a faculty member.

When searching for an MIS job, you should have some experience in a business setting. Many programs offer local internships to give you hands-on experience, which is particularly useful for systems analysis (which emphasizes analyzing business processes) and consulting (in which you may work with several industries).

Management information systems programs may emphasize different aspects of the curriculum. For example, some programs may focus on technology-related topics, while other programs may cover more managerial topics. You can usually determine a program's focus by looking at its course offerings.

Other majors you might like:
Business communications
E-commerce
Organizational behavior studies
Software engineering
Management science
Computer engineering technology
Emergency management/homeland security
Organizational communication
Information technology
Computer forensics
Health information management
Computer networking and telecommunications

Questions to ask colleges:
How many classes make use of computer labs (or other advanced facilities) as part of the course work? Practical experience is essential in this field.

Are the faculty members actively involved in research or the local business community? It's important for the faculty and the curriculum to keep up with the rapid change in this field.

Is the equipment in the computer labs kept current with changing technology and maintained with good tech support? Students should learn in a technical environment similar to the one they will work in professionally, so a fairly rapid upgrade/replacement cycle is necessary.

What sort of network access is available? Are the classrooms connected to the Internet and campus networks, either by "port per seat" or wireless networking?

Career options and trends:
Systems analyst/designer*; software developer (programmer)*; database administrator*; consultant; project manager; chief information officer (CIO); researcher.

Job opportunities are generally excellent for students with MIS knowledge and good business sense. Heightened concern over "cyber security" is also spurring demand for managers proficient in computer security issues; in fact, such knowledge is almost a prerequisite.

Students who have very specific interests and career goals ("information security analyst for medical information systems," for example) usually have excellent opportunities for specialization after they graduate. In addition, the job market rewards students who double-major and match MIS with finance, marketing, operations, or accounting.

For more info:
Association for Information Systems (AIS)
P.O. Box 2712
Atlanta, GA 30301-2712
(404) 413-7441
www.aisnet.org

Association for Computing Machinery (ACM)
2 Penn Plaza, Suite 701
New York, NY 10121-0701
(800) 342-6626
www.acm.org

Marketing

What it's about:

Marketing is concerned with the process of developing customer relationships, uncovering business opportunities, and delivering products and services to buyers. Marketing majors learn to analyze customers and their needs, and to make decisions about product design and quality, pricing, advertising, selling, and distribution.

Is this for you?

You might like this major if you also like: buying and selling; looking at quality TV commercials, magazine ads, and store window displays; online social networking; working in teams; involvement with student groups; volunteerism; part-time work; thinking about what motivates people; shopping.

Consider this major if you are good at: creativity; critical reading/thinking; leadership; persuading/influencing; quantitative analysis; research; teamwork *...or have...* initiative; verbal skills; writing skills.

Recommended high school prep:

English 4, math 3, lab science 3, social studies 3, and a foreign language 2–3. If available, take computer classes that teach word processing and spreadsheet applications.

Did you know...

...that marketing isn't just about advertising and sales? Actually, it is much broader and more strategic in focus, requiring a strong understanding of accounting, economics, finance, management, information technology, and other areas.

Typical courses in this major:

Principles of marketing
Retailing
Professional selling
Sales management
Consumer behavior
Marketing communications/promotion
E-commerce/Internet marketing
Services marketing
Product development and management
International marketing
Marketing research
Marketing management
Marketing strategy
Advertising principles

Concentrations:

Generally, none in college; but if you go on to grad school: market research; e-commerce; advertising management; product management.

What the study of this major is like:

Marketing focuses on important business measures that have a central role in company performance and success, such as customer satisfaction, sales revenue, and market share. As a major in marketing, you will explore the role of marketing in business performance and examine the functions of marketing professionals.

Questions you will ask include these: How does marketing affect society, and how does society affect marketing? In which ways is research important to marketing? On what basis do consumers and industrial buyers make purchasing decisions? How are products developed, priced, and distributed? How do organizations communicate with prospective customers through advertising, personal selling, social networking websites, and publicity? What are the steps involved in developing, conducting, and evaluating marketing strategies? What impact do international environments have on marketing?

Marketing is an intellectually stimulating and demanding subject. Analytical, creative, and communication skills are important to success in the profession. Consequently, marketing majors spend about half their time taking courses in the liberal arts. You must also take a number of business courses, including economics, statistics, accounting, finance, computer information systems, and management.

These courses may challenge you, but they are fundamental for exploring the field. For instance, you'll familiarize yourself with the two primary types of marketing. In business-to-business (B2B) marketing, products such as computers, copying machines, steel, and chemicals are sold to other businesses. In business-to-consumer (B2C) marketing, in contrast, individuals buy products (called, appropriately, "consumer products") such as appliances, cars, packaged goods (food, soap), and services such as insurance and banking. Courses in marketing principles and marketing management teach you to develop and implement plans to market products and services.

Other courses specialize in a single aspect of marketing management. Market research—usually required of all majors—teaches you to use surveys, experiments, test markets, and other techniques to obtain the information you need in making effective marketing decisions. In advertising management, you study the development, testing, execution, and monitoring of advertising campaigns. (Marketing majors are usually not involved in the creative aspects of advertising—design and production.) Courses in sales management focus on the psychology of effective selling and the recruiting, selecting, organizing, training, and motivating of salespeople. In marketing channels courses, you learn about the institutions (retailers, wholesalers, industrial distributors) that work as intermediaries between manufacturers and buyers.

Most marketing courses combine lecture with discussion. Majors usually complete a number of team and individual projects that involve research, analysis, critical thinking, creativity, information technology, writing skills, and oral presentations.

Strong marketing programs focus on ideas and theories while providing you with experiences and teaching you skills that can be easily applied in the workplace. Differences in programs may involve the relative emphasis on project-oriented, hands-on courses; the availability and use of technology; the availability of internships and student competitions; and the degree to which quantitative (math-related) skills are woven into the curriculum. Location, potential employers, and faculty members may add unique aspects to a program.

Other majors you might like:
Advertising
Fashion merchandising

Selling/sales operations
Family and consumer sciences
Economics
Public relations
Sociology
Political communications
Sports communications
Tourism promotion
Business statistics
Psychology

Career options and trends:

Sales representative*; sales manager; advertising and integrated marketing communications manager*; retail manager*; entrepreneur/business owner; product manager; marketing researcher; marketing consultant; customer service manager.

The broad nature of marketing leads to a positive job outlook. Since marketing is used in business, nonprofits, and government agencies, job opportunities can be found even during economic downturns. Marketers are generally paid well, and the field is especially lucrative for those who earn commissions or bonuses based on performance. Those who are adept at social media, web-based and mobile marketing will have the best prospects.

Job prospects for market researchers are projected to be fairly strong through 2022, driven by the increased availability and use of data to both devise and evaluate marketing strategies.

For more info:
American Marketing Association (AMA)
311 South Wacker Drive, Suite 5800
Chicago, IL 60606
(800) AMA-1150
www.marketingpower.com

Real estate

What it's about:

The real estate major provides you with an understanding of the economic and social principles that affect how real property—buildings and land—is developed, financed, operated, and traded.

Is this for you?

You might like this major if you also like: working independently; making decisions; interacting with people; building things; travel; buying and selling; playing Monopoly.

Consider this major if you are good at: caring/nurturing; critical reading/thinking; negotiating; organizing; persuading/influencing; teamwork ...*or have...* initiative; patience; verbal skills; writing skills.

Recommended high school prep:

English 4, math 3, lab science 3, social studies 3, a foreign language 2–3. If they are available, take a course in statistics and a course that teaches business fundamentals and/or general legal principles.

Did you know...

...that real estate is not simply about building, buying, or selling a home? Professionals who handle appraisals, valuation, investments, and similar activities for multimillion dollar projects around the world need sophisticated training. Think about it—all businesses must operate at some physical location that they either lease or own. In either case, someone must develop the property, and someone must handle the financial transactions.

Typical courses in this major:

Real estate principles and practices
Real estate law
Financing
Appraising
Real estate investments
Residential real estate
Commercial real estate
Taxation
International real estate
Computer applications for real estate analysis
Global perspectives in real estate
Management of income properties
Real estate securities and syndications
Real estate practicums (practical applications)

Concentrations:

Real property development; construction management; real estate finance and mortgage lending; international real estate; real estate law; real estate asset management; appraising; market analysis; and a combination of real estate and almost any other professional subject offered by a typical college of business.

What the study of this major is like:

In real estate, which is an interdisciplinary field, you study various areas of business and you learn to communicate well, both in speaking and in writing. As a major, you probably won't take real estate courses until after you complete course work in the liberal arts and introductory business courses such as accounting, economics, and statistics. Then you take an introductory course covering the language of real estate, ethics, brokerage (the buying and selling of real estate), appraisal (the valuation of real estate), contracts, and property management.

In higher-level courses, you learn about the law of property ownership, transfer, and land-use control; methods of financing property purchases and sales; the effect of tax laws on real estate investments; management of office buildings and apartment buildings; and marketing techniques. In addition, you gain development and redevelopment skills, including ways of salvaging abandoned properties. You might also have the opportunity to do a residential or commercial practicum, managing the construction or development of an actual piece of property.

Real estate classes typically follow a lecture-discussion format and use case studies and computer software as problem-solving tools. Some programs in real estate focus on physical elements (sites and structures) and have studio courses to teach physical planning and construction. Other programs concentrate on theory. Try to determine which type of program interests you the most. You might be attracted to theory-oriented programs if you are considering a job in planning or government. If you want to go into the real estate business, look for programs that emphasize real-world interaction between the real estate and business communities.

The real estate field, which is constantly changing, is a challenging area. To creatively meet the needs of owners, landlords, tenants, purchasers, financiers, and others involved in property transfers, real estate professionals must understand the many aspects of the business and work well with a variety of individuals and representatives. For example, you might have to locate a site for an office building; determine how to finance the transaction; figure out a tax-saving strategy; and work with teams of attorneys, accountants, and other professionals. Successful real estate professionals need initiative, patience, and stamina to see projects through; various technical skills; and an ability to see the "big picture" of a real estate deal.

Although many graduates work in established sectors of the industry, others establish their own businesses or manage their own investments. In addition to financial rewards, the real estate field can give you the chance to set your own flexible schedule.

Other majors you might like:
Construction management
Finance
Building/property maintenance
Urban, community, and regional planning
International business
Environmental studies
Landscape architecture
Architecture
Construction technology
Surveying technology
Housing and human environments
Historic preservation

Questions to ask colleges:
How well are the computer applications used in this major kept up-to-date with advances in technology in the current real estate market?

Can students combine a real estate major with another, such as accounting, finance, international business, or entrepreneurial studies?

What are the research opportunities, internships, or other ways for students to interact with faculty members and the real estate community as a way to gain practical experience?

Career options and trends:
Real estate broker or sales agent; appraiser; consultant; mortgage banker; financial analyst; developer; tax assessor; real estate asset manager.

In order to work as a real estate sales agent or broker, you must pass a state real estate licensing exam.

Opportunities in the real estate field can be found in global and international real estate, REITs (real estate investment trusts), corporate positions, investment houses, financial and tax planning organizations, low-income housing, and government agencies dealing with housing, building regulation, and property management. Because of an aging population, opportunities are also being created for those who can manage health care facilities and housing for the elderly.

The real estate field tends to be cyclical. Swings in the economy, especially interest rates, affect agents and brokers the most. The real estate market is slowly recovering from the financial crisis of 2008, but to varying extent across the country. The time it will take to recover will also vary by region.

However, there are a wide variety of employment opportunities in the industry. After all, everyone needs a place to live, and a place to work. With or without cycles, this fact won't change.

For more info:
National Association of Realtors (NAR)
430 North Michigan Ave.
Chicago, IL 60611-4087
(800) 874-6500
www.realtor.org

Communications

However you get the news—smart phone, twitter, the Web, TV, radio, or newspaper, you have already gotten the word that the communications media seems to be in permanent flux. All this change is affecting communications majors, too.

"Twenty years ago few people understood that telephones could also be cameras and texting devices and game consoles and appointment books" observes Professor Janet H. Murray of the Graduate Program in Digital Media at Georgia Tech. "It's exciting to see what my students create and how they talk about the advantages and limitations of the devices—tablets, websites, apps—they use every day."

A major in communications— which might be in advertising, digital media, journalism, pubic relations, radio and television, sports communications, or just communications in general—is a gateway to jobs on the content and business sides of broadcasting, telecommunications, and other media and sectors. You might become a writer, Webmaster, designer, producer, or announcer; or you might work in sales, management, human resources, the legal department, or research.

"Most students begin their post-baccalaureate work, not in the communications field but in general business and industry, usually sales," says Professor Bruce E. Gronbeck of the University of Iowa.

"Students considering broadcast media don't realize how satisfying it is to work in less visible positions which are crucial to the success of any media production," says Professor John Doolittle of American University. "News producers, radio sales staff, video shooters, and Web designers are in very demanding and rewarding jobs."

"Understanding business and the needs of the commercial world is integral to succeeding in the field," adds Professor Joel A. Kline of Lebanon Valley College. "Opportunities are also found in public relations and the government."

New jobs in communications are linked to the latest technologies. Emerging majors on campus get students up-to-date on Web-based, mobile, and interactive communications; visual journalism and video graphics; strategic communications; health communications; human interface design; social media strategies; multimedia arts; and Internet advertising and marketing. Many media are coming together so students will have to be familiar with a variety of methods of communication.

"To communicate requires writing skills, visual skills, and technological skills. When students master these perspectives, they can enter many different fields," Kline says.

Get the story on colleges

To choose a college, do some investigative reporting. Get out your notebook or video camera, burn some shoe leather, check their websites, read guidebooks; if possible, visit colleges and talk to people who may be helpful. Or send e-mails instead (look on a college's website for details). Either way, get the scoop about colleges, including schools of journalism, communications, mass communications, media studies, business, humanities, social sciences, liberal arts, and arts and sciences.

Colleges have many different ways of covering communications.

"The single most important dividing line is between programs that are practically oriented and those that are built around a liberal arts philosophy," explains Gronbeck. "Some colleges offer professionally oriented courses, believing that students are completing a business-type degree aimed at the communication industries. Others are constructed around the philosophy that 'communication' is such a general notion that training should be focused on the analytical and speaking/writing skills that students can bring to any entry-level position."

If you did a TV series on choosing a college, it would have five episodes: Faculty, Courses, Facilities, Internships, and Jobs. Here are some ideas for your script.

Episode One: Faculty. Are they experienced professionals? What are the backgrounds of instructors teaching the courses? Are professors easy to meet with outside class?

Episode Two: Courses. When must you declare your major and what are the required courses? Is the focus on technical skills or creative and thinking skills?

Episode Three: Facilities. What's in the computer lab? How new is the broadcast equipment like cameras and editing platforms? How often is the hardware and software updated? How much access will you have to the studios and labs? Can you work for the campus website, newspaper, radio or TV station, or other publications and outlets? Are they run by the faculty or independently?

Episode Four: Internships. What kinds of internship programs are offered and what are the typical assignments? Will the college help you land an internship at a broadcast or other outlet (on or off campus)? Is the campus near a city with lots of communications opportunities? Will you put together a portfolio of your projects to show your talents to future employers? (At this point in your script, cut to an interview with an expert like advertising maven Thomas A. Bowers, University of North Carolina at Chapel Hill.) "Potential employers will ask for samples of work the student did on campus publications or at internships. Having such experience is absolutely essential."

Episode Five: Jobs. Will you get help finding a job after graduation? Where are graduates working now and what kinds of work are they doing? How many go on to law school or graduate work in communication studies? (Show a graphic here of the top five careers for graduates, then cut to Gronbeck.) "A variety of career opportunities are available for people with skills in researching, writing, and presenting information clearly."

Fade to black and roll credits.

Advertising

What it's about:

Advertising majors learn to create and distribute paid messages in communication media in order to persuade people to accept an idea, change attitudes, or to take action. Your studies include analysis of customers, markets, and media, as well as advertising's history, regulation, and social and economic effects.

Is this for you?

You might like this major if you also like: writing; art and design; being curious about a wide variety of subjects; keeping up on current trends and current events.

Consider this major if you are good at: active listening; attention to detail; creativity; critical reading/thinking; meeting deadlines; quantitative analysis; teamwork *...or have...* initiative; verbal skills; writing skills.

Recommended high school prep:

English 4, math 3, lab science 3, social studies 3, and a foreign language 2–3. Courses in art, business, and computer applications are also recommended.

Did you know...

...that many advertising agencies hire copywriters and art directors who have attended portfolio-preparation schools that offer specialized, advanced training to college graduates? Such preparation has become essential for creative positions.

Typical courses in this major:

Fundamentals of ad design
Principles of advertising
Social and economic aspects of advertising
Copywriting
Media planning
Advertising campaigns
New media and e-commerce strategies
Market research
Account management and planning
Marketing principles
Creative strategies
Art of persuasion
Business to business advertizing
Retail advertising and promotion
Interactive design
Consumer behaviors and trends
Social media in a dynamic marketplace

Concentrations:

Copywriting; media planning; design; account management.

What the study of this major is like:

Successful advertising depends on a range of skill sets, and this major will give you the opportunity to develop those that suit you best. Coursework covers both the business and creative sides of the field. (You can see this mix in the list of typical courses above.) But "creative" in advertising is not just about producing compelling ad copy and visuals. The ability to approach a familiar problem from a fresh perspective is also important on the business side of advertising, such as media planning and account development.

This major is very project-based, and courses are a blend of theory and practical experience. You are introduced to the concepts, principles and strategies used to develop each aspects of an advertising campaign, and then learn by doing. All advertising courses stress clear, concise writing.

In most courses you will be expected to make oral presentations, an essential part of selling campaigns to clients. Because much of the work in advertising is done by teams of people, most projects are assigned to groups. The challenges of coordinating the work with your classmates will be excellent preparation for the real world.

Courses in the major cover such areas as copywriting, in which you learn to create the text of your ads; media planning, in which you decide where your ads will appear (the Web, TV, and so on); and research, in which you explore how to analyze e-commerce data that tracks consumer "clicks" and buying behaviors, conduct surveys, and other ways to learn about and target customers. You will also be trained on the various software programs that are used in Web-based advertising campaigns.

Advertising art is usually not a big part of this major at most colleges. If you have artistic talent and intend to pursue a career in advertising art, you might consider a visual arts major in digital art, illustration or graphic design instead.

You don't need to be an artist to do well in creative strategy, a core course in most advertising programs. You will be expected to write and design original ads, and again the idea is to learn by doing. Your professor will be looking for clear thinking that's part of an overall strategy to attract buyers.

Advertising programs are usually found in schools of journalism and mass communications and are influenced by the strong liberal arts emphasis in such institutions. Don't be surprised if you are required to take several humanities courses from outside the major, and you will most likely be advised or required to take at least one course in marketing, usually taught in a school of business.

To land a job in an ad agency, a portfolio that shows your best thinking and imagination is essential. Most programs will help you develop one from the results of your project assignments. You can also write copy or create ads for your school website or newspaper; or seek such opportunities through internships.

Other majors you might like:
E-Commerce
Graphic communications
Marketing
Commercial/advertising art
Public relations
Business administration and management
Family and consumer sciences
English
Graphic design
Photojournalism
Fashion merchandising
Retailing

Questions to ask colleges:
What is the professional experience of the faculty? In a strong program, the professors are engaged in the field of advertising.

What are the opportunities for internships and other hands-on experience?

Career options and trends:
Copywriter*; creative or graphic designer*; media planner*; account executive*; advertising salesperson; account planner.

After graduate study, you may pursue work as an advertising research specialist.

Employment is expected to grow in this field since advertising is essential for businesses seeking to grow their market share as the economy recovers. A decline in print advertising is being offset by new ways to target customers through e-commerce, digital media, mobile and location-sensitive applications and especially social media. If you understand how these various forms of media are evolving and can apply that understanding, you will be at an advantage.

Insider's viewpoint:
"I love the fact that our knowledge of human behavior will never be complete and that even the best advertising campaigns will not always be successful. Long live the independent-minded consumer!"

—Professor Thomas A. Bowers, University of North Carolina at Chapel Hill

For more info:
The American Advertising Federation (AAF)
1101 Vermont Ave., N.W.
Suite 500
Washington, DC 20005-6306
(202) 898-0089
www.aaf.org

Communications

What it's about:

Communications majors examine the many ways in which information and ideas are exchanged in modern society. You may study the history of political and religious speeches; write reviews of TV programs and films; evaluate the impact of mass media on individuals and society; and analyze how digital and social media are shaping communication practices.

Is this for you?

You might like this major if you also like: group discussions; blogging; research and writing; volunteering for political/service organizations; making videos; student government; making presentations; working on the school newspaper, website, or yearbook.

Consider this major if you are good at: active listening; critical reading/thinking; leadership; public speaking; teamwork *...or have...* verbal skills; writing skills.

Recommended high school prep:

English 4, math 3, lab science 3, social studies 3, and a foreign language 2–3. If possible, take courses in speech, journalism, debate, and theater. It is also valuable to work on the school yearbook or newspaper; at a radio station; as a DJ at dances; or community service organizations.

Did you know...

...that after college, most majors begin working in business and industry—usually in sales? Communications is one of the most popular gateways into a wide variety of jobs in business and industry.

Typical courses in this major:

Foundations of communication
History of communication
Interpersonal communications
Organizational communications
Communications theory and research
Communications management
Media and politics
Introduction to rhetoric
Media criticism
Radio/TV/film production
Introduction to digital media
Social media and society
Public speaking
Writing, reporting, and editing news
Mass media and society
Intercultural communications

Concentrations:

New media/Internet studies; journalism; advertising; public relations; political communications; broadcasting; film studies; media studies.

What the study of this major is like:

The study of communication is as old as the writings of the ancient Greeks on rhetoric and politics. Today, communication in all its forms, from political speeches to Facebook posts, is explored from historical, critical, theoretical, ethical, and sociological perspectives.

Typically, you begin the major with an introductory course that gives you an overview of the discipline. You might also be required to take core courses in fundamental topics such as the history of communication, research methods used in the field, and theories about how communication processes work.

In such courses you may read and discuss presidential speeches, First Amendment court cases, or other documents that call on your analytical skills. You are graded on your contributions to class discussions, your ability to analyze what you have read and observed, and the clarity and precision of your writing.

In courses in public speaking, interviewing, group communications, and argumentation, you learn to prepare and deliver messages and to listen carefully to what others have to say. Performance and production courses provide technical training in preproduction (planning and writing), production (recording/shooting/digitizing), and postproduction (editing).

What is learned in this major can be applied across many fields, including politics, health, business, sports, and entertainment. Most programs will allow you to concentrate your upper-level courses in an area that aligns with your interests and career goals, whether it be journalism, digital content production, filmmaking, public relations, or advertising. You can also pursue studies involving a particular media, such as print, radio, television, or online media.

Some programs encourage you to develop an area of focus by taking elective courses outside the major. For example, you might take courses in the social sciences to prepare for a career in the service industries, or political science electives if you are interested in government or politics.

Internships are an important feature of most communications programs. You may spend a few hours a week or an entire semester getting on-the-job experience in settings such as a radio station, an advertising firm, a digital media company, or a customer relations department. Given the variety of career options in the communications field, you may want to complete several internships to get a better sense of your preferred career path.

So many colleges offer this major that it can be challenging to sort through them all. The most important distinction to consider is how the colleges emphasize different areas of study. Some schools emphasize traditional print and broadcast journalism, while others offer courses on creating content for digital media. Some schools focus on public relations, marketing, and advertising, and emphasize using communication in the business world.

Programs that emphasize technical skills are generally aimed at the media industries. Other programs stress the analytical, speaking, and writing skills useful for entry-level positions in a wide variety of businesses and occupations.

Other majors you might like:
Health information management
Business communications
Media studies
Design/visual communications
Graphic design
Photography
English
Drama and theater arts

Technical and business writing
Speech/rhetorical studies
Web page/multimedia design

Questions to ask colleges:
Is the program more focused on traditional media (such as radio and newspapers) or new media (such as blogs and social media)?

What are the five careers that graduates most frequently pursue? How many majors each year go on to professional or graduate school?

Is there an internship program? If so, what are some typical assignments?

How does the program train students to work with the equipment and technology that they'll be using in the professional world?

Career options and trends:
Digital media producer*; advertising copywriter*; publicist*; writer/editor*; broadcast media production assistant; communications research specialist; communications consultant.

Communications majors also go on to careers in law, management, human resources, the telecommunications industry, public advocacy, and government agencies.

The ease with which you'll find that first job after graduation will depend in part on your career preferences. Job opportunities involving digital communications are expanding rapidly to meet demand for websites, webcasts, mobile devices, and apps. Your chances of finding a job in advertising, marketing, or public relations are also good, particularly if you have some experience with digital media.

You can improve your job prospects by honing your writing, editing, and media production skills. Internship or work experience in a relevant area will help strengthen your resume and provide you with contacts who can aid you in your job search.

For more info:
National Communication Association (NCA)
1765 N St., N.W.
Washington, DC 20036
(202) 464-4622
www.natcom.org

Digital media

Also known as:
New media design
Interactive media

What it's about:
Digital Media is an interdisciplinary study of new genres of information, entertainment, art, and communication supported by computer technologies. It combines the creativity of art and design with the technology of multimedia production for a wide range of media platforms and interactive applications.

Is this for you?
You might like this major if you also like: writing; video games; 3-D movies; visual and performing arts; designing websites; learning new computer programs; presenting ideas with writing and graphics.

Consider this major if you are good at: attention to detail; creativity; spacial thinking/analysis; teamwork *...or have...* initiative; math skills; mechanical aptitude; patience; writing skills.

Recommended high school prep:
English 4, math 3, lab science 3, social studies 3, and a foreign language 2–3. If possible, take an art class, an intro to computer science or programming class, and a website design or computer graphics course.

Did you know...
...that you don't need to be both artistically talented and a whiz with computers in order to succeed in this major? Almost anyone with an interest in communications, design or technology can be part of a team that creates digital media.

Typical courses in this major:
Fundamentals of design
Human-computer interaction
Writing for digital media
Graphics for digital media
Web-based media
Interactive and non-linear narrative

Experimental film and video
Visual communications technology
Integrated media
Game design
Web page design
Digital imaging
Multimedia design
Social media communications
Communicating with mobile technology
New media production

Concentrations:
In college: Web design, game studies, animation, digital art and design, writing for digital media.

If you go on to grad school: Game design, interactive narrative, information design, interaction design, civic media, educational computing.

What the study of this major is like:
Digital media is truly multi-faceted, blending technical, art and design, and language skills to enable you to use this dynamic and evolving form of communication to express ideas. You will learn underlying concepts and theories through reading and lectures, but most programs are primarily project-based where you learn through experience how to conceive and create digital content and interactive media.

Your introductory courses will cover topics such as how media affects society, media traditions, and how people perceive and react to interactive and multimedia formats. Other ways of approaching digital media, such as from the perspectives of business, law, and journalism, are usually presented in a lecture or discussion format.

You do much of the creative work—writing, art, and media programming—in a computer lab or studio. Here you transform an idea into a completed project. You will be introduced to the fundamentals of digital content creation, including basic programming, graphic design, digital imaging (photography, film/video, animation), and audio production, working with software and computer graphic programs used in the industry.

You will collaborate on these projects and learn how to work in a team. Don't be intimidated by classmates with different skill sets; programmers, writers, and artists are often painfully aware that they don't share the same abilities. This major requires that you learn skills outside your comfort zone. To succeed, everyone needs to become adept at sharing knowledge and asking for help from each other as well as their teachers.

Be prepared to work long hours because computers crash and software doesn't always perform as expected. You may have to redo your projects several times, especially if working with interactive programs where problems are only apparent once there is a working model.

The work you do on projects will feed your final senior year portfolio, a requirement of most programs.

What is taught in this major is evolving as new technologies emerge. Web design is always improving; mobile applications are increasingly important; tablets are changing the way we read, learn, and entertain ourselves; and the potential of social media is just beginning to be understood. A good digital media program will teach you skills that will enable you to adapt to these changes and lay the groundwork for continued lifelong learning, while at the same time providing the right mixture of skills for the immediate job market.

When researching colleges, look for this major among the communications, computer science, art and design, media studies, film studies, or liberal arts departments. The emphasis can range from practical production skills to media theory to social analysis, or the focus can be on a particular area, such as game design, Web design, educational computing, or cutting-edge technologies such as immersive virtual worlds, massive multiplayer platforms, or 3-D visualization. Two-year programs tend to provide technical training for a specific aspect of digital media, such as sound engineering or digital photography.

Schools often have a gallery of student work on their website. Check it out to see if the creative work of the program appeals to you.

Other majors you might like:
Game Design
Animation
Web page/multimedia design
Graphic design
Information technology
Computer graphics
Computer modeling, virtual environments and simulation
Digital art
Drafting and design technology
Educational/instructional technology
Management information systems
E-commerce

Questions to ask colleges:
Where are graduates working and what are their job titles? A game tester, for example, is a low level job though it might sound like fun. Lead game designer is a better job.

What types of projects do students work on?

What digital platforms do students work with? Look for a range of technologies, both established and emerging, and projects should focus on the creation of interactive media, not just traditional linear media that happen to be digital.

Career options and trends:
Website designer*, game designer, animator, digital technician, graphic designer, multimedia designer; information architect; website content manager; creative director, technology support specialist; user experience designer, art director.

There is demand for digital media specialists in all areas where communication is a primary function—marketing, public relations, advertising, government, education, the arts. Through 2022, job growth is projected to be faster than average in the areas of web design, social media and educational applications, and about average in the graphic design field.

For more info:
Interaction Design Association (IxDA)
www.ixda.org

Internet Society (ISOC)
1775 Wiehle Ave.
Suite 201
Reston, VA 20190-5108
(703) 439-2120
www.isoc.org

Journalism

What it's about:

Beginning with a broad introduction to the liberal arts and sciences, journalism majors learn how to find information and how to communicate their findings through writing, speech, and other forms of expression, including multimedia tools such as digital video. You also practice the skills you'll need for working with a newspaper, radio and TV station, advertising or public relations agency, and Web media.

Is this for you?

You might like this major if you also like: reading and writing; blogging; current events; history; politics; photography; sports; movies; networking; research; adventure; making presentations.

Consider this major if you are good at: attention to detail; creativity; critical reading/thinking; meeting deadlines; organizing; research ...*or have*... curiosity; initiative; perseverance; verbal skills; writing skills.

Recommended high school prep:

English 4, math 3, lab science 3, social studies 4, and a foreign language 3–4. Being active on your high school media—newspaper, yearbook, literary magazine, and/or, if available, television and radio—is also recommended. But many students enter college with little or no high school journalism experience and do very well.

Did you know...

...that despite the decline of the print news media, there are increasing opportunities for journalists? Wireless devices such as smart phones and tablets provide constant access to the news, generating huge demand for up-to-the-minute information. This demand has opened up a whole new realm of journalism jobs in a greater variety of media.

Typical courses in this major:

News reporting methods and techniques
Broadcast journalism
Writing for digital media
Multimedia and online journalism
News reporting, writing and editing
Photojournalism
Copyediting
Feature writing
Media law and ethics
The documentary
Sports writing and reporting
Political reporting
Covering the financial markets
Business and financial writing
Investigative reporting
Editorial and review writing

Concentrations:

In college: broadcast journalism; business journalism; public relations; newmedia technology; photojournalism.

If you go on to grad school: specialized reporting (such as political, financial, international, agricultural); investigative reporting; documentary studies.

What the study of this major is like:

Students considering journalism often say they have so many interests they can't decide on a major—they want to major in everything. If you have that level of curiosity and love of learning, it's a sign that this major is a good choice.

Majors typically take many courses in the liberal arts and sciences, to gain a broad understanding of history, geography, political science, economics, literature, and the natural sciences. This comprehensive background will help you understand the context of the information you will, as a journalist, gather and report.

There is a strong emphasis on writing skills in this major. You will be required to write, write, write in many contexts and for varying media. Overall, your course work will emphasize the fundamentals of reporting and technical skills, as well as professional practices and values. Assignments develop your ability to express yourself using language, computers, software, and recording equipment. You also take courses in media law and ethics.

Multi-platform distribution strategies that include mobile platforms such as smart phones and tablets along with traditional and online media are changing the ways news and stories are delivered. As the journalism field adapts to these changes, colleges are responding by adding courses in such areas as interactive journalism, multimedia, web development, data visualization, social media strategy, and web production alongside traditional courses.

But to succeed in this major, you must do more than merely go to class. You have to connect personally with faculty members, seek out mentors (instructors or others who give you guidance and support), make professional contacts, and get real-world experience through assignments, school media and internships.

For that reason journalism course work is very much project-based. You will probably have field assignments in most of your courses, every semester. Frequently, course projects involve helping local community groups to develop ad campaigns or publications. You are also encouraged to participate in one or more of the college media outlets; you might report for a student website, newspaper, magazine, or radio station. Most journalism programs arrange for you to intern with a professional media organization.

At some colleges, you can't become a journalism major until you have completed a certain number of credits, and you can't join a student media organization until a specified point in your academic progress. Other schools admit you as a major in your first year and encourage you to join student media organizations from day one. Generally, the policy depends on the size of the school; larger schools tend to be more restrictive.

Other majors you might like:
History
Radio and television
Urban studies
Community organization/advocacy
Public relations
Political science
Sports communications
Peace and conflict studies
Law enforcement investigation and interviewing

International relations
Media studies
Global studies

Questions to ask colleges:
What student media are available? How and when can a student join the college website, newspaper, radio station, or other type of media? Is there faculty supervision, or are the media outlets independent?

Is there an internship program? Is an internship required? Are students assisted in finding internships?

Are students and student organizations encouraged to enter regional and national competitions?

Career options and trends:
Print or online news reporter, editor, or photographer*; social media specialist; blogger; public relations manager*; magazine or Web editor; freelance writer (magazine, Web, newsletter); photojournalist; news outlet manager; Web designer. A major in journalism will prepare you for a wide variety of careers that require good writing and analytical skills.

Large media companies require 3 to 5 years of postgraduate experience and usually prefer job applicants who have a degree and/or experience in a specific subject area, such as economics, business, science, or politics.

Because of a decline in advertising, many newspapers, magazines, and other print media have downsized their newsroom staffs. The new forms of media taking their place require journalists to have both traditional and new media skill sets. Competition is stiff, but graduates with a variety of technical skills are entering an industry with a wide range of opportunity. Recent surveys of journalism graduates indicate that the best-paid entry-level jobs are with Internet organizations.

Insider's viewpoint:
"We came into class one morning, and the professor gave us the topic for a newspaper story and said we had an hour and a half to complete it. We had to run around campus gathering information and opinions, which is difficult at 8:30 a.m. because no one is awake yet. It was good experience, though."

—Courtney, senior, SUNY Binghamton

For more info:

American Society of Newspaper Editors (ASNE)
209 Reynolds Journalism Institute
Missouri School of Journalism
Columbia, MO 65211
(573) 884-2405
www.asne.org

American Society of Magazine Editors (ASME)
Magazine Publishers of America
810 Seventh Avenue, 24th Floor
New York, NY 10019
(212) 872-3700
www.magazine.org/asme

Public relations

Also known as:
Organizational communication

What it's about:
Public relations majors study how to manage the public image and communications of an organization (such as a corporation, sports team, or nonprofit organization). You learn how to shape the appropriate message and how to harness a variety of media, from television to Twitter, to get your message across.

Is this for you?
You might like this major if you also like: writing; public speaking; planning parties, club activities, or fund-raising events; team sports; working on the school yearbook; using social media.

Consider this major if you are good at: creativity; critical reading/thinking; organizing; persuading/influencing; research; teamwork *...or have...* initiative; verbal skills; writing skills; "people skills".

Recommended high school prep:
English 4, math 3, lab science 3, social studies 4, and a foreign language 3–4. If available, take courses in journalism, business, sociology, or speech.

Did you know...
...that strong writing skills are critical to success in public relations? Public relations professionals spend far more time writing and editing than organizing events or networking at social functions.

...that this field also involves technical and analytical skills? PR professionals must be able to show how their efforts affect the bottom line, which requires familiarity with statistics, research methods, finance, and communications technologies.

Typical courses in this major:
Fundamentals of public relations
Writing for mass media
Reporting
Media strategies
Principles of advertising
Public relations research
Public relations writing
Speech writing
Media law and ethics
Media campaigns
Visual communications and graphic design
Digital media production
New media and public relations
International public relations
Crisis management
Case studies in public relations management

Concentrations:
Corporate public relations; consumer relations; employee relations; health communications; nonprofit public relations; financial or investor relations; media relations; international public relations.

What the study of this major is like:
Public relations courses can be broadly divided into two types: those that teach technical skills, such as writing, design, and research—and those that address strategies, tactics, and managerial skills. The best programs provide a balanced blend of both types.

Excellent writing is the top-ranked skill in public relations, so most programs start with courses in media writing, reporting, and editing. In these courses you will sharpen your writing skills and learn the operations and formats of different media, ranging from newspapers to television to blogs.

You are also likely to take a core course in visual communications, learning the principles of design, layout, art, and typography. In both writing and visual communications courses, you develop skills for working with print materials and digital media, including social media and mobile apps.

Expect to take at least one research methods course, which introduces tools such as surveys and focus groups along with mathematical techniques for analyzing data. These skills are essential to obtain and evaluate feedback from the public. So yes, you will need to brush up your math skills.

In courses that focus on strategy and concepts, you explore the issues that inform public relations campaigns, often by analyzing real-world case studies. You learn how to incorporate public opinion into business strategies, and you develop expertise in strategic planning and problem solving. You also learn how to use common public relations tactics, such as news releases, media kits, brochures, position papers, speeches, newsletters, special events, and website articles.

A good program will offer an elective on strategies for adapting to new channels of communication, particularly social media, which enables and even demands two-way communication between an organization and the public. You might also take an elective in international or multicultural public relations, which will help you to work effectively in a global economy.

You will most likely be required to participate in a team capstone project, in which you plan, develop, implement, and evaluate a complete public relations campaign, often for a real client in the nearby community. At the end of the project you and your team will present the campaign in a written report and oral presentation just as you would in the workplace.

An important aspect of the major is an internship, which is typically required. In addition to providing real-world experience and contacts, an internship also helps you develop a portfolio of your work, which you'll need when looking for that first job after graduation. Writing for your college website, student newspaper, or TV or radio station is another excellent way to gain experience and material for your portfolio.

Other majors you might like:
Advertising
Business communications
Marketing
Music management
Public administration
Community organization/advocacy
Human resources management
Media studies
Graphic design
Organizational behavior studies

Hospitality administration and management
Meeting and event planning

Questions to ask colleges:
Is the program accredited by the Accrediting Council on Education in Journalism and Mass Communications (ACEJMC), or certified by the Certification in Education for Public Relations (CEPR) program?

Does the curriculum cover emerging technologies and communication platforms?

Career options and trends:
Public relations manager; corporate communications manager; publicist; media relations specialist; event planner; speech writer; public opinion researcher; public relations agency representative; promoter; nonprofit or educational fund-raiser.

Over the next decade or so, employment opportunities in the public relations field are expected to grow faster than in many other professions. The explosive growth of social media is driving demand for public relations specialists who can help organizations use these platforms to maintain their relationships with key constituents. Opportunities in international public relations are also expanding with the rising number of companies pursuing global markets.

Nevertheless, there will be stiff competition for entry-level jobs because the major is so popular. Prospects will be best for graduates who can exhibit strong writing and research skills, who are knowledgeable about current trends and technologies, and who have pursued a minor and/or internship in a relevant area.

For more info:
Public Relations Society of America (PRSA)
33 Maiden Lane
New York, NY 10038
(212) 460-1400
www.prsa.org

Accredting Council on Education in Journalism
    and Mass Communications (ACEJMC)
www.ku.edu/~acejmc

Radio and television

What it's about:

The radio and television major prepares you for a career in all areas of these two types of media, including writing, editing, production, performance, and sales. You learn to develop and deliver programming for both traditional broadcast and new media platforms.

Is this for you?

You might like this major if you also like: telling or writing stories; knowing about everyday events and issues; expressing your ideas and opinions; technology; taking pictures or making videos.

Consider this major if you are good at: attention to detail; creativity; critical reading/thinking; organizing; teamwork *...or have...* initiative; patience; verbal skills; writing skills.

Recommended high school prep:

English 4, math 3, lab science 3, social studies 3, and a foreign language 2–3. If possible, participate in student media activities such as radio and TV stations, newspapers, and yearbooks.

Did you know...

...that the demand for radio and TV content is on the rise? Mobile devices, webcasting, and on-demand platforms have allowed people to access radio and TV in more ways than ever before, with more control over the content they select. These changes have opened up new markets for TV and radio programming.

Typical courses in this major:

Introduction to mass media
History of broadcasting
Writing for electronic media
Fundamentals of video production
Media aesthetics and analysis
Production management
Mass media and society
New media technology
Media law and regulation
On-air performance
Interactive media
Sound design/production
Studio television production
Graphics and animation
Video editing

Concentrations:

Media production; audio production; broadcasting; production management; experimental/interactive/emerging media; scriptwriting.

What the study of this major is like:

The study of this major usually starts with an introductory course in media studies, which explores various cultural, legal, and economic aspects of mass media. Additional core courses focus on subjects such as media law, broadcasting history, and new technologies. A course in media writing may also be required. Many of these courses are conducted in a lecture format.

But this is not the kind of major where you spend a lot of time in a formal classroom. Working in computer editing labs, television and radio studios, and "on location" in the field are a vital part of the radio and TV major. In these venues you gain hands-on experience working on different types of programming, from documentaries to sports events to narrative stories, and you learn to use specialized equipment and software.

In production classes you work directly with television and radio equipment as you learn the different aspects of media production, such as multi-camera televising; sound and audio production; radio programming; and on-demand streaming. Elective performance courses help you hone your newscasting, announcing, and interviewing skills.

One thing you will quickly discover is that radio and television production requires lots of teamwork. In order for all the components of a production to come together, you need to cooperate with others and to be both a follower and a leader. The glamour this field might have for you can swiftly fade when you are faced with deadlines, difficult-to-follow scripts, and technical problems. These experiences prepare you for the kinds of challenges you are likely to face in the working world.

If you take this major at a college in or near a large city you are more likely to find opportunities for internships and part-time employment in the industry. On the other hand, TV and radio stations in rural or suburban communities may allow you to be more involved in productions. Student-run radio and television studios can also provide you with excellent outside-of-class experience.

Colleges with a tradition of media-related programs, such as journalism, advertising, and the arts, are likely to emphasize those areas in their radio and television offerings. Four-year programs usually require a capstone or thesis-level course in your final year, where you can integrate and demonstrate what you have learned throughout the program.

Other majors you might like:
Sports communications
Film/cinema studies
Electrical and communications engineering
Drama and theater arts
Recording arts
Animation
Photographic/film/video technology
Cinematography and film/video production
Media studies
Broadcast journalism
Photojournalism
Telecommunications technology

Questions to ask colleges:
What kinds of equipment are available for students to use? How soon do majors begin working directly with production equipment?

How does the curriculum reflect recent changes in the TV and radio industries, including the shift toward delivering more content online?

What kind of jobs do graduates of the program typically obtain?

Career options and trends:
Producer*; TV newscaster/sportscaster*; director*; station manager; production coordinator; camera operator; video editor; sound designer; lighting designer; radio DJ; sales executive.

Mergers, new technology, and the growth of alternative media sources are reshaping the radio and TV industries. Corporate media conglomerates now include cable and/or broadcast TV stations, film studios, radio stations, newspapers, magazines, and digital media outlets. Job losses resulting from this consolidation are being offset, however, by opportunities in the growth area of mobile and Internet based media distribution. At the local level, radio and TV stations are hiring fewer employees due to decreasing advertising revenue and automation.

All job seekers face keen competition in this field. If you have diversified skills and hands-on experience that can be applied to both content development and production, you may have a better chance of finding a job with a media company.

For more info:
Broadcast Education Association (BEA)
1771 N Street, NW
Washington, DC 20036-2891
(202) 429-3935
www.beaweb.org

College Broadcasters, Inc. (CBI)
UPS – Hershey Square Center
1152 Mae Street
Hummelstown, PA 17036
(855) 275-4224
www.askcbi.org

Sports communications

What it's about:

Students of sports communications prepare for careers as sports journalists or public relations professionals specializing in sports. In this major you will examine the relationships between sport, communication, and society, and study the impact of sports media. You will also learn practical skills in areas such as sports reporting, broadcasting, promotion, and various media production methods.

Is this for you?

You might like this major if you also like: all types of sports (not just those that are popular); writing; keeping a journal or blog; reading; coaching; describing or explaining things to others; fact-checking and research.

Consider this major if you are good at: attention to detail; creativity; critical reading/thinking; organizing; teamwork *...or have...* initiative; patience; verbal skills; writing skills.

Recommended high school prep:

English 4, math 3, lab science 3, social studies 4, and a foreign language 3. Courses in journalism and speech are helpful. If possible, participate in student media activities such as a school website, newspaper, or yearbook.

Did you know...

...that you don't have to be an athlete to excel in this major? In fact, the ability to look critically at sport is more likely to bring success. That requires a different perspective than that of a player or a fan.

...that this major focuses on writing? Students are often surprised by how much time they spend practicing their writing skills.

Typical courses in this major:

Introduction to journalism
Media writing
Sports reporting
Sports broadcasting
Sports and society

The business of sports media
Sports and film
Sports event management
History of sports media
Sports marketing
Sports and gender
Sports psychology
Sports law and ethics
Public and media relations in sports
Audio production and performance
Principles of television production

Concentrations:

Sports broadcasting; sports public relations.

What the study of this major is like:

Students sometimes come into this major thinking it is a "fun" major. In actuality, the major is demanding and takes lots of hard work. And you have to work when everyone else is having fun— attending sporting events.

You'll be held to strict newsroom standards, and deadlines are real, as they are in the real world. Most professors won't accept late assignments at all. They also tend to be sticklers for accuracy and good spelling, just like editors.

Sports communications involve a lot more than team scores and statistics. You will look at sports in new ways, examining the role of sports in society and considering issues such as gender, race, performance enhancing drugs, and other tough topics. You'll study the history, economics, psychology, and cultural significance of sports of all kinds. This major combines critical thinking with a deep understanding of the field.

Your studies begin with a broad foundation of courses that range from the theoretical to the applied. Most four-year programs require a solid grounding in the liberal arts and humanities in order to provide a broad cultural context. General introductory courses in communications, media, and journalism are often required.

Introductory courses provide an in-depth study of the field. You will study the practice and effects of sports communications and will likely write research papers on these topics. You will likely study the economics of sports media and examine sports marketing and management as well. Most of these courses will be taught in lecture and discussion classes.

In later courses you will move into more applied areas, such as sports reporting, sports public relations, and sports broadcasting. These courses usually start with lecture/discussion formats, and then focus more on field work and real world practice. For example, in a sports reporting course, students often attend, cover, and write about sporting events and write "game stories." You'll also try your hand at columns, features, and possibly in-depth investigative reporting. In a sports broadcasting course you learn production and postproduction methods along with play-by-play announcing. In all of these courses, writing will be emphasized.

In many schools, internships are an integral part of this major. You might intern with media organizations, sports organizations, sports advertising and promotion companies, and other groups that perform the many affiliated functions of sports communications. Some schools may also have a capstone class that allows students to work in-depth on a particular sports communication project.

As you explore colleges, you'll see a difference between schools that offer a B.A. (bachelor of arts) and a B.S. (bachelor of science) degree in this major. Those in the former will be geared toward journalism and focus more on the liberal arts. Those in the latter are usually geared more toward broadcasting and offer more technical classes. Some programs require a minor, concentration, or dual degree in kinesiology—the study of human movement.

Other majors you might like:
Radio and television
Broadcast journalism
Photojournalism
Media studies
Business communications
Athletic training
Physical education
Sports and fitness administration

Physical therapy
Hospitality/recreation marketing
Golf management
Parks, recreation, and leisure studies

Questions to ask colleges:
Does the school have broadcasting facilities or a studio? Is there a journalism lab?

Are there internship opportunities with off-campus sports organizations and events?

Does the school offer sports that interest you?

What kind of jobs do graduates of the program typically obtain?

Career options and trends:
Sports journalist*; sports broadcaster*; sports writer; sports marketing specialist; sports public relations specialist*; team publicist; statistician; event planner; promoter; sports information director*; production assistant; public address announcer.

There are few areas of public interest as popular as sports. The huge demand for sports information is fueling increased coverage on cable networks and the Internet, which in turn creates new jobs for sports communications professionals. At the same time, the information industry as a whole is in great flux as different media forms migrate online.

Competition for jobs is keen in all areas of sports communications. Sports journalists, broadcasters and writers who can work in an online environment and in multiple mediums will have the the best prospects.

For more info:
National Collegiate Baseball Writers Association (NCBWA); Football Writers Association of America (FWAA); United States Basketball Writers Association (USBWA)
www.sportswriters.net

Associated Press Sports Editors (APSE)
National Sports Journalism Center
Indiana University-Purdue University Indianapolis
535 West Michigan Street
Indianapolis, IN 46202
http://apsportseditors.org

Computer and information sciences

Computer science is making a comeback as college major. After years of declining enrollment, the Computing Research Association reports an increase in the number of students in computer science programs. This is good news for those in the industry who were worried about the nation's ability to compete in a global economy.

Apparently, fear of jobs going overseas were overblown, as more IT jobs are available in the United States today than at the height of the dot com boom, reports the Association for Computing Machinery.

The demand for workers in this field still far exceeds supply—in fact, computer occupations are consistently projected by the Department of Labor to be among the fastest-growing fields in the United States. Employment for software developers is expected to grow by nearly 30 percent through 2022.

"One thing I can say for sure is people with a good computer science education in the next 15 years will have tons and tons of opportunities to choose from," Microsoft Chairman Bill Gates told students at the University of Michigan. "If there's a great field to go into, this is it."

If you're leaning toward a computer major, you probably already have a good deal of experience using computers for communicating with friends, doing homework, and gaming. Maybe you've used graphics, animation, or multimedia systems. People probably come to you for help with their computers. You may also enjoy doing math and puzzles and building mechanical or electronic gadgets.

But how do you turn your familiarity with computers into a challenging and rewarding college education and career? First, get to know how the various computer sciences are taught and which areas of the field attract your interest.

Computer science provides a foundation in the theory and design of computer systems. The information sciences majors add an understanding of the way people use the technologies. After all, an information system includes not just the computers, programs, and networks but also the way individuals, organizations, and society use these powerful tools. Computer forensics blends computer science and law enforcement, while game design draws on both technical and artistic skills.

"One can view the world of computing as a continuum," explains Anne Marchant, Department of Applied Information Technology, George Mason University. "At one end, you have fields like computer science and electrical engineering that focus on the development of hardware and software. At the other end, you have fields like information science ... and management information systems. Information technology is in the middle. Practitioners in the field of IT integrate technologies to build and administer information infrastructure."

Since computers influence just about every profession, you may also be interested in other chapters in this book that discuss majors including management information systems, digital media, electrical and communications engineering, computer engineering technology, drafting and design technology, graphic design, and animation. Computer sciences are also applied to emerging areas of study such as bioinformatics, mobile/wireless computing, digital media design, and cognitive science.

The program for you

When you enter the workplace as a college grad, you'll need the latest skills and knowledge of sophisticated software, the Internet, networking and wireless technologies and a variety of programming tools and languages in order to make computers work for people.

Problem solving is a mission for computer programmers, according to Kate Stewart, Department of Technology and Professional Programs, Tallahassee Community College. "Students who truly enjoy the challenge of creating software that serves a user's needs are passionate and addicted to the process of design and development."

When you are comparing colleges, look for adequate lab facilities and a wide selection of courses. See if you'll have access, from your home or dormitory, to the Internet and the computer networks you'll need. Will you have to invest in hardware and software? Find out if research or internship opportunities are open to you. Also, be aware that colleges stress different aspects of computer science. Some colleges may be more theoretical, others more hands-on or business oriented. If possible, conduct some research on faculty members to see what they've published. Are their priorities similar to yours?

"Each orientation has its strength, and you should consider your overall goal—graduate school or employment. You should also consider the industry needs of the geographic area you hope to reside in," Stewart suggests.

Some concentrations in undergraduate majors include computer systems, database management, programming, robotics, interface design, systems analysis, information systems management, multimedia, data communications and networking, e-commerce, and Web development.

Learning never ends in these cutting-edge fields. Advanced and graduate studies include computer architecture, compilers, operating systems, programming languages, networks and security; advanced database applications, knowledge systems, artificial intelligence, medical or biological informatics; data mining, software engineering; algorithm analysis, programming languages, and artificial intelligence.

Look for these majors in colleges of computing, engineering, information technology, applied sciences, liberal arts and sciences, and in business schools. Also check colleges of engineering, because some programs combine electrical and computer engineering.

For more information, visit the Association for Computing Machinery (www.acm.org), the Institute of Electrical and Electronics Engineers (www.ieee.org), the Society for Industrial and Applied Mathematics (www.siam.org), and the Association for Information Systems (www.aisnet.org and www.itsworld.org).

Computer forensics

Also known as:
Digital forensics
Cyber forensics

What it's about:
Computer forensics majors learn how to analyze computer systems, networks, and data storage devices for evidence related to criminal acts; how to preserve and present digital evidence for legal actions; and how to troubleshoot computer security problems and protect against system intrusions.

Is this for you?
You might like this major if you also like: pursuing elusive clues, solving complex problems, open source software, trying new operating systems, law enforcement shows, math and science.

Consider this major if you are good at: attention to detail; quantitative analysis; research; teamwork; communicating with others ...*or have...* self reliance; initiative; patience; math skills; writing skills.

Recommended high school prep:
English 4, math 4 (including precalculus), lab science 3 (including physics), social studies 3, and a foreign language 2–3. If possible, take a course in criminal justice, and as many computer courses as you can.

Did you know...
...that computer forensics is not like the forensics made popular on TV? This major is not about using computers to examine physical evidence in criminal cases, but rather it focuses on digital evidence found on computers, computer networks and digital devices.

Typical courses in this major:
Criminal law and procedure
Introduction to criminal justice
Criminal evidence and investigation
Operating systems
Forensic science
Forensic accounting
Digital forensics I, II
Analysis of digital media
Investigative interviewing
Computer and network security
Network forensics
Cybercrime
Digital investigation
Statistics
Technical writing
E-discovery

Concentrations:
Network forensics, digital media analysis, network security, law enforcement, e-discovery.

What the study of this major is like:
This major combines the study of information systems, computer security, law, and criminal procedure with technical courses in the analysis and deconstruction of digital devices and data found on computer storage systems.

Students starting out in this major are often surprised by the number of criminal justice courses required. By the time you take your first technical digital forensic course, you will be well grounded in legal theory and practice as well as computer theory and operating systems.

After your foundation courses you will tackle the process of analyzing digital devices in order to find evidence pertaining to crimes. Most of these courses are a combination of lecture and laboratory, where you learn to apply theories and best practices to hand-on analysis of computer forensic images and traces. You will conduct computer lab projects both in class and for homework, and also participate in group projects.

You will also learn how to write detailed reports of your analysis of digital devices and to present your findings both orally and in writing. This may be another surprise if you think this major is only about technical skills. But the ability to express yourself clearly is vital, because digital forensic examiners must work collaboratively with detectives and prosecutors to present their case, and to explain how data on digital devices supports or contradicts findings. This often requires giving testimony in court.

Typically during your third and fourth years of study you will participate in an internship, obtaining real life experience working in a local digital forensics firm, laboratory or law enforcement agency. The length of your internship may vary depending on the program, but the experience is invaluable both for your training and your job prospects.

In upper level courses you will also be introduced to the subjects of forensic accounting and white collar crime. You'll probably study alongside business and accounting majors, learning the painstaking and detailed work involved in examining business accounts, personal financial transactions, and the methods used by criminals to launder money.

Seniors often conduct their own research in new and highly technical aspects of digital forensics. It's a good idea to also participate in computer forensics associations or clubs in order to broaden your knowledge outside the classroom and make connections in the field.

Many programs are very law enforcement centric, but there is another side to computer forensics relating to commerce, e-discovery (the disclosure in civil lawsuits of electronically held information) and computer security outside the prosecution of crimes. If you want to widen your career options, look for colleges with programs that cover both aspects of computer forensics or offer a minor or concentration in network security.

Other majors you might like:
Forensic science
Information systems
Computer/systems security
Emergency management/homeland security
Criminology
Behavioral sciences
Criminal justice and law enforcement
Police science
Information technology
Computer engineering technology
Management information systems
Health information management

Questions to ask colleges:
What other areas of the industry besides law enforcement can your program prepare me for?

Is the computer forensics major part of a larger division or school within the college? A program housed in the Computer Science department will be different than a program housed under Criminal Justice.

Does the program require or encourage an internship? What support does the college offer in finding internships?

What are the general education course requirements for this major?

Career options and trends:
Digital forensics examiner/analyst*; computer forensics technologist; information systems security officer*; systems analyst; system engineer; database analyst; computer forensics associate

Job prospects are good, especially in law enforcement, where the increase in computer and internet crime is forcing agencies to create technology task forces and to hire digital examiners. The FBI predicts that before long up to fifty percent of its cases will require a computer forensic expert.

The need for computer security is also pushing demand for digital media and systems analysts throughout all industries. The health care industry, for example, will need information security analysts to create safeguards as the use of electronic medical records expands. The Bureau of Labor Statistics projects employment of such analysts to grow much faster than average through 2022.

Applicants for law enforcement or government positions must pass security clearances and often undergo a lie detector test. Be aware that if you pursue a career in law enforcement, child pornography cases can be as much as seventy percent of the work load for state level digital forensic laboratories.

Insider's viewpoint:
"It is encouraging to see that President Obama has created a new cabinet position for Information Technology and Security. This is a clear message that this field is very important!"

— Professor Cristian Balan, Champlain College

For more info:

International Association of Financial Crimes
  Investigators
1020 Suncast Lane, Suite 102
El Dorado Hills, CA 95762
(916) 939-5000
www.iafci.org

American Academy of Forensic Sciences (AAFS)
410 North 21st Street
Colorado Springs, CO 80904
(719) 636-1100
www.aafs.org

Computer programming

What it's about:

Computer programming majors learn how to write various programming languages used for software development and operating systems. Topics covered include software installation and maintenance, program customization and linking, debugging, and prototype testing.

Is this for you?

You might like this major if you also like: puzzles and brain teasers; computer games; learning new technology; figuring out creative solutions to challenging problems.

Consider this major if you are good at: attention to detail; creativity; critical reading/thinking; math; organizing; teamwork ...*or have...* listening skills; patience; verbal skills; writing skills.

Recommended high school prep:

English 4, math 3, lab science 3 (including physics), social studies 3, and a foreign language 2–3. Take as many computer courses as you can. Courses that cover business and communication are also helpful

Did you know...

...that the core of computer programming is to figure out how to meet users' needs, not just to know how the computer works? That's why communication skills are important.

Typical courses in this major:

Computer literacy
Introduction to computer technology
Business communications
Operating systems
Networking essentials
C++ programming
Java programming
Object oriented programming
Visual basic programming
Database design
Database systems
Multimedia applications

Web page development
Scripting languages
Network security

Concentrations:

Generally, none available.

What the study of this major is like:

In this major you learn how to talk to computers—using programming languages to tell a computer how to do what you want it to. If you are interested in a higher-level study of the theory and design of computer systems, consider a major in computer science. But if you want to dive right into coding, this could be the major for you.

Course work in computer programming gives you an understanding of software design and development strategies; basic hardware principles; elementary network concepts; database design and implementation techniques; and a combination of Web, multimedia, and security concepts. Most of these topics are taught through a combination of lectures and lab work. Lectures cover techniques, strategies, vocabulary, and concepts. The lab time allows you to put into practice what you've learned.

It's not rote learning. Because a successful computer programmer must have the ability to analyze a user's needs and then develop an efficient piece of software that meets those needs, the program's emphasis is on building strong problem-solving and communication skills. Stress is also placed on cultivating habits of patience and attention to detail.

You will probably spend a lot of time outside of class acquiring these skills and habits. Each programming language and/or topic may present specific challenges. As might be expected, many students find that they are stronger in some areas than in others—for example, they have an easier time understanding hardware than programming concepts, or they have particular difficulty anticipating how changes in code will affect outcomes. In the beginning, some assignments will drive you nuts.

But if you are prepared at the outset to dedicate the extra time and effort required to patiently think about, design, implement, and debug your work, you should find that the rewards outweigh the frustrations. The satisfaction you get when a project is completed and functioning properly is addictive—as you encounter each assignment, problem solving becomes a mission. But there's no getting around the fact that this is a rigorous major. It takes practice, patience, and dedication.

This major is offered mostly at two-year (community) colleges and technical schools. If you come across a four-year program, it's most likely a higher-level computer science major. Colleges use many different names for their computer majors, so go by the description in the course catalogue, not the name.

As you explore colleges, you will notice that the major can vary widely in focus. At some schools, the concentration is on software (mostly programming); at others, the emphasis is on Web page design and management. Some majors are geared toward industry-recognized certifications (Cisco or Microsoft, for example); others are applications oriented (computer graphics, data entry, etc.); still others deal mostly with systems and networking. Examine the descriptions closely to see which programs best match your goals.

And as you think about your goals, remember that programmers can never stop learning; to stay employable, you'll have to keep up with the state of the art.

Other majors you might like:
Information technology
Mathematics
Computer engineering technology
Information systems
Computer science
Medical office computer specialist
Animation
Computer graphics
Database design/management
Management information systems

Career options and trends:
Computer programmer*; web developer/administrator*; database administrator; network administrator; help desk operator; PC support/technician; network support/technician*.

Industry-recognized vendor certifications, such as those offered by Cisco, Microsoft, CompTia, or C-Tech, are good credentials to take into the job market. Learning a variety of programming languages and tools for networking, database management, and Internet applications will also increase your chances of landing a job.

Job prospects are good for those with a bachelor's degree and experience with a variety of programming languages. Basic or routine programming jobs, however, continue to be shifted to countries with educated workers and low wages. For future job security, combine your technical savvy with knowledge of some other business or scientific field, so you'll know both how to use programming tools and how to apply them to a specific goal.

For more info:
Association for Computing Machinery (ACM)
2 Penn Plaza
Suite 701
New York, NY 10121-0701
(800) 342-6626
www.acm.org

Institute of Electrical and Electronics Engineers
  (IEEE)
3 Park Avenue
17th Fl.
New York, NY 10016-5997
(212) 419-7900
www.ieee.org

Computer science

What it's about:
The computer science major trains you in the theory and design of computing systems and software, as well as in important application areas. Your course work balances the need to keep up-to-date with the latest technology with the need to acquire a conceptual foundation that will last throughout your career.

Is this for you?
You might like this major if you also like: mathematical and logical puzzles; using programming to solve real-world problems or explore mathematics; giving precise and elegant explanations for how things work; building mechanical or electronic gadgets.

Consider this major if you are good at: active listening; attention to detail; creativity; critical reading/thinking; math; quantitative analysis; research; teamwork ...*or have...* mental stamina; writing skills.

Recommended high school prep:
English 4, math 4 (including precalculus), lab science 3, social studies 3, and a foreign language 2–3. If possible, take discrete mathematics, calculus, a computer science course, and physics (covering electricity and magnetism).

Did you know...
...that companies like Microsoft have more jobs for computer-science graduates with bachelor's degrees than they can fill? But while high-end computer jobs in the United States may be abundant, the Commerce Department confirms that the outsourcing of low-end, routine jobs is on the rise.

...that mathematical ability and logical thinking are the core skills you need for this major? You don't need to learn programming in high school. In fact, many students come to college thinking they know how to program, only to find that they have to relearn the subject from a more analytical perspective.

...that there are many interdisciplinary areas of study within the computer science major? Cognitive science connects computer science and psychology, linguistics, philosophy, and neuroscience. Bioinformatics and computational biology combine computer science and biology. Digital media design links computer science to the fine arts and communications.

Typical courses in this major:
Introduction to program design
Data structures
Computer system organization
Mathematics for computer science
Automata and formal language theory
Algorithms
Digital system design
Operating systems
Software engineering
Compilers
Principles of database design
Computer graphics
Artificial intelligence
Robotics

Concentrations:
In college: theoretical computer science; computer systems; artificial intelligence; databases; graphics; robotics; computational biology; computational linguistics; multimedia.

If you go on to grad school: computer architecture; compilers; operating systems; programming languages; networks and security; robotics and computer vision; natural language processing; algorithms and complexity; bioinformatics.

What the study of this major is like:
In this major you study many abstract concepts, and examine fundamental notions such as mathematical proof, knowledge, computability, and randomness in a new light. But computer science, of course, also focuses on the computer.

Because using a computer to communicate requires precision, you must learn to use precise programming languages. During your core training, you'll be asked to think about many questions: Why are programming languages designed the way they are? How do you translate a real-world problem into a carefully worded set of instructions—a program—that a computer can execute (or follow) to produce the solution? What goes on inside a computer when a program is being executed? How is the computer constructed to enable it to function? What impact do computers and programs have on a variety of fields?

Computer science programs vary in the amount of core training they provide. A solid foundation will help you solve problems in application areas. Some programs focus on skills that are immediately applicable, while others emphasize abstract, conceptual ideas to ensure that what you learn will be able to help you to adapt to rapid changes in technology. In addition, some programs assume that students have pretty sophisticated backgrounds in math and logic. In other programs, students aren't necessarily expected to have such in-depth, high-level preparation.

Designing and analyzing computer programs requires a mathematical creativity that you may find challenging. Furthermore, you will encounter a multitude of programming environments and languages and may struggle to master them. Projects and assignments typically require long hours of work. On the whole, the computer science major is intellectually demanding, but the field is young and full of possibilities. Once you acquire a mathematical and logical foundation, you can quickly reach the point where you are conceiving and evaluating ideas on your own. If you are attracted to abstract thinking as well as to practicality, computer science can offer you the best of both worlds.

Other majors you might like:
Computer engineering
Electrical and communications engineering
Computer hardware engineering
Computational mathematics
Cognitive science
Software engineering
Systems engineering
Robotics technology
Information technology
Computer engineering technology
Computer graphics
Digital media

Questions to ask colleges:
Does the computer science program include aspects of electrical engineering? If you are interested in the circuitry of computers, examine a school's course list carefully. Because schools may differ in the way they divide the content of electrical engineering and computer science, the circuitry of computers is not taught in all computer science departments.

Career options and trends:
Senior programmer*; systems analyst*; network administrator; database manager; software developer*; financial analyst*.

Job prospects are excellent, especially for computer system designers, database administrators, and computer security specialists, which are projected to be among the nation's fastest growing occupations for the forseeable future. There are minor fluctuations in the market and small ups and downs in the salaries for entry-level jobs. But the shortage of students choosing this field will increase demand for those that do.

Insider's viewpoint:
"Networking and Graphics are my favorite classes. Networking is the backbone for communications nowadays, and there is much to be done to increase security, speed, and availability. Graphics is simply fun. In my Graphics class, we created a video game, a flight simulator, and a ray tracer that produces highly realistic pictures."

—Amy, senior, University of Maryland

For more info:
Association of Computing Machinery (ACM)
2 Penn Plaza
Suite 701
New York, NY 10121-0701
(800) 342-6626
www.acm.org

Game design

Also known as:
Game development
Video game design

Game production
Game criticism
Multiplayer network programming

What it's about:
Game design and development blends art, science, and technical proficiency to produce computer games. In this major you learn how to design, program, test, and produce interactive games for a variety of platforms.

Is this for you?
You might like this major if you also like: telling stories (especially visually); intricate puzzles; comics; reading fiction, biography, history; experimentation; the give and take of working in group projects.

Consider this major if you are good at: teamwork; creativity; attention to detail; quantitative analysis; critical reading/thinking; time management ...*or have*...curiosity; initiative; leadership skills; writing skills; a strong visual imagination.

Recommended high school prep:
English 4, math 4 (including precalculus), lab science 3 (including physics), social studies 4, and a foreign language 2–3. If available, take courses in creative and technical writing, introductory programming, and art/media history.

Typical courses in this major:
Introduction to game development
Game design I, II
Sound and music for games
Computer animation
Fundamentals of 3D graphics
Simulation design
Digital game studies
Programming for games
Physics for games
Narrative writing for games
Story development for interactive media
Game culture
Engine-based design

Concentrations:
In college: game development, game sound design, game programming, game art/animation.

If you go on to grad school: game studies/theory, game production and management.

What the study of this major is like:
Courses in game design revolve around the five main components of a production team: design (fun and gameplay), art (2D and 3D animation, and interface), programming (game code and structure), sound (sound effects and music), and management (project scheduling and planning). The background of game culture (theory and criticism, sociology, marketing) is also covered.

Introductory classes focus on the fundamentals in each area, providing a foundation and framework for later classes. Some classes in the major are entirely focused on one topic, but more often the various components of game design and development are integrated.

This integrated approach will carry through in group projects as well. Game design is rarely a solo endeavor, so it is extremely important that you learn to work in a team that collectively provides the creative and technical expertise necessary to create a game that is not only fun and challenging, but also technically and artistically sound.

Classes combine theoretical presentation and discussion with hands-on practical instruction. You will be exposed to multiple game engines and production tools, and will be encouraged to experiment with new gameplay ideas and techniques. Classes are very often goal-oriented and focused on the completion of a final group project. Many classes also delve into problem-solving techniques specific to each stage of game development.

Class structure can be loose and informal, but demanding. The ability to think critically and to take and receive useful criticism is required. Participation and interaction are key to the learning process. That's because games are an active medium that requires thought and response. They must challenge the user to not just watch something happen, but to make decisions that change outcomes in surprising ways.

Most game design programs are focused on preparing the student for a career in game development, but more and more schools are offering another focus that emphasizes social-conscious games, sometimes referred to as "serious games." Some colleges, especially those with graduate programs, also teach the use of game engines and game technology for alternative applications, such as virtual environments. Games are also used in other areas such as in education, training, simulation, and advertising.

Two-year or certificate programs are usually focused on creating technically adept workers, especially in the areas of 3D animation and programming, but contain little creative or artistic emphasis. An associate degree will qualify you for an entry-level job, but a bachelor's will help you into higher-level design positions.

Other majors you might like:
Animation
Computer graphics
Digital media
Graphic communications
Graphic design
Cinematography and film/video production
Creative writing
Web page/multimedia design
Instructional media
Software engineering
Drafting and design technology
Computational mathematics

Questions to ask colleges:
How long has the college offered this major? Are your graduates finding jobs in the industry?

What kind of facilities and software library does the school have to support game studies?

Do faculty have game industry experience?

Are there internship opportunities?

How many team-oriented game projects do students typically work on? Is there a focus on portfolio development?

How much extra-curricular support is there for independent game production?

Career options and trends:
Game designer; game artist; game producer; game tester; game sound designer.

Even in a weak economy, the demand for computer and video games is expected to remain strong, and the need for skilled game designers is likely to increase. Nevertheless, the game industry is very competitive; so be prepared to present a wide variety of completed works (games, models, etc.) that show a range of abilities.

Insider's viewpoint:
"I love this field because of the creative possibilities. You can tell stories, visit odd places, be someone you can never be in real life and help save the day; and at the same time explore serious issues of social justice and cultural heritage."

—Professor Tom Dowd, Columbia College Chicago

For more info:
International Game Developers Association
19 Mantua Road
Mt. Royal, NJ 08061
(856) 423-2990
www.igda.org

Information systems

Also known as:
Information science

What it's about:
Information systems is about bringing computers and people together. Majors learn how to conceive, design, and implement computer applications, systems, and information technology (IT) that meet the specific needs of individuals, businesses, and many other types of organizations.

Is this for you?
You might like this major if you also like: using computers to solve problems or accomplish tasks; showing others how to use computers; having your own website; playing computer games; working on team projects; tutoring. If you enjoy working both with computers and with people, this major could be a good choice.

Consider this major if you are good at: attention to detail; communicating; critical reading/thinking; math; organizing; teamwork *...or have...* initiative; listening skills; writing skills.

Recommended high school prep:
English 4, math 4 (including precalculus), lab science 4 (including physics), social studies 3, and a foreign language 2–3. If available, take courses that cover computer science and applications, psychology or sociology, speech, and writing.

Did you know...
...that in this major, you learn the same technology skills as a computer science major, but you must also develop good communication skills? An ability to communicate well with nontechnical users and to write specifications accurately is essential for students in this field.

Typical courses in this major:
Introduction to programming
Introduction to data structures
Operating systems
Systems analysis
Information retrieval and data mining
Object-oriented programming
Web development and e-commerce
Human and computer interaction
Principles of database design
Database applications
Multimedia systems
Computer graphics
Simulation and modeling
Game design
Decision support systems
Advanced information systems

Concentrations:
In college: computer interface design; systems analysis and design; decision support systems; information systems management; multimedia, visualization, and graphics; data communications and networking; management information systems; e-commerce and Web development.

If you go on to grad school: networking and security; advanced database applications; information systems assurance (IS auditing and security); computer-mediated communications; knowledge systems; artificial intelligence and expert systems; medical or biological informatics.

What the study of this major is like:
This major prepares you to bring computers and people together to solve problems. Computers are fast and logical; people are slower and intuitive, but also creative and insightful. To develop useful information systems and computer applications for business, government, science, and society, you need to understand both the benefits and the dangers that can occur when humans interact with computers. You must learn how humans solve problems, as well as how organizational processes work.

Generally, about half your course work is devoted to general education—math, science, speech, writing, social sciences, humanities, and electives, most of which you complete during your first two years. The work is geared to help you explore the way people solve problems and the way group and organizational processes function. What you learn can be translated into the design and implementation of computer systems and applications.

The technical skills you'll learn are similar to those taught in the computer science major. Although computer studies begin in your first year, you take most computer courses in your third and fourth years. Core requirements are generally spread evenly over the following areas:

Computer and programming concepts. Basic information and skills you'll use for developing computer hardware, computer operating systems, and computer programs.

Data and file structures. Basic ideas and techniques you'll use in creating the logical and physical structures of data and files.

Database management. Instruction that enables you to design, construct, and use database systems.

Data communications. Basic ideas, terms, design, and applications you'll need for developing data communications and networks.

Systems analysis and design. Tools and techniques you'll use in analyzing and developing computer-based systems.

In the lab, you'll be taught a variety of computer languages and systems. You are usually required to learn at least one high-level computer language well enough so that you can create programs in it. Electives and advanced courses may be offered in interface design, multimedia systems, expert systems, e-commerce and Internet applications, and computer-aided modeling and systems engineering.

The field of information systems is rapidly evolving; new material is constantly being developed. Among the essential things you learn as a major is how to master the professional literature and how to keep up with new developments.

Leading information systems programs are accredited by the Computing Sciences Accreditation Board (CSAB). Ideally, a program should encourage you to pursue an area of concentration but not to overemphasize that area (that is, not to take more than about five courses in one application). In fact, most courses should concentrate on concepts that cut across application areas—and that can be useful in any number of situations.

Other majors you might like:
Computer science
Behavioral sciences
Communications
Web page/multimedia design
Health information management
E-commerce
Management information systems
Digital media
Electrical and communications engineering
Software engineering
Computer education
Emergency management/homeland security

Questions to ask colleges:

Are faculty members actively engaged in research? This is an important indicator of a good program. If instructors are doing research in areas that interest you, that's another good sign.

Are faculty members using the Web and group communications to extend discussions outside the classroom? If they are not, perhaps they are somewhat behind the times.

What types of computer networks are available on campus? Can the computer facilities be accessed from off-campus over the Internet? Are majors required to have their own laptops or other equipment?

Is this program accredited by the Computer Science Accreditation Board (CSAB)?

Career options and trends:

Systems analyst*; trainer/consultant; database administrator; information systems manager*; applications programmer.

Fear about computer jobs being outsourced overseas has discouraged many students from entering this field, but that fear is unjustified—more jobs are being created state-side than there are applicants to fill them. Employment of computer and information systems managers is expected to increase 15 percent through 2022, mostly due to a large number of new jobs being created. Because of advances in Internet and mobile technology, however, you should be prepared to continually upgrade your skills throughout your career in order to remain employable.

Insider's viewpoint:

"We study a lot about design issues, figuring out what users find attractive, what they think is the easiest to read on Web pages, things of that sort. We're learning how to make things simpler, more accessible, because people in the computer industry have a tendency to make things hard."

—Erin, junior, Florida State University

For more info:

Association for Information Systems (AIS)
P.O. Box 2712
Atlanta, GA 30301-2712
(404) 413-7444
www.aisnet.org

Association for Computing Machinery (ACM)
2 Penn Plaza
Suite 701
New York, NY 10121-0701
(800) 342-6626
www.acm.org

Information technology

What it's about:

As an information technology (IT) major, you'll study the ways in which information and computing systems support business, research, and communications needs.

Is this for you?

You might like this major if you also like: using computers to solve real-world problems; experimenting with computer hardware and software; playing computer games; being online.

Consider this major if you are good at: attention to detail; creativity; critical reading/thinking; math; organizing; research; teamwork *...or have...* patience; verbal skills; writing skills.

Recommended high school prep:

English 4, math 4 (including precalculus), lab science 4 (including physics), social studies 3, and a foreign language 2–3. If available, take courses that cover computer science and applications, Java programming, psychology or sociology, and business.

Did you know...

...that there are more IT jobs now than at the height of the dot-com boom? A recent report by the Association for Computing Machinery found that the 2 to 3 percent of IT jobs that are outsourced overseas each year are more than made up for by new jobs created in the U.S.

Typical courses in this major:

Fundamentals of programming
Computer systems and architecture
Database management
Web development
Information security
Introduction to computer science
Problem solving and algorithm design
Networking
Computer forensics
IT ethics and social issues
Probability and statistics
Discrete mathematics
Technical writing
Speech communication
Human and computer interaction
Systems analysis and design

Concentrations:

In college: Web development; networking; database management; digital communications; applications development.

If you go on to grad school: information security; data mining; computer forensics; medical information systems

What the study of this major is like:

Sometimes it's difficult to figure out how the IT major differs from other computer majors. It might help to imagine all the computer fields arranged along a line.

At one end are fields like computer science and computer engineering, which focus on the development of hardware and software. At the other end are topics like information systems, which explores the ways computers and people work together, and management information systems, which examines the application of computers to specific business processes, such as accounting or inventory control.

IT is in the middle, where technologies and concepts from both ends are integrated to build and administer an information infrastructure—systems, networks, applications, hardware, and software.

As a result, IT majors develop a breadth of knowledge through introductory courses in a range of subjects, including Web development, database management, networking, information security, programming, and human-computer interaction. They then acquire in-depth understanding by concentrating elective courses on a particular area.

For example, you may decide to specialize in Web development and take classes such as Web page design and database development for the Web. Or you may be drawn to digital communications and take classes in telecommunications networks.

Courses in discrete mathematics and probability and statistics are usually required. You won't need to take as much math as in other computer or engineering majors, but the work can still be challenging. Most programs also require supporting courses in natural science, business, speech, and writing. You will be encouraged to minor in a related field such as business, visual arts, or communication.

Classes usually combine lectures, hands-on lab experience, projects, presentations, and online applications. Teamwork is emphasized, along with writing, research, and presentation skills. In most four-year programs, you'll be expected to do a senior project in which you will collaborate with other students to solve an IT problem. This learning approach mirrors the real world of IT.

The academic lifestyle of an IT major is fast paced and energized. Most likely you'll be taught by instructors from the industry, who bring real-world experience to the classroom and are up-to-date on the latest developments.

A good IT program should offer a balance between theory and applied skills. You'll want to see plenty of hands-on lab experience, but not so much that you'll be acquiring only technical skills or short-term (vendor-specific) knowledge. Programs administered by schools of business may include more courses in finance, accounting, marketing, and management, while majors that have evolved from computer science departments may require more math and programming.

IT is available in many two-year programs at community colleges, where you can get a good grounding in the field. If you go that route, though, you should think about continuing on to a four-year program at some point—you'll have better career prospects with a bachelor's degree.

Other majors you might like:
Management information systems
Computer engineering technology
Systems engineering
Bioinformatics
Health information management
Software engineering
Library science
Communications
Applied mathematics
Medical office computer specialist
Behavioral sciences
E-commerce

Questions to ask colleges:
Are professors working in the field, applying the latest trends in information technology?

Will the college help me find an internship?

Is the program recognized by the Accreditation Board for Engineering and Technology (ABET)?

Career options and trends:
IT project manager; tech support; network administrator; Web developer; website administrator; information security analyst; database administrator; applications developer; software tester.

Job growth for IT professionals is predicted to remain strong through 2022. Businesses continue to depend heavily on networks and are particularly concerned about cyber-security. Some IT jobs (such as routine programming and customer support) are being outsourced overseas; but in diminishing numbers, relative to the number of new jobs being created. Jobs that require on site support or are security related will remain domestic. Job prospects are also better for those who can combine IT with other areas of business, such as e-commerce or supply chain management.

Women students are often attracted to IT because of the opportunities for collaborative work, particularly in health-related fields and in government.

For more info:
Association for Computing Machinery (ACM)
2 Penn Plaza
Suite 701
New York, NY 10121-0701
(800) 342-6626
www.acm.org

Education

To be an educator, you have to be educated. It makes sense that education is the field with the most graduate degrees awarded, both masters' and doctorates. It's second only to business in the number of all degrees earned.

Teaching is something you should know about already. You've seen teachers in action for many years now. You can probably think of a teacher who has influenced your vision of the future.

"This is truly a career where you can influence the hearts and minds of young teenagers, ensuring them a healthier and more productive adulthood," says Jeanneine Jones, a professor of middle school education at the University of North Carolina at Charlotte. "Students touch my life and I touch theirs; they teach me and I teach them. It's a wonderful relationship built on mutual respect and pervasive caring."

You may be wondering why a middle school teacher like Jones is working at a college. She became a university instructor so she can pass on her skills and knowledge to the next generation of teachers. To become a teacher isn't easy. To begin with, you have to prove that you're a good student in your first year or two of college. Then you may qualify to enter an education program. There you learn two big things—the subject you'll be teaching and how to teach it. You'll also have to work as a student teacher for a semester, under the watchful eye of an experienced educator. That's similar to the way doctors learn—by working for real. Finally, teachers take a test to get certified. Many states require another test to show that you know the subject(s) you'll be teaching.

Teaching may not be a breeze, but it can make you walk on air. "The sense of accomplishment that I feel after teaching a class is as good as climbing to the top of a mountain," says Professor Mary C. Clement of Berry College. "I feel that I have won the lottery when students 'get' the lesson presented and when something that they learned in my class helps them to attain success."

Making the Grade

In a way, you have already begun your teaching career by working hard in school to master a number of academic subjects.

"Studying to be a teacher involves learning the subject you plan to teach extremely well, so students must be prepared to complete a major or the equivalent if they are going to teach a subject like math, English, French, history, or physics," Clement advises.

Why not talk to some of your teachers about their college years and how they chose their schools? They may tell you that some universities have separate divisions of education, while others offer the education major as part of studies like arts or sciences.

When comparing education programs, you'll find that some emphasize teaching reading and literacy and that colleges use technology in different ways. However, the standards for a major are mostly set by the state in which the college is located. When you finish your bachelor's degree, you'll need to be certified in the state where you'll teach. Specific certifications go with particular types of teaching, like early childhood, elementary, middle school, secondary (high) school, special education, and physical education. In general, look for a program that's been approved by the National Council for Accreditation of Teacher Education (www.ncate.org). And be sure to ask the college about the percentage of its grads who become certified.

Of course, teaching isn't the only career that educators pursue. Other jobs include administrator (like your principal), school counselor, school psychologist, curriculum director, and education researcher; or you might be interested in becoming a corporate trainer to use your teaching skills in the business world.

Don't be discouraged by all the news about cutbacks in education budgets—long term, employment prospects are good. Even near term, teaching jobs are projected to increase at all grade levels. That's mostly because many teachers are expected to retire soon. Also, as states and schools try to improve education and boost course requirements for students, more and better-qualified teachers are needed. Job opportunities vary, of course, depending on the region and the subject. Teachers of foreign languages, math and science, and bilingual education are especially in demand.

Teachers often go to grad school to obtain certifications and credentials such as an "endorsement," which allows you to teach a particular subject, like reading. Other grad students in education focus on advanced work in their subjects so that they become experts in their field who can inspire and enlighten students.

"It is my philosophy that teachers are not just subject matter experts, but dispensers of hope for students of all ages," offers Clement.

With any luck, you've had a teacher like that. With hard work and dedication, you may become one.

Early childhood education

What it's about:

This major prepares you to teach infants and children through age eight, in all subjects through grade 3. You receive practicum/internship experience with small children in a variety of settings, such as day care, before- and after-school programs, pre-K (kindergarten) programs, early start, and K through grade 3 classrooms.

Is this for you?

You might like this major if you also like: working with very young children; watching them grow and change; volunteer or part-time work at day care or community centers; crafts; games; puppet shows; team sports; being creative; tutoring.

Consider this major if you are good at: active listening; caring/nurturing; coaching; communicating; critical reading/thinking; empathizing with children's thoughts and feelings; teamwork ...*or have...* an open mind; manual dexterity; patience; physical stamina.

Recommended high school prep:

English 4, math 3, lab science 3, social studies 3, and a foreign language 2–3. In addition, take a course in family and consumer science (home economics), especially if there is a child development component; and courses in psychology and sociology, if available.

Did you know...

...that early childhood is perhaps the most flexible field in education, with numerous areas in which to gain expertise? In fact, with just a few additional courses, you can pick up credentials in special education, child development, or literacy for early childhood along with your major, thus increasing your career possibilities.

Typical courses in this major:

Child development and learning
Parent–child relations
Curriculum methods in early education
Early childhood children's literature
Music methods
Arts and the child
Early childhood language arts
Early childhood mathematics
Social development and play
Educational psychology
Classroom management and behavior
Instructional resources and technology
Professional issues or foundations of education
Inclusion methods for special-needs students
Diversity of learners methods
Early childhood health and physical education

Concentrations:

Generally, none available.

What the study of this major is like:

Most early childhood education programs require a broad, general background in education; a core of professional courses that include education basics, knowledge of curriculum, and teaching methods; and opportunities to observe and student-teach in a variety of settings and at a variety of age and grade levels.

Because the early childhood curriculum focuses on a variety of subjects, you should take general education courses similar to those required in colleges of liberal arts and sciences. Your goal is to learn communication, critical-thinking, and problem-solving skills while you study the humanities, math, biological and physical sciences, social sciences, history, health, and physical education. You may be expected to complete a minor, or concentration, in one of the general education areas. If so, general education courses would make up between two-thirds and three-fourths of your undergraduate course work.

In professional education courses, you study the history and philosophy of early childhood education as well as early childhood growth and development. You also explore curriculum and classroom organization, by planning, putting into practice, and evaluating a program appropriate for young children. Since preschoolers learn through play, you learn how to introduce language arts, social skills, and basic math and science concepts through play and other hands-on activities. In addition, you learn how to introduce academics at the kindergarten and early primary grade levels. You may also take courses on teaching special-needs children in the regular classroom.

Your professional education includes fieldwork, called practicums, in which you observe and participate in programs for young children in settings such as elementary schools, child care centers, and Head Start programs. You conclude with student teaching or an internship, as you take on increasing responsibility for a class. Most programs require you to do a semester of student teaching in pre-K through grade 3 settings, or perhaps several student-teaching assignments at different age or grade levels.

As an early childhood education major, you will probably be taught in lectures, small-group interactive projects, discussions, demonstrations, and presentations. You may take part in distance-learning through video segments and hear expert speakers. In your third and fourth years, you will spend a great deal of (unpaid) time working with children in schools; keep that point in mind if you plan to hold a job during college. While you are student-teaching (also unpaid), you will have no time for a job, so plan to save money for that final semester.

Early childhood programs may emphasize different teaching philosophies. Many programs include all models and theories, and let you pick the approach that best suits you. Others may focus on one model, such as the Bank Street or the Montessori approach. In general, most quality programs follow standards set by the National Association for the Education of Young Children (NAEYC).

In all states, to be licensed to teach pre-K–3, you must have a four-year degree. Some states do not offer the early childhood teaching certificate but provide instead a "kindergarten endorsement" on an elementary teaching certificate. In these states, early childhood education may be a minor offered to elementary education majors. Some institutions offer teacher certification for early childhood education only at the graduate level. Many states are moving to requiring a master's degree or the equivalent for continued teacher certification.

Other majors you might like:
Elementary education
Middle school education
Special education
Teacher assistance
Communication disorders
Sociology
Human development and family studies
Behavioral sciences
Psychology
Social work
Child development
Child care management

Questions to ask colleges:
Where do students complete their fieldwork, practicum, internship, and student teaching? When do these projects occur in the program? How many hours are required? What kind of support do students receive in the assignments? What choices, if any, do students have in these placements? Are the settings rural, urban, suburban, metropolitan, or a mix?

What are the prerequisites for full admission into the early childhood major (e.g., required courses, GPA, cutoff scores on the SAT, ACT, or PRAXIS I exams)? Do I need a background check?

Career options and trends:
Teacher assistant or aide; pre-school teacher*; kindergarten teacher*; child care administrator; family service coordinator.

An associate degree is usually required for teacher aides or teacher paraprofessionals to work in public school classrooms. These persons may work with small children as well as older children with disabilities.

Center directors often have a master's degree, but it is not a requirement.

There is an increasing demand for preschool programs, and the population of children ages 3-5 is expected to increase as well. As a result the employment of early education teachers is projected to be quite strong through 2022. This will be especially true in the South (Florida, Georgia, and the Carolinas) and the West (Arizona, Texas, Nevada, and California). Job prospects continue to be better in urban and isolated rural areas.

In many regions, teachers who are willing to relocate and who hold more than one license/certification, such as in early childhood and special education or ESL (English as a second language), will have an advantage.

For more info:
National Association for the Education of Young
   Children (NAEYC)
1313 L St., N.W., Suite 500
Washington, DC 20005
(800) 424-2460
www.naeyc.org

Elementary education

What it's about:

Elementary education majors prepare to teach children in the elementary grades, which can range from K (kindergarten) through 8, depending on the school system. In addition to learning how to teach specific subjects, such as reading and math, you study the way children develop socially and intellectually, and you get hands-on professional experience in teaching and learning.

Is this for you?

You might like this major if you also like: working with children; tutoring; team sports; volunteer or community service; public speaking; problem solving.

Consider this major if you are good at: active listening; communicating; creativity; critical reading/thinking; organizing; persuading/influencing ...*or have...* enthusiasm; flexibility; patience; physical stamina.

Recommended high school prep:

English 4, math 3, lab science 3, social studies 3, and a foreign language 2-3. Take any computer science or applications courses available. Four years of Spanish is highly recommended, because fluency in that language would be a great asset for a teacher.

Typical courses in this major:

Child development and learning
History and philosophy of education
Curriculum methods in elementary education
Teaching language arts
Teaching mathematics
Teaching science
Teaching social studies
Reading fundamentals
Educational psychology
Classroom management and behavior
Educational assessment and measurement
Instructional resources and technology
Special education needs and issues
Schooling in a culturally diverse society

Concentrations:

Generally, none available.

What the study of this major is like:

Almost all elementary education programs offer a liberal arts foundation, a professional education core that includes course work in teaching methods, and a variety of student-teaching experiences in elementary school settings. The goal is to prepare you for state certification to teach in the elementary grades. States have different rules, and there may be special requirements for teaching kindergarten through third grade (K–3) or grades 6–8. In addition to completing the elementary education major, many states require students to pass tests in subject matter, communications, and knowledge of methods, in order to be certified. Some states also require a second major in a particular subject area (e.g., language arts) or specialty (e.g., reading).

Most elementary school teachers instruct one class in several subjects, using a wide range of tools, such as games, music, artwork, films, books, and computers. Therefore, you should probably take between 50 and 60 percent of your course work in the humanities, social sciences, natural sciences, technology, and mathematics—mostly during your first two years. Generally, you do not become fully admitted into the major until your second year, after you meet certain requirements. They vary among colleges, so be sure to find out what they are before you enroll in a program.

In methods courses, you focus on ways to instruct children, and you develop your capacity to solve problems that may arise as you introduce reading, language arts, mathematics, science, and social studies to young children. You also gain practice in planning lessons, evaluating learning, and managing the classroom. Some elementary education majors can minor in early childhood or special education.

Throughout the major, practical experiences in schools are typically interwoven with classroom studies. As you observe, assist, and teach elementary children, what you've learned in your classes becomes more meaningful and more useful. Student teaching, which normally occurs in your last semester, is often the high point of the elementary education major. This experience, under the supervision of both college and school instructors, gives you a big boost in your goal of becoming a teacher.

Other majors you might like:
Early childhood education
Middle school education
Special education
Teacher assistance
Reading teacher education
Communications
Family/consumer sciences education
Behavioral sciences
Psychology
Social work
Child development
Sociology

Questions to ask colleges:
Is the program accredited by the National Council for Accreditation of Teacher Education?

Career options and trends:
Besides teaching in the elementary schools, majors who pursue appropriate graduate training can become school administrators, educational researchers, curriculum specialists, reading specialists, or school counselors.

The Bureau of Labor Statistics projects employment for elementary school teachers will grow because of increasing enrollment and the large number of teachers retiring over the next ten years. However, these factors will vary by region. Fast-growing states in the South and West—particularly California, Texas, Georgia, Idaho, Hawaii, Alaska, and New Mexico—will experience the largest enrollment increases. Minority teachers and teachers who are bilingual in Spanish are in short supply, and demand for these will grow with the rising enrollment of minority and Spanish-speaking children.

While certification requirements vary by state, all states require a bachelor's degree and completion of an approved teacher education program with a prescribed number of subject and education credits as well as supervised student teaching. About one-third of the states also require technology training, and some require specific minimum grade point averages as well.

Insider's viewpoint:
"Most of the assignments focus on analyzing classroom practices—tell why you like it, how you'd change it. Then you plan your own lessons and implement those plans."

—Kau'i, senior, University of Hawaii

For more info:
National Association for the Education of Young Children (NAEYC)
1313 L St., N.W., Suite 500
Washington, DC 20005
(800) 424-2460
www.naeyc.org

Middle school education

Also known as:
Junior high education

What it's about:
This major prepares you for an entry-level license or certification to teach specific content areas (such as language arts, mathematics, social studies, or science) in middle school, intermediate school, or junior high school, which may include grades 4–9, depending on the school system.

Is this for you?
You might like this major if you also like: community service; working with youth; reading; writing; public speaking; tutoring; coaching; helping friends and others with their problems; leadership roles in high school.

Consider this major if you are good at: caring/nurturing; counseling; critical reading/thinking; leadership; organizing; persuading/influencing; teamwork *...or have...* patience; physical stamina; verbal skills.

Recommended high school prep:
English 4, math 3, lab science 3, social studies 3, and a foreign language 2–3. Course work that helps you develop your reading and communication skills is essential.

Did you know...
...that elementary school teachers teach children, and high school teachers teach content, but middle school teachers teach content to children?

...that the middle school years are commonly labeled the turning point in the life span? Middle school teachers can have a real impact on young people, encouraging them to become healthy, productive adults.

Typical courses in this major:
Introduction to middle school education
Early adolescent learners
Classroom management
Specific subject curriculum
Content methods
Philosophy of middle grades education
Curriculum of middle grades education
Reading and writing across subject areas
Research and analysis of middle grades education
Health and safety issues in middle schools
Instructional design and technology
Teaching students with special needs
Schooling in a culturally diverse society

Concentrations:
Specific content areas, such as science, math, language arts, social studies, and music.

What the study of this major is like:
As a middle school education major, you have the opportunity to make a real difference in the life of young adults. Although early adolescents are often portrayed as defiant and confused, people who work with middle school students generally agree that they are sensitive, stimulating, motivated, and eager to contribute to the world around them.

Majors study the developmental and learning styles of the 10- to 15-year-old and examine the ways in which students can be given structure and guidance, as well as a sense of independence and personal responsibility. You will also take about six to eight courses in one or two subject areas, such as language arts, mathematics, social studies, and science. As a whole, the program prepares you to enter a school knowing what to teach, how to teach, and the needs of your audience.

Although courses contain some lectures, they feature hands-on work experiences, called practicums or clinical hours, in local public and private schools. These are included in the course assignments and are a critical part of your workload. They are designed to help you transfer campus discussions and studies into successful classroom applications.

These experiences culminate in a full semester of student teaching in your last year. It will enable you to master the material you've been studying and to practice your presentation of it under the supervision of both college and middle school instructors. Perhaps even more important, your student-teaching semester will help you deal with the frustrations often associated with teaching, including enforcing classroom discipline, managing your time, and motivating unresponsive students.

While colleges vary, all strong programs should require the study of at least one content area. They should also communicate an in-depth understanding of adolescent development and middle school philosophy. Courses should cover lesson plan design, effective teacher behavior, and classroom management. Finally, you should be given opportunities to apply your course work in local schools and related community programs, especially in a challenging, well-supported student-teaching semester.

Other majors you might like:
Child development
Secondary education
Special education
ESL teacher education
Bilingual/bicultural education
Human development and family studies
Native American education
Liberal arts and sciences
Juvenile corrections
Youth ministry
Social work
Psychology

Questions to ask colleges:
Does this college have a clearly identified middle school program, which includes a professor to coordinate it? Do core faculty members have experience teaching in grades 6–8?

Does the surrounding region have strong middle schools for student-teaching work?

Career options and trends:
Middle school teacher*; secondary school teacher*; elementary school teacher; school counselor; school administrator*.

An additional, but related, license or certification is required for teaching at the elementary or secondary school level. An advanced degree is necessary for

positions as a school counselor, administrator, or supervisor.

This area of education is one of the most marketable in the country, but demand will vary by region and subject specialty. Currently, those most in demand are qualified to teach mathematics, science (especially chemistry and physics), bilingual education, foreign languages, and computer science.

Insider's viewpoint:
"Once I really, really know these children, they emerge as stimulating, and stimulated, young adults who are sensitive, capable, and productive citizens. They touch my life and I touch theirs, they teach me and I teach them. It's a wonderful relationship built on mutual respect and caring."

—Professor Jeanneine P. Jones, University of North Carolina at Charlotte

For more info:
Association for Middle Level Education
4151 Executive Parkway
Suite 300
Westerville, OH 43081
(800) 528-6672
www.amle.org

Physical education

What it's about:

Physical education majors prepare to teach physical education (PE) or to coach sports in public or private schools, kindergarten through twelfth grade (K–12).

Is this for you?

You might like this major if you also like: helping people; sports and competition; physical exercise; good health habits; coaching; tutoring; a sense of humor.

Consider this major if you are good at: caring/nurturing; coaching; critical reading/thinking; leadership; persuading/influencing; sports, gymnastics, or dance; teamwork ...*or have...* patience; physical stamina; verbal skills; writing skills.

Recommended high school prep:

English 4, math 3, lab science 3, social studies 3, and a foreign language 2–3. If possible, take extra physical education credits to enhance your skills, or serve as a physical education assistant in addition to participating in team sports. Knowledge of or fluency in a foreign language (especially Spanish) will make you more marketable.

Did you know...

...that this is not the easy major many people think it is! Learning to teach physical education means more than playing games. You must love sports and also enjoy teaching a variety of subjects to children and adolescents. In addition, you will be expected to continue your educational and professional development throughout your career.

Typical courses in this major:

Biology
Physics
Anatomy and physiology
Human growth and development
Motor learning and development
Observation and analysis of motor skills
Physical education teaching methods
Methods for teaching lifetime fitness

Physical education curriculum
Multicultural education
Educational psychology
History and philosophy of physical education
Tests and measures in physical education
Administration of physical education programs
Adapted physical education
Coaching effectiveness

Concentrations:

Elementary school physical education; secondary school physical education; adapted physical education; athletic coaching.

What the study of this major is like:

If you want to become a physical education teacher, you should generally enjoy many types of sports and exercise. Since few children and adolescents are elite athletes, knowing how to work with students at all skill levels is essential. Another plus is to feel comfortable speaking to groups and to be a skillful communicator. In addition, you should be warm and caring in your approach to young people. Good physical education teachers are role models of active, healthy lifestyles.

As a PE major, you take general education courses during your first two years. Then you enroll in science courses that focus on how the human body is affected by exercise and sports and how performance can be improved. Other courses include child development, psychology, and curriculum and instruction, and you'll have opportunities to work with children in supervised field settings. Although you will probably be required to take part in numerous recreational activities and sports, don't expect to get much academic credit. At the end of most programs, you'll do student teaching.

Many majors are challenged by the lab sciences that are often required (for example, anatomy and physiology and biology). In your third and fourth years, you typically take practicum courses, which give you extensive teaching practice in local schools. You'll learn to teach such subjects as sport skills, gymnastics, dance, lifetime activities, and fitness to diverse students in a range of settings. Practicum courses can be nerve-racking, though, because you teach real kids in real schools. After practicums, you usually do your student teaching. During this semester-long assignment, you gradually assume the full responsibilities of a teacher. Student teaching is often challenging, as you experience both the difficulties and the rewards of the profession.

Requirements for teaching certification vary from state to state. But programs that are approved by the National Council for Accreditation of Teacher Education (NCATE) meet the standards that ensure effective teaching preparation. In many states, to obtain a teaching certificate, you also need to earn acceptable scores on competency exams (for example, the PRAXIS I and II), and some physical education programs require you to pass competency exams in order to graduate. Most physical education programs will qualify you to be certified to teach K–12. However, in some programs you can major in elementary school physical education or secondary school physical education. If you enjoy working with young children, for example, you might seek out a program that specializes in elementary physical education.

Other majors you might like:
Athletic training
Exercise sciences
Sports and fitness administration
Parks, recreation, and leisure studies
Health teacher education
Physical therapy
Occupational therapy
Biology
Food and nutrition studies
Dance therapy
Recreational therapy
Community health services

Questions to ask colleges:
How much hands-on teaching experience is given in an actual school setting? Good programs should provide ample practical experience leading up to student teaching.

Is the program NCATE accredited?

Career options and trends:
Physical education teacher (K–12)*; recreation supervisor (community or private setting); aerobic dance instructor; physical trainer.

The demand for physical education teachers across the United States is not as high as it is for teachers in areas such as math and science, bilingual education, and special education. However, some districts (especially urban and rural) need teachers in all subject areas, including physical education.

Obtaining a minor in another teaching area or athletic coaching can really improve your career prospects. A physical education teacher who is dual certified (can teach physical education and an academic subject, or can teach physical education and coach a sport) is much more marketable. Increasing awareness of the growing problem of childhood obesity should also increase demand for PE teachers who can help combat this problem.

For more info:
American Alliance for Health, Physical Education, Recreation and Dance (AAHPERD)
1990 Association Drive
Reston, VA 20191-1598
800-213-7193
www.aahperd.org

Secondary education

Also known as:

High school teacher education

What it's about:

This major prepares you to be a high school teacher. You learn the curriculum and methods of teaching a specific subject (math, science, English, history, foreign language, and so forth), organization and management of a classroom, needs of diverse learners, and the role of high schools in today's society.

Is this for you?

You might like this major if you also like: Scouting; 4-H; extracurricular activities; sports; coaching; tutoring; working at summer camps; leading, not following. Idealism is a good attribute for teachers.

Consider this major if you are good at: caring/nurturing; creativity; organizing; persuading/influencing ...*or have*... initiative; patience; verbal skills; writing skills.

Recommended high school prep:

English 4, math 3, lab science 3, social studies 3, and a foreign language 2–3. Take a course in psychology, if one is offered. You should take a four-year sequence in the subject you plan to teach; if advanced or honors courses in that subject are available, taking those is highly recommended.

Did you know...

...that majoring in education as an undergraduate is generally the quickest way to become a teacher? If you decide after college to become a teacher, you will probably need to return to college for two more years.

...that in many states, you may have to undergo a criminal background check and be fingerprinted before observing or student-teaching in a public school district?

Typical courses in this major:

Introduction to secondary education

Issues and trends in secondary education

Adolescent behavior and development

Educational psychology

History and foundations of education

Educational technology

Specific subject curriculum

Specific subject instructional methods

Classroom management

Diversity/multicultural education

Teaching students with special needs

Testing in the classroom

Concentrations:

Generally, none available.

What the study of this major is like:

The secondary education major provides a foundation in the arts and sciences, in-depth study in a particular subject, and courses in teaching procedures. To achieve their goals, most students take a double major or the equivalent.

In introductory courses, which may include visits to schools to observe and interview teachers, you will explore the conditions of today's schools, the diversity of students, and the role of schools in today's society. Educational psychology courses focus on the way children and teenagers learn and provide strategies for motivating learners and for meeting the needs of all students, including those with disabilities, language deficiencies, and emotional problems. You will also take at least one special education course.

In content-based course work, you learn *what* to teach; how to prepare lesson plans, unit plans, and tests; and how to meet state and national teaching standards. In methods courses, you learn *how* to teach. For these upper-level courses, you may spend three to five hours a week in local schools before you begin student teaching.

A course in classroom management provides strategies for organizing time, space, and materials, as well as guidelines for creating a management style that suits your needs. In other courses you gain practice in giving lectures, doing demonstrations, running audio/visual equipment, and maintaining classroom discipline. Future science teachers learn how to supervise laboratory work; students interested in vocational education learn how to give students hands-on experience with tools and equipment.

Your final activity as a major is a semester of student teaching—working with a teacher, every school day for the entire day. You still pay full tuition and fees during student teaching, and you are not paid by the school district. You may also have to travel a considerable distance from campus, and it is difficult to hold a part-time job while you student-teach. Graduates say that this semester is the most challenging, but often the most useful, time of their college years.

At some colleges, you are required to double-major in the subject area you plan to teach; at others you major in your subject area and minor in secondary education or a teacher certification program. Many colleges gear their programs to the certification requirements of the state in which they are located; keep this point in mind when you are considering where to apply to college.

Other majors you might like:
Middle school education
Special education
ESL teacher education
Liberal arts and sciences
Agricultural education services
Human resources management
Juvenile corrections
Psychology
Social work
Sociology

Questions to ask colleges:
Is the program accredited by both the state body for teacher certification and by the National Council for Accreditation in Teacher Education (NCATE)?

How are student-teaching placements made? Are they assigned or do students have a choice? For how long is the full-time student-teaching placement, and how far away from campus may it be located?

Does this teacher education program require minimum exam scores for admission? Since some states require candidates to have a certain ACT, SAT, or PRAXIS I score in order to be granted a teaching license, many colleges now require such scores for admission to the major.

Career options and trends:
High school teacher*; school principal or assistant*; school superintendent or assistant; curriculum director; school counselor; educational writer; program director in Scouting, 4-H, youth programs, churches, or other organizations.

Although states have different certification requirements, most require you to have a bachelor's degree (and in some states, an additional year or a master's degree) in a program accredited by the state and by either the Teacher Education Accreditation Council (TEAC) or NCATE; to complete a major (or the equivalent) in your chosen subject area(s); and to pass a state exam, the Praxis II exam, or another test.

Additional licensing or certification and an advanced degree are necessary for a position as a principal, superintendent, or other upper-level administrator.

The acute shortage of math and science high school teachers in many parts of the United States is being called the "silent crisis." Shortages also exist for foreign languages, bilingual education, and special education. Teachers who earn certification in more than one subject are highly employable, and so are teachers who choose to work in non-English-speaking or disadvantaged communities. Graduates with ESL training are also in demand.

Through 2022, a significant number of high school teachers are expected to retire, creating job openings for new teachers.

For more info:
American Federation of Teachers (AFT)
555 New Jersey Ave. N.W.,
Washington, DC 20001
(202) 879-4400
www.aft.org

Special education

What it's about:

The special education major prepares you to meet the educational, social, emotional, and vocational needs of infants, children, and young adults with disabilities. Your professional preparation includes specialized course work, field experiences with children with disabilities, and student teaching.

Is this for you?

You might like this major if you also like: helping people, especially people who appear to be different; working with people one-on-one; multitasking.

Consider this major if you are good at: caring/nurturing; coaching; counseling; critical reading/thinking; leadership; organizing; teamwork *...or have...* initiative; patience; verbal skills.

Recommended high school prep:

English 4, math 3, lab science 3, social studies 3, and a foreign language 2–3.

Did you know...

...that special educators work in many settings, not just in schools? Settings include hospitals, private practice environments, health care centers, and correctional facilities.

...that many states and the federal government offer scholarships and loan forgiveness to students entering the special education field?

Typical courses in this major:

Introduction to psychology
Introduction to sociology
Statistics
Human development
Introduction to special education
Educational assessment
Behavior management
Curriculum and instruction
Speech/language development
Content area courses (e.g., reading, math)
Computers/technology for teachers
Educational policy and law
Integrated fieldwork
Student teaching

Concentrations:

In college: early childhood, elementary, or secondary special education; learning disabilities; autism; deaf/hard of hearing; visual impairments; severe/profound disabilities; emotional/behavioral disorders.

If you go on to grad school: policy studies; vocational training; transition to adult services; educational administration.

What the study of this major is like:

Special education refers to instruction that is specifically designed to meet the needs of students with varying types of disabilities and ranging in age from infancy to 21. In this major you develop skills in educational assessment and instruction for these students and in working with their families. Course work combines lectures and other class activities with field experiences, such as assisting in a special education classroom.

In your first and second years as a major, you will probably take introductory and core courses in education, psychology, and child development, along with general studies. In your third year, you explore the types of disabilities you are likely to encounter in your work. In addition, you observe classrooms and obtain supervised field placement experience.

In field placements, you receive hands-on experience working with children with disabilities in a special education setting, such as a regular classroom, resource room, self-contained classroom, vocational-technical school, or institution. During your first experiences you spend most of your time observing the teacher with whom you are placed; but as you progress, you gradually assume greater responsibility. In your fourth year, you take advanced courses in special education, along with electives, and do student teaching. By then, you will do most, if not all, of the teaching.

Being a special education teacher often means being an "educational manager"—the person who coordinates all the education and training a child receives. Many students with disabilities require the services of several professionals (such as school psychologists, speech therapists, occupational therapists). As a special educator, you need to know what role these professionals will play in a student's education and how their work relates to yours. In fact, you and the other service providers will function as a multidisciplinary team—each contributing professional and personal skills for the benefit of the child.

Several features distinguish special education programs. First, colleges vary in their approach to special education. For example, some colleges offer dual programs in elementary and special education, with less emphasis on special education than in a program focusing on that field alone. Further, some programs offer a generalized treatment of special education, while in others you can specialize by age level or type of disability. While some programs take four years to complete, others take five; some offer graduate credits and/or degrees in conjunction with the bachelor's program. Colleges also differ in the amount of required field experiences. Finally, special education programs may be distinguished by their philosophies. Programs may differ according to their emphasis on inclusion of individuals with disabilities in community settings and on using research to inform your teaching.

Majors are expected to demonstrate professional behavior from the first semester they are placed in classrooms. Professional behavior includes punctuality, time management, and the ability to interact as an adult with students, school staff, and students' parents. Opportunities to establish a network of potential job contacts begin the day you start your field placement. A career in special education is rewarding, exciting, and intellectually challenging.

Other majors you might like:
Communication disorders
Child development
Audiology/speech pathology
Education of learning disabled
Education of physically handicapped
Early childhood education
American sign language (ASL)
Art therapy
Occupational therapy

Physical therapy
Recreational therapy
Human development and family studies

Questions to ask colleges:
How much and which types of fieldwork are required? Where are students placed and who supervises field placements? What ages or disability types are students being prepared to teach?

Does the special education program have a more selective admissions process than other divisions of the college?

Which certification do students earn? Is certification transferable to other states?

Is the program focused on special education, or is training split between general and special education? Does the program provide graduate credits?

Career options and trends:
Special education teacher*; special education instructional assistant; special education advocate; educational administrator*; parent educator; psychologist; lobbyist; policy analyst; educational researcher.

The special education major prepares you to work in a school or institutional setting. With graduate study, students often pursue careers as administrators of special education. Advanced training may also lead to a career as a speech/language pathologist, audiologist, physical therapist, occupational therapist, school psychologist, school counselor, evaluation specialist, teacher trainer, parent/community coordinator, rehabilitation counselor, vocational/special needs teacher, or adaptive physical education instructor. A state certificate or license is required for teaching in public elementary and secondary schools.

Job opportunities in special education are excellent. All areas of special education are in the process of evolving, especially at the early childhood and secondary/transition levels. All regions of the country are experiencing shortages of special education teachers, and long-term projections indicate that the shortages will continue.

Insider's viewpoint:
"It is exciting to be in a profession that continually offers intellectual challenges, while serving individu-

als who have historically been relegated to the fringe of society."

—Dawn Eddy Molloy, University of Maryland

For more info:
American Association of Colleges for Teacher
    Education (AACTE)
1307 New York Ave., N.W.
Suite 300
Washington, DC 20005
(202) 293-2450
www.aacte.org

Engineering

Have you ever wondered how a touch screen works? Or what makes a metal magnetic? Do you enjoy brain teasers? Can you twist a wire hanger into something useful? Do you secretly love the math story problems that other students dread? You, my friend, might be an engineer.

But it's not enough to be mechanically inclined or have the ability to visualize in 3-D. To become an engineer takes an awful lot of work.

"Realize that engineering is not a 'party' major. You will have to work harder than your friends, but the rewards and satisfaction are worth it," says Lyle D. Feisel, a dean emeritus at the State University of New York at Binghamton.

Engineers design systems, components, and processes to make life better. Whenever a plane takes off, a computer boots up, the lights go on, a car is driven, a building constructed, a medical device used, a phone call made, a photo taken, or a product sold, it all comes down to engineering. When engineers show up for work, they may do research, development, production, construction, operations, quality improvement, management, technical sales, consulting, or teaching. Jobs in the field and studies of engineering cover materials, mining and metals, manufacturing, marine engineering, and mechanics—and those are just the ones that start with "m."

Anyone who goes into engineering can look forward to lifelong learning about leading-edge science—nuclear and alternative energy, information technologies, integrated circuits, aerospace and defense, global positioning systems, genetic research.

Colleges offer more than 40 engineering majors. The most common majors offered are electrical, mechanical, civil, chemical, and computer engineering. More than half of engineers find work in these areas. Some new majors include architectural engineering, biochemical engineering, robotics, environmental engineering, manufacturing engineering, nanotechnology, biomaterials, and energy management technology.

Did you know that engineers earn some of the highest salaries for people with a bachelor's degree? And that's not all; since fewer students are choosing engineering, overall job opportunities are expected to be good. Of course, jobs depend on how the economy is doing. But even during economic downturns, many engineering efforts—like building a bridge—are based on long-term plans that will continue through lean times.

Where will you go?

As you look at colleges of engineering, you'll see that many undergraduate programs look alike because standards are in place. If a program is good enough, it is "ABET-accredited" by the organization formerly known as the Accreditation Board for Engineering and Technology (but whose official name now is just the acronym).

How do colleges differ? Mostly in their approach. Some schools are more hands-on and mechanical, giving you a sort of job training through work in laboratories. Other colleges focus on theoretical concepts and abstract mathematical modeling to prepare you for graduate school. Graduate tracks include math, basic science, engineering sciences, design, and research. Some specific graduate areas are wireless engineering, hydrosystems, biochemical or pharmaceutical engineering, and software user interface design.

It's important to find out if the school is a research college that attracts talented professors. Also judge the quality of facilities like the design, computing, and testing laboratories and the libraries. Other factors to look at are admissions criteria, location, tuition and fees, and financial aid. How about work-study programs, part-time employment on campus, internships, or cooperative work to help finance your engineering education? It's okay to ask what recent graduates are doing. Have they gone on to grad school? Or have they taken jobs? If so, where? What percent of recent graduates got hired right away?

The one thing that will always come up is the need for strong math and science preparation on your part. Once you're at college, expect heavy math, statistics, basic science, and lab work for the first two years, followed by applied science and engineering courses later.

"Engineers are problem solvers, but many engineering students become disillusioned early in their studies because they fail to see the applicability of the abstract mathematical principles they encounter in their freshmen and sophomore years," warns Edward A. Hiler, a dean emeritus at Texas A&M University. "Perseverance is necessary, and is well rewarded later in college and in their careers."

Only about one-third of engineering graduates finish their degree in four years. Most students take nine or more semesters to graduate.

Studies often finish with a capstone course. That's a real-world project putting together everything you've learned. Ask the college about the types of projects students have done in the past.

Keep in mind that when you look up engineering majors in college catalogs and on the Internet, you might see some combinations and hybrids. Aerospace engineering and aviation might be called aeronautics. Industrial engineering is also known as industrial and systems engineering. Think it through.

Read more about the particular engineering majors in this section and about the field in general by going to the Junior Engineering Technical Society (www.jets.org), American Society for Engineering Education (www.asee.org), and ABET (www.abet.org).

Aeronautical/aerospace engineering

What it's about:

As an aeronautical/aerospace engineering major, you study the design and development of high-speed transportation vehicles such as aircraft, spacecraft, missiles, launch vehicles, deep space probes, dirigibles, hang gliders, unmanned aerial vehicles (UAVs), and space habitats. In addition, you examine the physics of the flow of air, water, and plasma around these vehicles.

Is this for you?

You might like this major if you also like: anything to do with aircraft, spacecraft, or space exploration; model aircraft building; flying; hang gliding; physics; astronomy; science fiction; computer programming; designing things; problem solving. If you instinctively look up when you hear an airplane, you know you have the aerospace bug.

Consider this major if you are good at: attention to detail; creativity; critical reading/thinking; leadership; math; organizing; quantitative analysis; spacial thinking/analysis; teamwork *...or have...* imagination; initiative.

Recommended high school prep:

English 4, math 4 (including precalculus), lab science 4, social studies 3, and a foreign language 2–3. If you must choose, take physics and chemistry over biology or earth science. Also, if possible, take a year of computer literacy, a computer programming course, and calculus.

Typical courses in this major:

Introduction to aerospace engineering
Thermodynamics
Strength of materials (with lab)
Aerodynamics (with lab)
Aerospace structures
Flight mechanics
Control systems
Aerospace propulsion
Flight controls
Space science and systems
Aerospace vehicle design
Robotics lab
Intelligent systems
Space mission design
Systems engineering
Computer-aided design (CAD)

Concentrations:

In college: aerodynamics; aerospace structures; propulsion; controls; aerospace vehicle design; intelligent systems; space science and systems.

If you go on to grad school: theoretical mechanics; heat transfer; numerical modeling.

What the study of this major is like:

For all engineers, the academic program usually consists of two years of science and engineering basics, followed by two years of specialty courses. In the aeronautical/aerospace engineering major, most of your general education electives and required courses (such as English, history, and social science) are taught in the lecture format, but some of the science courses also have labs. You will probably be required to take four semesters of calculus and analytic geometry, one semester of chemistry, two semesters of physics, one semester of differential equations, and courses in computer programming and in numerical methods.

Most likely, your engineering studies will begin with an overview course, often containing team projects and reports. You then take statics/dynamics, thermodynamics, electrical science, and materials science, courses that are normally taught as lectures, with homework and exams, and sometimes project reports. Advanced general engineering courses, such as computer programming, graphics, strength of materials, and controls, are also taught as lectures, but they often have lab sessions in which you work with a team on experimental or computer projects and on written reports. Most programs also require a fourth-year capstone course featuring a team experimental or vehicle design project.

You can probably specialize in either aeronautics (aircraft) or astronautics (spacecraft) at the undergraduate level. Although most programs cover both areas, usually with less emphasis on space, some colleges offer only one or the other. Aerospace courses, such as propulsion, flight mechanics, avionics, and vehicle/system design, have varied formats, but they often contain open-ended design projects (including reports) that you can do on your own or with a team. Technical and experimental electives—such as CAD, FEM (finite element method), courses from other engineering departments, and aerospace-specific courses such as space mission design and robotics lab—have varied formats featuring lectures, lab experiments, or design work.

As an aeronautical/aerospace engineering major, you need to sharpen your ability to visualize in three dimensions, in order to understand complex physical systems. The required work, as you would expect, is harder than in high school. New college students are not always good at budgeting their time, or at studying on their own; developing these skills in high school will give you a leg up. You must also learn how to work with a team. The demands of this major (including project reports and computer projects) leave little time for extracurricular activities. But if you have the time, you can usually join a technical society or a design/build/fly team. Tech societies often organize trips to aerospace companies or professional conferences.

There are four types of aeronautical/aerospace engineering programs approved by the Accreditation Board for Engineering and Technology (ABET): aeronautical engineering programs with a brief introduction to space; space programs with a short introduction to aeronautical engineering; aeronautics and astronautics programs that cover the two areas more or less equally; and aerospace options in fields such as mechanical engineering and engineering mechanics. Accredited programs regularly undergo standardized outside review. On the other hand, some of the best programs in the United States do not seek accreditation. Programs may also differ in their emphasis. Some colleges stress open-ended problems (design) rather than questions with specific answers (analysis). Some programs may include more hands-on experiences, and others, more computer simulations. Even standard aeronautical/aerospace engineering programs may sometimes set a particular emphasis, such as on intelligent systems, information technology, or space telecommunications.

Other majors you might like:
Aeronautics and aviation science
Aeronautical/aerospace engineering technology
Mechanical engineering technology
Astronomy
Astrophysics
Atmospheric sciences
Applied physics
Instrumentation technology
Marine engineering/naval architecture
Aviation management
Materials science
Nuclear engineering

Questions to ask colleges:
Which of the four ABET accredited aeronautical/aerospace engineering programs does this college offer?

Which facilities (such as wind tunnels, computer labs, and design labs) are available? What designing, building, and flying opportunities exist on a regular basis?

Career options and trends:
Design engineer*; project engineer*; fighter pilot; flight test engineer; research engineer.

Majors usually enter the aerospace industry, which loosely includes the prime aerospace contractors and their chief suppliers, the propulsion industry, academia, NASA, the Federal Aviation Administration, Department of Defense research and development (R&D), other government agencies, and the airlines (to be a pilot, you need rigorous training and licensing). Careers fall into the following areas: R&D, manufacturing, maintenance, marketing/planning, and computer applications technology. Engineers generally work in groups devoted to specific disciplines, such as systems engineering, structures, aerodynamics, controls, and human factors.

The aeronautical/aerospace engineering industry tends to be cyclical but is projected to slowly grow over the next decade or so: continued defense spending and the need to replace much of the commercial fleet with "next-generation" aircraft are creating job opportunities for graduates.

Those with training in modeling, simulation and robotics are especially in demand. The aerospace industry is distributed across the country, from the West Coast (Seattle, Los Angeles) to the Midwest (St. Louis and Forth Worth) and the South (Atlanta). Workplaces are normally in or near large cities and cultural centers.

Insider's viewpoint:

"I like building things that fly. I also like the fact that aero/astro is a combination of mechanical engineering, electrical engineering, and physics. I'm excited by the cutting edge stuff we do, the hands-on work."

—Stuart, senior, Massachusetts Institute of Technology

For more info:

American Institute of Aeronautics and
    Astronautics (AIAA)
1801 Alexander Bell Dr.
Suite 500
Reston, VA 20191-4344
(800) 639-2422
www.aiaa.org

Public Communications Office
NASA Headquarters
Suite 5K39
Washington, DC 20546-0001
(202) 358-0001
www.nasa.gov

Agricultural and biological engineering

Also known as:
Bioengineering
Biosystems engineering

What it's about:
Majors in agricultural and biological engineering learn to apply principles from the physical, biological, and engineering sciences to come up with improved methods of producing food, fiber, timber, and renewable energy sources; to preserve environmental quality; to tackle problems affecting plant and animal systems; and to develop products from biological resources.

Is this for you?
You might like this major if you also like: farming and agriculture; working on machinery and equipment; the outdoors; biology, chemistry, and math; scientific research; computers. If you are drawn to engineering, but would also like to do something about world hunger and environmental pollution, this major might be a good choice for you.

Consider this major if you are good at: creativity; critical reading/thinking; leadership; math; quantitative analysis; spacial thinking/analysis; teamwork *...or have...* a social conscience; initiative; verbal skills.

Recommended high school prep:
English 4, math 4 (including trigonometry and pre-calculus), lab science 4 (including biology, chemistry and physics), social studies 3, and a foreign language 2–3. Try to take as many math and science courses as possible, including life sciences, and if they are available, courses in calculus and computer science. You should also take courses in writing and speech, because all engineers must be able to communicate effectively.

Typical courses in this major:
Agricultural engineering design
Biochemistry
Water resources engineering
Power and machinery
Engineering properties of biological materials
Biological and agricultural energy systems
Soil science
Instrumentation and measurement
Transport processes
Bioenvironmental systems design
Hydrology
Food process engineering
Biosystems engineering
Electrical energy applications
Engineering mechanics
Fluid mechanics

Concentrations:
Agricultural process engineering; environmental and natural resources engineering; machine systems design; bioenvironmental controls; biomaterials systems; soil and water resources; food engineering; biochemical engineering.

What the study of this major is like:
The agricultural and biological engineering major, which focuses on theory, analysis, and design, includes supplementary lab work and project development. In core courses, you explore the nature of biological materials and study hydraulic systems, irrigation, agricultural machinery design, and erosion control. You take math, including calculus and differential equations; science, including biology, chemistry, physics, biochemistry, materials science, and plant and animal physiology; and basic engineering courses. In addition, you study the humanities and social sciences, and perhaps computer programming and numerical analysis. To enhance your ability to work with others, you sharpen your oral and written communication skills.

Some students become disillusioned because they don't see how the abstract mathematical principles they encounter in their first and second years apply to the major. But self-discipline, commitment, and perseverance pay off in the third and fourth years, when you explore practical applications in the upper-level courses.

Majors can generally concentrate in several areas, such as food engineering (which focuses on production, nutrition, packaging, factory design, and preservation); soil and water engineering (irrigation, soil science, drainage and hydraulic structure design, and erosion control); or machine design (various topics, such as the automation of animal feeding for large-scale farming). Many colleges offer cooperative education programs that provide opportunities for full-time employment during alternating academic terms. You will probably be eligible for these programs after completing the basic engineering course work. Most colleges include a capstone design course integrating concepts from previous courses.

Agricultural and biological engineering programs may vary in the emphasis they place on different areas of the field. For example, programs may stress natural resource and environmental engineering, food systems engineering, machinery systems engineering, or biological systems engineering. In addition, some programs prefer a hands-on, practical approach, while others are more academic.

Other majors you might like:
Aquaculture
Applied physics
Biomedical engineering
Forest engineering
Environmental engineering
Food science
Agronomy and crop science
Agricultural equipment technology
Environmental science
Biotechnology
Biochemistry
Genetics

Career options and trends:
Environmental engineer; design engineer; project engineer; product development engineer; soil and water conservationist; irrigation engineer; biomedical engineer; food engineer.

As the world's population grows and our global ecosystem becomes more fragile, the contributions of agricultural and biological engineers will be increasingly important to society. Employment growth for agricultural engineers will be generated by demand for more efficient crop production as well as the use of agriculture as renewable energy resources.

Opportunities for biomedical engineers is expected to grow much faster than average, as demand increases for more advanced medical equipment that can be used in a cost-effective manner. Career opportunities are also available in such related fields as medicine, pharmacy, and bioinstrumentation.

For more info:
American Society of Agricultural and Biological Engineers (ASABE)
2950 Niles Rd.
St. Joseph, MI 49085
(269)429-0300
www.asabe.org

Architectural engineering

What it's about:
Architectural engineering combines architecture and engineering to focus on the links between design and construction. Professionals in this discipline work with both architects and other engineers to ensure the timely, effective design and construction of buildings and other structures and systems.

Is this for you?
You might like this major if you also like: building things; discovering how things work; drawing; model making; working with your hands; working in teams; art; history; studying different architectural styles. If you are interested in architecture and have excellent math and science abilities, architectural engineering may be a good major for you.

Consider this major if you are good at: attention to detail; creativity; designing and drafting; math; quantitative analysis; spacial thinking/analysis; teamwork ...*or have...* patience; verbal skills; writing skills.

Recommended high school prep:
English 4, math 4 (including calculus or precalculus), lab science 4 (including physics and chemistry), social studies 3, and a foreign language 2–3. Take as many math, science, and English courses as possible. High school physics and chemistry are essential, but geology, biology, and environmental science are also relevant. Courses in computer skills, freehand drawing, CAD, and speech, if available, are good preparation, too.

Typical courses in this major:
Architectural design fundamentals
Thermal/fluid sciences
Energy conservation in buildings
Architectural history
Soil mechanics
Seismic analysis and design
Construction materials and methods
Architectural graphics
Steel and reinforced concrete design
Computer-aided design (CAD)
Lighting and power systems
Fire protection and plumbing design
Environmental systems design
Structural analysis
Construction finance and economics
Specifications and contracts

Concentrations:
Heating, ventilating, and air-conditioning (HVAC) systems; plumbing, piping, and fire protection; energy conservation and solar energy; electrical, lighting, communications, and control systems; structures; construction; acoustics; facility management.

What the study of this major is like:
Historically, architecture at most universities was housed in engineering schools, and architectural engineers were generally viewed as architects with a technical background. But in the late 1970s, many architecture programs, seeing themselves as more artistic than scientific, separated from engineering to form their own schools. Architectural engineering then redefined itself as a hybrid engineering discipline, focused on the analysis, design, and construction of building systems—functions that had once been part of architecture and civil, mechanical, and electrical engineering. But because architectural engineers still receive some architectural training, they are valuable links between architects and traditional engineers working on construction projects.

Both architecture and engineering are challenging fields that require dedication, passion, and stamina. If you are trying to decide between the two majors, architectural engineering might be a good solution. Typically, architectural engineering programs have competitive admissions standards. Therefore, you should take as many rigorous courses in high school as you can.

Even if you had introductory calculus in high school, you will probably be required to take engineering calculus courses in college. Majors typically complete four courses in advanced math, two in physics, one in chemistry, two in English, and several humanities electives. You can also expect to take a series of courses in structures—including statics, dynamics, strength of materials, and steel/concrete design—and some courses in mechanical and electrical systems and basic engineering sciences, such as circuits, thermodynamics, and fluid mechanics. While requirements may vary, most programs include at least one year's worth of architectural design and architectural history courses.

Course work includes lecture classes, lab sessions, and both independent and team projects. Because your work will be challenging, you must become excellent at time management and develop superior study skills. Summer internships are beneficial for obtaining that first full-time, post-graduation position.

All the programs approved by the Accreditation Board for Engineering and Technology (ABET) have similar basic requirements, usually covered in the first two years. However, colleges may differ in their emphasis on architecture, science, or engineering. If you are interested in design, you might choose a program that stresses architectural content, but if you are scientifically inclined, you may want to focus on engineering. Also, some programs include many electives that allow concentrations, whereas other programs are not as flexible. Architectural engineering courses are generally offered through a number of departments, so you may encounter a variety of philosophies and teaching styles.

Training to be a good architectural engineer is hard work. But careers in the field are often intellectually (and financially) rewarding—and you'll appreciate seeing your designs actually built!

Other majors you might like:
Drafting and design technology
Civil engineering
Structural engineering
Construction engineering
Marine engineering/naval architecture
Physics
Construction technology
Fire protection/safety technology
Heating/air conditioning/refrigeration technology
Urban, community, and regional planning

Environmental design
Architectural history/criticism

Questions to ask colleges:
How long will it take to earn a degree? Most bachelor's degree programs take four years, but a few take five years.

Is the program accredited by ABET? Most architectural engineers seek professional registration after graduation, and a degree from an accredited program is required.

Do undergraduates have open access to up-to-date design, computing, and testing laboratories? Are the facilities dedicated to the architectural engineering program, or are they shared with other engineering majors? Are design studios set aside for senior projects?

Career options and trends:
Consulting engineer*; analytical or design engineer*; architect*; engineering manager; construction manager.

Architectural education has become less technical and other engineering fields have become more general. As a result, architectural engineers are in demand because of the unique combination of design and analytical skills they possess. Graduates with concentrations in mechanical and electrical systems are in higher demand than grads with concentrations in construction and structural areas, who face competition from civil and construction engineers. Many architectural engineers move swiftly from design positions to project management and administration. Some soon start their own firms.

For more info:
Architectural Engineering Institute (AEI)
1801 Alexander Bell Dr.
Reston, VA 20191-4400
(800) 548-2723
www.asce.org/aei

Chemical engineering

What it's about:

Through the study of math and the natural sciences, chemical engineering majors learn to develop products for businesses, government, and consumers; they also look for solutions to regional or global problems, such as pollution. Like most engineers, chemical engineers turn technological advances in the lab into useful materials and services beyond the university walls.

Is this for you?

You might like this major if you also like: science and math (of course); exploring the basic nature of things; lab work and technology.

Consider this major if you are good at: attention to detail; creativity; critical reading/thinking; math; memorizing; organizing; quantitative analysis; teamwork ...*or have*... initiative; writing skills.

Recommended high school prep:

English 4, math 4 (including calculus or precalculus), lab science 4 (including biology, chemistry and physics), social studies 3, and a foreign language 2–3. If possible, take other advanced mathematics or science courses.

Did you know...

...that Frank Capra, the director of *It's a Wonderful Life*, earned a chemical engineering degree at Stanford?

Typical courses in this major:

General chemistry
Organic chemistry
Physical chemistry
Physics
Calculus
Differential equations
Computer programming
Statistics
Microbiology
Materials engineering
Energy and material balances
Thermodynamics
Heat mass and momentum transfer
Chemical and biological reaction engineering
Engineering economics
Chemical and pharmaceutical plant design

Concentrations:

Biochemical engineering; biomolecular engineering; biomedical engineering; environmental engineering; materials engineering; thin films and surface science; pharmaceutical engineering.

What the study of this major is like:

Chemical engineers convert the discoveries that physical or biological scientists make in the laboratory into products used by industry, the military, and ordinary consumers. In addition, they play an important role in the new areas of biotechnology (the development of medical treatments), nanotechnology (the science of miniaturization), and information technology. As a chemical engineering major, you are trained to design and develop many of the processes and products necessary for modern industrial society, including antibiotics and other medicines, natural and synthetic fibers, semiconductors, fuel cells, synthetic fuels, petroleum-based fuels and hydrogen, body parts and organ substitutes, and environmental pollution prevention and cleanup. In your work, the primary goal is to create products and processes that are safe and economical.

Chemical engineering programs in the United States are approved by the Accreditation Board for Engineering and Technology (ABET), in cooperation with the American Institute of Chemical Engineers (AIChE). These programs begin with courses in the natural sciences, math, and computer programming. In most programs, you will also be required to study speech and writing as well as the humanities and social sciences. Programs may vary in their focus; they may emphasize materials engineering, bioengineering, environmental concerns, modeling and computer applications, or some or all these areas. Physics and biochemistry or biophysics courses may be included as electives.

One of the most important courses you take as a major is energy and material balances—the basis for the design and evaluation of biological, chemical, energy, and environmental processes. Thermodynamics teaches you to determine the energy efficiency of chemical and biological processes, including those in the human body. In other courses, you learn about the economics of alternative designs, life-cycle analysis, and mathematical analysis by computer simulation. You'll need to get a good background in mathematics to do, for example, rigorous analyses of chemical plant processes. In a capstone course, you may design an entire process for the production of chemicals, fuels, electronic devices, or drinking water from the oceans; or you may design devices for kidney dialysis or blood oxygenators.

Other majors you might like:
Biotechnology
Biochemistry
Agricultural and biological engineering
Biomedical engineering
Materials engineering
Polymer/plastics engineering
Metallurgical engineering
Soil science
Environmental engineering
Chemical technology
Forensic science
Clinical/medical laboratory technology

Questions to ask colleges:
Does the college help students find internships while in school, and jobs after graduating?

Ask to see the facilities, particularly the computer rooms and student work areas. You should also ask for a list of graduate schools, companies, and government agencies that the previous 100–200 graduates enrolled in or were offered jobs by.

Career options and trends:
Consulting engineer; product designer/engineer; research and development engineer; production engineer or plant manager; sales representative; environmental engineer.

Careers are available in the environmental, pharmaceutical, materials, fuel, and specialty chemical industries. Favorable job prospects are projected through 2022, as many engineers in this field are reaching retirement age. Growth opportunities will be located in service-providing industries, such as professional, scientific, and technical services. Positions in the alternative energy, biotechnology and nanotechnology fields are also rapidly expanding. Engineering positions will require state certification in addition to the required degrees.

Insider's viewpoint:
"Go to class and get involved; just get through those first two years and you're golden."

—Travis, senior, Penn State

For more info:
American Institute of Chemical Engineers (AIChE)
3 Park Ave.
New York, NY 10016-5991
(800) 242-4363
www.aiche.org

Civil engineering

What it's about:

Civil engineering majors learn to apply the principles of science and math to the planning, construction, and maintenance of facilities, both public and private, that are essential to industrialized society. Civil engineers work on buildings; on such large-scale projects as bridges, dams, highways, environmental control systems, and water purification systems; and on other structures in both the urban and rural environments.

Is this for you?

You might like this major if you also like: learning how things work (building things, taking things apart); thinking big; brain teaser puzzles; math and science; achieving practical results; outdoor activities; watching construction sites. If you like to solve problems by dividing them up into logical parts (divide and conquer), then civil engineering might be a good choice. Projects tend to be large in scope, and you should have the patience for complexity and long-term commitments.

Consider this major if you are good at: attention to detail; math; organizing; quantitative analysis; research; spacial thinking/analysis; teamwork *...or have...* initiative; interpersonal skills; mechanical facility; verbal skills.

Recommended high school prep:

English 4, math 4 (including trigonometry, geometry, and calculus or precalculus), lab science 3–4 (including chemistry and physics), social studies 3, and a foreign language 2–3. Courses in computer applications, business, and economics are also helpful.

Typical courses in this major:

Engineering graphics
Structural analysis and design
Soil mechanics
Statics
Dynamics
Strength of materials
Surveying
Environmental engineering
Construction materials
Fluid mechanics
Water resources
Engineering economics
Transportation engineering
Geotechnical engineering
Construction management
Hydraulics and hydrology

Concentrations:

Structural engineering; geotechnical engineering; environmental engineering; construction; transportation engineering; hydrosystems (hydraulics, hydrology, water resources).

What the study of this major is like:

Civil engineers plan, analyze, design, and erect structures (such as buildings, bridges) and systems (transportation, water supply). Civil engineering is often called "the people-serving profession" because many of its projects serve the public good. To tackle complex problems, civil engineers use principles of math and science, as well as their creativity. Civil engineering works are generally large-scale, one-of-a-kind projects, usually requiring cooperation among professionals from a variety of disciplines.

Differences among civil engineering programs are minimal because of the requirements established by the Accreditation Board for Engineering and Technology (ABET). Programs include a broad range of courses in mathematics (especially calculus and differential equations); basic sciences (chemistry, physics, and possibly geology or biology); engineering sciences; engineering design; and the humanities and social sciences. In addition, programs may include courses in computers, English composition, speech, report writing, engineering economics, and statistics.

You can expect to take most professional courses during your last two years of study. In civil engineering, probably more than in any other engineering field, you can concentrate in a number of areas. Some typical concentrations include the following:

217

Structural engineering. The planning and design of large structures, including bridges, buildings, towers, dams, offshore drilling, and exploration facilities.

Environmental engineering. The planning and design of facilities for water purification; control of air and water pollution; solid water management; and disposal of hazardous materials.

Geotechnical engineering. The analysis and design of foundations and retaining walls; the development of excavation and construction techniques for tunnels, dams, and storage systems for hazardous materials.

Hydrosystems. The analysis and design of dams, floodwalls, pumping stations, aqueducts, canals, harbor and coastal facilities, irrigation and drainage systems, and navigable waterways.

Transportation engineering. The analysis and design of facilities for highways, airports, railways, aerospace systems, and pipelines.

Most courses are taught in lecture format, but some have lab components. In most technical courses, you learn primarily by solving "story problems": scenarios are described to the class, and you must determine which theories are applicable, which information is superfluous, which information is missing, and so on. Later courses often have open-ended problems, possibly involving teamwork or research. Like all engineering majors, this one is very demanding. Because many of your courses build on one another, you need to keep up with your studies.

Other majors you might like:
Mechanical engineering
Civil engineering technology
Industrial engineering
Materials science
Architecture
Architectural engineering
Construction management
Ocean engineering
Physics
Urban, community, and regional planning
Geology/earth science
Surveying technology

Questions to ask colleges:
Is there a student chapter of the American Society of Civil Engineers (ASCE) on campus?

Does the college offer a five-year combined bachelor's/master's degree program? (More than one-third of civil engineering graduates go on to earn a master's degree.)

Does the college offer a five-year cooperative study program in which you alternate periods of study with related employment?

Career options and trends:
Consulting engineer*; city engineer or official at a state or federal agency (e.g., EPA, Department of Transportation)*; construction engineer; researcher in a government laboratory, forensic engineering firm, or university.

Civil Engineers often need a professional engineer's (PE) license to practice. In some states, structural engineering (SE) has a separate licensure. Increasingly, a master's degree is required for entry-level positions or advancement.

Since many civil engineering projects are large in scope, they create numerous jobs that last a long time. As a result, employment may remain strong for some time after an economic downturn. Thus, hiring trends in civil engineering may lag behind national trends.

Insider's viewpoint:
"I love civil engineering because it is a field with a fascinating balance between the certainty of science and uncertainty of the natural environment."

—Professor Keith Hjelmstad, University of Illinois

For more info:
American Society of Civil Engineers (ASCE)
1801 Alexander Bell Drive
Reston, VA 20191-4400
(800) 548-2723
www.asce.org

Electrical and communications engineering

Also known as:
Electrical and computer engineering

What it's about:
Electrical and communications engineering deals with the design, manufacture, and operation of the range of devices and systems that depend on electricity—from wireless telephones to giant power generators. You examine superconductors, wave propagation, energy storage, fiber optics, reception, and amplification, from both a theoretical and an applied perspective.

Is this for you?
You might like this major if you also like: tinkering (putting things together, taking them apart, making them work); music; ham radio; computers.

Consider this major if you are good at: attention to detail; creativity; math; organizing; quantitative analysis; spacial thinking/analysis; teamwork; vsualization ...*or have...* initiative; writing skills.

Recommended high school prep:
English 4, math 4 (including precalculus or calculus), lab science 3–4 (including physics), social studies 3, and a foreign language 2–3. Advanced or honors courses in math and physics are recommended, as well as courses in computer applications and writing.

Did you know...
...that more engineers are employed in electrical engineering than in any other branch of engineering? According to the U.S. Bureau of Labor Statistics, nearly one-third work in California, Texas, New York, and New Jersey, where many large electronics firms are located.

Typical courses in this major:
Electric circuits and systems
Electromagnetics
Control systems
Electromechanical energy conversion
Digital circuits
Materials science
Microwaves and high-speed circuits
Signal processing
Semiconductor electronics
Instrumentation
Microprocessor systems
Fields, matter, and waves
Communications systems
Physics of electronic devices
Fiber optics and photonics
Electrical engineering practicum

Concentrations:
In college: communications systems; electric power; electronic design; electromagnetics; computer systems; digital systems; control systems; telecommunications.

If you go on to grad school: physical electronics; bioengineering; wireless engineering; electronics packaging; photonics; microwave engineering.

What the study of this major is like:
Most electrical and communications engineering programs begin with an introduction to the design process that stresses engineering fundamentals and suggests some of the careers you might pursue after graduation. You also start with mathematics, physics, and some chemistry courses that are the basis for many engineering courses you will take later on.

Your other courses cover engineering science and design, humanities, social sciences, and electives that correspond to your concentration. In humanities and social sciences courses, you see how the work that engineers do impacts society. You will probably participate in a significant design project in your fourth year, or perhaps earlier. Most students find the experience rewarding because it brings together what you've learned in various courses and helps you understand what engineering can accomplish. These projects, which are usually team efforts and may involve professional engineers and instructors, often require a written report and perhaps several oral presentations.

You learn by attending lectures and by working on computers, but especially by doing homework. Working through your homework problems and making sure you understand the concepts they illustrate is essential. Most engineering students do homework in small groups, but you should find out what your professors' policies are—sometimes instructors prefer that you work independently. You'll also take a number of lab courses, in which you explore abstract principles you learn in the classroom. Labs also provide opportunities to develop teamwork skills and your ability to write clear technical reports.

Your education does not necessarily take place entirely on campus. You will probably take a number of field trips to engineering labs and factories. You may also work as an engineering summer intern—an invaluable experience that can help when you seek your first job. In addition, many international programs allow engineering students to work or study abroad while earning academic credit.

Although there is much similarity among programs, there are also variations in coverage or emphasis. Some programs stress computer engineering; others may have more courses in digital communication technology and information science. All programs prepare graduates for entry into the profession, but some devote more attention to preparing students for graduate school. Graduates from these programs, which tend to emphasize theory over application, may need more on-the-job training before they can work independently in industry.

The ABET (Accreditation Board for Engineering and Technology) standards for approving engineering programs in the United States require that programs clearly state their objectives. These goals (published in college catalogs) might help you clarify a program's focus to see if it fits your interests. As in all areas of engineering, your education never really ends, because of the need to keep up with the rapid advances in electrical and communications technology.

Other majors you might like:
Mechanical engineering
Engineering physics
Systems engineering
Metallurgical engineering

Software engineering
Electrical engineering technologies
Rehabilitation engineering/assistive technology
Computer science
Physics
Neuroscience
Electrical drafting/CAD/CADD
Computer engineering technology

Questions to ask colleges:
Is computer engineering considered part of the electrical engineering major, or a separate major?

Are co-op educational experiences available?

How do you prepare graduates to work in an industry where outsourcing of engineering services is a growing trend?

Career options and trends:
Production engineer*; design engineer; engineering manager; systems analyst; consulting engineer*; field engineer; research engineer.

Licensure (or registration) as a professional engineer (PE) is often required of engineers working in the public sector (for instance, for power companies and government agencies) but not of engineers working for private firms. Although some electrical engineers (EEs) are licensed, most are not.

As the economy strengthens, job prospects are likely to be favorable, especially for graduates who have had engineering intern experience. Consulting engineering firms are expected to generate the fastest job growth. Because most products today involve electricity and electronics, EEs are found in almost every industry at every level, doing all kinds of work—from designing integrated circuits to performing instrumentation on a ship in the Antarctic Ocean.

Insider's viewpoint:
"In my first class, my partner and I designed the logic for a small, battery-powered vehicle to follow a path on the ground set by white tape. We used sensors on the vehicle to follow the tape and then send the correct signals to the motors and wheels. If anyone had told me before that I would be doing this my first semester, I probably would not have believed them."

—Ray, junior, University of Illinois at Urbana–Champaign

For more info:

The Institute of Electrical and Electronics
  Engineers (IEEE)
3 Park Avenue, 17th Fl.
New York, NY 10016-5997
(212) 419-7900
www.ieee.org

Association for Computer Machinery (ACM)
2 Penn Plaza
Suite 701
New York, NY 10121-0701
(212) 869-7440
www.acm.org

Industrial engineering

What it's about:

Industrial engineering is the most "people-oriented" of the engineering fields. As a major, you learn to plan, design, and implement complex systems for industry that take into account the needs and capabilities of individuals and groups, as well as the availability of information, equipment, and materials. Industrial engineers (IEs) find ways to increase both productivity and customer satisfaction in all kinds of organizations, from hospitals to steel foundries, and they are the only engineers educated as quality and productivity improvement professionals.

Is this for you?

You might like this major if you also like: helping people; working in teams; math and science; figuring out how to do things more easily; working with numbers; debating; solving puzzles and brain teasers.

Consider this major if you are good at: attention to detail; communicating ideas; creativity; critical reading/thinking; leadership; math; organizing; persuading/influencing; quantitative analysis *...or have...* initiative; listening skills.

Recommended high school prep:

English 4, math 4 (up to precalculus), lab science 4 (including biology, chemistry and physics), social studies 3, and a foreign language 2–3. English is important because industrial engineers must effectively communicate the ideas and procedures they develop. If available, courses in speech, psychology, and economics are also helpful.

Did you know...

...that industrial engineers are more widely distributed among manufacturing businesses than any other type of engineer? And IEs also work in unexpected places, like Disney World and other theme parks.

Typical courses in this major:

Production planning and control
Operations research
Quality control
Supply chain logistics
Human factors
Ergonomics
Facilities planning and design
Discrete event computer simulation
Engineering management
Engineering economics
Probability and statistics
Materials handling and control
Computer modeling
Information systems
Robotics
Safety management

Concentrations:

Generally, none in college; but if you go on to grad school: manufacturing; operations research; ergonomics; management systems.

What the study of this major is like:

While other engineers produce things, industrial engineers create or improve the systems and procedures used in making or doing things. The work that IEs do has been around a long time, and the profession has been recognized since the 1920s. In the early 1900s, two of industrial engineering's founders, Frank and Lillian Gilbreth, helped determine the "one best way" for hospitals to perform surgery and train doctors, nurses, and technicians. As a result, operating times dropped drastically and survival rates increased. Today, IEs serve as integration engineers, focusing on the way the numerous components of industrial or service systems work as a unit. In figuring out how to improve a procedure, IEs seek to reduce or eliminate the many areas of waste, especially of time, money, materials, and energy.

IEs concern themselves with the design of workplaces, ergonomic and safety studies, and productivity. They design factories (workstations, automated procedures, and robotics; material handling systems; and control systems) and determine the "best way" to manufacture goods. But the word "industrial" refers to more than just manufacturing; today, IEs work in (or with) providers of health care, lodging, and food service; in defense and government; and in such businesses as transportation and communications. A typical task might involve getting a package from San Francisco to Düsseldorf overnight.

Your first two years as a major are similar to those of most engineering students. You take courses in math, the physical sciences, and engineering sciences such as statics, thermodynamics, and electrical circuits. These two years can be intellectually challenging, and you may wonder whether you'll ever get to your chosen field of study, industrial engineering; perseverance and patience will pay off. In your third and fourth years, you explore topical areas of the major and take supporting math and statistics courses. Here, most students begin to identify their fields of interest.

You can expect to receive a diverse education in computer systems, design, and management, as well as in the physical and social sciences, including economics. Because IEs focus on organizations and the people in them, you will need to take arts and humanities courses. Your schedule will be full, with little room for electives.

Among different industrial engineering programs, requirements are similar and philosophies are fundamentally the same. Most programs stress manufacturing, operations research (applying mathematical modeling and analysis to problems), or "general" industrial engineering, which covers all or most topical areas. A few undergraduate programs have an in-depth focus on safety management, logistics, quality control, or human factors.

Other majors you might like:
Systems engineering
Business administration and management
Management science
Health information management
Industrial technology
Information systems
Psychology
Occupational safety/health technology
Management information systems
Human resources management
Economics
Organizational behavior studies

Questions to ask colleges:
How extensive and state-of-the-art are the computer lab facilities, and how accessible are they to undergrads? For industrial engineering majors, the computing equipment is essential because of the specialized (and often expensive) software they use.

Which types of research projects are under way? The answer will provide insight into the interests and strengths of the faculty.

Career options and trends:
Consulting industrial engineer*; manufacturing/production supervisor*; plant manager or chief operating officer; quality engineer; safety engineer; systems engineer; materials manager; operations analyst*; process engineer.

Because they are not as specialized as other engineers, industrial engineers are employed in a wide range of industries looking for new ways to reduce costs and raise productivity, and to make their operations more "green." IEs versatility allows them the ability to engage in activities useful to a number of businesses, such as supply chain management, quality assurance and project management.

For more info:
Institute of Industrial Engineers (IIE)
3577 Parkway Lane, Suite 200
Norcross, GA 30092
(800) 494-0460
www.iienet.org

Marine engineering/naval architecture

What it's about:

Marine engineers and naval architects design, build, operate, and maintain a wide variety of oceangoing vehicles, from recreational boats to ships at sea. Marine engineering concentrates on ship machinery, including propulsion, electrical, mechanical, and control systems. Naval architecture focuses on ship design, including hull shape, structure, power requirements, and performance.

Is this for you?

You might like this major if you also like: anything to do with ships and the sea; boating; competitive sailing; working with machinery; drawing, drafting, and design; model ship building; radio-controlled boat building; math and science.

Consider this major if you are good at: attention to detail; creativity; critical reading/thinking; making decisions; math; quantitative analysis; spacial thinking/analysis *...or have...* communication skills; initiative; patience.

Recommended high school prep:

English 4, math 4 (including trigonometry and calculus), lab science 3–4 (including chemistry and physics), social studies 3, and a foreign language 2–3. Take as much math and science as you can. Courses that prepare you to communicate well are also important. Knowledge of a foreign language would be useful, as the maritime industry is, by its nature, global. If possible, take courses in spreadsheet applications, manual graphics, and computer-assisted design (CAD).

Typical courses in this major:

Foundations of ship design
Hullform and hydrostatics
Intact and damaged stability
Ship structures
Resistance and powering
Seakeeping and maneuvering
Ship production
Marine power systems
Solid mechanics
Thermodynamics
Marine hydrodynamics
Marine electronics
Marine dynamics
Sailing craft design
Small craft design

Concentrations:

Generally, none in college; but if you go on to grad school: structural analysis; hydrodynamics; autonomous vehicles; maritime business; marine power systems; sailing yachts; energy conversion; nuclear propulsion; control systems; robotics.

What the study of this major is like:

Marine engineering and naval architecture has wide-ranging applications to ships and boats, from tankers to trawlers, submarines to sailboats, military ships to personal watercraft. It encompasses a variety of engineering challenges, including stability, seakeeping, engine selection, space utilization, structural design, model testing, propeller design, high-speed submarine dynamics, and historical ship performance.

The major usually stresses general technical content and design. Programs tend to be more applied than theoretical, although both facets are covered. Hands-on lab experiences are essential. As part of a long tradition, you take capstone courses in ship design. Field trips and practical work experience are also highly useful and instructive.

As a major, you will face challenges typical of any engineering program. Some students have a hard time with the spatial visualization of complex three-dimensional shapes. In addition, you may have to develop the ingenuity and patience needed in tackling the open-ended engineering problems that are often solved through repetitive trials. You should be prepared to spend plenty of time on your course work, especially on design courses. At the end of the program, you will be rewarded with comprehensive knowledge and a confidence in your ability to do the work. You will understand "the big picture" of the engineering and design of ships.

Although entry requirements are uniform, the various marine engineering and naval architecture programs reflect the expertise and interests of the teaching faculty. Some programs emphasize the analysis of marine vehicles; some, the design of marine vehicles; others, a particular category of ships or boats; and still others, a combination of these fields. In some programs, industry experience is incorporated into the curriculum. Also, some institutions consider their marine engineering and naval architecture programs to be subsets of larger engineering programs.

Other majors you might like:
Ocean engineering
Marine science/Merchant Marine
Electrical and communications engineering
Nuclear engineering
Oceanography
Mechanical engineering
Fishing and fisheries
Military technologies
Aircraft powerplant technology
Marine maintenance/fitter/ship repair
Drafting and design technology

Questions to ask colleges:
Do majors have access to a marine towing tank as an integral part of their academic program? Other facilities to inquire about: model basin, gravity wave tank, propeller tunnel, CAD computer laboratories.

How is the curriculum split between marine engineering and naval architecture studies? Does the school's marine engineering curriculum emphasize design or ship operations?

Is there a summer internship program in the marine industry?

Career options and trends:
Naval architect*; marine engineer*; yacht designer; naval officer; ship's officer (Merchant Marine); shipyard engineer.

Majors in marine engineering and naval architecture also pursue careers in ship operations and marine commerce. After additional professional or graduate study, you may find work in admiralty law or research. It is not necessary to be registered as a professional engineer (PE) to obtain employment, but it is a respected credential. Registration requirements vary, but they generally involve two examinations and a period of work experience.

Employment of marine engineers and naval architects is expected to improve through 2022, because of the need to design ships and systems to transport energy products, such as liquefied natural gas, and to modify the existing fleet of cargo ships to comply with emission and pollution control regulations. Demand will also increase for engineers needed to design and maintain oil rigs, offshore wind turbines and tidal power generators.

Good job prospects for marine engineers are also expected because of the need to replace workers and the limited number of students pursuing this field.

For more info:
Society of Naval Architects and Marine Engineers
  (SNAME)
601 Pavonia Ave.
Jersey City, NJ 07306
(800)798-2188
www.sname.org

American Society of Naval Engineers (ASNE)
1452 Duke St.
Alexandria, VA 22314-3458
(703) 836-6727
www.navalengineers.org

Materials engineering

Also known as:
Materials science and engineering

What it's about:
This major focuses on the materials used by all engineers: ceramics, metals, polymers, and combinations of these (composites). The major provides a rigorous exposure to the principles governing the fabrication, properties, and applications of these materials. Because a primary task of engineers is to create various types of products from a wide variety of ingredients, the study of materials is a gateway to almost any engineering field or project.

Is this for you?
You might like this major if you also like: chemistry, physics, and math; exploring the nature of things. Are you fascinated by the architecture of materials at the atomic and molecular levels? Do you wonder what things are made of—for example, computers, milk cartons, DVD players? Have you asked yourself, "Why are some plastics hard, while others are soft?" Would you rather work on a range of engineering projects than be limited to a particular field? If your answer is yes, read on.

Consider this major if you are good at: attention to detail; creativity; critical reading/thinking; math; organizing; quantitative analysis; spacial thinking/analysis; teamwork *...or have...* initiative; manual dexterity; writing skills.

Recommended high school prep:
English 4, math 4 (including precalculus), lab science 4 (including chemistry and physics), social studies 3, and a foreign language 2–3. If it is available, take a course that covers both integral and differential calculus. Courses that help you develop writing and speaking skills are essential in engineering.

Did you know...
...there are such things as "magnetic liquids" (magneto-rheological fluids), that you can morph from a fluid to a solid simply by moving your hand through them, and "memory metal" (Nitinol), which, after being bent and twisted, returns to its original shape with a blast of hot air? The discovery of materials like these, and the development of applications for them, is the fun part of materials engineering.

Typical courses in this major:
Introduction to materials
Thermodynamics of materials
Kinetics of materials
Physical metallurgy
Processing and properties of ceramics
Composites
Fundamentals of polymers
Polymer processing
Mechanical behavior of solids
Materials engineering design
Materials characterization laboratory
Engineering computational laboratory
Degradation of materials
Failure analysis
Phase equilibria
Senior design project

Concentrations:
In college: biomaterials; ceramic materials; composites; electronic materials; metals and alloys; nanomaterials; polymeric materials

If you go on to grad school: materials processing; process and microsection modeling; smart materials.

What the study of this major is like:
Materials are a common denominator among all branches of engineering because, without them, engineers cannot work. When designing systems, other engineers (civil, chemical, electrical, mechanical) frequently collaborate with materials engineers to select the most appropriate materials. Materials engineering can be done at the atomic level (as in fiber reinforcement to make a graphite fishing rod) or at the macroscopic level (as in the manufacture of appliances, cars, and bridges). In fact, everything we see and use—from skyscrapers to computers—

is made of materials derived from the earth. As a major, you learn to develop materials to meet specific needs.

Programs normally include math, communications, computer science, natural sciences (especially chemistry and physics), humanities, social sciences, engineering science, and engineering design courses. As a major, you study the physical and chemical properties of materials, transport phenomena, strength of materials, and tools for structural and chemical characterization. You use differential and integral calculus to solve equations governing the behavior of solids. In design courses, you gain practice in devising materials, components, systems, or processes to meet particular objectives. In various courses you will employ a variety of tools (such as electron microscopes, and software for modeling the behavior of materials and components) and ways of processing material (such as microgravity processing).

Typically, materials engineering classes are small (about 20 students), allowing for close interaction between students and faculty members. You learn primarily through lectures, presentations, and hands-on laboratories. You are encouraged to develop your oral and writing skills. Because much of the subject matter is conceptual, you must learn how to visualize solid materials in three dimensions.

Course requirements are similar at most colleges. All programs focus on the relation, in solids, of processing, microstructure, and property. Some colleges may stress mechanics of materials, thermodynamics, or kinetics. Other programs emphasize a particular material, such as ceramics or polymers. Differences in approach generally reflect faculty members' interest and expertise.

This major is often referred to as a science as well as an engineering discipline, because much of the science (chemistry and physics) of engineering materials is still being developed. You will find that most programs have a high ratio of graduate research students to undergraduate majors. This usually results in many opportunities for undergraduates to take part in important research on new materials, such as carbon nano tubes, for example.

Other majors you might like:
Materials science
Ceramic sciences/engineering
Polymer/plastics engineering
Metallurgical engineering
Mining and mineral engineering
Physics
Chemical engineering
Agricultural and biological engineering
Biotechnology
Manufacturing engineering
Industrial engineering
Hazardous materials technology

Questions to ask colleges:
Is the program accredited by the Accreditation Board for Engineering and Technology (ABET)?

Are faculty members engaged in research?

Is there a graduate program in materials science or engineering on campus? Are there opportunities for undergraduates to join in research, or to pursue independent study projects?

What types of lab facilities and equipment (such as electron microscopes) do undergrads have access to?

Career options and trends:
Applications engineer*; production engineer; metallurgist; polymer engineer*; industrial research and development staff member*; technical writer.

Every year, fewer than 1,000 students receive bachelor's degrees in this discipline. For this reason and because of the interdisciplinary nature of the field, there are a wide variety of job opportunities. While manufacturing in general is declining, job growth should be strong for materials engineers working on nanomaterials and biomaterials. Salaries are competitive with those in other fields of engineering.

Insider's viewpoint:
"It's a lot of fun; you get to break a lot of things. With materials you really get to delve into the nitty-gritty. Instead of mechanical engineers who look at how they can build a structure and how all the forces will act on the structure, we look at the little parts inside, what makes that structure."

—Tom, junior, Case Western Reserve University

For more info:

Materials Research Society (MRS)
506 Keystone Drive
Warrendale, PA 15086-7573
(724) 779-3003
www.mrs.org

The Minerals, Metals, and Materials Society (TMS)
184 Thorn Hill Rd.
Warrendale, PA 15086-7514
(800) 759-4867
www.tms.org

The Materials Information Society (ASM
    International)
9639 Kinsman Road
Materials Park, OH 44073-0002
(800) 336-5152
www.asminternational.org

Mechanical engineering

What it's about:

Mechanical engineering deals with the forces and energy at work in thermal and mechanical (solid and fluid) systems. You learn the engineering principles underlying the generation, transmission, and utilization of these energies, and the design, production, and application of mechanical devices and systems.

Is this for you?

You might like this major if you also like: mechanical devices; learning how things work; computers; cars; solving problems; math and science.

Consider this major if you are good at: attention to detail; creativity; organizing; quantitative analysis; research; spacial thinking/analysis ...*or have*... manual dexterity; verbal skills; writing skills.

Recommended high school prep:

English 4, math 4 (including precalculus), laboratory science 4 (including chemistry and physics), social studies 2, a foreign language 2–3. If it is available, take a computer science course.

Typical courses in this major:

Statics
Dynamics
Circuit analysis
Engineering graphics
Mechanical design fundamentals
Computer modeling
Mechanical vibrations
Solid mechanics
Energy systems
Mechanical systems
Fluid mechanics
Automatic controls
Thermodynamics
Materials science
Manufacturing systems
Heat transfer

Concentrations:

Automatic controls; energy systems; materials engineering, design, manufacturing systems; thermal systems; automotive engineering.

What the study of this major is like:

In mechanical engineering, you focus on mechanics (fluids and solids) and heat as forms of energy. You learn about the forces and motions that affect mechanical performance. Before you build a device, you use math to determine what the machine will do. You learn to model—to visualize a piece of equipment and to convey to others what it would do. And you learn what's involved in manufacturing the machinery you design—for example, a vehicle, an acoustic system, an engine.

All engineering disciplines start out the same way: with courses in math (calculus through differential equations) and numerical analysis; natural science (chemistry, physics, and perhaps biology or materials science); humanities and social science; and basic engineering science. In your second year, you will be introduced to mechanical engineering, in courses that include the design of thermal and mechanical systems. Training in engineering design, which is now largely computer-based, involves modeling, simulation, analysis, and synthesis.

Programs generally emphasize theory and analysis as well as design, with appropriate supporting labs and project work in such areas as these:

Engineering mechanics. Static and dynamic forces within and on structures; equivalent force systems; dynamics; stresses and strains; and strength of materials.

Materials. Properties of materials; physical metallurgy; and metallic and other materials including polymers, ceramics, and composites.

Electrical systems. Electrical circuits; direct and alternating current; electrical machinery; digital and analog electronic devices; circuits; and control systems.

Thermal systems. Fluid mechanics; thermodynamics; combustion; refrigeration; heat transfer; energy systems; and internal combustion engines.

Mechanical systems. Kinematics and mechanisms; modeling of multicomponent systems; control of mechanical systems; vibrations; component design and analysis; machine design; and dynamics of machinery.

Manufacturing systems. Modern manufacturing systems; robotics; computer-aided manufacturing systems; artificial intelligence; and computers integrated in manufacturing.

Specialty course work or technical electives typically include in-depth study of acoustics and noise control; advanced control system design; applied solar energy; automotive engineering; biomechanics and biomedical engineering; biotechnology; computer-aided design; composite materials; direct energy conversion; energy conservation; energy system analysis; environmental control systems; gas dynamics; heating, ventilating, and air conditioning; non-destructive testing; numerical modeling and simulation; packaging engineering; propulsion systems; polymer processing; robotics; and turbomachinery.

Because computers are used in the solution of many engineering problems, the major includes a great deal of programming and numerical analysis.

Many colleges offer cooperative education programs, which provide opportunities for full-time employment during alternating academic terms. Such programs are generally available after you have completed the basic engineering course work.

Other majors you might like:
Mechanical engineering technology
Aeronautical/aerospace engineering
Nuclear engineering
Robotics technology
Marine engineering/naval architecture
Electrical and communications engineering
Physics
Industrial engineering
Materials engineering
Drafting and design technology

Career options and trends:
Consulting engineer; industrial engineer; plastics fabrication engineer; safety engineer; test engineer; automotive engineer; manufacturing engineer; design engineer; research and development engineer.

Mechanical engineers are engaged in a wide range of careers in industry, business, government, and universities. They interact with people and machines in research, design, development, testing, manufacturing, operations, marketing, sales, and management. Continued demand for graduates trained in mechanical engineering is projected for the near future, especially in industries fostering emerging technologies. Job growth will also be spurred by the need for design of hybrid and electrical cars and clean emissions automobiles.

Insider's viewpoint:
"There is a lot of freedom in a mechanical engineering major. I feel like I'm learning a thought process as opposed to a trade, and this thought process is more powerful than anything you could memorize from a book."

—Alison, junior, Colorado State University

For more info:
American Society of Mechanical Engineers (ASME)
2 Park Avenue
New York, NY 10016-5990
(800) 843-2763
www.asme.org

Metallurgical engineering

What it's about:

In this major, you study the structure, properties, and performance of metals and alloys. Metallurgical engineering is a distinct discipline, although it is closely related to the more inclusive fields of materials science and materials engineering, which address similar relationships in all classes of materials (such as metals, ceramics, polymers, and fabrics).

Is this for you?

You might like this major if you also like: chemistry, physics, and math; exploring the nature of things. Have you ever asked yourself, "Why is glass transparent and steel shiny? Why do some steels rust and others don't? What makes some metals magnetic and other not?" If so, this major might interest you.

Consider this major if you are good at: attention to detail; creativity; critical reading/thinking; math; organizing data; quantitative analysis; spacial thinking/analysis; teamwork ...*or have...* initiative; patience; writing skills.

Recommended high school prep:

English 4, math 4 (including trigonometry and calculus or precalculus), lab science 3–4 (including chemistry and physics), social studies 3, and a foreign language 2–3.

Did you know...

...that most high school students considering metallurgical engineering envision a career in a steel mill or foundry? Such careers are actually in the minority. Many metallurgical engineers work in the aerospace industry, processing exotic alloys; in the microelectronics industry, contributing to advances in electro-optical materials; or in the biomedical industry, developing implants and biomedical sensors.

Typical courses in this major:

Structure and properties of materials
Mechanics of materials
Mechanical behavior of solids
Metallurgical thermodynamics
Physical metallurgy
Chemical metallurgy
Extractive metallurgy
Processing and properties of metals
Transport phenomena in metallurgy
Casting and solidification processing
Metallurgical engineering design
Degradation of materials
Engineering economics
Senior design project

Concentrations:

In college: physical metallurgy; extractive metallurgy.

If you go on to grad school: programs may focus on a specific alloy, processing technique, or application.

What the study of this major is like:

Although metallurgical engineering builds on a tradition of metalworking that is thousands of years old, it is sufficiently complex that materials and processes are continuously being discovered. Until fairly recently, high-temperature superconductivity, amorphous metals, buckyballs, and carbon nanotubes were unknown. Yet, if you consider the many elements on the periodic table, the ways in which they can be combined, and the possibilities for processing them to achieve novel structures, you will realize that the universe of achievable materials has barely been explored.

As an undergraduate in a program approved by ABET (Accreditation Board for Engineering and Technology), you must complete two years of math (including calculus and differential equations) and at least a year of both chemistry and physics. Majors typically take at least 48 semester credits of engineering-related courses, divided between general engineering courses (such as statics, design, and programming) and metallurgical core courses.

The core courses stress the relationships among the structure, properties, processing, and performance of metals and alloys. You study the structure of a metal on scales ranging from the bonding between individual atoms to the interaction of macroscopically visible components in engineered composites (such as fibers and particles). You use advanced techniques including optical and electron microscopy; X-ray diffraction; mechanical testing; thermal analysis; and electrical, magnetic, and optical characterization of materials.

Other courses cover the mechanical, chemical, and physical properties of alloys. Typically, you are required to take at least one course on mechanical properties and one course on physical properties (electrical, magnetic, optical). Often courses on electrochemical behavior of material (such as corrosion) are also required.

You study processing in courses that range from the thermodynamics of materials and the kinetic processes that govern movement of atoms and molecules, to the applied aspects of materials processing, such as sintering, casting, or vapor deposition of metals and alloys.

The desired performance of metals and alloys is governed by their properties, as well as factors such as cost, availability, and recyclability. Performance is usually incorporated into a number of courses and then emphasized in a major design project—which you probably undertake during your last year—that integrates knowledge and skills from earlier courses.

Most departments are relatively small and informal. Depending on the college, classes have from 10 to 50 students. Because metallurgical engineering depends on the application of advanced experimental techniques, you may take more lab classes than students in other engineering majors. Most majors get to know faculty members and fellow students, and many programs have student societies that help you become integrated into the profession before you graduate.

There are significant differences in emphasis among various departments across the United States. Some programs focus exclusively on metals; some include other classes of materials (ceramics, composites, and so on.). While some programs emphasize extractive processing of commodity metals, others concentrate on physical metallurgy and the application of engineering alloys. A careful examination of third- and fourth-year core and elective courses gives you a good indication of a program's emphasis.

Other majors you might like:
Materials engineering
Ceramic sciences/engineering
Chemical engineering
Electrical and communications engineering
Materials science
Chemistry
Physics
Metallurgical technology
Electrical engineering technology

Career options and trends:
Industrial metallurgist*; industrial researcher; research scientist at a university; quality control specialist; production engineer; production supervisor.

Because metallurgical and materials engineers work in all segments of the manufacturing economy, employment prospects for graduates tend to be less affected by downturns in a single industry than are some other engineering disciplines. Demand for metallurgical and materials engineers will likely be sustained by the need for fuel-efficient transportation; by advances in biomaterials, computers, and information technology; and by continued spending on national defense.

For more info:
The Minerals, Metals, and Materials Society (TMS)
184 Thorn Hill Rd.
Warrendale, PA 15086
(800) 759-4867
www.tms.org

Mining and mineral engineering

Also known as:
Natural resources engineering

What it's about:
Mining engineering is the application of scientific principles to the discovery, appraisal, and extraction of minerals from the earth and the sea. The engineer may work in underground mines or mines on the Earth's surface, overseeing the recovery of mineral resources from the natural environment; processing the extracted materials; ensuring safety; and restoring the land.

Is this for you?
You might like this major if you also like: rocks and rock collecting; fossil collecting; working outdoors rather than in an office; camping, fishing, hiking; the prospect of working with large, complex equipment.

Consider this major if you are good at: leadership; math; quantitative analysis; spacial thinking/analysis; teamwork *...or have...* initiative; patience; verbal skills; writing skills.

Recommended high school prep:
English 4, math 4 (including trigonometry, calculus or precalculus), lab science 3–4 (including chemistry and physics), social studies 3, and a foreign language 2–3. Courses in written and oral communication are also important.

Did you know...
...that according to the U.S. Bureau of Mines, for every American, every year, the equivalent of 40,000 pounds of new minerals, and energy equal to that produced by 30,000 pounds of coal, are harvested? With so much demand for extraction, mining engineers can choose to work in diverse environments, in many areas of the world. So if you're looking for a well-paid career with opportunities for advancement, then mining engineering could be a good major for you.

Typical courses in this major:
Physical geology
Structural geology
Engineering mechanics
Fluid mechanics
Thermodynamics
Ore and mineral deposits
Petrology
Mineral economics
Mining methods
Mine surveying
Mine planning and design
Ground control and rock mechanics
Rock blasting and fragmentation
Mineral or coal processing
Environmental reclamation
Mine health and safety

Concentrations:
In college: surface mining; underground mining; hard-rock mining; soft-rock (coal, phosphate, clays) mining; placer mining; quarry and industrial-minerals mining.

If you go on to grad school: rock mechanics; rock slope engineering; mine planning and design; geostatistical techniques; explosives engineering; mine health and safety; mine environment and reclamation; mine management.

What the study of this major is like:
Mining and mineral engineering is more hands-on than many other engineering fields. Like other areas of engineering, though, it is a highly technical field. These days, mining operations routinely use technologies such as global positioning, radio telemetry of data, satellite communications, computer-aided design, automation, and robotics. The equipment gets bigger and better; the industry's health and safety record continues to improve; and the productivity of miners in the United States (and, generally, worldwide) keeps increasing.

Mining engineers spend a considerable portion of their time out in the field. Accordingly, most majors consider themselves outdoorsy types. Often, students in the major started out in another science or engineering discipline. They took a summer internship at a mine operation, enjoyed the experience, and changed majors after returning to college in the fall.

Your course work generally includes math and science, basic engineering, mining engineering, geology, and the humanities and social sciences. Many courses, especially in mining and geology, are taught as a combination of lectures and laboratory experience. On the whole, though, most courses are still conducted as lectures. The greatest challenge most students encounter is to complete some of the other required engineering courses—for example, an electrical engineering course. Most programs in the United States are small, compared with better-known programs such as mechanical engineering. Therefore, students normally work in small groups with their instructors. Teamwork is emphasized; you'll get to know your colleagues and professors well.

Many of the eastern colleges offering degrees in mineral engineering specialize in coal mining, whereas western colleges tend to specialize in hard-rock mining. Graduates of eastern colleges most often find work in the coalfields of the eastern and central states, whereas their counterparts in western colleges usually find jobs in the central and western part of the country. Although some colleges have a practical orientation, a few emphasize undergrad research and the utilization of research conducted by faculty members and graduate students. Some programs have started offering specializations in areas such as quarry mining, underground construction, and management.

Other majors you might like:
Structural engineering
Geotechnical engineering
Environmental engineering
Natural resources and conservation
Mining technology
Surveying technology
Geology/earth science
Range science
Heavy/earthmoving equipment operation
Ocean engineering
Petroleum engineering
Geography

Questions to ask colleges:
Does the program specialize in a particular area of mining engineering?

Are summer internships or co-op education programs available?

Are field trips part of the curriculum, so that students can visit mines and gain real-world experience?

Career options and trends:
Mine engineer*; construction engineer*; mine manager*; environmental engineer; sales/technical representative.

In the United States, only about 125 students graduate each year with a degree in mining engineering. Recent studies have concluded that over 300 new graduates per year will be needed just to keep up with retirements. Starting salaries are expected to rise dramatically with this increase in demand.

Globalization is another trend affecting this field. Mining engineers frequently find opportunities overseas to introduce advances in technology or to assist in the development of the mining economy.

Insider's viewpoint:
"Mining engineering is as much of a lifestyle choice as a career choice."

—Professor Charles Kliche, South Dakota School of Mines and Technology

For more info:
Society for Mining, Metallurgy, and Exploration (SME)
12999 E. Adam Aircraft Circle
Englewood, CO 80112
(800) 763-3132
www.smenet.org

Nuclear engineering

Also known as:
Radiological engineering

What it's about:
Nuclear engineering focuses on the application of radioactive materials and radiation to meet many of society's needs. The generation of electricity by nuclear power plants typically receives the most attention, but other applications include nuclear medicine, space power, environmental research, and the use of radiation in industrial processes and research.

Is this for you?
You might like this major if you also like: math and science, especially physics; science fairs; science fiction; working in teams; building things.

Consider this major if you are good at: attention to detail; creativity; math; quantitative analysis; spacial thinking/analysis; teamwork ...*or have*... initiative; persistence; verbal skills; writing skills.

Recommended high school prep:
English 4, math 4 (including precalculus or calculus), lab science 3–4 (including chemistry and physics), social studies 3, and a foreign language 2–3. If available, courses in computer programming and technical writing would be valuable.

Did you know...
...that every year, two million nuclear medical procedures are performed in the United States? These procedures include cancer radiation treatments, nuclear magnetic resonance imaging (MRI), gamma knife surgery, boron neutron capture therapy, brain scans, and other applications to diagnose disease.

...that before its nuclear properties were discovered, uranium was used for coloring glass?

Typical courses in this major:
Introduction to nuclear science and engineering
Nuclear reactor theory
Nuclear fuel cycle
Radiation safety
Thermal hydraulics for nuclear plants
Radiation interactions with matter
Materials for nuclear applications
Radiation detection
Radiation shielding
Nuclear power systems
Nuclear engineering design
Engineering ethics

Concentrations:
In college: health physics; radiation protection.

If you go on to grad school: nuclear power; nuclear fusion; nuclear medicine; radioactive waste management; instrumentation and control; probabilistic safety assessment; nuclear reactor theory.

What the study of this major is like:
Nuclear engineers can work with radioactive materials and radiation in a variety of ways. Some are employed at large commercial power plants that produce electricity, while others work on smaller nuclear reactors that generate power for naval vessels, spacecraft, or equipment operating at remote locations. Some nuclear engineers focus on medical applications; others devote their efforts to radioactive waste disposal and environmental restoration of sites that have been contaminated.

As a nuclear engineering major, you will be introduced to these and other applications of radiation and radioactive materials. Primarily, though, you will learn the fundamentals that are essential for nuclear engineers preparing themselves for a number of possible careers. In your courses, more than likely, you will explore the nature of radiation and radioactive decay; naturally occurring radioactive materials; the detection of radiation; its interaction with matter (its effects on humans and other living things, as well as on materials in the power plant); the principles of radiation protection; the fuel cycle; and the environmental impact of nuclear facilities. At most colleges, courses contain some material that engineering students often consider to be soft science. But these topics (including ethics, economics, and regulation of nuclear facilities) are critical to professionals in the discipline.

Most of your courses are taught as lectures; you'll have a variety of out-of-class assignments, such as finding solutions to problems, developing or applying computer models to analyze reactors or other nuclear systems, and working on team research or design projects. Several courses have a laboratory component, in which you work with detection equipment and perhaps with a research reactor or a simulator (if your college has such equipment). Lab experiments are generally done in teams. You frequently spend one or more terms as a co-op or intern, working at a nuclear facility and learning firsthand what nuclear engineers do. Positions as co-ops, interns, or assistants on faculty research projects provide excellent opportunities to apply the theoretical material you learned.

A unique challenge students face is the public's ignorance about—and sometimes fear of—radiation, nuclear power, nuclear waste, and related topics. Professionals in this field need to educate themselves about the industry and learn to talk about it with laymen, in language they can understand. Most nuclear engineers belong to a professional organization, such as the American Nuclear Society. Nuclear engineering students are generally encouraged to begin participating in the ANS while they are still in college.

There are several areas in which nuclear engineering programs may vary among colleges. Some focus on nuclear power engineering; some focus on radiological engineering/health physics; and some include both subjects. At some colleges, the curriculum emphasizes theory, whereas others offer a good deal of practical application, including visits to nuclear facilities or hands-on lab courses. The curriculum may be geared toward students going on to graduate school, toward those who plan to work in the industry after completing a Bachelor of Science degree, or it may combine the two orientations.

Other majors you might like:
Radiation protection/health physics technology
Nuclear engineering technology
Hazardous materials technology
Applied math
Environmental engineering
Marine engineering/naval architecture
Nuclear medical technology
Nuclear power technology
Physics
Applied physics
Medical radiologic technology/radiation therapy
Radiologic technology/medical imaging

Questions to ask colleges:
What are the primary research areas of the nuclear engineering faculty members? Are undergraduate students encouraged to become involved in research?

What opportunities are available for co-op or intern positions in the nuclear industry, and what co-op and/or intern positions have recent students in the program held?

What lab facilities do undergrads have an opportunity to use?

Career options and trends:
Health physicist; radiation safety officer; nuclear reactor operator*; nuclear equipment design engineer; consulting engineer*; researcher at a national laboratory; government employee (U.S. Navy or Department of Energy)*; instrumentation design specialist; radioactive waste manager or environmental restoration specialist.

Approximately a third of the nuclear workforce is expected to retire in the next decade, and a shortage of new engineers is projected. While construction of new nuclear power is occurring primarily abroad, nuclear engineers will be needed in the U.S. to upgrade and operate existing plants. Nuclear engineers will also be needed in the areas of nuclear medicine technology, national defense, fusion research, waste management, and regulatory compliance. Salaries of nuclear engineers are among the highest for all engineers.

An exciting development in the nuclear industry is the worldwide effort to design a generation of nuclear power plants that are safer, more efficient, and more economical than existing plants. In addition to generating electricity, some of these plants are being designed to produce hydrogen to support the "hydrogen economy," desalinate water, provide industrial process heat, and burn nuclear waste.

For more info:

American Nuclear Society (ANS)
555 North Kensington Ave.
La Grange Park, IL 60526
(708) 352-6611
www.ans.org

Nuclear Energy Institute (NEI)
1201 F St., N.W.
Suite 1100
Washington, DC 20004-1218
(202) 739-8000
www.nei.org

Ocean engineering

Also known as:
Coastal engineering

What it's about:
Ocean engineers apply a variety of engineering disciplines to develop systems that operate in ocean and coastal waters. The profession includes such project areas as the construction and maintenance of facilities such as ports, harbors, and dikes; ocean drilling, dredging and salvage operations; underwater construction; and management of the ocean environment. This field should not be confused with marine engineering, which focuses primarily on the mechanics and operation of seagoing vessels.

Is this for you?
You might like this major if you also like: water sports (boating, diving, sailing, swimming, rowing, and surfing); math, science, and technology; designing and building things; the coastal and offshore environments.

Consider this major if you are good at: attention to detail; creativity; critical reading/thinking; math; quantitative analysis; research; spacial thinking/analysis; teamwork *...or have...* initiative; verbal skills.

Recommended high school prep:
English 4, math 4 (including precalculus), lab science 4 (earth science, biology, chemistry and physics), social studies 3, and a foreign language 2–3. If available, advanced or honors courses in math and physics are recommended. Since ocean engineering is, by its nature, a global discipline, facility with a foreign language can be valuable.

Typical courses in this major:
Marine structures
Coastal structures
Oceanography
Marine hydrodynamics
Mechanics of materials
Diving technology
Passive and active circuits
Fluid mechanics
Ocean measurements and instrumentation
Fundamentals of ocean mechanics
Wave mechanics and littoral (seashore) processes
Underwater acoustics
Engineering materials
Marine geomechanics
Ocean resources engineering
Nearshore environmental engineering

Concentrations:
Generally, none in college; but if you go on to grad school: ocean instrumentation and seafloor mapping; underwater acoustics; marine hydrodynamics and water wave mechanics; environmental engineering; marine geomechanics; coastal and offshore structures.

What the study of this major is like:
During your first two years as an ocean engineering major, you focus primarily on mathematics, chemistry, physics, and engineering fundamentals. You will probably take courses in calculus and analytic geometry; differential equations; statics/mechanics; electrical engineering; and engineering economics. Other general education requirements may be distributed throughout the curriculum. Electives, which will fill most of your third and fourth years, may include these:

Ocean acoustics. Sound is often the only way to sense the underwater environment or to transmit information underwater. You study the influence of water properties on sound speed and refraction; sonar systems; and sounds generated by ships and marine life.

Hydrodynamics. This field covers the behavior of water; floating and submerged objects; lift and drag forces; wave forces on beaches, vessels, and offshore platforms; and basic seakeeping.

Ocean measurements. You explore the principles of sensors, measurement, and electronics as applied to the ocean environment. You may also study seafloor mapping and underwater acoustics.

Ocean resources engineering. Here you examine systems to develop the energy, mineral, and living resources of the sea; the use of the ocean for waste disposal; and related environmental and economic issues.

Marine geomechanics. This focuses on the behavior of the seabed and sediments, dredging, cables and pipelines, and foundations for offshore and coastal structures.

Coastal engineering. Topics include ports and harbors, inlets, and barrier islands; nearshore environmental engineering; beach dynamics; flood hazards; and coastal structures such as piers.

Your fourth year will be dominated by a capstone project, in which you apply the knowledge and skills you've learned to a real-world design problem. It is usually a group project involving analysis, data collection, design, and a final presentation and report, and may also include scale-modeling, construction, and testing.

Programs are generally rigorous and comprehensive, requiring hardworking and dedicated students. Courses are typically taught as lectures, some with associated lab work and experimental projects. There is usually a great deal of fieldwork required, which most students enjoy. You may also take hands-on courses that focus on designing and building a system or structure, such as an autonomous underwater vehicle (AUV). Ocean engineering courses are sometimes supplemented by classes offered by other departments of engineering (chemical, civil, environmental, electrical, and/or mechanical), math, computer science, and grad schools of oceanography. Programs may be approved by the Accreditation Board for Engineering and Technology (ABET).

Other majors you might like:
Oceanography
Marine engineering/naval architecture
Environmental engineering
Marine biology
Marine science/Merchant Marine
Civil engineering
Water, wetlands, and marine management
Environmental science
Construction technology
Geology/earth science
Physics
Geography

Questions to ask colleges:
Are offshore or shoreline field experiences offered? What laboratory and experimental facilities are available? The extent of hands-on learning opportunities is a good indication of the strength of the program.

Career options and trends:
Coastal engineer*; civil engineer; underwater acoustician*; geotechnical engineer*; offshore engineer; marine engineer.

Job opportunities remain strong in the fields of coastal engineering; environmental engineering and pollution control; ocean instrumentation; dredging engineering; acoustics; ocean systems; and consulting. As nations increasingly rely on the oceans to meet the growing demand for resources, ocean engineers will be needed to meet these demands effectively and wisely.

For more info:
Marine Technology Society (MTS)
1100 H Street NW, Suite LL-100
Washington, DC 20005
(202) 717-8705
www.mtsociety.org

Association of Coastal Engineers
c/o Angie Gross, Executive Secretary
Erikson Consulting Engineers, Inc.
7201 Delainey Court
Sarasota, FL 34240
www.coastalengineers.org

Software engineering

What it's about:

As a software engineering major, you study the techniques used in constructing large, complex software systems. The discipline covers the analysis, specification, design, construction, testing, and maintenance of software systems. Software engineers build systems that empower users, increasing their capabilities and improving the way they work.

Is this for you?

You might like this major if you also like: solving puzzles and complex problems; abstract thinking; planning and organizing activities and events; explaining things; working in groups.

Consider this major if you are good at: attention to detail; creativity; critical reading/thinking; giving directions; logical reasoning; organizing; teamwork *...or have...* math skills; writing skills.

Recommended high school prep:

English 4, math 4 (including calculus or precalculus), lab science 3–4, social studies 3, and a foreign language 2–3. If possible, take advanced or additional classes in discrete mathematics, computer science, and writing.

Did you know...

...that software engineers don't have to be passionate, compulsive programmers? Many students who major in one of the computing fields never did computer programming in high school.

Typical courses in this major:

Fundamentals of software development
Introduction to computer science
Systems analysis
Programming language concepts
Discrete mathematics
Statistics
Software architecture and design
Software construction and evolution
Software requirements and specification
Database systems
Operating systems
Software testing and quality assurance
Software project management
Senior project/capstone experience

Concentrations:

In college: commercial applications; computer engineering; scientific computing; embedded systems.

If you go on to grad school: systems analysis; software development methodologies; software testing and quality assurance; software project management; software reengineering and evolution; user interface design; software metrics.

What the study of this major is like:

Software engineers do much more than program computers; they use their talents to help nonexperts benefit from the computer in their daily activities. They also create tools that enable computer users to work efficiently, economically, and effectively.

Most students don't realize that software engineering uses concepts from engineering, computer science, and mathematics, as well as from management, psychology, economics, politics, art, sociology, and language arts. To be successful in the discipline, you need good writing and oral presentation skills and the ability to use mathematical thinking (abstraction, logical reasoning), to work effectively in teams, and to understand computer programming. In addition, you must be able to learn new practices and procedures quickly, so that you can apply them soon after they are introduced.

In your first two years as a major, you take basic courses in computer science and math (including calculus and discrete mathematics) and other general education courses. Your last two years will focus on software engineering and related areas. Most programs have a capstone course in which you complete a software development project. The project requires you to put into practice what you have learned in previous courses, as a means of preparing you for a professional career. Courses in computer science and software engineering often involve group projects. Some courses have scheduled laboratories, but you can often do lab work at other times as well. If you delay your group project and lab assignments until just before the deadline, the result may be poor-quality work—and you will probably learn less as you play last-minute catch-up.

The earliest undergrad programs in software engineering date from the 1990s, and many colleges have not yet developed separate software engineering programs. Colleges may still offer numerous software engineering courses, however, provided by computer science, computer engineering, and/or electrical engineering programs. Software engineering, computer engineering, and computer science are not completely separate fields; they have significant amounts of overlap. Software engineering programs that are housed in electrical and computer engineering departments tend to focus on hardware issues. On the other hand, software engineering programs in departments of computer science (or math and computer science) tend to emphasize software, and their orientation is likely to be theoretical and mathematical.

As you study college catalogs, be aware that similarly named programs may actually contain different content—and programs with different names may, in fact, be very similar. Variation is to be expected in a field as new as software engineering.

Other majors you might like:
Computer science
Computer engineering
Digital media
Electrical and communications engineering
Management information systems
Game design
Animation
Artificial intelligence/robotics
E-commerce
Computer engineering technology
Bioinformatics
Applied mathematics

Questions to ask colleges:
What is the nature of the capstone course? What kinds of projects have been done in the past?

How good is the campus computer network? Are appropriate software tools available for software engineering students?

Do faculty members have experience building large software systems?

Are there any opportunities for summer internships or co-op work experiences? Are there opportunities for students to use their technical skills in campus jobs?

Career options and trends:
Software engineer*; software developer*; software or systems analyst*; senior programmer; systems programmer; database administrator.

Jobs in all computing fields are increasing at a good clip even during tough economic times. Software engineering opportunities are projected to be excellent, especially for those interested in cybersecurity and security software.

There is an important warning about entry-level jobs in computing fields: change in the computer industry is constant and rapid. A job you may want to prepare for as you begin college will probably be completely different by the time you graduate. Therefore, computer majors must be prepared for a life of constant learning.

For more info:
Association of Computing Machinery (ACM)
2 Penn Plaza
Suite 701
New York, NY 10121-0701
(800) 342-6626
www.acm.org

Institute of Electrical and Electronics Engineers
    Computer Society (IEEE-CS)
2001 L Street, N.W.
Suite 700
Washington, DC 20036-4928
(202) 371-0101
www.computer.org

Engineering technology

What's the difference between engineering (covered in the previous section) and engineering technology? To begin with, engineering programs always lead to bachelor's degrees and, often, graduate degrees. Engineering technology programs can lead to either an associate degree or a bachelor's degree (currently, most students earn associate degrees). Second, engineering is more theoretical and employs higher-level math and physics, to prepare you for a career in product design or systems research. Engineering technology gives you more practical experience with the installation, maintenance, and operation of components and instruments.

Let's look at a specific example from this section: telecommunications technology. "While engineering programs typically prepare you for equipment design, graduate school and research, telecommunications technology programs are usually oriented toward using existing equipment for system and network design," explains Professor Pierre Catala of Texas A&M University. "Telecom engineering technicians maintain all the networks and sophisticated gear that make the World Wide Web, satellite and space probe transmissions, and e-commerce possible."

In this case, the associate degree (technician) programs in engineering technology usually deal with the testing, operation, initial software configuration, and maintenance of telecommunications equipment. Bachelor's degree (technologist) programs in engineering technology expand into design, implementation, configuration, and management of telecommunications networks.

"Engineering technologists bridge the gap between technicians and engineers with an understanding of both operations and design," says Thomas M. Hall, Jr. a professor at Northwestern State University. "Engineering technology graduates solve the problems of today, while research engineers solve the problems of tomorrow."

Mechanical engineering technologists are another example. "Now that mechanical engineering technology and other branches of engineering technology are offered as four-year Bachelor of Science programs, the industry has begun to accept engineering technology graduates as full engineers," suggests Professor James Kamm, University of Toledo.

The same level of application-related education and training goes into other engineering technologies—computer, electrical, construction, drafting, and surveying.

"Electrical engineering technology programs apply math and science to the real world," Hall says of his specialty.

With these majors, you can make an immediate impact working in manufacturing, field service, systems engineering, and applied design. Jobs include technicians, salespeople, network administrators, support specialists, drafters, designers, computer-aided design (CAD) operators, project managers, field supervisors, and inspectors.

The employment outlook depends on the specific industry. For instance, jobs continue to be generated in the computer and software industries, while signals are mixed as to how jobs will fare in the manufacturing and construction sectors. Infrastructure projects should create job opportunities for all types of engineering technologists over the long term.

A bachelor's degree in one of the engineering technologies improves your chances. So do professional licenses and certifications.

Design for learning

If you choose one of these college majors, you won't have your nose in a book all day. "The hallmark of any engineering technology program is the extensive laboratory experience," says Hall. In addition to labs and class, some colleges offer field experience, and cooperative educational (co-op) programs, in which you combine your academic studies with on-the-job training.

When comparing colleges, get a feel for how much they stress fundamentals compared to the latest gizmos. You want to learn the state-of-the-art technology, but you'll also need to know the principles, because technologies are changing. The newest tracks include wireless communications, 3-D modeling and animation, geographic information systems, and environmental and energy management technologies.

Think about whether you're going for a two-year associate degree or a four-year bachelor's degree. The associate degree is for technical training, current technologies and hands-on, nuts-and-bolts preparation for an entry-level job. A bachelor's degree in engineering technology, like an engineering degree, means more math and science, to help you analyze complex problems. Some programs also delve into the business or management side. The B.S. degree can be a launching pad to graduate work in geomatics (three-dimensional computerized mapping), engineering economics, network engineering, and management information systems.

Here are some things to think about or to ask people: What is the college's philosophy and approach? Does the college see its role as preparing talent for local industry? If so, which companies are they and what kind of jobs are likely? What is the background of some of the professors? If they're from industry, the courses will probably be more practical; if the faculty members have academic backgrounds, the courses will be more theoretical and scientific.

Ask if the program is approved by the leading commission in the field, like the Accreditation Board for Engineering and Technology (www.abet.org) for some specialties. How large are the lab classes and what type of equipment is used? Is it the kind used in industry? Is the program equipped to teach how computers interface with engineering technology? What is the seating capacity of the lab facilities?

In most other majors, you want to know the ratio of students to faculty members, but in these majors you may also want to ask about the ratio of students to computers.

Computer engineering technology

What it's about:

The computer engineering technology major will prepare you for a career in a number of fields: computer networking, telecommunications, computer electronics, programming, wireless and data communications and networks, embedded system design, and robotics. Offered at both the associate and bachelor's degree levels, this major is designed to meet the needs of technically inclined students who prefer hands-on teaching and learning to the more theoretical, mathematics-oriented computer science and engineering disciplines.

Is this for you?

You might like this major if you also like: working and playing with computer hardware and software; electronics; math and science; figuring out why things work the way they do; mathematical and logical puzzles; solving complex problems.

Consider this major if you are good at: attention to detail; critical reading/thinking; math; memorizing; organizing; quantitative analysis; teamwork *...or have...* initiative; patience.

Recommended high school prep:

English 4, math 3–4, lab science 3 (including physics), social studies 3, and a foreign language 2–3. Precalculus, computer-aided design (CAD), and other computer programming and applications courses are also recommended, although not required.

Typical courses in this major:

Basic electricity and electronics
Digital systems and microprocessors
Object-oriented software development
Programming fundamentals I, II
Operating systems
Digital/communications
Computer architecture
Assembly language applications
Electronics computer-aided design
Data structures and file processing
Digital testing techniques
Wide-area networking
Local-area networking
Systems administration
Technical writing and communications

Concentrations:

Local-area and wide-area networking (LAN/WAN); systems administration; communications systems; microprocessors; programming languages; software engineering; hardware engineering; industrial automation systems; robotics.

What the study of this major is like:

This major provides you with practical training and skills in courses covering hardware and software, electronics, programming, and supporting topics. Most programs in computer engineering technology focus on both the hardware and the software aspects of the applications, including the interfacing of computers and systems; in contrast, most electrical engineering technology programs concentrate primarily on hardware and secondarily on related software.

Hands-on training in applications and equipment is the primary teaching method, but you'll also learn theoretical aspects to help you adapt to new technology in the future. You begin with the basics of electricity and electronics, including analog and digital circuit analysis. Then you'll be introduced to the fundamentals of microprocessors and operating systems; programming; and applications that use word processors, spreadsheets, and high-level and low-level computer languages.

Other required courses zero in on mathematical and communication skills, and you'll learn enough about the industrial and business environment to perform effectively on the job. In labs, you work on a variety of microprocessor systems and devices, as you gain experience in installing, diagnosing, operating, and servicing computer systems and related equipment.

Upper-level courses, in which you get an in-depth look at the hardware and software used in industry and business, are usually wide ranging enough to allow for specialization. Topics include networking technology and security; advanced programming; digital testing technology; data communications; hardware description languages; embedded system design; industrial instrumentation; and industrial automation systems.

Because many areas of computer application are important in industry and business, colleges vary in the aspects of the major that they emphasize. For instance, some programs may focus on computer-use topics such as programming, Internet technology, and database systems, while others may stress technical applications such as industrial networking, Web-based control, electronic devices, Web services, and other aspects of enterprise networking.

Two-year associate degree programs are more likely to focus on specific occupations or systems than are programs designed for a four-year bachelor's degree. In bachelor's programs, you'll study more math (in particular, differential equations, sets and logic, and calculus), alongside courses in the humanities and sciences. Coupled with business electives, a four-year degree will generally increase your employment options. Many students begin in the less-costly two-year program and then transfer into the last two years of a bachelor's program, usually with enough job skills to work as they continue their education.

In computer engineering technology, lifelong learning really counts—you have no choice but to continue your education if you want to remain employable. Technological advances come so rapidly that even people with good jobs have to keep their skills up-to-date. After all, employers are often looking to put the latest technologies to profitable use. Continuing education opportunities are plentiful, however, and many employers will help you take advantage of them.

Other majors you might like:
Game design
Software engineering
Digital media
Electrical and communications engineering
Management information systems
Health information management
Computational mathematics
Robotics technology

E-commerce
Information technology
Recording arts
Applied mathematics

Questions to ask colleges:
How often are the lab facilities upgraded with the latest hardware and software? Be sure that the new equipment includes various operating systems in the Microsoft, Apple, and Unix/Linux categories.

Is the program approved by the Technology Accreditation Commission of the Accreditation Board for Engineering and Technology (TAC/ABET)?

Are co-op education and internships available? If so, take advantage of them. Real-world experience will greatly enhance your employment opportunities.

How successful have graduates been in getting jobs in the specialty areas emphasized by the college?

Career options and trends:
Systems analyst; consulting engineer*; network administrator*; database administrator; systems administrator; software engineer (applications or systems); support specialist*.

Certification in a particular application, program language (such as JAVA), or system (Linux) may be of value to employers using them. Some vendors and software firms may require certification if you will be working with their products.

The job titles listed above are among the fastest-growing careers, according to the U.S. Bureau of Labor Statistics, which also projects computer and data processing services to be the most rapidly growing industry in the economy. The employment outlook is favorable for graduates who can set up and maintain computer networks, information and Internet technology, and computer-based electronic systems.

However, computer support, like many technical fields, is becoming increasingly competitive internationally. As a result of the expanding knowledge economy, countries in Eastern Europe and Asia are producing labor pools of relatively low-cost, highly trained computer specialists; and some computer support positions are being outsourced overseas.

But don't let that spook you—job creation is outpacing job destruction in this field, and you can prepare yourself for the competition by obtaining a broad-based education, developing interpersonal and business skills, and remaining alert to the areas of greatest demand, such as e-commerce and communications security.

For more info:

Institute of Electrical and Electronics Engineers
  (IEEE)
3 Park Avenue, 17th Fl.
New York, NY 10016-5997
(212) 752-4929
www.ieee.org

Association for Computer Machinery (ACM)
2 Penn Plaza
Suite 701
New York, NY 10121-0701
(800) 342-6626
www.acm.org

Construction technology

What it's about:

The construction technology major provides practical training and broad-based education in general, structural, and construction engineering principles; in planning and design; and in construction management.

Is this for you?

You might like this major if you also like: working in groups or teams; working with your hands; carpentry; the outdoors; achieving goals and results; watching construction sites.

Consider this major if you are good at: attention to detail; coaching; critical reading/thinking; leadership; math; organizing; persuading/influencing; spacial thinking/analysis; teamwork *...or have...* initiative.

Recommended high school prep:

English 4, math 3 (including trigonometry), lab science 3 (including physics and chemistry), social studies 3, industrial arts 2, and a foreign language 2. If they are available, take courses in computer-aided drafting (CAD) or mechanical drawing.

Did you know...

...that the construction industry is the second-largest employer in the United States, after the federal government?

Typical courses in this major:

Planning and scheduling
Safety, security, and environmental impact
Blueprint reading
Site surveying, planning, and design
Cost estimating
Architecture and urban form
Construction practices and methods
Computer-integrated construction (CIC)
Electrical systems
Groundwater hydrology
Soils and foundations
Construction materials and systems
Reinforced concrete design
Materials handling
Structural steel design
Technical report writing

Concentrations:

Structural design; construction management; construction engineering.

What the study of this major is like:

This major will provide you with a breadth of training, from management to carpentry, business law to asphalt paving. While the particular emphasis may vary, all programs feature hands-on, practical learning experiences in labs or in the field, in conjunction with classroom lectures.

You are encouraged to apply your skills through cooperative (co-op) experiences and independent studies. Most lecture classes use demonstrations and video aids, and in the labs you are introduced to construction methods and problems, which you work on either through simulations or with actual materials and equipment. Concepts and training come together in field experiences on construction sites.

Construction technology is usually taught in one of two ways. In one, the program follows the traditional engineering track: you apply mathematical theorics and equations to explain abstract engineering principles. Courses cover such topics as statics, applied thermodynamics, and fluid mechanics. The other method is to pattern the curriculum after business management courses, with emphasis on lectures, reading, and case studies. Programs feature course content in contract management, plans and specifications, estimation of costs, building codes, labor relations, team dynamics, project management, and environmental and land-use concerns. In programs that are geared toward construction management, most students earn a four-year Bachelor of Science degree.

Either approach will give you sufficient technical training to be familiar with the methods used in residential, commercial, industrial, and public-works construction. Architectural drafting and computer-aided design (CAD), blueprint reading, and the basics of surveying are also likely to be core requirements.

In a two-year associate degree program, which focuses on the technical aspects of construction, you will study the basics of structural design, construction methods and practices, and project management. Bachelor's degree programs include courses in mathematics, natural sciences, business, humanities, social sciences, and written and oral communications. In upper-level course work, you concentrate on advanced engineering, design, and management principles.

A valuable part of a strong construction technology program is co-op educational experience: you combine your academic studies with paid, on-the-job training, either during regular semesters or over the summer. Independent study opportunities—which are often available through student chapters of professional organizations such as the Associated Builders and Contractors, the Associated General Contractors of America, and the National Society of Professional Engineers—are another way to supplement your classroom and lab training.

Other majors you might like:
Civil engineering
Construction management
Structural engineering
Architectural engineering technology
Drafting and design technology
Historic preservation
Housing and human environments
Surveying technology
Heating/air conditioning/refrigeration technology
Heavy/earthmoving equipment operation
Parks, recreation, and leisure studies
Theater design and technology

Questions to ask colleges:
Do the lab facilities have enough computers and construction equipment to offer adequate training in the wide range of problems this program explores, such as soil analysis, materials testing, CAD, surveying?

Is the program approved by the Technology Accreditation Commission of the Accreditation Board for Engineering and Technology (TAC/ABET)?

Career options and trends:
Field engineer; job expeditor; project manager; field supervisor; site inspector; scheduler; contract administrator; estimator; designer.

Employment opportunities are expected to recover in the construction industry, because of a shortage of professionals who can handle the increasing complexity of projects, technology, and regulatory standards, and because of the need to replace much of the country's aging infrastructure. Job prospects will be best for graduates with a bachelor's degree and previous construction work experience.

For more info:
Associated Builders and Contractors (ABC)
4250 N. Fairfax Drive, 9th Fl.
Arlington, VA 22203
(703) 812-2000
www.abc.org

National Association of Women in Construction (NAWIC)
327 South Adams St.
Fort Worth, TX 76104
(800) 552-3506
www.nawic.org

Drafting and design technology

Also known as:
Computer Aided Drafting and Design (CADD)
Technical drawing and design

What it's about:
The major in drafting and design technology, which can lead to either an associate degree or a bachelor's degree, prepares you for a career in industry or in another design-related field. You learn how to make drawings, plans, and computer-aided drafting (CAD) models and simulations that will be used in constructing a building, manufacturing a product, or developing a creative project such as marketing materials.

Is this for you?
You might like this major if you also like: learning new tricks on the computer; being precise; working independently as well as in groups; contributing to large projects; drawing; making models; planning how things fit together.

Consider this major if you are good at: attention to detail; concentrating; creativity; critical reading/ thinking; math; organizing; spacial thinking/analysis ...*or have...* manual dexterity; patience.

Recommended high school prep:
English 4, math 3, lab science 3 (including physics), social studies 3, industrial arts 2, and a foreign language 2–3. If they are available, take courses in computer-aided drafting or mechanical drawing, computer applications, and a fine arts drawing class.

Did you know...
...that in this major, you learn another language—a graphic language? Known as the "the language of industry," drafting is a universal method of communication that is understood by technicians, engineers, designers, and architects all over the world.

Typical courses in this major:
Blueprint reading
Technical drawing
Computer-aided drafting (CAD) I, II
Engineering design graphics
Construction materials
Manufacturing processes
Solid modeling
Machine drafting
Architectural drafting
Business and technical writing
Geometric dimensioning and tolerancing
Descriptive geometry
Building codes
Architectural delineation
Electromechanical design
Product design

Concentrations:
Product design; architectural drafting.

What the study of this major is like:
Drafters and designers are important links between great ideas and actual products, buildings, processes, or services. As a drafting and design technology major, you study idea generation and sketching, product specification, working and assembly drawings, product realization and construction, and manufacturing processes and materials.

Few disciplines have been changed more by computers than drafting and design. You may be taught basic drafting on the drawing board, but you will certainly be trained to use computer-aided-drafting software and solid modeling software. "CAD" no longer refers just to drawing—it is now the first step in the programming of automated production equipment. Also, CAD is the principal ingredient in the trend away from making prototypes of products the old-fashioned way, by hand. More and more engineers are creating prototypes on modeling software and then testing them through computer simulation.

In most drafting and design courses the instructor will introduce a concept through a lecture and demonstration; then students complete an assignment to reinforce the concept. In a final project, you will show what you've learned: you'll develop an idea of your own choosing into a usable design. Your project and other work may be included in a portfolio that will be helpful during your job search.

What are the challenges? The ability to see an object in three dimensions is a skill that most majors must learn—it rarely comes naturally. Majors who are not familiar with computers may also have difficulty mastering CAD software while also learning the basics of computer operating systems.

The major is usually offered at two-year technical and community colleges. Programs may have different philosophies, requirements, and emphases. Philosophically, they may differ in the importance they place on teaching the fundamentals versus introducing students to the latest technology. Some colleges emphasize a theoretical, scientific orientation, while others focus on the "nuts and bolts" essentials that are needed for real-world jobs. Finally, programs may differ in the emphasis they place on certain industries. Community colleges in particular often reflect the local industries they serve. This emphasis can be seen in the types of courses and CAD software the program offers.

Other majors you might like:
Graphic design
Architectural technology
Surveying technology
Architectural engineering technology
Mechanical engineering technology
Industrial design
Medical illustrating
Digital media
Animation
Cartography
Computer science
Geology/earth science

Questions to ask colleges:
What types of computer software and hardware are used in the courses? Are they up-to-date? Is the software widely used in key industries? Is it used in the industry or geographic location you are considering?

What is the seating capacity of the lab facilities? Are the computers connected to a campus network? Are open labs available for homework and projects? What is the student-to-computer ratio?

Career options and trends:
CAD operator*; drafter or designer*; engineering technician; design engineer; CAD systems manager; technical illustrator.

Engineering positions such as design engineer usually require a four-year degree, although some designers earn these positions through progressive work experience.

The job outlook for drafting technicians is generally good. While the manufacturing base is declining, the number of industries and fields using CAD is expanding; as is the use of technical drawings and models in the production process. CAD modeling is also being used for product packaging and marketing activities.

Students who gain a strong understanding of the fundamentals and then keep up-to-date with the latest technology will be most likely to advance in their careers. But CADD systems are becoming more powerful and easier to use, making it easier for basic tasks to be handled by other workers or outsourced. This will reduce demand for lesser skilled drafters.

Insider's viewpoint:
"Drafting is a great field because of the opportunities it offers my students. What other field allows you to complete a degree or certificate program in two years or less, get a good-paying job, and continue your education while being paid for the valuable experience you are gaining?"

—Professor Paul Clarke, MiraCosta College

For more info:
American Design and Drafting Association (ADDA)
105 East Main St.
Newbern, TN 38059
(731) 627-0802
www.adda.org

Electrical engineering technology

Also known as:
Electrical and computer engineering technology

What it's about:
This major gives you practical training in a wide-ranging field of electrical engineering, including electronics, computers, communications, automatic controls, robotics, instrumentation, power systems, and computer-aided design (CAD). At the associate degree level, the focus is on operation, repair, and maintenance. At the bachelor's degree level, you also study the analysis, design, and development of electrical and electronic devices, systems, and processes.

Is this for you?
You might like this major if you also like: anything that involves math, science, electronics, and computers; tinkering and kit building; figuring out why things work the way they do.

Consider this major if you are good at: attention to detail; critical reading/thinking; math; organizing; quantitative analysis; spacial thinking/analysis; teamwork ...*or have...* initiative; patience.

Recommended high school prep:
English 4, math 3–4, lab science 3 (including physics), social studies 3, and a foreign language 2–3. Precalculus, calculus, computer-aided drafting, and other computer programming and applications courses are also recommended, although they are not required.

Did you know...
...that employers often prefer to hire engineering technologists rather than traditional engineers for positions in manufacturing, field service, systems engineering, and applied design? That's because engineering technologists combine an understanding of theory and design with hands-on operational experience.

Typical courses in this major:
Fundamentals of electricity
Control systems
Statics
Analog and digital electronics
Electronic system drafting (CAD)
Telecommunications systems
Electrical power and machines
Project management
Optical technology
Laser technology
Robotics
Data communications and computer networks
Technical writing
Transmission networks
Industrial electronics
Capstone project

Concentrations:
Electronics; electrical power and machinery; digital systems; computers and microprocessor systems; instrumentation; automation and control systems; telecommunications; information technology; electrical computer-aided drafting (CAD).

What the study of this major is like:
Students in electrical engineering technology (EET) programs like to build things, fix things, and make things work—or make them work better. They like to get their hands on the systems and the lab equipment. EET programs provide exactly that experience for you. The hallmark of any engineering technology program is the extensive laboratory experience—and EET is no exception.

EET programs apply math and science to the real world. Technical courses usually begin in your first year, along with general education courses in math, science, and the humanities. Sometimes students are surprised, and challenged, by the nontechnical course requirements; but employers expect EET graduates to acquire more than technical savvy. To prepare for a good job, you'll need to sharpen your skills in oral and written communication, teamwork, and project management; develop professional, ethical, and social responsibility; and be aware of contemporary issues.

In a bachelor's program, you are introduced to design concepts; and some courses stress calculus applications. Your first two years will lay a foundation in mathematics, chemistry, physics, and computer applications. In the third and fourth years, courses take an in-depth, technical approach and allow for specialization. You use software programs to simulate and design electrical systems and circuits, and to analyze complex problems.

Two-year associate degree programs provide technical training in circuit analysis, electronics, digital logic, microprocessors, communications, and control systems, with an emphasis on specific applications. The goal is to prepare you for entry-level employment as a technician.

The best students in EET programs learn, work, and play together. Often, student chapters of professional organizations, such as the Institute of Electrical and Electronics Engineers (IEEE) and the Instrumentation, Systems and Automation Society (ISA), offer a variety of programs and opportunities for students.

The field of EET is very broad. Typically, colleges with EET programs design a curriculum that is appropriate for both graduates and employers in the region. While all programs may touch on a range of topics, many emphasize one or more areas, such as robotics or industrial automated systems. In these areas of concentration, you get in-depth training and develop expertise; but be sure, when you are selecting a college, that its program matches your own interests.

Programs at various colleges can differ in other ways as well. Some rely heavily on the traditional classroom and laboratory settings; others make extensive use of field experience, co-op programs, or internships. In most programs, you will study with faculty members who have broad industrial experience. But in colleges that concentrate on theory and design, faculty members tend to have academic backgrounds.

Other majors you might like:
Computer engineering technology
Robotics technology
Applied mathematics
Telecommunications technology
Instrumentation technology

Electrocardiograph technology
Information technology
Laser/optical technology
Electrical drafting/CAD/CADD
Electrician
Avionics maintenance/technology
Radio and television

Questions to ask colleges:
Is the program approved by the Accreditation Board for Engineering and Technology (ABET)?

Does the program emphasize any particular areas within the broad field of EET?

Career options and trends:
Electrical/electronic technician; electrical engineering technologist; field service technician; systems technologist; communications engineer; design engineer; manufacturing process technologist; technical assistant; technical salesperson; technical writer.

According to the U.S. Bureau of Labor Statistics, employment for electrical engineering technologists is expected to grow at a moderate rate for the near future; job increases will be fueled by a demand for more sophisticated electrical and electronic products, controls, and processes. The decline in traditional manufacturing industries will be offset by increased demand for technicians in the computer systems design services industry, as computer and electronics systems become more integrated.

For more info:
Institute of Electrical and Electronics Engineers
 (IEEE)
3 Park Avenue, 17th Fl.
New York, NY 10016-5997
(212) 752-4929
www.ieee.org

Mechanical engineering technology

What it's about:

As a major in mechanical engineering technology, you will learn to apply engineering principles and technical skills to the design and development of a wide variety of projects involving mechanical systems and the products that they create.

Is this for you?

You might like this major if you also like: achieving practical results; working on something different every day; math and science.

Consider this major if you are good at: attention to detail; creativity; critical reading/thinking; math; quantitative analysis; spacial thinking/analysis *...or have...* initiative; patience; writing skills.

Recommended high school prep:

English 4, math 3, lab science 3 (including physics), social studies 3, and a foreign language 2–3. Your math classes should cover algebra and precalculus, and a class in computer-aided drafting or mechanical drawing would also be helpful.

Did you know...

...that math skills, rather than mechanical ability, are the most important indicator of success in this major? While high school calculus is not required, algebra and geometry are essential.

Typical courses in this major:

Fundamentals of mechanics
Computer-aided design (CAD)
Statics
Strength of materials
Thermodynamics
Fluid mechanics
Electrical circuits
Electromechanical control systems
Heating, ventilation, and air conditioning systems
Manufacturing processes
Stress and vibration analysis
Dynamics of systems
Machine design
Technical communications
Mechanical measurement and devices
Quality control systems

Concentrations:

In college: computer-aided design (CAD); thermodynamics; fluid mechanics; control systems; computer-controlled automation; materials science; machine design.

If you go on to grad school: engineering management; engineering economics.

What the study of this major is like:

Many people believe, incorrectly, that students who major in mechanical engineering technology must be amateur mechanics who love to work on, or under, cars. Although some majors do become automotive engineers or technicians, many others find good jobs as energy conservation engineers, plant managers, technical sales representatives, technical writers, robotics experts, and designers of alternative energy systems.

What's more, mechanical engineering technicians (METs) are no longer thought of simply as workers who simply assist mechanical engineers. Now that mechanical engineering technology and other branches of engineering technology are offered as four-year Bachelor's of Science programs, the industry has begun to accept graduates as full engineers. In fact, METs and mechanical engineers (MEs) often compete for the same jobs. Although MEs are more likely to get the jobs requiring a strong science background (for example, working with NASA or other research facilities), METs and MEs are usually considered equally qualified for a wide variety of jobs. There is even a procedure for METs to become registered as Professional Engineers (PEs).

The biggest difference between MEs and METs is in their education. MEs take more courses that require abstract thinking and heavy calculus loads; METs, on the other hand, take mostly applied, or practical, courses, with less calculus. At the undergraduate level, MEs prepare themselves for graduate school and employment as researchers, while METs are trained to get an engineering job—their only graduate school possibilities are in management or business. But the skills in design, application, and troubleshooting that METs and other engineering technology majors learn provide a significant career boost.

The mechanical engineering technology curriculum is diverse. You begin with physics; in your examination of machines, you'll observe the forces that are applied to mechanical devices and the forces that they generate. You'll learn, too, how engineers predict the way these forces are transmitted, multiplied, and/or reduced. You'll also study fluid mechanics: some machine systems rely on fluids to transmit either power or control. On the other hand, some fluid systems depend on machines, such as pumps, to distribute liquids (think of soup on an assembly line being poured into cans). In your class on thermodynamics, the science of heat, you'll concentrate on energy—how to make it work, how to use it more efficiently, how to find it in unexpected places (the sources of alternative energies). You study heat in automobile engines as well as in electric power plants. You also learn graphic arts by taking courses in computer-aided design (CAD) in both two- and three-dimensional formats.

Two-thirds of your courses deal primarily with problem solving—in the type of problem solving that engineers call "design," you'll use equations to determine important properties of a situation. For this work, you'll need a solid understanding of mathematics (including some calculus applications), as well as good critical-thinking skills, so that you can apply the math logically. You also take courses that develop your mechanical skills, usually by doing laboratory activities. Because, in some cases, laboratories simulate work environments, you'll have the chance to become familiar with instruments and equipment used in industry. Some equipment is based on cutting-edge technology, but most of the equipment in engineering labs is traditional, even timeless, such as pressure gauges, thermometers, material testers, and machine tools (metal cutting machines). Most programs end with a senior capstone design project.

Other majors you might like:
Biomedical technology
Robotics technology

Industrial technology
Aeronautical/aerospace engineering technology
Automotive engineering technology
Agricultural equipment technology
Drafting and design technology
Heavy equipment maintenance
Machine tool technology
Manufacturing technologies
Technical and business writing

Questions to ask colleges:
Is the program approved by the Accreditation Board for Engineering Technology (ABET)? If so, it will probably require an advanced level of calculus and have advanced courses that focus on abstract engineering, rather than on specific types of jobs in industry.

Career options and trends:
Plant manager; consulting engineer; manufacturing engineer; design engineer; sales engineer.

Consulting engineers typically are certified as Professional Engineers (PEs) by the state they work in. When you know where you'll be working, you should find out how a graduate of an engineering technology program becomes a PE in that state, since rules may differ from state to state.

Mechanical engineers and technicians are typically the most sought after of all the engineering disciplines, and entry-level salaries are good. Many graduates begin their careers performing CAD functions. Once they learn the product or service, they take on more responsibility for its actual design. Employment opportunities follow the national economy; sometimes jobs are more difficult to find or starting salaries are lower than normal, but graduates can almost always find a job. The two growing fields for mechanical engineering technicians are remanufacturing and alternative energy.

Insider's viewpoint:
"A career in mechanical engineering technology is full of options—it allows you to go to the community of your choice, anywhere in the United States, anywhere in the world, and find a good-paying and respected job; and it allows you to choose whether you want to travel or work a 9-to-5 job, carry tools or carry a laptop, or spend your days dealing with dozens of people or work in solitude in your own office."

—Professor James Kamm, University of Toledo

For more info:

American Society of Mechanical Engineers (ASME)
2 Park Ave.
New York, NY 10016-5990
(800) 843-2763
www.asme.org

Surveying technology

Also known as:
Geomatics engineering

What it's about:
Using specialized equipment and techniques, surveying technology majors learn how to measure the physical features of the earth. You gather data to determine land boundaries, locate existing and proposed engineering structures, make topographic maps of the earth's surface, and perform computations and computer-assisted drafting.

Is this for you?
You might like this major if you also like: drafting; drawing; working outdoors; geography and maps; solving practical problems; working with precision and detail.

Consider this major if you are good at: attention to detail; math; organizing; research; spacial thinking/ analysis; teamwork *...or have...* communication skills; initiative; manual dexterity; physical stamina.

Recommended high school prep:
English 4, math 3, lab science 3 (including physics), social studies 3, and a foreign language 2–3. Math courses should cover algebra, geometry, trigonometry, and perhaps precalculus. If possible, also take courses in drafting and computer science or computer applications.

Did you know...
...that surveyors can map in three dimensions? They use the computerized technology known as geomatics, which processes information received from satellites and from sensors and imaging systems in the air, sea, and ground. Geomatic surveying is important for the building and monitoring of large engineering projects.

Typical courses in this major:
Calculus and analytic geometry
Basic statistics
Physics
Surveying fundamentals
Advanced surveying
Engineering and construction surveying
Measurement error analysis and adjustment
Geodetic datums and coordinate systems
Photogrammetry
Land information systems
Real estate law
Boundary surveying principles
Technical writing
Soil mechanics
Statics and strength of materials
Hydrology and drainage

Concentrations:
In college: geodetic (large-area) surveying; mine surveying; hydrographic surveying; cartography; photogrammetry (aerial surveying); geographic information science.

If you go on to grad school: geomatics (three-dimensional computerized mapping); geodesy; remote sensing.

What the study of this major is like:
In this major, you study the technologies used in making accurate measurements on earth. These measurements include distances, directions, and elevations that can be calculated directly or indirectly with optical or electromechanical instruments. The most recognizable device is the tripod-mounted *theodolite*, which measures horizontal and vertical angles. You will also learn to gather measurements by using tools such as aerial photographs, global positioning system (GPS) satellites, geographic information systems (GIS), and satellite remote sensing imagery. In addition to taking measurements, you'll acquire skills in analyzing the information you collect and in making conclusions and recommendations.

Courses are laboratory-oriented. In outdoor lab work, you explore different surveying techniques and gain practice in using the equipment. In indoor labs, you use specialized software to do survey computations and related drafting. Because most survey technology programs have small enrollments, students often become a closely knit group whose members help each other. In most schools, organizations representing students in the major are affiliated with state or national professional surveying organizations.

This major is offered at either the associate (two-year) or the bachelor's (four-year) degree level, depending on the college. Many programs prepare students to obtain state licensure for professional practice. These programs usually consist of courses on boundary determination, land development, and related state and federal statutes. Programs at some colleges may emphasize engineering and construction surveying, while other programs may stress mapping and the management of geographic information. Although a bachelor's degree from any accredited surveying technology program will make you eligible to apply to graduate school, an undergraduate program that gives you a strong grounding in math may better prepare you for graduate studies.

After graduation, your work location and responsibilities may change as you progress in your career. Early on, you will probably work mostly outdoors, performing different types of surveys. Senior surveyors usually become partners in surveying/engineering companies and hold management positions.

There are several career tracks open to you, in addition to assisting professional surveyors as a technician. *Photogrammetrists* prepare detailed maps of remote or inaccessible areas, using aerial photographs and other imaging systems. *Geodetic surveyors* measure large areas of the earth's surface, using technology such as satellite remote sensing. *Geophysical surveyors* map prospecting sites for subsurface exploration. *Hydrographic surveyors* survey harbors, rivers, and other bodies of water to determine depths, shorelines, bottom topography, and other nautical features.

In most states, to become a professional land surveyor, you must have a license or registration. Requirements vary but generally include the completion of a two-part examination, conducted by the National Committee of Examiners for Engineering and Surveying, and a period of apprenticeship. An increasing number of states also require a bachelor's degree. Licensure is not required unless your practice includes work related to property boundaries. Certification as a survey technician is available through national professional societies.

Other majors you might like:
Cartography
Civil engineering
Drafting and design technology
Real estate
Forest engineering
Landscape architecture
Geology/earth science
Geography
Construction management
Land use planning
Mining and mineral engineering
Instrumentation technology

Questions to ask colleges:
Does the program offer an associate degree, a bachelor's degree, or both?

Is the program accredited? Most programs in this major are approved under one of three commissions of the Accreditation Board for Engineering and Technology (ABET): the Engineering Accreditation Commission, the Applied Science Accreditation Commission, or the Technology Accreditation Commission.

What surveying equipment is available for laboratory work? Are students trained in the latest surveying technologies?

Are the students required to purchase any supplies other than textbooks?

Career options and trends:
Surveying technician*; drafting technician; photogrammetric technician; professional land surveyor*; GIS manager; consultant.

Job growth for surveying technicians is projected to continue through 2022, according to the Bureau of Labor Statistics. Opportunities will be greatest for those who have a bachelor's degree and proficiency in advanced technologies such as GPS and GIS. Renewed growth in construction, which is also projected for the long term, should create demand for surveyors to lay out projects and to define areas in need of environmental protection.

Telecommunications technology

What it's about:

In the telecommunications technology major, students are trained in the installation, management, operation, and maintenance of telecommunications equipment and systems, such as those used in telephone, data, Internet, and wireless networks. Graduates of associate degree (technician) programs typically handle the testing, operation, initial software configuration, and maintenance of telecommunications equipment. Bachelor's degree (technologist) programs, in contrast, prepare you to design, implement, configure, and manage telecommunications networks.

Is this for you?

You might like this major if you also like: amateur or ham radio; working and playing with computers; connecting systems (computers, home entertainment systems); electronics.

Consider this major if you are good at: attention to detail; creativity; critical reading/thinking; math; memorizing; organizing; teamwork...*or have...* initiative; patience; verbal skills; writing skills.

Recommended high school prep:

English 4, math 3–4 (trigonometry and precalculus), lab science 3, social studies 3, and a foreign language 2–3. If they are available, take courses in computer office applications (word processing, spreadsheets, and databases) and introductory computer programming.

Did you know...

...that telecommunications covers a lot more than just communicating by phone, cell, or instant messaging? Telecom engineering technicians maintain all the networks and sophisticated gear that make the World Wide Web, satellite and space probe transmissions, and e-commerce possible. These networks form the fabric of the global economy.

Typical courses in this major:

Communication systems
Electrical circuits and systems
Data communications
Telephony
Digital transmission
Central offices
Local-area networks and wide-area networks
Internet protocols (IP) for data and voice
Fiber optics
Telecom testing techniques
Wireless systems
Radio frequency design
Network planning and design
Satellite networks
Microwave link design
Network management

Concentrations:

In college: data communications; local-area networks (LAN); wide-area networks (WAN); telephony (transmission and switching); wireless systems (wireless LAN, microwave links, satellites); fiber optics.

If you go on to grad school: network engineering; traffic engineering; telecom regulations; international telecommunications; management of information systems (MIS).

What the study of this major is like:

Telecommunications technology professionals design, install, manage, operate, and maintain the equipment and systems (such as telephone, data, Internet, and wireless networks) that make possible today's fast-paced exchange of information. Telecom technicians and technologists work to create the right balance between sophistication and cost effectiveness while setting up networks and ensuring that they function properly.

To become an engineering technologist, you must complete a four-year bachelor's degree program that prepares you to design, implement/configure, and manage telecommunications networks. Two-year associate degree programs, which train you to become a technician, typically cover the testing, operation, initial software configuration, and maintenance of telecommunications equipment.

As a major, you learn to design both local and long distance telecommunications networks (LANs and WANs). You also learn the principles of cellular telephone networks and receive a strong foundation in LAN administration.

Although the major is mostly system- or network-oriented, you generally take additional electronics and computers courses that cover basic electricity, solid-state fundamentals, digital concepts, and microprocessors. You learn about central office switching, analog and digital carrier circuits, broadband design and analysis, fiber optics, coaxial and twisted pair splicing, outside plant construction, and specific computer applications. And because communication skills are important, development of your writing and speaking abilities is an essential part of your training.

You are taught through lectures, webinars, and presentations from industry visitors. Almost all your courses have accompanying labs, in which you get hands-on experience, working with a variety of tools and electronic testing equipment. Starting in your second year, you work on many team projects. To prepare you for the industry, you write reports and term papers and give oral presentations to other students. In addition, you can join a telecom student society—the field trips and other interesting activities that such groups usually sponsor are good opportunities for you to meet industry professionals.

While most electrical engineering programs prepare you for graduate school, research, or a job designing new equipment, telecommunications technology programs train students to use existing equipment for system and network design. Telecom technology programs also have fewer math requirements but a much greater emphasis on hands-on experience. Some four-year programs focus on the business or management side of telecommunications.

Other majors you might like:
Electrical engineering technology
Radio and television
Recording arts
Information technology
Computer engineering technology
Communications
Electrical drafting/CAD/CADD
Communications systems installation/repair

Digital media
Medical records technology
Technical and business writing
Management information systems

Questions to ask colleges:
How large are the lab classes? What types of equipment are used? The ability to learn on up-to-date, accessible, "real-industry" equipment is an important factor in selecting a program.

How "wired"—and wireless—is the campus? How many types of network technologies are available?

Career options and trends:
Design engineer; network developer*; network administrator*; network applications support specialist; test engineer; radio frequency (RF) engineer*; sales engineer; facilities engineer; telecom manager.

The telecom industry is transitioning from wired to wireless, and introducing new technologies and services at a fast pace. Although this transition will create jobs, gains will be offset by declines in maintenance work—the new equipment doesn't require as much. The rapid pace of change and technological development in this industry will create the most opportunities for college-educated technologists with the training, knowledge, and skills to oversee these changes.

For more info:
IEEE Communications Society
3 Park Ave., 17th Fl.
New York, NY 10016
(212) 705-8900
www.comsoc.org

English language and literature

English is a major major, to borrow from Joseph Heller. More bachelor's degrees are earned in English than in any of the other liberal arts.

The English language dates back to Anglo-Saxon, yet it's perfectly suited to the digital age. English lends itself well to computer and multimedia communications because it's dense in meaning and conveys more ideas in less time and space than many other tongues do. The spread of American culture and business internationally has also popularized the language.

To study English is to grasp its Germanic roots and shake loose its literary leaves, from *Beowulf* to Weblogs. Students who choose to study English must be ready to read as many as 500 pages each week.

"One of the most important interests or activities for a creative writer is engaged reading—to try and understand how a text influences a reader's emotions or intellect," explains Jonathan Fink, a poet who teaches at Emory University.

Fortunately, if you like high school English, you're probably already an avid reader and a skilled writer. These talents aren't just for budding novelists, either. Corporations, nonprofit organizations, and government agencies all need good writers to take advantage of online communications, desktop publishing, and video editing tools.

"The discipline's emphasis on analytical skills and on careful writing prepares students for a variety of professions and occupations far beyond the world of teaching," says Professor Emeritus James G. Taaffe of the University of Alabama.

English majors go on to journalism, publishing, advertising, technical writing, management, law, and other careers. Graduate students specialize in genres, or types of literature, such as fiction, poetry, children's books, sci fi, and even hypertext—interactive fiction online. Other graduate areas include linguistics, film, and drama. Some grad students latch on to a specific historical period—say, nineteenth-century American literature. Multicultural literature, which might focus on works by African Americans or by women, is an emerging area these days. (See the section on Area, ethnic, and gender studies for related majors.)

"For a student, the number of possibilities for graduate study is encouraging; for a graduate, the competition for employment in creative writing can be daunting," cautions Fink. College English teaching positions are also hard to come by, so be flexible in planning a career using your English smarts. Technical or business writing may be an outlet if you're a good communicator with an interest in technology and multimedia.

"Increasingly, even liberal arts majors such as those in American literature are asked to have high-level technical skills," notes Professor Brett C. Millier of Middlebury College. "Many careers, ranging from magazine editing to investment banking, require strong research skills."

Read Up on Colleges

Look for these majors in colleges of arts and sciences or arts and letters, and in departments and schools of English, liberal arts, and humanities.

When comparing colleges, you should do some reading, research, and critical analysis of your own. You'll notice that two-year colleges usually prepare students for the workplace and technical communications jobs. If that's your goal, find out if you'll be ready for an entry-level job when you get your associate degree. Also for technical writers, scope out the software at the college and find out how widely it's used in the real world. See if the college has partnerships and internships with industry to get your foot in the door.

Most English majors go to four-year colleges, which have an academic slant.

"Inquire about whether the department is committed to a cultural studies approach or whether its focus is on critical theory," Taaffe advises. Cultural studies requires intense reading of literature to put it into a social or historical context. In critical theory, instead of reading and interpreting a work, you explore what other people, especially writers over the years, have said about it.

Other points to consider: Check out the college library, its books and journals. Is the library catalog online? Will you have access to the *Oxford English Dictionary* (*OED* to you), which traces how words have been used over the centuries? Can you access digitized materials offsite?

The faculty is most important. You want class time with the top profs. How many lower-division and upper-division courses are taught by graduate students instead? Are any of the leading professors called "emeritus"? That means they don't teach anymore.

Will you have the chance to work on a literary journal or publications? Does the university often host visiting writers on campus? Are other literary or cultural opportunities nearby?

If American lit is your passion, ask if it's a department of its own. How many courses are offered and in what depth? Are they huge lectures or smaller seminars? Keep in mind that you'll read modern writers, but even as an American literature major, you'll curl up with the masters of English literature—including Chaucer, Shakespeare, and Milton—during your college years.

American literature

What it's about:

As an American literature major, you study the principal literary movements and the fiction, nonfiction, poetry, and drama of the United States. You examine how American literature has developed historically and learn about the intellectual, economic, geographic, and social forces that have shaped U.S. culture.

Is this for you?

You might like this major if you also like: reading; expository and critical writing; contemporary literature; literature in its cultural and historical context; creative writing.

Consider this major if you are good at: active listening; attention to detail; creativity; critical reading/thinking; research *...or have...* initiative; verbal skills; writing skills.

Recommended high school prep:

English 4, math 3, lab science 3, social studies 3, and a foreign language 2–3.

Did you know...

...that even American literature majors should take Chaucer, Shakespeare, and Milton?

Typical courses in this major:

Survey of American literature
The American novel
American drama
Native American literature
Melville
Faulkner
The American Renaissance
American poetry
African-American literature
Literature by American women
American autobiography
American poetry
Senior seminar

Concentrations:

In college: comparative studies; creative writing.

If you go on to grad school: a particular historical era (e.g., 18th, 19th, 20th centuries); a particular genre (e.g., fiction, poetry).

What the study of this major is like:

Although American literature is comparatively young, its writings are rich and varied. The tradition began in the oral songs and tales of Native Americans and continued in the literature of European exploration and settlement, through the seventeenth century. In New England, the Puritans developed a prolific literary culture that included histories, biographies, poetry, and sermons. The Puritan influence was transformed, in the mid-nineteenth century, by Nathaniel Hawthorne, Ralph Waldo Emerson, Henry Thoreau, Emily Dickinson, and Harriet Beecher Stowe. Although New England dominated American writing until the Civil War, authors elsewhere in the North (Benjamin Franklin, James Fenimore Cooper, Herman Melville, and Walt Whitman) and in the South (William Byrd, Thomas Jefferson, and Edgar Allan Poe) created a distinctive, significant literature. Other lively, often subversive traditions flourished: fugitive slave narratives, Native American protest speeches, folk songs, and frontier humor.

Since the Civil War, American literature has undergone a cultural explosion. As an American literature major, you will follow the development of this legacy, by exploring the rise of realism in fiction (William Dean Howells, Henry James, Stephen Crane, Edith Wharton, Theodore Dreiser); the growth of midwestern, western, and southern regionalism (Willa Cather, Sherwood Anderson, Frank Norris, John Steinbeck, Flannery O'Connor, Eudora Welty); America's leadership in international modernism in poetry (Ezra Pound, T. S. Eliot, Marianne Moore, Wallace Stevens, William Carlos Williams); the modernist novels of Ernest Hemingway, F. Scott Fitzgerald, William Faulkner; the emergence of major dramatists (Eugene O'Neill, Arthur Miller, Tennessee Williams); the prominence of African-American literature (Langston Hughes, Zora Neale Hurston, Richard Wright, Ralph Ellison, James Baldwin); the self-conscious affirmations of post-World War II fiction (Saul Bellow, Vladimir Nabokov, Norman Mailer, John Updike); the grimness of post-World War II poetry (Robert Lowell, John Berryman, Elizabeth Bishop, Sylvia Plath); the revolt of the Beat Generation (Jack Kerouac). The course work also highlights the achievements in Native American writings in English (N. Scott Momaday, Leslie Silko, James Welch, Louise Erdrich); literature by and for women (Adrienne Rich, Ann Beattie, Joan Didion, Toni Morrison); and a powerful array of ethnic literatures.

If you major in American literature, you will probably take an introduction-to-literature course and then three or four courses covering (in historical order) the literary traditions of the United States. You may then take a seminar or two on a single author, and you elect your concentration—usually either comparative studies or creative writing. You also take several electives—in American poetry, or African-American literature, for example— in preparation for advanced study in your fourth year. Fourth-year work usually consists of a seminar or two, a comprehensive exam, and, if you are eligible, an honors thesis.

American literature is studied today basically as it has always been studied. While computers help you write papers more easily and have easier access to resource materials, you still do the important work by reading a book and your professor still lectures in front of a chalkboard. Your academic routine will be generally low-tech, quiet, and relatively solitary. You must read a great deal—sometimes 400 or 500 pages in a week—and typically write several papers for each course.

Not many colleges offer an American literature major, so most students study American literature within the context of an English major. English departments may vary as to how many courses in American literature are offered, and there may be gaps in historical sequence. Departments may also vary in their course offerings in emerging fields such as ethnic American literatures, or reject the idea of "cultural studies" of literature altogether.

Other majors you might like:
English
American studies
African-American studies
Publishing
Native American studies
American history (U.S.)
Media studies
English literature (British)
Comparative literature
Political science
Women's studies
Creative Writing

Questions to ask colleges:
Is American literature taught within an English department or on its own? If it is taught within an English department, how many courses in the field are offered in a typical year, and how much depth can students achieve?

How big are the courses—are they all large lecture courses, or are there also medium-size courses and seminars? Are there courses in emerging fields like African-American literature or ethnic American literatures?

Career options and trends:
High school teacher; journalist; editor; college professor.

American literature majors do well in a variety of fields because careers ranging from magazine editing to investment banking often require strong research skills.

For more info:
American Studies Association (ASA)
1120 19th St., N.W.
Suite 301
Washington, DC 20036
(202) 467-4783
www.theasa.net

Creative Writing

What it's about:
As a creative writing major, you study the creation and construction of poetry, fiction, drama, nonfiction, and screenwriting. You examine the works of established writers and develop your own original work (poems, stories, dramas, etc.), and submit your work to professors and peers for discussion and analysis.

Is this for you?
You might like this major if you also like: reading; drama; poetry; fiction; film; language; self-expression; the subtle meanings of words and sentences. Creative writing majors find pleasure in weighing, balancing, and selecting words for their ability to convey meaning through image, tone, rhythm, and scene.

Consider this major if you are good at: attention to detail; creativity; critical reading/thinking; organizing; persuading/influencing ...*or have...* emotional stamina/endurance; initiative; patience; perception; verbal skills; writing skills.

Recommended high school prep:
English 4, math 3, lab science 3, social studies 4, and a foreign language 4. If available, take courses that encourage you to write and to think about how art is constructed. Also, activities such as working on a student literary journal or newspaper are recommended.

Typical courses in this major:
Introduction to creative writing
Poetry writing
Fiction writing
Journalism
Composition
Playwriting
Screenwriting
Argumentation
Advanced creative writing
Expository writing
Memoir/creative non-fiction writing
Topics in English composition

Concentrations:
Poetry; fiction; playwriting; screenwriting; creative nonfiction.

What the study of this major is like:
The creative writing major closely resembles the English major. Much of the course work is similar, and you study works of drama, prose, and poetry, as well as composition. But in creative writing, you develop your own literary voice in workshops that are taught by practicing writers who know firsthand the challenges and struggles of the writing process.

In general, your course work is divided among writing workshops, literature courses, and liberal arts requirements in the sciences, mathematics, and other humanities. In most programs, your writing samples and performance in writing courses is examined before you are admitted into the workshops.

Most introductory creative writing courses combine several forms of writing. Similar to survey courses in the arts, an introductory course in creative writing usually encourages you to write fiction, poetry, and, often, drama. You will also examine the history of several forms of writing and analyze the works of contemporary authors.

"Forms" courses are similar to a traditional literature course, but with a focus on an aspect of writing not usually covered in core courses. The topics may range from contemporary short story or memoir to an examination of the struggles involved in revision. Most upper-level courses are divided by genre, which allows you to focus more in-depth on your own poetry, fiction, or drama. You will also probably be required to submit a thesis project—usually a collection of poems, stories, or essays.

Upper-level workshops also focus on a particular form. In essay writing, you study techniques of analysis and persuasion, explore the relation between voice and purpose, and learn how to design an argument. In poetry writing, you experiment with meter, image, tone, and organization. In fiction courses, you may focus on characterization, narrative, scene, dialogue, or plot. In most courses, members of the class analyze each other's work with guidance from the instructor. Because writing is such a solitary endeavor, most students consider this feedback to be the most valued aspect of the major.

Being a creative writing major requires maturity, patience, and determination. The challenges you are likely to face are generally those that all writers encounter: Where do I get ideas? How can I overcome writer's block? How can I choose the most appropriate way to express my ideas? You will also need to set writing and revision schedules for yourself; this task can be hard, because the amount of time creative work takes is often unpredictable. Unlike majors that have clearly mapped out paths to success, creative writing challenges you not only to follow the guidance of professionals, but also to rely heavily on your own initiative and conviction.

Creative writing may be offered as an independent major, as a concentration in the English major, or as an independent minor. Because content and approach vary widely in creative writing programs, you should examine the writing of professors at the colleges you are considering. Look for writers whose work addresses some of your own interests and concerns.

Other majors you might like:
English
Drama and theater arts
Journalism
Publishing
Comparative literature
Advertising
Philosophy
Psychology
Business communications
Radio and television
Fine/studio arts
Technical and business writing

Questions to ask colleges:
Does the college have a visiting-writers program that invites authors to campus?

What opportunities are there for students to become involved in literary journals or readings?

How many creative writing majors does the college currently enroll?

Career options and trends:
Freelance writer; copywriter for advertising or marketing; editor; content manager for a website or other electronic publishing venue.

Not many authors make a living from their writing, however the declining costs of self-publishing and the growing popularity of e-books have created opportunities for many freelancers to get their work published.

Creative writing majors do find employment, however, in related fields like teaching, advertising, journalism, television, radio, film, and publishing. The growing number of online publications and services are spurring demand for writers with web experience and who are comfortable working with digital media. Most university-level teaching positions require an advanced degree.

Recently, there has been an increase in the number of graduate creative writing programs. For a student, the increased possibilities for graduate study are encouraging; for a graduate, the competition for employment in the field of creative writing can be daunting.

Insider's viewpoint:
"The longer I struggle with the creation and motivation of my invented characters, the more I am able to translate that empathy to individuals I encounter in 'real' life."

—Professor Jonathan Fink, Emory University

For more info:
Associated Writing Programs
George Mason University
Mail Stop 1E3
Fairfax, VA 22030
(703) 993-4301
www.awpwriter.org

Poets & Writers, Inc.
90 Broad St.
Suite 2100
New York, NY 10004
(212) 226-3586
www.pw.org

English

What it's about:

English majors read, discuss, and write about literature. Literary works include poetry, prose, and drama but may also be drawn from film, journalism, and television. Study focuses on the critical, historical, linguistic, and cultural contexts of these works. In addition, you practice your own writing, developing your language-use and composition skills.

Is this for you?

You might like this major if you also like: reading; writing; discussion; languages; film; music; theater; dance; working independently.

Consider this major if you are good at: attention to detail; creativity; critical reading/thinking; persuading/influencing; research *...or have...* initiative; patience; verbal skills; writing skills.

Recommended high school prep:

English 4, math 3, lab science 3, social studies 3, and foreign language 3.

Did you know...

...that the major requires a lot of library research, as well as reading and writing assignments? Even if you are an avid reader, you must plan your time carefully in order to complete your work.

...that the study of English literature covers not just the text of a work but also its context—how, when, and why it was produced, as well as how it has influenced generations of readers?

Typical courses in this major:

Survey of English literature
Chaucer
Shakespeare
Milton
History of the English language
Medieval literature
Victorian literature
The Romantics
Modern English grammar
English drama
American literature
Continental literature
Critical theory
New voices in literature
Poetry
The modern short story

Concentrations:

Creative writing; critical theory; drama; film; linguistics; ethnic literatures; literature of a particular period.

What the study of this major is like:

An almost universal first-year requirement of this major is a semester- or year-long chronological (or thematic) survey of English and American literature, which lays the groundwork for further courses in particular genres or literary time periods. Classes are usually small, and you are expected to contribute to class discussion and to write term papers—usually two per course.

Upper-level courses present a more formal study of literature. You learn how to read critically, how to determine the contexts of literature, and how literature creates and reflects the culture from which it springs. In addition, you study point of view, explication, tone, irony, metaphor, image, structure, and allusion. You also explore the ways in which texts affect audiences' beliefs and emotions, and the ways in which literature sheds light on our lives.

Besides the core courses, most programs offer a broad selection of electives focusing on genre study, critical theory, individual authors, and other topics. Courses in writing encourage you to practice the techniques you learn by reading the works of others. You'll become increasingly sensitive to the subtleties of language and to the influences of what you read and hear. In both literature and writing courses, you will examine the logic of an argument, the ways experiences are organized, and reactions to psychological and emotional persuasion. Your studies may conclude with a seminar on a particular theme or subject approached from a variety of directions. And there will likely be a lengthy term project for that seminar.

In addition to classes, most programs provide opportunities to attend readings presented by guest speakers, topical seminars, and more formal lectures given by faculty members. It is also common for English majors with similar interests to meet informally outside of class (usually at the local watering hole) to discuss their work and to exchange ideas and opinions.

Other majors you might like:
Communications
Drama and theater arts
Chicano studies
African-American studies
Comparative literature
Public relations
Medieval and Renaissance studies
Film/cinema studies
English teacher education
History
Philosophy
Classics

Questions to ask colleges:
What are typical class sizes? Which classes have prerequisites? English classes are popular and often, especially at larger colleges, getting into classes is competitive. If you see a course in the catalog that you must take, be sure to ask about it, so you know you have at least a chance of being enrolled.

Does the college offer both U.S. and foreign library catalogs online? Does it offer access to the *Oxford English Dictionary* and *Early English Books Online*? You might research the college's holdings of books and journals to see what is available in the library and online.

Career options and trends:
Elementary, middle, or high school teacher; college professor; editor; journalist; technical writer.

The English major also prepares you for broad career options, including opportunities in publishing; radio, television, and online communications; social work; and management. With graduate or professional study, you can pursue a career in law, medicine, or other field.

A state certificate or license is required for teaching in public schools. College-level teaching positions in English are few and difficult to obtain.

Insider's viewpoint:
"Have an idea of where you want to go with the major. Many people choose English because they don't know what else to do or they think it's easy. Having a career goal, like journalism in my case, helps a lot."

—Courtney, senior, SUNY Binghamton

For more info:
Modern Language Association (MLA)
26 Broadway
3rd Floor
New York, NY 10004-1789
(646) 576-5000
www.mla.org

Technical and business writing

Also known as:
Professional writing

What it's about:
As a technical and business writing major, you learn how to adapt technical information to specific audiences and types of media (text, images, animation, audio, video). You also learn to manage the technical communication process—the steps you go through before, during, and after you write.

Is this for you?
You might like this major if you also like: working with computers; science and technology; reading; tutoring; working with different types of people; being precise; expressing yourself in writing and in person.

Consider this major if you are good at: attention to detail; concentrating; creativity; critical reading/thinking; organizing; research; teamwork...*or have...* initiative; verbal skills; writing skills.

Recommended high school prep:
English 4, math 3, lab science 3, social studies 3, and a foreign language 2–3. Courses in business and computer science or applications are also recommended.

Did you know...
...that you don't need technical expertise to go into technical and business writing? The "technical" part of the major isn't nearly as scary as some students think. And the major doesn't deal just with computers. What is most important is the ability to work with many different people and to communicate clearly and carefully.

Typical courses in this major:
Foundations in technical communications
Technical editing
Software documentation
Product documentation
Correspondence and report writing
Graphics for technical communications
Documentation process and management
Writing grant proposals
Web authoring
Science writing
Business writing
Multimedia for training and tutorials
Usability testing for technical communications
Internationalizing/localizing documentation

Concentrations:
Internet publishing; scientific writing; business writing; writing for the arts.

What the study of this major is like:
In this major you learn how to translate technical texts into "ordinary" language so that people with no special training can understand them. You also learn how to manage the overall process of technical communications—in particular, determining what type of work you are expected to create (such as a draft copy) and when you need to deliver the completed project. In addition, you gain practice in tracking and reviewing your work, and in writing up your decisions as documentation plans and proposals.

Courses on the internationalization and the localization of information focus on ways to make information understandable to a broad audience or to a specific audience. In other courses you study editing and usability testing, as well as financial, legal, and ethical issues. Most programs include a research component where you learn how to gather information from print and electronic sources, conduct interviews, and design surveys and questionnaires.

The curriculum also introduces you to "visual writing"—the use of layout and design, tables and graphs, illustrations, and other ways to highlight and structure text. By the time you graduate, you will have experience with desktop publishing, image editing, graphics, multimedia, and other types of software.

Your studies generally prepare you for entry-level technical communications jobs. Four-year programs may concentrate on theory and research, along with general education courses in the sciences and humanities. Two-year programs at community colleges and technical schools focus more on training you for entry into the workforce.

Other majors you might like:
Desktop publishing
Information systems
Web page/multimedia design
Creative Writing
Management information systems
Public relations
Design/visual communications
Drafting and design technology
Digital media
Business communications
Computer graphics
Health information management

Questions to ask colleges:
Is there an open lab where majors can use publishing software? Which software programs does the program make available, and how often are they upgraded? Are software applications used in various industries featured in the courses?

Does the program have partnerships and internships with local businesses?

Career options and trends:
Workplace technical communicator*; software documentation writer; website editor/writer; information architect; product planner; marketing technical communicator.

Employment of technical writers is expected to increase. As a result of rapid growth in technology and electronics, both at home and in the workplace, there will be more need to interpret technical information into users guides, training materials and instruction manuals.

The role of the technical communicator is evolving as businesses look for ways to manage content most effectively—that is, to enable one text to be published in different media forms. Also, the profession may join forces with related areas such as quality assurance and technical support.

For more info:
Society for Technical Communication (STC)
9401 Lee Highway, Suite 300
Fairfax, VA 22031
www.stc.org

Association for Computing Machinery (ACM)
2 Penn Plaza
Suite 701
New York, NY 10121-0701
(800) 342-6626
www.acm.org

Family and consumer sciences

People who study and work in the family and consumer sciences home in on living.

"A general major addresses the study of individuals, families, and communities to understand people's basic needs of food, clothing, shelter, and relationships—and to seek solutions to problems," says Professor Penny A. Ralston of Florida State University.

On the undergraduate and graduate levels, students specialize in the social and behavioral sciences, like child development and family relations, and in such fields as consumer economics, apparel design and merchandising, housing and living environments, and applied sciences in food, nutrition, and textiles. Those who choose family and consumer sciences tend to be creative, analytical, and caring. "The desire to help others and the opportunity to make a difference in people's lives" lead students to these majors, according to Professor Anne L. Sweaney of the University of Georgia.

Colleges have dozens of names for this category. The old name, "home economics," just doesn't cut it anymore. Instead, new and dynamic fields of family and consumer sciences are taught in schools, colleges, and departments of human sciences, human ecology, human resources, humanities and social science, business management, professional studies, arts and sciences, applied sciences, applied technology, or even education.

The majors differ at each college, so be sure to do your homework if you're planning to go into housing, human and family studies, apparel and textiles, or culinary arts. Find out if the program focuses on the industrial or the creative aspects of the field. In housing majors, for instance, the industrial approach emphasizes business functions like residential property management, while creative programs stress space design and planning. Culinary arts or apparel studies might also focus on one approach or the other.

Finding your college home

When choosing a college, see how many credits you'll take in general education courses in comparison with specific courses in your major. The issue here is, does the college mostly look at the "big picture" or does the program plunge into the occupation in a practical way?

"At some, especially larger, institutions, there may be more opportunity to specialize in one area of the major, while other colleges may treat the major in a more integrated and holistic manner, with broad, contextual courses," explains Professor Eva L. Essa of the University of Nevada, Reno.

Talk to an adviser on campus about what's important at that college. How much of your work will be in the classroom, and how much hands-on experience will you get? If you major in housing and human environments, will you work in the housing industry or do service work in the community to learn problem solving? Can you do an internship at a preschool if you're majoring in family studies, or at a restaurant if you're majoring in culinary arts? Will the college help you find the position? Will you be paid?

"Culinary arts programs will require students to complete internships in the field," says Paul Sorgule, a dean at Paul Smith's College. "These 'real-life' experiences can be a gateway to a permanent job after graduation."

Also ask how much real-world experience the faculty members have. As Sorgule puts it, "Not all chefs make the best teachers, but no teacher can be effective teaching the culinary arts without the experience to back up theory." That's good advice in many areas of study.

You might also find out what other courses you will take in college. Perhaps physical sciences to learn about foods or textiles? How about a foreign language as an academic and professional enhancement? For that matter, you might want to take courses at other parts of the university to learn topics from other colleges or departments. Ask if that's okay.

Other questions for colleges: What types of careers do their graduates pursue? What is the employment rate for graduates with the major you want?

Job prospects will differ depending on your major. For example, the apparel industry can go up or down with the economy and is extremely competitive. Production has moved overseas, where wages are low. Culinary and housing professionals enjoy fields with high employment even in shaky economic times. In addition to private industry, many of these fields of study can lead to work in the public sector and steady government jobs for teachers and social workers.

Family and consumer sciences are also great preparation for further studies in and outside of the field. Graduate students might specialize in adult development and the aging population. In apparel, graduate programs include textile engineering and retail marketing; housing grads might choose real estate or city and regional planning.

Two good general websites are those of the American Association of Family and Consumer Sciences (www.aafcs.org), and the National Council on Family Relations (www.ncfr.org). Also read about related majors in this book, including fashion merchandising and hospitality administration and management in the Business section, food science in the Agriculture section, and the majors in the section on Public administration.

Clothing, apparel, and textile studies

What it's about:

The apparel and textiles major includes the design, production, marketing, and use of garments, fabrics, and fibers. You learn about technology applications, manufacturing systems, product development, buying, promotional techniques, clothing and material design and customization, and quality control in the apparel and textiles industries.

Is this for you?

You might like this major if you also like: combining colors, fabrics, and shapes; using your imagination; sewing; drawing; sketching; shopping; history; fashion magazines; predicting trends.

Consider this major if you are good at: creativity; critical reading/thinking; leadership; math; persuading/influencing; quantitative analysis; research; teamwork ...*or have...* initiative.

Recommended high school prep:

English 4, math 2, lab science 2, social studies 3, and a foreign language 3. If possible, take courses in computer/graphic arts, photography, business, accounting, and family and consumer studies (for example, fashion design)

Did you know...

...that this major requires you to have a working knowledge of computer applications such as Excel, Access, and PowerPoint? Knowledge of creative software, such as PhotoShop and Publisher, is also helpful.

Typical courses in this major:

Textile fundamentals
Apparel design
Sociology of clothing
Clothing construction
Mass production of apparel
Figure and fashion illustration
Promotion and marketing principles
Historic textiles and costumes
Textiles in non-apparel uses
Tailoring
Product development
Advanced textile testing and analysis
Computer-aided design
Merchandise buying and management
Contemporary fashion designers
Textile and apparel economics

Concentrations:

In college: buying; product development; textile production; apparel design and production; fashion promotion and marketing; interior merchandising.

If you go on to grad school: retail marketing; costume design; textile design; textile science; historic costume and textiles; curating and preservation; textile economics.

What the study of this major is like:

This major is typically taught in laboratory, studio, and lecture settings. In most classes you apply what you learn by completing projects or papers. You will probably be expected to make presentations to the class, so good oral communications are an asset. Your work may occasionally be evaluated by industry professionals. Especially in senior-level courses, you will apply critical-thinking skills in analytical and persuasive writing. Many classes invite guest speakers to discuss up-to-date trends and requirements of the industry.

Understanding consumer behavior, likes, and wants will contribute to your potential success in this field. Therefore, many colleges require internships in which you earn credit while getting firsthand experience in the industry. You can also participate in field trips or off-campus study programs in manufacturing and fashion centers, including retail stores, design houses, textiles factories, museums, and historic sites in areas such as New York, Dallas, and Europe.

This major may be offered in a college of arts and sciences or in a college of family and consumer sciences (formerly home economics), and may lead either to a Bachelor of Science degree (with an emphasis on physical science) or a Bachelor of Arts (humanities). In some Bachelor of Science programs, you take chemistry to fulfill the science requirement. Bachelor of Arts programs usually require fewer core courses and more general education courses. Colleges that focus on retailing do not offer creative courses as part of the major. Programs in other colleges may focus on design, product development, or textiles. Many colleges require you to take two semesters of foreign language and at least one semester of economics, and to be proficient in computer systems.

Apparel and textiles majors tend to be outgoing and self-motivated. Most colleges host an industry-related organization like Fashion Group International. Depending on the campus, you might participate in the Student Marketing Association, Student Retail Federation, or the Advertising and Public Relations Club. Majors who are active in the community or have a part-time job may conduct fashion shows for fund-raisers, organize clothing drives, or set up programs to recycle textiles, apparel, and shoes.

Other majors you might like:
Fashion and apparel design
Textile science
Fashion merchandising
Textile sciences/engineering
Retailing
Marketing
Family and consumer sciences
Advertising
Fiber/textile arts
Theater design and technology
Interior design

Questions to ask colleges:
In what ways do faculty members and students become involved in related local industries? How many faculty members have had industry experience? How frequently do industry professionals serve as guest speakers in classes?

What types of off-campus study programs are available? Does the program require an internship prior to graduation?

What types of careers do graduates in this major pursue after graduation? Where do most graduates relocate to for their first industry job?

Career options and trends:
Buyer; product developer; product manager; market researcher; fashion coordinator; fashion reporter; fashion or textile designer; pattern maker; visual merchandising manager.

The apparel and textiles major can prepare you to work as a merchandise coordinator with a national-brand wholesale firm; an in-store sales associate or manager with a major retailer; a production assistant with a manufacturing firm; an educational representative for a fabric, pattern, sewing machine, or notions firm; a textile and apparel advertiser and promoter; or a quality control analyst. With specialized training, you may work as a textile chemist, textile engineer, or museum costume curator.

The apparel and textiles industries are strongly affected by the national economy and consumer spending. In good times, the industry expands so rapidly that firms have a difficult time hiring enough people; but when the economy suffers, the industry may not hire entry-level employees and may even close stores. Be aware that most of the labor-intensive activities (especially apparel manufacturing) have moved to developing countries, where wages are significantly lower.

For more info:
International Textile and Apparel Association (ITAA)
PO Box 70687
Knoxville, TN 37938-0687
(865) 992-1535
www.itaaonline.org

Fashion Group International, Inc. (FGI)
8 W. 40th St.
7th Floor
New York, NY 10018
(212) 302-5511
www.fgi.org

Culinary arts and chef training

What it's about:

Culinary arts and chef training programs prepare you for a career in the food service industry as a chef, executive chef, pastry chef, restaurant manager, food and beverage director, food service director, or restaurateur. Chefs today are managers of people, products, and facilities. They have a responsibility to provide quality food and experiences in a safe, sanitary environment.

Is this for you?

You might like this major if you also like: cooking and presenting different kinds of food; serving others; people of diverse backgrounds; expressing yourself in artistic ways; travel; creating something and receiving immediate feedback.

Consider this major if you are good at: coaching; counseling; leadership; multi-tasking; organizing; spacial thinking/analysis; teamwork *...or have...* initiative; manual dexterity; physical stamina.

Recommended high school prep:

English 4, math 3, lab science 3, social studies 3, and a foreign language 2–3. If possible, also take a basic computer applications course.

Did you know...

...there is much more to this major than cooking? Being a professional cook is a hands-on career, but chefs need a strong foundation in math applications, problem resolution, decision making, human resources management, team building, and critical-thinking skills.

Typical courses in this major:

Professional cooking
Foundations of baking
International cooking
Advanced cooking
Banquets and catering
Garde-manger (cold food preparation)
Fabrication and charcuterie
Nutrition
Food science
Restaurant management
Food service sanitation
Menu planning and purchasing
Food and beverage control
Human resources management

Concentrations:

Pastry arts; baking.

What the study of this major is like:

Training to be a chef requires discipline. The field demands a strong work ethic; empathy; a dedication to excellence; and self-assessment, organizational, multitasking, and timing abilities. A successful chef is good at following through on projects, always aware that the job must get done.

Like many academic programs, programs in culinary arts require dedication to research, reading, writing, and computation. However, as a chef-in-training, you must work long hours, under the critical eye of instructors and the dining public. Most colleges insist you follow the conservative uniform and grooming standards of the industry. In chef training programs, you work with others, performing as part of a team, and you are evaluated and receive critiques as a group member. At most colleges you will spend 15–40 hours a week in the kitchen (depending on the semester), beginning as early as 5 a.m. and often working into the evening. At the same time, you must complete assignments for courses in cooking, liberal arts, and management.

Training programs include internships that can be anywhere in the country. Traditionally, internships are paid positions, although some are not. Most students use these real-world experiences as a way to obtain permanent jobs after graduation.

Many colleges offer degrees in culinary arts and related services. As you investigate the schools you are considering, keep in mind their philosophies and methodologies. Most programs require hands-on experience, although some emphasize it more strongly than others. In some programs, general education courses are optional. Other programs include both cooking and liberal arts courses.

Recently, some colleges have started offering bachelor's degrees in culinary arts. Besides stressing the technical skills that can make you a successful chef, they encourage you to be a decision maker, team builder, manager, and leader.

If you think you'd like to be a chef, you should pursue a balanced education. A chef must understand the finances of an operation, be well read and able to design restaurant menus that match a profiled guest, know how environments affect human behavior, and be a good communicator.

Other majors you might like:
Restaurant/food services management
Food and nutrition studies
Food science
Dietetics
Hospitality administration and management
Baking/pastry arts
Nutrition sciences
Human resources management
Italian studies
Entreprencurial studies

Questions to ask colleges:
Which types of industry experience does the faculty have? Not all chefs make good teachers, but it is hard to be an effective teacher in the culinary arts without some experience to back up the theory.

Is the program accredited by the American Culinary Federation? How current are the facilities?

Career options and trends:
Cook; sous chef; executive chef; food and beverage director; restaurant manager; restaurateur.

Increasingly, serious chefs are seeking certification through the American Culinary Federation as chef de cuisine, executive chef, pastry chef, or master chef. A certificate in sanitation from the National Restaurant Association is also useful.

Since dining out has become essential to the American lifestyle, the culinary business continues to grow, even during tough economic times. Job opportunities are expected to be about average through 2022. Finding a position should not be difficult, although many positions are part-time, resulting in high turnover rates as people leave the profession for full-time positions. Competition should be keen for jobs in the top kitchens of higher end restaurants which pay better but have low turnover.

A bachelor's degree is becoming the standard for positions at the chef level, and within the next decade or so, a master's degree may be necessary. The major companies are winning the battle for customers, so even though 80 percent of the restaurants in the United States are privately owned, restaurant chains have the ability and cash flow to reward their employees. The chains are therefore likely to offer the most career opportunities.

Insider's viewpoint:
"Chefs are designers of experiences that are the basis for building relationships, mending disagreements, creating partnerships, confirming friendships, celebrating accomplishments, and recognizing personal and professional achievements."

—Paul Sorgule, Paul Smith's College

For more info:
American Culinary Federation (ACF)
180 Center Place Way
St. Augustine, FL 32095
(800) 624-9458
www.acfchefs.org

National Restaurant Association
2055 L St., N.W., Suite 700
Washington, DC 20036
(800) 424-5156
www.restaurant.org

Family and consumer sciences

Also known as:
Human sciences
Home economics

What it's about:
The major in family and consumer sciences focuses on individuals, families, and communities from ecological and interdisciplinary perspectives. The purpose of the major is to help you understand the problems they face—especially those related to the basic needs of food, clothing, shelter, and relationships—and to seek solutions.

Is this for you?
You might like this major if you also like: children and families; community service; leadership roles; helping people make decisions and solve problems.

Consider this major if you are good at: active listening; caring/nurturing; critical reading/thinking; leadership; research; teamwork *...or have...* initiative; verbal skills; writing skills.

Recommended high school prep:
English 4, math 3, lab science 4 (including biology and chemistry), social studies 3, and a foreign language 2–3. If possible, take at least one year of family and consumer sciences.

Did you know...
...that you need a background in chemistry to do well in courses like food science, nutrition, and textiles, which are usually included in the major?

Typical courses in this major:
Personal and family financial management
Child development
Family relations
Consumer economics
Housing and interior design
Food science
Fundamentals of nutrition
Nutrition in the life cycle
Community nutrition
Apparel production and analysis
Consumer textiles
Human development

Concentrations:
Child development; family relations; consumer economics (including personal finance); apparel design; fashion merchandising; textiles; housing and interiors; food and nutrition; family and consumer science education.

What the study of this major is like:
The family and consumer sciences major is the interdisciplinary study of factors that can affect the well-being of people of all ages. As you explore a range of subjects—from social and behavioral sciences, such as child development and family relations, to applied sciences, such as food science, nutrition, and textiles—you must be open to different approaches to understanding individuals, families, and communities.

The major begins with course work in the liberal arts. You then choose courses in areas such as family studies, housing, clothing and textiles, food science and nutrition, and personal/family finances and resource management.

The information you learn will be applied to individual and family concerns. For example, you might translate a family's nutritional problems into strategies for selecting better diets, or you may determine how children's developmental needs can be met in different settings, such as child care and community centers. For your last year, you will select a practicum, or internship, that will provide both the work experience and the contacts needed in any job search. Some programs offer opportunities for international or cross-cultural internships.

At large institutions the program may be located in divisions of human ecology, human sciences, or family and consumer sciences. Generally, the number of required courses depends on the size of the program. Larger programs usually provide more flexibility, so that you can focus on an area of your choice.

Family and consumer sciences majors gain not only an in-depth appreciation of the subject matter but also a broad understanding of the environments in which consumers and families live, work, and, sometimes, struggle. As a graduate, you'll have a variety of career options, particularly if you choose to specialize. Course work and internships or other supervised practical experiences prepare you for professional roles in business, government, education, and human services.

Other majors you might like:
Human services
Psychology
Environmental design
Culinary arts and chef training
Dietetics
Gerontology
Fashion and apparel design
Interior design
Business administration and management
Community health services
Sociology
Youth services

Questions to ask colleges:
How much access do majors have to advisers? Students pursuing the general major in family and consumer sciences often look for a flexible program. You'll need appropriate guidance on how to handle practicums, internships, honors, and undergraduate research.

Career options and trends:
High school teacher; child care professional; family services professional; community agency administrator; sales representative; product designer; financial planner.

With appropriate course work, you can become certified as a family life educator and, with an examination, as a family and consumer sciences professional.

In the light of increasing globalization, family and consumer sciences majors should consider international opportunities, including study abroad. The experience can lead to jobs with national or international health organizations and strengthen your credentials for human service and education positions. Also, there is a critical shortage of secondary school teachers in this field. With additional coursework, you can become certified to teach.

For more info:
American Association of Family and Consumer Sciences (AAFCS)
400 N. Columbus St.
Suite 202
Alexandria, VA 22314
(800) 424-8080
www.aafcs.org

National Council on Family Relations (NCFR)
1201 West River Parkway, Suite 200
Minneapolis, MN 55454-1115
(888) 781-9331
www.ncfr.org

Food and nutrition studies

What it's about:

The food and nutrition studies major covers the processing and preparation of food before it is eaten (food science) and the role of nutrients in human metabolism (nutrition). You study food safety, quality, and nutritional content; food product and recipe development; the planning of diets to maintain wellness and nutrition counseling.

Is this for you?

You might like this major if you also like: cooking, tasting, and experimenting with recipes; sports and exercise; helping others; science (especially biology and chemistry) and math; knowing what you eat and how it is made; working with others to tackle problems.

Consider this major if you are good at: attention to detail; caring/nurturing; critical reading/thinking; leadership; math; organizing; teamwork ...*or have...* initiative; verbal skills; writing skills.

Recommended high school prep:

English 4, math 3 (including trigonometry and pre-calculus), lab science 4 (including biology, chemistry, and physics), social studies 3, and a foreign language 2–3. If possible, also take speech.

Did you know...

...the differences between the food and nutrition studies major, the food science major, and the dietetics major? Food science primarily focuses on food production and safety—what happens before it gets into your kitchen. Dietetics programs prepare you to become a licensed health professional as either a registered dietician (RD) or a dietician technician (DTR). Food and nutrition studies spans much of what is covered in both, with a broader, interdisciplinary approach to healthy eating and living.

...that this major requires strong science and math skills? The basic courses are the same as those taken by biology or chemistry majors. Food and nutrition studies can be thought of as an applied biology or an applied chemistry major, with the focus on food, nutrition, and human health.

Typical courses in this major:

Biology
Biochemistry
Microbiology
Physiology
Chemistry
Physics
Mathematics
Statistics
Nutrition
Community nutrition
Food chemistry
Food microbiology
Food preparation
Food product development
Food processing
Sensory evaluation

Concentrations:

In college: consumer-related issues; food processing; food product development; food safety; wellness studies; clinical nutrition; community nutrition; pre–health professional track for entry into graduate or medical school.

If you go on to grad school: food chemistry; food microbiology; sensory and quality evaluation; nutritional biochemistry; nutritional toxicology.

What the study of this major is like:

The food and nutrition studies major is usually found at large universities in schools of home economics, agriculture, human ecology, family and consumer sciences, health and human services, or applied sciences. At some institutions, food science and nutrition are separate majors; at others, they are one major and you may specialize in either food science or nutrition. The breadth of the major can vary from narrow, emphasizing only food science, nutrition, or dietetics, to broad, covering many aspects of food and nutrition studies.

In your first two years, you take courses such as chemistry, biochemistry, physiology, and microbiology, often in large lecture classes that break into smaller discussion and laboratory sections. The science and math requirements are similar to most other science- or health-related majors. If you plan to focus on dietetics or nutrition education (working with individuals and families to promote health), you also take courses in education and communication. To prepare for work in the business world, you should take business administration, marketing, computers, and public relations courses. Courses in sociology and psychology are also helpful.

You'll likely enroll in an introductory nutrition or food science course during your first two years, but you probably won't take many courses in the major until you have completed the basic science courses. In the beginning, you may feel lost in large lecture classes. Because these courses are prerequisites for the major rather than part of it, you may wonder about their relevance; but you'll soon see how they relates to your career goals.

You may usually concentrate on either food science or nutrition or both. In food science, you learn about food preparation, processing, packaging, storage, and distribution. You also learn what makes food pleasing to our sense of sight, smell, and taste. In nutrition courses, you study food selection, preparation, consumption, and digestion. You take courses in food chemistry and in basic and advanced nutrition. Although emphasis is placed on the chemistry of these processes, you also study the psychological and behavioral aspects of eating.

In addition to lectures, most courses have laboratory work, to provide you with hands-on experience in, for example, identifying microorganisms in foods. In laboratory sessions, you often work in teams to conduct short-term experiments and independent projects. Upper-level class sizes are usually small. Courses may be taught as lectures or as discussion sections on subjects such as community nutrition, assessment methods, and nutrition and disease. Individual and team projects are often included.

Summer jobs or internships provide real-world experiences that relate to academic course work. You can also work with faculty members on research projects during the academic year; these experiences are valuable when you apply for jobs or acceptance into graduate school or internship programs. The Institute of Food Technologists and the American Dietetic Association approve or accredit undergraduate programs, but some colleges offer nonaccredited programs instead. The level of science courses required for the major varies and is usually lower in nonaccredited programs. The laboratory facilities also vary from one college to another.

Technology has drastically changed the way food is grown, harvested, packaged, transported, and sold. Our understanding of the relation of nutrition to health, especially in the causes and treatment of chronic diseases, has greatly increased and an enormous variety of products are available from all over the world. At the same time, fad diets, eating disorders, substance abuse, and nutrient-drug interactions threaten health and well-being. Careers in food and nutrition studies provide many opportunities for making important contributions to our world.

Other majors you might like:
Food science
Chemistry
Dietetics
Culinary arts and chef training
Nutrition sciences
Sports and fitness administration
Food service
Institutional food production
Pharmacy
Restaurant/food services management
Hospitality administration and management

Career options and trends:
Food purchasing manager; test kitchen/recipe developer*; product researcher/developer; dietitian*; nutrition counselor*; community nutritionist; food editor (for newspaper or magazine); inspector for the Food and Drug Administration or the Department of Agriculture.

To become a registered dietitian (RD), you must complete a prescribed set of undergraduate courses and a supervised internship program and take the registered dietitian's examination (see the description for the dietetics major in the section on Health).

The food industry itself, and the demand for all types of industry professionals, remain quite stable; population growth and the marketability of new food products provide more job opportunities. Because of current concerns, food safety specialists should have no trouble finding work. Because of the increasing interest in nutrition, the development of enhanced foods, the emergence of wellness programs, and an aging population, the demand for nutritionists and dietitians is projected to be strong.

Insider's viewpoint:

"Ever since I became a nutrition major, I am eating better, exercising more, and basically living a healthier lifestyle. I honestly believe that this lifestyle has aided me in my studying and my overall college performance."

—Kate, senior, Rutgers University

For more info:

Institute of Food Technologists (IFT)
525 West Van Buren, Suite 1000
Chicago, IL 60607
(312) 782-8424
www.ift.org

American Society for Nutrition (ASN)
9650 Rockville Pike
Suite 4500
Bethesda, MD 20814
(301) 634-7050
www.nutrition.org

Housing and human environments

What it's about:

As a housing and human environments major, you study various aspects of housing, including needs assessment, financing, legislation, equipment, energy conservation, and housing alternatives. Your goal is to gain an in-depth understanding of housing as a product, an environment, a service, and a process for sheltering a diverse, changing population adequately, accessibly, and affordably.

Is this for you?

You might like this major if you also like: helping others; community or volunteer service; interior design; working on team projects.

Consider this major if you are good at: caring/nurturing; critical reading/thinking; leadership; persuading/influencing; research *...or have...* initiative; patience; verbal skills; writing skills.

Recommended high school prep:

English 4, math 3, lab science 3, social studies 3, and a foreign language 2–3.

Typical courses in this major:

Housing in contemporary society
Advanced housing theories
Housing alternatives
Housing policy
Housing counseling
Household technology and systems
Family demographics and policy
Interiors and furnishings
Kitchen and bath design
Real estate
State and local developments
Special needs housing
Family resource management
Property management
Principles of family finance

Concentrations:

Property management; public policy; interiors.

What the study of this major is like:

All housing and human environment majors receive a background in liberal arts, mathematics, natural sciences, and social studies before choosing a concentration. You study housing issues (safety, types of dwellings, ownership) and learn how housing policies, particularly financial programs, government regulation, and taxation, affect families. You also study factors influencing family well being, such as poverty and access to health care, education, and other public services. You might examine consumer legislation and lobbying efforts by housing advocates. Economics and other business courses are often required.

Most programs emphasize learning through experience. You can often do an internship in your area of interest and earn a limited amount of course credit (and sometimes pay) for your work. A positive internship may even lead to a job offer. Another advantage is the mentoring you receive from your field supervisor—a relationship that may last beyond your internship. Guest speakers, field trips, and community service projects can also enhance your studies. For example, students in one program worked with AARP to publicize predatory lending practices. They delivered literature to senior citizens who were at risk of being targeted by dishonest lenders.

Every housing and human environments program is unique. Some focus on space planning and design, with courses in environmental or interior design, and in preparation for kitchen and bath certification. In others, where there is emphasis on the residential property management industry, you use your academic experience to tackle real-life problems that may occur among residents of multifamily dwellings. Still other programs focus on the socioeconomic and policy aspects of housing, where you take additional courses in political science or economics. Before you decide on a program, study the catalogs from different colleges to make sure your interests match a program's strengths.

This major provides you with opportunities to work in both public and private housing arenas. You will be able to apply what you learn in your personal as well as your professional life. Students seeking degrees in housing can be creative in designing programs and career paths to match their interests and abilities, but they all share the desire to help shape the present and future accommodations of our society.

Other majors you might like:
Real estate
Home furnishings
Construction technology
Social work
Historic preservation
Public administration
Urban, community, and regional planning
Construction management
Interior design
Sociology
Civil engineering

Questions to ask colleges:
Are there opportunities to take courses in other majors such as real estate, social work, journalism, and computer science?

What opportunities are there for students to work on service projects in the community, such as Habitat for Humanity, homeless shelters, or homebuilder shows? What kinds of internships are available?

Career options and trends:
Commercial real estate broker*; residential property manager*; construction project manager; residential home loan officer; area housing administrator*; housing counselor; mortgage originator; homebuilder; banking officer; research analyst.

Housing majors find jobs with real estate companies, state and federal agencies, public utilities, historic preservation firms, financial/mortgage institutions, and trade organizations.

Opportunities in this field may be closely related to strength of the housing market, though positions can be found even in tough economic times. As the population ages, there are many employment possibilities involving housing for older adults. Also, as the housing stock itself ages, many consumers are remodeling. These factors are providing good career opportunities for graduates of housing programs.

For more info:
Housing Education and Research Association
  (HERA)
Montana State University Extension Service
109 Taylor Hall
P.O. Box 173580
Bozeman, MT 59717-3580
(406) 994-3451
www.housingeducators.org

National Apartment Association (NAA)
4300 Wilson Blvd.
Suite 400
Arlington, VA 22203
(703) 518-6141
www.naahq.org

Human development and family studies

Also known as:
Human ecology

What it's about:
The human development and family studies major prepares you to investigate how individuals interact as members of a family and how individuals and families interact with the larger social and economic community. You also study the impact of life cycle changes on individuals, families, and societies.

Is this for you?
You might like this major if you also like: taking care of children or the elderly; learning family histories; helping people work out their problems.

Consider this major if you are good at: caring/nurturing; counseling; critical reading/thinking; leadership; organizing; teamwork ...*or have...* initiative; verbal skills; writing skills.

Recommended high school prep:
English 4, math 3, lab science 3, social studies 3, and a foreign language 2–3. If possible, take courses in economics, sociology, and psychology.

Typical courses in this major:
Lifespan human development
Child guidance and parenting
Family finance
Communications in human development
Early childhood education
Human sexuality
Administration of child and family services
Family education and intervention programs
Child socialization
Family interaction
Death and dying: a family and lifespan perspective
Children and families in a multiethnic society
Work and family systems
Families and public policy
Contemporary family issues
Issues in family health

Concentrations:
In college: early childhood education; child development; adolescent development; adult development and aging; family studies; consumer education; family resource management

If you go on to grad school: consumer economics; work and family studies; financial planning and counseling; marriage and family therapy.

What the study of this major is like:
If you major in human development and family studies, you explore the biological, psychological, and sociological development of individuals and families. Courses are designed to help you learn about people in various contexts (including communities and society) and to study them within appropriate theoretical frameworks. Theory and research are coordinated with supervised field experiences.

Generally, you take two introductory courses: one in lifespan development, which covers both continuity and change in individuals from conception to death; the other in the study of families. More advanced courses dealing with such subjects as death and dying and family interaction deepen your understanding. Other courses, such as family education and intervention programs, and the administration of child and family services, have a more practical purpose. Still others, on research and communication, are focused on auxiliary skills.

Professors in human development and family studies use a wide variety of teaching methods, including lecture, discussion, Web-based instruction, field study, and community internship. You are expected to build on and integrate the information and skills you learn as you progress in the program, and to develop your analytical skills and demonstrate good written and oral communication abilities. Most courses include written assignments, essay exams, and opportunities for discussion. An important element in most programs is the fourth-year internship, which is customized to help you consolidate your learning in a semester-long community-based experience.

At some institutions, especially the larger ones, you will probably have greater opportunity to focus your studies on a particular area. These colleges may concentrate on a specialized area such as infant development or family communication and, as a result, offer fewer courses that explore topics from a wider social perspective. Other colleges have a more integrated, holistic approach to human development and family studies, offering a broader, more comprehensive program.

Other majors you might like:
Psychology
Sociology
Early childhood education
Gerontology
Funeral services/mortuary science
Child care management
Occupational therapy
Adult development/aging
Child development
Food and nutrition studies
Work/family studies
Social work

Questions to ask colleges:
How available are supervised practicum sites, such as an infant program, a preschool, or a family-counseling center, where hands-on involvement and observation are carried out?

How many credits are required in general education, in the major, and in elective courses? How accessible and supportive is student advisement? To what extent do students have opportunities to design courses of study to meet their individual interests?

Career options and trends:
Counselor*; early childhood educator*; child care or youth program administrator*; human services agency administrator*; family life educator; family or consumer advocate; child care curriculum coordinator; senior center coordinator; family financial planner.

Human development and family studies majors also find work in child care licensing, Child Life programs, parent education, and human resources.

With a graduate degree, you can pursue counseling certification as a Marriage and Family Therapist (MFT). If you plan to work in parent education or as a family life educator, you will need to fulfill additional requirements and become a Certified Family Life Educator (CFLE).

The job outlook is very good. There will be strong demand for well-trained human service workers and teachers in this field for some time.

For more info:
National Council on Family Relations (NCFR)
1201 West River Parkway, Suite 200
Minneapolis, MN 55454-1115
(888) 781-9331
www.ncfr.org

Health

If you're looking for a major that leads to job security and satisfaction, you've come to the right place. Health care is a growth industry. Because the population is aging and people are living longer, total employment for occupations and industries related to healthcare is projected to increase 10.8 percent, or 15.6 million jobs, by 2022, according to the U.S. Bureau of Labor Statistics—more than any other field. And that's on top of the need to replace about 2 million health care workers who will retire or leave the profession. At the same time, fewer students are moving into the health professions and related sciences lately. Shortages of workers are expected across the board.

"With the shift from paper records to computers to manage health information, the need for health information managers and technicians has sky-rocked in importance," says Professor Valerie Watzlaf of the University of Pittsburgh's School of Health and Rehabilitation Sciences.

"This is an industry that truly combines high tech with high touch," notes Leonard H. Friedman of the Department of Public Health, Oregon State University. "I can think of no professional activity that is more important, worthwhile, or ultimately satisfying."

How will you prepare for a demanding and in-demand career as a clinician, therapist, technician, or other health professional? Look for colleges that specialize in health education. They include schools or divisions of medicine or allied health; nursing schools; colleges of pharmacy, health sciences or services, health occupations, or health professions; and schools of arts and sciences, professional studies, human environmental sciences, health and human sciences, or medical sciences.

The names of the colleges may vary, but the health studies in each field—respiratory therapy, for example—should be very much alike. That's because of groups like CoARC, ARC-PA, AUPHA, and CAPTE. What's with the alphabet soup? Those letters stand for the names of accrediting groups. For instance, more than 130 physician assistant programs nationwide have gotten a professional OK from the Accreditation Review Commission on Education for the Physician Assistant (but you can call it ARC-PA for short). Having standardized courses means that college programs cover similar material to prepare students for professional certification or licensing. Accreditation is the stamp of approval that you'll want your college to have.

Do you want to be a doctor, dentist, or veterinarian? Each field requires specific preprofessional undergraduate courses even though the fields aren't actually majors. That's right—you may know what you want to be but not know what to major in as an undergraduate! For example, premedical studies is a program of prerequisite courses for entrance into medical school. But premed students still have to pick an academic major, and most choose a science such as biology. A preprofessional adviser at college will help you choose a major, prepare for the graduate school entrance examination, arrange the interview, get letters of recommendation, and find volunteer or paid clinical, research, and community service opportunities.

Look for colleges with a strong record of placing students into medical, dental, or veterinary school. For other health studies, ask how long the program has had its gold star from the group that oversees education and training in the profession. (See the individual majors in this section for accrediting bodies.) Also, is it a full accreditation or just something pending? Is the college itself accredited or only the particular program?

Get a complete history

Even with standards in place to nail down core skills and knowledge, programs can differ. Some may take a clinical, practical, hands-on approach to teaching, while others are geared toward theory or research. Some go past the basics into cutting-edge science.

Ask about the three main types of studies you'll do: class/lecture, lab, and clinical internships. Find out about the credentials and experience of the faculty members. What is the ratio of students to teachers? Will the top professors actually do the teaching, or are most courses taught by grad students? Will you be able to do research? Are the labs and equipment up-to-date? What kind of fieldwork or clinical experience is the college set up to give you? Will you work in a hospital? Is it near campus? Will you need to take a licensing exam to work in your professional area? What percent of grads pass that exam?

Also, find out if you're looking at a two-year or a four-year degree program. Different levels of degrees prepare you for different types of work. A dental hygiene or laboratory technician program typically takes two years. Radiologic technicians need an associate degree but can add a bachelor's degree to learn a particular type of medical imaging technology. Veterinary technicians typically have two-year associate degrees.

Nurses at the baccalaureate level are qualified to work in nearly all health care settings, while two-year degrees prepare entry-level LPNs—licensed practical nurses—with lesser responsibilities that vary from state to state.

Is graduate school for you? Physicians, dentists, and veterinarians aren't the only health care professionals with advanced degrees. Pharmacy is a six-year doctoral (Pharm.D.) program starting with two years of preprofessional requirements. You'll need to go beyond a four-year degree for physical therapy programs; the doctorate has become the degree of choice to work in that field. Occupational therapists must also have at least a master's degree. Some nurses study at the graduate level to learn clinical specialties like neonatal (newborn) acute care.

If you're interested in health care but don't want to be a clinician or provide direct patient care, you might go into health care administration or work as a clinical or medical lab technician. Ten of the top 20 fastest growing occupations are healthcare related.

In many health specialties, you'll need continuing professional education to keep up with new technologies and therapies. State licenses may require it. If you want the career benefits of working in health care, your education is only just beginning.

Athletic training

Also known as:
Sports medicine

What it's about:
This major prepares you to become a certified athletic trainer (ATC), a health care professional who knows how to prevent, evaluate, and treat the injuries and related illnesses sustained by physically active people.

Is this for you?
You might like this major if you also like: helping people; sports and competition; problem solving; science and medicine; physical exercise; working with people; tutoring.

Consider this major if you are good at: caring/nurturing; organizing; persuading/influencing; teamwork *...or have...* a sense of humor; initiative; manual dexterity; physical stamina; verbal skills; writing skills.

Recommended high school prep:
English 4, math 3, lab science 4 (take all possible lab sciences), social studies 3, and a foreign language 2–3 (Greek or Latin would help with medical terminology). If available, take a course in anatomy or physiology, and try to obtain First Aid and CPR certification. If possible, work as a team manager, attend summer athletic training camps, or volunteer in sports medicine clinics.

Did you know...
...that more than 60 percent of certified athletic trainers have a master's degree or higher? While the minimum degree needed for many jobs is a bachelor's, you'll significantly improve your career prospects if you have one to two years of graduate school.

Typical courses in this major:
Prevention and care of athletic injuries
Assessment of extemity injuries
Assessment of illnesses
General medical conditions and disabilities
First Aid and emergency care
Therapeutic modalities
Therapeutic exercise and rehabilitation techniques
Human anatomy
Human physiology
Exercise physiology
Kinesiology or biomechanics
Nutrition
Strength and reconditioning
Pharmacology
Pathology
Psychosocial intervention

Concentrations:
Generally, none in college; but if you go on to grad school: health promotion; exercise physiology; biomechanics; exercise psychology; physical education teaching certification; anatomy.

What the study of this major is like:
As an athletic training major, you study academic and clinical sciences. You'll be trained to watch for injuries that may occur in the gym or on the field and to determine, through examination, whether an injury requires First Aid and whether a doctor or an ambulance should be called. You'll also prepare yourself to become a member of a health care team, so that (under a physician's direction), you can administer treatment: whirlpool baths, ultrasound, electrical stimulation, taping, splints, and exercise.

As you work with coaches, physicians, administrators, and athletes, you develop leadership and communication skills. When you complete the program and pass the required exam, you qualify for national certification—the entry-level standard for this profession.

Your first year or two of courses include general studies in the humanities, basic sciences (anatomy, physiology, and chemistry), and an introduction to athletic training. You also learn more about the profession and the major. In some colleges, you must then be accepted into the program. As a major, you are required to complete a minimum of four semesters of clinical experience, in addition to your course work. You'll probably receive at least 800 hours of directed clinical experience, usually in a range of sports: contact and noncontact; male and female; team and individual. Clinical settings are both on- and off-campus, or perhaps in sports medicine clinics in hospitals or private settings.

Most courses include both lecture and laboratory sessions. In lab and clinical courses, you develop practical application (psychomotor) skills and apply them in real-world situations. The biggest challenge most majors face involves time management. Your day might consist of classes during the morning, clinical work for several hours every afternoon, perhaps a class in the evening, and even sports competitions on weekends. You'll have to devote a lot of time to clinical work, but you won't want to neglect your other course assignments. Probably most important, you are responsible for keeping sensitive medical information confidential, and you must always act professionally.

The biggest difference among programs often depends on the orientation of the department that runs the major. Programs in a sports or exercise science department tend to require more science based courses; those housed in departments of kinesiology or physical education may require more courses in sports training; and programs in a health science or health education department may stress such areas as prevention of injuries. Philosophical differences among programs show up in the way students are selected and assigned to clinical experiences. In some programs, you begin clinical education during your first semester, while other programs require one or two years of courses and observation before you are admitted to the major and begin your clinical education. In addition, some programs offer many off-campus opportunities in sports medicine clinics and at local high schools, while others provide clinical opportunities only on campus.

Other majors you might like:
Physical therapy
Recreational therapy
Sports and fitness administration
Sports communications
Occupational therapy
Exercise sciences
Physical education
Health/physical fitness

Emergency medical technology (EMT paramedic)
Physician assistant
Parks, recreation, and leisure studies
Hospitality administration and management

Questions to ask colleges:
Is this program accredited by the Commission on Accreditation of Athletic Training Education (CAATE)? Only graduates of an accredited program are eligible to take the national certification exam.

What is the application process to be formally accepted into the major?

What is the school's passing rate on the Board of Certification exam?

Where are some of the graduates employed—in which settings, in which schools, and with which teams?

Where are clinical rotations completed?

Career options and trends:
High school athletic trainer*; college athletic trainer*; clinical athletic trainer (sports medicine clinic or hospital); industrial athletic trainer; professional sports athletic trainer; medical sales representative.

Very strong job growth is projected through 2022, mostly in the health care industry. The desire of employers to reduce worker injuries and insurance costs is also fueling demand for athletic trainers. Fitness and recreation sports centers continue to provide many new jobs, and opportunities are emerging in the armed services and performing arts.

Because of the growing awareness of the effects of sports-related injuries on young athletes, demand for athletic trainers is expected to increase in high schools, colleges, and youth leagues. However, many high schools require a teaching license in addition to the athletic training certification, and high-profile colleges and universities, as well as professional sports, have limited turnover.

Insider's viewpoint:
"This is a great major for people who love the human sciences because you get just enough of basic science but you are not inundated with chemical formulas and learning why starfish are in phylum Echinodermata."

—Caleb, sophomore, University of Southern California

For more info:

National Athletic Trainers' Association (NATA)
2952 Stemmons Freeway
Suite 200
Dallas, TX 75247-6916
(214) 637-6282
www.nata.org

Commission on Accreditation of Athletic Training
    Education (CAATE)
2201 Double Creek Drive
Suite 5006
Round Rock, TX 78664
(512) 733-9700
www.caate.net

Clinical/medical laboratory technology

What it's about:

Clinical/medical lab technicians examine blood and other body fluids to search for clues in the diagnosis of various diseases. In this major, you are trained to perform general tests in all medical laboratory areas, such as blood banking and hematology; clinical chemistry; urinalysis; immunology; and medical microbiology.

Is this for you?

You might like this major if you also like: solving problems; challenges; puzzles; computers; science and technology; knowing why and how things work; working with precision and accuracy.

Consider this major if you are good at: attention to detail; critical reading/thinking; organizing; quantitative analysis; spacial thinking/analysis; teamwork *...or have...* manual dexterity; patience; verbal skills.

Recommended high school prep:

English 4, math 3, lab science 3 (biology, chemistry, physics), social studies 3, and a foreign language 2–3. Take computer technology and advanced chemistry if available.

Did you know...

...that 70 to 80 percent of all medical decisions are based on laboratory data? The practice of medicine would be impossible without the tests performed by clinical/medical laboratory technicians.

...that the ability to communicate well, both in writing and in speaking, is important in this field? Technical skills alone do not get the job done—results must be communicated accurately and completely.

Typical courses in this major:

Introduction to the clinical laboratory
Clinical chemistry
Hematology
Immunology
Immunohematology
Microbiology
Quality assessment
Anatomy and physiology
College algebra
General chemistry and lab
English composition
Urinalysis/body fluids
Clinical internship

Concentrations:

In college: clinical chemistry; hematology; immunology; clinical microbiology; urinalysis.

If you go on to grad school: clinical/laboratory facilities management; molecular diagnostics.

What the study of this major is like:

A career in clinical/medical laboratory technology is an excellent choice if you want to work in health care, but not directly with patients. As a clinical/medical laboratory technician, you apply your knowledge of, and skills in, the basic sciences to testing in such settings as health care, research, industry, or government agencies.

Laboratory technicians work with medical teams of pathologists, other specialists, and scientists to determine the absence, presence, extent, or cause of disease, and to provide data for evaluating the effectiveness of treatment. The field offers opportunities to learn and grow. As procedures are developed to detect both old and new diseases, the laboratory remains in the forefront of medicine. In addition to an array of precision instruments and electronic equipment, successful laboratories need well-trained, responsible staff.

The clinical/medical laboratory technology major is offered as both a two-year associate degree and a four-year bachelor's degree. This major may be found in departments of biology, chemistry, natural sciences, or life sciences, and in schools of health professions, allied health and/or nursing, or medicine.

Because classes are usually small and labs generally have fewer than 18 students, teamwork and group learning are encouraged. To gain a sound foundation for your clinical studies, you are likely to begin with a number of science courses. You'll take courses in anatomy and/or physiology, genetics, and microbiology, and perhaps advanced cell physiology. In chemistry courses, you'll focus on inorganic and organic compounds and biochemistry. Algebra and statistics may also be also required; courses in chemical analysis and computer science are useful. Many students find the large amount of information presented in a two-year program a bit overwhelming, especially if they have not been full-time college students before entering the program.

In this major, the emphasis is on laboratory practice. Unlike traditional science majors, in which the lab work illustrates theories you learn in the classroom, clinical/medical laboratory technology uses theory to support the lab work. You learn by doing, in order to understand the theoretical and clinical significance of lab procedures. In most programs you spend the equivalent of one semester learning the theory, procedures, equipment, and practices of clinical laboratory science in a working laboratory. During this time, you learn to test body fluids and tissues and practice what you learn in class. Most majors find laboratory work the most exciting and interesting part of the program.

To be eligible for national certification exams, you should attend an accredited program—one that meets the standards set by the National Accrediting Agency for Clinical Laboratory Science (NAACLS). Programs at different colleges may meet the standards in different ways—for example, by teaching courses in a different order, making use of online programs or courses, or varying the required clinical internship from none to several hundred hours.

Other majors you might like:
Chemistry
Biochemistry
Biomedical technology
Molecular biology
Cytotechnology
Microbiology
Forensic science
Phlebotomy
Biotechnology
Dental laboratory technology
Clinical laboratory science
Radiologic technology/medical imaging

Questions to ask colleges:
Is the program accredited?

Are the lab facilities dedicated to this major?

In a two-year program, is there an articulation agreement with a four-year college to accept transfer credit for these courses?

Is space guaranteed in the clinical facility for the internship?

Career options and trends:
Clinical/medical laboratory technologist*; microbiologist*; laboratory director; forensic analyst; biotechnician; research technician; technical/marketing sales representative.

Clinical/medical laboratory technicians work in a variety of practice settings, such as hospitals, for-profit laboratories, clinics, nursing homes, public health facilities, business, and industry. Supervisory or management positions usually require Clinical Laboratory Scientist (CLS) certification.

The long-term employment for medical laboratory technicians looks bright. According to the Bureau of Labor Statistics, employment of medical laboratory technicians is projected to grow 30 percent by 2022, much faster than the average for all occupations.

For more info:
American Society for Clinical Laboratory Science (ASCLS)
1861 International Drive, Suite 200
McLean, VA 22102
(541) 748-3770
www.ascls.org

Communication disorders

What it's about:

At the undergraduate level, this major is primarily a preprofessional program designed to give training in the identification and treatment of human communication disorders, in preparation for professional training in a master's degree program in either speech-language pathology or audiology. You learn about the normal processes of human communication and the problems that may occur, including disorders of articulation, language, hearing, cognition, swallowing, and voice.

Is this for you?

You might like this major if you also like: helping people; problem solving; using technology; working with children; working with older adults.

Consider this major if you are good at: attention to detail; caring/nurturing; counseling; creativity; math; persuading/influencing ...*or have...* initiative; patience; verbal skills; writing skills.

Recommended high school prep:

English 4, math 3, lab science 3, social studies 3, and a foreign language 2–3. Take anatomy and psychology if they are available.

Typical courses in this major:

Survey of communication disorders
Phonetics
Normal speech and language development
Audiology
Anatomy and physiology
Articulation disorders
Language disorders
Aural rehabilitation
Diagnostics
Augmentative communication

Concentrations:

In college: childhood speech; language disorders.

If you go on to grad school: speech-language pathology; audiology; adult and neurological communication disorders; childhood and developmental communication disorders.

What the study of this major is like:

The major in communication disorders emphasizes both normal and abnormal growth and development. Professionals (such as speech-language pathologists and speech, language, and hearing scientists) deal with infants, children, adolescents, adults, and the elderly, in schools, hospitals, businesses, private practice, universities, research laboratories, and government agencies.

The undergraduate major prepares you for professional study at the master's degree level. As a major, you explore normal and defective hearing and speech, and then learn to identify and evaluate communication disorders and available treatment. The typical program is sequential—courses are based on the knowledge and skills you developed in previous course work.

In introductory courses, you study normal voice, speech, and language processes and the symptoms of disorders. Taking anatomy and physiology teaches you how people produce and perceive speech. You will read research reports on speech disorders, in order to apply findings to treatment programs and to determine what further research should be done. You may study stuttering, aphasia, and other common disorders.

While you pursue your major, you complete requirements in academic areas that support the core courses, including biology and physical sciences, behavioral and social sciences, and other liberal arts and sciences course work. Majors usually get clinical experience by working (under close supervision) in the college speech and hearing clinic with children and adults.

Although most courses follow the lecture format, you may also work with interactive computer instruction. Academic standards for the major are high, because the majority of students will continue on to a master's program. In fact, most states require an advanced degree for certification in this field. To be successful in this major, you need a strong background in math, science, and writing. Anatomy and neurology require a lot of memorization, and you may have difficulty managing your time as a result of heavy clinical requirements. But students in this major tend to bond into closely knit groups and assist each other through the program.

Other majors you might like:
Child development
Psychology
Gerontology
Special education
Education of speech impaired
Linguistics
Audiology/speech pathology
American sign language (ASL)
Anthropology
Speech teacher education
Education of deaf/hearing impaired
Speech/rhetorical studies

Questions to ask colleges:
What are the academic requirements for admission into the major, both at the undergraduate and at the graduate level? Are students admitted into the program as freshmen, or must they qualify for admission after their first or second year in college?

Is a combined bachelor's/graduate degree program available?

Is the undergraduate program broad-based, or is it geared toward either childhood disorders or adult disorders?

Career options and trends:
School speech/language therapist*; speech pathologist*; audiologist; speech scientist.

The American Speech–Language–Hearing Association (ASHA) sets standards for national certification in speech-language pathology or audiology (check their website for updates). Currently, this certificate requires a master's degree, passing a national exam, and at least 36 weeks of supervised professional employment in the field. State teacher certification is required for teaching students with speech and language disabilities in the public school system. Most states also have professional license requirements for speech pathologists employed in a health care setting.

Employment prospects in this field are expected to grow much faster than average through 2022. As awareness and identification of speech and language disorders in children becomes more prevalent, the number of positions available in educational settings will increase. Opportunities for speech-language pathologists in private practice should also increase as hospitals, schools, and nursing care facilities have begun contracting out for these services in an effort to control costs. Demand for audiologists will keep pace with the increasing population of older Americans facing hearing loss.

Insider's viewpoint:
"We're required to have a lot of clinical hours, and we have to get them in a lot of different areas, including adults and children, diagnostics, and treatment. So it's the fun part and it's also the hard part, to make sure you get all those hours in."

—Cara, graduate student, University of Pittsburgh

For more info:
American Speech–Language–Hearing Association (ASHA)
2200 Research Blvd.
Rockville, MD 20850-3289
(800) 638-8255
www.asha.org

Dental hygiene

What it's about:

As a major in dental hygiene, you obtain the knowledge and clinical skills needed to prevent and treat oral diseases in order to protect teeth and gums—and to preserve patients' general health. Courses in basic and dental sciences, as well as clinical training in patient care, prepare you to become a licensed dental hygienist.

Is this for you?

You might like this major if you also like: working with your hands; routines and schedules; working with people; detail-oriented activities; crafts.

Consider this major if you are good at: caring/nurturing; counseling; following directions; multitasking; organizing; teamwork ...*or have* manual dexterity; patience; verbal skills.

Recommended high school prep:

English 4, math 3, lab science 3 (including chemistry), social studies 3, and a foreign language 2–3. Take a basic computer/keyboarding course and a health course, if available.

Did you know...

...that while an associate degree in dental hygiene is offered at many two-year colleges, it may actually take longer than two years to complete? That's because most schools require you to take prerequisite courses before admission into the program.

Typical courses in this major:

Pharmacology
Histology
Pathology
Radiology
Microbiology
Chemistry
Dental anatomy
Preventive dentistry
Dental materials
Dental hygiene techniques
Nutrition
Office emergencies
Office management
Introduction to clinic procedures

Concentrations:

Generally, none available.

What the study of this major is like:

Registered dental hygienists are licensed health care professionals. To become licensed, you must graduate from an accredited dental hygiene program and pass state and national exams.

The primary responsibility of dental hygienists is to assist patients in maintaining oral and dental health. Majors in dental hygiene are therefore required to master a wide range of skills related to health and patient education. Although training differs among states, you are usually taught to perform patient assessments (including medical histories; blood pressure testing; head, neck, and mouth examinations; and oral cancer screenings); remove deposits from the teeth (oral prophylaxis); use agents such as fluoride to help prevent decay; work with dental X rays; and advise patients on maintaining healthy lifestyles.

You first take anatomy, physiology, and pathology to explore the functions of the human body, the process of disease, and the biological and physiological basis of health. Courses in dental hygiene sciences provide the foundation for dental hygiene care and clinical practice. Learning takes place in the classroom, in laboratories, and in clinical experiences. In your first year, you develop skills by practicing on models and then, under professional supervision, by treating patients. Your course work emphasizes providing dental hygiene services to diverse groups of patients in clinical settings. Because much of a dental hygienist's time is spent interacting one-on-one with patients, you take courses in psychology, speech, sociology, and patient management to develop strong communications and interpersonal skills.

Dental hygiene programs are full-time courses of study. Course material must be covered in a certain

301

sequence, because new courses build on past work. Throughout your clinical experience, you will continue to apply what you've learned in your courses. Outside experiences may include visits to patients in public health clinics, hospitals, child care centers, nursing homes, and correctional facilities. You may also participate in health fairs, health education presentations, and elementary school activities. Some programs send you to work in dental offices in the community to gain real-world experience.

Dental hygiene programs may be located in community colleges or four-year institutions. Some programs are affiliated with dental schools. In the two-year associate degree program, the curriculum should be accredited by the American Dental Association (ADA). The associate degree is the minimum required for entry-level certification. Bachelor's or master's degree programs prepare you to work in industry, education, or research. If you have dental assisting experience or are a graduate of an ADA-accredited dental-assisting program, some colleges give you transfer credit for your experience, so that you do not have to repeat material you have already covered.

Other majors you might like:
Clinical/medical laboratory technology
Dental laboratory technology
Physical therapy
Makeup artist
Public health education
Ophthalmic technology
Physician assistant
Radiologic technology/medical imaging
Medical records technology
Dietetics
Social work
American sign language (ASL)

Questions to ask colleges:
Is the program accredited by the ADA? If not, your degree will not be recognized by state licensing bodies and you will not be eligible to take the national board exam.

Which courses must be taken before entry into the program?

Where is the clinical component performed? Most programs have on-site clinical facilities, but some may require travel to nearby locations.

Career options and trends:
Dental hygiene practitioner*; clinical instructor; clinical researcher.

In order to become a registered dental hygienist and obtain a state license, you must pass a national written examination, and a state or regional clinical examination.

This field is consistently ranked among the fastest growing occupations. Most dental hygienists work in private dental offices, but many work in clinics, schools, nursing homes, hospitals, universities, managed health care organizations, and correctional institutions. As health care expands to include dental professionals as part of an interdisciplinary team of health care providers, practice settings available to dental hygienists will also expand.

For more info:
American Dental Hygienists' Association (ADHA)
444 North Michigan Ave., Suite 3400
Chicago, IL 60611
(312) 440-8900
www.adha.org

Dietetics

What it's about:

Dietetics prepares you to provide for the nutritional needs of people in conditions of both wellness and ill health. Your studies include the basic sciences, nutrition and food science, principles of management, and behavioral and social sciences. Bachelor degree programs prepare you to become a registered dietitian (RD), and associate degree programs prepare you to be a dietitian technician (DTR).

Is this for you?

You might like this major if you also like: cooking and eating; watching cooking shows on TV; reading about nutrition and health in magazines; science fairs and projects; sports; health and fitness activities; helping people.

Consider this major if you are good at: attention to detail; caring/nurturing; counseling; critical reading/thinking; science; teamwork ...*or have...* initiative; verbal skills.

Recommended high school prep:

English 4, math 3, lab science 4 (including chemistry and physics), social studies 3, and a foreign language 2–3. If possible, take advanced biology and chemistry; courses on health, foods, and nutrition are also recommended.

Did you know...

...that this is a great major for entrepreneurs? The food industry is the fourth largest in the world. Almost any food- or health-related setting needs dietitians, and nutrition is essential to health, from birth to old age.

Typical courses in this major:

Organic chemistry
Biochemistry
Anatomy and physiology
Microbiology
Food science
Food chemistry
Basic nutrition
Advanced nutrition and metabolism
Medical nutrition therapy
Maternal and child nutrition
Geriatric nutrition
Public health *or* Community nutrition
Quantity food production and procurement
Diet selection and management

Concentrations:

Clinical nutrition; health and fitness; institutional food management.

What the study of this major is like:

All dietetics programs must be approved by the Commission on Accreditation for Dietetics Education (CADE). To become a registered dietitian, you must complete an accredited program and earn at least a four-year Bachelor of Science degree. Your course work includes biochemistry, microbiology, and anatomy, as well as industry-related subjects such as culinary arts, food service systems management, and food and nutrition sciences. In courses like communications, computer science, and sociology, you learn the necessary business skills and "people skills."

You must also complete a supervised practice program in dietetics (typically 6 to 12 months)—either while you're in college or afterward—and pass an exam administered nationally by the Commission on Dietetic Registration (CDR). Programs that combine your degree work and the practice program are called coordinated programs in dietetics (CPD). Programs that postpone the supervised practice work until after you graduate are called didactic programs in dietetics (DPD). You should choose which program is best for you before you enroll.

If you plan to become a dietitian technician, you must complete a CADE-accredited dietetics program while you earn at least a two-year associate degree. You take courses in food and nutrition, food service systems management, and general science, together with at least 450 hours of supervised practice in a health care facility or food service organization. After you graduate, you must pass the CDR's nationally administered registration examination. If you think you might later want to become an RD, check with the dietitian program you are considering to see if it has formal arrangements (known as an articulation agreement) with CPD and DPD programs to accept some or all of your credits. Otherwise, check directly with the CPD or DPD programs you are considering to see if your courses will receive transfer credit.

Course work in the dietetics major includes lecture, labs, individual and group projects, and required practical experience and/or summer internships. In courses with labs, you'll be kept very busy, so you must organize your time efficiently. Programs may differ in aspects of the curriculum that work best for faculty members. For example, a program in a research-based university may emphasize science, whereas in a small college, it may stress food service systems management. As a result, some programs may be more academically challenging than others, and some may offer opportunities beyond the basic requirements. To find out about a program's emphasis, look at the catalog. Faculty members' areas of expertise will be reflected in the courses they teach.

Sometimes people confuse registered dietitians, dietitian technicians, and nutritionists. Although in some states you need to be licensed to call yourself a nutritionist, the definition often varies. In every state, however, only professionals who are certified by the Commission on Dietetic Registration (CDR) can legally use the titles "registered dietitian" and "dietitian technician."

Other majors you might like:
Culinary arts and chef training
Food and nutrition studies
Pharmacy
Sports and fitness administration
Physician assistant
Occupational therapy
Restaurant/food services management
Hospitality administration and management
Nutrition sciences
Public health education
Gerontology
Food science

Questions to ask colleges:
Does the program help identify opportunities for summer jobs and entry-level job?

What percent of the program's graduates pass the certification examination to become an RD?

What is the acceptance rate of graduates into dietetic practice programs?

Career options and trends:
Registered dietitian (RD) in clinical, administrative, or private practice*; registered dietitian technician (DTR) working in a school or health care facility*; restaurant manager; extension educator; research dietitian; chef; food industry representative.

According to the Bureau of Labor Statistics, job prospects for dietitians will increase faster than average over the next decade, especially in home health care and social services. Employment in hospitals is expected to show little change over the next decade or so because of anticipated slow growth and reduced length of patients' hospital stays. Faster growth, however, is anticipated in nursing homes, residential care facilities, and physician clinics. Rising public interest in nutrition and obesity disorders will also spur demand.

While job prospects are good for all dietetics majors, the best and most plentiful jobs go to graduates who are RDs.

For more info:
American Dietetic Association
120 South Riverside Plaza, Suite 2000
Chicago, IL 60606
(800) 877-1600
www.eatright.org

Emergency medical technology (EMT paramedic)

Also known as:
Emergency medical services (EMS)

What it's about:
In this major, you develop the problem-solving, critical-thinking, and management skills necessary to function independently in prehospital settings. You learn how to recognize, assess, and manage medical emergencies; to supervise ambulance personnel; and to carry out medical interventions, from basic responses such as bandaging to high-level techniques such as administering medication, providing cardiac care, and performing advanced airway measures.

Is this for you?
You might like this major if you also like: working with all types of people; helping people in times of crisis; fast action; sports; technology, science, and medicine; taking command.

Consider this major if you are good at: attention to detail; caring/nurturing; critical reading/thinking; organizing; persuading/influencing; teamwork; thinking on your feet ...*or have...* initiative; patience; self-confidence; verbal skills.

Recommended high school prep:
English 4, math 3, lab science 3–4 (biology and chemistry most important), social studies 3, and a foreign language 2–3. If available, take a course on anatomy or physiology; and try to obtain First Aid and CPR certification.

Did you know...
...that being a paramedic requires more responsibility than putting people into the back of an ambulance and driving them to the hospital? The job involves interacting with other community organizations, family members, and hospital personnel. In many communities, you are crossed-trained with other public safety responders, such as police officers and firefighters.

Typical courses in this major:
Anatomy and physiology
College math
Pathophysiology
Pharmacology
Bioterrorism
Medical and trauma assessment
Emergency care analysis and intervention
Communications and computer operations
Crisis scene management
Accounting and budgeting
Advanced cardiac life support
Prehospital field techniques
Vehicle rescue
Equipment operation and maintenance
Prehospital trauma life support
Professional standards

Concentrations:
In college: pharmacology; trauma assessment; anatomy and physiology; emergency care and analysis.

If you go on to grad school: emergency management; ambulatory care.

What the study of this major is like:
Emergency medical services (EMS) providers help people in life- or health-threatening situations. The most highly trained prehospital EMS providers are EMT (emergency medical technician) paramedics, who care for patients on site and then help get them to hospitals. As workers or volunteers for ambulance services, fire departments, hospitals, and government-based services, EMTs may be called in to help someone suffering from a broken toe one hour, and someone else having a massive heart attack the next.

If you major in emergency medical technology, you usually take courses such as anatomy and physiology, disease process, pharmacology, cardiology, medical and trauma assessment, hazardous material, bioterrorism, and vehicle rescue. Liberal arts courses teach you how to communicate and work with patients and with other health professionals. Courses are taught in a number of ways, ranging from lecture format to Web-based scenario practice. In classrooms and labs, you learn and practice skills such as intravenous (IV) insertion, intubations, and defibrillation.

In addition to course work, you do clinical rotations in hospitals and with paramedic units. During clinical rotations, you gain experience in making decisions, assessing patients' condition, and providing appropriate treatment—always under close supervision. Because paramedics must be familiar with all types of injury and illness, your clinical rotations cover a range of patients, including adult, pediatric, and geriatric patients, as well as a wide variety of conditions, including chest pain, respiratory distress, broken bones, and spinal cord injuries. You may work in a cardiac intensive care unit, an operating room, an emergency department, a trauma unit, a burn unit, or a behavioral unit.

In your paramedic unit rotation, you work in the field, answering calls with a qualified instructor. You learn how to care for patients under often-difficult conditions. Some programs require one paramedic field rotation, whereas others call for two—one in a suburban ambulance and one in an urban ambulance. Most EMT majors are enrolled full-time, and some find it hard to balance study time with clinical rotations and course work. Still, most majors find, in the end, that being well trained to help others is worth the effort they have put into studying.

Emergency medical technology programs are found in colleges, EMT academies, and hospitals. Most are similar, emphasizing critical-thinking, problem-solving, and clinical skills. Some programs provide training in entry-level management. Others focus on paramedic studies and do not include management or education courses. The majority of programs offer a two-year associate degree or certificate program; but if you plan to move up quickly into management or supervisory roles, you should consider pursuing a four-year Bachelor of Science degree.

Other majors you might like:
Physician assistant
Nursing (RN)
Athletic training
Community health/preventative medicine
Respiratory therapy
Occupational safety/health technology
Forensic science
Emergency management/homeland security
Hazardous materials technology
Fire protection and safety technology
Paralegal studies
Social work

Questions to ask colleges:
Where are the clinical rotations done (for instance, in trauma centers or in a local hospital)? Where are the prehospital rotations done?

What system is used to track and record the required number of student-patient contacts necessary for certification?

Are graduates of the program eligible to sit for the National Registry Examination for paramedics?

Career options and trends:
Paramedic*; emergency room technician; fire fighter; police officer; occupation health officer; state office of EMS employee; Federal Emergency Management Agency (FEMA) employee; infection control officer; EMS coordinator; EMS supervisor.

Most states require certification through the National Registry Examination for Paramedics, which makes it easier to relocate from state to state. Municipal or federal employment usually requires you to take a civil service exam as well.

EMS employment is projected to have a high growth rate through the year 2022, partly due to an increase in the number of age-related health emergencies, such as heart attacks and strokes, and also due to the increasing number of specialized medical facilities requiring the transfer of patients to these facilities for treatment.

For more info:
National Association of Emergency Medical
    Technicians (NAEMT)
P.O. Box 1400
Clinton, MS 39060-1400
(800) 34-NAEMT
www.naemt.org

Health care administration

What it's about:
The health care administration major prepares you to manage the business activities of a wide variety of organizations that make up the health care delivery system, such as hospitals, clinics, nursing homes, insurance companies, and public health agencies.

Is this for you?
You might like this major if you also like: organizing or leading a club or group activity; solving problems; team sports; working with different types of people; starting and running a business; debating; health and science issues; community service projects.

Consider this major if you are good at: active listening; attention to detail; leadership; organizing; persuading/influencing; quantitative analysis; teamwork ...*or have...* initiative; verbal skills; writing skills.

Recommended high school prep:
English 4, math 3, lab science 4, social studies 3, and a foreign language 2–3. While not a specific requirement, evidence of leadership either in high school or in the community is desirable. Additionally, a course in public speaking would be helpful.

Did you know...
...that the majority of undergraduates pursuing health administration are women?

Typical courses in this major:
Introduction to health care
Organizational behavior
Statistics
Epidemiology (disease contagion and control)
Health policy
Ethics
Strategic planning
Marketing health care
Economics of health care
Accounting
Management information systems
Public health
Health law
Health care management
Financial management
Human resources management

Concentrations:
Long-term health care; health information systems; physician practice management.

What the study of this major is like:
Healthcare administrators are needed just about everywhere health care is delivered, taking care of the important business end of things while doctors and nurses focus on the patients. In this major, you will learn how to make health care available to individuals and how to manage organizations such as nursing homes, clinics, welfare departments, rehabilitation centers, and hospitals. The program teaches you to manage finances, deal with personnel, understand and comply with the laws that affect health care delivery, and oversee other aspects of administration.

Health care administration is a "people business." As a health care administrator, you'll spend most of your time dealing with physicians, nurses, patients and their families, payers, regulators, government agencies, and media representatives. Although majors must be organized and willing to work hard, the most important quality health care administrators need is good interpersonal skills. To be successful, you should feel comfortable working with diverse groups of people; communicate well (writing, speaking, and listening); be able to assume a leadership role when necessary; accept criticism without taking it personally; juggle multiple demands; take into account information from a variety of sources when making decisions; and be ready to improve your organization.

Majors take courses in three broad areas—liberal arts, general management, and health services management. In liberal arts courses, you study communications (especially public speaking), mathematics (especially statistics), critical thinking, and social context (including philosophy, sociology, psychology, political science, and economics). For general management, you examine theories of management, the functional areas of management (such as accounting, computer applications, human resource management, marketing, and strategic management courses), and leadership skills. Health services management courses cover health and disease, health services organization and delivery, financial management, law and government regulation, and health policy.

Health services management courses begin in your third year. Your classes will primarily be lecture/discussion. Many courses use the case method: groups of students examine a question or a problem and come up with a number of solutions. Most programs require a supervised, field-based internship (in the summer or for a semester). Additional practicum experience is highly recommended. Experience in either paid or volunteer positions can make all the difference when you begin your job search.

There are two challenges that most majors face. The first is time management—courses (particularly at the upper level) are intense and require numerous papers and extensive reading. The second challenge is public speaking—an essential skill for health care professionals. In upper-level courses, you often work to overcome both challenges by participating in study groups.

Programs may have different emphases, depending on where they are housed. For example, programs in business schools stress finance and similar subjects, whereas programs in schools of public health or health sciences stress subjects like community response to infectious diseases. As a major, you should seek out courses that balance your studies. If your program has a business focus, be sure to enroll in courses in public health; similarly, if the program is in a health sciences/public health school, you should think about minoring in business.

Other majors you might like:
Business administration and management
Occupational health/industrial hygiene
Health information management
Funeral services/mortuary science
Health services administration
Biotechnology

Psychology
Public administration
Human services
Social work
Community health services
Management information systems

Questions to ask colleges:
Is the program a certified member or candidate member of the Association of University Programs in Health Administration? Certification by AUPHA indicates that the program has met national standards in facilities, program support, curriculum, and outcomes measures.

Are student chapters of health care professional organizations available on campus? These clubs give students valuable leadership and networking opportunities.

Career options and trends:
Health plan administrator; health policy analyst; hospital or health system management*; nurse management; nursing home administrator*; physician group practice administrator*; public health administrator; pharmaceutical sales representative.

State licensure is usually required to run a skilled-care nursing home. Administrators of public health departments or agencies typically have a clinical background either in nursing, social work, or equivalent field of practice.

As the healthcare industry expands and changes, more managers will be needed to ensure that business operations continue to run smoothly.

The Bureau of Labor Statistics projects faster than average growth in this field through 2022, which is not surprising considering that the entire health care industry is the fastest growing in the U.S. economy. The most significant trend for likely employment is in the areas of long-term care and physician group-practice management. The increasing number of acute care hospitals is also opening up employment opportunities. But keep in mind that to move up from an entry-level management position, you'll probably need a master's degree and at least five years' experience.

For more info:

Association of University Programs in Health
   Administration (AUPHA)
2000 14th St. North
Suite 780
Arlington, VA 22201
(703) 894-0940
www.aupha.org

American College of Healthcare Executives
   (ACHE)
One North Franklin, Suite 1700
Chicago, IL 60606
(312) 424-2800
www.ache.org

Medical Group Management Association (MGMA)
104 Iverness Terrace East
Englewood, CO 80112
(877) 275-6462
www.mgma.org

Health information management

Also known as:
Health informatics
Health information technology
Medical records administration/technology

What it's about:
Health information management (HIM) will prepare you to become a credentialed professional responsible for the information systems and data needed to deliver quality, cost-effective healthcare in all settings. Your studies will draw upon the fields of medicine, management, information technology, finance, law, and health sciences.

Is this for you?
You might like this major if you also like: science and technology; running a small business; organizing things efficiently; leading a club or group activity; debating; solving problems; team sports; working with numbers and databases.

Consider this major if you are good at: quantitative analysis; attention to detail; organizing; critical reading/thinking; leadership; teamwork *?or have?* initiative; computer skills; verbal skills; writing skills.

Recommended high school prep:
English 4, math 3, lab science 4, social studies 3, and a foreign language 2–3. If offered, courses in anatomy, statistics, computer applications, business or accounting would be helpful.

Did you know...
...that HIM is at the forefront of innovation in health care reform? The push towards electronic health records is spawning many new start-ups, developing apps that harness the power of both open and secure data to provide new ways to understand and deliver health care.

Typical courses in this major:
Management of health information systems
Statistics and health data analytics
Healthcare database design and development
Electronic health record systems
Legal aspects of health care
Medical terminology, coding, and classification systems
Privacy and security of health information
Quality and performance management
Healthcare finance and budgeting
Health information systems analysis
Health informatics
Epidemiology
Pharmacology
Professionalism and leadership
Senior capstone project (independent research)
Clinical internships (I–IV)

Concentrations:
Health information privacy and security; data analysis; electronic health record systems; data systems design and management; revenue management.

What the study of this major is like:
If you want to work in healthcare, but think you might rather work with computers than with patients, this major is a great choice. HIM combines interests in medicine, management, and information technology to prepare you for a vital role in support of direct patient care, disease control, public health, basic and applied research, and more.

Many HIM programs are offered on campus, online, or a combination of both. Usually this major is taught in small classes by faculty that are very accessible and close to their students. In most bachelor degree programs, you don't get accepted into the HIM major until after you've completed the first two years of college, and admission can be competitive. To be eligible, you'll have to take some pre-requisite courses in your freshman and sophomore years and maintain a certain GPA.

Prerequisite courses can include anatomy and physiology (with lab, which usually involves dissections); statistics; biology; chemistry; computer/information science; English composition; math; medical terminology; pathophysiology (study of human disease); psychology; and public speaking. Most colleges will provide an adviser to help you register for the right courses in the right sequence.

Once you enter the major, your courses will span a range of subjects, such as epidemiology (how diseases spread and are controlled); informatics (the study of how information is represented, processed, and communicated); and analytics (how data is used to generate insights and draw conclusions). You will learn coding—not computer coding, but the system for assigning code numbers to the diagnosis, procedures, and complications noted in a patient's medical record. These codes are not only used to determine reimbursement, but also make it possible to identify and track health issues across patient populations, determine trends, and make planning decisions.

Another area of training is how to implement and manage an Electronic Health Record (EHR) system, which enables a patient's complete and current medical history to be instantly accessed, even in remote locations via a mobile device (smart phone or tablet). Of course, how to maintain security and privacy in that environment will be an important part of what you learn.

But managing information systems is not the sole focus of this major—an HIM professional must also be a good communicator, so some courses will be writing-intensive. You'll also take courses on leadership, ethics, and human relations. The fundamentals of statistics, database design, accounting, and business management, as well as applicable legal and regulatory requirements, are also part of the curriculum.

Because HIM professionals must be able to fit into the workflow processes in many different situations, and often serve as a bridge connecting clinical, operational, and administrative functions, every accredited HIM program includes a Professional Practice Experience (PPE) component that provides hands-on experiences in a variety of settings, such as a hospital, insurance company, or doctor's office. Typically, you'll have four separate PPE internships, each with a different focus. In addition to participating in real world day-to-day operations, you'll complete special projects with the help of a mentor.

Two-year associate degree programs in HIM focus on the basic technical skills of the profession, such as coding and database management, and prepare you to be credentialed as a Registered Health Information Technician (RHIT). Four-year bachelor's degree programs focus on the administrative, leadership, and higher-level technical skills needed for the Registered Health Information Administrator (RHIA) credential, which offers greater career opportunities and earning potential.

It is essential that any HIM program you are considering be accredited by the Commission on Accreditation of Health Informatics and Information Management (CAHIIM), since only students from an accredited program are eligible to take the RHIA or RHIT credentialing exam.

Other majors you might like:
Management information systems
Information technology
Health communications
Bioinformatics
Industrial engineering
Database design/management
Computer and information systems security
Technical and business writing
Statistics
Medical office administration
Medical insurance specialist
Digital media

Questions to ask colleges:
Is the program accredited? You won't be eligible to take the RHIT or RHIA credentialing exam otherwise.

What is the school's passing rate on the credentialing exam? That's a good indication of how well the program prepares its students.

What is the job placement rate of HIM graduates? Since there is great demand for HIM professionals, the job placement rate should be fairly high.

Where do students go to fulfill PPE/internship requirements? Some colleges may have access to lots of healthcare sites and others may not. This is a key part of your education and can lead to a potential job, so ask to see a list of the places providing internships.

Career options and trends:
Systems analyst*; data analyst; coding specialist*; EHR implementation or training consultant*; HIM

director or assistant director; compliance manager; health information privacy and security officer*; data quality manager.

Although most new graduates find jobs in hospitals and clinics, employment can also be found in software companies, mental/behavioral health facilities, home and hospice care, government agencies, and long term/elder care facilities.

The job outlook is excellent. According to the Bureau of Labor Statistics, employment in this field is projected to grow much faster than average through 2022. And unlike many other health professions, state licensure is *not* required for HIM professionals. The RHIA/RHIT credentials are universally accepted in all states.

For more info:
American Health Information Management
    Association (AHIMA)
233 N. Michigan Avenue, 21st Floor
Chicago, IL 60601-5809
(3120 233-1100
www.ahima.org

Commission on Accreditation of Health
    Informatics and Information Management
    (CAHIIM)
www.cahiim.org

Licensed practical nursing

Also known as:
Vocational nursing

What it's about:
The practical nursing major is a one- or two-year program that prepares you to assist registered nurses and physicians in providing general nursing care. After you graduate, you will be eligible to take the National Council Licensing Examination for Practical Nurses (NCLEX-PN). Passing the exam allows you to be certified by a state board of nursing as a licensed practical/vocational nurse (LP/VN).

Is this for you?
You might like this major if you also like: working with others; caring for peoples' physical, psychological, and emotional needs; physical and social sciences; learning about the human body.

Consider this major if you are good at: caring/nurturing; communicating; critical reading/thinking; making decisions; math; organizing; teamwork ...*or have...* manual dexterity; patience; physical stamina; positive attitude.

Recommended high school prep:
English 4, math 3, lab science 3 (including biology and chemistry), social studies 3, and a foreign language 2–3.

Typical courses in this major:
Nursing (lecture and clinical courses)
Nutrition
Pharmacology
English composition
Chemistry
Anatomy and physiology
Microbiology
Psychology
Developmental psychology
Sociology

Concentrations:
Generally, none available.

What the study of this major is like:
Licensed practical nurses (LPNs)—also called licensed vocational nurses (LVNs) in some states—play an essential part in hospital care: monitoring patients' condition and reporting changes to nurses and physicians; taking temperature and blood pressure; helping patients do rehabilitative exercises; giving medications; bathing patients; changing bandages; and collecting laboratory samples. With the growing shortage of registered nurses (RNs) throughout the world, the role of the LPN continues to evolve. For example, intravenous (IV) therapy for patients used to be provided only by RNs. In some states, certified LPNs can now perform IV therapy.

The major includes general education, science, and nursing courses. Behavioral and social science courses stress the elements of human behavior, growth and development, interpersonal relationships, and cultural diversity. Nursing courses generally cover the nursing process, basic and advanced nursing skills, communication, disease, medications, dosage calculations, lab tests, treatments, ethics, legal/professional issues, and patient care from birth to death.

Behavioral and social science courses are typically in lecture format. Nursing and natural science courses include both lecture and laboratory/clinical experiences. Your initial lab courses allow you to safely practice your nursing skills. Before working with patients, you need to become knowledgeable, competent, and confident. You then move out into the real world for your clinical practice work, where you are supervised as you care for patients in acute care or long-term care facilities.

The most likely challenge you may face is to recognize how difficult the work can be and to devote the necessary time and effort to it. To participate actively in class, you must prepare the required class presentations and written work. Many programs expect you to maintain a minimum grade point average. After you graduate, you must complete a national exam.

To become an LPN, you can pursue either a one-year vocational program at a technical school or a two-year associate degree at a college. As you compare programs, consider your career plans. If you see yourself as a bedside nurse working under the supervision of a registered nurse, doctor, or dentist, then a one-year vocational program is enough. On the other hand, if you think you might want to advance further in nursing, you should start with an accredited two-year program where you can transfer credits to other programs. Because nursing courses vary among colleges, it may be hard to transfer—so if you need to transfer, meet with the director of the new program and provide a description of the courses you have completed. Try to get credit for what you have learned.

Other majors you might like:
Nursing (RN)
Dietetics
Physician assistant
Psychology
Dental hygiene
Physical therapy
Art therapy
Gerontology
Medical office administration
Human development and family studies
American sign language (ASL)
Emergency medical technology (EMT paramedic)

Questions to ask colleges:
Is the nursing program approved by the state board of nursing?

What are the admission, curriculum, progression, and graduation requirements? You should find out before you enroll, so you won't have any surprises later.

What percent of the school's graduating nurses pass the NCLEX-PN?

Career options and trends:
Specialty certification is available to LPNs in areas such as long-term care, pharmacology, I.V. therapy, and gerontology. To advance to higher levels of nursing—to become, say, a registered nurse or a certified nurse specialist in pediatrics, you will most likely need a bachelor's or master's degree, work experience in the particular area of nursing, and a passing grade on a certification exam.

Long term, employment prospects for LPNs are excellent because of a severe shortage of nurses worldwide and the large number of retirements expected over the next ten years. Nevertheless recent graduates are currently finding it hard to find jobs because the lingering effects of the jobs recession is causing older nurses to delay retirement. But that will necessarily ease up soon—over 25% of nurses are nearing retirement age.

The majority of LPNs work in hospitals, clinics, long-term-care and nursing home facilities; but other employment opportunities are available in rehabilitation centers, public health agencies, industrial/occupational health offices, private doctor's offices, and schools. Employment growth is expected in the areas of community and home health nursing, because insurance companies are mandating shorter hospital stays, and more patients will require nurses to aid recovery at home.

Insider's viewpoint:
"Nursing is not just medication administration; you are there for the patients when they are throwing up or have diarrhea. One must think about those things as well: can you handle that?"

—Josette, A.S. candidate, Riverside Community College

For more info:
National Federation of Licensed Practical Nurses (NFLPN)
111 West Main Street, Suite 100
Garner, NC 27529
(919) 779-0046
www.nflpn.org

National Association for Practical Nurse Education & Service (NAPNES)
1940 Duke St.
Suite 200
Alexandria, VA 22314
(703) 933-1003
www.napnes.org

Nursing (RN)

What it's about:

This major prepares students to be frontline providers of health care. Registered nurses design, manage, and coordinate care for individuals, families, groups, communities, and larger populations. Nursing students learn how to attend to the sick and the injured; how to rehabilitate, counsel, and educate patients; and how to work as part of a health care team in many settings.

Is this for you?

You might like this major if you also like: caregiving; volunteer work; making a difference in people's lives; science; autonomy and independence; a fast pace; working in groups; challenges.

Consider this major if you are good at: active listening, caring/nurturing; critical reading/thinking; leadership; math; organizing; problem solving; teamwork ...*or have...* initiative; patience; verbal skills.

Recommended high school prep:

English 4, math 4 (including precalculus, calculus, or statistics), lab science 3 (including biology and chemistry), social studies 3, and a foreign language 2–3. If available, courses in psychology, growth and development, nutrition and health are recommended, as are speech and writing courses. A computer applications course would also be helpful.

Did you know...

...that nurses aren't just doctors' helpers? Nurses are independent primary health care providers, whose responsibilities range from directly treating patients to developing and supervising complex nursing care systems. In the United States, RNs—who outnumber physicians by more than four to one—are involved in just about every type of health care service.

Typical courses in this major:

Psychology
Anatomy and physiology
Microbiology
Chemistry
Nutrition
Fundamentals of practice in nursing
Pharmacology
Physical assessment
Nursing leadership
Sociology
Mental health
Environmental and occupational health
Adult, pediatric, and geriatric care
Maternal/child and neonatal care
Medical and surgical care
Home health care

Concentrations:

Generally, none in college; but if you go on to grad school: family primary care; women's health; pediatrics; adult primary care; geriatrics; neonatal acute care; adult acute care.

What the study of this major is like:

Generally, you take courses in English, social sciences, the humanities, and the natural sciences during your first two years as a major. In your nursing program, you apply your education in liberal arts and sciences to learn the principles of nursing theory. You evaluate research to determine its benefit to nursing practice; examine nurse–client relationships and the organization of health care delivery; study ethical and practical issues related to terminal illness and death; and examine ways of providing health promotion services and illness care to culturally diverse communities.

Some programs require a fourth-year internship in which you receive academic credit while gaining clinical experience. You may work (under supervision) in hospitals, long-term care facilities, schools, community health organizations, mental health/psychiatric institutions, and other settings. There may also be opportunities for paid summer work experience.

You do not specialize at the undergraduate level. Graduates of nursing programs are generalists, able to assume roles in acute care, long-term care, and community-based facilities. After completing your undergraduate degree, you must pass the National Council Licensing Examination for Registered Nurses (NCLEX-RN) in order to work in the field.

Perhaps the biggest surprise for beginning students in nursing is the intensity and rigor of the subject matter and clinical practice requirements. Because nurses, who often work independently, must be responsible and accountable, they are expected to master a great deal of specialized (often technical) knowledge and theory.

Being a nursing major requires time management and a commitment to long hours of both course work and clinical practice. Usually you will need to study for several hours for every hour of class time. Clinical practice generally involves 16 hours a week of work in a variety of health care settings. Before and after clinical practice, you develop case studies, care plans, and education projects related to your client population. Also, early in your studies, you must begin preparation for the NCLEX-RN exam.

Programs can grant an associate degree in nursing (A.D.N.) or a Bachelor of Science degree in nursing (B.S.N.). For an A.D.N. (usually from a community college), you complete the program in two to three years and are prepared for entry-level registered nurse practice at the bedside.

The four-year B.S.N. prepares you to work in the full range of health care settings, including hospitals; critical care, long-term care, rehabilitation, outpatient care, public health, community health, and mental health facilities; private homes; and neighborhood clinics. It also prepares you for graduate work. In addition to the liberal arts and sciences courses, B.S.N. programs feature more in-depth nursing courses, including theory, research, pharmacology, pathophysiology, physical assessment, and nutrition. You also receive training in specific areas such as community and public health nursing, medical-surgical nursing, maternal-child nursing, pediatric nursing, mental health nursing, and nursing leadership and management.

Other majors you might like:
Education of physically handicapped
Human services
Communication disorders
Psychology
Licensed practical nursing
Physical therapy
Music therapy
Gerontology
Food and nutrition studies
Human development and family studies
American sign language (ASL)
Emergency medical technology (EMT paramedic)

Questions to ask colleges:
Is the program accredited by the Commission on Collegiate Nursing Education (CCNE) or the National League for Nursing Accrediting Commission (NLNAC)?

What is the NCLEX-RN passing rate for graduates?

What types of laboratories are available for the program, and how well equipped are they?

What are the types and locations of clinical sites used for student practice opportunities?

Career options and trends:
Advanced nurse practitioner*; nurse educator*; clinical nurse specialist; nurse anesthetist; nurse midwife; nurse researcher; nurse administrator*.

For advanced or specialty practice, a bachelor's or master's degree and certification based on examination and clinical practice requirements are essential.

Recent RN graduates are finding it hard to get jobs because the slow economic recovery is causing older nurses to delay retirement, while at the same time the number of RN grads is increasing each year. But the fact remains that the United States is in the midst of a national nursing shortage that is projected to intensify as the population ages and the demand for new health care services and technologies increases. It is projected by the Bureau of Labor Statistics that by the year 2022, employment of RN's will increase by nearly 20 percent, particularly in outpatient care centers and elder care settings.

Insider's viewpoint:
"Put on your seat belt; you are in for a wild ride. You will feel emotions you have never felt before."

—Jenn, senior, Golden West College

For more info:

American Association of Colleges of Nursing
  (AACN)
One Dupont Circle, N.W., Suite 530
Washington, DC 20036
(202) 463-6930
www.aacn.nche.edu

National Student Nurse Association (NSNA)
45 Main St., Suite 606
Brooklyn, NY 11201
(718) 210-0705
www.nsna.org

American Nurses Association (ANA)
8515 Georgia Avenue, Suite 400
Silver Spring, MD 20910
(800) 274-4262
www.ana.org

Occupational therapy

What it's about:

Occupational therapy is the use of "occupation" (work, self-care, and play/leisure) to help people who are affected by developmental, psychosocial, or physical problems to achieve or regain independent function, enhance development, and prevent injury. You must have a master's degree or higher in order to be certified as an occupational therapist. In college you take the prerequisite courses needed to be admitted into the graduate program.

Is this for you?

You might like this major if you also like: working with individuals from diverse backgrounds; hobbies, activities, or interests involving fine hand (motor) skills; solving problems or puzzles in creative ways, even when there are no right or wrong answers; technology; physical activity; working in groups.

Consider this major if you are good at: active listening; caring/nurturing; counseling; creativity; critical reading/thinking; organizing; teamwork *...or have...* initiative; manual dexterity; verbal skills; writing skills.

Recommended high school prep:

English 4, math 3–4, lab science 3 (including biology, chemistry, and physics), social studies 3, and a foreign language 2–3. Courses in the arts, music, and, if available, psychology or human behavior would be helpful

Did you know...

...that creativity and problem solving are important in this profession? After you learn the knowledge and skills to be an OT, you must be able to apply them to the unique situations and individuals you encounter in the various areas of practice that make up the profession.

Typical courses in this major:

Biology
English composition
Anatomy and physiology
General psychology
Developmental (life-span) psychology
Human development
Ergonomics
Statistics
Sociology
Anthropology
Mechanical physics
Kinesiology
Neuroscience
Gerontology
Leadership and management
Research methods

Concentrations:

Generally, none in college; but if you go on to grad school: occupational science; psychiatric disabilities; physical disabilities; pediatrics; rehabilitation technology

What the study of this major is like:

Occupational therapists help people who may have conditions that make it hard for them to function. These conditions may include developmental problems (such as learning disabilities), psychosocial issues (eating disorders), physical problems (arthritis or repetitive stress injury), the aging process (difficulty seeing or hearing), poverty, or cultural differences. OTs start by considering people's surroundings, evaluating their performance of everyday tasks, and assessing their personal goals. Then they use various activities to help the clients function with greater independence and to make the most of their abilities. Finally, OTs determine how well the therapy has worked.

To become an OT, you must pass the National Board for Certification in Occupational Therapy examination (NBCOT). Those who pass the exam are awarded the title "Occupational Therapist Registered" (OTR), and are eligible for state licensure.

As of January 1, 2007, in order to qualify for the exam, you must graduate from an accredited graduate program in OT, at either the master's or doctorate degree level. In college, this major is now primarily a preprofessional program made up of prerequisite courses that will prepare you for admission into a graduate program in OT.

These prerequisite courses generally include one year (two semesters) of anatomy and physiology, English, statistics, and sociology, and usually three semesters of general and developmental psychology. In addition, most graduate programs require you to be certified in CPR (cardiopulmonary resuscitation) and to have at least 50 hours of volunteer experience working with a licensed OTR. A course in mechanical physics (related to movement and/or principles of movement) is often recommended, although not required.

You can major in anything you want in college so long as you take the prerequisite courses, but the most popular majors are biology, psychology, sociology, anthropology, liberal arts, and anatomy. Quite a few colleges offer a combined bachelor's/master's program that allows you to enter as a college freshman, and continue straight through to the OT graduate degree in five years.

Once you get into the graduate program, the curriculum includes the study of normal maturation, development, and function; the effect of diseases, trauma, and aging; and the varied ways in which therapists can help people whose ability to do normal activities is threatened or impaired. Programs generally consist of lecture courses; lab courses, in which you practice and analyze skills; and fieldwork training in clinical settings.

In courses on occupational therapy theory and practice, you do closely supervised fieldwork, where you observe and then treat clients in hospitals, schools, or other facilities. As you advance in the program this fieldwork becomes full-time, for a minimum of 24 weeks; also under the supervision of a qualified occupational therapist.

Fieldwork is the most demanding part of your studies because you must apply, in a real-world setting, what you've learned in class and the lab. However, students typically enjoy fieldwork immensely, and their enthusiasm helps them complete the program.

Other majors you might like:
Physical therapy
Gerontology
Child development
Art, dance, or music therapy
Psychology
Special education
Athletic training
Recreational therapy
Human services
Exercise sciences
Human resources management
Biomedical engineering

Questions to ask colleges:
Is the program approved by the Accreditation Council for Occupational Therapy Education?

Is there a combined bachelor's/graduate degree option? If so, what are the requirements to move on into the graduate part of the program?

What kinds of internships or volunteer experiences working with OTs are available?

Career options and trends:
Occupational therapist*; researcher; industrial ergonomist; instructor; master clinician; health care administrator.

In addition to requiring successful completion of the NBCOT exam, most states have licensing standards. Practitioners must also renew their certification every three years.

Job prospects are excellent. The Bureau of Labor Statistics projects job growth in this field to increase much faster than average through 2022 and beyond. That's because as society ages, occupational therapists will be more in demand.

The largest number of occupational therapists are employed by hospitals, rehabilitation centers, long-term-care facilities, and also schools providing services for children with disabilities.

Because the profession has been underutilized, many areas of practice have yet to be developed. Emerging areas of practice include evaluation, rehabilitation, and training for driving skills; consultation on accessibility design and home modification; ergonomics and workplace modification; assistive device development; services for those with impaired vision; and private practice in community health services.

For more info:

American Occupational Therapy Association
   (AOTA)
4720 Montgomery Lane
P.O. Box 31220
Bethesda, MD 20824-1220
(800) 377-8555
www.aota.org

National Board for Certification in Occupational
   Therapy (NBCOT)
12 South Summit Ave.
Suite 100
Gaithersburg, MD 20877-4150
(301) 990-7979
www.nbcot.org

Pharmacy

What it's about:

Pharmacists apply a knowledge of medicines to patient needs. As a pharmacy student, you learn how to counsel patients, dispense drugs, monitor drug therapy, minimize side effects, and work with physicians, nurses, and other health care professionals. Pharmacy is no longer an undergraduate major. The entry-level degree is now the Doctor of Pharmacy (Pharm.D.) first-professional degree, a four-year program that usually follows two years of college-level prepharmacy courses.

Is this for you?

You might like this major if you also like: chemistry; community service activities; meeting different kinds of people; helping people; learning; reading; being independent.

Consider this major if you are good at: attention to detail; counseling; critical reading/thinking; multitasking; organizing; quantitative analysis; teamwork *...or have...* initiative; verbal skills; writing skills.

Recommended high school prep:

English 4, math 4 (including precalculus), lab science 4 (including biology, chemistry and physics), social studies 3, and a foreign language 2–3. Courses that develop communications skills (writing and speech) are also important. Latin can be helpful, but is not necessary. Computer skills are essential.

Did you know...

...that pharmacists do much more than fill prescriptions? While about half of all pharmacists work in community pharmacies, many others are employed as clinical education specialists, researchers, government agency employees (e.g., in the Food and Drug Administration), or work in the pharmaceutical industry as scientists, consultants, product development managers, or marketing reps.

Typical courses in this major:

Physiology
Pathophysiology
Biochemistry
Microbiology
Molecular biology
Pharmaceutics
Pharmacology/medicinal chemistry
Immunology
Nonprescription medications and self-care
Dietary supplements and herbal medicines
Biostatistics
Professional communication
Pharmaceutical care
Pharmacy law and ethics
Health systems management
Physical assessment

Concentrations:

Generally, none available.

What the study of this major is like:

Typically, the pharmacy (Pharm.D.) major is a six-year doctorate program that requires two undergraduate years of prepharmacy courses, followed by four academic years (or three calendar years in an accelerated program, with summer semesters) of professional education. The prepharmacy curriculum usually includes courses in writing and speech, biology, general chemistry, organic chemistry, microbiology, calculus, human anatomy and physiology, social and behavioral sciences, economics, English, and humanities. Some prepharmacy programs also require physics courses and computer competency.

But you do not have to do prepharmacy training in order to be accepted into the professional pharmacy program; you must simply complete the prerequisite courses in college. For example, many pharmacy applicants are chemistry, biochemistry, or biology majors, and their pharmacy prerequisites are usually covered by courses they took to complete their major. Be aware that admissions requirements may vary greatly among professional pharmacy programs. To be considered for admission in about half the programs, you must submit Pharmacy College Admission Test (PCAT) scores.

At the graduate level, you focus on the physiology and biochemistry of the body, and on appropriate medication therapy, to diagnose, treat, or prevent disease. In medicinal chemistry (biochemistry of medicinals, immunology, biotechnology) and pharmacology courses, you study the effects of various classes of medications on the body. In courses on pharmaceutics/drug delivery systems, you learn how drugs are administered to, absorbed into, and eliminated from the body. Pharmacotherapy focuses on choosing and implementing medication therapies, including patient evaluation and counseling; risk assessment; prescribing, preparing, and dispensing; symptom management; and evaluation of results. In pathophysiology courses, you examine the way disease affects the body; pharmacokinetics explores the body's reactions to medications over time, as well as the measurement of blood levels to determine dosage; and in pharmacognosy, you study drugs derived from plants.

You'll be trained to dispense medication safely and to educate patients about their prescription and non-prescription (over-the-counter) therapies. Further, you learn to work with, and advise, physicians on medication selection. You also take courses in pharmacy management, pharmacy law, pharmacoeconomics, managed care, and pharmaceutical marketing.

All professional programs have the equivalent of three years of classroom instruction involving lectures, discussion sessions, laboratories, and practice-related activities. Integrated into this time is an "Introductory Pharmacy Practice Experience" which continues in a progressive manner until the "Advanced Pharmacy Practice Experiences" (clerkship rotations) which occur during the fourth year. During your clerkship rotations you apply what you have learned, completing 1,500 hours or more of hands-on practice in hospitals, clinics, community pharmacies, or other patient care settings.

Some colleges offer a bachelor's degree in pharmaceutical sciences or pharmacology, which can prepare you for a career in the pharmaceutical industry or for graduate study or medical school; but such a degree will not make you eligible for licensure as a pharmacist. Another option is the two-year associate degree (or diploma or certificate, depending on the program) that trains you to become a pharmacy technician. Pharmacy technicians work under the close supervision of pharmacists, performing technical tasks such as stocking, packaging, and pricing medications, and maintaining records and inventories of prescriptions, medications, and supplies.

Other majors you might like:
Biochemistry
Clinical/medical laboratory technology
Chemistry
Substance abuse counseling
Health care administration
Pharmacy assistant
Public heath
Community health/preventative medicine
Microbiology
Medical records administration
Small business administration/management
Dietetics

Questions to ask colleges:
Does the college offer a six-year prepharmacy/Pharm.D. program for entering students? If so, what are the requirements (such as GPA) for continuing on into the professional program? What percentage of the prepharm students continue? If a state school, do in-state students get preference?

Are students required to take the PCAT before admission into the Pharm.D. program? If so, what is the score range for admission?

Do students get help in obtaining summer internship opportunities?

What is the range of clerkship opportunities available during the last professional year? How does the college assign students to these clerkships, and do students often have to relocate to attend them?

Career options and trends:
Community pharmacist*; hospital staff pharmacist*; long-term care facility pharmacist; managed care pharmacist; public health service pharmacist; clinical specialist; clinical drug researcher; quality control supervisor.

Every state requires a license to practice pharmacy. To qualify, you must serve an internship period and pass a national board exam and a state exam. Continuing professional education is required for license renewal.

Some positions in research, clinical pharmacy, teaching, or other specialty area may require an advanced graduate degree (master's or Ph.D.), and/or further training in a residency program or fellowship.

The job outlook is excellent, with good employment opportunities projected through 2022. Also, fewer Pharm.D. degrees are expected to be granted than the number of jobs created. The retail sector will be influenced by such trends as automated dispensing and wider use of pharmacy technicians to meet the growing demand at lower cost; expansion of chain drugstores and of mail order firms; and increased involvement by managed care and Medicare.

For more info:
American Association of Colleges of Pharmacy (AACP)
1727 King Street
Alexandria, VA 22314
(703) 739-2330
www.aacp.org

Physical therapy

What it's about:

Physical therapists (PTs) are licensed health care professionals who work to prevent, diagnose, and treat conditions that affect a person's movement and functional independence. Although you have to go to graduate school to earn a degree in physical therapy, a variety of undergraduate majors can prepare you for a professional PT program.

Is this for you?

You might like this major if you also like: helping people; sports and exercise; dance; gymnastics; science and technology; learning and discovery; problem solving; understanding other people's perspectives; seeking and using feedback.

Consider this major if you are good at: active listening; caring/nurturing; creativity; critical reading/thinking; organizing; persuading/influencing ...*or have...* initiative; patience; physical stamina; verbal skills.

Recommended high school prep:

English 4, math 3, lab science 3 (including biology and chemistry), social studies 3, and a foreign language 2–3. In addition, it may be helpful to participate in a job-shadowing program at a local hospital.

Did you know...

...that physical therapists have considerable flexibility in their career paths? You can serve as a clinician, teacher, researcher, consultant, administrator, or in some combination of these roles. Also, both full-time and part-time opportunities exist in physical therapy, so that you can pursue other personal and professional goals if you wish.

Typical courses in this major:

Biology
Human development
Anatomy
Physiology
Physics
General (inorganic) chemistry
Mathematics
Statistics
Psychology
Sociology
Ethics
Neuroanatomy
Orthopedics
Health policy
Physical therapy exercise
Kinesiology

Concentrations:

Generally, none available.

What the study of this major is like:

To become a physical therapist, you must complete the prerequisites in college and then take a full-time, three-year, graduate-level program. Some colleges offer "3 + 3" programs, which enable you to complete both college and graduate work in six years.

Currently, the professional degree in physical therapy is either a master's degree (M.S.P.T. or M.P.T.) or the Doctorate in Physical Therapy (D.P.T.). The D.P.T. emerged in response to a significant shift in the roles and responsibilities of the physical therapist; PT education now requires a depth and breadth like that in other professional health care fields, such as medicine, dentistry, and optometry. A large number of professional programs have either converted to the D.P.T. degree, or have indicated an intention to do so.

Although various undergraduate majors, including biology, psychology, chemistry, or engineering, may help you get into a professional physical therapy program, you must be interested in movement as a primary component of health, and be committed to the study and application of the science of movement in the context of health care. As an undergraduate, you should take courses in the natural sciences, social sciences, and humanities, as well as in quantitative and analytical fields. A broad liberal arts education will help you hone your interpersonal skills, think critically, provide evidence-based care, and learn how to serve diverse populations.

Prerequisite course work for admission to professional programs can include anatomy, kinesiology, athletic training, exercise science, neuropsychology, social psychology, human development, physiology, physical education, and special education. Many graduate PT programs also require computer literacy, certification in CPR, and competence in medical terminology (a knowledge of Latin and Greek roots). Many also require a certain number of hours of volunteer clinical experience. You should plan each semester in college to be sure that you fulfill all the requirements for admission to grad school.

What can you look forward to in grad school? Most programs begin with basic science courses such as anatomy (generally dissection-based), neuroscience and motor control, exercise physiology and pathophysiology, and the psychosocial aspects of health and disability. You then apply what you learn to clinical practice, through guided clinical experiences. The core of your curriculum involves studying clinical sciences in neurology, cardiology, pediatrics, and orthopedics and acquiring patient management skills that you can use in diagnosing problems, planning interventions, and assessing results. Your clinical competence will be judged by a variety of clinical internships that you must complete.

Other majors you might like:
Psychology
Biomedical engineering
Anthropology
Exercise sciences
Occupational therapy
Nursing (RN)
Athletic training
Sports and fitness administration
Dance therapy
Social work
Dietetics
Respiratory therapy

Questions to ask colleges:
Does the college offer a combined pre-PT/graduate program? If so, what are the requirements for admission and for continuing on into the professional program?

How are students advised about, and assisted in, meeting prerequisites for grad school?

What are the opportunities for volunteer experience in physical therapy settings?

Career options and trends:
Clinician; private practitioner; clinical administrator; clinical educator.

Physical therapists work in hospitals, extended-care facilities, home health agencies, public and private schools, industry, programs for people with developmental disabilities, and private clinics.

All states require physical therapists to pass a licensure exam before they can practice, after graduating from an accredited PT educational program. A number of states require continuing education to maintain licensure.

Physical therapy is now about prevention as well as rehabilitation. Clients include individuals in good health, as well as those at acute stages of illness; in schools and fitness facilities as well as in hospitals and nursing homes; and of both young and old ages. Therefore, the job outlook is excellent in all settings; health care, health promotion, and prevention opportunities abound.

For more info:
American Physical Therapy Association (APTA)
1111 N. Fairfax St.
Alexandria, VA 22314
(800) 999-2782
www.apta.org

Physician assistant

What it's about:
Physician assistants (PAs) are licensed to practice medicine under the supervision of a doctor. Working as part of a health care team, PAs take medical histories, examine and treat patients, order and interpret laboratory tests and X-rays, make diagnoses, and prescribe medications.

Is this for you?
You might like this major if you also like: working both independently and as part of a team; taking responsibility; solving problems for others; volunteer work in hospitals or clinics.

Consider this major if you are good at: active listening; attention to detail; caring/nurturing; critical reading/thinking; handling emergencies; leadership; organizing; teamwork; time management ...*or have...* initiative; self-confidence; verbal skills.

Recommended high school prep:
English 4, math 3–4 (statistics would be helpful), lab science 3–4 (biology and chemistry most important), social studies 3, and a foreign language 2–3.

Did you know...
...that in some programs, PA majors attend many of the same classes as medical students? PA education and physician education differ not so much in the curriculum but in the amount of training.

...that PAs often work autonomously? In rural or inner-city clinics, where a physician may be available only one or two days a week, PAs may be the principal care providers; they consult with the supervising physician as needed. PAs also make house calls and go to hospitals and nursing homes to check on patients and report back to the physician.

Typical courses in this major:
Anatomy
History taking and physical diagnosis
Pharmacology
Microbiology
Behavioral sciences
Clinical medicine
Obstetrics and gynecology
Pediatrics
Geriatrics
Psychiatry
Surgery
Critical care
Medical laboratory sciences
Radiology
Health care delivery
Ethics

Concentrations:
Generally, none available.

What the study of this major is like:
All states require that new PAs complete a program approved by the Accreditation Review Commission on Education for the Physician Assistant, Inc. (ARC-PA). PA programs are located within sponsoring institutions such as universities, four-year colleges, community colleges, and hospitals.

The credential offered by a program (certificate, associate degree, bachelor's degree, or master's degree) depends on the institution; more than half award a master's degree, and most PA graduates earn at least a bachelor's. No matter what degree is granted, every accredited PA program must meet the standards established by the ARC-PA, by offering courses in the basic medical sciences, behavioral and social sciences, clinical sciences, health policy, and professional practice, as well as supervised clinical practice. The average length of PA training is 26 months.

For admission, many PA programs require you to have completed at least two years of college and participated in some health care work. Many applicants enter PA programs from other health care professions, such as nursing and emergency medical technology. Prerequisites (including health care experience, courses, degree, and test scores) and application deadlines vary, so be sure to research PA programs well in advance.

In general, PA education includes one year of classroom studies followed by a year of supervised clinical experience (rotations) in health care institutions. You take courses in anatomy, microbiology, clinical medicine, clinical pharmacology, physical diagnosis, medical ethics, geriatric and home health care, biochemistry, pathology, and disease prevention. In addition to lectures, there are many opportunities for you to learn in small groups and refine your clinical skills under faculty supervision. During your second year, you spend at least 40 hours a week at your clinical rotation sites, including internal medicine, family medicine, emergency medicine, obstetrics and gynecology, pediatrics, general surgery, and psychiatry.

After completing the PA program, you must pass the national exam administered by the National Commission on Certification of Physician Assistants (NCCPA). In addition to national certification, you must then be licensed or registered by the state in which you practice. The profession is committed to lifelong learning, and PAs must recertify by examination every six years and complete 100 hours of continuing medical education every two years.

Other majors you might like:
Optometric assistant
Licensed practical nursing
Radiologic technology/medical imaging
Athletic training
Funeral services/mortuary science
Respiratory therapy
Medical records administration
Medical illustration
Forensic science
Biology
Biomedical engineering

Questions to ask colleges:
How much heath care experience is required for admission to the PA program? Which types of experiences qualify?

Does the program participate in the Central Application Service for Physician Assistants (CASPA)? This service collects and authenticates applicant materials for distribution to participating programs.

What is the first-time pass rate for recent graduates taking the Physician Assistants National Certifying Examination?

Career options and trends:
Many PAs work in primary care areas, such as internal medicine, pediatrics, and family medicine. Others work in specialty areas, such as general and thoracic surgery, emergency medicine, orthopedics, and geriatrics. PAs specializing in surgery provide pre- and postoperative care, and may work as assistants during major surgery.

Employment opportunities are excellent and projected to grow at an above-average pace, because of the nation's expanding health care needs and efforts to contain costs. Demand for PAs will be high in areas and settings where there is a shortage of physicians, such as rural and inner-city clinics. Technology that allows interactive consultations with off-site doctors ("telemedicine") will also increase the role of PAs.

For more info:
Physician Assistant Education Association (PAEA)
300 N. Washington St.
Suite 710
Alexandria, VA 22314-2544
(703) 548-5538
www.paeaonline.org

Predental

What it's about:

Predental studies consists of the courses you need to take in college in order to get into dental school. It's not a major by itself, so you have to choose a major in addition to completing the predental requirements. Predental programs also provide guidance to help you prepare for dental school.

Is this for you?

You might like this major if you also like: helping people of all kinds; science and technology; working with your hands; arts and crafts; model making; playing a musical instrument; problem solving.

Consider this major if you are good at: attention to detail; caring/nurturing; creativity; critical reading/thinking; math; memorizing ...*or have...* integrity; manual dexterity; motivation; verbal skills.

Recommended high school prep:

English 4, math 4 (including precalculus and calculus), lab science 4 (including biology, chemistry, and physics), social studies 4 (including economics), and a foreign language 3–4 (Spanish recommended). If available, courses in psychology, speech communication, business, and computer science are also recommended.

Did you know...

...that cleaning and filling teeth are just a few of the jobs a dentist performs? Since many medical conditions that affect the whole body are revealed in the mouth, dentists are on the forefront of the early detection of disease.

Typical courses in this major:

Inorganic (general) chemistry
Organic chemistry
Biology
Zoology
Biochemistry
Physics
Calculus
College mathematics
English
Psychology
Cell biology
Genetics
Anatomy and physiology
Speech communication
Computer science
Sculpture

Concentrations:

Generally, none available.

What the study of this major is like:

Sometimes students are surprised to learn that taking part in studio arts or playing a musical instrument is good preparation for a career in dentistry. But it makes sense—dentists must be able to visualize three-dimensional objects from diagrams, have good eye–hand coordination, and perform detailed tasks in very small spaces. Perhaps you didn't realize that it takes some artistic ability to give people beautiful smiles.

In a predental program, however, science rather than the sculptural arts will occupy most of your time. You must take two semesters each of biology, general chemistry, organic chemistry, and physics. Many dental schools also expect you to take calculus and biochemistry. Courses in English and perhaps psychology are in the mix too. On top of all that, you will have to fulfill the requirements for the major you select.

Most students choose a science major, since the courses dovetail with the predental requirements. However, you don't have to follow that path if you don't want to. Many predental students select a nonscience major, and dental school admissions offices are satisfied with that option; in fact, they like to accept students from a variety of academic backgrounds, as long as the applicants excelled in their science courses. Choosing a nonscience major, though, may create some course-scheduling conflicts that might make it difficult to graduate in four years. The trick is to keep your goal in mind, but also to follow your bliss—you'll do best in a major you like.

Your predental adviser will play a critical role in helping you navigate your undergraduate career. He or she will assist you in planning your course work, choosing a major, coping with difficulties that may arise, and finding internships or community service opportunities. You will appreciate your adviser's help most during the process of applying to dental school: evaluating your prospects, lining up interviews and letters of recommendations, and preparing for the Dental Admission Test (DAT).

What you do outside class is another important aspect of a predental program. It's a definite plus to get related experience, such as "job-shadowing" a dentist or volunteering in a dental office. Many communities have Healthcare for the Homeless organizations, which provide oral care to people who are unable to visit a dentist; these groups often use student volunteers. Successful dental school candidates usually devote 15–20 hours a week to such activities during the school year and 40–50 hours a week over the summer.

Just how hard is it to get into dental school? Nationally, the mean GPA of successful dental school applicants is in the 3.1–3.2 range. The percentage of students who are accepted depends on the number of applicants per year, but is usually between 40 and 60 percent. Most dental schools are state institutions that give preference to residents of their state.

Here's something to consider: more than half the dental schools in the United States cooperate with colleges to offer joint programs that enable you to achieve both a bachelor's degree and a dental degree in less time than if you pursued the two programs separately. If you are interested, look at the latest edition of the *Official Guide to Dental Schools*, published by the American Dental Education Association.

Other majors you might like:
Biology
Biochemistry
Chemistry
Dental laboratory technology
Biomedical technology
Entrepreneurial studies
Anthropology

Occupational therapy
Communication disorders
Medical office administration
Forensic science

Questions to ask colleges:
How many predental and premedical students does the institution have? (The premedical and predental populations are often considered as one.)

How many predental students get into dental school after one application? After two or more applications?

Is the predental adviser easily accessible, particularly when students apply to dental school?

Is there help to obtain dentistry-related internship or volunteer experiences, during both the school year and school breaks?

Does the college have a combined bachelor's/D.D.S. program or other special relationship with dental schools?

Is there a DAT prep course available on campus?

Career options and trends:
Dentist*; oral surgeon*; orthodontist; dental or medical laboratory technician.

During dental school you must pass Parts I and II of the National Board Dental Examination. After dental school you will have to become fully licensed in the state(s) in which you want to practice. Like most licensed professionals, dentists are required to complete a certain amount of continuing education credits each year.

The demand for dentists is strong and growing, because the population is increasing and improved public oral hygiene has enabled people to keep their teeth longer! Also, many dentists who were educated in the 1960's and '70's will be retiring soon.

For more info:
American Dental Education Association (ADEA)
1400 K St., N.W., Suite 1100
Washington, DC 20005
(202) 289-7201
www.adea.org

American Student Dental Association (ASDA)
211 E. Chicago Ave., Suite 700
Chicago, IL 60611
(800) 621-8099 ext. 2795
www.asdanet.org

Premedicine

What it's about:

If you want to be a medical doctor, osteopathic doctor, or podiatrist, you must go to medical school, and that means you have to take certain courses in college. Premedicine is not itself a major—just those prerequisite courses. It's also an advising program to help you get into medical school.

Is this for you?

You might like this major if you also like: helping people; science and technology; anatomy; learning and discovery; problem solving; *ER.* You will spend many years studying and training to become a doctor, so a desire to heal and prevent disease must be a strong motivator.

Consider this major if you are good at: attention to detail; counseling; critical reading/thinking; math; memorizing...*or have...* compassion; initiative; integrity; motivation; verbal skills.

Recommended high school prep:

English 4, math 4 (including precalculus and calculus), lab science 4 (including biology, chemistry, and physics), social studies 4, and a foreign language 3–4 (Spanish recommended). If available, courses in psychology, statistics, and computer science are also recommended. It is also advisable to do volunteer work at a local hospital or other health facility.

Did you know...

...that you don't need a 4.0 to get into medical school? You should be an excellent student, but medical schools look at applicants as more than the sum of their grade point averages and MCAT test scores.

...that some colleges offer a seven-year program that combines undergraduate and medical studies and culminates in an M.D.?

Typical courses in this major:

Inorganic chemistry
Biology
Calculus
Organic chemistry
Physics
Psychology
Cell Biology
Genetics
Sociology
English
Statistics
Biochemistry
Computer science
Bioethics
Neuroscience
Medicinal chemistry

Concentrations:

Generally, none available.

What the study of this major is like:

"Declaring" premed may be as simple as checking off a box on your college application or filling out a form during orientation. In any event, you should contact the premed adviser at your college as soon as you enroll.

The adviser's role is critical to your success in college. He or she will help you plan your premedical course work, choose a major, overcome any academic difficulties, and find internships or community service opportunities. You will also receive help applying to med school, preparing for the Medical College Application Test (MCAT), securing and sending letters of recommendation, preparing for interviews, and making a successful transition to medical school.

The premed science requirements include a full year (two semesters) each of general chemistry, biology, organic chemistry, and physics. Some medical schools also require either one or two semesters of calculus. Other courses that, although not required, will help you prepare for the MCAT and medical school are cell biology, biochemistry, genetics, molecular biology, and physiology. Because there is a two- to three-year sequence in the required science courses, you should take general chemistry and biology in your first year, no matter what you decide to major in.

It is important to know that premed is not just about science. Medical schools look for well-rounded students who possess a broad background in the humanities and social sciences. For example, English courses will provide an opportunity to sharpen your writing skills, a philosophy course will help you develop critical thinking skills and a moral compass, and psychology courses can help you understand the connection between mind and body. At most colleges you can usually fulfill the nonscience premed requirements by taking courses in the core liberal arts program.

Because the premed requirements emphasize science, the field in which their interests lie, most premed students choose a science major—but about 15 to 20 percent do not. Not only can students pursue a nonscience major, but most medical schools, seeking diversity, look with favor on applicants who take this route. If you are considering a nonscience major, however, you should realize that you must excel in the science courses you do take and that because of scheduling conflicts between premed and major-course requirements, you may not be able to graduate in four years.

During college you will need to pace yourself. Avoid taking more than two science and/or math courses per semester, and if you want to enter med school right after college, plan to complete your science/math requirements by the end of your third year, so that you can take the MCAT and then apply to med school during your fourth year. In addition, to be competitive you should consider taking honors and independent-study courses. Your premed advisor will help you juggle this challenging course load.

A premed program is not just about schoolwork, either. A successful premed student usually spends an average of 15–20 hours per week in extracurricular activities (clinical, research, or community service work) during the academic year, and 40–50 hours per week during school breaks. When selecting colleges, look to see if opportunities for such experiences are easily available nearby, and if you will receive help in obtaining them.

Other majors you might like:
Biology
Biochemistry
Chemistry
Music therapy
Physician assistant
Biomedical engineering
Psychology
Sociology
Anthropology
Health care administration
Emergency medical technology (EMT paramedic)
Neuroscience

Questions to ask colleges:
How many premed students are there at this college? How many are accepted into medical school?

Is the premed adviser easily accessible, particularly when students apply for medical school?

Is assistance available to obtain clinical, research, and community service experience during the school year and school breaks?

Is there an MCAT prep course available on campus?

Career options and trends:
Medical doctor*; osteopathic doctor*; podiatrist; physician assistant; physician/scientist*; optometrist; physical therapist; pharmacist; radiologist.

Medical school graduates must complete the United States Medical Licensing Examination (USMLE), Parts I–III. Physicians must be licensed in each state in which they want to practice; there are some interstate and regional agreements between and among states. In addition, in order to maintain their licenses, physicians must complete a certain amount of continuing medical education (CME) credits each year.

There is a particular need for general practitioners, geriatricians, psychiatrists, and podiatrists. In addition, because of a growing interest among patients in alternative cures and treatments, there is expected to be an increased demand for naturopathic physicians.

For more info:
Association of American Medical Colleges (AAMC)
2450 N Street, N.W.
Washington, DC 20037
www.aamc.org

The Student Doctor Network
26 Pinecrest Plaza #262
Southern Pinces, NC 28387
www.studentdoctor.net

Preveterinary

What it's about:

If you love animals and are good at science, you might be thinking you want to go to veterinary medical school after college. Because there are only twenty-eight vet schools in the United States, however, being accepted is a challenge. A program in preveterinary studies will help you become a competitive candidate by guiding you through the college courses and extracurricular experience that vet schools require. But keep in mind that prevet studies is not itself a major—you'll still have to pick one.

Is this for you?

You might like this major if you also like: all creatures great and small; people too; science and nature; volunteering at the local shelter or animal rescue center. Prevet students have a passion for animals, both sick and well, and the people who own them.

Consider this major if you are good at: attention to detail; caring/nurturing; critical reading/thinking; math; memorizing ...*or have...* integrity; motivation; patience; verbal skills.

Recommended high school prep:

English 4, math 4 (including precalculus and calculus), lab science 4 (including biology, chemistry, and physics), social studies 4, and a foreign language 3–4 (Spanish recommended). If available, courses in psychology, statistics, speech, and computer science are also recommended. It is strongly suggested that you have experience working with animals.

Did you know...

...that veterinary school is actually more competitive than medical school? That's because there are very few veterinary schools and many applicants. The prevet science requirements are the same as for premed, plus additional courses such as zoology, microbiology, or animal science. But don't be discouraged—you should be able to reach your goal if you have faith in yourself and stay focused.

Typical courses in this major:
Inorganic (general) chemistry
Organic chemistry
Biology
Biochemistry
Zoology
Physics
Calculus
Speech communication
Statistics
English
Animal science
Genetics
Comparative anatomy
Microbiology
Animal nutrition
Business management

Concentrations:
Generally, none available.

What the study of this major is like:

The preveterinary curriculum usually includes courses in biochemistry, biology, general chemistry, organic chemistry, physics, and English. Some veterinary schools require additional course work in microbiology, biochemistry, nutrition, or animal science. You may also be expected to take courses in the humanities and social sciences.

Nonscience courses are important because veterinary schools prefer well-rounded students. What is more, these courses help you develop the skills you'll need as a vet. For example, courses in psychology can help you understand the behavior of animals as well as that of their owners; business courses will be valuable if you, like most vets, run your own practice.

In addition to academics, you will need to acquire hands-on experience working with both small and large animals under the eye of a veterinarian. Practical experience might involve breeding, rearing, feeding, and showing various kinds of animals, including pets, livestock, laboratory animals, zoo animals, or wildlife. Some vet schools set a minimum number of hours for such work, usually 200, but successful applicants usually have much more than that.

At most colleges, preveterinary studies is not a major; it's an advising program—and the prevet adviser at your college will be a very important to you. You'll get assistance in selecting and scheduling courses, choosing a major, dealing with difficulties that may crop up, and finding internships and other extracurricular opportunities. Your adviser will also be a big help when you apply to veterinarian school.

You might wonder whether you can pursue a prevet program while taking a nonscience major. Yes, it is possible; but because veterinary schools require their students to become familiar with so many different species, a solid science background is strongly recommended. Students with a nonscience interest are usually encouraged to have a science major but a nonscience minor. If you are still committed to a nonscience major, go for it—but you might need more than four years to finish college.

About a third of the twenty-eight accredited vet schools in the United States offer joint programs with undergraduate colleges, ranging in length from six to eight years. Admission to these highly competitive programs is open to excellent students who, as high school seniors, are committed to pursuing a career as a veterinarian. If you are interested, review the latest edition of *Veterinary Medical School Admissions Requirements*, available from Purdue University Press.

Because managing the work load while maintaining academic excellence in all your courses is a challenge, you must be highly motivated and committed to your goal of becoming a veterinarian. Success also requires a four-year plan at the outset that allows you to fulfill all the requirements at a pace you can handle. But remember—college offers a wonderful opportunity to grow as a person and should not be a total grind. Your prevet adviser can help you achieve the right balance.

Other majors you might like:
Animal sciences
Biology
Zoology
Anthropology
Biochemistry
Chemistry
Wildlife and wilderness management
Agricultural and biological engineering

Genetics
Veterinary technology
Wildlife biology
Equestrian studies

Questions to ask colleges:
How many prevet students does the college have, as opposed to other pre–health profession students?

How many students are accepted into vet school after one application? After two or more applications?

Is there a knowledgeable prevet adviser who is easily accessible, particularly when students apply to vet school?

What kind of opportunities are available to gain practical experience working with animals, and where are these opportunities located?

Does the college have a combined D.V.M. program or other special relationship with vet schools?

Career options and trends:
About 75 percent of veterinarians today work in clinical practice. The rest are employed in a variety of areas, such as teaching at colleges and universities; conducting biomedical research or working for local, state, or federal agencies, departments of agriculture, and public health services that regulate or protect animals as well as people. Practice settings may also include race tracks, zoos, animal shelters, aquariums, and wildlife management facilities.

After graduating from veterinary school, you will have to meet the licensure requirements of the state(s) where you want to practice. In addition, like most licensed professionals, you must complete a certain amount of continuing education credits each year.

Job prospects are good, but also competitive because of an increasing number of graduates from veterinary schools. Competition will be strongest in the field of companion animal care in populated areas (where most pet owners live), since that's where most graduates want to work. There will be much less competition in rural areas where there is a great need for large animal care.

For more info:

Association of American Veterinary Medical
  Colleges
1101 Vermont Ave., N.W., Suite 301
Washington, DC 20005
(202) 371-9195
www.aavmc.org

American Veterinary Medical Association
1931 N. Meacham Rd., Suite 100
Schaumburg, IL 60173-4360
(800) 248-2862
www.avma.org

Radiologic technology/medical imaging

Also known as:
X ray technology

What it's about:
Radiologic technologists, also called radiographers, use X ray equipment to perform diagnostic imaging examinations of internal parts of the body. Experienced radiographers may perform more complex imaging procedures, such as computed tomography (CT) scans and magnetic resonance imaging (MRI).

Is this for you?
You might like this major if you also like: science and technology; art and photography (radiologic technology is said to be a combination of science and art); medical illustrations; working in teams; thinking about what's inside the human body.

Consider this major if you are good at: attention to detail; caring/nurturing; creativity; critical reading/thinking; organizing; quantitative analysis; spacial thinking/analysis; teamwork ...*or have...* initiative; manual dexterity; writing skills.

Recommended high school prep:
English 4, math 3, lab science 3 (including biology and physics), social studies 3, and a foreign language 2–3. Participating in a job-shadowing program in radiologic technology at a local hospital would be most helpful, and you will need CPR certification before you begin your clinical courses in college.

Did you know...
...that radiologic technology is not always neat and clean? Occasionally a technologist must perform unpleasant examinations, and sometimes physical stamina is required for lifting patients and positioning them properly.

...that radiation is natural? Each year, you are exposed to an amount of naturally occurring "background radiation" from the atmosphere, the Earth's crust, and cosmic rays, that is 50 times stronger than a typical dental X ray.

Typical courses in this major:
Radiologic physics
Radiographic positioning
Imaging equipment
Medical terminology
Human anatomy and physiology
Radiographic exposure
Radiobiology and protection
Radiographic pathology
Clinical practice
Cross-sectional anatomy
Health law and ethics
Principles of radiation exposure

Concentrations:
Radiation biology; fluoroscopy; and anatomical positioning.

What the study of this major is like:
Radiographers take X rays of parts of the body to create films that are used in diagnosing medical conditions. Closely following physicians' instructions and radiation-use regulations, radiographers prepare, position, and protect patients (for example, by using lead shields); position and operate radiographic equipment; and develop the film. In addition, they may help to decide which types of equipment to buy; maintain equipment; keep patient records; and manage an office or department.

If you choose to study radiologic technology/medical imaging, you can pursue a certificate, an associate degree, or a bachelor's degree. There are more two-year associate degree programs than four-year bachelor's programs, and some hospitals offer certificate programs. Most formal training programs are accredited by the Joint Review Committee on Education in Radiologic Technology (JRCERT) and have similar requirements in anatomy, physiology, algebra, and physical science. Bachelor's degree programs offer more concentrations in specialty areas, such as radiation therapy, nuclear medicine, ultrasound, CT scan, or MRI, than are available in associate degree programs.

As a major in radiologic technology/medical imaging, you split your time among classroom lectures, laboratory activities, and clinical internship work.

You must fulfill both general requirements (such as English, algebra, psychology, political science, sociology, and speech courses) and radiologic-specific course work. For the major, you study anatomy, physiology, biology, pathology, physics, radiation safety, patient care procedures, principles of imaging, medical ethics, and medical terminology. You learn to use computers and operate highly advanced medical equipment.

You must also develop your communication skills in order to work with patients and with other health care professionals as part of an effective team. In laboratories, you apply what you learn in the classroom, experimenting with patient positioning and X ray equipment. During hands-on clinical training, you work in actual radiology departments with physicians, nurses, and radiographers, again practicing what you learned in the classroom and laboratory.

Other majors you might like:
Laser/optical technology
Clinical/medical laboratory technology
Respiratory therapy
Electrical engineering technology
Computer science
Nuclear medical technology
Photographic/film/video technology
Physician assistant
Ophthalmic technology
Neuroscience
Animation
Radiation protection/health physics technology

Career options and trends:
There is an acute shortage of radiologic technologists that is expected to continue. As the population ages, the demand for diagnostic imaging will likely increase. This situation should not only guarantee employment but also generate improved compensation and working conditions.

In addition to becoming a staff X ray technician, you can—with on-the-job training, home study, and continuing education—go into a specialty area of radiography, such as heart catheterization; CT or MRI; ultrasound; mammography; nuclear medicine; radiation therapy; commercial sales; equipment repair; radiation health physics; education; or administration.

Although most jobs are found in hospitals, greater employment growth is projected in doctors' offices,

clinics, and diagnostic imaging centers, because of the strong shift toward outpatient care. Radiologic technologists who are qualified for more than one type of diagnostic imaging technology, such as radiography and sonography or nuclear medicine, will be the most sought after.

Depending on where you work, you may have to be certified, registered, or licensed; and the differences between these credentials can be confusing. Certification is awarded by the American Registry of Radiologic Technologists (ARRT) to those who complete the required education and training and pass the national exam. Certification qualifies you to practice anywhere in the U.S. and is generally required for employment. Registration, which is voluntary but preferred by many employers, is an annual renewal of the certificate; it indicates that you have complied with ARRT's continuing education requirements. Licensing is required by most states in order to practice. Each state administers its own licensing process, but most require only ARRT certification and a fee.

For more info:
American Society of Radiologic Technologist (ASRT)
15000 Central Ave., S.E.
Albuquerque, NM 87123-3917
(800) 444-2778
www.asrt.org

Respiratory therapy

What it's about:

This major trains you to work with physicians, nurses, and other health care professionals in the diagnosis, treatment, and rehabilitation of patients whose heart, circulation, or lungs are functioning abnormally. Working mostly in hospitals, respiratory therapists manage the ventilation of critically ill patients, or provide immediate and long-term care to patients with breathing disorders.

Is this for you?

You might like this major if you also like: helping people; working with technology; science.

Consider this major if you are good at: attention to detail; critical reading/thinking; math; organizing; persuading/influencing; teamwork...*or have...* initiative; manual dexterity; verbal skills.

Recommended high school prep:

English 4, math 3, lab science 3 (including biology, physics, and chemistry), social studies 3, and a foreign language 2–3. If they are available, take courses in health, sociology, psychology, interpersonal communications, and computer skills.

Typical courses in this major:

Human anatomy and physiology
Medical terminology
Cardiopulmonary pathophysiology
Pharmacology
Respiratory therapy procedures
Physical assessment
Mechanical ventilation
Neonatal and pediatric care
Critical care
Home care
Pulmonary function testing
Sleep disorders and their treatment
Microbiology
Pulmonary rehabilitation
Pulmonary diagnostics

Concentrations:

In college: neonatal/pediatric respiratory care; adult critical care; home care/extended care; polysomnography (sleep disorders, sleep medicine); cardiovascular technology; and pulmonary function testing.

If you go on to grad school: perfusion technology; extracorporeal circulation; health education; management/administration.

What the study of this major is like:

Respiratory therapists typically treat patients of all ages on all floors, in the emergency room, in clinics—in short, all over the hospital. They may attend to premature newborns; heart attack, stroke, drowning, or shock victims; and older patients with chronic diseases such as emphysema or asthma.

Respiratory therapists often deal with high-stress situations, working in intensive care units and participating in all cardiac resuscitations ("Code Blue"). They work with a variety of medical professionals and assist with other cardiac procedures such as pacemaker insertions, cardiac catheterization, and cardioversion. Besides hospitals, respiratory therapists can be employed in patients' homes, long-term-care facilities, diagnostic labs, and rehabilitation and educational facilities. And although sleep disorders have only recently become widely known, over half the professional staff in sleep labs now are respiratory therapists.

As a respiratory therapy major, you must fulfill general education requirements, including college algebra, chemistry, physics, English, computer and information literacy, communications, and social science (psychology or sociology). In the major, you take courses in anatomy, physiology, microbiology, pharmacology, diseases of the heart and lungs, and medical terminology, as well as technical courses that deal with procedures and clinical tests.

After examining the way the heart and lungs function, learning how to evaluate their condition, and determining which injuries, diseases, and disorders can seriously threaten cardiopulmonary (heart and lung) function, you are taught how to treat patients who have problems with their breathing and circulation. You gain practice in administering medications and using techniques and equipment (gases, humidity, equipment function and sterilization, arterial puncture and blood gas analysis, expansion therapies) to improve oxygen delivery to vital organs. You also spend time in hospitals applying what you have learned and providing patient care under supervision.

The program features lectures, laboratory work, and clinical practice. You learn theory in class, have hands-on experience with equipment in a laboratory setting, and then practice direct patient care under the supervision of faculty. Observing and caring for critically ill patients can be stressful and requires maturity. You will also have to adapt to the rigorous course work and the hours you must spend in the laboratory and clinical settings. You will be doing patient care during actual shifts, which are usually 12 hours long and may include afternoons and nights. You should therefore plan to attend classes, labs, and clinical courses full-time. As a result, you may not be able to have a job in addition; try to save money for your education before you enroll.

Respiratory therapy programs vary in length as well as in the degree or credential that graduates earn. Some programs offer two-year associate or four-year bachelor's degrees, preparing you for a career as a registered respiratory therapist (RRT). Shorter programs offer certificates and prepare you for work as an entry-level certified respiratory therapist (CRT).

Other majors you might like:
Cardiovascular technology
Physician assistant
Occupational therapy
Renal/dialysis technology
Clinical/medical laboratory technology
Licensed practical nursing
Gerontology
Biomedical technology
Social work
Recreational therapy
Radiologic technology/medical imaging

Questions to ask colleges:
Is the program approved by the Committee on Accreditation for Respiratory Care (CoARC)?

How many hospitals are used for clinical training, and where are they located?

After completing the program, are students eligible to take the National Registration Exam offered by the National Board for Respiratory Care (NBRC)? What is the first-time pass rate for recent graduates?

Career options and trends:
Respiratory therapist*; advanced-practice respiratory therapist; polysomnography technologist (sleep tech); cardiac ultrasound technician; perfusionist (operates bypass during heart surgery).

You must pass the NBRC examination to become a certified respiratory therapist, which allows you to practice as a CRT in every state that requires a license.

Respiratory therapists are employed in acute care hospitals, long-term care facilities, home health care, equipment and pharmaceutical sales, education, sleep laboratories, and health promotion. Employment forecasts for RTs show continuing strong demand for more therapists through 2022 and beyond, primarily due to an aging population. Therapists with cardiopulmonary care skills, or experience working with newborns and infants, will be especially in demand.

For more info:
American Association for Respiratory Care (AARC)
9425 N. MacArthur Blvd.
Suite 100
Irving, TX 75063
(972) 243-2272
www.aarc.org

Veterinary technology

Also known as:
Animal health technology

What it's about:
This major prepares you to work under the supervision of veterinarians, zoologists, and lab specialists to provide animal care and clinical assistance. Veterinary technicians (VTs) serve as receptionists, practice managers, radiologic/imaging technicians, medical and surgical nurses, anesthetists, pharmacy and laboratory technicians, animal behavior educators, and client liaisons.

Is this for you?
You might like this major if you also like: animal or pet training; the sciences; volunteering at the local shelter; 4H groups; farmwork; getting involved in animal welfare issues; meeting people; talking about animals.

Consider this major if you are good at: attention to detail; caring/nurturing; critical reading/thinking; organizing; problem solving; teamwork ...*or have...* initiative; patience; verbal skills.

Recommended high school prep:
English 4, math 3, lab science 4, social studies 3, and a foreign language 2–3. If your high school offers an advanced science track, try to take one or more of the following: anatomy and physiology, microbiology, nutrition, and genetics.

Did you know...
...that veterinary technicians spend a great deal of their time working not only with animals but with people? Students who find satisfaction in this field possess good "people skills" and can function well as team players.

Typical courses in this major:
Animal anatomy and physiology
Parasitology
Clinical laboratory techniques
Animal nutrition
Large animal clinical procedures
Small animal clinical procedures
Veterinary pharmacology and anesthesia
Animal disease
Veterinary radiology and surgical nursing
Lab animal science and exotics
Externship/internship

Concentrations:
Generally, none available.

What the study of this major is like:
VTs perform a wide range of activities, doing everything veterinarians do expect making diagnoses, performing surgery, and prescribing medicine. VTs assist veterinarians with client appointments, client education, and management of the practice. They work as medical and surgical animal nurses, animal physical therapists, animal dental hygienists (cleaning teeth), and diagnostic laboratory technicians (working with laboratory specimens). In laboratory animal medicine, VTs do experimental procedures, keep records, analyze data, write reports, and take care of animals. In the pet food industry, VTs work in sales, marketing, and research.

As a veterinary technology major, you would probably earn a two-year associate degree in applied science. Introduction to veterinary technology courses usually cover office procedures, vocational opportunities, regulatory issues, and client communication. In addition to other core courses, most programs require general education courses, in English, applied mathematics (algebra, statistics), social science, humanities, and biological science (microbiology). To be successful in this career, you need to do well in science. You should also develop computer and communication skills, as well as critical-thinking skills, such as patient assessment, and decision-making abilities.

In all programs, you must work as a student intern/extern for a minimum of 240 hours at specific types of veterinary sites. This experience allows you to explore various vocational opportunities (such as jobs in companion animal and large-animal care, and in biomedical research) and to develop the skills you learned during your early training. In your intern/externship, you are also exposed to specialized clinical areas such as cardiology, emergency medicine, and exotic animals.

Veterinary technology programs are career-oriented; if you complete the curriculum, you should be ready to work in a veterinary facility. Most programs incorporate traditional lecture format, computer self-study, guest speakers, "wet labs" (for hands-on work such as dentistry), and scheduled and open laboratory time. You also have opportunities to work with a variety of species and are usually responsible for caring for the animals housed on campus.

Programs accredited by the American Veterinary Medical Association Committee on Veterinary Technician Education and Activities (AVMA CVTEA) have a required content, to ensure that you are properly prepared for a career. But programs may vary. Some provide additional instruction in laboratory animal science and medicine, clinical diagnostic techniques, or large-animal or exotic species care. Programs may incorporate distance learning or online training into their curriculum or vary their scheduling (offering day and/or night courses). Some programs prepare you to become a veterinary assistant (VA); but take note that VAs do *not* receive an equivalent form of training as VTs.

Other majors you might like:
Biology
Animal sciences
Wildlife and wilderness management
Animal breeding
Equestrian studies
Dairy science
Zoology
Genetic
Biotechnology
Wildlife biology

Questions to ask colleges:
Is the program accredited by the American Veterinary Medical Association (AVMA)?

How many courses provide hands-on experience with animals, and which species of animals will students work with?

What kind of veterinary sites are offered to students for their externship experience, and where are they located?

Career options and trends:
Many states provide licensure for veterinary technicians. The terminology will vary (certified, registered, licensed), as will the requirements. Most states require that you graduate from an accredited program and pass the National Veterinary Technician Board Examination.

Job prospects in this field are excellent particularly in rural areas. There is currently a shortage of formally trained veterinary technicians, and demand is projected to increase in all veterinary practice areas and industrial fields.

Some of the areas in which graduates find job opportunities are small-animal and large-animal veterinary clinics; companion animal practice; pet food and pharmaceutical companies (technical research assistance or sales); laboratory animal research; animal diagnostic laboratories; zoos and wildlife centers; wildlife rehabilitation; and government regulatory agencies. Research and academic institutions usually require a bachelor's degree.

For more info:
National Association of Veterinary Technicians in America (NAVTA)
PO Box 1227
Albert Lea, MN 56007
(888) 996-2882
www.navta.net

Humanities

In the humanities, it's not so much *what* you know as *how* you know it. In these liberal arts majors, you'll learn how to learn by honing skills in research, reading, writing, and thinking.

"Liberal arts is a major for students who enjoy learning, who want to spend their college time getting an education and exploring new ideas, rather than strictly preparing for a specific career," says Professor Joseph Ugoretz, Manhattan Community College.

What are the humanities? You could write a whole term paper on that question. They cover history, philosophy, comparative literature, the classics, linguistics, and many other subjects, including the liberal arts. Perhaps in keeping with the spirit of these studies, their exact definition is open to interpretation.

When you search for colleges offering humanities majors, look for schools and divisions of arts and sciences, arts and letters, liberal arts, general studies, literature, science, and social sciences. Other sections in this book include related majors in Languages, English language and literature, Social sciences, and Religion and theology.

By now you may be worried that studying the humanities is like trying to nail Jell-O to the wall. But it's not. The fact is that more associate degrees are awarded in the humanities than any other major by far. And a college degree is something you really *can* hang on the wall!

It turns out that the humanities provide a wealth of understanding that can transfer to many other studies and careers. Liberal arts majors are able to "take advantage of openings in the job market that may be closed to others who are less broadly prepared," Ugoretz points out.

Many humanities students go on to advanced degrees and pursue careers in law, medicine, business, and teaching. History and the classics are two majors that often lead to a Master of Arts in Teaching degree.

Cross training for the mind

Some humanities, such as liberal arts, allow students to find themselves academically. (Examples of new liberal arts programs include multimedia design and writing for the Internet.) Other humanities majors are specialized. Linguistics, which teaches us how language works, is also a good place to sharpen your computer programming skills. "Linguistic training is excellent preparation for employment in high-tech industry, particularly when combined with computer science or information science training," says Professor Emeritus D. Terence Langendoen of the University of Arizona, Tucson. The humanities sometimes merge with each other and with other fields to create new areas of thought. For example, philosophy and computer science together give rise to the study of artificial intelligence. Linguistics and philosophy combine to become cognitive sciences. Whew! You won't find gut courses here.

Even though the humanities cover a lot of ground, colleges pretty much take the same approach to these majors. That means if you transfer from one college to another, your humanities credits will likely be accepted. But check to make sure the credits from your first college will go toward your degree at the second one, especially if you transfer from a two-year to a four-year college.

When choosing a college, always consider the faculty factor. Who teaches the undergrad classes? Is it the regular faculty (that's who you want) or graduate students (who may be less able to inspire you)?

"The best way to find out about a particular department's undergraduate curriculum is to talk to a current student, a recent graduate, or one of the faculty members," says Professor Richard T. Lee of Trinity College. "Even an e-mail correspondence with a faculty member will give the student some feel for the program."

Another issue: Does the major you want have its own department? That's a sure sign it's an important curriculum at the college. Also ask about class size. Will you have the opportunity to take small classes and seminars with fewer than 20 students?

Essential to these majors are the college's library, archives, and databases, to give you access to the storehouse of knowledge that the humanities encompass.

You may want the freedom to explore other subjects and courses, so find out how many electives you can take. If it's a big university, can you take courses at other colleges in the university system? If it's a small college, are any of the top profs planning a leave of absence or sabbatical during the time you plan to attend?

Speaking of leave of absence, you may want one yourself. To strengthen skills and enhance experience, humanities majors often take time to study abroad. See if the college has a strong program.

In a world that's changing rapidly, nobody knows exactly what skills and knowledge will be needed down the road. The humanities provide a kind of cross training for the mind that can prepare you for more specialized studies and career development later. Knowing how to know may be one of the most sought-after abilities in the workplace of the future.

Classics

Also known as:
Greek and Latin

What it's about:
Classics is the study of the languages, literatures, and civilization of the ancient Greco-Roman world, including both ancient Greek and Latin. Course work usually involves reading classical texts in these two languages (with discussion in English); but in some programs, the readings may be in English translation.

Is this for you?
You might like this major if you also like: the History Channel; archaeology; languages; debate; computer programming; music; theater.

Consider this major if you are good at: attention to detail; creativity; critical reading/thinking; memorizing; organizing; research *...or have...* initiative; linguistic ability; patience; verbal skills.

Recommended high school prep:
English 4, math 3, lab science 3, social studies 4, and a foreign language 4. If possible, take Latin. French, Italian, and German are also useful.

Did you know...
...that classics can appeal to both "techie" students and "fuzzy" students (those who like art, literature, and philosophy)? To master Latin and Greek, you develop the same kind of mental discipline that is typical of physicists or computer programmers. Some computer companies, in fact, hire classicists because they, like programmers, insist on obeying the language rules. Classicists even distinguished themselves as code breakers in World War II.

...that classics is a leader in the use of computer technology in the humanities? Because the discipline is based on intensive study of a set of texts, databases were developed to help classicists analyze these works. These databases are now part of the regular research tools for students and professionals.

Typical courses in this major:
Elementary Greek
Intermediate Greek (Plato, Homer)
Elementary Latin
Intermediate Latin (Caesar, Ovid)
Ancient philosophy
Classical art and archaeology
Greek and Roman civilization
Athenian democracy
Classical mythology
Tragedy and comedy
Elegiac poetry
Lyric poetry
Epic and lyric: Virgil and Horace
Livy and Tacitus
Homer
Herodotus

Concentrations:
In college: classics and philosophy; classics and archaeology; classics and religion; classics and ancient history; classics and art.

If you go on to grad school: Greek literature (in ancient Greek); Latin literature (in Latin); Latin teacher education.

What the study of this major is like:
"Classics" refers to the literature of the ancient Greeks and Romans. Its themes, forms, and images have inspired generations of readers and writers. In the classics major, you learn Latin, Greek, or both and, in the process, learn about language itself. You explore different methods of interpreting literature—methods that consider audience, context, transmission of the text, and modern theory. You also gain practice in distinguishing between reliable and unreliable sources and in using evidence to understand others' arguments and to create your own. These skills are useful in any career.

You will almost certainly study the oldest surviving classical text (and one of the oldest texts of Western literature): Homer's *Iliad*. Homer probably composed this epic in the ninth century B.C., but he incorporated songs and themes from far earlier times. Homer reveals a society just beginning to develop the intellectual, cultural, and political life of the Greek city-state.

You are introduced to the more lyrical works of later Greek poets, such as Sappho and Pindar. Aeschylus, Sophocles, and Euripides created tragedies, and Aristophanes wrote comedies for democratic Athens. Their plays are still powerful, beautiful, and funny. The works of other Greek writers—Herodotus, Thucydides, Plato, Aristotle, and Demosthenes—were devoted to history, philosophy, rhetoric, and literary theory. As a classics major, you'll consider the questions about human existence, knowledge, politics, ethics, and beauty that these writers asked and that still interest us today.

Latin literature begins with the lively comedies of Plautus in the third century B.C., when Rome was already a great power. Your reading of Latin works includes the comedies of Terence, the philosophical poetry of Lucretius, the love poetry of Catullus, Caesar's accounts of his conquest of Gaul (roughly, modern France), and the orations of Cicero; these works all are part of the turbulent culture of the late Roman Republic.

In the early years of the empire founded by Augustus in 29 B.C., the great Latin writers flourished: the poets Virgil, Horace, and Ovid; the satirist and poet Juvenal; the historians Livy and Tacitus; and the statesman and playwright Seneca. In addition to their works (and despite Horace's conviction that poetry is the most enduring of all monuments), you'll examine the practical Roman creations: architectural and civil engineering works, legal codes, and principles of governing. Like the literature, these achievements have shaped Western society.

In classics departments, classes are often small, so you should have regular contact with faculty members. Individual professors may offer different approaches. Some might emphasize the learning of the languages, whereas others may stress literary interpretation or the analysis of the social and intellectual contexts of the written works. It's helpful to have both sides represented in a department.

Although students often expect classics majors to be stuffy and conservative, most of them aren't. Qualities typical of classics majors are intellectual curiosity about the ancient world, a willingness to accept the challenge of learning no-longer-spoken languages, and an urge to do something unconventional. Most classics majors take their academic work

(but not necessarily themselves) seriously; learning Greek and Latin can be difficult. You will probably spend most of your time working alone, although students occasionally work together outside class—for example, upper-level students sometimes tutor lower-level students. Indeed, majors tend to have a shared feeling of enthusiasm and commitment. Beyond acting as curators of a great literary tradition, they discover new meaning in the works of the ancient Greeks and Romans, so that the classic texts remain alive and relevant.

Other majors you might like:
Comparative literature
Medieval and Renaissance studies
History
Philosophy
Archaeology
Linguistics
Liberal arts and sciences
Judaic studies
Ancient studies
Ancient Near Eastern/Biblical languages
Architectural history and criticism
Speech/rhetorical studies

Questions to ask colleges:
Do students have access to databases such as the *Thesaurus Linguae Graecae* and the L'Année philologique website?

Career options and trends:
A recent survey of business recruitment officers shows that employers appreciate the intellectual stamina, communication and analytical skills, ability to handle complex information, and broad perspective that Classics majors bring to the workplace. Classics majors pursue careers in law, medicine, journalism, education, finance and banking, marketing, management, government, computer programming, publishing, speechwriting, TV production, and the ministry.

Recently, Latin-class enrollments have increased significantly, and so has the demand for high school Latin teachers.

Insider's viewpoint:
"What most appeals to me is the intellectual challenge of tackling a text written in a complicated,

long-dead language, and the thrill of discovery in decoding it. Every time I meet with my Greek and Latin students it is to unravel something that was written over two thousand years ago."

—Professor Kenneth S. Rothwell Jr., University of Massachusetts Boston

For more info:
American Philological Association (APA)
University of Pennsylvania
220 S. 40th St., Suite 201E
Philadelphia, PA 19104-3512
(215) 898-4975
www.apaclassics.org

National Committee for Latin and Greek (NCLG)
www.promotelatin.org

American Classical League (ACL)
Miami University
422 Wells Mill Drive
Oxford, OH 45056
(513) 529-7741
www.aclclassics.org

Comparative literature

What it's about:

As a comparative literature major, you study the literature of different countries, cultures, and languages. You explore poetry, prose, and drama and consider the relation of literature to other arts and other fields of study. The major requires you to study at least two bodies of literature (one of which may be English) in their original languages.

Is this for you?

You might like this major if you also like: travel; literature; art; foreign languages; different cultures; debating; philosophy.

Consider this major if you are good at: active listening; attention to detail; creativity; critical reading/ thinking; research ...*or have...* initiative; linguistic ability; verbal skills; writing skills.

Recommended high school prep:

English 4, math 3, lab science 3, social studies 4, and a foreign language 4 (one language). If possible, take a year of world literature and all available world history courses.

Typical courses in this major:

Great books of Western culture
Medieval epic
Tragedy
Romanticism
Baroque and Neoclassicism
Proust, Mann, and Joyce
History and the novel
The novel of the self
Myths and legends
Literature of China and Japan
Literature of the Americas
Gender and interpretation
Narrative technique

Concentrations:

Literature of a particular nation or culture.

What the study of this major is like:

Comparative literature majors study subjects that cross national, historical, and language boundaries.

Topics include literary movements (for example, Romanticism), literary periods (the Renaissance), literary forms (the novel), literary issues (the treatment of science and technology), and literary theory and criticism. You'll study at least two bodies of literature (American students usually choose English or American literature as one of the fields) and at least one foreign language.

Then you'll focus on comparisons and contrasts between the two cultures and their literature. You may also explore the connections between literature and other artistic fields, such as painting, photography, film, or sculpture, or between literature and other academic areas, such as anthropology, psychology, or history. The field is strongly interdisciplinary, and the possibilities for comparative study are nearly endless. And if you'd enjoy reading works of literature from as many societies as you can, this is the major for you.

Most programs require one or more courses that introduce you to comparative analysis and to new approaches to reading. You may focus on the text alone; or on the society and the times in which it was written; or on the link between the text, its author, and its readers. Which traditions did an author draw upon? What influences can be seen underlying a poem, play, or novel?

In advanced courses you may read works in the language in which they were written. Most colleges offer the study of English, French, Spanish, German, Latin, and Greek language and literature; others offer Russian, Japanese, Chinese, Arabic, Polish, or others. Because you study these bodies of literature in their own language departments, you come across a variety of critical approaches. Many programs also require a capstone project—such as researching and writing a fourth-year thesis.

Comparative literature departments and classes are usually small, and tend to identify with a particular literary theory, interpretative tradition, and attitude toward language study. The major requires a lot of reading and writing, sometimes in a foreign language. Also, you should be ready, willing, and able to see the world from a perspective that differs from the one you are familiar with. Therefore, study abroad can be an exciting and important part of your college work. By graduation, most students have developed a powerful connection to at least one other culture—its literature, art, and unique view of life.

Other majors you might like:
Anthropology
Medieval and Renaissance studies
Area, ethnic, and gender studies
Linguistics
English
Philosophy
Film/cinema studies
Global studies
Art history
International business
Creative Writing
Religious studies

Questions to ask colleges:
Are the professors full-time comparative literature faculty members or are they borrowed from other departments?

Is a senior thesis required? If so, do students receive help from comparative literature faculty members?

Does the department have a club for majors? Do majors help plan events (such as speakers and readings)?

Career options and trends:
Comparative literature majors pursue jobs in journalism, business, cultural institutions, education, publishing, law, government, radio, television, and film. Graduate or professional school is also a popular option. Prospects are best for majors who have mastered another language.

Insider's viewpoint:
"In comparative literature the implicit nationalism of most programs of literary study is rare. Comparatists like to ride the fence, so to speak, which means that you have an investment in more than one place."

—Professor Tobin Siebers, University of Michigan

For more info:
American Comparative Literature Association
 (ACLA)
University of South Carolina
Dept of Languages, Literatures and Cultures
1620 College St Rm 813A
Columbia, SC 29208
(803) 777-3021
www.acla.org

History

What it's about:
History is the study of the record of past human experience. Working with written, oral, visual, and artifacts, history majors examine the causes, contexts, and chronologies of historical events to understand how human experiences have both remained the same and changed over time.

Is this for you?
You might like this major if you also like: reenactments; the History Channel; model building; museums; historical novels; collecting stamps, coins, etc.; other cultures and other times; genealogy and family history.

Consider this major if you are good at: attention to detail; critical reading/thinking; organizing; persuading/influencing; research ...*or have...* curiosity; initiative; patience; verbal skills; writing skills.

Recommended high school prep:
English 4, math 3, lab science 3, social studies 4, and a foreign language 4. If possible, take a year of both European and American history. One year of civics or government would also be beneficial.

Did you know...
...that the study of history is not confined to just books and documents? For example, to research the history of the blues, you might include such sources as posters, music recordings, photographs, oral histories, newspaper clippings, and business contracts.

Typical courses in this major:
Survey of European history
Western civilization
Ancient Greece
Tudor and Stuart England
Precolonial Africa
U.S. constitutional history
Modern Latin America
Renaissance and Reformation
French Revolution
East Asian civilization
Ancient Rome
Modern England
American history
U.S. economic history
Medieval history
Historical research

Concentrations:
Geographical regions (for example, European civilization, Russian history); time periods (medieval and early modern studies); themes (law and society, environmental history).

What the study of this major is like:
As a history major, you examine the causes, contexts, and narratives of past events. Historians now study a wide range of subjects, but most historians work with either political or social history. Although historians employ their own methods, they also make use of those of many other disciplines. Some "studies" majors include history; for instance, American studies generally has a literary or historical emphasis, whereas Russian/Slavic studies tends to focus on political science or international relations.

Courses usually focus on time periods, nations, geographic areas, historical perspectives, and themes, often in combination (for example, civil rights in the United States, or women in nineteenth-century Europe). Your course work helps you to understand the purposes, principles, and methods of the study of history, and to grasp both the particulars and the universals of societies past and present. You also explore questions of judgment and interpretation.

There are prerequisites for advanced work, but you do not necessarily have to take courses in a fixed, chronological order. You devise a program that meets your interests and also fulfills requirements found in most colleges: one or two introductory courses, one or more courses that acquaint you with cultures and histories other than your own, a course in historical methods, and a research seminar.

Some programs offer an introductory course that teaches the basics of history while featuring a particular topic, such as immigration in American history.

Other lower-level courses may cover the history of Europe, the United States, and, perhaps, the non-Western world. Upper-level courses are usually seminars in areas you find most interesting. There is generally a capstone course that may explore great historical writing, the different genres of the subject, or the construction of chronologies from the raw materials of human experience.

As a major, you read extensively and develop writing skills through essay exams, book reviews, and research papers (you must become familiar with computer-aided research, especially if your research project has a social science focus). Because history majors often do archival research and interviewing, and your classes rely on lectures and discussion, you'll need to sharpen your listening and speaking skills.

The main challenge you will face as a major is to find source material for your research studies. At first, you'll interpret documents presented to you. Eventually, though, you must choose a question you want to answer (such as, what was the route of the Underground Railroad?) and then decide how to locate the books and other sources that will help you come up with an answer. With the encouragement of instructors and others in the field, you should quickly become an independent historian.

Other majors you might like:
Classics
Medieval and Renaissance studies
European studies
Asian studies
Art history
Anthropology
International relations
Political science
Archaeology
African-American studies
Public history/archives
Journalism

Questions to ask colleges:
Is the curriculum heavily focused on European and American history, or are there courses on the non-Atlantic world?

What are the library's strengths and weaknesses? Which journals does the library subscribe to and which archives (if any) does it control? Does the library make online databases available and offer online access to journals?

What kinds of connections does the department have with local historical societies, museums, historical sites, or the history departments of other colleges in the area?

Career options and trends:
College professor; high school teacher*; lawyer; museum curator or archivist*; journalist.

History majors learn how to locate, synthesize, and present information—valuable training for almost any career. Graduate and professional schools also value the education history majors receive. Few majors actually become historians—and college level teaching positions are extremely competitive—but employment options are many and varied, including government service, business, teaching in elementary and secondary schools, law, medicine, and other professions.

Insider's viewpoint:
"I used to read every book I could get my hands on about the Holocaust, about sixteenth-century France. If you think about it, every novel you read, if it's not set in the present, is a historical novel. Studying history is an extension of that love of literature; it's like watching a very long movie."

—Emily, sophomore, Northwestern University

For more info:
American Historical Association (AHA)
400 A St., S.E.
Washington, DC 20003-3889
(202) 544-2422
www.historians.org

Liberal arts and sciences

What it's about:
The liberal arts and sciences major provides you with a well-rounded education in the sciences, humanities, mathematics, and languages. You gain the ability to reason critically, communicate effectively, and understand relationships across broad fields of knowledge. This generalist background prepares you for a wide range of endeavors rather than for a specific career.

Is this for you?
You might like this major if you also like: reading; writing; discussing new ideas; arguing; reasoning.

Consider this major if you are good at: creativity; critical reading/thinking; persuading/influencing; quantitative analysis; teamwork *...or have...* initiative; patience; verbal skills; writing skills.

Recommended high school prep:
English 4, math 3, lab science 3, social studies 3, art 1, and a foreign language 3.

Did you know...
...that liberal arts and sciences is not just another term for "undecided"? Choosing this major is a decision to prepare for a world in which new and unexpected careers are invented every day.

Typical courses in this major:
English literature
Biological concepts
Environmental science
American history since 1865
World religions
Philosophy
Psychology
Sociology
Fundamentals of economics
Cultural anthropology
Philosophy
Probability and statistics
Foreign language I, II
Communications
Music history
Art history

Concentrations:
A wide range is available; among them are gender studies, multicultural studies, social sciences, literature and linguistics, natural sciences.

What the study of this major is like:
If you enjoy learning and want to spend your college years exploring new ideas rather than preparing for a specific career, you might consider majoring in liberal arts. The liberal arts program is typically offered only as an undergraduate major. Most liberal arts courses include a great deal of reading, writing, and discussion, and classes tend to be small.

As a liberal arts major, you will be required to study a wide range of subjects, some of which may be new to you or may be in areas in which you have not excelled in the past. Even though you might prefer studying literature, you will have to take classes in history and mathematics. Science lovers will have to take classes in poetry and music.

Most liberal arts programs have a required "core"—meaning you must take at least an introductory course in each of certain designated areas (although you usually have a choice of courses in each area). The areas include the fine arts (such as art history, music, drama); social sciences (economics, sociology, history); natural sciences (chemistry, biology); mathematics; humanities (literature, philosophy); and a foreign language. Some programs also require a semester of study abroad, or some other cross-cultural experience.

In addition to a core of required courses, you will likely be offered a wide range of electives from a wide range of subjects. You might find this freedom to choose very liberating; or you might find it confusing or intimidating. In either case, you would be wise to ask your academic adviser for help in designing a course of study that is relevant to your talents and interests.

Because the liberal arts program includes basic college subjects, you will meet students from many disciplines and be exposed to the perspectives of many academic areas. For the liberal arts major, college is an opportunity to discover and refine goals rather than to work single-mindedly on a predetermined regimen. This major allows you to be flexible with your schedule and to follow specific interests over several semesters in various related courses. Although your reading and writing assignments tend to be heavy, the variety of the subject matter keeps your work fresh and interesting. You will have opportunities to see connections between different subjects and to broaden and deepen your learning.

As a survey of college subjects, the major tends not to vary much, in emphases, requirements, and philosophies, from one college to another. The similarity will come in handy if you should want to transfer to another institution. At the two-year or community college level, students intending to continue on to a four-year college usually prefer this major. Generally, most of your liberal arts credits will be accepted at other colleges, and you will be well prepared for upper-level courses.

Other majors you might like:
Humanities
Journalism
English
American studies
Mathematics
Natural sciences
Communications
Global studies
Environmental studies
Women's studies
Classics
Philosophy

Questions to ask colleges:
Is this major housed in its own department, or is it pulled together from different departments?

How easy is it to transfer to other majors?

Are students eligible to take classes at other colleges while they are enrolled in the program? Is there a study-abroad program?

Career options and trends:
Teacher*; lawyer*; doctor; journalist*; filmmaker.

Career paths for liberal arts and science majors are wide open: they include journalism, teaching, business and industry, sales, social work, government, film, entrepreneurship—almost any area of human endeavor. The major is also an excellent foundation for an advanced or professional degree leading to careers in law, medicine, engineering, or teaching.

For liberal arts majors, the job outlook is positive, even in difficult times. Because the curriculum is flexible in terms of career preparation, graduates can take advantage of openings in the job market (including jobs that don't even exist yet) that may be closed to others who are less broadly prepared.

For more info:
American Academy for Liberal Education
127 S. Peyton St., Suite 210
Alexandria, VA 22314
(703) 713-9719
www.aale.org

Linguistics

What it's about:

As a linguistics major, you learn what makes human languages special: how they are spoken, written, and understood. You'll also examine many of the world's languages—how they are related and how they have changed over time—as well as methods of analyzing languages for their characteristic and distinctive properties.

Is this for you?

You might like this major if you also like: learning new languages; traveling; exploring other cultures; your own heritage culture; crossword puzzles and word games like Scrabble; figuring out where people come from by their accent; word origins.

Consider this major if you are good at: active listening; attention to detail; creativity; critical reading/thinking; organizing; research *...or have...* initiative; patience; verbal skills.

Recommended high school prep:

English 4, math 3, lab science 3, social studies 3, and a foreign language 4. It may be helpful to divide your foreign language studies between two languages. If possible, take a year of computer programming.

Did you know...

...that there are more than 5,000 languages spoken in the world today and that many of them are threatened with extinction before the end of this century? Linguists are leading the efforts to document these languages and to help their speakers preserve them, in written and oral form, for future generations.

...that linguistic training is excellent preparation for employment in high-tech industry, particularly when combined with training in computer science or information science? Linguistics also prepares you for further study in any area in which knowledge of how language works is useful.

Typical courses in this major:

Introduction to linguistics
Phonetics
Phonology
Syntax
Semantics
Morphology
Dialectology
Languages of the world
Language and mind
Language and society
Historical linguistics
Writing systems
Structure of a particular language
Psycholinguistics

Concentrations:

In college: a language or group of languages, e.g., Germanic languages (such as English, German, Dutch); Romance languages (Spanish, Portuguese, French, Italian); Semitic languages; or East Asian languages. However, few undergraduate linguistics programs are large enough to support concentrations.

If you go on to grad school: phonetics/phonology; morphology/syntax; semantics; typology; psycholinguistics; sociolinguistics; computational linguistics; historical linguistics; structure of a language or group of languages.

What the study of this major is like:

Linguistics focuses on the similarities among the world's languages, as well as on the unique characteristics of individual languages, in order to understand those traits and the people who speak the languages. The major usually begins with an introductory course, followed by courses in phonetics and phonology (the study of speech sounds), morphology (the structure and function of words), syntax (the way words combine to form phrases or sentences), and semantics (meaning and use of words).

In addition, the major may include the study of specific languages, or families of languages, and the communities or societies that speak them. You might undertake comparative and historical studies of both well-known and little known languages and dialects. You might explore how children acquire language; how people produce and comprehend written, spoken, and signed language; how language disorders are diagnosed and treated; how languages can be taught most effectively; how the use of particular languages and dialects has been fostered (or discouraged) by government policy; and how computers can be programmed to recognize and produce language.

Most students find linguistics intellectually challenging—in a word, hard. In introductory courses, you will most likely be given samples from languages you don't know and be asked to describe the languages. Once you get the hang of it, you will probably enjoy such exercises and be ready for the next stage of training, in which you'll explore linguistic theories and their explanation of observed data. At first, this approach may be frustrating, because you won't understand how the theories work. But once you feel comfortable doing a linguistic experiment, you might begin a project for an advanced course or an undergraduate thesis. You may, in fact, find yourself working on cutting-edge studies while still an undergraduate.

There are two major approaches to the study of human language: formal and functional. Formal study emphasizes the structure of languages and requires good data-handling and reasoning skills. Functional study emphasizes the use of language and may involve laboratory or field research and statistics. Most linguistics programs stress one or the other of these approaches. A few (mostly larger) departments combine them successfully.

Other majors you might like:
Native American studies
Anthropology
Classics
Speech/rhetorical studies
Communications
Computer science
Foreign language teacher education
Language interpretation/translation
Philosophy
Psychology
Communication disorders
American sign language (ASL)

Questions to ask colleges:
Is the major offered by a linguistics department, by another department that includes linguistics, or as an interdisciplinary program? Are courses in the core areas of linguistics (phonology, syntax, semantics) regularly offered?

Is there a strong study-abroad program that enables students to learn a language or strengthen skills in one they already know?

Can students do independent research with a faculty member in linguistics, work in a linguistics lab, or do an industry internship (for example, in computational linguistics) as part of the undergraduate degree?

Career options and trends:
High school language teacher*; college professor*; translator; consultant.

The Bureau of Labor Statistics projects very strong job growth for interpreters and translators through 2022, due to an increasingly diverse U.S. population and growing international trade. Computerized translation technology is not expected to diminish those job prospects, although they will make the translator's job easier.

The linguistics major can also prepare you for jobs in international business, government service, public relations, software design, marketing, publishing, advertising, English as a second language (ESL) teaching and research, health-related professions (speech pathology and language disorders), industrial research and development (speech recognition, text analysis and interpretation, electronic dictionary preparation, artificial intelligence, and speech synthesis), and law. Some of these fields require graduate study.

Linguists are playing a prominent role in high-tech industry, primarily in information retrieval and analysis and in speech technology. While technology has made this work easier in some ways, it will never replace the need for individuals with strong language skills. As business and commerce becomes more international in the global economy, opportunites are expected to increase for translators and interpreters. Good language teachers are always needed in the United States and overseas (especially English teachers), as are speech and language therapists.

Insider's viewpoint:
"I volunteered as a conversation partner for foreign students, which was fun and provided some insight

into how people learn foreign languages. Anything that puts you in contact with native speakers of as many languages as possible is great, because for linguistics classes you very often need native consultants to provide data."

—Andrea, senior, University of Washington

For more info:
Linguistic Society of America (LSA)
1325 18th St., N.W.
Suite 211
Washington, DC 20036-6501
(202) 835-1714
www.lsadc.org

Center for Applied Linguistics (CAL)
4646 40th St., N.W.
Washington, DC 20016-1859
(202) 362-0700
www.cal.org

Philosophy

What it's about:

Philosophy is the study of the fundamental questions about the nature of being, knowledge, right and wrong, and our place in the physical world. You explore the key philosophical texts and traditions, and examine the nature of argument and reasoning. You'll also consider the ways philosophy affects other fields of inquiry, such as physics, religion, and computer science.

Is this for you?

You might like this major if you also like: puzzles and games; thinking about what life is about; debate and argument; science fiction or other imaginative literature; thinking differently from the way other people do.

Consider this major if you are good at: attention to detail; creativity; critical reading/thinking; organizing...*or have...* patience; verbal skills; writing skills.

Recommended high school prep:

English 4, math 3, lab science 3, social studies 4, and a foreign language 3–4. If possible, take a course in philosophy or a humanities course that includes philosophical works. Any course that requires a lot of reading will also be beneficial.

Did you know...

...that it is a rare and valuable ability to know what an argument is? Employers are often grateful to find someone who can write clear prose and think logically.

Typical courses in this major:

Problems of philosophy
History of philosophy
Ethics
Political theory
Logic
Epistemology
Philosophy of religion
Aristotle
Kant
Aesthetics
Metaphysics
Theory of knowledge
Philosophy of science
Plato
Locke
Hegel

Concentrations:

In college: history of philosophy; ethics; logic.

If you go on to grad school: epistemology; metaphysics.

What the study of this major is like:

Philosophy majors participate in a tradition of thought as old as civilization and as new as artificial intelligence. Philosophy is the most general field of study. Every religious or moral belief, every detail from science—even ordinary information—can be viewed as subject matter. Philosophy majors are encouraged to contemplate the universe, both human and nonhuman. At the same time, they are trained to become disciplined, imaginative thinkers who can persuasively support their positions.

Many questions that philosophers ask are often asked by children: How did the world begin? Do animals have their own language? Could I be someone else? Part of the fascination of philosophy is that it can reveal the complexity and subtlety of simple matters. On the other hand, philosophy tries to expose the muddled thinking we read and hear every day.

Beginning courses in philosophy are designed for students with little background, because few high schools teach philosophy. Most college programs have introductory courses in philosophical problems, which may include such topics as ethics (moral conduct), metaphysics (the nature of reality), logic, epistemology (the study of knowledge), and aesthetics (the nature of art). Another introductory course surveys the history of philosophy beginning with the Greeks, and usually takes one or two years to complete.

As you progress through the major, you will read works by Plato, Aristotle, Aquinas, Descartes, Hume, Kant, Hegel, Wittgenstein, John Dewey, and other important writers on such issues as the nature of consciousness, "truth," and social justice. Increasingly, though, you will be expected to think from a philosophical perspective on your own. A substantial paper or thesis is usually required in your senior year.

Philosophy can present you with ideas that may at first seem overly abstract, incomprehensible, or pure fantasy. You may also have trouble seeing the connection between the philosophical concepts you study and the issues that matter in your daily life. In addition, philosophy courses seldom begin with easy material and then progress to the more difficult. Philosophers circle back on questions again and again. When studying philosophy, you can expect to progress from confusion to some clarity, but not from one small but clear concept to another well-defined concept. This situation frustrates some students and excites others.

Most philosophy departments at large universities are strong in certain areas of philosophy, such as ethics and moral philosophy, philosophy of language, history of philosophy, or political philosophy. Some departments focus on the sciences, some on the humanities, and a few take a religious approach. Departments at colleges that do not have graduate programs tend not to be specialized. Most departments, however, offer undergraduates a full range of courses. You can generally assume that the more professors in the department, the greater the variety of subjects taught.

Other majors you might like:
English
Religious studies
Political science
History
Mathematics
Music, general
Physics
Classics
European studies
Asian studies
Legal studies
Theology

Questions to ask colleges:
Is there an opportunity to take small classes (under 20 students) and seminars? Is there a philosophy club? Do students have any role in the department's activities, such as helping to select outside speakers?

Career options and trends:
Philosophy majors find their training useful in a variety of fields. The analytic skills developed in college are easily transferable to a number of professional areas. Students of philosophy tend to have the flexibility and capacity for growth that employers find valuable. Many graduates accept jobs in business, journalism, computer science, public administration, teaching, publishing, and public relations.

Teaching positions at the college level are very competitive and require a Ph.D.

Insider's viewpoint:
"Philosophy unites living and thinking in a way that few other disciplines do. It is a matter of giving yourself over to a life of questioning and searching, with no holds barred. It rewards honesty, courage, and curiosity. Philosophy at its best is not a way to make a living, but a way to be alive."

—Professor Richard T. Lee, Trinity College

For more info:
The American Philosophical Association (APA)
University of Delaware
31 Amstel Ave.
Newark, DE 19716-4797
(302) 831-1112
www.apaonline.org

Languages

People don't realize that the United States has no official language. There's a movement afoot to give English the nod (and English has its own section in this book). But what about the 34.5 million Americans who speak Spanish at home? Or the 8.3 million who speak Asian tongues? Knowing more than one language is a valuable skill in business, government, and the nonprofit sectors here and around the world.

"More students would consider language majors if they knew how important proficiency in a foreign language is in the workplace today," says Professor Theresa A. Antes, University of Florida, Gainesville. "Many employers will hire an applicant who is proficient in a foreign language over one who is not."

Language skills are growing in importance because of Internet communications, global business, the integration of the European Union, unrest in the Middle East, and the emergence of China as a participant in international affairs and commerce.

Regarding China, Professor Scott Cook of Grinnell College says, "Students may not realize just how important China is in the world and how many job opportunities a Chinese degree may open up for them."

The significance of Arabic is not in doubt, with the Middle East so prominent in the news. "Knowledge of Arabic is indispensable for a firsthand acquaintance with events in the region," says Professor Michael Fishbein, University of California: Los Angeles.

The world is your oyster (and your ostra, Auster, huître, ostrica) if you master languages. Consider these pearls of opportunity: employment in international relations, diplomacy, intelligence gathering, journalism, law, medicine, tourism, and the arts; jobs as translators/interpreters, Foreign Service specialists, and environmental specialists; and positions in a nongovernmental organization, the computer industry, and international banking and business.

"It used to be assumed that all students pursued a degree in French in order to teach at the high school level, but demands of the global economy have changed that scenario," Antes says.

La Dolce Vita

Studying a language requires much more than memorizing vocabulary and learning grammar rules. And the rewards go beyond career enhancement.

"Learning to speak Italian enables one to combine good employment with fine living," notes Professor Robert E. Proctor, Connecticut College. "There's always something new to discover," he says of Italy.

"Once you take Russia as your focus," observes Professor Melissa Frazier of Sarah Lawrence College, "concepts like 'East' and 'West,' 'Europe' and 'Asia' become more tentative, and your understanding of the world around you much more complicated and also much more interesting."

Japanese is a subject of inexhaustible riches, according to H. Mack Horton, University of California, Berkeley. Sure, Japan is the world's second-largest economy, but he's talking about intellectual enrichment. "The Japanese major is a gold mine for anyone with an abiding curiosity about the human condition," he says.

Just as languages differ, so do college programs. At some colleges, you'll choose between studying the language/linguistics, or the literature/culture, of the countries where the language is spoken. By the way, there are also separate majors called area studies, which emphasize the history, culture, politics, and economics of a region rather than its language and literature. As an example, German (language/literature) is a different major from German studies. It's good if colleges offer both types. (See the chapter on Area, ethnic, and gender studies.)

Many graduate programs combine language studies with studies of other things, such as the arts, political science, religious studies, sociology, and economics. Graduate tracks in literature may concentrate on a particular period—classical or modern—or on a genre, such as poetry or drama. (Some colleges teach literature in translation, so find out if you'll be reading works in the original language.)

Here are some questions to ask: What are the possibilities for study abroad? Are the study-abroad programs offered through the university, so you can be sure credits will be transferred? Are tuition and fees the same as those for courses on campus?

How many faculty members are native speakers? What are their specializations? If you want to learn a particular dialect, make sure a faculty member teaches it. How big are the classes? To master a language, you'll want the chance to speak in class.

In choosing a college, look for facilities that include a library with computers and databases. Are computers set up to access the Web and handle word processing in the language? How good is the library's collection? What about language labs? Does the college receive news and other TV programming in the language?

Will your college experience include social opportunities to meet and converse with others who speak the language in dorms or the cafeteria? Is a community of native speakers nearby? Are activities and lectures offered to promote studies on and off campus?

Resources for more information include the Association for Asian Studies, at www.asian-studies.org; Modern Language Association, at www.mla.org; American Council on the Teaching of Foreign Languages, at www.actfl.org; Association of Professional Schools of International Affairs, at www.apsia.org; and National Foreign Affairs Training Center (Foreign Service Institute), at www.state.gov.

This section also covers American Sign Language. For more information about the classics and linguistics majors, turn to the Humanities chapter.

American Sign Language (ASL)

What it's about:

American Sign Language (ASL) is a visual language used by the Deaf community in the United States and Canada. In this major you learn how to sign, and study the literature, grammar, and history of this language and its use among members of the Deaf community in North America.

Is this for you?

You might like this major if you also like: taking risks; interacting with people from different cultures and with different points of view; helping others; breaking down barriers.

Consider this major if you are good at: critical reading/thinking; memorizing; spacial thinking/analysis ...*or have...* cultural sensitivity; initiative; manual dexterity; patience; physical stamina; verbal skills.

Recommended high school prep:

English 4, math 3, lab science 3, social studies 3, and a foreign language 3–4.

Did you know...

...that ASL is not based on English? Its syntax has more in common with Japanese, and is also completely different from British Sign Language.

...that there are cross-cultural issues you might not be aware of? Deaf Culture is a distinct group that has its own language and customs. Students who hear can sometimes cross invisible cultural lines without realizing it.

Typical courses in this major:

Comparative analysis of ASL and English
ASL literature
ASL classifiers
ASL incorporated numbers and fingerspelling
Introduction to methods of teaching ASL
Introduction to Deaf studies
Deaf Culture
History of the Deaf community
Communication in gestures
Senior thesis/seminar

Concentrations:

In college: ASL teacher education; ASL interpretation.

If you go on to grad school: ASL linguistics; Deaf studies with an emphasis on ASL.

What the study of this major is like:

When you begin learning American Sign Language, you can expect to be fascinated by it. Language acquisition research shows that picking up the basics of ASL shouldn't take you a long time. But although you may at first think that ASL is easy, you will probably realize, soon enough, that mastering the language can be a challenging, sometimes tedious experience.

ASL does not "mime" spoken English and is not structured like English at all. ASL has its own rules for the creation of words, phonetics, and grammar quite unlike those for spoken languages. ASL also involves more than hand gestures—facial movements are also part of the grammatical structure, and meaning is also derived from the signer's use of the surrounding space.

You may also have difficulty communicating with Deaf people because they sign quickly; for many, ASL is their native language. And after you become proficient in ASL, you may still feel stalled in your ability to interact with members of the Deaf community. But if you persevere and don't let yourself be discouraged by the frustrations of being unable to understand them at times and of occasionally being rejected, you will eventually qualify as a skilled interpreter.

Some colleges offer courses in Signed English, in the belief that this form of communication can enhance Deaf children's English literacy skills. This practice is not widely accepted in the Deaf community, however.

If you think you may want to become an ASL teacher, keep in mind that while this is not impossible, such training is intended, primarily, for Deaf students.

ASL-trained people who hear can more easily find jobs as general teachers of the Deaf, ASL interpreters, or counselors.

Other majors you might like:
Communication disorders
Education of Deaf/hearing impaired
Special education
Audiology/hearing sciences
Linguistics
Sign language interpretation
Anthropology
Human services
Foreign languages/literatures
Audiology/speech pathology
Child development

Questions to ask colleges:
Are there Deaf teachers? Are there adequate ASL labs?

Does the program provide interaction with the local Deaf community? Is there group support for students who are new to Deaf Culture and may experience culture shock?

Career options and trends:
ASL interpreter; high school teacher; ASL specialist.

The American Sign Language Teachers Association offers three levels of certification: Provisional, Qualified, and Professional. ASL interpreters earn certifications from the Registry of Interpreters for the Deaf or from the National Association of the Deaf.

Legislative mandates that incorporate ASL into foreign language curriculums is increasing the demand for ASL high school teachers all over the United States. In metropolitan areas, the job market for ASL interpreting is both very hot and very competitive. The hourly rates are excellent (but freelance interpreters receive no fringe benefits). The increasing use of video relay services, which allow individuals to conduct video calls using a sign language interpreter over an Internet connection, will also increase demand for interpreters.

Overall, the Bureau of Labor Statistics predicts that interpreters for the Deaf will have favorable job prospects due to a shortage of people with needed skill levels, especially in urban areas.

Insider's viewpoint:
"I enjoy watching my students acquiring the language. They appear to be intimidated on the first day of classes but by the end, they are animated with the use of their faces, hands, and bodies when they communicate."

—Professor Mike Kemp, Gallaudet University

For more info:
American Sign Language Teachers Association (ASLTA)
P.O. Box 92426
Rochester, NY 14692
www.aslta.org

National Association of the Deaf (NAD)
8630 Fenton St.
Suite 820
Silver Spring, MD 20910
(301) 587-1788
www.nad.org

Arabic

What it's about:

Arabic majors learn to understand, read, and speak Modern Standard Arabic; read and analyze the key works of classical and modern Arabic literature; and study Islam and Middle Eastern history.

Is this for you?

You might like this major if you also like: learning languages; Arabic and Islamic culture; history; travel; religious issues and thought.

Consider this major if you are good at: attention to detail; critical reading/thinking; memorizing; organizing; research ...*or have...* linguistic ability; patience; verbal skills; writing skills.

Recommended high school prep:

English 4, math 3, lab science 3, social studies 4, and a foreign language 3–4. If possible, take Arabic. Otherwise, take another language with a case system (where nouns and adjectives are inflected depending upon the grammar of the sentence), such as German, Russian, or Latin. World history, comparative religion, and literature courses are also helpful.

Did you know...

...that Arabic is the classical language of Islamic civilization and is the language preferred for religious expression by Muslims everywhere, whether or not their native language is Arabic? Much of classical Arabic literature also covers history, biography, travel literature, poetry, and philosophy from a nonreligious perspective.

Typical courses in this major:

Literary Arabic
Islamic texts
Classical Arabic texts
Philosophical and Kalam texts
Modern Arabic literature
Arabic media
Shi'ia in Islamic history
Contemporary Islamic thought
History of the Arabs
Spoken Egyptian Arabic
Spoken Moroccan Arabic
Western Islamic art
Survey of the Middle East from 500 to the present
Islamic civilization: premodern Islam
Islamic civilization: Islam and the modern world

Concentrations:

Generally, none in college; but if you go on to grad school: classical Arabic literature; Islamic texts; modern Arabic literature.

What the study of this major is like:

If you major in Arabic, you can expect to devote plenty of time to learning the language. According to the U.S. Foreign Service, Arabic, along with Chinese and Japanese, is among the languages that adults have most trouble learning. Arabic has a complicated phonetic system and grammar, as well as a system of usage that is not even remotely related to English. In addition, the formal Modern Standard Arabic is very different from informal, colloquial Arabic. Students often feel that they are learning two languages at the same time, so be prepared to work hard and to persevere.

To become proficient in listening to, speaking, reading, and writing Arabic, you'll have to study long hours outside class, completing homework assignments, reading and preparing texts for discussion, researching topics for reports and papers, and reviewing. Arabic courses may use videotapes and CDs, in addition to textbooks. You should gain as much exposure to the language as possible; for example, you can use the Web to access Arabic newspapers and radio broadcasts. An exciting development in recent years is the availability of up-to-the-minute journalism in Arabic online.

Undergraduate Arabic courses usually include language, literature, culture, history, and Islamics (the study of the religion). You should plan to spend at least one summer in an Arabic-speaking country, or possibly in a semester- or year-abroad program. Most American institutions have adopted the proficiency method of language teaching. In other words, Arabic is no longer taught purely as a classical language, with stress on grammar and translation. So even if you are interested primarily in modern or classical literature, you'll be expected to learn to pronounce the language correctly and to acquire a reasonable fluency in speaking.

Because only a few students major in Arabic, you'll have more opportunities to receive individual attention from faculty members than you would in most other majors. You will also have ample opportunity to meet other Arabic majors. Friendships often form across cultural borders: for example, between Muslim and Christian students or between students with a Middle Eastern background and those of European or African origin.

Other majors you might like:
Near and Middle Eastern studies
Linguistics
Ancient Near Eastern/Biblical languages
History
Religious studies
Art history
Musicology/ethnomusicology
Political science
Classics
Islamic studies
Judaic studies
International relations

Questions to ask colleges:
Does the program have a special focus? One program may emphasize modern literature, another linguistics, or Islamic thought. Look for a program that will satisfy your own interests.

Is the library committed to keeping the Arabic and Middle Eastern collections up-to-date? Library resources are extremely important for the study of Arabic.

Do computers have access to the Web in Arabic, and can they handle Arabic word processing?

Career options and trends:
College professor*; translator/interpreter*; Foreign Service Officer*; journalist.

Jobs in the U.S. Foreign Service are usually open only to U.S. citizens. To become a FSO, you must pass the Foreign Service Examination.

The importance of the Middle east in world affairs is pushing demand for speakers of Arabic. More jobs are available in intelligence, translation, and journalism for people with expertise in Arabic and the Middle East. More universities are establishing Arabic programs and are hiring faculty members in the field.

For more info:
American Association of Teachers of Arabic
   (AATA)
3416 Primm Lane
Birmingham, AL 35216
(205) 822-6800
www.aataweb.org

Middle East Studies Association of North America
University of Arizona
1219 North Santa Rita Ave.
Tuscon, AZ 85721
(520) 621-5850
www.mesana.org

Chinese language and literature

What it's about:

The Chinese major prepares you to interact with and understand the modern Chinese world, while introducing you to China's long and rich cultural tradition. It typically combines three to four years of language study (modern Mandarin) with courses in literature, philosophy, history, and other fields.

Is this for you?

You might like this major if you also like: Chinese culture; studying languages; history; travel; different ways of thinking about the world.

Consider this major if you are good at: attention to detail; creativity; critical reading/thinking; memorizing *...or have...* initiative; linguistic ability; patience; persistence; verbal skills; writing skills.

Recommended high school prep:

English 4, math 3, lab science 3, social studies 4, and a foreign language 4. Be sure to take as much foreign language as possible; Chinese is preferable but in no way required. World history courses are also recommended.

Did you know...

...that you don't need to know any Chinese before you begin college? If you have solid study habits, the language, as difficult as it may be, is highly learnable.

Typical courses in this major:

Elementary Chinese
Intermediate Chinese
Advanced Chinese
Advanced classical Chinese
Traditional Chinese literature
Modern Chinese fiction
Modern Chinese film
Modern Chinese theater
Chinese philosophy
Chinese religion
Chinese history
East Asian civilization
Chinese linguistics
Chinese gender and women's studies
Chinese music
Chinese art

Concentrations:

Chinese language; Chinese literature; Chinese calligraphy.

What the study of this major is like:

For English speakers, Chinese is easy to learn, but difficult to master. Once you learn the four tones and basic vocabulary, speaking the language should not be hard, because the grammar is user-friendly.

If you major in Chinese, be ready to immerse yourself in the language. Language courses typically meet five days a week and are often conducted in Chinese only. The classes may consist of alternating grammar and drill sessions. You learn to speak, listen, read, and write Chinese. In your first year or two, greater emphasis is placed on speaking and listening. Most language programs introduce Chinese written characters almost immediately, although some instructors wait until you establish a solid foundation in the spoken language.

By your third year, the emphasis will likely shift, to take in more written materials, such as newspaper articles and fairly simple literature. Your fourth-year courses usually include advanced literature and perhaps a course in classical Chinese. Although classical Chinese is grammatically different from modern Chinese, learning it will increase your understanding of Chinese as a whole. Language courses are supplemented by English-taught courses in literature, philosophy, and history. Such courses typically focus on lecture and discussion and require written papers in English.

As a Chinese major, you should expect a demanding workload, especially in the language courses, although your studies should be enjoyable if you are well prepared. Your greatest challenge will be to get off to a good start—to develop solid study habits and establish a strong foundation for future language study. You should advance quickly in your first year; but in your second year, your progress, though no less real, may be less noticeable. In your second year you focus on memorization and the acquisition of characters and vocabulary, which can be frustrating if you have not mentally prepared yourself for it. After the second year, students generally feel more confident as they begin to gain mastery of the language. For real fluency, you should study in a Chinese-speaking community or country for at least a semester, preferably a year.

The Chinese major may be housed in departments that teach only modern languages, teach East Asian languages and culture, teach East Asian languages and literature, teach comparative literature, teach linguistics, or offer second-language education, including bilingual education. The biggest difference among Chinese programs is the balance between courses in language study and in area studies (for example, the literature, religion, and history of a region). Often, if a program requires only two years of language study but offers a number of courses in area studies, the reason is not a matter of philosophy but rather of necessity. The program may not have enough professors to offer more than two or three years of Chinese. You would then take area studies courses from faculty members in other departments.

Other majors you might like:
Asian studies
Linguistics
Asian-American studies
Comparative literature
Foreign language teacher education
Philosophy
History
Chinese studies
East Asian studies
International relations
East Asian languages
Art history

Questions to ask colleges:
How many years of Chinese are offered on campus? A small liberal arts college that offers three or four years of the language should be considered to have, for its size, a substantial program.

How many other departments offer China-related courses? How many hours a week do language courses meet? A college that offers less than five hours per week at the first- and second-year levels is cutting corners.

How large is the Chinese community on campus? What kinds of activities promote Chinese studies on campus, including guest lecturers, Chinese tables, Chinese houses, or Lunar New Year celebrations?

Career options and trends:
Chinese language teacher*; ESL teacher; Foreign Service Officer; administrator or analyst for an international NGO (nongovermental organization); translator/interpreter; journalist.

An increasing number of Chinese language majors are hired by firms dealing with overseas markets. Various branches of government and international organizations need experts in Chinese languages and culture. The Foreign Service is usually open only to U.S. citizens who pass an exam.

As China prospers economically and grows in political importance, job opportunities related to China continue to increase. However, fluency in Chinese alone may not get you a foot in the door; you also need training in another field—for instance, if you want to do business in China, you should take economics courses, and preferably pursue an MBA degree later on. College faculty positions in Chinese are not easy to come by, so you should not consider seeking a doctorate in Chinese unless you have a deep commitment to the field.

For more info:
Association for Asian Studies (AAS)
825 Victors Way, Suite 310
Ann Arbor, MI 48108
(734) 665-2490
www.asian-studies.org/

French

What it's about:
Majors in French study the language, literature, and culture of France and other areas of the French-speaking world.

Is this for you?
You might like this major if you also like: French culture; studying languages; literature; art; traveling.

Consider this major if you are good at: active listening; attention to detail; critical reading/thinking; memorizing ...*or have*... linguistic ability; perseverance; verbal skills; writing skills.

Recommended high school prep:
English 4, math 3, lab science 3, social studies 4 (including European and world history), and French 4. If possible, also take a second foreign language; Spanish, Italian, and Latin are especially recommended.

Did you know...
...that there are many career opportunities available to French majors besides teaching? In addition to language and literature classes, you can often choose among topics such as French for business, French for medicine, cultural studies, or film studies to expand your options in the global economy.

...that, in many programs, the courses in elementary French are considered prerequisites and do not count toward your major? So if you can, take at least two years of high school French; then you can begin studying at the intermediate level in college.

Typical courses in this major:
French composition
French conversation
French grammar
Stylistics
French literature
French phonetics
Structure of French
French theater
Realism and naturalism
Twentieth-century poetry

Concentrations:
French literature and culture; French language and linguistics; foreign language education.

What the study of this major is like:
As a French major, you study the language, literature, and culture of the people of France and other French-speaking regions. Traditionally, Parisian French (the language spoken in France's capital) and the culture of France have dominated the major. But since World War II, the French major has broadened to include the language and cultures of nations formerly under French control, such as Algeria, the Ivory Coast, Lebanon, and Indochina (now Southeast Asia). The widened perspective reflects the importance of French, which has been an international language (one used in diplomacy and global trade) since the eighteenth century.

Most programs provide a combination of language and literature courses. While you work on fluency and accuracy in language courses, you learn about the culture by studying various French texts. In a series of grammar, composition, and conversation courses, you read, listen to, speak, and write French. In literature courses you may examine the classics: the theater of Molière, Corneille, and Racine; the poetry of the Renaissance; the novels of Flaubert. You may also view films or read newspapers, magazines, and technical reports.

To succeed as a French major, you must be willing to spend a good deal of time outside class memorizing word forms, listening to cassettes, working with multimedia materials, and doing other language-learning activities. In fact, you'll probably spend twice as much time preparing for class as you spend in class. Although many French majors have been exposed to the language before college, you can begin studying French in your first year and start your course work for your major in your third year. Generally, you must complete at least 12 semester-length courses in upper-level French.

Many students learning a foreign language in the United States face the challenge of working in a sort of intellectual vacuum. You're most likely to succeed in the French major if you seek out opportunities to practice the language with native speakers, attend French club meetings, eat dinner at a French table, or even live in a language house.

At many colleges, study abroad is strongly encouraged, in either a summer program or your third year. Many French departments also sponsor film series, lectures, theatrical performances, and informal social gatherings where you can speak and hear French. Keep in mind that you'll usually have to look for such opportunities yourself. Although they are essential for gaining proficiency in French, they are not necessarily required.

If you want to teach French in elementary or high school, the Bachelor of Science in Education is the logical choice; for all other careers or if you wish to go on to grad school, the Bachelor of Arts probably makes sense.

Other majors you might like:
Comparative literature
Linguistics
International relations
Latin
Business
Art history
History
French teacher education
Romance languages
European studies
European history
French studies

Questions to ask colleges:
How many faculty members are native or near-native speakers? When do students have contact with native speakers?

What is the variety of specializations among the faculty members? Is there one literature specialist who teaches all courses, or are there several, who specialize in different centuries or genres? Is there a linguist on the faculty?

Career options and trends:
High school teacher*; Foreign Service Officer*; interpreter/translator.

French majors also go on to jobs in tourism, international relations, the computer industry, international

business, journalism, and publishing. With appropriate graduate degrees, you can work in research, law, diplomacy, banking, and marketing. A state certificate or license is required for teaching in public elementary and secondary schools. Translation work usually requires that you get specially certified.

Many states are predicting a shortage of high school French teachers in the near future, due to the expected retirement of older teachers. To a lesser extent, a shortage of college faculty members is also expected. The computer industry has provided numerous jobs for linguists and translators, and this trend will probably continue. The Bureau of Labor Statistics projects demand will be strong for French language translators through 2022.

For more info:
Modern Language Association (MLA)
26 Broadway, 3rd Fl.
New York, NY 10004-1789
(646) 576-5000
www.mla.org

American Association of Teachers of French
Southern Illinois University
Mailcode 4510
Carbondale, IL 62901-4510
(618) 453-5731
www.frenchteachers.org

German

What it's about:
This major primarily teaches the language and literature of Germany, Austria, and much of Switzerland. By examining genres, literary movements, and individual authors and themes, you expand your capacity for literary analysis and appreciation.

Is this for you?
You might like this major if you also like: German culture and heritage; languages; travel; history; philosophy; literature; music; art; architecture; science.

Consider this major if you are good at: attention to detail; creativity; critical reading/thinking; memorizing; organizing *...or have...* initiative; patience; perseverance; verbal skills; writing skills.

Recommended high school prep:
English 4, math 3, lab science 3, social studies 4, and foreign language 4. If possible, social studies should include both European history and art history. Language should be German, and a year of Latin is useful. One year of classical music (orchestra, lessons) is also recommended.

Did you know...
...that beginning and intermediate language courses often do not count toward your major?

...that in almost every German department, there are opportunities, including stipends, for study abroad?

...that German is often required for graduate study in fields such as art, music history, and philosophy?

Typical courses in this major:
Introduction to German literature I, II
Conversation and composition
German history and thought
The age of Goethe
Romanticism
Realism
Fin-de-siècle Vienna
Thomas Mann
Franz Kafka
German drama
German women writers
Jewish contributions to German culture
Postwar literature
Migration literature
German film
Modern German literature

Concentrations:
German literature of a particular period; German cinema; German area studies; Germanic linguistics; German intellectual history.

What the study of this major is like:
If you major in German language and literature, you must first concentrate on the language. You need a good knowledge of grammar in order to write properly, so, even if you know how to speak German and have a wide vocabulary, be prepared to polish your skills. You then use the language to explore increasingly complex texts in courses that are taught in German and tend to have small enrollments.

Like other literature majors, German language and literature includes the study of literary theory. You are introduced not only to classical German literature but also to recent works. You read eighteenth- and nineteenth-century authors such as Goethe, Schiller, and Heine, and major figures from the early twentieth century such as Kafka, Rilke, Dürrenmatt, and Brecht. You also read contemporary writers such as Frisch, Sebald, Böll, and Grass. Many German departments teach the literature and film of postwar divided Germany (1945–89) or of recent immigrants (for example, Italian, Turkish). You thus explore questions of multiculturalism and diversity as they are emerging in Europe today.

Some colleges offer a German studies major—a more interdisciplinary approach that emphasizes cultural expressions other than literature, such as music, art, film, philosophy, science, and history. German studies may cover anything from the works of great philosophers such as Kant, Hegel, Nietzsche, and Marx, the writings of Freud, the German contribution to music and art, to the role of women in contemporary German culture.

The major typically includes time abroad, in either academic or work programs. Generally, colleges that have their own programs abroad offer courses taught by special staff; students live in dormitories, apartments, or local homes. Most of the stronger junior-year-abroad programs accept students from various institutions. Colleges without their own programs generally permit, or even encourage, qualified students to attend them. Many American colleges and other organizations can help you find vacation employment in German-speaking countries, to strengthen your command of the language and appreciation of the culture.

Other majors you might like:
Comparative literature
Linguistics
European studies
Music, general
Philosophy
History
Political science
German studies
Germanic languages
German teacher education

Questions to ask colleges:
Does the program teach literary works primarily in the original German or in translation? How will previous language training be credited?

Is there a German house or dormitory on campus that students can live in? Which types of study-abroad programs does the program offer? Does the program provide stipends?

Career options and trends:
College professor*; high school teacher*; interpreter/translator*; international lawyer.

German majors tend to pursue a rich variety of careers. Many enter jobs in government, business, library and information science, tourism, or journalism. With appropriate professional study, you can pursue a career in law or medicine. A mastery of German is valuable in almost any academic field, as well as in international business and diplomacy. A graduate degree is usually necessary for obtaining a

job in a German field. An additional state certificate or license is required for teaching in public elementary and secondary schools.

Insider's viewpoint:
"I took a class with a professor who made me realize that German was a new way in which I could communicate my life experiences and emotions. A lot of German literature tends to be highly emotionally charged, and it takes a strong person to deal with it."

—Sabrina, junior, Oberlin College

For more info:
Modern Language Association (MLA)
26 Broadway, 3rd Fl.
New York, NY 10004-1789
(646) 576-5000
www.mla.org

American Association of Teachers of German
 (AATG)
112 Haddontowne Court, #104
Cherry Hill, NJ 08034-3668
(856) 795-5553
www.aatg.org

Italian

What it's about:

As an Italian major, you study the language and literature of Italy, usually in the broader context of Italy's culture, history, and society.

Is this for you?

You might like this major if you also like: Italian culture and heritage; Romance languages; traveling; art; history; nature; food; architecture; music; film.

Consider this major if you are good at: active listening; caring/nurturing; critical reading/thinking; leadership; memorizing *...or have...* initiative; patience; verbal skills; writing skills.

Recommended high school prep:

English 4, math 3, lab science 3, social studies 4 (including European history and art history), and a foreign language 4. If possible, take Latin. If Latin is not available, take French or Italian.

Typical courses in this major:

Elementary Italian
Intermediate Italian
Advanced Italian
Italian composition and conversation
Masterworks of Italian literature
Dante's *Divine Comedy*
Twentieth-century literature
Italian theater
Italian civilization
Renaissance literature
Nineteenth-century literature
Italian cinema

Concentrations:

Italian language and literature; Italian culture and society; Italian and linguistics.

What the study of this major is like:

If you don't know the language, you begin with elementary Italian, a two-semester course in which you study basic grammar and learn to listen to, speak, read, and write Italian. After this course (or if you know basic Italian before entering college), you take intermediate Italian, a two-semester course usually taught in Italian, in which you review grammar and practice listening, speaking, reading, and writing.

Most intermediate courses include poetry and prose, and introduce you to Italian history, culture, and contemporary Italian society. Intermediate Italian also prepares you for a possible third year abroad, which all language majors are encouraged to pursue. Most study-abroad programs require two years of college Italian because the courses are taught entirely in Italian. In advanced Italian, which emphasizes conversation and composition, you discuss and write about historical and contemporary aspects of Italian culture and civilization.

Italy's greatest poet is Dante Alighieri, author of *The Divine Comedy*, a work in three parts that profoundly influenced the development of modern Italian. You are usually required to read either part or all of this poem in the original language. Most programs in Italian also include study of Italian Renaissance literature, especially the writings of Boccaccio and Petrarch, sometimes the epic poems of Ariosto and Tasso, and often the writings of Machiavelli and Galileo. Most colleges expect majors to explore the works of nineteenth-century Romantic writers, such as the novelist Alessandro Manzoni, author of *I promessi sposi* (*The Betrothed*).

Twentieth-century literature, a popular course among majors, includes the best Italian fiction writers of our time—Pirandello, D'Annunzio, Moravia, Pasolini, Ginsburg, and Calvino—and the poets Montale, Ungaretti, Saba, and Quasimodo. At some colleges you can take a course in masterworks of Italian literature, an in-depth examination of one or more great writers, or a survey course on writers from Dante to the present. In many programs, films are shown in the contemporary literature course; or a course in Italian cinema may be offered, devoted to the works of such famous directors as De Sica, Visconti, Fellini, Antonioni, Pasolini, and Bertolucci. You may also have one or more required courses in Italian opera.

Learning a language is like playing a musical instrument; you have to practice every day. Most students find that reading serious literature in Italian is a challenge, because building a vocabulary takes time and effort. But the more time you spend reading Italian, the sooner you will be able to read effortlessly. Colleges may offer different literature and cultural courses, depending on the interests of the faculty members, and may vary in the way they teach these subjects. Approaches can range from a textual and linguistic analysis, to a cultural and historical orientation, to interpretations of the text based on recent theories of art and literature, such as feminist literary theory.

Other majors you might like:

Linguistics
Romance languages
Classics
Art history
Comparative literature
Latin
Medieval and Renaissance studies
Culinary arts and chef training
Spanish
Italian studies
Music, general
European studies

Questions to ask colleges:

Who teaches the Italian language courses? Some colleges believe that teaching language and teaching literature and culture are separate specializations that require different instructors. Other colleges adopt a liberal arts approach that encourages each faculty member to teach all areas of Italian, from elementary language to Dante, and to introduce students to culture and literature when they teach language courses.

Career options and trends:

College professor*; high school teacher; art historian; interpreter/translator.

Italian majors also go on to careers in music, film, the arts, research, government, NGOs (nongovernmental organizations), diplomacy, law, fashion design, tourism, international politics, or international business. Graduate study is required for some of these careers.

Italy is "in." New York and Los Angeles are filled with upscale Italian restaurants. College students want to study in Italy; their parents want to vacation there. College enrollments in Italian courses continue to rise. More high schools are offering Italian. The need for people fluent in both English and Italian is growing; indeed the Bureau of Labor Statistics projects demand for Italian translation and interpretive services will be strong through 2022.

For more info:
National Italian American Foundation (NIAF)
1860 19th St., N.W.
Washington, DC 20009
(202) 387-0600
www.niaf.org

American Association of Teachers of Italian (AATI)
www.aati-online.org

Japanese

What it's about:
This major focuses on Japanese spoken and written language, often in both premodern and modern forms. Students are generally exposed to Japanese literature through reading primary texts in either the original or in English translation, as well as through secondary sources.

Is this for you?
You might like this major if you also like: Japanese culture; learning difficult languages; travel; anime and *manga*; word games; poetry; calligraphy; interacting with different cultures

Consider this major if you are good at: attention to detail; critical reading/thinking; memorizing; research *...or have...* Linguistic ability; Motivation; Self Discipline; patience; verbal skills; writing skills.

Recommended high school prep:
English 4, math 3, lab science 3, social studies 4, and a foreign language 4. Be sure to take as much foreign language as possible; Japanese is preferable but not required. World history courses and classes involving writing and research are also recommended.

Did you know...
...that the Japanese use several different writing systems? In earlier times, there was even one form of writing for men and another for women.

Typical courses in this major:
Elementary Japanese
Intermediate Japanese
Advanced Japanese
Reading Japanese—newspapers and periodicals
East Asian cultures
Survey of Japanese literature in translation
Introduction to Classical Japanese
Introduction to Japanese linguistics
Readings in modern Japanese literature
Japanese history
The world of premodern Japan
The Tale of Genji
Japanese theater: ghosts, masks and actors
Religion and philosophy in premodern Japan
Japanese cinema
Writers and thinkers: modern Japan in the world

Concentrations:
Generally, none in college; but if you go on to grad school: Premodern literature, modern literature, linguistics.

What the study of this major is like:
This major is for those who really like to challenge themselves. Modern Japanese is one of the most difficult languages to learn. Its grammar is the reverse of that of English, and its writing system is very complex, involving two different syllabary sets (*hiragana* and *katakana*) and between two thousand and three thousand characters (*kanji*), most with at least two different readings. Despite its difficulty, though, Japanese has become a highly popular language major.

Unless you have had experience speaking Japanese, you will spend the first year acquiring the basics of the grammar and writing system. In many colleges, lecture courses are taught in English and may meet once or twice a week; they are coupled with smaller practice or recitation classes, conducted in Japanese and meeting daily.

Often beginning Japanese courses focus on the everyday side of the language. You might learn how to talk about weather, food, shopping, or school, and how to read menus, street maps, signs, and letters to and from friends. You may even have an opportunity to send e-mail in Japanese. Since Japanese majors often go on to work in business, practical details like these are important.

During the first and perhaps second year, you will probably also take one or two literature survey courses in English translation, which will involve considerable reading, class discussion, quizzes and exams, and papers of varying length.

In the third and fourth years, you will spend more time with electives in your areas of interest, such as modern literature, drama, film, or courses built around specific themes or questions, such as love in classical and modern Japan, the life of the premodern warrior, and representations of gender in literature.

If Japanese is offered within a broader major in Asian or East Asian studies, as it is at many smaller colleges, the language requirement is often only two years. Courses relating to other Asian countries may be required as well.

You are unlikely to learn enough, even after two or three years of courses in the language, to read Japanese high school texts or newspapers easily, much less to work in business or as a translator. A year of study in Japan is extremely helpful for attaining conversational fluency. Keep in mind, however, that the university experience in Japan is very different from that in the United States; the academic year starts in April, and your credits may not all transfer.

Other majors you might like:
Asian studies
Linguistics
International relations
Comparative literature
International business
Asian-American studies
Anthropology
East Asian studies
Animation
Global studies
Geography

Questions to ask colleges:
How many full-time professors does the program have?

How many years of Japanese-language courses does the program offer?

Does the program offer a study-abroad or exchange program, or access to Japanese television and other media?

Career options and trends:
Japanese-language teacher*; ESL teacher; interpreter or translator; journalist; Foreign Service officer*.

Knowledge of Japanese is an asset for almost any career path. There is significant demand for people with good Japanese-language ability and knowledge of Japanese culture in the areas of international business and the travel industry, and those who possess a Ph.D. have a much better chance of obtaining a faculty position in a college or university than is true for other fields.

Japanese companies, either in Japan or elsewhere, often hire non-Japanese with good language ability for translation, writing, or research duties, although the growth potential in such positions may be limited.

Insider's viewpoint:
"There is so much to read, and so few people outside Japan who can read it; you can go into the library and peruse ancient Japanese works that may not have been read by anyone else at the university."

—Professor H. Mack Horton, University of California: Berkeley

For more info:
Association for Asian Studies (AAS)
825 Victors Way, Suite 310
Ann Arbor, MI 48108
(734) 665-2490
www.asian-studies.org/

Russian

What it's about:

In this major, you learn the Russian language and investigate the Russian-speaking world. You learn oral and written communication, and you explore the historical, geographic, and cultural factors that have contributed to the development of the Russian language.

Is this for you?

You might like this major if you also like: Russian literature; international politics; Russian culture; Russian/world film, dance, theater, and music.

Consider this major if you are good at: attention to detail; creativity; critical reading/thinking; learning languages; memorizing ...*or have...* initiative; patience; persistence; verbal skills; writing skills.

Recommended high school prep:

English 4, math 3, lab science 3, social studies 3 (including a year of world history), and a foreign language 4. Although any language experience is helpful, another inflected language (for example, Latin or German, whose nouns change form for gender) can be especially useful.

Did you know...

...that many opportunities exist for study abroad in Russia? There are now excellent programs in a variety of Russian locations.

Typical courses in this major:

Elementary Russian
Intermediate Russian
Advanced Russian
Russian theater and drama
The Russian short story
The Russian novel
Phonetics and intonation
Conversation and composition
Survey of Russian literature
Alexander Pushkin
Nikolai Gogol
Dostoyevsky and Tolstoy
Anton Chekhov

Concentrations:

In college: Russian literature; Russian language.

If you go on to grad school: Slavic literatures/languages/linguistics (such as Russian); non-Slavic Eurasian literature/language/linguistics (focusing on the Caucasus, Central Asia, and other areas); folklore; drama; literary theory; specific literary genres or periods.

What the study of this major is like:

Russian, the language of one of the world's greatest bodies of literature, is valuable in international relations, business, and science. Russian majors study the language and read the literature; you may also study Russian culture and civilization, Russian and European history, and related disciplines.

The Russian major usually requires three to four years of language study, or an equivalent combination of language study and advanced literature/culture courses in the original Russian, survey courses in Russian literature/culture in translation, or Russian-related courses in other departments. Lecture and seminar courses in Russian departments offer you the opportunity to read the classics of Russian literature, but they have also become increasingly interdisciplinary, incorporating, for example, the study of film, contemporary society, or intellectual history. Russian literature today is not studied in geographic isolation, and many departments offer you the option of studying the language, literature, and cultures of other eastern European, central European, and Eurasian countries. You can sometimes count courses in other literature programs toward your major.

During your first two years, you are usually required to take at least 5–6 hours a week of language classes and labs. Some colleges offer intensive language courses, which require 8–12 hours a week. In upper-level language courses, you learn to communicate effectively with Russian speakers on a variety of topics. The choice of courses at the advanced level depends on the department and the strength of its program. Several offerings allow you to pursue your own interests. During your fourth year, you may participate in a seminar on a literary topic.

As a major, you spend a significant amount of time studying a language that most English speakers don't find easy. Fortunately, your classes are likely to be small and your teachers and classmates a quirky, interesting, and highly motivated bunch. All Russian majors should seriously consider the option of studying for a summer, a semester, or, best of all, a year abroad. Although the culture shock can at first be extreme, students often find that their time in Russia is the most personally and intellectually rewarding experience of their college career.

Other majors you might like:
Linguistics
Comparative literature
History
Political science
Geography
Anthropology
International relations
International business
Russian/Slavic studies
Slavic languages
Central/Middle/Eastern European studies

Questions to ask colleges:
Are there student- or department-sponsored activities, such as Russian tables and Russian clubs, lectures, film screenings, musical gatherings, or dinners? Most good Russian departments have enthusiastic students looking for opportunities to satisfy, outside the classroom, their love of things Russian.

Career options and trends:
High school teacher; college professor; Foreign Service Officer; interpreter/translator.

Russian majors also enter the fields of international law, international business, health care, social work, environmental affairs, and journalism. Although strong language skills are most important for Russian majors looking for work in these areas, some employers may want you to have at least a master's degree. Russian translators are in great demand, but that work usually requires that you get specially certified. Careers in the Foreign Service are usually open only to U.S. citizens.

Politics always plays a role for Americans looking for work related to Russia, no matter how apolitical that work may seem. In the post-Soviet world, visa regulations, laws of international business, and the degree of U.S. involvement in the region are in a state of uncertainty and will remain so for some time. If you are looking for work in or with Russia, you should keep up-to-date on current events. A focus on Eurasia is of increasing importance for all jobs.

Insider's viewpoint:
"For me the defining marker of Russian-ness is the question 'what is Russia?'—a question that Russians are still trying to answer in a post-Soviet, postmodern world. The endlessly creative ways Russian writers have tried to resolve the issue of their own identity is fascinating for me as a literary scholar."

—Professor Melissa Frazier, Sarah Lawrence College

For more info:
American Association of Teachers of Slavic and Eastern European Languages (AATSEEL)
AATSEEL of U.S., Inc.
University of Southern California
3501 Trousdale Parkway
THH 255L
Los Angeles, CA 90089-4353
(213) 740-2734
www.aatseel.org

Association for Slavic, East European, an Eurasian Studies (ASEEES)
203C Bellefield Hall
University of Pittsburgh
Pittsburgh, PA 15260-6424
(412) 648-9911
www.aseees.org

Spanish

What it's about:

As a Spanish major, you learn the Spanish language and explore the literature and culture of Spain, Latin America, and the Latino communities living in the United States.

Is this for you?

You might like this major if you also like: Spanish culture and heritage; community service; travel; politics; history; languages; reading.

Consider this major if you are good at: attention to detail; creativity; critical reading/thinking; memorizing; persuading/influencing; teamwork *...or have...* patience; verbal skills; writing skills.

Recommended high school prep:

English 4, math 3, lab science 3, social studies 4, and a foreign language 4. Studying Spanish is, of course, useful, but any other Romance language (such as Italian, French, or Latin) is also highly recommended. If possible, take a year of Latin American history.

Did you know...

...that Spanish is the official language of more countries than any other language except English? Depending on the methodology used, Spanish is also ranked as either the second or third most spoken language on earth. It is unlikely to ever catch number one, however—Mandarin Chinese.

Typical courses in this major:

Elementary Spanish
Intermediate Spanish
Advanced Spanish
Spanish literature in translation
Culture and civilization
Business Spanish
Latin American novels
Applied linguistics
Spanish Renaissance
Miguel de Cervantes
Phonetics
Latin American literature in translation
Iberian peninsular literature

Concentrations:

Spanish literature; Latin American literature; Spanish and Portuguese literature; language teaching; international trade; translation.

What the study of this major is like:

During your first and second years in college, your primary focus is on learning and using the Spanish language. Almost all of your classes are conducted in Spanish, so you can hone your basic skills (speaking, listening, reading, writing) rapidly.

During your third and fourth years, you work on advanced speaking and writing skills, learning phonetics and doing creative writing in Spanish. You also study literature, usually that of both Spain and Latin America. The broad range of Spanish-language literature may include the medieval epic *El Cid* and the literature written when Christians, Jews, and Moors shared the Iberian Peninsula; the early Renaissance Spanish classic *La Celestina*; the picaresque novel *Lazarillo de Tormes*; the writings of the mystics; the great Spanish dramatists of the Golden Age (Lope de Vega, Tirso de Molina, Calderón de la Barca); the baroque masterpiece *Don Quixote*; and neoclassical, Romantic, realist, and modernist works. The literature of Latin America includes such authors as Borges, García Márques, Fuentes, and Vargas Llosa. You may also watch films produced in Spanish-speaking regions.

In general, you will be asked to do research and write papers on different topics. Oral practice is important when learning a language. This is accomplished outside of class by working in language labs, meeting with language assistants, doing field or community work, attending lectures and poetry readings in Spanish, or even participating in the construction or maintenance of a Spanish website.

Many Spanish departments have different styles and philosophies. Individual faculty members also vary in their approaches to teaching. Some stress grammar over oral communication or, when teaching literature, the social and intellectual context of a work over the literary aspects. The program may offer courses in teaching methods and applied linguistics, often in collaboration with the school of education. Many programs—responding to the number of students looking to use Spanish in their careers—offer business Spanish and medical Spanish, as well as courses in the history and culture of Spain and Latin America (independent of courses offered by the history department).

The biggest challenge you will encounter is to immerse yourself in the Spanish language without falling back on English when you don't know how to express your ideas. Almost all programs encourage you to spend a semester, a summer, or a year of study—often during your third year—in a Spanish-speaking country. The lifestyle of the Spanish major is one of its most appealing features. Latin culture offers good food, music, literature, and social life—and it usually influences class dynamics. Students tend to work in groups and find it rewarding as a way to relax and make friends.

Other majors you might like:
Comparative literature
Linguistics
Language interpretation/translation
ESL teacher education
European studies
Spanish/Iberian studies
Latin American studies
History
Linguistics
Chicano studies
Spanish teacher education
International business

Questions to ask colleges:
Does the program recognize the varieties of the language as spoken throughout the Spanish-speaking world, or does it focus only upon how Spanish is spoken in Spain?

Does the library provide access to computers and databases? How extensive is the library's catalog in the field?

Career options and trends:
College professor; interpreter/translator; high school teacher; ESL teacher.

Translating work usually requires that you get specially certified; the Bureau of Labor Statistics projects very strong demand for translators of Spanish through 2022. Spanish majors can also find jobs in business, banking, social services, government, and international organizations. A state certificate or license is required for teaching in public elementary and secondary schools. With appropriate advanced degrees, you may also work in medicine, law, and other professions, where you will be especially valued in bilingual Spanish/English-speaking communities.

For more info:
Modern Language Association (MLA)
26 Broadway, 3rd Fl.
New York, NY 10004-1789
(646) 576-5000
www.mla.org

Latin American Studies Association (LASA)
University of Pittsburgh
416 Bellefield Hall
Pittsburgh, PA 15260
(412) 648 7929
lasa.international.pitt.edu

Legal studies

Sometimes you have to know what something isn't before you can know what it is.

The programs in this chapter will not qualify you to take the bar exam and become a lawyer. To do that, you must go to law school to get a graduate degree called a juris doctor (J.D.), or doctor of jurisprudence (in simpler terms, doctor of law).

If you want to be an attorney, you can take nearly any undergraduate major, not just the ones in this chapter. That's true even if you take prelaw. "Students interested in legal careers major in every possible field. There is no required course of study for admission to law school," says Diane Curtis, prelaw adviser at the University of Massachusetts, Amherst.

"Prelaw is not a major or a specific course of study," Curtis explains. "At the overwhelming majority of colleges and universities, it is an advising program designed to assist students to explore future legal careers, and to help with the law school application process."

Okay. Now that you know what this chapter isn't, let's move on to what is. (See? You are thinking like a lawyer already.)

Whether you choose a prelaw program or not, if you are planning on going to law school, you must be prepared to take the most challenging undergraduate courses from the toughest professors and get good grades. "In your undergraduate classes, you need to acquire the core knowledge and skills upon which your legal education will be built," Curtis says. "Since law deals with a wide variety of human conflicts, the more you know about the diversity of human experience, the better prepared you will be to study law."

Legal studies is a major by itself, and can lead to any number of careers—lawyer, professor, teacher; legal assistant, paralegal, librarian, mediator, arbitrator; a job in the courts, or in other areas of government or politics; police or corrections work; business.

Is legal studies the right field for you? Students who gravitate toward the program tend to have leadership potential; analytical, problem-solving, and quantitative skills; a talent for persuasion or counseling; a powerful memory; research abilities; and a gift for communicating. Interests often include history, current events, politics, debating, student government, community service, and social justice.

Legal studies

"Legal studies is a fascinating field because...virtually every aspect of our lives is touched in some way by the law, and a knowledge and awareness of the legal system is beneficial regardless of the career path a student might take," says Jeffrey J. Davis, assistant professor of political science at the University of Maryland.

Legal Research

To find legal studies majors, look at a college's school of government or political science, or sociology department. For paralegal studies, check out colleges of arts and science or business and management.

Programs differ. Those geared toward training students to become paralegal and legal assistants offer more practice- and skills-oriented courses than programs that prepare you for law school, other graduate school, or for careers in government or business. Ask yourself if you're more likely to succeed in rigorous academic and theoretical courses or in hands-on training for law-related work. If you're considering a paralegal or legal assistant program, see if it's approved by the American Bar Association. Whether it's a two-year or four-year paralegal or legal assistant program, expect to study areas and foundations of the law in a very demanding environment requiring loads of reading and writing.

You may be bound for law school or for a legal career straight out of college. In either case, be sure to research the institution. Do your due diligence. Find out if the college's faculty members or advisers have law degrees themselves. Have they actually practiced law? Does the college arrange for graduates to have internships with attorneys and/or judges? Are participatory activities available, such as mock trial, moot court, or debate team?

For prelaw programs, it's a good idea to register with a prelaw adviser as early as possible in your college career, to get on track academically. Your adviser can also help you explore the different legal specialities and work environments. (A few examples: litigating criminal cases in court, doing corporate law at a big firm, devoting yourself to government service.) Ask what percentage of students who see an adviser gain admission to one or more law schools. See whether advisers will help you after you graduate. Is an LSAT prep course offered? Does the school have a network of attorney-alumni that undergraduates can contact? (Note that some institutions compress B.A. and J.D. curriculums into a joint six-year program.)

Recent graduates are facing one of the most challenging job markets in decades. Applications to law schools have dropped dramatically, and law schools are responding by providing more clinical experience and postgraduate training programs to make their graduates more employable. Some schools are even creating non-profit firms where graduates can learn skills while providing legal services to the poor. The goal is to address a paradox that exists across the country: heavily indebted law graduates without jobs and the large number of Americans without access to a lawyer.

For paralegals and legal assistants, job opportunities are projected to grow rapidly as employers try to reduce costs by hiring paralegals to perform tasks formerly done by lawyers.

For more information, visit the website of the American Bar Association (www.americanbar.org). Who knows? You may become a member of that organization one day.

Legal studies

What it's about:

This major examines the law and legal issues from the perspectives of the social sciences and the humanities. Taking a theoretical rather than a practical approach, students explore the origins, evolution, function, and effects of the law as a social phenomenon. Legal studies is not a prelaw program, and this major will not qualify you to take the bar examination or to work as a lawyer. If your goal is to become an attorney, you must attend law school after college.

Is this for you?

You might like this major if you also like: history; philosophy; current events; politics; debating; student government; community service activities; issues relating to social justice; reading and writing.

Consider this major if you are good at: attention to detail; counseling; creativity; critical reading/thinking; leadership; persuading/influencing; research *...or have...* initiative; verbal skills; writing skills.

Recommended high school prep:

English 4, math 3, lab science 2, social studies 4, and a foreign language 3–4. Other recommended courses include business law, philosophy, sociology, psychology, statistics, and comparative government and politics.

Did you know...

...that while legal studies is a good prelaw major, it won't increase your chances of getting into law school? Law schools don't favor any specific college major.

...that combining a science or technology major with a major or minor in legal studies is a good marriage for the career-minded? The areas are increasingly intertwined, in both law and business.

Typical courses in this major:

American politics and government
Philosophy of law
Civil rights and liberties
Legal and judicial process
Legal reasoning
Constitutional law
Law, crime, and social justice
International law
Comparative law
Business law
Legal history
Environmental law
Law and literature
Legal ethics
Legal research and writing
Women and the law

Concentrations:

Criminal justice; government and politics; international and comparative law; business and commercial law

What the study of this major is like:

Shortly after the September 11, 2001, terrorist attacks, President George W. Bush signed the Patriot Act. This law made it easier for the government to guard against terrorist activity by allowing such tactics as searches without notice. But many people believe that the measure endangers the civil rights and civil liberties of both citizens and immigrants.

Does it make sense to trade in some civil rights for greater protection against terrorism? Will the government's greater access to our private lives make us safer? As a legal studies major, you'll take an in-depth look at these and other important issues.

While legal studies is not a prelaw program, it is a good major for prelaw students because it will help you to develop your ability to think clearly and to analyze arguments critically. It is also an excellent major if you are leaning toward a career in public service or planning to study business or the social sciences in grad school.

The major is academically rigorous. It requires excellent reading comprehension skills and sharp analytical ability. Reading and writing assignments can be substantial. You should be ready to engage in intense discussion of thorny legal problems, study actual court cases, do computer research using legal databases, and write a senior thesis.

Course work, which is usually interdisciplinary, focuses on the legal process, legal institutions, and how they operate in society. For example, you might examine crime and punishment from the viewpoint of psychology, philosophy, and anthropology, or use legal doctrines to study international business models in a globalized economy. A course in comparative law will expose you to systems that differ from those in the United States, such as European civil law or Islamic Sharia. Legal studies is based on the idea that an understanding of the foundations of law and justice requires the application of a broad range of academic disciplines, as well as a critical analysis of human behavior and institutions.

In most programs you will have a chance to participate in moot courts (arguing an artificial appeal), mock trials (playing a role in an artificial trial) and to serve internships with judges, private lawyers, prosecutors, defense attorneys, or in government offices. This aspect of the major can give you a close perspective on a legal career prior to deciding on law school.

At some colleges this major emphasizes training for the paralegal and legal assistant professions. These programs, which may be available at the two-year, or associate degree, level, often provide practice-oriented courses in specific areas of law, such as real estate or contracts. Generally, four-year colleges that house the major prepare students for law school, for graduate school, or for careers in government and business. These programs offer courses in a variety of disciplines, and are usually more rigorous academically and more theoretical.

Other majors you might like:
Political science
Criminology
Sociology
History
Public policy analysis
Environmental studies
International relations
Labor studies

Behavioral sciences
Peace studies
Criminal justice and law enforcement
Public administration

Questions to ask colleges:
Do any of the faculty members have law degrees, and have they actually practiced law?

Does the school assist with internships with lawyers and/or judges in the area?

Is there a mock trial, moot court, or debate team?

Is there an active legal studies club?

Career options and trends:
Lawyer*; government official*; paralegal; public interest advocate; business executive; law enforcement officer; journalist.

To practice law, you must go to law school, pass a bar exam, and be certified by the bar of the state in which you will practice.

As a liberal arts program, legal studies can prepare you for a variety of careers in business and public service, as well as in the law. The major will also qualify you to apply to graduate school in the humanities and social sciences, or to professional school in teaching, public policy, business and health administration, and social work.

For more info:
American Bar Association
321 N. Clark St.
Chicago, IL 60654-7598
(800) 285-2221
www.americanbar.org

Paralegal studies

What it's about:

This major prepares you to conduct legal research; draft legal documents; and perform investigatory, record-keeping, and other administrative duties under the supervision of an attorney or a court officer. Paralegal education is not the equivalent of law school training and does not qualify you for, or make you eligible to take, a bar examination.

Is this for you?

You might like this major if you also like: public speaking; Mock Trial competitions; debate; student government; politics; public service; reading; research; social justice issues.

Consider this major if you are good at: attention to detail; critical reading/thinking; leadership; organizing; research; teamwork ...*or have...* initiative; patience; verbal skills; writing skills.

Recommended high school prep:

English 4, math 3, lab science 3, social studies 3, and a foreign language 2–3. If possible, take an introductory law or political science course.

Did you know...

...that the paralegal profession is one of the five fastest growing career fields in the United States? Today, paralegals perform much of the work that was once done by lawyers. As a result, paralegals have a great deal of responsibility and play an essential role in providing legal services to the public. Some paralegals even represent clients before local, state, and national administrative agencies.

Typical courses in this major:

Litigation/civil procedure
Criminal law and procedure
Computerized research
Legal writing
Real estate law
Business law
Wills, trusts, and probate law
Family law

Immigration law
Intellectual property law
Evidence
Ethics
Personal injury/tort law
Environmental law
Alternative dispute resolution
Elder law

Concentrations:

Generally, none available.

What the study of this major is like:

As a paralegal studies major, you learn practical, job-related skills along with the underlying legal theory. You study substantive law (the particular disciplines, or areas, you can practice) and procedural law (how you practice—such as rules of evidence and pre-trial paper work). Legal research and writing are essential parts of the curriculum and often are the most challenging elements for students. Your course work also stresses communication skills (oral, non-verbal, and interpersonal), computational and organizational skills, an ability to think critically, and an appreciation of legal ethics. You use computer-based resources to help you with your work.

You are encouraged to learn through hands-on work; therefore, internships, practicums, or clinical experience are highly recommended and sometimes required. Internships and similar experiences give you the chance to obtain firsthand knowledge about the practice of law and may even lead to a full-time position after graduation. Most paralegal programs have active student organizations, which build camaraderie among participants by organizing law-related events on or near the campus.

This major is offered at two-year, community and junior colleges; four-year colleges; and business and proprietary schools devoted solely to providing this training. Because there is no uniformly accepted educational standard for entry into the paralegal field, content, length, and admissions requirements vary among colleges.

The American Bar Association approves paralegal education programs that meet its guidelines. Although seeking ABA approval is voluntary on the part of the college, the bar association's standards are rigorous and, therefore, helpful in evaluating a program. However, there are some quality programs that have chosen not to seek ABA approval. A complete listing of paralegal education programs approved by the ABA is found on its website (www.abanet.org). Additionally, the American Association for Paralegal Education (AAPE) has a set of minimum program requirements that must be adhered to by member institutions and can be found on the AAPE website.

When deciding among programs, you may also want to consider local or regional standards, particularly with regard to future job opportunities. Check with your local or regional paralegal associations for additional information about educational standards for paralegals in your area.

Other majors you might like:
Criminal justice and law enforcement
Political science
Sociology
Office management
Physician assistant
Technical and business writing
Real estate
Social work
Insurance
Criminology
Legal studies
Labor studies

Questions to ask colleges:
Is the paralegal studies program approved by the American Bar Association? Is the institution a member of the American Association for Paralegal Education and therefore guided by its requirements?

Are faculty members practicing attorneys and/or paralegals?

Do students have access to the resources they need to do legal research (such as a law library)?

Are students taught how to use computerized legal research systems (WESTLAW or Lexis-Nexis)?

Career options and trends:
The Bureau of Labor Statistics projects strong growth in this field through 2020. Law firms will continue to be the largest employers of paralegals, with hiring increasing to rebuild support staff cutbacks during the recession. Many large corporations are also hiring paralegals for their in-house legal departments in order to cut costs.

Graduates also pursue careers as private investigators, law librarians, human resources personnel, court personnel, mediators, arbitrators, special advocates, estate and trust officers, real estate professionals, insurance agents, risk managers, contract managers, legal administrators, corporate compliance officers, and government workers.

Although there is no mandatory certification of paralegals, voluntary certification is sponsored by the two paralegal professional associations. The National Association of Legal Assistants sponsors a national certification exam, several state-specific exams, and certification for specialty areas of law. The National Federation of Paralegal Associations offers the Paralegal Advanced Competency Examination (PACE).

Many states, through the legislature, court system, or bar association, have issued ethics opinions dealing with a paralegal's use of title, the scope of duties, the unauthorized practice of law, and how clients may be billed for paralegal services. You should examine and review these opinions prior to obtaining employment as a paralegal.

For more info:
National Association of Legal Assistants (NALA)
1516 South Boston Ave., Suite 200
Tulsa, OK 74119
(918) 587-6828
www.nala.org

American Association for Paralegal Education
 (AAfPE)
19 Mantua Road
Mt. Royal, NJ 08061
(856) 423-2829
www.aafpe.org

Prelaw

What it's about:

Prelaw is not a major or a prescribed course of study, and it is not a requirement for law school. Rather, it is an advising program designed to help you prepare for law school while in college, explore future legal careers, and manage the law school application process. You must obtain a bachelor's degree to apply to law school, but you can major in anything you want.

Is this for you?

You might like this major if you also like: history; philosophy; current events; politics; debating; student government; community service activities; social justice issues; problem solving; reading and writing. The law plays a role in almost every field—from sports to music to banking—and many potential law students have a wide variety of hobbies and interests.

Consider this major if you are good at: attention to detail; critical reading/thinking; leadership; organizing; persuading/influencing; research ...*or have...* initiative; intellectual curiousity; verbal skills; writing skills.

Recommended high school prep:

English 4, math 3, lab science 2, social studies 4 (including economics and government, if available), and a foreign language 3–4. Other recommended courses include philosophy, sociology, psychology, statistics, and speech.

Did you know...

...that only one-third of law school applicants come directly from college? Many law schools like to see applicants that have gained some work experience after college.

Typical courses in this major:

Principles of economics
English composition
U.S. history to 1865
U.S. history from 1865 to present
Western philosophy
Introduction to psychology
Ethics
Logic
Social anthropology
Law and literature
American government and politics
Scientific methods
Computer science
English literature
Principles of accounting
Expository writing

Concentrations:

Generally, none available.

What the study of this major is like:

Because "prelaw" is not a major but an advising program, there are no admission requirements—just register with the prelaw adviser as early as you can. You will still have to pick a college major before the end of your second year.

While many prelaw students choose majors that are considered traditional preparation for law school, such as English, history, political science, legal studies, economics, or business, none of these disciplines are preferred by law schools. You can major in art, music, math, computer science, a foreign language—anything that will lead to a bachelor's degree. What matters is that you take courses that will help you develop the skills law schools are looking for and that will help you do well on the Law School Admission Test (LSAT).

Just what are those skills? According to the American Bar Association (ABA), a likely candidate for law school is good at critical thinking and reading; writing, speaking, and listening; research; and task management and organization. Law schools also look for applicants who value service and justice and who have an understanding of the historical, cultural, and political influences on society; of human behavior and sociology; and of basic math and science.

Your prelaw adviser will assist you in selecting courses and extracurricular activities that can give you the grounding you need. A useful approach is to choose challenging courses from demanding professors. Get as much practice as you can in critical thinking and writing. Seek out courses in which you will be expected to write several papers and will receive detailed feedback. Literature courses offer practice in close reading, and a course in logic is often recommended for reasoning and analysis.

If you like math or science, you might want to consider a major in one of those areas. Scientific or technical knowledge can make you marketable in specialized fields such as patent law or environmental law.

In evaluating an applicant's extracurricular activities or internships, law school admissions committees are flexible. Still, they favor activities that indicate a candidate's sense of service and justice and that helps reveal his or her interests and experiences. While a law-related internship will not give you an edge, it is an excellent way to see what lawyers do and to determine if their work is what you would enjoy doing.

If you choose prelaw, be prepared to take your college work seriously. Admission to law school is competitive, so aim for an above-average GPA—3.5 and higher is preferable, although 3.0 to 3.5 is still acceptable, if coupled with a good LSAT score. Other factors such as letters of recommendation and extracurricular activities are relatively minor compared with the GPA and the LSAT score. The higher these numbers are, the more options you will have when choosing law schools.

But don't worry about law school right now. Enjoy college, and be open to the ideas and options you will discover there. There will be plenty of time to focus on a legal career later. Major in what interests you—you will do better in classes that excite and challenge you.

Other majors you might like:
Accounting
English
Journalism
Environmental studies
Women's studies
Liberal arts and sciences
Peace and conflict studies
Philosophy
Criminal justice and law enforcement
Political science
Real estate
History

Questions to ask colleges:
How much individual attention is the prelaw adviser able to give each student? What kinds of services are offered?

What kind of resources does the school offer to students seeking law-related internships?

Does the school have a network of attorneys who graduated from the college that undergraduates can contact?

Do you offer LSAT preparation courses?

Career options and trends:
Private practice lawyer*; government attorney*; corporate attorney*; paralegal; legislative aid; journalist; business executive; public interest lawyer; public official; legal editor.

Prelaw advising helps prepare the student for law school, not for a career. To become a practicing attorney, you must obtain a J.D. degree from a law school, pass a state bar exam, and be admitted to the bar in a specific jurisdiction (state or federal). But there are many law-related careers that do not require admission to the bar.

Currently, the number of law school graduates is outpacing the number of job openings at law firms. New lawyers are increasingly finding work in less traditional areas where a law degree may be an asset, but not required.

While there will always be a need for lawyers, job prospects generally track the ups and downs of the economy. Certain areas of practice, such as real estate, are more likely than others to be affected by economic cycles.

Insider's viewpoint:
"I was an English major in college, and I think that major—or any that requires a great deal of careful reading and analytical writing—is useful if not essential preparation for law school."

—Sara, J.D. candidate, Columbia University

For more info:

American Bar Association
321 North Clark Street
Chicago, IL 60654-7598
(800) 285-2221
www.americanbar.org

The Council on Legal Education Opportunities
740 15th St., NW
9th Floor
Washington, DC 20005
(866) 886-4343
www.cleoscholars.com

Mathematics

Is the probability high that you will study mathematics? If so, you may be interested to know that the number of students getting bachelor's degrees in math continues to decline. But the silver lining may be that by studying math, you can rise above other students and job seekers.

"There is a steady, strong demand for math majors," says Professor David M. Bressoud of Macalester College. "Many employers (as well as graduate schools in professions such as law and medicine) will give preferential treatment to graduates with a degree in math."

Then why don't more students major in math? The work is intense. But students don't realize it's also very creative.

"Mathematics is not just learning a bunch of formulas," says Professor James Alexander of Case Western Reserve University. "Mathematics ranges from the purely theoretical studies to highly integrated with engineering and the physical and social sciences; and many majors, including applied mathematics, are available."

Professor Bressoud points out, "Mathematics is about understanding basic, abstract structures to discover progressively deeper and more refined patterns that give profound insights into the workings of the world around us."

And don't forget statistics. Virginia Tech's Michele Marini calls statistics "an undiscovered gem of a major."

As a likely math student, you'll choose from many colleges offering mathematics, applied mathematics, statistics, and related programs. Look for these majors in colleges, divisions, or schools of sciences, mathematical sciences, physical sciences, engineering, arts and sciences, and humanities.

You'll want a college that shares your interests. For instance, some colleges put more emphasis on applied mathematics to prepare you for the workplace, while other programs stress advanced topics in analysis, algebra, geometry, and related areas—rigorous preparation for grad school. Graduate tracks include statistics, applied mathematics, computational mathematics, algebra, number theory, analysis, logic, geometry, and topology (the bending and stretching of geometric forms). Other advanced studies cover computing/information science, operations research, and control theory; or industrial statistics, environmental statistics, and bioinformatics (computerized health and medical stats).

When comparing colleges, ask if computers are used in the classroom or if it's mostly "chalk and talk," as instructors like to call their lectures. Is statistics required for nonstatistics majors? How often are key courses like modern algebra taught? Do students enter math competitions? Or help the faculty members with research? Have any students been published as co-writers? What kind of capstone or senior project is required?

Also ask how many students go on to graduate school. How successful are students at getting jobs after graduation? What kinds of jobs are they getting?

Career permutations and combinations

You'll find that the job outlook is good for students with a math education.

"The study of mathematics is excellent preparation for a host of employment opportunities in business, finance, insurance, communications, electronics, scientific research of any type, and any field that has challenging problems to solve," Bressoud says. "Mathematics lies behind the models of the physical world that are used in predicting weather or in understanding subatomic particles. It lies at the root of economics as well as ecology. It provides the tools for analyzing medical, sociological, or psychological research. It explains electricity and magnetism, radio waves, and quantum tunneling, as well as the hidden patterns of business cycles."

If you major in applied math, you'll be preparing for a career in which you use your math skills in a particular industry or for a particular purpose.

"The Bachelor of Science degree in applied mathematics includes a solid foundation in mathematics as well as a professional core that is specific to computing and information science, operations research, systems engineering, control theory, and statistics," explains Alexander.

If you're going for applied math, see if you can shave college time through a five-year integrated program leading to a Bachelor of Science degree in math and a master's degree in your specialty.

Your math and statistics skills can be used in almost any type of business or research effort.

"I can work on a psychological problem one week, work on U.S. census data the next, and then work on health issues," says Marini.

"The importance of a math background is the ability to think abstractly and conceptually. This is especially important because technology changes rapidly and more specialized skills are likely to be outmoded soon," Alexander notes.

Careers in math include all sorts—engineering, business, and management consulting; high school or college teaching; working for a government agency; as a financial analyst; or as an actuary in the insurance industry. An advanced degree is an enhancement in nearly all math work.

For more information, visit the Mathematical Association of America (www.maa.org), the American Mathematical Society (www.ams.org), the American Statistical Association (www.amstat.org), and the Society for Industrial and Applied Mathematics (www.siam.org).

In this book, see also the sections on Computer and information sciences, Engineering, and Multi/interdisciplinary studies.

Applied mathematics

What it's about:

In the applied mathematics major, you receive a solid grounding in mathematics as well as professional training in your chosen area of application. Possible application areas are computing and information science, operations research, systems engineering, control theory, and statistics.

Is this for you?

You might like this major if you also like: seeing how math explains natural phenomena; understanding the theory behind the way computers and other mechanical things work.

Consider this major if you are good at: attention to detail; creativity; critical reading/thinking; math; organizing; quantitative analysis; teamwork *...or have...* initiative; patience; writing skills.

Recommended high school prep:

English 4, math 4, lab science 3, social studies 3, and a foreign language 2–3. Try to take as many mathematics classes as possible. Also, if available, take courses in computer programming and statistics.

Did you know...

...that you can become an applied mathematics major if you have an interest in math and in an application such as engineering—you don't necessarily have to decide between your two interests?

Typical courses in this major:

Calculus
Differential equations
Linear algebra
Discrete mathematics
Numerical analysis
Physics
Computer science
Probability theory
Logic design and computer architecture
Systems design
Signals, systems, and control engineering
Optimization theory and technique
Data analysis and linear models
Multivariate analysis and data mining
Theoretical statistics
Time series

Concentrations:

In college: computing/information science; systems engineering; statistics.

If you go on to grad school: operations research; control theory.

What the study of this major is like:

As an applied mathematics major, you have two homes. You spend plenty of time studying math—in your third and fourth year, you will most likely take at least two math courses per semester. In addition, you'll enroll in classes in the application area you choose. By searching for connections between math and its applications, you combine knowledge from your two bases. In a kind of conceptual loop, you apply abstract principles of math to your area of interest, and then translate functions of that application back into more general mathematics. For example, in a control theory course, you learn how to construct a feedback mechanism, such as a robot. In a math course, you explore the math behind the mechanism. Your task is to discover the link between what you've learned in the two courses.

The material in math courses and in many applications courses is presented in lecture formats. You are expected to spend considerable time outside class getting comfortable with the material. Some applications courses may involve laboratories or computer programming.

Although a Bachelor of Science degree prepares you to start a career, many professionals return for more specialized training by pursuing a master's degree. Some colleges offer a five-year integrated program leading to a Bachelor of Science degree in applied mathematics and a Master of Science degree in your chosen application area or in applied mathematics.

Colleges may also have different mathematics requirements. No matter which technical field you go into, a strong mathematical background—one that teaches you to think abstractly and conceptually—is essential. Because technology changes so rapidly, specific engineering skills can soon become out-of-date. If you have a good grounding in math, though, you should be able to adapt to advances in technology.

Other majors you might like:
Computer science
Management information systems
Aeronautical/aerospace engineering
Statistics
Systems engineering
Management science
Astrophysics
Applied physics
Mathematics/computer science
Computational mathematics
Information systems
Economics

Questions to ask colleges:
How are the different majors offered in the math department distinguished? Do they contain distinctly different content?

How well do relevant departments (such as physics and engineering) cooperate? Are there adequate facilities, particularly in the applications areas, for course work and research?

How easy is it to switch majors? You'll be introduced to many exciting disciplines during your course work, which may spark new interests.

Career options and trends:
Engineer*; statistician*; actuary; management consultant; financial mathematical analyst.

Demand is always strong for people who are strong in math. Traditionally, jobs requiring a math background have been found primarily in the technical and engineering fields; but going forward the best career prospects are for those who can apply math to the life and medical sciences.

Insider's viewpoint:
"As a mathematician, I'm excited about being able to bring my knowledge to bear on other areas of knowledge. I love having problems brought to me by researchers from a wide variety of disciplines, from science and engineering to social science and medicine."

—Professor James Alexander, Case Western Reserve University

For more info:
Society for Industrial and Applied Mathematics (SIAM)
3600 Market St., 6th Floor
Philadelphia, PA 19104-2688
(215) 382-9800
www.siam.org

Mathematical Association of America (MAA)
1529 18th St., N.W.
Washington, DC 20036
(800) 741-9415
www.maa.org

Mathematics

What it's about:

Math majors develop the ability to explore, conjecture, and reason logically, as well as to use mathematical methods to solve problems. Mathematics is both a discipline and a tool used extensively in the sciences, medicine, engineering, and industry.

Is this for you?

You might like this major if you also like: music, especially composition; art, especially as it relates to shape, balance, and design; playing with abstractions; intellectual challenges; solving puzzles; philosophy; writing that is succinct and precise.

Consider this major if you are good at: attention to detail; creativity; critical reading/thinking; math; organizing; quantitative analysis; spacial thinking/analysis ...*or have...* initiative; patience.

Recommended high school prep:

English 4, math 4 (including precalculus and trigonometry), lab science 4 (including physics), social studies 3, and a foreign language 2–3. Calculus and statistics would be helpful, but are not required.

Did you know...

...that high-level math is not about memorizing procedures? It is about understanding basic, abstract structures to discover deeper, more refined patterns that give insights into the workings of the world around us. Like music, math is the creative exploration of possibilities within prescribed rules and parameters.

Typical courses in this major:

Single-variable calculus
Multivariable calculus
Elementary statistics
Discrete mathematics
Linear algebra
Differential equations
Modern algebra
Modeling
Combinatorics
Number theory
Modern geometry
Topology
Complex analysis
Real analysis

Concentrations:

In college: statistics; applied mathematics; discrete mathematics; computational mathematics.

If you go on to grad school: number theory; functional analysis; geometric analysis; topology; logic.

What the study of this major is like:

Mathematics deals with how basic patterns and processes can be turned into abstract representations. As a math major, you work with increasingly abstract concepts in analytic, algebraic, and geometric math.

Analysis (the mathematics of dynamic change) begins with calculus. Calculus was developed in the seventeenth century to analyze changes in physical quantities—for example, the minimum distance between two planets or the maximum profit of a business enterprise. Through calculus, you can determine the lengths of curves and the volumes of solids, or investigate the acceleration of moving objects. Analysis continues with differential equations, in which you use the knowledge of the way things interact to predict their future state. Real analysis, complex analysis, and functional analysis provide tools that deal with unexpected phenomena.

Modern algebra involves integers, counting problems, and symmetries. It begins with linear algebra (probably the most useful undergrad course) and continues with combinatorics and number theory. You also study structures known as groups, rings, and fields, in order to explore such questions as "is pi rational?"

Discrete mathematics and combinatorics consider the finite nature of certain problems—for instance, in how many ways can a fixed number of vehicles visit multiple locations, and which schedule would be the least costly? Modern geometry and topology study the world of transformations and explore the deeper meaning of concepts such as shape, area, and distance.

Traditionally, math has been taught entirely through lectures, but this approach is changing. Many math courses now make use of computers; you do projects that help you explore a topic in depth; and in written assignments, you clarify difficult concepts. In addition, lectures themselves have changed. Today, many professors understand the importance of describing how particular mathematical concepts came about and of showing how mathematical insights can be applied outside the classroom.

Majoring in mathematics can be an intense experience. There are always new ideas to be mastered. Learning how to rely on precise definition, how to tackle an unfamiliar problem, and how to construct a proof is sometimes difficult. Many math majors find it helpful to form supportive study groups, in which participants share their struggles and insights. Activities such as annual COMAP modeling competitions are built on teamwork; good mathematics programs build strong camaraderie among majors.

Some colleges emphasize applied math or allow you to take an applied mathematics track. These programs typically replace advanced courses in analysis, algebra, and geometry with advanced work in statistics, operations research, and modeling. It is usually a less intense major that can be excellent preparation for the workplace.

Other majors you might like:
Engineering
Economics
Physics
Computer science
Accounting
Finance
Business statistics
Actuarial science
Mathematics teacher education
Information systems
Music theory and composition
Philosophy

Questions to ask colleges:
How does the program incorporate computers into math classes? Is there an emphasis on writing?

In which competitions do math students participate?

Do any of the faculty members use students to help with their research? Have any instructors published a joint paper with a student?

Is a capstone project or fourth-year thesis required?

Career options and trends:
Operations researcher*; business consultant; high school teacher*; statistician*; financial or securities analyst; college professor; actuary.

There is a steady, strong demand for math majors. Many employers (as well as graduate schools in professions such as law and medicine) will give preferential treatment to graduates with a degree in math. The study of mathematics is excellent preparation for a host of employment opportunities in business, finance, insurance, communications, electronics, scientific research of any type, and any field that has challenging problems to solve. Cloud computing is a growing field in need of those with master's degrees in mathematics.

Insider's viewpoint:
"Be careful; it's a difficult field. All the classes I'd ever taken before were 'standard' math, very real-world-based math, application-based math, which is a far cry from the abstract reality of a math major's world."

—John, sophomore, Case Western Reserve University

For more info:
The Mathematical Association of America (MAA)
1529 18th St., N.W.
Washington, DC 20036
(800) 741-9415
www.maa.org

Statistics

What it's about:

Statistics is the practical science of dealing with data—information in the form of numbers, often from many sources. In this major, you study the most efficient ways to collect data and to analyze and interpret it. Statistics, which forms the backbone of all research methods, includes the study of experimental design, regression analysis (the relationships between measurements), probability, and sampling theory.

Is this for you?

You might like this major if you also like: math; quantitative problems; figuring out how things work and how to make them work better; dealing with numbers; puzzles.

Consider this major if you are good at: active listening; attention to detail; critical reading/thinking; math; quantitative analysis; research; teamwork *...or have...* patience; writing skills.

Recommended high school prep:

English 4, math 4 (including calculus), lab science 3, social studies 3, and a foreign language 2–3. If possible, take statistics.

Did you know...

...that statistics includes much more than just tallying batting averages or shooting percentages? Using statistics, you can perform a wide range of tasks, such as deciding which people should fill out a certain survey or ensuring that a medication up for approval works better than medicines currently on the market.

...that statisticians are in high demand and are often well paid? Think of an area of study that interests you. You can usually find statisticians giving work-related advice to professionals in that field.

Typical courses in this major:

Statistical methods I, II
Statistical theory I, II
Experimental design and analysis of variance
Regression analysis
Statistical computing
Sample survey theory
Applied time series analysis
Technical writing
Probability
Statistical quality control
Calculus

Concentrations:

In college: actuarial science.

If you go on to grad school: industrial statistics; environmental statistics; bioinformatics.

What the study of this major is like:

Statistics is the science of handling data in the most effective way. It's not just a branch of mathematics, but a separate discipline that uses a great deal of math and relies heavily on computers. Most statistics departments are in colleges of liberal arts and sciences, but several are in business colleges and a few are in colleges of engineering or agriculture. Combined departments of mathematics and statistics also exist, primarily in small- to medium-size institutions.

If you want to complete an undergraduate degree (B.S.) in statistics, be prepared to take a fairly vigorous math curriculum. In your first year, you concentrate on general courses and mathematics, including a year of calculus. Introductory courses in statistics and computers most often begin in the second year, after you have developed sufficient math skills. In your third year, statistics becomes the dominant part of your studies.

Courses in the applied techniques of describing and analyzing data to extract information require strong skills in algebra and computing. For courses focusing on probability and the mathematical theory of statistics, you'll need to sharpen your abilities in calculus and in logic. In courses that deal with the preparation of sample surveys, small groups of students design a study, collect and analyze the data, and present a report of the results. If you plan on going to graduate school, you should study advanced calculus.

To be a successful statistician, you must understand both the theory and the application of statistics. In an important application, statisticians routinely advise scientists and researchers in business, government, nonprofit organizations, and industry on how to handle data in a wide variety of projects. The work that statisticians do demands not only mathematical tools but also communication, teamwork, and technical writing skills, as well as familiarity with the concepts and terminology of the business or organization they're assisting. In fact, statisticians must rely on the business executives or professionals in these organizations to supply the data they'll be examining. Therefore, courses in the natural sciences, humanities, and social sciences are essential. You are strongly encouraged to strengthen your oral and written communication skills by taking writing and speech courses or participating in related extracurricular activities.

Statistics programs that emphasize actuarial science tend to focus on preparing you for actuarial exams. Other programs concentrate on a particular discipline. For example, biostatistics is more likely to be taught in a college that has a medical education program. In still other programs, geared to preparing students to pursue advanced degrees, the math curriculum is usually much more rigorous.

Other majors you might like:
Accounting
Information systems
Genetics
Economics
Systems science/theory
Econometrics/quantitative economics
Computational mathematics
Actuarial science
Applied mathematics
Systems engineering
Operations research
Health information management

Career options and trends:
Actuary; data analyst*; statistician*; statistical analyst*; statistical programmer; professor*; project statistician.

The Bureau of Labor Statistics expects job prospects for those skilled in statistics to be very good through 2022, due to increasing use of statistical analysis to make informed business, healthcare, and policy decisions. In addition, the ability to gather "big data" from social media, mobile devices, and computerized government and corporate records is fueling demand for statisticians to analyze the data for both commercial and public purposes.

Statisticians work in a wide variety of areas, including manufacturing, pharmaceuticals, insurance, government agencies, consulting firms, and agricultural research. Statistics majors also find jobs in actuarial science, statistical programming, operations research, and mathematical analysis.

Graduates with a master's degree in statistics and with a strong background in a related field, such as finance, biology, engineering, or computer science, should have the most opportunities for employment.

Insider's viewpoint:
"I can work on a psychological problem one week, work on U.S. census data the next, and then work on health issues in an animal species. I have the constant opportunity to learn new things about subjects that I have no formal education in."

—Michele Marini, Instructor, Virginia Tech

For more info:
American Statistical Association (ASA)
732 North Washington St.
Alexandria, VA 22314-1943
(888) 231-3473
www.amstat.org

Multi/interdisciplinary studies

If you've ever written a college application essay, you've probably tried to tap your knowledge and experience in many areas in order to answer an interesting or important question. That's what multi/interdisciplinary studies are like. These majors take more than one path of learning to arrive at understanding.

The world is not just black and white. To get the flavor of multi/interdisciplinary studies, don't think chocolate or vanilla. Think swirl or twist. By mixing areas of study, we can effectively answer questions like these: Why do we think and behave the way we do? How does the mind relate to the body? Can we ever live in peace? If you want that broad perspective, you need to study the finer points of more than one subject. Each of these majors covers many topics and the majors are very different from one another. In this chapter you'll flash back to the fall of Rome and glimpse the future frontiers of science.

Multi/interdisciplinary fields include Medieval and Renaissance studies, neuroscience, gerontology, global studies, and peace studies. Gerontology, for example, looks at aging from many angles—biological, behavioral, and social.

"Almost every aspect of the human aging process impacts on most academic disciplines—arts and sciences, business administration, education, government, law, medicine, mental health, nursing, public health, public relations, and communication," says Professor Joseph F. Cimini, University of Scranton.

Global studies also casts a wide net. "The global studies major is based on new approaches to knowledge and combining political economy and cultural studies with comparative regional studies," explains Professor Eve Walsh Stoddard of St. Lawrence University. "It emphasizes the interconnections and interactions, as opposed to studying discrete, separate topics."

The same goes for neuroscience, which combines studies of the nervous system and behavior. Neuroscience is found within other sciences such as biology, chemistry, physics, and psychology, but also in mathematics, computer science, philosophy, economics, and cognitive science. "Neuroscience has a huge impact in many areas of science and beyond," says Professor Richard Lewis, Pomona College.

A glimpse at graduate studies in just three majors suggests how relevant multi/interdisciplinary studies can be. In gerontology, graduate tracks include elder law, geriatric nursing, personal care/assisted living, and retirement planning. In global studies, graduates might specialize in peace and conflict studies, international relations, or environmental issues. In neuroscience, graduate studies include behavioral or cognitive functions of the nervous system.

No easy questions

You can probably picture the reaction at the Thanksgiving table when you come home from college and tell everyone you're considering a multi/interdisciplinary major. "Huh?" they may ask. If that happens, calmly explain the importance of knowing about more than one thing—and that these majors combine various in-depth studies to meet a new need, like caring for a growing population of old people, or understanding a complex problem like war.

At that point, the focus should shift to the turkey. But if anyone's still listening, tell them how you carefully chose your college and your major.

Why would you choose an interdisciplinary major? Maybe you enjoy making connections between cultures or exploring the unknown. Perhaps you have good interpersonal skills, like to solve problems, are socially or politically active, or love to volunteer. Those are the types of students who are interested in these majors.

To pinpoint your multidisciplinary or interdisciplinary major requires a lot of legwork. You'll need to find out as much as you can about the major and how it fits into the college's courses. What is the history of the major at the college? What is the expertise of the faculty members? Is your major supported by related activities, speakers, or conferences? What exactly will your degree be in? Can you declare a double major, a minor, or a concentration in another subject? How about an independent study or self-guided learning in something that you're passionate about? What are graduates doing—going to professional or grad school, teaching, or pursuing business careers? What opportunities exist for off-campus and experiential study?

Just as there are no easy answers when you study these diverse fields, there are no easy questions when looking at colleges that offer them. You'll need to know if study abroad is required. If so, what are the costs and are they greater than studying on campus? Can your financial aid be applied toward study abroad? In a major that fuses two or more fields, is one stressed more than the other? Which department is the major under? Does the college offer career help, field experience, research opportunities, or a mentoring program to get real-world skills or find a job?

Students interested in these combined majors should look for colleges of arts and sciences, liberal arts, social sciences, or professional studies; schools of humanities; and divisions of interdisciplinary majors or life sciences. In this book, also read the sections on Area, ethnic, and gender studies; the Humanities; and the Social sciences.

Gerontology

Also known as:
Elder studies

What it's about:
Gerontology majors study the processes of aging and the resulting biological, behavioral, and social changes that affect older people's lives. The practical application of gerontology involves providing services to older adults and their families.

Is this for you?
You might like this major if you also like: helping people; community service activities; family relationships; interacting with older adults.

Consider this major if you are good at: caring/ nurturing; counseling; creativity; critical reading/ thinking; organizing ...*or have...* a sense of justice; initiative; interpersonal skills; patience; verbal skills; writing skills.

Recommended high school prep:
English 4, math 3, lab science 3, social studies 3, and a foreign language 2–3. If possible, take a service-learning class—one that combines community service experience with learning.

Did you know...
...that according to estimates, by the year 2030 there will be about 72 million older persons in the United States, more than twice as many as there were in 1997?

Typical courses in this major:
Social problems of aging
Aging around the world
Aging and the life cycle
Aging and human behavior
Aging and the community
Health and aging
Crime and aging
Social policy and aging
Aging and death
Special topics in gerontology
Psychology of aging
Housing needs of older adults
Physical activity programs
Services for older adults
Food for the elderly

Concentrations:
In college: health care; human services; long-term-care administration; social work.

If you go on to grad school: elder law; community advocacy; estate and financial planning; geriatric nursing; human development; nursing home administration; personal care/assisted living; recreation/ leisure; retirement planning.

What the study of this major is like:
The gerontology major prepares you to understand the process of aging and to work for organizations that serve older adults (such as Area Agencies on Aging; family services; long-term-care facilities; federal, state, and local government agencies; retirement communities; and business and industry institutions). If you plan to pursue a career administering or developing programs for a government agency, you should take courses in finance and accounting, and, probably, program planning and evaluation. In addition, oral and written communications skills and computer literacy are essential.

In this major, your course work will include both the liberal arts and preparation for an entry-level practice in human services or advanced work in gerontology/aging studies, social work, public administration, social welfare, or related fields. Your courses in the major are interdisciplinary and cover topics that explore what it is like to grow old, how an individual typically progresses through the life cycle, and what an aging population means to society.

In courses on the aging process, you examine, first, the physical and intellectual changes that occur from middle age to the end of life, including intellectual stability and Alzheimer's disease. Later courses deal with the influence of family and community on older people's quality of life; topics include the changing role that families play, ways in which members of minority and ethnic groups experience aging, and influences of social class on aging. Your third area of study will focus on the laws, programs, and institutions that help or hinder the process of aging in the United States and other countries. You examine programs such as Social Security, Medicare, and Medicaid, and the ways in which government influences private programs through tax incentives and regulation.

Some gerontology programs emphasize research and statistics. Others stress theory. Still others may focus on casework. The traditions of the college, as well as any religious affiliation, will likely determine the orientation of its gerontology program.

The gerontology major is not more, and not less, challenging than most social science programs. The subject matter is generally taught in lecture courses, with opportunities for service learning, internships, special-topic courses, guided independent study, and faculty-student research projects. As a major, you will probably spend substantial time volunteering or interning in both profit-making and not-for-profit agencies that provide services for the elderly in areas like housing, health, mental health, transportation, education, recreation, and social work. For example, you may visit senior citizen centers, volunteer in nursing homes, work part-time in retirement communities, or have field experiences in a government program.

Other majors you might like:
Urban, community, and regional planning
Human development and family studies
Exercise sciences
Health care administration
Human services
Nursing (RN)
Occupational therapy
Physical therapy
Psychology
Social work
Anthropology
Women's studies

Questions to ask colleges:
Are guided independent-study courses, community-service learning experiences, and internships available?

Can students declare double majors, a minor, or a concentration?

What library and electronic media resources support gerontology study?

How successful are graduates of the program in graduate and professional schools, as well as in careers?

Career options and trends:
Research gerontologist; geriatric physician; elder law attorney*; gerontology research assistant; long-term care administrator*; advocate for older adults; long-term care caseworker*; area agency on aging staff member*.

Additional employment possibilities for gerontology graduates include program development positions in recreation, education, and social services; administration of nursing homes, housing projects, and government programs; and service roles in multipurpose senior citizen centers, mental health agencies, and human resources departments of corporations and not-for-profit organizations.

Employment prospects are excellent in this field. An aging population with increasing life spans ensures continued demand for professionals knowledgeable in gerontology and elder care issues.

For more info:
Gerontological Society of America (GSA)
1220 L St., N.W.
Suite 901
Washington, DC 20005
(202) 842-1275
www.geron.org

Association for Gerontology in Higher Education
1220 L St., N.W.
Suite 901
Washington, DC 20005
(202) 289-9806
www.aghe.org

Global studies

What it's about:

Global studies is an interdisciplinary major that combines politics, economics, and cultural studies with comparative regional studies. You learn to view individuals, communities, states, economies, cultures, and ecologies in larger, internationally oriented contexts.

Is this for you?

You might like this major if you also like: current events; politics; international popular culture; world music; other cultures; travel; geography; history; peace and/or social justice movements.

Consider this major if you are good at: creativity; critical reading/thinking; leadership; research; spacial thinking/analysis *...or have...* initiative; verbal skills; writing skills.

Recommended high school prep:

English 4, math 3, lab science 3, social studies 4, and a foreign language 4. If possible, take courses in world history, economics, statistics, and world geography.

Typical courses in this major:

Introduction to global studies
Introduction to international relations
Introduction to anthropology
Modern world history
The international economy
The global environment
Ethnic conflict and nationalism
Comparative education
Topics in world literature
Global women's issues
Global social movements
Global climate change
Cultural geography
Intercultural studies
Regional perspectives

Concentrations:

Peace and conflict studies; international relations; international economics; gender issues; environmental issues; media and communications; specific regions.

What the study of this major is like:

The global studies major can be challenging, because the field is immense and it requires you to think in ways you might not be accustomed to. Your global studies course work combines aspects of history, economics, geography, and culture. As a major, you will move back and forth between two perspectives: the big-picture approach, in which you examine world systems and world history, and the case studies approach, in which you take an in-depth look at specific regions or nations.

Topics you'll consider include mass migrations, the effects of colonialism, and questions of cultural influence—for instance, can globalization be labeled a synonym for Americanization? Your courses will be taught in lecture or discussion format; students usually do research projects on areas they want to pursue. Language study and experiential learning (such as study-abroad) are important. You will also benefit from reading, and watching, the news and checking the Internet for alternative perspectives.

The global studies major may differ from college to college. Some colleges require you to study abroad and to learn the language of your host area; some have a capstone fourth-year independent project; and some allow you to design the focus of your major. Although certain programs have their own core courses and may have dedicated full-time faculty members, programs in other colleges may be a collection of courses from various departments, sometimes coordinated by only one faculty member.

Some colleges offer a broad range of international courses; others have a smaller number, perhaps restricted to fewer regions of the world. In some colleges, the cost of study abroad is the same as on-campus study; in others, you cannot take all your financial aid with you when you study abroad. Also, the types of concentrations offered can vary among colleges.

Other majors you might like:

International business
Peace and conflict studies
Geography
Sociology
Anthropology
Religious studies
Intercultural/diversity studies
International relations
Women's studies
Journalism
Economics
Linguistics

Questions to ask colleges:

What kinds of study-abroad opportunities are offered? For example, a strong global studies program should offer both on-campus studies of, and off-campus opportunities in, the developing countries outside Europe. Also, look for colleges that make it affordable to study abroad.

Does the program cover a range of topics? Most global studies programs include the social science disciplines (sociology, anthropology, politics, history, economics) within an international framework. But does the program also touch on the arts, communications, and ecology and climate?

Career options and trends:

High school teacher*; international NGO (non-governmental organization) worker*; Peace Corps volunteer; government/State Department worker*.

Global studies majors also go on to work in international business and international banking. A state certificate or license is required for teaching in secondary public schools. Working for the State Department usually requires language proficiency.

As political, social, economic, and environmental concerns continue to bring the world closer to us, job opportunities in the global studies field continue to grow. These days, it is crucial that you strengthen your qualifications by living abroad or learning to speak a second language.

For more info:

Global Studies Association (GSA)
c/o Department of Sociology
Manton Building,
Manchester Metropolitan University
Oxford Road
Manchester M15 6LL
United Kingdom
+44 (0) 161 247 1751
www.globalstudiesassociation.org

International Studies Association (ISA)
324 Social Sciences
University of Arizona
Tuscon, AZ 85721
(520) 621-7715
www.isanet.org

Social Science Research Council (SSRC)
One Pierrepont Plaza, 15th Floor
300 Cadman Plaza West
Brooklyn, NY 11201
(212) 377-2700
www.ssrc.org

Historic preservation

What it's about:

Majoring in historic preservation will teach you the theories and practices of preserving historically significant buildings, structures, and landscapes for future generations. You'll study the history of architecture, the principles of conservation and restoration, and the tools and techniques used in documenting, maintaining, and protecting cultural resources.

Is this for you?

You might like this major if you also like: exploring old buildings; antiquing; storytelling; detective work; reading about history and other cultures; travel; photography; visiting museums and historic sites

Consider this major if you are good at: attention to detail; creativity; critical reading/thinking; leadership; research; spacial thinking/analysis; teamwork *...or have...* initiative; verbal skills; writing skills.

Recommended high school prep:

English 4, math 3, lab science 4 (including physics), social studies 4, visual arts 2, and a foreign language 3–4. History courses offer the best preparation for this major. If they are available, courses in art history, photography, drafting/technical drawing, and speech communication are also recommended.

Typical courses in this major:

Foundations of architecture
Architectural history
American architecture
Documentation and recording
History and theory of preservation
Preservation planning and policy
Material resources of preindustrial America
Preservation law and finance
Landscape preservation
Researching historic structures and sites
Technology and materials for building
    conservation
Designing for an existing context
Exterior and interior rehabilitation
Social and cultural landscapes
Codes and requirements
Site development, interpretation, and management

Concentrations:

Building conservation; landscape preservation; documentation and research; preservation planning; site management

What the study of this major is like:

This major trains students to be the stewards of America's historic buildings, structures, and landscapes. The program, which involves a mix of lectures and hands-on experience, presents the theory and history of preservation and the tools and techniques used in documenting, maintaining, and protecting cultural resources.

You'll learn the nuts and bolts of the profession—investigation of the history of a building using local records and archives, analysis of its construction and style, and examination of physical evidence. By pulling all the information together, you'll be able to determine the significance of the structure. And you'll come to understand how preserving historic buildings and sites provides the community with a renewed appreciation of its heritage.

Your classes will cover a wide range of subjects, such as landscape architecture and urban planning, architectural history, conservation techniques, public relations, as well as land-use, real-estate, and tax policies. Then in individual and group projects, these interrelated topics will be applied to specific buildings, sites, structures, and objects as well as to the community as a whole.

The fieldwork is what distinguishes the historic preservation major. You deal directly with old stones, timbers, and documents. Some colleges have specialized laboratories for this work; most programs team with local or regional historic sites and agencies to supplement their on-campus facilities and to provide extended learning opportunities for their students.

All programs have similar core requirements that include courses on preservation theory and philosophy, architectural history, documentation techniques, and public policy principles. Programs differ in the amount of emphasis given to fieldwork and in the types and variety of elective courses and internship opportunities offered. The specific nature of each program usually depends on which academic department the historic preservation major is housed in and where the college itself is located.

Programs housed in schools of architecture tend to be more technically oriented—they emphasize the built environment through documentation and technology courses and through projects in adaptive use and design. Programs housed in planning departments focus more on public policy. If the major is in the history department, the emphasis will be on general research using documentation from the past. And the location of the college itself largely determines the types of internships and on-site fieldwork available. As might be expected, smaller communities have a feel and an influence that differ from those of urban areas.

One of the biggest challenges of this rewarding major is the research component. You'll use a variety of research techniques, including nontraditional primary sources such as the building itself. Time management is very important, because many projects require you to be self-motivated and self-directed. A keen sense of curiosity and a good dose of patience will serve you well as you work beyond the classroom and in your future career.

Other majors you might like:
American studies
Archaeology
Housing and human environments
Art history
Architectural history/criticism
Geography
Cultural resource management
History
Architectural engineering
Museum studies
Urban, community, and regional planning
Public policy analysis

Questions to ask colleges:
Are internships or fieldwork required for this major? What types are available, and how does the college help students obtain them?

Is the college connected to local preservation organizations, agencies, and historic sites?

What types of jobs have graduates of the program obtained?

Career options and trends:
Historic preservation consultant; cultural resource manager; historic site manager or curator; urban planner.

Planners and developers have come to realize that it is often more economical to restore than to build anew. Because of the growing trend to adapt and reuse historic buildings by modifying and repurposing the interiors, a greater number of skilled professionals with formal preservation training will be needed.

For more info:
National Trust for Historic Preservation
1785 Massachusetts Ave., N.W.
Washington, DC 20036 2117
(800) 944-6847
www.preservationnation.org

National Council for Preservation Education
www.ncpe.us

Medieval and Renaissance studies

What it's about:

Medieval and Renaissance studies explores the ideas, achievements, and practices of the period A.D. 500–1660. These eras comprise the heart of most modern cultures of the West and Near East, affecting current literature, philosophy, art, history, religion, and politics.

Is this for you?

You might like this major if you also like: the History Channel; drama; music; Renaissance fairs; foreign languages and cultures; Shakespeare; painting; sculpture; architecture; discovering the origins of social attitudes and practices.

Consider this major if you are good at: attention to detail; creativity; critical reading/thinking; organizing; research; spacial thinking/analysis ...*or have...* initiative; writing skills.

Recommended high school prep:

English 4, math 3, lab science 3, social studies 4, and a foreign language 3–4. If possible, take at least one European history class as well as an art history, music history, or theater history class.

Did you know...

...that this major offers you opportunities to do focused, original research based on your own interests? You might be drawn to examples of devout worship or bawdy storytelling. You may concentrate on a specific author or artist, and then study the society in which he or she worked. Or you might consider the social forces that shaped the hospital, the parliament, and the organization of work according to clock time; study the evolution of jury trials or the idea of human rights; or trace the spread of ideas after the printing press was invented.

Typical courses in this major:

The great cathedrals
Medieval art
Leonardo da Vinci
Classical drama
Dante and medieval theology
Religion of late antiquity
Arthurian legend
Science and Islam
Chaucer/Shakespeare/Milton
Age of the Baroque
Judaism in the Middle Ages
The Italian Renaissance
England: Reformation to revolution
Spanish medieval literature
Music and the Church
Medieval philosophy

Concentrations:

In college: a particular author, artist, nation, monarch (e.g., Elizabeth I), or cultural practice.

If you go on to grad school: the medieval period; the Renaissance; a particular religious tradition, philosophic tradition, or art form.

What the study of this major is like:

If you major in medieval and Renaissance studies, you will analyze the historical and cultural features of the sixth through seventeenth centuries in Europe and the Middle East; be able to read at least one relevant language; become familiar with the primary artistic, intellectual, and social developments of the period; and recognize medieval and Renaissance contributions to modern thought and culture.

In this major, you should take a variety of courses in a number of academic areas: architecture, art history, classics, religious studies, English, history, modern languages, music, philosophy, and theater arts, among others. Although some courses may be in lecture format, most are seminars highlighting student discussion, independent research, and presentations (as individuals and in groups). Several courses may be devoted to interdisciplinary topics, such as the medieval or Renaissance city, the iconographic tradition, Shakespeare's world, encounters with Islam, and voice and verse. Because many central documents of the period were written in languages other than English, a reading knowledge of

Latin, French, German, Spanish, or Italian—whichever suits your interests—is generally required.

Many programs have a strong focus on either English or history; others emphasize England or Europe; still others stress the Renaissance to the near-exclusion of the Middle Ages. Sometimes the focus of a program is evident in the basic course offerings or in specially presented topics or seminars. At other times, the focus is apparent only when you look into the faculty's research interests. If certain aspects of the major appeal to you, check into the emphases of the colleges you are considering to make sure you don't end up feeling frustrated or restricted.

Student and faculty gatherings are often an excellent source of information and community for medieval and Renaissance studies majors. At such meetings, you can hear about the latest research and get to know both professors and other students with similar interests. Many programs encourage you and your classmates to attend local stage and musical performances, museum exhibits, lectures, and conferences. As a medieval and Renaissance studies major, you can look forward to having stimulating exchanges with students and faculty members and to making genuine academic discoveries.

Other majors you might like:
English
History
Art history
Archaeology
Classics
Philosophy
Architectural history/criticism
Comparative literature
European studies
Religious studies
Italian studies
Drama and theater arts

Questions to ask colleges:
How many departments contribute to the medieval and Renaissance studies faculty? Is there an undergraduate research program? Is an undergraduate thesis required or encouraged? Which relevant study resources or activities are available on campus? Is there a larger academic community (such as a related graduate program) that undergraduate majors can easily access?

Career options and trends:
A degree in Medieval and Renaissance studies, like all liberal arts degrees, gives you a well-rounded education rather than training for a particular career. The degree is excellent preparation for graduate or professional school, and for careers in law, medicine, businesses, the arts, journalism, museology, and teaching.

For more info:
Medieval Academy of America (MAA)
104 Mount Auburn St., 5th Fl.
Cambridge, MA 02138
(617) 491-1622
www.medievalacademy.org

Renaissance Society of America (RSA)
CUNY Graduate Center
365 Fifth Ave., Room 5400
New York, NY 10016-4309
(212) 817-2130
www.rsa.org

Neuroscience

Also known as:
Psychobiology

What it's about:
Neuroscience is the interdisciplinary study of the nervous system and behavior. It covers issues such as the molecular and cellular basis of neuronal function, nervous system structure, systems of neurons as processors of information, the representation of functions in the brain, the evolutionary development of the nervous system, neural correlates of behavior, and mechanisms of nervous system disorders. The neuroscience major prepares you for graduate study in neuroscience or a related field and for careers requiring a solid foundation in science.

Is this for you?
You might like this major if you also like: thinking about how we think; anatomy; computers; science; exploring the unknown; probability-based reasoning; complex problems.

Consider this major if you are good at: attention to detail; creativity; critical reading/thinking; math; quantitative analysis; research; teamwork *...or have...* manual dexterity; verbal skills.

Recommended high school prep:
English 4, math 4 (including precalculus), lab science 4 (including biology, chemistry, and physics), social studies 4, and a foreign language 3–4. Your courses in English and social studies are just as important as your math and science courses.

Did you know...
...that areas of neuroscience are found not only in traditional science fields, such as biology, chemistry, physics, and psychology, but also in mathematics, computer science, philosophy, economics, and cognitive science?

...that the curriculum for neuroscience at most colleges parallels a pre-med program?

Typical courses in this major:
General chemistry
Organic chemistry
General biology
Calculus
Statistics
Physics
Introductory psychology
Introductory neuroscience
Neurobiology
Behavioral neuroscience
Cognitive neuroscience
Systems neuroscience
Neuropharmacology
Sensory neuroscience
Developmental neuroscience

Concentrations:
Neurobiology; comparative and evolutionary neuroscience; systems neuroscience; behavioral neuroscience; social neuroscience; cognitive neuroscience; computational neuroscience.

What the study of this major is like:
Neuroscience addresses interesting questions. How do we think? Why do we behave the way we do? What is the relationship between the mind and the brain? How does the brain give rise to consciousness? How do nature and nurture influence our behavior? But neuroscientists seek answers to these questions in the lab sciences.

You shouldn't think of becoming a neuroscience major unless you enjoy laboratory research approaches to exploring these issues. Like other life sciences majors, neuroscience students spend many hours in labs. All neuroscience programs will expect you to obtain a firm grounding in the basics, including biology, chemistry, physics, math, psychology, and statistics. Some students may be frustrated by taking so many courses that do not deal specifically with the major. But your understanding of the nervous system will depend on your familiarity with scientific fundamentals.

Neuroscience may be the broadest major that exists. It is based in the life sciences but has connections to the social sciences and humanities. To date, there is no agreed-on sense of what is essential for the neuroscience curriculum. Each program differs in some ways from all the others. At each school that offers the major, the nature of the program is determined by the faculty members who teach the courses. Few colleges have hired instructors specifically to develop undergraduate programs in neuroscience. Instead, professors develop departmental majors such as biology and psychology. Therefore, the major depends on which areas of neuroscience are valued in the departments that contribute faculty members to the program. Look carefully at course offerings to see if the courses in the major match your interests.

Neuroscience is in an exciting phase because techniques have been developed that provide new ways to explore the brain. The human brain is the most complex phenomenon in nature. Answers to many neuroscientists' questions are beginning to surface, but much remains unknown. If you expect final answers, you will be frustrated by the brain's complexity. If you are excited by a sense of discovery, then you should do well in neuroscience.

Other majors you might like:
Molecular biology
Psychology
Behavioral sciences
Chemistry
Philosophy
Biopsychology
Information systems
Neurobiology/physiology
Biomedical engineering
Robotics technology
Biological/physical sciences
Electroencephalograph technology

Questions to ask colleges:
What are the areas of faculty expertise?

Will students get a background in molecular and cellular aspects of neuroscience? Will students get training in neuroanatomy, neuropharmacology, neurophysiology, and neurochemistry?

How much emphasis is placed on behavior? How much emphasis is placed on cognitive neuroscience, social neuroscience, computational neuroscience, and comparative and evolutional neuroscience?

Career options and trends:
Physician*; college professor/researcher*; high school teacher; science writer; research technician (e.g., with a drug company or research lab); electroneurodiagnostic technician.

Neuroscience is becoming an important area within the sciences. Medical and academic prospects are relatively good in this field. Increasingly, universities are hiring in this area, especially in fields that have not had neuroscience representation, such as computer science, mathematics, and cognitive science.

Insider's viewpoint:
"I enjoy learning about the human brain and all of the bodily and spiritual connections to it, to help understand people around me as well as myself. Being able to spout off about the brain is also great at parties."

—Candace, senior, University of Rochester

For more info:
Society for Neuroscience (SfN)
1121 14th St., N.W.
Suite 1010
Washington, DC 20005
(202) 962-4000
www.sfn.org

Peace and conflict studies

What it's about:

As a peace and conflict studies major, you explore strategies for constructing a just and peaceful world. You study issues of war, sexism, racism, and poverty; nonviolent social change; and conflict resolution. The approach is both theoretical and experience-based.

Is this for you?

You might like this major if you also like: social and political activism; service-related activities; volunteer activities; creative writing; theater; art; community building; human rights issues.

Consider this major if you are good at: caring/nurturing; creativity; critical reading/thinking; leadership; organizing; persuading/influencing; teamwork *...or have...* initiative; people skills; verbal skills; writing skills.

Recommended high school prep:

English 4, math 3, lab science 3, social studies 4, and a foreign language 4.

Did you know...

...that peace and conflict studies is less about mastering material and more about learning a process of action and reflection? There is a substantial hands-on component to this major. Most students complete internships in the United States and abroad.

Typical courses in this major:

Theory and practice of nonviolence
History of nonviolence
The global political economy
Introduction to international relations
Philosophical inquiry: peace and justice
Contemporary social theory
Postcolonial theory
Conflict resolution
Methods of peacemaking
Philosophy of social science
International law
Theories of international relations
Issues before the United Nations
Marxism
Urban political economy
Feminism, ecology, and peace

Concentrations:

Interpersonal and intergroup conflict resolution; international war and peace; social, economic, and/or environmental justice.

What the study of this major is like:

As a peace and conflict studies major, you spend part of your time in class, learning theory and history, and part of your time in lab situations—in settings (such as internships) where you can develop peacemaking skills and put them to good use. Many courses require you to write papers and present oral reports based on group projects. You become accustomed to analyzing problems locally and globally.

Peace and conflict studies may be a program on its own or an interdepartmental major including courses from different departments. Many programs have been influenced by the traditional peace churches (Quakers, Mennonites, Church of the Brethren) or by Catholic social thought, although some are not affiliated with any religion.

Some programs are global in scope; others tend to focus on the United States. In either case you will be encouraged to explore a non-western culture and issues of human diversity. Some programs also require proficiency in a foreign language equivalent to two years of college-level study. Internships and hands-on learning are encouraged more on some campuses than on others; some programs even offer their own international, off-campus study programs.

Most peace and conflict studies majors take their education very seriously. You will have significant interaction with faculty members who serve as teachers and mentors both in and out of the classroom. Majors frequently make friends they keep long after graduation.

Other majors you might like:

International relations
Women's studies

Gay/lesbian studies
Environmental studies
Religious studies
Philosophy
Labor/industrial relations
Emergency management/homeland security
Legal studies
Intercultural/diversity studies
Political science
Near and Middle Eastern studies

Questions to ask colleges:
Does the program sponsor peace-related activities, speakers, conferences, and so on?

How many faculty members participate in the program?

Do the students have a say in the design of their education? What opportunities are there for off-campus and experience-based study?

Have graduates found work in peace and justice efforts?

Career options and trends:
College professor*; nongovernmental organization (NGO) worker*; lawyer*; minister or other member of the clergy*; government worker; public relations manager; international business consultant; human resources manager.

Peace and conflict studies majors also enter graduate and professional schools to become doctors, lawyers, teachers, and caregivers. Many people who eventually teach peace and conflict studies do not pursue graduate training in the field. Instead, they specialize in a discipline that lends itself to a peace perspective, such as sociology, economics, political science, history, or philosophy.

In the United States, mediation and conflict resolution are becoming increasingly promising fields. Also, a peace and conflict studies degree can be useful for positions in a wide range of nongovernmental organizations.

For more info:
Peace and Justice Studies Association (PJSA)
Prescott College
220 Grove Ave.
Prescott, AZ 86301
(928) 350-2008
www.peacejusticestudies.org

Natural resources and conservation

If you are considering the majors in this section, you probably already know about disappearing forests, threats to wildlife habitats, and other ways that humans hurt the environment. The good news is that, by learning about natural resources and conservation, you should be able to do something about these problems. "Students for whom environmental studies is the right major are those who take pleasure in making a difference," says Professor Michael Maniates of Allegheny College. "They have compelling interest in environmental issues and deep-felt concern about current patterns of assault on the environment and what this means for future generations."

If you the love the outdoors, enjoy camping trips or Scouting, or have a passion for bird watching, these majors may be right for you.

Many areas of study, including programs that mix several subjects, fall under this category. "Environmental science zips together a working knowledge of physics, chemistry, and biology," says Professor David E. Smith, University of Virginia. "Environmental *science* programs focus on the natural sciences, whereas environmental *studies* also emphasizes the social sciences as they relate to environmental issues."

Why should you study the social sciences if your interest is in the environment? "Many students enter natural resource and conservation programs in the belief or expectation that they will not be dealing with political, economic, or social areas of study," says Professor David K. Loomis, University of Massachusetts Amherst. "Managing natural resources is in many ways accomplished by managing people. There is no distinct separation between society and our natural resources."

As a professional in these fields (and forests, wetlands, and waterways!), you will spend a great deal of time working with the public. In fact, public awareness of the urgency to protect the environment increases funding and jobs in conservation. It's weird, but a healthy job outlook stems in part from an unhealthy environmental outlook.

"Americans are concerned about the environment, and this awareness has created a stable need for environmental professionals in both the government and private sector," Smith says.

Fields, forests, and fisheries

Careers in natural resources management and conservation include research, teaching, consulting, law, journalism, policymaking, government regulation, and advocacy. Some new areas of study and work include conservation biology and watershed management. Okay, now, get out the bug spray and consider these specific jobs: environmental consulting, engineering, and policy analysis; community recycling and energy-conservation projects; research in health risks from pollutants; or working as an outdoor educator, field naturalist, forester, or park ranger; endangered species officer; fisheries biologist, manager, or ecologist. To get a job in wildlife work, such as wildlife biologist or operations officer, you'll face more competition.

When you compare colleges, you'll see that they differ in the way they achieve balance between the scientific and the human pieces of the environmental puzzle.

"This difference is fine and welcome, so long as the program incorporates significant insight from other disciplines and features courses and projects that allow students to effectively combine the skills and ideas they're learning from different fields," advises Maniates.

The issues of accreditation and certification are also huge. That's because some jobs in conservation require specific credentials, like state certifications. See whether your area of interest has certifications and find out if the college degree comes with a certification or a way to earn it. Accreditation is different from certification: certification is for you, while accreditation is for the college. Look for college programs accredited by the professional association for your specialty.

Here are some other questions for colleges: What's the most important course in the program? The answer should reveal that college's priorities. Is your major a full-fledged degree area or just a concentration under another major—like wildlife under zoology? Are internships available for what you're studying? Are the laboratories up-to-date? Will you get field experience? Are good field sites near the university? The location of the college may suggest a strong program—for instance, in fisheries or regional forestry. Also ask about the variety of classes open to you and how many electives you can take. Explore where students go after graduation. But most of all, read the catalog descriptions of the faculty members.

"College and university programs are only as good as their faculties," Smith emphasizes. "The faculty should be fully engaged in all aspects of scholarship, both teaching and research." Look for opportunities to do supervised research and independent study in a topic that's important to you, especially if you're planning to go to grad school. Graduate studies include environmental policy and law; land use, sprawl, and urban planning; water, wetlands, and marine resources management; forest management/resources and wood science; and fisheries science and management.

For information, go to the Ecological Society of America (www.esa.org). Read about related majors in the sections on Agriculture; Parks and recreation; and the Physical sciences.

Environmental science

What it's about:
The interdisciplinary field of environmental science spotlights two concerns: the interaction of the physical and biological processes that shape our natural environment, and the application of scientific methods and research to environmental problems.

Is this for you?
You might like this major if you also like: complex puzzles; exploring the outdoors; using computers; taking a journey to an unknown destination; working on real-world problems; learning how the environment works.

Consider this major if you are good at: attention to detail; creativity; critical reading/thinking; math; organizing; quantitative analysis; research; teamwork *...or have...* initiative; patience; writing skills.

Recommended high school prep:
English 4, math 4 (including precalculus), lab science 4 (earth science, biology, chemistry, physics), social studies 3, and a foreign language 2–3. If they are available, take courses in environmental studies or sciences, ecology, computer applications, and calculus or statistics.

Did you know...
...how important a background in the physical sciences and the life sciences is in this field? If you were investigating the oxygen concentration in a lake or the impact of acid rain on a forest, you would have to evaluate both the physical and the biological processes, and their interaction, to show how the environment works.

Typical courses in this major:
Environmental modeling and methodology
Physical geology
Fundamentals of ecology
Hydrology and water resources
Atmosphere and weather
Population and the environment
Geographic information systems (GIS)
Remote sensing
Global biogeochemistry cycles
Climatological analysis
Biochemistry
Coastal processes
Management of forest ecosystems
Environmental impact assessment
Waste management systems
Marine biology/ecology

Concentrations:
Environmental biology; environmental chemistry; environmental geology; environmental physics; aquatic ecology; terrestrial ecology; environmental health; environmental protection; natural resource management.

What the study of this major is like:
Because problems that affect the environment are complex, environmental science requires an imaginative approach that includes a working knowledge of physics, chemistry, and biology. As a major, you will probably be expected to gain a clear understanding of a wide range of physical and biological processes. For example, you may be required to take classes that deal with the water cycle and its effect on sediments and rocks. You will also study atmospheric science, geoscience, ecology, environmental chemistry, hydrology, and land and resource analysis. When you complete the required subjects, you should be ready to construct a course of study that emphasizes your own strengths and interests.

Fieldwork, which is often an important part of your education, can offer intellectual challenges and the sort of real-world risks that laboratory research can't provide. You may have additional opportunities to do supervised research in which you work closely with faculty members in the field or the laboratory. Paid summer research internships or fellowships at research sites throughout the country are also available; these opportunities supplement your academic course work. For a variety of reasons, environmental science is collaborative; many individuals contribute their special talents as they work in research or investigative groups to solve problems. Therefore, you should develop your communication skills (writing, reading, speaking, listening) and learn the terminology, or distinct vocabulary, of the profession.

Computer skills are also essential; a strong program will provide experience with data analysis, digital mapping, remote sensing, and geographic information systems (GIS). The opportunity to conduct professional-level research in a senior capstone project is another indicator of a good program.

People sometimes confuse environmental science and environmental studies, but these programs differ in key ways. In general, environmental science focuses on the natural sciences (chemistry, biology, physics) as they relate to the environment, whereas environmental studies emphasizes the social sciences (such as economics, policy, or law) as they relate to environmental issues. Environmental science majors study the natural sciences on a deeper level, while environmental studies majors gain additional opportunities through their exposure to the social sciences. Be sure to investigate the programs that interest you to see that you understand the goals and requirements of each.

Other majors you might like:
Environmental engineering
Petroleum engineering
Ecology
Natural sciences
Soil science
Hazardous materials technology
Hydrology/water resources science
Geology/earth science
Geography
Atmospheric science
Oceanography
Environmental health

Questions to ask colleges:
Are the faculty members in this program engaged in both teaching and research? Professors who are active in research can, and do, incorporate aspects of their research into their teaching.

Are undergraduates given opportunities to participate in supervised research and/or independent study? These activities are valuable regardless of which career path you take after graduation.

Career options and trends:
Researcher; college professor or high school teacher; environmental consultant; environmental lawyer; resource manager in industry; regulatory compliance specialist; state or federal government regulator; staff member of an advocacy group.

A master's degree is required for most entry-level research and teaching positions, and a Ph.D. is usually necessary for high-level research.

Job prospects are generally very good in the government, academic, and private sectors for students with undergraduate and graduate degrees, although a master's degree is usually preferred. Because of increasing pressures on the environment from expanding populations and economic development, demand for environmental scientists in both government and industry is projected to grow, both in the United States and abroad. Opportunities should be especially strong in companies that provide regulatory compliance services.

Coupling a major in environmental science with a minor in business, public administration, or health will also improve your job prospects.

For more info:
Ecological Society of America (ESA)
1990 M St., N.W.
Suite 700
Washington, DC 20036
202-833-8773
www.esa.org

Environmental studies

What it's about:

Environmental studies integrates insights and tools from natural and engineering sciences, social sciences, and humanities to explore the effects of human activities on the natural world. In this major, you identify environmental problems, analyze their causes, and learn how to develop a range of solutions.

Is this for you?

You might like this major if you also like: community service; environmental causes; the outdoors; camping trips; Scouting; fishing; hunting; bird watching; working on problems without easy answers; making the world a better place.

Consider this major if you are good at: advocating; attention to detail; creativity; critical reading/thinking; organizing; quantitative analysis; teamwork ...*or have...* curiosity; initiative; writing skills.

Recommended high school prep:

English 4, math 3, lab science 3 (earth science, biology, chemistry), social studies 3, and a foreign language 2–3. If it is available, take a course in environmental science/studies or ecology.

Did you know...

...that most undergraduates majoring in environmental studies are women?

Typical courses in this major:

Introduction to environmental studies
Ecology
Conservation biology
Environmental chemistry
Geology
Environmental politics
Environmental philosophy and ethics
Environmental and ecological economics
Tools of environmental analysis
Wildlife management
Land use planning
Environmental education
Environmental history
Environmental health
Energy technologies, supply, and policy

Concentrations:

Environmental policy and law; terrestrial ecosystems; aquatic ecosystems; conservation biology and biodiversity; environmental education; environmental ethics and philosophy; environmental preservation; land use and urban planning; energy production and conservation.

What the study of this major is like:

The rapidly growing interest in environmental studies as an undergraduate major results from an increasing awareness of the human impact on the environment. Environmental studies differs from environmental science and environmental engineering in its greater emphasis on the social sciences and humanities. As an environmental studies major, you enroll in a number of academic subjects to examine the causes of, and possible solutions to, environmental problems.

Programs can differ greatly from college to college. Typically, you begin by taking introductory courses in the natural sciences and the social sciences, with at least half your courses in biology, chemistry, and geology. If you have a strong interest in natural science, you might combine a concentration in science with courses in environmental studies.

Many programs offer courses and projects that allow you to integrate, or combine, what you learn from different fields. Some may focus on the natural sciences, while others offer advanced courses in the social sciences, environmental economics, and environmental history. Economic analysis is often the basis of solutions to problems such as pollution and resource depletion (overuse). Classes in environmental politics will help you understand the context in which policies and programs are created and carried out. Some programs also cover environmental issues in foreign countries—for example, the erosion of beaches in the Caribbean islands—and global concerns like the greenhouse effect. In programs that include humanities, you are encouraged to take courses in environmental philosophy and ethics as well as in art, religion, and literature, as a way of examining the links between human activity and the environment.

Programs in environmental studies tend to argue that human society is undermining the ecological foundations of life and that we must fundamentally change behavior if we are to prosper as a species—we must go beyond recycling or planting trees in order to tackle looming environmental threats. For some students, this claim can be unsettling. Most programs value your ability to think critically about problems and to develop innovative solutions, but a problem-solving emphasis is likely to make certain demands on you. Instead of learning facts about specific environmental problems, you are encouraged to analyze them, because the environmental challenges we will face in twenty years will probably differ significantly from the ones that confront us today.

In environmental studies, your course work is often rewarding and eye-opening. You can get hands-on experience in responding to environmental threats through fieldwork, service-learning programs, and internships. However, careers in the field increasingly require technical training at advanced levels, usually graduate work. The liberal arts education in environmental studies does not replace specialized training, but it provides excellent preparation for such training.

Other majors you might like:
Geography
Political science
Economics
Environmental engineering
Global studies
Geology/earth science
Forestry
Urban, community, and regional planning
Sustainable agriculture
Ecology
Environmental health
Wildlife and wilderness management

Questions to ask colleges:
In which courses do you apply ideas from various fields to resolve environmental problems? Some programs ask you to take a variety of courses from different disciplines but offer few opportunities to integrate, or tie together, what you've learned.

What internships are available? How well do these internships complement, or enrich, the course offerings?

Has the number of students majoring in the program grown over the past few years and, if so, are faculty members being brought in to accommodate the increased interest?

Are there faculty members whose primary responsibility is teaching and advising environmental studies students? Sometimes the program's professors are "on loan" from other programs, which may hold first claim to the instructors' time.

What is the most important course in the curriculum? The answer will tell you about the focus of the program. Compare that focus with your own interests.

Where are recent graduates of the program working? If they have landed jobs that sound interesting, that's a good sign.

Career options and trends:
Environmental consultant*; environmental lobbyist; environmental engineer; park naturalist; specialist in environmental communications; specialist in regulations compliance; environmental educator.

As environmental problems are becoming more of a concern throughout the world, the job market is expanding. Career opportunities exist in toxic waste disposal, management of environmental organizations, journalism, community recycling and energy conservation, and environmental and economic development in nonindustrial countries. With appropriate graduate work, you can pursue a career in air or water quality planning, solid waste planning, land use planning, fisheries and wildlife management, policy analysis, environmental law, laboratory research, or resource economics.

Insider's viewpoint:
"I love the excitement of working directly on problems that scare us all at least a little bit. It's hard, as a professor or as a student, to be bored by the subject: the issues are too large, the stakes too high, the rewards too great."

—Professor Michael Maniates, Allegheny College

For more info:

National Wildlife Federation
11100 Wildlife Center Drive
Reston, VA 20190-5362
(800) 822-9919
www.nwf.org

Association for the Study of Literature and
    Environment (ASLE)
P.O. Box 502
Keene, NH 03431-0502
(603) 357-7411
www.asle.org

Fishing and fisheries

What it's about:

The major in fisheries explores the biology and ecology of fishes and other aquatic species; the bodies of water that are their habitats; and the human use, management, and production of aquatic species. Courses cover both basic science and applied aspects of commercial and recreational fishing activities.

Is this for you?

You might like this major if you also like: fishing, boating, or hiking; working with your hands as well as your mind; keeping an aquarium or raising live animals; learning about living creatures and natural ecosystems.

Consider this major if you are good at: attention to detail; creativity; critical reading/thinking; problem solving; quantitative analysis; spacial thinking/analysis; teamwork ...*or have...* initiative; verbal skills.

Recommended high school prep:

English 4, math 3, lab science 3, social studies 3, and a foreign language 2–3. Courses in advanced biology, environmental science, precalculus, and computer literacy are also recommended.

Typical courses in this major:

Evolutionary biology
Genetics
Fisheries techniques
Ichthyology
Fish ecology
Limnology
Aquatic animal nutrition
Economics
Aquatic entomology
Freshwater ecology
Statistics
Policies, laws, and regulations
Principles of aquaculture
Fisheries management

Concentrations:

Fisheries management; fisheries science; aquaculture.

What the study of this major is like:

Fisheries management is a science-based field that requires you to understand and apply principles of biology, ecology, statistics, and social sciences. Professionals who work in fisheries management do not simply sample, assess, and stock fish populations; they also improve habitats for certain species to protect biodiversity (for example, helping endangered species recover) and interact with the public. Fisheries managers must also be able to communicate technical information in person and in writing.

You begin your studies by establishing a strong foundation in fields such as biology, chemistry, mathematics, and English. You will also probably take an introductory course in natural resources management in your first year. Your second-year studies generally include plant and evolutionary biology, physical sciences, and social sciences, along with an introduction to principles of fisheries and wildlife management. Through your first two years, the prime method of instruction is lectures, supplemented by laboratories in biology and chemistry and some fieldwork in natural resources management. Many majors tend to feel most challenged by course work in chemistry and calculus.

In your third and fourth years, course content becomes more fisheries-oriented; fieldwork and hands-on learning is more important. Your third year generally includes foundation courses, such as field techniques, ichthyology (the study of fishes), and fish ecology. The fourth year usually features such key courses as freshwater ecology, human dimensions of fisheries and wildlife management, aquaculture, and a capstone course in fisheries management. The capstone course generally combines everything you have learned; groups of students devise action plans for solving real-world problems in fisheries management. In your third and fourth years, classes are smaller and you have more opportunities to interact personally with your professors and with other majors. In fact, majors typically study in groups and socialize after hours. Many of them enroll in the local chapter of a professional society and begin to feel part of the profession.

You will be encouraged to learn from practical experience by volunteering to help graduate students with fieldwork or laboratory work, by participating in internships in fisheries management agencies or nongovernmental organizations, or by conducting independent research projects. In these activities, you can identify and explore areas of technical specialization. You can also establish professional contacts that may prove helpful if you look for an entry-level position after graduation. Of students graduating with bachelor's degrees, roughly one-quarter move on to graduate studies and three-quarters obtain entry-level jobs in the field.

Some of the programs emphasize fisheries science, which encourage you to solve management problems by understanding fish ecology. Science-based programs are essential if you are considering going to graduate school and pursuing a challenging career in fisheries science. Other programs stress instruction in practical fisheries management and aim to produce entry-level managers for state or federal fisheries management agencies. Programs may also differ in the amount of hands-on learning available and in the opportunities for participation in research and internships. Often, universities with graduate programs in fisheries offer more opportunities for learning outside formal classes.

Other majors you might like:
Aquaculture
Marine biology
Ocean engineering
Parks, recreation, and leisure studies
Zoology
Aquatic biology/limnology
Marine engineering/naval architecture
Marine science/Merchant Marine
Underwater diving
Oceanography
Natural resources management/policy
Water, wetlands, and marine management

Questions to ask colleges:
What sorts of facilities are offered? Do they include laboratories, experimental ponds, raceways (canals), and aquaria, as well as access to nearby streams, rivers, or reservoirs?

Are there opportunities for doing hands-on learning and for gaining practical research experience? Is there a graduate program, so that undergraduates can learn by helping graduate students with their research? Are undergraduates encouraged to undertake independent research projects?

Career options and trends:
Fisheries manager*; conservation officer; fish ecologist; fish culturist*; endangered species management officer; environmental consultant; fisheries research scientist; fisheries and wildlife journalist.

Many state and federal fisheries management agencies require their employees to become certified fisheries scientists under the program administered by the American Fisheries Society. Certification requires formal education and professional experience. Although entry-level jobs can be obtained with a bachelor's degree, an advanced degree will lead to a more rewarding career.

Not all jobs focus on management of sport and commercial fisheries, and many address recovery of endangered species, public education, development of public policy, and other areas. Most jobs in fisheries combine physical work outdoors with intellectual engagement—the talents, skills, and energies of fisheries managers seldom go unused.

Private-sector employment has grown in response to our increased awareness of environmental issues. Fisheries professionals are employed by environmental consulting firms, forest products companies, public utilities, and conservation groups. Aquaculturists can work in both public agencies and private firms.

Employment of captains and crews in the fishing industry is declining, because of foreign competition, stock depletion, and habitat destruction. The good news is that these same factors should spur demand for professionals trained in fisheries science and management.

Insider's viewpoint:
"Fisheries management is maturing as a field of applied science, and it is exciting to witness and participate in its application. For example, during my own career, I have witnessed the restoration of Great Lakes fisheries, the rise of aquaculture, and the emergence of conservation science and manage-

ment. Many are the days that I smile inwardly and think, 'I get paid to do what I love.' "

—Professor Eric Hallerman, Virginia Polytechnic Institute and State University

For more info:
American Fisheries Society (AFS)
5410 Grosvenor Lane
Bethesda, MD 20814
(301) 897-8616
www.fisheries.org

World Aquaculture Society
143 J. M. Parker Coliseum
Louisiana State University
Baton Rouge, LA 70803
(225) 578-3137
www.was.org

Forestry

What it's about:

This major deals with the management, conservation, and preservation of forest ecosystems. Integrating what you learn in the physical, biological, and social sciences helps you appreciate the numerous benefits and resources of forests, including wood and fiber products, biodiversity, recreation, water, wilderness, and wildlife.

Is this for you?

You might like this major if you also like: the great outdoors; math and science; maps; geography; arboretums; building things; working with people; helping others accomplish their goals.

Consider this major if you are good at: critical reading/thinking; leadership; managing people; organizing; quantitative analysis; teamwork *...or have...* initiative; patience; verbal skills.

Recommended high school prep:

English 4, math 4 (including pre-calculus), lab science 4 (earth science, biology, chemistry, and physics), social studies 3, and a foreign language 2–3. If they are available, courses in statistics, environmental science or ecology, and computer applications are also recommended. Many agencies, such as county conservation boards, state and national parks, and the U.S. Forest Service, provide summer employment opportunities in forestry.

Did you know...

that the amount of forest land in the United States is down only about one-third from what it was when the Pilgrims landed, and is about the same as it was a century ago? Because of forest management policies, forest growth exceeds harvesting by 33 percent each year—a reassuring statistic, because, for every individual in the United States, the equivalent of a full-grown tree is turned into wood and paper each year.

Typical courses in this major:

Botany
Forest soils
Forest management and policy
Forest measurements
Forest economics
Silviculture
Forest ecology
Forest growth and yield
Wildlife management
Resource allocation
Aerial photo interpretation
Geographic information systems (GIS)
Harvesting and production technology
Hydrology
Wood science
Composite products

Concentrations:

In college: forest resource management; urban forestry; wood products; wood science; fire management.

If you go on to grad school: forest biology; forest economics; forest biometry; forest ecology.

What the study of this major is like:

Forestry programs begin with general course work in English, mathematics, chemistry, physics, speech, and statistics. In your first year, you generally take introductory forestry courses and do field studies conducted by forestry faculty members. Because forestry is a broad field, you typically have to choose an area of concentration. You may pick your concentration as early as your first year or as late as the end of your second year. You then begin course work in your chosen area. Nonforestry courses, such as business management, industrial engineering, and technical report writing, help you prepare for work in the field.

Many aspects of a forestry education are hands-on. Some courses are taught in the field so that you can experience for yourself the complexities of the forest and apply theories learned in the classroom to real situations. Most problems encountered in forestry represent new challenges, arising from new circumstances, and your task may be to come up with appropriate solutions. Therefore, critical thinking, analysis, and problem-solving skills are essential.

In laboratory sessions, you do statistical analysis of data collected in the field and study biological relationships among different species of trees, as well as between trees and other living organisms in the forest. You are encouraged to use your summers to work in forestry-related jobs. Many programs offer credit for these experiences, most of which are paid jobs in private industry; with county, state, or federal government agencies; or with other resource management agencies. Working in the field improves your understanding of forestry and your chances of finding a permanent job after graduation. You should also become active in professional organizations so you can practice the teamwork and leadership skills that are central to a successful forestry career.

There are four main types of forestry programs. Some programs train students to be forestry technicians and usually grant two-year degrees that allow graduates to work in field jobs related to forestry. Other programs prepare you for both field and supervisory work, such as being a district ranger, forest supervisor, regional forester, or chief forester with the U.S. Forest Service; a consulting forester; or a forester with a state department of natural resources. These are usually four-year Bachelor of Science programs. Other programs prepare you to work in wood science, with either a B.S. degree or an advanced degree. Still other programs are intended primarily for graduate students. And some forestry programs offer a combination of the four options. In addition, some programs focus on forestry in a particular region of the United States, while others offer a generic, broad-ranging approach.

Other majors you might like:
Botany
Wildlife and wilderness management
Forest resources production
Surveying technology
Landscape architecture
Horticulture
Environmental studies
Ecology
Land use planning
Wood science/pulp/paper technology
Entomology
Forest engineering

Questions to ask colleges:
Is the program accredited by the Society of American Foresters or the Society of Wood Science and Technology? If it is, then you know that the curriculum is reviewed periodically by an outside team of professionals, and that it meets accepted standards.

What types of field laboratory experiences are offered, and in what types of environments? What forestry-related facilities (research labs, habitats, remote sensing equipment, greenhouses, preserves) are on or near campus?

Career options and trends:
Forester with the U. S. Forest Service or state agency*; park ranger*; urban forester; industrial forester or timber manager*; arborist; wood product sales; consulting forester.

Generally, not much job growth is projected in the forestry field, and overall employment is expected to decline in the timber industry. Nevertheless, there is increasing demand for graduates in the areas of wood science, urban and community forestry, and natural resource conservation or interpretation. The growing public demand for protection and responsible management of forest resources should create opportunities in research, testing, and compliance services.

For more info:
Society of American Foresters (SAF)
5400 Grosvenor Lane
Bethesda, MD 20814-2198
(866) 897-8720
www.safnet.org

Society of Wood Science and Technology (SWST)
P.O. Box 6155
Monona, WI 53716-6155
(608) 577-1342
www.swst.org

Natural resources and conservation

What it's about:
Natural resources and conservation is a broad, interdisciplinary field of study that addresses the management, protection, use, restoration, and enjoyment of the Earth's resources. Training is provided in a number of academic areas, including biology and other natural sciences, social sciences, economics, and environmental studies.

Is this for you?
You might like this major if you also like: outdoor activities such as camping, fishing, hunting, hiking, and canoeing; traveling; photography; debating; getting involved in environmental causes; politics; business and economics; leading or organizing school activities.

Consider this major if you are good at: creativity; critical reading/thinking; integrative thinking; leadership; quantitative analysis; research; teamwork *...or have...* initiative; verbal skills; writing skills.

Recommended high school prep:
English 4, math 3, lab science 3, social studies 4, and a foreign language 2–3. If they are available, courses in environmental studies, economics, and computer applications are also recommended.

Did you know...
...that the management of natural resources is in many ways accomplished by the management of people? There is no distinct separation between society and the natural world. Many students begin this major expecting an in-depth examination of the environment. They soon learn, however, that they must also take courses in the social sciences, and that as professionals they will spend a great deal of time working with the public.

...that much of the work in this field is done indoors? This is especially true as you advance in your career.

Typical courses in this major:
Biology
Ecology
Chemistry
Plant and animal identification
Economics
Human dimensions
Natural resources management
Environmental policy
Conservation law
Wildlife and fisheries conservation
Geographic information systems (GIS)
Measurements and sampling techniques
Environmental communication
Soils and land use
Politics and ecology
Ecotourism

Concentrations:
Natural resources policy; outdoor recreation; resources management; environmental law and policy; environmental education; wildlife rehabilitation; wetlands restoration; coastal zone management.

What the study of this major is like:
Historically, professionals working in the natural resources and conservation field focused on specific academic areas, or disciplines, such as forestry or wildlife biology. Today, leading programs combine a range of courses; as a result, all majors become familiar with several fields, including forestry, wildlife, fisheries, physical sciences (such as chemistry), and social sciences (economics and political science). In addition, you take writing and, often, public speaking courses. Majors learn to integrate, or link, many disciplines and apply them to natural resource issues.

Many natural resources and conservation courses are taught in the traditional lecture and discussion format. Other courses focus on fieldwork, such as plant or animal identification and sampling techniques. Some courses combine the two, with a lecture/discussion session followed by fieldwork. An increasing number of courses require group projects, designed to prepare you for the type of work you may do after you graduate.

Natural resources and conservation programs vary a great deal in their emphases, degree requirements, and philosophies. Some programs have well-defined requirements that offer little flexibility, while others can accommodate almost any reasonable curriculum you want to pursue. At the same time, accreditation (offered by the Society of American Foresters) and individual certification (offered by SAF, the American Fisheries Society, and The Wildlife Society) ensure that all programs follow professional guidelines. All programs that are accredited must meet the same standards of quality and course requirements.

Some programs place more emphasis on either the biophysical or the socioeconomic aspects of natural resources and conservation. The combination of disciplines available at a college can also create differences among programs. For example, some programs cover only forestry or wildlife conservation. Even though such programs might be of high quality, your study and career options are somewhat limited. Other colleges have larger, integrated programs that offer you more possibilities. For instance, a college might combine wildlife and fisheries conservation, forestry, and natural resource studies into a single program.

Other majors you might like:
Biology
Geography
Geology/earth science
Political science
Oceanography
Range science
Agronomy and crop science
Emergency management/homeland security
Natural resources management/policy
Ecology
Sustainable agriculture
Mining and mineral engineering

Questions to ask colleges:
Which field experiences or other opportunities for hands-on learning are offered to undergraduates? Where do the activities take place? Is there access to nearby nature preserves, field stations, or research centers?

How flexible is the program regarding electives—can students design a course of study that reflects their interests?

Is the program accredited? What certification requirements can be fulfilled through this program?

Career options and trends:
Wildlife biologist; fisheries manager; forester; park ranger; conservation law enforcement officer; natural resources manager; government agency employee (EPA, state conservation department, etc.); natural resources policy analyst; environmental lawyer; environmental educator.

The various professional disciplines in this field have different certification requirements. You should investigate the certification options and their importance in the area of natural resources you are most interested in. Also, many careers in the discipline require graduate study.

While the rate of job growth has slowed recently, job trends remain promising. The broad nature of this field provides a variety of career options in both government and industry. Most students with a bachelor's degree will find employment, but prospects are better if you have a master's degree or higher. Also, many employees in public natural resources management agencies are reaching retirement age. As with any occupation, there are times of greater or lesser demand, but highly motivated, well-trained graduates should be able to find employment.

Insider's viewpoint:
"Economics and policy are an integral part of natural resources management; these 'practical' concerns are necessary to be able to effectively deal with natural resources in today's society. If you're not cut out for the economics, look somewhere else for a major."

—Zeb, senior, University of Delaware

For more info:
Society of American Foresters (SAF)
5400 Grosvenor Lane
Bethesda, MD 20814-2198
(866) 897-8720
www.safnet.org

The Wildlife Society (TWS)
5410 Grosvenor Lane
Suite 200
Bethesda, MD 20814-2144
(301) 897-9770
www.wildlife.org

Wildlife and wilderness management

Also known as:
Conservation biology

What it's about:
Wildlife and wilderness management is an area of applied ecology that deals with the conservation of animal populations, ranging from those that are regularly hunted to those that are considered endangered, and the habitats in which these animals are found.

Is this for you?
You might like this major if you also like: outdoor activities such as hiking, camping, fishing, and hunting; science; Scouting; caring for animals; bird watching; natural history museums; zoos; travel; learning about the natural world.

Consider this major if you are good at: attention to detail; creativity; critical reading/thinking; leadership; organizing; quantitative analysis; teamwork *...or have...* initiative; physical stamina; verbal skills; writing skills.

Recommended high school prep:
English 4, math 3, lab science 4, social studies 3, and a foreign language 2–3. Any course in environmental studies is recommended, if available. Advanced biology would also be a plus, but is not required.

Did you know...
...that this is the best major at most universities for students who have a strong interest in field-oriented ecology? Biology programs typically cater to premed students and emphasize "skin-in" biology. Wildlife programs attract students interested in animal populations and emphasize "skin-out" biology.

Typical courses in this major:
Biology
Anatomy
Chemistry, general and organic
Statistics
Principles of wildlife management
Terrestrial wildlife ecology

Wetlands wildlife ecology
Field methods for wildlife management
Ornithology (study of birds)
Mammalogy
Entomology (study of insects)
Conservation biology
Genetics
Behavioral ecology
Systematic botany
Conservation law and policy

Concentrations:
Wildlife biology; wildlife conservation; habitat management; wetlands conservation.

What the study of this major is like:
Wildlife and wilderness management programs began as game management programs in the 1950s. Back then, people thought game species (mostly birds and mammals) were the only wildlife that needed to be managed. But human population growth inevitably affects animal populations by loss or change of habitat, reduction of food supply, presence of pollutants, and other human-related factors. In recent years, more and more rare and endangered species have been added to the list of wildlife in need of active management.

Wildlife professionals have come to realize that many species that are neither hunted nor endangered are also in need of our attention. Examples include declining populations of amphibians, birds of prey, and neotropical migrant birds; they could all become endangered if they do not receive immediate assistance. As a result of changes in attitudes toward the natural world, many wildlife and wilderness programs study a much broader array of species, and teach the skills needed to protect them, than those traditionally covered in game management programs.

As a wildlife major, you study both resource management and biology. Most of your courses are in biology, but you must also take chemistry, mathematics (through elementary calculus), and statistics. Anatomy and vertebrate zoology courses, such as ornithology and mammalogy, are important, too. Because wildlife biologists must be able to identify plants, at least one plant taxonomy course is generally required. Most other courses in a wildlife and wilderness management program are field-oriented and deal with ecology.

You will probably have to take several lab courses each semester in order to graduate in four years. Most lab courses (beyond introductory biology and chemistry) are strongly field oriented. Wildlife and wilderness management deals with animals living in natural environments; you must therefore be prepared to work with animal populations and their habitats. In the field, you gain experience in identifying birds and mammals, estimating their populations, and analyzing their habitats—you acquire firsthand knowledge of how and where the animals that you study in the classroom live. At many colleges, summer courses give you an opportunity to work full-time on field projects.

If you are comparing wildlife and wilderness management programs, look carefully at the courses offered to see whether programs you are considering favor traditional game management, or whether their courses reflect a broader, more modern conservation-biology focus.

Other majors you might like:
Forestry
Zoology
Botany
Entomology
Range science
Veterinary technology
Animal sciences
Biology
Natural sciences
Land use planning
Wildlife biology
Ecology

Questions to ask colleges:
Is the wildlife program a full major, or just a concentration within another major, such as zoology or forestry?

Does the school offer (or require) a broad array of natural resources management courses beyond those in the wildlife major?

What opportunities are there to do course-related field experience or to become involved in graduate student or faculty research? Are there good field sites near the campus? Is there a study-abroad program in this major?

Do the courses required for the major satisfy The Wildlife Society's standards for certification?

Career options and trends:
Wildlife biologist; research biologist; environmental educator; environmental consultant; university professor; park or field naturalist; conservation biologist; wildlife manager.

The job outlook continues to be very competitive. Students hoping to enter this field should complete at least a four-year Bachelor's of Science degree. Field experience gained through internships and temporary jobs remains an important way to obtain a permanent job. A graduate program leading to a Master's of Science degree can enhance your marketability for full-time employment and for advancement in the field.

Insider's viewpoint:
"A challenge of the major is low pay. It's also a really competitive field. There are a lot of people wanting to go into it."

—Chad, Junior, Oregon State University

For more info:
The Wildlife Society (TWS)
5410 Grosvenor Lane
Suite 200
Bethesda, MD 20814-2144
(301) 897-9770
www.wildlife.org

Parks and recreation

If you choose to study parks and recreation, you will become something of an expert in leisure, and that may mean you'll get teased a bit.

"Students in this major should expect some 'razzing' regarding their chosen major," admits Professor Lowell Caneday of Oklahoma State University.

But you may end up laughing all the way to the bank, because several mega-trends suggest that working at playing will be a hot job market in the future. Employment in recreation, parks, and leisure services is expected to increase over the long term. One reason is that when economies rebound there is pent up demand for recreational activities. Also, folks are living longer, more active lives. Students seem to get it, because recreation and sports majors have been among the fastest growing over the last ten years.

Hmmm, let's see... A popular group of majors. A growing market segment. A college career devoted to studying what people do for fun. Sounds like a slam dunk. But these majors aren't just a walk in the park or a day at the beach. College is college, and you will have to buckle down.

The foundations for academic preparation in recreation, park, and leisure studies include behavioral sciences: human growth and development, normal and abnormal psychology, cultural and environmental sociology, learning and leadership theory, motivation and consumer behavior.

People in this field run programs and supervise and administer activities in many settings: state and national parks, campus recreational programs, hospitals, long-term-care facilities, youth service agencies, military recreational facilities, forest recreation, commercial settings, church outings, corporate and employee recreational destinations, resorts and cruise ships, and camps.

Graduate students dive into topics like leisure services management and therapeutic recreation, or follow business tracks in commercial recreation and tourism management.

Fans know that sports management is also big. Even if you can't swish a trey, you can become a pro at sports marketing, sports and the law, sports finance and business, college sports, events management, and labor relations.

Sports management "is concerned with the operation of many types of sports organizations, ranging from professional teams and leagues to national and international amateur sports organizations, federations, conferences, and associations," says Professor Stephen W. Jefferson, University of Massachusetts Amherst. Sports management is linked to professions including broadcasting, community relations, finance and accounting, law, licensing, and merchandising.

A park-like campus

Start your college search by looking at divisions and schools of education, physical education, and recreation; health and human services; arts and sciences; forestry and natural resources; and yes, business. Where the college stands in its approach to these majors may depend on where it sits.

"Since these programs may be found in a wide variety of academic units or divisions on college campuses, differences between programs can be expected depending upon the 'academic home,'" says Caneday. "Programs housed in education or human services divisions focus on human behavior, whereas programs offered by forestry or natural resources divisions emphasize the natural environment. Programs in business divisions will likely stress management, economics, finance, and business practices."

Compare schools by considering whether the program plays an important role in the college's family of offerings or is just an add-on to a department devoted to other majors. Does the college have diverse courses such as program design in leisure services; natural resource recreation; sport marketing, management, and law?

Is the program accredited? If so, it has passed an external review by the likes of the National Recreation and Park Association (www.nrpa.org) or other recognized body. Parks and recreation programs that are accredited must teach conceptual foundations, professional practices and service delivery, programming strategies, assessment, planning, evaluation, management, and legislative and legal issues. Accredited programs also offer field experience. There's more than one type of accreditation, so ask which kind the college has.

In addition to accreditation, you will need to be certified for some jobs in therapeutic recreation, so ask what the pass rate is for recent grads on their national certification examinations. (See, these majors aren't so easy after all.)

Other questions: What is the placement rate of graduates, and where are they finding jobs? What research are faculty members doing, and are undergraduates helping? Will regular faculty members teach your classes or will graduate assistants? You want the veterans, not the rookies.

In sports management programs particularly, find out if the college has a good network of graduates that gives you a chance to rub elbows with professionals, do networking, and find internships. An internship might be a tryout for a great job.

"A major in recreation, park, and leisure studies provides the foundation to work in a career focusing on improving the quality of life for all," Caneday observes.

That would certainly make the teasing worthwhile.

Parks, recreation, and leisure studies

Also known as:
Leisure sciences

What it's about:
This major focuses on the environments, behaviors, and experiences of people during recreation. You examine people's motivations for choosing a pastime, investigate the effects of their behaviors, and develop skills to manage a variety of recreation and leisure services, enterprises, and organizations.

Is this for you?
You might like this major if you also like: working with different types and ages of people; voluntary service programs such as Scouting, 4-H, YM/YWCA; sports; games that require physical and social interaction; leading or organizing group activities.

Consider this major if you are good at: active listening; caring/nurturing; counseling; creativity; leadership; organizing; persuading/influencing ...*or have...* initiative; verbal skills; writing skills.

Recommended high school prep:
English 4, math 3, lab science 3, social studies 3, and a foreign language 2–3. If possible, also take courses in writing, computer applications, communications (speech, drama, or debate), psychology, and sociology.

Did you know...
...that jobs related to parks, recreation, and leisure are among the fastest-growing areas of employment according to the United States Department of Labor? In addition, a career in this field is identified as one of the top ten most satisfying jobs among working people surveyed.

Typical courses in this major:
Introduction to parks, recreation, and leisure
History of leisure
Philosophy of leisure
Recreation for special populations
Recreation leadership
Program and event planning
Area and facility design
Computer applications in leisure services
Evaluation of leisure services
Administration of leisure services
Legal issues in leisure services
Marketing recreation enterprises
Outdoor recreation
Commercial recreation

Concentrations:
Leisure services management; therapeutic recreation; natural resources recreation; tourism; program management; commercial recreation.

What the study of this major is like:
"Leisure" is actually a complex, multifaceted concept that differs from person to person. As a major in parks, recreation, and leisure studies, you encounter many different aspects and applications, from the operation of community leisure services to the provision of therapeutic recreation. Your studies are generally built upon behavioral science courses, such as human growth and development, normal and abnormal psychology, cultural and environmental sociology, learning and leadership theory, and motivation and consumer behavior.

Professors may employ a variety of teaching techniques and learning styles. Most classes feature lectures supported by appropriate technology, questioning, and group interaction; in many classes, you'll do laboratory work, or applied experiences, in which you organize, deliver, and evaluate leisure services for specific populations. In fact, all accredited programs in the major require one or more fieldwork activities, either as part of your regular courses, as internships for credit, or as employment or voluntary service.

Parks, recreation, and leisure studies has been identified as a "discovery" major, meaning most students learn about it only after arriving at college; so you may find second- or third-year students beginning the major with you. The two biggest challenges of the major are, first, the combination of theory, applied learning, and service delivery experience that is necessary to develop a complete perspective; and second, time management. Don't be surprised by how demanding this major can be.

Programs in parks, recreation, and leisure studies may be found in a variety of academic divisions. Therefore, differences between programs may depend upon a program's academic home. Programs housed in education or human services divisions focus more on human behavior, whereas programs offered by forestry or natural resources divisions emphasize the natural environment. Programs in business divisions will likely stress management, economics, finance, and business practices.

Besides fieldwork, the accreditation standards require all students to learn conceptual foundations; professional and service delivery practices; programming and assessment strategies; planning; and evaluation, management, legislative, and legal issues. Concentrations can prepare you for service in therapeutic recreation, park and recreation management, not-for-profit management, military recreation, correctional leisure services, natural resources recreation, sports management, tourism management, and other specialties.

Other majors you might like:
Landscape architecture
Physical education
Tourism/travel management
Recreational therapy
Sports communications
Hospitality administration and management
Gerontology
Forestry
Athletic training
Sports and fitness administration
Exercise sciences
Family/community services

Questions to ask colleges:
Is the program accredited by The National Recreation and Park Association (NRPA)? If you are interested in a specific concentration, be sure to ask if that aspect of the program is also accredited.

Where do students complete their internships? What additional field experience is expected or required of students? What is the "pass rate" for recent graduates on the national certification exams?

Career options and trends:
Activities director (sports, aquatics, outdoor pursuits, etc.); program supervisor; department administrator; facilities manager; park ranger; certified therapeutic recreation specialist.

Majors find jobs in campus recreation, hospitals, long-term-care facilities, YM/YWCAs and other youth service agencies, commercial outfitters, corporate recreation services, resorts and cruise ships, camps, and similar areas.

Most public park and recreation agencies will expect you to have the certified park and recreation professional (CPRP) credential offered by the NRPA. Numerous skill-based certifications, in such areas as first aid, aquatic facility management, challenge-course programming, and outdoor/environmental education, may also be required.

Long-term trends that are fueling employment growth include a growing population; longer and more energetic retirement lives; expanding leisure opportunities through technology; and increased expectations of populations that have been underserved in the past. These trends are likely to continue well into this century.

For more info:
National Recreation and Park Association (NRPA)
22377 Belmont Ridge Rd.
Ashburn, VA 20148
(800) 626 6772
www.nrpa.org

Sport and fitness administration

What it's about:
The sports and fitness administration major prepares you to apply the principles of business, coaching, and physical education to the management of athletic programs, sports teams, fitness facilities and health clubs, and sport recreation.

Is this for you?
You might like this major if you also like: mathematical and logical puzzles; playing sports; managing fantasy league sports teams; attending sports events; interacting with athletes; tracking sports statistics.

Consider this major if you are good at: attention to detail; coaching; critical reading/thinking; leadership; math; teamwork ...*or have...* initiative; patience; verbal skills; writing skills.

Recommended high school prep:
English 4 (including a writing course), math 4 (including precalculus), lab science 3, social studies 3, and a foreign language 2–3. If possible, take an economics course and any business courses that are offered.

Did you know...
...that successfully managing athletes, sports teams, or sports facilities involves a lot of math, logic, and other business skills?

Typical courses in this major:
History of sports
Sociology of sports
Kinesiology (exercise science)
Human anatomy and physiology
Sports and fitness marketing
Sports communications
Sports finance
Sports law
Athletic program management
Fitness program management
Labor relations and professional sports
Facilities management
Media relations
Economics of sports
Community relations
Principles of coaching

Concentrations:
In college: professional sports; sports communication; sports broadcasting; fitness management; recreation and tourism; sports marketing; sports finance; sport agency; facilities and event management.

If you go on to grad school: social-historical foundations of modern sports; sports economics; sports organizational behavior and development; sports management policy; labor relations.

What the study of this major is like:
Sports are fun and exciting, but sports are also a business. Whatever aspect of sports and fitness administration you pursue, you will most likely need a solid business foundation. In most sports and fitness administration programs, you take courses in accounting, finance, management, economics, and marketing (and perhaps computer science and precalculus) before you begin sports-specific business courses.

Within the major, you generally take three types of courses. The first type is devoted to theory—the sociology, psychology, physiology, and history of sports. The second explores the fundamentals of business and management. The third type involves the application of management theory to specific aspects of the sports and fitness industry, such as marketing and public relations; sports law; business operations for sports, health, and fitness organizations; the organization of and management of events; media relations; broadcasting; and college athletics.

Because sports management is relatively difficult to break into, most programs include a fieldwork component or encourage you to get hands-on experience and to make valuable connections through internships. The types of internships offered by programs vary. Some colleges have connections to sport industries or are located near sports or broadcasting facilities that are willing to hire interns. You may also be able to work in facilities on campus or at college-sponsored events.

In addition, programs at different colleges may have different emphases. Some programs focus on college athletics—how to create and nurture competitive teams, meet budgets, and maybe even coach. In programs that focus on spectator sports, you learn how to attract and satisfy fans. Programs that stress participant sports and fitness teach you how to find and manage individual athletes, or how to manage and operate health clubs and spas. Fitness-oriented programs will stress health related courses such as anatomy and physiology, nutrition, injury prevention, and physical training.

Other majors you might like:
Athletic training
Physical education
Public relations
Business administration and management
Marketing
Sports communications
Physical therapy
Entrepreneurial studies
Equestrian studies
Fishing and fisheries
Hospitality administration and management
Tourism/travel management

Questions to ask colleges:
Are there adequate facilities for students to do hands-on activities as part of their course work? For example, are there places where students participate in selling tickets, running events, or marketing? The answers should help you determine the quality of the program.

Is the sports and fitness program offered as its own major or is it simply a minor (sometimes offered through a business school) or a concentration in some other field? The answer to this question can give you an idea of the size of the program as well as the college's commitment to it.

Does the curriculum include an internship track that might lead to job opportunities in the field? If so, are a wide variety of internships available, including positions in such areas as facility management,

events management, sports agency, or sports marketing? Check to see that the internship placement opportunities match your own interests.

Does the program have a strong alumni network? Often a good alumni network results in better internship opportunities and job openings.

Career options and trends:
Athletic director; health club manager; sports broadcaster; promoter; sports agent or scout; fitness program coordinator; general manager.

Sports managers are concerned with the operation of many types of organizations: professional teams and leagues, college athletic departments and conference offices, and national and international amateur sports organizations. Sports and fitness administration graduates also serve the sport industry through club and facilities management, marketing and event promotion, and sports clothing and equipment sales and distribution.

Job prospects are generally excellent—the sports and fitness industry is strong and growing. There are minor fluctuations from year to year and small ups and downs in salaries for entry-level jobs, but even in tighter markets, sports fitness and administration majors who have initiative are in demand.

For more info:
North American Society for Sport Management (NASSM)
NASSM Business Office,
135 Winterwood Dr.
Butler, PA 16001
(724) 482-6277
www.nassm.com

American Alliance for Health, Physical Education, Recreation and Dance (AAHPERD)
1900 Association Drive
Reston, VA 20191-1598
(800) 213-7193
www.aahperd.org

Physical sciences

If someone asked you why the sky is blue, would you tell them about wavelengths? If so, you know something about the laws of nature, and that's what the physical sciences are all about. Areas of study in this group include aeronautics and aviation science, astronomy, astrophysics, atmospheric science, chemistry, geology (earth science), oceanography, and physics. The most popular major is chemistry, where students earn more than half of all bachelor's degrees in the physical sciences.

"Chemistry is the entry point for many careers in science. Almost every interesting question has chemistry at its base," says Professor James N. Spencer, Franklin and Marshall College. "As we learn about life processes, drug action, synthetic fuels, and behavior, the more evident it is that chemical processes are vitally important to understanding."

Physics is another top major and a foundation for many of these studies. It covers the principles of mechanics (forces, energy, and the basic laws of motion), electricity and magnetism, quantum mechanics, and thermodynamics (the theory of heat).

"There are no limits on what physics can do for us, but there are serious challenges in what we can do with physics," says Professor Bahram Roughani, who teaches applied physics at Kettering University. "That is why preparing the next generation of physicists is crucial for society."

The physical sciences are exciting and exacting. How deep is the ocean? What will tomorrow's weather be? When did the world begin? Better get out your calculator to answer physical science questions.

"You are usually required to complete an introduction to probability and statistics course, and mathematics through first-year calculus," says Ronald E. Johnson, professor of oceanography at Old Dominion University. "You then apply this knowledge at increasingly complex levels."

The climate is the same in atmospheric science. "Most students don't realize that meteorology is an applied physical science that is mathematically intensive and challenging. It involves developing sophisticated quantitative and conceptual skills. Mathematics is heavily used," says Professor James P. Koermer, Plymouth State College.

"Astronomy is a quantitative physical science, and upper-level astronomy courses usually require substantial preparation in physics and mathematics," adds Professor Richard G. French of Wellesley College. "I love being able to reach into the toolkit of mathematics and physics to help untangle the mysterious objects that we see."

Make a quantum leap

You've worked hard in high school and studied all the math offered. Soon you'll be ready for the next level: choosing a college with a great physical sciences program. Look for these majors in colleges of arts and sciences or engineering, and schools or divisions of science. For aeronautics, look for schools of aviation or transportation.

Here are a few things to consider: Find out if you need to come in with stellar math skills or if the college will help you catch up. Ask if your major is in the physical sciences department or has its own department. The setup may affect the course sequence and which courses you can take. "A wide range of courses offered on a reasonable time schedule is a good indication of a quality program," Johnson says.

Every college is different, just as every student is different. Some departments put more emphasis on lab work than others. Ask if introductory courses have a lab component. Some colleges require undergrads to do a research project. Ask if you'll have the chance to do research with faculty members or if you'll work independently. See what recent projects students have done.

Try to get an idea of the college's approach. Is the program more about applying the science or learning it in an academic sense? "Some colleges may emphasize work in observational astronomy more than theoretical astrophysics, some may do the reverse. A good, balanced program is best," suggests Professor Neta A. Bahcall, Princeton University. "Evaluate the quality of the program—the faculty, facilities, teaching and research programs, as well as the mentorship available."

As for the faculty, how many professors have advanced degrees and will those professors be your teachers (or will your instructors be grad students)? Have a look at the faculty members' publications to see what they're researching. Find out if you'll be studying hot new majors like nanotechnology or environmental aspects of the physical sciences.

Also ask about the quality of the laboratories, computers, and other equipment. How much access will you have to the best stuff, like the most powerful telescope on or near campus? Will you go on expeditions like coastal field exercises in oceanography?

What are former students doing? Are graduates successful at landing jobs in government and industry? Jobs in the physical sciences include scientist, researcher, teacher or professor, policymaker, writer, data analyst, software developer, pilot, astronaut, broadcaster, and medical doctor. Be sure to explore your graduate school options for advanced sciences. (See the majors in this section for examples of graduate studies.)

Aeronautics and aviation science

Also known as:
Air transportation
Airline/commercial pilot

What it's about:
The aviation science major prepares you for a career as a flight crew member on commercial aircraft, a corporate pilot, or other type of pilot. In your training to become an aviation professional, you will be encouraged to develop your mathematical and problem-solving skills. Emphasis is placed on crew resource management, safety, and the principles involved in aircraft operations.

Is this for you?
You might like this major if you also like: flying; travel; mathematical and logical puzzles; working with machinery; interacting with people; looking up at every airplane that flies over.

Consider this major if you are good at: attention to detail; leadership; math; memorizing; spacial thinking/analysis; teamwork *...or have...* manual dexterity; mental stamina; verbal skills.

Recommended high school prep:
English 4, math 4 (including precalculus), lab science 3 (including a physics course that covers electricity and magnetism), social studies 3, and a foreign language 2–3. It is not necessary to have flight experience.

Did you know...
...that this major covers a variety of subjects? Math and physics are obviously important, but your course work will also help you acquire problem-solving and communication skills, as well as good judgment.

...that an increasing number of men and women enter professional flying careers directly out of college, without military training?

Typical courses in this major:
Aeronautics
Flight instruction
Meteorology
Aerodynamics
Aircraft performance
Aircraft engines
High speed, long range navigation
Aircraft systems and components
Flight physiology
Crew resource management
Jet transport systems
Flight safety
Flight technique analysis
Turbojet techniques and crew procedure
Electronic navigation and flight control systems
International flight operations

Concentrations:
In college: airline pilot; corporate pilot; law enforcement aviation; agricultural aviation; military pilot (ROTC).

If you go on to grad school: aviation education technology; aviation management; aviation/aerospace operations; safety systems; human factors in aviation systems; space studies.

What the study of this major is like:
As an aviation science major, you combine flight training and academic studies, preparing for a career as a professional flight crew member on a jet transport aircraft, a corporate pilot, or a military pilot. Generally, you spend your first two years learning basic physics, mathematics, and communications skills, as well as fundamental aeronautics. You study how aircraft are designed and how they work, including the function of flight systems and controls and of navigation systems. You also study the procedures and government regulations for flight crew operations, radio communications, air safety, air traffic, and navigation.

In your third and fourth years, you take advanced training courses and study high-level aeronautical science. With the aid of both aircraft trainers and simulator trainers, you practice flying, navigating, and operating aircraft. These exercises help you sharpen your abilities to react quickly and effectively, by analyzing situations and solving problems. As in all flight-related courses, the paramount emphasis is on safety.

In addition to flight training, some programs offer courses in the human factors of aviation, which may include cockpit resource management, aviation psychology, and aviation accident investigation and analysis. In conjunction with courses in business, economics, communications, and management, you are prepared for a variety of careers in the aviation industry besides flying. A few colleges (the University of North Dakota is one) offer training in unmanned aircraft systems operations, or drone piloting, for an emerging industry with increasing commercial applications.

Depending on the strength of the program, by the time you graduate you may be qualified to take commercial and airline crew examinations given by the Federal Aviation Administration, or you may have already earned FAA certification as an instrument-rated commercial pilot.

Other majors you might like:
Aviation management
Aeronautical/aerospace engineering
Atmospheric science
Physics
Transportation management
Geography
Air traffic control
Aircraft powerplant technology
Avionics maintenance/technology
Military technologies

Questions to ask colleges:
Are faculty members experienced in the aviation industry? Professionally experienced instructors can do more than teach you about aircraft and how to fly them; they can also give you valuable insights into the aviation industry.

Which FAA certifications (private pilot, multiengine, commercial, and others) and ratings do students qualify for at the completion of their training? How much of the costs of obtaining the certifications are covered by tuition?

How many and which types of aircraft and simulators are available for student flight training? You will need sufficient access to appropriate, well-maintained aircraft and adequate simulator time.

Is the program accredited by the Aviation Accreditation Board International (AABI)?

Career options and trends:
Passenger airline pilot*; corporate pilot*; military pilot*; aircraft dispatcher; flight instructor; natural resources pilot; firefighting pilot; law enforcement pilot; aerial applicator.

All pilots who are paid to transport passengers or cargo must have a commercial pilot's license with an instrument rating issued by the FAA, which requires a minimum of 250 hours of flight experience. Requirements for the airlines are much higher. You must have an airline transport pilot's license (minimum of 1,500 hours); obtain night, instrument, and multiengine ratings; and pass FAA written and flight examinations. Depending on the airline, you may have to be certified for specific types of aircraft and pass psychological and aptitude tests.

Jobs in the airline industry are closely tied to the economy. During times of recession, as well as decreased air travel for other reasons, airlines will be forced to lay off flight crews, normally for a few months only.

Competition for jobs is expected to be strong, even with a projected growth in passenger travel and the approaching retirement age of a considerable number of pilots. Globally however, there is an acute and growing need for airline pilots, especially in Asia. A recent report by Boeing forecasts that nearly half a million new pilots will be needed to fly all the new aircraft entering the world fleet over the next 20 years. Domestically, the fastest growth should occur among regional commuter airlines, although at lower pay scales.

More pilots with civilian rather than military training are entering the airline profession; but military pilots continue to have a competitive advantage because they usually have more flight experience in sophisticated equipment.

Insider's viewpoint:
"Aviation allows one to meet individuals from many cultures, and get paid to have a god's-eye view of humanity below."

—Professor David Esser, Embry-Riddle Aeronautical University

For more info:

Aviation Accreditation Board International (AABI)
3410 Skyway Drive
Auburn, AL 36830-6444
(334) 844-2431
www.aabi.aero

Federal Aviation Administration (FAA)
800 Independence Ave., S.W.
Washington, DC 20591
(866) 835-5322
www.faa.gov

Women in Aviation, International (WAI)
Morningstar Airport
3647 State Route 503 South
West Alexandria, OH 45381
(937) 839-4647
www.wai.org

Applied physics

Also known as:
Engineering physics

What it's about:
Applied physics combines pure physics with math, science, and engineering principles, and applies them to practical ends. It is especially geared toward advanced and emerging technologies such as nanotechnology, medical and advanced imaging, and renewable energies.

Is this for you?
You might like this major if you also like: learning how things work; working in teams; learning about new technologies; relating theoretical concepts to practical uses; participating in science fairs and competitions or summer science camps.

Consider this major if you are good at: thinking creatively; math; quantitative analysis; spatial thinking/analysis; attention to detail; research ...*or have...*initiative; curiosity; verbal skills; writing skills.

Recommended high school prep:
English 4, math 4 (including precalculus or calculus), lab science 4 (including physics and chemistry), social studies 3, and a foreign language 3. Take as many additional math and science courses as you can.

Did you know...
...that applied physicists usually don't design anything in particular? That's for the engineers. Rather, applied physicists use physics concepts or conduct research to develop new technologies or solve an engineering problem.

Typical courses in this major:
Calculus and analytic geometry
Classical mechanics
Quantum mechanics
Electricity and magnetism
Thermodynamics
Physics of waves
Optics

Acoustics
Materials science
Nanotechnology
Applied nuclear physics
Fiber optics
Optoelectronics
Solid state physics
Computer modeling
Statistical mechanics

Concentrations:
In college: acoustics; optics; nanotechnology; biophysics; computational physics; space science; environmental science; microelectronics.

If you go on to grad school: accelerator physics; biomedical and health physics; laser physics; microfluids; plasma physics; quantum information science.

What the study of this major is like:
Besides its "practical" emphasis, the principal way that this major differs from the traditional physics major is the greater breadth and flexibility that it offers. Introductory and upper-level courses integrate other related disciplines such as engineering, computer science, chemistry and biology, and you have a much greater choice of electives and concentrations.

For example, courses in applied optics may combine knowledge of fiber optics, lasers, and LEDs with electrical devices, controls, and communication systems in order to explore ways to increase data transfer rates or Internet bandwidth. Or, courses in applied materials could combine the physics of electronic, magnetic, and optical materials with the engineering behind materials processing to examine possible applications of nanotechnology.

Courses are often taught in a combination of approaches. The basic courses may be either a traditional lecture and lab or a combined lecture/lab setting. More advanced courses include group projects, independent research work, and a senior thesis

449

project. (More rigorous programs may require a high-level senior research thesis that makes an "original contribution" to the field.)

Ideally, course work is combined with extended work co-op or internships that provide hands-on experience, enabling you to see the connection between physics concepts and their application in real-world cases.

Among colleges there are varying requirements for an applied physics degree, ranging from two terms of elective lab courses added to a traditional physics program, to a more rigorous four-year plan. In the later case there may be a required sequence (concentration) of courses in a specific field of applied physics such as acoustics, optics, medical physics, and the like; plus a sequence of technical courses (minor) in a field outside physics such as engineering; plus a co-op experience or summer internship; plus a thesis.

As you consider this degree, be aware that a high level of preparation in high school mathematics is necessary to grasp the advanced physics concepts you will be facing. You should expect to engage in teamwork with other students in group projects, as well as individual problem solving and independent research. This is a challenging degree that requires a passion for learning, discipline, and good time management skills.

Other majors you might like:
Applied mathematics
Biophysics
Biomedical engineering
Architectural engineering
Environmental engineering
Nuclear engineering
Industrial design
Aeronautics and aviation science
Aeronautical/aerospace engineering
Radiologic technology/medical imaging
Robotics
Entrepreneurial studies

Questions to ask colleges:
How does your applied physics major differ from traditional physics or engineering majors?

Is there a co-op or internship requirement? If so, is there placement assistance?

Are there a thesis requirement for this degree?

What facilities and laboratories are available for each area of emphasis in applied physics?

Career options and trends:
Optical engineer*; medical physicist; researcher*; acoustics engineer*; materials scientist*; laser technologist.

The applied physics major will open the door to almost any technical industry, but most opportunities will require a master's degree. A bachelor's degree may qualify you for entry-level positions related to engineering, computer science, environmental science, and some nonscience fields, such as sales. There is also a strong demand for high school physics teachers, but most states require new teachers to obtain a master's degree within a certain time.

The Bureau of Labor Statistics projects favorable prospects through 2022 in applied research, development, and related technologies, particularly for physicists with good oral and written communication skills and some knowledge in areas outside of physics, such as economics, information technology, or business management.

The fastest job growth will be in the biomedical, environmental, alternative energy, and similar advanced and emerging technologies.

For more info:
American Institute of Physics (AIP)
One Physics Ellipse
College Park, MD 20740-3845
301-209-3100
www.aip.org

American Physical Society (APS)
One Physics Ellipse
College Park, MD 20740-3844
(301) 209-3200
www.aps.org

Astronomy

What it's about:

Astronomy majors study the universe beyond our atmosphere, beginning with the underlying physical principles. You observe and investigate the planets, stars, and galaxies, as you learn methods of inquiry such as optical astronomy, radio astronomy, and theoretical astronomy.

Is this for you?

You might like this major if you also like: observing the changing patterns in the sky—the constellations, phases of the moon, and eclipses; news about space exploration and technology; science museums; computers; taking things apart and putting them back together to see how they work.

Consider this major if you are good at: attention to detail; creativity; critical reading/thinking; math; quantitative analysis; research; spacial thinking/analysis; teamwork *...or have...* initiative; patience.

Recommended high school prep:

English 4, math 4 (including precalculus or calculus), lab science 4 (including physics), social studies 3, and a foreign language 2–3. If possible, take an introduction to computer science course and a writing course. Also, take as many advanced science courses as you can.

Did you know...

...that astronomers spend only a small part of their time looking through telescopes? In fact, astronomers spend most of their time analyzing data with computers. Most people think that astronomy is about stargazing, but it is actually a quantitative science with plenty of math and physics.

Typical courses in this major:

Stars, galaxies, and cosmology
Planetary astronomy
Observational astronomical techniques
Planetary geology
Archaeoastronomy and the history of astronomy
Computer science
Multiwavelength astronomy
Calculus
Quantum physics
Planetary physics
Galactic astronomy
Extragalactic astronomy and cosmology
Stellar structure and evolution
Astrophysical techniques
Observational radio astronomy
Observational optical astronomy

Concentrations:

In college: observational astronomy; planetary science; extragalactic astronomy and cosmology; multiwavelength astronomy.

If you go on to grad school: radio astronomy; interstellar processes; planetary physics; stars and stellar structure; dynamical astronomy; galactic structure; astronomical instrumentation.

What the study of this major is like:

Students of astronomy examine the key components of the universe, such as the stars and planets, and the physical and mathematical laws that govern them. In cosmology, you analyze current theories about the origins and future of the universe; planetary astronomy describes the surfaces and makeup of the planets and moons in the solar system. Usually, the solar system and stars, galaxies, and cosmology are covered in two separate courses. Most likely, you'll attend weekly laboratory sessions in which you study such topics as the constellations and the motions of the sky, the properties of gravity and of light, and the operation of telescopes.

Once you complete the survey courses, the pace quickens. If you are serious about majoring in astronomy, you should plan your program of study to ensure that you take the required upper-level courses in physics and mathematics. Typically, these courses are the equivalent of a major in physics and a minor in math.

Most astronomy departments offer at least one course in astrophysics; as the theoretical side of astronomy, it explores the formation and evolution of stars, galaxies, and the universe itself. Many students find this investigation to be challenging, because it requires fluency in the language of math and physics. To learn why a star shines, for example, you need a basic understanding of mechanics, electricity and magnetism, thermodynamics and statistical mechanics, quantum mechanics, special relativity, and nuclear physics.

Most astronomy departments offer upper-level courses in observation through telescopes. You may have opportunities to carry out independent projects, typically using a digital (CCD) camera and requiring computer analysis of the observations. Even on research projects, you can often get by with relatively small telescopes. For a taste of professional astronomy, you may be able to do research, during the summer, at national observatories, or at some universities and colleges.

Departments with a strong physics orientation might emphasize astrophysics rather than observational techniques; those with strong connections to a research observatory might stress the development of instrumentation and hands-on astronomy. At some colleges, planetary astronomy is offered in coordination with the departments of geology and/or atmospheric science. Some departments offer two tracks in the astronomy program: one leads to broad, general knowledge of the field; the other, which includes intensive work in physics and mathematics, prepares you for graduate study.

Other majors you might like:
Astrophysics
Planetary sciences
Atmospheric sciences
Computer science
Geology/earth science
Physics
Aeronautical/aerospace engineering
Mathematics
Aeronautics and aviation science

Questions to ask colleges:
What observing facilities are available on or near campus? Can undergraduates use the largest telescope? Is there a digital camera on the telescope? Are there computers that can be used to analyze the observations?

What opportunities are available for undergraduates to participate in research during the academic year or over the summer? Are there opportunities for independent study? What are some recent projects by astronomy majors? Is there an astronomy club?

Career options and trends:
Most astronomers working in the field do research at universities, observatories, or laboratories, or teach at the high school or college level. Research jobs depend primarily upon federal funding, so job prospects are impacted by federal budget constraints. A small number work in planetariums and science museums. An advanced degree is required.

The major in astronomy provides excellent preparation for careers in fields other than the physical sciences. Astronomy majors have become engineers, neurosurgeons, trial lawyers, insurance executives, and business leaders.

Insider's viewpoint:
"There's a lot of acronyms, special terminology for things. There's a lot of data: when people give talks they list names of stars, not "Rigel" or the sun, but they'll give the names and numbers. It takes a few years of experience to comprehend those."

—David, junior, University of Texas at Austin

For more info:
American Astronomical Society (AAS)
2000 Florida Ave., N.W.
Suite 400
Washington, DC 20009-1231
(202) 328-2010
www.aas.org

American Association of Variable Star Observers
49 Bay State Rd.
Cambridge, MA 02138
(617) 354-0484
www.aavso.org

Astrophysics

What it's about:

Astrophysics, which focuses on the theoretical side of astronomy, presents the basic physical laws of the formation, evolution, and behavior of stars, galaxies, and the universe itself.

Is this for you?

You might like this major if you also like: using a telescope; math; computers; science fiction; abstract thinking; logical solutions; working through complex problems.

Consider this major if you are good at: attention to detail; creativity; critical reading/thinking; math; quantitative analysis; research; spacial thinking/analysis ...*or have...* imagination; initiative.

Recommended high school prep:

English 4, math 4 (including precalculus or calculus), lab science 4 (earth science, biology, chemistry, and physics), social studies 3, and a foreign language 2–3. Take as much advanced math and science as you can. Courses in language arts and computer skills are also important.

Did you know...

...the difference between astrophysics and astronomy? Some people in the field say there isn't any, because all astronomers use physics to understand their findings. Basically, astronomy places greater emphasis on observing, measuring, and gathering data about celestial bodies and phenomena, while astrophysics concentrates on the physical processes of outer space and the origin and future of the universe.

Typical courses in this major:

Principles of astrophysics
Waves and particles
Quantum mechanics
Differential equations
Stars and star formation
Topics in modern astronomy
Galactic astronomy
Extragalactic astronomy
Cosmology
The early universe
Plasma astrophysics
The interstellar medium
High-energy astrophysics
General relativity

Concentrations:

Theoretical astrophysics; observational astronomy; cosmology; high-energy astrophysics.

What the study of this major is like:

Astrophysics is a rigorous major, with plenty of physics and mathematics (much like the physics major itself), especially in your first two years. You typically take courses in upper-level astronomy, astrophysics, physics, and math; you also do independent research projects in observational or theoretical astrophysics. Your course work generally includes topics such as stars and stellar evolution, galaxies and extragalactic astronomy, cosmology, relativity, and the physics of space plasma.

You should be prepared to spend time in an observational astronomy lab and perhaps to research and write a senior thesis. Most programs place a great deal of emphasis on both independent and collaborative research. Independent projects can cover any research topic in the field, from planets to the Big Bang. You use computers for all projects, including data analyses, investigation through telescopes, and theoretical modeling of the universe. If you are interested in the solar system, you should probably take additional geology courses.

Some colleges do not distinguish between astrophysics and astronomy; others design the astrophysics major primarily as a stepping-stone to graduate study in the field and offer astronomy as a less rigorous science major for liberal arts students. If you see yourself working with equations more than with telescopes to unlock the secrets of the universe, then a strong astrophysics program might be for you.

Other majors you might like:
Physics
Aeronautical/aerospace engineering
Astronomy
Planetary sciences
Geology/earth science
Geophysics//seismology
Nuclear engineering
Mathematics
Computer science
Aeronautical/aerospace engineering technology
Philosophy

Questions to ask colleges:
What opportunities are there for undergrads to work individually with faculty members on research projects?

Such opportunities are desirable for any science major, but they are particularly important for astrophysics majors because research is fundamental to the field.

Is the department of astronomy and astrophysics separate from the physics department?

Are the physics courses that are needed to fulfill requirements offered on a regular basis?

How much time do undergraduates get at either on-campus or off-campus observatories?

Career options and trends:
Professor*; researcher*; science teacher; software developer.

Most jobs are in basic research and development, and in college-level teaching; a doctoral degree is the usual educational requirement for these positions. A bachelor's or master's degree is sufficient for some jobs in applied research and development and in teaching at the high school level. A degree in astrophysics also prepares you for a wide variety of technical careers in industry, especially the computer science, space, and aeronautical fields.

Insider's viewpoint:
"It's very demanding, very time-consuming. The physics and math are really hard. It's a lot of late nights, problem sets, and labs. But I think it's worth it; it's so interesting. I don't want to go to college and not be challenged."

—Allison, sophomore, Harvard University

For more info:
American Astronomical Society (AAS)
2000 Florida Ave., N.W., Suite 400
Washington, DC 20009
(202) 328-2010
www.aas.org

Atmospheric science

Also known as:
Meteorology

What it's about:
In the atmospheric science major, you gain a broad understanding of the Earth's atmosphere, including its composition, structure, processes, and weather systems. Most programs are highly interdisciplinary and rely heavily on math, physics, and chemistry to develop the underlying theories and principles governing atmospheric behavior.

Is this for you?
You might like this major if you also like: the outdoors; computers; aviation; sailing; scientific inquiry and analysis; the Weather Channel; dealing with changing situations.

Consider this major if you are good at: attention to detail; critical reading/thinking; math; organizing; quantitative analysis; spacial thinking/analysis; teamwork *...or have...* a strong work ethic; initiative; patience.

Recommended high school prep:
English 4, math 4, lab science 4 (earth science, biology, chemistry, and physics), social studies 3, and a foreign language 2–3. If it is available, calculus is recommended, as are courses in communications, environmental science, and computer applications.

Did you know...
...that this major is not only about weather maps and TV forecasting? It is an applied physical science that requires you to develop sophisticated skills in math and in abstract thinking. Atmospheric science is essential in such fields as air pollution control, agriculture, air and sea transportation, defense, and the study of trends in the earth's climate, including global warming, droughts, or ozone depletion.

Typical courses in this major:
Climatology
Atmospheric thermodynamics
Observations and instrumentation
Weather communications
Weather analysis and forecasting
Atmospheric dynamics
Air pollution
Mesoscale meteorology
Micrometeorology
Tropical meteorology
Radar meteorology
Remote sensing systems
Stormwater hydrology
Atmospheric boundary layer
Biosphere and carbon cycle

Concentrations:
In college: broadcast meteorology; climatology; mesoscale meteorology; synoptic meteorology; air quality and pollution.

If you go on to grad school: atmospheric physics and dynamics; atmospheric modeling; air chemistry; climate change; cloud physics; tropical meteorology; paleoclimatology; remote sensing; satellite meteorology.

What the study of this major is like:
The major in atmospheric science builds on a core of mathematics, physics, and chemistry. (In fact, you might be required to take enough math courses to earn a math minor.) Your first two years generally include math every semester, a two-semester sequence in chemistry, and a two-semester sequence in physics. In some colleges, you take descriptive, introductory-level meteorology courses during your first few semesters. Other programs may hold off on meteorology until you complete the required math and science courses. In your third and fourth years, you apply math, physics, and chemistry to gain a scientific understanding of how the atmosphere works. Most weather analysis and forecasting courses are offered at this level. Many programs also offer internships, practicums, and research opportunities.

Although some meteorology courses are primarily in a lecture format, most of them usually have associated laboratories. As with other science and engineering majors, you can expect to spend more time in classes than students in nonscience disciplines, because of longer laboratory courses. Nonscience majors may spend 15 hours per week in class; science and/or engineering majors probably spend closer to 20 hours.

At first, many students are challenged by the math and chemistry requirements, especially if their backgrounds are weak in these areas. Perhaps the biggest hurdle to clear, though, is calculus-based physics, which is the most time-consuming course many students have taken. A solid understanding of physics takes patience and commitment—you should expect to do a great deal of work in this area. But once these potential stumbling blocks have been passed, most students can complete a meteorology program if they remain focused and continue to work hard.

A few colleges emphasize a particular area of atmospheric science, such as weather analysis and forecasting, theoretical meteorology, physical meteorology, or climatology. If you are interested in becoming a weather forecaster, choose a college that emphasizes weather analysis and instrumentation. If you might like to become a broadcast meteorologist for radio or TV, look for programs that will help you develop strong communication skills, with courses in speech, journalism, and related areas.

Other majors you might like:
Chemistry
Geology/earth science
Aeronautics and aviation science
Oceanography
Geography
Agronomy and crop science
Instrumentation technology
Environmental science
Aeronautical/aerospace engineering
Radio and television

Questions to ask colleges:
Does the program meet the minimum guidelines established by the American Meteorological Society? Do graduates possess the minimum requirements needed for entry-level forecasters with the National Weather Service?

Does the program have reliable access to real-time weather data? Does the program support weather visualization tools to access these data? If you are interested in broadcasting, you should also ask if the program has access to studio facilities.

Does the program have any student organizations, such as a student chapter of the American Meteorological Society or the National Weather Association?

Career options and trends:
Operational meteorologist*; certified consulting meteorologist (CCM); broadcast meteorologist*; researcher*; forensic meteorologist.

To be a CCM, you must be certified by the American Meteorological Society (AMS), which requires at least a B.S. degree, experience, a passing grade on AMS exams, and professional references.

Most atmospheric scientists work as weather forecasters, known professionally as operational meteorologists. As long as you are willing to relocate and be flexible, entry-level jobs in forecasting are generally available. A master's degree will improve your job prospects and chances for advancement; it is usually required for positions involving research and development.

Opportunities in broadcasting are rare and highly competitive. The federal government is the largest employer of atmospheric scientists, mostly to staff National Weather Service stations throughout the country. However government hiring overall is expected to decline.

This situation should be offset by increased opportunities in private industry, spurred by continuing improvements in weather forecasting. Demand is projected to grow for consulting firms that can give weather-sensitive industries more detailed and closely targeted information than the National Weather Service.

Insider's viewpoint:
"It's frustrating being a meteorology major and someone asking you 'What's the weather going to be like tomorrow?' and you have to say 'I don't know.' You have to pay your dues, but in the end you come out with a real good understanding of the atmosphere."

—Haddie, senior, University of Wisconsin–Madison

For more info:

American Meteorological Society (AMS)
45 Beacon St.
Boston, MA 02108-3693
(617) 227-2425
www.ametsoc.org

National Weather Association (NWA)
228 West Millbrook Rd.
Raleigh, NC 27609-4304
(919) 845-1546
www.nwas.org

Chemistry

What it's about:
Majors in chemistry study the composition, structure, and properties of matter, as well as the reactions that transform one form of matter into another. Because it is an experimental science, students learn to design and perform the investigations that will lead to a better understanding of the physical world.

Is this for you?
You might like this major if you also like: solving problems; lab experiments; taking things apart; working independently; using math; questioning why things are the way they are.

Consider this major if you are good at: attention to detail; critical reading/thinking; math; quantitative analysis; research; teamwork *...or have...* curiosity; initiative; perserverance; writing skills.

Recommended high school prep:
English 4, math 4 (including precalculus or calculus), lab science 4 (earth science, biology, chemistry and physics), social studies 3, and a foreign language 2–3. If it is available, also take a computer science course.

Did you know...
...that the chemistry major provides preparation for many careers, even outside science? The thorough grounding in math, critical thinking, and computers that the major offers can qualify you for work in areas you might not have expected, such as banking, business, and law.

Typical courses in this major:
General chemistry
Inorganic chemistry
Organic chemistry
Physical chemistry
Analytical chemistry
Biochemistry
Thermodynamics
Quantitative analysis
Instrumental analysis
Environmental chemistry
Spectroscopy and crystallography
Biochemistry
Polymer and materials chemistry

Concentrations:
In college: analytical chemistry; inorganic chemistry; organic chemistry; physical chemistry.

If you go on to grad school: physical and theoretical chemistry; polymer chemistry; materials chemistry; forensic chemistry; medicinal chemistry; environmental chemistry.

What the study of this major is like:
Chemists provide the expertise to create products you encounter every day, such as medicines, fabrics, and synthetic materials. As a major, for example, you learn ways to control the chemical reactions that produce ceramics, semiconductors, insulators, polymers with unusual properties, and molecules essential for life. In your examination of atoms bonding to form molecules, you observe how the properties of substances depend on which atoms are combined, and how.

Chemistry has traditionally been divided into four areas: organic, inorganic, physical, and analytical. Organic chemistry is the study of carbon compounds, whereas inorganic chemistry is the study of all other elements. Physical chemists investigate the structure and properties of matter, and analytical chemists devise the procedures used in identifying and measuring the individual components of complex mixtures.

Chemistry majors usually take a core curriculum that includes courses in all four areas before they concentrate in one area. Your concentration may require you to take advanced courses that explore the methods for synthesizing natural products; that introduce you to the instruments and techniques used in analyzing unknown compounds; or that show you how to use lasers to study a molecular collision. You will also be expected to take courses in math, physics, and, probably, biology.

All chemistry majors spend a great deal of time performing experiments in the laboratory. The lab experience teaches you to observe the world around you, to draw conclusions from these observations, and to challenge currently accepted beliefs. A typical week's classes consist of about three 50-minute classroom sessions and a two- to four-hour lab. Advanced students take independent study courses, in which they work with a professor on a research project. There is generally little time for electives. On top of lecture classes and lab work, you should expect to work on daily problem sets and put in considerable time studying and writing reports.

Some colleges award Bachelor of Arts degrees in chemistry; others award Bachelor of Science degrees; still others offer both. But regardless of which degree is offered, most chemistry programs emphasize critical-thinking and laboratory skills. The American Chemical Society specifies the course requirements that enable a bachelor's degree program to qualify graduates for ACS certification, which most employers look for.

Other majors you might like:
Atmospheric science
Environmental science
Clinical/medical laboratory technology
Soil science
Chemical engineering
Materials engineering
Biochemistry
Molecular biology
Chemical technology
Forensic science
Pharmacy
Chemistry teacher education

Questions to ask colleges:
Are research opportunities and equipment available for all students? Doing worthwhile research is especially important if you intend to go on to grad school.

What do most chemistry majors do after obtaining their degree—go to medical school or graduate school, or go into industry? If one area predominates, it may reflect a particular emphasis in the program.

Does the program qualify graduates for ACS certification?

Career options and trends:
Industrial or pharmaceutical research chemist*; physician, pharmacist, or other medical professional*; pharmaceutical sales representative; high school chemistry teacher*; chemical lab technician; food scientist; government inspector (for FDA or EPA); crime lab analyst or forensic chemist; occupational safety specialist; environmental consultant.

Graduates entering this field may find competition for jobs, particularly in the declining chemical manufacturing industry; job opportunities will be more plentiful in pharmaceutical and biotechnology firms. Research and testing firms will experience healthy growth as manufacturers outsource research and testing formerly done by in-house chemists. Another area of opportunity is environmental research and regulatory compliance. Chemists with a master's or doctorate degree will be in most demand, although those with a bachelor's degree should be able to find work as assistant research scientists in smaller firms.

Insider's viewpoint:
"I really enjoyed organic chemistry, despite the many horror stories I heard beforehand. There is a certain thought process that goes along with orgo and once that process is understood, it becomes logical. Understanding why reactions go the way they do simplifies many problems."

—Christina, junior, University of California: Davis

For more info:
American Chemical Society (ACS)
1155 16th St., N.W.
Washington, DC 20036
(800) 227-5558
www.acs.org

Geology/earth science

What it's about:

Geology/earth science is the study of the earth and the forces that act on it. Topics include the history and formation of planet Earth; the behavior of the solids, liquids, and gases that it is composed of; and the interaction between the biosphere—the living things that call the earth their home—and the planet's inorganic, or nonliving, substances.

Is this for you?

You might like this major if you also like: the outdoors; history; archaeology; gems; dinosaurs; rock climbing; hiking and camping; collecting; environmental issues; a broad range of scientific inquiry, from the unimaginably big to the very small.

Consider this major if you are good at: attention to detail; creativity; critical reading/thinking; math; quantitative analysis; spacial thinking/analysis; teamwork ...*or have...* initiative; patience; physical stamina; verbal skills; writing skills.

Recommended high school prep:

English 4, math 4 (including precalculus), lab science 4 (earth science, biology, chemistry, and physics), social studies 3, and a foreign language 2–3. Courses in computer science or applications are recommended, if available; and you will benefit if you can obtain a basic understanding of geographic information systems, either in school or on your own.

Did you know...

...that geology isn't just about rocks—it is a scientific discipline closely linked to chemistry, biology, and physics? It is not a place to avoid these other sciences, but rather a place to apply them. The field is becoming increasingly quantitative, so math skills are a definite advantage.

Typical courses in this major:

Physical geology
Historical geology
Paleontology
Structural geology
Mineralogy
Petrology
Surficial geology
Geophysics
Geochemistry
Hydrogeology
Field geology
Stratigraphy and sedimentation
Geologic hazards
Tectonics
Geographical information systems
Earth resources

Concentrations:

In college: geochemistry; geophysics; environmental geology.

If you go on to grad school: paleontology; petrology; petroleum geology; mineralogy; hydrology; tectonics; paleomagnetics; structural geology and tectonics; geological engineering; geochronology.

What the study of this major is like:

Geology/earth science students first take introductory courses in physical and/or historical geology that teach you basics: rock, mineral, and fossil identification; landform evolution; plate tectonics; and the geological time scale. Topical courses, such as environmental geology, planetary geology, or oceanography, may also serve as introductions to the major. Most introductory courses and upper-level courses have weekly three- to four-hour laboratories or field trips of various lengths. To learn other essential geology/earth science tools, you take yearlong courses in chemistry, physics, mathematics, and biology.

Upper-level courses are often arranged in sequence: you take courses in a specific order so that you learn the skills and knowledge needed to continue. For instance, a semester or year of mineralogy provides the analytic skills (such as the use of the petrographic microscope) essential for later courses in petrology. Paleontology, sedimentation, and stratigraphy often form a sequence covering the origin of sedimentary rocks and the fossil organisms they may contain. Geomorphology and glacial geology courses focus on processes that shape the earth's surface. Courses in resources—energy, minerals, and water—examine their origin, as well as the exploration, recovery, and use of these essential commodities.

A unique aspect of geology/earth science is its emphasis on the history of the earth—a recurring theme of many courses in the major. Another trademark is its reliance on fieldwork. Because the field is to a geologist what the library is to a historian, most geology/earth science courses include fieldwork as well as lab work. Some undergraduate departments require a semester-long or summer course in field geology, and most graduate departments require such a course for admission.

Many summer courses, which average four to five weeks and are based at permanent facilities in the western states, offer intensive training in geological mapping and in preparing reports. After completing the third year and a field course, the best-qualified majors may be able to find summer jobs as geological field assistants or interns in industry or government.

Visualizing in three dimensions, and comprehending the large scale of many geological phenomena, can be challenging at first. And although geologists are typically not regimented in their activities, you cannot afford to be undisciplined. Because deadlines in geology/earth science courses are usually farther apart than in many other majors, you must figure out a long-term time management plan.

The main philosophical differences among programs are in applied rather than purely academic geological science. If you are interested in using your geological training to tackle concrete problems, you will probably be more comfortable in a department that focuses on hydrogeology, petroleum geology, environmental geology, and exploration seismology. Such departments have more of an engineering perspective, and may even have a geological engineer or civil engineer on staff. In more academically focused departments, faculty members include petrologists, mineralogists, paleontologists, and tectonists.

Other majors you might like:
Atmospheric science
Geography
Oceanography
Soil science
Surveying technology
Environmental science
Mining and mineral engineering
Planetary sciences
Geological engineering
Petroleum engineering
Landscape architecture
Science teacher education

Questions to ask colleges:
Are field trips and field instruction built into most, if not all, of the courses?

How many geology majors take chemistry, biology, physics, or math beyond the minimum requirements?

How accessible are facilities and instrumentation housed in other departments, like chemistry, for use by geology majors?

Do any of the faculty members have experience working as professional geologists outside the academic setting (e.g., industry)?

Career options and trends:
Earth science teacher*; engineering geologist; environmental hydrologist*; petroleum geologist; government agency staff geologist; researcher*.

A Ph.D. degree is required for most research positions in colleges and universities and in government.

Many graduates work in the energy industry, particularly in the exploration and production of oil and natural gas. The petroleum industry is a cyclical business, with employment rising and falling with the price of energy. But over the long term there will be opportunities in the energy sector, especially for those willing to work overseas. In other industries, the need to comply with environmental regulations and to responsibly manage land and water will create opportunities for environmental geoscientists, especially hydrologists and engineering geologists.

The Bureau of Labor Statistics projects employment to grow much faster than average in this field, with job openings exceeding the number of jobseekers through 2022.

Insider's viewpoint:
"You don't look at a rock as having a life, but it really does. It's splitting and moving and changing

constantly. The rocks tell us a story about what happened in the past and what we can expect to happen in the future."

—Mona, junior, University of California: Berkeley

For more info:
Geological Society of America (GSA)
P.O. Box 9140
Boulder, CO 80301-9140
(303) 357-1000
www.geosociety.org

Oceanography

What it's about:

Oceanography majors study the oceans—their origins; movement; and biological, chemical, geological, and physical components. As an interdisciplinary science, oceanography draws on the natural sciences to increase our understanding of the ocean environments of planet Earth.

Is this for you?

You might like this major if you also like: the coast and the sea; science and math; exploring the unknown; water sports such as boating, diving, surfing, sailing; travel; environmental issues; asking questions such as "how did that bottle get to our beach?"

Consider this major if you are good at: attention to detail; creativity; critical reading/thinking; math; quantitative analysis; research; teamwork ...*or have...* initiative; writing skills.

Recommended high school prep:

English 4, math 4 (including precalculus or calculus), lab science 4 (earth science, biology, chemistry, and physics), social studies 3, and a foreign language 2–3. Courses in writing, computer science, and environmental science are also recommended, if available.

Typical courses in this major:

Physical oceanography
Chemical oceanography
Geological oceanography
Biological oceanography
Waves and tides
Fluid mechanics
Meteorology
Marine ecology
Environmental physiology of marine animals
Sedimentology
Marine pollution
Barrier islands and coastal lagoons
Oceanic and atmospheric processes
Polar oceanography
Estuarine oceanography
Sampling techniques and field studies

Concentrations:

Biological oceanography; chemical oceanography; geological oceanography; physical oceanography; marine resource management.

What the study of this major is like:

Scientists know more about the surface of the moon than they do about the depths of the oceans. Oceanography is an interdisciplinary science that makes use of principles of biology, chemistry, geology, physics, geophysics, mathematics, botany, zoology, meteorology, and geography.

You begin the major by taking math, physics, biology, geology, and chemistry. Usually you must complete an introduction to probability and statistics course, and mathematics through first-year calculus. (In some programs, an earth science education track requires only precalculus.) As you study oceanography at increasingly complex levels, you explore the methods and instruments of research and do fieldwork, collecting data to analyze and interpret.

In your third year, you will probably choose to concentrate in biological, chemical, geological, or physical oceanography. In biological oceanography, you study the distribution, abundance, and production of plants, animals, and nutrients in the oceanic ecosystem; the emphasis is on the investigation of bacteria, phytoplankton, zooplankton, and other organisms living at the bottom of the sea.

Chemical oceanography examines the complex chemistry, distribution, and cycling of dissolved substances, nutrients, and gases in seawater, especially the mechanisms that control these elements and compounds. Geological oceanography focuses on marine sediments, examines the theory of ocean basin formation, and surveys shoreline formation. In physical oceanography, you observe and predict the seas' motion, from small tidal changes to the giant circular currents. Important areas of research include the distribution of physical properties (temperature, salinity, sea ice), and air-sea interaction, with its effect on climate.

In accompanying laboratories, you apply lecture and reading material in a practical setting. By your fourth year, you are ready to do solid fieldwork and to assist faculty members in their research. Most programs finish with a yearlong capstone field study course in ocean and earth science.

Some oceanography majors have trouble completing the math requirements. It helps if you focus on math in high school and in your first two years of college—especially if you are thinking of concentrating in physical oceanography. It is also important to complete your introductory science courses during your first two years. Because oceanography is an integrated field, most of your concentration courses will include material from biology, chemistry, geology, and physics. And since oceanography requires a lot of fieldwork, you should learn, early on, how to translate the theoretical material in textbooks to the practical activities in the lab. Another recommendation is to do volunteer work on faculty research projects, both in the lab and in the field. Many majors experience field exercises, aboard a research ship bound for distant seas—a highlight of their college career.

Other majors you might like:
Marine biology
Ocean engineering
Fishing and fisheries
Marine engineering/naval architecture
Water, wetlands, and marine management
Geology/earth science
Atmospheric science
Environmental science
Geography
Aquaculture
Marine science/Merchant Marine
Underwater diving

Questions to ask colleges:
What types of offshore or coastal field exercises are offered to undergraduates? Are research opportunities with faculty members also available?

Does the program emphasize a particular concentration within oceanography? Some colleges stress physical oceanography, others take a biological or environmental slant, and some integrate oceanography and atmospheric science. A wide range of courses offered on a reasonable schedule indicates a quality program.

Career options and trends:
Middle school or high school earth science teacher; government, faculty, or industry researcher; government agency staff oceanographer (U.S. Geological Survey, National Oceanographic and Atmospheric Administration, state environmental protection agencies); marine technician.

The largest employers of oceanographers, besides colleges and universities, are the federal and state governments, where job prospects are subject to budget constraints. Careers in private industry are also available, primarily in engineering, geology, geophysics, environmental quality, marine policy, and marine fisheries. More students are entering this field than in the past, so competition is increasing, especially for biological oceanographers. Most jobs require an advanced degree. There is strong demand, however, for qualified earth science teachers in middle and high schools.

Insider's viewpoint:
"I went on a research cruise with Scripps (Institution of Oceanography) with kids from across the country. We sailed to Samoa for the quarter, dredging the bottom of the ocean to pick up volcanic rocks in hope of dating these submarine volcanoes. I worked the night shift, and even though there were hardships, I found that it pushed me."

—Teresa, junior, University of California: Los Angeles

For more info:
The Oceanography Society
P. O. Box 1931
Rockville, MD 20849-1931
(301) 251-7708
www.tos.org

Physics

What it's about:

Physics is the study of the basic laws of nature, including mechanics, sound, electricity and magnetism, optics, heat, and quantum theory. You explore matter and systems, and the particles within them to see how they exchange energy and momentum with their surroundings, exert forces on one another, and move under the influences of these forces.

Is this for you?

You might like this major if you also like: math; computers; electronics; tinkering with things to see how they work; learning about the natural world; abstract thinking; logical solutions; solving puzzles.

Consider this major if you are good at: attention to detail; creativity; critical reading/thinking; math; organizing; quantitative analysis; spacial thinking/analysis ...*or have...* imagination; manual dexterity; patience.

Recommended high school prep:

English 4, math 4 (including precalculus or calculus), lab science 4, social studies 3, and a foreign language 2–3. Take as many advanced science courses as possible, but don't neglect language arts and social studies.

Did you know...

...that a lot of math is required in this major? Your math courses will probably include calculus, linear algebra, differential equations, complex variables, and statistics.

Typical courses in this major:

Modern physics
Classical mechanics
Electricity and magnetism
Thermodynamics
Statistical mechanics
Quantum mechanics
Computational physics
Advanced laboratory
Solid-state physics
Electronics
Nuclear physics
Wave motion
Particle physics
Optics
Acoustics

Concentrations:

In college: applied physics; biophysics; computational physics.

If you go on to grad school: atomic/molecular physics; elementary particle physics; nuclear physics; condensed matter; optics; plasma physics; solid-state physics; astrophysics.

What the study of this major is like:

Physics courses examine phenomena as different as the structure and evolution of the universe, on the one hand, and the fundamental particles from which all matter is made, on the other. As a major, you begin with courses that introduce you to the principles of physics: mechanics (forces, energy, and the laws of motion); electricity and magnetism (the emission of electromagnetic radiation by charged particles); quantum mechanics (the particle nature of electromagnetic waves, the wave nature of particles, energy levels, and the effect of the uncertainties of nature on particle behavior); and probably thermodynamics (the theory of heat).

These courses emphasize the logical, mathematical structure of the principles of nature, as well as important applications of these principles. For example, you learn about the nature of light, atomic structure, and the properties of solids, including the semiconductors that have revolutionized our world. As you advance in the major, the math becomes more complex, so strong computation skills are imperative.

Physics courses stress problem-solving skills. You will be assigned homework sets consisting of increasingly difficult problems. Most courses are taught in lecture format, but there will be several laboratory courses as well. Physics is an experimental science, and your course work will show the relation between experiments and the theories derived from them.

Because some of the advanced material is conceptually and mathematically challenging, physics majors often work together. Collaborating with others is one of the highlights of physics study. In the end, of course, you must be able to work on your own, on exams and certain assignments. As a physics major, your goal is to become an independent thinker, a problem solver, and a researcher.

The main challenge most physics majors face is the conceptual complexity of the subject. You will have to visualize abstract concepts, some of which may not immediately make sense. Although the task can be hard, understanding a difficult concept can give you great satisfaction. Another challenge you may encounter is to find solutions to complicated problems. Simply selecting a formula won't help; you must comprehend the principles at work and determine a strategy for unraveling the puzzle. Solutions often require lengthy mathematical computations.

Most physics departments have an undergraduate organization that encourages you to take part in the life of the department. In these departments, interaction between faculty members and students is generally high, often providing the opportunity to participate in independent research with faculty members.

Although most physics programs have similar curricula, the sequence of courses might differ—for example, some programs introduce the modern fields of physics (relativity, quantum theory) earlier on than in other programs. In many programs the introductory courses are taught with combined lectures and labs. But some programs place more emphasis on laboratory work than others do. There may also be variations among departments in the use of technology in instruction. And in some programs, you must complete a research project as part of your degree requirements.

Other majors you might like:
Architecture
Mathematics
Astrophysics
Philosophy
Computer science
Engineering physics
Civil engineering
Aeronautical/aerospace engineering
Nuclear engineering
Radiologic technology/medical imaging
Technical and business writing
Nuclear medical technology

Questions to ask colleges:
Are the physics courses listed in the course catalog offered on a regular basis? Often they are not, so you should find out which courses will actually be available to you in your third and fourth years.

What are the opportunities for undergraduate research? This is an important consideration if you intend to go on to grad school.

How accessible are the computers in the physics labs and outside of class?

Is there an active SPS (Society of Physics Students) chapter on campus?

Career options and trends:
Researcher*; engineer*; high school teacher; professor; laboratory technician; computer programmer*; financial analyst.

Certification in education is required for teaching in public high schools; a Ph.D. is essential for teaching in college.

Most physicists work in research and development, in industry, government, or academia. A Ph.D. is generally required for basic research, but with a master's degree, you can get an entry-level position in manufacturing and applied research and development.

Nanotechnology is becoming an important field. In this discipline, physicists, chemists, and engineers explore the properties and applications of materials of increasingly small size ("nano" means "one-billionth"). In fact, physics in general is growing more interdisciplinary, as it overlaps with chemistry, engineering, biology, and other fields.

Students who double-major in physics and engineering or business, or pursue these areas in grad school, have greater job options. But a bachelor's degree in physics can open doors in many fields that value analytical skills. There is a strong demand for high school physics teachers.

Insider's viewpoint:
"Being a woman in physics now is not as weird because you learn to adapt to the culture. I just went to the CERN laboratories in Switzerland, and out of the eight people who were invited, I was the only woman. You just get used to that."

—Sarah, senior, Columbia University

For more info:
American Institute of Physics (AIP)
One Physics Ellipse
College Park, MD 20740-3843
(301) 209-3100
www.aip.org

PhysLink.com
5318 East Second St., #530
Long Beach, CA 90803
www.physlink.com

Protective services

Working in the protective services is not exactly like what you see in the movies or on some TV crime dramas. The detective doesn't crack the case alone, and the true hero in a disaster may not be a first responder, but someone working behind the scenes. It may not be glamorous but the contributions of professionals in protective services are just as essential as the TV shows depict.

"Both crime prevention and justice delivery are important matters for society at large," says Professor Dennis R. Longmire, Sam Houston State University. "Being able to engage in studies related to these important issues is both fulfilling and exciting." And while the challenges presented to emergency management planners "are as varied as the types of disasters any community may face," notes Daniel J. Klenow, a professor at North Dakota State University, "they are also opportunities to create a safer and more resilient community."

Criminal justice professionals work in a wide variety of settings, in both industry and government. Most work for federal, state, or local government, but some private firms, such as security companies or correctional service providers, receive government contracts for certain types of work.

What types of jobs are we talking about here? Criminal justice majors go on to become police officers, security officers, probation officers, parole officers, and other law enforcement agents. Those who major in emergency management/homeland security can become disaster response coordinators, business continuity analysts, or FEMA program managers. Forensic science majors, who learn to analyze evidence, work as evidence technicians, fingerprint analysts, firearms experts, and as scientists like chemists, DNA or dental experts, anthropologists, pathologists, and psychiatrists. Of course, the fire service is another important branch of public safety. Professionals in those ranks include fire protection consultants; fire marshals or inspectors; environmental, health, and safety experts; and loss control personnel, who often work in the insurance business.

For better or worse, many jobs are available in occupations that protect people and property. "Crime is a 'growth industry,'" Longmire says. "Any of the careers associated with it continue to experience increased demands for new and highly qualified workers."

Law enforcement and corrections agencies are regularly looking for police recruits and officers. If you want to be among the Finest, as the police are rightly known, or the Bravest—the firefighters—it helps to go to college. In many communities, you need a college degree to become a police officer.

"The field of criminal justice continues to become increasingly professionalized. What this means is that positions that were once filled by workers who only held high school degrees now require college-level workers who can exercise increasingly complex and demanding discretion," Longmire explains.

Several national trends contribute to the growing importance of these fields. Mandatory minimum prison sentences have swelled the prison population and created the need for workers in corrections agencies and industries. Other laws have increased the use of DNA and fingerprints, so hiring is also taking place in forensic sciences. The needs of the various agencies merged into the Department of Homeland Security keep the job market strong.

"There will always be demand for scientists in crime labs, police, and security agencies," predicts Professor Frank Vozzo of Russell Sage College.

First and second degrees

These majors reside in many types of colleges, and in divisions and departments within colleges. Look for criminal justice, public administration, social sciences, natural sciences, applied arts and sciences, applied arts and technology, behavioral science, anthropology, human services, engineering, and engineering technologies.

You'll notice that protective services majors are multidisciplinary—they require you to study many subjects to understand complex topics like criminal behavior or the way the justice system works. For instance, the criminal justice major mixes sociology, psychology, and public administration, and colleges strike different balances among those fields. Majors in emergency management/homeland security may focus more on natural disasters than on terrorism. Forensics combines science and the law with varying emphasis on each. The fire and safety programs may differ in whether they stress practical skills or theoretical studies.

Read up on the colleges of interest and their programs and ask some questions about finding work with an associate, bachelor's, or graduate (master's, doctorate, or law) degree. Look for schools that offer internship programs in agencies for your field. Ask about the professional and academic credentials of the faculty members. You can learn a lot from a former cop as an instructor, but you really need professors who are also highly educated and keep current with the latest trends and techniques in law enforcement and forensic sciences. Like the faculty, the college labs need to be up-to-date. Also find out if the program is accredited and if you will need professional certification.

Graduate tracks in criminal justice include criminological theory, private and public security, and criminal justice administration or management. Graduates in forensics specialize in administration, analytical chemistry, forensic toxicology (poisons), molecular biology, genetics or serology (blood) as they relate to forensics. In the fire service, grads may become professionals in industrial hygiene or in computer fire modeling.

Some of the newest majors in these fields include victim studies, international security studies, terrorism and security analysis, bioinformatics (clinical databases), and fire and emergency management.

"The field of criminal justice is filled with exciting and important issues that are constantly changing," says Longmire.

That's not just on TV, but in real life.

Criminal justice and law enforcement

What it's about:

The major in criminal justice and law enforcement administration focuses on how society responds to criminal behavior. Areas of study include policing, the courts, and the sentencing of both adult and juvenile violators. Don't confuse this major with criminology, which is primarily concerned with the sociopathic and psychological bases of criminal behavior.

Is this for you?

You might like this major if you also like: working with people; helping others; membership in religious or community groups; "service" activities; public speaking; debating; mystery games; crime stories.

Consider this major if you are good at: attention to detail; counseling; leadership; organizing; persuading/influencing; problem solving; teamwork *...or have...* composure during crises; initiative; patience; verbal skills; writing skills.

Recommended high school prep:

English 4, math 3, lab science 3, social studies 3, and a foreign language 2–3. If they are available, take courses in psychology and philosophy.

Did you know...

...that criminal justice professionals are primarily involved in the delivery of human services to their communities? Many courses you will take draw from psychology, social work, and public-service-related disciplines.

...that criminal justice professionals work in both the public and the private sectors? While most of them work for government agencies (federal, state, and local), some are employed by private security agencies, as well as by private correctional agencies that contract with the government. Criminal justice positions are also available in all branches of the military.

Typical courses in this major:

Introduction to the criminal justice system
Legal aspects of law enforcement
Criminology
Courts and criminal procedure
Fundamentals of criminal law
Human behavior
Comparative criminal justice systems
Law and society
White-collar crime
Research methods
Criminal profiles
Forensic sciences
Correctional systems and practices
Police systems and practices
Criminal investigation
Professionalism and ethics

Concentrations:

In college: law enforcement; forensic studies; corrections.

If you go on to grad school: criminological theory; private and public security; criminal justice administration; criminal justice management; research methods and statistics.

What the study of this major is like:

Course work in criminal justice includes the behavioral sciences, especially sociology, psychology, and social work. You examine theories about the causes of crime, as well as ways to organize public agencies for both crime prevention and crime control. Courses in research methods and criminal statistics are often required.

In most programs, you can concentrate in either law enforcement (policing) or corrections (including probation, prisons, and parole), but you must still take courses on a wide variety of subjects related to the administration of justice. All programs emphasize effective communication skills: the ability to speak well is essential, because there is extensive public contact in the criminal justice profession; you must know how to write well because written reports are an integral part of the work.

Since the discipline of criminal justice is actually a blend of sociology, psychology, and public administration, colleges may vary in the emphasis they place on these areas. Programs that developed out of sociology tend to stress theories of crime causation that focus on the problems that plague society. In contrast, programs that emerged from psychology tend to see crime primarily in terms of individual background, motivation, and behavior. And degree programs that evolved out of public administration are usually more interested in issues of law enforcement than in crime causation itself.

All programs require students to explore the constitutional and legal aspects of the administration of justice. However, some colleges place less emphasis on these courses than others. Those that do so tend to focus on the scientific study of crime causation and require students to take more courses in research methods and in statistics.

In general, courses involve classroom lectures, supplemented by out-of-class reading and other homework assignments. Many programs deliver some of their course work online, and some even offer complete degree programs through nontraditional, Web-based methods. Many programs will also allow you to accumulate academic credit through internships with criminal justice agencies, in which you work under the supervision of a professor as well as a criminal justice professional. Some programs provide the opportunity to travel to foreign countries to examine the cross-cultural and international issues facing criminal justice professionals around the world.

Other majors you might like:
Criminology
Corrections
Police science
Legal studies
Psychology
Security/loss prevention
Public administration
Forensic science
Human services
Juvenile corrections
Sociology
Security services management

Questions to ask colleges:
Does the program place students in internships with appropriate public or private agencies? Wide-rang-

ing experience in such agencies can help graduates seeking jobs in those agencies or similar organizations.

What are the academic and professional backgrounds of the faculty members? Some programs employ former law enforcement personnel who have had little or no academic training. Their teaching style often relies on the telling of "war stories." These instructors may be interesting, but they may not provide the most current and useful information in the field.

Career options and trends:
Police officer*; security officer; probation officer*; parole officer*; correctional counselor; federal law enforcement agent (FBI, Secret Service, etc.).

Special certification is usually required for positions involving "special-needs offenders," such as youthful, drug- and alcohol-addicted, and mentally challenged violators of the law. Often, your college course work can be counted as partial credit toward such certification.

The field of criminal justice has become increasingly professionalized—college degrees are required where high school diplomas would once have been enough. It is also becoming more globalized, as professionals from all over the world cooperate on significant issues and cases. Job applicants who are bilingual or multilingual, or who have military experience, have a competitive edge.

Employment opportunities in law enforcement are mostly determined by the level of government spending, so the number of job opportunities can vary from year to year. Layoffs are rare, but trained law enforcement officers who lose their jobs because of budget cuts usually find jobs quickly in other agencies.

Insider's viewpoint:
"My particular interest in the discipline is driven by the realization that issues associated with law enforcement and criminal justice are also associated with human rights and basic freedoms."

—Professor Dennis R. Longmire, Sam Houston State University

Emergency management/homeland security

Also known as:
Disaster management

What it's about:
This major studies natural as well as man-made catastrophes within a social, political, and environmental context. The interdisciplinary curriculum provides a broad overview of disaster preparedness, mitigation, response and recovery, and issues of homeland security.

Is this for you?
You might like this major if you also like: community service; working collaboratively; current affairs; learning about international issues. Students who are innovators, problem solvers, and who have leadership qualities would enjoy this major.

Consider this major if you are good at: organizing; critical reading/thinking; teamwork; attention to detail; persuading/influencing; caring/nurturing *...or have...* initiative; patience; verbal skills; writing skills.

Recommended high school prep:
English 4, math 3, lab science 3 (including chemistry), social studies 4 (including American government), and a foreign language 3–4. If available, courses in psychology, sociology, and computer applications are helpful.

Did you know...
...that this major is not about becoming a first responder? Rather, the focus is on managing disaster planning and recovery work at the organizational level, whether municipal, state, national, or international.

Typical courses in this major:
Principles of emergency management
American government
Organizational behavior
Introduction to homeland security
Disaster response and recovery
Emergency response preparedness and planning
Special populations in disasters
Sociology of disaster
Psychology of disaster
Meteorology
Chemical, biological, and radiological hazards
Geographic Information Systems (GIS)
Border and coastal security
Terrorism and anti-terrorism
Business continuity
Public policy issues in emergency management

Concentrations:
Generally, none in college; but if you go on to grad school: pandemic planning; disaster recovery; environmental hazard mitigation; homeland security management.

What the study of this major is like:
The term "emergency" has become the most common label for this major, but it can be misleading if you think it's mostly about the immediate response to a localized and unforeseen event, such as the attacks on 9/11. Some programs prefer the term "disaster management" as a better indicator that your studies will encompass events that significantly disrupt an entire social or ecological system, whether by surprise terror attack, devastating oil spill, viral outbreak, or natural disaster such as an earthquake or hurricane.

You won't be trained to be a hero—but rather as a planner and manager who can help enhance community preparedness, mitigate effects, and provide effective response and recovery efforts.

The typical teaching model involves a traditional emphasis on lectures, but your studies will be a blend of the theoretical and the practical. Many programs offer seminars that incorporate class interaction and student research. Courses that emphasize research methods and specific applications such as geographic information systems may have lab activities as well.

Since emergency management is an applied field, most programs will require some form of field experience or internship outside of class, which may be integrated into the academic year or experienced during the summer. Internship opportunities can include working with organizations (such as the local chapter of the Red Cross) and agencies involved with providing security or building community preparedness for floods, tornadoes, or public health crises.

How this major is taught at various colleges can vary significantly in terms of emphasis. Some programs focus on disaster management, government policy, and social topics related to natural and man-made disasters with little emphasis on terrorism. Others focus more directly on homeland security with specific attention to global and domestic terrorism and related events while still providing content on natural disasters. Programs that are more science oriented will focus on understanding and mitigating the effects of disasters and include courses such as meteorology, chemistry, geology, environmental science, computer modeling, and information systems.

In addition, this interdisciplinary major may be housed in a variety of academic departments which can influence its perspective, such as sociology, public policy and administration, public health, political science, or environmental studies.

Other majors you might like:
Urban, community, and regional planning
Emergency medical technology (EMT
paramedic)
Hazardous materials technology
Environmental studies
Natural resources management/policy
Criminal justice and law enforcement
Criminology
Computer forensics
Computer/systems security
Management information systems
International relations
Peace and conflict studies

Questions to ask colleges:
How long have you had an emergency management program?

What is the primary focus of the program – is it sociological, political, environmental? Natural disaster planning and recovery, or anti-terrorism?

What types of internship opportunities are available?

What types of organizations are employing your graduates? How successful are your graduates in the job market?

Has this program applied for accreditation from the Foundation of Higher Education for Disaster/Emergency Management and Homeland Security?

Career options and trends:
Emergency management planner, homeland security planner, disaster response coordinator, business continuity analyst/planner, geographic information systems specialist, city emergency manager, FEMA program manager.

This is a new and rapidly expanding field. Jobs are available at all levels of government, both locally and nationally; many non-governmental organizations and relief agencies need people trained in emergency management; and there is a wide-spread and growing need for trained disaster planners in the private business sector (particularly the insurance industry).

Jobs are increasingly going to candidates with specific education in emergency management. The addition of a minor (business, transportation logistics, sociology, communication, natural resource management, planning, political science, etc) to your plan of study can greatly enhance employment options.

For more info:
International Association of Emergency Managers (IAEM)
201 Park Washington Court
Falls Church, VA 22046
(703) 538-1795
www.iaem.com

Fire protection and safety technology

What it's about:
In this major, you learn to evaluate and reduce potential loss of property and life in the workplace and other settings. You explore three of the most likely threats to safety: fire, accidents, and exposure to hazardous materials.

Is this for you?
You might like this major if you also like: volunteer work; firefighting; change; working with people; helping others.

Consider this major if you are good at: attention to detail; creativity; critical reading/thinking; leadership; organizing; persuading/influencing; quantitative analysis ...*or have...* initiative; verbal skills.

Recommended high school prep:
English 4, math 4 (including precalculus or calculus), lab science 4 (including chemistry and physics), social studies 3, and a foreign language 2–3. Courses in computer applications and drafting are also recommended.

Did you know...
...that professionals in fire protection and safety technology are dedicated to protecting people in all types of employment from many kinds of hazards? The major is not limited to firefighting and fire service organizations.

...that there is a big demand for the services of loss control professionals? The opportunities for women and minorities are at an all-time high, and graduates are enjoying record placement rates of nearly 100 percent.

Typical courses in this major:
Fire safety and hazards recognition
Fire suppression and detection systems
Introduction to occupational safety techniques
Studies in loss control
Fire protection management
Design and analysis of sprinkler systems
Elements of industrial hygiene
Fire protection hydraulics and water supply
Industrial safety organization
Structural designs for fire and life safety
Human factors in accident prevention
Fire dynamics
Building electrical systems
Issues in local government and fire services
Disaster and fire defense planning
Hazardous materials management

Concentrations:
In college: fire protection systems; code compliance; fire dynamics and behavior; fire investigation; industrial safety; industrial hygiene.

If you go on to grad school: computer fire modeling.

What the study of this major is like:
Programs in fire protection and safety technology prepare you for a career in loss control. The profession is divided into three areas: loss from fire; loss from physical accidents; and loss from environmental exposure. As a major, you learn to predict threats to safety in the workplace and to take steps to prevent them—for example, by designing efficient evacuation routes; by identifying objects that could injure workers; and by controlling the use of toxic materials in factories.

The curriculum introduces you immediately to issues in fire protection and safety. Therefore, you can measure your interest in a fire protection and safety technology career early on in your studies. The program includes many courses in math and in the physical sciences. Two semesters of calculus are required, as well as two semesters of chemistry and one semester of physics. Computers are an essential tool in most courses. If you know that you want to pursue this major, you should try to take classes in high school that will prepare you for college-level math and science.

Some programs include plenty of hands-on work; you do numerous lab exercises to reinforce the facts and ideas that are taught in lectures. You might be expected to take at least two or three afternoon lab sessions each semester. Industry internships are frequently encouraged, because they provide valuable experience and let you apply, in a real-world setting, what you've learned.

A number of programs gear their curriculum toward careers in the fire service. The emphasis of these programs is on practical application—you put into use the techniques you've studied, but you may or may not learn the theories behind the techniques. Courses designed specifically for fire protection may not be easily transferred to more general programs. Therefore, you should be committed to a career in fire safety if you enroll in such a program.

Other majors you might like:
Architectural engineering
Industrial engineering
Fire services administration
Occupational safety/health technology
Firefighting/fire science
Security/loss prevention
Insurance
Civil engineering
Hazardous materials technology
Construction technology
Building inspection

Questions to ask colleges:
Is the program approved by an outside professional organization, such as the International Fire Service Accreditation Congress (IFSAC) or the Technology Accreditation Commission of the Accreditation Board for Engineering and Technology (ABET/TAC)? These organizations have set standards that can help you judge the quality of a program.

Does the college support internships and co-ops? Internships are especially valuable in the broad field of fire protection and safety.

Are there enough lab facilities available? Are the faculty members and students dedicated to safety? You may be able to get an indication of the program's commitment to safety by observing the college's own facilities.

Career options and trends:
Fire protection consultant*; environment, health, and safety engineer*; building code official/plans

examiner; loss control consultant (for insurance companies)*; industrial safety engineer; deputy fire marshal/inspector.

You can become certified as a certified fire protection specialist (CFPS), an associate safety professional (ASP), a certified safety professional (CSP), or an engineer-in-training/professional engineer (EIT/PE). You can also become state-licensed as a fire prevention officer.

Fire protection engineering activities are indirectly tied to the construction industry. Upturns in construction have a significant, positive impact on job opportunities. The effects of downturns are less dramatic; because of code requirements, structures must be maintained and retrofitted as necessary. Recent emphasis on homeland security is predicted to create substantial growth in the fire protection field.

The field of safety is more closely linked to manufacturing and industrial activities, which are subject to shifts in the global economy. Homeland security concerns are expected to increase activities in safety, security, and environmental monitoring.

Insider's viewpoint:
"Testing the response of materials and structures to the assault of fire is dramatic and interesting, and protecting firefighters and occupants from the effects of fire is challenging and rewarding."

—Professor Thomas J. Woodford, Oklahoma State University

For more info:
International Fire Service Accreditation Congress (IFSAC)
1700 West Tyler
Oklahoma State University
Stillwater, OK 74078-8075
(405) 744-8303
www.ifsac.org

Forensic science

What it's about:
Forensic science is an interdisciplinary major that applies knowledge of the natural sciences, the criminal justice system, and the law to the analysis and evaluation of evidence gathered from a crime or accident scene.

Is this for you?
You might like this major if you also like: science clubs; chemistry; computers; lab experiments; amateur sleuthing; detective stories and police shows; working with precision instruments.

Consider this major if you are good at: attention to detail; math; organizing; quantitative analysis; spacial thinking/analysis; teamwork *...or have...* manual dexterity; observational skills; patience; writing skills.

Recommended high school prep:
English 4, math 4 (including precalculus), lab science 4 (including biology, chemistry, and physics), social studies 3, and a foreign language 2–3.

Did you know...
...that forensic scientists, evidence technicians, crime scene investigators, and detectives are separate people who have taken separate career paths? TV shows can give the impression that one person does it all, from discovering trace evidence to cracking the case—but most forensic science takes place in the field or in the lab, as one part of an investigatory team process.

Typical courses in this major:
Introduction to criminal justice
Analytical chemistry
Human anatomy
Instrumental analysis
Genetics
Microbiology
Molecular biology
Criminal evidence and procedure
Criminalisitics
Crime scene investigation
Statistics
Care and preservation of evidence
Fire investigation
Toxicology
Forensic anthropology
Forensic entomology

Concentrations:
In college: toxicology; forensic anthropology; crime scene investigation; forensic chemistry; trace evidence; accident and fire investigation.

If you go on to grad school: criminalistics; forensic science administration; analytical chemistry; forensic molecular biology; forensic engineering; forensic entomology; forensic DNA/serology.

What the study of this major is like:
Although trace evidence may be tiny, it is often enough to establish the particulars of a crime and lead to its solution. The forensic science major teaches you how to use scientific analysis to tie pieces of evidence to particular sources. Because analytical techniques are constantly improving, forensic scientists can more easily protect the innocent and bring the guilty to justice. In fact, investigators can often crack cases that have gone unsolved for decades.

Your first two years in the Bachelor of Science program are typically like those of a chemistry major or a premed student. You take challenging courses in biology, general and inorganic chemistry, and physics, as well as college-level statistics and calculus. Since the chemistry, biology, and math courses have sequencing requirements, you must begin them in your first semester. You will also take introductory courses in criminal justice, the social sciences, and psychology.

In your third and fourth years, you enroll in specialized lab courses, taught by or in association with forensic scientists, where you apply the scientific principles and techniques from your earlier courses to forensics. These later courses, which sometimes include independent work (such as research projects or internships), provide you with professional skills and career information. In your final year, you usually participate in a field practicum and a capstone seminar project. Although the forensic science major prepares you for direct employment as a laboratory technician, you are generally encouraged to go on to graduate school for further specialization.

Most forensic science programs have developed from existing programs in criminal justice or the natural sciences. There is considerable variation as to which areas they cover in depth. The oldest and largest programs may offer a variety of concentrations, while newer and smaller programs generally focus on one or two of the following subdisciplines:

Forensic biology, which deals with the analysis of blood and other body fluids, physical wounds, and body positions; DNA analysis; forensic chemistry, which examines trace evidence such as hairs, fibers, paint, soil; forensic anthropology, which is concerned with skeletal remains; forensic entomology, which uses insect activity in decomposing bodies to determine place and time of death; forensic toxicology, which analyzes specimens of blood, urine, or tissue for drugs, alcohol, or poison. There are other specializations in such areas as computer crime, fingerprints, firearms and explosives, and footprint, tool, and tire impressions.

Two-year or certificate programs in forensic science prepare you for careers as crime scene or evidence technicians. Training may include the collection and preservation of evidence; crime scene photography; latent fingerprint processing; and/or composite drawing. Many of these positions require you to pass a certification exam given by the International Association for Identification (IAI). Not all jurisdictions use civilian technicians for these functions, so be sure to check the rules where you intend to work.

Other majors you might like:
Criminology
Psychology
Microbiology
Biochemistry
Anthropology
Criminal justice and law enforcement
Police science

Chemistry
Materials science
Computer forensics
Emergency medical technology (EMT paramedic)
Clinical/medical laboratory technology

Questions to ask colleges:
Are internships available in crime labs or related facilities?

What opportunities do undergraduates have for field research or other hands-on training?

Career options and trends:
Forensic lab technician*; crime scene investigator*; latent fingerprint analyst; forensic engineer; forensic chemist*; forensic DNA analyst*; law enforcement officer.

In some states, only uniformed law enforcement officers investigate crime scenes. Forensic pathologists, psychiatrists, and medical examiners are licensed physicians.

Demand for forensic science professionals is projected to increase because of new technologies in the field, the needs of homeland security, and legislation requiring DNA and fingerprint sampling from members of certain groups. Prospects are best for those who have a strong background in the basic sciences (especially chemistry) and who are willing to relocate.

Insider's viewpoint:
"Don't major in forensic science as an undergrad. Get a strong science background first. Make sure this is what you want to do. Nothing is worse than getting into a field after two or more years of higher learning and discovering it isn't your cup of tea."

—Elizabeth, M.S. candidate, John Jay College of Criminal Justice

For more info:
American Academy of Forensic Sciences (AAFS)
410 North 21st St.
Colorado Springs, CO 80904
(719) 636-1100
www.aafs.org

Public administration

What is public administration? Let's break it down. "Public" refers to the public sector, and that means government. "Administration" means the management of a program or an agency. So public administrators manage government programs, right? Well, that's true, but it's not the whole story. Public administration isn't just for your class treasurer. These majors also prepare students for work in non-profit organizations and for the private (business) sector. That's because more and more, the government is outsourcing—hiring outside companies to do government work.

Why does public administration have a whole chapter in this book? Because it is the largest category of civilian jobs in the federal government. And then there are the state, county, and local government employees, like those in public welfare agencies. But it's not the quantity, it's the quality of work that counts. Public administrators run the most critical services for the most vulnerable citizens.

"Public administration is a great field for those who want to make a difference in society," says Professor Danny Lee Balfour of Grand Valley State University.

What do public administrators do? In addition to providing direct service to individuals, they have management and supervisory responsibilities, in areas like human resources management, budgeting, and policy and planning. They might also do economic development, labor relations, and court administration—almost anything requiring organizational and time management skills and a concern for people.

In human services agencies, professionals and paraprofessionals help individuals and families become self-sufficient. Jobs include substance abuse counselors, probation officers, and mental health workers. Social work is another big part of public service, even bigger than you may think.

"Unfortunately, many students equate social work only with public assistance, and their vision of a social worker is that of a case worker," says Professor Irene Queiro-Tajalli, Indiana University-Purdue University Indianapolis. "Students need to realize the wide range of employment opportunities after graduation."

As you may know, many states and the federal government have had budget problems lately. In some cases, this has led to a reduction in the public workforce or to a hiring slowdown. On the plus side, the work that public administrators do is often essential and can't be cut because it helps people get the necessities of life. The job outlook for new graduates is buoyed by an expected wave of retirement of older government workers.

Know your goals

When you look for colleges, you'll find the public administration program in schools or divisions of social science, professional studies, health studies, anthropology, sociology, social work, and public affairs.

Some public administration programs are geared toward getting you ready to work at a specific level of government—local, state, or federal. If it's local government, for instance, you'll learn skills for community development and city management. It's good to know ahead of time what level of government you're interested in. It would also be great if you had a preference for direct service (one-to-one contact like social work) or management and supervisory work.

You may not be able to make all these decisions yet. But give some thought to what type of degree you're after, because you can pursue a public administration major (and later a career) at any degree level. If it's a certificate program, find out if your course work would be eligible for transfer credits toward a college degree later.

Think about style as well as substance: What is your learning style? You may want to get both theory (book learning) and practice (getting out there and doing it!). Also, find the class size and faculty-to-student ratio that works for you. Ask if you'll do an internship or community service project before graduation. If you're juggling many responsibilities, see if classes are offered in the day and in the evening. How about online?

For studies leading to social work, you want a program accredited by the Council on Social Work Education. Most accredited programs cover topics like human behavior and social policy, and there isn't a huge difference among colleges. However, the location of the college and the needs of its surrounding community may guide the way the college prepares students to help people.

Graduate studies in social work may be organized in several different ways: by who is served (individuals, families, communities); by fields of work, such as child welfare, aging, and mental health; or by particular social problems, such as poverty and homelessness. In other areas of public administration, specialties in graduate school include management and leadership, nonprofit administration, criminal justice, urban or regional affairs, and community health.

Find out more from the National Association of Schools of Public Affairs and Administration (www.naspaa.org), the American Society for Public Administration (www.aspanet.org), and the International City/County Management Association (www.icma.org).

Human services

What it's about:

The human service major prepares you to become an aide to a professional or to practice as a professional who helps individuals, families, or communities become self-sufficient. You learn about social service delivery systems and explore the reasons why many people are unable to obtain or hold on to the basic necessities of life.

Is this for you?

You might like this major if you also like: helping people from different backgrounds; improving people's lives; volunteering in your community; working both independently and in groups.

Consider this major if you are good at: caring/nurturing; counseling; creativity; critical reading/thinking; organizing; teamwork *...or have...* initiative; patience; social skills; verbal skills; writing skills.

Recommended high school prep:

English 4, math 3, lab science 3, social studies 3, and a foreign language 3–4. If possible, take courses in speech and computer literacy. Community volunteering experience is also helpful.

Did you know...

...that being able to speak a foreign language is particularly useful in the human services field? As immigration to the United States increases, social service professionals who can communicate with non-English-speaking populations are in great demand.

Typical courses in this major:

Group dynamics/process
Intake and referral
Introduction to counseling
Introduction to criminal justice
Local, state, and federal government
Multiculturalism
Social problems
Introduction to psychology
Ethics and the law
Introduction to sociology
Human services agencies and organizations
Organizational behavior
Human development
Legal issues in human services
Medical aspects of human services
Adult development

Concentrations:

In college: criminal justice; addiction studies (drug and alcohol); counseling; youth development; advocacy; human services management.

If you go on to grad school: organizing human services; human services management and leadership; community organization.

What the study of this major is like:

As a human services major, you study a range of topics. You will most likely examine the history of the human services delivery systems in the United States; counseling and service theories; and the various philosophical approaches to the human condition, team work, and social problems. Most courses are lecture based and often feature case studies, group work, games, and class discussion. Well-rounded programs provide you with the opportunity to participate in (and often require) internships, community service learning, or practicums. Strong bachelor's degree programs will also require course requirements outside the human services major.

Generally, the challenges you encounter involve managing your time, being organized, and working effectively in groups. As in any major, expect to spend a lot of time studying. But you may be asked to apply your newly learned skills and theories earlier in your academic career than your colleagues in other majors.

Because of the range of content and skills taught in human services, the major can be housed in various departments. You can also study human services at a variety of institutions that offer certification or degree options. Before you pick a program, you should think about the level of education you plan to attain. Courses in certificate programs might not be transferable if you later wish to earn a bachelor's degree. In addition, some programs focus on direct service (one-to-one contact) and others focus on human services management (supervisory skills). You should probably look for a program that offers a variety of courses, so that you can explore many tracks within the profession. You don't need to choose your area of specialization before you enter college.

Other majors you might like:
Criminal justice and law enforcement
Urban, community, and regional planning
Public policy analysis
Family/community services
Human development and family studies
Gerontology
Community organization/advocacy
Community health services
Health care administration
Substance abuse counseling
Anthropology
Behavioral sciences

Questions to ask colleges:
What are the different types of internship or community service learning experiences available? Is the program affiliated or in partnership with local organizations?

Career options and trends:
Residential counselor; drug/alcohol counselor; case manager; probation/parole officer; client advocate; child abuse worker; mental health worker; youth worker; rehabilitation case worker; social service worker.

Certification requirements for different careers vary from state to state. For example, some states require drug and alcohol counselors to have state certification in addition to a college degree. Most human services professions have a continuing education requirement.

The aging baby boomer population is creating a demand for human services workers and professionals skilled in working with older people. The restorative justice field (in which members of the community are brought into the criminal justice process,

such as sentencing and rehabilitation) is also expected to continue growing. In another trend, most states are funding drug treatment and counseling through departments of corrections, rather than the traditional human services areas. This development will further integrate the fields of human services and criminal justice.

For more info:
National Organization for Human Services (NOHS)
3760 Sixes Road, Ste. 126 # 262
Canton, GA 30114
(770) 924-8899
www.nationalhumanservices.org

Council for Standards in Human Service Education (CSHSE)
3337 Duke Street
Alexandria, VA 22314
www.cshse.org

Public administration

Also known as:
Public affairs

What it's about:
Public administration majors study the management of public and nonprofit organizations and the many aspects of public service and governance. Topics include political issues, group dynamics, public policy, health care delivery, economic development, human resources management, philanthropy, voluntarism, budgeting, public finance, information technologies, and neighborhood analysis.

Is this for you?
You might like this major if you also like: community service; student government; Boy or Girl Scouts; joining clubs or teams; environmental issues; organizing group activities.

Consider this major if you are good at: critical reading/thinking; leadership; organizing events; persuading/influencing; solving problems; teamwork *...or have...* initiative; patience; verbal skills; writing skills.

Recommended high school prep:
English 4, math 3, lab science 3, social studies 4 (including government and economics), and a foreign language 2–3. A business course is also recommended.

Typical courses in this major:
Introduction to public administration
Public budgeting and financial administration
Public human resources administration
Public policy and policy processes
Local politics and administration
Introduction to nonprofit management
Developing nonprofit resources
Volunteerism and the nonprofit sector
Public sector information technology
Grant writing
Organization theory
Community analysis

Economic development
Structure of state government
Public service ethics

Concentrations:
Public finance; economic development; community development; health administration; human resources; environmental policy; nonprofit administration; urban/regional affairs.

What the study of this major is like:
In this major you explore the ways that public administration professionals achieve managerial efficiency, program effectiveness, legal accountability, client-driven responsiveness, political representation, and organizational reform. You acquire practical skills, including analyzing agency budgets, supervising staff, designing Web pages and evaluation surveys, and writing grant proposals. You learn to recognize the moral, social, political, economic, and technical issues to consider as you design and lead programs in the public interest.

Upper-level courses deal with budgets, accounting, and financial management, as well as with specific executive and personal skills such as strategic planning, leadership, and ethical sensitivity. Majors are strongly encouraged to take a broad range of liberal arts courses, including English, history, communications, economics, political science, psychology, and sociology.

Courses frequently use case studies, simulations, and other activities to provide a sense of what real-world public administration is all about. Most programs require you do an internship, perhaps in Washington, D.C., or in a state capital, to gain experience in public or nonprofit agencies. At some institutions, cooperative programs allow you to alternate semesters (first studying in the classroom, then working in a government agency).

Programs at different colleges may vary in their organization, approach to public policy, or the level of government they emphasize. For example, some programs focus on local politics, economic and community development, and city management. Other programs prepare you for a career in state government or in the federal government. A few programs specialize in environmental policy, international development, regulatory policies, social policy, or other areas. A growing number of programs provide courses in nonprofit administration, including grant writing, volunteer management, fund-raising, and philanthropy.

A bachelor's degree opens doors to a variety of public service careers with government agencies, nonprofit organizations, and private sector firms. It also offers a good background for many graduate programs. You can enhance your marketability by taking part in paid or volunteer internships; gaining valuable skills in information technology, public relations, or planning; joining professional organizations; and developing your oral, written, and visual communication skills. The most successful students combine classroom study with real-world experience, and they network, or make contact, with professionals in the field. Increasingly, international study is playing an important role in public affairs, and you are encouraged to participate in study-abroad programs.

Other majors you might like:
Political science
Public policy analysis
Urban, community, and regional planning
Parks, recreation, and leisure studies
Public relations
Economics
Civil engineering
Urban studies
Emergency management/homeland security
Sociology
Health care administration
Environmental studies

Questions to ask colleges:
Does the program require or provide internship opportunities?

How active is the program in the field's professional associations?

Does the program specialize in particular areas? If so, which ones? Does the program focus on a level of government (local, state, or federal), or include nonprofit administration?

Career options and trends:
City manager; assistant city manager*; budget/financial officer; human resource manager; policy analyst; grant coordinator; program evaluator; volunteer coordinator; neighborhood planner; economic development coordinator.

The retirement of the baby boom generation should open up job opportunities, even at the coveted federal level. For example, the Office of Personnel Management projects that 282,000 of the executive branch's full-time civilian employees will leave within a few years.

Nonprofit organizations (neighborhood associations, religious organizations, schools, chambers of commerce, etc.) provide a good employment entry point because they offer many volunteer and internship positions through which you can acquire experience.

Insider's viewpoint:
"Public policy studies how to do things, how to use what we have to make a world. In many cases, we even try to be fair. It has amazed me to learn that there is a science, a precision, a balancing to be addressed with the precision and discipline of an artist."

—Kobi, senior, Columbia University

For more info:
American Society for Public Administration (ASPA)
1301 Pennsylvania Ave., N.W.
Suite 700
Washington, DC 20004
(202) 393-7878
www.aspanet.org

Social work

What it's about:

The social work major is a professional degree program that provides the knowledge, values, and skills needed for generalist social work practice. You learn to help individuals, families, groups, and communities prevent and respond to social problems. As a practicing social worker, you modify harmful social conditions, promote social and economic well being, and increase opportunities for people to live fulfilling, dignified lives.

Is this for you?

You might like this major if you also like: helping people in need; diversity; being a "people person"; working for social and economic justice.

Consider this major if you are good at: caring/ nurturing; counseling; creativity; critical reading/ thinking; leadership; organizing; teamwork ...*or have...* initiative; respect for others; verbal skills; writing skills.

Recommended high school prep:

English 4, math 3, lab science 3, social studies 4, and a foreign language 2–3. If you can, take classes in computer science and anthropology. Spanish is a useful language to learn because of the changing makeup of the U.S. population. Volunteer work or community service activities are strongly recommended.

Did you know...

...that social work covers more than just administering public assistance? Many students' idea of a social worker is that of a caseworker. Ironically, few caseworkers are trained social workers.

Typical courses in this major:

Human behavior and social environment
Introduction to psychology
Introduction to sociology
Social work research
Social work practice
Social policy and services

Values and ethics
Diversity
Modern social problems
Populations-at-risk
Social and economic justice
Community resources
Field internship

Concentrations:

Generally, none in college; but if you go on to grad school: child welfare; family welfare; aging; health; addictions; working with individuals, groups, families, or communities; poverty, homelessness, and other social problems; social administration; social work research.

What the study of this major is like:

As a social work major, you gain a foundation in the liberal arts, with an emphasis on the social sciences. In your first two years of college, you generally take sociology, political science, economics, psychology, and human biology. In your third and fourth years, you take most of your social work courses, learning how to conduct a generalist social work practice.

In courses in social welfare policy and services, which describe the laws, programs, and benefits available to meet human needs, you consider the way social programs are developed and changed. Research courses teach basic methods and stress the evaluation of social welfare programs. At most colleges, the major emphasizes the understanding and acceptance of diversity in ethnicity, race, culture, gender, and sexual orientation.

Typically, social work professors use a variety of approaches in their courses: lectures, teamwork, role-playing, research projects, field trips, and skill-building exercises. An attractive feature of the major is the combination of theory and hands-on experience. Your most important educational experience is a supervised practicum (field internship), most likely in a social service agency. All undergraduates earning a Bachelor's of Social Work (B.S.W.) must complete at least 400 hours of field experience under the supervision of a qualified social worker.

Early in your studies, you may have difficulty applying theoretical concepts to practical situations. Programs handle this challenge by closely supervising students as they complete their internships. You may also be troubled by differences between your personal values and those of the profession. In response, most programs encourage you to examine your values as well as those of social workers and society.

In many states, you must graduate from a program accredited by the Council on Social Work Education (CSWE) in order to be licensed and certified. Because of these standards, undergraduate social work programs tend to be very similar. Differences may exist in the number of courses offered, but the choices you have are usually based more on program resources or regional mission than on program philosophies.

The sense of calling and commitment that can lead you to choose social work as a profession may generate a spirit of camaraderie and dedication among students. Although healthy competition is part of academic life, social work students often develop projects cooperatively, make group presentations, and form long-lasting professional relationships. In recent years many nontraditional and older students have found social work an attractive choice for a major and a career.

Other majors you might like:
Sociology
Psychology
Native American studies
American sign language (ASL)
Funeral services/mortuary science
Human development and family studies
Community health services
Gerontology
Youth ministry
Emergency medical technology (EMT paramedic)
Nursing (RN)
Occupational therapy

Questions to ask colleges:
Is the program accredited by the CSWE?

Which types of agencies are available for students looking to fulfill their practicum requirements?

Career options and trends:
Generalist social work practitioner; clinician; administrator; case manager; social planner; researcher.

A bachelor's degree prepares you for generalist social work in a wide range of settings, such as child welfare and public welfare agencies, hospitals and other health care facilities, schools, developmental disabilities services, services for the aged, the juvenile and criminal justice systems, industry, and business. A master's degree is required for jobs involving supervision, administration, or complex research. All states license or regulate social workers, but regulations and procedures vary from state to state.

Job prospects are favorable for those going into social work and are expected to grow faster than average through 2022. Generally, there will be more opportunities in the areas of mental health and substance abuse than in child, family and school social work.

Insider's viewpoint:
"When my adviser suggested I take the introductory social work class I didn't want to because I never heard anything positive about it; I associated it with child protection services and doing the dirty work. But that was before my favorite professor introduced me to macro social work and the public policy side of it: legislation, community development and economic revitalization, that sort of thing."

—Melissa, junior, Michigan State University

For more info:
National Association of Social Workers (NASW)
750 First St., N.E.
Suite 700
Washington, DC 20002-4241
(202) 408-8600
www.naswdc.org

Religion and theology

The study of religion is not what you may think. It's not necessarily faith-based, or a form of worship. And it isn't always preparation for the clergy. Instead, the majors in this group often approach religion as an academic subject.

"The study of religion in the academic context is not the same as in some religious context (church, synagogue, mosque)," says Professor Emeritus Richard B. Pilgrim of Syracuse University.

"Once students realize that the study of religion does not favor or teach about a religion in order to convert or train a person in that tradition, then religion as an academic discipline begins," explains Professor John A. Grim, Bucknell University.

The academic approach to religion includes studies of civilization and society, history, language and texts, culture, music, and many other subjects.

Theology is just one of the majors in the universe of religion studies. "Theology" literally means "the study of God." This major often concentrates on a particular faith, and may have liturgical (worship) and counseling components to prepare students for graduate work in the ministry, among other careers.

"A major in theology typically includes courses in biblical studies, history of the church, history of Christian thought, ethics, and the moral life. It is also likely to include study of world religions," says Professor David G. Truemper of Valparaiso University.

Religion and theology majors are all about the big picture.

"The study of religion is only one aspect of Judaic studies," says Professor Shmuel Bolozky, University of Massachusetts Amherst. "It is also the study of the Jewish people, its role in civilization, and its interaction with the other members of society."

For its part, Islamic studies "involves a great deal of reading, researching, and writing," says Professor Kamran S. Aghaie, University of Texas at Austin. "It entails expanding one's perspective on the world and understanding different cultures."

Your Higher Education

Studying religion as part of a liberal arts education is a way to obtain skills in research, reading, writing, and thinking that are needed in

491

graduate school and in almost any career. When you look for an institution offering religion majors, consider colleges of liberal arts or humanities or arts and sciences, divinity schools, and schools of religion or theology.

How religion is taught depends on the college. Some colleges have been set up by a particular religion, so they are faith-based. If you are preparing for the ministry, consider a religion-affiliated university with a preministry program to guide you toward a major and graduate studies. "Through advising, internship experiences, and well-chosen curricula across the disciplines in courses from biblical literature to psychology to ethics, interested men and women can determine what types of ministry suits them," says Shelley Shepherd, preministerial studies adviser at Southern Methodist University.

At other colleges, including state universities, the approach is not religious but secular. Be sure you are entering the type of program you want and double-check that any state aid you will receive applies if you study religion. It may not.

Professor Pilgrim explains the primary distinction between religious and nonreligious colleges: "The difference is between private, paro-chial schools where religious indoctrination or advocacy may be the main thrust in a religion or theology major, and private or public colleges or universities where religious studies is clearly an academic, scholarly enterprise," he says. "It's not always easy to tell one from the other, but prospective students need to check closely about this."

Some programs are devoted to a particular tradition, like Buddhism, Christianity, Islam, or Judaism, or to an aspect of a tradition, like the Bible or Islamic law. Other programs specialize in theoretical approaches (such as ethics, psychology, philosophy, anthropology).

"A prospective student should look for balance across approaches and cultural traditions in a religion department. Look for courses in ethics, philosophy of religion, religion and ecology, or popular religion," Grim suggests. "A basic perspective is to look for courses in Judaism, Christianity, Islam, Buddhism, Hinduism, Confucianism, or Taoism to get a sense of the commitment of the department to teaching the full spectrum of cultural religious expressions."

Whatever your likely major, check out the courses and faculty members to see if their focus matches your interests. You can reach out to educators at the college. Ask how the school can help you connect personal religious faith with intellectual and academic work. How does the program help you relate to people of other faiths? Will your studies have a global dimension? Is there a religious community nearby to provide support and stimulation? Does the college have resources such as online library subscriptions, translations, and a language lab? Are grants and scholarships available? How about an internship, mission, or social service, if such an opportunity is right for you?

In choosing a college, think about your future. Most religion students are probably planning to work in education, law, business, medicine, social activism, or social service. If you envision a career in the clergy, or plan on graduate studies, see the individual majors in this section for graduate tracks. A good general resource is the American Academy of Religion, at www.aarweb.org.

Bible studies

What it's about:

As a Bible studies major, you explore the literature of the Bible, including the historical and cultural setting of the biblical world. Emphasis is placed on the content, concepts, and theological teachings of the Bible, as well as on ways to interpret biblical literature. Some programs may require you to study Greek and Hebrew.

Is this for you?

You might like this major if you also like: archaeology; history; volunteering and service activities; exploring your spirituality; reading the Bible and biblical literature.

Consider this major if you are good at: attention to detail; caring/nurturing; creativity; critical reading/thinking; organizing; research ...*or have...* patience; verbal skills; writing skills.

Recommended high school prep:

English 4, math 3, lab science 3, social studies 4, and a foreign language 3. If possible, take classes in ancient history, anthropology, classical Greek, Latin, philosophy, or world religions.

Did you know...

...that this major is much broader than you might think? It covers the rich heritage of Hebrew and Judeo-Christian religious traditions, often emphasizing interdisciplinary study. Majoring in Bible studies can lead to job opportunities for both women and men.

Typical courses in this major:

New Testament overview
Old Testament overview
Christian doctrine and systematic theology
Church history and historical theology
Biblical interpretation and hermeneutics
History of Greece
History of Rome
History of the ancient Near East
Biblical archaeology
Biblical criticism
Christian ethics
Literature of the Bible
Geography of the Bible
Contemporary social concerns
Global Christianity
Key figures in biblical or Church history

Concentrations:

In college: Church history; New Testament; Old Testament.

If you go on to grad school: apologetics; biblical criticism; biblical interpretation; biblical theology; Christian/spiritual formation; classical dogmatics; early Christianity; evangelism/missions; religion in America; systematic theology.

What the study of this major is like:

Bible studies majors encounter broad and diverse subject matter. Course work may cover biblical history, biblical literature and methods for interpreting it, key characters in the Bible, important eras and figures in Church history, historical or systematic theology and ethics, the original languages of the Bible, the culture of the biblical world, the contribution of archaeology to biblical studies, and world religions.

Bible studies is taught and learned in many ways, and classes may vary in size. Your classes may feature lectures, discussion, seminars, research, writing, oral and written examinations, special projects, and student presentations. Other learning opportunities may include independent or guided study with a small group of students (directed by a faculty member); special lectures, symposiums, and conferences conducted by guest speakers; study-abroad programs; archaeological field work; off-campus internships and social service projects; and language lab instruction in Greek or Hebrew.

The reading, research, and writing demanded by your course work will require time management, good study habits, and personal discipline. Challenges specific to the Bible studies major include mastering the subject matter; the interdisciplinary nature of the major; and the diversity of Christian thought and teaching that has emerged from Roman Catholic, Orthodox, and Protestant traditions over many centuries. You must also balance your intellectual pursuits, on the one hand, with your spiritual and religious needs and your desire to serve, on the other.

Bible studies programs may differ in their requirements. Some may emphasize the biblical languages of Greek and Hebrew. Others may require an internship or a missions or social service component. There is considerable variation in how much emphasis is given to liberal arts or interdisciplinary studies. Programs also differ in their selection of reading strategies and their choice of interpretive approaches to biblical and religious literature.

Differences in emphases and philosophies stem from several factors. The weight given to matters of history, literature, and theology often reflects the specialized training of the faculty members. Another consideration is whether the educational institution is a state-supported, public college or a private institution linked to a particular Christian denomination or other religious group. Keep in mind that each of the three branches of the Christian tradition (Roman Catholic, Orthodox, and Protestant) sustains college programs in Bible studies committed to its own historical and theological traditions—traditions that, in turn, are based on doctrines and beliefs, biblical teachings, worship practices, and the religious body's purpose in providing theological education.

Other majors you might like:
Anthropology
Archaeology
Youth ministry
Ancient studies
Preministerial studies
Sociology
Sacred music
Christian studies
Ancient Near Eastern/biblical languages
History
Missionary studies
Philosophy

Questions to ask colleges:
Does the major require biblical languages (Greek or Hebrew)?

Are faculty members involved in the ministry of the church, in social services, or in missions?

At what kinds of academic institutions (research universities, seminaries, or professional schools) did faculty members study or work?

Career options and trends:
Christian education director; youth minister; clergy member; chaplain (military, hospitals, prisons, retirement/nursing homes); college professor.

Many church denominations require those entering the clergy to be ordained. Most states require licensing for clergy conducting religious rites with civil implications, such as marriages, funerals, and burials, and some types of counseling.

Bible studies majors also pursue careers in church ministry, campus ministries, social service organizations, counseling ministries, home or overseas missions, religious education, religious publishing, religious administration, journalism, business, or law.

Insider's viewpoint:
"Jewish tradition has an expression for the love of the Hebrew Scriptures known as *simchah Torah* or 'the joy of Torah.' My passion for the study of the Bible was sparked by a professor who taught courses in Hebrew language and Old Testament studies with this sense of joy."

—Professor Andrew E. Hill, Wheaton College (IL)

For more info:
Council for Christian Colleges and Universities
  (C.C.C.U.)
321 Eighth Street, N.E.
Washington, DC 20002
(202) 546-8713
www.cccu.org

Islamic studies

What it's about:

As an Islamic studies major, you explore the history, culture, and interpretation of the Islamic faith. You may also be required to study Arabic, Persian, Turkish, or Urdu for the equivalent of two years.

Is this for you?

You might like this major if you also like: learning about Islamic culture and heritage; religious customs and writings; foreign languages and cultures; history; philosophy; understanding world events; community service activities.

Consider this major if you are good at: attention to detail; critical reading/thinking; leadership; organizing; persuading/influencing; research ...*or have...* an open mind; initiative; verbal skills; writing skills.

Recommended high school prep:

English 4, math 3, lab science 3, social studies 3, and a foreign language 2–3. If possible, take courses in the Arabic, Turkish, Persian, or Urdu language.

Did you know...

...that Islam is the fastest-growing religion in the United States?

...that most Muslims do not live in the Middle East and are not Arabs? Arabs make up less than 15 percent of the Muslim population. The nation with the largest Muslim population is Indonesia.

Typical courses in this major:

Prophet of Islam
The Qur'an
Islamic sciences
Sufism
Shi'ite Islam
Popular Islam
Modern political Islam
Islamic revolution of Iran
Women in Islam
Islamic art
Islamic architecture
Islamic law
Islamic theology
Islamic philosophy
Hadith
Muslim intellectual history

Concentrations:

Women and gender issues; Islam in America; Islamic art and architecture; Islam in South Asia (India and Pakistan); Islam in Iran; Sufism; Islamic law; modern political Islam and fundamentalism; Shi'ite Islam; popular Islam; Islamic theology and philosophy; Islamic history.

What the study of this major is like:

The Islamic studies major focuses on the diversity of Islamic society and culture found in many geographic areas, time periods, and branches of the faith (including Sunni, Shi'ia, and Ahmadiyya). Your studies begin in sixth-century Arabia with the teachings of the Prophet Muhammad and include interpretations and additions made by Islamic teachers and scholars over the centuries.

You learn about Islamic scripture, principally the Qur'an, and other texts (Hadith, Sirah, Sunnah, Tafsir) that interpret, describe, or illustrate the Qur'an and the life and teachings of the Prophet. In addition, you examine the mystical beliefs of Sufism, modern Islamic politics, gender issues in Islam, Islamic sciences, Islamic law, Islamic art, and Islamic architecture.

As an Islamic studies major, you are required to do a great deal of reading, researching, and writing. Some colleges teach Islam as a component of U.S. foreign policy studies. Others include Islamic studies in the context of comparative religions. In most colleges, though, Islam is taught from an "area studies" perspective; the focus is on culture and history rather than on religion. In all programs, you develop an understanding of different societies and expand your perspective on the world.

Other majors you might like:

Near and Middle Eastern studies
Religious studies

Arabic
Iranian/Persian languages
Asian studies
Anthropology
History
South Asian studies
Sociology
Peace and conflict studies
Medieval and Renaissance studies
Judaic studies

Questions to ask colleges:
Which approaches to Islam does the program offer?
Which specialties are the strongest?

Career options and trends:
College professor; teacher; journalist; Foreign Service Officer.

Majors in Islamic studies often go on to study at professional or graduate schools to prepare for careers in the clergy, law, medicine, or social work. They also find employment in the government; in nongovernmental organizations dealing with the Muslim world; and in business, education, and publishing.

Opportunities in all areas of Islamic studies have dramatically increased, especially positions in higher education (as college professors), research, government, and think tanks. For most jobs in the field, competence in an Islamic language is highly desirable.

For more info:
Middle Eastern Studies Associations of North
  America
University of Arizona
1219 North Santa Rita Ave.
Tuscon, AZ 85721
(520) 621-5850
www.mesa.arizona.edu

Judaic studies

Also known as:
Jewish studies

What it's about:
This major explores the culture and religion of the Jewish people over the course of its 3,500-year history, in both their ancestral land and the lands of dispersion (migration to Europe, North America, and Israel). Your studies are wide-ranging, including the Jewish religion, heritage, philosophy, and intellectual history; Hebrew and Yiddish languages and literature; anti-Semitism; Jewish-Gentile (non-Jewish) relations; the Holocaust; Zionism; and the State of Israel.

Is this for you?
You might like this major if you also like: foreign cultures and languages; the Bible and religion; learning about Jewish heritage; community service activities.

Consider this major if you are good at: attention to detail; creativity; critical reading/thinking; leadership; research; teamwork ...*or have...* initiative; verbal skills; writing skills.

Recommended high school prep:
English 4, math 3, lab science 3, social studies 4, and a foreign language 4. Hebrew is recommended if available, although it is not a prerequisite; knowledge of any other foreign language will help you learn Hebrew in college.

Did you know...
...that the study of religion is only one aspect of Judaic studies? The major also includes the history of the Jewish people, their role in civilization, and their interaction with other cultures. Because Jewish studies is interdisciplinary, you can explore areas suited to your interests and goals.

Typical courses in this major:
Elementary, intermediate, and advanced Hebrew
Biblical Hebrew
Ancient Israel and the ancient Near East

Judaism in the Middle Ages
Jewish law and society
Family and sexuality in Judaism
Women in Jewish history
Modern Jewish history
Anti-Semitism in historical perspective
Yiddish language and culture
The Holocaust
Jewish culture in America
Zionism and Israel
Hebrew/Israeli literature in translation
Jewish and Israeli film
Jewish mysticism

Concentrations:
In college: Jewish civilization in the ancient Near East; Rabbinical Hebrew and medieval Judaism; Jewish literature; modern Jewish religion and philosophy; Holocaust studies.

If you go on to grad school: ancient Jewish texts in related languages (Hebrew, Aramaic, Akkadian); Mishna/Talmud; medieval texts; modern Rabbinical writing; Jewish history of a particular period; Zionism and Israel studies; modern Hebrew language and literature.

What the study of this major is like:
This major allows Jewish students to explore their culture in an objective, academic setting, and it gives non-Jewish students the opportunity to broaden their understanding of Judaism, a central foundation of Western civilization, Christianity, and Islam. It is a demanding course of study; you must be willing to work hard in reading and analyzing classical texts, and in most programs you are required to obtain proficiency in the Hebrew language.

Areas covered include archaeology, Biblical times, Christian Europe, and the Islamic world. In-depth study is available in Rabbinical Hebrew and medieval Judaism, including the Mishna/Talmud and medieval Jewish philosophy. Of special interest is the modern period—the beginnings of secularization, the origins of Reform and Conservative Judaism, and the development of modern anti-Semitism, leading to the Holocaust. Examination of the State of Israel focuses on the gathering of exiles; the revival of Hebrew; the status of the Palestinians; and the historical, social, and political forces that have shaped the struggle to maintain a democracy in the Middle East.

Most classes are conducted as seminars, with plenty of outside reading and directed group discussion. A frequent attribute of programs is a close relationship between students and their professors and classmates. Majors tend to study in groups, and work together on projects. Advanced Hebrew language students often tutor beginning students (for practicum credit), an activity that fosters group interaction and friendships.

Study abroad is an important aspect of the major. Most overseas study takes place in Israel; however, travel advisories in times of conflict may require colleges to offer alternative locations, such as Prague or other European cities with strong Jewish communities. Internships in Jewish community centers, museums, synagogues, and Hillel (a prominent Jewish student organization) are also encouraged, or even required.

One significant difference among programs concerns the importance placed on achieving proficiency in Hebrew. Some departments insist that students who cannot read Hebrew documents in the original language cannot gain a genuine understanding of Jewish culture. Other programs believe that what really matters is the content, and reliable translations are sufficient. If you might want to continue your Judaic studies in graduate school, however, you will need at least intermediate-level skills in Hebrew or other Semitic language (such as Arabic or Aramaic).

Other majors you might like:
Religious studies
History
Philosophy
Archaeology
Anthropology
Hebrew
Near and Middle Eastern studies
Ancient Near Eastern/Biblical languages
Talmudic studies
Islamic studies

Linguistics
Sociology

Questions to ask colleges:
What resources does the library have in Judaic studies? Do they include online resources, educational DVDs, Israeli publications, and so on? Does the Judaica collection include both Yiddish and Hebrew texts? Is there access to Jewish and Israeli music and film?

Is there a language lab, and are there computer-assisted instructional materials for Hebrew?

Are there Judaica-related extracurricular activities on or near campus?

Career options and trends:
College professor*; teacher*; Rabbi*; director of religious education; journalist; community center administrator.

A teaching certificate is required for teaching in public school, but not necessarily for Hebrew day schools or religious schools.

Judaic studies can lead to careers in business, education, government service, social work, and other careers that require a liberal arts education. It is also sound preparation for a range of graduate or professional programs, such as law, medicine, Jewish scholarship, the rabbinate, or the cantorate.

Insider's viewpoint:
"Hebrew is a fascinating language, as all Semitic languages are, because of its special mechanisms for word formation, but also because of its revival as a spoken language in the last century. I love reading Hebrew texts, and enjoy imparting their internal beauty to my students."

—Professor Shmuel Bolozky, University of Massachusetts Amherst

For more info:

Association for Jewish Studies (AJS)
Center for Jewish History
15 West 16th St.
New York, NY 10011-6301
(917) 606-8249
www.ajsnet.org

American Academy for Jewish Research (AAJR)
202 S. Thayer Street
Ann Arbor, MI 48104-1608
(734) 615-6093
www.aajr.org

National Association of Professors of Hebrew
University of Wisconsin–Madison
1346 Van Hise Hall, 1220 Linden Drive
Madison, WI 53706
(608) 262-2997
vanhise.lss.wisc.edu/naph

Preministerial studies

What it's about:

A preministerial studies program will help you prepare to become an ordained Christian minister, priest, or other religious leader. At most colleges it is not a major but an advising program; students planning to enter a seminary, divinity school, or full-time ministerial work after college may pursue any major they choose.

Is this for you?

You might like this major if you also like: Bible study; public speaking; reflecting on spiritual issues and discussing them with others; being a friend to turn to; taking an active role in the church community. A true calling to the ministry is sometimes clear and sometimes not; but a deep religious faith and empathy for others are often found among those who are called.

Consider this major if you are good at: caring/nurturing; counseling; creativity; leadership; organizing...or have... Compassion; patience; verbal skills; writing skills.

Recommended high school prep:

English 4, math 3, lab science 3, social studies 4, and a foreign language 2–3. If available, a year of Latin or Greek would be helpful, and courses in psychology, philosophy, speech, and world religions are also recommended.

Typical courses in this major:

New Testament
Western philosophy
Old Testament/Hebrew Bible
Church history
World religions
Christian ethics
Sociology
Introductory psychology
Advanced Bible study
Expository writing
Homiletics (preaching)
Church organization and management
Evangelism
Dynamics of intercultural communication
Western civilization
Liturgical theology and practice

Concentrations:

Generally, none available.

What the study of this major is like:

Many preministerial programs are nondenominational, with no sectarian or religious requirements for admission. Most, however, are typically offered at colleges affiliated with a particular religion and focus on the history, rituals, traditions, and beliefs of that denomination. Each faith usually sets its own requirements for becoming a minister. Some religions require a graduate degree from a seminary or divinity school, while others do not; so where and how a candidate is educated varies from one faith to the next.

But common to all preministerial programs is the role of the adviser, who will help you to choose a major in line with your interests and to select courses that will prepare you for the ministry or for admission to divinity school or other graduate program—and who will, in addition, discuss with you how best to use your skills in the community. Although your adviser will assist primarily in the academic aspects of your education, he or she will be sensitive to your unique concerns as you contemplate a career in ministry.

In a typical preministerial program, the courses provide you with a strong background in biblical literature, as well as a look at the cultures that produced the sacred texts. A balanced curriculum that emphasizes the liberal arts will give you the well-rounded education you'll need as you prepare for the variety of challenges you will face as a minister. If you decide to go on to the graduate level, you will have the skills necessary there as well: how to make use of the library, do research, and write effectively.

Some preministerial programs are very flexible about what courses you can select, while other programs have specific requirements, which may include vocational experience courses and courses in cross-cultural understanding. Usually, programs with specific requirements are geared to a particular faith or tradition; so check out a school's affiliation and direction before you apply.

In addition to academic pursuits, you'll do one or more internships, practicing what you've been learning about the ministry. This experience can take a number of forms: you might visit congregation members' homes, work with young people at a Christian summer camp, teach Bible lessons, give sermons, or play sacred music.

You should also attend lectures and seminars and talk with clergy to familiarize yourself with current issues. A useful pursuit is to engage in volunteer work in the community, that will expose you to real-world problems such as poverty, homelessness, and substance abuse.

Preministerial programs are not abundant and are more likely to be found at religiously affiliated universities and colleges. It is not essential to come from a preministerial program in order to get into graduate school or enter the ministry. But a good preministerial program will give you the time to broaden your understanding, to participate in a multitude of experiences, and to determine who you are and what really matters to you.

Other majors you might like:
Religious studies
Bible studies
Judaic studies
Pastoral counseling
Philosophy
History
Sacred music
Social work
Psychology
Peace and conflict studies
Religious education
Youth ministry

Questions to ask colleges:
May I choose any major if I wish to pursue a preministerial studies path, or are there specific disciplines I must choose from?

Is there a faculty member or adviser to help students navigate the program and assist them in obtaining related internship or vocational experiences?

If the program is nondenominational, is there a club or other student organization on campus for my specific faith?

Career options and trends:
Minister; priest; religious education coordinator; theology professor; military chaplain; missionary.

Usually ministers, priests, and chaplains must go through a candidacy and ordination process through a church conference or diocese before they may become a minister. In some Christian denominations, students who wish to start the process toward ordination must secure the blessing of a bishop or other church authority well in advance of beginning a graduate program.

Fewer young people are entering the ministry as a first career these days. Job prospects are good, especially for those who have a graduate degree, or are willing to accept part-time positions or to work in rural areas. In some Christian denominations, you may have to relocate at the discretion of a bishop.

For more info:
Association for Biblical Higher Education
5850 T.G. Lee Blvd., Suite 130
Orlando, FL 32822-1781
(407) 207-0808
www.abhe.org

Association of Theological Schools (ATS)
10 Summit Park Drive
Pittsburgh, PA 15275-1110
(412) 788-6505
www.ats.edu

Religious studies

Also known as:
Comparative religion

What it's about:
In the religious studies major, you become familiar with many of the world's spiritual traditions, and learn to use a range of approaches—historical, textual, psychological, philosophical, sociological, and anthropological—to examine the variety of religious experience.

Is this for you?
You might like this major if you also like: philosophy; literature; the arts; other cultures, past and present; mythology; languages; thinking about religious themes and motivations.

Consider this major if you are good at: caring/nurturing; creativity; critical reading/thinking; memorizing; research; teamwork ...*or have...* an open mind; patience; writing skills.

Recommended high school prep:
English 4, math 3, lab science 3, social studies 4, and a foreign language 3–4. Take as many history courses as possible, including art history.

Did you know...
...that most religious studies majors do not intend to pursue careers as priests, imams, or rabbis? This major is mostly taught as an interdisciplinary liberal arts field that prepares you for many different career paths.

Typical courses in this major:
Introduction to religion
Judaism
Hinduism
Christianity
Buddhism
Islam
Religions of China
American religions
Existentialist theology
Religions of Japan
Religion and moral issues
Critiques of religion
Pilgrimage
Mysticism
New religious movements
Philosophy of religion

Concentrations:
In college: particular religions; groups of religions (for example, Asian); historical periods; cultural studies (Christianity in the Americas); comparative religions.

If you go on to grad school: psychology of religion; religious anthropology; ritual studies; language and scriptural studies (such as the Torah and Hebrew, the Sanskrit scriptures of Hinduism, or Taoist classics in Chinese); religion and science.

What the study of this major is like:
The study of religion includes many cultures and traditions. You learn the difference between *participating in* a religious tradition—its stories, rituals, symbols, beliefs, social and institutional structures, and customs—and *understanding* that tradition, regardless of whether or not you participate in it. By studying religion independently of participants' beliefs, you learn to think critically and imaginatively.

Your course work teaches you a variety of methods and approaches, including historical investigation, psychological inquiry, social analysis, anthropological and ethnological investigation, feminist criticism, and linguistic analysis. As you examine a range of religions, you begin to recognize and appreciate their similarities and differences.

Generally, you are not expected to enter college with a background in religion. The major typically begins with introductory courses that familiarize you with the basic elements of religion, such as myth, ritual, scripture, and symbols. You can usually choose from among courses in several areas: the Western traditions of Judaism, Christianity, and

Islam; the Asian traditions of Hinduism, Jainism, Sikhism, Buddhism, Confucianism, and Taoism; theoretical and philosophical approaches to the study of religion; and, occasionally, on indigenous traditions (for instance, the religious practices of Native American cultures).

Most programs require an entry-level course in at least two traditions and recommend that you take courses in both Western and non-Western traditions. At least one of your courses will examine theoretical approaches. In some programs, languages associated with religious traditions may be offered. Although you are not usually required to take a foreign language, such training is helpful, especially if you intend to continue religious studies in grad school.

Your course work examines key questions on such topics as ecology, science, gender relations, cultural and historical conflicts, the emergence of the universe, and conscious awareness. You explore the development of religious traditions over time, as well as the creativity that keeps religions relevant today. Areas that may prove difficult to deal with include unfamiliar worldviews and practices, and abstract theological and philosophical ideas. But learning to recognize other religious points of view will challenge, contradict, and then deepen your understanding.

Programs at different colleges may vary in their emphases. For example, some specialize in theoretical approaches, such as ethics, philosophy, or anthropology, while others may focus on a particular religion or an aspect of a religion (such as biblical studies or Islamic law/Shari'ah). Look for balance across approaches and traditions—for a good indication, look for courses in both Eastern and Western faiths. Also, some private colleges teach religious studies from a faith-based, rather than an academic, point of view. It is not always easy to tell, so if you have a preference, be sure to check.

Other majors you might like:
Anthropology
Peace and conflict studies
Theology
Near and Middle Eastern studies
Medieval and Renaissance studies
History
Archaeology

Philosophy
Psychology
Sociology
Global studies

Questions to ask colleges:
Which religious traditions are taught? Do course descriptions mention women, ritual, or indigenous peoples? Are topics such as the psychology of religion or science and religion covered in the curriculum?

Career options and trends:
High school teacher; college professor; social worker; journalist.

Majors in religious studies also go on to work in business, law, medicine, counseling, management, psychology, academic research, and religious vocations. Careers in many of these disciplines require graduate or professional study.

Insider's viewpoint:
"I wrote a paper on the anthropology of religious war. It really helped me see that, wow, maybe I can do this sort of thing and maybe it can be useful. I see a great need to make religious studies practical."

—Andy, junior, Cornell University

For more info:
American Academy of Religion (AAR)
825 Houston Mill Rd., N.E.
Suite 300
Atlanta, GA 30329
(404) 727-3049
www.aarweb.org

Council of Societies for the Study of Religion
c/o Rice University
P.O. Box 1892, MS-156
Houston, TX 77251-1892
(713) 348-5721
cohesion.rice.edu/CentersAndInst/CSSR/index.cfm

Sacred music

Also known as:
Religious music
Pastoral music

What it's about:
The sacred music major provides a broad base of information about music history, music theory, and performance skills as preparation for careers as minister of music, organist, or choir director in a place of worship. You develop a repertory of sacred music, grounded in both historical and contemporary forms of expression.

Is this for you?
You might like this major if you also like: singing; chorus; expressing your faith through music; playing an instrument; participating in worship-related activities; leading group activities; tutoring.

Consider this major if you are good at: caring/nurturing; coaching; creativity; leadership; musicianship; organizing; persuading/influencing; teamwork *...or have...* patience; verbal skills.

Recommended high school prep:
English 4, math 3, lab science 3, social studies 3, music 1–2, and a foreign language 2–3. Participation in high school chorus (2 or 3 years) is highly recommended. Basic keyboarding skills (piano or organ) are also expected.

Did you know...
...that success in this field requires more than just musical ability? Certainly a passion for sacred music is essential; but enthusiasm and a desire to work with people can be as important as musical skills.

Typical courses in this major:
Music theory
Music history
Composition
Choral conducting
Choir training methods
Sight singing
Sacred music history
Choral literature
Hymnology
Children's choir leadership
Church music administration
Applied voice, piano, or organ
College choir, vocal, or instrumental ensemble

Concentrations:
Organ studies; conducting; worship leadership

What the study of this major is like:
Throughout history, musicians have worked alongside the clergy to lead others in worship and praise. Many consider expressing faith through music to be one of the highest forms of worship. The sacred music major helps you develop the skills you need to be successful in the profession.

Besides training in music, professionals in sacred music need skills in areas such as arts management, program planning and organization, community building, and talent development. As a professional, you are responsible for bringing the music of the religious institution to life, developing musical resources, and guiding the congregation in praise and worship. The exploration of contemporary worship music, such as music from world cultures, keeps the profession fresh.

As a major, you study basic musicianship. Theory courses review the mechanics of music (such as rhythmic and pitch notation, key signatures, triads, and scales) and explore composition (harmonic activity and structure). In sacred music history courses, you examine the development of music in worship (in the West and in traditional Asian and African cultures), liturgy, the historical significance of the sections of a worship service, and the primary works of sacred music.

Because most majors plan to be musical leaders in congregations, programs include performance and ensemble participation, conducting, choir training, and choral literature. You also study hymnology (the history and techniques of congregational singing);

administrative skills; and applied instruction in voice, piano, or organ. Organ instruction is highly recommended, and some proficiency at the piano is generally expected. In addition, you may have opportunities to conduct children's and/or handbell choirs.

Because musicians serving congregations often function as performers, most programs encourage majors to participate in third-year and fourth-year solo recitals. In addition, you can attend concerts and recitals by ensembles, faculty members, and visiting artists, and perhaps intern in local houses of worship. Some programs offer workshops and conferences (on weekends or during the summer) that teach current trends and special aspects of the profession.

The sacred music program presents challenges beyond those of performance. Unlike other music programs, you are faced with questions about music's role in worship, its historical significance to modern liturgy, its place in contemporary society, and its function as "performance" or "offering." Also, at large conservatory programs, sacred music majors often find they are less respected than students majoring in performance or education. This can dishearten students who work just as hard as their peers in other concentrations do.

As a sacred music major, you earn either a Bachelor of Arts degree, which denotes a music specialty within a broad liberal arts program, or a Bachelor of Music degree, which focuses on performance and professional training. At a faith-based college, religious training may be just as important as musical training. At a music conservatory, the focus is on scholarly work and performance, and music study is offered at a more demanding level. You are expected to enter the program with considerable musical ability and to show achievement in performances throughout your college career. If the university is state-supported, certain sacred music courses may not be offered.

Other majors you might like:
Conducting
Piano/organ
Youth ministry
Music pedagogy
Music teacher education
Music history/literature

Recording arts
Music theory and composition
Voice/opera
Music management
Religious studies

Questions to ask colleges:
Are internships or other practical experiences available at local places of worship?

Does the program offer special campus activities, such as workshops/seminars/conferences related to sacred music, led by respected practitioners?

Is there ample access to organ or piano instruments for practice and rehearsals?

Career options and trends:
Choir director; organist in house of worship*; director of music ministries*; children's choir director; handbell choir director; parochial school music teacher.

Two issues present challenging opportunities for newcomers to the field: global music and contemporary worship music. Due to our growing appreciation of other cultures, the sacred music professional needs to be aware of the contributions and performance styles of other societies. Additionally, many mainstream denominations are including contemporary styles of worship, requiring the ability to blend praise choruses with traditional hymns or to incorporate instruments such as keyboards, guitar, and percussion into the worship service.

For more info:
American Guild of Organists
475 Riverside Drive
Suite 1260
New York, NY 10115
212-870-2310
www.agohq.org

Theology

What it's about:

Theology is the academic study of the beliefs and practices of a particular religion or religious community. You gain an understanding of its faith and practices by studying its history, literature, ethics, doctrines, and present-day situation. This major may also include a comparative study of world religions and practical courses in counseling, homiletics (preaching), and worship services.

Is this for you?

You might like this major if you also like: thinking about philosophical and spiritual matters; ritual and liturgy; music or drama; helping others; community activities.

Consider this major if you are good at: caring/nurturing; counseling; creativity; critical reading/thinking; leadership; research ...*or have...* initiative; patience; verbal skills; writing skills.

Recommended high school prep:

English 4, math 3, lab science 3, social studies 4, and a foreign language 2–3. If available, courses in psychology, sociology, and world literature are also recommended.

Did you know...

...that the study of theology can be both intellectually and spiritually demanding? It requires reflection on the relationship (even tension) between personal faith and critical thinking on fundamental religious questions.

Typical courses in this major:

Introduction to theology
The Old Testament
The New Testament
History of Christian thought
The early church
Medieval thought
The Reformation era
Biblical interpretation and hermeneutics
Studies in the Gospels
Studies in the Epistles
Christian doctrine
Liturgical theology and practice
Ethics
Systematic theology
Church history
World religions

Concentrations:

In college: biblical studies; history of religions; youth and family ministry; religious education; church history.

If you go on to grad school: theology and ministry; Hebrew Bible; New Testament/Christian origins; pastoral theology; liturgical studies.

What the study of this major is like:

Theological studies can be a rich and diverse major. It may be found in departments of theology, religion, philosophy and religion, or Bible studies. In most colleges, theology is taught not just as the beliefs of a particular religious community, but in a more all-encompassing spirit —that is, you learn about the theologies of your community, other communities, and the broader non-Christian world.

As a major, you explore the issues of justice, mercy, and the power attributed to God, and meditate on the problem of evil, suffering, and death in a world ruled by God. In Christian theology, you read the Bible, if possible in the original languages. By studying various religions, you learn how their followers perceive the moral life, and you evaluate the effect of faith on practical matters of worship and ethics.

Other Bible-oriented courses may examine how the books of the Bible came to be considered by Jews and Christians as sacred. Taking note of parables and metaphors in secular, or nonreligious, literature highlights the similarities and differences between the Bible and other literary works.

In church history courses, topics include the development of spirituality and worship; the relationship between religious institutions and civil governments

507

and secular society; the impact of believers on culture and politics; and the way social and political environments affect the church. In ethics, you study the personal and social teachings of the living faith, including the challenges of medical and economic technology, and consider the ways in which believers can participate in social action and political life.

Your college experience will include a lot of reading and reflection, intense and wide-ranging conversations with other students, and exploratory visits to worshiping communities from other traditions. You typically learn through a combination of reading, lecture, discussion, and, sometimes, formal debate. Fieldwork, internships, and practicums are regular features of theological studies programs, and service learning is becoming increasingly popular.

Between your third and fourth years, you are likely to do an internship. Practical/ministerial studies also include clinical experience and frank self-reflection. The biggest challenge you may face is to take an objective look at beliefs and ideas you may have accepted unquestioningly; students are often afraid of asking hard-driving questions about their faith.

Some colleges encourage this no-holds-barred inquiry into the faith, on the basis that critical questioning (when supported by a community of believing scholars) can deepen and strengthen your faith by helping you become mature and reflective. Other colleges focus on instilling faith and strengthening your conviction, contending that careful teaching of the faith can make you a mature believer, without causing you stress by questioning your basic convictions.

Other majors you might like:
Bible studies
Religious studies
Human services
Youth ministry
Preministerial studies
Philosophy
Religious education
Social work
Anthropology
Legal studies
Peace and conflict studies

Questions to ask colleges:
How does the program help students relate to persons of other faiths in a pluralistic society?

Is there a community of faith that can provide support and stimulation?

Career options and trends:
Priest or minister; teacher; youth minister; director of religious education; journalist; social worker; parish administrator; vocational counselor.

Like other liberal arts majors, theology prepares you for a variety of careers in education, business, government, public affairs, and social work. A theology degree is excellent preparation for graduate study in divinity, which enables you to work in pastoral positions. Most mainline Christian church bodies are suffering from severe shortages in pastoral and other ministry positions.

For more info:
American Academy of Religion (AAR)
825 Houston Mill Rd., N.E.
Suite 300
Atlanta, GA 30329-4205
(404) 727-3049
www.aarweb.org

Association of Theological Schools (ATS)
10 Summit Park Drive
Pittsburgh, PA 15275-1110
(412) 788-6505
www.ats.edu

Social sciences

Social sciences are the most popular academic majors in American four-year colleges and second only to business among all categories of majors chosen. More than 195,000 bachelor's degrees are given in the social sciences each year, including nearly 90,000 in psychology alone. It seems we can never know enough about our fellow human beings.

These majors cover the world inside and out, from archaeological digs that investigate the beginnings of humankind, to satellite global positioning systems that pinpoint where we are today. (You'll study GPS in the geography major.) Anthropology explores our origins, cultures, and evolution from prehistory to the present. Sociology, the study of groups of people, covers places, spaces, and races. Psychologists probe the way we behave and think. Economists track resources. Political scientists gauge power. And experts in international relations tackle global conflicts, poverty, oppression, and the flip side—peace, wealth, and freedom.

"I love this field because it addresses the 'big' issues, problems and challenges that confront humanity today to provide tools and insights that can help us create a more just, humane, and peaceful world," says Professor Andrew A. Latham of Macalester College.

These majors touch on many fields, and the knowledge and skills you'll learn can be applied later along many career paths.

"Economics graduates find jobs in education, government, industry, public policy, and planning. Many become business managers," says Professor John J. Siegfried, Vanderbilt University. "The field is also excellent preparation for law school, business school, and, more recently, medical school. Many students with a B.A. or a B.S. degree enter general management training in large corporations. Others start out in sales or analyst positions."

As is often the case, jobs are harder to get for students with just a bachelor's degree, if the economy is slow. But because the social sciences make students think, use numbers intelligently, write well, and understand people, these majors are good overall training for the workplace.

"More students would consider international relations if they knew how valuable this major is as a flexible basis for future careers," notes

Professor Robert Mandel, Lewis and Clark College, of his department, whose grads are likely to be in demand in today's global workplace.

"For political science majors," Latham says, "developing the intellectual tools necessary to understand politics equips students with some of the skills required for leadership in their chosen field."

Mixing art and science

These majors cover a lot of bases, so, in addition to schools of social sciences, look into colleges of humanities, liberal arts, arts and sciences, arts and letters, behavioral sciences, life sciences, and education, as well as preprofessional divisions. For economics, be sure to check out business programs.

But wait, are social sciences really humanities or are they really sciences?

"The study of political science can be both 'scientific' and 'humanistic,'" Latham explains. "Some schools favor methods that are more scientific or quantitative, some more humanistic or qualitative."

Another example of this blend is in geography. "Two main specializations within geography are physical geography and human geography," says Professor Gregory A. Elmes of West Virginia University. "Purely physical geography is akin to the natural sciences with emphasis on theory, laws, and experimental evidence. Within human geography are the more conventional systematic elements, such as cultural, economic, and urban studies."

When choosing a college program, ask if it's more about humankind or research, the people or the numbers. Are you mostly theorizing about the subject or analyzing it? Or both? Some majors, including psychology, can lead to either a Bachelor of Arts or a Bachelor of Science degree.

Ask colleges which electives you should take with your major, like history with international relations. How much math will you need to know? What are the degree requirements and what special courses can you take? Do most students in the major finish their degree in four years?

Learn the strengths of the faculty members. Do they know about other fields so they can help you draw connections to other disciplines? Are full professors teaching undergraduates? Do the profs also teach the labs and offer advising? What kind of research are the faculty members doing? Will you get a chance to do research with them? How big are the classes? Are libraries, book collections, journals, and computers and software adequate and up-to-date?

Are scholarships and internships available for undergrads? What kinds of jobs do grad students often get? Find out if your major has a graduate program, where you could go for a master's or a Ph.D. (See the individual majors in this section for graduate concentrations, careers, and sources of information.)

Also in this book, read about related majors in the sections on Area, ethnic, and gender studies; Business; Education; Engineering technology; Family and consumer sciences; Humanities; Multi/interdisciplinary studies; Natural resources and conservation; and Public administration. You see, the social sciences are everywhere.

Anthropology

What it's about:

Anthropology is the study of people—their origins, physical nature, and social behavior. Anthropology majors explore human cultural and biological evolution and the way all peoples, from prehistoric times to today, adapt to their environment; form families, clans, tribes, and nations; regulate behavior through laws and government; worship and celebrate; communicate; educate their young; and adapt to change.

Is this for you?

You might like this major if you also like: traveling; learning about different peoples and cultures; *National Geographic*; reading; history; geography.

Consider this major if you are good at: attention to detail; foreign languages; observing; research ...*or have...* initiative; verbal skills; writing skills.

Recommended high school prep:

English 4, math 3, lab science 3 (including biology), social studies 4, and a foreign language 3–4. If available, courses in sociology and government are also recommended.

Typical courses in this major:

Biological anthropology
Introduction to archaeology
Cultural anthropology
Primate behavior
Archaeological field methods
Religion and culture
Music and culture
Language and culture
Mythology
Human origins and evolution
Culture and personality
Native American cultures
Forensic anthropology
Human population genetics
Old World prehistory
Peoples and cultures of Africa, Asia, etc.

Concentrations:

Archaeology; physical/biological anthropology; linguistic anthropology; cultural anthropology; urban anthropology; applied anthropology; cultural resource management.

What the study of this major is like:

Majors in anthropology focus on the similarities and differences between human beings and other primates, as well as on the similarities and differences among human populations. Anthropologists are interested in all aspects of what it means to be human.

You learn how people in different parts of the world live their lives and adapt to their environments. Most programs require courses in each of the four main subdivisions of anthropology: physical anthropology, cultural anthropology, linguistic anthropology, and archaeology. Elective courses allow you to follow your interests—a specific country or cultural unit, such as Japan or Mexico, or a topic, such as political systems, child-rearing practices, music, or art.

Physical anthropology (also known as biological anthropology) investigates when and where human beings first appeared; you may even handle stone tools, skeletal materials, and plaster casts of the remains of people who lived many centuries ago. You may spend time in a local zoo observing chimpanzees and other primates to compare their actions with human behavior. In addition, you'll examine genetic evidence, as you trace human biological origins and evolutionary development.

Cultural anthropology explores specific cultures or concentrates on aspects shared by all cultures—religion, politics, law, or ecology. Cultural anthropologists study the diversity found in contemporary societies, from the few remaining peoples who hunt and gather roots and berries to those who shop in supermarkets and live in metropolitan areas such as Tokyo, New York, and London.

In linguistic anthropology, you examine the relationship of language to other aspects of culture. For instance, you study methods of communication—including body language, dialects, jargon, and slang;

you observe how the language people use reflects their perception of and interaction with the world around them.

Archaeology, which deals with excavating, analyzing, and interpreting physical and cultural remains, is increasingly studied as an independent major or graduate program. Most anthropology programs offer introductory courses and opportunities to study field methods during a summer session.

Some programs encourage students to apply what they learn to contemporary problems facing the United States or other industrial societies; this approach is usually called applied anthropology.

As a rule, instructors will have spent a year or more living and studying among the peoples they are teaching about; the firsthand experience of living for extended periods in other cultures is an important part of anthropological training. In fact, fieldwork in other cultures sets anthropology apart from other social sciences and usually results in engaging lectures.

Most colleges offer courses in the four main subdivisions of anthropology, but few have courses in all the specialized subjects or include all regions of the world with equal thoroughness. If you are interested in a specific society, such as Japan, or a specific topic, such as legal anthropology, you should read course catalogs carefully to see if a particular program covers the topics you want.

Other majors you might like:
Archaeology
Sociology
Linguistics
Classics
Genetics
Geography
History
Psychology
Native American studies
Human development and family studies
Religious studies
Urban studies

Questions to ask colleges:
Are majors encouraged to spend a semester or term abroad? The opportunity to relate what you have learned in your anthropology courses to your own experiences with another culture is the best way to grasp the theories and methods of anthropology. Some programs consider fieldwork so important that they make a term abroad a requirement.

Career options and trends:
Social worker; genetic counselor; field archaeologist; teacher of English as a second language (ESL); cultural artifact specialist; educator; national/state park interpreter; environmental impact assessment researcher; travel agent/guide/consultant; museum administrator or technician.

Some occupations, such as field archaeologist, genetic counselor, and museum technician, may require additional specialized training and experience; graduate study is usually required for research, social work, and teaching.

Anthropology provides good preparation for a wide variety of jobs—in government, business, social services, the news media, museums, and education—that require an understanding of cultural and national differences and the ability to work with people from a variety of backgrounds.

Insider's viewpoint:
"Come prepared to think. This isn't a major for people who like to sit back and listen to others talk. Also, you need an open mind to study anthropology, because part of what you have to learn is that the way other people think is no less developed, no less 'right,' than the way you think."

—Chris, senior, Williams College

For more info:
American Anthropological Association (AAA)
2200 Wilson Blvd.
Suite 600
Arlington, VA 22201
(703) 528-1902
www.aaanet.org

Archaeology

What it's about:
Archaeology majors investigate extinct societies and the history of living societies. By excavating, analyzing, and interpreting cultural remains, you reconstruct lifeways and study why and how human cultures have changed over the last 2.5 million years.

Is this for you?
You might like this major if you also like: Scouting; collecting; detecting; discovery; history; mummies; ancient civilizations.

Consider this major if you are good at: attention to detail; creativity; critical reading/thinking; organizing; research; spacial thinking/analysis *...or have...* curiosity/thirst for knowledge; initiative; patience; writing skills.

Recommended high school prep:
English 4, math 3, lab science 3, social studies 3, and a foreign language 3–4. Computer skills and an additional language are useful but not mandatory.

Did you know...
...that archaeological "digs," or investigations, require systematic and detailed data collection, often in remote locations? While there is excitement in discovery, the process can be slow and somewhat tedious, often based upon minute and fragmentary evidence.

Typical courses in this major:
Introduction to archaeological theory and
  methods
Survey of world prehistory
Greco-Roman studies
Egyptology
Chinese and Japenese dynastic history
Paleolithic cultures
Origins of New World civilizations
Sub-Saharan African cultures
Central Asian archaeology
Origins of Australian and Polynesian cultures
Megalithic and Celtic archaeology

Field excavation
Zooarchaeology
Paleoethnobotany
GIS (Geographic Information Systems)
Forensic archaeology

Concentrations:
In college: classical archaeology; anthropological archaeology.

If you go on to grad school: maritime archaeology; zooarchaeology; paleoethnobotany; environmental archaeology; aDNA (ancient DNA) analyses; forensic archaeology; cultural resources management; GIS (Geographic Information Systems) and spatial analysis; rock art analyses; and regional studies, such as Egyptology, Hittite archaeology, Mayan archaeology.

What the study of this major is like:
First- and second-year archaeology courses are survey lectures that provide the tools to get you involved in the more interesting aspects of the discipline. For example, you need to learn where and when a culture existed before you go out into the field and study it. Your third- and fourth-year courses, usually seminars of about 5 to 15 students, focus on specific issues, areas, and problems of anthropological or classical archaeology.

For anthropological archaeology, you take lab courses ranging from the preliminary analyses of excavation materials to advanced labs in specialty fields, such as zooarchaeology (the analysis of animal remains); geoarchaeology (the use of geologic methods to interpret an excavation site); paleoethnobotany (the analysis of plant remains); forensic archaeology (the recovery of buried criminal evidence); spatial analysis (use of GIS technology); or historical archaeology (the archaeologic record of historic events).

If you concentrate in classical archaeology, your work shifts to literature-and-language studies and intensive investigation of Greek, Roman, Egyptian, or Chinese cultures. In both trajectories, students often prepare an honors thesis, the product of an independent study.

Most students participate in one or more semester-abroad excavation projects, which sometimes take place during the summer. There are many possibilities; selecting the one best for you is often a challenge. For some, the issue is cost; to attend a field school, you must pay for room and board, transportation, and perhaps tuition. Also, if you need to work during the summer to help pay for school, field projects can interfere. Another consideration is the type of data you need to collect. Although the field school is a good place to do research for an honors thesis, you may have trouble knowing which kind of data your project requires. Your college advisers should provide you with suggestions.

Archaeology professors are often working on their own field research projects, so you may be able to help with the analysis of earlier excavations or participate in the excavations on a current project. If you develop an interest in a geographic area or an ancient culture other than those your instructors are pursuing, you might work on a project with some of their colleagues. Also, colleges with a grad program may allow you to work with master's or doctorate degree students on their research projects. Advanced students often make good mentors.

Working together in the field and on thesis projects can be fun and exciting. Students often develop a strong camaraderie and pick up on each other's enthusiasm. Most programs offer colloquiums, in which students meet to hear an undergrad, grad student, faculty member, or distinguished visitor give an informal presentation on work in progress.

Other majors you might like:

Art history
Anthropology
Geology/earth science
Classics
Environmental studies
Architectural history/criticism
History
Historic preservation
Bible studies
Medieval and Renaissance studies
Ancient studies
Classical/ancient Mediterranean/Near Eastern studies

Questions to ask colleges:

Does the program offer undergrad concentrations in classical and/or anthropological archaeology? Learning about both approaches provides you with a broader grasp of archaeology and may offer you more graduate and post-graduate opportunities.

Does the college have a grad program in archaeology? What kinds of archaeological labs are available? Are there opportunities for students to go on excavation projects? The presence of a grad program usually indicates a stronger program for undergraduates, with more facilities and field opportunities.

Where do the faculty members conduct their field research? If you are already interested in a particular region, you should go to a college that will allow you to work in that area.

Career options and trends:

College professor; museum curator; cultural resource management specialist; state or federal government archaeologist; park ranger.

If you go into cultural resource management or, to a lesser extent, other archaeological fields, you are strongly encouraged to meet the training and certification requirements of the Register of Professional Archaeologists (www.rpanet.org), which includes obtaining an advanced degree.

Employment prospects for archaeologists are strong. According to the Bureau of Labor Statistics, one factor encouraging job growth is the need to upgrade the nation's infrastructure. That's because such projects will require archaeologists to ensure compliance with historical preservation laws.

Less than half of all archaeologists work in traditional areas such as teaching and museums. The majority now work for state or federal government agencies or in the private sector. Probably as many as two-thirds of all archaeologists hold positions that did not exist a generation ago.

Insider's viewpoint:

"I thrill to the excitement of discovery, finding the first known example of geophagy (the practice of eating earth when food is scarce) in the Andes, discovering evidence for a new trade route, pulling the disparate pieces of the puzzle together and figuring out the lifeways of past human cultures."

—Professor David L. Browman, Washington University in St. Louis

For more info:

Society for American Archaeology (SAA)
1111 14th Street, NW, Suite 800
Washington, DC 20005-5622
(202) 789-8200
www.saa.org

Society for Historical Archaeology (SHA)
13017 Wisteria Drive
No. 395
Germantown, MD 20874
(301) 972-9684
www.sha.org

Economics

What it's about:

The economics major provides a framework for analyzing issues such as inflation, unemployment, monopoly, and economic growth. You learn how economic systems function to provide goods and services. As you study theory, policy, and trends, you explore ways to deal with the economic problems that confront individuals, businesses, and nations.

Is this for you?

You might like this major if you also like: Thinking about issues such as wealth, poverty, discrimination, the environment, and trends in the global economy; working with numbers; reading about current events in newspapers and news magazines; investment clubs.

Consider this major if you are good at: attention to detail; logical reasoning; math; organizing; quantitative analysis ...*or have...* initiative; writing skills.

Recommended high school prep:

English 4, math 4, lab science 3 (including physics), social studies 4 (including American/U.S. history, world history, government/civics, and economics), and a foreign language 2–3. If possible, take a computer science course.

Did you know...

...that economics is concerned with choices people make in all areas of their lives, not just choices related to financial matters?

Typical courses in this major:

Principles of microeconomics
Principles of macroeconomics
Economic statistics
Money and banking
Business and government
International trade
International finance
Urban economics
Environmental economics
Labor economics
Public economics
Industrial organization
Economic history
Poverty and discrimination
Health economics
Law and economics

Concentrations:

Generally, none in college; but if you go on to grad school: microeconomic theory; macroeconomic theory; econometrics; labor economics; monetary economics; industrial organization; public economics; international economics; economic history; economic development.

What the study of this major is like:

Economics is about choices and change. By investigating how people make decisions, economists can predict how people will react to change. Economics can help people to understand the causes of economic problems and to devise ways to avoid them. It is a practical discipline that plays an important role in the formulation of policies on such issues as taxation, energy policy, retirement security, international trade, health care, the environment, and the rate of inflation.

If you like rigorous analysis and problem solving, economics can be intellectually appealing. It uses simplified models to explain and predict economic behavior in a complicated, disorderly world. For example, when the interest rate goes down, what happens to mortgage rates and to the cost of new cars? Economics emphasizes insights derived from observation. It teaches you to isolate the most important facts and to focus on their implications.

As a major, you will probably begin with introductory and intermediate microeconomics (the study of individual firms, consumers, and workers) and macroeconomics (the study of economy-wide income, employment, and prices), and an economic statistics course. Later, in electives—such as international trade and finance, environmental economics, labor, public finance, or comparative economic systems—you see how basic principles come to bear in specific applied fields. Your standard tools of analysis are graphs and algebra. Most of your classes will be taught as lectures, and you can expect to do plenty of problem sets.

Some programs focus on theoretical analysis; others favor data analysis. Programs may also vary in their definition of economic practice. According to some professionals, an economist's main job is to model the economy as it might be—to develop theories that predict the consequences of policies. Other economists see their job as collecting data that describe the economy as it is. Still others examine the social, cultural, and political factors that influence the economy.

Although few economics departments have enough staff to offer courses in all the applied fields, most programs emphasize universal, fundamental principles. However, if you are interested in applying economics to a particular problem, be sure to choose a college that has the courses you'll need.

Other majors you might like:
Agricultural economics
Business administration and management
Accounting
Applied mathematics
Business/managerial economics
Finance
Psychology
Entrepreneurial studies
Statistics
Econometrics/quantitative economics
International business
International relations

Questions to ask colleges:
How much math do you need to succeed in the major? Is it enough to do well in algebra, or is calculus or even more advanced math necessary? The answers can help you plan what courses to take in both high school and college.

Is there a capstone experience such as a senior seminar, thesis, or independent-study project?

Career options and trends:
Business economist; economic consultant; government economist; investment banker; market researcher.

Graduates also find jobs in education, industry, public policy, and planning. In addition, the field is excellent preparation for law school, business school, and, recently, medical school. Many students with a B.A. or B.S. degree in economics enter training programs in large corporations and may become business managers. Others start out in sales or analyst positions. Economics majors can also consider teaching positions; high schools in particular are expected to have a growing need for economics instructors.

Insider's viewpoint:
"It's hard to understand and accept the fact that there are economic theories that support either conservative or liberal policies and that, although these theories contradict each other, they are both viable."

—David, senior, Cornell University

For more info:
Council for Economic Education
122 East 42 Street, Suite 2600
New York, NY 10168
(212) 730-7007
www.councilforeconed.org

Geography

What it's about:

Geography is the science of space and place on the earth's surface. You examine how people, regions, and environments interact to create and sustain the world in which we live. Using a multidisciplinary approach, you study local, regional, and global geography.

Is this for you?

You might like this major if you also like: maps; current affairs; *National Geographic*; travel; backpacking; biking; environmental issues; Model UN; computer graphics; other people and cultures.

Consider this major if you are good at: Integrating information from different sources; attention to detail; creativity; critical reading/thinking; research; spacial thinking/analysis ...*or have...* graphical skills; initiative; verbal skills; writing skills.

Recommended high school prep:

English 4, math 3, lab science 3, social studies 4, and a foreign language 2–3. If they are available, also take ecology and AP human geography.

Typical courses in this major:

Human geography
Physical geography
Urban geography
World regional geography
Cultural geography
Economic geography
Remote sensing
Political geography
Cartography
Natural resources
Energy and the environment
Urban and regional planning
Weather and climate
Social geography
Geographic Information Systems (GIS)
Human-environmental relations

Concentrations:

In college: physical geography; environmental geography; human geography; spatial skills (tools and techniques); regional or area studies.

If you go on to grad school: human-environment relations; geographic information science; environmental geoscience; atmospheric and climatic studies; geomorphology; urban and regional systems; development studies.

What the study of this major is like:

Geography includes much more than the memorization of place names, capitals, and longest rivers. It investigates the way people from a variety of localities relate to their environment and the way their surroundings shape their lives. As a major, you gain a broad understanding of the way humans have adapted to, changed, and organized their physical environments. Geography draws from related fields, such as anthropology, economics, political science, and biology.

Two main specializations in the major are physical geography and human geography and discussions often focus on their overlap. Physical geographers study climates, landforms, vegetation, soils, and water. In human geography, the emphasis is on people's perception, use, and modification of space, as individuals and communities create and sustain the places they call home. Topics the two groups examine include the effects, on both human activity and the natural world, of global warming, desertification, deforestation, loss of biodiversity, groundwater pollution, fire, and flooding.

The major begins with first-year courses that introduce you to facts, ideas, and tools. Besides human geography and physical geography, you take statistics, regional geography (such as courses on Africa or North America), and skills (such as cartography or remote sensing). Then you can concentrate in an area such as environmental geography, geographic education, or geographic information systems (GIS). You may be required to complete an independent research project—a capstone experience that pulls together numerous topics and skills. Sometimes you can meet the requirement by participating in a field course. You should also take courses in other departments that relate to your concentration.

Because geography is not usually emphasized in high school, few students begin college as geography majors. Many pick this major in their second or third year of college, so your classmates are often a mixture of upper- and lower-division students. Your course work includes a rich mixture of lectures, lab, and library and field research. As you progress, you spend more time in specialized computer labs for cartography, GIS, and remote sensing; and in labs for physical geography (soils, geomorphology, and fluvial and glacial processes).

Frequently, the best place to learn is in the field. For example, you can spend a semester collecting, analyzing, and presenting local data, or you can study overseas. Often, the hardest part of being a geography major is integrating varied subject matter and approaches. In particular, you need to appreciate the perspectives of both the natural and the social sciences.

Because of geography's roots in both the natural sciences and the humanities, programs are offered in a wide variety of divisions and schools. Undergrad programs are often influenced by the emphasis and philosophy of connected graduate programs. Some programs rely heavily on graduate teaching assistants and part-time faculty members. Many specialized courses—such as medical geography; social and physical planning; population and demographics; and race, ethnicity, and class—are based on the research interests of faculty members. But the most noticeable differences are among programs that stress either physical or human geography. Some colleges have successfully bridged the two by focusing on human-environment relations.

Other majors you might like:
Cartography
Environmental engineering
Urban, community, and regional planning
Global studies
Mining and mineral engineering
Landscape architecture
International relations
Area/ethnic/cultural studies
Wildlife and wilderness management
Surveying technology
Natural resources and conservation
Geology/earth science

Questions to ask colleges:
Are there labs for GIS, remote sensing, and cartography? How many computers are dedicated to geography majors?

Are there certificate programs in GIS, remote sensing, or applied geography? Where and how large is the library/map collection? Which digital data sources are available (for example, population census and aerial photographs)?

What field trips are required or recommended for graduation?

Career options and trends:
Cartographer; GIS manager; economic development analyst; energy analyst; environmental engineer; engineer in photogrammetry (aerial surverying); land use planner; land surveyor; remote sensing specialist; water resources planner.

The hottest job market in the field is for graduates with experience in geographic information systems and remote sensing.

Engineering jobs such as surveying require certification. Increasingly, certification is a requirement for GIS-related jobs. Planning jobs are available to geographers without specific qualifications, but a master's degree in planning is strongly recommended.

Insider's viewpoint:
"I do everything from calculus to paper writing to map analysis. There is incredible variety in the work involved in my major and that's one of the things I love about it. Things stay interesting."

—Carolyn, senior, Arizona State University

For more info:
Association of American Geographers (AAG)
1710 16th St., N.W.
Washington, DC 20009-3198
(202) 234-1450
www.aag.org

National Geographic Society (NGS)
1145 17th St. N.W.
Washington, DC 20036-4688
(800) 647-5463
www.nationalgeographic.com

International relations

What it's about:

International relations is the study of the causes, consequences, and efforts to resolve global patterns of conflict and peace, poverty and wealth, and freedom and oppression. As a major, you examine nations and international organizations to understand political, economic, military, and cultural interactions on the international level.

Is this for you?

You might like this major if you also like: world history; travel; maps; flags; "big picture" issues; stamp collecting; languages; politics.

Consider this major if you are good at: attention to detail; creativity; critical reading/thinking; leadership; persuading/influencing ...*or have...* initiative; patience; verbal skills; writing skills.

Recommended high school prep:

English 4, math 3, lab science 3, social studies 4 (especially world history), and a foreign language 4.

Typical courses in this major:

U.S. foreign policy
International organizations
International law
African politics
Latin American politics
European politics
Russian and East European politics
Northeast Asian politics
South Asian politics
Middle East politics
Global environmental issues
International relations theory
National security
International conflict
International political economy
Global human rights issues

Concentrations:

International law and organization; international business; human rights; international political econ-

omy; national security; international environmental issues; transnational studies; comparative and regional perspectives; U.S. foreign policy.

What the study of this major is like:

This major draws from many disciplines, such as political science, economics, history, sociology, and foreign languages.

You typically begin with an introduction to international relations (usually offered by the political science department), intro courses in micro- and macroeconomics, one or two courses in world history, and a course in sociology or anthropology. Generally, in your third and fourth years you take courses in U. S. foreign policy, international organizations (especially the United Nations), regional issues, diplomacy, national security, and in economics, law, the environment, and human rights, all from a global perspective.

Courses typically incorporate insights from several disciplines and focus on significant current issues. Other requirements may include a seminar in your area of concentration, as well as proficiency in a related foreign language. International travel is recommended to deepen your understanding of other societies.

Although much of the material is presented in lectures, you listen to, and may participate in, serious debate on how the theories of international relations can be most effectively applied. Global discussions, such as those at regional conferences, frequently involve controversial topics. In most colleges, therefore, you will encounter a wide variety of viewpoints on international issues. Exams generally stress interpretive essays rather than single-answer questions. In addition, you will be expected to write papers that combine solid research with independent thinking.

Many majors are overwhelmed, at first, by the broad scope of international relations and the rapidly changing state of world affairs. Because the discipline does not have a fixed body of absolute truths, you must make full use of your critical-thinking and analytical skills. You should expect ongoing challenge and a constant questioning of your views.

There are several differences in the way the major is taught. Often, the program is a multidisciplinary subject of study administered by a committee of professors from various departments. There are few actual departments of international relations, because most professors who teach the subject hold positions in political science, history, or economics departments. Programs may also vary in emphases. While most programs focus on political science, history, and economics, some emphasize language and literature. In addition, a few colleges stress the worldview of the United States, while most attempt to represent a more global perspective.

Some programs may require you to specialize in a global region, although most permit you to be a generalist with a functional, rather than a geographic, specialty (such as business/economics, security/conflict, or human rights). In other programs, the focus is almost entirely on sovereign states. Still others examine transnational and subnational forces (such as humanitarian organizations, terrorist groups, multinational corporations, and separatist groups like the Basques, the Tibetans, and the Tamils). A program may emphasize concepts and theories or practical cases in world affairs. Some programs cover most of the twentieth century, while others focus on recent issues.

Other majors you might like:
International business
Political science
History
Geography
Global studies
Comparative literature
Asian studies
Islamic studies
Peace and conflict studies
Linguistics
Journalism
Emergency management/homeland security

Questions to ask colleges:
Do students in the program pursue internships for undergraduate credit? How are overseas programs integrated into the major?

Career options and trends:
Graduates in international relations are usually eligible for entry-level positions in the federal Civil Service (especially the departments of State, Defense, Agriculture, and Treasury). Many graduates take positions with members of Congress, congressional committees, or the CIA. Other options are United Nations work, international journalism, paralegal positions with law firms and public service legal agencies; jobs in banks and other firms doing international business; and positions with humanitarian organizations such as Amnesty International. A graduate degree in international relations enhances your career options, especially in the Foreign Service and international business.

Graduates with international relations training are in high demand. Globalization is accelerating, and many jobs now have an international component. People who have cultural sensibilities and understand international political, economic, and military issues are much needed.

Insider's viewpoint:
"I just like the fact that the news is part of my major. What I learn in class I can apply to what I read in the news or on the Internet or see on TV. I like having a sense of what's outside the bubble of my university and the United States."

—Sean, senior, Baylor University

For more info:
International Studies Association (I.S.A.)
324 Social Sciences Building
University of Arizona
Tuscon, AZ 85721
(520) 621-7715
www.isanet.org

Political science

Also known as:
Government

What it's about:
As a political science major, you explore the origins, historical development, and functions of government and political power. You study the ways in which electoral, legislative, judicial, and administrative structures vary among countries; the reasons why governments change, fall, and engage in wars; and the behavior of public officials and other citizens who take part in politics.

Is this for you?
You might like this major if you also like: history; current events; politics; debating; student government; community service activities; issues relating to social justice.

Consider this major if you are good at: critical reading/thinking; leadership; quantitative analysis; research; teamwork *...or have...* initiative; verbal skills; writing skills.

Recommended high school prep:
English 4, math 4, lab science 2, social studies 4, and a foreign language 3–4.

Typical courses in this major:
U.S. government
Judicial processes
U.S. foreign policy
Public policy analysis
International law
Global issues
Political action groups
Comparative politics
Political theory
American political campaigns and elections
Politics of developing areas
Politics of ecological crisis
U.S. intelligence and policymaking
Contemporary political ideologies
Ethnic and racial politics
U.S. political thought

Concentrations:
U.S. politics; international relations; comparative politics; political theory.

What the study of this major is like:
The political science and government major deals with a range of domestic and international issues, including civil rights, health care, war and peace, economic development, democracy, the environment, and the role of race, ethnicity, and gender in political life.

You might begin the major with an intro course in political science or, more likely, with an intro to one or more subfields (for example, international relations). In addition, you'll probably take intro theory courses and a class on analytical methods and databased research. Intermediate and advanced courses may cover such topics as international security and global political economy, and U.S. institutions and constitutional law.

Most programs require you to minor in a related field, such as history, sociology, economics, or anthropology. You examine such issues as the principles of human behavior that underlie political activity, the actions of citizens, politicians, and public officials; overall social and economic structures and processes; the origins and development of individual political systems; and the physical and social geography in which governments exist and politics takes place. In some colleges, you study these and other subjects through the core curriculum. If there is no core curriculum, you should choose electives that cover these areas.

Many programs now require majors to complete a capstone project—usually a substantial piece of research in which you integrate the knowledge and skills you have learned, as you investigate questions that interest you. Designing a research project and writing a paper based on your research can be very rewarding.

Your classes may be in either a traditional (lectures) or an active (seminars, problem-based learning) format. You learn both individually and, especially in upper-division courses, in teams. College courses generally take an analytical approach, rather than the historical and current-events approach that students may be accustomed to in high school courses. Even at large colleges, courses above the intro level usually have relatively few students and provide opportunities for discussion among students and instructors.

Most programs offer academic and practical experience outside the classroom—for example, internships in public offices (such as those of state legislative committees, public defenders, and county attorneys) or in administrative agencies. You may spend a "Washington semester" working and studying in the nation's capital. Political science departments often participate in the college's study-abroad programs. Political science clubs and campus political organizations can also enhance the intellectual and social life of majors.

Political science programs differ widely; you should examine the description of the major at colleges you may apply to. Some colleges are more liberal, others more conservative. Some favor scientific or quantitative (math-based) approaches; others choose a humanistic or qualitative perspective.

Other majors you might like:
International relations
History
Criminal justice and law enforcement
Public administration
Public relations
American studies
Urban, community, and regional planning
Legal studies
Journalism
Peace and conflict studies
Urban studies
Military technologies

Career options and trends:
The study of political science and government can lead to careers in a wide range of fields including business, journalism, government service, public administration, nongovernmental organizations (NGOs), law, teaching, the Foreign Service, and the diplomatic corps.

Insider's viewpoint:
"A special commitment to understanding history and current events is helpful. More importantly, perhaps, political science majors should feel comfortable engaging with others on these issues, occasionally in heated debates. I love doing that."

—Brian, junior, Columbia University

For more info:
American Political Science Association (APSA)
1527 New Hampshire Ave., N.W.
Washington, DC 20036
(202) 483-2512
www.apsanet.org

Psychology

What it's about:

Psychology majors study the behavior and mental (emotional, learning, and thought) processes of animals and humans. You learn psychological principles, facts, and theories about individuals and groups, using experimental, observational, and case study methods.

Is this for you?

You might like this major if you also like: observing how animals and people act and respond; science; helping others; working with children or the elderly; working with numbers.

Consider this major if you are good at: critical reading/thinking; math; memorizing; research ...*or have...* empathy; initiative; motivation; people skills; writing skills.

Recommended high school prep:

English 4, math 4 (including trigonometry or precalculus), lab science 4 (including advanced biology or chemistry), social studies 3, and a foreign language 2–3. If possible, take computer science and statistics courses and a year of psychology. Participating in community service is also beneficial.

Did you know...

...that in psychology, animals are studied both to examine their behavior and to provide insights into human behavior?

...that this major requires you to learn scientific and statistical methods? Many students are surprised by this but then find it to be not that difficult.

...that for almost all work done as a professional psychologist, you need a graduate or professional degree?

Typical courses in this major:

Abnormal psychology
Social psychology
Personality development
Learning and memory
History of psychology
Tests and measurement
Cognitive psychology
Statistics
Child psychology
Perception
Physiological psychology
Experimental psychology
Industrial/organizational psychology
Developmental psychology
Research methods in psychology
Cross-cultural psychology

Concentrations:

In college: methodology/research; applied psychology; clinical psychology; child psychology; social psychology.

If you go on to grad school: ecological psychology; personality; sensation and perception; animal behavior; industrial and organizational psychology; sports psychology; forensic psychology.

What the study of this major is like:

The psychology major most often begins with a required one-semester intro course; continues with several other required core courses, such as in research methods, statistics, and experimental psychology; and concludes with a fourth-year capstone experience—perhaps a research seminar.

Most departments divide the major into concentrations—such as developmental psychology (which may include infant and child psychology, adolescence, gerontology, and the life span) and experimental psychology (learning, sensation and perception, and biological psychology)—and require you to take courses from each area. In addition, you can usually choose from a range of electives. You earn either a Bachelor of Science degree (which requires more math and science) or a Bachelor of Arts degree (requiring more humanities and a foreign language); otherwise, there may be little difference in course work between the two degrees.

The subject matter of psychology is diverse. An intro course may cover the basics of motivation, perception, learning, memory, social psychology, developmental psychology, abnormal psychology, counseling psychology, and language—topics that may also be covered, in depth, in intermediate and advanced courses. In undergraduate counseling psychology, you learn about psychotherapy. Clinical psychology adds psychological assessment (testing) and program evaluation and research skills.

Some courses feature lecture and discussion, and some have research components. Labs may involve working with sophisticated equipment, or with a rat, pigeon, or other animal colony. Doing research allows you to learn scientific methods and to differentiate between commonsense notions and research-based findings. In individual and group research, you may investigate attitudes and beliefs through questionnaires; observe people in social situations; or explore differences in responses between experimental groups and control groups.

The challenges you may face include mastering statistics and becoming familiar with the methods of scientific inquiry. Learning the terminology and basic concepts of psychology will probably require some no-nonsense studying. Presenting research at a forum or conference can be a rewarding, if intimidating, experience.

Departments may vary in whether they emphasize psychology as a liberal arts or as a preprofessional program. At some colleges, the emphasis is on pure research. At others, which stress the practical application of research, there may be more opportunities to do internships in the mental health/human service and industrial/organizational areas.

Other majors you might like:
Mental health services technology
Behavioral sciences
Gerontology
Industrial engineering
Neuroscience
Human development and family studies
Criminology
Sociology
Child development
Anthropology
Human resources management
Religious studies

Questions to ask colleges:
Can students take courses that give them experience with professional or applied psychology, such as counseling or industrial/organizational work? Which courses allow students to participate in labs and/or field research?

Do faculty members help students determine if they should go on to grad school? Ideally, full-time instructors are available as advisers throughout your undergraduate education.

Career options and trends:
Social worker; school psychologist; clinical psychologist; lawyer; counseling psychologist; physician (internist, psychiatrist, or other specialist); health care administrator; psychotherapist.

Psychology majors also pursue careers in a wide variety of public, private, profit, nonprofit, business, and service organizations, working in administration/management, community relations, program development, research, human resources, public relations, military service, advertising, market research, retail, and sales.

Jobs in health care administration, social work, industrial/organizational psychology, and medicine (including psychiatry) require graduate or professional degrees. Job growth will be strong for positions in school psychology, clinical psychology, and human services/mental health, which usually require either a master's or doctorate degree, state certification or licensure, and sometimes a one-year internship. Physicians must pass the state board exams to be licensed to practice in a particular state.

Many graduate programs that teach clinical skills (such as psychotherapy, assessment, and program evaluation) are discontinuing such training at the master's level; the doctorate is becoming the entry-level degree of choice.

Insider's viewpoint:
"Don't base your decision to major in psychology on Psych 101 because it is pretty broad and boring. I found classes in social, abnormal, and adolescent psychology to be the most interesting."

—Alison, senior, University of Virginia

For more info:

American Psychological Association (APA)
750 First St., N.E.
Washington, DC 20002-4242
(800) 374-2721
www.apa.org

Association for Psychological Science (APS)
1133 15th St., N.W.
Suite 1000
Washington, DC 20005
(202) 293-9300
www.psychologicalscience.org

Sociology

What it's about:

Sociology is the study of society and social behavior. By studying how individuals act in small and large groups, as well as how such groups are formed and function, you explore social problems and public policy. You investigate a range of topics, including the intimacies of family relationships; the demographics of urban and rural spaces; and the consequences of race, gender, and class divisions across societies.

Is this for you?

You might like this major if you also like: observing human behavior; reading; research; writing; community service activities; debating; computers; politics; exploring different perspectives on social issues such as gender and race.

Consider this major if you are good at: attention to detail; creativity; critical reading/thinking; organizing; quantitative analysis; research; teamwork *...or have...* initiative; patience; writing skills.

Recommended high school prep:

English 4, math 3, lab science 3, social studies 3, and a foreign language 2–3.

Did you know...

...how much scientific research is involved in sociology? Sociologists follow strict guidelines for the collection and analysis of information, including quantitative methods used for conducting surveys, qualitative methods used for interviews and observations, analytical procedures used for coding and interpreting field notes, and statistical procedures used to analyze data.

Typical courses in this major:

Introduction to sociology
Sociological theory
Research methods
Social stratification
Deviance
Socially complex organizations
Minority groups
Juvenile delinquency
Social problems
Gender roles
Social psychology
Sociology of education
Sociology of the family

Concentrations:

In college: racial and ethnic minorities; sex and gender; criminology and delinquency; family sociology; work and occupations; urban or rural affairs; stratification.

If you go on to grad school: demography; methodology; education; social movements; gerontology; medical sociology.

What the study of this major is like:

Course work ranges from case studies of the relationships among individuals in particular social settings, to scrutiny of governments and economic systems across time. Intro courses ask questions such as "How are rules of normality established? How do these rules change? How do social institutions (such as the family) influence our choices, our perceptions of reality, and our plans for the future?" To answer these questions, you may explore the issues from several perspectives (often drawn from disciplines such as history, economics, and political science) as you make progress in your studies.

Sociology is taught mostly through lectures, supplemented by presentations, films, guest speakers, and independent research. Required courses usually include introductory sociology, research methods, theory, and statistics. Probably you'll take courses in such related areas as geography, political science, religion, and economics. Many courses deal with social policy. For example, a course on social stratification (that is, how societies are divided up) may include discussion of policies designed to reduce inequality.

Most programs require you to learn the theories and research methods that prepare you for independent projects. You'll gain practice in using academic journals, computerized databases, and other materials available at most college libraries; or you might gather and analyze data yourself, through surveys, interviews, and observations. In many programs, you will have the opportunity to do an internship at a social service agency, where you can apply what you have learned in the classroom.

There are some challenges. First, the field is so wide that you may have difficulty narrowing your interests to a specific research topic. Second, the scientific method of conducting research, especially the emphasis on statistical analysis, can cause trouble for some students. But students who master data analysis are usually rewarded. Statistics makes their research work much more efficient, and many jobs that majors take after graduation require data analysis. Finally, there is a fair amount of reading, writing, studying terminology, and evaluating different perspectives and theories that are sometimes difficult. The independent research project that some colleges require takes time, initiative, patience, and, often, creativity. Despite the academic demands of this major, though, students rarely complain that the readings are uninteresting.

Programs may vary in the number of courses required for the major. Across colleges, concentrations may also vary according to faculty members' expertise, and areas of concentration may change as new topics emerge. You can get a feel for the differences among programs by comparing courses required and concentrations offered and by looking at the types of research the professors are doing.

Other majors you might like:
African-American studies
Political science
Anthropology
Community organization/advocacy
Criminal justice and law enforcement
Chicano studies
Media studies
Parks, recreation, and leisure studies
Human development and family studies
Social work
Urban, community, and regional planning
Gay/lesbian studies

Career options and trends:
The sociology major can lead to careers in marketing, consumer research, advertising, insurance,
human resources, teaching, nonprofit organizations, community development agencies, environmental groups, criminal justice (probation or parole officers), government research (in local, state, and federal agencies), law, urban planning, Foreign Service, and industrial sociology. Advanced degrees are required for work as college professors, lawyers, demographers, policy analysts, and research institute managers.

Insider's viewpoint:
"I've heard many people say statistics don't mean anything, they're just numbers, but to me they represent what goes on. When I took statistics in my first semester, I didn't understand why I had to, but in a lot of the classes it's 'ninety percent of these people...' or 'ninety-seven percent of kids...'"

—Liz, senior, San Jose State University

For more info:
American Sociological Association (ASA)
1430 K Street, NW
Suite 600
Washington, DC 20005
(202) 383-9005
www.asanet.org

Visual and performing arts

If you turned to this chapter first, you probably think of the arts as more than just entertainment or pretty pictures. You are not alone. The arts are popular majors for students who might like to pursue a career in painting, acting, dance, or other creative or expressive fields. The performing arts differ from the visual arts, so let's start with the performing arts.

If you're a singer, actor, dancer, or musician, you may already know that the intense competition for performance work limits jobs to the most accomplished artists in a given field.

"Very few performance majors are ever able to make a living through music performance alone," says Professor Sandra Billy of the Center for Sacred Music at Virginia Wesleyan College. (See the Religion and theology section for sacred music.)

Fortunately, you can break the stereotype of the starving artist. Many doors are open to trained artists. For instance, dancers and choreographers (who create dances) may not be able to break through the competition barrier, but dance teachers are needed. Arts management is another professional outlet.

"Despite limited job opportunities, there is always room for those who are highly talented and well prepared," says Jo Anne Caputo, a member of the faculty at the Cleveland Institute of Music.

You can parlay your talent and training in the arts into a rewarding career. Take another example. Theater majors are known for their ability to get ideas across. That skill is important in many professions—law, advertising, business, teaching, and even politics. President Ronald Reagan and California governor Arnold Schwarzenegger worked as movie actors before running for public office.

"Fine arts are excellent preparation for any field requiring careful thinking, synthesis, accurate observation and expression, not just art-related positions," assures Professor of Arts Studies Emeritus David B. Greene of North Carolina State University.

In the visual arts, a similar dynamic is at play, because few people earn their living from gallery exhibits and sales of their artwork. But visual and design skills can be transferred to jobs like interior and fashion design; photography; and graphic design for print, video, and the Internet. Many college programs, including interactive and digital art, multimedia, Web design, and animation, apply computer technologies to the visual arts. Composers of music use computers and digital musical instruments in their craft, leading to valuable workplace skills.

If you can use digital technologies or think visually, you have prized talents in a media-driven world. "In a knowledge economy, those who make information comprehensible are valued," explains Professor Meredith Davis of North Carolina State University.

The education landscape

If someone did a painting depicting all of the country's college art programs, it would look like a Pollock, not a Mondrian. "This is a complicated educational landscape...with wildly different degree offerings," cautions Professor Davis.

Choose wisely if you plan to study the arts in college. Especially if you're interested in the fine arts, ask yourself how competitive a school you really want. "Some performance students prefer and thrive in a hyper-competitive environment. Others may prefer a less intense, more nurturing setting. It is important to find the right fit," Caputo advises.

Here are some other things to think about in choosing visual or performing arts programs: Should you study near a city with lots of concerts and galleries? Does the college have its own collection, facilities, image archive, rehearsal instruments, and studios? Do you have to audition or submit a portfolio of your artwork to be accepted?

Are you going for a B.A. degree or a B.F.A (Bachelor of Fine Arts)? The B.A. is a broader approach to art. The B.F.A. gets you ready for a career in a specific art form and might require an audition or portfolio to get into college.

If you're headed for a teaching career, you'll want a higher degree. Graduate studies in the various arts focus on recording and studio production techniques, animation, creative art therapy, and performance art, to name a few. Fine arts grad students may study a particular period, region, or medium.

Also try to get an idea of the daily life of an arts major. How many hours per week will you be taking lessons or working in a studio or at a computer? Are computer lab fees included in your tuition? Will you set your own schedule or are rehcarsals preset? How crowded are studios or computer stations? Are they open late? Look at the studios, concert halls, galleries, and design technologies on campus. Nice facilities mean the school is committed to the arts.

The faculty is most important, especially in the performing arts, where students are guided by mentors. Your choice of a college may hinge on the availability of a master teacher.

In your search, you'll run across art programs in colleges of arts and sciences, liberal arts, mass communications, fine and performing arts, schools of design, schools or conservatories of music, and so on. A good website to get you going is www.arts-accredit.org. If you don't have a computer, ask your school counselor or local librarian to help you compare colleges and programs. Also see the Communications section for some related majors.

Animation

What it's about:

Animation majors learn a broad range of animation techniques, both traditional and contemporary. Your training covers a broad range of drawing, sound, acting, film, and storytelling skills, along with current software applications.

Is this for you?

You might like this major if you also like: filmmaking; photography; reading and writing stories; drama clubs; art clubs.

Consider this major if you are good at: attention to detail; creativity; critical reading/thinking; organizing; spacial thinking/analysis; teamwork ...*or have...* imagination.

Recommended high school prep:

English 4, math 3, lab science 3, social studies 3, and a foreign language 2–3. Take as many courses in art (including studio art and art history) and computer applications as you can. A strong background in language arts (literature and writing) is also recommended.

Did you know...

...that traditional art skills are still the most important quality that successful animators have? If you have these skills, you will have an edge over those who don't. Specific knowledge of software is not essential; you will learn computer techniques in the major.

...that an interest in literature and storytelling is also important? Knowing what makes a good story is just as significant as having technical skills.

Typical courses in this major:

Figure and animal drawing
Color theory
Storyboard and narrative
Screenwriting for animators
Acting for animators
History of animation
Character animation techniques
Stop-motion techniques
Experimental animation techniques
Layout and background design
Digital ink and paint
Special effects
Sound design
Digital compositing
Digital character modeling
3-D computer animation

Concentrations:

Computer animation; character animation; stop-motion animation; special effects.

What the study of this major is like:

Do you enjoy telling stories? Do you love to draw? Do you visualize the characters and settings in some of the works you read? If so, animation might be a good major for you. The field of animation offers many ways to use your imagination, including writing stories, designing characters, and re-creating the worlds that the characters inhabit.

As an animation major, you'll first receive a firm grounding in the principles of art, and you'll explore a variety of ways to develop and tell stories. You then learn the techniques (practical as well as creative) of cinema and how to apply these techniques to both traditional and computer-assisted filmmaking.

As you advance in the program, you are introduced to various animation software packages (for example, 3D Studio Max and Maya for three-dimensional modeling and animation; Flash, Photoshop, and After Effects for compositing; Toonz for digital ink and paint). These and other software systems become part of your toolkit as you gain experience in making your own films. You'll finish with a fourth-year thesis film.

Your courses consist of lectures and demonstrations, accompanied by many hours of practice in and out of the classroom. Early in the program, you concentrate on drawing, a skill that will help you master the more advanced techniques taught later on. Ideally, animation programs challenge you to enlarge your visual vocabulary and storytelling abilities. To do so, you should have a passion for your studies and a willingness to work long hours outside of class— qualities that will serve you well in the professional world.

All strong animation programs emphasize a solid foundation in art while also teaching skills and techniques that are in demand in the real world. Because there are a number of specializations within the animation business (for example, storyboard artist, character designer, and 3-D modeler), programs may differ in the concentrations they offer.

As you progress through the major, your assignments will become more complex and instructors will review your work periodically to see how well you are integrating the skills you have learned with your creative ideas. At some colleges, passing these reviews is a requirement for continuing in the major. Your final project, the thesis film, along with a portfolio, will serve as your "résumé" in the industry.

Other majors you might like:
Computer graphics
Game design
Illustration
Graphic design
Digital art
Digital media
Photographic/film/video technology
Make-up artist
Computer engineering technology
Drafting and design technology
Web page/multimedia design
Radio and television

Questions to ask colleges:
What is the student-to-instructor ratio? Are the instructors currently working in the animation industry? In a good program, you will receive close instruction from faculty members who are familiar with the latest technology and have helpful contacts in the industry.

Are there adequate studio facilities, and are they available around the clock, so that students have a chance to complete assignments? Do the hardware and software capabilities keep current with the industry?

Are internships or apprenticeships in the animation business part of curriculum?

Career options and trends:
Art director/production designer*; storyboard/concept artist*; background/layout designer; character designer; 3-D animator (computer)*; 2-D animator; stop-motion animator; game designer; production coordinator.

Jobs are increasingly freelance in nature, with staff hired from project to project. Some portions of productions are being outsourced overseas. Developing multiple skills will give you a competitive advantage, particularly during economic downturns. In addition to film, television, advertising, and advertising productions, there are opportunities in the creation of computer games and in Web design.

For more info:
Animation World Network (AWN)
6525 Sunset Blvd.
Garden Suite 10
Hollywood, CA 90028
(323) 606-4200
www.awn.com

International Animated Film Association (ASIFA)
www.asifa.net

StopMotionAnimation.com
www.stopmotionanimation.com

Art history

What it's about:

Art history majors study how works of art were created, how they were interpreted by their first audiences, and what they mean to us now. Through visual analysis and extensive reading and writing, majors achieve an understanding of the context of art—time, place, culture, influences, and traditions—and develop the ability to describe art and its meaning to others.

Is this for you?

You might like this major if you also like: visual arts and architecture; antiquing; museums and galleries; travel; model making; reading about history and other cultures; finding connections and relationships between things.

Consider this major if you are good at: active listening; attention to detail; creativity; critical reading/thinking; research; spacial thinking/analysis *...or have...* initiative; verbal skills; writing skills.

Recommended high school prep:

English 4, math 3, lab science 3, social studies 4, art 2, music 1, and a foreign language 3–4. English and social studies courses that teach writing, speech, critical analysis, and research skills are essential, and studio art classes give valuable insight.

Did you know...

...that while the study of art history is similar in many ways to the study of literature or other cultural fields, it is unique in that you rely primarily on visual perception and on your ability to translate a nonverbal language into a verbal one?

Typical courses in this major:

Art and civilization before 1400
Asian art and temple architecture
Greek and Roman art
Egyptian art and architecture
Medieval art and architecture
The Renaissance
Michelangelo
European Baroque
Early modern architecture
Impressionism and Postimpressionism
Picasso
Postmodernism
Abstract expressionism
American art
History of photography
Introduction to museology

Concentrations:

In college: a historical period, such as ancient, medieval, or modern; a medium, such as painting, architecture, or sculpture; or the arts of a specific culture, such as America, Byzantium, or Polynesia.

If you go on to grad school: a particular artist or movement; museology and curatorship.

What the study of this major is like:

This major teaches you to differentiate among artworks by their style, materials, workmanship, and other characteristics. You can then identify (and seek to understand) the artists, cultures, and/or periods that produced the works. In addition, you consider how individual works of art and groups of works may express or symbolize ideas or emotions. Like archaeologists and anthropologists examining artifacts, you explore what a work of art reveals about a society's culture, rituals, and other aspects of civilization. Often you discover that the art's original value and meaning resulted from its connection to specific religious, political, or social practices.

In your first and second years, you generally take introductory art history courses, along with liberal arts courses in science, English, math, and history. Because art varies widely among societies (both past and present), art is often studied in association with a particular time and place (for example, Renaissance art, East African art). Thus the study of art generally includes some account of the religious, political, economic, literary, and intellectual history of the culture in which a work was created. You will read about art patrons, critics, and viewers, as well as artists. Frequent field trips to local museums augment classroom slide presentations.

After the introductory courses, you take smaller lecture courses that explore art in more detail. Seminars help you develop and refine advanced skills in research and presentation. In your fourth year, you usually have the option of writing a thesis under the direction of a faculty member. Many art history majors also take courses in areas related to their particular interests, such as history, anthropology, or literature. In addition, many study two or more years of a foreign language as a way of understanding other cultures.

Art history majors usually enjoy the benefits of working in a relatively small department where your needs can be dealt with individually. Study-abroad programs are common, and you should have opportunities to participate in internships at museums, galleries, and historic sites. Keep in mind, however, that while internships in museums are attractive, many involve work in education departments that may be isolated from the museum's curatorial activity. Smaller museums often offer more interesting opportunities. Commercial galleries may hire some summer staff, although summer is generally their slow period.

Other majors you might like:
Museum studies
Architecture
Architectural history/criticism
Anthropology
Classics
Comparative literature
Area studies (European, Asian, etc.)
Historic preservation
Medieval and Renaissance studies
Archaeology
Arts management
Music history/literature

Questions to ask colleges:
What is the extent of the visual media collection (slides, digitized images, etc.)?

What opportunities are there to study original works of art in a university collection or nearby museum?

Career options and trends:
Teacher (college or high school); museum curator*; museum management/staff (education, installation, registrar, etc.)*; commercial gallery operator/assistant*; art editor; art appraiser.

Art history majors graduate with a liberal arts degree that has trained them in observation, analysis, and communication. This preparation may qualify you for many jobs in business and government. A master's degree is generally required for employment in museums, archives, auction houses, and galleries, and for teaching in high school; a Ph.D. is essential for positions as museum curators and directors, and as instructors at the college level. Art conservation usually requires specialized training and knowledge of chemistry.

Insider's viewpoint:
"It's fairly important to study a foreign language, especially if you want to go to grad school. I've been taking Italian, so I chose to concentrate on late-medieval and early-Renaissance art; I wanted to read primary documents in the original."

—Dilip, senior, Northwestern University

For more info:
College Art Association (CAA)
50 Broadway
21st Fl.
New York, NY 10004
(212) 691-1051
www.collegeart.org

Cinematography and film/video production

What it's about:

This major prepares you to work in all aspects of film and/or video production, including producing, media writing, production management, directing, lighting, cinematography and/or videography, editing, and sound recording and mixing. The major also provides a strong foundation in media literacy, history, and theory.

Is this for you?

You might like this major if you also like: movies and television; taking photographs and making videos; reading; storytelling and creative writing; painting and drawing; the theater and stagecraft; working with computers; using technology creatively. If you like to make things and can think in visual terms, this field may be for you.

Consider this major if you are good at: attention to detail; creativity; critical reading/thinking; organizing; spacial thinking/analysis; teamwork ...*or have*... discipline; initiative; verbal skills; writing skills.

Recommended high school prep:

English 4, math 3, lab science 3, social studies 3, and a foreign language 2–3. Take as many art courses as possible, especially those covering photography and media; theater and drama; and computer courses. If these subjects are not available in high school, extracurricular or community activities in these areas are highly recommended.

Did you know...

...that the digital revolution in this field has made skills in math, science, and computers increasingly important? Writing skills and social, cultural, and media literacy are also necessary—if you want to make meaningful films, you need something meaningful to say.

Typical courses in this major:

Introduction to film and video production
Advanced film and video production
Studio television production
Directing
Cinematography and/or videography
Digital editing
Screenwriting
Sound design/production
Animation and special effects
Production management
Lighting
Television programming
Media and society
Visual literacy and communication
Film history
Film, video, and television genres

Concentrations:

Directing; producing; editing; screenwriting; sound; cinematography/videography; animation; narrative production; documentary production; alternative/experimental production.

What the study of this major is like:

Terms used in film and/or video production can be confusing. Although "film" programs traditionally use motion picture cameras and celluloid (film) to capture images, they are increasingly incorporating digital video. "Video" generally refers to single-camera production using either analog or digital videotape, and is similar to filmmaking in the way its production is organized.

Most programs in cinematography/film/video provide a mix of media studies and production courses. In media studies, you explore film and video history, theory, and analysis. You learn the language, theories, and politics of using images and sound to communicate. Because media making is a social and cultural practice that overlaps with many other disciplines, most programs require a foundation in liberal arts. In production courses, you are taught basic techniques: the creative use of lenses, lighting, cameras, and film stock; the theory and practice of editing; and the art and technology of sound design and recording. Once you master the basics, you move on to intermediate and advanced production work. In many programs, your studies culminate in a thesis project, which often becomes part of a demo reel—a viewable collection of your work—that can help you in your job search.

Programs may offer concentrations in one or more areas, such as editing or cinematography. In all programs, you can expect to work as a crew member on other students' projects. By crewing for other students, you can focus in one area of production or expand your skills in several areas. For example, if you are interested in sound design, you can volunteer to record and mix students' projects. You should seek as much practical production experience as possible because anything you work on can be included in your demo reel.

In media studies, most courses consist of both lectures and screenings, and assignments include writing research papers. Typical production courses require two two-hour lectures and one two-hour lab per week. Labs, which have fewer students than lectures do, involve hands-on learning and the screening of student projects. You generally shoot required projects outside of class.

The cinematography and film/video production major is time-intensive. You often work on projects during the evenings and on weekends. Because you're most likely to get a job through skill and experience, you should take advantage of all on- and off-campus opportunities, such as volunteering at a public TV station, and also seek internships or media jobs in the summer. Students sometimes earn course credit for participation in extracurricular activities.

This major can be costly, because you will probably have to buy some of the gear. While all programs provide major equipment, most expect you to purchase your own light meter, computer hard drive, and film/tape stock, and to pay for film lab services. But there is always a market for used equipment, and you can often purchase items at reduced cost from graduating majors.

Some cinematography/film/video programs emphasize production for "the industry," while others focus on film/video as an art form. Commercially oriented programs use Hollywood production techniques and tend to stress narrative fiction or broadcast news; little attention is given to avant-garde work. An arts-oriented program, in contrast, challenges you to explore your own vision and may also emphasize experimental or documentary production. Most programs strive for a balance. Some programs emphasize individual production and require you to write, direct, and edit your own projects. Other programs operate on a crew-oriented basis: only a few student projects are picked for production, and the other students crew on these films.

Other majors you might like:
Radio and television
Photography
Digital art
Digital media
Web/multimedia management
Playwriting/screenwriting
Media studies
Theater design and technology
Animation
Photographic/film/video technology
Instructional media
Laser/optical technology

Questions to ask colleges:
What equipment does the department provide, and how available is the equipment? Are editing and sound labs open on evenings and weekends? Does the department have a television studio/sound stage?

When do students start doing actual production? (Some programs introduce students to production in the first or second year; others wait until the third year.) Do the students own the rights to the productions they produce? Who funds the productions? Does the college provide film stock, or tape, or lab services?

Does the department sponsor a film or video festival?

Career options and trends:
Independent film/videomaking*; camera operator, director of photography*; sound editor, designer, mixer; apprentice or assistant editor; production assistant*; producer; director or assistant director; production manager; screenwriter.

Employment in the industry depends on ability, as evidenced in a demo reel, or in previous jobs or internships, rather than on a college degree. However, college training is often the best way to acquire job-qualifying skills, contacts, hands-on experience, and a demo reel. Technical positions other than entry-level ones may require membership in a union or guild.

The job market in film/video is competitive. There are far more job seekers than positions, but that should not discourage you from pursing this major. Students who commit to the profession, who excel in their production skills, who develop a good work ethic, and who are attentive and enthusiastic do get jobs. Moreover, the field as a whole is projected to grow as the entertainment market expands and computers and the Internet provide opportunities for interactive productions.

Small or independent filmmakers may provide the best job prospects for beginners, because they are likely to grow more quickly as digital technology cuts production costs.

Many graduates do not hold full-time or staff jobs but work freelance; but even those who work on a television series can have months of downtime each year.

Insider's viewpoint:
"The hardest classes are critical studies in film. You've got to know the film terminology and be able to pull apart scenes and read into them. That's a little bit hard, reading what's going on behind what you see on the screen."

—Anthony, junior, San Francisco State University

For more info:
American Film Institute (AFI)
2021 North Western Ave.
Los Angeles, CA 90027
(323) 856-7600
www.afi.com

University Film and Video Association (UFVA)
www.ufva.org

Dance

What it's about:

Dance majors learn to use their bodies in motion as instruments of artistic expression. As a major, you receive intensive training in the art of dance, in a liberal arts context, to prepare you for a career as a dancer or a choreographer. You'll study dance from several perspectives: technical, choreographic, aesthetic, historical, anatomical, cultural, anthropological, psychological, and therapeutic.

Is this for you?

You might like this major if you also like: dance; music; theater; learning about different cultures. Dance students have a passion for this art form; dance is a part of their daily lives.

Consider this major if you are good at: active listening; attention to detail; creativity; critical reading/thinking; memorizing; organizing; spacial thinking/analysis; teamwork ...*or have...* perseverance; physical stamina; self-discipline.

Recommended high school prep:

English 4, math 3, lab science 3, social studies 3, and a foreign language 2–3. Your dance training should consist of ballet and modern dance, with integrated dance history and anatomy components, and courses in dance composition and motif description.

Did you know...

...that there are significant differences between a Bachelor of Arts degree in dance, in which you study dance in a liberal arts context, and a Bachelor of Fine Arts degree, in which you train for a professional career as a dancer? Since many dancers stop performing by their late thirties, these differences are important: with a B.A. rather than an B.F.A., you may have an easier time getting a job after you retire from dancing.

Typical courses in this major:

Dance technique (ballet, modern, and jazz)
Principles of choreography
Improvisation
Dance appreciation
Dance composition
Technical production for dance
Music for dance
Dance history
Motif description and labanotation
Anatomy and kinesiology for dance
Dance theory, philosophy, and criticism
Historic dances (Renaissance, Baroque, Ragtime)
The teaching of dance

Concentrations:

In college: technique and performance; choreography; dance education; dance history and criticism; dance therapy.

If you go on to grad school: dance kinesiology; dance and technology; labanotation (for scoring music and dance) and labanalysis (movement analysis)—terms named for Rudolf Laban, a dance theorist.

What the study of this major is like:

To pursue a B.F.A. degree in dance, you will take a number of studio courses in technique, choreography, partnering, company repertoire, mainstage performances, and notation—a curriculum that trains students to become performing and creative artists.

In contrast, a B.A. degree in dance, which emphasizes courses in liberal arts subjects such as English, history, literature, and music, can prepare you for a career as a performing and creative artist *and* as a dance educator, administrator, historian, or critic. The B.A. is usually stronger preparation if you plan to go on to grad school or simply want to have more career options.

The B.A. program usually requires a minimum of 12 credit hours in ballet, modern, and jazz dance technique courses. In-depth training in technique is essential, but a breadth of experience is also important. Technique courses may include other kinds of dance, such as ethnic, folk, social, tap, historic, or character dance.

Course work in anatomy and kinesiology (the anatomical study of movement) will enhance your technical skills by teaching you how the body moves and how to avoid injury. Courses in rhythmic analysis, percussion accompaniment, and music resources sharpen your sensitivity to rhythm and help you find or create appropriate accompaniment for your choreography. In dance notation courses, you analyze movement and record it, and read movement scores. In a course on dance philosophy, you may learn principles of aesthetics that you can apply to choreography. And when you study dance history, you'll be encouraged to develop an appreciation for dance as an innate (inborn) and universal form of human expression.

Dance majors should expect to choreograph throughout college—at first, simple dance studies and improvisations; then, later, at least one fully staged work. You learn to design costumes, to light dances, and to help produce concerts. You also learn to work cooperatively with others, to direct, to evaluate choreography (including your own), and to accept and benefit from criticism.

And you perform! Some performances are informal presentations for teachers and classmates; others are theater productions before the public. If possible, take advantage of courses on teaching methods. Although many professional dancers may not plan to teach, almost all eventually do.

Daily classes in dance technique, rehearsals, and performances will cut deeply into your study time for academic subjects. To be a successful dance major, you need to have time management and stress management skills, the ability to focus clearly on the task at hand, and a commitment to produce quality work under deadline pressure.

At some colleges, the dance major is housed in the department of physical education rather than a department of fine arts, dance, or theater. Such programs usually emphasize kinesiology, physiology of exercise, health science, nutrition, and physical therapy.

Other majors you might like:
Anthropology
Sociology
Physical therapy
Dance therapy

Physical education
Theater arts management
American sign language (ASL)
Athletic training
Fine/studio arts
Drama and theater arts
Communications
Creative Writing

Questions to ask colleges:
May both dance majors and nonmajors participate in the technical dance courses?

How many and what kinds of performance opportunities are offered each semester?

What is the audition policy? Do students have to audition for entrance into the dance major, for placement in technique classes, for opportunities to perform their own choreography or to select dancers for their own choreography, to perform in someone else's choreography, or to be in the dance company?

How many hours per week are devoted to technical instruction?

Are students able to control their own rehearsal schedule or is it predetermined?

Career options and trends:
Professional dancer and/or choreographer; dance teacher; dance critic; dance scientist/kinesiologist/ physical therapist; dance historian/reconstructor; dance arts administrator; dance therapist.

Certification is required for teaching, and physical therapists and dance therapists are licensed health professionals with graduate degrees in their fields.

The field is overcrowded with professional dancers and choreographers—only the most talented find regular employment. Many performance opportunities depend on funding from public and private organizations; such support is not expected to keep up with rising production costs. On the other hand, there is a great need for dance educators in public and private elementary and secondary schools. There are few positions in dance criticism or dance therapy; but opportunities are expanding in the fields of dance/arts administration, dance science, dance history and reconstruction, and dance kinesiology (which usually require a master's degree).

Insider's viewpoint:
"If you're constantly comparing yourself to others, you won't get anywhere. And don't always stand in

the back corner of your class; have enough confidence in yourself to stand in the front."

—Nicole, sophomore, University of Wisconsin

For more info:
National Dance Association (NDA)
American Alliance for Health, Physical Education,
    Recreation and Dance
1900 Association Drive
Reston, VA 20191-1598
(800) 213-7193
www.aahperd.org

Digital art

Also known as:
Computer art

What it's about:
Digital art majors use the computer as the primary means of making art, including interactive installations, digital photography, animation, sound and video. Students are trained in various software applications and technical skills along with the fundamentals of studio art, such as drawing, design, and color theory.

Is this for you?
You might like this major if you also like: computer games; movie special effects; art history and contemporary culture; drawing; stretching your imagination; experimenting; coming up with practical solutions; learning new computer programs.

Consider this major if you are good at: Attention to detail; creativity; drawing; memorization; organizing; spacial thinking/analysis; team work *...or have...* imagination; initiative; patience; verbal skills.

Recommended high school prep:
English 4, math 3, lab science 3, social studies 3, foreign language 2–3, art 1-2, computer science 1. Take as many courses in art and computer applications as you can.

Did you know...
...that most colleges offering this major require applicants to present a portfolio (examples of your work) that demonstrates traditional art skills as well as computer skills?

Typical courses in this major:
Drawing
Color theory
History of art and design
Multimedia design
2-D and 3-D animation
Sound design
Web design (static and dynamic)
Interactive media
Digital photography
Video art
Installation/performance media
Digital paint
3D computer modeling
Digital imaging
Scripting
Game design

Concentrations:
Computer modeling; animation; special effects; digital sound; digital design; graphic design; website design; digital photography; digital video; multimedia.

What the study of this major is like:
Digital artists make art in inventive ways, using any form of digital technology available. In this major you will gain both the artistic skills and the technological expertise you'll need to create hybrid art forms, and to stretch the boundaries of what art can be.

In a typical four-year program, the sequence of courses usually begins with foundation classes such as drawing, design, and color theory. You'll also take an intro course in which you study the history of the computer's use in art and learn basic programming skills.

In subsequent classes these foundational skills are incorporated with technologies that include interactive art and design, time-based media (sound, video and animation) and web design. Some programs offer internships as electives. Seniors usually take one or two capstone classes or complete a senior project, thesis or portfolio.

This is a time-intensive major—you should expect to work very long hours. Successful students usually spend most of the day and night working in the labs. Most courses are project based with a series of assignments that teach practical skills while you complete a finished product such as a video or animation.

Some classes involve team projects to simulate real world commercial jobs. Team projects also accelerate learning—when you work in the lab or studio with other students rather than on your own, you learn much more as you help each other solve problems. When everything works right you learn a little; when things go wrong and you have to figure out why, you learn a lot.

Like most other art programs, you will also learn from critiques of your work by peers and professors.

As you explore colleges, you'll see that some house this major in the computer science department. Such programs emphasize the programming side of the field, and usually require applicants to have strong math skills. Other colleges will house the major in the art department, and while computer proficiency is expected, they will be more interested in seeing a portfolio of your basic art skills.

Some programs combine courses from different academic departments. These programs incorporate aspects of visual and performing arts, computer science, and cultural theory. The goal of an interdisciplinary approach is to give you a broad-based artistic, technical and theoretical background that will prepare you to work in various media and adapt to rapidly changing technologies. Other programs focus more on providing training in current software applications or a particular media, such as computer animation, game art or computer music.

Most programs will allow you to specialize in a particular area or opt for a more comprehensive study of the discipline. Keep in mind that in the digital world, what is state-of-the-art today will be old hat tomorrow. It's best to look for a program that balances practical training with the fundamental concepts that will prepare you for a life-long career.

Two-year associate degree programs in digital art provide training in computer graphics, sound, and animation, and prepare you for technical support positions in the field or for transfer to four-year programs.

Other majors you might like:
Animation
Computer graphics
Game design
Digital media
Photographic/film/video technology
Drafting and design technology

Software engineering
Multimedia
Graphic design
Web page/multimedia design
Instructional media

Questions to ask colleges:
What studio and lab facilities are provided and when do students have access to them? Are there any lab fees?

How up-to-date is the equipment?

Is the program part of the Art Department? Is there a relationship with the Computer Science Department?

How does the curriculum balance the study of fine arts and technology—does it emphasize one over the other?

What are recent grads doing now?

Career options and trends:
Animator*; video artist; graphic artist/designer*; game designer*; illustrator; special effects artist; art director; web designer.

This field is expanding and always changing—many students end up doing things that they never heard of as freshmen. Until recently degree requirements were minimal to nonexistent in the game industry; but with more colleges offering this major, more companies will look for graduates with a degree in the field.

The U.S. Bureau of Labor Statistics (BLS) projects that through 2022, multimedia artists and animators should have more job opportunities than most other types of artists. A particular area of opportunity for digital artists is the growing demand for animation and graphics in games and apps for mobile devices, such as smart phones and tablets.

Insider's viewpoint:
"This field changes every day. I get to do whatever my imagination leads me to. It was fun when I started and still is 25 years later."

—Professor Sven Anderson, State University of New York at Oneonta

For more info:

Association for Computing Machinery's Special
Interest Group on Graphics and Interactive
Techniques (ACM SIGGRAPH)
www.siggraph.org

The National Association of Schools of Art and
Design (NASAD)
11250 Roger Bacon Drive
Suite 21
Reston, VA 20190-5248
(703) 437-0700
www.arts-accredit.org

Drama and theater arts

What it's about:

The major in drama and theater arts covers many aspects of staged plays, including theater history, literature, and criticism; acting and directing; lighting, scenery, and costume design; stage management; playwriting; and arts administration. You may specialize in one area while you obtain a broad foundation in many of the other areas.

Is this for you?

You might like this major if you also like: school and community drama clubs; speech and debate; music and art; expressing ideas and feelings; collaborating with others. Because theater encompasses many areas, a variety of personality types enjoy this major.

Consider this major if you are good at: creativity; critical reading/thinking; leadership; organizing; persuading/influencing; teamwork ...*or have...* initiative; physical stamina; verbal skills; writing skills.

Recommended high school prep:

English 4, math 3, lab science 3, social studies 4, and a foreign language 2–3. In addition to any drama/theater courses available, take courses covering Shakespeare and dramatic literature, art history, music appreciation, art studio, and industrial arts (woodworking, drafting, etc.). Participation in theater, dance, or musical activities is a must.

Did you know...

...that theatrical skills are practical as well as creative? Dramatic projects must be produced within the boundaries of time, money, and labor constraints. Theater majors learn to think creatively, speak well, motivate a group, sell an idea, and get a job done on time—achievements that look good on a résumé for almost any job.

Typical courses in this major:

Introduction to theater
Theater design
Theater history
Dramatic literature
Play analysis
Acting
Directing
Production laboratory
Stagecraft
Production fundamentals
Voice for the actor
Shakespeare
Lighting design
Costume design
Scenic design
Musical theater

Concentrations:

In college: acting; directing; theater studies (history, literature, criticism); lighting design; costume design; scenic design; stage management; theater technology; production management.

If you go on to grad school: playwriting; dramaturgy.

What the study of this major is like:

The first thing to decide is whether to pursue a Bachelor of Arts or a Bachelor of Fine Arts degree. In a B.A. program, you gain a broader education, but may have difficulty competing with B.F.A. graduates in the professional world. But although the B.F.A. prepares you more rigorously for a theatrical profession, you may be less able to explore other areas of interest while you're in college.

You can generally choose from a wide variety of theater-related courses. In dramatic art courses, you study dramatic style and structure, theories of criticism, and the functions of theater artists, technicians, and managers. Theater history and dramatic literature courses cover Western theater from ancient Greece to the twentieth century. In directing courses, you learn how to analyze a script's style, form, and action, with the goal of translating the text into a staged production.

Introductory acting courses teach the fundamentals of relaxation, trust, sensory awareness, group interaction, and reaction and response. Improvisations, group exercises, and monologues are usually included. In advanced acting courses, you generally do scene work of increasing complexity in various classical and contemporary styles.

In courses in speech and voice, you practice phrasing, dialect, and breath control. Stage movement (sometimes taught as dance) develops relaxation and expressiveness. Theater history and criticism courses, often taught as lectures, involve considerable reading, discussion, and paper writing. Design and production courses are typically more hands-on; usually the lecture portion is coordinated with a laboratory session in which you work with tools and materials. For a concentration in arts administration, you study business and public relations/communications, in addition to taking theater courses.

Theater students and faculty members are typically opinionated and creative; class discussions and projects can be high-spirited. To add to the excitement, you may study, in a single day, contemporary theater in an acting course, fencing in a stage movement course, Shakespeare in a voice course, and end by rehearsing a performance art piece.

But the wide range of work is not only a blessing; if you do not have good organizational skills and time management skills, it can also be a curse. The greatest challenge that majors face is being committed to too many production projects. You must be able to withstand the rigors of nightly rehearsals, while still participating fully in your classes. Developing time management skills and the ability to take care of yourself (proper eating and sleeping) may be the most important thing you can do to ensure success as a drama and theater arts major.

The presence of a graduate theater program at an institution may have both advantages and disadvantages. Faculty members connected with a graduate program tend to be more high-powered, and production standards tend to be more professional. On the other hand, the graduate program may overshadow the undergraduate program. The size of a program may also make a big difference: larger programs may offer a greater variety of courses and more chances to act, direct, and design, whereas at smaller colleges, there may be more production opportunities.

Other majors you might like:
Theater design and technology
Fashion and apparel design

Film/cinema studies
Cinematography and film/video production
Art history
Music management
Theater arts management
Communications
Radio and television
Digital media
Make-up artist
English

Questions to ask colleges:
What is the policy on crew hours and rehearsals? Sometimes working on a crew or attending rehearsal is tied to course work, sometimes to a noncredit requirement. There should be guidelines for time spent rehearsing and building a production.

Does the department provide assistance in obtaining internships and summer work?

Is there ample space for students to practice acting and directing? At least two performance sites are desirable.

Career options and trends:
Actor, director, technician, or designer*; drama teacher; business manager, marketer, or publicist for theater*; arts educator at regional theaters*.

Competition for jobs is fierce in the performance segment of the industry. Versatility is one way to expand your career possibilities. Although technicians and arts administrators usually find more work than actors, directors, and designers, all theater students should be able to multitask. For example, touring companies might hire actors who have the technical skills to set up and strike, or take down, a set. Regional theaters may hire graduates to teach in their educational programs or to participate in workshops or other short-term projects. Taking jobs in related areas can often open doors for future work in your specialty.

Insider's viewpoint:
"Some of the best theater I have witnessed has been in scene work for acting classes. Also, rarely produced classics, new plays, large cast shows, and alternative performance art pieces are often found on university stages, rather than in the commercial or regional theater that can't take the risk."

—Professor Diane Timmerman, Butler University

For more info:
University/Resident Theater Association
1560 Broadway, Suite 1103
New York, NY 10036
(212) 221-1130
www.urta.com

Fashion and apparel design

What it's about:

This major prepares you for a career as a designer of commercial fashions, clothing, and accessories. You are trained in all aspects of fashion design, including sketching, creative design, computer applications, draping, and flat pattern drafting. You also learn how to communicate design ideas through storyboards and fashion shows, and how to work effectively in a diversified, global industry.

Is this for you?

You might like this major if you also like: drawing; sewing; decorating; museums; pop culture; travel; fabrics; shopping; fashion magazines; art and photography; keeping up with trends.

Consider this major if you are good at: attention to detail; creativity; math; organizing; persuading/influencing; quantitative analysis; spacial thinking/analysis; teamwork *...or have...* manual dexterity; patience.

Recommended high school prep:

English 4, math 3, lab science 3, social studies 3, visual arts 2–3, and a foreign language 2–3. Also recommended, if they are available: vocational and family/home economics courses covering sewing, textiles, and apparel; drafting and design; and computer applications.

Did you know...

...that in this major, you need to feel comfortable with math? That's because you must have technical and analytical skills to design a garment from sketch to pattern to construction and finishing of the garment.

Typical courses in this major:

Fashion sketching
History of costume
Creative design theory and elements
Color and design theory
Computer-aided design
Computer pattern drafting
Computer grading, marking, and cutting
Draping
Industrial sewing techniques
Garment construction
Accessory design
Fashion industry survey
Collection development
Fashion show production
Professional practices
Portfolio development

Concentrations:

Film and TV costume design; theater costume design; footwear design.

What the study of this major is like:

The fashion and apparel design major is generally hands-on, immersing you in a working environment from day one. From sketching to pattern making, you explore the many areas of design, under the instruction of industry professionals.

In your lower-level courses, you are introduced to figure-sketching techniques and to pattern drafting. In later courses, you explore such topics as color and design theory; textiles; and industry practices, including fashion groups, storyboards, and the development of collections. In computer-aided design (CAD) work, you learn how to design garments and construct patterns using techniques that are widespread throughout the industry. Most programs require a capstone course in which you develop a complete collection. This is the final course you take, and it prepares you to begin interviewing for jobs. You should leave the program with a comprehensive portfolio and real-world experience.

Expect to work hard; majors sometimes have to pull all-nighters to complete their projects. Fashion and apparel design is a highly technical industry that requires attention to detail and patience. Measurements must be exact, sketches must be proportional, and patterns must be cut precisely. Majors often find that the technical requirements are the most challenging. But programs are developed with these challenges in mind, and you generally have step-by-step guidance.

You will find many two-year fashion design programs leading to an associate degree, and some four-year programs leading to a bachelor's degree. The fashion design curriculum is similar in the two programs, but the first two years of B.A. programs provide a broad liberal arts background.

Programs can also be categorized by type of approach: training-based and theory-based. Elements of both types are essential for success in the industry. In the training approach, you have more opportunity to practice the skills you study in the classroom. As you construct garments from start to finish, you absorb the nuances of design, discover and solve problems, and perfect your technique. A theory-based education, in contrast, gives you a broader understanding of the industry as a whole—its history and its future.

Other majors you might like:
Commercial/advertising art
Fashion merchandising
Marketing
Fiber/textile arts
Advertising
Interior design
Metal/jewelry arts
Theater design and technology
Anthropology
Family and consumer sciences
Apparel/textile marketing
Entrepreneurial studies

Questions to ask colleges:
What ties does the college have to the fashion industry? Are the instructors industry professionals?

Does the college use the latest industry technology? How accessible are computers, and design and production facilities, after class?

If this is a four-year bachelor's degree program, are students admitted into the major at the outset, or do they have to meet requirements (such as a portfolio or high academic standing) at the end of the second year in order to continue?

Career options and trends:
Designer or assistant designer; pattern maker; grader; visual merchandiser; textile designer; technical designer; illustrator; stylist; costume designer.

As the fashion industry incorporates computer technology into every aspect of design, traditional ways of creating garments are being revolutionized. Majors in fashion should become proficient in as many of the software programs used in the fashion industry as possible. Since two-thirds of salaried fashion designers work in either New York or California, a willingness to relocate may be necessary.

As in all design fields, fashion majors face a lot of competition. Demand for designers should remain strong, however, because style-conscious consumers will always want something new to wear. The best opportunities will be in design firms that specialize in stylish, affordable, mass market clothing; opportunities will be limited in firms that cater to more specialized, higher-end customers.

For more info:
Fashion Group International
8 W. 40th St., 7th Floor
New York, NY 10018
(212) 302-5511
www.fgi.org

Fine/studio arts

Also known as:
Visual arts

What it's about:
Students majoring in the fine and studio arts learn to create images, objects, and environments using a variety of techniques and media. As you work on a number of structured assignments and independent studio projects, you sharpen your visual understanding and enhance your critical-thinking skills. Most likely, you will begin with an introduction to design and then choose a medium, such as photography or ceramics, for focused study.

Is this for you?
You might like this major if you also like: handicrafts, especially sewing, woodworking, model building, or pottery; riddles and metaphors; cooking; museums and galleries; drawing and painting; manipulating digital images; working independently; taking risks.

Consider this major if you are good at: attention to detail; creativity; critical reading/thinking; relational thinking; research; spacial thinking/analysis *...or have...* manual dexterity; patience; persistence; verbal skills.

Recommended high school prep:
English 4, math 2, lab science 2, social studies 4, and a foreign language 3. If possible, take a variety of visual and performing arts classes, including as many object- and figure-drawing classes as you can. Some colleges will require a portfolio of your artwork for admission.

Did you know...
...that you don't need to think of yourself as "artistic" or "really creative" to major in art? Art can be taught; it need not be regarded as a mysterious gift that only a few possess. To be successful in this major, you should have a strong interest in studio art and a commitment to learning.

...that this major is work-intensive, with plenty of outside projects? Studio projects take more time to complete than regular academic assignments. To do well, you need to be disciplined, patient, attentive to detail, and good at managing your time.

Typical courses in this major:
Two- or three-dimensional basic design
Drawing
Art history
Painting
Jewelry
Illustration
Sculpture
Book arts
Digital imaging
Printmaking
Graphic design
Ceramics
Industrial design
Textile and fiber arts
Photography
Art theory

Concentrations:
In college: drawing; sculpture; printmaking; graphic design; illustration; painting; photography; book arts; textile and fiber arts; ceramics; animation; glass blowing; architecture; jewelry and metalsmithing; industrial design; film and video.

If you go on to grad school: historic preservation; performance art; art conservation; environmental works; art history; museum studies; landscape architecture; time-based media; city planning; urban design.

What the study of this major is like:
Art classes in this major take place in studios outfitted with the equipment you'll need for a particular medium, such as charcoal drawing or woodworking. Your instructors are practicing, exhibiting artists and designers. In most programs, a basic design course is a prerequisite for upper-level courses. You will probably be required to take a series of art history courses as well, although some colleges emphasize art history more than others. By designing and producing artworks of your own and by studying the

work of others, you learn to understand the ideas, values, motives, and vocabulary of artists, and you develop an appreciation of the way art was, and is, created and the important social and cultural role it plays.

Art schools offer a Bachelor of Fine Arts degree, while liberal arts colleges usually offer a Bachelor of Arts. Both degrees have their strengths. A B.F.A. program allows you to become immersed in art. Classes tend to be three or four hours long. After completing foundation courses in your first two years, you focus on your concentration (for example, painting, sculpture) for two or three years before graduating. In contrast, a B.A. program allows you to maintain a focus on art but also explore other serious interests—which are likely to serve as inspiration for the images and objects you will create. B.A. classes are generally shorter, around two hours. When you graduate, you might have done only one or two years of independent work (less than in the B.F.A. program), but you have benefited from an exposure to a multitude of issues and ideas.

Not all studio programs offer the same choices of media. Even in a single medium like painting, the philosophy of programs can differ greatly. Some colleges stress conceptual or contemporary references to shape the curriculum. Others might emphasize the traditional materials and techniques. It may be useful to review images of student and faculty work, which are often available on a college's website.

As a major, you balance structured, in-class assignments with independent, outside work. Instead of term papers and exams, you receive feedback through individual and group critiques and portfolio reviews, in which you learn to take and give criticism. You are encouraged to read art magazines and be aware of current exhibitions in galleries and museums. A good student learns to work steadily throughout the semester. In the studio, don't expect to cram to make up for lost time; creativity cannot be rushed. You spend long hours and many late nights working. In effect, the studio becomes your second home and part of your social life.

While in the program, you can seek employment in galleries, studio apprenticeships to artists, and internships in architecture firms or museums. Both the B.A. and B.F.A. prepare you for continuing work toward a Master of Arts or Master of Fine Arts. The major also provides preparation for a fulfilling career as a practicing artist or commercial designer.

Other majors you might like:
Arts management
Museum studies
Medical illustrating
Film/cinema studies
Theater design and technology
Architecture
Art therapy
Digital art
Commercial/advertising art
Graphic design
Classics
Medieval and Renaissance studies

Questions to ask colleges:
How crowded are the studios? How late are they open? What security is offered for late-night work? Is there an accessible collection of art (on slides or elsewhere)? How extensive is the library's collection of art and art history books? The availability and condition of resources and facilities often reflect the institution's commitment to teaching the arts.

How many students go on to graduate school or related professional opportunities? Art is highly competitive, and the number of students who continue on in the field may point to the seriousness and success of the program.

Career options and trends:
Art teacher*; commercial artist; museum curator; architect; gallery preparator*; art therapist; studio artist; art editor or critic; art restorer/conservator; art director or administrator*.

A master's degree is generally required for employment in museums and galleries, and a Ph.D. (usually in art history) is required for positions as museum curators and directors. A master's in art education is the usual requirement for teaching in high school, and a master of fine arts (M.F.A.) for teaching at the college level. Art restoration and conservation usually requires specialized training and knowledge of chemistry.

Making a living solely from producing art is extremely difficult; most working artists have a sideline. One source of employment is the growing number of city and county arts councils that need staff for a variety of positions, including management and teaching; art therapy is also a growing field, but it requires further specialized education.

The interface between computers and art is the most important trend, for both creating art and teaching art. Illustrators are increasingly using technology, which has created new opportunities to work with animators, game designers, and in broadcast media.

Insider's viewpoint:

"Majoring in visual arts was never an easy way out. I spent more time and effort on my painting projects than some people in premed spent studying. And in the end, I believe I learned more than any academic major could have taught me: how to see the world I live in and express it to others."

—James, senior, Fordham University

For more info:

College Art Association (CAA)
50 Broadway
21st Fl.
New York, NY 10004
(212) 691-1051
www.collegeart.org

Graphic design

What it's about:

The graphic design major is about visual communication—how it is created and how it is perceived. Graphic designers plan and create print, film, and electronic communications composed of images and typography; their work ranges from books to multimedia programs, CD covers to film titles, logos to websites.

Is this for you?

You might like this major if you also like: books, magazines, and comics; graphic novels; coming up with practical solutions; working on the school newspaper, yearbook, or literary and arts magazines; drawing; color; working with different types of people; computers; craftsmanship.

Consider this major if you are good at: Communicating; attention to detail; creativity; critical reading/thinking; organizing; persuading/influencing; spacial thinking/analysis ...*or have...* curiosity; imagination; patience; writing skills.

Recommended high school prep:

English 4, math 3, lab science 3, social studies 3, and a foreign language 2–3. Many colleges require a portfolio (examples of your work), and your high school art classes can help you prepare one. Many colleges also offer summer or Saturday design camps, where you can develop your portfolio and get a taste of college-level instruction in design.

Did you know...

...that historically, the graphic design profession arose from the typesetting and printing trades? Practitioners came into the field through apprenticeships, without a formal education in design. Today, the complexity of contemporary communications requires graphic designers to have a deeper knowledge of how visual information works.

...that this major is about design more than computers? While graphic designers use computers extensively, knowledge of computers and software applications is not the same as knowledge of design.

Typical courses in this major:

Design analysis and theory
Typography
2-D and 3-D graphics
Factors of human perception
Packaging and display
Technical and professional writing
Drawing and illustration
Photography
Web page design
History of visual communications
Text and images
Identity and symbols
Digital imagery
Multimedia design
Motion graphics
Advertising design

Concentrations:

Advertising; multimedia; computer graphics; motion graphics (film titles and animation); Web design; identity or symbol design; information design (charts and graphs); publications; packaging; environmental graphics (signs and signage systems).

What the study of this major is like:

Graphic design programs vary widely from college to college, and a course title in a catalog does not necessarily describe the course content. But regardless of content distribution or course names, the graphic design major should prepare you to solve design problems; understand audiences; handle tools and technology (including offset printing, photography, and interactive media); apply concepts such as visual organization, information hierarchy, symbolic representation, and aesthetics; understand design history, theory, and criticism from a variety of perspectives (including art history, linguistics, and communication and information theory); and know basic business practices (such as organizing design projects and working productively with teams).

If you expect to go into advertising, you should enroll in a program that includes additional course work in marketing, audience and/or user evaluation, art direction, copywriting, and communications theory. If you want to work in time-based or interactive media, select programs with additional courses in storyboarding, computer scripting, sound editing, and interface design. For a career in planning and strategy development, seek programs that teach team problem solving; systems analysis; writing for business; and the application of management, communications, and information theories.

As a graphic design major, you learn primarily by completing hands-on projects in classes of 15–25 students. Design majors work long hours and must be self-motivated. Assignments are usually open-ended, with many right answers; they require you to think through different approaches and a variety of solutions. Your work is then evaluated by your classmates and instructors, based on how well you fulfilled the requirement of the assignment and on whether you showed an understanding of the audience and the context for which the item was intended. This approach is frequently used in all design and studio courses, and you have to learn not to take the criticism personally.

Exhibitions, auctions of visual work, costume balls, and design competitions are extracurricular activities in most colleges. Most design programs have some affiliation with the graphic design profession through clubs, portfolio reviews, field trips, internships, sponsored projects, or conferences. Generally, design programs have strong networks of graduates who can help you make the transition from college to work.

According to the accreditation requirements of the National Association of Schools of Art and Design, a Bachelor of Fine Arts degree in graphic design requires at least 65 percent of your courses to be studio art and design instruction, with at least 25 percent of those courses to be specifically related to graphic design. The B.F.A. is considered to be the professional degree for graphic design practice. In Bachelor of Arts or Bachelor of Science programs (B.A., B.S.), you will find a higher percentage of general education/liberal arts courses, and a smaller percentage of graphic design courses as part of the total art and design requirements. Two-year associate degree programs prepare you for technical support positions in the field and for transfer to four-year programs in design.

Other majors you might like:
Animation
Computer graphics
Digital art
Digital media
Drafting and design technology
Illustration
Industrial design
Communications
Advertising
Desktop publishing
Web page/multimedia design
Instructional media

Questions to ask colleges:
What studio, computer resources, and lab facilities are provided and how many hours do students have access to them? Are there any lab fees?

Is there a graphic design slide collection? What other library resources support graphic design majors?

Do students have to buy their own computer equipment? Does the college provide technical assistance for student-owned computers and/or software? Are printers, scanners, digital cameras, video and sound equipment, or other peripherals available for student use?

Career options and trends:
Art director*; graphic designer in design group or studio*; interactive/multimedia designer*; Web designer*; illustrator; exhibition designer; advertising agent; package designer; design strategist/planner; print production pre-press designer.

In a knowledge-based economy, those who make information comprehensible are valued. Success in the field of graphic design depends on talent, education, and work ethic, and students who graduate at the top of their class find jobs. Rapid technological change has created specializations in the field; as a result, specialists are in demand and more graphic designers are likely to obtain a graduate degree.

Increasingly, basic layout and design work is being outsourced to design firms overseas. Higher-level graphic design jobs that focus on "strategic design"—developing communication strategies for clients and firms—require proximity and will remain in the United States. Graphic designers with skills in website design and animation will have the best opportunities, as will those with knowledge or experience in marketing and business.

For more info:
American Institute of Graphic Arts (AIGA)
164 Fifth Ave.
New York, NY 10010
(212) 807-1990
www.aiga.org

The National Association of Schools of Art and
   Design (NASAD)
11250 Roger Bacon Drive
Suite 21
Reston, VA 20190-5248
(703) 437-0700
www.arts-accredit.org

Interior design

What it's about:
This major provides academic preparation for professional practice as an interior designer. You learn how to create indoor environments that are both beautiful and functional: they are intended to improve the quality of life, increase productivity, and protect the health and safety of the public.

Is this for you?
You might like this major if you also like: tours of museums and historical buildings; art; theater; math; debate; community service; working with people; making things; learning about different cultures; travel.

Consider this major if you are good at: attention to detail; creativity; critical reading/thinking; math; organizing; research; spacial thinking/analysis; teamwork ...*or have...* initiative; verbal skills.

Recommended high school prep:
English 4, math 3, lab science 3, social studies 3, and a foreign language 2–3. Art and art history courses, if offered, are highly recommended. A course in computer-aided design (CAD) would be good but it is not a prerequisite. Taking part in theater or music activities can teach you disciplines and skills used by successful interior design students.

Did you know...
...that there is a difference between interior design and interior decorating? While both fields are concerned with aesthetics, decorators work only with surface adornment; they work with paint, fabric, furnishings, lighting, and other materials. Interior designers are professional space planners, who ensure that interiors meet code requirements and the practical, technical, and functional needs of a wide range of clients—commercial, industrial, and residential—in such facilities as hospitals, schools, hotels, and apartment complexes.

...that interior design is subject to government regulation? Almost half the states and the District of Columbia require interior designers to be licensed or registered after passing the National Council for Interior Design's qualification examination.

Typical courses in this major:
Principles of interior design
History of interiors and decorative arts
Drawing and design in two and three dimensions
Computer-aided design
Interior materials and finishes
Construction documents and specifications
Codes, public health, and safety
Residential interiors
Furniture design
Textiles
Acoustics and interior design
Lighting design and building systems
Environmental control systems
Interiors for special populations
Professional practice
Portfolio preparation

Concentrations:
In college: lighting design; furniture design; exhibition design; acoustics; fabric design.

If you go on to grad school: historic preservation; workplace design; institutional facilities; interior environmental health; construction management.

What the study of this major is like:
Interior design majors study all aspects of the built environment: scale, proportion, arrangement, light sources, acoustics, temperature, textures, colors, and materials. Because interior design projects are complex, you learn to employ a systematic process; you balance the client's needs and resources, on the one hand, with the goal of creating safe, attractive, and practical interiors, on the other.

To design successful interior environments, you must be trained in building construction, materials specification, lighting techniques, technical drawing, and business practices. You learn to analyze problem areas; develop detailed design solutions; and organize and oversee the project to completion.

You must be familiar with building codes and fire regulations. And because interior designers usually function as members of a team rather than as individual designers, you need to be able to work well with other professionals.

Programs usually consist of a series of design courses that culminate in a senior thesis. Generally, studio courses use a hands-on approach: the professor presents a problem and you work on a solution, discussing and evaluating your progress with the instructor. As you advance through the program, you will be expected to demonstrate increasing skill in tackling such problems.

Undergraduate majors receive a generalized education in interior design. Nevertheless, some programs may emphasize architecture or environmental design, whereas others stress fine arts or family and consumer science. Programs with an architectural focus generally concentrate on three-dimensional design, construction practices, and large-scale commercial projects. These programs tend to prepare you for work in large architectural and interior design firms. Programs that concentrate on fine arts or family and consumer sciences usually focus on the decorative aspects of the field—fixtures and furniture, selection and layout, and coordination of finishes. Also some programs feature residential design, while others highlight commercial and/or institutional design. However, standards ensure that all accredited programs prepare you for entry-level professional work in either residential or commercial/institutional design.

Other majors you might like:
Housing and human environments
Environmental design
Industrial design
Architectural history/criticism
Furniture design/manufacturing
Fashion and apparel design
Psychology
Anthropology
Theater design and technology
Drafting and design technology
Hotel/motel administration/management
Art history

Questions to ask colleges:
Is the program accredited by the Foundation of Interior Design Education and Research (FIDER)? Most states that license interior designers require graduation from a FIDER-accredited program.

Are students given their own desks in the studio for the entire semester? "Cold studios" are those in which students are given work spaces for the term; "hot studios" are more like typical classrooms with drawing tables. Colleges with cold studios generally have stronger design programs.

Are the computer laboratories accessible most hours of the day? Do they provide access plotters and printers? Gaining proficiency in computer-aided design applications is essential.

Career options and trends:
Interior designer*; furniture designer; lighting designer; facilities manager; real estate broker; trade show exhibit designer; product representative.

Interior designers work for interior design firms, architectural firms, department and home furnishing stores, theme parks and resorts, and hotel and restaurant chains. Some designers do freelance work full-time, part-time, or in addition to a salaried job. Beginning designers usually receive on-the-job training and normally need one to three years of apprenticeship before they advance to higher-level positions.

Ergonomics and "green design" are trends to watch. Ergonomic design is important for an aging population and workplace safety, and concerns for environmental quality and the needs of people with allergies and asthma are driving demand for green design.

For more info:
American Society of Interior Designers (ASID)
608 Massachusetts Ave., N.E.
Washington, DC 20002-6006
(202) 546-3480
www.asid.org

Music, general

What it's about:

This liberal arts major is for those who want a generalist approach, rather than a career-specific orientation, to the subject. You study music from various perspectives: the historical development of musical styles; ear training and musicianship; the structures and theory of music; composition; music technologies; performance instruction; and music teaching.

Is this for you?

You might like this major if you also like: playing, listening, and learning about music, of course; math; travel; working independently as well as in groups; using computers. Mere enjoyment of music is not enough for success in this major —you must have a real commitment and well-developed musical skills.

Consider this major if you are good at: attention to detail; concentration; creativity; critical reading/thinking; memorizing; quantitative analysis; spacial thinking/analysis *...or have...* patience; perseverance; physical stamina; self-discipline; verbal skills.

Recommended high school prep:

English 4, math 3, lab science 3, social studies 3, music 4, and a foreign language 3. Courses in music theory, music history, individual lessons on an instrument or in voice, and participation in performance ensembles (orchestra, band, jazz, chamber music) are highly recommended, whether available inside or outside high school. No matter what instrument you play or even if you don't intend to perform, all college music majors are expected to have basic knowledge of piano (keyboard). Even six months of lessons will help—a year is better.

Did you know...

...that this major isn't just about playing music? In some ways it is more demanding than many other majors, because you have to be both academic and musical.

Typical courses in this major:

Music history
Ethnomusicology
Music theory
Ear training and/or musicianship
Composition
Conducting
Orchestration
Keyboard competence
Sight singing
Lyric diction
Chamber ensemble
Wind ensemble
Chorus
Tonal counterpoint
Computer and electronic music
Jazz studies

Concentrations:

History or musicology; ethnomusicology; performance; conducting; theory; composition; music education.

What the study of this major is like:

Most music programs require at least four courses in music history, in which you study the musical styles and genres of different periods, as well as the most important composers. You may do advanced work in the music of a period or of a composer; the extent of change in music from one period to the next; and the connection between music and the society in which it was created. More and more colleges are teaching music produced outside Europe and North America—for example, traditional Chinese music and music of the West African coast.

Music theory courses assume that you are familiar with the fundamentals of music (rhythmic and pitch notation, key signatures, and scales). In a minimum of four theory courses, you learn the principles of four-part music. You then practice these principles in weekly writing exercises. Theory courses also teach methods of analyzing music in depth. You may do advanced work in counterpoint, analysis, or the history of music theory; or begin work in composition. In composition courses, you may use computer programs to synthesize music electronically.

The music major almost always includes work in basic musicianship—piano, sight singing, score reading, keyboard harmony, and melodic and harmonic dictation. All programs provide you with opportunities to perform in ensembles, and many require you to do so. Individual voice and instrumental lessons, as well as conducting courses, are available at many colleges. Some programs offer a music performance degree, which involves much more performance work (for example, in voice, violin, trumpet, or percussion). These programs often lead to the Bachelor of Music degree rather than to a liberal arts degree with a music major.

Instruction style may vary according to the aspect of music you are studying. Your courses may be research-oriented or lab-oriented, or you may work mostly one-on-one with your professors. The music major can be demanding, because it requires you to take numerous courses and spend many hours studying and rehearsing, both in and out of the classroom. But majors generally have a strong sense of community and of working toward a common goal. Because colleges sponsor recitals and concerts by faculty members and guest artists, students frequently meet and talk extensively with professional performers and also participate in the management of these concerts. Many colleges offer music majors the opportunity to present their own recitals when they are in their fourth year.

Colleges vary widely in their approach to the study of music. Some schools are conservatories that emphasize performance and composition. Other colleges focus on the historical and theoretical study of music. Still others seek a balance between practice and theory.

Other majors you might like:
Music management
Sacred music
Music history/literature
Music teacher education
Music therapy
Radio and television
Recording arts
Musical instrument fabrication/repair
Computer science
Electrical and communications engineering
Mathematics
Digital media

Questions to ask colleges:
Are auditions required for admission into or placement in the major? In many programs, candidates must be able to sing in tune and also take a written music exam.

What practice facilities are available and during what hours? Is digital recording equipment available?

What are the performance opportunities? What kinds of ensembles are available?

To what extent is non-Western music taught?

Career options and trends:
Professional or studio musician; composer; music teacher; recording engineer or mixer; art administrator; music publishing editor; film music editor; music therapist; music store manager; music software developer.

To become a music therapist or to teach in public schools, you must obtain certification and meet specific education requirements.

A general music major does not directly lead to careers in the profession, but like all liberal arts majors, it provides a broad, flexible foundation for a variety of occupations or for graduate school. Students at the top of their class who are willing to relocate may obtain music-related jobs after graduation, but the music industry is very competitive.

For more info:
College Music Society (CMS)
312 East Pine St.
Missoula, MT 59802
(406) 721-9616
www.music.org

Music management

What it's about:

This major provides a broad understanding of the fields of music and management. You take courses in music history, theory, and performance. In addition, you explore the methods, concepts, and principles of management, with specific focus on the music business.

Is this for you?

You might like this major if you also like: starting or running a business venture; managing or performing in a band; organizing or leading a club or group activity; solving problems; taking risks; competing; sports; helping others to succeed.

Consider this major if you are good at: attention to detail; critical reading/thinking; leadership; organizing; persuading/influencing; teamwork...*or have...* initiative; verbal skills; writing skills.

Recommended high school prep:

English 4, math 3, lab science 3, social studies 3, music 3–4, and a foreign language 3. If they are available, these are also recommended: statistics, computer applications, economics, accounting, business, psychology, and participation in music performance such as band or orchestra.

Typical courses in this major:

Introduction to the music business
Music publishing and copyright law
Recording and broadcast industries
Contracts and other legal issues
Accounting
Economics
Introduction to marketing
Fundamentals of management
Computer applications
Music history
Basic music theory and ear training
International marketing
Concert and tour promotion
Business statistics
Music technology
Recording techniques

Concentrations:

In college: recording and studio production techniques; marketing and merchandising; arts management.

If you go on to grad school: international marketing.

What the study of this major is like:

The music management major prepares you to enter the music business world. You learn about issues such as patronage, copyright laws, and musicians' union regulations, as well as fund-raising, grant-proposal writing, and advertising techniques.

There are two main approaches to the music management major. Some colleges focus on business or management, expecting you to learn only a minimal amount about music. In these programs, you generally take a core of courses that teach methods, concepts, and principles of music management and business. A number of other programs have strong offerings in music, with only a smattering of business and management courses. Industry experts have come to demand a greater balance between the two aspects of the major. Ideally, you should choose a program that provides maximum opportunities to study both music and business/management.

For a comprehensive or music-oriented program, you may be asked to demonstrate (through an audition) the ability to play an instrument or sing, and to take a music theory placement examination. To prepare yourself, you'll need some previous music training. Such colleges also require you to enroll in a sequence of music history and theory courses, in addition to the business and management courses. In all programs, you must participate in activities promoting music and art on campus and in the surrounding community (such as campus concerts and local civic organizations) to test out the concepts and strategies you study in class. Additionally, most colleges expect you to take 30–40 percent of your total course work in humanities, mathematics, and the sciences, to ensure that you receive a well-rounded education.

Upper-level courses often require at least two internships at off-campus establishments. These internships, often in cooperation with recording studios, music publishing houses, arts organizations, symphony orchestras, or television studios, provide a unique way for you to explore the professional field under the guidance of college mentors. The biggest challenge most students encounter involves time management—balancing the development of academic skills with practical fieldwork. You also need to cultivate good "people skills."

Other majors you might like:
Radio and television
Recording arts
Musicology/ethnomusicology
Jazz studies
Public relations
Business administration and management
Hospitality administration and management
Web/multimedia management
Information systems
Theater arts management
Music history/literature
Entrepreneurial studies

Questions to ask colleges:
Are there opportunities on campus to gain experience in promoting concerts and other arts events?

Does the college have a recording studio, or a radio and/or television station, and opportunities to develop skills in audio and video work?

What connections do the faculty members and the department have with the music industry?

Career options and trends:
Business manager*; recording industry promoter or producer*; orchestra manager; booking agent; artist representative or manager; music publishing executive or editor*; television and radio promoter*; A&R (artist and repertoire) administrator or coordinator; studio production manager; entertainment lawyer.

The field is becoming highly international, so knowledge of a foreign language (such as Spanish, French, or Japanese) is a big plus. Also, knowledge of digital technology and intellectual property rights is essential. As in all art-related fields, there is plenty of competition, but the business end of music is varied enough to provide greater opportunity. Internship experience, which is expected of job applicants in all music-related businesses, is an invaluable way to develop networking contacts and, sometimes, to receive job offers.

For more info:
American Society of Composers, Authors, and
    Publishers (ASCAP)
One Lincoln Plaza
New York, NY 10023
(212) 621-6000
www.ascap.com

American Federation of Musicians
1501 Broadway
Suite 600
New York, NY 10036
(212) 869-1330
www.afm.org

Music performance

Also known as:
Applied music

What it's about:
The music performance major allows you to achieve a high level of technical proficiency and musical sensitivity. You are trained to play a musical instrument or to sing professionally, both as a solo and ensemble performer.

Is this for you?
You might like this major if you also like: communicating through music; listening to music; performing outside school; reading music biographies. If you have strong encouragement from your music teachers, confidence in your abilities, and a commitment to succeed, you might consider this major.

Consider this major if you are good at: attention to detail; creativity; math; memorizing; organizing; teamwork *...or have...* aural skills; physical stamina; self-discipline.

Recommended high school prep:
English 4, math 3–4, lab science 3, social studies 3, music 3–4, and a foreign language 2–3. While not required, music courses covering large ensembles, small ensembles, solo performance, music theory, and music history are recommended. Regardless of your specific training (voice or instrument), you will be expected to have basic knowledge of the piano keyboard.

Did you know...
...that most auditions require you to sing? No matter what your instrument, you are expected to be able to use your voice intelligently and in tune.

Typical courses in this major:
Music theory
Aural skills
Music history
Individual instruction
Computer and/or electronic music
Vocal diction
Percussion
Strings
Brass
Woodwinds
Introduction to music literature
Accompanying
Instrumental ensemble
Vocal ensemble
Fundamentals of conducting
Pedagogy of the piano/voice/etc.

Concentrations:
Voice; piano; organ; individual orchestra or band instruments; jazz studies; early music; instrumental pedagogy; conducting.

What the study of this major is like:
Most music performance majors have already taken part in musical activities in high school, except perhaps for singers, whose "instruments" are not available until their voices mature. Most programs test new students to determine their background and skills. Tests may include an audition and both a written and an oral exam. If you lack necessary skills, you may have to enroll in catch-up courses.

In addition to performance work and related instruction, the major includes core courses in music theory, literature, and history. Traditionally, you attend weekly private lessons in your chosen instrument (or in voice) with your concentration instructor. You also participate in master classes, studio recitals, and solo recitals. Instrumentalists take part in chamber music coaching and performances; vocalists take part in opera coaching, workshops, and performances; and all students participate in rehearsals and large-ensemble performances.

In music theory and aural skills courses, you study harmony, rhythm, counterpoint, sight singing, ear training, melodic and harmonic dictation, improvisation, and analysis of musical structure. Mastering theory and aural skills helps you understand the way a piece of music is put together. In music history and literature courses, you will survey music through the ages and explore books and documents related to your concentration. Other courses may cover repertoire, music education, conducting, composition, and jazz studies.

Voice concentrates may need to take Italian, German, Russian, and/or French, the languages of many operas. Nonpiano concentrates must take an introduction to keyboard harmony. And almost all performance programs require you to do 25–50 percent of your course work in the liberal arts. Therefore, you must come to college with the same study skills, writing skills, and academic background as liberal arts majors.

For performance majors, time is precious; large blocks of it (besides the hours you spend in classes and studying) must be set aside for solitary practice. When you are not practicing and studying, you often perform both on and off campus and participate in competitions—leaving you very little free time. Your social life will probably center on a small group of friends who share your goals and serve as a support group.

Among various colleges, striking differences may exist in mission and atmosphere. For example, a single-purpose conservatory that enrolls top students will differ significantly from a four-year liberal arts college. Professionally oriented performance schools sometimes foster intense competition. Whereas some students thrive in such an environment, others prefer a less intense, more nurturing educational setting. You should examine your options carefully to find the right fit.

Other majors you might like:
Music management
Sacred music
Music theory and composition
Music teacher education
Music therapy
Radio and television
Recording arts
Jazz studies
Computer science
Electrical and communications engineering
Mathematics
Voice/opera

Questions to ask colleges:
What is the ratio of students to practice rooms?

How many hours of private instruction do students receive each week in their major? Can incoming students meet with the instructor to whom they will be assigned?

How will this program and the faculty members help undergraduates make the transition from student to professional life?

Career options and trends:
Orchestral musician; solo musician; ensemble musician (string quartet, jazz trio, etc.); church musician; orchestra or opera company manager; music technician/producer; music teacher (private); music teacher (public school or college); music therapist.

Performing arts are risky career choices, because they are highly competitive and compensation for artists is notoriously low. Symphony orchestras and opera companies are facing decreased contributions, endowment income, and ticket sales; and while digital radio, free downloads and streaming is making it easier for musicians and performers to gain visibility and build a fan base, these technological changes are also creating turmoil in the recording industry.

Longer term, the pendulum will swing the other way and conditions should improve all around. All signs point to a future with plenty of audience for the work of performers. Teaching music shows promise, as there has been no falloff in the desire to study music. The American String Teachers Association (ASTA) projects a need for 5,000 string teachers over the next several years.

For more info:
College Music Society (CMS)
312 East Pine St.
Missoula, MT 59802
(406) 721-9616
www.music.org

Music theory and composition

What it's about:

This major consists of two related areas of study—music theory is the study of the materials, processes, and structures of music; music composition is the art of writing music. In some institutions, the two are combined into a single major; in other institutions, they are separate.

Is this for you?

You might like this major if you also like: computer science; psychology; mathematics; audio recording; languages; art; drama.

Consider this major if you are good at: attention to detail; creativity; critical reading/thinking; organizing; quantitative analysis *...or have...* aural perception; initiative; patience; writing skills.

Recommended high school prep:

English 4, math 3–4, lab science 3, social studies 3, and a foreign language 2–3. Most colleges do not require or recommend any specific music courses at the high school level. But you must have a thorough knowledge of the fundamentals (intervals, scales, chords in treble and bass clef; simple rhythmic and metric notation) and skill in basic ear training (intervals, scales, triads; dictation of simple rhythmic, melodic, and harmonic examples). An ability to play a keyboard instrument is recommended. Courses that cover math, psychology, and computer science can be good background for music theory.

Typical courses in this major:

Aural skills
Music history
Schenkerian analysis
Analysis of twentieth-century music
Atonal music
Operatic literature
Symphonic literature
Composition seminar
Psychology of music
Music technology
Diction and song literature
Counterpoint
Piano pedagogy
Orchestration
Computer-assisted music notation
Senior thesis project

Concentrations:

Generally, none available.

What the study of this major is like:

As a music theory and composition major, you learn to understand and describe the forces that shape music. The discipline of music theory can be compared with subjects such as linguistics and psychology: you explore the principles that help determine the results, whether in music or in human behavior and language. Studying music composition is similar to studying creative writing: you combine knowledge of the principles and techniques with imagination to produce a work of art.

In beginning theory courses, you will read works on the topic by leading scholars (for example, Rameau, Schenker, Forte). When you first take composition, you may study under the guidance of a master teacher, who sets tasks or goals for you and then analyzes your work and suggests possible improvements. For both theory and music composition, you typically examine the literature—including scholarly writings and original scores—and enhance your musical skills. Advanced theory courses teach you how to formulate and test your own ideas through research; advanced composition courses usually offer you more opportunities for creative expression.

Musical skills courses include ear training and sight singing, and training in voice or in your instrument. Like all music majors, you will participate in a student ensemble, band, choir, or other group. You cannot become a good theorist or composer without also becoming a good musician.

Although some programs combine music theory and composition in a single major, other programs address them separately. But differences among individual professors of music theory and of composition are usually more significant than differences among programs. To figure out which program is probably best for you, you should talk to professors about their teaching style and expectations.

Other majors you might like:
Music performance
Jazz studies
Music history/literature
Musicology/ethnomusicology
Music management
Creative Writing
Mathematics
Linguistics
Computer science
Conducting

Questions to ask colleges:
Is the program accredited by the National Association of Schools of Music?

What opportunities does the program offer in music pedagogy?

Is electronic or computer music part of the curriculum?

Are there any audition requirements?

Career options and trends:
A bachelor's degree in this major does not prepare students for specific careers, except possibly as a private teacher, performer, or composer. Teaching in elementary, middle, and high school requires a music education degree and state certification, and teaching at the college level usually requires a doctorate degree.

For more info:
College Music Society (CMS)
312 East Pine St.
Missoula, MT 59802
(406) 721-9616
www.music.org

Society for Music Theory
University of Chicago
Department of Music
1010 East 59th St.
Chicago, IL 60637
(773) 834-3821
www.societymusictheory.org

Photography

What it's about:

The major in photography is for students interested in the art of communicating information, ideas, moods, and feelings through photographic images. You gain a broad background in both the technical and the aesthetic aspects of photography.

Is this for you?

You might like this major if you also like: nature studies; art and art classes; science and technology; working with equipment and chemicals; the school newspaper, yearbook, or photography club; working independently.

Consider this major if you are good at: attention to detail; creativity; organizing; spacial thinking/analysis; visualizing ideas or images *...or have...* initiative; patience; verbal skills; writing skills.

Recommended high school prep:

English 4, math 3, lab science 3 (including chemistry and physics), social studies 3, visual arts 3–4, and a foreign language 2–3. If available, a journalism course would be helpful, and computer applications courses are recommended.

Did you know...

...that often the same type of preparatory courses are required for photography as for other art disciplines—drawing, two-dimensional and three-dimensional design, and color theory?

Typical courses in this major:

Elementary photography
History of photography
Two-dimensional design
Black-and-white photography
Color photography
Digital photography
Materials and processes
Commercial and/or industrial photography
Portraiture
Photo editing
Studio photography
Photojournalism
Advanced photographic techniques
Lighting techniques
Biomedical and forensic practicum
Portfolio preparation

Concentrations:

In college: fine art photography; digital imaging; portraiture; biomedical photographic illustration; commercial photography; fashion photography; photojournalism.

If you go on to grad school: most graduate photography programs concentrate on fine art applications, and many are self-directed.

What the study of this major is like:

As a photography major, you begin by exploring the fundamentals of design, form, color, and composition. You learn about the nature of light and analyze how three-dimensional space is changed into two-dimensional images. In an introductory course, you study camera operation and controls (such as focus, shutter speed, and aperture setting) and their effects on photographic images; you also learn about types of cameras: digital, 35 mm, medium format, and large format field cameras that produce single negatives. You discuss contemporary issues in photography, as well as photographic history. Critiques (in which you evaluate the strengths and weaknesses of a photograph) are an essential part of your learning process.

In lower-level photography courses, your assignments center on depicting specific ideas or situations. As you progress through the major, you concentrate more on your own ideas of what to depict. You create portfolios (a group of photographs on a theme) and study many approaches to photography, such as studio techniques, color, digital applications, and alternative processes. Taking courses in other arts, such as drawing, sculpture, and painting, can enrich your work. If you are interested in documentary photography or photojournalism, you might take courses in journalism, English, and anthropology. Throughout your studies, you evaluate your strengths and interests in relation to a possible career. A final portfolio that showcases your work is the capstone to almost every degree program.

Most photography programs try to balance the technical and the creative aspects of the art. Programs often specialize in one or two areas of photography; fine arts and journalism are the most common. (Such courses may also be offered in conjunction with broader art or journalism programs.)

The biggest issue facing photography programs is the tension between traditional, "wet" darkroom practice and digital processes, so be aware of the technical practices of the programs you consider. Also, some colleges emphasize the practical, commercial aspects of photography; these programs train you to concentrate on meeting the demands of clients. Other programs, which are based in the fine arts, encourage you to express your personal point of view. Degree programs can range from two-year associate degrees to four-year Bachelor of Arts, Bachelor of Science, or Bachelor of Fine Arts degrees, each with its own emphasis.

Other majors you might like:
Cinematography and film/video production
Journalism
Graphic design
Advertising
Digital art
Fashion merchandising
Entrepreneurial studies
Photographic/film/video technology
Radiologic technology/medical imaging
Surveying technology
Computer graphics
Digital media

Questions to ask colleges:
Does the program offer training in digital technologies?

What equipment must students provide on their own, and what equipment is available for student checkout?

Is there sufficient darkroom space and access time? How many majors and nonmajors share darkroom facilities?

Career options and trends:
Photojournalist; fine art photographer; freelance photographer; commercial or industrial photographer; technical or medical photographer; digital image technician; wedding photographer; portrait photographer; animator; manager of a photo lab.

Most photographers are either working freelance or running their own businesses and studios; salaried jobs are increasingly hard to find. Competition is keen, especially for photojournalists and commercial photographers. Fine arts photographers face the same challenge as other artists: how to attract audiences who favor their particular type of work. In all areas, good business sense, creative talent, and technological savvy are necessary ingredients for success.

Insider's viewpoint:
"I like isolating segments of the environment through the frame of the camera's viewfinder. I tend to see my surroundings in a series of still images—like the stop-action aspect of a movie."

—Professor Fred Niles, University of Dayton

For more info:
Student Photographic Society
229 Peachtree St., N.E.
Suite 2200
Atlanta, GA 30303
(866) 886-5325
www.studentphoto.com

Society of Photographic Education (SPE)
2530 Superior Ave.
Suite 403
Cleveland, OH 44114
(216) 622-2733
www.spenational.org

Theater design and technology

Also known as:
Technical theater

What it's about:
This major covers the design and production of costumes, lighting, scenery, and sound for theater, opera, and dance. Typically housed in a theater or a performing arts department, the program enables students to specialize in one or more of these areas while they gain a broad foundation in the related disciplines of acting, directing, and theater history and theory.

Is this for you?
You might like this major if you also like: building things; working with your hands; decorating; art and literature; music; photography; working collaboratively with people; organizing events; solving problems. If you enjoy plays, movies, museums, and theme parks and would like to know how these attractions are produced, you might consider working behind the scenes in theater.

Consider this major if you are good at: attention to detail; creativity; critical reading/thinking; organizing; spacial thinking/analysis; teamwork ...*or have...* initiative; manual dexterity; patience; verbal skills.

Recommended high school prep:
English 4, math 3, lab science 3, social studies 3, foreign language 2–3, music 1–2, and visual arts 1–2. Courses that cover music appreciation, design (computer-aided if possible), and dramatic arts and literature are recommended, as is participation in extracurricular activities such as drama, art, and music clubs, and community organizations or summer theater companies. Industrial and/or vocational arts classes in woodworking, metalworking, drafting, and sewing are also helpful.

Did you know...
...that even though they work behind the scenes, majors in theater design and technology are often required to take performance classes such as acting or dance, and courses in theater history and theory? That's because the technician's job is to enhance the work of performers and directors, so an understanding of their craft is necessary.

Typical courses in this major:
Introduction to theater
Mechanical drafting
Scenographic techniques
Computer applications for theater
Sound
Stage management
Costume design and construction
Makeup for the stage
Lighting
Scene design and construction
Theater history
Theater graphics
Play analysis
Acting and performance courses
Art and art history courses
Portfolio development and presentation

Concentrations:
Lighting design; costume design (including makeup); scene design; technical direction; sound design; stage management.

What the study of this major is like:
This major is generally divided into design and production courses. The design component includes introductory and advanced courses in costume, lighting, scenery, and sound design. You'll study script analysis, historical research, fundamentals of visual art, drawing, rendering, and design presentation.

In the production courses, you'll learn how to pattern, drape, and fit costumes on an actor's body; construct, paint, and prop scenery; rig, hang, and focus lighting equipment; record sound effects; and place microphones or speakers for sound reinforcement. Introductory courses in these subjects teach basic vocabulary, tool usage, and procedures for design production.

Some departments offer specialty courses in period styles in clothing and architecture; drawing and painting techniques; and advanced crafts, such as millinery, fabric dyeing and modification, makeup, wig construction, scene painting, properties design and construction, model making, and structural engineering for scenery.

Many production courses consist of a lecture class that addresses theory and laboratory sessions in which you have the opportunity to practice what you learn. Labs often provide the labor to implement your designs for department plays. Faculty members evaluate each assignment to determine if you are ready for projects that are more challenging. Ideally, you progress through the program by taking more advanced classes and assuming greater responsibilities in the design and production of plays. Because you'll often have to spend hours doing work outside your course requirements, you should be prepared to balance your academic and production commitments.

Most theater design and technology programs offer either a Bachelor of Arts or a Bachelor of Fine Arts degree. The B.A. program provides a liberal arts education that gives you an understanding of the world that the theater attempts to reflect; the program also prepares you for jobs you can take while pursuing the goal of working full-time in theater. The B.F.A. program trains you for a professional career in theater by offering more specialized, intensive course work. Most B.F.A. programs require auditions and/or interviews for admission and yearly performance evaluations to remain in the program.

A few universities offer Bachelor of Science (B.S.) degrees in theater, which have stronger science and technology components than B.A. programs. A few junior and community colleges offer a two-year associate of arts (A.A.) degree in theater design and technology.

Other majors you might like:
Radio and television
Cinematography and film/video production
Architecture
Interior design
Theater history/criticism

Theater arts management
Fashion and apparel design
Structural engineering
Construction technology
Resort management
Interior design
Museum studies

Questions to ask colleges:
Is the program accredited by the National Association of Schools of Theater (NAST)?

Is there also a graduate program at this college? The presence of a graduate program has both advantages and disadvantages for undergrads—usually the quality of productions is high, but undergraduates may have to compete with grad students for the best design and production opportunities.

How many productions are offered per season and/or academic year? What types of theatrical works are produced (period plays, musicals, opera, dance)?

Do student designers and technicians have to audition and/or interview for positions on a production?

Career options and trends:
Regional/professional theater designer (costume, scenery, lighting, sound)*; theater technician (carpenter, scene painter, tailor or seamster, cutter/draper, electrician, sound engineer)*; technical director/production manager; art director/production designer for film and television; college or high school teacher in theater*.

The skills learned in this major are also useful in designing and working in theme parks, film, television, special effects, concerts, interior design, store and window display, cruise ship entertainment, architecture, and any business requiring the creation of an environment that people can view and interact with. New content delivery methods such as mobile apps and online TV may lead to more work opportunities in the future.

A bachelor's degree in Education and/or state certification is necessary to teach theater on a high school level. An advanced degree (MFA or Ph.D.) is mandatory for teaching at the college level. Technicians who have gained production experience can often find entry-level jobs with a bachelor's degree, but designers usually need to attend grad school for additional training.

Because theater is both an art and a business, it is subject to the ups and downs of local, state, and national economics and to trends in political ideology. While theater technicians enjoy more job security than actors, directors, and playwrights, they still must look for seasonal jobs at a variety of theaters.

Insider's viewpoint:

"If you're passionate about something you might as well go out and do it. Even if you're not famous or rich at least you'll be happy instead of being stuck in a cubicle. I'd rather be happy doing what I love, which is theater, than in a different job and making money."

—Emily, senior, San Jose State University

For more info:
Educational Theater Association (ETA)
2343 Auburn Ave.
Cincinnati, OH 45219
(513) 421-3900
www.edta.org

Part II: Brief Descriptions of Majors

About Part II

There are far more fields of study available at U.S. colleges and universities than are fully described in Part I of this book. To give you an idea of what they are about, Part II includes brief descriptions of the more than 1,200 majors recognized by the U.S. Department of Education and offered among the nation's undergraduate colleges, graduate schools, and first-professional schools.

Use the brief descriptions of majors in this Part in conjunction with Part III. They will help you get a better idea of what the colleges listed there are offering. These brief descriptions indicate the scope of the major and, where appropriate, the job or career for which it prepares you.

You won't find all of these majors at every institution. Some are very specialized fields, which are offered only by a few colleges. Some are vocational or technical in nature, and only offered by community colleges, technical institutes, or other two-year institutions. And some are only available as graduate degree programs.

Some of these briefly-described majors are mentioned in the "related majors" section of the full descriptions of majors that appear in Part I. All of these majors are listed in Part III of this book, showing which colleges and universities offer degrees for each major, and at what degree level.

If you think one of these majors sounds interesting, but you can't find a college listed in Part III that offers it at the degree level that's appropriate for you, keep in mind that there might still be ways you can study the subject in college. One way is to go to a college that offers a major in a related, broader field, and then concentrate or minor in your preferred subject. If you do this, you will then be well-prepared for a career or graduate study that focuses on the specialization you've chosen.

Brief descriptions of majors

Accounting. Includes instruction in various types of accounting, legal considerations, auditing, report procedures, planning and consulting, research methods, and professional standards and ethics.

Accounting/business management. A combined program in accounting and business management.

Accounting/computer science. A program that combines accounting with computer science and/or computer studies.

Accounting/finance. An integrated program that trains individuals to function as accountants and financial managers.

Accounting technology/bookkeeping. Prepares students to provide technical administrative support to financial management personnel.

Acoustics. Investigates the properties and behavior of sound waves under different conditions.

Acting. Prepares students to impart ideas and feelings through naturalistic and believable behavior in imaginary circumstances.

Actuarial science. Highlights the mathematical and statistical analysis of risk and its applications to insurance and other business management problems.

Acupuncture. Readies individuals to practice pulse diagnosis, acupuncture point selection, and needle insertion to treat health imbalances.

Administrative/secretarial services. Describes the duties of administrative assistants and/or secretaries and stenographers.

Adult/continuing education. Prepares students to instruct adult students in various types of educational programs.

Adult/continuing education administration. Readies individuals to serve the basic educational needs of undereducated adults or the needs of adults seeking further instruction.

Adult development/aging. Investigates aging populations and the needs of older individuals in family and institutional settings.

Adult health nursing. Informs registered nurses how to provide general care for adult patients.

Adult literacy instruction. Prepares students to serve as instructors and mentors for adults in literacy programs in school, institutional, community, and private settings.

Advertising. Focuses on commercial messages intended to promote and sell products, services, and brands.

Aeronautical/aerospace engineering. Studies the design, development, and operational evaluation of aircraft, missiles, space vehicles, and their systems.

Aeronautical/aerospace engineering technology. Covers the development, manufacturing, and testing of aircraft, spacecraft, and their systems.

Aeronautics and aviation science. The study of aviation, including in-flight and ground support operations.

Aesthetician/skin care. Prepares individuals to cleanse, depilate, massage, and beautify the human body.

African-American studies. Investigates the history, sociology, politics, culture, and economics of the North American peoples descended from Africa.

African languages. Focuses on one or more of the languages originating in Africa.

African studies. Explores the history, society, politics, culture, and economics of Africa.

Agribusiness operations. Investigates the management of agricultural businesses and agriculturally related operations within diversified corporations.

Agricultural business. Focuses on the organization, operation, and management of agricultural enterprises.

Agricultural business technology. Explores the operation of agricultural office equipment, software, and information systems.

Agricultural communications. Prepares students to apply journalistic, communication, and broadcasting principles to develop, produce, and transmit agricultural information.

Agricultural economics. The analysis of resource allocation, productivity, investments, and trends in the agricultural sector.

Agricultural education services. Features the provision of referral, consulting, technical assistance, and educational services to gardeners, farmers, ranchers, and agribusinesses.

Agricultural engineering. The study of systems used to produce, process, and store agricultural products and to improve agricultural methods.

Agricultural equipment technology. Provides instruction in the maintenance and repair of specialized farm, ranch, and agribusiness power equipment and vehicles.

Agricultural/food products processing. Readies individuals to receive, inspect, process, and package agricultural products for human consumption, animal or plant food, or other products.

Agricultural mechanization. Readies students to sell, select, and service agricultural or agribusiness technical equipment and facilities, including computers, power units, machinery, and utilities.

Agricultural power machinery operation. Highlights the operation of specialized farm, ranch, and agribusiness power equipment.

Agricultural production. Focuses on the general planning, economics, and use of facilities, natural resources, labor, and capital to produce plant and animal products.

Agricultural supplies. Highlights the purchasing, marketing, and selling of agricultural products.

Agricultural teacher education. Prepares students to teach vocational agricultural programs at various educational levels.

Agriculture, general. The study of agricultural research and production.

Agroecology/sustainable agriculture. The study of farming methods that enhance the environment and are compatible with the local ecology, economically viable, and socially responsible.

Agronomy and crop science. The study of the chemical, physical, and biological relationships of crops and soils.

Air traffic control. Prepares students to manage and control air traffic, usually with additional training at the FAA Flight Control Center in a cooperative education program.

Aircraft maintenance/technology. Prepares individuals to repair all aircraft components other than engines, propellers, avionics, and instruments.

Aircraft powerplant technology. Prepares students to repair, service, and maintain all types of aircraft power plant and related systems.

Airline/commercial pilot. Focuses on the flying and/or navigation of commercial fixed-wing aircraft.

Algebra/number theory. Prepares students to express quantities by means of symbols, vectors, matrices, equations, and integer properties.

Alternative/complementary medicine. Focuses on the theories, science, and practice of alternative and complementary medicine and medical systems.

Alternative fuel vehicle technology. Describes the maintenance of alternative fuel vehicles and the conversion of standard vehicles to AFV status.

American government/politics. Features the political institutions of the United States.

American history (U.S.). Focuses on the development of American society, culture, and institutions from the Pre-Columbian period to the present.

American literature. Features the literature of the United States from the colonial era to the present.

American Sign Language (ASL). Focuses on American Sign Language as a medium of communication for deaf individuals and Deaf culture.

American studies. The study of the history, society, politics, culture, and economics of the United States.

Analysis/functional analysis. Defines the properties of equations, multivariate solutions, functions, and dynamic systems.

Analytical chemistry. Prepares students to analyze and describe the composition of matter.

Anatomy. Highlights organs, tissues, and whole bodies together with their cellular and structural components.

Ancient Greek. Highlights the Greek language and literature from its origins through the fall of the Byzantine Empire, as a secular and/or theological subject.

Ancient Near Eastern/Biblical languages. The study of the extinct Semitic and/or Non-Semitic languages spoken in the ancient Near East, including those used to write historical Jewish and Christian religious texts.

Ancient studies. Focuses on Western and non-Western cultures and related topics in the periods of prehistory and antiquity.

Anesthesiologist assistant. Trains students to assist anesthesiologists and nurses in developing and implementing patient anesthesia care plans.

Animal-assisted therapy. Instructs health and human service professionals to integrate the use of animals into their treatment practices.

Animal behavior/ethology. Highlights the psychological and neurological processes of animals.

Animal breeding. Applies the principles of genetics and genetic engineering to the improvement of agricultural animal health and the development of new animal breeds.

Animal genetics. Features animal genetics from the experimental, comparative, veterinary, and medical viewpoints.

Animal health. Investigates the prevention and control of diseases in agricultural animals.

Animal husbandry. Features the selection, breeding, care, processing, and marketing of livestock and small farm animals.

Animal nutrition. Focuses on nutrition as related to animal health, and on the production of improved animal products.

Animal physiology. The study of internal function, development, and dynamics within animal species, with comparative applications to humans.

Animal sciences. Studies the scientific principles underlying the breeding and husbandry of agricultural animals; and the production and distribution of agricultural animal products.

Animal training. Prepares individuals to teach and exercise animals for leisure, sport, show, and professional purposes.

Animation. Prepares individuals to communicate simulated real-world content through the manipulation of film, video, photographs, digital copy, and soundtracks.

Anthropology. Describes human beings, their antecedents, and their cultural behavior and institutions in comparative perspective.

Apparel/accessories marketing. Prepares students to perform operations connected with the distribution and sale of apparel and accessories.

Apparel/textile manufacture. A program that focuses on the design, development, and production of textile products and related processes.

Apparel/textile marketing. Trains students to apply marketing research and management to the products of the apparel and textile industries.

Appliance installation and repair. Readies students to mend, install, and fix major gas, electric, and microwave appliances.

Applied behavior analysis. Prepares individuals to address the behavioral needs of individuals, especially those with developmental disabilities and autism.

Applied economics. Applies economics to the study of particular industries, activities, or the exploitation of particular resources.

Applied history. A program that applies history and administrative skills to the recording of public events and the management of related historical resources.

Applied linguistics. Focuses on language-related concerns in the everyday world, including language education, acquisition of first and additional languages, literacy, and language policy and planning.

Applied mathematics. Uses mathematics and statistics to find solutions to functional problems in fields such as engineering and the applied sciences.

Applied/professional ethics. Focuses on the systematic study of ethical issues in the workplace and public life.

Applied psychology. Applies psychological theories and methods to various real-world settings and problems.

Aquaculture. Prepares students to culture, propagate, harvest, and market domesticated fish, shellfish, and marine plants.

Aquatic biology/limnology. Highlights the ecology and behavior of microbes, plants, and animals inhabiting inland fresh waters.

Arabic. The study of the language, literature, and culture of Arabic-speaking peoples.

Archaeology. Explores societies via the excavation, analysis, and interpretation of their artifactual and human remains.

Architectural and building sciences. Studies the application of advanced technology and environmental principals to the design, construction, reconstruction, conservation and operation of buildings.

Architectural drafting/CAD/CADD. Highlights the technical skills used to develop working drawings and electronic simulations for architectural and related construction projects.

Architectural engineering. Features the mathematical and scientific principles applied to the design and development of materials, systems, and methods used to construct buildings for human habitation or other purposes.

Architectural engineering technology. Prepares students to support architects, engineers, and planners engaged in designing and developing buildings and urban complexes.

Architectural history/criticism. Studies the aesthetic, technical, and social development of the built environment and the architectural profession from ancient times to the present.

Architectural technology. Prepares students to assist architects in developing plans and documentation, and in performing office services.

Architecture. Prepares students for the professional practice of architecture, with instruction in architectural design, history, and theory; building structures; site planning; and construction.

Archival administration. Trains students to identify, manage, preserve, and manage records with long-term value for documentation, legal, research, and other purposes.

Aromatherapy. Readies individuals to provide therapeutic care through the preparation and application of essential oils.

Art. An introductory study and appreciation of the visual arts.

Art history. Studies the historical development of art as social and intellectual phenomenon, the analysis of art, and art conservation.

Art teacher education. Readies individuals to provide art and art appreciation programs at various educational levels.

Art therapy. Describes the use of art media to assess, treat, and rehabilitate individuals with physical, emotional, developmental, or mental disorders.

Artificial intelligence. Focuses on the simulation by computers of human learning and reasoning, and the computer modeling of human motor control and motion.

Arts, entertainment, and media management, general. Trains individuals to organize and manage various aspects of the visual arts, performing arts, and entertainment media industries.

Asian-American studies. Describes the history, sociology, politics, culture, and economics of Asian population groups who have immigrated to the United States and Canada.

Asian bodywork therapy. Readies students to provide relief and improved health through the traditional bodywork therapies of Asia.

Asian history. Examines the development of the societies, cultures, and institutions of the Asian continent from their origins to the present.

Asian studies. Studies the history, society, politics, culture, and economics of the Asian continent.

Astronomy. Focuses on the planetary, galactic, and stellar phenomena occurring in outer space.

Astrophysics. The theoretical study of the physical laws underlying the formation, evolution, and behavior of stars, galaxies, and the universe.

Athletic training. Instructs students on the prevention, evaluation, and treatment of sports injuries.

Atmospheric physics/dynamics. Features the processes governing the behavior of atmospheric, terrestrial, and solar phenomena.

Atmospheric science. Investigates the earth's atmosphere and its effect on terrestrial weather, and on related environment and climate problems.

Atomic/molecular physics. Investigates the behavior of matter-energy phenomena at the atomic and molecular levels.

Audiology/audiologist. Trains students to diagnose and treat hearing loss and other disorders involving the ear, advise patients on how to cope, and select and fit hearing aids.

Audiology/speech pathology. An integrated program that prepares individuals as audiologists and speech-language pathologists.

Auditing. Prepares individuals to evaluate organizational financial and operational activities, ensure regulatory compliance, safeguard assets, and promote resource allocation.

Australian/Oceanic/Pacific languages. Focuses on the languages native to Papua/New Guinea, Australia, New Zealand, and the island groups of the Pacific Ocean.

Auto body repair. Prepares individuals to repair, reconstruct, and finish automobile bodies, fenders, and external features.

Automation technology. Trains students to support engineers engaged in developing, installing, calibrating, modifying and maintaining automated systems.

Automotive engineering technology. Trains students in the development, manufacture, and testing of self-propelled ground vehicles and their systems.

Automotive technology. Describes the servicing and maintenance of all types of automobiles.

Aviation management. Emphasizes the management of aviation industry operations and services.

Avionics maintenance/technology. Trains individuals to maintain aircraft operating, control, and electronic systems.

Bacteriology. Features bacteria that are significant factors in causing human disease.

Baking/pastry arts. Describes bread and pastry making, decorating, marketing, counter display, and service.

Ballet. Trains individuals to express ideas and feelings through interpretation of classical dance choreography.

Banking/financial services. Describes a variety of customer services in banks, insurance agencies, and savings and loan companies.

Barbering. Focuses on facial shaving, hair cutting, styling art, facial and scalp massage, hairpiece fitting, equipment operation, and safety.

Bartending. Readies students to mix beverages and manage bars, lounges, and beverage services operations.

Behavioral aspects of health. Focuses on the biological, behavioral, and socio-cultural determinants of health and health behavior.

Behavioral sciences. Studies problems of human individual and social growth and behavior.

Bible studies. The study of the Christian and/or Jewish Bible, with an emphasis on interpreting the messages contained therein.

Bilingual/bicultural education. Focuses on the design and provision of teaching to bilingual/bicultural children or adults.

Biochemical engineering. Studies biochemical processes in living organisms, properties of biological materials, and processes using biochemical agents such as cells, enzymes, and antibodies.

Biochemistry. Focuses on living systems, their chemical substances and pathways, and information transfer systems.

Biochemistry and molecular biology. A program of study that combines the biological sub-disciplines of biochemistry and molecular biology.

Bioengineering/biomedical engineering. Studies the design and development of biomedical and health systems and products such as integrated biomedical systems, medical information systems, and artificial organs and prostheses.

Bioethics/medical ethics. A course of study that analyzes health care issues, clinical decision-making, and research procedures.

Bioinformatics. Applies computer-based technologies to biological, biomedical, and biotechnological research.

Biological/biosystems engineering. Prepares students to design, develop and manage biological systems.

Biological immunology. Describes the biological origination and development of disease and host responses to disease.

Biological/physical sciences. A program that is either a general synthesis of the biological and physical sciences, or a specialization that draws from the biological and physical sciences.

Biology. Introductory study of living organisms and their relations to their natural environments.

Biology lab technology. Prepares students to support biologists in research, industrial, and government settings.

Biology teacher education. Trains individuals to teach biology at various educational levels.

Biomedical sciences. The scientific study of biological issues related to health and medicine.

Biomedical technology. Readies students to support engineers engaged in developing biological or medical systems and products.

Biometrics. Applies various computational methods to the study of problems in the biological sciences and related fields in agriculture and natural resources.

Biophysics. Applies the principles of physics to the workings of biological processes and assemblies.

Biopsychology. Highlights linkages between biochemical and biophysical activity to central nervous system functioning.

Biostatistics. Prepares students to apply statistics to biomedical research and clinical, health, and industrial issues related to humans.

Biotechnology. Combines biological sciences, biochemistry, and genetics with engineering principles to prepare new agricultural, environmental, clinical, and industrial products.

Blasting. Prepares students to apply technical knowledge in using a variety of explosive materials to aid in the construction process.

Blood bank technology. Prepares individuals to administer blood testing procedures, process blood donations, and support other personnel administering transfusion therapy.

Boilermaking. Trains individuals to make and repair steam boiler components.

Botany. The study of plants, related organisms, and plant habitats and ecosystem relations.

Brass instruments. Trains students to master a brass instrument.

Broadcast journalism. Prepares students to report, produce, and deliver news via radio, television, and video/film media.

Buddhist studies. Explores the Buddhist faith; along with its intellectual, cultural, social, and ritual developments.

Building construction technology. Prepares students to apply technical knowledge and skills to residential and commercial building construction and remodeling.

Building inspection. The study of industrial, labor, and governmental standards to the oversight of construction projects and the maintenance of completed buildings.

Building/property maintenance. Prepares individuals to keep a building functioning and service a variety of structures.

Business administration and management. Prepares students to plan, organize, direct, and control the functions of a firm or organization.

Business/commerce. The general study of business, business organization, and accounting as used in profit-making and nonprofit public and private institutions and agencies.

Business communications. Prepares students to function in an organization as a composer, editor, and proofreader of business communications.

Business machine repair. Prepares individuals to install and maintain a variety of office machinery.

Business/managerial economics. The application of economic principles to the analysis of the organization and operation of business enterprises.

Business statistics. Features the description, analysis, and forecasting of business data.

Business teacher education. Prepares individuals to teach vocational business programs.

Cabinetmaking/millwright. Prepares students to set up, operate, and repair woodworking machinery, and to design and fabricate wooden items.

CAD/CADD drafting/design technology. Prepares individuals to create graphic representations and simulations in support of engineering projects.

Canadian studies. Describes the history, society, politics, culture, and economics of the Canadian people.

Cardiopulmonary technology. Readies individuals, under the supervision of physicians and nurses, to perform cardiovascular and pulmonary procedures.

Cardiovascular science. Highlights the heart, vascular system, and blood, and the disorders associated with the cardiovascular system.

Cardiovascular technology. Describes cardiovascular testing procedures used to aid in diagnoses and treatments.

Caribbean studies. Explores the history, society, politics, culture, and economics of the major islands and archipelagoes of the Caribbean Sea.

Carpentry. Prepares students to lay out, fabricate, install, and repair wooden structures and fixtures using hand and power tools.

Casino management. Prepares individuals to manage casinos and gaming establishments.

Cell biology and histology. Features the structure, function, and regulation of cells as individual units and as components of tissues and organs.

Cell physiology. Features the physiological processes, communications, and behavior of cells in the context of whole organisms.

Cellular/anatomical biology. Integrates the study of cell structure and function within the context of anatomical systems.

Cellular/molecular biology. Integrates the study of cells, cellular systems, and the molecular basis of cell structure and function.

Celtic languages. A program that focuses on the historical and modern languages spoken by the Celtic peoples of the British Isles, Continental Europe, and Asia Minor.

Central Asian studies. Focuses on the history, society, politics, culture, and economics of Inner/Central Asia, including the inhabitants of the Caspian, Amur, Tien Shan, Baikal, Gobi, Siberian, and Manchurian regions and the historical Silk Road.

Ceramic sciences/engineering. Prepares students to design, develop, and evaluate inorganic nonmetallic materials.

Ceramics. Studies the production of artwork out of clay and similar materials.

Chemical and biomolecular engineering. Integrates the study of chemical engineering and biology, with an emphasis at the molecular level.

Chemical engineering. The study of the design and development of systems employing chemical processes and the analysis of chemical problems such as corrosion, pollution, and energy loss.

Chemical engineering technology. Prepares students to support engineers engaged in the production and utilization of chemicals on an industrial scale.

Chemical physics. Combines the disciplines of physical chemistry and atomic/molecular physics to study structural phenomena.

Chemical process technology. Prepares students to operate chemical processing equipment in various industries.

Chemical technology. Prepares students to aid chemical and biochemical research and industrial operations.

Chemistry. Investigates the composition and behavior of matter, the processes of chemical change, and the laboratory simulation of these phenomena.

Chemistry teacher education. Prepares individuals to teach chemistry.

Chicano/Hispanic-American/Latino studies. The study of the Hispanic-American immigrant populations within the United States and Canada.

Child care management. Prepares individuals to plan, design, and manage child care facilities that meet children's developmental needs in a safe environment.

Child care service. Includes instruction in child development, nutrition, recreation, activities supervision, child abuse prevention, and parent-child relationships.

Child development. Features the intellectual, social, emotional, and biological development of children and the planning of related human services

Children's/adolescent literature. Studies children's and adolescent literature to enhance the work of teachers, librarians, publishers, booksellers, and creative writers.

Chinese. Features the Chinese language and its associated dialects and literature.

Chinese studies. Investigates the history, society, politics, culture, and economics of present-day China.

Chiropractic (D.C.). Readies students for the professional practice of chiropractic, including the application of noninvasive treatments and spinal adjustments to alleviate problems caused by vertebral misalignments.

Chiropractic assistant. Prepares students to assist chiropractors by providing patient management, examinations, and treatment services.

Christian studies. Features the teachings of Jesus Christ and the subsequent movements and institutions based on Christianity.

Cinematography and film/video production. Prepares students to communicate dramatic information, ideas, moods, and feelings through the creation and production of films and videos.

Civil engineering. Studies the design, development, and evaluation of public facilities, including structural, load-bearing, transportation, water resource, and material control systems.

Civil engineering drafting/CAD/CADD. Features the technical skills necessary to develop working drawings and electronic simulations in support of civil engineers and geological engineers.

Civil engineering technology. Trains individuals in the practical application of the design and execution of public works projects.

Classical/ancient Mediterranean/Near Eastern studies. Explores the cultures, environment, and history of the ancient Near East, Europe, and Mediterranean basin from the perspectives of the humanities, social sciences, and archaeology.

Classics. Focuses on the Greek and Latin languages and literatures.

Climatology. Describes the characteristics of atmospheric elements and processes in predictive, current, and historical contexts.

Clinical child psychology. Emphasizes the developmental processes of children and associated disorders.

Clinical laboratory science. Readies students to conduct medical tests, clinical trials and research, manage laboratories, and consult with physicians and researchers.

Clinical/medical laboratory assistant. Prepares students to assist laboratory teams by performing tests, phlebotomy, and other duties.

Clinical/medical laboratory technology. Trains individuals to engage in various medical laboratory procedures and tests and to record and analyze data.

Clinical/medical social work. Describes the professional practice of social work in hospitals and other health care facilities and organizations.

Clinical nurse leader. Readies registered nurses to work as part of an interdisciplinary team providing medical care based on evidence-based practice and research.

Clinical nurse specialist. Trains registered nurses to deliver direct patient care in clinical settings.

Clinical nutrition. Readies students to manage nutrition programs as part of clinical therapies, and oversee health care facility food services.

Clinical pastoral counseling. Prepares clergy and other counseling professionals to respond to the emotional and spiritual needs of patients and families in emergency or debilitating health care situations.

Clinical psychology. Describes the analysis, diagnosis, and clinical treatment of psychological disorders and behavioral pathologies.

Clinical research coordinator. Readies students to organize, coordinate and administer clinical research trials under the supervision of a principal investigator.

Clothing, apparel and textile studies. Highlights the development, distribution, and use of textile products in terms of the consumer's needs.

Cognitive psychology/psycholinguistics. Studies the processes of learning, thinking, and associated information systems.

Cognitive science. An interdisciplinary study of the mind and the nature of intelligence.

College student counseling. Studies the provision of counseling and administrative services to students in postsecondary educational institutions and adult education facilities.

Commercial/advertising art. Prepares students to communicate ideas and information to business and consumer audiences via illustrations and other media.

Commercial fishing. Prepares students to function as commercial fishermen or fishing operations supervisors.

Commercial photography. Focuses on artistic techniques for communicating ideas and information to business and consumer audiences, and recording events and people, by way of digital, film, still, and video images.

Communication disorders. The study of speech, language, hearing, and cognitive communication problems caused by disease, injury, or disability.

Communications. The comprehensive study of communication, spanning mass communications, old and new media, social and political applications, and theory.

Communications/speech/rhetoric. Focuses on the theory and practice of human communication, including speaking and listening, verbal and nonverbal interaction, rhetorical theory and criticism, argumentation and persuasion, and various contextual applications.

Communications systems installation/repair. Prepares students to assemble, operate, and fix one- and two-way communications equipment.

Communications technology. Prepares individuals to function within communications industries.

Community health/preventative medicine. Prepares individuals to plan and manage health services in local community settings.

Community health services. Readies students to link health care and related social services with affected recipient communities.

Community/junior college administration. Focuses on administration at community and junior colleges and related postsecondary systems.

Community organization/advocacy. Prepares individuals to provide services to communities, organize communities for social action, and serve as community liaisons to public agencies.

Community psychology. Trains students to analyze social problems and implement intervention strategies for addressing these problems.

Comparative/international education. Compares educational practices and institutions within different countries, states, and societies.

Comparative literature. The study of the literatures of different societies and linguistic groups from a comparative perspective.

Comparative psychology. Focuses on the behavior of group members and the relationship of those behaviors to the group's evolutionary origins.

Computational/applied mathematics. Applies mathematical and computational methods to modeling, analysis, algorithm development, and simulations for the solution of complex scientific and engineering problems.

Computational biology. Focuses on computational approaches to understanding biological systems.

Computational mathematics. Prepares students to apply mathematics to the theory, architecture, and design of computers, computational techniques, and algorithms.

Computational science. An interdisciplinary program that focuses on the study of scientific computing and its application.

Computer and information systems security. Readies students to assess the security needs of computer systems, recommend solutions, and manage security devices and procedures.

Computer education. A program that prepares individuals to teach computer education programs.

Computer engineering. Prepares individuals to design and develop computer systems and to analyze specific problems related to computer applications.

Computer engineering technology. Provides practical training in the design, development, and maintenance of computer systems, networks, and installations.

Computer forensics. Focuses on the techniques used to find, seize and analyze digital media and to conduct cyber investigations against improper, criminal or terrorist activity.

Computer graphics. Studies the software and hardware used to represent, display, and manipulate topological, two-, and three-dimensional objects on a computer screen.

Computer hardware engineering. Readies students to design, develop, and evaluate computer hardware.

Computer hardware technology. Highlights the design of computer hardware and peripheral systems.

Computer/information sciences, general. Focuses on computing, computer science, and information science as part of an interdisciplinary program.

Computer installation and repair. Describes the application of technical skills to install and maintain computers.

Computer modeling, virtual environments and simulation. Studies the principles of visual simulation technology and human-computer interaction.

Computer networking/telecommunications. Analyzes the management of linked computer systems, peripherals, and software to maximize efficiency and productivity.

Computer numerically controlled (CNC) machinist. Prepares students to operate computer numerically controlled (CNC) machine tools, such as lathes, mills, and precision measuring tools, and to perform machining functions.

Computer programming, general. Studies the writing and implementation of programs to drive operating systems and other applications, including instruction in software design, installation, and maintenance.

Computer programming, specific applications. Prepares individuals to devise customized solutions for problems presented by individual software users.

Computer science. Focuses on computer theory, computing problems and solutions, and the design of computer systems and user interfaces.

Computer software technology. Prepares students to aid in developing, implementing, and evaluating computer software and program applications.

Computer support specialist. Readies students to provide technical assistance to computer users by identifying and solving hardware and software problems.

Computer systems analysis. Trains students to design and implement large-scale computer applications and networking systems.

Computer systems technology. Includes instruction in basic computer design and architecture, programming, maintenance and inspection, and problem diagnosis and repair.

Computer typography. Prepares students to execute page formats, layouts, and text composition; and to make typographical selections using computer programs.

Concrete finishing. Trains individuals to prepare, construct, and finish buildings using masonry mixtures.

Condensed matter and materials physics. Focuses on macroscopic physical phenomena and properties that arise from basic microscopic interactions.

Conducting. Prepares students to lead bands, choirs, orchestras, and other ensembles in performance.

Conservation biology. Specifies conservation issues that result from advancing human social, economic, and industrial pressures.

Construction engineering. Studies the planning, design, and building of facilities and structures, including structural principles, site analysis, geology, materials, contracting, project management, and graphic communications.

Construction management. Readies students to coordinate the construction process from concept development through project completion on a timely and economical basis.

Construction site management. Prepares students to supervise, manage, and inspect construction sites and buildings.

Construction technology. Provides practical training in the planning, design, execution, and management of construction projects.

Construction trades. Focuses on the building, inspecting, and maintenance of structures.

Consumer economics. Prepares students to apply economic theories to consumer behavior and individual and family consumption of goods and services.

Consumer merchandising. Highlights product and service promotion from the consumer's perspective.

Consumer services/advocacy. Features the techniques needed to protect consumers from unsafe, unreliable, and/or unhealthy products and services.

Correctional facilities administration. Trains students to provide management services for institutional facilities that house and rehabilitate prisoners.

Corrections. The study of correctional science in preparation for becoming a corrections officer in an incarceration facility.

Cosmetic services. Trains students for licensed practice in hair cutting and styling, cosmetic preparations, manicures and pedicures, and facial treatments.

Cosmetology. Prepares grooming technicians to teach their specializations in schools of cosmetology and barbering.

Costume design. Prepares students to design and select costumes for characters in the performing arts.

Counseling psychology. Highlights the provision of therapeutic services to individuals and groups experiencing psychological problems and symptoms.

Counselor education. Prepares individuals to support student development and to organize guidance services within educational institutions.

Court reporting. Readies students to record examinations, testimony, judicial orders, and other proceedings via print or electronic methods.

Crafts/folk art/artisanry. Features the aesthetics and techniques for designing objects in the handcraft or folk art traditions.

Creative writing. Focuses on the process and techniques of original composition in various literary forms such as the short story, poetry, the novel, and others.

Credit management. Includes instruction in how to perform credit, collateral, and loan processing operations.

Criminal justice and law enforcement. Prepares students to apply theories and practices of criminal justice and organization management to the administration of public law enforcement agencies and operations.

Criminal justice studies. Focuses on the criminal justice system, its components and processes, and its legal and public policy contexts.

Criminalistics/criminal science. Highlights the reconstruction of crimes and the analysis of physical evidence.

Criminology. Highlights crime as a sociopathological phenomenon, the behavior of criminals, and the social institutions developed to respond to crime.

Critical care nursing. Readies students to provide specialized care to patients with life-threatening problems.

Critical incident response/special police operations. Studies the principles and techniques for dealing with police emergencies such as hostage situations, bomb threats, barricades and terrorist incidents.

Critical infrastructure protection. Studies the design, planning and management of systems and procedures for protecting critical national physical and cyber infrastructure from external threats, including terrorism.

Crop production. Prepares individuals to cultivate grain, fiber, forage, oilseed, fruits and nuts, vegetables, and other domesticated plant products.

Culinary arts and chef training. Prepares students to provide professional chef and related cooking services, with instruction in various cuisines, recipe and menu planning, cooking techniques, kitchen supervision, food supply management, and food presentation.

Culinary arts/related services. The general study of cooking and related culinary arts, including food preparation, cooking techniques, equipment operation, sanitation and safety, and food service management.

Culinary science/culinology. Integrates food science with the culinary arts to prepare students to work as research chefs in the food industry.

Cultural anthropology. The study of culture and the relationship of culture to other aspects of social life.

Cultural resource management. Readies students to preserve and protect cultural heritage sites and artifacts.

Cultural studies. An interdisciplinary analysis and critique of culture in its varied forms, including values, ideas, belief systems, expressions, and power structures.

Curriculum/instruction. Includes instruction in curriculum theory, design, planning, and evaluation, as well as instructional material design and evaluation.

Customer service management. Prepares students to monitor customer service performance and manage frontline customer support services.

Customer service support. Trains individuals to assist customers with inquiries and problems in call centers, help desks, teleservice centers, and online.

Cytogenetics/clinical genetics technology. Readies students to analyze human chromosomes for the research and diagnosis of genetic diseases, organ transplants, and cancer treatments.

Cytotechnology. Explores the change in body cells that may indicate the early development of cancers and other diseases.

Dairy husbandry. Prepares students to manage the selection and care of dairy animals and associated dairy farm facilities.

Dairy science. Prepares students to produce and manage dairy animals and products.

Dance. Explores the cultural effects of dance and prepares students to perform in one or more of the dance disciplines.

Dance therapy. A course of study that applies creative dance movement to promote client rehabilitation and physical, emotional, and mental health.

Danish. Highlights the Danish language and related dialects.

Data entry/applications. Prepares individuals to perform basic data and text entry using varied software products.

Data processing technology. Describes the use of computers and software packages for text processing, number processing, graphics, and database management.

Database design/management. Prepares individuals to design and manage databases, including the linking of data sets to create complex searchable databases and the use of analytical search tools.

Deaf studies. Focuses on the sociological, cultural, historical and linguistic aspects of the deaf and hearing impaired.

Demography/population studies. Emphasizes population models, population phenomena, and related problems of social structure and behavior.

Dental assistant. Focuses on the provision of patient care, the preparation for procedures, and the completion of office functions under the supervision of dental professionals.

Dental clinical services. Generally prepares dentists in one or more of the oral sciences and advanced/graduate dentistry specialties.

Dental hygiene. Prepares individuals to clean teeth, provide oral health education, identify oral pathologies, and manage dental hygiene practices.

Dental laboratory technology. Trains students, under the supervision of dentists, to design and construct dental prostheses.

Dentistry (D.D.S., D.M.D.). Prepares students for the professional practice of dentistry, including the evaluation, diagnosis, prevention, and treatment of diseases, disorders, and conditions of the teeth and mouth.

Design/visual communications. Focuses on effectively communicating ideas and information, and packaging products, to business and consumer audiences.

Desktop publishing. Trains students to design the layout and typography of printed and electronic graphic and textual products.

Development economics. Defines economic development and its application to the problems of specific countries and regions.

Developmental biology/embryology. The scientific study of the development and growth of animals and human beings from fertilization to birth.

Developmental/child psychology. The study of the psychological growth and development of individuals from infancy through adulthood.

Developmental services. Prepares students to support individuals with a variety of physical, mental or developmental disabilities in a family or community setting.

Diagnostic medical sonography. Features the utilization of medical ultrasound techniques to gather data used to diagnose a variety of conditions and diseases.

Diesel mechanics. Trains individuals to maintain diesel engines in vehicles, as well as stationary diesel engines in electrical generators.

Dietetic technician. Prepares individuals to implement nutritional and dietetic plans and to provide direct client services as certified dietitian technicians.

Dietetics. A program that trains students to design and manage effective nutrition programs in a variety of settings as a registered dietitian.

Dietician assistant. Trains students to assist in planning, preparing, and serving meals to individuals with specific dietary needs.

Digital arts. Focuses on the use of the computer as the primary means of creating works in the visual and performing arts, including animation, 3D visualization, music and sound design, web design and video.

Digital media. Prepares students to function as developers and managers of digital communications media.

Directing/theatrical production. Readies individuals to manage the planning, design, preparation, and production of theatrical entertainment programs.

Disability studies. Focuses on the nature, meaning, and consequences of what it is to be defined as disabled.

Dispute resolution. Provides students with skills in negotiating, mediating, and arbitrating disputes in a variety of settings.

Divinity/ministry (B.Div., M.Div.). Prepares individuals for ordination as ministers or priests in any of the Christian religious traditions.

Documentary production. Focuses on the production of nonfiction film and video.

Drafting and design technology. Features the application of technical skills to create working drawings and computer simulations for a variety of applications.

Drama and theater arts. Focuses on the general study of dramatic works and their performance.

Drama/dance teacher education. A program that prepares students to teach components of drama and/or dance.

Drawing. Highlights the expression of emotions, ideas, or inner visions through lines made on a surface.

Driver/safety education. The study of driver and safety education curricula.

Drywall installation. Describes how to install, tape, and plaster drywall installations in interior and exterior construction jobs.

Dutch/Flemish. Studies the Dutch language and related dialects.

E-commerce. Trains individuals to manage, supervise, and market electronic operations, products, and services provided on the Internet.

Early childhood education. Readies individuals to teach all relevant subject matter to students ranging in age from infancy through eight years.

Early childhood special education. A program that specifies teaching infants and preschool age children with special learning needs.

Earth science teacher education. Prepares students to teach earth science programs at various educational levels.

East Asian languages. Highlights one or more of the Sino-Tibetan, Japanese, and Korean languages of East Asia.

East Asian studies. Focuses on the history, society, politics, culture, and economics of China, Korea, Mongolia, Taiwan, Tibet, and related borderlands and island groups.

Ecology. Prepares students to relate small-scale biological systems, such as organisms, to complex and whole systems, and to the physical environment.

Ecology/evolutionary biology. Studies the relationships and interactions across levels of biological organization and how these change over time within an ecological context.

Econometrics/quantitative economics. Prepares students for the mathematical and statistical analysis of economic phenomena.

Economics. Covers the production, conservation, and allocation of resources, together with the organizational systems related to these processes.

Education, general. Covers learning and teaching, educational psychology, educational activities, and the social foundations of education.

Education of autistic. Prepares students to plan and implement educational services for children or adults who are autistic.

Education of blind/visually handicapped. Readies individuals to provide services for children or adults with visual disabilities.

Education of brain injured. Highlights educational services for students who are recovering from brain injuries that affect their cognitive, perceptive, and motor functions.

Education of Deaf/hearing impaired. Prepares students to provide educational services to Deaf and hard of hearing students at various grade levels.

Education of developmentally delayed. Readies individuals to provide educational services for students who exhibit slow social, physical, cognitive, or emotional growth patterns.

Education of emotionally handicapped. Readies students to provide educational services for individuals affected by emotional conditions.

Education of gifted/talented. Studies the provision of educational services and opportunities to individuals exhibiting exceptional intellectual or artistic talent, maturity, or social leadership skills.

Education of learning disabled. Characterizes various learning disabilities and the programs designed to address them.

Education of mentally handicapped. Characterizes mental disabilities that adversely affect educational performance and the programs designed to address them.

Education of multiple handicapped. Prepares students to design and provide educational services for individuals with multiple disabilities.

Education of physically handicapped. Describes orthopedic and other physical health impairments that affect students and their educational performance.

Education of speech impaired. Describes the design and provision of educational services for children or adults with speech impairments.

Education policy analysis. The systematic analysis of public policy issues related to education at the local, state, national, and international levels.

Educational assessment/testing. Prepares students to design, implement, and evaluate tests, and to assess teaching tools, strategies, and curricula.

Educational evaluation/research. Highlights procedures for generating information about educational programs, personnel and methods, and the analysis of such information for planning purposes.

Educational/instructional technology. Focuses on integrating technology into educational curricula and designing and producing educational software.

Educational leadership/administration. The description of techniques for administering a wide variety of schools, to prepare individuals as general administrators and supervisors.

Educational psychology. Studies learning environments, their effects on behavior, and the effects of nonschool experience on the educational process.

Educational statistics/research methods. The application of statistics to the analysis of educational research problems, and the development of technical designs for research studies.

Educational superintendency. Prepares students to lead and manage multi-school educational systems and school districts.

Educational supervision. Includes instruction in staffing and organization, personnel relations, and administrative duties at the school building, facility, or staff level.

Electrical and electronics engineering. Trains students to design, develop, and evaluate electrical and electronic systems and components.

Electrical drafting/CAD/CADD. Readies students to design working schematics and representations in support of electrical/electronic engineers and computer engineers.

Electrical engineering technology. Includes instruction in electrical circuitry, prototype testing, systems analysis and maintenance, instrument calibration, and report preparation.

Electrician. Prepares students to install, operate, maintain, and repair electric systems, as well as DC and AC motors, controls, and electrical distribution panels.

Electrocardiograph technology. Readies individuals to administer EKG and ECG examinations, and to report results to the treatment team.

Electroencephalograph technology. Prepares students, under the supervision of a physician, to study and record electrical activity in the brain and nervous system.

Electrolysis. Describes the process of hair removal from the human scalp, face, and body using specialized needle probes.

Electromechanical engineering. Focuses on combining electrical and mechanical components with special emphasis on manufacturing and automated processes.

Electromechanical technology. Prepares individuals to support engineers engaged in developing and testing automated, servomechanical, and other electromechanical systems.

Electronics/electrical equipment repair. The study of the operation, maintenance, and repair of electrical and electronic equipment.

Elementary education. Readies individuals to teach subject matter to students in grades kindergarten through grade eight.

Elementary/middle school administration. Prepares individuals to serve as principals and masters of elementary and middle schools.

Elementary special education. Describes the design and provision of educational services to elementary school children with special learning needs.

Emergency care attendant (EMT ambulance). Readies individuals to assist EMTs to transport patients and operate emergency vehicles and equipment.

Emergency/disaster management. An inter-disciplinary field drawing on the social, natural and applied sciences to prepare students for careers in disaster preparedness, response, and recovery.

Emergency medical technology (EMT paramedic). Prepares students to recognize, assess, and manage medical emergencies in prehospital settings, and to supervise ambulance personnel.

Emergency room/trauma nursing. Prepares registered nurses to deliver advanced, direct patient care in emergency and trauma settings.

Endocrinology. Covers the development and secretion of protein compounds by cells and glands, and the role of endocrine substances in bodily processes.

Energy systems technology. Readies students to support engineers engaged in the development of energy-efficient systems or monitoring energy use.

Engine machinist. Focuses on the construction of automotive and commercial vehicle engines.

Engineering chemistry. Prepares students to apply chemical principles to the analysis and evaluation of engineering problems.

Engineering design. Prepares students to coordinate and organize multiple systems and components, plan projects and procedures, resolve specification conflicts, and choose among competing theories and solutions.

Engineering, general. Prepares students to solve a wide variety of practical problems in industry, social organizations, public works and commerce.

Engineering/industrial management. Covers the planning and operational management of industrial and manufacturing operations.

Engineering mechanics. Investigates the behavior of structures, forces, and materials in engineering problems.

Engineering physics/applied physics. Combines fundamental physics, math, and engineering with a focus on specific technologies or fields, such as electrical engineering, chemistry, or computer science.

Engineering science. Focuses on the general application of various mathematical and scientific principles to the analysis and evaluation of engineering problems.

Engineering technology, general. A program that readies individuals to apply basic engineering principles and technical skills in support of engineers engaged in a wide variety of projects.

English language and literature. Explores the English language, including its history and structure, and the literature and culture of English-speaking peoples.

English literature (British). Studies the literature of the English speaking peoples of Britain and the British Commonwealth from the origins of the English language to the present.

English teacher education. Studies the teaching of English grammar, composition, and literature programs.

Entomology. The scientific study of insects.

Entrepreneurial studies. Prepares students to perform development, marketing, and management functions associated with owning a business, and to recognize, evaluate, and respond to new business opportunities.

Environmental biology. Focuses on living populations in relation to changing environmental processes.

Environmental chemistry. Uses chemistry to study natural systems (air, water, and soil), with an emphasis on pollutants and remediation.

Environmental design. Prepares students to design total environments and living systems, both indoor and outdoor.

Environmental education. Readies students to teach environmental education at various educational levels.

Environmental engineering. Studies the design, development, and evaluation of environmental systems, including pollution control, waste and hazardous material disposal, health and safety protection, and conservation.

Environmental engineering technology. Investigates the development and use of indoor and outdoor environmental pollution control systems.

Environmental health. The study of environmental factors affecting human health, safety, and related ecological issues.

Environmental psychology. Investigates ways in which to improve the behavioral interactions between human beings and the environment.

Environmental science. Applies various scientific principles to the study of the physical environment and the solution of environmental problems.

Environmental studies. Studies environment-related issues using a combination of scientific, social, or humanistic approaches.

Environmental toxicology. Focuses on the effects of exposure to toxic chemicals, pollutants, and biohazards; the management of environmental toxins, and the development of protective measures.

Epidemiology. Studies the distribution and prevention of disease across populations.

Equestrian studies. Focuses on the horse, horsemanship, and related businesses, facilities, and equipment, and the training of horses and riders.

ESL teacher education. Studies the principles and practice of teaching English to students who are not proficient in the language or who do not speak, read, or write English.

Ethics. Investigates the theory of moral good and its application to various theoretical and practical problems.

Ethnic studies, general. An interdisciplinary study of the various minority groups in the United States and the many meanings of diversity.

European history. Studies the development of European society, culture, and institutions from its origins to the present.

European studies. Focuses on the history, society, politics, culture, and economics of the European continent.

Evolutionary biology. Describes the emergence and changes of organisms and species over time.

Executive assistant. Trains individuals to function as special assistants and/or personal secretaries for business executives and top management.

Exercise physiology. Explores the processes involved in physical or motor activity.

Exercise sciences. Focuses on the anatomy, physiology, biochemistry, and biophysics of human movement, and applications to exercise and therapeutic rehabilitation.

Experimental psychology. Investigates behavior under experimental conditions and analyzes controlled behavioral responses.

Facial treatment. Studies massage and treatment of the face, scalp, and neck.

Facilities/event planning. Prepares students to become facility and event managers and workplace consultants.

Family and consumer sciences. Studies family, work, and community settings and how people relate to their physical, social, emotional, and intellectual environments.

Family/community services. Focuses on the development and implementation of support services for individuals, families, and localities.

Family/consumer business sciences. Investigates the relationship between the economy and the consuming individual and family.

Family/consumer sciences education. Readies students to teach vocational home economics programs.

Family practice nurse/nurse practitioner. Readies registered nurses to provide independent general care for family groups and individuals.

Family psychology. Readies students to provide therapeutic, evaluative, and research services to families and individuals in the family unit context.

Family resource management studies. Includes instruction in financial goal-setting and management, preventing and resolving financial difficulties, and the use of relevant public resources.

Family systems. Highlights the family in its development and its significance as a system that impacts individuals and society.

Farm and ranch management. Prepares individuals to manage farms, ranches, or similar enterprises.

Fashion and apparel design. Trains students to design commercial fashions, apparel, and accessories, and to manage fashion development projects.

Fashion/fabric consultant. Readies individuals to assist in fashion selection, style coordination, sales, fabric selection, clothing specifications, and purchasing.

Fashion merchandising. Readies students to promote fashion product lines/brands and to organize promotional campaigns to attract retailer interest, wholesale purchasing, and supply contracts.

Fashion modeling. Highlights the display of fashion apparel and accessories in wholesale and retail settings.

Fiber/textile arts. Readies students to construct designs from woven or nonwoven fabrics and fibrous materials.

Filipino/Tagalog. Emphasizes the modern Filipino/Tagalog language as used in the Philippines.

Film/cinema/video studies. The study of film/video arts, as well as the basic principles of filmmaking and film production.

Finance. Readies students to plan, manage, and analyze the financial aspects and performance of business enterprises or banking institutions.

Financial forensics and fraud investigation. Trains students to conduct investigations into illegal financial activity, and to use accounting data as evidence.

Financial mathematics. Applies mathematics and statistics to the finance industry, including the development, critique, and use of various financial models.

Financial planning. Prepares individuals to plan and manage the financial interests and growth of individuals and institutions.

Fine and studio arts management. Describes how to organize and manage fine and studio art organizations, operations, and facilities.

Fine/studio arts. Prepares individuals to function as creative artists in the visual and plastic media.

Fire/arson investigation and prevention. Studies fire combustion and behavior as applied to the analysis of fires and their causes.

Fire protection and safety technology. Applies fire science and technology to fire prevention and mitigation, substance removal, safety procedures, inspections and investigations.

Fire services administration. Focuses on the principles, theory, and practices associated with the management of fire operations, firefighting services, and community fire issues.

Fire systems technology. Focuses on firefighting systems, building construction and related resources as applied to fire prevention, control, and mitigation.

Firefighting/fire science. Readies individuals to perform the duties of firefighters.

Fishing and fisheries. The scientific study of the husbandry and production of fish and shellfish populations for commercial and recreational purposes, and the management of fishing and related product processing.

Flight attendant. Readies students to perform a variety of personal services conducive to the safety and comfort of airline passengers during flight.

Flight instructor. Prepares individuals to train pilots and flight crews to fly and/or operate commercial, corporate, agricultural, public service, or rescue aircraft.

Floriculture. Explores the operation and management of florist enterprises, supply and delivery services, and flower catering services.

Folklore studies. Examines the aesthetic expression in everyday life found in narratives, literature, performing arts, culture, work, family and community.

Food and nutrition studies. A general program that focuses on the role of foods and nutrition in human health and wellness.

Food preparation. Trains students to serve as kitchen support staff and food preparation workers.

Food science. Studies the conversion of raw agricultural products into processed forms suitable for human consumption.

Food service. Includes instruction in table and counter services, dining room operations, personnel supervision, safety, and sanitation.

Food technology/processing. Describes the manufacturing, packaging, storage, and distribution technologies and processes for food products.

Foreign language teacher education. Instructs individuals how to teach foreign languages other than French, German, or Spanish.

Foreign languages, general. A program that studies multiple foreign languages at the basic/elementary level.

Forensic chemistry. The application of chemical analysis to evaluate physical evidence in criminal investigations.

Forensic psychology. Prepares individuals to apply clinical, counseling, and neuropsychological skills to criminal investigations.

Forensic science. Trains students to apply physical, biomedical, and social sciences to analyze physical evidence, human testimony, and criminal suspects.

Forest engineering. Highlights the mechanical devices and processes used for efficient forest management, timber production, and related systems.

Forest management. Prepares individuals for the management and administration of forest lands and related resources.

Forest resources production. Prepares students to perform technical and managerial functions as they relate to the production, harvesting, and processing of forest resources.

Forest sciences/biology. The study of environmental factors affecting forests and the growth and management of forest resources.

Forest technology. Readies individuals to assist foresters in the management and production of forest resources.

Forestry. Features the management and development of forest areas for economic, recreational, and ecological purposes.

Franchise operations. Trains individuals to manage and operate franchises.

French. The study of the language and literature of French-speaking peoples, including related dialects and creoles.

French studies. Describes the history, society, politics, culture, and economics of France.

French teacher education. Describes how to teach French language programs.

Funeral direction. Prepares individuals for professional licensure as managers of funeral homes and cemeteries.

Funeral services/mortuary science. Describes the basic elements of mortuary science, the funeral service business, and counseling.

Furniture design/manufacturing. Readies individuals to design furniture projects; assemble, finish, and repair furniture articles; and use hand and power tools.

Game/interactive media design. Prepares students to apply the artistic and technical skills needed to design and develop computer games and other forms of interactive media.

Gay/lesbian studies. The study of homosexuality and the public policies and legal issues surrounding the gay and lesbian community.

Gene therapy. Describes the treatment of diseases and inherited abnormalities through the modification of gene expression.

General literature. Focuses on literature from one or more genres, cultures or traditions.

Genetic counseling. Readies students to counsel patients and families concerning inherited genetic disorders and diseases.

Genetics. The study of biological inheritance, development, disease, and evolution in all living organisms and viruses.

Genome sciences. The study of whole genome sequences and patterns of gene expression.

Geochemistry. Investigates the properties and behavior of the substances forming, and formed by, geomorphological processes of the earth and other planets.

Geochemistry/petrology. Explores the igneous, metamorphic, and hydrothermal processes within the earth and their resulting deposits.

Geographic information science and cartography. Focuses on map-making, geographic data analysis, geographic information systems, and the science of mapping geographic information.

Geography. Highlights the spatial distribution and interrelationships of people, natural resources, and plant and animal life.

Geography teacher education. Describes teaching geography at various grade levels.

Geological engineering. Prepares students to apply geological analysis to engineering problems, such as environmental recovery sites, or the geological forces acting upon structures.

Geology/earth science. The scientific study of the earth, the forces acting upon it, and the behavior of the solids, liquids, and gases comprising it.

Geophysics/seismology. The scientific study of the physics of solids and its application to the study of the earth.

Geotechnical/geoenvironmental engineering. Prepares students to design and build earth and earth supported structures to address environmental problems, such as waste containment, land fills, and soil improvement.

Geriatric nurse/nursing. Prepares registered nurses to provide health care to aging and elderly patients.

German. Highlights the German language and related dialects.

German studies. Focuses on the history, society, politics, culture, and economics of the Germanic peoples.

German teacher education. Prepares students to teach German language programs at various educational levels.

Germanic languages. A general program that focuses on one or more of the Germanic languages of Western, Central, and Northern Europe.

Gerontology. Investigates the aging process and aged human populations.

Geropsychology. Investigates the psychology of aging populations, with reference to growth and decline across the life span.

Glazier. Readies individuals to install and repair fixtures, sheets, windows, and skylights made of glass or Plexiglas.

Global studies. Investigates global and international issues from the perspective of the social sciences and social services.

Golf management. Prepares students to manage the operation of golf courses.

Graphic communications. Provides technical training in the manufacture, distribution, or transmission of graphic communications, including prepress, press, and postpress operations.

Graphic design. Readies students to use artistic and computer techniques to convey technical and commercial concepts through images and typography.

Graphic/printing production. Prepares students to apply technical knowledge to perform a variety of commercial and industrial graphic communications jobs.

Greenhouse operations. Investigates the production and storage of plant species in controlled indoor environments for sale or research purposes.

Gunsmithing. Highlights the making and modification of firearms.

Hair styling. Readies individuals to shampoo, style, and set hair, and apply hair cosmetics and wigs.

Hazardous materials information systems. Readies individuals to implement, monitor, and enforce hazardous materials management and removal.

Hazardous materials technology. Focuses on basic engineering principles to aid in identifying and disposing of hazardous materials.

Health aide. Readies individuals to provide supervised care to patients, and/or perform maintenance and general assistance in health care facilities.

Health and wellness, general. Prepares students to assume roles as health/wellness professionals in private business and industry, community organizations, and health care settings.

Health care administration. Readies individuals to develop, plan, and manage health care operations and services within health care facilities.

Health communications. Explores how people understand health and illness and the media's role in shaping health care messages.

Health information management. Prepares students to plan, design, and manage health information systems, processes, and facilities used to collect, store, analyze, and transmit electronic health records and related information.

Health information technology. Trains individuals to classify, construct, and secure medical records and health information systems under the supervision of health information managers.

Health management/clinical assistant. Prepares students to perform office services and clinical specialties under the supervision of physicians, nurses, or other health care professionals.

Health/medical psychology. Studies health, illness, and recovery, from the perspective that these phenomena arise from a combination of physical, behavioral, and social conditions.

Health occupations teacher education. Trains students to teach specific vocational health occupations programs.

Health/physical fitness. Readies students to promote physical fitness and athletic prowess, and to accomplish related research and service goals.

Health physics/radiologic health. A program of study that applies nuclear science and engineering physics to diagnostic, treatment, and therapeutic processes, and to public health protection.

Health policy analysis. The systematic analysis of public policy issues related to domestic and international health and health care systems.

Health services. Prepares for entry into specialized training programs or for concentrations in the allied health area.

Health services administration. Readies students to plan and manage health services delivery systems in the public and private sectors.

Health teacher education. Prepares individuals to educate students about health-related topics.

Health unit coordinator. Readies individuals to perform administrative and reception duties in a patient care unit.

Health unit manager. Prepares students to supervise and coordinate the operations of patient care units.

Hearing instrument specialist. Prepares students to test hearing and to select, fit and dispense appropriate hearing aids.

Heating/air conditioning/refrigeration maintenance. Describes the maintenance of heating, air conditioning, and refrigeration systems.

Heating/ventilation/air conditioning/refrigeration technology. Focuses on the development and installation of air conditioning, refrigeration, ventilation, and heating systems.

Heavy/earthmoving equipment operation. Trains students to operate and maintain heavy construction equipment involved in digging, sloping, grading, stripping, backfilling, clearing, and excavating.

Heavy equipment maintenance. Trains individuals to repair and overhaul heavy equipment.

Hebrew. Explores premodern and/or modern forms of the Hebrew language.

Hematology technology. Readies students, under the supervision of a laboratory scientist or physician, to perform tests and analyze blood samples.

Herbalism. A program that utilizes herbal medicines to prevent and cure illnesses and temporary physical disorders.

High performance/custom engine mechanic. Describes how to increase the power of engines; enhance the performance of automobiles; and repair, service, and maintain high performance vehicles.

Higher education administration. Prepares students to become administrators in four-year colleges, universities, and higher education systems.

Hispanic and Latin American languages. Studies the languages and literatures of the Spanish- and Portuguese-speaking areas of the world, including regional and Latin American dialects and Chicano literature.

Histologic assistant. Readies individuals to process tissue samples and perform routine histologic procedures and tests.

Histologic technology. Trains students to identify tissue and cell components and relate these findings to physiological functions and to the detection and diagnoses of diseases.

Historic preservation. Studies the process of saving and restoring old structures for contemporary use.

History. The study and interpretation of the past.

History of science/technology. Describes the historical evolution of scientific theories, applications and technologies, as well as the philosophy of science and its historical socio-economic context.

History teacher education. Prepares students to teach history programs at various educational levels.

Holistic health. Focuses on the interconnectedness of attributes and influences of well-being, and integrates aspects of Eastern and Western medicine to optimize health.

Holocaust studies. Investigates acts of genocide in human history with particular reference to twentieth-century genocides.

Home furnishings. Includes instruction in selecting, purchasing, designing, and decorating home furnishings; floral design; accessory construction; textiles; and upholstery.

Home health attendant. Highlights the provision of support services for homebound disabled, recovering, or elderly people.

Homeland security. Studies security policies, planning and operations dedicated to the protection of U.S. territory, assets, infrastructure, institutions and citizens from external threats.

Homeopathic medicine. Features a system that uses natural substances in highly diluted forms to mimic symptoms of illness and trigger autoimmune responses.

Horse husbandry/equine science. Trains students in the care and maintenance of horses and of horse farms, stables, and tracks.

Horticultural science. Focuses on the scientific principles related to the cultivation of garden and ornamental plants, including fruits, vegetables, flowers, and landscape and nursery plants.

Horticulture. Describes the production of domesticated plants, shrubs, flowers, trees, and groundcover, and the management of horticultural services.

Hospital/health care facilities administration. Prepares students to administer hospitals, clinics, nursing homes, and other health care facilities.

Hospitality administration/management. Prepares students to serve as general managers of hospitality operations in the travel, lodging, food service, and recreation industries.

Hospitality/recreation marketing. Focuses on the provision of marketing services in the hospitality and leisure fields.

Hotel/motel administration. Prepares individuals to oversee operations and facilities that provide lodging services to travelers.

Hotel/motel/restaurant management. Readies students to manage operations and facilities that provide food and/or lodging services to the traveling public.

Housing and human environments. The study of the behavioral, social, economic, functional, and aesthetic aspects of housing, interiors, and other environments.

Human biology. An interdisciplinary program that addresses contemporary issues related to biology and society, such as global health and disease, environmental policy, bioethics, and biotechnology.

Human computer interaction. An interdisciplinary program that focuses on the study of the interaction between people and technology.

Human development and family studies. Studies human development and behavioral characteristics of the individual within the context of the family.

Human/medical genetics. Describes human genetics as they relate to diagnosis, genetic engineering and therapy, transplantation, and diseases and their defense.

Human nutrition. Highlights the relationships between food consumption and human development and health.

Human resources development. Readies students to manage and evaluate programs to improve individual productivity, employability and job satisfaction, and organizational effectiveness.

Human resources management. Prepares students to manage the development of personnel in organizations, including recruitment, staffing, training, performance management, compensation, labor relations, and health and safety.

Human sciences communication. Focuses on communication of human sciences subject matter to various audiences through print and non-print media.

Human services. Explores the provision of human and social services to individuals and communities.

Humanities. Combined studies in the humanities, emphasizing languages, literatures, art, music, philosophy, and religion.

Hydraulics technology. Includes instruction in hydraulics principles, pipeline and pumping systems, operational testing, and inspection and maintenance procedures.

Hydrology/water resources science. The study of the circulation, distribution, chemical and physical properties, and environmental interaction of surface and subsurface waters.

Illustration. Highlights artistic techniques to portray the concepts of authors and designers to specifications.

Industrial and product design. Readies individuals to convey information through forms, shapes, and packaging for manufactured products.

Industrial electronics technology. Trains individuals to assemble, manage, and service industrial electrical/electronic equipment.

Industrial engineering. Prepares students to design systems for managing industrial production processes.

Industrial equipment maintenance/repair. Readies students to fix and sustain the operation of industrial machinery and equipment.

Industrial/organizational psychology. Examines individual and group behavior in industrial and organizational settings.

Industrial radiologic technology. Focuses on the operation of industrial and research testing equipment using radioisotopes.

Industrial safety technology. Prepares students to implement and enforce industrial safety standards.

Industrial technology. Includes instruction in organizational behavior, industrial planning, computer applications, and report and presentation preparation.

Informatics. Examines computer systems from a user-centered perspective and studies the structure, behavior and interactions of natural and artificial systems that store, process and communicate information.

Information resources management. Prepares students to plan, manage, and evaluate information services in organizations.

Information systems. Focuses on the theory and process of information collection, transmission, and utilization in traditional and electronic forms.

Information technology. Highlights the design of technological information systems as solutions to business, research, and communications support needs.

Information technology project management. Prepares students to design, develop, and manage information technology projects in a variety of companies and organizations.

Inorganic chemistry. Covers elements and their compounds, other than the hydrocarbons and their derivatives.

Institutional food production. Focuses on the management of food service operations in institutional settings.

Institutional food service. Provides instruction in the production and service used in institutional food establishments.

Instrumentation technology. Readies students to apply basic engineering principles in support of engineers engaged in developing measurement systems and procedures.

Insurance. Trains individuals to manage risk in organizational settings and provide insurance and risk-aversion services to businesses and individuals.

Integrated circuit design. Prepares students to design circuits in microelectronics.

Intercultural/diversity studies. Examines the social relations between and among majority and minority groups, and ways to promote cooperation, tolerance, and management of diversity issues.

Interior architecture. Prepares students to apply architectural principles in the design of structural interiors for living, working, and leisure purposes.

Interior design. Readies individuals to plan, design, equip, and furnish interior spaces.

International agriculture. Studies the problems of global food production and distribution, and the agricultural systems of other countries.

International business. Trains individuals to oversee international business operations.

International economics. Prepares individuals to analyze international commercial behavior and trade policy.

International finance. Trains students to manage international financial operations and related currency transactions.

International/intercultural communication. Provides specialized knowledge and skills needed for effective communication in the international community and among people of different cultures.

International marketing. Readies students to perform marketing techniques for enterprises engaged in exporting or importing goods and services in world markets.

International policy analysis. The systematic analysis of public policy issues related to relationships among nations and among governments and nongovernmental entities.

International public health. Focuses on public health problems in poor and developing countries and regions.

International relations. The study of international politics and institutions, and the conduct of diplomacy and foreign policy.

Investments/securities. A program that prepares students to oversee assets placed in capital markets.

Iranian languages. A program that focuses on the languages used in ancient, medieval, and modern Iran and its border regions.

Irish studies. Focuses on the history, society, politics, culture, and economics of Ireland.

Ironworking. Readies individuals to make and install ornamental and reinforcing metal structures and supports.

Islamic studies. The study of the history, culture, and interpretation of the Islamic faith.

Italian. Explores the Italian language and its applications in varied settings.

Italian studies. Highlights the history, society, politics, culture, and economics of modern Italy.

Japanese. The study of Japanese literature, language, and dialects.

Japanese studies. Features the history, society, politics, culture, and economics of Japan.

Jazz studies. Studies the performance and composition of jazz.

Journalism. Focuses on gathering, processing, and delivering news.

Judaic studies. Focuses on the history, culture, and religion of the Jewish people.

Junior high/middle school special education. Describes the design and provision of educational services to children with special learning needs in junior high/middle school.

Juvenile corrections. Studies the provision of correction services to underage populations.

Keyboard instruments. Trains students to master the piano, organ, or related keyboard instruments and to perform as solo, accompanist, or in ensemble.

Kindergarten/preschool education. Trains individuals to instruct students ranging in age from three to six years, in settings prior to beginning regular elementary school.

Kinesiotherapy. Readies individuals to treat the effects of disease, injury, and congenital disorders through exercise and education.

Knowledge management. The study of knowledge management in government agencies and corporations for the purpose of supporting stated goals and objectives.

Korean. The study of Korean literature, language, and dialects.

Korean studies. Examines the history, society, politics, culture, and economics of Korea.

Labor/industrial relations. The study of employee-management interactions and the management of issues regarding working conditions and worker benefit packages.

Labor studies. Highlights work, labor organization, policy, and movements from the perspective of the social sciences and history.

LAN/WAN management. A program that prepares students to oversee and regulate computer systems and performance requirements of an entire network of satellite users, including local and wide area networks.

Land use planning. Focuses on how land can be preserved, developed, and used for maximum social, economic, and environmental benefit.

Landscape architecture. Prepares students for the professional practice of landscape architecture, with instruction in geology and hydrology; soils, groundcovers, and horticultural elements; site planning; and landscape design.

Landscaping/groundskeeping. Describes the maintenance of ornamental and recreational plants and related conceptual designs.

Language interpretation/translation. Highlights the interpretation and/or translation of documents and data files, either from English or (Canadian) French into another language or vice versa.

Laser/optical engineering. Prepares students to design, develop and evaluate optical systems, lasers and related electronic devices.

Laser/optical technology. Readies individuals to support engineers in the development and use of lasers and other optical instruments for commercial or research purposes.

Latin. Features the Latin language and literature and its current ecclesiastical usage.

Latin American/Caribbean studies. An integrated program that focuses on the history, society, politics, culture, and economics of the peoples and countries of Latin America and the Caribbean.

Latin American studies. Features the history, society, politics, culture, and economics of the North and South American continents outside Canada and the United States.

Latin teacher education. A program that prepares individuals to teach Latin at various grade levels.

Law (J.D.). Preparation for the independent practice of law, taking bar examinations, and advanced research in jurisprudence.

Law enforcement intelligence analysis. Trains law enforcement personnel to perform intelligence and surveillance operations and to analyze and use data collected.

Law enforcement investigation and interviewing. Focuses on the principles, procedures, techniques, issues, and legalities associated with criminal investigations.

Law enforcement records/evidence management. Prepares students to manage records in police or other security offices, including storing and retrieving evidence and related data.

Lay ministry. Prepares non-ordained individuals to serve in positions open to the laity in local churches and other settings.

Learning sciences. Focuses on the various environmental and social dynamics of learning; cognition; learning strategies; educational psychology; testing and measurement; and statistical educational research.

Legal administrative assistance. Instruction includes legal terminology, research, and documentation; software applications; and office procedures.

Legal studies. Applies the social sciences and humanities to the study of law and legal issues.

Liberal arts and sciences. A program that is a structured combination of the arts, sciences, and humanities, emphasizing breadth of study.

Library assistance. Includes instruction in library operation and services; acquisition, storage, and display systems; and material retrieval.

Library science. Prepares individuals for professional service as librarians and information consultants.

Licensed midwifery. Readies individuals to provide for prenatal, natural birth, and immediate postpartum care to pregnant women.

Licensed practical nursing. Prepares students, under the direction of a registered nurse, physician, or dentist, to assist in providing general nursing care.

Lineworker. Describes how to install, operate, maintain, and repair electric power cables; erect and construct pole and tower lines; and install underground cables.

Linguistics. The study of language, language development, and the relationships among languages and language groups.

Livestock management. Readies individuals to produce and manage livestock animals and the production and handling of meat and other products.

Locksmithing. Trains students to open locks, make keys, enter and change lock and safe combinations, and install and repair safes.

Logic. The systematic study of valid inference, argument, and sound reasoning.

Logistics/materials/supply chain management. Prepares individuals to coordinate all logistical functions within an enterprise, such as acquisitions, receiving and handling, storage, allocation of resources, quality control, and delivery of output.

Long term care administration. Focuses on the management of term care facilities, settings and agencies serving the elderly and disabled.

Machine shop technology. Trains students to make and modify metal parts used in manufacturing, repair, or design activities.

Machine tool technology. Prepares individuals to manufacture, assemble, test, and repair parts, mechanisms, and machines.

Magnetic resonance imaging (MRI) technology. Trains AART-certified radiological technicians to utilize MRI technology.

Make-up artist. Prepares students to apply cosmetics and perform specialized makeovers including wig work, masking, and related costuming for professional, artistic, security, or leisure purposes.

Mammography technology. Trains registered radiographers to become registered mammographers.

Management information systems. Readies individuals to manage data systems for processing and retrieving internal business information, to select systems, and to train personnel.

Management science. Highlights the application of statistical modeling, data mining, forecasting, and operations research techniques to the analysis of business organization and performance problems.

Manicurist. Readies students to shape fingernails and toenails, remove unwanted skin, and apply polish and cosmetics to nails.

Manufacturing engineering. Includes instruction in the design, development, and implementation of manufacturing systems.

Manufacturing technologies. Covers the basic engineering principles used to identify and resolve production problems in the manufacturing process.

Marine biology. Emphasizes marine organisms and their interactions with the physical environment.

Marine engineering/naval architecture. Prepares individuals to design vessels operating on or under the water, and to analyze related engineering problems.

Marine maintenance/fitter/ship repair. Prepares students to repair vessel components and mechanical devices, maintain sails, and repair and balance propeller and drive shafts.

Marine sciences. An interdisciplinary study of biology, chemistry, geology and physics as applied to marine, estuarine and coastal environments.

Maritime studies. An interdisciplinary program that focuses on the history, science, policy issues, law and literature of the seas and other navigable waters.

Maritime technology/Merchant Marine. Prepares individuals to serve as captains, executive officers, engineers, and ranking mates on commercially licensed vessels.

Marketing. Prepares students to manage the development of consumer audiences and the delivery of products from producers to consumers.

Marketing research. A program that readies individuals to describe consumer behavior patterns and market environments to marketing managers.

Marriage/family therapy. Trains individuals to diagnose mental and emotional disorders within marriages and family systems, and to apply short- and long-term therapeutic strategies.

Masonry. Focuses on the laying or setting of brick, concrete block, hard tile, and marble, using hand tools.

Massage therapy. Prepares individuals to apply manual techniques for manipulating skin, muscles, and connective tissues.

Materials chemistry. Examines organic or inorganic materials and their electronic, magnetic, optical or mechanical properties.

Materials engineering. Focuses on the design, development and evaluation of materials used in manufacturing, the synthesis of new materials, and the analysis of materials requirements.

Materials science. Focuses on the analysis and evaluation of the characteristics and behavior of solids.

Maternal/child health. Emphasizes public health issues affecting women, children, and families.

Maternal/child health nursing. Informs registered nurses how to provide prenatal care to pregnant women and to mothers and their newborn infants.

Mathematical biology. Applies mathematics to the biological sciences and the analysis of biological systems.

Mathematical statistics/probability. Focuses on the mathematical theory underlying the use of statistical methods.

Mathematics. A general program that analyzes quantities, magnitudes, forms, and their relationships, using symbolic logic and language.

Mathematics/computer science. A program with a general synthesis of mathematics and computer science, or a specialization that draws from mathematics and computer science.

Mathematics/statistics. A program with a general synthesis of mathematics and statistics.

Mathematics teacher education. Prepares individuals to teach mathematical subjects.

Meat cutting. Prepares individuals to receive, cut, and package animal meat products in commercial establishments.

Mechanical drafting/CAD/CADD. Trains individuals to prepare working drawings and electronic simulations in support of mechanical and industrial engineers.

Mechanical engineering. Focuses on the design and development of mechanical devices and systems, including physical systems used in manufacturing; engines; power units; hydraulics; and the integration of computers and remote control with operating systems.

Mechanical engineering technology. Provides practical training in the design, development, and implementation of engineering projects involving mechanical systems.

Mechanics/repairers, general. Emphasizes the application of technical skills in the adjustment, maintenance, part replacement, and repair of tools, equipment, and machines.

Mechatronics/robotics/automation engineering. Focuses on computer controlled electromechanical systems and products with embedded electronics, sensors, and actuators, including robots and automation systems.

Media studies. Analyzes the criticism of media, how people understand media, and the roles of media in transforming culture.

Medical administrative assistant. Prepares students to provide administrative assistance to physicians and other health professionals.

Medical anthropology. Examines biological, sociocultural, psychological, and behavioral factors as they relate to health, illness, medical practices, and access to health care.

Medical claims examiner. Readies students to investigate, analyze, and evaluate medical/health insurance claims.

Medical/clinical assistant. Readies students to support physicians by providing assistance during patient consultations and examinations.

Medical illustrating. Focuses on the creation of visual materials to facilitate educational, research, and clinical purposes.

Medical informatics. Prepares individuals to apply computer science to medical research and clinical support, and to develop advanced imaging, database, and decision systems.

Medical insurance coding specialist. Trains students to conduct data entry, classification, and record-keeping procedures related to medical insurance documentation.

Medical insurance specialist. Covers the management of insurance operations in a medical office, facility, or organization.

Medical office administration. Focuses on the management of business functions in a medical or clinical office.

Medical office assistant. Trains individuals to perform routine administrative duties in a medical, clinical, or health care facility office.

Medical office computer specialist. Readies individuals to install, maintain, and upgrade medical software and associated hardware.

Medical radiologic technology/radiation therapy. Readies students to administer prescribed radiation treatments, manage patients, and maintain pertinent records.

Medical receptionist. Readies students to provide customer service, visitor reception, and patient services.

Medical scientist. Prepares clinicians to conduct clinical and translational research in various areas.

Medical staff services technology. Prepares individuals to provide personnel management, credentialing, and accreditation compliance services for health care facilities and organizations.

Medical transcription. Prepares students to execute verbatim medical minutes, reports, and orders.

Medication aide. Prepares students to administer prescribed medications, report patient reactions, and perform emergency and recording duties.

Medieval and Renaissance studies. Explores the medieval and Renaissance periods in Europe from the perspective of the humanities and social sciences.

Medium/heavy vehicle technology. Highlights the specialized maintenance of commercial and industrial vehicles, such as trucks and buses.

Meeting and event planning. Prepares individuals to plan, budget, and implement conferences, meetings, and other special events.

Mental health counseling. Trains students to evaluate, refer, and counsel people to prevent or mediate personal conflicts and emotional crises.

Mental health services technology. Prepares individuals to assist psychiatrists, psychologists, and nurses in patient care and treatment.

Merchandising/buying operations. Prepares students to function as professional buyers of resale products and product lines for stores, chains, and other retail enterprises.

Metal building assembly. Highlights the construction of metal structures using prefabricated framing and siding components.

Metal fabricator. Prepares students to fabricate metal plates or shapes, and to manufacture and/or install metal products as interpreted through technical drawings.

Metal/jewelry arts. Trains individuals to fashion artwork from gems and other stones and precious metals.

Metallurgical engineering. Covers the metal components of structural, power, transmission, and moving systems, and the analysis of engineering problems.

Metallurgical technology. Trains students to support metallurgists engaged in developing and using industrial metals and manufacturing processes.

Meteorology. Readies students to predict atmospheric motion and climate change.

Microbiology. The study of small organisms, including bacteria and viruses, as distinguished from the cellular material of larger organisms.

Microbiology and immunology. Investigates microorganisms that cause disease and the host immune response to them.

Middle Eastern and Semitic languages. Focuses on one or more of the Middle/Near Eastern and Semitic languages of the ancient and modern Middle/Near East, Western Asia, North Africa, and Europe.

Middle school education. Trains individuals to guide students in the middle, intermediate, or junior high grades.

Military history. Focuses on the history of warfare and military institutions in their operational, politico-economic and socio-cultural contexts.

Mining and mineral engineering. Studies the evaluation of mineral extraction and refining systems, including open shaft mines and prospecting equipment.

Mining technology. Prepares individuals to support engineers engaged in the development and operation of mines and related mineral processing facilities.

Missionary studies. The theory and practice of religious outreach, social service, and proselytization.

Modern Greek. A program that focuses on the development and use of the Greek language.

Molecular biochemistry. Describes the chemical processes of living organisms at the molecular level.

Molecular biology. Investigates the structure and function of biological macromolecules, with emphasis on proteins and nucleic acids, and processes such as metabolism, gene function and regulation, differentiation, and development.

Molecular biophysics. Applies physics principles to the study of living cells and organisms at the molecular level.

Molecular genetics. Covers the molecular structure and processes that regulate gene expression, information transfer, replication, and stability.

Molecular medicine. Focuses on the molecular and cellular basis of disease, and the development of clinical and diagnostic tools, medications, and therapies.

Molecular pharmacology. Highlights characteristics of drugs at the molecular level and their interaction with, and effects on, microbiological structures and processes.

Molecular physiology. Focuses on the scientific study of biochemical communications and processes at the subcellular level.

Molecular toxicology. Describes the interaction of toxic agents with biological systems at the molecular and cellular levels.

Montessori teacher education. Highlights the pedagogical principles and methods developed by Maria Montessori and her followers.

Mortuary science/embalming. Prepares students for licensure as embalmers and morticians, with instruction in embalming, restorative art, laws and regulations, and special services.

Motorcycle maintenance. Prepares students to fix motorcycles and other similarly powered vehicles.

Movement therapy. Prepares individuals to promote body awareness and optimal mental and physical functioning.

Multi/interdisciplinary studies, general. A program that integrates two or more distinct subjects or disciplines around a unifying theme or topic.

Multicultural education. Highlights the design and implementation of instructional and advising services for culturally diverse learning populations.

Multimedia. Prepares students to display ideas in either two or three dimensions, through the simultaneous use of a variety of materials and media.

Museum studies. Prepares individuals to develop, conserve, and retrieve artifacts, exhibits, and collections in museums and galleries.

Music, general. An introductory study and appreciation of music and the performing arts.

Music history/literature. Highlights the evolution of music, the development of musical instruments, and the analysis and criticism of musical literature.

Music management. Explores the organization and management of music operations, facilities, personnel, bands, ensembles, and individual artists.

Music pedagogy. Studies the provision of musical instruction and tutoring to clients in private and institutional settings.

Music performance. Trains individuals to master musical instruments or to sing, and to become solo and/or ensemble performers.

Music teacher education. Prepares individuals to teach music and music appreciation.

Music technology. Focuses on the creative aspects of blending music and technology, including composition, recording, performance, and software and multimedia development.

Music theory and composition. The study of the structures and processes of music, and the art of writing and arranging music.

Music therapy. Highlights the utilization of music to address patients' physical, psychological, cognitive, emotional, and social needs.

Musical instrument fabrication/repair. Describes the fabrication, repair, maintenance, and tuning of musical instruments.

Musical theater. Studies the principles and techniques for integrating theater, music, and dance into a unified production.

Musicology/ethnomusicology. The study of the forms, methods, and functions of music in Western and non-Western societies and cultures.

Mycology. The study of various fungi and their relationship to diseases in plants, animals, and humans, as well as to useful drug products.

Nanotechnology. Focuses on technical skills used to manipulate matter at the atomic and molecular level and to create nanoscale structures, devices, and systems.

National security policy studies. Focuses on the theory and application of intelligence, diplomacy, military power, and related tools of statecraft to national security policy.

Native American education. Prepares individuals to provide teaching and administrative services to American Indian, Alaska Native, and Hawaiian Native students that attend Tribal/First Nation schools.

Native American languages. A program that focuses on the languages native to the Western Hemisphere, with an emphasis on American Indian languages and literatures, but including other Native American languages.

Native American studies. Highlights the history, sociology, politics, culture, and economics of the American Indian, Aleut, Inuit, and Hawaiian peoples.

Natural resource economics. Applies economic concepts and methods to the analysis of issues such as pollution, land use planning, waste disposal, and conservation policies.

Natural resource recreation and tourism. Prepares students to plan, develop, and manage recreational activities and tourism in a natural resource setting.

Natural resources and conservation. Focuses on the natural environment and its conservation, use, and improvement.

Natural resources law enforcement. Trains students to enforce conservation and environmental protection laws, and to engage in emergency response and rescue procedures in natural resource areas.

Natural resources management/policy. Readies students to plan, manage, and evaluate programs to protect and regulate natural habitats and resources.

Natural sciences. A combined or undifferentiated focus on one or more of the physical and biological sciences.

Naturopathic medicine. Describes an approach that combines medical knowledge with noninvasive therapies and emphasizes disease prevention, wellness, and self-healing.

Near and Middle Eastern studies. Covers the history, society, politics, culture, and economics of North Africa, Southwestern Asia, Asia Minor, and the Arabian Peninsula.

Network/system administration. Trains individuals to control the system configurations and manage the computer operations of a specific site or network hub.

Neuroanatomy. Focuses on the scientific study of the structure and function of the brain and central nervous system.

Neurobiology/anatomy. Describes the structure and function of the central and peripheral nervous system in vertebrates and invertebrates.

Neurobiology/behavior. Studies the structure and function of the central and peripheral nervous system in vertebrates and invertebrates as it relates to control of behavior.

Neuropharmacology. Focuses on drugs that modify brain function, the human body, and behavior, and the development of treatment therapies.

Neuroscience. Investigates the molecular, structural, cognitive, and behavioral aspects of the brain and nervous system.

Nonprofit/public organization management. Readies individuals to manage the business affairs of foundations, educational institutions, associations, public agencies, or governmental operations.

Norwegian. The study of the language and related dialects of the Norwegian-speaking peoples.

Nuclear engineering. Focuses on systems for controlling and manipulating nuclear energy and the analysis of related engineering problems.

Nuclear engineering technology. Readies individuals to support engineers operating nuclear facilities and engaged in nuclear applications and safety procedures.

Nuclear medical technology. Features the employment of nuclides in evaluations and therapeutic applications, while monitoring for patient health and safety.

Nuclear physics. The scientific study of the properties and behavior of atomic nuclei.

Nuclear power technology. Readies individuals to support engineers in the running of nuclear reactors, and in nuclear materials processing and disposal.

Nurse anesthetist. Teaches registered nurses how to administer anesthetics and provide care for patients before, during, and after anesthesia.

Nurse midwifery. Readies registered nurses to independently deliver babies and treat mothers in the prenatal, delivery, and post-delivery periods.

Nursery operations. Studies the management of plant farms, nurseries, and facilities that develop domesticated plant products for propagation, harvesting, and transplantation.

Nursing (RN). Provides instruction in the knowledge, techniques, and procedures for promoting health and providing care for the sick and disabled, and preparation for licensure as a registered nurse.

Nursing administration. Prepares registered nurses to manage nursing personnel and services in hospitals and other health agencies.

Nursing assistant. Readies individuals, under the training and supervision of a registered nurse or licensed practical nurse, to provide nursing-related services to patients.

Nursing education. Prepares registered nurses to teach in academic and clinical settings, including staff development.

Nursing practice. A practice-focused program that prepares registered nurses for increasingly complex evidence-based nursing practice.

Nursing science. The study of clinical practices, research methodologies, and the administration of complex nursing services.

Nutrition sciences. Focuses on the utilization of food for human growth and metabolism in both normal and dysfunctional states.

Occupational/environmental health nursing. A program that prepares registered nurses to deliver nursing services to worker populations in clinical settings and at job sites.

Occupational health/industrial hygiene. Trains students to monitor and evaluate health and related safety standards in the workplace.

Occupational safety/health technology. Features the maintenance of job-related health and safety standards.

Occupational therapy. Prepares students to maximize patient independence and health through a mix of skills, motivation, environmental adaptations, and assistive technologies.

Occupational therapy assistant. Focuses on aiding occupational therapists by providing assistance during examinations and treatments and by keeping patient records.

Ocean engineering. Describes how to plan, design, and evaluate systems that monitor, control, and operate within coastal and ocean environments.

Oceanography. Features the chemical components, mechanisms, and movement of ocean waters and their interactions with terrestrial and atmospheric phenomena.

Office/clerical services. Prepares individuals, under the supervision of office managers, administrative assistants, and secretaries, to provide administrative support.

Office management. A program that prepares students to supervise and manage the operations and personnel of business offices and management-level divisions.

Office technology/data entry. Readies students to support businesses by using computer equipment for administrative purposes.

Oncology. Features the genetics, onset, and composition of cancer cells, as well as cancer behaviors and treatments.

Operations management. Readies students to direct the development, production, and manufacturing functions of an organization.

Operations research. Focuses on the development and application of simulation models to solve problems involving operational systems that are subject to human intervention.

Ophthalmic laboratory technology. Prepares individuals, under the supervision of an ophthalmologist or optometrist, to make corrective lenses and eyewear.

Ophthalmic technology. Prepares students to aid ophthalmologists and optometrists in examining and treating patients with vision disorders and eye diseases.

Opticianry/ophthalmic dispensing. Trains students to fit corrective eyewear, assist patients in selecting appropriate frames, and prepare work orders for ophthalmic technicians.

Optics. Covers light energy and its structure, properties, and behavior under different conditions.

Optometric assistant. Readies individuals to assist in providing patient care, administer examinations and treatments, and perform office functions.

Organic chemistry. Investigates the properties and behavior of hydrocarbon compounds and their derivatives.

Organizational behavior studies. Focuses on the scientific study of the behavior and motivations of individuals functioning in organized groups and its application to business and industrial settings.

Organizational communication. Includes instruction in group relations within organizations; decision-making and conflict management; symbolic messages; and human interaction with computer technology.

Organizational leadership. Focuses on leadership skills that can be applied to a business, government, non-profit, or educational enterprise.

Ornamental horticulture. Prepares students to breed, grow, and utilize ornamental plant varieties for commercial and aesthetic purposes.

Orthotics/prosthetics. Features the techniques used to design and fit orthoses and prostheses for patients with disabling conditions or limb deformity.

Outdoor education. Prepares students to work as an educator, instructor or facilitator for outdoor activities in parks, recreational facilities, camps and other outdoor settings.

Pacific area/rim studies. Describes the history, society, politics, culture, and economics of Australia, New Zealand, and the Pacific Islands.

Packaging science. Focuses on the development of packages and packaging materials, including production, design, distribution, recycling and reuse.

Painting. Readies individuals to impart ideas through the application of paints and chemical color substances to canvases.

Painting/wall covering. Prepares students to finish structural surfaces by applying protective or decorative coating materials, such as paint and wallpaper.

Paleontology. Features the reconstruction and analysis of ancient and extinct lifeforms, ecosystems, and geologic processes.

Palliative care nursing. Prepares registered nurses to provide therapies intended to comfort and support patients and their families living with life-threatening illness.

Paper science and engineering. Trains students to design, develop, and evaluate processes to manufacture pulp and paper products.

Paralegal studies. Prepares students to perform research, drafting, investigatory, record-keeping, and administrative functions under the supervision of an attorney or court.

Parasitology. Focuses on organisms that live on or within host organisms, and the role of parasites in causing injury, disease, and environmental damage.

Parks, recreation, and leisure studies. Investigates the practices involved in the provision of recreational facilities and services to the general public.

Parks/recreational/leisure facilities management. Prepares students to develop and manage park facilities and other recreational and leisure facilities.

Particle physics. Studies the basic elements of subatomic matter and energy, and the forces governing their fundamental processes.

Parts/warehousing operations. Prepares students to maintain inventory control, care for inventory, and make minor repairs to warehouse equipment.

Pastoral counseling. Prepares ordained clergy to provide nonclinical pastoral counseling.

Pathology assistant. Trains individuals to help pathologists by performing autopsies, obtaining and preparing surgical specimens, and writing autopsy reports.

Pathology, human/animal. The scientific study of tissue injury and disease, including death and disease infestation and transfer.

Peace and conflict studies. Emphasizes the origins, resolution, and prevention of international and inter-group conflicts.

Pediatric nursing. Prepares registered nurses to provide care for children from infancy through adolescence.

Percussion instruments. Trains students to master percussion instruments for a variety of musical settings.

Perfusion technology. Trains individuals to operate equipment that supports or replaces a patient's own respiratory or circulatory system.

Personal/culinary services. Focuses on professional services related to cosmetology, funeral services, and food service.

Personal/financial services marketing. Prepares students to perform marketing and operational tasks associated with the provision of personal and financial services.

Personality psychology. Focuses on characteristics that set the individual apart from other individuals and on how others respond to that individual.

Petroleum engineering. Readies students to develop systems for locating, extracting, processing, and refining crude oil and natural gas.

Petroleum technology. Readies individuals to implement the development and operation of oil and natural gas extraction and processing facilities.

Pharmaceutical marketing and management. Combines the study of basic and pharmaceutical sciences with marketing and management studies for careers in the pharmaceutical industry and related fields.

Pharmaceutical sciences. Focuses on the basic sciences that underlie drugs and drug therapy and prepares students for further study and/or careers in pharmaceuticals, biotechnology, and related fields.

Pharmacology. Emphasizes the interactions of drugs on organisms and their various uses.

Pharmacology/toxicology. The study of pharmacological and toxicological issues in biology and the biomedical sciences.

Pharmacy assistant. Prepares students, under the supervision of pharmacists, to prepare medications, provide medications to patients, and to manage pharmacy business and clinical operations.

Philosophy. Focuses on ideas and their structure, including arguments and investigations about abstract and real phenomena.

Philosophy and religious studies, general. Combines the study of philosophy and religious studies.

Phlebotomy technician. Trains students to draw blood samples from patients using a variety of intrusive procedures.

Photographic/film/video technology. Readies students to operate and maintain camera and lighting equipment; and produce finished still, video, and film products.

Photography. Describes the creation of images on photographic film, plates, and digital images.

Photojournalism. Describes the use of still and motion photography in journalism.

Physical/biological anthropology. Studies the adaptations, variability, and evolution of human beings and their living and fossil relatives.

Physical chemistry. Explores the behavior of chemical systems ranging from nuclear particles to macroscopic assemblies.

Physical education. Readies students to coach sports and/or teach physical education programs.

Physical fitness technician. Prepares students for instructional and administrative duties in health clubs, wellness centers, recreation facilities, hospitals, and fitness programs.

Physical sciences. The study of the topics, concepts, processes, and interrelationships of physical phenomena.

Physical therapy. Readies individuals to alleviate physical and functional impairments and limitations caused by injury or disease through the use of therapeutic interventions.

Physical therapy assistant. Trains individuals to support physical therapists to implement treatment plans, use equipment, and observe and record patient progress.

Physician assistant. Prepares students, under the supervision of a physician, to practice medicine.

Physics. The study of matter and energy, and the formulation and testing of the laws governing their behavior.

Physics teacher education. Focuses on the teaching of physics curricula.

Physiological psychology/psychobiology. Covers the biological bases of psychological functioning and their application to experimental and therapeutic research.

Physiology. The study of the functions, processes, and interactions of cells, tissues, and organs, such as respiration, circulation, digestion, sensory perception, and reproduction.

Pipefitting. Focuses on the design, installation, and testing of piping systems and automatic fire and exposure protections systems.

Planetary sciences. The scientific study of planets, small objects, and related gravitational systems.

Plant breeding. Applies genetics and genetic engineering to the improvement of agricultural plant health and populations and the development of new plant varieties.

Plant genetics. Highlights the relation of botanical research, comparative genetics, ecology, and evolutionary studies to the genetics of plants and fungi.

Plant molecular biology. Explores molecular structures, functions, and processes specific to plants and plant substances.

Plant pathology. Highlights plant diseases, plant health, and the development of disease control mechanisms.

Plant physiology. Investigates the internal workings and systems of plants, plant-environment interaction, and plant life cycles and processes.

Plant protection/pest management. Prepares students to control animal, insect and weed infestation of domesticated plant populations and crops; prevent/reduce economic loss; and control environmental pollution related to pest control measures.

Plant sciences. Highlights the breeding, cultivation, and production of plants and the processing and distribution of agricultural plant products.

Plasma/high-temperature physics. Highlights the properties and behavior of matter at high temperatures.

Plastics/polymer engineering technology. Includes instruction in the development and use of industrial plastics and polymers.

Platemaker/imager. Readies students to prepare film, digital data, and surfaces to reproduce printed or graphic images.

Playwriting/screenwriting. Describes the composition of written works for theater, film, and/or television.

Plumbing. Trains students to install and maintain piping fixtures and systems in home and business environments.

Polarity therapy. Includes instruction in energy-based anatomy and physiology; polarity processing, bodywork, and yoga; and energetic nutrition, evaluation, and assessment.

Police science. Prepares individuals to perform the duties of police and public security officers.

Polish. Highlights the Polish language and its use in literature.

Polish studies. Covers the history, society, politics, culture, and economics of Poland.

Political communications. Focuses on human and media communication in the political process and readies individuals to function as members of political and public affairs organizations, political campaign staffs, and related media entities.

Political economy. Highlights the interaction between politics and economics in the formation of public policy.

Political science. A general program that focuses on the study of political institutions and behavior.

Polymer chemistry. The study of synthesized macromolecules and their interactions with other substances.

Polymer/plastics engineering. Studies the design and development of synthesized macromolecular compounds and their application to specific engineering uses.

Polysomnography. Prepares students to assist a physician provide comprehensive evaluation and treatment of sleep disorders.

Population biology. Investigates the natural history, life cycle behavior, and ecosystem dynamics of single- and multi-species communities and the causes of diversity among such populations.

Portuguese. Focuses on the Portuguese language and related dialects.

Poultry science. Prepares students for the production and management of poultry animals and products.

Power/electrical transmission. Features the installation of indoor and outdoor residential, commercial, and industrial electrical systems and associated power transmission lines.

Pre-engineering. Prepares students for admission or transfer to a baccalaureate-level program in any of the fields of engineering.

Prechiropractic studies. Prepares undergraduates for admission to a doctoral-professional program in chiropractic medicine.

Precision production trades, general. A program that prepares individuals to apply technical knowledge in creating products using precision crafting and technical illustration.

Predental. Prepares undergraduates for admission to a doctoral-professional program in dentistry.

Prelaw. A four-year program, in virtually any major, that prepares individuals for admission to law school or a doctoral-professional (JD) law program.

Premedicine. Prepares undergraduates for admission to a doctoral-professional program in medicine, osteopathic medicine, or podiatric medicine.

Preministerial studies. Readies students to enter a seminary or other religious ordination program, or a related religious vocation.

Prenursing. Prepares students for admission to professional study in nursing.

Preoccupational therapy studies. Prepares undergraduates for admission to a doctoral-professional program in occupational therapy.

Preoperative/surgical nursing. Readies registered nurses to provide care to surgery patients and to provide tableside assistance to surgeons.

Preoptometry studies. Prepares undergraduates for admission to a doctoral-professional program in optometry.

Prepharmacy. Prepares undergraduates for admission to a doctoral-professional program in pharmacy.

Prephysical therapy studies. Prepares undergraduates for admission to a doctoral-professional program in physical therapy.

Preveterinary. Prepares undergraduates for admission to a doctoral-professional program in veterinary medicine.

Printing management. Analyzes the application of managerial skills to printing operations from design through finished product.

Printing press operator. The application of technical skills to set up, operate, and maintain printing presses.

Printmaking. Prepares individuals to render art concepts onto surfaces and transfer images, via ink or dyes, onto paper or fabric.

Project management. Readies students to manage projects in a wide range of fields and occupations.

Protective services operations. Instructs on providing physical/perimeter security protection in various environments and situations.

Psychiatric nursing. Describes the provision of nursing care to patients with mental, emotional, or behavioral disorders.

Psychoanalysis. Readies individuals to provide psychoanalytic counseling to individuals and groups.

Psychology. The study of individual and collective behavior, the bases of behavior, and the analysis and treatment of behavior problems and disorders.

Psychology teacher education. A program that prepares students to teach general psychology at the secondary school level.

Psychometrics/quantitative psychology. Explores psychological test construction and validation procedures; problems associated with behavior measurement; and quantitative methods used in research design.

Psychopharmacology. Describes the behavioral effects of drugs, nutrients, and chemicals in laboratory and clinical settings.

Public administration. Trains students to serve as managers in the executive arm of local, state, and federal government.

Public finance. Readies individuals to tend to the financial assets and budgets of public sector organizations.

Public health. Prepares individuals to plan, manage, and evaluate public health care services and to provide leadership in the field of public health.

Public health education. A program of study that promotes preventive health measures and the education of targeted populations on health issues.

Public health nursing. Prepares individuals, under the supervision of a public health agency, to provide nursing services for groups or communities.

Public policy analysis. The study of public policy issues and decision processes.

Public relations. Prepares students to manage the media image of an organization and communicate with clients and the general public.

Public relations/advertising/applied communication. A general program that prepares students to function in a wide range of public and private sector positions requiring the skills of persuasive communication.

Publishing. Describes the creation, publishing, and distribution of print and electronic books and other text products.

Purchasing/procurement/contracts. Readies individuals to manage the process of contracting goods and services for an organization.

Quality control technology. Highlights the maintenance of manufacturing and construction standards.

Rabbinical studies (M.H.L., Rav.). A program that prepares individuals for ordination as rabbis.

Radiation biology. Emphasizes the effects of radiation on organisms and biological systems.

Radiation protection/health physics technology. Prepares students to monitor and control radiation exposure and implement preventive measures in health care, work, and natural environments.

Radio and television. Studies the planning, production, and distribution of audio and video programs, and prepares students to function as staff, producers, directors, and managers of radio and television shows.

Radio/television broadcasting. Prepares students to apply technical knowledge to the production of radio and television programs.

Radiologic technology/medical imaging. Focuses on the provision of x-ray and other medical imaging services to patients and health care professionals.

Radiologist assistant. Trains students to assist physicians with patient assessment, patient management, selecting imaging procedures and initial observations of diagnostic images.

Railroad/railway transportation. Prepares students to operate railroads and other aspects of the railway industry, including railroad and rail yard service.

Range science. Studies rangelands, arid regions, and grasslands, and the principles of managing such resources for maximum benefit and environmental balance.

Reading teacher education. Describes how to diagnose reading difficulties and teach reading programs.

Real estate. Prepares individuals to develop, buy, sell, appraise, and manage real property.

Real estate development. Trains individuals to create and redevelop housing, offices, retail centers, and industrial sites.

Receptionist. Prepares students to perform frontline public relations duties for a business, organization, or answering service.

Recording arts. Prepares individuals to produce sound recordings as finished products or as components of other media productions.

Recreational therapy. Trains students to organize and direct recreational activities designed to promote health for patients who suffer from disabling conditions.

Regional studies. The study of the defined geographic subregions and subcultures within countries and societies.

Rehabilitation aide. Trains students perform routine functions in support of rehabilitation services under the supervision therapeutic professionals.

Rehabilitation engineering/assistive technology. Features the design and implementation of technological interventions and systems to promote patient rehabilitation and function.

Rehabilitation science. Examines human function, disability, and rehabilitation from the perspectives of the health sciences, social sciences, psychology, engineering, and related fields.

Reiki. Highlights the manipulation of the body's energy field to increase healing energy.

Religious education. Prepares individuals to provide religious educational services to members of faith communities.

Religious studies. Explores the nature of religious beliefs and specific religious and quasi-religious systems.

Renal/dialysis technology. Trains individuals to administer hemodialysis treatments to patients with renal failure.

Reproductive biology. The study of reproductive processes in animals and human beings.

Research and development management. Prepares students to manage projects, programs and organizations involving basic and applied research.

Research methodology. Focuses on the design of research studies, measurement of variables, data analysis, and formulation of models.

Resort management. Emphasizes the planning, management, and marketing of comprehensive vacation facilities, services, and products.

Respiratory therapy. Trains individuals to manage the ventilation of critically ill patients, provide respiratory care to patients with breathing disorders, and consult with other health care team members.

Respiratory therapy assistant. Highlights the administration of general respiratory care procedures under the supervision of respiratory therapists.

Restaurant/catering management. Readies individuals to plan, supervise, and manage food and beverage service operations, restaurant facilities, and catering services.

Restaurant/food services management. Trains students to manage restaurants, food services in hospitality establishments, chains and franchises, and restaurant suppliers.

Retail management. Describes how to manage the operations of a wide variety of retail businesses, including online businesses.

Retailing. Readies individuals to perform operations associated with retail sales in a variety of settings.

Rhetoric/composition. Studies grammar, morphology, syntax, and semantics, and the techniques used to express ideas in written forms.

Robotics technology. Prepares individuals to aid engineers and other professionals engaged in developing and using robots.

Romance languages. A general curriculum that focuses on the Romance languages of Western, Central, and Southern Europe.

Romanian. Highlights the Romanian language and related dialects.

Roofing. Readies individuals to prepare, install, and maintain exterior roofing materials and roofs.

Rural sociology. Focuses on the structure and function of rural societies.

Russian. The study of the languages, literatures, and cultures of Russian-speaking peoples.

Russian/Central and Eastern European/Eurasian studies. Highlights the history, society, politics, culture, and economics of Russia, Central Europe, Eastern Europe, and Eurasia.

Russian/Slavic studies. Focuses on the history, society, politics, culture, and economics of the Russian Federation.

Sacred music. Highlights the history, theory, composition, and performance of music for religious or sacred purposes.

Sales/distribution. Studies the process and techniques of direct wholesale and retail buying and selling operations and introduces individuals to related careers.

Sales/marketing education. Investigates the teaching of vocational sales, marketing, and distributive operations education programs.

Salon management. Trains individuals to manage beauty parlors, shops, and specialized salons.

Sanskrit/classical Indian languages. The study of Sanskrit and related ancient and classical Indo-Aryan languages.

Scandinavian languages. A program that characterizes one or more of the languages, literatures, and linguistics of the Scandinavian peoples.

Scandinavian studies. Studies the history, society, politics, culture, and economics of Denmark, Finland, Greenland, Iceland, Norway, and Sweden.

School librarian education. Prepares students to serve as librarians and media specialists in elementary and secondary schools.

School psychology. Prepares individuals to treat and diagnose student behavioral problems.

Science teacher education. Prepares students to teach general science subjects or a combination of biology and physical science.

Science technologies, general. Trains students to provide technical support for scientific research and development.

Science, technology, and society. Covers the relationship, ramifications, and ethical dimensions of science and technology to public policy.

Sculpture. Features the use of clay, plaster, wood, stone, and metal to create three-dimensional works of art.

Secondary education. Readies individuals to teach a comprehensive curriculum or specific subject matter to students at the secondary school level.

Secondary school administration. Prepares individuals to serve as principals and masters of junior high, secondary, or senior high schools.

Secondary special education. Describes the design and provision of educational services to secondary school children with special learning needs.

Security/loss prevention. Focuses on the performance of routine inspection, patrol, and crime prevention services for private clients.

Security services management. Readies individuals to plan, manage, and supervise services providing private security protection for people and property.

Security system installation/repair/inspection. Prepares individuals to install and repair household, business, and industrial security devices.

Selling/sales operations. Prepares individuals in the direct promotion of products and services to potential customers, and to function as sales representatives and managers.

Semiconductor manufacturing technology. Trains students to operate, monitor and maintain equipment for the fabrication of semiconductors or microchips.

Sheet metal technology. Focuses on the forming, shaping, bending, and folding of metal, including the creation of new products, using hand tools and machines.

Shoe/leather repair. Readies students to replace, mend, refinish, and dye leather goods and footwear.

Sign language interpretation. Prepares students to be simultaneous interpreters of American Sign Language and other sign language systems, both one-way and two-way.

Sign language linguistics. Explores American Sign Language and other visual signed languages as modes of communication within the Deaf community and in relation to spoken and written languages.

Slavic languages. A general program that focuses on one or more of the Slavic languages of Central and Eastern Europe.

Slavic studies. Analyzes the history, society, politics, culture, and economics of the Slavic peoples.

Slovak. The study of the Slovak language, dialects, and literature.

Small business administration/management. A program that prepares individuals to develop and manage independent small businesses.

Small engine mechanics. Readies students to service small internal-combustion engines used on portable power equipment.

Social/philosophical foundations of education. Studies education as a social and cultural institution, and the educational process as an object of humanistic inquiry.

Social psychology. Explores individual behavior in group contexts, group behavior, and associated phenomena.

Social science teacher education. Studies the teaching of specific social science subjects and programs.

Social sciences. The study of human social behavior and institutions using any of the methodologies common to the social sciences and/or history.

Social studies teacher education. Prepares students to teach general social studies programs.

Social work. Studies the provision of basic support services for vulnerable individuals and groups.

Sociology. The systematic study of human social institutions and social relationships.

Sociology and anthropology. Combines sociology and anthropology to study how society is organized and changes, the origins and development of social institutions, and race, class, gender and culture.

Software engineering. Prepares individuals to design, implement, validate, and maintain computer software systems using a variety of computer languages.

Soil chemistry/physics. The analysis of the nature, properties, conservation, and management of soils.

Soil science. The scientific classification of soils and soil properties, and the study of their relationship to agricultural crops.

Solar energy technology. Highlights the development of solar-powered energy systems.

Somatic bodywork. A course of study that encourages physical and emotional balance through the provision of skilled touch principles and techniques.

South Asian languages. Features one or more of the languages, literatures, and linguistics of the peoples speaking the languages of the Indian subcontinent.

South Asian studies. Analyzes the history, society, politics, culture, and economics of Afghanistan, India, the Maldives, Burma, Pakistan, and Sri Lanka.

Southeast Asian languages. Focuses on one or more of the modern or historical languages spoken or originating in mainland Southeast Asia and the Indonesian and Philippines Archipelagoes.

Southeast Asian studies. Covers the history, society, politics, culture, and economics of the peoples of Southeast Asia, defined as Brunei, Cambodia, Indonesia, Laos, Malaysia, The Philippines, Singapore, Thailand, and Viet Nam.

Spanish. Features the language, literature, and culture of Spanish-speaking peoples.

Spanish/Iberian studies. Analyzes the history, society, politics, culture, and economics of the peoples of the Iberian Peninsula.

Spanish teacher education. Readies individuals to teach the language, literature, and culture of Spanish-speaking peoples.

Special education. Describes the design and provision of educational services to children or adults with special learning needs.

Special education administration. Highlights the planning, supervision, and management of programs for exceptional students and their parents.

Special products marketing. Trains individuals to execute marketing and sales operations connected with the promotion of special products, including floristry, food, and home and office products.

Speech-language pathology assistant. Trains students to assist a licensed speech language pathologist with treatment of children and adults with communication disorders.

Speech pathology. Readies individuals to evaluate patients' speaking capabilities and develop rehabilitative solutions in consultation with related professionals.

Speech teacher education. Prepares students to teach speech and language arts at various educational levels.

Sports and fitness administration. Highlights the organization, administration, and management of athletic programs and teams, fitness/rehabilitation facilities, and sport recreation services.

Sports communications. The theoretical study of sport and communication combined with practical skills in sports reporting, broadcasting, and public relations.

Sports studies. Focuses on the psychological, sociological, and historical aspects of sport and physical activity.

Statistics. A study of the theory and proofs that form the basis of probability and inference, and of the methods of collecting, analyzing, and interpreting data.

Sterile processing technology. Trains students to clean, sterilize, and assemble surgical instruments, equipment, and supplies for use in medical and surgical facilities.

Stringed instruments. Trains students to master a stringed instrument, such as the violin, viola, or guitar.

Structural biology. The scientific study of molecular components and how they are organized into cells and tissues.

Structural engineering. Studies the design, analysis, and structural problems of load-bearing structures such as roads, bridges, and dams.

Substance abuse counseling. Focuses on intervention techniques and therapeutic services for persons suffering from addiction.

Surgical technology. Prepares students to maintain, monitor, and enforce the sterile field and aseptic technique by surgical personnel.

Surveying engineering. Readies individuals to determine the location, elevations, and alignment of natural and man-made topographic features.

Surveying technology. Trains students to determine, plan, and position land tracts and water boundaries, and to prepare related maps, charts, and reports.

Sustainability studies. A program that focuses on the concept of sustainability from an interdisciplinary perspective.

Swedish. Focuses on the Swedish language and related dialects.

Systems engineering. Trains individuals to design, develop, and evaluate total systems solutions to a wide variety of engineering problems.

Systems science/theory. Focuses on the solution of complex problems using data from the natural, social, technological, behavioral, and life sciences.

Talmudic studies. Prepares students for advanced Talmudic scholarship and entry to ordination programs and conventional graduate and professional schools.

Taxation. Prepares students to provide tax advice and management services to individuals and corporations.

Taxidermy. Trains individuals to reproduce life-like representations of living animals for permanent display and to manage taxidermy businesses.

Teacher assistance. Readies individuals to assist teachers in regular classroom settings or instruct and supervise special student populations.

Teacher education, multiple levels. Prepares individuals to teach students at more than one educational level.

Technical and business writing. The study of the methods and skills needed for professional, technical, business, and scientific writing.

Technical/scientific communication. Focuses on the communication of technical and scientific knowledge to a variety of audiences and through various media.

Technology/industrial arts education. Trains students to teach technology education/industrial arts programs at various levels.

Telecommunications engineering. Prepares students to design, develop, and maintain telecommunications technology, networks, and systems.

Telecommunications management. Prepares students to design, implement, and manage the voice, video, and data networking systems of organizations.

Telecommunications technology. Focuses on the design and implementation of telecommunications systems.

Terrorism/counterterrorism. The study of terrorism as a global and national threat and the methods for analyzing and countering it.

Textile science. Investigates the properties and processing of fibers, yarns, whole fabrics, dyes, and finishes.

Textile sciences/engineering. Focuses on systems that test and manufacture fiber products and the development of new and improved fibers, textiles, and their uses.

Theater arts management. Trains students to manage theaters and production companies.

Theater design and technology. Prepares students to communicate dramatic information, ideas, moods, and feelings through technical theater methods, including set design, lighting, sound, scene painting, costumes, and computer applications.

Theater history/criticism. Studies the literature, history, and analysis of theatrical productions and theater methods and organization.

Theological studies. The study of the beliefs and doctrines of a particular religious faith from the point of view of that faith.

Theoretical/mathematical physics. Prepares individuals to formulate and evaluate the physical laws governing matter-energy phenomena and to analyze experimental designs and results.

Tool and die technology. Prepares individuals to operate tools and make instruments used to form metal parts.

Tourism promotion. Trains students to perform marketing and sales operations connected with the promotion of tourism in a variety of settings.

Tourism/travel management. Readies individuals to manage travel-related enterprises and conventions and/or tour services.

Tourism/travel services. Features the provision of retail services to hotel and motel clients and customers in a variety of settings.

Toxicology. The study of toxic substances; their interaction with organisms; and their prevention, management, and counteraction.

Trade/industrial education. Prepares students to teach specific vocational trades and industries programs.

Traditional Chinese medicine/herbology. Highlights the use of natural products and prescribed medical formulae to treat health imbalances as defined in the Nei Ching Su Wen and other authorities.

Transportation. A program that prepares individuals to apply technical skills to perform services that facilitate the movement of people or materials.

Transportation/highway engineering. Focuses on the development of systems for the physical movement of people, materials, and information.

Transportation management. Readies students to coordinate physical transportation operations, networks, and systems.

Truck/bus/commercial vehicle operation. Trains individuals to drive or to train others to drive trucks and buses, delivery vehicles, for-hire and other commercial vehicles.

Turf management. Readies individuals to develop, plant, and manage grassed areas and produce and store turf used for transplantation.

Turkish. A program that focuses on the Turkish language in either or both of its premodern and modern variants.

Ukrainian. Focuses on the Ukrainian language and its applications in varied settings.

Underwater diving. Prepares students to function as professional deep-water or scuba divers, diving instructors, or support personnel.

Upholstery. Highlights the installation of springs, padding, covering, and finishing on furniture, seats, caskets, mattresses, and bedsprings.

Urban, community, and regional planning. The application of planning, analysis, and architecture to the development and improvement of urban areas.

Urban education. Describes issues specific to the educational needs of populations located in metropolitan areas and inner cities.

Urban forestry. Studies the development, care, and maintenance of trees and forested areas that are within or near areas of dense human habitation.

Urban ministry. Prepares the ordained clergy and other religious professionals to minister to individuals and groups in urban communities.

Urban studies. Emphasizes urban institutions and the forces influencing urban social and political life.

Vehicle emissions inspection/maintenance. Prepares individuals to test and service all vehicle emission systems in accordance with relevant laws and regulations.

Vehicle maintenance and repair technologies, general. Provides students technical knowledge and skills to adjust, maintain, and repair vehicles and mobile equipment.

Vehicle parts/accessories marketing. Prepares individuals to distribute and sell replacement parts and other supplies in the automotive, marine, and aviation industries.

Vendor/product certification. Prepares students to fulfill requirements set by vendors for professional qualification to install, customize, and maintain specific software products and/or processes.

Veterinary technology. Prepares students, under the supervision of veterinarians, to provide animal health care, clinical assistance, and owner communication.

Virology. Examines viruses that inhabit living cells in parasitical relationships and their role in causing disease.

Vision science. The study of vision, visual processes, clinical research, and forms of treatment.

Visual/performing arts. Highlights the visual and performing arts, and prepares individuals in any of the visual artistic media or performing disciplines.

Viticulture/enology. The study of the cultivation of grapes, the making of wine, and the wine business.

Vocational rehabilitation counseling. Prepares students to counsel and assist disabled individuals and recovering patients in order for them to have fulfilling and productive lives.

Vocational/technical education. Readies individuals to teach vocational technical education programs to students.

Voice/opera. Trains students to master the human voice and to perform in concerts, choirs, operas, or other forms of singing.

Warehousing/inventory management. Readies individuals to support warehouse operations, inventory control, parts identification, and counter services for customers.

Watch/jewelrymaking. Readies individuals to mend and maintain time-measuring devices and jewelry items.

Water quality/treatment/recycling technology. Prepares individuals to implement engineering designs for origination and use of water storage, waterpower, and wastewater treatment systems.

Water resource engineering. Describes systems for collecting, storing, moving, conserving, and controlling surface- and groundwater.

Water, wetlands, and marine management. Investigates the development, conservation, and management of freshwater and saltwater environments.

Web/multimedia management. Covers the development and maintenance of Web servers and Web pages at Web sites.

Web page/multimedia design. Readies students to produce and publish documents, images, graphics, sound, and multimedia projects on the World Wide Web.

Welding. Trains students to apply technical knowledge and skills to join or cut metal surfaces.

Welding engineering technology. Prepares students to design and implement welding and joining systems and processes.

Well drilling. Readies individuals to operate well-drilling equipment; locate, drill, and construct wells; and test and monitor wells.

Western European studies. Covers the history, society, politics, culture, and economics of historical Western Europe.

Wildland/forest firefighting. Applies fire science, firefighting and investigation techniques to the prevention, control and mitigation of wildland and forest fires.

Wildlife biology. A program that applies biological principles to the study of vertebrate wildlife and habitats in remote and urban areas.

Wildlife, fish and wilderness management. Describes the conservation and management of wildlife, fish and wilderness areas, and the management of wildlife reservations, aquarium and zoological facilities.

Wine steward/sommelier. Prepares students to manage the selection, storage, sales, and service of wine.

Women's health nurse/nursing. Prepares registered nurses to provide health care specific to women.

Women's studies. Focuses on the history, sociology, politics, culture, and economics of women and the development of modern feminism.

Wood science/pulp/paper technology. Describes the properties and behavior of wood and the development of processes for converting wood into paper and other products.

Woodwind instruments. Trains students to master a woodwind instrument.

Woodworking. Trains students to shape, mark, saw, carve, sand, and repair wooden products, and to use a variety of hand and power tools.

Word processing. Highlights typing, table construction, and document formatting on personal computers.

Work/family studies. Focuses on family and consumer science concepts and the various career paths open to interested students.

Writing, general. Focuses on writing skills and processes for applied and liberal arts purposes.

Yoga teacher/therapy. Trains students to provide spiritual and physical Yoga therapy in private, institutional, and clinical settings.

Youth ministry. Studies the provision of spiritual counseling and leadership services to children, adolescents, and young adults.

Youth services. Readies students to plan, manage, and implement social services for children, youth, and families.

Zoology. Emphasizes the anatomy, structure, and behavior of animals.

Part III: College Listings

About Part III

Once you have an idea of what you might want to study, you can use this Part to find colleges that offer the majors or academic programs you are interested in.

Colleges listed by major

All of the majors that are fully or briefly described in this book (over 1,200 in all) are presented here alphabetically, and under each is a state-by-state list of the colleges that teach it. After the college name you'll find letter symbols that designate the different degree levels at which the major is offered by that college:

C Certificate or diploma
A Associate degree
B Bachelor's degree
T Teacher certification
M Master's degree
D Doctorate
P Professional degree

Certificate or diploma. Certificates are awarded to students who complete nondegree programs, which usually take one year or less and are most frequently offered in technical and vocational fields of study.

Associate degree. Usually two years in length, associate degree programs are most often found at community colleges and technical schools, but they are also offered at many four-year colleges.

Bachelor's degree. Programs in which you earn a bachelor's degree usually take four years, but some programs can be completed in three years and some take five.

Teacher certification. Each state sets its own certification standards, and all colleges that prepare teachers are accredited by the state in which they are located. Students must meet both bachelor's degree requirements and state certification requirements. Most states require candidates to pass an examination in the field they plan to teach.

Master's degree. Master of arts (M.A.) and master of science (M.S.) programs are graduate degrees in the liberal arts and sciences, intended for students with B.A. or B.S. degrees, and usually take one or two years to complete. Among other master's degree programs are the master of business administration (MBA), the master of library science (M.L.S.), and the master of social work (M.S.W.) In some fields, such as law and medicine, the master's degree follows the first-professional degree (J.D., M.D.).

Doctorate. Doctoral programs usually consist of course work and independent research culminating in a dissertation or other formal presentation of the results of independent study. Length of study varies widely, and is usually self-determined.

Professional degree. These programs provide the academic prerequisites to become licensed in a recognized profession, such as medicine, law, or veterinary medicine. At least two years of prior college-level study are required for entrance into the program, and the total registered time of study must equal six academic years.

Special academic programs

In addition to majors, minors, and concentrations, many colleges offer other ways to enhance, focus, or further shape your undergraduate education. For each of the more common and popular programs, there is a state-by-state listing of colleges that offer it.

Colleges listed by major

Accounting

Alabama

Alabama Agricultural and Mechanical
   University *B*
Alabama State University *B, M*
Athens State University *B*
Auburn University *B, M*
Auburn University at Montgomery *B*
Birmingham-Southern College *B*
Bishop State Community College *A*
Calhoun Community College *A*
Chattahoochee Valley Community
   College *A*
Huntingdon College *B*
Jacksonville State University *B*
Lawson State Community College *A*
Miles College *B*
Oakwood University *B*
Samford University *B, M*
Troy University *B, M*
Tuskegee University *B*
University of Alabama *B, M, D*
University of Alabama
   Birmingham *B, M*
   Huntsville *B, M*
University of Mobile *B*
University of Montevallo *B*
University of North Alabama *B*
University of Phoenix
   Birmingham *B, M*
University of South Alabama *B, M*
University of West Alabama *B*
Virginia College
   Birmingham *A, B*
Wallace State Community College at
   Hanceville *A*

Alaska

Charter College *C, A*
Ilisagvik College *C, A*
University of Alaska
   Anchorage *A, B*
   Fairbanks *B*
   Southeast *C, B*

Arizona

Arizona State University *B, M*
Arizona Western College *C, A*
Brookline College
   Phoenix *C, A*
Brown Mackie College
   Tucson *A, B*
Central Arizona College *C, A*
Chandler-Gilbert Community
   College *A*
Coconino County Community
   College *C, A*
Everest College
   Phoenix *A*
GateWay Community College *C, A*
Glendale Community College *C*
Grand Canyon University *B, M*
Mohave Community College *C, A*
Northcentral University *B*
Northern Arizona University *B*
Northland Pioneer College *C, A*
Paradise Valley Community
   College *C, A*
Penn Foster College *A*
Phoenix College *C, A*
Pima Community College *C, A*
Rio Salado College *C, A*

Scottsdale Community College *C, A*
University of Arizona *B, M*
University of Phoenix
   Phoenix-Hohokam *B, M*
   Southern Arizona *B, M*
Western International
   University *C, B, M*
Yavapai College *C, A*

Arkansas

Arkansas Baptist College *B*
Arkansas Northeastern College *C*
Arkansas State University *B, M*
Arkansas Tech University *B*
Black River Technical College *A*
Central Baptist College *B*
College of the Ouachitas *C*
Harding University *B*
Henderson State University *B*
Hendrix College *B, M*
John Brown University *B*
Lyon College *B*
North Arkansas College *C*
Northwest Arkansas Community
   College *C, A*
Ouachita Baptist University *B*
South Arkansas Community
   College *C*
Southern Arkansas University *B*
University of Arkansas *B, M*
University of Arkansas
   Community College at Batesville *A*
   Little Rock *B, M*
   Monticello *B*
   Pine Bluff *B*
University of Central Arkansas *B, M*
University of the Ozarks *B*

California

Allan Hancock College *C, A*
American River College *C, A*
Azusa Pacific University *B*
Barstow Community College *C, A*
Biola University *B*
Butte College *C, A*
Cabrillo College *C, A*
California Baptist University *B*
California College San Diego *B*
California Lutheran University *B*
California Polytechnic State
   University: San Luis Obispo *M*
California State Polytechnic
   University: Pomona *M*
California State University
   Dominguez Hills *B*
   East Bay *B, M*
   Fresno *B*
   Fullerton *B, M*
   Long Beach *B*
   Los Angeles *M*
   Northridge *M*
   Sacramento *B, M*
   San Bernardino *B, M*
Canada College *C, A*
Carrington College California
   Citrus Heights *A*
   Pleasant Hill *A*
   San Jose *A*
   San Leandro *A*
Cerritos College *A*
Chabot College *A*
Chaffey College *C, A*
Chapman University *B*
Citrus College *C*

City College of San Francisco *C, A*
Claremont McKenna College *B*
Coastline Community College *C, A*
College of Alameda *A*
College of Marin *C, A*
College of San Mateo *C, A*
College of the Desert *C*
College of the Sequoias *C, A*
College of the Siskiyous *C, A*
Columbia College *C*
Copper Mountain College *C*
Cosumnes River College *C, A*
Crafton Hills College *C*
Cuyamaca College *C, A*
Cypress College *C, A*
De Anza College *C, A*
DeVry University
   Pomona *B, M*
Diablo Valley College *C, A*
Empire College *C, A*
Everest College
   Ontario Metro *A*
Evergreen Valley College *C*
Folsom Lake College *C, A*
Foothill College *C, A*
Fresno City College *C, A*
Fresno Pacific University *B*
Fullerton College *A*
Gavilan College *C*
Glendale Community College *C, A*
Golden Gate University *C, B, M*
Golden West College *C, A*
Hartnell College *C*
Heald College
   Concord *C, A*
   Roseville *C, A*
Holy Names University *B*
Humphreys College *A, B*
Institute of Technology: Clovis *A*
Irvine Valley College *C, A*
Kaplan College
   Riverside *A*
La Sierra University *B, M*
Lake Tahoe Community College *C, A*
Laney College *C, A*
Lassen Community College *A*
Long Beach City College *C, A*
Los Angeles City College *A*
Los Angeles Harbor College *A*
Los Angeles Mission College *A*
Los Angeles Pierce College *C, A*
Los Angeles Southwest College *A*
Los Angeles Trade and Technical
   College *C, A*
Los Angeles Valley College *C*
Los Medanos College *C, A*
Loyola Marymount University *B, M*
Master's College *B*
Mendocino College *C, A*
Menlo College *B*
Merced College *C, A*
MiraCosta College *C, A*
Mission College *A*
Modesto Junior College *C, A*
Monterey Peninsula College *C, A*
Moreno Valley College *C, A*
Mount St. Mary's College *A, B*
Mount San Antonio College *C, A*
Napa Valley College *A*
National University *C, B, M*
Norco College *C, A*
Ohlone College *C, A*
Orange Coast College *C, A*
Pacific States University *C, B, M*

Palo Verde College *C, A*
Pasadena City College *C, A*
Pepperdine University *B*
Point Loma Nazarene University *B*
Reedley College *C, A*
Rio Hondo College *A*
Riverside City College *C, A*
Sacramento City College *C, A*
Saddleback College *C, A*
St. Mary's College of California *B*
San Bernardino Valley College *C, A*
San Diego Miramar College
   San Diego Miramar College *C, A*
San Diego City College *C, A*
San Diego Mesa College *C, A*
San Diego State University *B, M*
San Jose City College *C, A*
San Jose State University *B, M*
Santa Ana College *C, A*
Santa Barbara City College *C, A*
Santa Clara University *B*
Santa Monica College *C, A*
Santa Rosa Junior College *C*
Santiago Canyon College *A*
Scripps College *B*
Shasta College *A*
Sierra College *C, A*
Simpson University *B*
Skyline College *C, A*
Solano Community College *C, A*
Southern California Institute of
   Technology *C*
Southwestern College *C, A*
Taft College *C, A*
University of California
   Irvine *M*
University of La Verne *B*
University of Phoenix
   Bay Area *B, M*
   Central Valley *B, M*
   Sacramento Valley *B, M*
   San Diego *B, M*
   Southern California *B, M*
University of Redlands *C, B*
University of San Diego *B, M*
University of San Francisco *B*
University of Southern
   California *B, M*
University of the West *B*
Vanguard University of Southern
   California *B*
Ventura College *C, A*
West Hills College: Coalinga *C, A*
West Los Angeles College *C, A*
West Valley College *A*
Woodbury University *B*
Woodland Community College *A*
Yuba College *C, A*

Colorado

Adams State University *B*
Aims Community College *C, A*
CollegeAmerica
   Colorado Springs *B*
   Fort Collins *B*
Colorado Christian University *B*
Colorado Mesa University *B*
Colorado Mountain College *C, A*
Colorado State University *B, M*
Colorado State University
   Pueblo *B*

Everest College
Aurora *A*
Colorado Springs *A*
Denver *C, A*
Fort Lewis College *B*
Lamar Community College *C*
Metropolitan State University of
Denver *B, M*
Morgan Community College *A*
National American University
Denver *A, B*
Regis University *B, M*
Trinidad State Junior College *A*
University of Colorado
Boulder *B, M*
Denver *M*
University of Denver *B, M*
University of Northern Colorado *M*
University of Phoenix
Denver *B, M*
Southern Colorado *B, M*
Western State Colorado University *B*
Westwood College
Denver North *B*

Connecticut

Albertus Magnus College *B*
Asnuntuck Community College *A*
Capital Community College *C, A*
Central Connecticut State
University *B*
Eastern Connecticut State
University *B, M*
Fairfield University *B, M*
Gateway Community College *A*
Housatonic Community College *A*
Manchester Community College *C, A*
Middlesex Community College *A*
Northwestern Connecticut
Community College *A*
Norwalk Community College *C, A*
Post University *C, A, B*
Quinebaug Valley Community
College *C, A*
Quinnipiac University *B, M*
Sacred Heart University *B*
Three Rivers Community
College *C, A*
Tunxis Community College *C, A*
University of Bridgeport *B, M*
University of Connecticut *B, M*
University of Hartford *B, M*
University of New Haven *B, M*
University of Saint Joseph *B*
Western Connecticut State
University *B*

Delaware

Delaware State University *B*
Delaware Technical Community
College
Jack F. Owens Campus *A*
Stanton/Wilmington Campus *A*
Terry Campus *A*
Goldey-Beacom College *A, B*
University of Delaware *B, M*
Wesley College *B*
Wilmington University *B*

District of Columbia

American University *B, M*
Catholic University of America *B, M*
Gallaudet University *B*
George Washington
University *B, M, D*
Georgetown University *B*
Howard University *B*
Strayer University *C, A, B, M*
University of Phoenix
Washington DC *M*
University of the District of
Columbia *B*
University of the Potomac *B*

Florida

Barry University *B, M*
Bethune-Cookman University *B*
Broward College *C, A*
Brown Mackie College
Miami *A*
Clearwater Christian College *B*
College of Business and Technology
Kendall *A*
College of Central Florida *C, A*
Daytona State College *C, A*
DeVry University
Miramar *B*
Eastern Florida State College *C*
Edison State College *C, A*
Everest University
Brandon *A, B*
Jacksonville *C, A, B*
Lakeland *B*
Largo *A, B*
Melbourne *A, B*
North Orlando *A, B*
Pompano Beach *A, B*
Tampa *A, B*
Flagler College *B*
Florida Agricultural and Mechanical
University *B*
Florida Atlantic University *B, M*
Florida Gulf Coast University *B, M*
Florida Institute of Technology *B*
Florida International University *B, M*
Florida Memorial University *B*
Florida National University *A, B*
Florida Southern College *B*
Florida State College at
Jacksonville *A*
Florida State University *B, M*
Fortis College
Winter Park *A*
Herzing University
Winter Park *C, A, B*
Hodges University *A, B*
Indian River State College *C, A*
Jacksonville University *B*
Jose Maria Vargas University *A*
Keiser University *A, B*
Miami Dade College *C, A*
Northwood University
Florida *B*
Nova Southeastern University *B, M*
Palm Beach Atlantic University *B*
Palm Beach State College *A*
Pensacola State College *C, A*
Rasmussen College
Fort Myers *A, B*
New Port Richey *A, B*
Ocala *A, B*
Pasco/Land O'Lakes *A, B*
Tampa/Brandon *A, B*
Saint Leo University *B*
Saint Thomas University *B, M*
Southeastern University *B*
Southwest Florida College *A, B*
State College of Florida, Manatee-
Sarasota *C, A*
Stetson University *B, M*
Tallahassee Community College *A*
University of Central Florida *B, M*
University of Florida *B, M*
University of Miami *B, M*
University of North Florida *B, M*
University of Phoenix
Central Florida *B, M*
North Florida *B, M*
South Florida *B, M*
West Florida *B, M*
University of South Florida *B, M*
University of South Florida
Saint Petersburg *B*
Sarasota-Manatee *B*
University of Tampa *B, M*
University of West Florida *B, M*
Webber International
University *A, B, M*

Georgia

Abraham Baldwin Agricultural
College *A*
Albany State University *B*
Altamaha Technical College *C, A*
Augusta Technical College *C, A*
Bainbridge College *C, A*
Berry College *B*
Brenau University *B, M*
Chattahoochee Technical
College *C, A*
Clark Atlanta University *B, M*
Clayton State University *B*
Columbus State University *B*
Columbus Technical College *C, A*
Dalton State College *B*
Emory University *B, D*
Fort Valley State University *B*
Georgia College and State
University *B, M*
Georgia Regents University *B*
Georgia Southern University *B, M*
Georgia Southwestern State
University *B*
Georgia State University *B, M, D*
Gwinnett College *C*
Kennesaw State University *B, M*
LaGrange College *B*
Mercer University *B, M*
Middle Georgia State College *A, B*
North Georgia Technical
College *C, A*
Oglethorpe University *B*
Point University *B*
Reinhardt University *B*
Savannah State University *B*
Shorter University *B*
South Georgia State College *A*
Southeastern Technical College *A*
Southern Crescent Technical
College *A*
Southern Polytechnic State
University *B, M*
Thomas University *B*
University of Georgia *B, M*
University of North Georgia *A, B*
University of Phoenix
Atlanta *B, M*
Augusta *B, M*
Columbus *B, M*
Savannah *B, M*
University of West Georgia *B, M*
Valdosta State University *B, M*
West Georgia Technical College *A*

Hawaii

Brigham Young University-Hawaii *B*
Chaminade University of
Honolulu *B, M*
Hawaii Pacific University *A, B*
Heald College
Honolulu *A*
University of Hawaii
Hawaii Community College *A*
Hilo *B*
Kapiolani Community College *C, A*
Kauai Community College *C, A*
Leeward Community College *C, A*
Manoa *B, M*
Maui College *A*
West Oahu *B*
University of Phoenix
Hawaii *M*

Idaho

Boise State University *B, M*
Brigham Young University-Idaho *B*
Broadview University
Boise *A, B*
College of Idaho *B*
College of Southern Idaho *A*
College of Western Idaho *A*
Eastern Idaho Technical College *C, A*
Idaho State University *B, M*

Northwest Nazarene University *B*
Stevens-Henager College
Boise *A, B*
University of Idaho *B, M*
University of Phoenix
Idaho *B, M*

Illinois

Augustana College *B*
Aurora University *B, M*
Benedictine University *B, M*
Black Hawk College *A*
Blackburn College *B*
Bradley University *B, M*
Carl Sandburg College *C, A*
Chicago State University *B*
City Colleges of Chicago
Harold Washington College *C, A*
Harry S. Truman College *C, A*
Kennedy-King College *C, A*
Olive-Harvey College *C, A*
Richard J. Daley College *C, A*
Wilbur Wright College *C, A*
College of DuPage *C, A*
College of Lake County *C*
Concordia University Chicago *B*
DePaul University *B, M*
DeVry University
Online *A*
Dominican University *B, M*
Eastern Illinois University *B, M*
Elgin Community College *A*
Elmhurst College *B, M*
Eureka College *B*
Governors State University *B, M*
Greenville College *B*
Harper College *C, A*
Heartland Community College *C*
Hebrew Theological College *B*
Highland Community College *C, A*
Illinois Central College *C, A*
Illinois College *B*
Illinois Eastern Community Colleges
Olney Central College *A*
Illinois State University *B, M*
Illinois Valley Community College *A*
Illinois Wesleyan University *B*
John Wood Community College *A*
Joliet Junior College *C, A*
Judson University *B*
Kaskaskia College *C, A*
Kishwaukee College *C, A*
Lewis University *B*
Lewis and Clark Community
College *A*
Lincoln College *A*
Lincoln Land Community College *A*
Loyola University Chicago *B, M*
MacMurray College *B*
McKendree University *B*
Midstate College *A, B*
Millikin University *B*
Monmouth College *B*
Morton College *A*
National-Louis University *C, B*
North Central College *B*
Northeastern Illinois University *B, M*
Northern Illinois University *B, M*
Northwestern College *A*
Northwestern University *M, D*
Oakton Community College *C, A*
Olivet Nazarene University *B*
Quincy University *B*
Rasmussen College
Aurora *A, B*
Mokena/Tinley Park *A, B*
Rockford *A, B*
Romeoville/Joliet *A, B*
Richland Community College *A*
Rock Valley College *A*
Rockford University *B*
Roosevelt University *B, M*
St. Augustine College *C, A*
Saint Xavier University *B*
Sauk Valley Community College *C, A*

Shawnee Community College *A*
South Suburban College of Cook
County *C, A*
Southern Illinois University
Carbondale *B, M*
Southern Illinois University
Edwardsville *B, M*
Southwestern Illinois College *A*
Spoon River College *C*
Trinity Christian College *B*
Trinity International University *B*
Triton College *A*
University of Illinois
Chicago *B, M*
Springfield *B, M*
Urbana-Champaign *B, M, D*
University of St. Francis *B*
Waubonsee Community College *C, A*
Western Illinois University *B, M*

Indiana

Anderson University *B, D*
Ball State University *B, M*
Bethel College *B*
Brown Mackie College
Fort Wayne *C*
Michigan City *C*
Butler University *B, M*
Calumet College of St. Joseph *C, A, B*
Franklin College *B*
Goshen College *B*
Grace College *B*
Harrison College
Indianapolis *C, A, B*
Huntington University *B*
Indiana Institute of Technology *A, B*
Indiana State University *B*
Indiana University
Bloomington *M*
Kokomo *C*
Purdue University Fort Wayne *B*
Purdue University Indianapolis *M*
South Bend *M*
Southeast *C*
Indiana Wesleyan University *A, B, M*
Manchester University *B*
Marian University *B*
Martin University *B*
National College
South Bend *A*
National College: Fort Wayne *A*
Oakland City University *A, B*
Purdue University *B*
Purdue University
Calumet *B, M*
Saint Joseph's College *B*
Saint Mary's College *B*
St. Mary-of-the-Woods College *A, B*
Taylor University *B*
Trine University *A, B*
University of Evansville *B*
University of Indianapolis *B, M*
University of Notre Dame *B, M*
University of Phoenix
Indianapolis *M*
University of St. Francis *B*
University of Southern Indiana *B, M*
Valparaiso University *B, M*

Iowa

AIB College of Business *A, B*
Ashford University *B*
Briar Cliff University *B*
Buena Vista University *B*
Central College *B*
Clarke University *B*
Clinton Community College *C*
Coe College *B*
Des Moines Area Community
College *A*
Dordt College *B*
Drake University *B, M*
Ellsworth Community College *A*
Graceland University *B*

Grand View University *C, B*
Hawkeye Community College *C, A*
Iowa Central Community
College *C, A*
Iowa Lakes Community College *A*
Iowa State University *B, M*
Iowa Wesleyan College *B*
Kirkwood Community College *C, A*
Loras College *B*
Luther College *B*
Marshalltown Community
College *C, A*
Mount Mercy University *B*
North Iowa Area Community
College *C, A*
Northeast Iowa Community
College *A*
Northwest Iowa Community
College *A*
Northwestern College *B*
St. Ambrose University *B, M*
Simpson College *B*
Southeastern Community
College *C, A*
Southwestern Community College *A*
University of Dubuque *B*
University of Iowa *B, M, D*
University of Northern Iowa *B, M*
University of Phoenix
Des Moines *M*
Upper Iowa University *B, M*
Wartburg College *B*
Western Iowa Tech Community
College *A*
William Penn University *B*

Kansas

Allen County Community College *A*
Baker University *B*
Barton County Community College *A*
Benedictine College *B*
Bethany College *B*
Brown Mackie College
Salina *A*
Butler Community College *A*
Central Christian College of
Kansas *A, B*
Coffeyville Community College *A*
Cowley County Community
College *A*
Dodge City Community College *A*
Donnelly College *A*
Emporia State University *B*
Fort Hays State University *B*
Friends University *B, M*
Haskell Indian Nations University *A*
Independence Community College *A*
Johnson County Community
College *A*
Kansas State University *B, M*
Kansas Wesleyan University *A, B*
Labette Community College *A*
McPherson College *B*
MidAmerica Nazarene University *B*
Neosho County Community
College *C, A*
Newman University *B*
Pittsburg State University *B*
Pratt Community College *C, A*
Seward County Community
College *C, A*
Southwestern College *B*
Tabor College *M*
University of Kansas *B, M*
University of St. Mary *B*
Washburn University *B, M*
Wichita State University *B, M*
Wright Career College
Overland Park *B*
Wichita *A*

Kentucky

Asbury University *B*
Ashland Community and Technical
College *A*

Bellarmine University *C, B*
Berea College *B*
Big Sandy Community and Technical
College *A*
Brescia University *B*
Brown Mackie College
Hopkinsville *C, A*
Campbellsville University *A, B*
Daymar College
Paducah *C*
Eastern Kentucky University *B*
Georgetown College *B*
Hopkinsville Community College *A*
Kentucky Wesleyan College *B*
Madisonville Community College *A*
Maysville Community and Technical
College *C, A*
Morehead State University *B*
Murray State University *B*
National College
Danville *C, A*
Florence *C, A*
Lexington *C, A*
Louisville *C, A*
Pikeville *C, A*
Richmond *C, A*
Northern Kentucky
University *C, B, M*
Spalding University *C, B*
Sullivan University *C, A, B*
Thomas More College *A, B*
Transylvania University *B*
Union College *B*
University of Kentucky *B, M*
University of Louisville *B, M*
University of the Cumberlands *B*
West Kentucky Community and
Technical College *A*
Western Kentucky University *B, M*

Louisiana

Centenary College of Louisiana *B*
Delta School of Business &
Technology *C, A*
Dillard University *B*
Grambling State University *B*
Herzing University
Kenner *A, B*
Louisiana College *B*
Louisiana State University
Shreveport *B*
Louisiana State University and
Agricultural and Mechanical
College *B, M, D*
Louisiana Tech University *B, M*
Loyola University New Orleans *B*
McNeese State University *B*
Nicholls State University *B*
Northwestern State University *B*
Our Lady of Holy Cross College *B*
Southeastern Louisiana University *B*
Southern University
Shreveport *A*
Southern University and Agricultural
and Mechanical College *B*
Tulane University *A, B, M*
University of Louisiana at Lafayette *B*
University of Louisiana at Monroe *B*
University of New Orleans *B, M*
University of Phoenix
Baton Rouge *B, M*
Lafayette *B, M*
Louisiana *B, M*
Shreveport *B, M*
Xavier University of Louisiana *B*

Maine

Beal College *A*
Central Maine Community College *A*
Husson University *A, B*
Kaplan University
South Portland *A, M*
Northern Maine Community
College *A*

Saint Joseph's College of Maine *B*
Thomas College *A, B*
University of Maine *B, M*
University of Maine
Augusta *B*
Machias *A, B*
University of Southern Maine *C, B, M*
York County Community College *A*

Maryland

Allegany College of Maryland *A*
Baltimore City Community College *A*
Frederick Community College *A*
Frostburg State University *B*
Harford Community College *C*
Kaplan University
Hagerstown *C, A, B, M*
Loyola University Maryland *B*
Morgan State University *B*
Mount St. Mary's University *B*
Prince George's Community
College *C, A*
Salisbury University *B*
Stevenson University *B*
Towson University *B, M*
University of Baltimore *B, M*
University of Maryland
College Park *B*
Eastern Shore *B*
University College *B*
Washington Adventist University *A, B*

Massachusetts

American International College *B, M*
Assumption College *B*
Babson College *B*
Bay Path College *B*
Bentley University *B, M, D*
Boston College *B, M*
Boston University *B*
Bridgewater State University *B, M, T*
Bristol Community College *A*
Bunker Hill Community College *C, A*
Cape Cod Community College *A*
Clark University *M*
College of the Holy Cross *B*
Dean College *C*
Eastern Nazarene College *B*
Elms College *B, M*
Endicott College *B*
Fisher College *A, B*
Fitchburg State University *B, M*
Gordon College *B*
Greenfield Community College *C, A*
Lasell College *B*
Marian Court College *A*
Massachusetts Bay Community
College *C, A*
Massachusetts College of Liberal
Arts *B*
Massasoit Community College *A*
Merrimack College *B*
Middlesex Community College *C, A*
New England College of Business and
Finance *C*
Newbury College *B*
Nichols College *B*
Northeastern University *B, M*
Northern Essex Community
College *C, A*
Quincy College *C, A*
Roxbury Community College *C, A*
Salem State University *B*
Simmons College *B*
Springfield Technical Community
College *A*
Stonehill College *B*
Suffolk University *B, M*
University of Massachusetts
Amherst *B, M*
Boston *M*
Dartmouth *B*
Lowell *M*

University of Phoenix
Boston *M*
Western New England
University *B, M*
Westfield State University *M*

Michigan

Adrian College *B*
Albion College *B*
Alma College *B*
Alpena Community College *A*
Andrews University *B*
Aquinas College *B*
Baker College
Allen Park *A*
Auburn Hills *A, B*
Cadillac *C, A, B*
Clinton Township *C, A, B*
Flint *C, A, B*
Jackson *C, A, B*
Muskegon *C, A, B*
Owosso *A, B*
Port Huron *C, A, B*
Bay de Noc Community College *C, A*
Calvin College *B*
Central Michigan University *B*
Cleary University *A, B, M*
Cornerstone University *B*
Davenport University *A, B, M*
Delta College *C, A*
Eastern Michigan University *B, M*
Ferris State University *B*
Finlandia University *B*
Glen Oaks Community College *C*
Gogebic Community College *A*
Grace Bible College *B*
Grand Valley State University *B, M*
Henry Ford Community College *A*
Hillsdale College *B*
Hope College *B*
Jackson College *C, A*
Kalamazoo Valley Community
College *C, A*
Kellogg Community College *C, A*
Kuyper College *B*
Lake Superior State University *B*
Macomb Community College *C, A*
Madonna University *C, B*
Marygrove College *C, A, B*
Michigan State University *B, M, D*
Michigan Technological University *B*
Monroe County Community
College *C, A*
Montcalm Community College *A*
Muskegon Community College *A*
North Central Michigan College *C, A*
Northern Michigan University *B*
Northwestern Michigan College *A*
Northwood University
Michigan *A, B*
Oakland University *B, M*
Rochester College *B*
Saginaw Valley State University *B*
Siena Heights University *A, B*
Spring Arbor University *B*
University of Detroit Mercy *B*
University of Michigan *M*
University of Michigan
Flint *B, M*
University of Phoenix
Metro Detroit *B, M*
West Michigan *B, M*
Walsh College of Accountancy and
Business Administration *B, M*
Washtenaw Community College *C, A*
Wayne State University *B, M*
West Shore Community College *A*
Western Michigan University *B, M*

Minnesota

Academy College *C, A, B*
Alexandria Technical and Community
College *A*
Anoka Technical College *A*

Anoka-Ramsey Community College *A*
Augsburg College *B*
Bemidji State University *B*
Capella University *B, M*
Central Lakes College *A*
Century College *C, A*
College of St. Benedict *B*
College of St. Scholastica *B*
Concordia College: Moorhead *B*
Concordia University St. Paul *B*
Dakota County Technical
College *C, A*
Globe University
Minneapolis *A, B*
Moorhead *A, B*
Woodbury *C, A, B*
Gustavus Adolphus College *B*
Hamline University *B*
Hennepin Technical College *C, A*
Herzing University
Minneapolis *B*
Inver Hills Community College *A*
Itasca Community College *A*
Lake Superior College *A*
Metropolitan State University *B*
Minneapolis Business College *A*
Minnesota School of Business
Blaine *C, A, B*
Brooklyn Center *A, B*
Elk River *A, B*
Lakeville *A, B*
Plymouth *C, A, B*
Richfield *C, A, B*
Rochester *A, B*
St. Cloud *A, B*
Shakopee *A, B*
Minnesota State College - Southeast
Technical *C, A*
Minnesota State Community and
Technical College *C, A*
Minnesota State University
Mankato *B*
Moorhead *B*
Minnesota West Community and
Technical College *A*
National American University
Bloomington *B*
Roseville *B*
Normandale Community College *A*
North Hennepin Community
College *C, A*
Pine Technical College *C, A*
Rasmussen College
Blaine *A, B*
Bloomington *A, B*
Brooklyn Park *A, B*
Eagan *A, B*
Lake Elmo/Woodbury *A, B*
Mankato *A, B*
Moorhead *A, B*
St. Cloud *A, B*
Ridgewater College *C, A*
Riverland Community College *C, A*
Rochester Community and Technical
College *A*
St. Catherine University *B*
Saint Cloud State University *B*
St. Cloud Technical and Community
College *C, A*
St. John's University *B*
St. Mary's University of
Minnesota *C, B, M*
St. Paul College *A*
South Central College *C, A*
Southwest Minnesota State
University *A, B*
University of Minnesota
Crookston *B*
Duluth *B*
Twin Cities *C, B*
University of Northwestern - St.
Paul *B*
University of Phoenix
Minneapolis-St. Paul *B, M*
University of St. Thomas *B, M*

Walden University *B, M*
Winona State University *B*

Mississippi

Alcorn State University *B*
Belhaven University *C, B*
Coahoma Community College *A*
Delta State University *B, M*
East Mississippi Community
College *A*
Hinds Community College *A*
Itawamba Community College *A*
Jackson State University *B, M*
Millsaps College *B, M*
Mississippi College *B*
Mississippi Delta Community
College *A*
Mississippi Gulf Coast Community
College *A*
Mississippi State University *B, M*
Mississippi University for Women *B*
Mississippi Valley State University *B*
Northeast Mississippi Community
College *A*
Northwest Mississippi Community
College *A*
University of Mississippi *B, M, D*
University of Phoenix
Jackson *M*
University of Southern
Mississippi *B, M*

Missouri

Avila University *B*
Central Methodist University *A, B*
College of the Ozarks *B*
Columbia College *B*
Culver-Stockton College *B*
Drury University *B*
Evangel University *A, B*
Grantham University *B*
Hannibal-LaGrange University *B*
Harris-Stowe State University *B*
Lincoln University *B*
Lindenwood University *B, M*
Maryville University of Saint Louis *B*
Metropolitan Community College -
Kansas City *C, A*
Mineral Area College *A*
Missouri Baptist University *B*
Missouri Southern State
University *A, B*
Missouri State University *B, M*
Missouri Valley College *B*
Missouri Western State University *B*
National American University
Kansas City *A, B*
North Central Missouri College *C, A*
Northwest Missouri State
University *B*
Park University *B*
St. Louis Community College *C, A*
Saint Louis University *B, M*
Southeast Missouri State University *B*
Southwest Baptist University *A, B*
State Fair Community College *A*
Three Rivers Community College *A*
Truman State University *B, M*
University of Central Missouri *B, M*
University of Missouri
Columbia *B, M, D*
Kansas City *B, M*
St. Louis *B, M*
University of Phoenix
Kansas City *M*
St. Louis *B, M*
Washington University in St.
Louis *B, M*
Webster University *B*
Westminster College *B*
William Jewell College *B*
William Woods University *B*

Montana

Carroll College *B*
Flathead Valley Community
College *C, A*
Fort Peck Community College *C*
Helena College University of
Montana *A*
Montana State University *M*
Montana State University
Great Falls College *A*
Rocky Mountain College *B*
University of Great Falls *B*
University of Montana *A, M, D*

Nebraska

Bellevue University *B, M*
Chadron State College *B*
Concordia University *B*
Creighton University *B*
Doane College *B*
Hastings College *B*
Herzing University
Omaha School of Massage Therapy
and Healthcare *C*
Kaplan University
Lincoln *A*
Omaha *A, B*
Metropolitan Community
College *C, A*
Midland University *A, B*
Nebraska Wesleyan University *B*
Northeast Community College *A*
Peru State College *B*
Union College *A, B*
University of Nebraska
Lincoln *B, M*
Omaha *B, M*
University of Phoenix
Omaha *M*
Western Nebraska Community
College *C, A*
Wright Career College
Omaha *B*
York College *B*

Nevada

College of Southern Nevada *A*
Great Basin College *C, A*
Morrison University *A, B*
Sierra Nevada College *B*
Truckee Meadows Community
College *A*
University of Nevada
Las Vegas *B, M*
Reno *B, M*
University of Phoenix
Las Vegas *B, M*
Northern Nevada *B, M*
Western Nevada College *A*

New Hampshire

Daniel Webster College *B*
Franklin Pierce University *A*
Great Bay Community College *C, A*
Lakes Region Community
College *C, A*
Manchester Community College *C, A*
Mount Washington College *A, B*
NHTI-Concord's Community
College *C, A*
Nashua Community College *C, A*
New England College *B, M*
Plymouth State University *B*
River Valley Community College *A*
Saint Anselm College *B*
Southern New Hampshire
University *C, A, B, M*
University of New Hampshire *M*
White Mountains Community
College *A*

New Jersey

Atlantic Cape Community College *A*
Berkeley College *A, B*

Bloomfield College *B, M*
Brookdale Community College *C*
Burlington County College *A*
Caldwell College *B, M*
Camden County College *A*
Centenary College *B, M*
College of New Jersey *B*
Cumberland County College *C, A*
Essex County College *C, A*
Fairleigh Dickinson University
   College at Florham *B*
   Metropolitan Campus *B, M*
Felician College *B*
Georgian Court University *C, B*
Gloucester County College *C, A*
Hudson County Community
   College *A*
Kean University *B, M*
Mercer County Community
   College *A*
Middlesex County College *A*
Montclair State University *M*
New Jersey City University *M*
Ocean County College *C*
Ramapo College of New Jersey *B*
Rider University *B, M*
Rowan University *B, M*
Rutgers, The State University of New
   Jersey
   Camden Campus *B, M*
   New Brunswick/Piscataway
      Campus *B, M*
   Newark Campus *B, M*
Saint Peter's University *B, M*
Seton Hall University *B, M*
Sussex County Community
   College *C, A*
Thomas Edison State College *C, B*
Warren County Community
   College *C, A*
William Paterson University of New
   Jersey *B*

New Mexico

Brookline College
   Albuquerque *A*
Central New Mexico Community
   College *C, A*
Eastern New Mexico University *B*
Eastern New Mexico University:
   Roswell *A*
Luna Community College *C, A*
National American University
   Albuquerque *B*
Navajo Technical University *C, A*
New Mexico Highlands University *B*
New Mexico Junior College *A*
New Mexico State University *B, M*
Northern New Mexico College *C, A*
Santa Fe Community College *A*
University of New Mexico *M*
University of Phoenix
   New Mexico *M*
University of the Southwest *B*
Western New Mexico University *B*

New York

Adelphi University *B, M*
Alfred University *B, M*
Berkeley College of New York
   City *A, B*
Bramson ORT College *C, A*
Briarcliffe College *A, B*
Bryant & Stratton College
   Albany *A*
   Henrietta *A*
   Rochester *A*
   Syracuse *A*
   Syracuse North *A*
Canisius College *B, M*
Cazenovia College *B*
City University of New York
   Baruch College *B, M*
   Bronx Community College *A*

Brooklyn College *B, M*
College of Staten Island *B, M*
Hostos Community College *A*
Hunter College *B*
Kingsborough Community
   College *A*
Lehman College *B, M*
Medgar Evers College *B*
Queens College *B, M*
Queensborough Community
   College *A*
York College *B*
Clinton Community College *A*
College of Saint Rose *B*
College of Westchester *C, A, B*
Columbia-Greene Community
   College *C, A*
Concordia College *B*
Cornell University *D*
Corning Community College *A*
D'Youville College *B*
Daemen College *C, B, M*
Dominican College of Blauvelt *B*
Dowling College *B*
Elmira Business Institute *C, A*
Elmira College *B*
Everest Institute
   Rochester *A*
Excelsior College *B*
Finger Lakes Community College *A*
Fordham University *B, M*
Genesee Community College *A*
Globe Institute of
   Technology *C, A, B*
Hartwick College *B*
Hilbert College *A, B*
Hofstra University *C, B, M*
Houghton College *B*
Hudson Valley Community
   College *C, A*
Iona College *B, M*
Ithaca College *B, M*
Jamestown Business College *A*
Keuka College *B*
Le Moyne College *B*
Long Island University
   LIU Brooklyn *B, M*
   LIU Post *B, M*
Manhattan College *B, M*
Manhattanville College *B*
Maria College *A*
Marist College *B, M*
Marymount Manhattan College *B*
Medaille College *B*
Mercy College *B, M*
Mildred Elley
   Albany *C*
Molloy College *B, M*
Monroe College *A, B*
Monroe Community College *A*
Mount Saint Mary College *C, B*
Nassau Community College *A*
Nazareth College *B*
New York Institute of
   Technology *A, B*
New York University *B, M, D*
Niagara County Community
   College *C, A*
Niagara University *B*
Nyack College *B*
Orange County Community
   College *A*
Pace University *C, B, M*
Pace University: Pleasantville/
   Briarcliff *C, B, M*
Plaza College *A*
Professional Business College *C, A*
Roberts Wesleyan College *B*
Rochester Institute of
   Technology *B, M*
Rockland Community College *A*
SUNY
   College at Brockport *B, M*
   College at Fredonia *B*
   College at Geneseo *B, M*

   College at New Paltz *B, M*
   College at Old Westbury *B, M*
   College at Oneonta *B*
   College at Oswego *B, M*
   College at Plattsburgh *B*
   College of Technology at Alfred *A*
   College of Technology at Delhi *A*
   Farmingdale State College *C*
   Institute of Technology at Utica/
      Rome *B, M*
   University at Albany *B, M*
   University at Binghamton *B, M*
   University at Buffalo *B, M*
Sage Colleges *B*
Saint Bonaventure University *B, M*
St. Francis College *B, M*
St. John Fisher College *B*
St. John's University *B, M*
St. Joseph's College New York:
   Suffolk Campus *B, M*
St. Joseph's College, New York *B, M*
St. Thomas Aquinas College *B*
Siena College *C, B, M, T*
Suffolk County Community College *A*
Syracuse University *B, M*
Touro College *C, A, B, M*
University of Rochester *M*
Utica College *B*
Utica School of Commerce *C, A*
Wagner College *B, M*
Westchester Community College *C, A*
Yeshiva University *B, M*

North Carolina

Alamance Community College *C, A*
Appalachian State University *B, M*
Asheville-Buncombe Technical
   Community College *A*
Barton College *D*
Beaufort County Community
   College *A*
Belmont Abbey College *B*
Bennett College for Women *B*
Blue Ridge Community College *A*
Caldwell Community College and
   Technical Institute *A*
Campbell University *B*
Catawba College *B*
Central Carolina Community
   College *A*
Central Piedmont Community
   College *A*
Cleveland Community College *A*
Craven Community College *C, A*
Davidson County Community
   College *C, A*
Durham Technical Community
   College *A*
East Carolina University *B, M*
Edgecombe Community College *A*
Elizabeth City State University *B*
Elon University *B*
Fayetteville State University *B*
Fayetteville Technical Community
   College *A*
Forsyth Technical Community
   College *A*
Gardner-Webb University *B, M*
Gaston College *A*
Greensboro College *C, B*
Guilford College *C, B*
Haywood Community College *C, A*
High Point University *B*
James Sprunt Community
   College *C, A*
Johnson & Wales University
   Charlotte *B*
Johnston Community College *C, A*
Lenoir Community College *C, A*
Lenoir-Rhyne University *B*
Livingstone College *B*
Mars Hill University *B*
Mayland Community College *C*
McDowell Technical Community
   College *A*

Meredith College *B*
Methodist University *B*
Miller-Motte College
   Wilmington *C, A*
Mitchell Community College *A*
Montgomery Community
   College *C, A*
Nash Community College *A*
North Carolina Agricultural and
   Technical State University *B*
North Carolina Central University *B*
North Carolina State University *B, M*
North Carolina Wesleyan College *B*
Pamlico Community College *A*
Pfeiffer University *B*
Piedmont Community College *A*
Pitt Community College *C, A*
Queens University of Charlotte *B*
Randolph Community College *C, A*
Richmond Community College *C, A*
Roanoke-Chowan Community
   College *C*
Rockingham Community
   College *C, A*
Rowan-Cabarrus Community
   College *C, A*
St. Augustine's University *B*
Salem College *B*
Sampson Community College *A*
Sandhills Community College *C, A*
South College *A*
South Piedmont Community
   College *C, A*
Southwestern Community
   College *C, A*
Stanly Community College *C, A*
Surry Community College *C, A*
Tri-County Community College *A*
University of North Carolina
   Asheville *B*
   Chapel Hill *M*
   Charlotte *B, M*
   Greensboro *B, M*
   Pembroke *B*
   Wilmington *B, M*
University of Phoenix
   Charlotte *M*
   Raleigh *M*
Vance-Granville Community
   College *A*
Wake Forest University *B, M*
Wake Technical Community
   College *A*
Wayne Community College *A*
Western Carolina University *B, M*
Western Piedmont Community
   College *C, A*
Wilkes Community College *C, A*
Wilson Community College *A*
Wingate University *B, M*
Winston-Salem State University *B*

North Dakota

Dickinson State University *B*
Minot State University *B*
North Dakota State University *B*
Rasmussen College
   Bismarck *A, B*
   Fargo *A, B*
University of Jamestown *B*
University of Mary *B*
University of North Dakota *B, M*

Ohio

Ashland University *B*
Baldwin Wallace University *C, B, M*
Belmont College *A*
Bluffton University *B*
Bowling Green State University *B, M*
Bowling Green State University:
   Firelands College *C, A*

Brown Mackie College
Akron *C, A*
Cincinnati *A*
North Canton *C, A*
Bryant & Stratton College
Eastlake *A*
Parma *A*
Capital University *B*
Case Western Reserve
University *B, M*
Cedarville University *B*
Central Ohio Technical College *A*
Central State University *B*
Cincinnati State Technical and
Community College *C, A*
Cleveland State University *B, M*
College of Mount St. Joseph *A, B*
Columbus State Community
College *C*
Cuyahoga Community College
Metropolitan *A*
Daymar College
Chillicothe *A*
Defiance College *B*
ETI Technical College of Niles *A*
Eastern Gateway Community
College *A*
Edison State Community College *C, A*
Fortis College
Ravenna *A*
Franciscan University of
Steubenville *A, B*
Franklin University *A, B, M*
Gallipolis Career College *A*
Harrison College
Grove City *A, B*
Heidelberg University *B*
Herzing University
Toledo *C, A, B*
John Carroll University *B, M*
Kent State University *B, M*
Lake Erie College *B*
Lakeland Community College *C, A*
Lorain County Community College *A*
Malone University *B*
Marietta College *B*
Marion Technical College *A*
Miami University
Middletown *C, A*
Oxford *B, M*
Miami-Jacobs Career College
Dayton *A*
Mount Vernon Nazarene University *B*
Muskingum University *B*
National College
Kettering *C*
Willoughby Hills *A*
North Central State College *A*
Northwest State Community
College *A*
Notre Dame College *B*
Ohio Business College
Sandusky *C, A*
Sheffield *C, A*
Ohio Dominican University *C, B*
Ohio Northern University *B*
Ohio State University
Columbus Campus *B, M, D*
Ohio University *B, M*
Ohio Wesleyan University *B*
Otterbein University *B, M*
Owens Community College
Toledo *C*
Shawnee State University *A*
Sinclair Community College *A*
Stark State College *A*
Stautzenberger College *A*
Terra State Community College *A*
Tiffin University *A, B*
Trumbull Business College *C, A*
University of Akron *B, M*
University of Akron: Wayne
College *A*
University of Cincinnati *B, M*
University of Dayton *B*

University of Findlay *A, B*
University of Mount Union *B*
University of Northwestern
Ohio *A, B*
University of Phoenix
Cleveland *M*
University of Rio Grande *B*
University of Toledo *A, B, M*
Urbana University *B*
Ursuline College *B*
Walsh University *A, B*
Washington State Community
College *A*
Wilberforce University *B*
Wilmington College *B*
Wittenberg University *B*
Wright State University *B, M*
Xavier University *B*
Youngstown State University *A, B, M*
Zane State College *C, A*

Oklahoma

Bacone College *A*
Cameron University *B*
Carl Albert State College *C, A*
Connors State College *A*
East Central University *B, M*
Eastern Oklahoma State College *A*
Langston University *B*
Mid-America Christian University *M*
Northeastern Oklahoma Agricultural
and Mechanical College *C, A*
Northeastern State University *B*
Northern Oklahoma College *A*
Northwestern Oklahoma State
University *B*
Oklahoma Baptist University *B*
Oklahoma Christian University *B*
Oklahoma City University *B, M*
Oklahoma Panhandle State
University *B*
Oklahoma State University *B, M*
Oral Roberts University *B*
Rogers State University *A*
St. Gregory's University *B*
Southeastern Oklahoma State
University *B*
Southern Nazarene University *B*
Southwestern Oklahoma State
University *B*
Tulsa Community College *A*
University of Central Oklahoma *B, M*
University of Oklahoma *B, M*
University of Phoenix
Oklahoma City *M*
Tulsa *M*
University of Tulsa *B, M*
Wright Career College
Oklahoma City *B*
Tulsa *B*

Oregon

Central Oregon Community
College *A*
Chemeketa Community College *C, A*
Clackamas Community College *C, A*
Clatsop Community College *A*
Corban University *B*
Everest College
Portland *A*
Linfield College *B*
Northwest Christian University *B*
Oregon Institute of Technology *B*
Oregon State University *B*
Pioneer Pacific College *A*
Portland Community College *C*
Portland State University *C, B*
Southern Oregon University *B*
Tillamook Bay Community College *A*
Umpqua Community College *A*
University of Oregon *B, M, D*
University of Portland *B*

Pennsylvania

Albright College *B*
Alvernia University *B*
Arcadia University *B*
Berks Technical Institute *A*
Bloomsburg University of
Pennsylvania *B*
Cabrini College *B*
California University of
Pennsylvania *A*
Cambria-Rowe Business College *A*
Cambria-Rowe Business College:
Indiana *A*
Carlow University *B*
Carnegie Mellon University *M, D*
Cedar Crest College *C, B*
Central Penn College *A, B*
Chatham University *B, M*
Chestnut Hill College *B*
Clarion University of Pennsylvania *C*
Community College of
Philadelphia *A*
Consolidated School of Business
Lancaster *A*
York *A*
DeSales University *C, B*
Delaware Valley College *B*
Drexel University *B*
Duquesne University *B, M*
Elizabethtown College *B*
Erie Business Center *A*
Erie Business Center South *A*
Fortis Institute
Erie *A*
Forty Fort *C*
Gannon University *B*
Geneva College *B*
Grove City College *B*
Gwynedd Mercy University *B*
Holy Family University *B*
Immaculata University *C, A, B*
Indiana University of Pennsylvania *B*
Juniata College *B, M*
Kaplan Career Institute
Pittsburgh *A*
Keystone College *B*
King's College *B*
La Roche College *B, M*
La Salle University *A, B*
Lackawanna College *A*
Lansdale School of Business *A*
Laurel Business Institute *A*
Lebanon Valley College *A, B*
Lehigh University *B, M*
Lincoln University *B*
Lock Haven University of
Pennsylvania *B*
Luzerne County Community
College *A*
Lycoming College *B*
Manor College *A*
Mansfield University of
Pennsylvania *B*
Marywood University *B*
McCann School of Business and
Technology
Hazleton *A*
Mercyhurst University *B*
Messiah College *B*
Misericordia University *B*
Moravian College *B*
Mount Aloysius College *A, B*
Muhlenberg College *C, A, B*
Neumann University *B*
Pace Institute *A*
Peirce College *B*
Penn Commercial Business and
Technical School *C*
Penn State
Abington *B*
Altoona *C, B*
Beaver *B*
Berks *B*
Brandywine *B*

DuBois *B*
Erie, The Behrend College *B*
Fayette, The Eberly Campus *B*
Greater Allegheny *B*
Harrisburg *B*
Hazleton *B*
Lehigh Valley *B*
Mont Alto *B*
New Kensington *B*
Schuylkill *B*
Shenango *B*
University Park *B, M*
Wilkes-Barre *C, B*
Worthington Scranton *C, B*
York *B*
Pennsylvania College of
Technology *B*
Pennsylvania Highlands Community
College *A*
Philadelphia University *C, A, B, M*
Point Park University *C, A, B*
Reading Area Community
College *C, A*
Robert Morris University *C, B*
Rosemont College *B*
St. Francis University *B*
Saint Joseph's University *B, M*
St. Vincent College *C, B, M*
Seton Hill University *B*
Shippensburg University of
Pennsylvania *B*
Slippery Rock University of
Pennsylvania *C, B*
South Hills School of Business &
Technology *A*
Susquehanna University *B*
Temple University *B, M*
Thiel College *A, B*
University of Pennsylvania *B, M, D*
University of Pittsburgh *B, M*
University of Pittsburgh
Bradford *B*
Greensburg *B*
Johnstown *B*
Titusville *A*
University of Scranton *C, B, M*
Villanova University *B, M*
Washington & Jefferson College *B*
Waynesburg University *B*
West Chester University of
Pennsylvania *B*
Westminster College *B*
Widener University *B, M*
Wilkes University *B*
Wilson College *A, B*
YTI Career Institute
York *A*
York College of Pennsylvania *B, M*
Yorktowne Business Institute *A*

Puerto Rico

American University of Puerto
Rico *A, B*
Atlantic University College *A, B*
Bayamon Central University *B, M*
Caribbean University *A, B*
Huertas College *A*
ICPR Junior College *A*
Inter American University of Puerto
Rico
Aguadilla Campus *A, B, M*
Arecibo Campus *A, B*
Barranquitas Campus *A, B*
Bayamon Campus *A, B*
Fajardo Campus *A, B*
Guayama Campus *A, B*
Metropolitan Campus *A, B, M*
Ponce Campus *A, B*
San German Campus *A, B, M*
Pontifical Catholic University of
Puerto Rico *B, M*
Turabo University *A, B, M*
Universidad Metropolitana *B, M*
Universidad del Este *B, M*
University College of San Juan *A, B*

University of Phoenix
Puerto Rico *M*
University of Puerto Rico
Aguadilla *B*
Arecibo *B*
Bayamon University College *B*
Cayey University College *B*
Humacao *B*
Mayaguez *B*
Ponce *B*
Rio Piedras *B, M*
Utuado *A, B*
University of the Sacred Heart *B*

Rhode Island

Bryant University *B, M*
Community College of Rhode
Island *C, A*
Johnson & Wales University
Providence *B, M*
Providence College *B*
Rhode Island College *B, M*
Roger Williams University *B*
Salve Regina University *B*
University of Rhode Island *B, M*

South Carolina

Aiken Technical College *C, A*
Benedict College *B*
Bob Jones University *B*
Central Carolina Technical College *A*
Charleston Southern University *B, M*
Clemson University *B, M*
Coastal Carolina University *B, M*
College of Charleston *B, M*
Columbia College *B*
Converse College *B*
Florence-Darlington Technical
College *A*
Forrest Junior College *A*
Francis Marion University *B*
Furman University *B*
Greenville Technical College *C, A*
Horry-Georgetown Technical
College *A*
Limestone College *B*
Midlands Technical College *C, A*
Newberry College *B*
North Greenville University *B*
Northeastern Technical College *A*
Orangeburg-Calhoun Technical
College *C, A*
Piedmont Technical College *C*
South Carolina State University *B*
Southern Wesleyan University *B*
Spartanburg Community College *C, A*
Technical College of the
Lowcountry *C*
Tri-County Technical College *C, A*
Trident Technical College *C, A*
University of South Carolina
Columbia *B, M*
Voorhees College *B*
Wofford College *B*
York Technical College *C, A*

South Dakota

Augustana College *B*
Black Hills State University *B*
Dakota State University *B*
Dakota Wesleyan University *B*
Globe University
Sioux Falls *A, B*
Kilian Community College *A*
Lake Area Technical Institute *A*
Mount Marty College *C, A, B*
National American University
Rapid City *A, B*
Northern State University *B*
Oglala Lakota College *B*
Sinte Gleska University *A*
Sisseton Wahpeton College *A*
Southeast Technical Institute *A*
University of Sioux Falls *B*

University of South Dakota *B, M*
Western Dakota Technical
Institute *C, A*

Tennessee

Belmont University *B, M*
Carson-Newman University *B*
Christian Brothers University *B, M*
Cumberland University *B*
Daymar Institute
Clarksville *A*
Murfreesboro *A*
Nashville *C, A*
East Tennessee State University *B, M*
Freed-Hardeman University *B*
Hiwassee College *A*
Jackson State Community College *A*
King University *B*
Lee University *B*
Lincoln Memorial University *B, M*
Lipscomb University *B, M*
Martin Methodist College *B*
Middle Tennessee State University *B*
Miller-Motte Technical College
Clarksville *A*
Milligan College *B*
Nashville State Community College *A*
National College of Business and
Technology
Bristol *C, A*
Knoxville *C, A*
Nashville *C, A*
Northeast State Community
College *C*
Rhodes College *M*
South College *A*
Southern Adventist
University *A, B, M*
Tennessee State University *A, B*
Tennessee Technological
University *B*
Tennessee Wesleyan College *B*
Trevecca Nazarene University *B*
Tusculum College *B*
Union University *B, T*
University of Memphis *B, M*
University of Phoenix
Chattanooga *B, M*
Knoxville *M*
Memphis *M*
Nashville *B, M*
University of Tennessee
Chattanooga *M*
Knoxville *B, M*
Martin *B*
Vanderbilt University *M*

Texas

Abilene Christian University *B, M*
Amarillo College *C, A*
Amberton University *B*
Angelina College *A*
Angelo State University *B, M*
Austin Community College *C*
Baylor University *B, M*
Blinn College *A*
Brazosport College *A*
Brookhaven College *C, A*
Clarendon College *A*
Coastal Bend College *C, A*
College of the Mainland *A*
Dallas Baptist University *B, M*
Eastfield College *C, A*
El Centro College *C, A*
El Paso Community College *C, A*
Everest College
Fort Worth *A*
Frank Phillips College *C, A*
Galveston College *C, A*
Grayson College *C, A*
Hallmark College of Technology *C, B*
Hardin-Simmons University *B*
Houston Baptist University *B, M*

Houston Community College
System *C, A*
Howard College *C, A*
Howard Payne University *B*
Huston-Tillotson University *B*
Kilgore College *C, A*
Lamar State College at Orange *C*
Lamar University *B*
Laredo Community College *C, A*
LeTourneau University *B*
Lee College *C, A*
Lone Star College System *C, A*
Lubbock Christian University *B*
McLennan Community College *C, A*
McMurry University *B*
Midwestern State University *B*
Mountain View College *C, A*
National American University
Austin *A, B*
Navarro College *C, A*
North Lake College *C, A*
Northeast Texas Community
College *A*
Northwood University
Texas *B*
Our Lady of the Lake University of
San Antonio *B*
Paris Junior College *A*
Paul Quinn College *B*
Prairie View A&M University *B, M*
Richland College *C, A*
St. Edward's University *B*
St. Mary's University *B, M*
St. Philip's College *A*
Sam Houston State University *B, M*
San Jacinto College *C, A*
Schreiner University *B*
South Plains College *A*
South Texas College *C, A*
Southern Methodist University *B, M*
Southwestern Adventist University *B*
Southwestern Assemblies of God
University *B*
Southwestern University *B*
Stephen F. Austin State
University *B, M*
Sul Ross State University *B*
Tarleton State University *B*
Texas A&M International
University *B, M*
Texas A&M University *B, M, D*
Texas A&M University
Commerce *B, M*
Corpus Christi *B, M*
Kingsville *B, M*
Texarkana *B, M*
Texas Christian University *B, M*
Texas Lutheran University *B, M*
Texas Southern University *B, M*
Texas State University *B, M*
Texas Tech University *B, M*
Texas Wesleyan University *B, M*
Texas Woman's University *B*
Trinity University *B, M*
Trinity Valley Community
College *C, A*
University of Dallas *M*
University of Houston *B, M*
University of Houston
Clear Lake *B, M*
Downtown *B*
Victoria *B*
University of Mary Hardin-Baylor *B*
University of North Texas *B, M, D*
University of Phoenix
Austin *B, M*
Dallas Fort Worth *B, M*
Houston Westside *B, M*
San Antonio *M*
University of St. Thomas *B, M*
University of Texas
Arlington *B, M, D*
Austin *B, M, D*
Brownsville *B*
Dallas *B, M*

El Paso *B, M*
Pan American *B, M*
Permian Basin *B, M*
San Antonio *B, M, D*
Tyler *B, M*
University of the Incarnate
Word *B, M*
Vernon College *A*
Weatherford College *C, A*
West Texas A&M University *B, M*
Western Texas College *C, A*
Wiley College *B*

Utah

Brigham Young University *B, M*
Broadview University
Layton *A, B*
Orem *A*
West Jordan *A, B*
Dixie State College *B*
LDS Business College *C, A*
Provo College *A*
Snow College *A*
Southern Utah University *B, M*
University of Phoenix
Utah *B, M*
University of Utah *B, M*
Utah State University *C, B, M*
Utah Valley University *C, A, B*
Weber State University *B, M*
Western Governors University *B*
Westminster College *B, M*

Vermont

Castleton State College *B, M*
Champlain College *C, A, B, M*
College of St. Joseph in
Vermont *A, B*
Community College of Vermont *A*
Lyndon State College *B*
Norwich University *B*
Saint Michael's College *B*
University of Vermont *M*

Virginia

American National University
Charlottesville *A*
Danville *C, A*
Harrisonburg *C, A*
Lynchburg *C, A*
Martinsville *C, A*
Salem *C, A, B, M*
Averett University *B*
Blue Ridge Community College *A*
Bluefield College *B*
Bryant & Stratton College
Richmond *A*
Virginia Beach *A*
Central Virginia Community
College *C, A*
Christopher Newport University *B*
College of William and Mary *M*
Danville Community College *A*
ECPI University *B*
Eastern Mennonite University *B*
Emory & Henry College *B*
Ferrum College *B*
George Mason University *B, M*
Germanna Community College *C*
Hampton University *B*
James Madison University *B, M*
Liberty University *B*
Lord Fairfax Community College *A*
Lynchburg College *B*
Mountain Empire Community
College *A*
New River Community College *C, A*
Norfolk State University *B*
Northern Virginia Community
College *A*
Old Dominion University *B, M*
Patrick Henry Community College *A*
Radford University *B*
Randolph-Macon College *B*

Rappahannock Community
College C, A
Regent University B
Southwest Virginia Community
College A
Thomas Nelson Community
College A
Tidewater Community College C, A
University of Phoenix
Northern Virginia M
Richmond B
University of Richmond B
University of Virginia M
University of Virginia's College at
Wise B
University of the Potomac B
Virginia Commonwealth
University B, M
Virginia Highlands Community
College C, A
Virginia Polytechnic Institute and
State University B, M
Virginia State University B
Virginia Union University B
Virginia Western Community
College A
Wytheville Community College A

Washington

Central Washington University B, M
Centralia College C, A
City University of Seattle C, B, M
DeVry University
Federal Way B, M
Eastern Washington University B
Everett Community College C, A
Gonzaga University B, M
Green River Community College C, A
Heritage University B
Highline Community College C, A
Lower Columbia College C, A
Peninsula College A
Saint Martin's University B
Seattle Central Community
College C, A
Seattle Pacific University B
Seattle University B, M
Skagit Valley College C, A
South Puget Sound Community
College C, A
South Seattle Community
College C, A
Spokane Community College A
University of Phoenix
Western Washington M
University of Washington B, M
University of Washington Bothell B
University of Washington Tacoma B
Walla Walla University B
Washington State University B, M, D
Western Washington University B
Whatcom Community College C, A
Whitworth University B

West Virginia

Alderson-Broaddus University B
American National University
Princeton C, A
American Public University
System B, M
Bethany College B
Blue Ridge Community and Technical
College A
Bluefield State College B
Bridgemont Community and
Technical College A
Concord University B
Davis and Elkins College B
Fairmont State University B
Kanawha Valley Community and
Technical College A
Marshall University B, M
Mountain State College A

New River Community and Technical
College A
Ohio Valley University B
Shepherd University B
Southern West Virginia Community
and Technical College A
University of Charleston B
West Liberty University B
West Virginia State University B
West Virginia University B, M
West Virginia Wesleyan College B
Wheeling Jesuit University B, M

Wisconsin

Blackhawk Technical College A
Bryant & Stratton College
Milwaukee A
Cardinal Stritch University B
Carroll University B
Carthage College B
Chippewa Valley Technical College A
College of Menominee Nation A
Concordia University Wisconsin B
Edgewood College B, M
Fox Valley Technical College A
Gateway Technical College A
Globe University
Appleton A, B
Eau Claire C, A, B
Green Bay A, B
La Crosse A, B
Madison East A, B
Middleton A, B
Wausau A, B
Herzing University
Kenosha C, B
Madison A, B
Lac Courte Oreilles Ojibwa
Community College A
Lakeland College B
Lakeshore Technical College C, A
Madison Area Technical College C, A
Maranatha Baptist Bible College B
Marian University B
Marquette University B, M
Mid-State Technical College A
Milwaukee Area Technical
College C, A
Moraine Park Technical College C, A
Mount Mary University B
Nicolet Area Technical College A
Northcentral Technical College A
Northeast Wisconsin Technical
College A
Rasmussen College
Appleton A, B
Green Bay A, B
Wausau A, B
St. Norbert College B
Silver Lake College of the Holy
Family B
Southwest Wisconsin Technical
College C, A
University of Phoenix
Milwaukee B, M
University of Wisconsin
Eau Claire B
Green Bay B
La Crosse B
Madison B, M
Milwaukee B
Oshkosh B
Parkside B
Platteville B
River Falls B
Stevens Point B
Superior B
Whitewater B, M
Viterbo University B
Waukesha County Technical
College A
Western Technical College A
Wisconsin Indianhead Technical
College A

Wyoming

Casper College A
Central Wyoming College A
Eastern Wyoming College A
Laramie County Community
College A
Northwest College A
University of Wyoming B, M
Western Wyoming Community
College C, A

Accounting/business
management

Alabama

University of Phoenix
Birmingham B

Alaska

Alaska Pacific University B
Charter College B

Arizona

Grand Canyon University M
ITT Technical Institute
Tempe B
University of Phoenix
Phoenix-Hohokam B
Southern Arizona B

California

Claremont McKenna College B
Heald College
Concord C, A
Fresno C, A
Hayward C, A
Rancho Cordova C, A
Salinas C, A
San Francisco C, A
San Jose C, A
Stockton C, A
Kaplan College
Riverside A
Santa Clara University B
University of Phoenix
Bay Area B
Central Valley B
Sacramento Valley B
San Diego B
Southern California B

Colorado

CollegeAmerica
Denver A, B
IntelliTec College: Grand Junction A
University of Phoenix
Denver B
Southern Colorado B

Connecticut

Mitchell College B

District of Columbia

Strayer University B
University of Phoenix
Washington DC B
University of the Potomac C, B

Florida

Herzing University
Winter Park B
Rasmussen College
Fort Myers B
New Port Richey B
Ocala B
Pasco/Land O'Lakes B
Tampa/Brandon B
University of Phoenix
Central Florida B
North Florida B
South Florida B
West Florida B
Valencia College C

Georgia

University of Phoenix
Atlanta B
Augusta B
Columbus B
Savannah B

Hawaii

University of Phoenix
Hawaii B

Idaho

University of Phoenix
Idaho B

Illinois

Elgin Community College C
Kaskaskia College C
Rasmussen College
Aurora B
Mokena/Tinley Park B
Rockford B
Romeoville/Joliet B
Sauk Valley Community College A
University of Illinois
Urbana-Champaign B
University of Phoenix
Chicago B

Indiana

Indiana University
Bloomington M
Purdue University Indianapolis M
National College
Indianapolis C, A, B
Purdue University B, M, D
University of Phoenix
Indianapolis B
Vincennes University C

Iowa

AIB College of Business A
Dordt College B
University of Phoenix
Des Moines B

Kansas

Colby Community College C
Kansas City Kansas Community
College A
Kansas State University A
Ottawa University B
Tabor College B

Kentucky

Spalding University B
University of Phoenix
Louisville B

Louisiana

Herzing University
Kenner B
University of Phoenix
Baton Rouge B
Lafayette B
Louisiana B
Shreveport B

Maine

Husson University B, M

Maryland

Towson University M
University of Phoenix
Maryland B

Massachusetts

Babson College B
Cape Cod Community College A
Eastern Nazarene College B
Elms College B
Lasell College B

University of Phoenix
Boston *B*

Michigan
Baker College
Muskegon *B*
Oakland Community College *A*
University of Phoenix
Metro Detroit *B*
West Michigan *B*

Minnesota
Augsburg College *B*
Minnesota West Community and
Technical College *A*
Rasmussen College
Blaine *B*
Bloomington *B*
Brooklyn Park *B*
Eagan *B*
Lake Elmo/Woodbury *B*
Mankato *B*
St. Cloud *B*
University of Phoenix
Minneapolis-St. Paul *B*
Walden University *M*

Mississippi
Mississippi College *M*
University of Phoenix
Jackson *B*

Missouri
Park University *A, B*
University of Missouri
Kansas City *B*
University of Phoenix
Kansas City *B*
St. Louis *B*

Montana
Rocky Mountain College *B, M*
University of Great Falls *B*

Nebraska
ITT Technical Institute
Omaha *B*
University of Phoenix
Omaha *B*

Nevada
University of Phoenix
Las Vegas *B*
Northern Nevada *B*

New Jersey
Eastwick College
Hackensack *C*
University of Phoenix
Jersey City *B*

New Mexico
National American University
Albuquerque *B*
University of Phoenix
New Mexico *B*

New York
ASA College *A*
Canisius College *M*
City University of New York
Brooklyn College *M*
Globe Institute of
Technology *C, A, B*
Mercy College *B*
Mount Saint Mary College *M*
Utica College *M*

North Carolina
Chowan University *B*
East Carolina University *B*
University of Mount Olive *B*

North Dakota
Dakota College at Bottineau *A*
Rasmussen College
Bismarck *B*
Fargo *B*
University of Mary *M*

Ohio
National College
Cincinnati *A*
Stow *A*
Stark State College *A*
University of Phoenix
Cleveland *B*
Urbana University *B*

Oklahoma
University of Phoenix
Oklahoma City *B*
Tulsa *B*

Oregon
Corban University *B*
George Fox University *B*
Heald College
Portland *C, A*
University of Phoenix
Oregon *B*

Pennsylvania
Chestnut Hill College *A, B*
DuBois Business College *A*
DuBois Business College
Huntingdon *A*
Oil City *A*
Harrisburg Area Community
College *A*
University of Phoenix
Harrisburg *B*
Philadelphia *B*
Pittsburgh *B*

Puerto Rico
National University College
Bayamon *A, B*
Rio Grande *A, B*

South Carolina
Miller-Motte Technical College *A*
University of Phoenix
Columbia *B*

South Dakota
Mitchell Technical Institute *A*
Mount Marty College *C*
National American University
Rapid City *B, M*

Tennessee
Bethel University *B*
Daymar Institute
Murfreesboro *A*
ITT Technical Institute
Memphis *B*
Nashville *B*
National College of Business and
Technology
Bartlett *C, A*
Madison *A*
Memphis *A*
University of Phoenix
Chattanooga *B*
Knoxville *B*
Memphis *B*
Nashville *B*

Texas
Cedar Valley College *C, A*
Northeast Texas Community
College *C, A*
University of Phoenix
Austin *B*
Dallas Fort Worth *B*

Houston Westside *B*
San Antonio *B*

Utah
University of Phoenix
Utah *B*

Vermont
Lyndon State College *B*

Virginia
Rappahannock Community
College *C, A*
University of Phoenix
Northern Virginia *B*
Richmond *B*
University of the Potomac *C*
Washington and Lee University *B*

Washington
University of Phoenix
Western Washington *B*

Wisconsin
Herzing University
Madison *B*
ITT Technical Institute
Green Bay *B*
Greenfield *B*
Maranatha Baptist Bible College *B*
Northcentral Technical College *A*
Rasmussen College
Appleton *B*
Green Bay *B*
Wausau *B*
University of Phoenix
Milwaukee *B*

Accounting/computer science

Arizona
Arizona Western College *C, A*
Paradise Valley Community College *C*

California
San Jose State University *B*

Colorado
Colorado Mountain College *A*

Connecticut
Three Rivers Community College *A*

Georgia
Georgia State University *M*

Illinois
McKendree University *B*
Rock Valley College *C*

Indiana
St. Mary-of-the-Woods College *B*

Iowa
Coe College *B*

Maine
Northern Maine Community
College *B, M*

Massachusetts
American International College *B, M*
Massasoit Community College *C*

Missouri
State Fair Community College *A*

New Hampshire
Southern New Hampshire
University *B*

New York
Schenectady County Community
College *A*

Ohio
Ashland University *B*

Oregon
Warner Pacific College *B*

Pennsylvania
Grove City College *B*

Texas
Houston Baptist University *B*
Texas State University *M*
University of Dallas *M*

Washington
Western Washington University *B*

Accounting/finance

Alabama
Faulkner University *B*

Arizona
DeVry University
Phoenix *M*

California
DeVry University
Pomona *M*
Westwood College
Anaheim *B*

Colorado
DeVry University
Westminster *M*

District of Columbia
Strayer University *M*

Florida
DeVry University
Miramar *M*
Orlando *M*

Illinois
City Colleges of Chicago
Wilbur Wright College *C*
DeVry University
Chicago *M*
Online *M*

Indiana
Huntington University *B*
Indiana University
Southeast *M*
Purdue University *B, M, D*

Iowa
AIB College of Business *A*
Maharishi University of
Management *M*

Maine
University of Southern Maine *B*

Maryland
University of Maryland
University College *M*

Massachusetts
Babson College *B*
Bentley University *B*
Bridgewater State University *B*
Eastern Nazarene College *B*
Lasell College *B*
New England College of Business and
Finance *M*
Salem State University *B*

Simmons College *B*
Western New England University *B*

Michigan

Aquinas College *B*
Ferris State University *B*
Northern Michigan University *B*

Minnesota

Bethel University *B*
Minnesota State University
　Moorhead *B*
Minnesota West Community and
　Technical College *A*

Missouri

DeVry University
　Kansas City *M*
University of Missouri
　Kansas City *B*
Webster University *B*

New Hampshire

Franklin Pierce University *B*
Granite State College *B*
Southern New Hampshire
　University *B, M*

New York

Clarkson University *B*
DeVry College of New York
　Midtown Campus *M*
Globe Institute of
　Technology *C, A, B*
Rochester Institute of Technology *M*
SUNY
　College at Oneonta *B*

North Dakota

University of North Dakota *B*

Ohio

DeVry University
　Columbus *M*
Hiram College *B*
Lourdes University *B*
Stark State College *A*

Oklahoma

Northeastern State University *M*
Oklahoma State University
　Oklahoma City *A*

Oregon

Corban University *B*

Pennsylvania

Albright College *B*
Bucknell University *B*
DeVry University
　Fort Washington *M*
Eastern University *B*
Holy Family University *B*
York College of Pennsylvania *M*

South Carolina

Voorhees College *B*
York Technical College *C*

Tennessee

Vanderbilt University *M*

Texas

DeVry University
　Houston *M*
　Irving *M*
North Lake College *C*
Our Lady of the Lake University of
　San Antonio *M*

Vermont

Lyndon State College *B*

Virginia

DeVry University
　Arlington *M*

Washington

DeVry University
　Federal Way *M*

Wisconsin

Herzing University
　Madison *B*
Northcentral Technical College *A*

Accounting technology/ bookkeeping

Alabama

Gadsden State Community College *A*
Herzing University
　Birmingham *C, A*
Jefferson Davis Community
　College *A*
Jefferson State Community
　College *C, A*
Northwest-Shoals Community
　College *C*

Alaska

University of Alaska
　Anchorage *C, A*
　Fairbanks *C, A*

Arizona

Brown Mackie College
　Tucson *A, B*
Central Arizona College *C, A*
Coconino County Community
　College *C*
Everest College
　Phoenix *A*
Glendale Community College *A*
Paradise Valley Community
　College *C, A*

Arkansas

Arkansas State University
　Beebe *C*
　Newport *C*
Black River Technical College *C*
Cossatot Community College of the
　University of Arkansas *C*
National Park Community
　College *C, A*
Pulaski Technical College *C*
Southeast Arkansas College *C*
University of Arkansas
　Community College at Hope *C*

California

Bakersfield College *C, A*
Canada College *C*
College of the Canyons *C, A*
College of the Siskiyous *C, A*
Columbia College *A*
Contra Costa College *C*
DeVry University
　Pomona *A*
Diablo Valley College *C, A*
East Los Angeles College *C, A*
Folsom Lake College *C*
Foothill College *C*
Imperial Valley College *C, A*
Kaplan College
　Riverside *A*
MTI College *C*
MiraCosta College *C, A*
Palomar College *C, A*
San Joaquin Delta College *C, A*
Santa Barbara City College *C, A*
Southwestern College *C*
West Hills College: Lemoore *C*

Colorado

Aims Community College *C, A*
Arapahoe Community College *C, A*
Colorado Mountain College *C, A*
Colorado Northwestern Community
　College *C, A*
Community College of Aurora *C, A*
Community College of Denver *C, A*
DeVry University
　Westminster *A*
Front Range Community College *C, A*
IBMC College
　Fort Collins *C, A*
Northeastern Junior College *C, A*
Pikes Peak Community College *C, A*
Pueblo Community College *C, A*
Red Rocks Community College *C, A*

Connecticut

Lincoln College of New England *A*
Naugatuck Valley Community
　College *C, A*

Delaware

Delaware Technical Community
　College
　Jack F. Owens Campus *C*
　Stanton/Wilmington Campus *C*
　Terry Campus *C*

District of Columbia

Strayer University *C, A*
University of the District of
　Columbia *A*
University of the Potomac *C, A*

Florida

College of Central Florida *A*
Daytona State College *A*
DeVry University
　Miramar *A*
　Orlando *A*
Florida Gateway College *C*
Gulf Coast State College *C, A*
Hillsborough Community College *A*
ITT Technical Institute
　Miami *B*
Northwest Florida State College *A*
Polk State College *C, A*
Rasmussen College
　Fort Myers *C*
　New Port Richey *C*
　Ocala *C*
　Pasco/Land O'Lakes *C*
　Tampa/Brandon *C*
Saint Johns River State College *C, A*
St. Petersburg College *C*
Seminole State College of
　Florida *C, A*
South Florida State College *C, A*
University of Miami *C*
Valencia College *A*

Georgia

Albany Technical College *C*
Athens Technical College *C, A*
Atlanta Technical College *C, A*
Central Georgia Technical
　College *C, A*
Georgia Highlands College *A*
Georgia Piedmont Technical
　College *C, A*
Gwinnett Technical College *C, A*
Savannah Technical College *C, A*
Southwest Georgia Technical
　College *C, A*

Hawaii

University of Hawaii
　Leeward Community College *C, A*

Idaho

College of Western Idaho *C, A*
Lewis-Clark State College *C, A, B*

Illinois

Black Hawk College *C*
College of DuPage *C, A*
College of Lake County *C, A*
Danville Area Community
　College *C, A*
DeVry University
　Online *A*
Harper College *C*
Highland Community College *C*
Illinois Central College *C, A*
Illinois Eastern Community Colleges
　Wabash Valley College *C, A*
Illinois Valley Community College *C*
John A. Logan College *C, A*
John Wood Community College *C, A*
Kankakee Community College *C*
McHenry County College *C, A*
Moraine Valley Community College *C*
Northwestern University *C*
Parkland College *C, A*
Prairie State College *C*
Rasmussen College
　Aurora *C*
　Mokena/Tinley Park *C*
　Rockford *C*
　Romeoville/Joliet *C*
Robert Morris University: Chicago *B*
Rock Valley College *C*
Triton College *C*
Waubonsee Community College *C*

Indiana

Brown Mackie College
　Michigan City *A*
　South Bend *A*
ITT Technical Institute
　Fort Wayne *B*
　Indianapolis *A, B*
International Business College *C, A*
International Business College:
　Indianapolis *C, A*
Ivy Tech Community College
　Bloomington *C, A*
　Central Indiana *C, A*
　Columbus *C, A*
　East Central *C, A*
　Kokomo *C, A*
　Lafayette *C, A*
　North Central *C, A*
　Northeast *C, A*
　Northwest *C, A*
　Richmond *C, A*
　South Central *C, A*
　Southeast *C, A*
　Southwest *C, A*
　Wabash Valley *C, A*
Vincennes University *A*

Iowa

Des Moines Area Community
　College *C, A*
North Iowa Area Community
　College *C*
Northeast Iowa Community
　College *C*
Western Iowa Tech Community
　College *C*

Kansas

Barton County Community College *A*
Highland Community College *C, A*
Hutchinson Community College *C, A*
Johnson County Community
　College *C*
Wichita Area Technical College *C, A*

Kentucky

Brown Mackie College
　North Kentucky *A*
Daymar College
　Bowling Green *C, A*
Jefferson Community and Technical
　College *C, A*

Somerset Community College *C*
Spencerian College *C, A*

Louisiana

Baton Rouge Community College *A*
Bossier Parish Community College *C*
Delgado Community College *C, A*

Maine

Kennebec Valley Community
College *A*

Maryland

Allegany College of Maryland *C, A*
Anne Arundel Community
College *C, A*
Carroll Community College *C, A*
Cecil College *C*
Chesapeake College *C, A*
College of Southern Maryland *C, A*
Community College of Baltimore
County *C, A*
Hagerstown Community College *A*
Harford Community College *C, A*
Howard Community College *C, A*
Montgomery College *C, A*
Wor-Wic Community College *C, A*

Massachusetts

Bristol Community College *C*
Bunker Hill Community College *C*
Holyoke Community College *C, A*
Mount Wachusett Community
College *C*
North Shore Community College *A*
Quinsigamond Community College *C*

Michigan

Baker College
Muskegon *C*
Port Huron *C*
Ferris State University *A, B*
Grand Rapids Community College *A*
Henry Ford Community College *C*
Kirtland Community College *C*
Lake Michigan College *A*
Lansing Community College *C, A*
Mid Michigan Community College *A*
Mott Community College *C, A*
Northwestern Michigan College *A*
Oakland Community College *C, A*
St. Clair County Community
College *A*
Schoolcraft College *C, A*
Southwestern Michigan College *A*
Wayne County Community
College *C, A*

Minnesota

Anoka Technical College *C*
Anoka-Ramsey Community
College *C, A*
Central Lakes College *C*
Century College *C*
Dakota County Technical College *C*
Hennepin Technical College *C, A*
Lake Superior College *C*
Minneapolis Community and
Technical College *C, A*
Minnesota State College - Southeast
Technical *C, A*
Minnesota State Community and
Technical College *C*
Minnesota West Community and
Technical College *C*
National American University
Roseville *A*
North Hennepin Community
College *C, A*
Northland Community & Technical
College *C, A*
Northwest Technical College *C, A*
Pine Technical College *C*

Rasmussen College
Blaine *C*
Bloomington *C*
Brooklyn Park *C*
Eagan *C*
Lake Elmo/Woodbury *C*
Mankato *C*
St. Cloud *C*
Ridgewater College *C*
Rochester Community and Technical
College *C*
St. Cloud Technical and Community
College *C*
St. Paul College *C*
South Central College *C, A*

Mississippi

Copiah-Lincoln Community
College *A*
Hinds Community College *C, A*
Northeast Mississippi Community
College *A*

Missouri

East Central College *A*
Moberly Area Community College *A*
Ozarks Technical Community
College *A*
St. Charles Community College *C, A*

Montana

Helena College University of
Montana *A*
Montana State University *C*
Montana State University
Billings *C, A*
Montana Tech of the University of
Montana *C, A*

Nevada

Western Nevada College *C*

New Jersey

Bergen Community College *A*
Brookdale Community College *A*
Burlington County College *C, A*
Essex County College *A*
Passaic County Community
College *C, A*
Raritan Valley Community College *A*
Union County College *A*

New Mexico

Central New Mexico Community
College *C*
Eastern New Mexico University:
Roswell *C*
National American University
Albuquerque *A*
New Mexico State University
Carlsbad *C*
San Juan College *C, A*
Santa Fe Community College *C*
Southwestern Indian Polytechnic
Institute *C, A*

New York

Adirondack Community College *A*
Broome Community College *A*
Cayuga Community College *C, A*
City University of New York
Borough of Manhattan Community
College *A*
Brooklyn College *C*
LaGuardia Community College *A*
New York City College of
Technology *A*
Dutchess Community College *C, A*
Elmira Business Institute: Vestal *C, A*
Fulton-Montgomery Community
College *A*
Genesee Community College *C, A*
Globe Institute of
Technology *C, A, B*

Herkimer County Community
College *A*
Jamestown Community College *A*
Jefferson Community College *C, A*
Mercy College *A*
Mohawk Valley Community
College *A*
New York Institute of Technology *A*
Onondaga Community College *A*
Orange County Community
College *C*
Pace University: Pleasantville/
Briarcliff *M*
Rockland Community College *C, A*
SUNY
College of Agriculture and
Technology at Cobleskill *A*
College of Agriculture and
Technology at Morrisville *A*
College of Technology at Alfred *A*
College of Technology at Canton *A*
Sullivan County Community
College *C, A*
Technical Career Institutes *A*
Tompkins Cortland Community
College *C, A*
Ulster County Community College *A*
Wood Tobe-Coburn School *C, A*

North Carolina

Blue Ridge Community College *C*
Cape Fear Community College *A*
Catawba Valley Community
College *C, A*
Central Piedmont Community
College *A*
Coastal Carolina Community
College *C, A*
Guilford Technical Community
College *C, A*
King's College *C, A*
Martin Community College *C, A*
Southeastern Community College *C*

North Dakota

Dakota College at Bottineau *A*
Rasmussen College
Bismarck *C*
Fargo *C*
Williston State College *A*

Ohio

Bradford School *C, A*
Brown Mackie College
Akron *A*
Findlay *A*
Cincinnati State Technical and
Community College *C*
Clark State Community College *C, A*
Columbus State Community
College *C, A*
Davis College *C, A*
Hocking College *C, A*
ITT Technical Institute
Norwood *A*
Strongsville *A*
James A. Rhodes State College *A*
Kent State University
Ashtabula *A*
East Liverpool *A*
Geauga *A*
Salem *A*
Trumbull *A*
Tuscarawas *A*
Miami University
Hamilton *C, A*
Oxford *A*
National College
Canton *C, A*
Willoughby Hills *C*
North Central State College *C*
Northwest State Community
College *C*

Ohio University
Lancaster Campus *A*
Southern Campus at Ironton *A*
Owens Community College
Toledo *C, A*
Sinclair Community College *C*
Southern State Community College *A*
Stark State College *A*
Stautzenberger College *A*
University of Akron *C, A*
University of Cincinnati
Blue Ash College *C, A*
Clermont College *C, A*
University of Rio Grande *A*
University of Toledo *A*
Youngstown State University *A*

Oklahoma

Oklahoma State University
Oklahoma City *A*
Rose State College *A*

Oregon

Blue Mountain Community
College *C, A*
Chemeketa Community College *C, A*
Clackamas Community College *C*
Klamath Community College *C, A*
Lane Community College *C, A*
Linn-Benton Community College *C, A*
Mt. Hood Community College *C, A*
Portland Community College *C, A*
Rogue Community College *A*
Southwestern Oregon Community
College *C, A*
Treasure Valley Community
College *C*
Umpqua Community College *A*

Pennsylvania

Bradford School: Pittsburgh *C, A*
Bucks County Community
College *C, A*
Butler County Community
College *C, A*
Community College of Allegheny
County *C, A*
Community College of Beaver
County *A*
Consolidated School of Business
Lancaster *A*
York *A*
Delaware County Community
College *C, A*
Everest Institute: Pittsburgh *A*
Gannon University *A*
Harrisburg Area Community
College *C, A*
Lansdale School of Business *C*
Lehigh Carbon Community
College *C, A*
Luzerne County Community
College *C, A*
Montgomery County Community
College *C, A*
Northampton Community
College *C, A*
Pace Institute *C*
Pennsylvania College of
Technology *A*
Pennsylvania Highlands Community
College *A*
Prism Career Institute *C, A*
South Hills School of Business &
Technology *C*
Westmoreland County Community
College *C, A*

South Carolina

Aiken Technical College *C*
York Technical College *C*

Tennessee

Chattanooga State Community
  College *A*
Daymar Institute
  Nashville *A*
ITT Technical Institute
  Memphis *B*
Pellissippi State Community
  College *A*
Southwest Tennessee Community
  College *C, A*

Texas

Austin Community College *C, A*
Brookhaven College *C*
Del Mar College *C, A*
ITT Technical Institute
  Austin *A*
  Richardson *A*
  San Antonio *A*
Lamar Institute of Technology *C, A*
Lamar State College at Orange *A*
Lamar State College at Port
  Arthur *C, A*
St. Edward's University *B*
St. Philip's College *C, A*
San Antonio College *C, A*
San Jacinto College *C*
Tarrant County College *C, A*
Tyler Junior College *C, A*

Utah

Salt Lake Community College *C, A*

Virginia

Piedmont Virginia Community
  College *A*
Southwest Virginia Community
  College *C*
Stratford University: Falls
  Church *C, A, B, M*

Washington

Bellevue College *C, A*
Bellingham Technical College *C, A*
Big Bend Community College *C, A*
Clark College *C, A*
Clover Park Technical College *C, A*
Columbia Basin College *C, A*
DeVry University
  Federal Way *A*
Edmonds Community College *C, A*
Grays Harbor College *C, A*
Heritage University *C*
Lake Washington Institute of
  Technology *C, A*
Lower Columbia College *C, A*
North Seattle Community
  College *C, A*
Olympic College *C, A*
Peninsula College *C, A*
Pierce College *C, A*
Renton Technical College *C, A*
Shoreline Community College *C, A*
Spokane Falls Community College *C*
Tacoma Community College *C, A*
Walla Walla Community College *C, A*
Wenatchee Valley College *C, A*
Yakima Valley Community
  College *C, A*

West Virginia

American National University
  Parkersburg *C*
American Public University System *A*
Blue Ridge Community and Technical
  College *C*
Davis and Elkins College *A*
Kanawha Valley Community and
  Technical College *A*

Wisconsin

Fox Valley Technical College *C*
Herzing University
  Madison *C*
Milwaukee Area Technical College *C*
Northcentral Technical College *C*
Rasmussen College
  Appleton *C*
  Green Bay *C*
  Wausau *C*
Southwest Wisconsin Technical
  College *C*
Western Technical College *C*
Wisconsin Indianhead Technical
  College *C*

Wyoming

Casper College *C, A*
Central Wyoming College *C, A*

Acoustics

Pennsylvania

Penn State
  University Park *M, D*

Acting

California

Academy of Art University *A, B, M*
American Academy of Dramatic Arts:
  West *C, A*
Chapman University *B*
College of the Desert *A*
Grossmont College *C, A*
Monterey Peninsula College *C, A*
Moorpark College *C, A*
Pacific Union College *A*
Pepperdine University *B*
University of Southern
  California *B, M*

Colorado

Colorado Mountain College *C*
Community College of Aurora *C*

Connecticut

University of Connecticut *B*
University of Hartford *B*
Yale University *M*

Florida

Daytona State College *A*
Florida Southern College *B*
Florida State University *B, M*
University of Miami *B*

Illinois

Bradley University *B*
Columbia College Chicago *B*
DePaul University *B, M*
Illinois Wesleyan University *B*
Roosevelt University *B, M*
University of Illinois
  Urbana-Champaign *B*

Indiana

Purdue University *B, M*

Iowa

Coe College *B*
Drake University *B*
University of Northern Iowa *B*

Maine

University of Southern Maine *B*

Maryland

Stevenson University *B*
Towson University *B*
University of Maryland
  Baltimore County *B*

Massachusetts

Bard College at Simon's Rock *B*
Boston University *B, M*
Emerson College *B*
Salem State University *B*

Michigan

Aquinas College *B*
Central Michigan University *B*
Michigan State University *B, M*
Oakland University *B*
Western Michigan University *B*

Minnesota

Saint Cloud State University *B*

Mississippi

Mississippi University for Women *M*

Missouri

Lindenwood University *B*
Northwest Missouri State
  University *B*
Webster University *B*

New Hampshire

Keene State College *B*

New Jersey

Cumberland County College *A*
Kean University *B*

New Mexico

Santa Fe University of Art and
  Design *B*

New York

American Academy of Dramatic
  Arts *A*
Bard College *B*
Cornell University *M*
Five Towns College *B*
Hofstra University *B*
Ithaca College *B*
Juilliard School *C*
Marymount Manhattan College *B*
Nazareth College *B*
Pace University *B*
SUNY
  College at Fredonia *B*
  University at Binghamton *B*
Syracuse University *B*

North Carolina

East Carolina University *B*
Elon University *B*

Ohio

Ashland University *B*
Baldwin Wallace University *B*
Ohio University *B, M*
Otterbein University *B*
Wright State University *B*
Youngstown State University *B*

Oklahoma

Oklahoma City University *B*
Oral Roberts University *B*

Pennsylvania

Arcadia University *B*
Lycoming College *B*
Montgomery County Community
  College *A*
Northampton Community College *A*
Penn State
  Abington *B*
  Altoona *B*
  Beaver *B*
  Berks *B*
  Brandywine *B*
  DuBois *B*
  Erie, The Behrend College *B*

Fayette, The Eberly Campus *B*
  Greater Allegheny *B*
  Harrisburg *B*
  Hazleton *B*
  Lehigh Valley *B*
  Mont Alto *B*
  New Kensington *B*
  Schuylkill *B*
  Shenango *B*
  University Park *B*
  Wilkes-Barre *B*
  Worthington Scranton *B*
  York *B*
Point Park University *M*
Seton Hill University *B*
Slippery Rock University of
  Pennsylvania *B*
Temple University *B, M*
University of the Arts *B*

South Carolina

Coker College *B*

Tennessee

Belmont University *B*
Chattanooga State Community
  College *C*
Freed-Hardeman University *B*

Texas

Baylor University *B*
St. Edward's University *B*
Texas Christian University *B*

Utah

Brigham Young University *B*

Vermont

Bennington College *B*

Virginia

Emory & Henry College *B*
Old Dominion University *B*
Regent University *M*
Shenandoah University *B*

Washington

Cornish College of the Arts *B*

Wyoming

Casper College *A*
Central Wyoming College *A*

Actuarial science

California

Master's College *B*

Connecticut

University of Connecticut *B*

Florida

Florida State University *B*

Georgia

Georgia State University *B, M*

Illinois

Aurora University *B*
Bradley University *B*
North Central College *B*
Roosevelt University *B*
University of Illinois
  Urbana-Champaign *B, M, D*
University of St. Francis *B*

Indiana

Ball State University *B, M*
Butler University *B*
Indiana University
  Northwest *B*
  South Bend *B*

Purdue University *B*
Valparaiso University *B*

Iowa
Central College *B*
Dordt College *B*
Drake University *B*
Northwestern College *B*
University of Iowa *B, M*

Kentucky
Bellarmine University *B*

Maine
University of Maine
Farmington *B*

Massachusetts
Bentley University *B*
Boston University *M*
Worcester Polytechnic Institute *B*

Michigan
Central Michigan University *B*
Eastern Michigan University *B*
Oakland University *B*
Spring Arbor University *B*
University of Michigan
Flint *B*

Minnesota
St. Mary's University of Minnesota *B*
University of Minnesota
Twin Cities *B*
University of St. Thomas *B*

Missouri
Maryville University of Saint
Louis *B, M*
University of Central Missouri *B*

Nebraska
University of Nebraska
Lincoln *B, M*

New York
City University of New York
Baruch College *B*
Queens College *B*
SUNY
University at Binghamton *B*
St. John's University *B*
Siena College *B*

North Carolina
Appalachian State University *B*
High Point University *B*

Ohio
Ashland University *B*
Bowling Green State University *B*
Ohio State University
Columbus Campus *B*
Ohio University *B*
Otterbein University *B, M*
Xavier University *B*

Oklahoma
University of Central Oklahoma *B*

Pennsylvania
Arcadia University *B*
Carnegie Mellon University *B, M*
Lebanon Valley College *B*
Lycoming College *B*
Mansfield University of
Pennsylvania *B*
Penn State
Abington *C*
Altoona *C*
Beaver *C*
Berks *C*
Brandywine *C*

DuBois *C*
Erie, The Behrend College *C*
Fayette, The Eberly Campus *C*
Greater Allegheny *C*
Harrisburg *C*
Hazleton *C*
Lehigh Valley *C*
Mont Alto *C*
New Kensington *C*
Schuylkill *C*
Shenango *C*
University Park *C*
Wilkes-Barre *C*
Worthington Scranton *C*
York *C*
Robert Morris University *B*
Saint Joseph's University *B*
Seton Hill University *B*
Slippery Rock University of
Pennsylvania *B*
Temple University *B, M*
Thiel College *B*
University of Pennsylvania *B*

Rhode Island
Bryant University *B*

South Carolina
Bob Jones University *B*

Texas
Texas Christian University *B*
University of Texas
Dallas *B, M*
San Antonio *B*

Utah
Brigham Young University *D*

Washington
Central Washington University *B*

Wisconsin
Carroll University *B*
Concordia University Wisconsin *B*
Milwaukee School of Engineering *B*
University of Wisconsin
Madison *B*
Milwaukee *B*

Acupuncture

California
Pacific College of Oriental Medicine:
San Diego *M, D*

Connecticut
University of Bridgeport *M*

Florida
Florida College of Natural Health
Pompano Beach *C*

Illinois
National University of Health
Sciences *M*

Minnesota
Northwestern Health Sciences
University *M*

Washington
Bastyr University *B, M, D*

Administrative/
secretarial services

Alabama
Alabama Southern Community
College *C, A*
Bevill State Community College *C, A*
Bishop State Community College *A*

Central Alabama Community
College *C, A*
Chattahoochee Valley Community
College *C, A*
Enterprise State Community
College *C, A*
Faulkner State Community
College *C, A*
Gadsden State Community
College *C, A*
George C. Wallace Community
College at Dothan *C, A*
George C. Wallace State Community
College at Selma *C, A*
Jefferson Davis Community
College *C, A*
Jefferson State Community
College *C, A*
Lawson State Community College *A*
Lurleen B. Wallace Community
College *A*
Northeast Alabama Community
College *C, A*
Northwest-Shoals Community
College *C, A*
Shelton State Community
College *C, A*
Snead State Community College *C, A*
Southern Union State Community
College *C, A*
Virginia College
Birmingham *A*
Huntsville *A*
Mobile *C, A*
Montgomery *A*
Wallace State Community College at
Hanceville *A*

Alaska
University of Alaska
Anchorage *C, A*
Fairbanks *C*
Southeast *A*

Arizona
Brown Mackie College
Tucson *A*
Central Arizona College *C, A*
Cochise College *A*
Dine College *C, A*
Eastern Arizona College *C, A*
GateWay Community College *A*
Glendale Community College *C, A*
Mesa Community College *C*
Mohave Community College *C, A*
Northland Pioneer College *C, A*
Paradise Valley Community
College *C, A*
Phoenix College *C, A*
Pima Community College *C, A*
Scottsdale Community College *A*
South Mountain Community
College *A*
Tohono O'odham Community
College *C*
Yavapai College *C, A*

Arkansas
Arkansas Northeastern College *A*
Arkansas State University
Mountain Home *A*
Arkansas Tech University *C, A*
Black River Technical College *C*
Cossatot Community College of the
University of Arkansas *C*
East Arkansas Community
College *C, A*
National Park Community College *A*
North Arkansas College *C*
Northwest Arkansas Community
College *A*
Philander Smith College *B*
Rich Mountain Community
College *C, A*

South Arkansas Community
College *C, A*
Southeast Arkansas College *C*
University of Arkansas
Community College at Batesville *A*
Monticello *C*

California
Allan Hancock College *C, A*
American River College *C, A*
Antelope Valley College *C, A*
Bakersfield College *C, A*
Barstow Community College *C*
Butte College *C, A*
Canada College *C, A*
Cerritos College *A*
Cerro Coso Community College *C, A*
Chabot College *C, A*
Chaffey College *C, A*
Citrus College *C, A*
City College of San Francisco *C, A*
Coastline Community College *C*
College of Alameda *C, A*
College of the Canyons *C, A*
College of the Redwoods *A*
College of the Sequoias *C, A*
College of the Siskiyous *C, A*
Columbia College *C, A*
Contra Costa College *C, A*
Crafton Hills College *C, A*
Cypress College *C, A*
De Anza College *C, A*
Diablo Valley College *C*
East Los Angeles College *C, A*
El Camino College *C, A*
Empire College *C, A*
Evergreen Valley College *A*
Feather River College *C, A*
Folsom Lake College *A*
Fresno City College *C, A*
Fullerton College *A*
Glendale Community College *C, A*
Golden West College *C, A*
Grossmont College *C, A*
Hartnell College *C, A*
Humphreys College *C, A, B*
Imperial Valley College *C, A*
Kaplan College
Riverside *C*
Laney College *C, A*
Lassen Community College *C, A*
Long Beach City College *C, A*
Los Angeles City College *C, A*
Los Angeles Harbor College *C, A*
Los Angeles Mission College *C, A*
Los Angeles Southwest College *A*
Los Angeles Trade and Technical
College *C, A*
Los Angeles Valley College *C, A*
Mendocino College *C, A*
Merced College *C, A*
MiraCosta College *C, A*
Mission College *A*
Modesto Junior College *C, A*
Mount San Antonio College *C, A*
Napa Valley College *C, A*
Ohlone College *C, A*
Orange Coast College *C, A*
Oxnard College *C, A*
Palomar College *C, A*
Pasadena City College *C, A*
Porterville College *A*
Sacramento City College *C, A*
Saddleback College *C, A*
San Bernardino Valley College *C*
San Deigo Miramar College
San Diego Miramar College *C, A*
San Diego City College *C, A*
San Joaquin Delta College *C*
San Jose City College *A*
Santa Barbara City College *C, A*
Santa Monica College *C, A*
Santa Rosa Junior College *C*
Shasta College *C, A*
Sierra College *C, A*

Skyline College *C, A*
Solano Community College *C, A*
Southern California Institute of
Technology *C*
Ventura College *C, A*
Victor Valley College *C, A*
West Hills College: Coalinga *C, A*
West Los Angeles College *C, A*
West Valley College *C, A*
Woodland Community College *C, A*
Yuba College *C, A*

Colorado

Aims Community College *C, A*
Arapahoe Community College *C, A*
Community College of Denver *C, A*
IBMC College
    Fort Collins *C, A*
Otero Junior College *A*
Pueblo Community College *C*

Connecticut

Capital Community College *C, A*
Gateway Community College *C, A*
Housatonic Community College *C, A*
Manchester Community College *C, A*
Middlesex Community College *A*
Naugatuck Valley Community
    College *C, A*
Quinebaug Valley Community
    College *C, A*
Tunxis Community College *C, A*

District of Columbia

University of the District of
    Columbia *A, B*

Florida

Broward College *C*
Eastern Florida State College *A*
Florida Gateway College *C*
Florida State College at
    Jacksonville *C, A*
Hobe Sound Bible College *A*
Indian River State College *A*
Lincoln College of Technology
    West Palm Beach *A*
Miami Dade College *C, A*
Pensacola State College *A*
Seminole State College of Florida *A*
South Florida State College *C*
Tallahassee Community College *C, A*
Virginia College
    Pensacola *A*

Georgia

Albany Technical College *C*
Athens Technical College *C, A*
Atlanta Technical College *C, A*
Augusta Technical College *A*
Bainbridge College *C, A*
Central Georgia Technical
    College *C, A*
Chattahoochee Technical College *A*
Clayton State University *A*
Columbus Technical College *C, A*
Darton College *A*
Georgia Piedmont Technical
    College *C, A*
Gwinnett College *C*
Gwinnett Technical College *C, A*
Savannah Technical College *C, A*
Southeastern Technical College *C*
Southern Crescent Technical
    College *A*
Southwest Georgia Technical
    College *C, A*
University of North Georgia *A*
Valdosta State University *B*
West Georgia Technical College *A*

Hawaii

University of Hawaii
    Hawaii Community College *C, A*
    Leeward Community College *C, A*

Idaho

College of Western Idaho *C, A*
Eastern Idaho Technical College *C, A*
Idaho State University *C, A, B*
Lewis-Clark State College *C, A, B*
North Idaho College *A*

Illinois

Black Hawk College *C, A*
Carl Sandburg College *C, A*
City Colleges of Chicago
    Kennedy-King College *C, A*
College of DuPage *C, A*
College of Lake County *C, A*
Danville Area Community College *C*
East-West University *A*
Elgin Community College *C*
Harper College *C*
Heartland Community College *C*
Highland Community College *C, A*
Illinois Central College *C, A*
Illinois Eastern Community Colleges
    Frontier Community College *C, A*
    Lincoln Trail College *C, A*
    Olney Central College *C, A*
    Wabash Valley College *C, A*
John Wood Community College *C, A*
Joliet Junior College *C, A*
Kankakee Community College *C, A*
Kaskaskia College *C*
Lake Land College *A*
Lincoln Land Community College *A*
McHenry County College *C, A*
Midstate College *A*
Moraine Valley Community
    College *C, A*
Morton College *C, A*
Oakton Community College *C*
Parkland College *C*
Prairie State College *C*
Rend Lake College *C, A*
Rock Valley College *C, A*
St. Augustine College *C, A*
Sauk Valley Community College *A*
South Suburban College of Cook
    County *C, A*
Southeastern Illinois College *C, A*
Spoon River College *C, A*
Triton College *C*

Indiana

Ball State University *A*
Harrison College
    Indianapolis *C, A*
International Business College *C, A*
International Business College:
    Indianapolis *C, A*
Ivy Tech Community College
    Northwest *A*
National College
    Indianapolis *A*
Vincennes University *C, A*

Iowa

Clinton Community College *C, A*
Dordt College *A*
Ellsworth Community College *A*
Faith Baptist Bible College and
    Theological Seminary *A, B*
Iowa Central Community
    College *C, A*
Iowa Lakes Community College *C*
Kirkwood Community College *C, A*
Marshalltown Community College *A*
North Iowa Area Community
    College *C, A*
Northeast Iowa Community
    College *C, A*
Northwest Iowa Community
    College *C*
Southeastern Community
    College *C, A*
Southwestern Community College *A*

Western Iowa Tech Community
    College *C, A*

Kansas

Allen County Community College *A*
Barton County Community College *A*
Cloud County Community
    College *C, A*
Coffeyville Community College *A*
Colby Community College *C, A*
Cowley County Community
    College *C, A*
Fort Hays State University *A*
Fort Scott Community College *C, A*
Garden City Community College *C*
Haskell Indian Nations University *A*
Highland Community College *C, A*
Hutchinson Community College *C, A*
Independence Community College *A*
Johnson County Community
    College *C, A*
Kansas City Kansas Community
    College *C, A*
Manhattan Area Technical
    College *C, A*
Neosho County Community
    College *C, A*
Seward County Community
    College *C, A*
Tabor College *A, B*
Washburn University *C, A*

Kentucky

Big Sandy Community and Technical
    College *A*
Bluegrass Community and Technical
    College *C, A*
Daymar College
    Owensboro *C, A*
    Paducah *C*
Eastern Kentucky University *A*
Henderson Community College *A*
Madisonville Community College *A*
National College
    Danville *C, A*
    Florence *C, A*
    Lexington *C, A*
    Louisville *A*
    Pikeville *C, A*
    Richmond *C, A*
Owensboro Community and
    Technical College *C*
Somerset Community College *C*
Southeast Kentucky Community and
    Technical College *C, A*
Spencerian College *C*
West Kentucky Community and
    Technical College *A*

Louisiana

Delgado Community College *C, A*
ITI Technical College *A*
Louisiana State University
    Eunice *C, A*
Nunez Community College *C*
Virginia College
    Baton Rouge *C*

Maine

Beal College *C, A*
Eastern Maine Community College *A*
Kaplan University
    South Portland *A*
Northern Maine Community
    College *A*

Maryland

Allegany College of Maryland *C, A*
Baltimore City Community College *A*
Carroll Community College *C*
College of Southern Maryland *C*
Community College of Baltimore
    County *C, A*
Harford Community College *C*

Howard Community College *C, A*
Kaplan University
    Hagerstown *A*
Prince George's Community
    College *C, A*
TESST College of Technology
    Towson *C*
Wor-Wic Community College *C, A*

Massachusetts

Cape Cod Community College *C, A*
Greenfield Community College *C, A*
Holyoke Community College *C, A*
Mount Wachusett Community
    College *C*
Northern Essex Community
    College *A*
Roxbury Community College *A*
Springfield Technical Community
    College *C, A*

Michigan

Baker College
    Auburn Hills *C, A*
    Cadillac *A*
    Clinton Township *C, A, B*
    Flint *C, A*
    Jackson *C, A*
    Muskegon *C, A, B*
    Owosso *A, B*
    Port Huron *C, A, B*
Bay de Noc Community College *C, A*
Delta College *C, A*
Glen Oaks Community College *C*
Henry Ford Community College *C*
Kalamazoo Valley Community
    College *C, A*
Kellogg Community College *C, A*
Kirtland Community College *C, A*
Lake Michigan College *A*
Macomb Community College *C, A*
Mid Michigan Community
    College *C, A*
Monroe County Community
    College *C, A*
Montcalm Community College *A*
Mott Community College *A*
Muskegon Community College *C, A*
North Central Michigan College *A*
Northern Michigan University *A*
Northwestern Michigan College *C*
Schoolcraft College *C, A*
Southwestern Michigan College *C*
Washtenaw Community College *C, A*
West Shore Community College *A*

Minnesota

Alexandria Technical and Community
    College *C*
Anoka Technical College *C, A*
Anoka-Ramsey Community College *C*
Central Lakes College *A*
Century College *A*
Dakota County Technical College *C*
Globe University
    Minneapolis *C*
    Moorhead *C*
    Woodbury *C*
Hibbing Community College *A*
Mesabi Range Community and
    Technical College *A*
Minneapolis Business College *A*
Minneapolis Community and
    Technical College *C*
Minnesota School of Business
    Blaine *C*
    Brooklyn Center *C*
    Elk River *C*
    Lakeville *C*
    Plymouth *C*
    Richfield *C*
    Rochester *C*
    St. Cloud *C*
    Shakopee *C*

Minnesota State College - Southeast
Technical *C, A*
Minnesota State Community and
Technical College *C, A*
Minnesota West Community and
Technical College *A*
Northland Community & Technical
College *C, A*
Northwest Technical College *C, A*
Ridgewater College *C*
Riverland Community College *C, A*
Rochester Community and Technical
College *C, A*
St. Cloud Technical and Community
College *A*
St. Paul College *C, A*
South Central College *C, A*

Mississippi

East Mississippi Community
College *C, A*
Hinds Community College *C, A*
Holmes Community College *C, A*
Itawamba Community College *A*
Meridian Community College *C, A*
Mississippi Delta Community
College *C, A*
Mississippi Gulf Coast Community
College *C, A*
Northeast Mississippi Community
College *C, A*

Missouri

Baptist Bible College *A, B*
Crowder College *C, A*
East Central College *C, A*
Jefferson College *A*
Metropolitan Community College -
Kansas City *C, A*
Mineral Area College *C, A*
Northwest Missouri State
University *B*
Ozarks Technical Community
College *A*
St. Louis Community College *C, A*
State Fair Community College *C*
Three Rivers Community College *A*

Montana

Chief Dull Knife College *C*
Dawson Community College *C, A*
Fort Peck Community College *C, A*
Helena College University of
Montana *A*
Miles Community College *A*
Montana State University
Billings *C, A*
Montana Tech of the University of
Montana *A*
Salish Kootenai College *C, A*
University of Montana *C, A*

Nebraska

Central Community College *C, A*
Kaplan University
Lincoln *A*
Metropolitan Community
College *C, A*
Midland University *A*
Northeast Community College *A*
Southeast Community College *C, A*
Western Nebraska Community
College *C, A*
Wright Career College
Omaha *C*

Nevada

College of Southern Nevada *A*
Everest College
Las Vegas *A*
Great Basin College *C, A*
Truckee Meadows Community
College *A*

New Hampshire

Great Bay Community College *C, A*
Lakes Region Community College *C*
Manchester Community College *C, A*
White Mountains Community
College *C, A*

New Jersey

Atlantic Cape Community College *A*
Bergen Community College *C, A*
Camden County College *C*
Cumberland County College *C, A*
Essex County College *A*
Gloucester County College *C, A*
Hudson County Community
College *C, A*
Mercer County Community
College *C, A*
Ocean County College *C*
Raritan Valley Community College *C*
Rider University *A*
Salem Community College *C*
Sussex County Community College *C*
Union County College *C, A*

New Mexico

Central New Mexico Community
College *C, A*
Clovis Community College *C*
Dona Ana Community College of
New Mexico State
University *C, A*
Eastern New Mexico University:
Roswell *C, A*
Luna Community College *C, A*
Navajo Technical University *C, A*
New Mexico Junior College *C, A*
New Mexico State University
Alamogordo *C, A*
Carlsbad *C, A*
Grants *C*
Northern New Mexico College *C, A*
San Juan College *C*
Santa Fe Community College *C*

New York

Bramson ORT College *A*
Briarcliffe College *A*
Broome Community College *C*
Bryant & Stratton College
Albany *A*
Buffalo *A*
Henrietta *A*
Rochester *C, A*
Syracuse *A*
Syracuse North *A*
City University of New York
Borough of Manhattan Community
College *A*
Bronx Community College *A*
Hostos Community College *A*
LaGuardia Community
College *C, A*
Queensborough Community
College *A*
Columbia-Greene Community
College *C, A*
Concordia College *A*
Corning Community College *C, A*
Finger Lakes Community
College *C, A*
Fulton-Montgomery Community
College *A*
Genesee Community College *C, A*
Globe Institute of Technology *C*
Hudson Valley Community College *A*
Jamestown Business College *C, A*
Jamestown Community College *C, A*
Jefferson Community College *C, A*
Mildred Elley
Albany *C*
Mohawk Valley Community
College *C, A*
Monroe Community College *C, A*

Nassau Community College *A*
Niagara County Community
College *C, A*
Orange County Community
College *C, A*
Rockland Community College *C*
SUNY
College of Agriculture and
Technology at Morrisville *A*
College of Technology at Delhi *A*
Sanford-Brown Institute
Melville *A*
Sullivan County Community
College *C, A*
Tompkins Cortland Community
College *C, A*
Trocaire College *A*
Utica School of Commerce *C, A*
Westchester Community College *C, A*
Wood Tobe-Coburn School *C, A*

North Carolina

Alamance Community College *A*
Asheville-Buncombe Technical
Community College *A*
Beaufort County Community
College *A*
Blue Ridge Community College *C, A*
Brunswick Community College *C, A*
Caldwell Community College and
Technical Institute *C, A*
Cape Fear Community College *A*
Carteret Community College *A*
Central Carolina Community
College *A*
Central Piedmont Community
College *A*
Coastal Carolina Community
College *C, A*
College of the Albemarle *A*
Durham Technical Community
College *C, A*
Edgecombe Community College *A*
Gaston College *A*
Haywood Community College *C, A*
King's College *C, A*
Mayland Community College *A*
Mitchell Community College *C, A*
Nash Community College *A*
Piedmont Community College *A*
Randolph Community College *A*
Richmond Community College *C, A*
Roanoke-Chowan Community
College *A*
Sampson Community College *A*
Sandhills Community College *A*
Southwestern Community
College *C, A*
Tri-County Community College *A*
Vance-Granville Community
College *C, A*
Wake Technical Community
College *A*
Western Piedmont Community
College *C, A*

North Dakota

Bismarck State College *C, A*
Cankdeska Cikana Community
College *A*
Dakota College at Bottineau *A*
Dickinson State University *A*
Fort Berthold Community College *C*
Lake Region State College *C, A*
North Dakota State College of
Science *C, A*
United Tribes Technical College *C, A*
Williston State College *C, A*

Ohio

Bowling Green State University:
Firelands College *A*

Bryant & Stratton College
Cleveland *A*
Eastlake *A*
Parma *A*
Columbus State Community
College *A*
Cuyahoga Community College
Metropolitan *C, A*
Davis College *A*
Daymar College
Chillicothe *A*
ETI Technical College of Niles *C, A*
Eastern Gateway Community
College *C, A*
Edison State Community College *C*
Fortis College
Centerville *A*
Gallipolis Career College *A*
God's Bible School and College *A*
Hocking College *C, A*
James A. Rhodes State College *A*
Kent State University
Ashtabula *A*
Salem *A*
Trumbull *A*
Tuscarawas *A*
Lakeland Community College *C, A*
Lorain County Community College *A*
Marion Technical College *C, A*
Miami University
Middletown *C, A*
Oxford *A*
Miami-Jacobs Career College
Dayton *A*
National College
Cincinnati *C, A*
Stow *A*
Willoughby Hills *C*
North Central State College *A*
Northwest State Community
College *A*
Ohio Business College
Sandusky *C, A*
Sheffield *C, A*
Ohio University
Chillicothe Campus *A*
Southern State Community College *A*
Stark State College *A*
Trumbull Business College *A*
University of Akron *C*
University of Akron: Wayne
College *C, A*
University of Cincinnati
Blue Ash College *A*
Clermont College *A*
University of Northwestern Ohio *A*
University of Rio Grande *C, A*
Wright State University *M*
Zane State College *C, A*

Oklahoma

Carl Albert State College *A*
Eastern Oklahoma State College *A*
Murray State College *A*
Northeastern Oklahoma Agricultural
and Mechanical College *C, A*
Oklahoma Wesleyan University *A*
Tulsa Community College *C, A*
Western Oklahoma State College *A*

Oregon

Blue Mountain Community
College *C, A*
Chemeketa Community College *A*
Clackamas Community College *C, A*
Lane Community College *C*
Linn-Benton Community College *A*
Portland Community College *C, A*
Southwestern Oregon Community
College *A*
Umpqua Community College *C, A*

Pennsylvania

Baptist Bible College of
Pennsylvania *A, B*
Bradford School: Pittsburgh *C, A*
Butler County Community College *A*
Cambria-Rowe Business College *A*
Cambria-Rowe Business College:
Indiana *A*
Career Training Academy:
Monroeville *C*
Clarion University of Pennsylvania *C*
Community College of Allegheny
County *C, A*
Community College of
Philadelphia *A*
Consolidated School of Business
Lancaster *A*
York *A*
DuBois Business College *C*
DuBois Business College
Huntingdon *C*
Oil City *C*
Erie Business Center *A*
Everest Institute: Pittsburgh *A*
Harrisburg Area Community
College *C, A*
Kaplan Career Institute
Pittsburgh *A*
Keystone Technical Institute *C, A*
Lackawanna College *A*
Lehigh Carbon Community College *C*
Luzerne County Community
College *C, A*
McCann School of Business and
Technology
Hazleton *A*
Montgomery County Community
College *C, A*
Northampton Community College *A*
Pace Institute *A*
Penn Commercial Business and
Technical School *A*
Pennsylvania Highlands Community
College *A*
Pennsylvania Institute of Health and
Technology *A*
Reading Area Community
College *C, A*
South Hills School of Business &
Technology *C*
Westmoreland County Community
College *C, A*
Yorktowne Business Institute *A*

Puerto Rico

American University of Puerto
Rico *A, B*
Atlantic University College *A, B*
Bayamon Central University *A, B*
Caribbean University *B*
Columbia Centro Universitario:
Caguas *A*
EDP University of Puerto Rico: Hato
Rey *A*
Huertas College *A*
Humacao Community College *A*
ICPR Junior College *C, A*
Inter American University of Puerto
Rico
Arecibo Campus *A, B*
Barranquitas Campus *A, B*
Fajardo Campus *A, B*
Metropolitan Campus *A, B*
Ponce Campus *A, B*
Pontifical Catholic University of
Puerto Rico *A, B*
Universal Technology College of
Puerto Rico *A*
Universidad Adventista de las
Antillas *A, B*
Universidad del Este *B*
University College of San Juan *C, A*

University of Puerto Rico
Arecibo *B*
Carolina Regional College *B*
Cayey University College *B*
Humacao *B*
Mayaguez *B*
Ponce *A, B*
Rio Piedras *B*
Utuado *A*

Rhode Island

Community College of Rhode
Island *A*

South Carolina

Aiken Technical College *C, A*
Central Carolina Technical
College *C, A*
Denmark Technical College *C*
Florence-Darlington Technical
College *C, A*
Forrest Junior College *A*
Greenville Technical College *C, A*
Horry-Georgetown Technical
College *C, A*
Midlands Technical College *C, A*
Northeastern Technical College *C, A*
Orangeburg-Calhoun Technical
College *A*
Piedmont Technical College *C, A*
Spartanburg Community College *C, A*
Technical College of the
Lowcountry *C, A*
Tri-County Technical College *C, A*
Trident Technical College *C, A*
University of South Carolina
Lancaster *A*
Virginia College
Florence *C*
Williamsburg Technical College *C, A*
York Technical College *C, A*

South Dakota

Globe University
Sioux Falls *C*
Mount Marty College *C*
Northern State University *A*
Southeast Technical Institute *C*

Tennessee

Chattanooga State Community
College *A*
Cleveland State Community
College *C, A*
Daymar Institute
Clarksville *A*
National College of Business and
Technology
Bartlett *A*
Bristol *C, A*
Knoxville *A*
Madison *A*
Memphis *A*
Nashville *C, A*
Northeast State Community
College *C, A*
Pellissippi State Community
College *A*
South College *C*
Southwest Tennessee Community
College *A*
Tennessee State University *A, B*
Tennessee Temple University *A, B*
Virginia College
School of Business and Health in
Chattanooga *A*
School of Business and Health in
Knoxville *A*
Volunteer State Community
College *C*
West Tennessee Business
College *C, A*

Texas

Alvin Community College *C*
Amarillo College *C, A*
Angelina College *C, A*
Austin Community College *C, A*
Blinn College *C*
Brazosport College *C, A*
Cedar Valley College *C, A*
Central Texas College *C, A*
Coastal Bend College *C, A*
College of the Mainland *C, A*
Collin County Community College
District *C, A*
Del Mar College *C, A*
El Centro College *C*
El Paso Community College *C, A*
Frank Phillips College *C, A*
Galveston College *C, A*
Grayson College *C, A*
Lamar Institute of Technology *C, A*
Lamar State College at Orange *C, A*
Lamar State College at Port
Arthur *C, A*
Laredo Community College *A*
Lee College *C, A*
Lone Star College System *C, A*
McLennan Community College *C*
Midland College *C*
Navarro College *C, A*
North Central Texas College *C, A*
North Lake College *C*
Northeast Texas Community
College *C, A*
Odessa College *C, A*
Palo Alto College *C, A*
Panola College *C*
Paris Junior College *C, A*
Ranger College *A*
Richland College *C, A*
St. Philip's College *C, A*
San Antonio College *C*
San Jacinto College *C, A*
South Plains College *A*
Southwest Texas Junior College *A*
Sul Ross State University *B*
Tarrant County College *C, A*
Temple College *C*
Texarkana College *C, A*
Texas State Technical College
Harlingen *C, A*
Texas Woman's University *B*
Trinity Valley Community
College *C, A*
Tyler Junior College *C, A*
Vernon College *A*
Victoria College *C, A*
Virginia College
Austin *C*
Weatherford College *C, A*
Western Texas College *C, A*
Wharton County Junior College *C*

Utah

LDS Business College *C*
Provo College *C, A*
Utah State University *C, A*
Utah Valley University *C*
Weber State University *A, B*

Virginia

American National University
Charlottesville *C, A*
Danville *C, A*
Harrisonburg *C, A*
Lynchburg *C, A*
Martinsville *C, A*
Salem *C, A*
Blue Ridge Community College *C, A*
Bryant & Stratton College
Richmond *A*
Virginia Beach *A*
Central Virginia Community
College *A*

Dabney S. Lancaster Community
College *A*
Danville Community College *A*
Lord Fairfax Community College *A*
New River Community College *A*
Northern Virginia Community
College *A*
Paul D. Camp Community College *A*
Piedmont Virginia Community
College *C*
Southside Virginia Community
College *A*
Southwest Virginia Community
College *C, A*
Tidewater Community College *A*
Virginia Baptist College *A*
Virginia Highlands Community
College *A*
Virginia Western Community
College *C, A*
Wytheville Community College *A*

Washington

Bates Technical College *C, A*
Bellevue College *C, A*
Clover Park Technical College *C*
Columbia Basin College *C*
Edmonds Community College *C*
Everett Community College *C, A*
Highline Community College *C, A*
Lake Washington Institute of
Technology *C, A*
Lower Columbia College *C, A*
North Seattle Community
College *C, A*
Olympic College *C, A*
Peninsula College *C, A*
Pierce College *A*
Renton Technical College *C, A*
Seattle Central Community
College *C, A*
Skagit Valley College *C, A*
South Puget Sound Community
College *C, A*
Spokane Community College *C, A*
Wenatchee Valley College *C*
Whatcom Community College *C*
Yakima Valley Community College *C*

West Virginia

American National University
Parkersburg *C*
Princeton *C, A*
Concord University *A*
Eastern West Virginia Community and
Technical College *C, A*
Kanawha Valley Community and
Technical College *A*
Mountain State College *A*
Potomac State College of West
Virginia University *A*
West Virginia Northern Community
College *C, A*

Wisconsin

Blackhawk Technical College *A*
Bryant & Stratton College
Milwaukee *A*
Chippewa Valley Technical College *A*
College of Menominee Nation *A*
Fox Valley Technical College *A*
Gateway Technical College *A*
Globe University
Appleton *C*
Eau Claire *C*
Green Bay *C*
La Crosse *C*
Madison East *C*
Middleton *C*
Wausau *C*
Lakeshore Technical College *A*
Madison Area Technical College *A*
Mid-State Technical College *A*

Milwaukee Area Technical
College *C, A*
Moraine Park Technical College *C, A*
Nicolet Area Technical College *A*
Northcentral Technical College *C, A*
Northeast Wisconsin Technical
College *A*
Southwest Wisconsin Technical
College *C, A*
Waukesha County Technical
College *A*
Western Technical College *A*
Wisconsin Indianhead Technical
College *C, A*

Wyoming

Casper College *C, A*
Central Wyoming College *A*
Eastern Wyoming College *A*
Northwest College *C, A*
Sheridan College *C, A*
Western Wyoming Community
College *C, A*

Adult/continuing education

Alabama

Auburn University *M, D*
Troy University *M*
University of West Alabama *M, T*

Arizona

Cochise College *A*

Arkansas

University of Arkansas *M, D*
University of Arkansas
Little Rock *M*

California

Patten University *B*
Whittier College *T*

Colorado

Colorado Christian University *B*
Colorado State University *M*
Regis University *M*

Connecticut

University of Connecticut *M, D, T*

Delaware

Delaware State University *D*

District of Columbia

George Washington University *M*

Florida

Florida International University *M, D*
University of South Florida *M*

Georgia

Armstrong Atlantic State
University *M*
University of Georgia *M, D, T*

Idaho

University of Idaho *M*

Illinois

Argosy University
Chicago *M*
National-Louis University *M, D*
University of Illinois
Urbana-Champaign *M*

Indiana

Ball State University *M, D*
Indiana University
Bloomington *M*

Iowa

University of Iowa *M, D*

Kansas

Kansas State University *M, D*

Kentucky

Morehead State University *M*
University of Louisville *M*
Western Kentucky University *M*

Louisiana

Louisiana State University and
Agricultural and Mechanical
College *B, M, D*
Northwestern State University *M*

Maine

University of Southern Maine *M*

Michigan

Michigan State University *M, D*
Robert B. Miller College *B*

Minnesota

Capella University *M, D*
University of Minnesota
Twin Cities *M, T*

Missouri

University of Central Missouri *M, T*
University of Missouri
St. Louis *M*

Nebraska

University of Nebraska
Lincoln *M*

Nevada

University of Nevada
Las Vegas *B, M*

New Jersey

Rutgers, The State University of New
Jersey
New Brunswick/Piscataway
Campus *M*

New York

Cornell University *D*
Elmira College *M*
SUNY
College at Buffalo *M*

North Carolina

North Carolina Agricultural and
Technical State University *M*

Ohio

Cleveland State University *M*

Oklahoma

Oklahoma State University *D*
University of Central Oklahoma *M*
University of Oklahoma *M, D*

Oregon

Oregon State University *M*
Portland State University *D*

Pennsylvania

Cheyney University of
Pennsylvania *M*
Indiana University of
Pennsylvania *M, T*
Penn State
Greater Allegheny *M*
Harrisburg *M, D*
University Park *M, D*

Texas

Midwestern State University *M*
Texas A&M University *M, D*

Texas A&M University
Commerce *M*
Texarkana *M*
Texas State University *M*

Virginia

James Madison University *M*
Regent University *M*
Virginia Commonwealth
University *M*

Washington

Eastern Washington University *M*
Seattle University *M*
Western Washington University *M*

Wisconsin

Alverno College *M*

Adult/continuing education administration

Alabama

Auburn University *M, D*

Arizona

Argosy University
Online *M*
University of Phoenix
Phoenix-Hohokam *M*
Southern Arizona *M*

Arkansas

University of Arkansas *M, D*

California

Trident University International *M*
University of Phoenix
Bay Area *M*
Central Valley *M*
Sacramento Valley *M*
San Diego *M*
Southern California *M*

Colorado

University of Phoenix
Denver *M*
Southern Colorado *M*

Florida

Nova Southeastern University *D*
University of Phoenix
Central Florida *M*
North Florida *M*
South Florida *M*
West Florida *M*

Georgia

Valdosta State University *M, D*

Hawaii

University of Phoenix
Hawaii *M*

Illinois

Bradley University *M*
Northern Illinois University *M, D*
University of Illinois
Urbana-Champaign *M, D*

Indiana

Ball State University *M*

Iowa

Drake University *M*
Iowa State University *M, D*

Maine

University of Southern Maine *M*

Maryland

Coppin State University *M*

Massachusetts

Harvard College *M, D*
Lesley University *M*

Michigan

Central Michigan University *M*
Grand Valley State University *M*
Marygrove College *M*
Michigan State University *M, D*
University of Phoenix
Metro Detroit *M*
West Michigan *M*

Minnesota

Walden University *M*

Mississippi

University of Southern Mississippi *M*

Missouri

University of Missouri
Columbia *M, D*
University of Phoenix
Kansas City *M*
St. Louis *M*

Nevada

University of Phoenix
Las Vegas *M*
Northern Nevada *M*

New Mexico

University of Phoenix
New Mexico *M*

New York

Fordham University *M, D*
SUNY
College at Buffalo *M*

North Carolina

East Carolina University *M*
North Carolina Agricultural and
Technical State University *M*
North Carolina State University *M, D*

Oregon

Oregon State University *M*

Pennsylvania

Penn State
University Park *M, D*
Widener University *M*

Puerto Rico

Universidad Metropolitana *M*
Universidad del Este *M*

South Dakota

University of South Dakota *M, D*

Tennessee

Tusculum College *M*
University of Phoenix
Chattanooga *M*
Nashville *M*

Texas

Argosy University
Dallas *M*
Texas A&M University
Kingsville *M*
Texas State University *D*
University of Phoenix
Austin *M*
Dallas Fort Worth *M*
Houston Westside *M*
San Antonio *M*

Virginia

University of Phoenix
Northern Virginia *M*
Richmond *M*

Wisconsin

Carroll University *M*

Adult development/aging

Alabama

University of Phoenix
Birmingham *M*

Arizona

Glendale Community College *C*
University of Phoenix
Phoenix-Hohokam *M*

Arkansas

University of Arkansas
Pine Bluff *C, B*

California

East Los Angeles College *C*
Folsom Lake College *C, A*
San Joaquin Delta College *C*
University of Phoenix
Bay Area *M*
Central Valley *M*
Sacramento Valley *M*
San Diego *M*
Southern California *M*

Colorado

University of Northern
Colorado *B, M*

Connecticut

Gateway Community College *C, A*

Florida

University of Phoenix
Central Florida *M*
North Florida *M*
South Florida *M*
West Florida *M*

Georgia

Georgia State University *C*
Southwest Georgia Technical
College *C*
University of Phoenix
Atlanta *M*
Augusta *M*
Columbus *M*
Savannah *M*

Hawaii

University of Phoenix
Hawaii *M*

Illinois

Spoon River College *C*

Iowa

Ashford University *B*

Kentucky

Western Kentucky University *C*

Louisiana

University of Phoenix
Baton Rouge *M*
Louisiana *M*
Shreveport *M*

Maryland

Notre Dame of Maryland
University *M*

Massachusetts

North Shore Community
College *C, A*

Michigan

Eastern Michigan University *M*
Ferris State University *C*
Grand Rapids Community College *C*
Lansing Community College *C*
Madonna University *C, A, B*
Oakland Community College *C, A*
University of Phoenix
Metro Detroit *M*
West Michigan *M*
Wayne County Community College *C*

Minnesota

University of Minnesota
Twin Cities *C*

New Jersey

Georgian Court University *C*

New York

City University of New York
LaGuardia Community College *A*
Genesee Community College *C*
Mercy College *C*
St. Joseph's College New York:
Suffolk Campus *C*
St. Joseph's College, New York *C*

Ohio

Bowling Green State University *B*
Cleveland State University *D*
Stark State College *A*
University of Cincinnati
Clermont College *C*

Oklahoma

University of Central Oklahoma *B*

Pennsylvania

Harrisburg Area Community
College *C*
Penn State
Abington *C*
Altoona *C*
Beaver *C*
Berks *C*
Brandywine *C*
DuBois *C*
Fayette, The Eberly Campus *C*
Greater Allegheny *C*
Harrisburg *C*
Hazleton *C*
Lehigh Valley *C*
Mont Alto *C*
New Kensington *C*
Schuylkill *C*
Shenango *C*
University Park *C*
Wilkes-Barre *C*
Worthington Scranton *C*
York *C*
Saint Joseph's University *M*

Rhode Island

Community College of Rhode
Island *A*

Tennessee

University of Phoenix
Chattanooga *M*

Texas

San Antonio College *C*
University of Phoenix
Austin *M*
Dallas Fort Worth *M*
Houston Westside *M*

Virginia

Virginia Commonwealth
University *M*

Adult health nursing

California

University of San Francisco *M*

Connecticut

Quinnipiac University *M, D*
Western Connecticut State
University *M*

Florida

Florida International University *M*
University of Tampa *M*

Illinois

DePaul University *M*
Loyola University Chicago *M*
Saint Anthony College of
Nursing *B, M*

Indiana

Goshen College *M*
Indiana University
Purdue University Indianapolis *M*

Iowa

Allen College *M*
University of Iowa *M*

Kansas

Washburn University *M*

Kentucky

Spalding University *M*

Louisiana

Louisiana State University
Health Sciences Center *M*

Massachusetts

Worcester State University *B*

Michigan

Madonna University *M*
Oakland University *M*
Wayne State University *M*

Minnesota

College of St. Scholastica *M*
Metropolitan State University *M*
Winona State University *M, D*

Missouri

Maryville University of Saint Louis *M*
Research College of Nursing *M*

Nebraska

Clarkson College *M*

New Jersey

Seton Hall University *M*

New York

Adelphi University *M*
City University of New York
College of Staten Island *M*
Hunter College *B, M*
College of New Rochelle *M*
Daemen College *M*
Long Island University
LIU Brooklyn *M*
Molloy College *M*
Mount Saint Mary College *M*
New York University *M, D*
SUNY
University at Binghamton *M*
University at Buffalo *M, D*
University at Stony Brook *M, D*

Sage Colleges *M*
University of Rochester *M*

Ohio

Case Western Reserve University *M*
University of Cincinnati *M*
University of Toledo *M*
Wright State University *M*
Youngstown State University *M*

Pennsylvania

Gwynedd Mercy University *M*
Neumann University *M*
Pennsylvania College of
Technology *B*
University of Pennsylvania *M*
University of Scranton *M*
Widener University *M*
York College of Pennsylvania *M*

South Carolina

Medical University of South
Carolina *M*

Tennessee

Southern Adventist University *M, D*
Vanderbilt University *M*

Virginia

James Madison University *M*

Wisconsin

Marian University *M*

Adult literacy instruction

Minnesota

University of Minnesota
Twin Cities *T*

Nevada

University of Nevada
Reno *M*

Advertising

Alabama

University of Alabama *B, M*

Arizona

Art Institute of Tucson *B*
Southwest University of Visual Arts *B*

Arkansas

Harding University *B*
University of Arkansas
Little Rock *B*

California

Academy of Art University *C, A, B, M*
Art Center College of Design *B*
Art Institute of California
San Diego *B*
California Lutheran University *B*
California State University
East Bay *B*
Fullerton *B*
Cosumnes River College *A*
Fullerton College *C*
Irvine Valley College *A*
La Sierra University *B*
Long Beach City College *C, A*
Los Angeles City College *A*
Los Angeles Southwest College *A*
Mount San Antonio College *A*
Orange Coast College *A*
Pacific Union College *B*
Palomar College *C, A*
Pepperdine University *B*
San Diego State University *B, M*
San Jose State University *B*

Santa Ana College *C, A*
University of San Francisco *B*

Colorado

Adams State University *B*
Trinidad State Junior College *A*
University of Denver *M*

Connecticut

Albertus Magnus College *B*
Middlesex Community College *C*
Quinnipiac University *B*
University of Bridgeport *B*

District of Columbia

University of the District of
Columbia *A*

Florida

Art Institute of Fort Lauderdale *B*
Barry University *B*
Florida State University *B*
Miami International University of Art
and Design *B*
Northwood University
Florida *B*
University of Central Florida *B*
University of Florida *B, M*
University of Miami *B*
University of Tampa *B*

Georgia

Art Institute of Atlanta *C, B*
University of Georgia *B*
Wesleyan College *B*

Hawaii

Hawaii Pacific University *B*

Idaho

Brigham Young University-Idaho *B*
University of Idaho *B*

Illinois

American Academy of Art *B*
Bradley University *B*
Columbia College Chicago *B*
Illinois Institute of Art
Chicago *A, B*
Schaumburg *B*
North Park University *B*
Northwestern University *C*
Oakton Community College *C*
University of Illinois
Urbana-Champaign *B, M, D*
University of St. Francis *B*

Indiana

Purdue University *B*
St. Mary-of-the-Woods College *B*
University of Southern Indiana *B*

Iowa

Drake University *B*
Iowa State University *B*
Morningside College *B*
St. Ambrose University *B*

Kansas

Independence Community College *A*

Kentucky

Murray State University *B*
Western Kentucky University *B*

Maryland

Harford Community College *C, A*
Montgomery College *C, A*

Massachusetts

American International College *B*
Babson College *B*
Boston University *B, M*

Emerson College *B, M*
Lasell College *B*
Salem State University *B*
Simmons College *B*
Suffolk University *B*

Michigan

Central Michigan University *B*
College for Creative Studies *B*
Ferris State University *B*
Grand Valley State University *B*
Michigan State University *B, M*
North Central Michigan College *C*
Northwood University
Michigan *B*
Spring Arbor University *B*
Western Michigan University *B*

Minnesota

Art Institutes International
Minnesota *B*
College of St. Scholastica *B*
Crown College *B*
Hennepin Technical College *C, A*
Metropolitan State University *B*
Minneapolis College of Art and
Design *B*
Minnesota State University
Moorhead *B*
North Hennepin Community
College *C*
Saint Cloud State University *B*
St. Cloud Technical and Community
College *C, A*
Winona State University *B*

Mississippi

East Mississippi Community
College *A*
Mississippi Delta Community
College *A*
University of Southern Mississippi *B*

Missouri

Drury University *B*
Fontbonne University *B*
Lindenwood University *B*
Northwest Missouri State
University *B*
Stephens College *B*
University of Missouri
Columbia *B*
Washington University in St. Louis *B*
Webster University *B, M*
Westminster College *B*

Nebraska

Hastings College *B*
University of Nebraska
Kearney *B*

New Hampshire

New England College *B*
Southern New Hampshire
University *B*

New Jersey

Rider University *B*
Rowan University *B*

New Mexico

Southwest University of Visual Arts *B*

New York

City University of New York
City College *B*
Fashion Institute of Technology *A, B*
Mohawk Valley Community
College *C, A*
Monroe Community College *A*
New York Institute of Technology *B*
New York University *M*
Pace University *B*

Pace University: Pleasantville/
Briarcliff *B*
Rochester Institute of Technology *B*
St. John's University *B*
St. Joseph's College New York:
Suffolk Campus *C*
St. Joseph's College, New York *C*
Syracuse University *B, M*

North Carolina

Alamance Community College *C*
Appalachian State University *B*
Campbell University *B*

North Dakota

Dakota College at Bottineau *C, A*

Ohio

Art Institute of Ohio: Cincinnati *B*
Ashland University *B*
Bowling Green State University *B*
Central Ohio Technical College *A*
Cincinnati State Technical and
Community College *C*
Kent State University *B*
Marietta College *B*
School of Advertising Art *A*
Xavier University *B*
Youngstown State University *B*

Oklahoma

Oklahoma Christian University *B*
Oklahoma City University *B*
University of Oklahoma *B*

Oregon

University of Oregon *B, M*

Pennsylvania

Art Institute of Philadelphia *B*
Art Institute of Pittsburgh *C, B*
Gannon University *B*
Luzerne County Community
College *C, A*
Penn State
Abington *C, B*
Altoona *C, B*
Beaver *C, B*
Berks *C, B*
Brandywine *C, B*
DuBois *C, B*
Erie, The Behrend College *C*
Fayette, The Eberly Campus *C, B*
Greater Allegheny *C, B*
Harrisburg *C, B*
Hazleton *C, B*
Lehigh Valley *C, B*
Mont Alto *C, B*
New Kensington *C, B*
Schuylkill *C, B*
Shenango *C, B*
University Park *B*
Wilkes-Barre *C, B*
Worthington Scranton *C, B*
York *C, B*
Point Park University *B*
Temple University *B*
University of Scranton *C*
Waynesburg University *B*

Puerto Rico

University of Puerto Rico
Carolina Regional College *B*
University of the Sacred Heart *B, M*

Rhode Island

Johnson & Wales University
Providence *B*

South Carolina

University of South Carolina
Columbia *B*

South Dakota

South Dakota State University *B*
Southeast Technical Institute *A*

Tennessee

Chattanooga State Community
College *A*
Lee University *B*
Southern Adventist University *B*
Union University *B*
University of Tennessee
Knoxville *B*

Texas

Amarillo College *A*
Dallas Baptist University *C*
Del Mar College *A*
Lamar University *B*
North Lake College *C*
Sam Houston State University *B*
Southern Methodist University *B*
Texas State University *B*
Texas Tech University *B*
University of Houston *B*
University of Texas
Arlington *B*
Austin *B, M, D*
El Paso *B*
West Texas A&M University *B*

Utah

Brigham Young University *B*

Virginia

Art Institute of Washington *B*
Hampton University *B*

Washington

Seattle Central Community
College *C, A*

West Virginia

Bethany College *B*
Concord University *B*
Kanawha Valley Community and
Technical College *C*
West Virginia University *B*

Wisconsin

Art Institute of Wisconsin *B*
Marquette University *B*

Aeronautical/
aerospace engineering

Alabama

Auburn University *B, M, D*
Tuskegee University *B*
University of Alabama *B, M, D*
University of Alabama
Huntsville *M, D*

Arizona

Arizona State University *B, M, D*
Embry-Riddle Aeronautical University
Prescott Campus *B*
University of Arizona *B, M, D*

California

California Institute of
Technology *M, D*
California Polytechnic State
University: San Luis Obispo *B, M*
California State Polytechnic
University: Pomona *B*
California State University
Long Beach *B, M*
Northridge *M*
San Diego State University *B, M*
San Jose State University *B, M*
Stanford University *M, D*

University of California
  Davis B
  Irvine B
  Los Angeles B, M, D
  San Diego B, M, D
University of Southern
  California B, M, D

Colorado
United States Air Force Academy B
University of Colorado
  Boulder B, M, D

Delaware
Delaware State University B
University of Delaware B

District of Columbia
George Washington University M, D

Florida
Embry-Riddle Aeronautical
  University B, M
Florida Institute of
  Technology B, M, D
University of Central Florida B, M
University of Florida B, M, D
University of Miami B

Georgia
Georgia Institute of
  Technology B, M, D

Idaho
Northwest Nazarene University B

Illinois
Illinois Institute of Technology B
University of Illinois
  Urbana-Champaign B, M, D

Indiana
Purdue University B, M, D
University of Notre Dame B, M

Iowa
Iowa State University B, M, D

Kansas
University of Kansas B, M, D
Wichita State University B, M, D

Maryland
United States Naval Academy B
University of Maryland
  College Park B, M, D

Massachusetts
Massachusetts Institute of
  Technology B, M, D
Worcester Polytechnic Institute B

Michigan
University of Michigan B, M, D
Western Michigan University B

Minnesota
University of Minnesota
  Twin Cities B, M, D

Mississippi
Mississippi State University B, M

Missouri
Missouri University of Science and
  Technology B, M, D
Saint Louis University B, M

New Hampshire
Daniel Webster College B

New Mexico
New Mexico State University B, M, D

New York
Clarkson University B
Cornell University M, D
Rensselaer Polytechnic
  Institute B, M, D
Rochester Institute of Technology B
SUNY
  University at Buffalo B, M, D
Syracuse University B

North Carolina
North Carolina State
  University B, M, D

Ohio
Case Western Reserve
  University B, M, D
Kent State University
  Ashtabula A
Ohio State University
  Columbus Campus B, M, D
University of Akron B
University of Cincinnati B, M, D
University of Dayton M, D

Oklahoma
Oklahoma State University B
Southeastern Oklahoma State
  University B
University of Oklahoma B, M, D

Pennsylvania
Penn State
  Abington B
  Altoona B
  Beaver B
  Berks B
  Brandywine B
  DuBois B
  Erie, The Behrend College B
  Fayette, The Eberly Campus B
  Greater Allegheny B
  Harrisburg B
  Hazleton B
  Lehigh Valley B
  Mont Alto B
  New Kensington B
  Schuylkill B
  Shenango B
  University Park C, B, M, D
  Wilkes-Barre B
  Worthington Scranton B
  York B

South Carolina
University of South Carolina
  Columbia M

Tennessee
University of Tennessee
  Knoxville B, M, D

Texas
Rice University M, D
Texas A&M University B, M, D
University of Houston M
University of Texas
  Arlington B, M, D
  Austin B, M, D

Utah
Utah State University M

Virginia
University of Virginia B
Virginia Polytechnic Institute and
  State University B, M, D

Washington
University of Washington B, M, D

West Virginia
West Virginia University B, M, D

Aeronautical/aerospace engineering technology

Alabama
Calhoun Community College A

Arizona
GateWay Community College A

Arkansas
Southern Arkansas University Tech C

California
Antelope Valley College C, A
Solano Community College A
University of California
  San Diego B

Delaware
Delaware Technical Community
  College
  Jack F. Owens Campus A

Georgia
Middle Georgia State College A

Hawaii
University of Hawaii
  Honolulu Community College A

Indiana
Purdue University A, B

Kansas
Wichita Area Technical College C, A

Maryland
Capitol College B
Prince George's Community
  College A

Missouri
Saint Louis University B

New York
Vaughn College of Aeronautics and
  Technology A

North Carolina
Lenoir Community College C, A

Ohio
Bowling Green State University B
Cincinnati State Technical and
  Community College C, A
Columbus State Community
  College A

Pennsylvania
Community College of Beaver
  County A

Texas
Laredo Community College A
LeTourneau University B

Washington
Bates Technical College C

West Virginia
Fairmont State University B

Aeronautics and aviation science

Alabama
Calhoun Community College A
Community College of the Air
  Force A

Arizona
Chandler-Gilbert Community
  College C, A
Embry-Riddle Aeronautical University
  Prescott Campus B

Arkansas
Henderson State University B
Northwest Arkansas Community
  College A

California
Chabot College A
City College of San Francisco C, A
Cypress College C, A
Glendale Community College C
Long Beach City College C, A
Mount San Antonio College A
Orange Coast College C, A
Pacific Union College A, B
San Diego Mesa College C
San Jose State University B
Santa Rosa Junior College C

Colorado
Colorado Northwestern Community
  College C, A

Connecticut
Naugatuck Valley Community
  College A
Three Rivers Community College A

Delaware
Delaware State University B
Wilmington University B

District of Columbia
University of the District of
  Columbia A, B

Florida
Broward College A
Embry-Riddle Aeronautical
  University B, M
Embry-Riddle Aeronautical University
  Worldwide Campus A, B, D
Everglades University
  Boca Raton B, M
Florida Institute of Technology B
Florida Memorial University B
Florida State College at
  Jacksonville A
Miami Dade College A
Palm Beach State College A

Indiana
Indiana State University A
Purdue University B

Iowa
Iowa Central Community
  College C, A
Iowa Lakes Community College A

Kansas
Central Christian College of Kansas A
Hesston College A
Kansas State University B

Kentucky
Eastern Kentucky University B

Louisiana
Louisiana Tech University B

Maryland
Cecil College C, A
Community College of Baltimore
  County C, A
University of Maryland
  Eastern Shore B

Massachusetts
Bridgewater State University *B*

Michigan
Andrews University *A, B*
Delta College *C, A*
Northwestern Michigan College *A*

Minnesota
Northland Community & Technical
    College *C*
University of Minnesota
    Crookston *B*

Mississippi
Delta State University *B*
Hinds Community College *C, A*

Montana
Montana State University *A*

Nebraska
University of Nebraska
    Omaha *B*

New Hampshire
Daniel Webster College *B*

New Jersey
County College of Morris *A*

New York
Dowling College *B*
Schenectady County Community
    College *A*
Vaughn College of Aeronautics and
    Technology *B*

North Carolina
Elizabeth City State University *B*

North Dakota
University of North Dakota *M, D*

Ohio
Kent State University *D*
Ohio State University
    Columbus Campus *B*
Ohio University *A, B*
Sinclair Community College *A*
University of Cincinnati
    Clermont College *A*

Oklahoma
Oklahoma City Community
    College *A*
Oklahoma State University *B*
Spartan College of Aeronautics and
    Technology *A*
University of Oklahoma *B*
Western Oklahoma State College *A*

Oregon
Umpqua Community College *A*

Pennsylvania
Lehigh Carbon Community College *A*

South Carolina
Greenville Technical College *C*
Trident Technical College *C*

South Dakota
South Dakota State University *B*

Tennessee
Middle Tennessee State University *B*

Texas
LeTourneau University *B*
Palo Alto College *A*
Texas Lutheran University *B*

Texas Southern University *B*
University of North Texas *B*

Utah
Westminster College *B*

Virginia
Averett University *B*
Liberty University *A, B*
Northern Virginia Community
    College *A*

Washington
Central Washington University *B*
Green River Community College *A*
Highline Community College *C, A*
South Seattle Community
    College *C, A*

West Virginia
American Public University
    System *C, B, M*
Fairmont State University *B*

Wyoming
Northwest College *A*

Aesthetician/skin care

Alabama
Gadsden State Community College *C*
Lurleen B. Wallace Community
    College *C*

California
Cerritos College *C, A*
San Jose City College *C*

Colorado
IBMC College
    Fort Collins *C*
Pueblo Community College *C*
Red Rocks Community College *C*
Trinidad State Junior College *C*

Florida
Indian River State College *C*
Pensacola State College *C*
Southeastern College
    Greenacres *C*

Georgia
Columbus Technical College *C*

Kansas
Johnson County Community
    College *C*

Kentucky
West Kentucky Community and
    Technical College *C*

Michigan
Mott Community College *C*

Minnesota
Minnesota State College - Southeast
    Technical *C*
Minnesota State Community and
    Technical College *C*
Ridgewater College *C*
St. Paul College *C, A*

New Mexico
Clovis Community College *C*

North Carolina
Brunswick Community College *C*
Cape Fear Community College *C*
Carteret Community College *C*
Central Carolina Community
    College *A*

Cleveland Community College *C*
Craven Community College *C*
Davidson County Community
    College *C*
Edgecombe Community College *C*
Fayetteville Technical Community
    College *C*
Isothermal Community College *C*
Miller-Motte College
    Cary *C*
    Wilmington *C*
Southeastern Community College *C*
Stanly Community College *C*

Puerto Rico
Caribbean University *C*

South Carolina
Horry-Georgetown Technical
    College *C*
Miller-Motte Technical College
    Conway *C*

Tennessee
Miller-Motte Technical College
    Chattanooga *C*

Texas
Panola College *C*

Virginia
Dabney S. Lancaster Community
    College *C*

Washington
Clover Park Technical College *C, A*
Olympic College *C*

Wisconsin
Southwest Wisconsin Technical
    College *C*

Wyoming
Eastern Wyoming College *C*

African-American studies

Alabama
Talladega College *B*
University of Alabama *B*
University of Alabama
    Birmingham *B*

Arizona
Arizona State University *B*
Mesa Community College *C*
University of Arizona *B*

Arkansas
Arkansas Baptist College *A, B*
University of Central Arkansas *B*

California
California State University
    Dominguez Hills *B*
    East Bay *B*
    Fresno *B*
    Fullerton *B*
    Long Beach *B*
    Los Angeles *B*
    Northridge *B*
    San Bernardino *B*
Claremont McKenna College *B*
College of Alameda *A*
Contra Costa College *A*
De Anza College *A*
El Camino College *A*
Fresno City College *A*
Laney College *A*
Los Angeles City College *A*
Los Angeles Southwest College *A*
Loyola Marymount University *B*

Merritt College *A*
Pitzer College *B*
Pomona College *B*
San Diego City College *A*
San Diego Mesa College *A*
San Diego State University *B*
San Francisco State University *B*
San Jose State University *B*
Santa Ana College *A*
Santa Barbara City College *A*
Scripps College *B*
Solano Community College *A*
Sonoma State University *B*
Southwestern College *A*
Stanford University *B*
University of California
    Berkeley *B, D*
    Davis *B*
    Irvine *B*
    Los Angeles *B, M*
    Riverside *B*
    Santa Barbara *B*
University of Southern California *B*

Colorado
Metropolitan State University of
    Denver *B*
University of Northern Colorado *B*

Connecticut
Trinity College *B*
University of Connecticut *B*
Wesleyan University *B*
Yale University *B, M, D*

District of Columbia
Howard University *B*

Florida
Florida Agricultural and Mechanical
    University *B*
Florida International University *M*
Florida State University *B*
University of Florida *B*
University of Miami *B*
University of South Florida *B*

Georgia
Atlanta Metropolitan College *A*
Clark Atlanta University *M, D*
Emory University *B*
Georgia State University *B, M*
Morehouse College *B*
University of Georgia *B*

Illinois
Chicago State University *B*
DePaul University *B*
Dominican University *B*
Eastern Illinois University *B*
Knox College *B*
Loyola University Chicago *B*
North Park University *B*
Northwestern University *B, D*
Roosevelt University *B*
Southern Illinois University
    Carbondale *B*
University of Chicago *B*
University of Illinois
    Chicago *B*
Western Illinois University *B*

Indiana
DePauw University *B*
Earlham College *B*
Indiana State University *B*
Indiana University
    Bloomington *B, M, D*
    Northwest *B*
    Purdue University
        Indianapolis *C, B*
Purdue University *B*
University of Notre Dame *B*

Iowa

Coe College *B*
Luther College *B*
University of Iowa *B, M*

Kentucky

Berea College *B*
University of Louisville *B, M, D*

Maine

Bates College *B*
Colby College *B*

Maryland

Morgan State University *B, M*
Prince George's Community
    College *A*
University of Maryland
    Baltimore County *B*
    College Park *B*
    Eastern Shore *B*

Massachusetts

Amherst College *B*
Bard College at Simon's Rock *B*
Boston University *M*
Brandeis University *B*
Hampshire College *B*
Harvard College *B, M*
Mount Holyoke College *B*
Northeastern University *B*
Smith College *B*
Tufts University *B*
University of Massachusetts
    Amherst *B, M, D*
    Boston *B*
Wellesley College *B*

Michigan

Eastern Michigan University *B, M*
Lansing Community College *A*
Michigan State University *B, M, D*
University of Detroit Mercy *C*
University of Michigan *B*
University of Michigan
    Flint *B*
Wayne State University *B*
Western Michigan University *B*

Minnesota

Carleton College *B*
University of Minnesota
    Twin Cities *B*

Mississippi

East Mississippi Community
    College *A*
University of Mississippi *B*

Missouri

Saint Louis University *B*
University of Missouri
    Columbia *B*
Washington University in St. Louis *B*

Nebraska

University of Nebraska
    Omaha *B*

New Hampshire

Dartmouth College *B*

New Jersey

Ramapo College of New Jersey *B*
Rutgers, The State University of New
    Jersey
    Camden Campus *B*
    New Brunswick/Piscataway
      Campus *B*
    Newark Campus *B*
Seton Hall University *B*
William Paterson University of New
    Jersey *B*

New Mexico

University of New Mexico *B*

New York

City University of New York
    Brooklyn College *B*
    City College *B*
    College of Staten Island *B*
    Hunter College *B*
    Lehman College *B*
    York College *B*
Colgate University *B*
Columbia University *B*
Columbia University
    School of General Studies *B*
Cornell University *B, M*
Fordham University *B*
Hamilton College *B*
Hobart and William Smith Colleges *B*
New York University *B, M*
SUNY
    College at Brockport *B*
    College at Cortland *B*
    College at Geneseo *B*
    College at New Paltz *B*
    College at Oneonta *B*
    University at Albany *B, M*
    University at Binghamton *B*
    University at Buffalo *B*
    University at Stony Brook *B*
Syracuse University *B*
University of Rochester *B*

North Carolina

Duke University *B*
East Carolina University *B*
Guilford College *B*
North Carolina State University *B*
St. Augustine's University *B*
University of North Carolina
    Chapel Hill *B*
    Charlotte *B*
    Greensboro *B*
Winston-Salem State University *B*

Ohio

Bowling Green State University *B*
College of Wooster *B*
Denison University *B*
Kent State University *B*
Miami University
    Oxford *B*
Oberlin College *B*
Ohio State University
    Columbus Campus *B, M*
Ohio University *B*
Ohio Wesleyan University *B*
University of Cincinnati *B*
University of Toledo *B*
Wright State University *B*
Youngstown State University *B*

Oklahoma

University of Oklahoma *B*

Pennsylvania

Franklin & Marshall College *B*
Gettysburg College *B*
Penn State
    Abington *B*
    Altoona *B*
    Beaver *B*
    Berks *B*
    Brandywine *B*
    DuBois *B*
    Erie, The Behrend College *D*
    Fayette, The Eberly Campus *B*
    Greater Allegheny *B*
    Harrisburg *B*
    Hazleton *B*
    Lehigh Valley *B*
    Mont Alto *B*
    New Kensington *B*
    Schuylkill *B*
    Shenango *B*
    University Park *B*
    Wilkes-Barre *B*
    Worthington Scranton *B*
    York *B*
Swarthmore College *B*
Temple University *B, M, D*
University of Pennsylvania *B*
University of Pittsburgh *B*

Rhode Island

Brown University *B*
Rhode Island College *B*
University of Rhode Island *B*

South Carolina

Claflin University *B*
Clemson University *B*
University of South Carolina
    Columbia *B*
Wofford College *B*

Tennessee

American Baptist College *A, B*
Rhodes College *B*
University of Memphis *B*
Vanderbilt University *B*

Texas

Southern Methodist University *B*
University of Texas
    Austin *B, M, D*

Vermont

Goddard College *B, M*

Virginia

College of William and Mary *B*
Old Dominion University *B*
University of Virginia *B*
Virginia Commonwealth University *B*

Washington

University of Washington *B*

Wisconsin

University of Wisconsin
    Madison *B, M*
    Milwaukee *B, D*

African languages

California

University of California
    Los Angeles *B*
Whittier College *B*

Massachusetts

Wellesley College *B*

Wisconsin

University of Wisconsin
    Madison *B, M, D*

African studies

California

Claremont McKenna College *B*
San Diego City College *A*
San Diego Mesa College *A*
Stanford University *M*
University of California
    Davis *B*
    Los Angeles *M*

Connecticut

Connecticut College *B*
Trinity College *B*
Yale University *B, M*

District of Columbia

Howard University *B, M, D*

Georgia

Agnes Scott College *B*
Emory University *B*
Kennesaw State University *B*
Mercer University *B*
Savannah State University *B*

Illinois

Augustana College *B*
Illinois Wesleyan University *B*
University of Chicago *B*
University of Illinois
    Urbana-Champaign *M*

Indiana

Indiana University
    Bloomington *M*

Iowa

University of Iowa *B*

Kansas

University of Kansas *B, M*

Kentucky

Kentucky State University *B*

Louisiana

Dillard University *B*
Tulane University *B*

Maine

Bowdoin College *B*

Maryland

Johns Hopkins University *B, D*

Massachusetts

Amherst College *B*
Hampshire College *B*
Simmons College *B*
Tufts University *B*
University of Massachusetts
    Amherst *C*
Wellesley College *B*

Minnesota

University of Minnesota
    Twin Cities *B*

New Hampshire

Dartmouth College *B*

New Jersey

Drew University *B*
Rowan University *B*
Rutgers, The State University of New
    Jersey
    Newark Campus *B*
William Paterson University of New
    Jersey *B*

New York

Bard College *B*
Barnard College *B*
City University of New York
    Queens College *B, T*
Colgate University *B*
Columbia University *B*
Columbia University
    School of General Studies *B*
Fordham University *B*
Hobart and William Smith Colleges *B*
Hofstra University *B*
Nassau Community College *A*
SUNY
    College at Brockport *B*
St. Lawrence University *B*
Syracuse University *M*
Union College *B*
United States Military Academy *B*
Vassar College *B*

North Carolina

Davidson College *B*

Ohio

Bowling Green State University *B*
College of Wooster *B*
Oberlin College *B*
Ohio University *B, M*
University of Akron *C*
University of Cincinnati *C*

Oregon

Portland State University *B*

Pennsylvania

Dickinson College *B*
Franklin & Marshall College *B*
Lafayette College *B*
Lehigh University *B*
University of Pennsylvania *B*

Rhode Island

Brown University *B*

Vermont

Middlebury College *B*

Virginia

University of Richmond *B*

Washington

University of Washington *B*

Agribusiness operations

Alabama

Alabama Agricultural and Mechanical
  University *M*

Arizona

Eastern Arizona College *A*
Mesa Community College *A*

Arkansas

Arkansas State University *B, M*
Arkansas State University
  Beebe *A*
Arkansas Tech University *B*
Cossatot Community College of the
  University of Arkansas *C, A*
Southern Arkansas University *A*
University of Arkansas *B*
University of Arkansas
  Monticello *B*
  Pine Bluff *B*

California

Allan Hancock College *C, A*
Bakersfield College *C, A*
California State University
  Fresno *B*
College of the Redwoods *A*
College of the Sequoias *C, A*
Hartnell College *C, A*
San Joaquin Delta College *C, A*
Santa Rosa Junior College *C, A*
Shasta College *C, A*

Colorado

Colorado State University *B*
Northeastern Junior College *C, A*

Delaware

University of Delaware *B*

Florida

Florida Agricultural and Mechanical
  University *B*
Miami Dade College *A*

Georgia

College of Coastal Georgia *A*
University of Georgia *B, M*

Idaho

Brigham Young University-Idaho *A*

Illinois

Kishwaukee College *A*

Indiana

Purdue University *M*

Iowa

Dordt College *B*
Iowa Central Community College *A*
Iowa State University *B*
Iowa Western Community College *A*
North Iowa Area Community
  College *A*
Northeast Iowa Community
  College *C, A*

Kansas

Barton County Community College *A*
Colby Community College *C, A*
Dodge City Community College *C, A*
Highland Community College *A*

Kentucky

Morehead State University *A*

Michigan

Michigan State University *C*

Minnesota

Ridgewater College *A*
South Central College *C, A*
Southwest Minnesota State
  University *A, B*
University of Minnesota
  Crookston *B*
  Twin Cities *B*

Mississippi

Hinds Community College *C, A*
Mississippi State University *B*
Northwest Mississippi Community
  College *A*

Missouri

Crowder College *A*
Missouri State University *B*
North Central Missouri College *C, A*
Northwest Missouri State
  University *B*
Southeast Missouri State University *B*
State Fair Community College *C, A*
William Woods University *M*

Montana

Montana State University
  Northern *A, B*

Nebraska

Nebraska College of Technical
  Agriculture *A*
Northeast Community College *A*

New Jersey

Burlington County College *A*
Salem Community College *A*

New Mexico

New Mexico State University *B*

New York

Cornell University *B*
SUNY
  College of Agriculture and
    Technology at Cobleskill *A, B*
  College of Agriculture and
    Technology at Morrisville *B*
  College of Technology at Alfred *A*

North Carolina

Bladen Community College *A*
James Sprunt Community College *A*
North Carolina State University *B*
Wayne Community College *C, A*

North Dakota

Dickinson State University *A*
North Dakota State University *B*
Sitting Bull College *A*

Ohio

Wilmington College *B*

Oklahoma

Northern Oklahoma College *A*
Northwestern Oklahoma State
  University *B*
Oklahoma Panhandle State
  University *B*

Pennsylvania

Delaware Valley College *B, M*
Harrisburg Area Community
  College *C, A*
Penn State
  Abington *B*
  Altoona *B*
  Beaver *B*
  Berks *B*
  Brandywine *B*
  DuBois *B*
  Erie, The Behrend College *B*
  Fayette, The Eberly Campus *B*
  Greater Allegheny *B*
  Harrisburg *B*
  Hazleton *B*
  Lehigh Valley *B*
  Mont Alto *B*
  New Kensington *B*
  Schuylkill *B*
  Shenango *B*
  University Park *B*
  Wilkes-Barre *B*
  Worthington Scranton *B*
  York *B*

Puerto Rico

University of Puerto Rico
  Mayaguez *B*

South Carolina

South Carolina State University *B*

South Dakota

Lake Area Technical Institute *A*
South Dakota State University *B*

Tennessee

Middle Tennessee State University *B*
Tennessee Technological
  University *B*

Texas

Abilene Christian University *B*
Sam Houston State University *B*
San Jacinto College *A*
Southwest Texas Junior College *A*
Stephen F. Austin State University *B*
Sul Ross State University *B, M*
Tarleton State University *B*
Texas A&M University *B, M*
Texas A&M University
  Commerce *B*
  Kingsville *B*
Texas State University *B*
West Texas A&M University *B, M*

Utah

Snow College *C, A*

Vermont

Vermont Technical College *A*

Virginia

Virginia Polytechnic Institute and
  State University *B*

Wisconsin

Fox Valley Technical College *C*
Northcentral Technical College *C, A*
Southwest Wisconsin Technical
  College *A*
University of Wisconsin
  Platteville *B*

Wyoming

Eastern Wyoming College *A*
Laramie County Community
  College *A*
Northwest College *A*
University of Wyoming *B*

Agricultural business

Alabama

Central Alabama Community
  College *A*
Faulkner State Community College *A*

Arizona

Arizona Western College *A*
Central Arizona College *C, A*
Cochise College *A*
University of Arizona *B*
Yavapai College *C, A*

Arkansas

Arkansas Northeastern College *C*
Cossatot Community College of the
  University of Arkansas *C, A*
Southern Arkansas University *B*

California

Butte College *C, A*
California Polytechnic State
  University: San Luis Obispo *B, M*
California State Polytechnic
  University: Pomona *B*
California State University
  Chico *C, B*
  Fresno *B*
College of the Desert *A*
College of the Redwoods *C*
Cosumnes River College *A*
Imperial Valley College *C, A*
Los Angeles Pierce College *C, A*
Merced College *A*
Modesto Junior College *A*
Mount San Antonio College *A*
Reedley College *C, A*
San Diego State University *B*
Santa Rosa Junior College *C*
Shasta College *A*
West Hills College: Coalinga *A*
Woodland Community College *C*
Yuba College *C, A*

Colorado

Adams State University *B*
Aims Community College *C, A*
Colorado Mesa University *A*
Lamar Community College *C, A*
Morgan Community College *C*

Delaware

Delaware State University *B*
Delaware Technical Community
  College
  Jack F. Owens Campus *A*
  Stanton/Wilmington Campus *A*
  Terry Campus *A*
University of Delaware *B*

Florida

College of Central Florida *A*
Florida Southern College *B*
Pensacola State College *A*

Georgia

Abraham Baldwin Agricultural
    College *A*
University of North Georgia *A*

Idaho

College of Southern Idaho *C, A*
University of Idaho *B*

Illinois

Black Hawk College *A*
Carl Sandburg College *A*
Danville Area Community College *A*
Highland Community College *A*
Illinois Central College *C, A*
John Wood Community College *A*
Kaskaskia College *C*
Kishwaukee College *C, A*
Lake Land College *C*
Parkland College *C, A*
Rend Lake College *A*
Richland Community College *A*
Sauk Valley Community College *A*
Shawnee Community College *A*
Spoon River College *A*
University of Illinois
    Urbana-Champaign *B, M, D*

Indiana

Purdue University *B, M*
Vincennes University *C, A*

Iowa

Dordt College *B*
Ellsworth Community College *C, A*
Graceland University *B*
Grand View University *B*
Iowa Western Community College *A*
Marshalltown Community College *A*
North Iowa Area Community
    College *A*
Southeastern Community College *A*
Southwestern Community College *A*

Kansas

Coffeyville Community College *A*
Dodge City Community College *A*
Fort Hays State University *B*
Fort Scott Community College *A*
Garden City Community College *A*
Independence Community College *A*
Kansas State University *B, M*
Pratt Community College *C, A*
Seward County Community
    College *A*

Kentucky

Henderson Community College *C*

Louisiana

Louisiana State University and
    Agricultural and Mechanical
    College *B*
Louisiana Tech University *B*
University of Louisiana at Monroe *B*

Maine

Northern Maine Community
    College *A*
University of Maine *B*

Maryland

Harford Community College *A*
University of Maryland
    Eastern Shore *B*

Massachusetts

Bristol Community College *C*

Michigan

Andrews University *A, B*
Delta College *A*
Lansing Community College *A*
Michigan State University *C, B*

Minnesota

Minnesota West Community and
    Technical College *A*
Ridgewater College *C, A*
University of Minnesota
    Twin Cities *B*

Mississippi

Alcorn State University *B*
Itawamba Community College *A*
Mississippi Delta Community
    College *A*
Mississippi State University *M*
Northeast Mississippi Community
    College *A*

Missouri

College of the Ozarks *B*
Lincoln University *B*
Missouri State University: West
    Plains *A*
Three Rivers Community College *A*
University of Central Missouri *B*
University of Missouri
    Columbia *B*

Montana

Dawson Community College *C, A*
Miles Community College *C, A*
Montana State University *B*
Rocky Mountain College *B*

Nebraska

Central Community College *C, A*
Concordia University *B*
Nebraska College of Technical
    Agriculture *C, A*
Northeast Community College *A*
Southeast Community College *A*
University of Nebraska
    Kearney *B*
    Lincoln *B*

New Jersey

County College of Morris *A*

New Mexico

Eastern New Mexico University *B*
Luna Community College *A*

New York

Cornell University *B*
SUNY
    College of Agriculture and
        Technology at Cobleskill *B*
    College of Agriculture and
        Technology at Morrisville *A*

North Carolina

Bladen Community College *A*
North Carolina State University *A*
University of Mount Olive *B*

North Dakota

Bismarck State College *A*
Dickinson State University *B*
Lake Region State College *A*
North Dakota State College of
    Science *A*

Ohio

Clark State Community College *A*
Ohio State University
    Agricultural Technical Institute *A*
    Columbus Campus *A, B*
Terra State Community College *A*

University of Northwestern

Ohio *C, A*
Wilmington College *B*

Oklahoma

Eastern Oklahoma State College *A*
Langston University *B*
Oklahoma State University *B*

Oregon

Blue Mountain Community College *A*
Chemeketa Community College *A*
Klamath Community College *A*
Linn-Benton Community College *A*
Oregon State University *B*
Treasure Valley Community
    College *C, A*

Puerto Rico

University of Puerto Rico
    Mayaguez *B*

South Carolina

Clemson University *B, M*

South Dakota

Oglala Lakota College *A*

Tennessee

Dyersburg State Community
    College *C*
Hiwassee College *A*
Jackson State Community College *A*
University of Tennessee
    Knoxville *B*
    Martin *M*

Texas

Clarendon College *A*
Frank Phillips College *C*
Hill College *A*
Howard College *A*
Navarro College *A*
Northeast Texas Community
    College *C, A*
South Plains College *A*
Southwest Texas Junior College *A*
Tarleton State University *B*
Texas A&M University *B, M, D*
Texas A&M University
    Kingsville *B, M*
Texas Tech University *B, M*
Trinity Valley Community College *A*
Weatherford College *C, A*
West Texas A&M University *B*

Utah

Snow College *A*
Utah State University *B*

Vermont

Vermont Technical College *A*

Virginia

Ferrum College *B*

Washington

Columbia Basin College *A*
Skagit Valley College *A*
Spokane Community College *A*
Walla Walla Community College *C, A*
Washington State University *B, M*
Wenatchee Valley College *C*
Yakima Valley Community
    College *C, A*

West Virginia

West Virginia University *B*

Wisconsin

Moraine Park Technical College *C*
Northcentral Technical College *C, A*

Northeast Wisconsin Technical

College *A*
Southwest Wisconsin Technical
    College *A*
University of Wisconsin
    Madison *B*
    River Falls *B*

Wyoming

Casper College *A*
Central Wyoming College *C, A*
Sheridan College *A*

Agricultural business technology

Arizona

University of Arizona *B*

Florida

Indian River State College *A*

Illinois

Illinois Eastern Community Colleges
    Wabash Valley College *A*

Kentucky

Henderson Community College *A*

Minnesota

South Central College *C, A*
University of Minnesota
    Crookston *B*

New York

SUNY
    College of Agriculture and
        Technology at Cobleskill *A, B*

Texas

Texas State Technical College
    Harlingen *A*
Wharton County Junior College *A*

Virginia

Tidewater Community College *A*

Washington

Edmonds Community College *C, A*
Washington State University *B*

West Virginia

Potomac State College of West
    Virginia University *A*

Wyoming

Laramie County Community
    College *A*

Agricultural communications

California

California Polytechnic State
    University: San Luis Obispo *B*

Georgia

University of Georgia *B*

Idaho

University of Idaho *B*

Illinois

University of Illinois
    Urbana-Champaign *B*

Indiana

Purdue University *B*

Kansas

Kansas State University *B*

Missouri
University of Missouri
Columbia *B*

Nebraska
University of Nebraska
Lincoln *B*

North Dakota
North Dakota State University *B*

Ohio
Ohio State University
Agricultural Technical Institute *A*

Oklahoma
Oklahoma State University *B, M*

South Dakota
South Dakota State University *B*

Texas
Texas A&M University *B*
Texas Tech University *B, M*
West Texas A&M University *B*

Utah
Utah State University *B*

Washington
Washington State University *B*

Wisconsin
University of Wisconsin
Madison *B, M*

Wyoming
Northwest College *A*
University of Wyoming *B*

Agricultural economics

Alabama
Auburn University *B, M, D*
Tuskegee University *M*

Arizona
University of Arizona *M*

Arkansas
University of Arkansas *M*

California
University of California
Berkeley *D*
Davis *M, D*

Colorado
Colorado State University *B, M, D*

Connecticut
University of Connecticut *B, M, D*

Delaware
University of Delaware *B, M*

Florida
University of Florida *B, M, D*

Georgia
Fort Valley State University *B*
University of Georgia *B, M, D*

Idaho
University of Idaho *B, M*

Illinois
Southern Illinois University
Carbondale *B, M*
University of Illinois
Urbana-Champaign *B, M, D*

Indiana
Purdue University *B, M, D*

Iowa
Iowa State University *M, D*

Kansas
Kansas State University *B, M, D*

Kentucky
Bluegrass Community and Technical
College *A*
University of Kentucky *B, M, D*

Louisiana
Louisiana State University and
Agricultural and Mechanical
College *M, D*

Maine
University of Maine *B, M*

Maryland
University of Maryland
College Park *B, M, D*

Massachusetts
University of Massachusetts
Amherst *B, M, D*

Michigan
Michigan State University *B, M, D*

Minnesota
Northland Community & Technical
College *C*
Ridgewater College *A*
South Central College *C, A*
University of Minnesota
Twin Cities *B, M, D*

Mississippi
Alcorn State University *B*
Mississippi Delta Community
College *A*
Mississippi State University *B*
Northwest Mississippi Community
College *A*

Missouri
Northwest Missouri State
University *B*
University of Central Missouri *B*
University of Missouri
Columbia *B, M, D*

Nebraska
University of Nebraska
Lincoln *B, M, D*

New Jersey
Rutgers, The State University of New
Jersey
New Brunswick/Piscataway
Campus *M*

New Mexico
New Mexico State University *M*

New York
Cornell University *B, M, D*

North Carolina
North Carolina Agricultural and
Technical State University *B, M*
North Carolina State University *M*

North Dakota
North Dakota State University *B, M*

Ohio
Ohio State University
Columbus Campus *C, B, M, D*

Oklahoma
Langston University *B*
Oklahoma State University *B, M, D*

Oregon
Oregon State University *B, M*
Treasure Valley Community
College *A*

Puerto Rico
University of Puerto Rico
Mayaguez *B, M*

South Carolina
Clemson University *B, M, D*

South Dakota
South Dakota State University *C, B*

Tennessee
Hiwassee College *A*
University of Tennessee
Knoxville *M*

Texas
Clarendon College *A*
Prairie View A&M University *M*
Tarleton State University *B*
Texas A&M University *B, M, D*
Texas Tech University *B, M, D*

Utah
Utah State University *B*

Virginia
Virginia Polytechnic Institute and
State University *M*

Washington
Washington State University *B, D*

West Virginia
West Virginia University *B, M, D*

Wisconsin
University of Wisconsin
Madison *B, M, D*
Platteville *B*

Wyoming
University of Wyoming *M*

Agricultural education services

Arkansas
University of Arkansas *B*

Colorado
Colorado State University *B, M*
Northeastern Junior College *C*

Georgia
University of Georgia *M*

Illinois
University of Illinois
Urbana-Champaign *B, M, T*

Indiana
Purdue University *M, D*

Iowa
Iowa State University *B*

New Mexico
New Mexico State University *B*

North Carolina
North Carolina State
University *B, M, D*

Ohio
Ohio State University
Columbus Campus *A, B*

Puerto Rico
University of Puerto Rico
Mayaguez *B, M*

Tennessee
University of Tennessee
Knoxville *B, M*

Texas
Tarleton State University *M*
Texas Tech University *D*

West Virginia
Potomac State College of West
Virginia University *A*

Agricultural engineering

Alabama
Auburn University *B, M, D*

Arizona
University of Arizona *M, D*

Arkansas
University of Arkansas *B, M*

California
California Polytechnic State
University: San Luis Obispo *B*
University of California
Los Angeles *B*

Colorado
Colorado State University *M, D*

Delaware
University of Delaware *B*

Florida
Florida Agricultural and Mechanical
University *B*
University of Florida *M, D*

Georgia
Abraham Baldwin Agricultural
College *A*
Fort Valley State University *B*
University of Georgia *B, M, D*

Hawaii
University of Hawaii
Manoa *B, M, D*

Illinois
Illinois Institute of Technology *M*
University of Illinois
Urbana-Champaign *B, M, D*

Indiana
Purdue University *B, M, D*
Vincennes University *A*

Iowa
Dordt College *B*
Iowa Lakes Community College *A*
Iowa State University *B, M, D*

Kansas
Kansas State University *B, M, D*

Kentucky
University of Kentucky B, M, D

Louisiana
Louisiana State University and
Agricultural and Mechanical
College M

Maine
University of Maine B, M

Maryland
University of Maryland
College Park B, M, D

Michigan
Michigan State University B, M, D

Minnesota
University of Minnesota
Twin Cities B, M, D

Missouri
University of Missouri
Columbia B, M, D

Nebraska
University of Nebraska
Lincoln B, M

New Jersey
New Jersey Institute of
Technology M
Rutgers, The State University of New
Jersey
New Brunswick/Piscataway
Campus B, M

New York
Cornell University B, M, D

North Carolina
North Carolina Agricultural and
Technical State University B
North Carolina State
University B, M, D

North Dakota
North Dakota State
University B, M, D

Ohio
Clark State Community College A
Ohio State University
Columbus Campus A, B, M, D

Oklahoma
Oklahoma State University B, M, D

Oregon
Oregon State University B, M, D

Pennsylvania
Penn State
Abington B
Altoona B
Beaver B
Berks B
Brandywine B
DuBois B
Erie, The Behrend College B
Fayette, The Eberly Campus B
Greater Allegheny B
Harrisburg B
Hazleton B
Lehigh Valley B
Mont Alto B
New Kensington B
Schuylkill B
Shenango B
University Park B, M, D
Wilkes-Barre B

Worthington Scranton B
York B

South Carolina
Clemson University B, M, D

South Dakota
South Dakota State University B, M

Tennessee
University of Tennessee
Knoxville B, M, D

Texas
Laredo Community College A
Texas A&M University B, M, D

Utah
Utah State University A, B, M, D

Virginia
Virginia Polytechnic Institute and
State University B, M, D

Washington
Washington State University M, D

Wisconsin
University of Wisconsin
Madison B, M, D

Agricultural equipment technology

Arizona
Central Arizona College C

California
San Joaquin Delta College C
Shasta College C

Georgia
Southwest Georgia Technical
College A

Illinois
Black Hawk College A
Illinois Eastern Community Colleges
Wabash Valley College C
Spoon River College A

Kansas
Garden City Community College A
Hutchinson Community College C, A
North Central Kansas Technical
College A

Minnesota
Minnesota West Community and
Technical College C, A
South Central College C

Nebraska
Northeast Community College A

New York
SUNY
College of Agriculture and
Technology at Cobleskill B
College of Agriculture and
Technology at Morrisville C, A

North Dakota
North Dakota State College of
Science A

Ohio
Ohio State University
Agricultural Technical Institute A

Oklahoma
Western Oklahoma State College A

South Dakota
Mitchell Technical Institute A

Washington
Walla Walla Community College C, A

Wisconsin
Fox Valley Technical College C
Northcentral Technical College C
University of Wisconsin
River Falls B

Agricultural/food products processing

Florida
University of Florida B

Indiana
Purdue University B, M, D

Iowa
Des Moines Area Community
College C
Northeast Iowa Community
College C, A

Kansas
Kansas State University B

Nebraska
University of Nebraska
Lincoln B

North Dakota
North Dakota State University M, D

Ohio
Ohio State University
Agricultural Technical Institute A
Columbus Campus A, B

Oklahoma
Eastern Oklahoma State College A

Texas
Texas A&M University B

Washington
Washington State University C, B
Wenatchee Valley College A

Wisconsin
University of Wisconsin
River Falls B

Agricultural mechanization

California
California Polytechnic State
University: San Luis Obispo B
Yuba College A

Colorado
Northeastern Junior College A

Idaho
University of Idaho B

Illinois
Black Hawk College C
Illinois Central College A
Parkland College C, A
Rend Lake College C, A
University of Illinois
Urbana-Champaign B, M, D

Indiana
Purdue University B

Iowa
Iowa State University B

Kansas
Fort Scott Community College A
Kansas State University B

Minnesota
Ridgewater College C
University of Minnesota
Crookston B

Nebraska
Northeast Community College A
University of Nebraska
Lincoln B, M

New York
SUNY
College of Agriculture and
Technology at Cobleskill A, B

North Carolina
Beaufort County Community
College A
North Carolina State University B

North Dakota
North Dakota State University B

Ohio
Ohio State University
Columbus Campus A
Owens Community College
Toledo A

South Dakota
South Dakota State University B

Texas
Sam Houston State University B
Stephen F. Austin State University B
Tarleton State University B

Utah
Utah State University C, A

Washington
Walla Walla Community College C, A
Washington State University B

Wisconsin
Fox Valley Technical College A

Agricultural power machinery operation

California
Shasta College C

Georgia
Southwest Georgia Technical
College A

Iowa
Hawkeye Community College A
Iowa Lakes Community College A
Kirkwood Community College A
Northeast Iowa Community
College A

Kansas
North Central Kansas Technical
College C

Minnesota
South Central College C, A
University of Minnesota
Crookston B

Montana
Dawson Community College C, A

New York

SUNY
College of Agriculture and
Technology at Cobleskill *A*

North Carolina

Guilford Technical Community
College *A*

Ohio

Ohio State University
Agricultural Technical Institute *A*
Columbus Campus *C, A*

Oklahoma

Western Oklahoma State College *A*

Wisconsin

Wisconsin Indianhead Technical
College *C*

Agricultural production

Alabama

Wallace State Community College at
Hanceville *C, A*

Arizona

Tohono O'odham Community
College *A*

Arkansas

University of Arkansas *M*

Colorado

Aims Community College *C, A*
Northeastern Junior College *C, A*

Illinois

Black Hawk College *A*
Highland Community College *C*
Illinois Eastern Community Colleges
Wabash Valley College *A*
Lincoln Land Community College *A*
Rend Lake College *C, A*

Indiana

Purdue University *B*

Iowa

Iowa Lakes Community College *A*
Kirkwood Community College *C, A*
North Iowa Area Community
College *A*
Northeast Iowa Community
College *C, A*
Southwestern Community College *A*

Kansas

Cloud County Community
College *C, A*
Garden City Community College *A*

Kentucky

Hopkinsville Community
College *C, A*
Owensboro Community and
Technical College *C, A*
Western Kentucky University *A*

Michigan

Michigan State University *C*

Minnesota

Minnesota West Community and
Technical College *A*
Northland Community & Technical
College *C*
Ridgewater College *C, A*
South Central College *C, A*

Missouri

Crowder College *A*
Mineral Area College *A*

Nebraska

Northeast Community College *A*

New Mexico

Eastern New Mexico University *C, A*

Ohio

Wilmington College *B*

Oregon

Blue Mountain Community College *A*

Puerto Rico

University of Puerto Rico
Utuado *A*

South Carolina

Piedmont Technical College *A*

South Dakota

Mitchell Technical Institute *A*

Texas

Stephen F. Austin State University *B*

Utah

Utah State University *B, M*

Virginia

Virginia Polytechnic Institute and
State University *A*

Washington

Big Bend Community College *A*
Walla Walla Community College *C, A*
Wenatchee Valley College *C, A*

Wisconsin

Fox Valley Technical College *C*
Mid-State Technical College *C*
Wisconsin Indianhead Technical
College *C*

Wyoming

Laramie County Community
College *A*
Northwest College *C, A*

Agricultural supplies

California

Modesto Junior College *A*

Illinois

Carl Sandburg College *C*
Joliet Junior College *C, A*
Kishwaukee College *A*

Iowa

Des Moines Area Community
College *C, A*
Hawkeye Community College *C, A*
Iowa Lakes Community College *A*
Kirkwood Community College *A*
North Iowa Area Community
College *A*
Southeastern Community College *A*
Western Iowa Tech Community
College *C, A*

Kansas

Cloud County Community College *A*
Coffeyville Community College *A*

Texas

Tarleton State University *B*
Texas A&M University *B*

Wisconsin

Fox Valley Technical College *A*
Madison Area Technical College *C*
Western Technical College *A*

Agricultural teacher education

Alabama

Auburn University *B, M, T*

Arizona

University of Arizona *M*

Arkansas

Arkansas Tech University *B*
Southern Arkansas University *B, T*
University of Arkansas *M*
University of Arkansas
Pine Bluff *B, T*

California

California Polytechnic State
University: San Luis
Obispo *B, M, T*
California State Polytechnic
University: Pomona *B*
California State University
Chico *M*
Fresno *B*
University of California
Davis *M, T*

Colorado

Colorado State University *B, T*

Connecticut

University of Connecticut *B, T*

Delaware

Delaware State University *B*
University of Delaware *B, T*

Florida

University of Florida *B, M, D*

Georgia

Fort Valley State University *B, T*
University of Georgia *B*

Idaho

University of Idaho *B, M, T*

Illinois

Elmhurst College *B*
University of Illinois
Urbana-Champaign *B, M, T*

Indiana

Purdue University *B*

Iowa

Ellsworth Community College *A*
Iowa State University *B, M, D, T*

Kansas

Colby Community College *A*
Kansas State University *B, T*

Louisiana

Louisiana State University and
Agricultural and Mechanical
College *B*
McNeese State University *T*
University of Louisiana at Lafayette *B*

Minnesota

University of Minnesota
Twin Cities *B, M*

Mississippi

Mississippi State University *B, M*
Northeast Mississippi Community
College *A*

Missouri

College of the Ozarks *B, T*
Missouri State University *B*
Northwest Missouri State
University *B, M, T*
Southeast Missouri State University *B*
University of Central Missouri *B*
University of Missouri
Columbia *B, M, D*

Montana

Montana State University *B, M*

Nebraska

University of Nebraska
Lincoln *B, M, T*

Nevada

Great Basin College *B*

New Mexico

Eastern New Mexico University *B*
New Mexico State University *B, M*

New York

Cornell University *B, M, D, T*
SUNY
College at Oswego *B*

North Carolina

North Carolina Agricultural and
Technical State
University *B, M, T*
North Carolina State
University *B, M, T*
University of Mount Olive *B*

North Dakota

North Dakota State
University *B, M, T*

Ohio

Ohio State University
Agricultural Technical Institute *A*
Columbus Campus *A, B, M, D*
Wilmington College *B*

Oklahoma

Eastern Oklahoma State College *A*
Northwestern Oklahoma State
University *B*
Oklahoma Panhandle State
University *B*
Oklahoma State University *B, M, D*

Oregon

Oregon State University *M*

Pennsylvania

Penn State
Abington *B*
Altoona *B*
Beaver *B*
Berks *B*
Brandywine *B*
DuBois *B*
Erie, The Behrend College *B*
Fayette, The Eberly Campus *B*
Greater Allegheny *B*
Harrisburg *B*
Hazleton *B*
Lehigh Valley *B*
Mont Alto *B*
New Kensington *B*
Schuylkill *B*
Shenango *B*
University Park *B, M, D*
Wilkes-Barre *B*

Worthington Scranton *B*
York *B*

Puerto Rico
Universidad Metropolitana *M*
University of Puerto Rico
Mayaguez *B, M*

South Carolina
Clemson University *B, M*

South Dakota
South Dakota State University *B*

Tennessee
Tennessee Technological
University *B, T*

Texas
Laredo Community College *A*
Lubbock Christian University *B*
Prairie View A&M University *M*
Sam Houston State University *M, T*
Stephen F. Austin State University *T*
Tarleton State University *M, T*
Texas A&M University *M, D*
Texas A&M University
Kingsville *B, M*
Texas State University *M, T*
Texas Tech University *M, D*
West Texas A&M University *T*

Utah
Utah State University *B*

Washington
Washington State University *B, T*

West Virginia
West Virginia University *B, M, T*

Wisconsin
University of Wisconsin
Platteville *B, T*
River Falls *B, M, T*

Wyoming
Northwest College *A*
University of Wyoming *B*

Agriculture, general

Alabama
Alabama Agricultural and Mechanical
University *B*
Faulkner State Community College *A*

Arizona
Arizona Western College *C, A*

Arkansas
Cossatot Community College of the
University of Arkansas *C, A*
East Arkansas Community College *A*
Mid-South Community College *A*
North Arkansas College *A*
Northwest Arkansas Community
College *A*
Phillips Community College of the
University of Arkansas *A*
Southern Arkansas University *M*

California
California Polytechnic State
University: San Luis Obispo *M*
California State Polytechnic
University: Pomona *M*
California State University
Chico *B*
Stanislaus *B*
Feather River College *C, A*
Fresno City College *C, A*
Hartnell College *C, A*

Imperial Valley College *C, A*
Lassen Community College *C, A*
Merced College *A*
Napa Valley College *C, A*
San Joaquin Delta College *A*
Shasta College *A*
Sierra College *C, A*
West Hills College: Coalinga *A*
Woodland Community College *A*

Colorado
Colorado State University *M*

Connecticut
University of Connecticut *B*

Delaware
Delaware State University *B, M*
University of Delaware *A*

Florida
Daytona State College *A*
Florida Agricultural and Mechanical
University *B, M*

Georgia
Abraham Baldwin Agricultural
College *B*
Andrew College *A*
Darton College *A*
East Georgia State College *A*
Georgia Highlands College *A*
Middle Georgia State College *A*
University of Georgia *B*
University of North Georgia *A*

Hawaii
University of Hawaii
Hawaii Community College *C, A*
Hilo *B*
Maui College *A*
Windward Community College *C*

Illinois
Black Hawk College *A*
Illinois State University *B, M*
Joliet Junior College *C, A*
Kaskaskia College *C, A*
Lake Land College *A*
Parkland College *A*
Sauk Valley Community College *A*
Southern Illinois University
Carbondale *B*
Western Illinois University *B*

Indiana
Ivy Tech Community College
Columbus *A*
East Central *C, A*
Kokomo *C, A*
Lafayette *A*
North Central *A*
Richmond *A*
Southwest *A*
Wabash Valley *A*
Purdue University *A, B*
Vincennes University *A*

Iowa
Iowa Western Community
College *C, A*
North Iowa Area Community
College *A*
Southeastern Community College *A*

Kansas
Barton County Community College *A*
Coffeyville Community College *A*
Garden City Community College *A*
Hutchinson Community College *A*
Pratt Community College *C, A*
Seward County Community
College *A*

Kentucky
Berea College *B*
Kentucky State University *B*
Morehead State University *B*
Murray State University *A, B, M, T*
Western Kentucky University *B, M, T*

Louisiana
McNeese State University *B*
University of Louisiana at Lafayette *B*

Maine
College of the Atlantic *B, M*

Maryland
Montgomery College *C, A*
University of Maryland
College Park *B, M, D*
Eastern Shore *B*

Massachusetts
Hampshire College *B*
North Shore Community College *C*

Minnesota
Minnesota West Community and
Technical College *A*
Ridgewater College *C, A*
South Central College *C, A*
University of Minnesota
Twin Cities *B, M*

Mississippi
Alcorn State University *B, M*
East Mississippi Community
College *A*
Hinds Community College *A*
Mississippi Gulf Coast Community
College *A*
Mississippi State University *B, M, D*

Missouri
Lincoln University *B*
Missouri State University *B*
Northwest Missouri State
University *B, M*
Truman State University *B*
University of Central Missouri *B*
University of Missouri
Columbia *B*

Montana
Little Big Horn College *A*
Montana State University *B*

Nebraska
Nebraska College of Technical
Agriculture *C, A*
Northeast Community College *A*
University of Nebraska
Lincoln *B, M*
Western Nebraska Community
College *A*

Nevada
Great Basin College *A, B*
University of Nevada
Reno *B*

New Jersey
Cumberland County College *C, A*
Rutgers, The State University of New
Jersey
New Brunswick/Piscataway
Campus *B*
Salem Community College *A*

New Mexico
Eastern New Mexico University *B*
Mesalands Community College *C, A*
Navajo Technical University *A*
New Mexico State University *B, M*

New York
Cornell University *B, M, D*
SUNY
College of Agriculture and
Technology at Cobleskill *A*
College of Agriculture and
Technology at Morrisville *A*
College of Technology at Alfred *A*

North Carolina
North Carolina Agricultural and
Technical State University *B*
North Carolina State University *A*

North Dakota
Cankdeska Cikana Community
College *A*
Dakota College at Bottineau *A*
North Dakota State University *B*
Turtle Mountain Community
College *C*
Williston State College *A*

Ohio
Ohio State University
Agricultural Technical
Institute *C, A*
Southern State Community College *A*

Oklahoma
Cameron University *B*
Eastern Oklahoma State College *A*
Murray State College *A*
Northeastern Oklahoma Agricultural
and Mechanical College *A*
Northwestern Oklahoma State
University *A*
Oklahoma Panhandle State
University *A*
Oklahoma State University *M*
Redlands Community College *A*

Oregon
Klamath Community College *A*
Linn-Benton Community College *C, A*
Oregon State University *B, M*
Treasure Valley Community
College *A*

Pennsylvania
Penn State
Abington *B*
Altoona *B*
Beaver *B*
Berks *B*
Brandywine *B*
DuBois *B*
Erie, The Behrend College *B*
Fayette, The Eberly Campus *B*
Greater Allegheny *B*
Harrisburg *B*
Hazleton *B*
Lehigh Valley *B*
Mont Alto *B*
New Kensington *B*
Schuylkill *B*
Shenango *B*
University Park *B*
Wilkes-Barre *B*
Worthington Scranton *B*
York *B*

Puerto Rico
University of Puerto Rico
Utuado *B*

South Dakota
Lake Area Technical Institute *A*
Sisseton Wahpeton College *A*
South Dakota State University *A, B*

Tennessee

Austin Peay State University *B*
University of Tennessee
  Knoxville *D*
  Martin *B*

Texas

Blinn College *A*
Brazosport College *A*
Clarendon College *A*
Howard College *A*
Kilgore College *A*
Laredo Community College *A*
Lubbock Christian University *A, B*
Odessa College *A*
Palo Alto College *A*
Paris Junior College *A*
Prairie View A&M University *B*
Sam Houston State University *B, M*
San Jacinto College *A*
Southwest Texas Junior College *A*
Stephen F. Austin State
  University *B, M*
Tarleton State University *B, M*
Texarkana College *A*
Texas A&M University *B*
Texas A&M University
  Commerce *B, M*
Texas State University *B*
Texas Tech University *B, M*
Tyler Junior College *C, A*
West Texas A&M University *B, M, D*

Utah

Southern Utah University *B*

Vermont

Sterling College *B*
University of Vermont *B*
Vermont Technical College *B*

Virginia

Virginia Polytechnic Institute and
  State University *B, M*
Virginia State University *B*

Washington

Washington State University *B, M*

West Virginia

Potomac State College of West
  Virginia University *A*
West Virginia University *M, D*

Wisconsin

Blackhawk Technical College *C*
Lac Courte Oreilles Ojibwa
  Community College *A*
Madison Area Technical College *A*
University of Wisconsin
  Platteville *M*
  River Falls *B*

Wyoming

Casper College *A*
Laramie County Community
  College *A*
Sheridan College *A*

Agroecology/ sustainable agriculture

Arizona

Prescott College *B*

Iowa

Iowa State University *M, D*

Kentucky

St. Catharine College *B*

Louisiana

Louisiana State University and
  Agricultural and Mechanical
  College *M, D*

Maine

Unity College *B*
University of Maine *B*

Massachusetts

University of Massachusetts
  Amherst *C*

Minnesota

University of Minnesota
  Crookston *B*

Montana

Montana State University *B*

New Hampshire

University of New Hampshire *B*

New York

SUNY
  College of Agriculture and
    Technology at Cobleskill *B*
  College of Technology at Alfred *A*

North Carolina

Central Carolina Community
  College *C, A*
Wayne Community College *A*

Ohio

Cincinnati State Technical and
  Community College *C*
Lorain County Community College *C*
Xavier University *B*

South Carolina

Piedmont Technical College *C*

Texas

Northeast Texas Community
  College *C, A*

Vermont

Green Mountain College *B, M*
Sterling College *B*

Washington

Evergreen State College *B*

Wisconsin

University of Wisconsin
  Madison *M*

Wyoming

University of Wyoming *B*

Agronomy and crop science

Arkansas

University of Arkansas *B, M, D*

California

Butte College *C, A*
California Polytechnic State
  University: San Luis Obispo *B*
California State University
  Fresno *B*
Merced College *A*
Modesto Junior College *A*
University of California
  Davis *B*

Colorado

Colorado State University *B, M, D*

Connecticut

University of Connecticut *B*

Delaware

University of Delaware *B*

Florida

University of Florida *M, D*

Georgia

University of Georgia *M, D*

Idaho

Brigham Young University-Idaho *B*

Illinois

University of Illinois
  Urbana-Champaign *B, M, D*

Indiana

Purdue University *B, M, D*

Iowa

Iowa State University *B, M*

Kansas

Garden City Community College *A*
Kansas State University *B, M, D*

Kentucky

University of Kentucky *B, M, D*

Michigan

Michigan State University *C*

Minnesota

Minnesota West Community and
  Technical College *A*
Northland Community & Technical
  College *C*
Ridgewater College *C, A*
Southwest Minnesota State
  University *B*
University of Minnesota
  Crookston *B*
  Twin Cities *B, M, D*

Mississippi

Mississippi State University *B*

Missouri

College of the Ozarks *B*
Missouri State University *B*
Northwest Missouri State
  University *B*
University of Missouri
  Columbia *M, D*

Nebraska

Northeast Community College *A*
University of Nebraska
  Lincoln *B, M, D*

New Mexico

New Mexico State University *B, M, D*

New York

Cornell University *M, D*
SUNY
  College of Technology at Alfred *A*

North Carolina

North Carolina Agricultural and
  Technical State University *M*
North Carolina State
  University *B, M, D*

North Dakota

North Dakota State University *M, D*

Ohio

Ohio State University
  Agricultural Technical Institute *A*
  Columbus Campus *A, B*
Wilmington College *B*

Oklahoma

Eastern Oklahoma State College *A*
Oklahoma Panhandle State
  University *A*
Oklahoma State University *D*
Redlands Community College *A*
Western Oklahoma State College *A*

Oregon

Oregon State University *B*
Treasure Valley Community
  College *A*

Pennsylvania

Delaware Valley College *B*
Penn State
  University Park *M, D*

Puerto Rico

University of Puerto Rico
  Mayaguez *B, M*

South Carolina

Clemson University *B, M, D*

South Dakota

South Dakota State University *B, D*

Tennessee

Tennessee Technological
  University *B*

Texas

Clarendon College *A*
Tarleton State University *B*
Texas A&M University *B, M, D*
Texas A&M University
  Kingsville *M*
Texas Tech University *B, M, D*
West Texas A&M University *B, M*

Vermont

University of Vermont *B*

Virginia

Virginia Polytechnic Institute and
  State University *B, M, D*

Washington

Washington State University *B, M, D*

West Virginia

Potomac State College of West
  Virginia University *A*
West Virginia University *B, M*

Wisconsin

Fox Valley Technical College *C*
University of Wisconsin
  Madison *B, M, D*
  Platteville *B*
  River Falls *B*

Wyoming

University of Wyoming *M, D*

Air traffic control

Alabama

Community College of the Air
  Force *A*

Alaska

University of Alaska
  Anchorage *A, B*

Arizona

Embry-Riddle Aeronautical University
Prescott Campus *B*

California

Mount San Antonio College *A*

Colorado

Aims Community College *A*

Florida

Embry-Riddle Aeronautical
University *B*
Florida State College at
Jacksonville *A*

Georgia

Middle Georgia State College *A*

Illinois

Lewis University *A, B*

Indiana

Purdue University *B*

Kansas

Kansas State University *C*

Maryland

Cecil College *C, A*

Minnesota

Minneapolis Community and
Technical College *A*
Saint Cloud State University *B*

New Hampshire

Daniel Webster College *B*

New Jersey

Thomas Edison State College *A, B*

New Mexico

Eastern New Mexico University:
Roswell *A*

New York

Vaughn College of Aeronautics and
Technology *C*

North Dakota

University of North Dakota *B*

Ohio

Sinclair Community College *C*

Pennsylvania

Community College of Beaver
County *C, A*

Texas

LeTourneau University *A*
Palo Alto College *A*
Texas State Technical College
Waco *C, A*

Aircraft maintenance/ technology

Alabama

Community College of the Air
Force *A*
Enterprise State Community
College *C, A*

Alaska

University of Alaska
Anchorage *C, A*
Fairbanks *C*

Arizona

Pima Community College *C, A*

Arkansas

Black River Technical College *C*
Pulaski Technical College *C*
Southern Arkansas University Tech *C*
University of Arkansas
Community College at
Batesville *C, A*

California

Antelope Valley College *C, A*
Chaffey College *A*
City College of San Francisco *C, A*
College of Alameda *C, A*
Cypress College *C, A*
Foothill College *C, A*
Gavilan College *C, A*
Glendale Community College *C, A*
Mount San Antonio College *A*
Orange Coast College *C, A*
Reedley College *C*
Sacramento City College *C, A*
San Bernardino Valley College *C*
San Deigo Miramar College
San Diego Miramar College *C, A*
San Joaquin Valley College *A*
Solano Community College *C, A*
West Los Angeles College *C, A*

Colorado

Colorado Northwestern Community
College *C, A*
Redstone College *C, A*

Connecticut

Housatonic Community College *A*

Delaware

Delaware Technical Community
College
Jack F. Owens Campus *C*

Florida

Florida State College at
Jacksonville *C*
St. Petersburg College *A*

Georgia

Atlanta Technical College *C*
Central Georgia Technical College *C*
Middle Georgia State College *A*
Savannah Technical College *C*

Hawaii

University of Hawaii
Honolulu Community College *C, A*

Illinois

Lewis University *C, A, B*
Lincoln Land Community
College *C, A*
Moody Bible Institute *B*
Rock Valley College *A*
Southwestern Illinois College *C, A*

Iowa

Iowa Western Community College *A*

Kansas

Central Christian College of Kansas *A*
Wichita Area Technical College *C, A*

Massachusetts

Middlesex Community College *A*

Michigan

Andrews University *B*
Lansing Community College *C, A*
Northern Michigan University *C, A*
Wayne County Community
College *C, A*

Minnesota

Northland Community & Technical
College *C, A*

Mississippi

Hinds Community College *C, A*

Missouri

Linn State Technical College *C, A*

Montana

Helena College University of
Montana *A*

Nebraska

Western Nebraska Community
College *C, A*

New Hampshire

Nashua Community College *A*

New Jersey

Thomas Edison State College *A, B*

New Mexico

Central New Mexico Community
College *C, A*
Eastern New Mexico University:
Roswell *C, A*

New York

Mohawk Valley Community
College *C, A*
Vaughn College of Aeronautics and
Technology *C, A, B*

North Carolina

Craven Community College *A*
Wayne Community College *C, A*

Ohio

Columbus State Community
College *C*
Sinclair Community College *C, A*

Oklahoma

Southeastern Oklahoma State
University *B*

Oregon

Lane Community College *C, A*
Portland Community College *C, A*

Pennsylvania

Pittsburgh Institute of
Aeronautics *C, A*

South Carolina

Trident Technical College *C, A*

South Dakota

Lake Area Technical Institute *A*

Texas

Amarillo College *C, A*
Del Mar College *C, A*
Hallmark College of Aeronautics *C, A*
LeTourneau University *B*
Midland College *C*
St. Philip's College *C, A*
Tarrant County College *C, A*
Texas State Technical College
Harlingen *C, A*
Waco *C, A*
West Texas *C, A*

Virginia

Hampton University *A*
Northern Virginia Community
College *A*

Washington

Big Bend Community College *C, A*
Edmonds Community College *C*
South Seattle Community
College *C, A*
Spokane Community College *A*

West Virginia

Pierpont Community and Technical
College *A*

Wisconsin

Fox Valley Technical College *C*
Milwaukee Area Technical College *C*

Aircraft powerplant technology

Alabama

Enterprise State Community
College *C, A*

Alaska

University of Alaska
Fairbanks *C, A*

Arkansas

Black River Technical College *C*
Pulaski Technical College *C, A*
Southern Arkansas University
Tech *C, A*

California

Antelope Valley College *C*
City College of San Francisco *C*
Long Beach City College *C, A*
Orange Coast College *C*

Florida

Embry-Riddle Aeronautical
University *A, B*
Embry-Riddle Aeronautical University
Worldwide Campus *A, B*

Georgia

Atlanta Technical College *C*
Savannah Technical College *C*

Idaho

Idaho State University *C, A, B*

Illinois

Lincoln Land Community College *C*
Rock Valley College *C*

Kansas

Wichita Area Technical College *C*

Kentucky

Somerset Community College *C, A*

Michigan

Lansing Community College *C, A*
Wayne County Community
College *C, A*

Missouri

Linn State Technical College *C, A*

Nebraska

Western Nebraska Community
College *C, A*

New Mexico

Central New Mexico Community
College *C*

New York

Vaughn College of Aeronautics and
Technology *C, A, B*

Ohio

Columbus State Community
    College *C*
Sinclair Community College *C*

Oregon

Portland Community College *C*

Pennsylvania

Pennsylvania College of
    Technology *C, A*
Pittsburgh Institute of
    Aeronautics *C, A*

South Carolina

Trident Technical College *C, A*

South Dakota

Lake Area Technical Institute *A*

Texas

Del Mar College *C, A*
Hallmark College of Aeronautics *A*
LeTourneau University *B*
Midland College *C*
St. Philip's College *C, A*
Tarrant County College *C, A*
Texas State Technical College
    Harlingen *C*
    Waco *C, A*
    West Texas *C*

Virginia

Liberty University *C*

Washington

South Seattle Community
    College *C, A*

Wisconsin

Milwaukee Area Technical College *C*

Airline/commercial pilot

Alabama

Wallace State Community College at
    Hanceville *A*

Alaska

University of Alaska
    Anchorage *A, B*
    Fairbanks *A*

Arizona

Cochise College *C, A*

Arkansas

Pulaski Technical College *A*

California

California Baptist University *B*
Cypress College *C, A*
Orange Coast College *C, A*
Palomar College *C, A*

Colorado

Aims Community College *C, A*
Metropolitan State University of
    Denver *B*

Florida

College of Central Florida *A*
Embry-Riddle Aeronautical
    University *B*
Embry-Riddle Aeronautical University
    Worldwide Campus *M*
Jacksonville University *B*
Polk State College *A*
Santa Fe College *A*

Hawaii

University of Hawaii
    Honolulu Community College *A*

Illinois

Lewis University *A*
Quincy University *B*
Southern Illinois University
    Carbondale *A*
University of Illinois
    Urbana-Champaign *C, B*

Indiana

Indiana State University *B*
Purdue University *B*
Vincennes University *C, A*

Iowa

University of Dubuque *B*

Kansas

Hutchinson Community College *A*

Kentucky

Bluegrass Community and Technical
    College *A*

Louisiana

University of Louisiana at Monroe *B*

Massachusetts

North Shore Community College *A*

Michigan

Baker College
    Muskegon *A*
Eastern Michigan University *B*
Northwestern Michigan College *A*
Oakland Community College *A*
Western Michigan University *B*

Minnesota

Academy College *A*
Lake Superior College *C, A*
Saint Cloud State University *B*
University of Minnesota
    Crookston *B*

Mississippi

Delta State University *B*

Missouri

Saint Louis University *B*

Montana

Rocky Mountain College *B*

New Jersey

Mercer County Community
    College *A*

New Mexico

Eastern New Mexico University:
    Roswell *A*

New York

Dutchess Community College *A*
SUNY
    Farmingdale State College *B*
Vaughn College of Aeronautics and
    Technology *A, B*

North Carolina

Guilford Technical Community
    College *C, A*
Lenoir Community College *C, A*

North Dakota

University of North Dakota *B*

Ohio

Sinclair Community College *C, A*

Oklahoma

Southeastern Oklahoma State
    University *B*

Oregon

Central Oregon Community
    College *A*
Lane Community College *A*
Portland Community College *A*
Treasure Valley Community
    College *A*
Umpqua Community College *C, A*

Pennsylvania

Community College of Allegheny
    County *A*
Lehigh Carbon Community College *A*
Luzerne County Community
    College *A*
Pennsylvania Highlands Community
    College *A*

Rhode Island

New England Institute of
    Technology *A*

Texas

Baylor University *B*
Central Texas College *C, A*
LeTourneau University *B*
Mountain View College *C, A*
Palo Alto College *A*
San Jacinto College *C, A*
Tarleton State University *B*
Tarrant County College *A*
Texas State Technical College
    Waco *C, A*

Utah

Salt Lake Community College *A*
Southern Utah University *A*
Utah State University *B*
Utah Valley University *A, B*

Virginia

Averett University *B*

Washington

Big Bend Community College *C, A*
Central Washington University *B*
Clover Park Technical College *C, A*

Wisconsin

Fox Valley Technical College *C, A*
Gateway Technical College *A*

Wyoming

Casper College *A*

Algebra/number theory

Virginia

Virginia Commonwealth
    University *M*

Alternative/complementary medicine

Puerto Rico

Turabo University *D*

Alternative fuel vehicle technology

Arkansas

Pulaski Technical College *C*

California

College of the Desert *C*
Long Beach City College *C, A*

Illinois

Morton College *C*

Kansas

Kansas City Kansas Community
    College *C*

Massachusetts

Benjamin Franklin Institute of
    Technology *A*

Michigan

Northwestern Michigan College *C, A*
Wayne County Community College *C*

New Mexico

Santa Fe Community College *C*

North Carolina

Central Carolina Community
    College *C, A*

American government/politics

Arizona

Arizona Christian University *B*

California

American Jewish University *B*
Master's College *B*
Mills College *B*
University of California
    San Diego *B*

District of Columbia

Catholic University of America *M*

Florida

Ave Maria University *B*
Florida State University *M*

Iowa

William Penn University *B*

Maine

College of the Atlantic *B*
Thomas College *B*

Massachusetts

Boston College *M, D*
Brandeis University *B*
Fitchburg State University *B*

Michigan

University of Michigan
    Flint *M*
Western Michigan University *B*

Missouri

Drury University *B*

New York

United States Military Academy *B*

North Carolina

Belmont Abbey College *B*
Meredith College *B*

Ohio

Ohio Wesleyan University *B*
University of Akron *B*

Pennsylvania

Gettysburg College *B*
La Salle University *B*
Lycoming College *B*
Misericordia University *B*

Texas

Wayland Baptist University *B*

Virginia
Emory & Henry College *B*

American history (U.S.)

California
Mills College *B*
Pitzer College *B*

Florida
Florida College *B*
Nova Southeastern University *B*

Iowa
Morningside College *B*
William Penn University *B*

Kentucky
Hopkinsville Community College *A*

Massachusetts
Bard College at Simon's Rock *B*
Elms College *B*
Harvard College *M, D*
Salem State University *B*

Michigan
Central Michigan University *M*
University of Michigan
  Flint *M*

New Hampshire
Keene State College *B*

New York
Bard College *B*
United States Military Academy *B*

Ohio
Ashland University *M*

Pennsylvania
Gettysburg College *B*
La Salle University *B*
Lycoming College *B*

Puerto Rico
University of Puerto Rico
  Rio Piedras *B*

South Carolina
Charleston Southern University *B*

Texas
Howard Payne University *B*

Virginia
Emory & Henry College *M*

American literature

California
California State University
  Bakersfield *B, M*
  East Bay *B*
College of the Desert *A*
University of California
  Los Angeles *B*
  San Diego *B, M, D*
Whittier College *B*

District of Columbia
American University *B*
George Washington University *M, D*

Florida
Miami Dade College *A*

Illinois
Illinois Valley Community College *A*
Lincoln College *A*
Richland Community College *A*

Kentucky
Northern Kentucky University *C*

Maine
University of Maine
  Fort Kent *B*

Maryland
Johns Hopkins University *D*

Massachusetts
Bard College at Simon's Rock *B*
Simmons College *B*
Tufts University *M, D*

Michigan
Cornerstone University *B*
Eastern Michigan University *M*
Michigan State University *D*
University of Michigan
  Flint *M*

Minnesota
Augsburg College *B*
Saint Cloud State University *B*

Missouri
Washington University in St.
  Louis *B, M, D*

Montana
Miles Community College *A*

New York
Bard College *B*
Columbia University *B*
New York University *B, M, D*
SUNY
  College at Purchase *B*
St. Lawrence University *B*

Ohio
Ohio Wesleyan University *B*

Pennsylvania
Gettysburg College *B*
La Salle University *B*
University of Pittsburgh
  Johnstown *B*
Westminster College *B, T*

Rhode Island
Brown University *B, M, D*

Texas
North Lake College *A*

Vermont
Bennington College *B*
Castleton State College *B*
Marlboro College *B*
Middlebury College *B*

American Sign Language (ASL)

Arizona
Phoenix College *C*

California
Antelope Valley College *A*
Bakersfield College *A*
California State University
  Sacramento *B*
Grossmont College *A*
Imperial Valley College *A*
Ohlone College *A*
San Diego Mesa College *A*
San Joaquin Delta College *C*
Santa Rosa Junior College *A*
Santiago Canyon College *A*
Sierra College *A*

District of Columbia
Gallaudet University *B*

Idaho
Idaho State University *A*

Indiana
Goshen College *B*
Indiana University
  Purdue University Indianapolis *C*
Vincennes University *A*

Kentucky
Western Kentucky University *C*

Maryland
Montgomery College *A*

Massachusetts
Bristol Community College *A*
Northeastern University *B*

Michigan
Madonna University *C, A, B*
Wayne County Community College *C*

Minnesota
Minnesota State Community and
  Technical College *C*
North Central University *B*
North Hennepin Community
  College *C*
St. Catherine University *B*
St. Paul College *C*

Missouri
William Woods University *B*

New Jersey
Union County College *A*

New York
Keuka College *B*
Nassau Community College *A*
Rochester Institute of
  Technology *A, B*
University of Rochester *B*

North Carolina
Gardner-Webb University *B*

Oregon
Portland Community College *A*

South Carolina
Spartanburg Community College *C*

South Dakota
Augustana College *B, T*

Tennessee
Maryville College *B*

Texas
University of Houston *B*

Utah
Utah Valley University *B*

Virginia
Liberty University *B*
Tidewater Community College *A*

American studies

Alabama
University of Alabama *B, M*

Arkansas
Hendrix College *B*
University of Arkansas *B*

California
California State University
  Fullerton *B, M*
  San Bernardino *B*
Claremont McKenna College *B*
Cosumnes River College *A*
El Camino College *A*
Folsom Lake College *A*
Foothill College *A*
Los Angeles Valley College *A*
Mills College *B*
Mount St. Mary's College *B*
Occidental College *B*
Pepperdine University *M*
Pitzer College *B*
Pomona College *B*
San Diego State University *B*
San Francisco State University *B*
Scripps College *B*
Southwestern College *A*
Stanford University *B*
University of California
  Berkeley *B*
  Davis *B*
  Santa Cruz *B*
University of San Francisco *B*
University of Southern
  California *B, M, D*

Connecticut
Connecticut College *B*
Fairfield University *B, M*
Trinity College *B, M*
University of Connecticut *B*
Wesleyan University *B*
Western Connecticut State
  University *B*
Yale University *B, M, D*

Delaware
Wesley College *B*

District of Columbia
American University *B*
George Washington
  University *B, M, D*
Georgetown University *B*

Florida
Eckerd College *B*
Miami Dade College *A*
Nova Southeastern University *B*
Rollins College *B*
Stetson University *B*
University of Miami *B*
University of South Florida *B, M*

Georgia
College of Coastal Georgia *B*
Emory University *B*
Kennesaw State University *C, M*
Oglethorpe University *B*

Hawaii
University of Hawaii
  Manoa *B, M, D*

Idaho
University of Idaho *B*

Illinois
DePaul University *D*
Dominican University *B*
Elmhurst College *B*
Illinois College *B*
Illinois Wesleyan University *B*
Knox College *B*
Lake Forest College *B*
Northwestern University *B*

Indiana

Franklin College *B*
Indiana University
Bloomington *B, D*
University of Notre Dame *B*
Valparaiso University *B*

Iowa

Coe College *B*
University of Iowa *B, M, D*
University of Northern Iowa *B*
Upper Iowa University *B*

Kansas

University of Kansas *B, M, D*

Kentucky

Georgetown College *B*
Lindsey Wilson College *B*

Louisiana

Tulane University *B*

Maine

Bates College *B*
Colby College *B*
University of Southern Maine *M*

Maryland

Anne Arundel Community College *A*
Goucher College *B*
Howard Community College *A*
Prince George's Community
College *A*
Towson University *B*
University of Maryland
Baltimore County *B*
College Park *B, M, D*
Washington College *B*

Massachusetts

American International College *B*
Amherst College *B*
Bard College at Simon's Rock *B*
Boston College *M*
Boston University *B, D*
Brandeis University *B*
Elms College *B*
Emmanuel College *B*
Hampshire College *B*
Lesley University *B, M*
Mount Ida College *B*
Simmons College *B*
Smith College *B*
Stonehill College *B*
Tufts University *B*
University of Massachusetts
Boston *B, M*
Lowell *B*
Wellesley College *B*
Wheaton College *B*
Wheelock College *B*
Williams College *B*

Michigan

Hillsdale College *B*
Lansing Community College *A*
Michigan State University *B, M, D*
Siena Heights University *B*
University of Michigan *B, M, D*
University of Michigan
Dearborn *B*

Minnesota

Carleton College *B*
St. Olaf College *B*
University of Minnesota
Twin Cities *B, M, D*

Mississippi

Mississippi Delta Community
College *A*
University of Southern Mississippi *B*

Missouri

Columbia College *B*
Lindenwood University *B, M*
Saint Louis University *B, M, D*
University of Missouri
Kansas City *B*
Washington University in St.
Louis *B, M*
Webster University *B*

Nebraska

Creighton University *B*
Midland University *B*

New Hampshire

Franklin Pierce University *B*
Keene State College *B*

New Jersey

College of St. Elizabeth *B*
Ramapo College of New Jersey *B*
Richard Stockton College of New
Jersey *M*
Rider University *B*
Rowan University *B*
Rutgers, The State University of New
Jersey
New Brunswick/Piscataway
Campus *B*
Newark Campus *B, M, D*
Saint Peter's University *B*

New Mexico

University of New Mexico *B, M, D*

New York

Bard College *B*
Barnard College *B*
City University of New York
Brooklyn College *B*
College of Staten Island *B*
Queens College *B*
Clarkson University *B*
College of New Rochelle *B*
College of Saint Rose *B*
Columbia University *B*
Columbia University
School of General Studies *B*
Cornell University *B*
Elmira College *B*
Fordham University *B*
Hamilton College *B*
Hobart and William Smith Colleges *B*
Hofstra University *B*
Long Island University
LIU Post *B*
Manhattanville College *B*
Marist College *B*
Nazareth College *B*
New York University *M, D*
Pace University *B*
SUNY
College at Fredonia *B*
College at Geneseo *B*
College at Old Westbury *B*
College at Oswego *B*
University at Buffalo *B, M, D*
University at Stony Brook *B*
Sage Colleges *B*
St. John Fisher College *B*
Siena College *B, T*
Skidmore College *B*
Syracuse University *B*
Union College *B*
University of Rochester *B*
Vassar College *B*
Wells College *B*

North Carolina

Lenoir-Rhyne University *B*
Montreat College *B*
Salem College *B*
University of North Carolina
Chapel Hill *B, M, D*

Ohio

Bowling Green State
University *B, M, D*
Case Western Reserve University *B*
Cedarville University *B*
Kenyon College *B*
Miami University
Oxford *B*
Oberlin College *B*
University of Dayton *B*
University of Mount Union *B*
University of Rio Grande *B*
University of Toledo *B*
Wittenberg University *B*
Youngstown State University *B, M*

Oklahoma

Northeastern State University *M*
Oklahoma City University *B*
Oklahoma State University *B*
Southern Nazarene University *B*

Oregon

Oregon State University *B*
Pacific University *B*
Reed College *B*
Warner Pacific College *B*
Willamette University *B*

Pennsylvania

Albright College *B*
Bucks County Community College *A*
Cabrini College *B*
Dickinson College *B*
Franklin & Marshall College *B*
Gettysburg College *B*
Lafayette College *B*
Lehigh University *M*
Lycoming College *B*
Muhlenberg College *C, B*
Penn State
Abington *B*
Brandywine *B*
Harrisburg *B, M, D*
Worthington Scranton *B*
St. Francis University *B*
Temple University *B*
University of Pennsylvania *B, M, D*
University of Pittsburgh
Greensburg *B*
Ursinus College *B*
West Chester University of
Pennsylvania *B*

Rhode Island

Brown University *B, M, D*
Bryant University *B*
Providence College *B*
Roger Williams University *B*
Salve Regina University *B*

South Carolina

Claflin University *B*
Erskine College *B*

Tennessee

Cumberland University *B*
King University *B, T*
Lincoln Memorial University *B*
Lipscomb University *B*
Sewanee: The University of the
South *B*
Tennessee Wesleyan College *B*
Vanderbilt University *B*

Texas

Austin College *B*
Baylor University *B, M*
Texas State University *B*
University of Dallas *M*
University of Texas
Austin *B, M, D*
Dallas *B*

Pan American *B*
San Antonio *B*

Utah

Brigham Young University *B*
Utah State University *B, M*

Vermont

Bennington College *B*
Goddard College *B, M*
Marlboro College *B*
Middlebury College *B*
Saint Michael's College *B*

Virginia

Christopher Newport University *B*
College of William and Mary *B, M, D*
University of Mary Washington *B*
University of Richmond *B*

Washington

Heritage University *B*
University of Washington Bothell *B*
University of Washington Tacoma *B*
Washington State University *M, D*
Western Washington University *B*
Whitworth University *B*

Wyoming

University of Wyoming *B, M*

Analysis/functional analysis

District of Columbia

American University *M*

New York

University of Rochester *M*

Analytical chemistry

Illinois

Governors State University *M*
Illinois Institute of Technology *M*
North Central College *B*

Iowa

Iowa State University *M, D*

Massachusetts

Tufts University *M, D*

Minnesota

University of Minnesota
Twin Cities *M, D*

Montana

University of Montana *M, D*

Pennsylvania

West Chester University of
Pennsylvania *B*

Anatomy

Arkansas

University of Arkansas
for Medical Sciences *M, D*

California

Loma Linda University *M, D*
University of California
Irvine *D*

Colorado

University of Colorado
Denver *M*

District of Columbia

Howard University *M, D*

Florida
Barry University *M*

Illinois
Rush University *M, D*
University of Chicago *D*

Indiana
Indiana University
  Bloomington *M, D*

Iowa
University of Iowa *M, D*

Kentucky
University of Kentucky *D*
University of Kentucky: College of
  Medicine *D*
University of Louisville *M, D*

Louisiana
Louisiana State University
  Health Sciences Center *D*
Tulane University *M, D*

Massachusetts
Boston University *M, D*
Tufts University *D*

Michigan
Wayne State University *M, D*

Minnesota
Minnesota State University
  Mankato *B*
University of Minnesota
  Twin Cities *M, D*

Mississippi
University of Mississippi Medical
  Center *M, D*

Missouri
Saint Louis University *M, D*

Nebraska
Creighton University *M*

New Jersey
Rutgers, The State University of New
  Jersey
  New Brunswick/Piscataway
    Campus *M, D*
  Newark Campus *M, D*

New York
SUNY
  University at Buffalo *M, D*
  University at Stony Brook *D*
  Upstate Medical University *M, D*

North Carolina
Duke University *B, M, D*

North Dakota
University of North Dakota *M, D*

Ohio
Case Western Reserve University *M*
Kent State University *D*
Ohio State University
  Columbus Campus *M, D*
Wright State University *M*

Pennsylvania
Lycoming College *B*

Puerto Rico
University of Puerto Rico
  Medical Sciences *M, D*

South Dakota
University of South Dakota *M, D*

Texas
University of Texas
  Health Science Center at
    Houston *M, D*

Utah
University of Utah *M, D*

Virginia
Virginia Commonwealth
  University *M, D*

Ancient Greek

Alabama
Samford University *B*

California
Loyola Marymount University *B*
Santa Clara University *B*
University of California
  Berkeley *B, M*
  Los Angeles *B, M*

Connecticut
Yale University *B*

District of Columbia
Howard University *B*

Florida
Florida State University *B, M*
University of Miami *B*

Georgia
Emory University *B*
University of Georgia *B*

Illinois
Augustana College *B*
Knox College *B*
Loyola University Chicago *B*
Monmouth College *B*
Moody Bible Institute *B*
Trinity International University *M*

Indiana
DePauw University *B*
Indiana University
  Bloomington *B*
University of Notre Dame *B*
Wabash College *B*

Iowa
University of Iowa *B, M*

Louisiana
Loyola University New Orleans *B*

Massachusetts
Amherst College *B*
Boston College *B, M*
Boston University *B*
Harvard College *B, D*
Mount Holyoke College *B*
Smith College *B*
Tufts University *B, M*
Wellesley College *B*

Michigan
Calvin College *B*
Grand Valley State University *B*
University of Michigan *B, M*

Minnesota
St. Olaf College *B*
University of Minnesota
  Twin Cities *B*

Missouri
Washington University in St.
  Louis *B, M*

Nebraska
Creighton University *B*

New Hampshire
University of New Hampshire *B*

New York
Bard College *B*
Barnard College *B*
Canisius College *B*
City University of New York
  Hunter College *B*
  Queens College *B*
Columbia University *B*
Fordham University *B, M, D*

North Carolina
Duke University *B*
Wake Forest University *B*

Ohio
John Carroll University *B*
Kenyon College *B*
Oberlin College *B*

Oregon
Multnomah University *B*

Pennsylvania
Bryn Mawr College *B, M, D*
Duquesne University *B*
Franklin & Marshall College *B*
Haverford College *B*
Swarthmore College *B*

Rhode Island
Brown University *B*

South Carolina
Furman University *B*

Tennessee
Sewanee: The University of the
  South *B*

Texas
Baylor University *B*
Howard Payne University *B*
Rice University *B*
Southwestern University *B, T*
University of Texas
  Austin *B*

Utah
Brigham Young University *B*

Vermont
University of Vermont *B*

Virginia
Hampden-Sydney College *B*
Randolph College *B*
Randolph-Macon College *B*
University of Richmond *B*

Washington
University of Washington *B*

Wisconsin
Lawrence University *B*
University of Wisconsin
  Madison *M*

Ancient Near Eastern/
Biblical languages

Arkansas
Ouachita Baptist University *B*

California
Concordia University Irvine *B*
Master's College *B*
Santa Clara University *M*

Connecticut
Yale University *B, M, D*

Delaware
University of Delaware *B*

District of Columbia
Catholic University of America *M, D*

Illinois
Concordia University Chicago *B*
University of Chicago *B, D*

Iowa
Luther College *B*

Michigan
Calvin College *B*
Concordia University *B*

Nebraska
Grace University *B*

New York
Columbia University *B*

Ohio
Ohio Wesleyan University *B*

Pennsylvania
Geneva College *B*
La Salle University *B*
Valley Forge Christian College *B*

South Carolina
Columbia International University *B*

Tennessee
Belmont University *B*

Texas
Baylor University *B*
Houston Baptist University *B*
Howard Payne University *B*

Utah
Brigham Young University *B*

Washington
University of Washington *M*

Wisconsin
Concordia University Wisconsin *B*
Maranatha Baptist Bible College *B*

Ancient studies

California
Loyola Marymount University *B*
Santa Clara University *B*
University of California
  Riverside *B*

Connecticut
Wesleyan University *B*
Yale University *B*

Florida
University of Miami *B*

Illinois
University of Chicago *M*

Iowa
University of Iowa *B, M*

Kansas
University of Kansas *B*

Maine
Bates College *B*
Bowdoin College *B*
Colby College *B*

Maryland
University of Maryland
Baltimore County *B*

Massachusetts
Hampshire College *B*
Mount Holyoke College *B*
Smith College *B*

Michigan
University of Michigan *B, M, D*

Minnesota
St. Olaf College *B*
University of Minnesota
Twin Cities *B*

Missouri
Missouri State University *M*
Washington University in St. Louis *B*

Nebraska
Creighton University *B*
University of Nebraska
Lincoln *B*

New Hampshire
Dartmouth College *B*

New Jersey
Rutgers, The State University of New
Jersey
Newark Campus *B*

New York
Barnard College *B*
Columbia University *B*
Columbia University
School of General Studies *B*
New York University *D*
Vassar College *B*

Ohio
Ohio State University
Columbus Campus *B*
Ohio Wesleyan University *B*

Pennsylvania
Lehigh University *B*

Rhode Island
Brown University *B*

Tennessee
Vanderbilt University *B*

Texas
University of Texas
Austin *B*

Anesthesiologist assistant

Colorado
University of Colorado
Denver *M*

Missouri
University of Missouri
Kansas City *M*

Ohio
Case Western Reserve University *M*

Texas
Sanford-Brown College
Houston *A*

Washington
Renton Technical College *A*

Wisconsin
Milwaukee Area Technical College *A*

Animal-assisted therapy

Arizona
Prescott College *M*

Wyoming
Casper College *C*

Animal behavior/ ethology

Arizona
Arizona State University *D*

California
University of California
Davis *D*

Maine
College of the Atlantic *B, M*
University of New England *B*

Massachusetts
Hampshire College *B*

New York
Canisius College *B*

Pennsylvania
Bucknell University *B, M*
Franklin & Marshall College *B*

Texas
Southwestern University *B*

Wisconsin
Carroll University *B*

Animal breeding

California
Modesto Junior College *A*

Illinois
Kishwaukee College *A*

Indiana
Purdue University *B*

Iowa
Iowa State University *M, D*

Minnesota
South Central College *C, A*

New York
Cornell University *M, D*
SUNY
College of Agriculture and
Technology at Cobleskill *B*

Ohio
Lake Erie College *B*

Texas
Texas A&M University *M, D*

Animal genetics

Minnesota
University of Minnesota
Twin Cities *M, D*

New Jersey
Rutgers, The State University of New
Jersey
New Brunswick/Piscataway
Campus *B*

New York
Cornell University *M, D*

South Carolina
Clemson University *B, M, D*

Washington
Washington State University *M, D*

Animal health

California
Los Angeles Pierce College *A*
San Diego Mesa College *A*

Colorado
Colorado Mountain College *A*
Front Range Community College *C, A*

Georgia
University of Georgia *B*

Indiana
Purdue University *B*

Iowa
Kirkwood Community College *C*

Nebraska
Nebraska College of Technical
Agriculture *C, A*
University of Nebraska
Lincoln *M*

North Carolina
North Carolina Agricultural and
Technical State University *M*

Texas
Sul Ross State University *B*

Animal husbandry

California
San Joaquin Delta College *C*
Santa Rosa Junior College *C*

Illinois
Black Hawk College *C*
John Wood Community College *C*
Parkland College *C, A*
University of Illinois
Urbana-Champaign *B, M, D*

Indiana
Purdue University *B*

Iowa
Ellsworth Community College *C*
Hawkeye Community College *C, A*
Iowa State University *M*

Kansas
Colby Community College *C*
Highland Community College *A*

Michigan
Michigan State University *C*

Minnesota
University of Minnesota
Twin Cities *B*

New York
Jefferson Community College *A*

North Carolina
James Sprunt Community
College *C, A*
North Carolina State University *A*
Wayne Community College *C, A*

Ohio
Ohio State University
Agricultural Technical Institute *A*
Columbus Campus *A, T*

Oregon
Blue Mountain Community College *A*

Puerto Rico
University of Puerto Rico
Utuado *A*

Texas
Angelo State University *B*
Paris Junior College *C*
Tarleton State University *B*
Texas A&M University *B*

Utah
Southern Utah University *C, A*

Wyoming
Casper College *A*

Animal nutrition

Georgia
University of Georgia *D*

Illinois
Joliet Junior College *C*

Indiana
Purdue University *B*

Oklahoma
Oklahoma State University *D*

Animal physiology

Arkansas
University of Arkansas
for Medical Sciences *M, D*

California
University of California
San Diego *B*

Colorado
Colorado State University *M, D*

Connecticut
University of Connecticut *B*

Idaho
University of Idaho *D*

Iowa
Iowa State University *M, D*

Maine
College of the Atlantic *B, M*

Minnesota
University of Minnesota
Twin Cities *M, D*

New York

Cornell University *M, D*

Ohio

Kent State University *M, D*

Pennsylvania

Penn State
University Park *M, D*

South Carolina

Clemson University *M, D*

Animal sciences

Alabama

Alabama Agricultural and Mechanical
University *B*
Auburn University *B, M, D*
Tuskegee University *B, M*

Arizona

University of Arizona *B, M, D*

Arkansas

Arkansas State University *B*
University of Arkansas *B, M, D*

California

Bakersfield College *C, A*
Butte College *C, A*
California Polytechnic State
University: San Luis Obispo *B*
California State Polytechnic
University: Pomona *B*
California State University
Chico *B*
Fresno *B, M*
College of the Redwoods *C, A*
College of the Sequoias *C*
Cosumnes River College *A*
Los Angeles Pierce College *C, A*
Merced College *C, A*
Modesto Junior College *A*
Moorpark College *C, A*
Mount San Antonio College *C, A*
Reedley College *C*
Santa Rosa Junior College *C*
University of California
Davis *B, M, D*
Yuba College *C*

Colorado

Colorado State University *B, M, D*
Otero Junior College *A*

Connecticut

University of Connecticut *A, B, M, D*

Delaware

University of Delaware *B, M, D*

Florida

University of Florida *B, M, D*

Georgia

Abraham Baldwin Agricultural
College *A*
Berry College *B*
Fort Valley State University *B, M*
University of Georgia *B, M, D*

Hawaii

University of Hawaii
Manoa *B, M*

Idaho

Brigham Young University-Idaho *A, B*
University of Idaho *B, M*

Illinois

John Wood Community College *A*
Kaskaskia College *C, A*
Southern Illinois University
Carbondale *B, M*
University of Illinois
Urbana-Champaign *B, M, D*

Indiana

Purdue University *B, M, D*

Iowa

Dordt College *B*
Iowa State University *B, M, D*

Kansas

Butler Community College *A*
Garden City Community College *A*
Kansas State University *C, B, M, D*
Pratt Community College *A*
Seward County Community
College *A*

Kentucky

University of Kentucky *B, M, D*

Louisiana

Louisiana State University and
Agricultural and Mechanical
College *B, M, D*
Louisiana Tech University *B*
Southern University and Agricultural
and Mechanical College *B*

Maine

University of Maine *B, M*

Maryland

University of Maryland
College Park *B, M, D*

Massachusetts

University of Massachusetts
Amherst *B, M, D*

Michigan

Andrews University *B*
Michigan State University *C, B, M, D*

Minnesota

University of Minnesota
Crookston *B*
Twin Cities *B, M, D*

Mississippi

East Mississippi Community
College *A*
Mississippi State University *B*
Northwest Mississippi Community
College *A*

Missouri

College of the Ozarks *B*
Missouri State University *B*
Northwest Missouri State
University *B*
Southeast Missouri State University *B*
University of Missouri
Columbia *B, M, D*

Montana

Montana State University *B*

Nebraska

Northeast Community College *A*
University of Nebraska
Lincoln *B, M, D*

New Hampshire

University of New
Hampshire *A, B, M, D*

New Jersey

Rutgers, The State University of New
Jersey
New Brunswick/Piscataway
Campus *B, M, D*

New Mexico

New Mexico State University *B, M, D*

New York

Cornell University *B, M, D*
Mercy College *B*
Niagara County Community
College *A*
SUNY
College of Agriculture and
Technology at Cobleskill *A*
College of Agriculture and
Technology at Morrisville *A, B*
College of Environmental Science
and Forestry *B, M, D*
College of Technology at Alfred *A*
Ulster County Community College *C*

North Carolina

North Carolina Agricultural and
Technical State University *B*
North Carolina State
University *B, M, D*
Sampson Community College *C*

North Dakota

North Dakota State
University *B, M, D*

Ohio

Ohio State University
Columbus Campus *B, M, D*
University of Findlay *B*
Wilmington College *B*

Oklahoma

Eastern Oklahoma State College *A*
Langston University *B*
Oklahoma Panhandle State
University *B*
Oklahoma State University *B, M*
Western Oklahoma State College *A*

Oregon

Linn-Benton Community College *A*
Oregon State University *B, M, D*
Treasure Valley Community
College *A*

Pennsylvania

Delaware Valley College *B*
Harcum College *A*
Penn State
Abington *B*
Altoona *B*
Beaver *B*
Berks *B*
Brandywine *B*
DuBois *B*
Erie, The Behrend College *B*
Fayette, The Eberly Campus *B*
Greater Allegheny *B*
Harrisburg *B*
Hazleton *B*
Lehigh Valley *B*
Mont Alto *B*
New Kensington *B*
Schuylkill *B*
Shenango *B*
University Park *B, M, D*
Wilkes-Barre *B*
Worthington Scranton *B*
York *B*

Puerto Rico

University of Puerto Rico
Mayaguez *B, M*

Rhode Island

University of Rhode Island *B, M*

South Carolina

Clemson University *B, M*

South Dakota

South Dakota State
University *B, M, D*

Tennessee

Hiwassee College *A*
Middle Tennessee State University *B*
Tennessee State University *B, M*
Tennessee Technological
University *B*
University of Tennessee
Knoxville *B, M, D*

Texas

Abilene Christian University *B*
Angelo State University *B, M*
Central Texas College *C*
Clarendon College *A*
Lubbock Christian University *B*
Prairie View A&M University *M*
Sam Houston State University *B*
Stephen F. Austin State University *B*
Sul Ross State University *B, M*
Tarleton State University *B*
Texas A&M University *B, M, D*
Texas A&M University
Commerce *B*
Kingsville *B, M*
Texas State University *B*
Texas Tech University *B, M, D*
West Texas A&M University *B, M*
Western Texas College *A*

Utah

Snow College *A*
Utah State University *B, M, D*

Vermont

University of Vermont *B, M, D*

Virginia

Blue Ridge Community College *C, A*
Virginia Polytechnic Institute and
State University *B, M, D*

Washington

Washington State University *B, M, D*

West Virginia

Potomac State College of West
Virginia University *A*
West Virginia University *B, M*

Wisconsin

Madison Area Technical College *A*
Northcentral Technical College *A*
University of Wisconsin
Madison *B, M, D*
Platteville *B*
River Falls *B*

Wyoming

Northwest College *A*
University of Wyoming *B, M, D*

Animal training

Colorado

Colorado Northwestern Community
College *C*
Lamar Community College *C, A*

Massachusetts

Becker College *A*

South Dakota

National American University
Rapid City *A*

Animation

Alabama

ITT Technical Institute
Birmingham *B*

Arizona

Art Institute of Phoenix *B*
Art Institute of Tucson *B*
Cochise College *C*
ITT Technical Institute
Tempe *B*
Tucson *B*
Southwest University of Visual Arts *B*
University of Advancing
Technology *A, B*

Arkansas

ITT Technical Institute
Little Rock *B*
University of Arkansas
Fort Smith *B*

California

Academy of Art University *C, A, B, M*
Allan Hancock College *A*
Art Center College of Design *B, M*
Art Institute of California
Hollywood *B*
Inland Empire *B*
Orange County *B*
Sacramento *B*
San Francisco *B, M*
Silicon Valley *B*
Canada College *C, A*
City College of San Francisco *C*
College of the Canyons *C, A*
College of the Siskiyous *C*
East Los Angeles College *C, A*
Ex'pression College *B*
ITT Technical Institute
Lathrop *B*
National City *B*
Oxnard *B*
Rancho Cordova *B*
San Bernardino *B*
Sylmar *B*
Torrance *B*
Long Beach City College *C*
Loyola Marymount University *B*
Otis College of Art and Design *B*
Palomar College *C, A*
Platt College
Ontario *B*
Santa Ana College *C*
Santa Monica College *C, A*
Santa Rosa Junior College *C*
Westwood College
Inland Empire *B*
Los Angeles *B*
South Bay *B*

Colorado

Aims Community College *C, A*
Colorado Mesa University *C, A*
Colorado Mountain College *A*
Front Range Community College *C, A*
Pikes Peak Community College *C, A*
Pueblo Community College *A*
Rocky Mountain College of Art &
Design *B*
Westwood College
Denver South *B*

Connecticut

Northwestern Connecticut
Community College *A*

Delaware

Delaware College of Art and
Design *A*

Florida

Art Institute of Fort Lauderdale *B*
Full Sail University *B*
Gulf Coast State College *B*
ITT Technical Institute
Lake Mary *B*
Tampa *B*
International Academy of Design and
Technology: Tampa *B*
Miami Dade College *A*
Miami International University of Art
and Design *B, M*
Ringling College of Art and Design *B*

Georgia

Art Institute of Atlanta *A, B*
Central Georgia Technical College *C*
Savannah College of Art and
Design *C, B, M*
Southwest Georgia Technical
College *C*

Hawaii

University of Hawaii
Leeward Community College *C, A*

Idaho

ITT Technical Institute
Boise *B*

Illinois

Bradley University *B*
City Colleges of Chicago
Harold Washington College *C, A*
Kennedy-King College *C*
Columbia College Chicago *B*
DePaul University *B, M*
Elgin Community College *C*
Moraine Valley Community College *C*
North Central College *B*
Oakton Community College *C*
Prairie State College *C*
School of the Art Institute of
Chicago *B, M*
Waubonsee Community College *C*

Indiana

ITT Technical Institute
Fort Wayne *B*
Indianapolis *B*
Newburgh *B*

Iowa

Western Iowa Tech Community
College *C, A*

Kansas

Johnson County Community
College *A*
Kansas City Kansas Community
College *C*

Kentucky

ITT Technical Institute
Louisville *B*
Sullivan College of Technology and
Design *A, B*

Louisiana

Bossier Parish Community College *C*
ITT Technical Institute
St. Rose *B*

Maryland

Cecil College *C, A*
Hagerstown Community College *C, A*
ITT Technical Institute
Owings Mills *B*
Montgomery College *C*

Massachusetts

ITT Technical Institute
Norwood *B*
Wilmington *B*
Mount Ida College *B*
New England Institute of Art *B*
Northeastern University *B*
School of the Museum of Fine
Arts *B, M*
Springfield Technical Community
College *A*

Michigan

College for Creative Studies *B*
Davenport University *B*
Ferris State University *B*
Henry Ford Community College *A*
ITT Technical Institute
Troy *B*
Kirtland Community College *A*
Lansing Community College *C, A*

Minnesota

Academy College *A*
Art Institutes International
Minnesota *B*
Century College *C*
ITT Technical Institute
Eden Prairie *B*
Minneapolis College of Art and
Design *B*
Minneapolis Community and
Technical College *C, A*
Minnesota School of Business
Richfield *C, A, B*
North Hennepin Community
College *C*
St. Paul College *A*
University of Northwestern - St.
Paul *B*

Missouri

Missouri State University: West
Plains *A*
Webster University *B*

Nebraska

ITT Technical Institute
Omaha *B*

Nevada

Art Institute of Las Vegas *B*
College of Southern Nevada *C, A*
ITT Technical Institute
Henderson *B*
Nevada State College *B*

New Jersey

Bergen Community College *A*
Brookdale Community College *A*
Burlington County College *A*
Montclair State University *B*
New Jersey Institute of Technology *B*
Raritan Valley Community College *A*
Union County College *A*

New Mexico

ITT Technical Institute
Albuquerque *B*
New Mexico State University *B*
New Mexico State University
Alamogordo *A*
Carlsbad *C*
Grants *C*
Southwest University of Visual Arts *B*

New York

Daemen College *C*
Fashion Institute of Technology *B*
Mildred Elley
Albany *C, A*
Pratt Institute *B*

Rochester Institute of
Technology *B, M*
School of Visual Arts *B*
Villa Maria College of Buffalo *B*

North Carolina

Central Piedmont Community
College *A*

Ohio

North Central State College *A*
Terra State Community College *C, A*
University of Cincinnati
Blue Ash College *C*
Washington State Community
College *A*

Oklahoma

Oklahoma Christian University *B*

Oregon

ITT Technical Institute
Portland *B*
Lane Community College *C, A*
Portland Community College *C*

Pennsylvania

Art Institute of Philadelphia *B*
Art Institute of Pittsburgh *A, B*
Art Institute of York *A, B*
Delaware County Community
College *A*
Lehigh Carbon Community College *A*
Philadelphia University *B, M*
Point Park University *B*

Puerto Rico

Colegio de Cinematografía, Artes y
Televisión *C*

Rhode Island

New England Institute of
Technology *A*

South Carolina

ITT Technical Institute
Greenville *B*

South Dakota

Southeast Technical Institute *A*

Tennessee

East Tennessee State University *B*
ITT Technical Institute
Knoxville *B*
Memphis *A*
Nashville *B*

Texas

Austin Community College *C, A*
Houston Community College
System *C, A*
North Lake College *C*
St. Philip's College *A*
Sam Houston State University *B*
Texas State Technical College
Waco *A*
University of the Incarnate Word *B*
Wharton County Junior College *A*

Utah

Brigham Young University *B*
Broadview University
Broadview Entertainment Arts
University *A*
Salt Lake Community College *A*

Vermont

Bennington College *B*

Virginia

Art Institute of Washington *B*
George Mason University *B*

ITT Technical Institute
Norfolk *B*
Richmond *B*
Regent University *B*
Virginia Polytechnic Institute and
State University *M*
Westwood College
Annandale *B*
Arlington Ballston *B*

Washington

Art Institute of Seattle *A*
DigiPen Institute of Technology *B, M*
ITT Technical Institute
Everett *B*
Seattle *B*
Spokane *B*
International Academy of Design and
Technology
Seattle *B*
Lake Washington Institute of
Technology *A*

Wisconsin

Art Institute of Wisconsin *B*
Herzing University
Madison *A, B*
ITT Technical Institute
Green Bay *B*
Greenfield *B*
Madison Media Institute *A*

Anthropology

Alabama

Auburn University *B*
Troy University *B*
University of Alabama *B, M, D*
University of Alabama
Birmingham *B*
University of South Alabama *B*

Alaska

University of Alaska
Anchorage *B, M*
Fairbanks *B, M, D*

Arizona

Arizona State University *B, D*
Coconino County Community
College *A*
Eastern Arizona College *A*
Northern Arizona University *B, M*
Pima Community College *A*
University of Arizona *B, M, D*

Arkansas

Hendrix College *B*
University of Arkansas *B, M, D*
University of Arkansas
Little Rock *B*

California

Bakersfield College *A*
Biola University *B*
Cabrillo College *A*
California Institute of Integral
Studies *M, D*
California State Polytechnic
University: Pomona *B*
California State University
Bakersfield *B*
Channel Islands *B*
Chico *B, M*
Dominguez Hills *B*
East Bay *B, M*
Fresno *B*
Fullerton *B, M*
Long Beach *B, M*
Los Angeles *B, M*
Northridge *B*
Sacramento *B, M*

San Bernardino *B*
Stanislaus *B*
Canada College *A*
Cerritos College *A*
Chaffey College *A*
College of Alameda *A*
College of the Desert *A*
College of the Siskiyous *A*
Contra Costa College *A*
Copper Mountain College *A*
Crafton Hills College *A*
Cypress College *A*
De Anza College *A*
East Los Angeles College *A*
El Camino College *A*
Foothill College *A*
Fresno City College *A*
Fullerton College *A*
Gavilan College *A*
Glendale Community College *A*
Golden West College *A*
Humboldt State University *B*
Imperial Valley College *A*
Irvine Valley College *A*
Lake Tahoe Community College *A*
Los Medanos College *A*
Merced College *A*
Mills College *B*
Monterey Peninsula College *A*
Ohlone College *C*
Orange Coast College *A*
Oxnard College *A*
Pitzer College *B*
Pomona College *B*
Saddleback College *A*
St. Mary's College of California *B*
San Diego City College *A*
San Diego Mesa College *A*
San Diego State University *B, M*
San Francisco State University *B, M*
San Jose State University *B*
Santa Ana College *A*
Santa Barbara City College *A*
Santa Clara University *B*
Santa Rosa Junior College *A*
Santiago Canyon College *A*
Scripps College *B*
Sonoma State University *B, M*
Southwestern College *A*
Stanford University *B, M, D*
University of California
Berkeley *B, D*
Davis *B, M, D*
Irvine *B, D*
Los Angeles *B, M, D*
Merced *B*
Riverside *B, M, D*
San Diego *B, D*
Santa Barbara *B, M, D*
Santa Cruz *B, D*
University of La Verne *B*
University of Redlands *B*
University of San Diego *B*
University of Southern
California *B, M, D*
Vanguard University of Southern
California *B*
West Los Angeles College *A*
Westmont College *B*
Whittier College *B*

Colorado

Colorado College *B*
Colorado State University *B, M*
Community College of Aurora *A*
Fort Lewis College *B*
Metropolitan State University of
Denver *B, T*
University of Colorado
Boulder *B, M, D*
Colorado Springs *B*
Denver *B, M*
University of Denver *B, M*
University of Northern Colorado *B*
Western State Colorado University *B*

Connecticut

Central Connecticut State
University *B*
Connecticut College *B*
Southern Connecticut State
University *B*
Trinity College *B*
University of Connecticut *B, M, D*
Wesleyan University *B, M*
Yale University *B, M, D*

Delaware

University of Delaware *B*

District of Columbia

American University *C, B, M, D*
Catholic University of America *B, M*
George Washington University *B, M*
Georgetown University *B*
Howard University *B*
University of the District of
Columbia *B*

Florida

Broward College *A*
Eckerd College *B*
Florida Atlantic University *B, M*
Florida Gulf Coast University *B*
Indian River State College *A*
Miami Dade College *A*
New College of Florida *B*
Palm Beach State College *A*
Rollins College *B*
University of Central Florida *B, M*
University of Florida *B, M, D*
University of Miami *B*
University of North Florida *B*
University of South Florida *B, M, D*
University of South Florida
Saint Petersburg *B*
University of West Florida *B, M*

Georgia

Darton College *A*
East Georgia State College *A*
Emory University *B, D*
Georgia Perimeter College *A*
Georgia Southern University *B*
Georgia State University *B, M*
Kennesaw State University *B*
Thomas University *B*
University of Georgia *B, M, D*
University of North Georgia *A*
University of West Georgia *B*

Hawaii

Hawaii Pacific University *C, B*
University of Hawaii
Hilo *B*
Manoa *B, M, D*
West Oahu *B*

Idaho

Boise State University *B*
College of Southern Idaho *A*
College of Western Idaho *A*
Idaho State University *B, M*
North Idaho College *A*
University of Idaho *B, M*

Illinois

Augustana College *B*
Chicago State University *B*
DePaul University *B*
Illinois State University *B*
Illinois Wesleyan University *B*
Knox College *B*
Loyola University Chicago *B*
Monmouth College *B*
National-Louis University *B*
North Central College *B*
Northeastern Illinois University *B*
Northern Illinois University *B, M*
Northwestern University *B, M, D*

Principia College *B*
Richland Community College *A*
South Suburban College of Cook
County *A*
Southern Illinois University
Carbondale *B, M, D*
Southern Illinois University
Edwardsville *B*
Southwestern Illinois College *A*
University of Chicago *B, D*
University of Illinois
Chicago *B, M, D*
Urbana-Champaign *B, M, D*
Wheaton College *B*

Indiana

Ball State University *B, M*
Butler University *B*
DePauw University *B*
Hanover College *B*
Indiana State University *B*
Indiana University
Bloomington *B, M, D*
Northwest *B*
Purdue University Fort Wayne *B*
Purdue University
Indianapolis *B, M*
South Bend *B*
Purdue University *B, M, D*
University of Indianapolis *B, M*
University of Notre Dame *B*
University of Southern Indiana *B*
Vincennes University *A*

Iowa

Central College *B*
Cornell College *B*
Drake University *B*
Grinnell College *B*
Iowa State University *B, M*
Luther College *B*
University of Iowa *B, M, D, T*
University of Northern Iowa *B*

Kansas

Barton County Community College *A*
Cowley County Community
College *A*
Kansas State University *B*
University of Kansas *B, M, D*
Washburn University *B*
Wichita State University *B, M*

Kentucky

Centre College *B*
Eastern Kentucky University *B*
Northern Kentucky University *B*
Transylvania University *B*
University of Kentucky *B, M, D*
University of Louisville *B, M*
Western Kentucky University *B*

Louisiana

Louisiana State University and
Agricultural and Mechanical
College *B, M*
Tulane University *B, M, D*
University of Louisiana at Lafayette *B*
University of New Orleans *B*

Maine

Bates College *B*
Bowdoin College *B*
Colby College *B*
College of the Atlantic *B, M*
University of Maine *B*
University of Southern Maine *B*

Maryland

Goucher College *B*
Harford Community College *A*
Howard Community College *A*
Johns Hopkins University *B, M, D*
St. Mary's College of Maryland *B*

University of Maryland
Baltimore County *B*
College Park *B, M, D*
Washington College *B*

Massachusetts

Amherst College *B*
Bard College at Simon's Rock *B*
Boston University *B, M, D*
Brandeis University *B, M, D*
Bridgewater State University *B*
College of the Holy Cross *B*
Hampshire College *B*
Harvard College *B, M, D*
Massachusetts Institute of
Technology *B*
Mount Holyoke College *B*
Smith College *B*
Tufts University *B*
University of Massachusetts
Amherst *B, M, D*
Boston *B*
Wellesley College *B*
Wheaton College *B*
Williams College *B*

Michigan

Albion College *B*
Andrews University *B*
Central Michigan University *B*
Eastern Michigan University *B*
Grand Valley State University *B*
Kalamazoo College *B*
Lansing Community College *A*
Michigan State University *B, M, D*
Michigan Technological University *B*
Oakland University *B*
University of Michigan *B, M, D*
University of Michigan
Dearborn *B*
Flint *B*
Wayne State University *B, M, D*
Western Michigan University *B, M*

Minnesota

Carleton College *B*
Gustavus Adolphus College *B*
Hamline University *B*
Macalester College *B*
Minnesota State University
Mankato *B, M*
Moorhead *B*
Saint Cloud State University *B*
University of Minnesota
Duluth *B*
Morris *B*
Twin Cities *B, M, D*

Mississippi

Mississippi State University *B, M*
University of Mississippi *B, M*
University of Southern
Mississippi *B, M*

Missouri

Lindenwood University *B*
Missouri State University *B*
Saint Louis University *B*
University of Missouri
Columbia *B, M, D*
St. Louis *B*
Washington University in St.
Louis *B, M, D*
Westminster College *B*

Montana

Montana State University *B*
University of Montana *B, M*
University of Montana: Western *B*

Nebraska

Creighton University *B*
University of Nebraska
Lincoln *B, M*

Western Nebraska Community
College *A*

Nevada

Truckee Meadows Community
College *C, A*
University of Nevada
Las Vegas *B, M, D*
Reno *B, M, D*

New Hampshire

Dartmouth College *B*
Franklin Pierce University *B*
Plymouth State University *B*
University of New Hampshire *B*

New Jersey

Drew University *B*
Monmouth University *B, M*
Montclair State University *B, M*
Princeton University *B, M, D*
Rutgers, The State University of New
Jersey
New Brunswick/Piscataway
Campus *B, M, D*
Newark Campus *B*
Seton Hall University *B*
Thomas Edison State College *B*
William Paterson University of New
Jersey *B*

New Mexico

Central New Mexico Community
College *A*
Eastern New Mexico University *B, M*
New Mexico Highlands University *B*
New Mexico State University *B, M*
University of New Mexico *B, M, D*

New York

Adelphi University *B*
Bard College *B*
Barnard College *B*
Canisius College *B*
City University of New York
Brooklyn College *B*
City College *B, M*
Hunter College *B, M*
Lehman College *B*
Queens College *B, T*
York College *B*
Colgate University *B*
Columbia University *B*
Columbia University
School of General Studies *B*
Cornell University *B, M, D*
Dowling College *B*
Fordham University *B*
Hamilton College *B*
Hartwick College *B*
Hobart and William Smith Colleges *B*
Hofstra University *B*
Ithaca College *B*
Long Island University
LIU Brooklyn *B, M*
Manhattanville College *B*
Nazareth College *B*
New York University *B, M, D*
SUNY
College at Brockport *B*
College at Buffalo *B*
College at Cortland *B*
College at Geneseo *B*
College at New Paltz *B*
College at Oneonta *B*
College at Oswego *B*
College at Plattsburgh *B*
College at Potsdam *B*
College at Purchase *B*
University at Albany *B, M, D*
University at Binghamton *B, M, D*
University at Buffalo *B, M, D*
University at Stony Brook *B, M, D*
St. John Fisher College *B*

St. John's University *B*
St. Lawrence University *B*
Skidmore College *B*
Syracuse University *B, M, D*
Union College *B*
University of Rochester *B*
Vassar College *B*
Wagner College *B*
Wells College *B*

North Carolina

Appalachian State University *B*
Davidson College *B*
Duke University *B, M, D*
East Carolina University *B, M*
Elon University *B*
Guilford College *B*
North Carolina State University *B, M*
University of North Carolina
Asheville *B*
Chapel Hill *B, M, D*
Charlotte *B*
Greensboro *B*
Wilmington *B*
Wake Forest University *B, M*
Western Carolina University *B*
William Peace University *B*

North Dakota

North Dakota State University *B, M*
University of North Dakota *B*

Ohio

Case Western Reserve
University *B, M, D*
Cleveland State University *B*
College of Wooster *B*
Denison University *B*
Franciscan University of
Steubenville *B*
Heidelberg University *B*
Kent State University *B, M*
Kenyon College *B*
Miami University
Middletown *A*
Oxford *B*
Muskingum University *B*
Oberlin College *B*
Ohio State University
Columbus Campus *B, M, D*
Ohio University *B*
Ohio Wesleyan University *B*
University of Akron *B*
University of Cincinnati *C, B, M*
University of Toledo *B*
Wright State University *B*
Youngstown State University *B*

Oklahoma

Oklahoma Baptist University *B*
University of Oklahoma *B, M, D*
University of Tulsa *B, M, D*

Oregon

Lewis & Clark College *B*
Linfield College *B, T*
Linn-Benton Community College *A*
Oregon State University *B, M, D*
Portland State University *B, M, D*
Reed College *B*
Southern Oregon University *B*
University of Oregon *B, M, D*
Western Oregon University *B*
Willamette University *B*

Pennsylvania

Albright College *B*
Bloomsburg University of
Pennsylvania *B*
Bryn Mawr College *B*
Bucknell University *B*
California University of
Pennsylvania *B*
Clarion University of Pennsylvania *B*

Delaware County Community
College *A*
Dickinson College *B*
Drexel University *B*
Edinboro University of
Pennsylvania *B*
Franklin & Marshall College *B*
Gettysburg College *B*
Haverford College *B, T*
Indiana University of Pennsylvania *B*
Juniata College *B*
Kutztown University of
Pennsylvania *B*
Lafayette College *B*
Lehigh University *B*
Lincoln University *B*
Lycoming College *B*
Mansfield University of
Pennsylvania *B*
Mercyhurst University *B*
Millersville University of
Pennsylvania *B*
Muhlenberg College *C, B*
Penn State
Abington *B*
Altoona *B*
Beaver *B*
Berks *B*
Brandywine *B*
DuBois *B*
Erie, The Behrend College *B*
Fayette, The Eberly Campus *B*
Greater Allegheny *B*
Harrisburg *B*
Hazleton *B*
Lehigh Valley *B*
Mont Alto *B*
New Kensington *B*
Schuylkill *B*
Shenango *B*
University Park *B, M, D*
Wilkes-Barre *B*
Worthington Scranton *B*
York *B*
St. Vincent College *B*
Susquehanna University *B*
Temple University *B, M, D*
University of Pennsylvania *A, B, M, D*
University of Pittsburgh *B, M, D*
University of Pittsburgh
Greensburg *B*
Ursinus College *B*
West Chester University of
Pennsylvania *B*
Widener University *B*

Puerto Rico

Inter American University of Puerto
Rico
Metropolitan Campus *B*
San German Campus *B*
University of Puerto Rico
Aguadilla *A*
Rio Piedras *B*

Rhode Island

Brown University *B, M, D*
Rhode Island College *B*
Roger Williams University *B*
University of Rhode Island *B*

South Carolina

Clemson University *B*
College of Charleston *B*
Furman University *B*
University of South Carolina
Columbia *B, M, D*

South Dakota

Augustana College *B*
University of South Dakota *B*

Tennessee

Lee University *B*
Middle Tennessee State University *B*
Rhodes College *B*
Sewanee: The University of the
    South *B*
University of Memphis *B, M*
University of Tennessee
    Knoxville *B, M, D*
Vanderbilt University *B, M, D*

Texas

Austin Community College *A*
Baylor University *B*
Galveston College *A*
Howard Payne University *B*
Rice University *B, M, D*
Southern Methodist
    University *B, M, D*
Southwestern University *B*
Texas A&M University *B, M, D*
Texas Christian University *B*
Texas State University *B, M*
Texas Tech University *B, M*
Trinity University *B*
University of Houston *B, M*
University of Houston
    Clear Lake *B*
University of North Texas *B, M*
University of Texas
    Arlington *B, M*
    Austin *B, M, D*
    El Paso *B*
    Pan American *B*
    San Antonio *B, M, D*

Utah

Brigham Young University *B, M*
Snow College *A*
University of Utah *B, M, D, T*
Utah State University *B, M*
Weber State University *B*

Vermont

Bennington College *B*
Johnson State College *B*
Marlboro College *B*
Saint Michael's College *B*
University of Vermont *B*

Virginia

College of William and Mary *B, M, D*
Emory & Henry College *B*
George Mason University *B, M*
James Madison University *B*
Longwood University *B*
Mary Baldwin College *B*
Radford University *B*
Sweet Briar College *B*
University of Mary Washington *B*
University of Richmond *B*
University of Virginia *B, M, D*
Virginia Commonwealth University *B*
Washington and Lee University *B*

Washington

Central Washington University *B*
Centralia College *A*
Eastern Washington University *B*
Highline Community College *A*
Pacific Lutheran University *B*
Saint Martin's University *B*
University of Washington *B, M, D*
Washington State University *B, M, D*
Western Washington University *D, M*
Whitman College *B*

Wisconsin

Beloit College *B*
Lawrence University *B*
Marquette University *B*
Ripon College *B*
St. Norbert College *B*

University of Wisconsin
    Madison *B, M, D*
    Milwaukee *B, M, D*
    Oshkosh *B*
    Parkside *T*
    River Falls *T*

Wyoming

Casper College *A*
Laramie County Community
    College *A*
Northwest College *A*
University of Wyoming *B, M, D*
Western Wyoming Community
    College *A*

Apparel/accessories marketing

Arizona

Art Institute of Phoenix *B*

California

Art Institute of California
    Inland Empire *B*
    Orange County *B*
Sierra College *C, A*

Florida

Miami International University of Art
    and Design *A, B*

Georgia

Gwinnett Technical College *C*

Iowa

Des Moines Area Community
    College *C, A*
Kirkwood Community College *C, A*

Massachusetts

Lasell College *B*

Michigan

Art Institute of Michigan *B*
Michigan State University *B, M*

New York

Fashion Institute of Technology *M*

Ohio

Art Institute of Ohio: Cincinnati *B*
Youngstown State University *B*

Oklahoma

University of Central Oklahoma *B*

Pennsylvania

Art Institute of Philadelphia *A, B*
Philadelphia University *B*

Rhode Island

University of Rhode Island *B*

Washington

Art Institute of Seattle *A, B*

Wisconsin

Art Institute of Wisconsin *B*

Apparel/textile manufacture

Alabama

Bishop State Community College *C*

Arizona

Mesa Community College *C*

California

Academy of Couture Art *A, B*
Canada College *C, A*
Fashion Institute of Design and
    Merchandising
    Los Angeles *A*
    San Diego *A*
    San Francisco *A*
Orange Coast College *C*

Iowa

Iowa State University *B*

Michigan

Michigan State University *B, M*

Minnesota

Minneapolis Community and
    Technical College *C*

New York

Fashion Institute of
    Technology *C, A, B*

Apparel/textile marketing

Alabama

Auburn University *B, M*

California

Allan Hancock College *C*
Canada College *C, A*
Fashion Institute of Design and
    Merchandising
    Los Angeles *A*
    San Diego *A*
    San Francisco *A*
Palomar College *A*
San Joaquin Delta College *C, A*
Santa Monica College *C, A*

Colorado

Colorado State University *B, M*

Georgia

Savannah College of Art and
    Design *B*

Hawaii

University of Hawaii
    Maui College *A*

Indiana

Indiana Institute of Technology *B*
Purdue University *B*

Iowa

Iowa State University *B*

Michigan

Michigan State University *B, M*
Wayne State University *B, M*

Mississippi

Hinds Community College *C*

Missouri

Northwest Missouri State
    University *B*

Nebraska

University of Nebraska
    Lincoln *B*

North Dakota

North Dakota State University *M*

Ohio

Ashland University *B*

Oregon

Oregon State University *M, D*

Pennsylvania

Philadelphia University *B, M*

South Dakota

South Dakota State University *B*

Texas

University of the Incarnate
    Word *A, B*

Washington

Central Washington University *B*

Appliance installation and repair

California

Los Medanos College *C*
Solano Community College *C, A*

Georgia

Columbus Technical College *C*

Kansas

Kansas City Kansas Community
    College *C*

Kentucky

Elizabethtown Community and
    Technical College *C, A*
Somerset Community College *C*

West Virginia

West Virginia Northern Community
    College *C*

Wisconsin

Milwaukee Area Technical College *C*

Applied behavior analysis

Alabama

Auburn University *M*

Connecticut

University of Saint Joseph *M*

Florida

Florida Institute of Technology *M, D*

Illinois

Aurora University *M*

Kentucky

Spalding University *M*

Massachusetts

Northeastern University *M*
Simmons College *M*
University of Massachusetts
    Dartmouth *M*
Western New England
    University *M, D*
Westfield State University *M*

Michigan

Western Michigan University *M, D*

Missouri

Saint Louis University *M*

Nebraska

University of Nebraska
    Omaha *M*

New Jersey
Caldwell College *M, D, T*
Georgian Court University *B*

Ohio
Youngstown State University *M*

Rhode Island
Salve Regina University *M*

Texas
University of North Texas *B*

Virginia
Shenandoah University *M*

Applied economics

Arizona
University of Arizona *B*

California
University of San Francisco *B*

District of Columbia
Georgetown University *M*

Florida
Florida State University *B*

Georgia
Georgia Southern University *M, T*

Illinois
DePaul University *M*

Iowa
University of Northern Iowa *B*

Kentucky
Western Kentucky University *M*

Maine
College of the Atlantic *B*

Massachusetts
University of Massachusetts
    Amherst *C*

Michigan
Eastern Michigan University *M*
Michigan Technological University *M*
University of Michigan *M*
Western Michigan University *M, D*

Minnesota
Augsburg College *B*
College of St. Scholastica *B*
Saint Cloud State University *M*
University of Minnesota
    Twin Cities *B, M, D*

New Jersey
Montclair State University *B, M*

New York
Ithaca College *B*
SUNY
    Farmingdale State College *B*
    University at Binghamton *B*

North Carolina
East Carolina University *M*

North Dakota
University of North Dakota *M*

Ohio
University of Akron *B*

Oklahoma
University of Central Oklahoma *B*

Oregon
Oregon State University *M, D*

Pennsylvania
Allegheny College *B*

Rhode Island
Bryant University *B*
University of Rhode Island *B, M, D*

Tennessee
Vanderbilt University *D*

Texas
Southern Methodist University *M*
University of Houston *M*

Utah
Utah State University *M*

Virginia
Virginia Polytechnic Institute and
    State University *B*

Washington
Washington State University *M*

Wisconsin
Marquette University *M*

Applied history

Arkansas
Arkansas Tech University *B*

California
California State University
    Sacramento *M, D*
San Diego State University *M*

Connecticut
Central Connecticut State
    University *M*

Georgia
Georgia Southern University *T*

Illinois
Loyola University Chicago *M*

Kentucky
Northern Kentucky University *C, M*
University of Louisville *C*

Maine
College of the Atlantic *B, M*

Maryland
Stevenson University *B*

Massachusetts
Salem State University *B*

Michigan
Western Michigan University *B, M*

Missouri
Southeast Missouri State University *M*

New York
City University of New York
    Queens College *T*
St. John's University *M*

North Carolina
East Carolina University *B*
North Carolina State University *M*
St. Andrews University *B*

North Dakota
North Dakota State University *B*

Pennsylvania
Duquesne University *M*

Rhode Island
Rhode Island College *C*

South Carolina
University of South Carolina
    Columbia *M*

Texas
McMurry University *B*
Texas Lutheran University *B*

Virginia
Emory & Henry College *B*

Applied linguistics

Arizona
Arizona State University *D*

California
National University *M*

Iowa
Ashford University *B*

Massachusetts
Boston University *M, D*

North Carolina
Mid-Atlantic Christian University *B*

Texas
Texas Tech University *M*
University of Houston *M*
University of Texas
    El Paso *M*

Applied mathematics

Alabama
Auburn University *B, M*
Oakwood University *B*
University of Alabama *D*
University of Alabama
    Birmingham *D*
    Huntsville *D*

Alaska
University of Alaska
    Fairbanks *B, M*

Arizona
Arizona State University *D*
University of Arizona *M, D*

Arkansas
University of Arkansas
    Little Rock *M*
University of Central Arkansas *M*

California
California State University
    East Bay *B, M*
    Fullerton *B, M*
    Long Beach *B, M, D*
    Northridge *B, M*
Fresno Pacific University *B*
Harvey Mudd College *B*
Loyola Marymount University *B*
Master's College *B*
Mount St. Mary's College *B*
San Diego City College *A*
San Diego State University *B, M*
San Francisco State University *B*
San Jose State University *B*
Santa Clara University *M*

University of California
    Berkeley *B, D*
    Davis *B, M, D*
    Los Angeles *B*
    Merced *B, M, D*
    Riverside *B, M*
    San Diego *B, M*
    Santa Barbara *M*
    Santa Cruz *M, D*
University of Southern
    California *B, M, D*
University of the Pacific *B*

Colorado
Colorado School of Mines *B*
Colorado State University *M*
University of Colorado
    Boulder *B, M, D*
    Colorado Springs *M*
    Denver *M, D*

Connecticut
Central Connecticut State
    University *M, T*
University of Connecticut *B, M*
University of New Haven *B*
Yale University *B, M, D*

Delaware
Delaware State University *M, D*

District of Columbia
American University *B*
George Washington University *B, M*

Florida
Florida Atlantic University *M*
Florida Gulf Coast University *M*
Florida Institute of
    Technology *B, M, D*
Florida International University *M*
Florida State University *B, M, D*
New College of Florida *B*
University of Central Florida *M, D*
University of Miami *B*
University of North Florida *M*

Georgia
Emory University *B*
Georgia Institute of Technology *B*
University of Georgia *M*
Valdosta State University *B*

Hawaii
Hawaii Pacific University *B*

Idaho
Boise State University *B*
College of Idaho *B*
University of Idaho *B*

Illinois
Augustana College *B*
DePaul University *M*
Illinois Institute of
    Technology *B, M, D*
Millikin University *B*
National-Louis University *B*
North Central College *B*
Northwestern University *B, M, D*
University of Chicago *B*
University of Illinois
    Urbana-Champaign *M*

Indiana
Franklin College *B*
Indiana University
    Purdue University Fort Wayne *M*
    South Bend *B*
Oakland City University *B*
Purdue University *B, M, D*
Saint Mary's College *B*

Taylor University *B*
University of Notre Dame *M*

Iowa

Grand View University *B*
Iowa State University *M, D*
University of Iowa *B, D*
University of Northern Iowa *B*
William Penn University *B*

Kansas

Independence Community College *A*

Kentucky

Berea College *B*
Brescia University *B*
University of Kentucky *M*
University of Louisville *D*

Louisiana

Tulane University *M, D*

Maine

University of New England *B*

Maryland

Bowie State University *M*
Howard Community College *A*
Johns Hopkins University *B, M, D*
Loyola University Maryland *B*
Stevenson University *B*
Towson University *M*
University of Maryland
    Baltimore County *M, D*
    College Park *M, D*

Massachusetts

Bard College at Simon's Rock *B*
Endicott College *B*
Fitchburg State University *B*
Harvard College *B, M, D*
Lasell College *B*
Northeastern University *M*
Tufts University *B, M*
University of Massachusetts
    Amherst *M*
    Lowell *B*
Wentworth Institute of Technology *B*
Worcester Polytechnic Institute *B, M*

Michigan

Ferris State University *B*
Kettering University *B*
Michigan State University *M, D*
Oakland University *M, D*
Saginaw Valley State University *B*
University of Detroit Mercy *B*
University of Michigan *M, D*
Wayne State University *M*
Western Michigan University *B*

Minnesota

Concordia University St. Paul *B*
Metropolitan State University *B*
University of Minnesota
    Duluth *M*
    Twin Cities *M*

Mississippi

Millsaps College *B*
Mississippi State University *D*

Missouri

Central Methodist University *A*
Maryville University of Saint Louis *B*
Missouri University of Science and
    Technology *B, M*
University of Missouri
    Columbia *M*
    St. Louis *B, D*
Washington University in St. Louis *B*

Montana

Carroll College *B*
University of Montana: Western *B*

Nebraska

Creighton University *B*

Nevada

University of Nevada
    Las Vegas *B, M, D*

New Jersey

Bloomfield College *B, T*
New Jersey Institute of
    Technology *B, M*
Princeton University *M, D*
Rutgers, The State University of New
    Jersey
    Newark Campus *B*
Stevens Institute of Technology *B, M*

New Mexico

New Mexico Institute of Mining and
    Technology *B, M, D*

New York

Barnard College *B*
City University of New York
    Hunter College *M*
    New York City College of
        Technology *B*
Clarkson University *B*
Columbia University *B, M, D*
Columbia University
    School of General Studies *B*
Cornell University *M, D*
Dowling College *B*
Hofstra University *M*
Iona College *B*
Long Island University
    LIU Post *B, M*
Marist College *B*
New York University *M*
Rensselaer Polytechnic Institute *M*
Rochester Institute of
    Technology *B, M*
SUNY
    College at Fredonia *B*
    College at Oswego *B*
    Farmingdale State College *B*
    Institute of Technology at Utica/
        Rome *B*
    University at Albany *B*
    University at Buffalo *B*
    University at Stony Brook *B, M, D*
St. Thomas Aquinas College *B*
University of Rochester *B, M*

North Carolina

Elon University *B*
North Carolina Agricultural and
    Technical State University *B, M*
North Carolina State
    University *B, M, D*
University of North Carolina
    Chapel Hill *B*
    Charlotte *D*
Western Carolina University *M*

North Dakota

University of Jamestown *B*

Ohio

Case Western Reserve
    University *B, M, D*
Kent State University *B, M, D*
Ohio University *B*
University of Akron *B, M*
University of Dayton *M*
Wright State University *M*

Oklahoma

East Central University *B*
University of Central Oklahoma *B, M*
University of Tulsa *B, M, D*

Oregon

Oregon Institute of Technology *B*

Pennsylvania

Carnegie Mellon University *B*
Geneva College *B*
Indiana University of Pennsylvania *M*
La Salle University *B, T*
Lehigh University *M, D*
Penn State
    Harrisburg *B*
Robert Morris University *B*
Temple University *B*
University of Pittsburgh *B, M*
University of Pittsburgh
    Bradford *B*
    Greensburg *B*

Puerto Rico

Inter American University of Puerto
    Rico
    San German Campus *M*
Universidad Metropolitana *B*
University of Puerto Rico
    Mayaguez *M*

Rhode Island

Brown University *B, M, D*
Bryant University *B*
University of Rhode Island *D*

South Carolina

Charleston Southern University *B*
Coastal Carolina University *B*
Presbyterian College *B, T*
University of South Carolina
    Aiken *B*
    Columbia *M*
    Upstate *B*

South Dakota

University of Sioux Falls *B*

Tennessee

Trevecca Nazarene University *B*
University of Tennessee
    Chattanooga *B*

Texas

Baylor University *B*
Lamar University *B, M*
Rice University *B, M, D*
Southwestern Adventist University *B*
Texas A&M University *B*
Texas State University *B, M*
University of Houston *M*
University of Houston
    Downtown *B*
University of St. Thomas *B*
University of Texas
    El Paso *B*
    San Antonio *M*

Utah

University of Utah *B*
Weber State University *B*

Virginia

Christopher Newport University *B*
Hampden-Sydney College *B*
Hampton University *M*
Mary Baldwin College *B*
Old Dominion University *M, D*

Washington

University of Washington *B, M, D*
Washington State University *B, M, D*

Western Washington University *B*
Whitworth University *B*

West Virginia

Alderson-Broaddus University *B*
West Virginia State University *B*

Wisconsin

Carroll University *B*
University of Wisconsin
    Madison *B*
    Milwaukee *B*
    Stout *B*

Applied/professional ethics

Arizona

Arizona State University *M*

California

Mount St. Mary's College *B*

Illinois

Loyola University Chicago *M*

Indiana

Valparaiso University *M*

Michigan

Western Michigan University *B*

Pennsylvania

Carnegie Mellon University *B*

Applied psychology

California

Mount St. Mary's College *B*
University of Southern California *M*

Connecticut

Sacred Heart University *M*

Florida

Florida Institute of Technology *M, D*
Lynn University *M*

Illinois

Loyola University Chicago *B*

Indiana

University of St. Francis *B*

Kansas

Kansas Wesleyan University *B*

Michigan

University of Michigan
    Flint *B*

New Jersey

Rider University *M*

New York

Pace University *B*
SUNY
    College of Agriculture and
        Technology at Cobleskill *B*
    College of Agriculture and
        Technology at Morrisville *B*
    College of Technology at Canton *B*
    Farmingdale State College *B*

North Carolina

Belmont Abbey College *B*

Ohio

Franklin University *B*

Rhode Island

Bryant University *B*

South Carolina

Columbia College *M*

Tennessee

Christian Brothers University *B*

Texas

Argosy University
 Dallas *D*

Aquaculture

Alabama

Auburn University *B, M, D*
Gadsden State Community College *C*

Arkansas

University of Arkansas
 Pine Bluff *M, D*

Delaware

Delaware Technical Community
 College
 Jack F. Owens Campus *C*

Florida

Hillsborough Community
 College *C, A*

Idaho

College of Southern Idaho *C, A*

Maine

University of New England *B*

Massachusetts

Bristol Community College *C*

New York

SUNY
 College of Agriculture and
  Technology at Morrisville *A*

North Carolina

Brunswick Community College *C, A*

South Carolina

Clemson University *B, M*

Texas

Texas A&M University
 Corpus Christi *M*
 Galveston *B*

West Virginia

New River Community and Technical
 College *A*

Wyoming

Eastern Wyoming College *C*
Sheridan College *C*

Aquatic biology/ limnology

California

University of California
 Santa Barbara *B*

Florida

Florida Institute of Technology *B*
Stetson University *B*

Kentucky

Murray State University *M*

Maine

College of the Atlantic *B, M*

Minnesota

Bemidji State University *B*
Saint Cloud State University *B*

New York

SUNY
 College at Brockport *B*
 College of Environmental Science
  and Forestry *B*

Rhode Island

Brown University *B*
University of Rhode Island *M*

Texas

Baylor University *M*
Texas A&M University
 Galveston *B*
Texas State University *B, M*

Wisconsin

University of Wisconsin
 Superior *B*

Arabic

California

Grossmont College *A*
Imperial Valley College *A*
National University *B*
University of California
 Los Angeles *B*

District of Columbia

Catholic University of America *M, D*
George Washington University *B*
Georgetown University *B, M, D*

Georgia

University of Georgia *B*

Illinois

DePaul University *B, M*

Indiana

University of Notre Dame *B*

Kentucky

Western Kentucky University *B*

Maryland

Howard Community College *A*
United States Naval Academy *B*
University of Maryland
 College Park *B*

Massachusetts

Wellesley College *B*

Michigan

Michigan State University *B*
University of Michigan *M*

Minnesota

University of Minnesota
 Twin Cities *B, M*

Missouri

Washington University in St.
 Louis *B, M*

New Hampshire

Dartmouth College *B*

New York

Bard College *B*
SUNY
 University at Binghamton *B*
United States Military Academy *B*

Ohio

Ohio State University
 Columbus Campus *B*

Oklahoma

University of Oklahoma *B*

Pennsylvania

California University of
 Pennsylvania *C, B*
Gettysburg College *B*

Texas

Baylor University *B*
University of Texas
 Austin *B, M, D*

Utah

Brigham Young University *B*
University of Utah *B, M, D*

Vermont

Middlebury College *B*

Washington

University of Washington *B*

Archaeology

California

California State University
 East Bay *B*
 San Bernardino *C*
Canada College *A*
Merced College *A*
Palomar College *C, A*
St. Mary's College of California *B*
Stanford University *B*
University of California
 Los Angeles *M, D*
 San Diego *B*
University of Southern California *B*

Connecticut

Norwalk Community College *C*
Wesleyan University *B*
Yale University *B, M*

District of Columbia

George Washington University *B*

Idaho

University of Idaho *C*

Illinois

Illinois State University *M*
Richland Community College *A*
Southwestern Illinois College *A*
Wheaton College *B, M*

Indiana

University of Evansville *B*
University of Indianapolis *B*

Iowa

Cornell College *B*

Maine

Bowdoin College *B*

Maryland

Johns Hopkins University *B*

Massachusetts

Boston University *B, M, D*
Tufts University *B*
Wellesley College *B*

Michigan

Michigan Technological
 University *M, D*

Minnesota

University of Minnesota
 Twin Cities *M, D*

Missouri

University of Missouri
 Columbia *B, M, D*
Washington University in St.
 Louis *B, M, D*

New York

City University of New York
 Hunter College *B*
Columbia University *B*
Columbia University
 School of General Studies *B*
Cornell University *B, M*
Hamilton College *B*
New York University *B*
SUNY
 College at Potsdam *B*

North Carolina

University of North Carolina
 Chapel Hill *B*

Ohio

College of Wooster *B*
University of Akron *C*
University of Cincinnati *M*
University of Rio Grande *B*

Pennsylvania

Bryn Mawr College *B, M, D*
Dickinson College *B*
Haverford College *B*
Indiana University of Pennsylvania *M*
Lycoming College *B*
Penn State
 Abington *D*
 Altoona *B*
 Beaver *B*
 Berks *B*
 Brandywine *B*
 DuBois *B*
 Erie, The Behrend College *B*
 Fayette, The Eberly Campus *B*
 Greater Allegheny *B*
 Harrisburg *B*
 Hazleton *B*
 Lehigh Valley *B*
 Mont Alto *B*
 New Kensington *B*
 Schuylkill *B*
 Shenango *B*
 University Park *B*
 Wilkes-Barre *B*
 Worthington Scranton *B*
 York *B*
University of Pennsylvania *M, D*

Rhode Island

Brown University *B, M, D*

Tennessee

Southern Adventist University *B*

Texas

University of Texas
 Austin *B*

Utah

Brigham Young University *B*
Weber State University *C, A*

Virginia

Sweet Briar College *B*

Washington

Western Washington University *B*

Wisconsin

University of Wisconsin
  La Crosse *B*

Wyoming

Northwest College *C, A*
Western Wyoming Community
  College *A*

Architectural and building sciences

California

University of Southern California *M*

Georgia

Georgia Institute of Technology *B, M*

Minnesota

South Central College *C, A*

Mississippi

Northeast Mississippi Community
  College *A*

Pennsylvania

Pennsylvania College of
  Technology *B*

Architectural drafting/ CAD/CADD

Alaska

University of Alaska
  Anchorage *C*

Arizona

Coconino County Community
  College *C, A*
Mesa Community College *C, A*
Phoenix College *C, A*
Pima Community College *C, A*
Scottsdale Community College *C, A*

California

Bakersfield College *C*
Carrington College California
  San Jose *C, A*
College of the Canyons *C, A*
College of the Desert *C, A*
Hartnell College *C*
Long Beach City College *C, A*
Palomar College *C, A*
Santa Rosa Junior College *C*
Shasta College *C, A*
Sierra College *C, A*
Southwestern College *C*
Westwood College
  Inland Empire *A*
  South Bay *A*

Colorado

IntelliTec College: Grand Junction *A*

Florida

College of Central Florida *A*
Indian River State College *A*
Lincoln College of Technology
  West Palm Beach *A*
Palm Beach State College *C*

Georgia

Albany Technical College *C*
Atlanta Technical College *C*
Central Georgia Technical College *C*
Clayton State University *A*
Southwest Georgia Technical
  College *C*

Hawaii

University of Hawaii
  Honolulu Community College *A*

Illinois

City Colleges of Chicago
  Harold Washington College *C, A*
  Wilbur Wright College *C, A*
Harper College *C, A*
Illinois Central College *C*
Illinois Valley Community College *C*
Kaskaskia College *C, A*
Lincoln Land Community
  College *C, A*
Triton College *C, A*
Waubonsee Community College *C*

Indiana

Indiana University
  Purdue University Indianapolis *A*
Vincennes University *A*

Iowa

Clinton Community College *C, A*
Des Moines Area Community
  College *C, A*
Kirkwood Community College *A*

Kansas

Hutchinson Community College *A*

Kentucky

Sullivan College of Technology and
  Design *A*
Western Kentucky University *A*

Maine

Southern Maine Community
  College *A*
York County Community
  College *C, A*

Maryland

Carroll Community College *C, A*
Community College of Baltimore
  County *C, A*
Hagerstown Community College *C*
Wor-Wic Community College *C*

Massachusetts

Springfield Technical Community
  College *C*

Michigan

Baker College
  Allen Park *A*
  Muskegon *A*
Grand Rapids Community
  College *C, A*
Oakland Community College *C*

Minnesota

Anoka Technical College *C, A*
Dakota County Technical
  College *C, A*
Globe University
  Woodbury *A*
Hennepin Technical College *C, A*
Lake Superior College *C, A*
Minneapolis Community and
  Technical College *C*
Minnesota State Community and
  Technical College *A*
Northland Community & Technical
  College *C, A*
Rochester Community and Technical
  College *C*
St. Cloud Technical and Community
  College *C, A*

Missouri

Jefferson College *C, A*

Nebraska

Metropolitan Community
  College *C, A*

Northeast Community College *A*
Southeast Community College *A*

Nevada

College of Southern Nevada *C*

New Mexico

Central New Mexico Community
  College *C, A*
Santa Fe Community College *C, A*

New York

City University of New York
  New York City College of
    Technology *A*
SUNY
  College of Agriculture and
    Technology at Morrisville *A*

North Carolina

Gaston College *C*

Ohio

Central Ohio Technical College *A*
Owens Community College
  Toledo *C, A*
University of Toledo *A*

Oklahoma

Oklahoma State University
  Oklahoma City *A*

Oregon

Chemeketa Community College *C*
Clackamas Community College *A*
Portland Community College *A*
Rogue Community College *C*

Pennsylvania

Butler County Community College *A*
Commonwealth Technical Institute *A*
Delaware County Community
  College *C, A*
Johnson College *A*
Keystone Technical Institute *A*
Luzerne County Community
  College *C, A*
Triangle Tech
  DuBois *A*
  Erie *A*
  Greensburg *A*
Westmoreland County Community
  College *A*

Puerto Rico

Turabo University *C, A*
Universidad del Este *C*

Rhode Island

New England Institute of
  Technology *A, B*

South Carolina

Spartanburg Community College *C*

Texas

Del Mar College *C*
Eastfield College *C*
St. Philip's College *C, A*
Wharton County Junior College *C*

Utah

Salt Lake Community College *A*

Washington

Bates Technical College *C*
Lake Washington Institute of
  Technology *C, A*
Olympic College *C*

West Virginia

Kanawha Valley Community and
  Technical College *A*

Wisconsin

Herzing University
  Madison *A, B*

Wyoming

Casper College *C*

Architectural engineering

Alabama

Auburn University *B, M*

California

California Polytechnic State
  University: San Luis Obispo *B*

Colorado

University of Colorado
  Boulder *B, M, D*

District of Columbia

University of the District of
  Columbia *A*

Florida

Miami Dade College *A*
University of Miami *B, M*

Illinois

Illinois Institute of Technology *B, M*
University of Illinois
  Urbana-Champaign *M*

Kansas

Independence Community College *A*
Kansas State University *B, M*
University of Kansas *B, M*

Kentucky

Sullivan College of Technology and
  Design *A*

Massachusetts

Springfield Technical Community
  College *A*
Tufts University *B*
Worcester Polytechnic Institute *B*

Michigan

Delta College *A*
Lawrence Technological
  University *B, M*
University of Detroit Mercy *B*

Mississippi

Holmes Community College *A*

Missouri

Missouri University of Science and
  Technology *B*

Nebraska

University of Nebraska
  Lincoln *B, M, D*

North Carolina

North Carolina Agricultural and
  Technical State University *B*

Ohio

Stark State College *A*
University of Cincinnati *B*

Oklahoma

Oklahoma State University *B*
University of Oklahoma *B*

Pennsylvania

Drexel University *B*
Penn State
  Abington *B*
  Altoona *B*
  Beaver *B*
  Berks *B*
  Brandywine *B*
  DuBois *B*
  Erie, The Behrend College *B*
  Fayette, The Eberly Campus *B*
  Greater Allegheny *B*
  Harrisburg *B*
  Hazleton *B*
  Lehigh Valley *B*
  Mont Alto *B*
  New Kensington *B*
  Schuylkill *B*
  Shenango *B*
  University Park *B, M, D*
  Wilkes-Barre *B*
  Worthington Scranton *B*
  York *B*
Philadelphia University *B*
Widener University *M*

Rhode Island

New England Institute of
  Technology *A, B*

Tennessee

Tennessee State University *B*

Texas

Laredo Community College *A*
University of Texas
  Austin *B, M*

Wisconsin

Milwaukee School of Engineering *B*

Wyoming

University of Wyoming *B*

Architectural engineering technology

Alabama

Lawson State Community
  College *C, A*

Alaska

University of Alaska
  Anchorage *A*

California

Allan Hancock College *A*
Chabot College *A*
Chaffey College *C, A*
College of the Desert *C, A*
College of the Sequoias *A*
Cuyamaca College *A*
Diablo Valley College *C*
El Camino College *C, A*
Fullerton College *C*
Golden West College *C, A*
Laney College *C, A*
Long Beach City College *C, A*
Los Angeles Harbor College *C, A*
Los Angeles Trade and Technical
  College *C, A*
Modesto Junior College *C, A*
Mount San Antonio College *C, A*
National University *C*
Orange Coast College *C, A*
Ventura College *C, A*

Colorado

Arapahoe Community College *C, A*
Front Range Community College *C, A*
Pikes Peak Community College *C, A*
Westwood College
  Denver North *A*

Connecticut

Capital Community College *A*
Norwalk Community College *A*
Three Rivers Community
  College *C, A*
University of Hartford *B*

Delaware

Delaware State University *B*
Delaware Technical Community
  College
  Jack F. Owens Campus *A*
  Stanton/Wilmington Campus *A*
  Terry Campus *A*

Florida

College of Central Florida *C*
Daytona State College *A*
Florida State College at
  Jacksonville *A*
Gulf Coast State College *C*
Hillsborough Community
  College *C, A*
Miami Dade College *A*
Northwest Florida State College *C, A*
Pensacola State College *C*
Seminole State College of
  Florida *C, A, B*
Valencia College *C*

Georgia

Southern Polytechnic State
  University *B*

Hawaii

University of Hawaii
  Hawaii Community College *C*

Idaho

Brigham Young University-Idaho *A*

Illinois

Joliet Junior College *C, A*
Morrison Institute of Technology *A*

Indiana

Indiana State University *B*
Indiana University
  Purdue University Fort Wayne *A*
  Purdue University Indianapolis *B*
Purdue University *A, B*
Purdue University
  Calumet *C, B*
  North Central *A, B*

Iowa

Iowa Western Community College *A*

Kansas

Colby Community College *A*
Independence Community College *A*

Kentucky

Eastern Kentucky University *B*
Northern Kentucky University *A, B*
Sullivan College of Technology and
  Design *A*

Louisiana

Delgado Community College *A*

Maryland

Montgomery College *A*

Massachusetts

Fitchburg State University *B*
Massasoit Community College *A*
Wentworth Institute of Technology *A*

Michigan

Baker College
  Auburn Hills *A*
  Flint *A*

Muskegon *A*
  Owosso *A*
Ferris State University *A, B*
Lansing Community College *A*
Monroe County Community
  College *C, A*
Mott Community College *C, A*
Oakland Community College *A*
St. Clair County Community
  College *C, A*

Mississippi

Hinds Community College *C, A*
Mississippi Delta Community
  College *A*
University of Southern Mississippi *B*

Missouri

University of Central Missouri *B*

Nebraska

Southeast Community College *A*

Nevada

Truckee Meadows Community
  College *C, A*

New Hampshire

Keene State College *B*
NHTI-Concord's Community
  College *A*

New Jersey

Essex County College *A*
Mercer County Community
  College *C, A*

New York

Dutchess Community College *A*
Erie Community College *A*
Finger Lakes Community College *A*
Institute of Design and
  Construction *A*
Orange County Community
  College *A*
SUNY
  College of Agriculture and
    Technology at Morrisville *A*
  College of Technology at
    Alfred *A, B*
  College of Technology at Delhi *A*
  Farmingdale State College *A, B*
Suffolk County Community College *A*

North Carolina

Cape Fear Community College *A*
Catawba Valley Community
  College *A*
Central Piedmont Community
  College *C, A*
Coastal Carolina Community
  College *C, A*
Durham Technical Community
  College *C, A*
Fayetteville Technical Community
  College *C, A*
Forsyth Technical Community
  College *A*
Gaston College *C, A*
Guilford Technical Community
  College *C, A*
Nash Community College *A*
Pitt Community College *A*
Sandhills Community College *A*
Wake Technical Community
  College *C, A*
Wilkes Community College *C, A*

North Dakota

North Dakota State College of
  Science *A*

Ohio

Cincinnati State Technical and
  Community College *A*
Columbus State Community
  College *C*
Cuyahoga Community College
  Metropolitan *A*
James A. Rhodes State College *C*
Lakeland Community College *C*
Owens Community College
  Toledo *C, A*
Sinclair Community College *A*
Stark State College *A*
Terra State Community College *C, A*

Oregon

Mt. Hood Community College *A*

Pennsylvania

Community College of
  Philadelphia *A*
Delaware County Community
  College *A*
Harrisburg Area Community
  College *C, A*
Northampton Community College *A*
Pennsylvania Highlands Community
  College *A*
Pennsylvania Institute of
  Technology *A*

South Carolina

Greenville Technical College *A*
Midlands Technical College *C, A*
Trident Technical College *C, A*

South Dakota

Southeast Technical Institute *A*

Tennessee

Middle Tennessee State University *B*
Nashville State Community College *A*
Southwest Tennessee Community
  College *C, A*

Texas

Del Mar College *A*
San Antonio College *C, A*
Tarrant County College *C, A*
Texas Tech University *B*

Vermont

Vermont Technical College *A, B*

Virginia

Central Virginia Community
  College *A*
New River Community College *A*
Norfolk State University *A*
Northern Virginia Community
  College *A*
Virginia Western Community
  College *A*

Washington

Clover Park Technical College *C, A*
Lake Washington Institute of
  Technology *C, A*
Spokane Community College *A*

West Virginia

Bluefield State College *A, B*
Fairmont State University *A, B*

Wisconsin

Madison Area Technical College *A*
Milwaukee Area Technical College *A*
Northeast Wisconsin Technical
  College *A*
Western Technical College *A*
Wisconsin Indianhead Technical
  College *A*

Architectural history/criticism

California
University of San Diego *B*

Georgia
Savannah College of Art and Design *B, M*

Illinois
DePaul University *B*
University of Illinois Urbana-Champaign *D*

Kansas
University of Kansas *B*

Massachusetts
Amherst College *B*
Boston University *B*
Northeastern University *B*

Michigan
Lawrence Technological University *B*

New York
Bard College *M*
Barnard College *B*
Columbia University School of General Studies *B*
Cornell University *B, M, D*

Rhode Island
Brown University *B, M, D*
Roger Williams University *B*

Texas
University of Texas Austin *M*

Virginia
University of Virginia *B, M*

Architectural technology

Alabama
Shelton State Community College *A*

Arizona
Arizona Western College *C, A*
Coconino County Community College *C, A*

California
Allan Hancock College *C, A*
Bakersfield College *A*
College of the Desert *C, A*
Diablo Valley College *C, A*
East Los Angeles College *C, A*
Los Angeles Harbor College *C, A*
Los Angeles Pierce College *C, A*
MiraCosta College *C, A*
Orange Coast College *C, A*
Palomar College *C, A*
San Joaquin Delta College *C, A*
Southwestern College *C, A*

Colorado
Westwood College Denver South *A*

Connecticut
Three Rivers Community College *C, A*

Florida
Miami Dade College *A*

Idaho
Brigham Young University-Idaho *A*

Illinois
Morrison Institute of Technology *A*
Rend Lake College *C, A*

Kentucky
Western Kentucky University *B*

Maine
University of Maine Augusta *A, B*

Maryland
Montgomery College *A*

Massachusetts
Benjamin Franklin Institute of Technology *A*
Fitchburg State University *B*
Roxbury Community College *A*

Michigan
Delta College *C, A*
Henry Ford Community College *A*
Lansing Community College *C, A*
Lawrence Technological University *C, B*
Washtenaw Community College *C, A*

Minnesota
Dunwoody College of Technology *A*
Minneapolis Community and Technical College *C*

Missouri
Washington University in St. Louis *B*

Nevada
College of Southern Nevada *A*

New York
City University of New York New York City College of Technology *B*
New York Institute of Technology *A, B*
Onondaga Community College *A*
SUNY College of Technology at Delhi *A*

North Carolina
College of the Albemarle *C, A*
Durham Technical Community College *C, A*
Gaston College *C, A*
Nash Community College *A*
Roanoke-Chowan Community College *A*
Sandhills Community College *A*

Pennsylvania
Pennsylvania College of Technology *A*
Thaddeus Stevens College of Technology *A*

Rhode Island
New England Institute of Technology *A, B*

South Dakota
Southeast Technical Institute *A*

Texas
Abilene Christian University *A*
North Lake College *C, A*
South Texas College *C, A*

Virginia
J. Sargeant Reynolds Community College *A*
John Tyler Community College *A*

Wisconsin
Milwaukee Area Technical College *A*
Northcentral Technical College *A*
Northeast Wisconsin Technical College *A*

Architecture

Alabama
Auburn University *B*
Tuskegee University *B*

Arizona
Arizona State University *B, M, D*
Phoenix College *A*
University of Arizona *B, M*

Arkansas
University of Arkansas *B*

California
Academy of Art University *B, M*
California Baptist University *M*
California College of the Arts *B, M*
California Polytechnic State University: San Luis Obispo *B, M*
California State Polytechnic University: Pomona *B, M*
Cerritos College *A*
College of San Mateo *A*
NewSchool of Architecture & Design *B, M*
Otis College of Art and Design *B*
Southern California Institute of Architecture *B, M*
University of California Berkeley *B, M, D*
Los Angeles *B, M, D*
University of San Francisco *B*
University of Southern California *B, M, D*
Woodbury University *B, M*

Colorado
University of Colorado Denver *B, M*

Connecticut
Connecticut College *B*
University of Hartford *M*
Yale University *B, M*

District of Columbia
Catholic University of America *B, M*
Howard University *B*
University of the District of Columbia *B*

Florida
Daytona State College *A*
Florida Agricultural and Mechanical University *B, M*
Florida Atlantic University *B*
Florida International University *M*
University of Central Florida *B*
University of Florida *B, M, D*
University of Miami *B, M*
University of South Florida *M*

Georgia
Georgia Institute of Technology *B, M, D*
Savannah College of Art and Design *B, M*
Southern Polytechnic State University *B*

Hawaii
University of Hawaii Manoa *D*

Idaho
University of Idaho *B, M*

Illinois
College of DuPage *C, A*
Illinois Institute of Technology *B, M, D*
Judson University *B, M*
School of the Art Institute of Chicago *M*
Southern Illinois University Carbondale *B, M*
University of Illinois Chicago *B, M*
Urbana-Champaign *B, M, D*

Indiana
Ball State University *B, M*
University of Notre Dame *B, M*

Iowa
Iowa State University *B, M*

Kansas
Kansas State University *M*
University of Kansas *M, D*

Kentucky
Hopkinsville Community College *A*
University of Kentucky *B, M*

Louisiana
Louisiana State University and Agricultural and Mechanical College *B, M*
Louisiana Tech University *B*
Tulane University *B, M*
University of Louisiana at Lafayette *B, M*

Maryland
Morgan State University *B, M*
University of Maryland College Park *B, M*

Massachusetts
Boston Architectural College *B, M*
College of the Holy Cross *B*
Hampshire College *B*
Harvard College *M, D*
Massachusetts Institute of Technology *B, M, D*
Mount Holyoke College *B*
Northeastern University *B, M*
University of Massachusetts Amherst *B, M*
Wellesley College *B*
Wentworth Institute of Technology *B, M*

Michigan
Andrews University *B, M*
Eastern Michigan University *B*
Grand Rapids Community College *A*
Lawrence Technological University *B, M*
University of Detroit Mercy *B, M*
University of Michigan *B, M, D*

Minnesota
University of Minnesota Twin Cities *B, M*

Mississippi
East Mississippi Community College *A*
Hinds Community College *A*
Mississippi State University *B, M*

Missouri
Drury University *B*
University of Missouri Kansas City *B*
Washington University in St. Louis *B, M*

Montana

Montana State University *M*

Nebraska

University of Nebraska
  Lincoln *B, M*

Nevada

University of Nevada
  Las Vegas *B, M*

New Hampshire

Keene State College *B*

New Jersey

Brookdale Community College *A*
New Jersey Institute of
  Technology *B, M*
Princeton University *B, M, D*

New Mexico

University of New Mexico *B, M*

New York

Barnard College *B*
City University of New York
  City College *B, M*
Columbia University *B*
Columbia University
  School of General Studies *B*
Cooper Union for the Advancement
  of Science and Art *B, M*
Cornell University *B, M*
Hobart and William Smith Colleges *B*
Ithaca College *B*
New York Institute of
  Technology *B, M*
Parsons The New School for
  Design *B, M*
Pratt Institute *B, M*
Rensselaer Polytechnic
  Institute *B, M, D*
Rochester Institute of Technology *M*
SUNY
  College of Technology at Delhi *B*
  University at Buffalo *B, M*
Syracuse University *B, M*

North Carolina

North Carolina State University *B, M*
University of North Carolina
  Charlotte *B, M, D*

North Dakota

North Dakota State University *M*

Ohio

Bowling Green State University *M*
Kent State University *B, M*
Miami University
  Oxford *B, M*
Ohio State University
  Columbus Campus *C, B, M*
University of Cincinnati *B, M, D*

Oklahoma

Oklahoma State University *B*
University of Oklahoma *B, M*

Oregon

Portland State University *B, M*
University of Oregon *B, M, D*

Pennsylvania

Carnegie Mellon University *B, M*
Drexel University *B*
Harrisburg Area Community
  College *A*
Lehigh University *B*
Marywood University *B, M*
Penn State
  University Park *B, M*
Philadelphia University *B*

Temple University *B*
University of Pennsylvania *B, M, D*

Puerto Rico

Pontifical Catholic University of
  Puerto Rico *B*
Turabo University *M*
Universidad Politecnica de Puerto
  Rico *B*
University of Puerto Rico
  Rio Piedras *M*

Rhode Island

Rhode Island School of Design *B, M*
Roger Williams University *B, M*

South Carolina

Clemson University *B, M*

South Dakota

South Dakota State University *B, M*

Tennessee

Tennessee State University *B*
University of Tennessee
  Knoxville *B, M*

Texas

Prairie View A&M University *B, M*
Rice University *B, M, D*
Texas A&M University *B, M, D*
Texas Tech University *B, M*
University of Houston *B, M*
University of Texas
  Arlington *B, M*
  Austin *B, M*
  San Antonio *B, M*

Utah

University of Utah *B, M*

Vermont

Bennington College *B*
Norwich University *B, M*

Virginia

Hampton University *M*
University of Virginia *B, M*
Virginia Polytechnic Institute and
  State University *B, M, D*

Washington

University of Washington *B, M*
Washington State University *B, M*

Wisconsin

University of Wisconsin
  Milwaukee *B, M, D*

Archival administration

California

Diablo Valley College *C, A*

Massachusetts

Simmons College *M*

Minnesota

Anoka-Ramsey Community College *C*

North Carolina

Central Carolina Community
  College *C, A*

Aromatherapy

Vermont

Goddard College *B, M*

Art

Alabama

Alabama Agricultural and Mechanical
  University *B*
Alabama State University *B*
Athens State University *B*
Auburn University at Montgomery *B*
Birmingham-Southern College *B*
Faulkner State Community College *A*
Gadsden State Community College *A*
Jacksonville State University *B*
Judson College *B*
Samford University *B*
Stillman College *B*
Troy University *B*
University of Alabama
  Birmingham *B*
  Huntsville *B*
University of Mobile *B*
University of Montevallo *B, T*
University of North Alabama *B*
University of South Alabama *B*

Alaska

University of Alaska
  Anchorage *B*
  Fairbanks *B, M*
  Southeast *C, B*

Arizona

Arizona State University *B, M*
Central Arizona College *A*
Cochise College *A*
Coconino County Community
  College *A*
Eastern Arizona College *A*
Glendale Community College *A*
Paradise Valley Community College *C*
Phoenix College *A*
Scottsdale Community College *C*
South Mountain Community
  College *A*
University of Arizona *M*

Arkansas

Arkansas State University *B*
Arkansas Tech University *B*
Black River Technical College *A*
Henderson State University *B*
Hendrix College *B*
Lyon College *B*
University of Arkansas *B, M*
University of Arkansas
  Fort Smith *B*
  Little Rock *B, M*
  Monticello *B*
  Pine Bluff *B*
University of Central Arkansas *B*

California

Allan Hancock College *A*
Azusa Pacific University *B*
Bakersfield College *A*
Berkeley City College *C, A*
Biola University *B*
Cabrillo College *A*
California College of the Arts *B*
California Lutheran University *B*
California State Polytechnic
  University: Pomona *B*
California State University
  Bakersfield *B*
  Channel Islands *B*
  Chico *B, M*
  Dominguez Hills *B*
  East Bay *B*
  Fresno *B, M*
  Fullerton *B, M*
  Long Beach *B, M*
  Los Angeles *B, M*
  Monterey Bay *B*
  Northridge *B, M*
  Sacramento *B, M*

San Bernardino *B, M*
  Stanislaus *B*
Canada College *A*
Cerritos College *A*
Cerro Coso Community College *A*
Chabot College *A*
Chaffey College *A*
Chapman University *B*
Citrus College *A*
Claremont McKenna College *B*
College of the Canyons *A*
College of the Desert *A*
College of the Sequoias *A*
College of the Siskiyous *C*
Columbia College *A*
Concordia University Irvine *B*
Copper Mountain College *A*
Cosumnes River College *A*
Crafton Hills College *A*
Cypress College *A*
De Anza College *A*
Dominican University of California *B*
El Camino College *A*
Folsom Lake College *A*
Foothill College *C, A*
Fresno City College *A*
Fresno Pacific University *B*
Fullerton College *A*
Gavilan College *A*
Golden West College *A*
Hartnell College *A*
Humboldt State University *B*
Imperial Valley College *A*
Irvine Valley College *A*
La Sierra University *B*
Lake Tahoe Community College *C, A*
Laney College *A*
Long Beach City College *A*
Los Angeles City College *A*
Los Angeles Harbor College *A*
Los Angeles Mission College *A*
Los Angeles Southwest College *A*
Los Angeles Valley College *A*
Mendocino College *C, A*
Mills College *B*
Mission College *C, A*
Modesto Junior College *A*
Monterey Peninsula College *C, A*
Mount St. Mary's College *A, B*
Mount San Jacinto College *A*
Notre Dame de Namur University *B*
Occidental College *B*
Orange Coast College *A*
Otis College of Art and Design *B, M*
Oxnard College *C, A*
Palomar College *A*
Pepperdine University *B*
Pitzer College *B*
Reedley College *A*
Saddleback College *A*
St. Mary's College of California *B*
San Diego Mesa College *C, A*
San Diego State University *B, M*
San Francisco State University *B, M*
San Joaquin Delta College *A*
San Jose City College *C*
San Jose State University *B, M*
Santa Barbara City College *A*
Santa Monica College *A*
Santa Rosa Junior College *C, A*
Santiago Canyon College *C, A*
Shasta College *A*
Sierra College *C, A*
Skyline College *A*
Southwestern College *A*
Stanford University *B, M, D*
Taft College *C, A*
University of California
  Berkeley *B, M*
  Davis *M*
  Los Angeles *B, M*
  Riverside *B*
  Santa Barbara *B*
  Santa Cruz *B*
University of La Verne *B*

University of Redlands *B*
University of San Diego *B*
University of Southern California *B*
University of the Pacific *B*
Victor Valley College *A*
West Hills College: Coalinga *A*
West Los Angeles College *C, A*
West Valley College *A*
Westmont College *B*
Whittier College *B*
Yuba College *A*

Colorado

Adams State University *A, B, M*
Colorado Mesa University *B*
Colorado Mountain College *A*
Colorado State University *B, M*
Community College of Aurora *C, A*
Metropolitan State University of
   Denver *B*
Morgan Community College *A*
Regis University *B*
University of Denver *B*
Western State Colorado University *B*

Connecticut

Albertus Magnus College *B*
Central Connecticut State
   University *B*
Middlesex Community College *A*
Naugatuck Valley Community
   College *A*
Sacred Heart University *B*
Trinity College *B*
University of Hartford *M*
Western Connecticut State
   University *B*
Yale University *B*

Delaware

Delaware State University *B*
University of Delaware *B*

District of Columbia

American University *B*
Catholic University of America *B*
Corcoran College of Art and
   Design *B*
Georgetown University *B*
Howard University *B, M*

Florida

Barry University *B*
Broward College *A*
Daytona State College *A*
Florida Atlantic University *B*
Florida Gulf Coast University *B*
Florida International University *B*
Indian River State College *A*
Jacksonville University *B*
Northwest Florida State College *A*
Pensacola State College *A*
Rollins College *B*
South Florida State College *A*
Stetson University *B*
University of Central Florida *B*
University of Miami *B, M*
University of North Florida *B*
University of South Florida *B*
University of South Florida
   Saint Petersburg *B*
University of Tampa *B*
University of West Florida *B*

Georgia

Armstrong Atlantic State University *B*
Atlanta Metropolitan College *A*
Berry College *B*
Clark Atlanta University *B*
College of Coastal Georgia *A*
Columbus State University *B*
Darton College *A*
East Georgia State College *A*

Georgia College and State
   University *B*
Georgia Highlands College *A*
Georgia Perimeter College *A*
Georgia Regents University *B*
Georgia Southern University *B*
Georgia Southwestern State
   University *B*
Gordon College *A*
Kennesaw State University *B*
Mercer University *B*
Middle Georgia State College *A*
Morehouse College *B*
Oglethorpe University *B*
Piedmont College *B, T*
Reinhardt University *A, B*
University of Georgia *B, M, D*
University of West Georgia *B*
Valdosta State University *B*
Young Harris College *B*

Hawaii

Brigham Young University-Hawaii *B*
University of Hawaii
   Hilo *B*
   Manoa *B, M*

Idaho

Boise State University *B, M*
Brigham Young University-Idaho *B*
College of Southern Idaho *A*
Idaho State University *B, M*
University of Idaho *B, M*

Illinois

Augustana College *B*
Aurora University *B*
Black Hawk College *A*
Blackburn College *B*
Bradley University *B, M*
Chicago State University *B*
City Colleges of Chicago
   Harold Washington College *A*
   Harry S. Truman College *A*
College of DuPage *A*
College of Lake County *A*
Columbia College Chicago *B*
Concordia University Chicago *B, T*
DePaul University *B*
Dominican University *B*
Eastern Illinois University *B, M, T*
Elgin Community College *A*
Elmhurst College *B, T*
Eureka College *B*
Governors State University *B, M*
Greenville College *B*
Illinois College *B, T*
Illinois Institute of Art
   Schaumburg *B*
Illinois State University *B, M, T*
Illinois Valley Community College *A*
Illinois Wesleyan University *B*
John A. Logan College *A*
John Wood Community College *A*
Joliet Junior College *A*
Judson University *B*
Kankakee Community College *A*
Kishwaukee College *A*
Lake Forest College *B*
Lewis University *B*
Lincoln College *A*
MacMurray College *B*
McHenry County College *A*
McKendree University *B*
Monmouth College *B, T*
National Louis University *B*
North Central College *B*
North Park University *B*
Northeastern Illinois University *B*
Northern Illinois University *B, M, D*
Northwestern University *B, M*
Olivet Nazarene University *B, T*
Parkland College *A*
Rend Lake College *A*

Richland Community College *A*
Rockford University *B*
Sauk Valley Community College *A*
School of the Art Institute of
   Chicago *B, M*
South Suburban College of Cook
   County *C*
Southern Illinois University
   Carbondale *B*
Southern Illinois University
   Edwardsville *B, T*
Southwestern Illinois College *A*
Spoon River College *A*
Western Illinois University *B*
Wheaton College *B, T*

Indiana

Ball State University *B, M*
Bethel College *B*
Earlham College *B*
Goshen College *B*
Grace College *B*
Holy Cross College *B*
Huntington University *B*
Indiana State University *B, M*
Indiana University
   Bloomington *B, M*
   East *B*
   Kokomo *B*
   Purdue University Fort Wayne *B*
   South Bend *B*
   Southeast *B*
Manchester University *B, T*
Marian University *B, T*
Oakland City University *A, B*
Purdue University *B*
Saint Mary's College *B*
St. Mary-of-the-Woods College *B*
Taylor University *B*
University of Evansville *B*
University of Indianapolis *B, M*
University of St. Francis *B*
University of Southern Indiana *B, T*
Valparaiso University *B*
Vincennes University *A*
Wabash College *B*

Iowa

Briar Cliff University *B*
Buena Vista University *B, T*
Central College *B, T*
Coe College *B*
Cornell College *B, T*
Dordt College *B*
Ellsworth Community College *A*
Graceland University *B, T*
Grinnell College *B*
Iowa State University *B*
Iowa Western Community College *A*
Luther College *B*
Mount Mercy University *B*
Northwestern College *B, T*
Simpson College *B*
University of Iowa *B, M, T*
University of Northern Iowa *B, M*
Upper Iowa University *B*
Wartburg College *B, T*

Kansas

Allen County Community College *A*
Barton County Community College *A*
Benedictine College *B*
Bethany College *B, T*
Butler Community College *A*
Central Christian College of Kansas *A*
Coffeyville Community College *A*
Cowley County Community
   College *A*
Dodge City Community College *A*
Emporia State University *B, T*
Fort Hays State University *B*
Friends University *B*
Garden City Community College *A*
Independence Community College *A*

McPherson College *B, T*
Neosho County Community
   College *A*
Newman University *B*
Ottawa University *B, T*
Pittsburg State University *B, M*
Seward County Community
   College *A*
Sterling College *B, T*
University of St. Mary *B*
Washburn University *B*
Wichita State University *B, M, T*

Kentucky

Berea College *B, T*
Brescia University *B*
Campbellsville University *B*
Centre College *B*
Eastern Kentucky University *B*
Kentucky Wesleyan College *B, T*
University of Louisville *M*
University of Pikeville *B*

Louisiana

Centenary College of Louisiana *B, T*
Dillard University *B*
Grambling State University *B*
Louisiana Tech University *B, M*
Loyola University New Orleans *B*
McNeese State University *B*
Northwestern State University *M*
Southeastern Louisiana University *B*
Tulane University *B*
University of Louisiana at Lafayette *B*
Xavier University of Louisiana *B*

Maine

Bates College *B*
Colby College *B*
Maine College of Art *B*
University of Maine
   Presque Isle *B*
University of Southern Maine *B*

Maryland

Allegany College of Maryland *A*
Baltimore City Community College *A*
Bowie State University *B*
Coppin State University *B*
Frederick Community College *A*
Hood College *B*
Howard Community College *A*
Loyola University Maryland *B*
McDaniel College *B*
Notre Dame of Maryland
   University *B*
St. Mary's College of Maryland *B*
Salisbury University *B*
University of Maryland
   Baltimore County *B*
Washington College *B, T*

Massachusetts

Anna Maria College *B, M*
Bristol Community College *C*
Bunker Hill Community College *A*
Clark University *B*
Framingham State University *B*
Gordon College *B*
Harvard College *M, D*
Holyoke Community College *A*
Lesley University *B, M*
Massachusetts Bay Community
   College *C*
Massachusetts College of Liberal
   Arts *B*
Mount Wachusett Community
   College *A*
Northeastern University *B*
Salem State University *B*
School of the Museum of Fine
   Arts *B, M, T*
Simmons College *B*
Smith College *B*

Springfield College *B*
University of Massachusetts
    Boston *B*
Westfield State University *B, T*

Michigan

Adrian College *A, B, T*
Albion College *B*
Andrews University *B*
Aquinas College *B, T*
Calvin College *B, T*
Central Michigan University *B, M*
Concordia University *B*
Delta College *A*
Eastern Michigan University *B*
Finlandia University *B*
Gogebic Community College *A*
Grand Rapids Community College *A*
Grand Valley State University *B*
Henry Ford Community College *A*
Hillsdale College *B*
Kalamazoo College *B*
Lake Michigan College *A*
Lansing Community College *A*
Marygrove College *B, T*
Michigan State University *B, M*
Mott Community College *C*
Northern Michigan University *A, B*
Northwestern Michigan College *A*
Oakland Community College *A*
Olivet College *B, T*
Saginaw Valley State University *B*
Siena Heights University *A, B*
Spring Arbor University *B*
University of Michigan *B, M*
Wayne County Community College *A*
Wayne State University *B, M*
Western Michigan University *B*

Minnesota

Bethel University *B*
College of St. Benedict *B*
College of St. Scholastica *B*
Concordia College: Moorhead *D*
Concordia University St. Paul *B*
Gustavus Adolphus College *B*
Macalester College *B*
Minneapolis College of Art and
    Design *B*
Minnesota State University
    Mankato *B, M*
    Moorhead *B*
Minnesota West Community and
    Technical College *A*
Ridgewater College *A*
Saint Cloud State University *B, M*
St. John's University *B*
St. Olaf College *B*
Southwest Minnesota State
    University *B, T*
University of Minnesota
    Duluth *B, M*
    Twin Cities *B, M*
Winona State University *B*

Mississippi

Belhaven University *B*
Hinds Community College *A*
Itawamba Community College *A*
Mississippi College *M*
Mississippi Gulf Coast Community
    College *A*
Northeast Mississippi Community
    College *A*
Tougaloo College *B*
William Carey University *B*

Missouri

Avila University *B*
Calvary Bible College and Theological
    Seminary *B*
College of the Ozarks *B*
Columbia College *B*
Crowder College *A*

Culver-Stockton College *B*
Fontbonne University *B, M, T*
Hannibal-LaGrange University *A, B*
Lindenwood University *B, M*
Missouri State University *B*
Missouri Valley College *B*
Missouri Western State University *B*
Southeast Missouri State University *B*
Southwest Baptist University *B*
Truman State University *B*
University of Central Missouri *B*
University of Missouri
    Columbia *B, M*
    Kansas City *B, M*
Washington University in St. Louis *B*
Webster University *C, B, M*
William Jewell College *B, T*
William Woods University *B, T*

Montana

Miles Community College *A*
Montana State University *B*
Montana State University
    Billings *B*
Rocky Mountain College *B*
Salish Kootenai College *A*
University of Great Falls *B*
University of Montana *B, M*
University of Montana: Western *B, T*

Nebraska

Bellevue University *B*
Chadron State College *B*
Concordia University *B*
Creighton University *B*
Doane College *B*
Hastings College *B, T*
Midland University *B, T*
Nebraska Wesleyan University *B*
Northeast Community College *A*
Union College *A*
University of Nebraska
    Kearney *B, M, T*
    Omaha *B*
Wayne State College *B*
Western Nebraska Community
    College *A*

Nevada

College of Southern Nevada *A*
University of Nevada
    Las Vegas *B, M*
    Reno *B, M*

New Hampshire

Colby-Sawyer College *B*
New England College *B*
Plymouth State University *B*
Rivier University *A*
Saint Anselm College *B*
University of New Hampshire *B*

New Jersey

Burlington County College *A*
Caldwell College *B*
College of New Jersey *B*
College of St. Elizabeth *B*
Cumberland County College *A*
Drew University *B*
Essex County College *A*
Felician College *B*
Georgian Court University *B*
Gloucester County College *A*
Kean University *B, T*
Monmouth University *B*
Montclair State University *B, M, T*
New Jersey City University *B, T*
New Jersey Institute of Technology *B*
Ramapo College of New Jersey *B*
Rider University *B*
Rowan University *C, B, T*

Rutgers, The State University of New
    Jersey
    Camden Campus *B, T*
    New Brunswick/Piscataway
        Campus *B, M*
    Newark Campus *B, T*
Sussex County Community College *A*
Thomas Edison State College *B*
William Paterson University of New
    Jersey *B*

New Mexico

Central New Mexico Community
    College *C*
Eastern New Mexico University *A, B*
New Mexico Highlands University *B*
New Mexico State University
    Grants *A*
Northern New Mexico College *A*
Santa Fe Community College *A*
Santa Fe University of Art and
    Design *B*
University of New Mexico *B, M*

New York

Cayuga Community College *A*
City University of New York
    Brooklyn College *B*
    City College *B*
    Queensborough Community
        College *A*
Colgate University *B*
Concordia College *B*
Daemen College *B*
Dutchess Community College *A*
Elmira College *B, T*
Fordham University *B*
Fulton-Montgomery Community
    College *A*
Genesee Community College *A*
Hartwick College *B, T*
Herkimer County Community
    College *A*
Houghton College *B*
Ithaca College *B*
Keuka College *B*
Marist College *B*
Marymount Manhattan College *B*
Mohawk Valley Community
    College *A*
Nassau Community College *A*
Nazareth College *B, T*
Pace University *B*
Pace University: Pleasantville/
    Briarcliff *B*
SUNY
    College at Brockport *B, M*
    College at Cortland *B*
    College at Fredonia *B*
    College at Oswego *B*
    College at Plattsburgh *B*
    College at Potsdam *B*
    University at Binghamton *B*
    University at Buffalo *B*
    University at Stony Brook *B, M*
St. Thomas Aquinas College *B, T*
Vassar College *B*
Villa Maria College of Buffalo *B*

North Carolina

Appalachian State University *B*
Brevard College *B*
Caldwell Community College and
    Technical Institute *A*
College of the Albemarle *A*
Davidson College *B*
East Carolina University *B, M*
Elon University *B*
Fayetteville State University *B*
Gardner-Webb University *B*
Guilford College *B*
Lees-McRae College *B*
Mars Hill University *B, T*
Methodist University *B*

North Carolina Agricultural and
    Technical State University *B, T*
North Carolina Central University *B*
Queens University of Charlotte *B*
St. Andrews University *B*
St. Augustine's University *B*
Sandhills Community College *A*
University of Mount Olive *B*
University of North Carolina
    Asheville *B, T*
    Charlotte *B*
    Greensboro *B*
Western Carolina University *B*
Western Piedmont Community
    College *A*
Winston-Salem State University *B*

North Dakota

Dickinson State University *B, T*
Minot State University *B*
North Dakota State University *B*
University of North Dakota *B, M*
Valley City State University *B*

Ohio

Ashland University *B*
Baldwin Wallace University *B*
Bluffton University *B*
Bowling Green State University *B, M*
Capital University *B*
Central State University *B*
Cleveland State University *B, T*
College of Mount St. Joseph *A, B, T*
Defiance College *A, B, T*
Edison State Community College *A*
Hocking College *C, A*
Lourdes University *A, B*
Miami University
    Oxford *B, M*
Mount Vernon Nazarene University *B*
Muskingum University *B*
Ohio Dominican University *B, T*
Ohio Northern University *B*
Ohio State University
    Columbus Campus *B, M*
Ohio University *B, M*
Otterbein University *B*
Sinclair Community College *A*
Tiffin University *B*
University of Findlay *B*
University of Rio Grande *A*
University of Toledo *B*
Virginia Marti College of Art and
    Design *A*
Wilmington College *B*
Wittenberg University *B*
Wright State University *B*
Xavier University *B*
Youngstown State University *B*

Oklahoma

Bacone College *A*
Cameron University *B*
Carl Albert State College *A*
Connors State College *A*
East Central University *B, T*
Langston University *B*
Northeastern Oklahoma Agricultural
    and Mechanical College *A*
Northeastern State University *B*
Northern Oklahoma College *A*
Oklahoma Baptist University *B, T*
Oklahoma Christian University *B*
Oklahoma Panhandle State
    University *B*
Oklahoma State University *B*
Oral Roberts University *B*
Redlands Community College *A*
St. Gregory's University *B*
Seminole State College *A*
Southeastern Oklahoma State
    University *B*
University of Central Oklahoma *B*

University of Science and Arts of Oklahoma *B, T*
University of Tulsa *B, M*
Western Oklahoma State College *A*

Oregon

Eastern Oregon University *B*
George Fox University *B*
Lewis & Clark College *B*
Linfield College *B, T*
Linn-Benton Community College *A*
Marylhurst University *B*
Mt. Hood Community College *A*
Oregon State University *B*
Pacific University *B*
Portland State University *B*
Reed College *B*
Southern Oregon University *B, T*
Treasure Valley Community College *A*
University of Oregon *B*
Western Oregon University *B*

Pennsylvania

Albright College *B*
Allegheny College *B*
Arcadia University *B*
California University of Pennsylvania *B*
Carnegie Mellon University *B, M*
Cedar Crest College *B*
Cheyney University of Pennsylvania *B*
Clarion University of Pennsylvania *B*
Community College of Allegheny County *A*
Community College of Philadelphia *A*
Edinboro University of Pennsylvania *B, M, T*
Gettysburg College *B*
Harrisburg Area Community College *A*
Immaculata University *C*
Indiana University of Pennsylvania *B*
Juniata College *B*
Kutztown University of Pennsylvania *B, M*
Lafayette College *B*
Lebanon Valley College *B, T*
Lehigh Carbon Community College *A*
Lehigh University *B*
Lock Haven University of Pennsylvania *B*
Lycoming College *B*
Mansfield University of Pennsylvania *B, T*
Millersville University of Pennsylvania *B, M, T*
Montgomery County Community College *A*
Moravian College *B, T*
Muhlenberg College *C, B*
Penn State
  Abington *B*
  Altoona *B*
  Beaver *B*
  Berks *B*
  Brandywine *B*
  DuBois *B*
  Erie, The Behrend College *B*
  Fayette, The Eberly Campus *B*
  Greater Allegheny *B*
  Harrisburg *B*
  Hazleton *B*
  Lehigh Valley *B*
  Mont Alto *B*
  New Kensington *B*
  Schuylkill *B*
  Shenango *B*
  University Park *B, M*
  Wilkes-Barre *B*
  Worthington Scranton *B*
  York *B*

Pennsylvania College of Art and Design *B*
Shippensburg University of Pennsylvania *B, T*
Slippery Rock University of Pennsylvania *B*
Susquehanna University *B*
Temple University *B*
Thiel College *B*
Ursinus College *B*
Washington & Jefferson College *B*
Waynesburg University *B*
West Chester University of Pennsylvania *B*
Westminster College *B*
Wilson College *B*

Puerto Rico

Turabo University *M*
University of Puerto Rico Rio Piedras *B*

Rhode Island

Community College of Rhode Island *A*
Roger Williams University *A, B*

South Carolina

Anderson University *B*
Benedict College *B*
Claflin University *B*
Clemson University *B, M*
Columbia College *B*
Converse College *B*
Erskine College *B*
Francis Marion University *B*
Furman University *B, T*
Lander University *B*
Newberry College *B*
Presbyterian College *B*
University of South Carolina Lancaster *A*
Winthrop University *B*

South Dakota

Augustana College *B, T*
Black Hills State University *B*
Dakota Wesleyan University *B*
Northern State University *B*
Oglala Lakota College *A*
University of Sioux Falls *B*
University of South Dakota *B, M*

Tennessee

Austin Peay State University *B*
Carson-Newman University *B, T*
East Tennessee State University *B, M, T*
Fisk University *B*
Freed-Hardeman University *B, T*
Jackson State Community College *A*
LeMoyne-Owen College *B*
Lincoln Memorial University *B, T*
Maryville College *B*
Memphis College of Art *B, M*
Middle Tennessee State University *B*
Rhodes College *B*
Southern Adventist University *B*
Tennessee Technological University *T*
University of Memphis *B, M*
University of Tennessee Chattanooga *B*
Watkins College of Art, Design & Film *B*

Texas

Alvin Community College *A*
Amarillo College *A*
Angelina College *A*
Angelo State University *B, T*
Austin College *B*
Austin Community College *A*
Brazosport College *A*
Central Texas College *A*

Clarendon College *A*
Dallas Baptist University *B, M*
Del Mar College *A*
El Paso Community College *A*
Galveston College *A*
Grayson College *A*
Howard College *A*
Howard Payne University *B*
Kilgore College *A*
Lamar University *B*
Laredo Community College *A*
Midland College *A*
Midwestern State University *B*
Navarro College *C, A*
Northeast Texas Community College *A*
Odessa College *A*
Our Lady of the Lake University of San Antonio *B*
Paris Junior College *A*
Rice University *B*
St. Edward's University *B*
St. Philip's College *A*
Sam Houston State University *B*
San Jacinto College *A*
Southwestern University *B, T*
Stephen F. Austin State University *B, M, T*
Sul Ross State University *B, M*
Temple College *A*
Texarkana College *A*
Texas A&M University Corpus Christi *T*
Texas Lutheran University *B*
Texas State University *B, T*
Texas Tech University *B, M*
Texas Woman's University *B, M*
Trinity University *B*
Trinity Valley Community College *A*
Tyler Junior College *A*
University of Houston *B, M*
University of North Texas *B, M, D*
University of Texas
  Arlington *B*
  Austin *B*
  Brownsville *B*
  El Paso *B, M*
  Permian Basin *B*
  San Antonio *B, M*
  Tyler *B*
University of the Incarnate Word *B*
Wayland Baptist University *B, T*
West Texas A&M University *B, M*
Western Texas College *A*
Wharton County Junior College *A*

Utah

Brigham Young University *B, M*
Snow College *A*
Southern Utah University *B*
University of Utah *B, M, T*
Utah State University *B, M*
Weber State University *B*
Westminster College *B*

Vermont

Castleton State College *B*
Green Mountain College *B*
Johnson State College *B*
Marlboro College *B*
Saint Michael's College *B*

Virginia

Averett University *B*
Bluefield College *B*
College of William and Mary *B*
Eastern Mennonite University *B*
Emory & Henry College *B, T*
Ferrum College *B*
Hampton University *B*
James Madison University *B, M, T*
Lynchburg College *B*
Mary Baldwin College *B*
Norfolk State University *B*

Old Dominion University *B*
Radford University *B, M*
Roanoke College *B, T*
Southern Virginia University *B*
University of Virginia *B*
University of Virginia's College at Wise *B, T*
Virginia Intermont College *B*
Virginia Polytechnic Institute and State University *B*
Virginia Union University *B*
Virginia Wesleyan College *B*

Washington

Central Washington University *B, M*
Centralia College *A*
Cornish College of the Arts *B*
Evergreen State College *B*
Highline Community College *A*
North Seattle Community College *C, A*
Pacific Lutheran University *B*
Seattle Pacific University *B*
University of Puget Sound *B, T*
University of Washington *B, M*
University of Washington Bothell *B*
Walla Walla University *B*
Western Washington University *B*
Whitworth University *B, T*

West Virginia

Bethany College *B*
Concord University *B*
Marshall University *B*
Shepherd University *B, T*
University of Charleston *B*
West Virginia University *B, M, T*
West Virginia Wesleyan College *B*

Wisconsin

Alverno College *B*
Cardinal Stritch University *B, M, T*
Carroll University *B*
Concordia University Wisconsin *B*
Edgewood College *B*
Lakeland College *B*
Lawrence University *B, T*
Mount Mary University *B, T*
Northland College *B*
Ripon College *T*
St. Norbert College *B*
Silver Lake College of the Holy Family *B*
University of Wisconsin
  Eau Claire *B*
  Green Bay *B, T*
  La Crosse *B, T*
  Madison *B, M*
  Milwaukee *B, M*
  Oshkosh *B*
  Parkside *B, T*
  Platteville *B*
  River Falls *B*
  Stevens Point *B*
  Superior *B, T*
  Whitewater *A, B, T*
Viterbo University *B, T*
Wisconsin Lutheran College *B*

Wyoming

Casper College *A*
Central Wyoming College *C, A*
Eastern Wyoming College *A*
Laramie County Community College *A*
Northwest College *A*
Sheridan College *A*
University of Wyoming *B*
Western Wyoming Community College *A*

Art history

Alabama

Auburn University *B*
Birmingham-Southern College *B*

University of Alabama *B, M*
University of Alabama
Birmingham *M*

Arizona

Arizona State University *D*
University of Arizona *B, M*

Arkansas

University of Arkansas
Little Rock *B*

California

Academy of Art University *B, M*
Berkeley City College *A*
California College of the Arts *M*
California State University
Dominguez Hills *B*
East Bay *B*
Fullerton *B, M*
Long Beach *B, M*
Northridge *B, M*
San Bernardino *B*
Chapman University *B*
College of San Mateo *C, A*
College of the Desert *A*
Cosumnes River College *A*
De Anza College *C, A*
Dominican University of California *B*
Folsom Lake College *A*
Foothill College *C, A*
Gavilan College *A*
Grossmont College *A*
Lassen Community College *A*
Los Angeles Southwest College *A*
Los Angeles Valley College *A*
Loyola Marymount University *B*
Merced College *A*
Mills College *B*
Monterey Peninsula College *A*
Occidental College *B*
Ohlone College *C*
Pepperdine University *B*
Pitzer College *B*
Pomona College *B*
San Diego City College *A*
San Diego State University *B, M*
San Francisco Art Institute *B, M*
San Jose State University *B, M*
Santa Barbara City College *A*
Santa Clara University *B*
Scripps College *B*
Sonoma State University *B*
University of California
Berkeley *B, D*
Davis *B, M*
Irvine *B*
Los Angeles *B, M, D*
Riverside *B, M*
San Diego *B*
Santa Barbara *B, M, D*
Santa Cruz *B*
University of La Verne *B*
University of Redlands *B*
University of San Diego *B*
University of San Francisco *B*
University of Southern
California *B, M, D*
Whittier College *B*

Colorado

Colorado College *B*
Metropolitan State University of
Denver *B*
Regis University *B*
University of Colorado
Boulder *B, M*
University of Denver *B, M*

Connecticut

Albertus Magnus College *B*
Connecticut College *B*
Fairfield University *B*

Southern Connecticut State
University *B*
Trinity College *B*
University of Connecticut *B, M*
University of Hartford *B*
University of Saint Joseph *B*
Wesleyan University *B*
Yale University *B, M, D*

Delaware

University of Delaware *B, M, D*

District of Columbia

American University *B, M*
Catholic University of America *B*
Corcoran College of Art and
Design *M*
Gallaudet University *B*
George Washington
University *B, M, D*
Georgetown University *B*
Howard University *B, M*

Florida

Flagler College *B*
Florida International University *B*
Florida Southern College *B*
Florida State University *B, M, D*
Jacksonville University *B*
New College of Florida *B*
Palm Beach State College *A*
Rollins College *B*
University of Florida *B, M, D*
University of Miami *B, M*
University of North Florida *B*
University of South Florida *B, M*
University of West Florida *B*

Georgia

Agnes Scott College *B*
Emory University *B, D*
Georgia State University *M*
Kennesaw State University *B*
Oglethorpe University *B*
Savannah College of Art and
Design *B, M*
University of Georgia *B, M*
Wesleyan College *B*

Hawaii

University of Hawaii
Manoa *M*

Idaho

Boise State University *B*

Illinois

Augustana College *B*
Bradley University *B*
Columbia College Chicago *B*
DePaul University *B*
Dominican University *B*
Illinois Valley Community College *A*
Knox College *B*
Lake Forest College *B*
Lincoln College *A*
Loyola University Chicago *B*
North Central College *B*
Northern Illinois University *B*
Northwestern University *B, M, D*
Principia College *B*
Richland Community College *A*
Rockford University *B*
Roosevelt University *B*
School of the Art Institute of
Chicago *B, M*
Southern Illinois University
Carbondale *M*
University of Chicago *B, D*
University of Illinois
Chicago *B, M, D*
Urbana-Champaign *B, M, D*

Indiana

DePauw University *B*
Franklin College *B*
Hanover College *B*
Indiana University
Bloomington *B, M, D*
Purdue University Indianapolis *B*
Marian University *B, T*
Purdue University *B*
University of Evansville *B*
University of Notre Dame *B, M*
University of St. Francis *B*

Iowa

Clarke University *A, B, T*
Coe College *B*
Cornell College *B*
Drake University *B*
University of Iowa *B, M, D*
University of Northern Iowa *B*

Kansas

Baker University *B*
University of Kansas *B, M, D*
Washburn University *B*
Wichita State University *B*

Kentucky

Berea College *B*
Bluegrass Community and Technical
College *A*
Thomas More College *A, B*
Transylvania University *B*
University of Kentucky *B, M*
University of Louisville *B, D*
Western Kentucky University *B*

Louisiana

Louisiana State University and
Agricultural and Mechanical
College *M*
Tulane University *B, M*
University of New Orleans *B*

Maine

Bowdoin College *B*
Colby College *B*
College of the Atlantic *B*
University of Maine *B*
University of Southern Maine *B*

Maryland

Goucher College *B*
Howard Community College *A*
Johns Hopkins University *B, D*
Maryland Institute College of Art *B*
McDaniel College *B*
Montgomery College *A*
Notre Dame of Maryland
University *B*
Towson University *B*
University of Maryland
College Park *B, M, D*

Massachusetts

Assumption College *B*
Bard College at Simon's Rock *B*
Boston College *B*
Boston University *B, M, D*
Brandeis University *B*
Clark University *B*
College of the Holy Cross *B*
Hampshire College *B*
Harvard University *B*
Massachusetts College of Art and
Design *B*
Merrimack College *B*
Mount Holyoke College *B*
Salem State University *B*
Smith College *B*
Stonehill College *B*
Tufts University *B, M*

University of Massachusetts
Amherst *B, M*
Dartmouth *B*
Wellesley College *B*
Wheaton College *B*
Williams College *B, M*

Michigan

Albion College *B*
Andrews University *B*
Aquinas College *B*
Calvin College *B*
Eastern Michigan University *B*
Ferris State University *B*
Grand Valley State University *B*
Hope College *B*
Kalamazoo College *B*
Lansing Community College *A*
Madonna University *B*
Michigan State University *B*
Northern Michigan University *B*
Oakland University *B*
University of Michigan *B, M, D*
Wayne State University *B, M*
Western Michigan University *B*

Minnesota

Augsburg College *B*
Carleton College *B*
Gustavus Adolphus College *B*
Hamline University *B*
Minnesota State University
Mankato *B*
St. Catherine University *B*
Saint Cloud State University *B*
St. Olaf College *B*
University of Minnesota
Duluth *B*
Morris *B*
Twin Cities *B, M, D*

Mississippi

Millsaps College *B*
University of Mississippi *B*

Missouri

Drury University *B*
Kansas City Art Institute *B*
Lindenwood University *B*
Missouri State University *B*
Saint Louis University *B*
Truman State University *B*
University of Missouri
Kansas City *B, M, D*
St. Louis *B*
Washington University in St.
Louis *B, M, D*

Montana

University of Montana *B, M*

Nebraska

Hastings College *B*
University of Nebraska
Kearney *B*
Lincoln *B, M*
Omaha *B*

Nevada

University of Nevada
Reno *B*

New Hampshire

Colby-Sawyer College *B*
Dartmouth College *B*
New England College *B*
Plymouth State University *B*

New Jersey

Drew University *B*
Kean University *B*
Princeton University *B, M, D*

Rutgers, The State University of New
Jersey
New Brunswick/Piscataway
Campus B, M, D
Seton Hall University B

New Mexico

Santa Fe Community College A
Santa Fe University of Art and
Design B
University of New Mexico B, M, D

New York

Adelphi University B
Bard College B, M, D
Barnard College B
Canisius College B
City University of New York
Brooklyn College B, M
City College B, M
Hunter College B, M
Lehman College B, M
Queens College B, M
York College B
Colgate University B
College of New Rochelle B, T
Columbia University B
Columbia University
School of General Studies B
Cornell University B, M, D
Fashion Institute of Technology B
Fordham University B
Hamilton College B
Hartwick College B
Hobart and William Smith Colleges B
Hofstra University B
Ithaca College B
Long Island University
LIU Post B
Manhattanville College B
Marist College B
Marymount Manhattan College B
Nazareth College B
New York University B, M, D
Pace University B
Pace University: Pleasantville/
Briarcliff B
Parsons The New School for
Design M
Pratt Institute B, M
SUNY
College at Buffalo B, M
College at Fredonia B
College at Geneseo B
College at New Paltz B
College at Oneonta B
College at Potsdam B
College at Purchase B, M
University at Albany B
University at Binghamton B, M, D
University at Buffalo B, M
University at Stony Brook B, M, D
Saint Bonaventure University B
School of Visual Arts B, M
Skidmore College B
Syracuse University B, M
University of Rochester B
Wells College B

North Carolina

Duke University B, D
East Carolina University B
Elon University B
North Carolina State University B
Queens University of Charlotte B
Salem College B
University of North Carolina
Chapel Hill B, M, D
Charlotte B
Wilmington B
Wake Forest University B

Ohio

Art Academy of Cincinnati B
Baldwin Wallace University B
Bowling Green State University B
Case Western Reserve
University B, M, D
College of Wooster B
Denison University B
Hiram College B
John Carroll University B
Kent State University B, M
Kenyon College B
Lourdes University B
Miami University
Oxford B
Oberlin College B
Ohio State University
Columbus Campus B, M, D
Ohio University B, M
Ohio Wesleyan University B
Terra State Community College A
University of Akron B
University of Cincinnati B, M
University of Dayton B
University of Toledo B
Ursuline College B
Virginia Marti College of Art and
Design A
Wright State University B
Youngstown State University B

Oklahoma

Oklahoma State University M
University of Central Oklahoma B
University of Oklahoma B, M, D
University of Tulsa B

Oregon

Art Institute of Portland B
Mt. Hood Community College A
Portland State University B
University of Oregon B, M, D
Willamette University B

Pennsylvania

Allegheny College B
Arcadia University B
Bloomsburg University of
Pennsylvania B
Bryn Mawr College B, M, D
Bucknell University B
Chatham University B
Duquesne University B
Edinboro University of
Pennsylvania B
Elizabethtown College B
Franklin & Marshall College B
Gettysburg College B
Haverford College B
Juniata College B
La Salle University B
Lehigh University B
Lycoming College B
Mansfield University of
Pennsylvania B
Messiah College B
Moore College of Art and Design B
Moravian College B
Penn State
Abington B
Altoona B
Beaver B
Berks B
Brandywine B
DuBois B
Erie, The Behrend College B
Fayette, The Eberly Campus B
Greater Allegheny B
Harrisburg B
Hazleton B
Lehigh Valley B
Mont Alto B
New Kensington B
Schuylkill B

Shenango B
University Park B, M, D
Wilkes-Barre B
Worthington Scranton B
York B
Rosemont College B
St. Vincent College B
Seton Hill University B
Susquehanna University B
Swarthmore College B
Temple University B, M, D
University of Pennsylvania B, M, D
University of Pittsburgh B, M, D
Ursinus College B
Villanova University B

Puerto Rico

University of Puerto Rico
Aguadilla A
Mayaguez B
Rio Piedras B

Rhode Island

Brown University B, M, D
Providence College B
Rhode Island College B
Roger Williams University B, M
Salve Regina University B
University of Rhode Island B

South Carolina

College of Charleston B
Converse College B
Furman University B
University of South Carolina
Columbia B, M
Winthrop University B

South Dakota

South Dakota State University C

Tennessee

Belmont University B
Middle Tennessee State University B
Sewanee: The University of the
South B
Tennessee State University B
University of Memphis B, M
University of Tennessee
Knoxville B
Vanderbilt University B

Texas

Baylor University B
Lamar University M
Rice University B
Southern Methodist University B, M
Southwestern University B
Stephen F. Austin State University B
Texas Christian University B, M
Texas Tech University M
Trinity University B
University of Dallas B
University of Houston B, M
University of North Texas B, M
University of Texas
Arlington B
Austin B, M, D
El Paso B
San Antonio B, M
University of the Incarnate Word B

Utah

Brigham Young University B, M
Southern Utah University B
University of Utah B, M

Vermont

Bennington College B
Marlboro College B
Middlebury College B
Saint Michael's College B
University of Vermont B

Virginia

George Mason University B, M
Hollins University B
James Madison University B
Old Dominion University B
Randolph University B
Randolph-Macon College B
Roanoke College B
Sweet Briar College B
University of Mary Washington B
University of Richmond B
University of Virginia M, D
Virginia Commonwealth
University B, M, D
Washington and Lee University B

Washington

Eastern Washington University B
Seattle University B
University of Washington B, M, D
Western Washington University B
Whitman College B

West Virginia

West Virginia University B

Wisconsin

Beloit College B
Carthage College B
Lawrence University B, T
Ripon College B
University of Wisconsin
Madison B, M, D
Milwaukee B, M
Superior B, M
Whitewater B, T

Art teacher education

Alabama

Alabama Agricultural and Mechanical
University B, M
Birmingham-Southern College B, T
University of Alabama
Birmingham M

Alaska

University of Alaska
Fairbanks T

Arizona

Cochise College A
Eastern Arizona College A
University of Arizona B, M, D

Arkansas

Arkansas Tech University B
Harding University B, T
Henderson State University B
Ouachita Baptist University B, T
University of Arkansas
Pine Bluff B, T
University of the Ozarks T
Williams Baptist College B

California

Academy of Art University B, M
Azusa Pacific University B, T
California Baptist University T
California Lutheran University B, T
California State University
Chico T
Long Beach B, T
Northridge B, T
San Bernardino T
Cuesta College A
Humboldt State University T
Mills College T
Mount St. Mary's College T
Point Loma Nazarene University B
San Diego State University T
San Francisco State University T
Sonoma State University T

University of San Diego *T*
University of San Francisco *M*
Westmont College *T*

Colorado

Adams State University *B, M, T*
Colorado State University *B, T*
Colorado State University
 Pueblo *T*
Metropolitan State University of
 Denver *T*
Rocky Mountain College of Art &
 Design *B*
Western State Colorado
 University *B, T*

Connecticut

Albertus Magnus College *B, T*
Central Connecticut State
 University *B, M, T*
Southern Connecticut State
 University *B, M*

Delaware

Delaware State University *B*

District of Columbia

Catholic University of America *M*
Corcoran College of Art and
 Design *B, M*
Gallaudet University *B, T*
George Washington University *M, T*
Howard University *B*
University of the District of
 Columbia *B*

Florida

Flagler College *B*
Florida International University *B, M*
Florida Southern College *B, T*
Florida State University *M, D, T*
Palm Beach Atlantic University *B, T*
Palm Beach State College *A*
Pensacola State College *A*
University of Central Florida *B*
University of Florida *B, M*
University of Miami *M*
University of North Florida *B*
University of South Florida *B, M*
University of West Florida *B*

Georgia

Armstrong Atlantic State University *B*
Berry College *M*
Brenau University *B*
Columbus State University *B, M*
Darton College *A*
Georgia State University *B, M*
Kennesaw State University *B*
Piedmont College *M, T*
Shorter University *B*
University of Georgia *M, D, T*
University of North Georgia *A, B, M*
Valdosta State University *B*

Hawaii

Brigham Young University-
 Hawaii *B, T*

Idaho

Boise State University *B, M, T*
Brigham Young University-Idaho *B, T*
Northwest Nazarene University *B*
University of Idaho *B, T*

Illinois

Augustana College *B, T*
Blackburn College *B, T*
Bradley University *B, M*
Chicago State University *B*
City Colleges of Chicago
 Harold Washington College *A*
Columbia College Chicago *B, M*
Concordia University Chicago *B*

DePaul University *B, M, T*
Dominican University *T*
Elmhurst College *B*
Illinois College *T*
John A. Logan College *A*
Knox College *T*
Lincoln College *A*
McKendree University *B*
Millikin University *B, T*
Monmouth College *T*
North Central College *B, T*
North Park University *T*
Northern Illinois University *B, M, T*
Olivet Nazarene University *B, T*
Parkland College *A*
Rockford University *T*
Saint Xavier University *B*
School of the Art Institute of
 Chicago *B, M*
Trinity Christian College *B, T*
University of Illinois
 Chicago *B*
 Urbana-Champaign *B, M, D, T*
University of St. Francis *B, M*

Indiana

Anderson University *B, T*
Calumet College of St. Joseph *T*
Goshen College *B, T*
Grace College *B*
Huntington University *B*
Indiana State University *B, T*
Indiana University
 Bloomington *B, M*
 Purdue University Fort Wayne *B, T*
 Purdue University
  Indianapolis *B, M, T*
Indiana Wesleyan University *B, T*
Manchester University *B*
Oakland City University *B*
Purdue University *B, M, D*
Saint Mary's College *T*
St. Mary-of-the-Woods College *B, T*
Taylor University *B, T*
University of Evansville *B, T*
University of Indianapolis *B, M, T*
University of St. Francis *B*
Valparaiso University *B*
Vincennes University *A*

Iowa

Briar Cliff University *B*
Buena Vista University *B, T*
Central College *T*
Coe College *B*
Cornell College *B, T*
Dordt College *B*
Drake University *T*
Graceland University *T*
Grand View University *B, T*
Iowa State University *T*
Iowa Wesleyan College *B, T*
Loras College *B*
Maharishi University of
 Management *T*
Morningside College *B*
Mount Mercy University *T*
Northwestern College *T*
St. Ambrose University *B, T*
Simpson College *T*
University of Iowa *M, D, T*
Upper Iowa University *T*
Wartburg College *B, T*

Kansas

Baker University *B, T*
Benedictine College *B*
Bethany College *B*
Bethel College *T*
Colby Community College *A*
Friends University *B*
Garden City Community College *A*
Independence Community College *A*
Kansas State University *B, T*

Kansas Wesleyan University *B, T*
McPherson College *B, T*
Pittsburg State University *B*
Sterling College *T*
University of Kansas *B, M, T*
Washburn University *B, T*
Wichita State University *B, M, T*

Kentucky

Asbury University *B, T*
Berea College *B, T*
Brescia University *B, T*
Campbellsville University *B*
Eastern Kentucky University *B*
Hopkinsville Community College *A*
Kentucky Wesleyan College *B, T*
Lindsey Wilson College *B, T*
Spalding University *M*
Thomas More College *B*
Transylvania University *T*
University of Kentucky *B, M*
University of Louisville *M*
University of the
 Cumberlands *B, M, T*
Western Kentucky University *M*

Louisiana

Centenary College of Louisiana *T*
Grambling State University *B*
Louisiana College *B, T*
Louisiana State University
 Shreveport *T*
Louisiana Tech University *B*
McNeese State University *T*
Nicholls State University *B*
Southeastern Louisiana University *B*
University of Louisiana at Lafayette *B*
Xavier University of Louisiana *B*

Maine

Maine College of Art *T*
University of Maine *B*
University of Maine
 Machias *T*
 Presque Isle *B*
University of New England *B*
University of Southern Maine *B, T*

Maryland

Bowie State University *M*
Hood College *T*
Maryland Institute College of
 Art *B, M, T*
Mount St. Mary's University *M, T*
Notre Dame of Maryland
 University *T*
Towson University *B, M*
University of Maryland
 College Park *B*
 Eastern Shore *B*

Massachusetts

Anna Maria College *B, M*
Assumption College *T*
Boston University *B, M*
Bridgewater State University *B, M, T*
Fitchburg State University *M*
Framingham State University *M*
Harvard College *M, D*
Lesley University *B, M*
Massachusetts College of Art and
 Design *B, M, T*
Montserrat College of Art *T*
School of the Museum of Fine
 Arts *M, T*
Springfield College *B*
Tufts University *M, T*
University of Massachusetts
 Dartmouth *B, M, T*

Michigan

Adrian College *B, T*
Alma College *T*
Andrews University *M*

Aquinas College *B, T*
Calvin College *B*
Central Michigan University *B*
Concordia University *B, T*
Delta College *A*
Eastern Michigan University *B, M*
Ferris State University *B*
Grand Valley State University *T*
Hope College *B, T*
Michigan State University *B*
Northern Michigan University *B, T*
Olivet College *B, T*
Spring Arbor University *B*
University of Michigan
 Dearborn *B*
 Flint *B, T*
Wayne State University *B, M, T*
Western Michigan University *B, M, T*

Minnesota

Augsburg College *T*
Bethel University *B*
College of St. Benedict *T*
Concordia College: Moorhead *B, T*
Concordia University St. Paul *B, T*
Gustavus Adolphus College *T*
Minnesota State University
 Mankato *B, M, T*
 Moorhead *T*
Ridgewater College *A*
St. Catherine University *B, M, T*
Saint Cloud State University *B*
St. John's University *T*
Southwest Minnesota State
 University *B, T*
University of Minnesota
 Duluth *B*
 Morris *B*
 Twin Cities *B, M*
University of Northwestern - St.
 Paul *B*
Winona State University *B, T*

Mississippi

Coahoma Community College *A*
Itawamba Community College *A*
Millsaps College *T*
Mississippi College *B, M*
Mississippi Delta Community
 College *A*
Mississippi Gulf Coast Community
 College *A*
Mississippi University for
 Women *B, T*
Northeast Mississippi Community
 College *A*
Northwest Mississippi Community
 College *A*
University of Southern Mississippi *M*
William Carey University *B, M*

Missouri

Avila University *T*
College of the Ozarks *B, T*
Culver-Stockton College *B, T*
Evangel University *B, T*
Hannibal-LaGrange University *B*
Lincoln University *B*
Lindenwood University *B*
Maryville University of Saint
 Louis *B, M, T*
Missouri Southern State
 University *B, T*
Missouri State University *B*
Missouri Western State University *B*
Northwest Missouri State
 University *B, T*
Park University *T*
Southeast Missouri State University *B*
Southwest Baptist University *B, T*
Truman State University *M*
University of Central Missouri *B*

University of Missouri
Columbia *B, M, D*
Kansas City *B*
St. Louis *B, M*
Washington University in St.
Louis *B, M, T*
William Jewell College *B, T*
William Woods University *B, T*

Montana

Montana State University
Billings *B, T*
Rocky Mountain College *B*
University of Great Falls *B*
University of Montana *B, T*
University of Montana: Western *B, T*

Nebraska

Chadron State College *B*
Concordia University *B, T*
Creighton University *T*
Hastings College *B, M, T*
Midland University *B, T*
Nebraska Wesleyan University *T*
Union College *B*
University of Nebraska
Kearney *B, M, T*
Omaha *B*
Wayne State College *B, T*
Western Nebraska Community
College *A*
York College *B, T*

New Hampshire

Franklin Pierce University *M, T*
New England College *B, T*
New Hampshire Institute of Art *B*
Plymouth State University *B, M, T*
University of New Hampshire *T*

New Jersey

College of New Jersey *B, T*
Cumberland County College *A*
Georgian Court University *T*
Kean University *M*
New Jersey City University *M, T*
Rowan University *M*
William Paterson University of New
Jersey *B, T*

New Mexico

New Mexico Highlands University *B*
University of New Mexico *B, M*
Western New Mexico University *B*

New York

Adelphi University *B, M*
Alfred University *B, T*
City University of New York
Brooklyn College *M*
City College *B, M, T*
Hunter College *B*
Lehman College *M*
Queens College *B, M, T*
College of New Rochelle *B, M, T*
College of Saint Rose *B, M, T*
Daemen College *B, T*
Dowling College *B*
Elmira College *B, T*
Fordham University *T*
Hofstra University *B, M, T*
Houghton College *B, T*
Ithaca College *B, T*
Long Island University
LIU Brooklyn *B, T*
LIU Post *B, M, T*
Manhattanville College *M, T*
Nazareth College *B, M, T*
New York University *B, M, D*
Pace University *M*
Pace University: Pleasantville/
Briarcliff *M, T*
Pratt Institute *B, M*
Roberts Wesleyan College *B*

Rochester Institute of Technology *M*
SUNY
College at Buffalo *B, M, T*
College at New Paltz *B, M, T*
College at Oswego *M*
Sage Colleges *M*
St. Lawrence University *T*
St. Thomas Aquinas College *B, T*
School of Visual Arts *M*
Syracuse University *B, M, T*

North Carolina

Appalachian State University *B, T*
Barton College *B, T*
East Carolina University *B, M*
Elizabeth City State University *B, T*
Fayetteville State University *B, T*
Greensboro College *B, T*
Lenoir-Rhyne University *B, T*
Mars Hill University *B, T*
Meredith College *B, T*
Methodist University *B, T*
North Carolina Central
University *B, T*
University of North Carolina
Charlotte *B*
Greensboro *B*
Pembroke *B, M*
Western Carolina University *B, T*
Wingate University *B, T*

North Dakota

Dickinson State University *B, T*
Minot State University *B*
Valley City State University *B, T*

Ohio

Art Academy of Cincinnati *M*
Ashland University *B, T*
Bluffton University *B*
Bowling Green State
University *B, M, T*
Capital University *T*
Case Western Reserve
University *B, M*
College of Mount St. Joseph *B, T*
Defiance College *B, T*
Hiram College *T*
Kent State University *B, M*
Malone University *B*
Miami University
Oxford *B, M, T*
Mount Vernon Nazarene
University *B, T*
Notre Dame College *T*
Ohio Dominican University *B, T*
Ohio Northern University *B, T*
Ohio State University
Columbus Campus *B, M, D*
Ohio Wesleyan University *B*
Otterbein University *B*
Shawnee State University *B*
University of Akron *B, M*
University of Cincinnati *M, T*
University of Dayton *B, M, T*
University of Findlay *B, M, T*
University of Mount Union *T*
University of Rio Grande *B, T*
University of Toledo *B, M, T*
Ursuline College *B, M, T*
Youngstown State University *B, M*

Oklahoma

East Central University *B*
Eastern Oklahoma State College *A*
Northeastern State University *B*
Oklahoma Baptist University *B, T*
Oklahoma Christian University *B, T*
Oklahoma City University *B*
Oral Roberts University *B, T*
Southeastern Oklahoma State
University *B, T*

Southwestern Oklahoma State
University *B, M, T*
University of Central Oklahoma *B*

Oregon

Linfield College *T*
Portland State University *T*
Southern Oregon University *T*

Pennsylvania

Albright College *B, T*
Arcadia University *B, M, T*
Carlow University *B, M, T*
Chatham University *M*
Holy Family University *B*
Keystone College *B, T*
Lebanon Valley College *T*
Lycoming College *T*
Mansfield University of
Pennsylvania *B, T*
Marywood University *B, M*
Mercyhurst University *B, T*
Messiah College *B, M, T*
Moore College of Art and
Design *B, M, T*
Moravian College *T*
Penn State
Abington *B*
Altoona *B*
Beaver *B*
Berks *B*
Brandywine *B*
DuBois *B*
Erie, The Behrend College *B*
Fayette, The Eberly Campus *B*
Greater Allegheny *B*
Harrisburg *B*
Hazleton *B*
Lehigh Valley *B*
Mont Alto *B*
New Kensington *B*
Schuylkill *B*
Shenango *B*
University Park *B, M, D*
Wilkes-Barre *B*
Worthington Scranton *B*
York *B*
Rosemont College *T*
Saint Joseph's University *B, M, T*
St. Vincent College *B*
Seton Hill University *B, T*
Temple University *B, M*
University of the Arts *M*
Washington & Jefferson College *B, T*
Waynesburg University *B*

Puerto Rico

Escuela de Artes Plasticas de Puerto
Rico *B*
Inter American University of Puerto
Rico
San German Campus *B*
Pontifical Catholic University of
Puerto Rico *B, T*
Turabo University *M*

Rhode Island

Rhode Island College *B, M*
Rhode Island School of Design *M*

South Carolina

Anderson University *B, T*
Claflin University *B*
Coker College *B, T*
Converse College *B, T*
Francis Marion University *B, T*
Furman University *T*
South Carolina State University *B, T*
University of South Carolina
Columbia *B, M*
Upstate *B, T*
Winthrop University *M, T*

South Dakota

Augustana College *B, T*
Northern State University *B, T*
South Dakota State University *B*
University of Sioux Falls *B*
University of South Dakota *T*

Tennessee

Belmont University *B, T*
Bethel University *T*
Freed-Hardeman University *B, T*
Lee University *B*
Lincoln Memorial University *B, T*
Lipscomb University *B, T*
Memphis College of Art *M, T*
Middle Tennessee State University *B*
Southern Adventist University *B*
Tennessee Technological University *T*
Tusculum College *B, T*
Union University *B, T*
University of Tennessee
Chattanooga *B, T*

Texas

Abilene Christian University *B, T*
Austin College *M*
Del Mar College *A*
Hardin-Simmons University *B, T*
Houston Baptist University *B, M*
Howard Payne University *B*
Kilgore College *A*
Lamar University *B, M, T*
Laredo Community College *A*
Lubbock Christian University *B*
McMurry University *B, T*
St. Edward's University *B, T*
St. Mary's University *D*
Sam Houston State University *M, T*
Southwestern University *T*
Stephen F. Austin State University *M*
Tarleton State University *T*
Texas A&M University
Kingsville *B, M*
Texas Christian University *B*
Texas College *B, T*
Texas Tech University *M*
University of Dallas *T*
University of Mary Hardin-Baylor *T*
University of North Texas *M, D, T*
University of Texas
Arlington *T*
Austin *M*
El Paso *M*
San Antonio *T*
University of the Incarnate
Word *B, T*
West Texas A&M University *T*

Utah

Dixie State College *B*
Southern Utah University *B*
Utah Valley University *B*
Weber State University *B*
Westminster College *M*

Vermont

Castleton State College *B, T*
Goddard College *B, M*
Green Mountain College *B, T*
Johnson State College *B*
Saint Michael's College *B, M, T*
University of Vermont *B, T*

Virginia

Averett University *B, M, T*
Bluefield College *B, T*
Bridgewater College *T*
Eastern Mennonite University *T*
Emory & Henry College *B*
George Mason University *M*
Hollins University *T*
Longwood University *T*
Northern Virginia Community
College *A*

Radford University *T*
Virginia Commonwealth
   University *B, M*
Virginia Intermont College *T*
Virginia Wesleyan College *B, T*

Washington
Central Washington University *B, T*
Eastern Washington University *B*
Heritage University *M*
Seattle Pacific University *B, T*
Western Washington University *B, M*
Whitworth University *M, T*

West Virginia
Bethany College *B*
Concord University *B, T*
Shepherd University *T*
West Liberty University *B*
West Virginia State University *B*
West Virginia University *T*
West Virginia Wesleyan College *B*

Wisconsin
Alverno College *B, T*
Beloit College *B, T*
Carroll University *B, T*
Carthage College *M, T*
Concordia University Wisconsin *B, M*
Edgewood College *B, T*
Lawrence University *T*
Marian University *B, T*
Mount Mary University *B, T*
Silver Lake College of the Holy
   Family *B, T*
University of Wisconsin
   Green Bay *T*
   Madison *B, M*
   Milwaukee *B, M, T*
   Platteville *B*
   River Falls *B, T*
   Stout *B, T*
   Superior *B, T*
   Whitewater *B*
Viterbo University *B, T*

Wyoming
Casper College *A*

Art therapy

Arizona
Prescott College *B, M*

California
Notre Dame de Namur
   University *M, D*
Pacific Union College *C*

Connecticut
Albertus Magnus College *B, M*

District of Columbia
George Washington University *M*

Florida
Florida State University *M*

Georgia
Georgia College and State
   University *M*

Illinois
Millikin University *B*
School of the Art Institute of
   Chicago *M*
Southern Illinois University
   Edwardsville *M*

Indiana
Indiana University
   Purdue University Indianapolis *M*
St. Mary-of-the-Woods College *M*

University of Indianapolis *B*
University of St. Francis *B*
Vincennes University *A*

Kansas
Bethany College *B*
Emporia State University *M*

Massachusetts
Anna Maria College *B*
Emmanuel College *B*
Lesley University *B, M, D*
Springfield College *B, M*

Michigan
Marygrove College *B*

New Jersey
Caldwell College *M*

New York
College of New Rochelle *B, M, T*
Hofstra University *M*
Long Island University
   LIU Post *B, M*
Nazareth College *M*
Pratt Institute *M*
St. Thomas Aquinas College *B*
School of Visual Arts *M*

North Carolina
Mars Hill University *B*

Ohio
Bowling Green State University *B*
Capital University *B*
Ursuline College *M*

Oregon
Marylhurst University *M*

Pennsylvania
Arcadia University *B*
Carlow University *B*
Cedar Crest College *B*
Marywood University *B, M*
Mercyhurst University *B*
Seton Hill University *B, M*

South Carolina
Converse College *B*

Tennessee
Southern Adventist University *B*

Vermont
Goddard College *M*

West Virginia
West Virginia Wesleyan College *B*

Wisconsin
Alverno College *B*
Edgewood College *B*
Mount Mary University *B, M, D*
University of Wisconsin
   Superior *B, M*

Artificial intelligence

Arizona
University of Advancing
   Technology *A, B, M*

Arkansas
East Arkansas Community College *C*

California
University of Southern California *M*

Georgia
Georgia Institute of Technology *D*
University of Georgia *M*

Illinois
College of Lake County *A*

Massachusetts
Worcester Polytechnic Institute *B*

Michigan
Henry Ford Community College *C*

New York
Globe Institute of Technology *A, B*
Rochester Institute of Technology *M*

Pennsylvania
Carnegie Mellon University *M, D*
University of Pittsburgh *M, D*

Texas
Texas State Technical College
   Marshall *A*

Arts, entertainment, and media management, general

Alabama
University of North Alabama *B*

California
National University *B*
San Diego State University *B, M*

Colorado
Colorado State University *M*

Georgia
Brenau University *B*

Illinois
Judson University *B*

Indiana
Butler University *B*
Valparaiso University *M*

Kentucky
University of Kentucky *B*

Massachusetts
Stonehill College *B*
Western New England University *B*

Michigan
Adrian College *B*
University of Michigan
   Flint *M*

Minnesota
Globe University
   Minneapolis *B*
   Woodbury *B*
Minnesota School of Business
   Brooklyn Center *B*
   Richfield *B*
   St. Cloud *B*
St. Mary's University of Minnesota *M*

Missouri
Webster University *M*

New York
Concordia College *B*
Syracuse University *M*

North Carolina
Bennett College for Women *B*

Ohio
University of Cincinnati *M*

Pennsylvania
Albright College *B*
Carnegie Mellon University *M*

Tennessee
Belmont University *B*

Texas
St. Edward's University *B*
University of Houston *M*

Utah
Southern Utah University *M*

Vermont
Champlain College *B*

Virginia
Shenandoah University *B, M*

Wisconsin
University of Wisconsin
   Green Bay *B*

Asian-American studies

Arizona
Arizona State University *B*

California
California State University
   East Bay *B*
   Fullerton *B*
Claremont McKenna College *B*
De Anza College *A*
El Camino College *A*
Los Angeles City College *A*
Pitzer College *B*
Pomona College *B*
San Francisco State University *B, M*
Scripps College *B*
Solano Community College *A*
Southwestern College *A*
Stanford University *B*
University of California
   Berkeley *B*
   Davis *B*
   Irvine *B*
   Los Angeles *B, M*
   Riverside *B*
University of Southern California *B*

Colorado
University of Denver *B*

New York
Columbia University *B*
SUNY
   University at Binghamton *B*
   University at Stony Brook *B*

Pennsylvania
Gettysburg College *B*

Washington
University of Washington *B*

Asian bodywork therapy

California
California University of Management
   and Sciences *A*

New York
Swedish Institute *A*

Asian history

Massachusetts
Harvard College *D*

New York
Bard College *B*

Ohio
University of Akron *C*

Pennsylvania
Gettysburg College *B*

Asian studies

Alabama
Samford University *B*

Arizona
Arizona State University *B*

California
Cabrillo College *A*
California State University
   Chico *B*
   Long Beach *B, M*
   Sacramento *B, M*
   San Bernardino *M*
Claremont McKenna College *B*
Cypress College *A*
Laney College *A*
Loyola Marymount University *B*
Pepperdine University *B*
Pitzer College *B*
Pomona College *B*
San Diego State University *B, M*
Scripps College *B*
Skyline College *C, A*
University of California
   Berkeley *B, M, D*
   Los Angeles *B, M*
   Riverside *B*
   Santa Barbara *B, M, D*
University of Redlands *B*
University of San Francisco *M*
University of the Pacific *B*

Colorado
Colorado College *B*
University of Colorado
   Boulder *B*
University of Northern Colorado *B*

Connecticut
Trinity College *B*

District of Columbia
American University *B*

Florida
Florida International University *B, M*
Florida State University *B, M*
Miami Dade College *A*
Rollins College *B*
University of Florida *B*

Hawaii
University of Hawaii
   Manoa *B, M*

Illinois
Augustana College *B*
Illinois Wesleyan University *B*
Knox College *B*
Lake Forest College *B*
Northwestern University *B*
University of Illinois
   Urbana-Champaign *M*

Indiana
Purdue University *B*

Iowa
Coe College *B*
University of Iowa *B, M*

Kentucky
Berea College *B*
University of Louisville *C*
Western Kentucky University *B*

Louisiana
Tulane University *B*

Maine
Bowdoin College *B*

Maryland
Howard Community College *A*
McDaniel College *B*
St. Mary's College of Maryland *B*
University of Maryland
   University College *B*

Massachusetts
Amherst College *B*
Bard College at Simon's Rock *B*
College of the Holy Cross *B*
Mount Holyoke College *B*
Northeastern University *B*
Smith College *B*
Suffolk University *B*
Tufts University *B, M*
University of Massachusetts
   Amherst *C*
   Boston *B*
Wellesley College *B*
Wheaton College *B*
Williams College *B*

Michigan
Calvin College *B*
Michigan State University *B, M, D*
University of Michigan *B*

Minnesota
Carleton College *B*
College of St. Benedict *B*
Macalester College *B*
St. John's University *B*
St. Olaf College *B*

Missouri
Washington University in St. Louis *B*

Montana
University of Montana *B*

Nevada
University of Nevada
   Las Vegas *B*

New Hampshire
Dartmouth College *B*

New Jersey
Kean University *B*
Seton Hall University *B, M*

New Mexico
University of New Mexico *B*

New York
Bard College *B*
Barnard College *B*
City University of New York
   City College *B*
Colgate University *B*
Columbia University *B*
Columbia University
   School of General Studies *B*
Cornell University *B, M*
Hamilton College *B*
Hobart and William Smith Colleges *B*
Manhattanville College *B*
Nazareth College *B*
New York University *B*
Pace University *B*
SUNY
   College at New Paltz *B*
   University at Albany *B*
   University at Binghamton *B, M*
   University at Buffalo *B*
   University at Stony Brook *B, T*
St. John's University *B*
St. Lawrence University *B*
Skidmore College *B*
Union College *B*
Vassar College *B*

North Carolina
Duke University *B*
St. Andrews University *B*
University of North Carolina
   Chapel Hill *B*

Ohio
Bowling Green State University *B*
Case Western Reserve University *B*
Marietta College *B*
Ohio University *B, M*
University of Cincinnati *C, B*
University of Mount Union *B*
University of Toledo *B*

Oregon
Pacific University *B*
University of Oregon *B, M*
Willamette University *B*

Pennsylvania
Gettysburg College *B*
Indiana University of Pennsylvania *B*
Lafayette College *B*
Lehigh University *B*
Penn State
   Abington *C, B*
   Altoona *C, B*
   Beaver *C, B*
   Berks *C, B*
   Brandywine *C, B*
   DuBois *C, B*
   Erie, The Behrend College *C*
   Fayette, The Eberly Campus *C, B*
   Greater Allegheny *C, B*
   Harrisburg *C, B*
   Hazleton *C, B*
   Lehigh Valley *C, B*
   Mont Alto *C, B*
   New Kensington *C, B*
   Schuylkill *C, B*
   Shenango *C, B*
   University Park *C, B*
   Wilkes-Barre *C, B*
   Worthington Scranton *C, B*
   York *C, B*
Saint Joseph's University *B*
Swarthmore College *B*
Temple University *B*

Rhode Island
Brown University *B*

South Carolina
Furman University *B*

Tennessee
Belmont University *B*
Sewanee: The University of the
   South *B*
Vanderbilt University *B*

Texas
Austin College *B*
Baylor University *B*
Rice University *B*
Texas State University *B*
Trinity University *B*

University of Texas
   Austin *B, M*

Utah
Brigham Young University *B*
University of Utah *B, M*
Utah State University *B*

Vermont
Bennington College *B*
Marlboro College *B*
University of Vermont *B*

Virginia
Mary Baldwin College *B*
Old Dominion University *B*
Randolph-Macon College *B*
University of Richmond *B*

Washington
Gonzaga University *B*
Seattle University *B*
University of Puget Sound *B*
University of Washington *B, M, D*
University of Washington Tacoma *B*
Washington State University *B*
Whitman College *B*

Wisconsin
Carthage College *B*
University of Wisconsin
   Madison *B*
   Milwaukee *C*

Astronomy

Arizona
Northern Arizona University *B*
University of Arizona *B, M, D*

California
College of San Mateo *C*
De Anza College *A*
El Camino College *A*
Fullerton College *A*
Gavilan College *A*
Golden West College *A*
Orange Coast College *A*
Palomar College *C, A*
Pomona College *B*
Saddleback College *A*
San Bernardino Valley College *A*
San Diego State University *B, M*
Southwestern College *A*
University of California
   Los Angeles *M, D*
   Santa Cruz *D*
University of Southern California *B*

Colorado
Colorado Mountain College *C*
University of Colorado
   Boulder *B*

Connecticut
Wesleyan University *B, M*
Yale University *B, M, D*

Delaware
University of Delaware *B*

District of Columbia
Howard University *M, D*

Florida
Daytona State College *A*
University of Florida *B, M, D*

Georgia
Emory University *B*
Georgia State University *D*
Gordon College *A*

University of Georgia *B*
Valdosta State University *B*

Hawaii

University of Hawaii
  Hilo *B*
  Manoa *M, D*

Idaho

North Idaho College *A*

Illinois

Kishwaukee College *A*
South Suburban College of Cook
  County *A*
Southwestern Illinois College *A*
University of Chicago *D*
University of Illinois
  Urbana-Champaign *B, M, D*

Indiana

Indiana University
  Bloomington *B, M, D*
Valparaiso University *B*

Iowa

Drake University *B*
University of Iowa *B, M, D*

Kansas

Benedictine College *B*
Central Christian College of Kansas *A*
University of Kansas *B*

Maryland

Johns Hopkins University *B, D*
University of Maryland
  College Park *B, M, D*

Massachusetts

Amherst College *B*
Boston University *B, M, D*
Hampshire College *B*
Harvard College *M, D*
Mount Holyoke College *B*
Smith College *B*
Stonehill College *B*
Tufts University *B*
University of Massachusetts
  Amherst *B, M, D*
Wellesley College *B*
Williams College *B*

Michigan

Central Michigan University *B*
Michigan State University *M, D*
University of Michigan *B, M, D*
Wayne State University *B*

Minnesota

Minnesota State University
  Mankato *B*
University of Minnesota
  Twin Cities *B, M*

New Hampshire

Dartmouth College *B*

New Mexico

New Mexico State University *M, D*

New York

Barnard College *B*
Colgate University *B*
Columbia University *B*
Columbia University
  School of General Studies *B*
Cornell University *B, M, D*
Rensselaer Polytechnic Institute *M*
SUNY
  College at New Paltz *B*
  University at Stony Brook *B*
Suffolk County Community College *A*

Union College *B*
Vassar College *B*

Ohio

Case Western Reserve
  University *B, M, D*
Ohio State University
  Columbus Campus *B, M, D*
Ohio Wesleyan University *B*
University of Toledo *B*
Wilmington College *B*
Youngstown State University *B*

Oklahoma

Tulsa Community College *A*
University of Oklahoma *B*

Pennsylvania

Bryn Mawr College *B*
Franklin & Marshall College *B*
Gettysburg College *B*
Haverford College *B*
Lehigh University *B*
Lycoming College *B*
Penn State
  Abington *B*
  Altoona *B*
  Beaver *B*
  Berks *B*
  Brandywine *B*
  DuBois *B*
  Fayette, The Eberly Campus *B*
  Greater Allegheny *B*
  Harrisburg *B*
  Hazleton *B*
  Lehigh Valley *B*
  Mont Alto *B*
  New Kensington *B*
  Schuylkill *B*
  Shenango *B*
  University Park *B, M, D*
  Wilkes-Barre *B*
  Worthington Scranton *B*
  York *B*
Swarthmore College *B*
University of Pittsburgh *B*
Villanova University *B*

South Carolina

College of Charleston *B*

Texas

Baylor University *B*
Rice University *B, M, D*
University of Texas
  Austin *B, M, D*

Utah

Brigham Young University *B, D*

Vermont

Bennington College *B*
Marlboro College *B*

Virginia

George Mason University *B*
University of Virginia *B, M, D*

Washington

Highline Community College *A*
University of Washington *B, M, D*
Whitman College *B*

Wisconsin

University of Wisconsin
  Madison *M, D*

Wyoming

University of Wyoming *B*

Astrophysics

Alaska

University of Alaska
  Fairbanks *M, D*

Arizona

Arizona State University *M, D*

California

California Institute of
  Technology *B, M, D*
Moorpark College *A*
University of California
  Berkeley *B, D*
  Los Angeles *B*
  Santa Cruz *B*

Colorado

University of Colorado
  Boulder *D*

Connecticut

Yale University *B*

Georgia

Agnes Scott College *B*

Indiana

Indiana University
  Bloomington *D*

Iowa

Iowa State University *M, D*

Massachusetts

Boston University *B*
Smith College *B*
Tufts University *B, M, D*
Wellesley College *B*
Williams College *B*

Michigan

Michigan State University *B, M, D*

Minnesota

University of Minnesota
  Twin Cities *B, M, D*

New Jersey

Princeton University *B, M, D*
Rutgers, The State University of New
  Jersey
  New Brunswick/Piscataway
    Campus *B*

New Mexico

New Mexico Institute of Mining and
  Technology *B, M, D*
University of New Mexico *B*

New York

Barnard College *B*
Colgate University *B*
Columbia University *B*
Columbia University
  School of General Studies *B*
Rochester Institute of
  Technology *M, D*

Ohio

Ohio University *B*
University of Cincinnati *B*

Oklahoma

University of Oklahoma *B*

Pennsylvania

Carnegie Mellon University *B*
Franklin & Marshall College *B*
Lehigh University *B*
Lycoming College *B*

Swarthmore College *B*
Villanova University *B*

South Carolina

College of Charleston *B*

Texas

Baylor University *B*
Rice University *B, M, D*
Texas Christian University *D*

Washington

University of Washington *B*
Whitman College *B*

Wisconsin

University of Wisconsin
  Madison *B*

Wyoming

University of Wyoming *B*

Athletic training

Alabama

Samford University *B*
Troy University *B*
University of Alabama *B*
University of Mobile *B*
University of West Alabama *B*
Wallace State Community College at
  Hanceville *A*

Arizona

Arizona Western College *C, A*
Carrington College
  Tucson *C*
Grand Canyon University *B*

Arkansas

Arkansas State University *B*
Harding University *B*
Henderson State University *B*
John Brown University *B*
Southern Arkansas University *B*
University of Arkansas *M*
University of Central Arkansas *B*

California

California Baptist University *M*
California Lutheran University *B*
California State University
  East Bay *B*
  Fresno *B*
  Fullerton *B*
  Northridge *M*
Carrington College California
  Pleasant Hill *C*
Chapman University *B*
College of the Canyons *A*
Concordia University Irvine *B*
Diablo Valley College *C, A*
Foothill College *C, A*
Fresno Pacific University *B*
Grossmont College *C, A*
Orange Coast College *C, A*
Pepperdine University *B*
Point Loma Nazarene University *B*
San Bernardino Valley College *C*
San Diego Christian College *B*
San Diego State University *B*
San Francisco State University *C*
Santa Barbara City College *C, A*
Santa Rosa Junior College *C*
University of La Verne *B*
University of the Pacific *B*
Vanguard University of Southern
  California *B*

Colorado

Colorado Mesa University *B*
Colorado State University *B*
Community College of Aurora *C*

Fort Lewis College *B*
Metropolitan State University of
  Denver *B*
University of Northern Colorado *B*

Connecticut

Central Connecticut State
  University *B*
Quinnipiac University *B*
Sacred Heart University *B*
Southern Connecticut State
  University *B*
University of Connecticut *B*

Delaware

University of Delaware *B*

Florida

Barry University *B*
Broward College *A*
Florida Gulf Coast University *B*
Florida International University *M*
Florida Southern College *B*
Florida State University *B*
Nova Southeastern University *B*
Palm Beach Atlantic University *B*
University of Central Florida *B*
University of Florida *B*
University of Miami *B*
University of North Florida *B*
University of South Florida *B*
University of Tampa *B*

Georgia

Abraham Baldwin Agricultural
  College *A*
Andrew College *A*
Armstrong Atlantic State
  University *M*
Columbus Technical College *C*
Darton College *C*
Georgia College and State
  University *B*
Georgia Southern University *B*
Piedmont College *B*
University of Georgia *B*
University of North Georgia *B*
Valdosta State University *B*

Hawaii

University of Hawaii
  Manoa *M*

Idaho

Boise State University *B, M*
Idaho State University *M*
University of Idaho *B, M, D*

Illinois

Aurora University *B*
City Colleges of Chicago
  Kennedy-King College *C*
  Malcolm X College *C*
Eastern Illinois University *B*
Illinois State University *B*
Illinois Valley Community College *A*
Kaskaskia College *C*
Lewis University *B*
McKendree University *B*
Millikin University *B*
North Central College *B*
North Park University *B*
Northern Illinois University *B*
Olivet Nazarene University *B*
Sauk Valley Community College *A*
Trinity International University *B*
University of Illinois
  Urbana-Champaign *B, M*
Western Illinois University *B*

Indiana

Anderson University *B*
DePauw University *B*
Franklin College *B*

Indiana State University *B, M*
Indiana University
  Bloomington *B*
Indiana Wesleyan University *B*
Manchester University *B, M*
Purdue University *B*
Saint Joseph's College *B*
University of Evansville *B, M*
University of Indianapolis *B*

Iowa

Buena Vista University *B*
Central College *B*
Clarke University *B*
Coe College *B*
Dordt College *B*
Ellsworth Community College *A*
Graceland University *B*
Iowa Western Community College *A*
Loras College *B*
Luther College *B*
Northwestern College *B*
Simpson College *B*
University of Iowa *B, M*
University of Northern Iowa *B, M*
Upper Iowa University *B*

Kansas

Barton County Community College *A*
Benedictine College *B*
Bethany College *B*
Bethel College *B*
Coffeyville Community College *A*
Dodge City Community College *A*
Emporia State University *B*
Garden City Community College *A*
Independence Community College *A*
Kansas State University *B*
MidAmerica Nazarene University *B*
Neosho County Community
  College *A*
Seward County Community
  College *A*
Southwestern College *B*
Sterling College *B*
Tabor College *B*
University of Kansas *B*
Washburn University *B*
Wichita State University *B*

Kentucky

Campbellsville University *B*
Eastern Kentucky University *M*
Georgetown College *B*
Murray State University *B*
Northern Kentucky University *B*
Union College *B*
University of Kentucky *M*

Louisiana

Louisiana College *B*
Louisiana State University and
  Agricultural and Mechanical
  College *B*
McNeese State University *B*
Nicholls State University *B*
Southeastern Louisiana University *B*
University of Louisiana at Lafayette *B*

Maine

University of Maine *B*
University of Maine
  Presque Isle *B*
University of New England *B*
University of Southern Maine *B*

Maryland

Howard Community College *A*
Salisbury University *B*
Towson University *B*

Massachusetts

Boston University *B, D*
Bridgewater State University *B, M*

Dean College *A*
Endicott College *B*
Lasell College *B*
Massachusetts College of Liberal
  Arts *B*
Merrimack College *B*
Mount Wachusett Community
  College *C*
Northeastern University *B*
Salem State University *B*
Springfield College *B, M*
Westfield State University *B*

Michigan

Adrian College *B, M*
Albion College *B*
Aquinas College *B*
Calvin College *B*
Central Michigan University *B*
Eastern Michigan University *B*
Grand Valley State University *B*
Hillsdale College *B*
Hope College *B*
Michigan State University *B*
Northern Michigan University *B*
Saginaw Valley State University *B*
University of Michigan *B*
Western Michigan University *B, M*

Minnesota

Bethel University *B*
Concordia University St. Paul *B*
Gustavus Adolphus College *B*
Lake Superior College *C*
Minnesota State University
  Mankato *B, M, T*
  Moorhead *B*
Ridgewater College *A*
St. Paul College *C, A*
University of Minnesota
  Duluth *B*
Winona State University *B*

Mississippi

Delta State University *B*
East Mississippi Community
  College *A*
Northeast Mississippi Community
  College *A*
University of Southern Mississippi *B*

Missouri

Central Methodist University *B*
Culver-Stockton College *B*
Lindenwood University *B*
Missouri State University *B*
Missouri Valley College *B*
Park University *B*
Saint Louis University *B, M*
Southeast Missouri State University *B*
Southwest Baptist University *B*
Truman State University *B*
William Woods University *B*

Montana

Montana State University
  Billings *B, M*
Rocky Mountain College *B*
University of Montana *B*

Nebraska

Midland University *B*
Nebraska Wesleyan University *B*
University of Nebraska
  Lincoln *B*
  Omaha *B, M*
Wayne State College *B*
Western Nebraska Community
  College *A*
Wright Career College
  Omaha *A*

Nevada

University of Nevada
  Las Vegas *B*

New Hampshire

Colby-Sawyer College *B*
Keene State College *B*
Plymouth State University *B, M*
University of New Hampshire *B*

New Jersey

Kean University *B*
Montclair State University *B*
Ocean County College *C*
Rowan University *B*
Seton Hall University *M*

New Mexico

Carrington College
  Albuquerque *C*
New Mexico Junior College *A*
New Mexico State University *B*

New York

Alfred University *B*
Canisius College *B*
Daemen College *M*
Dominican College of Blauvelt *B*
Finger Lakes Community College *A*
Hofstra University *B*
Ithaca College *B*
Long Island University
  LIU Brooklyn *B, M*
Marist College *B*
Rochester Institute of Technology *C*
SUNY
  College at Brockport *B*
  College at Cortland *B*
  University at Stony Brook *B*
Suffolk County Community College *A*

North Carolina

Appalachian State University *B*
Barton College *B*
Campbell University *B*
Catawba College *B*
Chowan University *B*
East Carolina University *B, M*
Gardner-Webb University *B*
Greensboro College *C, B*
Guilford College *B*
High Point University *B*
Lenoir-Rhyne University *B, M*
Mars Hill University *B*
Methodist University *B*
North Carolina Central University *B*
Shaw University *B*
University of North Carolina
  Charlotte *B*
  Pembroke *B*
  Wilmington *B*
Western Carolina University *B*
Wingate University *B*

North Dakota

North Dakota State University *M*
University of Mary *B*
University of North Dakota *B*

Ohio

Ashland University *B*
Baldwin Wallace University *B*
Bowling Green State University *B*
Capital University *B*
Cedarville University *B*
Cincinnati State Technical and
  Community College *C*
College of Mount St. Joseph *B*
Defiance College *C, B*
Heidelberg University *B*
Kent State University *B*
Lorain County Community
  College *C, A*
Marietta College *B*

Miami University
  Oxford *B*
Ohio Northern University *B*
Ohio State University
  Columbus Campus *B*
Ohio University *B, M*
Otterbein University *B, M*
Shawnee State University *B*
University of Akron *A, B, M*
University of Cincinnati *B*
University of Findlay *B, M*
University of Mount Union *B*
University of Toledo *B*
Urbana University *B*
Xavier University *B*
Youngstown State University *B*

Oklahoma

East Central University *B*
Northeastern Oklahoma Agricultural
  and Mechanical College *A*
Oklahoma Baptist University *B*
Oklahoma State University *B*
Southern Nazarene University *B*
Southwestern Oklahoma State
  University *B*
University of Central Oklahoma *B, M*
University of Tulsa *B*

Oregon

Concordia University *B*
George Fox University *B*
Linfield College *B*
Oregon State University *B*
Southern Oregon University *B*

Pennsylvania

Alvernia University *B*
Bloomsburg University of
  Pennsylvania *M*
California University of
  Pennsylvania *B, M*
Chestnut Hill College *C*
Duquesne University *B*
East Stroudsburg University of
  Pennsylvania *B*
Eastern University *B*
Indiana University of Pennsylvania *B*
King's College *B*
Lock Haven University of
  Pennsylvania *B*
Marywood University *B*
Mercyhurst University *B*
Messiah College *B*
Neumann University *B*
Northampton Community College *A*
Penn State
  Abington *B*
  Altoona *B*
  Beaver *B*
  Berks *B*
  Brandywine *B*
  DuBois *B*
  Fayette, The Eberly Campus *B*
  Greater Allegheny *B*
  Harrisburg *B*
  Hazleton *B*
  Lehigh Valley *B*
  Mont Alto *B*
  New Kensington *B*
  Schuylkill *B*
  Shenango *B*
  University Park *B*
  Wilkes-Barre *B*
  Worthington Scranton *B*
  York *B*
Slippery Rock University of
  Pennsylvania *B*
Temple University *B*
University of Pittsburgh
  Bradford *B*
Waynesburg University *B*
West Chester University of
  Pennsylvania *B, M*

Puerto Rico

Turabo University *D*
University of Puerto Rico
  Mayaguez *B*
  Ponce *B*

South Carolina

Charleston Southern University *B*
College of Charleston *B*
Erskine College *B*
Lander University *B*
Limestone College *B*
Winthrop University *B*

South Dakota

Augustana University *B*
Dakota Wesleyan University *B*
South Dakota State University *B, M*

Tennessee

Carson-Newman University *B*
King University *B*
Lee University *B*
Lincoln Memorial University *B*
Lipscomb University *B*
Middle Tennessee State University *B*
Tusculum College *B*
Union University *B*
University of Tennessee
  Chattanooga *M*

Texas

Angelo State University *B, T*
Baylor University *B*
East Texas Baptist University *B*
Hardin-Simmons University *B*
Howard College *A*
Howard Payne University *B*
Kilgore College *A*
Lubbock Christian University *B*
McMurry University *B*
Midwestern State University *B*
South Plains College *A*
Stephen F. Austin State University *M*
Texas A&M University *M*
Texas A&M University
  Commerce *B*
  Corpus Christi *B*
Texas Christian University *B*
Texas Lutheran University *B*
Texas State University *B, M, T*
Texas Tech University Health
  Sciences Center *M*
Texas Wesleyan University *B*
Texas Woman's University *M*
University of Houston *M*
University of Mary Hardin-Baylor *B*
University of Texas
  Arlington *B*
  Austin *B*
  Permian Basin *B*
University of the Incarnate Word *B*
West Texas A&M University *B*

Utah

Brigham Young University *B, M*
Southern Utah University *B*
University of Utah *B*
Weber State University *B, M*

Vermont

Castleton State College *B*
Johnson State College *B*
Lyndon State College *B*
Norwich University *B*
University of Vermont *B*

Virginia

Averett University *B*
Bridgewater College *B*
Emory & Henry College *B*
George Mason University *B*
James Madison University *B*
Liberty University *B*

Longwood University *B*
Lynchburg College *B*
Radford University *B*
Roanoke College *B*
Shenandoah University *M*
Virginia Commonwealth
  University *M*

Washington

Eastern Washington University *B*
Spokane Falls Community College *A*
Washington State University *B*
Whitworth University *B*

West Virginia

Alderson-Broaddus University *B*
Concord University *B*
Marshall University *B*
Potomac State College of West
  Virginia University *A*
University of Charleston *B*
West Virginia University *B, T*
West Virginia Wesleyan College *B, M*

Wisconsin

Carroll University *B*
Carthage College *B*
Concordia University Wisconsin *B*
Marquette University *B*
University of Wisconsin
  Eau Claire *B*
  La Crosse *B*
  Madison *B*
  Milwaukee *C, B*
  Stevens Point *B*

Wyoming

Casper College *A*
Central Wyoming College *A*
Northwest College *A*

Atmospheric physics/ dynamics

New Mexico

New Mexico Institute of Mining and
  Technology *B, M, D*

Atmospheric science

Alabama

Community College of the Air
  Force *A*
University of Alabama
  Huntsville *M, D*
University of South Alabama *B*

Alaska

University of Alaska
  Fairbanks *M, D*

Arizona

Embry-Riddle Aeronautical University
  Prescott Campus *B*
University of Arizona *M, D*

California

San Francisco State University *B*
San Jose State University *M*
Shasta College *A*
University of California
  Berkeley *B*
  Davis *B, M, D*
  Los Angeles *M, D*

Colorado

Colorado State University *M, D*
Metropolitan State University of
  Denver *B*
United States Air Force Academy *B*
University of Colorado
  Boulder *M, D*

Connecticut

Western Connecticut State
  University *B*

Delaware

University of Delaware *D*

District of Columbia

Howard University *M, D*

Florida

Embry-Riddle Aeronautical
  University *B*
Florida State University *B, M, D*
Miami Dade College *A*
University of Miami *B*

Illinois

Northern Illinois University *B*
University of Illinois
  Urbana-Champaign *B, M, D*

Indiana

Purdue University *B*
Valparaiso University *B*

Kansas

University of Kansas *B, M*

Kentucky

University of Louisville *B*

Louisiana

University of Louisiana at Monroe *B*

Maryland

University of Maryland
  College Park *B, M, D*

Massachusetts

Massachusetts Institute of
  Technology *M, D*

Michigan

Michigan Technological University *D*
University of Michigan *B, M, D*

Minnesota

Saint Cloud State University *B*

Mississippi

East Mississippi Community
  College *A*
Jackson State University *B*

Missouri

Saint Louis University *B, M, D*
University of Missouri
  Columbia *B, M, D*

Nebraska

Creighton University *C, B, M*
University of Nebraska
  Lincoln *B*

Nevada

University of Nevada
  Reno *B, M, D*

New Hampshire

Plymouth State University *B, M*

New Jersey

Princeton University *M, D*
Rutgers, The State University of New
  Jersey
  New Brunswick/Piscataway
    Campus *B, M, D*

New York

Cornell University *B, M, D*
SUNY
College at Brockport *B*
University at Albany *B, M, D*
University at Stony Brook *B*

North Carolina

North Carolina Agricultural and
Technical State University *B*
North Carolina State University *B*
University of North Carolina
Asheville *B*

North Dakota

University of North Dakota *B, M, D*

Ohio

Ohio State University
Columbus Campus *B, M, D*
Ohio University *B*

Oregon

Oregon State University *M*

Pennsylvania

Millersville University of
Pennsylvania *B*
Penn State
Abington *B*
Altoona *B*
Beaver *B*
Berks *B*
Brandywine *B*
DuBois *B*
Fayette, The Eberly Campus *B*
Greater Allegheny *B*
Harrisburg *B*
Hazleton *B*
Lehigh Valley *B*
Mont Alto *B*
New Kensington *B*
Schuylkill *B*
Shenango *B*
University Park *B, M, D*
Wilkes-Barre *B*
Worthington Scranton *B*
York *B*

South Dakota

South Dakota School of Mines and
Technology *B, M, D*

Texas

Texas A&M University *B, M, D*
Texas Tech University *M*
University of Houston *M, D*

Utah

University of Utah *B, M, D*

Vermont

Lyndon State College *B*

Virginia

George Mason University *D*

Washington

University of Washington *B, M, D*

Wisconsin

Mid-State Technical College *A*
University of Wisconsin
Madison *B, M, D*

Wyoming

University of Wyoming *M, D*

Atomic/molecular physics

California

San Diego State University *B*
University of California
San Diego *B*

Florida

Florida State University *D*

Massachusetts

Harvard College *B, M, D*

Minnesota

University of Minnesota
Twin Cities *M, D*

Ohio

Ohio State University
Columbus Campus *M, D*

Texas

Rice University *M, D*

Utah

University of Utah *D*

Virginia

Norfolk State University *M*

Audiology/audiologist

Alabama

University of Montevallo *B*
University of South Alabama *D*

Arizona

University of Arizona *D*

Arkansas

University of Arkansas
Little Rock *D*

California

San Diego State University *D*

Colorado

University of Colorado
Boulder *D*
University of Northern
Colorado *B, M, D*

Connecticut

University of Connecticut *D*

District of Columbia

Gallaudet University *D*

Florida

Nova Southeastern University *D*
University of South Florida *D*

Idaho

Idaho State University *D*

Illinois

Northern Illinois University *D*
Northwestern University *M, D*
Rush University *D*
University of Illinois
Urbana-Champaign *B, M, D*

Indiana

Ball State University *M*
Purdue University *B, M, D*

Iowa

University of Iowa *B, D*

Kansas

University of Kansas *D*
University of Kansas Medical
Center *M, D*

Kentucky

University of Louisville *D*

Louisiana

Louisiana State University
Health Sciences Center *D*

Maryland

Towson University *D*
University of Maryland
College Park *D*

Massachusetts

Boston University *M, D*
Elms College *B*
Emerson College *B, M*
Northeastern University *D*
University of Massachusetts
Amherst *D*

Michigan

Central Michigan University *D*
Michigan State University *D*
Wayne State University *D*
Western Michigan University *D*

Minnesota

University of Minnesota
Twin Cities *D*

Mississippi

University of Southern Mississippi *M*

Missouri

Missouri State University *D*
Washington University in St.
Louis *M, D*

Nebraska

University of Nebraska
Lincoln *D*

New Jersey

Montclair State University *D*

New York

City University of New York
Hunter College *M*
Hofstra University *D*
SUNY
University at Buffalo *D*

North Carolina

University of North Carolina
Chapel Hill *D*

Ohio

Cleveland State University *B, M*
Ohio State University
Columbus Campus *B, M, D*
University of Akron *D*
University of Cincinnati *D*

Oklahoma

University of Oklahoma *M, D*

Oregon

Portland State University *B, M*

Pennsylvania

Bloomsburg University of
Pennsylvania *D*
La Salle University *B, M*

Puerto Rico

University of Puerto Rico
Medical Sciences *D*

Tennessee

East Tennessee State University *D*
University of Memphis *D*
University of Tennessee
Knoxville *M, D*
Vanderbilt University *D*

Texas

Lamar University *M, D*
Stephen F. Austin State University *B*
Texas Tech University Health
Sciences Center *T*
University of North Texas *D*
University of Texas
Dallas *D*

Utah

University of Utah *M, D*
Utah State University *D*

Virginia

James Madison University *D*

Washington

University of Washington *M, D*

West Virginia

West Virginia University *D*

Wisconsin

University of Wisconsin
Madison *D*
Stevens Point *D*

Audiology/speech pathology

Alabama

Auburn University *B, M, D*
University of Alabama *B*

Arizona

Arizona State University *D*

Arkansas

Arkansas State University *B*
University of Arkansas *B, M*
University of Arkansas
Little Rock *B, M, D*
for Medical Sciences *M*
University of Central
Arkansas *B, M, D*

California

California State University
East Bay *B, M*
Northridge *M*
Sacramento *B, M*
University of Redlands *B, M*

Colorado

University of Northern Colorado *B*

Connecticut

Southern Connecticut State
University *B, M*
University of Connecticut *M, D*

District of Columbia

Gallaudet University *M*
George Washington University *B, M*

Florida

Florida Atlantic University *M*
Florida International University *M*
Florida State University *B, M, D, T*
University of Central Florida *B, M*
University of Florida *B, M, D*
University of Miami *B, M*
University of South Florida *B, M, D*

Hawaii

University of Hawaii
Manoa *B, M*

Idaho

College of Idaho *B*
Idaho State University *B*

Illinois

Illinois State University *B, M, D*
Northwestern University *D*
Southern Illinois University
    Edwardsville *B, M*
University of Illinois
    Urbana-Champaign *B, M, D*

Indiana

Ball State University *B, D*
Indiana State University *B, M, T*
Indiana University
    Bloomington *B, M, D*
    Purdue University Fort Wayne *B*
Purdue University *B, M, D*

Iowa

University of Iowa *B, M, D*

Kansas

Fort Hays State University *M*
Wichita State University *D*

Kentucky

Brescia University *B*
Murray State University *B, M, T*
University of Kentucky *B, M*
University of Louisville *M*
Western Kentucky University *M, T*

Louisiana

Louisiana State University
    Health Sciences Center *M*
Louisiana State University and
    Agricultural and Mechanical
    College *B, M, D*
Louisiana Tech University *B, M*
Nicholls State University *B*
Southeastern Louisiana University *B*
Southern University and Agricultural
    and Mechanical College *B, M*
University of Louisiana at
    Lafayette *B, M*
University of Louisiana at
    Monroe *B, M*

Maine

University of Maine *B, M*

Maryland

Loyola University Maryland *M*

Massachusetts

Boston University *M, D*
Elms College *B*
Emerson College *B*
Northeastern University *B, M*

Michigan

Andrews University *B*
Michigan State University *B, M, D*
Western Michigan University *B*

Minnesota

Minnesota State University
    Moorhead *B*
Saint Cloud State University *B*
University of Minnesota
    Twin Cities *B, M, D*

Mississippi

Delta State University *B*
University of Mississippi *B, M*
University of Southern
    Mississippi *B, M*

Missouri

Missouri State University *B, M*
Saint Louis University *B, M, D*
University of Central Missouri *M*
University of Missouri
    Columbia *B, M*

Washington University in St.
    Louis *M, D*

Nebraska

University of Nebraska
    Lincoln *M*

Nevada

University of Nevada
    Reno *M*

New Hampshire

University of New Hampshire *M*

New Jersey

Richard Stockton College of New
    Jersey *B*
William Paterson University of New
    Jersey *M*

New Mexico

Eastern New Mexico University *B, M*
University of New Mexico *B, M*

New York

Adelphi University *B, M, D*
City University of New York
    Brooklyn College *B*
    Lehman College *B, M*
College of Saint Rose *B, M, T*
Hofstra University *B*
Iona College *B*
Long Island University
    LIU Brooklyn *B, M*
    LIU Post *B, M*
Marymount Manhattan College *B*
Mercy College *B*
Molloy College *B, M*
New York University *B, M, D*
SUNY
    College at Cortland *B*
    College at Fredonia *B, M, T*
    College at Plattsburgh *B*
    University at Buffalo *B, M, D*
St. John's University *B, M, D*
Syracuse University *M, D*
Yeshiva University *B*

North Carolina

East Carolina University *B, M, D*
Shaw University *B*
University of North Carolina
    Chapel Hill *M, D*
    Greensboro *B, M*

Ohio

Bowling Green State University *B*
College of Wooster *B*
Kent State University *B, M, D*
Miami University
    Oxford *D, M*
Ohio University *B, M, D*
University of Akron *B, M*

Oklahoma

Northeastern State University *B*
University of Central Oklahoma *B*
University of Tulsa *B, M*

Pennsylvania

Bloomsburg University of
    Pennsylvania *B*
East Stroudsburg University of
    Pennsylvania *B, M, T*
Indiana University of
    Pennsylvania *B, M, D*
La Salle University *B, M*
Marywood University *B, M*
Temple University *B, M, D*
Thiel College *B*
University of Pittsburgh *B, M, D*
West Chester University of
    Pennsylvania *B, M*

Puerto Rico

Inter American University of Puerto
    Rico
    Barranquitas Campus *B*

South Carolina

South Carolina State University *B, M*
University of South Carolina
    Columbia *D*

South Dakota

University of South Dakota *D*

Tennessee

East Tennessee State University *M*
Tennessee State University *B*
University of Memphis *M, D*
University of Tennessee
    Knoxville *D*
Vanderbilt University *M, D*

Texas

Hardin-Simmons University *B*
Lamar University *B*
Texas Woman's University *M*
University of North Texas *B*
University of Texas
    Austin *D*
    Dallas *B, M*
    El Paso *M*

Utah

Brigham Young University *B, M*
University of Utah *B, M, D, T*

Virginia

Hampton University *B, M*
Longwood University *B, M*
Old Dominion University *B, M*
Radford University *M*
University of Virginia *B, M*

Washington

University of Washington *B, M, D*
Washington State University *B, M*
Western Washington University *B, M*

West Virginia

Marshall University *M*
West Virginia University *B*

Wisconsin

Marquette University *B*
University of Wisconsin
    Madison *B, M, D*
    Milwaukee *B, M*
    Stevens Point *B, M, T*
    Whitewater *M*

Wyoming

University of Wyoming *B, M*

Auditing

Illinois

University of Illinois
    Urbana-Champaign *B*

Massachusetts

Babson College *B*
New England College of Business and
    Finance *M*

Michigan

Eastern Michigan University *M*

North Dakota

Cankdeska Cikana Community
    College *A*

Pennsylvania

Carlow University *B*

Puerto Rico

Inter American University of Puerto
    Rico
    Bayamon Campus *B*

Australian/Oceanic/Pacific languages

Hawaii

University of Hawaii
    West Oahu *M*

Auto body repair

Alabama

Bevill State Community College *C*
Bishop State Community
    College *C, A*
Calhoun Community College *C*
Gadsden State Community College *C*
George C. Wallace Community
    College at Dothan *C*
Jefferson Davis Community
    College *C*
Lawson State Community College *C*
Northwest-Shoals Community
    College *C*
Shelton State Community College *C*
Southern Union State Community
    College *C, A*
Wallace State Community College at
    Hanceville *C, A*

Arizona

Central Arizona College *C*

Arkansas

Arkansas State University
    Beebe *C*
Arkansas Tech University *C*
Black River Technical College *C*
Cossatot Community College of the
    University of Arkansas *C*
North Arkansas College *C*
Pulaski Technical College *C*
University of Arkansas
    Community College at
    Morrilton *C, A*

California

Allan Hancock College *C, A*
Antelope Valley College *C, A*
Cerritos College *A*
Cerro Coso Community College *C, A*
Chabot College *A*
Chaffey College *C, A*
College of Marin *C, A*
Columbia College *C*
Contra Costa College *C, A*
Cuesta College *C, A*
Cypress College *C, A*
El Camino College *C, A*
Fresno City College *C, A*
Fullerton College *C, A*
Gavilan College *C*
Golden West College *C, A*
Hartnell College *C, A*
Imperial Valley College *C, A*
Lassen Community College *C, A*
Long Beach City College *C, A*
Los Angeles Pierce College *C, A*
Los Angeles Trade and Technical
    College *C, A*
Mendocino College *C, A*
Merced College *C, A*
Modesto Junior College *C, A*
Mount San Jacinto College *C*
Oxnard College *C, A*
Palomar College *C, A*
Pasadena City College *C, A*
Porterville College *C, A*
Rio Hondo College *C, A*
Riverside City College *C, A*

San Joaquin Delta College *C*
Santa Rosa Junior College *C*
Solano Community College *C, A*
WyoTech: Sacramento *C, A*
Yuba College *C*

Colorado

Aims Community College *C, A*
Morgan Community College *A*
Pikes Peak Community College *C, A*
Red Rocks Community College *C, A*
Trinidad State Junior College *C, A*

Florida

College of Central Florida *C*
Daytona State College *C*
Florida State College at
  Jacksonville *C*
Hillsborough Community College *C*
Palm Beach State College *C*
South Florida State College *C*

Georgia

Albany Technical College *C*
Athens Technical College *C*
Atlanta Technical College *C*
Central Georgia Technical College *C*
Columbus Technical College *C*
North Georgia Technical College *C*
Savannah Technical College *C, A*

Hawaii

University of Hawaii
  Hawaii Community College *C, A*
  Honolulu Community College *A*
  Kauai Community College *C, A*
  Maui College *A*

Idaho

College of Southern Idaho *C, A*
College of Western Idaho *C, A*
Idaho State University *C, A, B*
Lewis-Clark State College *C, A, B*
North Idaho College *C, A*

Illinois

Black Hawk College *C, A*
Carl Sandburg College *C, A*
City Colleges of Chicago
  Kennedy-King College *C*
College of Lake County *C*
Danville Area Community
  College *C, A*
Highland Community College *C, A*
Illinois Eastern Community Colleges
  Olney Central College *A*
John A. Logan College *C, A*
Joliet Junior College *C, A*
Kaskaskia College *C, A*
Kishwaukee College *C, A*
Lake Land College *C*
Lincoln Land Community
  College *C, A*
Parkland College *C, A*
Waubonsee Community College *C, A*

Indiana

Lincoln College of Technology
  Indianapolis *C, A*
Vincennes University *C, A*

Iowa

Des Moines Area Community
  College *C, A*
Hawkeye Community College *C, A*
Iowa Central Community
  College *C, A*
Iowa Lakes Community College *C*
Kirkwood Community College *C*
Northwest Iowa Community
  College *C, A*
Southeastern Community College *C*
Southwestern Community
  College *C, A*

Western Iowa Tech Community
  College *C, A*

Kansas

Butler Community College *C, A*
Coffeyville Community College *C*
Highland Community College *C, A*
Hutchinson Community College *C*
Kansas City Kansas Community
  College *C*
Manhattan Area Technical
  College *C, A*
Northwest Kansas Technical
  College *C, A*
Wichita Area Technical College *C*

Kentucky

Big Sandy Community and Technical
  College *C*
Bluegrass Community and Technical
  College *C*
Gateway Community and Technical
  College *C, A*
Maysville Community and Technical
  College *C*
Owensboro Community and
  Technical College *C, A*
Somerset Community College *C, A*
West Kentucky Community and
  Technical College *C*

Maine

Northern Maine Community
  College *C, A*

Michigan

Alpena Community College *C*
Kirtland Community College *C*
Lansing Community College *C, A*
Oakland Community College *C*
Washtenaw Community College *C, A*

Minnesota

Century College *C*
Dakota County Technical
  College *C, A*
Dunwoody College of
  Technology *C, A*
Hennepin Technical College *C, A*
Lake Superior College *C*
Minnesota State College - Southeast
  Technical *C, A*
Minnesota State Community and
  Technical College *C, A*
Minnesota West Community and
  Technical College *C, A*
Northland Community & Technical
  College *C, A*
Ridgewater College *C, A*
Riverland Community College *C*
St. Cloud Technical and Community
  College *C, A*
St. Paul College *C, A*
South Central College *C, A*

Mississippi

Coahoma Community College *C*
East Central Community College *C, A*
Hinds Community College *C*
Itawamba Community College *C*
Mississippi Gulf Coast Community
  College *C*
Northeast Mississippi Community
  College *C, A*
Northwest Mississippi Community
  College *C*
Pearl River Community College *C, A*

Missouri

Crowder College *C*
Linn State Technical College *C, A*
Metropolitan Community College -
  Kansas City *C, A*
Mineral Area College *C, A*

North Central Missouri College *A*
Ozarks Technical Community
  College *C, A*
Ranken Technical College *A*

Montana

Montana State University
  Billings *C, A*
  Northern *A*

Nebraska

Central Community College *C, A*
Metropolitan Community
  College *C, A*
Mid-Plains Community College *C, A*
Northeast Community College *A*
Southeast Community College *A*
Western Nebraska Community
  College *C, A*

New Hampshire

Nashua Community College *A*

New Mexico

Luna Community College *C*
San Juan College *C, A*

New York

Erie Community College *A*
SUNY
  College of Agriculture and
    Technology at Morrisville *A*
  College of Technology at Alfred *A*

North Carolina

Blue Ridge Community College *C*
Caldwell Community College and
  Technical Institute *C*
Cape Fear Community College *C*
Central Carolina Community
  College *C*
Central Piedmont Community
  College *C*
Cleveland Community College *C*
Coastal Carolina Community
  College *C*
Edgecombe Community College *C*
Fayetteville Technical Community
  College *C*
Forsyth Technical Community
  College *C*
Guilford Technical Community
  College *C, A*
Haywood Community College *C*
Isothermal Community College *C*
Lenoir Community College *C, A*
Mayland Community College *C*
McDowell Technical Community
  College *C*
Randolph Community College *C*
Sandhills Community College *C*
Surry Community College *C*
Tri-County Community College *C*
Wayne Community College *C, A*
Wilkes Community College *C*

North Dakota

Bismarck State College *C, A*
North Dakota State College of
  Science *C, A*

Ohio

Ohio Technical College *C, A*
Owens Community College
  Toledo *C*

Oklahoma

Oklahoma State University
  Institute of Technology:
    Okmulgee *A*
Western Oklahoma State College *A*

Oregon

Clackamas Community College *C, A*
Lane Community College *C, A*
Portland Community College *C, A*

Pennsylvania

Pennco Tech *C, A*
Pennsylvania College of
  Technology *C, A, B*
Thaddeus Stevens College of
  Technology *A*
WyoTech: Blairsville *C, A*

Rhode Island

New England Institute of
  Technology *A*

South Carolina

Greenville Technical College *C*

South Dakota

Southeast Technical Institute *A*
Western Dakota Technical
  Institute *C, A*

Tennessee

Chattanooga State Community
  College *C*
Lincoln College of Technology
  Nashville *C, A*

Texas

Amarillo College *C*
Central Texas College *C, A*
Del Mar College *C*
Eastfield College *C, A*
Grayson College *C, A*
Howard College *C*
Kilgore College *C, A*
Midland College *C*
Northeast Texas Community
  College *C, A*
St. Philip's College *C, A*
San Jacinto College *C, A*
South Plains College *C, A*
Tarrant County College *C, A*
Texarkana College *C*
Texas State Technical College
  Harlingen *C, A*
  Waco *C, A.*
  West Texas *C*
Trinity Valley Community College *C*

Utah

Salt Lake Community College *C, A*
Utah Valley University *C, A*

Virginia

Danville Community College *C*
Northern Virginia Community
  College *C*

Washington

Bates Technical College *C, A*
Bellingham Technical College *A*
Clover Park Technical College *C, A*
Green River Community College *C, A*
Lake Washington Institute of
  Technology *A*
Lower Columbia College *A*
Renton Technical College *C, A*
South Seattle Community
  College *C, A*
Spokane Community College *A*
Walla Walla Community College *C, A*

Wisconsin

Chippewa Valley Technical College *C*
Fox Valley Technical College *C, A*
Lakeshore Technical College *C*
Madison Area Technical College *C*
Milwaukee Area Technical College *C*
Moraine Park Technical College *C*

Northcentral Technical College *C*
Northeast Wisconsin Technical
    College *C*
Southwest Wisconsin Technical
    College *C*
Waukesha County Technical
    College *C*
Wisconsin Indianhead Technical
    College *C*

Wyoming
Casper College *C, A*
Laramie County Community
    College *C, A*
WyoTech: Laramie *C, A*

Automation technology

Arizona
Cochise College *C*

California
WyoTech: Long Beach *C*

Michigan
Southwestern Michigan College *C, A*

Minnesota
Alexandria Technical and Community
    College *C, A*
Northland Community & Technical
    College *C, A*
Northwest Technical College *C*
St. Cloud Technical and Community
    College *C, A*
South Central College *C, A*

Mississippi
Copiah-Lincoln Community
    College *C, A*

New Mexico
Clovis Community College *C, A*

Ohio
Sinclair Community College *A*

South Dakota
Mitchell Technical Institute *A*

Virginia
ECPI University *B*

Washington
Bates Technical College *C, A*

West Virginia
Blue Ridge Community and Technical
    College *C*

Wisconsin
Fox Valley Technical College *A*
Northeast Wisconsin Technical
    College *A*
Waukesha County Technical
    College *A*

Wyoming
Casper College *C*

Automotive engineering technology

Alabama
George C. Wallace Community
    College at Dothan *C, A*
Lawson State Community
    College *C, A*

California
Santa Barbara City College *C, A*

Colorado
Colorado State University
    Pueblo *B*

Florida
College of Central Florida *A*
Daytona State College *C*
Pensacola State College *A*
Santa Fe College *A*

Georgia
Columbus Technical College *C, A*

Illinois
Southern Illinois University
    Carbondale *B*

Indiana
Indiana State University *B*

Kansas
Pittsburg State University *B*

Kentucky
Northern Kentucky University *A*

Massachusetts
Benjamin Franklin Institute of
    Technology *A, B*
Massachusetts Bay Community
    College *A*
Springfield Technical Community
    College *C, A*

Michigan
Baker College
    Clinton Township *A*
Central Michigan University *B, M*
Ferris State University *B*
Gogebic Community College *C, A*
Grand Rapids Community College *A*
Montcalm Community College *C, A*

Minnesota
Hennepin Technical College *C, A*
Minnesota State University
    Mankato *B*

Mississippi
Copiah-Lincoln Community
    College *C, A*

New Jersey
Brookdale Community College *A*
Burlington County College *C, A*
Mercer County Community
    College *A*
Raritan Valley Community College *A*
Sussex County Community
    College *C, A*

New York
City University of New York
    Bronx Community College *C*
SUNY
    College of Technology at Alfred *A*
    Farmingdale State College *A, B*

Ohio
Cincinnati State Technical and
    Community College *C, A*
Columbus State Community
    College *C, A*
Owens Community College
    Toledo *C, A*
Sinclair Community College *C, A*
Terra State Community College *C, A*

Oklahoma
Oklahoma State University
    Institute of Technology:
    Okmulgee *A*
Western Oklahoma State College *A*

Pennsylvania
Community College of Allegheny
    County *C, A*
Pennsylvania College of
    Technology *B*

Puerto Rico
University of Puerto Rico
    Carolina Regional College *A*

Texas
Brookhaven College *C*
Lincoln College of Technology
    Grand Prairie *C, A*

Utah
Weber State University *C*

West Virginia
Blue Ridge Community and Technical
    College *A*

Automotive technology

Alabama
Bevill State Community College *C*
Bishop State Community
    College *C, A*
Calhoun Community College *C*
Gadsden State Community College *C*
Jefferson Davis Community
    College *C*
Lawson State Community College *C*
Lurleen B. Wallace Community
    College *C*
Northwest-Shoals Community
    College *C*
Shelton State Community College *C*
Southern Union State Community
    College *C*
Wallace State Community College at
    Hanceville *C, A*

Alaska
University of Alaska
    Anchorage *C, A*
    Fairbanks *C*
    Southeast *C, A*

Arizona
Arizona Western College *C, A*
Central Arizona College *C, A*
Cochise College *C, A*
Eastern Arizona College *C, A*
GateWay Community College *C, A*
Glendale Community College *C, A*
Mesa Community College *C*
Mohave Community College *A*
Northland Pioneer College *C, A*
Pima Community College *C, A*
Universal Technical Institute *C, A*
Yavapai College *C, A*

Arkansas
Arkansas Northeastern College *C*
Arkansas State University
    Beebe *C*
Arkansas Tech University *C*
Black River Technical College *C*
College of the Ouachitas *C*
Cossatot Community College of the
    University of Arkansas *C, A*
National Park Community College *C*
North Arkansas College *C*
Ozarka College *C*
South Arkansas Community
    College *C*
Southern Arkansas University Tech *C*
University of Arkansas
    Community College at
    Morrilton *C, A*
    Fort Smith *C*
    Monticello *C*

California
Allan Hancock College *C, A*
American River College *A*
Antelope Valley College *C, A*
Bakersfield College *C, A*
Barstow Community College *C, A*
Butte College *C, A*
Chabot College *C, A*
Chaffey College *C, A*
Citrus College *C, A*
College of the Canyons *C, A*
College of the Desert *C*
Columbia College *A*
Copper Mountain College *C, A*
Cypress College *C, A*
East Los Angeles College *C, A*
El Camino College *C, A*
Fresno City College *C, A*
Golden West College *C, A*
Hartnell College *C, A*
Imperial Valley College *C, A*
Lassen Community College *A*
Long Beach City College *C, A*
Los Angeles Harbor College *C, A*
Los Angeles Pierce College *C, A*
Los Medanos College *C, A*
Merced College *C*
MiraCosta College *C*
Modesto Junior College *C, A*
Mount San Jacinto College *C, A*
Oxnard College *C, A*
Palo Verde College *C, A*
Palomar College *C, A*
Rio Hondo College *C, A*
Riverside City College *C, A*
Saddleback College *C*
San Bernardino Valley College *C, A*
San Deigo Miramar College
    San Diego Miramar College *C, A*
San Joaquin Delta College *C, A*
Santa Ana College *C, A*
Santa Barbara City College *C, A*
Santa Rosa Junior College *C*
Santiago Canyon College *A*
Shasta College *C, A*
Sierra College *C, A*
Skyline College *C, A*
Southwestern College *C, A*
Taft College *C, A*
Ventura College *C, A*
Victor Valley College *C, A*
WyoTech: Fremont *C, A*
WyoTech: Long Beach *C, A*
WyoTech: Sacramento *C, A*
Yuba College *C, A*

Colorado
Aims Community College *C, A*
Arapahoe Community College *C, A*
Colorado Mesa University *C, A*
Colorado Mountain College *C*
Colorado Northwestern Community
    College *C*
Front Range Community College *C, A*
IntelliTec College: Grand Junction *A*
Lincoln College of Technology
    Denver *A*
Morgan Community College *C, A*
Northeastern Junior College *C, A*
Otero Junior College *C*
Pikes Peak Community College *C, A*
Red Rocks Community College *C, A*
Trinidad State Junior College *C, A*
Westwood College
    Denver North *A*

Connecticut
Gateway Community College *A*
Naugatuck Valley Community
    College *C, A*

Delaware
Delaware Technical Community
    College
    Jack F. Owens Campus *C, A*
    Stanton/Wilmington Campus *C, A*

Florida

Broward College *A*
College of Central Florida *C, A*
Daytona State College *C*
Eastern Florida State College *C*
Florida State College at
 Jacksonville *C, A*
Hillsborough Community College *C*
Indian River State College *C, A*
Lincoln College of Technology
 West Palm Beach *C, A*
Palm Beach State College *C, A*
Pensacola State College *A*
Santa Fe College *C*
Seminole State College of
 Florida *C, A*
South Florida State College *C*

Georgia

Albany Technical College *C*
Altamaha Technical College *C*
Athens Technical College *C*
Atlanta Technical College *C*
Central Georgia Technical College *C*
Chattahoochee Technical
 College *C, A*
Columbus Technical College *C, A*
Georgia Piedmont Technical
 College *C, A*
Gwinnett Technical College *C, A*
North Georgia Technical College *C*
Savannah Technical College *C, A*
South Georgia State College *A*
Southeastern Technical College *C, A*
Southwest Georgia Technical
 College *C*
West Georgia Technical College *C*

Hawaii

University of Hawaii
 Hawaii Community College *C, A*
 Honolulu Community College *A*
 Kauai Community College *C, A*
 Leeward Community College *C, A*
 Maui College *A*

Idaho

Brigham Young University-Idaho *A*
College of Southern Idaho *C, A*
College of Western Idaho *C, A*
Eastern Idaho Technical College *C, A*
Idaho State University *C, A, B*
Lewis-Clark State College *C, A, B*
North Idaho College *C, A*

Illinois

Black Hawk College *C, A*
City Colleges of Chicago
 Harry S. Truman College *C, A*
 Kennedy-King College *C, A*
College of DuPage *C, A*
College of Lake County *C, A*
Danville Area Community
 College *C, A*
Elgin Community College *C, A*
Highland Community College *C, A*
Illinois Central College *C, A*
Illinois Eastern Community Colleges
 Frontier Community College *C, A*
Illinois Valley Community
 College *C, A*
John A. Logan College *C, A*
Kankakee Community College *C, A*
Kaskaskia College *C, A*
Kishwaukee College *C, A*
Lewis and Clark Community
 College *A*
Lincoln Land Community
 College *C, A*
McHenry County College *C, A*
Moraine Valley Community
 College *C, A*
Morton College *C, A*
Oakton Community College *C, A*

Parkland College *C, A*
Prairie State College *C, A*
Rend Lake College *C, A*
Richland Community College *A*
Rock Valley College *C, A*
Spoon River College *C, A*
Triton College *C, A*
Waubonsee Community College *C, A*

Indiana

Ivy Tech Community College
 Central Indiana *C, A*
 Columbus *C, A*
 East Central *C, A*
 Kokomo *C, A*
 Lafayette *C, A*
 North Central *C, A*
 Northeast *C, A*
 Northwest *C, A*
 Richmond *C, A*
 South Central *C, A*
 Southwest *A*
 Wabash Valley *C, A*
Lincoln College of Technology
 Indianapolis *C, A*
Vincennes University *A*

Iowa

Des Moines Area Community
 College *C, A*
Hawkeye Community College *A*
Iowa Central Community College *A*
Iowa Lakes Community College *C*
Iowa Western Community
 College *C, A*
Kirkwood Community College *C, A*
North Iowa Area Community
 College *C, A*
Northeast Iowa Community
 College *C, A*
Northwest Iowa Community
 College *C, A*
Western Iowa Tech Community
 College *C, A*

Kansas

Barton County Community
 College *C, A*
Butler Community College *C, A*
Coffeyville Community College *C*
Cowley County Community
 College *C, A*
Highland Community College *C, A*
Hutchinson Community College *C, A*
Johnson County Community
 College *C, A*
Kansas City Kansas Community
 College *C*
Manhattan Area Technical
 College *C, A*
McPherson College *B*
North Central Kansas Technical
 College *C, A*
Northwest Kansas Technical
 College *C, A*
Pittsburg State University *C, A*
Pratt Community College *A*
Wichita Area Technical College *C, A*

Kentucky

Big Sandy Community and Technical
 College *C, A*
Bluegrass Community and Technical
 College *C, A*
Elizabethtown Community and
 Technical College *C, A*
Gateway Community and Technical
 College *C, A*
Hazard Community and Technical
 College *A*
Hopkinsville Community College *C*
Jefferson Community and Technical
 College *C, A*

Maysville Community and Technical
 College *C*
Owensboro Community and
 Technical College *C, A*
Somerset Community College *C, A*

Louisiana

Delgado Community College *C, A*

Maine

Central Maine Community College *A*
Eastern Maine Community
 College *A*
Northern Maine Community
 College *C, A*
Southern Maine Community
 College *A*
Washington County Community
 College *C*

Maryland

Allegany College of Maryland *C, A*
Community College of Baltimore
 County *C, A*
Montgomery College *C, A*

Massachusetts

Benjamin Franklin Institute of
 Technology *C, A, B*
Middlesex Community College *A*
Mount Wachusett Community
 College *C, A*
Quinsigamond Community
 College *C, A*

Michigan

Alpena Community College *C, A*
Baker College
 Clinton Township *A*
 Flint *A*
 Owosso *C, A*
Bay de Noc Community College *C, A*
Delta College *C, A*
Ferris State University *A*
Glen Oaks Community College *C*
Gogebic Community College *C, A*
Grand Rapids Community College *C*
Henry Ford Community College *C, A*
Jackson College *C, A*
Kalamazoo Valley Community
 College *C, A*
Kirtland Community College *C, A*
Lansing Community College *C, A*
Macomb Community College *C, A*
Mid Michigan Community
 College *C, A*
Mott Community College *C, A*
Northern Michigan University *C, A*
Northwestern Michigan College *C, A*
Oakland Community College *C, A*
Southwestern Michigan College *C, A*
Washtenaw Community College *C, A*
Wayne County Community
 College *C, A*

Minnesota

Anoka Technical College *C, A*
Central Lakes College *C, A*
Century College *C*
Dakota County Technical
 College *C, A*
Dunwoody College of
 Technology *C, A*
Hennepin Technical College *C, A*
Hibbing Community College *C*
Lake Superior College *C, A*
Mesabi Range Community and
 Technical College *C, A*
Minnesota State College - Southeast
 Technical *C*
Minnesota State Community and
 Technical College *C, A*
Minnesota State University
 Mankato *B*

Minnesota West Community and
 Technical College *C, A*
Northland Community & Technical
 College *C, A*
Northwest Technical College *C, A*
Pine Technical College *C, A*
Ridgewater College *C, A*
Riverland Community College *C, A*
Rochester Community and Technical
 College *C*
St. Cloud Technical and Community
 College *C, A*
St. Paul College *C, A*
South Central College *C, A*

Mississippi

Copiah-Lincoln Community
 College *C, A*
East Mississippi Community
 College *C, A*
Hinds Community College *C*
Itawamba Community College *A*
Meridian Community College *C*
Northeast Mississippi Community
 College *C, A*
Southwest Mississippi Community
 College *C, A*

Missouri

Crowder College *C, A*
East Central College *C, A*
Jefferson College *C, A*
Linn State Technical College *C, A*
Metropolitan Community College -
 Kansas City *C, A*
Mineral Area College *C, A*
Ozarks Technical Community
 College *C, A*
Ranken Technical College *A*
St. Louis Community College *C, A*
State Fair Community College *C, A*

Montana

Dawson Community College *A*
Fort Peck Community College *C, A*
Helena College University of
 Montana *A*
Montana State University
 Billings *C, A*
 Northern *A, B*
Montana Tech of the University of
 Montana *C*

Nebraska

Central Community College *C, A*
Metropolitan Community
 College *C, A*
Mid-Plains Community College *C, A*
Northeast Community College *A*
Southeast Community College *A*
Western Nebraska Community
 College *C, A*

Nevada

College of Southern Nevada *A*
Truckee Meadows Community
 College *A*
Western Nevada College *C, A*

New Hampshire

Great Bay Community College *C, A*
Lakes Region Community College *A*
Manchester Community College *C, A*
Nashua Community College *A*
White Mountains Community
 College *C, A*

New Jersey

Brookdale Community College *C*
Gloucester County College *A*
Middlesex County College *A*
Sussex County Community
 College *C, A*
Union County College *A*

New Mexico

Central New Mexico Community
College *C*
Clovis Community College *C, A*
Dona Ana Community College of
New Mexico State
University *C, A*
Eastern New Mexico University:
Roswell *C, A*
Luna Community College *C*
Mesalands Community College *C, A*
Navajo Technical University *C*
New Mexico Junior College *C, A*
New Mexico State University
Alamogordo *A*
Grants *A*
San Juan College *C, A*

New York

Columbia-Greene Community
College *C, A*
Corning Community College *C, A*
Erie Community College *A*
Fulton-Montgomery Community
College *C, A*
Monroe Community College *A*
Onondaga Community College *A*
Rockland Community College *A*
SUNY
College of Agriculture and
Technology at
Morrisville *C, A, B*
College of Technology at Alfred *A*
College of Technology at Canton *A*
College of Technology at
Delhi *C, A*
Farmingdale State College *A*
Suffolk County Community College *A*
Technical Career Institutes *A*
Westchester Community College *A*

North Carolina

Asheville-Buncombe Technical
Community College *C, A*
Beaufort County Community
College *A*
Bladen Community College *C*
Blue Ridge Community College *C*
Caldwell Community College and
Technical Institute *C*
Cape Fear Community College *A*
Catawba Valley Community
College *C, A*
Central Carolina Community
College *C, A*
Central Piedmont Community
College *C, A*
Coastal Carolina Community
College *C*
Craven Community College *A*
Davidson County Community
College *A*
Durham Technical Community
College *A*
Fayetteville Technical Community
College *C, A*
Forsyth Technical Community
College *A*
Guilford Technical Community
College *C, A*
Halifax Community College *C, A*
Haywood Community College *C, A*
Lenoir Community College *C, A*
Martin Community College *C, A*
Pitt Community College *C, A*
Randolph Community College *A*
Rowan-Cabarrus Community
College *C*
Sandhills Community College *C, A*
Southwestern Community
College *C, A*
Surry Community College *A*
Tri-County Community College *A*
Wayne Community College *C, A*

Wilkes Community College *C, A*
Wilson Community College *C, A*

North Dakota

Bismarck State College *C, A*
Cankdeska Cikana Community
College *C, A*
Lake Region State College *A*
North Dakota State College of
Science *C, A*
Williston State College *C, A*

Ohio

Cincinnati State Technical and
Community College *C, A*
Cuyahoga Community College
Metropolitan *A*
Ohio Technical College *C, A*
Sinclair Community College *C, A*
Stark State College *A*
University of Cincinnati
Blue Ash College *C, A*
University of Northwestern
Ohio *C, A*
Washington State Community
College *A*
Zane State College *A*

Oklahoma

Western Oklahoma State College *A*

Oregon

Central Oregon Community
College *C*
Chemeketa Community College *A*
Clackamas Community College *A*
Clatsop Community College *C, A*
Klamath Community College *A*
Lane Community College *C, A*
Linn-Benton Community College *C, A*
Mt. Hood Community College *C, A*
Portland Community College *C, A*
Rogue Community College *C, A*
Umpqua Community College *A*

Pennsylvania

Commonwealth Technical Institute *C*
Delaware County Community
College *C, A*
Harrisburg Area Community
College *C, A*
Johnson College *A*
Lincoln Technical Institute
Philadelphia *C, A*
Luzerne County Community
College *A*
New Castle School of Trades *A*
Northampton Community
College *C, A*
Pennco Tech *C, A*
Pennsylvania College of
Technology *C, A*
Rosedale Technical Institute *C, A*
Thaddeus Stevens College of
Technology *A*
WyoTech: Blairsville *C, A*

Puerto Rico

EDP University of Puerto Rico: Hato
Rey *A*

Rhode Island

New England Institute of
Technology *A*

South Carolina

Florence-Darlington Technical
College *C, A*
Greenville Technical College *C, A*
Midlands Technical College *C, A*
Orangeburg-Calhoun Technical
College *A*
Piedmont Technical College *C, A*
Spartanburg Community College *C, A*

Trident Technical College *C*
Williamsburg Technical College *C*
York Technical College *C, A*

South Dakota

Lake Area Technical Institute *A*
Southeast Technical Institute *A*

Tennessee

Lincoln College of Technology
Nashville *C, A*
Nashville State Community College *A*
Northeast State Community
College *C, A*
Southern Adventist University *C, A*
Southwest Tennessee Community
College *A*

Texas

Alvin Community College *C*
Amarillo College *C, A*
Angelina College *A*
Austin Community College *C, A*
Brazosport College *C, A*
Brookhaven College *C, A*
Central Texas College *C, A*
Del Mar College *C, A*
Eastfield College *C, A*
El Paso Community College *C*
Houston Community College
System *C, A*
Kilgore College *C, A*
Lamar State College at Port
Arthur *C, A*
Laredo Community College *C*
Lone Star College System *C, A*
Midland College *C, A*
Northeast Texas Community
College *C, A*
Odessa College *C, A*
St. Philip's College *C, A*
San Jacinto College *C, A*
South Plains College *C, A*
South Texas College *C, A*
Tarrant County College *C, A*
Texarkana College *C*
Texas State Technical College
Harlingen *C, A*
Waco *C, A*
West Texas *C, A*
Trinity Valley Community College *C*
Tyler Junior College *C, A*
Wharton County Junior College *C, A*

Utah

Dixie State College *C, A*
Salt Lake Community College *A*
Utah State University *C, A*
Utah Valley University *C, A*
Weber State University *C, A*

Vermont

Vermont Technical College *A*

Virginia

Advanced Technology Institute *C, A*
Blue Ridge Community College *C*
Danville Community College *C*
Germanna Community College *C*
J. Sargeant Reynolds Community
College *C, A*
New River Community College *A*
Northern Virginia Community
College *C, A*
Southside Virginia Community
College *C*
Thomas Nelson Community
College *C, A*
Tidewater Community College *A*

Washington

Bates Technical College *A*
Bellingham Technical College *C, A*
Big Bend Community College *C, A*

Clark College *C, A*
Clover Park Technical College *C, A*
Columbia Basin College *C, A*
Grays Harbor College *C, A*
Lake Washington Institute of
Technology *C, A*
Lower Columbia College *A*
Peninsula College *C, A*
Renton Technical College *C, A*
Shoreline Community College *C, A*
Skagit Valley College *C, A*
South Puget Sound Community
College *C, A*
South Seattle Community
College *C, A*
Walla Walla Community College *C, A*
Walla Walla University *B*
Wenatchee Valley College *C, A*
Yakima Valley Community College *A*

West Virginia

Blue Ridge Community and Technical
College *A*
West Virginia University at
Parkersburg *A*

Wisconsin

Blackhawk Technical College *C*
Chippewa Valley Technical College *C*
Fox Valley Technical College *C, A*
Gateway Technical College *C, A*
Lakeshore Technical College *C*
Mid-State Technical College *C*
Milwaukee Area Technical
College *C, A*
Moraine Park Technical College *C*
Nicolet Area Technical College *C*
Northcentral Technical College *C, A*
Northeast Wisconsin Technical
College *C*
Southwest Wisconsin Technical
College *C*
Waukesha County Technical
College *A*
Western Technical College *C*
Wisconsin Indianhead Technical
College *C*

Wyoming

Casper College *C, A*
Central Wyoming College *C, A*
Laramie County Community
College *C, A*
Western Wyoming Community
College *C, A*
WyoTech: Laramie *C, A*

Aviation management

Alabama

Auburn University *B*
Community College of the Air
Force *A*

Alaska

University of Alaska
Anchorage *A, B*

California

California Baptist University *B*
College of Alameda *C, A*
Cypress College *A*
Palomar College *C, A*
San Bernardino Valley College *A*

Colorado

Metropolitan State University of
Denver *B*

Delaware

Delaware State University *B*
Wilmington University *B*

Florida

Broward College *A*
Embry-Riddle Aeronautical University *B*
Embry-Riddle Aeronautical University Worldwide Campus *C, B, M*
Everglades University Boca Raton *B*
Florida Institute of Technology *B, M*
Florida State College at Jacksonville *A*
Jacksonville University *B*
Lynn University *B*
Miami Dade College *C, A*
Santa Fe College *A*

Hawaii

University of Hawaii Honolulu Community College *A*

Illinois

Kaskaskia College *C*
Lewis University *B, M*
Lincoln Land Community College *A*
Quincy University *B*
Southern Illinois University Carbondale *B*
University of Illinois Urbana-Champaign *B*

Indiana

Indiana State University *B*
Purdue University *B*

Iowa

University of Dubuque *B*

Kansas

Central Christian College of Kansas *A*
Kansas State University *C*

Kentucky

Northern Kentucky University *A, B*

Louisiana

Baton Rouge Community College *A*
Louisiana Tech University *B*
Southern University Shreveport *C, A*

Massachusetts

North Shore Community College *A*

Michigan

Baker College
Flint *A, B*
Muskegon *A, B*
Eastern Michigan University *B*
Lansing Community College *C*
Oakland Community College *A*
Schoolcraft College *C, A*
Western Michigan University *B*

Minnesota

Academy College *A*
Anoka Technical College *C, A*
Dakota County Technical College *A*
Minnesota State University Mankato *B*
Saint Cloud State University *B*

Mississippi

Delta State University *M*
Hinds Community College *A*

Missouri

Saint Louis University *B, M, D*
University of Central Missouri *B*

Montana

Rocky Mountain College *B*

New Hampshire

Daniel Webster College *B, M*

New Jersey

Mercer County Community College *A*

New Mexico

Eastern New Mexico University *B*

New York

City University of New York York College *B*
Dowling College *B, M*
SUNY Farmingdale State College *B*
Schenectady County Community College *A*
Vaughn College of Aeronautics and Technology *A, B*

North Carolina

Caldwell Community College and Technical Institute *A*

North Dakota

University of North Dakota *B*

Ohio

Ohio University *B*

Oklahoma

Southern Nazarene University *B*
Spartan College of Aeronautics and Technology *A, B*
Tulsa Community College *A*
Western Oklahoma State College *A*

Pennsylvania

Community College of Allegheny County *A*
Community College of Beaver County *A*
Luzerne County Community College *A*
Marywood University *B*

Puerto Rico

Inter American University of Puerto Rico Bayamon Campus *B*

Tennessee

Middle Tennessee State University *M*

Texas

LeTourneau University *B*
Lone Star College System *A*
Mountain View College *A*
Palo Alto College *A*
San Jacinto College *C, A*
Tarleton State University *B*
Texas Southern University *B*

Utah

Dixie State College *B*
Westminster College *B*

Virginia

Averett University *B*
Hampton University *B*

West Virginia

Fairmont State University *B*

Avionics maintenance/technology

Alabama

Enterprise State Community College *C, A*

Arizona

Cochise College *C, A*
Pima Community College *C*

Arkansas

Pulaski Technical College *C*
Rich Mountain Community College *C*

California

Orange Coast College *C, A*

Colorado

Redstone College *C*

Connecticut

Gateway Community College *C*

Georgia

Atlanta Technical College *C*

Illinois

Lewis University *B*
Southern Illinois University Carbondale *B*

Kansas

Wichita Area Technical College *C, A*

Michigan

Western Michigan University *B*

New York

Excelsior College *A*
Jamestown Community College *A*
Vaughn College of Aeronautics and Technology *A, B*

North Carolina

Guilford Technical Community College *C, A*

Ohio

Sinclair Community College *C*

Oklahoma

Spartan College of Aeronautics and Technology *A, B*
Tulsa Community College *A*

Pennsylvania

Pennsylvania College of Technology *B*

Puerto Rico

Universidad del Este *A*

Texas

Hallmark College of Aeronautics *A*
Texas State Technical College Waco *C, A*

Utah

Salt Lake Community College *C, A*
Utah State University *B*

West Virginia

Fairmont State University *A*

Wisconsin

Fox Valley Technical College *A*

Bacteriology

Alabama

Alabama State University *D*
Auburn University *B*

Arkansas

University of Arkansas for Medical Sciences *M, D*

California

Bakersfield College *A*
California Polytechnic State University: San Luis Obispo *B*
California State University
Long Beach *B, M*
Northridge *B*
Sacramento *B, M*
Cerritos College *A*
Crafton Hills College *A*
Fullerton College *A*
Loma Linda University *M, D*
University of California
Irvine *D*
San Diego *B*
Santa Barbara *B*

Colorado

Adams State University *B*
Regis University *M*

Connecticut

Yale University *M, D*

District of Columbia

George Washington University *M, D*
Georgetown University *M*

Florida

University of Florida *B, M, D*
University of South Florida *B, M*

Georgia

Georgia Regents University *M, D*

Hawaii

University of Hawaii Manoa *M, D*

Illinois

Chicago State University *B*

Kansas

University of Kansas Medical Center *M, D*

Kentucky

Eastern Kentucky University *B*
University of Kentucky *D*
University of Kentucky: College of Medicine *D*
University of Louisville *M, D*

Louisiana

Louisiana State University Health Sciences Center *D*
Tulane University *M, D*

Maine

University of Maine *B*

Massachusetts

Boston University *M, D*
Harvard College *D*
Tufts University *M, D*

Michigan

University of Michigan Dearborn *B*

Minnesota

Minnesota State University Mankato *B, T*
University of Minnesota Twin Cities *B, M, D*

Mississippi

Mississippi State University *B*
Mississippi University for Women *B*
University of Mississippi Medical Center *M, D*

Missouri

Missouri Southern State University *B*
University of Missouri
  Columbia *M, D*
Washington University in St. Louis *D*

Montana

Montana State University *B, M, D*
University of Montana *B, M, D*

New Hampshire

University of New Hampshire *M, D*

New Jersey

Rutgers, The State University of New
  Jersey
  New Brunswick/Piscataway
    Campus *B*
  Newark Campus *B*

New Mexico

New Mexico State University *B*

New York

Cornell University *M, D*
Dowling College *M*
SUNY
  University at Buffalo *M, D*
Wagner College *B, M*

North Carolina

Duke University *M, D*
East Carolina University *D*
University of North Carolina
  Chapel Hill *M, D*
Wake Forest University *B*

North Dakota

University of North Dakota *M, D*

Ohio

Bowling Green State University *B*
Case Western Reserve University *D*
Ohio Wesleyan University *B*
Wilmington College *B*
Wright State University *B, M*

Oklahoma

Eastern Oklahoma State College *A*
University of Oklahoma *M, D*

Pennsylvania

Drexel University *M, D*
Penn State
  Abington *B*
  Altoona *B*
  Beaver *B*
  Berks *B*
  Brandywine *B*
  DuBois *B*
  Erie, The Behrend College *B*
  Fayette, The Eberly Campus *B*
  Greater Allegheny *B*
  Harrisburg *B*
  Hazleton *B*
  Lehigh Valley *B*
  Mont Alto *B*
  New Kensington *B*
  Schuylkill *B*
  Shenango *B*
  University Park *B*
  Wilkes-Barre *B*
  Worthington Scranton *B*
  York *B*
University of Pittsburgh *M, D*

Puerto Rico

Inter American University of Puerto
  Rico
  Arecibo Campus *B*
University of Puerto Rico
  Arecibo *B*

Tennessee

University of Tennessee
  Knoxville *M, D*

Texas

Laredo Community College *A*
Texas Tech University Health
  Sciences Center *M, D*
University of Texas
  Health Science Center at
    Houston *M, D*

Utah

Snow College *A*

Virginia

University of Virginia *D*
Virginia Commonwealth
  University *M, D*

Washington

University of Washington *B, D*

West Virginia

West Liberty University *B*

Wisconsin

University of Wisconsin
  Oshkosh *B, M*

Baking/pastry arts

Alabama

Virginia College
  Birmingham *C*

Alaska

University of Alaska
  Fairbanks *C*

Arizona

Art Institute of Tucson *A*
Cochise College *C*
Phoenix College *C*

Arkansas

Pulaski Technical College *C*

California

Art Institute of California
  Inland Empire *C, A*
  Orange County *C*
  Silicon Valley *C*
Columbia College *C*
Contra Costa College *C, A*
Diablo Valley College *C, A*
Grossmont College *C, A*
Le Cordon Bleu College of Culinary
  Arts
  Los Angeles *C, A*
  San Francisco *C*
Long Beach City College *C, A*
Orange Coast College *C, A*
Santa Rosa Junior College *C*
Shasta College *C*

Colorado

Colorado Mountain College *C*
Johnson & Wales University
  Denver *A, B*

Florida

Art Institute of Fort Lauderdale *A*
Johnson & Wales University
  North Miami *A, B*
Le Cordon Bleu College of Culinary
  Arts
  Miami *C, A*
  Orlando *C, A*
Lincoln College of Technology
  West Palm Beach *C, A*

Miami International University of Art
  and Design *C, A*

Georgia

Art Institute of Atlanta *C, A*
Gwinnett Technical College *C*
North Georgia Technical College *C*

Illinois

City Colleges of Chicago
  Kennedy-King College *C, A*
Elgin Community College *C, A*
Harper College *C*
Illinois Institute of Art
  Chicago *C*
Kendall College *A*
Lexington College *A, B*
Lincoln Land Community College *C*
Moraine Valley Community
  College *C, A*
Triton College *C, A*

Indiana

Harrison College
  Indianapolis *A*

Iowa

Kirkwood Community College *C*

Kansas

Johnson County Community
  College *C*

Kentucky

Sullivan University *C, A*

Louisiana

Delgado Community College *C, A*

Maine

York County Community College *A*

Maryland

Anne Arundel Community
  College *C, A*
Howard Community College *C, A*

Massachusetts

Bristol Community College *C*
Massasoit Community College *C*
Newbury College *C*

Michigan

Art Institute of Michigan *C*
Baker College
  Muskegon *C*
Bay de Noc Community College *C*
Grand Rapids Community College *C*
Henry Ford Community College *C*
Mott Community College *A*
Oakland Community College *C*
Schoolcraft College *C*
Washtenaw Community College *C*

Minnesota

Art Institutes International
  Minnesota *C, A*
Le Cordon Bleu College of Culinary
  Arts
  Minneapolis-St. Paul *C, A*
Minneapolis Community and
  Technical College *C*
St. Paul College *C*

Missouri

Ozarks Technical Community
  College *C*

Nevada

Art Institute of Las Vegas *C, A*

New Hampshire

Southern New Hampshire
  University *C, A*
White Mountains Community
  College *C, A*

New Jersey

Brookdale Community College *C*
Burlington County College *C, A*
Hudson County Community
  College *C*

New Mexico

Central New Mexico Community
  College *C*
Navajo Technical University *C, A*

New York

Culinary Institute of America *A*
Erie Community College *C*
Niagara County Community
  College *C*
Paul Smith's College *C, A, B*
SUNY
  College of Technology at Alfred *A*
Suffolk County Community
  College *C, A*
Sullivan County Community
  College *A*

North Carolina

Central Piedmont Community
  College *C, A*
Chef's Academy *A*
Johnson & Wales University
  Charlotte *A, B*
Wilkes Community College *A*

Ohio

Art Institute of Ohio: Cincinnati *C*
Cincinnati State Technical and
  Community College *C, A*
Columbus State Community
  College *C*
Owens Community College
  Toledo *C*
Sinclair Community College *C*

Oregon

Central Oregon Community
  College *C, A*
Le Cordon Bleu College of Culinary
  Arts
  Portland *C, A*

Pennsylvania

Art Institute of Philadelphia *C*
Art Institute of Pittsburgh *C, A*
Bucks County Community College *A*
Harrisburg Area Community
  College *C*
Luzerne County Community
  College *C, A*
Montgomery County Community
  College *A*
Pennsylvania College of
  Technology *A*
Restaurant School at Walnut Hill
  College *A, B*
Westmoreland County Community
  College *C, A*
Yorktowne Business Institute *C*

Puerto Rico

Inter American University of Puerto
  Rico
  Aguadilla Campus *C*
  Ponce Campus *C*

Rhode Island

Johnson & Wales University
  Providence *A, B*

South Carolina

Trident Technical College *C, A*

Texas

Art Institute of Houston *A*
Central Texas College *C*
Collin County Community College
 District *C, A*
Culinary Institute LeNotre *C, A*
Del Mar College *C, A*
El Centro College *C, A*
Houston Community College
 System *C, A*
Le Cordon Bleu College of Culinary
 Arts
 Austin *C*
St. Philip's College *C, A*
San Jacinto College *C, A*

Vermont

New England Culinary Institute *C, A*

Virginia

Art Institute of Washington *A, B*
ECPI University *C, A*
J. Sargeant Reynolds Community
 College *C, A*
Stratford University: Falls Church *A*

Washington

Art Institute of Seattle *A*
Bellingham Technical College *C*
Clark College *C, A*
Clover Park Technical College *A*
Edmonds Community College *C, A*
Lake Washington Institute of
 Technology *A*
Renton Technical College *C*
Seattle Central Community
 College *C, A*
South Seattle Community
 College *C, A*

West Virginia

Blue Ridge Community and Technical
 College *C*

Wisconsin

Art Institute of Wisconsin *A*
Milwaukee Area Technical
 College *C, A*

Ballet

Indiana

Indiana University
 Bloomington *B*

Kansas

Friends University *B*

Texas

Texas Christian University *B, M*

Utah

Brigham Young University *B*
University of Utah *B, M*

Banking/financial services

Alaska

University of Alaska
 Fairbanks *C*

Arizona

GateWay Community College *A*
Phoenix College *C, A*
Rio Salado College *A*

Arkansas

National Park Community College *C*
Northwest Arkansas Community
 College *A*

California

Cabrillo College *A*
California State University
 Northridge *B*
Cerritos College *A*
Chabot College *A*
Fresno City College *C, A*
Hartnell College *C, A*
Imperial Valley College *C, A*
Laney College *C, A*
Los Angeles City College *C, A*
Los Angeles Pierce College *C*
Los Angeles Southwest College *A*
Los Angeles Valley College *C*
Mission College *A*
Mount San Antonio College *C, A*
Pasadena City College *C, A*
Porterville College *C, A*
San Joaquin Delta College *C, A*
San Jose City College *A*
Santa Barbara City College *A*
Shasta College *C*
Solano Community College *C, A*

Colorado

Arapahoe Community College *C, A*
Colorado Northwestern Community
 College *C, A*

Connecticut

Housatonic Community College *C*
Naugatuck Valley Community
 College *C, A*
Northwestern Connecticut
 Community College *A*
Three Rivers Community College *A*

Florida

Daytona State College *A*
Florida State College at
 Jacksonville *C, A*
Miami Dade College *C, A*
Northwood University
 Florida *B*
Pensacola State College *A*
St. Petersburg College *A*
Schiller International University *B*
Seminole State College of Florida *A*
Tallahassee Community College *A*
University of North Florida *B*

Georgia

Central Georgia Technical College *C*
Georgia Piedmont Technical
 College *C, A*
Gwinnett Technical College *C*

Hawaii

Hawaii Pacific University *B*

Illinois

Black Hawk College *C, A*
Carl Sandburg College *A*
City Colleges of Chicago
 Wilbur Wright College *C*
Harper College *C, A*
Illinois Central College *C, A*
Lewis and Clark Community
 College *A*
Prairie State College *C*
University of Illinois
 Urbana-Champaign *B, M*

Indiana

University of Indianapolis *A*

Iowa

Buena Vista University *B*

Kansas

Dodge City Community College *A*
Neosho County Community
 College *A*
Seward County Community
 College *C*
Wichita Area Technical College *C, A*

Kentucky

Ashland Community and Technical
 College *A*
Owensboro Community and
 Technical College *C*
Southeast Kentucky Community and
 Technical College *C, A*
West Kentucky Community and
 Technical College *A*

Louisiana

Louisiana State University
 Shreveport *B*
Southern University
 Shreveport *A*

Maine

Eastern Maine Community College *A*
Husson University *B*

Maryland

Baltimore City Community College *C*
Frederick Community College *C, A*

Massachusetts

Bristol Community College *A*
New England College of Business and
 Finance *C, A*

Michigan

Delta College *C*
Lansing Community College *C, A*
Monroe County Community
 College *C, A*

Minnesota

Minneapolis Community and
 Technical College *C*
Minnesota State University
 Mankato *B*
North Hennepin Community
 College *C*

Mississippi

East Mississippi Community
 College *A*
Hinds Community College *C, A*
Mississippi Gulf Coast Community
 College *A*

Missouri

Central Methodist University *B*
Mineral Area College *A*
St. Louis Community College *A*
University of Missouri
 Columbia *B*

Nebraska

Bellevue University *B*
Northeast Community College *A*
University of Nebraska
 Lincoln *B*
 Omaha *B*

Nevada

College of Southern Nevada *A*

New Jersey

Bergen Community College *A*
Camden County College *A*
Saint Peter's University *B*

New Mexico

New Mexico Junior College *A*
New Mexico State University
 Carlsbad *C*
Santa Fe Community College *A*

New York

Erie Community College *C*
Fordham University *M*
Globe Institute of
 Technology *C, A, B*
Mohawk Valley Community
 College *A*
SUNY
 College of Technology at Alfred *A*

North Carolina

Alamance Community College *A*
Catawba Valley Community
 College *C, A*
Cleveland Community College *A*
Fayetteville Technical Community
 College *C, A*
Forsyth Technical Community
 College *A*
Isothermal Community College *A*
Mitchell Community College *C*

Ohio

Lorain County Community College *A*
Miami University
 Hamilton *C*
Northwest State Community
 College *A*
Ohio Business College
 Sandusky *A*
Sinclair Community College *A*
Stautzenberger College *A*
Terra State Community College *C, A*
Youngstown State University *B, M*

Oklahoma

Oklahoma City Community College *C*

Oregon

Southwestern Oregon Community
 College *C, A*

Pennsylvania

Community College of Allegheny
 County *C, A*
Community College of
 Philadelphia *A*
Delaware County Community
 College *A*
Harrisburg Area Community
 College *C, A*
La Salle University *A, B*
Lackawanna College *A*
Luzerne County Community
 College *A*
Westmoreland County Community
 College *C, A*

Puerto Rico

Universidad Metropolitana *C, A*

Rhode Island

Community College of Rhode
 Island *A*

South Carolina

Trident Technical College *C*

South Dakota

Lake Area Technical Institute *A*
Northern State University *B*
Southeast Technical Institute *A*

Tennessee

Southern Adventist University *M*

Texas

Austin Community College *C, A*
College of the Mainland *A*
Del Mar College *C*
Houston Community College
    System *C, A*
North Lake College *C*
Sam Houston State University *B*
San Antonio College *C*
South Texas College *C, A*
Texas Southern University *B*
University of North Texas *B, M, D*
University of Texas
    Arlington *B, D*
University of the Incarnate Word *B*

Virginia

Dabney S. Lancaster Community
    College *C*
Germanna Community College *C*
Hampton University *B*
Tidewater Community College *A*

Washington

Gonzaga University *B*
Spokane Community College *C, A*
Walla Walla Community College *C, A*

West Virginia

Kanawha Valley Community and
    Technical College *C, A*
New River Community and Technical
    College *C, A*
West Liberty University *B*
West Virginia State University *B*

Wisconsin

Fox Valley Technical College *A*
Mid-State Technical College *C*
Milwaukee Area Technical College *A*
University of Wisconsin
    Whitewater *M*

Barbering

Alabama

Bevill State Community College *C*
Calhoun Community College *C*
Jefferson Davis Community
    College *C*
Lawson State Community College *C*

California

Santiago Canyon College *C*

Colorado

Trinidad State Junior College *C*

Florida

College of Central Florida *C*
Indian River State College *C*
Pensacola State College *C*

Georgia

Atlanta Technical College *C*
Central Georgia Technical College *C*
Savannah Technical College *C*

Kentucky

West Kentucky Community and
    Technical College *C*

Louisiana

Delgado Community College *C*

Minnesota

Minneapolis Community and
    Technical College *C*

Mississippi

Coahoma Community College *C*
Hinds Community College *C*

New Mexico

Luna Community College *C*
Northern New Mexico College *C*
San Juan College *C*

North Carolina

Central Carolina Community
    College *C*

Puerto Rico

Caribbean University *C*
Inter American University of Puerto
    Rico
    San German Campus *C*

Utah

Snow College *C, A*

Washington

Bates Technical College *C*
Clover Park Technical College *C*
Olympic College *C*

Bartending

California

Columbia College *C*
Shasta College *C*

Georgia

Art Institute of Atlanta *A*

Puerto Rico

Universidad del Este *C*

Texas

Weatherford College *C*

Behavioral aspects of health

California

University of Southern
    California *B, D*

Indiana

Indiana University
    Bloomington *D*
Taylor University *B*

Missouri

Washington University in St. Louis *M*

Tennessee

University of Tennessee
    Knoxville *M, D*

Behavioral sciences

Alabama

Columbia Southern University *A*
University of Phoenix
    Birmingham *B*

Arizona

Glendale Community College *A*
University of Phoenix
    Phoenix-Hohokam *B*
    Southern Arizona *B*
Western International University *B*

Arkansas

University of Phoenix
    Little Rock *B*
    Northwest Arkansas *B*

California

California Baptist University *B*
California State University
    Bakersfield *M*
    Dominguez Hills *B*

College of the Siskiyous *A*
Concordia University Irvine *B*
Contra Costa College *A*
Imperial Valley College *A*
Los Medanos College *A*
MiraCosta College *A*
Mount San Jacinto College *A*
San Diego City College *A*
San Jose State University *B*
Shasta College *A*
University of California
    Merced *M, D*
    San Diego *B*
University of La Verne *B*
University of Phoenix
    Bay Area *B*
    Central Valley *B*
    Sacramento Valley *B*
    San Diego *B*
    Southern California *B*

Colorado

Metropolitan State University of
    Denver *B*
United States Air Force Academy *B*
University of Colorado
    Denver *D*
University of Phoenix
    Denver *B*
    Southern Colorado *B*

Connecticut

Mitchell College *B*
Naugatuck Valley Community
    College *A*

Delaware

Wilmington University *B*

Florida

Nova Southeastern University *B*
University of Phoenix
    Central Florida *B*
    North Florida *B*
    South Florida *B*
    West Florida *B*

Georgia

University of Phoenix
    Atlanta *B*
    Augusta *B*
    Columbus *B*
    Savannah *B*

Hawaii

Chaminade University of Honolulu *B*
Hawaii Pacific University *B*
University of Phoenix
    Hawaii *B*

Idaho

Lewis-Clark State College *A*
University of Phoenix
    Idaho *B*

Illinois

National-Louis University *B*
Southeastern Illinois College *A*

Indiana

Ancilla College *A*
Purdue University
    North Central *B*
University of Phoenix
    Indianapolis *B*
Vincennes University *A*

Iowa

Ashford University *B*
Ellsworth Community College *A*

Kansas

Garden City Community College *A*
Tabor College *B*
University of Kansas *B, M, D*

Kentucky

University of Phoenix
    Louisville *B*

Louisiana

University of Phoenix
    Baton Rouge *B*
    Louisiana *B*
    Shreveport *B*

Maine

University of Maine
    Machias *B*
University of Southern Maine *B*

Maryland

Johns Hopkins University *B, D*

Massachusetts

Cape Cod Community College *A*

Michigan

Grand Valley State University *B*
Northern Michigan University *B*
University of Michigan
    Dearborn *B*
University of Phoenix
    Metro Detroit *B*
    West Michigan *B*

Minnesota

University of Phoenix
    Minneapolis-St. Paul *B*

Mississippi

University of Phoenix
    Jackson *B*

Missouri

Evangel University *M*
Missouri Baptist University *B*
University of Missouri
    Columbia *B*
University of Phoenix
    Kansas City *B*
    St. Louis *B*

Nebraska

Concordia University *B*
University of Nebraska
    Omaha *B*

Nevada

University of Phoenix
    Las Vegas *B*
    Northern Nevada *B*

New Hampshire

Granite State College *A, B*

New Jersey

Drew University *B*

New Mexico

University of Phoenix
    New Mexico *B*

New York

Concordia College *B*
SUNY
    Downstate Medical Center *D*

North Dakota

Dickinson State University *B*

Oklahoma

Mid-America Christian University *B*
Murray State College *A*

Oklahoma Wesleyan University *A, B*
Seminole State College *A*
Southern Nazarene University *B*
University of Phoenix
   Oklahoma City *B*
   Tulsa *B*

Oregon

George Fox University *B*
University of Phoenix
   Oregon *B*

Pennsylvania

Carnegie Mellon University *B, M, D*
Duquesne University *B*
Gettysburg College *B*
Neumann University *B*
Penn State
   Harrisburg *C*
Point Park University *B*
York College of Pennsylvania *B*

Puerto Rico

Carlos Albizu University: San Juan *B*
Universidad Metropolitana *M*

South Carolina

Anderson University *B*
Columbia College *B*

South Dakota

Dakota Wesleyan University *B*

Tennessee

Martin Methodist College *B*
Tennessee Wesleyan College *B*
Trevecca Nazarene University *B*
University of Phoenix
   Chattanooga *B*
   Knoxville *B*
   Memphis *B*
   Nashville *B*

Texas

Hill College *A*
Midland College *A*
Northwest Vista College *A*
San Jacinto College *A*
South Plains College *A*
University of Houston
   Clear Lake *B, M*
University of North Texas *B, M*
University of Phoenix
   Austin *B*
   Dallas Fort Worth *B*
   Houston Westside *B*
   San Antonio *B*

Utah

University of Phoenix
   Utah *B*

Vermont

College of St. Joseph in Vermont *B*

Virginia

Bluefield College *B*
University of Phoenix
   Northern Virginia *B*
   Richmond *B*

Washington

University of Phoenix
   Western Washington *B*

Wisconsin

Mount Mary University *B*
University of Phoenix
   Milwaukee *B*
University of Wisconsin
   Milwaukee *C*

Bible studies

Alabama

Amridge University *B, M*
Faulkner University *B, M*
Heritage Christian University *A, B, M*
Huntsville Bible College *C, A, B*
Oakwood University *A*
Southeastern Bible College *A, B*

Alaska

Alaska Bible College *C, A, B*

Arizona

Arizona Christian University *B*
Grand Canyon University *B*
International Baptist College *C, A, M*

Arkansas

Central Baptist College *B*
Ecclesia College *A, B*
Harding University *B, M*
Ouachita Baptist University *B*
Williams Baptist College *B*

California

Azusa Pacific University *B, M*
Bethesda University of
   California *B, M*
Biola University *B, M*
California Baptist University *B*
Fresno Pacific University *B, M*
Hope International University *C, A, B*
Horizon University *A, B*
King's University *C, A, B, M, D*
Life Pacific College *A, B*
Master's College *B, M*
Patten University *C, A*
Point Loma Nazarene University *B*
Providence Christian College *B*
SUM Bible College & Theological
   Seminary *A, B, M*
San Diego Christian College *B*
Shasta Bible College and Graduate
   School *C, A*
Simpson University *C, A, B*
Southern California Seminary *A, B, M*
Vanguard University of Southern
   California *B, M*
William Jessup University *C, A*
World Mission University *B*

Colorado

Colorado Christian University *C, B*
Nazarene Bible College *A, B*

District of Columbia

Catholic University of America *M, D*

Florida

Baptist College of Florida *B, M*
Clearwater Christian College *B*
Florida College *B*
Hobe Sound Bible College *C, A, B*
Johnson University: Florida *A, B*
Palm Beach Atlantic University *B*
Trinity Baptist College *M*
Trinity College of Florida *C, A*
Warner University *B*

Georgia

Beulah Heights University *A, B, M*
Brewton-Parker College *B*
Carver College *C, A, B*
Covenant College *B*
Point University *B*
Toccoa Falls College *C, B*

Idaho

Boise Bible College *C, A, B*
Northwest Nazarene University *B*

Illinois

Judson University *B*
Lincoln Christian University *A, B, M*
Moody Bible Institute *C, A, B, M*
North Park University *B*
Olivet Nazarene University *B*
Trinity International
   University *B, M, D*
Wheaton College *B*

Indiana

Anderson University *B*
Bethel College *A, B*
Grace College *C, A, B*
Huntington University *B*
Indiana Wesleyan University *A, B*
Taylor University *B*
University of Evansville *B*

Iowa

Emmaus Bible College *C, A, B*
Faith Baptist Bible College and
   Theological Seminary *A, B, M*
Shiloh University *A, B, M*

Kansas

Barclay College *C, A, B*
Manhattan Christian College *C, A, B*
Sterling College *B*
Tabor College *B*

Kentucky

Asbury University *B*
Campbellsville University *C, A, B*
Clear Creek Baptist Bible
   College *C, A, B*
Kentucky Christian University *B, M*
Mid-Continent University *C, B*
Southern Baptist Theological
   Seminary *A, B*
University of the Cumberlands *M*

Louisiana

New Orleans Baptist Theological
   Seminary *A, B, M, D*

Massachusetts

Boston Baptist College *C, A, B*
Boston College *D*
Boston University *M, D*
Northpoint Bible College *C, A, B, M*

Michigan

Andrews University *M, D*
Calvin College *B*
Concordia University *C*
Cornerstone University *C, A, B*
Grace Bible College *B*
Great Lakes Christian College *A, B*
Griggs University *B*
Kuyper College *C, A, B*
Manthano Christian College *C, A, B*
Rochester College *B*
Spring Arbor University *B*

Minnesota

Bethel University *B*
Crossroads College *A*
Crown College *C, B*
North Central University *C, A, B*
Oak Hills Christian College *C, A, B*
University of Northwestern - St.
   Paul *C, B*

Mississippi

Belhaven University *C, B*
Blue Mountain College *B*
Southeastern Baptist College *B*
William Carey University *B*

Missouri

Baptist Bible College *C*
Calvary Bible College and Theological
   Seminary *C, A, B, M*
Central Christian College of the
   Bible *C, A*
Evangel University *B*
Hannibal-LaGrange University *B*
Ozark Christian College *A, B*
St. Louis Christian College *B*
Southwest Baptist University *B*

Montana

Montana Bible College *C*

Nebraska

Grace University *C, A, B, M*
Nebraska Christian College *B*
York College *B*

New Jersey

Drew University *M, D*
Pillar College *C, A, B*

New York

Davis College *C, A*
Houghton College *B*
Nyack College *A, B, M*
Roberts Wesleyan College *B*

North Carolina

Carolina Christian College *C, A, B, M*
Gardner-Webb University *M*
Mid-Atlantic Christian University *A, B*
Montreat College *B*
Piedmont International
   University *C, A, B, M, D*
Shepherds Theological Seminary *M*
Southeastern Baptist Theological
   Seminary *A, B, M, D*

North Dakota

Trinity Bible College *C, A, B*

Ohio

Ashland University *M*
Bluffton University *B*
Cedarville University *C*
Cincinnati Christian University *B, M*
God's Bible School and College *A*
Malone University *B*
Mount Vernon Nazarene University *B*
Pontifical College Josephinum *M*
Rosedale Bible College *C, A*

Oklahoma

Family of Faith College *C, B*
Hillsdale Free Will Baptist
   College *A, B, M*
Mid-America Christian University *B*
Oklahoma Baptist University *B*
Oklahoma Christian University *B, M*
Oklahoma Wesleyan University *A, B*
Oral Roberts University *B, M*
Southwestern Christian University *B*

Oregon

Corban University *C, A, B, M, D*
George Fox University *B*
Mount Angel Seminary *M*
Multnomah University *B, M*
New Hope Christian College *C, B*
Northwest Christian University *B*

Pennsylvania

Baptist Bible College of
   Pennsylvania *C, D*
Cairn University *C, B, M*
Eastern University *B*
Geneva College *A, B*
Lancaster Bible College *C, A, B, M*
Messiah College *B*
Valley Forge Christian College *A, B*

Puerto Rico

Bayamon Central University *M*
Universidad Pentecostal Mizpa *B*

Rhode Island

Providence College *M*

South Carolina

Anderson University *B*
Bob Jones University *B, M*
Clinton Junior College *A*
Columbia International
   University *C, A, B, M*
Erskine College *C, M*
North Greenville University *B, M, D*
W.L. Bonner Bible College *C, B*

Tennessee

American Baptist College *A, B*
Belmont University *B*
Bryan University
   Dayton *B*
Freed-Hardeman University *B, M*
Hiwassee College *A*
Johnson University *C, A, B, M*
King University *B*
Lee University *B*
Lipscomb University *B, M*
Milligan College *B*
Southern Adventist University *A*
Tennessee Temple University *A, B*
Trevecca Nazarene University *M*
Welch College *A, B*

Texas

Abilene Christian University *B, M*
Arlington Baptist College *C, B, M*
Austin Graduate School of
   Theology *B*
Baptist University of the
   Americas *C, B*
College of Biblical Studies-
   Houston *C, A, B*
Criswell College *B, M*
Dallas Baptist University *A, B*
Dallas Christian College *B*
East Texas Baptist University *B*
Hardin-Simmons University *B*
Howard Payne University *C, A, B*
LeTourneau University *B*
Lubbock Christian University *B, M*
Southwestern Assemblies of God
   University *A, B, M*
Southwestern Baptist Theological
   Seminary *C*
Southwestern Christian College *A, B*
University of Mary Hardin-Baylor *B*

Virginia

Bluefield College *B*
Eastern Mennonite University *A, B*
Liberty University *B*
Regent University *B, M*
Virginia Baptist College *C*

Washington

Northwest University *C, B*
Trinity Lutheran College *C, A, B*

West Virginia

Appalachian Bible College *C, A, B, M*
Ohio Valley University *B*

Wisconsin

Concordia University Wisconsin *A, B*
Maranatha Baptist Bible College *B, M*
Northland International
   University *A, B, M*

Bilingual/bicultural education

Arizona

Northern Arizona University *M*

California

Butte College *A*
California Lutheran University *M*
California Polytechnic State
   University: San Luis Obispo *T*
California State University
   Dominguez Hills *M*
   East Bay *T*
   Fullerton *M, T*
   Long Beach *B, M, T*
   Northridge *M*
   Sacramento *M*
   San Bernardino *M*
   San Marcos *T*
Cerritos College *A*
Chapman University *T*
Fresno City College *A*
Fresno Pacific University *M, T*
Loyola Marymount University *M, T*
Sacramento City College *A*
San Diego City College *A*
San Diego State University *M, T*
San Francisco State University *T*
University of California
   San Diego *M*
University of La Verne *T*
University of San Francisco *M, D, T*

Colorado

Colorado Mountain College *A*

Connecticut

Fairfield University *M, T*
Southern Connecticut State
   University *M, T*

Delaware

Delaware Technical Community
   College
   Terry Campus *A*
University of Delaware *M*

District of Columbia

American University *M*

Florida

University of Miami *M*

Idaho

Boise State University *B, M, T*
College of Idaho *B*
College of Southern Idaho *A*
Northwest Nazarene University *M*

Illinois

Aurora University *B, M*
Chicago State University *M, T*
Columbia College Chicago *M*
DePaul University *M*
Loyola University Chicago *B*
North Central College *T*
North Park University *M*
Northeastern Illinois University *B*
University of Illinois
   Urbana-Champaign *M, D*
Western Illinois University *B*

Massachusetts

Boston University *B, M, T*
Eastern Nazarene College *M, T*
Elms College *B, M, T*
Salem State University *M*

Michigan

Aquinas College *B, T*
Calvin College *B, T*
Saginaw Valley State University *T*
Wayne State University *M, T*

Minnesota

Concordia University St. Paul *B, T*
Hamline University *T*

University of Minnesota
   Twin Cities *B, M, T*

Missouri

Northwest Missouri State
   University *M, T*
Rockhurst University *T*
University of Missouri
   Kansas City *B*

Montana

Blackfeet Community College *A*

New Jersey

Fairleigh Dickinson University
   Metropolitan Campus *M*
Georgian Court University *T*
Montclair State University *T*
New Jersey City University *T*
Seton Hall University *M*
William Paterson University of New
   Jersey *T*

New Mexico

University of the Southwest *B, M*
Western New Mexico University *T*

New York

Adelphi University *M, T*
Canisius College *M*
City University of New York
   Brooklyn College *M, T*
   City College *B, M, T*
   Hunter College *M, T*
   York College *T*
Hofstra University *M, T*
New York University *M, D, T*
SUNY
   College at Brockport *B, M, T*
   College at Buffalo *M*
   College at Old Westbury *B, T*
   University at Albany *M*
   University at Buffalo *M, T*
St. John's University *M, T*

North Carolina

Greensboro College *M*

Ohio

Ashland University *B*
University of Findlay *B, M, T*

Oklahoma

Oklahoma State University
   Oklahoma City *A*

Oregon

Treasure Valley Community
   College *A*
University of Oregon *T*
Western Oregon University *T*

Pennsylvania

Immaculata University *M, T*
La Salle University *B, M*

Puerto Rico

Inter American University of Puerto
   Rico
   Aguadilla Campus *M*
   Metropolitan Campus *B, M*
Turabo University *M*
University of the Sacred Heart *B*

Texas

Del Mar College *A*
Houston Baptist University *M*
Laredo Community College *A*
McMurry University *T*
Midwestern State University *B*
Our Lady of the Lake University of
   San Antonio *B*
Richland College *A*

Southern Methodist University *T*
Sul Ross State University *M*
Texas A&M International
   University *B, M, T*
Texas A&M University *M*
Texas A&M University
   Kingsville *B, M, D*
Texas Christian University *B*
Texas State University *M, T*
Texas Tech University *M*
Texas Wesleyan University *B, M, T*
University of St. Thomas *M*
University of Texas
   Brownsville *M*
   Pan American *M*
   Permian Basin *M*
   San Antonio *M*
West Texas A&M University *T*

Utah

Brigham Young University *D*

Washington

Central Washington University *T*
Heritage University *B*
University of Washington *M*
Washington State University *B, M, T*

Wisconsin

University of Wisconsin
   Madison *D*

Biochemical engineering

Colorado

Colorado School of Mines *B*
University of Colorado
   Boulder *B*

Georgia

University of Georgia *B, M*

New Jersey

New Jersey Institute of
   Technology *M*
Rowan University *B*

Pennsylvania

Drexel University *M*

Biochemistry

Alabama

Auburn University *B*
Huntingdon College *B*
Oakwood University *B*
Samford University *B*
Spring Hill College *B*

Arizona

Arizona State University *B, M, D*
University of Arizona *B, M, D*

Arkansas

Harding University *B*
John Brown University *B*
University of Arkansas
   for Medical Sciences *M, D*

California

Azusa Pacific University *B*
Biola University *B*
California Institute of
   Technology *M, D*
California Lutheran University *B*
California Polytechnic State
   University: San Luis Obispo *B*
California State University
   Chico *B*
   Dominguez Hills *B*
   East Bay *B, M*

Fullerton *B*
Long Beach *B, M*
Los Angeles *B*
Northridge *B*
San Bernardino *B*
San Marcos *B*
Chapman University *B*
Claremont McKenna College *B*
La Sierra University *B*
Loma Linda University *M, D*
Loyola Marymount University *B*
Mills College *B*
Mount St. Mary's College *B*
Notre Dame de Namur University *B*
Occidental College *B*
Pacific Union College *B*
Pepperdine University *B*
Pitzer College *B*
Point Loma Nazarene University *B*
St. Mary's College of California *B*
San Francisco State University *B*
San Jose State University *B*
Santa Clara University *B*
Scripps College *B*
Sonoma State University *B*
Stanford University *M, D*
University of California
　Berkeley *M, D*
　Irvine *M, D*
　Los Angeles *B, M, D*
　Riverside *B, M, D*
　San Diego *B, D*
　Santa Barbara *B, M, D*
University of Redlands *B*
University of San Diego *B*
University of Southern California *B*
University of the Pacific *B*
Vanguard University of Southern
　California *B*
Whittier College *B*

Colorado

Adams State University *B*
Colorado College *B*
Colorado State University *B, M, D*
Regis University *B*
University of Colorado
　Boulder *B, D*
　Colorado Springs *B*
University of Denver *B*

Connecticut

Central Connecticut State
　University *B*
Connecticut College *B*
Eastern Connecticut State
　University *B*
Fairfield University *B*
Quinnipiac University *B*
Trinity College *B*
University of Connecticut *M, D*
University of Saint Joseph *B, M*
Wesleyan University *B, D*
Yale University *B, M, D*

Delaware

University of Delaware *B, M, D*

District of Columbia

American University *B*
Catholic University of America *B*
George Washington University *M, D*
Georgetown University *B, M*
Howard University *M, D*
Trinity Washington University *B*

Florida

Ave Maria University *B*
Eckerd College *B*
Florida Institute of Technology *B*
Florida International University *D*
Florida State University *B*
New College of Florida *B*
Pensacola State College *A*

Rollins College *B*
Stetson University *B*
University of Miami *B, D*
University of Tampa *B*

Georgia

Agnes Scott College *B*
Berry College *B*
Emory University *D*
Georgia Institute of Technology *B*
Kennesaw State University *B*
LaGrange College *B*
Mercer University *B*
Spelman College *B*

Hawaii

Brigham Young University-Hawaii *B*

Idaho

Idaho State University *B*
Northwest Nazarene University *B*
University of Idaho *B*

Illinois

Augustana College *B*
Benedictine University *B*
Blackburn College *B*
Bradley University *B, T*
Chicago State University *B*
Illinois Institute of Technology *B*
Illinois State University *B*
Judson University *B*
Knox College *B*
Lewis University *B*
Loyola University Chicago *B, M, D*
Monmouth College *B*
North Central College *B*
Rockford University *B*
Roosevelt University *B*
Rush University *D*
University of Illinois
　Chicago *B*
　Urbana-Champaign *B, M, D*

Indiana

Anderson University *B*
DePauw University *B*
Earlham College *B*
Huntington University *B*
Indiana University
　Bloomington *B, M, D*
　East *B*
　Kokomo *B*
　Purdue University
　　Indianapolis *M, D*
　South Bend *B*
Manchester University *B*
Purdue University *B, M, D*
Rose-Hulman Institute of
　Technology *B*
Saint Joseph's College *A, B*
University of Evansville *B*
University of Notre Dame *B, M, D*
University of Southern Indiana *B*
Valparaiso University *B*
Vincennes University *A*
Wabash College *B*

Iowa

Buena Vista University *B*
Central College *B*
Clarke University *B*
Coe College *B*
Cornell College *B*
Drake University *B*
Grand View University *B*
Grinnell College *B*
Iowa State University *B, M, D*
Loras College *B*
Simpson College *B*
University of Iowa *B, M, D*
University of Northern Iowa *B, M*
Wartburg College *B*

Kansas

Benedictine College *B*
Kansas State University *B, M, D*
Newman University *B*
Southwestern College *B*
Tabor College *B*
University of Kansas *B*
Washburn University *B*
Wichita State University *B*

Kentucky

Asbury University *B*
Bluegrass Community and Technical
　College *A*
Centre College *B*
University of Kentucky *D*
University of Louisville *M, D*
Western Kentucky University *B*

Louisiana

Centenary College of Louisiana *B*
Louisiana State University
　Health Sciences Center *D*
Louisiana State University and
　Agricultural and Mechanical
　College *B, M, D*
Tulane University *B, M, D*
Xavier University of Louisiana *B*

Maine

Bates College *B*
Bowdoin College *B*
Colby College *B*
University of Maine *B, M, D*
University of New England *B*

Maryland

Hood College *B*
McDaniel College *B*
Montgomery College *A*
Mount St. Mary's University *B*
St. Mary's College of Maryland *B*
Stevenson University *B*
University of Maryland
　Baltimore County *M, D*
　College Park *B, M, D*
Washington Adventist University *B*

Massachusetts

American International College *B*
Bay Path College *B*
Boston College *B, M, D*
Boston University *B, M, D*
Brandeis University *B, M, D*
Clark University *B, M*
Eastern Nazarene College *B*
Emmanuel College *B*
Harvard College *B, M, D*
Merrimack College *B*
Mount Holyoke College *B*
Northeastern University *B*
Regis College *B*
Salem State University *B*
Simmons College *B*
Smith College *B*
Stonehill College *B*
Tufts University *B, D*
University of Massachusetts
　Boston *B*
Wellesley College *B*
Wheaton College *B*
Worcester Polytechnic Institute *B, M*

Michigan

Albion College *B*
Alma College *B*
Andrews University *B*
Calvin College *B*
Central Michigan University *B*
Eastern Michigan University *B*
Ferris State University *B*
Grand Valley State University *B*
Hillsdale College *B*
Kettering University *B*

Lawrence Technological University *B*
Madonna University *B*
Michigan State University *B, M, D*
Northern Michigan University *B, M*
Oakland University *B*
Olivet College *B*
Saginaw Valley State University *B*
Spring Arbor University *B*
University of Detroit Mercy *B*
University of Michigan *B, M, D*
University of Michigan
　Dearborn *B*
　Flint *B, M*
Western Michigan University *B*

Minnesota

College of St. Benedict *B*
College of St. Scholastica *B*
Gustavus Adolphus College *B*
Hamline University *B*
Minnesota State University
　Mankato *B*
St. Catherine University *B*
Saint Cloud State University *B*
St. John's University *B*
St. Mary's University of Minnesota *B*
University of Minnesota
　Duluth *B*
　Twin Cities *B, M, D*
University of Northwestern - St.
　Paul *B*
University of St. Thomas *B*
Winona State University *B*

Mississippi

East Mississippi Community
　College *A*
Millsaps College *B*
Mississippi College *B*
Mississippi State University *B*
University of Mississippi *B*
University of Mississippi Medical
　Center *M, D*

Missouri

Culver-Stockton College *B*
Maryville University of Saint Louis *B*
Missouri Baptist University *B*
Missouri Southern State University *B*
Missouri University of Science and
　Technology *B*
Missouri Western State University *B*
Rockhurst University *B*
Saint Louis University *B, D*
University of Missouri
　Columbia *B, M, D*
　St. Louis *B, M*
Washington University in St.
　Louis *B, D*
Westminster College *B*
William Jewell College *B*

Montana

Montana State University *M, D*
University of Montana *M, D*

Nebraska

Doane College *B*
Peru State College *B*
Union College *B*
University of Nebraska
　Lincoln *B, M, D*

Nevada

University of Nevada
　Reno *B, M, D*

New Hampshire

Dartmouth College *B, D*
Saint Anselm College *B*
University of New Hampshire *M, D*

New Jersey

College of St. Elizabeth *B*
Fairleigh Dickinson University
   College at Florham *B*
   Metropolitan Campus *B*
Georgian Court University *B*
Montclair State University *B*
New Jersey Institute of Technology *B*
Ramapo College of New Jersey *B*
Richard Stockton College of New
   Jersey *B*
Rider University *B*
Rowan University *B*
Rutgers, The State University of New
   Jersey
   New Brunswick/Piscataway
     Campus *B, M, D*
Saint Peter's University *B*
Seton Hall University *B*
Stevens Institute of
   Technology *B, M, D*

New Mexico

Eastern New Mexico University *B*
New Mexico Institute of Mining and
   Technology *B, M*
New Mexico State University *B*
University of New Mexico *B*

New York

Adelphi University *B*
Barnard College *B*
Canisius College *B*
City University of New York
   City College *B, M*
   College of Staten Island *B*
   Hunter College *M*
Colgate University *B*
College of Mount St. Vincent *B*
College of Saint Rose *B*
Columbia University *B*
Columbia University
   School of General Studies *B*
Cornell University *M, D*
Daemen College *B*
Elmira College *B*
Hamilton College *B*
Hartwick College *B*
Hobart and William Smith Colleges *B*
Hofstra University *B*
Houghton College *B*
Iona College *B*
Ithaca College *B*
Keuka College *B*
Le Moyne College *B*
Long Island University
   LIU Brooklyn *B*
Manhattan College *B, T*
Manhattanville College *B*
Marist College *B*
Nazareth College *B*
New York University *B, M, D*
Niagara University *B*
Pace University *B*
Pace University: Pleasantville/
   Briarcliff *B*
Roberts Wesleyan College *B*
Rochester Institute of Technology *B*
SUNY
   College at Brockport *B*
   College at Fredonia *B*
   College at Geneseo *B*
   College at New Paltz *B*
   College at Old Westbury *B*
   College at Oneonta *B*
   College at Plattsburgh *B*
   College at Potsdam *B*
   College of Environmental Science
     and Forestry *B*
   Downstate Medical Center *D*
   University at Albany *B, M, D*
   University at Binghamton *B*
   University at Buffalo *B, M, D*

University at Stony Brook *B*
   Upstate Medical University *M, D*
Sage Colleges *B*
Saint Bonaventure University *B*
St. Lawrence University *B*
Siena College *B*
Syracuse University *B*
Union College *B*
University of Rochester *B, M, D*
Vassar College *B*
Wells College *B*
Yeshiva University *B, M, D*

North Carolina

Campbell University *B*
Duke University *M, D*
East Carolina University *B, D*
Elon University *B*
High Point University *B*
North Carolina State
   University *B, M, D*
Queens University of Charlotte *B*
University of North Carolina
   Chapel Hill *M, D*
   Greensboro *B*
Wake Forest University *D*

North Dakota

North Dakota State University *M, D*
University of Jamestown *B*
University of North Dakota *M, D*

Ohio

Ashland University *B*
Bowling Green State University *B*
Capital University *B*
Case Western Reserve
   University *B, M, D*
College of Mount St. Joseph *B*
Denison University *B*
Hiram College *B*
John Carroll University *B*
Kenyon College *B*
Marietta College *B*
Miami University
   Oxford *B*
Notre Dame College *B*
Oberlin College *B*
Ohio Northern University *B*
Ohio State University
   Columbus Campus *A, B, M, D*
Ohio Wesleyan University *B*
Otterbein University *B*
University of Akron *B*
University of Cincinnati *B*
University of Dayton *B*
University of Mount Union *B*
University of Toledo *B*
Walsh University *B*
Wilmington College *B*
Wright State University *M*

Oklahoma

Oklahoma Baptist University *B*
Oklahoma Christian University *B*
Oklahoma City University *B*
Oklahoma State University *B, M, D*
Oral Roberts University *B*
Southern Nazarene University *B*
University of Oklahoma *B*
University of Tulsa *B, M*

Oregon

Lewis & Clark College *B*
Linfield College *B*
Mt. Hood Community College *A*
Pacific University *B*
Portland State University *B*
Reed College *B*
University of Oregon *B*

Pennsylvania

Albright College *B*
Allegheny College *B*

Alvernia University *B*
Bucknell University *B*
Cedar Crest College *B*
Chatham University *B*
Chestnut Hill College *B*
DeSales University *B*
Dickinson College *B*
Drexel University *M, D*
Duquesne University *B*
East Stroudsburg University of
   Pennsylvania *B*
Eastern University *B*
Elizabethtown College *B*
Franklin & Marshall College *B*
Geneva College *B*
Gettysburg College *B*
Grove City College *B*
Holy Family University *B*
Indiana University of Pennsylvania *B*
Juniata College *B*
Kutztown University of
   Pennsylvania *B*
La Salle University *B*
Lafayette College *B*
Lehigh University *B, D*
Mansfield University of
   Pennsylvania *B*
Mercyhurst University *B*
Messiah College *B*
Misericordia University *B*
Moravian College *B*
Muhlenberg College *B*
Penn State
   Abington *B*
   Altoona *B*
   Beaver *B*
   Berks *B*
   Brandywine *B*
   DuBois *B*
   Erie, The Behrend College *B*
   Fayette, The Eberly Campus *B*
   Greater Allegheny *B*
   Harrisburg *B*
   Hazleton *B*
   Lehigh Valley *B*
   Mont Alto *B*
   New Kensington *B*
   Schuylkill *B*
   Shenango *B*
   University Park *B, M, D*
   Wilkes-Barre *B*
   Worthington Scranton *B*
   York *B*
Philadelphia University *B*
Rosemont College *B*
Saint Joseph's University *B*
St. Vincent College *B*
Seton Hill University *B*
Slippery Rock University of
   Pennsylvania *B*
Susquehanna University *B*
Swarthmore College *B*
Temple University *B*
University of Pennsylvania *B*
University of Pittsburgh *M, D*
University of Scranton *B, M*
University of the Sciences *B, M, D*
Villanova University *B*
Washington & Jefferson College *B*
West Chester University of
   Pennsylvania *B*
Westminster College *B*
Widener University *B*
Wilkes University *B*

Puerto Rico

University of Puerto Rico
   Medical Sciences *M, D*

Rhode Island

Brown University *B, M, D*
Providence College *B*
University of Rhode Island *D*

South Carolina

Charleston Southern University *B*
Claflin University *B*
Clemson University *B, M, D*
Coastal Carolina University *B*
Columbia College *B*
Converse College *B*
Presbyterian College *B*

South Dakota

Augustana College *B*
Dakota Wesleyan University *B*
South Dakota State University *B*
University of South Dakota *M, D*

Tennessee

Christian Brothers University *B*
Freed-Hardeman University *B*
King University *B*
Lee University *B*
Lipscomb University *B*
Maryville College *B*
Sewanee: The University of the
   South *B*
Southern Adventist University *B*
Tennessee State University *B*
Tennessee Technological
   University *B*
University of Tennessee
   Knoxville *M, D*
Vanderbilt University *M, D*

Texas

Abilene Christian University *B*
Angelo State University *B*
Austin College *B*
Baylor University *B*
McMurry University *B*
Our Lady of the Lake University of
   San Antonio *B*
Rice University *B, M, D*
St. Edward's University *B*
St. Mary's University *B*
Schreiner University *B*
Southern Methodist University *B*
Southwestern University *B*
Stephen F. Austin State University *B*
Texas A&M University *B, M, D*
Texas Christian University *B*
Texas State University *B, M*
Texas Tech University *B*
Texas Wesleyan University *B*
Texas Woman's University *B*
Trinity University *B*
University of Dallas *B*
University of Houston *B, M, D*
University of North Texas *B, M, D*
University of St. Thomas *B*
University of Texas
   Arlington *B*
   Austin *B, M, D*
   Dallas *B*
   Health Science Center at
     Houston *M, D*
   San Antonio *B*
University of the Incarnate Word *B*

Utah

Brigham Young University *B, M, D*
University of Utah *M, D*
Utah State University *B, M, D*

Vermont

Marlboro College *B*
Middlebury College *B*
Norwich University *B*
Saint Michael's College *B*
University of Vermont *B*

Virginia

Eastern Mennonite University *B*
George Mason University *D*
Hampden-Sydney College *B*
Liberty University *B*

Marymount University *B*
Old Dominion University *B*
Roanoke College *B*
University of Virginia *D*
Virginia Commonwealth
University *M, D*
Virginia Polytechnic Institute and
State University *B*
Washington and Lee University *B*

Washington

Gonzaga University *B*
Seattle Pacific University *B*
Seattle University *B*
University of Puget Sound *B*
University of Washington *B, M, D*
Walla Walla University *B*
Washington State University *B, M, D*
Western Washington University *B*

West Virginia

Bethany College *B*
Ohio Valley University *B*
University of Charleston *B*
West Virginia University *B*

Wisconsin

Beloit College *B*
Carroll University *B*
Lakeland College *B*
Lawrence University *B*
Ripon College *B*
St. Norbert College *B*
University of Wisconsin
La Crosse *B*
Madison *B, M, D*
Milwaukee *B*
River Falls *B*
Stevens Point *B*
Viterbo University *B*
Wisconsin Lutheran College *B*

Biochemistry and molecular biology

Arizona

University of Arizona *D*

Arkansas

Harding University *B*
Hendrix College *B*

California

California Institute of
Technology *M, D*
University of California
Irvine *B, M, D*
Riverside *M, D*
University of Southern
California *M, D*

Colorado

University of Colorado
Denver *D*

Connecticut

Yale University *B, M, D*

Delaware

Wesley College *B*

Florida

Florida Southern College *B*
Rollins College *B*
University of Florida *M, D*

Georgia

Georgia Regents University *M, D*
University of Georgia *B, M, D*

Illinois

Northwestern University *D*
University of Illinois
Chicago *M, D*

Indiana

Indiana University
Bloomington *D*
Indiana Wesleyan University *B*
Purdue University *B, M, D*

Iowa

Cornell College *B*

Kansas

Emporia State University *B*
University of Kansas *M, D*
University of Kansas Medical
Center *M, D*

Kentucky

Bellarmine University *B*

Maryland

Goucher College *B*
University of Maryland
Baltimore *M, D*
Baltimore County *B*

Massachusetts

University of Massachusetts
Amherst *B, M*

Michigan

Michigan State University *B, M, D*
Michigan Technological University *B*
University of Michigan
Flint *B, M*
Wayne State University *M, D*

Minnesota

Bethel University *B*
Minnesota State University
Moorhead *B*
University of Minnesota
Twin Cities *M, D*

Nebraska

Nebraska Wesleyan University *B*
University of Nebraska
Medical Center *M, D*

New Hampshire

Dartmouth College *B*
University of New Hampshire *B*

New Jersey

Drew University *B*
Rutgers, The State University of New
Jersey
Newark Campus *M, D*

New York

Rensselaer Polytechnic
Institute *B, M, D*

North Dakota

North Dakota State University *B*

Ohio

College of Wooster *B*
University of Cincinnati *M, D*

Oklahoma

University of Oklahoma *M, D*

Oregon

Oregon Health & Science
University *M, D*
Oregon State University *B, M, D*

Pennsylvania

Lebanon Valley College *B*
University of Pennsylvania *M, D*

South Carolina

Medical University of South
Carolina *D*

Tennessee

Belmont University *B*
Rhodes College *B*
Vanderbilt University *M, D*

Texas

Hardin-Simmons University *B*

Vermont

Middlebury College *B*

Virginia

Christopher Newport University *B*
Sweet Briar College *B*

Washington

Evergreen State College *B*
Whitman College *B*

West Virginia

West Virginia University *D*

Wisconsin

Marquette University *B*

Bioengineering/ biomedical engineering

Alabama

University of Alabama
Birmingham *B, M, D*

Arizona

Arizona State University *B, M, D*
University of Arizona *B, M, D*

Arkansas

Harding University *B*
University of Arkansas *B*

California

California Institute of
Technology *B, M, D*
California Polytechnic State
University: San Luis Obispo *B, M*
California State University
Long Beach *B*
National University *B*
San Diego State University *M*
Santa Clara University *B, M*
Stanford University *M, D*
University of California
Berkeley *B, D*
Davis *B, M, D*
Irvine *B, M, D*
Los Angeles *M, D*
Merced *B, M, D*
Riverside *B, M, D*
San Diego *B, M, D*
Santa Cruz *B*
University of Southern
California *B, M, D*
University of the Pacific *B*

Colorado

Colorado State University *B, M, D*
University of Colorado
Denver *B, M, D*
University of Denver *M*

Connecticut

Trinity College *B*
University of Bridgeport *M*
University of Connecticut *B, M, D*

University of New Haven *C*
Yale University *B, M, D*

Delaware

Delaware State University *B*
University of Delaware *B, M, D*

District of Columbia

Catholic University of
America *B, M, D*
George Washington University *B*

Florida

Florida Agricultural and Mechanical
University *M, D*
Florida Atlantic University *M*
Florida Gulf Coast University *B*
Florida Institute of Technology *B*
Florida International
University *B, M, D*
Florida State University *M, D*
University of Florida *B, M, D*
University of Miami *B, M, D*
University of South Florida *M, D*

Georgia

Emory University *D*
Georgia Institute of
Technology *B, M, D*
Mercer University *B, M*

Illinois

DeVry University
Chicago *B*
Illinois Institute of Technology *B, D*
Northwestern University *B, M, D*
Southern Illinois University
Carbondale *M*
University of Illinois
Chicago *B, M, D*
Urbana-Champaign *B, M, D*

Indiana

Grace College *B*
Indiana Institute of Technology *B*
Indiana University
Purdue University
Indianapolis *B, M*
Purdue University *B, M, D*
Rose-Hulman Institute of
Technology *B, M*
Trine University *M*

Iowa

Dordt College *B*
University of Iowa *B, M, D*

Kansas

University of Kansas *M, D*
Wichita State University *B*

Kentucky

University of Kentucky *M, D*
University of Louisville *B, M*

Louisiana

Louisiana State University and
Agricultural and Mechanical
College *B*
Louisiana Tech University *B, D*
Tulane University *B, M, D*

Maine

University of Maine *B*

Maryland

Howard Community College *A*
Johns Hopkins University *B, M, D*
University of Maryland
College Park *M, D*

Massachusetts

Boston University *B, M, D*
Bunker Hill Community College *A*
Endicott College *B*
Massachusetts Institute of
    Technology *B, M, D*
Quinsigamond Community College *A*
Smith College *B*
Tufts University *B, M, D*
University of Massachusetts
    Dartmouth *B*
Wentworth Institute of Technology *B*
Western New England University *B*
Worcester Polytechnic
    Institute *B, M, D*

Michigan

Lawrence Technological University *B*
Michigan State University *B*
Michigan Technological
    University *B, D*
University of Michigan *B, M, D*
Wayne State University *B, M, D*

Minnesota

Anoka-Ramsey Community College *A*
University of Minnesota
    Twin Cities *B, M, D*

Mississippi

East Mississippi Community
    College *A*
Mississippi State University *B, M, D*

Missouri

Saint Louis University *B, M, D*
University of Missouri
    Columbia *B, M, D*
Washington University in St.
    Louis *B, M, D*

Nevada

University of Nevada
    Reno *M, D*

New Hampshire

Dartmouth College *B, M, D*

New Jersey

College of New Jersey *B*
New Jersey Institute of
    Technology *B, M, D*
Rutgers, The State University of New
    Jersey
    New Brunswick/Piscataway
        Campus *B, M, D*
    Newark Campus *B, M, D*
Stevens Institute of
    Technology *B, M, D*

New Mexico

University of New Mexico *M*

New York

Alfred University *B, M*
City University of New York
    City College *B, M, D*
Columbia University *B, M, D*
Cornell University *M, D*
Hofstra University *B*
Rensselaer Polytechnic
    Institute *B, M, D*
Rochester Institute of Technology *B*
SUNY
    University at Binghamton *B, M, D*
    University at Buffalo *B, M, D*
    University at Stony Brook *B, M, D*
Syracuse University *B, M, D*
Union College *B*
University of Rochester *B, M, D*

North Carolina

Duke University *B, M, D*
Elon University *B*
North Carolina Agricultural and
    Technical State University *B, M*
North Carolina State
    University *B, M, D*
University of North Carolina
    Chapel Hill *M, D*
Wake Forest University *M, D*

Ohio

Case Western Reserve
    University *B, M, D*
Cleveland State University *D*
Miami University
    Oxford *B*
Ohio State University
    Columbus Campus *B, M, D*
Ohio University *M*
University of Akron *B, M, D*
University of Cincinnati *B, M, D*
University of Toledo *B, M, D*
Wright State University *B, M*

Oklahoma

Oral Roberts University *B*
University of Central Oklahoma *B*
University of Oklahoma *M, D*

Oregon

Oregon Health & Science
    University *M, D*
Oregon State University *B*

Pennsylvania

Bucknell University *B*
Carnegie Mellon University *B, M, D*
Drexel University *B, M, D*
Gannon University *B*
Lehigh University *B, M, D*
Penn State
    Abington *B*
    Altoona *B*
    Beaver *B*
    Berks *B*
    Brandywine *B*
    DuBois *B*
    Erie, The Behrend College *B*
    Fayette, The Eberly Campus *B*
    Greater Allegheny *B*
    Harrisburg *B*
    Hazleton *B*
    Lehigh Valley *B*
    Mont Alto *B*
    New Kensington *B*
    Schuylkill *B*
    Shenango *B*
    University Park *B, M, D*
    Wilkes-Barre *B*
    Worthington Scranton *B*
    York *B*
Temple University *B, M*
University of Pennsylvania *B, M, D*
University of Pittsburgh *B, M, D*
Widener University *B, M*
Wilkes University *M*

Rhode Island

Brown University *B, M*
University of Rhode Island *B*

South Carolina

Clemson University *B, M, D*
University of South Carolina
    Columbia *B, M, D*

South Dakota

South Dakota School of Mines and
    Technology *M, D*
University of South Dakota *D*

Tennessee

University of Memphis *B, M, D*
University of Tennessee
    Knoxville *B, M, D*
Vanderbilt University *B, M, D*

Texas

Baylor University *M*
LeTourneau University *B*
Rice University *B, M, D*
Texas A&M University *B, M, D*
Texas Tech University *M*
University of Houston *B, M, D*
University of Texas
    Arlington *B, M, D*
    Austin *B, M, D*
    Dallas *B, M, D*
    San Antonio *M, D*

Utah

University of Utah *B, M, D*

Vermont

University of Vermont *D*

Virginia

George Mason University *B*
University of Virginia *B, M, D*
Virginia Commonwealth
    University *B, M, D*
Virginia Polytechnic Institute and
    State University *M, D*

Washington

University of Washington *B, M, D*
Walla Walla University *B*
Washington State University *D*

Wisconsin

Marquette University *B, M, D*
Milwaukee School of Engineering *B*
University of Wisconsin
    Madison *B, M, D*

Bioethics/medical ethics

California

American Jewish University *B*
Loma Linda University *M*
Loyola Marymount University *M*

Florida

University of Miami *B*
University of South Florida *M*

Georgia

Emory University *M*

Illinois

Loyola University Chicago *M, D*
Northwestern University *M*

Missouri

Saint Louis University *D*
University of Missouri
    Kansas City *B*

New Jersey

Drew University *M*

New York

Yeshiva University *M, T*

Ohio

Case Western Reserve
    University *M, D*

Pennsylvania

Duquesne University *M, D*
Saint Joseph's University *M*
Temple University *M*

University of Pennsylvania *M*
University of Pittsburgh *M*

Texas

University of Texas
    Medical Branch at Galveston *M, D*

Bioinformatics

Arizona

University of Arizona *M*

Arkansas

University of Arkansas
    Little Rock *M, D*
    for Medical Sciences *M, D*

California

Foothill College *A*
Pacific Union College *B*
San Diego State University *M*
Stanford University *M, D*
University of California
    Irvine *B*
    Los Angeles *M, D*
    San Diego *B*
    Santa Cruz *B, M, D*

Colorado

University of Denver *M*

Florida

University of South Florida *M*

Georgia

Georgia Institute of Technology *M, D*
University of Georgia *M, D*

Idaho

University of Idaho *M, D*

Illinois

Loyola University Chicago *B*
Northwestern University *M*
University of Illinois
    Chicago *M, D*
    Urbana-Champaign *M, D*

Indiana

Indiana University
    Bloomington *M*
    Purdue University Indianapolis *M*

Iowa

Iowa State University *B, M, D*

Kansas

University of Kansas *D*

Maryland

Howard Community College *A*
Morgan State University *M*
University of Maryland
    Baltimore County *B*

Massachusetts

Boston University *M, D*
Brandeis University *M*
Clark University *B*
Northeastern University *M*
Wheaton College *B*
Worcester Polytechnic Institute *B, M*

Michigan

Davenport University *B*
Eastern Michigan University *M*
Michigan Technological University *B*
University of Michigan *M, D*

Mississippi

Mississippi Valley State University *M*

Missouri
University of Missouri
   Kansas City *M*
Washington University in St. Louis *D*

Nebraska
University of Nebraska
   Omaha *B*

New Jersey
New Jersey Institute of
   Technology *B, M*
Ramapo College of New Jersey *B*
Rutgers, The State University of New
   Jersey
   Newark Campus *M*
Stevens Institute of Technology *B, M*

New Mexico
New Mexico State University *M*

New York
Canisius College *B*
City University of New York
   Hunter College *B, M*
   New York City College of
     Technology *B*
College of Saint Rose *B*
Rensselaer Polytechnic Institute *B*
Rochester Institute of
   Technology *B, M*
SUNY
   University at Buffalo *B, M*
Saint Bonaventure University *B*

North Carolina
North Carolina State University *M, D*
University of North Carolina
   Chapel Hill *D*
   Charlotte *M, D*

Ohio
University of Toledo *M*
Walsh University *B*

Oklahoma
Oklahoma City Community
   College *A*

Oregon
Oregon Health & Science
   University *M, D*
Pacific University *B*

Pennsylvania
Gannon University *B*
St. Vincent College *B*
University of Pennsylvania *B*
University of Pittsburgh *B, M, D*
University of the Sciences *B, M*

Puerto Rico
Inter American University of Puerto
   Rico
   Bayamon Campus *B*

South Carolina
Claflin University *B*

Tennessee
Vanderbilt University *M, D*

Texas
Baylor University *D*
St. Edward's University *B*
University of St. Thomas *B*
University of Texas
   Dallas *M*
   El Paso *M*

Utah
Brigham Young University *B*

Virginia
George Mason University *M*
Virginia Commonwealth
   University *B, M*
Virginia Polytechnic Institute and
   State University *D*

Wisconsin
Marquette University *M*
Mid-State Technical College *A*

Biological/biosystems engineering

Alabama
Auburn University *B, M, D*

Arizona
Arizona State University *D*
University of Arizona *B*

Florida
University of Florida *B*

Georgia
University of Georgia *B, M*

Idaho
University of Idaho *B, M*

Indiana
Purdue University *M, D*

Nebraska
University of Nebraska
   Lincoln *B, D*

South Dakota
South Dakota School of Mines and
   Technology *D*

Biological immunology

California
California Institute of
   Technology *M, D*
Stanford University *M, D*
University of California
   Davis *M, D*

Colorado
University of Colorado
   Denver *D*

Connecticut
Yale University *M, D*

Illinois
Loyola University Chicago *M, D*
Rush University *D*
University of Chicago *D*
University of Illinois
   Chicago *M, D*

Iowa
University of Iowa *D*

Maine
University of Southern Maine *M*

Massachusetts
Boston University *D*
Harvard College *M, D*

Michigan
University of Michigan *D*
Wayne State University *M, D*

Missouri
Washington University in St. Louis *D*

New York
Cornell University *M, D*
SUNY
   Downstate Medical Center *D*

North Carolina
North Carolina State University *M, D*

Ohio
University of Cincinnati *M, D*
University of Toledo *M, D*

Pennsylvania
Penn State
   University Park *M, D*
University of Pennsylvania *M, D*
University of Pittsburgh *M, D*

Washington
University of Washington *M, D*

West Virginia
West Virginia University *D*

Biological/physical sciences

Alabama
Troy University *B*
University of Alabama
   Birmingham *B*
   Huntsville *M*
University of South Alabama *M, D*
University of West Alabama *B*

Alaska
University of Alaska
   Anchorage *B*
   Fairbanks *B*

Arizona
Arizona Western College *A*
Central Arizona College *A*
Coconino County Community
   College *A*
Northland Pioneer College *A*

Arkansas
Southern Arkansas University *B*
University of Arkansas
   Little Rock *M*
   Monticello *B*
   for Medical Sciences *M, D*
University of Central Arkansas *B*

California
American River College *A*
California Lutheran University *B*
Canada College *A*
Cerro Coso Community College *A*
Citrus College *A*
College of the Canyons *A*
College of the Desert *A*
College of the Sequoias *A*
College of the Siskiyous *A*
Contra Costa College *A*
East Los Angeles College *A*
Folsom Lake College *A*
Fresno City College *A*
Glendale Community College *A*
Golden West College *A*
Imperial Valley College *A*
Laney College *A*
Lassen Community College *A*
Master's College *B*
National University *B*
Ohlone College *A*
Oxnard College *A*
Palomar College *A*
Pitzer College *B*
Porterville College *A*
San Joaquin Delta College *C*
Santa Monica College *A*

Scripps College *B*
Solano Community College *A*
University of California
   Santa Barbara *B*
University of La Verne *B*
University of the Pacific *B*
Vanguard University of Southern
   California *B*

Colorado
Colorado Christian University *B*
Colorado Mountain College *A*
Colorado State University *M*
Morgan Community College *A*
University of Colorado
   Colorado Springs *M*
   Denver *M*
University of Denver *B*

District of Columbia
American University *B, M*
Georgetown University *B*

Florida
Palm Beach State College *A*
University of South Florida *B*
University of West Florida *B*

Georgia
Covenant College *B*
Spelman College *B*
University of Georgia *B*

Illinois
Black Hawk College *A*
City Colleges of Chicago
   Harold Washington College *A*
   Harry S. Truman College *A*
   Kennedy-King College *A*
   Malcolm X College *A*
   Olive-Harvey College *A*
   Richard J. Daley College *A*
   Wilbur Wright College *A*
College of DuPage *A*
College of Lake County *A*
DePaul University *B, M*
Dominican University *B*
Heartland Community College *A*
Highland Community College *A*
Illinois Eastern Community Colleges
   Lincoln Trail College *A*
Illinois Valley Community College *A*
John A. Logan College *A*
John Wood Community College *A*
Kaskaskia College *A*
Kishwaukee College *A*
Lincoln Land Community College *A*
McHenry County College *A*
Moraine Valley Community College *A*
Morton College *A*
National-Louis University *B*
North Central College *T*
Northwestern University *B*
Olivet Nazarene University *B, T*
Parkland College *A*
Prairie State College *A*
Rend Lake College *A*
Rock Valley College *A*
Saint Xavier University *B*
Shawnee Community College *A*
Spoon River College *A*
Triton College *A*
University of Chicago *D*
Waubonsee Community College *A*

Indiana
Ball State University *M, D, T*
Grace College *B*
Indiana University
   Bloomington *M*
   Kokomo *B*
   Purdue University Indianapolis *B*
Purdue University *B*
University of Notre Dame *B*

University of Southern Indiana *B, T*
Valparaiso University *A*
Vincennes University *A*

Iowa

Briar Cliff University *B*
Coe College *B*
St. Ambrose University *B*
University of Iowa *B, M, D*
University of Northern Iowa *B, M*

Kansas

Fort Hays State University *B*
Pratt Community College *A*
Seward County Community
College *A*
Washburn University *A*

Kentucky

Alice Lloyd College *B*
Brescia University *B*
Spalding University *C, B*
Western Kentucky University *M*

Louisiana

Louisiana College *B, T*
Louisiana State University and
Agricultural and Mechanical
College *M*
Our Lady of Holy Cross College *B*

Maine

College of the Atlantic *B, M*
University of Maine *B, M*

Maryland

Baltimore City Community College *A*
Community College of Baltimore
County *A*
Montgomery College *A*
Notre Dame of Maryland
University *B*
St. Mary's College of Maryland *B*
University of Maryland
College Park *M, D*
Wor-Wic Community College *A*

Massachusetts

American International College *B*
Eastern Nazarene College *B*
Elms College *B*
University of Massachusetts
Amherst *B*
Dartmouth *M, D*
Wellesley College *B*
Worcester Polytechnic
Institute *B, M, D*

Michigan

Andrews University *B, M*
Calvin College *B*
Concordia University *B*
Eastern Michigan University *B, M*
Ferris State University *A*
Grand Valley State University *B*
Michigan State University *B*
Olivet College *B*
Rochester College *A*

Minnesota

College of St. Benedict *B*
Minnesota State University
Mankato *B*
St. John's University *B*
University of Minnesota
Twin Cities *B*

Mississippi

Delta State University *B, M*
Mississippi State University *B, M*
University of Southern
Mississippi *B, M, D*

Missouri

Avila University *B*
Maryville University of Saint Louis *B*
Missouri Valley College *B*
Northwest Missouri State
University *B*
Washington University in St.
Louis *B, M, D*

Montana

Montana State University
Billings *B*
Stone Child College *A*

New Hampshire

Keene State College *B*
Saint Anselm College *B*

New Jersey

Cumberland County College *A*
Fairleigh Dickinson University
Metropolitan Campus *B, M*
Gloucester County College *A*
Ramapo College of New Jersey *B*
Rutgers, The State University of New
Jersey
Camden Campus *M*
New Brunswick/Piscataway
Campus *M, D*
Newark Campus *M*
Saint Peter's University *B*
Sussex County Community College *A*

New Mexico

Northern New Mexico College *A*

New York

Adelphi University *B, M*
Alfred University *B*
City University of New York
Baruch College *B*
Clarkson University *M*
Colgate University *B*
College of New Rochelle *B, T*
Corning Community College *A*
Eugene Lang College The New
School for Liberal Arts *B*
Le Moyne College *B*
North Country Community College *A*
Paul Smith's College *B*
Rensselaer Polytechnic
Institute *B, M, D*
Roberts Wesleyan College *B*
SUNY
Empire State College *A, B*
St. Thomas Aquinas College *B, T*
Touro College *B*
Union College *B*

North Carolina

Brevard College *B*
East Carolina University *M, D*
Mars Hill University *B*

North Dakota

Fort Berthold Community College *A*

Ohio

Ashland University *B*
Baldwin Wallace University *B, T*
Bowling Green State University:
Firelands College *A*
Defiance College *B, T*
Heidelberg University *B*
Urbana University *B*
Walsh University *B*
Wilberforce University *B*
Wright State University *D*

Oklahoma

Eastern Oklahoma State College *A*
Oklahoma Christian University *B*
Oklahoma City University *B*

Oklahoma Panhandle State
University *B*
St. Gregory's University *B*

Oregon

Linn-Benton Community College *A*
Portland State University *B, M*
Southern Oregon University *B*
Southwestern Oregon Community
College *A*
University of Oregon *B*
Western Oregon University *B*

Pennsylvania

Allegheny College *B*
Alvernia University *B*
Arcadia University *B*
Cheyney University of
Pennsylvania *B, T*
Community College of Beaver
County *A*
Delaware County Community
College *A*
East Stroudsburg University of
Pennsylvania *B, M, T*
Edinboro University of
Pennsylvania *B*
Geneva College *B*
Gettysburg College *B*
Immaculata University *B*
Indiana University of Pennsylvania *B*
King's College *B, T*
Kutztown University of
Pennsylvania *B*
La Salle University *B*
Luzerne County Community
College *A*
Penn State
Abington *C, B*
Altoona *A, B*
Beaver *B*
Berks *B*
Brandywine *B*
DuBois *C, A, B*
Erie, The Behrend College *B*
Fayette, The Eberly Campus *A, B*
Greater Allegheny *A, B*
Harrisburg *B*
Hazleton *B*
Lehigh Valley *B*
Mont Alto *B*
New Kensington *B*
Schuylkill *B*
Shenango *C, A, B*
University Park *B*
Wilkes-Barre *B*
Worthington Scranton *B*
York *B*
St. Francis University *B*
University of Pittsburgh *B*
University of Pittsburgh
Bradford *B*
Ursinus College *B*
Villanova University *A, B*
West Chester University of
Pennsylvania *T*

Puerto Rico

Bayamon Central University *B*

Rhode Island

Brown University *B*
Community College of Rhode
Island *A*
University of Rhode Island *M, D*

South Carolina

North Greenville University *B, T*

Tennessee

Middle Tennessee State University *B*
Tennessee State University *B*

Texas

Central Texas College *A*
College of the Mainland *A*
Galveston College *A*
Navarro College *A*
North Central Texas College *A*
St. Mary's University *B*
Sam Houston State University *B*
Stephen F. Austin State University *M*
Texas A&M University
Galveston *B*
Texas Tech University *B*
University of Houston *M*
University of Houston
Downtown *B*
University of Texas
Arlington *M*
Austin *B*
Dallas *M, T*
Health Science Center at
Houston *M, D*
Medical Branch at Galveston *M*
San Antonio *B*
University of the Incarnate Word *M*
Wayland Baptist University *M*

Utah

Brigham Young University *B, M*
Snow College *A*

Vermont

Bennington College *B*
Castleton State College *B*
Lyndon State College *B*
Marlboro College *B*

Virginia

Danville Community College *A*
George Mason University *D*
J. Sargeant Reynolds Community
College *A*
Jefferson College of Health
Sciences *A*
Lord Fairfax Community College *A*
New River Community College *A*
Northern Virginia Community
College *A*
Paul D. Camp Community College *A*
Piedmont Virginia Community
College *A*
Southside Virginia Community
College *A*
Tidewater Community College *A*
University of Virginia *M*
Virginia Commonwealth University *B*
Virginia Highlands Community
College *A*
Virginia Western Community
College *A*
Wytheville Community College *A*

Washington

Evergreen State College *B*
University of Puget Sound *B, T*
University of Washington *M, D*
Washington State University *B*
Western Washington University *B, M*
Whitworth University *B*

West Virginia

Bethany College *B*
Bluefield State College *B*

Wisconsin

Madison Area Technical College *A*
Mount Mary University *B, T*
St. Norbert College *B*
University of Wisconsin
Green Bay *B*
River Falls *B, T*
Stevens Point *B, T*
Superior *B*
Viterbo University *B*

Wyoming

Laramie County Community
College *A*
Sheridan College *A*

Biology

Alabama

Alabama Agricultural and Mechanical
University *B*, *M*
Alabama State University *B*, *M*
Athens State University *B*
Auburn University *M*, *D*
Auburn University at Montgomery *B*
Birmingham-Southern College *B*
Calhoun Community College *A*
Faulkner State Community College *A*
Faulkner University *B*
Gadsden State Community College *A*
Huntingdon College *B*
Jacksonville State University *B*, *M*
Judson College *B*
Miles College *B*
Oakwood University *B*
Samford University *B*
Spring Hill College *B*, *T*
Stillman College *B*
Talladega College *B*
Troy University *B*
Tuskegee University *B*, *M*, *D*, *T*
University of Alabama *B*, *M*, *D*
University of Alabama
Birmingham *B*, *M*, *D*
Huntsville *B*, *M*
University of Mobile *B*
University of Montevallo *B*, *T*
University of North Alabama *B*
University of South Alabama *B*, *M*
University of West Alabama *B*, *T*

Alaska

University of Alaska
Anchorage *B*, *M*
Fairbanks *B*, *M*, *D*
Southeast *B*

Arizona

Arizona Christian University *B*
Arizona State University *B*, *M*, *D*
Arizona Western College *A*
Central Arizona College *A*
Cochise College *A*
Dine College *A*
Eastern Arizona College *A*
Grand Canyon University *B*
Mesa Community College *C*
Northern Arizona University *B*, *M*, *D*
South Mountain Community
College *A*
University of Arizona *B*

Arkansas

Arkansas State University *B*, *M*
Arkansas Tech University *B*
Central Baptist College *B*
Harding University *B*
Henderson State University *B*
Hendrix College *B*
John Brown University *B*
Lyon College *B*
Ouachita Baptist University *B*
Philander Smith College *B*
Phillips Community College of the
University of Arkansas *A*
Southern Arkansas University *B*
University of Arkansas *B*, *M*, *D*
University of Arkansas
Fort Smith *B*
Little Rock *B*, *M*
Monticello *B*
Pine Bluff *B*
University of Central Arkansas *B*, *M*
University of the Ozarks *B*
Williams Baptist College *B*

California

Allan Hancock College *A*
Antelope Valley College *A*
Azusa Pacific University *B*
Bakersfield College *A*
Biola University *B*
Cabrillo College *A*
California Baptist University *B*
California Institute of
Technology *B*, *M*, *D*
California Lutheran University *B*
California Polytechnic State
University: San Luis Obispo *B*, *M*
California State Polytechnic
University: Pomona *B*, *M*
California State University
Bakersfield *B*
Channel Islands *B*, *M*
Chico *B*, *M*
Dominguez Hills *B*, *M*
East Bay *B*, *M*
Fresno *B*, *M*
Fullerton *B*, *M*
Long Beach *B*, *M*
Los Angeles *B*, *M*
Monterey Bay *B*
Northridge *B*, *M*
Sacramento *B*, *M*
San Bernardino *B*, *M*
San Marcos *B*
Stanislaus *B*
Canada College *A*
Cerritos College *A*
Chabot College *A*
Chaffey College *A*
Chapman University *B*
City College of San Francisco *A*
Claremont McKenna College *B*
College of Alameda *A*
College of Marin *A*
College of San Mateo *A*
College of the Desert *A*
College of the Siskiyous *A*
Columbia College *A*
Concordia University Irvine *B*
Contra Costa College *A*
Crafton Hills College *A*
Cuesta College *A*
De Anza College *A*
Diablo Valley College *A*
Dominican University of California *B*
El Camino College *A*
Feather River College *A*
Folsom Lake College *A*
Foothill College *A*
Fresno Pacific University *B*
Fullerton College *A*
Gavilan College *A*
Glendale Community College *A*
Golden West College *A*
Grossmont College *A*
Hartnell College *A*
Harvey Mudd College *B*
Holy Names University *B*
Humboldt State University *B*, *M*
Imperial Valley College *A*
Irvine Valley College *A*
La Sierra University *B*
Lassen Community College *A*
Loma Linda University *M*, *D*
Long Beach City College *A*
Los Angeles City College *A*
Los Angeles Southwest College *A*
Los Angeles Valley College *A*
Los Medanos College *A*
Loyola Marymount University *B*
Master's College *B*
Mendocino College *A*
Merced College *A*
Mills College *B*
Mission College *A*
Monterey Peninsula College *A*
Moorpark College *A*
Mount St. Mary's College *B*

Mount San Antonio College *A*
National University *B*, *M*
Notre Dame de Namur University *B*
Occidental College *B*, *M*
Ohlone College *A*
Orange Coast College *A*
Oxnard College *A*
Pacific Union College *B*
Palomar College *C*, *A*
Pasadena City College *A*
Pepperdine University *B*
Pitzer College *B*
Point Loma Nazarene University *B*
Pomona College *B*
Porterville College *A*
Reedley College *A*
Rio Hondo College *A*
Saddleback College *A*
St. Mary's College of California *B*
San Bernardino Valley College *A*
San Deigo Miramar College
San Diego Miramar College *A*
San Diego Christian College *B*
San Diego City College *A*
San Diego Mesa College *A*
San Diego State University *B*, *M*, *D*
San Francisco State University *B*, *M*
San Jose State University *B*, *M*
Santa Ana College *A*
Santa Barbara City College *A*
Santa Clara University *B*
Santa Rosa Junior College *A*
Santiago Canyon College *A*
Scripps College *B*
Shasta College *A*
Sierra College *A*
Simpson University *B*
Solano Community College *A*
Sonoma State University *B*, *M*
Southwestern College *A*
Stanford University *B*, *M*, *D*
University of California
Berkeley *B*, *D*
Davis *B*
Irvine *B*, *D*
Los Angeles *B*, *M*, *D*
Merced *B*
Riverside *B*
San Diego *B*, *D*
Santa Barbara *B*, *M*, *D*
Santa Cruz *B*
University of La Verne *B*
University of Redlands *B*
University of San Diego *B*
University of San Francisco *B*, *M*
University of Southern
California *B*, *M*
University of the Pacific *B*, *M*
Vanguard University of Southern
California *B*
Ventura College *A*
West Hills College: Lemoore *A*
West Los Angeles College *A*
West Valley College *A*
Westmont College *B*
Whittier College *B*
William Jessup University *B*
Yuba College *A*

Colorado

Adams State University *B*
Colorado Christian University *B*
Colorado Mesa University *B*
Colorado Mountain College *B*
Colorado State University *B*
Colorado State University
Pueblo *B*
Community College of Aurora *A*
Fort Lewis College *B*
Metropolitan State University of
Denver *B*, *T*
Otero Junior College *A*
Regis University *B*
United States Air Force Academy *B*

University of Colorado
Colorado Springs *B*
Denver *B*, *M*
University of Denver *B*, *M*, *D*
University of Northern
Colorado *B*, *M*, *D*, *T*
Western State Colorado University *B*

Connecticut

Albertus Magnus College *B*
Central Connecticut State
University *B*, *M*, *T*
Connecticut College *B*
Eastern Connecticut State
University *B*
Fairfield University *B*
Naugatuck Valley Community
College *A*
Post University *B*
Quinnipiac University *B*
Sacred Heart University *B*
Southern Connecticut State
University *B*, *M*
Trinity College *B*
University of Bridgeport *B*
University of Connecticut *B*
University of Hartford *B*
University of New Haven *B*
University of Saint Joseph *B*, *M*
Wesleyan University *B*, *D*
Western Connecticut State
University *B*, *M*
Yale University *B*

Delaware

Delaware State University *B*, *M*
Delaware Technical Community
College
Jack F. Owens Campus *A*
Stanton/Wilmington Campus *A*
University of Delaware *B*, *M*, *D*
Wesley College *B*

District of Columbia

American University *B*, *M*
Catholic University of America *B*
Gallaudet University *B*
George Washington
University *B*, *M*, *D*
Georgetown University *B*, *M*, *D*
Howard University *B*, *M*, *D*
Trinity Washington University *B*
University of the District of
Columbia *B*, *M*, *T*

Florida

Ave Maria University *B*
Barry University *B*, *M*, *T*
Bethune-Cookman University *B*
Broward College *A*
Chipola College *A*, *B*
Clearwater Christian College *B*
Daytona State College *A*
Eckerd College *B*
Edward Waters College *B*
Florida Agricultural and Mechanical
University *B*, *M*
Florida Atlantic University *B*, *M*, *D*
Florida Gulf Coast University *B*
Florida Institute of Technology *B*, *D*
Florida International
University *B*, *M*, *D*
Florida Memorial University *B*
Florida Southern College *B*
Florida State University *B*, *M*, *D*
Indian River State College *A*
Jacksonville University *B*
Lynn University *B*
Miami Dade College *A*
New College of Florida *B*
Nova Southeastern University *B*
Palm Beach Atlantic University *B*
Palm Beach State College *A*
Pensacola State College *A*

Rollins College *B*
Saint Leo University *B*
St. Petersburg College *B*
Saint Thomas University *B*
South Florida State College *A*
Southeastern University *B*
Stetson University *B*
University of Central Florida *B, M*
University of Florida *B*
University of Miami *B, M, D*
University of North Florida *B, M*
University of South Florida *B, M, D*
University of South Florida
   Saint Petersburg *B*
   Sarasota-Manatee *B*
University of Tampa *A, B*
University of West Florida *B, M*
Warner University *A, B*

Georgia

Abraham Baldwin Agricultural
   College *A*
Agnes Scott College *B*
Albany State University *B*
Armstrong Atlantic State
   University *B, T*
Atlanta Metropolitan College *A*
Berry College *B*
Brenau University *B*
Brewton-Parker College *B*
Clark Atlanta University *B, M, D*
Clayton State University *B*
College of Coastal Georgia *A, B*
Columbus State University *B*
Columbus Technical College *A*
Covenant College *B*
Dalton State College *B*
Darton College *A*
East Georgia State College *A*
Emmanuel College *B*
Emory University *B, D*
Fort Valley State University *B*
Georgia College and State
   University *B, M*
Georgia Gwinnett College *B*
Georgia Highlands College *A*
Georgia Institute of
   Technology *B, M, D*
Georgia Military College *A*
Georgia Perimeter College *A*
Georgia Regents University *B*
Georgia Southern University *B, M*
Georgia Southwestern State
   University *B*
Georgia State University *B, M, D*
Gordon College *A, B, T*
Kennesaw State University *B, M*
LaGrange College *B*
Life University *B*
Mercer University *B*
Middle Georgia State College *A, B*
Morehouse College *B*
Oglethorpe University *B*
Paine College *B*
Piedmont College *B*
Point University *B*
Reinhardt University *B*
Savannah State University *B*
Shorter University *B*
South Georgia State College *A*
Southern Polytechnic State
   University *B*
Spelman College *B*
Thomas University *B*
Toccoa Falls College *B*
Truett-McConnell College *B*
University of Georgia *B*
University of North Georgia *B*
University of West Georgia *B, M*
Valdosta State University *B, M*
Wesleyan College *B*
Young Harris College *B*

Hawaii

Brigham Young University-Hawaii *B*
Chaminade University of Honolulu *B*
Hawaii Pacific University *B*
University of Hawaii
   Hilo *B*
   Manoa *B*

Idaho

Boise State University *B, M, T*
Brigham Young University-Idaho *A, B*
College of Idaho *B*
College of Southern Idaho *A*
College of Western Idaho *A*
Idaho State University *B, M, D*
Lewis-Clark State College *B*
North Idaho College *A*
Northwest Nazarene University *B*
University of Idaho *B, M, D*

Illinois

Augustana College *B*
Aurora University *B*
Benedictine University *B, T*
Benedictine University at
   Springfield *B*
Blackburn College *B*
Bradley University *B, M, T*
Chicago State University *B, T*
Concordia University Chicago *B, T*
DePaul University *B, M*
Dominican University *B*
Eastern Illinois University *B, M, T*
Elmhurst College *B, T*
Eureka College *B, T*
Governors State University *B, T*
Greenville College *B, T*
Illinois College *B, T*
Illinois Institute of
   Technology *B, M, D*
Illinois State University *B, M, D, T*
Illinois Valley Community College *A*
Illinois Wesleyan University *B*
John A. Logan College *A*
John Wood Community College *A*
Joliet Junior College *A*
Judson University *B*
Kankakee Community College *A*
Knox College *B*
Lake Forest College *B*
Lewis University *B*
Lincoln College *B*
Loyola University Chicago *B, M*
MacMurray College *B, T*
McKendree University *B, T*
Millikin University *B*
Monmouth College *B, T*
Moraine Valley Community College *A*
National-Louis University *B*
North Central College *B, T*
North Park University *B*
Northeastern Illinois University *B, M*
Northern Illinois
   University *B, M, D, T*
Northwestern University *B, M, D*
Olivet Nazarene University *B, T*
Principia College *B*
Quincy University *B, T*
Richland Community College *A*
Rockford University *B*
Roosevelt University *B, M*
Saint Xavier University *B*
Sauk Valley Community College *A*
South Suburban College of Cook
   County *A*
Southern Illinois University
   Carbondale *B, M*
Southern Illinois University
   Edwardsville *B, M*
Southwestern Illinois College *A*
Spoon River College *A*
Trinity Christian College *B*
Trinity International University *B*
University of Chicago *B*

University of Illinois
   Chicago *B, M, D*
   Springfield *B, M*
   Urbana-Champaign *B, M, D*
University of St. Francis *B*
Western Illinois University *B, M*
Wheaton College *B, T*

Indiana

Ancilla College *A*
Anderson University *B*
Ball State University *B, M, T*
Bethel College *B*
Butler University *B*
DePauw University *B*
Earlham College *B*
Franklin College *B*
Goshen College *B*
Grace College *B*
Hanover College *B*
Huntington University *B*
Indiana State University *B, M, D, T*
Indiana University
   Bloomington *B, M, D*
   East *B*
   Kokomo *B*
   Northwest *B*
   Purdue University Fort
     Wayne *B, M, T*
   Purdue University
     Indianapolis *B, M*
   South Bend *B*
   Southeast *B*
Indiana Wesleyan University *A, B*
Manchester University *B, T*
Marian University *B, T*
Martin University *B*
Oakland City University *B*
Purdue University *B, M, D*
Purdue University
   Calumet *B, M*
   North Central *B*
Rose-Hulman Institute of
   Technology *B*
Saint Joseph's College *B*
Saint Mary's College *B*
St. Mary-of-the-Woods College *B*
Taylor University *B*
Trine University *B*
University of Evansville *B*
University of Indianapolis *B, M*
University of Notre Dame *B, M, D*
University of St. Francis *B*
University of Southern Indiana *B, T*
Valparaiso University *B*
Vincennes University *A*
Wabash College *B*

Iowa

Ashford University *B*
Briar Cliff University *B*
Buena Vista University *B, T*
Central College *B, T*
Clarke University *A, B, T*
Coe College *B*
Cornell College *B, T*
Dordt College *B*
Drake University *B*
Ellsworth Community College *A*
Graceland University *B, T*
Grand View University *B*
Grinnell College *B*
Iowa State University *B*
Iowa Wesleyan College *B, T*
Iowa Western Community College *A*
Loras College *B*
Luther College *B*
Marshalltown Community College *A*
Morningside College *B*
Mount Mercy University *B, T*
Northwestern College *B, T*
St. Ambrose University *B*
Simpson College *B*
University of Dubuque *B*

University of Iowa *B, M, D, T*
University of Northern Iowa *B, M*
Upper Iowa University *B*
Waldorf College *B*
Wartburg College *B, T*
William Penn University *B*

Kansas

Allen County Community College *A*
Baker University *B, T*
Barton County Community College *A*
Benedictine College *B*
Bethany College *B, T*
Bethel College *B*
Central Christian College of Kansas *B*
Coffeyville Community College *A*
Colby Community College *A*
Cowley County Community
   College *A*
Dodge City Community College *A*
Donnelly College *A*
Emporia State University *B, M, T*
Fort Hays State University *B, M*
Friends University *B*
Garden City Community College *A*
Hutchinson Community College *A*
Independence Community College *A*
Kansas State University *B, M, D*
Kansas Wesleyan University *B, T*
Labette Community College *A*
McPherson College *B, T*
MidAmerica Nazarene University *B, T*
Neosho County Community
   College *A*
Newman University *B*
Ottawa University *B*
Pittsburg State University *B, M*
Pratt Community College *A*
Seward County Community
   College *A*
Southwestern College *B*
Sterling College *B, T*
Tabor College *B*
University of Kansas *B*
University of St. Mary *B*
Washburn University *B*
Wichita State University *B, M, T*

Kentucky

Alice Lloyd College *B*
Asbury University *B*
Bellarmine University *B, T*
Berea College *B*
Bluegrass Community and Technical
   College *A*
Brescia University *A, B*
Campbellsville University *B*
Centre College *B*
Eastern Kentucky University *B, M*
Georgetown College *B, T*
Hopkinsville Community College *A*
Kentucky Christian University *B*
Kentucky State University *B*
Kentucky Wesleyan College *B, T*
Lindsey Wilson College *A, B, T*
Midway College *B*
Morehead State University *B, M, T*
Murray State University *B, M, T*
Northern Kentucky University *B*
St. Catharine College *B*
Thomas More College *A, B*
Transylvania University *B*
Union College *B*
University of Kentucky *B, M, D*
University of Louisville *B, M, D*
University of Pikeville *B, T*
University of the Cumberlands *B, T*
Western Kentucky University *B, M, T*

Louisiana

Centenary College of Louisiana *B, T*
Dillard University *B*
Grambling State University *B*
Louisiana College *B, T*

Louisiana State University
  Alexandria *B*
  Eunice *A*
  Shreveport *B, M*
Louisiana State University and
  Agricultural and Mechanical
  College *B, M, D*
Louisiana Tech University *B, M*
Loyola University New Orleans *B*
McNeese State University *B*
Nicholls State University *B*
Northwestern State University *B*
Our Lady of Holy Cross College *B, T*
Our Lady of the Lake College *B*
Southeastern Louisiana
  University *B, M*
Southern University
  New Orleans *B*
  Shreveport *B*
Southern University and Agricultural
  and Mechanical College *B, M*
Tulane University *B, M, D*
University of Louisiana at
  Lafayette *B, M*
University of Louisiana at
  Monroe *B, M*
University of New Orleans *B, M*
Xavier University of Louisiana *B*

Maine

Bates College *B, T*
Bowdoin College *B*
Colby College *B*
College of the Atlantic *B, M*
Husson University *B*
Kennebec Valley Community
  College *A*
Saint Joseph's College of Maine *B*
University of Maine *B, M, D*
University of Maine
  Augusta *B*
  Farmington *B*
  Fort Kent *B*
  Machias *B, T*
  Presque Isle *B*
University of New England *B, M*
University of Southern Maine *B*

Maryland

Allegany College of Maryland *A*
Bowie State University *B*
Cecil College *A*
Coppin State University *B*
Frederick Community College *A*
Frostburg State University *B, T*
Goucher College *B*
Harford Community College *A*
Hood College *B, T*
Johns Hopkins University *B, M, D*
Loyola University Maryland *B*
McDaniel College *B*
Morgan State University *B*
Mount St. Mary's University *B*
Notre Dame of Maryland
  University *B*
Prince George's Community
  College *A*
St. Mary's College of Maryland *B*
Salisbury University *B, M*
Stevenson University *B*
Towson University *B, M*
University of Maryland
  Baltimore County *B, M, D*
  College Park *B, M, D*
  Eastern Shore *B*
Washington Adventist University *B*
Washington College *B, T*

Massachusetts

American International College *B*
Amherst College *B*
Anna Maria College *B*
Assumption College *B*
Bard College at Simon's Rock *B*

Bay Path College *B*
Becker College *B*
Boston College *B, M, D*
Boston University *B, M, D*
Brandeis University *B*
Bridgewater State University *B*
Bunker Hill Community College *A*
Clark University *B, M, D*
College of the Holy Cross *B*
Curry College *B*
Eastern Nazarene College *B*
Elms College *B*
Emmanuel College *B*
Fitchburg State University *B, M, T*
Framingham State University *B*
Gordon College *B*
Hampshire College *B*
Harvard College *B*
Lesley University *B*
Massachusetts College of Liberal
  Arts *B, T*
Massachusetts Institute of
  Technology *B, D*
Merrimack College *B*
Mount Holyoke College *B*
Mount Ida College *B*
Northeastern University *B, M, D*
Northern Essex Community
  College *A*
Pine Manor College *A, B*
Regis College *B*
Roxbury Community College *A*
Salem State University *B, M*
Simmons College *B*
Smith College *B, M, D*
Springfield College *B*
Springfield Technical Community
  College *A*
Stonehill College *B*
Suffolk University *B*
Tufts University *B, M, D*
University of Massachusetts
  Amherst *B*
  Boston *B, M, D*
  Dartmouth *B, M*
  Lowell *C, B, M*
Wellesley College *B*
Western New England University *B*
Westfield State University *B, M, T*
Wheaton College *B*
Williams College *B*
Worcester Polytechnic Institute *B, M*
Worcester State University *B*

Michigan

Adrian College *A, B, T*
Albion College *B, T*
Alma College *B, T*
Andrews University *B, M*
Aquinas College *B, T*
Calvin College *B, T*
Central Michigan University *B, M*
Concordia University *B*
Cornerstone University *B, T*
Delta College *A*
Eastern Michigan University *B, M*
Ferris State University *B*
Gogebic Community College *A*
Grand Rapids Community College *A*
Grand Valley State University *B, M*
Hillsdale College *B*
Hope College *B*
Kalamazoo College *B*
Lake Michigan College *A*
Lake Superior State University *B, T*
Lansing Community College *A*
Macomb Community College *A*
Madonna University *B*
Marygrove College *B, T*
Michigan State University *B, M*
Michigan Technological
  University *B, M, D*
Mid Michigan Community College *A*
Mott Community College *A*
Northern Michigan University *B, M*

Northwestern Michigan College *A*
Oakland University *B, M, D, T*
Olivet College *B*
Saginaw Valley State University *B*
Siena Heights University *A, B*
Spring Arbor University *B*
University of Detroit Mercy *B*
University of Michigan *B*
University of Michigan
  Dearborn *B*
  Flint *B, M, T*
Wayne State University *B, M, D*
West Shore Community College *A*
Western Michigan University *B, M, D*

Minnesota

Anoka-Ramsey Community College *A*
Augsburg College *B*
Bemidji State University *B, M*
Bethany Lutheran College *B*
Bethel University *B*
Carleton College *B*
College of St. Benedict *B*
College of St. Scholastica *B*
Concordia College: Moorhead *B*
Concordia University St. Paul *B*
Crown College *B*
Gustavus Adolphus College *B*
Hamline University *B*
Inver Hills Community College *A*
Macalester College *B*
Mesabi Range Community and
  Technical College *A*
Metropolitan State University *B*
Minneapolis Community and
  Technical College *A*
Minnesota State Community and
  Technical College *A*
Minnesota State University
  Mankato *B, M, T*
  Moorhead *B*
Minnesota West Community and
  Technical College *A*
North Hennepin Community
  College *A*
Ridgewater College *A*
St. Catherine University *B*
Saint Cloud State University *B, M*
St. John's University *B*
St. Mary's University of Minnesota *B*
St. Olaf College *B*
South Central College *A*
Southwest Minnesota State
  University *B, T*
University of Minnesota
  Crookston *B*
  Duluth *B, M*
  Morris *B*
  Twin Cities *B, M, D*
University of Northwestern - St.
  Paul *B*
University of St. Thomas *B*
Winona State University *B*

Mississippi

Alcorn State University *B, M*
Belhaven University *B, T*
Blue Mountain College *B*
Coahoma Community College *A*
Delta State University *B*
East Mississippi Community
  College *A*
Hinds Community College *A*
Jackson State University *B, M*
Millsaps College *B*
Mississippi College *B, M*
Mississippi Delta Community
  College *A*
Mississippi Gulf Coast Community
  College *A*
Mississippi State University *B, M, D*
Mississippi University for
  Women *B, T*
Mississippi Valley State University *B*

Northeast Mississippi Community
  College *A*
Rust College *B*
Tougaloo College *B*
University of Mississippi *B, M, D, T*
University of Southern
  Mississippi *B, M, D*
William Carey University *B*

Missouri

Avila University *B*
Central Methodist University *B*
College of the Ozarks *B*
Columbia College *B*
Crowder College *A*
Culver-Stockton College *B*
Drury University *B, T*
Evangel University *B*
Fontbonne University *B*
Hannibal-LaGrange University *B*
Harris-Stowe State University *B*
Lincoln University *B*
Lindenwood University *B*
Maryville University of Saint Louis *B*
Missouri Baptist University *B, T*
Missouri Southern State
  University *B, T*
Missouri State University *B, M*
Missouri University of Science and
  Technology *B*
Missouri Valley College *B*
Missouri Western State
  University *B, T*
Northwest Missouri State
  University *B, M*
Ozarks Technical Community
  College *A*
Park University *B*
Rockhurst University *B*
St. Charles Community College *A*
St. Louis Community College *A*
Saint Louis University *B, M, D*
Southeast Missouri State University *B*
Southwest Baptist University *B, T*
Stephens College *B*
Three Rivers Community College *A*
Truman State University *B, M*
University of Central Missouri *B, M*
University of Missouri
  Columbia *B, M, D*
  Kansas City *B, M*
  St. Louis *B, M, D*
Washington University in St.
  Louis *B, M, D*
Webster University *B*
Westminster College *B, T*
William Jewell College *B, T*
William Woods University *B, T*

Montana

Blackfeet Community College *A*
Carroll College *B*
Little Big Horn College *A*
Miles Community College *A*
Montana State University *B, M, D*
Montana State University
  Billings *B*
  Northern *A, B*
Montana Tech of the University of
  Montana *B*
Rocky Mountain College *B*
University of Great Falls *B*
University of Montana *B, M, D*
University of Montana: Western *A, B*

Nebraska

Bellevue University *B*
Chadron State College *B*
College of Saint Mary *B, T*
Concordia University *B, T*
Creighton University *B*
Doane College *B*
Hastings College *B*
Midland University *B, T*

Nebraska Wesleyan University *B*
Northeast Community College *A*
Peru State College *B*
Union College *B*
University of Nebraska
   Kearney *B, M, T*
   Lincoln *B, M, D*
   Omaha *B, M*
Wayne State College *B*
Western Nebraska Community
   College *A*
York College *B*

Nevada

College of Southern Nevada *A*
Nevada State College *B*
Sierra Nevada College *B*
University of Nevada
   Las Vegas *B, M, D*
   Reno *B, M, D*

New Hampshire

Colby-Sawyer College *B*
Dartmouth College *B, M, D, T*
Franklin Pierce University *B*
Keene State College *B*
New England College *B, T*
Plymouth State University *B, M*
Rivier University *B, T*
Saint Anselm College *B, T*
University of New Hampshire *B, M*
University of New Hampshire at
   Manchester *A, B*

New Jersey

Bergen Community College *A*
Bloomfield College *B, T*
Caldwell College *B*
Centenary College *B*
College of New Jersey *B, T*
College of St. Elizabeth *B*
Drew University *B*
Essex County College *A*
Fairleigh Dickinson University
   College at Florham *B, M*
   Metropolitan Campus *B, M*
Felician College *B*
Georgian Court University *B, M*
Gloucester County College *A*
Hudson County Community
   College *A*
Kean University *B, T*
Mercer County Community
   College *A*
Monmouth University *B*
Montclair State University *B, M, T*
New Jersey City University *B*
New Jersey Institute of
   Technology *B, M, D*
Ramapo College of New Jersey *B*
Richard Stockton College of New
   Jersey *B*
Rider University *B*
Rowan University *B, T*
Rutgers, The State University of New
   Jersey
   Camden Campus *B, M, T*
   New Brunswick/Piscataway
      Campus *B, T*
   Newark Campus *B, M, D, T*
Saint Peter's University *B*
Seton Hall University *B, M, T*
Sussex County Community College *A*
Thomas Edison State College *A, B*
Union County College *A*
Warren County Community
   College *A*
William Paterson University of New
   Jersey *B, M*

New Mexico

Central New Mexico Community
   College *A*
Eastern New Mexico University *B, M*

Eastern New Mexico University:
   Roswell *A*
Luna Community College *A*
New Mexico Highlands
   University *B, M*
New Mexico Institute of Mining and
   Technology *B, M*
New Mexico Junior College *A*
New Mexico State University *B, M, D*
Northern New Mexico College *B*
San Juan College *A*
Santa Fe Community College *A*
University of New Mexico *B, M, D*
University of the Southwest *B*
Western New Mexico University *B*

New York

Adelphi University *B, M*
Alfred University *B*
Bard College *B*
Barnard College *B*
Canisius College *B*
Cayuga Community College *A*
City University of New York
   Baruch College *B*
   Brooklyn College *B, M*
   City College *B, M*
   College of Staten Island *B, M, D*
   Hunter College *B, M*
   Kingsborough Community
      College *A*
   LaGuardia Community College *A*
   Lehman College *B, M*
   Medgar Evers College *A, B*
   Queens College *B, M*
   Queensborough Community
      College *A*
   York College *B*
Clarkson University *B*
Colgate University *B*
College of Mount St. Vincent *B, T*
College of New Rochelle *B, T*
College of Saint Rose *B*
Columbia University *B*
Columbia University
   School of General Studies *B*
Concordia College *B, T*
Cornell University *B*
D'Youville College *B*
Daemen College *B, T*
Dominican College of Blauvelt *B*
Dowling College *B*
Elmira College *B, T*
Excelsior College *B*
Fordham University *B, M, D*
Genesee Community College *A*
Hamilton College *B*
Hartwick College *B, T*
Hobart and William Smith Colleges *B*
Hofstra University *B, M*
Houghton College *B*
Iona College *B*
Ithaca College *B, T*
Jamestown Community College *A*
Keuka College *B*
Le Moyne College *B*
Long Island University
   LIU Brooklyn *B, M*
   LIU Post *B, M*
Manhattan College *B*
Manhattanville College *B*
Marist College *B*
Marymount Manhattan College *B*
Medaille College *B*
Mercy College *B*
Molloy College *B*
Monroe Community College *A*
Mount Saint Mary College *B, T*
Nazareth College *B*
New York Institute of Technology *B*
New York University *A, B, M, D*
Niagara University *B*
Pace University *B*
Pace University: Pleasantville/
   Briarcliff *B*

Paul Smith's College *B*
Rensselaer Polytechnic
   Institute *B, M, D*
Roberts Wesleyan College *B*
Rochester Institute of
   Technology *A, B*
SUNY
   College at Brockport *B, M, T*
   College at Buffalo *B, M*
   College at Cortland *B*
   College at Fredonia *B, M, T*
   College at Geneseo *B, T*
   College at New Paltz *B, M*
   College at Old Westbury *B, T*
   College at Oneonta *B, M*
   College at Oswego *B*
   College at Plattsburgh *B*
   College at Potsdam *B*
   College at Purchase *B*
   College of Technology at Alfred *A*
   Farmingdale State College *B*
   Institute of Technology at Utica/
      Rome *B*
   University at Albany *B, M, D*
   University at Binghamton *B, M, D*
   University at Buffalo *B, M, D*
   University at Stony Brook *B, M*
Sage Colleges *B*
Saint Bonaventure University *B, T*
St. Francis College *B*
St. John Fisher College *B*
St. John's University *B, M, D*
St. Joseph's College New York:
   Suffolk Campus *B*
St. Joseph's College, New York *B*
St. Lawrence University *B, T*
St. Thomas Aquinas College *B, T*
Siena College *B, T*
Skidmore College *B*
Suffolk County Community College *A*
Syracuse University *B, M, D*
Touro College *B*
Union College *B*
United States Military Academy *B*
University of Rochester *B, M, D*
Utica College *B*
Vassar College *B, M*
Wagner College *B, T*
Wells College *B*
Yeshiva University *B*

North Carolina

Appalachian State University *B, M*
Barton College *B*
Belmont Abbey College *B*
Bennett College for Women *B*
Brevard College *B*
Campbell University *B, T*
Catawba College *B, T*
Chowan University *B*
Davidson College *B*
Duke University *B, D*
East Carolina University *B, M*
Elizabeth City State University *B, M*
Elon University *B*
Fayetteville State University *B, M*
Gardner-Webb University *B*
Greensboro College *B, T*
Guilford College *B*
High Point University *B*
Johnson C. Smith University *B*
Lees-McRae College *B*
Lenoir-Rhyne University *B*
Livingstone College *B*
Louisburg College *A*
Mars Hill University *B, T*
Meredith College *B*
Methodist University *A, B, T*
Montreat College *B*
North Carolina Agricultural and
   Technical State University *B, M*
North Carolina Central
   University *B, M*
North Carolina State University *B*
North Carolina Wesleyan College *B*

Pfeiffer University *B*
Queens University of Charlotte *B*
St. Andrews University *B*
St. Augustine's University *B*
Salem College *B*
Sandhills Community College *A*
Shaw University *B*
Southeastern Community College *A*
University of Mount Olive *B*
University of North Carolina
   Asheville *B, T*
   Chapel Hill *B, M, D*
   Charlotte *B, M, D*
   Greensboro *B, M*
   Pembroke *B*
   Wilmington *B, M*
Wake Forest University *B, M, D*
Warren Wilson College *B*
Western Carolina University *B, M*
Western Piedmont Community
   College *A*
William Peace University *B*
Wingate University *B*
Winston-Salem State University *B*

North Dakota

Dakota College at Bottineau *A*
Dickinson State University *B*
Mayville State University *B, T*
Minot State University *B*
North Dakota State University *B, M*
University of Jamestown *B*
University of Mary *B*
University of North Dakota *B, M, D*
Valley City State University *B*

Ohio

Ashland University *B*
Baldwin Wallace University *B*
Bluffton University *B*
Bowling Green State
   University *B, M, D*
Capital University *B*
Case Western Reserve
   University *B, M, D*
Cedarville University *B*
Central State University *B*
Cincinnati State Technical and
   Community College *C, A*
Cleveland State University *B, M*
College of Mount St. Joseph *B, T*
College of Wooster *B*
Defiance College *B, T*
Denison University *B*
Eastern Gateway Community
   College *A*
Franciscan University of
   Steubenville *B*
Heidelberg University *B*
Hiram College *B*
John Carroll University *B, M*
Kent State University *B, M*
Kent State University
   Stark *B*
Kenyon College *B*
Lake Erie College *B*
Lorain County Community College *A*
Lourdes University *A, B*
Malone University *B*
Marietta College *B*
Mercy College of Ohio *B*
Miami University
   Oxford *B, D*
Mount Vernon Nazarene University *B*
Muskingum University *B*
Notre Dame College *B, T*
Oberlin College *B*
Ohio Dominican University *B*
Ohio Northern University *B*
Ohio State University
   Columbus Campus *B*
   Lima Campus *B*
Ohio University *B*
Ohio Wesleyan University *B*

Otterbein University *B*
Shawnee State University *C, A, B*
Sinclair Community College *A*
Terra State Community College *A*
University of Akron *C, B, M, D*
University of Cincinnati *C, B, M, D, T*
University of Cincinnati
  Blue Ash College *A*
  Clermont College *A*
University of Dayton *B, M, D*
University of Findlay *B*
University of Mount Union *B*
University of Rio Grande *A, B*
University of Toledo *B, M, D*
Ursuline College *B*
Walsh University *B*
Wilberforce University *B*
Wilmington College *B*
Wittenberg University *B*
Wright State University *A, B, M*
Wright State University: Lake
  Campus *A*
Xavier University *B*
Youngstown State University *B, M*

Oklahoma

Cameron University *B*
Carl Albert State College *A*
Connors State College *A*
East Central University *B*
Eastern Oklahoma State College *A*
Langston University *B*
Northeastern Oklahoma Agricultural
  and Mechanical College *A*
Northeastern State University *B*
Northern Oklahoma College *A*
Northwestern Oklahoma State
  University *B*
Oklahoma Baptist University *B, T*
Oklahoma Christian University *B*
Oklahoma City Community
  College *A*
Oklahoma City University *B*
Oklahoma Panhandle State
  University *B*
Oklahoma State University *B*
Oklahoma Wesleyan University *A, B*
Oral Roberts University *B*
Rogers State University *A, B*
Rose State College *A*
St. Gregory's University *B*
Southeastern Oklahoma State
  University *B*
Southern Nazarene University *B*
Southwestern Oklahoma State
  University *B*
University of Central Oklahoma *B, M*
University of Science and Arts of
  Oklahoma *B*
University of Tulsa *B, M, D*
Western Oklahoma State College *A*

Oregon

Central Oregon Community
  College *A*
Concordia University *B, T*
Eastern Oregon University *B*
George Fox University *B*
Lewis & Clark College *B*
Linfield College *B, T*
Linn-Benton Community College *A*
Mt. Hood Community College *A*
Oregon Institute of Technology *B*
Oregon State University *B*
Pacific University *B*
Portland State University *B, M*
Reed College *B*
Southern Oregon University *B, T*
Treasure Valley Community
  College *A*
University of Oregon *B, M, D*
University of Portland *B, T*
Warner Pacific College *B, T*

Western Oregon University *B*
Willamette University *B*

Pennsylvania

Albright College *B, T*
Allegheny College *B*
Alvernia University *B*
Arcadia University *B*
Bloomsburg University of
  Pennsylvania *B, M, T*
Bryn Athyn College *B*
Bryn Mawr College *B*
Bucknell University *B, M*
Butler County Community College *A*
Cabrini College *B*
California University of
  Pennsylvania *B, M*
Carlow University *B*
Carnegie Mellon University *B, M, D*
Cedar Crest College *B*
Chatham University *B, M*
Chestnut Hill College *B*
Cheyney University of
  Pennsylvania *B, M, T*
Clarion University of
  Pennsylvania *B, M*
Community College of Allegheny
  County *A*
Community College of Beaver
  County *A*
DeSales University *B, T*
Delaware Valley College *B*
Dickinson College *B*
Drexel University *B, M, D*
Duquesne University *B, M, D*
East Stroudsburg University of
  Pennsylvania *B, M*
Eastern University *B*
Edinboro University of
  Pennsylvania *B, M, T*
Elizabethtown College *B, T*
Franklin & Marshall College *B*
Gannon University *B*
Geneva College *B, T*
Gettysburg College *B*
Grove City College *B*
Gwynedd Mercy University *B*
Harrisburg Area Community
  College *A*
Haverford College *B, T*
Holy Family University *B*
Immaculata University *A, B*
Indiana University of
  Pennsylvania *B, M, T*
Juniata College *B*
Keystone College *B*
King's College *B, T*
Kutztown University of
  Pennsylvania *B*
La Roche College *B*
La Salle University *B, T*
Lackawanna College *A*
Lafayette College *B*
Lebanon Valley College *B, T*
Lehigh Carbon Community College *A*
Lehigh University *B*
Lincoln University *B*
Lock Haven University of
  Pennsylvania *B*
Lycoming College *B*
Mansfield University of
  Pennsylvania *B, T*
Marywood University *B*
Mercyhurst University *B, T*
Messiah College *B*
Millersville University of
  Pennsylvania *B, T*
Misericordia University *B*
Moravian College *B, T*
Mount Aloysius College *B*
Muhlenberg College *C, B*
Neumann University *B*
Northampton Community College *A*

Penn State
  Abington *B*
  Altoona *B*
  Beaver *B*
  Berks *B*
  Brandywine *B*
  DuBois *B*
  Erie, The Behrend College *B*
  Fayette, The Eberly Campus *B*
  Greater Allegheny *B*
  Harrisburg *B*
  Hazleton *B*
  Lehigh Valley *B*
  Mont Alto *B*
  New Kensington *B*
  Schuylkill *B*
  Shenango *B*
  University Park *B, M, D*
  Wilkes-Barre *B*
  Worthington Scranton *B*
  York *B*
Philadelphia University *B*
Point Park University *B*
Reading Area Community College *A*
Robert Morris University *B*
Rosemont College *B*
St. Francis University *B*
Saint Joseph's University *B, M*
St. Vincent College *B*
Seton Hill University *B, T*
Shippensburg University of
  Pennsylvania *B, M, T*
Slippery Rock University of
  Pennsylvania *B*
Susquehanna University *B, T*
Swarthmore College *B*
Temple University *B, M, D*
Thiel College *B*
University of Pennsylvania *B, M, D*
University of Pittsburgh *B, M, D*
University of Pittsburgh
  Bradford *B*
  Greensburg *B*
  Johnstown *B*
University of Scranton *B, T*
University of the Sciences *B*
Ursinus College *B, T*
Valley Forge Military College *A*
Villanova University *B, M*
Washington & Jefferson College *B*
Waynesburg University *B*
West Chester University of
  Pennsylvania *B, M, T*
Westminster College *B*
Widener University *B, T*
Wilkes University *B*
Wilson College *B*
York College of Pennsylvania *A, B, T*

Puerto Rico

Bayamon Central University *B*
Inter American University of Puerto
  Rico
  Aguadilla Campus *B*
  Arecibo Campus *B*
  Barranquitas Campus *B*
  Bayamon Campus *B*
  Guayama Campus *B*
  Metropolitan Campus *B*
  Ponce Campus *B*
  San German Campus *B*
Pontifical Catholic University of
  Puerto Rico *B*
Turabo University *B*
Universidad Adventista de las
  Antillas *B*
Universidad Metropolitana *B*
Universidad del Este *B*
University of Puerto Rico
  Aguadilla *B*
  Bayamon University College *B*
  Cayey University College *B*
  Humacao *B*
  Mayaguez *B, M*
  Medical Sciences *D*

Ponce *B*
Rio Piedras *B, M, D*
University of the Sacred Heart *B*

Rhode Island

Brown University *B, M, D*
Bryant University *B*
Providence College *B*
Rhode Island College *B, M*
Roger Williams University *B*
Salve Regina University *B*
University of Rhode Island *B*

South Carolina

Allen University *B*
Anderson University *B*
Benedict College *B*
Bob Jones University *B*
Charleston Southern University *B*
Citadel *B, M, T*
Claflin University *B*
Clemson University *B, M, D*
Coastal Carolina University *B*
Coker College *B*
College of Charleston *B, T*
Columbia College *B*
Converse College *B*
Erskine College *B*
Francis Marion University *B*
Furman University *B, T*
Lander University *B*
Limestone College *B*
Morris College *B*
Newberry College *B, T*
North Greenville University *B*
Presbyterian College *B, T*
South Carolina State University *B*
Southern Wesleyan University *B, T*
University of South Carolina
  Aiken *B*
  Beaufort *B*
  Columbia *B, M, D*
  Upstate *B*
Voorhees College *B*
Winthrop University *B, M*
Wofford College *B, T*

South Dakota

Augustana College *B, T*
Black Hills State University *B*
Dakota Wesleyan University *B*
Mount Marty College *B*
Northern State University *B*
Presentation College *A*
Sinte Gleska University *A*
South Dakota State
  University *B, M, D*
University of Sioux Falls *B*
University of South Dakota *B, M, D*

Tennessee

Austin Peay State University *B, M*
Belmont University *B, T*
Bethel University *B, T*
Bryan University
  Dayton *B, T*
Carson-Newman University *B, T*
Christian Brothers University *B*
Cumberland University *B*
Dyersburg State Community
  College *A*
East Tennessee State
  University *B, M, T*
Fisk University *B, M*
Freed-Hardeman University *B, T*
Hiwassee College *A*
Jackson State Community College *A*
King University *B, T*
Lane College *B*
LeMoyne-Owen College *B*
Lee University *B*
Lincoln Memorial University *B, M, T*
Lipscomb University *B*
Martin Methodist College *B*

Maryville College *B, T*
Middle Tennessee State
  University *B, M*
Milligan College *B, T*
Rhodes College *B*
Sewanee: The University of the
  South *B*
South College *B*
Southern Adventist University *B*
Tennessee State University *B, M, D*
Tennessee Technological
  University *B, M, T*
Tennessee Temple University *B*
Tennessee Wesleyan College *B*
Trevecca Nazarene University *B*
Tusculum College *B, T*
Union University *B, T*
University of Memphis *B, M, D*
University of Tennessee
  Chattanooga *B*
  Knoxville *B*
  Martin *B*
Vanderbilt University *B, M, D*
Victory University *B*
Welch College *A*

Texas

Abilene Christian University *B*
Alvin Community College *A*
Amarillo College *A*
Angelina College *A*
Angelo State University *B, M, T*
Austin College *B*
Austin Community College *A*
Baylor University *B, M, D*
Blinn College *A*
Brazosport College *A*
Central Texas College *A*
Clarendon College *A*
Coastal Bend College *A*
College of the Mainland *A*
Concordia University Texas *B*
Dallas Baptist University *B*
Del Mar College *A*
East Texas Baptist University *B*
El Paso Community College *A*
Frank Phillips College *A*
Galveston College *A*
Grayson College *A*
Hardin-Simmons University *B*
Hill College *A*
Houston Baptist University *B*
Howard College *A*
Howard Payne University *B*
Huston-Tillotson University *B*
Jarvis Christian College *B, T*
Kilgore College *A*
Lamar State College at Orange *A*
Lamar University *B, M*
Laredo Community College *A*
LeTourneau University *B*
Lubbock Christian University *B*
McMurry University *B*
Midland College *A*
Midwestern State University *B, M*
Navarro College *A*
Northeast Texas Community
  College *A*
Northwest Vista College *A*
Odessa College *A*
Our Lady of the Lake University of
  San Antonio *B*
Palo Alto College *A*
Paris Junior College *A*
Paul Quinn College *B*
Prairie View A&M University *B, M*
Rice University *B, M, D*
St. Edward's University *B*
St. Mary's University *B*
St. Philip's College *A*
Sam Houston State University *B, M*
San Jacinto College *A*
Schreiner University *B*
South Plains College *A*
South Texas College *A*

Southern Methodist
  University *B, M, D*
Southwestern Adventist
  University *B, T*
Southwestern University *B, T*
Stephen F. Austin State
  University *B, M, T*
Sul Ross State University *B, M*
Tarleton State University *B, M*
Temple College *A*
Texarkana College *A*
Texas A&M International
  University *B, T*
Texas A&M University *B, M, D*
Texas A&M University
  Commerce *B, M*
  Corpus Christi *B, M, T*
  Galveston *B*
  Kingsville *B, M*
  Texarkana *B, T*
Texas Christian University *B, M*
Texas College *B*
Texas Lutheran University *B*
Texas Southern University *B, M*
Texas State Technical College
  Harlingen *A*
Texas State University *B, M, T*
Texas Tech University *B, M, D*
Texas Wesleyan University *B, T*
Texas Woman's University *B, M*
Trinity University *B*
Trinity Valley Community College *A*
Tyler Junior College *A*
University of Dallas *B*
University of Houston *B, M, D*
University of Houston
  Clear Lake *B, M*
  Downtown *B*
  Victoria *B*
University of North Texas *B, M, D*
University of St. Thomas *B*
University of Texas
  Arlington *B*
  Austin *B*
  Brownsville *B, M*
  Dallas *B*
  El Paso *B, M, D*
  Medical Branch at Galveston *M, D*
  Pan American *B, M*
  Permian Basin *B, M*
  San Antonio *B, M*
  Tyler *B, M*
University of the Incarnate
  Word *B, M*
Wayland Baptist University *B, T*
West Texas A&M University *B, M*
Western Texas College *A*
Wharton County Junior College *A*
Wiley College *B*

Utah

Dixie State College *B*
Salt Lake Community College *A*
Snow College *A*
Southern Utah University *B*
University of Utah *B, M, D, T*
Utah State University *B, M, D*
Utah Valley University *A, B*
Westminster College *B*

Vermont

Bennington College *B*
Castleton State College *B*
Green Mountain College *B*
Johnson State College *B*
Marlboro College *B*
Middlebury College *B*
Norwich University *B*
Saint Michael's College *B*
Southern Vermont College *B*
University of Vermont *B, M, D*

Virginia

Averett University *B*
Bluefield College *B*
Bridgewater College *B*
Christopher Newport University *B*
College of William and Mary *B, M*
Eastern Mennonite University *B*
Emory & Henry College *B, T*
Ferrum College *B*
George Mason University *B, M*
Germanna Community College *A*
Hampden-Sydney College *B*
Hampton University *B, M*
Hollins University *B*
James Madison University *B, M, T*
Liberty University *B, T*
Longwood University *B*
Lynchburg College *B*
Mary Baldwin College *B*
Marymount University *B*
Mountain Empire Community
  College *A*
Norfolk State University *B*
Old Dominion University *B, M*
Radford University *B*
Randolph College *B*
Randolph-Macon College *B*
Roanoke College *B, T*
Shenandoah University *B*
Southern Virginia University *B*
Sweet Briar College *B*
University of Mary Washington *B*
University of Richmond *B*
University of Virginia *B, M, D*
University of Virginia's College at
  Wise *B, T*
Virginia Commonwealth
  University *B, M*
Virginia Intermont College *B*
Virginia Military Institute *B*
Virginia Polytechnic Institute and
  State University *B, M, D*
Virginia State University *B, M*
Virginia Union University *B*
Virginia Wesleyan College *B*
Washington and Lee University *B*

Washington

Cascadia Community College *A*
Central Washington University *B, M*
Centralia College *A*
Eastern Washington University *B, M*
Edmonds Community College *A*
Evergreen State College *B*
Gonzaga University *B*
Heritage University *C, B*
Northwest University *B*
Pacific Lutheran University *B*
Pierce College *A*
Saint Martin's University *B*
Seattle Pacific University *B*
Seattle University *B*
South Seattle Community College *A*
Tacoma Community College *A*
University of Puget Sound *B, T*
University of Washington *B*
University of Washington Bothell *B*
Walla Walla University *B, M*
Washington State University *B, M*
Western Washington University *B, M*
Whitman College *B*
Whitworth University *B, T*

West Virginia

Alderson-Broaddus University *B*
Bethany College *B*
Concord University *B*
Davis and Elkins College *B*
Fairmont State University *B*
Glenville State College *B*
Marshall University *B, M*
Ohio Valley University *A, B*
Potomac State College of West
  Virginia University *A*

Shepherd University *B, T*
University of Charleston *B*
West Liberty University *B*
West Virginia State University *B*
West Virginia University *B, M, D, T*
West Virginia University Institute of
  Technology *B*
West Virginia Wesleyan College *B*
Wheeling Jesuit University *B*

Wisconsin

Alverno College *B*
Beloit College *B, T*
Cardinal Stritch University *B, T*
Carroll University *B*
Carthage College *B*
College of Menominee Nation *A*
Concordia University Wisconsin *B*
Edgewood College *B*
Lakeland College *B*
Lawrence University *B, T*
Maranatha Baptist Bible College *B*
Marian University *B*
Marquette University *B, M, D*
Mount Mary University *B, T*
Northland College *B*
Ripon College *B*
St. Norbert College *B, T*
Silver Lake College of the Holy
  Family *B, T*
University of Wisconsin
  Eau Claire *B*
  Green Bay *B*
  La Crosse *B, T*
  Madison *B*
  Milwaukee *B, M, D*
  Oshkosh *B*
  Parkside *B*
  Platteville *B, T*
  River Falls *B, T*
  Stevens Point *B, M*
  Superior *B, T*
  Whitewater *B, T*
Viterbo University *B, T*
Wisconsin Lutheran College *B*

Wyoming

Casper College *A*
Central Wyoming College *A*
Eastern Wyoming College *A*
Laramie County Community
  College *A*
Northwest College *A*
Sheridan College *A*
University of Wyoming *B*
Western Wyoming Community
  College *A*

Biology lab technology

Arizona

Pima Community College *C*

California

Berkeley City College *C, A*
California Lutheran University *B*
City College of San Francisco *C*
College of the Canyons *C*
De Anza College *C, A*
East Los Angeles College *C*
Foothill College *C, A*
MiraCosta College *C, A*
San Diego City College *A*
Santa Barbara City College *A*
Skyline College *A*
Solano Community College *C, A*

Connecticut

Quinnipiac University *B*
University of New Haven *B*

Delaware

Delaware State University *B*
Delaware Technical Community
   College
    Jack F. Owens Campus *A*
    Stanton/Wilmington Campus *A*

Florida

Hillsborough Community
   College *C, A*
Santa Fe College *A*

Georgia

Athens Technical College *A*
Atlanta Technical College *C, A*
Gwinnett Technical College *C, A*

Illinois

City Colleges of Chicago
   Harry S. Truman College *A*
Elgin Community College *A*

Indiana

Ball State University *D*
Brown Mackie College
   Fort Wayne *A*

Iowa

Ellsworth Community College *A*

Kansas

Cloud County Community
   College *C, A*
Hutchinson Community College *C, A*

Kentucky

Owensboro Community and
   Technical College *C, A*

Louisiana

Bossier Parish Community College *C*

Maine

Kennebec Valley Community
   College *A*

Maryland

Frederick Community College *A*
Hagerstown Community College *C, A*
Harford Community College *C*
Montgomery College *A*

Massachusetts

Massachusetts Bay Community
   College *A*
Middlesex Community College *C, A*
North Shore Community College *A*
Quincy College *A*

Michigan

Delta College *A*

Missouri

East Central College *A*

Nebraska

Southeast Community College *A*

New Jersey

County College of Morris *A*
Mercer County Community
   College *A*
Middlesex County College *A*
Passaic County Community College *A*

New York

Erie Community College *C*
Finger Lakes Community College *A*
Jamestown Community College *A*
Manhattan College *M*
Monroe Community College *A*
Niagara University *B*

SUNY

   College at Brockport *B*
   College of Agriculture and
    Technology at Cobleskill *A*
Tompkins Cortland Community
   College *C, A*

North Carolina

Beaufort County Community
   College *A*
Central Carolina Community
   College *A*
Cleveland Community College *C, A*
Forsyth Technical Community
   College *A*
Pitt Community College *A*
Southeastern Community
   College *C, A*
Vance-Granville Community
   College *A*
Wayne Community College *A*
Wilson Community College *A*

Ohio

Cleveland State University *B*
Columbus State Community
   College *C*
Lakeland Community College *A*
Ohio State University
   Columbus Campus *C*
Sinclair Community College *A*
University of Cincinnati
   Blue Ash College *A*
Washington State Community
   College *A*

Pennsylvania

Bucks County Community College *A*
Harrisburg University of Science and
   Technology *B*
Lackawanna College *A*
Luzerne County Community
   College *A*
Montgomery County Community
   College *A*
Northampton Community College *C*
Penn State
   Abington *B*
   Altoona *B*
   Beaver *B*
   Berks *B*
   Brandywine *B*
   DuBois *B*
   Erie, The Behrend College *B*
   Fayette, The Eberly Campus *B*
   Greater Allegheny *B*
   Harrisburg *B*
   Hazleton *B*
   Lehigh Valley *B*
   Mont Alto *B*
   New Kensington *B*
   Schuylkill *B*
   Shenango *B*
   University Park *B*
   Wilkes-Barre *B*
   Worthington Scranton *B*
   York *B*
Thomas Jefferson University *B*
Westmoreland County Community
   College *A*

Puerto Rico

Turabo University *C*

Texas

Austin Community College *C, A*
Collin County Community College
   District *C*
El Centro College *C, A*
Houston Community College
   System *C, A*
Lone Star College System *C, A*
Mountain View College *C, A*
Northwest Vista College *A*

Temple College *C, A*
Texas State Technical College
   Waco *A*

Utah

Salt Lake Community College *A*
Weber State University *C, A*

Virginia

Piedmont Virginia Community
   College *C, A*

Washington

Bates Technical College *C, A*
Shoreline Community College *C, A*

Wisconsin

Blackhawk Technical College *C*
Fox Valley Technical College *A*
Madison Area Technical College *A*
Mid-State Technical College *A*
University of Wisconsin
   Milwaukee *C*

Biology teacher education

Alabama

Auburn University *M, T*
Birmingham-Southern College *T*
Faulkner University *B, M, T*
Huntingdon College *B, T*
Oakwood University *B*
Spring Hill College *B, T*
Talladega College *B*
Tuskegee University *B*
University of Mobile *B, T*

Arizona

Arizona Christian University *B*
Grand Canyon University *B*

Arkansas

Arkansas State University *B, M, T*
Arkansas Tech University *B*
Harding University *B, T*
Ouachita Baptist University *B, T*
University of Arkansas
   Fort Smith *B*
University of the Ozarks *B, T*

California

California Polytechnic State
   University: San Luis Obispo *T*
California State University
   Chico *T*
   Long Beach *T*
   San Bernardino *T*
Fresno Pacific University *B*
Humboldt State University *T*
Master's College *T*
Point Loma Nazarene University *M*
San Diego State University *T*
San Francisco State University *T*
Stanford University *M, T*
University of California
   Irvine *B, M*
University of San Diego *T*
Vanguard University of Southern
   California *T*

Colorado

Adams State University *B, T*
Colorado State University *B, T*
Colorado State University
   Pueblo *T*

Connecticut

Albertus Magnus College *B, T*
Fairfield University *T*
Quinnipiac University *B, M*
Sacred Heart University *T*

University of Connecticut *T*
University of Saint Joseph *T*

Delaware

Delaware State University *B, M*
University of Delaware *B, T*

Florida

Barry University *T*
Bethune-Cookman University *B, T*
Clearwater Christian College *B*
Daytona State College *B*
Florida Institute of Technology *B*
Palm Beach Atlantic University *B, T*
St. Petersburg College *B*
Southeastern University *B, T*
Stetson University *B*
University of Miami *M*

Georgia

Columbus State University *B*
Kennesaw State University *B*
Middle Georgia State College *B*
Paine College *B*
Piedmont College *B, M, T*
Reinhardt University *B*
Southern Polytechnic State
   University *B*

Hawaii

Brigham Young University-
   Hawaii *B, T*

Idaho

Boise State University *B, T*
Brigham Young University-Idaho *B, T*
Northwest Nazarene University *B*
University of Idaho *T*

Illinois

Augustana College *B, T*
Benedictine University *T*
Blackburn College *B, T*
Bradley University *B*
Chicago State University *B, T*
Concordia University Chicago *B, T*
DePaul University *M, T*
Dominican University *T*
Elmhurst College *B*
Eureka College *T*
Governors State University *B, T*
Greenville College *B, T*
Illinois College *T*
Illinois Wesleyan University *B*
Knox College *T*
MacMurray College *B, T*
McKendree University *B*
Millikin University *B, T*
North Park University *T*
Olivet Nazarene University *B, T*
Rockford University *T*
Saint Xavier University *B*
Trinity Christian College *B, T*
Trinity International University *B, T*
University of Illinois
   Chicago *B*
   Urbana-Champaign *B, M, T*

Indiana

Anderson University *B, T*
Bethel College *B*
Butler University *T*
Franklin College *B, T*
Goshen College *B, T*
Huntington University *D, M*
Indiana University
   Bloomington *B, T*
   Northwest *B*
   Purdue University Fort Wayne *B, T*
   South Bend *B, T*
   Southeast *B*
Indiana Wesleyan University *T*
Manchester University *B, T*
Oakland City University *B*

Purdue University *B, M, D*
Saint Mary's College *T*
St. Mary-of-the-Woods College *B, T*
University of Evansville *B, T*
University of Indianapolis *B, T*
University of St. Francis *B*
Valparaiso University *B*

Iowa

Briar Cliff University *B*
Buena Vista University *B, T*
Central College *T*
Cornell College *B, T*
Dordt College *B*
Drake University *M*
Ellsworth Community College *A*
Graceland University *T*
Grand View University *T*
Iowa State University *T*
Iowa Wesleyan College *B*
Loras College *T*
Maharishi University of
    Management *T*
Morningside College *B*
Mount Mercy University *T*
Northwestern College *B, T*
St. Ambrose University *B, T*
Simpson College *T*
University of Dubuque *B, T*
University of Iowa *T*
Upper Iowa University *B, T*
Wartburg College *T*

Kansas

Benedictine College *B*
Bethany College *B*
Bethel College *T*
Independence Community College *A*
McPherson College *B, T*
MidAmerica Nazarene University *B, T*
Pittsburg State University *B*
Sterling College *T*
Tabor College *B*
University of St. Mary *T*
Washburn University *B, T*

Kentucky

Alice Lloyd College *B*
Campbellsville University *B*
Eastern Kentucky University *B*
Kentucky Wesleyan College *B, T*
Lindsey Wilson College *B, T*
Midway College *M*

Louisiana

Centenary College of Louisiana *T*
Grambling State University *B*
Louisiana State University
    Shreveport *B*
McNeese State University *T*
Southeastern Louisiana University *B*
University of Louisiana at Lafayette *B*
University of Louisiana at Monroe *B*
Xavier University of Louisiana *B*

Maine

College of the Atlantic *T*
Husson University *B, T*
Saint Joseph's College of Maine *B*
University of Maine *B*
University of Maine
    Farmington *B, T*
    Machias *T*
University of Southern Maine *T*

Maryland

Coppin State University *B, T*
Hood College *T*
Mount St. Mary's University *T*
Notre Dame of Maryland
    University *T*

Massachusetts

Assumption College *T*
Bridgewater State University *B, M, T*
Eastern Nazarene College *B*
Elms College *T*
Fitchburg State University *B, M, T*
Framingham State University *M*
Merrimack College *B*
Salem State University *M*
Tufts University *T*
University of Massachusetts
    Dartmouth *T*
Western New England
    University *B, T*
Westfield State University *M, T*
Worcester State University *T*

Michigan

Adrian College *B, T*
Alma College *T*
Andrews University *M*
Aquinas College *B, T*
Calvin College *B*
Central Michigan University *B*
Concordia University *B, T*
Cornerstone University *B, T*
Eastern Michigan University *B, M*
Ferris State University *B*
Grand Valley State University *M, T*
Hope College *B, T*
Madonna University *B*
Michigan State University *B*
Michigan Technological University *T*
Northern Michigan University *B, T*
Spring Arbor University *B*
University of Detroit Mercy *B, M, T*
Western Michigan University *B, D*

Minnesota

Augsburg College *B, T*
Bethel University *B*
College of St. Scholastica *T*
Concordia College: Moorhead *B, T*
Concordia University St. Paul *B, T*
Gustavus Adolphus College *T*
Hamline University *T*
Metropolitan State University *B*
Minnesota State University
    Mankato *B, T*
    Moorhead *B*
St. Catherine University *T*
Saint Cloud State University *B, M, T*
St. Mary's University of Minnesota *B*
Southwest Minnesota State
    University *B, T*
University of Minnesota
    Morris *T*
    Twin Cities *B, M*
Winona State University *B, T*

Mississippi

Blue Mountain College *B*
Itawamba Community College *A*
Millsaps College *T*
Mississippi College *B, M*
Rust College *B*
William Carey University *B*

Missouri

Avila University *T*
Central Methodist University *B*
College of the Ozarks *B, T*
Lincoln University *B*
Lindenwood University *B*
Maryville University of Saint
    Louis *M, T*
Missouri Baptist University *T*
Missouri Southern State
    University *B, T*
Missouri State University *B*
Missouri Valley College *T*
Northwest Missouri State
    University *B, T*
Park University *T*

Southwest Baptist University *B, T*
University of Central Missouri *B, T*
University of Missouri
    Columbia *B*
    Kansas City *B*
Washington University in St.
    Louis *B, M*
William Jewell College *B, T*
William Woods University *T*

Montana

Carroll College *B*
Montana State University
    Billings *B, T*
Rocky Mountain College *B*
University of Great Falls *B*
University of Montana *B, M, T*
University of Montana: Western *B, T*

Nebraska

Chadron State College *B*
College of Saint Mary *B, T*
Concordia University *B, T*
Creighton University *T*
Hastings College *B, M, T*
Midland University *B, T*
Nebraska Wesleyan University *T*
Union College *B*
University of Nebraska
    Kearney *B, M, T*
    Lincoln *B, T*
Wayne State College *B, T*
York College *B, T*

Nevada

Great Basin College *B*
Nevada State College *B*

New Hampshire

Franklin Pierce University *M, T*
Keene State College *B, T*
New England College *B, T*
Rivier University *B, T*
Saint Anselm College *T*
University of New Hampshire *T*

New Jersey

College of New Jersey *B, T*
County College of Morris *A*
Georgian Court University *T*
Saint Peter's University *T*
William Paterson University of New
    Jersey *T*

New Mexico

New Mexico Highlands University *B*
New Mexico Institute of Mining and
    Technology *M*
Western New Mexico University *B*

New York

Adelphi University *M, T*
Alfred University *B, T*
City University of New York
    Brooklyn College *B, M*
    City College *B*
    College of Staten Island *B, M*
    Hunter College *B, M, T*
    Lehman College *M*
    Queens College *M, T*
Colgate University *M*
College of Mount St. Vincent *T*
College of Saint Rose *B, T*
Cornell University *M, T*
D'Youville College *M, T*
Dominican College of Blauvelt *B, T*
Dowling College *B, M*
Dutchess Community College *A*
Elmira College *B, T*
Fordham University *M, T*
Hobart and William Smith Colleges *T*
Hofstra University *B, M*
Houghton College *B, T*
Iona College *B, M, T*

Ithaca College *B, M, T*
Keuka College *B, T*
Le Moyne College *T*
Long Island University
    LIU Brooklyn *B, M, T*
    LIU Post *B, M, T*
Manhattan College *B, T*
Marist College *T*
Medaille College *B, M, T*
Medaille College: Amherst *M*
Molloy College *B, M*
Nazareth College *B, M, T*
New York University *B, M*
Niagara University *B, M, T*
Pace University *B, M, T*
Pace University: Pleasantville/
    Briarcliff *B, M, T*
Roberts Wesleyan College *B, M*
SUNY
    College at Brockport *B, M, T*
    College at Buffalo *B, M*
    College at Cortland *B, M*
    College at Fredonia *B, M, T*
    College at Geneseo *B, M, T*
    College at New Paltz *B, M, T*
    College at Old Westbury *B, M, T*
    College at Oneonta *B, T*
    College at Oswego *B, M*
    College at Plattsburgh *B*
    College at Potsdam *B, M*
    College of Environmental Science
        and Forestry *B, T*
    University at Albany *M, T*
    University at Binghamton *M*
    University at Buffalo *M, T*
    University at Stony Brook *T*
St. Francis College *B*
St. John Fisher College *B, M, T*
St. John's University *B, M, T*
St. Joseph's College New York:
    Suffolk Campus *B*
St. Joseph's College, New York *B*
St. Lawrence University *T*
St. Thomas Aquinas College *B, M, T*
Syracuse University *B, M, T*
Ulster County Community College *A*
University of Rochester *M*
Vassar College *T*
Wagner College *T*
Wells College *T*

North Carolina

Appalachian State University *T*
Campbell University *B, T*
Elizabeth City State University *B, T*
Gardner-Webb University *B*
Greensboro College *B, T*
Lenoir-Rhyne University *B*
Mars Hill University *T*
Meredith College *T*
Methodist University *A, B, T*
North Carolina Agricultural and
    Technical State University *B, T*
North Carolina Central
    University *B, M, T*
Sandhills Community College *A*
University of North Carolina
    Greensboro *B*
    Wilmington *T*
Wake Forest University *T*
Western Carolina University *M, T*
Wingate University *B, T*

North Dakota

Dickinson State University *B, T*
Mayville State University *B, T*
Minot State University *B*
North Dakota State University *B, T*
University of Jamestown *B*
University of Mary *B*
Valley City State University *B, T*

Ohio

Antioch University
  Midwest *M*
Ashland University *B, T*
Baldwin Wallace University *T*
Bluffton University *B*
Bowling Green State
  University *B, M, T*
Case Western Reserve University *T*
Cedarville University *B*
Defiance College *B, T*
Hiram College *T*
John Carroll University *T*
Miami University
  Oxford *B, M, T*
Mount Vernon Nazarene
  University *B, T*
Ohio Dominican University *B, T*
Ohio Northern University *B, T*
Ohio Wesleyan University *B*
Otterbein University *B*
University of Findlay *B, M, T*
University of Mount Union *T*
University of Rio Grande *B, T*
University of Toledo *M, T*
Urbana University *B*
Wilmington College *B*
Xavier University *B*
Youngstown State University *B, M*

Oklahoma

East Central University *B, T*
Eastern Oklahoma State College *A*
Oklahoma Baptist University *B, T*
University of Central Oklahoma *B*
University of Tulsa *T*

Oregon

Concordia University *B, M, T*
Corban University *B*
Linfield College *T*
Portland State University *T*
Southern Oregon University *T*
Western Oregon University *B, M, T*

Pennsylvania

Albright College *T*
Alvernia University *B*
Arcadia University *B, M, T*
Bucks County Community College *A*
Cabrini College *T*
Chatham University *M, T*
DeSales University *T*
Duquesne University *M, T*
Geneva College *T*
Gettysburg College *T*
Grove City College *B, T*
Holy Family University *B*
Juniata College *B, T*
King's College *T*
La Salle University *B, T*
Lebanon Valley College *T*
Lycoming College *T*
Mansfield University of
  Pennsylvania *B, T*
Marywood University *B*
Mercyhurst University *B, T*
Messiah College *B, T*
Misericordia University *B, T*
Moravian College *T*
Point Park University *B*
St. Francis University *B, T*
Saint Joseph's University *M, T*
St. Vincent College *T*
Seton Hill University *B, T*
Susquehanna University *T*
Thiel College *B*
University of Pittsburgh
  Greensburg *B, T*
  Johnstown *B, T*
University of Scranton *B*
Villanova University *T*
Washington & Jefferson College *T*
Waynesburg University *B, T*

Westminster College *T*
Widener University *T*
Wilkes University *M, T*
Wilson College *T*
York College of Pennsylvania *B, T*

Puerto Rico

Inter American University of Puerto
  Rico
  Aguadilla Campus *B*
  Arecibo Campus *B*
  Barranquitas Campus *B*
  Fajardo Campus *B, T*
  Ponce Campus *B, T*
  San German Campus *B*
Pontifical Catholic University of
  Puerto Rico *B, T*
Turabo University *B*

Rhode Island

Bryant University *M*
Rhode Island College *B*

South Carolina

Coker College *B, T*
Furman University *T*
Morris College *B, T*
Southern Wesleyan University *B, T*
Wofford College *T*

South Dakota

Augustana College *B, T*
Dakota State University *B, T*
Dakota Wesleyan University *B, T*
Mount Marty College *B*
University of Sioux Falls *T*
University of South Dakota *B, M, T*

Tennessee

Belmont University *T*
Bryan University
  Dayton *T*
Cumberland University *B, T*
Freed-Hardeman University *B, T*
King University *T*
Lee University *B*
Lincoln Memorial University *B, T*
Lipscomb University *B, T*
Martin Methodist College *B*
Maryville College *B, T*
Middle Tennessee State
  University *B, T*
Southern Adventist University *B*
Tennessee Technological University *T*
Tennessee Temple University *B*
Trevecca Nazarene University *B, T*
Tusculum College *B, T*
Union University *B, T*
Victory University *B, T*

Texas

Abilene Christian University *B, T*
East Texas Baptist University *B*
Houston Baptist University *T*
Howard Payne University *B*
Jarvis Christian College *B, T*
Kilgore College *A*
Lamar University *T*
Laredo Community College *A*
Lubbock Christian University *B*
McMurry University *B, T*
Our Lady of the Lake University of
  San Antonio *B*
St. Edward's University *B, T*
St. Mary's University *T*
Sam Houston State University *M, T*
Schreiner University *B*
Tarleton State University *T*
Texas A&M International
  University *B, T*
Texas A&M University
  Kingsville *T*
Texas College *B, T*
Texas State University *M, T*

Texas Wesleyan University *B, T*
University of Dallas *T*
University of Mary Hardin-Baylor *T*
University of Texas
  Arlington *T*
  San Antonio *T*
West Texas A&M University *T*

Utah

Brigham Young University *B*
Dixie State College *B*
Southern Utah University *B*
Utah State University *B*
Utah Valley University *B*
Weber State University *B*
Western Governors
  University *B, M, T*

Vermont

Castleton State College *B, T*
Green Mountain College *B, T*
Johnson State College *B*
Saint Michael's College *M, T*

Virginia

Averett University *B, M, T*
Bluefield College *B, T*
Bridgewater College *T*
Eastern Mennonite University *T*
Emory & Henry College *B*
Hampton University *M*
Hollins University *T*
Longwood University *T*
Radford University *T*
University of Virginia's College at
  Wise *T*
Virginia Intermont College *T*

Washington

Central Washington University *B, T*
Eastern Washington University *B*
Heritage University *B, M*
Northwest University *T*
University of Washington *M, T*
Washington State University *B, M, T*
Western Washington University *B*
Whitworth University *B, T*

West Virginia

Bethany College *B*
Concord University *B, M, T*
Shepherd University *T*
University of Charleston *B*
West Liberty University *B*
West Virginia Wesleyan College *B*
Wheeling Jesuit University *B*

Wisconsin

Carroll University *B, T*
Carthage College *T*
Concordia University Wisconsin *B*
Edgewood College *B*
Lakeland College *T*
Lawrence University *T*
Maranatha Baptist Bible College *B*
Marquette University *B*
Mount Mary University *B, T*
St. Norbert College *T*
University of Wisconsin
  Green Bay *T*
  Platteville *B*
  River Falls *T*
  Superior *B, T*
  Whitewater *B*
Viterbo University *B, T*

Biomedical sciences

Alabama

Auburn University *B, M, D*
Oakwood University *B*
Troy University *B*

University of Alabama
  Birmingham *M*
University of South Alabama *B*

Arizona

Northern Arizona University *B*

California

California State University
  East Bay *B*
Cerritos College *A*
College of San Mateo *A*
La Sierra University *B*
Loma Linda University *D*
San Francisco State University *M*
University of California
  Riverside *M, D*
  San Diego *M, D*

Colorado

Colorado State University *B, D*
Community College of Denver *A*
University of Colorado
  Denver *B, M*
University of Northern Colorado *M*

Connecticut

Quinnipiac University *B*
University of Connecticut *M, D*

District of Columbia

George Washington University *B*
Georgetown University *B, M, D*

Florida

Barry University *M*
Florida Atlantic University *M*
Florida Institute of Technology *B*
Florida International University *D*
Florida State College at
  Jacksonville *A, B*
Florida State University *D*
Nova Southeastern University *M*
University of Central Florida *B, M, D*
University of Miami *D*
University of South Florida *B*

Georgia

Darton College *A*
Emory University *D*

Hawaii

University of Hawaii
  Manoa *M, D*

Idaho

Stevens-Henager College
  Boise *B*

Illinois

Chicago State University *M*
Loyola University Chicago *M, D*
National University of Health
  Sciences *B*
South Suburban College of Cook
  County *A*

Iowa

University of Iowa *D*
University of Northern Iowa *B*

Kentucky

Spencerian College: Lexington *A*
University of Louisville *D*

Louisiana

Our Lady of the Lake College *B*

Maine

University of Maine *D*

Maryland

Hood College *M*

Massachusetts

Bay Path College *B*
Benjamin Franklin Institute of
    Technology *A*
Fitchburg State University *B*
Northeastern University *D*
University of Massachusetts
    Boston *M*
    Lowell *M, D*
Worcester Polytechnic Institute *M, D*

Michigan

Central Michigan University *B*
University of Michigan
    Flint *B, M*
Western Michigan University *B*

Minnesota

Rochester Community and Technical
    College *A*
University of Minnesota
    Duluth *B*

Mississippi

Mississippi College *B, M*

Missouri

Maryville University of Saint Louis *B*
Saint Louis University *D*
Washington University in St. Louis *M*

Montana

Fort Peck Community College *A*

Nebraska

Creighton University *M, D*
University of Nebraska
    Lincoln *D*

New Hampshire

University of New Hampshire *B*

New Jersey

Cumberland County College *A*
Rutgers, The State University of New
    Jersey
    Camden Campus *B*

New York

City University of New York
    Borough of Manhattan Community
        College *A*
Marist College *B*
Rochester Institute of Technology *B*
SUNY
    College at Cortland *B*
    University at Albany *M, D*
    University at Buffalo *B*
    University at Stony Brook *M*
St. Francis College *B*
University of Rochester *D*

North Carolina

East Carolina University *D*
North Carolina Wesleyan College *B*
St. Augustine's University *B*

Ohio

Hiram College *B*
Ohio State University
    Columbus Campus *B, D*
University of Akron *T*
University of Toledo *M*

Oklahoma

Oklahoma City University *B*
St. Gregory's University *B*

Oregon

Eastern Oregon University *B*

Pennsylvania

Drexel University *M, D*
Penn State
    University Park *M, D*
Slippery Rock University of
    Pennsylvania *B*
Temple University *M, D*
University of Pennsylvania *B, M, D*

Puerto Rico

Inter American University of Puerto
    Rico
    Metropolitan Campus *B*
    Ponce Campus *B*

South Carolina

Clemson University *B*
Medical University of South
    Carolina *M*
University of South Carolina
    Columbia *M, D*

South Dakota

Southeast Technical Institute *A*
University of South Dakota *B*

Tennessee

Christian Brothers University *B*
East Tennessee State University *M, D*

Texas

Baylor University *M, D*
Lubbock Christian University *B*
McMurry University *B*
Northeast Texas Community
    College *A*
Tarleton State University *B*
Texas A&M University *B, M, D*
Texas A&M University
    Baylor College of Dentistry *M, D*
    Corpus Christi *B*
    Galveston *B*
Texas Tech University Health
    Sciences Center *M, D*
University of Mary Hardin-Baylor *B, T*
University of Texas
    Austin *D*
    Medical Branch at Galveston *D*
    San Antonio *D*

Virginia

George Mason University *M*
Jefferson College of Health
    Sciences *B*
Liberty University *B*
Lynchburg College *B*
Old Dominion University *D*
Virginia Commonwealth
    University *M, D*

Washington

Washington State University *B*

West Virginia

Marshall University *M, D*
West Virginia University *M*

Wisconsin

Marquette University *B*

Wyoming

University of Wyoming *M, D*

Biomedical technology

Arizona

Brown Mackie College
    Tucson *A*
DeVry University
    Phoenix *B*

Arkansas

North Arkansas College *A*
Phillips Community College of the
    University of Arkansas *C, A*

California

American River College *C, A*
City College of San Francisco *C*
College of the Canyons *C*
DeVry University
    Pomona *B*
East Los Angeles College *C*
Foothill College *C, A*
Los Angeles City College *C, A*
Napa Valley College *C, A*
San Francisco State University *C*
Santa Barbara City College *C, A*

Colorado

Aims Community College *A*

Connecticut

Gateway Community College *A*
Quinebaug Valley Community
    College *A*

Delaware

Delaware Technical Community
    College
    Terry Campus *A*

Florida

DeVry University
    Miramar *B*
    Orlando *B*
Florida Gateway College *A*
Florida State College at
    Jacksonville *A*
Keiser University *A*
Santa Fe College *A*
South Florida State College *A*

Illinois

DeVry University
    Chicago *B*
Illinois Institute of Technology *M*

Indiana

Indiana University
    Purdue University
        Indianapolis *A, B*

Iowa

Western Iowa Tech Community
    College *C*

Louisiana

Delgado Community College *A*

Maryland

Frederick Community College *A*
Montgomery College *A*

Massachusetts

Benjamin Franklin Institute of
    Technology *A*
Northern Essex Community
    College *C, A*
Quinsigamond Community
    College *C, A*

Michigan

Schoolcraft College *C, A*

Minnesota

Anoka-Ramsey Community
    College *C, A*
Dakota County Technical
    College *C, A*
Minnesota State College - Southeast
    Technical *C, A*

St. Cloud Technical and Community
    College *A*
St. Paul College *A*

Missouri

Moberly Area Community College *A*
Ozarks Technical Community
    College *A*

New Jersey

DeVry University
    North Brunswick *B*
Thomas Edison State College *A, B*

New Mexico

New Mexico State University
    Alamogordo *A*

New York

DeVry College of New York
    Midtown Campus *B*

North Carolina

Central Carolina Community
    College *C, A*
Gaston College *C, A*
Rowan-Cabarrus Community
    College *A*
Stanly Community College *A*

Ohio

Cincinnati State Technical and
    Community College *A*
DeVry University
    Columbus *B*
Owens Community College
    Toledo *C, A*

Pennsylvania

Community College of
    Philadelphia *A*
DeVry University
    Fort Washington *B*
Johnson College *A*
Penn State
    Altoona *A*
    Berks *A*
    DuBois *A*
    Erie, The Behrend College *A*
    Fayette, The Eberly Campus *A*
    Hazleton *A*
    New Kensington *A*
    Schuylkill *A*
    Shenango *A*
    York *A*

South Dakota

Southeast Technical Institute *A*

Texas

DeVry University
    Irving *B*
Palo Alto College *C*
St. Philip's College *A*
Texas State Technical College
    Harlingen *A*
    Waco *A*

Washington

Bates Technical College *A*
Bellingham Technical College *A*
North Seattle Community College *A*

Wisconsin

Herzing University
    Madison *A*
Milwaukee Area Technical College *A*
Waukesha County Technical
    College *A*
Western Technical College *A*

Biometrics

California
La Sierra University *B*

Minnesota
University of Minnesota
Twin Cities *B, M, D*

New Jersey
Rutgers, The State University of New
Jersey
New Brunswick/Piscataway
Campus *B*

New York
Cornell University *B, M, D*
SUNY
University at Albany *M, D*
Yeshiva University *M*

North Carolina
Duke University *M*
East Carolina University *D*
North Carolina State University *M, D*

Ohio
Kent State University *M, D*

Pennsylvania
Carnegie Mellon University *B, M, D*

Texas
University of Texas
Health Science Center at
Houston *M, D*

Virginia
George Mason University *M, D*

Wisconsin
University of Wisconsin
Madison *M*

Biophysics

Arizona
Arizona State University *B*

California
La Sierra University *B*
Pacific Union College *B*
Pitzer College *B*
Stanford University *M, D*
University of California
Berkeley *D*
Davis *D*
Los Angeles *B, M, D*
San Diego *B, M, D*
University of San Diego *B*
University of Southern California *B*

Connecticut
University of Connecticut *B, M, D*

District of Columbia
George Washington University *B*
Georgetown University *B*

Illinois
Illinois Institute of
Technology *B, M, D*
Loyola University Chicago *B*
University of Chicago *D*
University of Illinois
Urbana-Champaign *B, M, D*

Indiana
Indiana University
Purdue University
Indianapolis *M, D*

University of Notre Dame *M, D*
University of Southern Indiana *B, T*

Iowa
Iowa State University *B, M, D*

Louisiana
Centenary College of Louisiana *B*

Maryland
Johns Hopkins University *B, M, D*
University of Maryland
College Park *M, D*

Massachusetts
Boston University *M, D*
Brandeis University *B, M, D*
Harvard College *D*
Northeastern University *B*
Tufts University *D*

Michigan
Andrews University *B*
Oakland University *B, D*
University of Michigan *B, D*

Minnesota
University of Minnesota
Twin Cities *M, D*

Missouri
Missouri University of Science and
Technology *B*
Washington University in St.
Louis *B, D*

New Jersey
New Jersey Institute of Technology *B*

New York
Barnard College *B*
City University of New York
Hunter College *B, M*
Columbia University *B*
Columbia University
School of General Studies *B*
Cornell University *M, D*
SUNY
College at Geneseo *B*
University at Albany *D*
University at Buffalo *B, M, D*
St. Lawrence University *B*
Syracuse University *D*
University of Rochester *M, D*

North Carolina
East Carolina University *D*
Elon University *B*
Forsyth Technical Community
College *A*

Ohio
Case Western Reserve University *D*
Miami University
Oxford *B*
Ohio State University
Columbus Campus *M, D*

Oklahoma
Southwestern Oklahoma State
University *B*

Pennsylvania
Carnegie Mellon University *D, D*
Temple University *B*
University of Pennsylvania *B, D*
University of Scranton *B*
Washington & Jefferson College *B*
Westminster College *B*

Rhode Island
Brown University *B, M, D*

Tennessee
King University *B*
Southern Adventist University *B*

Texas
St. Mary's University *B*
Texas Christian University *D*
University of Texas
El Paso *M*
Health Science Center at
Houston *M, D*

Utah
Brigham Young University *B*

Virginia
Hampden-Sydney College *B*
Regent University *B*
University of Virginia *D*

Washington
University of Washington *M, D*
Walla Walla University *B*
Whitworth University *B*

Wisconsin
University of Wisconsin
Madison *M, D*

Biopsychology

Alabama
Spring Hill College *B*

California
Holy Names University *B*
Mills College *B, M*
St. Mary's College of California *B*
University of California
Santa Barbara *B*

Georgia
Oglethorpe University *B*

Illinois
Monmouth College *B*
University of Chicago *D*

Iowa
Morningside College *B*

Maryland
Notre Dame of Maryland
University *B*

Michigan
Grand Valley State University *B*

Missouri
Northwest Missouri State
University *B*
Washington University in St. Louis *B*

Nebraska
Hastings College *B*

New Jersey
Rider University *B*

New York
SUNY
University at Albany *D*

Oregon
Warner Pacific College *B*

Pennsylvania
Arcadia University *B*
Carnegie Mellon University *B*
Immaculata University *B*
Messiah College *B*

Philadelphia University *B*
Westminster College *B*

Wisconsin
Ripon College *B*

Biostatistics

Alabama
University of Alabama
Birmingham *M, D*

Arizona
University of Arizona *M, D*

California
California State University
East Bay *M*
Loma Linda University *M*
National University *B*
University of California
Berkeley *M, D*
Davis *M, D*
Los Angeles *M, D*
University of Southern
California *M, D*

Colorado
University of Colorado
Denver *M, D*

Connecticut
Yale University *M*

District of Columbia
George Washington University *D*
Georgetown University *M*

Florida
Florida State University *M, D*
University of Florida *M, D*
University of Miami *M, D*

Georgia
Emory University *D*
Georgia Regents University *M, D*

Illinois
Northwestern University *M*

Indiana
Indiana University
Purdue University Indianapolis *D*

Iowa
University of Iowa *M, D*

Kansas
University of Kansas Medical
Center *M, D*

Kentucky
University of Louisville *M, D*

Louisiana
Louisiana State University
Health Sciences Center *M, D*
Tulane University *M, D*

Massachusetts
Boston University *M, D*
Emmanuel College *B*
Harvard College *M, D*
Simmons College *B*

Michigan
University of Michigan *M, D*

Minnesota
University of Minnesota
Twin Cities *B, M, D*

Missouri

Saint Louis University *M*
Washington University in St. Louis *M*

New Jersey

New Jersey Institute of
   Technology *M*
Rutgers, The State University of New
   Jersey
   New Brunswick/Piscataway
      Campus *M*
   Newark Campus *M*

New York

SUNY
   University at Albany *M, D*
   University at Buffalo *B, M, D*
University of Rochester *M*

North Carolina

University of North Carolina
   Chapel Hill *B, M, D*

Ohio

Case Western Reserve
   University *M, D*
Ohio State University
   Columbus Campus *D*
University of Cincinnati *M, D*

Oklahoma

University of Oklahoma *M, D*

Oregon

Oregon Health & Science
   University *M*

Pennsylvania

Drexel University *M*
University of Pennsylvania *M, D*
University of Pittsburgh *M, D*

Puerto Rico

University of Puerto Rico
   Medical Sciences *M*

South Carolina

Medical University of South
   Carolina *D*
University of South Carolina
   Columbia *M, D*

Tennessee

Vanderbilt University *M, D*

Texas

Southwestern Adventist University *B*

Utah

Brigham Young University *B*
University of Utah *M*

Vermont

University of Vermont *M*

Virginia

George Mason University *M*
Virginia Commonwealth
   University *M, D*

Washington

University of Washington *M, D*

Biotechnology

Alabama

University of Alabama
   Huntsville *D*

Arizona

Glendale Community College *A*
Mesa Community College *A*
University of Arizona *M*

Arkansas

Central Baptist College *B*

California

Berkeley City College *C, A*
California State Polytechnic
   University: Pomona *B, M*
California State University
   Channel Islands *B, M*
   Fresno *M*
   Fullerton *M*
   San Marcos *B*
College of San Mateo *C, A*
Contra Costa College *A*
Foothill College *A*
MiraCosta College *C, A*
Moorpark College *C, A*
Southwestern College *A*
University of California
   Davis *B*
   Irvine *M*
   San Diego *B*

Connecticut

Middlesex Community College *A*
Quinnipiac University *B*
University of Connecticut *M*

Delaware

Delaware State University *B, M*
University of Delaware *B*

District of Columbia

American University *M*
Georgetown University *M*

Florida

Florida Atlantic University *M*
Florida Gulf Coast University *B*
Florida Institute of Technology *M*
Miami Dade College *A*
State College of Florida, Manatee-
   Sarasota *A*
University of Central Florida *B, M*
University of South Florida *M*

Georgia

Athens Technical College *A*
Georgia Regents University *M, D*
Kennesaw State University *B*
University of Georgia *B, M*

Illinois

City Colleges of Chicago
   Harold Washington College *C*
Northwestern University *M*
Roosevelt University *M*
Southern Illinois University
   Edwardsville *M*
University of Illinois
   Chicago *M*
   Urbana-Champaign *B, M, D*

Indiana

Indiana University
   Bloomington *B, M*
   East *B*
Purdue University
   Indianapolis *C, B*
Ivy Tech Community College
   Bloomington *A*
   Central Indiana *A*
   Lafayette *A*
   North Central *A*
   Southwest *A*
   Wabash Valley *A*
Vincennes University *A*

Iowa

Des Moines Area Community
   College *A*
Ellsworth Community College *A*
Grand View University *B*
Kirkwood Community College *A*
University of Northern Iowa *M*
Western Iowa Tech Community
   College *A*

Kentucky

Bluegrass Community and Technical
   College *C*
University of Kentucky *B*

Maine

Southern Maine Community
   College *A*
University of Southern Maine *B*

Maryland

Baltimore City Community College *A*
Cecil College *C*
Howard Community College *A*
Johns Hopkins University *M*
Mount St. Mary's University *M*
Stevenson University *B*
University of Maryland
   University College *B, M*

Massachusetts

Assumption College *B*
Bay Path College *B*
Bristol Community College *C*
Endicott College *B*
Fitchburg State University *B*
Massachusetts College of Liberal
   Arts *B*
Massasoit Community College *C*
Middlesex Community College *A*
Mount Wachusett Community
   College *A*
Northeastern University *M*
Quinsigamond Community College *A*
Springfield Technical Community
   College *C, A*
University of Massachusetts
   Amherst *C*
   Boston *M*
Worcester Polytechnic
   Institute *B, M, D*
Worcester State University *B, M*

Michigan

Bay de Noc Community College *A*
Calvin College *B*
Delta College *A*
Ferris State University *B*
Lansing Community College *C, A*
Oakland Community College *A*
Wayne State University *M*

Minnesota

Minneapolis Community and
   Technical College *A*
Minnesota State University
   Mankato *B*
Saint Cloud State University *B*

Mississippi

Alcorn State University *M*
Mississippi Gulf Coast Community
   College *A*

Missouri

Missouri Baptist University *B*
Missouri Southern State University *B*
Northwest Missouri State
   University *M*
Washington University in St. Louis *M*

Montana

Montana State University *B*

Nebraska

University of Nebraska
   Omaha *B*

Nevada

University of Nevada
   Reno *B, M*

New Hampshire

Great Bay Community College *A*
Plymouth State University *B*

New Jersey

Bergen Community College *A*
Burlington County College *A*
Kean University *M*
Raritan Valley Community College *A*
Rutgers, The State University of New
   Jersey
   New Brunswick/Piscataway
      Campus *B*
Salem Community College *A*
William Paterson University of New
   Jersey *B, M*

New Mexico

Central New Mexico Community
   College *C, A*

New York

Albany College of Pharmacy and
   Health Sciences *M*
City University of New York
   Hunter College *B, M*
   York College *B*
Clarkson University *D*
Daemen College *M*
Finger Lakes Community College *A*
Manhattan College *M*
New York Institute of Technology *B*
Rochester Institute of Technology *B*
SUNY
   College at Brockport *B*
   College of Agriculture and
      Technology at Cobleskill *B*
   College of Environmental Science
      and Forestry *B*
   University at Buffalo *B, M*
Syracuse University *B*

North Carolina

Alamance Community College *A*
Bladen Community College *A*
Carteret Community College *A*
Durham Technical Community
   College *A*
Fayetteville State University *B*
Lenoir Community College *A*
North Carolina State University *M*
Piedmont Community College *A*
Rockingham Community College *A*
University of North Carolina
   Pembroke *B*
Winston-Salem State University *B*

North Dakota

North Dakota State University *B*

Ohio

Ashland University *B*
Kent State University *B*
Lakeland Community College *A*
North Central State College *A*
Owens Community College
   Toledo *C*
Ursuline College *B*

Oklahoma

Oklahoma City Community
   College *A*
Southeastern Oklahoma State
   University *B*
Tulsa Community College *C, A*

Oregon

Oregon State University *B, M*
Portland Community College *A*

Pennsylvania

Bucks County Community
College *C, A*
Carnegie Mellon University *M*
Drexel University *M*
Duquesne University *M*
East Stroudsburg University of
Pennsylvania *B*
Elizabethtown College *B*
Harrisburg University of Science and
Technology *B*
Lehigh Carbon Community College *A*
Marywood University *B, M*
Montgomery County Community
College *A*
Northampton Community College *A*
Penn State
University Park *M*
Pennsylvania Highlands Community
College *A*
Point Park University *B*
Temple University *M*
Thomas Jefferson University *B*
University of Pennsylvania *M*

Puerto Rico

Inter American University of Puerto
Rico
Aguadilla Campus *B*
Barranquitas Campus *B*
Bayamon Campus *B*
Guayama Campus *B*
Ponce Campus *B*
Turabo University *A*
Universidad del Este *B*
University of Puerto Rico
Mayaguez *B*

South Carolina

Claflin University *B, M*
Greenville Technical College *A*

South Dakota

South Dakota State University *B*

Tennessee

Southwest Tennessee Community
College *A*

Texas

San Jacinto College *A*
Stephen F. Austin State University *M*
Texas A&M University *M*
Texas Tech University *M*
Texas Tech University Health
Sciences Center *M*
University of Houston *B*
University of Houston
Clear Lake *M*
Downtown *B*
University of Texas
Dallas *M*
San Antonio *M*
West Texas A&M University *B*

Utah

Brigham Young University *B, M*
University of Utah *M*
Utah Valley University *B*

Virginia

James Madison University *B*
Virginia Western Community
College *A*

Washington

Seattle Central Community College *A*
Shoreline Community College *A*

West Virginia

West Liberty University *B*
West Virginia State University *M*

Wisconsin

University of Wisconsin
Madison *M*
River Falls *B*

Wyoming

Sheridan College *C*

Blasting

West Virginia

Bridgemont Community and
Technical College *A*

Blood bank technology

New Mexico

Eastern New Mexico University:
Roswell *C*

North Carolina

Wayne Community College *C*

Tennessee

Southwest Tennessee Community
College *C*

Wisconsin

Marquette University *M*

Boilermaking

Indiana

Ivy Tech Community College
Southwest *C, A*

Ohio

Columbus State Community
College *C*

Wisconsin

Milwaukee Area Technical College *C*

Botany

Alabama

Auburn University *B, M, D*

Alaska

University of Alaska
Fairbanks *M*

Arizona

Arizona State University *M, D*

California

California State University
Long Beach *B*
Cerritos College *A*
Citrus College *A*
El Camino College *A*
Humboldt State University *B*
San Diego State University *B, M*
University of California
Berkeley *B, D*
Davis *B, M, D*
Irvine *B*
Riverside *B, M, D*

Colorado

Colorado State University *M, D*

Connecticut

Connecticut College *B*

District of Columbia

George Washington University *M, D*

Florida

Daytona State College *A*
Pensacola State College *A*
University of Florida *B, M, D*

Georgia

University of Georgia *B, M, D*

Hawaii

University of Hawaii
Manoa *B, M, D*

Idaho

Idaho State University *B*
North Idaho College *A*

Illinois

Southern Illinois University
Carbondale *B, M, D*
University of Illinois
Urbana-Champaign *B, M, D*

Indiana

Indiana University
Bloomington *M, D*
Purdue University *B, M, D*

Iowa

Iowa Western Community College *A*
Marshalltown Community College *A*
University of Iowa *M*

Kansas

Independence Community College *A*
Pratt Community College *A*
University of Kansas *M, D*

Maine

College of the Atlantic *B, M*
University of Maine *B, M, D*

Massachusetts

University of Massachusetts
Amherst *M, D*

Michigan

Andrews University *B*
Michigan State University *B, M, D*
University of Michigan *B*

Minnesota

Minnesota State University
Mankato *B, T*
University of Minnesota
Twin Cities *B, M, D*

Missouri

Washington University in St. Louis *D*

Montana

University of Great Falls *B*
University of Montana *B*

Nebraska

University of Nebraska
Lincoln *B*

New Hampshire

University of New
Hampshire *B, M, D*

New Jersey

Rutgers, The State University of New
Jersey
New Brunswick/Piscataway
Campus *M, D*
Newark Campus *B*

New Mexico

Western New Mexico University *B*

New York

Cornell University *M, D*

North Carolina

Duke University *M, D*
Mars Hill University *B*
Methodist University *B*
North Carolina State
University *B, M, D*

North Dakota

Dakota College at Bottineau *A*
North Dakota State
University *B, M, D*

Ohio

Kent State University *B, M, D*
Miami University
Oxford *B, M, D, T*
Ohio State University
Columbus Campus *B, M, D*
Ohio University *B, M, D*
Ohio Wesleyan University *B*

Oklahoma

Oklahoma State University *B, M, D*
University of Oklahoma *B, M, D*

Oregon

Oregon State University *B*

Texas

Laredo Community College *A*
Texas A&M University *M, D*
Texas A&M University
Galveston *B*
University of Texas
Austin *M, D*

Utah

Snow College *A*
Utah Valley University *B*
Weber State University *B*

Vermont

Bennington College *B*
Marlboro College *B*
University of Vermont *B, M, D*

Washington

Centralia College *A*
University of Washington *B, M, D*
Washington State University *M, D*
Western Washington University *B*

Wisconsin

University of Wisconsin
Madison *B, M, D*
Superior *B*

Wyoming

University of Wyoming *B, M, D*

Brass instruments

California

University of Southern
California *B, M, D*

Kansas

University of Kansas *B, M*

Massachusetts

New England Conservatory of
Music *B, M, D*

Minnesota

McNally Smith College of Music *B, M*

New York

Houghton College *B, M*
Ithaca College *B*

Ohio

Ashland University *B*

Puerto Rico

Conservatory of Music of Puerto
Rico *B, M*

Tennessee

Vanderbilt University *B*

Broadcast journalism

Arizona

Grand Canyon University *B*

Arkansas

Harding University *B*
John Brown University *A, B*
University of the Ozarks *B*

California

Biola University *B*
Butte College *C, A*
California Lutheran University *B*
California State University
East Bay *B*
Long Beach *B*
Northridge *B, M*
Chabot College *A*
Chaffey College *C, A*
Chapman University *B*
City College of San Francisco *C*
College of San Mateo *C, A*
College of the Siskiyous *C, A*
Cosumnes River College *A*
Cuesta College *C, A*
Foothill College *C, A*
Fullerton College *A*
Glendale Community College *A*
Golden West College *C, A*
Grossmont College *C, A*
Laney College *C, A*
Long Beach City College *C, A*
Los Angeles City College *C, A*
Los Angeles Valley College *C, A*
Modesto Junior College *C, A*
Mount San Antonio College *C, A*
Ohlone College *C, A*
Pasadena City College *C, A*
Pepperdine University *B*
Point Loma Nazarene University *B*
Saddleback College *C, A*
San Diego City College *A*
Santa Ana College *C, A*
Santa Rosa Junior College *C*
Southwestern College *C, A*
University of Southern
California *B, M*

Colorado

Aims Community College *C, A*

Connecticut

Middlesex Community College *C, A*
Mitchell College *B*
Quinnipiac University *B*

Delaware

Delaware State University *B*

District of Columbia

Howard University *B*

Florida

Broward College *A*
City College
Fort Lauderdale *A*
Miami Dade College *A*
Palm Beach State College *A*
University of Miami *B*

Georgia

University of Georgia *B*

Hawaii

Chaminade University of Honolulu *B*

Idaho

Brigham Young University-Idaho *B*

Illinois

Chicago State University *B*
Columbia College Chicago *B, M*
Governors State University *B, M*
Illinois Central College *A*
Illinois Eastern Community Colleges
Wabash Valley College *A*
Lake Land College *A*
Northwestern University *B, M*
University of Illinois
Urbana-Champaign *B, M*
University of St. Francis *B*

Indiana

Franklin College *B*
Goshen College *B*
Huntington University *B*
Manchester University *B*
Purdue University *B*

Iowa

Dordt College *B*
Drake University *B*
Grand View University *B*
Iowa Lakes Community College *C, A*
Iowa Western Community College *A*
St. Ambrose University *B*
Wartburg College *B*
William Penn University *B*

Kansas

Coffeyville Community College *A*
Dodge City Community College *C, A*
Independence Community College *A*

Kentucky

Campbellsville University *B*
Eastern Kentucky University *B*
Northern Kentucky University *B*
Western Kentucky University *B*

Maine

New England School of
Communications *B*

Maryland

Frederick Community College *C*
Montgomery College *A*
Washington Adventist University *B*

Massachusetts

American International College *B*
Boston University *B, M*
Emerson College *B*
Massachusetts College of Liberal
Arts *B*
Northern Essex Community
College *A*
Springfield College *B*
Suffolk University *B*

Michigan

Grand Valley State University *B*
Henry Ford Community College *A*
Lansing Community College *A*
Macomb Community College *C, A*
Spring Arbor University *B*

Minnesota

Brown College
Mendota Heights *A*
Minnesota State University
Moorhead *B*
Saint Cloud State University *B*
Southwest Minnesota State
University *B*

Mississippi

Coahoma Community College *A*
Itawamba Community College *A*
Northwest Mississippi Community
College *A*
Rust College *B*

Missouri

College of the Ozarks *B*
Evangel University *A, B*
University of Central Missouri *B*
University of Missouri
Columbia *B*
Webster University *C, B*

Montana

University of Montana *B, M*

Nebraska

Hastings College *B*
University of Nebraska
Kearney *B*
Lincoln *B*

New Jersey

Felician College *B*
Montclair State University *B*
Ocean County College *A*

New Mexico

New Mexico State University
Carlsbad *C*

New York

Cayuga Community College *A*
City University of New York
Brooklyn College *B*
Kingsborough Community
College *A*
College of New Rochelle *B*
Finger Lakes Community College *A*
Five Towns College *B*
Herkimer County Community
College *A*
Ithaca College *B*
Manhattan College *B*
SUNY
College at Brockport *B*
College at Buffalo *B*
College at Oswego *B*
College of Agriculture and
Technology at Morrisville *B*
St. Thomas Aquinas College *B*
Suffolk County Community College *A*
Sullivan County Community
College *A*
Syracuse University *B, M*

North Carolina

Campbell University *B*
East Carolina University *B*
Elon University *B*
Gardner-Webb University *B*
Gaston College *A*
Lenoir-Rhyne University *B*

North Dakota

Minot State University *B*

Ohio

Ashland University *B*
Bluffton University *B*
Bowling Green State University *B*
Central State University *B*
Marietta College *B*
Mount Vernon Nazarene University *B*
Ohio University *B*
Ohio Wesleyan University *B*
Otterbein University *B*
University of Akron *B*
Washington State Community
College *A*

Oklahoma

Langston University *B*
Northern Oklahoma College *A*
Oklahoma Baptist University *B*
Oklahoma Christian University *B*
Oklahoma City Community
College *A*
Oklahoma City University *B*
Rose State College *A*
University of Central Oklahoma *B*
University of Oklahoma *B*

Oregon

Lane Community College *C, A*

Pennsylvania

Chatham University *B*
Edinboro University of
Pennsylvania *B*
La Salle University *B*
Lincoln University *B*
Mansfield University of
Pennsylvania *B*
Marywood University *B*
Point Park University *B*
Temple University *B*
Waynesburg University *B*
Westminster College *B*

South Carolina

North Greenville University *B*
Trident Technical College *A*
University of South Carolina
Columbia *B*
Voorhees College *B*

Tennessee

Belmont University *B*
Southern Adventist University *B*
Union University *B*

Texas

Amarillo College *A*
Central Texas College *C, A*
Laredo Community College *A*
Odessa College *A*
Our Lady of the Lake University of
San Antonio *B*
South Plains College *A*
Southwestern Adventist University *B*
University of North Texas *B*
West Texas A&M University *B*

Vermont

Champlain College *B*
Lyndon State College *B*

Virginia

Hampton University *B*
Regent University *M*

Washington

Centralia College *A*
Gonzaga University *B*
Green River Community College *C*
Shoreline Community College *A*

West Virginia

Bethany College *B*
Concord University *B*
West Virginia University *B*

Wisconsin

Concordia University Wisconsin *B*
University of Wisconsin
Oshkosh *B*
Superior *B*
Whitewater *B*

Wyoming

Northwest College *A*

Buddhist studies

California
University of California
Berkeley *D*
University of the West *D*

Massachusetts
University of Massachusetts
Amherst *C*

Missouri
Webster University *C*

Building construction technology

Alaska
University of Alaska
Anchorage *C*

Arizona
Arizona Western College *C*
Cochise College *A*
Pima Community College *C*

California
Bakersfield College *C, A*
Barstow Community College *C*

Colorado
Red Rocks Community College *C, A*

Massachusetts
University of Massachusetts
Amherst *B*
Wentworth Institute of Technology *A*

Michigan
Mott Community College *C*

Minnesota
Lake Superior College *C, A*

Montana
Blackfeet Community College *C, A*

New Mexico
Central New Mexico Community
College *A*
Santa Fe Community College *C*

New York
Institute of Design and
Construction *A*
SUNY
Farmingdale State College *B*

Ohio
Sinclair Community College *C*

Pennsylvania
New Castle School of Trades *A*

Rhode Island
New England Institute of
Technology *B*

South Carolina
Greenville Technical College *C*
Piedmont Technical College *C, A*

South Dakota
Mitchell Technical Institute *A*

Texas
Cedar Valley College *C, A*

Utah
Southern Utah University *C, A*

West Virginia
Bridgemont Community and
Technical College *A*

Wyoming
Sheridan College *C, A*

Building inspection

Arizona
Mesa Community College *C*
Phoenix College *C, A*
Scottsdale Community College *C, A*

California
Coastline Community College *C*
College of San Mateo *C, A*
College of the Canyons *C*
College of the Desert *C*
Diablo Valley College *C, A*
Palomar College *C, A*
Southwestern College *C, A*

Colorado
Arapahoe Community College *A*

Georgia
Gwinnett Technical College *C*

Illinois
Harper College *C*
McHenry County College *C, A*

Kentucky
Jefferson Community and Technical
College *C*

Michigan
Delta College *C*

Minnesota
North Hennepin Community
College *C*

Missouri
St. Louis Community College *C*

Ohio
Vatterott College
Cleveland *A*

Oregon
Chemeketa Community College *A*
Portland Community College *C, A*

Pennsylvania
Bucks County Community College *A*
Harrisburg Area Community
College *C, A*

South Carolina
Greenville Technical College *C*

Texas
Cedar Valley College *C*

Utah
Utah Valley University *C, A*

Washington
Bellingham Technical College *C*
Centralia College *A*
Edmonds Community College *C*

Building/property maintenance

Alaska
University of Alaska
Fairbanks *C*

Arizona
Eastern Arizona College *C*
GateWay Community College *C, A*
Northland Pioneer College *C*
Pima Community College *C, A*
Yavapai College *C, A*

California
Allan Hancock College *C*
Butte College *C, A*
Chabot College *A*
City College of San Francisco *C*
College of the Redwoods *C, A*
College of the Sequoias *C, A*
Cosumnes River College *C, A*
El Camino College *C, A*
Fresno City College *C, A*
Fullerton College *A*
Laney College *C, A*
Los Angeles Trade and Technical
College *C, A*
Modesto Junior College *C, A*
Orange Coast College *C, A*
Pasadena City College *C, A*
Porterville College *C*
Saddleback College *C*
Southwestern College *C, A*
Ventura College *C, A*
West Valley College *C, A*

Florida
Daytona State College *C*
Florida State College at
Jacksonville *A*
Miami Dade College *A*
Palm Beach State College *C, A*
Pensacola State College *A*
Seminole State College of Florida *C*
Tallahassee Community College *A*

Illinois
College of DuPage *A*
Lincoln Land Community
College *C, A*
Oakton Community College *A*
Parkland College *C*
Rend Lake College *C*
Sauk Valley Community College *C*
South Suburban College of Cook
County *A*
Southwestern Illinois College *C, A*
Waubonsee Community College *C*

Indiana
Ivy Tech Community College
Bloomington *C, A*
Central Indiana *C, A*
Columbus *C, A*
East Central *C, A*
Kokomo *C, A*
Lafayette *C, A*
North Central *C, A*
Northeast *C, A*
Northwest *C, A*
Richmond *C, A*
South Central *C, A*
Southwest *C, A*
Wabash Valley *C, A*
Vincennes University *C*

Iowa
Southeastern Community College *A*

Kansas
Coffeyville Community College *C*
Kansas City Kansas Community
College *C*

Maine
Central Maine Community
College *C, A*

Maryland
Hagerstown Community College *C*

Massachusetts
Cape Cod Community College *C*

Michigan
Delta College *C, A*
Henry Ford Community College *C*
Macomb Community College *C*
Northwestern Michigan College *C*
Washtenaw Community College *C, A*

Minnesota
Century College *C, A*
Hennepin Technical College *C, A*
Minnesota State University
Mankato *B*
Rochester Community and Technical
College *C, A*

Mississippi
Mississippi Delta Community
College *A*

Missouri
North Central Missouri College *A*
St. Louis Community College *A*

Montana
Miles Community College *A*
University of Montana *C, A*

Nebraska
Metropolitan Community
College *C, A*
Mid-Plains Community College *C, A*

Nevada
Truckee Meadows Community
College *A*

New Hampshire
Manchester Community College *C, A*

New Mexico
Dona Ana Community College of
New Mexico State University *A*
Eastern New Mexico University:
Roswell *C*
New Mexico State University
Carlsbad *C*
Northern New Mexico College *C, A*
Santa Fe Community College *C*

New York
Erie Community College *A*
Hudson Valley Community College *A*
Mohawk Valley Community
College *A*
Orange County Community
College *C*
Rockland Community College *A*
Technical Career Institutes *C, A*

North Carolina
Blue Ridge Community College *C*
Central Piedmont Community
College *C, A*
Cleveland Community College *C*
Guilford Technical Community
College *A*
Haywood Community College *C, A*
Western Piedmont Community
College *C, A*

Ohio
Eastern Gateway Community
College *A*
Vatterott College
Cleveland *C*

Pennsylvania
Commonwealth Technical Institute *C*
Community College of Allegheny
County *C, A*

Dean Institute of Technology *C*
Delaware County Community
    College *C, A*
Fortis Institute
    Erie *A*
Luzerne County Community
    College *C, A*
Orleans Technical Institute *C*

Rhode Island

Community College of Rhode
    Island *C*

South Carolina

Aiken Technical College *C*
Denmark Technical College *C*

South Dakota

Mitchell Technical Institute *C*

Texas

Del Mar College *C, A*
Laredo Community College *C*
North Lake College *C*
Odessa College *C, A*

Utah

Salt Lake Community College *A*
Utah Valley University *A*

Vermont

Vermont Technical College *A, B*

Virginia

John Tyler Community College *C*

Washington

Bates Technical College *C, A*
Bellingham Technical College *C, A*
Centralia College *A*
Edmonds Community College *C*
Pierce College *C, A*
Renton Technical College *C, A*

Wisconsin

Gateway Technical College *C*
University of Wisconsin
    Platteville *B*
Waukesha County Technical
    College *C*

Wyoming

Central Wyoming College *C, A*

Business administration and management

Alabama

Alabama Agricultural and Mechanical
    University *B, M*
Alabama State University *B*
Amridge University *B*
Athens State University *B*
Auburn University *B, M, D*
Auburn University at Montgomery *B*
Birmingham-Southern College *B*
Calhoun Community College *C, A*
Central Alabama Community
    College *A*
Chattahoochee Valley Community
    College *A*
Columbia Southern
    University *C, A, B, M, D*
Concordia College *B*
Enterprise State Community
    College *C, A*
Faulkner State Community College *A*
Faulkner University *B*
Gadsden State Community College *A*
George C. Wallace State Community
    College at Selma *A*
Herzing University
    Birmingham *A, B*

Huntingdon College *B*
ITT Technical Institute
    Birmingham *B*
Jacksonville State University *B, M*
Judson College *B*
Lawson State Community College *A*
Miles College *B*
Northeast Alabama Community
    College *A*
Oakwood University *B*
Samford University *B, M*
Selma University *B*
Spring Hill College *B, M*
Stillman College *B*
Talladega College *B*
Troy University *B, M*
Tuskegee University *B*
University of Alabama *B, M, D*
University of Alabama
    Birmingham *B, M*
    Huntsville *B, M*
University of Mobile *B, M*
University of Montevallo *B, M*
University of North Alabama *B, M*
University of Phoenix
    Birmingham *B, M*
University of South Alabama *B, M, D*
University of West Alabama *B*
Virginia College
    Birmingham *A, B, M*
    Huntsville *C, A*
    Mobile *A*
    Montgomery *A*
Wallace State Community College at
    Hanceville *A*

Alaska

Alaska Pacific University *C, A, B, M*
Charter College *A*
Ilisagvik College *C, A*
University of Alaska
    Anchorage *C, A, B, M*
    Fairbanks *C, A, B, M*
    Southeast *A*

Arizona

Anthem College
    Phoenix *A, B*
Argosy University
    Online *B, M, D*
    Phoenix *B, M, D*
Arizona Christian University *B*
Arizona State University *B, M, D*
Arizona Western College *A*
Brookline College
    Phoenix *C, A, B*
    Tempe *C, A*
    Tucson *A*
Brown Mackie College
    Tucson *A, B*
Central Arizona College *C, A*
Cochise College *A*
Coconino County Community
    College *C, A*
DeVry University
    Phoenix *B, M*
Dine College *A*
Eastern Arizona College *A*
Estrella Mountain Community
    College *A*
Everest College
    Phoenix *A, B*
Glendale Community College *A*
Golf Academy of America
    Phoenix *A*
Grand Canyon University *B, M, D*
ITT Technical Institute
    Tempe *B*
    Tucson *B*
Mesa Community College *C*
Mohave Community College *C, A*
Northcentral University *B, M, D*
Northern Arizona University *B, M*
Northland Pioneer College *C, A*

Paradise Valley Community
    College *C, A*
Phoenix College *C, A*
Rio Salado College *C, A*
South Mountain Community
    College *C, A*
Tohono O'odham Community
    College *A*
University of Arizona *M, D*
University of Phoenix
    Phoenix-Hohokam *B, M*
    Southern Arizona *B, M*
Western International
    University *A, B, M*
Yavapai College *C, A*

Arkansas

Arkansas Baptist College *A, B*
Arkansas State University *B, M*
Arkansas State University
    Mountain Home *C*
Arkansas Tech University *B, M*
Black River Technical College *A*
Central Baptist College *A, B*
College of the Ouachitas *C, A*
Crowley's Ridge College *B*
East Arkansas Community College *A*
Ecclesia College *B*
Harding University *B, M*
ITT Technical Institute
    Little Rock *B*
John Brown University *B, M*
Lyon College *B*
Northwest Arkansas Community
    College *A*
Ouachita Baptist University *B*
Ozarka College *A*
Philander Smith College *B*
Phillips Community College of the
    University of Arkansas *A*
South Arkansas Community
    College *A*
Southeast Arkansas College *C*
Southern Arkansas University *M*
Southern Arkansas University Tech *A*
University of Arkansas *B, M, D*
University of Arkansas
    Community College at Batesville *A*
    Fort Smith *C, A, B*
    Little Rock *B, M*
    Monticello *B*
    Pine Bluff *B*
University of Central
    Arkansas *A, B, M*
University of Phoenix
    Little Rock *B, M*
    Northwest Arkansas *B, M*
University of the Ozarks *B*
Williams Baptist College *B*

California

Allan Hancock College *C, A*
Alliant International
    University *B, M, D*
Antelope Valley College *C, A*
Argosy University
    Inland Empire *B, M, D*
    Los Angeles *B, M, D*
    Orange County *B, M, D*
    San Diego *B, M, D*
    San Francisco Bay Area *B, M, D*
Azusa Pacific University *B, M*
Bakersfield College *A*
Berkeley City College *C, A*
Biola University *B, M*
Butte College *A*
Cabrillo College *A*
California Baptist University *M*
California Coast University *A, B, M*
California College San Diego *A*
California College of the Arts *M*
California Lutheran University *B, M*
California Maritime Academy *B*

California Miramar
    University *A, B, M, D*
California National University for
    Advanced Studies *B, M*
California Polytechnic State
    University: San Luis Obispo *B, M*
California State Polytechnic
    University: Pomona *B, M*
California State University
    Bakersfield *B, M*
    Channel Islands *M*
    Chico *C, B, M*
    Dominguez Hills *B, M*
    East Bay *B, M*
    Fresno *B, M*
    Fullerton *B, M*
    Long Beach *M*
    Los Angeles *B, M*
    Monterey Bay *B, M*
    Northridge *B, M*
    Sacramento *B, M*
    San Bernardino *B, M*
    San Marcos *B, M*
    Stanislaus *B, M*
California University of Management
    and Sciences *B, M, D*
Canada College *C, A*
Cerritos College *A*
Cerro Coso Community College *C, A*
Chaffey College *C, A*
Chapman University *B, M*
Citrus College *C*
City College of San Francisco *A*
Coastline Community College *C, A*
Coleman University *M*
College of Alameda *A*
College of Marin *C, A*
College of San Mateo *A*
College of the Canyons *C, A*
College of the Desert *A*
College of the Siskiyous *A*
Columbia College *C, A*
Concordia University Irvine *B, M*
Contra Costa College *C, A*
Copper Mountain College *A*
Cosumnes River College *A*
Crafton Hills College *C, A*
Cuyamaca College *C, A*
Cypress College *A*
De Anza College *C, A*
DeVry University
    Pomona *B, M*
Diablo Valley College *C, A*
Dominican University of
    California *B, M*
East Los Angeles College *C, A*
El Camino College *A*
Everest College
    Ontario Metro *A, B*
Evergreen Valley College *C*
Foothill College *C, A*
Fresno City College *A*
Fresno Pacific University *B*
Fullerton College *A*
Golden Gate University *C, B, M, D*
Golden West College *C, A*
Grossmont College *C, A*
Hartnell College *C, A*
Heald College
    Concord *C, A*
    Fresno *C, A*
    Hayward *C, A*
    Rancho Cordova *C, A*
    Roseville *A*
    Salinas *C, A*
    San Francisco *C, A*
    San Jose *C, A*
    Stockton *C, A*
Holy Names University *B, M*
Hope International University *B, M*
Humboldt State University *B, M*
Humphreys College *A, B*
ITT Technical Institute
    Lathrop *B*
    National City *B*

Oxnard *B*
Rancho Cordova *B*
San Bernardino *B*
Sylmar *B*
Torrance *B*
Imperial Valley College *A*
Irvine Valley College *C, A*
John F. Kennedy University *B, M*
John Paul the Great Catholic
  University *M*
Kaplan College
  Riverside *A*
  San Diego *C, A*
La Sierra University *B, M*
Lassen Community College *A*
Lincoln University *B, M, D*
Long Beach City College *C, A*
Los Angeles City College *C, A*
Los Angeles Harbor College *C, A*
Los Angeles Mission College *A*
Los Angeles Pierce College *C, A*
Los Angeles Southwest College *A*
Los Angeles Trade and Technical
  College *A*
Loyola Marymount University *M*
Marymount California
  University *B, M*
Master's College *B*
Mendocino College *C, A*
Menlo College *B*
Merced College *A*
Mills College *M*
MiraCosta College *C, A*
Mission College *A*
Modesto Junior College *A*
Monterey Peninsula College *A*
Moorpark College *A*
Mount St. Mary's College *A, B, M*
Mount San Antonio College *C, A*
Mount San Jacinto College *C, A*
Mt. Sierra College *B*
National Hispanic University *A, B*
National University *A, B, M*
Northwestern Polytechnic
  University *B, M, D*
Notre Dame de Namur
  University *B, M*
Ohlone College *C, A*
Oxnard College *C, A*
Palo Verde College *C, A*
Palomar College *A*
Patten University *B, M*
Pepperdine University *B, M*
Point Loma Nazarene University *B, M*
Porterville College *A*
Providence Christian College *B*
Rio Hondo College *A*
Saddleback College *C, A*
St. Mary's College of California *B, M*
San Bernardino Valley College *C, A*
San Deigo Miramar College
  San Diego Miramar College *A*
San Diego Christian College *B*
San Diego City College *A*
San Diego Mesa College *C, A*
San Diego State University *B, M*
San Francisco State University *B, M*
San Joaquin Delta College *A*
San Joaquin Valley College *C, A*
San Jose City College *C*
San Jose State University *B, M*
Santa Ana College *C, A*
Santa Barbara Business College *B, M*
Santa Barbara Business College
  Bakersfield *B*
  Rancho Mirage *C, A, B*
  Ventura *C, A, B*
Santa Barbara City College *C, A*
Santa Clara University *M*
Santa Monica College *A*
Santa Rosa Junior College *A*
Santiago Canyon College *C, A*
Shasta College *A*
Sierra College *C, A*
Silicon Valley University *B, M*

Simpson University *B*
Skyline College *C, A*
Solano Community College *C, A*
Sonoma State University *B, M*
Southern California Institute of
  Technology *A, B*
Southwestern College *A*
Stanford University *M, D*
Taft College *A*
Trident University International *B, D*
University of California
  Berkeley *B, M, D*
  Davis *M*
  Irvine *B, M, D*
  Los Angeles *M, D*
  Merced *B*
  Riverside *B*
University of La Verne *B, M*
University of Phoenix
  Bay Area *B, M*
  Central Valley *B, M*
  Sacramento Valley *B, M*
  San Diego *B, M*
  Southern California *B, M*
University of Redlands *B, M*
University of San Diego *B, M*
University of San Francisco *B, M*
University of Southern
  California *B, M, D*
University of the Pacific *B, M*
University of the West *M*
Vanguard University of Southern
  California *B, M*
Ventura College *A*
Victor Valley College *C, A*
West Hills College: Coalinga *C, A*
West Hills College: Lemoore *C, A*
West Los Angeles College *C, A*
West Valley College *C, A*
Westwood College
  Anaheim *B*
  Los Angeles *B, M*
Whittier College *B*
William Jessup University *B*
Woodbury University *B, M*
Woodland Community College *A*
WyoTech: Long Beach *C*
Yuba College *C, A*

Colorado

Adams State University *B, M*
American Sentinel University *M*
Argosy University
  Denver *B, M, D*
Aspen University *B, M*
CollegeAmerica
  Colorado Springs *A, B*
  Denver *A, B*
Colorado Christian University *B, M*
Colorado Mountain College *C, A, B*
Colorado Northwestern Community
  College *C*
Colorado State University *B, M*
Colorado Technical
  University *B, M, D*
Community College of Aurora *A*
Community College of Denver *C, A*
DeVry University
  Westminster *B, M*
Everest College
  Aurora *A*
  Colorado Springs *A*
  Denver *A*
Fort Lewis College *B*
Front Range Community College *C, A*
IBMC College
  Fort Collins *C, A*
ITT Technical Institute
  Westminster *B*
Johnson & Wales University
  Denver *B*
Jones International
  University *A, B, M, D*
Metropolitan State University of
  Denver *B*

National American University
  Denver *A, B*
Northeastern Junior College *C*
Otero Junior College *A*
Pueblo Community College *C, A*
Red Rocks Community College *A*
Regis University *B, M*
Trinidad State Junior College *A*
United States Air Force Academy *B*
University of Colorado
  Boulder *B, M, D*
  Colorado Springs *B, M*
  Denver *B, M*
University of Denver *B, M*
University of Northern Colorado *B*
University of Phoenix
  Denver *B, M*
  Southern Colorado *B, M*
Western State Colorado University *B*
Westwood College
  Denver North *B*

Connecticut

Albertus Magnus College *C, A, B, M*
Asnuntuck Community College *C, A*
Capital Community College *C, A*
Central Connecticut State
  University *B*
Eastern Connecticut State
  University *B*
Fairfield University *B, M*
Gateway Community College *A*
Goodwin College *C, A, B*
Housatonic Community College *A*
Manchester Community College *A*
Middlesex Community College *A*
Mitchell College *B*
Naugatuck Valley Community
  College *C, A*
Northwestern Connecticut
  Community College *A*
Norwalk Community College *A*
Post University *C, A, B*
Quinebaug Valley Community
  College *C, A*
Quinnipiac University *B, M*
Southern Connecticut State
  University *B, M*
Three Rivers Community
  College *C, A*
Tunxis Community College *C, A*
United States Coast Guard
  Academy *B*
University of Bridgeport *A, M*
University of Connecticut *B, M, D*
University of Hartford *B, M*
University of New Haven *B, M*
University of Phoenix
  Fairfield County *B, M*
University of Saint Joseph *B, M*
Western Connecticut State
  University *B*
Yale University *M, D*

Delaware

Delaware State University *B, M*
Delaware Technical Community
  College
  Stanton/Wilmington Campus *C, A*
  Terry Campus *C, A*
Goldey-Beacom College *A, B, M*
University of Delaware *B, M*
Wesley College *A, B, M*
Wilmington University *M*

District of Columbia

American University *B, M*
Gallaudet University *B*
George Washington
  University *B, M, D*
Georgetown University *B, M*
Howard University *B, M*
Strayer University *C, A, B, M*
Trinity Washington University *B, M*

University of Phoenix
  Washington DC *B, M*
University of the District of
  Columbia *B, M*
University of the Potomac *B*

Florida

Argosy University
  Sarasota *C, B*
  Tampa *B, M, D*
Ave Maria University *B*
Baptist College of Florida *B*
Barry University *B, M*
Beacon College *A, B*
Bethune-Cookman University *B*
Broward College *C, A*
Brown Mackie College
  Miami *A, B*
Carlos Albizu University *M*
Chipola College *A, B*
City College
  Altamonte Springs *A*
  Fort Lauderdale *A, B*
  Gainesville *A, B*
  Miami *A, B*
Clearwater Christian College *B*
College of Business and Technology
  Cutler Bay *C, A*
  Flagler *C, A*
  Hialeah *C, A*
  Kendall *C, A, B*
College of Central Florida *C, A*
Daytona State College *A*
DeVry University
  Miramar *B, M*
  Orlando *B, M*
Eastern Florida State College *A*
Eckerd College *B*
Edison State College *A*
Edward Waters College *B*
Embry-Riddle Aeronautical
  University *B, M*
Embry-Riddle Aeronautical University
  Worldwide Campus *A, B, M*
Everest University
  Brandon *A, B, M*
  Jacksonville *A, B, M*
  Lakeland *B*
  Largo *A, B, M*
  Melbourne *A, B, M*
  North Orlando *A, B, M*
  Orange Park *A, B*
  Pompano Beach *A, B, M*
  South Orlando *A, B, M*
  Tampa *A, B, M*
Everglades University
  Boca Raton *B, M*
Flagler College *B*
Florida Agricultural and Mechanical
  University *B, M*
Florida Atlantic University *B, M, D*
Florida Career College
  Miami *B*
Florida College *B*
Florida Gateway College *A*
Florida Gulf Coast University *B, M*
Florida Institute of Technology *B, M*
Florida International
  University *B, M, D*
Florida Keys Community College *A*
Florida Memorial University *B, M*
Florida National University *A, B, M*
Florida Southern College *B, M*
Florida State College at
  Jacksonville *A, B*
Florida State University *B, M*
Florida Technical College
  Orlando *A*
Fortis College
  Orange Park *A*
  Winter Park *A*
Golf Academy of America
  Orlando *A*
Gulf Coast State College *C, A*

Herzing University
  Winter Park *A, B*
Hillsborough Community
  College *C, A*
Hodges University *A, B, M*
ITT Technical Institute
  Ft. Lauderdale *B*
  Jacksonville *B*
  Lake Mary *B*
  Miami *B*
Indian River State College *A*
Jacksonville University *B, M*
Johnson & Wales University
  North Miami *B*
Jones College *A, B*
Jose Maria Vargas University *B*
Keiser University *B, M, D*
Lake-Sumter State College *A, B*
Lynn University *B, M*
Miami Dade College *C, A*
Northwest Florida State College *C, A*
Northwood University
  Florida *B, M*
Nova Southeastern
  University *B, M, D*
Palm Beach Atlantic University *B, M*
Palm Beach State College *A*
Pasco-Hernando State College *C, A*
Pensacola State College *A*
Polk State College *A*
Rasmussen College
  Fort Myers *C, A, B*
  New Port Richey *C, A, B*
  Ocala *C, A, B*
  Pasco/Land O'Lakes *C, A, B*
  Tampa/Brandon *C, A, B*
Remington College
  Tampa *A*
Rollins College *M*
Saint Johns River State College *C, A*
Saint Leo University *B*
St. Petersburg College *C, A, B*
Saint Thomas University *B, M*
Santa Fe College *C, A*
Schiller International
  University *A, B, M*
Seminole State College of
  Florida *C, A*
South Florida State College *A*
Southeastern University *M*
Southwest Florida College *A, B*
State College of Florida, Manatee-
  Sarasota *A*
Stetson University *B, M*
Tallahassee Community College *A*
University of Central Florida *B, M, D*
University of Florida *B, M, D*
University of Miami *B, M, D*
University of North Florida *B, M*
University of Phoenix
  Central Florida *B, M*
  North Florida *B, M*
  South Florida *B, M*
  West Florida *B, M*
University of South Florida *B, M, D*
University of South Florida
  Sarasota-Manatee *B, M*
University of Southernmost
  Florida *C, A*
University of Tampa *B, M*
University of West Florida *B, M*
Valencia College *C, A*
Virginia College
  Jacksonville *B*
  Pensacola *A*
Warner University *A, B, M*
Webber International
  University *A, B, M*

Georgia

Abraham Baldwin Agricultural
  College *A*
Agnes Scott College *B*
Albany State University *B, M*
Altamaha Technical College *C, A*

Argosy University
  Atlanta *B*
Atlanta Metropolitan College *A*
Atlanta Technical College *C, A*
Berry College *B, M*
Central Georgia Technical College *C*
Clark Atlanta University *B, M*
Clayton State University *B, M*
College of Coastal Georgia *A, B*
Columbus State University *B, M*
Columbus Technical College *C, A*
Dalton State College *A, B*
Darton College *A*
East Georgia State College *A*
Emmanuel College *A, B*
Emory University *B, M, D*
Fort Valley State University *B*
Georgia College and State
  University *B*
Georgia Gwinnett College *B*
Georgia Highlands College *A*
Georgia Institute of
  Technology *B, M, D*
Georgia Military College *A*
Georgia Perimeter College *A*
Georgia Piedmont Technical
  College *C, A*
Georgia Regents University *B, M*
Georgia Southern University *B, M*
Georgia Southwestern State
  University *B, M*
Georgia State University *B, M, D*
Gordon College *A*
Gwinnett College *C, A*
Gwinnett Technical College *C, A*
Kennesaw State University *B, M, D*
LaGrange College *B*
Middle Georgia State College *A, B*
Morehouse College *B*
North Georgia Technical
  College *C, A*
Oglethorpe University *B*
Paine College *B*
Piedmont College *B, M*
Point University *A, B*
Reinhardt University *B, M*
Savannah State University *B*
Shorter University *B*
South Georgia State College *A*
Southeastern Technical College *A*
Southern Crescent Technical
  College *A*
Southwest Georgia Technical
  College *C, A*
Toccoa Falls College *A, B*
University of Georgia *B, M, D*
University of North Georgia *A, B, M*
University of Phoenix
  Atlanta *B, M*
  Augusta *B, M*
  Columbus *B, M*
  Savannah *B, M*
University of West Georgia *B, M*
Valdosta State University *B, M*
Wesleyan College *B, M*
West Georgia Technical College *A*

Hawaii

Argosy University
  Hawaii *B, M, D*
Brigham Young University-Hawaii *B*
Chaminade University of
  Honolulu *A, B, M*
Hawaii Pacific University *A, B, M*
Heald College
  Honolulu *A*
University of Hawaii
  Hilo *B*
  Leeward Community College *C, A*
  Manoa *B, M*
  West Oahu *B*
University of Phoenix
  Hawaii *B, M*

Idaho

Boise State University *M*
Brigham Young University-Idaho *B*
Broadview University
  Boise *A, B*
College of Idaho *B*
ITT Technical Institute
  Boise *B*
Idaho State University *B, M*
Lewis-Clark State College *B*
North Idaho College *A*
Northwest Nazarene University *B*
Stevens-Henager College
  Boise *A, B, M*
University of Idaho *C, B, M*
University of Phoenix
  Idaho *B, M*

Illinois

American InterContinental
  University *A, B, M*
Argosy University
  Chicago *B, M, D*
  Schaumburg *B*
Augustana College *B*
Aurora University *M*
Benedictine University *C, A, M*
Blackburn College *B*
Bradley University *B, M*
Carl Sandburg College *A*
Chicago State University *B*
City Colleges of Chicago
  Harold Washington College *C*
  Harry S. Truman College *C, A*
  Kennedy-King College *C, A*
  Olive-Harvey College *C, A*
  Richard J. Daley College *C, A*
  Wilbur Wright College *C, A*
College of DuPage *C, A*
College of Lake County *C, A*
Columbia College Chicago *B, M*
Concordia University Chicago *B, M*
DePaul University *B, M*
DeVry University
  Chicago *B, M*
  Online *B, M*
Dominican University *B, M*
East-West University *B*
Eastern Illinois University *B, M*
Elgin Community College *A*
Elmhurst College *B*
Eureka College *B*
Governors State University *B, M*
Greenville College *B, M*
Harper College *C, A*
Illinois Central College *A*
Illinois Eastern Community Colleges
  Olney Central College *C, A*
Illinois Institute of Technology *B, M*
Illinois State University *B, M*
Illinois Valley Community College *A*
Illinois Wesleyan University *B*
John A. Logan College *A*
John Wood Community College *C, A*
Joliet Junior College *A*
Judson University *B, M*
Kankakee Community College *C, A*
Kaskaskia College *C*
Kendall College *B*
Lewis University *B, M*
Lewis and Clark Community
  College *A*
Lincoln College *A, B*
Lincoln Land Community College *C*
Loyola University Chicago *M*
MacCormac College *A*
MacMurray College *A, B*
McHenry County College *C, A*
McKendree University *A, B, M*
Midstate College *B*
Millikin University *B, M*
Monmouth College *B*
Moraine Valley Community College *A*
Morton College *A*

National-Louis University *C, B, M*
North Central College *B, M*
North Park University *B, M*
Northeastern Illinois University *B, M*
Northern Illinois University *B, M*
Northwestern College *A*
Northwestern University *C, M*
Oakton Community College *A*
Olivet Nazarene University *B, M*
Parkland College *A*
Prairie State College *A*
Principia College *B*
Quincy University *B, M*
Rasmussen College
  Aurora *C, A, B*
  Mokena/Tinley Park *C, A, B*
  Rockford *C, A, B*
  Romeoville/Joliet *C, A, B*
Rend Lake College *C, A*
Robert Morris University:
  Chicago *A, B, M*
Rock Valley College *A*
Rockford University *B, M*
Roosevelt University *M*
St. Augustine College *A*
Saint Xavier University *M*
Southeastern Illinois College *A*
Southern Illinois University
  Carbondale *B, M, D*
Southern Illinois University
  Edwardsville *B, M*
Southwestern Illinois College *A*
Triton College *C, A*
University of Chicago *M, D*
University of Illinois
  Chicago *B, M, D*
  Springfield *B, M*
  Urbana-Champaign *C, B, M*
University of Phoenix
  Chicago *B, M*
University of St. Francis *B, M*
Waubonsee Community College *C, A*
Western Illinois University *B, M*

Indiana

Ancilla College *A*
Anderson University *B, M, D*
Ball State University *A, B, M*
Bethel College *B, M*
Brown Mackie College
  Fort Wayne *B*
  Merrillville *B*
  Michigan City *B*
  South Bend *B*
Butler University *M*
Calumet College of St. Joseph *C, A, B*
Crossroads Bible College *B*
Goshen College *B*
Grace College *B, M*
Harrison College
  Indianapolis *A, B*
Huntington University *A, B*
ITT Technical Institute
  Fort Wayne *B*
  Indianapolis *A, B, M*
  Newburgh *B*
Indiana Institute of Technology *A, B*
Indiana State University *B, M*
Indiana University
  East *M*
  Purdue University Fort
    Wayne *A, B, M*
  Southeast *C*
Indiana Wesleyan University *A, B, M*
International Business College *B*
Ivy Tech Community College
  Bloomington *C, A*
  Central Indiana *A*
  Columbus *C, A*
  East Central *C, A*
  Kokomo *C, A*
  Lafayette *C, A*
  North Central *C, A*
  Northeast *C, A*
  Northwest *C, A*

Richmond *A*
South Central *C, A*
Southeast *C, A*
Southwest *C, A*
Wabash Valley *A*
Manchester University *B*
Martin University *B*
National College
Indianapolis *C, A, B*
South Bend *A*
National College: Fort Wayne *A*
Oakland City University *A, B, M*
Purdue University *B, M, D*
Purdue University
Calumet *C, B, M*
North Central *M*
Saint Joseph's College *B*
Saint Mary's College *B*
St. Mary-of-the-Woods College *B*
Taylor University *A, B, M*
Trine University *A, B*
University of Evansville *B*
University of Indianapolis *A, B*
University of Notre Dame *M*
University of Phoenix
Indianapolis *B, M*
University of St. Francis *B, M*
University of Southern Indiana *B*
Valparaiso University *C, M*
Vincennes University *C, A*

Iowa

AIB College of Business *A, B*
Ashford University *B, M*
Briar Cliff University *B*
Buena Vista University *B*
Central College *B, T*
Clarke University *A, B, M*
Clinton Community College *C, A*
Coe College *B*
Des Moines Area Community
College *A*
Drake University *M*
Emmaus Bible College *B*
Graceland University *B*
Iowa Central Community College *A*
Iowa Lakes Community College *A*
Iowa State University *M*
Iowa Wesleyan College *B*
Iowa Western Community College *A*
Kirkwood Community College *C, A*
Loras College *B, M*
Luther College *B*
Maharishi University of
Management *C, B, M, D*
Marshalltown Community College *A*
Morningside College *B*
Mount Mercy University *B, M*
North Iowa Area Community
College *C, A*
Northeast Iowa Community
College *A*
Northwest Iowa Community
College *A*
Northwestern College *B, T*
St. Ambrose University *B, M, D*
Simpson College *B*
Southeastern Community College *A*
University of Dubuque *B, M*
University of Iowa *B, M*
University of Northern Iowa *B, M*
University of Phoenix
Des Moines *B, M*
Upper Iowa University *A, B, M*
Wartburg College *B*
Western Iowa Tech Community
College *A*
William Penn University *B*

Kansas

Allen County Community College *A*
Barclay College *B*
Barton County Community College *A*
Benedictine College *B, M*

Bethany College *B*
Brown Mackie College
Salina *A*
Bryan University
Topeka *C, A*
Butler Community College *C, A*
Central Christian College of
Kansas *A, B*
Cloud County Community
College *C, A*
Coffeyville Community College *A*
Colby Community College *C, A*
Cowley County Community
College *A*
Emporia State University *B, M*
Fort Hays State University *B, M*
Fort Scott Community College *C, A*
Friends University *B, M*
Haskell Indian Nations
University *A, B*
Highland Community College *A*
Independence Community College *A*
Johnson County Community
College *A*
Kansas City Kansas Community
College *A*
Kansas State University *B, M*
Kansas Wesleyan University *A, B, M*
Labette Community College *A*
Manhattan Christian College *B*
McPherson College *B*
MidAmerica Nazarene
University *B, M*
Neosho County Community
College *C, A*
Newman University *A, B, M*
North Central Kansas Technical
College *C*
Ottawa University *B, M*
Pittsburg State University *M*
Pratt Community College *C, A*
Seward County Community
College *A*
Southwestern College *B, M*
Sterling College *B*
Tabor College *B, M*
University of Kansas *B, M*
University of St. Mary *B, M*
Washburn University *B, M*
Wichita Area Technical College *C, A*
Wichita State University *B, M*
Wright Career College
Overland Park *A*
Wichita *A*

Kentucky

Alice Lloyd College *B*
Asbury University *B*
Ashland Community and Technical
College *C, A*
Beckfield College *A, B*
Bellarmine University *B, M*
Bluegrass Community and Technical
College *C, A*
Brescia University *B, M*
Brown Mackie College
Hopkinsville *C, A*
Louisville *B*
North Kentucky *C, A*
Campbellsville University *A, B, M*
Daymar College
Bowling Green *C, A, B*
Louisville *C, A, B*
Owensboro *C, A, B*
Eastern Kentucky University *B*
Elizabethtown Community and
Technical College *C, A*
Gateway Community and Technical
College *C, A*
Henderson Community College *A*
Hopkinsville Community
College *C, A*
ITT Technical Institute
Louisville *B*

Jefferson Community and Technical
College *C, A*
Kentucky Christian University *B*
Kentucky State University *M*
Kentucky Wesleyan College *B*
Lincoln College of Technology
Florence *A*
Lindsey Wilson College *A, B*
Madisonville Community
College *C, A*
Maysville Community and Technical
College *C, A*
Mid-Continent University *B*
Morehead State University *B*
Murray State University *B*
National College
Danville *C, A*
Florence *A*
Lexington *C, A, B*
Louisville *C, A, B*
Pikeville *C, A*
Richmond *C, A*
Northern Kentucky University *B*
Owensboro Community and
Technical College *C, A*
St. Catharine College *B*
Somerset Community College *A*
Southeast Kentucky Community and
Technical College *C, A*
Sullivan University *C, B*
Thomas More College *A, B, M*
Union College *B*
University of Phoenix
Louisville *B, M*
University of Pikeville *A, B, M*
University of the Cumberlands *M*
West Kentucky Community and
Technical College *C, A*
Western Kentucky
University *A, B, M, T*

Louisiana

Bossier Parish Community College *C*
Centenary College of Louisiana *B, M*
Delgado Community College *A*
Delta School of Business &
Technology *C, A*
Dillard University *B*
Grambling State University *B*
Herzing University
Kenner *A, B*
ITI Technical College *A*
ITT Technical Institute
St. Rose *B*
Louisiana College *B*
Louisiana State University
Alexandria *B*
Shreveport *B, M*
Louisiana State University and
Agricultural and Mechanical
College *B, M, D*
Louisiana Tech University *B, M, D*
Loyola University New Orleans *B*
McNeese State University *B, M*
Nicholls State University *B, M*
Northwestern State University *B*
Our Lady of Holy Cross College *B*
Remington College
Lafayette *A*
Shreveport *A*
Southeastern Louisiana
University *B, M*
Southern University
Shreveport *A*
Southern University and Agricultural
and Mechanical College *B, M*
Southwest University *A, B, M*
Tulane University *B, M, D*
University of Louisiana at
Lafayette *B, M*
University of Louisiana at
Monroe *B, M*
University of New Orleans *B, M*

University of Phoenix
Baton Rouge *B, M*
Lafayette *B, M*
Louisiana *B, M*
Shreveport *B, M*
Virginia College
Baton Rouge *B*
Shreveport *A, B*
Xavier University of Louisiana *B*

Maine

Beal College *C, A*
Central Maine Community
College *C, A*
Eastern Maine Community College *A*
Husson University *A, B, M*
Kaplan University
South Portland *A, B, M*
Maine Maritime Academy *B*
Northern Maine Community
College *A*
Saint Joseph's College of
Maine *A, B, M*
Southern Maine Community
College *A*
Thomas College *B, M*
University of Maine *B, M*
University of Maine
Augusta *A, B*
Fort Kent *A, B*
Machias *B*
Presque Isle *B*
University of New England *B*
University of Southern Maine *A, B, M*
Washington County Community
College *A*
York County Community College *A*

Maryland

Allegany College of Maryland *C, A*
Anne Arundel Community College *C*
Baltimore City Community College *A*
Bowie State University *B, M*
Capitol College *B*
Cecil College *C, A*
Chesapeake College *C, A*
College of Southern Maryland *C, A*
Community College of Baltimore
County *C, A*
Frederick Community College *A*
Frostburg State University *B, M*
Garrett College *C, A*
Goucher College *B*
Hagerstown Community College *C, A*
Harford Community College *C, A*
Hood College *B, M*
Howard Community College *A*
Kaplan University
Hagerstown *A, B, M*
Loyola University Maryland *M*
Maryland Institute College of Art *M*
McDaniel College *B*
Montgomery College *A*
Morgan State University *B, M, D*
Mount St. Mary's University *M*
Prince George's Community
College *C, A*
Salisbury University *B, M*
Sojourner-Douglass College *B*
Stevenson University *B*
Towson University *B, M*
University of Baltimore *B, M*
University of Maryland
College Park *M*
Eastern Shore *B*
University College *B, M*
University of Phoenix
Maryland *B, M*
Washington Adventist University *B*
Wor-Wic Community College *C, A*

Massachusetts

American International
College *A, B, M*

Anna Maria College *A, B, M*
Assumption College *B, M*
Babson College *B, M*
Bay Path College *A, B, M*
Bay State College *A, B*
Becker College *B*
Bentley University *B, M*
Berkshire Community College *A*
Boston College *B, M*
Boston University *B, M, D*
Bridgewater State University *M*
Bristol Community College *A*
Bunker Hill Community College *A*
Cape Cod Community College *A*
Clark University *B, M*
Curry College *B, M*
Dean College *A, B*
Eastern Nazarene College *B*
Elms College *B, M*
Emmanuel College *B, M*
Endicott College *B, M*
Fisher College *A, B*
Fitchburg State University *C, B, M*
Gordon College *B*
Greenfield Community College *A*
Holyoke Community College *A*
Lasell College *B*
Lesley University *B*
Marian Court College *A, B*
Massachusetts Bay Community
    College *C, A*
Massachusetts College of Liberal
    Arts *B, M, T*
Massachusetts Maritime Academy *M*
Massasoit Community College *A*
Merrimack College *B*
Middlesex Community College *A*
Mount Ida College *B*
Mount Wachusett Community
    College *C, A*
New England College of Business and
    Finance *A, B*
Newbury College *A, B*
Nichols College *B, M*
North Shore Community College *A*
Northeastern University *B, M*
Northern Essex Community
    College *A*
Pine Manor College *B*
Quincy College *A*
Quinsigamond Community College *A*
Regis College *M*
Roxbury Community College *A*
Salem State University *B, M*
Simmons College *B, M*
Springfield College *B, M*
Springfield Technical Community
    College *A*
Stonehill College *B*
Suffolk University *B, M*
University of Massachusetts
    Amherst *B, M, D*
    Boston *B, M*
    Dartmouth *B, M*
    Lowell *B, M*
University of Phoenix
    Boston *B, M*
Urban College of Boston *C*
Wentworth Institute of Technology *B*
Western New England
    University *B, M*
Worcester Polytechnic Institute *B, M*
Worcester State University *B, M*

Michigan

Adrian College *A, B, T*
Albion College *B*
Alma College *B, T*
Alpena Community College *A*
Andrews University *B, M*
Aquinas College *B, M*
Baker College
    Auburn Hills *A, B*
    Cadillac *A, B*
    Clinton Township *A, B, M*

Flint *A, B, M*
Jackson *A*
Muskegon *A, B*
Owosso *A, B*
Port Huron *A, B, M*
Bay Mills Community College *A*
Bay de Noc Community College *A*
Calvin College *B*
Central Michigan University *B, M*
Cleary University *A, B, M*
Concordia University *B*
Cornerstone University *B*
Davenport University *B, M*
Delta College *A*
Eastern Michigan University *B, M*
Ferris State University *C, A, B, M*
Finlandia University *B*
Glen Oaks Community College *C*
Gogebic Community College *A*
Grace Bible College *B*
Grand Rapids Community College *A*
Grand Valley State University *B, M*
Griggs University *B, M*
Henry Ford Community College *A*
Hillsdale College *B*
Hope College *B*
ITT Technical Institute
    Canton *A, B*
    Troy *A*
Jackson College *C, A*
Kalamazoo Valley Community
    College *C, A*
Kellogg Community College *C, A*
Kettering University *B, M*
Kirtland Community College *C, A*
Kuyper College *B*
Lake Michigan College *C, A*
Lake Superior State University *A, B*
Lansing Community College *C, A*
Lawrence Technological
    University *B, M, D*
Macomb Community College *C, A*
Madonna University *A, B, M*
Marygrove College *B*
Michigan Jewish Institute *A, B*
Michigan State University *B, M, D*
Michigan Technological
    University *B, M*
Mid Michigan Community College *A*
Monroe County Community
    College *C, A*
Montcalm Community College *A*
Mott Community College *C, A*
North Central Michigan College *C, A*
Northern Michigan University *B*
Northwestern Michigan College *A*
Northwood University
    Michigan *A, B, M*
Oakland Community College *A*
Oakland University *M*
Olivet College *B*
Robert B. Miller College *B*
Rochester College *B*
Saginaw Chippewa Tribal College *A*
Saginaw Valley State University *B, M*
St. Clair County Community
    College *C*
Schoolcraft College *A*
Southwestern Michigan College *A*
Spring Arbor University *B, M*
University of Detroit Mercy *B, M*
University of Michigan *B, M, D*
University of Michigan
    Dearborn *B, M*
    Flint *B, M*
University of Phoenix
    Metro Detroit *B, M*
    West Michigan *B, M*
Walsh College of Accountancy and
    Business Administration *B, M, D*
Washtenaw Community College *C, A*
Wayne County Community College *A*
Wayne State University *M, D*
Western Michigan University *M*

Minnesota

Academy College *A, B*
Alexandria Technical and Community
    College *C, A*
Anoka-Ramsey Community College *A*
Argosy University
    Twin Cities *A, B, M, D*
Augsburg College *B, M*
Bemidji State University *B*
Bethany Lutheran College *B*
Bethel University *B, M*
Brown College
    Brooklyn Center *B*
Capella University *B, M, D*
Central Lakes College *A*
Century College *A*
College of St. Benedict *B*
College of St. Scholastica *B*
Concordia College: Moorhead *B*
Concordia University St. Paul *B, M*
Crossroads College *B*
Crown College *A, B*
Dakota County Technical College *A*
Duluth Business University *A, B*
Dunwoody College of Technology *B*
Globe University
    Minneapolis *A, B, M, D*
    Moorhead *A, B*
    Woodbury *A, B, M*
Hamline University *B, M*
Herzing University
    Minneapolis *A, B*
Hibbing Community College *A*
ITT Technical Institute
    Eden Prairie *B*
Inver Hills Community College *A*
Itasca Community College *A*
Lake Superior College *A*
Leech Lake Tribal College *A*
Metropolitan State University *B, M, D*
Minneapolis Community and
    Technical College *A*
Minnesota School of Business
    Blaine *A, B*
    Brooklyn Center *A, B*
    Elk River *A, B*
    Lakeville *A, B*
    Plymouth *A, B*
    Richfield *A, B, M*
    Rochester *A, B*
    St. Cloud *A, B*
    Shakopee *A, B*
Minnesota State College - Southeast
    Technical *C, A*
Minnesota State Community and
    Technical College *C, A*
Minnesota State University
    Mankato *B, M*
    Moorhead *B*
Minnesota West Community and
    Technical College *A*
National American University
    Bloomington *B*
    Roseville *B*
Normandale Community College *C*
North Central University *A, B*
North Hennepin Community
    College *C, A*
Northland Community & Technical
    College *A*
Northwest Technical College *C*
Pine Technical College *A*
Rasmussen College
    Blaine *C, A, B*
    Bloomington *C, A, B*
    Brooklyn Park *C, A, B*
    Eagan *C, A, B*
    Lake Elmo/Woodbury *C, A, B*
    Mankato *C, A, B*
    Moorhead *A, B*
    St. Cloud *C, A, B*
Rochester Community and Technical
    College *C, A*
St. Catherine University *B, M*

Saint Cloud State University *B, M*
St. Cloud Technical and Community
    College *A*
St. John's University *B*
St. Mary's University of
    Minnesota *M, D*
St. Paul College *A*
South Central College *A*
Southwest Minnesota State
    University *A, B, M*
University of Minnesota
    Crookston *B*
    Duluth *C, B, M*
    Twin Cities *C, B, M, D*
University of Northwestern - St.
    Paul *B*
University of Phoenix
    Minneapolis-St. Paul *B, M*
University of St. Thomas *B, M*
Walden University *B, M, D*
White Earth Tribal and Community
    College *A*
Winona State University *B*

Mississippi

Alcorn State University *B, M*
Belhaven University *C, B, M*
Blue Mountain College *B*
Copiah-Lincoln Community
    College *A*
Delta State University *B, M*
Holmes Community College *A*
Jackson State University *B, M, D*
Millsaps College *B, M*
Mississippi College *B, M*
Mississippi Gulf Coast Community
    College *A*
Mississippi State University *B, M, D*
Mississippi University for Women *B*
Mississippi Valley State
    University *B, M*
Northeast Mississippi Community
    College *A*
Northwest Mississippi Community
    College *A*
Pearl River Community College *A*
Rust College *A, B*
Southeastern Baptist College *A*
University of Mississippi *B, M, D*
University of Phoenix
    Jackson *B, M*
University of Southern
    Mississippi *B, M*
William Carey University *B, M*

Missouri

Avila University *B, M*
Calvary Bible College and Theological
    Seminary *B*
Central Methodist University *B*
College of the Ozarks *B*
Columbia College *B*
Culver-Stockton College *B*
DeVry University
    Kansas City *B, M*
Drury University *B, M*
Evangel University *B*
Fontbonne University *B, M*
Grantham University *A, B, M*
Hannibal-LaGrange University *B*
Harris-Stowe State University *B*
Lincoln University *B, M*
Lindenwood University *B, M*
Maryville University of Saint Louis *B*
Metropolitan Community College -
    Kansas City *C, A*
Mineral Area College *A*
Missouri Baptist University *C, A, B, M*
Missouri State University *B, M*
Missouri University of Science and
    Technology *B, M*
Missouri Valley College *B*
Missouri Western State
    University *A, B*

National American University
  Kansas City *A, B, M*
North Central Missouri College *C, A*
Northwest Missouri State
  University *B, M*
Park University *A, B, M*
Ranken Technical College *B*
Rockhurst University *B, M*
Saint Louis University *B, M*
Southeast Missouri State
  University *B, M*
Southwest Baptist University *B, M*
State Fair Community College *A*
Stephens College *B, M*
Stevens Institute of Business &
  Arts *A, B*
Truman State University *B*
University of Central Missouri *B*
University of Missouri
  Columbia *B, M, D*
  Kansas City *B, M*
  St. Louis *B, M, D*
University of Phoenix
  Kansas City *B, M*
  St. Louis *B, M*
Washington University in St.
  Louis *C, B, M, D*
Webster University *B, M, D*
Westminster College *B, T*
William Jewell College *B*
William Woods University *B, M*

Montana

Blackfeet Community College *A*
Carroll College *A, B*
Chief Dull Knife College *A*
Flathead Valley Community
  College *C, A*
Fort Peck Community College *C, A*
Little Big Horn College *C, A*
Miles Community College *A*
Montana State University
  Great Falls College *C, A*
  Northern *A, B*
Rocky Mountain College *B*
Salish Kootenai College *A, B*
University of Great Falls *B*
University of Montana *B, M*
University of Montana: Western *A, B*

Nebraska

Bellevue University *B*
Central Community College *C, A*
Chadron State College *B, M*
Clarkson College *B, M*
College of Saint Mary *A, B, M*
Concordia University *B, M, T*
Creighton University *B, M*
Doane College *B*
Grace University *B*
Hastings College *B*
Herzing University
  Omaha School of Massage Therapy
    and Healthcare *B*
ITT Technical Institute
  Omaha *B*
Kaplan University
  Lincoln *A, B*
  Omaha *A, B, M*
Metropolitan Community College *A*
Mid-Plains Community College *C, A*
Midland University *B*
Nebraska Indian Community
  College *A*
Nebraska Wesleyan University *B*
Northeast Community College *A*
Southeast Community College *A*
Union College *A, B*
University of Nebraska
  Kearney *B, M*
  Lincoln *B, M*
  Omaha *B, M*
University of Phoenix
  Omaha *B, M*

Wayne State College *B, M*
Western Nebraska Community
  College *C, A*
Wright Career College
  Omaha *A*
York College *B*

Nevada

College of Southern Nevada *C, A*
Everest College
  Las Vegas *A*
Great Basin College *C, A, B*
ITT Technical Institute
  Henderson *B*
Morrison University *M*
Nevada State College *B*
Roseman University of Health
  Sciences *M*
Sierra Nevada College *B*
Truckee Meadows Community
  College *A*
University of Nevada
  Las Vegas *M*
  Reno *B, M*
University of Phoenix
  Las Vegas *B, M*
  Northern Nevada *B, M*
Western Nevada College *C, A*

New Hampshire

Colby-Sawyer College *B*
Daniel Webster College *A, B, M*
Dartmouth College *M*
Franklin Pierce University *A, B, M*
Granite State College *A, B, M*
Great Bay Community College *C, A*
Keene State College *B*
Lakes Region Community
  College *C, A*
Lebanon College *A*
Manchester Community College *C, A*
Mount Washington College *A, B*
NHTI-Concord's Community
  College *A*
Nashua Community College *A*
New England College *B, M*
Plymouth State University *B, M*
Rivier University *A, B, M*
Southern New Hampshire
  University *A, B, M*
University of New Hampshire *B*
University of New Hampshire at
  Manchester *A, B, M*
White Mountains Community
  College *C, A*

New Jersey

Atlantic Cape Community College *A*
Berkeley College *A, B*
Bloomfield College *B*
Brookdale Community College *A*
Burlington County College *A*
Caldwell College *B, M*
Camden County College *A*
Centenary College *B, M*
College of New Jersey *B*
College of St. Elizabeth *C, B, M*
County College of Morris *A*
Cumberland County College *A*
DeVry University
  North Brunswick *B, M*
Drew University *B*
Essex County College *C, A*
Fairleigh Dickinson University
  College at Florham *B, M*
  Metropolitan Campus *B, M*
Felician College *B*
Georgian Court University *B, M*
Gloucester County College *A*
Hudson County Community
  College *A*
Kean University *B*
Mercer County Community
  College *C, A*

Middlesex County College *A*
Monmouth University *B, M*
Montclair State University *B, M*
New Jersey City University *B*
New Jersey Institute of
  Technology *B, M*
Ocean County College *C, A*
Ramapo College of New Jersey *B*
Raritan Valley Community College *A*
Richard Stockton College of New
  Jersey *B, M*
Rider University *A, B, M*
Rowan University *B, M*
Rutgers, The State University of New
  Jersey
  Camden Campus *B, M*
  New Brunswick/Piscataway
    Campus *B, M, D*
  Newark Campus *B, M, D*
Saint Peter's University *A, B, M*
Salem Community College *A*
Seton Hall University *B, M*
Stevens Institute of Technology *B, M*
Sussex County Community College *A*
Thomas Edison State
  College *C, A, B, M*
Union County College *A*
University of Phoenix
  Jersey City *B*
William Paterson University of New
  Jersey *B, M*

New Mexico

Brookline College
  Albuquerque *C, A*
Central New Mexico Community
  College *C, A*
Dona Ana Community College of
  New Mexico State
  University *C, A*
Eastern New Mexico University *B, M*
Eastern New Mexico University:
  Roswell *C, A*
ITT Technical Institute
  Albuquerque *B*
Institute of American Indian Arts *C*
Luna Community College *A*
Mesalands Community College *A*
National American University
  Albuquerque *A, B*
New Mexico Highlands
  University *B, M*
New Mexico Institute of Mining and
  Technology *A, B*
New Mexico Junior College *A*
New Mexico State University *B, M, D*
Northern New Mexico
  College *C, A, B*
San Juan College *C, A*
Santa Fe Community College *A*
Santa Fe University of Art and
  Design *B, M*
Southwestern Indian Polytechnic
  Institute *C, A*
University of New Mexico *B, M*
University of Phoenix
  New Mexico *B, M*
University of the Southwest *B, M*
Western New Mexico
  University *A, B, M*

New York

ASA College *C, A*
Adelphi University *B, M*
Adirondack Community College *A*
Alfred University *B, M*
Berkeley College *A, B*
Berkeley College of New York
  City *A, B*
Boricua College *B*
Bramson ORT College *A*
Briarcliffe College *A, B*
Broome Community College *A*

Bryant & Stratton College
  Albany *A*
  Amherst *A, B*
  Buffalo *B*
  Rochester *A*
  Southtowns *C, A, B*
  Syracuse *A*
Canisius College *M*
Cayuga Community College *C, A*
Cazenovia College *C, A, B*
City University of New York
  Baruch College *B, M*
  Borough of Manhattan Community
    College *A*
  Brooklyn College *B*
  College of Staten Island *M*
  Guttman Community College *A*
  Hostos Community College *A*
  Kingsborough Community
    College *A*
  LaGuardia Community College *A*
  Lehman College *B*
  Medgar Evers College *A, B*
  Queensborough Community
    College *A*
  York College *B*
Clarkson University *B, M*
Clinton Community College *A*
College of Mount St. Vincent *B, M*
College of Saint Rose *B, M*
College of Westchester *C, A, B*
Columbia-Greene Community
  College *A*
Concordia College *A, B*
Cornell University *M, D*
Corning Community College *A*
D'Youville College *B*
Daemen College *B*
DeVry College of New York
  Midtown Campus *B, M*
Dominican College of Blauvelt *B, M*
Dowling College *B, M*
Dutchess Community College *A*
Elmira College *A, B, M*
Erie Community College *A*
Excelsior College *A, B, M*
Finger Lakes Community College *A*
Five Towns College *A, B*
Fordham University *B, M*
Fulton-Montgomery Community
  College *A*
Genesee Community College *C, A*
Globe Institute of
  Technology *C, A, B*
Hartwick College *B*
Herkimer County Community
  College *A*
Hilbert College *A, B*
Hofstra University *C, B, M*
Houghton College *B*
Hudson Valley Community College *A*
Iona College *B, M*
Ithaca College *B, M*
Jamestown Business College *A, B*
Jamestown Community College *A*
Jefferson Community College *A*
Keuka College *B, M*
King's College *B*
LIM College *B*
Le Moyne College *B, M*
Long Island University
  LIU Brooklyn *A, B, M*
  LIU Post *B, M*
Manhattan College *M*
Manhattanville College *B, M*
Maria College *A*
Marist College *B, M*
Marymount Manhattan College *B*
Medaille College *B, M*
Medaille College: Amherst *A, B, M*
Medaille College: Rochester *A, B, M*
Mercy College *C, A, B, M*
Metropolitan College of New
  York *B, M*

Mildred Elley
  Albany *A*
Molloy College *B, M*
Monroe College *A, B, M*
Mount Saint Mary College *C, B, M*
Nassau Community College *C, A*
New York Institute of
  Technology *A, B, M*
New York University *C, M, D*
Niagara County Community
  College *C, A*
Niagara University *M*
North Country Community College *A*
Nyack College *A, B, M*
Onondaga Community College *A*
Orange County Community
  College *A*
Pace University *M, D*
Pace University: Pleasantville/
  Briarcliff *B, M*
Paul Smith's College *B*
Plaza College *A, B*
Professional Business College *A*
Rensselaer Polytechnic
  Institute *B, M, D*
Roberts Wesleyan College *B, M*
Rochester Institute of
  Technology *B, M*
Rockland Community College *A*
SUNY
  College at Brockport *B*
  College at Buffalo *B*
  College at Fredonia *B*
  College at Geneseo *B*
  College at New Paltz *B, M*
  College at Old Westbury *B*
  College at Oswego *B, M*
  College at Plattsburgh *B*
  College at Potsdam *B*
  College of Agriculture and
    Technology at Cobleskill *A, B*
  College of Agriculture and
    Technology at Morrisville *A, B*
  College of Technology at
    Alfred *A, B*
  College of Technology at
    Canton *A, B*
  College of Technology at
    Delhi *A, B*
  Empire State College *M*
  Farmingdale State College *C, B*
  Institute of Technology at Utica/
    Rome *B*
  University at Albany *B, M*
  University at Binghamton *B, M, D*
  University at Buffalo *B, M, D*
  University at Stony Brook *B, M*
Sage Colleges *B, M*
Saint Bonaventure University *M*
St. Francis College *A, B*
St. John Fisher College *B, M*
St. John's University *A, B, M*
St. Joseph's College New York:
  Suffolk Campus *C, B, M*
St. Joseph's College, New
  York *C, B, M*
St. Thomas Aquinas College *A, B, M*
Sanford-Brown Institute
  Melville *A*
Siena College *B*
Suffolk County Community College *A*
Sullivan County Community
  College *A*
Syracuse University *B, M, D*
Technical Career Institutes *A*
Tompkins Cortland Community
  College *C, A*
Touro College *A, B*
Trocaire College *A*
Ulster County Community College *A*
United States Military Academy *B*
University of Rochester *B, M, D*
Utica College *B*
Utica School of Commerce *A*
Villa Maria College of Buffalo *A, B*

Wagner College *B, M*
Westchester Community College *A*
Yeshiva University *B*

North Carolina
Alamance Community College *C, A*
Appalachian State University *B, M*
Asheville-Buncombe Technical
  Community College *A*
Barton College *B*
Beaufort County Community
  College *A*
Belmont Abbey College *B*
Bennett College for Women *B*
Bladen Community College *C, A*
Brevard College *B*
Brunswick Community College *C, A*
Caldwell Community College and
  Technical Institute *A*
Campbell University *B, M*
Cape Fear Community College *C, A*
Catawba College *B*
Catawba Valley Community
  College *A*
Central Carolina Community
  College *A*
Central Piedmont Community
  College *C, A*
Chowan University *B*
Cleveland Community College *C, A*
Coastal Carolina Community
  College *C, A*
College of the Albemarle *A*
Craven Community College *C, A*
Davidson County Community
  College *C, A*
Duke University *M, D*
Durham Technical Community
  College *A*
East Carolina University *B, M*
Edgecombe Community College *A*
Elizabeth City State University *B*
Elon University *B, M*
Fayetteville State University *B, M*
Fayetteville Technical Community
  College *C, A*
Forsyth Technical Community
  College *A*
Gardner-Webb University *B, M*
Gaston College *A*
Guilford College *C, B*
Guilford Technical Community
  College *C, A*
Halifax Community College *C, A*
Haywood Community College *C, A*
High Point University *B, M*
Isothermal Community College *C, A*
James Sprunt Community College *A*
Johnson & Wales University
  Charlotte *B*
Johnson C. Smith University *B*
Johnston Community College *C, A*
Laurel University *B, M*
Lees-McRae College *B*
Lenoir Community College *C, A*
Livingstone College *B*
Mars Hill University *B*
Martin Community College *C, A*
Mayland Community College *C, A*
Meredith College *B, M*
Methodist University *A, B, M*
Miller-Motte College
  Wilmington *C, A, B*
Mitchell Community College *A*
Montgomery Community
  College *C, A*
Montreat College *C, A, B, M*
Nash Community College *A*
North Carolina Agricultural and
  Technical State University *B, M*
North Carolina Central
  University *B, M*
North Carolina State University *B, M*
North Carolina Wesleyan College *B*
Pamlico Community College *A*

Pfeiffer University *B, M*
Piedmont Community College *A*
Pitt Community College *C, A*
Queens University of Charlotte *B, M*
Randolph Community College *A*
Richmond Community College *C, A*
Roanoke-Chowan Community
  College *A*
Robeson Community College *A*
Rockingham Community
  College *C, A*
Rowan-Cabarrus Community
  College *C, A*
St. Andrews University *B, M*
St. Augustine's University *B*
Salem College *B*
Sampson Community College *A*
Sandhills Community College *A*
Shaw University *B*
South College *B*
South Piedmont Community
  College *C, A*
Southeastern Community
  College *C, A*
Southwestern Community
  College *C, A*
Stanly Community College *C, A*
Surry Community College *C, A*
Tri-County Community College *A*
University of Mount Olive *B, M*
University of North Carolina
  Asheville *B*
  Chapel Hill *B, M, D*
  Charlotte *B, M, D*
  Greensboro *B, M*
  Pembroke *B, M*
  Wilmington *B, M*
University of Phoenix
  Charlotte *B, M*
  Raleigh *B, M*
Vance-Granville Community
  College *C, A*
Wake Forest University *M*
Warren Wilson College *B*
Wayne Community College *C, A*
Western Carolina University *B, M*
Western Piedmont Community
  College *C, A*
Wilkes Community College *C, A*
William Peace University *B*
Wilson Community College *C, A*
Wingate University *B, M*
Winston-Salem State University *B, M*

North Dakota
Cankdeska Cikana Community
  College *A*
Dakota College at Bottineau *A*
Dickinson State University *B*
Fort Berthold Community
  College *C, A*
Lake Region State College *A*
Mayville State University *B*
Minot State University *B, M*
North Dakota State College of
  Science *A*
North Dakota State University *B, M*
Rasmussen College
  Bismarck *C, A, B*
  Fargo *C, A, B*
Sitting Bull College *A, B*
Turtle Mountain Community
  College *A*
United Tribes Technical College *A, B*
University of Jamestown *B*
University of Mary *B, M*
University of North Dakota *B, M*
Valley City State University *B*
Williston State College *C, A*

Ohio
Akron Institute of Herzing
  University *A, B*

Antioch University
  Midwest *B, M*
Ashland University *C, B, M*
Baldwin Wallace University *C, B, M*
Belmont College *A*
Bluffton University *B, M*
Bowling Green State University *B, M*
Bowling Green State University:
  Firelands College *C, A, B*
Brown Mackie College
  Akron *C, A*
  Findlay *A*
  North Canton *C, A, B*
Bryant & Stratton College
  Eastlake *B*
  Parma *A, B*
Capital University *B, M*
Case Western Reserve
  University *B, M, D*
Cedarville University *B*
Central Ohio Technical College *A*
Chatfield College *A*
Cincinnati State Technical and
  Community College *A*
Clark State Community College *C, A*
Cleveland State University *M, D*
College of Mount St. Joseph *A, B, M*
Columbus State Community
  College *C, A*
Cuyahoga Community College
  Metropolitan *A*
Davis College *A*
Daymar College
  Chillicothe *A*
DeVry University
  Columbus *B, M*
Defiance College *A, B, M*
Eastern Gateway Community
  College *C, A*
Edison State Community College *A*
Fortis College
  Cuyahoga *A*
  Ravenna *A*
Franciscan University of
  Steubenville *A, B, M*
Franklin University *A, B, M*
Gallipolis Career College *A*
Harrison College
  Grove City *A, B*
Heidelberg University *B, M*
Herzing University
  Toledo *A, B*
Hiram College *B*
ITT Technical Institute
  Dayton *A*
  Hilliard *A*
  Norwood *A*
  Strongsville *A*
  Youngstown *A*
John Carroll University *B, M*
Kent State University *B, M, D*
Kent State University
  Ashtabula *B*
  Geauga *B*
  Salem *B*
  Stark *B, M*
  Trumbull *B*
  Tuscarawas *B*
Lake Erie College *B, M*
Lakeland Community College *C, A*
Lincoln College of Technology
  Dayton *A*
Lorain County Community College *A*
Lourdes University *B, M*
Malone University *B, M*
Marion Technical College *C, A*
Miami University
  Hamilton *A*
  Middletown *C, A*
  Oxford *B, M*
Mount Vernon Nazarene
  University *A, B, M*
Muskingum University *B*

National College
Canton *C, A*
Cincinnati *A*
Kettering *C, A*
Stow *C, A*
Willoughby Hills *C*
Youngstown *C, A*
North Central State College *C, A*
Northwest State Community
College *A*
Notre Dame College *B*
Ohio Business College
Sandusky *A*
Sheffield *A*
Ohio Christian University *A, B, M*
Ohio Dominican University *A, B, M*
Ohio Mid-Western College *B*
Ohio Northern University *B*
Ohio State University
Agricultural Technical Institute *A*
Columbus Campus *B, M, D*
Mansfield Campus *B*
Marion Campus *B*
Newark Campus *B*
Ohio University *B, M*
Ohio University
Chillicothe Campus *A, B, M*
Lancaster Campus *A*
Southern Campus at Ironton *B*
Ohio Valley College of Technology *A*
Otterbein University *B, M*
Remington College
Cleveland *A*
Cleveland West *A*
Shawnee State University *A, B*
Sinclair Community College *C, A*
Southern State Community College *A*
Stark State College *A*
Stautzenberger College *A*
Terra State Community College *C, A*
Tiffin University *A, B, M*
Trumbull Business College *A*
Union Institute & University *B*
University of Akron *C, A, B, M*
University of Akron: Wayne
College *A*
University of Cincinnati *C, B, M, D*
University of Cincinnati
Blue Ash College *A*
Clermont College *A, B*
University of Dayton *B, M*
University of Findlay *B, M*
University of Mount Union *B*
University of Northwestern
Ohio *A, B, M*
University of Phoenix
Cleveland *B, M*
University of Rio Grande *B*
University of Toledo *A, B, M*
Urbana University *B, M*
Ursuline College *B*
Walsh University *A, B, M*
Washington State Community
College *A*
Wilberforce University *B*
Wilmington College *B*
Wright State University *A, B, M*
Wright State University: Lake
Campus *A, B*
Xavier University *C, A, B, M*
Youngstown State
University *C, A, B, M*
Zane State College *C, A*

Oklahoma

Bacone College *A, B*
Cameron University *A, B*
Carl Albert State College *A*
Connors State College *A*
East Central University *B*
Eastern Oklahoma State College *A*
Langston University *B*
Mid-America Christian
University *B, M*
Murray State College *A*

Northeastern Oklahoma Agricultural
and Mechanical College *A*
Northeastern State University *B, M*
Northern Oklahoma College *A*
Northwestern Oklahoma State
University *B*
Oklahoma Baptist University *B, M*
Oklahoma Christian University *B, M*
Oklahoma City University *B, M*
Oklahoma Panhandle State
University *A, B*
Oklahoma State University *B, M, D*
Oklahoma State University
Oklahoma City *A*
Oklahoma Wesleyan
University *A, B, M*
Oral Roberts University *B, M*
Redlands Community College *A*
Rogers State University *A, B*
Rose State College *A*
St. Gregory's University *A, B, M*
Seminole State College *A*
Southeastern Oklahoma State
University *B, M*
Southern Nazarene
University *A, B, M*
Southwestern Christian University *B*
Southwestern Oklahoma State
University *B, M*
Tulsa Community College *A*
University of Central Oklahoma *B, M*
University of Oklahoma *B, M, D*
University of Phoenix
Oklahoma City *B, M*
Tulsa *B, M*
University of Science and Arts of
Oklahoma *B, T*
University of Tulsa *B, M*
Western Oklahoma State College *A*
Wright Career College
Oklahoma City *A*
Tulsa *A*

Oregon

Blue Mountain Community College *A*
Central Oregon Community
College *A*
Chemeketa Community College *A*
Clackamas Community College *C, A*
Clatsop Community College *A*
Concordia University *B*
Corban University *A, B, M*
Eastern Oregon University *B, M*
Everest College
Portland *C, A*
George Fox University *B, M, D*
Heald College
Portland *C, A*
ITT Technical Institute
Portland *B*
Klamath Community College *C, A*
Linfield College *B*
Linn-Benton Community College *A*
Marylhurst University *B, M*
Mt. Hood Community College *A*
New Hope Christian College *B*
Northwest Christian University *B, M*
Oregon State University *B, M*
Pacific University *B*
Pioneer Pacific College *A, B*
Portland Community College *A*
Portland State University *B, D*
Rogue Community College *C, A*
Southern Oregon University *B, M*
Southwestern Oregon Community
College *A*
Tillamook Bay Community College *A*
Umpqua Community College *A*
University of Oregon *M, D*
University of Phoenix
Oregon *B, M*
University of Portland *B, M*
Warner Pacific College *B, M*
Willamette University *M*

Pennsylvania

Albright College *C, B*
Alvernia University *B*
Arcadia University *C, B, M*
Berks Technical Institute *A*
Bloomsburg University of
Pennsylvania *B, M*
Bucknell University *B*
Bucks County Community College *A*
Butler County Community College *A*
Cabrini College *B*
Cairn University *B*
California University of
Pennsylvania *B*
Cambria-Rowe Business College *A*
Cambria-Rowe Business College:
Indiana *A*
Carlow University *B, M*
Carnegie Mellon University *B, M, D*
Cedar Crest College *B*
Central Penn College *A, B*
Chatham University *B, M*
Chestnut Hill College *A, B*
Cheyney University of
Pennsylvania *B*
Clarion University of
Pennsylvania *A, B, M*
Community College of Allegheny
County *C, A*
Community College of Beaver
County *A*
Community College of
Philadelphia *C, A*
Consolidated School of Business
Lancaster *A*
York *A*
DeSales University *B, M*
DeVry University
Fort Washington *B, M*
Delaware County Community
College *A*
Delaware Valley College *B*
Douglas Education Center *A*
DuBois Business College *A*
DuBois Business College
Huntingdon *A*
Oil City *A*
Duquesne University *M*
East Stroudsburg University of
Pennsylvania *B*
Eastern University *B, M*
Edinboro University of
Pennsylvania *A, B*
Elizabethtown College *B*
Erie Business Center South *A*
Fortis Institute
Erie *A*
Franklin & Marshall College *B*
Gannon University *B, M*
Geneva College *A, B, M*
Gettysburg College *B*
Grove City College *B*
Gwynedd Mercy University *A, B, M*
Harcum College *A*
Harrisburg Area Community
College *A*
Holy Family University *B, M*
Immaculata University *C, A, B, M*
Indiana University of
Pennsylvania *B, M*
Juniata College *B*
Kaplan Career Institute
Harrisburg *A*
Pittsburgh *A*
Keystone College *A, B*
King's College *C, A, B*
Kutztown University of
Pennsylvania *B, M*
La Salle University *A, B, M*
Lackawanna College *A*
Laurel Business Institute *A*
Laurel Technical Institute *A*
Lebanon Valley College *A, B, M*
Lehigh Carbon Community College *A*

Lehigh University *M*
Lincoln University *B*
Lock Haven University of
Pennsylvania *A, B*
Luzerne County Community
College *A*
Lycoming College *B*
Manor College *A*
Mansfield University of
Pennsylvania *B*
Marywood University *B, M*
McCann School of Business and
Technology
Hazleton *A*
Mercyhurst University *B, T*
Messiah College *B*
Millersville University of
Pennsylvania *B*
Misericordia University *B, M*
Montgomery County Community
College *C, A*
Moravian College *B, M*
Mount Aloysius College *A, B, M*
Muhlenberg College *C, A, B*
Neumann University *B*
Northampton Community College *A*
Pace Institute *A*
Peirce College *A, B*
Penn Commercial Business and
Technical School *A*
Penn State
Abington *C*
Altoona *C*
Beaver *C, B*
Berks *C*
Brandywine *C, B*
DuBois *C, B*
Erie, The Behrend College *C, M*
Fayette, The Eberly Campus *C, B*
Greater Allegheny *C, B*
Harrisburg *C, B*
Hazleton *C, B*
Lehigh Valley *C, B*
Mont Alto *C, B*
New Kensington *C, B*
Schuylkill *C, B*
Shenango *C, B*
University Park *C, M, D*
Wilkes-Barre *C, B*
Worthington Scranton *C, B*
York *C, B*
Pennsylvania College of
Technology *A, B*
Pennsylvania Institute of
Technology *A*
Philadelphia University *A, B, M*
Point Park University *C, A, B, M*
Reading Area Community College *A*
Robert Morris University *B, M*
Rosemont College *B, M*
St. Francis University *A, B, M*
Saint Joseph's University *A, B, M*
St. Vincent College *C, B, M*
Sanford-Brown Institute
Pittsburgh *C, A*
Seton Hill University *B, M*
Shippensburg University of
Pennsylvania *B, M, T*
Slippery Rock University of
Pennsylvania *B, M*
Susquehanna University *A, B*
Temple University *M, D*
Thaddeus Stevens College of
Technology *A*
Thiel College *B*
University of Pennsylvania *B, M, D*
University of Phoenix
Harrisburg *B, M*
Philadelphia *B, M*
Pittsburgh *B, M*
University of Pittsburgh *M, D*
University of Pittsburgh
Bradford *B*
Greensburg *B*
University of Scranton *C, A, B, M*

Valley Forge Christian College *B*
Villanova University *B, M*
Waynesburg University *B, M*
West Chester University of
Pennsylvania *B, M*
Westminster College *B*
Westmoreland County Community
College *C, A*
Widener University *A, B, M*
Wilkes University *B, M*
Wilson College *A, B*
YTI Career Institute
Altoona *A*
York *A*
York College of Pennsylvania *A, B, M*
Yorktowne Business Institute *A*

Puerto Rico

American University of Puerto
Rico *B*
Atlantic University College *A, B*
Bayamon Central University *B, M*
Caribbean University *A, B*
Columbia Centro Universitario:
Caguas *C, A, B, M*
Columbia Centro Universitario:
Yauco *A, B*
EDP University of Puerto Rico: Hato
Rey *A, B*
Huertas College *A*
Humacao Community College *A, B*
ICPR Junior College *C, A*
Inter American University of Puerto
Rico
Aguadilla Campus *A*
Arecibo Campus *A, B*
Barranquitas Campus *A, B*
Bayamon Campus *A*
Fajardo Campus *B*
Guayama Campus *A, B*
Metropolitan Campus *A, B, M*
Ponce Campus *A, B*
San German Campus *A, B*
Pontifical Catholic University of
Puerto Rico *B, M, D*
Turabo University *A, B, M, D*
Universidad Metropolitana *B, M*
Universidad Politecnica de Puerto
Rico *B, M*
Universidad del Este *A, B, M*
University of Phoenix
Puerto Rico *B, M*
University of Puerto Rico
Arecibo *B*
Bayamon University College *B*
Carolina Regional College *B*
Cayey University College *B*
Humacao *B*
Mayaguez *B, M*
Ponce *A, B*
Utuado *A*
University of the Sacred Heart *B*

Rhode Island

Bryant University *B, M*
Community College of Rhode
Island *C, A*
Johnson & Wales University
Providence *B*
Providence College *C, A, B, M*
Rhode Island College *B*
Roger Williams University *A, B, M*
Salve Regina University *A, B, M*
University of Rhode Island *B, M, D*

South Carolina

Aiken Technical College *C, A*
Allen University *B*
Anderson University *B, M*
Benedict College *B*
Bob Jones University *B*
Charleston Southern University *B, M*
Citadel *B, M*
Claflin University *B, M*

Clemson University *B, M*
Coastal Carolina University *B, M*
College of Charleston *B, M*
Columbia College *B*
Erskine College *B*
Florence-Darlington Technical
College *C*
Forrest Junior College *A*
Francis Marion University *B, M*
Furman University *B*
Greenville Technical College *C, A*
Lander University *C, B*
Limestone College *A, B, M*
Midlands Technical College *A*
Miller-Motte Technical College *A*
Morris College *B*
Newberry College *B*
North Greenville University *B, M*
Northeastern Technical College *A*
Piedmont Technical College *C*
Presbyterian College *B*
South Carolina State University *B*
Southern Wesleyan University *B, M*
Spartanburg Community College *A*
Spartanburg Methodist College *A*
Technical College of the
Lowcountry *C*
Tri-County Technical College *C, A*
Trident Technical College *A*
University of Phoenix
Columbia *B, M*
University of South Carolina
Aiken *B*
Beaufort *B*
Columbia *B, M, D*
Lancaster *A*
Upstate *B*
Virginia College
Charleston *A, B*
Columbia *A*
Greenville *A*
Spartanburg *A*
Voorhees College *B*
Winthrop University *B, M*
York Technical College *A*

South Dakota

Augustana College *B*
Black Hills State University *B, M*
Dakota State University *A, B, M*
Globe University
Sioux Falls *A, B*
Kilian Community College *A*
Lake Area Technical Institute *A*
Mount Marty College *C, A, B, M*
National American University
Rapid City *A, B, M*
Northern State University *A, B*
Oglala Lakota College *C, A, B*
Presentation College *A, B*
Sinte Gleska University *A, B*
Sisseton Wahpeton College *A*
Southeast Technical Institute *A*
University of Sioux Falls *A, B*
University of South Dakota *B, M*
Western Dakota Technical
Institute *C, A*

Tennessee

American Baptist College *A, B*
Anthem Career College
Memphis *A*
Aquinas College *B*
Argosy University
Nashville *B, M*
Austin Peay State University *A, M*
Belmont University *B*
Bethel University *B, M*
Bryan University
Dayton *A, B, M*
Carson-Newman University *B*
Chattanooga State Community
College *A*
Christian Brothers University *B, M*

Cleveland State Community
College *C, A*
Columbia State Community
College *C, A*
Daymar Institute
Clarksville *A, B*
Nashville *C, A, B*
Dyersburg State Community
College *A*
East Tennessee State University *B, M*
Fisk University *B*
Freed-Hardeman University *B, M*
Hiwassee College *A*
ITT Technical Institute
Knoxville *B*
Memphis *B*
Nashville *B*
Jackson State Community College *A*
King University *B*
Lane College *B*
LeMoyne-Owen College *B*
Lee University *B, M*
Lincoln Memorial University *B, M*
Lipscomb University *B, M*
Martin Methodist College *B*
Maryville College *B*
Middle Tennessee State
University *B, M*
Miller-Motte Technical College
Clarksville *A*
Milligan College *B*
Motlow State Community College *A*
Nashville State Community College *A*
National College of Business and
Technology
Bartlett *A*
Bristol *C, A*
Knoxville *C, A*
Madison *C, A*
Memphis *C, A*
Nashville *C, A*
Northeast State Community
College *A*
Pellissippi State Community
College *A*
Remington College
Memphis *B*
Rhodes College *B*
Roane State Community College *A*
South College *A, B*
Southern Adventist
University *A, B, M*
Southwest Tennessee Community
College *A*
Tennessee State University *B, M*
Tennessee Temple University *A, B*
Tennessee Wesleyan College *B*
Trevecca Nazarene University *B, M*
Tusculum College *B, M*
Union University *B, M*
University of Memphis *B, M, D*
University of Phoenix
Chattanooga *B, M*
Knoxville *B, M*
Memphis *B, M*
Nashville *B, M*
University of Tennessee
Chattanooga *B, M*
Knoxville *B, M, D*
Martin *B, M*
Vanderbilt University *M, D*
Victory University *B*
Virginia College
School of Business and Health in
Chattanooga *A*
School of Business and Health in
Knoxville *A*
Volunteer State Community
College *A*
Walters State Community College *A*
Welch College *B*
West Tennessee Business
College *C, A*

Texas

Abilene Christian University *B*
Alvin Community College *C, A*
Amberton University *B, M*
Angelina College *C, A*
Angelo State University *B, M*
Argosy University
Dallas *B, M, D*
Austin Community College *C, A*
Baptist University of the Americas *B*
Baylor University *B, M*
Blinn College *C*
Brazosport College *C, A*
Brookhaven College *C, A*
Cedar Valley College *C, A*
Central Texas College *C, A*
Cisco College *C*
Coastal Bend College *A*
College of the Mainland *A*
Collin County Community College
District *C, A*
Concordia University Texas *B, M*
Dallas Baptist University *A, B, M, D*
Dallas Christian College *A, B*
DeVry University
Houston *B, M*
Irving *B, M*
Del Mar College *C, A*
Eastfield College *C, A*
El Centro College *C, A*
El Paso Community College *C, A*
Everest College
Arlington *A*
Dallas *A*
Fort Worth *A*
Frank Phillips College *A*
Galveston College *C, A*
Hallmark College of Technology *B, M*
Hardin-Simmons University *B, M*
Hill College *A*
Houston Baptist University *B, M*
Houston Community College
System *C, A*
Howard Payne University *B, M*
Huston-Tillotson University *B*
ITT Technical Institute
Arlington *B*
Austin *B*
Houston North *B*
Houston West *B*
Richardson *B*
San Antonio *B*
Webster *B*
Jarvis Christian College *B, T*
Kilgore College *C, A*
Lamar Institute of Technology *A*
Lamar State College at Orange *C, A*
Lamar State College at Port Arthur *A*
Lamar University *B, M*
LeTourneau University *B, M*
Lee College *C, A*
Lone Star College System *C, A*
Lubbock Christian University *B*
McMurry University *B*
Midland College *B*
Midwestern State University *B, M*
Mountain View College *C, A*
National American University
Austin *A, B*
Navarro College *C, A*
North Lake College *A*
Northeast Texas Community
College *C, A*
Northwest Vista College *A*
Northwood University
Texas *B, M*
Odessa College *C, A*
Our Lady of the Lake University of
San Antonio *B, M*
Palo Alto College *C, A*
Paris Junior College *A*
Paul Quinn College *B*
Prairie View A&M University *B, M*

Remington College
 Dallas *C, A*
 Fort Worth *A*
 Houston Southeast *A*
 North Houston *A*
Rice University *B, M*
Richland College *C, A*
St. Edward's University *B, M*
St. Mary's University *B, M*
St. Philip's College *C, A*
Sam Houston State University *B, M*
San Antonio College *C, A*
San Jacinto College *C, A*
Schreiner University *B*
South Plains College *A*
South Texas College *C, A*
Southern Methodist University *B, M*
Southwestern Adventist
 University *B, M*
Southwestern Assemblies of God
 University *A, B*
Stephen F. Austin State
 University *B, M*
Sul Ross State University *B, M*
Tarleton State University *B, M*
Tarrant County College *C, A*
Texarkana College *C, A*
Texas A&M International
 University *B, M*
Texas A&M University *B, M, D*
Texas A&M University
 Commerce *B, M*
 Corpus Christi *B, M*
 Galveston *B*
 Kingsville *M*
 Texarkana *B, M*
Texas Christian University *M*
Texas College *B*
Texas Lutheran University *B*
Texas Southern University *B, M*
Texas State University *B, M*
Texas Tech University *B, M, D*
Texas Wesleyan University *B, M*
Texas Woman's University *B, M*
Trinity University *B*
Trinity Valley Community College *A*
Tyler Junior College *C, A*
University of Dallas *B, M*
University of Houston *B, M*
University of Houston
 Clear Lake *B, M*
 Downtown *B, M*
 Victoria *B, M, T*
University of Mary Hardin-Baylor *B*
University of North Texas *M, D*
University of Phoenix
 Austin *B, M*
 Dallas Fort Worth *B, M*
 Houston Westside *B, M*
 San Antonio *B, M*
University of St. Thomas *B, M*
University of Texas
 Arlington *B, M, D*
 Austin *B, M, D*
 Brownsville *B, M*
 Dallas *M, D*
 El Paso *B, M*
 Pan American *B, M*
 Permian Basin *B, M*
 San Antonio *B, M, D*
 Tyler *B, M*
University of the Incarnate
 Word *A, B, M*
Victoria College *C, A*
Wayland Baptist University *A, B, M*
West Texas A&M University *D, M*
Western Texas College *A*
Wharton County Junior College *A*
Wiley College *B*

Utah

Argosy University
 Salt Lake City *B, M, D*
Brigham Young University *B, M*

Broadview University
 Layton *A, B*
 Orem *A, B*
 West Jordan *A, B, M*
LDS Business College *A*
Provo College *A*
Salt Lake Community College *C, A*
Snow College *A*
Southern Utah University *B, M*
University of Phoenix
 Utah *B, M*
University of Utah *B, M, D*
Utah State University *A, B, M*
Utah Valley University *C, A, B, M*
Weber State University *C, B, M*
Western Governors University *B, M*
Westminster College *B, M*

Vermont

Castleton State College *B*
Champlain College *C, B, M*
College of St. Joseph in
 Vermont *A, B, M*
Goddard College *B, M*
Johnson State College *A, B*
Landmark College *A*
Lyndon State College *A, B*
Norwich University *B, M*
Saint Michael's College *B, M*
Southern Vermont College *B*
University of Vermont *B, M*
Vermont Technical College *A, B*

Virginia

American National University
 Charlottesville *C, A*
 Danville *C, A, B*
 Harrisonburg *C, A, B*
 Lynchburg *C, A, B*
 Martinsville *C, A*
 Salem *C, A, B, M*
Argosy University
 Washington D.C. *B, M*
Averett University *A, B, M*
Blue Ridge Community College *A*
Bluefield College *B*
Bridgewater College *B*
Bryant & Stratton College
 Richmond *A, B*
 Virginia Beach *A, B*
Central Virginia Community
 College *A*
Christopher Newport University *B*
College of William and Mary *B, M*
Dabney S. Lancaster Community
 College *A*
Danville Community College *A*
DeVry University
 Arlington *B, M*
ECPI University *B*
Eastern Mennonite University *B, M*
Eastern Shore Community College *A*
Emory & Henry College *B*
Ferrum College *B*
George Mason University *B, M*
Germanna Community College *A*
Hampton University *B, M, D*
ITT Technical Institute
 Chantilly *B*
 Norfolk *B*
 Richmond *B*
 Springfield *B*
J. Sargeant Reynolds Community
 College *C*
James Madison University *B, M*
John Tyler Community College *A*
Liberty University *B, M*
Longwood University *B, M*
Lord Fairfax Community College *A*
Lynchburg College *B, M*
Mary Baldwin College *B*
Marymount University *B, M*
Mountain Empire Community
 College *A*

New River Community College *A*
Northern Virginia Community
 College *A*
Old Dominion University *B, M, D*
Patrick Henry Community College *A*
Paul D. Camp Community College *A*
Piedmont Virginia Community
 College *A*
Radford University *B, M*
Rappahannock Community College *A*
Regent University *A, B, M*
Roanoke College *B*
Shenandoah University *B, M*
Southern Virginia University *B*
Southside Virginia Community
 College *A*
Southwest Virginia Community
 College *A*
Stratford University: Falls
 Church *A, B, M*
Thomas Nelson Community
 College *A*
Tidewater Community College *A*
University of Management and
 Technology *C, A, B, M, D*
University of Mary Washington *B, M*
University of Phoenix
 Northern Virginia *B, M*
 Richmond *B, M*
University of Richmond *B, M*
University of Virginia *M, D*
University of Virginia's College at
 Wise *B*
University of the Potomac *B*
Virginia College
 Richmond *A*
Virginia Commonwealth
 University *M*
Virginia Highlands Community
 College *A*
Virginia Intermont College *B*
Virginia Polytechnic Institute and
 State University *B, M*
Virginia State University *B*
Virginia Union University *B*
Virginia University of Lynchburg *B*
Virginia Wesleyan College *B*
Virginia Western Community
 College *C, A*
Washington and Lee University *B*
Westwood College
 Annandale *B*
 Arlington Ballston *B*
Wytheville Community College *A*

Washington

Antioch University
 Seattle *M*
Argosy University
 Seattle *B, M, D*
Bates Technical College *C*
Bellevue College *C, A*
Bellingham Technical College *C*
Central Washington University *B*
Centralia College *A, B*
City University of Seattle *C, A, B, M*
Clark College *C, A*
Columbia Basin College *C, A, B*
DeVry University
 Federal Way *B, M*
Eastern Washington University *B, M*
Edmonds Community College *C, A*
Everett Community College *C, A*
Evergreen State College *B*
Gonzaga University *B, M*
Grays Harbor College *C, A*
Heritage University *C, B*
Highline Community College *C, A*
ITT Technical Institute
 Everett *B*
 Seattle *B*
 Spokane *B*
Lower Columbia College *A*
Northwest Indian College *C, A, B*
Northwest University *B, M*

Olympic College *C, A*
Pacific Lutheran University *B, M*
Peninsula College *C, A, B*
Pierce College *C, A*
Saint Martin's University *B, M*
Seattle University *B, M*
Shoreline Community College *A*
Skagit Valley College *C, A*
Spokane Community College *C, A*
Spokane Falls Community
 College *C, A*
Tacoma Community College *C, A*
Trinity Lutheran College *B*
University of Phoenix
 Western Washington *B, M*
University of Puget Sound *B*
University of Washington *B, M, D*
University of Washington
 Bothell *B, M*
University of Washington
 Tacoma *B, M*
Walla Walla Community College *C, A*
Walla Walla University *B*
Washington State University *B, M, D*
Wenatchee Valley College *C, A*
Western Washington University *B, M*
Whatcom Community College *C*
Whitworth University *B, M*
Yakima Valley Community College *A*

West Virginia

Alderson-Broaddus University *B*
American National University
 Parkersburg *C, A*
 Princeton *C, A, B*
American Public University
 System *C, B, M*
Blue Ridge Community and Technical
 College *A*
Bluefield State College *B*
Bridgemont Community and
 Technical College *A*
Concord University *B*
Davis and Elkins College *A, B*
Eastern West Virginia Community and
 Technical College *C, A*
Fairmont State University *B, M*
Glenville State College *B*
Kanawha Valley Community and
 Technical College *A*
Marshall University *B*
New River Community and Technical
 College *C*
Ohio Valley University *B*
Potomac State College of West
 Virginia University *A, B*
Shepherd University *B, M*
Southern West Virginia Community
 and Technical College *A*
University of Charleston *B*
West Liberty University *B*
West Virginia Junior College
 Bridgeport *A*
 Charleston *C, A*
West Virginia State University *B*
West Virginia University *B, D*
West Virginia University Institute of
 Technology *B*
West Virginia University at
 Parkersburg *B*
West Virginia Wesleyan College *B, M*
Wheeling Jesuit University *B, M*

Wisconsin

Alverno College *B, M*
Cardinal Stritch University *B, M*
Carroll University *B*
Carthage College *B*
Chippewa Valley Technical College *A*
College of Menominee Nation *A, B*
Concordia University
 Wisconsin *A, B, M*
Edgewood College *B, M*
Fox Valley Technical College *A*

Globe University
Appleton *A, B*
Eau Claire *A, B*
Green Bay *A, B*
La Crosse *A, B*
Madison East *A, B*
Middleton *A, B, M*
Wausau *A, B*
Herzing University
Brookfield *A, B*
Kenosha *B*
Madison *A, B, M*
ITT Technical Institute
Green Bay *A, B*
Greenfield *A, B*
Lac Courte Oreilles Ojibwa
Community College *A*
Lakeland College *B, M*
Lakeshore Technical College *A*
Madison Area Technical College *A*
Maranatha Baptist Bible College *B*
Marian University *B, M*
Marquette University *B, M*
Mid-State Technical College *A*
Milwaukee Area Technical College *A*
Milwaukee School of
Engineering *B, M*
Mount Mary University *B, M, T*
Nicolet Area Technical College *A*
Northcentral Technical College *C, A*
Northeast Wisconsin Technical
College *A*
Northland College *B*
Rasmussen College
Appleton *C, A, B*
Green Bay *C, A, B*
Wausau *C, A, B*
Ripon College *B*
St. Norbert College *B*
Silver Lake College of the Holy
Family *B, M*
Southwest Wisconsin Technical
College *A*
University of Phoenix
Milwaukee *B, M*
University of Wisconsin
Eau Claire *B, M*
Green Bay *B*
La Crosse *B, M*
Madison *B, M*
Manitowoc *C*
Milwaukee *M*
Oshkosh *M*
Parkside *B, M*
Platteville *B*
River Falls *B*
Stevens Point *B*
Stout *B*
Superior *B*
Whitewater *B, M*
Viterbo University *B, M*
Waukesha County Technical
College *A*
Western Technical College *A*
Wisconsin Indianhead Technical
College *A*
Wisconsin Lutheran College *B*

Wyoming

Casper College *A*
Central Wyoming College *A*
Eastern Wyoming College *A*
Laramie County Community
College *A*
Northwest College *A*
University of Wyoming *B, M*
Western Wyoming Community
College *A*

Business/commerce

Alabama

Alabama Southern Community
College *A*
Auburn University at
Montgomery *B, M*
Birmingham-Southern College *B*
Bishop State Community College *C*
Central Alabama Community
College *C, A*
Faulkner University *B*
Huntingdon College *B*
Jefferson Davis Community
College *C*
Southern Union State Community
College *C, A*
Troy University *A, B*
University of South Alabama *B*
Wallace State Community College at
Hanceville *A*

Alaska

University of Alaska
Anchorage *C, A*
Southeast *B*

Arizona

American Indian College of the
Assemblies of God *A*
Arizona State University *M*
Arizona Western College *A*
Central Arizona College *C, A*
Chandler-Gilbert Community
College *A*
Cochise College *C*
Coconino County Community
College *C, A*
GateWay Community College *A*
Glendale Community College *C, A*
Mesa Community College *C, A*
Northcentral University *B, M, D*
Northland Pioneer College *A*
Paradise Valley Community
College *C, A*
Penn Foster College *A, B*
Phoenix College *C, A*
Pima Community College *C, A*
Rio Salado College *C, A*
Scottsdale Community College *C, A*
University of Arizona *B*
Western International University *B*

Arkansas

Arkansas Northeastern College *A*
Arkansas State University
Beebe *C, A*
Mountain Home *A*
Newport *A*
Bryan University
Rogers *C, A*
College of the Ouachitas *A*
Cossatot Community College of the
University of Arkansas *C, A*
Henderson State University *B, M*
National Park Community College *A*
North Arkansas College *A*
Phillips Community College of the
University of Arkansas *A*
Pulaski Technical College *A*
Rich Mountain Community College *A*
South Arkansas Community
College *A*
Southeast Arkansas College *A*
Southern Arkansas University *A, B*
University of Arkansas *B*
University of Arkansas
Community College at
Batesville *C, A*
Community College at Hope *A*
Community College at
Morrilton *C, A*
University of Central Arkansas *B*

California

Allan Hancock College *A*
American Jewish University *B*
Antelope Valley College *C, A*
Azusa Pacific University *B*
Bakersfield College *C*
Barstow Community College *C, A*
Butte College *C, A*
Cabrillo College *C, A*
California Baptist University *B*
California Coast University *A, B, M*
California Lutheran University *B*
California State University
Channel Islands *B*
Dominguez Hills *B, M*
East Bay *B*
Long Beach *B*
Carrington College California
Citrus Heights *A*
Pleasant Hill *A*
San Jose *A*
San Leandro *A*
Cerritos College *A*
Cerro Coso Community College *C, A*
Chabot College *A*
Citrus College *A*
Coastline Community College *C, A*
College of Alameda *C, A*
College of Marin *C, A*
College of San Mateo *C, A*
College of the Redwoods *A*
College of the Sequoias *A*
College of the Siskiyous *C, A*
Columbia College *A*
Cosumnes River College *A*
Cuesta College *C, A*
Cypress College *A*
DeVry University
Pomona *B, M*
Diablo Valley College *C, A*
El Camino College *C, A*
Feather River College *C, A*
Folsom Lake College *A*
Fremont College *A*
Fresno City College *C, A*
Fresno Pacific University *B*
Gavilan College *C, A*
Glendale Community College *A*
Golden West College *C, A*
Grossmont College *C, A*
Humboldt State University *B*
Humphreys College *A, B*
ITT Technical Institute
Lathrop *A*
National City *A*
Oxnard *A*
Rancho Cordova *A*
San Bernardino *A*
Sylmar *A*
Torrance *A*
Irvine Valley College *A*
John Paul the Great Catholic
University *B*
Lake Tahoe Community College *A*
Laney College *C, A*
Long Beach City College *C, A*
Los Angeles Harbor College *C, A*
Los Angeles Pierce College *C, A*
Los Angeles Southwest College *A*
Los Angeles Trade and Technical
College *A*
Los Angeles Valley College *C, A*
Mendocino College *C, A*
Merced College *C, A*
Merritt College *C, A*
Mission College *C, A*
Modesto Junior College *A*
Monterey Peninsula College *A*
Moorpark College *A*
Moreno Valley College *C, A*
Mount St. Mary's College *B*
Mount San Antonio College *A*
Napa Valley College *A*
Norco College *C, A*
Ohlone College *A*
Orange Coast College *C, A*
Pacific Union College *A, B*
Palomar College *A*
Pasadena City College *A*
Porterville College *A*
Rio Hondo College *C*
Riverside City College *C, A*
Sacramento City College *A*
Saddleback College *A*
St. Mary's College of California *B, M*
San Diego City College *C, A*
San Diego Mesa College *A*
San Diego State University *B, M*
San Joaquin Delta College *C, A*
San Jose City College *C*
Santa Barbara Business College *C, A*
Santa Barbara Business College
Bakersfield *C, A*
Santa Maria *C, A*
Santa Barbara City College *C, A*
Shasta College *A*
Sierra College *C, A*
Taft College *A*
Touro University Worldwide *B, M*
University of Redlands *B*
University of San Francisco *B*
Vanguard University of Southern
California *B*
Ventura College *C, A*
Victor Valley College *A*
West Hills College: Coalinga *C, A*
West Hills College: Lemoore *A*
West Los Angeles College *C, A*
West Valley College *A*
Westmont College *B*

Colorado

Adams State University *A, B*
Arapahoe Community College *C*
CollegeAmerica
Fort Collins *B*
Colorado Mesa University *B, M*
Colorado Mountain College *C, A*
Colorado State University
Pueblo *M*
Community College of Aurora *C*
Fort Lewis College *B*
Morgan Community College *A*
Regis University *B*
Trinidad State Junior College *A*
University of Denver *B, M*
Westwood College
Denver North *B*

Connecticut

Goodwin College *C, A*
Housatonic Community College *C, A*
Norwalk Community College *A*
Post University *C*
Quinnipiac University *B, M*
Sacred Heart University *A, B, M*
University of Bridgeport *B, M*
University of Connecticut *B, M*
Western Connecticut State
University *M*

Delaware

Delaware Technical Community
College
Jack F. Owens Campus *C, A*
Stanton/Wilmington Campus *A*
Goldey-Beacom College *B, M*

District of Columbia

Catholic University of America *B*
Gallaudet University *B*
Strayer University *C, A, B*
University of the District of
Columbia *A, M*

Florida

Broward College *A*
Carlos Albizu University *B*
DeVry University
Miramar *B*
Everest University
North Orlando *A, B*
Pompano Beach *A, B*
Tampa *A, B*

Herzing University
Winter Park *A, B*
Jacksonville University *B*
Lincoln College of Technology
West Palm Beach *A*
Nova Southeastern University *B*
Palm Beach State College *A*
Pensacola State College *A*
Rollins College *B*
Saint Johns River State College *B*
Saint Leo University *A, M*
Saint Thomas University *M*
Schiller International University *B*
South Florida State College *A*
Southeastern University *B*
Tallahassee Community College *A*
Trinity College of Florida *B*
University of Central Florida *B, M*
University of Miami *B, M*
University of South Florida *B, M*
University of South Florida
Saint Petersburg *M*
Sarasota-Manatee *B*
University of West Florida *B*
Webber International University *B*

Georgia

Andrew College *A*
Bainbridge College *A*
Brenau University *B, M*
Brewton-Parker College *B*
Chattahoochee Technical College *A*
Clayton State University *B*
Columbus State University *B*
Covenant College *A, B*
Fort Valley State University *B*
Georgia College and State
University *B, M*
Georgia Regents University *B, M*
Georgia State University *M*
Life University *B*
Mercer University *B, M*
Reinhardt University *B*
Savannah State University *M*
Shorter University *A*
Thomas University *A, B, M*
Truett-McConnell College *B*
University of Georgia *B*
University of North Georgia *A*

Hawaii

Brigham Young University-Hawaii *A*
Hawaii Pacific University *A, B*
University of Hawaii
Kapiolani Community College *A*
Manoa *B*
Maui College *C, A*

Idaho

College of Southern Idaho *A*
College of Western Idaho *A*
Idaho State University *A, B*

Illinois

Aurora University *B*
DeVry University
Chicago *B*
Online *B*
Eureka College *B*
Hebrew Theological College *B*
Illinois Central College *A*
John Wood Community College *A*
Kaskaskia College *A*
Kishwaukee College *A*
Lake Forest College *D*
Lake Land College *A*
Lewis University *B*
Lewis and Clark Community
College *A*
Lincoln College *A*
Lincoln Land Community College *A*
MacCormac College *A*
Midstate College *A*

Moraine Valley Community
College *C, A*
North Park University *B, M*
Northeastern Illinois University *B*
Northern Illinois University *B*
Northwestern University *M*
Olivet Nazarene University *A, B*
Parkland College *A*
Prairie State College *C*
Richland Community College *A*
Rock Valley College *C*
Roosevelt University *B*
Saint Xavier University *B*
Sauk Valley Community College *A*
Shawnee Community College *A*
South Suburban College of Cook
County *A*
Southwestern Illinois College *A*
Spoon River College *A*
Trinity Christian College *B*
Trinity International University *B*
University of Illinois
Urbana-Champaign *B, M, D*

Indiana

Ball State University *B, M*
Bethel College *A*
Brown Mackie College
Fort Wayne *A*
Merrillville *C, A*
South Bend *A*
Calumet College of St. Joseph *B, M*
Franklin College *B*
Grace College *B*
Holy Cross College *B*
Huntington University *B*
Indiana Institute of Technology *M*
Indiana University
Bloomington *C, B, M, D*
East *C, B*
Kokomo *C, B, M*
Northwest *A, B, M*
Purdue University Fort
Wayne *C, B, M*
Purdue University
Indianapolis *C, B, M*
South Bend *C, B, M*
Southeast *C, B, M*
International Business College *A, B*
Manchester University *B*
Marian University *B*
Martin University *B*
Oakland City University *A, B*
Purdue University
Calumet *B*
Saint Joseph's College *M*
St. Mary-of-the-Woods College *A, B*
University of Notre Dame *B*
University of Southern Indiana *B, M*
Valparaiso University *C*
Vincennes University *A*

Iowa

Dordt College *A, B*
Drake University *B*
Ellsworth Community College *A*
Grand View University *B, M*
Iowa State University *B*
Iowa Wesleyan College *B*
Loras College *B*
Marshalltown Community College *A*
Mount Mercy University *B*
St. Ambrose University *B*
Southeastern Community College *A*
Southwestern Community College *A*
Upper Iowa University *A, B*
Waldorf College *B*
William Penn University *M*

Kansas

Baker University *B, T*
Barclay College *B*
Barton County Community
College *C, A*

Bethel College *B*
Central Christian College of Kansas *A*
Coffeyville Community College *A*
Cowley County Community
College *A*
Dodge City Community College *A*
Donnelly College *A*
Fort Hays State University *B*
Fort Scott Community College *A*
Garden City Community College *A*
Haskell Indian Nations University *A*
Hesston College *A*
Hutchinson Community College *A*
Independence Community College *A*
Kansas State University *B*
MidAmerica Nazarene
University *A, B*
North Central Kansas Technical
College *A*
Pittsburg State University *B*
Seward County Community
College *C, A*
University of Kansas *B, M, D*
University of St. Mary *B*
Washburn University *B*

Kentucky

Asbury University *B*
Berea College *B*
Brescia University *A, B*
Campbellsville University *A, B*
Eastern Kentucky University *B, M*
Georgetown College *B*
Hopkinsville Community College *A*
Kentucky State University *B*
Kentucky Wesleyan College *B*
Maysville Community and Technical
College *C, A*
Midway College *A, B, M*
Morehead State University *M*
Murray State University *A, B, M*
Northern Kentucky
University *A, B, M*
St. Catharine College *A*
Spalding University *A, B, M*
Sullivan University *M*
Thomas More College *A*
Transylvania University *B*
University of Kentucky *B, M, D*
University of Louisville *M*
University of the Cumberlands *B*

Louisiana

Baton Rouge Community
College *C, A*
Baton Rouge School of
Computers *C, A*
Bossier Parish Community
College *C, A*
Delgado Community College *A*
Louisiana College *B*
Louisiana State University
Eunice *A*
Loyola University New Orleans *M*
Northwestern State University *A*
Nunez Community College *A*
South Louisiana Community
College *A*
Tulane University *C, A, B, M, D*

Maine

Eastern Maine Community College *A*
Husson University *B*
Maine Maritime Academy *B, M*
Thomas College *A*
University of Maine *B*
University of Maine
Fort Kent *A, B*
Machias *B*
University of Southern Maine *B, M*

Maryland

Allegany College of Maryland *C, A*
Anne Arundel Community
College *C, A*

Baltimore City Community College *A*
Carroll Community College *A*
Cecil College *A*
Chesapeake College *A*
College of Southern Maryland *A*
Community College of Baltimore
County *A*
Garrett College *A*
Hagerstown Community College *A*
Harford Community College *A*
Johns Hopkins University *B, M*
Loyola University Maryland *B*
Montgomery College *A*
Mount St. Mary's University *B*
Notre Dame of Maryland
University *B*
University of Baltimore *B, M*
University of Maryland
College Park *B, M, D*
University College *D*
Washington College *B*
Wor-Wic Community College *A*

Massachusetts

American International College *B*
Babson College *B*
Bentley University *B, M, D*
Berkshire Community College *A*
Brandeis University *B*
Bristol Community College *A*
Cambridge College *B, M*
Clark University *B, M*
Dean College *C, A*
Eastern Nazarene College *A, B*
Endicott College *A*
Framingham State University *B, M*
Greenfield Community College *A*
Harvard College *M, D*
Massachusetts Bay Community
College *A*
Massachusetts Institute of
Technology *B, M, D*
Mount Wachusett Community
College *A*
New England College of Business and
Finance *A*
Nichols College *M, T*
Northeastern University *B*
Northern Essex Community
College *A*
Quinsigamond Community
College *C, A*
Regis College *B*
Springfield Technical Community
College *A*
University of Massachusetts
Dartmouth *B*
Lowell *A*
Western New England University *B*
Westfield State University *B, T*
Wheaton College *B*

Michigan

Andrews University *A*
Baker College
Auburn Hills *B*
Cadillac *A*
Flint *A*
Jackson *B*
Muskegon *A*
Owosso *A*
Port Huron *A, B*
Bay de Noc Community College *A*
Davenport University *A, D*
Delta College *A*
Eastern Michigan University *B*
Ferris State University *B*
Glen Oaks Community College *A*
Gogebic Community College *C, A*
Grace Bible College *A, B*
Grand Rapids Community College *A*
Henry Ford Community College *A*
Hillsdale College *B*
Jackson College *C, A*

Kalamazoo College *B*
Lake Superior State University *A, B*
Lansing Community College *A*
Macomb Community College *C, A*
Marygrove College *A, B*
Mott Community College *A*
North Central Michigan College *C, A*
Northern Michigan University *A, B*
Northwestern Michigan College *A*
Oakland University *B*
Saginaw Valley State University *B*
St. Clair County Community
  College *C, A*
Schoolcraft College *C, A*
Siena Heights University *A, B*
Walsh College of Accountancy and
  Business Administration *B*
West Shore Community College *A*
Western Michigan University *B*

Minnesota

Anoka-Ramsey Community
  College *C, A*
Brown College
  Mendota Heights *B*
Capella University *M, D*
College of St. Scholastica *M*
Crown College *A, B*
Gustavus Adolphus College *B*
ITT Technical Institute
  Eden Prairie *A*
Inver Hills Community College *A*
Mesabi Range Community and
  Technical College *A*
Minnesota State Community and
  Technical College *A*
Minnesota State University
  Mankato *B*
Minnesota West Community and
  Technical College *A*
National American University
  Bloomington *A, B, M*
North Hennepin Community
  College *C*
Northwest Technical College *C*
Rasmussen College
  Moorhead *C*
Ridgewater College *A*
Saint Cloud State University *B*
St. Mary's University of Minnesota *B*
St. Paul College *C, A*
University of Minnesota
  Duluth *B*
  Twin Cities *B*
Vermilion Community College *A*

Mississippi

Coahoma Community College *A*
Delta State University *B*
East Mississippi Community
  College *A*
Hinds Community College *A*
Itawamba Community College *A*
Mississippi Gulf Coast Community
  College *A*
Mississippi State University *M*
Southeastern Baptist College *C, A*

Missouri

Avila University *B*
Central Methodist University *B*
Columbia College *A, B, M*
Crowder College *C, A*
DeVry University
  Kansas City *B*
East Central College *C, A*
Evangel University *B*
Hannibal-LaGrange University *B*
Jefferson College *C, A*
Lindenwood University *B, M*
Maryville University of Saint
  Louis *B, M*
Metropolitan Community College -
  Kansas City *A*

Mineral Area College *C, A*
Missouri Southern State
  University *A, B*
Missouri State University *B*
Missouri State University: West
  Plains *A*
Missouri University of Science and
  Technology *B*
St. Louis Community College *A*
Southwest Baptist University *A*
Stephens College *B*
University of Missouri
  Columbia *B, M, D*
  Kansas City *B, M, D*
  St. Louis *B, M*
Washington University in St. Louis *B*

Montana

Aaniiih Nakoda College *A*
Dawson Community College *A*
Fort Peck Community College *A*
Montana State University *B*
Montana State University
  Billings *A, B*
Montana Tech of the University of
  Montana *B*
Stone Child College *A*
University of Montana *B, M*
University of Montana: Western *A, B*

Nebraska

Bellevue University *B, M*
Clarkson College *B, M*
Concordia University *B*
Little Priest Tribal College *A*
Metropolitan Community College *A*
Midland University *B*
University of Nebraska
  Omaha *B*
Vatterott College
  Spring Valley *A*
Western Nebraska Community
  College *C, A*

Nevada

College of Southern Nevada *A*
Great Basin College *A*
Sierra Nevada College *B*
Truckee Meadows Community
  College *C, A*
University of Nevada
  Reno *B*

New Hampshire

Daniel Webster College *B*
Great Bay Community College *C, A*
Mount Washington College *A*
Plymouth State University *B*
River Valley Community College *A*
Saint Anselm College *B*
University of New
  Hampshire *A, B, M*

New Jersey

Brookdale Community College *A*
Burlington County College *A*
College of St. Elizabeth *C*
Gloucester County College *A*
Mercer County Community
  College *C, A*
Ocean County College *A*
Passaic County Community
  College *C, A*
Raritan Valley Community College *A*
Saint Peter's University *C*
Union County College *A*
Warren County Community
  College *C, A*

New Mexico

Central New Mexico Community
  College *C, A*
ITT Technical Institute
  Albuquerque *A*

New Mexico Junior College *A*
New Mexico State University *A, B*
New Mexico State University
  Alamogordo *A*
  Carlsbad *A*
  Grants *A*
Northern New Mexico College *A*
Southwestern Indian Polytechnic
  Institute *A*

New York

Berkeley College *B*
Broome Community College *C*
Bryant & Stratton College
  Buffalo *A*
  Syracuse North *A*
City University of New York
  Baruch College *B, M*
  Bronx Community College *A*
  CUNY Online *B, M*
  City College *B*
  College of Staten Island *A, B*
  Hostos Community College *A*
  Medgar Evers College *B*
  Queensborough Community
    College *A*
College of Mount St. Vincent *A, B*
College of New Rochelle *B*
Concordia College *B*
D'Youville College *B*
Everest Institute
  Rochester *A*
Excelsior College *A, B*
Finger Lakes Community College *A*
Fordham University *B, M*
Fulton-Montgomery Community
  College *A*
Globe Institute of
  Technology *C, A, B*
Hofstra University *B*
Houghton College *B*
Hudson Valley Community College *A*
Ithaca College *B*
Long Island Business Institute *A*
Manhattan College *B*
Maria College *A*
Medaille College *B*
Medaille College: Amherst *A, B*
Medaille College: Rochester *A, B*
Mercy College *C*
Metropolitan College of New
  York *A, B, M*
Molloy College *B*
Monroe Community College *A*
Nazareth College *B, M*
New York University *A, B*
Niagara University *A*
North Country Community College *A*
Orange County Community
  College *A*
Pace University *C, B, M*
Pace University: Pleasantville/
  Briarcliff *B*
Paul Smith's College *B*
Professional Business College *C*
SUNY
  College at Buffalo *B*
  College at Geneseo *B*
  College at New Paltz *B, M*
  College at Plattsburgh *B*
  Empire State College *A, B*
  Institute of Technology at Utica/
    Rome *B, M*
  University at Albany *M*
St. Thomas Aquinas College *B*
Schenectady County Community
  College *A*
Siena College *T*
Skidmore College *B*
Suffolk County Community College *A*
Sullivan County Community
  College *C*
Touro College *A, B*
Ulster County Community
  College *C, A*

University of Rochester *B*
Utica School of Commerce *A*
Vaughn College of Aeronautics and
  Technology *B, M*
Westchester Community College *C*

North Carolina

Alamance Community College *C, A*
Blue Ridge Community College *A*
Campbell University *B*
Carteret Community College *A*
Gardner-Webb University *B, M*
Lenoir-Rhyne University *M*
Louisburg College *A*
Mars Hill University *B*
McDowell Technical Community
  College *A*
Piedmont Community College *A*
St. Andrews University *B*
Wake Forest University *B*
Wake Technical Community
  College *A*

North Dakota

Bismarck State College *A*
Cankdeska Cikana Community
  College *C, A*
Dickinson State University *B*
Mayville State University *A*
Trinity Bible College *A, B*

Ohio

Ashland University *C, B*
Belmont College *A*
Bowling Green State University *B*
Bowling Green State University:
  Firelands College *A*
Brown Mackie College
  Akron *C, A*
Bryant & Stratton College
  Cleveland *A*
  Eastlake *A*
Central State University *B*
Cuyahoga Community College
  Metropolitan *A*
Defiance College *B*
Edison State Community College *C*
Hocking College *A*
Kent State University
  Ashtabula *A*
  East Liverpool *A*
  Geauga *A*
  Salem *A*
  Trumbull *A*
  Tuscarawas *A*
Lorain County Community College *A*
Lourdes University *A*
Miami University
  Middletown *A*
  Oxford *A, M*
North Central State College *A*
Ohio Christian University *A, B*
Ohio State University
  Columbus Campus *B*
  Lima Campus *B*
Ohio University *M*
Ohio University
  Lancaster Campus *A*
Otterbein University *B*
Owens Community College
  Toledo *A*
Sinclair Community College *A*
Southern State Community College *A*
Stark State College *A*
Stautzenberger College: Brecksville *A*
Terra State Community College *A*
University of Akron *B*
University of Akron: Wayne
  College *A*
University of Cincinnati
  Blue Ash College *C, A*
  Clermont College *A*
University of Dayton *B*
University of Findlay *A, B*

University of Rio Grande *A*
University of Toledo *A, B*
Walsh University *A, B*
Washington State Community
 College *A*
Wilmington College *C*
Wittenberg University *B*
Wright State University *A, M*
Wright State University: Lake
 Campus *A, M*
Xavier University *B*
Youngstown State University *A, B, M*

Oklahoma

Cameron University *M*
Carl Albert State College *A*
Connors State College *A*
East Central University *B*
Eastern Oklahoma State College *A*
Hillsdale Free Will Baptist College *B*
Northern Oklahoma College *A*
Oklahoma Baptist University *B*
Oklahoma Christian University *B, M*
Oklahoma City Community
 College *A*
Oklahoma State University
 Institute of Technology:
 Okmulgee *A*
Oklahoma Wesleyan University *B*
Rose State College *A*
Southern Nazarene University *B, M*
Southwestern Oklahoma State
 University *A, B, M*
Tulsa Community College *A*

Oregon

Concordia University *B*
Corban University *B*
Eastern Oregon University *B*
Lane Community College *A*
Marylhurst University *B, M*
Portland Community College *A*
Portland State University *B, M*
Rogue Community College *A*
Southern Oregon University *B*
Treasure Valley Community
 College *A*
Umpqua Community College *A*
University of Oregon *B, M*
Western Oregon University *B*

Pennsylvania

Alvernia University *A, B*
Arcadia University *B*
Bloomsburg University of
 Pennsylvania *B, M, T*
Bryn Athyn College *B*
Bucks County Community College *A*
Butler County Community College *C*
Cambria-Rowe Business College *A*
Community College of
 Philadelphia *A*
DeSales University *C, B, M*
Delaware Valley College *A*
Drexel University *B, M, D*
Gannon University *A*
Harcum College *A*
Harrisburg Area Community
 College *A*
Indiana University of
 Pennsylvania *B, M*
Juniata College *B*
La Salle University *B*
Lackawanna College *A*
Lehigh Carbon Community
 College *C, A*
Luzerne County Community
 College *A*
Montgomery County Community
 College *A*
Northampton Community College *A*
Penn Commercial Business and
 Technical School *A*

Penn State
 Abington *A, B*
 Altoona *C, A, B*
 Beaver *C, A*
 Berks *C, A, B*
 Brandywine *C, A*
 DuBois *C, A*
 Erie, The Behrend College *C, A*
 Fayette, The Eberly Campus *C, A*
 Greater Allegheny *C, A*
 Harrisburg *A*
 Hazleton *C, A*
 Lehigh Valley *C, A, B*
 Mont Alto *C, A*
 New Kensington *C, A*
 Schuylkill *C, A*
 Shenango *C, A*
 University Park *C, A*
 Wilkes-Barre *C, A*
 Worthington Scranton *C, A*
 York *C, A*
Pennsylvania Highlands Community
 College *A*
Pennsylvania Institute of Health and
 Technology *A*
Reading Area Community
 College *C, A*
Rosemont College *B*
Saint Joseph's University *M*
Temple University *B*
University of Pittsburgh
 Bradford *B*
 Johnstown *C, B*
 Titusville *A*
Valley Forge Christian College *B*
Valley Forge Military College *A*
Washington & Jefferson College *B*
Waynesburg University *B*

Puerto Rico

American University of Puerto
 Rico *B*
Bayamon Central University *A, B, M*
Caribbean University *B*
Columbia Centro Universitario:
 Caguas *A, B*
ICPR Junior College *C*
Inter American University of Puerto
 Rico
 Barranquitas Campus *B*
 Fajardo Campus *A, B*
Pontifical Catholic University of
 Puerto Rico *A, B, M*
Universidad Adventista de las
 Antillas *A, B*
Universidad Politecnica de Puerto
 Rico *B*
University of Puerto Rico
 Aguadilla *B*
 Cayey University College *B*
 Mayaguez *M*
 Rio Piedras *B, M*

Rhode Island

Community College of Rhode
 Island *A*
New England Institute of
 Technology *A, B*
Rhode Island College *B*
University of Rhode Island *B*

South Carolina

Anderson University *B*
Clinton Junior College *A*
Coker College *B*
Denmark Technical College *A*
Forrest Junior College *A*
Horry-Georgetown Technical
 College *C, A*
Midlands Technical College *C*
Orangeburg-Calhoun Technical
 College *A*
Piedmont Technical College *C, A*
South Carolina State University *M*

Southern Wesleyan University *A*
Technical College of the
 Lowcountry *C, A*
Tri-County Technical College *C*
Trident Technical College *C, A*
Voorhees College *B*
Williamsburg Technical College *A*
York Technical College *A*

South Dakota

Augustana College *B*
Dakota Wesleyan University *A, B, M*
Northern State University *B*
Sinte Gleska University *A*
University of Sioux Falls *M*

Tennessee

Austin Peay State University *B*
Belmont University *B, M*
Bethel University *M*
Carson-Newman University *B, T*
Christian Brothers University *B*
Cumberland University *A, B, M*
Hiwassee College *A*
Lincoln Memorial University *B, M, T*
Lipscomb University *M*
Martin Methodist College *B*
Southwest Tennessee Community
 College *A*
Tennessee Technological
 University *B, M*
Tennessee Temple University *B*
Welch College *A*

Texas

Alvin Community College *A*
Amarillo College *C, A*
Amberton University *B, M*
Angelina College *C, A*
Austin College *B*
Austin Community College *A*
Baylor University *B*
Brazosport College *A*
Brookhaven College *A*
Cisco College *C, A*
Clarendon College *A*
Coastal Bend College *A*
College of the Mainland *A*
Concordia University Texas *B*
DeVry University
 Houston *B*
 Irving *B*
Del Mar College *C, A*
East Texas Baptist University *B*
El Paso Community College *C, A*
Frank Phillips College *C, A*
Grayson College *A*
Houston Baptist University *B*
Howard College *C, A*
Howard Payne University *B*
ITT Technical Institute
 Arlington *A*
 Houston West *A*
 Richardson *A*
 San Antonio *A*
Kilgore College *C, A*
Lamar State College at Orange *A*
Lamar University *B, M*
Laredo Community College *A*
LeTourneau University *B*
McLennan Community College *C, A*
McMurry University *B*
Midland College *C, A*
Midwestern State University *B*
Mountain View College *A*
Navarro College *A*
North Central Texas College *A*
Odessa College *A*
Panola College *C, A*
Paris Junior College *A*
St. Mary's University *B*
St. Philip's College *C, A*
Sam Houston State University *B*
San Jacinto College *C, A*

South Plains College *C*
Southern Methodist University *B*
Southwestern Assemblies of God
 University *A, B*
Southwestern University *B*
Stephen F. Austin State University *B*
Sul Ross State University *B*
Tarleton State University *B, T*
Tarrant County College *C, A*
Temple College *C, A*
Texarkana College *A*
Texas A&M University
 Commerce *B*
 Corpus Christi *B*
 Kingsville *B*
 Texarkana *B*
Texas Lutheran University *B*
Texas Tech University *B*
Tyler Junior College *A*
University of Houston *D*
University of Houston
 Clear Lake *B*
 Downtown *B*
 Victoria *B*
University of Mary Hardin-
 Baylor *B, M*
University of North Texas *B*
University of Texas
 Austin *C, B, M, D*
 Brownsville *B*
 Dallas *B*
 El Paso *B*
 Pan American *D*
 San Antonio *B*
Vernon College *C, A*
Weatherford College *C, A*
West Texas A&M University *B*
Western Texas College *A*

Utah

Brigham Young University *B*
Dixie State College *B*
LDS Business College *A*
Salt Lake Community College *A*
Snow College *C, A*
Southern Utah University *A*
University of Utah *B, M*
Utah State University *A*
Westminster College *B*

Vermont

Castleton State College *A, B*
Champlain College *A, B*
Community College of Vermont *C, A*
Johnson State College *B*
Vermont Technical College *A, B*

Virginia

Blue Ridge Community College *C*
Central Virginia Community
 College *A*
Danville Community College *A*
Germanna Community College *A*
Hollins University *B*
Liberty University *B, T*
Lord Fairfax Community College *C*
Marymount University *M*
Mountain Empire Community
 College *A*
Norfolk State University *B*
Randolph College *B*
Southwest Virginia Community
 College *A*
Stratford University: Falls
 Church *A, B, M*
Sweet Briar College *B*
University of Virginia *B, M*
Virginia Commonwealth
 University *B, M, D*
Virginia Polytechnic Institute and
 State University *D*
Virginia Western Community
 College *A*

Washington

Bellevue College *A*
Big Bend Community College *A*
Centralia College *A*
Columbia Basin College *A*
DeVry University
　Federal Way *B*
Edmonds Community College *A*
Everett Community College *C, A*
Grays Harbor College *A*
Heritage University *A, B*
Highline Community College *C, A*
ITT Technical Institute
　Everett *A*
　Seattle *A*
　Spokane *A*
Lake Washington Institute of
　Technology *A*
North Seattle Community College *A*
Pierce College *A*
Seattle University *B*
South Puget Sound Community
　College *A*
South Seattle Community College *A*
Spokane Community College *C, A*
Spokane Falls Community College *A*
Tacoma Community College *A*
University of Washington Tacoma *B*
Walla Walla University *A*
Washington State University *B*
Whatcom Community College *A*
Yakima Valley Community College *A*

West Virginia

Alderson-Broaddus University *A*
American Public University System *A*
Bethany College *B*
Blue Ridge Community and Technical
　College *C, A*
Concord University *B*
Glenville State College *A, B*
Marshall University *M*
New River Community and Technical
　College *A*
West Liberty University *B*
West Virginia Northern Community
　College *C, A*
West Virginia State University *B*
West Virginia University *B, M*

Wisconsin

Bryant & Stratton College
　Milwaukee *A, B*
Cardinal Stritch University *A, B*
Concordia University Wisconsin *B*
Edgewood College *B*
Milwaukee School of Engineering *B*
St. Norbert College *B*
University of Wisconsin
　Madison *B, M, D*
　Milwaukee *C, B*
　Parkside *B*
　Platteville *B*
　Richland *C*
　Superior *B*
　Whitewater *B*

Wyoming

Central Wyoming College *A*
Laramie County Community
　College *A*
Northwest College *A*
Sheridan College *C, A*

Business communications

Alaska

University of Alaska
　Anchorage *C*

California

Foothill College *C*
Holy Names University *B*
National University *B*
Ohlone College *C*
Point Loma Nazarene University *B*
Saddleback College *C*

Colorado

Jones International University *B, M*

Connecticut

Quinnipiac University *B*

District of Columbia

University of the District of
　Columbia *A*

Florida

Florida State College at
　Jacksonville *C*
Saint Leo University *B*
Schiller International University *M*

Hawaii

Hawaii Pacific University *B*

Illinois

Concordia University Chicago *B*
Trinity Christian College *B*

Iowa

Morningside College *B*

Kansas

MidAmerica Nazarene University *B*

Kentucky

Northern Kentucky University *C*

Maine

University of Maine
　Presque Isle *B*
University of New England *B*

Maryland

Stevenson University *B*
University of Baltimore *B*

Massachusetts

Babson College *B*
Bentley University *B, M*
Emerson College *B, M*
Nichols College *B*

Michigan

Aquinas College *B*
Calvin College *B*
Cleary University *B*
Macomb Community College *C*

Minnesota

Anoka-Ramsey Community College *C*
North Hennepin Community
　College *C*
University of St. Thomas *M*
Walden University *B*

Missouri

Lindenwood University *B, M*
Rockhurst University *B*

Montana

Flathead Valley Community College *C*

Nebraska

Concordia University *B*

New York

City University of New York
　Baruch College *B*
　CUNY Online *C*

Globe Institute of Technology *C*
Saint Bonaventure University *M*

North Carolina

East Carolina University *C*

North Dakota

North Dakota State University *B*
University of Mary *B*

Ohio

Marietta College *B*
Ohio Dominican University *B*
Stark State College *A*
Urbana University *B*
Walsh University *B*

Oregon

Corban University *B*
Marylhurst University *B, M*

Pennsylvania

Chestnut Hill College *A, B*
Community College of Beaver
　County *C*
Duquesne University *B*
La Salle University *B*
Lycoming College *B*
Montgomery County Community
　College *C, A*
Penn State
　Abington *B*
　Fayette, The Eberly Campus *C*
　Greater Allegheny *C*
　Hazleton *C*
　Lehigh Valley *B*
Rosemont College *B*
Thiel College *B*

Puerto Rico

Pontifical Catholic University of
　Puerto Rico *B*

South Carolina

Forrest Junior College *A*

South Dakota

Augustana College *B*

Tennessee

Christian Brothers University *B*

Texas

Houston Community College
　System *C, A*
Southwestern Adventist University *B*
University of Houston *B*

Virginia

Dabney S. Lancaster Community
　College *A*
Thomas Nelson Community
　College *C*

West Virginia

Blue Ridge Community and Technical
　College *C*

Wisconsin

Madison Area Technical College *C, A*

Business machine repair

California

Yuba College *C*

Georgia

Athens Technical College *C*

Pennsylvania

Community College of Allegheny
　County *A*

Business/managerial economics

Alabama

Auburn University *B, M*
Auburn University at Montgomery *B*
Jacksonville State University *B*
Samford University *B*
Troy University *B*
University of Alabama *B, M, D*
University of Alabama
　Birmingham *B*
　Huntsville *B*
University of North Alabama *B*

Arizona

Northern Arizona University *B*
University of Arizona *B*

Arkansas

Arkansas State University *B*
Arkansas Tech University *B*
University of Arkansas *B*
University of Arkansas
　Little Rock *B*

California

California Institute of Technology *B*
California Lutheran University *B*
California State University
　East Bay *B, M*
　Fullerton *B, M*
　Long Beach *B*
　Northridge *B*
　San Bernardino *B*
Chapman University *B*
Claremont McKenna College *B*
College of the Desert *A*
College of the Redwoods *A*
Lincoln University *B*
Mills College *B*
Point Loma Nazarene University *B*
Santa Clara University *B*
Santiago Canyon College *A*
University of California
　Irvine *B*
　Los Angeles *B*
　Riverside *B*
　Santa Cruz *B*
University of La Verne *B*
University of Redlands *B*
University of San Diego *B*
University of San Francisco *B*

Colorado

Colorado State University
　Pueblo *B*
University of Denver *B*

Connecticut

Albertus Magnus College *B*
Quinnipiac University *B*
Sacred Heart University *B*

Delaware

Delaware State University *B*
University of Delaware *M, D*

Florida

Jacksonville University *B*
Stetson University *B*
University of Central Florida *B*
University of Miami *B, M, D*
University of North Florida *B*
University of South Florida *B, M*
University of South Florida
　Saint Petersburg *B*
University of West Florida *B*

Georgia

Berry College *B*
Clark Atlanta University *B, M*

Georgia College and State
    University B
Georgia Highlands College A
Georgia Institute of Technology B, M
Georgia Southern University B
Georgia State University B, M
Kennesaw State University B
Oglethorpe University B
Shorter University B
University of Georgia B, M, D
University of West Georgia B
Valdosta State University B

Hawaii

Hawaii Pacific University A, B

Idaho

Boise State University B
University of Idaho B

Illinois

Benedictine University B, T
Bradley University B
DePaul University B
Illinois College B
Lewis University B
Loyola University Chicago B
Monmouth College B
Northwestern University M, D
Southern Illinois University
    Carbondale B
Southern Illinois University
    Edwardsville B
Spoon River College A
Western Illinois University B
Wheaton College B

Indiana

Anderson University B
Ball State University B
Huntington University B
Indiana University
    Purdue University Fort Wayne B
    Southeast C
Indiana Wesleyan University B, M
Taylor University B
University of Indianapolis B

Iowa

Ashford University B
Buena Vista University B
Drake University B
Iowa State University B
Northwestern College B
University of Iowa B, D

Kansas

Bethany College B
Washburn University B

Kentucky

Eastern Kentucky University B
Morehead State University B
Northern Kentucky University C, B
University of Kentucky B
University of Louisville B
Western Kentucky University B

Louisiana

Centenary College of Louisiana B
Grambling State University B
Louisiana State University
    Shreveport B
Louisiana State University and
    Agricultural and Mechanical
    College B
Louisiana Tech University B
Loyola University New Orleans B
University of Louisiana at Lafayette B
University of New Orleans M, D

Maine

Husson University B
University of Maine
    Farmington B

Maryland

Allegany College of Maryland A
University of Baltimore B

Massachusetts

American International College B
Babson College B
Bentley University B, M
Boston College B
Harvard College M, D
Nichols College B
Salem State University B

Michigan

Andrews University B, M
Eastern Michigan University B
Grand Valley State University B
Hope College B
Lake Superior State University B
Northwood University
    Michigan A, B
Oakland University B
Olivet College B
Saginaw Valley State University B
Spring Arbor University B
Western Michigan University B

Mississippi

Jackson State University B
Mississippi State University B, M, D
University of Mississippi B
University of Southern
    Mississippi B, M

Missouri

College of the Ozarks B
Northwest Missouri State
    University B
Park University B
Saint Louis University B
Washington University in St. Louis B
William Jewell College B
William Woods University B

Nebraska

University of Nebraska
    Lincoln B
    Omaha B

Nevada

Morrison University A, B
Sierra Nevada College B
University of Nevada
    Las Vegas B, M
    Reno B, M, D

New Hampshire

Saint Anselm College B

New Jersey

Drew University B
Fairleigh Dickinson University
    College at Florham B
    Metropolitan Campus B
Rider University B
Saint Peter's University B
Seton Hall University B
William Paterson University of New
    Jersey B

New Mexico

Eastern New Mexico University B

New York

Canisius College B
City University of New York
    Baruch College B
Elmira College B

Fordham University B, M
Hofstra University B
Manhattan College B
New York University B, M, D
Niagara University B
Pace University M
Pace University: Pleasantville/
    Briarcliff M
SUNY
    College at Oneonta B
    College at Potsdam B
Touro College B
Ulster County Community College A
Utica College B
Wagner College B
Wells College B

North Carolina

Greensboro College B
North Carolina State University B
University of North Carolina
    Charlotte B, M
    Greensboro B, M, D
    Wilmington B

North Dakota

University of Jamestown B
University of North Dakota B

Ohio

Capital University B
Cleveland State University B
College of Wooster B
John Carroll University B
Kent State University B, M, D
Miami University
    Oxford B
Muskingum University B
Ohio State University
    Columbus Campus B
Ohio University B
Ohio Wesleyan University B
Otterbein University B
University of Dayton B
Urbana University B
Wilberforce University B
Wright State University B, M
Xavier University B
Youngstown State University B

Oklahoma

Oklahoma City University B, M
Oklahoma State University B, M, D
Tulsa Community College A
University of Central Oklahoma B
University of Oklahoma B

Pennsylvania

Allegheny College B
Carnegie Mellon University B, M, D
Chatham University B
Clarion University of Pennsylvania B
Duquesne University B
Grove City College B
La Salle University B
Lehigh University B, M, D
Lycoming College B
Mercyhurst University B
Penn State
    Erie, The Behrend College B
Rosemont College B
Susquehanna University B
University of Pittsburgh
    Johnstown B
Villanova University B
West Chester University of
    Pennsylvania B
Westminster College B
Widener University B

Puerto Rico

Inter American University of Puerto
    Rico
    Bayamon Campus B
    Metropolitan Campus B

Pontifical Catholic University of
    Puerto Rico B
Universidad Metropolitana B
University of Puerto Rico
    Rio Piedras B, M

Rhode Island

Providence College B
Rhode Island College B

South Carolina

Coastal Carolina University B
Converse College B
Forrest Junior College A
Francis Marion University B
Limestone College B
South Carolina State University B
University of South Carolina
    Columbia B
Wofford College B

South Dakota

Northern State University A
University of South Dakota B

Tennessee

Belmont University B
Carson-Newman University B
East Tennessee State University B
Hiwassee College A
Lincoln Memorial University B
Lipscomb University B
Middle Tennessee State University B
Tennessee State University B
Tennessee Technological
    University B
Union University B
University of Memphis B
University of Tennessee
    Knoxville B, M, D
    Martin B

Texas

Baylor University B, M
Houston Baptist University B
Lamar University B
Midwestern State University B
Sam Houston State University B
Stephen F. Austin State University B
Tarleton State University B
Texas A&M International
    University B
Texas A&M University
    Corpus Christi B
    Kingsville B
Texas State University B
Tyler Junior College A
University of North Texas B
University of Texas
    Arlington B
    El Paso B, M
    Permian Basin B
    San Antonio B, M
    Tyler B
University of the Incarnate Word B
West Texas A&M University B

Utah

Brigham Young University B
Snow College A
Weber State University C, B
Westminster College B

Vermont

Green Mountain College B, M

Virginia

Hampden-Sydney College B
Hampton University B
James Madison University B
Old Dominion University B
Patrick Henry College B
Randolph-Macon College B

Southwest Virginia Community
College *A*
Virginia Commonwealth
University *B, M*
Virginia Polytechnic Institute and
State University *B*
Virginia State University *B, M*
Wytheville Community College *A*

Washington
Eastern Washington University *B*
Gonzaga University *B*
Seattle University *B*

West Virginia
Concord University *B*
Marshall University *B*
West Liberty University *B*
West Virginia University *B, M, D*
West Virginia Wesleyan College *B*

Wisconsin
Beloit College *B*
Marquette University *B*
University of Wisconsin
Whitewater *B*

Wyoming
University of Wyoming *B, M, D*

Business statistics

Colorado
University of Denver *B, M*

Iowa
Iowa State University *B*

Maryland
University of Maryland
University College *M*

Massachusetts
Babson College *B*
Bentley University *M*

Michigan
Ferris State University *B*
Michigan Technological University *C*

New Hampshire
Southern New Hampshire
University *B, M*

New York
City University of New York
Baruch College *B, M*
Manhattan College *B*

Ohio
Bowling Green State University *M*
Cleveland State University *B*

Pennsylvania
La Salle University *B*

Puerto Rico
University of Puerto Rico
Rio Piedras *B, M*

Tennessee
University of Tennessee
Knoxville *B, M*

Texas
Texas A&M University *B*
University of Texas
Arlington *D*

Utah
Brigham Young University *B*

Business teacher education

Alabama
Alabama Agricultural and Mechanical
University *B, M*
Auburn University *B, M, T*
Faulkner State Community College *A*
Oakwood University *B*

Arizona
Arizona Christian University *B*
Eastern Arizona College *A*

Arkansas
Arkansas State University *B, M, T*
Arkansas Tech University *B*
Henderson State University *B*
Ouachita Baptist University *B, T*
Philander Smith College *B*
University of Arkansas
Pine Bluff *B, T*
University of Central Arkansas *B, M*
University of the Ozarks *B, T*

California
Azusa Pacific University *B, T*
California Baptist University *T*
California State University
Dominguez Hills *B*
Northridge *B, T*
Fresno Pacific University *B, T*
Fullerton College *A*
Humboldt State University *T*
Merritt College *A*
Mount St. Mary's College *T*
University of San Diego *T*

Colorado
Adams State University *B, M, T*
Colorado State University *B, M, T*

Connecticut
Albertus Magnus College *B, T*
Central Connecticut State
University *M*

Delaware
Delaware State University *B, M*

District of Columbia
University of the District of
Columbia *B*

Florida
Bethune-Cookman University *B, T*
St. Petersburg College *B*
University of South Florida *B, M*

Georgia
Darton College *A*
East Georgia State College *A*
Emmanuel College *B*
University of West Georgia *B, M, T*
Valdosta State University *B, M*

Hawaii
Brigham Young University-
Hawaii *B, T*

Idaho
Boise State University *T*
North Idaho College *A*
University of Idaho *T*

Illinois
Benedictine University *T*
Chicago State University *B*
Illinois State University *B, T*
McKendree University *B*
Northern Illinois University *M*
Trinity Christian College *B, T*

Indiana
Ball State University *B, M, T*
Calumet College of St. Joseph *T*
Goshen College *B, T*
Grace College *B*
Huntington University *B*
Indiana State University *B, T*
Indiana Wesleyan University *B*
Oakland City University *B*
University of Indianapolis *B, T*
University of St. Francis *B*
University of Southern Indiana *B*
Vincennes University *A*

Iowa
Ashford University *B*
Buena Vista University *B, T*
Central College *T*
Dordt College *B*
Drake University *M, T*
Ellsworth Community College *A*
Maharishi University of
Management *T*
Mount Mercy University *T*
Northwestern College *B, T*
St. Ambrose University *B, T*
Simpson College *T*
University of Northern Iowa *B*
Upper Iowa University *T*

Kansas
Bethany College *B*
Butler Community College *A*
Colby Community College *A*
Emporia State University *M, T*
Fort Hays State University *B, T*
Friends University *B*
Garden City Community College *A*
Labette Community College *A*
McPherson College *B, T*
Tabor College *B*

Kentucky
Eastern Kentucky University *B*
Morehead State University *B*
Northern Kentucky University *B*
Spalding University *M*
Thomas More College *B*
University of the Cumberlands *M, T*
Western Kentucky University *B, T*

Louisiana
Louisiana College *B, T*
McNeese State University *T*
Nicholls State University *B*
Our Lady of Holy Cross College *B*
University of Louisiana at Lafayette *B*

Maine
University of Maine
Fort Kent *B*

Maryland
Mount St. Mary's University *T*
Prince George's Community
College *A*
University of Maryland
Eastern Shore *B*

Massachusetts
Eastern Nazarene College *B*
Northern Essex Community
College *A*
University of Massachusetts
Dartmouth *T*
Western New England
University *B, T*

Michigan
Alma College *T*
Central Michigan University *B*
Delta College *A*
Eastern Michigan University *B, M*

Ferris State University *B*
Siena Heights University *B, T*
University of Michigan
Dearborn *B*
Western Michigan University *B*

Minnesota
Concordia College: Moorhead *B, T*
Minnesota State University
Mankato *B, M, T*
Minnesota West Community and
Technical College *A*
Ridgewater College *A*
St. Catherine University *B*
University of Minnesota
Twin Cities *B, M, T*
Winona State University *B, T*

Mississippi
Coahoma Community College *A*
Hinds Community College *A*
Itawamba Community College *A*
Millsaps College *T*
Mississippi College *B, M*
Mississippi Delta Community
College *A*
Mississippi Gulf Coast Community
College *A*
Mississippi State University *B*
Northeast Mississippi Community
College *A*
Northwest Mississippi Community
College *A*
Rust College *B*
University of Southern Mississippi *B*

Missouri
Avila University *T*
Evangel University *B, T*
Hannibal-LaGrange University *B*
Lincoln University *B*
Lindenwood University *B*
Missouri Baptist University *B, T*
Missouri Southern State
University *B, T*
Missouri State University *B*
Northwest Missouri State
University *B, M, T*
Southeast Missouri State University *B*
University of Central
Missouri *B, M, T*
University of Missouri
Columbia *B*

Montana
University of Montana *B, T*
University of Montana: Western *B, T*

Nebraska
Chadron State College *B, M*
Concordia University *B, T*
Grace University *B*
Hastings College *B, M, T*
Midland University *B, T*
Union College *B*
University of Nebraska
Kearney *B, M, T*
Lincoln *B, T*
Wayne State College *B, T*
York College *B, T*

Nevada
Great Basin College *B*

New Hampshire
Southern New Hampshire
University *B, M*

New Jersey
Montclair State University *B, M, T*
Rider University *B, M*
Saint Peter's University *T*

New Mexico

Eastern New Mexico University *B*
Western New Mexico University *B*

New York

Alfred University *B, T*
Canisius College *M, T*
D'Youville College *M, T*
Dowling College *B, M*
Hofstra University *B, M*
Nazareth College *B, M, T*
New York University *B, M, D, T*
Niagara University *B, M, T*
Pace University *M*
Pace University: Pleasantville/
    Briarcliff *B, M, T*
SUNY
    College at Buffalo *B, M, T*
    College at Oswego *B*

North Carolina

Appalachian State University *B, T*
East Carolina University *B*
Lenoir-Rhyne University *T*
North Carolina Agricultural and
    Technical State
    University *B, M, T*

North Dakota

Dickinson State University *B, T*
Minot State University *B*
University of Mary *B*
University of North Dakota *B*
Valley City State University *B, T*

Ohio

Ashland University *T*
Bowling Green State
    University *B, M, T*
Defiance College *B, T*
Mount Vernon Nazarene
    University *B, T*
University of Rio Grande *B, T*
University of Toledo *B, M, T*
Wright State University *B, T*
Youngstown State University *B, M*

Oklahoma

Eastern Oklahoma State College *A*
Oklahoma Panhandle State
    University *B*
Oklahoma Wesleyan University *B*
Oral Roberts University *B, T*
Southwestern Oklahoma State
    University *B*
University of Central Oklahoma *B*

Oregon

Concordia University *B, M, T*
Corban University *B*
Portland State University *T*

Pennsylvania

Community College of
    Philadelphia *A*
Gwynedd Mercy University *B, T*
Immaculata University *B*
Mercyhurst University *B, T*
Reading Area Community College *A*
Robert Morris University *B, M*
St. Vincent College *B*
Seton Hill University *T*

Puerto Rico

Caribbean University *B, T*
Inter American University of Puerto
    Rico
    Metropolitan Campus *M*
    San German Campus *M, D*
Pontifical Catholic University of
    Puerto Rico *B, D, T*
University of Puerto Rico
    Mayaguez *T*

Rhode Island

Bryant University *M*
Johnson & Wales University
    Providence *T*

South Carolina

South Carolina State University *B, T*

South Dakota

Dakota State University *B, T*
Northern State University *B, T*

Tennessee

Lee University *B*
Lincoln Memorial University *B, T*
Martin Methodist College *B*
Middle Tennessee State
    University *B, M, T*
Trevecca Nazarene University *B, T*
Tusculum College *B, T*
Union University *B, T*
Victory University *B, T*

Texas

Hardin-Simmons University *B, T*
Howard Payne University *B*
Jarvis Christian College *B*
Lamar University *T*
Laredo Community College *A*
LeTourneau University *B, T*
Lubbock Christian University *B*
McMurry University *T*
St. Mary's University *T*
Tarleton State University *T*
Texas A&M University
    Kingsville *T*
University of Mary Hardin-Baylor *T*
Wayland Baptist University *B*
West Texas A&M University *T*

Utah

Snow College *A*
Southern Utah University *B*
Utah Valley University *B*
Weber State University *B*

Virginia

Bluefield College *B, T*
Emory & Henry College *B*
Norfolk State University *B*
University of Virginia's College at
    Wise *T*
Virginia State University *B*

Washington

Eastern Washington University *B*
Pierce College *A*
Renton Technical College *A*
Walla Walla University *B*

West Virginia

Concord University *B, T*
Davis and Elkins College *B*
Wheeling Jesuit University *B*

Wisconsin

Concordia University Wisconsin *B, T*
Edgewood College *B, T*
Lakeland College *T*
Maranatha Baptist Bible College *B*
Mount Mary University *B, T*
University of Wisconsin
    Whitewater *B, M, T*
Viterbo University *B, T*

Wyoming

Eastern Wyoming College *A*

Cabinetmaking/ millwright

Alabama

George C. Wallace Community
    College at Dothan *C*

Jefferson Davis Community
    College *C*
Northwest-Shoals Community
    College *C*
Southern Union State Community
    College *C*

Arizona

Pima Community College *C*

California

Bakersfield College *C, A*
Long Beach City College *C, A*
Palomar College *C, A*
San Joaquin Delta College *C*

Florida

Palm Beach State College *C*

Georgia

Central Georgia Technical College *C*
Columbus Technical College *C*
Savannah Technical College *C*

Illinois

Prairie State College *C*

Indiana

Ivy Tech Community College
    Bloomington *C, A*
    Central Indiana *C, A*
    Lafayette *C, A*
    North Central *C, A*
    Northwest *C, A*
    South Central *C, A*
    Southwest *C, A*

Iowa

Des Moines Area Community
    College *C*

Kentucky

Jefferson Community and Technical
    College *C*

Minnesota

Minnesota State College - Southeast
    Technical *C*
St. Cloud Technical and Community
    College *C*
St. Paul College *C*

New Mexico

Central New Mexico Community
    College *C*

North Carolina

Tri-County Community College *C*

Ohio

Columbus State Community
    College *A*

Pennsylvania

Bucks County Community
    College *C, A*
Harrisburg Area Community
    College *C, A*
Thaddeus Stevens College of
    Technology *A*

Utah

Salt Lake Community College *C*
Utah Valley University *C, A*

Washington

Bates Technical College *C, A*
Clover Park Technical College *C*

Wisconsin

Fox Valley Technical College *C*
Milwaukee Area Technical College *C*

CAD/CADD drafting/ design technology

Alabama

ITT Technical Institute
    Birmingham *A*
Virginia College
    Birmingham *A*

Alaska

University of Alaska
    Anchorage *C*

Arizona

Arizona Western College *C, A*
Cochise College *C*
Coconino County Community
    College *A*
Glendale Community College *C, A*
ITT Technical Institute
    Tempe *A*
    Tucson *A*
Mesa Community College *C*
Phoenix College *C*

Arkansas

Arkansas Northeastern College *C*
East Arkansas Community
    College *C, A*
ITT Technical Institute
    Little Rock *A*
North Arkansas College *C*
Southern Arkansas University Tech *C*
University of Arkansas
    Fort Smith *C, A*

California

Bakersfield College *C*
College of San Mateo *C*
ITT Technical Institute
    Lathrop *A*
    National City *A*
    Oxnard *A*
    Rancho Cordova *A*
    San Bernardino *A*
    Sylmar *A*
    Torrance *A*
Ohlone College *A*
Orange Coast College *C, A*
Southwestern College *C, A*

Colorado

Colorado Northwestern Community
    College *C*
Front Range Community College *C, A*
ITT Technical Institute
    Westminster *A*
Pikes Peak Community College *C, A*

Connecticut

Naugatuck Valley Community
    College *C, A*
Quinebaug Valley Community
    College *A*
Three Rivers Community
    College *C, A*

Delaware

Delaware Technical Community
    College
    Stanton/Wilmington Campus *C, A*
    Terry Campus *C*

Florida

ITT Technical Institute
    Ft. Lauderdale *A*
    Jacksonville *A*
    Lake Mary *A*
    Tampa *A*
Pasco-Hernando State College *C*
Tallahassee Community College *C*

Georgia

Atlanta Technical College *C*
Central Georgia Technical College *C*
Gwinnett Technical College *C*
Savannah Technical College *C*
Southwest Georgia Technical
   College *C*

Idaho

ITT Technical Institute
   Boise *A*
Idaho State University *C, A, B*

Illinois

Black Hawk College *C*
City Colleges of Chicago
   Wilbur Wright College *C*
College of Lake County *C*
Danville Area Community College *A*
Elgin Community College *C, A*
Heartland Community College *C, A*
Illinois Central College *C*
Illinois Valley Community
   College *C, A*
Kaskaskia College *C*
Lincoln Land Community College *C*
Moraine Valley Community College *C*
Morrison Institute of Technology *A*
Morton College *C, A*
Prairie State College *C*
Sauk Valley Community College *C*
Triton College *C*
Waubonsee Community College *C, A*

Indiana

ITT Technical Institute
   Fort Wayne *A*
   Indianapolis *A*
   Newburgh *A*

Iowa

Hamilton Technical College *A*

Kansas

Barton County Community College *C*
Brown Mackie College
   Salina *A*
Highland Community College *C, A*
Johnson County Community
   College *C, A*
Kansas City Kansas Community
   College *C, A*
Manhattan Area Technical
   College *C, A*

Kentucky

ITT Technical Institute
   Louisville *A*
Murray State University *B*
Sullivan College of Technology and
   Design *A*

Louisiana

ITT Technical Institute
   St. Rose *A*

Maine

Kennebec Valley Community
   College *A*

Maryland

College of Southern Maryland *C*
Frederick Community College *C, A*
Harford Community College *C, A*
Howard Community College *C, A*
ITT Technical Institute
   Owings Mills *A*

Massachusetts

ITT Technical Institute
   Norwood *A*
   Wilmington *A*

Quinsigamond Community College *C*
Roxbury Community College *A*

Michigan

Baker College
   Muskegon *A*
Eastern Michigan University *B, M*
Ferris State University *A*
Gogebic Community College *A*
Henry Ford Community College *C, A*
ITT Technical Institute
   Canton *A*
   Troy *A*
Lake Michigan College *C, A*
Northern Michigan University *A*
West Shore Community College *A*

Minnesota

Anoka Technical College *C*
Century College *C, A*
Dunwoody College of Technology *A*
ITT Technical Institute
   Eden Prairie *A*
Lake Superior College *C, A*
Minnesota State College - Southeast
   Technical *C, A*
Ridgewater College *C, A*
Rochester Community and Technical
   College *C, A*

Mississippi

Mississippi Gulf Coast Community
   College *A*

Missouri

Metropolitan Community College -
   Kansas City *A*
Mineral Area College *C, A*
Missouri Southern State University *A*
State Fair Community College *C, A*

Montana

Montana State University *A*

Nebraska

ITT Technical Institute
   Omaha *A*

Nevada

College of Southern Nevada *C, A*
ITT Technical Institute
   Henderson *A*

New Jersey

Burlington County College *A*
Thomas Edison State College *A*

New Mexico

Central New Mexico Community
   College *C*
ITT Technical Institute
   Albuquerque *A*
Southwestern Indian Polytechnic
   Institute *C*

New York

Erie Community College *A*
ITT Technical Institute
   Albany *A*
   Getzville *A*
   Liverpool *A*
Jamestown Community College *C*
Mohawk Valley Community
   College *C, A*
Niagara County Community
   College *C, A*
Rockland Community College *C*
SUNY
   College of Agriculture and
      Technology at Morrisville *A*
   College of Technology at Alfred *A*
Vaughn College of Aeronautics and
   Technology *A*
Westchester Community College *C*

North Carolina

Edgecombe Community College *C*
Gaston College *C*

Ohio

Bryant & Stratton College
   Cleveland *A*
Central Ohio Technical College *C*
ITT Technical Institute
   Dayton *A*
   Hilliard *A*
   Norwood *A*
   Strongsville *A*
   Youngstown *A*
James A. Rhodes State College *C*
Kent State University
   Tuscarawas *A*
Marion Technical College *C*
Miami University
   Hamilton *C*
Northwest State Community
   College *C, A*
Shawnee State University *C, A*
Southern State Community College *A*
Terra State Community College *C*
University of Cincinnati
   Clermont College *C, A*

Oklahoma

Northeastern Oklahoma Agricultural
   and Mechanical College *C, A*

Oregon

Central Oregon Community
   College *C, A*
Clackamas Community College *C, A*
ITT Technical Institute
   Portland *A*

Pennsylvania

Community College of
   Philadelphia *C, A*
Delaware County Community
   College *C, A*
ITT Technical Institute
   Pittsburgh *A*
   Plymouth Meeting *A*
Luzerne County Community
   College *C, A*
Northampton Community College *A*
Thaddeus Stevens College of
   Technology *A*
YTI Career Institute
   York *A*

Puerto Rico

Inter American University of Puerto
   Rico
   Aguadilla Campus *C*
   San German Campus *C*

South Carolina

ITT Technical Institute
   Greenville *A*

Tennessee

ITT Technical Institute
   Knoxville *A*
   Memphis *A*
   Nashville *A*
Pellissippi State Community
   College *A*
Vatterott College
   Memphis *C, A*

Texas

Del Mar College *C*
ITT Technical Institute
   Arlington *A*
   Austin *A*
   Houston North *A*
   Houston West *A*
   Richardson *A*

San Antonio *A*
Webster *A*
San Antonio College *C*

Utah

Southern Utah University *A*
Utah State University *C*

Virginia

ITT Technical Institute
   Chantilly *A*
   Norfolk *A*
   Richmond *A*
   Springfield *A*
J. Sargeant Reynolds Community
   College *C*
John Tyler Community College *C*
Mountain Empire Community
   College *A*
Norfolk State University *B*
Thomas Nelson Community
   College *A*
Tidewater Community College *A*
Westwood College
   Annandale *A*
   Arlington Ballston *A*

Washington

Bates Technical College *C*
Clark College *C*
ITT Technical Institute
   Everett *A*
   Seattle *A*
   Spokane *A*
Lake Washington Institute of
   Technology *C*
Renton Technical College *C, A*
Shoreline Community College *C, A*
South Seattle Community
   College *C, A*

West Virginia

Blue Ridge Community and Technical
   College *C*
Bridgemont Community and
   Technical College *A*

Wisconsin

Herzing University
   Madison *A, B*
ITT Technical Institute
   Green Bay *A*
   Greenfield *A*
Southwest Wisconsin Technical
   College *A*
Western Technical College *C*

Wyoming

Northwest College *C, A*
Sheridan College *C, A*

Canadian studies

Kentucky

Eastern Kentucky University *B*
Western Kentucky University *C*

New York

St. Lawrence University *B*

Washington

University of Washington *B, M*
Western Washington University *B*

Cardiopulmonary technology

Massachusetts

Northeastern University *B, M*

North Carolina

Johnston Community College *C, A*

Cardiovascular science

Ohio
University of Toledo *M, D*

Wisconsin
Milwaukee School of Engineering *M*

Cardiovascular technology

Alabama
Community College of the Air
    Force *A*

Arkansas
Arkansas Tech University *A*

California
Butte College *A*
City College of San Francisco *C*
Grossmont College *C, A*
Orange Coast College *C, A*

Connecticut
St. Vincent's College *A*

Delaware
Delaware Technical Community
    College
    Stanton/Wilmington Campus *A*

Florida
Barry University *B*
Broward College *A*
Edison State College *A*
Polk State College *A*
Sanford-Brown Institute
    Jacksonville *A*
    Tampa *C, A*
Santa Fe College *A*

Georgia
Augusta Technical College *A*
Columbus Technical College *C, A*
Darton College *A*
Gwinnett Technical College *A*

Illinois
City Colleges of Chicago
    Harry S. Truman College *C*
Harper College *C, A*

Kentucky
Daymar College
    Bowling Green *C, A*
Spencerian College *A*

Louisiana
Louisiana State University
    Health Sciences Center *B*

Maine
Southern Maine Community
    College *A*

Maryland
Howard Community College *C, A*

Massachusetts
Bunker Hill Community College *C, A*

Michigan
Kirtland Community College *A*

Minnesota
Northland Community & Technical
    College *A*
Rochester Community and Technical
    College *A*
St. Cloud Technical and Community
    College *A*

Nebraska
BryanLGH College of Health
    Sciences *A, B*
Nebraska Methodist College of
    Nursing and Allied Health *A, B*

North Carolina
Caldwell Community College and
    Technical Institute *C, A*
Central Piedmont Community
    College *A*
Forsyth Technical Community
    College *C, A*
Johnston Community College *C, A*
Stanly Community College *C*

Ohio
Mercy College of Ohio *A*

Oklahoma
Bacone College *A*
Oklahoma State University
    Oklahoma City *A*

Pennsylvania
Community College of Allegheny
    County *A*
Drexel University *B*
Gwynedd Mercy University *C, A*
Harrisburg Area Community
    College *A*
Pennsylvania College of Health
    Sciences *A*
Pennsylvania College of
    Technology *B*
Thomas Jefferson University *B*

Puerto Rico
Pontifical Catholic University of
    Puerto Rico *B*
Universidad Metropolitana *B*

South Carolina
Medical University of South
    Carolina *B*
Piedmont Technical College *A*
University of South Carolina
    Columbia *B*

South Dakota
Southeast Technical Institute *A*

Tennessee
Chattanooga State Community
    College *C*
Northeast State Community
    College *A*

Texas
Alvin Community College *C, A*
El Centro College *A*
Houston Community College
    System *C, A*
Sanford-Brown College
    Houston *A*

Virginia
Northern Virginia Community
    College *C*

Washington
Spokane Community College *A*

Wisconsin
Milwaukee Area Technical College *A*

Caribbean studies

California
Pitzer College *B*

Georgia
Emory University *B*

Illinois
University of Chicago *M*
University of Illinois
    Urbana-Champaign *M*

New Hampshire
Dartmouth College *B*

New Jersey
Rutgers, The State University of New
    Jersey
    New Brunswick/Piscataway
        Campus *B*
William Paterson University of New
    Jersey *B*

New York
City University of New York
    Brooklyn College *B*
    City College *B*
Columbia University
    School of General Studies *B*
Hofstra University *B*
SUNY
    University at Albany *B, M*

Carpentry

Alabama
Bishop State Community College *C*
Calhoun Community College *C*
Gadsden State Community College *C*
Jefferson Davis Community
    College *C*
Lawson State Community College *C*
Northwest-Shoals Community
    College *C*

Alaska
Ilisagvik College *C*
University of Alaska
    Fairbanks *C, A*

Arizona
Arizona Western College *C, A*
Central Arizona College *C*
Cochise College *C*
Coconino County Community
    College *A*
Eastern Arizona College *C*
GateWay Community College *C, A*
Northland Pioneer College *C, A*
Tohono O'odham Community
    College *C, A*

Arkansas
Cossatot Community College of the
    University of Arkansas *A*
National Park Community College *C*
North Arkansas College *C*

California
Bakersfield College *C, A*
Barstow Community College *C*
College of the Sequoias *C, A*
Fresno City College *C, A*
Fullerton College *A*
Hartnell College *C*
Laney College *A*
Long Beach City College *C, A*
Los Angeles Trade and Technical
    College *C, A*
Palomar College *C, A*
Pasadena City College *C, A*
Porterville College *C, A*
Santa Rosa Junior College *C*
Santiago Canyon College *A*
Sierra College *C, A*
Victor Valley College *A*

Colorado
Aims Community College *C*
Trinidad State Junior College *C*

Florida
Florida State College at
    Jacksonville *C*
Hillsborough Community College *C*
Indian River State College *C*
Palm Beach State College *C*
Santa Fe College *C*

Georgia
Albany Technical College *C, A*
Atlanta Technical College *C*
Central Georgia Technical College *C*
Columbus Technical College *C*
Gwinnett Technical College *C*
Savannah Technical College *C*
West Georgia Technical College *C*

Hawaii
University of Hawaii
    Hawaii Community College *C, A*
    Honolulu Community College *C, A*
    Kauai Community College *C, A*
    Maui College *A*

Idaho
Idaho State University *C, A, B*
North Idaho College *C, A*

Illinois
Black Hawk College *C, A*
City Colleges of Chicago
    Kennedy-King College *C*
John A. Logan College *A*
Kaskaskia College *C, A*
Southeastern Illinois College *C*
Southwestern Illinois College *C, A*

Indiana
Ivy Tech Community College
    Central Indiana *C, A*
    East Central *C, A*
    Lafayette *C, A*
    North Central *C, A*
    Northwest *C, A*
    Southwest *C, A*
    Wabash Valley *C, A*

Iowa
Des Moines Area Community
    College *C*
Ellsworth Community College *C, A*
Hawkeye Community College *A*
Iowa Central Community College *C*
Iowa Lakes Community College *C*
Kirkwood Community College *C*
North Iowa Area Community
    College *C*
Northeast Iowa Community
    College *C, A*
Northwest Iowa Community
    College *C, A*
Southeastern Community
    College *C, A*
Southwestern Community
    College *C, A*
Western Iowa Tech Community
    College *C*

Kansas
Coffeyville Community College *C*
Fort Scott Community College *A*
Hutchinson Community College *C, A*
Kansas City Kansas Community
    College *C*
Manhattan Area Technical
    College *C, A*

Kentucky

Bluegrass Community and Technical College *C, A*
Elizabethtown Community and Technical College *C*
Hopkinsville Community College *C*
Jefferson Community and Technical College *C*
Maysville Community and Technical College *C*
Owensboro Community and Technical College *C, A*
Somerset Community College *C, A*
West Kentucky Community and Technical College *C*

Louisiana

Delgado Community College *C*
Nunez Community College *C*

Maine

Eastern Maine Community College *A*
Northern Maine Community College *C, A*
Washington County Community College *C*

Michigan

Delta College *A*
Gogebic Community College *A*
Lansing Community College *C, A*
Northwestern Michigan College *C, A*
Oakland Community College *C, A*
Southwestern Michigan College *C, A*

Minnesota

Alexandria Technical and Community College *C*
Hennepin Technical College *C, A*
Lake Superior College *C*
Leech Lake Tribal College *C*
Mesabi Range Community and Technical College *A*
Minnesota State College - Southeast Technical *C, A*
Minnesota State Community and Technical College *C, A*
Minnesota West Community and Technical College *C*
Northland Community & Technical College *C*
Northwest Technical College *C*
Ridgewater College *C, A*
Riverland Community College *C*
Rochester Community and Technical College *C*
St. Cloud Technical and Community College *C, A*
St. Paul College *C*

Mississippi

Coahoma Community College *C*
East Mississippi Community College *C*
Hinds Community College *C*
Mississippi Gulf Coast Community College *C*
Pearl River Community College *C, A*
Southwest Mississippi Community College *C*

Missouri

Ranken Technical College *A*
St. Louis Community College *A*

Montana

Aaniiih Nakoda College *C*
Flathead Valley Community College *C*
Helena College University of Montana *C, A*
Miles Community College *C, A*
Montana State University
  Great Falls College *C*
  Northern *A*

Montana Tech of the University of Montana *C, A*

Nebraska

Nebraska Indian Community College *C, A*

Nevada

Truckee Meadows Community College *C, A*

New Mexico

Central New Mexico Community College *C*
Luna Community College *C*
Navajo Technical University *C*
New Mexico State University Carlsbad *C*
San Juan College *C, A*

New York

Hudson Valley Community College *A*
Mohawk Valley Community College *C*
SUNY
  College of Technology at Alfred *A*
  College of Technology at Delhi *C, A*

North Carolina

Alamance Community College *C*
Asheville-Buncombe Technical Community College *C*
Bladen Community College *C*
Blue Ridge Community College *C*
Cape Fear Community College *C*
Cleveland Community College *C*
Fayetteville Technical Community College *C*
Forsyth Technical Community College *C*
Guilford Technical Community College *C*
Martin Community College *C*
McDowell Technical Community College *C*
Piedmont Community College *C*
Rowan-Cabarrus Community College *C*
Sampson Community College *C, A*
Surry Community College *C, A*
Vance-Granville Community College *C*

North Dakota

Bismarck State College *C, A*
Cankdeska Cikana Community College *A*
Sitting Bull College *C, A*
Williston State College *C, A*

Ohio

Hocking College *A*

Oregon

Treasure Valley Community College *C, A*

Pennsylvania

Community College of Allegheny County *C*
Delaware County Community College *C*
Harrisburg Area Community College *C*
Johnson College *A*
Orleans Technical Institute *C*
Thaddeus Stevens College of Technology *A*
Triangle Tech
  Bethlehem *A*
  DuBois *A*
  Erie *A*
  Greensburg *A*

Pittsburgh *A*
Sunbury *A*
Williamson Free School of Mechanical Trades *A*

Rhode Island

New England Institute of Technology *A*

South Carolina

York Technical College *C*

South Dakota

Lake Area Technical Institute *C*
Oglala Lakota College *A*
Sisseton Wahpeton College *A*

Texas

Austin Community College *C, A*
Central Texas College *C*
Houston Community College System *C*
Howard College *C*
Laredo Community College *C*
North Lake College *A*
Odessa College *C, A*
St. Philip's College *A*

Utah

Salt Lake Community College *C, A*

Virginia

Liberty University *A*
Southwest Virginia Community College *C*
Wytheville Community College *C, A*

Washington

Bates Technical College *C, A*
Edmonds Community College *C*
Grays Harbor College *C, A*
Green River Community College *A*
Peninsula College *C*
Seattle Central Community College *C, A*
Spokane Community College *C, A*
Walla Walla Community College *C, A*

Wisconsin

Chippewa Valley Technical College *C*
College of Menominee Nation *C*
Fox Valley Technical College *C*
Gateway Technical College *C*
Lac Courte Oreilles Ojibwa Community College *C*
Lakeshore Technical College *C*
Mid-State Technical College *C*
Milwaukee Area Technical College *C*
Waukesha County Technical College *C*
Wisconsin Indianhead Technical College *C*

Wyoming

Central Wyoming College *C, A*

Casino management

California

National University *C, B*

Illinois

Roosevelt University *B, M*

Maryland

Howard Community College *C, A*

Michigan

Lake Michigan College *C, A*

New Jersey

Burlington County College *A*

New York

Niagara County Community College *C, A*

Oklahoma

Oklahoma State University Institute of Technology: Okmulgee *A*

Washington

Northwest Indian College *C*
Olympic College *C*

Cell biology and histology

Alabama

University of Alabama Birmingham *D*

California

California State University
  Dominguez Hills *B*
  Long Beach *B*
  Northridge *B*
San Francisco State University *M*
University of California
  Davis *B, M, D*
  San Diego *B*
  Santa Barbara *B, M, D*

Connecticut

Quinnipiac University *M*
University of Connecticut *M, D*
Yale University *M, D*

District of Columbia

Catholic University of America *M, D*

Florida

University of Miami *M, D*

Georgia

University of Georgia *B, M, D*

Illinois

University of Illinois Urbana-Champaign *B, D*

Indiana

University of Indianapolis *B*

Iowa

Iowa State University *M, D*

Louisiana

Tulane University *B, M, D*

Maine

Colby College *B*

Maryland

Johns Hopkins University *B, M, D*
University of Maryland Baltimore County *D*

Massachusetts

Boston University *D*
Harvard College *M, D*
Tufts University *D*

Minnesota

Southwest Minnesota State University *B*
University of Minnesota
  Duluth *B*
  Twin Cities *B, M, D*

Missouri

Washington University in St. Louis *D*

Montana

Salish Kootenai College *B*

New Hampshire

Dartmouth College *B*

New Jersey

Rutgers, The State University of New
Jersey
New Brunswick/Piscataway
Campus *B, M, D*

New York

College of Saint Rose *B*
New York University *M, D*
SUNY
College at Plattsburgh *B*
University at Albany *M, D*
University of Rochester *B*
Yeshiva University *M, D*

North Carolina

Duke University *M, D*
East Carolina University *D*
University of North Carolina
Chapel Hill *M, D*

Ohio

Case Western Reserve University *D*
Kent State University *M, D*

Oklahoma

Oklahoma City University *B*
University of Oklahoma *M, D*

Oregon

Oregon Health & Science
University *D*

Pennsylvania

Mansfield University of
Pennsylvania *B*
Pennsylvania Highlands Community
College *A*
University of Pittsburgh *M, D*

Rhode Island

Brown University *B, M, D*

Texas

University of Texas
Health Science Center at
Houston *M, D*

Vermont

Johnson State College *B*
Marlboro College *B*

Virginia

University of Virginia *D*

Washington

University of Washington *M, D*
Western Washington University *B*

Wisconsin

University of Wisconsin
Superior *B*

Cell physiology

California

University of California
Davis *M, D*

Indiana

Indiana University
Purdue University
Indianapolis *M, D*

Ohio

Case Western Reserve University *D*
University of Cincinnati *D*

West Virginia

West Virginia University *D*

Cellular/anatomical biology

Alabama

Huntingdon College *B*

Georgia

Georgia Regents University *M, D*

Illinois

Loyola University Chicago *M, D*
University of Illinois
Chicago *M, D*

Indiana

Indiana University
Purdue University
Indianapolis *M, D*

Iowa

University of Iowa *M, D*

Kansas

University of Kansas Medical
Center *M, D*

Minnesota

Saint Cloud State University *B*

Nebraska

University of Nebraska
Medical Center *M, D*

Pennsylvania

Washington & Jefferson College *B*

South Carolina

Medical University of South
Carolina *D*

Texas

Dallas Baptist University *B*
University of Texas
Health Science Center at
Houston *M, D*

Cellular/molecular biology

Arizona

Arizona State University *D*
University of Arizona *B, M, D*

Arkansas

Arkansas State University *D*
University of Arkansas *M, D*

California

California Institute of
Technology *M, D*
Stanford University *M, D*
University of California
Berkeley *B, M, D*
Irvine *B, M, D*
Los Angeles *B, M, D*
Merced *M, D*
Riverside *M, D*
Santa Cruz *B, M, D*
University of Southern
California *M, D*

Colorado

Adams State University *B*
Colorado College *B*

Colorado State University *M, D*
University of Colorado
Boulder *B, D*
Denver *D*

Connecticut

Connecticut College *B*
University of Connecticut *B, M, D*
University of New Haven *M*
Yale University *M, D*

District of Columbia

Georgetown University *D*

Florida

Florida Institute of Technology *M*
University of Florida *M, D*
University of Miami *M, D*

Hawaii

University of Hawaii
Manoa *M, D*

Illinois

Bradley University *B*
University of Illinois
Urbana-Champaign *B, M, D*

Indiana

Bethel College *B*
Purdue University *B, M, D*

Iowa

Drake University *B*

Kansas

University of Kansas *M, D*

Maryland

Johns Hopkins University *B*
University of Maryland
College Park *M, D*

Massachusetts

Boston University *M, D*
Harvard College *M, D*
University of Massachusetts
Amherst *M, D*

Michigan

Grand Valley State University *B*
Michigan State University *M, D*
University of Michigan *B, M, D*

Minnesota

University of Minnesota
Duluth *B*

Missouri

Missouri State University *B, M*
Washington University in St. Louis *D*

Montana

University of Montana *B*
University of Montana: Western *B*

Nevada

University of Nevada
Reno *M, D*

New Jersey

Rutgers, The State University of New
Jersey
New Brunswick/Piscataway
Campus *M, D*
Newark Campus *M, D*

New Mexico

Western New Mexico University *B*

New York

SUNY
College at Brockport *B*
College at Oneonta *B*
University at Binghamton *B*
University at Stony Brook *D*

North Carolina

Methodist University *B*
Wake Forest University *M, D*

North Dakota

North Dakota State University *D*

Ohio

Cedarville University *B*
John Carroll University *B*
Ohio University *B, D*
University of Cincinnati *M, D*

Oregon

Oregon Health & Science
University *D*
Oregon State University *M, D*

Pennsylvania

Bucknell University *B*
Drexel University *M, D*
Penn State
University Park *M, D*
University of Pennsylvania *M, D*
University of the Sciences *M, D*

Rhode Island

University of Rhode Island *B*

South Carolina

Limestone College *B*

Tennessee

Union University *B*
Vanderbilt University *M, D*

Texas

Texas A&M University *B*
Texas Tech University *B*
University of Texas
Austin *M, D*
Dallas *M, D*
Health Science Center at
Houston *M, D*
Medical Branch at Galveston *M, D*
San Antonio *D*

Utah

University of Utah *D*

Vermont

Bennington College *B*
Southern Vermont College *B*
University of Vermont *M, D*

Virginia

Christopher Newport University *B*
Liberty University *B*
Marymount University *B, T*

Washington

University of Puget Sound *B*
Western Washington University *B*

Wyoming

University of Wyoming *D*

Celtic languages

California

University of California
Berkeley *B*

Massachusetts

Boston College *M*
Harvard College *M, D*

Central Asian studies

Indiana

Indiana University
  Bloomington *M, D*

Massachusetts

Harvard College *D*

Ceramic sciences/engineering

Illinois

University of Illinois
  Urbana-Champaign *B, M, D*

Missouri

Missouri University of Science and
  Technology *B, M, D*

New Jersey

Rutgers, The State University of New
  Jersey
  New Brunswick/Piscataway
    Campus *B, M, D*

New York

Alfred University *B, M, D*

South Carolina

Clemson University *B, M, D*

Washington

University of Washington *B*

Ceramics

California

Butte College *C, A*
California College of the Arts *B, M*
California State University
  East Bay *B*
  Long Beach *B, M*
  Northridge *B, M*
Chabot College *A*
Citrus College *C*
De Anza College *C, A*
Glendale Community College *C*
Grossmont College *A*
Laney College *A*
Monterey Peninsula College *C, A*
Ohlone College *C*
Palomar College *A*
Pasadena City College *C, A*
Santa Rosa Junior College *C*
Ventura College *C, A*
West Los Angeles College *C, A*

Colorado

Adams State University *B*

Connecticut

University of Hartford *B*

District of Columbia

George Washington University *M*

Florida

University of Miami *B*

Idaho

Northwest Nazarene University *B*

Illinois

Bradley University *B*
Lincoln College *A*
Richland Community College *A*

School of the Art Institute of
  Chicago *B, M*

Indiana

Indiana Wesleyan University *B*

Iowa

Coe College *B*
University of Iowa *B, M*

Kansas

Allen County Community College *A*
Pratt Community College *A*
Seward County Community
  College *A*
University of Kansas *B, M*

Kentucky

Eastern Kentucky University *B*

Maine

College of the Atlantic *B*
Maine College of Art *B*

Maryland

Cecil College *C*
Hood College *M*
Maryland Institute College of Art *B*

Massachusetts

Massachusetts College of Art and
  Design *B, M*
School of the Museum of Fine
  Arts *B, M*
University of Massachusetts
  Dartmouth *B, M*

Michigan

Andrews University *B*
Aquinas College *B*
College for Creative Studies *B*
Finlandia University *B*
Grand Valley State University *B*
Northern Michigan University *B*
Oakland Community College *C, A*
Siena Heights University *B*
University of Michigan *B*

Minnesota

Minnesota State University
  Mankato *B, M*
Saint Cloud State University *B*

Missouri

Columbia College *B*
Kansas City Art Institute *B*
Washington University in St.
  Louis *B, M*

Nevada

Sierra Nevada College *B*

New Hampshire

New Hampshire Institute of Art *B*
Plymouth State University *B*

New Jersey

Cumberland County College *C, A*

New York

Alfred University *B, M*
Hofstra University *B*
Rochester Institute of
  Technology *B, M*
SUNY
  College at Fredonia *B*
  College at New Paltz *B, M*
Syracuse University *B, M*

North Carolina

East Carolina University *B*
Elon University *B*
Gardner-Webb University *B*

Haywood Community College *A*
Methodist University *B*

Ohio

Bowling Green State University *B*
Cleveland Institute of Art *B*
Ohio University *B, M*
University of Akron *B*

Oregon

Mt. Hood Community College *A*
Oregon College of Art & Craft *C, B*
University of Oregon *B*

Pennsylvania

Arcadia University *B*
Marywood University *B, M*
Seton Hill University *B*
Temple University *B, M*

Puerto Rico

Inter American University of Puerto
  Rico
  San German Campus *M*

Rhode Island

Providence College *B*
Rhode Island School of Design *B, M*
Salve Regina University *B*

South Dakota

South Dakota State University *C*

Tennessee

Tennessee Technological
  University *B*

Texas

Texas Christian University *B*
University of Dallas *B, M*
University of Texas
  El Paso *B, M*
Western Texas College *A*

Utah

Brigham Young University *M*
Dixie State College *B*

Vermont

Bennington College *B*
Marlboro College *B*

Virginia

Lord Fairfax Community College *C*

Washington

University of Washington *B, M*
Western Washington University *B*

West Virginia

West Virginia State University *B*
West Virginia Wesleyan College *B*

Wyoming

Western Wyoming Community
  College *A*

Chemical and biomolecular engineering

Illinois

University of Chicago *D*

Massachusetts

Massachusetts Institute of
  Technology *B*

Michigan

University of Michigan *M*

Nebraska

University of Nebraska
  Lincoln *D*

Pennsylvania

Lehigh University *M*

Wisconsin

Milwaukee School of Engineering *B*

Chemical engineering

Alabama

Auburn University *B, M, D*
Tuskegee University *B*
University of Alabama *B, M, D*
University of Alabama
  Huntsville *B*
University of South Alabama *B, M*

Arizona

Arizona State University *B, M, D*
University of Arizona *B, M, D*

Arkansas

University of Arkansas *B, M*

California

California Baptist University *B*
California Institute of
  Technology *B, M, D*
California State Polytechnic
  University: Pomona *B*
California State University
  Long Beach *B*
  Northridge *B, M*
San Jose State University *B, M*
Stanford University *B, M, D*
University of California
  Berkeley *B, M, D*
  Davis *B, M, D*
  Irvine *B, M, D*
  Los Angeles *B, M, D*
  Riverside *B*
  San Diego *B, M, D*
  Santa Barbara *B, M, D*
University of Southern
  California *B, M, D*

Colorado

Colorado School of Mines *B, M, D*
Colorado State University *B, M, D*
University of Colorado
  Boulder *B, M, D*

Connecticut

University of Connecticut *B, M, D*
University of New Haven *B*
Yale University *B, M, D*

Delaware

University of Delaware *B, M, D*

District of Columbia

Howard University *B, M*

Florida

Florida Agricultural and Mechanical
  University *B, M, D*
Florida Institute of
  Technology *B, M, D*
Florida State University *B, M, D*
University of Florida *B, M, D*
University of South Florida *B, M, D*

Georgia

Georgia Institute of
  Technology *B, M, D*

Idaho

North Idaho College *A*
Northwest Nazarene University *B*
University of Idaho *B, M, D*

Illinois

Illinois Institute of
Technology *B, M, D*
Northwestern University *B, M, D*
University of Illinois
Chicago *B, M, D*
Urbana-Champaign *B, M, D*

Indiana

Purdue University *B, M, D*
Rose-Hulman Institute of
Technology *B, M*
Trine University *B*
University of Notre Dame *B, M, D*

Iowa

Dordt College *B*
Iowa State University *B, M, D*
University of Iowa *B, M, D*

Kansas

Independence Community College *A*
Kansas State University *B, M, D*
University of Kansas *B, M*

Kentucky

University of Kentucky *B, M, D*
University of Louisville *B, M, D*

Louisiana

Louisiana State University and
Agricultural and Mechanical
College *B, M, D*
Louisiana Tech University *B*
Tulane University *B, M, D*
University of Louisiana at
Lafayette *B, M*

Maine

University of Maine *B, M, D*

Maryland

Johns Hopkins University *B, M, D*
University of Maryland
Baltimore County *B, M, D*
College Park *B, M, D*

Massachusetts

Massachusetts Institute of
Technology *B, M, D*
Northeastern University *B, M, D*
Smith College *B*
Tufts University *B, M, D*
University of Massachusetts
Amherst *B, M, D*
Lowell *B, M*
Worcester Polytechnic
Institute *B, M, D*

Michigan

Calvin College *B*
Kettering University *B*
Michigan State University *B, M, D*
Michigan Technological
University *B, M, D*
University of Michigan *B, M, D*
Wayne State University *B, M, D*
Western Michigan University *B, M*

Minnesota

University of Minnesota
Duluth *B*
Twin Cities *B, M, D*

Mississippi

Mississippi State University *B, M*
University of Mississippi *B*

Missouri

Missouri University of Science and
Technology *B, M, D*
University of Missouri
Columbia *B, M, D*

Washington University in St.
Louis *B, M, D*

Montana

Montana State University *B, M*

Nebraska

University of Nebraska
Lincoln *B, M*

Nevada

University of Nevada
Reno *B, M, D*

New Hampshire

University of New
Hampshire *B, M, D*

New Jersey

New Jersey Institute of
Technology *B, M, D*
Princeton University *B, M, D*
Rowan University *B, M*
Rutgers, The State University of New
Jersey
New Brunswick/Piscataway
Campus *B, M, D*
Stevens Institute of
Technology *B, M, D*

New Mexico

New Mexico Institute of Mining and
Technology *B*
New Mexico State University *B, M*
University of New Mexico *B, M*

New York

City University of New York
City College *B, M, D*
Hostos Community College *A*
Clarkson University *B, M, D*
Columbia University *B, M, D*
Cooper Union for the Advancement
of Science and Art *B, M*
Cornell University *B, M, D*
Manhattan College *B, M*
New York University *B*
Pace University *B*
Rensselaer Polytechnic
Institute *B, M, D*
Rochester Institute of Technology *B*
SUNY
University at Buffalo *B, M, D*
University at Stony Brook *B*
Syracuse University *B, M, D*
United States Military Academy *B*
University of Rochester *B, M, D*

North Carolina

Bennett College for Women *B*
Elon University *B*
North Carolina Agricultural and
Technical State University *B, M*
North Carolina State
University *B, M, D*

North Dakota

University of North Dakota *B, M, D*

Ohio

Case Western Reserve
University *B, M, D*
Cleveland State University *B, M, D*
Miami University
Oxford *B*
Ohio State University
Columbus Campus *B, M, D*
Ohio University *B, M, D*
University of Akron *C, B, M, D*
University of Cincinnati *B, M, D*
University of Dayton *B, M*
University of Toledo *B, M*
Wilberforce University *B*

Xavier University *B*
Youngstown State University *B, M*

Oklahoma

Oklahoma State University *B, M, D*
University of Oklahoma *B, M, D*
University of Tulsa *B, M, D*

Oregon

Oregon State University *B, M, D*

Pennsylvania

Bucknell University *B, M*
Carnegie Mellon University *B, M, D*
Drexel University *B, M, D*
Geneva College *B*
Lafayette College *B*
Lehigh University *B, M, D*
Penn State
Abington *B*
Altoona *B*
Beaver *B*
Berks *B*
Brandywine *B*
DuBois *B*
Erie, The Behrend College *B*
Fayette, The Eberly Campus *B*
Greater Allegheny *B*
Harrisburg *B*
Hazleton *B*
Lehigh Valley *B*
Mont Alto *B*
New Kensington *B*
Schuylkill *B*
Shenango *B*
University Park *B, M, D*
Wilkes-Barre *B*
Worthington Scranton *B*
York *B*
University of Pennsylvania *B, M, D*
University of Pittsburgh *B, M, D*
University of Pittsburgh
Bradford *B*
Villanova University *B, M*
Widener University *B*

Puerto Rico

Universidad Politecnica de Puerto
Rico *B*
University of Puerto Rico
Mayaguez *B, M, D*
Ponce *A*

Rhode Island

Brown University *B, M, D*
University of Rhode Island *B, M, D*

South Carolina

Clemson University *B, M, D*
University of South Carolina
Columbia *B, M, D*

South Dakota

South Dakota School of Mines and
Technology *B, M, D*

Tennessee

Christian Brothers University *B*
Tennessee Technological
University *B, M, D*
University of Tennessee
Chattanooga *B*
Knoxville *B, M, D*
Vanderbilt University *B, M, D*

Texas

Kilgore College *A*
Lamar University *B, M, D*
Prairie View A&M University *B*
Rice University *B, M, D*
Texas A&M University *B, M, D*
Texas A&M University
Kingsville *B, M*
Texas Tech University *B, M, D*

University of Houston *B, M, D*
University of Texas
Austin *B, M, D*

Utah

Brigham Young University *B, M, D*
University of Utah *B, M, D*
Utah State University *A*

Virginia

Hampton University *B*
University of Virginia *B, M, D*
Virginia Commonwealth University *B*
Virginia Polytechnic Institute and
State University *B, M, D*
Washington and Lee University *B*

Washington

Bellevue College *A*
Edmonds Community College *A*
Spokane Falls Community College *A*
University of Washington *B, M, D*
Washington State University *B, M, D*

West Virginia

West Virginia University *B, M, D*
West Virginia University Institute of
Technology *B*

Wisconsin

University of Wisconsin
Madison *B, M, D*

Wyoming

University of Wyoming *B, M, D*

Chemical engineering technology

North Carolina

Cape Fear Community College *C*

Oklahoma

Northeastern Oklahoma Agricultural
and Mechanical College *A*

Chemical physics

Arkansas

Hendrix College *B*

California

University of California
San Diego *B*
University of Southern California *D*

Colorado

Adams State University *B*
University of Colorado
Boulder *D*

Florida

Florida State University *M, D*

Illinois

Lewis University *B*
University of Illinois
Urbana-Champaign *M, D*

Indiana

Indiana University
Bloomington *D*

Iowa

University of Iowa *M*

Kentucky

Centre College *B*

Maine

Bowdoin College *B*

Maryland

University of Maryland
College Park *M, D*

Michigan

Michigan State University *B, D*
Saginaw Valley State University *B*

Mississippi

Mississippi College *B*

Nevada

University of Nevada
Reno *D*

New York

Columbia University *B*
Hamilton College *B*

Ohio

College of Wooster *B*

Pennsylvania

Carnegie Mellon University *B*
Swarthmore College *B*

Rhode Island

Brown University *B*

Tennessee

Union University *B*

Texas

Rice University *B*

Chemical process technology

Louisiana

ITI Technical College *A*

Texas

San Jacinto College *C, A*

Chemical technology

Alabama

Calhoun Community College *A*
Jefferson Davis Community
College *C*
Northwest-Shoals Community
College *C*

California

Ohlone College *C*

Delaware

Delaware Technical Community
College
Stanton/Wilmington Campus *A*

Florida

Pensacola State College *A*

Illinois

City Colleges of Chicago
Harry S. Truman College *A*

Indiana

Ball State University *A*
Indiana University
Purdue University Fort Wayne *A*

Iowa

Iowa Central Community College *A*

Kentucky

Jefferson Community and Technical
College *C, A*
Murray State University *M*

Louisiana

ITI Technical College *A*

Massachusetts

Massachusetts Bay Community
College *A*

Michigan

Delta College *C, A*
Ferris State University *A*
Grand Rapids Community College *A*
Lansing Community College *A*
Lawrence Technological University *A*

Minnesota

North Hennepin Community
College *C*
St. Paul College *A*

Missouri

East Central College *A*

New Jersey

Burlington County College *A*
Essex County College *C, A*

New York

City University of New York
New York City College of
Technology *A*
Corning Community College *A*
Excelsior College *A*
Mohawk Valley Community
College *A*

North Carolina

Guilford Technical Community
College *A*

Ohio

Cincinnati State Technical and
Community College *A*
University of Cincinnati
Blue Ash College *A*

Oklahoma

Tulsa Community College *A*

Pennsylvania

Bidwell Training Center *A*
Bucks County Community College *A*
Community College of Allegheny
County *A*
Community College of
Philadelphia *A*
Lehigh Carbon Community College *A*
Westmoreland County Community
College *A*

Puerto Rico

University of Puerto Rico
Humacao *A*

Rhode Island

Community College of Rhode
Island *C, A*

South Carolina

Midlands Technical College *C*
York Technical College *C*

Tennessee

Chattanooga State Community
College *C*

Texas

Alvin Community College *C, A*
Del Mar College *C, A*
Houston Community College
System *C, A*
Lamar Institute of Technology *A*
Lamar State College at Orange *C, A*

Lamar State College at Port
Arthur *C, A*
San Jacinto College *C, A*
Texas State Technical College
Harlingen *A*
Waco *C, A*
Wharton County Junior College *A*

Utah

Salt Lake Community College *A*
Weber State University *C, A*

Washington

Big Bend Community College *C*
Edmonds Community College *A*
Lake Washington Institute of
Technology *C, A*

Wisconsin

Milwaukee Area Technical College *A*

Chemistry

Alabama

Alabama Agricultural and Mechanical
University *B*
Alabama State University *B*
Athens State University *B*
Auburn University *B, M, D*
Birmingham-Southern College *B*
Calhoun Community College *A*
Faulkner State Community College *A*
Gadsden State Community College *A*
Huntingdon College *B*
Jacksonville State University *B*
Judson College *B*
Miles College *B*
Oakwood University *B*
Samford University *B*
Spring Hill College *B, T*
Talladega College *B*
Troy University *B*
Tuskegee University *B, M*
University of Alabama *B, M, D*
University of Alabama
Birmingham *B, M, D*
Huntsville *B, M*
University of Montevallo *B, T*
University of North Alabama *B*
University of South Alabama *B*
University of West Alabama *B, T*

Alaska

University of Alaska
Anchorage *B*
Fairbanks *B, M, D*

Arizona

Arizona State University *B, M, D*
Arizona Western College *A*
Central Arizona College *A*
Cochise College *A*
Eastern Arizona College *A*
Northern Arizona University *B, M*
South Mountain Community
College *A*
University of Arizona *B, M, D*

Arkansas

Arkansas State University *B, M*
Arkansas Tech University *B*
Harding University *B*
Henderson State University *B*
Hendrix College *B*
John Brown University *B*
Lyon College *B*
Ouachita Baptist University *B*
Philander Smith College *B*
Phillips Community College of the
University of Arkansas *A*
Southern Arkansas University *A, B*
University of Arkansas *B, M, D*

University of Arkansas
Fort Smith *B*
Little Rock *B, M*
Monticello *B*
Pine Bluff *B*
University of Central Arkansas *B*
University of the Ozarks *B*

California

Allan Hancock College *A*
Azusa Pacific University *B*
Bakersfield College *A*
Biola University *B*
Cabrillo College *A*
California Baptist University *B*
California Institute of
Technology *B, M, D*
California Lutheran University *B*
California Polytechnic State
University: San Luis Obispo *B*
California State Polytechnic
University: Pomona *B, M*
California State University
Bakersfield *B*
Channel Islands *B*
Chico *C, B*
Dominguez Hills *B*
East Bay *B, M*
Fresno *B, M*
Fullerton *B, M*
Long Beach *B, M*
Los Angeles *B, M*
Northridge *B, M*
Sacramento *B, M*
San Bernardino *B*
San Marcos *B*
Stanislaus *B*
Canada College *A*
Cerritos College *A*
Chaffey College *A*
Chapman University *B*
Citrus College *A*
City College of San Francisco *A*
Claremont McKenna College *B*
College of Marin *A*
College of San Mateo *A*
College of the Desert *A*
College of the Siskiyous *A*
Columbia College *A*
Concordia University Irvine *B*
Contra Costa College *A*
Crafton Hills College *C, A*
Cuesta College *C, A*
Cypress College *A*
De Anza College *A*
Dominican University of California *B*
El Camino College *A*
Foothill College *A*
Fresno City College *A*
Fresno Pacific University *B*
Fullerton College *A*
Gavilan College *A*
Glendale Community College *A*
Golden West College *A*
Grossmont College *C, A*
Hartnell College *A*
Harvey Mudd College *B*
Humboldt State University *B*
Irvine Valley College *A*
La Sierra University *B*
Los Angeles City College *A*
Los Angeles Southwest College *A*
Los Angeles Valley College *A*
Los Medanos College *A*
Loyola Marymount University *B*
Merced College *A*
Mills College *B*
Mission College *A*
Monterey Peninsula College *A*
Moorpark College *A*
Mount St. Mary's College *B*
Occidental College *B*
Orange Coast College *A*
Pacific Union College *B*
Palomar College *C, A*

Pepperdine University *B*
Pitzer College *B*
Point Loma Nazarene University *B*
Pomona College *B*
Porterville College *A*
St. Mary's College of California *B*
San Bernardino Valley College *A*
San Deigo Miramar College
  San Diego Miramar College *A*
San Diego City College *A*
San Diego Mesa College *C, A*
San Diego State University *B, M, D*
San Francisco State University *B, M*
San Jose State University *B, M*
Santa Ana College *A*
Santa Barbara City College *A*
Santa Clara University *B*
Santa Rosa Junior College *A*
Santiago Canyon College *A*
Scripps College *B*
Sierra College *A*
Solano Community College *A*
Sonoma State University *B*
Southwestern College *A*
Stanford University *B, M, D*
University of California
  Berkeley *B, M, D*
  Davis *B, M, D*
  Irvine *B, M, D*
  Los Angeles *B, M, D*
  Merced *B*
  Riverside *B, M, D*
  San Diego *B, D*
  Santa Barbara *B, M, D*
  Santa Cruz *B, M, D*
University of La Verne *B*
University of Redlands *B*
University of San Diego *B*
University of San Francisco *B, M*
University of Southern
  California *B, M, D*
University of the Pacific *B*
Vanguard University of Southern
  California *B*
West Los Angeles College *C, A*
West Valley College *A*
Westmont College *B*
Whittier College *B*

Colorado

Adams State University *B*
Colorado College *B*
Colorado Mountain College *A*
Colorado School of Mines *B, M, D*
Colorado State University *B, M, D*
Colorado State University
  Pueblo *B*
Community College of Aurora *A*
Fort Lewis College *B*
Metropolitan State University of
  Denver *B*
Otero Junior College *A*
Regis University *B*
United States Air Force Academy *B*
University of Colorado
  Boulder *B, D*
  Colorado Springs *B, M*
  Denver *B, M*
University of Denver *B, M, D*
University of Northern
  Colorado *B, M*
Western State Colorado University *B*

Connecticut

Albertus Magnus College *B*
Central Connecticut State
  University *B*
Connecticut College *B*
Fairfield University *B*
Quinnipiac University *B*
Sacred Heart University *B, M*
Southern Connecticut State
  University *B, M*

Trinity College *B*
University of Connecticut *B, M, D*
University of Hartford *B*
University of New Haven *B*
University of Saint Joseph *B, M*
Wesleyan University *B, M, D*
Western Connecticut State
  University *B*
Yale University *B, M, D*

Delaware

Delaware State University *B, M, D*
University of Delaware *B, M, D*

District of Columbia

American University *B, M*
Catholic University of America *B, M*
Gallaudet University *B*
George Washington
  University *B, M, D*
Georgetown University *B, M, D*
Howard University *B, M, D*
Trinity Washington University *B*
University of the District of
  Columbia *B*

Florida

Barry University *B*
Bethune-Cookman University *B*
Broward College *A*
Daytona State College *A*
Eckerd College *B*
Florida Agricultural and Mechanical
  University *B, M*
Florida Atlantic University *B, M, D*
Florida Gulf Coast University *B*
Florida Institute of
  Technology *B, M, D*
Florida International
  University *B, M, D*
Florida Southern College *B*
Florida State University *B, M, D*
Indian River State College *A*
Jacksonville University *B*
Miami Dade College *A*
New College of Florida *B*
Nova Southeastern University *B*
Palm Beach State College *A*
Pensacola State College *A*
Rollins College *B*
Saint Thomas University *B*
South Florida State College *A*
Stetson University *B*
University of Central Florida *B, M, D*
University of Florida *B, M, D*
University of Miami *B, M, D*
University of North Florida *B*
University of South Florida *B, M, D*
University of Tampa *A, B*
University of West Florida *B*

Georgia

Abraham Baldwin Agricultural
  College *A*
Agnes Scott College *B*
Albany State University *B*
Armstrong Atlantic State
  University *B, T*
Atlanta Metropolitan College *A*
Berry College *B*
Clark Atlanta University *B, M, D*
Clayton State University *B*
College of Coastal Georgia *A*
Columbus State University *B*
Covenant College *B*
Dalton State College *B*
Darton College *A*
East Georgia State College *A*
Emory University *B, D*
Fort Valley State University *B*
Georgia College and State
  University *B*
Georgia Highlands College *A*

Georgia Institute of
  Technology *B, M, D*
Georgia Perimeter College *A*
Georgia Regents University *B*
Georgia Southern University *B*
Georgia Southwestern State
  University *B*
Georgia State University *B, M, D*
Gordon College *A*
Kennesaw State University *B, M*
LaGrange College *B*
Mercer University *B*
Middle Georgia State College *A*
Morehouse College *B*
Oglethorpe University *B*
Paine College *B*
Piedmont College *B*
Savannah State University *B*
Shorter University *B*
South Georgia State College *A*
Southern Polytechnic State
  University *B*
Spelman College *B*
University of Georgia *B, M, D*
University of North Georgia *A, B*
University of West Georgia *B*
Valdosta State University *B*
Wesleyan College *B*
Young Harris College *B*

Hawaii

University of Hawaii
  Hilo *B*
  Manoa *B, M, D*

Idaho

Boise State University *B, T*
Brigham Young University-Idaho *B*
College of Idaho *B*
College of Southern Idaho *A*
Idaho State University *B, M*
Lewis-Clark State College *B*
North Idaho College *A*
Northwest Nazarene University *B*
University of Idaho *B, M, D*

Illinois

Augustana College *B*
Benedictine University *B, T*
Blackburn College *B*
Bradley University *B, M, T*
Chicago State University *B, T*
Concordia University Chicago *B, T*
DePaul University *B, M*
Dominican University *B*
Eastern Illinois University *B, M, T*
Elmhurst College *B, T*
Eureka College *B*
Governors State University *B, T*
Greenville College *B, T*
Illinois Central College *A*
Illinois College *B*
Illinois Institute of
  Technology *B, M, D*
Illinois State University *B, M, T*
Illinois Valley Community College *A*
Illinois Wesleyan University *B*
John A. Logan College *A*
Joliet Junior College *A*
Judson University *B*
Kankakee Community College *A*
Kishwaukee College *A*
Knox College *B*
Lake Forest College *B*
Lewis University *B*
Lincoln College *A*
Loyola University Chicago *B, M, D*
MacMurray College *B*
McKendree University *B*
Millikin University *B*
Monmouth College *B, T*
North Central College *B, T*
North Park University *B*
Northeastern Illinois University *B, M*

Northern Illinois
  University *B, M, D, T*
Northwestern University *B, M, D*
Olivet Nazarene University *B, T*
Principia College *B*
Quincy University *B*
Rockford University *B*
Roosevelt University *B*
Saint Xavier University *B*
Sauk Valley Community College *A*
South Suburban College of Cook
  County *A*
Southern Illinois University
  Carbondale *B, M, D*
Southern Illinois University
  Edwardsville *B, M*
Southwestern Illinois College *A*
Trinity Christian College *B, T*
Trinity International University *B*
University of Chicago *B*
University of Illinois
  Chicago *B, M, D*
  Springfield *B*
  Urbana-Champaign *B, M, D*
Western Illinois University *B, M*
Wheaton College *B, T*

Indiana

Anderson University *B*
Ball State University *B, M, T*
Bethel College *B*
Butler University *B*
DePauw University *B*
Earlham College *B*
Franklin College *B*
Goshen College *B*
Hanover College *B*
Huntington University *B*
Indiana State University *B, T*
Indiana University
  Bloomington *B, M, D*
  Kokomo *B*
  Northwest *B*
  Purdue University Fort Wayne *B, T*
  Purdue University
    Indianapolis *A, B, M*
  South Bend *B*
  Southeast *B*
Indiana Wesleyan University *A, B*
Manchester University *B, T*
Marian University *B, T*
Martin University *B*
Purdue University *B, M, D*
Purdue University
  Calumet *B*
Rose-Hulman Institute of
  Technology *B*
Saint Joseph's College *B*
Saint Mary's College *B, T*
Taylor University *B*
Trine University *B*
University of Evansville *B*
University of Indianapolis *A, B*
University of Notre Dame *B, M, D*
University of St. Francis *A, B*
University of Southern Indiana *B, T*
Valparaiso University *B*
Vincennes University *A*
Wabash College *B*

Iowa

Briar Cliff University *B*
Buena Vista University *B, T*
Central College *B, T*
Clarke University *B, T*
Coe College *B*
Cornell College *B, T*
Dordt College *B*
Drake University *B*
Ellsworth Community College *A*
Graceland University *B, T*
Grinnell College *B*
Iowa State University *B, M, D*
Iowa Wesleyan College *B*

Iowa Western Community College A
Loras College B
Luther College B
Morningside College B
Northwestern College B, T
St. Ambrose University B
Simpson College B
University of Iowa B, M, D, T
University of Northern Iowa B, M
Upper Iowa University B
Wartburg College B, T

Kansas

Allen County Community College A
Baker University B, T
Barton County Community College A
Benedictine College B
Bethany College B, T
Bethel College B
Butler Community College A
Central Christian College of
    Kansas A, B
Coffeyville Community College A
Colby Community College A
Cowley County Community
    College A
Dodge City Community College A
Emporia State University B, T
Fort Hays State University B
Friends University B
Garden City Community College A
Independence Community College A
Kansas State University B, M, D
Kansas Wesleyan University B, T
McPherson College B, T
MidAmerica Nazarene University B
Neosho County Community
    College A
Newman University B
Pittsburg State University B, M
Pratt Community College A
Seward County Community
    College A
Southwestern College B
Sterling College B, T
Tabor College B
University of Kansas B, M, D
University of St. Mary B
Washburn University B
Wichita State University B, M, D, T

Kentucky

Asbury University B, T
Bellarmine University B, T
Berea College B, T
Bluegrass Community and Technical
    College A
Brescia University B
Campbellsville University B
Centre College B
Eastern Kentucky University B, M
Georgetown College B, T
Hopkinsville Community College A
Kentucky State University B
Kentucky Wesleyan College B, T
Lindsey Wilson College A
Morehead State University B
Murray State University B, M, T
Northern Kentucky University A, B
Thomas More College A, B
Transylvania University B, T
Union College B
University of Kentucky B, M, D
University of Louisville B, M, D
University of Pikeville B, T
University of the Cumberlands B, T
Western Kentucky University B, M

Louisiana

Centenary College of Louisiana B
Dillard University B
Grambling State University B
Louisiana College B, T

Louisiana State University
    Shreveport B
Louisiana State University and
    Agricultural and Mechanical
    College B, M, D
Louisiana Tech University B, M
Loyola University New Orleans B
McNeese State University B
Nicholls State University B
Our Lady of Holy Cross College T
Southeastern Louisiana University B
Southern University
    Shreveport A
Southern University and Agricultural
    and Mechanical College B
Tulane University B, M, D
University of Louisiana at Lafayette B
University of New Orleans B, M, D
Xavier University of Louisiana B

Maine

Bates College B
Bowdoin College B
Colby College B
College of the Atlantic B
Husson University B
Saint Joseph's College of Maine B, T
University of Maine B, M, D
University of New England B
University of Southern Maine B

Maryland

Allegany College of Maryland A
Coppin State University B
Frederick Community College A
Frostburg State University B, T
Goucher College B
Harford Community College A
Hood College B, T
Johns Hopkins University B, M, D
Loyola University Maryland B
McDaniel College B
Morgan State University B
Mount St. Mary's University B
Notre Dame of Maryland
    University B
Prince George's Community
    College A
St. Mary's College of Maryland B
Salisbury University B
Stevenson University B
Towson University B
United States Naval Academy B
University of Maryland
    Baltimore County B, M, D
    College Park B, M, D
    Eastern Shore B
Washington Adventist University B
Washington College B, T

Massachusetts

American International College B
Amherst College B
Assumption College B
Bard College at Simon's Rock B
Boston College B, M, D
Boston University B, M, D
Brandeis University B, M, D
Bridgewater State University B
Bunker Hill Community College A
Clark University B, M, D
College of the Holy Cross B
Eastern Nazarene College B
Elms College B
Emmanuel College B
Framingham State University B
Gordon College B
Hampshire College B
Harvard University B, M, D
MCPHS University B
Massachusetts College of Liberal
    Arts B
Massachusetts Institute of
    Technology B, D

Merrimack College B
Mount Holyoke College B
Northeastern University B, M, D
Regis College B
Salem State University B
Simmons College B
Smith College B
Springfield Technical Community
    College A
Stonehill College B
Suffolk University B
Tufts University B, M, D
University of Massachusetts
    Amherst B, M, D
    Boston B, M, D
    Dartmouth B, M, D
    Lowell B, M, D
Wellesley College B
Western New England
    University B, T
Westfield State University B, T
Wheaton College B
Williams College B
Worcester Polytechnic
    Institute B, M, D
Worcester State University B

Michigan

Adrian College B, T
Albion College B, T
Alma College B, T
Andrews University B
Aquinas College B, T
Calvin College B, T
Central Michigan University B, M
Delta College A
Eastern Michigan University B, M
Ferris State University B
Gogebic Community College A
Grand Rapids Community College A
Grand Valley State University B
Henry Ford Community College A
Hillsdale College B
Hope College B
Kalamazoo College B
Kettering University B
Lake Michigan College A
Lake Superior State University A, B
Lansing Community College A
Lawrence Technological University B
Macomb Community College A
Madonna University B
Marygrove College B, T
Michigan State University B, M, D
Michigan Technological
    University B, M, D
Mid Michigan Community College A
Northern Michigan University B
Oakland University B, M, T
Olivet College B, T
Saginaw Valley State University B
Siena Heights University A, B
Spring Arbor University B
University of Detroit Mercy B, M
University of Michigan B, M, D
University of Michigan
    Dearborn B
    Flint B
Wayne State University B, M, D
Western Michigan University B, M, D

Minnesota

Augsburg College B
Bemidji State University B
Bethany Lutheran College B
Bethel University B
Carleton College B
College of St. Benedict B
College of St. Scholastica B
Concordia College: Moorhead B
Gustavus Adolphus College B
Hamline University B
Inver Hills Community College A
Macalester College B

Metropolitan State University B
Minneapolis Community and
    Technical College A
Minnesota State University
    Mankato B
    Moorhead B
Minnesota West Community and
    Technical College A
North Hennepin Community
    College A
Ridgewater College A
St. Catherine University B
Saint Cloud State University B
St. John's University B
St. Mary's University of Minnesota B
St. Olaf College B
Southwest Minnesota State
    University B
University of Minnesota
    Duluth B, M
    Morris B
    Twin Cities B, M, D
University of St. Thomas B
Winona State University B

Mississippi

Alcorn State University B
Belhaven University B
Coahoma Community College A
Delta State University B
East Mississippi Community
    College A
Hinds Community College A
Itawamba Community College A
Jackson State University B, M, D
Millsaps College B
Mississippi College B, M
Mississippi State University B, M, D
Mississippi University for
    Women B, T
Mississippi Valley State University B
Northeast Mississippi Community
    College A
Rust College B
Tougaloo College B
University of Mississippi B, M, D
University of Southern
    Mississippi B, M, D
William Carey University B

Missouri

Central Methodist University A, B
College of the Ozarks B
Columbia College B
Crowder College A
Drury University B, T
Evangel University B
Lincoln University B
Lindenwood University B
Maryville University of Saint Louis B
Missouri Baptist University B, T
Missouri Southern State
    University B, T
Missouri State University B, M
Missouri University of Science and
    Technology B, M, D, T
Missouri Western State
    University B, T
Northwest Missouri State
    University B
Ozarks Technical Community
    College A
Park University B
Rockhurst University B
St. Charles Community College A
St. Louis Community College A
Saint Louis University B, M, D
Southeast Missouri State
    University B, M
Southwest Baptist University B, T
State Fair Community College A
Three Rivers Community College A
Truman State University B
University of Central Missouri B

University of Missouri
Columbia *B, M, D*
Kansas City *B, M, D*
St. Louis *B, M, D*
Washington University in St.
Louis *B, M, D*
Westminster College *B*
William Jewell College *B, T*

Montana

Carroll College *B*
Montana State University *B, M, D*
Montana State University
Billings *B, T*
Northern *B*
Montana Tech of the University of
Montana *B*
Rocky Mountain College *B*
University of Great Falls *B*
University of Montana *B, M, D*
University of Montana: Western *A, B*

Nebraska

Chadron State College *B*
College of Saint Mary *B, T*
Concordia University *B, T*
Creighton University *B*
Doane College *B*
Hastings College *B*
Midland University *B, T*
Nebraska Wesleyan University *B*
Northeast Community College *A*
Peru State College *B*
Union College *B*
University of Nebraska
Kearney *B*
Lincoln *B, M, D*
Omaha *B*
Wayne State College *B*
Western Nebraska Community
College *A*

Nevada

University of Nevada
Las Vegas *B, M*
Reno *B, M, D*
Western Nevada College *A*

New Hampshire

Dartmouth College *B, M, D, T*
Keene State College *B*
Plymouth State University *B*
Saint Anselm College *B, T*
University of New
Hampshire *B, M, D*

New Jersey

Bergen Community College *A*
Bloomfield College *B, T*
College of New Jersey *B, T*
College of St. Elizabeth *B*
Drew University *B*
Essex County College *A*
Fairleigh Dickinson University
College at Florham *B, M*
Metropolitan Campus *B, M*
Georgian Court University *B*
Gloucester County College *A*
Hudson County Community
College *A*
Kean University *B, T*
Middlesex County College *A*
Monmouth University *B*
Montclair State University *B, M*
New Jersey City University *B*
New Jersey Institute of
Technology *B, M, D*
Princeton University *B, M, D*
Ramapo College of New Jersey *B*
Richard Stockton College of New
Jersey *B*
Rider University *B*
Rowan University *B*

Rutgers, The State University of New
Jersey
Camden Campus *B, M, T*
New Brunswick/Piscataway
Campus *B, M, D*
Newark Campus *B, M, D*
Saint Peter's University *B*
Salem Community College *A*
Seton Hall University *B, M, D, T*
Stevens Institute of
Technology *B, M, D*
Sussex County Community College *A*
Union County College *A*
Warren County Community
College *A*
William Paterson University of New
Jersey *B*

New Mexico

Eastern New Mexico University *B, M*
New Mexico Highlands
University *B, M*
New Mexico Institute of Mining and
Technology *B, M, D*
New Mexico Junior College *A*
New Mexico State University *B, M, D*
San Juan College *A*
University of New Mexico *B, M, D*
Western New Mexico University *B*

New York

Adelphi University *B*
Albany College of Pharmacy and
Health Sciences *B*
Alfred University *B*
Bard College *B*
Barnard College *B*
Canisius College *B*
Cayuga Community College *A*
City University of New York
Brooklyn College *B, M*
City College *B, M*
College of Staten Island *B, D*
Hunter College *B, M*
Kingsborough Community
College *A*
Lehman College *B*
Queens College *B, M, T*
Queensborough Community
College *A*
York College *B*
Clarkson University *B, M, D*
Colgate University *B*
College of Mount St. Vincent *B, T*
College of New Rochelle *B, T*
College of Saint Rose *B*
Columbia University *B*
Columbia University
School of General Studies *B*
Cornell University *B, M, D*
D'Youville College *B*
Dowling College *B*
Elmira College *B, T*
Excelsior College *B*
Finger Lakes Community College *A*
Fordham University *B, M, D*
Hamilton College *B*
Hartwick College *B, T*
Hobart and William Smith Colleges *B*
Hofstra University *B*
Houghton College *B*
Hudson Valley Community College *A*
Iona College *B*
Ithaca College *B, T*
Le Moyne College *B*
Long Island University
LIU Brooklyn *B, M*
LIU Post *B*
Manhattan College *B*
Manhattanville College *B*
Marist College *B*
Monroe Community College *A*
Mount Saint Mary College *B, T*
Nazareth College *B*

New York Institute of Technology *B*
New York University *B, M, D*
Niagara University *B*
Pace University *B*
Pace University: Pleasantville/
Briarcliff *B*
Rensselaer Polytechnic
Institute *B, M, D*
Roberts Wesleyan College *B*
Rochester Institute of
Technology *B, M*
SUNY
College at Brockport *B, T*
College at Buffalo *B, M*
College at Cortland *B*
College at Fredonia *B, M, T*
College at Geneseo *B, T*
College at New Paltz *B*
College at Old Westbury *B, T*
College at Oneonta *B*
College at Oswego *B, M*
College at Plattsburgh *B*
College at Potsdam *B*
College at Purchase *B*
College of Environmental Science
and Forestry *B*
University at Albany *B, M, D*
University at Binghamton *B, M, D*
University at Buffalo *B, M, D*
University at Stony Brook *B, M, D*
Sage Colleges *B*
Saint Bonaventure University *B*
St. Francis College *B*
St. John Fisher College *B*
St. John's University *B, M*
St. Joseph's College New York:
Suffolk Campus *B*
St. Joseph's College, New York *B*
St. Lawrence University *B, T*
St. Thomas Aquinas College *B, T*
Siena College *B, T*
Skidmore College *B*
Suffolk County Community College *A*
Syracuse University *B, M, D*
Touro College *B*
Union College *B*
United States Military Academy *B*
University of Rochester *B, M, D*
Utica College *B*
Vassar College *B, M*
Wagner College *B, T*
Wells College *B*
Yeshiva University *B*

North Carolina

Appalachian State University *B*
Barton College *B*
Bennett College for Women *B*
Campbell University *B*
Catawba College *B, T*
Davidson College *B*
Duke University *B, M, D*
East Carolina University *B, M*
Elizabeth City State University *B*
Elon University *B*
Fayetteville State University *B*
Gardner-Webb University *B*
Greensboro College *B*
Guilford College *B*
High Point University *B*
Johnson C. Smith University *B*
Lenoir-Rhyne University *B*
Livingstone College *B*
Mars Hill University *B, T*
Meredith College *B*
Methodist University *A, B, T*
North Carolina Agricultural and
Technical State University *B, M*
North Carolina Central
University *B, M*
North Carolina State
University *B, M, D*
North Carolina Wesleyan College *B*
Pfeiffer University *B*
Queens University of Charlotte *B*

St. Andrews University *B*
St. Augustine's University *B*
Salem College *B*
Shaw University *B*
Southeastern Community College *A*
University of Mount Olive *B*
University of North Carolina
Asheville *B, T*
Chapel Hill *B, M, D*
Charlotte *B, M*
Greensboro *B, M*
Pembroke *B*
Wilmington *B, M*
Wake Forest University *B, M, D*
Warren Wilson College *B*
Western Carolina University *B, M*
Western Piedmont Community
College *A*
Wingate University *B*
Winston-Salem State University *B*

North Dakota

Dickinson State University *B*
Mayville State University *B, T*
Minot State University *B*
North Dakota State
University *B, M, D, T*
University of Jamestown *B*
University of North Dakota *B, M, D*
Valley City State University *B*

Ohio

Ashland University *B*
Baldwin Wallace University *B*
Bluffton University *B*
Bowling Green State University *B, M*
Capital University *B*
Case Western Reserve
University *B, M, D*
Cedarville University *B*
Central State University *B*
Cleveland State University *B, M, D, T*
College of Mount St. Joseph *B, T*
College of Wooster *B*
Denison University *B*
Franciscan University of
Steubenville *B*
Heidelberg University *B*
Hiram College *B*
John Carroll University *B*
Kent State University *B, M, D*
Kenyon College *B*
Lake Erie College *B*
Malone University *B*
Marietta College *B*
Miami University
Middletown *A*
Oxford *B, M, D*
Mount Vernon Nazarene University *B*
Muskingum University *B*
Notre Dame College *B, T*
Oberlin College *B*
Ohio Dominican University *A, B*
Ohio Northern University *B*
Ohio State University
Columbus Campus *B, M, D*
Ohio University *B, M, D*
Ohio Wesleyan University *B*
Otterbein University *B*
Shawnee State University *B*
Sinclair Community College *A*
Terra State Community College *A*
University of Akron *B, M, D*
University of Cincinnati *C, B, M, D*
University of Cincinnati
Blue Ash College *A*
Clermont College *A*
University of Dayton *B, M*
University of Mount Union *B*
University of Rio Grande *A, B, T*
University of Toledo *B, M, D*
Walsh University *B*
Wilberforce University *B*
Wilmington College *B*

Wittenberg University *B*
Wright State University *A, B, M, T*
Wright State University: Lake
  Campus *A*
Xavier University *B*
Youngstown State University *B, M*

Oklahoma

Cameron University *B*
Connors State College *A*
East Central University *B, T*
Eastern Oklahoma State College *A*
Langston University *B*
Northeastern State University *B*
Northern Oklahoma College *A*
Northwestern Oklahoma State
  University *B*
Oklahoma Baptist University *B, T*
Oklahoma Christian University *B*
Oklahoma City Community
  College *A*
Oklahoma City University *B*
Oklahoma Panhandle State
  University *B*
Oklahoma State University *B, M, D*
Oklahoma Wesleyan University *A, B*
Oral Roberts University *B*
Rose State College *A*
Southeastern Oklahoma State
  University *B*
Southern Nazarene University *B*
Southwestern Oklahoma State
  University *B*
Tulsa Community College *A*
University of Central Oklahoma *B*
University of Oklahoma *B, M, D*
University of Science and Arts of
  Oklahoma *B*
University of Tulsa *B, M, D*

Oregon

Concordia University *B*
Eastern Oregon University *B*
George Fox University *B*
Lewis & Clark College *B*
Linfield College *B, T*
Linn-Benton Community College *A*
Mt. Hood Community College *A*
Oregon State University *B, M, D*
Pacific University *B*
Portland State University *B, M*
Reed College *B*
Southern Oregon University *B*
Treasure Valley Community
  College *A*
University of Oregon *B, M, D*
University of Portland *B*
Western Oregon University *B*
Willamette University *B*

Pennsylvania

Albright College *B, T*
Allegheny College *B*
Alvernia University *B*
Arcadia University *B*
Bloomsburg University of
  Pennsylvania *B, T*
Bryn Mawr College *B, M, D*
Bucknell University *B, M*
Cabrini College *B*
California University of
  Pennsylvania *B, M*
Carlow University *B*
Carnegie Mellon University *B, M, D*
Cedar Crest College *B*
Chatham University *B*
Chestnut Hill College *B*
Cheyney University of
  Pennsylvania *B, T*
Clarion University of Pennsylvania *B*
Community College of Allegheny
  County *A*
DeSales University *B, T*
Delaware Valley College *B*

Dickinson College *B*
Drexel University *B, M, D*
Duquesne University *B, M, D*
East Stroudsburg University of
  Pennsylvania *B, T*
Eastern University *B*
Edinboro University of
  Pennsylvania *B, T*
Elizabethtown College *B, T*
Franklin & Marshall College *B*
Gannon University *B*
Geneva College *B, T*
Gettysburg College *B*
Grove City College *B*
Harrisburg Area Community
  College *A*
Harrisburg University of Science and
  Technology *B*
Haverford College *B, T*
Immaculata University *A, B*
Indiana University of
  Pennsylvania *B, M*
Juniata College *B*
King's College *B, T*
Kutztown University of
  Pennsylvania *B*
La Roche College *B*
La Salle University *B*
Lafayette College *B*
Lebanon Valley College *B, T*
Lehigh Carbon Community College *A*
Lehigh University *B, M, D*
Lincoln University *B*
Lock Haven University of
  Pennsylvania *B*
Lycoming College *B*
Mansfield University of
  Pennsylvania *B, T*
Mercyhurst University *B*
Messiah College *B*
Millersville University of
  Pennsylvania *B, T*
Misericordia University *B*
Moravian College *B, T*
Muhlenberg College *C, B*
Northampton Community College *A*
Penn State
  Abington *B*
  Altoona *B*
  Beaver *B*
  Berks *B*
  Brandywine *B*
  DuBois *B*
  Erie, The Behrend College *B*
  Fayette, The Eberly Campus *B*
  Greater Allegheny *B*
  Harrisburg *B*
  Hazleton *B*
  Lehigh Valley *B*
  Mont Alto *B*
  New Kensington *B*
  Schuylkill *B*
  Shenango *B*
  University Park *B, M, D*
  Wilkes-Barre *B*
  Worthington Scranton *B*
  York *B*
Philadelphia University *B*
Rosemont College *B*
St. Francis University *B*
Saint Joseph's University *B*
St. Vincent College *B*
Seton Hill University *B, T*
Shippensburg University of
  Pennsylvania *B, T*
Slippery Rock University of
  Pennsylvania *B*
Susquehanna University *B, T*
Swarthmore College *B*
Temple University *B, M, D*
Thiel College *B*
University of Pennsylvania *B, M, D*
University of Pittsburgh *B, M, D*

University of Pittsburgh
  Bradford *B*
  Greensburg *B*
  Johnstown *B*
University of Scranton *B, M, T*
University of the Sciences *B, M, D*
Ursinus College *B, T*
Villanova University *B, M*
Washington & Jefferson College *B*
Waynesburg University *B*
West Chester University of
  Pennsylvania *B, T*
Westminster College *B*
Widener University *B*
Wilkes University *B*
Wilson College *B*
York College of Pennsylvania *A, B*

Puerto Rico

Bayamon Central University *B*
Inter American University of Puerto
  Rico
  Arecibo Campus *B*
  Metropolitan Campus *B*
  San German Campus *B*
Pontifical Catholic University of
  Puerto Rico *B, M*
Turabo University *B*
Universidad Adventista de las
  Antillas *B*
Universidad Metropolitana *B*
University of Puerto Rico
  Cayey University College *B*
  Humacao *B*
  Mayaguez *B, M, D*
  Rio Piedras *B, M, D*
University of the Sacred Heart *B*

Rhode Island

Brown University *B, M, D*
Providence College *B*
Rhode Island College *B*
Roger Williams University *B*
Salve Regina University *B*
University of Rhode Island *B, M, D*

South Carolina

Allen University *B*
Benedict College *B*
Bob Jones University *B*
Charleston Southern University *B*
Citadel *B, T*
Claflin University *B*
Clemson University *B, M, D*
Coastal Carolina University *B*
Coker College *B*
College of Charleston *B, T*
Columbia College *B*
Converse College *B*
Erskine College *B, T*
Francis Marion University *B*
Furman University *B, M, T*
Lander University *B*
Limestone College *B*
Newberry College *B, T*
Presbyterian College *B*
South Carolina State University *B*
Southern Wesleyan University *B*
University of South Carolina
  Aiken *B*
  Columbia *B, M, D*
  Upstate *B*
Winthrop University *B*
Wofford College *B, T*

South Dakota

Augustana College *B, T*
Black Hills State University *B*
Mount Marty College *B*
Northern State University *B*
South Dakota School of Mines and
  Technology *B, M*
South Dakota State
  University *B, M, D*

University of Sioux Falls *B*
University of South Dakota *B, M*

Tennessee

Austin Peay State University *B*
Belmont University *B, T*
Bethel University *B*
Carson-Newman University *B, T*
Christian Brothers University *B*
East Tennessee State
  University *B, M, T*
Fisk University *B, M*
Freed-Hardeman University *B*
Hiwassee College *A*
Jackson State Community College *A*
King University *B, T*
Lane College *B*
LeMoyne-Owen College *B*
Lee University *B*
Lincoln Memorial University *B, T*
Lipscomb University *B*
Maryville College *B, T*
Middle Tennessee State
  University *B, M, D*
Milligan College *B, T*
Rhodes College *B*
Sewanee: The University of the
  South *B*
Southern Adventist University *B*
Tennessee State University *B, M*
Tennessee Technological
  University *B, M, T*
Tennessee Wesleyan College *B*
Trevecca Nazarene University *B*
Union University *B, T*
University of Memphis *B, M, D*
University of Tennessee
  Chattanooga *B*
  Knoxville *B, M, D*
  Martin *B*
Vanderbilt University *B, M, D*

Texas

Abilene Christian University *B*
Amarillo College *A*
Angelo State University *B*
Austin College *B*
Austin Community College *A*
Baylor University *B, M, D*
Blinn College *A*
Brazosport College *A*
Central Texas College *A*
Clarendon College *A*
Coastal Bend College *A*
College of the Mainland *A*
Del Mar College *A*
East Texas Baptist University *B*
El Paso Community College *A*
Frank Phillips College *A*
Galveston College *A*
Grayson College *A*
Hardin-Simmons University *B*
Hill College *A*
Houston Baptist University *B*
Howard College *A*
Howard Payne University *B*
Huston-Tillotson University *B*
Jarvis Christian College *B, T*
Kilgore College *A*
Lamar University *B, M*
Laredo Community College *A*
LeTourneau University *B*
Lubbock Christian University *B*
McMurry University *B*
Midland College *A*
Midwestern State University *B*
Navarro College *A*
Northeast Texas Community
  College *A*
Northwest Vista College *A*
Odessa College *A*
Our Lady of the Lake University of
  San Antonio *B*
Palo Alto College *A*

Paris Junior College *A*
Prairie View A&M University *B, M*
Rice University *B, M, D*
St. Edward's University *B*
St. Mary's University *B*
St. Philip's College *A*
Sam Houston State University *B, M*
San Jacinto College *A*
Schreiner University *B*
South Plains College *A*
South Texas College *A*
Southern Methodist
    University *B, M, D*
Southwestern Adventist
    University *B, T*
Southwestern University *B, T*
Stephen F. Austin State
    University *B, T*
Sul Ross State University *B*
Tarleton State University *B, T*
Texarkana College *A*
Texas A&M International
    University *B*
Texas A&M University *B, M, D*
Texas A&M University
    Commerce *B, M*
    Corpus Christi *B, T*
    Kingsville *B, M*
Texas Christian University *B, M, D*
Texas Lutheran University *B*
Texas Southern University *B, M*
Texas State University *B, M, T*
Texas Tech University *B, M, D*
Texas Wesleyan University *B*
Texas Woman's University *B, M*
Trinity University *B*
Trinity Valley Community College *A*
Tyler Junior College *A*
University of Dallas *B*
University of Houston *B, M, D*
University of Houston
    Clear Lake *B, M*
    Downtown *B*
University of Mary Hardin-Baylor *B, T*
University of North Texas *B, M, D*
University of St. Thomas *B*
University of Texas
    Arlington *B, M, D*
    Austin *B, M, D*
    Brownsville *B*
    Dallas *B, M, D*
    El Paso *B, M, D*
    Pan American *B*
    Permian Basin *B*
    San Antonio *B, M, D*
    Tyler *B*
University of the Incarnate
    Word *A, B*
Wayland Baptist University *B, T*
West Texas A&M University *B, M*
Western Texas College *A*
Wharton County Junior College *A*
Wiley College *B*

Utah

Brigham Young University *B, M, D*
Salt Lake Community College *A*
Snow College *A*
Southern Utah University *B*
University of Utah *B, M, D, T*
Utah State University *B, M, D*
Utah Valley University *B*
Weber State University *B*
Westminster College *B*

Vermont

Bennington College *B*
Castleton State College *A*
Marlboro College *B*
Middlebury College *B*
Norwich University *B*
Saint Michael's College *B*
University of Vermont *B, M, D*

Virginia

Bluefield College *B*
Bridgewater College *B*
Christopher Newport University *B*
College of William and Mary *B, M*
Eastern Mennonite University *B*
Emory & Henry College *B, T*
Ferrum College *B*
George Mason University *B, M*
Hampden-Sydney College *B*
Hampton University *B, M*
Hollins University *B*
James Madison University *B, M*
Liberty University *B*
Longwood University *B*
Lynchburg College *B*
Mary Baldwin College *B*
Norfolk State University *B*
Old Dominion University *B, M, D*
Radford University *B*
Randolph College *B*
Randolph-Macon College *B*
Roanoke College *B, T*
Shenandoah University *B*
Sweet Briar College *B*
University of Mary Washington *B*
University of Richmond *B*
University of Virginia *B, M, D*
University of Virginia's College at
    Wise *B, T*
Virginia Commonwealth
    University *B, M, D*
Virginia Military Institute *B*
Virginia Polytechnic Institute and
    State University *B, M, D*
Virginia State University *B*
Virginia Union University *B*
Virginia Wesleyan College *B*
Washington and Lee University *B*

Washington

Cascadia Community College *A*
Central Washington University *B, M*
Centralia College *A*
Eastern Washington University *B*
Gonzaga University *B*
Heritage University *B*
Pacific Lutheran University *B*
Saint Martin's University *B*
Seattle Pacific University *B*
Seattle University *B*
South Seattle Community College *A*
University of Puget Sound *B, T*
University of Washington *B, M, D*
Walla Walla University *B*
Washington State University *B, M, D*
Western Washington University *B, M*
Whitman College *B*
Whitworth University *B, T*

West Virginia

Alderson-Broaddus University *B*
Bethany College *B*
Concord University *B*
Davis and Elkins College *B*
Fairmont State University *B*
Glenville State College *B*
Marshall University *B, M*
Potomac State College of West
    Virginia University *A*
Shepherd University *B, T*
University of Charleston *B*
West Liberty University *B*
West Virginia State University *B*
West Virginia University *B, M, D, T*
West Virginia University Institute of
    Technology *B*
West Virginia Wesleyan College *B*
Wheeling Jesuit University *B*

Wisconsin

Alverno College *B*
Beloit College *B*
Cardinal Stritch University *B, T*

Carroll University *B*
Carthage College *B*
Edgewood College *B*
Lakeland College *B*
Lawrence University *B*
Marian University *B*
Marquette University *B, M, D*
Mount Mary University *B, T*
Northland College *B*
Ripon College *B*
St. Norbert College *B, T*
University of Wisconsin
    Eau Claire *B*
    Green Bay *B*
    La Crosse *B, T*
    Madison *B, M, D*
    Milwaukee *B, M, D*
    Oshkosh *B*
    Parkside *B*
    Platteville *B, T*
    River Falls *B*
    Stevens Point *B, T*
    Superior *B, T*
    Whitewater *B, T*
Viterbo University *B, T*
Wisconsin Lutheran College *B*

Wyoming

Casper College *A*
Laramie County Community
    College *A*
Northwest College *A*
University of Wyoming *B, M, D*
Western Wyoming Community
    College *A*

Chemistry teacher education

Alabama

Auburn University *M, T*
Birmingham-Southern College *T*
Huntingdon College *B, T*
Oakwood University *B*

Arizona

Grand Canyon University *B*

Arkansas

Arkansas State University *B, M, T*
Ouachita Baptist University *B, T*
University of Arkansas
    Fort Smith *B*

California

Azusa Pacific University *T*
California Polytechnic State
    University: San Luis Obispo *T*
California State University
    Chico *T*
    Long Beach *T*
    San Bernardino *T*
Pepperdine University *B*
San Diego State University *T*
San Francisco State University *T*
Stanford University *M, T*
University of San Diego *T*
Vanguard University of Southern
    California *T*

Colorado

Adams State University *B, T*
Colorado State University *B, T*
Colorado State University
    Pueblo *T*

Connecticut

Albertus Magnus College *B, T*
Fairfield University *T*
Quinnipiac University *B, M*
Sacred Heart University *T*
University of Connecticut *T*
University of Saint Joseph *T*

Delaware

Delaware State University *B*
University of Delaware *B, T*

Florida

Bethune-Cookman University *B, T*
Daytona State College *B*
Florida Institute of Technology *B*
University of Miami *B, M*

Georgia

Columbus State University *B*
Piedmont College *B, T*
Southern Polytechnic State
    University *B*

Hawaii

Brigham Young University-
    Hawaii *B, T*

Idaho

Boise State University *B, T*
Brigham Young University-Idaho *B, T*
Northwest Nazarene University *B*
University of Idaho *T*

Illinois

Augustana College *B, T*
Benedictine University *T*
Bradley University *B*
Chicago State University *B*
Concordia University Chicago *B, T*
DePaul University *M, T*
Dominican University *T*
Elmhurst College *B*
Governors State University *B, T*
Greenville College *B, T*
Illinois State University *M, T*
Illinois Wesleyan University *B*
Knox College *T*
McKendree University *B*
Millikin University *B, T*
North Park University *T*
Olivet Nazarene University *B, T*
Rockford University *T*
Trinity Christian College *B, T*
University of Illinois
    Chicago *B*
    Urbana-Champaign *B, M, T*

Indiana

Anderson University *B, T*
Bethel College *B*
Butler University *T*
Franklin College *B, T*
Goshen College *B, T*
Huntington University *B, M*
Indiana University
    Bloomington *B, T*
    Northwest *B*
    Purdue University Fort Wayne *B, T*
    South Bend *B, T*
Indiana Wesleyan University *T*
Manchester University *B, T*
Purdue University *B, M, D*
Saint Mary's College *T*
University of Evansville *B, T*
University of Indianapolis *B, T*
University of St. Francis *B*
Valparaiso University *B*
Vincennes University *A*

Iowa

Briar Cliff University *B*
Buena Vista University *B, T*
Central College *T*
Cornell College *B, T*
Dordt College *B*
Drake University *M, T*
Ellsworth Community College *A*
Graceland University *T*
Grand View University *T*
Iowa State University *T*
Iowa Wesleyan College *B, T*

Loras College *T*
Maharishi University of
Management *T*
Morningside College *B*
Northwestern College *T*
St. Ambrose University *B, T*
Simpson College *A*
University of Dubuque *B, T*
University of Iowa *T*
Upper Iowa University *B, T*
Wartburg College *T*

Kansas

Benedictine College *B*
Bethany College *B*
Bethel College *T*
Garden City Community College *A*
Independence Community College *A*
McPherson College *B, T*
Pittsburg State University *B*
Sterling College *T*
Tabor College *B*
University of St. Mary *T*
Washburn University *B, T*

Kentucky

Campbellsville University *B*
Kentucky Wesleyan College *B, T*

Louisiana

Centenary College of Louisiana *T*
Louisiana State University
Shreveport *B*
McNeese State University *T*
Our Lady of Holy Cross College *T*
Southeastern Louisiana University *B*
University of Louisiana at Lafayette *B*
University of Louisiana at Monroe *D*
Xavier University of Louisiana *B*

Maine

University of Maine *B*
University of Maine
Farmington *B, T*
University of Southern Maine *T*

Maryland

Anne Arundel Community College *A*
Carroll Community College *A*
Chesapeake College *A*
Community College of Baltimore
County *A*
Coppin State University *B, T*
Harford Community College *A*
Hood College *T*
Howard Community College *A*
Notre Dame of Maryland
University *T*

Massachusetts

Assumption College *T*
Boston University *B*
Bridgewater State University *T*
Eastern Nazarene College *B*
Elms College *T*
Merrimack College *B*
Salem State University *M*
Tufts University *T*
University of Massachusetts
Dartmouth *T*
Western New England
University *B, T*
Westfield State University *M, T*
Worcester State University *T*

Michigan

Alma College *T*
Aquinas College *B, T*
Calvin College *B*
Central Michigan University *B, M*
Eastern Michigan University *B*
Ferris State University *B*
Grand Valley State University *M, T*
Hope College *B, T*

Madonna University *B*
Michigan State University *B*
Michigan Technological University *T*
Northern Michigan University *B, T*
Olivet College *B, T*
Spring Arbor University *B*
University of Detroit Mercy *B, M, T*
University of Michigan
Dearborn *B*
Western Michigan University *B, D*

Minnesota

Augsburg College *T*
Bethel University *B*
College of St. Scholastica *T*
Concordia College: Moorhead *B, T*
Concordia University St. Paul *B, T*
Gustavus Adolphus College *T*
Hamline University *T*
Minnesota State University
Mankato *B, T*
Moorhead *B*
Saint Cloud State University *B, T*
St. Mary's University of Minnesota *B*
Southwest Minnesota State
University *B, T*
University of Minnesota
Morris *T*
Twin Cities *M*
University of St. Thomas *B*
Winona State University *B, T*

Mississippi

Itawamba Community College *A*
Millsaps College *T*
Mississippi College *B*

Missouri

Central Methodist University *B*
College of the Ozarks *B, T*
Lincoln University *B*
Lindenwood University *B*
Maryville University of Saint Louis *M*
Missouri Baptist University *T*
Missouri Southern State
University *B, T*
Missouri State University *B*
Northwest Missouri State
University *B, T*
Park University *T*
Southwest Baptist University *B, T*
University of Central Missouri *B*
University of Missouri
Columbia *B*
Kansas City *B*
Washington University in St.
Louis *B, M, T*
William Jewell College *B, T*

Montana

Carroll College *B*
Montana State University
Billings *B*
University of Great Falls *B*
University of Montana *M, T*
University of Montana: Western *B, T*

Nebraska

Chadron State College *B*
College of Saint Mary *B, T*
Concordia University *B, T*
Creighton University *B, T*
Hastings College *B, M, T*
Midland University *B, T*
Nebraska Wesleyan University *T*
Union College *B*
University of Nebraska
Kearney *B*
Lincoln *B, T*
Wayne State College *B, T*

New Hampshire

Keene State College *B, T*
Saint Anselm College *T*
University of New Hampshire *T*

New Jersey

College of New Jersey *B, T*
County College of Morris *A*
Saint Peter's University *T*

New Mexico

New Mexico Institute of Mining and
Technology *M*
Western New Mexico University *B*

New York

Adelphi University *M, T*
Alfred University *B, T*
City University of New York
Brooklyn College *B, M*
City College *B*
College of Staten Island *B*
Hunter College *B, M, T*
Queens College *M, T*
Colgate University *M*
College of Mount St. Vincent *T*
College of Saint Rose *B, T*
Cornell University *M, T*
D'Youville College *M, T*
Dowling College *B, M*
Dutchess Community College *A*
Elmira College *B, T*
Fordham University *M, T*
Hofstra University *B, M*
Houghton College *B, T*
Iona College *M, T*
Ithaca College *B, M, T*
Le Moyne College *T*
Long Island University
LIU Brooklyn *B, M, T*
LIU Post *B, T*
Manhattan College *B, T*
Marist College *B*
Medaille College *M, T*
Medaille College: Amherst *M*
Nazareth College *B, M, T*
New York University *B, M*
Niagara University *B, M, T*
Pace University *B, M, T*
Pace University: Pleasantville/
Briarcliff *B, M, T*
Roberts Wesleyan College *B, M*
SUNY
College at Brockport *B, M, T*
College at Buffalo *B, M*
College at Cortland *B, M*
College at Fredonia *B, M, T*
College at Geneseo *B, T*
College at New Paltz *B, M, T*
College at Old Westbury *B, M, T*
College at Oneonta *B, T*
College at Oswego *B, T*
College at Plattsburgh *B*
College at Potsdam *B, M*
College of Environmental Science
and Forestry *B, T*
University at Albany *M, T*
University at Binghamton *M*
University at Buffalo *M, T*
University at Stony Brook *T*
St. Francis College *B*
St. John Fisher College *B, M, T*
St. Joseph's College, New York *B*
St. Lawrence University *T*
St. Thomas Aquinas College *B, M, T*
Syracuse University *B, M, T*
Ulster County Community College *A*
University of Rochester *M*
Vassar College *T*
Wagner College *T*
Wells College *T*

North Carolina

Appalachian State University *T*
Catawba College *T*
Elizabeth City State University *B, T*
Gardner-Webb University *B*
Lenoir-Rhyne University *B*
Mars Hill University *T*

Meredith College *T*
Methodist University *A, B, T*
North Carolina Agricultural and
Technical State University *B, T*
North Carolina Central
University *B, M, T*
Sandhills Community College *A*
University of North Carolina
Wilmington *B*
Wake Forest University *T*

North Dakota

Dickinson State University *B, T*
Mayville State University *B, T*
Minot State University *B*
North Dakota State University *B, T*
University of Jamestown *B*
Valley City State University *B, T*

Ohio

Ashland University *B, T*
Bluffton University *B*
Bowling Green State
University *B, M, T*
Case Western Reserve University *T*
Cedarville University *B*
Defiance College *B*
Hiram College *T*
John Carroll University *T*
Kent State University *B*
Miami University
Oxford *B, M, T*
Mount Vernon Nazarene
University *B, T*
Ohio Dominican University *B, T*
Ohio Northern University *B, T*
Ohio Wesleyan University *B*
Otterbein University *B*
University of Findlay *T*
University of Mount Union *T*
University of Rio Grande *B, T*
University of Toledo *M, T*
Wilmington College *B*
Xavier University *B*
Youngstown State University *B, M*

Oklahoma

East Central University *B, T*
Eastern Oklahoma State College *A*
Oklahoma Baptist University *B, T*
University of Central Oklahoma *B*
University of Tulsa *B, T*

Oregon

Concordia University *B, M, T*
Linfield College *T*
Portland State University *T*
Western Oregon University *B, M, T*

Pennsylvania

Albright College *T*
Alvernia University *B*
Arcadia University *B, M, T*
Bucks County Community College *A*
Cabrini College *T*
Chatham University *M, T*
DeSales University *T*
Duquesne University *M, T*
Geneva College *T*
Gettysburg College *T*
Grove City College *B, T*
Holy Family University *B*
Juniata College *B, T*
King's College *T*
La Salle University *B, T*
Lebanon Valley College *T*
Lycoming College *T*
Mansfield University of
Pennsylvania *B, T*
Mercyhurst University *B, T*
Messiah College *B, T*
Misericordia University *B, T*
Moravian College *T*
St. Francis University *B, T*

Saint Joseph's University *M, T*
St. Vincent College *T*
Seton Hill University *B, T*
Susquehanna University *T*
Thiel College *B*
University of Pittsburgh
  Greensburg *B, T*
  Johnstown *B, T*
University of Scranton *B*
Villanova University *T*
Washington & Jefferson College *T*
Waynesburg University *B, T*
Westminster College *T*
Widener University *T*
Wilkes University *M, T*
Wilson College *T*

Puerto Rico

Inter American University of Puerto
    Rico
  Arecibo Campus *B*
  Metropolitan Campus *B*
  San German Campus *B*
Pontifical Catholic University of
    Puerto Rico *B, T*
Turabo University *B*

Rhode Island

Rhode Island College *B*

South Carolina

Coker College *B, T*
Furman University *T*

South Dakota

Mount Marty College *B*
University of Sioux Falls *T*
University of South Dakota *B, M, T*

Tennessee

Belmont University *T*
King University *T*
Lee University *B*
Lincoln Memorial University *B, T*
Lipscomb University *B, T*
Maryville College *B, T*
Southern Adventist University *B*
Tennessee Technological University *T*
Trevecca Nazarene University *B, T*
Union University *B, T*

Texas

East Texas Baptist University *B*
Houston Baptist University *T*
Kilgore College *A*
Lamar University *T*
Laredo Community College *A*
Lubbock Christian University *B*
McMurry University *B, T*
St. Edward's University *B, T*
St. Mary's University *B*
Sam Houston State University *M, T*
Schreiner University *B*
Tarleton State University *T*
Texas A&M University
  Kingsville *T*
University of Dallas *T*
University of Mary Hardin-Baylor *T*
University of Texas
  Arlington *T*
  San Antonio *T*
West Texas A&M University *T*

Utah

Brigham Young University *B*
Southern Utah University *B*
Utah State University *B*
Utah Valley University *B*
Weber State University *B*
Western Governors
    University *B, M, T*

Vermont

Castleton State College *B, T*
Saint Michael's College *M, T*

Virginia

Averett University *B, M, T*
Bluefield College *B, T*
Bridgewater College *T*
Eastern Mennonite University *T*
Emory & Henry College *B*
Hampton University *M*
Hollins University *T*
Longwood University *T*
Radford University *T*
University of Virginia's College at
    Wise *T*

Washington

Central Washington University *B, T*
Eastern Washington University *B*
Heritage University *B*
Washington State University *B, M, T*
Western Washington University *B*
Whitworth University *B, T*

West Virginia

Bethany College *B*
Concord University *B, M, T*
Shepherd University *T*
West Liberty University *B*
West Virginia Wesleyan College *B*
Wheeling Jesuit University *B*

Wisconsin

Carroll University *B, T*
Carthage College *T*
Edgewood College *B*
Lakeland College *T*
Lawrence University *T*
Marquette University *B*
Mount Mary University *B, T*
St. Norbert College *T*
University of Wisconsin
  Green Bay *T*
  Platteville *B*
  River Falls *T*
  Superior *B, T*
  Whitewater *B*
Viterbo University *B, T*

Chicano/Hispanic-American/Latino studies

Arizona

Arizona State University *B*
Phoenix College *C*
University of Arizona *B, M, D*

California

California State University
  Channel Islands *B*
  Dominguez Hills *B*
  East Bay *B*
  Fresno *B*
  Fullerton *B*
  Long Beach *B*
  Los Angeles *B, M*
  Northridge *B*
  San Bernardino *B*
Cerritos College *A*
Claremont McKenna College *B*
Contra Costa College *A*
De Anza College *A*
El Camino College *A*
Fresno City College *A*
Loyola Marymount University *B*
Mills College *B*
Pitzer College *B*
Pomona College *B*
San Diego Mesa College *A*
San Diego State University *B*
San Francisco State University *B*

San Jose State University *M*
Santa Ana College *A*
Santa Barbara City College *A*
Scripps College *B*
Solano Community College *A*
Sonoma State University *B*
Southwestern College *A*
Stanford University *B*
University of California
  Berkeley *B*
  Davis *B*
  Irvine *B*
  Los Angeles *B, M, D*
  Riverside *B*
  Santa Barbara *B, M, D*
University of Southern California *B*

Colorado

Colorado College *B*
Fort Lewis College *B*
Metropolitan State University of
    Denver *B*
University of Northern Colorado *B*

Connecticut

Connecticut College *B*

Florida

University of Miami *B*

Illinois

University of Illinois
  Chicago *M*

Maine

University of Southern Maine *B*

Massachusetts

Boston College *B*

Michigan

Michigan State University *D*
University of Michigan *B*

Minnesota

University of Minnesota
  Twin Cities *B*

New Hampshire

Dartmouth College *B*

New Jersey

Rutgers, The State University of New
    Jersey
  New Brunswick/Piscataway
      Campus *B*
  Newark Campus *B*

New Mexico

University of New Mexico *C, B*
Western New Mexico University *B*

New York

City University of New York
  Brooklyn College *B*
Columbia University *B*
Columbia University
  School of General Studies *B*
Hobart and William Smith Colleges *B*
SUNY
  College at Oneonta *B*

Ohio

Bowling Green State University *B*
Pontifical College Josephinum *B*

Oregon

Lewis & Clark College *B*
Oregon State University *M*

Pennsylvania

Cedar Crest College *B*
University of Scranton *B*

Puerto Rico

Pontifical Catholic University of
    Puerto Rico *B, M*

Rhode Island

Brown University *B, M, D*

Texas

Our Lady of the Lake University of
    San Antonio *B*
Palo Alto College *A*
Rice University *B, M*
San Jacinto College *A*
South Texas College *A*
Southern Methodist University *B*
Texas A&M University *M, D*
University of Texas
  Austin *M*
  El Paso *D*
  Pan American *B*
  San Antonio *B, M*

Washington

University of Washington *B*
University of Washington Tacoma *B*

Child care management

Alabama

Bevill State Community College *C, A*
Bishop State Community
    College *C, A*
Calhoun Community College *C, A*
Chattahoochee Valley Community
    College *C*
Gadsden State Community College *C*
George C. Wallace Community
    College at Dothan *C, A*
Jefferson State Community
    College *C, A*
Lawson State Community College *C*
Lurleen B. Wallace Community
    College *C, A*
Northeast Alabama Community
    College *C, A*
Northwest-Shoals Community
    College *C, A*
Shelton State Community College *C*
Snead State Community College *C, A*
Southern Union State Community
    College *C, A*
Wallace State Community College at
    Hanceville *A*

Alaska

University of Alaska
  Southeast *C, A*

Arizona

Glendale Community College *C*
Mesa Community College *C*
Northland Pioneer College *C, A*
Phoenix College *C, A*
Scottsdale Community College *A*

Arkansas

Arkansas State University *M*
College of the Ouachitas *A*
Cossatot Community College of the
    University of Arkansas *A*
East Arkansas Community College *A*
National Park Community College *A*
Northwest Arkansas Community
    College *C, A*
Pulaski Technical College *C, A*
University of Arkansas
  Community College at Hope *A*
  Monticello *C*

California

American River College *C, A*
Antelope Valley College *C, A*
Barstow Community College *C*

Butte College *A*
Cabrillo College *C, A*
California State University
  Northridge *B*
Cerro Coso Community College *C, A*
Chabot College *A*
Chaffey College *C, A*
Citrus College *C*
City College of San Francisco *C*
College of the Canyons *C*
College of the Desert *A*
College of the Sequoias *C, A*
College of the Siskiyous *C, A*
Cuyamaca College *C, A*
Diablo Valley College *C*
Folsom Lake College *C*
Foothill College *C*
Fresno City College *C, A*
Fullerton College *C, A*
Glendale Community College *A*
Grossmont College *C, A*
Long Beach City College *C, A*
Los Angeles City College *C, A*
Los Angeles Harbor College *C, A*
Los Angeles Southwest College *C, A*
Los Medanos College *C*
Merritt College *C, A*
MiraCosta College *C, A*
Modesto Junior College *C, A*
Moorpark College *C, A*
Ohlone College *C, A*
Orange Coast College *C, A*
Palomar College *C, A*
Porterville College *C, A*
Reedley College *C*
Rio Hondo College *C*
Sacramento City College *C, A*
Saddleback College *C*
San Bernardino Valley College *C*
San Diego City College *C*
Santa Barbara City College *C, A*
Santa Rosa Junior College *C*
Shasta College *A*
Sierra College *A*
Southwestern College *C, A*
University of La Verne *B*
West Hills College: Lemoore *C*
West Valley College *C, A*

Colorado

Colorado Northwestern Community
  College *C, A*
Trinidad State Junior College *C, A*

Connecticut

Asnuntuck Community College *C, A*
Gateway Community College *C*
Goodwin College *C, A*
Housatonic Community College *C, A*
Middlesex Community College *C, A*
Norwalk Community College *C*
Post University *C, A*

Delaware

University of Delaware *B*

Florida

Broward College *A*
Eastern Florida State College *C*
Hillsborough Community College *A*
Indian River State College *C*
Miami Dade College *C*
Palm Beach State College *A*
Pensacola State College *A*
Polk State College *A*
Seminole State College of Florida *A*

Georgia

Abraham Baldwin Agricultural
  College *A*
Albany Technical College *C*
Atlanta Technical College *C*
Augusta Technical College *C*

Chattahoochee Technical
  College *C, A*
Fort Valley State University *B*
Gwinnett Technical College *C*
Savannah Technical College *C*
South Georgia State College *A*
University of North Georgia *C, A*

Hawaii

University of Hawaii
  Honolulu Community College *C, A*

Idaho

College of Western Idaho *C, A*

Illinois

Carl Sandburg College *A*
City Colleges of Chicago
  Harry S. Truman College *C*
College of DuPage *C, A*
Illinois Central College *A*
Illinois Eastern Community Colleges
  Wabash Valley College *A*
Illinois Valley Community College *A*
John Wood Community College *A*
Kishwaukee College *A*
Lake Land College *C, A*
Lewis and Clark Community
  College *A*
Rock Valley College *C, A*
South Suburban College of Cook
  County *C*
Southeastern Illinois College *A*
Southwestern Illinois College *C, A*

Indiana

Purdue University
  Calumet *C*
Vincennes University *A*

Iowa

Iowa Western Community College *A*
Marshalltown Community
  College *C, A*
Southeastern Community College *A*

Kansas

Allen County Community College *C*
Barton County Community
  College *C, A*
Butler Community College *C, A*
Cloud County Community
  College *C, A*
Colby Community College *A*
Cowley County Community
  College *A*
Dodge City Community College *C, A*
Garden City Community College *A*
Highland Community College *A*
Hutchinson Community College *C, A*
Independence Community
  College *C, A*
Johnson County Community
  College *A*
Kansas City Kansas Community
  College *A*
Neosho County Community
  College *C*

Kentucky

Eastern Kentucky University *A*
Somerset Community College *C, A*

Louisiana

Nicholls State University *A*

Maryland

Anne Arundel Community College *A*
Carroll Community College *A*
Cecil College *A*
Chesapeake College *C, A*
College of Southern Maryland *C, A*
Community College of Baltimore
  County *A*

Frederick Community College *C, A*
Hagerstown Community College *C, A*
Montgomery College *C, A*
Prince George's Community
  College *C, A*
Wor-Wic Community College *C, A*

Massachusetts

Bristol Community College *A*
Holyoke Community College *C, A*
Massachusetts Bay Community
  College *C, A*
Massasoit Community College *A*
Mount Wachusett Community
  College *A*
Northern Essex Community
  College *A*
Roxbury Community College *A*
Wheelock College *B, M*

Michigan

Baker College
  Muskegon *C*
  Owosso *C, A*
Bay de Noc Community College *A*
Ferris State University *A, B*
Glen Oaks Community College *C, A*
Gogebic Community College *C*
Grand Rapids Community College *A*
Kellogg Community College *C, A*
Macomb Community College *A*
Monroe County Community
  College *A*
Montcalm Community College *C, A*
Oakland Community College *A*
St. Clair County Community
  College *A*
Schoolcraft College *C, A*
Wayne County Community
  College *C, A*

Minnesota

Central Lakes College *C, A*
Dakota County Technical College *A*
Minnesota West Community and
  Technical College *A*
Pine Technical College *C, A*
Rochester Community and Technical
  College *A*
St. Cloud Technical and Community
  College *C, A*
St. Paul College *C, A*
South Central College *C, A*
University of Minnesota
  Twin Cities *B, M*

Mississippi

Coahoma Community College *A*
Copiah-Lincoln Community
  College *A*
Itawamba Community College *A*
Rust College *B*

Missouri

East Central College *A*
Jefferson College *C, A*
Metropolitan Community College -
  Kansas City *C, A*
Mineral Area College *C*
Missouri State University: West
  Plains *C, A*
Moberly Area Community
  College *C, A*
Northwest Missouri State
  University *A*
St. Charles Community College *C, A*
St. Louis Community College *A*
Southeast Missouri State University *A*
State Fair Community College *A*

Nebraska

Central Community College *C, A*
Metropolitan Community
  College *C, A*

Mid-Plains Community College *C, A*
Southeast Community College *A*

Nevada

Truckee Meadows Community
  College *C, A*

New Hampshire

Great Bay Community College *C, A*
Lakes Region Community College *C*
Nashua Community College *C*
River Valley Community College *C*

New Jersey

County College of Morris *C*
Hudson County Community
  College *C, A*

New Mexico

Dona Ana Community College of
  New Mexico State University *C*
Eastern New Mexico University *A*
Eastern New Mexico University:
  Roswell *C, A*

New York

Broome Community College *C, A*
Corning Community College *C, A*
Dutchess Community College *C, A*
Erie Community College *A*
Fulton-Montgomery Community
  College *C, A*
Genesee Community College *C*
Hudson Valley Community College *A*
Jamestown Community College *C*
Nassau Community College *C*
Orange County Community
  College *A*
SUNY
  College of Agriculture and
    Technology at Morrisville *A*
  College of Technology at Canton *A*
Tompkins Cortland Community
  College *A*
Trocaire College *C*
Westchester Community College *C, A*

North Carolina

Asheville-Buncombe Technical
  Community College *C, A*
Beaufort County Community
  College *A*
Blue Ridge Community College *C, A*
Cape Fear Community College *C, A*
Carteret Community College *C, A*
Central Carolina Community
  College *C, A*
Central Piedmont Community
  College *C, A*
Edgecombe Community College *A*
Halifax Community College *A*
Haywood Community College *C, A*
Mayland Community College *C, A*
Nash Community College *A*
Randolph Community College *A*
Richmond Community College *C, A*
Roanoke-Chowan Community
  College *A*
Sandhills Community College *A*
Southeastern Community College *A*
Southwestern Community College *A*
Vance-Granville Community
  College *C, A*
Western Piedmont Community
  College *C, A*

North Dakota

Mayville State University *B*

Ohio

Cincinnati State Technical and
  Community College *C*
Columbus State Community
  College *C*

Cuyahoga Community College
Metropolitan *A*
Lakeland Community College *A*
Mount Vernon Nazarene University *A*
North Central State College *C*
Northwest State Community
College *A*
Youngstown State University *A*
Zane State College *A*

Oklahoma

Connors State College *C, A*
Eastern Oklahoma State College *A*
Murray State College *A*
Oklahoma City Community
College *C, A*
Oklahoma State University
Oklahoma City *A*
Redlands Community College *A*
Rose State College *C, A*
Tulsa Community College *C, A*
Western Oklahoma State College *A*

Oregon

Central Oregon Community
College *C*
Chemeketa Community College *C, A*
Clackamas Community College *C, A*
Portland Community College *C, A*
Rogue Community College *C, A*
Southwestern Oregon Community
College *C, A*
Umpqua Community College *A*

Pennsylvania

Bucks County Community College *C*
Chestnut Hill College *A, B*
Community College of
Philadelphia *A*
Gannon University *M*
Laurel Business Institute *A*
Messiah College *B*
Montgomery County Community
College *A*
Northampton Community College *C*
Pennsylvania Highlands Community
College *C*
Reading Area Community
College *C, A*
Sanford-Brown Institute
Pittsburgh *A*
Seton Hill University *C, B*

South Carolina

Denmark Technical College *C*
Florence-Darlington Technical
College *C*
Forrest Junior College *C, A*
Greenville Technical College *A*
Horry-Georgetown Technical
College *A*
Midlands Technical College *C*
Northeastern Technical College *C*
Orangeburg-Calhoun Technical
College *C*
Piedmont Technical College *C, A*
Tri-County Technical College *C*
Trident Technical College *C, A*

South Dakota

Southeast Technical Institute *A*

Tennessee

Belmont University *B*
Northeast State Community
College *C*

Texas

Amarillo College *C, A*
Angelina College *C*
Blinn College *C, A*
Brazosport College *C, A*
Brookhaven College *C*
Central Texas College *C, A*

Coastal Bend College *C, A*
College of the Mainland *A*
Del Mar College *C, A*
Eastfield College *C*
El Paso Community College *C, A*
Houston Community College
System *C*
Howard College *C, A*
Kilgore College *C, A*
Lamar Institute of Technology *C*
Laredo Community College *C, A*
McLennan Community College *C, A*
Navarro College *A*
Odessa College *C, A*
San Antonio College *C*
San Jacinto College *C*
South Plains College *C, A*
Tarrant County College *C*
Temple College *C*
Trinity Valley Community
College *C, A*
Tyler Junior College *C, A*
University of Texas
Pan American *B*
University of the Incarnate Word *B*
Vernon College *C*
Victoria College *C*
Wharton County Junior College *C*

Utah

Snow College *A*
Utah State University *C, A*

Virginia

Central Virginia Community
College *C*
Danville Community College *C*
Lord Fairfax Community College *C*
Southwest Virginia Community
College *C*
Thomas Nelson Community
College *C*
Virginia Western Community
College *A*
Wytheville Community College *C, A*

Washington

Highline Community College *C, A*
Peninsula College *A*
Renton Technical College *C, A*
Shoreline Community College *C*
Walla Walla Community College *C*
Yakima Valley Community
College *C, A*

West Virginia

American Public University System *B*
Southern West Virginia Community
and Technical College *A*

Wisconsin

Blackhawk Technical College *C*
Gateway Technical College *A*
Madison Area Technical College *A*
Milwaukee Area Technical College *C*
Moraine Park Technical College *C, A*
Nicolet Area Technical College *C, A*
Northcentral Technical College *C*
Northeast Wisconsin Technical
College *C, A*
Southwest Wisconsin Technical
College *C, A*
Western Technical College *A*
Wisconsin Indianhead Technical
College *A*

Wyoming

Central Wyoming College *A*
University of Wyoming *C*

Child care service

Alaska

University of Alaska
Anchorage *C, A*
Fairbanks *C, A*

Arizona

Arizona Western College *C*
Central Arizona College *C, A*

Arkansas

Arkansas Northeastern College *C, A*
Arkansas State University
Beebe *C*
College of the Ouachitas *C*
National Park Community College *C*
Southeast Arkansas College *C, A*
Southern Arkansas University
Tech *A*
University of Arkansas
Community College at Hope *C*

California

Antelope Valley College *C, A*
Bakersfield College *C, A*
Barstow Community College *C*
Canada College *C*
City College of San Francisco *C*
College of Marin *C, A*
College of the Canyons *C, A*
College of the Siskiyous *C, A*
East Los Angeles College *C*
Feather River College *C, A*
Folsom Lake College *C*
Foothill College *C*
Los Medanos College *C*
Merced College *C*
MiraCosta College *C, A*
Monterey Peninsula College *A*
Palomar College *C, A*
Rio Hondo College *C, A*
San Joaquin Delta College *C, A*
Santa Rosa Junior College *C*
Southwestern College *C, A*
Taft College *C*
West Hills College: Lemoore *C*

Colorado

Aims Community College *C, A*
Colorado Mesa University *C*

Connecticut

Goodwin College *A*
Naugatuck Valley Community
College *C*

Florida

College of Central Florida *C, A*
Daytona State College *A*
Gulf Coast State College *C, A*
Hillsborough Community College *C*
Lake-Sumter State College *A*
Northwest Florida State College *C, A*
Palm Beach State College *C*
Pensacola State College *C, A*
Polk State College *C*
Rasmussen College
Fort Myers *C*
New Port Richey *C*
Ocala *C*
Pasco/Land O'Lakes *C*
Tampa/Brandon *C*
Santa Fe College *A*
Tallahassee Community College *A*

Georgia

Albany Technical College *C*
Atlanta Technical College *C*
Gwinnett Technical College *C*
Savannah Technical College *C, A*
Southwest Georgia Technical
College *C, A*

Idaho

Idaho State University *C, A, B*

Illinois

Black Hawk College *C, A*
City Colleges of Chicago
Harold Washington College *C, A*
Harry S. Truman College *C, A*

Kennedy-King College *C, A*
Malcolm X College *C, A*
Olive-Harvey College *C, A*
Richard J. Daley College *C, A*
Danville Area Community
College *C, A*
Elgin Community College *C*
Harper College *C, A*
Heartland Community College *C, A*
Highland Community College *C, A*
Illinois Central College *C, A*
Illinois Valley Community College *A*
Kaskaskia College *A*
Lincoln Land Community
College *C, A*
McHenry County College *C, A*
Moraine Valley Community College *A*
Morton College *C, A*
Parkland College *C, A*
Prairie State College *C, A*
Rasmussen College
Aurora *C*
Mokena/Tinley Park *C*
Rockford *C*
Romeoville/Joliet *C*
Sauk Valley Community College *C, A*
Triton College *C, A*
Waubonsee Community College *C, A*

Indiana

Vincennes University *C*

Iowa

Des Moines Area Community
College *C, A*
Hawkeye Community College *C, A*
Iowa Lakes Community College *C, A*
Kirkwood Community College *C, A*
Northeast Iowa Community
College *C*
Western Iowa Tech Community
College *C, A*

Kansas

Kansas City Kansas Community
College *C*

Kentucky

Ashland Community and Technical
College *C*
Bluegrass Community and Technical
College *C, A*
Campbellsville University *A*
Elizabethtown Community and
Technical College *C, A*
Gateway Community and Technical
College *C, A*
Hopkinsville Community
College *C, A*
Jefferson Community and Technical
College *C, A*
Madisonville Community
College *C, A*
Owensboro Community and
Technical College *C, A*
St. Catharine College *C, A*
Somerset Community College *C, A*
Western Kentucky University *C*

Louisiana

Bossier Parish Community College *A*
Delgado Community College *A*
Nunez Community College *C, A*
South Louisiana Community
College *A*

Maine

Beal College *A*

Maryland

Community College of Baltimore
County *C*

Massachusetts

Cape Cod Community College *C*
Massasoit Community College *C, A*
Mount Wachusett Community
  College *C*
North Shore Community
  College *C, A*
Pine Manor College *A*

Michigan

Baker College
  Allen Park *C*
  Muskegon *C*
  Port Huron *C*
Bay de Noc Community College *C*
Lansing Community College *C, A*
Mott Community College *C, A*
Oakland Community College *A*

Minnesota

Alexandria Technical and Community
  College *C*
Central Lakes College *C*
Dakota County Technical
  College *C, A*
Fond du Lac Tribal and Community
  College *C*
Inver Hills Community College *C*
Minneapolis Community and
  Technical College *C*
Minnesota State Community and
  Technical College *C*
Minnesota West Community and
  Technical College *C*
Northwest Technical College *C, A*
Rasmussen College
  Blaine *C*
  Bloomington *C*
  Brooklyn Park *C*
  Eagan *C*
  Lake Elmo/Woodbury *C*
  Mankato *C*
  Moorhead *C*
  St. Cloud *C*
Ridgewater College *C*
Rochester Community and Technical
  College *C*
St. Cloud Technical and Community
  College *C*
St. Paul College *C*
South Central College *C*

Mississippi

Hinds Community College *C, A*
Northeast Mississippi Community
  College *C, A*

Missouri

North Central Missouri College *A*
Ozarks Technical Community
  College *C, A*

Nebraska

Wayne State College *B*

New Hampshire

River Valley Community College *A*

New Jersey

Raritan Valley Community College *C*

New Mexico

Central New Mexico Community
  College *C*
San Juan College *C, A*
Santa Fe Community College *C*

New York

Monroe Community College *C, A*
Onondaga Community College *C*

North Carolina

Bladen Community College *C, A*
Blue Ridge Community College *C*
Carteret Community College *C, A*
South Piedmont Community
  College *C, A*

North Dakota

Dakota College at Bottineau *A*
Lake Region State College *C, A*
Mayville State University *A*
Rasmussen College
  Bismarck *C*
  Fargo *C*
Turtle Mountain Community
  College *C*

Ohio

Cincinnati State Technical and
  Community College *C*
North Central State College *C*
Stark State College *A*

Oklahoma

Northeastern Oklahoma Agricultural
  and Mechanical College *C*
Western Oklahoma State College *C*

Oregon

Clatsop Community College *C*
Lane Community College *C, A*

Pennsylvania

Bucks County Community College *A*
Harcum College *A*
Harrisburg Area Community
  College *A*
Keystone Technical Institute *A*
Lackawanna College *A*
Montgomery County Community
  College *C*
Northampton Community College *C*
Pennsylvania College of
  Technology *A*
Pennsylvania Highlands Community
  College *A*
Westmoreland County Community
  College *C, A*

Puerto Rico

Inter American University of Puerto
  Rico
  Aguadilla Campus *C*
  Bayamon Campus *C*
  Metropolitan Campus *C*
  Ponce Campus *C*
  San German Campus *C*

South Carolina

Aiken Technical College *G*
Greenville Technical College *C*
Horry-Georgetown Technical
  College *C*
Midlands Technical College *C*
Piedmont Technical College *C*
Spartanburg Community College *C*
Technical College of the
  Lowcountry *C, A*
Tri-County Technical College *C, A*
Williamsburg Technical College *C*

South Dakota

Southeast Technical Institute *C*

Tennessee

Trevecca Nazarene University *A*

Texas

Brookhaven College *C*
Cisco College *C, A*
Collin County Community College
  District *C, A*
Del Mar College *C*

Eastfield College *C*
Houston Community College
  System *C*
Lamar Institute of Technology *C, A*
San Antonio College *C*
Tarrant County College *C*
Weatherford College *C, A*

Vermont

Community College of Vermont *C*

Virginia

J. Sargeant Reynolds Community
  College *C, A*
John Tyler Community College *C, A*

Washington

Bates Technical College *C, A*
Bellingham Technical College *C*
Centralia College *C, A*
Peninsula College *C, A*

West Virginia

American Public University System *C*
Eastern West Virginia Community and
  Technical College *C, A*

Wisconsin

Chippewa Valley Technical College *A*
Lakeshore Technical College *C*
Northcentral Technical College *C, A*
Rasmussen College
  Appleton *C*
  Green Bay *C*
  Wausau *C*

Child development

Alabama

Calhoun Community College *A*
Gadsden State Community College *A*

Alaska

University of Alaska
  Fairbanks *B*

Arizona

Arizona State University *M*
Arizona Western College *C, A*
Central Arizona College *C, A*
Mesa Community College *A*
Phoenix College *C*
Pima Community College *C, A*

Arkansas

Arkansas Tech University *A*
Cossatot Community College of the
  University of Arkansas *C*
Harding University *B*
Henderson State University *B*
Rich Mountain Community College *C*
University of Arkansas
  Community College at
  Morrilton *C, A*

California

Alliant International University *B*
Antelope Valley College *A*
Barstow Community College *C, A*
California State University
  San Bernardino *B*
City College of San Francisco *A*
Columbia College *C, A*
East Los Angeles College *C, A*
Foothill College *C, A*
Grossmont College *C, A*
Hartnell College *C, A*
Imperial Valley College *C, A*
Long Beach City College *C, A*
Los Medanos College *A*
Merced College *C, A*
Mills College *B*
MiraCosta College *C, A*

Monterey Peninsula College *A*
Mount St. Mary's College *B*
Oxnard College *C, A*
Palo Verde College *C, A*
Point Loma Nazarene University *B*
San Diego Mesa College *C, A*
Santa Barbara City College *C*
Santa Monica College *C*
Santa Rosa Junior College *C*
Shasta College *A*
Southwestern College *C, A*
Taft College *C*
Ventura College *C, A*
West Hills College: Lemoore *C*

Colorado

Aims Community College *C, A*
Arapahoe Community College *A*
Community College of Denver *C, A*
Northeastern Junior College *C, A*

Connecticut

Goodwin College *C, A, B*
Naugatuck Valley Community
  College *C, A*
Post University *B*
University of Saint Joseph *B*

District of Columbia

Gallaudet University *B*

Florida

Indian River State College *C*
Miami Dade College *A*
Nova Southeastern University *M, D*

Georgia

Columbus Technical College *C*
Fort Valley State University *B*
Point University *B*

Idaho

Lewis-Clark State College *A, B*

Illinois

Rend Lake College *C, A*
Spoon River College *C*
University of Illinois
  Chicago *M*
  Urbana-Champaign *B, M, D*

Iowa

Ashford University *B*

Kansas

Kansas State University *B*
University of St. Mary *B*

Louisiana

Grambling State University *A, B*

Maine

Kennebec Valley Community
  College *A*
York County Community
  College *C, A*

Maryland

Bowie State University *B*
Towson University *M*

Massachusetts

Lesley University *B*
Mount Wachusett Community
  College *A*
Wheelock College *B, M*

Michigan

Central Michigan University *B*
Delta College *C, A*
Henry Ford Community College *A*
Madonna University *A, B*
Michigan State University *B, M*

Northern Michigan University *A*
Schoolcraft College *C, A*
Western Michigan University *B*

Minnesota
Alexandria Technical and Community
College *A*
Concordia University St. Paul *C, B*
Dakota County Technical College *A*
Hennepin Technical College *C, A*
Minneapolis Community and
Technical College *A*
Northwest Technical College *A*
Rochester Community and Technical
College *A*
St. Paul College *A*
South Central College *C, A*

Mississippi
Alcorn State University *B*
Mississippi Gulf Coast Community
College *C*

Missouri
Central Methodist University *B*
College of the Ozarks *B*
Mineral Area College *C, A*
Missouri Baptist University *B*
Missouri State University *M*
Park University *B*
University of Central Missouri *B*

Nevada
University of Nevada
Reno *B*

New Hampshire
Southern New Hampshire
University *B, M*

New Jersey
Passaic County Community College *C*

New York
SUNY
College at Oswego *B*

North Carolina
Appalachian State University *B*
Beaufort County Community
College *A*
Campbell University *B*
Carteret Community College *C, A*
Central Piedmont Community
College *C*
Cleveland Community College *C*
Craven Community College *C*
East Carolina University *B*
Fayetteville Technical Community
College *C*
Isothermal Community College *C*
James Sprunt Community College *C*
Johnston Community College *C*
Lenoir Community College *C*
Meredith College *B*
Montgomery Community College *C*
North Carolina Agricultural and
Technical State University *B*
University of North Carolina
Greensboro *B*
Wayne Community College *C*
William Peace University *B*

Ohio
Bowling Green State University *B*
Edison State Community College *C, A*
James A. Rhodes State College *C, A*
Ohio University *A*
Ohio University
Lancaster Campus *A*
Southern Campus at Ironton *A*
Union Institute & University *B*
University of Akron *B, M*
University of Dayton *M*

Oklahoma
Cameron University *B*
Redlands Community College *C, A*
Rose State College *A*
University of Central Oklahoma *B*
Western Oklahoma State College *A*

Pennsylvania
Community College of Allegheny
County *C, A*
Penn State
Abington *C*
Altoona *C*
Beaver *C*
Berks *C*
Brandywine *C*
DuBois *C*
Erie, The Behrend College *C*
Fayette, The Eberly Campus *C*
Greater Allegheny *C*
Harrisburg *C*
Hazleton *C*
Lehigh Valley *C*
Mont Alto *C*
New Kensington *C*
Schuylkill *C*
Shenango *C*
University Park *C*
Wilkes-Barre *C*
Worthington Scranton *C*
York *C*
Seton Hill University *B*

South Carolina
Midlands Technical College *A*
York Technical College *C*

Tennessee
Cleveland State Community
College *C, A*
Columbia State Community
College *C*
Dyersburg State Community
College *C, A*
East Tennessee State University *B*
Jackson State Community College *A*
Motlow State Community College *C*
Northeast State Community
College *C, A*
Pellissippi State Community
College *A*
Southwest Tennessee Community
College *C, A*
Vanderbilt University *B, M*
Volunteer State Community
College *A*
Walters State Community College *A*

Texas
Alvin Community College *C, A*
Angelina College *C, A*
Angelo State University *B*
Austin Community College *C, A*
Brookhaven College *C, A*
Del Mar College *C, A*
Eastfield College *A*
Houston Baptist University *B*
Houston Community College
System *C, A*
Midland College *C, A*
Odessa College *A*
St. Philip's College *C, A*
San Antonio College *C, A*
San Jacinto College *C, A*
South Texas College *A*
Tarrant County College *C, A*
Temple College *C, A*
Texarkana College *C, A*
Texas Southern University *B*
Texas Tech University *B*
Texas Woman's University *B, M, D*
University of Texas
Arlington *B*
University of the Incarnate Word *B*

Victoria College *C*
Wharton County Junior College *C, A*

Utah
Dixie State College *A*
Southern Utah University *A*
Weber State University *A, B*

Vermont
Bennington College *B*

Virginia
Danville Community College *A*

Washington
Eastern Washington University *B*
Lower Columbia College *C, A*
Washington State University *C*
Western Washington University *B*

West Virginia
West Virginia University *B*

Wisconsin
Northcentral Technical College *C*

Children's/adolescent literature

Maine
College of the Atlantic *B, M*

Chinese

California
California State University
Los Angeles *B*
Claremont McKenna College *B*
Foothill College *A*
Los Angeles City College *A*
National University *B*
Pitzer College *B*
Pomona College *B*
San Francisco State University *B, M*
San Joaquin Delta College *A*
San Jose State University *B*
Scripps College *B*
Stanford University *B, M, D*
University of California
Berkeley *B, M, D*
Davis *B*
Los Angeles *B*
Riverside *B*
Santa Barbara *B*
Whittier College *B*

Colorado
University of Colorado
Boulder *B*

Connecticut
Connecticut College *B*
Trinity College *B*
Wesleyan University *B*
Yale University *B*

District of Columbia
George Washington University *B*
Georgetown University *B*

Florida
Florida State University *B*
New College of Florida *B*

Georgia
Emory University *B*
University of Georgia *B*

Hawaii
University of Hawaii
Manoa *B, M, D*

Illinois
DePaul University *M*
North Central College *B*

Indiana
Indiana University
Bloomington *M, D*
University of Notre Dame *B*

Iowa
Grinnell College *B*
University of Iowa *B, M, T*

Kentucky
Western Kentucky University *B*

Maine
Bates College *B, T*

Maryland
United States Naval Academy *B*
University of Maryland
College Park *B*

Massachusetts
Boston University *B*
College of the Holy Cross *B*
Tufts University *B*
University of Massachusetts
Amherst *B, M*
Wellesley College *B*
Williams College *B*

Michigan
Calvin College *B*
Madonna University *C*
Michigan State University *B*
Michigan Technological University *T*

Minnesota
Concordia College: Moorhead *B*
Macalester College *B*
University of Minnesota
Twin Cities *B, M, D*

Mississippi
University of Mississippi *B*

Missouri
Washington University in St.
Louis *B, M, D*

New Hampshire
Dartmouth College *B*

New Jersey
Drew University *B*
Rutgers, The State University of New
Jersey
New Brunswick/Piscataway
Campus *B, M*
Seton Hall University *T*

New York
Bard College *B*
City University of New York
Hunter College *B*
Queens College *B, T*
Columbia University *B*
Hamilton College *B*
Hobart and William Smith Colleges *B*
Hofstra University *B*
Nazareth College *B*
Union College *B*
United States Military Academy *B*
Vassar College *B*

North Carolina
Wake Forest University *B*

Ohio
Ohio State University
Columbus Campus *B*

Oklahoma
University of Oklahoma *B*
University of Tulsa *B*

Oregon
Pacific University *B*
Portland State University *B*
Reed College *B*
University of Oregon *B*

Pennsylvania
Carnegie Mellon University *B*
Gettysburg College *B*
Haverford College *T*
Lehigh University *B*
Messiah College *B*
Penn State
 Abington *B*
 Altoona *B*
 Beaver *B*
 Berks *B*
 Brandywine *B*
 DuBois *B*
 Erie, The Behrend College *B*
 Fayette, The Eberly Campus *B*
 Greater Allegheny *B*
 Harrisburg *B*
 Hazleton *B*
 Lehigh Valley *B*
 Mont Alto *B*
 New Kensington *B*
 Schuylkill *B*
 Shenango *B*
 University Park *B*
 Wilkes-Barre *B*
 Worthington Scranton *B*
 York *B*
Swarthmore College *B*
University of Pittsburgh *B*

Rhode Island
Bryant University *B*
University of Rhode Island *B*

South Carolina
Wofford College *B*

Texas
Southwestern University *T*
Trinity University *B*
University of Houston *B*

Utah
Brigham Young University *B*
University of Utah *B*

Vermont
Bennington College *B*
Middlebury College *B, M, D*
Norwich University *B*
University of Vermont *B*

Virginia
College of William and Mary *B*

Washington
Central Washington University *B*
Pacific Lutheran University *B*
University of Puget Sound *B*
University of Washington *B*

Wisconsin
Beloit College *B*
Carthage College *B*
Lawrence University *B*
University of Wisconsin
 Madison *B, M, D*

Chinese studies

California
Skyline College *C*
University of California
 Irvine *B*
 San Diego *B*

Georgia
Emory University *B*

Illinois
DePaul University *B*

Indiana
Indiana University
 Purdue University Indianapolis *C*
Valparaiso University *M*

Massachusetts
Bard College at Simon's Rock *B*

Michigan
Grand Valley State University *B*

Minnesota
Inver Hills Community College *C*
University of Minnesota
 Duluth *B*

Missouri
Lindenwood University *B*

New York
City University of New York
 College of Staten Island *C*
Columbia University *B*
SUNY
 University at Albany *B*
St. John's University *M*

North Dakota
University of North Dakota *B*

Oklahoma
University of Tulsa *B*

Virginia
University of Richmond *B*

Washington
University of Washington *B, M*

Wisconsin
Lawrence University *B*
Wisconsin Lutheran College *B*

Chiropractic (D.C.)

California
Cleveland Chiropractic College: Los
 Angeles *P*
Life Chiropractic College West *P*
Los Angeles College of
 Chiropractic *P*
Palmer College of Chiropractic-
 West *P*

Connecticut
University of Bridgeport College of
 Chiropractic *P*

Georgia
Life College *P*

Illinois
National University of Health
 Sciences: First Professional *P*

Iowa
Palmer College of Chiropractic *P*

Minnesota
Northwestern College of
 Chiropractic *P*

Missouri
Cleveland Chiropractic College:
 Kansas City *P*
Logan University *P*

New York
New York Chiropractic College *P*

Oregon
University of Western States *P*

South Carolina
Sherman College of Straight
 Chiropractic *P*

Texas
Parker University *P*
Texas Chiropractic College *P*

Chiropractic assistant

Illinois
National University of Health
 Sciences *C*

Christian studies

Alabama
Faulkner University *B, M*

Arizona
Grand Canyon University *B, M*

California
California Baptist University *B*
Epic Bible College *A*
Santa Clara University *M*
Simpson University *B*
Vanguard University of Southern
 California *B*

Georgia
Brewton-Parker College *B*
Mercer University *B*
Truett-McConnell College *B*

Illinois
Loyola University Chicago *M*
Trinity International University *M*

Indiana
Bethel College *B*
University of Notre Dame *M*

Iowa
Iowa Wesleyan College *B*

Kansas
Bethany College *B*
Friends University *B*

Kentucky
Lindsey Wilson College *B*
Mid-Continent University *D*

Louisiana
Loyola University New Orleans *B*
New Orleans Baptist Theological
 Seminary *A, B*

Massachusetts
Gordon College *B*
Stonehill College *B*

Michigan
Hillsdale College *B*
Spring Arbor University *B*

Minnesota
College of St. Scholastica *B*
Crown College *A, M*
North Central University *B*
St. Mary's University of Minnesota *B*

Mississippi
Mississippi College *B*

Missouri
Lindenwood University *B*
Missouri Baptist University *C, B*

New Jersey
Pillar College *C, A, B*

North Carolina
Montreat College *C, B*
Southeastern Baptist Theological
 Seminary *C, A, B, M, D*

Ohio
Cincinnati Christian
 University *A, B, M*
Ursuline College *B*

Oklahoma
Oklahoma Baptist University *C*
Oklahoma Christian University *B*
Oklahoma Wesleyan University *B*

Oregon
New Hope Christian College *C, B*

South Carolina
Anderson University *B*

Tennessee
Bethel University *B*
Bryan University
 Dayton *B*
Lee University *B*
Tennessee Wesleyan College *B*
Union University *C, A, B*

Texas
Hardin-Simmons University *B, M*
Houston Baptist University *B*
Howard Payne University *B*
McMurry University *B*
Southwestern Assemblies of God
 University *A, B, M*
Texas Wesleyan University *B*
University of Mary Hardin-Baylor *B*
Wayland Baptist University *A, B, M*

Virginia
Bluefield College *B*
Liberty University *B*
Regent University *A*
Roanoke College *B*

Washington
Trinity Lutheran College *A, B*

West Virginia
Alderson-Broaddus University *B*

Wisconsin
Marquette University *M*

Cinematography and film/video production

Arizona
Art Institute of Phoenix *B*
Art Institute of Tucson *B*
Glendale Community College *A*
Grand Canyon University *B*
Pima Community College *C, A*
Scottsdale Community College *C, A*
Yavapai College *C*

Arkansas
Southern Arkansas University Tech *C*
University of Central Arkansas *B, M*

California
Academy of Art University *C, A, B, M*
Allan Hancock College *C*
Antelope Valley College *C, A*

Art Center College of Design *B, M*
Art Institute of California
   Los Angeles *A, B*
   Sacramento *B*
   Silicon Valley *B*
Biola University *B*
Brooks Institute *B*
California College of the Arts *B, M*
California Institute of the
   Arts *C, B, M*
California State University
   Long Beach *B*
   Sacramento *B*
Chapman University *B, M*
City College of San Francisco *A*
College of the Canyons *A*
Cosumnes River College *A*
De Anza College *C, A*
Ex'pression College *B*
Grossmont College *C, A*
Los Angeles City College *C, A*
Los Angeles Valley College *C*
Loyola Marymount University *B, M*
Modesto Junior College *A*
Moorpark College *A*
Mount St. Mary's College *B, M*
National University *M*
Orange Coast College *A*
Pacific Union College *A, B*
Pitzer College *B*
San Francisco Art Institute *B, M*
Southwestern College *A*
University of California
   Santa Barbara *B*
University of Southern
   California *B, M*
Vanguard University of Southern
   California *B*

Colorado
Community College of Aurora *C, A*
Red Rocks Community College *C, A*

Connecticut
University of Hartford *B*

District of Columbia
American University *B, M*

Florida
Art Institute of Fort Lauderdale *A, B*
Everest University
   Melbourne *A*
   North Orlando *A*
   Pompano Beach *A*
Florida State College at
   Jacksonville *A*
Florida State University *B, M*
Full Sail University *B*
Gulf Coast State College *C, A*
Hillsborough Community
   College *C, A*
Lynn University *B*
Miami Dade College *A, B*
Miami International University of Art
   and Design *B, M*
Palm Beach State College *A*
Ringling College of Art and Design *B*
University of Central Florida *B, M*
University of Miami *B, M*
Valencia College *C, A*

Georgia
Art Institute of Atlanta *B*
Savannah College of Art and
   Design *B, M*

Illinois
Columbia College Chicago *B, M*
DePaul University *B, M*
Judson University *B*
School of the Art Institute of
   Chicago *B, M*

Southern Illinois University
   Carbondale *B*
University of Illinois
   Chicago *B, M*

Indiana
Huntington University *B*
Taylor University *B*

Iowa
University of Iowa *B, M*
Western Iowa Tech Community
   College *C, A*

Kentucky
Bluegrass Community and Technical
   College *C*

Louisiana
Baton Rouge Community College *A*
Centenary College of Louisiana *B*

Maine
College of the Atlantic *B*

Maryland
Cecil College *C*
Howard Community College *A*

Massachusetts
Bard College at Simon's Rock *B*
Boston University *B, M*
Emerson College *B*
Fitchburg State University *B*
Massachusetts College of Art and
   Design *B, M*
School of the Museum of Fine
   Arts *B, M*

Michigan
Calvin College *B*
College for Creative Studies *B*
Lansing Community College *C, A*
Mott Community College *C, A*
Northern Michigan University *B*
Wayne State University *B*

Minnesota
Art Institutes International
   Minnesota *B*
Minneapolis Community and
   Technical College *C, A*

Missouri
Calvary Bible College and Theological
   Seminary *B*
Kansas City Art Institute *B*
Webster University *B*

Montana
Montana State University *B*
University of Montana *M*

Nevada
Art Institute of Las Vegas *B*

New Hampshire
Keene State College *B*

New Jersey
Cumberland County College *A*
Fairleigh Dickinson University
   College at Florham *B*
Montclair State University *B*
Raritan Valley Community College *C*
Rutgers, The State University of New
   Jersey
   Newark Campus *B*

New Mexico
Central New Mexico Community
   College *C*
Eastern New Mexico University *B*

Eastern New Mexico University:
   Roswell *C, A*
Luna Community College *A*
New Mexico State University *B*
New Mexico State University
   Carlsbad *C*
Santa Fe University of Art and
   Design *C, B*

New York
Art Institute of New York City *A*
Bard College *B, M*
City University of New York
   Brooklyn College *C, B*
   City College *B, M*
   College of Staten Island *B*
   Hunter College *B*
   New York City College of
     Technology *C*
Five Towns College *B*
Ithaca College *B*
Long Island University
   LIU Post *B*
New York University *B, M, D*
Pratt Institute *B*
Rochester Institute of
   Technology *B, M*
SUNY
   College at Purchase *B*
   University at Binghamton *B*
Syracuse University *B, M*

North Carolina
Cape Fear Community College *A*
East Carolina University *B*
Piedmont Community College *A*
St. Augustine's University *B*
University of North Carolina
   School of the Arts *B, M*
   Wilmington *B*

Ohio
Art Institute of Ohio: Cincinnati *A, B*
Cleveland Institute of Art *B*
Cleveland State University *B*
Ohio University *B, M*

Oklahoma
Oklahoma City University *B*

Oregon
Art Institute of Portland *B*
George Fox University *B*
Portland Community College *C*

Pennsylvania
Art Institute of Philadelphia *A, B*
Art Institute of Pittsburgh *A, B*
Bucks County Community College *A*
Douglas Education Center *A*
Drexel University *B*
La Salle University *B*
Messiah College *B*
Point Park University *B*
University of the Arts *B*

Puerto Rico
Colegio de Cinematografía, Artes y
   Televisión *C, A*
Columbia Centro Universitario:
   Caguas *C*

Rhode Island
New England Institute of
   Technology *A*
University of Rhode Island *B*

South Carolina
Bob Jones University *B*
Trident Technical College *C*

Tennessee
Belmont University *B*
Pellissippi State Community
   College *A*
Southern Adventist University *B*
Watkins College of Art, Design &
   Film *C*

Texas
El Paso Community College *C, A*
Houston Community College
   System *C, A*
North Lake College *A*
South Plains College *A*
Southern Methodist University *M*

Utah
Dixie State College *B*

Vermont
Bennington College *B*
Burlington College *C*
Marlboro College *B*

Virginia
George Mason University *B*
Liberty University *B*
Regent University *B, M*
Virginia Commonwealth University *B*

Washington
Art Institute of Seattle *A, B*
Cornish College of the Arts *B*
Evergreen State College *B*
Shoreline Community College *A*

West Virginia
Wheeling Jesuit University *B*

Wisconsin
University of Wisconsin
   Oshkosh *B*
Wisconsin Lutheran College *B*

Wyoming
Northwest College *A*

Civil engineering

Alabama
Alabama Agricultural and Mechanical
   University *B*
Auburn University *B, M, D*
University of Alabama *B, M, D*
University of Alabama
   Birmingham *B, M, D*
   Huntsville *B, D*
University of South Alabama *B, M*

Alaska
University of Alaska
   Anchorage *B, M*
   Fairbanks *B, M*

Arizona
Arizona State University *B, M, D*
Northern Arizona University *B*
University of Arizona *B*

Arkansas
Arkansas State University *B*
University of Arkansas *B, M*

California
California Baptist University *B*
California Institute of
   Technology *M, D*
California Polytechnic State
   University: San Luis Obispo *B, M*
California State Polytechnic
   University: Pomona *B, M*

California State University
   Chico *B*
   Fresno *B, M*
   Fullerton *B, M*
   Long Beach *B, M*
   Los Angeles *B, M*
   Northridge *B, M*
   Sacramento *B, M*
Loyola Marymount University *B, M*
San Diego State University *B, M*
San Francisco State University *B*
San Jose State University *B, M*
Santa Clara University *B, M*
Stanford University *B, M, D*
University of California
   Berkeley *B, M, D*
   Davis *B*
   Irvine *B, M, D*
   Los Angeles *B, M, D*
University of Southern
      California *B, M, D*
University of the Pacific *B*

Colorado

Colorado School of Mines *B, M, D*
Colorado State University *B, M, D*
United States Air Force Academy *B*
University of Colorado
   Boulder *B, M, D*
   Denver *B, M, D*

Connecticut

Central Connecticut State
      University *B*
Quinnipiac University *B*
United States Coast Guard
      Academy *B*
University of Connecticut *B, M, D*
University of Hartford *B, M*
University of New Haven *B*

Delaware

Delaware State University *B*
University of Delaware *B, M, D*

District of Columbia

Catholic University of
      America *B, M, D*
George Washington
      University *B, M, D*
Howard University *B, M*
University of the District of
      Columbia *B*

Florida

Broward College *A*
Edison State College *A*
Embry-Riddle Aeronautical
      University *B*
Florida Agricultural and Mechanical
      University *B, M, D*
Florida Atlantic University *B, M*
Florida Gulf Coast University *B*
Florida Institute of
      Technology *B, M, D*
Florida International
      University *B, M, D*
Florida State College at
      Jacksonville *A*
Florida State University *B, M, D*
Miami Dade College *A*
Pensacola State College *A*
State College of Florida, Manatee-
      Sarasota *A*
Tallahassee Community College *A*
University of Central Florida *B, M, D*
University of Florida *B, M, D*
University of Miami *B, M, D*
University of North Florida *B, M*
University of South Florida *B, M, D*

Georgia

Georgia Institute of
      Technology *B, M, D*

Georgia Southern University *B*
Middle Georgia State College *A*
Southern Polytechnic State
      University *B*
University of Georgia *B*

Hawaii

University of Hawaii
   Manoa *B, M, D*

Idaho

Boise State University *B, M*
College of Southern Idaho *A*
Idaho State University *B, M*
North Idaho College *A*
Northwest Nazarene University *B*
University of Idaho *B, M, D*

Illinois

Bradley University *B, M*
Illinois Institute of
      Technology *B, M, D*
Lake Land College *A*
Northwestern University *B, M, D*
Southern Illinois University
      Carbondale *B, M*
Southern Illinois University
      Edwardsville *B, M*
University of Illinois
   Chicago *B, M, D*
   Urbana-Champaign *B, M, D*

Indiana

Grace College *B*
Indiana University
   Purdue University Fort Wayne *B*
Purdue University *B, M, D*
Purdue University
   Calumet *B*
Rose-Hulman Institute of
      Technology *B, M*
Trine University *B, M*
University of Evansville *B*
University of Notre Dame *B, M, D*
Valparaiso University *B*
Vincennes University *A*

Iowa

Dordt College *B*
Iowa State University *B, M, D*
University of Iowa *B, M, D*

Kansas

Independence Community College *A*
Kansas State University *B, M, D*
University of Kansas *B, M, D*

Kentucky

Hopkinsville Community College *A*
University of Kentucky *B, M, D*
University of Louisville *B, M, D*
Western Kentucky University *B*

Louisiana

Louisiana State University and
      Agricultural and Mechanical
      College *B, M, D*
Louisiana Tech University *B*
Southern University and Agricultural
      and Mechanical College *B*
University of Louisiana at
      Lafayette *B, M*
University of New Orleans *B*

Maine

University of Maine *B, M, D*

Maryland

Johns Hopkins University *B, M, D*
Montgomery College *A*
Morgan State University *B, M*
University of Maryland
   Baltimore County *M, D*
   College Park *B, M, D*

Massachusetts

Massachusetts Institute of
      Technology *B, M, D*
Merrimack College *B*
Northeastern University *B, M, D*
Smith College *B*
Tufts University *B, M, D*
University of Massachusetts
   Amherst *B, M, D*
   Dartmouth *B, M*
   Lowell *B, M*
Wentworth Institute of Technology *B*
Western New England University *B*
Worcester Polytechnic
      Institute *B, M, D*

Michigan

Calvin College *B*
Lawrence Technological
      University *B, M, D*
Michigan State University *B, M, D*
Michigan Technological
      University *B, M, D*
University of Detroit Mercy *B, M, D*
University of Michigan *B, M, D*
Wayne State University *B, M, D*
Western Michigan University *B, M*

Minnesota

Minnesota State University
   Mankato *B*
University of Minnesota
   Duluth *B, M*
   Twin Cities *B, M, D*

Mississippi

Jackson State University *B*
Mississippi State University *B, M*
University of Mississippi *B*

Missouri

Missouri University of Science and
      Technology *B, M, D*
St. Charles Community College *A*
Saint Louis University *B*
University of Missouri
   Columbia *B, M, D*
   Kansas City *B, M*
   St. Louis *B*

Montana

Carroll College *B*
Montana State University *B, M*

Nebraska

University of Nebraska
   Lincoln *B, M, D*

Nevada

University of Nevada
   Las Vegas *B, M, D*
   Reno *B, M, D*

New Hampshire

New England College *B*
University of New
      Hampshire *B, M, D*

New Jersey

College of New Jersey *B*
Essex County College *A*
Middlesex County College *A*
New Jersey Institute of
      Technology *B, M, D*
Princeton University *B, M, D*
Rowan University *B, M*
Rutgers, The State University of New
      Jersey
   New Brunswick/Piscataway
      Campus *B, M, D*
Stevens Institute of
      Technology *B, M, D*

New Mexico

New Mexico Institute of Mining and
      Technology *B*
New Mexico State University *B, M*
University of New Mexico *B, M*

New York

City University of New York
   City College *B, M, D*
   LaGuardia Community College *A*
Clarkson University *B, M, D*
Columbia University *B, M, D*
Cooper Union for the Advancement
      of Science and Art *B, M*
Cornell University *B, M, D*
Hofstra University *B*
Manhattan College *B, M*
New York University *B*
Rensselaer Polytechnic
      Institute *B, M, D*
SUNY
   University at Buffalo *B, M, D*
   University at Stony Brook *B*
Syracuse University *B, M, D*
United States Military Academy *B*

North Carolina

Central Carolina Community
      College *A*
Duke University *B, M, D*
North Carolina Agricultural and
      Technical State University *B, M*
North Carolina State
      University *B, M, D*
University of North Carolina
      Charlotte *B, M*
Western Piedmont Community
      College *A*

North Dakota

North Dakota State
      University *B, M, D*
University of North Dakota *B, M*

Ohio

Belmont College *A*
Case Western Reserve
      University *B, M, D*
Cleveland State University *B, M, D*
Ohio Northern University *B*
Ohio State University
   Columbus Campus *B, M, D*
Ohio University *B, M, D*
Stark State College *A*
University of Akron *B, M, D*
University of Cincinnati *B, M, D*
University of Dayton *B, M*
University of Mount Union *B*
University of Toledo *B, M*
Wilberforce University *B*
Youngstown State University *B, M*

Oklahoma

Oklahoma State University *B, M, D*
University of Oklahoma *B, M, D*

Oregon

George Fox University *B*
Oregon Institute of Technology *B*
Oregon State University *B, M, D*
Portland State University *B, M, D*
University of Portland *B, M*

Pennsylvania

Bucknell University *B, M*
Carnegie Mellon University *B, M, D*
Drexel University *B, M, D*
Lafayette College *B*
Lehigh University *B, M, D*
Penn State
   Abington *B*
   Altoona *B*
   Beaver *B*
   Berks *B*

Brandywine *B*
DuBois *B*
Erie, The Behrend College *B*
Fayette, The Eberly Campus *B*
Greater Allegheny *B*
Harrisburg *B*
Hazleton *B*
Lehigh Valley *B*
Mont Alto *B*
New Kensington *B*
Schuylkill *B*
Shenango *B*
University Park *C, B, M, D*
Wilkes-Barre *B*
Worthington Scranton *B*
York *B*
Temple University *B, M*
University of Pittsburgh *B, M, D*
University of Pittsburgh
  Bradford *B*
Villanova University *B, M*
Widener University *B, M*

Puerto Rico

Caribbean University *B*
Turabo University *B*
Universidad Politecnica de Puerto
  Rico *B, M*
University of Puerto Rico
  Mayaguez *B, M, D*
  Ponce *A*

Rhode Island

Brown University *B*
University of Rhode Island *B, M, D*

South Carolina

Citadel *B*
Clemson University *B, M, D*
University of South Carolina
  Columbia *B, M, D*

South Dakota

South Dakota School of Mines and
  Technology *B, M*
South Dakota State University *B, M*

Tennessee

Christian Brothers University *B*
Tennessee State University *B*
Tennessee Technological
  University *B, M, D*
University of Memphis *B, M*
University of Tennessee
  Chattanooga *B*
  Knoxville *B, M, D*
Vanderbilt University *B, M, D*

Texas

Kilgore College *A*
Lamar University *B, M*
Northeast Texas Community
  College *A*
Palo Alto College *A*
Prairie View A&M University *B*
Rice University *B, M, D*
Southern Methodist
  University *B, M, D*
Texas A&M University *B, M, D*
Texas A&M University
  Kingsville *B, M*
Texas Tech University *B, M, D*
University of Houston *B, M, D*
University of Texas
  Arlington *B, M, D*
  Austin *B, M, D*
  El Paso *B, M, D*
  Pan American *B*
  San Antonio *B, M*
  Tyler *B, M*
West Texas A&M University *B*

Utah

Brigham Young University *B, M, D*
University of Utah *B, M, D*
Utah State University *A, B, M, D*

Vermont

Norwich University *B, M*
University of Vermont *B, M, D*

Virginia

George Mason University *B, M, D*
J. Sargeant Reynolds Community
  College *A*
Lord Fairfax Community College *A*
Northern Virginia Community
  College *A*
Old Dominion University *B*
University of Virginia *B, M, D*
Virginia Military Institute *B*
Virginia Polytechnic Institute and
  State University *B, M, D*

Washington

Gonzaga University *B*
Saint Martin's University *B, M*
Seattle University *B*
Shoreline Community College *A*
University of Washington *B, M, D*
Walla Walla University *B*
Washington State University *B, M, D*

West Virginia

Potomac State College of West
  Virginia University *A*
West Virginia University *B, M, D*
West Virginia University Institute of
  Technology *B*

Wisconsin

Chippewa Valley Technical College *A*
Marquette University *B, M, D*
Milwaukee School of
  Engineering *B, M*
University of Wisconsin
  Madison *B, M, D*
  Milwaukee *B*
  Platteville *B*

Wyoming

University of Wyoming *B, M, D*

Civil engineering drafting/CAD/CADD

Alabama

Gadsden State Community
  College *C, A*

Alaska

University of Alaska
  Anchorage *C*

California

Santa Rosa Junior College *C*
Sierra College *C, A*

Colorado

Colorado Northwestern Community
  College *C*

Delaware

Delaware Technical Community
  College
  Stanton/Wilmington Campus *A*

Kentucky

Somerset Community College *C*

Ohio

Central Ohio Technical College *A*
Columbus State Community
  College *C*

Texas

Tyler Junior College *C, A*

Utah

Salt Lake Community College *A*
Southern Utah University *C*

Washington

Bates Technical College *C, A*
Lake Washington Institute of
  Technology *C*
North Seattle Community
  College *C, A*
Olympic College *C*

West Virginia

Bridgemont Community and
  Technical College *A*

Wisconsin

Herzing University
  Madison *A, B*

Civil engineering technology

Alabama

Bishop State Community College *A*
Gadsden State Community
  College *C, A*

Arizona

Arizona Western College *C*
Eastern Arizona College *A*
Penn Foster College *A*
Phoenix College *C, A*

California

Allan Hancock College *A*
Butte College *C, A*
California State University
  Long Beach *B*
Chabot College *A*
Santa Rosa Junior College *C, A*
Shasta College *C, A*
University of the Pacific *B*

Colorado

Arapahoe Community College *C*
Colorado Northwestern Community
  College *C, A*
Colorado State University
  Pueblo *B*
Metropolitan State University of
  Denver *B*
Pueblo Community College *C, A*
Trinidad State Junior College *C, A*

Connecticut

Central Connecticut State
  University *B*
Three Rivers Community College *A*

Delaware

Delaware State University *B*
Delaware Technical Community
  College
  Jack F. Owens Campus *A*
  Stanton/Wilmington Campus *C*
  Terry Campus *C, A*

Florida

Broward College *A*
Florida State College at
  Jacksonville *A*
Gulf Coast State College *A*
Indian River State College *A*
Miami Dade College *A*
Pensacola State College *A*
State College of Florida, Manatee-
  Sarasota *A*

Tallahassee Community College *A*
Valencia College *A*

Georgia

Middle Georgia State College *A*
Savannah State University *B*
Southern Polytechnic State
  University *B*

Idaho

Idaho State University *C, A, B*

Illinois

College of Lake County *C, A*
Morrison Institute of Technology *A*

Indiana

Indiana University
  Purdue University Fort Wayne *A*
Purdue University
  Calumet *C*

Iowa

Des Moines Area Community
  College *A*
Hawkeye Community College *A*
Iowa Western Community College *A*

Kansas

Independence Community College *A*
Johnson County Community
  College *A*

Kentucky

Bluegrass Community and Technical
  College *A*
Murray State University *A, B*

Louisiana

Baton Rouge Community College *C*
Delgado Community College *A*
Louisiana Tech University *B*

Maine

Central Maine Community College *A*
University of Maine *B*

Maryland

Community College of Baltimore
  County *C*
Montgomery College *A*
University of Maryland
  Eastern Shore *B*

Massachusetts

Northern Essex Community
  College *C*
Springfield Technical Community
  College *A*
University of Massachusetts
  Lowell *A, B*

Michigan

Ferris State University *A*
Lansing Community College *C, A*
Macomb Community College *C, A*

Minnesota

Dakota County Technical College *A*
Dunwoody College of
  Technology *C, A*
Lake Superior College *C, A*
Minnesota State Community and
  Technical College *A*
North Hennepin Community
  College *C*
St. Cloud Technical and Community
  College *C, A*
South Central College *A*

Mississippi

Northeast Mississippi Community
  College *A*

Northwest Mississippi Community
College *C, A*

Missouri

Lincoln University *B*
Linn State Technical College *A*
Mineral Area College *A*
Three Rivers Community College *A*

Montana

Montana State University
Northern *A, B*
Montana Tech of the University of
Montana *A*

Nebraska

Metropolitan Community
College *C, A*
Southeast Community College *A*

New Hampshire

NHTI-Concord's Community
College *A*
University of New Hampshire *A*

New Jersey

Burlington County College *A*
Essex County College *A*
Fairleigh Dickinson University
Metropolitan Campus *B*
Gloucester County College *C, A*
Middlesex County College *A*
Union County College *A*

New York

Broome Community College *A*
City University of New York
New York City College of
Technology *C, A*
Erie Community College *A*
Hudson Valley Community College *A*
Mohawk Valley Community
College *A*
Monroe Community College *C, A*
Nassau Community College *A*
Rochester Institute of Technology *B*
SUNY
College of Technology at
Canton *A, B*
Institute of Technology at Utica/
Rome *B*
Technical Career Institutes *A*
United States Military Academy *B*
Westchester Community College *A*

North Carolina

Asheville-Buncombe Technical
Community College *A*
Central Piedmont Community
College *C, A*
Fayetteville Technical Community
College *A*
Gaston College *C, A*
Guilford Technical Community
College *C, A*
Sandhills Community College *A*
University of North Carolina
Charlotte *B*
Wake Technical Community
College *A*

North Dakota

North Dakota State College of
Science *A*

Ohio

Central Ohio Technical College *A*
Cincinnati State Technical and
Community College *C, A*
Columbus State Community
College *A*
James A. Rhodes State College *C, A*
Lakeland Community College *A*

Owens Community College
Toledo *C*
Sinclair Community College *A*
Stark State College *A*
University of Toledo *C, B*
Youngstown State University *A, B*

Oklahoma

Oklahoma State University
Institute of Technology:
Okmulgee *B*
Oklahoma City *A*
Tulsa Community College *C, A*

Oregon

Blue Mountain Community
College *C, A*
Chemeketa Community College *A*
Linn-Benton Community College *C*
Mt. Hood Community College *A*
Portland Community College *C, A*
Umpqua Community College *A*

Pennsylvania

Butler County Community College *A*
Community College of Allegheny
County *A*
Harrisburg Area Community
College *C, A*
Pennsylvania College of
Technology *A, B*
Pennsylvania Institute of
Technology *A*
Point Park University *A, B*
Temple University *B*
University of Pittsburgh
Johnstown *B*

Puerto Rico

University of Puerto Rico
Bayamon University College *A*
Ponce *A*

South Carolina

Florence-Darlington Technical
College *A*
Horry-Georgetown Technical
College *A*
Midlands Technical College *A*
South Carolina State University *B*
Technical College of the
Lowcountry *C, A*
Trident Technical College *A*

South Dakota

Southeast Technical Institute *A*

Tennessee

Chattanooga State Community
College *A*
Nashville State Community College *A*
Pellissippi State Community
College *A*

Texas

Kilgore College *A*
Laredo Community College *A*
San Antonio College *C, A*
Texas Southern University *B*
University of Houston
Downtown *B*

Vermont

Vermont Technical College *A*

Virginia

Central Virginia Community
College *A*
J. Sargeant Reynolds Community
College *C*
John Tyler Community College *C*
Northern Virginia Community
College *C, A*

Tidewater Community College *A*
Virginia Western Community
College *A*

Washington

Bates Technical College *C, A*
Bellingham Technical College *A*
Centralia College *A*
Shoreline Community College *A*
South Seattle Community College *A*
Spokane Community College *A*
Walla Walla Community College *C, A*
Yakima Valley Community College *C*

West Virginia

Bluefield State College *A, B*
Bridgemont Community and
Technical College *A*
Fairmont State University *A, B*
West Virginia University Institute of
Technology *B*

Wisconsin

Chippewa Valley Technical College *A*
Gateway Technical College *A*
Herzing University
Madison *A, B*
Madison Area Technical College *A*
Milwaukee Area Technical College *A*
Moraine Park Technical College *A*
Northeast Wisconsin Technical
College *A*

Classical/ancient Mediterranean/Near Eastern studies

California

University of California
Berkeley *B, M, D*
Davis *B*
Irvine *B*
Los Angeles *B*

Georgia

Emory University *B*

Illinois

University of Chicago *M, T*
University of Illinois
Chicago *B*

Kansas

Wichita State University *B*

Maine

Bowdoin College *B*

Massachusetts

Harvard College *B, D*
Wellesley College *B*

Michigan

Calvin College *B*
Michigan State University *B*
University of Michigan *B*

Minnesota

University of St. Thomas *B*

New Hampshire

Dartmouth College *B*

New York

Columbia University *B*
Syracuse University *B*

Pennsylvania

Bryn Mawr College *B, M, D*
Lycoming College *B*

Texas

Rice University *B*

Virginia

Randolph-Macon College *B*
University of Richmond *B*

Wisconsin

University of Wisconsin
Milwaukee *C*

Classics

Alabama

Samford University *B*

Arizona

University of Arizona *B, M*

Arkansas

Hendrix College *B*
University of Arkansas *B*

California

California State University
Long Beach *B*
Claremont McKenna College *B*
Loyola Marymount University *B*
Pitzer College *B*
Pomona College *B*
St. Mary's College of California *B*
San Diego State University *B*
San Francisco State University *B, M*
Santa Clara University *B*
Scripps College *B*
Stanford University *B, M, D*
University of California
Berkeley *B, M, D*
Irvine *B, M, D*
Los Angeles *M, D*
Riverside *B, M, D*
San Diego *B*
Santa Barbara *B, M, D*
Santa Cruz *B*
University of Southern
California *B, M, D*

Colorado

Colorado College *B*
University of Colorado
Boulder *B, M, D*

Connecticut

Connecticut College *B*
Trinity College *B*
University of Connecticut *B*
Wesleyan University *B*
Yale University *B, M, D*

Delaware

University of Delaware *B*

District of Columbia

Catholic University of America *B, M*
George Washington University *B*
Georgetown University *B*
Howard University *B*

Florida

Ave Maria University *B*
Florida State University *D*
New College of Florida *B*
Rollins College *B*
University of Florida *B, M, D*
University of Miami *B*
University of South Florida *B, M*

Georgia

Agnes Scott College *B*
Emory University *B*
Mercer University *B*
University of Georgia *B, M*

Hawaii

University of Hawaii
  Manoa *B*

Illinois

Augustana College *B*
Illinois Wesleyan University *B*
Knox College *B*
Loyola University Chicago *B, M, D*
Monmouth College *B, T*
North Central College *B*
Northwestern University *B, M, D*
Rockford University *B*
Southern Illinois University
  Carbondale *B*
University of Chicago *B, D*
University of Illinois
  Chicago *B*
  Urbana-Champaign *B, M*
Wheaton College *B*

Indiana

Ball State University *B, T*
DePauw University *B*
Earlham College *B*
Hanover College *B*
Indiana University
  Bloomington *B, M, D*
Purdue University *B*
University of Evansville *B*
University of Notre Dame *B*
Valparaiso University *B*
Wabash College *B*

Iowa

Coe College *B*
Cornell College *B*
Grinnell College *B*
Luther College *B*
University of Iowa *B, M, D*

Kansas

University of Kansas *B, M*

Kentucky

Asbury University *B, T*
Centre College *B*
Transylvania University *B*
University of Kentucky *B, M*

Louisiana

Tulane University *B, M*

Maine

Bowdoin College *B*
Colby College *B*
University of Southern Maine *B*

Maryland

Johns Hopkins University *B, M, D*
Loyola University Maryland *B*
Notre Dame of Maryland
  University *B*
University of Maryland
  College Park *B, M*

Massachusetts

Amherst College *B*
Assumption College *B*
Bard College at Simon's Rock *B*
Boston College *B*
Boston University *B, M, D*
Brandeis University *B, M*
Clark University *B*
College of the Holy Cross *B*
Harvard College *B, M, D*
Mount Holyoke College *B*
Smith College *B*
Tufts University *B, M*
University of Massachusetts
  Amherst *B, M*
  Boston *B, M*
Wellesley College *B*

Wheaton College *B*
Williams College *B*

Michigan

Calvin College *B*
Grand Valley State University *B*
Hillsdale College *B*
Hope College *B*
Kalamazoo College *B*
University of Michigan *B, D*
Wayne State University *B, M*

Minnesota

Carleton College *B*
College of St. Benedict *B*
Concordia College: Moorhead *B*
Gustavus Adolphus College *B*
Macalester College *B*
St. John's University *B*
St. Olaf College *B*
University of Minnesota
  Twin Cities *B, M, D*
University of St. Thomas *B*

Mississippi

East Mississippi Community
  College *A*
Millsaps College *B*
University of Mississippi *B*

Missouri

Truman State University *B*
University of Missouri
  Columbia *B, M, D*
Washington University in St.
  Louis *B, M*

Montana

Carroll College *B*
University of Montana *B*

Nebraska

Creighton University *B*
University of Nebraska
  Lincoln *M*

New Hampshire

Dartmouth College *B*
Saint Anselm College *B*
University of New Hampshire *B*

New Jersey

Drew University *B*
Montclair State University *B*
Princeton University *B, M, D*
Rutgers, The State University of New
  Jersey
  New Brunswick/Piscataway
    Campus *B, M, D*
Saint Peter's University *B*
Seton Hall University *B*

New Mexico

University of New Mexico *B*

New York

Barnard College *B*
Canisius College *B*
City University of New York
  Brooklyn College *B*
  Hunter College *B*
Colgate University *B*
College of New Rochelle *B, T*
Columbia University *B*
Columbia University
  School of General Studies *B*
Cornell University *B, M, D*
Fordham University *B, M, D*
Hamilton College *B*
Hobart and William Smith Colleges *B*
Hofstra University *B*
New York University *B, M, D*

SUNY

University at Binghamton *B*
University at Buffalo *B, M, D*
Saint Bonaventure University *B*
Siena College *B*
Skidmore College *B*
Syracuse University *B*
Union College *B*
University of Rochester *B*

North Carolina

Davidson College *B*
Duke University *B, M, D*
University of North Carolina
  Asheville *B, T*
  Chapel Hill *B, M, D*
  Greensboro *B*
Wake Forest University *B*

North Dakota

North Dakota State University *B*
University of North Dakota *B*

Ohio

Bowling Green State University *B*
Case Western Reserve University *B*
College of Wooster *B*
Denison University *B*
Franciscan University of
  Steubenville *B*
Hiram College *B*
Kenyon College *B*
Miami University
  Oxford *B*
Oberlin College *B*
Ohio University *B*
Ohio Wesleyan University *B*
University of Akron *B*
University of Cincinnati *B, M, D*
Wright State University *B, M, D, T*
Xavier University *B*

Oklahoma

University of Oklahoma *B*

Oregon

Lewis & Clark College *B*
Reed College *B*
University of Oregon *B, M*
Willamette University *B*

Pennsylvania

Bryn Mawr College *B, M, D*
Bucknell University *B*
Carnegie Mellon University *B*
Dickinson College *B*
Duquesne University *B*
Franklin & Marshall College *B*
Gettysburg College *B*
Haverford College *B*
La Salle University *B*
Lehigh University *B*
Moravian College *B*
Penn State
  Abington *B*
  Altoona *B*
  Beaver *B*
  Berks *B*
  Brandywine *B*
  DuBois *B*
  Erie, The Behrend College *B*
  Fayette, The Eberly Campus *B*
  Greater Allegheny *B*
  Harrisburg *B*
  Hazleton *B*
  Lehigh Valley *B*
  Mont Alto *B*
  New Kensington *B*
  Schuylkill *B*
  Shenango *B*
  University Park *B*
  Wilkes-Barre *B*
  Worthington Scranton *B*
  York *B*

Swarthmore College *B*
Temple University *B*
University of Pennsylvania *B, M, D*
University of Pittsburgh *B, M, D*
University of Scranton *B*
Ursinus College *B, T*
Villanova University *B, M*
Westminster College *B*

Rhode Island

Brown University *B, M, D*
University of Rhode Island *B*

South Carolina

College of Charleston *B, T*
University of South Carolina
  Columbia *B*

Tennessee

Belmont University *B*
Rhodes College *B*
Sewanee: The University of the
  South *B*
University of Tennessee
  Knoxville *B*
Vanderbilt University *B, M*

Texas

Austin College *B*
Baylor University *B*
Rice University *B*
Southwestern University *B, T*
Texas A&M University *B*
Texas Tech University *B, M*
Trinity University *B*
University of Dallas *B*
University of St. Thomas *M*
University of Texas
  Austin *B, M, D*
  San Antonio *B*

Utah

Brigham Young University *B*
University of Utah *B*

Vermont

Middlebury College *B*
Saint Michael's College *B*
University of Vermont *B, M*

Virginia

Christendom College *B*
Christopher Newport University *B*
College of William and Mary *B*
Hampden-Sydney College *B*
Hollins University *B*
Randolph College *B*
Randolph-Macon College *B*
Sweet Briar College *B*
University of Mary Washington *B*
University of Virginia *B, M, D*
Washington and Lee University *B*

Washington

Evergreen State College *B*
Pacific Lutheran University *B*
Seattle Pacific University *B*
University of Puget Sound *B*
University of Washington *B, M, D*
Whitman College *B*

Wisconsin

Beloit College *B*
Carthage College *B*
Lawrence University *B*
Marquette University *B*
Ripon College *B*
University of Wisconsin
  Madison *B, M, D*
  Milwaukee *B*

Climatology

California

Shasta College *A*

New Jersey

Rutgers, The State University of New Jersey
  New Brunswick/Piscataway Campus *B*

Vermont

Lyndon State College *B*

Clinical child psychology

Kansas

University of Kansas *M, D*

New York

Pace University *D*
Pace University: Pleasantville/ Briarcliff *M*
St. John's University *D*

Ohio

Case Western Reserve University *D*

Texas

Prairie View A&M University *D*

Clinical laboratory science

Alabama

Auburn University *B*
Central Alabama Community College *A*
Faulkner State Community College *A*
Oakwood University *B*
Tuskegee University *B, M*
University of Alabama Birmingham *B, M*

Alaska

University of Alaska Anchorage *B*

Arizona

DeVry University Phoenix *B*
GateWay Community College *A*
Grand Canyon University *B*

Arkansas

Arkansas State University *A, B*
Arkansas Tech University *B*
Bryan University Rogers *A*
Harding University *B*
Henderson State University *B*
Southern Arkansas University *B, M*
University of Arkansas for Medical Sciences *B*
University of Central Arkansas *B*

California

California State University Dominguez Hills *B*
City College of San Francisco *A*
Fullerton College *A*
Loma Linda University *B*
National University *B*
University of California Davis *M*

Colorado

Colorado State University *M, D*

Connecticut

University of Bridgeport *B*
University of Connecticut *B*
University of Hartford *B*
Western Connecticut State University *B*

Delaware

University of Delaware *B*
Wesley College *B*

District of Columbia

Catholic University of America *B*
Howard University *B*

Florida

Barry University *B*
Bethune-Cookman University *B*
Florida Gulf Coast University *B*
Florida Memorial University *B*
Saint Leo University *B*
Santa Fe College *B*
University of Central Florida *B*
University of South Florida *B*
University of West Florida *B*

Georgia

Armstrong Atlantic State University *B*
Dalton State College *A*
Darton College *A*
Georgia Regents University *B, M*

Hawaii

University of Hawaii Manoa *B*

Idaho

College of Idaho *B*
Idaho State University *B, M*
University of Idaho *B*

Illinois

Aurora University *B*
Benedictine University *B*
Blackburn College *B*
Bradley University *B*
DePaul University *B*
DeVry University Chicago *B*
Eastern Illinois University *B*
Illinois State University *B*
Loyola University Chicago *B*
National-Louis University *B*
North Park University *B*
Northern Illinois University *B*
Quincy University *B*
Roosevelt University *B*
Rush University *B, M*
University of Illinois Springfield *B*
University of St. Francis *B*
Western Illinois University *B*

Indiana

Ball State University *B*
Harrison College Indianapolis *A*
Indiana State University *B*
Indiana University East *C*
  Purdue University Fort Wayne *B*
  Purdue University Indianapolis *C, B*
  Southeast *B*
Manchester University *B*
Purdue University *B*
Purdue University Calumet *B*
Saint Joseph's College *B*
St. Mary-of-the-Woods College *B*
University of Evansville *B*
University of Indianapolis *B*
University of St. Francis *B*

Iowa

Allen College *B*
Briar Cliff University *B*
Dordt College *B*
Mercy College of Health Sciences *C*
Morningside College *B*
Mount Mercy University *B*
Northwestern College *B*
University of Iowa *B*
Wartburg College *B*

Kansas

Pittsburg State University *B*
University of Kansas Medical Center *B*
Washburn University *B*
Wichita State University *B*

Kentucky

Bellarmine University *B*
Brescia University *B*
Eastern Kentucky University *B*
Madisonville Community College *A*
Thomas More College *B*
University of Kentucky *B, M, D*
Western Kentucky University *B*

Louisiana

Louisiana State University Alexandria *A*
  Health Sciences Center *B*
Louisiana Tech University *B*
McNeese State University *B*
Our Lady of the Lake College *A, B*
University of Louisiana at Monroe *B*

Maine

University of Maine *B, M*

Maryland

Salisbury University *B*
Stevenson University *B*
University of Maryland Baltimore *B, M*

Massachusetts

Northeastern University *B*
Salem State University *B*
University of Massachusetts Dartmouth *B*

Michigan

Andrews University *B, M*
Baker College Allen Park *A*
Central Michigan University *B*
Delta College *A*
Eastern Michigan University *B*
Ferris State University *A, B*
Gogebic Community College *A*
Grand Rapids Community College *A*
Grand Valley State University *B*
Lake Superior State University *B*
Madonna University *B*
Michigan State University *B, M*
Michigan Technological University *B*
Northern Michigan University *A, B*
Oakland University *B*
Saginaw Valley State University *B*
University of Michigan Flint *B*
Wayne State University *B*

Minnesota

Argosy University Twin Cities *B*
Augsburg College *B*
Bemidji State University *B*
Minnesota State University Moorhead *B*
St. Catherine University *A*
Saint Cloud State University *B*
St. Mary's University of Minnesota *B*

University of Minnesota Twin Cities *B, M*
Winona State University *B*

Mississippi

Blue Mountain College *B*
Coahoma Community College *A*
Copiah-Lincoln Community College *A*
East Mississippi Community College *A*
Hinds Community College *A*
Mississippi Gulf Coast Community College *A*
Mississippi State University *B*
University of Mississippi *B*
University of Mississippi Medical Center *B*
University of Southern Mississippi *B, M*

Missouri

Lincoln University *B*
Maryville University of Saint Louis *B*
Missouri State University *B*
Northwest Missouri State University *B*
Rockhurst University *B*
St. Louis Community College *A*
Saint Louis University *B*
Southeast Missouri State University *B*
Southwest Baptist University *B*
University of Missouri Kansas City *B*

Montana

University of Montana *B*

Nebraska

Union College *B*
University of Nebraska Medical Center *B*

Nevada

University of Nevada Las Vegas *B*

New Jersey

Caldwell College *B*
College of St. Elizabeth *B*
Fairleigh Dickinson University College at Florham *B*
  Metropolitan Campus *B, M*
Felician College *A*
Georgian Court University *B*
Kean University *B*
Monmouth University *B*
New Jersey City University *B*
Ramapo College of New Jersey *B*
Rutgers, The State University of New Jersey
  Camden Campus *B*
  Newark Campus *B*
Saint Peter's University *B*
Thomas Edison State College *A, B*

New Mexico

Eastern New Mexico University *B*
University of New Mexico *M*

New York

Albany College of Pharmacy and Health Sciences *B, M*
Canisius College *B*
City University of New York College of Staten Island *B*
  Hunter College *B*
  York College *B*
College of Saint Rose *B*
Elmira College *B*
Hartwick College *B*
Hudson Valley Community College *A*
Keuka College *B, M*

Long Island University
  LIU Brooklyn *B*
  LIU Post *B, M*
Marist College *B*
Mercy College *B*
Mount Saint Mary College *B*
Orange County Community
  College *A*
Pace University: Pleasantville/
  Briarcliff *B*
Rochester Institute of Technology *M*
SUNY
  College at Plattsburgh *B*
  University at Buffalo *B*
  University at Stony Brook *B*
  Upstate Medical University *B, M*
St. Francis College *B*
St. John's University *B*
St. Joseph's College New York:
  Suffolk Campus *B*
St. Joseph's College, New York *B*
Suffolk County Community College *A*

North Carolina

College of the Albemarle *A*
East Carolina University *B*
Lenoir-Rhyne University *B*
Southwestern Community College *A*
University of North Carolina
  Chapel Hill *B, M*
  Charlotte *B*
  Greensboro *B*
Wake Forest University *B*
Western Carolina University *B*
Winston-Salem State University *B*

North Dakota

Mayville State University *B*
Minot State University *B*
North Dakota State University *B*
University of Jamestown *B*
University of Mary *B*
University of North Dakota *B, M*

Ohio

Bowling Green State University *B*
Cedarville University *B*
Kent State University *B*
Malone University *B*
Miami University
  Oxford *B*
Mount Vernon Nazarene University *B*
Ohio Northern University *B*
Ohio State University
  Columbus Campus *C, B*
Shawnee State University *A*
University of Cincinnati *C, B*
University of Mount Union *B*
Wright State University *B*
Xavier University *B*
Youngstown State University *B*

Oklahoma

Cameron University *B*
East Central University *B*
Northeastern State University *B*
Oklahoma Christian University *B*
Oral Roberts University *B*
University of Central Oklahoma *B*

Oregon

Oregon Health & Science
  University *B*
Oregon Institute of Technology *B*

Pennsylvania

Bloomsburg University of
  Pennsylvania *B*
Cheyney University of
  Pennsylvania *B*
DeSales University *B*
East Stroudsburg University of
  Pennsylvania *B*
Gannon University *B*

Holy Family University *B*
Indiana University of Pennsylvania *B*
King's College *B*
Lebanon Valley College *B*
Mansfield University of
  Pennsylvania *B*
Marywood University *B*
Misericordia University *B*
Reading Area Community College *A*
Seton Hill University *B*
Thomas Jefferson University *B, M*
University of Scranton *B*
University of the Sciences *B*
Wilkes University *B*
York College of Pennsylvania *B*

Puerto Rico

Inter American University of Puerto
  Rico
  Metropolitan Campus *B, M*
  San German Campus *B*
Pontifical Catholic University of
  Puerto Rico *B*
University of Puerto Rico
  Medical Sciences *B, M*

Rhode Island

Rhode Island College *B*
Salve Regina University *B*
University of Rhode Island *B, M*

South Carolina

Coker College *B*
Winthrop University *B*

South Dakota

Augustana College *B*
Mount Marty College *B*
Northern State University *B*
South Dakota State University *B*
University of South Dakota *M*

Tennessee

Austin Peay State University *B*
Belmont University *B*
King University *B*
Lincoln Memorial University *B*
Southern Adventist University *B*
Tusculum College *B*
Union University *B*
University of Tennessee
  Knoxville *B*

Texas

Amarillo College *A*
Angelo State University *B*
Baylor University *B*
Grayson College *A*
Lamar University *B*
Midwestern State University *B*
Odessa College *A*
Prairie View A&M University *B*
St. Edward's University *B*
San Jacinto College *A*
Tarleton State University *A, B*
Texas A&M University
  Corpus Christi *B*
Texas Southern University *B*
Texas State University *B*
Texas Tech University Health
  Sciences Center *B*
Texas Woman's University *B*
University of Mary Hardin-Baylor *B*
University of North Texas *B*
University of Texas
  Arlington *B*
  Austin *B*
  El Paso *B*
  Medical Branch at Galveston *B, M*
  Pan American *B*
  San Antonio *M*

Utah

Brigham Young University *B*
Snow College *A*
University of Utah *B, M*
Utah State University *B*
Weber State University *B*

Vermont

University of Vermont *B*

Virginia

Eastern Mennonite University *B*
Ferrum College *B*
George Mason University *B*
Mary Baldwin College *B*
Norfolk State University *B*
Old Dominion University *B*
University of Virginia's College at
  Wise *B*
Virginia Commonwealth
  University *B, M*

Washington

Seattle University *B*
University of Washington *B, M*

West Virginia

Concord University *B*
Marshall University *B*
West Liberty University *B*
West Virginia University *B*

Wisconsin

Carroll University *B*
Marquette University *B*
University of Wisconsin
  La Crosse *B*
  Milwaukee *B, M*
  Stevens Point *B*

Clinical/medical
laboratory assistant

Alabama

Gadsden State Community College *A*

Alaska

University of Alaska
  Anchorage *C*
  Fairbanks *A*

Arizona

Phoenix College *C*
Pima Community College *C, A*

Arkansas

South Arkansas Community
  College *C*

California

De Anza College *C*
Diablo Valley College *C, A*

Delaware

Delaware Technical Community
  College
  Jack F. Owens Campus *A*

Florida

Broward College *A*

Georgia

Southeastern Technical College *A*

Idaho

North Idaho College *A*

Illinois

Oakton Community College *A*
Southwestern Illinois College *A*

Kansas

Seward County Community
  College *A*

Kentucky

Eastern Kentucky University *B*
Madisonville Community College *C*
Somerset Community College *A*
Southeast Kentucky Community and
  Technical College *A*
Spencerian College *C*

Louisiana

Bossier Parish Community College *C*

Maine

University of Maine
  Augusta *A*

Massachusetts

Bunker Hill Community College *C*

Michigan

Baker College
  Owosso *A*
Monroe County Community
  College *C*
Northern Michigan University *C, A*

Minnesota

St. Catherine University *C*

Nevada

College of Southern Nevada *A*

New Mexico

New Mexico Junior College *A*

New York

Elmira Business Institute *C, A*
Elmira Business Institute: Vestal *C, A*
Mildred Elley
  New York City *C*

North Carolina

Alamance Community College *A*
Carolinas College of Health
  Sciences *C*
Central Piedmont Community
  College *A*
Mars Hill University *B*
South Piedmont Community
  College *C*
Stanly Community College *A*
Western Piedmont Community
  College *A*

Ohio

Columbus State Community
  College *C*
Stark State College *A*
Washington State Community
  College *A*
Youngstown State University *A*

Oklahoma

Rose State College *A*
Tulsa Community College *A*

Oregon

Clackamas Community College *C*
Rogue Community College *C*

Pennsylvania

Edinboro University of
  Pennsylvania *B*
Sanford-Brown Institute
  Pittsburgh *A*

Rhode Island

New England Institute of
  Technology *A*

South Carolina

Aiken Technical College *C*
Forrest Junior College *C, A*
Orangeburg-Calhoun Technical
    College *C, A*
Spartanburg Community College *C*

Tennessee

Miller-Motte Technical College
    Clarksville *C*
Northeast State Community
    College *A*

Texas

Central Texas College *C, A*
El Paso Community College *C*
Tyler Junior College *A*

Vermont

Community College of Vermont *C*

Virginia

Jefferson College of Health
    Sciences *C*
Northern Virginia Community
    College *A*
Virginia Highlands Community
    College *A*

Washington

Centralia College *C*
Clover Park Technical College *A*
North Seattle Community College *C*
Shoreline Community College *C, A*
Wenatchee Valley College *A*

Wisconsin

Blackhawk Technical College *C, A*
Northcentral Technical College *A*

Clinical/medical laboratory technology

Alabama

Faulkner State Community College *A*
Gadsden State Community College *A*
Jefferson State Community College *A*
Wallace State Community College at
    Hanceville *A*

Alaska

University of Alaska
    Anchorage *A*

Arizona

Brookline College
    Phoenix *A*
    Tempe *A*
    Tucson *A*
Carrington College
    Phoenix Westside *A*
    Tucson *A*
Phoenix College *A*
Pima Community College *A*

Arkansas

Arkansas State University
    Beebe *A*
National Park Community College *A*
North Arkansas College *A*
South Arkansas Community
    College *A*

California

California State University
    East Bay *B*
    Sacramento *B, M*
Chabot College *A*
Folsom Lake College *A*
Fresno City College *A*
Hartnell College *A*
La Sierra University *C*

Los Angeles Southwest College *A*
Pasadena City College *A*
Southwestern College *A*

Colorado

Arapahoe Community College *A*

Connecticut

Manchester Community College *A*

Delaware

Delaware State University *B*
University of Delaware *B*

District of Columbia

George Washington University *A, B*

Florida

Broward College *A*
Eastern Florida State College *A*
Florida State College at
    Jacksonville *A*
Indian River State College *A*
Keiser University *A*
Miami Dade College *A*
Palm Beach State College *A*
St. Petersburg College *A*

Georgia

Augusta Technical College *A*
Central Georgia Technical College *A*
College of Coastal Georgia *A*
Georgia Piedmont Technical
    College *A*
Georgia Regents University *M*
North Georgia Technical College *A*
South Georgia State College *A*
Southeastern Technical College *A*
Southwest Georgia Technical
    College *A*
Wiregrass Georgia Technical
    College *A*

Hawaii

University of Hawaii
    Kapiolani Community College *A*

Illinois

Elgin Community College *A*
Illinois Central College *A*
Illinois Eastern Community Colleges
    Lincoln Trail College *A*
    Olney Central College *A*
John A. Logan College *A*
John Wood Community College *A*
Kankakee Community College *A*
Kaskaskia College *A*
Rend Lake College *A*
Southeastern Illinois College *A*
Southwestern Illinois College *A*
Triton College *A*

Indiana

Indiana University
    Purdue University Fort Wayne *B*
Ivy Tech Community College
    North Central *A*
    South Central *A*
    Wabash Valley *A*
University of Indianapolis *B*
University of St. Francis *A*

Iowa

Des Moines Area Community
    College *A*
Dordt College *B*
Hawkeye Community College *A*
Iowa Central Community College *A*
North Iowa Area Community
    College *A*
Northeast Iowa Community
    College *A*
St. Luke's College *C*

Kansas

Barton County Community College *A*
Bryan University
    Topeka *A*
Hutchinson Community College *A*
Seward County Community
    College *A*

Kentucky

Eastern Kentucky University *A, B*
Henderson Community College *A*
Madisonville Community College *A*
Owensboro Community and
    Technical College *C*
Somerset Community College *A*
Spencerian College *A*
West Kentucky Community and
    Technical College *A*

Louisiana

Delgado Community College *A*
Louisiana College *B*
Southern University
    Shreveport *A*

Maine

University of Maine
    Presque Isle *A*

Maryland

Allegany College of Maryland *A*
Anne Arundel Community College *A*
College of Southern Maryland *A*
Community College of Baltimore
    County *A*
Howard Community College *A*

Massachusetts

Boston University *B*
Bristol Community College *A*
Mount Wachusett Community
    College *A*
Quincy College *A*
Springfield Technical Community
    College *A*

Michigan

Baker College
    Owosso *A*
    Port Huron *A*
Ferris State University *A*
Kellogg Community College *A*

Minnesota

Alexandria Technical and Community
    College *A*
Argosy University
    Twin Cities *A*
Hibbing Community College *A*
Lake Superior College *A*
Minnesota State Community and
    Technical College *A*
Minnesota West Community and
    Technical College *A*
North Hennepin Community
    College *A*
Rasmussen College
    Lake Elmo/Woodbury *A*
    Mankato *A*
    Moorhead *A*
    St. Cloud *A*
St. Paul College *A*
South Central College *A*

Mississippi

Copiah-Lincoln Community
    College *A*
Hinds Community College *A*
Meridian Community College *A*
Mississippi Delta Community
    College *A*
Mississippi Gulf Coast Community
    College *A*

Northeast Mississippi Community
    College *A*

Missouri

Evangel University *B*
Mineral Area College *A*
Missouri Southern State University *A*
Missouri Western State University *B*
Three Rivers Community College *A*

Montana

University of Montana *A*

Nebraska

Central Community College *A*
Mid-Plains Community College *A*
Southeast Community College *A*

Nevada

College of Southern Nevada *A*

New Hampshire

River Valley Community College *A*

New Jersey

Bergen Community College *A*
Brookdale Community College *A*
Camden County College *A*
County College of Morris *A*
Mercer County Community
    College *A*
Middlesex County College *A*
Rutgers, The State University of New
    Jersey
    New Brunswick/Piscataway
        Campus *A*
    Newark Campus *B*
Sussex County Community College *A*

New Mexico

Central New Mexico Community
    College *A*
New Mexico Junior College *A*
San Juan College *A*
University of New Mexico *C, B*
Western New Mexico University *B*

New York

Broome Community College *A*
City University of New York
    Bronx Community College *A*
    Hunter College *B*
    Queensborough Community
        College *A*
    York College *B*
Dutchess Community College *A*
Erie Community College *A*
Hudson Valley Community College *A*
Orange County Community
    College *A*
SUNY
    College at Brockport *B*
    College at Fredonia *B*
    Farmingdale State College *A, B*

North Carolina

Alamance Community College *A*
Asheville-Buncombe Technical
    Community College *A*
Beaufort County Community
    College *A*
Coastal Carolina Community
    College *A*
Davidson County Community
    College *A*
Halifax Community College *A*
Salem College *B*
Sandhills Community College *A*
Southeastern Community College *A*
Southwestern Community College *A*
Wake Technical Community
    College *A*
Wayne Community College *C*

North Dakota

Bismarck State College *A*

Ohio

Cincinnati State Technical and
    Community College *A*
Clark State Community College *A*
Columbus State Community
    College *A*
Cuyahoga Community College
    Metropolitan *A*
Defiance College *B*
Eastern Gateway Community
    College *A*
Edison State Community College *A*
Lakeland Community College *A*
Lorain County Community College *A*
Marion Technical College *A*
Muskingum University *B*
Stark State College *A*
University of Rio Grande *A*
Youngstown State University *A*
Zane State College *A*

Oklahoma

Northeastern Oklahoma Agricultural
    and Mechanical College *A*
Seminole State College *A*
Southern Nazarene University *B*
Southwestern Oklahoma State
    University *A, B*
Tulsa Community College *A*

Oregon

Portland Community College *A*

Pennsylvania

California University of
    Pennsylvania *B*
Clarion University of Pennsylvania *B*
Community College of Allegheny
    County *A*
Community College of
    Philadelphia *A*
Harcum College *A*
Harrisburg Area Community
    College *C, A*
Mansfield University of
    Pennsylvania *B*
Montgomery County Community
    College *A*
Mount Aloysius College *A*
Penn State
    Hazleton *A*
    Schuylkill *A*
Pennsylvania College of Health
    Sciences *C*
St. Francis University *B*
Sanford-Brown Institute
    Pittsburgh *A*
Thiel College *B*

Puerto Rico

University of Puerto Rico
    Medical Sciences *B*

Rhode Island

Community College of Rhode
    Island *A*

South Carolina

Erskine College *B*
Florence-Darlington Technical
    College *A*
Forrest Junior College *A*
Greenville Technical College *A*
Midlands Technical College *A*
Orangeburg-Calhoun Technical
    College *A*
Spartanburg Community College *A*
Tri-County Technical College *A*
Trident Technical College *A*
York Technical College *A*

South Dakota

Augustana College *B*
Lake Area Technical Institute *A*
Mitchell Technical Institute *A*
Presentation College *A*

Tennessee

Jackson State Community College *A*
Lincoln Memorial University *B*
Southwest Tennessee Community
    College *A*
Volunteer State Community
    College *A*

Texas

Amarillo College *A*
Austin Community College *C, A*
Central Texas College *A*
Del Mar College *A*
El Centro College *A*
El Paso Community College *A*
Houston Community College
    System *C, A*
Kilgore College *A*
Lamar State College at Orange *A*
Laredo Community College *A*
McLennan Community College *A*
Northeast Texas Community
    College *A*
Panola College *C, A*
St. Philip's College *A*
San Jacinto College *C, A*
Sanford-Brown College
    Houston *A*
Southwestern Adventist University *B*
Victoria College *A*

Utah

Weber State University *A, B*

Virginia

Central Virginia Community
    College *A*
J. Sargeant Reynolds Community
    College *A*
Northern Virginia Community
    College *A*
Rappahannock Community College *C*
Southside Virginia Community
    College *A*
Wytheville Community College *A*

Washington

Columbia Basin College *A*
Spokane Community College *A*
Spokane Falls Community College *A*

West Virginia

Blue Ridge Community and Technical
    College *A*
Marshall University *A*
Potomac State College of West
    Virginia University *A*
Southern West Virginia Community
    and Technical College *A*

Wisconsin

Chippewa Valley Technical College *A*
Gateway Technical College *A*
Lakeshore Technical College *A*
Madison Area Technical College *A*
Milwaukee Area Technical College *A*
Northcentral Technical College *A*
Rasmussen College
    Green Bay *A*
Southwest Wisconsin Technical
    College *A*
University of Wisconsin
    Oshkosh *B*
Viterbo University *B*
Waukesha County Technical
    College *A*
Western Technical College *A*

Wyoming

Casper College *A*

Clinical/medical social work

California

Loma Linda University *D*

Indiana

University of Southern Indiana *M*

Maine

University of Southern Maine *M*

Michigan

Michigan State University *M*

Mississippi

University of Mississippi *M*
University of Southern Mississippi *M*

Montana

Dawson Community College *A*

New Mexico

Eastern New Mexico University *B*

Puerto Rico

Inter American University of Puerto
    Rico
    Metropolitan Campus *M*
Universidad del Este *M*

South Dakota

University of South Dakota *M, D*

Wisconsin

Concordia University Wisconsin *B*

Clinical nurse leader

Alabama

Spring Hill College *M*

California

University of San Diego *M*

Connecticut

Sacred Heart University *M*
Southern Connecticut State
    University *M*

Massachusetts

Curry College *M*

Missouri

Research College of Nursing *M*

New Jersey

Seton Hall University *M*

New York

City University of New York
    Hunter College *M*
Daemen College *M*

Ohio

Cleveland State University *M*
University of Toledo *M*
Walsh University *M*
Xavier University *M*

Tennessee

Vanderbilt University *M*

Texas

Texas Christian University *M*
University of Texas
    Medical Branch at Galveston *M*
University of the Incarnate Word *M*

Virginia

Lynchburg College *M*

Clinical nurse specialist

Arizona

Grand Canyon University *M*

California

Mount St. Mary's College *M*
University of San Diego *M, D*
University of San Francisco *M*

Florida

Florida Southern College *M*

Georgia

Georgia Southern University *M*
Mercer University *M*

Illinois

Loyola University Chicago *M*

Massachusetts

Worcester State University *M*

Michigan

Saginaw Valley State University *M*

Minnesota

College of St. Scholastica *M*

Missouri

Maryville University of Saint Louis *M*

New York

Molloy College *M*
Mount Saint Mary College *M*
New York University *M*
Pace University: Pleasantville/
    Briarcliff *M*
SUNY
    University at Binghamton *D*
    University at Buffalo *D*
    Upstate Medical University *M*
St. John Fisher College *M, D*

Ohio

Case Western Reserve University *M*
University of Cincinnati *M*
Ursuline College *M*

Pennsylvania

DeSales University *M*
Robert Morris University *D*
University of Pennsylvania *M*
University of Pittsburgh *M, D*

South Carolina

University of South Carolina
    Columbia *M*

Tennessee

Vanderbilt University *M*

Texas

Angelo State University *M*
Texas A&M University
    Corpus Christi *B*
Texas Christian University *M*
Texas Woman's University *M*
University of Texas
    El Paso *M*
    Pan American *M*
University of the Incarnate Word *M*

Utah

Brigham Young University *M*

Wisconsin

Marian University *M*

Clinical nutrition

Alabama

University of Alabama
   Birmingham *M*

Arizona

Central Arizona College *A*
Chandler-Gilbert Community
   College *A*

California

Loma Linda University *M, D*
MiraCosta College *A*

Florida

University of Miami *M*

Illinois

Loyola University Chicago *B*

Maryland

Howard Community College *A*

Massachusetts

Boston University *B, M*

Michigan

Madonna University *B*

New Jersey

Rutgers, The State University of New
   Jersey
   New Brunswick/Piscataway
      Campus *M, D*
   Newark Campus *M, D*

North Carolina

East Carolina University *B*

North Dakota

University of North Dakota *B, M*

Ohio

Kent State University *B, M*
University of Cincinnati
   Blue Ash College *A*

Oregon

Oregon Health & Science
   University *M*

Pennsylvania

Immaculata University *M*
Marywood University *M*
Messiah College *B*

Tennessee

East Tennessee State University *M*
University of Memphis *M*

Virginia

George Mason University *M*

Washington

Bastyr University *M*

Clinical pastoral counseling

Arizona

Argosy University
   Online *D*

California

Loma Linda University *M*

Florida

Argosy University
   Tampa *M*

Indiana

University of St. Francis *M*

Maryland

Loyola University Maryland *M, D*

Ohio

University of Dayton *M*

Texas

Southwestern Assemblies of God
   University *B, M*

Virginia

Virginia Commonwealth
   University *M*

Washington

Seattle University *M*

Clinical psychology

Alabama

Alabama Agricultural and Mechanical
   University *M*
Auburn University *M, D*

Alaska

University of Alaska
   Anchorage *M*

Arizona

Argosy University
   Phoenix *D*

California

Alliant International University *M, D*
Antioch University
   Los Angeles
   Santa Barbara *M, D*
Argosy University
   Inland Empire *D*
   Los Angeles *D*
   Orange County *D*
   San Diego *D*
   San Francisco Bay Area *D*
Azusa Pacific University *M, D*
Biola University *M, D*
California Institute of Integral
   Studies *D*
California Lutheran University *M, D*
California State University
   Bakersfield *M*
   Dominguez Hills *M*
   East Bay *M*
   San Bernardino *M*
John F. Kennedy University *M*
Notre Dame de Namur University *M*
Pepperdine University *M*
San Diego State University *M, D*
San Jose State University *M*
Southern California Seminary *D*
University of La Verne *M*
Vanguard University of Southern
   California *M*

Colorado

University of Denver *M, D*

Connecticut

University of Hartford *M, D*

Delaware

University of Delaware *M, D*

District of Columbia

American University *D*
Catholic University of America *M, D*
Gallaudet University *D*
George Washington University *D*

Florida

Barry University *M*
Carlos Albizu University *D*
Florida Institute of Technology *M, D*
Florida State University *D*
Nova Southeastern University *D*
University of Central Florida *M, D*

Georgia

Emory University *D*
Georgia Southern University *D*
Mercer University *D*

Idaho

Idaho State University *D*

Illinois

Argosy University
   Chicago *M, D*
Benedictine University *M*
DePaul University *M, D*
Dominican University *B*
Eastern Illinois University *M*
Loyola University Chicago *M, D*
Northwestern University *D*
Roosevelt University *M, D*
Wheaton College *M, D*

Indiana

Ball State University *M*
Indiana State University *D*
Indiana University
   Purdue University Indianapolis *D*
University of Indianapolis *M, D*

Iowa

Loras College *M*
University of Iowa *D*
University of Northern Iowa *M*

Kansas

Emporia State University *M*
Washburn University *M*
Wichita State University *D*

Kentucky

Eastern Kentucky University *M*
Morehead State University *M*
Murray State University *M*
Spalding University *M, D*
Union College *M*
University of Kentucky *M, D*
University of Louisville *D*

Louisiana

Northwestern State University *M*

Maine

University of Maine *D*

Maryland

Loyola University Maryland *M, D*

Massachusetts

American International College *M*
Clark University *M, D*
Eastern Nazarene College *B*
Suffolk University *D*
University of Massachusetts
   Boston *M, D*
   Dartmouth *M*

Michigan

Central Michigan University *D*
Eastern Michigan University *M, D*
Madonna University *M*
University of Detroit Mercy *M, D*
Western Michigan University *D*

Minnesota

Argosy University
   Twin Cities *D*
Capella University *M, D*

Minnesota State University
   Mankato *M*
Saint Cloud State University *M*
Walden University *M*

Mississippi

Jackson State University *D*

Missouri

Evangel University *M*
Missouri State University *M*
University of Missouri
   Columbia *M, D*
Washington University in St.
   Louis *M, D*

New Hampshire

Keene State College *B*
New England College *B*

New Jersey

Fairleigh Dickinson University
   College at Florham *M*
   Metropolitan Campus *M, D*
Montclair State University *M*
Rutgers, The State University of New
   Jersey
   New Brunswick/Piscataway
      Campus *D*
Seton Hall University *D*

New Mexico

New Mexico Highlands University *M*

New York

Adelphi University *D*
City University of New York
   Queens College *M*
Fordham University *M, D*
Hofstra University *M, D*
Long Island University
   LIU Brooklyn *D*
   LIU Post *D*
New York University *B, D*
SUNY
   University at Albany *D*
   University at Binghamton *D*
   University at Buffalo *D*
   University at Stony Brook *D*
St. John's University *D*
Syracuse University *D*
University of Rochester *D*
Yeshiva University *M, D*

North Carolina

Duke University *M, D*
East Carolina University *M*
University of North Carolina
   Charlotte *M*

North Dakota

North Dakota State University *D*
University of North Dakota *D*

Ohio

Case Western Reserve University *D*
Kent State University *M, D*
Ohio University *M, D*
Union Institute & University *D*
University of Dayton *M*
Wright State University *M, D*
Xavier University *D*

Oklahoma

University of Tulsa *M, D*

Oregon

George Fox University *M, D*
Pacific University *D*

Pennsylvania

Bryn Mawr College *M, D*
Chestnut Hill College *M, D*

Drexel University *D*
Duquesne University *D*
Immaculata University *D*
Indiana University of Pennsylvania *D*
La Salle University *D*
Marywood University *M, D*
Millersville University of
   Pennsylvania *M*
Penn State
   Harrisburg *M*
West Chester University of
   Pennsylvania *M*
Widener University *D*

Puerto Rico

Carlos Albizu University: San
   Juan *M, D*
Pontifical Catholic University of
   Puerto Rico *M, D*
University of Puerto Rico
   Rio Piedras *M*

Rhode Island

Roger Williams University *B, M*
University of Rhode Island *D*

South Carolina

Francis Marion University *M*
University of South Carolina
   Columbia *M, D*

South Dakota

University of South Dakota *D*

Tennessee

Southern Adventist University *B*

Texas

Abilene Christian University *M*
Argosy University
   Dallas *D*
Baylor University *M, D*
Houston Baptist University *M*
Our Lady of the Lake University of
   San Antonio *M*
Sam Houston State University *M, D*
Southern Methodist University *D*
Southwestern Assemblies of God
   University *M*
Texas Tech University *D*
University of Houston *D*
University of Houston
   Clear Lake *M*
University of North Texas *D*
University of Texas
   Austin *D*
   El Paso *M*
   Pan American *M*
   Tyler *M*

Utah

Brigham Young University *D*

Vermont

College of St. Joseph in Vermont *M*
Goddard College *M*
Saint Michael's College *M*

Virginia

Norfolk State University *D*
Old Dominion University *D*
Regent University *M, D*
University of Virginia *D*
Virginia Commonwealth University *D*

Washington

Seattle Pacific University *D*
University of Washington *D*

West Virginia

Marshall University *D*

Wisconsin

Marquette University *M, D*

Clinical research coordinator

California

National University *M*

Indiana

Grace College *M*

Minnesota

Anoka-Ramsey Community College *C*

Wisconsin

Mid-State Technical College *A*

Clothing, apparel and textile studies

Alabama

University of Alabama *B*

Arizona

Phoenix College *C*

Arkansas

University of Arkansas *B*

California

Antelope Valley College *C, A*
California State Polytechnic
   University: Pomona *B*
California State University
   Long Beach *B*
   Northridge *B*
Cerritos College *A*
Chabot College *A*
Chaffey College *C*
El Camino College *C*
Fashion Institute of Design and
   Merchandising
   Los Angeles *A*
   San Diego *A*
   San Francisco *A*
Fresno City College *C, A*
Glendale Community College *A*
Los Angeles Mission College *A*
Los Angeles Trade and Technical
   College *C, A*
Mendocino College *C*
Modesto Junior College *A*
Monterey Peninsula College *A*
Mount San Antonio College *A*
Orange Coast College *C, A*
Sacramento City College *C, A*
Saddleback College *C*
San Francisco State University *B*
Santa Rosa Junior College *C*
University of California
   Davis *B, M*

Colorado

Colorado State University *M*

Delaware

Delaware State University *B*

Florida

Florida State College at
   Jacksonville *A*
Florida State University *B, M*

Georgia

Georgia Southern University *B*
University of Georgia *M*

Hawaii

University of Hawaii
   Manoa *B*

Idaho

University of Idaho *B*

Illinois

Joliet Junior College *A*
Northern Illinois University *B*
Southern Illinois University
   Carbondale *B*

Indiana

Indiana State University *B*
Indiana University
   Bloomington *B, M*
Purdue University *B, M, D*

Iowa

Ellsworth Community College *A*
Iowa State University *B, M, D*
University of Northern Iowa *B*

Kansas

Kansas State University *B, M*

Kentucky

University of Kentucky *B*
Western Kentucky University *B*

Maryland

Baltimore City Community
   College *C, A*

Massachusetts

Fisher College *A*
Framingham State University *B*

Michigan

Michigan State University *B, M*
Western Michigan University *B*

Minnesota

Minnesota State University
   Mankato *B, M*
University of Minnesota
   Twin Cities *B*

Mississippi

Northeast Mississippi Community
   College *A*
University of Southern Mississippi *B*

Missouri

Fontbonne University *B*
Missouri State University *B*
Stephens College *B*
University of Central Missouri *B*
University of Missouri
   Columbia *B, M*

Nebraska

University of Nebraska
   Kearney *B*
   Lincoln *B, M*

New Mexico

New Mexico State University *B*

New York

Fashion Institute of Technology *A, B*
SUNY
   College at Buffalo *B*
   College at Oneonta *B*

North Carolina

Appalachian State University *B*
East Carolina University *B*
University of North Carolina
   Greensboro *B, M, D*

North Dakota

North Dakota State University *B*

Ohio

Bowling Green State University *B, M*
Ohio State University
   Columbus Campus *B, M, D*
Ohio University *B, M*
University of Akron *B, M*
Youngstown State University *B*

Oklahoma

Langston University *B*

Oregon

Oregon State University *B*

Pennsylvania

Cheyney University of
   Pennsylvania *B*
Philadelphia University *B, M*

Rhode Island

Rhode Island School of Design *B*
University of Rhode Island *B, M*

South Carolina

Tri-County Technical College *A*

Tennessee

Carson-Newman University *B*
Hiwassee College *A*
Lipscomb University *B*
Middle Tennessee State University *B*
Tennessee State University *B*
Tennessee Technological
   University *B*

Texas

Lamar University *B*
Texas A&M University
   Kingsville *B*
Texas Southern University *M*
University of Texas
   Austin *C, B, M*

Utah

Dixie State College *A*
Snow College *A*
Utah State University *B*

Virginia

Liberty University *B*

Washington

Seattle Pacific University *B*
Washington State University *B, M*

Wisconsin

University of Wisconsin
   Madison *B*
   Stout *B*

Cognitive psychology/ psycholinguistics

California

California State University
   Stanislaus *B*
University of California
   San Diego *D*
   Santa Cruz *B*
University of Southern California *D*

Connecticut

University of Connecticut *B, M, D*

Delaware

University of Delaware *M, D*

District of Columbia

George Washington University *D*

Florida

Florida State University *D*

Georgia

Emory University *D*

Illinois

Loyola University Chicago *D*
Northwestern University *B*

Massachusetts

Fitchburg State University *B*
Tufts University *M, D*

Missouri

University of Missouri
  Columbia *M, D*

Nebraska

University of Nebraska
  Omaha *M*

New York

SUNY
  University at Albany *D*
  University at Binghamton *D*
  University at Buffalo *D*

Rhode Island

Brown University *M, D*

Texas

Rice University *M, D*

Cognitive science

California

California State University
  Fresno *B*
  Stanislaus *B*
Occidental College *B*
Pomona College *B*
University of California
  Berkeley *B*
  Irvine *B*
  Los Angeles *B*
  Merced *B, M, D*
  San Diego *B*
University of Southern California *B*

Colorado

University of Colorado
  Boulder *D*
  Denver *D*

Connecticut

Yale University *B*

Georgia

University of Georgia *B*

Illinois

University of Chicago *D*

Indiana

Indiana University
  Bloomington *B, D*
University of Evansville *B*

Louisiana

University of Louisiana at Lafayette *D*

Maine

College of the Atlantic *B, M*

Maryland

Johns Hopkins University *B, D*

Massachusetts

Hampshire College *B*
Massachusetts Institute of
  Technology *B, D*

Michigan

Central Michigan University *B*
Michigan Technological
  University *M, D*

Minnesota

Carleton College *B*

Mississippi

Mississippi State University *C*

New York

Rensselaer Polytechnic Institute *M, D*
SUNY
  College at Oswego *B*
United States Military Academy *B*
Vassar College *B*

Ohio

Case Western Reserve
  University *B, M*

Oregon

George Fox University *B*

Pennsylvania

Carnegie Mellon University *B*
Lehigh University *B*
University of Pennsylvania *B*

Rhode Island

Brown University *B, M, D*

Tennessee

Vanderbilt University *B*

Texas

Rice University *B*
University of Texas
  Dallas *B, M*

Virginia

University of Richmond *B*

Wisconsin

Lawrence University *B*
University of Wisconsin
  Stout *B*

College student counseling

Arkansas

Arkansas State University *M*
Arkansas Tech University *M*
Southern Arkansas University *M*
University of Central Arkansas *M*

California

California State University
  Fresno *M*
University of Southern California *M*

Connecticut

University of Connecticut *T*

Delaware

University of Delaware *M*

Florida

University of Florida *M*
University of West Florida *M*

Georgia

University of Georgia *M, D*

Illinois

Eastern Illinois University *M*
Illinois State University *M*
Loyola University Chicago *M*

University of Illinois
  Urbana-Champaign *M, D*
Western Illinois University *M*

Indiana

Ball State University *M*
Indiana State University *M, T*
Indiana University
  Bloomington *M*

Iowa

Iowa State University *T*
University of Iowa *M, D*
University of Northern Iowa *M*

Kentucky

Eastern Kentucky University *M*
Western Kentucky University *M*

Louisiana

Northwestern State University *M*

Maine

University of Southern Maine *M*

Massachusetts

Northeastern University *M*
Springfield College *M*

Michigan

Eastern Michigan University *M*
Michigan State University *M*
Western Michigan University *M, T*

Minnesota

Minnesota State University
  Mankato *M*
Saint Cloud State University *M*

Mississippi

Mississippi State University *D*

Missouri

Southeast Missouri State University *M*
University of Missouri
  Columbia *M, D*

Nebraska

Wayne State College *M*

New Hampshire

Rivier University *M*

New Jersey

Rutgers, The State University of New
  Jersey
  New Brunswick/Piscataway
    Campus *M*
Seton Hall University *M*

New York

Canisius College *M*
Fordham University *M, D*
SUNY
  College at Plattsburgh *M, T*
Saint Bonaventure University *M*
Syracuse University *M*
University of Rochester *M, D*

North Carolina

Appalachian State University *M*
North Carolina Agricultural and
  Technical State University *M*
North Carolina Central University *M*
North Carolina State University *M*
University of North Carolina
  Charlotte *M*
  Greensboro *M, D*
  Pembroke *M*
Western Carolina University *M*

North Dakota

University of Mary *M*

Ohio

Bowling Green State University *B, M*
Miami University
  Oxford *M, D*
Ohio University *M*
University of Dayton *M*
Youngstown State University *M*

Pennsylvania

Holy Family University *M*
Indiana University of Pennsylvania *M*
Kutztown University of
  Pennsylvania *M*
Penn State
  University Park *M*
Shippensburg University of
  Pennsylvania *M*
Villanova University *M*
Widener University *M, T*

South Carolina

University of South Carolina
  Columbia *M*

South Dakota

South Dakota State University *M*

Tennessee

Hiwassee College *A*
Lee University *M*
University of Tennessee
  Knoxville *M, D*

Texas

Angelo State University *M*
Stephen F. Austin State University *M*

Utah

Brigham Young University *D*

Vermont

Johnson State College *M*

Washington

Seattle University *M*
Walla Walla University *M*
Western Washington University *M*

Wisconsin

University of Wisconsin
  La Crosse *M*

Commercial/ advertising art

Alabama

Calhoun Community College *A*
Faulkner State Community
  College *C, A*
Lawson State Community College *C*
Oakwood University *A*

Arizona

Art Institute of Phoenix *B*
Eastern Arizona College *A*
Phoenix College *C, A*
Yavapai College *C, A*

Arkansas

Arkansas State University *B*
National Park Community College *A*
Northwest Arkansas Community
  College *A*
Southern Arkansas University Tech *C*
University of Arkansas
  Community College at Morrilton *A*

California

Academy of Art University *C, A, B, M*
Allan Hancock College *A*
Art Center College of Design *B, M*

Art Institute of California
  Los Angeles *A, B*
  Orange County *A, B*
  San Diego *B*
  San Francisco *A, B*
  Silicon Valley *B*
Butte College *A*
California Lutheran University *B*
California State University
  East Bay *B*
  Long Beach *B*
  Los Angeles *B*
  Northridge *B*
  Sacramento *B, M*
  San Bernardino *B*
Cerro Coso Community College *C*
Chabot College *A*
Chaffey College *C, A*
Citrus College *C*
College of the Redwoods *C, A*
College of the Sequoias *C, A*
Cypress College *A*
De Anza College *C, A*
Evergreen Valley College *A*
Foothill College *C, A*
Fullerton College *A*
Glendale Community College *C, A*
Golden West College *C, A*
Laguna College of Art and
  Design *C, B*
Laney College *C, A*
Long Beach City College *C, A*
Los Angeles City College *A*
Los Angeles Pierce College *C, A*
Los Angeles Southwest College *A*
Los Angeles Trade and Technical
  College *A*
Los Angeles Valley College *C, A*
Los Medanos College *C, A*
Mission College *C, A*
Modesto Junior College *C, A*
Moorpark College *C, A*
Mount St. Mary's College *A*
Ohlone College *C, A*
Orange Coast College *C, A*
Palomar College *A*
Pasadena City College *C, A*
Platt College
  Los Angeles *C, A*
  Ontario *C, A, B*
  San Diego *C, A, B*
Porterville College *C, A*
Rio Hondo College *A*
Saddleback College *C, A*
San Bernardino Valley College *C, A*
San Diego City College *C, A*
Santa Ana College *A*
Santa Barbara City College *C, A*
Santa Rosa Junior College *C, A*
Santiago Canyon College *A*
Shasta College *A*
Solano Community College *A*
University of San Francisco *B*
University of the Pacific *B*
Ventura College *C, A*
West Hills College: Coalinga *C, A*
Westwood College
  Inland Empire *A*
Woodbury University *B*

Colorado

Colorado Mountain College *C, A*
Trinidad State Junior College *C, A*
Westwood College
  Denver North *A, B*
  Denver South *A, B*

Connecticut

Albertus Magnus College *B*
Asnuntuck Community College *C*
Housatonic Community College *C, A*
Manchester Community College *C, A*
Mitchell College *A*
Norwalk Community College *C, A*

Tunxis Community College *C, A*
University of Hartford *B*
University of New Haven *A, B*

Delaware

Delaware Technical Community
  College
  Terry Campus *A*
University of Delaware *B*

District of Columbia

Gallaudet University *B*
George Washington University *M*

Florida

Eastern Florida State College *A*
Everest University
  Tampa *A*
Florida State College at
  Jacksonville *A*
Indian River State College *A*
Jacksonville University *B*
Lake-Sumter State College *A*
Miami Dade College *A*
Northwest Florida State College *C, A*
Palm Beach State College *A*
Pensacola State College *A*
Ringling College of Art and Design *B*
Seminole State College of
  Florida *C, A*
Tallahassee Community College *A*
Valencia College *C*

Georgia

Art Institute of Atlanta *C, B*
Atlanta Technical College *C, A*
Savannah College of Art and
  Design *B, M*
University of North Georgia *B*

Hawaii

University of Hawaii
  Honolulu Community College *C, A*

Idaho

Boise State University *B*
College of Southern Idaho *A*
North Idaho College *A*

Illinois

American Academy of Art *B*
Chicago State University *B*
Columbia College Chicago *B*
Concordia University Chicago *B*
DePaul University *B*
Dominican University *B*
Illinois Institute of Art
  Chicago *A, B*
  Schaumburg *B*
Lewis University *B*
Millikin University *B*
Oakton Community College *A*
Parkland College *A*
Rend Lake College *C, A*
Robert Morris University: Chicago *A*

Indiana

Indiana University
  Purdue University Fort Wayne *B*
Marian University *B*
University of Indianapolis *B*
Vincennes University *A*

Iowa

Ashford University *B*
Buena Vista University *B*
Des Moines Area Community
  College *C, A*
Dordt College *B*
Drake University *B*
Ellsworth Community College *A*
Graceland University *B*
Iowa Lakes Community College *A*
Iowa State University *B, M*

St. Ambrose University *B*
Upper Iowa University *B*
Wartburg College *B*

Kansas

Haskell Indian Nations University *C*
Highland Community College *A*
Johnson County Community
  College *A*
Labette Community College *A*
Pratt Community College *A*
Tabor College *B*

Kentucky

Bluegrass Community and Technical
  College *A*
Northern Kentucky University *B*
Spencerian College: Lexington *A*

Louisiana

Louisiana College *B*
Louisiana Tech University *B*
Loyola University New Orleans *B*

Maine

College of the Atlantic *B, M*

Maryland

Anne Arundel Community
  College *C, A*
College of Southern Maryland *C*
Community College of Baltimore
  County *C, A*
Frostburg State University *B*
Hagerstown Community College *C, A*
Montgomery College *A*
Prince George's Community
  College *A*
University of Baltimore *M*
University of Maryland
  Eastern Shore *B*

Massachusetts

Boston University *B, M*
Bristol Community College *C*
Cape Cod Community College *A*
Greenfield Community College *A*
Holyoke Community College *C*
Middlesex Community College *C, A*
Northern Essex Community
  College *C, A*
Salem State University *B*
Simmons College *B*
Springfield Technical Community
  College *A*
University of Massachusetts
  Dartmouth *B, M*
  Lowell *C*

Michigan

Andrews University *B*
Baker College
  Auburn Hills *A*
  Clinton Township *A*
  Flint *A, B*
  Muskegon *A*
  Owosso *A*
  Port Huron *A*
College for Creative Studies *B*
Finlandia University *B*
Gogebic Community College *A*
Grand Rapids Community College *A*
Grand Valley State University *B*
Henry Ford Community College *C, A*
Kalamazoo Valley Community
  College *C, A*
Kellogg Community College *A*
Macomb Community College *C, A*
Muskegon Community College *C, A*
Northwestern Michigan College *A*
Oakland Community College *A*
St. Clair County Community
  College *A*
Siena Heights University *B*

Minnesota

Alexandria Technical and Community
  College *C, A*
Art Institutes International
  Minnesota *A, B*
Bemidji State University *B*
Central Lakes College *C, A*
Dakota County Technical
  College *C, A*
Duluth Business University *A*
Mesabi Range Community and
  Technical College *C*
Minneapolis Business College *A*
Minnesota State University
  Mankato *B*
  Moorhead *B*
South Central College *C, A*
University of Minnesota
  Duluth *B*
  Twin Cities *C, B*

Mississippi

Mississippi Gulf Coast Community
  College *A*
Northwest Mississippi Community
  College *A*

Missouri

East Central College *C, A*
Metropolitan Community College -
  Kansas City *A*
St. Charles Community College *C, A*
Southwest Baptist University *B*
University of Central Missouri *B*
Washington University in St.
  Louis *B, M*

Montana

Montana State University
  Northern *A, B*

Nebraska

Central Community College *C, A*
Metropolitan Community College *A*
Midland University *B*
Southeast Community College *C, A*
Union College *A, B*
University of Nebraska
  Kearney *B*
Vatterott College
  Spring Valley *C*

Nevada

College of Southern Nevada *A*

New Hampshire

Franklin Pierce University *B*
Keene State College *B*
Lakes Region Community
  College *C, A*
Manchester Community College *C, A*

New Jersey

Bergen Community College *A*
Centenary College *B*
College of New Jersey *B*
Cumberland County College *A*
Essex County College *A*
Gloucester County College *C, A*
Mercer County Community
  College *C, A*
Middlesex County College *A*
Ocean County College *C*
Seton Hall University *B*
Sussex County Community
  College *C, A*

New Mexico

Clovis Community College *C, A*
New Mexico Junior College *C, A*
San Juan College *A*

New York

Alfred University *M*
Briarcliffe College *A*
City University of New York
  Bronx Community College *A*
  City College *B*
  Kingsborough Community
    College *A*
  Lehman College *B*
  New York City College of
    Technology *A, B*
College of Saint Rose *B*
College of Westchester *C, A*
Dutchess Community College *A*
Fashion Institute of Technology *A, B*
Finger Lakes Community College *A*
Fulton-Montgomery Community
  College *A*
Jamestown Community College *A*
Mercy College *A, B*
Mohawk Valley Community
  College *A*
Monroe Community College *A*
New York Institute of Technology *B*
New York University *M*
Pace University *C*
Pace University: Pleasantville/
  Briarcliff *A*
Rochester Institute of Technology *B*
Rockland Community College *C, A*
SUNY
  College at Buffalo *B*
  College at Cortland *B*
  College at Oswego *B*
  College at Purchase *B*
School of Visual Arts *B, M*
Suffolk County Community College *A*
Sullivan County Community
  College *A*
Syracuse University *B*
Tompkins Cortland Community
  College *A*
Ulster County Community College *A*
Villa Maria College of Buffalo *A, B*
Westchester Community College *C*

North Carolina

Campbell University *B*
Catawba Valley Community
  College *A*
Central Piedmont Community
  College *C, A*
Fayetteville Technical Community
  College *C, A*
Gaston College *C*
Guilford Technical Community
  College *C, A*
Halifax Community College *A*
Isothermal Community College *A*
James Sprunt Community
  College *C, A*
Johnston Community College *C, A*
McDowell Technical Community
  College *A*
Pitt Community College *A*
Randolph Community College *A*
South Piedmont Community
  College *C, A*
Southwestern Community College *A*
Surry Community College *C, A*

North Dakota

Bismarck State College *C, A*

Ohio

Antonelli College
  Cincinnati *A*
Ashland University *B*
Bowling Green State University *B*
Cincinnati State Technical and
  Community College *A*
Clark State Community College *A*
Columbus College of Art and
  Design *B*
Cuyahoga Community College
  Metropolitan *A*
Defiance College *B*
Edison State Community College *A*
Kent State University *B, M*
Lakeland Community College *A*
Marietta College *B*
Miami University
  Oxford *B*
Ohio Northern University *B*
Owens Community College
  Toledo *C, A*
School of Advertising Art *A*
Sinclair Community College *C, A*
University of Cincinnati *B*
University of Findlay *B*
Virginia Marti College of Art and
  Design *A*
Wilmington College *B*
Youngstown State University *B*

Oklahoma

Oklahoma Christian University *B*
Oklahoma City Community
  College *A*
Oklahoma State University
  Oklahoma City *A*
Oral Roberts University *B*
Southwestern Oklahoma State
  University *B*

Oregon

Art Institute of Portland *B*
Lane Community College *C, A*
Linn-Benton Community College *C, A*
Portland Community College *A*
Portland State University *B*

Pennsylvania

Arcadia University *B*
Art Institute of Pittsburgh *A, B*
Art Institute of York *A*
Berks Technical Institute *A*
Bucks County Community College *A*
California University of
  Pennsylvania *A, B*
Community College of Allegheny
  County *C, A*
Community College of
  Philadelphia *A*
Delaware County Community
  College *A*
Douglas Education Center *A*
Hussian School of Art *A*
Kutztown University of
  Pennsylvania *B*
Luzerne County Community
  College *C*
Lycoming College *B*
Marywood University *M*
Pennsylvania College of Art and
  Design *B*
Pennsylvania College of
  Technology *A, B*
Seton Hill University *C, B*
Temple University *B*
Thiel College *B*
Westmoreland County Community
  College *A*
York College of Pennsylvania *B*

Puerto Rico

Atlantic University College *A, B*

South Carolina

Greenville Technical College *C*
Midlands Technical College *A*
Piedmont Technical College *C*
Spartanburg Community College *C*
Trident Technical College *C, A*
University of South Carolina
  Upstate *B*

South Dakota

Black Hills State University *B*
Northern State University *A*
Southeast Technical Institute *A*

Tennessee

Chattanooga State Community
  College *A*
Lipscomb University *B*
Memphis College of Art *B*
Nashville State Community College *A*
Nossi College of Art *A*
O'More College of Design *B*
Pellissippi State Community
  College *A*
Southern Adventist University *A, B*
Southwest Tennessee Community
  College *A*
University of Tennessee
  Knoxville *B*

Texas

Amarillo College *C, A*
Austin Community College *C, A*
Clarendon College *A*
Coastal Bend College *A*
Collin County Community College
  District *C, A*
El Paso Community College *A*
Grayson College *A*
Kilgore College *C, A*
Lamar University *B*
Navarro College *A*
Sam Houston State University *B*
San Jacinto College *C, A*
Schreiner University *B*
South Plains College *A*
Tarrant County College *A*
Texas State Technical College
  Harlingen *A*
  Waco *C, A*
Tyler Junior College *C, A*
University of North Texas *B*

Utah

Provo College *A*
Weber State University *B*

Vermont

Lyndon State College *B*

Virginia

Central Virginia Community
  College *A*
Hampton University *B*
Northern Virginia Community
  College *A*
Thomas Nelson Community
  College *A*
Tidewater Community College *A*
Virginia Western Community
  College *A*

Washington

Central Washington University *B*
Centralia College *A*
Cornish College of the Arts *B*
Highline Community College *A*
Shoreline Community College *C, A*
Skagit Valley College *C, A*
Spokane Falls Community
  College *C, A*
University of Washington *B, M*
Western Washington University *B*
Whatcom Community College *A*

West Virginia

Concord University *B*
Fairmont State University *B*
West Liberty University *B*
West Virginia State University *B*

Wisconsin

Cardinal Stritch University *B*
Carroll University *B*
Concordia University Wisconsin *B*
Madison Area Technical College *A*
Mount Mary University *B*
St. Norbert College *B*
University of Wisconsin
  Platteville *B*

Wyoming

Northwest College *A*

Commercial fishing

Texas

Texas A&M University
  Galveston *B*

Commercial photography

Alabama

Oakwood University *A*

Arizona

Art Institute of Phoenix *B*
Phoenix College *C, A*

California

Academy of Art University *C, A, B, M*
Allan Hancock College *A*
Art Center College of Design *B*
Butte College *A*
Cosumnes River College *C, A*
Lake Tahoe Community College *C*
Long Beach City College *C, A*
Modesto Junior College *A*
Orange Coast College *C, A*
Pasadena City College *C, A*
Sacramento City College *C, A*
Saddleback College *A*
Santa Monica College *C, A*
Solano Community College *C, A*

Colorado

Colorado Mountain College *A*

Florida

Art Institute of Fort Lauderdale *A, B*
Miami International University of Art
  and Design *B*

Georgia

Art Institute of Atlanta *A, B*
Gwinnett Technical College *C, A*
North Georgia Technical
  College *C, A*

Illinois

College of DuPage *C, A*
Prairie State College *C, A*
Triton College *A*
Waubonsee Community College *C*

Iowa

Des Moines Area Community
  College *C*
Hawkeye Community College *A*
Western Iowa Tech Community
  College *C*

Kansas

Highland Community College *A*

Maryland

Cecil College *C, A*
Montgomery College *A*

Massachusetts

Mount Wachusett Community
  College *C*

Springfield Technical Community
College *C, A*

Michigan

Art Institute of Michigan *B*
College for Creative Studies *B*
Kirtland Community College *A*
Washtenaw Community College *A*

Minnesota

Art Institutes International
Minnesota *B*
Central Lakes College *C*
Dakota County Technical College *C*
Minneapolis Community and
Technical College *C, A*
Minnesota State Community and
Technical College *C*
Ridgewater College *C, A*
Rochester Community and Technical
College *C*
St. Paul College *C*

Missouri

Webster University *C*

Nebraska

Metropolitan Community College *A*

Nevada

College of Southern Nevada *A*

New Jersey

Middlesex County College *A*

New York

City University of New York
LaGuardia Community
College *C, A*
Fashion Institute of Technology *A, B*
Mohawk Valley Community
College *A*
Rockland Community College *A*
Sullivan County Community
College *A*

North Carolina

Alamance Community College *C*
Appalachian State University *B*
McDowell Technical Community
College *A*
Randolph Community College *A*

Ohio

Antonelli College
Cincinnati *A*
Columbus State Community
College *C, A*
Kaplan College
Dayton *A*
Ohio University *M*
Owens Community College
Toledo *C, A*

Oregon

Mt. Hood Community College *A*

Pennsylvania

Art Institute of Philadelphia *A, B*
Art Institute of Pittsburgh *A, B*
Bucks County Community
College *C, A*
Community College of
Philadelphia *A*
Indiana University of Pennsylvania *C*
Pennsylvania College of Art and
Design *B*

Tennessee

Nossi College of Art *A*

Texas

Amarillo College *A*
Austin Community College *C, A*
El Paso Community College *A*
Kilgore College *C, A*
North Central Texas College *A*
Odessa College *C, A*

Virginia

Northern Virginia Community
College *A*

Washington

Art Institute of Seattle *A, B*
Edmonds Community College *A*
Seattle Central Community College *A*
Spokane Falls Community
College *C, A*

Wisconsin

Madison Area Technical College *A*
Milwaukee Area Technical College *A*

Wyoming

Central Wyoming College *A*
Northwest College *C, A*

Communication disorders

Alabama

Auburn University *B, M*
University of South Alabama *B, D*

Arizona

Arizona State University *B, D*
University of Arizona *B, M, D*

Arkansas

Harding University *B*
Ouachita Baptist University *B*
University of Arkansas
Little Rock *D*

California

Biola University *B*
California Baptist University *B*
California State University
Chico *B*
Fresno *B, M*
Fullerton *B, M*
Los Angeles *B, M*
Chapman University *M*
San Diego State University *B, M, D*
San Francisco State University *B, M*
San Jose State University *B*

Colorado

Metropolitan State University of
Denver *B*
University of Colorado
Boulder *B, M, D*

District of Columbia

Howard University *M, D*

Florida

University of South Florida
Sarasota-Manatee *B*

Georgia

Armstrong Atlantic State
University *B, M*
University of Georgia *B, M, D, T*

Illinois

Augustana College *B*
Eastern Illinois University *B, M*
Northern Illinois University *B, M*
Northwestern University *B, M, D*

Southern Illinois University
Carbondale *B, M*
Western Illinois University *B, M*

Indiana

Butler University *B*
Saint Mary's College *B*

Kansas

Kansas State University *B*
University of Kansas *B*
Wichita State University *B, M, D*

Kentucky

Western Kentucky University *B*

Maine

University of Maine *B, M*

Maryland

University of Maryland
College Park *B, D*

Massachusetts

Boston University *B, M*
Bridgewater State University *B*
Elms College *B, M*
Emerson College *B, M, D*
University of Massachusetts
Amherst *B, M, D*
Worcester State University *B*

Michigan

Central Michigan University *B*
Michigan State University *B, D*
Wayne State University *B, M, D*

Minnesota

Minnesota State University
Mankato *B, M*
Saint Cloud State University *B, M*
University of Minnesota
Duluth *B, M*
Twin Cities *B, M, D*

Mississippi

Jackson State University *M*
University of Mississippi *B*

Missouri

Maryville University of Saint Louis *B*
Southeast Missouri State
University *C, B, M*
Truman State University *B, M*
University of Missouri
Columbia *M, D*

Nebraska

University of Nebraska
Kearney *B, M*

New Hampshire

University of New Hampshire *M*

New Jersey

Montclair State University *M*

New York

City University of New York
Queens College *B*
Ithaca College *B*
Nazareth College *B*
Pace University *B*
Pace University: Pleasantville/
Briarcliff *B*
SUNY
College at Fredonia *B*
College at New Paltz *B, M*
Syracuse University *B*
Touro College *B*

North Carolina

Appalachian State University *B*
North Carolina Central University *M*
Western Carolina University *B, M*

North Dakota

Minot State University *B, M*
University of North Dakota *B, M, D*

Ohio

Ashland University *B*
Baldwin Wallace University *B*
Bowling Green State
University *B, M, D*
Case Western Reserve
University *B, M, D*
University of Akron *B*
University of Cincinnati *B, M, D*

Oklahoma

University of Oklahoma *B*
University of Tulsa *B*

Oregon

University of Oregon *B, M, D*

Pennsylvania

California University of
Pennsylvania *B, M*
Edinboro University of
Pennsylvania *B*
Penn State
Abington *B*
Altoona *B*
Beaver *B*
Berks *B*
Brandywine *B*
DuBois *B*
Fayette, The Eberly Campus *B*
Greater Allegheny *B*
Harrisburg *B*
Hazleton *B*
Lehigh Valley *B*
Mont Alto *B*
New Kensington *B*
Schuylkill *B*
Shenango *B*
University Park *B, M, D*
Wilkes-Barre *B*
Worthington Scranton *B*
York *B*

Rhode Island

University of Rhode Island *B*

South Carolina

Bob Jones University *B*
Winthrop University *B*

South Dakota

Augustana College *B*
University of South Dakota *B, M*

Texas

Baylor University *B, M*
Our Lady of the Lake University of
San Antonio *B, M*
Stephen F. Austin State University *B*
Texas State University *B, M*
Texas Tech University Health
Sciences Center *B, M, D*
University of Houston *B, M*
University of Texas
Austin *B, M, D*
Dallas *D*
Pan American *D, M*
West Texas A&M University *B, M*

Utah

Utah State University *B, M*

Vermont

University of Vermont *B, M*

Virginia

Hampton University *B*
Radford University *B*

West Virginia

West Virginia University *D*

Wisconsin

University of Wisconsin
  Eau Claire *B, M*
  River Falls *B, M*
  Whitewater *M*

Communications

Alabama

Huntingdon College *B*
Spring Hill College *B*
Tuskegee University *B*
University of Mobile *B*
University of Phoenix
  Birmingham *B*

Arizona

Arizona Christian University *B*
University of Phoenix
  Phoenix-Hohokam *B*
  Southern Arizona *B*

Arkansas

Arkansas State University *B*
Henderson State University *B*
University of Arkansas
  Fort Smith *B*
  Little Rock *M*
University of Phoenix
  Little Rock *B*

California

California Baptist University *M*
California State University
  Los Angeles *C*
College of San Mateo *C, A*
Columbia College *A*
Concordia University Irvine *B*
National University *A, B, M*
Pacific Union College *B*
Providence Christian College *B*
Skyline College *A*
Stanford University *B, M, D*
University of Phoenix
  Bay Area *B*
  Central Valley *B*
  Sacramento Valley *B*
  San Diego *B*
  Southern California *B*
University of San Diego *B*
West Hills College: Coalinga *A*
Woodland Community College *A*

Colorado

University of Colorado
  Colorado Springs *B, M*
University of Phoenix
  Denver *B*
  Southern Colorado *B*

Connecticut

Sacred Heart University *M*

District of Columbia

University of Phoenix
  Washington DC *B*

Florida

Eckerd College *B*
Florida College *B*
Florida Institute of Technology *B*
Lynn University *B*
Rollins College *B*
Southeastern University *B*
Stetson University *B*
University of Miami *B*

University of Phoenix
  Central Florida *B*
  North Florida *B*
  South Florida *B*
  West Florida *B*
University of Tampa *B*
Valencia College *C*

Georgia

Dalton State College *A*
Georgia Military College *A*
Georgia Regents University *B*
Paine College *B*
Toccoa Falls College *B*
University of Phoenix
  Atlanta *B*
  Augusta *B*
  Columbus *B*
  Savannah *B*

Idaho

College of Western Idaho *A*

Illinois

Benedictine University at
  Springfield *B*
DePaul University *B*
DeVry University
  Chicago *B*
  Online *B*
Eastern Illinois University *B, M*
Quincy University *B*
Roosevelt University *B*
Spoon River College *A*
University of Illinois
  Springfield *B, M*

Indiana

Goshen College *B*
Holy Cross College *B*
Indiana Wesleyan University *A, B*
University of Evansville *B*
University of Phoenix
  Indianapolis *B*
University of St. Francis *B*
University of Southern Indiana *M*

Iowa

Clarke University *B*
Iowa Wesleyan College *B*
Iowa Western Community College *A*
University of Dubuque *B*
William Penn University *B*

Kansas

Central Christian College of Kansas *A*
Colby Community College *A*
Friends University *B*
Pittsburg State University *B, M*
Southwestern College *B*

Kentucky

Asbury University *B*
University of Phoenix
  Louisville *B*

Louisiana

University of Phoenix
  Baton Rouge *B*
  Louisiana *B*
  Shreveport *B*

Maine

College of the Atlantic *B*
University of Maine *B, M*

Maryland

Hood College *B*
Johns Hopkins University *M*
Notre Dame of Maryland
  University *B*

Massachusetts

Curry College *B*
Massachusetts College of Liberal
  Arts *B, T*
Middlesex Community College *A*
Springfield College *B*
University of Massachusetts
  Boston *B*
Western New England University *B*

Michigan

Albion College *B*
Aquinas College *B, T*
Bay de Noc Community College *A*
Concordia University *B*
Lake Michigan College *A*
Spring Arbor University *B, M*
University of Michigan
  Flint *B*
University of Phoenix
  Metro Detroit *B*
  West Michigan *B*
Western Michigan University *M*

Minnesota

Bethel University *B*
Concordia College: Moorhead *B*
Crown College *B*
University of Minnesota
  Crookston *B*
  Duluth *B*
University of St. Thomas *B*
Walden University *B*

Mississippi

East Mississippi Community
  College *A*
Mississippi College *B*
University of Phoenix
  Jackson *B*

Missouri

DeVry University
  Kansas City *B*
Drury University *B, M*
University of Phoenix
  Kansas City *B*
  St. Louis *B*

Nebraska

Bellevue University *B*
Concordia University *B*
Grace University *B*

Nevada

University of Phoenix
  Northern Nevada *B*

New Hampshire

Granite State College *B*
University of New Hampshire at
  Manchester *B*

New Jersey

College of New Jersey *B*
Fairleigh Dickinson University
  College at Florham *M*
Passaic County Community College *A*

New Mexico

Central New Mexico Community
  College *A*
New Mexico State University *B, M*

New York

Fordham University *B, M*
Hamilton College *B*
Le Moyne College *B*
Marist College *B, M*
Nyack College *B*
Rochester Institute of Technology *B*

SUNY
  College at Fredonia *B*
  College at Oneonta *B*
St. John Fisher College *B*

North Carolina

Elon University *B*
High Point University *B, M*
Lenoir-Rhyne University *B*
Pfeiffer University *B*
Queens University of Charlotte *B, M*
Western Piedmont Community
  College *A*

North Dakota

University of North Dakota *B, M, D*

Ohio

Ashland University *B*
College of Mount St. Joseph *A, B*
John Carroll University *B, M*
Xavier University *B*
Youngstown State University *M*

Oklahoma

University of Central Oklahoma *B, M*

Oregon

University of Phoenix
  Oregon *B*

Pennsylvania

Albright College *B*
Carlow University *B*
DeSales University *B*
DeVry University
  Fort Washington *B*
Drexel University *B, M*
Keystone College *A, B*
Lycoming College *B*
Misericordia University *B*
Neumann University *B*
Reading Area Community College *A*
Saint Joseph's University *B*

South Carolina

Bob Jones University *B, M*
Columbia International University *B*
Newberry College *B*

Tennessee

University of Tennessee
  Chattanooga *B*

Texas

DeVry University
  Irving *B*
Northeast Texas Community
  College *A*
St. Philip's College *A*
Stephen F. Austin State University *M*
Texas A&M University *B, M, D*
University of Houston
  Clear Lake *B*
  Downtown *B*
University of Phoenix
  Austin *B*
  Dallas Fort Worth *B*
  Houston Westside *B*
  San Antonio *B*
University of Texas
  Arlington *M*
  El Paso *B, M*
  Pan American *M*
  Tyler *M*
West Texas A&M University *M*

Utah

University of Phoenix
  Utah *B*
University of Utah *B*

Vermont

Bennington College *B*
Southern Vermont College *B*

Virginia

Bluefield College *B*
Eastern Mennonite University *B*
Lynchburg College *B*
Marymount University *B*
Randolph-Macon College *B*
Roanoke College *B*
University of Phoenix
    Northern Virginia *B*
Virginia Polytechnic Institute and
    State University *M*

Washington

Central Washington University *B*
DeVry University
    Federal Way *B*

West Virginia

West Virginia University *B, M, D*
West Virginia Wesleyan College *B*
Wheeling Jesuit University *B*

Wisconsin

Edgewood College *B*
Marquette University *M*
Northcentral Technical College *C*
University of Phoenix
    Milwaukee *B*
University of Wisconsin
    Whitewater *B*

Wyoming

Sheridan College *A*

Communications/
speech/rhetoric

Alabama

Auburn University at Montgomery *B*
Miles College *B*
Oakwood University *B*
Samford University *B*
Troy University *B*
University of Alabama *B, M*
University of Alabama
    Birmingham *B, M*
    Huntsville *B*
University of North Alabama *B*
University of South Alabama *B, M*

Alaska

University of Alaska
    Fairbanks *B, M*
    Southeast *B*

Arizona

Arizona State University *B, M, D*
Arizona Western College *A*
Cochise College *A*
Grand Canyon University *B*
Northern Arizona University *B, M*
South Mountain Community
    College *C*
University of Arizona *B, M, D*
Western International University *B*

Arkansas

Arkansas Tech University *B*
Harding University *B*
John Brown University *B*
Ouachita Baptist University *B*
University of Arkansas *B, M*
University of Arkansas
    Little Rock *B*
    Monticello *B*
University of Central Arkansas *B*

California

Azusa Pacific University *B*
Bakersfield College *C, A*
Biola University *B*
California Baptist University *B*
California Lutheran University *B*
California Polytechnic State
    University: San Luis Obispo *B*
California State Polytechnic
    University: Pomona *B*
California State University
    Bakersfield *B*
    Channel Islands *B*
    Chico *M*
    Dominguez Hills *B*
    East Bay *B*
    Fresno *B, M*
    Fullerton *B, M*
    Los Angeles *B, M*
    Northridge *M*
    Sacramento *B, M*
    San Bernardino *B, M, T*
    San Marcos *B*
    Stanislaus *B*
Canada College *A*
Chaffey College *A*
Chapman University *B*
City College of San Francisco *C*
College of the Desert *A*
College of the Sequoias *A*
College of the Siskiyous *A*
Contra Costa College *A*
Copper Mountain College *A*
Cuesta College *C, A*
De Anza College *A*
Diablo Valley College *C, A*
Dominican University of California *B*
Foothill College *C, A*
Fresno City College *A*
Fresno Pacific University *B*
Fullerton College *A*
Gavilan College *A*
Grossmont College *A*
Humboldt State University *B*
Imperial Valley College *A*
La Sierra University *B*
Los Angeles Pierce College *C*
Loyola Marymount University *B*
Mendocino College *C, A*
Merced College *A*
Modesto Junior College *C, A*
Monterey Peninsula College *A*
Moorpark College *A*
Notre Dame de Namur University *B*
Palomar College *A*
Pasadena City College *C, A*
Pepperdine University *B, M*
Point Loma Nazarene University *B*
St. Mary's College of California *B*
San Bernardino Valley College *C, A*
San Deigo Miramar College
    San Diego Miramar College *A*
San Diego Christian College *B*
San Diego State University *B, M*
San Joaquin Delta College *A*
San Jose State University *M*
Santa Ana College *C, A*
Santa Barbara City College *A*
Santa Clara University *B*
Santa Rosa Junior College *C*
Santiago Canyon College *A*
Shasta College *A*
Simpson University *B*
Solano Community College *A*
Sonoma State University *B*
Southwestern College *A*
University of California
    Davis *B, M*
    San Diego *B, M, D*
    Santa Barbara *B, M, D*
University of La Verne *B*
University of San Francisco *B*
University of Southern
    California *B, M, D*

University of the Pacific *B, M*
Vanguard University of Southern
    California *B*
Westmont College *B*

Colorado

Colorado Christian University *B*
Colorado State University *B, M*
Metropolitan State University of
    Denver *B*
Regis University *B*
University of Colorado
    Boulder *B, M, D*
    Denver *B, M*
University of Denver *B, M, D*
University of Northern
    Colorado *B, M, T*
Western State Colorado University *B*
Westwood College
    Denver North *B*

Connecticut

Albertus Magnus College *B*
Central Connecticut State
    University *B*
Eastern Connecticut State
    University *B*
Fairfield University *B*
Middlesex Community College *A*
Norwalk Community College *A*
Quinnipiac University *B, M*
Southern Connecticut State
    University *B*
Tunxis Community College *C*
University of Bridgeport *B*
University of Connecticut *B, M*
University of Hartford *B, M*
University of New Haven *B*
Western Connecticut State
    University *B*

Delaware

University of Delaware *B, M*

District of Columbia

Catholic University of America *B*
Gallaudet University *B*
George Washington University *B*
Howard University *B, M, D*
Trinity Washington University *B*

Florida

Barry University *B*
Bethune-Cookman University *B*
Chipola College *A*
City College
    Fort Lauderdale *A*
Edward Waters College *B*
Embry-Riddle Aeronautical
    University *B*
Florida Atlantic University *B*
Florida International University *B*
Florida Southern College *B*
Florida State University *D*
Jacksonville University *B*
Nova Southeastern University *B*
Palm Beach Atlantic University *B*
Pensacola State College *A*
Saint Thomas University *B*
Seminole State College of Florida *A*
University of Central Florida *B*
University of Miami *B, M, D*
Warner University *B*
Webber International University *B*

Georgia

Abraham Baldwin Agricultural
    College *A*
Andrew College *A*
Atlanta Metropolitan College *A*
Bainbridge College *A*
Brewton-Parker College *A*
Clayton State University *B*
College of Coastal Georgia *A*

Emmanuel College *B*
Georgia Highlands College *A*
Georgia Perimeter College *A*
Georgia Regents University *B*
Georgia State University *B, M, D*
Gordon College *A*
Kennesaw State University *B*
Mercer University *B*
Oglethorpe University *B*
Reinhardt University *B*
Shorter University *B*
South Georgia State College *A*
University of Georgia *B, M, D*
Wesleyan College *B*

Hawaii

Chaminade University of Honolulu *B*
Hawaii Pacific University *B, M*
University of Hawaii
    Hilo *B*
    Manoa *B, M*

Idaho

Boise State University *B, M, T*
Brigham Young University-Idaho *B*
College of Southern Idaho *A*
Idaho State University *B*
Lewis-Clark State College *B*
North Idaho College *A*
Northwest Nazarene University *B*
University of Phoenix
    Idaho *B*

Illinois

Augustana College *B*
Aurora University *B*
Benedictine University *B*
Blackburn College *B*
Bradley University *B*
Concordia University Chicago *B*
DePaul University *B, M*
Dominican University *B*
East-West University *B*
Elmhurst College *B*
Eureka College *B*
Governors State University *B, M*
Illinois State University *M, T*
Illinois Valley Community College *A*
John Wood Community College *A*
Judson University *B*
Kishwaukee College *A*
Lake Forest College *B*
Lewis University *B*
Lincoln College *A*
Loyola University Chicago *C, B*
McKendree University *B*
Millikin University *B*
Monmouth College *B*
Moody Bible Institute *B*
North Central College *B*
North Park University *B*
Northern Illinois University *B, M*
Northwestern University *B, M, D*
Olivet Nazarene University *B*
Saint Xavier University *B*
Sauk Valley Community College *A*
Southwestern Illinois College *A*
Trinity Christian College *B*
Trinity International University *B*
University of Illinois
    Chicago *B, M, D*
    Urbana-Champaign *B, D*
Western Illinois University *B, M*
Wheaton College *B*

Indiana

Bethel College *B*
Butler University *B*
Grace College *B*
Hanover College *B*
Huntington University *B*
Indiana Institute of Technology *B*
Indiana State University *B, M, T*

Indiana University
Bloomington *B, M, D*
East *B*
Kokomo *B*
Northwest *B*
Purdue University Fort
Wayne *B, M, T*
Purdue University
Indianapolis *B, M*
South Bend *B*
Southeast *B*
Indiana Wesleyan University *B*
Ivy Tech Community College
Kokomo *A*
Manchester University *B, T*
Marian University *B*
Purdue University *B, M, D*
Purdue University
Calumet *B, M*
North Central *C, B*
Saint Joseph's College *B*
Saint Mary's College *B*
Taylor University *B*
Trine University *A, B*
University of Indianapolis *B*
Valparaiso University *B*

Iowa

AIB College of Business *B*
Ashford University *B*
Buena Vista University *B*
Central College *B*
Coe College *B*
Dordt College *B*
Drake University *B*
Ellsworth Community College *A*
Graceland University *B*
Iowa State University *B*
Iowa Wesleyan College *B*
Luther College *B*
Mount Mercy University *B*
St. Ambrose University *B*
University of Dubuque *M*
University of Iowa *B, M, D, T*
University of Northern Iowa *B, M*
Upper Iowa University *B*
Waldorf College *B*
Wartburg College *B*

Kansas

Baker University *B*
Barton County Community College *A*
Bethany College *B*
Central Christian College of
Kansas *A, B*
Coffeyville Community College *A*
Cowley County Community
College *A*
Emporia State University *B*
Fort Hays State University *B, M*
Fort Scott Community College *A*
Garden City Community College *A*
Haskell Indian Nations University *A*
Hutchinson Community College *A*
Independence Community College *A*
Kansas State University *B, M*
Kansas Wesleyan University *B, T*
McPherson College *B*
MidAmerica Nazarene University *B*
Neosho County Community
College *A*
Ottawa University *B*
Pratt Community College *A*
Seward County Community
College *A*
Southwestern College *B*
Sterling College *B*
Tabor College *B*
University of Kansas *B, M, D*
Washburn University *B*
Wichita State University *B, M*

Kentucky

Bellarmine University *B, M*
Bluegrass Community and Technical
College *A*
Campbellsville University *B*
Eastern Kentucky University *B*
Henderson Community College *A*
Hopkinsville Community College *A*
Kentucky Mountain Bible College *B*
Kentucky Wesleyan College *B*
Lindsey Wilson College *B*
Morehead State University *B, M*
Murray State University *M*
Northern Kentucky University *B, M*
Thomas More College *A, B*
Transylvania University *B*
Union College *B*
University of Kentucky *B, M, D*
University of Louisville *B, M*
University of Pikeville *B*
University of the Cumberlands *B, T*
West Kentucky Community and
Technical College *A*
Western Kentucky University *B, M*

Louisiana

Centenary College of Louisiana *B*
Dillard University *B*
Louisiana College *B*
Louisiana State University and
Agricultural and Mechanical
College *B, M, D*
Loyola University New Orleans *B*
Northwestern State University *B*
Southeastern Louisiana University *B*
University of Louisiana at
Lafayette *B, M*
University of Louisiana at
Monroe *B, M*

Maine

University of Southern Maine *B*

Maryland

Allegany College of Maryland *A*
Frederick Community College *A*
Frostburg State University *B*
Howard Community College *A*
Loyola University Maryland *B, M*
McDaniel College *B*
Mount St. Mary's University *B*
Salisbury University *B*
Towson University *B*
University of Maryland
College Park *B, M, D*
University College *B*
Washington Adventist University *B*

Massachusetts

Boston College *B*
Boston University *B, M*
Bridgewater State University *B*
Bristol Community College *A*
Bunker Hill Community College *A*
Cape Cod Community College *A*
Clark University *B, M*
Dean College *A*
Elms College *B*
Emerson College *C, B, M*
Emmanuel College *B*
Fitchburg State University *B, M*
Gordon College *B*
Hampshire College *B*
Massachusetts Bay Community
College *C, A*
Newbury College *B*
Northeastern University *B, M*
Regis College *B*
Salem State University *B*
Simmons College *B, M*
Stonehill College *B*
Suffolk University *B, M*
University of Massachusetts
Amherst *B, M, D*

Western New England University *B*
Westfield State University *B*
Worcester State University *B*

Michigan

Adrian College *A, B, T*
Albion College *B*
Andrews University *B, M*
Baker College
Jackson *A*
Calvin College *B*
Central Michigan University *B, M*
Cornerstone University *B*
Eastern Michigan University *B, M*
Ferris State University *B*
Grand Valley State University *B, M*
Hillsdale College *B*
Hope College *B*
Kuyper College *B*
Lake Superior State University *B*
Lansing Community College *A*
Lawrence Technological University *B*
Macomb Community College *C, A*
Michigan State University *B, M, D*
Northern Michigan University *B*
Northwestern Michigan College *A*
Oakland University *B, M*
Rochester College *B*
Saginaw Valley State University *B, T*
Siena Heights University *B*
Spring Arbor University *B*
University of Detroit Mercy *B*
University of Michigan *B, M, D*
University of Michigan
Dearborn *B*
Flint *B*
Wayne State University *B, M, D*
Western Michigan University *B, M*

Minnesota

Augsburg College *B*
Bethany Lutheran College *B*
Brown College
Mendota Heights *B*
Century College *C*
College of St. Scholastica *B*
Concordia College: Moorhead *B*
Gustavus Adolphus College *B*
Hamline University *B*
Minnesota State University
Mankato *B, M*
Moorhead *B*
Minnesota West Community and
Technical College *A*
Ridgewater College *A*
St. Catherine University *B*
Saint Cloud State University *B*
Southwest Minnesota State
University *B*
University of Minnesota
Morris *B*
Twin Cities *C*
University of Northwestern - St.
Paul *A, B*
Winona State University *B*

Mississippi

Belhaven University *B*
Hinds Community College *A*
Millsaps College *B*
Mississippi College *B, M*
Mississippi Delta Community
College *A*
Mississippi Gulf Coast Community
College *A*
Mississippi State University *B*
Mississippi University for Women *B*
Mississippi Valley State University *B*
Northeast Mississippi Community
College *A*
University of Southern
Mississippi *B, M, D*
William Carey University *B*

Missouri

Avila University *B*
Central Methodist University *B*
College of the Ozarks *B*
Columbia College *B*
Culver-Stockton College *B*
Drury University *B, M, T*
Evangel University *A, B*
Fontbonne University *B*
Hannibal-LaGrange University *B*
Lindenwood University *B, M*
Missouri Southern State University *B*
Missouri State University *B, M*
Missouri Western State University *B*
Northwest Missouri State
University *B*
Park University *B, M*
Rockhurst University *B*
St. Louis Community College *A*
Saint Louis University *B, M*
Southeast Missouri State University *B*
Southwest Baptist University *B*
Truman State University *B*
University of Central Missouri *B, M*
University of Missouri
Columbia *B, M, D*
Kansas City *B*
St. Louis *B, M*
Webster University *B, M*
William Jewell College *B*
William Woods University *B*

Montana

Carroll College *A, B*
Montana State University
Billings *B*
Rocky Mountain College *B*
University of Montana *B, M*
University of Montana: Western *B*

Nebraska

Creighton University *C, B*
Hastings College *B*
Midland University *B*
Nebraska Wesleyan University *B*
Union College *B*
University of Nebraska
Kearney *B*
Lincoln *B, M, D*
Omaha *B, M*
Wayne State College *B*
York College *B*

Nevada

College of Southern Nevada *A*
University of Nevada
Las Vegas *B, M*
Reno *B*

New Hampshire

Keene State College *B*
New England College *B*
Plymouth State University *B*
University of New Hampshire *B*

New Jersey

Bergen Community College *A*
Caldwell College *B*
Centenary College *B*
College of St. Elizabeth *B*
County College of Morris *C*
Fairleigh Dickinson University
College at Florham *B*
Felician College *B*
Georgian Court University *B*
Gloucester County College *A*
Kean University *B*
Middlesex County College *A*
Monmouth University *B*
Montclair State University *M*
New Jersey City University *B*
Ramapo College of New Jersey *B*
Richard Stockton College of New
Jersey *B*

Rider University *B*
Rutgers, The State University of New Jersey
  New Brunswick/Piscataway Campus *B, M, D*
Saint Peter's University *B*
Seton Hall University *B, M*
Thomas Edison State College *A, B*
William Paterson University of New Jersey *B, M*

New Mexico

Eastern New Mexico University *B, M*
New Mexico Junior College *A*

New York

Alfred University *B*
Broome Community College *A*
Canisius College *B*
Cazenovia College *B*
City University of New York
  Brooklyn College *B*
  City College *B*
  College of Staten Island *B*
  Hunter College *M*
  LaGuardia Community College *A*
  Lehman College *B*
  York College *B*
Clarkson University *B*
College of Mount St. Vincent *B*
College of New Rochelle *B, M*
College of Saint Rose *B, M*
Cornell University *B, M, D*
Dowling College *B*
Dutchess Community College *A*
Erie Community College *A*
Excelsior College *B*
Finger Lakes Community College *A*
Fulton-Montgomery Community College *A*
Genesee Community College *A*
Hofstra University *B, M*
Houghton College *B*
Iona College *B*
Ithaca College *B, M*
Jamestown Community College *A*
Keuka College *B*
Long Island University
  LIU Brooklyn *B, M*
Manhattan College *B*
Manhattanville College *B*
Marymount Manhattan College *B*
Molloy College *B*
Monroe Community College *A*
Nassau Community College *A*
Nazareth College *B*
New York University *B, M, D*
Niagara County Community College *A*
Niagara University *B*
Onondaga Community College *A*
Orange County Community College *A*
Pace University *B*
Pace University: Pleasantville/Briarcliff *B*
Rensselaer Polytechnic Institute *B, M, D*
Roberts Wesleyan College *B*
Rochester Institute of Technology *B*
Rockland Community College *A*
SUNY
  College at Brockport *B*
  College at Buffalo *B*
  College at Cortland *B*
  College at Geneseo *B*
  College at New Paltz *B*
  College at Old Westbury *B*
  College at Oswego *B*
  College of Agriculture and Technology at Cobleskill *A*
  University at Albany *B, M*
  University at Buffalo *B, M, D*
St. Francis College *B*

St. John's University *B*
St. Lawrence University *B*
St. Thomas Aquinas College *B*
Suffolk County Community College *A*
Sullivan County Community College *A*
Syracuse University *B, M*
Tompkins Cortland Community College *A*
Touro College *B*
Ulster County Community College *A*
Utica College *B*
Westchester Community College *A*

North Carolina

Appalachian State University *B*
Catawba College *B*
East Carolina University *B, M*
Elizabeth City State University *B*
Fayetteville State University *B*
Gardner-Webb University *B*
Lees-McRae College *B*
Lenoir-Rhyne University *B*
Meredith College *B, T*
Methodist University *A, B*
North Carolina State University *B*
St. Augustine's University *B*
Salem College *B*
Southeastern Community College *A*
University of North Carolina
  Chapel Hill *B, M, D*
  Charlotte *B, M*
  Greensboro *B, M*
  Wilmington *B*
Wake Forest University *B, M*
Western Carolina University *B*
William Peace University *B*
Wingate University *B*

North Dakota

Dickinson State University *B*
Mayville State University *B*
North Dakota State University *M, D*
University of Jamestown *B*
Valley City State University *B*

Ohio

Baldwin Wallace University *B*
Bluffton University *B*
Bowling Green State University *B, M, D*
Capital University *B*
Cedarville University *B*
Cincinnati Christian University *A*
Cleveland State University *B, M*
College of Wooster *B*
Defiance College *B*
Denison University *B*
Edison State Community College *A*
Franciscan University of Steubenville *B*
Heidelberg University *B*
Hiram College *B*
International College of Broadcasting *C, A*
Kent State University *B, M, D*
Kent State University
  Ashtabula *B*
  East Liverpool *B*
  Salem *B*
  Stark *B*
  Trumbull *B*
  Tuscarawas *B*
Lake Erie College *B*
Malone University *B*
Marietta College *B*
Miami University
  Middletown *A*
Mount Vernon Nazarene University *B*
Muskingum University *B*
Notre Dame College *B, T*
Ohio Dominican University *C, B*
Ohio Northern University *B*

Ohio State University
  Columbus Campus *B, M, D*
Ohio University *B, M, D*
Ohio University
  Southern Campus at Ironton *B*
Otterbein University *B*
Sinclair Community College *C, A*
Tiffin University *B*
University of Akron *B, M*
University of Cincinnati *B, M*
University of Cincinnati
  Blue Ash College *A*
University of Dayton *M*
University of Findlay *B*
University of Mount Union *B, T*
University of Rio Grande *A, B*
University of Toledo *B*
Urbana University *B*
Walsh University *B*
Wilmington College *B*
Wittenberg University *B*
Wright State University *A, B*
Wright State University: Lake Campus *A*
Youngstown State University *B*

Oklahoma

Connors State College *A*
East Central University *B*
Langston University *B*
Northeastern State University *B, M*
Oklahoma Baptist University *B*
Oklahoma Christian University *B, T*
Oklahoma Wesleyan University *B*
Oral Roberts University *B*
St. Gregory's University *B*
Southeastern Oklahoma State University *B*
Southern Nazarene University *A, B*
Southwestern Oklahoma State University *B*
University of Oklahoma *B, M, D*
University of Science and Arts of Oklahoma *B*
University of Tulsa *B*

Oregon

Central Oregon Community College *A*
Corban University *B*
George Fox University *B*
Lewis & Clark College *B*
Linfield College *B*
Marylhurst University *B*
Northwest Christian University *B*
Oregon Institute of Technology *B*
Oregon State University *B*
Pacific University *B*
Southern Oregon University *B*
Treasure Valley Community College *A*
Warner Pacific College *B*
Western Oregon University *B*

Pennsylvania

Albright College *B*
Allegheny College *B*
Alvernia University *B*
Arcadia University *C, B*
Baptist Bible College of Pennsylvania *B*
Bloomsburg University of Pennsylvania *B, T*
Bucks County Community College *A*
Cabrini College *B*
California University of Pennsylvania *B, M*
Carnegie Mellon University *M*
Cedar Crest College *B*
Central Penn College *A, B*
Chatham University *B*
Cheyney University of Pennsylvania *B*

Delaware County Community College *A*
Duquesne University *B, M*
East Stroudsburg University of Pennsylvania *B, T*
Eastern University *B*
Edinboro University of Pennsylvania *B, M*
Geneva College *B, T*
Gettysburg College *B*
Grove City College *B*
Gwynedd Mercy University *B*
Immaculata University *C, A, B*
Indiana University of Pennsylvania *B*
Juniata College *B*
La Salle University *A, B, M*
Lehigh Carbon Community College *A*
Lincoln University *B*
Lycoming College *B*
Manor College *A*
Mansfield University of Pennsylvania *B*
Mercyhurst University *B*
Messiah College *B*
Millersville University of Pennsylvania *B*
Montgomery County Community College *B*
Muhlenberg College *C, B*
Northampton Community College *A*
Penn State
  Abington *B*
  Altoona *B*
  Beaver *B*
  Berks *B*
  Brandywine *B*
  DuBois *B*
  Erie, The Behrend College *B*
  Fayette, The Eberly Campus *B*
  Greater Allegheny *B*
  Harrisburg *B, M*
  Hazleton *B*
  Lehigh Valley *B*
  Mont Alto *B*
  New Kensington *B*
  Schuylkill *B*
  Shenango *B*
  University Park *B, M, D*
  Wilkes-Barre *B*
  Worthington Scranton *B*
  York *B*
Pennsylvania Highlands Community College *A*
Robert Morris University *B*
Rosemont College *B, M*
St. Francis University *B*
Saint Joseph's University *B*
St. Vincent College *B*
Seton Hill University *B*
Shippensburg University of Pennsylvania *M*
Slippery Rock University of Pennsylvania *B*
Susquehanna University *A, B, T*
Thiel College *B*
University of Pennsylvania *B, M, D*
University of Pittsburgh
  Greensburg *B*
  Johnstown *B*
University of Scranton *B, T*
Ursinus College *B*
Villanova University *M*
Washington & Jefferson College *B*
Waynesburg University *B*
West Chester University of Pennsylvania *T*
Widener University *B*
Wilkes University *B*
York College of Pennsylvania *B*

Puerto Rico

American University of Puerto Rico *A, B*
Pontifical Catholic University of Puerto Rico *B*

Turabo University *B*
University of the Sacred Heart *B*

Rhode Island

Bryant University *B, M*
Rhode Island College *B*
University of Rhode Island *B, M*

South Carolina

Anderson University *B*
Coastal Carolina University *B*
Coker College *B*
College of Charleston *B*
Columbia College *B*
Furman University *B*
Southern Wesleyan University *B*
University of South Carolina
　Aiken *B*
　Beaufort *B*
　Upstate *B*

South Dakota

Augustana College *B*
Dakota Wesleyan University *B*
Northern State University *B, T*
Presentation College *B*
South Dakota State University *B*
University of South Dakota *B*

Tennessee

Belmont University *B*
Bryan University
　Dayton *B*
Carson-Newman University *B*
East Tennessee State University *M*
Freed-Hardeman University *B*
Hiwassee College *A*
Jackson State Community College *A*
Lane College *B*
Lee University *B*
Lincoln Memorial University *B*
Milligan College *B*
Tennessee State University *B*
Tennessee Technological
　University *B*
Trevecca Nazarene University *B*
Union University *B, T*
University of Tennessee
　Knoxville *B*
　Martin *B*
Vanderbilt University *B*

Texas

Abilene Christian University *B, M*
Amarillo College *A*
Angelina College *A*
Angelo State University *B, M, T*
Austin College *B*
Baylor University *B, M*
Brazosport College *A*
Brookhaven College *A*
Clarendon College *A*
Coastal Bend College *A*
Collin County Community College
　District *A*
Concordia University Texas *B*
Dallas Baptist University *B*
El Paso Community College *A*
Hardin-Simmons University *B*
Houston Baptist University *B*
Howard Payne University *B*
Kilgore College *A*
Lamar University *B*
Laredo Community College *A*
Lone Star College System *A*
McLennan Community College *A*
Midland College *A*
Navarro College *A*
North Lake College *C, A*
Northwest Vista College *A*
Our Lady of the Lake University of
　San Antonio *B*
Palo Alto College *A*
Prairie View A&M University *B*

St. Mary's University *B, M, T*
St. Philip's College *A*
San Jacinto College *A*
Schreiner University *B*
South Plains College *A*
Southwestern Adventist University *B*
Southwestern Assemblies of God
　University *A*
Southwestern University *B, T*
Sul Ross State University *B*
Tarleton State University *B*
Texas A&M International
　University *B*
Texas A&M University
　Corpus Christi *B*
　Kingsville *B*
Texas Christian University *B, M*
Texas Lutheran University *B*
Texas Southern University *B, M*
Texas Wesleyan University *B*
Trinity University *B*
Trinity Valley Community College *A*
University of Houston *B*
University of Houston
　Victoria *B, M*
University of Mary Hardin-Baylor *B*
University of St. Thomas *B*
University of Texas
　Austin *B*
　Brownsville *B*
　El Paso *B*
　Pan American *B*
　Permian Basin *B*
　San Antonio *B, M*
University of the Incarnate
　Word *B, M*
Wayland Baptist University *B*
Weatherford College *A*
West Texas A&M University *B*

Utah

Salt Lake Community College *A*
Southern Utah University *B, M*
University of Utah *B, M, D, T*
Utah Valley University *A, B*
Weber State University *B, M*
Westminster College *B, M*

Vermont

Champlain College *B*
Lyndon State College *A, B*

Virginia

Christopher Newport University *B*
George Mason University *B, M*
Hollins University *B*
James Madison University *B*
Liberty University *B*
Longwood University *B*
Lord Fairfax Community College *A*
Mary Baldwin College *B*
Northern Virginia Community
　College *A*
Radford University *B, M*
Randolph College *B*
Regent University *B, M, D*
Shenandoah University *B*
Thomas Nelson Community
　College *C*
University of Virginia's College at
　Wise *B*
Virginia Polytechnic Institute and
　State University *B*
Virginia Wesleyan College *B*

Washington

City University of Seattle *B*
Eastern Washington
　University *C, B, M*
Green River Community College *C*
Highline Community College *A*
Northwest University *B*
Pacific Lutheran University *B*
Seattle Central Community College *A*

Seattle Pacific University *B*
Skagit Valley College *A*
University of Puget Sound *B*
University of Washington *B, M, D*
University of Washington Tacoma *B*
Walla Walla University *B*
Washington State University *D*
Western Washington University *B*
Whitman College *B*
Whitworth University *B*

West Virginia

Alderson-Broaddus University *B*
American Public University System *A*
Bethany College *B*
Concord University *B*
Fairmont State University *B*
Kanawha Valley Community and
　Technical College *A*
Shepherd University *B*
West Liberty University *B*
West Virginia State University *B, M*
West Virginia University *B, M, D*

Wisconsin

Alverno College *B*
Cardinal Stritch University *B*
Carroll University *B*
Carthage College *B*
Concordia University Wisconsin *B*
Marian University *B*
Milwaukee School of Engineering *B*
Mount Mary University *B*
Ripon College *B*
St. Norbert College *B, T*
University of Wisconsin
　Eau Claire *B*
　Green Bay *B*
　La Crosse *B*
　Madison *B, M, D*
　Milwaukee *B, M, D*
　Oshkosh *B*
　Parkside *B, T*
　Platteville *B*
　River Falls *B, T*
　Stevens Point *B, M*
　Superior *B, M*
　Whitewater *B, M*
Wisconsin Lutheran College *B*

Wyoming

Casper College *A*
Eastern Wyoming College *A*
Laramie County Community
　College *A*
Northwest College *A*
University of Wyoming *B, M*
Western Wyoming Community
　College *A*

Communications systems installation/ repair

Georgia

Georgia Piedmont Technical
　College *C*

Idaho

College of Western Idaho *C, A*
Idaho State University *C, A*

Illinois

College of DuPage *A*
Illinois Central College *C*
Sauk Valley Community College *C*

Iowa

Des Moines Area Community
　College *C, A*

Kansas

Washburn University *A*

Kentucky

Big Sandy Community and Technical
　College *C*

Minnesota

Lake Superior College *C*
Minnesota State College - Southeast
　Technical *C*
Minnesota West Community and
　Technical College *C*
St. Paul College *C*

Mississippi

Meridian Community College *A*

New York

Dutchess Community College *A*
Erie Community College *A*
Mohawk Valley Community
　College *A*
Vaughn College of Aeronautics and
　Technology *A, B*

North Carolina

Central Carolina Community
　College *C*

Pennsylvania

Orleans Technical Institute *C*

Puerto Rico

Inter American University of Puerto
　Rico
　Guayama Campus *M*

Texas

Del Mar College *C, A*

Washington

Bates Technical College *C, A*
Bellingham Technical College *A*

Wisconsin

Herzing University
　Madison *A, B*
Wisconsin Indianhead Technical
　College *C*

Communications technology

Alabama

Community College of the Air
　Force *A*

Arizona

Northland Pioneer College *C, A*

California

Berkeley City College *C, A*
Butte College *C, A*
Chabot College *C, A*
City College of San Francisco *A*
College of San Mateo *C, A*
Cosumnes River College *A*
Cuyamaca College *A*
El Camino College *A*
Laney College *C, A*
Long Beach City College *C, A*
Los Angeles City College *C, A*
Los Angeles Southwest College *A*
Los Angeles Trade and Technical
　College *C, A*
Los Angeles Valley College *C*
Moorpark College *A*
Mount San Antonio College *C, A*
Napa Valley College *C, A*
Pasadena City College *C, A*
Rio Hondo College *A*
San Diego City College *A*
San Jose City College *C, A*
Santa Barbara City College *C, A*

Santa Monica College *A*
Skyline College *C, A*
Southwestern College *C, A*

Colorado

Aims Community College *C, A*
Arapahoe Community College *C, A*
Colorado Mesa University *A*
Pueblo Community College *C, A*

Connecticut

Asnuntuck Community College *A*
Manchester Community College *C*
Naugatuck Valley Community
College *C*
Sacred Heart University *B*

Florida

Miami Dade College *A*
Pensacola State College *A*
Polk State College *C*
Seminole State College of Florida *A*
Valencia College *C, A*

Illinois

College of DuPage *C, A*
Governors State University *M*
Southwestern Illinois College *C, A*

Iowa

AIB College of Business *A*
Dordt College *B*
Iowa Central Community College *A*
Marshalltown Community College *A*

Kansas

Coffeyville Community College *A*
Northwest Kansas Technical
College *C, A*

Kentucky

Jefferson Community and Technical
College *C, A*

Louisiana

ITI Technical College *C, A*

Maine

New England School of
Communications *B*

Maryland

Allegany College of Maryland *A*
Anne Arundel Community.
College *C, A*
Frederick Community College *A*

Massachusetts

Lesley University *B*
Newbury College *A*
Northern Essex Community
College *A*

Michigan

Andrews University *B*
Delta College *A*
Eastern Michigan University *B*
Kalamazoo Valley Community
College *C, A*
Kellogg Community College *A*
Lawrence Technological
University *C, M*
Michigan State University *B*
Mott Community College *C, A*

Minnesota

Hennepin Technical College *C, A*

Mississippi

Northwest Mississippi Community
College *A*

Missouri

Evangel University *B*
Metropolitan Community College -
Kansas City *C*
Ozarks Technical Community
College *A*
Ranken Technical College *A*

Nebraska

Grace University *B*
Hastings College *B*
University of Nebraska
Lincoln *D*

New Hampshire

NHTI-Concord's Community
College *C, A*

New Jersey

Bergen Community College *C*
County College of Morris *A*

New York

Cayuga Community College *A*
City University of New York
Queensborough Community
College *A*
York College *B*
Monroe Community College *A*
New York University *M, D*
SUNY
College of Agriculture and
Technology at Cobleskill *B*
Suffolk County Community College *A*

North Dakota

Minot State University *B*

Ohio

Bowling Green State University:
Firelands College *A*
Cedarville University *B*
Cuyahoga Community College
Metropolitan *A*

Oklahoma

Langston University *B*
Southern Nazarene University *B*
Tulsa Community College *A*

Oregon

Clackamas Community College *C, A*

Pennsylvania

Community College of Beaver
County *A*
East Stroudsburg University of
Pennsylvania *A, B*
Philadelphia University *M*
Point Park University *M*

Puerto Rico

American University of Puerto
Rico *B*
Inter American University of Puerto
Rico
Bayamon Campus *B*
University of Puerto Rico
Humacao *A*

Tennessee

Nashville State Community College *A*
Southern Adventist University *B*
Tennessee Technological
University *B*

Texas

Amarillo College *A*
Art Institute of Houston *A*
El Paso Community College *A*
Northwest Vista College *C, A*
Richland College *C, A*

Texas State Technical College
Marshall *C, A*
West Texas *A*
University of Houston
Clear Lake *M*

Vermont

Lyndon State College *B*

Virginia

Virginia Western Community
College *A*

Washington

North Seattle Community
College *C, A*
University of Washington *M*
Yakima Valley Community College *C*

West Virginia

New River Community and Technical
College *A*

Wisconsin

Madison Media Institute *A*
University of Wisconsin
Milwaukee *C*

Community health/
preventative medicine

California

East Los Angeles College *A*
National University *A, B, M*
University of California
Los Angeles *M*

Florida

Florida Gulf Coast University *B*
University of Florida *B, M*
University of North Florida *M*

Georgia

Georgia College and State
University *B*

Illinois

Southern Illinois University
Carbondale *M*
University of Illinois
Urbana-Champaign *B, M, D*

Indiana

Indiana University
Bloomington *B, M*

Iowa

University of Iowa *M, D*

Kentucky

Murray State University *B*
Western Kentucky University *B, T*

Louisiana

Louisiana State University
Health Sciences Center *D*

Minnesota

Anoka-Ramsey Community College *A*
Bemidji State University *B*
Minnesota State University
Moorhead *B*

Nebraska

Concordia University *B*
University of Nebraska
Medical Center *D*

New York

Adelphi University *M*
City University of New York
Hostos Community College *A*

Hofstra University *B, M*
Ithaca College *B*
Long Island University
LIU Brooklyn *M*
SUNY
University at Buffalo *M, D*

Ohio

University of Cincinnati
Blue Ash College *A*
University of Toledo *M*
Youngstown State University *B*

Pennsylvania

Moravian College *B*

Texas

University of Texas
El Paso *M*
Health Science Center at
Houston *M, D*
Medical Branch at Galveston *M, D*

Utah

Utah Valley University *A, B*

Vermont

Goddard College *B, M*

Virginia

George Mason University *B*

Wisconsin

University of Wisconsin
La Crosse *B, M*
Madison *M, D*

Community health
services

Alabama

Faulkner University *B*

Alaska

University of Alaska
Fairbanks *C, A*

Arizona

Pima Community College *C*
University of Arizona *B*

Arkansas

University of Central Arkansas *B, M*

California

Berkeley City College *C, A*
California State University
Fresno *B*
City College of San Francisco *C*

Connecticut

Quinebaug Valley Community
College *A*
Southern Connecticut State
University *M*
Western Connecticut State
University *B*

District of Columbia

Trinity Washington University *M*

Florida

College of Central Florida *C*
Hillsborough Community College *C*
University of Miami *M*
University of West Florida *B, M*

Georgia

Darton College *C, A*

Illinois
Illinois Central College *A*
McHenry County College *C*
Northeastern Illinois University *B*
Northern Illinois University *B*
Waubonsee Community College *C, A*

Indiana
Indiana State University *B*
Indiana University
  Purdue University Fort Wayne *B*
Indiana Wesleyan University *M*

Iowa
Mount Mercy University *M*

Kansas
University of Kansas *B*
Washburn University *C*

Kentucky
Northern Kentucky University *C*
University of the Cumberlands *B*

Maine
University of Maine
  Farmington *B*

Massachusetts
Berkshire Community College *C*
Mount Wachusett Community College *C*
Northeastern University *C*
University of Massachusetts Lowell *B*
Worcester State University *B, M, T*

Michigan
Michigan State University *B, M*
Mott Community College *A*
Northern Michigan University *B*
Oakland Community College *A*

Minnesota
Inver Hills Community College *C*
Minneapolis Community and Technical College *C*
Northwest Technical College *C*
Rochester Community and Technical College *C*
Saint Cloud State University *B*
South Central College *C*
University of Minnesota Twin Cities *M*

Montana
Carroll College *B*
Little Big Horn College *A*

Nebraska
University of Nebraska Omaha *B*

New Mexico
Eastern New Mexico University: Roswell *C*
New Mexico State University *B*

New York
Adelphi University *M*
Canisius College *M*
City University of New York
  Brooklyn College *M*
  Kingsborough Community College *M*
Dutchess Community College *C*
Erie Community College *A*
SUNY
  College at Cortland *M*

North Carolina
Johnson C. Smith University *B*

Ohio
Ashland University *M*
Cincinnati State Technical and Community College *C*
Cleveland State University *M*
Muskingum University *B*
North Central State College *C*
Ohio University *B*
University of Dayton *M*
Youngstown State University *B*

Oklahoma
University of Oklahoma *M*

Pennsylvania
Duquesne University *M*
University of Pennsylvania *B*

Rhode Island
Brown University *B*
Rhode Island College *B*

South Carolina
Morris College *B*

Texas
St. Mary's University *M*
Texas A&M University *B*
Texas Woman's University *M*
University of Texas
  Health Science Center at Houston *M, D*

Vermont
Goddard College *B, M*

Virginia
James Madison University *B*
Longwood University *B*
Old Dominion University *M*

Washington
Clark College *C*
Eastern Washington University *B*
Edmonds Community College *C, A*
Western Washington University *B*

West Virginia
West Virginia University *M*

Wisconsin
Marian University *M*

Community/junior college administration

California
California Lutheran University *M*
San Diego State University *M*

Colorado
Colorado State University *D*

Illinois
Argosy University Chicago *D*
Chicago State University *M*
University of Illinois Urbana-Champaign *M, D*

Massachusetts
Springfield College *D*

Michigan
Central Michigan University *M*
Eastern Michigan University *T*
Ferris State University *D*

Minnesota
University of Minnesota Twin Cities *M*

Mississippi
Alcorn State University *M*
Mississippi State University *M, D*

Missouri
Missouri Baptist University *D*

North Carolina
Western Carolina University *M*

Virginia
George Mason University *D*
Old Dominion University *D*

Washington
University of Washington *M, D*

Community organization/advocacy

Alaska
University of Alaska
  Fairbanks *C, A, B, M*

Arkansas
Southern Arkansas University *B*
University of Central Arkansas *M*

California
Foothill College *C*
Humphreys College *B*
Los Angeles Trade and Technical College *C, A*
Merritt College *C, A*
University of California
  Santa Cruz *B*

Connecticut
Manchester Community College *C, A*
University of Bridgeport *B*
University of Hartford *B*

Florida
Saint Leo University *B*

Georgia
Mercer University *B*

Hawaii
University of Hawaii
  Honolulu Community College *C, A*

Illinois
DePaul University *C, B*
Lewis University *B*
Northwestern University *B, M*
University of Illinois
  Urbana-Champaign *M, D*

Iowa
Des Moines Area Community College *C, A*
Marshalltown Community College *A*

Kentucky
Henderson Community College *A*
Murray State University *M*
Northern Kentucky University *C*
Western Kentucky University *M*

Maine
College of the Atlantic *B, M*

Maryland
Notre Dame of Maryland University *B*

Massachusetts
Berkshire Community College *A*
Brandeis University *M*
Clark University *M*
Holyoke Community College *C*

Merrimack College *M*
Springfield College *B, M*
University of Massachusetts Boston *C, B*

Michigan
Aquinas College *B*
Central Michigan University *B*
Lansing Community College *C, A*
Madonna University *C*
University of Michigan *M*

Minnesota
Minneapolis Community and Technical College *A*
University of Minnesota Twin Cities *B*

Mississippi
Delta State University *M*

Missouri
Rockhurst University *B*

Montana
Montana State University Northern *A, B*
University of Montana *C*

New Hampshire
University of New Hampshire *A*

New Jersey
Montclair State University *M*
Salem Community College *A*

New Mexico
New Mexico State University *B*
University of New Mexico *B*

New York
City University of New York
  Borough of Manhattan Community College *A*
  John Jay College of Criminal Justice *M*
College of New Rochelle *C*
Cornell University *M, D*
Erie Community College *C*
Genesee Community College *C, A*
Herkimer County Community College *A*
Hudson Valley Community College *A*
Jefferson Community College *A*
Metropolitan College of New York *A, B*
New York University *B*
Pace University: Pleasantville/Briarcliff *B*
SUNY
  College at Cortland *B*
  College of Agriculture and Technology at Morrisville *A*
  College of Technology at Alfred *A*
  Empire State College *A, B*
St. Joseph's College New York: Suffolk Campus *C*
St. Joseph's College, New York *C*
Sullivan County Community College *A*
Tompkins Cortland Community College *C, A*
Ulster County Community College *A*

North Carolina
University of North Carolina Greensboro *M*

Ohio
Cleveland State University *M*
James A. Rhodes State College *C*
University of Akron *C, A*
Urbana University *B*

Oregon

Clackamas Community College *A*
Corban University *B*
Lane Community College *C, A*

Pennsylvania

Penn State
    University Park *M*
Saint Joseph's University *M*
University of Pennsylvania *M*

Rhode Island

Bryant University *B*
Providence College *C, B*

South Dakota

Black Hills State University *B*
Northern State University *B*

Tennessee

Chattanooga State Community
    College *A*
Cumberland University *M*
Pellissippi State Community
    College *A*
University of Tennessee
    Chattanooga *B*
Vanderbilt University *M*
Volunteer State Community
    College *A*

Utah

Westminster College *M*

Virginia

Emory & Henry College *B*

Washington

Saint Martin's University *B*

West Virginia

West Virginia University Institute of
    Technology *B*

Wisconsin

Alverno College *B*
Northland College *B*
University of Wisconsin
    Milwaukee *C*

Community psychology

Alabama

Troy University *M*

California

Marymount California University *M*
University of La Verne *D*

Colorado

Adams State University *M*

Connecticut

Mitchell College *B*
University of New Haven *M*

District of Columbia

George Washington University *M*

Florida

Florida Agricultural and Mechanical
    University *M*
University of Miami *B, M, D*

Georgia

Clayton State University *B, M*
University of North Georgia *M*
University of West Georgia *D*

Illinois

DePaul University *M, D*
Northwestern University *B*

Indiana

Martin University *M*

Kansas

University of St. Mary *B*
Wichita State University *D*

Massachusetts

Boston University *M*
Cambridge College *B*

Michigan

Andrews University *M*

Minnesota

Saint Cloud State University *B*

New Hampshire

New England College *M*

New Jersey

Fairleigh Dickinson University
    College at Florham *M*

New York

College of New Rochelle *M*

Ohio

Kent State University *M*

Oklahoma

Rogers State University *B*

Pennsylvania

Penn State
    Harrisburg *M*
Point Park University *M*

Puerto Rico

University of Puerto Rico
    Rio Piedras *M*

South Carolina

Clemson University *M*
Francis Marion University *M*
University of South Carolina
    Aiken *M*

Tennessee

Vanderbilt University *M, D*

Texas

Lamar University *M*
Texas A&M University *D*

Vermont

Goddard College *M*

Virginia

Norfolk State University *M*

Washington

University of Washington Bothell *B*

Wisconsin

Mount Mary University *M*

Comparative/ international education

California

Stanford University *M, D*

District of Columbia

American University *M*
George Washington University *M*
Howard University *M*

Florida

Florida International University *M*
Florida State University *M, D*
University of Miami *B*

Illinois

Loyola University Chicago *M*
University of Illinois
    Urbana-Champaign *M, D*

Indiana

Indiana University
    Bloomington *M*

Massachusetts

Endicott College *M*
Harvard College *M, D*

Minnesota

Bethel University *T*

New Jersey

College of New Jersey *M*

New York

SUNY
    University at Albany *M, D*

Pennsylvania

Lehigh University *M, D*

Tennessee

Vanderbilt University *M*

Vermont

Goddard College *M*

Virginia

University of Virginia *M, D*

Comparative literature

Arkansas

University of Arkansas *M, D*

California

California State University
    Fullerton *B*
    Long Beach *B*
    Northridge *B*
Mills College *B*
National University *B*
San Diego State University *B*
San Francisco State University *B, M*
Stanford University *B, M, D*
University of California
    Berkeley *B, M, D*
    Davis *B, M, D*
    Irvine *B, D*
    Los Angeles *B, M, D*
    Merced *B*
    Riverside *B*
    San Diego *M, D*
    Santa Barbara *B, M, D*
University of La Verne *B*
University of San Francisco *B*
University of Southern
    California *B, M, D*
Whittier College *B*

Colorado

Colorado College *B*
University of Colorado
    Boulder *M, D*

Connecticut

Trinity College *B*
University of Connecticut *M, D*
Yale University *M, D*

Delaware

University of Delaware *B*

District of Columbia

Georgetown University *B*

Florida

Eckerd College *B*

Georgia

Emory University *B, D*
University of Georgia *B, M, D*

Hawaii

Hawaii Pacific University *B*

Illinois

Northwestern University *B, M, D*
University of Chicago *B, D*
University of Illinois
    Urbana-Champaign *B, M, D*

Indiana

Earlham College *B*
Indiana University
    Bloomington *B, M, D*
Manchester University *A*
Purdue University *B, M*
University of Notre Dame *D*

Iowa

University of Iowa *B*

Louisiana

Louisiana State University and
    Agricultural and Mechanical
    College *D*

Maine

University of Maine
    Fort Kent *B*

Maryland

University of Maryland
    College Park *D*

Massachusetts

Brandeis University *B*
Clark University *B*
College of the Holy Cross *B*
Harvard College *B, M, D*
Salem State University *B*
Smith College *B*
Tufts University *B, M, D*
University of Massachusetts
    Amherst *B, M, D*
Wellesley College *B*
Williams College *B*

Michigan

Hillsdale College *B*
Michigan State University *D*
University of Michigan *B, M, D*

Minnesota

University of Minnesota
    Twin Cities *B, M, D*
University of St. Thomas *B*

Missouri

Washington University in St.
    Louis *B, M, D*

New Hampshire

Dartmouth College *B, M*
New England College *B*

New Jersey

Princeton University *B, M, D*
Ramapo College of New Jersey *B*
Rutgers, The State University of New
    Jersey
    New Brunswick/Piscataway
    Campus *B, M, D*

New Mexico
University of New Mexico *B, M*

New York
Bard College *B*
Barnard College *B*
City University of New York
    Brooklyn College *B*
    City College *B*
    Hunter College *B*
    Lehman College *B*
    Queens College *B*
Columbia University *B*
Columbia University
    School of General Studies *B*
Concordia College *B*
Cornell University *B, M, D*
Eugene Lang College The New
    School for Liberal Arts *B*
Fordham University *B*
Hamilton College *B*
Hobart and William Smith Colleges *B*
Hofstra University *B*
New York University *B, M, D*
SUNY
    College at Geneseo *B*
    College at Old Westbury *B*
    University at Binghamton *B, M, D*
    University at Buffalo *M, D*
    University at Stony Brook *B, M, D*
Syracuse University *B*
University of Rochester *B, M*

North Carolina
Duke University *M, D*
University of North Carolina
    Chapel Hill *B, M, D*

Ohio
Case Western Reserve
    University *B, M*
College of Wooster *B*
John Carroll University *B*
Oberlin College *B*
Ohio State University
    Columbus Campus *B*
Ohio Wesleyan University *B*
Wilberforce University *B*

Oregon
Reed College *B*
University of Oregon *B, M, D*
Willamette University *B*

Pennsylvania
Bryn Mawr College *B*
Gettysburg College *B*
Haverford College *B, T*
La Salle University *B*
Penn State
    Abington *B*
    Altoona *B*
    Beaver *B*
    Berks *B*
    Brandywine *B*
    DuBois *B*
    Erie, The Behrend College *B*
    Fayette, The Eberly Campus *B*
    Greater Allegheny *B*
    Harrisburg *B*
    Hazleton *B*
    Lehigh Valley *B*
    Mont Alto *B*
    New Kensington *B*
    Schuylkill *B*
    Shenango *B*
    University Park *B, M, D*
    Wilkes-Barre *B*
    Worthington Scranton *B*
    York *B*
Swarthmore College *B*
University of Pennsylvania *B, M, D*

Puerto Rico
University of Puerto Rico
    Mayaguez *B*
    Rio Piedras *B, M*

Rhode Island
Brown University *B, M, D*

South Carolina
University of South Carolina
    Columbia *B, M, D*

Tennessee
Vanderbilt University *M*

Texas
University of Texas
    Austin *M, D*
    Dallas *B*

Utah
Brigham Young University *B*
University of Utah *B*

Vermont
Johnson State College *B*
Marlboro College *B*
Middlebury College *B*

Virginia
University of Virginia *B*

Washington
Gonzaga University *B*
University of Washington *B, M, D*

Wisconsin
Beloit College *B*
University of Wisconsin
    Madison *B, M, D*
    Milwaukee *B*

Comparative psychology

Washington
Western Washington University *M*

Computational/applied mathematics

California
University of Southern California *B*

Michigan
Michigan Technological University *D*
Western Michigan University *M*

New York
City University of New York
    Brooklyn College *B*
Rochester Institute of Technology *M*

Oklahoma
University of Central Oklahoma *M*

Rhode Island
Bryant University *B*

Texas
University of Texas
    Austin *M, D*

West Virginia
American Public University System *B*

Computational biology

California
Harvey Mudd College *B*
University of Southern California *D*

Colorado
University of Colorado
    Denver *D*

Connecticut
Yale University *M, D*

Maine
Colby College *B*

Massachusetts
Massachusetts Institute of
    Technology *B, M, D*

New Jersey
Princeton University *D*
Rutgers, The State University of New
    Jersey
    Camden Campus *B, M, D*

New York
New York University *D*

Ohio
Case Western Reserve
    University *B, M, D*

Pennsylvania
University of Pittsburgh *D*

Texas
University of Texas
    Arlington *D*

Computational mathematics

Arizona
Arizona State University *B*

California
Allan Hancock College *A*
California Institute of
    Technology *B, M, D*
University of California
    Davis *B*
    Los Angeles *B*

District of Columbia
American University *B*

Florida
Embry-Riddle Aeronautical
    University *B*
Florida State University *B, M, D*

Illinois
DePaul University *M*
University of Illinois
    Urbana-Champaign *B*

Indiana
Indiana University
    Purdue University Fort Wayne *B*

Kentucky
Asbury University *B*

Louisiana
Loyola University New Orleans *B*

Michigan
Hillsdale College *B*
Michigan State University *B*

Missouri
Missouri Southern State University *B*

New York
Rochester Institute of
    Technology *B, M*

North Carolina
University of North Carolina
    Greensboro *D*

Ohio
Ashland University *B*
University of Dayton *M*

Pennsylvania
Carnegie Mellon University *B, D*

Puerto Rico
University of Puerto Rico
    Humacao *B*

South Carolina
University of South Carolina
    Beaufort *B*

South Dakota
South Dakota State University *D*

Texas
North Lake College *A*
Southern Methodist University *M, D*
Southwestern University *B, T*

Utah
University of Utah *M*

Washington
Seattle Pacific University *B*

Wisconsin
Marquette University *B*

Computational science

Indiana
Valparaiso University *M*

Minnesota
College of St. Benedict *B*
St. John's University *B*

New Jersey
Richard Stockton College of New
    Jersey *B, M*

New York
Canisius College *B*
Siena College *B*

Ohio
Central Ohio Technical College *A*

Texas
Texas A&M University
    Commerce *M*
University of Texas
    El Paso *M, D*

Computer and information systems security

Alabama
Auburn University at Montgomery *M*
ITT Technical Institute
    Birmingham *B*
University of Alabama
    Huntsville *B*
University of Phoenix
    Birmingham *B*
Virginia College
    Birmingham *M*

Alaska
Charter College *C, A*

Arizona

Anthem College
  Phoenix *A*
Cochise College *A*
Glendale Community College *C, A*
ITT Technical Institute
  Tempe *B*
  Tucson *B*
South Mountain Community
  College *C, A*
University of Advancing
  Technology *A, B, M*
University of Phoenix
  Phoenix-Hohokam *B*
  Southern Arizona *B*

Arkansas

ITT Technical Institute
  Little Rock *B*
Rich Mountain Community College *C*
University of Phoenix
  Little Rock *B*
  Northwest Arkansas *B*

California

Coleman University *B*
Foothill College *C*
Heald College
  Concord *A*
  Hayward *C, A*
  Rancho Cordova *C, A*
  Roseville *A*
  San Francisco *A*
  San Jose *A*
ITT Technical Institute
  Lathrop *B*
  National City *B*
  Oxnard *B*
  Rancho Cordova *B*
  San Bernardino *B*
  Sylmar *B*
  Torrance *B*
Mt. Sierra College *B*
National University *M*
Santa Rosa Junior College *C*
University of Phoenix
  Bay Area *C, B*
  Central Valley *B*
  Sacramento Valley *C, B*
  San Diego *B*
  Southern California *B*
University of San Francisco *M*
University of Southern California *M*
Westwood College
  Anaheim *B*
  Los Angeles *B*
  South Bay *B*

Colorado

Aspen University *M*
Colorado Technical University *M*
ITT Technical Institute
  Westminster *B*
University of Colorado
  Colorado Springs *B*
University of Phoenix
  Denver *B*
  Southern Colorado *B*
Westwood College
  Denver North *B*
  Denver South *B*

Connecticut

Charter Oak State College *C, B*
University of Phoenix
  Fairfield County *B*

District of Columbia

Howard University *C*
University of Phoenix
  Washington DC *B*
University of the Potomac *C, A, B*

Florida

ITT Technical Institute
  Ft. Lauderdale *B*
  Jacksonville *B*
  Lake Mary *B*
  Miami *B*
  Tampa *B*
Nova Southeastern University *M*
Pasco-Hernando State College *A*
Rasmussen College
  Fort Myers *B*
  New Port Richey *B*
  Ocala *B*
  Pasco/Land O'Lakes *B*
  Tampa/Brandon *B*
University of Miami *B*
University of Phoenix
  Central Florida *B*
  North Florida *B*
  South Florida *B*
  West Florida *B*

Georgia

Atlanta Technical College *C*
Georgia Institute of Technology *M*
Gwinnett Technical College *C, A*
Kennesaw State University *B*
University of Phoenix
  Atlanta *B*
  Augusta *B*
  Columbus *B*
  Savannah *B*

Hawaii

University of Phoenix
  Hawaii *B*

Idaho

College of Western Idaho *C, A*
ITT Technical Institute
  Boise *B*
University of Phoenix
  Idaho *B*

Illinois

DePaul University *B, M*
Elgin Community College *C, A*
Heartland Community College *C*
Lewis University *B, M*
Loyola University Chicago *B*
Moraine Valley Community
  College *C, A*
Rasmussen College
  Aurora *B*
  Mokena/Tinley Park *B*
  Rockford *B*
  Romeoville/Joliet *B*
Rock Valley College *C, A*
University of Illinois
  Urbana-Champaign *B, M, D*
University of Phoenix
  Chicago *B*

Indiana

ITT Technical Institute
  Fort Wayne *B*
  Indianapolis *B*
  Newburgh *B*
Indiana Institute of Technology *B*
Indiana University
  Bloomington *M*
  Purdue University Indianapolis *C*
Ivy Tech Community College
  Bloomington *C*
  Central Indiana *C*
  Columbus *C*
  East Central *C*
  Kokomo *C*
  Lafayette *C*
  North Central *C*
  Northeast *C*
  Northwest *C*
  Richmond *C*
  South Central *C*

Purdue University *M, D*
University of Phoenix
  Indianapolis *B*

Iowa

Iowa Lakes Community College *C*
Iowa State University *M*
Iowa Western Community College *A*
St. Ambrose University *B*

Kansas

Cowley County Community
  College *A*
Emporia State University *B*

Kentucky

ITT Technical Institute
  Louisville *B*
Northern Kentucky University *M*
Sullivan College of Technology and
  Design *A, B*
Sullivan University *M*
University of Louisville *C*
University of Phoenix
  Louisville *B*
University of the Cumberlands *M*
Western Kentucky University *C*

Louisiana

Bossier Parish Community College *C*
ITT Technical Institute
  St. Rose *B*
University of Phoenix
  Baton Rouge *B*
  Lafayette *B*
  Louisiana *B*
  Shreveport *B*

Maryland

Anne Arundel Community
  College *C, A*
Chesapeake College *A*
College of Southern Maryland *A*
Community College of Baltimore
  County *C, A*
Frostburg State University *B*
Harford Community College *C, A*
ITT Technical Institute
  Owings Mills *B*
Johns Hopkins University *M*
University of Maryland
  University College *B, M*
University of Phoenix
  Maryland *B*

Massachusetts

Boston University *D*
Brandeis University *M*
Bristol Community College *C*
Bunker Hill Community College *A*
Holyoke Community College *C*
ITT Technical Institute
  Norwood *B*
  Wilmington *B*
Quinsigamond Community
  College *C, A*
Springfield Technical Community
  College *A*
University of Massachusetts
  Lowell *C*
University of Phoenix
  Boston *B*

Michigan

Baker College
  Port Huron *M*
Cleary University *B*
Davenport University *A, B*
Eastern Michigan University *M*
Ferris State University *B, M*
Henry Ford Community College *A*
ITT Technical Institute
  Canton *B*
  Troy *B*

Mott Community College *C*
Oakland Community College *C, A*
University of Phoenix
  Metro Detroit *B*
  West Michigan *B*
Washtenaw Community College *C, A*

Minnesota

Alexandria Technical and Community
  College *C*
Anoka-Ramsey Community College *C*
Capella University *B, M, D*
Century College *C, A*
Hennepin Technical College *C, A*
Hibbing Community College *A*
ITT Technical Institute
  Eden Prairie *B*
Inver Hills Community College *C*
Metropolitan State University *B*
Minneapolis Community and
  Technical College *C, A*
Minnesota State Community and
  Technical College *C, A*
Rasmussen College
  Blaine *B*
  Bloomington *B*
  Brooklyn Park *B*
  Eagan *B*
  Lake Elmo/Woodbury *B*
  Mankato *B*
  Moorhead *B*
  St. Cloud *B*
Saint Cloud State University *B*
University of Phoenix
  Minneapolis-St. Paul *B*
University of St. Thomas *B*

Mississippi

Hinds Community College *A*
University of Phoenix
  Jackson *B*

Missouri

Jefferson College *C, A*
Southeast Missouri State University *B*
University of Phoenix
  Kansas City *B*
  St. Louis *B*

Montana

University of Great Falls *B*

Nebraska

Bellevue University *M*
ITT Technical Institute
  Omaha *B*
University of Nebraska
  Omaha *B, M*

Nevada

ITT Technical Institute
  Henderson *B*
University of Phoenix
  Las Vegas *B*
  Northern Nevada *B*

New Jersey

Atlantic Cape Community College *C*
New Jersey Institute of
  Technology *M*
Stevens Institute of Technology *B, M*
University of Phoenix
  Jersey City *B*

New Mexico

Eastern New Mexico University:
  Roswell *C*
ITT Technical Institute
  Albuquerque *B*
University of Phoenix
  New Mexico *B*

New York

Erie Community College *C*
Globe Institute of
 Technology *C, A, B*
Marist College *C*
Mercy College *B*
Mildred Elley
 Albany *C*
Mohawk Valley Community
 College *C, A*
Rochester Institute of
 Technology *C, B, M*
Rockland Community College *A*
SUNY
 College of Technology at Alfred *B*
St. John's University *C, A, B*
Westchester Community College *C, A*

North Carolina

Central Piedmont Community
 College *A*
Cleveland Community College *C, A*
Durham Technical Community
 College *C, A*
Fayetteville Technical Community
 College *A*
Isothermal Community College *A*
Stanly Community College *C, A*
University of Phoenix
 Charlotte *B*
 Raleigh *B*
Vance-Granville Community
 College *A*
Wilson Community College *C, A*

North Dakota

North Dakota State College of
 Science *C*
Rasmussen College
 Bismarck *B*
 Fargo *B*

Ohio

Akron Institute of Herzing
 University *A*
Belmont College *A*
Bryant & Stratton College
 Parma *A*
Edison State Community College *A*
Franklin University *B*
ITT Technical Institute
 Dayton *B*
 Hilliard *B*
 Norwood *B*
 Youngstown *B*
James A. Rhodes State College *C, A*
Northwest State Community
 College *A*
Owens Community College
 Toledo *A*
Sinclair Community College *C, A*
Stark State College *A*
University of Akron *C*
University of Cincinnati *C*
University of Phoenix
 Cleveland *B*

Oklahoma

Oklahoma City Community
 College *A*
Oklahoma State University
 Institute of Technology:
 Okmulgee *B*
University of Phoenix
 Oklahoma City *B*
 Tulsa *B*
Wright Career College
 Oklahoma City *A*
 Tulsa *A*

Oregon

ITT Technical Institute
 Portland *B*
Southern Oregon University *B*

Pennsylvania

Bucks County Community College *C*
Butler County Community College *A*
Carnegie Mellon University *M, D*
Community College of
 Philadelphia *A*
Drexel University *B*
East Stroudsburg University of
 Pennsylvania *B*
Harrisburg Area Community
 College *C, A*
Kaplan Career Institute
 Pittsburgh *A*
Lackawanna College *A*
Lehigh Carbon Community College *A*
Luzerne County Community
 College *C, A*
Northampton Community College *A*
Peirce College *C*
Penn State
 Altoona *C, B*
 Berks *B*
Pennsylvania College of
 Technology *B*
Robert Morris University *M*
Temple University *M*
University of Phoenix
 Philadelphia *B*
 Pittsburgh *B*
Westmoreland County Community
 College *C, A*
YTI Career Institute
 Capital Region *A*

Puerto Rico

Atlantic University College *B*
Inter American University of Puerto
 Rico
 Guayama Campus *M*
Universidad del Este *M*

Rhode Island

Community College of Rhode
 Island *C*

South Carolina

ITT Technical Institute
 Greenville *B*
Limestone College *B*
University of Phoenix
 Columbia *B*
York Technical College *C*

South Dakota

Dakota State University *B, M*
National American University
 Rapid City *A, B*

Tennessee

Chattanooga State Community
 College *C*
Fountainhead College of
 Technology *B*
ITT Technical Institute
 Knoxville *B*
 Memphis *B*
 Nashville *B*
University of Phoenix
 Chattanooga *B*
 Knoxville *B*
 Memphis *B*
 Nashville *B*

Texas

Brookhaven College *C*
Central Texas College *C, A*
Del Mar College *A*
Eastfield College *C*
ITT Technical Institute
 Arlington *B*
 Houston North *B*
 Houston West *B*
 Richardson *B*

San Antonio *B*
 Webster *B*
North Lake College *C, A*
St. Philip's College *C, A*
Sam Houston State University *M*
San Antonio College *C, A*
South Texas College *A*
Texas State Technical College
 Waco *C, A*
University of Dallas *M*
University of Houston *M*
University of Phoenix
 Dallas Fort Worth *B*
 Houston Westside *B*
 San Antonio *B*
University of Texas
 San Antonio *B*

Utah

LDS Business College *C*
University of Phoenix
 Utah *B*
Weber State University *C, B*
Western Governors University *B, M*

Vermont

Champlain College *B*
Norwich University *B, M*

Virginia

ECPI University *B*
George Mason University *M*
ITT Technical Institute
 Chantilly *B*
 Norfolk *B*
 Richmond *B*
 Springfield *B*
Lord Fairfax Community College *C*
Marymount University *M*
Skyline College: Roanoke *B*
University of Management and
 Technology *A, B, M*
University of Phoenix
 Northern Virginia *B*
 Richmond *B*
University of the Potomac *C, A, B*
Virginia Commonwealth
 University *M*
World College *B*

Washington

Bellevue College *C, A*
Clover Park Technical College *C, A*
Edmonds Community College *C, A*
Green River Community College *C, A*
ITT Technical Institute
 Everett *B*
 Seattle *B*
 Spokane *B*
Olympic College *C*
Spokane Falls Community College *C*
University of Phoenix
 Western Washington *B*
University of Washington Tacoma *B*

West Virginia

American Public University
 System *C, B*
Blue Ridge Community and Technical
 College *C*

Wisconsin

Blackhawk Technical College *A*
ITT Technical Institute
 Green Bay *B*
 Greenfield *B*
Nicolet Area Technical College *C*
Northcentral Technical College *C*
Rasmussen College
 Appleton *B*
 Green Bay *B*
 Wausau *B*
University of Phoenix
 Milwaukee *B*

Wyoming

Casper College *C, A*
Sheridan College *C, A*

Computer education

Arizona

Northern Arizona University *M*

California

California Baptist University *T*
Fresno Pacific University *M*

Florida

Barry University *M*
Florida Institute of Technology *M*

Hawaii

Hawaii Pacific University *M*

Illinois

Concordia University
 Chicago *B, M, T*
DePaul University *M*

Indiana

Indiana Wesleyan University *T*
University of Indianapolis *T*

Iowa

Buena Vista University *B, T*
Loras College *T*

Kansas

Independence Community College *A*
McPherson College *B, T*
University of St. Mary *T*

Louisiana

Southeastern Louisiana University *B*

Maine

Thomas College *M*

Massachusetts

Lesley University *M*

Michigan

Alma College *T*
Eastern Michigan University *B*
Grand Valley State University *T*
Michigan State University *B*
Michigan Technological University *T*
Saginaw Valley State University *M, T*

Minnesota

Minnesota State University
 Mankato *B, M, T*

Mississippi

Millsaps College *T*

Missouri

Fontbonne University *M, T*
Northwest Missouri State
 University *M, T*

Montana

Montana State University
 Billings *T*
University of Montana: Western *T*

Nebraska

College of Saint Mary *T*
Concordia University *B, T*
Hastings College *M, T*
Union College *B*
University of Nebraska
 Lincoln *B, T*

Nevada

University of Nevada
Las Vegas *B*

New Hampshire

Keene State College *B, T*

New Jersey

Saint Peter's University *M, T*

New Mexico

New Mexico Institute of Mining and
Technology *M*

New York

College of Mount St. Vincent *T*
Long Island University
LIU Post *B, M*
Manhattan College *B, T*
Nazareth College *M*
Pace University: Pleasantville/
Briarcliff *B, T*
SUNY
College at Buffalo *M*
College at Plattsburgh *B, M*

North Dakota

Dickinson State University *B, T*

Ohio

Bowling Green State
University *B, M, T*
University of Findlay *M, T*
Wright State University *M*
Youngstown State University *B, M*

Oklahoma

Eastern Oklahoma State College *A*
Southwestern Oklahoma State
University *T*

Oregon

Western Oregon University *T*

Pennsylvania

Arcadia University *M*
Duquesne University *B, M, T*
Gwynedd Mercy University *M*

South Dakota

Dakota State University *B, T*

Tennessee

Bryan University
Dayton *T*

Texas

Abilene Christian University *B, T*
Hardin-Simmons University *B, T*
Howard Payne University *B*
Lamar University *T*
Laredo Community College *A*
LeTourneau University *B, T*
Lubbock Christian University *B*
McMurry University *B, T*
St. Mary's University *T*
Tarleton State University *T*
University of Mary Hardin-Baylor *T*
University of North Texas *D*
University of Texas
San Antonio *T*
West Texas A&M University *T*

Virginia

Eastern Mennonite University *T*
Hollins University *T*

Washington

Eastern Washington University *M*
Heritage University *B*

West Virginia

Wheeling Jesuit University *B*

Wisconsin

Cardinal Stritch University *M*
Carroll University *T*
Edgewood College *B*
Lawrence University *T*
Marian University *M*
University of Wisconsin
Whitewater *B, T*

Computer engineering

Alabama

Auburn University *B, M, D*
University of Alabama
Birmingham *D*
Huntsville *B, M, D*
University of South Alabama *B*

Alaska

University of Alaska
Fairbanks *B, M*

Arizona

Arizona State University *B, M, D*
Embry-Riddle Aeronautical University
Prescott Campus *B*

Arkansas

Harding University *B*
University of Arkansas *B, M*

California

California Baptist University *B*
California Polytechnic State
University: San Luis Obispo *B*
California State Polytechnic
University: Pomona *B*
California State University
Chico *B, M*
Fresno *B*
Fullerton *B*
Long Beach *B, M*
Northridge *B, M*
Sacramento *B, M*
Cuyamaca College *A*
De Anza College *A*
Heald College
Concord *A*
Northwestern Polytechnic
University *D*
San Diego State University *B, D*
San Francisco State University *B*
San Jose State University *B, M*
Santa Barbara City College *A*
Santa Clara University *B, M, D*
Sonoma State University *B, M*
University of California
Davis *B*
Irvine *B, M, D*
Los Angeles *B*
Merced *B*
Riverside *B*
San Diego *B, M, D*
Santa Barbara *B, M, D*
Santa Cruz *B, M, D*
University of Southern
California *B, M, D*
University of the Pacific *B*
Westwood College
Los Angeles *A*

Colorado

Colorado State University *B*
Colorado Technical University *B, M*
United States Air Force Academy *B*
University of Colorado
Boulder *B*
Colorado Springs *B*
University of Denver *B, M*
Westwood College
Denver North *A*

Connecticut

Fairfield University *B*
University of Bridgeport *B, M, D*
University of Connecticut *B, M, D*
University of Hartford *B*
University of New Haven *B*

Delaware

University of Delaware *B*

District of Columbia

George Washington
University *B, M, D*
Howard University *B*

Florida

Bethune-Cookman University *B*
Broward College *A*
Chipola College *A*
Daytona State College *A*
Eastern Florida State College *A*
Embry-Riddle Aeronautical
University *B*
Florida Agricultural and Mechanical
University *B*
Florida Atlantic University *B, M, D*
Florida Career College
Miami *A*
Florida Institute of
Technology *B, M, D*
Florida International University *B, M*
Florida State College at
Jacksonville *A*
Florida State University *B*
Keiser University *A*
Pensacola State College *A*
State College of Florida, Manatee-
Sarasota *A*
University of Central Florida *B, M, D*
University of Florida *B, M, D*
University of Miami *B, M*
University of South Florida *B, M, D*
University of West Florida *B*

Georgia

Georgia Institute of Technology *B*
Georgia Piedmont Technical
College *A*
Mercer University *B, M*
Middle Georgia State College *A*
University of Georgia *B*

Hawaii

University of Hawaii
Honolulu Community College *A*

Idaho

Brigham Young University-Idaho *B*
College of Southern Idaho *A*
University of Idaho *B, M*

Illinois

Bradley University *B*
Illinois Institute of
Technology *B, M, D*
Lewis University *B*
Northwestern University *B*
Southern Illinois University
Carbondale *B*
Southern Illinois University
Edwardsville *B*
University of Illinois
Chicago *B*
Urbana-Champaign *B, M, D*

Indiana

Indiana Institute of Technology *B*
Indiana University
Purdue University Fort Wayne *B*
Purdue University Indianapolis *B*
Purdue University *B*
Purdue University
Calumet *B*

Iowa

Dordt College *B*
Iowa State University *B, M, D*
University of Iowa *M, D*

Kansas

Kansas State University *B*
University of Kansas *B, M*
Wichita State University *B*

Kentucky

Bellarmine University *B*
University of Kentucky *B*
University of Louisville *B, M, D*

Louisiana

Louisiana State University and
Agricultural and Mechanical
College *B*
University of Louisiana at
Lafayette *B, M, D*
Xavier University of Louisiana *B*

Maine

University of Maine *B, M*

Maryland

Capitol College *A, B*
Carroll Community College *A*
Howard Community College *A*
Johns Hopkins University *B*
University of Maryland
Baltimore County *B, M, D*
College Park *B*

Massachusetts

Boston University *B, M, D*
Eastern Nazarene College *B*
Merrimack College *B*
Northeastern University *B, M, D*
Smith College *B*
Suffolk University *B*
Tufts University *B, M, D*
University of Massachusetts
Amherst *B*
Boston *B*
Dartmouth *B, M*
Lowell *M*
Wentworth Institute of Technology *B*
Western New England University *B*

Michigan

Kettering University *B, M*
Lake Superior State University *B*
Lawrence Technological University *B*
Michigan State University *B, M, D*
Michigan Technological
University *B, M, D*
Oakland University *B*
University of Detroit Mercy *B*
University of Michigan *B, M, D*
University of Michigan
Dearborn *B, M*
Flint *B*
Wayne State University *M, D*
West Shore Community College *A*
Western Michigan University *B, M*

Minnesota

Mesabi Range Community and
Technical College *A*
Minnesota State University
Mankato *B*
Saint Cloud State University *B, M*

Rose-Hulman Institute of
Technology *B*
Taylor University *B*
Trine University *B*
University of Evansville *B*
University of Notre Dame *B, M, D*
Valparaiso University *B*

University of Minnesota
Duluth *M*
Twin Cities *B, M*

Mississippi

Jackson State University *B*
Mississippi State University *B, M, D*

Missouri

Missouri University of Science and
Technology *B, M, D*
Saint Louis University *B, M*
University of Missouri
Columbia *B, M, D*
Washington University in St.
Louis *B, M, D*

Montana

Montana State University *B*
Salish Kootenai College *B*

Nebraska

University of Nebraska
Lincoln *B*

Nevada

University of Nevada
Las Vegas *B*
Reno *B, M, D*

New Hampshire

University of New Hampshire *B*

New Jersey

College of New Jersey *B*
Fairleigh Dickinson University
Metropolitan Campus *M*
New Jersey Institute of
Technology *B, M, D*
Princeton University *B, M, D*
Stevens Institute of
Technology *B, M, D*

New Mexico

University of New Mexico *B, M*

New York

City University of New York
City College *B, M*
Queensborough Community
College *A*
Clarkson University *B*
Columbia University *B, M, D*
Hofstra University *B*
Manhattan College *B, M*
New York Institute of Technology *B*
New York University *B*
Rensselaer Polytechnic
Institute *B, M, D*
Rochester Institute of
Technology *B, M*
SUNY
College at New Paltz *B*
University at Binghamton *B, M*
University at Buffalo *B, M*
University at Stony Brook *B, M, D*
Syracuse University *B, M, D*

North Carolina

Central Carolina Community
College *A*
College of the Albemarle *C, A*
Elon University *B*
Haywood Community College *A*
Johnson C. Smith University *B*
North Carolina Agricultural and
Technical State University *B*
North Carolina State
University *B, M, D*
Southwestern Community College *A*
Surry Community College *A*
University of North Carolina
Charlotte *B*

Western Piedmont Community
College *A*

North Dakota

North Dakota State University *B*

Ohio

Capital University *B*
Case Western Reserve
University *B, M, D*
Cedarville University *B*
Cleveland State University *B*
Miami University
Oxford *B*
Northwest State Community
College *A*
Ohio Northern University *B*
Ohio State University
Columbus Campus *B, M, D*
University of Akron *B, D*
University of Cincinnati *B, M, D*
University of Dayton *B, M*
University of Toledo *B*
Wright State University *B, M, D*
Youngstown State University *B*

Oklahoma

Oklahoma Christian University *B*
Oklahoma State University *B*
Oral Roberts University *B*
University of Oklahoma *B*
University of Tulsa *D*

Oregon

George Fox University *B*
Oregon Health & Science
University *M, D*
Oregon State University *B, M, D*
Portland State University *B, D*
University of Portland *B*

Pennsylvania

Bucknell University *B*
Carnegie Mellon University *B, M, D*
Drexel University *B, M*
Elizabethtown College *B*
Gannon University *M*
Kaplan Career Institute
Pittsburgh *A*
Lehigh University *B, M, D*
Penn State
Abington *B*
Altoona *B*
Beaver *B*
Berks *B*
Brandywine *B*
DuBois *B*
Erie, The Behrend College *B*
Fayette, The Eberly Campus *B*
Greater Allegheny *B*
Harrisburg *B*
Hazleton *B*
Lehigh Valley *B*
Mont Alto *B*
New Kensington *B*
Schuylkill *B*
Shenango *B*
University Park *B*
Wilkes-Barre *B*
Worthington Scranton *B*
York *B*
University of Pennsylvania *B*
University of Pittsburgh *B, M, D*
University of Scranton *A, B*
Villanova University *B, M*
York College of Pennsylvania *B*

Puerto Rico

Inter American University of Puerto
Rico
Bayamon Campus *B, M*
Turabo University *B*
Universidad Politecnica de Puerto
Rico *B, M*

University of Puerto Rico
Mayaguez *B, M, D*
Ponce *A*

Rhode Island

Brown University *B*
Johnson & Wales University
Providence *B*
University of Rhode Island *B*

South Carolina

Aiken Technical College *A*
Benedict College *B*
Clemson University *B, M, D*
University of South Carolina
Columbia *B, M, D*

South Dakota

South Dakota School of Mines and
Technology *B, M*

Tennessee

Christian Brothers University *B*
Lipscomb University *B*
Tennessee State University *M, D*
Tennessee Technological
University *B, M, D*
University of Memphis *B*
University of Tennessee
Knoxville *B, M, D*
Vanderbilt University *B*

Texas

Amarillo College *A*
LeTourneau University *B*
Prairie View A&M University *B*
Rice University *B, M, D*
St. Mary's University *B, M*
Southern Methodist
University *B, M, D*
Texas A&M University *B, M, D*
Texas A&M University
Kingsville *B, M*
Texas Tech University *B*
University of Houston *B*
University of Houston
Clear Lake *B, M*
University of North Texas *B, M*
University of Texas
Arlington *B, M, D*
Dallas *B, M, D*
El Paso *M, D*
Pan American *B*
San Antonio *M*

Utah

Brigham Young University *B*
University of Utah *B*
Utah State University *B, M*

Virginia

Christopher Newport University *B*
George Mason University *B, M, D*
Hampton University *B*
Liberty University *B*
New River Community College *A*
Old Dominion University *B*
University of Virginia *B, M, D*
Virginia Commonwealth University *B*
Virginia Polytechnic Institute and
State University *B, M, D*
Virginia State University *B*

Washington

DigiPen Institute of Technology *B*
Gonzaga University *B*
Pacific Lutheran University *B*
Seattle Pacific University *B*
University of Washington *B, M*
Walla Walla University *B*
Washington State University *B*

West Virginia

West Virginia University *B, D*

Wisconsin

Marquette University *B*
Milwaukee School of Engineering *B*
University of Wisconsin
Madison *B*
Milwaukee *B*
Stout *B*

Wyoming

University of Wyoming *B*

Computer engineering technology

Arizona

DeVry University
Phoenix *B*
Eastern Arizona College *C*
Pima Community College *C*

Arkansas

Arkansas State University
Newport *A*
University of Arkansas
Little Rock *B*

California

DeVry University
Pomona *B*
Heald College
San Francisco *A*
Santa Barbara City College *C, A*
Southwestern College *C, A*

Colorado

Arapahoe Community College *A*
DeVry University
Westminster *B*

Connecticut

Central Connecticut State
University *B*
Naugatuck Valley Community
College *C*
University of Hartford *A, B*

Delaware

Delaware Technical Community
College
Stanton/Wilmington Campus *A*
Terry Campus *A*

Florida

DeVry University
Miramar *B*
Orlando *B*
Polk State College *A*
Saint Johns River State College *C, A*
St. Petersburg College *A*
South Florida State College *A*

Georgia

Middle Georgia State College *A*
Savannah State University *B*
Southern Polytechnic State
University *B*

Illinois

DeVry University
Chicago *B*
Online *B*
Lincoln Land Community College *C*
Moraine Valley Community College *C*
Prairie State College *C*

Indiana

Indiana State University *B*
Indiana University
Purdue University Fort Wayne *B*
Purdue University Indianapolis *B*
Martin University *B*
Purdue University *A, B*

Kansas

Kansas City Kansas Community
College *A*

Kentucky

Southeast Kentucky Community and
Technical College *C, A*
Spencerian College: Lexington *C, A*
Sullivan College of Technology and
Design *A*

Maine

Southern Maine Community
College *A*

Maryland

Frederick Community College *C, A*

Massachusetts

Benjamin Franklin Institute of
Technology *A*
Massachusetts Bay Community
College *A*
Quinsigamond Community
College *C, A*
Springfield Technical Community
College *C, A*
University of Massachusetts
Lowell *C*
Wentworth Institute of Technology *B*

Michigan

Eastern Michigan University *B*
Northern Michigan University *C, A*

Minnesota

Minnesota State Community and
Technical College *C, A*
Minnesota State University
Mankato *B*
Minnesota West Community and
Technical College *A*
Rochester Community and Technical
College *C*

Mississippi

University of Southern Mississippi *B*

Missouri

DeVry University
Kansas City *B*
Grantham University *B*
Missouri Western State
University *A, B*

New Hampshire

NHTI-Concord's Community
College *C, A*

New York

Broome Community College *A*
Cayuga Community College *C*
City University of New York
New York City College of
Technology *B*
Corning Community College *A*
DeVry College of New York
Midtown Campus *B*
Fulton-Montgomery Community
College *C, A*
Rochester Institute of Technology *B*
SUNY
College of Agriculture and
Technology at Morrisville *A*
College of Technology at
Alfred *A, B*
Farmingdale State College *B*
Institute of Technology at Utica/
Rome *B*

North Carolina

Catawba Valley Community
College *A*

Central Piedmont Community
College *C, A*
College of the Albemarle *C*
Forsyth Technical Community
College *A*
Gaston College *A*
Isothermal Community College *C, A*
Lenoir Community College *C, A*
Nash Community College *A*
Sandhills Community College *C, A*
Stanly Community College *C, A*
Wilkes Community College *A*

Ohio

Bowling Green State University:
Firelands College *A*
Cincinnati State Technical and
Community College *A*
DeVry University
Columbus *B*
ITT Technical Institute
Strongsville *A*
Miami University
Hamilton *A*
North Central State College *A*
Northwest State Community
College *C*
Owens Community College
Toledo *C, A*
Shawnee State University *B*
University of Cincinnati *B*
University of Dayton *B*

Oregon

Oregon Institute of Technology *B*

Pennsylvania

California University of
Pennsylvania *A, B*
Community College of
Philadelphia *A*
DeVry University
Fort Washington *B*
Montgomery County Community
College *A*
University of Pittsburgh
Johnstown *B*
Westmoreland County Community
College *A*

Rhode Island

Community College of Rhode
Island *A*

South Carolina

Aiken Technical College *A*
York Technical College *A*

Tennessee

Southwest Tennessee Community
College *C, A*

Texas

Brookhaven College *C, A*
DeVry University
Houston *B*
Irving *B*
Houston Community College
System *C, A*
LeTourneau University *B*
Mountain View College *A*
North Lake College *C*
Prairie View A&M University *B*
Texas Southern University *B*
University of Houston *B, M*
University of Houston
Downtown *B*

Utah

Salt Lake Community College *A*
Weber State University *A, B*

Vermont

Vermont Technical College *A, B*

Virginia

American National University
Salem *C*
DeVry University
Arlington *B*
Norfolk State University *B*

Washington

Bates Technical College *C, A*
DeVry University
Federal Way *B*

Wisconsin

Herzing University
Madison *A, B*
Western Technical College *A*

Computer forensics

Arizona

University of Advancing
Technology *A, B*

District of Columbia

University of the Potomac *B*

Florida

Keiser University *B*
Southwest Florida College *B*

Illinois

Harper College *C, A*

Maryland

Stevenson University *M*
University of Maryland
University College *M*

Massachusetts

Bay Path College *M*

New York

City University of New York
John Jay College of Criminal
Justice *M*
Excelsior College *M*

North Carolina

Stanly Community College *C, A*

Ohio

Defiance College *B*
Sinclair Community College *C, A*
Tiffin University *B*

Oregon

Chemeketa Community College *C*

Pennsylvania

Bloomsburg University of
Pennsylvania *B*
Chestnut Hill College *C*
Robert Morris University *B*

Rhode Island

New England Institute of
Technology *B*

South Carolina

Southern Wesleyan University *B*

Tennessee

Christian Brothers University *B*

Vermont

Champlain College *B, M*

Virginia

George Mason University *M*
University of the Potomac *B*

West Virginia

American Public University System *C*

Computer graphics

Alabama

Calhoun Community College *A*
Faulkner State Community
College *C, A*

Arizona

Arizona Western College *A*
Art Institute of Phoenix *B*
Estrella Mountain Community
College *C*
Glendale Community College *C*
Northland Pioneer College *C, A*
Phoenix College *C, A*

California

Antelope Valley College *C, A*
Art Institute of California
Inland Empire *B*
Los Angeles *A, B*
Orange County *A, B*
San Diego *B*
San Francisco *B*
Silicon Valley *A, B*
California Lutheran University *B*
California State University
Chico *B*
Canada College *C*
Carrington College California
San Jose *C, A*
Chaffey College *C*
City College of San Francisco *C*
Coleman University *A, B*
Coleman University: San Marcos *C*
College of the Siskiyous *C*
Cypress College *C*
Diablo Valley College *C*
Ex'pression College *B*
Fashion Institute of Design and
Merchandising
San Francisco *A*
Foothill College *C, A*
Fullerton College *C*
Gavilan College *C, A*
Golden West College *C*
Los Angeles Southwest College *C, A*
Modesto Junior College *C, A*
Ohlone College *C, A*
Orange Coast College *C, A*
Palomar College *C, A*
Platt College
Los Angeles *C, A*
Ontario *C, A, B*
Saddleback College *C*
Santa Ana College *C*
Santa Barbara City College *C*
Santa Rosa Junior College *C*
University of California
Irvine *D*
Westwood College
Anaheim *A*
Los Angeles *B*

Colorado

CollegeAmerica
Colorado Springs *A, B*
Denver *A*
Fort Collins *A*
Colorado Mountain College *A*
Colorado Technical University *C*
Morgan Community College *C*
Rocky Mountain College of Art &
Design *B*
Westwood College
Denver North *A, B*
Denver South *A, B*

Connecticut

Norwalk Community College *C*
Quinnipiac University *B*
Tunxis Community College *C, A*

Florida

Art Institute of Fort Lauderdale *B*
Broward College *A*
Digital Media Arts College *B, M*
Florida Gateway College *A*
Florida State College at
  Jacksonville *A*
Herzing University
  Winter Park *C*
Indian River State College *A*
International Academy of Design and
  Technology
  Orlando *A, B*
Keiser University *A*
Miami International University of Art
  and Design *B*
Saint Johns River State College *A*
Seminole State College of Florida *A*
Tallahassee Community College *A*
University of Miami *B*

Georgia

Middle Georgia State College *C*
Southeastern Technical College *C*

Hawaii

University of Hawaii
  Hawaii Community College *C*
  Honolulu Community College *A*

Idaho

College of Southern Idaho *C, A*

Illinois

American Academy of Art *B*
DePaul University *B, M*
Lewis and Clark Community
  College *A*
Moraine Valley Community College *A*
Richland Community College *A*

Indiana

Indiana Institute of Technology *A*
Indiana Wesleyan University *B*
Purdue University *A, B, M*

Iowa

Ellsworth Community College *A*
Southeastern Community College *A*
University of Dubuque *B*

Kansas

Northwest Kansas Technical
  College *C, A*
Seward County Community
  College *C, A*

Kentucky

Spencerian College: Lexington *A*
Sullivan College of Technology and
  Design *A*

Maryland

Baltimore City Community
  College *C, A*
Carroll Community College *C, A*
Frederick Community College *C*
Kaplan University
  Hagerstown *A, B*
Montgomery College *A*

Massachusetts

Hampshire College *B*
Mount Wachusett Community
  College *C, A*
Newbury College *B*
Northern Essex Community
  College *A*

Quinsigamond Community College *A*
Springfield College *B*

Michigan

Art Institute of Michigan *B*
Baker College
  Auburn Hills *A*
  Clinton Township *A*
  Muskegon *A*
  Owosso *A, B*
  Port Huron *C, A*
Bay de Noc Community College *A*
Jackson College *C, A*
Kalamazoo Valley Community
  College *A*
Schoolcraft College *C, A*
Washtenaw Community College *C, A*

Minnesota

Art Institutes International
  Minnesota *A, B*
Capella University *B*
Hennepin Technical College *C, A*
St. Paul College *A*

Missouri

Lindenwood University *B*

Montana

Fort Peck Community College *A*
Miles Community College *A*
University of Great Falls *B*

Nebraska

Vatterott College
  Spring Valley *A*

Nevada

Art Institute of Las Vegas *B*
College of Southern Nevada *C, A*
Great Basin College *A*

New Hampshire

Southern New Hampshire
  University *B*

New Jersey

Bergen Community College *C, A*
Burlington County College *A*
Camden County College *A*
Cumberland County College *C*
Essex County College *C*
Gloucester County College *C, A*
Middlesex County College *A*
Salem Community College *A*

New Mexico

Dona Ana Community College of
  New Mexico State University *A*
New Mexico Junior College *A*
New Mexico State University
  Carlsbad *C*

New York

Columbia-Greene Community
  College *C*
Globe Institute of
  Technology *C, A, B*
Island Drafting and Technical
  Institute *A*
New York Institute of
  Technology *B, M*
North Country Community
  College *C, A*
Pratt Institute *B, M*
Rochester Institute of
  Technology *B, M*
Rockland Community College *A*
Suffolk County Community College *A*
Sullivan County Community
  College *A*

North Carolina

Alamance Community College *C*
Campbell University *B*
Methodist University *B*
Stanly Community College *A*
Wake Technical Community
  College *C, A*
Western Piedmont Community
  College *C*
Wilkes Community College *A*

Ohio

Art Institute of Cincinnati *A, B*
Belmont College *A*
Central Ohio Technical College *A*
ITT Technical Institute
  Dayton *A*
  Norwood *A*
  Strongsville *A*
James A. Rhodes State College *C*
School of Advertising Art *A*
Stark State College *A*
University of Cincinnati
  Blue Ash College *C, A*
Washington State Community
  College *A*

Oklahoma

Oklahoma State University
  Oklahoma City *A*
Rogers State University *B*

Oregon

Art Institute of Portland *B*

Pennsylvania

Arcadia University *C*
Art Institute of Philadelphia *B*
Art Institute of Pittsburgh *B*
Berks Technical Institute *A*
Carnegie Mellon University *B, M*
Eric Business Center *A*
La Salle University *B*
Lansdale School of Business *C, A*
Luzerne County Community
  College *A*
University of Pennsylvania *B*

South Carolina

Aiken Technical College *C*
York Technical College *C*

South Dakota

Dakota State University *B*

Tennessee

Memphis College of Art *B*

Texas

Amarillo College *C, A*
Midland College *C, A*
North Lake College *C*
Remington College
  Fort Worth *A*
Texas A&M University *B, M*
Trinity Valley Community
  College *C, A*
University of Houston *B*
University of Mary Hardin-Baylor *B*

Utah

Brigham Young University *B*
Dixie State College *B*

Vermont

Champlain College *B*
Lyndon State College *B*

Virginia

Central Virginia Community
  College *C*
New River Community College *A*

Thomas Nelson Community
  College *A*

Washington

Art Institute of Seattle *B*
Bellevue College *C, A*
Edmonds Community College *C, A*
Everett Community College *C*
Lake Washington Institute of
  Technology *C*
Pierce College *A*
Walla Walla University *B*

Wisconsin

Herzing University
  Madison *A, B*
Lakeshore Technical College *A*
Milwaukee Area Technical College *A*
Nicolet Area Technical College *A*
St. Norbert College *B*

Computer hardware engineering

Illinois

Illinois Institute of Technology *M*
University of Illinois
  Urbana-Champaign *B, M, D*

Maryland

United States Naval Academy *B*

Michigan

Oakland University *M*

New York

SUNY
  University at Stony Brook *B*

Rhode Island

New England Institute of
  Technology *A, B*

Utah

Utah Valley University *B*

Washington

Seattle University *B*

Computer hardware technology

Arizona

South Mountain Community
  College *C*

California

City College of San Francisco *C*
MTI College *C*

Colorado

IntelliTec College: Grand Junction *A*

Delaware

Delaware Technical Community
  College
  Terry Campus *C*

Florida

Florida Career College
  Miami *C*
St. Petersburg College *C*

Kentucky

Sullivan College of Technology and
  Design *A*

Maryland

Frederick Community College *C, A*

Massachusetts

Benjamin Franklin Institute of
Technology *A*

Michigan

Baker College
Muskegon *C*
Oakland Community College *C, A*

Minnesota

Anoka Technical College *C*
South Central College *C*

Mississippi

Pearl River Community College *C*

New York

Cayuga Community College *A*
SUNY
College of Technology at Alfred *A*
Farmingdale State College *C*

North Carolina

Forsyth Technical Community
College *C, A*

Ohio

Lakeland Community College *C*
Miami University
Hamilton *C*

Rhode Island

Community College of Rhode
Island *C*
New England Institute of
Technology *A, B*

South Dakota

Southeast Technical Institute *C, A*

Texas

North Lake College *C*

Virginia

Mountain Empire Community
College *A*

Washington

Bates Technical College *C, A*

Wisconsin

Herzing University
Madison *A, B*

Computer/information sciences, general

Alabama

Alabama Agricultural and Mechanical
University *B, M*
Amridge University *B*
Athens State University *B*
Auburn University *B*
Bevill State Community College *A*
Birmingham-Southern College *B*
Bishop State Community College *A*
Calhoun Community College *C, A*
Central Alabama Community
College *C, A*
Chattahoochee Valley Community
College *C, A*
Community College of the Air
Force *A*
Enterprise State Community
College *A*
Faulkner State Community College *A*
Faulkner University *A, B*
Gadsden State Community
College *C, A*
George C. Wallace Community
College at Dothan *C, A*

George C. Wallace State Community
College at Selma *C, A*
Jacksonville State University *B, M*
Jefferson State Community
College *C, A*
Lurleen B. Wallace Community
College *C, A*
Miles College *B*
Northeast Alabama Community
College *C, A*
Northwest-Shoals Community
College *A*
Oakwood University *B*
Snead State Community College *A*
Southern Union State Community
College *C, A*
Talladega College *B*
Troy University *A, B, M*
Tuskegee University *B*
University of Alabama *B, M, D*
University of Alabama
Birmingham *B, M, D*
Huntsville *B, M, D*
University of Mobile *B*
University of North Alabama *B*
University of South Alabama *M*
Wallace State Community College at
Hanceville *A*

Alaska

Charter College *C*
University of Alaska
Anchorage *B*
Fairbanks *B, M*
Southeast *C, A*

Arizona

Arizona State University *B*
Arizona Western College *C, A*
Central Arizona College *C, A*
Chandler-Gilbert Community
College *A*
Dine College *A*
GateWay Community College *C, A*
Glendale Community College *C, A*
Mesa Community College *A*
Mohave Community College *A*
Northcentral University *B, M, D*
Northland Pioneer College *C, A*
Paradise Valley Community
College *C, A*
Penn Foster College *A*
Phoenix College *C, A*
Pima Community College *C, A*
Rio Salado College *C, A*
Scottsdale Community College *C, A*
South Mountain Community
College *C, A*
University of Arizona *B*
University of Phoenix
Phoenix-Hohokam *B*
Western International
University *A, B, M*
Yavapai College *C, A*

Arkansas

Arkansas State University *B, M*
Arkansas Tech University *B*
College of the Ouachitas *C, A*
Henderson State University *B*
Mid-South Community College *A*
National Park Community College *C*
North Arkansas College *C, A*
Northwest Arkansas Community
College *A*
Southeast Arkansas College *A*
Southern Arkansas University *B, M*
Southern Arkansas University
Tech *C, A*
University of Arkansas *B, M, D*
University of Arkansas
Community College at Batesville *A*
Community College at Hope *C, A*
Fort Smith *A, B*

Little Rock *B, M*
Monticello *C*
Pine Bluff *B, M*
University of Central Arkansas *B*
Williams Baptist College *B*

California

Allan Hancock College *C, A*
American River College *C, A*
Antelope Valley College *C, A*
Azusa Pacific University *B, M*
Berkeley City College *C, A*
Butte College *C, A*
Cabrillo College *A*
California Institute of
Technology *B, M, D*
California Lutheran University *B, M*
California State University
Channel Islands *B, M*
East Bay *B, M*
Long Beach *B, M*
Los Angeles *B*
Northridge *B, M*
Sacramento *B, M*
San Marcos *B*
California University of Management
and Sciences *M*
Cerritos College *A*
Cerro Coso Community College *C, A*
Chabot College *A*
Chaffey College *C, A*
Chapman University *B*
Citrus College *C, A*
City College of San Francisco *C, A*
Coastline Community College *C, A*
College of Marin *C, A*
College of San Mateo *C, A*
College of the Desert *C, A*
College of the Redwoods *C, A*
College of the Sequoias *C*
College of the Siskiyous *C, A*
Columbia College *C, A*
Contra Costa College *A*
Copper Mountain College *C, A*
Crafton Hills College *C, A*
Cypress College *C, A*
De Anza College *A*
DeVry University
Pomona *B*
Diablo Valley College *C, A*
El Camino College *C, A*
Evergreen Valley College *A*
Folsom Lake College *A*
Foothill College *C, A*
Fresno City College *C, A*
Fullerton College *A*
Gavilan College *C, A*
Glendale Community College *C, A*
Golden West College *A*
Grossmont College *C, A*
Harvey Mudd College *B*
Heald College
Concord *C, A*
Fresno
Hayward *C, A*
Rancho Cordova *A*
San Francisco *A*
San Jose
Stockton *C, A*
Humphreys College *A, B*
Imperial Valley College *C, A*
Irvine Valley College *C, A*
Kaplan College
Riverside *C*
Lake Tahoe Community College *C, A*
Laney College *C, A*
Los Angeles City College *C, A*
Los Angeles Harbor College *C, A*
Los Angeles Mission College *A*
Los Angeles Pierce College *C, A*
Los Angeles Southwest College *A*
Los Angeles Trade and Technical
College *C, A*
Los Medanos College *C*
Loyola Marymount University *B*

Master's College *B*
Mendocino College *C, A*
Merced College *A*
Merritt College *C, A*
Mills College *C, B, M*
MiraCosta College *C, A*
Mission College *C*
Modesto Junior College *A*
Monterey Peninsula College *C, A*
Moorpark College *A*
Mount San Jacinto College *C, A*
Mt. Sierra College *B*
Napa Valley College *A*
National Hispanic University *B*
Notre Dame de Namur
University *B, M*
Orange Coast College *C, A*
Pacific States University *B*
Palo Verde College *C, A*
Pepperdine University *B*
Platt College
Los Angeles *C, A*
Ontario *A*
Porterville College *A*
Reedley College *A*
Rio Hondo College *A*
Riverside City College *C, A*
Sacramento City College *C, A*
Saddleback College *C, A*
San Deigo Miramar College
San Diego Miramar College *C, A*
San Diego City College *C, A*
San Joaquin Delta College *C*
San Jose City College *A*
Santa Ana College *C, A*
Santa Barbara City College *C, A*
Shasta College *A*
Skyline College *C, A*
Solano Community College *A*
Southwestern College *C, A*
Stanford University *B, M, D*
Trident University International *B*
University of California
Irvine *B, M, D*
Los Angeles *B, M, D*
San Diego *B, M, D*
Santa Barbara *B, M, D*
Santa Cruz *B, M, D*
University of La Verne *B*
University of Phoenix
Sacramento Valley *B*
Southern California *B*
University of San Francisco *B, M*
Ventura College *C, A*
West Hills College: Coalinga *C, A*
West Hills College: Lemoore *C, A*
West Valley College *C, A*
Yuba College *C, A*

Colorado

American Sentinel University *M*
Anthem College
Aurora *A*
CollegeAmerica
Fort Collins *B*
Colorado Christian University *B*
Colorado Mesa University *B*
Colorado Mountain College *A*
Colorado State University *B, M, D*
Colorado Technical
University *B, M, D*
Community College of Aurora *C, A*
Community College of Denver *C, A*
Everest College
Colorado Springs *A*
Front Range Community College *C, A*
IntelliTec College *A*
Lamar Community College *C, A*
Otero Junior College *C, A*
Pikes Peak Community College *C, A*
Pueblo Community College *C, A*
Regis University *C, B*
Trinidad State Junior College *A*

University of Colorado
   Colorado Springs *B, M, D*
   Denver *B, M, D*
Westwood College
   Denver North *A, B*

Connecticut

Asnuntuck Community College *A*
Capital Community College *A*
Central Connecticut State
   University *B, M*
Eastern Connecticut State
   University *B*
Fairfield University *B*
Housatonic Community College *C, A*
Naugatuck Valley Community
   College *A*
Norwalk Community College *C, A*
Quinebaug Valley Community
   College *C, A*
Quinnipiac University *B, M*
Sacred Heart University *B, M*
Southern Connecticut State
   University *B, M*
Three Rivers Community
   College *C, A*
Trinity College *B*
Tunxis Community College *C*
University of Bridgeport *B, M, D*
University of Hartford *B*
University of New Haven *B, M*
Wesleyan University *B, M*
Western Connecticut State
   University *B*
Yale University *B, M, D*

Delaware

Delaware Technical Community
   College
   Jack F. Owens Campus *A*
   Stanton/Wilmington Campus *A*
   Terry Campus *A*
University of Delaware *B, M, D*
Wilmington University *B, M*

District of Columbia

American University *B, M*
Catholic University of
   America *B, M, D*
Gallaudet University *B*
George Washington University *B, M*
University of the District of
   Columbia *A, B*
University of the Potomac *B*

Florida

Anthem College
   Orlando *A*
Barry University *B*
Beacon College *A, B*
Broward College *C, A*
Chipola College *A*
City College
   Altamonte Springs *A*
   Gainesville *A*
Daytona State College *A*
Eckerd College *B*
Edison State College *A*
Everest University
   Lakeland *B*
   Largo *A, B*
   Melbourne *A, B*
   North Orlando *A, B*
   Tampa *A, B*
Florida Agricultural and Mechanical
   University *B, M*
Florida Atlantic University *B, M, D*
Florida Career College
   Miami *A*
Florida Gateway College *A*
Florida Gulf Coast University *B*
Florida International
   University *B, M, D*
Florida Keys Community College *A*

Florida Memorial University *B*
Florida National University *A*
Florida State College at
   Jacksonville *A*
Florida State University *B, M, D*
Indian River State College *A*
Jacksonville University *B*
Jones College *A, B*
Keiser University *A*
Miami Dade College *C, A*
Northwood University
   Florida *A*
Nova Southeastern
   University *B, M, D*
Palm Beach State College *A*
Pensacola State College *A*
Rollins College *B*
Saint Leo University *B*
Saint Thomas University *B*
Seminole State College of Florida *A*
South Florida State College *A*
Southeastern College
   Greenacres *C, A*
Stetson University *B*
University of Central Florida *B, M, D*
University of Florida *B, M*
University of North Florida *B, M*
University of Phoenix
   South Florida *B*
University of South Florida *B*
University of Southernmost
   Florida *C, A*
University of Tampa *A, B*
University of West Florida *B, M*
Webber International University *B*

Georgia

Abraham Baldwin Agricultural
   College *A*
Albany State University *B*
Armstrong Atlantic State
   University *B, M*
Atlanta Metropolitan College *A*
Atlanta Technical College *A*
Bainbridge College *C, A*
Brewton-Parker College *B*
Chattahoochee Technical
   College *C, A*
Clark Atlanta University *B*
Columbus State University *B, M*
Covenant College *B*
Dalton State College *A*
Darton College *A*
Fort Valley State University *B*
Georgia Highlands College *A*
Georgia Institute of
   Technology *B, M, D*
Georgia Military College *A*
Georgia Piedmont Technical
   College *C, A*
Georgia Regents University *B*
Georgia Southern University *B*
Georgia State University *B, M, D*
Kennesaw State University *B, M*
LaGrange College *B*
Middle Georgia State College *A*
Morehouse College *B*
Shorter University *B*
South Georgia State College *A*
Southern Crescent Technical
   College *A*
Spelman College *B*
University of North Georgia *C, A, B*
University of West Georgia *B*
Valdosta State University *B*
West Georgia Technical College *A*
Wiregrass Georgia Technical
   College *C, A*

Hawaii

Chaminade University of
   Honolulu *A, B*
Hawaii Pacific University *C, B*

Heald College
   Honolulu *A*
Remington College
   Honolulu *A, B*
University of Hawaii
   Honolulu Community College *A*
   Leeward Community College *C, A*
   Manoa *B*

Idaho

Brigham Young University-Idaho *A, B*
College of Idaho *B*
Idaho State University *B*
Lewis-Clark State College *A, B*
North Idaho College *A*
Stevens-Henager College
   Boise *A, B*

Illinois

Aurora University *B*
Carl Sandburg College *A*
Chicago State University *B*
Concordia University Chicago *B*
DePaul University *M, D*
East-West University *A, B*
Eastern Illinois University *B*
Eureka College *B*
Governors State University *B, M*
Greenville College *B*
Harper College *A*
Illinois Central College *A*
Illinois Eastern Community Colleges
   Frontier Community College *C, A*
   Lincoln Trail College *A*
Illinois Institute of Technology *B*
Illinois Valley Community College *A*
Illinois Wesleyan University *B*
John A. Logan College *A*
Joliet Junior College *C, A*
Lake Land College *C*
Lewis and Clark Community
   College *A*
Loyola University Chicago *C, B*
MacMurray College *B*
McKendree University *B*
Midstate College *A*
Moraine Valley Community College *C*
Northwestern University *B*
Oakton Community College *A*
Olivet Nazarene University *B*
Principia College *B*
Richland Community College *A*
Rockford University *B*
St. Augustine College *C, A*
Saint Xavier University *B*
South Suburban College of Cook
   County *C, A*
Southwestern Illinois College *C, A*
University of Chicago *B*
University of Illinois
   Urbana-Champaign *B*
Western Illinois University *B, M*

Indiana

Ball State University *A, B, M*
Brown Mackie College
   Fort Wayne *A*
Butler University *B*
Calumet College of St. Joseph *A, B*
Earlham College *B*
Franklin College *B*
Hanover College *B*
Huntington University *B*
Indiana State University *B, M*
Indiana University
   Purdue University Fort Wayne *B*
   Purdue University Indianapolis *M*
Ivy Tech Community College
   Bloomington *C, A*
   Central Indiana *C, A*
   Columbus *C, A*
   East Central *C, A*
   Kokomo *C, A*
   Lafayette *C, A*

North Central *C, A*
Northeast *C, A*
Northwest *C, A*
Richmond *C, A*
South Central *C, A*
Southeast *C, A*
Southwest *C, A*
Wabash Valley *C, A*
Manchester University *B*
Purdue University *B, M, D*
Saint Joseph's College *B*
St. Mary-of-the-Woods College *B*
Taylor University *B*
University of Evansville *M*
University of Indianapolis *B*
University of Notre Dame *B*
University of Southern Indiana *B*
Vincennes University *A*

Iowa

AIB College of Business *A*
Briar Cliff University *B*
Central College *B*
Clarke University *B*
Dordt College *B*
Drake University *B*
Ellsworth Community College *A*
Emmaus Bible College *B*
Graceland University *B*
Grand View University *B*
Iowa State University *B, M, D*
Marshalltown Community
   College *C, A*
Mount Mercy University *B*
Northwestern College *B*
St. Ambrose University *C, B*
University of Dubuque *B*
University of Iowa *B, M, D*
University of Northern Iowa *B, M*
Wartburg College *B*
William Penn University *B*

Kansas

Allen County Community College *A*
Butler Community College *C, A*
Coffeyville Community College *A*
Colby Community College *A*
Cowley County Community
   College *A*
Dodge City Community College *A*
Emporia State University *B*
Fort Hays State University *B*
Fort Scott Community College *C, A*
Friends University *B*
Garden City Community College *A*
Hesston College *A*
Hutchinson Community College *C, A*
Independence Community
   College *C, A*
Kansas State University *B, M, D*
Kansas Wesleyan University *A, B*
Labette Community College *A*
Manhattan Area Technical College *A*
Neosho County Community
   College *A*
Pittsburg State University *B*
Seward County Community
   College *C, A*
University of Kansas *B, M, D*
Washburn University *A, B*
Wichita State University *B, M*

Kentucky

Bellarmine University *B*
Berea College *B*
Bluegrass Community and Technical
   College *C, A*
Brescia University *B*
Brown Mackie College
   Louisville *A*
   North Kentucky *A*
Campbellsville University *A, B*

Daymar College
  Bowling Green *C, A*
  Owensboro *C, A*
Eastern Kentucky University *B*
Elizabethtown Community and
  Technical College *C, A*
Georgetown College *B*
Hazard Community and Technical
  College *A*
Henderson Community College *C*
Hopkinsville Community
  College *C, A*
Jefferson Community and Technical
  College *C, A*
Kentucky State University *B, M*
Kentucky Wesleyan College *B*
Lincoln College of Technology
  Florence *C, A*
Lindsey Wilson College *A*
Madisonville Community
  College *C, A*
Maysville Community and Technical
  College *C, A*
Midway College *A, B*
Morehead State University *A, B*
Northern Kentucky University *B*
Owensboro Community and
  Technical College *C, A*
Somerset Community College *C, A*
Southeast Kentucky Community and
  Technical College *A*
Thomas More College *A, B*
Transylvania University *B*
Union College *B*
University of Kentucky *B, M, D*
University of Pikeville *B*
West Kentucky Community and
  Technical College *C, A*
Western Kentucky University *B, M*

Louisiana

Baton Rouge Community College *A*
Baton Rouge School of
  Computers *C, A*
Delta College of Arts &
  Technology *C*
Louisiana State University
  Eunice *A*
Remington College
  Baton Rouge *A*
  Lafayette *A*
Southern University
  Shreveport *A*
Xavier University of Louisiana *B*

Maine

Husson University *A, B*
Kaplan University
  South Portland *A*
Thomas College *B*
University of Maine
  Augusta *A, B*
  Fort Kent *B*
University of Southern Maine *B*

Maryland

Allegany College of Maryland *A*
Anne Arundel Community
  College *C, A*
Baltimore City Community College *A*
College of Southern Maryland *A*
Community College of Baltimore
  County *A*
Frederick Community College *A*
Frostburg State University *C, B, M*
Hagerstown Community College *A*
Harford Community College *A*
Hood College *M*
Johns Hopkins University *B, M, D*
Loyola University Maryland *B*
McDaniel College *B*
Montgomery College *A*
Mount St. Mary's University *B*

Notre Dame of Maryland
  University *B*
Prince George's Community
  College *C, A*
St. Mary's College of Maryland *B*
Salisbury University *B*
Towson University *B, M*
United States Naval Academy *B*
University of Baltimore *B, M*
University of Maryland
  Baltimore County *B, M, D*
  College Park *B, M, D*
  Eastern Shore *B, M*
  University College *B*
University of Phoenix
  Maryland *B*
Washington Adventist University *B*
Wor-Wic Community College *A*

Massachusetts

Assumption College *B*
Babson College *B*
Benjamin Franklin Institute of
  Technology *A*
Bentley University *B*
Berkshire Community College *A*
Boston College *B*
Boston University *B, M, D*
Bristol Community College *A*
Cape Cod Community College *A*
Clark University *B*
College of the Holy Cross *B*
Curry College *B*
Dean College *A*
Elms College *C, B*
Fisher College *A, B*
Fitchburg State University *C, B*
Framingham State University *B*
Greenfield Community College *C, A*
Massachusetts Bay Community
  College *A*
Massachusetts College of Liberal
  Arts *B*
Massachusetts Institute of
  Technology *M*
Massasoit Community College *A*
Mount Wachusett Community
  College *A*
Newbury College *B*
North Shore Community College *A*
Northeastern University *B, M, D*
Northern Essex Community
  College *C, A*
Roxbury Community College *C, A*
Salem State University *B*
Simmons College *B*
Springfield College *B*
Suffolk University *B, M*
Tufts University *B*
University of Massachusetts
  Boston *C, B*
  Dartmouth *B, M*
  Lowell *C*
Urban College of Boston *C*
Wellesley College *B*
Worcester State University *B*

Michigan

Alpena Community College *C, A*
Andrews University *B*
Aquinas College *B*
Baker College
  Auburn Hills *A*
  Cadillac *A*
  Clinton Township *A, B*
  Flint *B, M*
  Jackson *A*
  Muskegon *B*
  Owosso *A, B*
  Port Huron *A, B*
Delta College *C, A*
Eastern Michigan University *B*
Grace Bible College *B*
Grand Rapids Community College *A*

Grand Valley State University *B*
Henry Ford Community College *A*
Hope College *B*
ITT Technical Institute
  Canton *A*
Kalamazoo College *B*
Lake Superior State University *A, B*
Lansing Community College *A*
Macomb Community College *C, A*
Marygrove College *C, B*
Michigan Jewish Institute *B*
Michigan State University *B, M, D*
Monroe County Community
  College *C, A*
Montcalm Community College *A*
Muskegon Community College *C, A*
North Central Michigan College *C, A*
Northern Michigan University *B*
Northwood University
  Michigan *B*
Oakland University *B, M*
Rochester College *B*
Saginaw Valley State University *B*
Schoolcraft College *A*
Siena Heights University *A, B*
University of Detroit Mercy *B, M*
University of Michigan *B*
University of Michigan
  Dearborn *B*
  Flint *B, M*
University of Phoenix
  Metro Detroit *B*
Washtenaw Community College *C, A*
Wayne State University *B, M, D*

Minnesota

Academy College *B*
Bethel University *B*
College of St. Scholastica *B, M*
Gustavus Adolphus College *B*
Hennepin Technical College *C, A*
Hibbing Community College *A*
Macalester College *B*
Mesabi Range Community and
  Technical College *C, A*
Minnesota State University
  Mankato *B, M*
Minnesota West Community and
  Technical College *A*
National American University
  Bloomington *A*
Rasmussen College
  Moorhead *B*
Ridgewater College *C, A*
Riverland Community College *A*
St. Catherine University *B*
Saint Cloud State University *B*
Southwest Minnesota State
  University *B*
University of Minnesota
  Twin Cities *M, D*
Walden University *B, M, D*
White Earth Tribal and Community
  College *A*

Mississippi

Alcorn State University *B, M*
Coahoma Community College *A*
East Central Community College *A*
East Mississippi Community
  College *A*
Hinds Community College *A*
Holmes Community College *C, A*
Itawamba Community College *A*
Jackson State University *D, M*
Meridian Community College *A*
Mississippi College *B*
Mississippi Gulf Coast Community
  College *A*
Mississippi State University *B, M, D*
Mississippi Valley State University *B*
Northeast Mississippi Community
  College *A*

Northwest Mississippi Community
  College *A*
University of Mississippi *B*
University of Southern
  Mississippi *B, M*

Missouri

Avila University *B*
Columbia College *A, B*
Crowder College *A*
Evangel University *B*
Fontbonne University *B*
Hannibal-LaGrange University *B*
Jefferson College *C, A*
Lincoln University *A*
Lindenwood University *B*
Metropolitan Community College -
  Kansas City *C, A*
Missouri Southern State University *B*
Missouri State University: West
  Plains *A*
Missouri University of Science and
  Technology *B, M, D*
Missouri Valley College *B*
Missouri Western State University *B*
Northwest Missouri State
  University *B, M*
Park University *B*
Ranken Technical College *A*
St. Louis Community College *A*
Saint Louis University *B, M*
Southeast Missouri State University *B*
Southwest Baptist University *B*
University of Central Missouri *B*
University of Missouri
  Columbia *B, M, D*
Washington University in St.
  Louis *B, M, D*
Webster University *B, M*
Westminster College *B*

Montana

Aaniiih Nakoda College *A*
Blackfeet Community College *A*
Dawson Community College *A*
Miles Community College *A*
Montana State University
  Billings *A*
Rocky Mountain College *B*
University of Great Falls *B, M*
University of Montana: Western *A*

Nebraska

Bellevue University *B, M*
Central Community College *C, A*
Doane College *B*
Grace University *B*
Hastings College *B*
Little Priest Tribal College *C, A*
Metropolitan Community
  College *C, A*
Midland University *B*
Northeast Community College *A*
Union College *B*
University of Nebraska
  Kearney *B*
  Lincoln *B, M, D*
Wayne State College *B*
Western Nebraska Community
  College *C, A*

Nevada

Great Basin College *C, A*
Truckee Meadows Community
  College *A*
University of Nevada
  Reno *B, M*
University of Phoenix
  Las Vegas *B*
Western Nevada College *A*

New Hampshire

Keene State College *B*
Lakes Region Community
  College *C, A*

Manchester Community College *A*
Nashua Community College *C, A*
New England College *B*
Southern New Hampshire
University *A, B, M*
University of New
Hampshire *B, M, D*
University of New Hampshire at
Manchester *B, M*
White Mountains Community
College *C, A*

New Jersey

Bergen Community College *C, A*
Bloomfield College *B*
Brookdale Community College *A*
Caldwell College *C, B*
Camden County College *C, A*
Centenary College *B*
College of New Jersey *B*
College of St. Elizabeth *C*
County College of Morris *A*
Cumberland County College *A*
Eastwick College
Hackensack *C*
Essex County College *C, A*
Fairleigh Dickinson University
College at Florham *B*
Felician College *B*
Gloucester County College *C, A*
Hudson County Community
College *C*
Kean University *B, M*
Mercer County Community
College *C*
Middlesex County College *A*
Monmouth University *C, B, M*
Montclair State University *B, M*
New Jersey City University *B*
New Jersey Institute of
Technology *B, M, D*
Ocean County College *A*
Passaic County Community College *A*
Ramapo College of New Jersey *B*
Rider University *B*
Rutgers, The State University of New
Jersey
New Brunswick/Piscataway
Campus *B, M, D*
Newark Campus *B*
Saint Peter's University *B*
Seton Hall University *B*
Stevens Institute of
Technology *B, M, D*
Sussex County Community
College *C, A*
Warren County Community
College *C, A*
William Paterson University of New
Jersey *B*

New Mexico

Central New Mexico Community
College *C, A*
Clovis Community College *C, A*
Eastern New Mexico University *B*
Eastern New Mexico University:
Roswell *A*
Luna Community College *C, A*
Navajo Technical University *C, A, B*
New Mexico Institute of Mining and
Technology *B, M, D*
New Mexico Junior College *C, A*
New Mexico State University *B, M, D*
Northern New Mexico College *A*
Santa Fe Community College *A*
University of New Mexico *B, M, D*
University of Phoenix
New Mexico *B*

New York

ASA College *C*
Adelphi University *B*
Barnard College *B*

Bramson ORT College *C, A*
Broome Community College *A*
Bryant & Stratton College
Albany *A*
Amherst *A*
Buffalo *A*
Southtowns *A*
Syracuse *A*
Cayuga Community College *A*
City University of New York
Baruch College *B, M*
Borough of Manhattan Community
College *A*
Brooklyn College *B*
Hunter College *B*
Lehman College *B, M*
New York City College of
Technology *A*
Queensborough Community
College *A*
York College *B*
Clinton Community College *A*
Colgate University *B*
College of Saint Rose *B, M*
College of Westchester *C, A*
Columbia University
School of General Studies *B*
Columbia-Greene Community
College *C*
Cornell University *B, D*
Corning Community College *A*
Dominican College of Blauvelt *B*
Dowling College *B*
Dutchess Community College *C, A*
Erie Community College *A*
Excelsior College *B*
Finger Lakes Community
College *C, A*
Fordham University *B*
Fulton-Montgomery Community
College *A*
Globe Institute of
Technology *C, A, B*
Hamilton College *B*
Hartwick College *B*
Herkimer County Community
College *A*
Hobart and William Smith Colleges *B*
Ithaca College *B*
Jamestown Business College *A*
Jefferson Community College *A*
Le Moyne College *B*
Long Island University
LIU Brooklyn *B, M*
Manhattan College *B*
Manhattanville College *B*
Marist College *B, M*
Medaille College *B*
Mercy College *C, B*
Mohawk Valley Community
College *A*
Molloy College *B*
Monroe College *A, B*
Nassau Community College *C, A*
New York Institute of
Technology *B, M*
New York University *C, B, M, D*
Niagara County Community
College *A*
Niagara University *C, B*
Onondaga Community College *A*
Orange County Community
College *A*
Pace University *B, D*
Pace University: Pleasantville/
Briarcliff *B*
Roberts Wesleyan College *B*
Rochester Institute of
Technology *A, B, M, D*
SUNY
College at Brockport *B, M*
College at Buffalo *B*
College at Fredonia *B*
College at New Paltz *B, M*
College at Old Westbury *B*

College at Plattsburgh *B*
College at Potsdam *B*
College of Agriculture and
Technology at Cobleskill *A, B*
College of Agriculture and
Technology at Morrisville *A*
College of Technology at Alfred *A*
Farmingdale State College *C*
Institute of Technology at Utica/
Rome *B, M*
University at Albany *B, M, D*
University at Binghamton *B*
University at Buffalo *M, D*
Saint Bonaventure University *B*
St. John Fisher College *B*
St. John's University *A, B*
St. Joseph's College New York:
Suffolk Campus *C*
St. Joseph's College, New York *C*
St. Lawrence University *B*
St. Thomas Aquinas College *B*
Schenectady County Community
College *A*
Siena College *C, B*
Skidmore College *B*
Suffolk County Community
College *C, A*
Sullivan County Community
College *A*
Syracuse University *B, M, D*
Tompkins Cortland Community
College *A*
Touro College *B*
Union College *B*
United States Military Academy *B*
Utica College *B*
Utica School of Commerce *A*
Vassar College *B*
Westchester Community College *A*
Yeshiva University *B*

North Carolina

Barton College *B*
Bennett College for Women *B*
Bladen Community College *C, A*
Carteret Community College *C, A*
Catawba College *B*
Central Carolina Community
College *A*
College of the Albemarle *A*
Duke University *B, M, D*
Edgecombe Community College *A*
Elon University *B*
Fayetteville State University *B*
Forsyth Technical Community
College *A*
Gardner-Webb University *B*
Gaston College *C*
Guilford College *B*
Halifax Community College *A*
Johnson C. Smith University *B*
Lenoir Rhyne University *B*
Livingstone College *B*
Meredith College *B*
Methodist University *A, B*
Miller-Motte College
Wilmington *C, A*
Montreat College *C, B*
North Carolina Wesleyan College *B*
Pfeiffer University *B*
St. Augustine's University *B*
Sampson Community College *A*
Sandhills Community College *C, A*
Shaw University *B*
South Piedmont Community
College *A*
Southeastern Community
College *C, A*
Southwestern Community
College *C, A*
University of North Carolina
Charlotte *D*
Wilmington *M*
University of Phoenix
Charlotte *B*

Wake Technical Community
College *C, A*
Winston-Salem State University *M*

North Dakota

Cankdeska Cikana Community
College *C, A*
Mayville State University *B*
Minot State University *B*
North Dakota State College of
Science *C, A*
University of Mary *B*
University of North Dakota *B*
Valley City State University *B*

Ohio

Antonelli College
Cincinnati *A*
Belmont College *A*
Bowling Green State University *B, M*
Bryant & Stratton College
Eastlake *A*
Case Western Reserve
University *B, M, D*
Cincinnati State Technical and
Community College *A*
Cleveland State University *B, M*
College of Wooster *B*
Columbus State Community
College *C, A*
Cuyahoga Community College
Metropolitan *A*
Denison University *B*
Eastern Gateway Community
College *C, A*
Edison State Community College *C, A*
Fortis College
Centerville *A*
Franciscan University of
Steubenville *B*
Gallipolis Career College *A*
Heidelberg University *B*
Hiram College *B*
James A. Rhodes State College *A*
John Carroll University *B*
Kent State University *B, M*
Lincoln College of Technology
Dayton *A*
Lorain County Community
College *C, A*
Marietta College *B*
Marion Technical College *A*
Miami University
Hamilton *A*
Middletown *A, B*
Oxford *B, M*
Miami-Jacobs Career College
Dayton *C, A*
Mount Vernon Nazarene University *B*
Muskingum University *D*
National College
Kettering *C, A*
North Central State College *C, A*
Oberlin College *B*
Ohio State University
Columbus Campus *B*
Ohio University *B*
Ohio Wesleyan University *B*
Sinclair Community College *C, A*
Stark State College *A*
Tiffin University *B*
University of Cincinnati *B, M*
University of Cincinnati
Blue Ash College *A*
Clermont College *C, A*
University of Dayton *B*
University of Findlay *A, B*
University of Northwestern Ohio *A*
University of Rio Grande *A, B*
University of Toledo *B*
Wilberforce University *B*
Wilmington College *B*
Wright State University *B, M*

Youngstown State University *A, B, M*
Zane State College *A*

Oklahoma

Bacone College *A*
Connors State College *A*
East Central University *B*
Eastern Oklahoma State College *C, A*
Langston University *A*
Murray State College *A*
Northeastern Oklahoma Agricultural and Mechanical College *A*
Northern Oklahoma College *A*
Northwestern Oklahoma State University *B*
Oklahoma Baptist University *B*
Oklahoma Christian University *B*
Oklahoma City Community College *A*
Oklahoma City University *M*
Oklahoma Panhandle State University *B*
Oklahoma State University *B, M, D*
Oklahoma Wesleyan University *A, B*
Oral Roberts University *B*
Redlands Community College *A*
Rogers State University *A*
Rose State College *A*
Southeastern Oklahoma State University *B*
Southern Nazarene University *B*
Southwestern Oklahoma State University *B*
Tulsa Community College *C, A*
University of Central Oklahoma *B*
University of Tulsa *B*
Western Oklahoma State College *A*

Oregon

Central Oregon Community College *C, A*
Chemeketa Community College *A*
Eastern Oregon University *B*
Everest College
Portland *C, A*
George Fox University *B*
Heald College
Portland *C, A*
Linn-Benton Community College *A*
Mt. Hood Community College *A*
Northwest Christian University *B*
Pacific University *B*
Rogue Community College *C, A*
Southern Oregon University *B*
Treasure Valley Community College *C, A*
University of Oregon *B, M, D*
Western Oregon University *B*
Willamette University *B*

Pennsylvania

Albright College *B*
Arcadia University *C, B*
Berks Technical Institute *A*
Bloomsburg University of Pennsylvania *B*
Bucknell University *B*
Bucks County Community College *A*
Butler County Community College *A*
California University of Pennsylvania *A, B*
Cedar Crest College *C, B*
Chestnut Hill College *B*
Cheyney University of Pennsylvania *B*
Clarion University of Pennsylvania *B*
Community College of Philadelphia *A*
DeSales University *B*
Delaware County Community College *A*
Delaware Valley College *A, B*
Dickinson College *B*

East Stroudsburg University of Pennsylvania *B, M*
Edinboro University of Pennsylvania *A, B*
Elizabethtown College *B*
Erie Business Center South *A*
Erie Institute of Technology *C, A*
Fortis Institute
Erie *A*
Gannon University *B, M*
Geneva College *B*
Gettysburg College *B*
Harrisburg Area Community College *C, A*
Harrisburg University of Science and Technology *B*
Haverford College *B*
Indiana University of Pennsylvania *B*
Juniata College *B*
Kaplan Career Institute
Pittsburgh *A*
King's College *C, A, B*
Kutztown University of Pennsylvania *B*
La Roche College *B*
La Salle University *B, M*
Lafayette College *B*
Lehigh Carbon Community College *A*
Lincoln University *B*
Lock Haven University of Pennsylvania *B*
Luzerne County Community College *A*
Lycoming College *B*
Mansfield University of Pennsylvania *A, B*
McCann School of Business and Technology
Hazleton *A*
Mercyhurst University *B*
Millersville University of Pennsylvania *B*
Misericordia University *B*
Muhlenberg College *C, A, B*
Neumann University *B*
Penn State
Abington *C, B*
Altoona *C, B*
Beaver *C, B*
Berks *C, B*
Brandywine *C, B*
DuBois *C, B*
Fayette, The Eberly Campus *C, B*
Greater Allegheny *C, B*
Harrisburg *C, B, M*
Hazleton *C, B*
Lehigh Valley *C, B*
Mont Alto *C, B*
New Kensington *C, B*
Schuylkill *C, B*
Shenango *C, B*
University Park *C, B*
Wilkes-Barre *C, B*
Worthington Scranton *C, B*
York *C, B*
Pennsylvania Highlands Community College *A*
St. Francis University *B*
Saint Joseph's University *B, M*
St. Vincent College *C, B*
Sanford-Brown Institute
Pittsburgh *C*
Shippensburg University of Pennsylvania *B, M, T*
Swarthmore College *B*
Temple University *B, M, D*
Thiel College *B*
University of Pennsylvania *B, M, D*
University of Phoenix
Philadelphia *B*
University of Pittsburgh
Johnstown *B*
Waynesburg University *B*
West Chester University of Pennsylvania *B, M*

Westminster College *B*
Widener University *A, B, M*
Wilkes University *B*
YTI Career Institute
Lancaster *C*
Yorktowne Business Institute *A*

Puerto Rico

Bayamon Central University *A*
Caribbean University *A, B*
ICPR Junior College *A*
Inter American University of Puerto Rico
Arecibo Campus *A, B*
Barranquitas Campus *A, B*
Fajardo Campus *A, M*
Metropolitan Campus *B*
Universidad Adventista de las Antillas *A, B*
University College of San Juan *C, A, B*
University of Puerto Rico
Bayamon University College *A, B*
Mayaguez *B, M*
Ponce *A, B*

Rhode Island

Bryant University *B*
Community College of Rhode Island *C, A*
New England Institute of Technology *A, B*
Rhode Island College *B*
University of Rhode Island *B, M, D*

South Carolina

Benedict College *B*
Charleston Southern University *B*
Citadel *B*
Clemson University *B, M, D*
Coastal Carolina University *B*
College of Charleston *B*
Columbia College *B*
Denmark Technical College *C*
Forrest Junior College *C, A*
Francis Marion University *B*
Horry-Georgetown Technical College *C*
Lander University *B*
South Carolina State University *B*
Southern Wesleyan University *B*
University of South Carolina
Columbia *B, D*
Upstate *B*
Voorhees College *B*
Williamsburg Technical College *A*
Winthrop University *B*
York Technical College *C*

South Dakota

Dakota State University *C, B, M*
Kilian Community College *A*
Lake Area Technical Institute *A*
Mount Marty College *B*
National American University
Rapid City *A, B*
Northern State University *B, M*
Oglala Lakota College *B*
Sisseton Wahpeton College *C, A*
South Dakota State University *B, M*
Southeast Technical Institute *A*
University of Sioux Falls *B*
University of South Dakota *B, M*

Tennessee

Austin Peay State University *B, M*
Belmont University *B*
Carson-Newman University *B*
Daymar Institute
Clarksville *C, A*
Murfreesboro *A*
East Tennessee State University *B, M*
Freed-Hardeman University *B*
Hiwassee College *A*

Jackson State Community College *A*
Lane College *B*
Lee University *B*
Lincoln Memorial University *B*
Maryville College *B*
Middle Tennessee State University *B*
Miller-Motte Technical College
Clarksville *C, A*
Milligan College *B*
Nashville State Community College *A*
National College of Business and Technology
Nashville *A*
Northeast State Community College *C, A*
Roane State Community College *C*
Sewanee: The University of the South *B*
Southwest Tennessee Community College *A*
Tennessee Technological University *B*
Tennessee Wesleyan College *B*

Texas

Alvin Community College *A*
Amarillo College *C, A*
Angelina College *A*
Angelo State University *B, T*
Austin Community College *C, A*
Brazosport College *A*
Central Texas College *C, A*
Cisco College *C, A*
Clarendon College *A*
Coastal Bend College *C, A*
College of the Mainland *A*
Collin County Community College District *C, A*
Dallas Baptist University *B*
Eastfield College *C, A*
El Paso Community College *C, A*
Frank Phillips College *C, A*
Galveston College *A*
Grayson College *C, A*
Hill College *C, A*
Howard College *C, A*
Howard Payne University *B*
Huston-Tillotson University *B*
Kilgore College *A*
Lamar Institute of Technology *C, A*
Lamar State College at Orange *C, A*
Lamar University *B*
Laredo Community College *A*
LeTourneau University *B*
Lee College *C, A*
Lone Star College System *C, A*
Lubbock Christian University *B*
McLennan Community College *C, A*
McMurry University *B, T*
Midland College *A*
Midwestern State University *B, M*
Navarro College *C, A*
North Central Texas College *A*
North Lake College *A*
Northeast Texas Community College *C, A*
Northwest Vista College *A*
Our Lady of the Lake University of San Antonio *B, M*
Palo Alto College *C, A*
Panola College *C, A*
Paris Junior College *C, A*
Prairie View A&M University *B, M*
Ranger College *C, A*
Remington College
Houston *A*
Richland College *C, A*
St. Edward's University *B*
St. Mary's University *B, M*
St. Philip's College *C, A*
Sam Houston State University *B, M*
San Jacinto College *C, A*
South Plains College *A*
South Texas College *A*
Southwest Texas Junior College *A*

Southwestern Adventist University *B*
Southwestern University *B, T*
Stephen F. Austin State
   University *B, T*
Sul Ross State University *B*
Tarleton State University *B, T*
Tarrant County College *C, A*
Temple College *C, A*
Texarkana College *C, A*
Texas A&M University
   Commerce *B, M*
   Corpus Christi *B, M*
   Texarkana *B*
Texas Christian University *B*
Texas College *B*
Texas Lutheran University *B*
Texas Southern University *B*
Texas State University *B, M*
Texas Tech University *B, M, D*
Texas Woman's University *B, T*
Trinity University *B*
Trinity Valley Community
   College *C, A*
Tyler Junior College *C, A*
University of Houston *B, M, D*
University of Houston
   Clear Lake *B, M*
   Downtown *B*
   Victoria *B, T*
University of Mary Hardin-Baylor *B*
University of North Texas *B, M, D*
University of Texas
   Arlington *M, D*
   Austin *C, B, M, D*
   Brownsville *B*
   Dallas *B, M, D*
   El Paso *B, M*
   Pan American *B*
   Permian Basin *B, M*
   San Antonio *B, M*
   Tyler *B, M*
University of the Incarnate Word *B*
Victoria College *C, A*
Weatherford College *C, A*
Western Technical College: Diana
   Drive *C, A*
Western Texas College *A*
Wharton County Junior College *C, A*

Utah

LDS Business College *C, A*
Provo College *A*
Salt Lake Community College *C, A*
Snow College *A*
Southern Utah University *B*
University of Utah *M, D*
Utah State University *B, M, D*
Utah Valley University *A*
Weber State University *B*

Vermont

Bennington College *B*
Castleton State College *B*
Community College of Vermont *C, A*
Lyndon State College *A, B*
Marlboro College *B, M*
Vermont Technical College *A, B*

Virginia

American National University
   Lynchburg *A*
Blue Ridge Community College *C, A*
Bryant & Stratton College
   Virginia Beach *A*
College of William and Mary *B, M, D*
Dabney S. Lancaster Community
   College *A*
Danville Community College *A*
ECPI University *B, M*
Eastern Shore Community
   College *C, A*
George Mason University *B, M, D*
Hampton University *B*
James Madison University *B, M*

John Tyler Community College *A*
Liberty University *B, T*
Lord Fairfax Community College *A*
Lynchburg College *B*
Mary Baldwin College *B*
Miller-Motte Technical College
   Lynchburg *A*
Mountain Empire Community
   College *A*
Norfolk State University *B, M*
Northern Virginia Community
   College *A*
Old Dominion University *B, M, D*
Patrick Henry Community College *A*
Paul D. Camp Community
   College *C, A*
Piedmont Virginia Community
   College *C, A*
Randolph-Macon College *B*
Rappahannock Community College *C*
Roanoke College *B*
Skyline College: Roanoke *A*
Southern Virginia University *B*
Southside Virginia Community
   College *C, A*
Southwest Virginia Community
   College *A*
Stratford University: Falls
   Church *A, B, M*
Thomas Nelson Community
   College *C, A*
Tidewater Community College *A*
University of Management and
   Technology *A, B, M*
University of Mary Washington *B*
University of Phoenix
   Northern Virginia *B*
University of Richmond *B*
University of Virginia *B, M, D*
University of the Potomac *A, B*
Virginia Commonwealth
   University *B, M*
Virginia Highlands Community
   College *A*
Virginia Polytechnic Institute and
   State University *B, M, D*
Virginia Union University *B*
Virginia Western Community
   College *C, A*
Westwood College
   Annandale *A, B*

Washington

Bellevue College *C, A*
Cascadia Community College *A*
Centralia College *C, A*
City University of Seattle *M*
Columbia Basin College *A*
Eastern Washington University *B, M*
Evergreen State College *B*
Heritage University *A, B*
Highline Community College *A*
Lower Columbia College *A*
Peninsula College *A*
Renton Technical College *C*
Seattle Central Community
   College *C, A*
Shoreline Community College *C, A*
Skagit Valley College *C, A*
Spokane Falls Community College *A*
University of Washington *B, M, D*
University of Washington
   Bothell *B, M*
University of Washington Tacoma *B*
Walla Walla University *B*
Washington State University *B*
Western Washington University *B, M*
Whitworth University *B*
Yakima Valley Community College *A*

West Virginia

Alderson-Broaddus University *C*
Bethany College *B*
Bluefield State College *B*

Bridgemont Community and
   Technical College *A*
Concord University *B*
Fairmont State University *B*
Marshall University *B*
Mountain State College *A*
New River Community and Technical
   College *A*
Shepherd University *B*
West Virginia Junior College
   Charleston *C, A*
West Virginia University Institute of
   Technology *B*
West Virginia Wesleyan College *B*

Wisconsin

Alverno College *B*
Carroll University *B*
Chippewa Valley Technical College *A*
College of Menominee Nation *A*
Concordia University Wisconsin *B*
Edgewood College *B*
Herzing University
   Madison *A, B*
Lac Courte Oreilles Ojibwa
   Community College *C*
Lawrence University *B*
Madison Area Technical College *A*
Marquette University *B, M*
Nicolet Area Technical College *A*
Northeast Wisconsin Technical
   College *C, A*
University of Wisconsin
   Eau Claire *B*
   La Crosse *B, T*
   Madison *B, M, D*
   Parkside *M*
   River Falls *B*
   Stevens Point *B*
   Whitewater *B, T*
Viterbo University *B*
Wisconsin Indianhead Technical
   College *A*

Wyoming

Sheridan College *A*
Western Wyoming Community
   College *A*

Computer installation and repair

Alaska

University of Alaska
   Anchorage *A*
   Fairbanks *C, A*

Arizona

Cochise College *C*
Paradise Valley Community College *C*

Arkansas

Arkansas State University
   Mountain Home *C*
College of the Ouachitas *C*
Mid-South Community College *C*
University of Arkansas
   Fort Smith *C*
   Monticello *C*

California

East Los Angeles College *C*
Los Medanos College *C*
Orange Coast College *C*
Solano Community College *C, A*

Florida

Daytona State College *C*
Florida Technical College
   Orlando *A*
Miami Dade College *C*
Polk State College *A*
Saint Johns River State College *C*

Georgia

Albany Technical College *C*
Atlanta Technical College *C*
Gwinnett Technical College *C*
Savannah Technical College *C*

Illinois

Black Hawk College *C*
City Colleges of Chicago
   Malcolm X College *C*
   Richard J. Daley College *C*
   Wilbur Wright College *C*
College of Lake County *C, A*
Highland Community College *C*
Illinois Eastern Community Colleges
   Frontier Community College *C*
   Lincoln Trail College *C*
   Olney Central College *C*
   Wabash Valley College *C*
Morton College *C*
Prairie State College *C*
Sauk Valley Community College *C*
Spoon River College *C*

Kansas

Coffeyville Community College *C*
Kansas City Kansas Community
   College *C*

Kentucky

Bluegrass Community and Technical
   College *C*
Eastern Kentucky University *A*
Jefferson Community and Technical
   College *C*
Sullivan College of Technology and
   Design *A*
Sullivan University *A*

Louisiana

Delgado Community College *C*

Massachusetts

Cape Cod Community College *C*
Massasoit Community College *C*

Michigan

Baker College
   Muskegon *C*
Montcalm Community College *C, A*
Mott Community College *C*
Schoolcraft College *C*

Mississippi

Hinds Community College *C, A*

New Jersey

Brookdale Community College *C*

New York

City University of New York
   LaGuardia Community College *A*
Onondaga Community College *C*

North Carolina

Beaufort County Community
   College *A*
Central Carolina Community
   College *C*

North Dakota

Lake Region State College *C, A*

Ohio

Cincinnati State Technical and
   Community College *C*
University of Akron: Wayne
   College *C*
University of Cincinnati
   Blue Ash College *C, A*

Pennsylvania

Harrisburg Area Community
  College *C, A*
Northampton Community
  College *C, A*
Westmoreland County Community
  College *C*

Puerto Rico

Inter American University of Puerto
  Rico
  Aguadilla Campus *A*
  Bayamon Campus *A, B*
  Guayama Campus *A, B*
Universidad Metropolitana *C, A*
Universidad del Este *C*

South Carolina

Midlands Technical College *C*
York Technical College *C*

Texas

St. Philip's College *C, A*
Temple College *C, A*
Western Texas College *C*

Washington

Northwest Indian College *C*
Walla Walla Community College *A*

West Virginia

Bridgemont Community and
  Technical College *A*

Wisconsin

Blackhawk Technical College *C*
Herzing University
  Madison *A, B*

Wyoming

Laramie County Community
  College *C*

Computer modeling, virtual environments and simulation

Alabama

University of Alabama
  Huntsville *M, D*
Virginia College
  Huntsville *B*

California

Ex'pression College *B*

Colorado

University of Colorado
  Colorado Springs *B*

Idaho

University of Idaho *B*

Indiana

Purdue University
  Calumet *M*

Kansas

Johnson County Community
  College *A*

Maryland

University of Baltimore *B*

New Hampshire

Daniel Webster College *B*

New York

Rochester Institute of
  Technology *B, M*

Pennsylvania

Albright College *B*
Pennsylvania College of
  Technology *B*
Robert Morris University *B, M*

Virginia

ECPI University *A, B*

Washington

DigiPen Institute of Technology *B*

Computer networking/ telecommunications

Alabama

Community College of the Air
  Force *A*
Gadsden State Community College *A*
Herzing University
  Birmingham *C, A, B*
ITT Technical Institute
  Birmingham *A*
University of Phoenix
  Birmingham *B*
Virginia College
  Birmingham *A, B*

Alaska

University of Alaska
  Anchorage *C, A*
  Southeast *C, A*

Arizona

Arizona Western College *C*
Brown Mackie College
  Tucson *C, A*
Chandler-Gilbert Community
  College *A*
Cochise College *C, A*
DeVry University
  Phoenix *A, B, M*
GateWay Community College *C, A*
Glendale Community College *C, A*
ITT Technical Institute
  Tempe *B*
  Tucson *B*
Mesa Community College *C, A*
Northland Pioneer College *A*
Paradise Valley Community
  College *C, A*
Phoenix College *C*
Pima Community College *C, A*
University of Advancing
  Technology *A, B, M*
University of Phoenix
  Phoenix-Hohokam *B*
  Southern Arizona *B*

Arkansas

Arkansas Northeastern College *C*
Arkansas State University
  Mountain Home *C*
Bryan University
  Rogers *C, A*
East Arkansas Community College *C*
ITT Technical Institute
  Little Rock *A*
Mid-South Community College *C*
National Park Community College *C*
North Arkansas College *C*
Southeast Arkansas College *C, A*

California

Allan Hancock College *C*
American River College *C, A*
Butte College *C, A*
California College San Diego *A*
California State University
  East Bay *C, B, M*
Chaffey College *C*
City College of San Francisco *C*
Coastline Community College *C*

Coleman University *A, B*
College of the Canyons *C, A*
College of the Siskiyous *C*
Contra Costa College *C, A*
DeVry University
  Pomona *A, B, M*
Diablo Valley College *C, A*
Foothill College *C*
ITT Technical Institute
  Lathrop *A*
  National City *A*
  Oxnard *A*
  Rancho Cordova *A*
  San Bernardino *A*
  Sylmar *A*
  Torrance *A*
Institute of Technology: Clovis *C*
Irvine Valley College *C, A*
Los Medanos College *C, A*
MTI College *A*
Mt. Sierra College *B*
Oxnard College *C, A*
Palomar College *C, A*
Platt College
  Ontario *A*
Saddleback College *C*
San Joaquin Delta College *C, A*
San Jose City College *C, A*
Shasta College *C, A*
Sierra College *C, A*
Silicon Valley University *C*
Southwestern College *C, A*
University of California
  Irvine *M, D*
University of Phoenix
  Bay Area *B*
  Central Valley *B*
  Sacramento Valley *B*
  San Diego *B*
  Southern California *B*
University of Southern California *M*
Westwood College
  Anaheim *A, B*
  Los Angeles *B*

Colorado

Arapahoe Community College *C, A*
CollegeAmerica
  Denver *A*
Colorado Mountain College *A*
Colorado Technical University *C*
Community College of Aurora *C, A*
Community College of Denver *C*
DeVry University
  Westminster *A, B, M*
Everest College
  Colorado Springs *C, A*
Front Range Community College *C*
ITT Technical Institute
  Westminster *A*
Pikes Peak Community College *C, A*
Red Rocks Community College *C, A*
University of Phoenix
  Denver *B*
  Southern Colorado *B*
Westwood College
  Denver North *A, B*
  Denver South *A, B*

Connecticut

Gateway Community College *C, A*
Manchester Community College *A*
Naugatuck Valley Community
  College *A*

Delaware

Delaware Technical Community
  College
  Stanton/Wilmington Campus *A*
  Terry Campus *C, A*

District of Columbia

University of Phoenix
  Washington DC *B*

Florida

College of Business and Technology
  Flagler *C, A*
DeVry University
  Miramar *A, B, M*
  Orlando *A, B, M*
Edison State College *C*
Everest University
  South Orlando *A*
Florida State College at
  Jacksonville *A, B*
Florida Technical College
  Orlando *C, A*
Herzing University
  Winter Park *C, A*
ITT Technical Institute
  Ft. Lauderdale *A*
  Jacksonville *A*
  Lake Mary *A*
  Miami *A*
  Tampa *A*
Lincoln College of Technology
  West Palm Beach *C, A*
Pasco-Hernando State College *A*
Saint Johns River State College *A*
Santa Fe College *A*
Seminole State College of
  Florida *C, A*
South Florida State College *C*
Southwest Florida College *A, B*
State College of Florida, Manatee-
  Sarasota *A*
Tallahassee Community College *C, A*
University of Phoenix
  Central Florida *B*
  North Florida *B*
  South Florida *B*
  West Florida *B*

Georgia

Albany Technical College *C, A*
Altamaha Technical College *C, A*
Athens Technical College *C, A*
Atlanta Technical College *C, A*
Central Georgia Technical
  College *C, A*
Clayton State University *C, A*
Darton College *A*
Georgia Piedmont Technical
  College *C, A*
Gwinnett Technical College *C, A*
North Georgia Technical
  College *C, A*
Savannah Technical College *C, A*
Southeastern Technical College *A*
Southwest Georgia Technical
  College *C, A*
University of Phoenix
  Atlanta *B*
  Augusta *B*
  Columbus *B*
  Savannah *B*
West Georgia Technical College *C, A*

Hawaii

Remington College
  Honolulu *A*
University of Phoenix
  Hawaii *B*

Idaho

Broadview University
  Boise *A*
College of Western Idaho *C, A*
Eastern Idaho Technical College *C, A*
ITT Technical Institute
  Boise *A*
Idaho State University *C, A, B*
University of Phoenix
  Idaho *B*

Illinois

Black Hawk College *C*
City Colleges of Chicago
  Harold Washington College *C*
  Harry S. Truman College *C, A*
  Richard J. Daley College *C, A*
College of Lake County *A*
Danville Area Community
  College *C, A*
DePaul University *B, M*
DeVry University
  Chicago *A, B*
  Online *A, B, M*
Harper College *C*
Heartland Community College *C, A*
Illinois Central College *C, A*
Illinois Eastern Community Colleges
  Lincoln Trail College *C, A*
Illinois Institute of Technology *M*
Illinois State University *B*
Illinois Valley Community College *C*
Kaskaskia College *C*
Lake Land College *A*
Lincoln Land Community
  College *C, A*
McHenry County College *C*
Moraine Valley Community College *C*
Morton College *C*
Parkland College *C, A*
Prairie State College *C*
Robert Morris University: Chicago *A*
Rock Valley College *C, A*
Sauk Valley Community College *C*
Spoon River College *C*
Triton College *A*
Western Illinois University *B*

Indiana

Harrison College
  Indianapolis *A*
ITT Technical Institute
  Fort Wayne *A*
  Indianapolis *A*
  Newburgh *A*
Indiana Institute of Technology *A, B*
International Business College *A*
International Business College:
  Indianapolis *A*
Purdue University *A, B*
Purdue University
  North Central *C, A, B*
University of Phoenix
  Indianapolis *B*
Vincennes University *C, A*

Iowa

Hawkeye Community College *C, A*
Iowa Central Community College *C*
Iowa Lakes Community College *A*
Marshalltown Community College *A*
Northwest Iowa Community
  College *A*
Southeastern Community College *A*
University of Northern Iowa *B*

Kansas

Barton County Community
  College *C, A*
Brown Mackie College
  Salina *A*
Bryan University
  Topeka *C, A*
Coffeyville Community College *C, A*
Cowley County Community
  College *A*
Garden City Community College *A*
Highland Community College *C, A*
Hutchinson Community College *A*
Independence Community
  College *C, A*
Johnson County Community
  College *A*
Kansas City Kansas Community
  College *C, A*

Labette Community College *C, A*
North Central Kansas Technical
  College *A*
Wichita State University *M*

Kentucky

Big Sandy Community and Technical
  College *C, A*
Daymar College
  Louisville *A*
  Owensboro *A*
ITT Technical Institute
  Louisville *A*

Louisiana

Baton Rouge Community College *C*
Delgado Community College *A*
Herzing University
  Kenner *B*
ITT Technical Institute
  St. Rose *A*
University of Phoenix
  Baton Rouge *B*
  Lafayette *B*
  Louisiana *B*
  Shreveport *B*

Maryland

Anne Arundel Community College *C*
Community College of Baltimore
  County *C, A*
Garrett College *C*
Howard Community College *A*
ITT Technical Institute
  Owings Mills *A*
Johns Hopkins University *B*
Morgan State University *B*
Stevenson University *B, M*
TESST College of Technology
  Beltsville *C*
  Towson *C*
University of Maryland
  University College *M*
University of Phoenix
  Maryland *B*

Massachusetts

Becker College *B*
Boston University *M*
Bristol Community College *C, A*
Bunker Hill Community College *C, A*
Cape Cod Community College *C, A*
Holyoke Community College *C*
ITT Technical Institute
  Norwood *A*
  Wilmington *A*
Middlesex Community College *A*
Northeastern University *M*
Quinsigamond Community College *C*
Roxbury Community College *C*
University of Phoenix
  Boston *B*
Wentworth Institute of Technology *B*

Michigan

Alpena Community College *A*
Baker College
  Allen Park *A*
  Cadillac *A*
  Clinton Township *A*
  Muskegon *C, A*
  Owosso *A*
  Port Huron *C, A*
Bay de Noc Community College *A*
Davenport University *A, B*
Delta College *C, A*
Ferris State University *B*
Henry Ford Community College *C*
ITT Technical Institute
  Canton *A*
  Troy *A*
Kirtland Community College *C*
Lansing Community College *C, A*
Macomb Community College *C, A*

Michigan Technological University *B*
Mid Michigan Community College *A*
Mott Community College *A*
Northern Michigan University *B*
Oakland Community College *C*
St. Clair County Community
  College *A*
Schoolcraft College *C*
Southwestern Michigan College *A*
University of Phoenix
  Metro Detroit *B*
  West Michigan *B*
Washtenaw Community College *C, A*

Minnesota

Alexandria Technical and Community
  College *A*
Anoka-Ramsey Community College *A*
Brown College
  Brooklyn Center *A*
Capella University *M, D*
Central Lakes College *A*
Century College *C, A*
Dakota County Technical
  College *C, A*
Dunwoody College of
  Technology *C, A*
Globe University
  Minneapolis *A*
  Moorhead *A*
  Woodbury *A*
ITT Technical Institute
  Eden Prairie *A*
Inver Hills Community College *C, A*
Lake Superior College *C*
Minneapolis Community and
  Technical College *C*
Minnesota School of Business
  Blaine *A*
  Brooklyn Center *A*
  Elk River *A*
  Lakeville *A*
  Plymouth *A*
  Richfield *A*
  Rochester *A*
  St. Cloud *A*
  Shakopee *A*
Minnesota State College - Southeast
  Technical *C, A*
Minnesota State Community and
  Technical College *C, A*
National American University
  Bloomington *B*
Northland Community & Technical
  College *C, A*
Northwest Technical College *C, A*
Ridgewater College *C, A*
Saint Cloud State University *B*
St. Cloud Technical and Community
  College *C, A*
St. Mary's University of Minnesota *M*
St. Paul College *A*
South Central College *C, A*
University of Minnesota
  Duluth *B*
  Twin Cities *C, B*
University of Phoenix
  Minneapolis-St. Paul *B*

Mississippi

Copiah-Lincoln Community
  College *A*
East Mississippi Community
  College *A*
Hinds Community College *A*
Northwest Mississippi Community
  College *A*

Missouri

DeVry University
  Kansas City *A, B, M*
East Central College *C, A*
Grantham University *B*
Linn State Technical College *C, A*

Mineral Area College *C, A*
Missouri Southern State University *A*
Ozarks Technical Community
  College *A*
State Fair Community College *A*

Montana

Blackfeet Community College *A*
Montana State University
  Billings *A*
  Great Falls College *C, A*
Montana Tech of the University of
  Montana *C, A, B*
University of Great Falls *B*
University of Montana: Western *B*

Nebraska

ITT Technical Institute
  Omaha *B*
Metropolitan Community
  College *C, A*

Nevada

College of Southern Nevada *C, A*
Great Basin College *A*
ITT Technical Institute
  Henderson *A*
University of Phoenix
  Las Vegas *B*
  Northern Nevada *B*

New Hampshire

NHTI-Concord's Community
  College *C*
Nashua Community College *C, A*

New Jersey

Berkeley College *A*
Bloomfield College *C, B*
Cumberland County College *C, A*
DeVry University
  North Brunswick *A, B*
Kean University *B*
Mercer County Community
  College *C, A*
New Jersey Institute of
  Technology *M*
Raritan Valley Community College *C*
Stevens Institute of
  Technology *B, M, D*
University of Phoenix
  Jersey City *B*

New Mexico

ITT Technical Institute
  Albuquerque *A*
New Mexico State University
  Alamogordo *C*
University of Phoenix
  New Mexico *B*

New York

ASA College *C, A*
Adirondack Community College *A*
Briarcliffe College *A, B*
City University of New York
  Borough of Manhattan Community
    College *A*
  LaGuardia Community College *A*
Clinton Community College *A*
Corning Community College *A*
DeVry College of New York
  Midtown Campus *A, B*
Globe Institute of
  Technology *C, A, B*
Hudson Valley Community College *A*
ITT Technical Institute
  Albany *A*
  Getzville *A*
  Liverpool *A*
Iona College *B*
Marist College *C*
Monroe Community College *A*
New York University *C*

Pace University *C, A, M*
Pace University: Pleasantville/
   Briarcliff *M*
Rochester Institute of
   Technology *B, M*
SUNY
   College of Technology at Alfred *B*
Syracuse University *M*
Wood Tobe-Coburn School *A*

North Carolina

Beaufort County Community
   College *A*
Central Carolina Community
   College *A*
Central Piedmont Community
   College *A*
Cleveland Community College *C, A*
College of the Albemarle *A*
Davidson County Community
   College *C, A*
Durham Technical Community
   College *C, A*
Edgecombe Community College *A*
Fayetteville Technical Community
   College *C, A*
Forsyth Technical Community
   College *C, A*
Haywood Community College *C, A*
Isothermal Community College *C, A*
Johnston Community College *A*
King's College *A*
Lenoir Community College *C, A*
Montgomery Community College *C*
North Carolina State University *M*
Randolph Community College *A*
Richmond Community College *C, A*
South Piedmont Community
   College *C*
Southeastern Community
   College *C, A*
Southwestern Community College *A*
Stanly Community College *C, A*
University of North Carolina
   Greensboro *B, M*
Vance-Granville Community
   College *A*
Wayne Community College *C, A*
Wilson Community College *C, A*

North Dakota

Bismarck State College *C, A*
North Dakota State College of
   Science *A*
United Tribes Technical College *C, A*

Ohio

Akron Institute of Herzing
   University *C*
Baldwin Wallace University *B*
Bradford School *A*
Brown Mackie College
   Akron *A*
   North Canton *A*
Clark State Community College *A*
Davis College *A*
DeVry University
   Columbus *A, B, M*
Edison State Community College *C, A*
Herzing University
   Toledo *C, A*
Hocking College *C, A*
ITT Technical Institute
   Dayton *A*
   Hilliard *A*
   Norwood *A*
   Strongsville *A*
   Youngstown *A*
James A. Rhodes State College *A*
Kaplan College
   Dayton *A*
Lorain County Community College *A*
Marion Technical College *A*

Miami University
   Hamilton *A*
Miami-Jacobs Career College
   Dayton *C, A*
Mount Vernon Nazarene University *B*
Ohio University *B, M*
Owens Community College
   Toledo *C*
Remington College
   Cleveland *A*
   Cleveland West *A*
Sinclair Community College *C*
Stark State College *A*
Stautzenberger College *C, A*
Terra State Community College *A*
University of Akron *C, A, B*
University of Akron: Wayne
   College *A*
University of Cincinnati *C*
University of Cincinnati
   Clermont College *A*

Oklahoma

Oklahoma State University *M*
Rose State College *A*
Southern Nazarene University *B*
University of Phoenix
   Oklahoma City *B*
   Tulsa *B*

Oregon

Central Oregon Community
   College *A*
Clackamas Community College *C, A*
ITT Technical Institute
   Portland *A*
Lane Community College *A*
Mt. Hood Community College *C, A*

Pennsylvania

Berks Technical Institute *A*
Bradford School: Pittsburgh *A*
Bucks County Community
   College *C, A*
Community College of Beaver
   County *A*
Community College of
   Philadelphia *A*
DeVry University
   Fort Washington *A, B, M*
Delaware County Community
   College *A*
DuBois Business College *C*
DuBois Business College
   Huntingdon *C*
Erie Business Center *A*
Harrisburg Area Community
   College *C, A*
ITT Technical Institute
   Pittsburgh *A*
   Plymouth Meeting *A*
Johnson College *A*
Kaplan Career Institute
   Harrisburg *A*
Lehigh Carbon Community College *A*
Lincoln Technical Institute
   Northeast Philadelphia *C*
Northampton Community College *A*
Penn Commercial Business and
   Technical School *A*
Pennsylvania College of
   Technology *B*
Pennsylvania Highlands Community
   College *C, A*
Pennsylvania Institute of
   Technology *A*
Reading Area Community College *A*
Thaddeus Stevens College of
   Technology *A*
University of Pennsylvania *B, M*
University of Phoenix
   Philadelphia *B*
   Pittsburgh *B*
University of Pittsburgh *M*

Waynesburg University *B*
Westmoreland County Community
   College *C, A*

Puerto Rico

Inter American University of Puerto
   Rico
   Aguadilla Campus *B*
   Bayamon Campus *B*
   Metropolitan Campus *C*
National University College
   Arecibo *A, B*
   Rio Grande *A, B*
Universidad del Este *C*

Rhode Island

Community College of Rhode
   Island *C, A*

South Carolina

ITT Technical Institute
   Greenville *A*
Midlands Technical College *C*
Trident Technical College *C, A*
York Technical College *C*

South Dakota

National American University
   Rapid City *B*
Northern State University *A*
Southeast Technical Institute *A*
Western Dakota Technical
   Institute *C, A*

Tennessee

Daymar Institute
   Nashville *C, A*
Fountainhead College of
   Technology *C, A, B*
ITT Technical Institute
   Knoxville *B*
   Memphis *A*
   Nashville *B*
University of Phoenix
   Chattanooga *B*
   Knoxville *B*
   Memphis *B*
   Nashville *B*
University of Tennessee
   Chattanooga *C*

Texas

Angelina College *C, A*
Austin Community College *C, A*
Brookhaven College *C*
Cedar Valley College *C, A*
Central Texas College *C, A*
DeVry University
   Houston *A, B*
   Irving *A, B*
Eastfield College *C, A*
Hallmark College of Technology *A*
Houston Community College
   System *C, A*
ITT Technical Institute
   Arlington *A*
   Austin *A*
   Houston North *A*
   Houston West *A*
   Richardson *A*
   San Antonio *A*
Lamar State College at Port
   Arthur *C, A*
Mountain View College *C, A*
North Lake College *C, A*
Northeast Texas Community
   College *A*
Northwest Vista College *C, A*
Remington College
   Dallas *A*
   Fort Worth *A*
   Houston *A*
   Houston Southeast *A*
St. Philip's College *C, A*

South Texas College *A*
Tarrant County College *C, A*
Texas State Technical College
   Harlingen *C, A*
   Marshall *C, A*
   West Texas *C, A*
University of Phoenix
   Dallas Fort Worth *B*
   Houston Westside *B*
   San Antonio *B*
Victoria College *C, A*
Wharton County Junior College *C, A*

Utah

Broadview University
   Layton *A*
   Orem *A*
   West Jordan *A*
University of Phoenix
   Utah *B*
Utah Valley University *C, B*
Weber State University *C, A, B*

Vermont

Champlain College *C, B*

Virginia

DeVry University
   Arlington *A, B, M*
George Mason University *M*
Germanna Community College *C*
Hampton University *B*
ITT Technical Institute
   Chantilly *A*
   Norfolk *A*
   Richmond *A*
   Springfield *A*
J. Sargeant Reynolds Community
   College *C, A*
Lord Fairfax Community College *C, A*
Mountain Empire Community
   College *A*
Stratford University: Falls
   Church *A, B, M*
Thomas Nelson Community
   College *A*
Tidewater Community College *A*
University of Management and
   Technology *A, B, M*
University of Phoenix
   Northern Virginia *B*
   Richmond *B*
Virginia Western Community
   College *C*

Washington

Bates Technical College *A*
Bellevue College *C, A*
Bellingham Technical College *C, A*
Cascadia Community College *C*
Centralia College *C, A*
Clark College *C, A*
Clover Park Technical College *A*
Columbia Basin College *A*
DeVry University
   Federal Way *A, B, M*
Edmonds Community College *C, A*
Green River Community College *C, A*
ITT Technical Institute
   Everett *A*
   Seattle *A*
   Spokane *B*
Lake Washington Institute of
   Technology *A*
Lower Columbia College *A*
North Seattle Community
   College *C, A*
Northwest Indian College *C*
Olympic College *C, A*
Peninsula College *A*
Pierce College *C, A*
Renton Technical College *C, A*
Shoreline Community College *C, A*
Spokane Falls Community College *C*

Tacoma Community College *C, A*
University of Phoenix
    Western Washington *B*
Walla Walla Community College *C, A*
Wenatchee Valley College *C, A*
Yakima Valley Community College *C*

West Virginia

Blue Ridge Community and Technical
    College *C*

Wisconsin

Chippewa Valley Technical College *A*
Fox Valley Technical College *A*
Gateway Technical College *A*
Globe University
    Eau Claire *A*
    Green Bay *A*
    La Crosse *A*
    Madison East *A*
    Middleton *A*
    Wausau *A*
Herzing University
    Brookfield *A, B*
    Kenosha *B*
    Madison *A, B*
ITT Technical Institute
    Green Bay *A*
    Greenfield *B*
Lakeshore Technical College *A*
Mid-State Technical College *A*
Milwaukee Area Technical College *A*
Nicolet Area Technical College *A*
Northcentral Technical College *C, A*
Northeast Wisconsin Technical
    College *A*
Southwest Wisconsin Technical
    College *A*
University of Phoenix
    Milwaukee *B*
University of Wisconsin
    Stout *B*
Waukesha County Technical
    College *A*
Western Technical College *A*

Computer numerically controlled (CNC) machinist

California

Bakersfield College *C*

Georgia

Columbus Technical College *C*
North Georgia Technical College *C*

Kansas

Cowley County Community
    College *A*

Maryland

Community College of Baltimore
    County *C*

Massachusetts

Springfield Technical Community
    College *C*

Michigan

Lake Michigan College *C*
Wayne County Community College *A*

Minnesota

Anoka Technical College *C, A*
Dunwoody College of Technology *C*
Lake Superior College *C, A*

New Mexico

San Juan College *C*

North Carolina

Randolph Community College *C*

Ohio

Sinclair Community College *C*

South Carolina

Midlands Technical College *C*

Washington

Grays Harbor College *C*

Wisconsin

Lakeshore Technical College *C*

Computer programming, general

Alabama

Calhoun Community College *A*
Enterprise State Community
    College *C*
Gadsden State Community College *A*
ITT Technical Institute
    Birmingham *A, B*
Northwest-Shoals Community
    College *A*
University of Phoenix
    Birmingham *B*
Wallace State Community College at
    Hanceville *A*

Alaska

University of Alaska
    Southeast *C, A*

Arizona

Central Arizona College *C, A*
Cochise College *C, A*
Eastern Arizona College *C*
GateWay Community College *C*
ITT Technical Institute
    Tempe *A*
    Tucson *A*
Mesa Community College *C*
Mohave Community College *C*
Paradise Valley Community College *C*
South Mountain Community
    College *C*
University of Phoenix
    Phoenix-Hohokam *B*
    Southern Arizona *B*

Arkansas

ITT Technical Institute
    Little Rock *A*
North Arkansas College *C*
Northwest Arkansas Community
    College *A*
University of Arkansas
    Little Rock *A*
University of Phoenix
    Little Rock *B*
    Northwest Arkansas *B*

California

American River College *A*
Antelope Valley College *C, A*
Bakersfield College *C, A*
California College San Diego *A*
California Lutheran University *B*
Cerritos College *A*
Chabot College *A*
City College of San Francisco *C*
Coleman University *A, B*
College of San Mateo *C*
College of the Redwoods *C*
College of the Siskiyous *C, A*
Columbia College *A*
Cosumnes River College *C, A*
Crafton Hills College *C, A*
Cypress College *C*
De Anza College *C, A*
Diablo Valley College *C*
East Los Angeles College *C*
Evergreen Valley College *C*

Folsom Lake College *C*
Foothill College *C, A*
Fresno City College *A*
Gavilan College *C*
Grossmont College *C, A*
Hartnell College *C, A*
ITT Technical Institute
    Sylmar *A, B*
Irvine Valley College *C, A*
Los Angeles Mission College *C*
Los Angeles Pierce College *C, A*
Los Angeles Southwest College *A*
MiraCosta College *C, A*
Modesto Junior College *A*
Monterey Peninsula College *A*
Moreno Valley College *C, A*
Norco College *C*
Ohlone College *C, A*
Orange Coast College *C, A*
Pacific Union College *A*
Palomar College *C, A*
Pasadena City College *C, A*
Riverside City College *C, A*
Saddleback College *C, A*
San Diego Mesa College *C, A*
San Joaquin Delta College *C*
San Jose City College *C, A*
Santa Barbara City College *C*
Santa Monica College *C, A*
Santa Rosa Junior College *C*
Sierra College *C, A*
Solano Community College *C, A*
Sonoma State University *B*
Southwestern College *C, A*
University of Phoenix
    Bay Area *B*
    Central Valley *B*
    Sacramento Valley *B*
    San Diego *B*
    Southern California *B*
Victor Valley College *C*
West Valley College *C, A*
Westwood College
    Anaheim *A*
    Los Angeles *A*

Colorado

Aspen University *M*
CollegeAmerica
    Denver *A*
Colorado Mountain College *A*
Colorado Technical University *C*
Community College of Denver *C*
ITT Technical Institute
    Westminster *A, B*
Red Rocks Community College *C, A*
Trinidad State Junior College *A*
University of Phoenix
    Denver *B*
    Southern Colorado *B*
Westwood College
    Denver North *A*

Connecticut

Capital Community College *C*
Gateway Community College *A*
Northwestern Connecticut
    Community College *C*
Norwalk Community College *A*
Tunxis Community College *C*
University of Phoenix
    Fairfield County *B*

Delaware

Wilmington University *B, M*

District of Columbia

University of Phoenix
    Washington DC *B*

Florida

Broward College *C, A*
Eastern Florida State College *A*
Edison State College *A*

Everest University
    Tampa *A, B*
Florida Gateway College *A*
Florida Keys Community College *A*
Florida State College at
    Jacksonville *C, A*
Florida Technical College
    Orlando *A*
Herzing University
    Winter Park *A*
ITT Technical Institute
    Lake Mary *A*
Indian River State College *A*
Keiser University *A*
Lake-Sumter State College *A*
Lincoln College of Technology
    West Palm Beach *A*
Palm Beach State College *A*
Pasco-Hernando State College *C, A*
Pensacola State College *A*
Polk State College *A*
Saint Johns River State College *C, A*
St. Petersburg College *A*
Seminole State College of Florida *A*
South Florida State College *A*
State College of Florida, Manatee-
    Sarasota *C, A*
Tallahassee Community College *C, A*
University of Phoenix
    Central Florida *B*
    North Florida *B*
    South Florida *B*
    West Florida *B*

Georgia

Athens Technical College *C, A*
Atlanta Technical College *C, A*
Georgia Piedmont Technical
    College *C, A*
Gwinnett Technical College *C, A*
Middle Georgia State College *A*
South Georgia State College *A*
University of Phoenix
    Atlanta *B*
    Augusta *B*
    Columbus *B*
    Savannah *B*

Hawaii

University of Phoenix
    Hawaii *B*

Idaho

ITT Technical Institute
    Boise *A, B*
North Idaho College *A*
University of Phoenix
    Idaho *B*

Illinois

Black Hawk College *C*
Danville Area Community College *C*
DePaul University *B, M*
Harper College *C, A*
Heartland Community College *C*
Illinois Central College *A*
Illinois Valley Community College *C*
Joliet Junior College *A*
Lincoln Land Community
    College *C, A*
Moraine Valley Community College *C*
Morton College *C*
Olivet Nazarene University *B*
Prairie State College *C*
Richland Community College *A*
South Suburban College of Cook
    County *C*
Southwestern Illinois College *A*
Triton College *C*
University of Illinois
    Urbana-Champaign *B, M, D*
University of Phoenix
    Chicago *B*
Waubonsee Community College *C, A*

Indiana

ITT Technical Institute
  Fort Wayne *A, B*
  Indianapolis *A, B*
  Newburgh *A, B*
Indiana University
  South Bend *C*
Indiana Wesleyan University *B*
International Business College *A*
International Business College:
  Indianapolis *A*
Purdue University *B*
University of Phoenix
  Indianapolis *B*
Valparaiso University *C*
Vincennes University *A*

Iowa

AIB College of Business *A*
Ellsworth Community College *A*
Grand View University *B*
Iowa Western Community College *A*
Morningside College *B*
Southeastern Community College *A*

Kansas

Donnelly College *C, A*
Friends University *B*
Independence Community
  College *C, A*
Kansas State University *M*
Labette Community College *A*
Seward County Community
  College *C, A*

Kentucky

Big Sandy Community and Technical
  College *C, A*
Northern Kentucky University *C*
University of Phoenix
  Louisville *B*

Louisiana

ITT Technical Institute
  St. Rose *A, B*
University of Phoenix
  Baton Rouge *B*
  Lafayette *B*
  Louisiana *B*
  Shreveport *B*

Maine

Eastern Maine Community College *C*
Kaplan University
  South Portland *A*
Northern Maine Community
  College *A*
University of Southern Maine *B*

Maryland

College of Southern Maryland *A*
Hagerstown Community College *C*
Howard Community College *A*
Montgomery College *C, A*
Prince George's Community
  College *C, A*
University of Maryland
  University College *M*
University of Phoenix
  Maryland *B*

Massachusetts

Benjamin Franklin Institute of
  Technology *A*
Berkshire Community College *C*
Bristol Community College *A*
Bunker Hill Community College *C*
Fitchburg State University *C*
ITT Technical Institute
  Norwood *A*
Massasoit Community College *A*
North Shore Community
  College *C, A*

Northern Essex Community
  College *C, A*
Tufts University *B*
University of Phoenix
  Boston *B*

Michigan

Baker College
  Auburn Hills *A*
  Cadillac *A*
  Clinton Township *A*
  Flint *A*
  Jackson *A*
  Muskegon *A*
  Owosso *A*
  Port Huron *A*
Davenport University *B*
Delta College *A*
Grand Rapids Community
  College *C, A*
Grand Valley State University *B*
ITT Technical Institute
  Canton *B*
  Troy *A, B*
Jackson College *C, A*
Kalamazoo Valley Community
  College *A*
Kellogg Community College *C, A*
Lake Michigan College *C, A*
Macomb Community College *C, A*
Mid Michigan Community College *A*
Monroe County Community
  College *A*
Mott Community College *C, A*
Oakland Community College *C, A*
St. Clair County Community
  College *A*
Schoolcraft College *C, A*
Southwestern Michigan College *A*
University of Michigan
  Dearborn *B*
University of Phoenix
  Metro Detroit *B*
  West Michigan *B*
Washtenaw Community College *C, A*
Wayne County Community College *A*

Minnesota

Academy College *A*
Anoka-Ramsey Community College *C*
Central Lakes College *A*
Dakota County Technical
  College *C, A*
Hennepin Technical College *C, A*
ITT Technical Institute
  Eden Prairie *A, B*
Inver Hills Community College *A*
Mesabi Range Community and
  Technical College *C, A*
Minneapolis Community and
  Technical College *C, A*
Minnesota School of Business
  Richfield *A, B*
  St. Cloud *A, B*
Minnesota State College - Southeast
  Technical *A*
Minnesota State Community and
  Technical College *A*
National American University
  Roseville *B*
Pine Technical College *A*
St. Cloud Technical and Community
  College *A*
St. Paul College *A*
University of Phoenix
  Minneapolis-St. Paul *B*

Mississippi

East Central Community College *A*
Hinds Community College *A*
Holmes Community College *A*
Itawamba Community College *A*
Meridian Community College *A*

Mississippi Delta Community
  College *A*
Northeast Mississippi Community
  College *A*
Northwest Mississippi Community
  College *A*
University of Phoenix
  Jackson *B*

Missouri

Linn State Technical College *A*
Metropolitan Community College -
  Kansas City *C, A*
Mineral Area College *A*
Missouri Southern State
  University *A, B*
Moberly Area Community
  College *C, A*
Ozarks Technical Community
  College *A*
St. Charles Community College *C, A*
St. Louis Community College *A*
University of Phoenix
  Kansas City *B*
  St. Louis *B*

Montana

Helena College University of
  Montana *C, A*
University of Great Falls *B*

Nebraska

Bellevue University *B*
Midland University *B*
Northeast Community College *A*
Union College *B*
Western Nebraska Community
  College *A*

Nevada

College of Southern Nevada *A*
Truckee Meadows Community
  College *A*
University of Phoenix
  Las Vegas *B*
  Northern Nevada *B*

New Hampshire

Great Bay Community College *C, A*
Lakes Region Community
  College *C, A*
NHTI-Concord's Community
  College *C*
Southern New Hampshire
  University *C*

New Jersey

Atlantic Cape Community College *A*
Essex County College *A*
Fairleigh Dickinson University
  Metropolitan Campus *C*
Mercer County Community
  College *A*
Middlesex County College *A*
Saint Peter's University *C, A, B*
University of Phoenix
  Jersey City *B*

New Mexico

New Mexico Junior College *A*
New Mexico State University
  Alamogordo *C, A*
  Grants *A*
University of Phoenix
  New Mexico *B*

New York

ASA College *C, A*
Bramson ORT College *A*
Briarcliffe College *A, B*
Cayuga Community College *C*
City University of New York
  College of Staten Island *A*
  LaGuardia Community College *A*

Medgar Evers College *A*
Queensborough Community
  College *C, A*
College of Saint Rose *C*
Dutchess Community College *C*
Excelsior College *A*
Finger Lakes Community College *A*
Globe Institute of
  Technology *C, A, B*
Ithaca College *B*
Jamestown Community College *C*
Le Moyne College *B*
Marist College *C*
Mohawk Valley Community
  College *A*
Monroe Community College *A*
Nassau Community College *A*
Pace University *C*
Rockland Community College *A*
SUNY
  College at Buffalo *B*
  College of Agriculture and
    Technology at Morrisville *A, B*
  Farmingdale State College *C, A, B*
Schenectady County Community
  College *C, A*
Sullivan County Community
  College *A*
Utica School of Commerce *A*
Wood Tobe-Coburn School *A*

North Carolina

Beaufort County Community
  College *A*
Bladen Community College *C, A*
Blue Ridge Community College *A*
Brunswick Community College *C, A*
Caldwell Community College and
  Technical Institute *A*
Catawba Valley Community
  College *A*
Central Carolina Community
  College *A*
Central Piedmont Community
  College *C, A*
College of the Albemarle *A*
Davidson County Community
  College *C, A*
Durham Technical Community
  College *C, A*
Fayetteville Technical Community
  College *C, A*
Gaston College *C, A*
Isothermal Community College *C, A*
Johnston Community College *A*
King's College *A*
Mayland Community College *A*
McDowell Technical Community
  College *A*
Piedmont Community College *A*
Rowan-Cabarrus Community
  College *C, A*
Sandhills Community College *C, A*
Southwestern Community
  College *C, A*
University of Phoenix
  Charlotte *B*
  Raleigh *B*
Wake Technical Community
  College *C, A*
Wilkes Community College *C, A*

North Dakota

Minot State University *C*
North Dakota State College of
  Science *A*

Ohio

Belmont College *A*
Bowling Green State University:
  Firelands College *A*
Brown Mackie College
  Akron *C, A*
Central Ohio Technical College *A*

Cincinnati Christian University *B*
Cleveland Institute of
  Electronics *C, A*
Columbus State Community
  College *C*
Edison State Community College *C, A*
Hocking College *A*
ITT Technical Institute
  Dayton *A*
  Hilliard *A*
  Norwood *A*
  Strongsville *A*
  Youngstown *A*
James A. Rhodes State College *C, A*
Lakeland Community College *C, A*
Marion Technical College *A*
Miami-Jacobs Career College
  Dayton *C, A*
North Central State College *A*
Northwest State Community
  College *A*
Ohio Business College
  Sandusky *A*
Sinclair Community College *C, A*
Southern State Community College *A*
Stark State College *A*
Terra State Community College *C, A*
Tiffin University *A*
University of Cincinnati
  Clermont College *A*
University of Mount Union *B*
University of Phoenix
  Cleveland *B*
University of Toledo *A*
Washington State Community
  College *A*
Youngstown State University *A, B, M*

Oklahoma

Eastern Oklahoma State College *A*
Northeastern Oklahoma Agricultural
  and Mechanical College *C, A*
Oklahoma Christian University *B*
Oklahoma City Community
  College *A*
Tulsa Community College *C, A*
University of Phoenix
  Oklahoma City *B*
  Tulsa *B*
Western Oklahoma State College *A*

Oregon

Eastern Oregon University *C*
ITT Technical Institute
  Portland *A*
Lane Community College *C, A*
Northwest Christian University *B*
Southern Oregon University *B*
University of Phoenix
  Oregon *B*

Pennsylvania

Arcadia University *B*
Berks Technical Institute *A*
Bradford School: Pittsburgh *A*
Community College of
  Philadelphia *A*
Delaware Valley College *C, A*
Erie Business Center *A*
Fortis Institute
  Erie *A*
Gannon University *B*
Kaplan Career Institute
  Franklin Mills *A*
  Pittsburgh *A*
La Salle University *A, B*
Lehigh Carbon Community College *A*
Northampton Community
  College *C, A*
Pace Institute *C, A*
Reading Area Community College *A*
St. Francis University *B*

University of Phoenix
  Philadelphia *B*
  Pittsburgh *B*
Westminster College *B*
Westmoreland County Community
  College *A*

Puerto Rico

American University of Puerto
  Rico *A, B*
Atlantic University College *A*
Columbia Centro Universitario:
  Caguas *A*
Columbia Centro Universitario:
  Yauco *A*
EDP University of Puerto Rico: Hato
  Rey *A, B*
Pontifical Catholic University of
  Puerto Rico *A*
Universal Technology College of
  Puerto Rico *A*
Universidad Metropolitana *C*

Rhode Island

Johnson & Wales University
  Providence *A*
New England Institute of
  Technology *A, B*

South Carolina

Aiken Technical College *C*
Central Carolina Technical College *A*
Clemson University *M*
Greenville Technical College *C*
Limestone College *A, B*
Orangeburg-Calhoun Technical
  College *A*
Piedmont Technical College *C*
Trident Technical College *C*
University of Phoenix
  Columbia *B*
York Technical College *A*

South Dakota

Dakota State University *C, A*
Lake Area Technical Institute *A*
National American University
  Rapid City *A, B*
Southeast Technical Institute *A*

Tennessee

Chattanooga College *A*
Fountainhead College of
  Technology *A, B*
ITT Technical Institute
  Knoxville *A*
  Memphis *A*
  Nashville *A*
Northeast State Community
  College *C*
Southern Adventist University *B*
University of Phoenix
  Chattanooga *B*
  Knoxville *B*
  Memphis *B*
  Nashville *B*

Texas

Alvin Community College *C, A*
Amarillo College *C, A*
Austin Community College *C, A*
Brazosport College *C, A*
Brookhaven College *C, A*
Cedar Valley College *C, A*
Central Texas College *A*
Coastal Bend College *C, A*
College of the Mainland *A*
Del Mar College *C*
Eastfield College *C, A*
El Centro College *C, A*
El Paso Community College *A*
Galveston College *C, A*
Grayson College *A*
Hardin-Simmons University *B*

Hill College *A*
Houston Community College
  System *A*
ITT Technical Institute
  Arlington *A, B*
  Austin *A, B*
  Houston North *A, B*
  Houston West *A, B*
  Richardson *A, B*
  San Antonio *A, B*
  Webster *A, B*
Kilgore College *A*
Lamar State College at Port
  Arthur *C, A*
Laredo Community College *A*
Lee College *C, A*
McLennan Community College *A*
Midland College *A*
Mountain View College *C, A*
North Lake College *C, A*
Northeast Texas Community
  College *C*
Northwest Vista College *C, A*
Odessa College *C, A*
Remington College
  Houston *A*
St. Philip's College *C, A*
San Antonio College *C, A*
Tarrant County College *C, A*
Temple College *C, A*
Texas State Technical College
  Harlingen *A*
  Waco *A*
  West Texas *A*
Trinity Valley Community
  College *C, A*
University of Phoenix
  Dallas Fort Worth *B*
  San Antonio *B*
Victoria College *C, A*
Weatherford College *A*
Western Texas College *A*
Wharton County Junior College *C*

Utah

Provo College *A*
University of Phoenix
  Utah *B*
Utah Valley University *C*

Vermont

Champlain College *A, B*
Vermont Technical College *A, B*

Virginia

Blue Ridge Community College *A*
Danville Community College *A*
ECPI University *A, B*
ITT Technical Institute
  Chantilly *A*
  Norfolk *A, B*
  Richmond *A, B*
  Springfield *A, B*
J. Sargeant Reynolds Community
  College *C, A*
New River Community College *A*
Northern Virginia Community
  College *A*
Patrick Henry Community College *A*
Thomas Nelson Community
  College *C, A*
University of Phoenix
  Northern Virginia *B*
  Richmond *B*

Washington

Bates Technical College *C, A*
Bellevue College *C, A*
Cascadia Community College *C*
Centralia College *A*
City University of Seattle *C, B*
Clark College *C, A*
Clover Park Technical College *C, A*
Columbia Basin College *C, A*

Edmonds Community College *C*
ITT Technical Institute
  Everett *A, B*
  Seattle *A, B*
Lower Columbia College *A*
Olympic College *C*
Renton Technical College *A*
Seattle Central Community
  College *C, A*
Skagit Valley College *A*
University of Phoenix
  Western Washington *B*
Walla Walla University *A*

West Virginia

West Virginia Northern Community
  College *C, A*
West Virginia University Institute of
  Technology *B*

Wisconsin

Chippewa Valley Technical College *A*
Fox Valley Technical College *A*
Gateway Technical College *A*
Herzing University
  Madison *A, B*
ITT Technical Institute
  Green Bay *A*
  Greenfield *A*
Madison Area Technical College *A*
Mid-State Technical College *A*
Milwaukee Area Technical College *A*
Nicolet Area Technical College *A*
Northcentral Technical College *A*
Southwest Wisconsin Technical
  College *A*
University of Phoenix
  Milwaukee *B*
Wisconsin Indianhead Technical
  College *A*

Wyoming

Casper College *A*
Laramie County Community
  College *C, A*

Computer programming, specific applications

Alabama

Calhoun Community College *A*
Gadsden State Community College *C*
Northwest-Shoals Community
  College *C, A*

Alaska

University of Alaska
  Anchorage *A*
  Southeast *C, A*

Arizona

Central Arizona College *C, A*
Estrella Mountain Community
  College *C, A*
GateWay Community College *C*
South Mountain Community
  College *C*

Arkansas

North Arkansas College *C*

California

Butte College *C, A*
Cerritos College *A*
Chabot College *A*
Chaffey College *C, A*
Chapman University *M*
City College of San Francisco *C*
College of San Mateo *C, A*
Contra Costa College *C, A*
De Anza College *C, A*
Diablo Valley College *C*

Evergreen Valley College *A*
Fullerton College *A*
Grossmont College *C, A*
Irvine Valley College *C, A*
Long Beach City College *C, A*
Los Angeles City College *A*
Los Angeles Harbor College *C, A*
Los Angeles Pierce College *C, A*
Los Angeles Southwest College *A*
Los Angeles Valley College *C, A*
Mission College *A*
Moorpark College *A*
Mount San Antonio College *C*
Pasadena City College *A*
Saddleback College *C*
San Diego City College *C, A*
San Jose City College *C, A*
Southwestern College *C, A*
West Hills College: Coalinga *C, A*
Westwood College
    Inland Empire *A*

Colorado
Aims Community College *C*
Aspen University *C*
Colorado Mountain College *A*
Community College of Denver *C, A*
National American University
    Denver *A, B*
Westwood College
    Denver North *A*

Connecticut
Asnuntuck Community College *C*
Capital Community College *C*
Norwalk Community College *C, A*
Quinnipiac University *B*
Three Rivers Community
    College *C, A*
Tunxis Community College *C, A*
Yale University *B*

Delaware
Delaware Technical Community
    College
    Terry Campus *C*

Florida
Daytona State College *A*
Edison State College *C*
Everest University
    Brandon *A*
Florida State College at
    Jacksonville *A*
Gulf Coast State College *A*
Hillsborough Community
    College *C, A*
Indian River State College *A*
Miami Dade College *C, A*
Northwest Florida State College *C, A*
Palm Beach State College *A*
Pensacola State College *A*
Saint Johns River State College *C, A*
Seminole State College of Florida *A*
South Florida State College *C*
Valencia College *C*

Georgia
Abraham Baldwin Agricultural
    College *A*
Athens Technical College *C, A*
Atlanta Technical College *C*
Augusta Technical College *C, A*
Chattahoochee Technical
    College *C, A*
Dalton State College *C*
Georgia Piedmont Technical
    College *C*
Gwinnett Technical College *C*
Middle Georgia State College *A*
Southern Polytechnic State
    University *B*

Idaho
Idaho State University *A, B*
North Idaho College *A*

Illinois
College of DuPage *C, A*
Danville Area Community College *A*
DePaul University *B, M*
Harper College *C, A*
Illinois Central College *C, A*
Illinois Valley Community College *A*
Kishwaukee College *A*
Lincoln Land Community College *A*
McHenry County College *C, A*
Moraine Valley Community College *C*
National-Louis University *C*
Parkland College *C, A*
Rend Lake College *C, A*
Rock Valley College *C*
Southwestern Illinois College *C, A*

Indiana
Indiana University
    South Bend *A*

Iowa
Clinton Community College *C, A*
Des Moines Area Community
    College *C*
Iowa Lakes Community College *A*
Kirkwood Community College *C, A*
Northeast Iowa Community
    College *A*
Southeastern Community College *C*
Southwestern Community College *A*

Kansas
Johnson County Community
    College *C, A*
Seward County Community
    College *C, A*

Kentucky
Northern Kentucky University *C*
West Kentucky Community and
    Technical College *A*

Louisiana
Southern University
    Shreveport *A*

Maine
Northern Maine Community
    College *A*
University of Southern Maine *B*

Maryland
Community College of Baltimore
    County *C*
Frederick Community College *C, A*
Hagerstown Community College *C*
Harford Community College *C*

Massachusetts
Bristol Community College *C*
Bunker Hill Community College *C, A*
Cape Cod Community College *A*
Holyoke Community College *A*
Quinsigamond Community
    College *C, A*
Roxbury Community College *A*
Springfield Technical Community
    College *C, A*

Michigan
Baker College
    Cadillac *A*
    Muskegon *A*
    Port Huron *A*
Grand Rapids Community College *A*
Jackson College *C, A*
Lansing Community College *C, A*
Mid Michigan Community College *A*

Monroe County Community
    College *C, A*
Mott Community College *C, A*
Schoolcraft College *A*
Washtenaw Community College *C, A*

Minnesota
Hennepin Technical College *C, A*
Minneapolis Business College *A*
Minneapolis Community and
    Technical College *C*
Minnesota State College - Southeast
    Technical *C*
North Hennepin Community
    College *C*
Ridgewater College *C*
St. Paul College *C*

Mississippi
East Central Community College *A*
Northwest Mississippi Community
    College *A*
Pearl River Community College *A*

Missouri
St. Charles Community College *A*
State Fair Community College *A*

Montana
University of Great Falls *B*

New Hampshire
NHTI-Concord's Community
    College *C*
Nashua Community College *A*

New Jersey
Bergen Community College *A*
Burlington County College *C*
Camden County College *C*
Middlesex County College *A*
Passaic County Community College *C*
Sussex County Community College *A*

New Mexico
New Mexico Junior College *A*
New Mexico State University
    Carlsbad *C*
Northern New Mexico College *C*

New York
Bramson ORT College *A*
Everest Institute
    Rochester *C*
Globe Institute of
    Technology *C, A, B*
Marist College *C*
SUNY
    Farmingdale State College *C*

North Carolina
Asheville-Buncombe Technical
    Community College *A*
Beaufort County Community
    College *A*
Bladen Community College *C, A*
Caldwell Community College and
    Technical Institute *C, A*
Campbell University *A*
Central Carolina Community
    College *C*
College of the Albemarle *A*
Durham Technical Community
    College *C, A*
Forsyth Technical Community
    College *A*
Gaston College *A*
Haywood Community College *C, A*
McDowell Technical Community
    College *A*
Piedmont Community College *A*
Pitt Community College *C, A*
Sampson Community College *A*
Sandhills Community College *A*

South Piedmont Community
    College *C*
Surry Community College *C*
Wake Technical Community
    College *C, A*

North Dakota
Cankdeska Cikana Community
    College *C, A*
Sitting Bull College *A*

Ohio
Cincinnati State Technical and
    Community College *A*
Clark State Community College *C, A*
Columbus State Community
    College *A*
Eastern Gateway Community
    College *C*
James A. Rhodes State College *C*
Kent State University
    Ashtabula *A*
    East Liverpool *A*
    Geauga *A*
    Salem *A*
    Trumbull *A*
    Tuscarawas *A*
Marion Technical College *A*
Miami University
    Middletown *C, A*
Miami-Jacobs Career College
    Dayton *C, A*
North Central State College *A*
Owens Community College
    Toledo *C, A*
Southern State Community College *A*
Stark State College *A*
University of Akron: Wayne
    College *A*
University of Cincinnati
    Clermont College *A*
University of Northwestern
    Ohio *C, A*
University of Rio Grande *B*

Oklahoma
Oklahoma Baptist University *B*
Oklahoma State University
    Oklahoma City *A*
Tulsa Community College *A*

Oregon
Art Institute of Portland *B*
Chemeketa Community College *A*
Clackamas Community College *C, A*
Lane Community College *C*
Linn-Benton Community College *C*
Portland Community College *C, A*
Southwestern Oregon Community
    College *C, A*

Pennsylvania
Bucks County Community College *A*
Butler County Community College *A*
Community College of Beaver
    County *A*
Community College of
    Philadelphia *A*
Delaware County Community
    College *A*
Kaplan Career Institute
    Pittsburgh *A*
La Salle University *B, M*
Lehigh Carbon Community College *A*
Luzerne County Community
    College *C, A*
Manor College *A*
McCann School of Business and
    Technology
    Hazleton *A*
University of Pittsburgh
    Bradford *B*
Westmoreland County Community
    College *C*

Puerto Rico

ICPR Junior College *C, A*
Universidad del Este *A*

Rhode Island

Community College of Rhode
  Island *C, A*

South Carolina

York Technical College *A*

South Dakota

Southeast Technical Institute *A*

Tennessee

Fountainhead College of
  Technology *A*
Southwest Tennessee Community
  College *C*

Texas

Blinn College *C*
Del Mar College *A*
Eastfield College *A*
Hill College *A*
Houston Community College
  System *A*
North Lake College *C, A*
Remington College
  Houston *A*
Richland College *C, A*
South Texas College *A*
Tyler Junior College *A*

Vermont

Champlain College *A, B*

Washington

DigiPen Institute of Technology *B, M*
Heritage University *C*
Peninsula College *A*
Renton Technical College *C, A*
Seattle Central Community
  College *C, A*
Skagit Valley College *A*
South Puget Sound Community
  College *C, A*
Spokane Community College *C, A*
University of Washington Bothell *B*

West Virginia

American Public University System *C*
Mountain State College *A*
New River Community and Technical
  College *C*
Shepherd University *B*

Wisconsin

Chippewa Valley Technical College *A*
Herzing University
  Madison *A, B*
Moraine Park Technical College *C, A*
Northcentral Technical College *C*

Wyoming

Eastern Wyoming College *C*

Computer science

Alabama

Bevill State Community College *A*
Birmingham-Southern College *B*
Central Alabama Community
  College *C, A*
Faulkner University *B*
Gadsden State Community College *A*
Lawson State Community
  College *C, A*
Oakwood University *B*
Samford University *B*
University of South Alabama *B*

Alaska

Charter College *C, A*
University of Alaska
  Fairbanks *B, M*

Arizona

Arizona State University *B, M, D*
Brown Mackie College
  Tucson *B*
Chandler-Gilbert Community
  College *A*
Cochise College *A*
Dine College *A*
GateWay Community College *C*
Mohave Community College *C*
Northern Arizona University *B*
Paradise Valley Community College *C*
University of Arizona *B, M, D*

Arkansas

Harding University *B*
Hendrix College *B*
Ouachita Baptist University *B*
Philander Smith College *B*
Phillips Community College of the
  University of Arkansas *A*
University of Central Arkansas *M*

California

Allan Hancock College *A*
Antelope Valley College *C, A*
Azusa Pacific University *B*
Bakersfield College *C, A*
Barstow Community College *C, A*
Biola University *B*
California College San Diego *B*
California Lutheran University *B, M*
California National University for
  Advanced Studies *B*
California Polytechnic State
  University: San Luis Obispo *B, M*
California State Polytechnic
  University: Pomona *B, M*
California State University
  Bakersfield *B*
  Channel Islands *B*
  Chico *B, M*
  Dominguez Hills *B, M*
  East Bay *B, M*
  Fresno *B, M*
  Fullerton *B, M*
  Long Beach *B, M*
  San Bernardino *B, M*
  San Marcos *B, M*
Canada College *A*
Chabot College *A*
Chapman University *B*
City College of San Francisco *A*
Claremont McKenna College *B*
College of Marin *A*
College of the Canyons *A*
College of the Desert *A*
College of the Sequoias *C, A*
College of the Siskiyous *C, A*
Columbia College *C*
Contra Costa College *A*
Copper Mountain College *C, A*
Cuesta College *C, A*
De Anza College *A*
Diablo Valley College *C, A*
El Camino College *C, A*
Foothill College *C, A*
Fresno City College *C, A*
Golden West College *C*
Grossmont College *C, A*
Humboldt State University *B*
Imperial Valley College *A*
La Sierra University *B*
Los Angeles Pierce College *C, A*
Los Angeles Southwest College *C, A*
Los Angeles Trade and Technical
  College *C, A*
Los Medanos College *C*
Mills College *B, M*

MiraCosta College *A*
Mission College *A*
Modesto Junior College *A*
Napa Valley College *C*
National University *B, M*
Pacific States University *M*
Pacific Union College *B*
Point Loma Nazarene University *B*
Pomona College *B*
Reedley College *B*
Saddleback College *A*
San Bernardino Valley College *C, A*
San Diego State University *B, M*
San Francisco State University *B, M*
San Jose State University *B, M*
Santa Ana College *C, A*
Santa Barbara City College *C, A*
Santa Monica College *C, A*
Santa Rosa Junior College *C, A*
Santiago Canyon College *A*
Scripps College *B*
Silicon Valley University *B, M*
Skyline College *A*
Sonoma State University *B*
Southern California Institute of
  Technology *B*
Southwestern College *C, A*
Stanford University *B, M, D*
University of California
  Berkeley *B, M, D*
  Davis *B, M, D*
  Irvine *B, M, D*
  Riverside *B, M, D*
  San Diego *B, M, D*
University of San Diego *B*
University of San Francisco *B, M*
University of Southern
  California *B, M, D*
University of the Pacific *B*
Westmont College *B*
Yuba College *C, A*

Colorado

Adams State University *B*
American Sentinel University *M*
CollegeAmerica
  Colorado Springs *A, B*
  Denver *B*
Colorado College *B*
Colorado School of Mines *B, M, D*
Colorado Technical
  University *B, M, D*
Community College of Aurora *C, A*
IntelliTec College *A*
Metropolitan State University of
  Denver *B*
Regis University *B*
Trinidad State Junior College *A*
United States Air Force Academy *B*
University of Colorado
  Boulder *B, M, D*
  Colorado Springs *B, M*
University of Denver *B, M, D*

Connecticut

Connecticut College *B*
Gateway Community College *C, A*
Quinnipiac University *B, M*
Sacred Heart University *B, M*
Trinity College *B*
University of Connecticut *B*
University of New Haven *A, B, M*

Delaware

Delaware State University *B, M*

District of Columbia

Gallaudet University *B*
Georgetown University *B, M, D*
Howard University *M*
University of the District of
  Columbia *B, M*

Florida

Barry University *B*
Bethune-Cookman University *B*
Broward College *A*
Chipola College *A*
Embry-Riddle Aeronautical
  University *B*
Florida Institute of
  Technology *B, M, D*
Florida Memorial University *B*
Florida Southern College *B*
Florida State University *B, M, D*
Herzing University
  Winter Park *A*
Nova Southeastern
  University *B, M, D*
Palm Beach Atlantic University *B*
Pensacola State College *A*
Rasmussen College
  Fort Myers *B*
  New Port Richey *B*
  Ocala *B*
  Pasco/Land O'Lakes *B*
  Tampa/Brandon *B*
Saint Thomas University *B*
Seminole State College of Florida *A*
Stetson University *B*
University of Miami *B, M, D*

Georgia

Abraham Baldwin Agricultural
  College *A*
Andrew College *A*
Atlanta Metropolitan College *A*
Clark Atlanta University *B, M*
Clayton State University *B*
College of Coastal Georgia *A*
Darton College *A*
East Georgia State College *A*
Emory University *B, D*
Georgia College and State
  University *B*
Georgia Institute of Technology *M, D*
Georgia Perimeter College *A*
Georgia Southern University *M*
Georgia Southwestern State
  University *B, M*
Georgia State University *B, M, D*
Gordon College *A*
Kennesaw State University *B, M*
Mercer University *B*
Middle Georgia State College *A*
South Georgia State College *A*
Southern Polytechnic State
  University *B, M*
University of Georgia *B, M, D*
University of West Georgia *M*

Hawaii

Brigham Young University-Hawaii *B*
Chaminade University of Honolulu *B*
Hawaii Pacific University *B*
University of Hawaii
  Hilo *B*
  Manoa *B, M, D*

Idaho

Boise State University *B, M*
Brigham Young University-Idaho *B*
College of Southern Idaho *A*
Lewis-Clark State College *B*
Northwest Nazarene University *B*
University of Idaho *B, M, D*

Illinois

Augustana College *B*
Aurora University *B*
Benedictine University *B*
Blackburn College *B*
Bradley University *B, M*
DePaul University *B, M, D*
Dominican University *B*
Elmhurst College *B*
Eureka College *B*

Governors State University *B, M*
Harper College *A*
Illinois College *B*
Illinois Institute of
	Technology *B, M, D*
Illinois State University *B, M*
Knox College *B*
Lake Forest College *B*
Lewis University *B*
Lewis and Clark Community
	College *A*
Lincoln College *A*
Loyola University Chicago *M*
MacMurray College *B*
McKendree University *B*
Monmouth College *B*
North Central College *B*
Northeastern Illinois University *B, M*
Northern Illinois University *B, M*
Northwestern University *B, M, D*
Olivet Nazarene University *B*
Principia College *B*
Quincy University *B*
Rasmussen College
	Aurora *B*
	Mokena/Tinley Park *B*
	Rockford *B*
	Romeoville/Joliet *B*
Richland Community College *A*
Roosevelt University *B, M*
Saint Xavier University *B*
Southern Illinois University
	Carbondale *B, M, D*
Southern Illinois University
	Edwardsville *B, M*
Southwestern Illinois College *C, A*
Trinity Christian College *B*
University of Chicago *M, D*
University of Illinois
	Chicago *B, M, D*
	Springfield *B, M*
	Urbana-Champaign *B, M, D*
University of St. Francis *B*
Wheaton College *B*

Indiana

Anderson University *B*
DePauw University *B*
Franklin College *B*
Huntington University *B*
Indiana Institute of Technology *B*
Indiana University
	Bloomington *B, M, D*
	Northwest *C, B*
	Purdue University Indianapolis *B*
	South Bend *B*
	Southeast *B*
Indiana Wesleyan University *B*
Manchester University *B*
Purdue University *C, B, M, D*
Purdue University
	Calumet *B, M*
Rose-Hulman Institute of
	Technology *B*
Taylor University *B*
Trine University *B*
University of Evansville *B*
University of Indianapolis *B*
University of Southern Indiana *B*
Valparaiso University *B*
Vincennes University *A*

Iowa

Ashford University *B*
Briar Cliff University *B*
Buena Vista University *B*
Coe College *B*
Cornell College *B*
Dordt College *B*
Drake University *B*
Ellsworth Community College *A*
Grinnell College *B*
Iowa Western Community College *A*
Loras College *B*

Luther College *B*
Maharishi University of
	Management *B, M*
Mount Mercy University *B*
Northwestern College *B*
St. Ambrose University *B*
Simpson College *B*
University of Iowa *B, M, D*
University of Northern Iowa *B*

Kansas

Allen County Community College *A*
Baker University *B*
Barton County Community College *A*
Benedictine College *B*
Butler Community College *A*
Dodge City Community College *A*
Garden City Community College *A*
Independence Community College *A*
Kansas Wesleyan University *A, B*
Seward County Community
	College *A*
Southwestern College *B*
Wichita State University *B, M*

Kentucky

Centre College *B*
Eastern Kentucky University *B, M*
Murray State University *B*
National College
	Danville *A*
	Florence *A*
	Lexington *A*
	Louisville *A*
	Richmond *A*
Northern Kentucky University *M*

Louisiana

Dillard University *B*
Grambling State University *B*
Herzing University
	Kenner *A*
Louisiana State University
	Shreveport *B, M*
Louisiana State University and
	Agricultural and Mechanical
	College *B, D*
Louisiana Tech University *B, M*
McNeese State University *B*
Nunez Community College *A*
Southeastern Louisiana University *B*
Southern University
	Shreveport *A*
Southern University and Agricultural
	and Mechanical College *B, M*
University of Louisiana at
	Lafayette *B, M, D*
University of Louisiana at Monroe *B*
University of New Orleans *B, M*
Xavier University of Louisiana *B*

Maine

Bowdoin College *B*
Colby College *B*
Kaplan University
	South Portland *A*
Southern Maine Community
	College *A*
Thomas College *B*
University of Maine *B, M, D*
University of Maine
	Farmington *B*
	Fort Kent *A*
University of Southern Maine *B, M*

Maryland

Allegany College of Maryland *A*
Baltimore City Community College *A*
Bowie State University *B, M*
Capitol College *B, M*
Coppin State University *B*
Frederick Community College *A*
Goucher College *B*
Harford Community College *A*

Hood College *B, M*
Howard Community College *A*
Loyola University Maryland *M*
Montgomery College *A*
Morgan State University *B*
Notre Dame of Maryland
	University *B*
Prince George's Community
	College *A*
University of Maryland
	Baltimore County *B, M, D*
Washington Adventist University *A, B*
Washington College *B*

Massachusetts

American International College *B*
Amherst College *B*
Bard College at Simon's Rock *B*
Boston College *B*
Boston University *B, M, D*
Brandeis University *B, M, D*
Bridgewater State University *B, M*
Bristol Community College *A*
Bunker Hill Community College *A*
Cape Cod Community College *A*
Clark University *B*
Endicott College *B*
Fitchburg State University *B, M*
Gordon College *B*
Hampshire College *B*
Harvard College *B, M, D*
Massachusetts Bay Community
	College *A*
Massachusetts Institute of
	Technology *B, M, D*
Merrimack College *B*
Middlesex Community College *A*
Mount Holyoke College *B*
Newbury College *B*
North Shore Community College *A*
Northern Essex Community
	College *C, A*
Quincy College *C, A*
Quinsigamond Community College *A*
Smith College *B*
Springfield Technical Community
	College *A*
Stonehill College *B*
Suffolk University *B*
Tufts University *B, M, D*
University of Massachusetts
	Amherst *B, M, D*
	Boston *M, D*
	Lowell *B, M, D*
Wellesley College *B*
Wentworth Institute of Technology *B*
Western New England University *B*
Westfield State University *B*
Wheaton College *B*
Williams College *B*
Worcester Polytechnic
	Institute *B, M, D*

Michigan

Baker College
	Cadillac *B*
	Clinton Township *B*
	Flint *A*
	Muskegon *B*
	Owosso *A, B*
	Port Huron *A, B*
Calvin College *B*
Central Michigan University *B, M*
Delta College *A*
Eastern Michigan University *B, M*
Gogebic Community College *A*
Grand Valley State University *B*
Hillsdale College *B*
Kettering University *B*
Lake Michigan College *A*
Lawrence Technological
	University *C, B, M*
Madonna University *A, B*

Michigan Technological
	University *B, M, D*
Mid Michigan Community College *A*
Olivet College *B*
Spring Arbor University *B*
University of Detroit Mercy *B, M*
University of Michigan
	Flint *B, M*
Washtenaw Community College *C, A*
Western Michigan University *B, M, D*

Minnesota

Anoka-Ramsey Community College *A*
Augsburg College *B*
Bemidji State University *B*
Carleton College *B*
Century College *A*
College of St. Benedict *B*
Gustavus Adolphus College *B*
Inver Hills Community College *A*
Metropolitan State University *B*
Minnesota State University
	Mankato *B, M*
	Moorhead *B*
Normandale Community College *A*
North Hennepin Community
	College *A*
Rasmussen College
	Blaine *B*
	Bloomington *B*
	Brooklyn Park *B*
	Eagan *B*
	Lake Elmo/Woodbury *B*
	Mankato *B*
	Moorhead *B*
	St. Cloud *B*
Ridgewater College *A*
Rochester Community and Technical
	College *A*
Saint Cloud State University *B, M*
St. John's University *B*
St. Mary's University of Minnesota *B*
St. Olaf College *B*
University of Minnesota
	Duluth *B, M*
	Morris *B*
	Twin Cities *B, M, D*
University of St. Thomas *B*
Winona State University *B*

Mississippi

Coahoma Community College *A*
Holmes Community College *A*
Itawamba Community College *A*
Mississippi College *B, M*
Rust College *B*

Missouri

Calvary Bible College and Theological
	Seminary *B*
Central Methodist University *A, B*
College of the Ozarks *B*
Columbia College *B*
Drury University *B*
Grantham University *A, B*
Lindenwood University *B*
Maryville University of Saint Louis *B*
Missouri Southern State University *B*
Missouri State University *B, M*
Missouri University of Science and
	Technology *B, M, D*
Park University *A, B*
Southwest Baptist University *A, B*
Truman State University *B*
University of Missouri
	Columbia *B, M, D*
	Kansas City *B, M*
	St. Louis *B, M*
Washington University in St.
	Louis *B, M, D*
Webster University *B*

Montana

Carroll College *A, B*
Montana State University *B, M, D*
Montana Tech of the University of
Montana *B*
Rocky Mountain College *B*
Salish Kootenai College *C, A, B*
University of Great Falls *B*
University of Montana *B, M*

Nebraska

Concordia University *B*
Creighton University *C, A, B*
Doane College *B*
Hastings College *B*
Herzing University
Omaha School of Massage Therapy
and Healthcare *A*
Midland University *B*
Northeast Community College *A*
Union College *B*
University of Nebraska
Omaha *B, M*
Western Nebraska Community
College *A*

Nevada

Morrison University *A*
University of Nevada
Las Vegas *B, M, D*
Reno *B, M*

New Hampshire

Daniel Webster College *B*
Dartmouth College *B, M, D*
Nashua Community College *C, A*
Plymouth State University *B*
River University *M*
Saint Anselm College *B*
University of New Hampshire *M, D*
University of New Hampshire at
Manchester *B*

New Jersey

Burlington County College *A*
College of St. Elizabeth *B*
Cumberland County College *A*
Drew University *B*
Fairleigh Dickinson University
College at Florham *M*
Metropolitan Campus *B, M*
Felician College *B*
Gloucester County College *A*
Hudson County Community
College *A*
Montclair State University *B, M*
New Jersey Institute of
Technology *B, M, D*
Rowan University *B*
Rutgers, The State University of New
Jersey
Camden Campus *B, M*
Saint Peter's University *B*
Salem Community College *A*
Thomas Edison State College *C, A, B*
Union County College *A*
William Paterson University of New
Jersey *B*

New Mexico

Dona Ana Community College of
New Mexico State University *A*
New Mexico Highlands
University *B, M*
New Mexico Institute of Mining and
Technology *B, M, D*

New York

Adirondack Community College *A*
Bard College *B*
Barnard College *B*
Canisius College *B*
Cayuga Community College *A*

City University of New York
Baruch College *B, M*
Borough of Manhattan Community
College *A*
Bronx Community College *A*
Brooklyn College *M*
City College *B, M*
College of Staten Island *B, M, D*
Kingsborough Community
College *A*
LaGuardia Community College *A*
New York City College of
Technology *A*
Queens College *B, M*
York College *B*
Clarkson University *B, M, D*
Colgate University *B*
Columbia University *B, M, D*
Columbia University
School of General Studies *B*
Columbia-Greene Community
College *A*
Cornell University *B, M, D*
Dowling College *B*
Everest Institute
Rochester *A*
Finger Lakes Community College *A*
Globe Institute of
Technology *C, A, B*
Hobart and William Smith Colleges *B*
Hofstra University *B, M*
Houghton College *B*
Iona College *B, M*
Ithaca College *B*
Jefferson Community College *A*
Long Island University
LIU Post *B, M*
Manhattan College *B*
Marist College *B*
Monroe Community College *A*
Nassau Community College *A*
New York University *B, M, D*
Niagara County Community
College *A*
Niagara University *C, B*
Nyack College *B*
Onondaga Community College *A*
Pace University *B, M, D*
Pace University: Pleasantville/
Briarcliff *B, M*
Rensselaer Polytechnic
Institute *B, M, D*
Roberts Wesleyan College *B*
Rochester Institute of
Technology *A, B, M*
SUNY
College at Brockport *B*
College at Fredonia *B*
College at Oneonta *B*
College at Oswego *B*
College at Potsdam *B*
College of Technology at Alfred *A*
Farmingdale State College *A*
University at Binghamton *B, M, D*
University at Buffalo *C, B*
University at Stony Brook *B, M, D*
Saint Bonaventure University *B*
Schenectady County Community
College *A*
Suffolk County Community College *A*
Ulster County Community College *A*
University of Rochester *B, M, D*
Wagner College *B*
Wells College *B*
Westchester Community College *A*

North Carolina

Appalachian State University *B, M*
Campbell University *B*
East Carolina University *B, M*
Elizabeth City State University *B*
Elon University *B*
Gardner-Webb University *B*
High Point University *B*
Lees-McRae College *B*

Mars Hill University *B*
Meredith College *B*
Methodist University *A, B*
North Carolina Agricultural and
Technical State University *B, M*
North Carolina Central University *B*
North Carolina State
University *B, M, D*
St. Augustine's University *B*
Sandhills Community College *A*
Shaw University *B*
University of North Carolina
Asheville *B*
Chapel Hill *B, M, D*
Charlotte *B, M*
Greensboro *B, M*
Pembroke *B*
Wilmington *B*
Wake Forest University *B, M*
Western Carolina University *B*
Western Piedmont Community
College *A*
Winston-Salem State University *B*

North Dakota

Dickinson State University *B*
North Dakota State
University *B, M, D*
Rasmussen College
Bismarck *B*
Fargo *B*
Turtle Mountain Community
College *C, A*
University of Jamestown *B*
University of North Dakota *M, D*

Ohio

Ashland University *B*
Baldwin Wallace University *B*
Brown Mackie College
Cincinnati *C, A*
Capital University *B*
Case Western Reserve
University *B, M, D*
Cedarville University *B*
Central State University *B*
Fortis College
Centerville *A*
Franciscan University of
Steubenville *B*
Franklin University *A, B, M*
Heidelberg University *B*
Herzing University
Toledo *A*
Hiram College *B*
John Carroll University *B*
Malone University *B*
Marietta College *B*
Muskingum University *B*
Ohio Northern University *B*
Ohio University *B, M*
Ohio University
Southern Campus at Ironton *A*
Ohio Wesleyan University *B*
Otterbein University *B*
Stark State College *A*
University of Akron *C, B, M*
University of Dayton *B, M*
University of Findlay *A, B*
University of Rio Grande *A, B*
Virginia Marti College of Art and
Design *A*
Walsh University *A, B*
Wilmington College *B*
Wittenberg University *B*
Xavier University *B*
Youngstown State University *C, B*
Zane State College *C, A*

Oklahoma

Cameron University *B*
Carl Albert State College *A*
Eastern Oklahoma State College *A*
Murray State College *A*

Northeastern State University *B*
Oklahoma Baptist University *B*
Oklahoma Christian University *B*
Oklahoma City Community
College *A*
Oklahoma Wesleyan University *B*
Oral Roberts University *B*
Seminole State College *A*
Southwestern Oklahoma State
University *B*
University of Oklahoma *B, M, D*
University of Tulsa *B, M, D*
Western Oklahoma State College *A*

Oregon

Central Oregon Community
College *A*
Lewis & Clark College *B*
Linfield College *B*
Oregon State University *B, M, D*
Portland State University *B, M, D*
Southern Oregon University *B*
Southwestern Oregon Community
College *A*
University of Portland *B*

Pennsylvania

Albright College *B*
Allegheny College *B*
Arcadia University *B*
Berks Technical Institute *A*
Bloomsburg University of
Pennsylvania *B*
Bryn Mawr College *B*
Carnegie Mellon University *B, M, D*
Central Penn College *A, B*
Drexel University *B, M, D*
Duquesne University *B*
Fortis Institute
Erie *A*
Franklin & Marshall College *B*
Gettysburg College *B*
Grove City College *B*
Harrisburg Area Community
College *A*
King's College *B*
Kutztown University of
Pennsylvania *M*
La Roche College *B*
La Salle University *B, M*
Lebanon Valley College *B*
Lehigh University *B, M, D*
Mansfield University of
Pennsylvania *B*
Messiah College *B*
Montgomery County Community
College *A*
Moravian College *B*
Northampton Community College *A*
Penn State
Erie, The Behrend College *B*
University Park *M, D*
Pennsylvania Institute of
Technology *A*
St. Francis University *B*
Seton Hill University *C, B*
Slippery Rock University of
Pennsylvania *B*
South Hills School of Business &
Technology *C, A*
Susquehanna University *B*
University of Pittsburgh *B, M, D*
University of Pittsburgh
Bradford *B*
University of Scranton *B*
University of the Sciences *B*
Ursinus College *B*
Villanova University *B, M*
Waynesburg University *B*
Westminster College *B*
Westmoreland County Community
College *A*
Widener University *B*
York College of Pennsylvania *B*

Puerto Rico

Atlantic University College *A*
Huertas College *A*
Inter American University of Puerto
    Rico
    Aguadilla Campus *A, B*
    Arecibo Campus *A, B*
    Barranquitas Campus *C, A, B*
    Bayamon Campus *C, A, B*
    Ponce Campus *A, B*
    San German Campus *A, B*
Universidad Adventista de las
    Antillas *A, B*
Universidad Metropolitana *A, B*
Universidad Politecnica de Puerto
    Rico *B*
University of Puerto Rico
    Arecibo *B*
    Mayaguez *B, M*
    Rio Piedras *B*
University of the Sacred Heart *B*

Rhode Island

Brown University *B, M, D*
New England Institute of
    Technology *A, B*
Providence College *B*
Roger Williams University *B*

South Carolina

Benedict College *B*
Bob Jones University *B*
Charleston Southern University *B*
Citadel *M*
Claflin University *B*
Coker College *B*
College of Charleston *M*
Furman University *B*
Midlands Technical College *C, A*
Voorhees College *B*
Wofford College *B*

South Dakota

Augustana College *B*
Mount Marty College *B*
Sinte Gleska University *B*
South Dakota School of Mines and
    Technology *B, M*
University of Sioux Falls *B*

Tennessee

Bryan University
    Dayton *B*
Christian Brothers University *B*
Fisk University *B*
LeMoyne-Owen College *B*
Lipscomb University *B*
Middle Tennessee State
    University *B, M*
National College of Business and
    Technology
    Bristol *C, A*
Pellissippi State Community
    College *A*
Rhodes College *B*
Sewanee: The University of the
    South *B*
Southern Adventist University *B, M*
Tennessee State University *B*
Tennessee Technological
    University *B*
Tennessee Temple University *B*
Union University *B*
University of Memphis *B, M, D*
University of Tennessee
    Chattanooga *B, M*
    Knoxville *B, M, D*
    Martin *B*
Vanderbilt University *B, M, D*

Texas

Abilene Christian University *B*
Austin College *B*
Baylor University *B, M*

Coastal Bend College *A*
Concordia University Texas *B*
Dallas Baptist University *B*
Eastfield College *C, A*
El Paso Community College *A*
Galveston College *A*
Hill College *C, A*
Howard Payne University *B*
Huston-Tillotson University *B*
Laredo Community College *A*
LeTourneau University *B*
Mountain View College *A*
North Lake College *C, A*
Northwest Vista College *A*
Odessa College *A*
Palo Alto College *A*
Rice University *B, M, D*
St. Edward's University *B*
St. Mary's University *B, M*
St. Philip's College *A*
South Plains College *A*
South Texas College *A*
Southern Methodist
    University *B, M, D*
Southwestern Adventist University *B*
Texas A&M University *B, M, D*
Texas Lutheran University *B*
Texas Southern University *M*
Texas Wesleyan University *B*
University of Houston
    Clear Lake *B, M*
University of Mary Hardin-Baylor *B*
University of St. Thomas *B*
University of Texas
    Arlington *B*
    El Paso *D*
    Pan American *B, M*
    San Antonio *D*
West Texas A&M University *B*
Western Texas College *A*
Wiley College *B*

Utah

Brigham Young University *B, M, D*
Dixie State College *B*
Neumont University *B, M*
Salt Lake Community College *A*
Snow College *A*
Southern Utah University *B*
University of Utah *B, M, D*
Utah Valley University *A, B*
Weber State University *A, B*
Westminster College *B*

Vermont

Bennington College *B*
Champlain College *B*
Lyndon State College *A*
Marlboro College *B, M*
Middlebury College *B*
Norwich University *B*
Saint Michael's College *B*
University of Vermont *B, M, D*

Virginia

American National University
    Charlottesville *C, A*
    Danville *C, A*
    Harrisonburg *C, A*
    Lynchburg *C, A*
    Martinsville *C, A*
Averett University *B*
Bridgewater College *B*
Christopher Newport University *B*
Danville Community College *A*
Eastern Mennonite University *B*
George Mason University *B*
Hampden-Sydney College *B*
Hampton University *B*
J. Sargeant Reynolds Community
    College *A*
Longwood University *B*
Northern Virginia Community
    College *A*

Radford University *B*
Roanoke College *B, T*
Thomas Nelson Community
    College *A*
University of Management and
    Technology *A, B, M*
University of Virginia's College at
    Wise *B*
Virginia Military Institute *B*
Virginia State University *B, M*
Virginia Wesleyan College *B*
Washington and Lee University *B*

Washington

Central Washington University *B, M*
Centralia College *A*
Gonzaga University *B*
Lower Columbia College *A*
Pacific Lutheran University *B*
Renton Technical College *C, A*
Saint Martin's University *B*
Seattle Pacific University *B*
Seattle University *B, M*
University of Puget Sound *B*
University of Washington *B, M, D*
Walla Walla University *B*
Washington State University *B, M, D*
Whatcom Community College *A*
Whitworth University *B*

West Virginia

Alderson-Broaddus University *A, B*
American National University
    Princeton *C, A*
Bethany College *B*
Concord University *B*
Davis and Elkins College *B*
Kanawha Valley Community and
    Technical College *A*
West Virginia State University *B*
West Virginia University *B, M, D*
West Virginia University Institute of
    Technology *B*
West Virginia Wesleyan College *B*
Wheeling Jesuit University *B*

Wisconsin

Beloit College *B*
Cardinal Stritch University *A, B*
Carthage College *B*
Herzing University
    Kenosha *A*
    Madison *A, B*
Lakeland College *B*
Nicolet Area Technical College *A*
Rasmussen College
    Appleton *B*
    Green Bay *B*
    Wausau *B*
Ripon College *B*
St. Norbert College *B*
Silver Lake College of the Holy
    Family *C, B, T*
University of Wisconsin
    Green Bay *B*
    Milwaukee *B*
    Oshkosh *B*
    Parkside *B*
    Platteville *B, M*
    Superior *B*
    Whitewater *B*
Wisconsin Lutheran College *B*

Wyoming

Central Wyoming College *A*
Laramie County Community
    College *A*
University of Wyoming *B, M, D*
Western Wyoming Community
    College *A*

Computer software technology

Arizona

Coconino County Community
    College *A*
ITT Technical Institute
    Tempe *B*
    Tucson *B*
South Mountain Community
    College *C, A*

Colorado

IntelliTec College: Grand Junction *A*

Connecticut

Three Rivers Community College *C*

Delaware

Delaware Technical Community
    College
    Jack F. Owens Campus *C*
Wilmington University *B*

Florida

Brown Mackie College
    Miami *C, A*
ITT Technical Institute
    Miami *B*
Palm Beach State College *C*

Illinois

Prairie State College *C*

Kansas

Kansas City Kansas Community
    College *C, A*

Maryland

Frederick Community College *C, A*

Massachusetts

Bristol Community College *C*
Bunker Hill Community College *C*

Missouri

Metropolitan Community College -
    Kansas City *A*

Nebraska

Metropolitan Community College *A*

Nevada

ITT Technical Institute
    Henderson *B*

New York

Technical Career Institutes *A*

Ohio

Cleveland State University *M*
ITT Technical Institute
    Dayton *A*
    Strongsville *A*
    Youngstown *A*

Oregon

Oregon Institute of Technology *B*
Rogue Community College *A*

Puerto Rico

Universidad del Este *A*

Rhode Island

New England Institute of
    Technology *A, B*

Tennessee

ITT Technical Institute
    Memphis *A*

Texas

North Lake College *C*

Virginia

University of Virginia's College at
    Wise *B*

Washington

Bates Technical College *C, A*

Wisconsin

Herzing University
    Madison *A, B*
ITT Technical Institute
    Green Bay *B*
    Greenfield *B*

Computer support specialist

Arizona

Mesa Community College *C*
University of Phoenix
    Phoenix-Hohokam *A*
    Southern Arizona *B*

Arkansas

University of Phoenix
    Little Rock *B*

California

Contra Costa College *C, A*
Diablo Valley College *C, A*
Los Medanos College *C, A*
San Joaquin Valley College *A*
Shasta College *C*
University of Phoenix
    Sacramento Valley *B*
    San Diego *A*

Colorado

IBMC College
    Fort Collins *A*
University of Phoenix
    Denver *A*

District of Columbia

Strayer University *A*

Florida

College of Business and Technology
    Hialeah *C*
    Kendall *C*
Pasco-Hernando State College *C*
Rasmussen College
    Fort Myers *C, A*
    New Port Richey *C, A*
    Ocala *C, A*
    Pasco/Land O'Lakes *C, A*
    Tampa/Brandon *C, A*
Saint Johns River State College *C*
University of Phoenix
    Central Florida *B*
    North Florida *B*
    South Florida *B*

Georgia

Altamaha Technical College *C, A*
Columbus Technical College *C, A*
Dalton State College *C, A*
Georgia Piedmont Technical
    College *C, A*
Southeastern Technical College *A*

Idaho

College of Western Idaho *C, A*

Illinois

Rasmussen College
    Aurora *C, A*
    Mokena/Tinley Park *C, A*

Rockford *C, A*
    Romeoville/Joliet *C, A*
Sauk Valley Community College *C*

Indiana

Brown Mackie College
    South Bend *A*
Kaplan College
    Indianapolis *C*

Iowa

Iowa Western Community College *C*

Kentucky

Western Kentucky University *C*

Maryland

Howard Community College *A*

Massachusetts

Bristol Community College *C*
Bunker Hill Community College *C*
Quinsigamond Community College *C*

Michigan

Baker College
    Allen Park *C*
Cleary University *C*
Lake Superior State University *C*
University of Phoenix
    Metro Detroit *A, B*
Wayne County Community
    College *C, A*

Minnesota

Anoka-Ramsey Community College *C*
Century College *C*
Dakota County Technical College *C*
Inver Hills Community College *C, A*
Lake Superior College *C*
National American University
    Bloomington *A*
    Roseville *A*
Northland Community & Technical
    College *A*
Northwest Technical College *C*
Rasmussen College
    Blaine *C, A*
    Bloomington *C, A*
    Brooklyn Park *C, A*
    Eagan *C, A*
    Lake Elmo/Woodbury *C, A*
    Mankato *C, A*
    Moorhead *C, A*
    St. Cloud *C, A*
St. Cloud Technical and Community
    College *A*
South Central College *C*

Missouri

National American University
    Kansas City *C*

Nebraska

Northeast Community College *A*

Nevada

Kaplan College
    Las Vegas *C*

New Jersey

Passaic County Community College *A*
University of Phoenix
    Jersey City *B*

New Mexico

National American University
    Albuquerque *C, A*
University of Phoenix
    New Mexico *B*

New York

Clinton Community College *C*
Genesee Community College *C*
Herkimer County Community
    College *A*
Rockland Community College *A*
Tompkins Cortland Community
    College *A*

North Carolina

Central Carolina Community
    College *C*

North Dakota

North Dakota State College of
    Science *C*
Rasmussen College
    Bismarck *C, A*
    Fargo *C*

Ohio

Brown Mackie College
    Akron *C*
Central Ohio Technical College *A*
Cincinnati State Technical and
    Community College *A*
Kaplan College
    Dayton *C*
Miami University
    Hamilton *A*
Sinclair Community College *C*

Pennsylvania

Cambria-Rowe Business College *A*
Cambria-Rowe Business College:
    Indiana *A*
DuBois Business College *A*
DuBois Business College
    Huntingdon *A*
    Oil City *A*
Keystone Technical Institute *C, A*
Lansdale School of Business *C*
McCann School of Business and
    Technology
    Hazleton *A*
Peirce College *C*

Puerto Rico

Inter American University of Puerto
    Rico
    San German Campus *C*

Rhode Island

Community College of Rhode
    Island *C, A*

South Carolina

University of Phoenix
    Columbia *B*
York Technical College *C*

South Dakota

Mitchell Technical Institute *A*
National American University
    Rapid City *A*

Tennessee

Fountainhead College of
    Technology *A, B*
University of Phoenix
    Memphis *B*
    Nashville *B*

Texas

Central Texas College *C*
Lamar Institute of Technology *C*
South Texas College *C, A*
Texas State Technical College
    Waco *C*

Washington

Bellevue College *C, A*
Columbia Basin College *A*

Edmonds Community College *C*
Everett Community College *C*
Olympic College *C*
Pierce College *A*
Spokane Falls Community College *A*
Tacoma Community College *C*

West Virginia

New River Community and Technical
    College *C*

Wisconsin

Fox Valley Technical College *C*
Gateway Technical College *A*
Lakeshore Technical College *A*
Milwaukee Area Technical College *A*
Northcentral Technical College *C, A*
Rasmussen College
    Appleton *C, A*
    Green Bay *C, A*
    Wausau *C, A*
Waukesha County Technical
    College *A*
Western Technical College *A*
Wisconsin Indianhead Technical
    College *A*

Computer systems analysis

Alabama

Faulkner State Community
    College *C, A*
University of Phoenix
    Birmingham *B*

Arizona

DeVry University
    Phoenix *B*
GateWay Community College *C, A*
Glendale Community College *C, A*
Mesa Community College *C, A*
Mohave Community College *C*
Northern Arizona University *B*
Paradise Valley Community College *C*
Phoenix College *C, A*
Pima Community College *C, A*
South Mountain Community
    College *C, A*
University of Phoenix
    Phoenix-Hohokam *B*
    Southern Arizona *B*

Arkansas

Arkansas Tech University *B*
University of Phoenix
    Little Rock *B*
    Northwest Arkansas *B*

California

California Polytechnic State
    University: San Luis Obispo *B*
California State University
    San Bernardino *B*
Cerritos College *A*
De Anza College *C, A*
DeVry University
    Pomona *B*
Diablo Valley College *C*
Foothill College *C*
Glendale Community College *C*
Irvine Valley College *C, A*
Platt College
    Ontario *A*
San Bernardino Valley College *C, A*
San Diego City College *A*
San Jose State University *B*
University of California
    San Diego *B, M, D*
University of Phoenix
    Bay Area *B*
    Central Valley *B*
    Sacramento Valley *B*

San Diego *B*
Southern California *B*

Colorado
Colorado Technical
    University *B, M, D*
DeVry University
    Westminster *B*
IntelliTec College *A*
University of Denver *B*
University of Phoenix
    Denver *B*
    Southern Colorado *B*
Westwood College
    Denver North *A*

Connecticut
Northwestern Connecticut
    Community College *A*
Norwalk Community College *A*
University of Phoenix
    Fairfield County *B*

District of Columbia
Howard University *B*
University of Phoenix
    Washington DC *B*

Florida
Art Institute of Fort Lauderdale *A*
Broward College *A*
College of Central Florida *C*
Daytona State College *C, A*
DeVry University
    Miramar *B*
    Orlando *B*
Eastern Florida State College *A*
Florida State College at
    Jacksonville *A*
Gulf Coast State College *C*
Herzing University
    Winter Park *C*
Hillsborough Community
    College *C, A*
Indian River State College *A*
Lake-Sumter State College *A*
Northwest Florida State College *A*
Palm Beach State College *A*
Pasco-Hernando State College *A*
Pensacola State College *A*
Saint Johns River State College *A*
Seminole State College of Florida *A*
State College of Florida, Manatee-
    Sarasota *C, A*
University of Miami *B*
University of Phoenix
    Central Florida *B*
    North Florida *B*
    South Florida *B*
    West Florida *B*
Valencia College *C, A*

Georgia
Clayton State University *B*
University of Phoenix
    Atlanta *B*
    Augusta *B*
    Columbus *B*
    Savannah *B*

Hawaii
University of Phoenix
    Hawaii *B*

Idaho
University of Phoenix
    Idaho *B*

Illinois
DePaul University *M*
DeVry University
    Chicago *B*
    Online *B*

University of Illinois
    Springfield *B, M*
University of Phoenix
    Chicago *B*

Indiana
Purdue University *B*
Taylor University *B*
University of Phoenix
    Indianapolis *B*
Valparaiso University *C*

Iowa
Marshalltown Community College *A*
St. Ambrose University *B*

Kansas
Hutchinson Community College *A*
Pittsburg State University *B*
Wright Career College
    Overland Park *B*
    Wichita *B*

Kentucky
Daymar College
    Owensboro *A*
University of Phoenix
    Louisville *B*

Louisiana
University of Phoenix
    Baton Rouge *B*
    Lafayette *B*
    Louisiana *B*
    Shreveport *B*

Maryland
Baltimore City Community College *A*
Frederick Community College *A*
Prince George's Community
    College *A*
University of Phoenix
    Maryland *B*
Wor-Wic Community College *C, A*

Massachusetts
Bristol Community College *A*
Quinsigamond Community College *A*
University of Phoenix
    Boston *B*

Michigan
Baker College
    Muskegon *B*
Davenport University *A*
Kirtland Community College *C, A*
Oakland Community College *C, A*
Saginaw Valley State University *B*
University of Phoenix
    Metro Detroit *B*
    West Michigan *B*

Minnesota
Capella University *M*
Hennepin Technical College *C, A*
Mesabi Range Community and
    Technical College *A*
University of Phoenix
    Minneapolis-St. Paul *B*

Mississippi
University of Phoenix
    Jackson *B*

Missouri
DeVry University
    Kansas City *B*
Missouri Southern State University *A*
Northwest Missouri State
    University *M*
St. Louis Community College *A*

University of Phoenix
    Kansas City *B*
    St. Louis *B*

Montana
University of Great Falls *B*

Nebraska
Wright Career College
    Omaha *B*

Nevada
College of Southern Nevada *A*
University of Phoenix
    Las Vegas *B*
    Northern Nevada *B*

New Hampshire
Daniel Webster College *B*

New Jersey
DeVry University
    North Brunswick *B*
University of Phoenix
    Jersey City *B*

New Mexico
Central New Mexico Community
    College *C, A*
University of Phoenix
    New Mexico *B*

New York
City University of New York
    Baruch College *M*
DeVry College of New York
    Midtown Campus *B*
Globe Institute of
    Technology *C, A, B*
Monroe Community College *A*
New York University *C*
Pace University: Pleasantville/
    Briarcliff *B, M*
Rochester Institute of
    Technology *B, M*
SUNY
    College at Fredonia *B*

North Carolina
Durham Technical Community
    College *C, A*
Mayland Community College *A*
University of Phoenix
    Charlotte *B*
    Raleigh *B*
Western Piedmont Community
    College *C, A*

North Dakota
University of North Dakota *B*

Ohio
Baldwin Wallace University *B*
Cincinnati State Technical and
    Community College *A*
DeVry University
    Columbus *B*
Kent State University *B, M, D*
Miami University
    Middletown *A, B*
Southern State Community College *A*
Stark State College *A*
University of Akron *C, A*
University of Findlay *B*
University of Phoenix
    Cleveland *B*

Oklahoma
Eastern Oklahoma State College *A*
Oklahoma Baptist University *B*
Oklahoma City Community
    College *A*

University of Phoenix
    Oklahoma City *B*
    Tulsa *B*
Wright Career College
    Oklahoma City *B*
    Tulsa *B*

Pennsylvania
DeVry University
    Fort Washington *B*
Kaplan Career Institute
    Pittsburgh *A*
Robert Morris University *M*
Shippensburg University of
    Pennsylvania *B*
University of Phoenix
    Philadelphia *B*
    Pittsburgh *B*
YTI Career Institute
    York *A*

Puerto Rico
Caribbean University *B*
University of Puerto Rico
    Mayaguez *B*

Rhode Island
Johnson & Wales University
    Providence *B*
New England Institute of
    Technology *A, B*

South Carolina
University of Phoenix
    Columbia *B*

South Dakota
National American University
    Rapid City *A, B*

Tennessee
Fountainhead College of
    Technology *A, B*
University of Phoenix
    Chattanooga *B*
    Knoxville *B*
    Memphis *B*
    Nashville *B*

Texas
DeVry University
    Houston *B*
    Irving *B*
El Paso Community College *A*
Kilgore College *C, A*
North Lake College *C, A*
Remington College
    Houston *A*
Texas Christian University *B*
University of Houston *B*
University of Phoenix
    Dallas Fort Worth *B*
    Houston Westside *B*
    San Antonio *B*

Utah
University of Phoenix
    Utah *B*

Vermont
University of Vermont *B*

Virginia
Blue Ridge Community College *C, A*
DeVry University
    Arlington *B*
Tidewater Community College *A*
University of Management and
    Technology *A, B, M*
University of Phoenix
    Northern Virginia *B*
    Richmond *B*

Washington

DeVry University
  Federal Way *B*
Renton Technical College *C*
University of Phoenix
  Western Washington *B*
University of Washington Bothell *B*
University of Washington
  Tacoma *B, M*
Whatcom Community College *A*

Wisconsin

Bryant & Stratton College
  Milwaukee *A*
Fox Valley Technical College *A*
Lac Courte Oreilles Ojibwa
  Community College *A*
Southwest Wisconsin Technical
  College *A*
University of Phoenix
  Milwaukee *B*
University of Wisconsin
  Whitewater *B*
Wisconsin Indianhead Technical
  College *A*

Wyoming

Laramie County Community
  College *C*

Computer systems technology

Alabama

Gadsden State Community College *A*

Alaska

University of Alaska
  Anchorage *A*

Arizona

Coconino County Community
  College *C, A*

Arkansas

Arkansas State University
  Beebe *C, A*
College of the Ouachitas *C*
Southeast Arkansas College *C*
University of Arkansas
  Community College at
    Morrilton *C, A*
  Monticello *C*

California

Cuyamaca College *C, A*
Los Angeles Harbor College *A*
Westwood College
  Inland Empire *A*

Colorado

Colorado State University *B*

Delaware

Delaware Technical Community
  College
  Jack F. Owens Campus *C, A*
  Terry Campus *C, A*

Florida

Chipola College *C, A*
College of Central Florida *A*
Daytona State College *C, A, B*
Hillsborough Community
  College *C, A*
Lake-Sumter State College *A*
Northwest Florida State College *A*
Valencia College *C, A*

Idaho

College of Southern Idaho *C, A*

Illinois

Harper College *C*
Heartland Community College *C*
Illinois Central College *C*
Lincoln Land Community College *C*
Morton College *C*
Parkland College *C, A*
Triton College *C, A*

Indiana

Indiana University
  Purdue University Fort Wayne *C*
National College
  Indianapolis *A*

Kansas

Neosho County Community
  College *A*

Kentucky

Spencerian College: Lexington *A*
Sullivan University *B*

Louisiana

Nunez Community College *C*

Maryland

Frederick Community College *C, A*
Garrett College *C*

Massachusetts

Benjamin Franklin Institute of
  Technology *A*
Bristol Community College *C*
Newbury College *B*

Michigan

Bay de Noc Community College *A*
Central Michigan University *B*
Lansing Community College *C, A*
Oakland Community College *C, A*
Wayne County Community College *A*
Wayne State University *B*

Minnesota

Anoka Technical College *A*
Central Lakes College *C, A*
Century College *C, A*
Lake Superior College *A*
Minnesota State Community and
  Technical College *C, A*
Normandale Community College *C, A*
Rochester Community and Technical
  College *C, A*

Missouri

Metropolitan Community College -
  Kansas City *C*
Southeast Missouri State University *A*

New Hampshire

River Valley Community College *A*
White Mountains Community
  College *C, A*

New Jersey

Hudson County Community
  College *A*

New York

Corning Community College *A*
Erie Community College *A*
Genesee Community College *C*
Nassau Community College *C, A*
SUNY
  Farmingdale State College *C, B*
Sanford-Brown Institute
  Melville *A*
Technical Career Institutes *A*

North Carolina

Cape Fear Community College *C, A*

Ohio

James A. Rhodes State College *C, A*
Miami University
  Hamilton *A*
  Middletown *A*
National College
  Cincinnati *A*
  Stow *A*
  Youngstown *A*
Ohio Business College
  Sandusky *C*
Southern State Community College *A*
University of Cincinnati
  Clermont College *C, A*
University of Rio Grande *A*

Oregon

Linn-Benton Community College *C*

Pennsylvania

Bucks County Community College *C*
Butler County Community College *A*
Commonwealth Technical Institute *A*
Community College of
  Philadelphia *A*
Luzerne County Community
  College *A*
Metropolitan Career Center
  Computer Technology
  Institute *A*
Penn Commercial Business and
  Technical School *A*

Rhode Island

New England Institute of
  Technology *A, B*

South Carolina

York Technical College *A*

Tennessee

National College of Business and
  Technology
  Bartlett *A*
  Knoxville *C*
  Madison *A*
  Memphis *A*

Texas

Alvin Community College *C*
Brookhaven College *C, A*
Clarendon College *C, A*
Kilgore College *C*
Lamar Institute of Technology *C, A*
St. Philip's College *C, A*
Tarrant County College *C, A*
Texas State Technical College
  Harlingen *C, A*
  Waco *C, A*

Utah

Salt Lake Community College *C, A*

Virginia

American National University
  Salem *C, A*
ECPI University *A, B*

Washington

Bates Technical College *C, A*
Bellingham Technical College *A*
Edmonds Community College *C*
Spokane Falls Community College *C*

West Virginia

Blue Ridge Community and Technical
  College *C*
Bridgemont Community and
  Technical College *A*

Wisconsin

Herzing University
  Madison *A, B*

ITT Technical Institute
  Green Bay *A*
Mid-State Technical College *A*
Milwaukee Area Technical College *A*
Wisconsin Indianhead Technical
  College *A*

Wyoming

Central Wyoming College *C, A*

Computer typography

California

City College of San Francisco *C*
Santa Barbara City College *A*

Nevada

College of Southern Nevada *C, A*

Pennsylvania

Luzerne County Community
  College *C*

Concrete finishing

Illinois

Black Hawk College *C, A*

Indiana

Ivy Tech Community College
  Lafayette *C*

Wisconsin

Waukesha County Technical
  College *C*
Western Technical College *C*

Condensed matter and materials physics

Massachusetts

Tufts University *M, D*

New York

SUNY
  University at Albany *M, D*

Conducting

California

Azusa Pacific University *M*
Bethesda University of
  California *B, M*
California State University
  Long Beach *B, M*
Chapman University *B*
San Francisco Conservatory of
  Music *M*
University of Southern California *M*

Colorado

Colorado State University *B, M*

Connecticut

University of Hartford *M*

District of Columbia

Catholic University of America *M, D*
Howard University *B*

Florida

Florida State University *M*
University of Miami *M, D*

Georgia

Mercer University *B, M*

Illinois

Northwestern University *M, D*
University of Illinois
  Urbana-Champaign *M, D*

Indiana

Butler University *M*
Indiana University
　Purdue University Fort Wayne *T*

Iowa

University of Northern Iowa *M*

Kansas

Central Christian College of Kansas *A*
University of Kansas *M, D*

Kentucky

Campbellsville University *B, M*

Maryland

Johns Hopkins University: Peabody
　Conservatory of Music *M, D*

Massachusetts

Boston Conservatory *M*
New England Conservatory of
　Music *M, D*

Michigan

Central Michigan University *M*
Michigan State University *M, D*
Oakland University *M*
University of Michigan *M, D*
Western Michigan University *M*

Minnesota

Saint Cloud State University *M*

Mississippi

Mississippi College *M*

Missouri

University of Missouri
　Kansas City *M, D*

New Jersey

Rider University *M*
Rowan University *M*

New York

Bard College *B, M*
Eastman School of Music of the
　University of Rochester *M, D*
Houghton College *M*
Ithaca College *M*
Juilliard School *M*
Mannes College The New School for
　Music *B, M*
Syracuse University *M*
University of Rochester *M*

Ohio

Cleveland Institute of Music *M*
Oberlin College *B, M*
Terra State Community College *C*
University of Akron *M*
University of Cincinnati *B, M, D*

Oklahoma

Oklahoma City University *M*

Oregon

Portland State University *M*
University of Oregon *M*

Pennsylvania

Carnegie Mellon University *M*
Penn State
　University Park *M*
Temple University *M*

South Carolina

University of South Carolina
　Columbia *M, D*

Tennessee

Lee University *M*

Texas

Baylor University *M*
Concordia University Texas *B*
McMurry University *B*
Rice University *M*
Southern Methodist University *M*
Texas Christian University *M, D*
University of Texas
　Austin *D*

Utah

Brigham Young University *M*

Virginia

Shenandoah University *M*

Washington

University of Washington *M, D*

Conservation biology

Arizona

Prescott College *B*

California

San Francisco State University *M*
San Jose State University *B, M*

Colorado

Colorado State University *M*

Connecticut

University of Connecticut *M*

Florida

Florida Institute of Technology *B*
University of Central Florida *M, D*

Idaho

University of Idaho *B*

Louisiana

University of Louisiana at Lafayette *B*

Maine

College of the Atlantic *B, M*

Maryland

University of Maryland
　College Park *M*

Massachusetts

Boston University *B*

Michigan

Central Michigan University *M*

Minnesota

Ridgewater College *A*

Missouri

Missouri Southern State University *B*
University of Missouri
　Columbia *B, M, D*

New York

SUNY
　College of Environmental Science
　　and Forestry *B*
　University at Albany *M*
St. Lawrence University *B*

North Carolina

Methodist University *A, B*

Ohio

Muskingum University *B*

Pennsylvania

Gettysburg College *B*

Rhode Island

University of Rhode Island *M*

Tennessee

Union University *B*

Utah

Brigham Young University *B*
Utah State University *B*

Vermont

Sterling College *B*

Wisconsin

University of Wisconsin
　Madison *B*

Construction engineering

Alabama

University of Alabama *B*

Arizona

Arizona State University *B, M*

Arkansas

University of Arkansas
　Little Rock *B*

California

National University *B*

Georgia

Southern Polytechnic State
　University *B*

Illinois

Bradley University *B*
Illinois Institute of Technology *M*
University of Illinois
　Urbana-Champaign *B, M, D*

Indiana

Purdue University *B*

Iowa

Dordt College *B*
Iowa State University *B*

Massachusetts

Worcester Polytechnic Institute *M*

Michigan

Baker College
　Flint *A*
Ferris State University *C*
Lawrence Technological University *M*
University of Michigan *M*

Missouri

Washington University in St. Louis *M*

Nebraska

University of Nebraska
　Lincoln *B, M*

New Hampshire

Daniel Webster College *B*

New Jersey

Stevens Institute of Technology *M*

New Mexico

University of New Mexico *M*

North Carolina

North Carolina State University *B*

North Dakota

North Dakota State University *B*

Ohio

Eastern Gateway Community
　College *A*

Oregon

Oregon State University *B, M*

Pennsylvania

Carnegie Mellon University *M*

Texas

Texas A&M University
　Commerce *B*
Texas Tech University *B*

Virginia

George Mason University *M*
Virginia Polytechnic Institute and
　State University *B*

Wisconsin

Marquette University *B*

Construction management

Alabama

ITT Technical Institute
　Birmingham *B*

Alaska

Charter College *B*
University of Alaska
　Anchorage *A, B*
　Fairbanks *A*

Arizona

Arizona State University *B, M, D*
Coconino County Community
　College *C, A*
ITT Technical Institute
　Tempe *B*
　Tucson *B*
Northern Arizona University *B*
Phoenix College *C, A*

Arkansas

ITT Technical Institute
　Little Rock *B*
John Brown University *B*

California

Cabrillo College *C, A*
College of the Desert *C, A*
Diablo Valley College *C*
Heald College
　Hayward *A*
　Rancho Cordova *A*
　Salinas *C, A*
　San Francisco *A*
　San Jose *A*
　Stockton *A*
ITT Technical Institute
　Lathrop *B*
　National City *B*
　Oxnard *B*
　Rancho Cordova *B*
　San Bernardino *B*
　Sylmar *B*
　Torrance *B*
National University *C, B*
NewSchool of Architecture &
　Design *B, M*
San Joaquin Valley College *A*
Southwestern College *C, A*
University of Southern California *M*

Colorado

Colorado State University *B, M*
ITT Technical Institute
  Westminster *B*
University of Denver *B*

Connecticut

Central Connecticut State
  University *B*
Three Rivers Community
  College *C, A*

Delaware

Delaware Technical Community
  College
  Jack F. Owens Campus *C, A*
  Stanton/Wilmington Campus *C, A*

Florida

Everglades University
  Boca Raton *B*
ITT Technical Institute
  Ft. Lauderdale *B*
  Lake Mary *B*
  Miami *B*
  Tampa *B*
University of Miami *B*

Georgia

Atlanta Technical College *C*
Gwinnett Technical College *C, A*
Savannah Technical College *C, A*
Southern Polytechnic State
  University *C, B, M*

Idaho

Boise State University *B*
ITT Technical Institute
  Boise *B*

Illinois

City Colleges of Chicago
  Kennedy-King College *A*
Illinois State University *B*
Kankakee Community College *C, A*
Kaskaskia College *A*
Rock Valley College *C, A*
Triton College *C, A*
Waubonsee Community College *C, A*
Western Illinois University *B*

Indiana

ITT Technical Institute
  Fort Wayne *B*
  Indianapolis *B*
  Newburgh *B*
Purdue University *B*

Iowa

Kirkwood Community College *C, A*
Southeastern Community College *A*
University of Northern Iowa *B*

Kansas

Pittsburg State University *B*
University of Kansas *M*

Kentucky

ITT Technical Institute
  Louisville *B*

Louisiana

Baton Rouge Community College *A*
Delgado Community College *A*
ITT Technical Institute
  St. Rose *B*
Louisiana State University and
  Agricultural and Mechanical
  College *B, M*
University of Louisiana at Monroe *B*

Maryland

ITT Technical Institute
  Owings Mills *B*
Montgomery College *C, A*

Massachusetts

Wentworth Institute of
  Technology *A, B, M*

Michigan

Delta College *A*
Eastern Michigan University *B*
Ferris State University *B*
ITT Technical Institute
  Canton *B*
  Troy *B*
Lansing Community College *C, A*
Lawrence Technological University *B*
Michigan State University *B, M, D*
Michigan Technological University *B*
Montcalm Community College *C, A*
Oakland Community College *C, A*

Minnesota

Dunwoody College of Technology *C*
Inver Hills Community College *A*
Minnesota State Community and
  Technical College *A*
Minnesota State University
  Moorhead *B*

Mississippi

Mississippi State University *B*

Missouri

Missouri State University *B*

Nebraska

ITT Technical Institute
  Omaha *B*

Nevada

ITT Technical Institute
  Henderson *B*

New Mexico

Central New Mexico Community
  College *C, A*
ITT Technical Institute
  Albuquerque *B*

New York

City University of New York
  New York City College of
  Technology *C*
Erie Community College *A*
Nassau Community College *C*
New York University *M*
Pratt Institute *A, B*
SUNY
  College of Environmental Science
  and Forestry *B, M, D*

North Carolina

Appalachian State University *B*

North Dakota

North Dakota State University *B, M*

Ohio

ITT Technical Institute
  Strongsville *B*
  Youngstown *B*
Kent State University *B*
Ohio Northern University *B*
Ohio State University
  Columbus Campus *A*
Stark State College *A*

Oklahoma

Oklahoma State University
  Oklahoma City *A*
University of Oklahoma *B, M*

Oregon

Heald College
  Portland *A*
ITT Technical Institute
  Portland *B*

Pennsylvania

Delaware County Community
  College *A*
Drexel University *B, M*
Northampton Community College *A*
Philadelphia University *M*
Temple University *C*

South Carolina

Clemson University *B, M*
York Technical College *C*

South Dakota

Southeast Technical Institute *A*

Tennessee

ITT Technical Institute
  Knoxville *B*
  Memphis *B*
  Nashville *B*

Texas

ITT Technical Institute
  Arlington *B*
  Austin *B*
  Houston North *B*
  Houston West *B*
  Richardson *B*
  San Antonio *B*
  Webster *B*
North Lake College *C*
University of Texas
  San Antonio *M*
  Tyler *B*

Utah

Brigham Young University *B, M*
Utah Valley University *A, B*

Virginia

ITT Technical Institute
  Chantilly *B*
  Norfolk *B*
  Richmond *B*
  Springfield *B*
Virginia Polytechnic Institute and
  State University *B, M*
Westwood College
  Annandale *A, B*
  Arlington Ballston *B*

Washington

Central Washington University *B*
Edmonds Community College *C, A*
ITT Technical Institute
  Everett *B*
  Seattle *B*
  Spokane *B*
Lake Washington Institute of
  Technology *A*
University of Washington *B, M*
Washington State University *B*

Wisconsin

ITT Technical Institute
  Green Bay *B*
  Greenfield *B*
Milwaukee School of Engineering *B*
University of Wisconsin
  Stout *B*

Wyoming

Casper College *A*

Construction site management

Arizona

Arizona Western College *A*
Tohono O'odham Community
  College *C, A*

California

City College of San Francisco *A*
College of the Canyons *C, A*
College of the Sequoias *C*
Diablo Valley College *C, A*
Hartnell College *C, A*
Heald College
  Roseville *A*
San Joaquin Delta College *C*

Colorado

Aims Community College *C, A*

Connecticut

Three Rivers Community College *C*

Georgia

Columbus Technical College *C*

Hawaii

Heald College
  Honolulu *A*

Illinois

Triton College *A*

Indiana

Ivy Tech Community College
  Kokomo *A*
  Northeast *A*
  Northwest *A*
  Southwest *A*

Kansas

Johnson County Community
  College *C*

Louisiana

Bossier Parish Community College *C*

Maine

University of Southern Maine *B*

Maryland

Community College of Baltimore
  County *C, A*

Massachusetts

Wentworth Institute of Technology *A*

Minnesota

Anoka Technical College *C*
Dunwoody College of Technology *A*
Inver Hills Community College *C*
Minnesota State Community and
  Technical College *A*
North Hennepin Community
  College *C, A*
South Central College *A*

Missouri

State Fair Community College *A*

Nevada

Western Nevada College *A, B*

New Jersey

Cumberland County College *C, A*

New York

Pratt Institute *A, B*
SUNY
  College of Technology at Canton *A*
Utica College *B*

North Carolina

Cape Fear Community College *A*
Surry Community College *C, A*

Ohio

Ohio Northern University *B*

Oregon

Portland Community College *A*

Pennsylvania

Community College of
    Philadelphia *A*
Delaware County Community
    College *C*
Harrisburg Area Community
    College *C*
Lehigh Carbon Community College *A*
Pennsylvania College of
    Technology *B*

Rhode Island

Roger Williams University *B*

South Carolina

York Technical College *C*

South Dakota

Southeast Technical Institute *A*

Texas

San Jacinto College *C, A*
University of Texas
    San Antonio *B*

Utah

Salt Lake Community College *A*
Southern Utah University *B*

Virginia

J. Sargeant Reynolds Community
    College *A*

Washington

Centralia College *A*
Pierce College *C, A*

Wisconsin

Fox Valley Technical College *A*

Construction technology

Alabama

Alabama Agricultural and Mechanical
    University *B*
Community College of the Air
    Force *A*
Jefferson State Community
    College *C, A*
Lawson State Community
    College *C, A*
Tuskegee University *B*

Arizona

Coconino County Community
    College *A*

Arkansas

University of Arkansas
    Little Rock *B*

California

Antelope Valley College *C, A*
Butte College *C, A*
California Baptist University *B*
California State Polytechnic
    University: Pomona *B*
California State University
    Chico *B*
    Fresno *B*

Long Beach *B*
Sacramento *B, M*
College of the Desert *C*
College of the Redwoods *A*
College of the Sequoias *C, A*
El Camino College *C, A*
Los Angeles Pierce College *A*
Saddleback College *C*
San Bernardino Valley College *C*
San Diego Mesa College *C, A*
San Diego State University *B*
Santa Rosa Junior College *C*
Shasta College *C, A*

Colorado

Colorado Mesa University *B*
Colorado State University *B, M*
Trinidad State Junior College *A*

Connecticut

Norwalk Community College *A*

Florida

Florida Agricultural and Mechanical
    University *B*
Florida Institute of Technology *B*
Florida International University *B, M*
Florida State College at
    Jacksonville *A*
Gulf Coast State College *C, A*
Indian River State College *A*
Palm Beach State College *A*
Pensacola State College *C, A*
Santa Fe College *A*
Seminole State College of
    Florida *A, B*
State College of Florida, Manatee-
    Sarasota *A*
Tallahassee Community College *A*
University of Florida *B, M*
University of North Florida *B*
Valencia College *C, A*

Georgia

Georgia Southern University *B*

Idaho

Brigham Young University-Idaho *B*

Illinois

College of Lake County *C, A*
Danville Area Community College *C*
Joliet Junior College *C, A*
Lincoln Land Community College *A*
Morrison Institute of Technology *A*
Rock Valley College *C, A*
South Suburban College of Cook
    County *C, A*
Southern Illinois University
    Edwardsville *B*
Southwestern Illinois College *C, A*
Triton College *A*

Indiana

Indiana University
    Purdue University Fort Wayne *B*
Purdue University *A, B*

Iowa

Southeastern Community College *A*

Kansas

Kansas State University *B*
Pittsburg State University *B*

Kentucky

Maysville Community and Technical
    College *C*
Western Kentucky University *B*

Louisiana

Bossier Parish Community
    College *C, A*

Maine

Eastern Maine Community
    College *C, A*

Massachusetts

Bristol Community College *C*
Cape Cod Community College *C*
Fitchburg State University *B*

Michigan

Alpena Community College *A*
Baker College
    Allen Park *C, A*
Central Michigan University *B*
Eastern Michigan University *M*
Ferris State University *A*
Gogebic Community College *C, A*
Kalamazoo Valley Community
    College *C*
Lawrence Technological University *A*
Macomb Community College *C, A*
Michigan State University *B, M, D*
Northern Michigan University *B*
Washtenaw Community College *A*
Wayne State University *B*

Minnesota

Hennepin Technical College *C, A*

Mississippi

Hinds Community College *A*
Northeast Mississippi Community
    College *A*

Missouri

Mineral Area College *C, A*
Missouri Western State
    University *A, B*
University of Central Missouri *B*

Montana

Blackfeet Community College *C, A*
Helena College University of
    Montana *A*
Montana State University *B*
Montana State University
    Northern *A*

Nebraska

University of Nebraska
    Lincoln *B*

Nevada

University of Nevada
    Las Vegas *B*

New Jersey

Burlington County College *A*
Cumberland County College *C, A*
Essex County College *A*
Fairleigh Dickinson University
    Metropolitan Campus *B*
Raritan Valley Community College *A*
Thomas Edison State College *B*

New Mexico

Santa Fe Community College *C, A*
Western New Mexico University *C, A*

New York

City University of New York
    College of Staten Island *A*
    New York City College of
        Technology *C, A*
Mohawk Valley Community
    College *C*
Monroe Community College *A*
Onondaga Community College *A*
SUNY
    College of Technology at
        Alfred *A, B*
    College of Technology at Delhi *A*

Suffolk County Community College *A*
Ulster County Community College *A*

North Carolina

Central Carolina Community
    College *C*
East Carolina University *B, M*
Mitchell Community College *C, A*
Vance-Granville Community
    College *C*
Western Carolina University *B, M*
Western Piedmont Community
    College *C, A*

North Dakota

North Dakota State College of
    Science *A*

Ohio

Bowling Green State University *B*
Columbus State Community
    College *C, A*
Eastern Gateway Community
    College *A*
Hocking College *A*
Lakeland Community College *C*
Ohio State University
    Agricultural Technical Institute *A*
    Columbus Campus *C, A*
Owens Community College
    Toledo *C, A*
Sinclair Community College *C, A*
Stark State College *A*
University of Akron *C, A, B*
University of Toledo *B*
Youngstown State University *C*

Oklahoma

Oklahoma State University *B*
Oklahoma State University
    Institute of Technology:
        Okmulgee *A*
    Oklahoma City *A*
Western Oklahoma State College *A*

Oregon

Lane Community College *C, A*
Portland Community College *C, A*
Rogue Community College *C, A*

Pennsylvania

Community College of Allegheny
    County *C*
Community College of
    Philadelphia *A*
Harrisburg Area Community
    College *C, A*
Penn State
    Fayette, The Eberly Campus *A*
Pennsylvania College of
    Technology *C, A*

Rhode Island

New England Institute of
    Technology *A*

South Carolina

Aiken Technical College *C*
Greenville Technical College *A*
Horry-Georgetown Technical
    College *A*
Midlands Technical College *C*
Piedmont Technical College *C, A*
Technical College of the
    Lowcountry *C*
Trident Technical College *C*

South Dakota

South Dakota State University *B*
Southeast Technical Institute *A*

Tennessee

Nashville State Community College *A*

Texas

Brazosport College *C, A*
Houston Community College
　System *C, A*
Howard College *C, A*
Prairie View A&M University *B*
St. Philip's College *C, A*
Sam Houston State University *B*
San Jacinto College *A*
Texas A&M University *B*
Texas A&M University
　Commerce *B*
Texas State Technical College
　Harlingen *C, A*
　West Texas *C, A*
Texas State University *B*
University of Houston *B*
University of North Texas *B*
Wharton County Junior College *A*

Vermont

Vermont Technical College *A, B*

Virginia

Lord Fairfax Community College *C*
Norfolk State University *B*

Washington

Bates Technical College *C, A*
Central Washington University *B*
Clark College *C, A*
Spokane Community College *C, A*
Yakima Valley Community College *C*

Wisconsin

Northeast Wisconsin Technical
　College *C*

Construction trades

Alabama

Lawson State Community
　College *C, A*

Alaska

University of Alaska
　Southeast *C, A*

Arizona

Arizona Western College *C, A*
Mohave Community College *C*
Northland Pioneer College *C, A*
Tohono O'odham Community
　College *C*

Arkansas

North Arkansas College *C*
Pulaski Technical College *C, A*

California

City College of San Francisco *C*
Diablo Valley College *C, A*
Foothill College *C*
Hartnell College *C*
National University *B*
Orange Coast College *C, A*
Palo Verde College *C, A*
San Jose City College *C, A*
Shasta College *C, A*
Sierra College *C*
Westwood College
　South Bay *B*

Colorado

Arapahoe Community College *C, A*
Colorado Mesa University *C, A*
Lamar Community College *C, A*
Red Rocks Community College *C, A*

Georgia

Columbus Technical College *C*

Illinois

Illinois Central College *A*
Illinois Eastern Community Colleges
　Frontier Community College *C, A*
　Lincoln Trail College *C, A*
Kaskaskia College *C*
Parkland College *C, A*
Rock Valley College *C*
Triton College *C, A*

Indiana

Ivy Tech Community College
　Northeast *C*
　Northwest *C*
Vincennes University *C, A*

Iowa

Iowa Central Community
　College *C, A*
Iowa Western Community College *A*
Kirkwood Community College *A*
Northeast Iowa Community
　College *A*

Kansas

Neosho County Community
　College *C*

Kentucky

Maysville Community and Technical
　College *C*

Maine

Southern Maine Community
　College *C, A*

Maryland

Frederick Community College *C, A*

Massachusetts

Middlesex Community College *A*

Michigan

Bay Mills Community College *A*
Delta College *C, A*
Gogebic Community College *C, A*
Henry Ford Community College *A*
Northern Michigan University *A*
Northwestern Michigan College *C, A*

Minnesota

Minnesota West Community and
　Technical College *C, A*
Northwest Technical College *C*
South Central College *C, A*

Mississippi

Meridian Community College *C*

Missouri

East Central College *C, A*
Ozarks Technical Community
　College *C, A*

Montana

Flathead Valley Community
　College *C, A*
Montana State University
　Billings *A*
Stone Child College *C*

Nebraska

Central Community College *C, A*
Southeast Community College *A*

New Mexico

Eastern New Mexico University:
　Roswell *C*
Mesalands Community College *C, A*
Navajo Technical University *C*

New York

Fulton-Montgomery Community
　College *A*
Monroe Community College *A*
Nassau Community College *C*
SUNY
　College of Agriculture and
　　Technology at Morrisville *A*
Tompkins Cortland Community
　College *C, A*

North Carolina

Edgecombe Community College *C*
Isothermal Community College *C, A*
Wilkes Community College *C, A*

North Dakota

Fort Berthold Community College *A*
Turtle Mountain Community
　College *C, A*

Oklahoma

Northeastern Oklahoma Agricultural
　and Mechanical College *A*

Oregon

Clackamas Community College *C, A*
Mt. Hood Community College *C, A*
Portland Community College *C, A*
Rogue Community College *C, A*
Umpqua Community College *C*

Pennsylvania

Community College of Allegheny
　County *C, A*
Fortis Institute
　Erie *A*
Harrisburg Area Community
　College *C, A*
Lehigh Carbon Community
　College *C, A*
New Castle School of Trades *C*
Penn Commercial Business and
　Technical School *C*
Triangle Tech
　Bethlehem *A*
　Sunbury *A*

South Carolina

York Technical College *A*

South Dakota

Oglala Lakota College *C*

Tennessee

Southern Adventist University *A*

Texas

Central Texas College *C, A*
Cisco College *C, A*
Texas State Technical College
　Waco *C, A*

Utah

Snow College *C, A*

Virginia

Piedmont Virginia Community
　College *C*
Southwest Virginia Community
　College *C*
Virginia Western Community
　College *C*

Washington

Clover Park Technical College *C*
Northwest Indian College *C*

Wisconsin

Northcentral Technical College *C*
Southwest Wisconsin Technical
　College *C*

Wyoming

Casper College *C, A*

Consumer economics

California

Long Beach City College *C, A*

Delaware

Delaware State University *B*

Georgia

University of Georgia *B*

Illinois

University of Illinois
　Urbana-Champaign *B, M, D*

New York

Cornell University *M, D*

South Dakota

South Dakota State University *B*

Tennessee

University of Memphis *M*
University of Tennessee
　Knoxville *B*

Utah

University of Utah *B*

Consumer merchandising

California

Fashion Institute of Design and
　Merchandising
　Los Angeles *A*
　San Diego *A*
　San Francisco *A*

Georgia

Savannah College of Art and
　Design *B, M*

Illinois

Bradley University *B*

Indiana

Purdue University *M, D*

Kentucky

University of Kentucky *M*

Massachusetts

Simmons College *B*

Michigan

Madonna University *C, A, B*

New York

Syracuse University *B*

Oregon

Oregon State University *B*

Texas

Texas State University *M*
University of Houston *M*

Virginia

J. Sargeant Reynolds Community
　College *A*

Consumer services/ advocacy

Florida

Pensacola State College *A*

Pennsylvania

Penn State
Abington *C*
Altoona *C*
Beaver *C*
Berks *C*
Brandywine *C*
DuBois *C*
Erie, The Behrend College *C*
Fayette, The Eberly Campus *C*
Greater Allegheny *C*
Harrisburg *C*
Hazleton *C*
Lehigh Valley *C*
Mont Alto *C*
New Kensington *C*
Schuylkill *C*
Shenango *C*
University Park *C*
Wilkes-Barre *C*
Worthington Scranton *C*
York *C*

South Dakota

South Dakota State University *M*

Texas

Texas State University *B*

Correctional facilities administration

Arizona

Pima Community College *C*

Connecticut

Asnuntuck Community College *C*

Hawaii

University of Hawaii
Hawaii Community College *C*

Illinois

Triton College *C*

Massachusetts

Bunker Hill Community College *C*
Salem State University *C*

Michigan

Baker College
Muskegon *C, A*
Kirtland Community College *C, A*

Montana

University of Great Falls *M*

Nebraska

Bellevue University *B*

New York

Excelsior College *B*

North Dakota

University of Mary *B*

Pennsylvania

Mount Aloysius College *M*

Puerto Rico

Inter American University of Puerto
Rico
Metropolitan Campus *B*

West Virginia

American Public University System *C*

Wyoming

Eastern Wyoming College *A*

Corrections

Alaska

University of Alaska
Anchorage *C*

Arizona

Central Arizona College *C, A*
Coconino County Community
College *C*
Pima Community College *C*

Arkansas

Arkansas Baptist College *B*
Arkansas State University
Beebe *C*
University of Arkansas
Monticello *C*

California

Bakersfield College *A*
California State University
East Bay *B*
Fresno *B*
Sacramento *B*
College of the Redwoods *C*
Contra Costa College *C, A*
Diablo Valley College *C*
East Los Angeles College *C*
Fresno City College *C, A*
Gavilan College *C, A*
Grossmont College *C, A*
Hartnell College *C, A*
Heald College
Roseville *A*
Imperial Valley College *C, A*
Lassen Community College *A*
Sacramento City College *C, A*
San Deigo Miramar College
San Diego Miramar College *C, A*
San Joaquin Delta College *C, A*
San Joaquin Valley College *A*
Taft College *C, A*
Woodland Community College *A*

Delaware

Wilmington University *M*

District of Columbia

University of the District of
Columbia *A*

Florida

Chipola College *C*
College of Central Florida *C*
Daytona State College *C*
Florida Gateway College *C*
Florida Keys Community College *C*
Hillsborough Community College *C*
Northwest Florida State College *C*
Palm Beach State College *C*
Pasco-Hernando State College *C*
Polk State College *C*
Saint Johns River State College *C*
Santa Fe College *C*
Seminole State College of Florida *C*
South Florida State College *C*
Tallahassee Community College *C*
Valencia College *C*

Idaho

Lewis-Clark State College *B*

Illinois

Danville Area Community
College *C, A*
Heartland Community College *C*
Illinois Central College *A*
Illinois Valley Community College *A*
John A. Logan College *A*
Rend Lake College *C, A*
Sauk Valley Community College *C, A*

Kansas

Barton County Community College *A*
Cowley County Community
College *A*
Hutchinson Community College *C*
Kansas City Kansas Community
College *C, A*
Labette Community College *A*
Washburn University *B*

Kentucky

Eastern Kentucky University *A, B*

Maryland

Baltimore City Community
College *C, A*
Cecil College *C*
Chesapeake College *C, A*
Community College of Baltimore
County *C*
Garrett College *A*

Massachusetts

Bristol Community College *C*
Bunker Hill Community College *A*
Mount Wachusett Community
College *A*

Michigan

Alpena Community College *C, A*
Baker College
Flint *C, A*
Port Huron *C, A*
Bay Mills Community College *A*
Bay de Noc Community College *C, A*
Delta College *C, A*
Glen Oaks Community College *C*
Gogebic Community College *C*
Grand Rapids Community College *A*
Henry Ford Community College *C*
Kellogg Community College *C, A*
Lake Michigan College *A*
Lake Superior State University *B*
Lansing Community College *C, A*
Mid Michigan Community College *A*
Oakland Community College *C, A*
St. Clair County Community
College *A*
Schoolcraft College *A*
Washtenaw Community College *A*
Wayne County Community College *A*

Minnesota

Century College *C*
Minnesota State Community and
Technical College *C*
Minnesota State University
Mankato *B*
Minnesota West Community and
Technical College *A*
University of Minnesota
Crookston *B*
Winona State University *B*

Missouri

College of the Ozarks *B*
Metropolitan Community College -
Kansas City *C, A*
Saint Louis University *B*
Southeast Missouri State University *B*

Montana

Dawson Community College *C*
University of Great Falls *B*

Nebraska

Hastings College *B*
Northeast Community College *A*

Nevada

College of Southern Nevada *A*
Great Basin College *A*

Truckee Meadows Community
College *A*
Western Nevada College *C*

New Hampshire

Mount Washington College *A*

New Jersey

Bergen Community College *A*
Burlington County College *C*
Cumberland County College *A*
Middlesex County College *A*
Passaic County Community
College *C, A*
Raritan Valley Community College *C*

New Mexico

New Mexico Junior College *C*
New Mexico State University
Grants *C*
University of New Mexico *B*

New York

Broome Community College *A*
Cayuga Community College *C, A*
Herkimer County Community
College *C*
Jamestown Community College *C*
Monroe Community College *C, A*
Westchester Community College *A*

North Carolina

Central Piedmont Community
College *A*

Ohio

Bowling Green State University *B*
Clark State Community College *A*
Cuyahoga Community College
Metropolitan *A*
Hocking College *C, A*
James A. Rhodes State College *A*
Lakeland Community College *C, A*
Lorain County Community College *A*
Northwest State Community
College *A*
Sinclair Community College *C, A*
Southern State Community College *A*
Tiffin University *B*
University of Cincinnati
Clermont College *A*
Washington State Community
College *A*
Xavier University *A*
Youngstown State University *A, B, M*

Oklahoma

Langston University *B*
University of Central Oklahoma *B*
Western Oklahoma State College *A*

Oregon

Chemeketa Community College *C*
Clackamas Community College *C, A*
Lane Community College *C*
Southwestern Oregon Community
College *A*
Treasure Valley Community
College *C*
Western Oregon University *B*

Pennsylvania

Bucks County Community College *A*
Butler County Community College *C*
Community College of Allegheny
County *A*
Fortis Institute
Forty Fort *C*
Harrisburg Area Community
College *C*
Kaplan Career Institute
Harrisburg *A*
Pittsburgh *A*
Lehigh Carbon Community College *C*

Mount Aloysius College *A*
University of Pittsburgh *B*
University of Pittsburgh
  Bradford *B*
Westmoreland County Community
  College *C*

South Carolina

Trident Technical College *C*

South Dakota

Lake Area Technical Institute *A*

Tennessee

Daymar Institute
  Murfreesboro *A*

Texas

Alvin Community College *C, A*
Amarillo College *A*
Angelina College *A*
Austin Community College *A*
Central Texas College *C, A*
Coastal Bend College *C, A*
Del Mar College *A*
El Paso Community College *C, A*
Hill College *C, A*
Howard College *C, A*
Lamar State College at Orange *C, A*
Northeast Texas Community
  College *C, A*
Sam Houston State University *B*
San Antonio College *A*
San Jacinto College *C*
Stephen F. Austin State University *B*
Texas State University *B*
University of Texas
  Brownsville *B*
Weatherford College *A*

Utah

Weber State University *B*

Virginia

Bluefield College *B*
Mountain Empire Community
  College *A*
Southwest Virginia Community
  College *C, A*

Washington

Centralia College *C*
Peninsula College *C, A*
Spokane Community College *C, A*
Walla Walla Community College *C, A*
Yakima Valley Community College *C*

West Virginia

Glenville State College *A*
New River Community and Technical
  College *A*

Wisconsin

Mid-State Technical College *A*
Moraine Park Technical College *A*

Wyoming

Eastern Wyoming College *C*
Laramie County Community
  College *A*

Cosmetic services

Alabama

Alabama Southern Community
  College *A*
Bevill State Community College *C, A*
Bishop State Community
  College *C, A*
Calhoun Community College *C*
Central Alabama Community
  College *A*
Gadsden State Community College *C*

George C. Wallace Community
  College at Dothan *C*
George C. Wallace State Community
  College at Selma *C*
Lurleen B. Wallace Community
  College *C*
Northeast Alabama Community
  College *C*
Northwest-Shoals Community
  College *C*
Shelton State Community College *C*
Southern Union State Community
  College *C, A*
Virginia College
  Huntsville *C*
  Montgomery *C*
Wallace State Community College at
  Hanceville *C*

Arizona

Eastern Arizona College *C, A*
Northland Pioneer College *C, A*

Arkansas

Arkansas Tech University *C*
College of the Ouachitas *C*
Phillips Community College of the
  University of Arkansas *C*
Pulaski Technical College *C*
South Arkansas Community
  College *C*
Southern Arkansas University Tech *C*

California

Allan Hancock College *C, A*
Butte College *C, A*
Cerritos College *C, A*
Citrus College *C, A*
College of the Sequoias *C, A*
Contra Costa College *A*
El Camino College *C, A*
Fullerton College *A*
Gavilan College *C, A*
Golden West College *C, A*
Laney College *C, A*
MTI College *C*
Napa Valley College *C*
Riverside City College *C, A*
Sacramento City College *C, A*
Saddleback College *C*
San Jose City College *C, A*
Santa Barbara City College *C, A*
Santa Monica College *C, A*
Santiago Canyon College *A*
Skyline College *C, A*
Solano Community College *C, A*

Colorado

Colorado Northwestern Community
  College *C, A*
IBMC College
  Fort Collins *C*
Lamar Community College *C*
Northeastern Junior College *C*
Otero Junior College *C*
Pueblo Community College *C, A*
Red Rocks Community College *C, A*
Trinidad State Junior College *C*

Florida

College of Central Florida *C*
Daytona State College *C*
Eastern Florida State College *C*
Florida College of Natural Health
  Maitland *A*
Florida Gateway College *C*
Florida State College at
  Jacksonville *C*
Fortis College
  Winter Park *C, A*
Indian River State College *C*
Lincoln College of Technology
  West Palm Beach *C*
Palm Beach State College *C*

Pensacola State College *C*
South Florida State College *C*

Georgia

Albany Technical College *C*
Altamaha Technical College *C*
Athens Technical College *C*
Atlanta Technical College *C*
Augusta Technical College *C*
Central Georgia Technical College *C*
Chattahoochee Technical College *C*
Columbus Technical College *C*
Georgia Piedmont Technical
  College *C*
Gwinnett Technical College *C*
North Georgia Technical College *C*
Savannah Technical College *C*
South Georgia State College *A*
Southeastern Technical College *C*
Southwest Georgia Technical
  College *C*
Wiregrass Georgia Technical
  College *C*

Hawaii

University of Hawaii
  Honolulu Community College *C, A*

Idaho

Idaho State University *C*

Illinois

City Colleges of Chicago
  Harry S. Truman College *C*
College of DuPage *C, A*
Highland Community College *C*
Illinois Eastern Community Colleges
  Olney Central College *C*
John A. Logan College *C, A*
Kaskaskia College *C*
Lake Land College *C*
Lincoln Land Community College *C*
Rend Lake College *C*

Indiana

Vincennes University *A*

Iowa

Iowa Central Community College *A*
Northeast Iowa Community
  College *C, A*

Kansas

Cowley County Community
  College *C, A*
Garden City Community College *C*
Independence Community
  College *C, A*
Johnson County Community
  College *C, A*
Kansas City Kansas Community
  College *C*

Kentucky

Gateway Community and Technical
  College *C, A*
Jefferson Community and Technical
  College *C*
West Kentucky Community and
  Technical College *C*

Louisiana

Delgado Community College *C*
Virginia College
  Baton Rouge *C*

Massachusetts

North Shore Community College *C*
Springfield Technical Community
  College *C*

Michigan

Gogebic Community College *C*
Kirtland Community College *C, A*
Montcalm Community College *C, A*
Mott Community College *C*
Northern Michigan University *C*
Oakland Community College *A*

Minnesota

Century College *C, A*
Minnesota State College - Southeast
  Technical *C, A*
Minnesota State Community and
  Technical College *C*
Ridgewater College *A*
St. Paul College *C, A*

Mississippi

Coahoma Community College *C*
East Central Community College *C*
East Mississippi Community
  College *C*
Hinds Community College *C*
Holmes Community College *C*
Meridian Community College *C*
Mississippi Gulf Coast Community
  College *A*
Pearl River Community College *C*
Southwest Mississippi Community
  College *C*

Montana

University of Montana *C*

Nebraska

Vatterott College
  Spring Valley *C*
Western Nebraska Community
  College *C, A*

New Mexico

Central New Mexico Community
  College *A*
Clovis Community College *C, A*
Luna Community College *C*
New Mexico Junior College *C, A*
Northern New Mexico College *C, A*
San Juan College *C, A*

North Carolina

Alamance Community College *C*
Beaufort County Community
  College *C*
Bladen Community College *C, A*
Blue Ridge Community College *C*
Brunswick Community College *C, A*
Caldwell Community College and
  Technical Institute *C*
Cape Fear Community College *C, A*
Carteret Community College *C*
Catawba Valley Community
  College *C*
Central Carolina Community
  College *A*
Cleveland Community College *C*
Coastal Carolina Community
  College *C*
College of the Albemarle *C*
Craven Community College *C*
Davidson County Community
  College *C*
Edgecombe Community College *C*
Fayetteville Technical Community
  College *C, A*
Gaston College *A*
Guilford Technical Community
  College *C, A*
Haywood Community College *C, A*
Isothermal Community College *C, A*
James Sprunt Community
  College *C, A*
Johnston Community College *C*
Lenoir Community College *C*
Martin Community College *C, A*

Mayland Community College *C, A*
Miller-Motte College
    Fayetteville *A*
    Wilmington *C, A*
Mitchell Community College *C*
Nash Community College *C*
Piedmont Community College *C*
Pitt Community College *C, A*
Randolph Community College *C, A*
Roanoke-Chowan Community
    College *C*
Robeson Community College *C*
Rockingham Community College *C*
Sampson Community College *A*
Sandhills Community College *C, A*
Southeastern Community
    College *C, A*
Southwestern Community
    College *C, A*
Stanly Community College *C, A*
Surry Community College *A*
Vance-Granville Community
    College *C*
Virginia College in Greensboro *C, A*
Wayne Community College *C*
Wilson Community College *C*

Oregon

Mt. Hood Community College *A*
Umpqua Community College *A*

Pennsylvania

Butler County Community College *A*
Douglas Education Center *A*
Fortis Institute
    Erie *A*
Laurel Business Institute *A*
Laurel Technical Institute *C, A*

Puerto Rico

Caribbean University *C*
Inter American University of Puerto
    Rico
    Bayamon Campus *C*
    San German Campus *C*

South Carolina

Denmark Technical College *C*
Florence-Darlington Technical
    College *C*
Greenville Technical College *C*
Horry-Georgetown Technical
    College *C*
Miller-Motte Technical College
    Conway *C*
Technical College of the
    Lowcountry *C*
Trident Technical College *C*
Virginia College
    Florence *C*
Williamsburg Technical College *C*

Tennessee

Miller-Motte Technical College
    Chattanooga *C, A*
Remington College
    Nashville *C*
Virginia College
    School of Business and Health in
        Chattanooga *C*
    School of Business and Health in
        Knoxville *C*

Texas

Central Texas College *C*
Cisco College *C*
Clarendon College *C*
Del Mar College *C*
Frank Phillips College *C*
Grayson College *C*
Hill College *C, A*
Houston Community College
    System *C, A*
Howard College *C*

Kilgore College *C*
Lamar State College at Port
    Arthur *C, A*
Lee College *C*
Lone Star College System *C, A*
McLennan Community College *C*
Midland College *C*
Northeast Texas Community
    College *C, A*
Odessa College *C, A*
Panola College *C*
Paris Junior College *C*
Ranger College *C*
Remington College
    Dallas *C*
    Fort Worth *C*
    Houston Southeast *C*
    North Houston *C*
San Jacinto College *C, A*
Texarkana College *C, A*
Trinity Valley Community College *C*
Vernon College *C*
Weatherford College *C, A*
Wharton County Junior College *C*

Utah

Salt Lake Community College *C, A*
Snow College *C, A*
Utah State University *C, A*

Washington

Clover Park Technical College *C, A*
Olympic College *A*
Shoreline Community College *C, A*
Spokane Community College *C, A*
Walla Walla Community College *C, A*

West Virginia

Southern West Virginia Community
    and Technical College *A*

Wisconsin

Chippewa Valley Technical College *C*
Gateway Technical College *C*
Madison Area Technical College *A*
Moraine Park Technical College *C*
Nicolet Area Technical College *C*
Southwest Wisconsin Technical
    College *C*

Wyoming

Eastern Wyoming College *A*

Cosmetology

Alabama

Lawson State Community College *C*
Virginia College
    Birmingham *C*

Arkansas

Pulaski Technical College *C*

California

Santiago Canyon College *C*
Yuba College *C, A*

Colorado

IBMC College
    Fort Collins *C*

Florida

Chipola College *C*

Georgia

Savannah Technical College *C*
Southeastern Technical College *C*
West Georgia Technical College *C*

Illinois

Kaskaskia College *C, A*

Kansas

Seward County Community
    College *C, A*

Kentucky

Somerset Community College *A*

Louisiana

Delgado Community College *C*

Michigan

Mott Community College *C*
Northern Michigan University *C*

Mississippi

Copiah-Lincoln Community
    College *C, T*
Hinds Community College *C*
Meridian Community College *C*

New Mexico

San Juan College *C*

North Carolina

Brunswick Community College *C*
Cape Fear Community College *C*
Central Carolina Community
    College *A*
Cleveland Community College *C*
Isothermal Community College *C*
James Sprunt Community College *C*
Lenoir Community College *C*
Miller-Motte College
    Wilmington *C*
Pamlico Community College *C*

Pennsylvania

Laurel Business Institute *C*

Tennessee

West Tennessee Business College *C*

Texas

Cisco College *C*
Houston Community College
    System *C*
Lamar State College at Port
    Arthur *C, A*
Lone Star College System *C, A*
Panola College *C*
Paris Junior College *C*
San Jacinto College *C, A*

Utah

Snow College *C, A*

Washington

Everett Community College *C, A*
Olympic College *C*
Walla Walla Community College *A*

Costume design

Missouri

Webster University *B*

Pennsylvania

Albright College *B*
Carnegie Mellon University *M*

Virginia

Shenandoah University *B*

Counseling psychology

Alabama

Alabama Agricultural and Mechanical
    University *M*
Auburn University *D*
Oakwood University *B*
Troy University *M*
University of North Alabama *M*

Alaska

Alaska Pacific University *M*

Arizona

Argosy University
    Online *D*
    Phoenix *D*
Arizona Christian University *B*
Grand Canyon University *M*
Prescott College *B, M*

Arkansas

John Brown University *M*
University of Central Arkansas *M*

California

Alliant International University *M*
Argosy University
    Inland Empire *D*
    Los Angeles *D*
    Orange County *D*
    San Diego *D*
    San Francisco Bay Area *D*
California Baptist University *M*
California Institute of Integral
    Studies *M*
California State University
    Bakersfield *M*
    East Bay *M*
    Long Beach *M*
    San Bernardino *M*
Dominican University of California *M*
Golden Gate University *M*
Holy Names University *M*
Hope International University *M*
John F. Kennedy University *M*
Mount St. Mary's College *M*
National University *M*
Santa Clara University *M*
Southern California Seminary *M*
University of California
    Santa Barbara *M, D*
University of La Verne *M*
University of San Francisco *M*

Colorado

Adams State University *M, D*
Argosy University
    Denver *D*
Colorado Christian University *M*
Fort Lewis College *B*
Johnson & Wales University
    Denver *B*
Naropa University *M*
Regis University *M*
University of Denver *M, D*
University of Northern
    Colorado *M, D*

Connecticut

University of Hartford *M*
University of Saint Joseph *M*

Delaware

Wilmington University *M*

District of Columbia

George Washington University *M*
Howard University *M, D*

Florida

Bethune-Cookman University *M*
Carlos Albizu University *M*
Nova Southeastern University *M*
Palm Beach Atlantic University *M*
Saint Thomas University *M*
Southeastern University *M*
Trinity College of Florida *B*
University of Florida *D*
University of Miami *M, D*

Georgia

Mercer University *M, D*
Toccoa Falls College *B*
University of Georgia *D*

Hawaii

Chaminade University of Honolulu *M*
Hawaii Pacific University *M*
University of Hawaii
   Hilo *M*

Illinois

Argosy University
   Chicago *M, D*
Chicago State University *M*
Concordia University Chicago *M*
Governors State University *M, D*
Illinois State University *M*
Lewis University *M*
Loyola University Chicago *M, D*
McKendree University *M*
Northwestern University *M, D*
Olivet Nazarene University *M*
Roosevelt University *M*
Saint Xavier University *M*
Trinity Christian College *M*
Trinity International University *M*
University of Chicago *B, D*
University of Illinois
   Springfield *M*

Indiana

Ball State University *M, D, T*
Grace College *M*
Huntington University *M*
Indiana State University *M*
Indiana Wesleyan University *M*
Martin University *B*
Valparaiso University *M*

Iowa

Emmaus Bible College *B*
Morningside College *B*
University of Iowa *D*
University of Northern Iowa *M*

Kansas

Kansas Wesleyan University *B*
MidAmerica Nazarene University *M*
Newman University *B*
University of Kansas *M, D*

Kentucky

Kentucky Christian University *B*
Lindsey Wilson College *M*
Mid-Continent University *B*
Union College *M*
University of Kentucky *M, D*
University of the Cumberlands *M*
Western Kentucky University *M*

Louisiana

Louisiana State University
   Shreveport *M*
Louisiana Tech University *D*
Nicholls State University *M*

Maine

University of Maine *M, D*

Maryland

Bowie State University *M*
Coppin State University *M*
Frostburg State University *M*
Loyola University Maryland *M*
University of Baltimore *M*
Washington Adventist
   University *B, M*

Massachusetts

Anna Maria College *M*
Assumption College *M*
Boston University *D*
Cambridge College *M*
Eastern Nazarene College *B, M*
Emmanuel College *B*
Framingham State University *M*
Lesley University *M*
Northeastern University *M, D*
Salem State University *M*
Springfield College *M, D*
Tufts University *B, M*
Westfield State University *M*

Michigan

Andrews University *D*
Spring Arbor University *M*
Wayne State University *M*
Western Michigan University *M, D*

Minnesota

Bethel University *M*
Capella University *M, D*
Crossroads College *B*
Crown College *B*
Minnesota State University
   Mankato *M*
Saint Cloud State University *M*
St. Mary's University of
   Minnesota *M, D*
University of St. Thomas *M, D*

Mississippi

Mississippi College *D*
William Carey University *M*

Missouri

Avila University *M*
Lindenwood University *M*
Northwest Missouri State
   University *M*
University of Central Missouri *M*
University of Missouri
   Columbia *M, D*
   Kansas City *D*
Webster University *M*

Montana

University of Great Falls *M*

Nebraska

Chadron State College *M*
Doane College *M*
Wayne State College *B*

Nevada

University of Nevada
   Las Vegas *M*

New Hampshire

Rivier University *M, D*

New Jersey

Caldwell College *M, T*
Centenary College *M*
College of St. Elizabeth *M*
Fairleigh Dickinson University
   College at Florham *M*
Felician College *M*
Georgian Court University *M*
Monmouth University *M*
New Jersey City University *M*
Rider University *M*
Seton Hall University *M, D*

New Mexico

Eastern New Mexico University *M*
New Mexico State University *D*
University of New Mexico *D*

New York

College of New Rochelle *M*
Fordham University *M, D*
Mercy College *M*
New York University *D*

SUNY
   College at Old Westbury *M*
   College at Oswego *M*
   University at Albany *D*
   University at Buffalo *D*
Saint Bonaventure University *M*
St. Lawrence University *M*

North Carolina

Campbell University *M*
Gardner-Webb University *M*
Mid-Atlantic Christian University *B*

North Dakota

University of North Dakota *D*

Ohio

Ashland University *M*
Cleveland State University *D*
Franciscan University of
   Steubenville *M*
Heidelberg University *M*
John Carroll University *M*
Kent State University *M*
Union Institute & University *M*
University of Akron *M, D*
Wright State University *M*

Oklahoma

Cameron University *M*
East Central University *M*
Mid-America Christian University *M*
Northwestern Oklahoma State
   University *M*
Southeastern Oklahoma State
   University *M*
Southern Nazarene University *M*
University of Central Oklahoma *M*
University of Oklahoma *D*

Oregon

George Fox University *M*
Lewis & Clark College *M*
Northwest Christian University *M*
Pacific University *M*
University of Oregon *D*

Pennsylvania

Arcadia University *M*
Baptist Bible College of
   Pennsylvania *B, M*
Carlow University *M, D*
Chatham University *M*
Chestnut Hill College *M*
Delaware Valley College *B*
Eastern University *M*
Geneva College *M*
Holy Family University *M*
Immaculata University *M*
Indiana University of Pennsylvania *M*
Kutztown University of
   Pennsylvania *M*
La Salle University *M*
Lehigh University *D*
Rosemont College *M*
Slippery Rock University of
   Pennsylvania *M*
Temple University *M, D*
University of Pennsylvania *M*
Villanova University *M*
Waynesburg University *M*

Puerto Rico

Inter American University of Puerto
   Rico
   Aguadilla Campus *M*
   Metropolitan Campus *M, D*
   San German Campus *M, D*
Turabo University *B, M*

Rhode Island

Johnson & Wales University
   Providence *B*
Rhode Island College *M*
Salve Regina University *M*

South Carolina

Bob Jones University *B, M*
Coker College *B*
Columbia International University *M*

South Dakota

South Dakota State University *M*

Tennessee

Freed-Hardeman University *M*
Johnson University *B, M*
Lipscomb University *M*
Southern Adventist University *M*
Tennessee Technological
   University *M*
Victory University *M*

Texas

Abilene Christian University *M*
Amberton University *M*
Angelo State University *M*
Arlington Baptist College *B*
Dallas Baptist University *M*
East Texas Baptist University *M*
Lamar University *M*
Lubbock Christian University *M*
Midwestern State University *M*
Sam Houston State University *M*
Southwestern Assemblies of God
   University *M*
Tarleton State University *M*
Texas A&M International
   University *M*
Texas A&M University *D*
Texas A&M University
   Kingsville *M*
   Texarkana *M*
Texas State University *M, T*
Texas Tech University *M, D*
Texas Wesleyan University *M*
Texas Woman's University *M, D*
University of Houston *D*
University of Houston
   Victoria *M*
University of North Texas *M, D*
University of Texas
   Pan American *M*
   Tyler *M*
Wayland Baptist University *M*
West Texas A&M University *M*

Utah

Argosy University
   Salt Lake City *D*
Westminster College *M*

Vermont

College of St. Joseph in Vermont *M*
Goddard College *M*
Johnson State College *M*

Virginia

Eastern Mennonite University *M*
Liberty University *M*
Marymount University *M*
Radford University *D*
Regent University *M, D*
Virginia Commonwealth University *D*

Washington

Central Washington University *M, T*
City University of Seattle *M*
Eastern Washington University *M*
Gonzaga University *M*
Northwest University *M*
Saint Martin's University *M*
Western Washington University *M*

West Virginia

West Virginia University *D*

Wisconsin

Concordia University Wisconsin *M*
Lakeland College *M*
Marquette University *D*
University of Wisconsin
  Madison *M, D*
  Whitewater *M*

Counselor education

Alabama

Alabama Agricultural and Mechanical
  University *B, M*
Auburn University *M, D, T*
Auburn University at Montgomery *M*
Jacksonville State University *M, T*
Troy University *T*
University of Alabama *M, D*
University of Alabama
  Birmingham *M*
University of Montevallo *M*
University of North Alabama *M*
University of South Alabama *M, T*
University of West Alabama *M*

Alaska

University of Alaska
  Anchorage *M, T*
  Fairbanks *M, T*

Arizona

Arizona State University *M, D*
Northern Arizona University *M*
University of Phoenix
  Southern Arizona *M*

Arkansas

Arkansas State University *M, T*
Arkansas Tech University *M*
Harding University *M*
Henderson State University *M*
John Brown University *M*
Southern Arkansas University *M, T*
University of Arkansas *M, D*
University of Arkansas
  Little Rock *M*
University of Central Arkansas *M*

California

Azusa Pacific University *M*
California Baptist University *T*
California Lutheran University *M*
California State University
  Bakersfield *M*
  Chico *T*
  Dominguez Hills *M, T*
  East Bay *M, T*
  Fresno *M*
  Fullerton *M, T*
  Long Beach *M*
  Los Angeles *M*
  Northridge *M*
  Sacramento *M*
  San Bernardino *M*
Chapman University *M, T*
Concordia University Irvine *M*
Fresno Pacific University *M, T*
Humboldt State University *T*
La Sierra University *M*
Loma Linda University *M*
Loyola Marymount University *M, T*
Mount St. Mary's College *M*
National University *M*
St. Mary's College of California *M*
San Diego State University *M, T*
San Francisco State University *M, T*
San Jose State University *M*
Sonoma State University *M*
University of California
  Santa Barbara *M, D*
University of La Verne *M*
University of Redlands *M, T*
University of San Diego *T*

University of San Francisco *T*
University of Southern California *M*
Whittier College *M*

Colorado

Adams State University *M*
Colorado State University *M*
University of Colorado
  Colorado Springs *M*
  Denver *M*
University of Northern
  Colorado *M, D*
University of Phoenix
  Denver *M*

Connecticut

Central Connecticut State
  University *M*
Fairfield University *M, T*
Southern Connecticut State
  University *M, T*
University of Bridgeport *M*
University of Connecticut *T*
University of Hartford *M, T*
University of Saint Joseph *M*
Western Connecticut State
  University *M*

Delaware

University of Delaware *M*
Wilmington University *M*

District of Columbia

Gallaudet University *M*
George Washington University *M, D*
Howard University *M*
Trinity Washington University *M*
University of the District of
  Columbia *M*

Florida

Barry University *M*
Carlos Albizu University *M*
Florida Atlantic University *M, D, T*
Florida Gulf Coast University *M*
Florida International University *M*
Florida State University *T*
Nova Southeastern University *M*
Saint Thomas University *M*
Southeastern University *M*
Stetson University *M*
University of Central Florida *M*
University of Florida *M, D*
University of Miami *M*
University of North Florida *M*
University of South Florida *M*

Georgia

Albany State University *M*
Clark Atlanta University *M*
Columbus State University *M*
Fort Valley State University *M*
Georgia Regents University *M*
Georgia Southern University *M*
Georgia State University *M, D, T*
Mercer University *M*
University of Georgia *M, T*
University of West Georgia *M, D*
Valdosta State University *M*

Hawaii

University of Hawaii
  Manoa *M*

Idaho

Boise State University *M*
Idaho State University *M*
University of Idaho *M*

Illinois

Bradley University *M*
Chicago State University *M*
Concordia University Chicago *M*
DePaul University *M*

Eastern Illinois University *M*
Governors State University *M, D*
Lewis University *M*
Loyola University Chicago *M*
Northeastern Illinois University *M*
Northern Illinois University *M, D*
Roosevelt University *M*
Western Illinois University *M*

Indiana

Butler University *M*
Indiana State University *M, D, T*
Indiana University
  Bloomington *M, D*
  Purdue University Fort Wayne *M*
  Purdue University Indianapolis *M*
  South Bend *M*
  Southeast *M*
Indiana Wesleyan University *M*
University of St. Francis *M*
Valparaiso University *M*

Iowa

Buena Vista University *M*
Drake University *M*
Iowa State University *M, T*
University of Iowa *M, D*
University of Northern Iowa *M*

Kansas

Emporia State University *M*
Fort Hays State University *M*
Independence Community College *A*
Kansas State University *M, D*
Pittsburg State University *M*
Wichita State University *M*

Kentucky

Eastern Kentucky University *M*
Morehead State University *M*
Murray State University *M, T*
Northern Kentucky University *M*
Spalding University *M*
University of Louisville *M, D*
University of the Cumberlands *M, T*

Louisiana

Louisiana State University and
  Agricultural and Mechanical
  College *M*
Louisiana Tech University *M*
Loyola University New Orleans *M*
McNeese State University *M, T*
Nicholls State University *M*
Northwestern State University *M*
Our Lady of Holy Cross College *B, M*
Southeastern Louisiana University *M*
Southern University and Agricultural
  and Mechanical College *M*
University of Louisiana at Lafayette *M*
University of New Orleans *M, D*
Xavier University of Louisiana *M*

Maine

Husson University *M*
University of Maine *M, D*
University of Southern Maine *M*

Maryland

Bowie State University *M*
Frostburg State University *M*
Loyola University Maryland *M*
McDaniel College *M*
University of Maryland
  College Park *M, D*
  Eastern Shore *M*

Massachusetts

Assumption College *M*
Boston College *M, D*
Boston University *M, D, T*
Bridgewater State University *M, T*
Fitchburg State University *M, T*
Lesley University *M*

Salem State University *M*
Springfield College *M*
Suffolk University *M*
University of Massachusetts
  Boston *M*

Michigan

Andrews University *M, D*
Central Michigan University *M*
Eastern Michigan University *M*
Michigan State University *M*
Northern Michigan University *M*
Oakland University *M, D*
Siena Heights University *M*
University of Detroit Mercy *M*
Wayne State University *M, D*
Western Michigan University *M, D, T*

Minnesota

Capella University *M, D*
Minnesota State University
  Mankato *M*
  Moorhead *M*
Saint Cloud State University *M*
Walden University *M*
Winona State University *M*

Mississippi

Delta State University *M*
Jackson State University *M*
Mississippi College *M*
Mississippi State University *M, D*
University of Mississippi *M, D*
University of Southern Mississippi *M*

Missouri

Evangel University *M*
Lincoln University *M*
Lindenwood University *M*
Missouri Baptist University *M, T*
Missouri State University *M*
Northwest Missouri State
  University *M, T*
Saint Louis University *M, D*
Southeast Missouri State University *M*
Stephens College *M*
Truman State University *M*
University of Central Missouri *M*
University of Missouri
  Columbia *M, D*
  Kansas City *M*
  St. Louis *M*

Montana

Montana State University
  Billings *M*
  Northern *M*
University of Montana *M, D*

Nebraska

Chadron State College *M*
Creighton University *M*
Grace University *M*
University of Nebraska
  Kearney *M, T*
  Omaha *M*
Wayne State College *M*

Nevada

University of Nevada
  Las Vegas *M*
  Reno *M*
University of Phoenix
  Las Vegas *M*
  Northern Nevada *M*

New Hampshire

Keene State College *M*
Plymouth State University *M, T*
Rivier University *M*

New Jersey

College of New Jersey *M*
Kean University *M, T*

Monmouth University *M*
Montclair State University *M*
Rider University *M*
Rowan University *M*
Rutgers, The State University of New
Jersey
New Brunswick/Piscataway
Campus *M, D*
Seton Hall University *M*
William Paterson University of New
Jersey *M*

New Mexico

Eastern New Mexico University *M*
New Mexico Highlands University *M*
New Mexico State University *M*
University of New Mexico *M, D*
University of Phoenix
New Mexico *M*
University of the Southwest *M*
Western New Mexico University *M*

New York

Alfred University *M*
Canisius College *M*
City University of New York
Brooklyn College *M, T*
Hunter College *M*
Lehman College *M*
Queens College *M*
College of New Rochelle *M, T*
Hofstra University *M, T*
Long Island University
LIU Brooklyn *M*
LIU Post *M*
Manhattan College *M*
Mercy College *M*
New York Institute of Technology *M*
New York University *M, D, T*
Niagara University *M*
Roberts Wesleyan College *M*
SUNY
College at Brockport *M*
College at Buffalo *M*
College at Oneonta *M*
College at Oswego *M*
College at Plattsburgh *M, T*
University at Albany *M*
University at Buffalo *M, D, T*
Sage Colleges *M*
St. John's University *M*
St. Lawrence University *M*
Syracuse University *M, D, T*
University of Rochester *M, D*

North Carolina

Appalachian State University *M*
Campbell University *M*
East Carolina University *M, D*
Gardner-Webb University *M*
Lenoir-Rhyne University *M*
North Carolina Agricultural and
Technical State University *M*
North Carolina Central University *M*
North Carolina State University *M, D*
University of North Carolina
Chapel Hill *M*
Charlotte *M, D*
Greensboro *M, D*
Pembroke *M*
Wake Forest University *M, T*
Western Carolina University *M*

North Dakota

North Dakota State University *M*
University of Mary *M*
University of North Dakota *M*

Ohio

Bowling Green State
University *B, M, T*
Cleveland State University *D*
Heidelberg University *M*
John Carroll University *M*

Kent State University *M, D*
Malone University *M*
Ohio University *M, D*
University of Akron *M, D*
University of Cincinnati *D*
University of Dayton *M, T*
Walsh University *M*
Wright State University *M, T*
Xavier University *M*
Youngstown State University *M*

Oklahoma

East Central University *M, T*
Northeastern State University *M*
Northwestern Oklahoma State
University *M*
Oklahoma State University *M*
Southeastern Oklahoma State
University *M, T*
Southwestern Oklahoma State
University *M, T*
University of Central Oklahoma *M*
University of Oklahoma *M*

Oregon

George Fox University *M*
Lewis & Clark College *M*
Northwest Christian University *M*
Oregon State University *M, D*
Portland State University *M, D, T*

Pennsylvania

Arcadia University *M*
Baptist Bible College of
Pennsylvania *M*
Bloomsburg University of
Pennsylvania *M*
Bucknell University *M*
Cairn University *M*
California University of
Pennsylvania *M*
Carlow University *M*
Chatham University *T*
Duquesne University *M, D, T*
Eastern University *M*
Edinboro University of
Pennsylvania *M*
Gwynedd Mercy University *M, T*
Holy Family University *M*
Indiana University of Pennsylvania *M*
Kutztown University of
Pennsylvania *M*
Lancaster Bible College *M*
Lehigh University *M*
Marywood University *M*
Millersville University of
Pennsylvania *M, T*
Penn State
University Park *M, D*
Shippensburg University of
Pennsylvania *M, T*
Slippery Rock University of
Pennsylvania *M*
University of Pennsylvania *M*
University of Scranton *M*
Villanova University *M*
West Chester University of
Pennsylvania *M, T*
Westminster College *M*
Widener University *M, D, T*

Puerto Rico

Bayamon Central University *M*
Inter American University of Puerto
Rico
Metropolitan Campus *M*
San German Campus *M, D*
Pontifical Catholic University of
Puerto Rico *D*
Turabo University *M*
University of Phoenix
Puerto Rico *M*
University of Puerto Rico
Rio Piedras *M, D*

Rhode Island

Providence College *M*
Rhode Island College *M*

South Carolina

Citadel *M*
Clemson University *M*
South Carolina State University *M*
University of South Carolina
Columbia *M, D*
Winthrop University *M, T*

South Dakota

Northern State University *M*
South Dakota State University *M*
University of South Dakota *M, D*

Tennessee

Austin Peay State University *M*
Belmont University *T*
Carson-Newman University *M*
East Tennessee State University *M, T*
Freed-Hardeman University *M*
Lincoln Memorial University *M, D*
Middle Tennessee State University *M*
Tennessee State University *M*
Tennessee Technological
University *M*
University of Memphis *M, D*
University of Tennessee
Chattanooga *M*
Martin *M*
Vanderbilt University *M*

Texas

Angelo State University *M*
Dallas Baptist University *M*
Hardin-Simmons University *M*
Houston Baptist University *M*
Lamar University *B, M, T*
Lubbock Christian University *M*
Midwestern State University *M*
Our Lady of the Lake University of
San Antonio *M*
Prairie View A&M University *M*
St. Mary's University *D*
Sam Houston State University *M, D*
Sul Ross State University *M*
Tarleton State University *M*
Texas A&M International
University *M, T*
Texas A&M University
Commerce *M, D*
Corpus Christi *M, D, T*
Kingsville *M*
Texas Christian University *M, D*
Texas Southern University *M, D*
Texas Tech University *M, D*
Texas Woman's University *M*
University of Houston *M*
University of Houston
Clear Lake *M, T*
Victoria *M*
University of Mary Hardin-Baylor *M*
University of North Texas *M, D, T*
University of St. Thomas *M*
University of Texas
Brownsville *M*
El Paso *M*
Pan American *M*
Permian Basin *M*
San Antonio *M, D*
West Texas A&M University *M, T*

Utah

University of Phoenix
Utah *M*

Vermont

College of St. Joseph in Vermont *M*
Goddard College *M*
Johnson State College *M*
Lyndon State College *M*
University of Vermont *M*

Virginia

College of William and Mary *M, D*
George Mason University *M*
Hampton University *M*
James Madison University *M, T*
Lynchburg College *M*
Marymount University *D*
Old Dominion University *M*
Radford University *M*
University of Virginia *M, D*
Virginia Commonwealth
University *M*
Virginia Polytechnic Institute and
State University *M, D*
Virginia State University *M*

Washington

Central Washington University *M, T*
City University of Seattle *M*
Eastern Washington University *C*
Gonzaga University *M*
Heritage University *M*
Saint Martin's University *T*
Seattle Pacific University *M*
Seattle University *M*
University of Puget Sound *M*
Washington State University *M, D, T*
Western Washington University *M*
Whitworth University *M, T*

West Virginia

American Public University System *M*
Marshall University *B, M*
West Virginia University *M, T*

Wisconsin

Carthage College *M, T*
Concordia University Wisconsin *M*
Marquette University *M*
University of Wisconsin
La Crosse *M*
Oshkosh *M*
Platteville *M*
River Falls *M*
Stout *M*
Superior *M*
Whitewater *M*

Wyoming

University of Wyoming *M, D*

Court reporting

Alabama

Faulkner State Community College *A*
Gadsden State Community College *A*

Arizona

GateWay Community College *C, A*

California

Bryan College: Sacramento *A*
Bryan University: Los Angeles *C, A*
Butte College *C, A*
Cerritos College *C, A*
Chabot College *A*
College of Marin *C, A*
College of the Redwoods *C*
Cypress College *C, A*
Humphreys College *C, A, B*
Sage College *C, A*
Shasta College *C*
Taft College *C, A*
West Valley College *A*

Colorado

Prince Institute *A*

Florida

Broward College *A*
Eastern Florida State College *A*
Key College *A*

Miami Dade College *A*
Stenotype Institute: Jacksonville *A*

Illinois
Illinois Central College *C, A*
MacCormac College *A*
Midstate College *B*
South Suburban College of Cook
County *C, A*

Indiana
College of Court Reporting *A*

Iowa
AIB College of Business *A, B*

Kentucky
West Kentucky Community and
Technical College *A*

Michigan
Oakland Community College *C, A*

Minnesota
Anoka Technical College *C, A*

Mississippi
Hinds Community College *C, A*
Mississippi Gulf Coast Community
College *A*
Northwest Mississippi Community
College *A*

Nevada
Truckee Meadows Community
College *C*

New Mexico
Central New Mexico Community
College *C, A*

New York
Business Informatics Center *A*
Erie Community College *C*
Long Island Business Institute *C, A*
Monroe Community College *C*
New York Career Institute *C, A*
SUNY
College of Technology at
Alfred *C, A*

Ohio
Clark State Community College *A*
Cuyahoga Community College
Metropolitan *A*
Miami-Jacobs Career College
Columbus *A*
Dayton *A*
Sharonville *A*
Stark State College *A*
Stautzenberger College *A*
Stautzenberger College: Brecksville *A*

Pennsylvania
Harrisburg Area Community
College *C, A*
Luzerne County Community
College *A*
Orleans Technical Institute *A*

South Carolina
Midlands Technical College *C, A*

Tennessee
Chattanooga State Community
College *A*

Texas
Alvin Community College *C, A*
Amarillo College *C, A*
Court Reporting Institute of Dallas *A*
Del Mar College *C, A*

El Paso Community College *A*
San Antonio College *C*

Washington
Green River Community College *A*

Wisconsin
Fox Valley Technical College *A*
Gateway Technical College *A*
Lakeshore Technical College *A*
Madison Area Technical College *A*
Wisconsin Indianhead Technical
College *A*

Crafts/folk art/artisanry

Alaska
Ilisagvik College *C*

California
California College of the Arts *B, M*
California State University
Northridge *B*
Fresno City College *C, A*
Pasadena City College *A*
Santiago Canyon College *A*

Illinois
University of Illinois
Urbana-Champaign *B, M*

Indiana
Indiana University
Purdue University Fort Wayne *B*

Kansas
Allen County Community College *A*

Maine
College of the Atlantic *B*

Massachusetts
Montserrat College of Art *B*

Michigan
College for Creative Studies *B*

Montana
Miles Community College *A*

North Carolina
Montgomery Community
College *C, A*

Ohio
Bowling Green State University *B*
Kent State University *B, M*

Oregon
Oregon College of Art &
Craft *C, B, M*

Pennsylvania
Harrisburg Area Community
College *A*
Kutztown University of
Pennsylvania *B*
University of the Arts *B*

Virginia
Southwest Virginia Community
College *C*
Virginia Commonwealth University *B*

Washington
Northwest Indian College *C*

Creative writing

Alabama
Faulkner University *B*
University of Alabama *M*

Alaska
University of Alaska
Anchorage *M*
Fairbanks *M*

Arizona
Arizona State University *M*
Glendale Community College *C*
Mesa Community College *C*
Northern Arizona University *M*
Paradise Valley Community College *C*
Phoenix College *C*
Prescott College *B*
University of Arizona *B, M*

Arkansas
Arkansas Tech University *B*
University of Arkansas *M*
University of Central Arkansas *B, M*

California
Antioch University
Los Angeles *M*
Berkeley City College *C*
Biola University *B*
California College of the Arts *B, M*
California Institute of Integral
Studies *M*
California State University
Fresno *M*
Long Beach *B, M*
Northridge *B*
Sacramento *M*
San Bernardino *B*
Chapman University *B, M*
Dominican University of California *B*
Foothill College *A*
Fresno Pacific University *B*
Grossmont College *C, A*
Holy Names University *M*
Loyola Marymount University *M*
Mills College *B, M*
Mount St. Mary's College *M*
National University *A, M*
Otis College of Art and Design *M*
Pepperdine University *B*
Pitzer College *B*
St. Mary's College of California *M*
San Diego State University *M*
San Francisco State University *M*
San Jose State University *M*
University of California
Irvine *M*
Riverside *B, M*
University of La Verne *C*
University of Redlands *B*
University of San Francisco *M*
University of Southern
California *B, M, D*

Colorado
Adams State University *B*
Colorado College *B*
Colorado State University *B, M*
Naropa University *M*
University of Colorado
Boulder *M*

Connecticut
Albertus Magnus College *B*
Fairfield University *M*
Southern Connecticut State
University *M*
Trinity College *B*
University of Bridgeport *B*
Western Connecticut State
University *B, M*

District of Columbia
American University *M*
Corcoran College of Art and
Design *B*

Florida
Eckerd College *B*
Florida Atlantic University *M*
Florida International University *M*
Florida Southern College *B*
Florida State University *B, D*
Saint Leo University *B*
University of Central Florida *M*
University of Florida *B*
University of Miami *B, M*
University of South Florida *M*

Georgia
Agnes Scott College *B*
Emory University *B*
Georgia College and State
University *M*
Georgia State University *M, D*
Kennesaw State University *M*
Mercer University *B*
Young Harris College *B*

Idaho
Boise State University *M*
College of Idaho *B*
Lewis-Clark State College *B*
University of Idaho *B, M*

Illinois
Augustana College *B*
Columbia College Chicago *B, M*
DePaul University *B, M*
Eureka College *B*
Knox College *B*
McKendree University *B*
Millikin University *B*
North Central College *B*
Northwestern University *B, M*
Roosevelt University *M*
School of the Art Institute of
Chicago *B, M*
Southern Illinois University
Carbondale *M*
University of Illinois
Urbana-Champaign *M*

Indiana
Butler University *B, M*
Indiana University
Bloomington *M*
Purdue University *B*
Saint Joseph's College *B*
Saint Mary's College *B*
St. Mary-of-the-Woods College *B*
University of Evansville *B*
University of Indianapolis *B*
Valparaiso University *B*

Iowa
Briar Cliff University *B*
Coe College *B*
Cornell College *B*
Loras College *B*
Northwestern College *B*
University of Iowa *M*
Waldorf College *B*

Kansas
Cowley County Community
College *A*
Southwestern College *B*
University of Kansas *M*
Wichita State University *M*

Kentucky
Asbury University *B*
Berea College *B*
Morehead State University *B*
Murray State University *B, M*
Northern Kentucky University *C*
Spalding University *B, M*

Louisiana

Louisiana State University and
    Agricultural and Mechanical
    College *M*
Loyola University New Orleans *B*
McNeese State University *M*
University of New Orleans *M*

Maine

Colby College *B*
College of the Atlantic *B, M*
University of Maine
    Farmington *B*
University of Southern Maine *M*

Maryland

Goucher College *M*
Johns Hopkins University *B, M*
Loyola University Maryland *B*
University of Maryland
    College Park *M*

Massachusetts

Bard College at Simon's Rock *B*
Boston University *M*
Brandeis University *B*
Eastern Nazarene College *B*
Emerson College *B, M*
Hampshire College *B*
Lesley University *M*
Massachusetts College of Liberal
    Arts *B*
Massachusetts Institute of
    Technology *B*
Middlesex Community College *A*
Salem State University *B*
University of Massachusetts
    Amherst *M*
    Boston *M*
Western New England University *B*
Wheaton College *B*

Michigan

Albion College *B*
Aquinas College *B*
Central Michigan University *B, M*
Eastern Michigan University *B, M*
Grand Valley State University *B*
Kalamazoo College *B*
Lake Superior State University *B*
Lansing Community College *A*
Northern Michigan University *B, M*
Oakland University *B*
Saginaw Valley State University *B*
Siena Heights University *B*
Spring Arbor University *B*
University of Detroit Mercy *B*
University of Michigan *B, M*
University of Michigan
    Flint *M*
Western Michigan University *B, M, D*

Minnesota

Anoka-Ramsey Community College *A*
Augsburg College *B*
Bemidji State University *B*
Concordia University St. Paul *B*
Hamline University *B, M*
Metropolitan State University *B*
Minnesota State University
    Mankato *B, M*
    Moorhead *B*
Normandale Community College *A*
Saint Cloud State University *B*
Southwest Minnesota State
    University *B*
University of Minnesota
    Twin Cities *M*
University of St. Thomas *B*

Mississippi

Belhaven University *B*
University of Mississippi *M*

Missouri

Calvary Bible College and Theological
    Seminary *B*
Kansas City Art Institute *B*
Lindenwood University *B, M*
Missouri Southern State University *B*
Missouri State University *M*
Rockhurst University *C*
Stephens College *B*
Truman State University *B*
University of Missouri
    Kansas City *M*
    St. Louis *M*
Washington University in St. Louis *M*

Montana

Rocky Mountain College *B*
University of Montana *M*
University of Montana: Western *B*

Nebraska

Creighton University *B, M*
Hastings College *B*
Union College *B*
University of Nebraska
    Omaha *B, M*

Nevada

University of Nevada
    Las Vegas *M*

New Hampshire

Colby-Sawyer College *B*
New England College *B, M*
New Hampshire Institute of Art *B*
Southern New Hampshire
    University *B*
University of New Hampshire *M*

New Jersey

Fairleigh Dickinson University
    College at Florham *B, M*
Rutgers, The State University of New
    Jersey
    Camden Campus *M*
    Newark Campus *M*
Seton Hall University *B*

New Mexico

Institute of American Indian
    Arts *A, B*
New Mexico Highlands University *B*
New Mexico State University *M*
Santa Fe Community College *C*
Santa Fe University of Art and
    Design *B*
University of New Mexico *M*

New York

Adelphi University *M*
Adirondack Community College *A*
Bard College *B, M*
Canisius College *B*
City University of New York
    Brooklyn College *B, M*
    City College *M*
    Hunter College *B, M*
    Lehman College *M*
    Queens College *M*
College of Saint Rose *M*
Columbia University *B*
Columbia University
    School of General Studies *B*
Cornell University *M*
D'Youville College *B*
Hamilton College *B*
Hofstra University *B, M*
Ithaca College *B*
Manhattanville College *M*
New York University *M*
Pratt Institute *B*
SUNY
    College at Brockport *B, M*
    College at Potsdam *B*

College at Purchase *B*
University at Albany *D*
University at Binghamton *B*
University at Stony Brook *M*
St. Lawrence University *B*
St. Thomas Aquinas College *B*
Sarah Lawrence College *M*
Syracuse University *M*
Tompkins Cortland Community
    College *C, A*
University of Rochester *B*
Villa Maria College of Buffalo *B*
Yeshiva University *B*

North Carolina

Elon University *B*
Gardner-Webb University *B*
North Carolina State University *M*
Queens University of Charlotte *B, M*
St. Andrews University *B*
Salem College *B*
University of North Carolina
    Greensboro *M*
    Wilmington *B, M*
Warren Wilson College *B, M*

North Dakota

Dickinson State University *B*

Ohio

Antioch University
    Midwest *M*
Ashland University *B, M*
Baldwin Wallace University *B*
Bowling Green State University *B, M*
Capital University *B*
Cleveland State University *M*
Hiram College *B*
John Carroll University *B*
Kent State University *M*
Malone University *B*
Miami University
    Oxford *B*
Oberlin College *B*
Ohio Northern University *B*
Ohio University *B*
Ohio Wesleyan University *B*
Otterbein University *B*
Sinclair Community College *A*
University of Akron *M*
University of Cincinnati *C, B*
University of Findlay *B*
University of Mount Union *B*
Youngstown State University *M*

Oklahoma

Oklahoma Christian University *B*
Oklahoma City University *M*
Oklahoma State University *M*
University of Central Oklahoma *B, M*
University of Oklahoma *M*

Oregon

Linfield College *B*
Oregon State University *M*
Pacific University *B, M*
Portland State University *M*
Reed College *B*
University of Oregon *M*

Pennsylvania

Allegheny College *B*
Arcadia University *B, M*
Bucknell University *B*
Carlow University *B, M*
Carnegie Mellon University *B*
Cedar Crest College *M*
Chatham University *B, M*
Franklin & Marshall College *B*
Gettysburg College *B*
Lycoming College *B*
Moravian College *B*
Penn State
    Erie, The Behrend College *B*

Rosemont College *M*
Saint Joseph's University *M*
Seton Hill University *M*
Slippery Rock University of
    Pennsylvania *B*
Susquehanna University *B*
Temple University *M*
University of Pittsburgh *B*
University of Pittsburgh
    Bradford *B*
    Johnstown *B*
University of the Arts *M*
Waynesburg University *B*
Westminster College *B, T*
Widener University *B, T*
Wilkes University *M*

Rhode Island

Brown University *M*
Providence College *B*
Rhode Island College *B, M*
Roger Williams University *B*

South Carolina

Bob Jones University *B*
Coastal Carolina University *M*
Converse College *B, M*
University of South Carolina
    Columbia *M*
Wofford College *B*

South Dakota

Dakota Wesleyan University *B*

Tennessee

Christian Brothers University *B*
Sewanee: The University of the
    South *M*
Vanderbilt University *M*
Victory University *B*

Texas

Austin Community College *A*
Houston Baptist University *B*
Lubbock Christian University *B*
McMurry University *B*
Southern Methodist University *B*
Stephen F. Austin State University *B*
Texas Christian University *B*
Texas State University *M*
Texas Wesleyan University *B*
University of Houston *B, M, D*
University of North Texas *M*
University of Texas
    Austin *M*
    El Paso *B, M*
    Pan American *M*

Utah

Brigham Young University *M*
University of Utah *M*
Weber State University *B*

Vermont

Bennington College *B, M*
Goddard College *B, M*
Green Mountain College *B*
Marlboro College *B*
Southern Vermont College *B*

Virginia

Emory & Henry College *B*
George Mason University *B, M*
Hollins University *B, M*
Old Dominion University *M*
Randolph College *B*
Roanoke College *B*
Sweet Briar College *B*
University of Virginia *M*
Virginia Commonwealth
    University *M*
Virginia Polytechnic Institute and
    State University *M*

Washington

Eastern Washington University *M*
Pacific Lutheran University *M*
Seattle Pacific University *M*
Seattle University *B*
University of Washington *M*
Western Washington University *B*

West Virginia

Marshall University *B*
West Virginia University *M*
West Virginia Wesleyan College *B*
Wheeling Jesuit University *B*

Wisconsin

Beloit College *B*
Cardinal Stritch University *B*
Carroll University *B*
Northland College *B*
St. Norbert College *B*
University of Wisconsin
　Madison *M*
　River Falls *B*

Wyoming

University of Wyoming *M*

Credit management

Illinois

Harper College *C*

Minnesota

St. Cloud Technical and Community
　College *C, A*

New York

Globe Institute of Technology *C*

Texas

St. Mary's University *B*

Criminal justice and law enforcement

Alabama

Alabama Agricultural and Mechanical
　University *B*
Bishop State Community College *A*
Columbia Southern University *M*
Gadsden State Community College *A*
Herzing University
　Birmingham *A*
ITT Technical Institute
　Birmingham *A, B*
Judson College *B*
Remington College
　Mobile *A*
Troy University *M*
University of North Alabama *B, M*
University of Phoenix
　Birmingham *B*
University of South Alabama *B*
Virginia College
　Birmingham *A, B, M*
　Huntsville *B*

Alaska

Charter College *A, B*
University of Alaska
　Fairbanks *M*
　Southeast *C*

Arizona

Argosy University
　Online *B*
　Phoenix *B*
Arizona Western College *A*
Brookline College
　Phoenix *A, B*
　Tempe *A*
　Tucson *A, B*

Eastern Arizona College *A*
Grand Canyon University *B*
ITT Technical Institute
　Tempe *B*
　Tucson *B*
Northcentral University *B, M, D*
Pima Community College *C*
Rio Salado College *C, A*
Scottsdale Community College *C, A*
University of Phoenix
　Phoenix-Hohokam *B, M*
　Southern Arizona *B, M*
Yavapai College *C, A*

Arkansas

Arkansas State University *A*
Arkansas State University
　Beebe *C, A*
　Mountain Home *A*
Arkansas Tech University *C*
Bryan University
　Rogers *A*
College of the Ouachitas *C*
Cossatot Community College of the
　University of Arkansas *C, A*
ITT Technical Institute
　Little Rock *A, B*
Mid-South Community College *C, A*
North Arkansas College *C, A*
Northwest Arkansas Community
　College *A*
Ozarka College *A*
Phillips Community College of the
　University of Arkansas *C, A*
Pulaski Technical College *C, A*
Remington College
　Little Rock *A*
Southeast Arkansas College *C, A*
Southern Arkansas University *C, A*
Southern Arkansas University Tech *C*
University of Arkansas
　Community College at Hope *C, A*
　Community College at
　　Morrilton *C, A*
　Fort Smith *C, A, B*
　Monticello *C, A*
　Pine Bluff *C, A*
University of Phoenix
　Little Rock *B, M*
　Northwest Arkansas *B*

California

Alliant International University *B*
California Baptist University *B*
California State University
　East Bay *B*
　Los Angeles *B, M*
　Sacramento *B, M*
　San Bernardino *C, B, M*
Citrus College *C, A*
College of the Desert *C, A*
College of the Redwoods *C, A*
College of the Sequoias *C, A*
College of the Siskiyous *A*
Contra Costa College *C, A*
Copper Mountain College *C, A*
Cosumnes River College *A*
Crafton Hills College *C, A*
Cuesta College *C, A*
De Anza College *A*
Diablo Valley College *A*
El Camino College *C, A*
Folsom Lake College *A*
Fresno City College *C, A*
Gavilan College *C*
Glendale Community College *A*
Golden West College *C, A*
Hartnell College *C, A*
Heald College
　Concord *C, A*
　Hayward *C*
　Roseville *A*
　Salinas *A*
　Stockton *C, A*

ITT Technical Institute
　Lathrop *A, B*
　National City *A, B*
　Oxnard *A, B*
　Rancho Cordova *A, B*
　San Bernardino *A, B*
　Sylmar *A, B*
　Torrance *A, B*
Imperial Valley College *C, A*
Irvine Valley College *C, A*
La Sierra University *B*
Lake Tahoe Community College *C, A*
Lassen Community College *A*
Long Beach City College *C, A*
Los Medanos College *C*
Mendocino College *C, A*
Modesto Junior College *A*
Monterey Peninsula College *C, A*
National University *C, A, B, M*
Ohlone College *C, A*
Palo Verde College *C, A*
San Bernardino Valley College *C, A*
San Deigo Miramar College
　San Diego Miramar College *C, A*
San Jose City College *A*
Santa Barbara City College *C, A*
Shasta College *A*
Skyline College *C, A*
Sonoma State University *B*
Southwestern College *C, A*
University of Phoenix
　Bay Area *B, M*
　Central Valley *B, M*
　Sacramento Valley *B, M*
　San Diego *B, M*
　Southern California *B, M*
Victor Valley College *C, A*
West Hills College: Lemoore *A*
Westwood College
　Los Angeles *B*

Colorado

Aims Community College *A*
Arapahoe Community College *C, A*
Argosy University
　Denver *B*
Aspen University *B, M*
Colorado Christian University *C, A, B*
Colorado Mesa University *A*
Colorado Northwestern Community
　College *C, A*
Community College of Aurora *C, A*
Everest College
　Denver *A*
ITT Technical Institute
　Westminster *A, B*
Johnson & Wales University
　Denver *B*
Metropolitan State University of
　Denver *B*
Northeastern Junior College *C, A*
Pikes Peak Community College *C, A*
Pueblo Community College *C, A*
Trinidad State Junior College *A*
University of Colorado
　Colorado Springs *B, M*
　Denver *B, M*
University of Phoenix
　Denver *B, M*
　Southern Colorado *B, M*
Westwood College
　Denver North *B*
　Denver South *B*

Connecticut

Goodwin College *A*
Lincoln College of New England *B*
Northwestern Connecticut
　Community College *A*
Norwalk Community College *A*
Quinebaug Valley Community
　College *C*
Sacred Heart University *B, M*
Three Rivers Community College *A*

Tunxis Community College *C*
University of New Haven *A, B, D*
Western Connecticut State
　University *M*

Delaware

Delaware Technical Community
　College
　Jack F. Owens Campus *A*
　Stanton/Wilmington Campus *A*
　Terry Campus *C, A*

District of Columbia

George Washington University *M*
Strayer University *B*
Trinity Washington University *B*
University of Phoenix
　Washington DC *B*
University of the District of
　Columbia *A*

Florida

Bethune-Cookman University *B, M*
Brown Mackie College
　Miami *A, B*
Chipola College *C, A*
City College
　Gainesville *A*
Clearwater Christian College *B*
College of Central Florida *A*
Daytona State College *A*
Edison State College *A*
Edward Waters College *B*
Everest University
　Brandon *A, B, M*
　Jacksonville *A, B, M*
　Lakeland *M*
　Orange Park *A, B*
Florida Atlantic University *M*
Florida Gateway College *C, A*
Florida Keys Community College *C*
Florida State College at
　Jacksonville *A*
Florida Technical College
　Orlando *A*
Gulf Coast State College *C, A*
Hillsborough Community College *A*
Hodges University *M*
ITT Technical Institute
　Ft. Lauderdale *A, B*
　Jacksonville *A, B*
　Lake Mary *A, B*
　Miami *A, B*
　Tampa *A, B*
Johnson & Wales University
　North Miami *B*
Keiser University *A, B, M*
Lake-Sumter State College *A*
Lynn University *B*
Miami Dade College *C, A*
Northwest Florida State College *A*
Pasco-Hernando State College *A*
Pensacola State College *A*
Polk State College *C, A*
Remington College
　Tampa *B*
Saint Johns River State College *A*
St. Petersburg College *A*
Santa Fe College *A*
Seminole State College of Florida *A*
South Florida State College *A*
Southeastern University *B*
Southwest Florida College *A, B*
Tallahassee Community College *A*
University of Phoenix
　Central Florida *B, M*
　North Florida *B, M*
　South Florida *B, M*
　West Florida *B, M*
University of South Florida *M*
University of South Florida
　Sarasota-Manatee *M*
Valencia College *A*

Georgia

Athens Technical College *C, A*
Atlanta Metropolitan College *A*
Bainbridge College *A*
College of Coastal Georgia *A*
Columbus Technical College *C, A*
Georgia College and State
   University *B, M*
Georgia Military College *A*
Georgia Northwestern Technical
   College *C, A*
Georgia Perimeter College *A*
Kennesaw State University *M*
North Georgia Technical
   College *C, A*
Savannah State University *B*
Savannah Technical College *C*
Southeastern Technical College *A*
Southern Crescent Technical
   College *A*
University of Georgia *B*
University of Phoenix
   Atlanta *B, M*
   Augusta *B, M*
   Columbus *B, M*
   Savannah *B, M*

Hawaii

Chaminade University of Honolulu *M*
Hawaii Pacific University *A, B*
Heald College
   Honolulu *A*
University of Hawaii
   Hawaii Community College *A*
   Honolulu Community College *A*
   West Oahu *B*
University of Phoenix
   Hawaii *B, M*

Idaho

Boise State University *A, B, M*
Broadview University
   Boise *A, B*
College of Southern Idaho *C, A*
ITT Technical Institute
   Boise *A, B*
University of Phoenix
   Idaho *B, M*

Illinois

American InterContinental
   University *A, B*
Bradley University *B*
Carl Sandburg College *A*
Elmhurst College *B*
Eureka College *B*
Greenville College *B*
Illinois Valley Community
   College *C, A*
Joliet Junior College *C, A*
Kankakee Community College *A*
Kaskaskia College *C, A*
Lincoln College *A, B*
McKendree University *B*
North Park University *B*
Northwestern College *A*
Southeastern Illinois College *C*
Southern Illinois University
   Carbondale *B, M*
Spoon River College *A*
Triton College *C, A*
University of Phoenix
   Chicago *B*
University of St. Francis *B*
Western Illinois University *B, M*

Indiana

Ancilla College *A*
Bethel College *A, B*
Calumet College of St. Joseph *M*
Grace College *B*
Harrison College
   Indianapolis *A, B*

ITT Technical Institute
   Fort Wayne *A, B*
   Indianapolis *A, B*
   Newburgh *A, B*
Indiana Institute of Technology *B, M*
Indiana University
   East *B*
Purdue University *B*
University of Indianapolis *A, B*
University of Phoenix
   Indianapolis *B*

Iowa

Ashford University *B*
Briar Cliff University *B*
Ellsworth Community College *A*
Iowa Wesleyan College *B*
Marshalltown Community College *A*
Mount Mercy University *B*
Southeastern Community College *A*
Waldorf College *B*

Kansas

Brown Mackie College
   Salina *A*
Cowley County Community
   College *C, A*
Fort Scott Community College *C, A*
Garden City Community College *A*
Kansas Wesleyan University *B*
Labette Community College *A*
MidAmerica Nazarene University *B*
Newman University *B*
Seward County Community
   College *A*
Washburn University *A, B, M*

Kentucky

Beckfield College *A, B*
Campbellsville University *B*
Daymar College
   Bowling Green *C, A, B*
Eastern Kentucky University *A*
Elizabethtown Community and
   Technical College *A*
Hopkinsville Community
   College *C, A*
ITT Technical Institute
   Louisville *A, B*
Lincoln College of Technology
   Florence *A*
Madisonville Community College *A*
Owensboro Community and
   Technical College *C, A*
St. Catharine College *B*
Somerset Community College *C, A*
Sullivan University *C*
Union College *B*
University of Louisville *C, B, M*
University of Phoenix
   Louisville *B*
University of the Cumberlands *M*

Louisiana

ITT Technical Institute
   St. Rose *A, B*
Louisiana College *B*
Remington College
   Lafayette *A*
   Shreveport *A*
Southern University
   Shreveport *A*
Southwest University *A, B, M*
University of Phoenix
   Baton Rouge *B, M*
   Lafayette *B*
   Louisiana *B, M*
   Shreveport *B, M*

Maine

Central Maine Community College *A*
Husson University *A, B, M*
Kaplan University
   South Portland *A, B, M*

Thomas College *B*
University of Maine
   Augusta *B*
   Fort Kent *A*

Maryland

Anne Arundel Community
   College *C, A*
Baltimore City Community College *A*
Chesapeake College *C, A*
College of Southern Maryland *C, A*
Frostburg State University *B*
Kaplan University
   Hagerstown *A*
Montgomery College *A*
Stevenson University *B*
TESST College of Technology
   Towson *A*

Massachusetts

American International College *B*
Anna Maria College *B, M*
Becker College *B*
Boston University *B, M*
Bristol Community College *C*
Bunker Hill Community College *C, A*
Cape Cod Community College *C, A*
Curry College *M*
Dean College *A*
Eastern Nazarene College *B*
Lasell College *B*
Marian Court College *A, B*
Massachusetts Bay Community
   College *A*
Massasoit Community College *C*
Merrimack College *B*
Middlesex Community College *C, A*
Mount Wachusett Community
   College *C, A*
Newbury College *B*
Quincy College *C, A*
Roxbury Community College *A*
Salem State University *B, M*
Springfield College *B*
University of Massachusetts
   Lowell *A, B*

Michigan

Adrian College *A, B*
Alpena Community College *A*
Bay de Noc Community College *A*
Concordia University *B*
Delta College *A*
Ferris State University *B, M*
Finlandia University *A*
Gogebic Community College *A*
Grand Rapids Community College *A*
Grand Valley State University *B, M*
Henry Ford Community College *A*
ITT Technical Institute
   Canton *A, B*
   Troy *A, B*
Kalamazoo Valley Community
   College *A*
Kirtland Community College *A*
Lake Superior State University *A, B*
Michigan State University *B, M, D*
Muskegon Community College *C, A*
Northern Michigan University *A*
Northwestern Michigan College *A*
Oakland Community College *C, A*
St. Clair County Community
   College *A*
Spring Arbor University *B*
University of Detroit Mercy *B, M*
University of Michigan
   Flint *B, M*
University of Phoenix
   Metro Detroit *B, M*
   West Michigan *B, M*
Washtenaw Community College *A*
Wayne County Community College *A*
West Shore Community College *A*

Minnesota

Concordia University St. Paul *M*
Globe University
   Minneapolis *A, B*
   Woodbury *A, B*
ITT Technical Institute
   Eden Prairie *A, B*
Minnesota School of Business
   Blaine *A, B*
   Brooklyn Center *A, B*
   Elk River *A, B*
   Lakeville *A, B*
   Richfield *A, B*
   Rochester *A, B*
   St. Cloud *A, B*
   Shakopee *A, B*
Minnesota State University
   Mankato *C, B*
Minnesota West Community and
   Technical College *A*
Saint Cloud State University *M*
Southwest Minnesota State
   University *B*
University of Minnesota
   Crookston *B*
University of Phoenix
   Minneapolis-St. Paul *B, M*
University of St. Thomas *M*
Walden University *B, M*

Mississippi

Mississippi College *B, M*
Mississippi Delta Community
   College *A*
Mississippi Valley State University *M*
University of Mississippi *B, M*
University of Phoenix
   Jackson *B*

Missouri

Calvary Bible College and Theological
   Seminary *B*
Central Methodist University *B*
Columbia College *A, B, M*
Culver-Stockton College *B*
Drury University *M*
Grantham University *A, B*
Hannibal-LaGrange University *A, B*
Jefferson College *A*
Lincoln University *A, B*
Lindenwood University *M*
Metropolitan Community College
   Kansas City *C, A*
Missouri Southern State
   University *A, B*
Missouri Valley College *B*
Park University *C, A, B*
Rockhurst University *B*
St. Louis Community College *C*
Saint Louis University *B*
Southwest Baptist University *B*
University of Central Missouri *B, M*
University of Missouri
   Kansas City *B, M*
University of Phoenix
   Kansas City *B*
   St. Louis *B, M*

Montana

Dawson Community College *C, A*
University of Great Falls *M*

Nebraska

Bellevue University *M*
ITT Technical Institute
   Omaha *A*
York College *B*

Nevada

ITT Technical Institute
   Henderson *A, B*
Kaplan College
   Las Vegas *C, A*
Nevada State College *B*

Truckee Meadows Community
   College *A*
University of Phoenix
   Las Vegas *B, M*
   Northern Nevada *B*

New Hampshire

Great Bay Community College *A*
Mount Washington College *A, B*
NHTI-Concord's Community
   College *A*
White Mountains Community
   College *C, A*

New Jersey

Berkeley College *B*
College of New Jersey *B*
Essex County College *A*
Fairleigh Dickinson University
   Metropolitan Campus *B*
Felician College *B*
Kean University *B, M*
Middlesex County College *A*
Raritan Valley Community College *A*
Rutgers, The State University of New
   Jersey
   New Brunswick/Piscataway
      Campus *B*
Thomas Edison State College *B*
Union County College *C, A*

New Mexico

Brookline College
   Albuquerque *A*
Central New Mexico Community
   College *C, A*
ITT Technical Institute
   Albuquerque *A, B*
Mesalands Community College *C, A*
New Mexico State University
   Grants *A*
University of Phoenix
   New Mexico *B, M*
Western New Mexico University *C, B*

New York

Berkeley College *B*
Berkeley College of New York City *B*
Briarcliffe College *A*
Bryant & Stratton College
   Albany *A*
   Henrietta *A*
Canisius College *B*
Cayuga Community College *C*
City University of New York
   John Jay College of Criminal
      Justice *B, M*
   Kingsborough Community
      College *A*
   LaGuardia Community College *A*
Clinton Community College *A*
College of Saint Rose *B*
Columbia-Greene Community
   College *A*
Corning Community College *A*
Excelsior College *B*
Genesee Community College *C, A*
Herkimer County Community
   College *A*
Hilbert College *M*
ITT Technical Institute
   Getzville *A*
Iona College *B, M*
Jamestown Community College *C*
Jefferson Community College *C, A*
Keuka College *B*
Long Island University
   LIU Post *B, M*
Marist College *B*
Medaille College: Amherst *B*
Mercy College *B*
Mohawk Valley Community
   College *A*
Molloy College *B, M*

Monroe College *B*
Monroe Community College *C*
Nassau Community College *A*
New York Institute of Technology *B*
Niagara County Community
   College *A*
Onondaga Community College *A*
Orange County Community
   College *C*
Pace University *B*
Pace University: Pleasantville/
   Briarcliff *B*
Roberts Wesleyan College *B*
Rochester Institute of
   Technology *B, M*
SUNY
   College of Agriculture and
      Technology at Morrisville *B*
   College of Technology at Canton *B*
   Farmingdale State College *C, A*
Sage Colleges *B*
St. John's University *A, B, M*
St. Joseph's College New York:
   Suffolk Campus *C, B*
St. Joseph's College, New York *C, B*
St. Thomas Aquinas College *B*
Tompkins Cortland Community
   College *C, A*
Ulster County Community College *A*

North Carolina

Alamance Community College *A*
Bladen Community College *A*
Brevard College *B*
Catawba College *B*
Chowan University *B*
College of the Albemarle *A*
Mars Hill University *B*
Methodist University *B, M*
Miller-Motte College
   Fayetteville *A*
   Wilmington *A, B*
North Carolina Central University *B*
Rockingham Community College *A*
South College *A*
Southeastern Community
   College *C, A*
Surry Community College *A*
Vance-Granville Community
   College *A*

North Dakota

Sitting Bull College *A*
United Tribes Technical College *C, A*

Ohio

Ashland University *B*
Bowling Green State University *B*
Brown Mackie College
   Findlay *A*
Bryant & Stratton College
   Cleveland *C*
   Eastlake *A*
   Parma *A, B*
Cedarville University *B*
Central Ohio Technical College *A*
Clark State Community College *A*
Franklin University *B*
Harrison College
   Grove City *A*
Heidelberg University *B*
Herzing University
   Toledo *A*
ITT Technical Institute
   Norwood *B*
   Youngstown *A*
Kaplan College
   Dayton *A*
Lake Erie College *B*
Lincoln College of Technology
   Dayton *A*
Marion Technical College *A*

Miami University
   Hamilton *A*
   Oxford *A, B*
Miami-Jacobs Career College
   Dayton *A*
Mount Vernon Nazarene University *B*
North Central State College *A*
Northwest State Community
   College *A*
Ohio Northern University *B*
Ohio University
   Southern Campus at Ironton *A*
Owens Community College
   Toledo *A*
Remington College
   Cleveland West *A*
Sinclair Community College *A*
Tiffin University *A, B, M*
Union Institute & University *B*
University of Cincinnati
   Clermont College *A*
University of Findlay *B*
Urbana University *B*
Washington State Community
   College *A*
Youngstown State University *A, B, M*

Oklahoma

Eastern Oklahoma State College *A*
Northeastern State University *B, M*
Northern Oklahoma College *A*
Oklahoma City University *M*
Rogers State University *B*
University of Central Oklahoma *B, M*
University of Oklahoma *B*
University of Phoenix
   Oklahoma City *B, M*
   Tulsa *B*

Oregon

ITT Technical Institute
   Portland *A, B*
Klamath Community College *C, B*
Portland State University *B*
Southern Oregon University *B*
University of Phoenix
   Oregon *B*
Western Oregon University *B, M*

Pennsylvania

Alvernia University *B*
Berks Technical Institute *A*
Bucks County Community College *A*
Butler County Community College *A*
Chestnut Hill College *A, B*
Clarion University of Pennsylvania *A*
Delaware Valley College *B*
Drexel University *B*
Fortis Institute
   Erie *A*
Harcum College *A*
Harrisburg Area Community
   College *A*
ITT Technical Institute
   Pittsburgh *A*
   Plymouth Meeting *A*
Kaplan Career Institute
   Harrisburg *A*
   Pittsburgh *A*
Keystone College *B*
Lehigh Carbon Community College *A*
Lock Haven University of
   Pennsylvania *A, B*
Mansfield University of
   Pennsylvania *A, B*
Marywood University *M*
Mercyhurst University *M*
Mount Aloysius College *B*
Peirce College *A*
Penn State
   Abington *B*
   Altoona *C, B*
   Beaver *B*
   Berks *B*

Brandywine *B*
DuBois *B*
Fayette, The Eberly Campus *B*
Greater Allegheny *B*
Harrisburg *B*
Hazleton *C, B*
Lehigh Valley *B*
Mont Alto *B*
New Kensington *B*
Schuylkill *C, B*
Shenango *B*
University Park *C, B*
Wilkes-Barre *C, B*
Worthington Scranton *B*
York *B*
Pennsylvania Highlands Community
   College *A*
Reading Area Community College *A*
University of Phoenix
   Harrisburg *B*
   Philadelphia *B*
   Pittsburgh *B*
University of Pittsburgh
   Bradford *B*
   Greensburg *B*
   Johnstown *B*
Villanova University *B, M*
Waynesburg University *B*
Widener University *B, M*
YTI Career Institute
   Lancaster *A*
York College of Pennsylvania *A, B*

Puerto Rico

Inter American University of Puerto
   Rico
   Barranquitas Campus *B*
   Guayama Campus *B*
   Ponce Campus *B, M*
   San German Campus *B*
National University College
   Arecibo *A, B*
   Bayamon *A, B*
   Rio Grande *A, B*
Turabo University *M*
Universidad del Este *A, M*
University of Phoenix
   Puerto Rico *B*
University of Puerto Rico
   Aguadilla *A*
   Carolina Regional College *B*

Rhode Island

Johnson & Wales University
   Providence *B*
New England Institute of
   Technology *A, B*
Roger Williams University *A, B, M*
Salve Regina University *A, B, M*

South Carolina

Anderson University *B*
Benedict College *B*
Citadel *B*
Claflin University *B*
ITT Technical Institute
   Greenville *A, B*
Lander University *B*
Limestone College *B*
Morris College *B*
South Carolina State University *B*
Spartanburg Methodist College *A*
Trident Technical College *C, A*
University of Phoenix
   Columbia *B*
University of South Carolina
   Columbia *B, M*

South Dakota

Globe University
   Sioux Falls *A, B*
Lake Area Technical Institute *A*
Southeast Technical Institute *A*

Tennessee

Austin Peay State University B
Daymar Institute
    Clarksville C, A, B
    Murfreesboro B
East Tennessee State University B, M
ITT Technical Institute
    Memphis A, B
Lincoln Memorial University B
Martin Methodist College B
Middle Tennessee State
    University B, M
Remington College
    Nashville A
Tennessee State University M
Trevecca Nazarene University B
University of Memphis B, M
University of Phoenix
    Chattanooga B, M
    Knoxville B
    Memphis B
    Nashville B
University of Tennessee
    Chattanooga B, M
    Martin B
Virginia College
    School of Business and Health in
        Chattanooga B

Texas

Abilene Christian University B
Argosy University
    Dallas B
Cedar Valley College C, A
Central Texas College C, A
Concordia University Texas B
East Texas Baptist University B
Everest College
    Arlington A
Grayson College A
Hill College C, A
Howard College C, A
Kilgore College A
Lubbock Christian University B
McLennan Community College C, A
National American University
    Austin A, B
Northeast Texas Community
    College A
Remington College
    Dallas A
    North Houston A
Sam Houston State University M
South Plains College A
South Texas College A
Sul Ross State University M
Tarleton State University B, M
Texarkana College C, A
Texas College B
Texas Southern University B, M, D
Texas State University M, D
Trinity Valley Community
    College C, A
University of Houston
    Victoria B
University of Mary Hardin-Baylor B
University of Phoenix
    Austin B, M
    Dallas Fort Worth B, M
    Houston Westside B, M
    San Antonio B, M
University of Texas
    Brownsville B
    Dallas M
    Pan American B, M
    Permian Basin M
Wayland Baptist University A, B
Weatherford College A
Wiley College A, B

Utah

Argosy University
    Salt Lake City B

Broadview University
    Layton A, B
    Orem A, B
    West Jordan A, B
Provo College A
Snow College A
University of Phoenix
    Utah B
Utah Valley University C, A, B

Vermont

College of St. Joseph in
    Vermont A, B

Virginia

Averett University B
Blue Ridge Community College C
Bluefield College B
Bryant & Stratton College
    Virginia Beach A, B
Central Virginia Community
    College A
Danville Community College A
Everest College
    McLean A
George Mason University M, D
Hampton University B
ITT Technical Institute
    Chantilly A, B
    Norfolk A, B
    Richmond A, B
    Springfield A, B
J. Sargeant Reynolds Community
    College C, A
John Tyler Community College C, A
Marymount University B, M
Mountain Empire Community
    College A
New River Community College A
Northern Virginia Community
    College C, A
Rappahannock Community
    College C, A
Regent University A, B
Shenandoah University B
Thomas Nelson Community
    College A
University of Management and
    Technology A, B, M
University of Phoenix
    Northern Virginia B, M
    Richmond B, M
Virginia Commonwealth
    University B, M
Westwood College
    Annandale B

Washington

Bellevue College A
Centralia College A
Columbia Basin College A
ITT Technical Institute
    Everett A, B
    Seattle A, B
    Spokane A, B
Lower Columbia College A
Peninsula College C, A
Pierce College C, A
Seattle University B
Shoreline Community College A
Skagit Valley College C, A
Spokane Community College A
Tacoma Community College C, A
University of Phoenix
    Western Washington B
Washington State University B, M, D
Yakima Valley Community
    College C, A

West Virginia

American Public University System C
New River Community and Technical
    College A

Potomac State College of West
    Virginia University A, B
University of Charleston B
West Virginia University Institute of
    Technology B
West Virginia Wesleyan College B

Wisconsin

Bryant & Stratton College
    Milwaukee A
Globe University
    Appleton A, B
    Eau Claire A, B
    Green Bay A, B
    La Crosse A, B
    Madison East A, B
    Middleton A, B
    Wausau A, B
ITT Technical Institute
    Greenfield A, B
Lakeland College B
Marian University M
University of Phoenix
    Milwaukee B
University of Wisconsin
    Platteville B, M

Wyoming

Central Wyoming College A
Eastern Wyoming College A
Laramie County Community
    College A
Northwest College A
Sheridan College C, A
Western Wyoming Community
    College A

Criminal justice studies

Alabama

Alabama State University B
Athens State University B
Auburn University at
    Montgomery B, M
Community College of the Air
    Force A
Faulkner University A, B, M
Jacksonville State University B, M
Troy University B
University of Alabama B, M
University of Alabama
    Birmingham B, M

Arizona

Brown Mackie College
    Tucson A
Central Arizona College A
Chandler-Gilbert Community
    College C
Coconino County Community
    College A
Estrella Mountain Community
    College C, A
Everest College
    Phoenix A, B
Glendale Community College A
Grand Canyon University M
Mesa Community College C, A
Northland Pioneer College A
Paradise Valley Community College A
Phoenix College C, A
Pima Community College A
Scottsdale Community College A

Arkansas

Arkansas State University M
Arkansas State University
    Beebe A
Arkansas Tech University A
College of the Ouachitas A
Harding University B
Northwest Arkansas Community
    College A
Southeast Arkansas College A

Southern Arkansas University B
University of Arkansas B
University of Arkansas
    Community College at Batesville A
    Little Rock B, M, D
    Monticello A
    Pine Bluff B

California

California State University
    Bakersfield B
    Chico B
    Dominguez Hills B, M
    Fresno B
    Fullerton B
    Long Beach B, M
    Stanislaus B, M
Carrington College California
    Antioch A
    Citrus Heights A
    Pleasant Hill A
    San Jose A
Citrus College A
College of the Redwoods C
College of the Siskiyous A
Diablo Valley College C
Golden West College C, A
Kaplan College
    Salida A
    Vista A
Loma Linda University M
Los Angeles Mission College C, A
Saddleback College C
San Diego State University B, M
San Francisco State University B
San Jose State University B, M
Santa Barbara Business College A, B
Santa Barbara Business College
    Bakersfield A, B
    Rancho Mirage A, B
    Santa Maria C, A, B
    Ventura A, B
Shasta College A
Sierra College A
Southwestern College A
Taft College A
Ventura College C, A
West Valley College A
Westwood College
    South Bay B
Yuba College A

Colorado

Colorado Mesa University B
Colorado Mountain College A
Everest College
    Aurora A
    Colorado Springs A
Metropolitan State University of
    Denver B
Trinidad State Junior College A
University of Northern
    Colorado B, M
Western State Colorado University B

Connecticut

Albertus Magnus College B
Central Connecticut State
    University M
Goodwin College B
Mitchell College B
Post University A, B
Quinnipiac University B
Three Rivers Community
    College C, A
University of Bridgeport C, B
University of New Haven M

Delaware

Delaware State University B
University of Delaware B
Wilmington University B

District of Columbia

American University B, M, D
George Washington University B, M

Florida

Broward College A
City College
Gainesville A
Edison State College A, B
Everest University
Lakeland B
Orange Park A, B
Tampa A, B
Florida Agricultural and Mechanical
University B
Florida Atlantic University B
Florida Gulf Coast University B, M
Florida International University B, M
Florida National University A, B
Florida State College at
Jacksonville A
Florida State University B, M, D
Herzing University
Winter Park B
Hodges University A, B
Indian River State College A
Nova Southeastern
University B, M, D
Polk State College B
Rasmussen College
Fort Myers A, B
New Port Richey A, B
Ocala A, B
Pasco/Land O'Lakes A, B
Tampa/Brandon A, B
Saint Leo University B, M
Saint Thomas University C, B
South Florida State College A
State College of Florida, Manatee-
Sarasota A
Tallahassee Community College A
University of Central Florida B, M
University of Miami B, M, D
University of North Florida B, M
University of West Florida B, M

Georgia

Albany State University B
Albany Technical College C, A
Armstrong Atlantic State University C
Atlanta Technical College C
Central Georgia Technical
College C, A
Chattahoochee Technical
College C, A
Clark Atlanta University B, M
Clayton State University B
Columbus State University C, A, B
Darton College A
East Georgia State College A
Georgia Piedmont Technical
College C, A
Georgia Regents University A, B
Georgia Southern University B
Georgia State University B, M, D
Gordon College A
Gwinnett Technical College C, A
Kennesaw State University B
Mercer University B
Middle Georgia State College C, A
Piedmont College B
Point University B
Savannah Technical College C, A
Southwest Georgia Technical
College C, A
Thomas University A, B
University of North Georgia A, B, M
Valdosta State University B, M
West Georgia Technical College C, A

Hawaii

Remington College
Honolulu A, B

University of Hawaii
Hilo B
Honolulu Community College A

Idaho

College of Western Idaho A
Idaho State University A
Lewis-Clark State College B
North Idaho College A

Illinois

Aurora University B, M
Blackburn College B
Carl Sandburg College C
City Colleges of Chicago
Harold Washington College C, A
Harry S. Truman College C, A
Kennedy-King College C, A
Olive-Harvey College C, A
Richard J. Daley College C, A
Wilbur Wright College C
Elmhurst College B
Governors State University B, M
Heartland Community College A
Illinois Central College A
Illinois State University B, M
John A. Logan College C, A
Judson University C, B
Lewis University B, M
Lewis and Clark Community
College A
Lincoln Land Community College C
Loyola University Chicago B, M
Northeastern Illinois University B
Olivet Nazarene University B
Quincy University B
Rasmussen College
Aurora A, B
Mokena/Tinley Park A, B
Rockford A, B
Romeoville/Joliet A, B
Richland Community College A
Roosevelt University B
Saint Xavier University B
South Suburban College of Cook
County C, A
Southern Illinois University
Edwardsville B
Trinity Christian College B
University of Illinois
Chicago B, M, D
Springfield B

Indiana

Anderson University A, B
Ball State University A, B
Brown Mackie College
Merrillville A, B
Michigan City A, B
South Bend A, B
Butler University B
Indiana Institute of Technology A
Indiana University
Bloomington B, M, D
Kokomo C, B
Northwest C, A, B
Purdue University
Indianapolis B, M
South Bend B
Southeast B
Indiana Wesleyan University A, B
Ivy Tech Community College
Bloomington A
Central Indiana A
Columbus A
East Central A
Kokomo A
Lafayette A
North Central A
Northeast A
Northwest A
Richmond A
South Central A
Southeast A

Southwest A
Wabash Valley A
Manchester University B
Martin University B
Oakland City University A, B
Saint Joseph's College B
Trine University A, B
University of Evansville B
University of Southern Indiana B

Iowa

Ashford University B
Buena Vista University B
Ellsworth Community College A
Graceland University B
Grand View University B
Loras College B
St. Ambrose University B, M, T
Simpson College B, M
University of Dubuque B
Upper Iowa University B

Kansas

Bethany College B
Bryan University
Topeka B
Butler Community College A
Fort Hays State University B
Friends University B
Pittsburg State University B
Washburn University A, B
Wichita State University C, B, M

Kentucky

Bellarmine University B
Campbellsville University A
Eastern Kentucky University M
Gateway Community and Technical
College C, A
Kentucky State University B
Kentucky Wesleyan College B
Lindsey Wilson College B
Murray State University B
Northern Kentucky University A, B
Sullivan University A, B
Thomas More College A, B
University of Pikeville A, B
University of the Cumberlands B

Louisiana

Blue Cliff College
Metairie A
Bossier Parish Community College A
Grambling State University B, M
Herzing University
Kenner B
Louisiana State University
Eunice A
Shreveport B
Loyola University New Orleans B, M
McNeese State University B, M
Northwestern State University B
South Louisiana Community
College A
Southeastern Louisiana University B
Southern University
New Orleans B, M
Southern University and Agricultural
and Mechanical College B, M
University of Louisiana at Lafayette B
University of Louisiana at
Monroe B, M

Maine

Husson University A, B
Kaplan University
South Portland A, B, M
Saint Joseph's College of Maine B
Thomas College B
University of Maine
Augusta A
Fort Kent A
Presque Isle A, B
York County Community College A

Maryland

Coppin State University B, M
Frederick Community College A
Howard Community College A
Kaplan University
Hagerstown A
Prince George's Community
College C, A
University of Baltimore B, M
University of Maryland
University College B

Massachusetts

American International College B
Bay State College A, B
Becker College B
Berkshire Community College A
Bridgewater State University B, M
Bristol Community College A
Cape Cod Community College A
Curry College B
Dean College A
Eastern Nazarene College B
Endicott College B
Fitchburg State University B
Holyoke Community College C, A
Mount Ida College B
Nichols College B
North Shore Community
College C, A
Northeastern University B, M, D
Northern Essex Community
College C, A
Suffolk University M
University of Massachusetts
Amherst C
Boston B
Lowell M
Western New England University B
Westfield State University B, M
Worcester State University B

Michigan

Bay de Noc Community College A
Jackson College C, A
Lake Superior State University B
Madonna University C, A, B, M
Michigan State University B, M, D
Montcalm Community College C, A
Northern Michigan
University A, B, M
Olivet College B
Saginaw Valley State University B
Siena Heights University A, B
Southwestern Michigan College A
University of Detroit Mercy B, M
Wayne State University B, M
Western Michigan University B

Minnesota

Bemidji State University B
Brown College
Mendota Heights A, B
Capella University B, M, D
Central Lakes College C, A
Century College A
Concordia University St. Paul B, M
Gustavus Adolphus College B
Hamline University B
Inver Hills Community College C, A
Metropolitan State University B, M
Minneapolis Community and
Technical College A
Minnesota State College - Southeast
Technical A
Minnesota State Community and
Technical College A
Minnesota State University
Moorhead B
National American University
Bloomington A, B
Roseville A, B
Normandale Community College A

North Hennepin Community
College *A*
Rasmussen College
Blaine *A, B*
Bloomington *A, B*
Brooklyn Park *A, B*
Eagan *A, B*
Lake Elmo/Woodbury *A, B*
Mankato *A, B*
Moorhead *A, B*
St. Cloud *A, B*
Ridgewater College *A*
Rochester Community and Technical
College *A*
Saint Cloud State University *B, M*
Southwest Minnesota State
University *B*
University of Minnesota
Twin Cities *M*
University of Northwestern - St.
Paul *B*

Mississippi

Alcorn State University *B*
Coahoma Community College *A*
Delta State University *B, M*
Hinds Community College *A*
Itawamba Community College *A*
Jackson State University *B, M*
Mississippi Gulf Coast Community
College *A*
Mississippi Valley State University *B*
Northeast Mississippi Community
College *A*
University of Southern
Mississippi *B, M, D*

Missouri

Evangel University *B*
Harris-Stowe State University *B*
Lindenwood University *B*
Metropolitan Community College -
Kansas City *A*
Missouri Baptist University *B, M*
Missouri Western State University *B*
North Central Missouri College *C, A*
St. Louis Community College *C*
Southeast Missouri State University *M*
Truman State University *B*
University of Missouri
Kansas City *B*

Montana

Blackfeet Community College *A*
Flathead Valley Community
College *A*
Montana State University
Billings *B*
University of Great Falls *A, B*

Nebraska

Central Community College *C, A*
Herzing University
Omaha School of Massage Therapy
and Healthcare *B*
Kaplan University
Lincoln *A*
Omaha *A, B*
Southeast Community College *A*
University of Nebraska
Kearney *B*
Omaha *B, M, D*
Wayne State College *B*

Nevada

College of Southern Nevada *C, A*
Truckee Meadows Community
College *C, A*

New Hampshire

Franklin Pierce University *A, B*
Granite State College *B*
Lebanon College *C, A*
New England College *B, M*

Plymouth State University *B, M*
Saint Anselm College *B*

New Jersey

Caldwell College *B*
Centenary College *B*
College of St. Elizabeth *M*
Cumberland County College *A*
Essex County College *A*
Fairleigh Dickinson University
Metropolitan Campus *M*
Georgian Court University *B*
Hudson County Community
College *A*
Monmouth University *B, M*
New Jersey City University *M*
Richard Stockton College of New
Jersey *M*
Rowan University *B, M*
Rutgers, The State University of New
Jersey
Camden Campus *B, M*
Newark Campus *B, M, D*
Seton Hall University *B*
Sussex County Community College *A*
Thomas Edison State College *A, B*
Warren County Community
College *A*

New Mexico

Eastern New Mexico University *B*
Eastern New Mexico University:
Roswell *A*
Luna Community College *C, A*
National American University
Albuquerque *A, B*
New Mexico Highlands University *B*
New Mexico Junior College *A*
New Mexico State University *B, M*
New Mexico State University
Alamogordo *A*
Carlsbad *A*
Northern New Mexico College *A*
Santa Fe Community College *A*
University of the Southwest *B*
Western New Mexico University *A, B*

New York

ASA College *A*
Adelphi University *B*
Alfred University *B*
Canisius College *B*
Cazenovia College *A, B*
City University of New York
Hostos Community College *A*
John Jay College of Criminal
Justice *B*
Columbia-Greene Community
College *A*
Elmira College *B*
Finger Lakes Community
College *C, A*
Fulton-Montgomery Community
College *A*
Herkimer County Community
College *A*
Hilbert College *A, B*
Monroe Community College *A*
Niagara University *B, M*
North Country Community College *A*
Nyack College *B*
Onondaga Community College *A*
Orange County Community
College *A*
SUNY
College at Buffalo *B, M*
College at Fredonia *B*
College at Oneonta *B*
College at Plattsburgh *B*
College at Potsdam *B*
College of Agriculture and
Technology at Morrisville *A*
University at Albany *B, M, D*
St. Francis College *A, B*

Schenectady County Community
College *A*
Utica College *B, M*

North Carolina

Alamance Community College *A*
Appalachian State University *B, M*
Barton College *B*
Beaufort County Community
College *A*
Belmont Abbey College *B*
Campbell University *B*
Carteret Community College *A*
Catawba Valley Community
College *A*
Central Carolina Community
College *A*
Central Piedmont Community
College *C, A*
Cleveland Community College *C, A*
Craven Community College *C, A*
Davidson County Community
College *A*
East Carolina University *B, M*
Edgecombe Community College *A*
Elizabeth City State University *B*
Elon University *B*
Fayetteville State University *B, M*
Fayetteville Technical Community
College *C, A*
Forsyth Technical Community
College *C, A*
Guilford College *B*
Guilford Technical Community
College *A*
Haywood Community College *A*
High Point University *B*
Isothermal Community College *C, A*
James Sprunt Community College *A*
Johnston Community College *A*
Lees-McRae College *B*
Lenoir Community College *A*
Livingstone College *B*
Methodist University *A, B*
Montgomery Community College *A*
North Carolina Agricultural and
Technical State University *B*
North Carolina Central University *M*
North Carolina Wesleyan College *B*
Piedmont Community College *A*
Pitt Community College *A*
Roanoke-Chowan Community
College *A*
Robeson Community College *C, A*
Rowan-Cabarrus Community
College *A*
St. Augustine's University *B*
Sandhills Community College *A*
Shaw University *A, B*
South Piedmont Community
College *C, A*
Southwestern Community College *A*
Stanly Community College *C, A*
University of Mount Olive *B*
University of North Carolina
Charlotte *B, M*
Pembroke *B*
Wilmington *B*
Wayne Community College *A*
Western Carolina University *B*
Western Piedmont Community
College *A*
Wilkes Community College *C, A*
Wilson Community College *A*
Winston-Salem State University *B*

North Dakota

Bismarck State College *A*
Minot State University *B, M*
North Dakota State
University *B, M, D*
Rasmussen College
Bismarck *A, B*
Fargo *A, B*

University of Jamestown *B*
University of Mary *B*
University of North Dakota *B, D*

Ohio

Baldwin Wallace University *B*
Bluffton University *B*
Bowling Green State University *B, M*
Bowling Green State University:
Firelands College *A, B*
Brown Mackie College
Akron *A*
North Canton *C, A, B*
Central State University *B*
ITT Technical Institute
Dayton *A, B*
Hilliard *A, B*
Norwood *A*
Strongsville *A, B*
Kent State University *B*
Kent State University
Ashtabula *A, B*
East Liverpool *A, B*
Salem *A, B*
Stark *A, B*
Trumbull *A, B*
Tuscarawas *A, B*
Lourdes University *A, B*
Mount Vernon Nazarene University *B*
North Central State College *A*
Northwest State Community
College *A*
Ohio Dominican University *B*
Ohio Northern University *B*
Ohio University
Chillicothe Campus *B*
Southern Campus at Ironton *B*
Remington College
Cleveland West *A*
University of Akron *B*
University of Cincinnati *B, M, D*
University of Cincinnati
Blue Ash College *A*
Clermont College *A*
University of Dayton *B*
University of Toledo *B, M*
Urbana University *B*
Wilmington College *B*
Xavier University *A, B, M*
Youngstown State University *A, B, M*

Oklahoma

Bacone College *A, B*
Carl Albert State College *A*
Eastern Oklahoma State College *A*
Northeastern Oklahoma Agricultural
and Mechanical College *A*
St. Gregory's University *B*
Southeastern Oklahoma State
University *B*
Southern Nazarene University *B*
Southwestern Oklahoma State
University *B*
Tulsa Community College *A*
University of Central Oklahoma *B*
University of Oklahoma *M*

Oregon

Central Oregon Community
College *A*
Chemeketa Community College *C, A*
Corban University *B*
Lane Community College *A*
Linn-Benton Community College *A*
Pioneer Pacific College *A, B*
Portland Community College *C, A*
Portland State University *B, M*
Southern Oregon University *B*
Southwestern Oregon Community
College *A*
Treasure Valley Community
College *A*

Pennsylvania

Bloomsburg University of
    Pennsylvania *B*
Bucks County Community College *A*
California University of
    Pennsylvania *C, A, B*
Central Penn College *A, B*
DeSales University *B, M, T*
Edinboro University of
    Pennsylvania *A, B*
Gannon University *A, B*
Holy Family University *B, M*
Immaculata University *B*
Kaplan Career Institute
    Franklin Mills *A*
    Harrisburg *A*
    Pittsburgh *A*
King's College *A, B*
Kutztown University of
    Pennsylvania *B*
La Roche College *B*
La Salle University *A, B*
Lackawanna College *A*
Lansdale School of Business *C*
Lehigh Carbon Community
    College *C, A*
Lincoln University *B*
Luzerne County Community
    College *A*
Lycoming College *B*
Marywood University *B*
Mercyhurst University *B, M*
Messiah College *B*
Moravian College *B*
Neumann University *B*
Northampton Community College *A*
Penn State
    Abington *B*
    Altoona *A, B*
    Beaver *B*
    Fayette, The Eberly Campus *B*
    Harrisburg *B, M*
    New Kensington *B*
    Schuylkill *B*
    Shenango *B*
    University Park *M, D*
    Wilkes-Barre *B*
Point Park University *B, M*
Rosemont College *B*
Seton Hill University *B*
Shippensburg University of
    Pennsylvania *B, M*
Slippery Rock University of
    Pennsylvania *M*
South Hills School of Business &
    Technology *C, A*
Temple University *B, M, D*
Thiel College *B*
University of Scranton *A, B*
Valley Forge Christian College *B*
Valley Forge Military College *A*
West Chester University of
    Pennsylvania *B, M*
Westminster College *B*
Westmoreland County Community
    College *A*
Wilkes University *B*
YTI Career Institute
    Altoona *A*

Puerto Rico

American University of Puerto
    Rico *A, B, M*
Inter American University of Puerto
    Rico
    Aguadilla Campus *A, B, M*
    Arecibo Campus *A, B*
    Fajardo Campus *B*
    Metropolitan Campus *B, M*
Universidad Metropolitana *C, A, B*
Universidad del Este *C, B*

Rhode Island

Rhode Island College *B*

South Carolina

Aiken Technical College *C, A*
Bob Jones University *B*
Charleston Southern University *B, M*
Florence-Darlington Technical
    College *A*
Greenville Technical College *A*
Horry-Georgetown Technical
    College *C, A*
Midlands Technical College *C, A*
Northeastern Technical College *C*
Orangeburg-Calhoun Technical
    College *A*
Piedmont Technical College *A*
Southern Wesleyan University *B*
Technical College of the
    Lowcountry *C, A*
Tri-County Technical College *C, A*
University of South Carolina
    Lancaster *A*
    Upstate *B*

South Dakota

Dakota Wesleyan University *A, B*
Kilian Community College *A*
Mount Marty College *A, B*
University of Sioux Falls *B*
University of South Dakota *B*

Tennessee

Chattanooga College *A*
Cumberland University *A, B*
Daymar Institute
    Nashville *C, A*
Freed-Hardeman University *B*
Hiwassee College *A*
ITT Technical Institute
    Knoxville *A, B*
    Nashville *A, B*
Lane College *B*
Northeast State Community
    College *A*
Remington College
    Memphis *A*
Roane State Community College *A*
South College *A, B, M*
Tennessee State University *B, M*
Tennessee Wesleyan College *B*

Texas

Alvin Community College *C, A*
Angelina College *A*
Angelo State University *B*
Blinn College *C, A*
Cisco College *C, A*
Clarendon College *A*
Coastal Bend College *A*
Dallas Baptist University *C, B, M*
Del Mar College *C, A*
Eastfield College *C, A*
El Paso Community College *A*
Everest College
    Arlington *A*
    Dallas *A*
    Fort Worth *A*
Galveston College *C, A*
Hardin-Simmons University *B*
Howard Payne University *B*
Huston-Tillotson University *B*
Jarvis Christian College *B*
Kilgore College *C, A*
Lamar State College at Orange *A*
Lamar State College at Port Arthur *A*
Lamar University *B, M*
Laredo Community College *A*
Midwestern State University *B*
Mountain View College *C, A*
Navarro College *A*
North Central Texas College *A*
Our Lady of the Lake University of
    San Antonio *A*
Palo Alto College *A*
Paris Junior College *A*
Prairie View A&M University *B*

Remington College
    Fort Worth *A*
St. Edward's University *B*
St. Mary's University *B*
St. Philip's College *A*
Sam Houston State
    University *B, M, D*
San Antonio College *A*
Sul Ross State University *B*
Tarleton State University *B, M*
Tarrant County College *A*
Temple College *C, A*
Texarkana College *A*
Texas A&M International
    University *B, M*
Texas A&M University
    Commerce *B*
    Corpus Christi *B*
    Texarkana *B*
Texas Christian University *B, M*
Texas State University *B*
Texas Wesleyan University *B*
Texas Woman's University *B*
Tyler Junior College *A*
University of Houston
    Downtown *B, M*
University of North Texas *B, M*
University of Texas
    Arlington *B, M*
    Brownsville *B*
    El Paso *B*
    Permian Basin *B*
    San Antonio *B, M*
    Tyler *B, M*
Vernon College *C, A*
West Texas A&M University *B, M*

Utah

Dixie State College *C, A*
Salt Lake Community College *A*
Utah State University *A*
Weber State University *A, B, M*
Westminster College *B*

Vermont

Castleton State College *A, B*
Champlain College *B*
Community College of Vermont *A*
Lyndon State College *B*
Norwich University *B*

Virginia

Bryant & Stratton College
    Richmond *A, B*
Dabney S. Lancaster Community
    College *A*
ECPI University *B*
Ferrum College *B*
Liberty University *B*
Longwood University *B*
Mountain Empire Community
    College *A*
Norfolk State University *M*
Radford University *B, M*
Roanoke College *B*
University of Richmond *B*
University of Virginia's College at
    Wise *B*
Virginia State University *B, M*
Virginia Wesleyan College *B*
Virginia Western Community
    College *A*

Washington

Central Washington University *B*
Columbia Basin College *C*
Gonzaga University *B*
Heritage University *B*
Saint Martin's University *B*
Seattle University *B, M*
Walla Walla Community College *A*
Yakima Valley Community College *A*

West Virginia

American Public University
    System *A, B, M*
Blue Ridge Community and Technical
    College *C, A*
Bluefield State College *B*
Fairmont State University *B, M*
Marshall University *B, M*
Potomac State College of West
    Virginia University *A*
Southern West Virginia Community
    and Technical College *C, A*
West Liberty University *B*
West Virginia State University *B*
West Virginia University at
    Parkersburg *C, A, B*
Wheeling Jesuit University *B*

Wisconsin

Carroll University *B*
Concordia University Wisconsin *A, B*
Edgewood College *B*
Herzing University
    Brookfield *B*
    Kenosha *B*
    Madison *B*
ITT Technical Institute
    Green Bay *A, B*
Mount Mary University *B*
Rasmussen College
    Appleton *A, B*
    Green Bay *A, B*
    Wausau *A, B*
University of Wisconsin
    Eau Claire *B*
    Milwaukee *B, M*
    Parkside *B*
    Superior *B*
Viterbo University *B*

Wyoming

Casper College *A*
Eastern Wyoming College *A*
Sheridan College *C, A*
University of Wyoming *B*

Criminalistics/criminal science

California

Fresno Pacific University *B*
ITT Technical Institute
    Lathrop *A*
    National City *A*
    Oxnard *A*
    Rancho Cordova *A*
    San Bernardino *A*
    Sylmar *A*
    Torrance *A*

Florida

Florida Gulf Coast University *B, M*
Saint Leo University *B*

Hawaii

Chaminade University of
    Honolulu *A, B*

Illinois

City Colleges of Chicago
    Wilbur Wright College *C*

Indiana

ITT Technical Institute
    Fort Wayne *A*
Indiana Institute of Technology *B*

Iowa

St. Ambrose University *B*

Massachusetts

Bay Path College *B*

Michigan

Ferris State University C
Lake Superior State University B
Oakland Community College C, A

Minnesota

Central Lakes College A
Century College A
ITT Technical Institute
  Eden Prairie A

New York

Niagara County Community
  College A

Ohio

University of Mount Union B

Pennsylvania

Drexel University M
Harrisburg Area Community
  College C, A
Penn State
  Erie, The Behrend College C

Puerto Rico

Inter American University of Puerto
  Rico
  Bayamon Campus B

Texas

Del Mar College C

Washington

ITT Technical Institute
  Everett A
  Seattle A
  Spokane A
Seattle University B

West Virginia

West Virginia University B

Criminology

Alabama

Auburn University B
Enterprise State Community
  College C

Arizona

Central Arizona College A
Northern Arizona University B, M
Western International University B

Arkansas

Arkansas State University B

California

California Coast University A, B
California Lutheran University B
California State University
  Bakersfield B
  Fresno B, M
Cerritos College A
Chabot College A
Fresno City College A
Holy Names University B
Institute of Technology: Clovis A
Los Angeles Pierce College A
Mount St. Mary's College B
Porterville College A
San Diego State University M
San Jose State University M
University of California
  Irvine B, M, D
University of La Verne B
West Hills College: Coalinga A

Colorado

Adams State University B
Community College of Aurora A

Regis University B
Trinidad State Junior College A
University of Denver B

Connecticut

Central Connecticut State
  University A
Mitchell College B
Quinnipiac University B
University of Bridgeport B

Delaware

Delaware State University B
University of Delaware M, D

District of Columbia

Gallaudet University B

Florida

Barry University B
Florida Southern College B
Florida State University B, M, D
University of Florida B, M, D
University of Miami B
University of South Florida B, M, D
University of South Florida
  Saint Petersburg B
  Sarasota-Manatee B
University of Tampa B

Georgia

Brewton-Parker College B
East Georgia State College A
University of West Georgia B, M

Illinois

Benedictine University at
  Springfield B
Concordia University Chicago B
Dominican University B
Elmhurst College B
Kishwaukee College A
Southern Illinois University
  Carbondale D

Indiana

Ancilla College A
Butler University B
Franklin College B
Indiana State University B, M
St. Mary-of-the-Woods College B
Valparaiso University B

Iowa

Ellsworth Community College A
North Iowa Area Community
  College A
University of Northern Iowa B
Upper Iowa University B
William Penn University B

Kansas

Benedictine College B
University of St. Mary B

Kentucky

Western Kentucky University M

Louisiana

Loyola University New Orleans B, M

Maine

Husson University B, M
University of Southern Maine B

Maryland

Mount St. Mary's University B
Notre Dame of Maryland
  University B
University of Maryland
  College Park B, M, D
  Eastern Shore M

Massachusetts

American International College B
Stonehill College B
Suffolk University M
University of Massachusetts
  Dartmouth B

Michigan

Eastern Michigan University B, M

Minnesota

Ridgewater College A
University of Minnesota
  Duluth B, M
  Twin Cities B
University of St. Thomas B

Mississippi

East Mississippi Community
  College A
Mississippi State University B

Missouri

Avila University B
Drury University B, M
Evangel University B
Lindenwood University B, M
Maryville University of Saint Louis B
Missouri State University B, M
Saint Louis University M
University of Missouri
  Kansas City B
  St. Louis B, M, D

Montana

University of Montana B, M

Nebraska

Midland University B
York College B

Nevada

University of Nevada
  Reno B, M

New Hampshire

University of New Hampshire B, M

New Jersey

Fairleigh Dickinson University
  College at Florham B
Richard Stockton College of New
  Jersey B
Salem Community College A

New Mexico

Central New Mexico Community
  College A
New Mexico Highlands University B

New York

City University of New York
  John Jay College of Criminal
  Justice B
Dominican College of Blauvelt B
Hofstra University B
Keuka College B, M
Le Moyne College B
Niagara University B
Rochester Institute of
  Technology B, M
SUNY
  College at Cortland B
  College at Old Westbury B
St. John Fisher College B
St. John's University M

North Carolina

Johnson C. Smith University B
North Carolina State University B
Wingate University B

Ohio

Capital University B
Cleveland State University B
College of Mount St. Joseph B
Defiance College A, B
John Carroll University B
Notre Dame College B
Ohio State University
  Columbus Campus B
Ohio University B
Tiffin University B, M
University of Akron B
University of Mount Union B
Walsh University B
Wright State University B
Wright State University: Lake
  Campus B

Oregon

Southern Oregon University B

Pennsylvania

Albright College B
Arcadia University B
Cabrini College B
Carlow University B
Cedar Crest College B
Indiana University of
  Pennsylvania B, M, D
Juniata College B
La Salle University B
Lebanon Valley College B
Lycoming College B
Penn State
  DuBois C
  Shenango C
Reading Area Community College A
Saint Joseph's University B, M
Slippery Rock University of
  Pennsylvania B
University of Pennsylvania M, D
University of Pittsburgh
  Greensburg B

Puerto Rico

Inter American University of Puerto
  Rico
  Ponce Campus B
Pontifical Catholic University of
  Puerto Rico B, M
Turabo University B
Universidad del Este A

South Carolina

Coker College B
University of South Carolina
  Columbia D

South Dakota

Northern State University B

Tennessee

Hiwassee College A

Texas

Howard Payne University B
North Central Texas College A
Paris Junior College A
St. Edward's University B
St. Mary's University B
South Plains College A
Texas A&M University
  Commerce M
University of Houston
  Clear Lake B
University of Texas
  Dallas B, M, D
  Permian Basin B
Wharton County Junior College A

Utah

Dixie State College B

Vermont

Castleton State College *B*

Virginia

Lynchburg College *B*
Old Dominion University *B, D*
Virginia Union University *B*

Washington

Eastern Washington University *B*

West Virginia

Alderson-Broaddus University *B*
Davis and Elkins College *A, B*
Ohio Valley University *B*

Wisconsin

Marquette University *B*

Wyoming

Western Wyoming Community
College *A*

Critical care nursing

Florida

Florida State College at
Jacksonville *B*
University of Miami *M*

Illinois

Loyola University Chicago *M*

Iowa

Allen College *M*

Kentucky

University of Louisville *M*

Massachusetts

Northeastern University *M*

Minnesota

Winona State University *M, D*

New York

New York University *M, D*
SUNY
University at Buffalo *M*
University of Rochester *M*

Ohio

Case Western Reserve University *M*

Pennsylvania

University of Pennsylvania *M*

Puerto Rico

Universidad Metropolitana *M, D*

Tennessee

Vanderbilt University *M*

Critical incident response/special police operations

Florida

Rasmussen College
Fort Myers *B*
New Port Richey *B*
Ocala *B*
Pasco/Land O'Lakes *B*
Tampa/Brandon *B*

Illinois

Rasmussen College
Aurora *B*
Mokena/Tinley Park *B*
Rockford *B*
Romeoville/Joliet *B*

Minnesota

Rasmussen College
Blaine *B*
Bloomington *B*
Brooklyn Park *B*
Eagan *B*
Lake Elmo/Woodbury *B*
Mankato *B*
Moorhead *B*
St. Cloud *B*

North Dakota

Rasmussen College
Bismarck *B*
Fargo *B*

Ohio

Tiffin University *B*

Wisconsin

Rasmussen College
Appleton *B*
Green Bay *B*
Wausau *B*

Critical infrastructure protection

Ohio

Notre Dame College *M*

Rhode Island

Roger Williams University *M*

Virginia

George Mason University *M*

Crop production

Arizona

Arizona Western College *A*

California

Bakersfield College *C, A*
San Joaquin Delta College *C*

Illinois

Black Hawk College *A*
College of Lake County *C, A*
John Wood Community College *C*

Indiana

Purdue University *B*

Iowa

Des Moines Area Community
College *C*
Iowa State University *M, D*
Northeast Iowa Community
College *C, A*

Massachusetts

University of Massachusetts
Amherst *A*

Michigan

Northwestern Michigan College *A*

Minnesota

University of Minnesota
Crookston *B*
Twin Cities *B*

North Carolina

North Carolina State University *A*

North Dakota

North Dakota State University *B*

Ohio

Ohio State University
Agricultural Technical Institute *A*
Columbus Campus *A*

Oregon

Blue Mountain Community College *A*
Chemeketa Community College *C*
Clackamas Community College *C*

Pennsylvania

Delaware Valley College *B*

Washington

Washington State University *B*
Wenatchee Valley College *C*

Wisconsin

University of Wisconsin
River Falls *B*

Wyoming

Northwest College *A*

Culinary arts and chef training

Alabama

Lurleen B. Wallace Community
College *C*
Shelton State Community
College *C, A*
Virginia College
Birmingham *C*
Wallace State Community College at
Hanceville *A*

Alaska

University of Alaska
Anchorage *A*
Fairbanks *C, A*

Arizona

Art Institute of Phoenix *A, B*
Cochise College *A*
Estrella Mountain Community
College *C, A*
Mohave Community College *C, A*
Phoenix College *A*

Arkansas

Pulaski Technical College *C, A*

California

Allan Hancock College *C, A*
Art Institute of California
Hollywood *A, B*
Inland Empire *A*
Los Angeles *A, B*
Orange County *A*
San Diego *A*
San Francisco *A, B*
Silicon Valley *A*
City College of San Francisco *A*
College of the Desert *C*
Diablo Valley College *C*
Lake Tahoe Community College *C*
Le Cordon Bleu College of Culinary
Arts
Los Angeles *C, A*
Los Angeles Harbor College *C*
Santa Rosa Junior College *C*
Shasta College *C, A*

Colorado

Colorado Mountain College *A*
Johnson & Wales University
Denver *A, B*
Red Rocks Community College *C, A*
Westwood College
Denver North *A*

Connecticut

Gateway Community College *A*

Delaware

Delaware Technical Community
College
Stanton/Wilmington Campus *A*
Terry Campus *A*

Florida

Art Institute of Fort Lauderdale *C, A*
College of Central Florida *A*
Hillsborough Community College *C*
Johnson & Wales University
North Miami *A, B*
Le Cordon Bleu College of Culinary
Arts
Miami *C, A*
Orlando *C, A*
Lincoln College of Technology
West Palm Beach *C, A*
Miami International University of Art
and Design *C, A*
Pensacola State College *C*
South Florida State College *C*
Valencia College *C*

Georgia

Albany Technical College *C, A*
Art Institute of Atlanta *A, B*
Athens Technical College *C*
Atlanta Technical College *C, A*
Gwinnett Technical College *A*
North Georgia Technical
College *C, A*
Savannah Technical College *C, A*

Idaho

College of Western Idaho *C, A*
Idaho State University *C, A, B*

Illinois

City Colleges of Chicago
Kennedy-King College *C, A*
College of DuPage *C, A*
College of Lake County *C*
Danville Area Community College *C*
Elgin Community College *C, A*
Harper College *C*
Illinois Central College *C, A*
Illinois Institute of Art
Chicago *C*
John Wood Community College *C*
Kaskaskia College *C, A*
Kendall College *A, B*
Lexington College *A, B*
McHenry County College *C, A*
Rend Lake College *C, A*
Robert Morris University: Chicago *A*
St. Augustine College *C, A*
Triton College *C, A*

Indiana

Vincennes University *C, A*

Iowa

Des Moines Area Community
College *C, A*
Kirkwood Community College *C, A*

Kansas

Johnson County Community
College *A*

Kentucky

Elizabethtown Community and
Technical College *C*
Jefferson Community and Technical
College *C, A*
Maysville Community and Technical
College *C*
Sullivan University *C, A*

Louisiana

Bossier Parish Community College *C*
Delgado Community College *C, A*
Nicholls State University *A, B*
Nunez Community College *C, A*

Maine

Southern Maine Community
College *A*
York County Community
College *C, A*

Maryland

Allegany College of Maryland *A*
Anne Arundel Community
College *C, A*
Chesapeake College *C*

Massachusetts

Berkshire Community College *C*
Bunker Hill Community College *C*
Holyoke Community College *C*
Massasoit Community College *A*
Newbury College *A, B*
North Shore Community
College *C, A*

Michigan

Art Institute of Michigan *C, A*
Baker College
Muskegon *A*
Grand Rapids Community College *A*
Henry Ford Community College *C, A*
Mott Community College *A*
Northwestern Michigan College *A*
Oakland Community College *A*
Schoolcraft College *C, A*

Minnesota

Art Institutes International
Minnesota *C, A*
Hennepin Technical College *C, A*
Minneapolis Community and
Technical College *C, A*
St. Cloud Technical and Community
College *C*
St. Paul College *C, A*
South Central College *C, A*

Mississippi

East Central Community College *A*

Missouri

College of the Ozarks *B*
East Central College *C, A*
Jefferson College *C, A*
Ozarks Technical Community
College *A*

Montana

Flathead Valley Community
College *A*

Nebraska

Northeast Community College *A*

Nevada

Art Institute of Las Vegas *A*
College of Southern Nevada *C, A*

New Hampshire

Southern New Hampshire
University *C, A, B*
White Mountains Community
College *C, A*

New Jersey

Atlantic Cape Community College *A*
Bergen Community College *C, A*
Brookdale Community College *C, A*
Burlington County College *C, A*
Hudson County Community
College *A*

New Mexico

Central New Mexico Community
College *C, A*
Eastern New Mexico University:
Roswell *C*
Luna Community College *C*
Santa Fe Community College *C, A*

New York

Culinary Institute of America *A*
Erie Community College *A*
Mohawk Valley Community
College *C*
Niagara County Community
College *C, A*
Paul Smith's College *A, B*
SUNY
College of Agriculture and
Technology at Cobleskill *A, B*
College of Technology at Delhi *A*
Schenectady County Community
College *C*
Suffolk County Community
College *C, A*
Sullivan County Community
College *A*
Tompkins Cortland Community
College *A*

North Carolina

Central Carolina Community
College *A*
Central Piedmont Community
College *C, A*
Chef's Academy *A*
Fayetteville Technical Community
College *C, A*
Johnson & Wales University
Charlotte *A, B*
Lenoir Community College *C, A*
Montgomery Community College *C*
Wilkes Community College *C, A*
Wilson Community College *A*

North Dakota

North Dakota State College of
Science *C, A*

Ohio

Art Institute of Ohio:
Cincinnati *C, A, B*
Central Ohio Technical College *C, A*
Cincinnati State Technical and
Community College *C, A*
Columbus State Community
College *A*
Hocking College *C, A*
Lorain County Community
College *C, A*
Sinclair Community College *A*
University of Akron *C, A*

Oregon

Central Oregon Community
College *A*
Le Cordon Bleu College of Culinary
Arts
Portland *C, A*
Linn-Benton Community College *A*
Pioneer Pacific College *C, A*
Tillamook Bay Community College *A*
Umpqua Community College *C*

Pennsylvania

Art Institute of Philadelphia *C, A*
Art Institute of Pittsburgh *C, A*
Bidwell Training Center *C*
Bucks County Community
College *C, A*
Commonwealth Technical Institute *A*
Community College of Allegheny
County *C, A*
Community College of Beaver
County *C, A*

Community College of
Philadelphia *A*
Delaware Valley College *C, A*
Drexel University *B*
Harrisburg Area Community
College *C, A*
Indiana University of Pennsylvania *C*
Keystone College *A*
Keystone Technical Institute *A*
Montgomery County Community
College *A*
Northampton Community
College *C, A*
Pennsylvania College of
Technology *A*
Restaurant School at Walnut Hill
College *A, B*
Westmoreland County Community
College *C, A*
Yorktowne Business Institute *A*

Puerto Rico

Universidad del Este *C, A*

Rhode Island

Johnson & Wales University
Providence *A, B*

South Carolina

Bob Jones University *A*
Greenville Technical College *A*
Horry-Georgetown Technical
College *A*
Spartanburg Community College *C*
Technical College of the
Lowcountry *C*
Trident Technical College *C, A*

South Dakota

Mitchell Technical Institute *A*

Tennessee

Virginia College
School of Business and Health in
Chattanooga *C*
Walters State Community
College *C, A*

Texas

Alvin Community College *C, A*
Austin Community College *C, A*
Central Texas College *C, A*
Collin County Community College
District *C, A*
Culinary Institute LeNotre *C, A*
Del Mar College *C, A*
El Centro College *C, A*
Houston Community College
System *C, A*
Howard College *C*
Le Cordon Bleu College of Culinary
Arts
Austin *C, A*
Northeast Texas Community
College *C, A*
Odessa College *C, A*
Remington College
Dallas *A*
St. Philip's College *C, A*
San Jacinto College *C, A*
Tarrant County College *C, A*
Texas State Technical College
Waco *C, A*
West Texas *C, A*

Utah

Salt Lake Community College *A*
Utah Valley University *A*

Vermont

New England Culinary
Institute *C, A, B*

Virginia

Art Institute of Washington *A, B*
ECPI University *C, A*
Stratford University: Falls Church *A*

Washington

Art Institute of Seattle *A*
Bates Technical College *C, A*
Bellingham Technical College *C, A*
Clark College *C, A*
Clover Park Technical College *C, A*
Edmonds Community College *C, A*
Lake Washington Institute of
Technology *C*
Olympic College *C, A*
Renton Technical College *C, A*
Seattle Central Community
College *C, A*
South Seattle Community
College *C, A*
Walla Walla Community College *C, A*

West Virginia

Blue Ridge Community and Technical
College *C*
Bridgemont Community and
Technical College *C*
West Virginia Northern Community
College *A*

Wisconsin

Fox Valley Technical College *A*
Milwaukee Area Technical College *C*
Southwest Wisconsin Technical
College *C, A*

Wyoming

Central Wyoming College *C, A*
Sheridan College *C, A*

Culinary arts/related services

Alabama

Bishop State Community
College *C, A*
Faulkner State Community
College *C, A*
Virginia College
Birmingham *A*

Arizona

Art Institute of Phoenix *A, B*
Art Institute of Tucson *A, B*
Central Arizona College *C*
Estrella Mountain Community
College *C, A*
Le Cordon Bleu College of Culinary
Arts
Scottsdale *C, A, B*
Scottsdale Community College *C, A*

Arkansas

Ozarka College *C, A*
Rich Mountain Community College *C*

California

American River College *C, A*
Art Institute of California
Los Angeles *C, A*
Orange County *C, A, B*
Silicon Valley *C*
Bakersfield College *C, A*
Chaffey College *C*
City College of San Francisco *C*
College of the Canyons *C*
Columbia College *A*
Cypress College *C, A*
Diablo Valley College *C*
Glendale Community College *C, A*
Grossmont College *C, A*
Institute of Technology: Clovis *A*
Lake Tahoe Community College *C, A*

Laney College *C, A*
Le Cordon Bleu College of Culinary Arts
  San Francisco *A*
Long Beach City College *C, A*
Los Angeles Mission College *C, A*
Los Angeles Trade and Technical College *C, A*
Modesto Junior College *C, A*
Orange Coast College *C, A*
Oxnard College *C, A*
Saddleback College *C*
San Diego Mesa College *C, A*
San Joaquin Delta College *C, A*
Santa Barbara City College *C*
Santa Rosa Junior College *C*
Shasta College *C, A*
Yuba College *C, A*

Colorado

Colorado Mesa University *C, A*
Colorado Mountain College *A*
Johnson & Wales University
  Denver *A, B*
Pikes Peak Community College *C, A*
Pueblo Community College *C, A*

Connecticut

Lincoln College of New England *C, A*
Manchester Community College *C*
Naugatuck Valley Community College *C, A*
Norwalk Community College *C*

District of Columbia

University of the District of Columbia *A*

Florida

Chipola College *A*
Eastern Florida State College *C*
Florida State College at Jacksonville *A*
Indian River State College *C*
Johnson & Wales University
  North Miami *A, B*
Palm Beach State College *C*

Georgia

Altamaha Technical College *C, A*
Art Institute of Atlanta *C, A, B*
Chattahoochee Technical College *C, A*
West Georgia Technical College *C*

Hawaii

University of Hawaii
  Kapiolani Community College *A*
  Kauai Community College *C, A*
  Leeward Community College *C, A*

Idaho

College of Southern Idaho *C, A*
North Idaho College *C*

Illinois

College of DuPage *C, A*
Joliet Junior College *C, A*
Southwestern Illinois College *C, A*

Indiana

Harrison College
  Indianapolis *A*

Iowa

Iowa Central Community College *A*
Iowa Western Community College *A*

Kentucky

West Kentucky Community and Technical College *A*

Maine

Central Maine Community College *C*
Eastern Maine Community College *C, A*
Washington County Community College *C*

Maryland

Anne Arundel Community College *C, A*
Baltimore City Community College *C*
Frederick Community College *C, A*
Howard Community College *C, A*

Massachusetts

Cape Cod Community College *C*
Middlesex Community College *C, A*
Newbury College *C, A, B*

Michigan

Baker College
  Muskegon *A, B*
Macomb Community College *C, A*
Monroe County Community College *C, A*
Northwestern Michigan College *A*
Washtenaw Community College *C, A*

Minnesota

Art Institutes International Minnesota *C, A*
Hennepin Technical College *C, A*
Hibbing Community College *C*
Minnesota State Community and Technical College *C*

Mississippi

East Mississippi Community College *C*
Hinds Community College *C, A*
Mississippi University for Women *B*
Northeast Mississippi Community College *C, A*

Missouri

Jefferson College *C, A*
St. Louis Community College *A*

Montana

University of Montana *C, A*

Nebraska

Metropolitan Community College *C, A*

Nevada

University of Nevada
  Las Vegas *B*

New Hampshire

Lakes Region Community College *C, A*

New Jersey

Hudson County Community College *C, A*
Mercer County Community College *C, A*
Middlesex County College *C*

New Mexico

Central New Mexico Community College *C*
Dona Ana Community College of New Mexico State University *C*
Navajo Technical University *C, A*

New York

Adirondack Community College *C, A*
Culinary Institute of America *C*
Paul Smith's College *C, A, B*
Rockland Community College *C*

SUNY
  College of Technology at Alfred *A*
  College of Technology at Delhi *A*
Schenectady County Community College *C*
Suffolk County Community College *C, A*
Sullivan County Community College *A*
Westchester Community College *A*

North Carolina

Alamance Community College *C, A*
Cape Fear Community College *C, A*
College of the Albemarle *C*
Nash Community College *A*
Piedmont Community College *C*
Robeson Community College *A*
Sandhills Community College *A*
Southwestern Community College *A*
Vance-Granville Community College *A*
Wake Technical Community College *C, A*

Ohio

Bradford School *C, A*
Cuyahoga Community College Metropolitan *A*
Zane State College *A*

Oregon

Central Oregon Community College *C*
Southwestern Oregon Community College *A*

Pennsylvania

Butler County Community College *C*
JNA Institute of Culinary Arts *A*
Reading Area Community College *A*

Rhode Island

Community College of Rhode Island *C*
Johnson & Wales University
  Providence *A, B*

South Carolina

Denmark Technical College *C*
Trident Technical College *C, A*

Tennessee

Nashville State Community College *A*

Texas

Art Institute of Dallas *C*
Central Texas College *C, A*
El Paso Community College *C, A*
Galveston College *C, A*
Kilgore College *C, A*
Odessa College *C*
Trinity Valley Community College *C*

Vermont

New England Culinary Institute *C, A, B*

Virginia

Art Institute of Washington *A, B*
J. Sargeant Reynolds Community College *A*
Northern Virginia Community College *C*
Rappahannock Community College *C*
Stratford University, Falls Church *A*
Tidewater Community College *C, A*
Virginia Western Community College *C, A*

Washington

Lake Washington Institute of Technology *C, A*

Seattle Central Community College *C, A*
Skagit Valley College *C, A*
South Puget Sound Community College *C, A*
Spokane Community College *A*

West Virginia

University of Charleston *A, B*

Wisconsin

Blackhawk Technical College *A*
Madison Area Technical College *C, A*
Moraine Park Technical College *C, A*
Nicolet Area Technical College *C, A*
Southwest Wisconsin Technical College *C, A*

Culinary science/culinology

Connecticut

Naugatuck Valley Community College *C, A*

Georgia

Columbus Technical College *C*

Mississippi

Mississippi State University *B*

New York

Culinary Institute of America *A*

Pennsylvania

Drexel University *B*

South Carolina

Horry-Georgetown Technical College *C*

Washington

Bastyr University *B*

Cultural anthropology

Iowa

Ashford University *B*

Maine

College of the Atlantic *B, M*

Missouri

Webster University *B*

Pennsylvania

Arcadia University *B*

Vermont

Goddard College *B, M*

Cultural resource management

California

California State University
  Dominguez Hills *B*

Georgia

University of Georgia *M*

Kentucky

Western Kentucky University *C*

Michigan

Eastern Michigan University *M*

Nevada

Great Basin College *B*

Pennsylvania

Carnegie Mellon University *B, D*

Utah

Utah State University *A*

Cultural studies

Arizona

Northern Arizona University *B*

California

University of California
Irvine *D*

Florida

University of Tampa *B*

Kentucky

Western Kentucky University *B*

Maine

College of the Atlantic *B, M*

Maryland

Maryland Institute College of Art *M*

Massachusetts

Bard College at Simon's Rock *B*
Hampshire College *B*

Rhode Island

Bryant University *B*

Texas

Howard Payne University *B*

West Virginia

American Public University System *B*

Curriculum/instruction

Alabama

Auburn University *D*

Arizona

Argosy University
Online *M, D*
Phoenix *M, D*
Arizona State University *M, D*
Grand Canyon University *M*
Northcentral University *M, D*
Northern Arizona University *D*
University of Phoenix
Phoenix-Hohokam *M*
Southern Arizona *M*

Arkansas

Arkansas State University *M, T*
Henderson State University *M*
University of Arkansas *M, D*

California

Argosy University
Inland Empire *M, D*
Los Angeles *M, D*
Orange County *M, D*
San Diego *M, D*
San Francisco Bay Area *M, D*
Azusa Pacific University *M*
California Coast University *M*
California Lutheran University *M*
California State University
Dominguez Hills *M*
East Bay *M*
Fresno *M*
Northridge *M*
Sacramento *M*
San Bernardino *M*
Chapman University *D*
Concordia University Irvine *M*
Dominican University of California *M*

Fresno Pacific University *M*
Holy Names University *M*
La Sierra University *M, D*
Mills College *M*
St. Mary's College of California *M*
San Diego State University *M*
Sonoma State University *M*
Stanford University *M, D*
University of California
San Diego *M*
University of Redlands *M*
University of San Diego *M*
University of San Francisco *M, D*
University of the Pacific *M, D*

Colorado

Argosy University
Denver *M, D*
Colorado Christian University *M*
Regis University *M*
University of Colorado
Boulder *M, D*
Colorado Springs *M*
Denver *M*
University of Denver *M, D*

Connecticut

University of Connecticut *M, D, T*
Western Connecticut State
University *M*

Delaware

Delaware State University *M*
University of Delaware *M, D*
Wesley College *M*
Wilmington University *M*

District of Columbia

American University *M*
George Washington University *M, D*
Howard University *M*

Florida

Argosy University
Tampa *M, D*
Barry University *M, D*
Florida Atlantic University *M, D, T*
Florida Gulf Coast University *M*
Florida International University *M, D*
University of Florida *M, D*
University of Phoenix
Central Florida *M*
North Florida *M*
South Florida *M*
West Florida *M*
University of South Florida *M, D*
University of Tampa *M*
University of West Florida *M, D, T*
Warner University *M*

Georgia

Berry College *M*
Covenant College *M*
Georgia College and State
University *M, T*
Georgia Regents University *M*
Georgia Southern University *M, D*
LaGrange College *M*
Mercer University *D*
Piedmont College *D, T*
Valdosta State University *M, D*

Hawaii

University of Hawaii
Manoa *M*

Idaho

Boise State University *M, D*
Northwest Nazarene University *M*
University of Idaho *M*

Illinois

Aurora University *M, D*
Benedictine University *M*

Bradley University *M*
Chicago State University *M, T*
Concordia University Chicago *M, D*
DePaul University *M, D*
Dominican University *M*
Governors State University *M*
Illinois State University *M, D*
Lewis University *M*
Loyola University Chicago *M, D*
National-Louis University *M*
North Central College *M*
Northeastern Illinois University *M*
Northern Illinois University *M, D*
Olivet Nazarene University *M*
Rockford University *M*
Saint Xavier University *M*
Southern Illinois University
Carbondale *M, D*
University of Illinois
Chicago *D*
Urbana-Champaign *M, D*
University of St. Francis *M*

Indiana

Anderson University *M*
Ball State University *M, D, T*
Huntington University *M*
Indiana State University *M, D, T*
Indiana University
Bloomington *D*
Indiana Wesleyan University *M*
Purdue University *M, D*
University of Indianapolis *M*

Iowa

Buena Vista University *M*
Dordt College *M*
Drake University *B*
Iowa State University *M, D*
University of Iowa *M, D*
University of Northern Iowa *D*
Upper Iowa University *M*

Kansas

Emporia State University *M*
Kansas State University *D*
Newman University *M*
Southwestern College *M*
University of Kansas *M, D*
University of St. Mary *M*
Washburn University *M, T*
Wichita State University *M*

Kentucky

Brescia University *M*
Campbellsville University *M*
Georgetown College *M*
Morehead State University *M*
Spalding University *M*
Thomas More College *M*
University of Kentucky *M*
University of Louisville *D*
University of the Cumberlands *M*

Louisiana

Grambling State University *M, D*
Louisiana State University
Shreveport *M*
Louisiana State University and
Agricultural and Mechanical
College *M, D*
Louisiana Tech University *M, D*
McNeese State University *M*
Nicholls State University *M*
Northwestern State University *M*
Southeastern Louisiana University *M*
University of Louisiana at Lafayette *M*
University of Louisiana at
Monroe *M, D*
University of New Orleans *M, D*
Xavier University of Louisiana *M*

Maine

University of Maine *M*
University of New England *M*
University of Southern Maine *M*

Maryland

Coppin State University *M*
Frostburg State University *M*
Hood College *M*
Loyola University Maryland *M*
McDaniel College *M*
University of Maryland
College Park *M, D*

Massachusetts

Boston College *M, D*
Boston University *M, D*
Cambridge College *T*
Curry College *M*
Eastern Nazarene College *M, T*
Fitchburg State University *M*
Framingham State University *M*
Gordon College *M*
Harvard College *M, D*
Lesley University *M*
Tufts University *M*
University of Massachusetts
Lowell *M*
Western New England University *M*

Michigan

Andrews University *M, D*
Calvin College *M, T*
Concordia University *M*
Eastern Michigan University *M*
Ferris State University *M*
Madonna University *M*
Michigan State University *M, D*
Oakland University *M*
University of Detroit Mercy *M*
University of Michigan
Flint *M*
Wayne State University *D*

Minnesota

Argosy University
Twin Cities *M, D*
Bemidji State University *M*
Capella University *M, D*
College of St. Scholastica *M*
Concordia University St. Paul *M*
Minnesota State University
Mankato *B, M, T*
Moorhead *M*
Saint Cloud State University *M*
St. Mary's University of Minnesota *M*
University of Minnesota
Twin Cities *M, D*
University of St. Thomas *M, D*
Walden University *B, M*

Mississippi

Mississippi State University *D*
Mississippi University for Women *M*
University of Mississippi *M*
University of Southern Mississippi *M*

Missouri

Columbia College *M*
Maryville University of Saint
Louis *M, T*
Missouri Baptist University *M*
Northwest Missouri State
University *B*
University of Central Missouri *M*
University of Missouri
Columbia *M, D*
Kansas City *M*
St. Louis *M*
William Woods University *M*

Montana

Montana State University
Billings *B, M*

University of Great Falls *M*
University of Montana *M, D*

Nebraska

Bellevue University *M*
Concordia University *M*
Creighton University *M*
Doane College *M*
Grace University *M*
University of Nebraska
  Kearney *M*
  Lincoln *M*
Wayne State College *M*

Nevada

University of Nevada
  Las Vegas *M, D, T*
University of Phoenix
  Las Vegas *M*
  Northern Nevada *M*

New Hampshire

Franklin Pierce University *M, T*
Keene State College *M*
Rivier University *M*
Southern New Hampshire
  University *M*

New Jersey

Caldwell College *M*
Rider University *M*
Seton Hall University *M*

New Mexico

New Mexico Highlands University *M*
New Mexico State University *D*
University of New Mexico *D, T*
University of the Southwest *M*

New York

College of Saint Rose *M*
Fordham University *M, D*
Jewish Theological Seminary of
  America *M, D*
New York University *D*
SUNY
  College at Fredonia *M*
  College at Potsdam *M*
  University at Albany *M, D*
  University at Buffalo *D*
St. John's University *D*
Syracuse University *M, D*
University of Rochester *M, D*

North Carolina

Appalachian State University *M*
Campbell University *M*
Elon University *B, T*
North Carolina Central University *M*
North Carolina State University *M, D*
Shaw University *M*
University of North Carolina
  Chapel Hill *D*
  Charlotte *M, D*
  Greensboro *M, D*
  Wilmington *M*

North Dakota

University of Jamestown *M*

Ohio

Ashland University *M*
Baldwin Wallace University *M*
Bowling Green State University *M*
Cleveland State University *M*
Franklin University *M*
John Carroll University *M*
Kent State University *M, D*
Kent State University
  Stark *M*
Lake Erie College *B, M*
Malone University *M*
Mount Vernon Nazarene
  University *M*

Ohio Dominican University *M*
Ohio University *M, D*
Otterbein University *M*
Shawnee State University *M*
University of Cincinnati *M, D*
University of Findlay *B, M*
University of Toledo *M, D*
Urbana University *M*
Ursuline College *M*
Wright State University *M, T*
Youngstown State University *M*

Oklahoma

Northeastern State University *M*
Oklahoma City University *M*
Oklahoma State University *M*
Oral Roberts University *M*
Southern Nazarene University *M*
University of Central Oklahoma *B*

Oregon

Concordia University *M*
George Fox University *M*
Portland State University *M, D*

Pennsylvania

Bloomsburg University of
  Pennsylvania *M*
Bucknell University *M*
Gannon University *M*
King's College *M*
Penn State
  Harrisburg *M*
  University Park *M, D*
  York *M*
Point Park University *M*
Robert Morris University *M, D, T*
St. Vincent College *M*
Shippensburg University of
  Pennsylvania *M, T*
University of Pennsylvania *M, D*
University of Scranton *M*
Westminster College *M*
Widener University *D*

Puerto Rico

Caribbean University *M*
Inter American University of Puerto
  Rico
  Barranquitas Campus *M*
  Metropolitan Campus *D*
  San German Campus *D*
Pontifical Catholic University of
  Puerto Rico *M, D*
Turabo University *M*
Universidad Adventista de las
  Antillas *M*
Universidad Metropolitana *M*
Universidad del Este *M*
University of Puerto Rico
  Rio Piedras *M, D*

South Carolina

Clemson University *D*
Columbia International University *M*
North Greenville University *M, T*
University of South Carolina
  Columbia *D*
Winthrop University *T*

South Dakota

Black Hills State University *M*
Dakota Wesleyan University *M*
Mount Marty College *M*
South Dakota State University *M*
University of South Dakota *M, D, T*

Tennessee

Argosy University
  Nashville *M*
Austin Peay State University *M*
Carson-Newman University *M*
Freed-Hardeman University *B, M, T*
Lincoln Memorial University *M*

Lipscomb University *M, T*
Middle Tennessee State
  University *M, T*
Southern Adventist University *M*
Tennessee State University *M, D*
Tennessee Technological
  University *M*
Tennessee Temple University *M*
Tennessee Wesleyan College *M*
Trevecca Nazarene University *M*
Union University *D*
University of Memphis *M, D*
Vanderbilt University *M*

Texas

Angelo State University *M*
Argosy University
  Dallas *M*
Arlington Baptist College *M*
Baylor University *M, D*
Dallas Baptist University *M*
Houston Baptist University *M*
Midwestern State University *M*
Our Lady of the Lake University of
  San Antonio *M*
Prairie View A&M University *M*
St. Mary's University *B, M*
Sam Houston State University *M*
Southwestern Assemblies of God
  University *M*
Texas A&M University *M, D*
Texas A&M University
  Commerce *M*
  Corpus Christi *M, D, T*
  Texarkana *M*
Texas Christian University *M, D*
Texas Southern University *M, D*
Texas Tech University *M, D*
Texas Wesleyan University *D*
University of Houston *M, D*
University of Houston
  Clear Lake *M, T*
  Downtown *M*
University of Mary Hardin-Baylor *M*
University of North Texas *M, D*
University of St. Thomas *M*
University of Texas
  Arlington *M, T*
  Austin *M, D*
  Brownsville *M, D*
  El Paso *M, D*
  San Antonio *M*
  Tyler *M*
Wayland Baptist University *M*
West Texas A&M University *M*

Utah

Brigham Young University *D*
Utah State University *D*
Utah Valley University *M*
Western Governors University *M*

Vermont

Castleton State College *M, T*
Goddard College *B, M*
Johnson State College *M*
Lyndon State College *M*
Saint Michael's College *M, T*
Sterling College *B*
University of Vermont *M, T*

Virginia

Averett University *M*
College of William and Mary *D*
Eastern Mennonite University *M*
George Mason University *M*
Longwood University *T*
Lynchburg College *M*
Sweet Briar College *M*
University of Virginia *M, D*
Virginia Commonwealth
  University *M*

Virginia Polytechnic Institute and
  State University *M, D*
Virginia State University *M*

Washington

City University of Seattle *M*
Eastern Washington University *M*
Gonzaga University *M*
Seattle Pacific University *M*
Seattle University *M*
University of Puget Sound *M*
University of Washington *D*
Walla Walla University *M*
Washington State University *M, D*
Western Washington University *M*

West Virginia

Ohio Valley University *M*
Shepherd University *M*
West Virginia University *D*

Wisconsin

Alverno College *M*
Carroll University *M*
Concordia University Wisconsin *M*
Marian University *D*
University of Wisconsin
  Madison *M, D*
  Milwaukee *M*
  Whitewater *M*

Wyoming

University of Wyoming *D*

Customer service management

Arizona

Pima Community College *C*

California

Santa Rosa Junior College *C*

Colorado

Community College of Aurora *M*

Connecticut

Goodwin College *C*

Delaware

Delaware Technical Community
  College
  Stanton/Wilmington Campus *C, A*

Illinois

Illinois Valley Community College *C*
Saint Xavier University *M*

Iowa

Ashford University *B*

Michigan

Henry Ford Community College *C*

Minnesota

Art Institutes International
  Minnesota *B*
Inver Hills Community College *C*
Northland Community & Technical
  College *C*
Rochester Community and Technical
  College *C*

Missouri

Drury University *B*
Metropolitan Community College -
  Kansas City *C*
Southwest Baptist University *B*

Nebraska

Bellevue University *B*

New York

Bryant & Stratton College
    Rochester *A*
Genesee Community College *A*
Globe Institute of
    Technology *C, A, B*
Professional Business College *C*
Trocaire College *C*

North Carolina

Catawba Valley Community
    College *A*
Randolph Community College *A*

Ohio

Ohio University *B*

Oregon

Central Oregon Community
    College *A*

Pennsylvania

Drexel University *B*
Penn State
    Abington *C*
    Altoona *C*
    Beaver *C*
    Berks *C*
    Brandywine *C*
    DuBois *C*
    Erie, The Behrend College *C*
    Fayette, The Eberly Campus *C*
    Greater Allegheny *C*
    Harrisburg *C*
    Hazleton *C*
    Lehigh Valley *C*
    Mont Alto *C*
    New Kensington *C*
    Schuylkill *C*
    University Park *C*
    Wilkes-Barre *C*
    Worthington Scranton *C*
    York *C*

Rhode Island

Community College of Rhode
    Island *C, A*

South Carolina

York Technical College *C*

Washington

Bellingham Technical College *C*
North Seattle Community College *C*

Customer service support

Arizona

Paradise Valley Community
    College *C, A*
South Mountain Community
    College *C, A*

California

East Los Angeles College *C*
Santa Rosa Junior College *C*

Colorado

Colorado Technical University *A*

Connecticut

Three Rivers Community College *C*

Delaware

Delaware Technical Community
    College
    Jack F. Owens Campus *A*
    Stanton/Wilmington Campus *A*

Florida

College of Central Florida *C*
Everest University
    Largo *C*

Georgia

Albany Technical College *C*
Atlanta Technical College *C*
Central Georgia Technical College *C*
Columbus Technical College *C*
Georgia Piedmont Technical
    College *C*
Southwest Georgia Technical
    College *C*

Kansas

Cowley County Community
    College *C, A*

Maine

University of Maine
    Augusta *C*

Massachusetts

Bristol Community College *C*

Michigan

Glen Oaks Community College *C*
Lake Michigan College *C*
Lansing Community College *A*

Minnesota

Rasmussen College
    Blaine *A*
    Moorhead *A*

Missouri

Metropolitan Community College -
    Kansas City *A*

New Jersey

Union County College *A*

New York

Globe Institute of Technology *C*
Westchester Community College *C*

North Carolina

Isothermal Community College *C, A*

Ohio

Lorain County Community College *C*

Rhode Island

Community College of Rhode
    Island *C*

South Carolina

York Technical College *C*

Texas

Brookhaven College *C*
Northwest Vista College *C*
Palo Alto College *C*

Washington

Olympic College *C*

West Virginia

New River Community and Technical
    College *C*

Wyoming

Central Wyoming College *A*
Laramie County Community
    College *C*

Cytogenetics/clinical genetics technology

Alabama

Calhoun Community College *A*

Michigan

Northern Michigan University *B*

Cytotechnology

Alabama

Oakwood University *B*
University of Alabama
    Birmingham *B*

Arkansas

University of Arkansas
    for Medical Sciences *B*

California

La Sierra University *C*
Loma Linda University *C, B*

Connecticut

University of Connecticut *B*

District of Columbia

George Washington University *B*

Florida

Barry University *B*

Indiana

Indiana University
    Purdue University Indianapolis *B*

Kansas

University of Kansas Medical
    Center *B*

Massachusetts

Massachusetts College of Liberal
    Arts *B*

Michigan

Oakland University *B*

Minnesota

Minnesota State University
    Mankato *B, M*
St. Mary's University of Minnesota *B*
Winona State University *B*

Mississippi

University of Mississippi Medical
    Center *B*

Missouri

Saint Louis University *B*

New Jersey

Felician College *B*
Saint Peter's University *B*

New York

Albany College of Pharmacy and
    Health Sciences *M*
Long Island University
    LIU Brooklyn *B*
SUNY
    College at Plattsburgh *B*

North Carolina

Central Piedmont Community
    College *A*

North Dakota

University of North Dakota *B*

Pennsylvania

Slippery Rock University of
    Pennsylvania *B*
Thiel College *B*
Thomas Jefferson University *B, M*

Tennessee

University of Tennessee
    Knoxville *M*

Texas

University of North Texas *B*

West Virginia

Marshall University *B*

Wisconsin

Edgewood College *B*
Marian University *B*

Dairy husbandry

Iowa

Northeast Iowa Community
    College *C, A*

Michigan

Michigan State University *C*

New York

SUNY
    College of Agriculture and
        Technology at Cobleskill *A*
    College of Agriculture and
        Technology at Morrisville *A, B*

Vermont

Vermont Technical College *A, B*

Wisconsin

Fox Valley Technical College *C*
Lakeshore Technical College *C*
University of Wisconsin
    River Falls *B*
Wisconsin Indianhead Technical
    College *C*

Dairy science

California

California Polytechnic State
    University: San Luis Obispo *B*
College of the Sequoias *C*
Modesto Junior College *A*

Georgia

University of Georgia *B, M*

Indiana

Purdue University *B*

Iowa

Iowa State University *B*

Michigan

Michigan State University *C*

Minnesota

Ridgewater College *C, A*
University of Minnesota
    Twin Cities *M, D*

Mississippi

Northwest Mississippi Community
    College *A*

Nebraska

Northeast Community College *C*

New Hampshire

University of New Hampshire *B*

New Mexico

Eastern New Mexico University *B*

New York

SUNY
College of Agriculture and
Technology at Morrisville *A, B*
College of Technology at Alfred *A*

Ohio

Ohio State University
Agricultural Technical Institute *A*
Columbus Campus *C, A*

Pennsylvania

Delaware Valley College *B*

South Carolina

Clemson University *M*

South Dakota

South Dakota State University *B*

Vermont

Vermont Technical College *A*

Virginia

Virginia Polytechnic Institute and
State University *B, M*

Washington

Skagit Valley College *A*

Wisconsin

Northcentral Technical College *C, A*
Southwest Wisconsin Technical
College *C*
University of Wisconsin
Madison *B, M, D*
River Falls *B*

Dance

Alabama

Birmingham-Southern College *B*
Troy University *B*
University of Alabama *B*

Alaska

University of Alaska
Anchorage *B*

Arizona

Arizona State University *B, M*
Scottsdale Community College *A*
University of Arizona *B, M*

Arkansas

University of Arkansas
Little Rock *B*

California

Allan Hancock College *C, A*
Cabrillo College *A*
California Institute of the
Arts *C, B, M*
California State University
East Bay *B*
Fullerton *B*
Long Beach *B, M*
Northridge *B*
Canada College *A*
Chabot College *A*
Chaffey College *A*
Chapman University *B*
Citrus College *A*
City College of San Francisco *C*
Claremont McKenna College *B*
College of Marin *A*
College of San Mateo *A*
College of the Desert *A*
Cypress College *A*
Dominican University of California *B*
El Camino College *A*
Fresno City College *C, A*

Fullerton College *A*
Glendale Community College *C, A*
Golden West College *A*
Grossmont College *C, A*
Humboldt State University *B*
Irvine Valley College *A*
Lake Tahoe Community College *A*
Laney College *A*
Long Beach City College *A*
Loyola Marymount University *B*
Mills College *B, M*
MiraCosta College *A*
Monterey Peninsula College *A*
Mount San Jacinto College *A*
Orange Coast College *C, A*
Palomar College *C, A*
Pitzer College *B*
Pomona College *B*
Rio Hondo College *A*
Saddleback College *A*
St. Mary's College of California *B*
San Diego State University *B*
San Francisco State University *B*
San Joaquin Delta College *A*
San Jose State University *B*
Santa Ana College *C, A*
Santa Monica College *A*
Santa Rosa Junior College *C*
Santiago Canyon College *A*
Scripps College *B*
Skyline College *A*
Southwestern College *A*
University of California
Berkeley *B*
Irvine *B, M*
Los Angeles *B, M*
San Diego *B*
Santa Barbara *B, M*

Colorado

Colorado College *B*
Colorado State University *B*
University of Colorado
Boulder *B, M*

Connecticut

Connecticut College *B*
Naugatuck Valley Community
College *C, A*
Trinity College *B*
University of Hartford *B*
Wesleyan University *B*

District of Columbia

George Washington University *B*
Howard University *B*

Florida

Daytona State College *A*
Florida Southern College *B*
Florida State University *B, M*
Indian River State College *A*
Jacksonville University *B*
Miami Dade College *A*
Nova Southeastern University *B*
Palm Beach Atlantic University *B*
Palm Beach State College *A*
University of Florida *B*
University of Miami *B*
University of South Florida *B*
Valencia College *A*

Georgia

Agnes Scott College *B*
Brenau University *B*
Darton College *A*
Emory University *D*
Kennesaw State University *B*
University of Georgia *B*
Valdosta State University *B*

Hawaii

University of Hawaii
Manoa *B, M*

Idaho

University of Idaho *B*

Illinois

Columbia College Chicago *B*
Illinois Central College *A*
Lincoln College *A*
Loyola University Chicago *B*
Northwestern University *B*
University of Illinois
Urbana-Champaign *B, M*

Indiana

Anderson University *B*
Ball State University *B*
Butler University *B*
University of St. Francis *A, B*

Iowa

Luther College *B*
University of Iowa *B, M*

Kansas

Barton County Community College *A*
Friends University *B*
University of Kansas *B*

Kentucky

Western Kentucky University *B*

Louisiana

Tulane University *B*

Maine

Bates College *B*

Maryland

Goucher College *B*
Howard Community College *A*
Montgomery College *A*
Towson University *B*
University of Maryland
Baltimore County *B*
College Park *B, M*

Massachusetts

Amherst College *B*
Bard College at Simon's Rock *B*
Boston Conservatory *B*
Cape Cod Community College *A*
Dean College *A, B*
Hampshire College *B*
Mount Holyoke College *B*
Smith College *B, M*
Springfield College *B*
University of Massachusetts
Amherst *B*

Michigan

Alma College *B*
Eastern Michigan University *B*
Grand Valley State University *B*
Hope College *B*
Marygrove College *B, T*
Oakland University *B*
University of Michigan *B, M*
Wayne State University *B, T*
Western Michigan University *B*

Minnesota

Carleton College *B*
Gustavus Adolphus College *B*
Rochester Community and Technical
College *C*
St. Olaf College *B*
University of Minnesota
Twin Cities *B*

Mississippi

Belhaven University *C, B*
Hinds Community College *A*
University of Southern Mississippi *B*

Missouri

Lindenwood University *B*
Missouri State University *B*
Missouri Valley College *B*
Stephens College *B*
University of Missouri
Kansas City *B*
Washington University in St. Louis *B*
Webster University *B*

Montana

University of Montana *B*

Nebraska

University of Nebraska
Lincoln *B*

Nevada

University of Nevada
Las Vegas *B*

New Hampshire

Franklin Pierce University *B*
Keene State College *B*

New Jersey

Georgian Court University *B*
Middlesex County College *A*
Montclair State University *B*
Raritan Valley Community College *A*
Rider University *B*
Rowan University *B*
Rutgers, The State University of New
Jersey
New Brunswick/Piscataway
Campus *B, M*

New Mexico

New Mexico State University *B*
Santa Fe University of Art and
Design *B*
University of New Mexico *B, M*

New York

Adelphi University *B*
Bard College *B*
Barnard College *B*
City University of New York
Hunter College *B*
Queensborough Community
College *A*
Columbia University *B*
Columbia University
School of General Studies *B*
Cornell University *B*
Fordham University *B*
Hamilton College *B*
Hobart and William Smith Colleges *B*
Hofstra University *B*
Ithaca College *B*
Juilliard School *B*
Long Island University
LIU Brooklyn *B*
LIU Post *B*
Manhattanville College *B*
Marymount Manhattan College *B*
New York University *B, M, D*
SUNY
College at Brockport *B, M*
College at Fredonia *B*
College at Potsdam *B*
College at Purchase *B, M*
University at Buffalo *B*
Skidmore College *B*

North Carolina

Appalachian State University *B*
Duke University *B*
East Carolina University *B*
Elon University *B*
Meredith College *B*

University of North Carolina
Charlotte *B*
Greensboro *B, M*
School of the Arts *C, B*

Ohio

Case Western Reserve
University *B, M*
College of Wooster *B*
Denison University *B*
Kent State University *B*
Kenyon College *B*
Lake Erie College *B*
Oberlin College *B*
Ohio State University
Columbus Campus *C, B, M, D*
Ohio University *B*
Ohio Wesleyan University *B*
Sinclair Community College *C*
University of Akron *B*
University of Cincinnati *B*
Wright State University *B*
Youngstown State University *B*

Oklahoma

Oklahoma City University *B*
Oral Roberts University *B*
St. Gregory's University *B*
University of Central Oklahoma *B*
University of Oklahoma *B, M*

Oregon

University of Oregon *B, M*
Western Oregon University *B*

Pennsylvania

Cedar Crest College *B*
DeSales University *B*
Dickinson College *B*
Drexel University *B*
Eastern University *B*
Franklin & Marshall College *B*
La Roche College *B*
Mercyhurst University *B*
Messiah College *B*
Montgomery County Community
College *A*
Muhlenberg College *C, B*
Point Park University *B*
Slippery Rock University of
Pennsylvania *B*
Swarthmore College *B*
Temple University *B, M, D*
University of the Arts *C, B*
Ursinus College *B*
West Chester University of
Pennsylvania *B*

Rhode Island

Rhode Island College *B*
Roger Williams University *B*

South Carolina

Coker College *B*
Columbia College *B*
University of South Carolina
Columbia *B*
Winthrop University *B*

Texas

Austin Community College *A*
Kilgore College *A*
Lamar University *B*
Palo Alto College *A*
St. Philip's College *A*
Sam Houston State University *B, M*
San Jacinto College *A*
Southern Methodist University *B, M*
Stephen F. Austin State
University *B, T*
Texas Christian University *B, M*
Texas State University *B, T*
Texas Tech University *B*
Texas Woman's University *B, M, D*

Tyler Junior College *A*
University of Houston *B*
University of North Texas *B*
University of Texas
Austin *B, M*
El Paso *B*
Pan American *B*
West Texas A&M University *B*

Utah

Brigham Young University *B, M*
Snow College *A*
Southern Utah University *B*
University of Utah *B, M, T*
Utah Valley University *A, B*
Weber State University *B*

Vermont

Bennington College *B, M*
Johnson State College *B*
Marlboro College *B*
Middlebury College *B*

Virginia

George Mason University *B, M*
Hollins University *B, M*
Radford University *B*
Randolph College *B*
Shenandoah University *B*
Sweet Briar College *B*
University of Richmond *B*
Virginia Commonwealth University *B*

Washington

Cornish College of the Arts *B*
University of Washington *B, M*
Western Washington University *B*

West Virginia

West Virginia University *B*

Wisconsin

Beloit College *B*
University of Wisconsin
Madison *B, M*
Milwaukee *B, T*
Stevens Point *B*
Whitewater *B, T*

Wyoming

Casper College *A*
Western Wyoming Community
College *A*

Dance therapy

Illinois
Columbia College Chicago *M*

Massachusetts
Lesley University *M, D*

New York
Pratt Institute *M*

Vermont
Goddard College *M*

Danish

Washington
University of Washington *B*

Data entry/applications

Alabama
Gadsden State Community College *C*

Arizona
Arizona Western College *C, A*
Chandler-Gilbert Community
College *A*

Estrella Mountain Community
College *C, A*
GateWay Community College *C*
Glendale Community College *A*

California

Glendale Community College *C*
Kaplan College
Riverside *C*
Los Angeles Harbor College *C, A*
Orange Coast College *C, A*
San Diego City College *A*
San Joaquin Delta College *C*
San Jose City College *C, A*
Santa Monica College *C, A*
Santa Rosa Junior College *C*
Sierra College *C, A*
WyoTech: Fremont *C*

Colorado

Aims Community College *C*
Arapahoe Community College *A*
Community College of Denver *C*

Connecticut

Manchester Community College *C, A*
Three Rivers Community College *C*

Florida

College of Central Florida *C*
Florida Career College
Miami *C*
Herzing University
Winter Park *C*

Georgia

Albany Technical College *C*
Atlanta Technical College *C*
Central Georgia Technical College *C*
Gwinnett College *C*
Gwinnett Technical College *C*
Middle Georgia State College *A*
Savannah Technical College *C*
Southwest Georgia Technical
College *C, A*
West Georgia Technical College *C, A*

Illinois

Elgin Community College *A*
Heartland Community College *A*
John A. Logan College *A*
Kankakee Community College *C*
Richland Community College *A*
Sauk Valley Community College *C, A*
Waubonsee Community College *C*

Indiana

Brown Mackie College
Merrillville *A*
Michigan City *C, A*

Kansas

Johnson County Community
College *C*
Seward County Community
College *C, A*

Maryland

Chesapeake College *A*
TESST College of Technology
Beltsville *A*

Massachusetts

Bristol Community College *C*
Bunker Hill Community College *A*
Fitchburg State University *C*
Massasoit Community College *C*
Roxbury Community College *C*
Springfield Technical Community
College *C*

Michigan

Baker College
Muskegon *A*
Macomb Community College *C, A*

Minnesota

Central Lakes College *C*
North Hennepin Community
College *C*
Riverland Community College *C*

Mississippi

Copiah-Lincoln Community
College *A*

Montana

Montana State University
Billings *A*

Nebraska

Nebraska Indian Community
College *C, A*

New Hampshire

Mount Washington College *A*
Nashua Community College *A*

New Jersey

Burlington County College *C*
Mercer County Community
College *C*

New York

City University of New York
LaGuardia Community College *A*
Everest Institute
Rochester *C*
Globe Institute of Technology *C*
Pace University *C, A*
Pace University: Pleasantville/
Briarcliff *M*
Westchester Community College *C*

North Carolina

Beaufort County Community
College *C*

North Dakota

North Dakota State College of
Science *C, A*

Ohio

Belmont College *A*
Brown Mackie College
Akron *A*
Northwest State Community
College *A*
Ohio Business College
Sandusky *A*
Stark State College *A*
Stautzenberger College *A*
University of Cincinnati
Clermont College *C, A*

Oregon

Lane Community College *C*
Portland Community College *C*

Pennsylvania

Consolidated School of Business
Lancaster *A*
Delaware County Community
College *C, A*
Harrisburg Area Community
College *C*
Lansdale School of Business *C, A*
Pace Institute *C*
Westmoreland County Community
College *C*

Rhode Island

Community College of Rhode
Island *C*

South Carolina

Williamsburg Technical College C
York Technical College C

Tennessee

South College C, A

Texas

Northeast Texas Community
College C, A
St. Philip's College C, A
Temple College C, A

Virginia

Germanna Community College C

Washington

Bellingham Technical College C, A
Centralia College C
Clark College C, A
Clover Park Technical College C
Edmonds Community College C
Grays Harbor College C
Heritage University C
Lake Washington Institute of
Technology C, A
Lower Columbia College A
Peninsula College A
Spokane Falls Community College C
Walla Walla Community College C, A
Yakima Valley Community College C

West Virginia

American National University
Parkersburg C

Wisconsin

Northcentral Technical College C, A

Wyoming

Western Wyoming Community
College C

Data processing technology

Alabama

Gadsden State Community College C
Wallace State Community College at
Hanceville A

Arizona

Central Arizona College A
Eastern Arizona College C
GateWay Community College C
Mohave Community College C
Northland Pioneer College C, A
Pima Community College C
Tohono O'odham Community
College C

Arkansas

Arkansas State University B
Central Baptist College B

California

Antelope Valley College A
Cabrillo College A
Cerritos College A
Chabot College C, A
Citrus College A
College of the Redwoods C
Cypress College C, A
Diablo Valley College C
Foothill College C
Fresno City College C, A
Fullerton College C, A
Gavilan College C
Long Beach City College C, A
Los Angeles Mission College C
Los Angeles Pierce College C, A
Los Angeles Valley College C, A

Monterey Peninsula College C, A
Mount San Antonio College C, A
Orange Coast College C
Pasadena City College C, A
Porterville College C
San Diego City College C, A
Santa Ana College C, A
Santa Barbara City College C, A
Shasta College A
Skyline College C, A
Victor Valley College C
Yuba College C

Colorado

Colorado Mountain College C
National American University
Denver A

Connecticut

Gateway Community College C, A
Three Rivers Community College C

Delaware

Delaware State University B

Florida

Broward College A
Everest University
North Orlando A
Florida Keys Community College C
Florida State College at
Jacksonville C, A
Indian River State College C
Keiser University A
Miami Dade College C
Seminole State College of
Florida C, A
Tallahassee Community College C
University of Miami B

Georgia

Abraham Baldwin Agricultural
College A
Albany Technical College C, A
Athens Technical College C, A
Atlanta Technical College C
Central Georgia Technical
College C, A
Gwinnett Technical College C
Savannah Technical College C, A
Southwest Georgia Technical
College C, A

Hawaii

Hawaii Pacific University A
University of Hawaii
Kapiolani Community College C, A

Illinois

Chicago State University B
City Colleges of Chicago
Wilbur Wright College C
Harper College C
Kishwaukee College C
Lewis and Clark Community
College A
Oakton Community College C, A
Southwestern Illinois College A

Indiana

International Business College C
International Business College:
Indianapolis C
Vincennes University C

Iowa

Dordt College A
Ellsworth Community College A
Southeastern Community
College C, A
University of Dubuque B

Kansas

Dodge City Community College C, A
Donnelly College C, A
Haskell Indian Nations University A
Highland Community College A
Labette Community College A
Seward County Community
College C, A

Kentucky

Bluegrass Community and Technical
College A
Daymar College
Owensboro C, A
Eastern Kentucky University A
Henderson Community College A
Jefferson Community and Technical
College A
Northern Kentucky University A
Owensboro Community and
Technical College A
Southeast Kentucky Community and
Technical College A
Western Kentucky University A

Louisiana

Delgado Community College A
ITI Technical College A
Louisiana State University
Alexandria A

Maine

Kaplan University
South Portland A
Northern Maine Community
College A

Maryland

Allegany College of Maryland C
Chesapeake College C, A
Kaplan University
Hagerstown A, B

Massachusetts

Bristol Community College A

Michigan

Baker College
Auburn Hills A
Clinton Township A
Flint A
Jackson A
Muskegon A
Port Huron A
Bay de Noc Community College C, A
Glen Oaks Community College C
Jackson College C, A
Kalamazoo Valley Community
College A
Montcalm Community College C, A
Muskegon Community College C, A
Oakland Community College C, A
St. Clair County Community
College C, A
Washtenaw Community College C, A
West Shore Community College C, A

Minnesota

Central Lakes College A
Hennepin Technical College C, A
Minneapolis Business College C
Pine Technical College C, A
South Central College A

Mississippi

East Central Community College A
Itawamba Community College A
Northwest Mississippi Community
College A
Pearl River Community College A
Southwest Mississippi Community
College A
University of Southern Mississippi B

Missouri

St. Louis Community College C, A
University of Central Missouri B
Washington University in St. Louis B

Montana

Fort Peck Community College C, A
Miles Community College A
Montana Tech of the University of
Montana C
University of Great Falls B
University of Montana A

Nebraska

Kaplan University
Omaha A, B

Nevada

College of Southern Nevada A
Truckee Meadows Community
College A

New Hampshire

Lakes Region Community
College C, A
Nashua Community College C, A
River Valley Community College C

New Jersey

Atlantic Cape Community College A
Burlington County College C, A
Essex County College C
Gloucester County College C, A
Hudson County Community
College C, A
Ocean County College C
Saint Peter's University A

New Mexico

Central New Mexico Community
College C, A
Dona Ana Community College of
New Mexico State University A
Eastern New Mexico University:
Roswell C, A
New Mexico State University
Alamogordo C, A
Carlsbad C
San Juan College C, A

New York

Bramson ORT College A
Broome Community College A
Cayuga Community College C
City University of New York
Bronx Community College A
Brooklyn College C
Kingsborough Community
College A
Queensborough Community
College A
College of Saint Rose C
Globe Institute of Technology C
Hudson Valley Community
College C, A
Jamestown Business College A
Jamestown Community College C, A
Marist College C
New York University C
Orange County Community
College A
Pace University A
Pace University: Pleasantville/
Briarcliff B
Rockland Community College C, A
SUNY
College of Technology at Alfred A
College of Technology at
Delhi C, A, B
Farmingdale State College C, A
Sullivan County Community
College C, A
Utica School of Commerce A
Wood Tobe-Coburn School C

North Carolina

Caldwell Community College and
Technical Institute *A*
Central Carolina Community
College *C*
Central Piedmont Community
College *C, A*
Durham Technical Community
College *C, A*
King's College *C*
Stanly Community College *C*
Western Piedmont Community
College *C, A*

North Dakota

Mayville State University *C*

Ohio

Belmont College *C*
Bradford School *C*
Cincinnati Christian University *B*
Eastern Gateway Community
College *C*
Fortis College
Centerville *C*
Miami University
Oxford *A*
Miami-Jacobs Career College
Dayton *A*
Mount Vernon Nazarene University *A*
National College
Canton *C*
Willoughby Hills *C*
Northwest State Community
College *C*
Stark State College *A*
Terra State Community College *A*
University of Akron: Wayne
College *A*
University of Cincinnati
Clermont College *C, A*
Washington State Community
College *A*

Oklahoma

Connors State College *A*
Oklahoma City Community
College *A*

Pennsylvania

Bradford School: Pittsburgh *C*
Community College of
Philadelphia *A*
Consolidated School of Business
Lancaster *A*
York *A*
Reading Area Community College *A*
Westmoreland County Community
College *C*
Yorktowne Business Institute *A*

South Carolina

Aiken Technical College *A*
Florence-Darlington Technical
College *A*
Greenville Technical College *C, A*
Horry-Georgetown Technical
College *C, A*
Midlands Technical College *C, A*
Northeastern Technical College *C, A*
Orangeburg-Calhoun Technical
College *C, A*
Piedmont Technical College *C, A*
Spartanburg Community College *C, A*
Technical College of the
Lowcountry *C, A*
Tri-County Technical College *A*
Trident Technical College *C, A*

South Dakota

Lake Area Technical Institute *A*
Sinte Gleska University *A*
Southeast Technical Institute *C*

Tennessee

Chattanooga College *C*

Texas

Angelina College *C, A*
Brookhaven College *C*
Cedar Valley College *C, A*
Central Texas College *C*
Coastal Bend College *C, A*
Eastfield College *A*
El Centro College *C, A*
El Paso Community College *C, A*
Frank Phillips College *C*
Galveston College *C*
Hill College *C, A*
Howard College *C*
Lee College *C, A*
McLennan Community College *C, A*
Midland College *A*
Mountain View College *C, A*
North Central Texas College *A*
South Plains College *A*
Southwest Texas Junior College *A*
Trinity Valley Community College *A*
Tyler Junior College *C*
Vernon College *C, A*
Weatherford College *C, A*
Western Texas College *C, A*

Utah

Utah State University *C*

Virginia

Mountain Empire Community
College *C*
Virginia Highlands Community
College *A*

Washington

Bellevue College *C*
Centralia College *A*
Columbia Basin College *A*
Edmonds Community College *A*
Everett Community College *A*
Grays Harbor College *C*
Lake Washington Institute of
Technology *C, A*
Lower Columbia College *C, A*
Peninsula College *A*
Renton Technical College *C*
Shoreline Community College *C, A*
South Puget Sound Community
College *C, A*
Spokane Community College *C, A*
Tacoma Community College *C*
Walla Walla Community College *C, A*
Walla Walla University *B*
Whatcom Community College *C, A*
Yakima Valley Community College *C*

West Virginia

American National University
Parkersburg *C*
American Public University System *A*

Wisconsin

Lac Courte Oreilles Ojibwa
Community College *C*
Moraine Park Technical College *C, A*
Nicolet Area Technical College *A*
Southwest Wisconsin Technical
College *C*

Wyoming

Northwest College *C*
Western Wyoming Community
College *C, A*

Database design/
management

Alabama

University of Phoenix
Birmingham *B*

Arizona

University of Phoenix
Phoenix-Hohokam *B*
Southern Arizona *B*

California

American River College *C, A*
Diablo Valley College *C*
Foothill College *C, A*
National University *M*
Santa Monica College *C, A*
University of Phoenix
Bay Area *B*
Central Valley *B*
Sacramento Valley *B*
San Diego *B*
Southern California *B*

Colorado

Colorado Technical University *C*
Red Rocks Community College *C, A*
University of Phoenix
Denver *B*
Southern Colorado *B*

Connecticut

Norwalk Community College *C*

District of Columbia

University of Phoenix
Washington DC *B*

Florida

St. Petersburg College *C*
University of Phoenix
Central Florida *B*
North Florida *B*
South Florida *B*
West Florida *B*

Georgia

Atlanta Technical College *C, A*
University of Phoenix
Atlanta *B*
Augusta *B*
Columbus *B*
Savannah *B*

Hawaii

University of Phoenix
Hawaii *B*

Idaho

University of Phoenix
Idaho *B*

Illinois

DePaul University *M*
Moraine Valley Community College *C*

Indiana

Indiana University
Purdue University Indianapolis *C*
Ivy Tech Community College
Bloomington *C*
Central Indiana *C*
Columbus *C*
East Central *C*
Kokomo *C*
Lafayette *C*
North Central *C*
Northeast *C*
Northwest *C*
Richmond *C*
South Central *C*
University of Phoenix
Indianapolis *B*

Kansas

Cowley County Community
College *A*
Johnson County Community
College *C*

Kentucky

University of Louisville *C*

Louisiana

University of Phoenix
Baton Rouge *B*
Lafayette *B*
Louisiana *B*
Shreveport *B*

Maryland

University of Phoenix
Maryland *B*

Massachusetts

Brandeis University *M*
Bristol Community College *C*
Fitchburg State University *C*
Quinsigamond Community College *C*
University of Phoenix
Boston *B*

Michigan

Central Michigan University *M*
Oakland Community College *C*
University of Phoenix
Metro Detroit *B*
West Michigan *B*
Wayne County Community College *A*

Minnesota

Dakota County Technical
College *C, A*
Minneapolis Community and
Technical College *C*
University of Phoenix
Minneapolis-St. Paul *B*

Montana

Salish Kootenai College *A*

Nevada

College of Southern Nevada *C, A*
University of Phoenix
Las Vegas *B*
Northern Nevada *B*

New Jersey

University of Phoenix
Jersey City *B*

New Mexico

University of Phoenix
New Mexico *B*

New York

City University of New York
CUNY Online *M*
Globe Institute of
Technology *C, A, B*
Rochester Institute of
Technology *B, M*

North Carolina

Central Piedmont Community
College *C, A*
College of the Albemarle *C*
North Carolina State University *M*

Ohio

Clark State Community College *A*
Sinclair Community College *C*
Stark State College *A*
University of Akron *C*
University of Cincinnati *C*
University of Phoenix
Cleveland *B*
University of Rio Grande *C*

Oklahoma

University of Phoenix
Oklahoma City *B*
Tulsa *B*

Oregon
Mt. Hood Community College *C, A*

Pennsylvania
La Salle University *B, M*
Pennsylvania College of
  Technology *B*
University of Phoenix
  Philadelphia *B*
Westmoreland County Community
  College *A*

Puerto Rico
Inter American University of Puerto
  Rico
  Metropolitan Campus *M*

Rhode Island
Bryant University *B*

South Carolina
University of Phoenix
  Columbia *B*

Tennessee
University of Phoenix
  Chattanooga *B*
  Knoxville *B*
  Memphis *B*
  Nashville *B*

Texas
University of Phoenix
  Dallas Fort Worth *B*
  Houston Westside *B*
  San Antonio *B*

Utah
University of Phoenix
  Utah *B*

Virginia
Lord Fairfax Community College *C, A*
University of Phoenix
  Northern Virginia *B*
  Richmond *B*

Washington
Bates Technical College *C, A*
Bellevue College *A*
Clark College *C*
Edmonds Community College *C, A*
Green River Community College *A*
Shoreline Community College *C, A*
University of Phoenix
  Western Washington *B*
Yakima Valley Community College *C*

West Virginia
American Public University System *C*

Wisconsin
Northcentral Technical College *C*
University of Phoenix
  Milwaukee *B*

Deaf studies

California
Sierra College *A*

Indiana
Bethel College *A*

Maryland
Towson University *B*

Massachusetts
Boston University *B, M, D*
Quinsigamond Community College *A*

New York
Rochester Institute of Technology *C*

Oregon
Western Oregon University *B*

Pennsylvania
Valley Forge Christian College *B*

Demography/ population studies

California
University of California
  Berkeley *M, D*
  Irvine *M*

Florida
Florida State University *M*

Maine
University of New England *B*

Massachusetts
University of Massachusetts
  Amherst *C*

Ohio
Bowling Green State University *M*

Pennsylvania
University of Pennsylvania *M, D*
University of Pittsburgh
  Bradford *B*

Puerto Rico
University of Puerto Rico
  Medical Sciences *M*

Texas
University of Texas
  San Antonio *D*

Dental assistant

Alabama
Calhoun Community College *C, A*
Community College of the Air
  Force *A*
Faulkner State Community
  College *C, A*
Lawson State Community College *C*
University of Alabama
  Birmingham *C*
Wallace State Community College at
  Hanceville *C, A*

Alaska
Charter College *C*
University of Alaska
  Anchorage *C, A*
  Fairbanks *C, A*

Arizona
Brookline College
  Phoenix *C*
  Tempe *C*
Carrington College
  Mesa *C*
  Phoenix *C*
  Tucson *C*
Mohave Community College *C*
Phoenix College *A*
Pima Community College *C*
Rio Salado College *C*

Arkansas
Arkansas Northeastern College *C*
Northwest Arkansas Community
  College *C*
Pulaski Technical College *C*

California
Allan Hancock College *C, A*
Carrington College California
  Antioch *C, A*
  Citrus Heights *C, A*
  Pleasant Hill *C*
  Sacramento *C*
  San Jose *C*
  San Leandro *C*
  Stockton *C, A*
Cerritos College *C, A*
Chaffey College *C, A*
Citrus College *C, A*
City College of San Francisco *C, A*
College of Alameda *A*
College of Marin *C, A*
College of San Mateo *C, A*
College of the Redwoods *C*
Concorde Career College
  Garden Grove *C*
  North Hollywood *C*
  San Bernardino *C*
  San Diego *C*
Cypress College *C, A*
Diablo Valley College *C, A*
Foothill College *C, A*
Heald College
  Concord *C, A*
  Hayward *A*
  Stockton *C, A*
Kaplan College
  Palm Springs *C*
  Salida *C*
La Sierra University *C*
Modesto Junior College *A*
Monterey Peninsula College *C, A*
Orange Coast College *C, A*
Oxnard College *C*
Palomar College *C, A*
Pasadena City College *C, A*
Reedley College *C, A*
Sacramento City College *C, A*
San Diego Mesa College *C, A*
San Joaquin Valley College *A*
San Jose City College *C, A*
Santa Rosa Junior College *C, A*

Colorado
Concorde Career College
  Aurora *C*
Front Range Community College *C*
IBMC College
  Fort Collins *C, A*
IntelliTec College: Grand Junction *C*
Pikes Peak Community College *C, A*
Pueblo Community College *C, A*

Connecticut
Tunxis Community College *C*

Florida
Broward College *C*
College of Central Florida *C*
Daytona State College *C*
Eastern Florida State College *C*
Edison State College *C*
Everest University
  Largo *C*
Florida National University *C*
Florida State College at
  Jacksonville *C*
Gulf Coast State College *C*
Indian River State College *C*
Lincoln College of Technology
  West Palm Beach *C*
Northwest Florida State College *C*
Palm Beach State College *C*
Pasco-Hernando State College *C*
Pensacola State College *C*
Sanford-Brown Institute
  Tampa *C*
Santa Fe College *C*
South Florida State College *C*
Tallahassee Community College *C*

Georgia
Albany Technical College *C*
Athens Technical College *A*
Atlanta Technical College *C*
Augusta Technical College *C*
Columbus Technical College *C*
Gwinnett Technical College *C*
Savannah Technical College *C*

Hawaii
Heald College
  Honolulu *A*
University of Hawaii
  Kapiolani Community College *C, A*
  Maui College *C*

Idaho
Carrington College
  Boise *C, A*
College of Southern Idaho *C*
College of Western Idaho *C, A*
Eastern Idaho Technical College *C*

Illinois
Black Hawk College *C*
City Colleges of Chicago
  Harry S. Truman College *C*
  Wilbur Wright College *C*
Elgin Community College *C*
Illinois Central College *C*
Illinois Valley Community College *C*
John A. Logan College *C*
Kaskaskia College *C*
Lewis and Clark Community
  College *C*

Indiana
Fortis College
  Indianapolis *C*
Indiana University
  Northwest *C*
  Purdue University Fort Wayne *C*
  Purdue University Indianapolis *C*
International Business College:
  Indianapolis *A*
Ivy Tech Community College
  Columbus *C*
  East Central *C*
  Kokomo *C*
  Lafayette *C*
University of Southern Indiana *C, A*

Iowa
Clinton Community College *C*
Des Moines Area Community
  College *C*
Hawkeye Community College *C*
Iowa Western Community College *C*
Kirkwood Community College *C, A*
Marshalltown Community College *C*
Northeast Iowa Community
  College *C*
Western Iowa Tech Community
  College *C*

Kansas
Johnson County Community
  College *C, A*
Wichita Area Technical College *C, A*

Kentucky
Jefferson Community and Technical
  College *C*
West Kentucky Community and
  Technical College *C*

Louisiana
Blue Cliff College
  Metairie *C*

Maine
University of Maine
  Augusta *C, A*

Maryland

Hagerstown Community College *C*

Massachusetts

Massasoit Community College *C*
Middlesex Community College *C, A*
Mount Wachusett Community
College *C*
Northern Essex Community
College *C*
Quinsigamond Community College *C*
Springfield Technical Community
College *C*

Michigan

Baker College
Auburn Hills *A*
Port Huron *A*
Delta College *C, A*
Grand Rapids Community
College *C, A*
Lake Michigan College *C, A*
Mott Community College *C*
Northwestern Michigan College *C, A*
Washtenaw Community College *C*
Wayne County Community College *C*

Minnesota

Central Lakes College *C*
Century College *C, A*
Dakota County Technical
College *C, A*
Hennepin Technical College *C, A*
Herzing University
Minneapolis *C, A*
Hibbing Community College *A*
Minneapolis Community and
Technical College *C*
Minnesota State Community and
Technical College *A*
Minnesota West Community and
Technical College *A*
Northwest Technical College *C, A*
Rochester Community and Technical
College *C, A*
St. Cloud Technical and Community
College *C, A*
South Central College *C, A*
University of Minnesota
Twin Cities *C*

Mississippi

Hinds Community College *C, A*
Meridian Community College *C*

Missouri

Metropolitan Community College -
Kansas City *C, A*
Ozarks Technical Community
College *C, A*
St. Louis Community College *A*

Montana

Montana State University
Great Falls College *C*
Salish Kootenai College *C, A*

Nebraska

Central Community College *C, A*
Kaplan University
Omaha *C*
Metropolitan Community College *C*
Mid-Plains Community College *C, A*
Southeast Community College *C*
Vatterott College
Spring Valley *C*

Nevada

Truckee Meadows Community
College *C, A*

New Hampshire

NHTI-Concord's Community
College *C*

New Jersey

Brookdale Community College *C*
Camden County College *C, A*
Essex County College *C*
Ocean County College *A*
Raritan Valley Community College *C*
Thomas Edison State College *C*
Union County College *C*

New Mexico

Carrington College
Albuquerque *C*
Central New Mexico Community
College *C*
Eastern New Mexico University:
Roswell *C*
Luna Community College *C*
Santa Fe Community College *C, A*

New York

Erie Community College *C*
Monroe Community College *C*

North Carolina

Alamance Community College *C*
Asheville-Buncombe Technical
Community College *C*
Cape Fear Community College *C*
Central Piedmont Community
College *C*
Coastal Carolina Community
College *C*
Fayetteville Technical Community
College *C*
Guilford Technical Community
College *C*
Halifax Community College *C*
Martin Community College *C*
Miller-Motte College
Wilmington *C*
Montgomery Community College *C*
Rowan-Cabarrus Community
College *C*
University of North Carolina
Chapel Hill *C*
Wake Technical Community
College *C*
Wayne Community College *C*
Western Piedmont Community
College *C*
Wilkes Community College *C*

North Dakota

North Dakota State College of
Science *C*

Ohio

Akron Institute of Herzing
University *C, A*
Cuyahoga Community College
Metropolitan *C, A*
Eastern Gateway Community
College *C, A*
Fortis College
Cuyahoga *C*
Kaplan College
Dayton *C*
Miami-Jacobs Career College
Columbus *C, A*
Sharonville *A*
Ohio Business College
Hilliard *C*
Ohio Valley College of Technology *A*
Owens Community College
Toledo *C*
Remington College
Cleveland West *C*

Oklahoma

Rose State College *C, A*

Oregon

Blue Mountain Community College *C*
Central Oregon Community
College *C*
Chemeketa Community College *C, A*
Clackamas Community College *C*
Lane Community College *C*
Linn-Benton Community College *C*
Portland Community College *C*
Rogue Community College *C*
Umpqua Community College *C*

Pennsylvania

Bradford School: Pittsburgh *A*
Commonwealth Technical Institute *C*
Community College of
Philadelphia *C*
Fortis Institute
Erie *A*
Harcum College *C, A*
Harrisburg Area Community
College *C*
Keystone Technical Institute *C, A*
Luzerne County Community
College *C, A*
Manor College *A*
Westmoreland County Community
College *C*
YTI Career Institute
Altoona *C*
Capital Region *C*
York *C*
Yorktowne Business Institute *A*

Puerto Rico

Huertas College *A*
Humacao Community College *A*
National University College
Arecibo *A*
Bayamon *A*
Rio Grande *A*
University of Puerto Rico
Medical Sciences *A*

Rhode Island

Community College of Rhode
Island *C*

South Carolina

Aiken Technical College *C*
Florence-Darlington Technical
College *C*
Greenville Technical College *C*
Horry-Georgetown Technical
College *C*
Midlands Technical College *C, A*
Spartanburg Community College *C*
Tri-County Technical College *C*
Trident Technical College *C*
York Technical College *C*

South Dakota

Lake Area Technical Institute *C*

Tennessee

Anthem Career College
Nashville *C*
Chattanooga College *C, A*
Chattanooga State Community
College *C*
Daymar Institute
Murfreesboro *A*
Nashville *C, A*
Miller-Motte Technical College
Chattanooga *C, A*
Northeast State Community
College *C*
Remington College
Nashville *C*
Volunteer State Community
College *C*

Texas

Amarillo College *C*
Del Mar College *C, A*
El Paso Community College *C, A*
Grayson College *C*
Houston Community College
System *C*
Lamar State College at Orange *C*
Remington College
Houston Southeast *C*
San Antonio College *C*
Texas State Technical College
Harlingen *C*
Waco *C*

Utah

Provo College *C, A*

Virginia

ECPI University *A*
J. Sargeant Reynolds Community
College *C*
Wytheville Community College *C*

Washington

Bates Technical College *C, A*
Bellingham Technical College *C, A*
Carrington College
Spokane *C*
Centralia College *C*
Clover Park Technical College *C, A*
Columbia Basin College *C*
Highline Community College *A*
Lake Washington Institute of
Technology *C, A*
Renton Technical College *C, A*
South Puget Sound Community
College *C, A*
Spokane Community College *C, A*
Yakima Valley Community College *C*

West Virginia

West Virginia Junior College
Bridgeport *A*

Wisconsin

Blackhawk Technical College *C*
Chippewa Valley Technical College *C*
Fox Valley Technical College *C*
Gateway Technical College *C*
Lakeshore Technical College *C*
Madison Area Technical College *C*
Milwaukee Area Technical College *C*
Northcentral Technical College *C*
Northeast Wisconsin Technical
College *C*
Southwest Wisconsin Technical
College *C*
Waukesha County Technical
College *C*
Western Technical College *C*
Wisconsin Indianhead Technical
College *C*

Wyoming

Central Wyoming College *C*

Dental clinical services

Alabama

University of Alabama
Birmingham *M*

California

University of California
Los Angeles *M, D*
University of Southern
California *M, D*

Colorado

University of Colorado
Denver *M*

Connecticut

University of Connecticut *M*

Florida

Nova Southeastern University *M*
University of Florida *M*

Illinois

Northwestern University *M, D*

Indiana

Indiana University
 Purdue University
  Indianapolis *M, D*

Iowa

University of Iowa *M*

Kentucky

University of Kentucky *M*
University of Louisville *M*

Maryland

University of Maryland
 Baltimore *M, D*

Minnesota

Metropolitan State University *M*
University of Minnesota
 Twin Cities *M, D*

Missouri

University of Missouri
 Kansas City *M, D*

Nebraska

University of Nebraska
 Medical Center *M, D*

New Jersey

Rutgers, The State University of New
 Jersey
 New Brunswick/Piscataway
  Campus *M*
 Newark Campus *M*

New York

SUNY
 University at Buffalo *M*
University of Rochester *M*

North Carolina

University of North Carolina
 Chapel Hill *M, D*

Ohio

Case Western Reserve University *M*
Ohio State University
 Columbus Campus *D*
University of Toledo *M*

Oregon

Oregon Health & Science
 University *M*

Pennsylvania

University of Pittsburgh *M*

Tennessee

University of Tennessee
 Knoxville *M*

Texas

Texas A&M University
 Baylor College of Dentistry *M, D*

Virginia

Virginia Commonwealth
 University *M*

West Virginia

West Virginia University *M*

Wisconsin

Marquette University *M*

Dental hygiene

Alabama

Wallace State Community College at
 Hanceville *A*

Alaska

University of Alaska
 Anchorage *A, B*
 Fairbanks *A*

Arizona

Carrington College
 Mesa *A*
Mesa Community College *A*
Mohave Community College *A*
Northern Arizona University *B*
Phoenix College *A*
Pima Community College *A*
Rio Salado College *A*

Arkansas

University of Arkansas
 Fort Smith *A*
 for Medical Sciences *A, B*

California

Cabrillo College *C, A*
Carrington College California
 Sacramento *A*
 San Jose *A*
Cerritos College *C, A*
Chabot College *C, A*
Cypress College *C, A*
Diablo Valley College *C, A*
Foothill College *A*
Fresno City College *A*
Hartnell College *A*
La Sierra University *C*
Loma Linda University *A, B*
Moreno Valley College *A*
Oxnard College *A*
Pasadena City College *C, A*
Sacramento City College *C, A*
San Joaquin Valley College *A*
Santa Rosa Junior College *C, A*
Shasta College *A*
Southwestern College *A*
Taft College *C, A*
University of Southern California *B*
University of the Pacific *B*
West Coast University: Orange
 County *B*
West Los Angeles College *C, A*

Colorado

Colorado Northwestern Community
 College *A*
Community College of Denver *A*
Pueblo Community College *C, A*

Connecticut

Gateway Community College *A*
Goodwin College *A*
Tunxis Community College *A*
University of Bridgeport *A, B, M*
University of New Haven *A, B*

Delaware

Delaware Technical Community
 College
 Stanton/Wilmington Campus *A*

District of Columbia

Howard University *C*

Florida

Broward College *A*
Daytona State College *A*
Eastern Florida State College *A*

Edison State College *A*
Florida National University *A*
Florida State College at
 Jacksonville *A*
Gulf Coast State College *A*
Hillsborough Community College *A*
Indian River State College *A*
Miami Dade College *A*
Palm Beach State College *A*
Pasco-Hernando State College *A*
Pensacola State College *A*
St. Petersburg College *A, B*
Sanford-Brown Institute
 Jacksonville *A*
Santa Fe College *A*
South Florida State College *A*
State College of Florida, Manatee-
 Sarasota *A*
Tallahassee Community College *A*
Valencia College *A*

Georgia

Abraham Baldwin Agricultural
 College *A*
Athens Technical College *A*
Atlanta Technical College *A*
Central Georgia Technical College *A*
Clayton State University *B*
Columbus Technical College *A*
Dalton State College *A*
Darton College *A*
Georgia Highlands College *A*
Georgia Perimeter College *A*
Georgia Regents University *B*
Gordon College *A*
Savannah Technical College *A*
South Georgia State College *A*
Southeastern Technical College *A*
University of North Georgia *A*
Valdosta State University *A*

Hawaii

University of Hawaii
 Kapiolani Community College *A*
 Manoa *B*

Idaho

Carrington College
 Boise *A*
College of Southern Idaho *A*
Idaho State University *B, M*

Illinois

City Colleges of Chicago
 Kennedy-King College *A*
College of DuPage *A*
College of Lake County *A*
Harper College *A*
Illinois Central College *A*
John A. Logan College *A*
Lake Land College *A*
Lewis University *B*
Lewis and Clark Community
 College *A*
Parkland College *A*
Prairie State College *A*
Rock Valley College *A*
Southern Illinois University
 Carbondale *B*

Indiana

Indiana University
 Northwest *A, B*
 Purdue University Fort Wayne *A*
 Purdue University Indianapolis *A*
 South Bend *A, B*
University of Southern Indiana *A, B*

Iowa

Clinton Community College *A*
Des Moines Area Community
 College *A*
Hawkeye Community College *A*
Iowa Central Community College *A*

Iowa Western Community College *A*
Kirkwood Community College *A*
Western Iowa Tech Community
 College *A*

Kansas

Colby Community College *A*
Johnson County Community
 College *A*
Seward County Community
 College *A*
Wichita State University *B*

Kentucky

Big Sandy Community and Technical
 College *A*
Bluegrass Community and Technical
 College *C, A*
Elizabethtown Community and
 Technical College *A*
Henderson Community College *C*
Hopkinsville Community College *A*
University of Louisville *B*
Western Kentucky University *A, B*

Louisiana

Louisiana State University
 Health Sciences Center *B*
Southern University
 Shreveport *A*
University of Louisiana at Lafayette *B*
University of Louisiana at Monroe *B*

Maine

University of Maine
 Augusta *A, B*
University of New England *A, B*

Maryland

Allegany College of Maryland *A*
Baltimore City Community College *A*
Community College of Baltimore
 County *A*
Howard Community College *A*
University of Maryland
 Baltimore *B, M*

Massachusetts

Bristol Community College *A*
Cape Cod Community College *A*
MCPHS University *B*
Middlesex Community College *A*
Mount Ida College *A*
Mount Wachusett Community
 College *A*
Quinsigamond Community College *A*
Springfield Technical Community
 College *A*

Michigan

Baker College
 Auburn Hills *A*
 Port Huron *A*
Delta College *A*
Ferris State University *A, B*
Grand Rapids Community College *A*
Kalamazoo Valley Community
 College *A*
Kellogg Community College *A*
Lansing Community College *A*
Mott Community College *A*
Oakland Community College *A*
University of Detroit Mercy *B*
University of Michigan *B, M*
Wayne County Community College *A*

Minnesota

Argosy University
 Twin Cities *A*
Century College *A*
Herzing University
 Minneapolis *A*
Lake Superior College *A*
Metropolitan State University *B*

Minnesota State Community and
  Technical College
Minnesota State University
  Mankato *B*
Normandale Community College *A*
Rochester Community and Technical
  College *A*
St. Cloud Technical and Community
  College *A*
University of Minnesota
  Twin Cities *B, M*

Mississippi

East Mississippi Community
  College *A*
Hinds Community College *A*
Meridian Community College *A*
Mississippi Delta Community
  College *A*
Northeast Mississippi Community
  College *A*
University of Mississippi Medical
  Center *B*

Missouri

Missouri Southern State University *A*
Ozarks Technical Community
  College *A*
St. Louis Community College *A*
State Fair Community College *A*
University of Missouri
  Kansas City *B, M*

Montana

Montana State University
  Great Falls College *A*

Nebraska

Central Community College *C, A*
Creighton University *B*
University of Nebraska
  Medical Center *B*

Nevada

College of Southern Nevada *A, B*
Truckee Meadows Community
  College *A*

New Hampshire

NHTI-Concord's Community
  College *A*

New Jersey

Bergen Community College *A*
Brookdale Community College *A*
Burlington County College *A*
Camden County College *A*
Essex County College *A*
Middlesex County College *A*
Ocean County College *A*
Raritan Valley Community College *A*
Rutgers, The State University of New
  Jersey
  New Brunswick/Piscataway
    Campus *A*
  Newark Campus *A*
Thomas Edison State College *A, B*
Union County College *A*

New Mexico

Eastern New Mexico University:
  Roswell *A*
San Juan College *A*
University of New Mexico *B, M*

New York

Broome Community College *A*
City University of New York
  Hostos Community College *A*
  New York City College of
    Technology *A*
Erie Community College *A*
Hudson Valley Community College *A*
Monroe Community College *A*

New York University *A, B*
Orange County Community
  College *A*
SUNY
  College of Technology at
    Canton *A, B*
  Farmingdale State College *A, B*

North Carolina

Asheville-Buncombe Technical
  Community College *A*
Blue Ridge Community College *A*
Cape Fear Community College *A*
Catawba Valley Community
  College *A*
Central Carolina Community
  College *A*
Central Piedmont Community
  College *A*
Coastal Carolina Community
  College *A*
Fayetteville Technical Community
  College *A*
Forsyth Technical Community
  College *A*
Guilford Technical Community
  College *A*
Halifax Community College *A*
University of North Carolina
  Chapel Hill *C, B*
Wake Technical Community
  College *A*
Wayne Community College *A*

North Dakota

North Dakota State College of
  Science *A*

Ohio

Columbus State Community
  College *C, A*
Cuyahoga Community College
  Metropolitan *A*
Lakeland Community College *A*
Lorain County Community College *A*
Ohio State University
  Columbus Campus *B, M*
Owens Community College
  Toledo *C, A*
Shawnee State University *A*
Sinclair Community College *C, A*
Stark State College *A*
University of Cincinnati
  Blue Ash College *A*
Youngstown State University *A, B*

Oklahoma

Rose State College *A*
Tulsa Community College *A*
University of Oklahoma *B*

Oregon

Lane Community College *A*
Mt. Hood Community College *A*
Oregon Institute of Technology *A, B*
Portland Community College *A*
Treasure Valley Community
  College *A*

Pennsylvania

Community College of
  Philadelphia *A*
Fortis Institute
  Erie *A*
Harcum College *A*
Harrisburg Area Community
  College *A*
Luzerne County Community
  College *A*
Manor College *A*
Montgomery County Community
  College *A*
Northampton Community College *A*

Pennsylvania College of
  Technology *A, B*
University of Pittsburgh *B*
Westmoreland County Community
  College *A*

Puerto Rico

University of Puerto Rico
  Medical Sciences *A*

Rhode Island

Community College of Rhode
  Island *A*
Rhode Island College *B*

South Carolina

Aiken Technical College *C*
Florence-Darlington Technical
  College *A*
Greenville Technical College *A*
Horry-Georgetown Technical
  College *C, A*
Midlands Technical College *A*
Orangeburg-Calhoun Technical
  College *C*
Piedmont Technical College *C*
Spartanburg Community College *C*
Tri-County Technical College *C*
Trident Technical College *A*
York Technical College *A*

South Dakota

University of South Dakota *A, B*

Tennessee

Chattanooga State Community
  College *A*
East Tennessee State University *B*
Roane State Community College *A*
Southern Adventist University *A*
Tennessee State University *A, B*
University of Tennessee
  Knoxville *B, M*

Texas

Amarillo College *A*
Austin Community College *A*
Coastal Bend College *A*
Collin County Community College
  District *A*
Del Mar College *A*
El Paso Community College *A*
Houston Community College
  System *A*
Howard College *A*
Lamar Institute of Technology *A*
Lone Star College System *A*
Midwestern State University *B*
Northeast Texas Community
  College *A*
Tarrant County College *A*
Temple College *A*
Texas A&M University
  Baylor College of Dentistry *B, M*
Texas State Technical College
  Harlingen *A*
Texas Woman's University *B*
Tyler Junior College *A*
University of Texas
  Health Science Center at
    Houston *C, B*
Wharton County Junior College *A*

Utah

Dixie State College *A, B*
Salt Lake Community College *A*
Utah Valley University *A, B*
Weber State University *A, B*

Vermont

Vermont Technical College *A, B*

Virginia

Danville Community College *A*
Germanna Community College *A*
Lord Fairfax Community College *A*
Northern Virginia Community
  College *A*
Old Dominion University *B, M*
Virginia Commonwealth University *B*
Virginia Highlands Community
  College *A*
Virginia Western Community
  College *A*
Wytheville Community College *A*

Washington

Bellingham Technical College *A*
Clark College *A*
Columbia Basin College *A*
Eastern Washington University *B, M*
Everett Community College *A*
Lake Washington Institute of
  Technology *A*
Pierce College *A*
Shoreline Community College *A*
University of Washington *B*
Yakima Valley Community College *A*

West Virginia

Bridgemont Community and
  Technical College *A*
Southern West Virginia Community
  and Technical College *A*
West Liberty University *A, B*
West Virginia University *B, M*

Wisconsin

Chippewa Valley Technical College *A*
Fox Valley Technical College *A*
Herzing University
  Madison *A*
Lakeshore Technical College *A*
Madison Area Technical College *A*
Milwaukee Area Technical College *A*
Northcentral Technical College *A*
Northeast Wisconsin Technical
  College *A*
Waukesha County Technical
  College *A*

Wyoming

Laramie County Community
  College *A*
Sheridan College *A*
University of Wyoming *B*

Dental laboratory
technology

Alabama

Community College of the Air
  Force *A*

Arizona

Pima Community College *C, A*

California

Cypress College *A*
Diablo Valley College *C, A*
Los Angeles City College *C, A*
Pasadena City College *C, A*
San Diego Mesa College *A*

Florida

Florida National University *A*
Indian River State College *A*

Georgia

Atlanta Technical College *C*
Gwinnett Technical College *C*

Illinois

Triton College *C*

Indiana

Indiana University
  Purdue University Fort Wayne *A*

Iowa

Kirkwood Community College *A*

Kentucky

Bluegrass Community and Technical
  College *C, A*

Louisiana

Louisiana State University
  Health Sciences Center *A*

Massachusetts

Boston University *B*
Middlesex Community College *A*

New York

City University of New York
  New York City College of
    Technology *A*
Erie Community College *A*
New York University *M*

North Carolina

Durham Technical Community
  College *C, A*

Ohio

Cuyahoga Community College
  Metropolitan *C, A*

Oregon

Portland Community College *C, A*

Pennsylvania

Commonwealth Technical Institute *A*

Tennessee

Northeast State Community
  College *C, A*

Texas

Howard College *C, A*
Texas State Technical College
  Harlingen *C, A*

Virginia

J. Sargeant Reynolds Community
  College *C, A*

Washington

Bates Technical College *C, A*

Wisconsin

Milwaukee Area Technical
  College *C, A*

Dentistry (D.D.S., D.M.D.)

Alabama

University of Alabama at Birmingham:
  School of Dentistry *P*

California

Loma Linda University: School of
  Dentistry *P*
University of California Los Angeles:
  School of Dentistry *P*
University of California San Francisco:
  School of Dentistry *P*
University of Southern California:
  School of Dentistry *P*
University of the Pacific: School of
  Dentistry *P*

Colorado

University of Colorado Health
  Sciences Center: School of
  Dentistry *P*

Connecticut

University of Connecticut: School of
  Dentistry *P*

District of Columbia

Howard University: College of
  Dentistry *P*

Florida

University of Florida: College of
  Dentistry *P*

Georgia

Medical College of Georgia: School of
  Dentistry *P*

Illinois

Northwestern University: Dental
  School *P*
Southern Illinois University: School of
  Dentistry *P*
University of Illinois at Chicago:
  College of Dentistry *P*

Indiana

Indiana University School of
  Dentistry *P*

Iowa

University of Iowa College of
  Dentistry *P*

Kentucky

University of Kentucky: College of
  Dentistry *P*
University of Louisville: School of
  Dentistry *P*

Louisiana

Louisiana State University Health
  Sciences Center: School of
  Dentistry *P*

Maryland

University of Maryland at Baltimore:
  School of Dentistry *P*

Massachusetts

Boston University: Goldman School
  of Dental Medicine *P*
Harvard University: School of Dental
  Medicine *P*
Tufts University: School of Dental
  Medicine *P*

Michigan

University of Detroit Mercy: School
  of Dentistry *P*
University of Michigan: School of
  Dentistry *P*

Minnesota

University of Minnesota Twin Cities:
  School of Dentistry *P*

Mississippi

University of Mississippi Medical
  Center: School of Dentistry *P*

Missouri

University of Missouri Kansas City:
  School of Dentistry *P*

Nebraska

Creighton University: School of
  Dentistry *P*

University of Nebraska Medical
  Center: College of Dentistry *P*

New Jersey

University of Medicine and Dentistry
  of New Jersey
  New Jersey Dental School *P*

New York

Columbia University
  College of Dental Medicine *P*
New York University: College of
  Dentistry *P*
State University of New York Health
  Sciences Center at Stony Brook:
  School of Dentistry *P*
State University of New York at
  Buffalo: School of Dentistry *P*

North Carolina

University of North Carolina at
  Chapel Hill: School of
  Dentistry *P*

Ohio

Case Western Reserve University:
  School of Dentistry *P*
Ohio State University Columbus
  Campus: College of Dentistry *P*

Oklahoma

University of Oklahoma Health
  Sciences Center: College of
  Dentistry *P*

Oregon

Oregon Health Sciences University:
  School of Dentistry *P*

Pennsylvania

Temple University: School of
  Dentistry *P*
University of Pennsylvania: School of
  Dental Medicine *P*
University of Pittsburgh: School of
  Dental Medicine *P*

Puerto Rico

University of Puerto Rico Medical
  Sciences Campus: School of
  Dentistry *P*

South Carolina

Medical University of South Carolina:
  College of Dental Medicine *P*

Tennessee

Meharry Medical College: School of
  Dentistry *P*
University of Tennessee Memphis:
  College of Dentistry *P*

Texas

University of Texas Health Science
  Center: Dental School *P*
University of Texas Health Sciences
  Center-Dental Branch *P*

Virginia

Virginia Commonwealth University:
  School of Dentistry *P*

Washington

University of Washington: School of
  Dentistry *P*

West Virginia

West Virginia University: School of
  Dentistry *P*

Wisconsin

Marquette University: School of
  Dentistry *P*

Design/visual communications

Alabama

Auburn University *B*
Chattahoochee Valley Community
  College *C, A*
ITT Technical Institute
  Birmingham *A*
Wallace State Community College at
  Hanceville *A*

Arizona

Arizona State University *M*
ITT Technical Institute
  Tempe *A*
  Tucson *A*
Mesa Community College *C, A*
Northern Arizona University *B*
Pima Community College *A*
Yavapai College *C*

Arkansas

ITT Technical Institute
  Little Rock *A*

California

Academy of Art University *C, A, B, M*
Allan Hancock College *A*
Art Institute of California
  Los Angeles *A, B*
  San Diego *A*
Bethesda University of California *B*
California Institute of the
  Arts *C, B, M*
California State University
  Chico *C, B*
  Long Beach *B*
  Monterey Bay *B*
Chaffey College *C, A*
Fashion Institute of Design and
  Merchandising
  Los Angeles *A*
  San Diego *A*
  San Francisco *A*
Fullerton College *A*
ITT Technical Institute
  Lathrop *A*
  National City *A*
  Oxnard *A*
  Rancho Cordova *A*
  San Bernardino *A*
  Sylmar *A*
  Torrance *A*
Laney College *C, A*
Long Beach City College *A*
Mount San Antonio College *A*
Otis College of Art and Design *B*
Palomar College *A*
Platt College
  Los Angeles *B*
  Ontario *C, A, B*
Saddleback College *C, A*
San Francisco Art Institute *B, M*
San Francisco State University *B*
University of California
  Davis *B*
University of Redlands *B*
University of San Francisco *B*
Westwood College
  Anaheim *A, B*
  Inland Empire *B*
  Los Angeles *B*

Colorado

Colorado Mountain College *A*
Colorado State University *M*
ITT Technical Institute
  Westminster *A*
Rocky Mountain College of Art &
  Design *M*
Westwood College
  Denver North *B*
  Denver South *B*

Connecticut

Central Connecticut State
University *B, M*
University of Hartford *B*

District of Columbia

American University *B*
Howard University *B*

Florida

Florida State College at
Jacksonville *A*
ITT Technical Institute
Ft. Lauderdale *A*
Jacksonville *A*
Lake Mary *A*
Miami *A*
Tampa *A*
Jacksonville University *B, M*
Miami International University of Art
and Design *B, M*
University of Miami *B*

Georgia

Art Institute of Atlanta *C*
Atlanta Technical College *C, A*
Savannah College of Art and
Design *M*

Idaho

ITT Technical Institute
Boise *A*

Illinois

American Academy of Art *B*
Black Hawk College *C, A*
College of DuPage *C, A*
Columbia College Chicago *B*
Elgin Community College *C, A*
Heartland Community College *A*
Illinois Central College *A*
Illinois Institute of Art
Schaumburg *C, A, B*
Lewis University *B*
School of the Art Institute of
Chicago *B, M*
Southern Illinois University
Carbondale *B*
Triton College *C, A*
University of Chicago *M*

Indiana

Anderson University *B*
ITT Technical Institute
Fort Wayne *A*
Indianapolis *A*
Newburgh *A*
Indiana University
Purdue University Indianapolis *M*
Ivy Tech Community College
Central Indiana *A*
Columbus *A*
Kokomo *A*
North Central *A*
South Central *A*
Southwest *A*
Wabash Valley *A*
Purdue University *B*
St. Mary-of-the-Woods College *B*
University of Evansville *B*
University of Indianapolis *B*
University of Notre Dame *B, M*
University of St. Francis *A, B*

Iowa

Dordt College *B*
Graceland University *B*
Iowa State University *B, M*
Iowa Wesleyan College *B*
Loras College *B*

Kansas

Cowley County Community
College *A*

Hutchinson Community College *A*
University of Kansas *B, M*

Kentucky

ITT Technical Institute
Louisville *A*

Louisiana

ITT Technical Institute
St. Rose *A*

Maine

College of the Atlantic *B, M*
University of New England *B*
York County Community College *A*

Maryland

Cecil College *C, A*
Harford Community College *C, A*
ITT Technical Institute
Owings Mills *A*
Maryland Institute College of Art *M*
Stevenson University *B*

Massachusetts

Bristol Community College *A*
Bunker Hill Community College *A*
Endicott College *B*
Hampshire College *B*
Massachusetts College of Art and
Design *B, M*
Northeastern University *M*
Northern Essex Community
College *A*
School of the Museum of Fine
Arts *C, B, M*
University of Massachusetts
Dartmouth *B, M*

Michigan

Alma College *B*
Andrews University *B*
College for Creative Studies *B*
Ferris State University *B*
Finlandia University *B*
ITT Technical Institute
Canton *A*
Troy *A*
Lawrence Technological University *B*
Madonna University *C, B*
Michigan State University *B, M*
Spring Arbor University *B*
University of Michigan
Flint *B*

Minnesota

Art Institutes International
Minnesota *A, B*
Brown College
Mendota Heights *B*
Concordia University St. Paul *B*
ITT Technical Institute
Eden Prairie *A*
Minneapolis Community and
Technical College *C, A*
University of Minnesota
Twin Cities *B*

Missouri

Kansas City Art Institute *B*
Missouri State University *B*
Washington University in St.
Louis *B, M*
William Woods University *B*

Nebraska

ITT Technical Institute
Omaha *A*

Nevada

Art Institute of Las Vegas *B*
ITT Technical Institute
Henderson *A*

Truckee Meadows Community
College *A*

New Hampshire

Rivier University *B*

New Jersey

Kean University *B*

New Mexico

Eastern New Mexico University:
Roswell *C, A*
ITT Technical Institute
Albuquerque *A*
Northern New Mexico College *A*
Santa Fe Community College *C, A*

New York

Adirondack Community College *C, A*
Broome Community College *C*
Bryant & Stratton College
Rochester *A*
Cazenovia College *B*
City University of New York
New York City College of
Technology *B*
Concordia College *B*
Houghton College *B*
ITT Technical Institute
Albany *A*
Getzville *A*
Liverpool *A*
Nazareth College *B*
Parsons The New School for
Design *C, A, B, M*
Pratt Institute *B, M*
SUNY
College at Oneonta *B*
Farmingdale State College *B*
University at Buffalo *M, D*
Syracuse University *B*

North Carolina

Duke University *B*
North Carolina State University *B, M*
University of Mount Olive *B*
William Peace University *B*

Ohio

Art Academy of Cincinnati *B*
Art Institute of Cincinnati *A, B*
Bowling Green State University *B*
College of Mount St. Joseph *B*
Columbus State Community
College *C*
Edison State Community College *C*
ITT Technical Institute
Dayton *A*
Hilliard *A*
Norwood *A*
Strongsville *A*
Youngstown *A*
Lakeland Community College *C*
Northwest State Community
College *A*
Ohio State University
Columbus Campus *B*
University of Cincinnati
Blue Ash College *C, A*
Virginia Marti College of Art and
Design *A*

Oklahoma

Northeastern State University *B*
Oklahoma Christian University *B*
Oral Roberts University *B*
University of Central Oklahoma *M*

Oregon

Art Institute of Portland *B*
Chemeketa Community College *A*
ITT Technical Institute
Portland *A*
Linfield College *B*

Mt. Hood Community College *A*
Portland Community College *C, A*
Portland State University *B*

Pennsylvania

Art Institute of Pittsburgh *A, B*
Carnegie Mellon University *B, M, D*
Drexel University *M*
Harrisburg Area Community
College *A*
ITT Technical Institute
Pittsburgh *A*
Plymouth Meeting *A*
La Roche College *B*
Lehigh University *B*
Pennsylvania College of Art and
Design *B*
Robert Morris University *B*

Puerto Rico

Escuela de Artes Plasticas de Puerto
Rico *B*

Rhode Island

Bryant University *B*

South Carolina

Horry-Georgetown Technical
College *A*
ITT Technical Institute
Greenville *A*
Piedmont Technical College *C*
Spartanburg Community College *C*
University of South Carolina
Upstate *B*
Winthrop University *M*

South Dakota

Dakota State University *C*

Tennessee

Belmont University *B*
Freed-Hardeman University *B*
ITT Technical Institute
Knoxville *A*
Nashville *A*
Maryville College *B*
Memphis College of Art *B*
O'More College of Design *B*

Texas

Amarillo College *C, A*
Angelina College *C, A*
Blinn College *A*
Brookhaven College *C, A*
Cedar Valley College *C, A*
ITT Technical Institute
Arlington *A*
Austin *A*
Houston North *A*
Houston West *A*
Richardson *A*
San Antonio *A*
Webster *A*
International Academy of Design and
Technology
San Antonio *B*
Lubbock Christian University *B*
St. Philip's College *A*
San Jacinto College *C, A*
Schreiner University *B*
South Plains College *A*
Texas State Technical College
West Texas *A*
Texas State University *B, M*
University of North Texas *M*
University of Texas
Austin *B, M*
Wade College *A, B*

Utah

Brigham Young University *B*
Salt Lake Community College *A*

Utah Valley University *C, A, B*
Weber State University *B*

Vermont
Bennington College *B*
Lyndon State College *B*

Virginia
ITT Technical Institute
  Chantilly *A*
  Norfolk *A*
  Richmond *A*
  Springfield *A*
Radford University *B*
Virginia Commonwealth
  University *M*
Westwood College
  Annandale *B*

Washington
Cornish College of the Arts *B*
ITT Technical Institute
  Everett *A*
  Spokane *A*
Lake Washington Institute of
  Technology *B*
Northwest College of Art & Design *B*
Shoreline Community College *C, A*
Western Washington University *B*
Yakima Valley Community College *A*

West Virginia
Bethany College *B*
West Virginia University *B*

Wisconsin
ITT Technical Institute
  Green Bay *A*
Madison Area Technical College *A*
Viterbo University *B*
Western Technical College *A*

Desktop publishing

Arizona
Central Arizona College *C, A*
Chandler-Gilbert Community
  College *C*
Coconino County Community
  College *C*

California
Academy of Art University *C, A, B*
Antelope Valley College *C*
California Baptist University *B*
California State University
  Chico *C*
Cerritos College *A*
City College of San Francisco *C*
East Los Angeles College *C, A*
Long Beach City College *C, A*
MiraCosta College *C*
Ohlone College *A*
Palomar College *C, A*
Platt College
  Ontario *A*

Colorado
Westwood College
  Denver South *A, B*

Connecticut
Manchester Community College *C*

Idaho
Idaho State University *C, A, B*

Illinois
Harper College *C*
Highland Community College *C*
Illinois Central College *C*
John Wood Community College *C*
Kankakee Community College *C, A*

Moraine Valley Community College *C*
Morton College *C*
Prairie State College *C*
Sauk Valley Community College *A*
School of the Art Institute of
  Chicago *B, M*
South Suburban College of Cook
  County *C*
Spoon River College *C*

Iowa
Des Moines Area Community
  College *C, A*
Graceland University *B*
Iowa Central Community
  College *C, A*
Northeast Iowa Community
  College *A*
Southeastern Community College *A*
Western Iowa Tech Community
  College *C, A*

Kansas
Kansas City Kansas Community
  College *C, A*

Kentucky
Sullivan College of Technology and
  Design *A, B*

Maryland
Montgomery College *C, A*

Massachusetts
Bristol Community College *C*
Middlesex Community College *C, A*
Springfield Technical Community
  College *C*

Michigan
Baker College
  Muskegon *A*
Ferris State University *A*
International Academy of Design and
  Technology
  Detroit *B*

Minnesota
Dakota County Technical College *C*
Dunwoody College of
  Technology *C, A*
Hennepin Technical College *C, A*
North Hennepin Community
  College *C*
Ridgewater College *C, A*
Riverland Community College *C*
St. Mary's University of Minnesota *B*

Nevada
College of Southern Nevada *C*

New Hampshire
Manchester Community College *C, A*

New Jersey
Bergen Community College *C*
Passaic County Community
  College *C, A*

New York
City University of New York
  New York City College of
  Technology *C*
Rochester Institute of
  Technology *C, B*
Touro College *A*

Ohio
Cincinnati State Technical and
  Community College *C, A*
Davis College *C*
Sinclair Community College *C*
Terra State Community College *A*

University of Cincinnati
  Blue Ash College *C*

Oklahoma
Oklahoma City Community
  College *A*

Pennsylvania
La Salle University *B*

Puerto Rico
Universidad del Este *C*

Rhode Island
New England Institute of
  Technology *A*

Texas
Blinn College *C*
Del Mar College *A*
Eastfield College *C*
Houston Community College
  System *C*
Tarrant County College *C*

Utah
Salt Lake Community College *C*

Washington
Bellevue College *C*
Clark College *C*
Clover Park Technical College *C, A*
Walla Walla Community College *C, A*

Wisconsin
Art Institute of Wisconsin *A, B*

Wyoming
Northwest College *C, A*

Development economics

Arizona
University of Arizona *M*

Arkansas
Harding University *B*
John Brown University *M*

California
Hope International University *M*
Point Loma Nazarene University *B*
University of California
  Los Angeles *B*
University of San Francisco *B*
University of Southern California *M*

Colorado
University of Denver *M*

Connecticut
Mitchell College *B*
Yale University *M*

District of Columbia
Georgetown University *M*

Indiana
Taylor University *B*

Maine
College of the Atlantic *B, M*

Massachusetts
Boston University *M*
Brandeis University *M*
Northeastern University *B*

Michigan
Andrews University *B, M*
Calvin College *B*

Minnesota
St. Mary's University of Minnesota *M*

Mississippi
University of Southern Mississippi *D*

New Hampshire
Southern New Hampshire
  University *M, D*

New Mexico
New Mexico State University *D*

New York
Colgate University *B*
Houghton College *B*
SUNY
  College at Oneonta *B*

North Dakota
North Dakota State University *M*

Ohio
University of Akron *C*

Pennsylvania
Messiah College *B*

Rhode Island
Brown University *B*

Tennessee
Vanderbilt University *M*

Texas
University of St. Thomas *B*

Vermont
University of Vermont *B, M*

Virginia
Eastern Mennonite University *B*

Wisconsin
University of Wisconsin
  Madison *D*

Developmental biology/embryology

California
California Institute of
  Technology *M, D*

Illinois
Northwestern University *M*
University of Chicago *D*

Iowa
University of Iowa *M, D*

Maine
College of the Atlantic *B, M*

Missouri
Washington University in St. Louis *D*

New York
University of Rochester *B*

Ohio
Case Western Reserve University *D*
University of Cincinnati *M, D*

Developmental/child psychology

California
California State University
  East Bay *M*
  San Bernardino *M*

Mount St. Mary's College *B*
St. Mary's College of California *B*

Colorado
Metropolitan State University of
Denver *B*

Connecticut
Mitchell College *B*
University of Connecticut *M, D*

District of Columbia
George Washington University *D*

Florida
University of Miami *B*

Georgia
Savannah State University *B*
University of Georgia *D*

Illinois
DePaul University *M*
Loyola University Chicago *M, D*

Indiana
University of St. Francis *B, M*

Iowa
University of Iowa *D*

Kansas
Emporia State University *M*
University of Kansas *B*

Massachusetts
Bay Path College *B, M*
Clark University *M, D*
Eastern Nazarene College *B*
Emmanuel College *B*
Fitchburg State University *B*
Tufts University *M, D*
Wheelock College *M*

Michigan
Northern Michigan University *B, M*
University of Detroit Mercy *B*

Minnesota
Metropolitan State University *B*
University of Minnesota
Twin Cities *B, M, D*

Missouri
University of Missouri
Columbia *M, D*

Montana
University of Montana *M, D*

Nebraska
University of Nebraska
Omaha *M, D*

New Hampshire
Colby-Sawyer College *B*
Keene State College *B*
New England College *B*

New York
Cornell University *M, D*
University of Rochester *D*
Yeshiva University *D*

North Dakota
North Dakota State University *D*

Ohio
Case Western Reserve University *D*

Oregon
Warner Pacific College *B*

Pennsylvania
Duquesne University *M*
University of Pennsylvania *M*

Tennessee
Lee University *M*
Maryville College *B*
Vanderbilt University *B*

Texas
East Texas Baptist University *B*
Texas Christian University *B, M*
University of Houston *D*
University of Texas
Dallas *B, M*

Vermont
Goddard College *M*

Washington
Eastern Washington University *B*
Western Washington University *B*

Developmental services

Minnesota
Anoka Technical College *C, A*

New Mexico
Eastern New Mexico University:
Roswell *C*

Diagnostic medical sonography

Alabama
Community College of the Air
Force *A*
Lurleen B. Wallace Community
College *C, A*
Virginia College
Birmingham *A*
Wallace State Community College at
Hanceville *A*

Alaska
University of Alaska
Anchorage *A*

Arizona
GateWay Community College *A*

Arkansas
Arkansas State University *A*

California
Foothill College *A*
Lincoln University *A*
Orange Coast College *A*
Santa Barbara City College *A*

Colorado
Red Rocks Community College *A*

Connecticut
Gateway Community College *A*

Delaware
Delaware Technical Community
College
Jack F. Owens Campus *A*
Stanton/Wilmington Campus *A*

District of Columbia
George Washington University *B*

Florida
Adventist University of Health
Sciences *A, B*
Barry University *B*
Broward College *A*
Florida National University *A*
Florida State College at
Jacksonville *A*
Gulf Coast State College *A*
Hillsborough Community College *A*
Keiser University *A*
Nova Southeastern University *B*
Pensacola State College *A*
Polk State College *A*
Sanford-Brown Institute
Tampa *A*
Santa Fe College *A*
Southwest Florida College *A*
University of Miami *B*
Valencia College *A*

Georgia
Armstrong Atlantic State University *B*
Athens Technical College *A*
Darton College *A*
Georgia Regents University *B*
Gordon College *A*
Gwinnett Technical College *A*

Hawaii
University of Hawaii
Kapiolani Community College *A*

Illinois
Benedictine University *B*
Harper College *A*
John A. Logan College *A*
Lewis University *B*
Triton College *A*

Iowa
Allen College *B*
Clinton Community College *A*
Mercy College of Health Sciences *A*
St. Luke's College *C*

Kansas
Fort Hays State University *B*
Newman University *B*
Washburn University *B*

Kentucky
Jefferson Community and Technical
College *A*
St. Catharine College *A*
West Kentucky Community and
Technical College *A*

Maryland
Carroll Community College *A*
Howard Community College *A*
Montgomery College *A*

Massachusetts
Bunker Hill Community College *A*
MCPHS University *B*
Middlesex Community College *A*
Springfield Technical Community
College *A*

Michigan
Baker College
Owosso *A*
Port Huron *A*
Delta College *A*
Ferris State University *A*
Jackson College *A*
Kirtland Community College *A*
Lake Michigan College *A*
Lansing Community College *A*
Oakland Community College *A*

Minnesota
Argosy University
Twin Cities *A*
St. Catherine University *A*
St. Cloud Technical and Community
College *A*

Mississippi
Hinds Community College *A*
Itawamba Community College *A*

Missouri
St. Louis Community College *A*
State Fair Community College *A*
University of Missouri
Columbia *B, M*

Nebraska
BryanLGH College of Health
Sciences *A, B*
Nebraska Methodist College of
Nursing and Allied Health *A, B*
University of Nebraska
Medical Center *B*

New Hampshire
NHTI-Concord's Community
College *A*

New Jersey
Bergen Community College *A*
Brookdale Community College *A*
Burlington County College *A*
Eastern International College *A*
Eastwick College *A*
Gloucester County College *A*
Union County College *A*

New Mexico
Central New Mexico Community
College *A*

New York
Long Island University
LIU Brooklyn *B*
Rochester Institute of Technology *B*
SUNY
Downstate Medical Center *B*
Upstate Medical University *B*

North Carolina
Caldwell Community College and
Technical Institute *A*
Cape Fear Community College *A*
Forsyth Technical Community
College *A*
Pitt Community College *A*
South Piedmont Community
College *A*
Southwestern Community College *A*

Ohio
Bowling Green State University:
Firelands College *A*
Central Ohio Technical College *A*
Cincinnati State Technical and
Community College *A*
Kettering College *B*
Lorain County Community College *A*
Owens Community College
Toledo *A*
University of Rio Grande *A, B*

Oklahoma
Bacone College *A*
Oklahoma State University
Oklahoma City *A*
University of Oklahoma *B*

Oregon
Oregon Institute of Technology *B*

Pennsylvania
Community College of Allegheny
County *A*
Harrisburg Area Community
College *A*
Lackawanna College *A*
Misericordia University *B*
Northampton Community College *A*

Pennsylvania College of Health
 Sciences *A*
Sanford-Brown Institute
 Pittsburgh *A*
South Hills School of Business &
 Technology *A*
Thomas Jefferson University *B*

Puerto Rico

EDIC College *A*
ICPR Junior College *A*
Universidad Metropolitana *A*
Universidad del Este *A, B*

Rhode Island

Community College of Rhode
 Island *A*

South Carolina

Greenville Technical College *A*

South Dakota

Southeast Technical Institute *A*

Tennessee

Baptist College of Health Sciences *B*

Texas

Alvin Community College *A*
Angelina College *A*
Austin Community College *A*
Del Mar College *A*
El Centro College *A*
Hill College *A*
Lamar Institute of Technology *A*
Lone Star College System *A*
Midland College *A*
St. Philip's College *A*
San Jacinto College *A*
Sanford-Brown College
 Houston *A*
Temple College *A*
Tyler Junior College *A*
Weatherford College *A*

Utah

Weber State University *B*

Virginia

ECPI University *A*
Piedmont Virginia Community
 College *A*

Washington

Bellevue College *A*
Centralia College *A*
Columbia Basin College *A*
Seattle University *B*
Tacoma Community College *A*
Wenatchee Valley College *A*

West Virginia

University of Charleston *B*

Wisconsin

Blackhawk Technical College *A*
Chippewa Valley Technical College *A*
Mount Mary University *B*

Wyoming

Laramie County Community
 College *A*

Diesel mechanics

Alabama

Bevill State Community College *C*
Bishop State Community
 College *C, A*
Gadsden State Community College *C*
Lawson State Community College *C*
Lurleen B. Wallace Community
 College *C*

Shelton State Community College *C*
Wallace State Community College at
 Hanceville *C, A*

Alaska

University of Alaska
 Fairbanks *C*
 Southeast *C, A*

Arizona

Central Arizona College *C, A*
Eastern Arizona College *C*
Universal Technical Institute *C*

Arkansas

Arkansas State University
 Beebe *C*
 Newport *C*
Mid-South Community College *C*
Pulaski Technical College *C*
University of Arkansas
 Community College at Hope *C*
 Fort Smith *C*

California

Allan Hancock College *C, A*
Cerritos College *C*
Citrus College *C, A*
Golden West College *A*
Hartnell College *C, A*
Long Beach City College *C, A*
Los Angeles Trade and Technical
 College *C, A*
Merced College *C, A*
Palomar College *C, A*
San Bernardino Valley College *C, A*
San Deigo Miramar College
 San Diego Miramar College *C, A*
San Joaquin Delta College *C, A*
Santa Ana College *A*
Santa Rosa Junior College *C*
Shasta College *C, A*
WyoTech: Sacramento *C*
Yuba College *C*

Colorado

Colorado Northwestern Community
 College *C*
Community College of Aurora *C*
Lincoln College of Technology
 Denver *C, A*
Northeastern Junior College *C, A*
Pikes Peak Community College *C*
Trinidad State Junior College *C, A*

Florida

Florida State College at
 Jacksonville *C*

Georgia

Albany Technical College *C*
Altamaha Technical College *C, A*
Atlanta Technical College *C*
Georgia Piedmont Technical
 College *C*

Hawaii

University of Hawaii
 Hawaii Community College *C, A*
 Honolulu Community College *C, A*

Idaho

College of Southern Idaho *C, A*
College of Western Idaho *C, A*
Eastern Idaho Technical College *C, A*
Idaho State University *C, A, B*
Lewis-Clark State College *C, A, B*
North Idaho College *C, A*

Illinois

Black Hawk College *C, A*
Illinois Eastern Community Colleges
 Wabash Valley College *A*

Kishwaukee College *C, A*
Parkland College *A*
Rend Lake College *C, A*
Southeastern Illinois College *C, A*
Triton College *C, A*

Indiana

Lincoln College of Technology
 Indianapolis *C, A*
Vincennes University *A*

Iowa

Des Moines Area Community
 College *C, A*
Hawkeye Community College *A*
Iowa Central Community College *A*
Iowa Western Community
 College *C, A*
Kirkwood Community College *A*
Northeast Iowa Community
 College *C*
Northwest Iowa Community
 College *A*
Western Iowa Tech Community
 College *C*

Kansas

Highland Community College *C, A*
North Central Kansas Technical
 College *C, A*
Northwest Kansas Technical
 College *C, A*

Kentucky

Big Sandy Community and Technical
 College *C*
Bluegrass Community and Technical
 College *C*
Elizabethtown Community and
 Technical College *C, A*
Gateway Community and Technical
 College *C, A*
Maysville Community and Technical
 College *C*
Owensboro Community and
 Technical College *C, A*
Somerset Community College *C, A*
West Kentucky Community and
 Technical College *C*

Louisiana

Delgado Community College *C*

Maine

Northern Maine Community
 College *C, A*
Washington County Community
 College *C*

Massachusetts

Massasoit Community College *A*

Michigan

Baker College
 Owosso *C, A*
Kirtland Community College *C*

Minnesota

Alexandria Technical and Community
 College *C, A*
Central Lakes College *C*
Hennepin Technical College *C, A*
Hibbing Community College *C*
Minnesota State Community and
 Technical College *C, A*
Minnesota West Community and
 Technical College *C, A*
Riverland Community College *C*

Mississippi

Copiah-Lincoln Community
 College *C, A*
Hinds Community College *C, A*

Itawamba Community College *C, A*
Northeast Mississippi Community
 College *C, A*
Southwest Mississippi Community
 College *C, A*

Missouri

Crowder College *C, A*
Ozarks Technical Community
 College *C, A*
St. Louis Community College *C*

Montana

Helena College University of
 Montana *A*
Montana State University
 Billings *C, A*
 Northern *A, B*
University of Montana *A*

Nebraska

Central Community College *C, A*
Mid-Plains Community College *C, A*
Northeast Community College *A*
Southeast Community College *A*

Nevada

Great Basin College *C, A*
Truckee Meadows Community
 College *A*

New Hampshire

White Mountains Community
 College *C, A*

New Jersey

Raritan Valley Community College *A*

New Mexico

Central New Mexico Community
 College *C*
Mesalands Community College *C, A*
San Juan College *C, A*

New York

SUNY
 College of Agriculture and
 Technology at Cobleskill *A*
 College of Agriculture and
 Technology at Morrisville *A*
 College of Technology at Alfred *A*

North Carolina

Beaufort County Community
 College *A*
Cape Fear Community College *C*
Central Piedmont Community
 College *C, A*
Forsyth Technical Community
 College *C*
Johnston Community College *C, A*
Wilkes Community College *C, A*

North Dakota

North Dakota State College of
 Science *C, A*
Williston State College *C, A*

Ohio

University of Northwestern
 Ohio *C, A*
Washington State Community
 College *A*

Oklahoma

Oklahoma State University
 Institute of Technology:
 Okmulgee *A*
Western Oklahoma State College *A*

Oregon

Klamath Community College *A*
Lane Community College *C, A*

Linn-Benton Community College *C, A*
Mt. Hood Community College *A*
Portland Community College *C, A*
Rogue Community College *C, A*

Pennsylvania

Johnson College *A*
Lincoln Technical Institute
    Philadelphia *C, A*
Pennsylvania College of
    Technology *C, A*
Rosedale Technical Institute *C, A*
WyoTech: Blairsville *C, A*

South Carolina

Greenville Technical College *C*

South Dakota

Lake Area Technical Institute *A*
Southeast Technical Institute *A*

Tennessee

Lincoln College of Technology
    Nashville *C, A*

Texas

Angelina College *C*
Cedar Valley College *C*
Central Texas College *C, A*
College of the Mainland *C, A*
Del Mar College *C, A*
Houston Community College
    System *C*
Kilgore College *C, A*
Lamar Institute of Technology *C, A*
Lincoln College of Technology
    Grand Prairie *C*
Midland College *C, A*
North Central Texas College *A*
Odessa College *C, A*
St. Philip's College *C, A*
San Jacinto College *C, A*
South Plains College *C, A*
South Texas College *C, A*
Texarkana College *C*
Texas State Technical College
    Waco *C, A*
    West Texas *C, A*

Utah

Salt Lake Community College *C, A*
Utah State University *A*
Utah Valley University *C, A*
Weber State University *A*

Vermont

Vermont Technical College *A*

Virginia

Advanced Technology Institute *C, A*
J. Sargeant Reynolds Community
    College *C*
Southside Virginia Community
    College *C*
Southwest Virginia Community
    College *C*

Washington

Bates Technical College *C, A*
Bellingham Technical College *C, A*
Centralia College *A*
Clark College *C, A*
Grays Harbor College *C, A*
Lake Washington Institute of
    Technology *C, A*
Lower Columbia College *A*
Peninsula College *C, A*
Skagit Valley College *C, A*
South Seattle Community
    College *C, A*
Spokane Community College *A*
Walla Walla Community College *C*

West Virginia

Bridgemont Community and
    Technical College *A*

Wisconsin

Blackhawk Technical College *C*
Fox Valley Technical College *C, A*
Milwaukee Area Technical College *C*
Northeast Wisconsin Technical
    College *C*

Wyoming

Casper College *C, A*
Laramie County Community
    College *C, A*
Sheridan College *C, A*
Western Wyoming Community
    College *C, A*
WyoTech: Laramie *C, A*

Dietetic technician

Arizona

Central Arizona College *A*
Chandler-Gilbert Community
    College *A*
Paradise Valley Community College *A*

California

College of the Desert *A*
Long Beach City College *A*
Orange Coast College *A*

Connecticut

Gateway Community College *A*

Illinois

Harper College *A*

Indiana

Purdue University *B*

Louisiana

Delgado Community College *A*

Maine

Southern Maine Community
    College *A*

Massachusetts

North Shore Community College *A*

Minnesota

Normandale Community College *A*

Montana

Montana State University
    Great Falls College *A*

New York

City University of New York
    LaGuardia Community College *A*
Mohawk Valley Community
    College *A*
SUNY
    College of Agriculture and
        Technology at Morrisville *A*
Suffolk County Community College *A*

North Carolina

Gaston College *A*

Ohio

Youngstown State University *A*

Pennsylvania

Westmoreland County Community
    College *A*

Wisconsin

Milwaukee Area Technical College *A*

Dietetics

Alabama

Oakwood University *B*
University of Alabama *B*

Alaska

University of Alaska
    Anchorage *B*

Arkansas

Arkansas State University *B*
Harding University *B*
Ouachita Baptist University *B*

California

California Baptist University *B*
California Polytechnic State
    University: San Luis Obispo *B*
California State Polytechnic
    University: Pomona *B*
California State University
    Chico *B, M*
Loma Linda University *B, M*
Point Loma Nazarene University *B*
San Diego State University *B, M*
San Francisco State University *B*
San Jose State University *B, M*

Colorado

Colorado State University *M*
University of Northern Colorado *B*

Connecticut

University of Connecticut *B*
University of New Haven *B, M*

Florida

Florida International
    University *B, M, D*
Florida State University *B*
Palm Beach State College *A*
University of North Florida *B, M*

Georgia

Georgia Southern University *T*
Georgia State University *B*
Life University *B*
University of Georgia *B*

Idaho

Idaho State University *B*

Illinois

Bradley University *B*
Dominican University *B*
Eastern Illinois University *M*
Loyola University Chicago *M*
Northern Illinois University *B, M*
Olivet Nazarene University *B*
University of Illinois
    Chicago *B, M, D*
    Urbana-Champaign *B*

Indiana

Ball State University *B, M*
Indiana University
    Purdue University Indianapolis *M*
Purdue University *B*
Vincennes University *A*

Iowa

Iowa State University *B*

Kansas

Barton County Community College *A*
Kansas State University *B*

Louisiana

Nicholls State University *B*
University of Louisiana at Lafayette *B*

Maryland

Howard Community College *A*

Massachusetts

Laboure College *A*
Simmons College *B*

Michigan

Andrews University *B*
Central Michigan University *B*
Delta College *A*
Eastern Michigan University *B, M*
Ferris State University *A*
Michigan State University *B*
Wayne State University *B*
Western Michigan University *B*

Minnesota

College of St. Benedict *B*
St. Catherine University *B*
St. John's University *B*
University of Minnesota
    Twin Cities *B*

Mississippi

University of Mississippi *B*
University of Southern Mississippi *B*

Missouri

College of the Ozarks *B*
Fontbonne University *B*
Missouri State University *B*
Northwest Missouri State
    University *B*
University of Missouri
    Columbia *B*

Nebraska

Northeast Community College *A*

New Hampshire

Keene State College *B*

New Jersey

College of St. Elizabeth *B*
Rutgers, The State University of New
    Jersey
    New Brunswick/Piscataway
        Campus *B*
Thomas Edison State College *B*

New Mexico

New Mexico State University *B*

North Carolina

Appalachian State University *B, M*
East Carolina University *B*
Meredith College *B*
Western Carolina University *B*

North Dakota

North Dakota State University *B*
University of North Dakota *B*

Ohio

Ashland University *B*
Bowling Green State University *B*
Case Western Reserve
    University *B, M, D*
Cincinnati State Technical and
    Community College *A*
Miami University
    Oxford *B*
Ohio State University
    Columbus Campus *B*
Ohio University *B*
Owens Community College
    Toledo *A*
Sinclair Community College *A*
University of Akron *B*
University of Cincinnati *B*
University of Cincinnati
    Blue Ash College *A*

University of Dayton *B*
Youngstown State University *B*

Oklahoma
University of Oklahoma *M*

Oregon
Oregon Health & Science
University *M*

Pennsylvania
Harrisburg Area Community
College *A*
Immaculata University *B*
Marywood University *B*
Seton Hill University *B*
University of Pittsburgh *B*
West Chester University of
Pennsylvania *B*

Rhode Island
University of Rhode Island *B*

South Dakota
South Dakota State University *B, M*

Tennessee
Lipscomb University *B*
Southern Adventist University *A*

Texas
Abilene Christian University *B*
El Paso Community College *A*
Sam Houston State University *M*
Texas Christian University *B*
Texas Southern University *B*
Texas Tech University *B*
Texas Woman's University *B*
University of Texas
Pan American *B*
San Antonio *B, M*

Utah
Brigham Young University *B*
Utah State University *M*

Vermont
University of Vermont *B, M*

Washington
Shoreline Community College *A*

West Virginia
Marshall University *B, M*

Wisconsin
Mount Mary University *B, M*
University of Wisconsin
Stout *B*
Viterbo University *B*

Dietician assistant

Arizona
Arizona Western College *C*

Arkansas
University of Arkansas
Community College at Morrilton *C*

Florida
Hillsborough Community College *A*

Illinois
Harper College *C*

Iowa
Des Moines Area Community
College *C*

Kansas
Barton County Community College *C*
Coffeyville Community College *C*
Colby Community College *C*
Highland Community College *C*

New York
Broome Community College *C*
Erie Community College *A*
SUNY
College of Agriculture and
Technology at Morrisville *A*

Tennessee
Southwest Tennessee Community
College *A*

Texas
Tarrant County College *C, A*

Digital arts

Alabama
Huntingdon College *B*

Alaska
University of Alaska
Anchorage *A*

Arizona
Arizona State University *B*
Grand Canyon University *B*
Pima Community College *C*
Sessions College for Professional
Design *C*

California
Art Institute of California
Silicon Valley *B*
Berkeley City College *C, A*
College of San Mateo *C, A*
College of the Siskiyous *C*
Diablo Valley College *C, A*
Ex'pression College *B*
Fashion Institute of Design and
Merchandising
Los Angeles *A*
San Francisco *A*
Grossmont College *A*
Lassen Community College *C, A*
MiraCosta College *C, A*
Mt. Sierra College *B*
NewSchool of Architecture &
Design *B*
University of Southern
California *B, M*

Colorado
Colorado Mountain College *C*

District of Columbia
Corcoran College of Art and
Design *C*

Florida
International Academy of Design and
Technology: Tampa *B*
Polk State College *C*
Rasmussen College
Fort Myers *B*
New Port Richey *B*
Ocala *B*
Pasco/Land O'Lakes *B*
Tampa/Brandon *B*
Stetson University *B*
University of Central Florida *B, M*
University of Florida *B, M*
University of Tampa *B*

Illinois
DePaul University *B, M*
Rasmussen College
Aurora *B*
Mokena/Tinley Park *B*

Rockford *B*
Romeoville/Joliet *B*
School of the Art Institute of
Chicago *B, M*

Indiana
St. Mary-of-the-Woods College *B*
University of St. Francis *B*

Kansas
Southwestern College *B*

Louisiana
Louisiana State University
Shreveport *B*

Maine
College of the Atlantic *B, M*

Maryland
Goucher College *M*
Harford Community College *A*

Massachusetts
Montserrat College of Art *B*

Michigan
Lawrence Technological University *B*
Northern Michigan University *B*

Minnesota
Academy College *B*
Bethany Lutheran College *B*
Dakota County Technical College *C*
Hamline University *B*
Rasmussen College
Blaine *B*
Bloomington *B*
Brooklyn Park *B*
Eagan *B*
Lake Elmo/Woodbury *B*
Mankato *B*
Moorhead *B*
St. Cloud *B*
Rochester Community and Technical
College *C*
St. Paul College *C, A*
University of Northwestern - St.
Paul *B*

Missouri
Kansas City Art Institute *B*

New Hampshire
Great Bay Community College *C*

New Mexico
Santa Fe University of Art and
Design *B*
University of New Mexico *B*

New York
City University of New York
Hostos Community College *A*
LaGuardia Community College *C*
Daemen College *B*
Genesee Community College *C*
Jamestown Community College *C*
Long Island University
LIU Brooklyn *B, M*
LIU Post *B*
Mohawk Valley Community
College *A*
Nassau Community College *A*
Pratt Institute *A, B, M*
SUNY
College at Oneonta *B*
College of Technology at
Alfred *A, B*
Syracuse University *B, M*

North Carolina
Elon University *B*

North Dakota
Cankdeska Cikana Community
College *A*
Rasmussen College
Bismarck *B*
Fargo *B*

Ohio
Art Academy of Cincinnati *B*
Ashland University *B*
Bowling Green State University *B*
Cleveland Institute of Art *B*
Trumbull Business College *A*

Oregon
Mt. Hood Community College *A*
Pacific Northwest College of Art *B*
University of Oregon *B*

Pennsylvania
Albright College *B*
Pennsylvania College of Art and
Design *B*

Rhode Island
Providence College *B*

South Dakota
South Dakota State University *C*

Tennessee
Memphis College of Art *B*

Vermont
Champlain College *B*
Lyndon State College *B*

Washington
International Academy of Design and
Technology
Seattle *B*
Seattle University *B*

Wisconsin
Rasmussen College
Appleton *B*
Green Bay *B*
Wausau *B*
University of Wisconsin
Milwaukee *C*
Whitewater *B*
Waukesha County Technical
College *A*

Digital media

Alabama
Oakwood University *B*

Arizona
Arizona State University *D*
Cochise College *A*
Pima Community College *C, A*

Arkansas
Arkansas Tech University *M*
Harding University *B*
John Brown University *B*

California
Art Institute of California
Orange County *A, B*
Berkeley City College *C, A*
California State University
Dominguez Hills *B*
City College of San Francisco *C*
College of San Mateo *C, A*
College of the Siskiyous *C, A*
Diablo Valley College *C, A*
Grossmont College *C, A*
Hartnell College *C, A*
Holy Names University *B*

Long Beach City College *C*
Marymount California University *B*
Moorpark College *C, A*
National University *A, B, M*
Ohlone College *C, A*
San Diego State University *B*
Santa Barbara City College *C, A*
Santa Monica College *C, A*
Sierra College *C, A*
University of California
   San Diego *B*
Vanguard University of Southern
   California *B*
Westwood College
   Inland Empire *A, B*

Colorado

Aims Community College *A*
Colorado Technical University *C*
Pikes Peak Community College *C*
Red Rocks Community College *C, A*
University of Denver *B, M*

Connecticut

Manchester Community College *A*
Mitchell College *B*
Naugatuck Valley Community
   College *C, A*
Quinnipiac University *B*
University of Connecticut *B, M*

Delaware

Delaware Technical Community
   College
   Terry Campus *A*
Wesley College *B*

District of Columbia

American University *B, M*
Corcoran College of Art and
   Design *A, B*

Florida

Florida Atlantic University *B*
Florida Gulf Coast University *B*
Florida State College at
   Jacksonville *B*
Gulf Coast State College *C*
University of Miami *B*
University of Tampa *B*

Georgia

Art Institute of Atlanta *C, A, B*
Georgia Institute of
   Technology *B, M, D*
Georgia Southern University *B*
Kennesaw State University *C*
Middle Georgia State College *B*
Savannah College of Art and
   Design *B, M*
University of Georgia *B*

Idaho

University of Idaho *B*

Illinois

Harper College *C*
Lewis University *B*
Loyola University Chicago *B, M*
Northwestern University *M, D*
Prairie State College *C*
School of the Art Institute of
   Chicago *B, M*

Indiana

Butler University *B*
Huntington University *B*
Indiana University
   Bloomington *B, M*
   Kokomo *B*
   Purdue University
     Indianapolis *A, B, M*
Taylor University *B*
Valparaiso University *B, M*

Iowa

Briar Cliff University *B*
Buena Vista University *B*
Dordt College *B*
Hawkeye Community College *A*
Mount Mercy University *B*
Southeastern Community College *A*
University of Northern Iowa *B*
William Penn University *B*

Kansas

Southwestern College *B*

Louisiana

Centenary College of Louisiana *B*

Maine

New England School of
   Communications *B*
Saint Joseph's College of Maine *B*
Southern Maine Community
   College *A*

Maryland

Frederick Community College *C*
Notre Dame of Maryland
   University *B*
Stevenson University *B*

Massachusetts

Endicott College *B*
Fitchburg State University *B*
Lasell College *B*
Massachusetts Institute of
   Technology *M, D*
Western New England University *B*

Michigan

Calvin College *B*
Central Michigan University *M*
College for Creative Studies *B*
Cornerstone University *B*
Northern Michigan University *B*
Oakland Community College *C*
Saginaw Valley State University *M*
Wayne County Community
   College *C, A*

Minnesota

Art Institutes International
   Minnesota *A, B*
Century College *C, A*
Crown College *B*
Dakota County Technical College *A*
Hennepin Technical College *C, A*
Minnesota State University
   Moorhead *B*
Northland Community & Technical
   College *C, A*
Ridgewater College *C*
Rochester Community and Technical
   College *A*
St. Cloud Technical and Community
   College *C, A*

Mississippi

Hinds Community College *A*
University of Mississippi *B*

Missouri

Lindenwood University *B*
Webster University *C, B*

Nebraska

Central Community College *C, A*

New Hampshire

Granite State College *B*

New Jersey

Felician College *B*
Raritan Valley Community
   College *C, A*
Sussex County Community College *C*

New Mexico

New Mexico State University
   Grants *A*

New York

Canisius College *B*
Clarkson University *B*
Dominican College of Blauvelt *M*
Herkimer County Community
   College *A*
Hilbert College *B*
Houghton College *B*
Ithaca College *B*
Manhattanville College *B*
Monroe Community College *C*
New York University *M*
Niagara County Community
   College *C, A*
Pace University *C*
Rensselaer Polytechnic Institute *B*
Rochester Institute of
   Technology *B, M*
SUNY
   College at New Paltz *B*
   College of Technology at
     Alfred *A, B*
St. Francis College *B*
Technical Career Institutes *A*
Tompkins Cortland Community
   College *A*
University of Rochester *B*

North Carolina

Elon University *M*
Lenoir-Rhyne University *B*
Queens University of Charlotte *B*
University of North Carolina
   Chapel Hill *M*

North Dakota

North Dakota State University *B*

Ohio

Ashland University *B*
Baldwin Wallace University *B*
Denison University *B*
Franklin University *B*
Miami University
   Oxford *B*
Muskingum University *B*
North Central State College *A*
Notre Dame College *B*
Ohio University *B*
Ohio University
   Zanesville Campus *A*
Sinclair Community College *A*
Tiffin University *B*
University of Cincinnati
   Blue Ash College *C, A*
University of Dayton *B*
University of Mount Union *B*
Virginia Marti College of Art and
   Design *A*

Oregon

Clackamas Community College *A*
Lane Community College *C, A*

Pennsylvania

Albright College *B*
Art Institute of Pittsburgh *C*
Butler County Community College *A*
Carnegie Mellon University *B*
Cedar Crest College *B*
Community College of Beaver
   County *A*
Juniata College *B*
Kutztown University of
   Pennsylvania *B*
La Salle University *B*
Lebanon Valley College *B*
Lycoming College *B*
Marywood University *B*
Messiah College *B*

Montgomery County Community
   College *A*
Penn State
   Abington *C*
   Altoona *C*
   Beaver *C*
   Berks *C*
   Brandywine *C*
   DuBois *C*
   Erie, The Behrend College *C*
   Fayette, The Eberly Campus *C*
   Greater Allegheny *C*
   Harrisburg *C*
   Hazleton *C*
   Lehigh Valley *C*
   Mont Alto *C*
   New Kensington *C*
   Schuylkill *C*
   Shenango *C*
   University Park *C*
   Wilkes-Barre *C*
   Worthington Scranton *C*
   York *C*
Philadelphia University *B, M*
Point Park University *B*
Slippery Rock University of
   Pennsylvania *B*
University of Scranton *B*
Valley Forge Christian College *B, M*
Waynesburg University *B*
Wilkes University *B*

Puerto Rico

Inter American University of Puerto
   Rico
   Bayamon Campus *B*
Universidad Metropolitana *B*
Universidad del Este *B*
University of Puerto Rico
   Rio Piedras *B*

Rhode Island

New England Institute of
   Technology *A, B*

South Carolina

Columbia International University *B*

Tennessee

King University *B*
Lee University *B*
Trevecca Nazarene University *B*
Union University *B*
Visible Music College *B*

Texas

Abilene Christian University *B*
Baylor University *B*
Dallas Baptist University *B*
Howard Payne University *B*
Lubbock Christian University *B*
North Lake College *C*
Northwest Vista College *C*
St. Edward's University *B*
San Jacinto College *A*
Texas A&M University *B*
University of Texas
   Arlington *B*
   Dallas *B, M*
   El Paso *B*
University of the Incarnate Word *B*

Utah

Dixie State College *B*
Salt Lake Community College *C, A*

Vermont

Bennington College *B*
Castleton State College *B*
Champlain College *M*

Virginia

Art Institute of Washington *A, B*
Eastern Mennonite University *B*
George Mason University *M*

Washington

Evergreen State College *B*
Washington State University *B*

West Virginia

Wheeling Jesuit University *B*

Wisconsin

Concordia University Wisconsin *B*
Madison Media Institute *A*
Marquette University *B*

Wyoming

Laramie County Community
College *A*

Directing/theatrical production

California

California Institute of the Arts *M*
Monterey Peninsula College *C, A*
Moorpark College *C, A*
University of Southern California *M*

Connecticut

Yale University *M*

Florida

Florida State University *M*
University of Miami *B*

Illinois

Bradley University *B*
Columbia College Chicago *B*
DePaul University *M*
Roosevelt University *M*
University of Chicago *B*
University of Illinois
Urbana-Champaign *B*

Indiana

Saint Joseph's College *B*

Iowa

Coe College *B*
Drake University *B*
University of Iowa *M*

Maine

University of Southern Maine *B*

Massachusetts

Boston University *B, M*
Emerson College *B*

Michigan

Aquinas College *B*

Missouri

Lindenwood University *B*
University of Missouri
Kansas City *M*
Webster University *B*

New Hampshire

Keene State College *B*

New Jersey

Rider University *B*

New York

Bard College *B*
Hofstra University *B*
Pace University *M*
SUNY
University at Binghamton *B*

North Carolina

East Carolina University *B*
Elon University *B*

Ohio

Baldwin Wallace University *B*
Ohio University *M*

Pennsylvania

Carnegie Mellon University *B, M*
Juniata College *B*
Lycoming College *B*
Temple University *M*
University of the Arts *B*

Tennessee

Belmont University *B*

Texas

Baylor University *M*
Texas Christian University *B*

Vermont

Bennington College *B*

Virginia

Emory & Henry College *B*
Regent University *M*

Washington

Cornish College of the Arts *B*

Disability studies

Alaska

Prince William Sound Community
College *C, A*

California

California Baptist University *M*

Dispute resolution

California

San Francisco State University *C*

Illinois

Dominican University *M*

Michigan

Wayne State University *M*

Nebraska

Creighton University *M*

New York

City University of New York
John Jay College of Criminal
Justice *C*
Yeshiva University *M*

Vermont

Champlain College *M*

Virginia

George Mason University *M*

Wisconsin

Marquette University *M*
University of Wisconsin
Milwaukee *C*

Divinity/ministry (B.Div., M.Div.)

Alabama

Beeson Divinity School at Samford
University *P*

California

American Baptist Seminary of the
West *P*
Azusa Pacific University: School of
Theology *P*
Church Divinity School of the
Pacific *P*
Claremont School of Theology *P*
Dominican School of Philosophy and
Theology *P*
Franciscan School of Theology *P*
Fuller Theological Seminary *P*
Golden Gate Baptist Theological
Seminary *P*
International School of Theology *P*
Jesuit School of Theology at
Berkeley: Professional *P*
Mennonite Brethren Biblical
Seminary *P*
Pacific Lutheran Theological
Seminary *P*
Pacific School of Religion *P*
St. John's Seminary *P*
St. Patrick's Seminary *P*
San Francisco Theological
Seminary *P*
Starr King School for the Ministry *P*
Talbot School of Theology of Biola
University *P*
Westminster Theological Seminary in
California *P*

Colorado

Denver Conservative Baptist
Seminary *P*
Iliff School of Theology *P*

Connecticut

Yale University: Divinity School *P*

District of Columbia

Catholic University of America:
School of Theology *P*
Dominican House of Studies *P*
Howard University: Divinity School *P*
Washington Theological Union *P*
Wesley Theological Seminary *P*

Florida

St. Vincent De Paul Regional
Seminary *P*

Georgia

Candler School of Theology *P*
Columbia Theological Seminary *P*
Interdenominational Theological
Center *P*

Illinois

Catholic Theological Union *P*
Chicago Theological Seminary *P*
Garrett-Evangelical Theological
Seminary *P*
Lincoln Christian Seminary *P*
Lutheran School of Theology at
Chicago *P*
McCormick Theological Seminary *P*
Meadville-Lombard Theological
School *P*
North Park Theological Seminary *P*
Northern Baptist Theological
Seminary *P*
Seabury-Western Theological
Seminary *P*
Trinity Evangelical Divinity School *P*
University of Chicago: Divinity
School *P*
University of St. Mary of the Lake–
Mundelein Seminary *P*

Indiana

Anderson University: School of
Theology *P*

Associated Mennonite Biblical
Seminary *P*
Bethany Theological Seminary *P*
Bethel College: Elkhart *P*
Christian Theological Seminary *P*
Concordia Theological Seminary *P*
Earlham School of Religion *P*
St. Meinrad School of Theology *P*
University of Notre Dame: School of
Theology *P*

Iowa

Faith Baptist Bible College and
Theological Seminary:
Theological Professions *P*
University of Dubuque: School of
Theology *P*
Wartburg Theological Seminary *P*

Kansas

Central Baptist Theological
Seminary *P*

Kentucky

Asbury Theological Seminary *P*
Lexington Theological Seminary *P*
Louisville Presbyterian Theological
Seminary *P*
Southern Baptist Theological
Seminary *P*

Louisiana

New Orleans Baptist Theological
Seminary *P*
Notre Dame Seminary School of
Theology *P*

Maine

Bangor Theological Seminary *P*

Maryland

Mount St. Mary's College: Seminary *P*

Massachusetts

Andover Newton Theological
School *P*
Boston University: School of
Theology *P*
Episcopal Divinity School *P*
Gordon-Conwell Theological
Seminary *P*
Harvard University: Divinity School *P*
Holy Cross Greek Orthodox School
of Theology *P*
Pope John XXIII National Seminary *P*
St. John's Seminary *P*
Weston Jesuit School of Theology *P*

Michigan

Andrews University Seminary *P*
Calvin Theological Seminary *P*
Grand Rapids Baptist Seminary *P*
Sacred Heart Major Seminary *P*
Western Theological Seminary *P*

Minnesota

Bethel Theological Seminary *P*
St. John's University: School of
Theology *P*
University of St. Thomas: School of
Divinity *P*

Mississippi

Reformed Theological Seminary *P*
Wesley Biblical Seminary *P*

Missouri

Assemblies of God Theological
Seminary *P*
Concordia Seminary *P*
Eden Theological Seminary *P*
Kenrick-Glennon Seminary *P*

Midwestern Baptist Theological
Seminary *P*
Nazarene Theological Seminary *P*
St. Paul School of Theology *P*

New Jersey

Drew University: School of
Theology *P*
Immaculate Conception Seminary of
Seton Hall University *P*
New Brunswick Theological
Seminary *P*
Princeton Theological Seminary *P*

New York

Alliance Theological Seminary *P*
Christ The King Seminary *P*
Colgate Rochester Divinity School-
Bexley Crozer Theological
Seminary *P*
General Theological Seminary *P*
New York Theological Seminary *P*
St. Bernard's Institute *P*
St. John's University: Graduate School
of Arts and Sciences *P*
St. Joseph's Seminary and College *P*
St. Vladimir's Orthodox Theological
Seminary *P*
Seminary of the Immaculate
Conception *P*
Union Theological Seminary:
Theological Professions *P*

North Carolina

Duke University: Divinity School *P*
Hood Theological Seminary *P*
Southeastern Baptist Theological
Seminary: Theological
Professions *P*

Ohio

Ashland Theological Seminary *P*
Athenaeum of Ohio *P*
Methodist Theological School in
Ohio *P*
Pontifical College Josephinum: First
Professional *P*
St. Mary Seminary *P*
Trinity Lutheran Seminary *P*
United Theological Seminary *P*
Winebrenner Seminary *P*

Oklahoma

Phillips Theological Seminary *P*

Oregon

Western Seminary *P*

Pennsylvania

Academy of the New Church *P*
Biblical Theological Seminary *P*
Lancaster Theological Seminary *P*
Lutheran Theological Seminary at
Gettysburg *P*
Lutheran Theological Seminary at
Philadelphia *P*
Moravian Theological Seminary *P*
Palmer Theological Seminary *P*
Pittsburgh Theological Seminary *P*
Reformed Presbyterian Theological
Seminary *P*
St. Charles Borromeo Seminary-
Overbrook *P*
St. Vincent Seminary *P*
Trinity Episcopal School for
Ministry *P*
Westminster Theological Seminary *P*

Puerto Rico

Evangelical Seminary of Puerto
Rico *P*

South Carolina

Columbia Biblical Seminary and
Graduate School of Missions *P*
Erskine Theological Seminary *P*
Lutheran Theological Southern
Seminary *P*

South Dakota

North American Baptist Seminary *P*

Tennessee

Church of God Theological
Seminary *P*
Emmanuel School of Religion *P*
Harding University Graduate School
of Religion *P*
Memphis Theological Seminary *P*
Mid-America Baptist Theological
Seminary *P*
Temple Baptist Seminary: Theological
Professions *P*
University of the South: School of
Theology *P*
Vanderbilt University: The Divinity
School *P*

Texas

Abilene Christian University: College
of Biblical Studies *P*
Austin Presbyterian Theological
Seminary *P*
Baptist Missionary Association
Theological Seminary:
Theological Professions *P*
Episcopal Theological Seminary of
the Southwest *P*
Houston Graduate School of
Theology *P*
Oblate School of Theology *P*
Southern Methodist University:
Perkins School of Theology *P*
Southwestern Baptist Theological
Seminary: Theological
Professions *P*
Texas Christian University: Brite
Divinity School *P*
University of St. Thomas: School of
Theology *P*

Virginia

Eastern Mennonite Seminary *P*
Liberty Baptist Theological
Seminary *P*
Regent University: School of
Divinity *P*
Union Theological Seminary in
Virginia *P*
Virginia Theological Seminary *P*
Virginia Union University: The
Samuel DeWitt Proctor School of
Theology *P*

Washington

Gonzaga University: Department of
Religious Studies *P*
Seattle University: School of
Theology and Ministry *P*

Wisconsin

Sacred Heart School of Theology *P*
St. Francis Seminary *P*

Documentary production

California

Mount St. Mary's College *B*

Maine

College of the Atlantic *B, M*

Missouri

Webster University *C*

New York

Ithaca College *B*
Syracuse University *B*

Vermont

Burlington College *C, B*

Drafting and design technology

Alabama

Bevill State Community College *A*
Bishop State Community College *A*
Calhoun Community College *C, A*
Central Alabama Community
College *A*
Gadsden State Community College *C*
George C. Wallace Community
College at Dothan *C, A*
George C. Wallace State Community
College at Selma *C, A*
Jefferson Davis Community
College *C, A*
Lawson State Community
College *C, A*
Northeast Alabama Community
College *C, A*
Northwest-Shoals Community
College *C, A*
Remington College
Mobile *C*
Shelton State Community
College *C, A*
Southern Union State Community
College *C, A*
Wallace State Community College at
Hanceville *C, A*

Alaska

Charter College *A*
University of Alaska
Fairbanks *C, A*

Arizona

Anthem College
Phoenix *A*
Central Arizona College *C*
Eastern Arizona College *C, A*
Mesa Community College *C*
Northland Pioneer College *C*
Pima Community College *C*

Arkansas

Arkansas State University
Beebe *C, A*
Cossatot Community College of the
University of Arkansas *C*
North Arkansas College *C*
Northwest Arkansas Community
College *C, A*
Phillips Community College of the
University of Arkansas *C, A*
Pulaski Technical College *C, A*
Southeast Arkansas College *C, A*
University of Arkansas
Community College at
Morrilton *C, A*

California

American River College *A*
Antelope Valley College *C, A*
Bakersfield College *A*
Butte College *C, A*
Cabrillo College *C*
Cerritos College *A*
Cerro Coso Community College *C, A*
Chabot College *C, A*
Chaffey College *C, A*
Citrus College *C, A*
City College of San Francisco *C*
College of the Desert *C, A*
College of the Redwoods *C, A*
College of the Sequoias *C, A*

Cosumnes River College *C, A*
Cuyamaca College *A*
De Anza College *A*
Diablo Valley College *C*
East Los Angeles College *C, A*
El Camino College *C, A*
Evergreen Valley College *A*
Fresno City College *C, A*
Fullerton College *C, A*
Glendale Community College *C, A*
Golden West College *C, A*
Hartnell College *A*
ITT Technical Institute
Lathrop *A*
National City *A*
Oxnard *A*
Rancho Cordova *A*
San Bernardino *A*
Sylmar *A*
Torrance *A*
Irvine Valley College *C, A*
Long Beach City College *C, A*
Los Angeles City College *A*
Los Angeles Harbor College *A*
Los Angeles Pierce College *C, A*
Los Angeles Southwest College *C, A*
Los Angeles Trade and Technical
College *C, A*
Los Angeles Valley College *C*
Merced College *C, A*
Mission College *C, A*
Modesto Junior College *A*
Monterey Peninsula College *C, A*
Mount San Antonio College *C, A*
Napa Valley College *C, A*
Orange Coast College *C, A*
Palomar College *C, A*
Pasadena City College *C, A*
Porterville College *C, A*
Rio Hondo College *A*
Sacramento City College *C, A*
Saddleback College *C, A*
San Diego City College *C, A*
San Joaquin Delta College *A*
San Jose City College *A*
Santa Ana College *C, A*
Santa Barbara City College *C, A*
Santa Monica College *C, A*
Santiago Canyon College *A*
Sierra College *C, A*
Solano Community College *C, A*
Southwestern College *C, A*
Ventura College *C, A*
West Valley College *C, A*
Westwood College
Inland Empire *A*

Colorado

Aims Community College *C*
Community College of Denver *C, A*
IntelliTec College *A*
Otero Junior College *C*
Red Rocks Community College *C, A*
Trinidad State Junior College *A*
Westwood College
Denver North *A*

Connecticut

Gateway Community College *C*
Three Rivers Community
College *C, A*

Delaware

Delaware Technical Community
College
Jack F. Owens Campus *A*
Stanton/Wilmington Campus *A*
Terry Campus *A*

Florida

College of Central Florida *A*
Daytona State College *C, A*
Eastern Florida State College *A*

Florida State College at
Jacksonville *A*
Florida Technical College
Orlando *C, A*
Gulf Coast State College *C, A*
Hillsborough Community College *C*
Keiser University *A*
Key College *A*
North Florida Community College *C*
Northwest Florida State College *C, A*
Palm Beach State College *A*
Pasco-Hernando State College *A*
Pensacola State College *C, A*
Saint Johns River State College *C*
St. Petersburg College *C*
Seminole State College of
Florida *C, A*
State College of Florida, Manatee-
Sarasota *A*
Tallahassee Community College *C, A*
Valencia College *C, A*

Georgia

Albany Technical College *C, A*
Altamaha Technical College *C, A*
Athens Technical College *A*
Atlanta Technical College *C*
Augusta Technical College *C*
Central Georgia Technical
College *C, A*
Chattahoochee Technical College *C*
Columbus Technical College *C, A*
Dalton State College *C, A*
Georgia Highlands College *A*
Georgia Piedmont Technical
College *C, A*
Gwinnett Technical College *C, A*
Middle Georgia State College *C*
Savannah Technical College *C*
Southern Crescent Technical
College *C*
Southwest Georgia Technical
College *C*
West Georgia Technical College *C*
Wiregrass Georgia Technical
College *C, A*

Hawaii

University of Hawaii
Honolulu Community College *A*
Maui College *A*

Idaho

Brigham Young University-Idaho *A*
College of Southern Idaho *C, A*
College of Western Idaho *C, A*
Lewis-Clark State College *A, B*
North Idaho College *C, A*

Illinois

Carl Sandburg College *C, A*
College of DuPage *C, A*
Heartland Community College *C*
Illinois Central College *C*
Illinois Eastern Community Colleges
Lincoln Trail College *A*
Illinois Valley Community College *A*
John A. Logan College *C, A*
Joliet Junior College *A*
Kankakee Community College *C, A*
Kishwaukee College *A*
Lake Land College *C*
Lewis and Clark Community
College *A*
Oakton Community College *A*
Rend Lake College *C*
Richland Community College *A*
Robert Morris University: Chicago *A*
Sauk Valley Community College *C*
Shawnee Community College *C, A*
South Suburban College of Cook
County *C, A*
Southwestern Illinois College *C, A*

Indiana

ITT Technical Institute
Fort Wayne *A*
Ivy Tech Community College
Bloomington *A*
Central Indiana *C*
Columbus *A*
East Central *A*
Kokomo *C, A*
Lafayette *C, A*
North Central *A*
Northeast *C, A*
Northwest *C, A*
Richmond *A*
South Central *C, A*
Southeast *A*
Southwest *A*
Wabash Valley *A*

Iowa

Clinton Community College *A*
Iowa Lakes Community College *A*
Marshalltown Community College *A*
Northeast Iowa Community
College *C*
Southeastern Community
College *C, A*
Southwestern Community
College *C, A*

Kansas

Allen County Community College *A*
Butler Community College *C, A*
Cowley County Community
College *C, A*
Garden City Community College *A*
Hutchinson Community College *A*
Independence Community
College *C, A*
Johnson County Community
College *C, A*
Neosho County Community
College *A*
Wichita Area Technical College *C, A*

Kentucky

Bluegrass Community and Technical
College *C*
Eastern Kentucky University *A*
Elizabethtown Community and
Technical College *C*
Gateway Community and Technical
College *C, A*
Hopkinsville Community College *C*
Kentucky State University *A*
Madisonville Community College *A*
Owensboro Community and
Technical College *C, A*
Spencerian College: Lexington *C, A*
Sullivan College of Technology and
Design *A*

Louisiana

Bossier Parish Community College *C*
Delgado Community College *C, A*
Delta School of Business &
Technology *A*
Grambling State University *B*
Herzing University
Kenner *A*
ITI Technical College *A*

Maine

Kennebec Valley Community
College *C, A*
Northern Maine Community
College *A*

Maryland

Anne Arundel Community College *A*
Baltimore City Community
College *C, A*
Chesapeake College *C, A*
Montgomery College *A*

Prince George's Community
College *C, A*
Wor-Wic Community College *C, A*

Massachusetts

Bristol Community College *C*
Massachusetts Bay Community
College *C*
Middlesex Community College *C, A*
Northern Essex Community
College *C*
Roxbury Community College *A*

Michigan

Alpena Community College *A*
Baker College
Auburn Hills *A*
Clinton Township *A*
Flint *A*
Muskegon *A*
Owosso *A*
Port Huron *A*
Delta College *C, A*
Glen Oaks Community College *C*
Henry Ford Community College *A*
Kalamazoo Valley Community
College *C, A*
Kellogg Community College *A*
Macomb Community College *C, A*
Monroe County Community
College *C, A*
Montcalm Community College *C, A*
Mott Community College *C, A*
Muskegon Community College *C, A*
North Central Michigan College *C*
Northern Michigan University *B*
Northwestern Michigan College *A*
Oakland Community College *C, A*
Schoolcraft College *C, A*
Washtenaw Community College *C, A*
Western Michigan University *B*

Minnesota

Anoka Technical College *C*
Hennepin Technical College *C, A*
ITT Technical Institute
Eden Prairie *A*
Minnesota State College - Southeast
Technical *C*
Ridgewater College *C, A*
South Central College *C, A*

Mississippi

Copiah-Lincoln Community
College *A*
East Central Community College *A*
East Mississippi Community
College *A*
Hinds Community College *C, A*
Holmes Community College *A*
Itawamba Community College *C*
Meridian Community College *A*
Mississippi Gulf Coast Community
College *A*
Northeast Mississippi Community
College *A*
Northwest Mississippi Community
College *A*
Pearl River Community College *A*

Missouri

East Central College *C, A*
Jefferson College *C, A*
Lincoln University *A*
Linn State Technical College *A*
Missouri Southern State
University *C, A*
Moberly Area Community
College *C, A*
Ozarks Technical Community
College *C, A*
St. Charles Community College *C, A*
St. Louis Community College *A*

Three Rivers Community College *A*
University of Central Missouri *B*

Montana

Montana State University
Billings *C, A*
Northern *A, B*
Montana Tech of the University of
Montana *C, A*

Nebraska

Central Community College *C, A*
Metropolitan Community
College *C, A*
Southeast Community College *A*

Nevada

College of Southern Nevada *C, A*
Truckee Meadows Community
College *C, A*

New Hampshire

Great Bay Community College *C, A*
Manchester Community College *C, A*
Nashua Community College *C, A*

New Jersey

Bergen Community College *A*
Brookdale Community College *C, A*
Camden County College *C, A*
County College of Morris *C*
Gloucester County College *C, A*
Mercer County Community
College *C*
Middlesex County College *C*

New Mexico

Dona Ana Community College of
New Mexico State
University *C, A*
Eastern New Mexico University:
Roswell *C, A*
ITT Technical Institute
Albuquerque *A*
Luna Community College *A*
New Mexico Junior College *C, A*
Northern New Mexico College *C, A*
San Juan College *C, A*
Santa Fe Community College *C, A*
Western New Mexico University *C, A*

New York

Cayuga Community College *C*
City University of New York
Queensborough Community
College *A*
Corning Community College *C*
Dutchess Community College *C*
Genesee Community College *C, A*
Hudson Valley Community College *A*
Institute of Design and
Construction *A*
Island Drafting and Technical
Institute *A*
Orange County Community
College *C*
SUNY
College of Technology at
Delhi *C, A*
Suffolk County Community College *A*
Ulster County Community
College *C, A*

North Carolina

Alamance Community College *C, A*
Asheville-Buncombe Technical
Community College *A*
Beaufort County Community
College *A*
Blue Ridge Community College *C, A*
Caldwell Community College and
Technical Institute *C, A*
Central Carolina Community
College *C*

College of the Albemarle *C*
Durham Technical Community
College *C, A*
East Carolina University *B*
Forsyth Technical Community
College *A*
Gaston College *C*
Mitchell Community College *C, A*
Piedmont Community College *C*
Richmond Community College *C*
Rowan-Cabarrus Community
College *A*
Sandhills Community College *C, A*
Surry Community College *C, A*
Wake Technical Community
College *C, A*

Ohio

Belmont College *C*
Brown Mackie College
Akron *A*
Cincinnati *A*
Clark State Community College *C, A*
Cuyahoga Community College
Metropolitan *C, A*
Eastern Gateway Community
College *A*
Hocking College *C, A*
James A. Rhodes State College *C*
Lakeland Community College *C*
Lorain County Community College *C*
Miami University
Middletown *C*
North Central State College *C, A*
Sinclair Community College *C*
Southern State Community College *A*
University of Akron *C, A*
University of Rio Grande *C, A*
Washington State Community
College *A*
Wright State University *A*
Wright State University Lake
Campus *A*
Youngstown State University *A*
Zane State College *A*

Oklahoma

Langston University *A*
Northern Oklahoma College *A*
Oklahoma City Community
College *A*
Tulsa Community College *A*
Western Oklahoma State College *A*

Oregon

Blue Mountain Community
College *C, A*
Central Oregon Community
College *C, A*
Chemeketa Community College *C, A*
Clackamas Community College *A*
Clatsop Community College *C*
Lane Community College *C, A*
Linn-Benton Community College *A*
Portland Community College *C*
Treasure Valley Community
College *C, A*

Pennsylvania

Berks Technical Institute *A*
Lehigh Carbon Community College *A*
Luzerne County Community
College *C*
Montgomery County Community
College *A*
Penn Commercial Business and
Technical School *A*
Thaddeus Stevens College of
Technology *A*
Triangle Tech
Pittsburgh *A*

Puerto Rico

Caribbean University *A*
Universal Technology College of
Puerto Rico *C*
Universidad Metropolitana *C, A*

Rhode Island

Johnson & Wales University
Providence *A, B*
New England Institute of
Technology *A*

South Carolina

Aiken Technical College *C*
Central Carolina Technical College *A*
Florence-Darlington Technical
College *C, A*
Northeastern Technical College *C*
Orangeburg-Calhoun Technical
College *A*
Piedmont Technical College *A*
Tri-County Technical College *C, A*
Trident Technical College *C*
Williamsburg Technical College *C, A*
York Technical College *A*

South Dakota

Southeast Technical Institute *A*
Western Dakota Technical
Institute *C, A*

Tennessee

Chattanooga State Community
College *C, A*
Northeast State Community
College *C, A*

Texas

Alvin Community College *C, A*
Amarillo College *C, A*
Angelina College *C, A*
Austin Community College *C, A*
Brazosport College *C, A*
Central Texas College *C, A*
Coastal Bend College *A*
College of the Mainland *A*
Collin County Community College
District *C, A*
Del Mar College *C, A*
Eastfield College *C, A*
El Paso Community College *C, A*
Grayson College *C, A*
Houston Community College
System *C, A*
Howard College *C, A*
ITT Technical Institute
Arlington *A*
Houston West *A*
Richardson *A*
San Antonio *A*
Kilgore College *C, A*
Lamar Institute of Technology *C, A*
Lamar State College at Port Arthur *C*
LeTourneau University *A*
Lee College *C, A*
Midland College *C, A*
Mountain View College *C, A*
Navarro College *A*
North Central Texas College *A*
North Lake College *C*
Odessa College *C, A*
Paris Junior College *C, A*
Prairie View A&M University *B*
Sam Houston State University *B*
San Jacinto College *C, A*
South Plains College *C, A*
South Texas College *C, A*
Tarrant County College *C, A*
Temple College *C, A*
Texarkana College *C, A*
Texas Southern University *B*

Texas State Technical College
Harlingen *A*
Waco *C, A*
West Texas *C, A*
Trinity Valley Community
College *C, A*
Tyler Junior College *C, A*
Vernon College *C, A*
Wharton County Junior College *C, A*

Utah

Salt Lake Community College *C, A*
Snow College *A*
Utah Valley University *A*
Weber State University *A, B*

Virginia

Blue Ridge Community College *C*
Central Virginia Community
College *C*
Danville Community College *A*
Eastern Shore Community College *C*
Lord Fairfax Community College *C*
New River Community College *A*
Northern Virginia Community
College *C, A*
Patrick Henry Community College *A*
Paul D. Camp Community
College *C, A*
Southside Virginia Community
College *C, A*
Tidewater Community College *A*
Virginia Highlands Community
College *C, A*
Virginia Western Community
College *C*

Washington

Columbia Basin College *C*
Everett Community College *C, A*
Grays Harbor College *C*
Green River Community College *A*
Highline Community College *A*
ITT Technical Institute
Everett *A*
Seattle *A*
Spokane *A*
Lake Washington Institute of
Technology *C, A*
Olympic College *C, A*
Pierce College *C*
Renton Technical College *C, A*
Seattle Central Community College *A*
Shoreline Community College *C, A*
South Puget Sound Community
College *C, A*
South Seattle Community
College *C, A*
Spokane Community College *C*
Tacoma Community College *C*
Walla Walla Community College *C*
Wenatchee Valley College *C*
Yakima Valley Community
College *C, A*

West Virginia

Bridgemont Community and
Technical College *A*
Kanawha Valley Community and
Technical College *A*

Wisconsin

Blackhawk Technical College *A*
Chippewa Valley Technical College *A*
Herzing University
Madison *A, B*
Madison Area Technical College *C*
Moraine Park Technical College *C*
Northcentral Technical College *A*
Northeast Wisconsin Technical
College *A*
Southwest Wisconsin Technical
College *A*

Wyoming

Casper College *A*
Laramie County Community
College *C, A*
Sheridan College *C*

Drama and theater arts

Alabama

Alabama State University *B*
Auburn University *B*
Birmingham-Southern College *B*
Faulkner University *B*
Jacksonville State University *B*
Samford University *B*
Spring Hill College *B*
University of Alabama *B, M*
University of Alabama
Birmingham *B*
University of Montevallo *B, T*
University of South Alabama *B*

Arizona

Arizona State University *B, M, D*
Arizona Western College *A*
Central Arizona College *A*
Cochise College *A*
Eastern Arizona College *A*
Glendale Community College *A*
Grand Canyon University *B*
Northern Arizona University *B*
Paradise Valley Community College *A*
Phoenix College *A*
Scottsdale Community College *A*
University of Arizona *B, M*

Arkansas

Arkansas State University *B*
Harding University *B*
Henderson State University *B*
Hendrix College *B*
Lyon College *B*
Ouachita Baptist University *B*
Southern Arkansas University *B*
University of Arkansas *B, M*
University of Arkansas
Fort Smith *B*
Little Rock *B*
University of Central Arkansas *B*
University of the Ozarks *B*

California

Allan Hancock College *C*
American River College *A*
Azusa Pacific University *B*
Bakersfield College *A*
Biola University *B*
California Baptist University *B*
California Lutheran University *B*
California Polytechnic State
University: San Luis Obispo *B*
California State Polytechnic
University: Pomona *B*
California State University
Bakersfield *B*
Chico *B*
Dominguez Hills *B*
East Bay *B*
Fresno *B*
Fullerton *B, M*
Long Beach *B, M*
Los Angeles *B, M*
Northridge *B, M*
Sacramento *B, M*
San Bernardino *B*
Stanislaus *B*
Canada College *A*
Cerritos College *A*
Chabot College *A*
Chaffey College *A*
Chapman University *B*
Claremont McKenna College *B*
College of Marin *A*
College of the Canyons *A*

College of the Desert *A*
College of the Sequoias *A*
College of the Siskiyous *C, A*
Concordia University Irvine *B*
Cosumnes River College *A*
Crafton Hills College *A*
Cypress College *C, A*
East Los Angeles College *A*
El Camino College *A*
Foothill College *A*
Fresno City College *A*
Fresno Pacific University *B*
Fullerton College *A*
Gavilan College *A*
Glendale Community College *C*
Golden West College *A*
Hartnell College *C, A*
Humboldt State University *B, M*
Irvine Valley College *A*
Lake Tahoe Community College *C, A*
Laney College *C, A*
Long Beach City College *A*
Los Angeles City College *C, A*
Los Angeles Pierce College *A*
Los Angeles Southwest College *A*
Loyola Marymount University *B*
Mendocino College *A*
Merced College *A*
Modesto Junior College *A*
Monterey Peninsula College *C, A*
Moorpark College *A*
Mount San Jacinto College *A*
Notre Dame de Namur University *B*
Occidental College *B*
Orange Coast College *A*
Palomar College *A*
Pepperdine University *B*
Pitzer College *B*
Point Loma Nazarene University *B*
Pomona College *B*
Reedley College *A*
Rio Hondo College *A*
Sacramento City College *A*
Saddleback College *A*
St. Mary's College of California *B*
San Diego Christian College *B*
San Diego City College *A*
San Diego Mesa College *A*
San Diego State University *B, M*
San Francisco State University *B, M*
San Joaquin Delta College *A*
San Jose State University *B, M*
Santa Ana College *A*
Santa Barbara City College *A*
Santa Clara University *B*
Santa Monica College *A*
Santa Rosa Junior College *C, A*
Scripps College *B*
Shasta College *C, A*
Sierra College *A*
Solano Community College *A*
Sonoma State University *B*
Southwestern College *A*
Stanford University *B, M, D*
University of California
  Berkeley *B, M, D*
  Davis *B, M, D*
  Irvine *B, M, D*
  Los Angeles *B, M, D*
  Riverside *B*
  San Diego *B, M*
  Santa Barbara *B, M, D*
  Santa Cruz *B*
University of La Verne *B*
University of Redlands *B*
University of San Diego *B, M*
University of Southern California *B*
University of the Pacific *B*
Vanguard University of Southern
  California *B*
Ventura College *C, A*
West Valley College *A*
Westmont College *B*
Whittier College *B*
Yuba College *A*

Colorado

Adams State University *A, B*
Colorado College *B*
Colorado Mesa University *B*
Colorado Mountain College *A*
Colorado State University *B*
Fort Lewis College *B*
Metropolitan State University of
  Denver *B*
Otero Junior College *A*
University of Colorado
  Boulder *B, M, D*
  Denver *B*
University of Denver *B*
University of Northern
  Colorado *B, M, T*

Connecticut

Central Connecticut State
  University *B*
Connecticut College *B*
Fairfield University *B*
Naugatuck Valley Community
  College *A*
Quinnipiac University *B*
Southern Connecticut State
  University *B*
Trinity College *B*
University of Connecticut *B, M*
University of Hartford *B*
University of New Haven *B*
Wesleyan University *B*
Western Connecticut State
  University *B*
Yale University *B, M*

Delaware

University of Delaware *M*

District of Columbia

American University *B*
Catholic University of America *B, M*
Gallaudet University *B*
George Washington University *B, M*
Georgetown University *B*
University of the District of
  Columbia *B*

Florida

Barry University *B*
Broward College *A*
Eckerd College *B*
Flagler College *B*
Florida Agricultural and Mechanical
  University *B, T*
Florida Atlantic University *B, M*
Florida Gulf Coast University *B*
Florida International University *B*
Florida Southern College *B*
Florida State College at
  Jacksonville *B*
Florida State University *B, M, D*
Indian River State College *A*
Jacksonville University *B*
Lynn University *B*
Miami Dade College *A*
Nova Southeastern University *B*
Palm Beach Atlantic University *B*
Palm Beach State College *A*
Pensacola State College *A*
Rollins College *B*
Southeastern University *B*
Stetson University *B*
University of Central Florida *B, M*
University of Florida *B, M*
University of Miami *B, M*
University of South Florida *B*
University of Tampa *B*
University of West Florida *B*

Georgia

Agnes Scott College *B*
Andrew College *A*
Armstrong Atlantic State University *B*
Brenau University *B*
Clayton State University *B*
Columbus State University *B*
Covenant College *B*
Darton College *C, A*
Emory University *B*
Georgia College and State
  University *B*
Georgia Perimeter College *A*
Georgia Southern University *B*
Georgia Southwestern State
  University *B*
Gordon College *A*
Kennesaw State University *B*
LaGrange College *B*
Mercer University *B*
Middle Georgia State College *A*
Morehouse College *B*
Piedmont College *B*
Savannah College of Art and
  Design *B, M*
Shorter University *B*
South Georgia State College *A*
Spelman College *B*
University of Georgia *B, M, D*
University of North Georgia *A*
University of West Georgia *B*
Wesleyan College *B*

Hawaii

University of Hawaii
  Manoa *B, M, D*

Idaho

Boise State University *B*
College of Idaho *B*
College of Southern Idaho *A*
Idaho State University *B, M*
University of Idaho *B, M*

Illinois

Augustana College *B*
Aurora University *B*
Bradley University *B, T*
City Colleges of Chicago
  Kennedy-King College *A*
Columbia College Chicago *B*
Concordia University Chicago *B*
DePaul University *B*
Dominican University *B*
Eastern Illinois University *B, T*
Elmhurst College *B*
Eureka College *B*
Greenville College *B*
Illinois Central College *A*
Illinois College *B*
Illinois State University *B, M, T*
Illinois Valley Community College *A*
Illinois Wesleyan University *B*
John A. Logan College *A*
Kishwaukee College *A*
Knox College *B*
Lewis University *B*
Lincoln College *A*
Loyola University Chicago *C, B*
MacMurray College *B*
Millikin University *B*
Monmouth College *B, T*
National-Louis University *B*
North Central College *B*
Northern Illinois University *B, M*
Northwestern University *B, M, D*
Principia College *B*
Rockford University *B*
Roosevelt University *B, M*
South Suburban College of Cook
  County *A*
Southern Illinois University
  Carbondale *B, M*
Southern Illinois University
  Edwardsville *B*
Southwestern Illinois College *A*
University of Illinois
  Chicago *B, M*
  Urbana-Champaign *B, M, D*
Western Illinois University *B, M*

Indiana

Anderson University *B*
Ball State University *B, T*
Bethel College *B*
Butler University *B*
DePauw University *B*
Earlham College *B*
Franklin College *B*
Goshen College *B*
Grace College *B*
Hanover College *B*
Huntington University *B*
Indiana State University *B*
Indiana University
  Bloomington *B, M, D*
  Northwest *B*
  Purdue University Fort Wayne *B*
  South Bend *B*
Purdue University *B*
Saint Mary's College *B*
Taylor University *B*
University of Evansville *B*
University of Indianapolis *B*
University of Notre Dame *B*
University of Southern Indiana *B*
Valparaiso University *B*
Vincennes University *A*
Wabash College *B*

Iowa

Briar Cliff University *B*
Central College *B*
Clarke University *A, B, T*
Coe College *B*
Cornell College *B, T*
Dordt College *B*
Drake University *B, T*
Ellsworth Community College *A*
Graceland University *B*
Grand View University *B*
Grinnell College *B*
Luther College *B*
Morningside College *B*
Northwestern College *B, T*
St. Ambrose University *B*
Simpson College *B*
University of Iowa *B, M*
University of Northern Iowa *B*
Waldorf College *B*
Wartburg College *B*

Kansas

Baker University *B, T*
Barton County Community College *A*
Benedictine College *B*
Butler Community College *A*
Coffeyville Community College *A*
Cowley County Community
  College *A*
Emporia State University *B*
Friends University *B*
Garden City Community College *A*
Independence Community College *A*
Kansas State University *B, M*
Kansas Wesleyan University *B*
McPherson College *B, T*
Neosho County Community
  College *A*
Ottawa University *B, T*
Pratt Community College *A*
Seward County Community
  College *A*
Southwestern College *B*
Sterling College *B, T*
University of Kansas *B, M, D*
University of St. Mary *B*
Washburn University *B*
Wichita State University *B*

Kentucky

Asbury University *B*
Bellarmine University *B*
Berea College *B*
Bluegrass Community and Technical College *A*
Brescia University *B*
Campbellsville University *B*
Centre College *B*
Eastern Kentucky University *B*
Georgetown College *B*
Morehead State University *B*
Murray State University *B*
Northern Kentucky University *B*
Owensboro Community and Technical College *C, A*
Thomas More College *A, B*
Transylvania University *B*
Union College *B*
University of Kentucky *B, M*
University of Louisville *B, M*
University of the Cumberlands *B*
Western Kentucky University *B*

Louisiana

Centenary College of Louisiana *B*
Dillard University *B*
Grambling State University *B*
Louisiana College *B*
Louisiana State University Shreveport *B*
Louisiana State University and Agricultural and Mechanical College *B, M, D*
Loyola University New Orleans *B*
Northwestern State University *B*
Tulane University *B, M*
University of New Orleans *B, M*

Maine

Bates College *B*
Colby College *B*
University of Maine *B, M*
University of Southern Maine *B*

Maryland

Bowie State University *B*
Frederick Community College *A*
Frostburg State University *B*
Goucher College *B*
Howard Community College *A*
McDaniel College *B*
Morgan State University *B, M*
Prince George's Community College *C*
St. Mary's College of Maryland *B*
Salisbury University *B*
Towson University *B, M*
University of Maryland Baltimore County *B*
College Park *B*
Washington College *B, T*

Massachusetts

Amherst College *B*
Bard College at Simon's Rock *B*
Boston College *B*
Brandeis University *B, M*
Bunker Hill Community College *A*
Cape Cod Community College *A*
Clark University *B*
College of the Holy Cross *B*
Dean College *A, B*
Eastern Nazarene College *B*
Emerson College *B, M*
Fitchburg State University *B*
Gordon College *B*
Hampshire College *B*
Massasoit Community College *A*
Merrimack College *B*
Middlesex Community College *A*
Mount Holyoke College *B*
Northeastern University *B*
Salem State University *B*

Smith College *B*
Suffolk University *B*
University of Massachusetts Amherst *B, M*
Boston *B*
Wellesley College *B*
Westfield State University *B*
Williams College *B*

Michigan

Adrian College *A, B*
Albion College *B*
Alma College *B*
Aquinas College *B*
Calvin College *B*
Central Michigan University *B, M*
Delta College *A*
Eastern Michigan University *B, M*
Grand Rapids Community College *A*
Grand Valley State University *B*
Henry Ford Community College *A*
Hillsdale College *B*
Hope College *B*
Kalamazoo College *B, T*
Kuyper College *B*
Lake Michigan College *A*
Lansing Community College *C, A*
Michigan State University *B, M*
Mid Michigan Community College *A*
Northern Michigan University *B*
Northwestern Michigan College *A*
Oakland University *B*
Saginaw Valley State University *B*
Siena Heights University *B*
Spring Arbor University *B*
University of Detroit Mercy *B*
University of Michigan *B*
University of Michigan Flint *B, T*
Wayne State University *B, M*

Minnesota

Anoka-Ramsey Community College *A*
Augsburg College *B*
Bethany Lutheran College *B*
Bethel University *B*
Carleton College *B*
College of St. Benedict *B*
Concordia College: Moorhead *B*
Concordia University St. Paul *B*
Gustavus Adolphus College *B*
Hamline University *B*
Inver Hills Community College *A*
Macalester College *B*
Metropolitan State University *B*
Minneapolis Community and Technical College *A*
Minnesota State University Mankato *B, M*
Moorhead *B*
Normandale Community College *A*
North Central University *A, B*
North Hennepin Community College *A*
St. Catherine University *B*
Saint Cloud State University *B*
St. John's University *B*
St. Mary's University of Minnesota *B*
St. Olaf College *B*
Southwest Minnesota State University *B*
University of Minnesota Duluth *B*
Morris *B*
Twin Cities *B, M, D*
University of Northwestern - St. Paul *B*
Winona State University *B*

Mississippi

Belhaven University *B*
Hinds Community College *A*
University of Mississippi *B*

University of Southern Mississippi *B, M*
William Carey University *B*

Missouri

Avila University *B*
Calvary Bible College and Theological Seminary *B*
Central Methodist University *B*
College of the Ozarks *B*
Culver-Stockton College *B*
Drury University *B*
Evangel University *A, B*
Fontbonne University *B*
Hannibal-LaGrange University *B*
Lindenwood University *B, M*
Missouri Baptist University *B*
Missouri Southern State University *B, T*
Missouri State University *B, M*
Missouri Valley College *B*
Northwest Missouri State University *B*
Park University *B*
St. Charles Community College *A*
Saint Louis University *B*
Southeast Missouri State University *B*
Southwest Baptist University *B*
Stephens College *B*
Truman State University *B*
University of Central Missouri *B, M*
University of Missouri Columbia *B, M, D*
Kansas City *B, M*
St. Louis *B*
Washington University in St. Louis *B, M*
Webster University *B*
William Jewell College *B*
William Woods University *B, T*

Montana

Miles Community College *A*
Montana State University Billings *B*
Rocky Mountain College *B*
University of Montana *B, M*
University of Montana: Western *B*

Nebraska

Chadron State College *B*
Concordia University *B, T*
Creighton University *B*
Doane College *B*
Hastings College *B, T*
Midland University *B, T*
Nebraska Wesleyan University *B*
Northeast Community College *A*
University of Nebraska Kearney *B, T*
Lincoln *B, M*
Omaha *B, M*
Wayne State College *B*

Nevada

Truckee Meadows Community College *C, A*
University of Nevada Las Vegas *B, M*
Reno *B*

New Hampshire

Dartmouth College *B*
Franklin Pierce University *B*
New England College *B*
Plymouth State University *B*
University of New Hampshire *B*

New Jersey

Centenary College *B*
Cumberland County College *A*
Drew University *B*
Essex County College *A*

Fairleigh Dickinson University College at Florham *B*
Gloucester County College *A*
Kean University *B*
Middlesex County College *A*
Monmouth University *B*
Montclair State University *B, M*
Ramapo College of New Jersey *B*
Rutgers, The State University of New Jersey
Camden Campus *B, T*
New Brunswick/Piscataway Campus *B, M*
Newark Campus *B*
Seton Hall University *B*
Thomas Edison State College *B*

New Mexico

Eastern New Mexico University *B*
New Mexico State University *B*
Santa Fe University of Art and Design *B*
University of New Mexico *B, M*

New York

Adelphi University *B*
Alfred University *B*
Bard College *B*
Barnard College *B*
City University of New York
Brooklyn College *B, M*
City College *B*
College of Staten Island *B*
Hunter College *B, M*
LaGuardia Community College *A*
Queens College *B*
Queensborough Community College *A*
York College *B*
Colgate University *B*
Columbia University *B*
Columbia University School of General Studies *B*
Cornell University *B, M, D*
Daemen College *B*
Elmira College *B*
Finger Lakes Community College *A*
Five Towns College *B*
Fordham University *B, M*
Genesee Community College *A*
Hamilton College *B*
Hartwick College *B*
Hobart and William Smith Colleges *B*
Hofstra University *B*
Ithaca College *B*
Juilliard School *B*
Le Moyne College *B*
Long Island University LIU Post *B, M*
Manhattanville College *B*
Marymount Manhattan College *B*
Molloy College *B*
Nazareth College *B*
New York University *B, M, D*
Niagara County Community College *A*
Niagara University *B*
Pace University: Pleasantville/Briarcliff *B*
Rockland Community College *A*
SUNY
College at Brockport *B*
College at Buffalo *B*
College at Fredonia *B*
College at Geneseo *B*
College at New Paltz *B*
College at Oneonta *B*
College at Oswego *B*
College at Plattsburgh *B*
College at Potsdam *B*
College at Purchase *B*
University at Binghamton *B, M*
University at Buffalo *B, M, D*
University at Stony Brook *B, M*

Sage Colleges *B*
Saint Bonaventure University *B*
St. John's University *B*
Sarah Lawrence College *M*
Siena College *C*
Skidmore College *B*
Suffolk County Community College *A*
Syracuse University *B, M*
Ulster County Community College *A*
Vassar College *B*
Wagner College *B*
Westchester Community College *A*

North Carolina

Appalachian State University *B*
Barton College *B*
Blue Ridge Community College *A*
Brevard College *B*
Campbell University *B*
Catawba College *B, T*
College of the Albemarle *A*
Davidson College *B*
Duke University *B*
East Carolina University *B*
Elon University *B*
Fayetteville State University *B*
Gardner-Webb University *B*
Greensboro College *C, B, T*
Guilford College *B*
High Point University *B*
Lees-McRae College *B, T*
Lenoir-Rhyne University *B, T*
Livingstone College *B*
Mars Hill University *B*
Meredith College *B*
North Carolina Agricultural and
    Technical State University *B*
North Carolina Central University *B*
North Carolina Wesleyan College *B*
Queens University of Charlotte *B*
University of North Carolina
    Asheville *B, T*
    Chapel Hill *B, M*
    Charlotte *B*
    Greensboro *B, M*
    Pembroke *B*
    School of the Arts *C, B*
    Wilmington *B*
Wake Forest University *B*
Western Carolina University *B*
Western Piedmont Community
    College *A*

North Dakota

Dickinson State University *B*
Minot State University *B*
North Dakota State University *B*
Trinity Bible College *B*
University of Jamestown *B*
University of North Dakota *B, M*

Ohio

Ashland University *B*
Bowling Green State
    University *B, M, D*
Capital University *B*
Case Western Reserve
    University *B, M*
Cedarville University *B*
Cleveland State University *B*
College of Wooster *B*
Denison University *B*
Edison State Community College *A*
Franciscan University of
    Steubenville *B*
Hiram College *B, T*
Kent State University *B, M*
Kenyon College *B*
Malone University *B*
Marietta College *B*
Miami University
    Oxford *B, M*
Mount Vernon Nazarene University *B*
Muskingum University *B*

Oberlin College *B*
Ohio Northern University *B*
Ohio State University
    Columbus Campus *C, B, M, D*
    Lima Campus *B*
Ohio University *B, M*
Ohio Wesleyan University *B*
Otterbein University *B*
Sinclair Community College *A*
University of Akron *B, M*
University of Cincinnati *B*
University of Dayton *B*
University of Findlay *B*
University of Mount Union *B*
University of Toledo *B*
Wilmington College *B*
Wright State University *B*
Xavier University *B*
Youngstown State University *B*

Oklahoma

Carl Albert State College *A*
East Central University *B*
Eastern Oklahoma State College *A*
Northeastern Oklahoma Agricultural
    and Mechanical College *A*
Northeastern State University *B*
Northwestern Oklahoma State
    University *B*
Oklahoma Baptist University *B, T*
Oklahoma Christian University *B*
Oklahoma City University *B*
Oklahoma State University *B, M*
Oral Roberts University *B*
Southeastern Oklahoma State
    University *B*
Tulsa Community College *A*
University of Central Oklahoma *B*
University of Oklahoma *B, M*
University of Science and Arts of
    Oklahoma *B, T*
University of Tulsa *B*

Oregon

Eastern Oregon University *B*
George Fox University *B*
Lewis & Clark College *B*
Linfield College *B*
Linn-Benton Community College *A*
Mt. Hood Community College *A*
Pacific University *B*
Portland State University *B, M*
Reed College *B*
Southern Oregon University *B, T*
University of Oregon *B, M, D*
University of Portland *B, M*
Western Oregon University *B*
Willamette University *B*

Pennsylvania

Albright College *B*
Allegheny College *B*
Alvernia University *B*
Arcadia University *B*
Bloomsburg University of
    Pennsylvania *B*
Bucknell University *B*
Bucks County Community College *A*
California University of
    Pennsylvania *B*
Carnegie Mellon University *B, M*
Cedar Crest College *B*
Cheyney University of
    Pennsylvania *B*
Clarion University of Pennsylvania *B*
Community College of
    Philadelphia *A*
DeSales University *B, T*
Dickinson College *B*
Duquesne University *B*
East Stroudsburg University of
    Pennsylvania *B*
Edinboro University of
    Pennsylvania *B*

Elizabethtown College *B*
Franklin & Marshall College *B*
Gannon University *B*
Gettysburg College *B*
Harrisburg Area Community
    College *A*
Indiana University of Pennsylvania *B*
Juniata College *B*
King's College *B*
Lehigh University *B*
Lock Haven University of
    Pennsylvania *B*
Lycoming College *B*
Mansfield University of
    Pennsylvania *B*
Marywood University *B*
Messiah College *B*
Muhlenberg College *C, B*
Neumann University *B*
Penn State
    University Park *M*
Point Park University *B*
St. Vincent College *B*
Seton Hill University *B*
Susquehanna University *B*
Swarthmore College *B*
University of Pennsylvania *B*
University of Pittsburgh *B, M, D*
University of Pittsburgh
    Johnstown *B*
University of Scranton *B*
Ursinus College *B*
Villanova University *M*
West Chester University of
    Pennsylvania *B*
Westminster College *B, T*
Wilkes University *B*
York College of Pennsylvania *B*

Puerto Rico

University of Puerto Rico
    Aguadilla *A*
    Rio Piedras *B*
University of the Sacred Heart *B*

Rhode Island

Brown University *B, M, D*
Community College of Rhode
    Island *A*
Rhode Island College *B, M*
Roger Williams University *B*
Salve Regina University *B*
University of Rhode Island *B*

South Carolina

Anderson University *B*
Bob Jones University *B, M*
Coastal Carolina University *B*
Coker College *B*
College of Charleston *B*
Converse College *B*
Francis Marion University *B*
Furman University *B*
Limestone College *B*
Newberry College *B*
North Greenville University *B*
Presbyterian College *B*
South Carolina State University *B*
University of South Carolina
    Columbia *B, M*
Winthrop University *B*
Wofford College *B*

South Dakota

Augustana College *B, T*
Dakota Wesleyan University *B*
Mount Marty College *B*
South Dakota State University *B*
University of Sioux Falls *B*
University of South Dakota *B, M*

Tennessee

Belmont University *B*
Bethel University *B*

Bryan University
    Dayton *B*
Freed-Hardeman University *T*
Hiwassee College *A*
Lee University *B*
Lipscomb University *B*
Maryville College *B*
Middle Tennessee State University *B*
Milligan College *T*
Rhodes College *B*
Sewanee: The University of the
    South *B*
Tennessee State University *B*
Trevecca Nazarene University *B*
Union University *B, T*
University of Memphis *B, M*
University of Tennessee
    Chattanooga *B*
    Knoxville *B, M*
Vanderbilt University *B*

Texas

Abilene Christian University *B*
Alvin Community College *A*
Amarillo College *A*
Angelina College *A*
Angelo State University *B, T*
Austin Community College *A*
Baylor University *B, M*
Blinn College *A*
Brazosport College *A*
Clarendon College *A*
College of the Mainland *A*
Del Mar College *A*
East Texas Baptist University *B*
El Paso Community College *A*
Galveston College *A*
Grayson College *A*
Hardin-Simmons University *B*
Hill College *A*
Howard College *A*
Howard Payne University *B*
Kilgore College *A*
Lamar State College at Port Arthur *A*
Lamar University *B, M*
Laredo Community College *A*
Lee College *A*
McMurry University *B, T*
Midland College *A*
Midwestern State University *B*
Navarro College *A*
Northeast Texas Community
    College *A*
Our Lady of the Lake University of
    San Antonio *B*
Palo Alto College *A*
Paris Junior College *A*
Prairie View A&M University *B*
St. Edward's University *B*
St. Philip's College *A*
Sam Houston State University *B*
San Jacinto College *A*
Schreiner University *B*
South Plains College *A*
Southern Methodist University *B, M*
Southwestern University *B, T*
Stephen F. Austin State
    University *B, T*
Sul Ross State University *B*
Tarleton State University *B*
Texarkana College *A*
Texas A&M University *B*
Texas A&M University
    Commerce *B, M*
    Corpus Christi *T*
    Kingsville *B, T*
Texas Christian University *B*
Texas Lutheran University *B*
Texas Southern University *B*
Texas State University *B, M, T*
Texas Tech University *B, M*
Texas Woman's University *B, M*
Trinity University *B*
Trinity Valley Community College *A*
Tyler Junior College *A*

University of Dallas *B, T*
University of Houston *B, M*
University of North Texas *B, M*
University of St. Thomas *B*
University of Texas
  Arlington *B*
  Austin *B, M, D*
  El Paso *B*
  Pan American *B, M*
University of the Incarnate Word *B*
Wayland Baptist University *B, T*
West Texas A&M University *B*
Western Texas College *A*
Wharton County Junior College *A*

Utah

Brigham Young University *B*
Southern Utah University *B*
University of Utah *B, M, D, T*
Utah State University *B, M*
Utah Valley University *A, B*
Weber State University *B*
Westminster College *B*

Vermont

Bennington College *B*
Castleton State College *B*
Johnson State College *B*
Marlboro College *B*
Middlebury College *B*
Saint Michael's College *B*
University of Vermont *B*

Virginia

Averett University *B*
Bluefield College *B*
Christopher Newport University *B*
College of William and Mary *B*
Eastern Mennonite University *B*
Emory & Henry College *B*
Ferrum College *B*
George Mason University *B*
Hampton University *B*
Hollins University *B, M*
James Madison University *B, T*
Liberty University *B*
Lynchburg College *B*
Mary Baldwin College *B, M*
Old Dominion University *B*
Radford University *B*
Randolph College *B*
Randolph-Macon College *B*
Regent University *M*
Roanoke College *B, T*
Shenandoah University *B*
Southern Virginia University *B*
Sweet Briar College *B*
University of Virginia *B, M*
University of Virginia's College at
  Wise *B, T*
Virginia Commonwealth
  University *B, M*
Virginia Intermont College *B*
Virginia Polytechnic Institute and
  State University *B, M*
Virginia Wesleyan College *B*
Washington and Lee University *B*

Washington

Central Washington University *B*
Centralia College *A*
Cornish College of the Arts *B*
Eastern Washington University *B*
Evergreen State College *B*
Gonzaga University *B*
Highline Community College *A*
North Seattle Community
  College *C, A*
Saint Martin's University *B*
Seattle Pacific University *B*
Seattle University *B*
University of Puget Sound *B*
University of Washington *B, M, D*

Western Washington University *B, M*
Whitman College *B*

West Virginia

Bethany College *B*
Concord University *B*
Davis and Elkins College *B*
Fairmont State University *B*
West Virginia University *B, M*
West Virginia Wesleyan College *B*
Wheeling Jesuit University *B*

Wisconsin

Beloit College *B*
Cardinal Stritch University *B*
Carroll University *B*
Carthage College *B, T*
Edgewood College *B*
Lawrence University *B*
Marquette University *B*
Ripon College *B, T*
St. Norbert College *B*
University of Wisconsin
  Eau Claire *B*
  Green Bay *B, T*
  La Crosse *B*
  Madison *B, M, D*
  Milwaukee *B, T*
  Oshkosh *B*
  Parkside *B, T*
  Platteville *B, T*
  Stevens Point *B*
  Superior *B, M*
  Whitewater *B*
Viterbo University *B, T*
Wisconsin Lutheran College *B*

Wyoming

Central Wyoming College *A*
Sheridan College *A*
University of Wyoming *B*
Western Wyoming Community
  College *A*

Drama/dance teacher education

Alabama

Birmingham-Southern College *T*
Faulkner University *B, T*

Arizona

Grand Canyon University *B*

Arkansas

Ouachita Baptist University *B, T*

California

California State University
  Long Beach *T*
Orange Coast College *A*
San Francisco State University *T*

Colorado

Adams State University *B*
Colorado State University *B, T*

District of Columbia

Catholic University of America *M*
George Washington University *T*

Florida

Jacksonville University *B, M*
University of Miami *B*
University of South Florida *B*

Georgia

Brenau University *B*
Columbus State University *B*
Darton College *A*
Piedmont College *B, T*

Idaho

Brigham Young University-Idaho *B, T*

Illinois

Bradley University *B*
North Park University *T*
Rockford University *T*

Indiana

Anderson University *B, T*
University of Evansville *B, T*
Valparaiso University *B*

Iowa

Central College *T*
Dordt College *B*
Drake University *T*
Simpson College *T*
University of Iowa *T*

Kansas

Bethel College *T*
Hutchinson Community College *A*
Sterling College *T*
University of St. Mary *T*

Louisiana

Centenary College of Louisiana *T*

Massachusetts

Boston University *B, M*
Bridgewater State University *B*
Emerson College *B, M*
Tufts University *T*

Michigan

Hope College *B, T*

Minnesota

Hamline University *T*
Minnesota State University
  Mankato *B, T*
Saint Cloud State University *B, T*
Southwest Minnesota State
  University *B, T*
University of Minnesota
  Morris *T*

Mississippi

Millsaps College *T*
William Carey University *B*

Missouri

Missouri Baptist University *B, T*
Washington University in St.
  Louis *B, M, T*
William Jewell College *B, T*

Montana

Montana State University
  Billings *T*
University of Montana *T*
University of Montana: Western *T*

Nebraska

Chadron State College *B*
Hastings College *B, T*
Wayne State College *B, T*
York College *B, T*

New Hampshire

Keene State College *B*

New Jersey

County College of Morris *A*
Montclair State University *B*
Rutgers, The State University of New
  Jersey
  New Brunswick/Piscataway
    Campus *M*

New York

City University of New York
  Hunter College *B, T*
Hofstra University *B*
SUNY
  College at Potsdam *B*

North Carolina

East Carolina University *B*
Greensboro College *B, T*
Lees-McRae College *B, T*
Meredith College *B, T*
North Carolina Central
  University *B, M, T*
University of North Carolina
  Charlotte *B*
  Greensboro *B, M*

North Dakota

Dickinson State University *B, T*

Ohio

Bowling Green State University *B, M*
Ohio State University
  Columbus Campus *M*
Ohio Wesleyan University *B*
University of Akron *B, M*
University of Findlay *B, M, T*

Oklahoma

East Central University *B, T*
Eastern Oklahoma State College *A*
University of Central Oklahoma *B*

Oregon

Portland State University *T*

Pennsylvania

Point Park University *B*

South Carolina

Columbia College *B, T*
Furman University *T*

South Dakota

University of Sioux Falls *T*
University of South Dakota *B, M, T*

Tennessee

Belmont University *B, T*
Lee University *B*
Lipscomb University *B, T*
Maryville College *B, T*
Trevecca Nazarene University *B, T*

Texas

Austin College *M*
East Texas Baptist University *B*
Hardin-Simmons University *B, T*
Howard Payne University *B*
Lamar University *T*
Lubbock Christian University *B*
St. Edward's University *B, T*
Sam Houston State University *M, T*
Tarleton State University *T*
Texas A&M University
  Kingsville *T*
University of Dallas *T*
West Texas A&M University *T*

Utah

Brigham Young University *B*
Southern Utah University *B*
Utah Valley University *B*
Weber State University *B*

Vermont

Castleton State College *B, T*
Johnson State College *B*

Virginia

Bridgewater College *T*
Eastern Mennonite University *T*

Longwood University *T*
Virginia Highlands Community
College *A*
Virginia Intermont College *T*

Washington
Central Washington
University *B, M, T*
Western Washington University *B*
Whitworth University *T*

West Virginia
Davis and Elkins College *B*

Wisconsin
Carroll University *T*
Edgewood College *B*
University of Wisconsin
Green Bay *T*
Whitewater *B*
Viterbo University *B, T*

Drawing

Alabama
Birmingham-Southern College *B*

California
Academy of Art University *C, A, B, M*
Berkeley City College *C*
Biola University *B*
California College of the Arts *B, M*
California State University
East Bay *B*
Long Beach *B, M*
Northridge *B, M*
Chabot College *A*
College of the Desert *A*
Grossmont College *A*
Hartnell College *C*
Laguna College of Art and
Design *C, B, M*
Long Beach City College *A*
Monterey Peninsula College *C, A*
Ohlone College *C*
Oxnard College *A*
Palomar College *A*
Pasadena City College *A*
Santa Rosa Junior College *C*
Solano Community College *A*

Colorado
Adams State University *B*

Connecticut
Lyme Academy College of Fine
Arts *B*
University of Hartford *B*

District of Columbia
American University *M*
Corcoran College of Art and
Design *C*

Georgia
Albany State University *B*
Georgia State University *B, M*

Illinois
American Academy of Art *B*
Bradley University *B*
Lewis University *B*
Lincoln College *A*
Richland Community College *A*
School of the Art Institute of
Chicago *B, M*

Indiana
Grace College *B*
Indiana University
Purdue University Fort Wayne *B*
Indiana Wesleyan University *B*

Iowa
Drake University *B*
University of Iowa *B, M*

Kansas
Allen County Community College *A*
Central Christian College of Kansas *A*
Kansas Wesleyan University *B*
Pratt Community College *A*

Kentucky
Eastern Kentucky University *B*

Maine
College of the Atlantic *B, M*
University of Southern Maine *B*

Maryland
Cecil College *A*
Maryland Institute College of Art *B*

Massachusetts
Boston University *B*
Salem State University *B*
School of the Museum of Fine
Arts *B, M*
University of Massachusetts
Dartmouth *M*

Michigan
Aquinas College *B*
College for Creative Studies *B*
Ferris State University *B*
Finlandia University *B*
Northern Michigan University *B*
Oakland University *B, T*
Siena Heights University *B*
University of Michigan *B*

Minnesota
Minneapolis College of Art and
Design *B*
Minnesota State University
Mankato *B, M*
Saint Cloud State University *B*

Missouri
Kansas City Art Institute *B*
Washington University in St.
Louis *B, M*

Nevada
Sierra Nevada College *B*

New York
Pratt Institute *A*
Rochester Institute of Technology *M*
SUNY
College at Fredonia *B*
College at Oneonta *B*
College at Purchase *B*

North Carolina
East Carolina University *B*
Gardner-Webb University *B*

Ohio
Art Academy of Cincinnati *B*
Bowling Green State University *B*
Cleveland Institute of Art *B*
Sinclair Community College *C*

Oregon
Mt. Hood Community College *A*
Oregon College of Art & Craft *C, B*
Portland State University *B*

Pennsylvania
Pennsylvania Academy of the Fine
Arts *C, B, M*
Pennsylvania College of Art and
Design *B*

Seton Hill University *B*
University of the Arts *B*

Puerto Rico
Inter American University of Puerto
Rico
San German Campus *M*
University of Puerto Rico
Rio Piedras *B*

Rhode Island
Providence College *B*

South Carolina
Trident Technical College *C*

Tennessee
Memphis College of Art *B, M*
Tennessee Technological
University *B*

Texas
University of Texas
El Paso *B, M*
Western Texas College *A*

Utah
Dixie State College *B*

Vermont
Bennington College *B*
Marlboro College *B*

Washington
Cornish College of the Arts *B*
North Seattle Community College *C*
Western Washington University *B*

West Virginia
Marshall University *M*
West Virginia State University *B*
West Virginia Wesleyan College *B*

Wisconsin
Milwaukee Institute of Art &
Design *B*

Driver/safety education

Illinois
McKendree University *T*

Iowa
Grand View University *T*
Iowa State University *T*

Minnesota
Saint Cloud State University *B*

Missouri
Missouri Baptist University *T*
Missouri Western State University *T*

Montana
Montana State University
Northern *T*

New York
New York University *B, M, D*

North Carolina
North Carolina Agricultural and
Technical State
University *B, M, T*

Ohio
University of Findlay *B, M, T*

Oklahoma
Northeastern State University *T*
Southwestern Oklahoma State
University *T*

South Dakota
Northern State University *T*

Texas
Lamar University *T*
Texas State University *T*

Virginia
Radford University *T*
University of Virginia's College at
Wise *T*

West Virginia
Marshall University *M*
West Virginia University *T*

Wisconsin
University of Wisconsin
Whitewater *B*

Drywall installation

California
Palomar College *C, A*

Indiana
Ivy Tech Community College
Lafayette *C*

Kentucky
Big Sandy Community and Technical
College *C*

Dutch/Flemish

California
University of California
Berkeley *B*

Iowa
Dordt College *B*

Michigan
Calvin College *B*

E-commerce

Alabama
University of Phoenix
Birmingham *B*

Arizona
ITT Technical Institute
Tempe *B*
Tucson *B*
Northcentral University *B, M, D*
University of Phoenix
Phoenix-Hohokam *B*
Southern Arizona *B*

California
California State University
Fullerton *M*
College of the Siskiyous *C*
Foothill College *C*
ITT Technical Institute
Oxnard *B*
MiraCosta College *C*
National University *M*
Palomar College *C, A*
San Jose City College *C*
University of La Verne *B*
University of Phoenix
Bay Area *B*
Central Valley *B*
Sacramento Valley *B*
Southern California *B*
University of San Francisco *M*
Westwood College
Inland Empire *B*
Los Angeles *B*

Colorado

CollegeAmerica
Fort Collins *A*
Colorado Technical
University *C, A, B*
University of Phoenix
Denver *B*
Westwood College
Denver North *B*
Denver South *B*

Delaware

Delaware Technical Community
College
Jack F. Owens Campus *A*
Stanton/Wilmington Campus *C*
Terry Campus *A*

District of Columbia

University of Phoenix
Washington DC *B*

Florida

Pasco-Hernando State College *C, A*
University of Phoenix
Central Florida *B*
North Florida *B*
South Florida *B*
West Florida *B*

Georgia

Central Georgia Technical College *C*
Gwinnett Technical College *C*
University of Phoenix
Atlanta *B*
Augusta *B*
Columbus *B*
Savannah *B*

Hawaii

University of Phoenix
Hawaii *B*

Idaho

University of Phoenix
Idaho *B*

Illinois

DePaul University *B, M*
DeVry University
Online *B*
Lewis University *B*
Lincoln Land Community College *C*
Moraine Valley Community College *C*
Northwestern University *M*
Prairie State College *C*
Saint Xavier University *M*
University of Phoenix
Chicago *B*

Indiana

ITT Technical Institute
Fort Wayne *B*
Indianapolis *B*
Indiana University
Purdue University Indianapolis *C*
University of Phoenix
Indianapolis *B*

Iowa

Ashford University *B*

Kansas

Friends University *B*

Kentucky

ITT Technical Institute
Louisville *B*
Maysville Community and Technical
College *A*
University of Phoenix
Louisville *B*

Louisiana

University of Phoenix
Baton Rouge *B*
Louisiana *B*
Shreveport *B*

Maine

University of Maine
Fort Kent *B*

Maryland

ITT Technical Institute
Owings Mills *B*
University of Maryland
University College *M*
University of Phoenix
Maryland *B*

Massachusetts

Bristol Community College *C*
Bunker Hill Community College *C*
North Shore Community College *C*
University of Phoenix
Boston *B*

Michigan

Eastern Michigan University *M*
Ferris State University *C*
Lansing Community College *C, A*
Madonna University *C, M*
University of Phoenix
Metro Detroit *B*
West Michigan *B*
Wayne County Community
College *C, A*

Minnesota

Bemidji State University *B*
Capella University *B*
Century College *A*
Inver Hills Community College *C*
North Hennepin Community
College *C*
South Central College *C*
University of Phoenix
Minneapolis-St. Paul *B*

Mississippi

University of Phoenix
Jackson *B*

Missouri

Maryville University of Saint Louis *B*
University of Phoenix
Kansas City *B*
St. Louis *B*

Nebraska

University of Phoenix
Omaha *B*

Nevada

University of Phoenix
Las Vegas *B*

New Jersey

Bergen Community College *C*
Bloomfield College *B*
Passaic County Community College *C*
University of Phoenix
Jersey City *B*

New Mexico

ITT Technical Institute
Albuquerque *B*
University of Phoenix
New Mexico *B*
Western New Mexico University *A*

New York

Finger Lakes Community College *A*
Globe Institute of Technology *C*

Orange County Community
College *C, A*
Pace University: Pleasantville/
Briarcliff *B*
Rochester Institute of Technology *C*
Westchester Community College *C*

North Carolina

Brunswick Community College *C*
Catawba Valley Community
College *C, A*
Isothermal Community College *C, A*
Piedmont Community College *C*
Pitt Community College *A*
Sandhills Community College *A*
University of Phoenix
Charlotte *B*
Raleigh *B*

North Dakota

North Dakota State College of
Science *C, A*

Ohio

Lakeland Community College *C, A*
Stark State College *A*
Tiffin University *B*
University of Akron *B*
University of Phoenix
Cleveland *B*
University of Toledo *B*
Urbana University *B*
Washington State Community
College *A*

Oklahoma

Northwestern Oklahoma State
University *B*
University of Phoenix
Oklahoma City *B*

Oregon

Clackamas Community College *C, A*
Lane Community College *C*
Portland Community College *C*

Pennsylvania

DeSales University *B*
Delaware County Community
College *C, A*
Harrisburg University of Science and
Technology *B*
Penn State
Abington *C*
Altoona *C*
Beaver *C*
Berks *C*
Brandywine *C*
DuBois *C*
Erie, The Behrend College *C*
Fayette, The Eberly Campus *C*
Greater Allegheny *C*
Harrisburg *C*
Hazleton *C*
Lehigh Valley *C*
Mont Alto *C*
New Kensington *C*
Schuylkill *C*
Shenango *C*
University Park *C*
Wilkes-Barre *C*
Worthington Scranton *C*
York *C*
Thiel College *B*
University of Pennsylvania *B, M*
University of Phoenix
Pittsburgh *B*
University of Scranton *B*

Puerto Rico

Universidad del Este *M*

South Carolina

Limestone College *B*
University of Phoenix
Columbia *B*
Winthrop University *B*

Tennessee

Chattanooga State Community
College *C*
ITT Technical Institute
Knoxville *B*
Memphis *B*
Nashville *B*
Pellissippi State Community
College *A*
Trevecca Nazarene University *B*
University of Phoenix
Chattanooga *B*
Memphis *B*
Nashville *B*

Texas

Brookhaven College *C, A*
Eastfield College *C, A*
Kilgore College *C, A*
North Lake College *C*
Texas State Technical College
Marshall *C, A*
University of Dallas *M*
University of North Texas *B*
University of Phoenix
Austin *B*
Dallas Fort Worth *B*
Houston Westside *B*
San Antonio *B*

Utah

University of Phoenix
Utah *B, M*

Virginia

Germanna Community College *C*
ITT Technical Institute
Norfolk *B*
University of Phoenix
Northern Virginia *B*

Washington

Edmonds Community College *C, A*
ITT Technical Institute
Everett *B*
University of Phoenix
Western Washington *B*
Yakima Valley Community College *A*

Wisconsin

ITT Technical Institute
Green Bay *B*
Greenfield *B*
University of Phoenix
Milwaukee *B*

Early childhood education

Alabama

Alabama Agricultural and Mechanical
University *B, M*
Auburn University *B, M, D, T*
Birmingham-Southern College *B, T*
Bishop State Community
College *C, A*
Concordia College *B*
Faulkner State Community College *A*
Gadsden State Community College *A*
Samford University *M, T*
Shelton State Community College *C*
Spring Hill College *B, M, T*
Troy University *B, M, T*
University of Alabama *B, M*
University of Alabama
Birmingham *B, M, D, T*
University of Mobile *B, M, T*

University of South Alabama *B, M, T*
University of West Alabama *M, T*

Alaska

University of Alaska
    Anchorage *B, T*

Arizona

Arizona State University *B*
Arizona Western College *C, A*
Central Arizona College *C, A*
Cochise College *A*
Coconino County Community
    College *A*
Dine College *A*
Glendale Community College *C, A*
Grand Canyon University *B, M*
Mesa Community College *C*
Northcentral University *M, D*
Northern Arizona University *B, M*
Northland Pioneer College *C, A*
Paradise Valley Community
    College *C, A*
Penn Foster College *A*
Pima Community College *C, A*
Prescott College *T*
Scottsdale Community College *C, A*
South Mountain Community
    College *C, A*
University of Phoenix
    Phoenix-Hohokam *M*
    Southern Arizona *M*
Yavapai College *C, A*

Arkansas

Arkansas Northeastern College *A*
Arkansas State University *B, M, T*
Arkansas State University
    Beebe *A*
    Mountain Home *A*
Arkansas Tech University *B*
Black River Technical College *A*
College of the Ouachitas *A*
Harding University *B, M, T*
Henderson State University *B*
John Brown University *B, T*
Lyon College *A*
Northwest Arkansas Community
    College *A*
Ouachita Baptist University *B, T*
Ozarka College *C*
Phillips Community College of the
    University of Arkansas *C, A*
Pulaski Technical College *A*
South Arkansas Community
    College *C*
Southern Arkansas University *B, T*
University of Arkansas
    Community College at Batesville *A*
    Fort Smith *A, B*
    Little Rock *B, M*
    Pine Bluff *B, M*
University of Central Arkansas *M*
University of the Ozarks *B, T*
Williams Baptist College *B*

California

Allan Hancock College *C, A*
Bethesda University of
    California *C, B*
Butte College *C, A*
California Baptist University *B, T*
California Lutheran University *B, M*
California State University
    Bakersfield *B*
    Channel Islands *B*
    Chico *B*
    Dominguez Hills *B*
    Fresno *B*
    Fullerton *B, T*
    Long Beach *M, T*
    Northridge *M*
    Stanislaus *B*
Canada College *C, A*

Cerritos College *A*
Cerro Coso Community College *C, A*
Chabot College *C, A*
Chaffey College *C, A*
City College of San Francisco *C*
College of the Desert *C, A*
College of the Redwoods *C, A*
College of the Sequoias *C*
College of the Siskiyous *C*
Contra Costa College *C, A*
Copper Mountain College *C*
Cosumnes River College *C, A*
Crafton Hills College *C, A*
Cuesta College *C, A*
De Anza College *C, A*
Diablo Valley College *C, A*
El Camino College *C, A*
Folsom Lake College *C, A*
Foothill College *C, A*
Fresno City College *C, A*
Gavilan College *C*
Glendale Community College *C, A*
Humboldt State University *B*
Imperial Valley College *C, A*
Irvine Valley College *C, A*
Lake Tahoe Community College *C, A*
Lassen Community College *A*
Long Beach City College *C*
Los Angeles Pierce College *C, A*
Los Angeles Southwest College *A*
Loyola Marymount University *M*
Merced College *C, A*
Merritt College *C, A*
Mills College *M, T*
Moorpark College *C, A*
Moreno Valley College *C, A*
Mount St. Mary's College *A*
Mount San Jacinto College *C, A*
Napa Valley College *C, A*
National University *A, B, T*
Norco College *C, A*
Ohlone College *C, A*
Orange Coast College *C, A*
Pacific Oaks College *T*
Pacific Union College *A, B*
Pasadena City College *C, A*
Patten University *A, B*
Reedley College *C, A*
Riverside City College *C, A*
Saddleback College *C, A*
St. Mary's College of California *M*
San Deigo Miramar College
    San Diego Miramar College *C, A*
San Diego Christian College *B, T*
San Diego State University *B, M, T*
San Francisco State University *B, T*
San Joaquin Delta College *C*
San Jose City College *C, A*
San Jose State University *B, M*
Santa Ana College *C, A*
Santa Barbara City College *C, A*
Santa Rosa Junior College *C, A*
Shasta Bible College and Graduate
    School *C, A*
Shasta College *A*
Sierra College *C, A*
Skyline College *C, A*
Solano Community College *C, A*
Sonoma State University *M, T*
Southwestern College *C, A*
Taft College *C, A*
University of California
    Santa Barbara *M*
University of La Verne *B, M, T*
Vanguard University of Southern
    California *C, T*
Ventura College *C, A*
West Hills College: Coalinga *C, A*
West Valley College *A*
Whittier College *B, T*
Woodland Community College *A*
World Mission University *C*
Yuba College *C, A*

Colorado

Adams State University *A*
Aims Community College *C, A*
Aspen University *A, B*
Colorado Christian University *C, B*
Colorado Mountain College *C, A*
Colorado Northwestern Community
    College *C, A*
Colorado State University *B, T*
Community College of Aurora *C, A*
Front Range Community College *C, A*
Metropolitan State University of
    Denver *T*
Morgan Community College *C*
Naropa University *B*
Northeastern Junior College *C, A*
Otero Junior College *C, A*
Pikes Peak Community College *C, A*
Pueblo Community College *C, A*
Red Rocks Community College *C, A*
University of Colorado
    Denver *M*
University of Northern
    Colorado *M, T*
University of Phoenix
    Denver *M*

Connecticut

Asnuntuck Community College *C, A*
Capital Community College *C, A*
Eastern Connecticut State
    University *B, M, T*
Fairfield University *T*
Gateway Community College *C, A*
Housatonic Community College *A*
Manchester Community College *A*
Middlesex Community College *C, A*
Mitchell College *A, B*
Northwestern Connecticut
    Community College *C, A*
Norwalk Community College *C, A*
Quinebaug Valley Community
    College *C, A*
Southern Connecticut State
    University *B, T*
Three Rivers Community
    College *C, A*
Tunxis Community College *C, A*
University of Hartford *B, M*
University of Saint Joseph *T*

Delaware

Delaware State University *B*
Delaware Technical Community
    College
    Jack F. Owens Campus *C, A*
    Stanton/Wilmington Campus *A*
    Terry Campus *C, A*
University of Delaware *B, T*
Wilmington University *A, B*

District of Columbia

Catholic University of America *B, M*
Gallaudet University *B, T*
George Washington University *M*
Howard University *M*
Trinity Washington University *M*
University of the District of
    Columbia *A, B, M, T*

Florida

Barry University *B, M, T*
Broward College *A*
College of Central Florida *C, A, B*
Eastern Florida State College *A*
Florida Agricultural and Mechanical
    University *B, T*
Florida Gateway College *A*
Florida Gulf Coast University *B*
Florida International University *B, M*
Florida State College at
    Jacksonville *C, B*
Florida State University *B, M, D, T*
Indian River State College *A*

Jose Maria Vargas
    University *C, A, B, M*
Lake-Sumter State College *A*
Miami Dade College *C, A*
Nova Southeastern University *A, B*
Palm Beach State College *A*
Pensacola State College *A*
Rasmussen College
    Pasco/Land O'Lakes *A*
Saint Johns River State College *B*
St. Petersburg College *A*
Santa Fe College *A, B*
Southwest Florida College *A, B*
State College of Florida, Manatee-
    Sarasota *A, B*
Tallahassee Community College *A*
University of Central Florida *B, M*
University of Florida *M*
University of Miami *B, M*
University of North Florida *B*
University of Phoenix
    Central Florida *M*
    North Florida *M*
    South Florida *M*
    West Florida *M*
University of South Florida *B, M*
University of South Florida
    Sarasota-Manatee *B*
University of West Florida *B, T*

Georgia

Abraham Baldwin Agricultural
    College *A*
Albany State University *B, M*
Albany Technical College *C, A*
Altamaha Technical College *C, A*
Armstrong Atlantic State University *B*
Athens Technical College *C, A*
Atlanta Technical College *C, A*
Bainbridge College *C, A*
Berry College *B, M*
Brenau University *B, M*
Brewton-Parker College *B*
Central Georgia Technical
    College *C, A*
Clark Atlanta University *B*
Columbus State University *B, M*
Columbus Technical College *C, A*
Dalton State College *A, B*
Darton College *A*
Georgia College and State
    University *B, M, T*
Georgia Military College *A*
Georgia Piedmont Technical
    College *C, A*
Georgia Regents University *B*
Georgia Southern University *M*
Georgia State University *M*
Gordon College *B*
Gwinnett Technical College *C, A*
Kennesaw State University *B, D*
Mercer University *B*
Middle Georgia State College *A, B*
Morehouse College *B*
Oglethorpe University *M*
Piedmont College *B, M, T*
Point University *B*
Reinhardt University *B, M*
Savannah Technical College *C, A*
South Georgia State College *A*
Southeastern Technical College *A*
Southwest Georgia Technical
    College *C, A*
Spelman College *B, T*
Thomas University *B*
Truett-McConnell College *B*
University of Georgia *B, M, D, T*
University of North Georgia *A, B, M*
Valdosta State University *B*
Wesleyan College *B, M*
West Georgia Technical College *C, A*
Wiregrass Georgia Technical
    College *C, A*

Hawaii

Chaminade University of
  Honolulu *B, M, T*
University of Hawaii
  Hawaii Community College *C, A*
  Honolulu Community College *C, A*
  Kauai Community College *C, A*
  Maui College *C, A*
  West Oahu *B*

Idaho

Boise State University *A, M, T*
Brigham Young University-Idaho *A*
College of Southern Idaho *A*
College of Western Idaho *A*
Idaho State University *B*
North Idaho College *A*
University of Idaho *T*

Illinois

Black Hawk College *A*
Bradley University *B, T*
Chicago State University *B, M, T*
City Colleges of Chicago
  Harold Washington College *C, A*
  Kennedy-King College *C, A*
College of DuPage *A*
Columbia College Chicago *B*
Concordia University
  Chicago *B, M, D, T*
DePaul University *B, M, T*
Dominican University *B, M, T*
Elmhurst College *B*
Governors State University *B, M, T*
Greenville College *B, T*
Highland Community College *A*
Illinois College *B, T*
Illinois Valley Community College *A*
John A. Logan College *C, A*
Joliet Junior College *A*
Judson University *B*
Kankakee Community College *C, A*
Kendall College *B, T*
Kishwaukee College *A*
Lewis University *B, M*
Lewis and Clark Community
  College *C, A*
Lincoln Christian University *A*
Loyola University Chicago *B*
Millikin University *B, T*
Morton College *A*
National-Louis University *B, M, T*
North Park University *B, M, T*
Northeastern Illinois University *B, M*
Northern Illinois University *B, M, T*
Oakton Community College *A*
Olivet Nazarene University *B, T*
Rockford University *B, M, T*
Roosevelt University *B, M*
St. Augustine College *C, A*
Saint Xavier University *M*
Sauk Valley Community College *C, A*
South Suburban College of Cook
  County *A*
Southern Illinois University
  Carbondale *B*
Southern Illinois University
  Edwardsville *B, T*
Southwestern Illinois College *A*
Spoon River College *A*
Triton College *C, A*
University of Illinois
  Urbana-Champaign *B, M, D, T*

Indiana

Ancilla College *A*
Bethel College *A, B*
Butler University *B, T*
Indiana University
  Bloomington *B, T*
  Kokomo *B*
Indiana Wesleyan University *T*

Ivy Tech Community College
  Bloomington *C, A*
  Central Indiana *C, A*
  Columbus *C, A*
  East Central *C, A*
  Kokomo *C, A*
  Lafayette *C, A*
  North Central *C, A*
  Northeast *C, A*
  Northwest *C, A*
  Richmond *C, A*
  South Central *C, A*
  Southeast *C, A*
  Southwest *C, A*
  Wabash Valley *C, A*
Manchester University *A*
Martin University *B*
Oakland City University *C, A, B*
Purdue University *B*
Purdue University
  North Central *B*
St. Mary-of-the-Woods College *A, B, T*
Taylor University *A, T*
University of Southern Indiana *B*
Vincennes University *A*

Iowa

Ashford University *A, B*
Central College *T*
Drake University *M, T*
Graceland University *T*
Iowa State University *B, T*
Iowa Wesleyan College *B*
Loras College *B*
Mount Mercy University *T*
North Iowa Area Community
  College *A*
Northwestern College *T*
St. Ambrose University *B, T*
Simpson College *T*
University of Iowa *M*
Upper Iowa University *B, T*
Wartburg College *T*

Kansas

Butler Community College *A*
Coffeyville Community College *A*
Cowley County Community
  College *A*
Friends University *B*
Garden City Community College *A*
Hesston College *A*
Independence Community College *A*
Johnson County Community
  College *C, A*
Kansas Wesleyan University *A*
Labette Community College *A*
McPherson College *B, T*
Pratt Community College *A*
Southwestern College *B, M*
University of Kansas *B, T*
Washburn University *A, B, T*
Wichita State University *B*

Kentucky

Campbellsville University *A, B*
Elizabethtown Community and
  Technical College *A*
Gateway Community and Technical
  College *A*
Hazard Community and Technical
  College *A*
Henderson Community College *A*
Madisonville Community College *A*
Maysville Community and Technical
  College *C, A*
Morehead State University *B*
Murray State University *B, M, T*
Northern Kentucky University *C*
Spalding University *B*
Sullivan University *C, A*
University of Kentucky *B*
University of Louisville *M*

Western Kentucky
  University *A, B, M, T*

Louisiana

Delgado Community College *C*
Dillard University *B, T*
Grambling State University *B*
Louisiana State University
  Alexandria *A*
  Eunice *A*
  Shreveport *B*
Louisiana State University and
  Agricultural and Mechanical
  College *B*
Louisiana Tech University *B*
McNeese State University *B, T*
Nicholls State University *B*
Northwestern State University *B, M*
Southeastern Louisiana University *B*
Southern University
  New Orleans *B*
  Shreveport *A*
University of Louisiana at Lafayette *B*
University of New Orleans *B, M*
Xavier University of Louisiana *B*

Maine

Beal College *A*
Central Maine Community
  College *C, A*
Eastern Maine Community
  College *C, A*
Kaplan University
  South Portland *A, B*
Northern Maine Community
  College *C, A*
Southern Maine Community
  College *A*
Thomas College *B*
University of Maine
  Farmington *B, M, T*
Washington County Community
  College *A*

Maryland

Allegany College of Maryland *A*
Baltimore City Community
  College *C, A*
Carroll Community College *A*
Chesapeake College *A*
College of Southern Maryland *A*
Community College of Baltimore
  County *A*
Coppin State University *B*
Frederick Community College *A*
Frostburg State University *B, T*
Garrett College *A*
Hagerstown Community College *A*
Harford Community College *A*
Hood College *B, T*
Howard Community College *A*
Montgomery College *C, A*
Notre Dame of Maryland
  University *B*
Prince George's Community
  College *C*
Salisbury University *B*
Towson University *B, M*
Washington Adventist University *A*
Wor-Wic Community College *A*

Massachusetts

American International
  College *C, B, M, T*
Anna Maria College *B, M*
Bay Path College *A, B*
Bay State College *A*
Becker College *B*
Berkshire Community College *C*
Boston College *M, T*
Boston University *B, M, T*
Bridgewater State University *B, M, T*
Bristol Community College *C*
Bunker Hill Community College *C*

Cambridge College *M*
Cape Cod Community College *C, A*
Curry College *B*
Dean College *C, A*
Eastern Nazarene College *A, B, M, T*
Elms College *B, M, T*
Endicott College *B, M*
Fisher College *T*
Fitchburg State University *B, M, T*
Framingham State University *B, M*
Gordon College *B*
Greenfield Community College *C, A*
Lasell College *B, T*
Lesley University *B, M*
Massachusetts College of Liberal
  Arts *T*
Merrimack College *B, M*
Middlesex Community College *C, A*
Mount Ida College *B, T*
North Shore Community
  College *C, A*
Northern Essex Community
  College *A*
Pine Manor College *T*
Quincy College *C, A*
Roxbury Community College *A*
Salem State University *B, M*
Simmons College *B*
Springfield College *B, M, T*
Springfield Technical Community
  College *A*
Tufts University *B, M, T*
University of Massachusetts
  Boston *B*
Urban College of Boston *C, A*
Wellesley College *T*
Wheaton College *T*
Wheelock College *B, M*
Worcester State University *B, M, T*

Michigan

Alma College *T*
Aquinas College *T*
Baker College
  Cadillac *A*
  Clinton Township *A*
  Muskegon *C, A*
  Owosso *A*
  Port Huron *C, A*
Bay Mills Community College *A*
Calvin College *B, T*
Central Michigan University *B, M*
Cornerstone University *A, B*
Eastern Michigan University *M*
Glen Oaks Community College *C, A*
Gogebic Community College *A*
Grace Bible College *B*
Grand Valley State University *M*
Henry Ford Community College *A*
Hillsdale College *B*
Jackson College *A*
Lake Michigan College *C, A*
Lake Superior State University *A, B*
Madonna University *B*
Marygrove College *C, B, M, T*
Michigan State University *B*
Mid Michigan Community
  College *C, A*
Monroe County Community
  College *C, A*
Mott Community College *C, A*
Muskegon Community College *C, A*
North Central Michigan College *C, A*
Oakland University *M, D*
Rochester College *B*
Saginaw Valley State University *M, T*
Southwestern Michigan College *A*
Spring Arbor University *B*
University of Michigan
  Dearborn *B*
  Flint *B, M, T*
Washtenaw Community College *C, A*
Wayne State University *M*
West Shore Community College *C, A*
Western Michigan University *B, M, T*

Minnesota

Augsburg College *B, T*
Bethel University *B*
Capella University *M*
Concordia University St. Paul *B, M, T*
Crown College *B*
Itasca Community College *C, A*
Leech Lake Tribal College *A*
Martin Luther College *B*
Metropolitan State University *B*
Minnesota State College - Southeast
 Technical *C, A*
Minnesota State University
 Mankato *B, M*
 Moorhead *B*
St. Catherine University *B, T*
Saint Cloud State University *B, T*
Southwest Minnesota State
 University *B, T*
University of Minnesota
 Crookston *B*
 Duluth *B*
 Morris *B*
 Twin Cities *B, M*
University of Northwestern - St.
 Paul *B*
University of St. Thomas *M*
Walden University *M*
White Earth Tribal and Community
 College *A*

Mississippi

Coahoma Community College *A*
Meridian Community College *A*
Mississippi Valley State
 University *B, T*
Rust College *A*
Tougaloo College *A*

Missouri

Central Methodist University *B*
College of the Ozarks *B, T*
Culver-Stockton College *T*
Evangel University *A, B, T*
Fontbonne University *B, T*
Hannibal-LaGrange University *B*
Harris-Stowe State University *B*
Jefferson College *C, A*
Lincoln University *A*
Lindenwood University *B*
Maryville University of Saint
 Louis *B, M, T*
Missouri Baptist University *B, T*
Missouri Southern State
 University *B, M, T*
Missouri State University *B*
Missouri Valley College *T*
Northwest Missouri State
 University *M, T*
Park University *B*
Southeast Missouri State University *B*
Southwest Baptist University *T*
Stephens College *B, T*
Truman State University *M*
University of Missouri
 Columbia *B, M, D*
 Kansas City *B*
 St. Louis *B, M*
Washington University in St. Louis *M*
Webster University *B, M*
William Woods University *T*

Montana

Aaniiih Nakoda College *A*
Blackfeet Community College *A*
Dawson Community College *C, A*
Flathead Valley Community
 College *A*
Montana State University
 Billings *A, M*
Salish Kootenai College *A, B*
University of Great Falls *A, B*
University of Montana:
 Western *C, A, B*

Nebraska

College of Saint Mary *A, B, T*
Concordia University *B, M, T*
Grace University *B*
Hastings College *B, M*
Little Priest Tribal College *C*
Midland University *B, T*
Nebraska Indian Community
 College *C, A*
Northeast Community College *C, A*
University of Nebraska
 Kearney *B, T*
Wayne State College *B, T*
Western Nebraska Community
 College *C, A*

Nevada

College of Southern Nevada *A*
Great Basin College *C, A*
Truckee Meadows Community
 College *C, A*
University of Nevada
 Las Vegas *B*
Western Nevada College *C, A*

New Hampshire

Colby-Sawyer College *B, T*
Granite State College *A, B, T*
Great Bay Community College *C, A*
Keene State College *B, T*
Lakes Region Community
 College *C, A*
Manchester Community College *C, A*
Mount Washington College *C, A*
NHTI-Concord's Community
 College *C, A*
Nashua Community College *C, A*
Plymouth State University *B, T*
Rivier University *C, A, B, M, T*
Southern New Hampshire
 University *C, B, M*
University of New Hampshire *M*
White Mountains Community
 College *C, A*

New Jersey

Bergen Community College *A*
College of New Jersey *B, T*
County College of Morris *A*
Cumberland County College *C, A*
Felician College *B*
Gloucester County College *A*
Hudson County Community
 College *C, A*
New Jersey City University *B, M*
Passaic County Community College *A*
Rutgers, The State University of New
 Jersey
 Camden Campus *T*
 New Brunswick/Piscataway
 Campus *T*
 Newark Campus *T*
Salem Community College *C, A*
Sussex County Community
 College *C, A*
Warren County Community
 College *C, A*
William Paterson University of New
 Jersey *B, T*

New Mexico

Central New Mexico Community
 College *A*
Clovis Community College *C, A*
Dona Ana Community College of
 New Mexico State University *A*
Eastern New Mexico University *B*
Luna Community College *C, A*
Navajo Technical University *A*
New Mexico Highlands University *B*
New Mexico Junior College *A*
New Mexico State University *B*

New Mexico State University
 Alamogordo *A*
 Carlsbad *A*
Northern New Mexico College *A*
Santa Fe Community College *T*
Southwestern Indian Polytechnic
 Institute *C, A*
University of New Mexico *B*
University of the Southwest *M*
Western New Mexico
 University *C, A, B*

New York

Adelphi University *M, T*
Adirondack Community College *C*
Barnard College *T*
Canisius College *B, T*
Cayuga Community College *C, A*
Cazenovia College *B*
City University of New York
 Brooklyn College *B, M, T*
 City College *B, M, T*
 Hostos Community College *A*
 Hunter College *B, M, T*
 Kingsborough Community
 College *A*
 Queens College *B, M, T*
College of Mount St. Vincent *T*
College of New Rochelle *M*
Corning Community College *C, A*
D'Youville College *M, T*
Daemen College *B, M, T*
Dominican College of Blauvelt *M*
Dowling College *B, M*
Dutchess Community College *A*
Hofstra University *B, M*
Jamestown Community College *A*
Keuka College *B, M, T*
Long Island University
 LIU Post *B, M*
Manhattan College *B, T*
Manhattanville College *M, T*
Maria College *A*
Monroe Community College *C*
Mount Saint Mary College *B, M*
Nassau Community College *A*
Nazareth College *M, T*
New York University *B, M*
Niagara University *B, T*
Nyack College *B*
Orange County Community
 College *C*
Pace University *B, M, T*
Pace University: Pleasantville/
 Briarcliff *B, M, T*
Roberts Wesleyan College *B*
SUNY
 College at Brockport *M, T*
 College at Buffalo *B, T*
 College at Fredonia *B, T*
 College at Geneseo *B, M, T*
 College at Oneonta *A*
 College at Plattsburgh *B*
 College of Technology at Delhi *A*
 University at Buffalo *M*
St. John's University *M, T*
St. Joseph's College New York:
 Suffolk Campus *T*
Schenectady County Community
 College *C, A*
Suffolk County Community College *A*
Tompkins Cortland Community
 College *A*
Trocaire College *A*
University of Rochester *M*
Utica College *B*
Vassar College *T*
Wagner College *B, M, T*
Westchester Community College *C, A*
Yeshiva University *B*

North Carolina

Alamance Community College *C, A*
Beaufort County Community
 College *A*

Bladen Community College *C*
Brunswick Community College *C, A*
Caldwell Community College and
 Technical Institute *A*
Campbell University *B, M*
Catawba Valley Community
 College *C, A*
Central Carolina Community
 College *C, A*
Central Piedmont Community
 College *C, A*
Cleveland Community College *C, A*
Coastal Carolina Community
 College *C, A*
College of the Albemarle *C, A*
Craven Community College *C, A*
Davidson County Community
 College *C, A*
Durham Technical Community
 College *C, A*
Edgecombe Community College *C, A*
Elon University *B*
Fayetteville State University *B, T*
Fayetteville Technical Community
 College *C, A*
Forsyth Technical Community
 College *A*
Gaston College *C, A*
Greensboro College *C, B, T*
Guilford Technical Community
 College *C, A*
Halifax Community College *A*
High Point University *T*
Isothermal Community College *C, A*
James Sprunt Community
 College *A*
Johnston Community College *C, A*
Lenoir Community College *C, A*
Lenoir-Rhyne University *B, M, T*
Martin Community College *C, A*
Mayland Community College *C, A*
Meredith College *T*
Mitchell Community College *A*
Montgomery Community
 College *C, A*
Nash Community College *A*
North Carolina Agricultural and
 Technical State University *B, T*
Pamlico Community College *C, A*
Piedmont International University *A*
Pitt Community College *A*
Roanoke-Chowan Community
 College *A*
Rockingham Community
 College *C, A*
Rowan-Cabarrus Community
 College *A*
Sampson Community College *C, A*
Sandhills Community College *A*
South Piedmont Community
 College *C, A*
Southeastern Community College *A*
Southwestern Community
 College *C, A*
Stanly Community College *C, A*
Surry Community College *C, A*
University of Mount Olive *B*
University of North Carolina
 Chapel Hill *B*
 Greensboro *B, M*
Vance-Granville Community
 College *C, A*
Wake Technical Community
 College *C, A*
Wayne Community College *C, A*
Western Piedmont Community
 College *C, A*
Wilkes Community College *C, A*
William Peace University *B*
Wilson Community College *C, A*

North Dakota

Cankdeska Cikana Community
 College *A*
Dickinson State University *B, T*

Mayville State University *B, T*
Sitting Bull College *A, B*
Turtle Mountain Community
  College *A, B*
United Tribes Technical College *C, A*
University of Jamestown *B*
University of Mary *B*
University of North Dakota *B, M*

Ohio

Antioch University
  Midwest *B, M*
Ashland University *B, T*
Baldwin Wallace University *B, T*
Belmont College *A*
Bluffton University *B*
Bowling Green State University:
  Firelands College *B*
Capital University *B*
Cedarville University *B*
Central Ohio Technical College *A*
Central State University *B*
Chatfield College *A*
Cincinnati Christian University *B, T*
Cincinnati State Technical and
  Community College *C, A*
Clark State Community College *A*
Cleveland State University *B*
College of Mount St. Joseph *B, T*
Cuyahoga Community College
  Metropolitan *A*
Davis College *A*
Defiance College *B*
Franciscan University of
  Steubenville *A*
Hiram College *T*
James A. Rhodes State College *C, A*
John Carroll University *M, T*
Kent State University *B, M*
Kent State University
  Salem *B*
  Tuscarawas *B*
Lakeland Community College *A*
Lorain County Community
  College *C, A*
Lourdes University *B*
Malone University *B*
Marietta College *B*
Miami University
  Oxford *B, T*
Mount Vernon Nazarene
  University *B, T*
Muskingum University *B, T*
North Central State College *A*
Notre Dame College *B, T*
Ohio Christian University *B*
Ohio Northern University *B, T*
Ohio University *B, T*
Ohio University
  Chillicothe Campus *B*
  Southern Campus at Ironton *M*
  Zanesville Campus *B*
Ohio Wesleyan University *B*
Otterbein University *B*
Owens Community College
  Toledo *C, A*
Shawnee State University *B*
Sinclair Community College *A*
Southern State Community College *A*
Stark State College *A*
University of Akron *C, B*
University of Cincinnati *C, A, B, M, T*
University of Cincinnati
  Blue Ash College *A*
  Clermont College *A*
University of Dayton *B, M, T*
University of Findlay *B, M, T*
University of Mount Union *B, T*
University of Rio Grande *A, B*
Ursuline College *B, M, T*
Walsh University *B*
Wilmington College *B*
Wittenberg University *B*
Wright State University *B, M, T*

Wright State University: Lake
  Campus *B*
Xavier University *A, B, M*
Youngstown State University *B, M*

Oklahoma

Bacone College *B*
Cameron University *B*
Carl Albert State College *C*
Connors State College *A*
East Central University *B, T*
Mid-America Christian University *B*
Northeastern Oklahoma Agricultural
  and Mechanical College *A*
Northeastern State University *B, M*
Northwestern Oklahoma State
  University *B*
Oklahoma Baptist University *B, T*
Oklahoma Christian University *B, T*
Oklahoma City University *B*
Oral Roberts University *B, T*
Seminole State College *C*
Southern Nazarene University *B, M*
Southwestern Oklahoma State
  University *B, M, T*
University of Central Oklahoma *B, M*
University of Oklahoma *B, T*
University of Science and Arts of
  Oklahoma *B, T*
University of Tulsa *B, T*

Oregon

Blue Mountain Community
  College *C, A*
Clackamas Community College *A*
Clatsop Community College *A*
Concordia University *B, M, T*
George Fox University *M, T*
Klamath Community College *C, A*
Linfield College *T*
Linn-Benton Community College *C, A*
Mt. Hood Community College *C, A*
Oregon State University *M*
Portland Community College *C, A*
Portland State University *T*
Umpqua Community College *C, A*
Warner Pacific College *M, T*
Western Oregon University *B, M, T*
Willamette University *M*

Pennsylvania

Albright College *B, M, T*
Alvernia University *B*
Arcadia University *B, M, T*
Baptist Bible College of
  Pennsylvania *A, B*
Bloomsburg University of
  Pennsylvania *B, M, T*
Bucknell University *B, T*
Bucks County Community College *A*
Cairn University *B, T*
California University of
  Pennsylvania *C*
Carlow University *B, M*
Cedar Crest College *B, T*
Chatham University *B, M, T*
Chestnut Hill College *B, M, T*
Cheyney University of
  Pennsylvania *B, T*
Clarion University of
  Pennsylvania *A, B, T*
DeSales University *B, T*
Delaware County Community
  College *C, A*
Duquesne University *B, M, T*
East Stroudsburg University of
  Pennsylvania *B, T*
Eastern University *B, T*
Edinboro University of
  Pennsylvania *B, M*
Elizabethtown College *B, T*
Gannon University *A, B*
Grove City College *B, T*
Harcum College *A*

Harrisburg Area Community
  College *C, A*
Holy Family University *B, M, T*
Indiana University of
  Pennsylvania *B, M*
Keystone College *A, B, T*
King's College *B, T*
Kutztown University of
  Pennsylvania *B*
La Salle University *B, M, T*
Laurel Business Institute *A*
Laurel Technical Institute *A*
Lebanon Valley College *B*
Lehigh Carbon Community
  College *C, A*
Lincoln University *M, T*
Manor College *A*
Mansfield University of
  Pennsylvania *B, T*
McCann School of Business and
  Technology
  Hazleton *A*
Mercyhurst University *B, T*
Messiah College *B, T*
Millersville University of
  Pennsylvania *B, M, T*
Misericordia University *B, T*
Mount Aloysius College *A, B*
Neumann University *B, T*
Northampton Community
  College *C, A*
Penn State
  Abington *B*
  Altoona *B*
  Beaver *B*
  Berks *B*
  Brandywine *B*
  DuBois *C, B*
  Erie, The Behrend College *B*
  Fayette, The Eberly Campus *C, B*
  Greater Allegheny *B*
  Harrisburg *B*
  Hazleton *B*
  Lehigh Valley *C, B*
  Mont Alto *C, B*
  New Kensington *B*
  Schuylkill *B*
  Shenango *B*
  University Park *B*
  Wilkes-Barre *B*
  Worthington Scranton *B*
  York *B*
Point Park University *A, B*
Prism Career Institute *C*
Reading Area Community College *A*
Robert Morris University *T*
Rosemont College *T*
St. Vincent College *T*
Seton Hill University *T*
Shippensburg University of
  Pennsylvania *B, T*
Susquehanna University *B, T*
University of Pennsylvania *M*
University of Pittsburgh *T*
University of Pittsburgh
  Greensburg *B, T*
University of Scranton *B, M*
Valley Forge Christian College *A, B*
Washington & Jefferson College *T*
West Chester University of
  Pennsylvania *B, M, T*
Widener University *B, M, T*
York College of Pennsylvania *B, T*

Puerto Rico

Bayamon Central University *B, M*
EDIC College *C*
Inter American University of Puerto
  Rico
  Arecibo Campus *B*
  Barranquitas Campus *B*
  Fajardo Campus *B, T*
  Ponce Campus *B*
  San German Campus *B*

National University College
  Arecibo *B*
  Bayamon *B*
  Rio Grande *B*
Pontifical Catholic University of
  Puerto Rico *B, M*
Turabo University *B*
Universidad Metropolitana *B, M*
Universidad del Este *B*
University of Phoenix
  Puerto Rico *M*
University of Puerto Rico
  Rio Piedras *M*

Rhode Island

Community College of Rhode
  Island *C*
Rhode Island College *B, M*
Salve Regina University *B*

South Carolina

Anderson University *B, T*
Benedict College *B*
Bob Jones University *A, B*
Charleston Southern University *B*
Claflin University *B*
Clemson University *B*
Clinton Junior College *A*
Coastal Carolina University *B, T*
Coker College *B, T*
College of Charleston *B, M, T*
Columbia College *B, T*
Columbia International University *M*
Converse College *B, M, T*
Erskine College *B, T*
Forrest Junior College *A*
Francis Marion University *B, M, T*
Furman University *M, T*
Lander University *B, T*
Limestone College *B*
Morris College *B, T*
Newberry College *B, T*
North Greenville University *B, T*
Presbyterian College *B, T*
South Carolina State
  University *B, M, T*
Southern Wesleyan University *B, T*
University of South Carolina
  Aiken *B, T*
  Beaufort *B*
  Columbia *B, M, D*
  Upstate *B, M, T*
Voorhees College *B*
Williamsburg Technical College *C, A*
Winthrop University *B, M, T*
York Technical College *C, A*

South Dakota

Kilian Community College *A*
Northern State University *B, T*
Oglala Lakota College *C, A*
Sisseton Wahpeton College *A*
South Dakota State University *B*
University of South Dakota *B*

Tennessee

Belmont University *B, T*
Carson-Newman University *B*
Christian Brothers University *B*
Cumberland University *B, T*
East Tennessee State University *M, T*
Freed-Hardeman University *B, T*
Hiwassee College *A*
LeMoyne-Owen College *B*
Lee University *B*
Lincoln Memorial University *B, T*
Middle Tennessee State
  University *B, M, T*
Milligan College *B, M, T*
Nashville State Community College *A*
Roane State Community College *A*
Tennessee State University *B*
Tennessee Technological
  University *B, M, D, T*

Tennessee Temple University *T*
Tennessee Wesleyan College *B, T*
Trevecca Nazarene University *B, T*
Tusculum College *B, T*
University of Tennessee
    Chattanooga *B, T*
Vanderbilt University *B, D, T*
Welch College *A, B*

Texas

Alvin Community College *C, A*
Austin Community College *A*
Baylor University *T*
Brookhaven College *C, A*
Collin County Community College
    District *A*
Dallas Baptist University *B, M, T*
Dallas Christian College *B, T*
Del Mar College *A*
Hardin-Simmons University *B, T*
Houston Baptist University *B, M*
Jarvis Christian College *B, T*
Lamar University *B, M, T*
Laredo Community College *A*
Lubbock Christian University *B*
McMurry University *B*
Midland College *C, A*
Midwestern State University *B*
Mountain View College *A*
Our Lady of the Lake University of
    San Antonio *M*
Panola College *C, A*
Paris Junior College *A*
St. Philip's College *C, A*
Schreiner University *B*
South Texas College *C, A*
Southwestern Assemblies of God
    University *A, B, M*
Southwestern University *T*
Stephen F. Austin State University *M*
Tarleton State University *T*
Tarrant County College *A*
Texas A&M International
    University *B, M, T*
Texas A&M University
    Commerce *M, T*
    Corpus Christi *M, T*
    Kingsville *M*
    Texarkana *T*
Texas Christian University *B, M*
Texas College *A, T*
Texas Woman's University *M*
Trinity Valley Community
    College *C, A*
Tyler Junior College *C, A*
University of Houston
    Clear Lake *M, T*
University of Mary Hardin-Baylor *T*
University of North Texas *M, D, T*
University of Texas
    Arlington *T*
    Brownsville *M*
    Pan American *M*
    San Antonio *T*
Wayland Baptist University *B*
West Texas A&M University *T*
Western Texas College *C, A*
Wharton County Junior College *A*

Utah

Brigham Young University *B*
Dixie State College *A*
Snow College *A*
Utah State University *B*
Utah Valley University *A*
Weber State University *B*
Western Governors University *B*
Westminster College *B*

Vermont

Champlain College *B*
Community College of Vermont *C, A*
Goddard College *B, M*
Johnson State College *M*

Lyndon State College *B*
University of Vermont *B, T*

Virginia

Dabney S. Lancaster Community
    College *C*
Eastern Mennonite University *T*
Germanna Community College *C*
Hollins University *T*
J. Sargeant Reynolds Community
    College *C, A*
James Madison University *T*
Longwood University *T*
Lord Fairfax Community College *C*
New River Community College *C, A*
Northern Virginia Community
    College *C, A*
Paul D. Camp Community College *C*
Piedmont Virginia Community
    College *C*
Radford University *T*
Southwest Virginia Community
    College *C, A*
Thomas Nelson Community
    College *C, A*
Tidewater Community College *C, A*
Virginia Baptist College *A*
Virginia Western Community
    College *C, A*

Washington

Bellevue College *C, A*
Bellingham Technical College *C*
Big Bend Community College *C, A*
Central Washington University *B, T*
Centralia College *C, A*
Clark College *C, A*
Clover Park Technical College *C, A*
Columbia Basin College *C, A*
Eastern Washington University *B*
Edmonds Community College *C, A*
Everett Community College *C, A*
Grays Harbor College *C*
Green River Community College *C, A*
Heritage University *C, A, B*
Lake Washington Institute of
    Technology *C, A*
North Seattle Community
    College *C, A*
Northwest Indian College *A*
Olympic College *C, A*
Peninsula College *C, A*
Pierce College *C, A*
Renton Technical College *C, A*
Seattle Central Community College *C*
Shoreline Community College *A*
Skagit Valley College *C, A*
South Puget Sound Community
    College *C, A*
Spokane Falls Community College *A*
Trinity Lutheran College *B*
University of Washington Tacoma *T*
Walla Walla Community College *C, A*
Walla Walla University *A*
Washington State University *B, T*
Wenatchee Valley College *C, A*
Whatcom Community College *C, A*
Yakima Valley Community
    College *C, A*

West Virginia

Concord University *B, T*
Marshall University *M*
Pierpont Community and Technical
    College *A*
Potomac State College of West
    Virginia University *A*
Shepherd University *T*
West Liberty University *B*
West Virginia State University *B*
West Virginia University *T*
Wheeling Jesuit University *B*

Wisconsin

Beloit College *T*
Carroll University *B*
Chippewa Valley Technical College *A*
College of Menominee Nation *A*
Concordia University Wisconsin *B, T*
Edgewood College *B, T*
Fox Valley Technical College *A*
Gateway Technical College *A*
Lac Courte Oreilles Ojibwa
    Community College *A*
Lakeshore Technical College *C, A*
Maranatha Baptist Bible College *A, B*
Marian University *B, T*
Mid-State Technical College *A*
Milwaukee Area Technical
    College *A*
Mount Mary University *B, T*
Nicolet Area Technical College *A*
Northcentral Technical College *C, A*
Northeast Wisconsin Technical
    College *A*
Rasmussen College
    Green Bay *A*
Ripon College *T*
St. Norbert College *B, T*
Silver Lake College of the Holy
    Family *B, T*
University of Wisconsin
    Green Bay *T*
    Oshkosh *M*
    Platteville *B, T*
    River Falls *T*
    Stevens Point *B, T*
    Stout *B, T*
    Superior *T*
    Whitewater *B, T*
Viterbo University *T*
Waukesha County Technical
    College *A*
Western Technical College *A*
Wisconsin Lutheran College *B*

Wyoming

Central Wyoming College *A*
Eastern Wyoming College *C, A*
Laramie County Community
    College *A*
Sheridan College *C, A*

Early childhood special education

Alabama

Auburn University *B, M, D, T*

Arizona

Brown Mackie College
    Tucson *A*
Prescott College *B*
Tohono O'odham Community
    College *A*

Arkansas

Harding University *B, M, T*
Henderson State University *M, T*

California

California Baptist University *T*
College of the Siskiyous *A*
Mills College *M, T*
National University *T*
Palomar College *A*
Santa Monica College *A*

Connecticut

University of Saint Joseph *M*

Florida

University of Miami *M*

Georgia

Brenau University *B*
South Georgia State College *A*

Illinois

City Colleges of Chicago
    Kennedy-King College *A*
Judson University *B*
University of Illinois
    Urbana-Champaign *B, M, T*

Indiana

Brown Mackie College
    Michigan City *A*
Purdue University *B*

Iowa

Upper Iowa University *T*

Kansas

Newman University *B*

Louisiana

Dillard University *B*
Nicholls State University *B*
Southeastern Louisiana University *M*
University of Louisiana at Lafayette *B*
University of New Orleans *M*

Maine

University of Maine
    Farmington *B, T*

Maryland

Howard Community College *A*

Massachusetts

Lesley University *B, M*

Minnesota

Saint Cloud State University *M*
Winona State University *B, M, T*

Missouri

Lindenwood University *B*
Missouri Baptist University *T*

New Hampshire

Granite State College *T*

New Jersey

Felician College *B*
Georgian Court University *T*
Montclair State University *M*

New York

Adelphi University *M, T*
Canisius College *B, M, T*
City University of New York
    Brooklyn College *M, T*
    Queens College *M*
College of New Rochelle *M*
Elmira College *B, T*
Hofstra University *M, T*
Pace University *M*
Roberts Wesleyan College *B*
Rockland Community College *A*
SUNY
    College at Brockport *M*
    College at New Paltz *M, T*
St. John's University *M, T*
St. Joseph's College New York:
    Suffolk Campus *M, T*
St. Joseph's College, New York *T*
Syracuse University *B, M*
University of Rochester *M*

North Carolina

Surry Community College *A*

North Dakota

University of North Dakota *M*

Ohio

Ashland University *B, T*
Bowling Green State University *B*
Brown Mackie College
  Akron *A*
University of Akron *B, M*
University of Findlay *B, M, T*

Oregon

Portland State University *D*

Pennsylvania

Carlow University *M*
Gwynedd Mercy University *B*
Indiana University of Pennsylvania *B*
Juniata College *B, T*
Keystone College *B, T*
La Salle University *B, M, T*
Lock Haven University of
  Pennsylvania *B*
Washington & Jefferson College *T*
York College of Pennsylvania *B, T*

Puerto Rico

Atlantic University College *B*
Inter American University of Puerto
  Rico
  Aguadilla Campus *B*
  Guayama Campus *B, M*

Tennessee

Union University *B, T*

Texas

Del Mar College *A*

Utah

Salt Lake Community College *A*
Utah State University *B*

Vermont

University of Vermont *B, T*

Virginia

Radford University *T*

Washington

Eastern Washington University *B*
University of Washington Tacoma *T*

Wisconsin

Edgewood College *B*
Silver Lake College of the Holy
  Family *B, T*
University of Wisconsin
  Superior *M*

Earth science teacher education

Florida

Daytona State College *B*
Florida Institute of Technology *B*

Illinois

Augustana College *B, T*

Maine

University of Maine
  Farmington *B, T*

Michigan

Calvin College *B*
Central Michigan University *B*
University of Michigan
  Flint *B, T*
Western Michigan University *B, D, T*

Minnesota

Minnesota State University
  Moorhead *B*

University of Minnesota
  Duluth *B*
Winona State University *B, T*

Nebraska

College of Saint Mary *B, T*

New York

City University of New York
  Brooklyn College *B, M*
College of Saint Rose *B, T*
Cornell University *T*
Long Island University
  LIU Post *B, M, D*
New York University *B*
Pace University *B, M, T*
SUNY
  College at Fredonia *B, M, T*
  College at Oneonta *B, T*
  College at Potsdam *M*
  University at Stony Brook *T*
Syracuse University *M*

North Dakota

North Dakota State University *B, T*

Ohio

Ashland University *B, T*

East Asian languages

Arizona

Arizona State University *B, M, D*

California

University of California
  Irvine *D*
University of Southern
  California *B, M, D*

Colorado

University of Colorado
  Boulder *M, D*

Connecticut

Wesleyan University *B*
Yale University *M, D*

Illinois

Northwestern University *B*
University of Chicago *B, D*
University of Illinois
  Urbana-Champaign *B*

Indiana

Indiana University
  Bloomington *B*
Purdue University *B*

Kansas

University of Kansas *B, M*

Massachusetts

Northeastern University *B*
Smith College *B*

Michigan

Michigan State University *B*
University of Michigan *D*

Missouri

University of Missouri
  Columbia *B*

New Jersey

Rutgers, The State University of New
  Jersey
  New Brunswick/Piscataway
    Campus *M*

New York

Columbia University *B*
Cornell University *M, D*

North Carolina

Duke University *B*

Oregon

University of Oregon *M, D*

Pennsylvania

University of Pennsylvania *B, M, D*

Texas

Austin College *B*
University of Texas
  Austin *B, M, D*

Virginia

Washington and Lee University *B*

Washington

University of Puget Sound *B*
University of Washington *B*

Wisconsin

Lawrence University *B*

East Asian studies

Arizona

University of Arizona *B, M, D*

California

Occidental College *B*
Stanford University *B, M*
University of California
  Davis *B*
  Irvine *B*
  Los Angeles *B, M*
University of Southern
  California *B, M*

Connecticut

Connecticut College *B*
University of Bridgeport *B*
Wesleyan University *B*
Yale University *B, M*

District of Columbia

Georgetown University *M*

Florida

Eckerd College *B*

Georgia

Emory University *B*

Illinois

North Central College *B*
University of Chicago *B, D*
University of Illinois
  Urbana-Champaign *B, D*

Indiana

DePauw University *B*
Indiana University
  Bloomington *B, M*
Valparaiso University *B*

Maine

Bates College *B*
Colby College *B*

Maryland

Johns Hopkins University *B, D*

Massachusetts

Bard College at Simon's Rock *B*
Boston University *B*
Brandeis University *B*
Hampshire College *B*
Harvard College *B, M, D*
Mount Holyoke College *B*
Simmons College *B*

Tufts University *B*
Wellesley College *B*

Michigan

Oakland University *B*
University of Michigan *M*
Wayne State University *B*

Minnesota

Augsburg College *B*
Hamline University *B*
Minnesota State University
  Moorhead *B*
University of Minnesota
  Twin Cities *B, M*

Missouri

University of Missouri
  Columbia *B*
Washington University in St.
  Louis *B, M*

Nebraska

Creighton University *M*

New Jersey

Princeton University *B, M, D*
Rutgers, The State University of New
  Jersey
  New Brunswick/Piscataway
    Campus *B*

New York

City University of New York
  Queens College *B*
Columbia University *B*
Columbia University
  School of General Studies *B*
Hofstra University *B*
New York University *B, M, D*
SUNY
  University at Albany *B*
  University at Binghamton *B*
St. John's University *M*
United States Military Academy *B*
University of Rochester *B*

Ohio

College of Wooster *B*
Denison University *B*
John Carroll University *B*
Miami University
  Oxford *B*
Oberlin College *B*
Ohio State University
  Columbus Campus *M*
Ohio Wesleyan University *B*
Wittenberg University *B*

Oregon

Lewis & Clark College *B*
Portland State University *B*

Pennsylvania

Bryn Mawr College *B*
Bucknell University *B*
Dickinson College *B*
Gettysburg College *B*
Haverford College *B, T*
University of Pennsylvania *B, M, D*
University of Pittsburgh *M*
Ursinus College *B*

Rhode Island

Brown University *B*

Tennessee

Vanderbilt University *B*

Texas

Dallas Baptist University *M*

Vermont

Marlboro College *B*
Middlebury College *B*

Virginia

Emory & Henry College *B*
University of Virginia *M*
Washington and Lee University *B*

Washington

University of Washington *M*
Western Washington University *B*

Wisconsin

Lawrence University *B*

Ecology

Alabama

Tuskegee University *B, M*

Arizona

Prescott College *B*

California

California State University
   Dominguez Hills *B*
   Stanislaus *M*
Gavilan College *A*
Irvine Valley College *A*
Orange Coast College *A*
San Diego State University *B, M, D*
San Francisco State University *M*
University of California
   Davis *M, D*
   Los Angeles *B*
   San Diego *B*
   Santa Barbara *B, M, D*
   Santa Cruz *B*

Colorado

Colorado State University *B, M, D*
Fort Lewis College *B*
University of Denver *B*

Connecticut

University of Connecticut *B, D*
University of New Haven *B, M*

Florida

Florida Institute of Technology *M*
University of Florida *M, D*
University of Miami *B*

Georgia

University of Georgia *B, M, D*

Idaho

Idaho State University *B*
Northwest Nazarene University *B*

Illinois

Northwestern University *B*
University of Chicago *D*

Iowa

Cornell College *B*
Iowa State University *M, D*
University of Northern Iowa *B, M*

Kentucky

Eastern Kentucky University *B*
Midway College *B*

Louisiana

Tulane University *B, M, D*

Maine

College of the Atlantic *B, M*
University of Maine *B, M, D*
University of Maine
   Machias *B*

Maryland

Frostburg State University *M*
Salisbury University *B*
Towson University *B, M*
University of Maryland
   College Park *B*
   Eastern Shore *B*

Massachusetts

Bard College at Simon's Rock *B*
Boston University *B*
Salem State University *B*
Tufts University *B, M*

Michigan

Michigan Technological University *M*
Northern Michigan University *B*
University of Michigan
   Dearborn *B*
   Flint *B*

Minnesota

Minnesota State University
   Mankato *B, M, T*
Saint Cloud State University *B, M*
Southwest Minnesota State
   University *B*
University of Minnesota
   Twin Cities *B, M, D*

Missouri

Missouri Southern State University *B*
Washington University in St.
   Louis *B, D*

Montana

University of Montana *M, D*

Nevada

Sierra Nevada College *B*

New Hampshire

Dartmouth College *B*

New Jersey

Rutgers, The State University of New
   Jersey
   New Brunswick/Piscataway
      Campus *M, D*

New Mexico

New Mexico State University *B*

New York

Columbia University *B*
Concordia College *B*
Cornell University *B, M, D*
Le Moyne College *B*
Molloy College *B*
New York University *B*
SUNY
   College at Oneonta *B*
   College at Plattsburgh *B*
   College at Purchase *B*
   University at Buffalo *B, M, D*
   University at Stony Brook *B, M, D*
University of Rochester *B*

North Carolina

Appalachian State University *B*
Gardner-Webb University *B*
Methodist University *A, B*
University of North Carolina
   Chapel Hill *M, D*

Ohio

Kent State University *M, D*
Ohio State University
   Columbus Campus *M, D*
Ohio University *B*
University of Akron *B*

Oklahoma

Oklahoma State University *M, D*

Pennsylvania

Clarion University of Pennsylvania *B*
East Stroudsburg University of
   Pennsylvania *B*
Lycoming College *B*
Penn State
   University Park *M, D*
Susquehanna University *B*
Westminster College *B*

South Dakota

Northern State University *B*

Tennessee

Christian Brothers University *B*
University of Tennessee
   Knoxville *M, D*

Texas

Angelo State University *B*
Rice University *B, M, D*
Texas State University *M*

Utah

Utah State University *M, D*

Vermont

Bennington College *B*
Marlboro College *B*
Southern Vermont College *B*
Sterling College *B*

Virginia

Averett University *B*
Old Dominion University *D*

Washington

Evergreen State College *B*
University of Washington *B, M, D*
Western Washington University *B*

Wisconsin

Beloit College *B*
University of Wisconsin
   Superior *B*

Wyoming

University of Wyoming *D*
Western Wyoming Community
   College *A*

Ecology/evolutionary biology

Arizona

University of Arizona *B, M, D*

California

University of California
   Irvine *B, M, D*
   Riverside *M, D*

Colorado

Colorado College *B*
University of Colorado
   Boulder *B, M, D*

Indiana

Indiana University
   Bloomington *M, D*

Kansas

University of Kansas *M, D*

Maine

Colby College *B*

Michigan

University of Michigan *B, M, D*

New Jersey

Princeton University *B, M, D*

Oklahoma

University of Oklahoma *D*

Pennsylvania

University of Pittsburgh *B*

Tennessee

Sewanee: The University of the
   South *B*
Vanderbilt University *B*

Texas

University of Texas
   Austin *M, D*

Econometrics/ quantitative economics

California

Scripps College *B*
University of California
   Irvine *B*
   Santa Barbara *B*
University of San Francisco *M*

Colorado

Colorado College *B*

Iowa

University of Northern Iowa *B*

Kentucky

Western Kentucky University *B*

Maine

Bowdoin College *B*

Maryland

United States Naval Academy *B*

Minnesota

Saint Cloud State University *B*
University of Minnesota
   Twin Cities *B*
University of St. Thomas *B*

New York

Hofstra University *B*
Ithaca College *B*
SUNY
   College at Oswego *B*
St. Lawrence University *B*

North Carolina

High Point University *B*
Wake Forest University *B*

Ohio

Baldwin Wallace University *B*
University of Cincinnati *M*
University of Dayton *B*
Youngstown State University *B*

Pennsylvania

Bucknell University *B*
Carnegie Mellon University *B*
Lafayette College *B*
Lycoming College *B*

Rhode Island

Providence College *B*
University of Rhode Island *B*

Texas

Southern Methodist University *B, M*

Utah

University of Utah *M*
Utah State University *M*
Weber State University *B*

Virginia

Hampden-Sydney College *B*

Economics

Alabama

Auburn University *B, M*
Birmingham-Southern College *B*
Jacksonville State University *B*
Troy University *B*
Tuskegee University *B*

Alaska

University of Alaska
  Anchorage *B*
  Fairbanks *B*

Arizona

Arizona State University *B, D*
Cochise College *A*
University of Arizona *B, M, D*

Arkansas

Arkansas State University *B*
Black River Technical College *A*
Harding University *B*
Hendrix College *B*
Lyon College *B*
University of Arkansas *B, M, D*
University of Arkansas
  Little Rock *B*
University of Central Arkansas *B*
University of the Ozarks *B*

California

Bakersfield College *A*
Cabrillo College *A*
California Institute of Technology *B*
California Lutheran University *B*
California Polytechnic State
  University: San Luis Obispo *B, M*
California State Polytechnic
  University: Pomona *B, M*
California State University
  Bakersfield *B*
  Channel Islands *B*
  Chico *B*
  East Bay *B, M*
  Fresno *B*
  Fullerton *B, M*
  Long Beach *B, M*
  Los Angeles *B, M*
  Northridge *B*
  Sacramento *B, M*
  San Bernardino *B*
  San Marcos *B*
  Stanislaus *B*
Canada College *A*
Cerritos College *A*
Chaffey College *A*
Claremont McKenna College *B*
College of Alameda *A*
College of the Desert *A*
Concordia University Irvine *B*
Contra Costa College *A*
Copper Mountain College *A*
Crafton Hills College *A*
Cypress College *A*
De Anza College *A*
El Camino College *A*
Foothill College *A*
Fullerton College *A*
Gavilan College *A*
Glendale Community College *A*
Golden West College *A*
Grossmont College *A*
Humboldt State University *B*
Irvine Valley College *A*

Los Angeles Valley College *A*
Loyola Marymount University *B*
Mills College *B*
Monterey Peninsula College *A*
Occidental College *B*
Orange Coast College *A*
Oxnard College *A*
Palomar College *C, A*
Pepperdine University *B*
Pitzer College *B*
Pomona College *B*
Saddleback College *A*
St. Mary's College of California *B*
San Diego State University *B, M*
San Francisco State University *B, M*
San Jose State University *B, M*
Santa Ana College *A*
Santa Barbara City College *A*
Santa Clara University *B*
Santa Rosa Junior College *A*
Santiago Canyon College *A*
Scripps College *B*
Sonoma State University *B*
Southwestern College *A*
Stanford University *B, M, D*
University of California
  Berkeley *B, D*
  Davis *B, M, D*
  Irvine *B, M, D*
  Los Angeles *B, M, D*
  Merced *B*
  Riverside *B, M, D*
  San Diego *B, D*
  Santa Barbara *B, M, D*
  Santa Cruz *B, M*
University of La Verne *B*
University of Redlands *B*
University of San Diego *B*
University of San Francisco *B, M*
University of Southern
  California *B, M, D*
University of the Pacific *B*
West Los Angeles College *A*
Westmont College *B*
Whittier College *B*

Colorado

Adams State University *B*
Colorado College *B*
Colorado School of Mines *B, M, D*
Colorado State University *B, M, D*
Fort Lewis College *B*
Metropolitan State University of
  Denver *B, T*
Regis University *B*
United States Air Force Academy *B*
University of Colorado
  Boulder *B, D*
  Colorado Springs *B*
  Denver *B, M*
University of Denver *B, M*
University of Northern Colorado *B*
Western State Colorado University *B*

Connecticut

Central Connecticut State
  University *B*
Connecticut College *B*
Eastern Connecticut State
  University *B*
Fairfield University *B*
Quinnipiac University *B*
Southern Connecticut State
  University *B*
Trinity College *B, M*
University of Connecticut *B, M, D*
University of Hartford *B*
University of New Haven *B*
Wesleyan University *B, M*
Western Connecticut State
  University *B*
Yale University *B, M, D*

Delaware

Goldey-Beacom College *B*
University of Delaware *B*

District of Columbia

American University *B, M, D*
Catholic University of America *B*
Gallaudet University *B*
George Washington
  University *B, M, D*
Georgetown University *B, M, D*
Howard University *B, M, D*
Strayer University *A, B*
Trinity Washington University *B*
University of the District of
  Columbia *B*

Florida

Ave Maria University *B*
Broward College *A*
Daytona State College *A*
Eckerd College *B*
Flagler College *B*
Florida Agricultural and Mechanical
  University *B*
Florida Atlantic University *B, M*
Florida Gulf Coast University *B*
Florida International
  University *B, M, D*
Florida Southern College *B*
Florida State University *B, M, D*
Indian River State College *A*
Jacksonville University *B*
Miami Dade College *A*
New College of Florida *B*
Nova Southeastern University *B*
Rollins College *B*
Stetson University *B*
University of Central Florida *B*
University of Florida *B, M, D*
University of Miami *B*
University of North Florida *B*
University of South Florida *B*
University of South Florida
  Saint Petersburg *B*
University of Tampa *A, B*
University of West Florida *B*

Georgia

Agnes Scott College *B*
Armstrong Atlantic State University *B*
Covenant College *B*
Darton College *A*
Emory University *B, D*
Fort Valley State University *B*
Georgia Southern University *B*
Georgia State University *B, M, D*
Mercer University *B*
Middle Georgia State College *A*
Morehouse College *B*
Oglethorpe University *B*
Spelman College *B*
University of West Georgia *B*
Wesleyan College *B*

Hawaii

Hawaii Pacific University *B*
University of Hawaii
  Hilo *B*
  Manoa *B, M, D*
  West Oahu *B*

Idaho

Boise State University *B, T*
Brigham Young University-Idaho *B*
College of Southern Idaho *A*
Idaho State University *B*
University of Idaho *B*

Illinois

Augustana College *B*
Benedictine University *B*
Bradley University *B*
Chicago State University *B*

DePaul University *B, M*
Dominican University *B*
Eastern Illinois University *B, M*
Elmhurst College *B*
Illinois College *B*
Illinois State University *B, M*
Illinois Wesleyan University *B*
John A. Logan College *A*
John Wood Community College *A*
Kishwaukee College *A*
Knox College *B*
Lake Forest College *B*
Lake Land College *A*
Lincoln College *B*
McKendree University *B*
Monmouth College *B*
National-Louis University *B*
North Central College *B*
Northeastern Illinois University *B*
Northern Illinois University *B, M, D*
Northwestern University *B, M, D*
Olivet Nazarene University *B*
Principia College *B*
Richland Community College *A*
Rockford University *B*
Roosevelt University *B, M*
Sauk Valley Community College *A*
South Suburban College of Cook
  County *A*
Southern Illinois University
  Carbondale *B, M, D*
Southern Illinois University
  Edwardsville *B, M*
Southwestern Illinois College *A*
University of Chicago *B, D*
University of Illinois
  Chicago *B, M, D*
  Springfield *B*
  Urbana-Champaign *B, M, D*
Western Illinois University *B, M*
Wheaton College *B*

Indiana

Ball State University *B, T*
Butler University *B*
DePauw University *B*
Earlham College *B*
Franklin College *B*
Hanover College *B*
Indiana State University *B*
Indiana University
  Bloomington *B, M, D*
  Northwest *B*
  Purdue University Fort Wayne *B*
  Purdue University
    Indianapolis *B, M, D*
  South Bend *B*
  Southeast *B*
Indiana Wesleyan University *A, B*
Manchester University *B*
Marian University *B*
Purdue University *M, D*
Rose-Hulman Institute of
  Technology *B*
Saint Joseph's College *B*
Saint Mary's College *B*
Taylor University *B*
University of Evansville *B*
University of Indianapolis *B*
University of Notre Dame *B, M, D*
University of Southern Indiana *B, T*
Valparaiso University *B*
Vincennes University *A*
Wabash College *B*

Iowa

Central College *B, T*
Coe College *B*
Cornell College *B, T*
Drake University *B*
Graceland University *B*
Grinnell College *B*
Iowa State University *B, M, D*
Loras College *B*

Luther College *B*
Northwestern College *B*
St. Ambrose University *B, T*
Simpson College *B*
University of Iowa *B, D, T*
University of Northern Iowa *B*
Wartburg College *B, T*

Kansas

Allen County Community College *A*
Baker University *B*
Barton County Community College *A*
Benedictine College *B*
Bethany College *B*
Butler Community College *A*
Coffeyville Community College *A*
Dodge City Community College *A*
Emporia State University *B, T*
Fort Hays State University *B*
Independence Community College *A*
Kansas State University *B, M, D*
Pittsburg State University *B*
Seward County Community
    College *A*
University of Kansas *B, M, D*
Washburn University *B*
Wichita State University *B, M*

Kentucky

Bellarmine University *B*
Berea College *B*
Campbellsville University *B*
Centre College *B*
Eastern Kentucky University *B*
Georgetown College *B*
Hopkinsville Community College *A*
Murray State University *B, M, T*
Thomas More College *A, B*
Transylvania University *B*
University of Kentucky *B, M, D*
University of Louisville *B*
Western Kentucky University *B*

Louisiana

Centenary College of Louisiana *B*
Dillard University *B*
Louisiana College *B*
Louisiana State University and
    Agricultural and Mechanical
    College *B, M, D*
Loyola University New Orleans *B*
Tulane University *B, M*

Maine

Bates College *B*
Bowdoin College *B*
Colby College *B*
College of the Atlantic *B, M*
University of Maine *B, M*
University of Southern Maine *B*

Maryland

Allegany College of Maryland *A*
Frederick Community College *A*
Frostburg State University *B*
Goucher College *B*
Hood College *B*
Johns Hopkins University *B, M, D*
Loyola University Maryland *B*
McDaniel College *B*
Morgan State University *B, M*
Mount St. Mary's University *B*
Notre Dame of Maryland
    University *B*
St. Mary's College of Maryland *B*
Salisbury University *B*
Towson University *B*
United States Naval Academy *B*
University of Maryland
    Baltimore County *B, M*
    College Park *B, M, D*
Washington College *B*

Massachusetts

American International College *B*
Amherst College *B*
Assumption College *B*
Boston College *B, M, D*
Boston University *B, M, D*
Brandeis University *B, D*
Bridgewater State University *B*
Clark University *B, M, D*
College of the Holy Cross *B*
Fitchburg State University *B*
Framingham State University *B*
Gordon College *B*
Hampshire College *B*
Harvard College *B, M, D*
Massachusetts Institute of
    Technology *B, M, D*
Merrimack College *B*
Mount Holyoke College *B*
Nichols College *B*
Northeastern University *B, M, D*
Salem State University *B*
Simmons College *B*
Smith College *B*
Stonehill College *B*
Suffolk University *B, M, D*
Tufts University *B, M*
University of Massachusetts
    Amherst *B, M, D*
    Boston *B, M*
    Dartmouth *B*
    Lowell *B*
Wellesley College *B*
Western New England University *B*
Westfield State University *B*
Wheaton College *B*
Williams College *B, M*
Worcester Polytechnic Institute *B*
Worcester State University *B*

Michigan

Adrian College *A, B, T*
Albion College *B*
Alma College *B, T*
Andrews University *B*
Aquinas College *B*
Calvin College *B*
Central Michigan University *B, M*
Delta College *A*
Eastern Michigan University *B, M*
Grand Rapids Community College *A*
Grand Valley State University *B*
Hillsdale College *B*
Hope College *B*
Kalamazoo College *B*
Lansing Community College *A*
Michigan State University *B, M, D*
Michigan Technological University *B*
Northern Michigan University *B*
Oakland University *B*
University of Detroit Mercy *B, M*
University of Michigan *B, M, D*
University of Michigan
    Dearborn *B*
    Flint *B*
Wayne State University *B, M, D*
Western Michigan University *B*

Minnesota

Augsburg College *B*
Bemidji State University *B*
Bethel University *B*
Carleton College *B*
College of St. Benedict *B*
Gustavus Adolphus College *B*
Hamline University *B*
Macalester College *B*
Metropolitan State University *B*
Minnesota State University
    Mankato *B*
    Moorhead *B*
Minnesota West Community and
    Technical College *A*
Ridgewater College *A*

St. Catherine University *B*
Saint Cloud State University *B*
St. John's University *B*
St. Olaf College *B*
University of Minnesota
    Duluth *B*
    Morris *B*
    Twin Cities *B, M, D*
University of St. Thomas *B*
Winona State University *B*

Mississippi

East Mississippi Community
    College *A*
Itawamba Community College *A*
Millsaps College *B*
Mississippi State University *B*
Tougaloo College *B*
University of Mississippi *B, M, D*

Missouri

Drury University *B*
Lindenwood University *B*
Missouri State University *B*
Missouri University of Science and
    Technology *B, T*
Missouri Valley College *B*
Missouri Western State University *B*
Northwest Missouri State
    University *B*
Park University *B*
Rockhurst University *B*
St. Charles Community College *A*
Southeast Missouri State University *B*
Three Rivers Community College *A*
Truman State University *B*
University of Central Missouri *B*
University of Missouri
    Columbia *B, M, D*
    Kansas City *B, M, D*
    St. Louis *B, M*
Washington University in St.
    Louis *B, M, D*
Webster University *B*
Westminster College *B*

Montana

Miles Community College *A*
Montana State University *B, M*
University of Montana *B, M*

Nebraska

Creighton University *B*
Doane College *B*
Hastings College *B*
Midland University *B*
Nebraska Wesleyan University *B*
University of Nebraska
    Kearney *B*
    Lincoln *B, M, D*
    Omaha *B, M*
Western Nebraska Community
    College *A*

Nevada

Nevada State College *B*
Sierra Nevada College *B*

New Hampshire

Dartmouth College *B*
Keene State College *B*
Saint Anselm College *B*
Southern New Hampshire
    University *B*
University of New
    Hampshire *B, M, D*

New Jersey

Bergen Community College *A*
Caldwell College *B*
College of New Jersey *B*
College of St. Elizabeth *B*
Drew University *B*

Fairleigh Dickinson University
    College at Florham *B, M*
    Metropolitan Campus *B*
Kean University *B, T*
Montclair State University *B*
New Jersey City University *B*
Princeton University *B, M, D*
Ramapo College of New Jersey *B*
Richard Stockton College of New
    Jersey *B*
Rider University *B*
Rowan University *B*
Rutgers, The State University of New
    Jersey
    Camden Campus *B*
    New Brunswick/Piscataway
        Campus *B, M, D*
    Newark Campus *B, M*
Saint Peter's University *R*
Seton Hall University *B*
Thomas Edison State College *B*
William Paterson University of New
    Jersey *B*

New Mexico

New Mexico State University *B, M*
University of New Mexico *B, M, D*

New York

Adelphi University *B*
Alfred University *B*
Bard College *B*
Barnard College *B*
Canisius College *B*
City University of New York
    Baruch College *B, M*
    Brooklyn College *B, M*
    City College *B, M*
    College of Staten Island *B*
    Hunter College *B, M*
    John Jay College of Criminal
        Justice *B*
    Lehman College *B*
    Queens College *B, T*
    York College *B*
Colgate University *B*
College of Mount St. Vincent *B*
College of New Rochelle *B*
Columbia University *B*
Columbia University
    School of General Studies *B*
Cornell University *B, M, D*
Dominican College of Blauvelt *B*
Dowling College *B*
Elmira College *B*
Eugene Lang College The New
    School for Liberal Arts *B*
Excelsior College *B*
Fordham University *B, M, D*
Hamilton College *B*
Hartwick College *B*
Hobart and William Smith Colleges *B*
Hofstra University *B*
Iona College *B*
Ithaca College *B*
Le Moyne College *B*
Long Island University
    LIU Brooklyn *B, M*
    LIU Post *B*
Manhattan College *B*
Manhattanville College *B*
Marist College *B*
Nazareth College *B*
New York University *C, B, M, D*
Pace University *B*
Pace University: Pleasantville/
    Briarcliff *B*
Rensselaer Polytechnic
    Institute *B, M, D*
Rochester Institute of Technology *B*
SUNY
    College at Buffalo *B, M*
    College at Cortland *B*
    College at Fredonia *B*

College at Geneseo *B*
College at New Paltz *B*
College at Oneonta *B*
College at Oswego *B*
College at Plattsburgh *B*
College at Potsdam *B*
College at Purchase *B*
Empire State College *A, B*
University at Albany *B, M, D*
University at Binghamton *B, M, D*
University at Buffalo *B, M, D*
University at Stony Brook *B, M, D*
St. Francis College *B*
St. John Fisher College *B*
St. John's University *B*
St. Lawrence University *B*
Siena College *B, T*
Skidmore College *B*
Suffolk County Community College *A*
Syracuse University *B, M, D*
Touro College *B*
Union College *B*
United States Military Academy *B*
University of Rochester *B, M, D*
Utica College *B*
Vassar College *B*
Wagner College *B*
Wells College *B*
Yeshiva University *B*

North Carolina

Appalachian State University *B*
Campbell University *B*
Davidson College *B*
Duke University *B, M, D*
East Carolina University *B*
Elon University *B*
Guilford College *B*
Johnson C. Smith University *B*
Lenoir-Rhyne University *B, T*
Meredith College *B*
North Carolina Agricultural and
   Technical State University *B*
North Carolina State University *M, D*
Pfeiffer University *B*
Salem College *B*
University of North Carolina
   Asheville *B, T*
   Chapel Hill *B, M, D*
   Charlotte *B*
   Greensboro *B*
   Wilmington *B*
Wake Forest University *B*
Warren Wilson College *B*
Winston-Salem State University *B*

North Dakota

Minot State University *B*
North Dakota State University *B*
University of North Dakota *B, M*

Ohio

Ashland University *B*
Baldwin Wallace University *B*
Bluffton University *B*
Bowling Green State University *B, M*
Capital University *B*
Case Western Reserve University *B*
Central State University *B*
Cleveland State University *B, M*
College of Wooster *B*
Denison University *B*
Franciscan University of
   Steubenville *B*
Franklin University *B*
Heidelberg University *B*
Hiram College *B, T*
John Carroll University *B*
Kenyon College *B*
Marietta College *B*
Miami University
   Oxford *B, M*
Muskingum University *B*
Notre Dame College *T*

Oberlin College *B*
Ohio Dominican University *B*
Ohio State University
   Columbus Campus *B, M*
Ohio University *B, M*
Ohio Wesleyan University *B*
Otterbein University *B*
Terra State Community College *A*
University of Akron *B, M*
University of Cincinnati *B, T*
University of Cincinnati
   Blue Ash College *A*
University of Dayton *B*
University of Findlay *B*
University of Mount Union *B*
University of Rio Grande *B*
University of Toledo *B, M*
Wilberforce University *B*
Wilmington College *B*
Wittenberg University *B*
Wright State University *B*
Xavier University *B*
Youngstown State University *B, M*

Oklahoma

Langston University *B*
Oklahoma City University *B*
Oklahoma State University *B*
Tulsa Community College *A*
University of Central Oklahoma *B, M*
University of Oklahoma *B, M, D*
University of Science and Arts of
   Oklahoma *B*
University of Tulsa *B*

Oregon

George Fox University *B*
Lewis & Clark College *B*
Linfield College *B*
Linn-Benton Community College *A*
Mt. Hood Community College *A*
Oregon State University *B*
Pacific University *B*
Portland State University *B, M, D*
Reed College *B*
Southern Oregon University *B*
University of Oregon *B, M, D*
Western Oregon University *B*
Willamette University *B*

Pennsylvania

Albright College *B*
Allegheny College *B*
Bloomsburg University of
   Pennsylvania *B*
Bryn Mawr College *B*
Bucknell University *B*
Carnegie Mellon University *B, M, D*
Chatham University *B*
Cheyney University of
   Pennsylvania *B*
Clarion University of Pennsylvania *B*
Dickinson College *B*
Drexel University *B, D*
Duquesne University *B*
East Stroudsburg University of
   Pennsylvania *B*
Edinboro University of
   Pennsylvania *B*
Elizabethtown College *B*
Franklin & Marshall College *B*
Gettysburg College *B*
Grove City College *B*
Haverford College *B, T*
Immaculata University *A, B*
Indiana University of Pennsylvania *B*
Juniata College *B*
King's College *B*
La Salle University *B*
Lafayette College *B*
Lebanon Valley College *B*
Lincoln University *B*
Lycoming College *B*

Mansfield University of
   Pennsylvania *B, T*
Messiah College *B*
Millersville University of
   Pennsylvania *B*
Moravian College *B*
Muhlenberg College *C, B*
Penn State
   Abington *B*
   Altoona *B*
   Beaver *B*
   Berks *B*
   Brandywine *B*
   DuBois *B*
   Erie, The Behrend College *B*
   Fayette, The Eberly Campus *B*
   Greater Allegheny *B*
   Harrisburg *B*
   Hazleton *B*
   Lehigh Valley *B*
   Mont Alto *B*
   New Kensington *B*
   Schuylkill *B*
   Shenango *B*
   University Park *B, M, D*
   Wilkes-Barre *B*
   Worthington Scranton *B*
   York *B*
Point Park University *B*
Robert Morris University *B*
Rosemont College *B*
St. Francis University *B*
Saint Joseph's University *B*
St. Vincent College *B*
Seton Hill University *B*
Shippensburg University of
   Pennsylvania *B*
Slippery Rock University of
   Pennsylvania *B*
Susquehanna University *B*
Swarthmore College *B*
Temple University *B, M, D*
University of Pennsylvania *B, M, D*
University of Pittsburgh *B, M, D*
University of Pittsburgh
   Bradford *B*
   Johnstown *B*
University of Scranton *B*
Ursinus College *B*
Villanova University *B*
Washington & Jefferson College *B*
Westminster College *B*
Widener University *B*
Wilson College *B*
York College of Pennsylvania *B*

Puerto Rico

University of Puerto Rico
   Aguadilla *A*
   Cayey University College *B*
   Mayaguez *B*
   Rio Piedras *B, M*

Rhode Island

Brown University *B, M, D*
Bryant University *B*
Providence College *B*
Rhode Island College *B*
Roger Williams University *B*
Salve Regina University *B*
University of Rhode Island *B*

South Carolina

Benedict College *B*
Charleston Southern University *B*
Clemson University *B, M*
Coastal Carolina University *B*
College of Charleston *B*
Converse College *B*
Francis Marion University *B*
Furman University *B*
University of South Carolina
   Columbia *B, M, D*

Winthrop University *B*
Wofford College *B*

South Dakota

Augustana College *B, T*
Northern State University *B*
South Dakota State University *B, M*
University of South Dakota *B*

Tennessee

Carson-Newman University *B*
East Tennessee State University *B, T*
Hiwassee College *A*
King University *B*
Maryville College *B, T*
Middle Tennessee State
   University *B, M, D*
Rhodes College *B*
Sewanee: The University of the
   South *B*
Tennessee Technological
   University *B*
Union University *B, T*
University of Memphis *B, M*
University of Tennessee
   Chattanooga *B*
   Knoxville *B*
Vanderbilt University *B, M, D*

Texas

Austin College *B*
Austin Community College *A*
Brazosport College *A*
Clarendon College *A*
College of the Mainland *A*
Galveston College *A*
Hardin-Simmons University *B*
Houston Baptist University *B*
Lamar University *B*
Laredo Community College *A*
Lubbock Christian University *B*
Northwest Vista College *A*
Palo Alto College *A*
Rice University *B, M, D*
St. Edward's University *B*
St. Mary's University *B*
St. Philip's College *A*
Southern Methodist
   University *B, M, D*
Southwestern University *B*
Stephen F. Austin State University *B*
Tarleton State University *B, T*
Texas A&M University *B, M, D*
Texas A&M University
   Commerce *B, M*
   Corpus Christi *B*
Texas Christian University *B*
Texas Lutheran University *B*
Texas Southern University *B*
Texas State University *B, T*
Texas Tech University *B, M, D*
Trinity University *B*
University of Dallas *B*
University of Houston *B, M, D*
University of North Texas *B, M*
University of St. Thomas *B*
University of Texas
   Arlington *B, M*
   Austin *B, M, D*
   Dallas *B, M, D*
   Pan American *B*
   San Antonio *M*
Western Texas College *A*

Utah

Brigham Young University *B*
Salt Lake Community College *A*
Snow College *A*
Southern Utah University *B*
University of Utah *B, M, D, T*
Utah State University *B, M, D*
Utah Valley University *B*
Weber State University *B*
Westminster College *B*

Vermont

Marlboro College *B*
Middlebury College *B*
Norwich University *B*
Saint Michael's College *B*
University of Vermont *B*

Virginia

Bridgewater College *B*
Christopher Newport University *B*
College of William and Mary *B*
Eastern Mennonite University *B*
Emory & Henry College *B*
George Mason University *B, M, D*
Hampden-Sydney College *B*
Hollins University *B*
James Madison University *B*
Longwood University *B*
Lynchburg College *B*
Mary Baldwin College *B*
Marymount University *B*
Old Dominion University *B, M*
Radford University *B*
Randolph College *B*
Randolph-Macon College *B*
Roanoke College *B*
Sweet Briar College *B*
University of Mary Washington *B*
University of Richmond *B*
University of Virginia *B, M, D*
University of Virginia's College at Wise *B, T*
Virginia Military Institute *B*
Virginia Polytechnic Institute and State University *B, M, D*
Washington and Lee University *B*

Washington

Central Washington University *B*
Centralia College *A*
Eastern Washington University *B*
Gonzaga University *B*
Highline Community College *A*
Pacific Lutheran University *B*
Seattle Pacific University *B*
Seattle University *B*
University of Puget Sound *B*
University of Washington *B, M, D*
Washington State University *B, D*
Western Washington University *B*
Whitman College *B*
Whitworth University *B*

West Virginia

Bethany College *B*
Davis and Elkins College *B*
Marshall University *B*
Potomac State College of West Virginia University *A*
Shepherd University *B*
West Virginia State University *B*
West Virginia University *B*
West Virginia Wesleyan College *B*

Wisconsin

Beloit College *B*
Carthage College *B, T*
Concordia University Wisconsin *B*
Edgewood College *B*
Lawrence University *B*
Marquette University *B*
Ripon College *B*
St. Norbert College *B, T*
University of Wisconsin
  Eau Claire *B*
  Green Bay *B, T*
  La Crosse *B, T*
  Madison *B, M, D*
  Milwaukee *B, M, D*
  Oshkosh *B*
  Parkside *B, T*
  Platteville *B*
  River Falls *B, T*
  Stevens Point *B, T*
  Superior *B*
  Whitewater *B, T*

Wyoming

Casper College *A*
Eastern Wyoming College *A*
Laramie County Community College *A*

Education, general

Alabama

Alabama Agricultural and Mechanical University *T*
Auburn University *M*
Birmingham-Southern College *B*
Bishop State Community College *A*
Calhoun Community College *A*
Central Alabama Community College *A*
Gadsden State Community College *A*
Jacksonville State University *T*
Judson College *B*
Troy University *M, T*
Tuskegee University *B, T*
University of Alabama Birmingham *D, T*
University of Montevallo *M, T*
University of North Alabama *T*
Wallace State Community College at Hanceville *A*

Alaska

University of Alaska
  Anchorage *M*
  Fairbanks *B, M*
  Southeast *M*

Arizona

Arizona Western College *A*
Central Arizona College *A*
Coconino County Community College *A*
Dine College *A*
Estrella Mountain Community College *A*
Grand Canyon University *M*
Harrison Middleton University *B, M, D*
Mohave Community College *A*
Northland Pioneer College *A*
Phoenix College *A*
Pima Community College *A*
South Mountain Community College *A*
University of Arizona *M, D*

Arkansas

Arkansas Tech University *M*
Central Baptist College *A, B*
Crowley's Ridge College *A*
Harding University *M*
Ozarka College *A*
Phillips Community College of the University of Arkansas *A*
South Arkansas Community College *A*
University of Arkansas *B*
University of Central Arkansas *M*
Williams Baptist College *B*

California

Alliant International University *M, D*
American Jewish University *M*
Antioch University
  Los Angeles *M*
  Santa Barbara *M, T*
Azusa Pacific University *M, D*
Biola University *B, M, T*
Butte College *A*
California Baptist University *M*
California Coast University *M*
California Lutheran University *B, M*
California Polytechnic State University: San Luis Obispo *M*
California State Polytechnic University: Pomona *M*
California State University
  Bakersfield *M, T*
  Channel Islands *M*
  Chico *M*
  Dominguez Hills *M*
  East Bay *M*
  Fresno *B, M*
  Los Angeles *M*
  Monterey Bay *M*
  Sacramento *B, M*
  San Bernardino *M*
  San Marcos *M*
  Stanislaus *M*
Chaffey College *A*
Chapman University *B, M*
College of the Siskiyous *A*
Cypress College *A*
Dominican University of California *M*
Holy Names University *M*
Humboldt State University *M*
Humphreys College *A, B, M*
John F. Kennedy University *M*
Laney College *A*
Lassen Community College *A*
Los Angeles Southwest College *A*
Loyola Marymount University *M*
Master's College *B, M*
Merritt College *A*
Mount St. Mary's College *B, M*
Napa Valley College *A*
National Hispanic University *M, T*
National University *A, M, T*
Notre Dame de Namur University *M, T*
Pacific Union College *M*
Palomar College *A*
Patten University *M*
Pepperdine University *B, M*
Point Loma Nazarene University *M*
Porterville College *A*
St. Mary's College of California *M*
San Diego Christian College *B*
San Diego State University *M, D*
San Francisco State University *M*
Santa Rosa Junior College *A*
Simpson University *M, T*
Sonoma State University *M*
Southwestern College *A*
Stanford University *M, D*
University of California
  Berkeley *M, D, T*
  Davis *M, D, T*
  Irvine *D, T*
  Los Angeles *M, D*
  Riverside *M, D, T*
  Santa Barbara *M, D*
  Santa Cruz *M, D*
University of La Verne *B, M, T*
University of Redlands *M, T*
University of San Francisco *M*
University of Southern California *M, D*
University of the Pacific *B*
Vanguard University of Southern California *M, T*
Westmont College *B*
Whittier College *B, M, T*

Colorado

Adams State University *B*
Aspen University *M, D*
Colorado Christian University *B*
Colorado Mesa University *M*
Colorado Mountain College *A*
Colorado State University *B, T*
Colorado State University
  Pueblo *M*
Jones International University *M, D, T*
Metropolitan State University of Denver *M*
Morgan Community College *A*
National American University Denver *A*
Otero Junior College *A*
Regis University *M, T*
University of Colorado Denver *B*
University of Northern Colorado *M*

Connecticut

Albertus Magnus College *B, T*
Central Connecticut State University *M*
Fairfield University *M, T*
Post University *M*
Sacred Heart University *M*
Trinity College *B, T*
University of Connecticut *M, T*
University of New Haven *M*
University of Saint Joseph *M*
Western Connecticut State University *M*

Delaware

Delaware State University *B, M, D*
University of Delaware *B, T*
Wilmington University *B, M, D*

District of Columbia

Catholic University of America *B, M*
Gallaudet University *B*
Howard University *M, D*
Strayer University *M*
Trinity Washington University *B, M*

Florida

Broward College *A*
Chipola College *A*
Daytona State College *A*
Edward Waters College *B*
Florida Atlantic University *B, M*
Florida Gulf Coast University *B, M*
Florida National University *A*
Florida Southern College *M, D*
Indian River State College *A*
Jacksonville University *B, M, T*
Nova Southeastern University *M*
Pensacola State College *A*
Stetson University *M*
University of Central Florida *M, D*
University of Miami *B, M, D*
University of South Florida *B, M, D*
University of South Florida Sarasota-Manatee *M*

Georgia

Abraham Baldwin Agricultural College *A*
Andrew College *A*
Bainbridge College *A*
Clark Atlanta University *B*
College of Coastal Georgia *A*
East Georgia State College *A*
Emory University *B, M, D*
Georgia Gwinnett College *B*
Georgia Highlands College *A*
Georgia Military College *A*
Georgia Perimeter College *A*
Georgia Regents University *M*
Georgia State University *D*
Reinhardt University *A, B, M*
Shorter University *M*
South Georgia State College *A*
Thomas University *M*
University of Georgia *M*
University of North Georgia *A, B*
Young Harris College *B, T*

Hawaii

University of Hawaii
  Hilo *T*
  Manoa *D*

Idaho

Boise State University *B, M*
Idaho State University *M*
North Idaho College *A*
Northwest Nazarene University *B, M*
University of Idaho *B, M, D, T*

Illinois

Augustana College *B*
Aurora University *M*
Chicago State University *B*
Columbia College Chicago *M*
Concordia University Chicago *B, T*
Dominican University *M*
Elmhurst College *B*
Eureka College *B*
Governors State University *M*
Illinois College *M*
Illinois Valley Community College *A*
Illinois Wesleyan University *B*
Kankakee Community College *A*
Kishwaukee College *A*
Lake Forest College *B, M*
Lake Land College *A*
Lewis and Clark Community
　College *A*
Lincoln College *A*
McKendree University *B, M, D*
Monmouth College *B, T*
Moody Bible Institute *B*
National-Louis University *M*
North Central College *B*
North Park University *M*
Northern Illinois University *B, M*
Northwestern University *B*
Olivet Nazarene University *M*
Quincy University *M, T*
Richland Community College *A*
Rockford University *B, M*
Saint Xavier University *B, M*
South Suburban College of Cook
　County *A*
Southeastern Illinois College *A*
Spoon River College *A*
Trinity International University *D*
Triton College *A*
University of Chicago *M, D*
University of Illinois
　Urbana-Champaign *M, D*

Indiana

Ancilla College *A*
Anderson University *B*
Bethel College *M*
Butler University *M*
Calumet College of St.
　Joseph *B, M, T*
Earlham College *M*
Goshen College *B*
Grace College *M*
Huntington University *B, M*
Indiana University
　Kokomo *M*
Ivy Tech Community College
　Bloomington *A*
　Central Indiana *A*
　Columbus *A*
　East Central *A*
　Kokomo *A*
　Lafayette *A*
　North Central *A*
　Northeast *A*
　Northwest *A*
　Richmond *A*
　South Central *A*
　Southeast *A*
　Southwest *A*
　Wabash Valley *A*
Manchester University *B, T*
Martin University *B*
Purdue University *B, M, D, T*
Purdue University
　Calumet *B*
Taylor University *B*

University of Evansville *B*
University of Indianapolis *B*
University of St. Francis *B, M, T*
Valparaiso University *M*

Iowa

Ashford University *B, M*
Briar Cliff University *B, M*
Coe College *B, M*
Cornell College *B, T*
Dordt College *B*
Drake University *D*
Ellsworth Community College *A*
Graceland University *M*
Iowa State University *B, M, D*
Iowa Wesleyan College *B*
Iowa Western Community College *A*
Loras College *B, M*
Marshalltown Community College *A*
North Iowa Area Community
　College *A*
Northwestern College *B, T*
St. Ambrose University *B, M, T*
Simpson College *B, M*
Southwestern Community College *A*
University of Northern Iowa *M, D*
Upper Iowa University *B*

Kansas

Barton County Community College *A*
Benedictine College *M*
Bethany College *B, T*
Coffeyville Community College *A*
Colby Community College *A*
Cowley County Community
　College *A*
Dodge City Community College *A*
Fort Scott Community College *A*
Friends University *M*
Garden City Community College *A*
Haskell Indian Nations University *B*
Hutchinson Community College *A*
Independence Community College *A*
Labette Community College *A*
McPherson College *B, M, T*
MidAmerica Nazarene University *M*
Neosho County Community
　College *A*
Newman University *B*
Pratt Community College *A*
Seward County Community
　College *A*
Tabor College *B*
University of St. Mary *M*
Washburn University *B*
Wichita State University *B*

Kentucky

Bellarmine University *M, D*
Berea College *B*
Campbellsville University *A, B*
Eastern Kentucky University *D*
Madisonville Community College *A*
Morehead State University *M*
Northern Kentucky University *M*
Somerset Community College *A*
Spalding University *B*
Western Kentucky University *M*

Louisiana

Baton Rouge Community College *A*
Bossier Parish Community College *A*
Delgado Community College *A*
Louisiana College *B, M*
Louisiana State University
　Alexandria *B*
Louisiana State University and
　Agricultural and Mechanical
　College *M, T*
Nunez Community College *A*
Xavier University of Louisiana *B*

Maine

Thomas College *M*
University of Maine *B, M, D*
University of Maine
　Farmington *M*
　Fort Kent *B*
　Presque Isle *B*
University of New England *B*
York County Community College *A*

Maryland

Anne Arundel Community College *A*
Baltimore City Community College *A*
Carroll Community College *A*
Cecil College *A*
Chesapeake College *A*
College of Southern Maryland *A*
Community College of Baltimore
　County *A*
Frederick Community College *A*
Frostburg State University *M*
Garrett College *A*
Hagerstown Community College *A*
Harford Community College *A*
McDaniel College *M, T*
Montgomery College *A*
Notre Dame of Maryland
　University *M, D*
St. Mary's College of Maryland *M*
Salisbury University *M, T*
Towson University *M*
University of Maryland
　Baltimore County *M*
Washington Adventist University *B*
Washington College *B*
Wor-Wic Community College *A*

Massachusetts

Anna Maria College *B, M*
Boston University *B, M, D, T*
Brandeis University *B*
Bunker Hill Community College *A*
Cambridge College *M*
Cape Cod Community College *A*
Clark University *M*
Curry College *B*
Eastern Nazarene College *B, M, T*
Elms College *B, M*
Fitchburg State University *B, M, T*
Hampshire College *B*
Harvard College *M, D*
Lesley University *B, M, D*
Massachusetts College of Liberal
　Arts *B, M, T*
Merrimack College *B, M*
Mount Holyoke College *B, M*
Salem State University *B, M*
Simmons College *B, M, D*
Smith College *B, M*
Springfield College *M*
Stonehill College *B*
Suffolk University *M*
Tufts University *M*
University of Massachusetts
　Amherst *B, M, D*
　Boston *M, D*
Western New England
　University *B, T*
Westfield State University *M*
Worcester State University *M, T*

Michigan

Alma College *B*
Alpena Community College *A*
Aquinas College *B, M, T*
Baker College
　Auburn Hills *B*
Bay de Noc Community College *A*
Central Michigan University *M*
Cornerstone University *M*
Eastern Michigan University *T*
Gogebic Community College *A*
Grand Valley State University *M, T*
Hillsdale College *B*

Kalamazoo Valley Community
　College *A*
Marygrove College *B*
Michigan State University *B, M*
Northwestern Michigan College *A*
Olivet College *B, M, T*
Rochester College *B*
Schoolcraft College *A*
Spring Arbor University *M*
University of Detroit Mercy *B, M*
University of Michigan *M, D*
University of Michigan
　Dearborn *B, M, D, T*
　Flint *B, M*
West Shore Community College *A*

Minnesota

Augsburg College *B*
Bemidji State University *M*
Bethel University *M*
Capella University *M, D*
Century College *A*
Concordia College: Moorhead *B*
Gustavus Adolphus College *B*
Hamline University *M, D*
Hibbing Community College *A*
Inver Hills Community College *A*
Itasca Community College *A*
Macalester College *B*
Martin Luther College *M*
Mesabi Range Community and
　Technical College *A*
Minneapolis Community and
　Technical College *A*
Minnesota State University
　Mankato *B, M*
Minnesota West Community and
　Technical College *A*
Ridgewater College *A*
St. Catherine University *B*
St. Mary's University of Minnesota *M*
Southwest Minnesota State
　University *B, M*
University of Minnesota
　Duluth *B, M*
　Twin Cities *B, M, D, T*
Walden University *B, M, D*
White Earth Tribal and Community
　College *A*
Winona State University *B, M, T*

Mississippi

Belhaven University *M*
Coahoma Community College *A*
Delta State University *D*
East Central Community College *A*
Millsaps College *T*
Mississippi Delta Community
　College *A*
Mississippi Gulf Coast Community
　College *A*
Mississippi State University *D*
Northwest Mississippi Community
　College *A*
Southeastern Baptist College *A*
University of Mississippi *D*
University of Southern Mississippi *D*

Missouri

Avila University *B, M*
Calvary Bible College and Theological
　Seminary *M*
Central Methodist University *T*
Culver-Stockton College *B*
Drury University *B, M*
East Central College *A*
Evangel University *A*
Fontbonne University *M, T*
Hannibal-LaGrange University *B*
Harris-Stowe State University *B*
Maryville University of Saint
　Louis *M, T*
Metropolitan Community College -
　Kansas City *A*

Missouri Baptist University *B*
Missouri Southern State University *B*
Missouri State University: West
    Plains *A*
Missouri University of Science and
    Technology *A*
National American University
    Kansas City *A*
North Central Missouri College *A*
Park University *M*
Rockhurst University *M*
St. Louis Christian College *B*
Saint Louis University *B, M*
Southwest Baptist University *M*
Stephens College *B*
Three Rivers Community College *A*
University of Missouri
    Columbia *B*
    Kansas City *B, M, D*
    St. Louis *B, M, D*
Washington University in St.
    Louis *B, M, D, T*
Webster University *B, M, T*
William Woods University *B, T*

Montana

Fort Peck Community College *A*
Little Big Horn College *A*
Miles Community College *A*
Montana State University *M, D*
Montana State University
    Billings *B, M, T*
    Northern *A*
Salish Kootenai College *A, B*
University of Montana *B, M, D*
University of Montana:
    Western *A, B, T*

Nebraska

Bellevue University *B*
Concordia University *B, M, T*
Grace University *A*
Hastings College *B, M, T*
Little Priest Tribal College *A*
Midland University *B, T*
Union College *B*
University of Nebraska
    Kearney *B, M, T*
Western Nebraska Community
    College *A*
York College *B, T*

Nevada

University of Nevada
    Reno *D*

New Hampshire

Colby-Sawyer College *B*
Franklin Pierce University *B, M, T*
Keene State College *T*
NHTI-Concord's Community
    College *A*
Rivier University *A, B, M, T*
Southern New Hampshire
    University *B, M*

New Jersey

Bergen Community College *A*
Bloomfield College *B, T*
Brookdale Community College *A*
Centenary College *B*
Essex County College *A*
Felician College *M*
Georgian Court University *M*
Gloucester County College *A*
Middlesex County College *A*
Monmouth University *B, M*
Montclair State University *M, D*
Rutgers, The State University of New
    Jersey
    New Brunswick/Piscataway
        Campus *D*
Saint Peter's University *M*
Salem Community College *A*

Seton Hall University *M*
Warren County Community
    College *A*
William Paterson University of New
    Jersey *B, M*

New Mexico

Dona Ana Community College of
    New Mexico State University *A*
Eastern New Mexico University *M*
Eastern New Mexico University:
    Roswell *A*
Mesalands Community College *A*
New Mexico Junior College *A*
New Mexico State University *B, M, D*
New Mexico State University
    Alamogordo *A*
    Carlsbad *A*
    Grants *A*
Santa Fe Community College *A, T*
University of New Mexico *M*
University of the Southwest *B*

New York

Adelphi University *M*
Barnard College *T*
Canisius College *M*
City University of New York
    Hunter College *B, M, T*
    Queens College *T*
Colgate University *B, M*
College of New Rochelle *B, M, T*
Columbia University *B*
Concordia College *B, T*
Cornell University *M, D*
D'Youville College *D, T*
Dominican College of Blauvelt *B*
Dowling College *B*
Eugene Lang College The New
    School for Liberal Arts *B*
Fordham University *T*
Hofstra University *D*
Houghton College *B*
Jewish Theological Seminary of
    America *M, D*
Le Moyne College *M*
Manhattan College *B*
Manhattanville College *B, M*
Medaille College *B, M, T*
Metropolitan College of New York *M*
Nazareth College *M, T*
New York University *M, T*
Niagara University *B, M, T*
Orange County Community
    College *A*
SUNY
    College at Brockport *B, M, T*
    College at Buffalo *B*
    College at Fredonia *B, M, T*
    College at Oswego *M*
    Empire State College *A, B, M*
    University at Binghamton *M, D*
    University at Buffalo *B*
St. John Fisher College *B, M*
St. Joseph's College New York:
    Suffolk Campus *B*
St. Joseph's College, New York *B*
St. Lawrence University *M*
St. Thomas Aquinas College *B, M, T*
Siena College *T*
Skidmore College *B*
Touro College *M*
University of Rochester *M, D*
Wagner College *B, M*

North Carolina

Beaufort County Community
    College *A*
Belmont Abbey College *B*
Bladen Community College *A*
Campbell University *A, B, M, T*
Cape Fear Community College *A*
Carteret Community College *A*

Central Carolina Community
    College *A*
Chowan University *B*
College of the Albemarle *A*
East Carolina University *M*
Elon University *B*
Gardner-Webb University *B, M*
Greensboro College *B, T*
Guilford College *B, T*
Guilford Technical Community
    College *A*
Mars Hill University *B, M, T*
Martin Community College *A*
McDowell Technical Community
    College *A*
Methodist University *A, B*
Montreat College *A*
Nash Community College *A*
North Carolina Agricultural and
    Technical State University *B, T*
North Carolina State University *B*
North Carolina Wesleyan College *B*
Pamlico Community College *A*
Sampson Community College *A*
Southeastern Baptist Theological
    Seminary *D*
Southwestern Community College *A*
University of North Carolina
    Asheville *T*
    Chapel Hill *M, D*
Vance-Granville Community
    College *A*
Western Carolina University *M*
Wingate University *D*

North Dakota

Dakota College at Bottineau *A*
Minot State University *A*
United Tribes Technical College *A, T*
University of North Dakota *M*

Ohio

Antioch University
    Midwest *B, M*
Baldwin Wallace University *M*
Bluffton University *B*
Bowling Green State University *B, M*
Cedarville University *M*
Clark State Community College *A*
Cleveland State University *B, D*
College of Mount St. Joseph *M, T*
Defiance College *B, M, T*
Denison University *B*
Eastern Gateway Community
    College *A*
Edison State Community College *A*
Heidelberg University *M*
Hiram College *B*
Kent State University *B*
Lake Erie College *B, M*
Marietta College *B, M*
Mount Vernon Nazarene
    University *B, M*
Muskingum University *M*
Ohio Mid-Western College *B*
Ohio Northern University *B*
Ohio State University
    Columbus Campus *B, M, D, T*
    Lima Campus *B, M, T*
    Newark Campus *B, M, T*
Ohio University
    Eastern Campus *M*
Ohio Wesleyan University *B*
Otterbein University *B*
Shawnee State University *B*
Terra State Community College *A*
Tiffin University *B, M*
Union Institute & University *B*
University of Cincinnati
    Blue Ash College *A*
University of Findlay *B, M*
University of Rio Grande *B, M, T*
Urbana University *B*
Walsh University *M*

Washington State Community
    College *A*
Wilmington College *B*
Wittenberg University *B, M*
Wright State University *T*
Youngstown State University *B, M*

Oklahoma

Cameron University *M*
Langston University *B*
Northwestern Oklahoma State
    University *B, M*
Oklahoma City Community
    College *A*
Oklahoma City University *B*
Oklahoma State University *B, D*
Oral Roberts University *M*
Redlands Community College *A*
St. Gregory's University *A, B*
Seminole State College *A*
Southern Nazarene University *B*
Southwestern Christian University *B*
Southwestern Oklahoma State
    University *M, T*
Tulsa Community College *A*
University of Central Oklahoma *B, M*
University of Tulsa *M, T*

Oregon

Central Oregon Community
    College *A*
Concordia University *B, M, T*
Corban University *B*
Eastern Oregon University *A*
George Fox University *M*
Lewis & Clark College *M*
Linfield College *T*
Marylhurst University *M*
Oregon State University *B, M, D*
Pacific University *B, M, T*
Portland State University *M*
Southern Oregon University *B, M, T*
Umpqua Community College *A*
University of Oregon *B*
University of Portland *M*
Warner Pacific College *M, T*
Western Oregon University *B, M*

Pennsylvania

Allegheny College *B*
Alvernia University *B*
Arcadia University *B, M*
Bryn Athyn College *B*
Bucknell University *B, M*
Bucks County Community College *A*
Butler County Community College *A*
Cabrini College *B, M*
Cairn University *M*
California University of
    Pennsylvania *B*
Chatham University *M*
Clarion University of
    Pennsylvania *M, T*
Community College of Beaver
    County *A*
Community College of
    Philadelphia *A*
Duquesne University *B*
Gratz College *M*
Holy Family University *M, T*
Juniata College *B, T*
La Salle University *B, M, T*
Lackawanna College *A*
Lehigh Carbon Community College *A*
Luzerne County Community
    College *A*
Mansfield University of
    Pennsylvania *M*
Messiah College *M*
Misericordia University *M*
Moravian College *M*
Neumann University *M, D, T*
Pennsylvania Highlands Community
    College *A*

Reading Area Community College *A*
St. Francis University *B, M*
Saint Joseph's University *M*
St. Vincent College *T*
Swarthmore College *B*
Temple University *M, D*
University of Pennsylvania *B, M, D*
University of Pittsburgh *M, D, T*
University of Pittsburgh
  Bradford *B*
University of the Arts *M*
Villanova University *B, M*
Washington & Jefferson College *B*
Westminster College *B, M*
Widener University *M, D*
York College of Pennsylvania *M*

Puerto Rico

American University of Puerto
  Rico *B*
Inter American University of Puerto
  Rico
  Barranquitas Campus *B*
  Fajardo Campus *B, M*
  San German Campus *B*
University of Puerto Rico
  Ponce *A*
  Utuado *A*
University of the Sacred Heart *B*

Rhode Island

Brown University *B, M, T*
Johnson & Wales University
  Providence *D, T*
Rhode Island College *M, D*
Roger Williams University *B*
University of Rhode Island *M, D*

South Carolina

Anderson University *M*
Clemson University *M*
Coastal Carolina University *M*
Coker College *B*
Converse College *B, T*
Furman University *B*
Northeastern Technical College *A*
Southern Wesleyan University *M*
University of South Carolina
  Columbia *D*
Wofford College *B*

South Dakota

Dakota Wesleyan University *B, T*
Kilian Community College *A*
Northern State University *B*
Oglala Lakota College *A*
Sinte Gleska University *A, B, M*

Tennessee

American Baptist College *B*
Aquinas College *M*
Austin Peay State University *M*
Bethel University *M*
Bryan University
  Dayton *B*
Chattanooga State Community
  College *A*
Christian Brothers University *B, M, T*
Cleveland State Community
  College *A*
Columbia State Community
  College *A*
Cumberland University *B, M*
Dyersburg State Community
  College *A*
Hiwassee College *A*
Jackson State Community College *A*
Lee University *B, M*
Lincoln Memorial University *B, T*
Maryville College *B, T*
Milligan College *B, T*
Motlow State Community College *A*
Roane State Community College *A*

Southwest Tennessee Community
  College *A*
Tennessee State University *B*
Tennessee Technological
  University *B*
Tusculum College *M*
Union University *B, M, T*
University of Memphis *M, T*
University of Tennessee
  Knoxville *M, D*
Vanderbilt University *B*
Victory University *B, T*
Volunteer State Community
  College *A*
Walters State Community College *A*

Texas

Abilene Christian University *M*
Amarillo College *A*
Arlington Baptist College *B*
Baylor University *M*
Brazosport College *A*
Central Texas College *A*
Cisco College *A*
Clarendon College *A*
Coastal Bend College *A*
Concordia University Texas *M*
Dallas Baptist University *B, M, T*
Dallas Christian College *B, T*
East Texas Baptist University *B, M*
Frank Phillips College *A*
Grayson College *A*
Hill College *A*
Houston Community College
  System *A*
Howard College *A*
Huston-Tillotson University *B*
Jarvis Christian College *B*
Kilgore College *A*
Lamar State College at Orange *A*
Laredo Community College *A*
Navarro College *A*
Northwest Vista College *A*
Odessa College *A*
Our Lady of the Lake University of
  San Antonio *B, M*
Panola College *A*
Paris Junior College *A*
St. Mary's University *B*
St. Philip's College *A*
Schreiner University *M*
South Plains College *A*
Southern Methodist University *T*
Southwest Texas Junior College *A*
Southwestern Assemblies of God
  University *A*
Southwestern University *B, T*
Tarleton State University *M*
Texas A&M University
  Commerce *M*
  Kingsville *B, M*
  Texarkana *M*
Texas State University *M, D, T*
Texas Wesleyan University *B, M, D, T*
Texas Woman's University *M*
Trinity Valley Community College *A*
Tyler Junior College *A*
University of Dallas *B, T*
University of Houston
  Victoria *B*
University of St. Thomas *B, M*
University of Texas
  Arlington *M, T*
  El Paso *M*
  San Antonio *M*
University of the Incarnate
  Word *M, D*
Wayland Baptist University *M*
West Texas A&M University *M*
Western Texas College *A*

Utah

Snow College *A*
Southern Utah University *M*

University of Utah *B*
Westminster College *B, M*

Vermont

Bennington College *B*
Castleton State College *M, T*
College of St. Joseph in Vermont *M*
Community College of Vermont *A*
Goddard College *B, M*
Johnson State College *B, M*
Lyndon State College *B, M*
Norwich University *M*
University of Vermont *B, M, T*

Virginia

Bluefield College *B, M*
Central Virginia Community
  College *A*
Christopher Newport University *M*
Eastern Shore Community College *A*
Ferrum College *B*
George Mason University *D*
Germanna Community College *A*
Hampton University *B*
Hollins University *M, T*
James Madison University *M, T*
Longwood University *M*
Lord Fairfax Community College *A*
Mary Baldwin College *M, T*
Mountain Empire Community
  College *A*
New River Community College *A*
Norfolk State University *M*
Paul D. Camp Community College *A*
Piedmont Virginia Community
  College *A*
Radford University *M*
Randolph College *M*
Regent University *B, M, D*
Shenandoah University *M*
Southside Virginia Community
  College *A*
Southwest Virginia Community
  College *A*
Tidewater Community College *A*
University of Mary Washington *M*
University of Virginia *M, D*
Virginia Commonwealth
  University *M, D*
Virginia Highlands Community
  College *A*
Virginia Wesleyan College *B, T*
Virginia Western Community
  College *A*
Wytheville Community College *A*

Washington

Antioch University
  Seattle *M*
Central Washington University *M*
Centralia College *A*
Evergreen State College *B*
Gonzaga University *M*
Heritage University *B, M*
Highline Community College *A*
North Seattle Community College *A*
Northwest University *M*
Seattle Central Community College *A*
University of Washington *M, D, T*
University of Washington
  Bothell *B, M*
University of Washington
  Tacoma *M, T*
Walla Walla University *B*
Washington State
  University *B, M, D, T*
Whatcom Community College *A*
Whitworth University *B, M, T*
Yakima Valley Community College *A*

West Virginia

Alderson-Broaddus University *A*
American Public University System *M*
Bethany College *B, M*

Concord University *B, M, T*
Fairmont State University *B, M*
Marshall University *D*
New River Community and Technical
  College *A*
Ohio Valley University *B*
University of Charleston *B*
West Liberty University *M*
West Virginia State University *B*
West Virginia University *D*
West Virginia Wesleyan College *B*
Wheeling Jesuit University *B, T*

Wisconsin

Alverno College *B, M, T*
Beloit College *B*
Cardinal Stritch University *B, M*
Carroll University *B, M*
Concordia University Wisconsin *B*
Edgewood College *M, T*
Lakeland College *M*
Mount Mary University *B, M, T*
Ripon College *B*
St. Norbert College *M, T*
Silver Lake College of the Holy
  Family *M*
University of Wisconsin
  Green Bay *M*
  La Crosse *M*
  Milwaukee *B, D, T*
  Platteville *M*
  Stevens Point *M*
  Stout *M*
  Superior *M*
  Whitewater *B, M, T*
Viterbo University *M, T*
Wisconsin Lutheran College *B, M*

Wyoming

Laramie County Community
  College *A*
University of Wyoming *M, D*
Western Wyoming Community
  College *A*

Education of autistic

California

National University *T*

Illinois

University of Illinois
  Urbana-Champaign *M*

Kansas

University of Kansas *M*

Massachusetts

Emerson College *B, M*
Endicott College *M*

Michigan

Central Michigan University *M*
Madonna University *M*

Minnesota

Concordia University St. Paul *M, T*
Southwest Minnesota State
  University *M*
University of Minnesota
  Twin Cities *M*
University of St. Thomas *M*

Ohio

Ashland University *B*
Youngstown State University *B, M*

Pennsylvania

Holy Family University *M, T*

Puerto Rico

Bayamon Central University *M*

Wisconsin
University of Wisconsin
Whitewater *T*

Education of blind/visually handicapped

California
San Francisco State University *T*

Florida
Florida State University *M*

Illinois
University of Illinois
Urbana-Champaign *M*

Iowa
University of Northern Iowa *M*

Massachusetts
Boston College *M*

Michigan
Eastern Michigan University *B, M*
Western Michigan University *M, T*

New Jersey
College of New Jersey *M, T*

New York
City University of New York
Hunter College *M, T*
Dominican College of Blauvelt *M, T*
St. Francis College *B*

North Carolina
North Carolina Central University *M*

North Dakota
University of North Dakota *M*

Ohio
University of Toledo *T*

Oklahoma
Northeastern State University *T*

Oregon
Portland State University *T*

Pennsylvania
Kutztown University of
Pennsylvania *B*
University of Pittsburgh *T*

Puerto Rico
Inter American University of Puerto
Rico
Barranquitas Campus *B*

South Carolina
University of South Carolina
Upstate *M, T*

Tennessee
Trevecca Nazarene University *M*

Virginia
Radford University *T*
University of Mary Washington *T*

West Virginia
West Virginia University *T*

Wisconsin
Silver Lake College of the Holy
Family *T*

Education of brain injured

Illinois
University of Illinois
Urbana-Champaign *M*

Education of Deaf/hearing impaired

California
California State University
Northridge *M*
National University *M*
San Francisco State University *T*
University of San Diego *T*

District of Columbia
Gallaudet University *B, M, D*

Florida
Daytona State College *A*
Flagler College *B*
Hillsborough Community College *A*

Georgia
Valdosta State University *B, M*

Idaho
Idaho State University *M*

Illinois
Judson University *B*
MacMurray College *B, T*
University of Illinois
Urbana-Champaign *M, D*

Kansas
University of Kansas *M*

Kentucky
Eastern Kentucky University *B*

Louisiana
University of New Orleans *M*

Maryland
McDaniel College *M*

Massachusetts
Boston College *M*
Boston University *B, M, T*
Elms College *B, M, T*
Emerson College *B, M*
Smith College *M*

Michigan
Eastern Michigan University *B, M*
Grand Valley State University *M, T*
Michigan State University *B*

Mississippi
University of Southern Mississippi *B*

Missouri
Fontbonne University *B, M, T*
Washington University in St. Louis *M*

Nebraska
University of Nebraska
Lincoln *B, T*

Nevada
College of Southern Nevada *A*
Nevada State College *B*

New Jersey
College of New Jersey *B, M, T*
William Paterson University of New
Jersey *M*

New York
Canisius College *M*
City University of New York
Hunter College *M, T*
Ithaca College *B, M, T*
Nazareth College *T*
New York University *M, D, T*
Rochester Institute of Technology *M*

North Carolina
Barton College *B, T*
Lenoir-Rhyne University *B, T*
University of North Carolina
Greensboro *B*

North Dakota
Minot State University *B*

Ohio
Bowling Green State University *B, T*

Oklahoma
University of Science and Arts of
Oklahoma *B, T*
University of Tulsa *B, T*

Oregon
Lewis & Clark College *M*
Western Oregon University *M, T*

Pennsylvania
Bloomsburg University of
Pennsylvania *M*
Indiana University of Pennsylvania *B*
Rosemont College *T*

South Carolina
Converse College *B, T*

South Dakota
Augustana College *T*

Tennessee
Tennessee Temple University *B*
Vanderbilt University *M*

Texas
Del Mar College *A*
Lamar University *B, M, D*
Texas Christian University *B*
Texas Woman's University *M*

Utah
Utah Valley University *B*

Virginia
Hampton University *M*
Radford University *T*

Education of developmentally delayed

Illinois
University of Illinois
Urbana-Champaign *M*

Indiana
Purdue University *B*
St. Mary-of-the-Woods College *B, T*

Iowa
Upper Iowa University *T*

Kansas
Tabor College *B*

New Jersey
William Paterson University of New
Jersey *T*

New York
College of New Rochelle *M, T*
SUNY
College at Brockport *B, M*

Ohio
Ashland University *B*
University of Findlay *B, M, T*

Pennsylvania
La Salle University *B, M, T*

Texas
Del Mar College *A*

Wisconsin
University of Wisconsin
Superior *M*

Education of emotionally handicapped

California
California Lutheran University *M*
California State University
Northridge *M*
Sonoma State University *M*

District of Columbia
George Washington University *M, D*

Florida
Daytona State College *B*
University of Miami *M*
University of South Florida *B, M*

Georgia
Valdosta State University *M*

Illinois
Chicago State University *M*
DePaul University *M*
MacMurray College *B, T*
National-Louis University *M*
University of Illinois
Urbana-Champaign *M, D*

Iowa
Loras College *B*
Morningside College *M*

Kansas
Tabor College *B*
University of Kansas *M*

Michigan
Central Michigan University *B*
Eastern Michigan University *B, M*
Grand Valley State University *M, T*
Hope College *B, T*
Northern Michigan University *B, T*
Olivet College *B, T*
University of Detroit Mercy *B, M*
Western Michigan University *B*

Minnesota
Augsburg College *B*
Concordia University St. Paul *M, T*
Minnesota State University
Mankato *M*
University of St. Thomas *M*

New Hampshire
Franklin Pierce University *M, T*
Granite State College *T*
Rivier University *M*

New York
City University of New York
City College *M, T*
Fordham University *M*

Manhattan College *M*
Nazareth College *T*
New York University *M*
SUNY
College at Buffalo *B, M*

North Carolina
Greensboro College *B, T*
North Carolina Central University *M*
University of North Carolina
Charlotte *M*
Wilmington *B*

North Dakota
University of Mary *M*
University of North Dakota *M*

Ohio
University of Findlay *B, M, T*
University of Toledo *T*
Walsh University *B*
Youngstown State University *B, M*

Pennsylvania
La Salle University *B, T*

South Carolina
Converse College *B, T*
Furman University *M, T*

South Dakota
Augustana College *B, T*

Texas
West Texas A&M University *T*

Virginia
University of Virginia's College at
Wise *T*

Wisconsin
Silver Lake College of the Holy
Family *T*
University of Wisconsin
Oshkosh *B, M, T*

Education of gifted/talented

Alabama
Samford University *M, T*

Arizona
Northcentral University *M, D*

Arkansas
Arkansas State University *M, T*
University of Arkansas
Little Rock *M*

California
California State University
Fresno *M*
Northridge *M*
National University *M*

Delaware
Delaware State University *B*

Florida
Daytona State College *B*
University of South Florida *M*

Georgia
Valdosta State University *M*

Illinois
Chicago State University *M*
Northeastern Illinois University *M*
University of Illinois
Urbana-Champaign *M, D*

Iowa
Buena Vista University *M*
University of Northern Iowa *M*

Louisiana
Louisiana State University and
Agricultural and Mechanical
College *M*
University of Louisiana at Lafayette *M*

Michigan
Grand Valley State University *M*

Minnesota
Minnesota State University
Mankato *M*
University of Minnesota
Twin Cities *T*
University of St. Thomas *M*

Mississippi
Mississippi University for Women *M*
William Carey University *M*

Missouri
Maryville University of Saint
Louis *M, T*
Missouri Baptist University *T*
University of Missouri
Columbia *M, D*

Montana
University of Great Falls *B*

Nebraska
University of Nebraska
Kearney *M, T*

New Jersey
Montclair State University *M*

New York
Canisius College *M*
College of New Rochelle *M, T*
Dowling College *T*
Hofstra University *T*
Manhattanville College *M, T*
Saint Bonaventure University *M*

North Carolina
Elon University *M*
University of North Carolina
Charlotte *M, T*

Ohio
Ashland University *B, M, T*
Muskingum University *T*
University of Toledo *D*
Wright State University *M, T*
Youngstown State University *M*

Pennsylvania
Chatham University *T*
Millersville University of
Pennsylvania *M, T*

South Carolina
Converse College *M, T*

Texas
Hardin-Simmons University *M, T*
Southern Methodist University *T*
Texas A&M International
University *M, T*
University of Texas
Pan American *M*

Vermont
Johnson State College *M*

Virginia
College of William and Mary *M*
University of Mary Washington *T*

Washington
Whitworth University *M*

West Virginia
West Virginia State University *B*
West Virginia University *T*

Wisconsin
Carthage College *M, T*

Education of learning disabled

Arizona
Prescott College *B, T*

California
California Lutheran University *M*
California State University
Long Beach *T*
Northridge *M*
Holy Names University *M, T*
San Jose State University *M*
Sonoma State University *M, T*
University of San Francisco *T*

District of Columbia
American University *M*

Florida
Bethune-Cookman University *B, T*
Florida State University *M*
University of Miami *M, D*
University of South Florida *B, M*

Georgia
Valdosta State University *M*

Illinois
Bradley University *B, M*
Chicago State University *M*
DePaul University *M*
Highland Community College *A*
Judson University *B*
MacMurray College *B, T*
National-Louis University *M*
Northwestern University *B, M, D*
Rockford University *M, T*
Saint Xavier University *M*
University of Illinois
Urbana-Champaign *M*

Indiana
Ball State University *M*
University of Indianapolis *T*

Iowa
Iowa State University *T*
Northwestern College *T*

Kansas
Bethany College *T*
Southwestern College *M*
Tabor College *B*
University of Kansas *M*
Washburn University *M, T*

Massachusetts
Cambridge College *M*

Michigan
Aquinas College *B, T*
Calvin College *M, T*
Eastern Michigan University *M*
Grand Valley State University *M, T*
Hope College *B, T*
Madonna University *M*
Michigan State University *B*
Northern Michigan University *M*
University of Detroit Mercy *M*

Minnesota
Concordia University St. Paul *M, T*
Minnesota State University
Mankato *M*
University of St. Thomas *M*
Winona State University *B, M, T*

Mississippi
Mississippi College *M*

Missouri
Avila University *B, T*
Northwest Missouri State
University *T*
University of Missouri
Columbia *M, D*
William Woods University *T*

Nebraska
Hastings College *T*
University of Nebraska
Kearney *B, M, T*

New Hampshire
Franklin Pierce University *M, T*
Granite State College *T*
New England College *B, T*
Rivier University *M*

New Jersey
Fairleigh Dickinson University
Metropolitan Campus *M*
Georgian Court University *T*
Montclair State University *M*
Rowan University *M*
William Paterson University of New
Jersey *M*

New York
Canisius College *B, M*
City University of New York
Hunter College *M, T*
Fordham University *M*
Manhattanville College *M, T*
Nazareth College *T*
SUNY
College at New Paltz *B, M, T*

North Carolina
Appalachian State University *B, T*
Barton College *B, T*
East Carolina University *B, M*
Fayetteville State University *M*
Greensboro College *B, T*
North Carolina Central University *M*
North Carolina State University *T*
Salem College *M, T*
University of North Carolina
Charlotte *M*
Wilmington *B*

North Dakota
Minot State University *M*
University of Mary *M*
University of North Dakota *M*

Ohio
Ashland University *B*
Baldwin Wallace University *B, M, T*
Bowling Green State University *B, T*
Hiram College *T*
Malone University *B, M*
Muskingum University *T*
Notre Dame College *M, T*
University of Findlay *B, M, T*
University of Toledo *T*
Wright State University *M*
Youngstown State University *B, M*

Oklahoma
East Central University *M*
Northeastern State University *B*
Oklahoma Baptist University *B, T*

Southwestern Oklahoma State
University *B*

Oregon

Western Oregon University *M, T*

Pennsylvania

Immaculata University *T*

South Carolina

Francis Marion University *M*
Furman University *M, T*

South Dakota

Augustana College *B, T*

Texas

Lubbock Christian University *M, T*
Southern Methodist University *T*
West Texas A&M University *T*

Virginia

Hampton University *M*
Marymount University *M*
Radford University *T*
University of Virginia's College at
Wise *T*
Virginia Wesleyan College *B, T*

Washington

Central Washington University *M*

West Virginia

Bethany College *B*
Concord University *B, T*
West Virginia University *T*
West Virginia Wesleyan College *B*

Wisconsin

Silver Lake College of the Holy
Family *B, T*
University of Wisconsin
Oshkosh *B, M, T*
Superior *M*
Whitewater *B, T*

Education of mentally handicapped

California

California Lutheran University *M*
California State University
Northridge *M*
San Francisco State University *T*
Sonoma State University *M*

Florida

Florida State University *M, T*
University of South Florida *B, M*
University of West Florida *B*

Georgia

Brenau University *B*
Valdosta State University *B, M*

Illinois

Bradley University *B, T*
Chicago State University *B, M*
University of Illinois
Urbana-Champaign *M, D*

Indiana

Manchester University *B, T*

Iowa

Iowa State University *T*
Loras College *B*
Morningside College *M*
Northwestern College *T*

Kansas

Tabor College *B*
University of Kansas *M*

Louisiana

University of New Orleans *M*

Michigan

Central Michigan University *B*
Eastern Michigan University *B, M*
Grand Valley State University *M, T*
Northern Michigan University *B, T*
Western Michigan University *B*

Minnesota

Minnesota State University
Mankato *M*
University of St. Thomas *M*

Missouri

Northwest Missouri State
University *T*
University of Missouri
Columbia *M, D*
William Woods University *T*

Nebraska

University of Nebraska
Kearney *B, M, T*

New Hampshire

Granite State College *T*

New Jersey

William Paterson University of New
Jersey *M*

New York

City University of New York
City College *M, T*
Fordham University *M*
Manhattan College *M*
Nazareth College *T*
SUNY
College at Buffalo *B, M*

North Carolina

Bennett College for Women *B*
East Carolina University *M*
Greensboro College *B, T*
North Carolina Central University *M*
University of North Carolina
Wilmington *B*

North Dakota

Minot State University *B*
University of Mary *B*
University of North Dakota *M*

Ohio

Bowling Green State University *B, T*
Hiram College *T*
University of Findlay *B, M, T*
University of Toledo *T*
Walsh University *B*
Youngstown State University *B*

Oklahoma

Oklahoma Baptist University *B, T*
Southwestern Oklahoma State
University *B*

Oregon

Western Oregon University *M, T*

Pennsylvania

La Salle University *B, T*
University of Pittsburgh *T*

South Carolina

Converse College *B, M, T*
Furman University *M, T*

South Dakota

Augustana College *B, T*

Texas

Texas A&M University
Kingsville *M*
Texas Woman's University *M*
West Texas A&M University *T*

Virginia

Radford University *T*
University of Virginia's College at
Wise *T*

West Virginia

Concord University *B, T*
West Liberty University *B*
West Virginia State University *B*
West Virginia University *T*

Wisconsin

Silver Lake College of the Holy
Family *B, T*
University of Wisconsin
Oshkosh *B, M, T*

Education of multiple handicapped

California

California State University
Fresno *M*
Long Beach *T*
San Francisco State University *T*
Sonoma State University *M*

District of Columbia

Gallaudet University *B, M, T*

Florida

University of Miami *M*

Georgia

Georgia State University *M*

Illinois

Bradley University *T*
National-Louis University *M*
University of Illinois
Urbana-Champaign *B, M, D, T*

Indiana

Ball State University *B, T*

Iowa

Iowa State University *T*
Northwestern College *T*
St. Ambrose University *M, T*

Kansas

Tabor College *B*
University of Kansas *M*

Massachusetts

Boston College *M*
Endicott College *M*
Westfield State University *M, T*

Minnesota

Minnesota State University
Mankato *M*

Mississippi

William Carey University *M*

Missouri

Missouri Baptist University *T*
Missouri Valley College *B, T*
Northwest Missouri State
University *B, M, T*
University of Missouri
Columbia *B*

Nebraska

University of Nebraska
Kearney *B, M, T*

New York

City University of New York
Hunter College *M, T*
Dominican College of
Blauvelt *B, M, T*
Hofstra University *T*
Nazareth College *T*
New York University *T*
SUNY
College at Cortland *M*
University at Binghamton *M*

North Carolina

Greensboro College *B, T*
University of North Carolina
Wilmington *B*

North Dakota

Minot State University *M*

Ohio

Ashland University *B, M, T*
Bowling Green State University *B, T*
Muskingum University *T*
Ohio Dominican University *B, T*
University of Findlay *B, M, T*
University of Toledo *T*
Walsh University *B*
Wright State University *M, T*
Youngstown State University *B*

Oregon

Portland State University *T*
Western Oregon University *M, T*

Virginia

Norfolk State University *M*

West Virginia

Bethany College *B*
West Virginia University *T*

Education of physically handicapped

California

California State University
Northridge *M*
Fresno Pacific University *M, T*
San Francisco State University *T*

Florida

University of Miami *B*

Georgia

Georgia State University *M*

Illinois

University of Illinois
Urbana-Champaign *M*

Louisiana

Louisiana College *B, T*

Massachusetts

Springfield College *M, T*

Michigan

Aquinas College *B, T*
Eastern Michigan University *B, M*

Nebraska

University of Nebraska
Kearney *B, M, T*

New Jersey

William Paterson University of New
Jersey *M*

New York

City University of New York
Hunter College *T*
SUNY
College at Buffalo *B, M*

Ohio

Ashland University *M, T*
University of Toledo *T*

Oregon

Western Oregon University *M, T*

Pennsylvania

Cheyney University of
Pennsylvania *T*
La Salle University *B, T*
University of Pittsburgh *T*

Puerto Rico

University of Puerto Rico
Bayamon University College *B*

South Dakota

Augustana College *B, T*

Texas

Texas Woman's University *M*
West Texas A&M University *T*

Education of speech impaired

Alabama

Alabama Agricultural and Mechanical
University *B*

California

California State University
Chico *T*
Long Beach *T*
Northridge *B, M*
San Francisco State University *T*
University of Redlands *B, M*
University of San Francisco *M*

Georgia

Armstrong Atlantic State
University *B, M*
Georgia State University *M*
South Georgia State College *A*

Illinois

University of Illinois
Urbana-Champaign *M, T*

Kentucky

Eastern Kentucky University *B, M*
Hopkinsville Community College *A*

Louisiana

Louisiana Tech University *B*

Massachusetts

Emerson College *B, M, D*

Michigan

Eastern Michigan University *B, M*
Wayne State University *B, T*

Minnesota

Minnesota State University
Mankato *M*

Nebraska

University of Nebraska
Kearney *B, M, T*
Omaha *B, M, T*

New Jersey

Kean University *M*
William Paterson University of New
Jersey *M*

New Mexico

New Mexico State University *B, M*

New York

City University of New York
Hunter College *M, T*
College of New Rochelle *M, T*
Elmira College *B, T*
Hofstra University *M; T*
Ithaca College *B, M, T*
Long Island University
LIU Brooklyn *B, T*
Nazareth College *B, M, T*
New York University *B, M, D, T*
Pace University *B*
Pace University: Pleasantville/
Briarcliff *B*
SUNY
College at Buffalo *B, M*
College at Cortland *B*
College at Fredonia *B, M, T*
Syracuse University *M*

North Dakota

Minot State University *B, M*

Ohio

Ashland University *B*
University of Toledo *M, T*

Oregon

Chemeketa Community College *C, A*
Portland State University *T*

Pennsylvania

West Chester University of
Pennsylvania *T*

Puerto Rico

Carlos Albizu University: San Juan *B*

South Dakota

Augustana College *B, T*

Texas

Our Lady of the Lake University of
San Antonio *B, M*

Virginia

Hampton University *M*
Radford University *T*

West Virginia

West Virginia University *T*

Wisconsin

University of Wisconsin
River Falls *B, T*
Whitewater *M*

Education policy analysis

Arizona

Arizona State University *D*

Maine

College of the Atlantic *B, M*

Tennessee

Vanderbilt University *M*

Educational assessment/testing

California

California State University
Northridge *M*
Stanford University *M, D*

Connecticut

University of Connecticut *T*

Delaware

University of Delaware *M, D*

Illinois

University of Illinois
Chicago *M*
Urbana-Champaign *M, D*

Iowa

Iowa State University *M*
University of Iowa *M, D*

Maryland

University of Maryland
College Park *M, D*

Massachusetts

Tufts University *M*

Michigan

Eastern Michigan University *T*
Michigan State University *D*

Minnesota

Walden University *M*

New Mexico

University of the Southwest *M*

New York

Fordham University *M, D*
SUNY
University at Albany *M, D*

North Carolina

University of North Carolina
Greensboro *M, D*

Ohio

Kent State University *M, D*
University of Findlay *B, M*

Pennsylvania

University of Pennsylvania *M*

Texas

Lubbock Christian University *M, T*
Sul Ross State University *M*
University of St. Thomas *M*
Wayland Baptist University *M*

Utah

Western Governors University *M*

Washington

University of Washington *M, D*
Washington State University *M, D*

Educational evaluation/research

Colorado

University of Colorado
Boulder *D*
Colorado Springs *D*

Florida

University of Miami *M, D*

Georgia

Georgia State University *D*
University of Georgia *D*

Illinois

Loyola University Chicago *M*
Northern Illinois University *M*
University of Illinois
Urbana-Champaign *M, D*

Indiana

Indiana University
Bloomington *D*

Kentucky

University of Kentucky *M, D*

Massachusetts

Boston College *M, D*

Michigan

Michigan State University *D*
Wayne State University *M, D*
Western Michigan University *M, D, T*

Minnesota

University of Minnesota
Twin Cities *T*

Missouri

University of Missouri
Columbia *M, D*
Kansas City *M*

North Carolina

North Carolina State University *D*

North Dakota

North Dakota State University *D*

Ohio

Ohio University *M, D*
University of Findlay *B, M*

Pennsylvania

Penn State
University Park *M*

Puerto Rico

University of Puerto Rico
Rio Piedras *M*

South Carolina

University of South Carolina
Columbia *M, D*

South Dakota

University of South Dakota *M, D*

Texas

Texas Tech University *M, D*

Vermont

Goddard College *M*

Washington

Washington State University *M, D*

Educational/instructional technology

Alabama

Auburn University *M, T*
Jacksonville State University *M, T*
Miles College *B*
University of South Alabama *M, D, T*
University of West Alabama *M, T*

Arizona

Arizona State University *M, D*
Grand Canyon University *M*
Paradise Valley Community College *A*
University of Arizona *M*

Arkansas

Arkansas Tech University *M*
Southern Arkansas University *M, T*
University of Arkansas *M*
University of Arkansas
Little Rock *M*
University of Central Arkansas *M*

California

California State University
    Dominguez Hills *M*
    Fullerton *M, T*
    Monterey Bay *M*
    Sacramento *M*
    San Bernardino *M*
Fresno Pacific University *M, T*
National University *B, M, T*
San Diego State University *M, D*
San Jose State University *M*
Stanford University *M, D*
University of San Francisco *M*

Colorado

Aims Community College *A*
Red Rocks Community College *A*
Regis University *M*
Rocky Mountain College of Art &
    Design *M*
University of Northern
    Colorado *M, D, T*

Connecticut

Central Connecticut State
    University *M*
Fairfield University *M, T*
University of Bridgeport *M*
University of Connecticut *M*

Delaware

Wilmington University *M*

District of Columbia

Gallaudet University *M*

Florida

Full Sail University *M*
Nova Southeastern University *M, D*
Saint Leo University *M*
University of Central Florida *M*
University of Miami *M*
University of West Florida *M*

Georgia

Georgia College and State
    University *M, T*
Georgia Southern University *M*
Georgia State University *M, D*
Kennesaw State University *M, D*
Southern Polytechnic State
    University *M*
University of Georgia *M, D, T*
University of West Georgia *M*
Valdosta State University *M*

Hawaii

University of Hawaii
    Manoa *M*

Idaho

Boise State University *M*
Idaho State University *M, D*

Illinois

Aurora University *M*
DeVry University
    Online *M*
Illinois State University *M*
National-Louis University *M*
Northern Illinois University *M, D*
Southern Illinois University
    Edwardsville *M*
University of Illinois
    Urbana-Champaign *M, D*
Western Illinois University *B, M*

Indiana

Indiana State University *M, T*
Indiana University
    Bloomington *M, D, T*

Iowa

Ashford University *B*
Iowa State University *T*
University of Northern Iowa *M*

Kansas

Emporia State University *M*
Pittsburg State University *M*
University of Kansas *M*

Kentucky

Gateway Community and Technical
    College *A*
University of Kentucky *M*
Western Kentucky University *M*

Louisiana

McNeese State University *M*
Southeastern Louisiana University *M*

Maine

University of Maine *M*

Maryland

McDaniel College *M*
Towson University *M, D*
University of Maryland
    University College *M*

Massachusetts

Boston University *M, T*
Bridgewater State University *M, T*
Cambridge College *M*
Lesley University *M*
Salem State University *M*
University of Massachusetts
    Boston *M*

Michigan

Aquinas College *M, T*
Central Michigan University *M*
Eastern Michigan University *M, T*
Lawrence Technological University *M*
Michigan State University *M*
University of Michigan
    Flint *M*
Wayne State University *M, D*
Western Michigan University *M, T*

Minnesota

Capella University *M, D*
Concordia University St. Paul *M*
Minnesota State University
    Mankato *M*
Ridgewater College *A*
Saint Cloud State University *B, M*
St. Mary's University of Minnesota *M*
University of Minnesota
    Twin Cities *T*

Mississippi

University of Southern Mississippi *M*

Missouri

Missouri Baptist University *M*
Missouri State University *M*
Webster University *M*

New Hampshire

Southern New Hampshire
    University *M*

New Jersey

College of St. Elizabeth *M*
Georgian Court University *T*
Montclair State University *M*
Richard Stockton College of New
    Jersey *M*
Rowan University *M*
Rutgers, The State University of New
    Jersey
    New Brunswick/Piscataway
        Campus *T*

William Paterson University of New
    Jersey *T*

New York

Canisius College *M*
College of Saint Rose *M, T*
Dominican College of Blauvelt *M*
Long Island University
    LIU Post *M, T*
Rochester Institute of Technology *M*
SUNY
    College at Oneonta *M*
    College at Potsdam *M*
    University at Albany *M*
    University at Buffalo *M*
Syracuse University *M, D*

North Carolina

Appalachian State University *M*
East Carolina University *M*
North Carolina Agricultural and
    Technical State University *M*
North Carolina Central University *M*
North Carolina State University *M*
University of North Carolina
    Charlotte *M*
    Wilmington *M*

North Dakota

University of North Dakota *M*
Valley City State University *B*

Ohio

Ashland University *M, T*
Bowling Green State
    University *B, M, T*
John Carroll University *M*
Kent State University *M*
Miami University
    Oxford *M*
Ohio University *M, D*
University of Akron *M*
University of Toledo *M*

Oklahoma

Cameron University *A, B*
Oklahoma State University *M*
University of Central Oklahoma *B, M*
University of Oklahoma *M*

Oregon

Northwest Christian University *M*
Portland State University *M, T*
Western Oregon University *B*

Pennsylvania

Bloomsburg University of
    Pennsylvania *M*
Chestnut Hill College *M, T*
DeSales University *M, T*
Drexel University *M, T*
Duquesne University *M, D, T*
East Stroudsburg University of
    Pennsylvania *M, T*
Harrisburg University of Science and
    Technology *M*
Kutztown University of
    Pennsylvania *M*
La Salle University *M*
Lehigh University *M, D*
Penn State
    University Park *M, D*
Philadelphia University *M*
Saint Joseph's University *M, T*
Seton Hill University *M*
University of Pittsburgh *T*
Widener University *M*
Wilkes University *M*

Puerto Rico

Bayamon Central University *B*
Caribbean University *M*

Inter American University of Puerto
    Rico
    Metropolitan Campus *M*
Turabo University *M*
University of the Sacred Heart *M*

South Carolina

University of South Carolina
    Aiken *M*
    Columbia *M*

South Dakota

Dakota State University *M*
University of South Dakota *M*

Tennessee

East Tennessee State University *M, T*
Trevecca Nazarene University *M*

Texas

Angelo State University *M*
Dallas Baptist University *M*
Lone Star College System *A*
Midwestern State University *M*
Prairie View A&M University *M*
Texas A&M University *M*
Texas A&M University
    Commerce *M*
    Corpus Christi *M, T*
    Texarkana *M*
Texas State Technical College
    Waco *A*
Texas State University *M, T*
Texas Tech University *M, D*
University of Houston
    Clear Lake *M, T*
University of North Texas *M*
University of Texas
    Brownsville *M*
West Texas A&M University *M*

Utah

Brigham Young University *M, D*
Utah State University *M, D*
Western Governors University *M*

Washington

Eastern Washington University *M, T*
Walla Walla University *M*
Washington State University *T*

West Virginia

West Virginia University *M, D*

Wisconsin

University of Wisconsin
    La Crosse *M*

Educational leadership/
administration

Alabama

Alabama Agricultural and Mechanical
    University *M*
Alabama State University *M, D*
Auburn University *M, D, T*
Auburn University at
    Montgomery *M, D*
Jacksonville State University *M, T*
Samford University *M, D, T*
Troy University *M, T*
University of Alabama *M, D*
University of Alabama
    Birmingham *M, D, T*
University of Montevallo *M, T*
University of North Alabama *M*
University of South Alabama *M, T*
University of West Alabama *M*

Alaska

University of Alaska
    Anchorage *M*

Arizona

Argosy University
  Online *M, D*
  Phoenix *M, D*
Arizona State University *D*
Grand Canyon University *M, D*
Northcentral University *M, D*
Northern Arizona University *M, D*
University of Arizona *M, D*
University of Phoenix
  Phoenix-Hohokam *M*
  Southern Arizona *M*

Arkansas

Arkansas State University *D, T*
Arkansas Tech University *M*
Harding University *M, D*
Henderson State University *M, T*
Southern Arkansas University *M, T*
University of Arkansas *M, D*
University of Arkansas
  Little Rock *M, D*
  Monticello *M*

California

Alliant International
  University *M, D, T*
Antioch University
  Los Angeles *M*
Argosy University
  Inland Empire *M, D*
  Los Angeles *M, D*
  Orange County *M, D*
  San Diego *M, D*
  San Francisco Bay Area *M, D*
Azusa Pacific University *M, D*
California Baptist University *M, T*
California Coast University *M, D*
California Lutheran University *M, D*
California State Polytechnic
  University: Pomona *D*
California State University
  Chico *T*
  Dominguez Hills *M*
  East Bay *M, D, T*
  Fresno *D*
  Fullerton *M, D, T*
  Long Beach *M, D, T*
  Los Angeles *M*
  Northridge *M, D*
  Sacramento *M, D*
  San Bernardino *M, D*
  San Marcos *M*
  Stanislaus *D*
Concordia University Irvine *M*
DeVry University
  Pomona *M*
Fresno Pacific University *M, T*
La Sierra University *M, D*
Loyola Marymount
  University *M, D, T*
Mills College *M, D*
Mount St. Mary's College *M*
National University *M, T*
Notre Dame de Namur
  University *M, T*
Pepperdine University *M, D*
St. Mary's College of California *M, D*
San Diego State University *M, D, T*
San Francisco State University *D, T*
San Jose State University *M*
Santa Clara University *M*
Simpson University *M*
Soka University of America *M*
Sonoma State University *M*
Stanford University *M, D*
Trident University International *M, D*
University of California
  Berkeley *T*
  Irvine *D*
  Los Angeles *D*
University of La Verne *M, D*

University of Phoenix
  Bay Area *M*
  Central Valley *M*
  Sacramento Valley *M*
  San Diego *M*
  Southern California *M*
University of Redlands *M, D, T*
University of San Diego *M, D, T*
University of San Francisco *M, D, T*
University of Southern California *D*
University of the Pacific *M, D, T*
Whittier College *T*

Colorado

Adams State University *M*
Argosy University
  Denver *M, D*
Colorado State University *M, D*
Fort Lewis College *M*
Regis University *M*
University of Colorado
  Colorado Springs *M*
  Denver *M, D, T*
University of Denver *M, D*
University of Northern
  Colorado *M, D, T*
University of Phoenix
  Denver *M*
  Southern Colorado *M*

Connecticut

Central Connecticut State
  University *M, D*
Fairfield University *M, T*
Sacred Heart University *M, T*
Southern Connecticut State
  University *D, T*
University of Bridgeport *D*
University of Connecticut *M, T*
University of Hartford *M, D, T*
University of New Haven *M*
Western Connecticut State
  University *D*

Delaware

Delaware State University *D*
University of Delaware *M, D*
Wilmington University *M*

District of Columbia

Catholic University of America *M, D*
Gallaudet University *M*
George Washington University *M*
Howard University *M*
Trinity Washington University *M*
University of the District of
  Columbia *M*

Florida

Argosy University
  Tampa *M, D*
Barry University *M, D, T*
Clearwater Christian College *M*
Florida Agricultural and Mechanical
  University *M, D, T*
Florida Atlantic University *M, D, T*
Florida Gulf Coast University *M*
Florida International University *M, D*
Florida State University *M, D, T*
Jacksonville University *M*
Keiser University *M, D*
Lynn University *M, D*
Nova Southeastern University *D*
Saint Leo University *M*
Saint Thomas University *M, D*
Southeastern University *M*
Stetson University *M*
University of Central Florida *M, D*
University of Florida *M, D*
University of Miami *M, D*
University of North Florida *M, D*
University of Phoenix
  Central Florida *M*
  North Florida *M*

South Florida *M*
West Florida *M*
University of South Florida *M, D*
University of South Florida
  Saint Petersburg *M*
  Sarasota-Manatee *M*
University of West Florida *M, T*

Georgia

Albany State University *M*
Clark Atlanta University *M, D, T*
Columbus State University *M*
Covenant College *M*
Georgia College and State
  University *M, T*
Georgia Regents University *M*
Georgia Southern University *M, D*
Georgia State University *M, T*
Kennesaw State University *M, D*
Mercer University *M, D*
University of Georgia *M, D, T*
University of North Georgia *M*
University of West Georgia *M*
Valdosta State University *M, D*

Hawaii

Argosy University
  Hawaii *M*
University of Hawaii
  Manoa *M*
University of Phoenix
  Hawaii *M*

Idaho

Boise State University *M*
Idaho State University *M, D, T*
Northwest Nazarene University *M*
University of Idaho *M*
University of Phoenix
  Idaho *M*

Illinois

Argosy University
  Chicago *M, D*
Aurora University *M, D*
Benedictine University *M*
Bradley University *M*
Chicago State University *M, D*
Concordia University Chicago *M, D*
DePaul University *M, D, T*
DeVry University
  Online *M*
Dominican University *M*
Eastern Illinois University *M*
Governors State University *M*
Illinois State University *M, D*
Lewis University *M, D*
Loyola University Chicago *M, D*
National-Louis University *M*
North Central College *M*
Northeastern Illinois University *M*
Northern Illinois University *M, D*
Northwestern University *D*
Olivet Nazarene University *D*
Roosevelt University *M, D*
Saint Xavier University *M*
Southern Illinois University
  Carbondale *M, D*
Southern Illinois University
  Edwardsville *M, D*
University of Illinois
  Springfield *M*
  Urbana-Champaign *M, D, T*
University of St. Francis *M*
Western Illinois University *M, D*

Indiana

Anderson University *M*
Ball State University *M, D, T*
Butler University *M*
Indiana State University *M, D, T*
Indiana University
  Bloomington *M, D*
  East *M*

Northwest *M*
Purdue University Fort Wayne *M*
Purdue University Indianapolis *M*
Indiana Wesleyan University *D*
Oakland City University *D*
University of Notre Dame *M*
University of Phoenix
  Indianapolis *M*

Iowa

Drake University *M, D*
Grand View University *M*
Iowa State University *M, D*
Loras College *M*
St. Ambrose University *M*
University of Iowa *M, D*
University of Northern Iowa *D*
Upper Iowa University *M*

Kansas

Benedictine College *M*
Emporia State University *M*
Kansas State University *M, D*
Newman University *M*
Pittsburg State University *M*
Southwestern College *D*
University of Kansas *D*
Washburn University *M, T*
Wichita State University *M, D*

Kentucky

Asbury University *M*
Northern Kentucky University *D*
University of Kentucky *M, D*
Western Kentucky University *D*

Louisiana

Grambling State University *M, D*
Louisiana State University
  Shreveport *M*
Louisiana State University and
  Agricultural and Mechanical
  College *M, D*
Louisiana Tech University *D*
McNeese State University *M, T*
Nicholls State University *M*
Northwestern State University *M, T*
Our Lady of Holy Cross College *M*
Southeastern Louisiana
  University *M, D*
Southern University and Agricultural
  and Mechanical College *M*
University of Louisiana at
  Lafayette *M, D*
University of Louisiana at
  Monroe *M, D*
University of New Orleans *M, D*
Xavier University of Louisiana *M*

Maine

Thomas College *M*
University of Maine *M, D*
University of New England *M, D*
University of Southern Maine *M*

Maryland

Bowie State University *M*
Frostburg State University *M, D*
Hood College *M*
Loyola University Maryland *M*
McDaniel College *M*
Morgan State University *M, D, T*
Mount St. Mary's University *M*
Notre Dame of Maryland
  University *M*
Salisbury University *M*
University of Maryland
  Baltimore County *M*
  College Park *M, D*
  Eastern Shore *D*

Massachusetts

Boston College *M, D*
Boston University *M, D*

Bridgewater State University *M, T*
Cambridge College *M, D, T*
Eastern Nazarene College *M, T*
Emmanuel College *M*
Endicott College *D*
Fitchburg State University *M*
Framingham State University *M*
Lesley University *M, D*
Regis College *D*
Salem State University *M*
Simmons College *M, D*
Springfield College *M*
University of Massachusetts
  Boston *M*
  Lowell *M, D*
Westfield State University *M*
Wheelock College *M*
Worcester State University *M*

Michigan

Andrews University *M, D*
Central Michigan University *M, D*
Concordia University *M*
Eastern Michigan University *M, D*
Ferris State University *M*
Grand Valley State University *M*
Madonna University *M*
Marygrove College *M*
Michigan State University *M, D*
Northern Michigan University *M*
Oakland University *M, D*
Saginaw Valley State University *M, T*
University of Detroit Mercy *M*
University of Michigan
  Flint *M, D*
University of Phoenix
  Metro Detroit *M*
  West Michigan *M*
Wayne State University *D*
Western Michigan University *M, D, T*

Minnesota

Argosy University
  Twin Cities *M, D*
Bethel University *D*
Capella University *M, D*
Concordia University St. Paul *M*
Crown College *M*
Minnesota State University
  Mankato *M*
  Moorhead *M*
Saint Cloud State University *M, T*
St. Mary's University of
  Minnesota *M, D*
University of Minnesota
  Twin Cities *M, D, T*
University of St. Thomas *M, D*
Winona State University *M, T*

Mississippi

Delta State University *M*
Jackson State University *M, D*
Mississippi College *M, D*
Mississippi State University *M*
University of Mississippi *M*
University of Southern Mississippi *M*

Missouri

Lincoln University *M*
Lindenwood University *M, D*
Maryville University of Saint
  Louis *M, T*
Missouri State University *M*
Northwest Missouri State
  University *M*
Saint Louis University *M, D*
Southwest Baptist University *M*
University of Central Missouri *M*
University of Missouri
  Columbia *M, D*
  Kansas City *M*
  St. Louis *M*

University of Phoenix
  Kansas City *M*
  St. Louis *M*
Webster University *M, T*
William Woods University *M, D*

Montana

Rocky Mountain College *M*
University of Great Falls *M*
University of Montana *M, D*

Nebraska

College of Saint Mary *M, D*
Creighton University *M, D*
Doane College *M*
University of Nebraska
  Kearney *M*
  Lincoln *M, D*
  Omaha *M, D, T*
Wayne State College *M*

Nevada

University of Nevada
  Las Vegas *M, D*
  Reno *M, D*
University of Phoenix
  Las Vegas *M*
  Northern Nevada *M*

New Hampshire

Franklin Pierce University *D*
Keene State College *M*
New England College *M*
Plymouth State University *M, D, T*
Rivier University *M, D*
Southern New Hampshire
  University *M*
University of New Hampshire at
  Manchester *M*

New Jersey

Caldwell College *M, T*
Centenary College *M*
College of New Jersey *M*
College of St. Elizabeth *M, D*
Fairleigh Dickinson University
  College at Florham *M*
  Metropolitan Campus *M*
Georgian Court University *T*
Kean University *M, T*
Monmouth University *M*
Montclair State University *M*
New Jersey City University *M*
Ramapo College of New Jersey *M*
Richard Stockton College of New
  Jersey *M*
Rider University *M*
Rowan University *D*
Rutgers, The State University of New
  Jersey
  New Brunswick/Piscataway
    Campus *D, T*
Saint Peter's University *M, D*
Seton Hall University *M, D*
Thomas Edison State College *M*

New Mexico

New Mexico Highlands University *M*
New Mexico State University *M, D*
University of New Mexico *M, D, T*
University of Phoenix
  New Mexico *M*
University of the Southwest *M*
Western New Mexico University *M*

New York

Adelphi University *M, T*
Canisius College *M*
City University of New York
  Baruch College *M*
  Brooklyn College *M, T*
  City College *M*
  College of Staten Island *T*
  Lehman College *M*

College of New Rochelle *M, T*
College of Saint Rose *M*
Dowling College *D, T*
Fordham University *M, D*
Hofstra University *M, D, T*
Iona College *M*
Le Moyne College *M*
Long Island University
  LIU Post *M*
Manhattan College *M*
Manhattanville College *M, D*
New York University *M, D, T*
Niagara University *M*
Pace University *M*
Pace University: Pleasantville/
  Briarcliff *M*
SUNY
  College at Brockport *M*
  College at Fredonia *T*
  College at New Paltz *M*
  College at Oswego *M*
  University at Albany *M, D*
  University at Buffalo *M, D, T*
Sage Colleges *D*
Saint Bonaventure University *M*
St. John Fisher College *M*
St. John's University *M, D*
St. Lawrence University *M*
St. Thomas Aquinas College *M*
Syracuse University *M, D, T*
Touro College *M*
University of Rochester *M, D*
Wagner College *M*

North Carolina

Appalachian State University *D*
Campbell University *M*
East Carolina University *M, D*
Elizabeth City State University *M*
Fayetteville State University *M, D*
Gardner-Webb University *M, D*
High Point University *M, D*
North Carolina Agricultural and
  Technical State University *M*
North Carolina State University *M, D*
Queens University of Charlotte *M*
University of North Carolina
  Chapel Hill *D*
  Charlotte *M, D, T*
  Greensboro *M, D, T*
  Wilmington *M*
Western Carolina University *M, D*
Wingate University *D*

North Dakota

North Dakota State University *M*
University of North Dakota *M, D*

Ohio

Antioch University
  Midwest *M*
Ashland University *M, T*
Baldwin Wallace University *M*
Bowling Green State
  University *M, D, T*
Cleveland State University *M, D*
Franciscan University of
  Steubenville *M*
John Carroll University *M*
Lake Erie College *M*
Malone University *M*
Miami University
  Oxford *M, D*
Muskingum University *M*
Ohio University *M, D*
Ohio University
  Chillicothe Campus *M*
Union Institute & University *D*
University of Akron *M, D*
University of Cincinnati *M*
University of Dayton *M, D*
University of Findlay *M*
University of Mount Union *M*
University of Rio Grande *M*

University of Toledo *M, D, T*
Wright State University *M, T*
Xavier University *M*
Youngstown State University *M, D*

Oklahoma

Cameron University *M*
East Central University *M, T*
Northeastern State University *M, T*
Oklahoma State University *M, D*
Oral Roberts University *M*
Southeastern Oklahoma State
  University *M*
Southwestern Oklahoma State
  University *M, T*
University of Central Oklahoma *M*
University of Oklahoma *M, D*

Oregon

Concordia University *M*
George Fox University *M, D*
Lewis & Clark College *M, D*
Portland State University *D, T*
University of Oregon *M, D*

Pennsylvania

Alvernia University *D*
Arcadia University *M*
Bucknell University *M*
Cabrini College *T*
Cairn University *M*
California University of
  Pennsylvania *M*
Chestnut Hill College *M, T*
Cheyney University of
  Pennsylvania *M*
Delaware Valley College *M*
Drexel University *D*
Duquesne University *M, D*
Edinboro University of
  Pennsylvania *M*
Gannon University *D*
Gratz College *M*
Gwynedd Mercy University *M, T*
Holy Family University *M, D*
Immaculata University *M, D, T*
Indiana University of
  Pennsylvania *D, T*
Lehigh University *M, D*
Marywood University *M*
Millersville University of
  Pennsylvania *M, T*
Neumann University *D*
Penn State
  University Park *M, D*
Point Park University *M*
St. Francis University *M*
Saint Joseph's University *M, D, T*
St. Vincent College *M*
Shippensburg University of
  Pennsylvania *T*
Slippery Rock University of
  Pennsylvania *M*
Temple University *M, D*
University of Pennsylvania *M, D*
University of Pittsburgh *M, D*
University of Scranton *M*
Westminster College *M*
Widener University *M, D, T*
Wilkes University *D*
York College of Pennsylvania *M, T*

Puerto Rico

Bayamon Central University *M*
Caribbean University *M*
Inter American University of Puerto
  Rico
  Aguadilla Campus *M*
  Metropolitan Campus *M, D*
  San German Campus *M, D*
National University College
  Bayamon *M*
Pontifical Catholic University of
  Puerto Rico *M*

Turabo University *M, D*
Universidad Adventista de las
   Antillas *M*
Universidad Metropolitana *M*
Universidad del Este *M*
University of Phoenix
   Puerto Rico *M*
University of Puerto Rico
   Rio Piedras *M, D*

Rhode Island

Johnson & Wales University
   Providence *D*
Rhode Island College *M*

South Carolina

Anderson University *M*
Bob Jones University *M*
Citadel *M*
Clemson University *M, D*
Coastal Carolina University *M*
Columbia International
   University *M, D*
Furman University *M*
South Carolina State University *D*
Southern Wesleyan University *M*
University of South Carolina
   Columbia *M, D*
Winthrop University *M, T*

South Dakota

Dakota Wesleyan University *M*
Oglala Lakota College *M*
South Dakota State University *M*
University of South Dakota *M, D*

Tennessee

Austin Peay State University *M*
Christian Brothers University *M, T*
East Tennessee State
   University *M, D, T*
Freed-Hardeman University *M*
Lee University *M*
Lincoln Memorial University *M, D*
Lipscomb University *M, T*
Middle Tennessee State
   University *M, T*
Southern Adventist University *M*
Tennessee Technological
   University *M*
Tennessee Temple University *M*
Trevecca Nazarene University *M*
Union University *D*
University of Memphis *M, D*
University of Phoenix
   Chattanooga *M*
   Memphis *M*
   Nashville *M*
University of Tennessee
   Chattanooga *M, D*
   Knoxville *M, D*
   Martin *M*
Vanderbilt University *M, D*

Texas

Abilene Christian University *M*
Angelo State University *M*
Argosy University
   Dallas *M, D*
Arlington Baptist College *M*
Baylor University *M*
Dallas Baptist University *M, D*
Houston Baptist University *M*
Howard Payne University *M*
Lamar University *M, D, T*
Lubbock Christian University *M*
Midwestern State University *M*
Our Lady of the Lake University of
   San Antonio *M*
Prairie View A&M University *M, D*
St. Mary's University *M*
Sam Houston State University *M, D*
Southwestern Assemblies of God
   University *M*

Stephen F. Austin State
   University *M, D*
Sul Ross State University *M*
Tarleton State University *M, D*
Texas A&M International
   University *M, T*
Texas A&M University *M, D*
Texas A&M University
   Commerce *M, D*
   Corpus Christi *M, D, T*
   Kingsville *M*
   Texarkana *M*
Texas Christian University *M, D*
Texas Southern University *M, D*
Texas State University *M, D, T*
Texas Tech University *M, D*
Texas Wesleyan University *D*
Texas Woman's University *M*
Trinity University *M*
University of Houston *M, D*
University of Houston
   Clear Lake *M, D, T*
   Victoria *M*
University of Mary Hardin-
   Baylor *M, D*
University of North Texas *D*
University of Phoenix
   Austin *M*
   Dallas Fort Worth *M*
   Houston Westside *M*
   San Antonio *M*
University of St. Thomas *M*
University of Texas
   Arlington *M, D, T*
   Austin *M, D*
   Brownsville *M*
   El Paso *M, D*
   Pan American *M, D*
   Permian Basin *M*
   San Antonio *M, D*
   Tyler *M*
West Texas A&M University *M, T*

Utah

Argosy University
   Salt Lake City *M, D*
Brigham Young University *M, D*
University of Phoenix
   Utah *M*
University of Utah *M, D*
Western Governors University *M*

Vermont

Castleton State College *M*
Goddard College *M*
Johnson State College *M*
Saint Michael's College *M, T*
University of Vermont *M, D, T*

Virginia

College of William and Mary *M, D*
George Mason University *M*
Lynchburg College *M*
Marymount University *M*
Old Dominion University *M*
Radford University *M*
Regent University *M*
Shenandoah University *M, D*
University of Phoenix
   Northern Virginia *M*
   Richmond *M*
University of Virginia *M, D*
Virginia Commonwealth
   University *M, D*
Virginia Polytechnic Institute and
   State University *M, D*
Virginia State University *M, D*

Washington

Central Washington University *M, T*
City University of Seattle *M, D*
DeVry University
   Federal Way *M*
Eastern Washington University *M*

Gonzaga University *M, D*
Heritage University *M*
Pacific Lutheran University *M*
Saint Martin's University *T*
Seattle Pacific University *M, D*
Seattle University *M, D*
University of Washington *M, D*
University of Washington Bothell *M*
Walla Walla University *M*
Washington State University *M, D*
Whitworth University *M*

West Virginia

Concord University *M*
Marshall University *M*
West Virginia University *M, D*
Wheeling Jesuit University *M*

Wisconsin

Alverno College *M, T*
Carthage College *M, T*
Concordia University Wisconsin *M*
Edgewood College *D, T*
Marian University *M, D*
Marquette University *M, D*
Silver Lake College of the Holy
   Family *M*
University of Wisconsin
   Madison *M, D*
   Milwaukee *M*
   Superior *M*
   Whitewater *M*
Viterbo University *M*

Educational psychology

Alabama

Auburn University *D*
University of Alabama *M, D*

Arizona

Arizona State University *M, D*
Northern Arizona University *D*
University of Arizona *M, D*

California

Alliant International University *D*
Azusa Pacific University *M*
California Lutheran University *M*
California State University
   East Bay *M, T*
   Long Beach *M*
   Northridge *M*
   Sacramento *M*
Fresno Pacific University *M, T*
La Sierra University *M*
University of California
   Santa Barbara *M, D*
University of San Francisco *M, D*
University of the Pacific *M, D, T*

Colorado

University of Colorado
   Boulder *M, D*
   Denver *M, D*
University of Northern
   Colorado *M, D*

Connecticut

University of Connecticut *M, D, T*

Delaware

University of Delaware *M, T*

District of Columbia

Catholic University of America *D*
Howard University *M, D*

Florida

Florida State University *M, D*

Georgia

Georgia State University *M, D*
University of Georgia *M, D, T*
Valdosta State University *M*

Hawaii

University of Hawaii
   Manoa *M, D*

Idaho

Idaho State University *M*

Illinois

DePaul University *B*
Loyola University Chicago *M, D*
National-Louis University *M, D*
Northern Illinois University *M, D*
Southern Illinois University
   Carbondale *M, D*
University of Illinois
   Chicago *D*
   Urbana-Champaign *M, D*

Indiana

Ball State University *M, D, T*
Indiana University
   Bloomington *M, D*

Iowa

Iowa State University *T*
University of Iowa *M, D*
University of Northern Iowa *M*

Kansas

Fort Hays State University *M*
University of Kansas *M, D*
Wichita State University *M*

Kentucky

University of Kentucky *M, D*

Louisiana

Louisiana Tech University *M*
Nicholls State University *M*

Maryland

University of Maryland
   College Park *M, D*

Massachusetts

American International College *M, D*
Harvard College *M, D*
Tufts University *M, T*

Michigan

Andrews University *M, D*
Eastern Michigan University *M*
Michigan State University *D*
Wayne State University *M, D*

Minnesota

Capella University *M, D*
University of Minnesota
   Twin Cities *M, D*

Mississippi

Mississippi State University *B, M, D*

Missouri

University of Missouri
   Columbia *M, D*
Webster University *M*

Nebraska

University of Nebraska
   Kearney *M*
   Lincoln *D*

Nevada

University of Nevada
   Las Vegas *M, D*

New Jersey

Montclair State University *M*
New Jersey City University *M*
Rutgers, The State University of New
   Jersey
   New Brunswick/Piscataway
     Campus *M, D*

New Mexico

University of New Mexico *M, D*

New York

College of Saint Rose *M*
Marist College *M*
New York University *M, D*
SUNY
   University at Albany *M, D*
   University at Buffalo *M, D*
Touro College *M*

Ohio

Bowling Green State University *M, D*
John Carroll University *M*
Kent State University *M, D*
Miami University
   Oxford *M*
University of Toledo *M*
Youngstown State University *M*

Oklahoma

Oklahoma State University *M, D*
University of Oklahoma *D*

Pennsylvania

Edinboro University of
   Pennsylvania *M*
Indiana University of Pennsylvania *M*
Penn State
   University Park *M, D*
St. Vincent College *B*
Temple University *M*
University of Pittsburgh *B, M, D*
Widener University *M*

Puerto Rico

Pontifical Catholic University of
   Puerto Rico *M*

Rhode Island

Rhode Island College *M*

Tennessee

Tennessee State University *D*
Tennessee Technological
   University *M, D*
University of Tennessee
   Knoxville *M, D*

Texas

Argosy University
   Dallas *M*
Baylor University *M, D*
Tarleton State University *M*
Texas A&M University *M, D*
Texas A&M University
   Commerce *D*
Texas Tech University *M, D*
University of Houston *M, D*
University of North Texas *M*
University of Texas
   Arlington *M*
   Austin *M, D*

Utah

University of Utah *M, D*

Vermont

Goddard College *M*

Virginia

George Mason University *M*
University of Virginia *M, D*

West Virginia

West Virginia University *M, D*

Wisconsin

Marquette University *M*
University of Wisconsin
   Eau Claire *M*
   Madison *M, D*
   Milwaukee *M, D*
   Whitewater *M*

Educational statistics/research methods

Alabama

University of Alabama *D*

Arkansas

University of Arkansas *D*

California

San Diego State University *M*
Stanford University *M, D*

Colorado

University of Denver *M, D*
University of Northern
   Colorado *M, D*

Florida

University of Florida *M, D*
University of Miami *D*

Georgia

Georgia State University *M, T*

Illinois

Loyola University Chicago *M, D*
University of Illinois
   Urbana-Champaign *M, D*

Michigan

Michigan State University *D*

New Jersey

Rutgers, The State University of New
   Jersey
   New Brunswick/Piscataway
     Campus *M, D*

New York

Fordham University *M, D*
SUNY
   University at Albany *M, D*

Ohio

University of Toledo *M*

Pennsylvania

University of Pennsylvania *M*

Texas

University of North Texas *D*

Utah

Brigham Young University *D*

Virginia

Virginia Polytechnic Institute and
   State University *D*

Educational superintendency

Alaska

University of Alaska
   Anchorage *T*

Arizona

Grand Canyon University *M*

Arkansas

University of Central Arkansas *M*

Connecticut

Central Connecticut State
   University *T*
Southern Connecticut State
   University *T*
University of Connecticut *T*

Georgia

Berry College *M*

Illinois

Aurora University *D*
University of Illinois
   Urbana-Champaign *D, T*
University of St. Francis *D*
Western Illinois University *M*

Maryland

Bowie State University *D*

Michigan

Michigan State University *M, D*

Minnesota

Hamline University *T*

Missouri

Lindenwood University *M*
Maryville University of Saint
   Louis *D, T*
Missouri Baptist University *T*
Northwest Missouri State
   University *M*
Southwest Baptist University *M, D*
University of Missouri
   Columbia *M, D*
Webster University *M*

Nebraska

Wayne State College *M*

New Hampshire

New England College *M*
Plymouth State University *T*

New Jersey

William Paterson University of New
   Jersey *M*

New York

City University of New York
   Brooklyn College *M*
   City College *M, T*
   College of Staten Island *T*
Le Moyne College *M*
SUNY
   College at New Paltz *M*
   University at Stony Brook *M, T*
Saint Bonaventure University *M*

Ohio

University of Akron *M*
University of Findlay *M, T*
Youngstown State University *D*

Oregon

University of Oregon *T*

Pennsylvania

Edinboro University of
   Pennsylvania *M*
University of Scranton *M*

South Dakota

University of South Dakota *M, D*

Vermont

Saint Michael's College *M*

Washington

City University of Seattle *T*
University of Washington *D, T*
Washington State University *D, T*

Wisconsin

Marian University *D*
University of Wisconsin
   Superior *M*
   Whitewater *M*

Educational supervision

Alabama

Samford University *M, T*
University of Alabama *D*

Arizona

Grand Canyon University *D*
Northcentral University *M, D*

California

California Coast University *M*
California Lutheran University *M*
Mills College *M*
Mount St. Mary's College *M*
National University *M*
St. Mary's College of California *M*

Delaware

University of Delaware *M, D*

District of Columbia

Catholic University of America *M*
George Washington University *M*
Howard University *M*
University of the District of
   Columbia *M*

Florida

Nova Southeastern University *M*
University of Central Florida *M*
University of Miami *D*

Georgia

Georgia State University *D*
Kennesaw State University *D*
Valdosta State University *M*

Illinois

Argosy University
   Chicago *M, D*
Loyola University Chicago *M, D*
McKendree University *M*
National-Louis University *D*
University of Illinois
   Chicago *M, D*
   Springfield *M*
   Urbana-Champaign *M, D*

Indiana

Ball State University *D*
Purdue University *M, D*

Kansas

Emporia State University *M*

Kentucky

Eastern Kentucky University *M*

Louisiana

Centenary College of Louisiana *M*

Maine

University of Maine *M, D*

Massachusetts

Eastern Nazarene College *M*
Springfield College *M*

Michigan

Central Michigan University *M*
Northern Michigan University *M*
Wayne State University *M*
Western Michigan University *M, T*

Minnesota

Bethel University *M*
Minnesota State University
   Mankato *M*
Saint Cloud State University *T*
University of Minnesota
   Twin Cities *T*

Missouri

Northwest Missouri State
   University *M*

Montana

University of Great Falls *M*

Nebraska

University of Nebraska
   Kearney *M*

New Hampshire

New England College *M*
Plymouth State University *T*
University of New Hampshire *M*

New Jersey

Caldwell College *T*
Georgian Court University *M*
Rowan University *M*

New York

Canisius College *M*
City University of New York
   Baruch College *M*
College of Saint Rose *M*
Dowling College *T*
Fordham University *M, D*
Le Moyne College *M*
Long Island University
   LIU Post *M*
Mercy College *M*
New York Institute of Technology *T*
New York University *M*
Pace University *M*
SUNY
   College at Plattsburgh *M, T*
   University at Albany *D*
St. John's University *M*

North Carolina

Fayetteville State University *M*
North Carolina Agricultural and
   Technical State University *M*
University of North Carolina
   Greensboro *M*
Western Carolina University *M*

North Dakota

University of Mary *M*

Ohio

John Carroll University *M*
Otterbein University *M*
Wright State University *M, T*

Pennsylvania

Carlow University *M, T*
Gwynedd Mercy University *M*
Marywood University *M*
Millersville University of
   Pennsylvania *T*
St. Francis University *M*
Saint Joseph's University *M, T*
Shippensburg University of
   Pennsylvania *T*
Villanova University *M*
Widener University *M, D*

Puerto Rico

Turabo University *D*

South Carolina

Furman University *M*
Winthrop University *T*

Tennessee

Tennessee State University *M*
Tennessee Technological
   University *M*
Trevecca Nazarene University *M*
Vanderbilt University *M, D*

Texas

Lamar University *M*
Prairie View A&M University *M*
Sam Houston State University *M*
Sul Ross State University *M*
Texas A&M International University *T*
Texas A&M University
   Kingsville *M*
Texas Woman's University *M*
University of Houston
   Victoria *M*
University of Texas
   Brownsville *M*

Vermont

Johnson State College *M*

Washington

Washington State University *M, D*
Western Washington University *M*

West Virginia

Wheeling Jesuit University *M*

Wisconsin

University of Wisconsin
   Oshkosh *M, T*
   River Falls *M*
   Superior *M*

Electrical and electronics engineering

Alabama

Alabama Agricultural and Mechanical
   University *B*
Alabama Southern Community
   College *A*
Auburn University *B, M, D*
Lawson State Community College *C*
Tuskegee University *B, M*
University of Alabama *B, M, D*
University of Alabama
   Birmingham *B, M, D*
   Huntsville *B, D*
University of South Alabama *B, M*
Wallace State Community College at
   Hanceville *A*

Alaska

University of Alaska
   Anchorage *B*
   Fairbanks *B, M*

Arizona

Anthem College
   Phoenix *A*
Arizona State University *B, M, D*
Embry-Riddle Aeronautical University
   Prescott Campus *B*
Northern Arizona University *B*

Arkansas

Arkansas State University *B*
Arkansas Tech University *B*
Harding University *B*
University of Arkansas *B, M*

California

California Institute of
   Technology *B, M, D*
California Polytechnic State
   University: San Luis Obispo *B, M*
California State Polytechnic
   University: Pomona *B, M*
California State University
   Chico *B*
   Fresno *B, M*
   Fullerton *B, M*
   Long Beach *B, M*
   Los Angeles *B, M*
   Northridge *B, M*
   Sacramento *B, M*
College of the Redwoods *A*
Cuesta College *A*
Cuyamaca College *A*
De Anza College *A*
Los Angeles Harbor College *A*
Los Angeles Southwest College *A*
Loyola Marymount University *B*
Merritt College *A*
Modesto Junior College *A*
National University *B*
Northwestern Polytechnic
   University *B, M*
San Diego State University *B, M*
San Francisco State University *B*
San Jose State University *B, M*
Santa Clara University *B, M, D*
Southern California Institute of
   Technology *A, R*
Stanford University *B, M, D*
University of California
   Berkeley *B, M, D*
   Davis *B, M, D*
   Irvine *B, M, D*
   Los Angeles *B, M, D*
   Riverside *B, M, D*
   San Diego *B, M, D*
   Santa Barbara *B, M, D*
   Santa Cruz *B, M, D*
University of San Diego *B*
University of Southern
   California *B, M, D*
University of the Pacific *B*

Colorado

Colorado School of Mines *B, M, D*
Colorado State University *B, M, D*
Colorado Technical University *B, M*
IntelliTec College: Grand Junction *A*
United States Air Force Academy *B*
University of Colorado
   Boulder *B, M, D*
   Colorado Springs *B, M*
   Denver *B, M*
University of Denver *B, M*
Westwood College
   Denver North *A, B*

Connecticut

Capital Community College *A*
Central Connecticut State
   University *B*
Fairfield University *B, M*
Trinity College *B*
United States Coast Guard
   Academy *B*
University of Bridgeport *M*
University of Connecticut *B, M, D*
University of Hartford *B, M*
University of New Haven *B, M*
Yale University *B, M, D*

Delaware

Delaware State University *B*
University of Delaware *B, M, D*

District of Columbia

Catholic University of
   America *B, M, D*

George Washington
   University *B, M, D*
Howard University *B, M, D*
University of the District of
   Columbia *B, M*

Florida

Broward College *A*
Embry-Riddle Aeronautical
   University *B, M*
Florida Agricultural and Mechanical
   University *B, M, D*
Florida Atlantic University *B, M, D*
Florida Institute of
   Technology *B, M, D*
Florida International
   University *B, M, D*
Florida State University *B, M, D*
Jacksonville University *B*
Miami Dade College *A*
Palm Beach State College *A*
Pensacola State College *A*
Seminole State College of Florida *A*
University of Central Florida *B, M, D*
University of Florida *B, M, D*
University of Miami *B, M, D*
University of North Florida *B, M*
University of South Florida *B, M, D*
University of West Florida *B*

Georgia

Georgia Institute of
   Technology *B, M, D*
Georgia Piedmont Technical
   College *A*
Georgia Southern University *B*
Mercer University *B, M*
Middle Georgia State College *A*
Southern Polytechnic State
   University *B*
University of Georgia *B*

Hawaii

University of Hawaii
   Manoa *B, M, D*

Idaho

Boise State University *B, M, D*
Brigham Young University-Idaho *A*
College of Southern Idaho *A*
Idaho State University *B*
North Idaho College *A*
Northwest Nazarene University *B*
University of Idaho *B, M, D*

Illinois

Bradley University *B, M*
DeVry University
   Chicago *B*
   Online *M*
Illinois Central College *A*
Illinois Institute of
   Technology *B, M, D*
Joliet Junior College *A*
Northern Illinois University *B, M*
Northwestern University *B, M, D*
Southern Illinois University
   Carbondale *B, M, D*
Southern Illinois University
   Edwardsville *B, M*
University of Illinois
   Chicago *B, M, D*
   Urbana-Champaign *B, M, D*
Western Illinois University *B*

Indiana

Indiana Institute of Technology *B*
Indiana University
   Purdue University Fort Wayne *B*
Purdue University
   Indianapolis *B, D*
Purdue University *B, M, D*

Purdue University
  Calumet *B*
  North Central *B*
Rose-Hulman Institute of
  Technology *B, M*
Trine University *B*
University of Evansville *B, M*
University of Notre Dame *B, M, D*
Valparaiso University *B*
Vincennes University *A*

Iowa
Dordt College *B*
Iowa State University *B, M, D*
Loras College *B*
Southeastern Community College *A*
University of Iowa *B, M, D*

Kansas
Allen County Community College *A*
Kansas State University *B, M, D*
University of Kansas *B, M, D*
Wichita State University *B, M, D*

Kentucky
Daymar College
  Paducah *A*
Spencerian College: Lexington *A*
University of Kentucky *B, M, D*
University of Louisville *B, M, D*
Western Kentucky University *B*

Louisiana
Louisiana State University and
  Agricultural and Mechanical
  College *B, M, D*
Louisiana Tech University *B*
Southern University and Agricultural
  and Mechanical College *B*
University of Louisiana at Lafayette *B*
University of New Orleans *B*

Maine
University of Maine *B, M, D*
University of Southern Maine *B*

Maryland
Capitol College *A, B*
Carroll Community College *A*
Garrett College *A*
Howard Community College *A*
Johns Hopkins University *B, M, D*
Loyola University Maryland *B*
Morgan State University *B, M*
United States Naval Academy *B*
University of Maryland
  Baltimore County *M, D*
  College Park *B, M, D*

Massachusetts
Boston University *B, M, D*
Eastern Nazarene College *B*
Franklin W. Olin College of
  Engineering *B*
Massachusetts Institute of
  Technology *B, M, D*
Merrimack College *B*
Northeastern University *B, M, D*
Smith College *B*
Suffolk University *B*
Tufts University *B, M, D*
University of Massachusetts
  Amherst *B, M, D*
  Boston *B*
  Dartmouth *B, M, D*
  Lowell *B, M, D*
Wentworth Institute of Technology *B*
Western New England
  University *B, M*
Worcester Polytechnic
  Institute *B, M, D*

Michigan
Andrews University *B*
Baker College
  Muskegon *A*
Calvin College *B*
Central Michigan University *B*
Grand Valley State University *B*
Kettering University *B, M*
Lake Superior State University *B*
Lawrence Technological
  University *B, M*
Michigan State University *B, M, D*
Michigan Technological
  University *B, M, D*
Monroe County Community
  College *A*
Oakland University *B, M, D*
Saginaw Valley State University *B*
University of Detroit Mercy *B, M, D*
University of Michigan *B, M, D*
University of Michigan
  Dearborn *B, M*
Wayne State University *B, M, D*
Western Michigan University *B, M, D*

Minnesota
Minnesota State University
  Mankato *B, M*
Saint Cloud State University *B, M*
University of Minnesota
  Duluth *B, M*
  Twin Cities *B, M, D*
University of St. Thomas *B*

Mississippi
Holmes Community College *A*
Itawamba Community College *A*
Jackson State University *B*
Mississippi State University *B, M, D*
University of Mississippi *B*

Missouri
Missouri University of Science and
  Technology *B, M, D*
Saint Louis University *B*
University of Missouri
  Columbia *B, M, D*
  Kansas City *B, M*
  St. Louis *B*
Washington University in St.
  Louis *B, M, D*

Montana
Montana State University *B, M*
Montana Tech of the University of
  Montana *B, M*

Nebraska
University of Nebraska
  Lincoln *B, M, D*

Nevada
College of Southern Nevada *A*
University of Nevada
  Las Vegas *B, M, D*
  Reno *B, M, D*

New Hampshire
Daniel Webster College *B*
Nashua Community College *A*
University of New
  Hampshire *B, M, D*

New Jersey
College of New Jersey *B*
Essex County College *A*
Fairleigh Dickinson University
  Metropolitan Campus *B, M*
New Jersey Institute of
  Technology *B, M, D*
Princeton University *B, M, D*
Rowan University *B, M*

Rutgers, The State University of New
  Jersey
  New Brunswick/Piscataway
  Campus *B, M, D*
Stevens Institute of
  Technology *B, M, D*

New Mexico
Dona Ana Community College of
  New Mexico State University *A*
New Mexico Institute of Mining and
  Technology *B, M*
New Mexico State University *B, M*
University of New Mexico *B, M*

New York
Alfred University *M*
Bramson ORT College *A*
City University of New York
  City College *A*
  Hostos Community College *A*
  LaGuardia Community College *A*
Clarkson University *B, M, D*
Columbia University *B, M, D*
Cooper Union for the Advancement
  of Science and Art *B, M*
Cornell University *B, M, D*
Hofstra University *B*
Island Drafting and Technical
  Institute *A*
Manhattan College *B, M*
Nassau Community College *A*
New York Institute of
  Technology *B, M*
New York University *B*
Rensselaer Polytechnic
  Institute *B, M, D*
Rochester Institute of
  Technology *B, M*
SUNY
  College at New Paltz *B, M*
  Institute of Technology at Utica/
  Rome *B*
  Maritime College *B*
  University at Binghamton *B, M, D*
  University at Buffalo *B, M, D*
  University at Stony Brook *B, M, D*
Suffolk County Community College *A*
Syracuse University *B, M, D*
Union College *B*
United States Military Academy *B*
University of Rochester *B, M, D*

North Carolina
Alamance Community College *A*
Bennett College for Women *B*
Blue Ridge Community College *A*
Duke University *B, M, D*
Durham Technical Community
  College *A*
Mayland Community College *C, A*
Mitchell Community College *A*
Nash Community College *A*
North Carolina Agricultural and
  Technical State
  University *B, M, D*
North Carolina State
  University *B, M, D*
Pamlico Community College *A*
Richmond Community College *A*
Rockingham Community College *A*
Southwestern Community College *A*
Surry Community College *A*
University of North Carolina
  Charlotte *B, M, D*
Vance-Granville Community
  College *A*
Western Carolina University *B*
Western Piedmont Community
  College *A*

North Dakota
North Dakota State
  University *B, M, D*
University of North Dakota *B, M*

Ohio
Belmont College *A*
Bowling Green State University:
  Firelands College *A*
Brown Mackie College
  Akron *A*
Case Western Reserve
  University *B, M, D*
Cedarville University *B*
Cleveland State University *B, M, D*
Eastern Gateway Community
  College *A*
Fortis College
  Centerville *A*
Lorain County Community College *A*
Miami University
  Oxford *B*
Ohio Northern University *B*
Ohio State University
  Columbus Campus *B, M, D*
Ohio University *B, M, D*
Stark State College *A*
University of Akron *B, M, D*
University of Cincinnati *B, M, D*
University of Dayton *B, M, D*
University of Toledo *B, M*
Washington State Community
  College *A*
Wilberforce University *B*
Wright State University *B, M*
Youngstown State University *B, M*

Oklahoma
Oklahoma Christian University *B*
Oklahoma State University *B, M, D*
Oral Roberts University *B*
University of Central Oklahoma *B*
University of Oklahoma *B, M, D*
University of Tulsa *B, M*

Oregon
Chemeketa Community College *A*
George Fox University *B*
Oregon Health & Science
  University *M, D*
Oregon Institute of Technology *B*
Oregon State University *B, M, D*
Portland State University *B, M, D*
University of Portland *B, M*

Pennsylvania
Bloomsburg University of
  Pennsylvania *B*
Bucknell University *B, M*
Carnegie Mellon University *B, M, D*
Drexel University *B, M, D*
Gannon University *B, M*
Grove City College *B*
Lafayette College *B*
Lehigh University *B, M, D*
Pace Institute *A*
Penn State
  Abington *C, B*
  Altoona *C, B*
  Beaver *C, B*
  Berks *C, B*
  Brandywine *C, B*
  DuBois *C, B*
  Erie, The Behrend College *C, B*
  Fayette, The Eberly Campus *C, B*
  Greater Allegheny *C, B*
  Harrisburg *C, B, M*
  Hazleton *C, B*
  Lehigh Valley *C, B*
  Mont Alto *C, B*
  New Kensington *C, B*
  Schuylkill *C, B*
  Shenango *C, B*
  University Park *B, M, D*
  Wilkes-Barre *C, B*
  Worthington Scranton *C, B*
  York *C, B*
Reading Area Community College *A*
Temple University *B, M*

University of Pennsylvania *B, M, D*
University of Pittsburgh *B, M, D*
University of Pittsburgh
 Bradford *B*
University of Scranton *A, B*
Villanova University *B, M*
Widener University *B, M*
Wilkes University *B, M*
York College of Pennsylvania *B*

Puerto Rico

Caribbean University *B*
Inter American University of Puerto
 Rico
 Bayamon Campus *B*
Turabo University *B*
Universidad Politecnica de Puerto
 Rico *B, M*
University of Puerto Rico
 Mayaguez *B, M*

Rhode Island

Brown University *B, M, D*
Johnson & Wales University
 Providence *B*
New England Institute of
 Technology *A, B*
University of Rhode Island *B, M, D*

South Carolina

Aiken Technical College *A*
Benedict College *B*
Citadel *B*
Clemson University *B, M, D*
Horry-Georgetown Technical
 College *A*
University of South Carolina
 Columbia *B, M, D*
Williamsburg Technical College *A*

South Dakota

South Dakota School of Mines and
 Technology *B, M*
South Dakota State
 University *B, M, D*

Tennessee

Christian Brothers University *B*
Tennessee State University *B*
Tennessee Technological
 University *B, M, D*
Union University *B*
University of Memphis *B, M*
University of Tennessee
 Chattanooga *B*
 Knoxville *B, M, D*
Vanderbilt University *B, M, D*

Texas

Baylor University *B, M, D*
Del Mar College *A*
Lamar University *B, M*
Laredo Community College *A*
LeTourneau University *B*
Northeast Texas Community
 College *A*
Prairie View A&M University *B, M, D*
Remington College
 Houston *A*
Rice University *B, M, D*
St. Mary's University *B, M*
Southern Methodist
 University *B, M, D*
Southwest Institute of Technology *A*
Texas A&M University *B, M, D*
Texas A&M University
 Kingsville *B, M*
 Texarkana *B*
Texas State University *B*
Texas Tech University *B, M, D*
University of Houston *B, M, D*
University of North Texas *B, M*

University of Texas
 Arlington *B, M, D*
 Austin *B, M, D*
 Dallas *B, M, D*
 El Paso *B, M*
 Pan American *B, M*
 San Antonio *B, M, D*
 Tyler *B, M*

Utah

Brigham Young University *B, M, D*
Salt Lake Community College *A*
University of Utah *B, M, D*
Utah State University *A, B, M, D*

Vermont

Norwich University *B*
University of Vermont *B, M, D*

Virginia

Eastern Shore Community College *A*
George Mason University *B, M, D*
Hampton University *B*
Liberty University *B*
Lord Fairfax Community College *A*
Mountain Empire Community
 College *A*
Norfolk State University *B*
Old Dominion University *B*
Southwest Virginia Community
 College *A*
Thomas Nelson Community
 College *A*
University of Virginia *B, M, D*
Virginia Commonwealth University *B*
Virginia Military Institute *B*
Virginia Polytechnic Institute and
 State University *B, M, D*

Washington

Bellevue College *A*
Eastern Washington University *B*
Edmonds Community College *A*
Gonzaga University *B*
Renton Technical College *A*
Seattle Pacific University *B*
Seattle University *B*
Spokane Falls Community College *A*
Tacoma Community College *A*
University of Washington *B, M, D*
University of Washington Bothell *B*
Walla Walla University *B*
Washington State University *B, M, D*

West Virginia

Potomac State College of West
 Virginia University *A*
West Virginia University *B, M, D*
West Virginia University Institute of
 Technology *B*

Wisconsin

Blackhawk Technical College *A*
Marquette University *B*
Milwaukee School of Engineering *B*
Northcentral Technical College *A*
University of Wisconsin
 Madison *B, M, D*
 Milwaukee *C, B*
 Platteville *B*

Wyoming

University of Wyoming *B, M, D*

Electrical drafting/CAD/CADD

Alaska

University of Alaska
 Anchorage *C*

Arizona

Pima Community College *C*

California

Palomar College *C, A*

Florida

Chipola College *C*
Miami Dade College *C, A*
Palm Beach State College *C*

Illinois

Kaskaskia College *C*
Oakton Community College *C, A*

Minnesota

Dunwoody College of
 Technology *C, A*

New Mexico

Central New Mexico Community
 College *A*

Ohio

Lakeland Community College *C, A*

Oregon

Chemeketa Community College *C*
Clackamas Community College *A*

Texas

Eastfield College *C*

Washington

Bates Technical College *C*

Wisconsin

Herzing University
 Madison *A, B*

Electrical engineering technology

Alabama

Alabama Agricultural and Mechanical
 University *B*
Alabama Southern Community
 College *A*
Bishop State Community College *A*
Central Alabama Community
 College *A*
Community College of the Air
 Force *A*
Faulkner State Community College *C*
Gadsden State Community
 College *C, A*
ITT Technical Institute
 Birmingham *A, B*
Jacksonville State University *B*
Lawson State Community
 College *C, A*
Troy University *B*

Alaska

University of Alaska
 Fairbanks *C*

Arizona

Central Arizona College *C, A*
Cochise College *A*
DeVry University
 Phoenix *A, B*
ITT Technical Institute
 Tempe *A, B*
 Tucson *A, B*
Mesa Community College *C, A*
Northland Pioneer College *C, A*
Penn Foster College *A*

Arkansas

Arkansas Tech University *C*
East Arkansas Community College *C*
ITT Technical Institute
 Little Rock *A, B*
North Arkansas College *C, A*

Northwest Arkansas Community
 College *A*
Phillips Community College of the
 University of Arkansas *C*
Southern Arkansas University Tech *C*
University of Arkansas
 Community College at Hope *A*
 Little Rock *A*

California

Allan Hancock College *C, A*
American River College *C, A*
Butte College *C, A*
California State Polytechnic
 University: Pomona *B*
California State University
 Long Beach *B*
Cerritos College *C, A*
Cerro Coso Community College *C, A*
Chabot College *A*
College of San Mateo *C, A*
College of the Redwoods *C*
College of the Sequoias *C, A*
Cuyamaca College *A*
DeVry University
 Pomona *A, B*
Diablo Valley College *C, A*
Evergreen Valley College *C*
Foothill College *C, A*
Fullerton College *C, A*
Heald College
 San Jose *C, A*
ITT Technical Institute
 Lathrop *A, B*
 National City *A, B*
 Oxnard *A, B*
 Rancho Cordova *A, B*
 San Bernardino *A, B*
 Sylmar *A, B*
 Torrance *A, B*
Irvine Valley College *C, A*
Los Angeles City College *C, A*
Los Angeles Harbor College *C, A*
Los Angeles Pierce College *C, A*
Los Angeles Southwest College *C, A*
Los Angeles Trade and Technical
 College *C, A*
Los Angeles Valley College *C, A*
Merced College *C, A*
Moorpark College *C, A*
Mount San Antonio College *C, A*
Napa Valley College *C, A*
Ohlone College *A*
Orange Coast College *C, A*
Saddleback College *C*
San Bernardino Valley College *C, A*
San Diego City College *C, A*
San Jose City College *C, A*
Santa Barbara City College *C, A*
Santa Rosa Junior College *C, A*
Shasta College *A*
Solano Community College *C, A*
University of the Pacific *B*
West Valley College *C, A*
Yuba College *C, A*

Colorado

Aims Community College *A*
Arapahoe Community College *C, A*
Colorado Technical University *A, B*
Community College of Aurora *C*
DeVry University
 Westminster *A, B*
ITT Technical Institute
 Westminster *A, B*
Metropolitan State University of
 Denver *B*
Pikes Peak Community College *C, A*
Pueblo Community College *C, A*
Westwood College
 Denver North *A, B*

Connecticut

Gateway Community College *A*
Naugatuck Valley Community
  College *A*
Three Rivers Community College *A*
University of Hartford *A, B, M*

Delaware

Delaware State University *B*
Delaware Technical Community
  College
  Jack F. Owens Campus *C, A*
  Stanton/Wilmington Campus *C, A*
  Terry Campus *A*

District of Columbia

University of the District of
  Columbia *A, M*

Florida

Daytona State College *A, B*
DeVry University
  Miramar *A, B*
  Orlando *A, B*
Eastern Florida State College *C, A*
Florida Agricultural and Mechanical
  University *B*
Florida State College at
  Jacksonville *A*
Hillsborough Community
  College *C, A*
ITT Technical Institute
  Ft. Lauderdale *A, B*
  Jacksonville *A, B*
  Lake Mary *A, B*
  Miami *A, B*
  Tampa *A, B*
Indian River State College *A*
Lake-Sumter State College *C, A*
Miami Dade College *C, A, B*
Northwest Florida State College *A*
Palm Beach State College *A*
Pensacola State College *C, A*
Remington College
  Tampa *A*
St. Petersburg College *C*
Seminole State College of Florida *C*
South Florida State College *C*
State College of Florida, Manatee-
  Sarasota *A*
Tallahassee Community College *C*
Valencia College *C, A, B*

Georgia

Augusta Technical College *C, A*
Bainbridge College *C, A*
Chattahoochee Technical College *A*
Fort Valley State University *A, B*
Georgia Piedmont Technical
  College *C, A*
Savannah State University *B*
Savannah Technical College *A*
Southern Crescent Technical
  College *A*
Southern Polytechnic State
  University *B*
University of North Georgia *C, A*

Hawaii

Heald College
  Honolulu *A*
University of Hawaii
  Hawaii Community College *A*
  Honolulu Community College *C, A*
  Kauai Community College *C, A*

Idaho

Brigham Young University-Idaho *A*
College of Western Idaho *C, A*
ITT Technical Institute
  Boise *A, B*
Idaho State University *A, B*

Illinois

College of DuPage *C, A*
College of Lake County *C, A*
DeVry University
  Chicago *A, B*
  Online *A, B*
East-West University *A, B*
Harper College *A*
Heartland Community College *C, A*
Illinois Central College *A*
Illinois Valley Community College *A*
John A. Logan College *C*
Joliet Junior College *A*
Kaskaskia College *C, A*
Kishwaukee College *C, A*
Lincoln Land Community
  College *C, A*
McHenry County College *C, A*
Moraine Valley Community College *C*
Oakton Community College *C, A*
Parkland College *C*
Prairie State College *A*
Rend Lake College *C*
Rock Valley College *C, A*
Sauk Valley Community College *A*
Shawnee Community College *A*
South Suburban College of Cook
  County *C, A*
Southern Illinois University
  Carbondale *B*
Waubonsee Community College *C, A*

Indiana

ITT Technical Institute
  Fort Wayne *A, B*
  Indianapolis *A, B*
  Newburgh *A*
Indiana State University *A, B, M*
Indiana University
  Purdue University Fort
    Wayne *C, A, B*
  Purdue University Indianapolis *B*
Ivy Tech Community College
  Bloomington *A*
  Central Indiana *A*
  Columbus *A*
  East Central *A*
  Lafayette *A*
  North Central *A*
  Northwest *A*
  Richmond *A*
  South Central *A*
  Southeast *A*
  Southwest *A*
  Wabash Valley *A*
Purdue University *A, B*
Purdue University
  Calumet *C, B*
  North Central *A*
Vincennes University *C, A*

Iowa

Clinton Community College *C, A*
Des Moines Area Community
  College *A*
Hamilton Technical College *A, B*
Hawkeye Community College *C, A*
Iowa Central Community College *A*
Iowa Western Community College *A*
Kirkwood Community College *C, A*
North Iowa Area Community
  College *A*
Northeast Iowa Community
  College *A*
Northwest Iowa Community
  College *A*
Southeastern Community College *A*
Southwestern Community College *A*

Kansas

Allen County Community College *C*
Hutchinson Community College *A*
Johnson County Community
  College *C, A*

North Central Kansas Technical
  College *A*
Northwest Kansas Technical
  College *C, A*
Pittsburg State University *B*

Kentucky

Bluegrass Community and Technical
  College *A*
Brown Mackie College
  Louisville *A*
Daymar College
  Paducah *A*
Gateway Community and Technical
  College *A*
Henderson Community College *A*
ITT Technical Institute
  Louisville *A, B*
Kentucky State University *A*
Maysville Community and Technical
  College *C, A*
Northern Kentucky University *A, B*
Owensboro Community and
  Technical College *A*
Spencerian College: Lexington *C, A*
Sullivan College of Technology and
  Design *A*

Louisiana

Delgado Community College *A*
Grambling State University *B*
ITI Technical College *C, A*
ITT Technical Institute
  St. Rose *A, B*
Louisiana Tech University *B*
Northwestern State University *A, B*
Remington College
  Lafayette *C*
  Shreveport *C*
Southern University
  Shreveport *A*
Southern University and Agricultural
  and Mechanical College *B*

Maine

Eastern Maine Community College *A*
Kennebec Valley Community
  College *A*
Northern Maine Community
  College *A*
Southern Maine Community
  College *C, A*
University of Maine *B*
University of Southern Maine *B*

Maryland

Anne Arundel Community
  College *C, A*
Baltimore City Community
  College *C, A*
Capitol College *A, B*
College of Southern Maryland *C, A*
Howard Community College *C, A*
ITT Technical Institute
  Owings Mills *A, B*
Montgomery College *A*
Prince George's Community
  College *C, A*
TESST College of Technology
  Baltimore *C, A*
  Towson *A*
Wor-Wic Community College *C, A*

Massachusetts

Benjamin Franklin Institute of
  Technology *C, A*
Berkshire Community College *A*
Fitchburg State University *B*
ITT Technical Institute
  Norwood *B*
  Wilmington *A, B*
Massachusetts Bay Community
  College *C, A*
Massasoit Community College *A*

Northern Essex Community
  College *C, A*
Quinsigamond Community
  College *C, A*
Springfield Technical Community
  College *C, A*
University of Massachusetts
  Lowell *C, A, B*
Wentworth Institute of Technology *B*

Michigan

Baker College
  Flint *A, B*
  Muskegon *A*
  Owosso *A*
  Port Huron *C*
Bay de Noc Community College *C, A*
Central Michigan University *B*
Delta College *C, A*
Eastern Michigan University *B*
Ferris State University *B*
Glen Oaks Community College *C*
Grand Rapids Community College *A*
Henry Ford Community College *C, A*
ITT Technical Institute
  Canton *A, B*
  Troy *A, B*
Jackson College *C, A*
Kalamazoo Valley Community
  College *C, A*
Kellogg Community College *C, A*
Kirtland Community College *C, A*
Lake Superior State University *A, B*
Lawrence Technological University *A*
Macomb Community College *C, A*
Michigan Technological University *B*
Monroe County Community
  College *A*
Montcalm Community College *C, A*
Mott Community College *C, A*
Muskegon Community College *C, A*
Northern Michigan University *A, B*
Northwestern Michigan College *C, A*
Oakland Community College *C, A*
St. Clair County Community
  College *C, A*
Schoolcraft College *A*
Washtenaw Community College *A*
Wayne County Community
  College *C, A*
Wayne State University *B*
West Shore Community College *A*

Minnesota

Anoka Technical College *C, A*
Dunwoody College of
  Technology *C, A*
Hennepin Technical College *C, A*
ITT Technical Institute
  Eden Prairie *A, B*
Lake Superior College *C, A*
Minnesota State College - Southeast
  Technical *C, A*
Minnesota State University
  Mankato *B, M*
Northland Community & Technical
  College *C*
Ridgewater College *C, A*
St. Cloud Technical and Community
  College *C, A*
St. Paul College *C, A*

Mississippi

Coahoma Community College *A*
East Central Community College *A*
East Mississippi Community
  College *C, A*
Hinds Community College *C, A*
Itawamba Community College *A*
Mississippi Delta Community
  College *A*
Mississippi Gulf Coast Community
  College *T*

Northeast Mississippi Community College *A*
Northwest Mississippi Community College *A*
Pearl River Community College *C, A*
University of Southern Mississippi *B*

Missouri

Crowder College *C, A*
DeVry University
    Kansas City *A, B*
Grantham University *A, B*
Jefferson College *C, A*
Linn State Technical College *A*
Metropolitan Community College - Kansas City *A*
Mineral Area College *C, A*
Missouri Western State University *A, B*
Moberly Area Community College *C, A*
Ozarks Technical Community College *C, A*
Ranken Technical College *A*
St. Louis Community College *A*
University of Central Missouri *B*

Montana

Montana State University Northern *A, B*
University of Montana *A*

Nebraska

Central Community College *C, A*
ITT Technical Institute Omaha *A, B*
Metropolitan Community College *C, A*
Mid-Plains Community College *C, A*
Northeast Community College *A*
Southeast Community College *A*

Nevada

Career College of Northern Nevada *C, A*
College of Southern Nevada *A*
Great Basin College *C, A*
ITT Technical Institute Henderson *A, B*

New Hampshire

NHTI-Concord's Community College *C, A*
Nashua Community College *A*
University of New Hampshire *B*
University of New Hampshire at Manchester *B*

New Jersey

Bergen Community College *A*
Brookdale Community College *A*
Burlington County College *A*
Camden County College *A*
County College of Morris *A*
Cumberland County College *C, A*
DeVry University North Brunswick *A, B*
Essex County College *A*
Fairleigh Dickinson University Metropolitan Campus *B*
Hudson County Community College *C, A*
Mercer County Community College *C, A*
Middlesex County College *A*
Passaic County Community College *A*
Thomas Edison State College *C, A, B*

New Mexico

Central New Mexico Community College *C, A*
Dona Ana Community College of New Mexico State University *C, A*

Eastern New Mexico University: Roswell *C, A*
ITT Technical Institute Albuquerque *A, B*
Luna Community College *A*
New Mexico State University Alamogordo *A*
    Grants *A*
Northern New Mexico College *C, A*
San Juan College *A*
Santa Fe Community College *C*

New York

Briarcliffe College *A*
Broome Community College *A*
Cayuga Community College *C, A*
City University of New York
    Bronx Community College *A*
    College of Staten Island *A*
    New York City College of Technology *A*
    Queensborough Community College *A*
Clinton Community College *A*
Corning Community College *A*
DeVry College of New York Midtown Campus *A, B*
Dutchess Community College *A*
Erie Community College *A*
Excelsior College *A*
Fulton-Montgomery Community College *C, A*
Hudson Valley Community College *A*
ITT Technical Institute
    Albany *A*
    Getzville *A*
    Liverpool *A*
Island Drafting and Technical Institute *A*
Jamestown Community College *C, A*
Mohawk Valley Community College *A*
Monroe Community College *C, A*
Nassau Community College *A*
New York Institute of Technology *A*
Onondaga Community College *A*
Orange County Community College *A*
Rochester Institute of Technology *A, B, M*
Rockland Community College *A*
SUNY
    College at Buffalo *B*
    College of Agriculture and Technology at Morrisville *A*
    College of Technology at Alfred *A, B*
    College of Technology at Canton *A, B*
    Farmingdale State College *B*
    Institute of Technology at Utica/Rome *B*
Suffolk County Community College *A*
Technical Career Institutes *C, A*
Tompkins Cortland Community College *C, A*
Vaughn College of Aeronautics and Technology *A, B*
Westchester Community College *A*

North Carolina

Asheville-Buncombe Technical Community College *A*
Beaufort County Community College *A*
Bladen Community College *C, A*
Blue Ridge Community College *C, A*
Caldwell Community College and Technical Institute *A*
Cape Fear Community College *C, A*
Catawba Valley Community College *A*
Central Carolina Community College *C, A*

Central Piedmont Community College *C, A*
Cleveland Community College *C, A*
College of the Albemarle *C, A*
Craven Community College *C, A*
Davidson County Community College *C, A*
Durham Technical Community College *C, A*
Edgecombe Community College *C, A*
Fayetteville Technical Community College *C, A*
Gaston College *C, A*
Guilford Technical Community College *C, A*
Haywood Community College *A*
Isothermal Community College *A*
Johnston Community College *C*
Mitchell Community College *C, A*
Nash Community College *A*
Pamlico Community College *C, A*
Pitt Community College *C, A*
Randolph Community College *A*
Richmond Community College *A*
Robeson Community College *A*
Rowan-Cabarrus Community College *A*
Southeastern Community College *A*
Southwestern Community College *A*
Stanly Community College *C, A*
Surry Community College *C*
University of North Carolina Charlotte *B*
Vance-Granville Community College *C, A*
Wake Technical Community College *C, A*
Wayne Community College *A*
Western Carolina University *B*
Wilkes Community College *C, A*

North Dakota

Bismarck State College *C, A*

Ohio

Bowling Green State University *B*
Bowling Green State University: Firelands College *A*
Bryant & Stratton College Cleveland *A, B*
Central Ohio Technical College *A*
Cincinnati State Technical and Community College *C, A*
Cleveland Institute of Electronics *C, A*
Cleveland State University *B*
Columbus State Community College *A*
Cuyahoga Community College Metropolitan *A*
DeVry University Columbus *A, B*
ETI Technical College of Niles *C, A*
Eastern Gateway Community College *C, A*
Edison State Community College *A*
Hocking College *C, A*
ITT Technical Institute
    Dayton *A*
    Hilliard *B*
    Norwood *A*
    Strongsville *A*
    Youngstown *A*
James A. Rhodes State College *C, A*
Lakeland Community College *C, A*
Lorain County Community College *C, A*
Marion Technical College *A*
Miami University
    Hamilton *A*
    Middletown *C, A, B*
North Central State College *A*
Northwest State Community College *C, A*

Owens Community College Toledo *C, A*
Remington College Cleveland *C*
Sinclair Community College *C, A*
Southern State Community College *A*
Stark State College *A*
Terra State Community College *A*
University of Akron *C, A, B*
University of Cincinnati *B*
University of Dayton *B*
Washington State Community College *A*
Youngstown State University *A, B*
Zane State College *A*

Oklahoma

Cameron University *A*
Oklahoma City Community College *A*
Oklahoma State University *B*
Oklahoma State University Oklahoma City *A*
Tulsa Community College *C, A*

Oregon

Blue Mountain Community College *C, A*
Central Oregon Community College *A*
Chemeketa Community College *C, A*
Clackamas Community College *C, A*
ITT Technical Institute Portland *A*
Lane Community College *A*
Oregon Institute of Technology *B*
Portland Community College *C, A*
Rogue Community College *C, A*

Pennsylvania

Butler County Community College *A*
California University of Pennsylvania *A, B*
Community College of Allegheny County *C, A*
Community College of Philadelphia *C, A*
DeVry University Fort Washington *A, B*
Delaware County Community College *A*
Erie Institute of Technology *C, A*
Harrisburg Area Community College *C, A*
ITT Technical Institute
    Pittsburgh *A*
    Plymouth Meeting *A*
Johnson College *A*
Kaplan Career Institute Franklin Mills *C*
Lehigh Carbon Community College *A*
Luzerne County Community College *C, A*
Montgomery County Community College *C, A*
Northampton Community College *A*
Penn State
    Erie, The Behrend College *A*
    Fayette, The Eberly Campus *A*
    York *A*
Pennsylvania College of Technology *A*
Pennsylvania Institute of Technology *A*
Reading Area Community College *A*
Triangle Tech Sunbury *A*
University of Pittsburgh Johnstown *B*
Westmoreland County Community College *A*
YTI Career Institute York *A*

Puerto Rico

EDP University of Puerto Rico: Hato Rey A
Humacao Community College C, A
Inter American University of Puerto Rico
  Aguadilla Campus A, B
  San German Campus A, B
National University College
  Arecibo A
  Bayamon A
  Rio Grande A
Turabo University A
Universal Technology College of Puerto Rico C
Universidad del Este A
University College of San Juan A
University of Puerto Rico
  Aguadilla A, B
  Bayamon University College A, B
  Humacao A

Rhode Island

Johnson & Wales University
  Providence B
New England Institute of Technology A, B

South Carolina

Aiken Technical College C, A
Benedict College B
Florence-Darlington Technical College A
Greenville Technical College A
Horry-Georgetown Technical College A
ITT Technical Institute
  Greenville A, B
Midlands Technical College C, A
Northeastern Technical College C, A
Orangeburg-Calhoun Technical College A
Piedmont Technical College A
South Carolina State University B
Spartanburg Community College A
Tri-County Technical College A
Trident Technical College C, A
York Technical College A

South Dakota

South Dakota State University B
Southeast Technical Institute A

Tennessee

Chattanooga College A
Chattanooga State Community College A
Dyersburg State Community College C, A
Fountainhead College of Technology A, B
ITT Technical Institute
  Knoxville A, B
  Memphis A, B
  Nashville A, B
Nashville State Community College A
Northeast State Community College C, A
Pellissippi State Community College A
Remington College
  Memphis A
Southwest Tennessee Community College C, A

Texas

Alvin Community College C, A
Amarillo College C, A
Angelina College C, A
Austin Community College C, A
Brazosport College C, A
College of the Mainland A
Collin County Community College District C, A

DeVry University
  Houston A, B
  Irving A, B
Del Mar College C, A
Eastfield College C, A
El Paso Community College C, A
Grayson College C, A
Houston Community College System C, A
ITT Technical Institute
  Arlington A, B
  Austin A, B
  Houston North A, B
  Houston West A, B
  Richardson A, B
  San Antonio A, B
  Webster A, B
Kilgore College C, A
Lamar State College at Port Arthur C, A
LeTourneau University B
Lee College A
Lincoln College of Technology
  Grand Prairie C
Lone Star College System C, A
Mountain View College A
North Central Texas College A
North Lake College A
Panola College C
Paris Junior College C, A
Prairie View A&M University B
Richland College C, A
St. Philip's College A
Sam Houston State University B
San Antonio College C, A
San Jacinto College C, A
Tarrant County College C, A
Texarkana College C, A
Texas A&M University B
Texas A&M University
  Corpus Christi B
Texas Southern University B
Texas State Technical College
  Waco C, A
  West Texas C, A
University of Houston B
University of North Texas B
University of Texas
  Brownsville B
Victoria College C, A
Weatherford College C, A
Western Technical College: Diana Drive C, A
Wharton County Junior College A

Utah

Salt Lake Community College C
Utah State University C, A
Weber State University A, B

Vermont

Vermont Technical College A, B

Virginia

Blue Ridge Community College A
Central Virginia Community College A
Dabney S. Lancaster Community College C, A
Danville Community College C
ITT Technical Institute
  Chantilly A, B
  Norfolk A, B
  Richmond A, B
  Springfield A, B
John Tyler Community College C
Lord Fairfax Community College C, A
Mountain Empire Community College A
New River Community College A
Norfolk State University B
Northern Virginia Community College C, A
Paul D. Camp Community College A

Rappahannock Community College C, A
Southside Virginia Community College A
Southwest Virginia Community College A
Thomas Nelson Community College A
Virginia Highlands Community College A
Virginia State University B
Virginia Western Community College C, A
World College B

Washington

Bates Technical College A
Central Washington University B
Centralia College A
Columbia Basin College A
DeVry University
  Federal Way A, B
Edmonds Community College C, A
Green River Community College A
ITT Technical Institute
  Everett A, B
  Seattle A, B
  Spokane A, B
Lake Washington Institute of Technology C, A
Lower Columbia College A
North Seattle Community College C, A
Olympic College C, A
South Puget Sound Community College C, A
Spokane Community College C, A
University of Washington Bothell B
Western Washington University B

West Virginia

Bluefield State College A, B
Bridgemont Community and Technical College A
Fairmont State University A, B
Kanawha Valley Community and Technical College A
Southern West Virginia Community and Technical College C, A
West Virginia University Institute of Technology B

Wisconsin

Chippewa Valley Technical College A
Fox Valley Technical College A
Gateway Technical College A
Herzing University
  Madison A, B
ITT Technical Institute
  Green Bay A, B
  Greenfield A, B
Mid-State Technical College A
Milwaukee Area Technical College A
Milwaukee School of Engineering B
Moraine Park Technical College C
Northcentral Technical College A
Northeast Wisconsin Technical College A
Southwest Wisconsin Technical College A
Waukesha County Technical College A

Wyoming

Casper College C, A

Electrician

Alabama

Bevill State Community College C, A
Bishop State Community College C
Calhoun Community College A
George C. Wallace Community College at Dothan C, A

George C. Wallace State Community College at Selma C, A
Jefferson Davis Community College C
Lawson State Community College C
Northwest-Shoals Community College C
Shelton State Community College C, A

Alaska

Ilisagvik College C

Arizona

Arizona Western College C
Cochise College C
GateWay Community College C, A
Mohave Community College C
Northland Pioneer College C, A
Refrigeration School C
Tohono O'odham Community College C, A

Arkansas

Cossatot Community College of the University of Arkansas C

California

Allan Hancock College C
Bakersfield College C, A
Barstow Community College C, A
Foothill College C, A
Fresno City College C, A
Hartnell College C
Los Angeles Trade and Technical College C, A
Merced College C
Modesto Junior College C, A
Palomar College C, A
Santiago Canyon College A
Southern California Institute of Technology C
WyoTech: Fremont C
WyoTech: Long Beach C, A
WyoTech: Sacramento C

Colorado

Aims Community College C
Red Rocks Community College C, A

Florida

College of Business and Technology
  Flagler C, A
  Hialeah C, A
Daytona State College C
Florida State College at Jacksonville C
Gulf Coast State College C
Hillsborough Community College C
Indian River State College C
Palm Beach State College C
Santa Fe College C
Seminole State College of Florida C
South Florida State College C

Georgia

Albany Technical College C
Athens Technical College C
Atlanta Technical College C
Bainbridge College C, A
Central Georgia Technical College C
Columbus Technical College C
Gwinnett Technical College C
Savannah Technical College C
Southeastern Technical College A
Southwest Georgia Technical College C
West Georgia Technical College C

Hawaii

University of Hawaii
  Honolulu Community College C, A
  Kauai Community College C, A

Illinois

Black Hawk College *C, A*
City Colleges of Chicago
   Richard J. Daley College *A*
College of Lake County *A*
Danville Area Community
   College *C, A*
Heartland Community College *A*
Illinois Valley Community
   College *C, A*
John Wood Community College *C, A*
Kaskaskia College *C*
Parkland College *A*
Prairie State College *C, A*
Rend Lake College *C*
Richland Community College *A*
Rock Valley College *C, A*
Southwestern Illinois College *C, A*
Waubonsee Community College *C, A*

Indiana

Ivy Tech Community College
   Bloomington *C, A*
   Central Indiana *C, A*
   East Central *C, A*
   Kokomo *C, A*
   Lafayette *C, A*
   North Central *C, A*
   Northeast *C, A*
   Northwest *C, A*
   Richmond *C, A*
   South Central *C, A*
   Southwest *C, A*
   Wabash Valley *C, A*

Iowa

Des Moines Area Community
   College *C*
Northeast Iowa Community
   College *C, A*
Western Iowa Tech Community
   College *C*

Kansas

Coffeyville Community College *C*
Highland Community College *C*
Kansas City Kansas Community
   College *C*

Kentucky

Big Sandy Community and Technical
   College *C*
Bluegrass Community and Technical
   College *C, A*
Elizabethtown Community and
   Technical College *C, A*
Gateway Community and Technical
   College *C, A*
Hazard Community and Technical
   College *C*
Hopkinsville Community College *C*
Jefferson Community and Technical
   College *C*
Owensboro Community and
   Technical College *C, A*
Somerset Community College *C, A*
West Kentucky Community and
   Technical College *C, A*

Louisiana

Delgado Community College *C*
ITI Technical College *C*
Nunez Community College *C*

Maine

Eastern Maine Community College *C*
Kennebec Valley Community
   College *C, A*
Northern Maine Community
   College *C, A*
Washington County Community
   College *C*

Maryland

College of Southern Maryland *A*

Massachusetts

Benjamin Franklin Institute of
   Technology *A*

Michigan

Delta College *C, A*
Jackson College *C, A*
Kellogg Community College *C, A*
Lansing Community College *C, A*
Macomb Community College *C*
Michigan State University *C*
Mott Community College *C*
Northwestern Michigan College *C*
Oakland Community College *C, A*

Minnesota

Anoka Technical College *C*
Dakota County Technical
   College *C, A*
Dunwoody College of
   Technology *C, A*
Hennepin Technical College *C, A*
Hibbing Community College *C*
Lake Superior College *C, A*
Leech Lake Tribal College *C*
Minneapolis Community and
   Technical College *C*
Minnesota State Community and
   Technical College *C*
Minnesota West Community and
   Technical College *A*
Northland Community & Technical
   College *C*
Northwest Technical College *C*
Ridgewater College *C, A*
Riverland Community College *C*
St. Cloud Technical and Community
   College *C, A*
St. Paul College *C, A*

Mississippi

East Mississippi Community
   College *C, A*
Hinds Community College *C, A*
Itawamba Community College *A*
Northeast Mississippi Community
   College *C*

Missouri

Linn State Technical College *C, A*
St. Louis Community College *A*

Montana

Flathead Valley Community
   College *C, A*
Montana State University
   Northern *A*

Nebraska

Central Community College *C, A*
Mid-Plains Community College *C, A*
Northeast Community College *A*

Nevada

Great Basin College *C, A*

New Hampshire

Lakes Region Community
   College *C, A*

New Mexico

Central New Mexico Community
   College *C*
Dona Ana Community College of
   New Mexico State University *A*
Luna Community College *C*
Navajo Technical University *C*
Northern New Mexico College *C, A*

New York

Dutchess Community College *A*
SUNY
   College of Technology at Alfred *A*
   College of Technology at
     Delhi *C, A*

North Carolina

Beaufort County Community
   College *A*
Bladen Community College *C*
Blue Ridge Community College *C*
Cape Fear Community College *C, A*
Catawba Valley Community
   College *C*
Central Piedmont Community
   College *C, A*
Cleveland Community College *C, A*
Coastal Carolina Community
   College *C*
Fayetteville Technical Community
   College *C, A*
Forsyth Technical Community
   College *C*
Guilford Technical Community
   College *C, A*
Haywood Community College *C*
Isothermal Community College *C, A*
James Sprunt Community College *C*
Martin Community College *C, A*
Montgomery Community
   College *C, A*
Pitt Community College *C, A*
Randolph Community College *C, A*
Rockingham Community College *C*
Southwestern Community College *C*
Stanly Community College *C*
Surry Community College *C*
Tri-County Community College *A*
Vance-Granville Community
   College *C*
Wilkes Community College *A*
Wilson Community College *C, A*

Ohio

Hocking College *A*
Kaplan College
   Dayton *A*
Sinclair Community College *A*
Vatterott College
   Cleveland *C*

Oregon

Lane Community College *C, A*

Pennsylvania

Community College of Allegheny
   County *A*
Dean Institute of Technology *A*
Delaware County Community
   College *C*
Harrisburg Area Community
   College *C, A*
Kaplan Career Institute
   Franklin Mills *C*
Lehigh Carbon Community College *C*
Luzerne County Community
   College *C, A*
New Castle School of Trades *A*
Northampton Community College *A*
Orleans Technical Institute *C*
Pennco Tech *C*
Pennsylvania College of
   Technology *C, A*
Rosedale Technical Institute *C, A*
Thaddeus Stevens College of
   Technology *C*
Triangle Tech
   Bethlehem *A*
   DuBois *A*
   Erie *A*
   Greensburg *A*
   Pittsburgh *A*

Puerto Rico

Inter American University of Puerto
   Rico
   San German Campus *C*
Turabo University *A*

Rhode Island

New England Institute of
   Technology *A*

South Carolina

Aiken Technical College *C*
Greenville Technical College *C*
Trident Technical College *C*
York Technical College *C*

South Dakota

Mitchell Technical Institute *A*
Oglala Lakota College *C*
Western Dakota Technical Institute *A*

Tennessee

Northeast State Community
   College *C, A*
Vatterott College
   Memphis *C*

Texas

Brazosport College *C, A*
Houston Community College
   System *C*
Laredo Community College *C*
Northeast Texas Community
   College *C*
Paris Junior College *C*
St. Philip's College *C, A*
South Plains College *C*
Texarkana College *C*

Utah

Salt Lake Community College *A*
Utah State University *C, A*
Weber State University *A*

Virginia

Central Virginia Community
   College *C*
Liberty University *A*
Paul D. Camp Community College *C*
Rappahannock Community College *C*
Southside Virginia Community
   College *C*
Southwest Virginia Community
   College *C*
Thomas Nelson Community
   College *C*
Virginia Highlands Community
   College *C*
Virginia Western Community
   College *C*
Wytheville Community College *C, A*

Washington

Bates Technical College *C, A*
Bellingham Technical College *A*
Big Bend Community College *C, A*
Renton Technical College *C*
South Seattle Community College *A*
Yakima Valley Community College *A*

Wisconsin

Blackhawk Technical College *C*
Chippewa Valley Technical College *C*
Fox Valley Technical College *C*
Gateway Technical College *C*
Lakeshore Technical College *C*
Mid-State Technical College *C*
Northeast Wisconsin Technical
   College *C*
Waukesha County Technical
   College *C*
Western Technical College *C*

Wyoming

Northwest College *C, A*
Western Wyoming Community
College *C*

Electrocardiograph technology

California

City College of San Francisco *C*
De Anza College *C*
Orange Coast College *C*

Delaware

Delaware Technical Community
College
Stanton/Wilmington Campus *A*

Florida

Florida National University *C*

Illinois

College of DuPage *C*
Harper College *C*

Kentucky

Jefferson Community and Technical
College *C, A*

Louisiana

Bossier Parish Community College *C*
ITI Technical College *C*

Maryland

Anne Arundel Community College *C*

Michigan

Baker College
Auburn Hills *A*
Muskegon *C*
Port Huron *C*
Lansing Community College *C*
Monroe County Community
College *C*

Minnesota

St. Mary's University of Minnesota *B*

Ohio

Columbus State Community
College *C*
Lakeland Community College *C*
North Central State College *C*
Sinclair Community College *C*

Pennsylvania

Pennsylvania College of Health
Sciences *A*

Electroencephalograph technology

Alabama

Wallace State Community College at
Hanceville *C*

Arizona

GateWay Community College *C, A*
Phoenix College *C*

California

Orange Coast College *C, A*

Colorado

Community College of Denver *C, A*

Georgia

Gwinnett Technical College *C*

Illinois

Black Hawk College *A*
East-West University *C*
Parkland College *C*

Iowa

Clinton Community College *A*
Kirkwood Community College *A*

Maryland

Harford Community College *A*

Michigan

Oakland Community College *A*

Minnesota

Minneapolis Community and
Technical College *C, A*
Rochester Community and Technical
College *A*

New Jersey

DeVry University
North Brunswick *A*

North Carolina

Catawba Valley Community
College *A*

Pennsylvania

Community College of Allegheny
County *C*
Harcum College *A*

South Dakota

Southeast Technical Institute *A*

Texas

Alvin Community College *C, A*
Collin County Community College
District *C, A*

Wisconsin

Milwaukee Area Technical College *A*

Electrolysis

Ohio

Lorain County Community
College *C, A*

Electromechanical engineering

Massachusetts

Wentworth Institute of Technology *B*

Michigan

Michigan Technological University *C*

Electromechanical technology

Arizona

Mesa Community College *C, A*
Refrigeration School *C*

Arkansas

John Brown University *A*
University of Arkansas
Monticello *C*

California

Allan Hancock College *C, A*
Ohlone College *A*

Delaware

Delaware State University *B*
Delaware Technical Community
College
Terry Campus *A*

Idaho

Idaho State University *C, A, B*

Illinois

Black Hawk College *C*

Indiana

Purdue University
Calumet *B*

Kentucky

Hopkinsville Community College *C*
Jefferson Community and Technical
College *A*
Madisonville Community College *A*
Maysville Community and Technical
College *C, A*
Murray State University *B*
Owensboro Community and
Technical College *C*

Louisiana

Bossier Parish Community College *C*

Massachusetts

Bristol Community College *A*
Quinsigamond Community College *A*
Springfield Technical Community
College *A*

Michigan

Kirtland Community College *A*
Lansing Community College *C, A*
Northern Michigan University *A*
Oakland Community College *A*
Wayne State University *B*

Nebraska

Northeast Community College *A*

New Jersey

Union County College *A*

New Mexico

Eastern New Mexico University:
Roswell *C, A*
Mesalands Community College *C, A*

New York

City University of New York
New York City College of
Technology *A*
Corning Community College *A*
Excelsior College *A*
Rochester Institute of Technology *B*
SUNY
College at Buffalo *B*
College of Technology at
Alfred *A, B*

North Carolina

Cape Fear Community College *C*
Catawba Valley Community
College *A*
Guilford Technical Community
College *C*

Ohio

Bowling Green State University *B*
Cincinnati State Technical and
Community College *C, A*
Columbus State Community
College *A*
Edison State Community College *C, A*
Marion Technical College *A*
Miami University
Hamilton *A*
Shawnee State University *A*
Sinclair Community College *C*
Southern State Community College *A*
University of Toledo *B*

Pennsylvania

Montgomery County Community
College *A*
Northampton Community
College *C, A*
Pennsylvania College of
Technology *A*

Rhode Island

Community College of Rhode
Island *A*

South Carolina

Aiken Technical College *A*
York Technical College *A*

Texas

Angelina College *C, A*
Clarendon College *C, A*
Midland College *C, A*
Palo Alto College *C*
Paris Junior College *C, A*
Texas State Technical College
Harlingen *A*
Waco *C, A*

Virginia

Rappahannock Community
College *C, A*
Tidewater Community College *A*

West Virginia

Blue Ridge Community and Technical
College *A*
Bridgemont Community and
Technical College *A*

Wisconsin

Chippewa Valley Technical College *A*
Fox Valley Technical College *A*
Gateway Technical College *A*
Northeast Wisconsin Technical
College *A*
Southwest Wisconsin Technical
College *A*
Western Technical College *A*

Electronics/electrical equipment repair

Alabama

Alabama Southern Community
College *C, A*
Bishop State Community College *A*
Community College of the Air
Force *A*
Gadsden State Community College *A*
George C. Wallace Community
College at Dothan *C, A*
Jefferson Davis Community
College *C*
Lawson State Community College *C*

Arizona

Arizona Western College *A*
GateWay Community College *A*
Northland Pioneer College *C*
Refrigeration School *C*

Arkansas

College of the Ouachitas *C*
Pulaski Technical College *C, A*
University of Arkansas
Community College at Batesville *A*
Fort Smith *A*

California

Allan Hancock College *C, A*
Antelope Valley College *C, A*
Bakersfield College *C, A*
Cerritos College *C*
Chabot College *A*
Chaffey College *C, A*

Citrus College C, A
Coastline Community College C, A
College of the Redwoods C
College of the Sequoias C, A
Contra Costa College C
Cypress College C, A
Diablo Valley College C, A
East Los Angeles College C
El Camino College C, A
Fresno City College C, A
Hartnell College C, A
Long Beach City College C, A
Los Angeles City College A
Los Angeles Harbor College C, A
Los Angeles Mission College C, A
Los Angeles Trade and Technical
    College C, A
Los Medanos College A
Mendocino College C, A
Merced College C, A
Modesto Junior College C, A
Mount San Antonio College C, A
National University C
Ohlone College C, A
Orange Coast College C, A
Oxnard College C, A
Sacramento City College C, A
Saddleback College C
San Bernardino Valley College C, A
San Joaquin Delta College C
San Jose City College A
Santa Barbara City College C, A
Sierra College C, A
Southwestern College C, A
Victor Valley College C, A
Yuba College C, A

Colorado

IntelliTec College A
Redstone College A
Westwood College
    Denver North A, B

Connecticut

Gateway Community College C

Florida

Florida State College at
    Jacksonville C
Indian River State College C
Seminole State College of Florida C

Georgia

Albany Technical College C, A
Altamaha Technical College C, A
Athens Technical College C
Atlanta Technical College C
Augusta Technical College C
Central Georgia Technical College C
Chattahoochee Technical College C
Georgia Piedmont Technical
    College C, A
Middle Georgia State College A
South Georgia State College A
Southwest Georgia Technical
    College C
West Georgia Technical College A

Hawaii

University of Hawaii
    Hawaii Community College A
    Honolulu Community College A

Idaho

Lewis-Clark State College C, A, B

Illinois

College of DuPage C, A
Harper College C
Illinois Eastern Community Colleges
    Frontier Community College C
    Lincoln Trail College C, A
    Olney Central College C
    Wabash Valley College C

John A. Logan College C, A
Joliet Junior College C
Richland Community College A
Sauk Valley Community College C
Southwestern Illinois College C, A

Indiana

Ivy Tech Community College
    Central Indiana A
Lincoln College of Technology
    Indianapolis C, A

Iowa

Southwestern Community
    College C, A

Kansas

Allen County Community College A
Butler Community College A
Dodge City Community College C, A
Hutchinson Community College A
Johnson County Community
    College C, A
North Central Kansas Technical
    College A
Pittsburg State University C, A

Kentucky

Spencerian College: Lexington C, A

Louisiana

Delta School of Business &
    Technology C, A
ITI Technical College C
Nunez Community College C

Maine

Central Maine Community
    College C, A
Northern Maine Community
    College A

Maryland

Anne Arundel Community
    College C, A

Michigan

Baker College
    Cadillac A
Delta College C, A
Glen Oaks Community College C
Grand Rapids Community College C
Jackson College A
Macomb Community College C, A
Montcalm Community College C, A
Northwestern Michigan College C, A
Schoolcraft College C
Washtenaw Community College A

Minnesota

Hennepin Technical College C, A
Riverland Community College C
St. Paul College C

Mississippi

Copiah-Lincoln Community
    College A
East Mississippi Community
    College C
Hinds Community College A
Itawamba Community College A
Meridian Community College A
Mississippi Delta Community
    College C
Mississippi Gulf Coast Community
    College A
Pearl River Community College C

Missouri

Linn State Technical College C, A
North Central Missouri College A
Ranken Technical College A

Montana

Montana State University
    Northern A, B

Nebraska

Metropolitan Community College C
Mid-Plains Community College C, A

New Hampshire

Manchester Community College C
Nashua Community College A

New Mexico

Dona Ana Community College of
    New Mexico State
    University C, A
Western New Mexico University A

New York

Erie Community College C
Hudson Valley Community College A
Island Drafting and Technical
    Institute A
SUNY
    College of Technology at Alfred A
Sullivan County Community
    College A

North Carolina

Alamance Community College A
Asheville-Buncombe Technical
    Community College A
Beaufort County Community
    College A
Bladen Community College C, A
Central Carolina Community
    College C
Coastal Carolina Community
    College C, A
College of the Albemarle C
Durham Technical Community
    College C, A
Forsyth Technical Community
    College C
Gaston College C
McDowell Technical Community
    College A
Piedmont Community College C, A
Pitt Community College C, A
Richmond Community College C
Rockingham Community
    College C, A
South Piedmont Community
    College C, A
Tri-County Community College A
Vance-Granville Community
    College C, A
Wake Technical Community
    College C, A

Ohio

Eastern Gateway Community
    College A
North Central State College A
Ohio Technical College C
Stark State College A

Oklahoma

Tulsa Community College A
Western Oklahoma State College A

Oregon

Clackamas Community College C, A
Umpqua Community College A

Pennsylvania

Fortis Institute
    Erie A
Johnson College A
Lincoln Technical Institute
    Allentown A

Puerto Rico

EDP University of Puerto Rico: Hato
    Rey C
Huertas College C, A
University College of San Juan C

Rhode Island

New England Institute of
    Technology A

South Carolina

Aiken Technical College C
Central Carolina Technical College C
Denmark Technical College A
Florence-Darlington Technical
    College C
Midlands Technical College C
Northeastern Technical College C
Orangeburg-Calhoun Technical
    College A
Piedmont Technical College C, A
Tri-County Technical College C
Trident Technical College C
York Technical College C, A

South Dakota

Lake Area Technical Institute A
Southeast Technical Institute A

Tennessee

Southwest Tennessee Community
    College A

Texas

Amarillo College C, A
Central Texas College C, A
Collin County Community College
    District C, A
El Paso Community College C, A
Grayson College C, A
Kilgore College C, A
Laredo Community College C, A
Lee College C, A
Midland College A
Odessa College C, A
St. Philip's College C, A
South Plains College C, A
Temple College C, A
Vernon College C, A

Utah

Salt Lake Community College A

Virginia

Danville Community College C
Eastern Shore Community
    College C, A
Mountain Empire Community
    College A
Northern Virginia Community
    College C, A
Paul D. Camp Community College A
Southwest Virginia Community
    College C
Virginia Highlands Community
    College C

Washington

Bates Technical College A
Centralia College C, A
Peninsula College C, A
Renton Technical College C, A
Skagit Valley College C, A
Spokane Community College A

Wisconsin

Herzing University
    Madison A, B
Madison Area Technical College C, A
Milwaukee Area Technical College C
Moraine Park Technical College C, A
Southwest Wisconsin Technical
    College A

Wyoming

Western Wyoming Community
College *C, A*

Elementary education

Alabama

Alabama Agricultural and Mechanical
University *B, M*
Alabama State University *B*
Athens State University *B*
Auburn University *B, M, D, T*
Auburn University at
Montgomery *B, M*
Birmingham-Southern College *B, T*
Concordia College *B*
Faulkner State Community College *A*
Faulkner University *B, M, T*
Gadsden State Community College *A*
Huntingdon College *B, T*
Jacksonville State University *B, M, T*
Judson College *B*
Miles College *B*
Oakwood University *B*
Samford University *M, T*
Spring Hill College *B, M, T*
Stillman College *B, T*
Troy University *B, M, T*
Tuskegee University *B, T*
University of Alabama *B, M, D*
University of Alabama
Birmingham *B, M*
Huntsville *B*
University of Mobile *B, M, T*
University of Montevallo *B, M, T*
University of North Alabama *B, M*
University of South Alabama *B, M, T*
University of West Alabama *B, M, T*

Alaska

Alaska Pacific University *A, B, M, T*
University of Alaska
Anchorage *B, T*
Fairbanks *B, T*
Southeast *B, M, T*

Arizona

American Indian College of the
Assemblies of God *B*
Arizona Christian University *B*
Arizona State University *B, M*
Arizona Western College *A*
Central Arizona College *A*
Chandler-Gilbert Community
College *A*
Cochise College *A*
Coconino County Community
College *A*
Dine College *A, B*
Eastern Arizona College *A*
Glendale Community College *A*
Grand Canyon University *B, M*
Northern Arizona University *B, M*
Northland Pioneer College *A*
Paradise Valley Community College *A*
Phoenix College *A*
Prescott College *B, M, T*
Tohono O'odham Community
College *A*
University of Arizona *B*
University of Phoenix
Phoenix-Hohokam *B, M*
Southern Arizona *B, M*

Arkansas

Arkansas State University *M, T*
Arkansas Tech University *M*
Black River Technical College *A*
Cossatot Community College of the
University of Arkansas *A*
Harding University *B, M, T*
Ozarka College *A*
Phillips Community College of the
University of Arkansas *A*

Southern Arkansas University *M, T*
University of Arkansas *B, M*
University of Arkansas
Little Rock *B, M, T*
Pine Bluff *M*
University of the Ozarks *B*
Williams Baptist College *B*

California

Allan Hancock College *A*
Alliant International University *T*
Antioch University
Los Angeles *T*
Azusa Pacific University *B, T*
Biola University *B, T*
California Baptist University *T*
California Lutheran University *B, M*
California State University
Channel Islands *T*
Chico *T*
East Bay *T*
Fullerton *M, T*
Long Beach *B, M, T*
Los Angeles *M*
Northridge *T*
San Bernardino *M, T*
San Marcos *T*
Chapman University *M, T*
Concordia University Irvine *M, T*
Cypress College *A*
Fresno Pacific University *B, T*
Holy Names University *T*
Hope International University *B, M*
Humboldt State University *B, T*
La Sierra University *M, T*
Loyola Marymount University *M, T*
Master's College *B, T*
Mills College *T*
Mount St. Mary's College *M*
National University *B, M*
Notre Dame de Namur University *T*
Pacific Union College *B, M, T*
Patten University *T*
Point Loma Nazarene University *B*
St. Mary's College of California *M*
San Diego Christian College *B, T*
San Diego State University *M, T*
San Francisco State University *T*
San Jose State University *M*
Shasta College *A*
Simpson University *T*
Sonoma State University *M, T*
Southwestern College *A*
Stanford University *M, T*
University of California
Santa Barbara *T*
University of La Verne *B, M, T*
University of Phoenix
Bay Area *B, M*
Central Valley *B, M*
Sacramento Valley *B, M*
San Diego *B, M*
Southern California *B, M*
University of Redlands *B, T*
University of San Diego *T*
University of San Francisco *T*
Vanguard University of Southern
California *M, T*
Westmont College *T*
Whittier College *T*
William Jessup University *B*

Colorado

Adams State University *A, B, M, T*
Colorado Christian University *B*
Colorado College *M*
Colorado State University
Pueblo *B*
Metropolitan State University of
Denver *T*
Otero Junior College *A*
Regis University *B, T*
University of Colorado
Boulder *T*

University of Northern
Colorado *M, D, T*
University of Phoenix
Denver *B, M*
Southern Colorado *B, M*
Western State Colorado
University *M, T*

Connecticut

Central Connecticut State
University *B, M*
Eastern Connecticut State
University *B, M, T*
Fairfield University *M, T*
Quinnipiac University *B, M*
Sacred Heart University *M, T*
Southern Connecticut State
University *B, M, T*
University of Bridgeport *M, T*
University of Connecticut *B, T*
University of Hartford *B, M*
University of New Haven *M*
University of Saint Joseph *T*
Western Connecticut State
University *B, M*

Delaware

Delaware State University *B*
Delaware Technical Community
College
Jack F. Owens Campus *A*
Stanton/Wilmington Campus *A*
Terry Campus *A*
University of Delaware *B, T*
Wesley College *B*
Wilmington University *B, M*

District of Columbia

American University *B, M, T*
Catholic University of America *B*
Gallaudet University *B, T*
George Washington University *M*
Trinity Washington University *B, T*
University of the District of
Columbia *B, T*

Florida

Baptist College of Florida *B*
Barry University *B, M, T*
Bethune-Cookman University *B, T*
Broward College *A*
Carlos Albizu University *B, M*
Chipola College *B*
Clearwater Christian College *B*
College of Central Florida *A*
Daytona State College *B*
Flagler College *B*
Florida Agricultural and Mechanical
University *B, M, T*
Florida Atlantic University *B, M*
Florida College *B*
Florida Gulf Coast University *B*
Florida International University *B*
Florida Memorial University *B, M, T*
Florida Southern College *B, T*
Florida State College at
Jacksonville *A*
Florida State University *B, M, D, T*
Hobe Sound Bible College *B, T*
Indian River State College *A*
Jacksonville University *B, M, T*
Johnson University: Florida *B*
Jones College *B*
Lynn University *B*
Miami Dade College *A*
Northwest Florida State College *B*
Nova Southeastern University *B*
Palm Beach Atlantic University *B*
Palm Beach State College *A*
Pensacola State College *A*
Rollins College *B, M, T*
Saint Leo University *B, M*
St. Petersburg College *B*
Saint Thomas University *B, T*

South Florida State College *A*
Southeastern University *B, M, T*
Stetson University *B*
Trinity Baptist College *B*
Trinity College of Florida *B*
University of Central Florida *B, M*
University of Florida *B, M*
University of Miami *B, M*
University of North Florida *B, M*
University of Phoenix
Central Florida *B, M*
North Florida *B, M*
South Florida *B, M*
West Florida *B, M*
University of South Florida *B, M*
University of South Florida
Saint Petersburg *M*
Sarasota-Manatee *B, M*
University of Tampa *B, T*
University of West Florida *B, T*
Warner University *B*

Georgia

Armstrong Atlantic State
University *M*
Brenau University *B*
College of Coastal Georgia *A, B*
Covenant College *B, T*
Emmanuel College *B*
Fort Valley State University *B, M, T*
Georgia Southern University *B*
Georgia Southwestern State
University *B, M*
Kennesaw State University *B, M*
LaGrange College *B*
Mercer University *B, M, T*
Middle Georgia State College *A*
Oglethorpe University *M*
Paine College *B*
Reinhardt University *A, B, M*
Shorter University *B, T*
Thomas University *B*
Toccoa Falls College *B, T*
University of Georgia *D*
University of North Georgia *A, B*
University of West Georgia *B, M, T*
Young Harris College *B*

Hawaii

Brigham Young University-
Hawaii *B, T*
Chaminade University of
Honolulu *B, M, T*
Hawaii Pacific University *B, M*
University of Hawaii
Hilo *T*
Manoa *B*
West Oahu *B*
University of Phoenix
Hawaii *B, M*

Idaho

Boise State University *B, M, T*
Brigham Young University-Idaho *B*
College of Idaho *B*
College of Southern Idaho *A*
College of Western Idaho *A*
Idaho State University *B*
Lewis-Clark State College *B, T*
North Idaho College *A*
Northwest Nazarene University *B*
University of Idaho *B, T*
University of Phoenix
Idaho *M*

Illinois

Augustana College *B, T*
Aurora University *B, M*
Benedictine University *B, M, T*
Benedictine University at
Springfield *B*
Blackburn College *B, T*
Bradley University *B, T*
Chicago State University *B, M, T*

Columbia College Chicago *M*
Concordia University
  Chicago *B, M, T*
DePaul University *B, M, T*
Dominican University *B, M, T*
Eastern Illinois University *B, M, T*
Elmhurst College *B*
Eureka College *B*
Governors State University *B, T*
Greenville College *B, M, T*
Hebrew Theological College *B*
Illinois Central College *A*
Illinois College *B, T*
Illinois State University *B, M, T*
Illinois Wesleyan University *B*
John A. Logan College *A*
Joliet Junior College *A*
Judson University *B*
Kankakee Community College *A*
Kishwaukee College *A*
Knox College *B, T*
Lake Forest College *T*
Lewis University *B, M*
Lincoln College *A*
Loyola University Chicago *B*
MacMurray College *B, T*
McKendree University *B*
Millikin University *B, T*
Monmouth College *B, T*
Moraine Valley Community College *A*
National-Louis University *B, M, T*
North Central College *B, T*
North Park University *B, M*
Northeastern Illinois University *B*
Northern Illinois University *B, M, T*
Olivet Nazarene University *B, M, T*
Principia College *B, T*
Quincy University *B, T*
Rockford University *B, M, T*
Roosevelt University *B, M*
Saint Xavier University *M*
Sauk Valley Community College *A*
Southern Illinois University
  Carbondale *B*
Southern Illinois University
  Edwardsville *B, M, T*
Southwestern Illinois College *A*
Spoon River College *A*
Trinity Christian College *B, T*
Trinity International
  University *B, M, T*
University of Illinois
  Chicago *B*
  Urbana-Champaign *B, M, D, T*
University of St. Francis *B, M*
Western Illinois University *B, M*
Wheaton College *B, M, T*

Indiana

Ancilla College *A*
Anderson University *B, T*
Ball State University *B, M, D, T*
Bethel College *B, M*
Butler University *B, M*
Calumet College of St. Joseph *B, T*
DePauw University *T*
Franklin College *B, T*
Goshen College *B, T*
Grace College *B*
Hanover College *B*
Holy Cross College *B*
Huntington University *B, M*
Indiana Institute of Technology *B*
Indiana State University *B, M, T*
Indiana University
  Bloomington *B, M, T*
  East *B*
  Kokomo *B*
  Northwest *B, M, T*
  Purdue University Fort
    Wayne *B, M, T*
  Purdue University
    Indianapolis *B, M, T*
  South Bend *B, M, T*
  Southeast *B, M*

Indiana Wesleyan University *B, T*
Manchester University *B, T*
Marian University *B*
Oakland City University *A, B, M*
Purdue University *B, M*
Purdue University
  Calumet *B*
  North Central *B, M, T*
Saint Joseph's College *B*
Saint Mary's College *B, T*
St. Mary-of-the-Woods College *B, T*
Taylor University *B, T*
Trine University *B, T*
University of Evansville *B, T*
University of Indianapolis *B, M, T*
University of Phoenix
  Indianapolis *B, M*
University of St. Francis *B*
University of Southern Indiana *B, M*
Valparaiso University *B, M, T*
Vincennes University *A*

Iowa

Ashford University *B*
Briar Cliff University *B*
Buena Vista University *B, T*
Central College *B, T*
Clarke University *B, T*
Coe College *B*
Cornell College *B, T*
Dordt College *B, T*
Drake University *B, M*
Ellsworth Community College *A*
Emmaus Bible College *B*
Faith Baptist Bible College and
  Theological Seminary *B, T*
Graceland University *B, T*
Grand View University *B, T*
Iowa State University *B, M, T*
Iowa Wesleyan College *B*
Loras College *B*
Luther College *B*
Maharishi University of
  Management *B, M*
Marshalltown Community College *A*
Morningside College *B*
Mount Mercy University *B, T*
Northwestern College *B, T*
St. Ambrose University *B, T*
Simpson College *B, T*
University of Dubuque *B, T*
University of Iowa *B, M, D, T*
University of Northern Iowa *B, M*
Upper Iowa University *B, T*
Waldorf College *B*
Wartburg College *B, T*
William Penn University *B*

Kansas

Baker University *B, T*
Barclay College *B*
Benedictine College *B*
Bethany College *B, T*
Bethel College *B, T*
Butler Community College *A*
Central Christian College of Kansas *B*
Coffeyville Community College *A*
Colby Community College *A*
Cowley County Community
  College *A*
Dodge City Community College *A*
Donnelly College *A*
Emporia State University *B, M*
Fort Hays State University *B, M, T*
Friends University *B, T*
Garden City Community College *A*
Haskell Indian Nations
  University *A, B*
Independence Community College *A*
Kansas State University *B, T*
Kansas Wesleyan University *B, T*
Labette Community College *A*
McPherson College *B, T*
MidAmerica Nazarene University *B, T*

Newman University *B, T*
Ottawa University *B, T*
Pittsburg State University *B, M*
Pratt Community College *A*
Southwestern College *B*
Sterling College *B*
Tabor College *B*
University of Kansas *B, T*
University of St. Mary *B, T*
Washburn University *B, T*
Wichita State University *B, M, T*

Kentucky

Alice Lloyd College *B*
Asbury University *B, T*
Bellarmine University *B, M, T*
Berea College *B, T*
Brescia University *B, T*
Campbellsville University *B*
Centre College *B, T*
Eastern Kentucky University *B, M*
Georgetown College *B, M*
Hopkinsville Community College *A*
Kentucky Christian University *B, T*
Kentucky Mountain Bible College *B*
Kentucky State University *B*
Kentucky Wesleyan College *B, T*
Lindsey Wilson College *B, T*
Mid-Continent University *B*
Midway College *B*
Morehead State University *B, M, T*
Murray State University *B, M, T*
Northern Kentucky University *B, M*
St. Catharine College *B*
Spalding University *B, M*
Thomas More College *B*
Transylvania University *B, T*
Union College *B, M*
University of Kentucky *B, M*
University of Louisville *B, M*
University of Pikeville *B*
University of the
  Cumberlands *B, M, T*
Western Kentucky University *B, M, T*

Louisiana

Centenary College of Louisiana *M, T*
Dillard University *B, T*
Grambling State University *B*
Louisiana College *B, T*
Louisiana State University
  Alexandria *B*
  Shreveport *B*
Louisiana State University and
  Agricultural and Mechanical
  College *B, M*
Louisiana Tech University *B*
McNeese State University *B, M, T*
Nicholls State University *B, M*
Northwestern State University *B, M*
Our Lady of Holy Cross College *B*
Southeastern Louisiana
  University *B, M*
Southern University
  New Orleans *B*
Southern University and Agricultural
  and Mechanical College *B*
University of Louisiana at Lafayette *B*
University of Louisiana at
  Monroe *B, M*
University of New Orleans *B, M*
Xavier University of Louisiana *B, M*

Maine

College of the Atlantic *T*
Husson University *B, T*
Saint Joseph's College of Maine *B*
Thomas College *B*
University of Maine *B, M*
University of Maine
  Farmington *B, T*
  Fort Kent *B*
  Machias *B*
  Presque Isle *B*

University of New England *B*
University of Southern Maine *B, T*

Maryland

Allegany College of Maryland *A*
Anne Arundel Community College *A*
Bowie State University *B, M*
Carroll Community College *A*
Cecil College *A*
Chesapeake College *A*
College of Southern Maryland *A*
Community College of Baltimore
  County *A*
Coppin State University *B*
Frostburg State University *B, M, T*
Garrett College *A*
Goucher College *B, M*
Hagerstown Community College *A*
Harford Community College *A*
Hood College *T*
Howard Community College *A*
Loyola University Maryland *B, T*
McDaniel College *M, T*
Morgan State University *B, M*
Mount St. Mary's University *B, M, T*
Notre Dame of Maryland
  University *B*
Prince George's Community
  College *A*
Salisbury University *B*
Stevenson University *B*
Towson University *B*
University of Maryland
  College Park *B, T*
Washington Adventist University *B, T*
Wor-Wic Community College *A*

Massachusetts

American International
  College *B, M, T*
Anna Maria College *B, M, T*
Assumption College *T*
Bay Path College *B*
Becker College *B*
Boston College *B, M, T*
Boston University *B, M, T*
Bridgewater State University *B, M, T*
Bristol Community College *A*
Cambridge College *M*
Clark University *M*
Curry College *B*
Eastern Nazarene College *B, M, T*
Elms College *B, M, T*
Emmanuel College *B, M*
Endicott College *B, M*
Fitchburg State University *B, M, T*
Framingham State University *B, M*
Gordon College *B*
Hellenic College/Holy Cross *B*
Lasell College *B, M, T*
Lesley University *B, M*
Massachusetts College of Liberal
  Arts *T*
Massasoit Community College *A*
Merrimack College *B, M*
North Shore Community College *A*
Northeastern University *M*
Pine Manor College *T*
Quincy College *A*
Regis College *M*
Salem State University *B, M*
Simmons College *B, M*
Smith College *M*
Springfield College *B, M, T*
Springfield Technical Community
  College *A*
Tufts University *M, T*
University of Massachusetts
  Dartmouth *M, T*
Wellesley College *T*
Western New England
  University *B, M, T*
Westfield State University *B, M, T*
Wheaton College *T*

Wheelock College *B, M*
Worcester State University *B, M, T*

Michigan

Albion College *T*
Alma College *B, T*
Andrews University *B, M*
Aquinas College *B, T*
Baker College
  Allen Park *B*
  Auburn Hills *B*
  Clinton Township *B*
  Flint *B*
  Jackson *B*
  Muskegon *B*
  Owosso *B*
Calvin College *B, T*
Central Michigan University *B, M*
Concordia University *B, T*
Cornerstone University *B*
Delta College *A*
Eastern Michigan University *B, M, T*
Ferris State University *A, B*
Finlandia University *B*
Gogebic Community College *A*
Grace Bible College *B*
Grand Rapids Community College *A*
Grand Valley State University *M, T*
Henry Ford Community College *A*
Hillsdale College *B*
Kuyper College *B*
Lake Michigan College *A*
Lake Superior State University *B, T*
Madonna University *B, T*
Marygrove College *T*
Michigan State University *B*
Mid Michigan Community College *A*
Northern Michigan
  University *B, M, T*
Oakland University *B, M*
Robert B. Miller College *B*
Rochester College *B*
Saginaw Valley State University *B, T*
Siena Heights University *B, M, T*
Spring Arbor University *B*
University of Detroit Mercy *B, M, T*
University of Michigan *B, T*
University of Michigan
  Dearborn *T*
  Flint *B, M, T*
Washtenaw Community College *A*
Wayne County Community College *A*
Wayne State University *B, M, T*
Western Michigan University *B, T*

Minnesota

Augsburg College *B, T*
Bemidji State University *B, T*
Bethany Lutheran College *B*
Bethel University *B*
College of St. Benedict *B*
College of St. Scholastica *B, T*
Concordia College: Moorhead *B, T*
Concordia University St. Paul *B, T*
Crown College *B*
Gustavus Adolphus College *B*
Hamline University *B, T*
Martin Luther College *B*
Metropolitan State University *B*
Minnesota State University
  Mankato *B, M, T*
  Moorhead *B*
Minnesota West Community and
  Technical College *A*
Normandale Community College *A*
North Central University *B*
Ridgewater College *A*
St. Catherine University *B, M, T*
Saint Cloud State University *B, T*
St. John's University *B*
St. Mary's University of Minnesota *B*
Southwest Minnesota State
  University *B, T*

University of Minnesota
  Duluth *B*
  Morris *B*
  Twin Cities *B, M*
University of Northwestern - St.
  Paul *B*
University of St. Thomas *B, M*
Winona State University *B, T*

Mississippi

Alcorn State University *B, M*
Belhaven University *B, M, T*
Blue Mountain College *B, M*
Coahoma Community College *A*
Delta State University *B, M*
East Mississippi Community
  College *A*
Hinds Community College *A*
Holmes Community College *A*
Itawamba Community College *A*
Jackson State University *B, M*
Millsaps College *B, T*
Mississippi College *B, M*
Mississippi Delta Community
  College *A*
Mississippi Gulf Coast Community
  College *A*
Mississippi State University *B, M, D*
Mississippi University for
  Women *B, T*
Mississippi Valley State
  University *B, M, T*
Northeast Mississippi Community
  College *A*
Northwest Mississippi Community
  College *A*
Rust College *B*
Tougaloo College *B, T*
University of Mississippi *B, T*
University of Southern Mississippi *B*
William Carey University *B, M*

Missouri

Avila University *B, T*
Baptist Bible College *B*
Calvary Bible College and Theological
  Seminary *B*
Central Methodist University *B*
College of the Ozarks *B, T*
Crowder College *A*
Culver-Stockton College *B, T*
Drury University *B, T*
Evangel University *B, T*
Fontbonne University *B, T*
Hannibal-LaGrange University *B*
Harris-Stowe State University *B*
Lincoln University *B, M*
Lindenwood University *B, M*
Maryville University of Saint
  Louis *B, M, T*
Missouri Baptist University *B, T*
Missouri Southern State
  University *B, T*
Missouri State University *B, M*
Missouri Valley College *B, T*
Missouri Western State University *B*
Northwest Missouri State
  University *B, M, T*
Ozark Christian College *A*
Park University *B*
Rockhurst University *B*
Saint Louis University *B, T*
Southeast Missouri State
  University *B, M*
Southwest Baptist University *B, T*
Stephens College *B, T*
University of Central Missouri *B, M*
University of Missouri
  Columbia *B, M, D*
  Kansas City *B*
  St. Louis *B, M*
University of Phoenix
  Kansas City *B, M*
  St. Louis *B, M*

Washington University in St.
  Louis *B, M, T*
Webster University *B, M*
Westminster College *B, T*
William Jewell College *B, T*
William Woods University *B, T*

Montana

Aaniiih Nakoda College *A*
Blackfeet Community College *A*
Carroll College *B*
Montana State University *B*
Montana State University
  Billings *B, T*
  Northern *B*
Rocky Mountain College *B*
Salish Kootenai College *A, B*
Stone Child College *A*
University of Great Falls *B*
University of Montana *B, M*
University of Montana: Western *B, T*

Nebraska

Chadron State College *B, M*
College of Saint Mary *B, T*
Concordia University *B, T*
Creighton University *B*
Doane College *B*
Grace University *A, B*
Hastings College *B, M, T*
Midland University *B, T*
Nebraska Wesleyan University *B*
Northeast Community College *A*
Union College *B*
University of Nebraska
  Kearney *B, M, T*
  Lincoln *B, M*
  Omaha *B, M, T*
Wayne State College *B, T*
Western Nebraska Community
  College *A*
York College *B, T*

Nevada

Great Basin College *A, B*
Nevada State College *B*
Sierra Nevada College *B*
Truckee Meadows Community
  College *A*
University of Nevada
  Las Vegas *B, T*
  Reno *M*
University of Phoenix
  Las Vegas *B, M*
  Northern Nevada *B, M*

New Hampshire

Dartmouth College *T*
Franklin Pierce University *B, M, T*
Granite State College *B, T*
Keene State College *B, T*
New England College *B, T*
Plymouth State University *B, M, T*
Rivier University *B, M, T*
Southern New Hampshire
  University *B, M*
University of New Hampshire *T*
University of New Hampshire at
  Manchester *M, T*

New Jersey

Caldwell College *B, T*
Centenary College *T*
College of New Jersey *B, M, T*
Essex County College *A*
Felician College *B*
Georgian Court University *B, T*
Kean University *B, M, T*
Monmouth University *M*
New Jersey City University *B, T*
Rider University *B*
Rowan University *M*

Rutgers, The State University of New
  Jersey
  Camden Campus *T*
  New Brunswick/Piscataway
    Campus *M, D, T*
  Newark Campus *T*
Saint Peter's University *B, T*
Seton Hall University *B, M, T*
Sussex County Community College *A*
William Paterson University of New
  Jersey *B, M, T*

New Mexico

Eastern New Mexico University *B*
New Mexico Highlands
  University *A, B, M*
New Mexico Junior College *A*
New Mexico State University *B*
Northern New Mexico College *A*
San Juan College *A, T*
Santa Fe Community College *T*
University of New Mexico *B, M*
University of Phoenix
  New Mexico *B, M*
University of the Southwest *B, T*
Western New Mexico
  University *B, M, T*

New York

Adelphi University *M, T*
Alfred University *B, T*
Barnard College *T*
Boricua College *B, M*
Canisius College *B, M, T*
City University of New York
  Brooklyn College *B, M, T*
  City College *B, M, T*
  College of Staten Island *M*
  Hunter College *B, M, T*
  Kingsborough Community
    College *A*
  Lehman College *T*
  Medgar Evers College *B*
  Queens College *B, M, T*
  York College *T*
Colgate University *T*
College of Mount St. Vincent *T*
College of New Rochelle *B, M, T*
College of Saint Rose *B, M, T*
Columbia University
  School of General Studies *T*
Concordia College *B, T*
Corning Community College *A*
D'Youville College *M, T*
Daemen College *B, M, T*
Dominican College of Blauvelt *B, T*
Dowling College *B, M*
Dutchess Community College *A*
Elmira College *B, M, T*
Erie Community College *A*
Finger Lakes Community College *A*
Five Towns College *B, M*
Fordham University *M, T*
Fulton-Montgomery Community
  College *A*
Hobart and William Smith Colleges *T*
Hofstra University *B, M*
Houghton College *B, T*
Iona College *B, M, T*
Ithaca College *M, T*
Jamestown Community College *A*
Le Moyne College *M, T*
Long Island University
  LIU Brooklyn *B, M, T*
  LIU Post *B, M, T*
Manhattan College *B, T*
Manhattanville College *M, T*
Medaille College *B, M, T*
Medaille College: Amherst *M*
Mercy College *M, T*
Molloy College *B, M*
Monroe College *B*
Nassau Community College *A*
Nazareth College *B, M, T*

New York Institute of
Technology *B, T*
New York University *B, M, D, T*
Niagara County Community
College *A*
Niagara University *B, M, T*
Nyack College *B, M*
Orange County Community
College *A*
Pace University *B, M, T*
Pace University: Pleasantville/
Briarcliff *T*
Roberts Wesleyan College *M*
Rockland Community College *A*
SUNY
College at Brockport *B, M, T*
College at Buffalo *B, M, T*
College at Cortland *B, M*
College at Fredonia *B, M, T*
College at Geneseo *B, M, T*
College at New Paltz *B, T*
College at Old Westbury *B, T*
College at Oneonta *B*
College at Oswego *B, M, T*
College at Plattsburgh *B, M*
College at Potsdam *B, M*
College of Agriculture and
Technology at Morrisville *A*
College of Technology at Delhi *A*
University at Binghamton *M*
University at Buffalo *M, D, T*
Sage Colleges *B, M, T*
Saint Bonaventure University *B, M*
St. Francis College *B*
St. John Fisher College *B, M, T*
St. John's University *B, M, T*
St. Joseph's College New York:
Suffolk Campus *B, T*
St. Joseph's College, New York *B, T*
St. Thomas Aquinas College *B, M, T*
Sarah Lawrence College *M*
Skidmore College *B, T*
Syracuse University *M, T*
Ulster County Community College *A*
University of Rochester *M*
Utica College *B, M*
Vassar College *T*
Wagner College *M, T*
Wells College *T*
Yeshiva University *B, M*

North Carolina

Appalachian State University *B, M, T*
Barton College *B, M, T*
Belmont Abbey College *B*
Bennett College for Women *B*
Campbell University *B, M, T*
Catawba College *B, M, T*
Chowan University *B, M, T*
Craven Community College *A*
East Carolina University *B, M*
Elizabeth City State
University *B, M, T*
Elon University *B, M, T*
Fayetteville State University *B, M, T*
Fayetteville Technical Community
College *A*
Gardner-Webb University *B, M*
Greensboro College *B, T*
Guilford College *B, T*
High Point University *B, M, T*
Isothermal Community College *A*
James Sprunt Community College *A*
Laurel University *B, M*
Lees-McRae College *B, T*
Lenoir-Rhyne University *B, M, T*
Livingstone College *B*
Mars Hill University *B, T*
Martin Community College *A*
Meredith College *M, T*
Methodist University *A, B, T*
Mid-Atlantic Christian University *B*
Montreat College *B, M*

North Carolina Agricultural and
Technical State
University *B, M, T*
North Carolina Central
University *B, M, T*
North Carolina State
University *B, M, T*
North Carolina Wesleyan College *B*
Pfeiffer University *B, M, T*
Piedmont International University *B*
Queens University of Charlotte *B, M*
St. Andrews University *B*
St. Augustine's University *B*
Salem College *B, M, T*
Sandhills Community College *A*
Shaw University *B, T*
South Piedmont Community
College *A*
Southeastern Community College *A*
Stanly Community College *A*
University of Mount Olive *B*
University of North Carolina
Asheville *T*
Chapel Hill *B*
Charlotte *B, M*
Greensboro *B*
Pembroke *B, M*
Wilmington *B, M*
Wake Forest University *B, T*
Wayne Community College *A*
Western Carolina University *B, T*
Western Piedmont Community
College *A*
Wilkes Community College *A*
Wilson Community College *A*
Wingate University *B, M, T*
Winston-Salem State University *B, M*

North Dakota

Dickinson State University *B, T*
Fort Berthold Community
College *A, B*
Mayville State University *B, T*
Minot State University *B, M*
Sitting Bull College *A, B*
Trinity Bible College *B, T*
Turtle Mountain Community
College *B*
United Tribes Technical College *A, B*
University of Jamestown *B*
University of Mary *B*
University of North Dakota *B, M*
Valley City State University *B, M, T*

Ohio

Bluffton University *B*
Bowling Green State
University *B, M, T*
Cedarville University *B*
Cincinnati Christian University *B*
Cleveland State University *B, M, T*
College of Wooster *T*
Defiance College *B, T*
Franciscan University of
Steubenville *B, M*
God's Bible School and College *A, B*
Heidelberg University *T*
Hiram College *B, T*
John Carroll University *B, M, T*
Lake Erie College *B, M*
Marietta College *B*
Miami University
Middletown *B*
Oxford *M, T*
Muskingum University *B, M, T*
Notre Dame College *B, T*
Ohio Christian University *B*
Ohio Dominican University *B, T*
Ohio Mid-Western College *B*
Ohio State University
Columbus Campus *M*
Lima Campus *B*
Mansfield Campus *B, M, T*
Marion Campus *B, M, T*

Ohio University *M*
Ohio University
Eastern Campus *B*
Lancaster Campus *A*
Ohio Wesleyan University *B*
Otterbein University *B*
Sinclair Community College *A*
Union Institute & University *B*
University of Akron *M, D*
University of Cincinnati *T*
University of Cincinnati
Blue Ash College *A*
Clermont College *A*
University of Rio Grande *B, T*
University of Toledo *M, T*
Urbana University *B*
Walsh University *B*
Washington State Community
College *A*
Wilmington College *B*
Wright State University *M, T*
Wright State University: Lake
Campus *B*
Xavier University *B, M*
Youngstown State University *B, M*

Oklahoma

Bacone College *B*
Cameron University *B*
Carl Albert State College *A*
Connors State College *A*
East Central University *B, M, T*
Eastern Oklahoma State College *A*
Langston University *B, M*
Mid-America Christian University *B*
Murray State College *A*
Northeastern State University *B*
Northern Oklahoma College *A*
Northwestern Oklahoma State
University *B*
Oklahoma Baptist University *B, T*
Oklahoma Christian University *B, T*
Oklahoma City University *B*
Oklahoma Panhandle State
University *B*
Oklahoma State University *B*
Oklahoma Wesleyan University *B, T*
Oral Roberts University *B, T*
Rogers State University *A*
St. Gregory's University *B*
Seminole State College *A*
Southeastern Oklahoma State
University *B, M, T*
Southern Nazarene University *B, M*
Southwestern Oklahoma State
University *B, M, T*
University of Central Oklahoma *B, M*
University of Oklahoma *B, T*
University of Science and Arts of
Oklahoma *B, T*
University of Tulsa *B, T*

Oregon

Concordia University *B, M, T*
Corban University *B, M*
George Fox University *B, M, T*
Lewis & Clark College *M*
Linfield College *B, T*
Linn-Benton Community College *A*
Multnomah University *B*
Northwest Christian University *B, M*
Oregon State University *M*
Portland State University *T*
Southern Oregon University *M, T*
Treasure Valley Community
College *A*
University of Oregon *M, T*
University of Portland *B, M, T*
Warner Pacific College *B, T*
Western Oregon University *B, T*
Willamette University *M*

Pennsylvania

Albright College *B, M, T*
Alvernia University *B*
Arcadia University *B, M, T*
Baptist Bible College of
Pennsylvania *B, M*
Bucknell University *B, T*
Butler County Community College *A*
Cabrini College *B, T*
Cairn University *B, T*
California University of
Pennsylvania *B, M*
Cedar Crest College *B, T*
Chatham University *B, M, T*
Chestnut Hill College *B, M, T*
Cheyney University of
Pennsylvania *B, M, T*
Clarion University of
Pennsylvania *B, M, T*
Community College of Allegheny
County *A*
DeSales University *B, M, T*
Drexel University *B, T*
Duquesne University *M, T*
East Stroudsburg University of
Pennsylvania *B, M, T*
Eastern University *B, T*
Edinboro University of
Pennsylvania *B, M, T*
Gannon University *T*
Geneva College *B, T*
Grove City College *B, T*
Gwynedd Mercy University *B*
Holy Family University *B, M, T*
Immaculata University *B*
Indiana University of
Pennsylvania *B, D*
King's College *B, T*
Kutztown University of
Pennsylvania *M*
La Roche College *B*
La Salle University *B, M, T*
Lancaster Bible College *B*
Lehigh University *M*
Lincoln University *M, T*
Lycoming College *T*
Manor College *A*
Mansfield University of
Pennsylvania *B, M, T*
Marywood University *B, M*
Mercyhurst University *B, T*
Messiah College *B, T*
Millersville University of
Pennsylvania *M, T*
Misericordia University *B, T*
Montgomery County Community
College *A*
Moravian College *T*
Muhlenberg College *T*
Neumann University *B*
Penn State
Abington *B*
Altoona *B*
Beaver *B*
Berks *B*
Brandywine *B*
DuBois *B*
Erie, The Behrend College *B*
Fayette, The Eberly Campus *B*
Greater Allegheny *B*
Harrisburg *B*
Hazleton *B*
Lehigh Valley *B*
Mont Alto *B*
New Kensington *B*
Schuylkill *B*
Shenango *B*
University Park *B*
Wilkes-Barre *B*
Worthington Scranton *B*
York *B*
Point Park University *B*
Reading Area Community College *A*
Robert Morris University *B, T*

Rosemont College *B, M, T*
St. Francis University *B, T*
Saint Joseph's University *B, M, T*
St. Vincent College *B, T*
Seton Hill University *M, T*
Shippensburg University of
    Pennsylvania *T*
Slippery Rock University of
    Pennsylvania *B, M, T*
Susquehanna University *B, T*
Temple University *B, M*
Thiel College *B*
University of Pennsylvania *B, M, T*
University of Pittsburgh *T*
University of Pittsburgh
    Bradford *B*
    Greensburg *B, T*
    Johnstown *B, T*
University of Scranton *B, M*
Valley Forge Christian College *B*
Washington & Jefferson College *T*
Waynesburg University *B, T*
West Chester University of
    Pennsylvania *B, T*
Westminster College *B, M, T*
Widener University *B, M, T*
Wilkes University *B, T*
Wilson College *A, B, M, T*

Puerto Rico

American University of Puerto
    Rico *B, T*
Bayamon Central University *B, M*
Caribbean University *B*
Inter American University of Puerto
    Rico
    Aguadilla Campus *B, M*
    Arecibo Campus *B*
    Barranquitas Campus *B*
    Fajardo Campus *B, T*
    Guayama Campus *B*
    Metropolitan Campus *B, M*
    Ponce Campus *B, M*
    San German Campus *B, M*
Pontifical Catholic University of
    Puerto Rico *B, D*
Turabo University *B, M*
Universidad Adventista de las
    Antillas *B*
Universidad Metropolitana *B*
University of Puerto Rico
    Aguadilla *B, T*
    Arecibo *B*
    Humacao *B*
    Ponce *B*
    Rio Piedras *B*
    Utuado *B*
University of the Sacred Heart *B*

Rhode Island

Rhode Island College *B, M, T*
Roger Williams University *B, M*
Salve Regina University *B*
University of Rhode Island *B*

South Carolina

Anderson University *B, T*
Benedict College *B*
Bob Jones University *B*
Charleston Southern University *B, M*
Claflin University *B*
Clemson University *B, M*
Coastal Carolina University *B, T*
Coker College *B, T*
College of Charleston *B, M, T*
Columbia College *B, T*
Columbia International
    University *B, M*
Converse College *B, M, T*
Erskine College *B, T*
Francis Marion University *B, M, T*
Furman University *T*
Lander University *B, M, T*
Limestone College *B*

Morris College *B, T*
Newberry College *B, T*
North Greenville University *B, T*
Presbyterian College *B, T*
South Carolina State
    University *B, M, T*
Southern Wesleyan University *B, T*
University of South Carolina
    Aiken *B, T*
    Beaufort *B*
    Columbia *B, M*
    Upstate *B, M, T*
Winthrop University *B, M, T*

South Dakota

Augustana College *B, T*
Black Hills State University *B*
Dakota State University *B, T*
Dakota Wesleyan University *B, T*
Mount Marty College *B*
Northern State University *B, M, T*
Oglala Lakota College *B*
Sinte Gleska University *B*
University of Sioux Falls *B, M, T*
University of South Dakota *B, M, T*

Tennessee

Aquinas College *B, M*
Belmont University *B, M, T*
Bethel University *B, M, T*
Bryan University
    Dayton *T*
Carson-Newman University *B, M, T*
Christian Brothers University *M, T*
Cumberland University *B, T*
East Tennessee State University *M, T*
Fisk University *T*
Freed-Hardeman University *B, T*
Hiwassee College *A*
Johnson University *B, M, T*
King University *T*
Lee University *B*
Lincoln Memorial University *B, T*
Lipscomb University *B, T*
Martin Methodist College *B*
Motlow State Community College *A*
South College *B, M*
Southern Adventist University *B*
Tennessee State University *M, T*
Tennessee Technological
    University *M, T*
Tennessee Temple University *B, M, T*
Tennessee Wesleyan College *B, T*
Trevecca Nazarene University *B, M, T*
Tusculum College *B, T*
Union University *B, T*
University of Phoenix
    Chattanooga *B, M*
    Memphis *B, M*
    Nashville *B, M*
University of Tennessee
    Chattanooga *M*
Vanderbilt University *B, M, T*
Victory University *B, T*
Welch College *B*

Texas

Abilene Christian University *B, T*
Amarillo College *A*
Arlington Baptist College *B, T*
Austin College *A*
Baylor University *B, T*
Brazosport College *A*
Clarendon College *A*
Coastal Bend College *A*
College of the Mainland *A*
Concordia University Texas *B*
Dallas Baptist University *B, M*
Dallas Christian College *B, T*
Del Mar College *A*
East Texas Baptist University *B*
El Paso Community College *A*
Frank Phillips College *A*
Galveston College *A*

Grayson College *A*
Howard Payne University *B*
Huston-Tillotson University *T*
Jarvis Christian College *B, T*
Lamar University *B, M, T*
Laredo Community College *A*
LeTourneau University *B, T*
Lubbock Christian University *B, M, T*
McMurry University *B*
Midwestern State University *M*
Navarro College *A*
North Lake College *A*
Our Lady of the Lake University of
    San Antonio *M*
Paul Quinn College *B*
Prairie View A&M University *M*
St. Edward's University *T*
St. Mary's University *T*
San Jacinto College *A*
South Texas College *A*
Southwestern Adventist
    University *B, M, T*
Southwestern Assemblies of God
    University *B, M*
Southwestern University *T*
Stephen F. Austin State
    University *M, T*
Sul Ross State University *B, M, T*
Temple College *A*
Texas A&M International
    University *B, M, T*
Texas A&M University
    Commerce *D, T*
    Corpus Christi *M, T*
    Kingsville *B, M*
    Texarkana *T*
Texas Christian University *M*
Texas College *B, T*
Texas Lutheran University *B, T*
Texas State University *M, T*
Texas Tech University *M*
Texas Woman's University *M*
Trinity University *B, M*
Trinity Valley Community College *A*
University of Dallas *B, T*
University of Houston
    Victoria *M*
University of Mary Hardin-Baylor *B, T*
University of St. Thomas *B*
University of Texas
    Brownsville *B*
    Pan American *M*
    San Antonio *M, T*
University of the Incarnate
    Word *B, M, T*
Wayland Baptist University *B, M, T*
West Texas A&M University *T*
Wharton County Junior College *A*
Wiley College *B*

Utah

Brigham Young University *B*
Dixie State College *B*
Snow College *A*
Southern Utah University *B*
University of Phoenix
    Utah *B, M*
University of Utah *B*
Utah State University *B, M*
Utah Valley University *B*
Weber State University *A, B, M*
Western Governors
    University *B, M, T*
Westminster College *B*

Vermont

Castleton State College *B, M*
Champlain College *B*
College of St. Joseph in Vermont *M*
Goddard College *B, M*
Green Mountain College *B, T*
Johnson State College *B, M*
Lyndon State College *B*
Middlebury College *T*

Norwich University *T*
Saint Michael's College *B, M, T*
University of Vermont *B, T*

Virginia

Averett University *M, T*
Bluefield College *B, T*
Bridgewater College *T*
College of William and Mary *M, T*
Germanna Community College *A*
Hampton University *M*
Hollins University *T*
James Madison University *T*
Longwood University *T*
Lynchburg College *B*
Mary Baldwin College *T*
Marymount University *B, M*
Old Dominion University *M*
Radford University *T*
Randolph College *B*
Randolph-Macon College *T*
Regent University *M*
University of Mary Washington *M*
University of Virginia's College at
    Wise *T*
Virginia Baptist College *A, B*
Virginia Intermont College *T*
Virginia Wesleyan College *B, T*

Washington

Bellevue College *A*
Cascadia Community College *A*
Central Washington
    University *B, M, T*
City University of Seattle *B, M, T*
Eastern Washington University *M, T*
Edmonds Community College *A*
Gonzaga University *T*
Heritage University *B, M*
Lower Columbia College *A*
Northwest University *B*
Pacific Lutheran University *B*
Pierce College *A*
Renton Technical College *A*
Saint Martin's University *B, T*
Spokane Falls Community College *A*
Tacoma Community College *A*
University of Puget Sound *T*
University of Washington *M, T*
Walla Walla University *B, T*
Washington State University *B, M, T*
Western Washington University *B, M*
Whitworth University *B, M, T*

West Virginia

Alderson-Broaddus University *B*
American Public University System *M*
Appalachian Bible College *B*
Bethany College *B*
Bluefield State College *B*
Concord University *B, M, T*
Davis and Elkins College *B*
Glenville State College *B*
Marshall University *B, M*
Ohio Valley University *B*
Potomac State College of West
    Virginia University *A*
Shepherd University *B, T*
University of Charleston *B*
West Liberty University *B*
West Virginia State University *B*
West Virginia University *B, M, T*
West Virginia University at
    Parkersburg *A, B*
West Virginia Wesleyan College *B*
Wheeling Jesuit University *B*

Wisconsin

Alverno College *B, M, T*
Beloit College *T*
Carroll University *B, T*
Carthage College *B, T*
Concordia University Wisconsin *B, T*
Edgewood College *B, T*

Lakeland College *B*
Lawrence University *T*
Maranatha Baptist Bible College *B*
Marian University *B, M, T*
Marquette University *B*
Mount Mary University *B, T*
Northland International University *B*
Ripon College *T*
St. Norbert College *B, T*
Silver Lake College of the Holy
  Family *B, T*
University of Wisconsin
  Eau Claire *B, M*
  Green Bay *B, T*
  La Crosse *B, M, T*
  Madison *B*
  Oshkosh *B, M, T*
  Platteville *B, T*
  River Falls *B, M, T*
  Stevens Point *B, M, T*
  Superior *B, M, T*
  Whitewater *B, T*
Viterbo University *B, M, T*
Wisconsin Lutheran College *B*

Wyoming
Casper College *A*
Central Wyoming College *A*
Eastern Wyoming College *A*
Northwest College *A*
Sheridan College *A*
University of Wyoming *B*
Western Wyoming Community
  College *A*

Elementary/middle school administration

Alabama
University of Alabama *D*

Alaska
University of Alaska
  Anchorage *M*

Arkansas
Arkansas State University *M, T*
Henderson State University *M*

California
California State University
  Channel Islands *M*

Illinois
McKendree University *M*
University of Illinois
  Urbana-Champaign *M, D, T*

Iowa
University of Northern Iowa *M*

Kentucky
University of Louisville *M*

Louisiana
Xavier University of Louisiana *M*

Massachusetts
Lesley University *M*
Westfield State University *M*

Michigan
Marygrove College *M*
Michigan State University *M, D*

Minnesota
Hamline University *T*

Mississippi
Mississippi State University *D*

Missouri
Lincoln University *M*
Lindenwood University *M*
Missouri Baptist University *M, T*
Northwest Missouri State
  University *M*
Southeast Missouri State University *M*
Southwest Baptist University *M*
University of Missouri
  Columbia *M, D*

Montana
University of Great Falls *M*

Nebraska
Concordia University *M, T*
Creighton University *M*
Wayne State College *M*

New Hampshire
New England College *M*

New Jersey
Rowan University *M*
Rutgers, The State University of New
  Jersey
  New Brunswick/Piscataway
    Campus *M*
William Paterson University of New
  Jersey *M*

New York
Le Moyne College *M*
SUNY
  College at New Paltz *M*
Saint Bonaventure University *M*
St. John Fisher College *M, T*

North Carolina
Wingate University *M, T*

North Dakota
University of Mary *M*

Ohio
Antioch University
  Midwest *M*
Lake Erie College *M*
University of Findlay *M, T*
Wright State University *M, T*
Youngstown State University *M*

Pennsylvania
East Stroudsburg University of
  Pennsylvania *T*
St. Francis University *M*
Shippensburg University of
  Pennsylvania *M, T*
Widener University *M, T*
Wilkes University *M*
York College of Pennsylvania *M, T*

Puerto Rico
Inter American University of Puerto
  Rico
  Barranquitas Campus *M*

Rhode Island
Providence College *M*

South Carolina
Charleston Southern University *M*

South Dakota
University of South Dakota *M, D*

Texas
University of North Texas *M*

Vermont
Saint Michael's College *M, T*

Washington
City University of Seattle *M, T*
Seattle University *M*
University of Washington *M, D, T*
Washington State University *M, T*
Western Washington University *M*
Whitworth University *M*

West Virginia
Wheeling Jesuit University *M*

Wisconsin
Cardinal Stritch University *M, D*
University of Wisconsin
  Superior *M*

Elementary special education

California
Alliant International University *M, T*
Antioch University
  Los Angeles *T*

Georgia
Brenau University *B*

Illinois
Spoon River College *A*

Indiana
Purdue University *B*

Iowa
Upper Iowa University *M*

Maryland
Howard Community College *A*

Massachusetts
Merrimack College *B, M*

Nebraska
Concordia University *B, T*

Nevada
Nevada State College *B*

New York
Canisius College *B*
City University of New York
  Brooklyn College *M, T*
  College of Staten Island *M, T*
College of New Rochelle *M*
Nyack College *M*
St. John's University *M, T*
St. Joseph's College New York:
  Suffolk Campus *M, T*
St. Joseph's College, New York *T*
Syracuse University *B, M*

Ohio
Shawnee State University *B*

Pennsylvania
Alvernia University *B*

Puerto Rico
Universidad Metropolitana *B*

Wyoming
University of Wyoming *B*

Emergency care attendant (EMT ambulance)

Alabama
Virginia College
  Birmingham *A*

Wallace State Community College at
  Hanceville *C, A*

Arizona
Mohave Community College *C*

Arkansas
South Arkansas Community
  College *C*
University of Arkansas
  Community College at Hope *C*

California
Copper Mountain College *C*
La Sierra University *C*
San Jose City College *C*
Santa Rosa Junior College *C*

Colorado
Colorado Mountain College *C*
Colorado Northwestern Community
  College *C*
Lamar Community College *C*

Delaware
Delaware Technical Community
  College
  Stanton/Wilmington Campus *A*

Florida
City College
  Gainesville *A*
Pasco-Hernando State College *C*
Pensacola State College *C*
South Florida State College *C*
State College of Florida, Manatee-
  Sarasota *A*

Georgia
Altamaha Technical College *C*
Darton College *C*
Southeastern Technical College *C*

Illinois
City Colleges of Chicago
  Harold Washington College *C*
  Malcolm X College *C*
  Wilbur Wright College *C*
Harper College *C*
Heartland Community College *C*
Illinois Eastern Community Colleges
  Frontier Community College *C, A*
Kankakee Community College *C*
Lincoln Land Community College *C*
Loyola University Chicago *C*
Prairie State College *C, A*
Southeastern Illinois College *C*
Waubonsee Community College *C, A*

Kansas
Cloud County Community College *C*
Colby Community College *C*
Cowley County Community
  College *A*
Garden City Community College *C*
Highland Community College *C*
Hutchinson Community College *C*
Independence Community College *C*
Kansas City Kansas Community
  College *C*

Maryland
Carroll Community College *A*

Massachusetts
Bristol Community College *C*
Mount Wachusett Community
  College *C*

Michigan
Baker College
  Muskegon *C, A*

Minnesota

Anoka Technical College *C*
Central Lakes College *C*
Century College *C*
Northwest Technical College *C*
Vermilion Community College *C*

New Mexico

Clovis Community College *C, A*

North Carolina

Carteret Community College *A*
Sandhills Community College *A*

Ohio

Lakeland Community College *C*
North Central State College *C*
Sinclair Community College *C*
University of Cincinnati
    Clermont College *A*

Oregon

Clackamas Community College *C*
Klamath Community College *C*
Tillamook Bay Community College *C*

Pennsylvania

Delaware County Community
    College *C*
Penn State
    Fayette, The Eberly Campus *C*
Pennsylvania College of
    Technology *C*

South Carolina

York Technical College *C*

Texas

Howard College *C, A*
Tyler Junior College *C, A*
Weatherford College *C*

Utah

Dixie State College *C*

Virginia

J. Sargeant Reynolds Community
    College *C*

Washington

Clark College *C*
Columbia Basin College *A*
Tacoma Community College *C*

Wisconsin

Milwaukee Area Technical College *C*
Northcentral Technical College *C*

Emergency/disaster management

Alabama

Columbia Southern University *M*
University of Phoenix
    Birmingham *B*

Alaska

University of Alaska
    Fairbanks *B*

Arizona

Glendale Community College *A*
Grand Canyon University *B*
University of Phoenix
    Phoenix-Hohokam *C, B*
    Southern Arizona *B*

Arkansas

Arkansas State University *A, B, M*
Arkansas Tech University *B, M*

University of Phoenix
    Little Rock *B*
    Northwest Arkansas *B*

California

University of Phoenix
    Bay Area *B*
    Central Valley *C, B*
    Sacramento Valley *B*
    San Diego *B*
    Southern California *C, B*

Colorado

Community College of Aurora *C, A*
Pikes Peak Community College *C, A*
Red Rocks Community College *C, A*
University of Phoenix
    Denver *B*
    Southern Colorado *B*

District of Columbia

Georgetown University *M*
University of Phoenix
    Washington DC *B*

Florida

University of Phoenix
    Central Florida *B*
    North Florida *B*
    South Florida *B*
    West Florida *B*

Georgia

University of Phoenix
    Atlanta *B*
    Augusta *B*
    Columbus *B*
    Savannah *B*

Hawaii

University of Phoenix
    Hawaii *B*

Idaho

Idaho State University *A, B*
University of Idaho *C*

Illinois

University of Chicago *M*

Indiana

Indiana University
    Purdue University Indianapolis *C*
University of Phoenix
    Indianapolis *B*

Kansas

Kansas City Kansas Community
    College *C*
Kansas Wesleyan University *B*

Kentucky

Midway College *B*
University of Phoenix
    Louisville *B*

Louisiana

University of New Orleans *C*
University of Phoenix
    Baton Rouge *B*
    Lafayette *B*
    Louisiana *B*
    Shreveport *B*

Michigan

Oakland Community College *C*
University of Phoenix
    Metro Detroit *B*
    West Michigan *B*

Minnesota

Capella University *B, M, D*
University of Phoenix
    Minneapolis-St. Paul *B*
Walden University *M*

Missouri

University of Phoenix
    Kansas City *B*
    St. Louis *B*

Nebraska

University of Nebraska
    Omaha *B*

Nevada

University of Phoenix
    Las Vegas *B*
    Northern Nevada *B*

New Jersey

Burlington County College *C*

New Mexico

Eastern New Mexico University *C*
Eastern New Mexico University:
    Roswell *C*

New York

Adelphi University *B, M*
Elmira College *M*
Long Island Business Institute *C, A*
Nassau Community College *A*
Rochester Institute of Technology *C*
Sullivan County Community
    College *A*

North Carolina

Fayetteville Technical Community
    College *A*
Wayne Community College *C, A*

North Dakota

North Dakota State
    University *B, M, D*

Ohio

Cincinnati State Technical and
    Community College *A*
Union Institute & University *B*
University of Phoenix
    Cleveland *B*

Oklahoma

University of Phoenix
    Tulsa *B*

Pennsylvania

Bucks County Community
    College *C, A*
Millersville University of
    Pennsylvania *M*
Pennsylvania College of
    Technology *B*
Temple University *C*
University of Phoenix
    Harrisburg *B*
    Philadelphia *B*
    Pittsburgh *B*

Puerto Rico

Turabo University *A*

Rhode Island

Community College of Rhode
    Island *A*

South Carolina

University of Phoenix
    Columbia *B*
Voorhees College *B*

Tennessee

University of Phoenix
    Chattanooga *B*
    Knoxville *B*
    Memphis *B*

Texas

Texas Southern University *B*
University of North Texas *B*
University of Phoenix
    Austin *B*
    Dallas Fort Worth *B*
    Houston Westside *B*
    San Antonio *B*

Utah

University of Phoenix
    Utah *C, B*

Vermont

Community College of Vermont *A*

Virginia

University of Phoenix
    Northern Virginia *C, B*
    Richmond *B*

Washington

Clover Park Technical College *C, A*
Edmonds Community College *C, A*
Pierce College *C, A*
University of Phoenix
    Western Washington *B*

West Virginia

American Public University
    System *C, B, M*

Wisconsin

University of Phoenix
    Milwaukee *B*

Wyoming

Casper College *A*

Emergency medical technology (EMT paramedic)

Alabama

Bevill State Community College *C, A*
Bishop State Community
    College *C, A*
Calhoun Community College *C, A*
Central Alabama Community
    College *A*
Chattahoochee Valley Community
    College *C*
Enterprise State Community
    College *A*
Faulkner State Community College *A*
Gadsden State Community College *A*
George C. Wallace Community
    College at Dothan *C, A*
Herzing University
    Birmingham *C*
Jefferson Davis Community
    College *C*
Jefferson State Community
    College *C, A*
Lawson State Community College *C*
Lurleen B. Wallace Community
    College *C, A*
Northeast Alabama Community
    College *C, A*
Northwest-Shoals Community
    College *C, A*
Southern Union State Community
    College *C, A*
University of Alabama
    Birmingham *C*
University of South Alabama *C, B*

Wallace State Community College at
   Hanceville *C, A*

Alaska

University of Alaska
   Fairbanks *A*

Arizona

Arizona Western College *C, A*
Central Arizona College *C, A*
Cochise College *C, A*
Eastern Arizona College *C, A*
Glendale Community College *C, A*
Mesa Community College *C, A*
Northland Pioneer College *A*
Paradise Valley Community
   College *C, A*
Phoenix College *C, A*
Pima Community College *C, A*
Scottsdale Community College *C, A*
Yavapai College *C*

Arkansas

Arkansas Northeastern College *C*
Arkansas State University
   Beebe *C, A*
   Mountain Home *C, A*
   Newport *A*
Arkansas Tech University *C*
Cossatot Community College of the
   University of Arkansas *C*
East Arkansas Community
   College *C, A*
National Park Community
   College *C, A*
North Arkansas College *C, A*
Northwest Arkansas Community
   College *C, A*
Ozarka College *C*
Rich Mountain Community College *C*
South Arkansas Community
   College *C, A*
Southeast Arkansas College *C, A*
University of Arkansas
   Community College at Batesville *A*
   Community College at Hope *C, A*
   Community College at Morrilton *C*
   Monticello *C*
   for Medical Sciences *C, A, B*

California

Allan Hancock College *C*
Bakersfield College *C*
Barstow Community College *C*
Butte College *A*
California State University
   Chico *C*
City College of San Francisco *A*
College of the Desert *C*
College of the Sequoias *C*
College of the Siskiyous *C, A*
Columbia College *C*
Contra Costa College *C*
Cosumnes River College *C*
Crafton Hills College *C, A*
East Los Angeles College *C*
Foothill College *C*
Imperial Valley College *C, A*
Loma Linda University *B*
Long Beach City College *C*
Los Angeles Harbor College *C*
Los Medanos College *C*
Modesto Junior College *C*
Mount San Antonio College *C, A*
National University *C*
Pacific Union College *A*
Palo Verde College *C*
Palomar College *C, A*
Saddleback College *C*
San Joaquin Valley College *A*
San Jose City College *C*
Santa Barbara City College *C*
Santa Rosa Junior College *C, A*
Shasta College *A*

Skyline College *C*
Southwestern College *C, A*
Ventura College *C, A*
Victor Valley College *C, A*

Colorado

Aims Community College *C, A*
Arapahoe Community College *C*
Colorado Mesa University *C, A*
Colorado Mountain College *C, A*
Colorado Northwestern Community
   College *C, A*
Community College of Aurora *C, A*
Community College of Denver *C*
Front Range Community College *C, A*
Morgan Community College *C*
Northeastern Junior College *C*
Pikes Peak Community College *C, A*
Pueblo Community College *C, A*
Red Rocks Community College *C, A*

Connecticut

Capital Community College *C, A*
Goodwin College *C*
Norwalk Community College *C*

Delaware

Delaware Technical Community
   College
   Jack F. Owens Campus *A*
   Stanton/Wilmington Campus *A*
   Terry Campus *A*

Florida

Broward College *C, A*
City College
   Fort Lauderdale *A*
College of Central Florida *C, A*
Daytona State College *C, A*
Eastern Florida State College *C, A*
Edison State College *C, A*
Florida Gateway College *C, A*
Florida Keys Community College *C*
Florida State College at
   Jacksonville *C, A*
Gulf Coast State College *C, A*
Hillsborough Community
   College *C, A*
Indian River State College *C, A*
Lake-Sumter State College *A*
Miami Dade College *C, A*
Northwest Florida State College *C, A*
Palm Beach State College *C, A*
Pensacola State College *C, A*
Polk State College *C, A*
Saint Johns River State College *C, A*
St. Petersburg College *C, A*
Santa Fe College *C, A*
Seminole State College of
   Florida *C, A*
South Florida State College *C, A*
Tallahassee Community College *C, A*

Georgia

Albany Technical College *C*
Athens Technical College *C*
Atlanta Technical College *C*
Augusta Technical College *C, A*
Bainbridge College *C*
Central Georgia Technical College *C*
Darton College *C, A*
Georgia Piedmont Technical
   College *C*
Gwinnett Technical College *C, A*
North Georgia Technical College *C*
Savannah Technical College *C, A*
South Georgia State College *A*
Southeastern Technical College *C*
Southwest Georgia Technical
   College *C*
University of North Georgia *A*
West Georgia Technical College *C*

Hawaii

University of Hawaii
   Kapiolani Community College *C, A*

Idaho

Brigham Young University-Idaho *A*
College of Southern Idaho *C, A*
Idaho State University *C, A*

Illinois

Black Hawk College *C, A*
City Colleges of Chicago
   Kennedy-King College *C*
   Malcolm X College *C, A*
   Olive-Harvey College *C*
   Wilbur Wright College *C*
College of DuPage *C, A*
College of Lake County *C*
Concordia University Chicago *B*
Elgin Community College *C*
Harper College *C, A*
Heartland Community College *C*
Highland Community College *C, A*
Illinois Central College *C, A*
Illinois Eastern Community Colleges
   Frontier Community College *C*
Illinois Valley Community College *C*
John A. Logan College *C*
John Wood Community College *A*
Kankakee Community College *C, A*
Kaskaskia College *C, A*
Lincoln Land Community College *C*
McHenry County College *C, A*
Moraine Valley Community
   College *C, A*
Parkland College *C*
Prairie State College *C*
Rend Lake College *C, A*
Richland Community College *C, A*
Rock Valley College *C*
Sauk Valley Community College *C, A*
South Suburban College of Cook
   County *C*
Southeastern Illinois College *C*
Southwestern Illinois College *C, A*
Triton College *C, A*

Indiana

Indiana University
   Purdue University Indianapolis *A*
Ivy Tech Community College
   Bloomington *A*
   Central Indiana *A*
   Columbus *A*
   Kokomo *A*
   North Central *A*
   Northeast *A*
   Northwest *A*
   Richmond *A*
   Southwest *A*
   Wabash Valley *A*
Purdue University
   Calumet *C, A*
Saint Joseph's College *A*
University of St. Francis *A*
Vincennes University *C, A*

Iowa

Clinton Community College *C, A*
Des Moines Area Community
   College *C*
Iowa Central Community
   College *C, A*
Iowa Lakes Community College *C, A*
Kirkwood Community College *A*
Mercy College of Health
   Sciences *A*
North Iowa Area Community
   College *A*
Northeast Iowa Community
   College *C, A*
Southeastern Community College *A*
Southwestern Community College *C*

Western Iowa Tech Community
   College *C, A*

Kansas

Allen County Community College *A*
Barton County Community College *A*
Coffeyville Community College *A*
Cowley County Community
   College *A*
Dodge City Community College *C*
Garden City Community College *A*
Hutchinson Community College *A*
Independence Community
   College *C, A*
Johnson County Community
   College *C, A*
Kansas City Kansas Community
   College *A*
Neosho County Community
   College *C*

Kentucky

Eastern Kentucky University *C, A, B*
Gateway Community and Technical
   College *C, A*
Jefferson Community and Technical
   College *C*
Owensboro Community and
   Technical College *C*
Somerset Community College *C*
Spalding University *A*
Western Kentucky University *A*

Louisiana

Bossier Parish Community
   College *C, A*
Delgado Community College *C, A*
Nunez Community College *C*
South Louisiana Community
   College *C, A*

Maine

Eastern Maine Community College *C*
Kennebec Valley Community
   College *C, A*
Southern Maine Community
   College *A*

Maryland

Anne Arundel Community College *C*
Baltimore City Community
   College *C, A*
Cecil College *A*
Chesapeake College *C, A*
College of Southern Maryland *C, A*
Community College of Baltimore
   County *C, A*
Hagerstown Community College *C, A*
Howard Community College *C, A*
Prince George's Community
   College *C, A*
University of Maryland
   Baltimore County *B, M*
Wor-Wic Community College *C, A*

Massachusetts

Cape Cod Community College *C, A*
Greenfield Community College *C*
Massachusetts Bay Community
   College *C*
Northern Essex Community
   College *A*
Quinsigamond Community
   College *C, A*
Springfield College *B*

Michigan

Baker College
   Cadillac *C*
   Clinton Township *C*
   Muskegon *C, A*
Glen Oaks Community College *C*
Gogebic Community College *A*
Henry Ford Community College *A*

Jackson College *C, A*
Kalamazoo Valley Community
   College *C*
Kellogg Community College *C, A*
Kirtland Community College *A*
Lake Michigan College *C, A*
Lake Superior State University *C*
Lansing Community College *C, A*
Macomb Community College *C, A*
Montcalm Community College *C*
Mott Community College *A*
North Central Michigan College *A*
Oakland Community College *C, A*
Schoolcraft College *C, A*
Wayne County Community
   College *C, A*
West Shore Community College *A*

Minnesota
Century College *C, A*
Hennepin Technical College *A*
Inver Hills Community College *C, A*
Mesabi Range Community and
   Technical College *C*
Northland Community & Technical
   College *A*
Rochester Community and Technical
   College *A*
St. Cloud Technical and Community
   College *A*
South Central College *C, A*

Mississippi
Coahoma Community College *A*
Copiah-Lincoln Community
   College *C*
East Mississippi Community
   College *C, A*
Hinds Community College *C, A*
Itawamba Community College *A*
Mississippi Delta Community
   College *A*
Mississippi Gulf Coast Community
   College *A*
University of Mississippi Medical
   Center *C*

Missouri
Crowder College *C*
Drury University *B*
East Central College *C, A*
Jefferson College *C, A*
Metropolitan Community College -
   Kansas City *A*
Mineral Area College *C*
Missouri Southern State University *C*
Moberly Area Community College *C*
North Central Missouri College *A*
Ozarks Technical Community
   College *C, A*
St. Charles Community College *A*
St. Louis Community College *A*
Southwest Baptist University *A*
Three Rivers Community College *C*

Montana
Flathead Valley Community
   College *A*
Montana State University
   Billings *A*
   Great Falls College *C, A*

Nebraska
Creighton University *C, A, B, M*
Northeast Community College *A*
Western Nebraska Community
   College *C*

Nevada
College of Southern Nevada *A*

New Hampshire
NHTI-Concord's Community
   College *A*

New Jersey
Essex County College *A*
Hudson County Community
   College *C*
Union County College *C, A*

New Mexico
Central New Mexico Community
   College *C, A*
Dona Ana Community College of
   New Mexico State
   University *C, A*
Eastern New Mexico University:
   Roswell *C, A*
New Mexico Junior College *A*
New Mexico State University
   Alamogordo *C*
   Carlsbad *C*
San Juan College *C, A*
Santa Fe Community College *C*
University of New Mexico *B*

New York
Broome Community College *A*
City University of New York
   Borough of Manhattan Community
     College *A*
   LaGuardia Community College *A*
Corning Community College *A*
Dutchess Community College *C, A*
Erie Community College *C, A*
Finger Lakes Community
   College *C, A*
Herkimer County Community
   College *A*
Hudson Valley Community College *C*
Jefferson Community College *C, A*
Mohawk Valley Community
   College *A*
Rockland Community College *A*
SUNY
   College of Agriculture and
     Technology at Cobleskill *C, A*
Suffolk County Community College *A*
Ulster County Community
   College *C, A*
Westchester Community College *C, A*

North Carolina
Asheville-Buncombe Technical
   Community College *A*
Blue Ridge Community College *A*
Catawba Valley Community
   College *A*
Coastal Carolina Community
   College *A*
Davidson County Community
   College *C, A*
Durham Technical Community
   College *A*
Fayetteville Technical Community
   College *C, A*
Forsyth Technical Community
   College *A*
Gaston College *C, A*
Guilford Technical Community
   College *A*
Lenoir Community College *C, A*
Robeson Community College *A*
Sandhills Community College *A*
Southwestern Community College *A*
Stanly Community College *A*
Tri-County Community College *C, A*
Wake Technical Community
   College *C, A*
Western Carolina University *B*

North Dakota
Bismarck State College *C, A*
Dakota College at Bottineau *C, A*
North Dakota State College of
   Science *C, A*
Turtle Mountain Community
   College *C*

Ohio
Belmont College *C, A*
Central Ohio Technical College *C, A*
Cincinnati State Technical and
   Community College *C, A*
Clark State Community College *C, A*
Columbus State Community
   College *C, A*
Cuyahoga Community College
   Metropolitan *A*
Eastern Gateway Community
   College *C, A*
Hocking College *C, A*
James A. Rhodes State College *C, A*
Kent State University
   Trumbull *A*
Lakeland Community College *C*
Lorain County Community College *C*
Mercy College of Ohio *C*
Northwest State Community
   College *C*
Shawnee State University *C, A*
Sinclair Community College *C, A*
Stark State College *C*
University of Akron *A*
University of Cincinnati
   Blue Ash College *C, A*
   Clermont College *C, A*
Youngstown State University *C, A*

Oklahoma
Oklahoma City Community
   College *C, A*
Oklahoma State University
   Oklahoma City *C, A*
Redlands Community College *C, A*
Rogers State University *A*

Oregon
Central Oregon Community
   College *A*
Chemeketa Community College *A*
Clackamas Community College *C*
Lane Community College *C, A*
Linn-Benton Community College *C*
Mt. Hood Community College *A*
Oregon Health & Science
   University *B*
Oregon Institute of Technology *A*
Portland Community College *C, A*
Rogue Community College *C, A*
Southwestern Oregon Community
   College *C*
Treasure Valley Community
   College *C*
Umpqua Community College *A*

Pennsylvania
Delaware County Community
   College *C, A*
Harrisburg Area Community
   College *C, A*
Lackawanna College *C*
Luzerne County Community
   College *C, A*
Northampton Community College *C*
Pennsylvania College of
   Technology *A*
Pennsylvania Highlands Community
   College *A*
University of Pittsburgh
   Johnstown *A*

Puerto Rico
Centro de Estudios
   Multidisciplinarios *C*
EDP University of Puerto Rico: Hato
   Rey *A*
Inter American University of Puerto
   Rico
   Aguadilla Campus *C*
   Metropolitan Campus *C, A*
   San German Campus *C*

Universal Technology College of
   Puerto Rico *C*
Universidad Metropolitana *C*

South Carolina
Central Carolina Technical College *C*
Greenville Technical College *A*
Horry-Georgetown Technical
   College *C, A*
Piedmont Technical College *C*
Spartanburg Community College *C*
Trident Technical College *C, A*

South Dakota
Western Dakota Technical Institute *A*

Tennessee
Chattanooga State Community
   College *C*
Cleveland State Community
   College *C*
Columbia State Community
   College *C*
Dyersburg State Community
   College *C, A*
Jackson State Community College *C*
Northeast State Community
   College *C*
Roane State Community College *C*
Southwest Tennessee Community
   College *C, A*
Volunteer State Community
   College *C*
Walters State Community
   College *C, A*

Texas
Alvin Community College *C, A*
Amarillo College *C, A*
Angelina College *C, A*
Austin Community College *C, A*
Blinn College *C*
Brookhaven College *C, A*
Clarendon College *A*
Collin County Community College
   District *C, A*
Del Mar College *C, A*
El Centro College *C*
El Paso Community College *C*
Galveston College *C, A*
Grayson College *C, A*
Hill College *C, A*
Houston Community College
   System *C, A*
Kilgore College *C, A*
Lamar Institute of Technology *C, A*
Lamar State College at Orange *C, A*
Laredo Community College *A*
Lee College *C, A*
Lone Star College System *C, A*
McLennan Community College *A*
Midland College *C, A*
Navarro College *C*
North Central Texas College *A*
Northeast Texas Community
   College *C, A*
Odessa College *C, A*
Paris Junior College *C, A*
San Antonio College *C*
San Jacinto College *C, A*
South Plains College *C, A*
South Texas College *C, A*
Tarrant County College *C, A*
Temple College *C, A*
Texarkana College *C, A*
Texas State Technical College
   Harlingen *C, A*
   West Texas *C, A*
Trinity Valley Community College *C*
Tyler Junior College *C, A*
Victoria College *C, A*
Weatherford College *C, A*
Western Texas College *C, A*
Wharton County Junior College *C, A*

Utah

Dixie State College C, A
Snow College C, A
Utah Valley University C
Weber State University A

Virginia

J. Sargeant Reynolds Community
College C
Jefferson College of Health
Sciences B
John Tyler Community College C
Mountain Empire Community
College C, A
Northern Virginia Community
College A
Piedmont Virginia Community
College C, A
Rappahannock Community College C
Southwest Virginia Community
College C, A
Tidewater Community College A
Virginia Western Community
College C

Washington

Bellingham Technical College A
Central Washington University B
Clark College A
Columbia Basin College A
North Seattle Community College C
Spokane Community College C, A
Spokane Falls Community College C
Tacoma Community College C, A

West Virginia

American National University
Parkersburg C, A
Blue Ridge Community and Technical
College C, A
Kanawha Valley Community and
Technical College A
New River Community and Technical
College C
Southern West Virginia Community
and Technical College A

Wisconsin

Blackhawk Technical College C
Chippewa Valley Technical
College C, A
Fox Valley Technical College C, A
Gateway Technical College C
Lakeshore Technical College C, A
Madison Area Technical College C, A
Mid-State Technical College C, A
Milwaukee Area Technical College C
Moraine Park Technical College C, A
Nicolet Area Technical College C
Northcentral Technical College C, A
Waukesha County Technical
College C, A
Western Technical College C, A
Wisconsin Indianhead Technical
College C, A

Wyoming

Casper College A
Central Wyoming College C
Laramie County Community
College C, A

Emergency room/ trauma nursing

Pennsylvania

Widener University M

Tennessee

Vanderbilt University M

Endocrinology

California

University of California
Berkeley M, D

Wisconsin

University of Wisconsin
Madison M, D

Energy systems technology

Alabama

Northwest-Shoals Community
College C

Alaska

University of Alaska
Anchorage C

Arizona

Refrigeration School A

California

Santa Monica College C, A

Colorado

Colorado Mountain College C
Colorado Northwestern Community
College C, A
Ecotech Institute A
Front Range Community College A
Lamar Community College C, A
Pikes Peak Community College A
Pueblo Community College C, A
Red Rocks Community College C, A

Connecticut

Naugatuck Valley Community
College C, A
Norwalk Community College C

Florida

State College of Florida, Manatee-
Sarasota B

Idaho

Eastern Idaho Technical College C
Idaho State University A, B

Illinois

Black Hawk College C
City Colleges of Chicago
Wilbur Wright College C
Danville Area Community College A
Illinois Central College A
Illinois Eastern Community Colleges
Wabash Valley College C, A
Illinois State University B
Illinois Valley Community College C
Sauk Valley Community College C
Waubonsee Community College C

Iowa

Hawkeye Community College A
Iowa Central Community College A
Iowa Lakes Community College C, A
Kirkwood Community College A
Northeast Iowa Community
College C, A
Western Iowa Tech Community
College C, A

Kentucky

Gateway Community and Technical
College C, A
Maysville Community and Technical
College C, A

Maine

Unity College B

Massachusetts

Fitchburg State University B
Mount Wachusett Community
College A
North Shore Community College C
Quinsigamond Community
College C, A

Michigan

Alpena Community College C
Ferris State University B
Henry Ford Community College C, A
Lake Michigan College C, A
Lansing Community College C, A
Lawrence Technological University C
Mott Community College C
St. Clair County Community
College C, A
Schoolcraft College C

Minnesota

Century College A
Dakota County Technical
College C, A
Fond du Lac Tribal and Community
College C
Lake Superior College C
Northwest Technical College C, A
St. Cloud Technical and Community
College A
South Central College A

Missouri

North Central Missouri College C, A

Montana

Montana State University
Great Falls College C, A

Nebraska

Creighton University B
Northeast Community College A

New Jersey

Brookdale Community College A
Burlington County College A
Salem Community College A

New York

New York Institute of Technology M

North Carolina

Cape Fear Community College C, A
Central Carolina Community
College C, A
Central Piedmont Community
College C, A
Lenoir Community College C, A
University of North Carolina
Charlotte M
Wayne Community College A

North Dakota

North Dakota State College of
Science C, A
Sitting Bull College A

Ohio

Cincinnati State Technical and
Community College A
Columbus State Community
College C
Edison State Community College C
Hocking College A
Northwest State Community
College C, A
Owens Community College
Toledo C, A
Sinclair Community College C, A

Oklahoma

University of Tulsa B

Oregon

Lane Community College A
Oregon Institute of Technology B
Rogue Community College C

Pennsylvania

Delaware County Community
College A
Harrisburg Area Community
College A
Luzerne County Community
College C
Williamson Free School of
Mechanical Trades A

Rhode Island

Community College of Rhode
Island C

South Dakota

Mitchell Technical Institute C, A

Tennessee

Walters State Community
College C, A

Texas

Texas State Technical College
Waco C

Washington

Grays Harbor College C, A
Lake Washington Institute of
Technology C

Wisconsin

Fox Valley Technical College A
Mid-State Technical College A
Milwaukee Area Technical College A
Northeast Wisconsin Technical
College A
Western Technical College A
Wisconsin Indianhead Technical
College A

Wyoming

Casper College C, A
Laramie County Community
College C, A

Engine machinist

Arkansas

Pulaski Technical College C

Minnesota

Pine Technical College C

Mississippi

Hinds Community College C

Engineering chemistry

Michigan

West Shore Community College A

Engineering design

Florida

Florida Institute of Technology D

Pennsylvania

Carnegie Mellon University M

Rhode Island

Johnson & Wales University
Providence B

Engineering, general

Alabama

Central Alabama Community
    College A
Gadsden State Community College A
Snead State Community College A
University of Alabama
    Birmingham M
    Huntsville M
Wallace State Community College at
    Hanceville A

Alaska

University of Alaska
    Anchorage B
    Fairbanks B, D

Arizona

Anthem College
    Phoenix A
Arizona State University M
Arizona Western College A
Cochise College A
Coconino County Community
    College A
Embry-Riddle Aeronautical University
    Prescott Campus B
GateWay Community College A
Northern Arizona University M
University of Arizona M

Arkansas

Arkansas State University B, M
Arkansas Tech University M
John Brown University B
Phillips Community College of the
    University of Arkansas A
University of Arkansas M, D

California

Allan Hancock College A
Antelope Valley College A
Biola University B
California Baptist University B
California Institute of Technology B
California National University for
    Advanced Studies B, M
California Polytechnic State
    University: San Luis Obispo M
California State Polytechnic
    University: Pomona B, M
California State University
    Fresno B, M
    Fullerton B
    Long Beach B, M
    Los Angeles B
    Northridge B, M
Canada College A
Chabot College A
Chaffey College A
Citrus College A
City College of San Francisco A
Claremont McKenna College B
College of San Mateo A
College of the Sequoias A
College of the Siskiyous A
Contra Costa College C, A
Cuyamaca College A
Cypress College A
De Anza College A
El Camino College A
Foothill College A
Fresno City College A
Fullerton College A
Hartnell College A
Harvey Mudd College B
Imperial Valley College A
Long Beach City College A
Los Angeles City College A
Los Angeles Pierce College A
Los Angeles Southwest College A
Los Angeles Trade and Technical
    College A

Los Medanos College A
Merced College A
Mills College B
Mission College A
Modesto Junior College A
Moorpark College A
Mount San Antonio College A
Orange Coast College A
Pacific Union College C, A
Pepperdine University B
Saddleback College A
San Diego City College A
San Diego Mesa College A
San Diego State University B
San Francisco State University M
San Jose State University B, M
Santa Ana College A
Santa Barbara City College A
Santa Clara University B
Santa Rosa Junior College A
Santiago Canyon College A
Shasta College A
Sierra College A
Southwestern College A
Stanford University B, M
University of California
    Davis M, D
    Irvine B, M
    Los Angeles M
University of the Pacific B
Ventura College A
West Hills College: Lemoore A
West Los Angeles College A
West Valley College A

Colorado

Colorado School of Mines B, M, D
Colorado State University B
Colorado State University
    Pueblo B
Ecotech Institute A
Fort Lewis College B
Trinidad State Junior College A
United States Air Force Academy B
University of Colorado
    Boulder M
    Colorado Springs B, M, D
    Denver M
University of Denver B, D

Connecticut

Norwalk Community College A
Trinity College B
University of Connecticut M
University of Hartford B
University of New Haven B

District of Columbia

Catholic University of America B, M
George Washington
    University B, M, D

Florida

Broward College A
Chipola College A
Daytona State College A, B
Eastern Florida State College A
Edison State College A
Embry-Riddle Aeronautical
    University M
Florida Institute of Technology B
Florida State College at
    Jacksonville A
Indian River State College A
Palm Beach State College A
Pensacola State College A
Tallahassee Community College A
University of Miami B
University of South Florida B, M, D

Georgia

Abraham Baldwin Agricultural
    College A
Andrew College A

College of Coastal Georgia A
Georgia Perimeter College A
LaGrange College B
Mercer University B
Middle Georgia State College A
Spelman College B
University of Georgia M, D
University of North Georgia A

Hawaii

University of Hawaii
    Hilo B

Idaho

Brigham Young University-Idaho A
North Idaho College A

Illinois

City Colleges of Chicago
    Harold Washington College A
    Harry S. Truman College A
    Richard J. Daley College A
    Wilbur Wright College A
College of DuPage A
College of Lake County A
Danville Area Community College A
Dominican University B
Eastern Illinois University B
Elgin Community College A
Eureka College B
Harper College A
Heartland Community College A
Highland Community College A
Illinois Central College A
Illinois Eastern Community Colleges
    Frontier Community College A
    Lincoln Trail College A
    Olney Central College A
    Wabash Valley College A
Illinois Valley Community College A
John A. Logan College A
John Wood Community College A
Kankakee Community College A
Kaskaskia College A
Kishwaukee College A
Lake Land College A
Lincoln Land Community College A
MacMurray College B
McHenry County College A
Moraine Valley Community College A
Northwestern University B
Oakton Community College A
Olivet Nazarene University B
Parkland College A
Rend Lake College A
Richland Community College A
Rock Valley College A
Sauk Valley Community College A
South Suburban College of Cook
    County A
Southern Illinois University
    Carbondale D
Southwestern Illinois College A
University of Illinois
    Chicago M
    Urbana-Champaign B
Waubonsee Community College A
Wheaton College B

Indiana

Anderson University B
Ball State University B
Bethel College B
Indiana University
    Purdue University Fort Wayne M
    Purdue University Indianapolis B
Ivy Tech Community College
    Northwest A
    Southwest A
Manchester University B
Purdue University
    Calumet B
University of Notre Dame M
University of Southern Indiana B

Iowa

Dordt College B
Ellsworth Community College A
Iowa State University B
Marshalltown Community College A
University of Iowa B

Kansas

Barton County Community College A
Benedictine College B
Butler Community College A
Coffeyville Community College A
Cowley County Community
    College A
Dodge City Community College A
Donnelly College A
Garden City Community College A
Hutchinson Community College A
Independence Community College A
Pratt Community College A
Seward County Community
    College A
Wichita State University B

Kentucky

Brescia University A
Hopkinsville Community College A

Louisiana

Bossier Parish Community College A
Delgado Community College A
Louisiana Tech University M, D
McNeese State University B, M
Southern University and Agricultural
    and Mechanical College M

Maine

Bates College B
Southern Maine Community
    College A
University of Maine B, M

Maryland

Allegany College of Maryland A
Anne Arundel Community College A
Baltimore City Community College A
College of Southern Maryland A
Community College of Baltimore
    County C, A
Frederick Community College A
Frostburg State University B
Hagerstown Community College A
Harford Community College A
Howard Community College A
Johns Hopkins University B
Loyola University Maryland B, M
Montgomery College A
Morgan State University B, M, D
Notre Dame of Maryland
    University B
Prince George's Community
    College A
United States Naval Academy B
University of Maryland
    Baltimore County B
    College Park M
    Eastern Shore B
Washington Adventist University A

Massachusetts

Berkshire Community College A
Boston University B, M
Bristol Community College A
Bunker Hill Community College A
Cape Cod Community College A
Eastern Nazarene College B
Franklin W. Olin College of
    Engineering B
Holyoke Community College A
Massachusetts Maritime Academy B
Merrimack College B, M
Mount Wachusett Community
    College A
North Shore Community College A

Northeastern University *B, M, D*
Smith College *B*
Springfield Technical Community
  College *C, A*
Tufts University *B*
University of Massachusetts
  Lowell *C*
Wellesley College *B*
Wentworth Institute of Technology *B*

Michigan

Alpena Community College *A*
Andrews University *B*
Calvin College *B*
Delta College *A*
Ferris State University *A*
Gogebic Community College *A*
Grand Rapids Community College *A*
Henry Ford Community College *A*
Hope College *B*
Kalamazoo Valley Community
  College *A*
Lake Superior State University *A*
Michigan State University *B*
Michigan Technological
  University *B, M*
Northwestern Michigan College *A*
Oakland Community College *A*
St. Clair County Community
  College *A*
Schoolcraft College *A*
University of Detroit Mercy *B, M*
University of Michigan *B, M, D*
University of Michigan
  Dearborn *B*
Washtenaw Community College *A*

Minnesota

Augsburg College *B*
Central Lakes College *A*
Hibbing Community College *A*
Itasca Community College *A*
Minnesota State Community and
  Technical College *A*
Minnesota State University
  Mankato *B, M*
Minnesota West Community and
  Technical College *A*
North Hennepin Community
  College *A*
Rochester Community and Technical
  College *A*
University of Minnesota
  Duluth *M*
University of Northwestern - St.
  Paul *B*
University of St. Thomas *B*

Mississippi

East Mississippi Community
  College *A*
Hinds Community College *A*
Holmes Community College *A*
Itawamba Community College *A*
Jackson State University *M*
Mississippi Delta Community
  College *A*
Mississippi Gulf Coast Community
  College *A*
Mississippi State University *M, D*
Northeast Mississippi Community
  College *A*
University of Mississippi *B*

Missouri

Crowder College *A*
East Central College *A*
Jefferson College *A*
Metropolitan Community College -
  Kansas City *A*
Missouri Southern State University *A*
Moberly Area Community College *A*
Ozarks Technical Community
  College *A*

St. Charles Community College *A*
St. Louis Community College *A*
Saint Louis University *B, M, D*
State Fair Community College *A*
University of Missouri
  Columbia *M*
  Kansas City *D*

Montana

Blackfeet Community College *A*
Dawson Community College *A*
Miles Community College *A*
Montana State University *D*
Montana Tech of the University of
  Montana *B, M*

Nebraska

Northeast Community College *A*
Union College *A*
University of Nebraska
  Lincoln *B, M, D*
Western Nebraska Community
  College *A*

Nevada

Great Basin College *A*
Western Nevada College *A*

New Hampshire

Dartmouth College *M, D*
Saint Anselm College *B*

New Jersey

Bergen Community College *A*
Brookdale Community College *A*
Cumberland County College *A*
Essex County College *A*
Gloucester County College *A*
Ocean County College *A*
Rowan University *M*
Stevens Institute of
  Technology *B, M, D*
Union County College *A*

New Mexico

Luna Community College *A*
Mesalands Community College *A*
New Mexico Institute of Mining and
  Technology *B*
New Mexico Junior College *A*
New Mexico State University *D*
New Mexico State University
  Carlsbad *A*
San Juan College *A*
Santa Fe Community College *A*
Southwestern Indian Polytechnic
  Institute *A*
University of New Mexico *D*

New York

Adirondack Community College *A*
City University of New York
  Borough of Manhattan Community
    College *A*
  College of Staten Island *A, B*
  Kingsborough Community
    College *A*
Clarkson University *B*
Cooper Union for the Advancement
  of Science and Art *B*
Cornell University *B*
Dutchess Community College *A*
Erie Community College *A*
Finger Lakes Community College *A*
Fulton-Montgomery Community
  College *A*
Hudson Valley Community College *A*
Jamestown Community College *A*
Jefferson Community College *A*
Mohawk Valley Community
  College *A*
Nassau Community College *A*
Orange County Community
  College *A*

Rensselaer Polytechnic Institute *B, D*
Rochester Institute of
  Technology *A, M, D*
Rockland Community College *A*
SUNY
  College of Agriculture and
    Technology at Morrisville *A*
  College of Environmental Science
    and Forestry *B*
  College of Technology at Alfred *A*
  College of Technology at
    Canton *A, T*
  Maritime College *A*
  University at Binghamton *B*
  University at Buffalo *B, M*
  University at Stony Brook *B*
Syracuse University *B*
Tompkins Cortland Community
  College *A*
Ulster County Community College *A*
University of Rochester *B*
Westchester Community College *A*

North Carolina

Blue Ridge Community College *C*
East Carolina University *B*
Elon University *B*
Livingstone College *B*
North Carolina Agricultural and
  Technical State University *B*
North Carolina State University *B, M*
St. Augustine's University *B*
University of North Carolina
  Asheville *B*
  Charlotte *M*
Western Piedmont Community
  College *A*

North Dakota

North Dakota State University *D*
University of Mary *B*
University of North Dakota *D*

Ohio

Case Western Reserve
  University *B, M*
Cleveland State University *D*
James A. Rhodes State College *C, A*
Lorain County Community College *A*
Miami University
  Oxford *B*
Muskingum University *B*
Ohio Northern University *B*
Ohio State University
  Columbus Campus *M*
Ohio University *M*
Sinclair Community College *A*
Terra State Community College *A*
University of Akron *B, M, D*
University of Cincinnati *B*
University of Dayton *M*
Washington State Community
  College *A*
Wright State University *D*
Youngstown State University *B, M*

Oklahoma

Eastern Oklahoma State College *A*
Oklahoma Christian University *M*
Oklahoma City Community
  College *A*
Oral Roberts University *B*
Rose State College *A*
Southwestern Oklahoma State
  University *B*
Tulsa Community College *A*
University of Oklahoma *B, M, D*

Oregon

Central Oregon Community
  College *A*
George Fox University *B*
Linn-Benton Community College *A*

Southwestern Oregon Community
  College *A*
Treasure Valley Community
  College *A*

Pennsylvania

Arcadia University *B*
Butler County Community College *A*
Carnegie Mellon University *B, M, D*
Chatham University *B*
Community College of
  Philadelphia *A*
Delaware County Community
  College *A*
Drexel University *B, M*
Elizabethtown College *B*
Geneva College *A, B*
Harrisburg Area Community
  College *A*
Lafayette College *B*
Lehigh Carbon Community College *A*
Lincoln University *B*
Messiah College *B*
Northampton Community College *A*
Penn State
  Abington *B*
  Altoona *C*
  Berks *C*
  Brandywine *C, B*
  DuBois *B*
  Fayette, The Eberly Campus *C*
  Harrisburg *C*
  Hazleton *C, B*
  University Park *C*
  Wilkes-Barre *C*
Philadelphia University *B*
Reading Area Community College *A*
Robert Morris University *D*
St. Francis University *B*
St. Vincent College *B*
Seton Hill University *B*
Swarthmore College *B*
Temple University *B, D*
University of Pittsburgh
  Bradford *B*
Valley Forge Military College *A*
Waynesburg University *B*
Westminster College *B*
Widener University *B, M*

Puerto Rico

Inter American University of Puerto
  Rico
  Barranquitas Campus *B*
University of Puerto Rico
  Mayaguez *B*
  Ponce *A*

Rhode Island

Community College of Rhode
  Island *A*
Roger Williams University *B*

South Carolina

Bob Jones University *B*

South Dakota

South Dakota State University *M*

Tennessee

Jackson State Community College *A*
Maryville College *B*
Southern Adventist University *A*
Tennessee State University *B, M*
University of Memphis *D*
University of Tennessee
  Chattanooga *B, M*
  Martin *B*

Texas

Abilene Christian University *B*
Amarillo College *A*
Angelina College *A*
Austin Community College *A*

Baylor University *B, M*
Brazosport College *A*
Central Texas College *A*
Clarendon College *A*
Coastal Bend College *A*
College of the Mainland *A*
Collin County Community College
 District *A*
El Paso Community College *A*
Galveston College *A*
Grayson College *A*
Hill College *A*
Kilgore College *A*
Lamar University *B, M, D*
Laredo Community College *A*
LeTourneau University *B*
Lubbock Christian University *B*
Midwestern State University *B*
Navarro College *A*
Paris Junior College *A*
Prairie View A&M University *M*
St. Mary's University *M*
San Antonio College *A*
San Jacinto College *A*
Schreiner University *B*
South Plains College *A*
South Texas College *A*
Southern Methodist University *M, D*
Tarrant County College *A*
Temple College *A*
Texarkana College *A*
Texas A&M University *M, D*
Texas A&M University
 Kingsville *M*
Texas Christian University *B*
Texas State Technical College
 Harlingen *A*
Texas Tech University *M*
Trinity Valley Community College *A*
Tyler Junior College *A*
University of Texas
 El Paso *M*
Western Texas College *A*

Utah

Snow College *A*
University of Utah *B*
Utah State University *A*
Weber State University *A, B*

Vermont

Saint Michael's College *B*
University of Vermont *B*

Virginia

Danville Community College *A*
Hampton University *B*
J. Sargeant Reynolds Community
 College *A*
James Madison University *B*
John Tyler Community College *A*
Lord Fairfax Community College *A*
New River Community College *A*
Old Dominion University *B, M, D*
Piedmont Virginia Community
 College *A*
Southwest Virginia Community
 College *A*
Thomas Nelson Community
 College *A*
Tidewater Community College *A*
University of Virginia *B*
Virginia Commonwealth
 University *M, D*
Virginia Western Community
 College *C, A*

Washington

Centralia College *A*
Gonzaga University *B*
Highline Community College *A*
Lower Columbia College *A*
Shoreline Community College *A*
South Seattle Community College *A*

University of Washington *B, M*
Walla Walla University *B*
Washington State University *M*
Whitman College *B*
Whitworth University *B*
Yakima Valley Community College *A*

West Virginia

Marshall University *B, M*
West Virginia University *M, D*

Wisconsin

Beloit College *B*
Milwaukee School of
 Engineering *B, M*
Northland College *B*
University of Wisconsin
 Madison *M*
 Milwaukee *C, B, M, D*
 Platteville *B, M*

Wyoming

Casper College *A*
Central Wyoming College *A*
Laramie County Community
 College *A*
Northwest College *A*
Sheridan College *A*
Western Wyoming Community
 College *A*

Engineering/industrial management

Arizona

Arizona State University *B*
Central Arizona College *A*
GateWay Community College *C*
University of Arizona *B, M*

Arkansas

Arkansas State University *M*
University of Arkansas *M*

California

California Polytechnic State
 University: San Luis Obispo *M*
California State Polytechnic
 University: Pomona *M*
California State University
 Chico *B*
 East Bay *B, M*
National University *M*
Santa Clara University *M*
Stanford University *B, M, D*
University of the Pacific *B*

Colorado

University of Denver *M*

Connecticut

Naugatuck Valley Community
 College *A*
University of Bridgeport *M, D*
University of New Haven *M*

Delaware

Delaware Technical Community
 College
 Stanton/Wilmington Campus *A*

District of Columbia

Catholic University of America *M*
George Washington University *M, D*

Florida

Florida Institute of Technology *M*
Palm Beach State College *A*
Tallahassee Community College *A*
University of Central Florida *M*
University of Miami *M, D*

Georgia

Georgia Southern University *T*

Illinois

Illinois Institute of Technology *B, M*
Northern Illinois University *M*
Northwestern University *M*
University of Illinois
 Chicago *B*

Indiana

Indiana Institute of Technology *M*
Indiana University
 Purdue University Fort Wayne *M*
 Purdue University Indianapolis *M*
Purdue University *A, B*
Rose-Hulman Institute of
 Technology *M*

Kansas

Kansas State University *B, M*
Pittsburg State University *B*
University of Kansas *M*
Washburn University *A*
Wichita State University *M*

Kentucky

Northern Kentucky University *C*
University of Louisville *M*
Western Kentucky University *M*

Louisiana

Louisiana Tech University *M*
University of New Orleans *M*

Massachusetts

Massachusetts Maritime Academy *B*
University of Massachusetts
 Amherst *M*
Western New England
 University *M, D*
Worcester Polytechnic Institute *B*

Michigan

Baker College
 Muskegon *B*
Central Michigan University *M*
Eastern Michigan University *B, M*
Lake Superior State University *B*
Lawrence Technological
 University *B, M*
Northern Michigan University *M*
Oakland University *M*
University of Michigan
 Dearborn *M*
Wayne State University *M*
Western Michigan University *B, M*

Minnesota

Saint Cloud State University *M*
University of Minnesota
 Duluth *M*
University of St. Thomas *M*

Missouri

Grantham University *A, B*
Missouri State University *B, M*
Missouri University of Science and
 Technology *B, M, D*
Southeast Missouri State University *M*
Washington University in St. Louis *M*

Montana

Montana State University *M*

New Jersey

New Jersey Institute of
 Technology *M*
Stevens Institute of
 Technology *B, M, D*

New Mexico

New Mexico Institute of Mining and
 Technology *M*

New York

Clarkson University *B, M*
Columbia University *B*
Cornell University *M*
New York Institute of Technology *M*
Rensselaer Polytechnic Institute *B, M*
Rochester Institute of Technology *M*
SUNY
 College at Fredonia *B*
 College of Technology at Canton *B*
Syracuse University *M*
United States Merchant Marine
 Academy *M*
United States Military Academy *B*

North Carolina

Central Piedmont Community
 College *C, A*
Haywood Community College *A*
Mitchell Community College *A*
North Carolina Agricultural and
 Technical State University *B*
Pitt Community College *C, A*
University of North Carolina
 Charlotte *M*

Ohio

Bowling Green State University *M*
Case Western Reserve University *M*
Miami University
 Oxford *B*
Northwest State Community
 College *A*
Ohio University
 Chillicothe Campus *M*
Terra State Community College *C*
University of Dayton *M*

Oklahoma

Northeastern State University *M*
University of Tulsa *M*

Oregon

Portland State University *M, D*

Pennsylvania

Drexel University *M*
Gannon University *M*
Grove City College *B*
Philadelphia University *M*
Point Park University *M*
Robert Morris University *M*
University of Scranton *B*
Wilkes University *B, M*

Puerto Rico

Turabo University *B*
University of Puerto Rico
 Mayaguez *M*

South Carolina

Citadel *M*
University of South Carolina
 Upstate *B*

South Dakota

South Dakota School of Mines and
 Technology *M*
South Dakota State University *B, M*

Tennessee

Christian Brothers University *M*
Middle Tennessee State University *B*
University of Tennessee
 Chattanooga *B, M*

Texas

Lamar University *B, M*
St. Mary's University *B, M*

Southern Methodist University *M, D*
Texas A&M University
  Kingsville *B, M*
University of Houston
  Clear Lake *M*
University of Texas
  Arlington *M*
  Austin *M*
  Pan American *M*
  Tyler *M*
University of the Incarnate Word *B*

Virginia
Sweet Briar College *B*
University of Management and
  Technology *A, B, M*

Washington
Saint Martin's University *M*
Washington State University *M*

West Virginia
West Virginia University at
  Parkersburg *A, B*

Wisconsin
Northeast Wisconsin Technical
  College *A*
University of Wisconsin
  Stout *M*

Engineering mechanics

Alabama
University of Alabama *M*

California
California State University
  Northridge *B, M*
University of California
  San Diego *B, M, D*

Colorado
United States Air Force Academy *B*

Georgia
Georgia Institute of Technology *M*

Illinois
Northwestern University *M, D*
University of Illinois
  Urbana-Champaign *B, M, D*

Iowa
Iowa State University *M, D*
Southeastern Community College *A*

Maryland
Johns Hopkins University *B*

Massachusetts
Boston University *M*
Smith College *B*

Michigan
Michigan State University *M, D*
Michigan Technological University *M*
Washtenaw Community College *A*

Missouri
Missouri University of Science and
  Technology *B, M, D*

Nebraska
University of Nebraska
  Lincoln *M*

New York
Columbia University *B, M, D*
Cornell University *M, D*
Rensselaer Polytechnic Institute *M, D*

Ohio
Case Western Reserve University *M*
Cleveland State University *M*
Ohio State University
  Columbus Campus *M*
University of Cincinnati *M, D*
University of Dayton *M*

Pennsylvania
Carnegie Mellon University *M, D*
Lehigh University *B*
Penn State
  University Park *M*

South Carolina
Clemson University *M, D*

Tennessee
Lipscomb University *B*

Texas
San Jacinto College *A*
University of Texas
  Austin *M, D*

Utah
University of Utah *M*

Virginia
Virginia Polytechnic Institute and
  State University *B, M, D*

Wisconsin
Northcentral Technical College *A*
University of Wisconsin
  Madison *B, M, D*

Engineering physics/
applied physics

Alabama
Samford University *B*

Arkansas
Arkansas Tech University *B*
Henderson State University *B*

California
California Institute of
  Technology *B, M, D*
California State University
  San Marcos *B*
Loyola Marymount University *B*
Point Loma Nazarene University *B*
Santa Clara University *B*
University of California
  Berkeley *B*
  Davis *B*
  San Diego *B, M, D*
University of the Pacific *B*
Westmont College *B*
Whittier College *B*

Colorado
Adams State University *B*
Colorado School of Mines *B, M, D*
Colorado State University *B*
Fort Lewis College *B*
University of Colorado
  Boulder *B*

Connecticut
University of Connecticut *B*
Yale University *B, M, D*

Delaware
Delaware State University *B*

Florida
Embry-Riddle Aeronautical
  University *B, M, D*
Jacksonville University *B*

Georgia
Emory University *B*
Morehouse College *B*

Idaho
Northwest Nazarene University *B*

Illinois
Augustana College *B*
Bradley University *B*
Illinois Institute of Technology *B, M*
University of Illinois
  Chicago *B*
  Urbana-Champaign *B, M, D*

Indiana
Rose-Hulman Institute of
  Technology *B*
Taylor University *B*

Iowa
Loras College *B*
Morningside College *B*
St. Ambrose University *B*
University of Northern Iowa *B*

Kansas
University of Kansas *B*

Kentucky
Murray State University *B, T*

Louisiana
Tulane University *B, M, D*

Maine
University of Maine *B, M*

Maryland
Morgan State University *B*

Massachusetts
Eastern Nazarene College *B*
Gordon College *B*
Tufts University *B*
University of Massachusetts
  Boston *B*
Worcester Polytechnic Institute *B*

Michigan
Eastern Michigan University *B*
Kettering University *B*
Lansing Community College *A*
Michigan Technological University *D*
Oakland University *B*
University of Michigan *B*
University of Michigan
  Flint *B*

Minnesota
St. Mary's University of Minnesota *B*

Mississippi
Mississippi College *B*

Missouri
Drury University *B, T*
Saint Louis University *B*
Southeast Missouri State University *B*

Nevada
University of Nevada
  Reno *B*

New Hampshire
Dartmouth College *B*
Saint Anselm College *B*

New Jersey
Stevens Institute of Technology *B, M*

New Mexico
New Mexico State University *B*

New York
Barnard College *B*
Columbia University *M, D*
Cornell University *B, M, D*
Houghton College *B*
Rensselaer Polytechnic
  Institute *B, M, D*
SUNY
  University at Buffalo *B*

North Carolina
Elon University *B*

Ohio
Case Western Reserve University *B*
John Carroll University *B*
Miami University
  Oxford *B*
Ohio State University
  Columbus Campus *B*
Wright State University *B*
Xavier University *B*

Oklahoma
Oral Roberts University *B*
Southwestern Oklahoma State
  University *B*
University of Central Oklahoma *B, M*
University of Oklahoma *B, M, D*
University of Tulsa *B, M*

Oregon
Linfield College *B*
Oregon State University *B*

Pennsylvania
Carnegie Mellon University *D*
Juniata College *B*
Lehigh University *B*
University of Pittsburgh *B*

Rhode Island
Brown University *B*
Providence College *B*

South Dakota
Augustana College *B*

Tennessee
Belmont University *B*
Carson-Newman University *B*
Christian Brothers University *B*
Trevecca Nazarene University *B*
Union University *B*

Texas
Angelo State University *B*
Tarleton State University *B*
University of Texas
  Brownsville *B*

Virginia
Randolph College *B*
Randolph-Macon College *B*
University of Virginia *M, D*
Washington and Lee University *B*

Washington
Whitworth University *B*

Wisconsin
Carroll University *B*
University of Wisconsin
  Madison *B*
  Platteville *B*

Engineering science

Arizona
Arizona State University *M*
Northern Arizona University *D*

California
California Polytechnic State
    University: San Luis Obispo *B*
San Diego State University *D*
University of California
    Berkeley *B*
    San Diego *B*

Colorado
Colorado State University *B*
University of Colorado
    Denver *D*

Connecticut
Asnuntuck Community College *A*
Gateway Community College *A*
Manchester Community College *A*
Middlesex Community College *A*
Tunxis Community College *A*
Yale University *B*

District of Columbia
George Washington University *M, D*

Florida
State College of Florida, Manatee-
    Sarasota *A*
University of Miami *B*

Georgia
Morehouse College *B*

Idaho
Idaho State University *D*

Illinois
Benedictine University *B*
Northwestern University *B, M*
Principia College *B*
South Suburban College of Cook
    County *A*

Indiana
Bethel College *B*

Iowa
Wartburg College *B*

Kansas
Garden City Community College *A*
University of Kansas *M, D*

Kentucky
Eastern Kentucky University *B*

Louisiana
Louisiana State University and
    Agricultural and Mechanical
    College *M, D*
University of New Orleans *M, D*

Massachusetts
Boston University *D*
Bristol Community College *A*
Greenfield Community College *A*
Harvard College *B, M, D*
Middlesex Community College *A*
Northern Essex Community
    College *A*
Smith College *B*
Tufts University *B*
University of Massachusetts
    Dartmouth *D*

Michigan
Glen Oaks Community College *A*
University of Michigan *B*

University of Michigan
    Flint *B*
Washtenaw Community College *A*

Minnesota
Bethel University *B*
Concordia University St. Paul *B*

Mississippi
University of Mississippi *M, D*

New Hampshire
Dartmouth College *B*

New Jersey
Camden County College *A*
College of New Jersey *B*
County College of Morris *A*
Gloucester County College *A*
Hudson County Community
    College *A*
Middlesex County College *A*
New Jersey Institute of
    Technology *B, M*
Passaic County Community College *A*
Raritan Valley Community College *A*
Rutgers, The State University of New
    Jersey
    New Brunswick/Piscataway
        Campus *B*

New Mexico
University of New Mexico *B*

New York
Broome Community College *A*
Clarkson University *M, D*
Corning Community College *A*
Finger Lakes Community College *A*
Hofstra University *B*
Hudson Valley Community College *A*
Monroe Community College *A*
Onondaga Community College *A*
Rensselaer Polytechnic
    Institute *B, M, D*
Rochester Institute of Technology *A*
Suffolk County Community College *A*
University of Rochester *B*
Westchester Community College *A*

Ohio
Cleveland State University *B*
Miami University
    Oxford *M*
Muskingum University *B*
University of Toledo *M, D*
Wright State University *B, M*

Oklahoma
Western Oklahoma State College *A*

Pennsylvania
Carnegie Mellon University *M*
Montgomery County Community
    College *A*
Penn State
    Abington *B*
    Altoona *B*
    Beaver *B*
    Berks *B*
    Brandywine *B*
    DuBois *B*
    Erie, The Behrend College *B*
    Fayette, The Eberly Campus *B*
    Greater Allegheny *B*
    Harrisburg *B, M*
    Hazleton *B*
    Lehigh Valley *B*
    Mont Alto *B*
    New Kensington *B*
    Schuylkill *B*
    Shenango *B*
    University Park *B, M, D*
    Wilkes-Barre *B*

Worthington Scranton *B*
York *B*
University of Pittsburgh *B*
University of Pittsburgh
    Bradford *B*
Valley Forge Military College *A*

South Carolina
University of South Carolina
    Columbia *B*

Tennessee
Lipscomb University *B*
University of Tennessee
    Knoxville *M, D*
Vanderbilt University *B*

Texas
Abilene Christian University *B*
Houston Community College
    System *A*
St. Mary's University *B*
Texas Tech University *D*
Trinity University *B*

Utah
Southern Utah University *B*

Virginia
Sweet Briar College *B*

Washington
Pacific Lutheran University *B*
Seattle Pacific University *B*
Washington State University *D*

West Virginia
Wheeling Jesuit University *B*

Engineering technology, general

Alabama
Jefferson State Community
    College *C, A*
Northeast Alabama Community
    College *C, A*
Snead State Community College *A*

Arizona
Chandler-Gilbert Community
    College *A*
Glendale Community College *A*

Arkansas
East Arkansas Community College *C*
Ozarka College *A*

California
Allan Hancock College *A*
American River College *A*
Bakersfield College *A*
California Maritime Academy *B*
California State Polytechnic
    University: Pomona *B*
Cerro Coso Community College *C, A*
City College of San Francisco *A*
Hartnell College *A*
National University *A*
Norco College *A*
Ohlone College *C*
San Joaquin Delta College *A*
Santa Barbara City College *C, A*

Colorado
Aims Community College *C, A*
Arapahoe Community College *C, A*
Pueblo Community College *C, A*

Connecticut
Central Connecticut State
    University *M*

Middlesex Community College *C, A*
Naugatuck Valley Community
    College *C, A*
Northwestern Connecticut
    Community College *A*
Norwalk Community College *A*
Three Rivers Community College *A*
University of Hartford *B*

Florida
Gulf Coast State College *C, A*
Hillsborough Community College *A*
Miami Dade College *C, A*
Polk State College *A*
St. Petersburg College *C, A*
South Florida State College *A*
Tallahassee Community College *C*
University of West Florida *B*

Georgia
Atlanta Metropolitan College *A*
Berry College *B*
Darton College *A*
Middle Georgia State College *A*
North Georgia Technical College *A*
Southern Polytechnic State
    University *C, B, M*

Illinois
Illinois State University *B*
Northern Illinois University *B*
Southern Illinois University
    Carbondale *B*

Indiana
Grace College *B*
Indiana University
    Purdue University Fort Wayne *M*
Trine University *A, B*
Vincennes University *A*

Iowa
Dordt College *B*
William Penn University *B*

Kansas
Colby Community College *A*
Kansas State University *A, B*
Northwest Kansas Technical
    College *C, A*
Pittsburg State University *M*

Kentucky
Bluegrass Community and Technical
    College *C, A*
Elizabethtown Community and
    Technical College *C, A*
Gateway Community and Technical
    College *C, A*
Hopkinsville Community
    College *C, A*
Jefferson Community and Technical
    College *C, A*
Lindsey Wilson College *A*
Madisonville Community
    College *C, A*
Murray State University *M*
Northern Kentucky University *A, M*
Owensboro Community and
    Technical College *C, A*

Louisiana
McNeese State University *B*
Southeastern Louisiana University *B*

Maine
Maine Maritime Academy *B*

Maryland
Community College of Baltimore
    County *C*
Harford Community College *A*

University of Maryland
   Eastern Shore *B*

Massachusetts

Quinsigamond Community College *A*
Wentworth Institute of
   Technology *A, B*

Michigan

Bay de Noc Community College *A*
Eastern Michigan University *M, D*
Glen Oaks Community College *C*
Grand Rapids Community College *A*
Lawrence Technological University *B*
Michigan Technological
   University *A, B*
Mid Michigan Community College *A*
Saginaw Valley State University *B*
Southwestern Michigan College *A*
Spring Arbor University *B*
Wayne State University *M*

Minnesota

Bemidji State University *B*
Itasca Community College *A*
Ridgewater College *C, A*
Saint Cloud State University *C*

Mississippi

University of Southern Mississippi *M*

Missouri

Drury University *B*
Lincoln University *A*
Metropolitan Community College -
   Kansas City *A*
Southeast Missouri State University *B*

Montana

Stone Child College *C*

Nebraska

Wayne State College *B*

Nevada

College of Southern Nevada *A*

New Jersey

Bergen Community College *A*
Cumberland County College *C, A*
New Jersey Institute of Technology *B*

New Mexico

Eastern New Mexico University *B*
New Mexico State University *A, B*
San Juan College *A*

New York

New York Institute of Technology *B*

North Carolina

Western Carolina University *B*

North Dakota

Bismarck State College *A*
Lake Region State College *C, A*

Ohio

Bowling Green State University:
   Firelands College *A*
Cleveland State University *B*
Columbus State Community
   College *C*
James A. Rhodes State College *A*
Kent State University *B, M*
Kent State University
   Tuscarawas *A*
Lorain County Community College *A*
Miami University
   Hamilton *B*
   Oxford *A, B*
University of Dayton *B*
University of Toledo *A*

Wright State University *A*
Wright State University: Lake
   Campus *A*
Youngstown State University *A, B*

Oklahoma

Oklahoma State University
   Institute of Technology:
      Okmulgee *A*
   Oklahoma City *A*

Pennsylvania

Bucks County Community College *A*
California University of
   Pennsylvania *B, M*
Carnegie Mellon University *M*
Drexel University *B, M*
Edinboro University of
   Pennsylvania *B*
Pennsylvania Highlands Community
   College *A*
Pennsylvania Institute of
   Technology *A*
Temple University *B*

Puerto Rico

University of Puerto Rico
   Arecibo *A*

Rhode Island

Roger Williams University *B*

South Carolina

Piedmont Technical College *C, A*
Technical College of the
   Lowcountry *C*
Tri-County Technical College *A*
York Technical College *A*

Tennessee

Austin Peay State University *B*
Chattanooga State Community
   College *A*
East Tennessee State University *B, M*
Middle Tennessee State University *B*
University of Memphis *B, M*

Texas

Collin County Community College
   District *A*
North Lake College *C, A*
Tarleton State University *B*
Texas State University *B*
Texas Tech University *B*
University of Houston *M*
University of North Texas *M*
West Texas A&M University *B, M*

Utah

Brigham Young University *M*
Southern Utah University *A, B*

Virginia

Germanna Community College *C*
John Tyler Community College *C*
Old Dominion University *B*
Rappahannock Community College *A*
Southwest Virginia Community
   College *A*
Virginia State University *B*

Washington

Clover Park Technical College *C, A*
Columbia Basin College *A*
Edmonds Community College *A*
Lake Washington Institute of
   Technology *A*
Northwest Indian College *C*

West Virginia

West Virginia University Institute of
   Technology *B*

West Virginia University at
   Parkersburg *C, A*

Wisconsin

College of Menominee Nation *A*
University of Wisconsin
   Stout *B*

English language and literature

Alabama

Alabama Agricultural and Mechanical
   University *B*
Alabama State University *B*
Athens State University *B*
Auburn University *B, M, D*
Auburn University at Montgomery *B*
Birmingham-Southern College *B*
Calhoun Community College *A*
Faulkner State Community College *A*
Faulkner University *B, T*
Gadsden State Community College *A*
Huntingdon College *B*
Jacksonville State University *B, M*
Judson College *B*
Miles College *B*
Oakwood University *B*
Samford University *B*
Spring Hill College *B, T*
Stillman College *B*
Talladega College *B*
Troy University *B*
Tuskegee University *B*
University of Alabama *B, M, D*
University of Alabama
   Birmingham *B, M*
   Huntsville *B, M*
University of Mobile *B*
University of Montevallo *B, M, T*
University of North Alabama *B, M*
University of South Alabama *B, M*
University of West Alabama *B, T*

Alaska

University of Alaska
   Anchorage *B, M*
   Fairbanks *B, M*
   Southeast *B*

Arizona

Arizona State University *B, M, D*
Arizona Western College *A*
Central Arizona College *A*
Cochise College *A*
Eastern Arizona College *A*
Grand Canyon University *B*
Mohave Community College *A*
Northern Arizona University *B, M*
South Mountain Community
   College *A*
University of Arizona *B, M, D*

Arkansas

Arkansas State University *B, M*
Arkansas Tech University *B, M*
Central Baptist College *B*
Harding University *B*
Henderson State University *B*
Hendrix College *B*
John Brown University *B*
Lyon College *B*
Ouachita Baptist University *B*
Philander Smith College *B*
Phillips Community College of the
   University of Arkansas *A*
Southern Arkansas University *B*
University of Arkansas *B, M, D*
University of Arkansas
   Fort Smith *B*
   Little Rock *B*
   Monticello *B*
   Pine Bluff *B*

University of Central Arkansas *B, M*
University of the Ozarks *B, T*
Williams Baptist College *B*

California

Allan Hancock College *A*
Azusa Pacific University *B*
Bakersfield College *A*
Berkeley City College *A*
Biola University *B*
Butte College *A*
Cabrillo College *A*
California Baptist University *B*
California Institute of Technology *B*
California Lutheran University *B*
California Polytechnic
   University: San Luis Obispo *B, M*
California State Polytechnic
   University: Pomona *B, M*
California State University
   Bakersfield *B, M*
   Channel Islands *B*
   Chico *C, B, M*
   Dominguez Hills *B, M*
   East Bay *B, M*
   Fresno *B, M*
   Fullerton *B, M, T*
   Long Beach *B, M, T*
   Los Angeles *B, M*
   Northridge *B, M*
   Sacramento *B, M*
   San Bernardino *B*
   San Marcos *B, M*
   Stanislaus *B, M*
Canada College *A*
Cerritos College *A*
Chabot College *A*
Chaffey College *A*
Chapman University *B, M*
Citrus College *C, A*
Claremont McKenna College *B*
College of Alameda *A*
College of Marin *A*
College of San Mateo *A*
College of the Canyons *A*
College of the Desert *A*
College of the Sequoias *A*
College of the Siskiyous *A*
Columbia College *A*
Concordia University Irvine *B*
Contra Costa College *A*
Copper Mountain College *A*
Crafton Hills College *A*
Cypress College *A*
De Anza College *A*
Diablo Valley College *A*
Dominican University of California *B*
El Camino College *A*
Feather River College *A*
Folsom Lake College *A*
Foothill College *A*
Fresno City College *A*
Fullerton College *A*
Gavilan College *A*
Glendale Community College *A*
Golden West College *A*
Grossmont College *A*
Hartnell College *A*
Holy Names University *B*
Hope International University *B*
Humboldt State University *B, M*
Imperial Valley College *A*
La Sierra University *B, M*
Lake Tahoe Community College *A*
Laney College *A*
Lassen Community College *A*
Long Beach City College *A*
Los Angeles City College *A*
Los Angeles Mission College *A*
Los Angeles Southwest College *A*
Los Angeles Valley College *A*
Loyola Marymount University *B, M*
Master's College *B*
Mendocino College *A*
Merced College *A*

Merritt College *A*
Mills College *B, M*
Modesto Junior College *A*
Monterey Peninsula College *A*
Mount St. Mary's College *B*
Napa Valley College *A*
National University *B, M*
Notre Dame de Namur
     University *B, M*
Occidental College *B*
Orange Coast College *A*
Oxnard College *A*
Pacific Union College *C, B, T*
Palo Verde College *A*
Palomar College *A*
Pepperdine University *B*
Pitzer College *B*
Point Loma Nazarene University *B*
Pomona College *B*
Porterville College *A*
Providence Christian College *B*
Reedley College *A*
Rio Hondo College *A*
Saddleback College *A*
St. Mary's College of California *B*
San Deigo Miramar College
     San Diego Miramar College *A*
San Diego Christian College *B*
San Diego City College *A*
San Diego State University *B, M*
San Francisco State University *B, M*
San Joaquin Delta College *A*
San Jose State University *B, M*
Santa Ana College *A*
Santa Barbara City College *A*
Santa Clara University *B*
Santa Rosa Junior College *A*
Santiago Canyon College *A*
Scripps College *B*
Sierra College *A*
Simpson University *B*
Skyline College *A*
Solano Community College *A*
Sonoma State University *B, M*
Southwestern College *A*
Stanford University *B, M, D*
Taft College *A*
University of California
     Berkeley *B, D*
     Davis *B, M, D*
     Irvine *B, M, D*
     Los Angeles *B, M, D*
     Merced *B*
     Riverside *B, M, D*
     San Diego *B*
     Santa Barbara *B, M, D*
     Santa Cruz *B, M, D*
University of La Verne *B*
University of Phoenix
     Bay Area *B*
     Central Valley *B*
     Sacramento Valley *B*
     San Diego *B*
University of Redlands *B*
University of San Diego *B*
University of San Francisco *B*
University of Southern
     California *B, M, D*
University of the Pacific *B*
University of the West *B*
Vanguard University of Southern
     California *B*
West Los Angeles College *A*
West Valley College *A*
Westmont College *B*
Whittier College *B*
William Jessup University *B*
Woodland Community College *A*
Yuba College *A*

Colorado

Adams State University *B*
Colorado Christian University *B*
Colorado College *B*
Colorado Heights University *C*

Colorado Mesa University *B*
Colorado Mountain College *A*
Colorado State University *B, M*
Colorado State University
     Pueblo *B*
Fort Lewis College *B*
Metropolitan State University of
     Denver *B, T*
Naropa University *B*
Regis University *B*
United States Air Force Academy *B*
University of Colorado
     Boulder *B, M, D*
     Colorado Springs *B*
     Denver *B, M*
University of Denver *B, M, D*
University of Northern
     Colorado *B, M, T*
University of Phoenix
     Denver *B*
Western State Colorado University *B*

Connecticut

Albertus Magnus College *B*
Central Connecticut State
     University *B, M*
Connecticut College *B*
Eastern Connecticut State
     University *B*
Fairfield University *B*
Quinnipiac University *B*
Sacred Heart University *B*
Southern Connecticut State
     University *B, M*
Trinity College *B, M*
University of Bridgeport *B*
University of Connecticut *B, M, D*
University of Hartford *B*
University of New Haven *B*
University of Saint Joseph *B*
Wesleyan University *B*
Western Connecticut State
     University *B, M*
Yale University *B, M, D*

Delaware

Delaware State University *B*
Goldey-Beacom College *B*
University of Delaware *B, M, D*
Wesley College *B*

District of Columbia

American University *M*
Catholic University of
     America *B, M, D*
Gallaudet University *B*
George Washington University *B*
Georgetown University *B, M*
Howard University *B, M, D*
Trinity Washington University *B*
University of the District of
     Columbia *B, M*

Florida

Ave Maria University *B*
Baptist College of Florida *B*
Barry University *B*
Bethune-Cookman University *B*
Broward College *A*
Clearwater Christian College *B*
Eckerd College *B*
Flagler College *B*
Florida Agricultural and Mechanical
     University *B*
Florida Atlantic University *B, M*
Florida Gulf Coast University *B, M*
Florida International University *B, M*
Florida Memorial University *B*
Florida Southern College *B*
Florida State University *M, D*
Indian River State College *A*
Jacksonville University *B*
Miami Dade College *A*
New College of Florida *B*

Nova Southeastern University *B*
Palm Beach Atlantic University *B*
Palm Beach State College *A*
Pensacola State College *A*
Rollins College *B*
Saint Leo University *B*
Saint Thomas University *B*
South Florida State College *A*
Southeastern University *B*
Stetson University *B, M*
University of Central Florida *B, M*
University of Florida *B, M, D*
University of Miami *B, M, D*
University of North Florida *B, M*
University of Phoenix
     Central Florida *B*
     North Florida *B*
     South Florida *B*
     West Florida *B*
University of South Florida *B, M, D*
University of South Florida
     Saint Petersburg *B*
     Sarasota-Manatee *B*
University of Tampa *A, B*
University of West Florida *B, M*
Warner University *B*

Georgia

Abraham Baldwin Agricultural
     College *A*
Agnes Scott College *B*
Albany State University *B*
Armstrong Atlantic State University *B*
Atlanta Metropolitan College *A*
Bainbridge College *A*
Berry College *B*
Brenau University *B*
Brewton-Parker College *B*
Clark Atlanta University *B, M, D*
Clayton State University *B*
College of Coastal Georgia *A*
Columbus State University *B*
Covenant College *B*
Dalton State College *B*
Darton College *A*
East Georgia State College *A*
Emmanuel College *B*
Emory University *B, D*
Fort Valley State University *B*
Georgia College and State
     University *B, M*
Georgia Gwinnett College *B*
Georgia Highlands College *A*
Georgia Perimeter College *A*
Georgia Regents University *B*
Georgia Southern University *B, M*
Georgia Southwestern State
     University *B, T*
Georgia State University *B, M, D*
Gordon College *A*
Kennesaw State University *B*
LaGrange College *B*
Mercer University *B*
Middle Georgia State College *A, B*
Morehouse College *B*
Oglethorpe University *B*
Paine College *B*
Piedmont College *B*
Point University *B*
Reinhardt University *B*
Savannah State University *B*
Shorter University *B, T*
South Georgia State College *A*
Spelman College *B*
Thomas University *B*
Toccoa Falls College *B*
Truett-McConnell College *B*
University of Georgia *B, M, D*
University of North Georgia *A, B*
University of West Georgia *B, M*
Valdosta State University *B, M*
Wesleyan College *B*
Young Harris College *B*

Hawaii

Brigham Young University-Hawaii *B*
Chaminade University of Honolulu *B*
Hawaii Pacific University *B*
University of Hawaii
     Hilo *B*
     Manoa *B, M, D*
     West Oahu *B*

Idaho

Boise State University *B, M, T*
Brigham Young University-Idaho *B*
College of Idaho *B*
College of Southern Idaho *A*
College of Western Idaho *A*
Idaho State University *B, M, D*
Lewis-Clark State College *B*
North Idaho College *A*
Northwest Nazarene University *B*
University of Idaho *B, M*
University of Phoenix
     Idaho *B*

Illinois

Augustana College *B*
Aurora University *B*
Benedictine University *B, T*
Blackburn College *B*
Bradley University *B, M, T*
Chicago State University *B, M, T*
Concordia University Chicago *B*
DePaul University *B, M*
Dominican University *B*
Eastern Illinois University *B, M, T*
Elmhurst College *B*
Eureka College *B*
Governors State University *B, M, T*
Greenville College *B, T*
Harper College *A*
Hebrew Theological College *B*
Illinois Central College *A*
Illinois College *B, T*
Illinois State University *B, M, D, T*
Illinois Valley Community College *A*
Illinois Wesleyan University *B*
John A. Logan College *A*
Joliet Junior College *A*
Judson University *B*
Kankakee Community College *A*
Kishwaukee College *A*
Knox College *B*
Lake Forest College *B*
Lewis University *B*
Lincoln College *A*
Loyola University Chicago *B, M, D*
MacMurray College *B, T*
McKendree University *B*
Millikin University *B*
Monmouth College *B, T*
Morton College *A*
National-Louis University *B*
North Central College *B, T*
North Park University *B*
Northeastern Illinois University *B, M*
Northern Illinois University *B, M, D*
Northwestern University *B, M, D*
Olivet Nazarene University *B, T*
Principia College *B*
Quincy University *B, T*
Richland Community College *A*
Rockford University *B*
Roosevelt University *B*
Saint Xavier University *B*
Sauk Valley Community College *A*
South Suburban College of Cook
     County *A*
Southern Illinois University
     Carbondale *B, M, D*
Southern Illinois University
     Edwardsville *B, M*
Southwestern Illinois College *A*
Spoon River College *A*
Trinity Christian College *B*
Trinity International University *B*

University of Chicago *B, D*
University of Illinois
   Chicago *B, M, D*
   Springfield *B, M*
   Urbana-Champaign *B, M, D*
University of St. Francis *B*
Western Illinois University *B, M*
Wheaton College *B, T*

Indiana

Anderson University *B*
Ball State University *B, M, D, T*
Bethel College *B*
Butler University *B, M*
Calumet College of St. Joseph *A, B*
DePauw University *B*
Earlham College *B*
Franklin College *B*
Goshen College *B*
Grace College *B*
Hanover College *B*
Holy Cross College *B*
Indiana State University *B, M, T*
Indiana University
   Bloomington *B, M, D*
   East *B, M*
   Kokomo *B*
   Northwest *B*
   Purdue University Fort Wayne *B, T*
   Purdue University
      Indianapolis *B, M*
   South Bend *B, M*
   Southeast *B*
Indiana Wesleyan University *B*
Manchester University *B, T*
Marian University *B, T*
Oakland City University *B*
Purdue University *B, M, D*
Purdue University
   Calumet *B, M*
   North Central *B*
Saint Joseph's College *B*
St. Mary-of-the-Woods College *B*
Taylor University *B*
University of Evansville *B*
University of Indianapolis *B, M*
University of Notre Dame *B, M, D*
University of St. Francis *B*
University of Southern Indiana *B, T*
Valparaiso University *B, M*
Vincennes University *A*
Wabash College *B*

Iowa

Ashford University *B*
Briar Cliff University *B*
Buena Vista University *B, T*
Central College *B, T*
Clarke University *A, B, T*
Coe College *B*
Cornell College *B, T*
Dordt College *B*
Drake University *B*
Ellsworth Community College *A*
Graceland University *B, T*
Grand View University *B*
Grinnell College *B*
Iowa State University *B*
Iowa Wesleyan College *B, T*
Loras College *B*
Luther College *B*
Maharishi University of
   Management *B*
Marshalltown Community College *A*
Morningside College *B*
Mount Mercy University *B, T*
Northwestern College *B, T*
St. Ambrose University *B, T*
Simpson College *B*
University of Dubuque *B*
University of Iowa *B, M, D*
University of Northern Iowa *B, M*
Upper Iowa University *B*
Waldorf College *B*

Wartburg College *B, T*
William Penn University *B*

Kansas

Baker University *B, T*
Barton County Community College *A*
Benedictine College *B*
Bethany College *B*
Bethel College *B*
Central Christian College of
   Kansas *A, B*
Coffeyville Community College *A*
Colby Community College *A*
Cowley County Community
   College *A*
Donnelly College *A*
Emporia State University *B, M, T*
Fort Hays State University *B, M*
Friends University *B*
Garden City Community College *A*
Haskell Indian Nations University *A*
Hutchinson Community College *A*
Independence Community College *A*
Kansas State University *B, M*
Kansas Wesleyan University *B, T*
Labette Community College *A*
McPherson College *B, T*
MidAmerica Nazarene University *B*
Neosho County Community
   College *A*
Newman University *B*
Ottawa University *B*
Pittsburg State University *B, M*
Pratt Community College *A*
Seward County Community
   College *A*
Sterling College *B, T*
Tabor College *B*
University of Kansas *B, M, D*
University of St. Mary *B*
Washburn University *B*
Wichita State University *B, M, T*

Kentucky

Alice Lloyd College *B*
Asbury University *B, T*
Bellarmine University *B, T*
Berea College *B*
Bluegrass Community and Technical
   College *A*
Brescia University *B*
Campbellsville University *B*
Centre College *B*
Eastern Kentucky University *B, M*
Georgetown College *B, T*
Hopkinsville Community College *A*
Kentucky State University *B*
Kentucky Wesleyan College *B*
Lindsey Wilson College *B, T*
Mid-Continent University *B*
Midway College *B*
Morehead State University *B, M*
Murray State University *B, M, T*
Northern Kentucky University *B, M*
St. Catharine College *B*
Thomas More College *A, B*
Transylvania University *B*
Union College *B*
University of Kentucky *B, M, D*
University of Louisville *B, M*
University of Pikeville *B, T*
University of the Cumberlands *B, T*
Western Kentucky University *B, M, T*

Louisiana

Centenary College of Louisiana *B, T*
Dillard University *B*
Grambling State University *B*
Louisiana College *B, T*
Louisiana State University
   Shreveport *B*
Louisiana State University and
   Agricultural and Mechanical
   College *B, M, D*

Louisiana Tech University *B, M*
Loyola University New Orleans *B*
McNeese State University *B, M*
Nicholls State University *B*
Northwestern State University *B, M*
Our Lady of Holy Cross College *B*
Southeastern Louisiana
   University *B, M*
Southern University
   New Orleans *B*
Southern University and Agricultural
   and Mechanical College *B*
Tulane University *B, M, D*
University of Louisiana at
   Lafayette *M, D*
University of Louisiana at
   Monroe *B, M*
University of New Orleans *B, M*
University of Phoenix
   Baton Rouge *B*
   Louisiana *B*
   Shreveport *B*
Xavier University of Louisiana *B*

Maine

Bates College *B, T*
Bowdoin College *B*
Colby College *B*
College of the Atlantic *B, M*
Husson University *B*
Saint Joseph's College of Maine *B*
Thomas College *B*
University of Maine *B, M*
University of Maine
   Augusta *B*
   Farmington *B*
   Fort Kent *B*
   Machias *B, T*
   Presque Isle *B*
University of New England *B*
University of Southern Maine *B*

Maryland

Allegany College of Maryland *A*
Bowie State University *B, M*
Coppin State University *B*
Frederick Community College *A*
Frostburg State University *B, T*
Goucher College *B*
Harford Community College *A*
Hood College *B, T*
Howard Community College *A*
Johns Hopkins University *B, M, D*
Loyola University Maryland *B*
McDaniel College *B*
Morgan State University *B, M, D*
Mount St. Mary's University *B, T*
Notre Dame of Maryland
   University *B, M*
St. Mary's College of Maryland *B*
Salisbury University *B, M*
Stevenson University *B*
Towson University *B*
United States Naval Academy *B*
University of Baltimore *B*
University of Maryland
   Baltimore County *B*
   College Park *B, M, D*
   Eastern Shore *B*
   University College *B*
Washington Adventist University *B*
Washington College *B, M, T*

Massachusetts

American International College *B*
Amherst College *B*
Anna Maria College *B*
Assumption College *B*
Bard College at Simon's Rock *B*
Bentley University *B*
Boston College *B, M, D*
Boston University *B, M, D*
Brandeis University *B, M, D*
Bridgewater State University *B, M*

Bunker Hill Community College *A*
Cape Cod Community College *A*
Clark University *B, M*
College of the Holy Cross *B*
Curry College *B*
Eastern Nazarene College *B*
Elms College *B*
Emmanuel College *B*
Endicott College *B*
Fitchburg State University *B, M, T*
Framingham State University *B*
Gordon College *B*
Hampshire College *B*
Harvard College *B, M, D*
Lasell College *B*
Lesley University *B*
Massachusetts College of Liberal
   Arts *B, T*
Massachusetts Institute of
   Technology *B*
Merrimack College *B*
Mount Holyoke College *B*
Mount Ida College *B*
Nichols College *B*
Northeastern University *B, M, D*
Pine Manor College *B*
Regis College *B*
Roxbury Community College *A*
Salem State University *B, M*
Simmons College *B, M*
Smith College *B*
Springfield College *B*
Stonehill College *B*
Suffolk University *B*
Tufts University *B, M, D*
University of Massachusetts
   Amherst *B, M, D*
   Boston *B, M*
   Dartmouth *B*
   Lowell *C, B*
Wellesley College *B*
Western New England University *B*
Westfield State University *B, M, T*
Wheaton College *B*
Williams College *B*
Worcester State University *B, M*

Michigan

Adrian College *A, B, T*
Albion College *B, T*
Alma College *B, T*
Andrews University *B, M*
Aquinas College *B, T*
Calvin College *B*
Central Michigan University *B, M*
Concordia University *B*
Cornerstone University *B*
Delta College *A*
Eastern Michigan University *B, M*
Finlandia University *B*
Grand Rapids Community College *A*
Grand Valley State University *B*
Hillsdale College *B*
Hope College *B*
Kalamazoo College *B*
Kellogg Community College *A*
Lake Michigan College *A*
Lake Superior State University *B*
Lansing Community College *A*
Lawrence Technological University *B*
Madonna University *A, B*
Marygrove College *B, M*
Michigan State University *B, M, D*
Michigan Technological University *B*
Northern Michigan University *B, M*
Northwestern Michigan College *A*
Oakland University *B, M, T*
Rochester College *B*
Saginaw Valley State University *B*
Siena Heights University *B*
Spring Arbor University *B*
University of Detroit Mercy *B*
University of Michigan *B, M, D*

University of Michigan
   Dearborn *B*
   Flint *B, M, T*
University of Phoenix
   West Michigan *B*
Wayne State University *B, M, D*
Western Michigan University *B, M, D*

Minnesota

Augsburg College *B*
Bemidji State University *B, M*
Bethany Lutheran College *B*
Bethel University *B*
Carleton College *B*
College of St. Benedict *B*
College of St. Scholastica *B*
Concordia College: Moorhead *B, T*
Concordia University St. Paul *B*
Crown College *B*
Gustavus Adolphus College *B*
Hamline University *B*
Hibbing Community College *A*
Macalester College *B*
Metropolitan State University *B*
Minnesota State University
   Mankato *B, M*
   Moorhead *B*
Minnesota West Community and
   Technical College *A*
North Central University *B*
Ridgewater College *A*
St. Catherine University *B*
Saint Cloud State University *B, M*
St. John's University *B*
St. Olaf College *B*
Southwest Minnesota State
   University *B, T*
University of Minnesota
   Duluth *B, M*
   Morris *B*
   Twin Cities *B, M, D*
University of Northwestern - St.
   Paul *B*
University of St. Thomas *B, M*
Winona State University *B, M*

Mississippi

Alcorn State University *B*
Belhaven University *B*
Blue Mountain College *B*
Delta State University *B*
East Mississippi Community
   College *A*
Hinds Community College *A*
Jackson State University *B, M*
Millsaps College *B*
Mississippi College *B, M*
Mississippi Delta Community
   College *A*
Mississippi State University *B, M*
Mississippi University for
   Women *B, T*
Mississippi Valley State University *B*
Rust College *B*
Tougaloo College *B*
University of Mississippi *B, M, D*
University of Southern
   Mississippi *B, M, D*
William Carey University *B*

Missouri

Avila University *B*
Calvary Bible College and Theological
   Seminary *B*
Central Methodist University *B*
College of the Ozarks *B*
Columbia College *B*
Cottey College *A*
Culver-Stockton College *B*
Drury University *B, T*
Evangel University *B, T*
Fontbonne University *B, T*
Hannibal-LaGrange University *A, B*
Lincoln University *B*

Lindenwood University *B*
Maryville University of Saint Louis *B*
Mineral Area College *A*
Missouri Baptist University *C, B*
Missouri Southern State University *B*
Missouri State University *B, M*
Missouri University of Science and
   Technology *B, T*
Missouri Valley College *B*
Missouri Western State University *B*
Northwest Missouri State
   University *B, M*
Park University *B*
Rockhurst University *B*
St. Charles Community College *A*
Saint Louis University *B, M, D*
Southeast Missouri State
   University *B, M*
Southwest Baptist University *B, T*
Stephens College *B*
Three Rivers Community College *A*
Truman State University *B, M*
University of Central Missouri *B*
University of Missouri
   Columbia *B, M, D*
   Kansas City *B, M, D*
   St. Louis *B, M*
University of Phoenix
   St. Louis *B*
Washington University in St.
   Louis *B, M, D*
Webster University *B*
Westminster College *B, T*
William Jewell College *B, T*
William Woods University *B, T*

Montana

Carroll College *A, B*
Miles Community College *A*
Montana State University *B, M*
Montana State University
   Billings *B, T*
   Northern *B*
Rocky Mountain College *B*
University of Great Falls *B*
University of Montana *B, M*
University of Montana: Western *B*

Nebraska

Bellevue University *B, M*
Chadron State College *B*
College of Saint Mary *B*
Concordia University *B*
Creighton University *B, M*
Doane College *B*
Hastings College *B*
Little Priest Tribal College *A*
Midland University *B, T*
Nebraska Wesleyan University *B*
Northeast Community College *A*
Peru State College *B*
Union College *B*
University of Nebraska
   Kearney *B, M, T*
   Lincoln *B, M, D*
   Omaha *B, M*
Wayne State College *B*
Western Nebraska Community
   College *A*
York College *B*

Nevada

College of Southern Nevada *A*
Nevada State College *B*
Sierra Nevada College *B*
University of Nevada
   Las Vegas *B, M, D*
   Reno *B, M, D*
University of Phoenix
   Las Vegas *B*
   Northern Nevada *B*

New Hampshire

Colby-Sawyer College *B*
Dartmouth College *B, T*
Franklin Pierce University *B*
Granite State College *T*
Keene State College *B*
New England College *B*
Plymouth State University *B*
Rivier University *B, M*
Saint Anselm College *B, T*
Southern New Hampshire
   University *B, M*
University of New
   Hampshire *B, M, D*
University of New Hampshire at
   Manchester *B*

New Jersey

Bergen Community College *A*
Bloomfield College *B, T*
Caldwell College *B*
Centenary College *B, M*
College of New Jersey *B, M*
College of St. Elizabeth *B*
Cumberland County College *A*
Drew University *B*
Fairleigh Dickinson University
   College at Florham *B*
   Metropolitan Campus *B, M*
Felician College *B*
Georgian Court University *B*
Gloucester County College *A*
Kean University *B, T*
Monmouth University *B, M*
Montclair State University *B, M*
New Jersey City University *B*
Passaic County Community College *A*
Princeton University *B, M, D*
Raritan Valley Community College *A*
Richard Stockton College of New
   Jersey *B*
Rider University *B*
Rowan University *B*
Rutgers, The State University of New
   Jersey
   Camden Campus *B, M, T*
   New Brunswick/Piscataway
      Campus *B, M, D, T*
   Newark Campus *B, M, T*
Saint Peter's University *B*
Salem Community College *A*
Seton Hall University *B, M, T*
Stevens Institute of Technology *B*
Sussex County Community College *A*
Thomas Edison State College *B*
Warren County Community
   College *A*
William Paterson University of New
   Jersey *B, M*

New Mexico

Central New Mexico Community
   College *A*
Eastern New Mexico University *B, M*
New Mexico Highlands
   University *B, M*
New Mexico State University *B, M*
University of New Mexico *B, M, D*
University of Phoenix
   New Mexico *B*
University of the Southwest *B*
Western New Mexico University *B*

New York

Adelphi University *B*
Alfred University *B*
Bard College *B*
Barnard College *B*
Canisius College *B*
Cazenovia College *B*
City University of New York
   Baruch College *B*
   Borough of Manhattan Community
      College *A*

Brooklyn College *B, M*
City College *B, M, T*
College of Staten Island *B, M*
Hunter College *B, M*
John Jay College of Criminal
   Justice *B*
LaGuardia Community College *A*
Lehman College *B, M*
Medgar Evers College *B*
Queens College *B, M, T*
York College *B*
Colgate University *B*
College of Mount St. Vincent *B*
College of New Rochelle *B, T*
College of Saint Rose *B, M*
Columbia University *B*
Columbia University
   School of General Studies *B*
Concordia College *B, T*
Cornell University *B, M, D*
D'Youville College *B*
Daemen College *B, T*
Dominican College of Blauvelt *B*
Dowling College *B*
Elmira College *B, T*
Fordham University *B, M, D*
Hamilton College *B*
Hartwick College *B*
Hilbert College *B*
Hobart and William Smith Colleges *B*
Hofstra University *B, M*
Houghton College *B*
Iona College *B, M*
Ithaca College *B, T*
Keuka College *B*
Le Moyne College *B*
Long Island University
   LIU Brooklyn *B, M*
   LIU Post *B, M*
Manhattanville College *B*
Marist College *B*
Marymount Manhattan College *B*
Medaille College *B*
Mercy College *B*
Molloy College *B*
Mount Saint Mary College *B, T*
Nazareth College *B*
New York Institute of Technology *B*
New York University *B, M, D, T*
Niagara University *B*
Nyack College *B*
Pace University *B*
Pace University: Pleasantville/
   Briarcliff *B*
Roberts Wesleyan College *B*
SUNY
   College at Brockport *B, M*
   College at Buffalo *B, M*
   College at Cortland *B, M*
   College at Fredonia *B, M, T*
   College at Geneseo *B, T*
   College at New Paltz *B, M*
   College at Old Westbury *B*
   College at Oneonta *B*
   College at Oswego *B, M*
   College at Plattsburgh *B*
   College at Potsdam *B, M*
   University at Albany *B, M, D*
   University at Binghamton *B, M, D*
   University at Buffalo *C, B, M, D*
   University at Stony Brook *B, M, D*
Sage Colleges *B*
Saint Bonaventure University *B, T*
St. Francis College *B*
St. John Fisher College *B*
St. John's University *B, M, D*
St. Joseph's College New York:
   Suffolk Campus *B*
St. Joseph's College, New York *B*
St. Thomas Aquinas College *B*
Siena College *B, T*
Skidmore College *B*
Syracuse University *B, M, D*
Touro College *B*
Union College *B*

University of Rochester *B, M, D*
Utica College *B*
Vassar College *B*
Wagner College *B*
Wells College *B*
Yeshiva University *B*

North Carolina

Appalachian State University *B, M*
Barton College *B*
Belmont Abbey College *B*
Bennett College for Women *B*
Brevard College *B*
Campbell University *B, T*
Catawba College *B*
Chowan University *B*
Davidson College *B*
Duke University *B, D*
East Carolina University *B, M*
Elizabeth City State University *B*
Elon University *B, T*
Fayetteville State University *B, M*
Gardner-Webb University *B*
Greensboro College *B*
Guilford College *B, T*
High Point University *B*
Johnson C. Smith University *B*
Lees-McRae College *B*
Lenoir-Rhyne University *B*
Livingstone College *B*
Mars Hill University *B, T*
Meredith College *B*
Methodist University *A, B*
Montreat College *B*
North Carolina Agricultural and
    Technical State
    University *B, M, T*
North Carolina Central
    University *B, M*
North Carolina State University *B, M*
North Carolina Wesleyan College *B*
Pfeiffer University *B*
Queens University of Charlotte *B*
St. Andrews University *B*
St. Augustine's University *B*
Salem College *B*
Shaw University *B*
Southeastern Community College *A*
University of Mount Olive *B*
University of North Carolina
    Asheville *B*
    Chapel Hill *B, M, D*
    Charlotte *B, M*
    Greensboro *B, M, D*
    Pembroke *B*
    Wilmington *B, M*
Wake Forest University *B, M*
Warren Wilson College *B*
Western Carolina University *B, M*
Western Piedmont Community
    College *A*
William Peace University *B*
Wingate University *B*
Winston-Salem State University *B*

North Dakota

Dakota College at Bottineau *A*
Dickinson State University *B, T*
Mayville State University *B, T*
Minot State University *B*
North Dakota State
    University *B, M, T*
University of Jamestown *B*
University of Mary *B*
University of North Dakota *B, M, D*
Valley City State University *B*

Ohio

ATS Institute of Technology *C*
Ashland University *B*
Baldwin Wallace University *B*
Bluffton University *B*
Bowling Green State
    University *B, M, D*

Capital University *B*
Case Western Reserve
    University *B, M, D*
Cedarville University *B*
Central State University *B*
Clark State Community College *A*
Cleveland State University *B, M, T*
College of Mount St. Joseph *B, T*
College of Wooster *B*
Defiance College *B, T*
Denison University *B*
Franciscan University of
    Steubenville *B*
Heidelberg University *B*
Hiram College *B*
John Carroll University *B, M*
Kent State University *B, M, D*
Kent State University
    Ashtabula *B*
    East Liverpool *B*
    Geauga *B*
    Salem *B*
    Stark *B*
    Trumbull *B*
    Tuscarawas *B*
Kenyon College *B*
Lake Erie College *B*
Lourdes University *A, B*
Malone University *B*
Marietta College *B*
Miami University
    Middletown *A*
    Oxford *B, M, D, T*
Mount Vernon Nazarene University *B*
Muskingum University *B*
Notre Dame College *B*
Oberlin College *B*
Ohio Dominican University *B*
Ohio Northern University *B*
Ohio State University
    Columbus Campus *B, M, D*
    Lima Campus *B*
    Mansfield Campus *B*
    Marion Campus *B*
    Newark Campus *B*
Ohio University *B, M, D*
Ohio Wesleyan University *B*
Otterbein University *B*
Pontifical College Josephinum *B*
Shawnee State University *B*
Sinclair Community College *A*
Terra State Community College *A*
Tiffin University *B*
University of Akron *C, B, M*
University of Cincinnati *C, M, D, T*
University of Dayton *B, M*
University of Findlay *B*
University of Mount Union *B*
University of Rio Grande *B*
University of Toledo *B, M*
Urbana University *B*
Ursuline College *B*
Walsh University *B*
Wilberforce University *B*
Wilmington College *B*
Wittenberg University *B*
Wright State University *B, M*
Wright State University: Lake
    Campus *B*
Xavier University *A, B, M*
Youngstown State University *B, M*

Oklahoma

Cameron University *B*
Carl Albert State College *A*
Connors State College *A*
East Central University *B*
Eastern Oklahoma State College *A*
Langston University *B*
Mid-America Christian University *B*
Murray State College *A*
Northeastern Oklahoma Agricultural
    and Mechanical College *A*
Northeastern State University *B, M*
Northern Oklahoma College *A*

Northwestern Oklahoma State
    University *B*
Oklahoma Baptist University *B, T*
Oklahoma Christian University *B*
Oklahoma City University *B*
Oklahoma Panhandle State
    University *B*
Oklahoma State University *B, M, D*
Oklahoma Wesleyan University *B*
Oral Roberts University *B*
Redlands Community College *A*
Rose State College *A*
St. Gregory's University *A, B*
Southeastern Oklahoma State
    University *B*
Southern Nazarene University *B*
Southwestern Christian University *B*
Southwestern Oklahoma State
    University *B*
Tulsa Community College *A*
University of Central Oklahoma *B, M*
University of Oklahoma *B, M, D*
University of Phoenix
    Oklahoma City *B*
    Tulsa *B*
University of Science and Arts of
    Oklahoma *B, T*
University of Tulsa *B, M, D*
Western Oklahoma State College *A*

Oregon

Central Oregon Community
    College *A*
Concordia University *B*
Corban University *B*
Eastern Oregon University *B*
George Fox University *B*
Lewis & Clark College *B*
Linfield College *B*
Linn-Benton Community College *A*
Mt. Hood Community College *A*
Multnomah University *B*
Northwest Christian University *B*
Oregon State University *B, M*
Pacific University *B*
Portland State University *B, M*
Reed College *B*
Southern Oregon University *B, T*
Treasure Valley Community
    College *A*
University of Oregon *B, M, D*
University of Portland *B*
Warner Pacific College *B, T*
Western Oregon University *B*
Willamette University *B*

Pennsylvania

Albright College *B, T*
Allegheny College *B*
Alvernia University *B*
Arcadia University *B, M*
Bloomsburg University of
    Pennsylvania *B, T*
Bryn Athyn College *B*
Bryn Mawr College *B*
Bucknell University *B, M*
Butler County Community College *A*
Cabrini College *B*
California University of
    Pennsylvania *B, M*
Carlow University *B, T*
Carnegie Mellon University *B, M, D*
Cedar Crest College *B*
Chatham University *B*
Chestnut Hill College *B*
Cheyney University of
    Pennsylvania *B*
Clarion University of Pennsylvania *B*
Community College of Beaver
    County *A*
DeSales University *B, T*
Delaware Valley College *B*
Dickinson College *B*
Drexel University *B*

Duquesne University *B, M, D*
East Stroudsburg University of
    Pennsylvania *B, T*
Edinboro University of
    Pennsylvania *B, T*
Elizabethtown College *B, T*
Franklin & Marshall College *B*
Geneva College *B*
Gettysburg College *B*
Gwynedd Mercy University *B*
Haverford College *B, T*
Holy Family University *B, T*
Immaculata University *A, B*
Indiana University of
    Pennsylvania *B, M, D*
Juniata College *B*
King's College *B, T*
Kutztown University of
    Pennsylvania *B, M*
La Roche College *B*
La Salle University *B, M, T*
Lafayette College *B*
Lebanon Valley College *B*
Lehigh University *B, M, D*
Lincoln University *B*
Lock Haven University of
    Pennsylvania *B*
Lycoming College *B*
Mansfield University of
    Pennsylvania *A, B, T*
Marywood University *B*
Mercyhurst University *B, T*
Messiah College *B*
Millersville University of
    Pennsylvania *B, M, T*
Misericordia University *B*
Moravian College *B*
Mount Aloysius College *B*
Muhlenberg College *C, B*
Neumann University *B, T*
Penn State
    Abington *B*
    Altoona *B*
    Beaver *B*
    Berks *B*
    Brandywine *B*
    DuBois *B*
    Erie, The Behrend College *B*
    Fayette, The Eberly Campus *B*
    Greater Allegheny *B*
    Harrisburg *B*
    Hazleton *B*
    Lehigh Valley *B*
    Mont Alto *B*
    New Kensington *B*
    Schuylkill *B*
    Shenango *B*
    University Park *B, M, D*
    Wilkes-Barre *B*
    Worthington Scranton *B*
    York *B*
Point Park University *B*
Robert Morris University *B*
Rosemont College *B, M*
St. Francis University *B*
Saint Joseph's University *B*
St. Vincent College *B*
Seton Hill University *B, T*
Shippensburg University of
    Pennsylvania *B, T*
Slippery Rock University of
    Pennsylvania *B, T*
Susquehanna University *B*
Swarthmore College *B*
Temple University *B, M, D*
Thiel College *B*
University of Pennsylvania *B, M, D*
University of Pittsburgh *M, D*
University of Pittsburgh
    Bradford *B*
    Greensburg *B*
University of Scranton *B, T*
Ursinus College *B*
Valley Forge Christian College *B*
Villanova University *B, M*

Washington & Jefferson College *B*
Waynesburg University *B*
West Chester University of
     Pennsylvania *B, M, T*
Westminster College *B, M, T*
Widener University *B, T*
Wilkes University *B*
Wilson College *B*
York College of Pennsylvania *B*

Puerto Rico

Bayamon Central University *B*
Inter American University of Puerto
     Rico
     San German Campus *B*
Pontifical Catholic University of
     Puerto Rico *B*
University of Puerto Rico
     Cayey University College *B*
     Mayaguez *B*
     Rio Piedras *B, M, D*

Rhode Island

Brown University *B, M, D*
Bryant University *B*
Providence College *B*
Rhode Island College *B, M*
Salve Regina University *B*
University of Rhode Island *B, M, D*

South Carolina

Allen University *B*
Anderson University *B*
Benedict College *B*
Bob Jones University *B, M*
Charleston Southern University *B*
Citadel, *B, M*
Claflin University *B*
Clemson University *B, M*
Coastal Carolina University *B*
Coker College *B*
College of Charleston *B, M, T*
Columbia College *B, T*
Columbia International University *B*
Converse College *B*
Erskine College *B, T*
Francis Marion University *B, T*
Furman University *B, T*
Lander University *B, T*
Limestone College *B*
Morris College *B*
Newberry College *B, T*
North Greenville University *B*
Presbyterian College *B, T*
South Carolina State University *B*
Southern Wesleyan University *B, T*
University of South Carolina
     Aiken *B*
     Beaufort *B*
     Columbia *B, M, D*
     Upstate *B*
Voorhees College *B*
Winthrop University *B, M*
Wofford College *B, T*

South Dakota

Augustana College *B, T*
Black Hills State University *B*
Dakota Wesleyan University *B*
Mount Marty College *B*
Northern State University *B*
Presentation College *A*
South Dakota State University *B, M*
University of Sioux Falls *B*
University of South Dakota *B, M, D*

Tennessee

Aquinas College *B*
Austin Peay State University *B, M*
Belmont University *B, M*
Bethel University *B*
Bryan University
     Dayton *B*
Carson-Newman University *B, T*

Christian Brothers University *B*
Cumberland University *B*
East Tennessee State
     University *B, M, T*
Fisk University *B*
Freed-Hardeman University *B, T*
Hiwassee College *A*
Jackson State Community College *A*
King University *B*
Lane College *B*
LeMoyne-Owen College *B*
Lee University *B*
Lincoln Memorial University *B, T*
Lipscomb University *B*
Martin Methodist College *B*
Maryville College *B, T*
Middle Tennessee State
     University *B, M, D*
Milligan College *B*
Rhodes College *R*
Sewanee: The University of the
     South *B*
Southern Adventist University *B*
Tennessee State University *B, M*
Tennessee Technological
     University *B, M, T*
Tennessee Temple University *B*
Tennessee Wesleyan College *B*
Trevecca Nazarene University *B*
Tusculum College *B*
Union University *B, T*
University of Memphis *B, M, D*
University of Tennessee
     Chattanooga *B, M*
     Knoxville *B, M, D*
     Martin *B*
Vanderbilt University *B, M, D*
Victory University *B*
Welch College *B*

Texas

Abilene Christian University *B, M*
Amarillo College *A*
Angelo State University *B, M, T*
Austin College *B*
Baylor University *B, M, D*
Blinn College *A*
Brazosport College *A*
Clarendon College *A*
Coastal Bend College *A*
Concordia University Texas *B*
Dallas Baptist University *B, M*
Del Mar College *A*
East Texas Baptist University *B*
El Paso Community College *A*
Frank Phillips College *A*
Galveston College *A*
Hardin-Simmons University *B, M*
Hill College *A*
Houston Baptist University *B*
Howard College *A*
Howard Payne University *B*
Jarvis Christian College *B*
Kilgore College *A*
Lamar University *B, M*
Laredo Community College *A*
LeTourneau University *B*
Lee College *A*
Lubbock Christian University *B*
McMurry University *B, T*
Midland College *A*
Midwestern State University *B, M*
Navarro College *A*
North Lake College *A*
Northeast Texas Community
     College *A*
Northwest Vista College *A*
Our Lady of the Lake University of
     San Antonio *B, M*
Palo Alto College *A*
Paris Junior College *A*
Prairie View A&M University *B, M*
Rice University *B, M, D*
St. Edward's University *B*
St. Mary's University *B, M*

St. Philip's College *A*
Sam Houston State University *B, M*
San Jacinto College *A*
Schreiner University *B*
South Plains College *A*
South Texas College *A*
Southern Methodist
     University *B, M, D*
Southwestern Adventist
     University *B, T*
Southwestern Assemblies of God
     University *A, B*
Southwestern University *B, T*
Stephen F. Austin State
     University *B, M*
Sul Ross State University *B, M, T*
Tarleton State University *B, M*
Texas A&M International
     University *B, M, T*
Texas A&M University *B, M, D*
Texas A&M University
     Commerce *B, M, D*
     Corpus Christi *B, M, T*
     Kingsville *B, M*
     Texarkana *B, M*
Texas Christian University *B, M, D*
Texas College *B*
Texas Lutheran University *B, T*
Texas Southern University *B, M*
Texas State University *B, M, T*
Texas Tech University *B, M, D*
Texas Wesleyan University *B*
Texas Woman's University *B, M*
Trinity University *B*
Trinity Valley Community College *A*
University of Dallas *B, M, D*
University of Houston *B, M, D*
University of Houston
     Clear Lake *B, M*
     Downtown *B*
     Victoria *B, T*
University of Mary Hardin-Baylor *B, T*
University of North Texas *B, M, D*
University of Phoenix
     Austin *B*
     Dallas Fort Worth *B*
     Houston Westside *B*
     San Antonio *B*
University of St. Thomas *B*
University of Texas
     Arlington *B, M, D*
     Austin *B, M, D*
     Brownsville *B, M*
     El Paso *B, M*
     Pan American *B, M*
     Permian Basin *B, M*
     San Antonio *B, M, D*
     Tyler *B, M*
University of the Incarnate Word *B*
Wayland Baptist University *B, T*
West Texas A&M University *B, M*
Western Texas College *A*
Wharton County Junior College *A*
Wiley College *B*

Utah

Brigham Young University *B, M*
Salt Lake Community College *A*
Snow College *A*
Southern Utah University *B*
University of Phoenix
     Utah *B*
University of Utah *B, M, D, T*
Utah State University *B, M*
Utah Valley University *A, B*
Weber State University *B, M*
Westminster College *B*

Vermont

Bennington College *B*
Castleton State College *B*
College of St. Joseph in Vermont *B*
Goddard College *B, M*
Green Mountain College *B*

Johnson State College *B*
Lyndon State College *B*
Marlboro College *B*
Middlebury College *B, M*
Norwich University *B*
Saint Michael's College *B*
Southern Vermont College *B*
University of Vermont *B, M*

Virginia

Averett University *B*
Bluefield College *B*
Bridgewater College *B*
Christendom College *B*
Christopher Newport University *B*
College of William and Mary *B*
Eastern Mennonite University *B*
Emory & Henry College *B*
Ferrum College *B*
George Mason University *B*
Hampden-Sydney College *B*
Hampton University *B*
Hollins University *B*
James Madison University *B, M, T*
Liberty University *B, M, T*
Longwood University *B, M*
Lynchburg College *B, M*
Mary Baldwin College *B*
Marymount University *B, M, T*
Norfolk State University *B*
Old Dominion University *B, M, D*
Patrick Henry College *B*
Radford University *B, M*
Randolph College *B*
Randolph-Macon College *B*
Regent University *B*
Roanoke College *B, T*
Shenandoah University *B*
Southern Virginia University *B*
Sweet Briar College *B*
University of Mary Washington *B*
University of Phoenix
     Northern Virginia *B*
University of Richmond *B*
University of Virginia *B, M, D*
University of Virginia's College at
     Wise *B, T*
Virginia Commonwealth
     University *B, M*
Virginia Intermont College *B*
Virginia Military Institute *B*
Virginia Polytechnic Institute and
     State University *B, M*
Virginia State University *B, M*
Virginia Union University *B*
Virginia Wesleyan College *B, T*
Washington and Lee University *B*

Washington

Central Washington University *B, M*
Centralia College *A*
Eastern Washington University *B, M*
Evergreen State College *B*
Gonzaga University *B, M*
Heritage University *B*
Highline Community College *A*
Lower Columbia College *A*
Northwest University *B*
Pacific Lutheran University *B*
Saint Martin's University *B*
Seattle Pacific University *B*
Seattle University *B*
University of Puget Sound *B, T*
University of Washington *B*
Walla Walla University *B*
Washington State University *B, M, D*
Western Washington University *B, M*
Whitman College *B*
Whitworth University *B, T*

West Virginia

Alderson-Broaddus University *B*
American Public University System *B*
Bethany College *B*

Concord University *B*
Davis and Elkins College *B*
Fairmont State University *B*
Glenville State College *B*
Marshall University *B, M*
Ohio Valley University *B*
Potomac State College of West
Virginia University *A*
Shepherd University *B, T*
West Liberty University *B*
West Virginia State University *B*
West Virginia University *B, M, D*
West Virginia Wesleyan College *B*
Wheeling Jesuit University *B*

Wisconsin

Alverno College *B*
Beloit College *B*
Cardinal Stritch University *B, T*
Carroll University *B*
Carthage College *B, T*
Concordia University Wisconsin *B*
Edgewood College *B*
Lakeland College *B*
Lawrence University *B*
Maranatha Baptist Bible College *B*
Marian University *B*
Marquette University *B, M, D*
Mount Mary University *B, M, T*
Northland College *B*
Northland International University *B*
Ripon College *B, T*
St. Norbert College *B, T*
Silver Lake College of the Holy
Family *B, T*
University of Wisconsin
Eau Claire *B, M*
Green Bay *B*
La Crosse *B, T*
Madison *B, M, D*
Milwaukee *B, M, D, T*
Oshkosh *B*
Parkside *B, T*
Platteville *B*
River Falls *B*
Stevens Point *B, M, T*
Superior *B*
Whitewater *B*
Viterbo University *B, T*
Wisconsin Lutheran College *B*

Wyoming

Casper College *A*
Central Wyoming College *A*
Eastern Wyoming College *A*
Laramie County Community
College *A*
Northwest College *A*
Sheridan College *A*
University of Wyoming *B, M*
Western Wyoming Community
College *A*

English literature (British)

California

California State University
East Bay *B*
Northridge *B*
Irvine Valley College *A*
Mills College *B, M*
Saddleback College *A*
Stanford University *B*
University of California
San Diego *B, M, D*
Whittier College *B*

Connecticut

Albertus Magnus College *B*

District of Columbia

American University *B*
George Washington University *M, D*

Indiana

Indiana University
Purdue University Fort Wayne *B*
Saint Mary's College *B*

Kentucky

Berea College *B*

Maine

University of Maine
Fort Kent *B*

Maryland

Johns Hopkins University *D*

Massachusetts

Simmons College *B, M*
Tufts University *M, D*

Michigan

University of Michigan
Flint *M*

Missouri

Washington University in St.
Louis *B, M, D*

New York

Bard College *B*
City University of New York
Hunter College *B*
Columbia University *B*
Elmira College *B, T*
Excelsior College *B*
Hofstra University *M*
Mercy College *M*
New York University *B, M, D*
Pace University *B*
SUNY
College at Purchase *B*
Saint Bonaventure University *B, M*
St. Lawrence University *B*

North Carolina

Duke University *B*

Ohio

Denison University *B*
Ohio Northern University *B*
Ohio Wesleyan University *B*

Pennsylvania

Gannon University *B, M*
Gettysburg College *B*
La Salle University *B*
University of Pittsburgh *B*
University of Pittsburgh
Johnstown *B*
Waynesburg University *B*
Westminster College *B, T*

Rhode Island

Brown University *B, M, D*
Roger Williams University *B*

Vermont

Bennington College *B*
Marlboro College *B*

Virginia

George Mason University *M*
Randolph College *B*

West Virginia

Concord University *B*
Wheeling Jesuit University *B*

Wisconsin

Marian University *B*

English teacher education

Alabama

Auburn University *B, M, D*
Birmingham-Southern College *T*
Faulkner University *B, M, T*
Huntingdon College *B, T*
Judson College *B*
Miles College *B*
Oakwood University *B*
Samford University *B*
Spring Hill College *B, M, T*
Talladega College *B*
University of Mobile *B, T*

Arizona

Arizona Christian University *B*
Grand Canyon University *B*

Arkansas

Arkansas State University *B, M, T*
Arkansas Tech University *B, M*
Harding University *B, T*
John Brown University *B, T*
Ouachita Baptist University *B, T*
University of Arkansas
Fort Smith *B*
Pine Bluff *B, M, T*
University of the Ozarks *T*
Williams Baptist College *B*

California

Azusa Pacific University *T*
California Baptist University *T*
California Lutheran University *B, T*
California Polytechnic State
University: San Luis Obispo *T*
California State University
Chico *T*
Long Beach *B, M, T*
Northridge *B, T*
San Bernardino *T*
Fresno Pacific University *B, T*
Humboldt State University *T*
Master's College *T*
Mills College *T*
Mount St. Mary's College *T*
National University *B, M*
Pepperdine University *B*
San Diego Christian College *B, T*
San Diego State University *B*
San Francisco State University *T*
Simpson University *B, T*
Sonoma State University *T*
Stanford University *M, T*
University of San Diego *T*
University of San Francisco *T*
Vanguard University of Southern
California *T*
Westmont College *T*

Colorado

Adams State University *B, M, T*
Colorado Christian University *B*
Colorado State University *B, T*
Colorado State University
Pueblo *T*
Metropolitan State University of
Denver *T*
University of Colorado
Boulder *T*
Western State Colorado
University *B, T*

Connecticut

Albertus Magnus College *B, M*
Central Connecticut State
University *M*
Fairfield University *T*
Quinnipiac University *B, M*
Sacred Heart University *T*
University of Connecticut *T*
University of Saint Joseph *T*

Delaware

Delaware State University *B*
University of Delaware *B, T*

District of Columbia

Catholic University of America *B*
George Washington University *M, T*
Howard University *B*
Trinity Washington University *B, M*

Florida

Barry University *T*
Bethune-Cookman University *B, T*
Clearwater Christian College *B*
Flagler College *B*
Florida Agricultural and Mechanical
University *B, T*
Florida Atlantic University *B*
Florida State University *B, M, D*
Hobe Sound Bible College *B, T*
Palm Beach Atlantic University *B, T*
South Florida State College *A*
Southeastern University *B, T*
Stetson University *B*
University of Central Florida *B*
University of Florida *M*
University of Miami *B, M*
University of South Florida *B, M*
University of South Florida
Saint Petersburg *B*
Sarasota-Manatee *M*
University of West Florida *B*
Warner University *B*

Georgia

Albany State University *M*
Berry College *M*
Clayton State University *M*
Columbus State University *B, M*
Covenant College *B, T*
Darton College *A*
Emmanuel College *B*
Fort Valley State University *B, T*
Georgia Southwestern State
University *M*
Georgia State University *M*
Kennesaw State University *B*
Middle Georgia State College *B*
Paine College *B*
Piedmont College *B, M, T*
Reinhardt University *B*
Shorter University *T*
Toccoa Falls College *B, T*
University of Georgia *B, M, T*
University of North Georgia *M*

Hawaii

Brigham Young University-
Hawaii *B, T*
Hawaii Pacific University *M*

Idaho

Boise State University *B, M, T*
Brigham Young University-Idaho *B, T*
Lewis-Clark State College *B, T*
Northwest Nazarene University *B*
University of Idaho *B, T*

Illinois

Augustana College *B, T*
Benedictine University *T*
Blackburn College *B, T*
Bradley University *B, M*
Chicago State University *B*
Columbia College Chicago *M*
Concordia University Chicago *B, T*
DePaul University *M, T*
Dominican University *T*
Elmhurst College *B*
Eureka College *T*
Governors State University *B, M, T*
Greenville College *B, T*
Illinois College *T*
Illinois Wesleyan University *B*

Knox College *T*
Loyola University Chicago *M*
MacMurray College *B, T*
McKendree University *B*
Millikin University *B, T*
Monmouth College *T*
National-Louis University *M*
North Park University *T*
Olivet Nazarene University *B, T*
Rockford University *T*
Saint Xavier University *M*
Trinity Christian College *B, T*
Trinity International University *B, T*
University of Illinois
  Chicago *B*
  Urbana-Champaign *B, M, T*
University of St. Francis *B, M*

Indiana

Anderson University *B, T*
Bethel College *B*
Butler University *T*
Franklin College *B, T*
Goshen College *B, T*
Grace College *B*
Huntington University *B, M*
Indiana University
  Bloomington *B, T*
  Northwest *B*
  Purdue University Fort
    Wayne *B, M*
  Purdue University
    Indianapolis *B, T*
  South Bend *B, T*
  Southeast *B*
Indiana Wesleyan University *B, T*
Manchester University *B, T*
Oakland City University *B*
Saint Mary's College *T*
Taylor University *B, T*
Trine University *B, T*
University of Evansville *B, T*
University of Indianapolis *B, M, T*
University of St. Francis *B*
Valparaiso University *B*
Vincennes University *A*

Iowa

Briar Cliff University *B*
Buena Vista University *B, T*
Central College *T*
Cornell College *B, T*
Dordt College *B*
Drake University *T*
Faith Baptist Bible College and
  Theological Seminary *B, T*
Graceland University *T*
Grand View University *B, T*
Iowa State University *T*
Iowa Wesleyan College *B*
Loras College *T*
Maharishi University of
  Management *T*
Morningside College *B*
Mount Mercy University *T*
Northwestern College *B, T*
St. Ambrose University *B, T*
Simpson College *T*
University of Dubuque *B, T*
University of Iowa *M, D, T*
Upper Iowa University *T*
Wartburg College *T*

Kansas

Bethany College *B*
Bethel College *T*
Central Christian College of Kansas *B*
Friends University *B*
Independence Community College *A*
Kansas Wesleyan University *B, T*
McPherson College *B, T*
MidAmerica Nazarene University *B, T*
Newman University *T*
Pittsburg State University *B*

Southwestern College *B*
Sterling College *T*
Tabor College *B*
University of Kansas *B, T*
University of St. Mary *T*
Washburn University *B*

Kentucky

Alice Lloyd College *B*
Campbellsville University *B*
Kentucky Christian University *B, T*
Kentucky Wesleyan College *B, T*
Lindsey Wilson College *B, T*
Midway College *M*

Louisiana

Centenary College of Louisiana *T*
Grambling State University *B*
Louisiana College *B, T*
Louisiana State University
  Shreveport *B*
McNeese State University *T*
Nicholls State University *B*
Northwestern State University *B*
Our Lady of Holy Cross College *B*
Southeastern Louisiana University *B*
University of Louisiana at Lafayette *B*
University of Louisiana at Monroe *B*
Xavier University of Louisiana *B*

Maine

Husson University *B*
Saint Joseph's College of Maine *B*
University of Maine *B, M*
University of Maine
  Farmington *B, T*
  Fort Kent *B*
  Machias *T*
University of Southern Maine *T*

Maryland

Anne Arundel Community College *A*
Carroll Community College *A*
Cecil College *A*
Chesapeake College *A*
Frostburg State University *B, T*
Harford Community College *A*
Hood College *T*
Howard Community College *A*
Mount St. Mary's University *T*
Notre Dame of Maryland
  University *T*
Washington Adventist University *B*

Massachusetts

Anna Maria College *B, M, T*
Assumption College *T*
Boston University *B, M, T*
Bridgewater State University *B, M, T*
Eastern Nazarene College *B*
Elms College *B, M, T*
Fitchburg State University *B, M, T*
Framingham State University *M*
Lasell College *B, T*
Lesley University *B, M*
Merrimack College *B, M*
Smith College *M*
Springfield College *T*
Tufts University *M, T*
University of Massachusetts
  Dartmouth *T*
Western New England
  University *B, M, T*

Michigan

Adrian College *B, T*
Alma College *T*
Andrews University *M*
Aquinas College *B, T*
Calvin College *B*
Central Michigan University *B*
Concordia University *B, T*
Cornerstone University *B*
Eastern Michigan University *B, T*

Ferris State University *B*
Grand Valley State University *M, T*
Hope College *B, T*
Madonna University *B*
Michigan State University *M*
Michigan Technological University *T*
Northern Michigan
  University *B, M, T*
Rochester College *B*
Saginaw Valley State University *B*
Siena Heights University *T*
Spring Arbor University *B*
University of Michigan
  Flint *B, T*
Wayne State University *B, M, T*
Western Michigan University *B, M, T*

Minnesota

Augsburg College *T*
Bemidji State University *B, M, T*
Bethel University *B*
College of St. Benedict *T*
College of St. Scholastica *B*
Concordia University St. Paul *B, T*
Crown College *B*
Gustavus Adolphus College *T*
Hamline University *T*
Martin Luther College *B*
Metropolitan State University *B*
Minnesota State University
  Mankato *B, M, T*
  Moorhead *B*
St. Catherine University *B, T*
Saint Cloud State University *B, M, T*
St. John's University *T*
St. Mary's University of Minnesota *B*
University of Minnesota
  Morris *T*
  Twin Cities *B, M*
University of Northwestern - St.
  Paul *B*
University of St. Thomas *B*
Winona State University *B, M, T*

Mississippi

Blue Mountain College *B*
Delta State University *B*
Millsaps College *T*
Mississippi College *B, M*
Northeast Mississippi Community
  College *A*
Rust College *B*
University of Mississippi *B, T*
William Carey University *B, M*

Missouri

Avila University *T*
College of the Ozarks *B, T*
Culver-Stockton College *T*
Evangel University *B, T*
Hannibal-LaGrange University *B*
Lincoln University *B*
Maryville University of Saint
  Louis *M, T*
Missouri Baptist University *T*
Missouri Southern State
  University *B, T*
Missouri State University *B*
Missouri Valley College *T*
Missouri Western State University *B*
Northwest Missouri State
  University *B, M, T*
Park University *T*
Saint Louis University *T*
Southeast Missouri State University *B*
Southwest Baptist University *B, T*
Truman State University *M*
University of Central Missouri *B, M*
University of Missouri
  Columbia *B*
  Kansas City *B*
Washington University in St. Louis *B*
William Jewell College *B, T*
William Woods University *B, T*

Montana

Carroll College *B*
Montana State University
  Billings *B, T*
Rocky Mountain College *B*
University of Great Falls *B*
University of Montana *B, T*
University of Montana: Western *B, T*

Nebraska

Chadron State College *B, M*
College of Saint Mary *B, T*
Concordia University *B, T*
Creighton University *T*
Grace University *B*
Hastings College *B, M, T*
Midland University *B, T*
Nebraska Wesleyan University *B*
Union College *B*
University of Nebraska
  Kearney *B, M, T*
  Lincoln *B, T*
Wayne State College *B, T*
York College *B, T*

Nevada

Great Basin College *B*
Nevada State College *B*

New Hampshire

Franklin Pierce University *M, T*
Granite State College *B*
Keene State College *B, T*
New England College *B, T*
Plymouth State University *M, T*
Rivier University *B, M, T*
Saint Anselm College *T*
Southern New Hampshire
  University *B*
University of New Hampshire *T*
University of New Hampshire at
  Manchester *M*

New Jersey

Centenary College *T*
College of New Jersey *B, M, T*
Georgian Court University *T*
Rowan University *T*
Rutgers, The State University of New
  Jersey
  New Brunswick/Piscataway
    Campus *M, T*
Saint Peter's University *T*
William Paterson University of New
  Jersey *T*

New Mexico

University of the Southwest *B, T*

New York

Adelphi University *M*
Alfred University *B, T*
Bard College *M*
City University of New York
  Brooklyn College *B, M, T*
  City College *B, M*
  College of Staten Island *B, M*
  Hunter College *B, M, T*
  Lehman College *M, T*
  Queens College *M, T*
Colgate University *M*
College of Saint Rose *B, T*
Cornell University *M*
D'Youville College *M, T*
Dominican College of Blauvelt *B, T*
Dowling College *B, M*
Dutchess Community College *A*
Elmira College *B, T*
Fordham University *M, T*
Hobart and William Smith Colleges *T*
Hofstra University *B, M*
Houghton College *B, T*
Iona College *B, M, T*
Ithaca College *B, M, T*

Keuka College *B, T*
Le Moyne College *T*
Long Island University
    LIU Brooklyn *B, M, T*
    LIU Post *B, M, T*
Manhattan College *B, T*
Manhattanville College *M, T*
Marist College *B*
Medaille College *B, M, T*
Medaille College: Amherst *M*
Molloy College *B*
Nazareth College *B, M, T*
New York University *B, M*
Niagara University *B, M, T*
Nyack College *B*
Pace University *B, M, T*
Pace University: Pleasantville/
    Briarcliff *B, M, T*
Roberts Wesleyan College *B, M*
SUNY
    College at Brockport *B, M, T*
    College at Buffalo *B, M*
    College at Cortland *B, M*
    College at Fredonia *B, M, T*
    College at Geneseo *B, M, T*
    College at New Paltz *B, M, T*
    College at Oneonta *B*
    College at Oswego *B, M*
    College at Plattsburgh *B, M*
    College at Potsdam *B, M*
    University at Albany *M, T*
    University at Binghamton *M*
    University at Buffalo *M, D, T*
    University at Stony Brook *T*
Saint Bonaventure University *M*
St. Francis College *B*
St. John Fisher College *B, M, T*
St. John's University *B, M, T*
St. Joseph's College New York:
    Suffolk Campus *B*
St. Joseph's College, New York *B*
St. Lawrence University *T*
St. Thomas Aquinas College *B, T*
Syracuse University *B, M, T*
Ulster County Community College *A*
University of Rochester *M*
Vassar College *T*
Wells College *T*

North Carolina

Appalachian State University *B, T*
Bennett College for Women *B*
Campbell University *B, T*
Catawba College *T*
Chowan University *B, T*
Davidson College *T*
East Carolina University *B, M*
Elizabeth City State University *B, T*
Elon University *T*
Gardner-Webb University *B, M*
Greensboro College *B, T*
Lenoir-Rhyne University *B, T*
Livingstone College *T*
Mars Hill University *B, T*
Meredith College *T*
Methodist University *B, T*
North Carolina Agricultural and
    Technical State
    University *B, M, T*
North Carolina Central
    University *B, M, T*
North Carolina State
    University *B, M, T*
Piedmont International University *B*
Shaw University *B, T*
University of Mount Olive *B*
University of North Carolina
    Charlotte *B, M*
    Greensboro *B, M*
    Pembroke *B, M*
    Wilmington *B*
Wake Forest University *T*
Western Carolina University *B, M, T*
Wingate University *B, T*
Winston-Salem State University *B*

North Dakota

Dickinson State University *B, T*
Mayville State University *B, T*
Minot State University *B, M*
North Dakota State University *B, T*
University of Jamestown *B*
University of Mary *B*
Valley City State University *B, T*

Ohio

Antioch University
    Midwest *M*
Ashland University *B, T*
Baldwin Wallace University *T*
Bluffton University *B*
Bowling Green State
    University *B, M, T*
Capital University *T*
Case Western Reserve University *T*
Cedarville University *B*
Defiance College *B, T*
God's Bible School and College *B*
Hiram College *T*
John Carroll University *T*
Malone University *B*
Miami University
    Oxford *B, M, T*
Mount Vernon Nazarene
    University *B, T*
Ohio Dominican University *B, T*
Ohio Northern University *B, T*
Ohio State University
    Columbus Campus *B*
Ohio University *D, T*
Otterbein University *B*
Tiffin University *B*
University of Akron *B, M*
University of Cincinnati *M*
University of Findlay *B, M, T*
University of Mount Union *T*
University of Rio Grande *B, T*
University of Toledo *B, M, T*
Urbana University *B*
Ursuline College *B, M, T*
Walsh University *B*
Wilmington College *B*
Youngstown State University *B, M*

Oklahoma

Cameron University *B*
East Central University *B, T*
Mid-America Christian University *B*
Northeastern State University *B*
Northwestern Oklahoma State
    University *B*
Oklahoma Baptist University *B, T*
Oklahoma Christian University *B, T*
Oklahoma City University *B*
Oklahoma Wesleyan University *B*
Oral Roberts University *B, T*
Southeastern Oklahoma State
    University *B, T*
Southern Nazarene University *B, M*
Southwestern Oklahoma State
    University *B, M, T*
University of Oklahoma *B, T*
University of Tulsa *T*

Oregon

Concordia University *B, M, T*
Corban University *B*
Linfield College *T*
Oregon State University *M*
Portland State University *T*
Southern Oregon University *T*
Warner Pacific College *T*

Pennsylvania

Albright College *T*
Alvernia University *B*
Arcadia University *B, M, T*
Bryn Athyn College *B*
Cabrini College *T*
Cairn University *B, T*
Chatham University *M, T*
DeSales University *T*
Duquesne University *B, M, T*
Geneva College *T*
Gettysburg College *T*
Grove City College *T*
Holy Family University *B*
Juniata College *B, T*
Keystone College *B*
King's College *T*
La Roche College *B*
La Salle University *B, T*
Lebanon Valley College *T*
Lycoming College *T*
Mansfield University of
    Pennsylvania *B, T*
Marywood University *B*
Mercyhurst University *B, T*
Messiah College *B, T*
Misericordia University *B, T*
Moravian College *T*
Point Park University *B*
St. Francis University *B, T*
Saint Joseph's University *M, T*
St. Vincent College *T*
Seton Hill University *B, T*
Susquehanna University *T*
Temple University *B*
Thiel College *B*
University of Pennsylvania *M, T*
University of Pittsburgh
    Greensburg *B, T*
    Johnstown *B, T*
University of Scranton *B*
Villanova University *T*
Washington & Jefferson College *T*
Waynesburg University *B, T*
Westminster College *B, T*
Widener University *M, D, T*
Wilkes University *M, T*
Wilson College *T*
York College of Pennsylvania *B, T*

Puerto Rico

Bayamon Central University *B*
Caribbean University *B, T*
Inter American University of Puerto
    Rico
    Barranquitas Campus *B, T*
    San German Campus *B*
Pontifical Catholic University of
    Puerto Rico *B, T*
Turabo University *B*
University of Puerto Rico
    Aguadilla *B, T*
    Cayey University College *B*
    Mayaguez *M*

Rhode Island

Bryant University *M*
Rhode Island College *B, M*

South Carolina

Anderson University *B, T*
Bob Jones University *B*
Charleston Southern University *B*
Claflin University *B*
Coker College *B, T*
Francis Marion University *B, T*
Furman University *T*
Limestone College *B*
Morris College *B, T*
North Greenville University *B, M, T*
Southern Wesleyan University *B, T*
Wofford College *T*

South Dakota

Augustana College *B, T*
Dakota State University *B, T*
Dakota Wesleyan University *B, T*
Mount Marty College *B*
Northern State University *B, T*
Presentation College *A*
University of Sioux Falls *B, T*
University of South Dakota *B, T*

Tennessee

Aquinas College *B*
Belmont University *T*
Bethel University *B, T*
Bryan University
    Dayton *T*
Cumberland University *B*
Freed-Hardeman University *B, T*
King University *T*
Lee University *B*
Lincoln Memorial University *B, T*
Lipscomb University *B, T*
Martin Methodist College *B*
Maryville College *B*
Southern Adventist University *B*
Tennessee Technological
    University *B, T*
Tennessee Temple University *B*
Trevecca Nazarene University *B, T*
Tusculum College *B, T*
Union University *B, T*
Victory University *B, T*

Texas

Abilene Christian University *B, T*
Arlington Baptist College *B, T*
Baylor University *B, T*
Dallas Christian College *B, T*
Del Mar College *A*
East Texas Baptist University *B*
Hardin-Simmons University *B, T*
Houston Baptist University *B*
Howard Payne University *B*
Jarvis Christian College *B, T*
Lamar University *T*
Laredo Community College *A*
LeTourneau University *B, T*
McMurry University *B, T*
Midwestern State University *B*
Our Lady of the Lake University of
    San Antonio *B*
Prairie View A&M University *M*
St. Mary's University *T*
Sam Houston State University *M, T*
Schreiner University *B*
Southwestern Assemblies of God
    University *B*
Tarleton State University *T*
Texas A&M International
    University *B, M, T*
Texas Christian University *B*
Texas Lutheran University *B, T*
Texas Wesleyan University *B, T*
University of Dallas *T*
University of Mary Hardin-Baylor *B, T*
University of Texas
    Arlington *T*
    El Paso *M*
    San Antonio *T*
Wayland Baptist University *B*
West Texas A&M University *T*

Utah

Brigham Young University *B*
Dixie State College *B*
Southern Utah University *B*
Utah State University *B*
Utah Valley University *B*
Weber State University *B*

Vermont

Castleton State College *B, T*
College of St. Joseph in
    Vermont *B, M, T*
Goddard College *B, M*
Green Mountain College *B, T*
Johnson State College *B*
Lyndon State College *B*
Saint Michael's College *M*
University of Vermont *B, T*

Virginia

Averett University *B, M, T*
Bluefield College *B, T*
Bridgewater College *T*
Eastern Mennonite University *T*
Emory & Henry College *B, M*
Hampton University *M*
Hollins University *T*
Longwood University *T*
Radford University *T*
University of Virginia's College at
    Wise *T*
Virginia Intermont College *T*

Washington

Central Washington
    University *B, M, T*
Eastern Washington
    University *B, M, T*
Heritage University *B, M*
Northwest University *T*
Seattle Pacific University *B, T*
Washington State University *B, M, T*
Western Washington University *B*
Whitworth University *M, T*

West Virginia

Bethany College *B*
Concord University *B, M, T*
Ohio Valley University *B*
Shepherd University *T*
University of Charleston *B*
West Liberty University *B*
West Virginia State University *B*
West Virginia University *T*
West Virginia Wesleyan College *B*
Wheeling Jesuit University *B*

Wisconsin

Alverno College *B, T*
Carroll University *B, T*
Carthage College *M, T*
Concordia University Wisconsin *B*
Edgewood College *B, T*
Lakeland College *T*
Lawrence University *T*
Maranatha Baptist Bible College *B*
Marian University *B, T*
Mount Mary University *B, T*
St. Norbert College *T*
University of Wisconsin
    Green Bay *T*
    Milwaukee *T*
    Platteville *B, T*
    River Falls *T*
    Superior *B, T*
    Whitewater *B*
Viterbo University *B, T*

Entomology

Alabama

Auburn University *M, D*

Arizona

University of Arizona *M, D*

Arkansas

University of Arkansas *M, D*

California

University of California
    Davis *B, M, D*
    Riverside *B, M, D*

Colorado

Colorado State University *M, D*

Delaware

University of Delaware *B, M*

Florida

Florida Agricultural and Mechanical
    University *D*
University of Florida *B, M, D*

Georgia

University of Georgia *B, M, D*

Hawaii

University of Hawaii
    Manoa *M, D*

Idaho

University of Idaho *M, D*

Illinois

University of Illinois
    Urbana-Champaign *B, M, D*

Indiana

Purdue University *B, M, D*

Iowa

Iowa State University *B, M, D*

Kansas

Kansas State University *M, D*
University of Kansas *M, D*

Kentucky

University of Kentucky *M, D*

Louisiana

Louisiana State University and
    Agricultural and Mechanical
    College *M, D*

Maine

College of the Atlantic *B, M*
University of Maine *M*

Maryland

University of Maryland
    College Park *M, D*

Michigan

Michigan State University *B, M, D*

Minnesota

University of Minnesota
    Twin Cities *B, M, D*

Missouri

University of Missouri
    Columbia *M, D*

Montana

Montana State University *M*

Nebraska

University of Nebraska
    Lincoln *B, M, D*

New Hampshire

University of New Hampshire *B*

New Jersey

Rutgers, The State University of New
    Jersey
    New Brunswick/Piscataway
        Campus *M, D*

New York

Cornell University *B, M, D*

North Carolina

North Carolina State University *M, D*

North Dakota

North Dakota State University *M, D*

Ohio

Ohio State University
    Columbus Campus *B, M, D*

Oklahoma

Eastern Oklahoma State College *A*
Oklahoma State University *B, M, D*

Oregon

Oregon State University *M, D*

Pennsylvania

Penn State
    University Park *M, D*

South Carolina

Clemson University *M, D*

Texas

Texas A&M University *B, M, D*
Texas Tech University *M*

Virginia

Virginia Polytechnic Institute and
    State University *D*

Washington

Washington State University *M, D*

Wisconsin

University of Wisconsin
    Madison *B, M, D*

Wyoming

University of Wyoming *M, D*

Entrepreneurial studies

Alabama

Auburn University *B*
Samford University *B*
University of Phoenix
    Birmingham *B*
Wallace State Community College at
    Hanceville *A*

Alaska

University of Alaska
    Anchorage *C, A, B*

Arizona

Arizona State University *B*
Arizona Western College *C*
Central Arizona College *C*
Eastern Arizona College *C, A*
GateWay Community College *C*
Glendale Community College *C*
Grand Canyon University *B*
Northland Pioneer College *C*
Rio Salado College *C*
University of Arizona *B*
University of Phoenix
    Phoenix-Hohokam *B*
    Southern Arizona *B*

Arkansas

Arkansas State University
    Beebe *C*
East Arkansas Community College *C*
North Arkansas College *C*
Northwest Arkansas Community
    College *C*
Southeast Arkansas College *C*
Southern Arkansas University Tech *C*
University of Central Arkansas *B*

California

Azusa Pacific University *M*
Cabrillo College *C, A*

California State University

Dominguez Hills *B*
East Bay *B, M*
Fullerton *B, M*
Coastline Community College *A*
Cogswell Polytechnical College *M*
College of Alameda *C, A*
Cosumnes River College *A*
Diablo Valley College *C, A*
Fullerton College *C*
Lake Tahoe Community College *C, A*
Lincoln University *M*
Los Angeles City College *C, A*
Los Angeles Pierce College *C*
Los Angeles Trade and Technical
    College *A*
Los Medanos College *C, A*
Loyola Marymount University *B*
Marymount California University *B*
Mendocino College *C, A*
Menlo College *B*
MiraCosta College *C, A*
Mount St. Mary's College *C*
Mount San Antonio College *C, A*
Mount San Jacinto College *C*
Mt. Sierra College *B*
Pasadena City College *A*
Point Loma Nazarene University *B*
San Diego State University *M*
San Jose City College *C, A*
Santa Ana College *C, A*
Shasta College *A*
Southwestern College *C, A*
University of Phoenix
    Bay Area *B*
    Central Valley *B*
    Sacramento Valley *B*
    Southern California *B*
University of San Francisco *B, M*
Yuba College *C, A*

Colorado

Aspen University *M*
Colorado Mesa University *C*
Colorado Northwestern Community
    College *A*
Pueblo Community College *C, A*
University of Phoenix
    Denver *B*

Connecticut

Asnuntuck Community College *C*
Quinebaug Valley Community
    College *C*
Quinnipiac University *B*
University of Bridgeport *M*
University of Hartford *B*

Delaware

Delaware State University *B*
Delaware Technical Community
    College
    Jack F. Owens Campus *C, A*
    Stanton/Wilmington Campus *C*
    Terry Campus *C, A*

District of Columbia

Gallaudet University *B*

Florida

College of Central Florida *C*
Daytona State College *C*
Florida Keys Community College *C*
Hillsborough Community College *C*
Lake-Sumter State College *C*
Lynn University *B*
Northwest Florida State College *C*
Polk State College *C, A*
Rasmussen College
    Fort Myers *C*
    New Port Richey *C*
    Ocala *C*
    Pasco/Land O'Lakes *C*
    Tampa/Brandon *C*

Saint Johns River State College *C*
St. Petersburg College *C*
Santa Fe College *C*
South Florida State College *C*
Stetson University *B*
Tallahassee Community College *C, A*
University of Miami *B*
University of Phoenix
　Central Florida *B*
　North Florida *B*
　South Florida *B*
　West Florida *B*
University of South Florida *M*
University of South Florida
　Saint Petersburg *B*
University of Tampa *B*
Valencia College *C*

Georgia

Albany Technical College *C*
Georgia State University *C*
Gwinnett Technical College *C*
Southern Polytechnic State
　University *B, M*
University of Phoenix
　Atlanta *B*
　Augusta *B*
　Columbus *B*
　Savannah *B*

Hawaii

University of Phoenix
　Hawaii *B*

Idaho

University of Phoenix
　Idaho *B*

Illinois

Bradley University *B*
College of Lake County *C*
Danville Area Community College *C*
Elgin Community College *C, A*
Heartland Community College *C*
Kaskaskia College *C*
Kishwaukee College *C*
Loyola University Chicago *B*
McHenry County College *B*
Millikin University *B*
Northwestern University *M*
Parkland College *C*
Prairie State College *C*
Rasmussen College
　Aurora *B*
　Mokena/Tinley Park *C*
　Rockford *C*
　Romeoville/Joliet *C*
Rock Valley College *C*
Trinity Christian College *B*
Triton College *C*
University of Illinois
　Chicago *B*
　Urbana-Champaign *B, M, D, T*
University of Phoenix
　Chicago *B*
University of St. Francis *B*

Indiana

Anderson University *B*
Ball State University *B*
Huntington University *B*
Indiana Wesleyan University *B*
Trine University *B*
University of Indianapolis *B*
University of Phoenix
　Indianapolis *B*
University of Southern Indiana *B*
Vincennes University *C*

Iowa

Ashford University *B*
Buena Vista University *B*
Grand View University *B*

North Iowa Area Community
　College *C, A*

Kansas

Coffeyville Community College *A*
Cowley County Community
　College *A*
Johnson County Community
　College *C, A*
Kansas State University *B*
Pratt Community College *C, A*
Washburn University *C*
Wichita Area Technical College *C, A*
Wichita State University *B*

Kentucky

Northern Kentucky University *C, B*
University of Louisville *D*
University of Phoenix
　Louisville *B*
Western Kentucky University *B*

Louisiana

Delgado Community College *C*
Herzing University
　Kenner *B*
Southern University
　New Orleans *B*
University of Phoenix
　Baton Rouge *B*
　Louisiana *B*
　Shreveport *B*

Maine

College of the Atlantic *B, M*
Husson University *B*
Maine Maritime Academy *B*
Northern Maine Community
　College *C*
Washington County Community
　College *C*

Maryland

Anne Arundel Community
　College *C, A*
Harford Community College *C, A*
Howard Community College *C, A*
University of Baltimore *B*

Massachusetts

Babson College *B*
Bentley University *M*
Boston University *B*
Bristol Community College *A*
Endicott College *B*
Hampshire College *B*
Holyoke Community College *C*
Lasell College *B*
Marian Court College *A*
Massachusetts College of Liberal
　Arts *B*
Middlesex Community College *C*
Northeastern University *B, M*
Salem State University *B*
Suffolk University *B*
Tufts University *M*
University of Massachusetts
　Lowell *B, M*
University of Phoenix
　Boston *B*
Western New England University *B*

Michigan

Andrews University *B*
Bay de Noc Community College *C*
Central Michigan University *B*
Cleary University *B*
Eastern Michigan University *B, M*
Gogebic Community College *A*
Grand Rapids Community College *C*
Lake Superior State University *B*
Lansing Community College *C*
Mid Michigan Community College *A*
Montcalm Community College *C, A*

Mott Community College *C, A*
North Central Michigan College *C*
Northern Michigan University *B*
Northwood University
　Michigan *A, B*
Oakland Community College *C, A*
Schoolcraft College *A*
University of Michigan *M*
University of Michigan
　Flint *B*
University of Phoenix
　Metro Detroit *B*
　West Michigan *B*
Wayne County Community College *C*
Wayne State University *C*

Minnesota

Capella University *M*
Century College *C*
Crown College *B*
Dakota County Technical College *C*
Minneapolis College of Art and
　Design *B*
Minnesota State Community and
　Technical College *C, A*
Minnesota State University
　Moorhead *B*
North Hennepin Community
　College *C, A*
Northland Community & Technical
　College *C*
Northwest Technical College *C*
Rasmussen College
　Blaine *C*
　Bloomington *C*
　Brooklyn Park *C*
　Eagan *C*
　Lake Elmo/Woodbury *C*
　Mankato *C*
　Moorhead *A*
　St. Cloud *C*
Saint Cloud State University *B*
St. Mary's University of Minnesota *B*
St. Paul College *C, A*
University of Minnesota
　Crookston *B*
University of Phoenix
　Minneapolis-St. Paul *B*
University of St. Thomas *B*

Mississippi

Jackson State University *B*
University of Phoenix
　Jackson *B*

Missouri

Avila University *B*
Central Methodist University *B*
Lindenwood University *B, M*
Missouri State University *B*
Missouri State University: West
　Plains *C, A*
Missouri Valley College *A*
Saint Louis University *M*
Three Rivers Community College *A*
University of Missouri
　Kansas City *B, M, D*
University of Phoenix
　Kansas City *B*
　St. Louis *B*
Washington University in St. Louis *B*
Webster University *C*

Montana

Blackfeet Community College *A*
Flathead Valley Community College *C*
Helena College University of
　Montana *C*
Montana State University
　Great Falls College *A*

Nebraska

Creighton University *B*
Northeast Community College *A*

University of Phoenix
　Omaha *B*

Nevada

Great Basin College *C, A*
Sierra Nevada College *B*
University of Nevada
　Reno *B*
University of Phoenix
　Las Vegas *B*

New Hampshire

New England College *B*
White Mountains Community
　College *C*

New Jersey

Bergen Community College *C*
Berkeley College *B*
Burlington County College *C*
Eastwick College
　Hackensack *A*
Fairleigh Dickinson University
　College at Florham *B*
　Metropolitan Campus *B*
Mercer County Community
　College *C*
Ocean County College *C*
Rider University *B*
Rowan University *B*
Thomas Edison State College *B*
University of Phoenix
　Jersey City *B*
Warren County Community
　College *C, A*

New Mexico

Santa Fe Community College *C*
University of Phoenix
　New Mexico *B*

New York

Canisius College *B*
City University of New York
　Baruch College *M*
　Kingsborough Community
　　College *C*
Clarkson University *B*
Erie Community College *C*
Herkimer County Community
　College *C, A*
Hofstra University *B*
Jamestown Community College *C*
Mohawk Valley Community
　College *C*
Pace University *B, M*
Pace University: Pleasantville/
　Briarcliff *B, M*
Paul Smith's College *B*
Rockland Community College *C, A*
SUNY
　College at Plattsburgh *B*
　College of Agriculture and
　　Technology at Morrisville *B*
　College of Technology at
　　Alfred *C, A*
　University at Binghamton *B*
Syracuse University *B, M*
Tompkins Cortland Community
　College *A*
Ulster County Community College *A*
University of Rochester *M*

North Carolina

Cleveland Community College *C, A*
Craven Community College *C, A*
Elon University *B*
Isothermal Community College *C, A*
Lenoir-Rhyne University *B*
Stanly Community College *C*
Western Carolina University *B, M*

North Dakota

Rasmussen College
  Bismarck *B*
  Fargo *C*
Sitting Bull College *A*
University of North Dakota *C, B*

Ohio

Ashland University *B*
Baldwin Wallace University *B*
Belmont College *A*
Bowling Green State University:
  Firelands College *C*
Case Western Reserve University *M*
Columbus State Community
  College *C, A*
Cuyahoga Community College
  Metropolitan *A*
Kent State University *B*
Lake Erie College *B*
Lakeland Community College *C*
Lorain County Community College *A*
Northwest State Community
  College *A*
Sinclair Community College *C, A*
Southern State Community College *A*
Stautzenberger College *A*
University of Akron *M*
University of Dayton *B*
University of Findlay *B*
University of Phoenix
  Cleveland *B*
University of Toledo *B, M*
Xavier University *B*
Youngstown State University *C*

Oklahoma

Northeastern State University *B*
Oklahoma State University *B, M*

Oregon

George Fox University *B*
Mt. Hood Community College *C, A*
Portland Community College *C*
Southwestern Oregon Community
  College *A*

Pennsylvania

Carnegie Mellon University *B*
Central Penn College *A*
Community College of Allegheny
  County *C, A*
Delaware County Community
  College *C, A*
Drexel University *B*
Duquesne University *B*
Eastern University *B*
Gannon University *B*
Grove City College *B*
Juniata College *B*
Lehigh Carbon Community College *C*
Montgomery County Community
  College *C*
Northampton Community College *C*
Penn State
  Abington *C*
  Altoona *C*
  Beaver *C*
  Berks *C*
  Brandywine *C*
  DuBois *C*
  Erie, The Behrend College *C*
  Fayette, The Eberly Campus *C*
  Greater Allegheny *C*
  Harrisburg *C*
  Hazleton *C*
  Lehigh Valley *C*
  Mont Alto *C*
  New Kensington *C*
  Schuylkill *C*
  Shenango *C*
  University Park *C*
  Wilkes-Barre *C*

Worthington Scranton *C*
  York *C*
Seton Hill University *C, B*
Temple University *B, M*
University of Phoenix
  Pittsburgh *B*
University of Pittsburgh
  Bradford *B*
Valley Forge Christian College *B*
Wilkes University *B*
York College of Pennsylvania *B*

Puerto Rico

ICPR Junior College *C*
Inter American University of Puerto
  Rico
  Aguadilla Campus *B*
  Bayamon Campus *B*
  Metropolitan Campus *B*
  San German Campus *B*
National University College
  Arecibo *A*
  Bayamon *A*
  Rio Grande *A*
Pontifical Catholic University of
  Puerto Rico *B*
Universidad Metropolitana *C*
Universidad del Este *C*

Rhode Island

Bryant University *B*
Community College of Rhode
  Island *C*
Johnson & Wales University
  Providence *B*

South Carolina

Florence-Darlington Technical
  College *A*
Greenville Technical College *C*
Horry-Georgetown Technical
  College *C*
Piedmont Technical College *C*
Trident Technical College *C*
University of Phoenix
  Columbia *B*
York Technical College *C*

South Dakota

South Dakota State University *C, B*
Southeast Technical Institute *A*

Tennessee

Belmont University *B*
Southern Adventist University *M*
Tusculum College *B*
University of Phoenix
  Chattanooga *B*
  Memphis *B*
  Nashville *B*

Texas

Baylor University *B*
Dallas Baptist University *M*
East Texas Baptist University *M*
Galveston College *C, A*
Houston Baptist University *B*
Richland College *A*
St. Edward's University *B*
St. Mary's University *B*
San Jacinto College *C, A*
Southern Methodist University *M*
University of Dallas *M*
University of Houston *B*
University of Houston
  Victoria *M*
University of Phoenix
  Austin *B*
  Dallas Fort Worth *B*
  Houston Westside *B*
  San Antonio *B*
University of Texas
  Austin *C*
  Brownsville *B*

Dallas *M*
San Antonio *B*

Utah

Brigham Young University *B*
LDS Business College *C, A*
University of Phoenix
  Utah *B*
University of Utah *B*
Utah State University *B*
Weber State University *C*
Westminster College *B*

Vermont

Champlain College *C*
Lyndon State College *A, B*
Southern Vermont College *B*
University of Vermont *B*

Virginia

Northern Virginia Community
  College *C*
Shenandoah University *B*
Stratford University: Falls Church *M*
University of Phoenix
  Northern Virginia *B*

Washington

Bellevue College *C*
Edmonds Community College *C*
Grays Harbor College *C, A*
Heritage University *B*
Lake Washington Institute of
  Technology *C*
North Seattle Community College *C*
Seattle University *M*
Tacoma Community College *C*
University of Phoenix
  Western Washington *B*
Washington State University *B*
Yakima Valley Community College *A*

West Virginia

American Public University
  System *B, M*
Blue Ridge Community and Technical
  College *C, A*
Bridgemont Community and
  Technical College *C*
West Virginia Northern Community
  College *C*

Wisconsin

Carthage College *B*
Herzing University
  Brookfield *B*
  Kenosha *B*
  Madison *B*
Madison Area Technical College *C*
Marquette University *B*
Moraine Park Technical College *C*
Northland College *B*
Rasmussen College
  Appleton *B*
  Green Bay *C*
  Wausau *C*
University of Phoenix
  Milwaukee *B*
University of Wisconsin
  Milwaukee *C*
  Platteville *B*
  Whitewater *B*
Viterbo University *B*

Wyoming

Casper College *A*
Central Wyoming College *C, A*
Eastern Wyoming College *C*
Laramie County Community
  College *C, A*

Environmental biology

Arizona

Arizona State University *D*
Arizona Western College *A*
Eastern Arizona College *A*

California

California State Polytechnic
  University: Pomona *B*
College of Marin *A*
Master's College *B*
University of La Verne *B*

Connecticut

Mitchell College *B*

District of Columbia

Georgetown University *B*

Georgia

Mercer University *B*

Illinois

Blackburn College *B*
Chicago State University *B*
Eureka College *B*
Governors State University *M*
Greenville College *B*
Illinois College *B*

Indiana

Bethel College *B*
Grace College *B*
Manchester University *B*

Iowa

Northwestern College *B*

Kansas

Central Christian College of Kansas *A*
Friends University *B*

Louisiana

University of Louisiana at Lafayette *D*

Maine

College of the Atlantic *B, M*
Unity College *B*

Maryland

Hood College *M*
McDaniel College *B*
Morgan State University *D*

Massachusetts

Fitchburg State University *B*

Michigan

Cornerstone University *B*
Ferris State University *B*
Michigan State University *B*

Minnesota

St. Mary's University of Minnesota *B*

Missouri

Lindenwood University *B*
Washington University in St. Louis *B*

New Hampshire

Plymouth State University *B*

New Jersey

Centenary College *B*
Monmouth University *B*
Passaic County Community College *A*

New York

Barnard College *B*
Columbia University *B*
Corning Community College *A*

Houghton College *B*
Iona College *B*
SUNY
   College at Brockport *B*
   College of Environmental Science
    and Forestry *B, M, D*

North Carolina
Wingate University *B*

North Dakota
North Dakota State University *M, D*
United Tribes Technical College *A*

Ohio
Cedarville University *B*
Heidelberg University *B*
Notre Dame College *B*
University of Dayton *B*
Wilmington College *B*

Pennsylvania
Cedar Crest College *B*
Clarion University of Pennsylvania *B*
Eastern University *B*
Elizabethtown College *B*
Keystone College *B*
Philadelphia University *B*
University of Pennsylvania *M*
Waynesburg University *B*

Puerto Rico
Inter American University of Puerto
  Rico
   Bayamon Campus *M*
   San German Campus *M*

Tennessee
Lee University *B*

Texas
Baylor University *M*
Texas A&M University *B*

Vermont
Bennington College *B*
Southern Vermont College *B*
Sterling College *B*

Virginia
Christopher Newport University *B*
Liberty University *B*
Virginia Intermont College *B*

Washington
Whitman College *B*

Wisconsin
Beloit College *B*
University of Wisconsin
  Superior *B*

Wyoming
Eastern Wyoming College *A*

Environmental chemistry

Colorado
University of Denver *B*

Georgia
University of Georgia *B*

Maine
Colby College *B*

Michigan
Lawrence Technological University *B*
Oakland University *D*

Ohio
Ashland University *B*

South Dakota
Sisseton Wahpeton College *A*

Tennessee
Sewanee: The University of the
  South *B*

Texas
St. Edward's University *B*

Wisconsin
Beloit College *B*
University of Wisconsin
  Madison *M, D*

Environmental design

Alabama
Auburn University *B*

Arizona
Arizona State University *M*
Prescott College *B*
Scottsdale Community College *C, A*
Yavapai College *C, A*

California
Art Center College of Design *B, M*
City College of San Francisco *A*
College of Marin *A*
Cosumnes River College *C, A*
Otis College of Art and Design *B*
Rio Hondo College *C, A*

Colorado
Ecotech Institute *C*
University of Colorado
  Boulder *B*
  Denver *D*

Connecticut
Yale University *M*

District of Columbia
Catholic University of America *M*

Florida
Florida Atlantic University *B*
Florida State College at
  Jacksonville *A*

Georgia
Georgia Institute of Technology *M*
Middle Georgia State College *A*

Indiana
Ball State University *B*

Kansas
Kansas State University *D*

Maryland
Morgan State University *B, M*

Massachusetts
Massachusetts College of Art and
  Design *B, M*
Northeastern University *M*
University of Massachusetts
  Amherst *B*

Michigan
Lawrence Technological
  University *B, M*
Michigan State University *M*

Minnesota
University of Minnesota
  Twin Cities *B*

Missouri
Ranken Technical College *A, B*

Montana
Montana State University *B, M*

New Jersey
Rutgers, The State University of New
  Jersey
   New Brunswick/Piscataway
    Campus *B*

New Mexico
University of New Mexico *B*

New York
Cornell University *B, M, D*
Pratt Institute *M*
SUNY
  University at Buffalo *B*
  University at Stony Brook *B*
Suffolk County Community College *A*

North Carolina
North Carolina State University *B, D*

North Dakota
North Dakota State University *B*

Ohio
Bowling Green State University *B*
Stark State College *A*

Oklahoma
University of Oklahoma *B*

Oregon
Portland Community College *C*

Pennsylvania
Carnegie Mellon University *B*
Marywood University *B, M*
University of Pennsylvania *B*

Puerto Rico
University of Puerto Rico
  Rio Piedras *B*

Tennessee
University of Memphis *B, M*

Texas
Texas Tech University *D*
University of Houston *B*
University of Texas
  Austin *M*

Utah
Utah State University *B*

Vermont
Bennington College *B*

Virginia
University of Virginia *D*
Virginia Polytechnic Institute and
  State University *D*

Environmental education

Arizona
Prescott College *B, M*

Florida
Florida Institute of Technology *M*

Indiana
Goshen College *M*

Iowa
University of Dubuque *B, T*

Louisiana
McNeese State University *T*

Minnesota
University of Minnesota
  Crookston *B*
  Duluth *M*

Nevada
Nevada State College *B*

New York
New York University *M*

Pennsylvania
Washington & Jefferson College *T*

Puerto Rico
Universidad Metropolitana *M*

West Virginia
Potomac State College of West
  Virginia University *A*

Environmental engineering

Alabama
University of Alabama *M*
University of Alabama
  Birmingham *D*

Alaska
University of Alaska
  Anchorage *M*
  Fairbanks *M*

Arizona
Northern Arizona University *B*
University of Arizona *M, D*

Arkansas
Northwest Arkansas Community
  College *A*
University of Arkansas *M*

California
California Institute of
  Technology *B, M, D*
California Polytechnic State
  University: San Luis Obispo *B*
California State University
  Fresno *B*
  Fullerton *M*
Humboldt State University *B*
National University *M*
San Diego State University *B, M*
Stanford University *B*
University of California
  Berkeley *B*
  Irvine *B, M, D*
  Merced *B*
  Riverside *B*
University of Southern
  California *B, M, D*

Colorado
Colorado School of Mines *B, M, D*
Colorado State University *B*
United States Air Force Academy *B*
University of Colorado
  Boulder *B*

Connecticut
University of Connecticut *B, M, D*
University of Hartford *M*
University of New Haven *M*
Yale University *B, M, D*

Delaware

University of Delaware *B*

Florida

Florida Gulf Coast University *B*
Florida International University *B, M*
Florida State University *B*
University of Central Florida *B, M, D*
University of Florida *B, M, D*
University of Miami *B, M*
University of South Florida *M*

Georgia

Georgia Institute of
    Technology *B, M, D*
Mercer University *M*
University of Georgia *B, M*

Idaho

Idaho State University *M*
University of Idaho *M*

Illinois

Illinois Institute of Technology *M, D*
Northwestern University *B*
University of Illinois
    Urbana-Champaign *B, M, D*

Indiana

Indiana Institute of Technology *B*
Rose-Hulman Institute of
    Technology *M*
Taylor University *B*
University of Notre Dame *B*

Kansas

University of Kansas *M, D*

Kentucky

University of Louisville *C*

Louisiana

Louisiana State University and
    Agricultural and Mechanical
    College *B*

Maryland

Johns Hopkins University *B, M, D*

Massachusetts

Bristol Community College *A*
Massachusetts Institute of
    Technology *B, M, D*
Smith College *B*
Suffolk University *B*
Tufts University *B, M*
University of Massachusetts
    Amherst *M*
Worcester Polytechnic Institute *B, M*

Michigan

Michigan State University *M, D*
Michigan Technological
    University *B, M, D*
University of Michigan *B, M, D*
University of Michigan
    Flint *B*

Missouri

Missouri University of Science and
    Technology *B, M*
Washington University in St.
    Louis *M, D*

Montana

Montana State University *M*
Montana Tech of the University of
    Montana *B, M*

Nebraska

University of Nebraska
    Lincoln *M*

Nevada

University of Nevada
    Reno *B, M, D*

New Hampshire

University of New Hampshire *B*

New Jersey

New Jersey Institute of
    Technology *B, M, D*
Rutgers, The State University of New
    Jersey
    New Brunswick/Piscataway
        Campus *M, D*
Stevens Institute of
    Technology *B, M, D*

New Mexico

Central New Mexico Community
    College *A*
New Mexico Institute of Mining and
    Technology *B, M*
New Mexico State University *M*
University of New Mexico *M*

New York

Clarkson University *B, M, D*
Columbia University *B, M, D*
Cornell University *B*
Manhattan College *M*
Rensselaer Polytechnic
    Institute *B, M, D*
SUNY
    College of Environmental Science
        and Forestry *B, M*
    University at Buffalo *B*
Syracuse University *B, M*
United States Military Academy *B*

North Carolina

Elon University *B*
North Carolina State University *B*

North Dakota

North Dakota State University *M*
University of North Dakota *B, M*

Ohio

Central State University *B*
Ohio State University
    Columbus Campus *B*
Stark State College *A*
University of Akron *C*
University of Cincinnati *B, M, D*

Oklahoma

Oklahoma State University *M*
Oral Roberts University *B*
University of Oklahoma *B, M, D*

Oregon

Oregon State University *B, M, D*
University of Portland *B*

Pennsylvania

Bucknell University *B*
Carnegie Mellon University *M, D*
Drexel University *B, M, D*
Gannon University *B*
Lehigh University *B, M, D*
Penn State
    Abington *B*
    Altoona *B*
    Beaver *B*
    Berks *B*
    Brandywine *B*
    DuBois *B*
    Erie, The Behrend College *B*
    Fayette, The Eberly Campus *B*
    Greater Allegheny *B*
    Harrisburg *B, M*
    Hazleton *B*
    Lehigh Valley *B*

Mont Alto *B*
New Kensington *B*
Schuylkill *B*
Shenango *B*
University Park *B, M, D*
Wilkes-Barre *B*
Worthington Scranton *B*
York *B*
St. Francis University *B*
University of Pennsylvania *B*
Villanova University *M*
Wilkes University *B*

South Carolina

Benedict College *B*
Clemson University *M, D*

South Dakota

South Dakota School of Mines and
    Technology *B*

Tennessee

University of Tennessee
    Knoxville *M*
Vanderbilt University *M, D*

Texas

Lamar University *B, M*
Rice University *B, M, D*
Southern Methodist University *B, M*
Tarleton State University *B*
Texas Tech University *B, M*
University of Houston *M, D*
University of Texas
    Austin *M*
    El Paso *M, D*
    San Antonio *D*
West Texas A&M University *B*

Utah

University of Utah *M, D*
Utah State University *A, B*

Vermont

Norwich University *B*
University of Vermont *B*

Virginia

Old Dominion University *B*
Virginia Polytechnic Institute and
    State University *M*

Washington

University of Washington *B*
Washington State University *M*

West Virginia

West Virginia University *M, D*

Wisconsin

Marquette University *B*
Milwaukee School of Engineering *M*
University of Wisconsin
    Platteville *B*

Wyoming

Central Wyoming College *C, A*
University of Wyoming *M*

Environmental engineering technology

Alabama

Northwest-Shoals Community
    College *C, A*

Arizona

Pima Community College *C*

Arkansas

East Arkansas Community
    College *C, A*

Northwest Arkansas Community
    College *C, A*
Pulaski Technical College *A*
Southern Arkansas University Tech *A*

California

Allan Hancock College *C, A*
Rio Hondo College *C*

Connecticut

Naugatuck Valley Community
    College *C, A*
Three Rivers Community
    College *C, A*
University of Hartford *B*

Delaware

Delaware Technical Community
    College
    Stanton/Wilmington Campus *C*

Illinois

Black Hawk College *C, A*
City Colleges of Chicago
    Olive-Harvey College *A*
    Wilbur Wright College *C, A*

Iowa

Clinton Community College *C, A*
Iowa Lakes Community College *A*

Kentucky

Bluegrass Community and Technical
    College *C, A*

Maryland

College of Southern Maryland *C, A*
Wor-Wic Community College *C, A*

Massachusetts

Bristol Community College *A*
Holyoke Community College *A*
Tufts University *C, B, M, D*

Michigan

Bay de Noc Community College *A*
Lansing Community College *A*
Schoolcraft College *A*
Wayne County Community College *C*

Missouri

Metropolitan Community College -
    Kansas City *C, A*

Nevada

College of Southern Nevada *A*

New York

City University of New York
    New York City College of
        Technology *A*
New York Institute of Technology *M*
Onondaga Community College *A*
Rochester Institute of
    Technology *B, M*
United States Military Academy *B*

North Carolina

North Carolina State University *B*

North Dakota

Dakota College at Bottineau *A*

Ohio

Cincinnati State Technical and
    Community College *C, A*
James A. Rhodes State College *A*
Kent State University
    Trumbull *A*
Ohio University
    Chillicothe Campus *A, B*
Owens Community College
    Toledo *C, A*

Shawnee State University *B*
Sinclair Community College *A*
University of Toledo *A*

Oklahoma

Rose State College *C, A*

Oregon

Mt. Hood Community College *C, A*

Pennsylvania

Bucknell University *M*
Community College of Allegheny
County *A*
Community College of
Philadelphia *A*
Delaware County Community
College *C*
Penn State
Harrisburg *M*
University Park *M*
Temple University *M*

Puerto Rico

University of Puerto Rico
Aguadilla *B*

South Carolina

Trident Technical College *C*
York Technical College *C*

Tennessee

Chattanooga State Community
College *A*
Middle Tennessee State University *B*

Texas

Austin Community College *C, A*
Panola College *C*
Texas State Technical College
Waco *A*

Utah

Salt Lake Community College *C, A*

Virginia

Danville Community College *C*

Washington

Clover Park Technical College *A*

West Virginia

Glenville State College *A*
West Virginia University Institute of
Technology *B*

Wyoming

Sheridan College *A*

Environmental health

Alabama

University of Alabama
Birmingham *D*

Arizona

University of Arizona *M, D*

Arkansas

University of Arkansas
Little Rock *B*
for Medical Sciences *M*

California

California State University
East Bay *B*
Fresno *B*
San Bernardino *B*
Loma Linda University *M*
San Diego State University *B*

University of California
Berkeley *M, D*
Irvine *M, D*
Los Angeles *M, D*
University of Southern California *B*

Colorado

Colorado State University *B, M, D*

Connecticut

Gateway Community College *A*

Florida

University of Florida *M*
University of Miami *B*

Georgia

Paine College *B*
University of Georgia *B, M, D*

Idaho

Boise State University *B*

Illinois

Illinois State University *B*
University of Illinois
Urbana-Champaign *B*

Indiana

Indiana University
Bloomington *D*
University of St. Francis *M*
Vincennes University *A*

Iowa

University of Iowa *M, D*
University of Northern Iowa *M*

Kentucky

Western Kentucky University *B*

Louisiana

Tulane University *M, D*

Maine

University of Southern Maine *B*

Maryland

University of Maryland
University College *M*

Massachusetts

Boston University *M, D*
University of Massachusetts
Lowell *B*

Michigan

Oakland University *B*
University of Michigan *M, D*
University of Michigan
Flint *B*

Minnesota

University of Minnesota
Twin Cities *M, D*

Mississippi

Mississippi Valley State
University *B, M*

Missouri

Crowder College *A*
Missouri Southern State University *B*
Saint Louis University *M*

Montana

Little Big Horn College *A*

New York

City University of New York
Queensborough Community
College *A*
York College *B*

New York University *M*
SUNY
University at Albany *M, D*
University of Rochester *M*

North Carolina

Durham Technical Community
College *A*
East Carolina University *B, M*
University of North Carolina
Chapel Hill *B*
Western Carolina University *B*

Ohio

Bowling Green State University *B*
Case Western Reserve University *M*
Ohio University *B*
University of Cincinnati *M, D*
University of Findlay *B*
University of Toledo *M*
Wright State University *B, D*

Oklahoma

East Central University *B*
Oklahoma State University
Oklahoma City *A*
University of Oklahoma *M, D*

Oregon

Oregon State University *B, M*

Pennsylvania

Temple University *M*
University of Pennsylvania *M*
University of Pittsburgh *M, D*

Puerto Rico

Universidad Metropolitana *B*
University of Puerto Rico
Medical Sciences *M*

South Carolina

University of South Carolina
Columbia *D*

Tennessee

Chattanooga State Community
College *A*
East Tennessee State
University *B, M, D*
Roane State Community College *A*

Texas

Baylor University *B*
Texas Southern University *B*
Texas State Technical College
Marshall *A*

Utah

University of Utah *D*

Vermont

Goddard College *B, M*

Washington

University of Washington *B, M*

Wisconsin

University of Wisconsin
Eau Claire *B*

Environmental psychology

Arizona

Prescott College *B*

Florida

Embry-Riddle Aeronautical
University *B, M*

Maine

College of the Atlantic *B, M*

Environmental science

Alabama

Auburn University *B*
Miles College *B*
Samford University *B*
Troy University *B*
University of Alabama *B*
University of Mobile *B*

Alaska

Alaska Pacific University *B, M*
University of Alaska
Southeast *B*

Arizona

Arizona Western College *A*
Coconino County Community
College *A*
Dine College *A*
Glendale Community College *C*
Mesa Community College *C*
Northern Arizona University *B, M*
University of Arizona *B*

Arkansas

Arkansas State University *M*
Arkansas State University
Beebe *A*
John Brown University *B*
Northwest Arkansas Community
College *C*
University of Arkansas *B*

California

California Baptist University *B*
California Lutheran University *B*
California State University
Channel Islands *B*
Chico *B, M*
Dominguez Hills *M*
Fresno *B*
Fullerton *M*
Monterey Bay *B*
Claremont McKenna College *B*
College of the Desert *A*
Columbia College *A*
Fresno Pacific University *B*
Humboldt State University *M*
La Sierra University *B*
Loma Linda University *B*
Los Medanos College *A*
Loyola Marymount University *B, M*
Mills College *B*
Moorpark College *C, A*
National University *B*
Pitzer College *B*
Point Loma Nazarene University *B*
St. Mary's College of California *B*
San Diego State University *B*
Santa Clara University *B*
Santa Monica College *C, A*
Stanford University *B, M, D*
Trident University International *B*
University of California
Irvine *B*
Los Angeles *B, D*
Merced *M, D*
Riverside *B, M, D*
San Diego *B*
University of La Verne *B*
University of Redlands *B*
University of San Francisco *B*
University of Southern California *B*
University of the Pacific *B*

Colorado

Colorado College *B*
Colorado Mesa University *B*
Colorado School of Mines *B, M, D*

Regis University *B*
University of Colorado
Denver *M*
University of Denver *B*

Connecticut

Eastern Connecticut State
University *B*
Gateway Community College *A*
Middlesex Community College *A*
Naugatuck Valley Community
College *A*
Sacred Heart University *M*
Three Rivers Community
College *C, A*
Trinity College *B*
University of Connecticut *B*
University of New Haven *B, M*
Wesleyan University *B*
Yale University *M, D*

Delaware

Delaware State University *B*
Wesley College *M*

District of Columbia

American University *B, M*

Florida

Bethune-Cookman University *B, M*
Broward College *A*
Florida Agricultural and Mechanical
University *B, M, D*
Florida Atlantic University *M*
Florida Gateway College *A*
Florida Gulf Coast University *M*
Florida Institute of
Technology *B, M, D*
Florida State University *B*
Lake-Sumter State College *A*
Miami Dade College *A*
Nova Southeastern University *B, M*
Stetson University *B*
University of Florida *B*
University of Miami *D*
University of South Florida
Saint Petersburg *M*
University of West Florida *B, M*

Georgia

Berry College *B*
Columbus State University *M*
Georgia College and State
University *B*
Gordon College *A*
Mercer University *B*
North Georgia Technical College *A*
Piedmont College *B*
South Georgia State College *A*
Spelman College *B*
University of Georgia *B*
University of West Georgia *B*
Valdosta State University *B*

Hawaii

Hawaii Pacific University *B*
University of Hawaii
Hilo *B, M*
Manoa *B*

Idaho

Brigham Young University-Idaho *B*
Idaho State University *B*
University of Idaho *B, M, D*

Illinois

Benedictine University *B*
Bradley University *B*
Concordia University Chicago *B*
DePaul University *B*
Dominican University *B*
Lewis University *B*
Loyola University Chicago *C, B*
Monmouth College *B*

Northwestern University *B*
Southern Illinois University
Edwardsville *M*
University of Chicago *B*
University of Illinois
Springfield *M*
Urbana-Champaign *B, M, D*
University of St. Francis *B*
Wheaton College *B*

Indiana

DePauw University *B*
Earlham College *B*
Goshen College *B, M*
Grace College *B*
Hanover College *B*
Indiana University
Bloomington *B, M, D*
Purdue University
Indianapolis *B, D*
Southeast *C*
Martin University *B*
Purdue University *B*
Taylor University *B, M*
University of Evansville *B*
University of Indianapolis *B*
University of Notre Dame *B*
University of St. Francis *A, B*
University of Southern Indiana *B*
Valparaiso University *B*

Iowa

Ashford University *B*
Briar Cliff University *B*
Buena Vista University *B*
Coe College *B*
Drake University *B*
Iowa State University *B, M, D*
Simpson College *B*
University of Dubuque *B*
University of Iowa *B, M, D*
University of Northern Iowa *B, M*
Upper Iowa University *B*
Wartburg College *B*

Kansas

Kansas Wesleyan University *B*

Kentucky

Bellarmine University *B*
Midway College *B*
Northern Kentucky University *B*
Thomas More College *B*

Louisiana

Louisiana State University and
Agricultural and Mechanical
College *B, M, D*
Loyola University New Orleans *B*
Tulane University *B*

Maine

Colby College *B*
College of the Atlantic *B, M*
Saint Joseph's College of Maine *B*
Unity College *B*
University of Maine *B, M, D*
University of Maine
Farmington *B*
Fort Kent *B*
University of New England *B*
University of Southern Maine *B*

Maryland

Anne Arundel Community College *A*
Chesapeake College *A*
Harford Community College *A*
Hood College *B*
Howard Community College *A*
McDaniel College *B*
Salisbury University *B*
Stevenson University *B*

University of Maryland
Baltimore County *B*
College Park *B, M, D*

Massachusetts

Anna Maria College *B*
Assumption College *B*
Berkshire Community College *A*
Boston University *B, M*
Cape Cod Community College *A*
Clark University *B, M*
Curry College *B*
Dean College *A*
Eastern Nazarene College *B*
Endicott College *B*
Greenfield Community College *A*
Merrimack College *B*
Northeastern University *B*
Simmons College *B*
Suffolk University *B*
University of Massachusetts
Amherst *B*
Westfield State University *B*
Wheaton College *B*

Michigan

Adrian College *B*
Albion College *B*
Andrews University *B*
Aquinas College *B*
Calvin College *B*
Central Michigan University *B*
Delta College *A*
Hope College *B*
Lake Michigan College *A*
Lake Superior State University *B*
Madonna University *B*
Marygrove College *B*
Michigan State University *B*
Michigan Technological University *B*
Northern Michigan University *B*
Oakland University *B*
Olivet College *B*
University of Michigan
Flint *B*
Wayne State University *B*

Minnesota

Anoka-Ramsey Community College *A*
Bethel University *B*
Fond du Lac Tribal and Community
College *A*
Rochester Community and Technical
College *A*
Saint Cloud State University *B*
St. John's University *B*
Southwest Minnesota State
University *B*
University of Minnesota
Duluth *B*
University of St. Thomas *B*

Mississippi

Jackson State University *M, D*

Missouri

Central Methodist University *B*
Columbia College *B*
Drury University *B*
Lincoln University *B, M*
Lindenwood University *B*
Maryville University of Saint Louis *B*
Saint Louis University *B*
Southeast Missouri State
University *B, M*
University of Missouri
Kansas City *D*
Washington University in St. Louis *B*
Westminster College *B*

Montana

Blackfeet Community College *A*
Montana State University *B, D*
Rocky Mountain College *B*

Salish Kootenai College *A, B*
University of Montana: Western *A, B*

Nebraska

Concordia University *B*
Creighton University *B*
University of Nebraska
Omaha *B*

Nevada

Nevada State College *B*
Sierra Nevada College *B*
University of Nevada
Reno *B*

New Hampshire

Franklin Pierce University *B*
NHTI-Concord's Community
College *A*
New England College *B*
Saint Anselm College *B*
University of New Hampshire *B*
White Mountains Community
College *A*

New Jersey

Bergen Community College *A*
Fairleigh Dickinson University
Metropolitan Campus *B, M*
New Jersey Institute of
Technology *B, M, D*
Ocean County College *A*
Ramapo College of New Jersey *B*
Richard Stockton College of New
Jersey *M*
Rutgers, The State University of New
Jersey
New Brunswick/Piscataway
Campus *B*
Newark Campus *B, M, D*
Thomas Edison State College *A, B*
William Paterson University of New
Jersey *B*

New Mexico

Eastern New Mexico University *B*
Navajo Technical University *C, A*
New Mexico State University *B*
University of New Mexico *B*

New York

Barnard College *B*
Canisius College *B*
City University of New York
College of Staten Island *M*
LaGuardia Community College *A*
Queens College *B*
Clarkson University *B*
Columbia University *B*
Columbia University
School of General Studies *B*
Columbia-Greene Community
College *A*
Erie Community College *A*
Fordham University *B*
Ithaca College *B*
Keuka College *B*
Long Island University
LIU Post *B*
Nazareth College *B*
Pace University *B, M*
Pace University: Pleasantville/
Briarcliff *M*
Paul Smith's College *A, B*
Rensselaer Polytechnic Institute *B*
Rochester Institute of
Technology *B, M*
Rockland Community College *A*
SUNY
College at Brockport *B, M*
College at Fredonia *B*
College at Oneonta *B*
College at Plattsburgh *B*
College at Purchase *B*

College of Environmental Science and Forestry *B, M, D*
College of Technology at Alfred *A*
University at Albany *B*
Skidmore College *B*
Suffolk County Community College *A*
United States Military Academy *B*
University of Rochester *B*

North Carolina

Appalachian State University *B*
Barton College *B*
Catawba College *B*
Elon University *B*
Gardner-Webb University *B*
Meredith College *B*
North Carolina Agricultural and Technical State University *D*
North Carolina Central University *B*
North Carolina State University *B, M*
North Carolina Wesleyan College *B*
Queens University of Charlotte *B*
Roanoke-Chowan Community College *A*
Southeastern Community College *A*
University of North Carolina
Chapel Hill *B, M, D*
Pembroke *B*
Wilmington *B*
Western Carolina University *B*

North Dakota

Sitting Bull College *A*

Ohio

Ashland University *B*
Capital University *B*
Cedarville University *B*
Cleveland State University *B, M*
John Carroll University *B*
Lourdes University *B*
Marietta College *B*
Miami University
Oxford *B, M*
Muskingum University *B*
Ohio State University
Agricultural Technical Institute *A*
Columbus Campus *A, B*
University of Dayton *B*
University of Mount Union *B*
University of Toledo *B*
Walsh University *B*
Xavier University *B*
Youngstown State University *B, M*

Oklahoma

Oklahoma City University *B*
Oklahoma State University *B, M, D*
Rose State College *A*
University of Oklahoma *B, M, D*

Oregon

Klamath Community College *A*
Oregon Health & Science University *M, D*
Oregon Institute of Technology *B*
Oregon State University *B, M, D*
Pacific University *B*
University of Oregon *B, D*
University of Portland *B*
Willamette University *B*

Pennsylvania

Albright College *B*
Allegheny College *B*
Bucknell University *B*
Bucks County Community College *A*
California University of Pennsylvania *B, M*
Carnegie Mellon University *B*
Cedar Crest College *B*
Chatham University *B*
Chestnut Hill College *B*

Clarion University of Pennsylvania *B, T*
Dickinson College *B*
Drexel University *B, M, D*
Duquesne University *B, M*
Edinboro University of Pennsylvania *B*
Franklin & Marshall College *B*
Gannon University *B*
Geneva College *B*
Gettysburg College *B*
Harrisburg Area Community College *A*
Harrisburg University of Science and Technology *B*
Juniata College *B*
King's College *B*
Kutztown University of Pennsylvania *B*
La Salle University *B*
Lackawanna College *A*
Lehigh Carbon Community College *A*
Lincoln University *B*
Marywood University *B*
Messiah College *B*
Moravian College *B*
Muhlenberg College *C, B*
Northampton Community College *A*
Point Park University *B*
Robert Morris University *B*
Rosemont College *B*
St. Francis University *B*
St. Vincent College *B*
Susquehanna University *B, T*
Temple University *B*
University of Pennsylvania *M*
University of Scranton *B*
University of the Sciences *B*
Villanova University *B*
Widener University *B*
Wilson College *B*

Puerto Rico

Inter American University of Puerto Rico
Bayamon Campus *B*
San German Campus *B, M*
Turabo University *D*
Universidad Metropolitana *B*
University of Puerto Rico
Rio Piedras *B, M*

Rhode Island

Brown University *B*
Bryant University *B, M*
Roger Williams University *B*
University of Rhode Island *M, D*

South Carolina

Benedict College *B*
Claflin University *B*
Lander University *B*
South Carolina State University *M*
University of South Carolina
Columbia *B*
Winthrop University *B*
York Technical College *C*

South Dakota

Lake Area Technical Institute *A*
South Dakota State University *D*

Tennessee

Belmont University *B*
Lincoln Memorial University *B*
Lipscomb University *B, M*
Rhodes College *B*
University of Tennessee
Chattanooga *B, M*

Texas

Abilene Christian University *B*
Baylor University *B, M, D*
Central Texas College *A*

Clarendon College *A*
Dallas Baptist University *B*
Hardin-Simmons University *B*
Midland College *A*
Midwestern State University *B*
Northeast Texas Community College *A*
Rice University *M*
St. Mary's University *B*
St. Philip's College *A*
Sam Houston State University *B*
San Jacinto College *A*
Southern Methodist University *M*
Stephen F. Austin State University *B, M*
Tarleton State University *M*
Texas A&M University *B*
Texas A&M University
Commerce *B*
Texas Christian University *B, M*
Texas State Technical College
West Texas *A*
Texas State University *B, M, T*
Texas Tech University *M*
Tyler Junior College *A*
University of Houston *B*
University of Houston
Clear Lake *B, M*
University of North Texas *M, D*
University of St. Thomas *B*
University of Texas
Arlington *M, D*
Brownsville *B*
El Paso *B, M*
Pan American *B*
San Antonio *B, M*
University of the Incarnate Word *B*
Wayland Baptist University *B*
West Texas A&M University *B, M*

Utah

Brigham Young University *B, M*
Utah Valley University *B*

Vermont

Bennington College *B*
Castleton State College *B*
Community College of Vermont *C, A*
Lyndon State College *B*
Norwich University *B*
University of Vermont *B*

Virginia

Averett University *B*
Bridgewater College *B*
Christopher Newport University *M*
Emory & Henry College *B*
Ferrum College *B*
George Mason University *B, M, D*
Hampton University *B*
Lynchburg College *B*
Mountain Empire Community College *A*
Sweet Briar College *B*
University of Virginia *B, M, D*
Virginia Polytechnic Institute and State University *B*

Washington

Cascadia Community College *A*
Eastern Washington University *C, B*
Evergreen State College *B*
Heritage University *B*
Northwest University *B*
Pacific Lutheran University *B*
Seattle University *B*
Skagit Valley College *C, A*
University of Washington Bothell *B*
University of Washington Tacoma *B*
Washington State University *B, M, D*
Western Washington University *B, M*

West Virginia

Alderson-Broaddus University *B*
American Public University System *B*
Davis and Elkins College *B*
Marshall University *B, M*
New River Community and Technical College *A*

Wisconsin

Alverno College *B*
Carroll University *B*
Carthage College *B*
St. Norbert College *B*
University of Wisconsin
Green Bay *B*
Madison *B*
Milwaukee *B*
River Falls *B*
Whitewater *B*
Wisconsin Lutheran College *B*

Wyoming

Casper College *A*
Central Wyoming College *A*

Environmental studies

Alabama

Birmingham-Southern College *B*
Columbia Southern University *C, B*
University of Phoenix
Birmingham *B*

Alaska

University of Alaska
Anchorage *B*
Fairbanks *C*
Southeast *C, A, B*

Arizona

Arizona State University *B, M, D*
Northern Arizona University *B*
Prescott College *B, M*
University of Arizona *B, M*
University of Phoenix
Southern Arizona *B*

Arkansas

Arkansas State University *D*
Hendrix College *B*
University of Central Arkansas *B*
University of the Ozarks *B*

California

Allan Hancock College *A*
California State University
East Bay *B*
Monterey Bay *B*
Sacramento *B, M*
San Bernardino *B*
Chaffey College *A*
Claremont McKenna College *B*
College of the Desert *C, A*
Feather River College *C, A*
Fresno Pacific University *B*
Humboldt State University *B, M*
Mills College *B*
Pacific Union College *B*
Pitzer College *B*
Pomona College *B*
Saddleback College *A*
St. Mary's College of California *B*
San Diego State University *B*
San Francisco State University *B*
San Jose State University *B, M*
Santa Barbara City College *C, A*
Santa Clara University *B*
Santa Monica College *C, A*
Santa Rosa Junior College *A*
Sierra College *A*
Sonoma State University *B*
Southwestern College *C, A*

University of California
  Berkeley *B, M, D*
  Davis *B*
  Irvine *B, D*
  San Diego *B*
  Santa Barbara *B*
  Santa Cruz *B, D*
University of Phoenix
  Bay Area *B*
  Sacramento Valley *B*
  San Diego *B*
  Southern California *B*
University of Redlands *B*
University of San Diego *B*
University of San Francisco *B, M*
University of Southern California *M*
University of the Pacific *B*

Colorado

Colorado College *B*
Fort Lewis College *B*
Metropolitan State University of
  Denver *B*
Naropa University *B*
Regis University *B*
University of Colorado
  Boulder *B, M, D*
University of Denver *B*
University of Northern Colorado *B*
University of Phoenix
  Denver *B*
Western State Colorado
  University *B, M*

Connecticut

Connecticut College *B*
Goodwin College *C, A, B*
Mitchell College *B*
Post University *B*
University of Connecticut *B*
Yale University *B, M*

Delaware

Wesley College *B*

District of Columbia

American University *B*
George Washington University *B, M*

Florida

Eckerd College *B*
Florida Gulf Coast University *B*
Florida International University *B, M*
Florida Southern College *B*
Indian River State College *A*
Lynn University *B*
New College of Florida *B*
Nova Southeastern University *B*
Rollins College *B*
Saint Leo University *B*
Saint Thomas University *B*
University of Miami *B*
University of South Florida
  Saint Petersburg *B*
University of Tampa *B*

Georgia

Darton College *A*
Emory University *B*
Mercer University *B*
Shorter University *B*
University of North Georgia *B*
University of West Georgia *B*

Hawaii

Chaminade University of Honolulu *B*
Hawaii Pacific University *B*
University of Hawaii
  Hilo *B*

Idaho

Boise State University *B*
College of Idaho *B*

University of Phoenix
  Idaho *B*

Illinois

Augustana College *B*
Blackburn College *B*
DePaul University *B*
Illinois Wesleyan University *B*
Judson University *B*
Knox College *B*
Lake Forest College *B*
Lincoln College *A*
McKendree University *B*
Northeastern Illinois University *B*
Northern Illinois University *B*
Northwestern University *B*
Olivet Nazarene University *B*
University of Chicago *B, M*
University of Illinois
  Springfield *B, M*

Indiana

Earlham College *B*
Grace College *B*
Manchester University *B*
University of Evansville *B*

Iowa

Ashford University *B*
Central College *B*
Coe College *B*
Cornell College *B*
Dordt College *B*
Iowa Lakes Community College *A*
Iowa State University *B*
Luther College *B*
University of Iowa *B, M, D*
Wartburg College *B*
William Penn University *B*

Kansas

Friends University *M*
Kansas State University *B*
Kansas Wesleyan University *B*
Tabor College *B*
University of Kansas *B*

Kentucky

Bellarmine University *B*
Kentucky State University *M*

Louisiana

Delgado Community College *C*
Tulane University *B, M*

Maine

Bates College *B*
Bowdoin College *B*
Colby College *B*
College of the Atlantic *B, M*
Saint Joseph's College of Maine *B*
University of Maine
  Machias *B*
  Presque Isle *B*
University of New England *B*
University of Southern Maine *B*

Maryland

Frostburg State University *B*
Goucher College *B*
Harford Community College *C, A*
Johns Hopkins University *M*
Mount St. Mary's University *B*
University of Baltimore *B*
University of Maryland
  Baltimore County *B*
Washington College *B*

Massachusetts

Amherst College *B*
Anna Maria College *B*
Bard College at Simon's Rock *B*
Boston University *M*
Brandeis University *B*

Bristol Community College *A*
Cape Cod Community College *C, A*
Clark University *B, M*
College of the Holy Cross *B*
Eastern Nazarene College *B*
Framingham State University *B*
Hampshire College *B*
Harvard College *B*
Lasell College *B*
Lesley University *B, M*
Massachusetts College of Liberal
  Arts *B, T*
Mount Holyoke College *B*
Mount Wachusett Community
  College *A*
Northeastern University *B*
Springfield College *B*
Stonehill College *B*
Tufts University *B*
University of Massachusetts
  Boston *M, D*
Wellesley College *B*
Worcester Polytechnic Institute *B*

Michigan

Adrian College *B*
Albion College *B*
Alma College *B*
Aquinas College *B*
Calvin College *B*
Central Michigan University *B*
Henry Ford Community College *A*
Michigan State University *B*
University of Michigan *B*
University of Michigan
  Dearborn *B*
University of Phoenix
  Metro Detroit *B*
Western Michigan University *B*

Minnesota

Augsburg College *B*
Bemidji State University *B, M*
Bethel University *B*
Carleton College *B*
College of St. Benedict *B*
Concordia College: Moorhead *B*
Gustavus Adolphus College *B*
Hamline University *B*
Macalester College *B*
Minnesota State Community and
  Technical College *A*
Minnesota State University
  Mankato *B, M*
  Moorhead *B*
Saint Cloud State University *B*
St. Olaf College *B*
University of Minnesota
  Duluth *B*
  Morris *B*
  Twin Cities *B*
University of Phoenix
  Minneapolis-St. Paul *B*
University of St. Thomas *B*
White Earth Tribal and Community
  College *A*

Missouri

Columbia College *A*
Cottey College *B*
Drury University *B*
Maryville University of Saint Louis *B*
University of Missouri
  Kansas City *B*
University of Phoenix
  St. Louis *B*
Washington University in St.
  Louis *B, M*
Webster University *M*
Westminster College *B*

Montana

Carroll College *B*
Montana State University
  Billings *B*
Rocky Mountain College *B*

Nebraska

Concordia University *B*
Doane College *B*
University of Nebraska
  Lincoln *B*

Nevada

Truckee Meadows Community
  College *A*
University of Nevada
  Las Vegas *B*

New Hampshire

Colby-Sawyer College *B*
Dartmouth College *B*
Keene State College *B*
Plymouth State University *B, M*
Southern New Hampshire
  University *B*
University of New Hampshire *M, D*

New Jersey

Drew University *B*
Montclair State University *M*
Ramapo College of New Jersey *B, M*
Richard Stockton College of New
  Jersey *B*
Rider University *B*
Rowan University *B*
Rutgers, The State University of New
  Jersey
  New Brunswick/Piscataway
    Campus *B*
Seton Hall University *B*
Sussex County Community College *A*
Thomas Edison State College *B*
Warren County Community
  College *A*

New Mexico

New Mexico Institute of Mining and
  Technology *B*
Santa Fe Community College *C, A*
University of Phoenix
  New Mexico *B*
Western New Mexico University *B*

New York

Adelphi University *B, M*
Alfred University *B*
Bard College *B, M*
Barnard College *B*
Canisius College *B*
Cazenovia College *B*
City University of New York
  Brooklyn College *B*
  Medgar Evers College *B*
  Queens College *B*
Clarkson University *M*
Colgate University *B*
College of New Rochelle *B*
Elmira College *B*
Eugene Lang College The New
  School for Liberal Arts *B*
Finger Lakes Community College *A*
Genesee Community College *A*
Hamilton College *B*
Hobart and William Smith Colleges *B*
Hofstra University *B*
Hudson Valley Community College *A*
Ithaca College *B*
Le Moyne College *B*
Manhattanville College *B*
Niagara County Community
  College *A*
Pace University *B*
Pace University: Pleasantville/
  Briarcliff *B*
Parsons The New School for
  Design *B*
SUNY
  College at Brockport *B*
  College at Potsdam *B*
  College at Purchase *B*

College of Environmental Science
and Forestry *B, M, D*
University at Binghamton *B*
University at Stony Brook *B*
Sage Colleges *B*
St. John's University *B*
St. Lawrence University *B*
Siena College *B*
Skidmore College *B*
Suffolk County Community College *A*
Tompkins Cortland Community
College *A*
Ulster County Community College *A*
United States Military Academy *B*
University of Rochester *B*
Vassar College *B*
Wells College *B*

North Carolina

Appalachian State University *B*
Brevard College *B*
Catawba College *B*
Davidson College *B*
Elon University *B*
Guilford College *B*
Lenoir-Rhyne University *B*
Meredith College *B*
Montreat College *B*
North Carolina State University *M*
Pfeiffer University *B*
Queens University of Charlotte *B*
University of North Carolina
Asheville *B*
Chapel Hill *B*
Pembroke *B*
Wilmington *B*
Warren Wilson College *B*

North Dakota

Dakota College at Bottineau *A*
University of North Dakota *B, M, D*

Ohio

Bowling Green State University *B*
Case Western Reserve University *B*
Cleveland State University *B, M*
Defiance College *B*
Hiram College *B*
John Carroll University *B*
Lake Erie College *B*
Marietta College *B*
Oberlin College *B*
Ohio Dominican University *B*
Ohio Northern University *B*
Ohio State University
Agricultural Technical Institute *A*
Columbus Campus *A*
Ohio University *B, M*
Ohio Wesleyan University *B*
Otterbein University *B*
Stark State College *A*
University of Cincinnati *A, M, D*
University of Rio Grande *B*
University of Toledo *B*
Wittenberg University *B*

Oklahoma

Eastern Oklahoma State College *A*
University of Oklahoma *B*
University of Phoenix
Oklahoma City *B*
Tulsa *B*
University of Tulsa *B*

Oregon

Lane Community College *A*
Lewis & Clark College *B*
Linfield College *B*
Marylhurst University *B*
Pacific University *B*
Reed College *B*
Southern Oregon University *B, M*
Southwestern Oregon Community
College *A*

University of Oregon *B, M*
University of Portland *B*

Pennsylvania

Albright College *B*
Allegheny College *B*
Arcadia University *B, M*
Bucknell University *B*
Carnegie Mellon University *B*
Chatham University *B, T*
Delaware Valley College *C*
Dickinson College *B*
Drexel University *B*
Franklin & Marshall College *B*
Gannon University *M*
Gettysburg College *B*
Harrisburg Area Community
College *A*
Immaculata University *B*
Juniata College *B*
King's College *B*
Lackawanna College *A*
Lehigh University *B*
Mansfield University of
Pennsylvania *B*
Moravian College *B*
Penn State
Abington *B*
Altoona *B*
Beaver *B*
Berks *B*
Brandywine *B*
DuBois *B*
Erie, The Behrend College *B*
Fayette, The Eberly Campus *B*
Greater Allegheny *B*
Harrisburg *B*
Hazleton *B*
Lehigh Valley *B*
Mont Alto *B*
New Kensington *B*
Schuylkill *B*
Shenango *B*
University Park *B*
Wilkes-Barre *B*
Worthington Scranton *B*
York *B*
Philadelphia University *B*
Point Park University *M*
St. Francis University *B*
Saint Joseph's University *B*
Shippensburg University of
Pennsylvania *B, M*
Temple University *B*
Thiel College *B*
University of Pennsylvania *B, M*
University of Pittsburgh
Bradford *B*
Johnstown *B*
Ursinus College *B*
Villanova University *B*
Washington & Jefferson College *B*
Wilson College *B*

Puerto Rico

Inter American University of Puerto
Rico
Metropolitan Campus *M*
Pontifical Catholic University of
Puerto Rico *B*
Turabo University *M*
Universidad Politecnica de Puerto
Rico *M*

Rhode Island

Brown University *B, M*
Salve Regina University *B*
University of Rhode Island *B*

South Carolina

College of Charleston *M*
Winthrop University *B*
Wofford College *B*

South Dakota

Lake Area Technical Institute *A*

Tennessee

Maryville College *B*
Sewanee: The University of the
South *B*
Tennessee Wesleyan College *B*
Tusculum College *B*

Texas

Austin College *B*
Baylor University *B, M*
Concordia University Texas *B*
Lamar University *B*
Panola College *C*
St. Edward's University *B*
Southern Methodist University *B*
Southwestern University *B*
Texas A&M University *B*
Texas Southern University *B*
University of Phoenix
Austin *B*
Dallas Fort Worth *B*
Houston Westside *B*
San Antonio *B*
University of St. Thomas *B*
University of Texas
Austin *C*
Wayland Baptist University *B*

Utah

University of Phoenix
Utah *B*
University of Utah *B*
Utah State University *B*
Westminster College *B*

Vermont

Bennington College *B*
Champlain College *B*
Goddard College *B, M*
Green Mountain College *B, M*
Johnson State College *B*
Marlboro College *B*
Middlebury College *B*
Saint Michael's College *B*
Sterling College *B*
University of Vermont *B*

Virginia

College of William and Mary *B*
Eastern Mennonite University *B*
Emory & Henry College *B*
Hollins University *B*
Lynchburg College *B*
Randolph College *B*
Randolph-Macon College *B*
Roanoke College *B*
Shenandoah University *B*
Southwest Virginia Community
College *A*
Sweet Briar College *B*
Tidewater Community College *A*
University of Phoenix
Northern Virginia *B*
University of Richmond *B*
University of Virginia's College at
Wise *B*
Virginia Commonwealth
University *B, M*
Virginia Polytechnic Institute and
State University *B*
Virginia Wesleyan College *B*
Washington and Lee University *B*

Washington

Antioch University
Seattle *M, T*
Central Washington University *B*
Evergreen State College *B, M*
Gonzaga University *B*
Seattle University *B*
University of Washington Bothell *B*

University of Washington Tacoma *B*
Western Washington University *B*
Whitman College *B*

West Virginia

American Public University System *M*
Bethany College *B*
Potomac State College of West
Virginia University *A*
Shepherd University *B*
West Virginia Wesleyan College *B*

Wisconsin

Beloit College *B*
Concordia University Wisconsin *B*
Lawrence University *B*
Northland College *B*
Ripon College *B*
University of Phoenix
Milwaukee *B*
University of Wisconsin
Green Bay *B, T*
Madison *B*
Richland *C*
Wisconsin Lutheran College *B*

Wyoming

University of Wyoming *B, M*
Western Wyoming Community
College *A*

Environmental
toxicology

Alabama

University of South Alabama *M*

California

University of California
Davis *B*
Irvine *M, D*
Riverside *M, D*
Santa Cruz *M, D*

Louisiana

Southern University and Agricultural
and Mechanical College *D*

Michigan

Michigan State University *D*

Nebraska

University of Nebraska
Medical Center *M, D*

New York

Clarkson University *B*
Cornell University *M, D*

Ohio

University of Cincinnati *M, D*

Wisconsin

University of Wisconsin
Madison *M, D*

Epidemiology

Alabama

University of Alabama
Birmingham *D*

Arizona

University of Arizona *M, D*

California

Loma Linda University *M, D*
Stanford University *M, D*
University of California
Berkeley *M, D*
Davis *M, D*

Irvine *M, D*
Los Angeles *M, D*
University of Southern California *D*

Colorado
Colorado State University *M, D*
University of Colorado
Denver *M, D*

District of Columbia
George Washington University *D*

Florida
University of Florida *M, D*
University of Miami *M, D*

Georgia
Emory University *M, D*
University of Georgia *D*

Hawaii
University of Hawaii
Manoa *D*

Indiana
Indiana University
Bloomington *D*
Purdue University Indianapolis *D*

Iowa
University of Iowa *M, D*

Kentucky
University of Kentucky *M*
University of Louisville *M*

Louisiana
Louisiana State University
Health Sciences Center *D*
Tulane University *M, D*

Maryland
University of Maryland
Baltimore *M, D*
College Park *D*

Massachusetts
Boston University *M, D*

Michigan
Michigan State University *M, D*
University of Michigan *M, D*

Minnesota
University of Minnesota
Twin Cities *M, D*

Missouri
Washington University in St. Louis *M*

New York
SUNY
University at Albany *M, D*
University at Buffalo *M, D*
University of Rochester *D*

North Carolina
University of North Carolina
Chapel Hill *M, D*
Wake Forest University *M*

Ohio
Case Western Reserve
University *M, D*
University of Cincinnati *M, D*

Pennsylvania
Drexel University *D*
Temple University *M*
University of Pennsylvania *M, D*
University of Pittsburgh *M, D*

Puerto Rico
University of Puerto Rico
Medical Sciences *M*

South Carolina
Clemson University *M*
Medical University of South
Carolina *D*
University of South Carolina
Columbia *M, D*

Tennessee
University of Tennessee
Knoxville *M*
Vanderbilt University *M, D*

Texas
University of Texas
Health Science Center at
Houston *M, D*

Virginia
Virginia Commonwealth University *D*

Washington
University of Washington *M*

Wisconsin
University of Wisconsin
Madison *M, D*

Equestrian studies

Alabama
Judson College *B*

Arizona
Cochise College *C*
Scottsdale Community College *C, A*

California
Cosumnes River College *A*
Los Angeles Pierce College *C, A*
Mount San Antonio College *C*
Santa Rosa Junior College *C, A*
Shasta College *C, A*

Colorado
Colorado Northwestern Community
College *C, A*
Colorado State University *B*

Connecticut
Post University *C, B*

Florida
College of Central Florida *C, A*

Georgia
Savannah College of Art and
Design *B*

Idaho
College of Southern Idaho *A*

Illinois
Black Hawk College *A*
South Suburban College of Cook
County *C*

Indiana
St. Mary-of-the-Woods College *A, B*

Iowa
Ellsworth Community College *A*

Kansas
Cowley County Community
College *A*
Dodge City Community College *C, A*

Kentucky
Asbury University *B*
Bluegrass Community and Technical
College *C, A*
Midway College *A, B*

Maryland
Harford Community College *A*

Massachusetts
Becker College *B*
Mount Ida College *B*
University of Massachusetts
Amherst *A*

Minnesota
Minnesota State Community and
Technical College *C*
Rochester Community and Technical
College *C, A*

Missouri
William Woods University *B*

Montana
Dawson Community College *A*
Rocky Mountain College *B*
University of Montana: Western *A, B*

Nebraska
Nebraska College of Technical
Agriculture *A*

New Hampshire
University of New Hampshire *B*

New Jersey
Centenary College *B*

New York
Cazenovia College *C*
Houghton College *B*
SUNY
College of Agriculture and
Technology at Cobleskill *A*
College of Agriculture and
Technology at Morrisville *A*

North Carolina
Martin Community College *C, A*
St. Andrews University *B*

North Dakota
North Dakota State University *B*

Ohio
Hocking College *C, A*
Lake Erie College *B*
Ohio University
Southern Campus at Ironton *A*
Otterbein University *B*
University of Findlay *A, B*

Oklahoma
Connors State College *C, A*
Northeastern Oklahoma Agricultural
and Mechanical College *C, A*
Redlands Community College *A*

Pennsylvania
Delaware Valley College *A*
Wilson College *B*

Rhode Island
Johnson & Wales University
Providence *B*

Texas
Central Texas College *A*
Clarendon College *A*
Frank Phillips College *C, A*
North Central Texas College *A*

Sul Ross State University *B*
West Texas A&M University *B*

Vermont
Vermont Technical College *B*

Virginia
Averett University *B*
Lord Fairfax Community College *C*
Virginia Intermont College *B*

West Virginia
Bethany College *B*
Potomac State College of West
Virginia University *A*

Wisconsin
University of Wisconsin
River Falls *B*

Wyoming
Central Wyoming College *C, A*
Laramie County Community
College *A*
Northwest College *C, A*

ESL teacher education

Alabama
Auburn University *M, T*
University of Alabama *M*

Arizona
Arizona State University *M*
Grand Canyon University *M*
Mesa Community College *C*
Northcentral University *M, D*
Northern Arizona University *M*
University of Arizona *M, D*

Arkansas
Arkansas Tech University *M*
Henderson State University *T*
University of Arkansas *M*
University of Arkansas
Fort Smith *C*
Little Rock *M*

California
Alliant International
University *B, M, D*
Azusa Pacific University *C, M*
California State University
Chico *T*
Dominguez Hills *M*
East Bay *M*
Fresno *M*
Fullerton *M, T*
Long Beach *T*
Los Angeles *M*
Sacramento *M*
Fresno Pacific University *M*
Holy Names University *M, T*
Loyola Marymount University *M, T*
Master's College *B*
Pacific Union College *C*
San Jose State University *M*
University of California
San Diego *M*
University of San Francisco *M*
University of Southern California *T*

Colorado
Front Range Community College *C*
Regis University *C*

Connecticut
Central Connecticut State
University *M, T*
Fairfield University *M, T*

Delaware

Delaware State University *M*
University of Delaware *B, M, T*

District of Columbia

American University *M*
Catholic University of America *B*
George Washington University *A*
Georgetown University *M*
Trinity Washington University *M*

Florida

Barry University *T*
Carlos Albizu University *D*
Florida Atlantic University *M*
University of Central Florida *M*
University of Miami *M*
University of South Florida *D*

Georgia

Georgia Southern University *T*
Georgia State University *M, D*
Kennesaw State University *M*
University of Georgia *M*

Hawaii

Brigham Young University-
    Hawaii *B, T*
Hawaii Pacific University *B, M*
University of Hawaii
    Manoa *B*

Idaho

Boise State University *T*
University of Idaho *M, T*

Illinois

City Colleges of Chicago
    Harold Washington College *A*
DePaul University *M, T*
Dominican University *M*
Lincoln Christian University *C, M*
Moody Bible Institute *B*
Northeastern Illinois University *M*
Southern Illinois University
    Carbondale *M*
Southern Illinois University
    Edwardsville *M*
Spoon River College *A*
University of Illinois
    Urbana-Champaign *M, T*
Wheaton College *M*

Indiana

Ball State University *M, T*
Goshen College *B, T*
Indiana State University *M, T*
Indiana University
    Bloomington *M*
    Purdue University Indianapolis *T*
University of Evansville *T*
Valparaiso University *M*

Iowa

Buena Vista University *M*
Iowa State University *M, T*
Northwestern College *T*
University of Iowa *M, D, T*
University of Northern Iowa *B, M*

Kansas

Emporia State University *M*
McPherson College *T*
Newman University *M*
Pittsburg State University *M*
Wichita State University *B*

Kentucky

Asbury University *M, T*
Campbellsville University *B, M*
Murray State University *B, M*

Louisiana

Delgado Community College *C*
Northwestern State University *C*

Maryland

McDaniel College *M*
Notre Dame of Maryland
    University *M*
Salisbury University *B, T*

Massachusetts

Boston University *M, T*
Bridgewater State University *T*
Clark University *T*
Elms College *B, M, T*
Framingham State University *M*
Merrimack College *M*
Salem State University *M*
Simmons College *B, M*
University of Massachusetts
    Lowell *C*

Michigan

Andrews University *M*
Aquinas College *B, T*
Central Michigan University *M*
Cornerstone University *A*
Eastern Michigan University *M, T*
Madonna University *B, M*
Michigan State University *M*
Northern Michigan University *T*

Minnesota

Bethel University *B*
Concordia University St. Paul *B, T*
Crown College *B, T*
Hamline University *M, T*
Minneapolis Community and
    Technical College *C*
Minnesota State University
    Mankato *M, T*
    Moorhead *B*
North Central University *B*
Saint Cloud State University *M*
Southwest Minnesota State
    University *B*
University of Minnesota
    Twin Cities *B, M, T*
University of Northwestern - St.
    Paul *B*
Winona State University *B, T*

Mississippi

University of Mississippi *C*

Missouri

Avila University *T*
Missouri Southern State University *B*
Southeast Missouri State University *M*
University of Central Missouri *M*
Webster University *M*

Montana

Carroll College *B*
University of Montana *T*

Nebraska

Concordia University *B, M, T*
Doane College *B*
Grace University *B*
Hastings College *T*
Union College *B*
University of Nebraska
    Kearney *B, T*
    Lincoln *B*
    Omaha *T*

New Hampshire

Granite State College *B, T*
NHTI-Concord's Community
    College *C*
Plymouth State University *C*

Southern New Hampshire
    University *M*

New Jersey

College of New Jersey *M, T*
Georgian Court University *T*
Montclair State University *T*
New Jersey City University *T*
Rutgers, The State University of New
    Jersey
    Camden Campus *T*
William Paterson University of New
    Jersey *T*

New Mexico

Santa Fe Community College *T*
University of the Southwest *M*
Western New Mexico University *B*

New York

Adelphi University *M, T*
City University of New York
    Hunter College *M, T*
    Lehman College *M, T*
    Queens College *B, M, T*
College of New Rochelle *M, T*
Cornell University *M, T*
D'Youville College *M*
Dowling College *B*
Hofstra University *M, D, T*
Houghton College *B, T*
Le Moyne College *T*
Long Island University
    LIU Brooklyn *M, T*
    LIU Post *M, T*
Manhattanville College *M*
Mercy College *M, T*
Molloy College *T*
Nazareth College *M*
New York University *B, M, D, T*
Nyack College *B, M*
SUNY
    College at Cortland *B, M*
    College at Fredonia *M, T*
    College at New Paltz *M, T*
    University at Albany *M*
    University at Buffalo *M*
    University at Stony Brook *M, T*
St. John's University *M, T*
Syracuse University *M*
University of Rochester *M*
Utica College *B*

North Carolina

Lenoir-Rhyne University *B*
Meredith College *M, T*
University of North Carolina
    Charlotte *M*
Western Carolina University *B*
Winston-Salem State University *M*

North Dakota

University of North Dakota *M*

Ohio

Cedarville University *T*
Kent State University *B, M*
Miami University
    Oxford *C*
Ohio Dominican University *M, T*
Ohio State University
    Columbus Campus *M*
Union Institute & University *B*
University of Akron *C*
University of Cincinnati *C*
University of Findlay *B, M, T*
University of Toledo *M, T*
Wright State University *M*

Oklahoma

Langston University *M*
Oklahoma Christian University *B, T*
Oklahoma City University *M*

Oral Roberts University *M*
University of Central Oklahoma *B*

Oregon

Concordia University *M*
George Fox University *M, T*
Northwest Christian University *C*
Portland State University *M, T*
Southern Oregon University *T*
University of Oregon *T*
Western Oregon University *M, T*

Pennsylvania

Bloomsburg University of
    Pennsylvania *T*
DeSales University *T*
Duquesne University *M, T*
Holy Family University *M, T*
King's College *T*
Millersville University of
    Pennsylvania *T*
Penn State
    University Park *M*
Saint Joseph's University *M, T*
Temple University *C*
University of Pennsylvania *M*
University of Pittsburgh *T*
University of Scranton *M*
West Chester University of
    Pennsylvania *M*
Widener University *T*

Puerto Rico

American University of Puerto
    Rico *B, T*
Inter American University of Puerto
    Rico
    Aguadilla Campus *B*
    Fajardo Campus *B, T*
    Guayama Campus *B*
    Metropolitan Campus *B, M*
    Ponce Campus *B, M, T*
    San German Campus *B, M*
Pontifical Catholic University of
    Puerto Rico *B, M, T*
Turabo University *M*
Universidad Adventista de las
    Antillas *M*
Universidad del Este *B*
University of Puerto Rico
    Humacao *B*
    Rio Piedras *M*

Rhode Island

Rhode Island College *M*

South Carolina

Columbia International University *M*
University of South Carolina
    Upstate *T*

Tennessee

Belmont University *T*
Carson-Newman University *M*
Lipscomb University *B, M, T*
Maryville College *B, T*
Tennessee Technological University *T*
Trevecca Nazarene University *M, T*
Union University *B, T*
University of Memphis *T*
Vanderbilt University *M, T*

Texas

Dallas Baptist University *M*
Houston Baptist University *T*
Howard Payne University *B*
Lamar University *T*
McMurry University *T*
North Lake College *A*
Sam Houston State University *M, T*
Southern Methodist University *T*
Texas A&M University
    Commerce *T*
University of North Texas *M*

University of St. Thomas *M*
University of Texas
   Arlington *M, T*
   Brownsville *M*
   Pan American *M*
   San Antonio *M, T*
West Texas A&M University *T*

Utah

Brigham Young University *M, T*
Snow College *A*
Utah State University *M*
Western Governors University *M*

Vermont

Saint Michael's College *M, T*

Virginia

Bridgewater College *T*
Eastern Mennonite University *M, T*
Liberty University *B*
Longwood University *T*
Marymount University *M*
Regent University *M, T*
Shenandoah University *M*

Washington

Central Washington University *B, T*
Eastern Washington University *M*
Gonzaga University *M*
Heritage University *B, M*
Northwest University *T*
Seattle Pacific University *M*
Seattle University *M*
University of Washington *T*
Washington State
   University *B, M, D, T*
Whitworth University *B, M, T*

Wisconsin

St. Norbert College *T*
University of Wisconsin
   Green Bay *T*
   Milwaukee *C, T*
   River Falls *B, T*

Ethics

Colorado

Colorado Christian University *C*

District of Columbia

American University *M*

Florida

Pensacola State College *A*
University of North Florida *M*

Georgia

Kennesaw State University *C*

Indiana

Valparaiso University *M*

Iowa

Drake University *B*

Maryland

University of Maryland
   Baltimore County *M*

Massachusetts

Bard College at Simon's Rock *B*

Michigan

University of Michigan
   Flint *B*

Missouri

Webster University *C, B*

Montana

Carroll College *B*

Nevada

University of Nevada
   Las Vegas *M*

New Jersey

College of St. Elizabeth *C*
Stevens Institute of Technology *M*

New York

Syracuse University *B*

North Carolina

Southeastern Baptist Theological
   Seminary *M, D*
University of North Carolina
   Charlotte *M*

Oregon

Oregon State University *M*

Pennsylvania

Carnegie Mellon University *B*

Tennessee

Union University *B*

Texas

University of Texas
   Austin *C*

Washington

University of Washington Bothell *B*

Ethnic studies, general

California

Bakersfield College *A*
College of Marin *A*
College of San Mateo *A*
Mills College *B*
Palomar College *C*
San Francisco State University *M*
Santa Ana College *A*
Santa Monica College *C, A*
University of California
   Riverside *B*
University of San Diego *B*

Colorado

Colorado State University *B, M*
University of Colorado
   Boulder *B*
   Colorado Springs *B*
   Denver *B*

Hawaii

University of Hawaii
   Hawaii Community College *C*

Idaho

Boise State University *B*

Illinois

University of Chicago *B*

Indiana

Indiana University
   Northwest *C*

Kansas

Kansas State University *B*
Wichita State University *B*

Maine

College of the Atlantic *B, M*

Massachusetts

Hampshire College *B*
Simmons College *M*
Westfield State University *B*

Michigan

Albion College *B*

Minnesota

Metropolitan State University *B*
Minnesota State University
   Moorhead *B*
St. Olaf College *B*

New York

New York University *B*

Ohio

University of Cincinnati
   Clermont College *C*

Oregon

Lewis & Clark College *B*
University of Oregon *B*

Pennsylvania

Messiah College *B*

Texas

Baptist University of the Americas *A*
University of Texas
   Austin *B*

Vermont

Goddard College *B, M*

Virginia

College of William and Mary *B*

Washington

Green River Community College *C*

Wisconsin

Edgewood College *B*

European history

California

Pitzer College *B*

Massachusetts

Elms College *B*
Salem State University *B*

Michigan

Central Michigan University *M*

New Hampshire

Keene State College *B*

New York

Bard College *B*

Pennsylvania

Gettysburg College *B*
Lycoming College *B*

Puerto Rico

University of Puerto Rico
   Aguadilla *A*
   Rio Piedras *B*

South Carolina

Charleston Southern University *B*

Tennessee

Southern Adventist University *B*

Texas

Howard Payne University *B*

Wisconsin

Carroll University *B*

European studies

California

California State University
   Fullerton *B*
Claremont McKenna College *B*
Loyola Marymount University *B*
Pepperdine University *B*
Pitzer College *B*
St. Mary's College of California *B*
San Diego State University *B*
Scripps College *B*
University of California
   Irvine *B*
   Los Angeles *B*
Westmont College *B*

Connecticut

Yale University *B, M, D*

District of Columbia

George Washington University *B*

Florida

New College of Florida *B*

Georgia

Armstrong Atlantic State University *C*
Georgia Southern University *C*

Illinois

Northwestern University *B*

Kansas

University of Kansas *B*

Kentucky

Georgetown College *B*

Massachusetts

Amherst College *B*
Bard College at Simon's Rock *B*
Boston University *B*
Brandeis University *B*
Hampshire College *B*
Tufts University *B*
Wellesley College *B*

Michigan

Central Michigan University *B*
Hillsdale College *B*

Minnesota

University of Minnesota
   Morris *B*
   Twin Cities *B*

Mississippi

Millsaps College *B*

Missouri

University of Missouri
   Columbia *B*
Washington University in St.
   Louis *B, M*
Webster University *B*

New Hampshire

University of New Hampshire *B*

New Jersey

Rutgers, The State University of New
   Jersey
   New Brunswick/Piscataway
     Campus *B*

New Mexico

University of New Mexico *B*

New York

Barnard College *B*
Canisius College *B*
Columbia University *B*
Hobart and William Smith Colleges *B*
New York University *B, M*
SUNY
   University at Stony Brook *B*
United States Military Academy *B*

North Carolina

University of North Carolina
   Chapel Hill *B*

Ohio

Bowling Green State University *B*
Ohio University *B*
University of Cincinnati *C*
University of Toledo *B*

Oregon

Portland State University *B*

Pennsylvania

Carnegie Mellon University *B*
Saint Joseph's University *B*

Rhode Island

Brown University *B*

South Carolina

University of South Carolina
   Columbia *B*

Tennessee

Belmont University *B*
Vanderbilt University *B*

Texas

Texas State University *B*
Trinity University *B*
University of Texas
   Austin *B*

Utah

Brigham Young University *B*

Vermont

Bennington College *B*
Goddard College *B, M*
Marlboro College *B*
Middlebury College *B*
University of Vermont *B*

Virginia

Emory & Henry College *B*

Washington

Gonzaga University *B*
Seattle Pacific University *B*
University of Washington *B, M*

Wisconsin

Carroll University *B*

Evolutionary biology

Arizona

Arizona State University *D*

California

San Diego State University *D*
University of California
   Davis *B*
   San Diego *B*
University of Southern California *D*

Connecticut

Yale University *M, D*

Illinois

University of Chicago *D*

Louisiana

Tulane University *B, M, D*

Maine

College of the Atlantic *B, M*

Massachusetts

Harvard College *B, D*
University of Massachusetts
   Amherst *M, D*

Missouri

Washington University in St. Louis *D*

New Hampshire

Dartmouth College *B*

New York

Columbia University *B*
Columbia University
   School of General Studies *B*
Cornell University *M, D*
University of Rochester *B*

Ohio

Case Western Reserve University *B*

Pennsylvania

Lehigh University *D*

Texas

Angelo State University *B*
Rice University *B, M, D*

Vermont

Bennington College *B*

Washington

Western Washington University *B*

Executive assistant

Alabama

Virginia College
   Birmingham *A*
   Mobile *A*

Arkansas

University of Arkansas
   Fort Smith *C, A*

California

Grossmont College *C, A*
Shasta College *A*

Colorado

Lamar Community College *C, A*

Florida

College of Central Florida *C, A*
Daytona State College *C, A*
Hillsborough Community
   College *C, A*
Lake-Sumter State College *A*
Northwest Florida State College *C, A*
Saint Johns River State College *C, A*
Valencia College *C, A*

Georgia

West Georgia Technical College *A*

Illinois

Danville Area Community College *A*
Elgin Community College *A*
Illinois Eastern Community Colleges
   Frontier Community College *C, A*
   Wabash Valley College *C*
John A. Logan College *A*
John Wood Community College *A*
Kaskaskia College *A*
Moraine Valley Community College *C*

Parkland College *A*
Waubonsee Community College *C, A*

Indiana

Ivy Tech Community College
   Bloomington *C, A*
   Central Indiana *C, A*
   Columbus *C, A*
   East Central *C, A*
   Kokomo *C, A*
   Lafayette *C, A*
   North Central *C, A*
   Northeast *C, A*
   Northwest *C, A*
   Richmond *C, A*
   South Central *C, A*
   Southeast *C, A*
   Southwest *C, A*
   Wabash Valley *C, A*

Iowa

Hawkeye Community College *C, A*
Southeastern Community College *A*

Kansas

Manhattan Area Technical
   College *C, A*

Kentucky

Bluegrass Community and Technical
   College *C, A*
Elizabethtown Community and
   Technical College *C, A*
Gateway Community and Technical
   College *C, A*
Hopkinsville Community
   College *C, A*
Jefferson Community and Technical
   College *C, A*
Maysville Community and Technical
   College *C, A*
Owensboro Community and
   Technical College *C, A*
Somerset Community College *A*
Spencerian College *C*
West Kentucky Community and
   Technical College *C*
Western Kentucky University *A*

Louisiana

ITI Technical College *A*
Virginia College
   Shreveport *A*

Maryland

Hagerstown Community College *C*

Massachusetts

Cape Cod Community College *C, A*
North Shore Community College *A*
Quinsigamond Community College *A*

Michigan

Grand Rapids Community College *A*
Henry Ford Community College *C, A*
Kuyper College *A*
Montcalm Community College *A*
Northwestern Michigan College *C*
St. Clair County Community
   College *A*
Schoolcraft College *A*
Southwestern Michigan College *A*

Minnesota

Dakota County Technical College *A*
Minnesota West Community and
   Technical College *A*

Montana

Flathead Valley Community
   College *A*

New Jersey

Ocean County College *C*

New York

Broome Community College *A*
Globe Institute of Technology *C*
Utica School of Commerce *A*

North Carolina

Forsyth Technical Community
   College *C, A*
Guilford Technical Community
   College *A*
Martin Community College *C, A*
Wilson Community College *C, A*

Ohio

Bowling Green State University *B*
Cincinnati State Technical and
   Community College *A*
Edison State Community College *C, A*
Northwest State Community
   College *A*
Owens Community College
   Toledo *C, A*
Stark State College *A*
Terra State Community College *C, A*
University of Cincinnati
   Blue Ash College *A*

Oregon

Chemeketa Community College *A*
Mt. Hood Community College *A*
Umpqua Community College *A*

Pennsylvania

Consolidated School of Business
   Lancaster *A*
   York *A*
DuBois Business College *A*
DuBois Business College
   Huntingdon *A*
   Oil City *A*
Laurel Business Institute *A*
Westmoreland County Community
   College *A*

Puerto Rico

National University College
   Arecibo *B*
   Ponce *B*
   Rio Grande *B*
Universidad del Este *A*
University of Puerto Rico
   Aguadilla *B*
   Bayamon University College *B*
   Utuado *B*

Texas

Alvin Community College *A*
Brookhaven College *A*
Eastfield College *A*
El Centro College *A*
Kilgore College *C, A*
Texas State Technical College
   Harlingen *A*

Utah

LDS Business College *C, A*

Virginia

Danville Community College *A*

Washington

Bellingham Technical College *C, A*
Clark College *C, A*
Walla Walla Community College *C, A*

West Virginia

Bridgemont Community and
   Technical College *A*
Southern West Virginia Community
   and Technical College *C, A*

West Virginia University at
Parkersburg *C, A*

Exercise physiology

Arizona
Grand Canyon University *B*

California
Bryan College: Sacramento *A*
Notre Dame de Namur University *B*
University of California
Davis *B, M*

Colorado
Colorado State University *D*

Connecticut
Sacred Heart University *B, M*

Florida
University of Florida *B, M, D*
University of Miami *B, M, D*

Georgia
Georgia Institute of Technology *D*

Indiana
Indiana Wesleyan University *B*

Kansas
Central Christian College of Kansas *B*

Massachusetts
Fitchburg State University *B*
Gordon College *B*
Quincy College *C, A*
University of Massachusetts
Amherst *B, M, D*

Michigan
Eastern Michigan University *M*
Western Michigan University *M*

Minnesota
Bethany Lutheran College *B*
College of St. Scholastica *B, M*

Missouri
Drury University *B*
University of Missouri
Columbia *M, D*

New York
Ithaca College *B, M*
SUNY
College at Brockport *B*
University at Buffalo *B, M, D*

North Carolina
East Carolina University *B*
Methodist University *B*

Ohio
Ashland University *B, M*
Baldwin Wallace University *B*
Kent State University *M, D*
Ohio Northern University *B*

Oklahoma
Hillsdale Free Will Baptist College *B*

Oregon
Northwest Christian University *B*

Pennsylvania
Mercyhurst University *B, M*

Puerto Rico
University of Puerto Rico
Rio Piedras *M*

Texas
Baylor University *B*
Midwestern State University *B, M*

Utah
Brigham Young University *B*

Virginia
Bluefield College *B*
Lynchburg College *B*
Virginia Commonwealth University *D*

Washington
Central Washington University *B*
Washington State University *M*

West Virginia
West Virginia University *B, M, D*

Wisconsin
Concordia University Wisconsin *B*

Exercise sciences

Alabama
Auburn University *B, M, D*
Huntingdon College *B*
Samford University *B*
United States Sports Academy *M*
University of Alabama *D*

Arizona
Arizona State University *B, D*
Central Arizona College *C, A*
Glendale Community College *C, A*
Mesa Community College *C, A*
Northern Arizona University *B*
Scottsdale Community College *C*

Arkansas
Arkansas State University *B, M*
Harding University *B*
John Brown University *B*
Ouachita Baptist University *B*
Southern Arkansas University *B*
University of Arkansas *M, D*
University of Central Arkansas *B, M*

California
Biola University *B*
California Baptist University *B, M*
California State University
Chico *C, B*
East Bay *B, M*
Fresno *B, M*
San Bernardino *B, M*
Canada College *A*
Cerritos College *A*
College of San Mateo *C*
Contra Costa College *A*
Diablo Valley College *C*
Folsom Lake College *A*
Fremont College *A*
Grossmont College *C, A*
La Sierra University *B*
Occidental College *B*
Palomar College *A*
Pepperdine University *B*
Point Loma Nazarene University *B*
St. Mary's College of California *B*
San Diego Christian College *B*
San Diego State University *M*
San Francisco State University *B, M*
Santa Ana College *A*
Santa Barbara City College *A*
Skyline College *A*
University of San Francisco *B*
University of Southern
California *B, M, D*
Vanguard University of Southern
California *B*
Westmont College *B*

Whittier College *B*
William Jessup University *B*

Colorado
Adams State University *B, M*
Colorado Mesa University *B*
Colorado State University *B, M*
Colorado State University
Pueblo *B*
Fort Lewis College *B*
Metropolitan State University of
Denver *B*
Regis University *B*
University of Northern
Colorado *B, M, D, T*
Western State Colorado
University *B, T*

Connecticut
Manchester Community College *A*
Southern Connecticut State
University *M*
University of Connecticut *M, D*

Delaware
Delaware Technical Community
College
Stanton/Wilmington Campus *A*
University of Delaware *B, M, D*
Wesley College *B*

District of Columbia
George Washington University *B, M*

Florida
Barry University *B, M*
Clearwater Christian College *B*
Florida Atlantic University *B*
Florida Gulf Coast University *B*
Florida Southern College *B*
Jacksonville University *B*
Keiser University *A*
Lincoln College of Technology
West Palm Beach *C, A*
Miami Dade College *A*
South Florida State College *A*
University of Miami *B*
University of Tampa *B*
Warner University *B*

Georgia
Berry College *B*
Columbus State University *B*
Darton College *A*
East Georgia State College *A*
Emmanuel College *B*
Georgia Gwinnett College *B*
Georgia Regents University *B, M*
Georgia Southern University *B, M*
Georgia State University *D*
Kennesaw State University *B, M*
LaGrange College *B*
Life University *B, M*
Morehouse College *B*
Point University *B*
University of Georgia *B, M, D*

Hawaii
Brigham Young University-Hawaii *B*
University of Hawaii
Hilo *B*
Manoa *B, M*

Idaho
Boise State University *B, M*
College of Idaho *B*
College of Western Idaho *A*
Lewis-Clark State College *B*
Northwest Nazarene University *B*

Illinois
Benedictine University *B, M*
Concordia University Chicago *B*
DePaul University *B*

Eastern Illinois University *B, M, T*
Elmhurst College *B*
Greenville College *B*
Illinois State University *B*
Moraine Valley Community College *C*
North Central College *B*
North Park University *B*
Northeastern Illinois University *M*
Olivet Nazarene University *B*
Prairie State College *C, A*
Southern Illinois University
Carbondale *B, M*
Southern Illinois University
Edwardsville *B*
Trinity Christian College *B*
Triton College *C*
University of Illinois
Chicago *B, M, D*
Urbana-Champaign *B, M, D*
Waubonsee Community College *C*
Western Illinois University *B, M*

Indiana
Anderson University *B*
Bethel College *B*
DePauw University *B*
Franklin College *B*
Hanover College *B*
Huntington University *B*
Indiana University
Bloomington *B, M*
Purdue University
Indianapolis *B, M*
Ivy Tech Community College
Bloomington *A*
Manchester University *B*
Purdue University *B, M, D*
Taylor University *B*
University of Evansville *B*
University of Indianapolis *B*
University of Southern Indiana *B*
Valparaiso University *B*

Iowa
Briar Cliff University *B*
Buena Vista University *B*
Central College *B, T*
Cornell College *B*
Dordt College *B*
Iowa State University *B, M, D*
Iowa Wesleyan College *B*
Loras College *B*
Northwestern College *B*
St. Ambrose University *B*
Simpson College *B*
University of Iowa *B, M, D*
William Penn University *B*

Kansas
Baker University *B*
Barton County Community College *A*
Central Christian College of
Kansas *A, B*
Colby Community College *A*
Kansas State University *B, M*
Kansas Wesleyan University *B*
MidAmerica Nazarene University *B*
Neosho County Community
College *A*
Ottawa University *B*
Pittsburg State University *B*
Seward County Community
College *A*
University of Kansas *B*
Washburn University *B*
Wichita State University *B, M*
Wright Career College
Wichita *A*

Kentucky
Alice Lloyd College *B*
Bellarmine University *B*
Berea College *B*
Campbellsville University *B*

Hopkinsville Community College *A*
Morehead State University *B*
Murray State University *B*
Transylvania University *B, T*
University of Kentucky *M, D*
University of Louisville *M*
Western Kentucky University *B*

Louisiana

Centenary College of Louisiana *B*
McNeese State University *B, M*
University of Louisiana at
 Monroe *B, M*

Maine

Saint Joseph's College of Maine *B*
University of New England *B*
University of Southern Maine *B*

Maryland

Carroll Community College *A*
Frostburg State University *B*
McDaniel College *B*
Montgomery College *A*
Salisbury University *B*
Towson University *B, M*
University of Maryland
 College Park *B, M, D*
 Eastern Shore *B*

Massachusetts

Boston University *M*
Endicott College *B*
Fitchburg State University *B*
Lasell College *B*
Northeastern University *M*
Salem State University *B*
Simmons College *B*
Smith College *M*
Springfield College *B, M, D*

Michigan

Adrian College *B*
Albion College *B*
Alma College *B*
Calvin College *B*
Central Michigan University *B, M*
Concordia University *B*
Cornerstone University *D*
Henry Ford Community College *A*
Hope College *B*
Kuyper College *B*
Lake Superior State University *B*
Michigan State University *B, M, D*
Michigan Technological University *B*
Northern Michigan University *B, M*
Oakland Community College *C, A*
Oakland University *M*
Saginaw Valley State University *B*
University of Michigan *B, M, D*
Wayne State University *D*
Western Michigan University *B*

Minnesota

Bemidji State University *B*
Bethel University *B*
Concordia University St. Paul *B*
Dakota County Technical College *C*
Inver Hills Community College *A*
Mesabi Range Community and
 Technical College *A*
Minnesota State University
 Mankato *B, M, T*
 Moorhead *B*
St. Catherine University *B*
Saint Cloud State University *M*
St. Olaf College *B*
Southwest Minnesota State
 University *B*
University of Minnesota
 Duluth *B*
 Twin Cities *B, M, D*

University of Northwestern - St.
 Paul *B*
Winona State University *B*

Mississippi

Belhaven University *B*
Blue Mountain College *B*
East Mississippi Community
 College *A*
Mississippi College *B, M*
University of Mississippi *B, M, D*

Missouri

Avila University *B*
Drury University *B*
Lindenwood University *B*
Missouri Baptist University *B*
Missouri State University *B*
Missouri Valley College *B*
Rockhurst University *B*
Saint Louis University *B*
Truman State University *B*
University of Missouri
 Columbia *B, M, D*
Westminster College *B*

Montana

Rocky Mountain College *B*
University of Montana *B, M*

Nebraska

Concordia University *B*
Creighton University *B*
Hastings College *B*
Nebraska Wesleyan University *B*
Union College *B*
University of Nebraska
 Omaha *B, D*

Nevada

University of Nevada
 Las Vegas *B, M*

New Hampshire

Colby-Sawyer College *B*
Keene State College *B*
Manchester Community College *C, A*
New England College *B*
University of New Hampshire *B, M*

New Jersey

Bergen Community College *C*
Georgian Court University *B*
Gloucester County College *A*
Kean University *M*
Mercer County Community
 College *A*
Ocean County College *C*
Raritan Valley Community College *A*
Rutgers, The State University of New
 Jersey
 New Brunswick/Piscataway
  Campus *B, M, D*
William Paterson University of New
 Jersey *B, T*

New Mexico

New Mexico State University *B*

New York

City University of New York
 Brooklyn College *B, M*
 Kingsborough Community
  College *C, A*
 Queens College *B, M*
Ithaca College *B*
Long Island University
 LIU Brooklyn *B, M*
Orange County Community
 College *A*
SUNY
 College at Cortland *B, M*
 College of Agriculture and
  Technology at Morrisville *A, B*

Skidmore College *B*
Syracuse University *B, M*
United States Military Academy *B*

North Carolina

Appalachian State University *B, M*
Brevard College *B*
Campbell University *B*
Chowan University *B*
East Carolina University *B, M*
Elon University *B*
Gardner-Webb University *B*
Greensboro College *C, B*
Guilford College *B*
High Point University *B*
Meredith College *B*
Methodist University *B*
North Carolina Wesleyan College *B*
Pfeiffer University *B*
Queens University of Charlotte *B*
Shaw University *B*
University of Mount Olive *B*
University of North Carolina
 Chapel Hill *B*
 Greensboro *B, M, D*
Wake Forest University *B, M*
Winston-Salem State University *B*

North Dakota

North Dakota State University *B*
University of Jamestown *B*
University of Mary *B*
University of North Dakota *B, M*

Ohio

Capital University *B*
Cedarville University *B*
Cleveland State University *M*
Columbus State Community
 College *A*
Kent State University *B*
Malone University *B*
Miami University
 Oxford *B, M*
Mount Vernon Nazarene University *B*
Ohio Northern University *B*
Ohio State University
 Columbus Campus *B*
Ohio University *B, M*
Sinclair Community College *A*
University of Dayton *B, M*
University of Findlay *B*
University of Mount Union *B*
University of Toledo *B, M, D*
Urbana University *B*
Youngstown State University *B*

Oklahoma

Bacone College *B*
East Central University *B*
Northeastern State University *B, M*
Oklahoma Baptist University *B*
Oklahoma City University *B*
Oklahoma Wesleyan University *B*
Oral Roberts University *B*
Redlands Community College *A*
St. Gregory's University *B*
Southern Nazarene University *B*
University of Central Oklahoma *B, M*
University of Oklahoma *B, M, D*
University of Tulsa *B*

Oregon

Linfield College *B*
Oregon State University *M*
Pacific University *B*
Warner Pacific College *B*
Willamette University *B*

Pennsylvania

Bloomsburg University of
 Pennsylvania *M*
Cabrini College *B*
Chatham University *B*

DeSales University *B*
East Stroudsburg University of
 Pennsylvania *B*
Eastern University *B*
Gannon University *B, M*
Gettysburg College *B*
Grove City College *B*
Immaculata University *B*
Messiah College *B*
Penn State
 Abington *B*
 Altoona *B*
 Beaver *B*
 Berks *B*
 Brandywine *B*
 DuBois *B*
 Fayette, The Eberly Campus *B*
 Greater Allegheny *B*
 Harrisburg *B*
 Hazleton *B*
 Lehigh Valley *B*
 Mont Alto *B*
 New Kensington *B*
 Schuylkill *B*
 Shenango *B*
 University Park *B, M, D*
 Wilkes-Barre *B*
 Worthington Scranton *B*
 York *B*
Shippensburg University of
 Pennsylvania *B*
Slippery Rock University of
 Pennsylvania *B*
Temple University *B, M, D*
University of Scranton *B*
University of the Sciences *B*
Waynesburg University *B*
West Chester University of
 Pennsylvania *M*
Wilson College *B*

Rhode Island

University of Rhode Island *B, M*

South Carolina

Anderson University *B*
Citadel *M*
Coastal Carolina University *B*
Coker College *B*
Lander University *B*
University of South Carolina
 Aiken *B*
 Columbia *B, M, D*
Winthrop University *B*

South Dakota

Augustana College *B*
Dakota State University *B*
University of Sioux Falls *B*

Tennessee

Belmont University *B*
Bryan University
 Dayton *B, T*
Carson-Newman University *B*
Freed-Hardeman University *B*
Lipscomb University *B, M*
Maryville College *B*
Middle Tennessee State University *M*
Southern Adventist University *B*
Union University *B*
University of Memphis *B, M*
University of Tennessee
 Chattanooga *B, M*
 Knoxville *B, M, D*
Welch College *B*

Texas

Baylor University *D*
Blinn College *A*
Clarendon College *A*
Concordia University Texas *B*
Hardin-Simmons University *B*
Houston Baptist University *B*

Lamar State College at Port Arthur *A*
LeTourneau University *B*
McMurry University *B*
Midland College *A*
Midwestern State University *B, M*
Northwest Vista College *A*
Our Lady of the Lake University of San Antonio *B*
Rice University *B*
St. Edward's University *B*
St. Mary's University *B, T*
St. Philip's College *A*
Schreiner University *B*
South Texas College *A*
Southwestern University *B, T*
Stephen F. Austin State University *B, M, T*
Tarleton State University *B, M*
Texas A&M University *B, M, D*
Texas A&M University Commerce *B, M*
Texas Christian University *M*
Texas Lutheran University *B*
Texas Southern University *B*
Texas State University *B, M*
Texas Tech University *B, M*
Texas Wesleyan University *B*
Tyler Junior College *A*
University of Houston *B, M, D*
University of Houston Clear Lake *B, M*
University of North Texas *B, M*
University of Texas
  Arlington *B, M*
  Austin *B, M, D*
  Pan American *B, M*
  Permian Basin *B, M*
  San Antonio *M*
  Tyler *B, M*
University of the Incarnate Word *B, M*
West Texas A&M University *B, M*
Wharton County Junior College *A*

Utah

Brigham Young University *M, D*
Southern Utah University *M*
University of Utah *B, M, D, T*

Vermont

Castleton State College *B*
Johnson State College *B*
Lyndon State College *B*
University of Vermont *B*

Virginia

College of William and Mary *B*
Jefferson College of Health Sciences *B*
Liberty University *B*
Norfolk State University *B*
Roanoke College *B*
University of Virginia *B, M, D*

Washington

Bastyr University *B*
Central Washington University *B, M*
Eastern Washington University *B*
Seattle Pacific University *B*
Seattle University *B*
University of Puget Sound *B*
Washington State University *B, M*

West Virginia

American Public University System *B*
Davis and Elkins College *B*
Fairmont State University *B*
Marshall University *B, M*
West Liberty University *B*
West Virginia University *B, M, D*
West Virginia Wesleyan College *B*

Wisconsin

Carroll University *B*
Carthage College *B*
Ripon College *B*
University of Wisconsin
  Eau Claire *B*
  La Crosse *B, M*
  Madison *B, M, D*
  Milwaukee *C, B, M*
Viterbo University *B*
Wisconsin Lutheran College *B*

Wyoming

Sheridan College *A*
University of Wyoming *B, M*
Western Wyoming Community College *C, A*

Experimental psychology

Alabama

Auburn University *D*

California

California State University San Bernardino *B*
St. Mary's College of California *B*

Connecticut

University of Connecticut *M, D*
University of Hartford *M*

District of Columbia

Catholic University of America *M, D*

Florida

Florida Atlantic University *D*

Illinois

DePaul University *M, D*
Loyola University Chicago *D*

Iowa

University of Iowa *D*

Kentucky

University of Kentucky *M, D*
University of Louisville *D*

Maine

University of Maine *M, D*

Massachusetts

Tufts University *M, D*

Michigan

Central Michigan University *D*
Northern Michigan University *B, M*
University of Michigan *B, D*

Missouri

University of Missouri Columbia *M, D*

New Hampshire

Keene State College *B*

New Jersey

Seton Hall University *M*

New York

City University of New York Brooklyn College *M*
Fordham University *D*
New York University *D*
St. John's University *M*
Syracuse University *D*
University of Rochester *B, M, D*

North Carolina

Duke University *M, D*

Ohio

Case Western Reserve University *D*
Kent State University *M, D*
Ohio University *M, D*
Tiffin University *B*
University of Dayton *M*

Oklahoma

University of Central Oklahoma *M*

Rhode Island

University of Rhode Island *M, D*

South Carolina

University of South Carolina Columbia *B, M, D*

Texas

Texas State University *M*
Texas Tech University *M, D*
University of North Texas *M, D*
University of Texas
  Arlington *D*
  Dallas *M, D*
  El Paso *M*
  Pan American *M*

Washington

Central Washington University *M*

Wisconsin

University of Wisconsin Oshkosh *M*

Facial treatment

Colorado

IBMC College Fort Collins *C*

Florida

College of Central Florida *C*
Palm Beach State College *C*
Pensacola State College *C*

North Carolina

Cape Fear Community College *C*

Pennsylvania

Laurel Business Institute *C*

Texas

Houston Community College System *C*
Lamar State College at Port Arthur *C*
Lone Star College System *C, A*
San Jacinto College *C*

Facilities/event planning

California

California State University East Bay *C*

Connecticut

Naugatuck Valley Community College *A*

Massachusetts

Fitchburg State University *M*

Michigan

Eastern Michigan University *B*

Missouri

Missouri State University *B*
Southeast Missouri State University *C*

New York

City University of New York New York City College of Technology *B*

Ohio

Sinclair Community College *C*

Puerto Rico

Universidad del Este *C, B*

Utah

Brigham Young University *B*

Family and consumer sciences

Alabama

Alabama Agricultural and Mechanical University *B, M*
Faulkner State Community College *A*
Jacksonville State University *B*
Oakwood University *B*
University of Alabama *B, M*
University of Montevallo *B, T*
University of North Alabama *B*

Arizona

Arizona Western College *C, A*
Phoenix College *A*
South Mountain Community College *A*

Arkansas

Harding University *B, T*
Henderson State University *B*
University of Arkansas *B, M*
University of Arkansas Pine Bluff *B*
University of Central Arkansas *B, M*

California

Allan Hancock College *A*
American River College *C, A*
Antelope Valley College *A*
Butte College *C, A*
Cabrillo College *C, A*
California State University
  Fresno *B, M*
  Long Beach *B, M*
  Northridge *B, M*
  Sacramento *B, M*
Cerritos College *A*
Chaffey College *C, A*
College of the Sequoias *A*
El Camino College *A*
Fresno City College *A*
Fullerton College *A*
Glendale Community College *A*
Long Beach City College *C, A*
Los Angeles City College *A*
Los Angeles Valley College *A*
Master's College *B*
Merced College *A*
Modesto Junior College *A*
Monterey Peninsula College *A*
Moorpark College *A*
Mount San Antonio College *A*
Orange Coast College *A*
Palomar College *C, A*
Point Loma Nazarene University *B*
Riverside City College *C, A*
Sacramento City College *C, A*
Saddleback College *C, A*
San Diego State University *B, M*
San Francisco State University *B, M*
San Joaquin Delta College *C, A*
Santiago Canyon College *C, A*
Shasta College *A*
Sierra College *A*
Skyline College *C, A*
Solano Community College *C, A*
Ventura College *C, A*

Colorado

Colorado State University *B*

Connecticut

University of Saint Joseph *B*

Delaware

Delaware State University *M*
University of Delaware *B*

District of Columbia

University of the District of
    Columbia *B*

Florida

Palm Beach State College *A*
University of Miami *B*

Georgia

Abraham Baldwin Agricultural
    College *A*
East Georgia State College *A*
Fort Valley State University *B*
University of Georgia *M*

Hawaii

University of Hawaii
    Manoa *B*

Idaho

Idaho State University *B*
University of Idaho *M*

Illinois

Bradley University *B*
Eastern Illinois University *B, M*
Illinois Central College *A*
Illinois State University *B, M, T*
Kishwaukee College *A*
Lake Land College *A*
Olivet Nazarene University *B, T*
Western Illinois University *B*

Indiana

Ball State University *B, M*
Indiana State University *B, M, T*
Purdue University *B, M, D*
Vincennes University *A*

Iowa

Ellsworth Community College *A*
Iowa State University *B, M*
Marshalltown Community College *A*
North Iowa Area Community
    College *A*

Kansas

Coffeyville Community College *A*
Garden City Community College *A*
Hutchinson Community College *A*
Kansas State University *B, D*
Neosho County Community
    College *A*
Pittsburg State University *B*

Kentucky

Berea College *B*
University of Kentucky *B*

Louisiana

Louisiana State University and
    Agricultural and Mechanical
    College *B, M, D*
Louisiana Tech University *M*
Nicholls State University *B*
Northwestern State University *B*
Southeastern Louisiana University *B*
Southern University and Agricultural
    and Mechanical College *B*
University of Louisiana at Lafayette *M*

Maryland

Hood College *M*
Towson University *B*
University of Maryland
    Eastern Shore *B*

Massachusetts

Framingham State University *B*

Michigan

Madonna University *B*
Michigan State University *B, D*

Minnesota

Minnesota State University
    Mankato *B, M, T*
St. Catherine University *B*
University of Minnesota
    Twin Cities *B, M, D*

Mississippi

Delta State University *B*
Hinds Community College *A*
Itawamba Community College *A*
Mississippi Delta Community
    College *A*
Mississippi State University *B*
Northeast Mississippi Community
    College *A*

Missouri

College of the Ozarks *B*
Southeast Missouri State University *B*
University of Central Missouri *B*
University of Missouri
    Columbia *D*

Montana

Miles Community College *A*
Montana State University *B, M*

Nebraska

Central Community College *C, A*
Chadron State College *B*
University of Nebraska
    Kearney *B*
Wayne State College *B*

New Hampshire

River Valley Community College *A*

New Jersey

Montclair State University *B, M, T*

New Mexico

Eastern New Mexico University *B*
University of New Mexico *B, M, D*

New York

City University of New York
    Queens College *B, T*
SUNY
    College at Oneonta *B*
Syracuse University *B*

North Carolina

Meredith College *B*
North Carolina Agricultural and
    Technical State University *B, T*
North Carolina Central
    University *B, M*
Stanly Community College *C, A*

Ohio

Bowling Green State University *B, M*
Mount Vernon Nazarene
    University *A, B*
Muskingum University *B*
Youngstown State University *B*

Oklahoma

Connors State College *A*
Langston University *B*

Northeastern State University *B*
Oklahoma State University *M, D*
Rose State College *A*
Southwestern Christian University *B*
University of Central Oklahoma *B*

Oregon

George Fox University *B*
Linn-Benton Community College *A*

Pennsylvania

Indiana University of Pennsylvania *B*
Keystone College *B*
Seton Hill University *B*
University of Pittsburgh
    Titusville *A*

Puerto Rico

Pontifical Catholic University of
    Puerto Rico *B*
University of Puerto Rico
    Rio Piedras *B, M*

South Carolina

South Carolina State University *B*

Tennessee

East Tennessee State University *B, T*
Hiwassee College *A*
Lipscomb University *B*
Middle Tennessee State University *M*
Tennessee State University *B, M*
Tennessee Technological
    University *B, T*
University of Tennessee
    Martin *B, M*

Texas

Baylor University *B*
Brazosport College *A*
Coastal Bend College *A*
Del Mar College *C*
Lamar University *B, M*
Laredo Community College *A*
Lubbock Christian University *M*
Prairie View A&M University *M*
Sam Houston State University *B, M*
South Plains College *A*
Stephen F. Austin State
    University *B, M*
Tarleton State University *B, T*
Texas A&M University
    Kingsville *B, M*
Texas Southern University *B, M*
Texas State University *B, T*
Texas Tech University *B*
Texas Woman's University *B*
University of Texas
    Austin *B*

Utah

Brigham Young University *B, M, D*
Snow College *A*
Southern Utah University *B*
Utah State University *B, M*

Virginia

Bridgewater College *B*
Liberty University *B, T*

Washington

Central Washington University *B, M*
Highline Community College *A*
Washington State University *B*

West Virginia

Fairmont State University *B*
Marshall University *B, M*
Shepherd University *B, T*

Wisconsin

University of Wisconsin
    Madison *M, D*

Wyoming

University of Wyoming *B, M*

Family/community services

Alabama

Faulkner University *B*

Arizona

Arizona State University *M*
Glendale Community College *A*
Phoenix College *C, A*

Arkansas

Harding University *B*
John Brown University *B*

California

California State University
    Northridge *B*
College of the Siskiyous *C, A*
Diablo Valley College *C*
Fresno City College *C*
Loma Linda University *M, D*
Merritt College *C, A*
Modesto Junior College *A*
Monterey Peninsula College *A*
Palomar College *C, A*
Sacramento City College *C, A*
Santa Ana College *A*
Southwestern College *C*
Yuba College *C, A*

Delaware

University of Delaware *B, M, D*

Florida

University of Florida *B, M*
University of Miami *B*

Georgia

Toccoa Falls College *B*

Illinois

Judson University *C*
Olivet Nazarene University *B, T*
Shawnee Community College *A*

Indiana

Indiana University
    Purdue University Indianapolis *C*
Purdue University *B, M, D*

Iowa

Ellsworth Community College *A*
Iowa State University *B*
University of Northern Iowa *B*

Maine

Beal College *A*

Maryland

Stevenson University *B*
University of Maryland
    College Park *B, M, D*

Michigan

Michigan State University *B, M*

Minnesota

Capella University *M, D*
Minnesota State University
    Mankato *B, M, T*

North Carolina

East Carolina University *B, M*

Ohio

Bowling Green State University *B*
Columbus State Community
    College *C*

Sinclair Community College *C*
Youngstown State University *B*

Pennsylvania
Community College of
  Philadelphia *C*
La Roche College *B*
Messiah College *B*

Rhode Island
Roger Williams University *B*

South Carolina
Clemson University *D*

South Dakota
South Dakota State University *M*

Tennessee
Carson-Newman University *B, T*
Tennessee Technological
  University *B*

Texas
Lamar University *B*
Lubbock Christian University *M*
Texas Tech University *B*
University of Texas
  Austin *C*

Utah
Snow College *C, A*
University of Utah *M*

Washington
Washington State University *C*

Wisconsin
University of Wisconsin
  Madison *B*
  Stevens Point *M*

Family/consumer business sciences

California
California State University
  Northridge *B*
Skyline College *C, A*

Illinois
Northern Illinois University *M*

Nebraska
University of Nebraska
  Kearney *B*

Oklahoma
Connors State College *A*

Texas
Our Lady of the Lake University of
  San Antonio *B, M*
University of Houston *B, M*

Virginia
Virginia Polytechnic Institute and
  State University *B*

Family/consumer sciences education

Alabama
Oakwood University *B*

Arizona
Arizona Western College *A*

Arkansas
Harding University *B, T*
University of Arkansas
  Pine Bluff *B*
University of Central Arkansas *B*

California
California State University
  Long Beach *B, T*
  Northridge *B, T*
Master's College *T*
Saddleback College *A*
San Francisco State University *T*
University of San Diego *T*

Colorado
Colorado State University *B, T*

Connecticut
University of Saint Joseph *T*

Delaware
University of Delaware *B, T*

District of Columbia
Gallaudet University *B, T*

Georgia
Fort Valley State University *B, T*
University of Georgia *B*

Idaho
Brigham Young University-Idaho *B, T*
University of Idaho *T*

Illinois
Bradley University *B, M*
Northern Illinois University *B*
Olivet Nazarene University *B, T*

Indiana
Purdue University *B, M, D*
Vincennes University *A*

Iowa
Ellsworth Community College *A*
Grand View University *T*
Iowa State University *B, M, D, T*

Kansas
Kansas State University *B, T*
Pittsburg State University *B*

Kentucky
Berea College *B, T*
Eastern Kentucky University *B*
Western Kentucky University *B, T*

Louisiana
McNeese State University *T*
Northwestern State University *B*
Southeastern Louisiana University *B*
University of Louisiana at Lafayette *B*

Massachusetts
Bridgewater State University *T*

Michigan
Central Michigan University *B*
Michigan State University *B*
Western Michigan University *B, M*

Minnesota
Minnesota State University
  Mankato *B, M, T*
St. Catherine University *B, T*
University of Minnesota
  Twin Cities *B, M*

Mississippi
Northeast Mississippi Community
  College *A*

Northwest Mississippi Community
  College *A*

Missouri
Fontbonne University *B, M, T*
Missouri State University *B*
Northwest Missouri State
  University *B, T*
Southeast Missouri State
  University *B, M*
University of Central Missouri *B*

Nebraska
Chadron State College *B*
University of Nebraska
  Kearney *B*
Wayne State College *B, T*

New Jersey
Saint Peter's University *T*

New Mexico
New Mexico State University *B*

New York
City University of New York
  Queens College *B, M, T*
Cornell University *M*
Hofstra University *M*
New York University *B, M, D, T*
SUNY
  College at Oneonta *B, T*

North Carolina
Appalachian State University *B, T*
East Carolina University *B*
Meredith College *T*
North Carolina Agricultural and
  Technical State University *B, T*
North Carolina Central
  University *B, M, T*

North Dakota
North Dakota State
  University *B, M, T*

Ohio
Ashland University *B, T*
Bowling Green State University *B*
Mount Vernon Nazarene
  University *B, T*
Ohio State University
  Columbus Campus *B, M*
Ohio University *B, T*
University of Akron *B, M*
Youngstown State University *B, M*

Oklahoma
East Central University *B*
Langston University *B*
University of Central Oklahoma *B*

Oregon
Oregon State University *M*

Pennsylvania
Immaculata University *B*
Marywood University *B*
Messiah College *B, T*
Seton Hill University *B, T*

Puerto Rico
Pontifical Catholic University of
  Puerto Rico *B, T*
University of Puerto Rico
  Río Piedras *B, M*

South Carolina
South Carolina State University *B, T*
Winthrop University *B*

South Dakota
South Dakota State University *B, M*

Tennessee
Carson-Newman University *B*
Tennessee Technological University *T*

Texas
Lamar University *B, M, T*
Laredo Community College *A*
Prairie View A&M University *M*
Sam Houston State University *M, T*
Texas A&M University
  Kingsville *B*
Texas Tech University *M, D*

Utah
Brigham Young University *B*
Snow College *A*
Southern Utah University *B*
Utah State University *B*

Virginia
Bridgewater College *T*

Washington
Central Washington University *B, T*
Washington State University *B, M, T*

West Virginia
Shepherd University *T*

Wisconsin
University of Wisconsin
  Stevens Point *B, T*
  Stout *B, M, T*

Family practice nurse/ nurse practitioner

Alabama
Samford University *M*

Alaska
University of Alaska
  Anchorage *M*

Arizona
Grand Canyon University *M*
University of Phoenix
  Phoenix-Hohokam *M*
  Southern Arizona *M*

California
Azusa Pacific University *B*
Holy Names University *M*
Samuel Merritt University *M*
University of Phoenix
  Sacramento Valley *M*
  Southern California *M*
University of San Diego *M, D*
University of San Francisco *D*

Colorado
Regis University *M*
University of Northern
  Colorado *B, M, D*

Connecticut
Quinnipiac University *M, D*
Sacred Heart University *M*
Southern Connecticut State
  University *M*

Delaware
Wilmington University *M*

Florida
Florida International University *M*
University of Miami *M*
University of Tampa *M*

Georgia

Emory University *D*
Georgia College and State
   University *M*
Georgia Regents University *M*
Georgia Southern University *M*
Kennesaw State University *M*
Mercer University *M*
University of North Georgia *M*

Illinois

DePaul University *M*
Loyola University Chicago *M*
Southern Illinois University
   Edwardsville *M*

Indiana

Goshen College *M*
Indiana University
   Purdue University Indianapolis *M*
   South Bend *M*
   Southeast *M*
Indiana Wesleyan University *M, D*
University of Indianapolis *M*
University of St. Francis *M*

Iowa

Allen College *M*
Clarke University *M*
Graceland University *M*

Kansas

Washburn University *M*

Kentucky

Bellarmine University *D*
Spalding University *M*

Louisiana

Grambling State University *M*
Louisiana State University
   Health Sciences Center *M*
Loyola University New Orleans *M, D*
Southern University and Agricultural
   and Mechanical College *M*

Maine

Husson University *M*
University of Southern Maine *M*

Michigan

Grand Valley State University *M*
Michigan State University *B, M*
Oakland University *M*
Saginaw Valley State
   University *B, M, D*
University of Detroit Mercy *M*
University of Michigan
   Flint *M, D*

Minnesota

College of St. Scholastica *M*
Winona State University *M, D*

Missouri

Maryville University of Saint
   Louis *M, D*
Research College of Nursing *M*

Nebraska

Clarkson College *M*

New Hampshire

Rivier University *M*

New Jersey

Felician College *M*

New York

City University of New York
   Hunter College *B, M*
College of New Rochelle *M*
Dominican College of Blauvelt *M*

Long Island University
   LIU Post *M*
Molloy College *M*
New York University *M*
Pace University *M, D*
Pace University: Pleasantville/
   Briarcliff *M*
SUNY
   Downstate Medical Center *M*
   Institute of Technology at Utica/
     Rome *M*
   University at Binghamton *M, D*
   University at Buffalo *M, D*
   University at Stony Brook *M, D*
   Upstate Medical University *M*
Sage Colleges *M*
St. John Fisher College *M, D*
University of Rochester *M*

North Carolina

Pfeiffer University *B*
University of North Carolina
   Wilmington *M*
Winston-Salem State University *M*

North Dakota

North Dakota State University *D*
University of Mary *M*

Ohio

Case Western Reserve University *M*
University of Cincinnati *M*
University of Toledo *M*
Ursuline College *M*
Wright State University *M*

Oklahoma

Oklahoma City University *M*

Oregon

Oregon Health & Science
   University *M, D*

Pennsylvania

Carlow University *M*
DeSales University *M*
Duquesne University *M*
Gwynedd Mercy University *M*
Millersville University of
   Pennsylvania *M, T*
Misericordia University *M*
University of Pennsylvania *M*
University of Scranton *M*
Widener University *D*

Puerto Rico

Turabo University *M*

South Dakota

South Dakota State University *D*

Tennessee

King University *M*
Southern Adventist University *M*
University of Tennessee
   Chattanooga *D*
   Knoxville *D*
Vanderbilt University *M*

Texas

Baylor University *M*
Hardin-Simmons University *M*
McMurry University *M*
Midwestern State University *M*
Prairie View A&M University *M*
Texas A&M University
   Corpus Christi *B*
Texas State University *M*
Texas Tech University Health
   Sciences Center *M*
Texas Woman's University *M*
University of Texas
   Arlington *M*
   Austin *M*

El Paso *M*
   Medical Branch at Galveston *M*
   Pan American *M*
   Tyler *M*
West Texas A&M University *M*

Utah

Brigham Young University *M*
Westminster College *M*

Virginia

Marymount University *M*
Radford University *D*

Washington

Gonzaga University *M*
Seattle University *M*

West Virginia

Marshall University *M*
West Virginia University *D*
Wheeling Jesuit University *M*

Wisconsin

Alverno College *M*
Concordia University Wisconsin *M*
Viterbo University *M*

Family psychology

Arizona

Arizona Christian University *B*
Northcentral University *M, D*

California

Golden Gate University *M*
Touro University Worldwide *M*

Illinois

Northeastern Illinois University *M*

Kansas

Kansas Wesleyan University *B*

Michigan

Cornerstone University *B*

New Jersey

Seton Hall University *D*

Tennessee

Lee University *M*

Texas

Hardin-Simmons University *M*
Texas Wesleyan University *M*

Vermont

Goddard College *M*

Family resource management studies

Alabama

University of Alabama *B*

Arizona

Arizona State University *B, M*
University of Arizona *M, D*

California

Antelope Valley College *C, A*
Long Beach City College *C, A*

Georgia

University of Georgia *B*

Illinois

Prairie State College *C*
Triton College *C*

Iowa

Ashford University *B*
Iowa State University *B*

Missouri

University of Missouri
   Columbia *B, M*

New Mexico

New Mexico State University *B, M*

Ohio

Ohio State University
   Columbus Campus *B, M, D*
   Lima Campus *B*
Ohio University *B*

South Dakota

South Dakota State University *C*

Tennessee

Middle Tennessee State University *B*

Texas

Texas Tech University *B, M*

Family systems

California

Azusa Pacific University *D*

Connecticut

Goodwin College *A, B*
University of Connecticut *B, D*

Illinois

Harper College *C*
Prairie State College *C*
Triton College *C*

Indiana

Anderson University *B*

Kentucky

University of Kentucky *D*

Maryland

Towson University *B*

Michigan

Central Michigan University *B*
Cornerstone University *B*
Michigan State University *M*
Western Michigan University *B*

Minnesota

University of Minnesota
   Twin Cities *B, M*

Mississippi

East Mississippi Community
   College *A*
Mississippi University for
   Women *B, T*
University of Southern
   Mississippi *B, M*

Nebraska

Concordia University *M*

North Carolina

Mid-Atlantic Christian University *C, B*

Ohio

Bowling Green State University *B*
University of Akron *C, B*

Oklahoma

University of Central Oklahoma *B, M*

Tennessee

Lipscomb University *B*
Southern Adventist University *B*
Union University *B*

Texas

Lubbock Christian University *B*

Utah

Brigham Young University *B*
Weber State University *B*

Virginia

Southern Virginia University *B*

Washington

Central Washington University *B*

West Virginia

Alderson-Broaddus University *B*
American Public University System *C*

Farm and ranch management

Arizona

Central Arizona College *C*

Colorado

Colorado Mountain College *C*
Colorado Northwestern Community
College *C*
Northeastern Junior College *C, A*
Otero Junior College *C*
Trinidad State Junior College *C*

Georgia

Fort Valley State University *B*

Idaho

College of Western Idaho *C*

Indiana

Purdue University *B*

Iowa

Ellsworth Community College *C, A*
Iowa State University *B*
North Iowa Area Community
College *A*

Kansas

Allen County Community College *A*
Butler Community College *A*
Colby Community College *A*
Cowley County Community
College *A*
Dodge City Community College *C, A*
Fort Scott Community College *C*
Garden City Community College *A*
Highland Community College *A*
Hutchinson Community College *A*
Pratt Community College *C, A*
Seward County Community
College *A*

Minnesota

Alexandria Technical and Community
College *C*
Central Lakes College *C*
Minnesota West Community and
Technical College *C, A*
Northland Community & Technical
College *C*
Ridgewater College *C, A*
Riverland Community College *C*
St. Cloud Technical and Community
College *C*
South Central College *C, A*
Southwest Minnesota State
University *B*

University of Minnesota
Crookston *B*

Mississippi

Mississippi Delta Community
College *A*

Missouri

Crowder College *A*
Northwest Missouri State
University *C*

Montana

Dawson Community College *A*

Nebraska

Northeast Community College *A*

North Dakota

Bismarck State College *A*
Dickinson State University *C*

Ohio

Lake Erie College *B*
University of Findlay *B*
Wilmington College *B*

Oklahoma

Eastern Oklahoma State College *A*
Langston University *B*
Northeastern Oklahoma Agricultural
and Mechanical College *C, A*

Oregon

Blue Mountain Community College *A*
Treasure Valley Community
College *A*

Rhode Island

Johnson & Wales University
Providence *B*

South Dakota

Mitchell Technical Institute *C*

Texas

Central Texas College *C, A*
Clarendon College *C, A*
Frank Phillips College *A*
Navarro College *A*
North Central Texas College *A*
Northeast Texas Community
College *A*
Southwest Texas Junior College *C, A*
Texas A&M University *B*
Texas Christian University *C, B*
Trinity Valley Community
College *C, A*
Tyler Junior College *C, A*
Vernon College *C, A*
Weatherford College *C, A*

Utah

Snow College *A*

Vermont

Vermont Technical College *A*

Virginia

Virginia Highlands Community
College *C, A*

Wisconsin

Chippewa Valley Technical College *C*
Fox Valley Technical College *C*
Lakeshore Technical College *C*
Moraine Park Technical College *C*
Northeast Wisconsin Technical
College *A*
Southwest Wisconsin Technical
College *C*
Western Technical College *C*

Wisconsin Indianhead Technical
College *C*

Wyoming

Eastern Wyoming College *C, A*
Northwest College *A*

Fashion and apparel design

Arizona

Art Institute of Tucson *B*
Mesa Community College *C*
Phoenix College *C, A*

California

Academy of Art University *C, A, B, M*
Academy of Couture Art *C, A, B*
Allan Hancock College *C, A*
Art Institute of California
Hollywood *A, B*
Inland Empire *B*
Orange County *B*
San Diego *B*
San Francisco *A, B*
Silicon Valley *B*
Bethesda University of California *B*
Butte College *C, A*
California College of the Arts *B*
Canada College *C, A*
Chaffey College *C, A*
City College of San Francisco *C*
Fashion Institute of Design and
Merchandising
Los Angeles *A*
San Diego *A*
San Francisco *A*
Fullerton College *A*
International Academy of Design and
Technology
Sacramento *C, A, B*
Long Beach City College *C, A*
Los Angeles Southwest College *A*
Los Angeles Trade and Technical
College *A*
Modesto Junior College *C, A*
Orange Coast College *C, A*
Otis College of Art and Design *B*
Palomar College *A*
Saddleback College *C, A*
San Joaquin Delta College *C, A*
Santa Ana College *C, A*
Santa Monica College *C, A*
Santa Rosa Junior College *C, A*
Santiago Canyon College *A*
Ventura College *C, A*
West Valley College *C, A*
Westwood College
Los Angeles *A, B*
Woodbury University *B*

Connecticut

Sacred Heart University *B*

Delaware

University of Delaware *B*

Florida

Art Institute of Fort Lauderdale *A, B*
International Academy of Design and
Technology: Tampa *B*
Miami International University of Art
and Design *A, B*

Georgia

Art Institute of Atlanta *B*
Brenau University *B*
Clark Atlanta University *B*
Savannah College of Art and
Design *B, M*

Hawaii

University of Hawaii
Honolulu Community College *C, A*

Illinois

Columbia College Chicago *B*
Dominican University *B*
Illinois Institute of Art
Chicago *A, B*
School of the Art Institute of
Chicago *B, M*

Indiana

Indiana University
Bloomington *B*
Purdue University *B*

Iowa

Iowa State University *B*

Kansas

Johnson County Community
College *A*

Maryland

Baltimore City Community
College *C, A*
Stevenson University *B*

Massachusetts

Bay State College *A, B*
Lasell College *B*
Massachusetts College of Art and
Design *C, B*
Mount Ida College *B*

Michigan

Ferris State University *B*
Finlandia University *B*
International Academy of Design and
Technology
Detroit *A, B*
Michigan State University *B, M*

Minnesota

St. Catherine University *B*
University of Minnesota
Twin Cities *B*

Missouri

Lindenwood University *B*
Metropolitan Community College -
Kansas City *A*
Stephens College *B*
Washington University in St.
Louis *B, M*

Nevada

Art Institute of Las Vegas *B*
International Academy of Design and
Technology
Henderson *A, B*

New Jersey

Burlington County College *C, A*
Centenary College *B*
Montclair State University *B*

New Mexico

Santa Fe Community College *C*

New York

Art Institute of New York City *A*
Cazenovia College *B*
Cornell University *B*
Fashion Institute of Technology *A, B*
Marist College *B*
Pace University: Pleasantville/
Briarcliff *A*
Parsons The New School for
Design *C, A, B*
Pratt Institute *B*

SUNY
College at Buffalo *B*
Syracuse University *B*
Villa Maria College of Buffalo *B*
Wood Tobe-Coburn School *A*

North Carolina
Mars Hill University *B*
Meredith College *B*

Ohio
Bowling Green State University *B*
Columbus College of Art and
Design *B*
Kent State University *B, M*
University of Cincinnati *B*
Ursuline College *B*
Virginia Marti College of Art and
Design *A*

Oregon
Art Institute of Portland *A, B*

Pennsylvania
Albright College *B*
Art Institute of Philadelphia *A, B*
Drexel University *B, M*
Harcum College *A*
Lehigh Carbon Community College *A*
Moore College of Art and Design *B*
Philadelphia University *B*

Puerto Rico
Escuela de Artes Plasticas de Puerto
Rico *B*
Pontifical Catholic University of
Puerto Rico *A*
Turabo University *A*
Universal Technology College of
Puerto Rico *C*

South Carolina
Bob Jones University *B*

Tennessee
O'More College of Design *B*

Texas
Baylor University *B*
El Centro College *C, A*
El Paso Community College *A*
Houston Community College
System *C, A*
Texas Tech University *B*
Texas Woman's University *B*
University of North Texas *B*
University of the Incarnate Word *B*

Utah
Salt Lake Community College *C*

Vermont
Bennington College *B*

Virginia
Marymount University *B*
Virginia Commonwealth University *B*

Washington
Art Institute of Seattle *A, B*
International Academy of Design and
Technology
Seattle *A, B*

Wisconsin
Art Institute of Wisconsin *B*
Mount Mary University *B*

Fashion/fabric consultant

California
Academy of Art University *A, B, M*
Allan Hancock College *C, A*

City College of San Francisco *C*
Fashion Institute of Design and
Merchandising
Los Angeles *A*
San Diego *A*
San Francisco *A*
Monterey Peninsula College *A*

Illinois
Harper College *C, A*

Massachusetts
Fisher College *A*

Fashion merchandising

Alabama
Lawson State Community College *C*

Arizona
Art Institute of Tucson *B*
Mesa Community College *A*
Phoenix College *C, A*
Pima Community College *C, A*
Scottsdale Community College *C, A*

Arkansas
Harding University *B*

California
American River College *C, A*
Art Institute of California
Hollywood *A, B*
San Francisco *A, B*
Silicon Valley *B*
Butte College *C, A*
California State University
Long Beach *B*
Canada College *C, A*
Chaffey College *C, A*
City College of San Francisco *C, A*
College of Alameda *C, A*
Evergreen Valley College *A*
Fashion Institute of Design and
Merchandising
Los Angeles *A*
San Diego *A*
San Francisco *A*
Fresno City College *C, A*
Fullerton College *A*
Long Beach City College *C, A*
Los Angeles Trade and Technical
College *C, A*
Los Angeles Valley College *C, A*
Modesto Junior College *C, A*
Mount San Antonio College *C, A*
Orange Coast College *C, A*
Pasadena City College *C, A*
Point Loma Nazarene University *B*
Saddleback College *C, A*
San Diego Mesa College *C, A*
Santa Ana College *C, A*
Santa Rosa Junior College *C*
Ventura College *C, A*
West Valley College *C, A*
Westwood College
Los Angeles *A, B*
Woodbury University *B*

Colorado
Johnson & Wales University
Denver *B*
Westwood College
Denver South *B*

Connecticut
Gateway Community College *A*
Lincoln College of New England *A*
Sacred Heart University *B*
Tunxis Community College *C, A*
University of Bridgeport *A, B*

Delaware
University of Delaware *B*

District of Columbia
Howard University *B*

Florida
Art Institute of Fort Lauderdale *B*
Florida State College at
Jacksonville *A*
International Academy of Design and
Technology
Orlando *B*
Johnson & Wales University
North Miami *B*
Lynn University *B*
Miami International University of Art
and Design *A, B*

Georgia
Abraham Baldwin Agricultural
College *A*
Brenau University *B*
Middle Georgia State College *C*
University of Georgia *B*

Hawaii
University of Hawaii
Honolulu Community College *C, A*

Illinois
Chicago State University *B*
College of DuPage *A*
Columbia College Chicago *B*
Dominican University *B*
Harper College *C, A*
Illinois Institute of Art
Chicago *A, B*
Schaumburg *B*
Olivet Nazarene University *B*
South Suburban College of Cook
County *C, A*

Indiana
Purdue University *B, M, D*
Vincennes University *A*

Iowa
Ellsworth Community College *C, A*
Iowa Western Community College *A*

Kansas
Seward County Community
College *C, A*

Kentucky
Eastern Kentucky University *B*

Louisiana
Louisiana State University and
Agricultural and Mechanical
College *B*
University of Louisiana at Lafayette *B*

Maryland
Baltimore City Community College *A*
Stevenson University *B*

Massachusetts
Bay State College *A, B*
Bristol Community College *C*
Fisher College *A, B*
Lasell College *B*
Marian Court College *A*
Middlesex Community College *A*
Mount Ida College *B*
Newbury College *B*

Michigan
Art Institute of Michigan *C, A*
Central Michigan University *B*
Eastern Michigan University *B, M*
Grand Rapids Community College *A*

Lansing Community College *C, A*
Michigan State University *B, M*
Northwood University
Michigan *A, B*
Oakland Community College *A*

Minnesota
Alexandria Technical and Community
College *A*
Art Institutes International
Minnesota *A*
Ridgewater College *C*
St. Catherine University *B*
University of Minnesota
Twin Cities *B*

Mississippi
Hinds Community College *C, A*
Holmes Community College *A*
Mississippi Gulf Coast Community
College *A*
Northwest Mississippi Community
College *A*

Missouri
Metropolitan Community College -
Kansas City *A*
Stephens College *B*
Stevens Institute of Business &
Arts *A, B*

Nevada
International Academy of Design and
Technology
Henderson *B*

New Hampshire
Southern New Hampshire
University *A*

New Jersey
Berkeley College *A, B*
Brookdale Community College *A*
Middlesex County College *A*

New Mexico
Dona Ana Community College of
New Mexico State University *A*

New York
Berkeley College *A, B*
Berkeley College of New York
City *A, B*
Cazenovia College *B*
City University of New York
Kingsborough Community
College *A*
New York City College of
Technology *A*
Fashion Institute of
Technology *C, A, B*
Genesee Community College *A*
Herkimer County Community
College *A*
LIM College *A, B, M*
Nassau Community College *A*
Parsons The New School for
Design *C, A, B*
SUNY
College at Buffalo *B*
College at Oneonta *B*
Wood Tobe-Coburn School *A*

North Carolina
Johnson & Wales University
Charlotte *B*
Meredith College *B*

Ohio
Art Institute of Ohio: Cincinnati *A*
Ashland University *B*
Bowling Green State University *B*
Davis College *A*

Kent State University *B*
University of Akron *A*
Ursuline College *B*
Virginia Marti College of Art and
    Design *A*
Youngstown State University *B*

Oklahoma

Tulsa Community College *C, A*

Oregon

Art Institute of Portland *B*

Pennsylvania

Albright College *B*
Art Institute of Pittsburgh *B*
Art Institute of York *A, B*
Community College of
    Philadelphia *C, A*
Harcum College *A*
Immaculata University *A, B*
Indiana University of Pennsylvania *B*
Kaplan Career Institute
    Pittsburgh *A*
Mercyhurst University *B*
Pace Institute *A*
Philadelphia University *B*

Rhode Island

Johnson & Wales University
    Providence *B*

Tennessee

Lipscomb University *B*

Texas

Baylor University *B*
El Paso Community College *C, A*
Houston Community College
    System *C, A*
International Academy of Design and
    Technology
    San Antonio *A*
Laredo Community College *A*
Sam Houston State University *B*
South Plains College *A*
Stephen F. Austin State University *B*
Texas Christian University *B*
Texas State University *B*
Texas Tech University *B*
Texas Woman's University *B*
University of North Texas *B*

Virginia

Marymount University *B*

Washington

Edmonds Community College *C*
Highline Community College *A*
International Academy of Design and
    Technology
    Seattle *A, B*
Pierce College *C*
Seattle Central Community College *A*
Shoreline Community College *A*
Spokane Falls Community College *A*

Wisconsin

Madison Area Technical College *A*
Milwaukee Area Technical College *A*
Mount Mary University *B*

Fashion modeling

Illinois

Harper College *A*

New York

Fashion Institute of Technology *A*

Fiber/textile arts

California

Academy of Art University *C, A, B, M*
California College of the Arts *B, M*
California State University
    Long Beach *B, M*
Fashion Institute of Design and
    Merchandising
    Los Angeles *A*
    San Diego *A*
    San Francisco *A*
University of California
    Davis *M*

Georgia

Savannah College of Art and
    Design *B, M*

Illinois

School of the Art Institute of
    Chicago *B, M*

Kansas

University of Kansas *B, M*

Maryland

Maryland Institute College of Art *B*

Massachusetts

Massachusetts College of Art and
    Design *B, M*
University of Massachusetts
    Dartmouth *B, M*

Michigan

College for Creative Studies *B*
Finlandia University *B*
University of Michigan *B*

Minnesota

Minnesota State University
    Mankato *B, M*

Missouri

Kansas City Art Institute *B*

New Mexico

Northern New Mexico College *C, A*

New York

Cornell University *B, M, D*
SUNY
    College at Buffalo *B*

North Carolina

East Carolina University *B*
Haywood Community College *A*

Ohio

Bowling Green State University *B*

Oregon

Oregon College of Art & Craft *C, B*
University of Oregon *B*

Pennsylvania

Marywood University *M*
Philadelphia University *B, M*
Temple University *B, M*
University of the Arts *B*

Rhode Island

Rhode Island School of Design *B, M*

Tennessee

Tennessee Technological
    University *B*

Washington

University of Washington *B, M*
Western Washington University *B*

West Virginia

West Virginia State University *B*

Filipino/Tagalog

Hawaii

University of Hawaii
    Manoa *B*

Film/cinema/video studies

Alaska

University of Alaska
    Fairbanks *B*

Arizona

Arizona State University *B*
Scottsdale Community College *C*
University of Arizona *B*

California

Allan Hancock College *A*
Art Institute of California
    San Francisco *B*
Biola University *B*
Brooks Institute *B*
California Baptist University *B*
Chapman University *B, M*
La Sierra University *B*
Long Beach City College *A*
Los Angeles City College *A*
Los Angeles Pierce College *C*
National University *M*
Orange Coast College *C, A*
Palomar College *C, A*
Pitzer College *B*
San Francisco State University *B, M*
Santa Barbara City College *C, A*
Santa Monica College *A*
University of California
    Berkeley *B*
    Davis *B*
    Irvine *B*
    Los Angeles *B, M, D*
    Santa Barbara *B, M, D*
University of Southern
    California *B, M, D*

Colorado

Colorado College *B*
University of Colorado
    Boulder *B*
University of Denver *B*

Connecticut

Connecticut College *B*
Trinity College *B*
University of Hartford *B*
Wesleyan University *B*
Yale University *B, D*

District of Columbia

American University *B, M*
Georgetown University *B*
Howard University *M*

Florida

International Academy of Design and
    Technology: Tampa *A, B*
Jacksonville University *B*
Southeastern University *B*
Tallahassee Community College *A*
University of Miami *B, M*
University of Tampa *B*

Georgia

Emory University *B, M*
Georgia Perimeter College *A*
Georgia State University *B*

Savannah College of Art and
    Design *M*
University of Georgia *B*

Illinois

Columbia College Chicago *B*
Dominican University *B*
Governors State University *M*
Northwestern University *D*
University of Chicago *B, D*
University of Illinois
    Urbana-Champaign *B*

Indiana

DePauw University *B*
Grace College *B*
Huntington University *B*
Purdue University *B*

Iowa

Briar Cliff University *B*
Coe College *B*
University of Iowa *B, M, D*

Kansas

Southwestern College *B*
University of Kansas *B, M, D*

Kentucky

University of Pikeville *B*

Louisiana

University of Louisiana at Lafayette *B*

Maine

College of the Atlantic *B*

Maryland

Howard Community College *A*
Johns Hopkins University *B*
Maryland Institute College of Art *B*
McDaniel College *B*
Stevenson University *B*
University of Maryland
    College Park *B*

Massachusetts

Bard College at Simon's Rock *B*
Boston College *B*
Brandeis University *B*
Clark University *B*
Emerson College *B*
Hampshire College *B*
Massachusetts College of Art and
    Design *B, M*
Mount Holyoke College *B*
New England Institute of Art *B*
Northeastern University *B*
Smith College *B*
University of Massachusetts
    Amherst *C*
Wheaton College *B*

Michigan

Calvin College *B*
College for Creative Studies *B*
Eastern Michigan University *B*
Grand Valley State University *B*
Oakland Community College *A*
Oakland University *B*
Spring Arbor University *B*
University of Michigan *B, M, D*
Wayne State University *B*
Western Michigan University *B*

Minnesota

Art Institutes International
    Minnesota *B*
Augsburg College *B*
Carleton College *B*
Minneapolis Community and
    Technical College *C*

Minnesota State University
  Moorhead *B*
Saint Cloud State University *B*
University of Minnesota
  Twin Cities *B*

Missouri

Stephens College *B*
Washington University in St. Louis *B*
Webster University *B*

Nebraska

University of Nebraska
  Lincoln *B*

Nevada

International Academy of Design and
  Technology
  Henderson *B*
University of Nevada
  Las Vegas *B*

New Hampshire

Dartmouth College *B*
Keene State College *B*

New Jersey

Bergen Community College *A*
Kean University *B*

New Mexico

Santa Fe University of Art and
  Design *B*
University of New Mexico *B*

New York

Bard College *B, M*
Barnard College *B*
City University of New York
  City College *B, M*
  College of Staten Island *B, M*
  Hunter College *B*
  Queens College *B*
Columbia University *B*
Columbia University
  School of General Studies *B*
Cornell University *B*
Five Towns College *B*
Fordham University *B*
Ithaca College *B*
Pace University *B*
SUNY
  University at Buffalo *B*
  University at Stony Brook *B*
University of Rochester *B*
Vassar College *B*

Ohio

Baldwin Wallace University *B*
Bowling Green State University *B*
Denison University *B*
Malone University *B*
Oberlin College *B*
Ohio State University
  Columbus Campus *B*
University of Cincinnati *C*
University of Toledo *B*
Wright State University *B*

Oklahoma

Oklahoma City University *B*
University of Oklahoma *B*
University of Tulsa *B*

Oregon

University of Oregon *B*
Willamette University *B*

Pennsylvania

Carnegie Mellon University *B*
DeSales University *B*
Gettysburg College *B*
La Salle University *B*

Muhlenberg College *C, B*
Penn State
  Abington *B*
  Altoona *B*
  Beaver *B*
  Berks *B*
  Brandywine *B*
  DuBois *B*
  Erie, The Behrend College *B*
  Fayette, The Eberly Campus *B*
  Greater Allegheny *B*
  Harrisburg *B*
  Hazleton *B*
  Lehigh Valley *B*
  Mont Alto *B*
  New Kensington *B*
  Schuylkill *B*
  Shenango *B*
  University Park *B*
  Wilkes-Barre *B*
  Worthington Scranton *B*
  York *B*
Temple University *B, M*
University of Pennsylvania *B*
University of Pittsburgh *B, M, D*
University of the Arts *B*

Rhode Island

Rhode Island College *B*

South Carolina

University of South Carolina
  Columbia *B*

Tennessee

Vanderbilt University *B*
Watkins College of Art, Design &
  Film *B*

Texas

San Jacinto College *A*
Southern Methodist University *B*
University of Texas
  Austin *C*

Utah

Brigham Young University *B, M, D*
University of Utah *B, M*

Vermont

Bennington College *B*
Burlington College *A, B*
Champlain College *B*
Lyndon State College *A*
Marlboro College *B*
Middlebury College *B*
University of Vermont *B*

Virginia

Hollins University *B*
Regent University *M*
University of Richmond *B*

Washington

Eastern Washington University *B*
Evergreen State College *B*
Seattle University *B*

Wisconsin

University of Wisconsin
  Milwaukee *B*

Finance

Alabama

Alabama Agricultural and Mechanical
  University *B*
Auburn University *B*
Auburn University at Montgomery *B*
Birmingham-Southern College *B*
Columbia Southern University *C*
Faulkner State Community College *A*
Jacksonville State University *B*

Oakwood University *B*
Samford University *B*
Troy University *B*
Tuskegee University *B*
University of Alabama *B, M, D*
University of Alabama
  Birmingham *B*
  Huntsville *B*
University of Montevallo *B*
University of North Alabama *B*
University of Phoenix
  Birmingham *B*
University of South Alabama *B*
Wallace State Community College at
  Hanceville *A*

Alaska

University of Alaska
  Anchorage *B*

Arizona

Arizona State University *B*
Coconino County Community
  College *A*
Grand Canyon University *B*
Mohave Community College *C, A*
Northcentral University *M, D*
Northern Arizona University *B*
Penn Foster College *A*
Scottsdale Community College *C*
University of Arizona *B, M*
University of Phoenix
  Phoenix-Hohokam *B, M*
  Southern Arizona *B*
Western International
  University *B, M*

Arkansas

Arkansas State University *B*
East Arkansas Community College *A*
Harding University *B*
University of Arkansas *B*
University of Arkansas
  Little Rock *B*
University of Central Arkansas *B*
Williams Baptist College *B*

California

Azusa Pacific University *B, M*
California Lutheran University *B, M*
California State University
  Dominguez Hills *B*
  East Bay *B, M*
  Fresno *B*
  Fullerton *B, M*
  Long Beach *B*
  Northridge *M*
  Sacramento *B, M*
  San Bernardino *B, M*
  Stanislaus *M*
Claremont McKenna College *B, M*
Cosumnes River College *C, A*
Golden Gate University *C, B, M*
Holy Names University *M*
La Sierra University *B, M*
Lake Tahoe Community College *A*
Lincoln University *M*
Los Angeles Pierce College *C*
Loyola Marymount University *B*
Master's College *B*
Menlo College *B*
Modesto Junior College *A*
National University *C, B, M*
Pacific States University *M*
Pepperdine University *B*
Point Loma Nazarene University *B*
St. Mary's College of California *B*
San Diego State University *B, M*
San Jose State University *B*
Santa Barbara City College *C, A*
Santa Clara University *B*
Southwestern College *A*

University of Phoenix
  Bay Area *B*
  Central Valley *B*
  Sacramento Valley *B*
  San Diego *B*
  Southern California *B*
University of San Diego *B*
University of San Francisco *B*
University of the West *M*
Vanguard University of Southern
  California *B*

Colorado

Adams State University *B*
Aspen University *M*
Colorado State University *B*
Metropolitan State University of
  Denver *B*
Regis University *B*
University of Colorado
  Boulder *B*
  Denver *M*
University of Denver *B, M*
University of Phoenix
  Denver *B*
  Southern Colorado *B*

Connecticut

Albertus Magnus College *B*
Central Connecticut State
  University *B*
Fairfield University *B, M*
Post University *C, B*
Quinnipiac University *B, M*
Sacred Heart University *B*
Tunxis Community College *A*
University of Bridgeport *B, M*
University of Connecticut *B*
University of Hartford *B*
University of New Haven *B*
Western Connecticut State
  University *B*

Delaware

Delaware State University *B*
Goldey-Beacom College *B, M*
University of Delaware *B*
Wilmington University *B*

District of Columbia

American University *B, M*
Catholic University of America *B*
George Washington University *B, M*
Georgetown University *B*
Howard University *B*
University of Phoenix
  Washington DC *B*
University of the District of
  Columbia *B*

Florida

Barry University *B*
Bethune-Cookman University *B*
Broward College *A*
Edison State College *A*
Florida Atlantic University *B, M*
Florida Gulf Coast University *B*
Florida International University *B, M*
Florida State University *B, M, D*
Jacksonville University *B*
Northwood University
  Florida *B*
Nova Southeastern University *B*
Palm Beach Atlantic University *B*
Palm Beach State College *A*
Polk State College *A*
Rasmussen College
  Fort Myers *B*
  New Port Richey *B*
  Ocala *B*
  Pasco/Land O'Lakes *B*
  Tampa/Brandon *B*
Saint Johns River State College *A*
Saint Thomas University *B*

Schiller International University *B*
Southeastern University *B*
Stetson University *B*
University of Central Florida *B*
University of Florida *B, M*
University of Miami *B, D*
University of North Florida *B*
University of Phoenix
  Central Florida *B*
  North Florida *B*
  South Florida *B*
  West Florida *B*
University of South Florida *B, M*
University of South Florida
  Saint Petersburg *B*
  Sarasota-Manatee *B*
University of Tampa *B, M*
University of West Florida *B*
Webber International University *A, B*

Georgia

Berry College *B*
Columbus State University *B*
Emory University *B, D*
Georgia Regents University *B*
Georgia Southern University *B*
Georgia State University *B, M, D*
Kennesaw State University *B*
Mercer University *B, M*
University of Georgia *B*
University of North Georgia *B*
University of Phoenix
  Atlanta *B*
  Augusta *B*
  Columbus *B*
  Savannah *B*
University of West Georgia *B*
Valdosta State University *B*

Hawaii

Hawaii Pacific University *A, B*
University of Hawaii
  Manoa *B*
University of Phoenix
  Hawaii *B*

Idaho

Boise State University *B*
Idaho State University *B*
University of Idaho *B*
University of Phoenix
  Idaho *B*

Illinois

Augustana College *B*
Aurora University *B*
Benedictine University *B*
Benedictine University at
  Springfield *B*
Bradley University *B*
Chicago State University *B*
DePaul University *B, M*
Dominican University *B*
Eastern Illinois University *B*
Elmhurst College *B*
Eureka College *B*
Illinois College *B*
Illinois Institute of Technology *M*
Illinois State University *B*
Lake Forest College *B*
Lewis University *B, M*
Loyola University Chicago *B, M*
MacMurray College *B*
Millikin University *B*
North Central College *B*
Northeastern Illinois University *B*
Northern Illinois University *B*
Northwestern University *M, D*
Olivet Nazarene University *B*
Quincy University *B*
Rasmussen College
  Aurora *B*
  Mokena/Tinley Park *B*

Rockford *B*
Romeoville/Joliet *B*
Roosevelt University *B*
Saint Xavier University *M*
South Suburban College of Cook
  County *C, A*
Southern Illinois University
  Carbondale *B*
Trinity Christian College *B*
University of Illinois
  Chicago *B, M*
  Urbana-Champaign *B, M, D*
University of Phoenix
  Chicago *B*
University of St. Francis *B*
Western Illinois University *B*

Indiana

Anderson University *B, D*
Ball State University *B*
Butler University *B*
Franklin College *B*
Grace College *B*
Indiana State University *B*
Indiana University
  Purdue University Fort Wayne *B*
  Southeast *C*
Indiana Wesleyan University *B*
Manchester University *B*
Marian University *B*
Taylor University *B*
Trine University *B*
University of Evansville *B*
University of Notre Dame *B*
University of Phoenix
  Indianapolis *B*
University of Southern Indiana *B*
Valparaiso University *B*

Iowa

AIB College of Business *A*
Ashford University *B*
Drake University *B*
Grand View University *B*
Iowa State University *B*
Kirkwood Community College *A*
Loras College *B*
Mount Mercy University *B*
Northwestern College *B*
St. Ambrose University *B*
University of Iowa *B, D*
University of Northern Iowa *B*
University of Phoenix
  Des Moines *B*
Upper Iowa University *B, M*
Wartburg College *B*
Western Iowa Tech Community
  College *A*

Kansas

Benedictine College *B*
Bethany College *B*
Kansas State University *B*
McPherson College *B*
Pittsburg State University *B*
Seward County Community
  College *A*
Southwestern College *B*
University of Kansas *B*
University of St. Mary *M*
Washburn University *B*
Wichita State University *B*

Kentucky

Bellarmine University *B*
Berea College *B*
Eastern Kentucky University *B*
Madisonville Community College *A*
Morehead State University *B*
Murray State University *B*
Northern Kentucky University *C, B*
Southeast Kentucky Community and
  Technical College *C, A*
Sullivan University *B*

University of Kentucky *B*
University of Louisville *B*
University of Phoenix
  Louisville *B*
Western Kentucky University *B*

Louisiana

Centenary College of Louisiana *B*
Dillard University *B*
Louisiana College *B*
Louisiana State University and
  Agricultural and Mechanical
  College *B, M*
Louisiana Tech University *B*
Loyola University New Orleans *B*
McNeese State University *B*
Nicholls State University *B*
Southeastern Louisiana University *B*
Southern University and Agricultural
  and Mechanical College *B*
Tulane University *B, M*
University of Louisiana at Lafayette *B*
University of Louisiana at Monroe *B*
University of New Orleans *B*
University of Phoenix
  Baton Rouge *B*
  Lafayette *B*
  Louisiana *B*
  Shreveport *B*
Xavier University of Louisiana *B*

Maine

Husson University *B*
Saint Joseph's College of Maine *B*
Thomas College *B*
University of Maine *B*
University of Southern Maine *B, M*

Maryland

Kaplan University
  Hagerstown *M*
Loyola University Maryland *M*
Morgan State University *B, M*
Notre Dame of Maryland
  University *B*
Salisbury University *B*
University of Baltimore *B*
University of Maryland
  College Park *B*
  University College *B*
Washington Adventist University *M*

Massachusetts

American International College *B, M*
Babson College *B*
Bentley University *B, M*
Boston College *B, M, D*
Boston University *B, M*
Brandeis University *M*
Bridgewater State University *M*
Bunker Hill Community College *A*
Clark University *M*
Endicott College *B*
Fitchburg State University *B*
Gordon College *B*
Lasell College *B*
Merrimack College *B*
New England College of Business and
  Finance *M*
Nichols College *B*
Northeastern University *B, M*
Northern Essex Community
  College *C, A*
Salem State University *B*
Simmons College *B*
Springfield Technical Community
  College *A*
Stonehill College *B*
Suffolk University *B, M*
University of Massachusetts
  Amherst *B*
  Boston *M*
  Dartmouth *B*

University of Phoenix
  Boston *B*
Western New England University *B*

Michigan

Albion College *B*
Andrews University *B*
Central Michigan University *B*
Cleary University *B*
Davenport University *A, B, M*
Eastern Michigan University *B, M*
Ferris State University *B*
Glen Oaks Community College *C*
Grand Valley State University *B*
Hillsdale College *B*
Jackson College *C, A*
Lake Superior State University *B*
Michigan State University *B, M, D*
Michigan Technological University *B*
Northern Michigan University *B*
Northwood University
  Michigan *B*
Oakland University *B*
Saginaw Valley State University *B*
Spring Arbor University *B*
University of Michigan
  Flint *B, M*
University of Phoenix
  Metro Detroit *B*
  West Michigan *B*
Walsh College of Accountancy and
  Business Administration *B, M*
Wayne State University *B*
Western Michigan University *B*

Minnesota

Augsburg College *B*
Capella University *B, M*
College of St. Scholastica *B*
Concordia University St. Paul *B*
Fond du Lac Tribal and Community
  College *A*
Hamline University *B*
Metropolitan State University *B*
Minnesota State University
  Mankato *B*
  Moorhead *B*
National American University
  Roseville *B*
North Hennepin Community
  College *A*
Rasmussen College
  Blaine *B*
  Bloomington *B*
  Brooklyn Park *B*
  Eagan *B*
  Lake Elmo/Woodbury *B*
  Mankato *B*
  St. Cloud *B*
Saint Cloud State University *B*
St. Mary's University of Minnesota *B*
Southwest Minnesota State
  University *B*
University of Minnesota
  Duluth *B*
  Twin Cities *B*
University of Northwestern - St.
  Paul *B*
University of Phoenix
  Minneapolis-St. Paul *B*
University of St. Thomas *B*
Winona State University *B*

Mississippi

Delta State University *B*
Jackson State University *B*
Mississippi College *B, M*
Mississippi State University *B*
University of Mississippi *B*
University of Phoenix
  Jackson *B*
University of Southern Mississippi *B*

Missouri

Avila University *B*
Columbia College *B*
Culver-Stockton College *B*
Drury University *B*
Hannibal-LaGrange University *B*
Lindenwood University *B, M*
Missouri Southern State University *B*
Missouri State University *B*
Missouri Western State University *B*
Northwest Missouri State
  University *B*
Saint Louis University *B, M*
Southeast Missouri State University *B*
Southwest Baptist University *B*
University of Central Missouri *B*
University of Missouri
  Kansas City *B, M*
  St. Louis *B, M*
University of Phoenix
  Kansas City *B*
  St. Louis *B*
Washington University in St.
  Louis *B, M*
Webster University *B, M*

Montana

University of Montana *B*

Nebraska

Chadron State College *B*
Creighton University *C, B*
Union College *B*
University of Nebraska
  Lincoln *B*
  Omaha *B*
University of Phoenix
  Omaha *B*
York College *B*

Nevada

Sierra Nevada College *B*
University of Nevada
  Las Vegas *B*
  Reno *B, M*
University of Phoenix
  Las Vegas *B*
  Northern Nevada *B*

New Hampshire

New England College *B*
Plymouth State University *B*
Saint Anselm College *B*
Southern New Hampshire
  University *M*

New Jersey

Fairleigh Dickinson University
  Metropolitan Campus *B*
Gloucester County College *A*
Kean University *B*
Princeton University *M*
Rider University *B*
Rowan University *B, M*
Rutgers, The State University of New
  Jersey
  Camden Campus *B*
  New Brunswick/Piscataway
    Campus *B, M*
  Newark Campus *B*
Saint Peter's University *A, B, M*
Seton Hall University *B*
Thomas Edison State College *C, B*
University of Phoenix
  Jersey City *B*
William Paterson University of New
  Jersey *B*

New Mexico

Eastern New Mexico University *B*
National American University
  Albuquerque *B*
New Mexico Highlands University *B*
New Mexico State University *B*

University of Phoenix
  New Mexico *B*

New York

Adelphi University *B, M*
Alfred University *B*
Canisius College *B*
City University of New York
  Baruch College *B, M*
  CUNY Online *C*
  Queens College *B, M*
Clinton Community College *C*
Concordia College *B*
Dominican College of Blauvelt *B*
Dowling College *B, M*
Elmira College *B*
Excelsior College *B*
Fordham University *B, M*
Globe Institute of
  Technology *C, A, B*
Hofstra University *C, B, M*
Hudson Valley Community College *A*
Iona College *B, M*
Le Moyne College *B*
Long Island University
  LIU Brooklyn *B*
  LIU Post *B*
Manhattan College *B*
Manhattanville College *B, M*
Mercy College *M*
Metropolitan College of New York *M*
Mohawk Valley Community
  College *C*
Molloy College *B, M*
Nazareth College *B*
New York Institute of
  Technology *B, M*
New York University *B, M, D*
Niagara University *B*
Orange County Community
  College *A*
Pace University *B, M*
Pace University: Pleasantville/
  Briarcliff *B, M*
Rochester Institute of
  Technology *B, M*
SUNY
  College at Brockport *B*
  College at Fredonia *B*
  College at New Paltz *B, M*
  College at Old Westbury *B*
  College at Oswego *B*
  College at Plattsburgh *B*
  College of Technology at Alfred *A*
  College of Technology at Canton *B*
  University at Albany *M*
  University at Binghamton *B*
  University at Buffalo *M*
Saint Bonaventure University *B, M*
St. John Fisher College *B*
St. John's University *B*
St. Thomas Aquinas College *B*
Siena College *B, T*
Suffolk County Community College *A*
Syracuse University *B, M*
Wagner College *B*
Yeshiva University *B*

North Carolina

Appalachian State University *B*
East Carolina University *B*
Elon University *B*
Fayetteville State University *B*
Gardner-Webb University *B*
Lenoir-Rhyne University *B*
Mars Hill University *B*
Methodist University *B*
North Carolina Agricultural and
  Technical State University *B*
Queens University of Charlotte *B*
University of North Carolina
  Charlotte *B*
  Greensboro *B*
  Wilmington *B*

Wake Forest University *B*
Western Carolina University *B*
Western Piedmont Community
  College *C*
Wingate University *B*
Winston-Salem State University *B*

North Dakota

Dickinson State University *B*
Minot State University *B*
North Dakota State University *B*
Rasmussen College
  Bismarck *B*
  Fargo *B*
University of Jamestown *B*
University of Mary *B*
University of North Dakota *B*

Ohio

Ashland University *B*
Baldwin Wallace University *B*
Bowling Green State University *B*
Case Western Reserve
  University *B, M*
Cedarville University *B*
Cleveland State University *B, D*
Franklin University *A, B*
John Carroll University *B*
Kent State University *B*
Marietta College *B*
Miami University
  Middletown *A*
  Oxford *B*
Mount Vernon Nazarene University *B*
North Central State College *C*
Ohio Dominican University *B*
Ohio Northern University *B*
Ohio State University
  Columbus Campus *B, M*
Ohio University *B*
Otterbein University *B*
Tiffin University *B*
University of Akron *B, M*
University of Cincinnati *B, M*
University of Dayton *B*
University of Findlay *A, B*
University of Phoenix
  Cleveland *B*
University of Toledo *B, M*
Wilberforce University *B*
Wright State University *B, M*
Xavier University *B*
Youngstown State University *A, B, M*

Oklahoma

East Central University *B*
Northeastern State University *B*
Oklahoma Baptist University *B*
Oklahoma Christian University *B*
Oklahoma City Community
  College *C, A*
Oklahoma City University *B, M*
Oklahoma State University *B*
Oral Roberts University *B*
St. Gregory's University *B*
Southeastern Oklahoma State
  University *B*
Southern Nazarene University *B*
Tulsa Community College *A*
University of Central Oklahoma *B*
University of Oklahoma *B*
University of Phoenix
  Oklahoma City *B*
  Tulsa *B*
University of Tulsa *B, M*

Oregon

Corban University *B*
George Fox University *B*
Linfield College *B*
Oregon State University *B*
Portland State University *B, M*
University of Oregon *M, D*
University of Portland *B*

Pennsylvania

Albright College *B*
Arcadia University *B*
Cabrini College *B*
Carnegie Mellon University *B, M, D*
Clarion University of Pennsylvania *B*
DeSales University *B*
Drexel University *B, M*
Duquesne University *B*
Gannon University *B*
Gettysburg College *B*
Grove City College *B*
Holy Family University *B*
Immaculata University *B*
Indiana University of Pennsylvania *B*
Juniata College *B*
King's College *B*
La Roche College *B*
La Salle University *B*
Lehigh University *B, M*
Lincoln University *B*
Lycoming College *B*
Mercyhurst University *B*
Muhlenberg College *C, A, B*
Penn State
  Abington *B*
  Altoona *B*
  Beaver *B*
  Berks *B*
  Brandywine *B*
  DuBois *B*
  Erie, The Behrend College *B*
  Fayette, The Eberly Campus *B*
  Greater Allegheny *B*
  Harrisburg *B*
  Hazleton *B*
  Lehigh Valley *B*
  Mont Alto *B*
  New Kensington *B*
  Schuylkill *B*
  Shenango *B*
  University Park *B*
  Wilkes-Barre *B*
  Worthington Scranton *B*
  York *B*
Philadelphia University *B*
Robert Morris University *B*
St. Francis University *B*
Saint Joseph's University *B, M*
St. Vincent College *B*
Shippensburg University of
  Pennsylvania *B*
Slippery Rock University of
  Pennsylvania *B*
Temple University *B, M*
University of Pennsylvania *B, M, D*
University of Phoenix
  Harrisburg *B*
  Philadelphia *B*
  Pittsburgh *B*
University of Pittsburgh *B*
University of Pittsburgh
  Johnstown *B*
University of Scranton *B, M*
Villanova University *B, M*
Waynesburg University *B*
West Chester University of
  Pennsylvania *B*
Westminster College *B*
Widener University *B*
Wilkes University *B*
York College of Pennsylvania *B, M*

Puerto Rico

Bayamon Central University *B, M*
Inter American University of Puerto
  Rico
  Aguadilla Campus *M*
  Bayamon Campus *B*
  Metropolitan Campus *B, M*
  Ponce Campus *B, M*
  San German Campus *B, M*
Pontifical Catholic University of
  Puerto Rico *B, M*

Universidad Metropolitana *M*
University of Puerto Rico
  Aguadilla *B*
  Arecibo *B*
  Bayamon University College *B*
  Carolina Regional College *B*
  Mayaguez *B, M*
  Ponce *B*
  Rio Piedras *B, M, D*

Rhode Island

Bryant University *B, M*
Johnson & Wales University
  Providence *B*
Providence College *B*
Rhode Island College *B*
Roger Williams University *B*
Salve Regina University *B*
University of Rhode Island *B*

South Carolina

Anderson University *B*
Charleston Southern University *B, M*
Clemson University *B*
Coastal Carolina University *B*
Converse College *B*
Francis Marion University *B*
Limestone College *B*
University of Phoenix
  Columbia *B*
University of South Carolina
  Columbia *B*
Wofford College *B*

South Dakota

Dakota State University *B*
Lake Area Technical Institute *A*
Northern State University *B*
University of South Dakota *B, M*

Tennessee

Belmont University *B*
Christian Brothers University *B*
Cleveland State Community
  College *C*
East Tennessee State University *B*
Freed-Hardeman University *B*
Hiwassee College *A*
Lipscomb University *M*
Maryville College *B*
Middle Tennessee State University *B*
Southern Adventist University *B*
Tennessee Technological
  University *B*
Tennessee Wesleyan College *B*
University of Memphis *B*
University of Phoenix
  Chattanooga *B*
  Knoxville *B*
  Memphis *B*
  Nashville *B*
University of Tennessee
  Knoxville *B*
  Martin *B*
Vanderbilt University *M*

Texas

Abilene Christian University *B*
Amarillo College *A*
Angelo State University *B*
Baylor University *B*
Brazosport College *A*
Clarendon College *A*
Dallas Baptist University *B, M*
Del Mar College *C, A*
El Paso Community College *A*
Hardin-Simmons University *B*
Houston Baptist University *B*
Howard Payne University *B*
Lamar University *B*
Laredo Community College *C, A*
LeTourneau University *B*
Lubbock Christian University *B*
McMurry University *B*

Midwestern State University *B*
Our Lady of the Lake University of
  San Antonio *M*
Prairie View A&M University *B*
St. Edward's University *B*
St. Mary's University *B*
Sam Houston State University *B, M*
Schreiner University *B*
Southern Methodist University *B, M*
Southwestern Adventist University *B*
Stephen F. Austin State University *B*
Sul Ross State University *B*
Tarleton State University *B*
Texas A&M International
  University *B*
Texas A&M University *B, M, D*
Texas A&M University
  Commerce *B, M*
  Corpus Christi *B*
  Kingsville *B*
  Texarkana *B*
Texas Christian University *B*
Texas State University *B*
Texas Tech University *B*
Texas Wesleyan University *B*
Texas Woman's University *B*
Trinity University *B*
University of Houston *B, M*
University of Houston
  Clear Lake *B, M*
  Downtown *B*
University of Mary Hardin-Baylor *B*
University of North Texas *M*
University of Phoenix
  Austin *B*
  Dallas Fort Worth *B*
  Houston Westside *B, M*
  San Antonio *B*
University of St. Thomas *B, M*
University of Texas
  Arlington *M*
  Austin *B, M, D*
  Brownsville *B*
  Dallas *B, M*
  El Paso *B*
  Pan American *B*
  Permian Basin *B*
  San Antonio *B, M, D*
  Tyler *B*
West Texas A&M University *B, M*

Utah

Brigham Young University *B*
Dixie State College *B*
Salt Lake Community College *C, A*
Southern Utah University *B*
University of Phoenix
  Utah *B*
University of Utah *B, M*
Utah State University *B, M*
Utah Valley University *B*
Weber State University *B*
Westminster College *B*

Vermont

Lyndon State College *B*

Virginia

Averett University *B*
Central Virginia Community
  College *A*
Christopher Newport University *B*
Dabney S. Lancaster Community
  College *C*
Ferrum College *B*
George Mason University *B*
Hampton University *B*
James Madison University *B*
Old Dominion University *B*
Radford University *B*
University of Phoenix
  Northern Virginia *B*
  Richmond *B*

Virginia Highlands Community
  College *C*
Virginia Polytechnic Institute and
  State University *B*
Virginia Union University *B*

Washington

City University of Seattle *M*
Eastern Washington University *B*
Seattle University *B, M*
University of Phoenix
  Western Washington *B*
University of Washington *B*
University of Washington Tacoma *B*
Walla Walla University *B*
Washington State University *B, D*
Western Washington University *B*

West Virginia

Bethany College *B*
Concord University *B*
Davis and Elkins College *B*
Kanawha Valley Community and
  Technical College *A*
Marshall University *B*
University of Charleston *B*
West Virginia University *B, M*

Wisconsin

Carroll University *B*
Carthage College *B*
Concordia University Wisconsin *B*
Madison Area Technical College *A*
Marian University *B*
Marquette University *B*
Rasmussen College
  Appleton *B*
  Green Bay *B*
  Wausau *B*
St. Norbert College *B*
University of Phoenix
  Milwaukee *B*
University of Wisconsin
  Eau Claire *B*
  La Crosse *B*
  Madison *B, M*
  Milwaukee *B*
  Oshkosh *B*
  Parkside *B*
  Platteville *B*
  Superior *B*
  Whitewater *B*
Western Technical College *A*
Wisconsin Indianhead Technical
  College *A*

Wyoming

University of Wyoming *B, M*

Financial forensics and fraud investigation

Minnesota

Globe University
  Minneapolis *B*
  Woodbury *B*
Minnesota School of Business
  Blaine *B*
  Elk River *B*
  Plymouth *B*
  Richfield *B*
  Rochester *B*
  Shakopee *B*

New York

Canisius College *M*
Genesee Community College *A*

Pennsylvania

Carlow University *M*

Vermont

Champlain College *B*

Wisconsin

Globe University
  Appleton *B*
  Middleton *B*

Financial mathematics

California

University of Southern
  California *B, M*

Connecticut

University of Connecticut *M*

District of Columbia

American University *B*

Georgia

Georgia Institute of Technology *M*

Illinois

Illinois Institute of Technology *M*
Knox College *B*

Kentucky

Asbury University *B*
University of Kentucky *B*

Maryland

Johns Hopkins University *M*

Massachusetts

Boston University *M, D*

Michigan

University of Michigan *M*

Minnesota

Concordia College: Moorhead *B*

New York

City University of New York
  Brooklyn College *B*

North Carolina

University of North Carolina
  Charlotte *M*

Ohio

University of Cincinnati *B*
University of Mount Union *B*

Oklahoma

Oklahoma State University *M*

Pennsylvania

Carnegie Mellon University *B, M, D*
Lehigh University *M*

Tennessee

Trevecca Nazarene University *B*

Financial planning

California

Golden Gate University *M*
San Diego State University *B, M*
Southwestern College *C, A*
University of San Francisco *M*

Connecticut

Manchester Community College *C*
Norwalk Community College *A*
University of Connecticut *B*

Florida

Florida State College at
  Jacksonville *C, A*
Schiller International University *M*

Georgia

Columbus Technical College *C*
Georgia State University *M*

Illinois

DePaul University *M*
Saint Xavier University *M*
Triton College *A*
University of Illinois
   Urbana-Champaign *B, M, D*

Indiana

Grace College *B*
Purdue University *B*

Kansas

Barton County Community College *C*

Kentucky

Northern Kentucky University *C*
Western Kentucky University *C*

Louisiana

Louisiana State University
   Shreveport *B*

Maine

University of Maine
   Augusta *A, B*

Maryland

Howard Community College *C, A*
University of Maryland
   Eastern Shore *C*

Massachusetts

Bentley University *M*
New England College of Business and
   Finance *C*
Salem State University *M*

Michigan

Central Michigan University *B*
Cleary University *B, M*
Cornerstone University *B*
Northern Michigan University *B*
Olivet College *B*
Western Michigan University *B*

Minnesota

Minnesota State University
   Mankato *B*

Missouri

Missouri Southern State University *B*

New Jersey

Berkeley College *A, B*
Raritan Valley Community College *C*

New York

Berkeley College of New York
   City *A, B*
Bramson ORT College *A*
Broome Community College *A*
Globe Institute of Technology *C*
Pace University *M*
Pace University: Pleasantville/
   Briarcliff *M*
SUNY
   College of Agriculture and
      Technology at Cobleskill *C, B*
   College of Technology at Alfred *B*

North Carolina

Campbell University *B, M*
Rockingham Community College *A*

North Dakota

University of Jamestown *B*

Ohio

Cincinnati State Technical and
   Community College *A*
Franklin University *B*
Ohio State University
   Lima Campus *B*
University of Akron *C, B*
University of Cincinnati
   Blue Ash College *C, A*
Youngstown State University *B*

Pennsylvania

Marywood University *B, M*
Penn State
   Erie, The Behrend College *C*
   Harrisburg *C*
   University Park *C*
Saint Joseph's University *B, M*
Widener University *B, M*

Rhode Island

Bryant University *B*
Community College of Rhode
   Island *C*
University of Rhode Island *B*

South Carolina

York Technical College *C*

Texas

Baylor University *B*
Lamar State College at Orange *C*
Lubbock Christian University *B*
St. Mary's University *B*
Southern Methodist University *B, M*
Texas Tech University *D*
University of Dallas *M*
University of North Texas *B*

Utah

Utah Valley University *B*

Washington

City University of Seattle *C*

Wisconsin

University of Wisconsin
   Madison *B*
   Milwaukee *C*

Fine and studio arts management

Alabama

Spring Hill College *B*

California

California State University
   East Bay *B*
La Sierra University *B*
Santa Rosa Junior College *C*
University of San Francisco *B*

Delaware

Delaware State University *B*

District of Columbia

American University *M*
Howard University *B*

Florida

Florida State University *M*
Ringling College of Art and Design *B*

Georgia

Brenau University *B*
Savannah College of Art and
   Design *M*

Illinois

Benedictine University *B*
Columbia College Chicago *B, M*

DePaul University *B*
Eureka College *B*
School of the Art Institute of
   Chicago *M*

Indiana

Indiana University
   Bloomington *B, M*

Iowa

Buena Vista University *B*
University of Iowa *B, M, D*
Upper Iowa University *B*

Kentucky

Bellarmine University *B*
Bluegrass Community and Technical
   College *A*

Louisiana

Dillard University *B*
Southeastern Louisiana University *B*
University of New Orleans *M*

Maine

University of Southern Maine *B*

Maryland

Goucher College *M*
Maryland Institute College of Art *M*

Massachusetts

Anna Maria College *B*
Dean College *B*
Lasell College *B*
Massachusetts College of Liberal
   Arts *B*
Simmons College *B*

Michigan

Adrian College *B*
Aquinas College *B*
Eastern Michigan University *B*
University of Michigan
   Flint *M*

Minnesota

Art Institutes International
   Minnesota *B*

Mississippi

Belhaven University *B*

Missouri

Culver-Stockton College *B*
Drury University *B*
Lindenwood University *B, M*

Nebraska

Concordia University *B*

New Hampshire

Franklin Pierce University *B*

New Jersey

Rider University *B*

New Mexico

Santa Fe Community College *A*
Santa Fe University of Art and
   Design *B*

New York

City University of New York
   Baruch College *B*
Daemen College *B, M*
Fashion Institute of Technology *B, M*
Ithaca College *B*
Long Island University
   LIU Post *B*
Pratt Institute *M*

SUNY

   College at Purchase *B*
   University at Buffalo *M*
Wagner College *B*

North Carolina

Appalachian State University *B*
Catawba College *B*
Lees-McRae College *B*
Lenoir-Rhyne University *B*
North Carolina State University *B*
Pfeiffer University *B*
Queens University of Charlotte *B*
Salem College *B*
University of North Carolina
   Charlotte *M*

North Dakota

Minot State University *B*
United Tribes Technical College *C, A*

Ohio

Ohio State University
   Columbus Campus *M, D*
Tiffin University *B*

Oklahoma

University of Tulsa *B*

Oregon

Art Institute of Portland *B*
University of Oregon *M*

Pennsylvania

Albright College *B*
Carnegie Mellon University *M*
Chatham University *B*
Drexel University *M*
Mercyhurst University *M*
Messiah College *B*
St. Vincent College *B*
Seton Hill University *B*
Waynesburg University *B*

Puerto Rico

University of Puerto Rico
   Rio Piedras *M*

South Carolina

College of Charleston *B*
Winthrop University *M*

South Dakota

University of South Dakota *B*

Texas

El Paso Community College *C*
Southern Methodist University *M*

Utah

Westminster College *B*

Virginia

George Mason University *M*
Mary Baldwin College *B*
Randolph-Macon College *B*

Washington

Seattle University *D*

West Virginia

West Virginia Wesleyan College *B*

Wisconsin

University of Wisconsin
   Madison *M*
   Milwaukee *C*
   Stevens Point *B*
Viterbo University *B*

Fine/studio arts

Alabama

Auburn University *B*
Faulkner State Community College *A*
Huntingdon College *B*
Spring Hill College *B*
Talladega College *B*
University of Alabama *B, M*

Arizona

Arizona Western College *A*
Dine College *A*
Eastern Arizona College *A*
Glendale Community College *A*
Northern Arizona University *B*
Phoenix College *A*
Prescott College *B*
Scottsdale Community College *A*
Sessions College for Professional
　Design *C*
Southwest University of Visual
　Arts *B, M*
University of Arizona *B*

Arkansas

Harding University *B*
Ouachita Baptist University *B, T*
Southern Arkansas University *B*
University of the Ozarks *B*
Williams Baptist College *B*

California

Academy of Art University *C, A, B, M*
Art Center College of Design *B, M*
Azusa Pacific University *B, M*
Biola University *B*
Butte College *A*
Cabrillo College *A*
California College of the Arts *B, M*
California Institute of the
　Arts *C, B, M*
California Polytechnic State
　University: San Luis Obispo *B*
California State University
　Chico *B, M*
　East Bay *B*
　Fullerton *B, M*
　Long Beach *B, M*
　San Bernardino *B*
　Stanislaus *B*
Chabot College *A*
Chaffey College *A*
Chapman University *B*
Citrus College *A*
College of Alameda *A*
College of Marin *A*
College of San Mateo *A*
College of the Desert *A*
College of the Sequoias *A*
Cosumnes River College *A*
Diablo Valley College *C, A*
El Camino College *A*
Foothill College *C, A*
Gavilan College *A*
Golden West College *A*
Irvine Valley College *A*
John F. Kennedy University *B, M*
La Sierra University *B*
Lake Tahoe Community College *A*
Lassen Community College *A*
Los Angeles Pierce College *A*
Los Medanos College *A*
Loyola Marymount University *B*
Mills College *B, M*
Modesto Junior College *A*
Monterey Peninsula College *C, A*
Moorpark College *A*
Mount St. Mary's College *B*
Notre Dame de Namur University *B*
Ohlone College *A*
Orange Coast College *A*
Otis College of Art and Design *B, M*
Pacific Union College *B*

Pasadena City College *A*
Pepperdine University *B*
Pitzer College *B*
Pomona College *B*
Porterville College *C, A*
Sacramento City College *A*
Saddleback College *A*
San Deigo Miramar College
　San Diego Miramar College *A*
San Diego City College *A*
San Diego Mesa College *A*
San Diego State University *B, M*
San Francisco State University *M*
San Jose City College *A*
San Jose State University *B, M*
Santa Barbara City College *C, A*
Santa Clara University *B*
Scripps College *B*
Shasta College *A*
Sierra College *A*
Solano Community College *A*
Sonoma State University *B*
Stanford University *B*
University of California
　Davis *B*
　Irvine *B, M*
　Riverside *B*
　San Diego *B*
　Santa Barbara *B, M*
　Santa Cruz *M*
University of Redlands *B*
University of San Francisco *B*
University of Southern
　California *B, M*
University of the Pacific *B*
Ventura College *C, A*
West Hills College: Coalinga *A*
Yuba College *A*

Colorado

Adams State University *B*
Colorado Christian University *B*
Colorado College *B*
Colorado State University *B, M*
Colorado State University
　Pueblo *B*
Community College of Aurora *A*
Fort Lewis College *B*
Metropolitan State University of
　Denver *B*
Naropa University *B*
Rocky Mountain College of Art &
　Design *B*
University of Colorado
　Boulder *B, M*
　Denver *B*
University of Northern
　Colorado *B, M, T*
Western State Colorado University *B*

Connecticut

Albertus Magnus College *B*
Capital Community College *C*
Connecticut College *B*
Eastern Connecticut State
　University *B*
Fairfield University *B*
Gateway Community College *A*
Housatonic Community College *A*
Middlesex Community College *A*
Mitchell College *A*
Naugatuck Valley Community
　College *C*
Northwestern Connecticut
　Community College *C*
Norwalk Community College *A*
Paier College of Art *C, B*
Quinebaug Valley Community
　College *C, A*
Southern Connecticut State
　University *B*
Trinity College *B*
University of Connecticut *B, M*
University of New Haven *B*

Wesleyan University *B*
Western Connecticut State
　University *M*
Yale University *M*

Delaware

Delaware College of Art and
　Design *A*
Delaware State University *B*
University of Delaware *B, M*

District of Columbia

American University *B*
Corcoran College of Art and
　Design *A, B*
Gallaudet University *B*
George Washington University *B*
Trinity Washington University *B*
University of the District of
　Columbia *B*

Florida

Beacon College *A, B*
Daytona State College *A*
Eckerd College *B*
Flagler College *B*
Florida Agricultural and Mechanical
　University *B, T*
Florida Atlantic University *M*
Florida International University *B, M*
Florida Southern College *B*
Florida State University *B, M*
Jacksonville University *B*
Miami Dade College *A*
New College of Florida *B*
Nova Southeastern University *B*
Palm Beach Atlantic University *B*
Palm Beach State College *A*
Ringling College of Art and Design *B*
Rollins College *B*
University of Central Florida *B, M*
University of Florida *B, M*
University of Miami *B*
University of North Florida *B*
University of South Florida *B, M*
University of West Florida *B*

Georgia

Abraham Baldwin Agricultural
　College *A*
Agnes Scott College *B*
Brenau University *B*
Georgia Southern University *M*
Oglethorpe University *B*
Piedmont College *B*
Reinhardt University *B*
Shorter University *B*
Spelman College *B*
University of Georgia *B*
University of North Georgia *A, B*
Wesleyan College *B*

Hawaii

Brigham Young University-Hawaii *B*

Idaho

College of Idaho *B*
North Idaho College *A*
University of Idaho *B*

Illinois

American Academy of Art *B, M*
Benedictine University *B*
Bradley University *B, M, T*
Columbia College Chicago *B*
Dominican University *B*
Elgin Community College *C*
Harper College *A*
Illinois Central College *B*
Illinois College *B*
Illinois State University *B, M*
Illinois Valley Community College *A*
Judson University *B, D*
Knox College *B*

Lake Land College *A*
Lewis and Clark Community
　College *A*
Lincoln College *A*
Lincoln Land Community College *A*
Loyola University Chicago *C, B*
Millikin University *B*
Monmouth College *B*
Morton College *A*
Northern Illinois University *B, M*
Prairie State College *A*
Principia College *B*
Saint Xavier University *B*
Sauk Valley Community College *A*
School of the Art Institute of
　Chicago *B, M*
South Suburban College of Cook
　County *A*
Southern Illinois University
　Carbondale *B, M*
Southern Illinois University
　Edwardsville *B, M*
Southwestern Illinois College *A*
Trinity Christian College *B*
Triton College *A*
University of Illinois
　Chicago *B, M*
　Springfield *B*
　Urbana-Champaign *B, M*
Waubonsee Community College *C, A*
Western Illinois University *B*

Indiana

Anderson University *B*
Calumet College of St. Joseph *C, B*
DePauw University *B*
Franklin College *B*
Hanover College *B*
Huntington University *B*
Indiana State University *B, M*
Indiana University
　Bloomington *B, M*
　Kokomo *B*
　Northwest *B*
　Purdue University Fort Wayne *B*
　Purdue University Indianapolis *B*
　South Bend *B*
　Southeast *B*
Indiana Wesleyan University *A, B*
Purdue University *B, M*
Saint Joseph's College *B*
Saint Mary's College *B*
University of Notre Dame *B, M*
University of St. Francis *A, B, M*

Iowa

Clarke University *A, B, T*
Coe College *B*
Cornell College *B*
Ellsworth Community College *A*
Grand View University *B*
Iowa Wesleyan College *B*
Maharishi University of
　Management *B*
Marshalltown Community College *A*
Morningside College *B*
St. Ambrose University *B*
Simpson College *B*
University of Iowa *B*
University of Northern Iowa *B*
Upper Iowa University *B*
William Penn University *B*

Kansas

Allen County Community College *A*
Baker University *B, T*
Bethel College *B*
Coffeyville Community College *A*
Cowley County Community
　College *A*
Fort Hays State University *M*
Independence Community College *A*
Kansas State University *B, M*
Labette Community College *A*

Neosho County Community
  College *A*
Pratt Community College *A*
Seward County Community
  College *A*
Tabor College *B*
University of Kansas *B, M*
Washburn University *B*
Wichita State University *B, M*

Kentucky

Asbury University *B*
Bellarmine University *B, T*
Berea College *B, T*
Bluegrass Community and Technical
  College *A*
Campbellsville University *B*
Eastern Kentucky University *B*
Georgetown College *B*
Hopkinsville Community College *A*
Kentucky State University *B*
Kentucky Wesleyan College *B*
Lindsey Wilson College *A, B, T*
Morehead State University *B, M*
Murray State University *B, T*
Northern Kentucky University *B*
Owensboro Community and
  Technical College *A*
Thomas More College *A, B*
Transylvania University *B, T*
University of Kentucky *B, M*
University of Louisville *B*
University of the Cumberlands *B*
Western Kentucky University *B*

Louisiana

Centenary College of Louisiana *B*
Delgado Community College *A*
Louisiana College *B*
Louisiana State University
  Eunice *A*
Louisiana State University and
  Agricultural and Mechanical
  College *B, M*
Loyola University New Orleans *B*
Nicholls State University *B*
Northwestern State University *B*
Tulane University *B, M*
University of Louisiana at Monroe *B*
University of New Orleans *B, M*

Maine

Bowdoin College *B*
Colby College *B*
College of the Atlantic *B, M*
Maine College of Art *B, M*
Unity College *B*
University of Maine *B*
University of Maine
  Augusta *A, B*
  Presque Isle *B*
University of Southern Maine *B*

Maryland

Carroll Community College *A*
Cecil College *A*
Frostburg State University *B, T*
Goucher College *B*
Harford Community College *A*
Montgomery College *A*
Morgan State University *B*
Notre Dame of Maryland
  University *B*
Prince George's Community
  College *A*
Salisbury University *B*
Towson University *B, M*
University of Maryland
  Baltimore County *B*
  College Park *B, M*

Massachusetts

Amherst College *B*
Assumption College *B*

Bard College at Simon's Rock *B*
Boston College *B*
Boston University *M*
Brandeis University *B*
Bridgewater State University *B*
Bristol Community College *A*
Clark University *B*
College of the Holy Cross *B*
Curry College *B*
Elms College *B*
Emmanuel College *B*
Endicott College *B*
Hampshire College *B*
Lesley University *B, M*
Massachusetts College of Art and
  Design *B*
Massasoit Community College *A*
Middlesex Community College *C, A*
Montserrat College of Art *B*
Mount Holyoke College *B*
Northeastern University *B, M*
Quincy College *A*
School of the Museum of Fine
  Arts *C, B, M, T*
Smith College *B*
Springfield Technical Community
  College *A*
Stonehill College *B*
Tufts University *B*
University of Massachusetts
  Amherst *B, M*
  Dartmouth *B, M*
Wellesley College *B*
Wheaton College *B*
Williams College *B*

Michigan

Adrian College *B*
Albion College *B*
Andrews University *B*
Aquinas College *B*
Calvin College *B*
Central Michigan University *B, M*
College for Creative Studies *B*
Eastern Michigan University *M*
Ferris State University *B, M*
Finlandia University *B*
Grand Rapids Community College *A*
Grand Valley State University *B*
Henry Ford Community College *A*
Hope College *B*
Lake Superior State University *B*
Madonna University *A, B*
Marygrove College *B*
Monroe County Community
  College *A*
Northwestern Michigan College *A*
Oakland University *B, T*
Saginaw Valley State University *B*
St. Clair County Community
  College *A*
Siena Heights University *B*
University of Michigan
  Flint *B*
Western Michigan University *B, M*

Minnesota

Anoka-Ramsey Community College *A*
Augsburg College *B*
Bethany Lutheran College *B*
Bethel University *B*
Carleton College *B*
Century College *A*
Concordia University St. Paul *B*
Fond du Lac Tribal and Community
  College *A*
Hamline University *B*
Inver Hills Community College *A*
Lake Superior College *A*
Minneapolis College of Art and
  Design *B, M*
Minneapolis Community and
  Technical College *A*

Minnesota State Community and
  Technical College *A*
Minnesota State University
  Mankato *B, M*
  Moorhead *C*
Normandale Community College *A*
North Hennepin Community
  College *A*
Ridgewater College *A*
Rochester Community and Technical
  College *A*
St. Catherine University *B*
Saint Cloud State University *B*
St. Mary's University of Minnesota *B*
University of Minnesota
  Duluth *B*
  Morris *B*
  Twin Cities *B, M*
University of Northwestern - St.
  Paul *B*

Mississippi

Millsaps College *B*
Mississippi College *B, M*
Mississippi Delta Community
  College *A*
Mississippi Valley State University *B*
University of Mississippi *B, M*
University of Southern Mississippi *M*
William Carey University *B*

Missouri

College of the Ozarks *B*
Drury University *B, T*
East Central College *A*
Evangel University *B*
Fontbonne University *B, M, T*
Lincoln University *B*
Lindenwood University *B, M*
Maryville University of Saint Louis *B*
Missouri Southern State
  University *B, T*
Northwest Missouri State
  University *B*
Park University *B*
St. Louis Community College *A*
Saint Louis University *B*
Three Rivers Community College *A*
University of Central Missouri *B*
University of Missouri
  Kansas City *B, M*
  St. Louis *B*
Washington University in St.
  Louis *B, M*
William Woods University *B, T*

Montana

Montana State University
  Northern *B*
University of Montana: Western *B*

Nebraska

College of Saint Mary *B, T*
Concordia University *B*
Creighton University *B*
Metropolitan Community College *A*
Midland University *B*
Nebraska Wesleyan University *B*
Peru State College *B*
Union College *B*
University of Nebraska
  Kearney *B, M, T*
  Lincoln *B, M*
  Omaha *B*

Nevada

College of Southern Nevada *A*
Sierra Nevada College *B*
University of Nevada
  Las Vegas *B, M*

New Hampshire

Colby-Sawyer College *B*
Dartmouth College *B*

Franklin Pierce University *B*
Keene State College *B*
Lakes Region Community College *A*
Plymouth State University *B*
Rivier University *B*
Southern New Hampshire
  University *M*
University of New Hampshire *B*
University of New Hampshire at
  Manchester *A*

New Jersey

Brookdale Community College *A*
College of New Jersey *B, T*
Cumberland County College *A*
Essex County College *A*
Felician College *B*
Hudson County Community
  College *A*
Kean University *B*
Middlesex County College *A*
Monmouth University *B*
Montclair State University *M*
New Jersey City University *B, M*
Raritan Valley Community College *A*
Richard Stockton College of New
  Jersey *B*
Rider University *B*
Rowan University *B*
Rutgers, The State University of New
  Jersey
  New Brunswick/Piscataway
    Campus *M*
Saint Peter's University *B*
Sussex County Community College *A*
Warren County Community
  College *A*

New Mexico

Clovis Community College *A*
Institute of American Indian
  Arts *A, B*
New Mexico Highlands University *B*
New Mexico Junior College *A*
New Mexico State University *B, M*
New Mexico State University
  Alamogordo *A*
Northern New Mexico College *A*
Santa Fe University of Art and
  Design *B*
Southwest University of Visual Arts *B*
Western New Mexico University *B*

New York

Alfred University *B*
Bard College *B, M*
Canisius College *B*
Cayuga Community College *A*
Cazenovia College *B*
City University of New York
  Brooklyn College *B, M*
  City College *B*
  College of Staten Island *B*
  Hunter College *B*
  Kingsborough Community
    College *A*
  LaGuardia Community College *A*
  Queens College *B, M, T*
  York College *B*
Colgate University *B*
College of New Rochelle *B, M, T*
College of Saint Rose *B, M*
Columbia University *B*
Columbia University
  School of General Studies *B*
Columbia-Greene Community
  College *A*
Cooper Union for the Advancement
  of Science and Art *C, B*
Cornell University *B*
Daemen College *B*
Eugene Lang College The New
  School for Liberal Arts *B*
Fashion Institute of Technology *A, B*

Finger Lakes Community College *A*
Fordham University *B*
Hamilton College *B*
Hobart and William Smith Colleges *B*
Hofstra University *B*
Houghton College *B*
Ithaca College *B*
Jamestown Community College *A*
Long Island University
   LIU Brooklyn *B*
   LIU Post *B, M*
Manhattanville College *B*
Marist College *C, B*
Marymount Manhattan College *B*
Monroe Community College *A*
Nazareth College *B, T*
New York University *C, B, M, T*
Niagara County Community
   College *A*
Pace University *B*
Pace University: Pleasantville/
   Briarcliff *A*
Parsons The New School for
   Design *B, M*
Pratt Institute *B, M*
Rensselaer Polytechnic
   Institute *B, M, D*
Roberts Wesleyan College *B*
Rochester Institute of
   Technology *B, M*
Rockland Community College *A*
SUNY
   College at Brockport *B, M*
   College at Buffalo *B*
   College at Cortland *B*
   College at Fredonia *B*
   College at Oneonta *B*
   College at Oswego *M*
   Empire State College *A, B*
   University at Albany *B, M*
   University at Buffalo *B, M*
Sage Colleges *B*
St. Lawrence University *B*
St. Thomas Aquinas College *B*
School of Visual Arts *B, M*
Suffolk County Community College *A*
Syracuse University *B, M*
Union College *B*
University of Rochester *B*
Villa Maria College of Buffalo *A*
Wagner College *B*

North Carolina

Appalachian State University *B*
Barton College *B*
Campbell University *B*
Chowan University *B*
East Carolina University *B, M*
Elizabeth City State University *B*
Gardner-Webb University *B*
Greensboro College *C, B*
High Point University *B*
Meredith College *B*
Methodist University *B*
Mitchell Community College *A*
Piedmont Community College *A*
Randolph Community College *A*
Rockingham Community College *A*
Salem College *B*
Southeastern Community College *A*
University of North Carolina
   Asheville *B*
   Chapel Hill *B, M*
   Charlotte *B*
   Greensboro *B, M*
   Pembroke *B*
   Wilmington *B*
Wake Forest University *B*
Western Carolina University *B, M*
Western Piedmont Community
   College *A*

North Dakota

Cankdeska Cikana Community
   College *A*

Dickinson State University *B*
University of Jamestown *B*

Ohio

Art Academy of Cincinnati *B*
Ashland University *B*
Baldwin Wallace University *B*
Bowling Green State University *B*
Cedarville University *B*
College of Mount St. Joseph *B*
College of Wooster *B*
Columbus College of Art and
   Design *B*
Denison University *B*
Hiram College *B, T*
Kenyon College *B*
Lake Erie College *B*
Malone University *B*
Marietta College *B*
Notre Dame College *B*
Oberlin College *B*
Ohio Northern University *B*
Ohio University *B*
Ohio Wesleyan University *B*
Shawnee State University *B*
Terra State Community College *A*
University of Akron *B*
University of Cincinnati *B, M*
University of Dayton *B*
University of Mount Union *B*
Ursuline College *B*
Wilberforce University *B*
Xavier University *B*
Youngstown State University *B*

Oklahoma

Oklahoma Baptist University *B*
Oklahoma Christian University *B*
Oklahoma City Community
   College *A*
Oklahoma City University *B, M*
Oral Roberts University *B*
University of Central Oklahoma *B*
University of Oklahoma *B, M*
University of Science and Arts of
   Oklahoma *B, T*
University of Tulsa *M*

Oregon

Central Oregon Community
   College *A*
Lewis & Clark College *B*
Linfield College *B*
Marylhurst University *B*
Mt. Hood Community College *A*
Pacific Northwest College of Art *B*
Portland State University *B, M*
University of Oregon *B, M*
Western Oregon University *B, M*
Willamette University *B*

Pennsylvania

Albright College *B*
Allegheny College *B*
Arcadia University *B*
Bloomsburg University of
   Pennsylvania *B*
Bryn Mawr College *B*
Bucknell University *B*
Carlow University *B*
Cedar Crest College *B*
Chatham University *B*
Chestnut Hill College *B*
Community College of Beaver
   County *A*
Delaware County Community
   College *A*
Dickinson College *B*
Edinboro University of
   Pennsylvania *B, M*
Elizabethtown College *B, T*
Franklin & Marshall College *B*
Gettysburg College *B*
Haverford College *B*

Holy Family University *B*
Indiana University of Pennsylvania *B*
Juniata College *B*
Keystone College *A, B*
Kutztown University of
   Pennsylvania *B*
La Salle University *B*
Lafayette College *B*
Lincoln University *B*
Lock Haven University of
   Pennsylvania *B*
Lycoming College *B*
Mansfield University of
   Pennsylvania *B*
Marywood University *M*
Mercyhurst University *B, T*
Messiah College *B*
Moore College of Art and
   Design *B, M*
Moravian College *B*
Northampton Community College *A*
Pennsylvania College of Art and
   Design *B*
Rosemont College *B*
St. Vincent College *B*
Seton Hill University *B*
Slippery Rock University of
   Pennsylvania *B, T*
Swarthmore College *B*
University of Pennsylvania *B, M*
University of Pittsburgh *B*
University of the Arts *B, M*
West Chester University of
   Pennsylvania *B*
Westminster College *B*
Widener University *B*
York College of Pennsylvania *A, B*

Puerto Rico

Pontifical Catholic University of
   Puerto Rico *B*
University of Puerto Rico
   Mayaguez *B*
   Rio Piedras *B*

Rhode Island

Brown University *B*
Providence College *B*
Rhode Island College *B*
Roger Williams University *B*
Salve Regina University *B*
University of Rhode Island *B*

South Carolina

Bob Jones University *B*
Claflin University *B*
Coastal Carolina University *B*
Coker College *B*
College of Charleston *B*
Columbia College *B, T*
Converse College *B, M*
Limestone College *B*
North Greenville University *B*
South Carolina State University *B*
University of South Carolina
   Aiken *B*
   Beaufort *B*
   Columbia *B, M*
Winthrop University *B*
Wofford College *B*

South Dakota

South Dakota State University *B*
University of South Dakota *B, M*

Tennessee

Belmont University *B*
Christian Brothers University *B*
Cumberland University *B*
Lee University *B*
Lipscomb University *B*
Maryville College *B*
Memphis College of Art *B, M*

Sewanee: The University of the
   South *B*
Tennessee Technological
   University *B*
Union University *B*
University of Tennessee
   Knoxville *B, M*
Vanderbilt University *B*
Watkins College of Art, Design &
   Film *B*

Texas

Abilene Christian University *B*
Angelo State University *B*
Art Institute of Dallas *B*
Baylor University *B*
Coastal Bend College *A*
College of the Mainland *A*
El Paso Community College *C*
Hardin-Simmons University *B*
Hill College *A*
Houston Baptist University *B*
Howard Payne University *B*
Lamar State College at Port Arthur *A*
McMurry University *B*
Midwestern State University *B*
Mountain View College *A*
Palo Alto College *A*
Paris Junior College *A*
Rice University *B, M*
St. Philip's College *A*
Sam Houston State University *B*
South Texas College *A*
Southern Methodist University *B, M*
Tarleton State University *B*
Texas A&M University
   Commerce *B, M*
   Corpus Christi *B*
   Kingsville *B, M, T*
Texas Christian University *B, M*
Texas College *B*
Texas Southern University *B, M*
Texas State University *B*
Tyler Junior College *A*
University of Houston
   Clear Lake *B*
University of Mary Hardin-Baylor *B, T*
University of North Texas *B, M*
University of St. Thomas *B*
University of Texas
   Arlington *B, M*
   Austin *B, M*
   El Paso *B, M*
   Pan American *B, M*
   San Antonio *B*
   Tyler *M*
University of the Incarnate Word *B*
West Texas A&M University *B, M*

Utah

Brigham Young University *B, M*
Southern Utah University *B*

Vermont

Bennington College *B*
Burlington College *B*
Green Mountain College *B*
Johnson State College *B, M*
Marlboro College *B*
Middlebury College *B*
Saint Michael's College *B*
University of Vermont *B*

Virginia

Blue Ridge Community College *C*
Bridgewater College *B*
Christopher Newport University *B*
Germanna Community College *C*
Hampden-Sydney College *B*
Hollins University *B*
Liberty University *B*
Lord Fairfax Community College *C*
Marymount University *B, T*

Northern Virginia Community
College *A*
Randolph College *B*
Randolph-Macon College *B*
Regent University *M*
Sweet Briar College *B*
Thomas Nelson Community
College *A*
Tidewater Community College *A*
University of Richmond *B*
Virginia Commonwealth
University *M*
Virginia Western Community
College *A*
Washington and Lee University *B*

Washington

Central Washington University *B, M*
Centralia College *A*
Cornish College of the Arts *B*
Eastern Washington University *B*
Evergreen State College *B*
Gonzaga University *B*
North Seattle Community
College *C, A*
Pacific Lutheran University *B*
Seattle University *B*
Washington State University *B, M*
Whitman College *B*

West Virginia

Alderson-Broaddus University *B*
Bethany College *B*
Concord University *B*
Fairmont State University *B*
West Virginia State University *B*
West Virginia Wesleyan College *B*
Wheeling Jesuit University *B*

Wisconsin

Cardinal Stritch University *B, T*
Carroll University *B*
Carthage College *B*
Lawrence University *B, T*
Marian University *B*
Milwaukee Institute of Art &
Design *B*
Ripon College *B*
University of Wisconsin
Oshkosh *B*
River Falls *B*
Superior *B, M, T*
Viterbo University *B*

Wyoming

Casper College *A*
Western Wyoming Community
College *A*

Fire/arson investigation
and prevention

Arizona

Arizona Western College *C*

Kansas

Kansas City Kansas Community
College *C*

Minnesota

Hennepin Technical College *C*

Fire protection and
safety technology

Alabama

Calhoun Community College *A*
Community College of the Air
Force *A*

Arizona

Arizona Western College *C*
Central Arizona College *C, A*

California

Allan Hancock College *C, A*
American River College *A*
Antelope Valley College *C, A*
Bakersfield College *C, A*
Butte College *C, A*
Cerro Coso Community College *C, A*
City College of San Francisco *C, A*
College of San Mateo *C, A*
College of the Canyons *C, A*
College of the Desert *C, A*
College of the Sequoias *C, A*
College of the Siskiyous *C, A*
Columbia College *C, A*
Copper Mountain College *C, A*
Cosumnes River College *C, A*
El Camino College *C, A*
Fresno City College *C*
Glendale Community College *C, A*
Long Beach City College *C, A*
Mission College *C, A*
Monterey Peninsula College *C, A*
Palomar College *C, A*
Rio Hondo College *C, A*
Riverside City College *C, A*
San Joaquin Delta College *C, A*
Santa Ana College *A*
Santa Rosa Junior College *C*
Santiago Canyon College *A*
Shasta College *C, A*
Sierra College *C, A*
Victor Valley College *C, A*
Yuba College *C, A*

Colorado

Colorado Mountain College *C*

Connecticut

Capital Community College *A*
Naugatuck Valley Community
College *A*
Three Rivers Community College *A*
University of New Haven *C, A, B, M*

Delaware

Delaware State University *B*
Delaware Technical Community
College
Stanton/Wilmington Campus *C, A*

Florida

College of Central Florida *A*
Daytona State College *A*
Florida State College at
Jacksonville *A*
Gulf Coast State College *A*
Hillsborough Community
College *C, A*
Indian River State College *A*
Lake-Sumter State College *A*
Polk State College *A*
Saint Johns River State College *A*
Santa Fe College *A*
Seminole State College of Florida *A*
South Florida State College *A*

Hawaii

University of Hawaii
Honolulu Community College *C, A*

Idaho

College of Southern Idaho *A*

Illinois

College of DuPage *C, A*
College of Lake County *C, A*
Illinois Central College *A*
John Wood Community College *A*
Kishwaukee College *C, A*

Lincoln Land Community College *C*
Moraine Valley Community College *A*
Parkland College *C*
Prairie State College *C*
Rock Valley College *C*
Sauk Valley Community College *C*

Iowa

Des Moines Area Community
College *C, A*

Kansas

Hutchinson Community College *A*
Kansas City Kansas Community
College *C, A*

Kentucky

Bluegrass Community and Technical
College *A*
Eastern Kentucky University *C, A, B*
Northern Kentucky University *A*

Louisiana

Louisiana State University
Eunice *C, A*

Maryland

Anne Arundel Community College *A*

Massachusetts

Bristol Community College *C*
Cape Cod Community College *A*
Middlesex Community College *A*
Mount Wachusett Community
College *A*
North Shore Community
College *C, A*
Springfield Technical Community
College *A*

Michigan

Delta College *A*
Kellogg Community College *C, A*
Lake Superior State University *A, B*
Macomb Community College *A*
Mott Community College *A*
Wayne County Community College *C*

Minnesota

Hennepin Technical College *A*
Lake Superior College *A*
Northland Community & Technical
College *A*
Northwest Technical College *C*

Mississippi

Mississippi Gulf Coast Community
College *A*

Missouri

Jefferson College *C, A*
St. Louis Community College *C, A*

Montana

Montana State University
Billings *A*

Nebraska

Southeast Community College *A*

Nevada

College of Southern Nevada *A*

New Hampshire

Lakes Region Community College *A*

New Jersey

Camden County College *A*
Mercer County Community
College *C, A*
Ocean County College *C, A*
Passaic County Community
College *C, A*

Thomas Edison State College *A, B*
Union County College *A*

New Mexico

Eastern New Mexico University:
Roswell *A*

New York

Jamestown Community College *C, A*
Monroe Community College *A*
Onondaga Community College *A*
Rockland Community College *A*
Sullivan County Community
College *A*

North Carolina

Blue Ridge Community College *A*
Catawba Valley Community
College *A*
Central Piedmont Community
College *C, A*
Cleveland Community College *C, A*
Coastal Carolina Community
College *C, A*
Davidson County Community
College *C, A*
Fayetteville Technical Community
College *A*
Forsyth Technical Community
College *A*
Gaston College *A*
Guilford Technical Community
College *C, A*
Rowan-Cabarrus Community
College *A*
Wilson Community College *C, A*

Ohio

Cuyahoga Community College
Metropolitan *A*
Owens Community College
Toledo *A*
Sinclair Community College *C, A*
University of Akron *C, A*

Oklahoma

Oklahoma State University *B*
Oklahoma State University
Oklahoma City *C*
Tulsa Community College *A*

Oregon

Chemeketa Community College *A*
Rogue Community College *C, A*
Treasure Valley Community
College *C, A*

Pennsylvania

Bucks County Community College *A*
Community College of Allegheny
County *A*
Community College of
Philadelphia *A*
Luzerne County Community
College *C, A*
Montgomery County Community
College *C, A*
Westmoreland County Community
College *C, A*

Texas

Amarillo College *C, A*
Austin Community College *A*
Cisco College *C*
College of the Mainland *A*
Collin County Community College
District *C, A*
Del Mar College *C, A*
El Paso Community College *A*
Galveston College *C, A*
Houston Community College
System *C, A*
Lamar Institute of Technology *A*
Laredo Community College *A*

Midland College *C*
Navarro College *C, A*
Odessa College *C, A*
San Antonio College *C, A*
San Jacinto College *C, A*
South Plains College *C, A*
Tarrant County College *C, A*
Tyler Junior College *A*

Virginia
Northern Virginia Community
　College *C, A*

West Virginia
Blue Ridge Community and Technical
　College *C, A*

Wisconsin
Blackhawk Technical College *A*
Moraine Park Technical College *C, A*
Northcentral Technical College *C*
Northeast Wisconsin Technical
　College *A*
Waukesha County Technical
　College *A*
Western Technical College *A*

Fire services administration

Alabama
Calhoun Community College *C*
Chattahoochee Valley Community
　College *C, A*
Columbia Southern University *B*
Jefferson Davis Community
　College *C*
Jefferson State Community
　College *C, A*
Lawson State Community College *C*
Northwest-Shoals Community
　College *C*
Southern Union State Community
　College *C*

Arizona
Arizona Western College *C*

Arkansas
Southern Arkansas University Tech *A*

California
California Polytechnic State
　University: San Luis Obispo *M*
California State University
　Los Angeles *B*
College of the Siskiyous *A*
Fresno City College *C*
Santa Ana College *A*
Shasta College *C, A*

Colorado
Aims Community College *A*
Colorado Mountain College *C*
Colorado State University *B*
Community College of Aurora *C, A*

Connecticut
Gateway Community College *A*

Delaware
Delaware Technical Community
　College
　Stanton/Wilmington Campus *C, A*

District of Columbia
University of the District of
　Columbia *A, B*

Florida
Florida State College at
　Jacksonville *A*

Miami Dade College *A*
Palm Beach State College *A*

Georgia
Albany State University *B*
Atlanta Technical College *A*
Gwinnett Technical College *A*

Hawaii
University of Hawaii
　Honolulu Community College *A*

Illinois
Black Hawk College *A*
College of DuPage *C*
Elgin Community College *C, A*
Illinois Eastern Community Colleges
　Frontier Community College *A*
Lewis University *B*
Lincoln Land Community College *C*
Rend Lake College *C, A*
Southern Illinois University
　Carbondale *B, M*
Waubonsee Community College *C*

Iowa
North Iowa Area Community
　College *A*
Waldorf College *B*

Kansas
Kansas City Kansas Community
　College *C*

Maryland
Frederick Community College *C, A*
University of Maryland
　University College *B*

Massachusetts
Cape Cod Community College *C*
Quinsigamond Community College *A*
Salem State University *B*

Michigan
Delta College *A*
Wayne County Community College *A*

Minnesota
Hennepin Technical College *C*
Minnesota State Community and
　Technical College *C*
Southwest Minnesota State
　University *B*

Missouri
Columbia College *A*
Lindenwood University *B*
Park University *B*

Nebraska
Metropolitan Community College *A*
University of Nebraska
　Omaha *B*

New Hampshire
Lakes Region Community College *A*

New Jersey
Burlington County College *C*

New York
City University of New York
　John Jay College of Criminal
　Justice *B*
Dutchess Community College *A*
Erie Community College *A*
Jefferson Community College *A*
Mohawk Valley Community
　College *A*
Rockland Community College *A*

North Carolina
Fayetteville State University *B*
University of North Carolina
　Charlotte *B*

Ohio
Bowling Green State University *B*
Sinclair Community College *C, A*
University of Cincinnati *B*

Oklahoma
Oklahoma State University *M, D*

Oregon
Eastern Oregon University *B*
Western Oregon University *B*

Pennsylvania
Holy Family University *B*
Northampton Community College *A*
Point Park University *C*

South Carolina
Trident Technical College *A*
York Technical College *A*

Virginia
Hampton University *B*
Northern Virginia Community
　College *C, A*
Thomas Nelson Community
　College *A*

Washington
Bellevue College *C, A*
Edmonds Community College *A*
Pierce College *A*
Spokane Community College *A*
Yakima Valley Community College *A*

West Virginia
American Public University
　System *C, B*

Fire systems technology

Arizona
Arizona Western College *C*

Illinois
Sauk Valley Community College *C*

Texas
Hill College *C*

Washington
Bates Technical College *C, A*
Clover Park Technical College *C, A*

Firefighting/fire science

Alabama
Alabama Southern Community
　College *C, A*
Columbia Southern University *C, A*

Alaska
University of Alaska
　Fairbanks *A*

Arizona
Arizona Western College *C, A*
Central Arizona College *A*
Cochise College *C, A*
Coconino County Community
　College *A*
Eastern Arizona College *C*
Glendale Community College *C, A*
Grand Canyon University *B, M*
Mesa Community College *C*
Mohave Community College *C, A*

Northland Pioneer College *C, A*
Paradise Valley Community
　College *C, A*
Penn Foster College *A*
Phoenix College *C, A*
Pima Community College *C, A*
Scottsdale Community College *C, A*
Yavapai College *C, A*

Arkansas
Northwest Arkansas Community
　College *A*
Southern Arkansas University
　Tech *C, A*

California
Allan Hancock College *C*
Bakersfield College *C*
Cabrillo College *C, A*
Chabot College *C, A*
College of the Sequoias *C*
College of the Siskiyous *C, A*
Crafton Hills College *C, A*
East Los Angeles College *C, A*
El Camino College *C*
Folsom Lake College *A*
Fresno City College *C, A*
Hartnell College *C, A*
Imperial Valley College *C, A*
Lake Tahoe Community College *C, A*
Los Angeles Harbor College *C, A*
Los Medanos College *C, A*
Merced College *C, A*
Modesto Junior College *C, A*
Moreno Valley College *C, A*
Mount San Antonio College *C, A*
Oxnard College *C, A*
Palo Verde College *C, A*
Pasadena City College *A*
Porterville College *C*
San Deigo Miramar College
　San Diego Miramar College *C, A*
Santa Ana College *A*
Santa Rosa Junior College *C, A*
Shasta College *C, A*
Sierra College *C, A*
Solano Community College *C, A*
Southwestern College *C, A*
Woodland Community College *C*
Yuba College *C*

Colorado
Aims Community College *C, A*
Colorado Mountain College *A*
Community College of Aurora *C, A*
Northeastern Junior College *C, A*
Pikes Peak Community College *C, A*
Pueblo Community College *C, A*
Red Rocks Community College *C, A*

Delaware
Delaware Technical Community
　College
　Stanton/Wilmington Campus *A*

District of Columbia
University of the District of
　Columbia *A*

Florida
Broward College *A*
Chipola College *C, A*
Daytona State College *C*
Eastern Florida State College *C, A*
Edison State College *A*
Florida State College at
　Jacksonville *C, A*
Gulf Coast State College *A*
Hillsborough Community College *C*
Indian River State College *C*
Lake-Sumter State College *A*
Miami Dade College *C*
Northwest Florida State College *C*
Palm Beach State College *C, A*

Pensacola State College *C, A*
St. Petersburg College *C, A*
Seminole State College of
    Florida *C, A*
State College of Florida, Manatee-
    Sarasota *C, A*
University of Florida *B, M*
Valencia College *C, A*

Georgia

Albany Technical College *C*
Atlanta Technical College *C*
Georgia Piedmont Technical
    College *C*
Gwinnett Technical College *C*
Reinhardt University *A*
Savannah Technical College *C, A*
West Georgia Technical College *C, A*
Wiregrass Georgia Technical
    College *C, A*

Hawaii

University of Hawaii
    Hawaii Community College *C, A*
    Honolulu Community College *C, A*

Idaho

College of Western Idaho *A*
Eastern Idaho Technical College *C, A*
Idaho State University *A, B*
Lewis-Clark State College *A, B*

Illinois

Carl Sandburg College *C, A*
City Colleges of Chicago
    Harold Washington College *A*
College of DuPage *C*
Danville Area Community
    College *C, A*
Elgin Community College *C*
Harper College *A*
Illinois Eastern Community Colleges
    Frontier Community College *C, A*
Joliet Junior College *C*
Kishwaukee College *C, A*
Lewis and Clark Community
    College *A*
Lincoln Land Community
    College *C, A*
McHenry County College *C, A*
Moraine Valley Community College *A*
Oakton Community College *C, A*
Prairie State College *C, A*
Rasmussen College
    Romeoville/Joliet *A*
Rend Lake College *C*
Richland Community College *A*
Rock Valley College *A*
Sauk Valley Community College *C, A*
Southeastern Illinois College *C*
Southwestern Illinois College *C, A*
Triton College *C, A*
Waubonsee Community College *C, A*

Indiana

Vincennes University *C, A*

Iowa

Clinton Community College *A*
Iowa Central Community College *A*
Iowa Western Community College *A*
Kirkwood Community College *C, A*
Northeast Iowa Community
    College *A*
Western Iowa Tech Community
    College *C, A*

Kansas

Barton County Community
    College *C, A*
Butler Community College *C, A*
Dodge City Community College *A*
Garden City Community College *C, A*

Johnson County Community
    College *A*
Kansas City Kansas Community
    College *A*
Labette Community College *C, A*

Kentucky

Bluegrass Community and Technical
    College *C, A*
Elizabethtown Community and
    Technical College *C, A*
Jefferson Community and Technical
    College *C, A*
Owensboro Community and
    Technical College *C, A*
Somerset Community College *C*

Louisiana

Delgado Community College *C, A*

Maine

Eastern Maine Community College *A*
Southern Maine Community
    College *C, A*

Maryland

Cecil College *A*
College of Southern Maryland *A*
Montgomery College *A*

Massachusetts

Anna Maria College *B, M*
Berkshire Community College *A*
Bristol Community College *A*
Cape Cod Community College *A*
Massasoit Community College *A*
Springfield Technical Community
    College *C*

Michigan

Delta College *A*
Henry Ford Community College *A*
Kalamazoo Valley Community
    College *C, A*
Kellogg Community College *C*
Lake Superior State University *A, B*
Lansing Community College *C, A*
Macomb Community College *C, A*
Madonna University *C, A, B*
Mid Michigan Community College *A*
Oakland Community College *C, A*
Schoolcraft College *C, A*
Southwestern Michigan College *C, A*

Minnesota

Century College *C*
Minnesota State Community and
    Technical College *C*
Northland Community & Technical
    College *C*

Mississippi

Meridian Community College *C, A*

Missouri

East Central College *C, A*
Mineral Area College *C, A*
Missouri Southern State University *C*
Missouri State University: West
    Plains *A*
Ozarks Technical Community
    College *A*
St. Charles Community College *A*
Three Rivers Community College *C*

Montana

Helena College University of
    Montana *A*
Montana State University
    Great Falls College *A*

Nebraska

Mid-Plains Community College *C, A*

Nevada

College of Southern Nevada *A*
Truckee Meadows Community
    College *C, A*

New Hampshire

Lakes Region Community College *A*

New Jersey

Burlington County College *C, A*
Essex County College *A*
Middlesex County College *A*
New Jersey City University *B*
Sussex County Community
    College *C, A*

New Mexico

Central New Mexico Community
    College *A*
Clovis Community College *C, A*
Dona Ana Community College of
    New Mexico State University *A*
Eastern New Mexico University:
    Roswell *A*
Luna Community College *C, A*
New Mexico Junior College *C*
New Mexico State University
    Carlsbad *C*
San Juan College *C, A*

New York

Broome Community College *A*
City University of New York
    John Jay College of Criminal
    Justice *B*
Finger Lakes Community College *C*
Nassau Community College *A*
Onondaga Community College *C*
Suffolk County Community College *A*

North Carolina

Alamance Community College *A*
Tri-County Community College *C*

Ohio

Central Ohio Technical College *A*
Cincinnati State Technical and
    Community College *C, A*
Columbus State Community
    College *A*
Hocking College *C, A*
Lakeland Community College *C, A*
Lorain County Community College *A*
Owens Community College
    Toledo *C, A*
Sinclair Community College *C*
Stark State College *A*
University of Cincinnati *A*

Oklahoma

Oklahoma State University
    Oklahoma City *A*
Western Oklahoma State College *A*

Oregon

Central Oregon Community
    College *C, A*
Chemeketa Community College *A*
Clackamas Community College *C, A*
Clatsop Community College *A*
Portland Community College *A*
Southwestern Oregon Community
    College *C, A*
Treasure Valley Community
    College *A*
Umpqua Community College *A*

Pennsylvania

Butler County Community College *C*
Harrisburg Area Community
    College *C, A*
Northampton Community
    College *C, A*

Rhode Island

Community College of Rhode
    Island *A*
Providence College *A*

South Carolina

Greenville Technical College *C, A*
Horry-Georgetown Technical
    College *C*

South Dakota

Lake Area Technical Institute *A*
Western Dakota Technical Institute *A*

Tennessee

Chattanooga State Community
    College *A*
Volunteer State Community
    College *C, A*

Texas

Angelina College *C*
Austin Community College *C*
Blinn College *C, A*
Central Texas College *C*
Cisco College *C*
Del Mar College *C, A*
Houston Community College
    System *C*
Lamar Institute of Technology *C*
Lone Star College System *C, A*
Midland College *A*
Northeast Texas Community
    College *C*
Odessa College *C, A*
San Jacinto College *C, A*
South Plains College *A*
Temple College *C*
Trinity Valley Community
    College *C, A*
Vernon College *C*
Victoria College *C*
Weatherford College *C, A*
Wharton County Junior College *C*

Utah

Utah Valley University *C, A, B*

Virginia

Germanna Community College *C*
J. Sargeant Reynolds Community
    College *C, A*
Southside Virginia Community
    College *C*
Southwest Virginia Community
    College *C*
Tidewater Community College *A*
Virginia Highlands Community
    College *C*
Virginia Western Community
    College *C*

Washington

Bates Technical College *C, A*
Bellevue College *C, A*
Columbia Basin College *A*
Everett Community College *C, A*
Skagit Valley College *A*
South Puget Sound Community
    College *C, A*
Walla Walla Community College *C, A*
Yakima Valley Community
    College *C, A*

West Virginia

Blue Ridge Community and Technical
    College *A*

Wisconsin

Chippewa Valley Technical College *A*
Fox Valley Technical College *A*
Gateway Technical College *A*
Lakeshore Technical College *A*

Milwaukee Area Technical College *A*
Northcentral Technical College *A*
Waukesha County Technical
  College *C*

Wyoming
Casper College *C, A*
Central Wyoming College *C, A*
Laramie County Community
  College *C, A*

Fishing and fisheries

Alaska
University of Alaska
  Fairbanks *B, M, D*
  Southeast *A*

Arkansas
University of Arkansas
  Pine Bluff *B*

California
College of the Redwoods *C, A*
Fullerton College *A*
Humboldt State University *B, M*

Colorado
Trinidad State Junior College *C, A*

Delaware
Delaware State University *B*

Florida
University of Florida *M, D*

Idaho
North Idaho College *A*
University of Idaho *B*

Indiana
Purdue University *B*

Iowa
Iowa State University *M, D*

Kentucky
Kentucky State University *M*

Maryland
Frostburg State University *B, M*
University of Maryland
  Eastern Shore *M*

Massachusetts
Bristol Community College *C*

Michigan
Lake Superior State University *B*
Michigan State University *B, M, D*

Minnesota
University of Minnesota
  Twin Cities *B, M, D*

Mississippi
Mississippi Gulf Coast Community
  College *A*

Missouri
University of Missouri
  Columbia *B, M, D*

New York
Paul Smith's College *B*
SUNY
  College of Agriculture and
    Technology at Cobleskill *A, B*
  College of Environmental Science
    and Forestry *B, M, D*

North Carolina
Haywood Community College *A*

Ohio
Hocking College *A*
Ohio State University
  Columbus Campus *B*

Oregon
Mt. Hood Community College *A*
Oregon State University *B, M, D*

Pennsylvania
Mansfield University of
  Pennsylvania *B*

Rhode Island
University of Rhode Island *B*

Tennessee
Tennessee Technological
  University *B*

Texas
Texas A&M University *B*
Texas A&M University
  Galveston *B*
Texas Tech University *M, D*

Utah
Utah State University *B, M, D*

Virginia
Virginia Polytechnic Institute and
  State University *M, D*

Washington
Bellingham Technical College *C, A*
Heritage University *C, A*
Peninsula College *A*
University of Washington *B, M, D*

Wisconsin
University of Wisconsin
  Stevens Point *B*

Flight attendant

California
Chabot College *A*
Cypress College *C, A*
Mount San Antonio College *A*
Orange Coast College *C, A*
San Bernardino Valley College *C*

New Jersey
Mercer County Community
  College *A*

North Carolina
Asheville-Buncombe Technical
  Community College *C, A*

Ohio
Sinclair Community College *C*

Virginia
Liberty University *A*

Flight instructor

Illinois
University of Illinois
  Urbana-Champaign *C*

Kansas
Central Christian College of Kansas *A*

Minnesota
Central Lakes College *C*
Saint Cloud State University *B*

New Jersey
Mercer County Community
  College *C*

North Dakota
University of North Dakota *B*

Ohio
University of Cincinnati
  Clermont College *A*

South Dakota
South Dakota State University *B*

Texas
Tarrant County College *C*

Floriculture

California
City College of San Francisco *A*
Santa Rosa Junior College *C*
Southwestern College *C, A*

Georgia
Albany Technical College *C*
Gwinnett Technical College *C*

Illinois
City Colleges of Chicago
  Richard J. Daley College *C*
Danville Area Community
  College *C, A*
Illinois Valley Community College *A*

Iowa
Kirkwood Community College *C*

Kansas
Johnson County Community
  College *C*

Minnesota
Hennepin Technical College *C, A*

New Mexico
Eastern New Mexico University:
  Roswell *C*

New York
SUNY
  College of Agriculture and
    Technology at Cobleskill *A*

North Dakota
Dakota College at Bottineau *A*

Ohio
Ohio State University
  Agricultural Technical Institute *A*

Pennsylvania
Westmoreland County Community
  College *A*

Texas
Palo Alto College *C*

Virginia
J. Sargeant Reynolds Community
  College *A*

Folklore studies

Indiana
Indiana University
  Bloomington *B, M, D*

Kentucky
Western Kentucky University *M*

Oregon
University of Oregon *B, M*

Food and nutrition studies

Alabama
Lawson State Community College *C*
Oakwood University *B*
Samford University *B*
Tuskegee University *B, M*

Alaska
University of Alaska
  Fairbanks *C*

Arizona
Arizona Western College *C, A*
Central Arizona College *C*
Glendale Community College *C*
Mesa Community College *C*

Arkansas
University of Arkansas *B*
University of Central Arkansas *B*

California
Antelope Valley College *A*
California State University
  Long Beach *B, M*
  Los Angeles *B, M*
  Northridge *B*
  San Bernardino *B*
College of the Desert *A*
College of the Sequoias *C*
Feather River College *A*
Fresno City College *C, A*
Glendale Community College *A*
Los Angeles Mission College *A*
Master's College *B*
Merritt College *C*
Modesto Junior College *A*
Ohlone College *C, A*
Orange Coast College *C, A*
Pepperdine University *B*
Point Loma Nazarene University *B*
Reedley College *C*
Riverside City College *C, A*
Saddleback College *C, A*
Santa Ana College *C, A*
Santa Rosa Junior College *C*

Colorado
Colorado State University *B, M, D*
Johnson & Wales University
  Denver *B*
Pikes Peak Community College *C*

Connecticut
Gateway Community College *A*
Naugatuck Valley Community
  College *C*
University of Saint Joseph *B, M*

Delaware
Delaware State University *B, M*
University of Delaware *B, M*

District of Columbia
University of the District of
  Columbia *B, M*

Florida
Broward College *A*
Miami Dade College *A*
Pensacola State College *C, A*

Georgia
Fort Valley State University *B*
Georgia Southern University *B*
University of Georgia *B, M, D*

Hawaii

University of Hawaii
  Hawaii Community College *C*
  Maui College *A*

Idaho

Brigham Young University-Idaho *B*
University of Idaho *B*

Illinois

Benedictine University *B, M*
Dominican University *B*
Illinois Central College *A*
Lexington College *A, B*
Northern Illinois University *B, M*
Rush University *M*
Shawnee Community College *C, A*
Southern Illinois University
  Carbondale *B, M*

Indiana

Indiana State University *B*
Purdue University *B, M, D*

Iowa

Graceland University *B*
Iowa State University *B*
Waldorf College *B*

Kansas

Kansas State University *M*

Kentucky

Eastern Kentucky University *B*
Hopkinsville Community College *A*
Murray State University *B, M*
University of Kentucky *B, M*

Maryland

Morgan State University *B*

Massachusetts

Framingham State University *B, M*
Simmons College *M*

Michigan

Andrews University *B, M*
Eastern Michigan University *M*
Madonna University *A, B*
Northern Michigan University *B*
Wayne State University *B, M, D*

Minnesota

Minnesota State University
  Mankato *B, M, T*
St. Catherine University *B*
University of Minnesota
  Twin Cities *B*

Mississippi

Alcorn State University *B*
Mississippi State University *M, D*
University of Mississippi *M*
University of Southern
  Mississippi *M, D*

Missouri

College of the Ozarks *B*
Lincoln University *B*
St. Louis Community College *C, A*
Saint Louis University *B, M, D*
University of Missouri
  Columbia *B, M, D*

Nebraska

University of Nebraska
  Lincoln *B, M*
Wayne State College *B*
Western Nebraska Community
  College *A*

Nevada

University of Nevada
  Reno *M*

New Jersey

Montclair State University *B, M, T*

New Mexico

New Mexico State University *B*
Santa Fe Community College *C*
University of New Mexico *B, M*

New York

City University of New York
  Brooklyn College *B, M*
  Hunter College *B, M*
  Lehman College *B, M*
Nassau Community College *A*
New York University *B, M, D*
Rochester Institute of
  Technology *A, B*
SUNY
  College at Buffalo *B*
  College at Oneonta *B, M*
  College at Plattsburgh *B*
Suffolk County Community College *A*
Westchester Community College *A*

North Carolina

East Carolina University *M*
Meredith College *B*
North Carolina Agricultural and
  Technical State University *B, M*
University of North Carolina
  Chapel Hill *B*

North Dakota

North Dakota State University *M*

Ohio

Bluffton University *B*
Bowling Green State University *B, M*
Ohio State University
  Columbus Campus *B*
Ohio University *B, M*
University of Akron *B, M*
University of Cincinnati
  Blue Ash College *A*
University of Dayton *B*
Youngstown State University *A, B*

Oklahoma

Eastern Oklahoma State College *C*
Langston University *B*
Oklahoma State University *B, M*
University of Central Oklahoma *B, M*

Oregon

Oregon State University *B, M, D*

Pennsylvania

Cedar Crest College *B*
Chatham University *M*
Indiana University of
  Pennsylvania *B, M*
Mansfield University of
  Pennsylvania *B*

Puerto Rico

University of Puerto Rico
  Rio Piedras *B*

Rhode Island

University of Rhode Island *M*

South Carolina

South Carolina State University *B, M*

South Dakota

South Dakota State University *C, B*

Tennessee

Carson-Newman University *B*
Chattanooga State Community
  College *C, A*
Hiwassee College *A*
Middle Tennessee State University *B*
Southern Adventist University *A*
Tennessee State University *B*
Tennessee Technological
  University *B*
Trevecca Nazarene University *B*
University of Tennessee
  Knoxville *B, M, D*

Texas

Lamar University *B*
Prairie View A&M University *B*
Sam Houston State University *B*
Stephen F. Austin State University *B*
Texas A&M University *B*
Texas A&M University
  Kingsville *B*
Texas Southern University *B, M*
Texas State University *B*
Texas Tech University *B, M, D*
Texas Woman's University *B*
University of Texas
  Austin *B*

Utah

Dixie State College *A*
Snow College *A*
Utah State University *C, B, M, D*

Virginia

Bridgewater College *B*
James Madison University *B*
Radford University *B*
Virginia Polytechnic Institute and
  State University *B, M, D*

Washington

Bastyr University *B*
Highline Community College *A*
Seattle Pacific University *B*
Shoreline Community College *A*
Washington State University *B*

West Virginia

West Virginia University *D*

Wisconsin

Lac Courte Oreilles Ojibwa
  Community College *A*
Madison Area Technical College *A*
Northeast Wisconsin Technical
  College *C*
University of Wisconsin
  Stevens Point *M*

Food preparation

Arizona

Arizona Western College *C*
Central Arizona College *A*
Cochise College *C*
Phoenix College *C*
Pima Community College *C*

California

Art Institute of California
  Los Angeles *A, B*
Contra Costa College *C, A*
Long Beach City College *C*
Santa Rosa Junior College *C*
Shasta College *C*

Colorado

Colorado Mountain College *A*

Connecticut

Gateway Community College *A*

Florida

Art Institute of Fort Lauderdale *C*
Le Cordon Bleu College of Culinary
  Arts
  Miami *C, A*

Georgia

Albany Technical College *C*
Art Institute of Atlanta *C*
Atlanta Technical College *C*
Gwinnett Technical College *C*
Savannah Technical College *C*

Illinois

Black Hawk College *C*
Elgin Community College *C*
Harper College *C*
Kaskaskia College *C*

Indiana

Vincennes University *C*

Kansas

Kansas City Kansas Community
  College *C*
North Central Kansas Technical
  College *C*
Washburn University *A*

Maryland

Anne Arundel Community College *C*

Minnesota

Hennepin Technical College *A*
St. Paul College *C*

Missouri

Jefferson College *C, A*

New Mexico

Eastern New Mexico University:
  Roswell *C*
Southwestern Indian Polytechnic
  Institute *C*

New York

Monroe Community College *C*
Onondaga Community College *C*
Paul Smith's College *A*

North Carolina

Cape Fear Community College *C*

Oregon

Lane Community College *C*
Portland Community College *C*

Pennsylvania

Commonwealth Technical Institute *C*
JNA Institute of Culinary Arts *C*
Pennsylvania Highlands Community
  College *A*

Texas

Central Texas College *C, A*
San Jacinto College *C*
South Texas College *C*

Vermont

New England Culinary
  Institute *C, A, B*

Virginia

Dabney S. Lancaster Community
  College *A*
ECPI University *C*
J. Sargeant Reynolds Community
  College *C*
Stratford University: Falls Church *A*

Washington

South Seattle Community
  College *C, A*

West Virginia

West Virginia Northern Community
College *C*

Wisconsin

Fox Valley Technical College *C*
Waukesha County Technical
College *C*
Western Technical College *C*

Food science

Alabama

Alabama Agricultural and Mechanical
University *B, M, D*
Auburn University *B, M, D*

Arizona

Arizona Western College *C*

Arkansas

Arkansas Northeastern College *A*
University of Arkansas *B, M, D*

California

California Polytechnic State
University: San Luis Obispo *B*
California State Polytechnic
University: Pomona *B*
California State University
Fresno *B, M*
Fresno City College *C, A*
Mission College *C, A*
Modesto Junior College *C, A*
Reedley College *C*
San Jose State University *T*
University of California
Davis *B, M, D*

Colorado

Colorado Mountain College *A*

Delaware

Delaware State University *B, M*
University of Delaware *B, M*

Florida

University of Florida *B, M, D*

Georgia

University of Georgia *B, M, D*

Hawaii

University of Hawaii
Manoa *M*

Idaho

University of Idaho *B, M, D*

Illinois

Dominican University *B*
University of Illinois
Urbana-Champaign *B, M, D*

Indiana

Purdue University *B, M, D*
Vincennes University *A*

Iowa

Iowa State University *M, D*

Kansas

Kansas State University *C, B, M, D*

Kentucky

University of Kentucky *B*

Louisiana

Louisiana State University and
Agricultural and Mechanical
College *M, D*

Maine

Eastern Maine Community
College *C, A*
University of Maine *B, M, D*

Maryland

Howard Community College *A*
University of Maryland
College Park *B, M, D*
Eastern Shore *M, D*

Massachusetts

Framingham State University *B, M*
Simmons College *B, M*
University of Massachusetts
Amherst *B, M, D*

Michigan

Michigan State University *C, B, M, D*

Minnesota

Minnesota State University
Mankato *B*
Normandale Community College *A*
Southwest Minnesota State
University *B*
University of Minnesota
Twin Cities *B, M, D*

Mississippi

Mississippi Gulf Coast Community
College *C, A*
Mississippi State University *B*
Northwest Mississippi Community
College *A*

Missouri

Missouri State University: West
Plains *C, A*
University of Missouri
Columbia *B, M, D*

Nebraska

University of Nebraska
Lincoln *B, M, D*

New Jersey

Rutgers, The State University of New
Jersey
New Brunswick/Piscataway
Campus *B, M, D*

New York

Cornell University *B, M, D*

North Carolina

North Carolina State
University *B, M, D*

North Dakota

North Dakota State University *B*

Ohio

Ohio State University
Columbus Campus *B, M, D*

Oklahoma

Eastern Oklahoma State College *A*
Oklahoma State University *B, M, D*

Oregon

Oregon State University *B*

Pennsylvania

Delaware Valley College *C, B*
Drexel University *M*
Penn State
Abington *B*
Altoona *B*
Beaver *B*
Berks *B*
Brandywine *B*
DuBois *B*

Erie, The Behrend College *B*
Fayette, The Eberly Campus *B*
Greater Allegheny *B*
Harrisburg *B*
Hazleton *B*
Lehigh Valley *B*
Mont Alto *B*
New Kensington *B*
Schuylkill *B*
Shenango *B*
University Park *B, M, D*
Wilkes-Barre *B*
Worthington Scranton *B*
York *B*

Puerto Rico

Inter American University of Puerto
Rico
Barranquitas Campus *C*
University of Puerto Rico
Mayaguez *M*

South Carolina

Clemson University *B, D*

Tennessee

Hiwassee College *A*
University of Tennessee
Knoxville *B, M, D*

Texas

North Lake College *C*
Sul Ross State University *B*
Texas A&M University *M, D*
Texas A&M University
Kingsville *B, M*
Texas Tech University *B, M*

Utah

Brigham Young University *B, M*

Virginia

Virginia Polytechnic Institute and
State University *B*

Washington

Washington State University *B, M, D*

Wisconsin

Northeast Wisconsin Technical
College *A*
University of Wisconsin
Madison *B, M, D*
River Falls *B*

Wyoming

University of Wyoming *M*

Food service

California

City College of San Francisco *C*
Columbia College *C*
Santa Rosa Junior College *C*
Shasta College *C*

Colorado

Johnson & Wales University
Denver *B*

Connecticut

Three Rivers Community
College *C, A*

Florida

College of Central Florida *C*
Johnson & Wales University
North Miami *B*

Georgia

Art Institute of Atlanta *B*

Hawaii

University of Hawaii
Hawaii Community College *C, A*
Maui College *C, A*

Illinois

College of Lake County *C*
Harper College *C*
Kaskaskia College *C*

Maryland

Montgomery College *C, A*

Massachusetts

Newbury College *A, B*

Michigan

Henry Ford Community College *C*

Mississippi

Copiah-Lincoln Community
College *C, A*

Missouri

Jefferson College *C, A*

New York

Nassau Community College *A*
Paul Smith's College *A*
Schenectady County Community
College *A*

Ohio

Columbus State Community
College *C*

Pennsylvania

Northampton Community College *C*
Westmoreland County Community
College *C*

Rhode Island

Johnson & Wales University
Providence *B*

Texas

Del Mar College *C, A*

Vermont

New England Culinary Institute *A, B*

Washington

Clark College *C*
Edmonds Community College *C*

Food technology/ processing

Arkansas

Arkansas State University *A*

Colorado

Colorado Mountain College *A*

Georgia

University of Georgia *M*

Illinois

University of Illinois
Urbana-Champaign *B*

Indiana

Vincennes University *A*

Kansas

Kansas State University *M, D*

Kentucky

Western Kentucky University *C*

New Mexico

New Mexico State University *B*

Ohio

Southern State Community College *A*

Oregon

Oregon State University *M, D*

Puerto Rico

Inter American University of Puerto
 Rico
 Barranquitas Campus *C*
 Bayamon Campus *B*
University of Puerto Rico
 Utuado *A*

Foreign language teacher education

Alabama

Auburn University *B, M*
Birmingham-Southern College *T*

Alaska

University of Alaska
 Anchorage *T*

Arkansas

Arkansas State University *B, T*
Arkansas Tech University *B*
Harding University *T*
Ouachita Baptist University *B, T*

California

Azusa Pacific University *T*
California Lutheran University *B, T*
California State University
 Chico *M*
 Long Beach *B, T*
 Northridge *B, T*
 San Bernardino *T*
Humboldt State University *T*
Los Angeles Southwest College *A*
Mills College *T*
Mount St. Mary's College *T*
San Francisco State University *T*
Sonoma State University *T*
Stanford University *M, T*
Vanguard University of Southern
 California *T*

Colorado

Colorado State University
 Pueblo *T*
Metropolitan State University of
 Denver *T*
University of Colorado
 Boulder *T*
Western State Colorado
 University *B, T*

Connecticut

Central Connecticut State
 University *T*
Quinnipiac University *B, M*
University of New Haven *M*

Delaware

University of Delaware *B, T*

District of Columbia

George Washington University *M, T*

Florida

Florida International University *M*
Florida State University *M*
Stetson University *B*
University of Central Florida *B*
University of Miami *B, M*
University of South Florida *B, M*
University of West Florida *B*

Georgia

Darton College *A*
Fort Valley State University *B, T*
University of Georgia *B, M*
Valdosta State University *B*

Idaho

University of Idaho *T*

Illinois

Augustana College *B, T*
DePaul University *M*
Dominican University *T*
McKendree University *B*
North Park University *T*
Olivet Nazarene University *B, T*
University of Illinois
 Urbana-Champaign *B, M, T*

Indiana

Bethel College *B*
Butler University *T*
Indiana University
 Bloomington *B, T*
Manchester University *B, T*
Purdue University *B, M, D*
Saint Mary's College *T*
University of Indianapolis *B, T*
Valparaiso University *B*

Iowa

Central College *T*
Cornell College *B, T*
Dordt College *B*
Graceland University *T*
Iowa State University *T*
St. Ambrose University *B, T*
Simpson College *T*
University of Northern Iowa *B*

Kansas

McPherson College *B, T*
University of Kansas *B, T*

Kentucky

Northern Kentucky University *B*

Louisiana

Centenary College of Louisiana *T*
Louisiana College *B*
McNeese State University *T*
Xavier University of Louisiana *B*

Maine

University of Maine *B*
University of Southern Maine *T*

Maryland

Notre Dame of Maryland
 University *T*

Massachusetts

Boston University *M, T*
Brandeis University *M*
Tufts University *M, T*
University of Massachusetts
 Dartmouth *T*

Michigan

Andrews University *M*
Aquinas College *T*
Calvin College *B*
Eastern Michigan University *B*
University of Michigan
 Dearborn *B*
Wayne State University *M, T*

Minnesota

College of St. Benedict *T*
Concordia College:
 Moorhead *B, M, T*
Gustavus Adolphus College *T*

Minnesota State University
 Mankato *B, M, T*
St. Catherine University *B*
Saint Cloud State University *B*
St. John's University *T*
University of Minnesota
 Duluth *B*
 Morris *T*
 Twin Cities *M*

Mississippi

Millsaps College *T*
Northeast Mississippi Community
 College *A*
University of Mississippi *B, T*
University of Southern Mississippi *M*

Missouri

Central Methodist University *B*
Evangel University *B*
Missouri Southern State
 University *B, T*
Northwest Missouri State
 University *T*
Southeast Missouri State University *B*
Truman State University *M*
University of Central Missouri *B*
University of Missouri
 Columbia *B, M, D*
 Kansas City *B*
William Jewell College *B, T*

Montana

Montana State University
 Billings *B, T*
University of Montana *T*

Nebraska

Creighton University *T*
Hastings College *B, M, T*
University of Nebraska
 Kearney *B, M, T*
 Lincoln *B, T*
Wayne State College *B, T*

New Hampshire

Rivier University *B, M, T*
University of New Hampshire *T*

New Jersey

Rutgers, The State University of New
 Jersey
 New Brunswick/Piscataway
  Campus *M, D, T*
Saint Peter's University *T*

New York

City University of New York
 City College *B, T*
 Hunter College *B, M, T*
 Queens College *M, T*
College of Mount St. Vincent *T*
D'Youville College *M, T*
Dowling College *B, M*
Elmira College *B, T*
Fordham University *T*
Hobart and William Smith Colleges *T*
Hofstra University *B, M*
Houghton College *B, T*
Iona College *B, M, T*
Ithaca College *B, T*
Long Island University
 LIU Post *B, T*
Manhattan College *B, T*
Manhattanville College *M, T*
Nazareth College *B, M, T*
New York University *B, M*
Pace University *B, M, T*
Pace University: Pleasantville/
 Briarcliff *T*
SUNY
 College at Buffalo *B, T*
 College at Fredonia *B, T*
 College at Oneonta *M*

College at Plattsburgh *B*
University at Albany *M, T*
University at Buffalo *M, D*
University at Stony Brook *T*
St. Lawrence University *T*
St. Thomas Aquinas College *B, T*
Vassar College *T*
Wells College *T*

North Carolina

Davidson College *T*
Gardner-Webb University *B*
Lenoir-Rhyne University *T*
Meredith College *T*
Methodist University *A, B, T*
North Carolina Agricultural and
 Technical State University *B, T*

North Dakota

Minot State University *B*

Ohio

Bowling Green State University *B, T*
Hiram College *T*
Miami University
 Oxford *B, M, T*
Ohio Northern University *B, T*
Ohio State University
 Columbus Campus *B*
Ohio Wesleyan University *B*
Otterbein University *B*
University of Dayton *B*
University of Findlay *B, M, T*
University of Mount Union *T*
Wright State University *T*
Youngstown State University *B, M*

Oklahoma

Cameron University *B*
Oklahoma Baptist University *B, T*
Oral Roberts University *B, T*
University of Oklahoma *B, T*
University of Tulsa *T*

Oregon

Linfield College *T*
Western Oregon University *T*

Pennsylvania

King's College *T*
La Salle University *B, T*
Lycoming College *T*
Mansfield University of
 Pennsylvania *B, T*
Mercyhurst University *B, T*
Moravian College *T*
Penn State
 Abington *B*
 Altoona *B*
 Beaver *B*
 Berks *B*
 Brandywine *B*
 DuBois *B*
 Erie, The Behrend College *B*
 Fayette, The Eberly Campus *B*
 Greater Allegheny *B*
 Harrisburg *B*
 Hazleton *B*
 Lehigh Valley *B*
 Mont Alto *B*
 New Kensington *B*
 Schuylkill *B*
 Shenango *B*
 University Park *B*
 Wilkes-Barre *B*
 Worthington Scranton *B*
 York *B*
Rosemont College *T*
St. Francis University *B, T*
Saint Joseph's University *M, T*
St. Vincent College *T*
Seton Hill University *B, T*
Susquehanna University *T*
Temple University *B*

University of Pennsylvania *M, T*
University of Scranton *B*
Washington & Jefferson College *T*
Westminster College *B, T*
Widener University *M*

Rhode Island

Bryant University *M*
Rhode Island College *B, M*

South Carolina

College of Charleston *M*
Converse College *T*
Furman University *T*

South Dakota

Northern State University *B, T*
University of South Dakota *B, T*

Tennessee

Christian Brothers University *M, T*
Middle Tennessee State
   University *M, T*
Tennessee Technological University *T*
Union University *B, T*
Vanderbilt University *B*

Texas

Baylor University *T*
Del Mar College *A*
Lamar University *T*
Laredo Community College *A*
Sam Houston State University *M, T*
University of St. Thomas *M*
University of Texas
   Austin *M, D*
West Texas A&M University *T*

Vermont

Bennington College *M*
Castleton State College *B, T*
Saint Michael's College *M, T*
University of Vermont *B, T*

Virginia

Longwood University *T*
University of Virginia's College at
   Wise *T*

Washington

Central Washington University *B, T*
Washington State University *B, M, T*
Western Washington University *M*
Whitworth University *T*

West Virginia

Bethany College *B*
West Virginia University *T*
Wheeling Jesuit University *B*

Wisconsin

Carroll University *B*
Carthage College *M, T*
Lawrence University *T*
Mount Mary University *B, T*
St. Norbert College *T*

Foreign languages, general

Alabama

Auburn University at Montgomery *B*
Jacksonville State University *B*
Samford University *B*
University of Alabama *B*
University of Alabama
   Birmingham *B*
   Huntsville *B*
University of Montevallo *B*
University of North Alabama *B*
University of South Alabama *B*

Alaska

University of Alaska
   Anchorage *B*
   Fairbanks *B*

Arizona

Eastern Arizona College *A*
Northern Arizona University *B*

Arkansas

Arkansas State University *B*
Arkansas Tech University *B*
University of Arkansas
   Monticello *B*
University of Central Arkansas *B*

California

Cabrillo College *A*
California Lutheran University *B*
California Polytechnic State
   University: San Luis Obispo *B*
College of Marin *A*
College of the Sequoias *A*
Crafton Hills College *A*
Fresno City College *A*
Fullerton College *A*
Glendale Community College *A*
Golden West College *A*
Imperial Valley College *A*
Long Beach City College *A*
Los Angeles Southwest College *A*
Modesto Junior College *A*
Monterey Peninsula College *A*
Occidental College *B*
Palomar College *A*
Pitzer College *B*
Reedley College *A*
Saddleback College *A*
St. Mary's College of California *B*
San Diego City College *A*
Santa Ana College *A*
Santiago Canyon College *A*
Scripps College *B*
Shasta College *A*
Solano Community College *A*
University of California
   Riverside *B*
   San Diego *B*
   Santa Cruz *B*
West Valley College *A*

Colorado

Colorado State University *B, M*
Colorado State University
   Pueblo *B*
Metropolitan State University of
   Denver *B, T*
University of Northern
   Colorado *B, M, T*

Connecticut

Central Connecticut State
   University *M*
Trinity College *B*
University of Hartford *B*

Delaware

University of Delaware *B, M*

District of Columbia

George Washington University *B*
Howard University *M*

Florida

Broward College *A*
Indian River State College *A*
Miami Dade College *A*
New College of Florida *B*

Georgia

Abraham Baldwin Agricultural
   College *A*
Atlanta Metropolitan College *A*

Bainbridge College *A*
College of Coastal Georgia *A*
Columbus State University *B*
Darton College *A*
Georgia Highlands College *A*
Georgia Institute of Technology *B*
Georgia Perimeter College *A*
Georgia Regents University *B*
Gordon College *A*
Middle Georgia State College *A*
Reinhardt University *B*
South Georgia State College *A*
University of West Georgia *B*

Idaho

College of Southern Idaho *A*
North Idaho College *A*
University of Idaho *B*

Illinois

Eastern Illinois University *B, T*
Illinois Central College *A*
Illinois State University *M*
Illinois Valley Community College *A*
Kishwaukee College *A*
Knox College *B*
Olivet Nazarene University *B*
Principia College *B*
Sauk Valley Community College *A*
Southern Illinois University
   Carbondale *M*
Southern Illinois University
   Edwardsville *B*
Southwestern Illinois College *A*
Triton College *A*

Indiana

Grace College *B*
Manchester University *B, T*
Purdue University *B, M, D*
Purdue University
   Calumet *B*
Vincennes University *A*

Iowa

Cornell College *B*
Iowa State University *B*

Kansas

Barton County Community College *A*
Benedictine College *B*
Butler Community College *A*
Coffeyville Community College *A*
Cowley County Community
   College *A*
Emporia State University *B, T*
Fort Hays State University *B*
Hutchinson Community College *A*
Independence Community College *A*
Kansas State University *B, M*
McPherson College *B, T*
Neosho County Community
   College *A*
Wichita State University *B*

Kentucky

Eastern Kentucky University *B*
University of Kentucky *M*

Louisiana

Dillard University *B*
Louisiana College *B*
Loyola University New Orleans *B*
McNeese State University *B*
University of Louisiana at Lafayette *B*
University of Louisiana at Monroe *B*
University of New Orleans *B*

Maine

University of Maine *B*
University of Maine
   Fort Kent *B*
University of Southern Maine *B*

Maryland

Frostburg State University *B*
Notre Dame of Maryland
   University *B*
St. Mary's College of Maryland *B*
Towson University *B*
University of Maryland
   Baltimore County *B*

Massachusetts

Assumption College *B*
Boston University *B*
Bunker Hill Community College *A*
Cape Cod Community College *A*
Clark University *B*
Framingham State University *B*
Gordon College *B*
Massachusetts Institute of
   Technology *B*
Middlesex Community College *A*
Stonehill College *B*
Suffolk University *B*
Tufts University *B, M*
Wellesley College *B*

Michigan

Delta College *A*
Grand Rapids Community College *A*
Lake Michigan College *A*
Oakland University *B*
Wayne State University *B, M, D*

Minnesota

University of Minnesota
   Twin Cities *B, M*

Mississippi

Delta State University *B*
East Mississippi Community
   College *A*
Jackson State University *B*
Mississippi State University *B, M*
Northeast Mississippi Community
   College *A*
University of Southern Mississippi *B*

Missouri

St. Charles Community College *A*
Three Rivers Community College *A*
University of Missouri
   Columbia *D*
   Kansas City *M*
Washington University in St.
   Louis *B, M, D*
Webster University *B*

Montana

Miles Community College *A*
Montana State University *B*
University of Montana *M*

Nebraska

Hastings College *B*
Union College *B*
University of Nebraska
   Lincoln *M, D*
   Omaha *B*
Wayne State College *B*

Nevada

University of Nevada
   Las Vegas *M*
   Reno *M*

New Jersey

Bergen Community College *A*
Cumberland County College *A*
Monmouth University *B*
Richard Stockton College of New
   Jersey *B*

Rutgers, The State University of New Jersey
  Camden Campus *M*
  New Brunswick/Piscataway Campus *B*
Saint Peter's University *B*
Seton Hall University *B*
Thomas Edison State College *B*

New Mexico

New Mexico State University *B*
University of New Mexico *B*

New York

Bard College *B*
City University of New York
  City College *B, M*
  Hunter College *B*
College of Mount St. Vincent *B*
Dowling College *B*
Elmira College *B*
Eugene Lang College The New School for Liberal Arts *B*
Excelsior College *B*
Hamilton College *B*
Ithaca College *B*
Jewish Theological Seminary of America *B, M, D*
Long Island University
  LIU Brooklyn *B*
  LIU Post *B*
New York University *B, M, D, T*
Orange County Community College *A*
Pace University *B*
Pace University: Pleasantville/ Briarcliff *B*
SUNY
  College at Brockport *B*
  College at Purchase *B*
  University at Stony Brook *D*
St. Thomas Aquinas College *B, T*
Syracuse University *B*
Touro College *B*
Union College *B*
University of Rochester *B*
Utica College *B*
Wells College *B*

North Carolina

Elon University *B*
Gardner-Webb University *B*
North Carolina State University *M*
University of North Carolina Chapel Hill *B*

North Dakota

Minot State University *B*
University of North Dakota *B*

Ohio

College of Wooster *B*
Kenyon College *B*
Lake Erie College *B*
Sinclair Community College *A*
Wright State University *B, M, T*
Youngstown State University *B*

Oklahoma

Cameron University *B*
Oklahoma Baptist University *B, T*
Rose State College *A*

Oregon

Central Oregon Community College *A*
Lewis & Clark College *B*
Linn-Benton Community College *A*
Pacific University *B*
Portland State University *M*
Southern Oregon University *B*
Treasure Valley Community College *A*

Pennsylvania

Bloomsburg University of Pennsylvania *B, T*
California University of Pennsylvania *B*
Community College of Allegheny County *A*
Duquesne University *B*
Gannon University *B*
Juniata College *B*
La Salle University *B, T*
Mercyhurst University *B, T*
Millersville University of Pennsylvania *T*
Muhlenberg College *B*
Penn State
  Berks *B*
  Lehigh Valley *B*
Rosemont College *B*
St. Francis University *B*
West Chester University of Pennsylvania *T*
Westminster College *B*
Widener University *B*

Puerto Rico

University of Puerto Rico
  Rio Piedras *B*

Rhode Island

Roger Williams University *B*

South Carolina

Citadel *B, T*
Clemson University *B*
Converse College *B*
Presbyterian College *B*
South Carolina State University *B*
University of South Carolina
  Columbia *M*
Winthrop University *B*

South Dakota

Augustana College *B*

Tennessee

Austin Peay State University *B*
East Tennessee State University *B, T*
King University *B*
Middle Tennessee State University *B*
Southern Adventist University *B*
University of Memphis *B*
University of Tennessee
  Chattanooga *B*
  Knoxville *D*

Texas

Austin Community College *A*
Blinn College *A*
Brazosport College *A*
Central Texas College *A*
Clarendon College *A*
Del Mar College *A*
El Paso Community College *A*
Hill College *A*
Howard College *A*
Laredo Community College *A*
Lee College *A*
Midland College *A*
Northwest Vista College *A*
Odessa College *A*
Paris Junior College *A*
St. Philip's College *A*
San Jacinto College *A*
Southwestern Assemblies of God University *A*
Stephen F. Austin State University *B*
Texarkana College *A*
Texas A&M University *M*
Texas Tech University *B, M*
Tyler Junior College *A*
University of Houston *B*

University of Texas
  Arlington *B, M*
  San Antonio *B*
  Tyler *B*
Western Texas College *A*

Utah

Brigham Young University *B*
Snow College *A*
University of Utah *M, D*

Vermont

Bennington College *B*
Marlboro College *B*

Virginia

Averett University *B*
George Mason University *B, M*
James Madison University *B, T*
Longwood University *B*
Old Dominion University *B*
Radford University *B*
Sweet Briar College *B*
University of Mary Washington *B*
University of Virginia's College at Wise *B*
Virginia Commonwealth University *B*
Virginia Military Institute *B*
Virginia Polytechnic Institute and State University *B, M*
Virginia Wesleyan College *B*

Washington

Centralia College *A*
Evergreen State College *B*
Highline Community College *A*
Seattle University *B*
University of Puget Sound *B*
Washington State University *B*
Western Washington University *B*

West Virginia

Marshall University *B*
Potomac State College of West Virginia University *A*
West Virginia University *B, M*

Wisconsin

Beloit College *B*
Marquette University *M*
Ripon College *B, T*
University of Wisconsin
  Milwaukee *M*

Wyoming

Casper College *A*
Eastern Wyoming College *A*
Sheridan College *A*

Forensic chemistry

Delaware

Delaware State University *B*

Florida

Palm Beach Atlantic University *B*

Illinois

Western Illinois University *B*

Indiana

University of St. Francis *B*

Kansas

Kansas Wesleyan University *B*
Newman University *B*

Massachusetts

Emmanuel College *B*
Western New England University *B*

Michigan

Lake Superior State University *B*
Northern Michigan University *B*

Mississippi

University of Mississippi *B*

Missouri

Maryville University of Saint Louis *B*
Missouri Baptist University *B*

New Mexico

New Mexico Highlands University *B*

North Carolina

Methodist University *B*

Ohio

Ashland University *B*

Pennsylvania

Chestnut Hill College *B*
Slippery Rock University of Pennsylvania *B*

Rhode Island

University of Rhode Island *B*

Texas

St. Edward's University *B*
St. Mary's University *B*

Forensic psychology

California

Alliant International University *B, D*
California Baptist University *M*
Holy Names University *M, T*

Colorado

University of Denver *M*

Florida

Florida Institute of Technology *B*

Iowa

St. Ambrose University *B*

Maine

Thomas College *B*

Massachusetts

American International College *M*
Bay Path College *B*

Michigan

Madonna University *C*

Minnesota

Concordia University St. Paul *M*
Walden University *B, M*

New Jersey

College of St. Elizabeth *M*
Fairleigh Dickinson University Metropolitan Campus *M*

New York

Canisius College *B*
City University of New York
  John Jay College of Criminal Justice *B, M*
College of Saint Rose *B*

North Dakota

University of North Dakota *M*

Ohio

Tiffin University *B, M*

Oklahoma
University of Central Oklahoma *M*

Pennsylvania
Rosemont College *T*

Rhode Island
Roger Williams University *M*

Texas
Prairie View A&M University *M*

Virginia
Marymount University *M*

Forensic science

Alabama
University of Alabama
 Birmingham *M*

Arizona
Grand Canyon University *B*
Mesa Community College *C*
Phoenix College *C, A*
Pima Community College *C*
Scottsdale Community College *C*

Arkansas
Arkansas State University *A*
Arkansas State University
 Beebe *C, A*
College of the Ouachitas *C, A*
Cossatot Community College of the
 University of Arkansas *C, A*
Mid-South Community College *C, A*
North Arkansas College *C, A*
Northwest Arkansas Community
 College *C, A*
Phillips Community College of the
 University of Arkansas *C, A*
Pulaski Technical College *C, A*
Southeast Arkansas College *C, A*
Southern Arkansas University *C, A*
University of Arkansas
 Community College at Hope *C, A*
 Community College at
  Morrilton *C, A*
 Fort Smith *C, A*
 Monticello *C, A*
 Pine Bluff *C, A*

California
East Los Angeles College *C*
Grossmont College *C, A*
National University *M*
Palomar College *A*
San Jose State University *B*
Southwestern College *C, A*
University of California
 Davis *M*

Connecticut
Tunxis Community College *C*
University of New Haven *C, B, M*

Florida
Edison State College *A*
Florida International University *M*
Gulf Coast State College *C*
Hillsborough Community College *C*
Keiser University *A, B*
Lynn University *B*
Miami Dade College *C, A*
St. Petersburg College *C, A*
Tallahassee Community College *C*
University of Central Florida *B, M*
University of Tampa *B*

Georgia
Albany State University *B*
Darton College *A*
Savannah State University *B*

Hawaii
Chaminade University of Honolulu *B*

Illinois
Illinois Valley Community College *A*
Lewis University *B*
Loyola University Chicago *B*
Quincy University *B*
University of Illinois
 Chicago *M*

Indiana
Indiana University
 Purdue University
  Indianapolis *B, M*
Saint Joseph's College *M*
Trine University *B*

Iowa
Iowa Wesleyan College *B*
Iowa Western Community
 College *C, A*
Simpson College *B*

Kansas
Central Christian College of Kansas *A*
Newman University *B*
Washburn University *B*
Wichita State University *B*

Kentucky
Eastern Kentucky University *B*
Thomas More College *B*

Louisiana
Loyola University New Orleans *B*

Maryland
Carroll Community College *A*
Kaplan University
 Hagerstown *A*
Prince George's Community
 College *C, A*
Stevenson University *M*
Towson University *B, M*
University of Baltimore *B*
University of Maryland
 University College *B*

Massachusetts
Anna Maria College *B*
Bay Path College *B, M*
Becker College *B*
Bunker Hill Community College *C*
Eastern Nazarene College *B*
Holyoke Community College *C*
Massachusetts Bay Community
 College *A*
Mount Ida College *B*
Western New England University *B*

Michigan
Lake Superior State University *B*
Macomb Community College *A*
Madonna University *C, B*
Michigan State University *M*
Mott Community College *C*
Wayne County Community College *C*

Minnesota
Hamline University *B*

Mississippi
East Mississippi Community
 College *A*
University of Southern
 Mississippi *B, M*

Missouri
Columbia College *B*
Missouri Southern State University *B*

Montana
University of Great Falls *B*

Nebraska
Nebraska Wesleyan University *C, M*
University of Nebraska
 Lincoln *B*

New Jersey
Cumberland County College *A*
Salem Community College *A*

New Mexico
Eastern New Mexico University *B*
New Mexico Highlands University *B*

New York
City University of New York
 Borough of Manhattan Community
  College *A*
 Hostos Community College *A*
 John Jay College of Criminal
  Justice *B, M*
College of New Rochelle *C*
College of Saint Rose *B*
Erie Community College *C*
Herkimer County Community
 College *A*
Hilbert College *B*
Hofstra University *B, M*
Hudson Valley Community College *A*
Long Island University
 LIU Post *B*
Onondaga Community College *A*
Pace University *B, M*
Pace University: Pleasantville/
 Briarcliff *B, M*
Roberts Wesleyan College *B*
SUNY
 College at Buffalo *B*
 College of Technology at Alfred *B*
Sage Colleges *B*
St. Thomas Aquinas College *B*
Sullivan County Community
 College *A*
Syracuse University *B, M*
Tompkins Cortland Community
 College *A*
Touro College *M*

North Carolina
Catawba Valley Community
 College *A*
Central Carolina Community
 College *A*
Fayetteville State University *B*
Fayetteville Technical Community
 College *C, A*
Forsyth Technical Community
 College *A*
Guilford College *B*
Methodist University *B*
St. Augustine's University *B*
Wayne Community College *A*
Western Carolina University *B*

North Dakota
University of North Dakota *B*

Ohio
Ashland University *B*
Cedarville University *B*
Central Ohio Technical College *A*
Defiance College *B*
Ohio Northern University *B*
Tiffin University *B*
University of Akron *C*
University of Cincinnati
 Clermont College *C, A*
Youngstown State University *B*

Oklahoma
University of Central Oklahoma *B, M*

Pennsylvania
Alvernia University *B*
Arcadia University *M*
Cedar Crest College *B, M*
Chatham University *B*
Chestnut Hill College *B*
Community College of
 Philadelphia *A*
Drexel University *M*
Duquesne University *M*
Keystone College *B*
Mercyhurst University *B, M*
Penn State
 Abington *B*
 Altoona *B*
 Beaver *B*
 Berks *B*
 Brandywine *B*
 DuBois *B*
 Fayette, The Eberly Campus *B*
 Greater Allegheny *B*
 Harrisburg *B*
 Hazleton *B*
 Lehigh Valley *B*
 Mont Alto *B*
 New Kensington *B*
 Schuylkill *B*
 Shenango *B*
 University Park *B, M*
 Wilkes-Barre *B*
 Worthington Scranton *B*
 York *B*
Point Park University *B*
Seton Hill University *B*
University of Scranton *B*
Waynesburg University *B*
York College of Pennsylvania *B*

Puerto Rico
ICPR Junior College *A*
Inter American University of Puerto
 Rico
 Aguadilla Campus *B*
 Bayamon Campus *B*
 Ponce Campus *B*
Turabo University *M*
University of Puerto Rico
 Carolina Regional College *B*
 Ponce *B*

Rhode Island
Bryant University *B*
Roger Williams University *B*

South Carolina
Southern Wesleyan University *B*
Trident Technical College *C*

South Dakota
Mount Marty College *B*

Tennessee
Northeast State Community
 College *A*
Tennessee Wesleyan College *B*

Texas
East Texas Baptist University *C*
Howard College *C, A*
Lamar Institute of Technology *A*
St. Edward's University *B*
St. Mary's University *B*
Sam Houston State University *M*
Texas A&M University *B*
Texas Tech University *M*

Utah
Southern Utah University *B*
Utah Valley University *B*
Weber State University *B*

Virginia
Bluefield College *B*
George Mason University *B, M*

Marymount University *C, B*
New River Community College *A*
Virginia Commonwealth
    University *B, M*

Washington
Centralia College *A*
Seattle University *B*

West Virginia
American Public University
    System *C, B*
Blue Ridge Community and Technical
    College *C*
Fairmont State University *B*
Marshall University *M*
West Virginia University *B, M*
West Virginia University Institute of
    Technology *B*

Wisconsin
Carroll University *B*
Fox Valley Technical College *A*
Marian University *B*
University of Wisconsin
    Milwaukee *C*

Wyoming
Casper College *A*

Forest engineering

Oregon
Oregon State University *B, M, D*

Washington
University of Washington *B*

Forest management

Arkansas
University of Arkansas
    Monticello *M*

California
University of California
    Berkeley *B*

Connecticut
Yale University *M*

Florida
Pensacola State College *A*

Georgia
Abraham Baldwin Agricultural
    College *A*

Idaho
University of Idaho *C, B*

Maine
University of Maine *M, D*

Maryland
Allegany College of Maryland *C, A*

Michigan
Michigan Technological
    University *C, M*

Minnesota
Leech Lake Tribal College *A*
University of Minnesota
    Twin Cities *B, M*

Nevada
University of Nevada
    Reno *B*

New Mexico
New Mexico Highlands University *B*

New York
Paul Smith's College *B*
SUNY
    College of Environmental Science
    and Forestry *B, M, D*

North Carolina
North Carolina State University *B*

Ohio
Hocking College *A*

Oregon
Oregon State University *B*

Pennsylvania
Elizabethtown College *B*
Keystone College *A*
Penn State
    University Park *M, D*
St. Francis University *B*

South Carolina
Clemson University *A, B*

Texas
Stephen F. Austin State University *B*

West Virginia
Potomac State College of West
    Virginia University *A*
West Virginia University *B*

Forest resources production

Alabama
Lurleen B. Wallace Community
    College *C, A*

Florida
Pensacola State College *A*

Louisiana
Louisiana Tech University *B*

New York
Paul Smith's College *A, B*
SUNY
    College of Environmental Science
    and Forestry *B, M, D*

North Carolina
Haywood Community College *C, A*

South Carolina
Orangeburg-Calhoun Technical
    College *A*

Tennessee
Hiwassee College *A*

Virginia
Mountain Empire Community
    College *C*
Virginia Polytechnic Institute and
    State University *M, D*

Washington
Spokane Community College *A*
University of Washington *B*

Forest sciences/biology

Alabama
Auburn University *B, M, D*

Arizona
Northern Arizona University *B, M, D*

Colorado
Colorado State University *B, M, D*

Florida
Chipola College *A*

Georgia
University of Georgia *M, D*

Idaho
University of Idaho *B, D*

Illinois
University of Illinois
    Urbana-Champaign *B, M, D*

Kentucky
Bluegrass Community and Technical
    College *A*
Hopkinsville Community College *A*
University of Kentucky *B, M*

Maine
University of Maine *B*

Massachusetts
Harvard College *M*

Michigan
Michigan Technological University *D*

Minnesota
University of Minnesota
    Twin Cities *B*

New York
Paul Smith's College *B*
SUNY
    College of Environmental Science
    and Forestry *B*

Oregon
Oregon State University *M, D*

Pennsylvania
Penn State
    Abington *B*
    Altoona *B*
    Beaver *B*
    Berks *B*
    Brandywine *B*
    DuBois *B*
    Erie, The Behrend College *B*
    Fayette, The Eberly Campus *B*
    Greater Allegheny *B*
    Harrisburg *B*
    Hazleton *B*
    Lehigh Valley *B*
    Mont Alto *B*
    New Kensington *B*
    Schuylkill *B*
    Shenango *B*
    University Park *B*
    Wilkes-Barre *B*
    Worthington Scranton *B*
    York *B*

South Carolina
Clemson University *B, M*

West Virginia
West Virginia University *D*

Wisconsin
University of Wisconsin
    Madison *B*

Forest technology

California
Columbia College *C, A*
Shasta College *C*

Colorado
Colorado Mountain College *C*

Georgia
Abraham Baldwin Agricultural
    College *A*

Maine
Kennebec Valley Community
    College *C, A*

Michigan
Bay de Noc Community College *C*

Mississippi
East Mississippi Community
    College *A*
Mississippi State University *D*

Montana
Salish Kootenai College *A, B*

New Hampshire
University of New Hampshire *A, B*

New York
Paul Smith's College *A*
SUNY
    College of Environmental Science
    and Forestry *A*

North Carolina
Montgomery Community College *A*
Southeastern Community College *A*
Wayne Community College *A*

Oregon
Central Oregon Community
    College *C, A*
Mt. Hood Community College *A*

Pennsylvania
Penn State
    Mont Alto *A*
Pennsylvania College of
    Technology *A*

South Carolina
Clemson University *M, D*
Horry-Georgetown Technical
    College *A*

Washington
Green River Community College *C*

West Virginia
Glenville State College *A*

Forestry

Alabama
Alabama Agricultural and Mechanical
    University *B*
Faulkner State Community College *A*
Tuskegee University *B*

Arizona
Eastern Arizona College *A*
Northern Arizona University *M*

Arkansas
University of Arkansas
    Monticello *B*

California
Bakersfield College *C, A*
California Polytechnic State
    University: San Luis Obispo *B, M*
Citrus College *C, A*
College of the Redwoods *C, A*
Columbia College *C, A*
Feather River College *C, A*

Fullerton College *A*
Humboldt State University *B*
Modesto Junior College *C, A*
Mount San Antonio College *C, A*
Reedley College *A*
Shasta College *C*
University of California
  Berkeley *B, M*

Colorado

Colorado Mountain College *A*

Connecticut

Yale University *M, D*

Delaware

Delaware State University *B*

Florida

Miami Dade College *A*
Pensacola State College *A*
University of Florida *B, M, D*

Georgia

Abraham Baldwin Agricultural
  College *A*
Albany Technical College *C, A*
Andrew College *A*
Darton College *A*
Gordon College *A*
Middle Georgia State College *A*
Southeastern Technical College *C, A*
University of Georgia *B*
University of North Georgia *A*

Idaho

College of Southern Idaho *A*
North Idaho College *A*

Illinois

Joliet Junior College *C*
Shawnee Community College *A*
Southern Illinois University
  Carbondale *B, M*

Indiana

Purdue University *B, M, D*

Iowa

Iowa State University *B, M, D*
Marshalltown Community College *A*
Upper Iowa University *B*

Kansas

Barton County Community College *A*
Colby Community College *A*
Garden City Community College *A*
Seward County Community
  College *A*

Louisiana

Louisiana Tech University *B*

Maine

University of Maine *B, M*
University of Maine
  Fort Kent *A*

Michigan

Delta College *A*
Gogebic Community College *A*
Grand Rapids Community College *A*
Michigan State University *B, M, D*
Michigan Technological
  University *B, M*

Minnesota

Itasca Community College *A*
Northwest Technical College *C*
University of Minnesota
  Twin Cities *B, M, D*

Mississippi

East Mississippi Community
  College *A*
Hinds Community College *A*
Holmes Community College *A*
Itawamba Community College *A*
Mississippi Delta Community
  College *A*
Mississippi Gulf Coast Community
  College *A*
Mississippi State University *B, M*
Northeast Mississippi Community
  College *A*

Missouri

University of Missouri
  Columbia *B, M, D*

Montana

Miles Community College *A*
University of Montana *B, M, D*

Nebraska

Western Nebraska Community
  College *A*

New Hampshire

University of New Hampshire *B, M*

New Mexico

Northern New Mexico College *A*

New York

Paul Smith's College *A, B*
SUNY
  College of Environmental Science
    and Forestry *B, M, D*

North Carolina

Duke University *M, D*
Haywood Community College *C, A*
Lenoir-Rhyne University *B*
North Carolina State
  University *B, M, D*

Oklahoma

Eastern Oklahoma State College *A*
Northeastern Oklahoma Agricultural
  and Mechanical College *A*
Oklahoma State University *B*

Oregon

Oregon State University *M, D*

Pennsylvania

Gettysburg College *B*
St. Francis University *B*

Tennessee

Hiwassee College *A*
Sewanee: The University of the
  South *B*
University of Tennessee
  Knoxville *B, M*

Texas

Baylor University *B*
Stephen F. Austin State
  University *B, M, D*
Texas A&M University *B, M, D*

Utah

Snow College *A*
Utah State University *B, M, D*

Vermont

University of Vermont *B*

Virginia

Dabney S. Lancaster Community
  College *A*
Mountain Empire Community
  College *C, A*

Virginia Polytechnic Institute and
  State University *B*

Washington

Grays Harbor College *C, A*
Heritage University *C, A*
Spokane Community College *A*
University of Washington *B, M, D*

West Virginia

West Virginia University *M*

Wisconsin

Beloit College *B*
University of Wisconsin
  Madison *M, D*
  Stevens Point *B*

Franchise operations

New York

Hilbert College *A*

Oregon

Central Oregon Community
  College *A*

French

Alabama

Auburn University *B*
Birmingham-Southern College *B*
Oakwood University *B*
Samford University *B*

Alaska

University of Alaska
  Anchorage *B*

Arizona

Arizona State University *B, M*
University of Arizona *B, M*

Arkansas

Harding University *B*
Hendrix College *B*
University of Arkansas *B, M*
University of Arkansas
  Little Rock *B*

California

Bakersfield College *A*
Cabrillo College *A*
California Lutheran University *B*
California State University
  Chico *B*
  East Bay *B*
  Fresno *B*
  Fullerton *B*
  Long Beach *B, M*
  Los Angeles *B, M*
  Northridge *B*
  Sacramento *B, M*
  San Bernardino *B, T*
Cerritos College *A*
Chabot College *A*
Chaffey College *A*
Chapman University *B*
Claremont McKenna College *B*
College of Marin *A*
College of the Canyons *A*
College of the Desert *A*
College of the Sequoias *A*
Crafton Hills College *A*
Cypress College *A*
De Anza College *A*
El Camino College *A*
Foothill College *A*
Glendale Community College *A*
Golden West College *A*
Grossmont College *A*
Humboldt State University *B*
Imperial Valley College *A*

Irvine Valley College *A*
Los Angeles City College *A*
Los Angeles Pierce College *A*
Los Angeles Southwest College *A*
Los Angeles Valley College *A*
Loyola Marymount University *B*
Mendocino College *A*
Merced College *A*
Merritt College *A*
Mills College *B*
Mount St. Mary's College *B*
Occidental College *B*
Orange Coast College *A*
Palomar College *A*
Pepperdine University *B*
Pitzer College *B*
Point Loma Nazarene University *B*
Pomona College *B*
St. Mary's College of California *B*
San Diego City College *A*
San Diego Mesa College *A*
San Diego State University *B, M*
San Francisco State University *B, M*
San Joaquin Delta College *A*
San Jose State University *B, M*
Santa Barbara City College *A*
Santa Clara University *B*
Santiago Canyon College *A*
Scripps College *B*
Solano Community College *A*
Sonoma State University *B*
Southwestern College *A*
Stanford University *B, M, D*
University of California
  Berkeley *B, M, D*
  Davis *B, D*
  Irvine *B*
  Los Angeles *B, M, D*
  Riverside *B, M, D*
  San Diego *B, M*
  Santa Barbara *B, M, D*
University of La Verne *B*
University of Redlands *B*
University of San Diego *B*
University of San Francisco *B*
University of Southern California *B*
University of the Pacific *B*
West Los Angeles College *A*
Westmont College *B*
Whittier College *B*

Colorado

Colorado College *B*
Colorado State University *B, M*
Regis University *B*
University of Colorado
  Boulder *B, M, D*
  Denver *B*
University of Denver *B*

Connecticut

Central Connecticut State
  University *B*
Connecticut College *B*
Fairfield University *B*
Southern Connecticut State
  University *B*
Trinity College *B*
University of Connecticut *B*
Wesleyan University *B*
Yale University *B, M, D*

Delaware

Delaware State University *B, M*
University of Delaware *B, M, T*

District of Columbia

American University *B*
Catholic University of America *B*
Gallaudet University *B*
George Washington University *B*
Georgetown University *B*
Howard University *B, M, D*

University of the District of
   Columbia *B*

Florida

Barry University *B*
Eckerd College *B*
Florida Atlantic University *B, M*
Florida International University *B*
Florida State University *B, M, D*
Jacksonville University *B*
New College of Florida *B*
Rollins College *B*
Schiller International University *B*
Stetson University *B*
University of Central Florida *B*
University of Florida *B, M*
University of Miami *B, M, D*
University of South Florida *B, M*
University of Tampa *A*
University of West Florida *B*

Georgia

Agnes Scott College *B*
Berry College *B*
Clark Atlanta University *B, M*
Covenant College *B*
Emory University *B, D*
Georgia College and State
   University *B*
Georgia State University *B, M, T*
Mercer University *B*
Morehouse College *B*
Oglethorpe University *B*
Shorter University *B*
Spelman College *B*
University of Georgia *B, M*
University of North Georgia *B*
Valdosta State University *B*
Wesleyan College *B*

Hawaii

University of Hawaii
   Manoa *B, M*

Idaho

Boise State University *B, T*
Idaho State University *B*
University of Idaho *B*

Illinois

Augustana College *B*
Bradley University *B, T*
DePaul University *B, M*
Dominican University *B*
Elmhurst College *B, T*
Illinois College *B, T*
Illinois State University *B, T*
Illinois Wesleyan University *B*
Kishwaukee College *A*
Knox College *B*
Lake Forest College *B*
Loyola University Chicago *B*
MacMurray College *B*
Monmouth College *B, T*
North Central College *B, T*
North Park University *B*
Northeastern Illinois University *B*
Northern Illinois University *B, M, T*
Northwestern University *B, M, D*
Principia College *B*
Richland Community College *A*
Rockford University *B*
Southern Illinois University
   Carbondale *B*
Triton College *A*
University of Illinois
   Chicago *B, M*
   Urbana-Champaign *B, M, D*
Western Illinois University *B*
Wheaton College *B, T*

Indiana

Anderson University *B*
Ball State University *B, T*
Butler University *B*
DePauw University *B*
Earlham College *B*
Franklin College *B*
Grace College *B*
Hanover College *B*
Indiana University
   Bloomington *B, M, D*
   Northwest *B*
   Purdue University Fort Wayne *B, T*
   Purdue University Indianapolis *B*
   South Bend *B*
   Southeast *B*
Manchester University *B, T*
Marian University *B, T*
Purdue University *B*
Saint Mary's College *B*
St. Mary-of-the-Woods College *B*
Taylor University *B*
University of Evansville *B*
University of Indianapolis *B*
University of Notre Dame *B, M*
University of Southern Indiana *B, T*
Valparaiso University *B*
Wabash College *B*

Iowa

Central College *B, T*
Coe College *B*
Cornell College *B, T*
Grinnell College *B*
Luther College *B*
St. Ambrose University *B, T*
Simpson College *B*
University of Iowa *B, M, D, T*
Wartburg College *B, T*

Kansas

Baker University *D, T*
Independence Community College *A*
Pittsburg State University *B*
University of Kansas *B, M, D*
Washburn University *B*
Wichita State University *B, T*

Kentucky

Asbury University *B, T*
Berea College *B, T*
Bluegrass Community and Technical
   College *A*
Centre College *B*
Eastern Kentucky University *B*
Georgetown College *B*
Morehead State University *B*
Murray State University *B, T*
Northern Kentucky University *B*
Thomas More College *A*
Transylvania University *B, T*
University of Kentucky *B, M*
University of Louisville *B, M*
Western Kentucky University *B, T*

Louisiana

Centenary College of Louisiana *B, T*
Grambling State University *B*
Louisiana College *B, T*
Louisiana State University and
   Agricultural and Mechanical
   College *B, M, D*
Louisiana Tech University *B*
Loyola University New Orleans *B*
Tulane University *B, M, D*
University of Louisiana at
   Lafayette *M, D*
Xavier University of Louisiana *B*

Maine

Bates College *B, T*
Bowdoin College *B*
Colby College *B*
University of Maine *B, M*
University of Maine
   Fort Kent *B*
University of Southern Maine *B*

Maryland

Frostburg State University *T*
Goucher College *B*
Hood College *B, T*
Johns Hopkins University *B, M, D*
Loyola University Maryland *B*
McDaniel College *B*
Mount St. Mary's University *B, T*
Notre Dame of Maryland
   University *B*
Salisbury University *B*
University of Maryland
   College Park *B, M, D*
Washington College *B, T*

Massachusetts

Amherst College *B*
Assumption College *B*
Bard College at Simon's Rock *B*
Boston College *B, M, D*
Boston University *B, M, D*
Clark University *B*
College of the Holy Cross *B*
Gordon College *B*
Merrimack College *B*
Mount Holyoke College *B*
Northeastern University *B*
Roxbury Community College *A*
Simmons College *B, M*
Smith College *B*
Stonehill College *B*
Suffolk University *B*
Tufts University *B, M*
University of Massachusetts
   Amherst *B, M*
   Boston *B*
   Dartmouth *B*
Wellesley College *B*
Williams College *B*

Michigan

Adrian College *A, B, T*
Albion College *B, T*
Alma College *B, T*
Andrews University *B*
Aquinas College *B, T*
Calvin College *B, T*
Central Michigan University *B*
Eastern Michigan University *B, M*
Grand Valley State University *B*
Hillsdale College *B*
Hope College *B*
Kalamazoo College *B*
Lake Superior State University *B*
Lansing Community College *A*
Michigan State University *B, M, D*
Michigan Technological University *T*
Northern Michigan University *B*
Oakland University *B, T*
Saginaw Valley State University *B, T*
University of Michigan *B, M, D*
University of Michigan
   Dearborn *B*
   Flint *B, T*
Western Michigan University *B*

Minnesota

Augsburg College *B*
College of St. Benedict *B*
Concordia College: Moorhead *B, T*
Gustavus Adolphus College *B*
Macalester College *B*
Minnesota State University
   Mankato *B, M, T*
St. Catherine University *B*
Saint Cloud State University *B*
St. John's University *B*
St. Olaf College *B*
University of Minnesota
   Duluth *B*
   Morris *B*
   Twin Cities *B, M, D*
University of St. Thomas *B*

Mississippi

Itawamba Community College *A*
Mississippi College *B*
University of Mississippi *B*

Missouri

Drury University *B, T*
Lindenwood University *B*
Missouri Southern State University *B*
Missouri State University *B*
Missouri Western State
   University *B*
Rockhurst University *B*
St. Charles Community College *A*
Saint Louis University *B, M*
Truman State University *B*
University of Central Missouri *B*
University of Missouri
   Columbia *B, M*
   Kansas City *B*
   St. Louis *B*
Washington University in St.
   Louis *B, M, D*
Webster University *B*
Westminster College *B*
William Jewell College *B*

Montana

Carroll College *B*
Montana State University
   Northern *B*
University of Montana *B, M*

Nebraska

Creighton University *B*
Doane College *B*
Nebraska Wesleyan University *B*
University of Nebraska
   Kearney *B, M, T*
   Lincoln *B*
Western Nebraska Community
   College *A*

Nevada

University of Nevada
   Las Vegas *B*
   Reno *B*

New Hampshire

Dartmouth College *B, T*
Keene State College *B*
Plymouth State University *B*
Saint Anselm College *B, T*
University of New Hampshire *B*

New Jersey

Drew University *B*
Fairleigh Dickinson University
   College at Florham *B*
   Metropolitan Campus *B*
Montclair State University *B, M, T*
Princeton University *B, M, D*
Rider University *B*
Rutgers, The State University of New
   Jersey
   Camden Campus *B, T*
   New Brunswick/Piscataway
     Campus *B, M, D, T*
   Newark Campus *B, T*
Seton Hall University *B, T*
William Paterson University of New
   Jersey *B*

New Mexico

University of New Mexico *B, M, D*

New York

Adelphi University *B*
Bard College *B*
Barnard College *B*
Canisius College *B*
City University of New York
   Brooklyn College *B, M*
   City College *B*

Hunter College *B, M*
Lehman College *B*
Queens College *B, M, T*
York College *B*
Colgate University *B*
College of Mount St. Vincent *B, T*
College of New Rochelle *B, T*
Columbia University *B*
Columbia University
  School of General Studies *B*
Cornell University *B*
Daemen College *B, T*
Elmira College *T*
Fordham University *B, M, D*
Hamilton College *B*
Hartwick College *B, T*
Hobart and William Smith Colleges *B*
Hofstra University *B*
Iona College *B*
Ithaca College *B, T*
Le Moyne College *B*
Long Island University
  LIU Post *B*
Manhattan College *B*
Manhattanville College *B*
Marist College *B*
Nazareth College *B*
New York University *B, M, D*
Niagara University *B*
Orange County Community
  College *A*
Pace University: Pleasantville/
  Briarcliff *B*
SUNY
  College at Brockport *B, T*
  College at Buffalo *B*
  College at Cortland *B*
  College at Fredonia *B, T*
  College at Geneseo *B, T*
  College at New Paltz *B*
  College at Oneonta *B*
  College at Oswego *B*
  College at Plattsburgh *B*
  College at Potsdam *B*
  University at Binghamton *B, M*
  University at Buffalo *B, M, D*
  University at Stony Brook *B*
Saint Bonaventure University *B*
St. John Fisher College *B*
St. John's University *B*
St. Lawrence University *B, T*
St. Thomas Aquinas College *B*
Siena College *B, T*
Skidmore College *B*
Syracuse University *B, M*
Union College *B*
United States Military Academy *B*
University of Rochester *B, M*
Vassar College *B*
Wagner College *B*

North Carolina

Catawba College *B*
Davidson College *B*
Duke University *B, M, D*
East Carolina University *B*
Elon University *B*
Gardner-Webb University *B*
Greensboro College *B*
Guilford College *B, T*
High Point University *B*
Johnson C. Smith University *B*
Lenoir-Rhyne University *B*
Methodist University *A, B, T*
North Carolina Agricultural and
  Technical State University *B, T*
North Carolina Central University *B*
North Carolina State University *B, M*
Queens University of Charlotte *B*
Salem College *B*
University of North Carolina
  Asheville *B, T*
  Charlotte *B*
  Greensboro *B*
  Wilmington *B*

Wake Forest University *B*
Western Carolina University *B*

North Dakota

Minot State University *B*
North Dakota State University *B, T*
University of Jamestown *B*
University of North Dakota *B*

Ohio

Ashland University *B*
Baldwin Wallace University *B*
Bowling Green State University *B, M*
Capital University *B*
Case Western Reserve
  University *B, M*
Cleveland State University *B*
College of Wooster *B*
Denison University *B*
Franciscan University of
  Steubenville *B*
Hiram College *B, T*
John Carroll University *B*
Kent State University *B, M*
Kenyon College *B*
Lake Erie College *B*
Miami University
  Oxford *B, M*
Muskingum University *B*
Oberlin College *B*
Ohio Northern University *B*
Ohio State University
  Columbus Campus *B*
Ohio University *B, M*
Ohio Wesleyan University *B*
Otterbein University *B*
University of Akron *B*
University of Cincinnati *B, M, T*
University of Dayton *B*
University of Mount Union *B*
University of Toledo *B, M*
Walsh University *B*
Wittenberg University *B*
Wright State University *B, M, T*
Xavier University *A, B*
Youngstown State University *B*

Oklahoma

Oklahoma Baptist University *B, T*
Oklahoma City Community
  College *A*
Oklahoma City University *B*
Oklahoma State University *B*
Oral Roberts University *B*
Tulsa Community College *A*
University of Central Oklahoma *B*
University of Oklahoma *B, M, D*
University of Tulsa *B*

Oregon

Linfield College *B, T*
Oregon State University *B*
Pacific University *B*
Portland State University *B, M*
Reed College *B*
University of Oregon *B, M*
University of Portland *B, T*
Western Oregon University *T*
Willamette University *B*

Pennsylvania

Albright College *B, T*
Allegheny College *B*
Arcadia University *B*
Bloomsburg University of
  Pennsylvania *T*
Bryn Mawr College *B, M*
Bucknell University *B*
Cabrini College *B*
California University of
  Pennsylvania *B*
Carnegie Mellon University *B*
Chatham University *B*
Chestnut Hill College *B*

Cheyney University of
  Pennsylvania *B*
Clarion University of Pennsylvania *B*
Dickinson College *B*
East Stroudsburg University of
  Pennsylvania *B, T*
Elizabethtown College *B*
Franklin & Marshall College *B*
Gettysburg College *B*
Grove City College *B, T*
Haverford College *B, T*
Immaculata University *B, T*
Juniata College *B*
King's College *B, T*
La Salle University *B, T*
Lafayette College *B*
Lebanon Valley College *B*
Lehigh University *B*
Lincoln University *B*
Lycoming College *B*
Mansfield University of
  Pennsylvania *T*
Marywood University *B*
Messiah College *B*
Millersville University of
  Pennsylvania *B, M, T*
Moravian College *B, T*
Muhlenberg College *B*
Penn State
  Abington *B*
  Altoona *B*
  Beaver *B*
  Berks *B*
  Brandywine *B*
  DuBois *B*
  Erie, The Behrend College *B*
  Fayette, The Eberly Campus *B*
  Greater Allegheny *B*
  Harrisburg *B*
  Hazleton *B*
  Lehigh Valley *B*
  Mont Alto *B*
  New Kensington *B*
  Schuylkill *B*
  Shenango *B*
  University Park *B, M, D*
  Wilkes-Barre *B*
  Worthington Scranton *B*
  York *B*
Rosemont College *B*
Saint Joseph's University *B*
St. Vincent College *B*
Seton Hill University *T*
Shippensburg University of
  Pennsylvania *B, T*
Slippery Rock University of
  Pennsylvania *B, T*
Susquehanna University *B, T*
Swarthmore College *B*
Temple University *B*
University of Pennsylvania *B*
University of Pittsburgh *B, M, D*
University of Scranton *B, T*
Ursinus College *B, T*
Villanova University *B*
Washington & Jefferson College *B*
West Chester University of
  Pennsylvania *B, M, T*
Westminster College *B*
Widener University *B, T*
Wilson College *B*

Puerto Rico

University of Puerto Rico
  Aguadilla *A*
  Mayaguez *B*
  Rio Piedras *B*

Rhode Island

Brown University *B, M, D*
Bryant University *B*
Providence College *B*
Rhode Island College *B*

Salve Regina University *B*
University of Rhode Island *B*

South Carolina

College of Charleston *B, T*
Columbia College *B*
Erskine College *B*
Francis Marion University *B*
Furman University *B, T*
Presbyterian College *B*
University of South Carolina
  Columbia *B, M*
Wofford College *B, T*

South Dakota

Augustana College *B, T*
Northern State University *B*
South Dakota State University *B*
University of South Dakota *B*

Tennessee

Belmont University *B*
Carson-Newman University *B, T*
Hiwassee College *A*
King University *B, T*
Lane College *B*
Lee University *B*
Lipscomb University *B*
Milligan College *T*
Rhodes College *B*
Sewanee: The University of the
  South *B*
Southern Adventist University *B*
Tennessee State University *B*
Tennessee Technological
  University *B, T*
Union University *B, T*
University of Tennessee
  Knoxville *B, M*
  Martin *B*
Vanderbilt University *B, M, D*

Texas

Angelo State University *B, T*
Austin College *B*
Austin Community College *A*
Baylor University *B*
Blinn College *A*
Houston Baptist University *B*
Lamar University *B*
Paris Junior College *A*
Rice University *B, M, D*
St. Edward's University *B*
St. Mary's University *B*
Sam Houston State University *B*
South Plains College *A*
Southern Methodist University *B*
Southwestern University *B, T*
Stephen F. Austin State University *T*
Texas A&M University *B*
Texas Christian University *B*
Texas Southern University *B*
Texas State University *B, T*
Texas Tech University *B*
Trinity University *B*
University of Dallas *B*
University of Houston *B*
University of North Texas *B, M*
University of St. Thomas *B*
University of Texas
  Arlington *B*
  Austin *B, M, D*
  El Paso *B*
  Pan American *B*

Utah

Brigham Young University *B, M*
Snow College *A*
Southern Utah University *B*
University of Utah *B*
Utah State University *B*
Weber State University *B*

Vermont

Bennington College *B*
Middlebury College *B, M, D*
Saint Michael's College *B*
University of Vermont *B*

Virginia

Bridgewater College *B*
Christopher Newport University *B*
College of William and Mary *B*
Emory & Henry College *B, T*
Hampden-Sydney College *B*
Hollins University *B*
Lynchburg College *B*
Mary Baldwin College *B*
Randolph College *B*
Randolph-Macon College *B*
Roanoke College *B, T*
Sweet Briar College *B*
University of Richmond *B*
University of Virginia *B, M, D*
University of Virginia's College at
   Wise *B, T*
Virginia Wesleyan College *B*
Washington and Lee University *B*

Washington

Central Washington University *B*
Centralia College *A*
Eastern Washington University *B*
Gonzaga University *B*
Highline Community College *A*
Pacific Lutheran University *B*
Seattle Pacific University *B*
Seattle University *B*
University of Puget Sound *B*
University of Washington *B*
Walla Walla University *B*
Washington State University *B*
Western Washington University *D*
Whitman College *B*
Whitworth University *B, T*

West Virginia

Fairmont State University *B*
West Virginia University *T*
Wheeling Jesuit University *B*

Wisconsin

Beloit College *B*
Carthage College *B*
Edgewood College *B*
Lawrence University *B*
Marquette University *B*
Ripon College *B, T*
St. Norbert College *B, T*
University of Wisconsin
   Eau Claire *B*
   Green Bay *B, T*
   La Crosse *B, T*
   Madison *B, M, D*
   Milwaukee *B*
   Oshkosh *B*
   Parkside *B, T*
   River Falls *B*
   Stevens Point *B, T*
   Whitewater *B, T*

Wyoming

Northwest College *A*
University of Wyoming *B, M*

French studies

California

Mills College *B*
Scripps College *B*

Colorado

Colorado College *B*

Connecticut

Wesleyan University *B*

District of Columbia

American University *B*

Florida

New College of Florida *B*
University of North Florida *B*

Georgia

Emory University *B, D*

Indiana

Purdue University *B*

Iowa

Coe College *B*

Louisiana

University of Louisiana at Lafayette *D*

Maine

University of Southern Maine *B*

Massachusetts

Bard College at Simon's Rock *B*
Boston University *B*
Brandeis University *B*
Suffolk University *B*
Wellesley College *B*
Wheaton College *B*

Minnesota

Carleton College *B*
Minnesota State University
   Mankato *B, M*

New Hampshire

University of New Hampshire *B*

New Jersey

William Paterson University of New
   Jersey *B*

New York

Bard College *B*
Barnard College *B*
Columbia University *B*
Columbia University
   School of General Studies *B*
Skidmore College *B*

Ohio

Case Western Reserve University *B*

Oregon

Lewis & Clark College *B*
Linfield College *B*

Pennsylvania

Arcadia University *B*
Saint Joseph's University *B*
University of Scranton *B*

Rhode Island

Brown University *B, M, D*
Rhode Island College *B*

Tennessee

Sewanee: The University of the
   South *B*

Utah

Brigham Young University *B*

Virginia

Emory & Henry College *B*

Washington

University of Washington *B, M*

Wisconsin

University of Wisconsin
   Milwaukee *C*
   Parkside *B*

French teacher education

Alabama

Auburn University *B, M, T*
Birmingham-Southern College *T*

Arkansas

Harding University *B, T*
Ouachita Baptist University *B, T*

California

California State University
   Long Beach *T*
   San Bernardino *T*
Humboldt State University *T*
San Francisco State University *T*
Stanford University *M, T*
University of San Diego *T*

Colorado

Colorado State University *B, T*

Connecticut

Fairfield University *T*
University of Connecticut *T*
University of Saint Joseph *T*

Delaware

Delaware State University *B*
University of Delaware *B, T*

District of Columbia

Catholic University of America *B*

Florida

Stetson University *B*

Georgia

Fort Valley State University *B, T*
Valdosta State University *B*

Idaho

Boise State University *B, T*
University of Idaho *T*

Illinois

Augustana College *B, T*
Bradley University *B*
DePaul University *M, T*
Dominican University *T*
Elmhurst College *B*
Illinois College *T*
Illinois Wesleyan University *B*
Knox College *T*
North Park University *T*
Rockford University *T*
University of Illinois
   Chicago *B*
   Urbana-Champaign *B, M, T*

Indiana

Anderson University *B, T*
Franklin College *B, T*
Grace College *B*
Indiana University
   Bloomington *B, T*
   Northwest *B*
   Purdue University Fort Wayne *B, T*
   Purdue University
      Indianapolis *B, T*
   South Bend *B, T*
Indiana Wesleyan University *T*
Manchester University *B, T*
Purdue University *B, M, D*
Saint Mary's College *T*
Taylor University *B, T*

University of Evansville *B, T*
University of Indianapolis *B, T*
Valparaiso University *B*

Iowa

Central College *T*
Cornell College *B, T*
Iowa State University *T*
Northwestern College *T*
St. Ambrose University *B, T*
Simpson College *T*
University of Iowa *T*
Wartburg College *T*

Kansas

Benedictine College *B*
Pittsburg State University *B*
Washburn University *B, T*

Kentucky

University of the Cumberlands *T*

Louisiana

Centenary College of Louisiana *T*
Grambling State University *B*
Louisiana College *B, T*
Louisiana Tech University *B*
University of Louisiana at Lafayette *B*
Xavier University of Louisiana *B*

Maine

University of Maine *B*
University of Southern Maine *T*

Maryland

Hood College *T*
Mount St. Mary's University *T*
Notre Dame of Maryland
   University *T*

Massachusetts

Assumption College *T*
Elms College *T*
Merrimack College *B*
Tufts University *T*
University of Massachusetts
   Dartmouth *T*

Michigan

Adrian College *B, T*
Alma College *T*
Aquinas College *B, T*
Calvin College *B*
Central Michigan University *B*
Eastern Michigan University *B*
Grand Valley State University *T*
Hope College *B, T*
Michigan State University *B*
Northern Michigan University *B, T*
University of Michigan
   Flint *B, T*
Western Michigan University *B*

Minnesota

Augsburg College *T*
Bethel University *B*
College of St. Benedict *T*
Concordia College: Moorhead *B, T*
Gustavus Adolphus College *T*
Hamline University *T*
Minnesota State University
   Mankato *B, M, T*
St. Catherine University *T*
Saint Cloud State University *B, T*
St. John's University *T*
University of Minnesota
   Duluth *B*
   Morris *T*
   Twin Cities *M*
University of St. Thomas *B*

Mississippi

Itawamba Community College *A*
Millsaps College *T*

Missouri

Lindenwood University *B*
Missouri Southern State
   University *B, T*
Missouri State University *B*
Missouri Western State University *B*
Northwest Missouri State
   University *T*
University of Central Missouri *B*
University of Missouri
   Columbia *M*
   Kansas City *B*
Washington University in St.
   Louis *B, M, T*
William Jewell College *B, T*

Montana

University of Montana *T*

Nebraska

Creighton University *T*
Nebraska Wesleyan University *T*
University of Nebraska
   Kearney *B, T*
   Lincoln *B, T*

New Hampshire

Keene State College *B, T*
Saint Anselm College *T*
University of New Hampshire *T*

New Jersey

County College of Morris *A*
Rowan University *T*

New York

Alfred University *B, T*
City University of New York
   Brooklyn College *B, M, T*
   City College *B*
   Hunter College *B, M, T*
   Queens College *M, T*
College of Mount St. Vincent *T*
D'Youville College *M, T*
Dutchess Community College *A*
Elmira College *B, T*
Fordham University *M, T*
Hobart and William Smith Colleges *T*
Hofstra University *B, M*
Iona College *B*
Ithaca College *B, M, T*
Le Moyne College *T*
Long Island University
   LIU Post *B, T*
Manhattan College *B, T*
Marist College *B*
Medaille College *M, T*
Medaille College: Amherst *M*
New York University *B, M, T*
Niagara University *B, M, T*
Pace University: Pleasantville/
   Briarcliff *B, M, T*
SUNY
   College at Brockport *T*
   College at Buffalo *B*
   College at Cortland *B*
   College at Fredonia *B, T*
   College at Geneseo *B, M, T*
   College at New Paltz *B, T*
   College at Oneonta *B, T*
   College at Oswego *B, M*
   College at Plattsburgh *B*
   College at Potsdam *B*
   University at Albany *M, T*
   University at Binghamton *M*
   University at Buffalo *M, T*
   University at Stony Brook *T*
Saint Bonaventure University *M*
St. John Fisher College *B, M, T*
St. Lawrence University *M*
University of Rochester *M*
Vassar College *T*
Wells College *T*

North Carolina

Campbell University *B, T*
Davidson College *T*
East Carolina University *B*
Elon University *T*
Gardner-Webb University *B*
Meredith College *T*
North Carolina Agricultural and
   Technical State University *B, T*
North Carolina Central
   University *B, T*
North Carolina State University *B, T*
Salem College *T*
University of North Carolina
   Greensboro *B*
   Wilmington *B*
Wake Forest University *T*

North Dakota

Minot State University *B*
North Dakota State University *B, T*

Ohio

Ashland University *B, T*
Baldwin Wallace University *T*
Bowling Green State University *M, T*
Case Western Reserve University *T*
Hiram College *T*
Miami University
   Oxford *B, T*
Ohio Northern University *B, T*
Ohio University *B, T*
Ohio Wesleyan University *B*
Otterbein University *B*
University of Akron *B, M*
University of Dayton *B*
University of Mount Union *T*
University of Toledo *B, M, T*
Youngstown State University *B*

Oklahoma

Oklahoma Baptist University *B, T*
Oklahoma City University *B*
University of Central Oklahoma *B*
University of Tulsa *T*

Oregon

Linfield College *T*
Portland State University *T*
Western Oregon University *T*

Pennsylvania

Albright College *T*
Cabrini College *T*
Gettysburg College *T*
Grove City College *T*
Holy Family University *B*
Juniata College *B, T*
King's College *T*
La Salle University *B, T*
Lebanon Valley College *T*
Lycoming College *T*
Mansfield University of
   Pennsylvania *B, T*
Marywood University *B*
Messiah College *B, T*
Moravian College *T*
Rosemont College *T*
St. Francis University *B, T*
Saint Joseph's University *M, T*
St. Vincent College *T*
Seton Hill University *T*
Susquehanna University *T*
University of Scranton *B*
Villanova University *T*
Washington & Jefferson College *T*
Westminster College *T*
Widener University *T*

Rhode Island

Rhode Island College *B, M*

South Carolina

Furman University *T*
Wofford College *T*

South Dakota

Augustana College *B, T*
University of South Dakota *B, M, T*

Tennessee

Belmont University *T*
King University *T*
Lee University *B*
Lipscomb University *B, T*
Southern Adventist University *B*
Tennessee Technological University *T*
Union University *B, T*

Texas

Houston Baptist University *T*
Lamar University *T*
St. Mary's University *T*
Texas A&M University
   Kingsville *T*
University of Dallas *T*
University of Texas
   Arlington *T*
   San Antonio *T*

Utah

Brigham Young University *B*
Southern Utah University *B*
Utah State University *B*
Weber State University *B*

Vermont

Bennington College *M*
Saint Michael's College *M, T*

Virginia

Bridgewater College *T*
Emory & Henry College *B*
Hollins University *T*
Longwood University *T*
University of Virginia's College at
   Wise *T*

Washington

Central Washington University *B, T*
Eastern Washington University *B, M*
Washington State University *B, M, T*
Whitworth University *B, T*

West Virginia

Bethany College *B*
Wheeling Jesuit University *B*

Wisconsin

Carthage College *T*
Edgewood College *B*
Lawrence University *T*
St. Norbert College *T*
University of Wisconsin
   Green Bay *T*
   River Falls *T*
   Whitewater *B*

Funeral direction

Arkansas

University of Arkansas
   Community College at Hope *C*

Georgia

Gupton Jones College of Funeral
   Service *A*

Michigan

Wayne State University *B*

Mississippi

Mississippi Gulf Coast Community
   College *A*

Missouri

Lindenwood University *B*

North Carolina

Rowan-Cabarrus Community
   College *C*

Pennsylvania

Pittsburgh Institute of Mortuary
   Science *A*

Tennessee

John A. Gupton College *C, A*

Texas

San Antonio College *C*

Washington

Lake Washington Institute of
   Technology *A*

Funeral services/ mortuary science

Alabama

Bishop State Community College *A*
Jefferson State Community
   College *C, A*

Arizona

Mesa Community College *A*

Arkansas

Arkansas State University
   Mountain Home *A*
University of Arkansas
   Community College at Hope *A*

California

American River College *A*
Cypress College *C, A*

Colorado

Arapahoe Community College *A*

Connecticut

Lincoln College of New England *B*

District of Columbia

University of the District of
   Columbia *A*

Florida

Florida State College at
   Jacksonville *A*
Miami Dade College *C, A*
St. Petersburg College *A*

Georgia

Gupton Jones College of Funeral
   Service *A*

Illinois

Carl Sandburg College *A*
Southern Illinois University
   Carbondale *B*

Indiana

Ivy Tech Community College
   Central Indiana *A*
   Northwest *A*
Mid-America College of Funeral
   Service *A, B*
Vincennes University *A*

Iowa

Des Moines Area Community
   College *C*
Marshalltown Community College *A*
North Iowa Area Community
   College *A*
Upper Iowa University *B*

Kansas

Barton County Community College *A*
Kansas City Kansas Community
College *A*

Louisiana

Delgado Community College *A*

Maryland

Community College of Baltimore
County *A*

Massachusetts

Bristol Community College *C*
Mount Ida College *A, B*

Michigan

Delta College *A*
Eastern Michigan University *B*
Ferris State University *A*
Gogebic Community College *A*
Grand Rapids Community College *A*

Minnesota

University of Minnesota
Twin Cities *B*

Mississippi

East Mississippi Community
College *A*

Missouri

Lindenwood University *B*
St. Louis Community College *C, A*

New Jersey

Eastwick College
Hackensack *A*
Hudson County Community
College *A*
Mercer County Community
College *C, A*

New York

American Academy McAllister
Institute of Funeral Service *A*
Hudson Valley Community College *A*
Nassau Community College *A*
St. John's University *B*

North Carolina

Edgecombe Community College *A*
Fayetteville Technical Community
College *C, A*
Forsyth Technical Community
College *C*
Pitt Community College *A*

Ohio

Cincinnati College of Mortuary
Science *A, B*
University of Cincinnati
Blue Ash College *A*

Oklahoma

University of Central Oklahoma *C, B*

Oregon

Mt. Hood Community College *A*

Pennsylvania

Gannon University *B*
Luzerne County Community
College *A*
Northampton Community College *A*
Pittsburgh Institute of Mortuary
Science *A*
Point Park University *A, B*
Thiel College *B*

South Carolina

Florence-Darlington Technical
College *A*
Piedmont Technical College *A*

Tennessee

John A. Gupton College *A*

Texas

Amarillo College *A*
Commonwealth Institute of Funeral
Service *C, A*
Dallas Institute of Funeral
Service *C, A*
San Antonio College *A*

Virginia

John Tyler Community College *C, A*

Wisconsin

Milwaukee Area Technical College *A*

Furniture design/manufacturing

Michigan

College for Creative Studies *B*

Minnesota

Dakota County Technical College *C*
Minneapolis College of Art and
Design *B*

New Mexico

Northern New Mexico College *C, A*

New York

Rochester Institute of
Technology *A, B, M*

Ohio

University of Rio Grande *C*

Oregon

Oregon College of Art & Craft *C, B*

Pennsylvania

Thaddeus Stevens College of
Technology *A*

Rhode Island

Rhode Island School of Design *B, M*

Vermont

Burlington College *C*

Game/interactive media design

Arizona

ITT Technical Institute
Tucson *B*
Pima Community College *A*
Sessions College for Professional
Design *C*
University of Advancing
Technology *A, B, M*

Arkansas

Southern Arkansas University *B*

California

Academy of Art University *A, B*
Art Institute of California
Los Angeles *B*
Sacramento *B*
San Diego *B*
Silicon Valley *B*
California College of the Arts *B*
College of the Siskiyous *C*

DeVry University
Pomona *B*
Ex'pression College *B*
Foothill College *C*
Mt. Sierra College *B*
National University *A, M*
University of California
Irvine *B*
Santa Cruz *B*
University of Southern
California *B, M*

Colorado

Red Rocks Community College *C, A*

Connecticut

Quinnipiac University *B*
Sacred Heart University *B, M*

Florida

Art Institute of Fort Lauderdale *B*
Florida Gateway College *C*
Full Sail University *B, M*
International Academy of Design and
Technology
Orlando *B*
International Academy of Design and
Technology: Tampa *B*
Keiser University *A*
Miami International University of Art
and Design *B*
Rasmussen College
Fort Myers *C, A, B*
New Port Richey *C, A, B*
Ocala *C, A, B*
Pasco/Land O'Lakes *C, A, B*
Tampa/Brandon *C, A, B*
Ringling College of Art and Design *B*
University of Miami *M*

Georgia

Savannah College of Art and
Design *B, M*

Illinois

Bradley University *B*
Columbia College Chicago *B*
DeVry University
Online *B*
Illinois Institute of Art
Schaumburg *B*
McKendree University *B*
Rasmussen College
Aurora *C, A, B*
Mokena/Tinley Park *C, A, B*
Rockford *C, A, B*
Romeoville/Joliet *C, A, B*

Indiana

Indiana Wesleyan University *B*

Kansas

Johnson County Community
College *A*
Southwestern College *B*

Maryland

Howard Community College *A*
Maryland Institute College of Art *B*
Montgomery College *A*
University of Baltimore *B*

Massachusetts

Becker College *B*
ITT Technical Institute
Wilmington *B*
Worcester Polytechnic Institute *B, M*

Michigan

College for Creative Studies *B*
International Academy of Design and
Technology
Detroit *B*

Minnesota

Brown College
Brooklyn Center *B*
Rasmussen College
Blaine *C, A, B*
Bloomington *C, A, B*
Brooklyn Park *C, A, B*
Eagan *C, A, B*
Lake Elmo/Woodbury *C, A, B*
Mankato *C, A, B*
Moorhead *C, A, B*
St. Cloud *C, A, B*
St. Paul College *A*

Mississippi

Hinds Community College *C, A*

Missouri

Kansas City Art Institute *B*

Nebraska

University of Nebraska
Omaha *B*

Nevada

Art Institute of Las Vegas *B*
International Academy of Design and
Technology
Henderson *B*

New Hampshire

Daniel Webster College *B*

New Jersey

Union County College *A*

New York

College of Saint Rose *C*
Sullivan County Community
College *A*

North Carolina

Blue Ridge Community College *C, A*
Central Piedmont Community
College *A*
Fayetteville Technical Community
College *C, A*
Stanly Community College *C, A*
Surry Community College *A*
Wayne Community College *A*
Wilson Community College *A*

North Dakota

Rasmussen College
Bismarck *C, A, B*
Fargo *C, A, B*

Ohio

Cleveland Institute of Art *B*
Franklin University *B*
Shawnee State University *B*

Oklahoma

Oklahoma Christian University *B*

Oregon

Mt. Hood Community College *A*

Pennsylvania

Albright College *B*
Art Institute of Pittsburgh *B*
Carnegie Mellon University *M*
Lehigh Carbon Community College *A*
Pennsylvania College of Art and
Design *B*
University of the Arts *B*

Puerto Rico

Atlantic University College *B*
Inter American University of Puerto
Rico
Bayamon Campus *B*

South Dakota

Dakota State University *B*

Tennessee

ITT Technical Institute
Memphis *B*

Texas

Abilene Christian University *B*
Collin County Community College
District *C, A*
Panola College *C*
St. Edward's University *B*
San Antonio College *C*
Texas State Technical College
Waco *A*
University of Texas
Dallas *B, M, D*

Utah

Broadview University
Broadview Entertainment Arts
University *B*
Neumont University *B*
University of Utah *M*

Vermont

Champlain College *B*

Virginia

Art Institute of Washington *B*
New River Community College *A*
Westwood College
Annandale *B*
Arlington Ballston *B*

Washington

Art Institute of Seattle *B*
Cascadia Community College *C*
International Academy of Design and
Technology
Seattle *B*

Wisconsin

Herzing University
Madison *B*
ITT Technical Institute
Greenfield *B*
Milwaukee Area Technical College *A*
Northcentral Technical College *C*
Rasmussen College
Appleton *A, B*
Green Bay *C, A, B*
Wausau *C, A, B*

Gay/lesbian studies

California

Claremont McKenna College *B*
Mills College *B*

Connecticut

Trinity College *B*
Wesleyan University *B*

Maine

College of the Atlantic *B, M*

Massachusetts

Hampshire College *B*
University of Massachusetts
Amherst *C*

New Jersey

Drew University *B*

New York

Cornell University *B*
Hobart and William Smith Colleges *B*

Ohio

Denison University *B*

Rhode Island

Bryant University *B*

Vermont

Bennington College *B*
Goddard College *B, M*

Wisconsin

University of Wisconsin
Milwaukee *C*

Gene therapy

Connecticut

University of Connecticut *B*

General literature

Alaska

University of Alaska
Anchorage *B*

Connecticut

Yale University *B*

Florida

Ave Maria University *B*

Indiana

Huntington University *B*

Iowa

Iowa Western Community College *A*

Kansas

Southwestern College *B*

Maine

College of the Atlantic *B, M*

Massachusetts

Bard College at Simon's Rock *B*
Hampshire College *B*
Massachusetts College of Liberal
Arts *B*
Middlesex Community College *A*

Michigan

Calvin College *B*

Minnesota

Concordia University St. Paul *B*
St. Mary's University of Minnesota *B*

Mississippi

Mississippi College *B*

Missouri

Washington University in St.
Louis *B, M, D*

New York

Canisius College *B*
Eugene Lang College The New
School for Liberal Arts *B*
Yeshiva University *B*

North Carolina

Elon University *B*

Oklahoma

University of Central Oklahoma *M*

Pennsylvania

Duquesne University *B*
Grove City College *B*

Rhode Island

Bryant University *B*

Texas

Lubbock Christian University *B*

Utah

Dixie State College *B*

Virginia

Bluefield College *B*

West Virginia

Marshall University *B*

Wisconsin

University of Wisconsin
River Falls *B*

Genetic counseling

California

California State University
Stanislaus *M*
University of California
Irvine *M*

Colorado

University of Colorado
Denver *M*

Illinois

Northwestern University *M*

Indiana

Martin University *B*

Maryland

University of Maryland
Baltimore *M*

Michigan

Wayne State University *M*

New York

Long Island University
LIU Post *M*
Sarah Lawrence College *M*

Ohio

Case Western Reserve University *M*
Ohio State University
Columbus Campus *M*

Oklahoma

University of Oklahoma *M*

Pennsylvania

Arcadia University *M*
University of Pittsburgh *M*

South Carolina

University of South Carolina
Columbia *M*

Utah

University of Utah *M*

Virginia

Virginia Commonwealth
University *M*

Genetics

Arizona

University of Arizona *M, D*

California

California Institute of
Technology *M, D*
San Diego State University *M, D*
Stanford University *M, D*

University of California
Davis *B, M, D*
Irvine *B*
Riverside *M, D*

Connecticut

University of Connecticut *M, D*
Yale University *M, D*

District of Columbia

George Washington University *M, D*
Howard University *M, D*

Florida

University of Florida *D*

Georgia

University of Georgia *B, M, D*

Illinois

University of Chicago *D*

Indiana

Indiana University
Bloomington *D*

Iowa

Iowa State University *B, M, D*
University of Iowa *D*

Kansas

Kansas State University *M, D*

Louisiana

Tulane University *M, D*

Maine

College of the Atlantic *B, M*

Massachusetts

Boston University *D*
Harvard College *D*
Tufts University *M, D*

Michigan

Michigan State University *M, D*

Minnesota

Minnesota State University
Mankato *B*

Missouri

Missouri Southern State University *B*
University of Missouri
Columbia *D*
Washington University in St. Louis *D*

New Hampshire

Dartmouth College *B, D*
University of New
Hampshire *B, M, D*

New Jersey

Rutgers, The State University of New
Jersey
New Brunswick/Piscataway
Campus *B*

New Mexico

New Mexico State University *B*

New York

SUNY
University at Stony Brook *D*
University of Rochester *M, D*
Yeshiva University *M*

North Carolina

North Carolina State
University *B, M, D*
University of North Carolina
Chapel Hill *M, D*

Ohio

Ohio Wesleyan University *B*

Pennsylvania

Cedar Crest College *B*
Penn State
  University Park *M, D*

Vermont

Marlboro College *B*

Washington

University of Washington *M, D*
Washington State University *B*

West Virginia

Concord University *B*
West Virginia University *M, D*

Wisconsin

University of Wisconsin
  Madison *B, M, D*

Genome sciences

New York

SUNY
  University at Buffalo *M, D*

North Dakota

North Dakota State University *M, D*

Geochemistry

California

California Institute of
  Technology *B, M, D*
California State University
  Fullerton *M*
University of California
  Los Angeles *M, D*

Colorado

Colorado School of Mines *M, D*

Florida

University of Miami *B*

Maine

University of Maine
  Farmington *B*

Massachusetts

Bridgewater State University *B*

Michigan

Grand Valley State University *B*
Western Michigan University *B*

Missouri

Missouri University of Science and
  Technology *B, M, D*

New Mexico

New Mexico Institute of Mining and
  Technology *M, D*

New York

College of Saint Rose *B*
Columbia University *B*
SUNY
  College at Geneseo *B*
  College at New Paltz *B*
  College at Oswego *B*

Ohio

Bowling Green State University *B*

Rhode Island

Brown University *B*

Geochemistry/ petrology

Colorado

Colorado School of Mines *M, D*

Geographic information science and cartography

Arizona

Arizona State University *M*
Coconino County Community
  College *C*
Northern Arizona University *M*
University of Arizona *M*

Arkansas

East Arkansas Community College *C*

California

American River College *A*
Los Angeles Pierce College *C*
Palo Verde College *C*
Palomar College *C, A*
University of Southern California *M*

Colorado

Colorado Mesa University *C*
Front Range Community College *C*

Georgia

Kennesaw State University *C, B*

Illinois

DePaul University *C*
Eastern Illinois University *M*

Indiana

Indiana University
  Purdue University
    Indianapolis *M, T*

Iowa

Iowa Lakes Community College *A*

Kansas

North Central Kansas Technical
  College *A*

Kentucky

Western Kentucky University *C, B*

Louisiana

Louisiana Tech University *M*

Maine

University of Maine
  Presque Isle *C*

Maryland

College of Southern Maryland *C*
Johns Hopkins University *M*
Montgomery College *C*

Massachusetts

Salem State University *B*
University of Massachusetts
  Boston *C*

Michigan

Central Michigan University *B, M*
Michigan Technological University *C*
Northern Michigan University *C, A, B*

Minnesota

Fond du Lac Tribal and Community
  College *C*
Saint Cloud State University *M*
St. Mary's University of Minnesota *M*
South Central College *C*

University of Minnesota
  Duluth *B*

Mississippi

Hinds Community College *C, A*
University of Mississippi *C*

Missouri

Missouri State University *C*
Northwest Missouri State
  University *B, M*
Saint Louis University *C*

Montana

University of Montana *B, M*

New Jersey

Burlington County College *C, A*
Monmouth University *C*
Rowan University *B*

New Mexico

Central New Mexico Community
  College *C, A*
New Mexico State University
  Grants *C*
San Juan College *C*
Southwestern Indian Polytechnic
  Institute *C, A*

New York

Cayuga Community College *A*
City University of New York
  Hunter College *M*
SUNY
  College at Oneonta *B*
  University at Binghamton *B*

North Carolina

Southeastern Community College *C*
University of North Carolina
  Wilmington *C*

North Dakota

Bismarck State College *C, A*

Ohio

Lorain County Community College *C*
Miami University
  Hamilton *C*
Ohio State University
  Columbus Campus *B*
Sinclair Community College *C*
University of Akron *C, A, B, M*
University of Cincinnati *C, B*

Oklahoma

East Central University *B*
Oklahoma State University *C*
University of Oklahoma *B*

Oregon

Clackamas Community College *C, A*

Pennsylvania

Harrisburg Area Community
  College *C, A*
Lehigh Carbon Community
  College *C, A*

South Carolina

Greenville Technical College *C, A*
Midlands Technical College *C*

South Dakota

Mitchell Technical Institute *A*
South Dakota State University *C, B*

Tennessee

Pellissippi State Community
  College *A*
Roane State Community College *C, A*

Texas

Austin Community College *C, A*
Brookhaven College *C, A*
Collin County Community College
  District *C, A*
Houston Community College
  System *C*
Lamar Institute of Technology *C, A*
Lone Star College System *C, A*
Stephen F. Austin State University *B*
Tarrant County College *C, A*
Temple College *C, A*
Texas A&M University *B*
Texas State Technical College
  Waco *C, A*
Texas State University *B, M, D*
University of Texas
  Dallas *B, M, D*

Utah

Brigham Young University *B, M*
Southern Utah University *C*
University of Utah *B, M, D, T*

Virginia

George Mason University *M*
Radford University *B*
University of Mary Washington *C*

Washington

Everett Community College *C*
Olympic College *C*

Wisconsin

University of Wisconsin
  Madison *B, M*
  Milwaukee *C*

Wyoming

Casper College *C, A*

Geography

Alabama

Auburn University *B, M*
Jacksonville State University *B*
Samford University *C, B*
University of Alabama *B, M*
University of North Alabama *B*
University of South Alabama *C, B*

Alaska

University of Alaska
  Fairbanks *B, M*

Arizona

Arizona State University *B, M, D*
Mesa Community College *C, A*
Northern Arizona University *B*
University of Arizona *B, M, D*

Arkansas

Arkansas State University *B*
University of Arkansas *B, M*
University of Central Arkansas *B*

California

Cabrillo College *A*
California State Polytechnic
  University: Pomona *B*
California State University
  Chico *B*
  Dominguez Hills *B*
  East Bay *B, M*
  Fresno *B*
  Fullerton *B, M*
  Long Beach *B, M*
  Los Angeles *B, M*
  Northridge *B*
  Sacramento *B, M*
  San Bernardino *B*
  Stanislaus *B*
Canada College *A*

Cerritos College *A*
Chabot College *A*
Chaffey College *A*
College of Alameda *A*
College of Marin *A*
College of the Canyons *A*
College of the Desert *A*
Contra Costa College *A*
Crafton Hills College *A*
Cypress College *A*
De Anza College *A*
Diablo Valley College *A*
El Camino College *A*
Foothill College *A*
Fresno City College *A*
Fullerton College *A*
Gavilan College *A*
Grossmont College *A*
Humboldt State University *B*
Irvine Valley College *A*
Los Angeles Southwest College *A*
Los Angeles Valley College *A*
Ohlone College *C*
Orange Coast College *A*
Saddleback College *A*
San Bernardino Valley College *A*
San Diego City College *A*
San Diego State University *B, M, D*
San Francisco State University *B, M*
San Jose State University *B, M*
Santa Ana College *A*
Santa Barbara City College *A*
Santa Rosa Junior College *A*
Santiago Canyon College *A*
Sierra College *C*
Sonoma State University *B*
Southwestern College *A*
University of California
    Berkeley *B, D*
    Davis *M, D*
    Los Angeles *B, M, D*
    Santa Barbara *B, M, D*
University of Southern
    California *B, M, D*
West Hills College: Coalinga *A*
West Los Angeles College *A*

Colorado

United States Air Force Academy *B*
University of Colorado
    Boulder *B, M, D*
    Colorado Springs *B, M*
    Denver *B*
University of Denver *B, M, D*
University of Northern Colorado *B, T*

Connecticut

Central Connecticut State
    University *B, M*
Southern Connecticut State
    University *B*
University of Connecticut *B, M, D*

Delaware

University of Delaware *B, M*

District of Columbia

George Washington University *B, M*

Florida

Broward College *A*
Daytona State College *A*
Florida Atlantic University *B, M*
Florida International University *B*
Florida State University *D, M, D*
Jacksonville University *B*
Palm Beach State College *A*
Stetson University *B*
University of Florida *B, M, D*
University of Miami *B, M*
University of South Florida *B, M*
University of Tampa *A*

Georgia

Darton College *A*
Georgia College and State
    University *B*
Georgia Southern University *B*
Georgia State University *B*
Kennesaw State University *B*
Southern Polytechnic State
    University *C*
University of Georgia *B, M, D*
University of West Georgia *B*

Hawaii

University of Hawaii
    Hilo *B*
    Manoa *B, M, D*

Idaho

College of Southern Idaho *A*
College of Western Idaho *A*
University of Idaho *C, B, M, D*

Illinois

Augustana College *B*
Chicago State University *B, M, T*
Concordia University Chicago *B*
DePaul University *B*
Eastern Illinois University *B, T*
Elmhurst College *B, T*
Illinois State University *B, T*
Lincoln College *A*
Northeastern Illinois University *B*
Northern Illinois University *B, M, D*
Northwestern University *B*
Richland Community College *A*
South Suburban College of Cook
    County *A*
Southern Illinois University
    Carbondale *B, M*
Southern Illinois University
    Edwardsville *B, M*
Southwestern Illinois College *A*
University of Chicago *B, D*
University of Illinois
    Chicago *M*
    Urbana-Champaign *B, M, D*
Western Illinois University *B, M*

Indiana

Ball State University *B, M, T*
Indiana State University *C, B, M, D, T*
Indiana University
    Bloomington *B, M, D*
    Purdue University Indianapolis *B*
    Southeast *B*
Taylor University *B*
Valparaiso University *B*
Vincennes University *A*

Iowa

North Iowa Area Community
    College *A*
University of Iowa *B, M, D, T*
University of Northern Iowa *B, M*

Kansas

Allen County Community College *A*
Kansas State University *B, M, D*
Pittsburg State University *B*
University of Kansas *B, M, D*

Kentucky

Eastern Kentucky University *B*
Morehead State University *B*
Northern Kentucky University *C, B*
University of Kentucky *B, M, D*
University of Louisville *B, M*
Western Kentucky University *B, M*

Louisiana

Louisiana State University and
    Agricultural and Mechanical
    College *B, M, D*
Louisiana Tech University *B*

Maine

University of Maine
    Farmington *B*
University of Southern Maine *B*

Maryland

Community College of Baltimore
    County *C, A*
Frostburg State University *B*
Johns Hopkins University *B, M, D*
Salisbury University *B, M*
Towson University *B, M*
University of Maryland
    Baltimore County *B, M, D*
    College Park *B, M, D*

Massachusetts

Bard College at Simon's Rock *B*
Boston University *B, M, D*
Bridgewater State University *B*
Clark University *B, M, D*
Fitchburg State University *B*
Framingham State University *B*
Mount Holyoke College *B*
Salem State University *B, M*
University of Massachusetts
    Amherst *B, M*
Worcester State University *B*

Michigan

Aquinas College *B, T*
Calvin College *B, T*
Central Michigan University *B*
Delta College *A*
Eastern Michigan University *B, M*
Grand Rapids Community College *A*
Grand Valley State University *B*
Lake Michigan College *A*
Lansing Community College *A*
Michigan State University *B, M, D*
Northern Michigan University *B*
Western Michigan University *B, M*

Minnesota

Bemidji State University *B*
Gustavus Adolphus College *B*
Itasca Community College *C, A*
Macalester College *B*
Minnesota State University
    Mankato *B, M, T*
Minnesota West Community and
    Technical College *A*
Saint Cloud State University *B, M*
University of Minnesota
    Duluth *B*
    Twin Cities *B, M, D*
University of St. Thomas *B*

Mississippi

Mississippi State University *C*
University of Southern
    Mississippi *B, M, D*

Missouri

Metropolitan Community College -
    Kansas City *C*
Missouri State University *B*
Northwest Missouri State
    University *B*
Park University *B*
Three Rivers Community College *A*
University of Central Missouri *B*
University of Missouri
    Columbia *B, M*
    Kansas City *B*

Montana

Montana State University
    Billings *T*
University of Montana *B, M*

Nebraska

Concordia University *B, T*
University of Nebraska
    Kearney *B, T*
    Lincoln *B, M, D*
    Omaha *B, M*
Wayne State College *B*
Western Nebraska Community
    College *A*

Nevada

University of Nevada
    Reno *B, M, D*

New Hampshire

Dartmouth College *B*
Keene State College *B*
Plymouth State University *B*
University of New Hampshire *B*

New Jersey

Montclair State University *B*
Rowan University *B, M*
Rutgers, The State University of New
    Jersey
    New Brunswick/Piscataway
        Campus *B, M, D*
William Paterson University of New
    Jersey *B*

New Mexico

New Mexico State University *B, M*
University of New Mexico *B, M*

New York

Barnard College *B*
City University of New York
    Hunter College *B, M*
    Lehman College *B*
Colgate University *B*
Erie Community College *C*
Excelsior College *B*
Hofstra University *B*
Long Island University
    LIU Post *B*
SUNY
    College at Buffalo *B*
    College at Cortland *B*
    College at Geneseo *B*
    College at New Paltz *B*
    College at Oneonta *B*
    College at Plattsburgh *B*
    University at Albany *B, M*
    University at Binghamton *B, M*
    University at Buffalo *B, M, D*
Syracuse University *B, M, D*
United States Military Academy *B*
Vassar College *B*

North Carolina

Appalachian State University *B, M*
East Carolina University *B, M*
Fayetteville State University *B*
North Carolina Central University *B*
North Carolina State University *B*
University of North Carolina
    Chapel Hill *B, M, D*
    Charlotte *B, M, T*
    Greensboro *B, M, D*
    Wilmington *B*
Western Carolina University *B*

North Dakota

Minot State University *B*
University of North Dakota *B, M*

Ohio

Bowling Green State University *B, M*
Central State University *B*
Kent State University *B, M, D*
Miami University
    Middletown *A*
    Oxford *C, B, M*

Ohio State University
  Columbus Campus *B, M, D*
Ohio University *B, M*
Ohio Wesleyan University *B*
Sinclair Community College *A*
University of Akron *B, M*
University of Cincinnati *B, M, D, T*
University of Toledo *B, M*
Wright State University *A, B*
Youngstown State University *B*

Oklahoma
Langston University *B*
Northeastern State University *B*
Oklahoma State University *B, M, D*
Tulsa Community College *A*
University of Central Oklahoma *B*
University of Oklahoma *B, M, D*

Oregon
Mt. Hood Community College *A*
Oregon State University *M, D*
Portland State University *B, M*
Southern Oregon University *B*
University of Oregon *B, M, D*
Western Oregon University *B*

Pennsylvania
Bucknell University *B*
California University of
  Pennsylvania *B, M*
Community College of
  Philadelphia *A*
East Stroudsburg University of
  Pennsylvania *B*
Edinboro University of
  Pennsylvania *B*
Harrisburg University of Science and
  Technology *B*
Indiana University of
  Pennsylvania *B, M*
Kutztown University of
  Pennsylvania *B*
Mansfield University of
  Pennsylvania *A, B, T*
Millersville University of
  Pennsylvania *B*
Penn State
  Abington *B*
  Altoona *B*
  Beaver *B*
  Berks *B*
  Brandywine *B*
  DuBois *B*
  Erie, The Behrend College *B*
  Fayette, The Eberly Campus *B*
  Greater Allegheny *B*
  Harrisburg *B*
  Hazleton *B*
  Lehigh Valley *B*
  Mont Alto *B*
  New Kensington *B*
  Schuylkill *B*
  Shenango *B*
  University Park *B, M, D*
  Wilkes-Barre *B*
  Worthington Scranton *B*
  York *B*
Shippensburg University of
  Pennsylvania *B, T*
Slippery Rock University of
  Pennsylvania *B*
Temple University *B, M, D*
University of Pittsburgh *M*
University of Pittsburgh
  Johnstown *B*
Villanova University *B*
West Chester University of
  Pennsylvania *B, M, T*

Puerto Rico
University of Puerto Rico
  Aguadilla *A*
  Rio Piedras *B*

Rhode Island
Rhode Island College *B*

South Carolina
University of South Carolina
  Columbia *B, M, D*

South Dakota
South Dakota State University *B, M*

Tennessee
East Tennessee State University *B, T*
University of Memphis *B*
University of Tennessee
  Knoxville *B, M, D*

Texas
Austin Community College *A*
Baylor University *B*
Galveston College *A*
Sam Houston State University *B*
Stephen F. Austin State
  University *B, T*
Texas A&M University *B, M, D*
Texas Christian University *B*
Texas State University *B, M, D, T*
Texas Tech University *B, M*
University of Houston
  Clear Lake *B*
University of North Texas *B, M*
University of Texas
  Austin *B, M, D*
  San Antonio *B*
Western Texas College *A*

Utah
Brigham Young University *B, M*
Salt Lake Community College *A*
Snow College *A*
Utah State University *B, M*
Weber State University *C, B*

Vermont
Middlebury College *B*
University of Vermont *B*

Virginia
Emory & Henry College *B*
George Mason University *B, M*
James Madison University *B*
Old Dominion University *B*
Radford University *B*
University of Mary Washington *B*
University of Richmond *B*
Virginia Polytechnic Institute and
  State University *B, M, D*

Washington
Central Washington University *B*
Eastern Washington University *B*
Highline Community College *A*
University of Washington *B, M, D*
Western Washington University *B, M*

West Virginia
Concord University *B*
Marshall University *B, M*
West Virginia University *B, M, D*

Wisconsin
Carthage College *B*
University of Wisconsin
  Eau Claire *B*
  La Crosse *B, T*
  Madison *B, M, D*
  Milwaukee *B, M, D*
  Oshkosh *B*
  Parkside *B, T*
  Platteville *B, T*
  River Falls *B, T*
  Stevens Point *B, T*
  Whitewater *B, T*

Wyoming
University of Wyoming *B, M*

Geography teacher education

California
Stanford University *M, T*

Delaware
University of Delaware *B, T*

Idaho
University of Idaho *T*

Illinois
Augustana College *B, T*
DePaul University *M*
University of Illinois
  Urbana-Champaign *M*

Indiana
Valparaiso University *B*

Iowa
University of Iowa *T*

Kentucky
Eastern Kentucky University *B*

Massachusetts
Fitchburg State University *B*

Michigan
Aquinas College *B, T*
Central Michigan University *B*
Eastern Michigan University *M*
Michigan State University *B*
Northern Michigan University *B, T*
Western Michigan University *B, D*

Minnesota
University of Minnesota
  Morris *T*

Missouri
University of Missouri
  Kansas City *B*

Nebraska
Concordia University *B, T*
Wayne State College *B, T*

New York
City University of New York
  Hunter College *B, T*

North Dakota
Mayville State University *B, T*

Ohio
University of Findlay *B, M, T*
University of Toledo *M, T*

Rhode Island
Rhode Island College *B*

Texas
West Texas A&M University *T*

Utah
Utah State University *B*

Wisconsin
Carroll University *B, T*
Carthage College *T*

Geological engineering

Alaska
University of Alaska
  Fairbanks *B, M*

California
University of California
  Berkeley *B*
  Los Angeles *B*

Colorado
Colorado School of Mines *B, M, D*

Idaho
University of Idaho *M*

Michigan
Michigan Technological
  University *B, M, D*
University of Michigan *B*

Minnesota
University of Minnesota
  Twin Cities *B, M, D*

Mississippi
Northeast Mississippi Community
  College *A*
University of Mississippi *B*

Missouri
Missouri University of Science and
  Technology *B, M, D*

Montana
Montana Tech of the University of
  Montana *B, M*

Nevada
University of Nevada
  Reno *B, M, D*

New Jersey
New Jersey Institute of Technology *B*
Rutgers, The State University of New
  Jersey
  Newark Campus *B*

New York
Columbia University *B, M, D*
Cornell University *M*
University of Rochester *B*

North Dakota
University of North Dakota *B, M*

Oklahoma
University of Oklahoma *M, D*

Pennsylvania
Drexel University *M*
University of Pennsylvania *M*

South Dakota
South Dakota School of Mines and
  Technology *B, M, D*

Utah
University of Utah *B, M, D*

Wisconsin
University of Wisconsin
  Madison *B, M, D*

Geology/earth science

Alabama
Auburn University *B, M*
University of Alabama *B, M, D*
University of South Alabama *B*

Alaska

Alaska Pacific University *B*
University of Alaska
    Anchorage *B*
    Fairbanks *B, M, D*

Arizona

Arizona State University *B, M, D*
Arizona Western College *A*
Eastern Arizona College *A*
Northern Arizona University *B, M*
University of Arizona *B, M, D*

Arkansas

Arkansas Tech University *B*
University of Arkansas *B, M, D*
University of Arkansas
    Little Rock *B*

California

Bakersfield College *A*
California Institute of
    Technology *B, M, D*
California Lutheran University *B*
California Polytechnic State
    University: San Luis Obispo *B*
California State Polytechnic
    University: Pomona *B, M*
California State University
    Bakersfield *B, M*
    Chico *B, M*
    Dominguez Hills *B*
    East Bay *B, M*
    Fresno *B, M*
    Fullerton *B, M*
    Long Beach *B, M*
    Los Angeles *B, M*
    Northridge *B, M*
    Sacramento *B, M*
    San Bernardino *B*
    Stanislaus *B*
Canada College *A*
Cerritos College *A*
Chaffey College *A*
College of San Mateo *A*
College of the Desert *A*
Contra Costa College *A*
Crafton Hills College *C, A*
Cypress College *A*
De Anza College *A*
El Camino College *A*
Folsom Lake College *A*
Foothill College *A*
Fullerton College *A*
Gavilan College *A*
Golden West College *A*
Grossmont College *A*
Hartnell College *A*
Humboldt State University *B, M*
Irvine Valley College *A*
Lake Tahoe Community College *A*
Loma Linda University *B, M, D*
Los Angeles Southwest College *A*
Los Angeles Valley College *A*
Merced College *A*
Moorpark College *A*
National University *B*
Occidental College *B*
Orange Coast College *A*
Palomar College *A*
Pomona College *B*
Saddleback College *A*
San Bernardino Valley College *A*
San Diego City College *A*
San Diego State University *B, M, D*
San Francisco State University *B, M*
San Joaquin Delta College *A*
San Jose State University *B, M*
Santa Ana College *A*
Santa Barbara City College *A*
Santiago Canyon College *A*
Scripps College *B*
Shasta College *A*
Sierra College *A*

Sonoma State University *B*
Southwestern College *A*
Stanford University *B, M, D*
University of California
    Berkeley *B, M, D*
    Davis *B, M, D*
    Irvine *B, D*
    Los Angeles *B, M, D*
    Merced *B*
    Riverside *B, M, D*
    Santa Barbara *B, M, D*
    Santa Cruz *B, M, D*
University of Southern
    California *B, M, D*
University of the Pacific *B*
West Los Angeles College *C, A*
West Valley College *A*

Colorado

Adams State University *A, B*
Colorado College *B*
Colorado Mountain College *A*
Colorado School of Mines *B, M, D*
Colorado State University *B, M, D, T*
Fort Lewis College *B*
University of Colorado
    Boulder *B, M, D*
University of Northern
    Colorado *B, M, T*
Western State Colorado
    University *B, T*

Connecticut

Central Connecticut State
    University *B*
Southern Connecticut State
    University *B*
University of Connecticut *B, M, D*
Wesleyan University *B*
Western Connecticut State
    University *B, M*
Yale University *B, M, D*

Delaware

University of Delaware *B, M, D*

District of Columbia

George Washington
    University *B, M, D*

Florida

Florida Atlantic University *B, M, D*
Florida International
    University *B, M, D*
Florida State University *B, M, D*
Miami Dade College *A*
Pensacola State College *A*
University of Florida *B, M, D*
University of Miami *B, M, D*
University of South Florida *B, M, D*

Georgia

Columbus State University *B*
East Georgia State College *A*
Georgia Highlands College *A*
Georgia Perimeter College *A*
Georgia Southern University *B*
Georgia Southwestern State
    University *B*
Georgia State University *B, M*
Middle Georgia State College *A*
University of Georgia *B, M, D*
University of North Georgia *A*
University of West Georgia *B*

Hawaii

University of Hawaii
    Hilo *B*
    Manoa *B, M, D*

Idaho

Boise State University *B, M, D, T*
Brigham Young University-Idaho *B*
College of Southern Idaho *A*

College of Western Idaho *A*
Idaho State University *B, M*
North Idaho College *A*
University of Idaho *B, M, D*

Illinois

Augustana College *B*
Concordia University Chicago *B*
Eastern Illinois University *B, T*
Illinois Central College *A*
Illinois State University *B, T*
Illinois Valley Community College *A*
Northeastern Illinois University *B, M*
Northern Illinois University *B, M, D*
Northwestern University *B, M, D*
Olivet Nazarene University *B*
South Suburban College of Cook
    County *A*
Southern Illinois University
    Carbondale *B, M, D*
University of Illinois
    Chicago *B, M, D*
    Urbana-Champaign *B, M, D, T*
Western Illinois University *B*
Wheaton College *B, T*

Indiana

Ball State University *B, M*
DePauw University *B*
Earlham College *B*
Hanover College *B*
Indiana State University *B, M, T*
Indiana University
    Bloomington *B, M, D*
    Northwest *B*
    Purdue University Fort Wayne *B*
    Purdue University
        Indianapolis *B, M*
Purdue University *B, M, D*
Taylor University *B*
University of Indianapolis *B*
University of Southern Indiana *B*
Valparaiso University *B*
Vincennes University *A*

Iowa

Cornell College *B, T*
Iowa State University *B, M, D*
University of Iowa *B, M, D, T*
University of Northern Iowa *B*

Kansas

Colby Community College *A*
Emporia State University *B, T*
Fort Hays State University *B, M*
Kansas State University *B, M*
University of Kansas *B, M, D*
Wichita State University *B*

Kentucky

Bluegrass Community and Technical
    College *A*
Eastern Kentucky University *B, M*
Hopkinsville Community College *A*
Morehead State University *B*
Murray State University *B, M*
Northern Kentucky University *B*
University of Kentucky *B, M, D*
Western Kentucky University *B*

Louisiana

Centenary College of Louisiana *B*
Louisiana State University and
    Agricultural and Mechanical
    College *B, M, D*
Louisiana Tech University *B*
Tulane University *B, M, D*
University of Louisiana at
    Lafayette *B, M*
University of New Orleans *B, M*

Maine

Bates College *B*
Bowdoin College *B*

Colby College *B*
University of Maine *B, M, D*
University of Maine
    Farmington *B*
    Presque Isle *B*
University of Southern Maine *B*

Maryland

Johns Hopkins University *B, M, D*
Salisbury University *B*
Towson University *B*
University of Maryland
    College Park *B, M, D*

Massachusetts

Amherst College *B*
Boston College *B, M*
Boston University *B, M, D*
Bridgewater State University *B*
Hampshire College *B*
Harvard College *B, M, D*
Massachusetts Institute of
    Technology *B, M, D*
Mount Holyoke College *B*
Northeastern University *B*
Salem State University *B*
Smith College *B*
Tufts University *B*
University of Massachusetts
    Amherst *B, M, D*
    Boston *B*
Wellesley College *B*
Williams College *B*

Michigan

Adrian College *A, B*
Albion College *B, T*
Calvin College *B, T*
Central Michigan University *B, M*
Delta College *A*
Eastern Michigan University *B*
Grand Rapids Community College *A*
Grand Valley State University *B*
Hope College *B*
Lake Michigan College *A*
Lake Superior State University *B, T*
Michigan State University *B, M, D*
Michigan Technological
    University *B, M, D*
Northern Michigan University *B*
University of Michigan *B, M, D*
Wayne State University *B, M*
Western Michigan University *B, M*

Minnesota

Carleton College *B*
Gustavus Adolphus College *B*
Macalester College *B*
Minnesota State University
    Moorhead *B*
Ridgewater College *A*
Saint Cloud State University *B*
University of Minnesota
    Duluth *B, M*
    Morris *B*
    Twin Cities *B, M, D*
University of St. Thomas *B*

Mississippi

East Mississippi Community
    College *A*
Hinds Community College *A*
Itawamba Community College *A*
Jackson State University *B*
Millsaps College *B*
Mississippi State University *B, M*
University of Mississippi *B*
University of Southern Mississippi *B*

Missouri

Missouri State University *B*
Missouri University of Science and
    Technology *B, M, D*

Northwest Missouri State
University *B*
Saint Louis University *B, M*
University of Central Missouri *B*
University of Missouri
Columbia *B, M, D*
Kansas City *B*
Washington University in St.
Louis *B, M, D*

Montana

Helena College University of
Montana *C*
Rocky Mountain College *B*
University of Montana *B, M, D*
University of Montana: Western *A, B*

Nebraska

University of Nebraska
Lincoln *B, M, D*
Omaha *B*

Nevada

University of Nevada
Las Vegas *B, M, D*
Reno *B, M, D*

New Hampshire

Dartmouth College *B, M, D*
Keene State College *B*
University of New
Hampshire *B, M, D*

New Jersey

Kean University *B, T*
Montclair State University *B, M, T*
New Jersey City University *B*
Princeton University *B, M, D*
Richard Stockton College of New
Jersey *B*
Rider University *B*
Rutgers, The State University of New
Jersey
New Brunswick/Piscataway
Campus *B, M, D*
Newark Campus *B, M*

New Mexico

Eastern New Mexico University *B*
Mesalands Community College *A*
New Mexico Highlands University *B*
New Mexico Institute of Mining and
Technology *B, M, D*
New Mexico State University *B, M*
San Juan College *A*
University of New Mexico *B, M, D*

New York

Alfred University *B*
Cayuga Community College *A*
City University of New York
Brooklyn College *B, M*
City College *B, M*
Lehman College *B*
Queens College *B, M, T*
York College *B*
Colgate University *B*
Columbia University *B*
Columbia University
School of General Studies *B*
Concordia College *B*
Cornell University *B, M, D*
Excelsior College *B*
Hamilton College *B*
Hartwick College *B*
Hobart and William Smith Colleges *B*
Hofstra University *B*
Long Island University
LIU Post *B, M*
Pace University: Pleasantville/
Briarcliff *B*
Rensselaer Polytechnic
Institute *B, M, D*

SUNY

College at Brockport *B*
College at Buffalo *B*
College at Cortland *B*
College at Fredonia *B, T*
College at Geneseo *B, T*
College at New Paltz *B*
College at Oneonta *B*
College at Oswego *B*
College at Plattsburgh *B*
College at Potsdam *B*
University at Binghamton *B, M, D*
University at Buffalo *B, M, D*
University at Stony Brook *B, M, D*
St. Lawrence University *B, T*
Skidmore College *B*
Suffolk County Community College *A*
Syracuse University *B, M, D*
Union College *B*
University of Rochester *B, M, D*
Vassar College *B*

North Carolina

Appalachian State University *B*
Duke University *B, M, D*
East Carolina University *B, M*
Elizabeth City State University *B*
Guilford College *B*
North Carolina Central University *M*
North Carolina State University *B*
University of North Carolina
Chapel Hill *B, M, D*
Charlotte *B, M*
Wilmington *B, M*
Western Carolina University *B*

North Dakota

Minot State University *B*
North Dakota State University *B, T*
University of North Dakota *B, M, D*

Ohio

Ashland University *B*
Bowling Green State University *B, M*
Case Western Reserve
University *B, M, D*
Cedarville University *B*
Central State University *B*
Cleveland State University *B*
College of Wooster *B*
Denison University *B*
Kent State University *B, M, D*
Marietta College *B*
Miami University
Oxford *B, M, D*
Muskingum University *B*
Oberlin College *B*
Ohio State University
Columbus Campus *B, M, D*
Ohio University *B, M*
Ohio Wesleyan University *B*
Sinclair Community College *A*
University of Akron *B, M*
University of Cincinnati *B, M, D, T*
University of Dayton *B*
University of Mount Union *B*
University of Toledo *B, M*
Wilmington College *B*
Wittenberg University *B*
Wright State University *A, B, M, T*
Wright State University: Lake
Campus *A*
Youngstown State University *B*

Oklahoma

Oklahoma State University *B, M, D*
Rose State College *A*
Tulsa Community College *A*
University of Oklahoma *B, M, D*
University of Tulsa *B, M, D*

Oregon

Linn-Benton Community College *A*
Mt. Hood Community College *A*

Oregon State University *M, D*
Portland State University *B, M*
Southern Oregon University *B*
Treasure Valley Community
College *A*
University of Oregon *B, M, D*
Western Oregon University *B*

Pennsylvania

Allegheny College *B*
Bloomsburg University of
Pennsylvania *B, T*
Bryn Mawr College *B*
Bucknell University *B*
California University of
Pennsylvania *B, M*
Clarion University of Pennsylvania *B*
Dickinson College *B*
East Stroudsburg University of
Pennsylvania *B, T*
Edinboro University of
Pennsylvania *B*
Franklin & Marshall College *B*
Haverford College *B*
Indiana University of Pennsylvania *B*
Juniata College *B*
Keystone College *B*
Kutztown University of
Pennsylvania *B*
La Salle University *B*
Lafayette College *B*
Lock Haven University of
Pennsylvania *B*
Mansfield University of
Pennsylvania *B*
Mercyhurst University *B*
Millersville University of
Pennsylvania *B, T*
Moravian College *B*
Penn State
Abington *B*
Altoona *B*
Beaver *B*
Berks *B*
Brandywine *B*
DuBois *C, B*
Fayette, The Eberly Campus *B*
Greater Allegheny *B*
Harrisburg *B*
Hazleton *B*
Lehigh Valley *B*
Mont Alto *B*
New Kensington *B*
Schuylkill *B*
Shenango *B*
University Park *B, M, D*
Wilkes-Barre *B*
Worthington Scranton *B*
York *B*
Shippensburg University of
Pennsylvania *B, T*
Slippery Rock University of
Pennsylvania *B, T*
Temple University *B, M*
University of Pennsylvania *B, M, D*
University of Pittsburgh *B, M, D*
University of Pittsburgh
Johnstown *B*
West Chester University of
Pennsylvania *B, M, T*
Wilkes University *B*

Puerto Rico

University of Puerto Rico
Mayaguez *B, M*

Rhode Island

Brown University *B, M, D*
University of Rhode Island *B*

South Carolina

Clemson University *B*
College of Charleston *B*
Furman University *B*

University of South Carolina
Columbia *B, M, D*

South Dakota

South Dakota School of Mines and
Technology *B, M, D*
University of South Dakota *B, M*

Tennessee

Austin Peay State University *B*
Middle Tennessee State University *B*
Sewanee: The University of the
South *B*
Tennessee Technological
University *B*
University of Memphis *B, M, D*
University of Tennessee
Chattanooga *B*
Knoxville *B, M, D*
Martin *B*
Vanderbilt University *B, M*

Texas

Amarillo College *A*
Austin Community College *A*
Baylor University *B, M, D*
Central Texas College *A*
Clarendon College *A*
Coastal Bend College *A*
Del Mar College *A*
El Paso Community College *A*
Galveston College *A*
Grayson College *A*
Hardin-Simmons University *B*
Lamar University *B*
Laredo Community College *A*
Midland College *A*
Midwestern State University *B*
Odessa College *A*
Palo Alto College *A*
Rice University *B, M, D*
St. Mary's University *B, T*
St. Philip's College *A*
Sam Houston State University *B*
San Jacinto College *A*
South Plains College *A*
Southern Methodist
University *B, M, D*
Stephen F. Austin State
University *B, M*
Sul Ross State University *B, M*
Tarleton State University *B*
Texas A&M University *B, M, D*
Texas A&M University
Corpus Christi *B, T*
Galveston *B*
Kingsville *B, M, T*
Texas Christian University *B, M*
Texas Tech University *B, M, D*
Trinity University *B*
Tyler Junior College *A*
University of Houston *B, M, D*
University of Texas
Arlington *B*
Austin *B, M, D*
Dallas *B, M, D*
El Paso *B, M, D*
Permian Basin *B, M*
San Antonio *B, M*
Wayland Baptist University *B, T*
West Texas A&M University *B*
Western Texas College *A*

Utah

Brigham Young University *B, M*
Salt Lake Community College *A*
Snow College *A*
Southern Utah University *B*
University of Utah *B, M, D, T*
Utah State University *B, M, D*
Utah Valley University *B*
Weber State University *B*

Vermont

Bennington College *B*
Castleton State College *B*
Middlebury College *B*
Norwich University *B*
University of Vermont *B, M*

Virginia

College of William and Mary *B*
George Mason University *B, M*
James Madison University *B, T*
Radford University *B*
Virginia Polytechnic Institute and
    State University *B, M, D*
Washington and Lee University *B*

Washington

Cascadia Community College *A*
Central Washington University *B, M*
Centralia College *A*
Eastern Washington University *B*
Highline Community College *A*
Pacific Lutheran University *B*
University of Puget Sound *B, T*
University of Washington *B, M, D*
Washington State University *B, M, D*
Western Washington University *B, M*
Whitman College *B*

West Virginia

Concord University *B*
Marshall University *B*
Potomac State College of West
    Virginia University *A*
West Virginia University *B, M, D*

Wisconsin

Beloit College *B*
Lawrence University *B, T*
Northland College *B*
St. Norbert College *B, T*
University of Wisconsin
    Eau Claire *B*
    Madison *B, M, D*
    Milwaukee *B, M, D* *
    Oshkosh *B*
    Parkside *B, T*
    River Falls *B*
    Stevens Point *B*

Wyoming

Casper College *A*
Central Wyoming College *A*
University of Wyoming *B, M, D*
Western Wyoming Community
    College *A*

Geophysics/seismology

Alaska

University of Alaska
    Fairbanks *M, D*

California

California Institute of
    Technology *B, M, D*
California State University
    Northridge *B*
Occidental College *B*
San Diego State University *D*
Stanford University *B, M, D*
University of California
    Berkeley *B*
    Los Angeles *B, M, D*
    Riverside *B*
    Santa Barbara *B, M*

Colorado

Colorado School of Mines *B, M, D*
University of Colorado
    Boulder *D*

Delaware

University of Delaware *B*

Idaho

Boise State University *B, M, D*
Idaho State University *M*

Illinois

University of Chicago *B, D*

Massachusetts

Boston College *B, M*
Boston University *B*
Massachusetts Institute of
    Technology *M, D*

Michigan

Eastern Michigan University *B*
Michigan State University *B*
Michigan Technological
    University *B, M, D*
Western Michigan University *B*

Minnesota

University of Minnesota
    Twin Cities *B, M, D*

Missouri

Missouri University of Science and
    Technology *B, M, D*
Saint Louis University *B, M, D*
Washington University in St. Louis *B*

Nevada

University of Nevada
    Reno *B, M, D*

New Mexico

New Mexico Institute of Mining and
    Technology *B, M, D*

New York

Columbia University *B*
Columbia University
    School of General Studies *B*
SUNY
    College at Fredonia *B*
    College at Geneseo *B*
St. Lawrence University *B*

Ohio

Bowling Green State University *B, M*
University of Akron *B, M*
Wright State University *M*

Oklahoma

University of Oklahoma *B, M, D*
University of Tulsa *B, M*

Rhode Island

Brown University *B*

South Carolina

University of South Carolina
    Columbia *B*

Texas

Baylor University *B*
Rice University *B, M*
Southern Methodist
    University *B, M, D*
Texas A&M University *B, M, D*
University of Houston *B, M, D*
University of Texas
    Austin *B*
    El Paso *D, M*

Utah

University of Utah *B, M, D*

Washington

University of Washington *M, D*
Western Washington University *B*

Wyoming

University of Wyoming *M, D*

Geotechnical/
geoenvironmental
engineering

Alaska

University of Alaska
    Anchorage *C*

Illinois

Illinois Institute of Technology *M*
University of Illinois
    Urbana-Champaign *B, M, D*

New Jersey

Stevens Institute of Technology *M*

Ohio

University of Akron *C*

Geriatric nurse/nursing

Colorado

Regis University *C*

Illinois

Spoon River College *C, A*

Michigan

Oakland University *M, D*
University of Michigan *M*

Minnesota

College of St. Scholastica *M*

New Jersey

Seton Hall University *M*

New York

City University of New York
    College of Staten Island *M*
Le Moyne College *M*
New York University *M, D*
SUNY
    University at Buffalo *M*
Sage Colleges *M*

Ohio

Case Western Reserve University *M*
University of Akron *M*

Oregon

Oregon Health & Science
    University *M*

Pennsylvania

Gwynedd Mercy University *M*

Puerto Rico

Caribbean University *M*

South Dakota

National American University
    Rapid City *B*

Washington

Seattle University *M*

Wisconsin

Northeast Wisconsin Technical
    College *A*

German

Alabama

Auburn University *B*
Birmingham-Southern College *B*
Samford University *B*
University of Alabama *M*

Alaska

University of Alaska
    Anchorage *B*

Arizona

Arizona State University *B, M*
University of Arizona *B, M*

Arkansas

Hendrix College *B*
University of Arkansas *B, M*
University of Arkansas
    Little Rock *B*

California

Cabrillo College *A*
California Lutheran University *B*
California State University
    Chico *B*
    Long Beach *B, M*
    Northridge *B*
Cerritos College *A*
Chabot College *A*
Chaffey College *A*
Claremont McKenna College *B*
College of the Desert *A*
Cypress College *A*
De Anza College *A*
El Camino College *A*
Golden West College *A*
Grossmont College *A*
Los Angeles City College *A*
Los Angeles Valley College *A*
Merced College *A*
Orange Coast College *A*
Pepperdine University *B*
Pitzer College *B*
St. Mary's College of California *B*
San Diego State University *B*
San Francisco State University *B, M*
San Joaquin Delta College *A*
San Jose State University *B*
Santa Clara University *B*
Scripps College *B*
Solano Community College *A*
Sonoma State University *B*
Stanford University *B, M, D*
University of California
    Berkeley *B, M, D*
    Davis *B, M, D*
    Irvine *D*
    Los Angeles *B*
    Riverside *B, M, D*
    San Diego *B, M*
    Santa Barbara *B, M, D*
University of La Verne *B*
University of Redlands *B*
University of Southern
    California *B, M, D*

Colorado

Colorado College *B*
Colorado State University *B, M*
University of Denver *B*

Connecticut

Central Connecticut State
    University *B*
Connecticut College *B*
Fairfield University *B*
Southern Connecticut State
    University *B*
Trinity College *B*
University of Connecticut *B*
Wesleyan University *B*
Yale University *B, M, D*

Delaware

Delaware State University *B*
University of Delaware *B, M, T*

District of Columbia

American University *B*
Catholic University of America *B*

George Washington University *B*
Georgetown University *B, M, D*
Howard University *B*

Florida

Florida State University *B, M*
New College of Florida *B*
Schiller International University *B*
Stetson University *B*
University of Florida *B, M, D*
University of Miami *B*
University of South Florida *B*
University of Tampa *A*

Georgia

Agnes Scott College *B*
Berry College *B*
Emory University *B*
Georgia State University *B, M, T*
Mercer University *B*
University of Georgia *B, M*

Hawaii

University of Hawaii
  Manoa *B*

Idaho

Boise State University *B, T*
Idaho State University *B*

Illinois

Augustana College *B*
Bradley University *B, T*
DePaul University *B, M*
Elmhurst College *B, T*
Illinois College *B, T*
Illinois State University *B, T*
Illinois Wesleyan University *B*
Knox College *B*
North Central College *B*
Northern Illinois University *B, T*
Northwestern University *B, M, D*
Richland Community College *A*
Southern Illinois University
  Carbondale *B*
University of Illinois
  Urbana-Champaign *B, M, D*
Wheaton College *B, T*

Indiana

Ball State University *B, T*
Butler University *B*
DePauw University *B*
Earlham College *B*
Hanover College *B*
Indiana University
  Purdue University Fort Wayne *B, T*
  Purdue University Indianapolis *B*
  South Bend *B*
  Southeast *B*
Purdue University *B*
University of Evansville *B*
University of Indianapolis *B*
University of Notre Dame *B, M*
University of Southern Indiana *B, T*
Valparaiso University *B*
Wabash College *B*

Iowa

Central College *B, T*
Coe College *B*
Cornell College *B, T*
Grinnell College *B*
Luther College *B*
St. Ambrose University *B, T*
Simpson College *B*
University of Iowa *B, M, D, T*
Wartburg College *B, T*

Kansas

Baker University *B, T*
Washburn University *B*

Kentucky

Berea College *B, T*
Bluegrass Community and Technical
  College *A*
Centre College *B*
Eastern Kentucky University *B*
Georgetown College *B*
Murray State University *B, T*
Northern Kentucky University *B*
Transylvania University *B*
University of Kentucky *B, M*
Western Kentucky University *B, T*

Louisiana

Tulane University *B*

Maine

Bates College *B, T*
Bowdoin College *B*
Colby College *B*
University of Maine *B*

Maryland

Hood College *B*
Johns Hopkins University *B, M, D*
Loyola University Maryland *B*
McDaniel College *B*
Mount St. Mary's University *B, T*
University of Maryland
  College Park *B, M, D*
Washington College *B, T*

Massachusetts

Amherst College *B*
Bard College at Simon's Rock *B*
Boston College *B*
Boston University *B*
College of the Holy Cross *B*
Gordon College *B*
Harvard College *B, M, D*
Smith College *B*
Tufts University *B, M*
Wellesley College *B*
Wheaton College *B*
Williams College *B*

Michigan

Adrian College *A, B, T*
Albion College *B, T*
Alma College *B, T*
Aquinas College *B, T*
Calvin College *B, T*
Central Michigan University *B*
Eastern Michigan University *B, M*
Grand Valley State University *B*
Hillsdale College *B*
Hope College *B*
Kalamazoo College *B*
Michigan State University *B, M, D*
Michigan Technological University *T*
Oakland University *B, T*
University of Michigan *B, M, D*
Wayne State University *B, M*
Western Michigan University *B*

Minnesota

Augsburg College *B*
Carleton College *B*
College of St. Benedict *B*
Concordia College: Moorhead *B, T*
Gustavus Adolphus College *B*
Hamline University *B*
Macalester College *B*
Minnesota State University
  Mankato *B, M, T*
Saint Cloud State University *B*
St. John's University *B*
St. Olaf College *B*
University of Minnesota
  Duluth *B*
  Morris *B*
  Twin Cities *B, M, D*
University of St. Thomas *B*

Mississippi

University of Mississippi *B*

Missouri

Drury University *B, T*
Missouri Southern State University *B*
Missouri State University *B*
Missouri Western State University *T*
Saint Louis University *B*
Truman State University *B*
University of Central Missouri *B*
University of Missouri
  Columbia *B, M*
  Kansas City *B*
  St. Louis *B*
Washington University in St.
  Louis *B, M, D*
Webster University *B*

Montana

University of Montana *B, M*

Nebraska

Creighton University *B*
Doane College *B*
Hastings College *B*
Nebraska Wesleyan University *B*
Union College *B*
University of Nebraska
  Kearney *B, M, T*
  Lincoln *B*

Nevada

University of Nevada
  Las Vegas *B*

New Hampshire

Dartmouth College *B*
Saint Anselm College *B*
University of New Hampshire *B*

New Jersey

Drew University *B*
Montclair State University *B*
Princeton University *B, M, D*
Rider University *B*
Rutgers, The State University of New
  Jersey
  Camden Campus *B, T*
  New Brunswick/Piscataway
    Campus *B, M, D, T*
  Newark Campus *B*

New Mexico

University of New Mexico *B, M*

New York

Bard College *B*
Barnard College *B*
City University of New York
  Hunter College *B*
  Queens College *B, T*
Colgate University *B*
Columbia University *B*
Columbia University
  School of General Studies *B*
Cornell University *B*
Fordham University *B*
Hartwick College *B, T*
Hofstra University *B*
Ithaca College *B, T*
Nazareth College *B*
New York University *B, M, D*
SUNY
  College at New Paltz *B*
  College at Oswego *B*
  University at Binghamton *B*
  University at Buffalo *B, M, D*
  University at Stony Brook *B, M*
St. Lawrence University *B, T*
Skidmore College *B*
Syracuse University *B*
Union College *B*

United States Military Academy *B*
University of Rochester *B, M*
Vassar College *B*

North Carolina

Davidson College *B*
Duke University *B, M, D*
East Carolina University *B*
Guilford College *B, T*
Lenoir-Rhyne University *B*
Methodist University *A*
University of North Carolina
  Asheville *B, T*
  Chapel Hill *M, D*
  Charlotte *B*
  Greensboro *B*
  Wilmington *B*
Wake Forest University *B*
Western Carolina University *B*

North Dakota

Minot State University *B*
University of Jamestown *B*
University of North Dakota *B*

Ohio

Baldwin Wallace University *B*
Bowling Green State University *B, M*
Case Western Reserve University *B*
College of Wooster *B*
Denison University *B*
Franciscan University of
  Steubenville *B*
Heidelberg University *B*
Hiram College *B, T*
John Carroll University *B*
Kent State University *B, M*
Kenyon College *B*
Lake Erie College *B*
Miami University
  Oxford *B*
Muskingum University *B*
Oberlin College *B*
Ohio Northern University *B*
Ohio State University
  Columbus Campus *B, M, D*
Ohio University *B, M*
Ohio Wesleyan University *B*
University of Cincinnati *B, M, D, T*
University of Dayton *B*
University of Mount Union *B*
University of Toledo *B, M*
Wittenberg University *B*
Wright State University *B*
Xavier University *A, B*

Oklahoma

Oklahoma Baptist University *B, T*
Oklahoma State University *B*
Tulsa Community College *A*
University of Central Oklahoma *B*
University of Tulsa *B*

Oregon

Linfield College *B, T*
Oregon State University *B*
Pacific University *B*
Portland State University *B, M*
Reed College *B*
University of Oregon *B, M, D*
University of Portland *B, T*
Western Oregon University *T*
Willamette University *B*

Pennsylvania

Allegheny College *B*
Bloomsburg University of
  Pennsylvania *T*
Bryn Mawr College *B*
Bucknell University *B*
California University of
  Pennsylvania *B*
Carnegie Mellon University *B*
Dickinson College *B*

Edinboro University of
    Pennsylvania *B, T*
Elizabethtown College *B*
Franklin & Marshall College *B*
Gettysburg College *B*
Haverford College *B, T*
Immaculata University *B*
Juniata College *B*
La Salle University *B*
Lafayette College *B*
Lebanon Valley College *B*
Lehigh University *B*
Lycoming College *B*
Messiah College *B*
Millersville University of
    Pennsylvania *B, M, T*
Moravian College *B, T*
Muhlenberg College *B*
Penn State
  Abington *B*
  Altoona *B*
  Beaver *B*
  Berks *B*
  Brandywine *B*
  DuBois *B*
  Erie, The Behrend College *B*
  Fayette, The Eberly Campus *B*
  Greater Allegheny *B*
  Harrisburg *B*
  Hazleton *B*
  Lehigh Valley *B*
  Mont Alto *B*
  New Kensington *B*
  Schuylkill *B*
  Shenango *B*
  University Park *B, M, D*
  Wilkes-Barre *B*
  Worthington Scranton *B*
  York *B*
Rosemont College *B*
Saint Joseph's University *B*
Susquehanna University *B, T*
Swarthmore College *B*
Temple University *B*
University of Pennsylvania *B, M, D*
University of Pittsburgh *B, M, D*
University of Scranton *B, T*
Ursinus College *B, T*
Villanova University *B*
Washington & Jefferson College *B*
West Chester University of
    Pennsylvania *B, M, T*
Westminster College *B*

Rhode Island

Brown University *B, M, D*
University of Rhode Island *B*

South Carolina

College of Charleston *B, T*
Francis Marion University *B*
Furman University *B, T*
University of South Carolina
  Columbia *B, M*
Wofford College *B*

South Dakota

Augustana College *B, T*
Northern State University *B*
South Dakota State University *B*
University of South Dakota *B*

Tennessee

Belmont University *B*
Lipscomb University *B*
Rhodes College *B*
Sewanee: The University of the
  South *B*
Tennessee Technological
  University *B, T*
University of Tennessee
  Knoxville *B, M*
Vanderbilt University *B, M, D*

Texas

Angelo State University *B, T*
Austin College *B*
Austin Community College *A*
Baylor University *B*
Blinn College *A*
Paris Junior College *A*
Rice University *B*
Southern Methodist University *B*
Southwestern University *B, T*
Texas A&M University *B*
Texas Christian University *B*
Texas State University *B, T*
Texas Tech University *B, M*
Trinity University *B*
University of Dallas *B*
University of North Texas *B*
University of Texas
  Arlington *B*
  Austin *B*

Utah

Brigham Young University *B*
Southern Utah University *B*
Utah State University *B*
Weber State University *B*

Vermont

Middlebury College *B, M, D*
University of Vermont *B, M*

Virginia

Christopher Newport University *B*
College of William and Mary *B*
Hampden-Sydney College *B*
Randolph-Macon College *B*
Roanoke College *T*
Sweet Briar College *B*
University of Virginia *B, M, D*
Virginia Wesleyan College *B*
Washington and Lee University *B*

Washington

Central Washington University *B*
Centralia College *A*
Highline Community College *A*
Pacific Lutheran University *B*
Seattle Pacific University *B*
University of Puget Sound *B*
University of Washington *B, M, D*
Western Washington University *B*
Whitman College *B*

West Virginia

West Virginia University *T*

Wisconsin

Beloit College *B*
Carthage College *B*
Concordia University Wisconsin *B*
Lakeland College *B*
Lawrence University *B, T*
Marquette University *B*
Ripon College *B, T*
St. Norbert College *B, T*
University of Wisconsin
  Green Bay *B, T*
  La Crosse *B, T*
  Oshkosh *B*
  Parkside *B, T*
  Platteville *B*
  River Falls *B*
  Stevens Point *B, T*
  Whitewater *B, T*
Wisconsin Lutheran College *B*

Wyoming

University of Wyoming *B, M*

German studies

Arizona

University of Arizona *D*

California

Pomona College *B*
Scripps College *B*
Stanford University *B, M, D*
University of California
  Irvine *B*
  Riverside *B, M, D*
  San Diego *B*
  Santa Cruz *B*

Connecticut

Wesleyan University *B*
Yale University *B*

District of Columbia

American University *B*

Florida

New College of Florida *B*

Georgia

Emory University *B*

Illinois

University of Chicago *B, D*
University of Illinois
  Chicago *B, M, D*

Indiana

Purdue University *B*

Iowa

Coe College *B*
Cornell College *B*

Kentucky

Georgetown College *B*

Louisiana

Tulane University *B*

Massachusetts

Bard College at Simon's Rock *B*
Brandeis University *B*
College of the Holy Cross *B*
Mount Holyoke College *B*
University of Massachusetts
  Amherst *B, M, D*
Wellesley College *B*

Michigan

Northern Michigan University *B*

Minnesota

Minnesota State University
  Mankato *B*

Missouri

Washington University in St. Louis *B*

New Hampshire

Dartmouth College *B*

New York

Bard College *B*
Barnard College *B*
Columbia University *B*
Columbia University
  School of General Studies *B*
Cornell University *B, M, D*
Hamilton College *B*

North Carolina

North Carolina State University *B*

Ohio

Case Western Reserve University *B*

Oregon

Lewis & Clark College *B*
Linfield College *B*

Pennsylvania

Kutztown University of
  Pennsylvania *B*
Moravian College *B*
Muhlenberg College *C, B*
University of Pittsburgh *B*
University of Scranton *B*

Rhode Island

Brown University *B, M, D*

Texas

Rice University *B*

Utah

Brigham Young University *B, M*

Virginia

Sweet Briar College *B*
University of Richmond *B*

Washington

University of Washington *B, M*

Wisconsin

University of Wisconsin
  Milwaukee *C*
  Parkside *B*

German teacher education

Alabama

Auburn University *B, T*
Birmingham-Southern College *T*

California

California State University
  Long Beach *T*
Humboldt State University *T*
San Francisco State University *T*
Stanford University *M, T*

Colorado

Colorado State University *B, T*

Connecticut

Fairfield University *T*
University of Connecticut *T*

Delaware

Delaware State University *B*
University of Delaware *B, T*

District of Columbia

Catholic University of America *B*

Florida

Stetson University *B*

Idaho

Boise State University *B, T*

Illinois

Augustana College *B, T*
Bradley University *B*
DePaul University *M, T*
Elmhurst College *B*
Illinois College *T*
North Park University *T*
University of Illinois
  Chicago *B*
  Urbana-Champaign *B, M, T*

Indiana

Indiana University
  Bloomington *B, T*
  Purdue University Fort Wayne *B, T*
  Purdue University
    Indianapolis *B, T*
  South Bend *B, T*
Purdue University *B, M, D*

University of Evansville *B, T*
University of Indianapolis *T*
Valparaiso University *B*

Iowa

Central College *T*
Cornell College *B, T*
Iowa State University *T*
St. Ambrose University *B, T*
Simpson College *T*
University of Iowa *T*
Wartburg College *T*

Kansas

Bethel College *T*
Washburn University *B, T*

Louisiana

Centenary College of Louisiana *T*
University of Louisiana at Lafayette *B*

Maryland

Mount St. Mary's University *T*

Massachusetts

Tufts University *T*

Michigan

Adrian College *B, T*
Alma College *T*
Calvin College *B*
Central Michigan University *B*
Eastern Michigan University *B*
Grand Valley State University *T*
Hope College *B, T*
Michigan State University *B*
Western Michigan University *B*

Minnesota

Augsburg College *T*
College of St. Benedict *T*
Concordia College: Moorhead *B, T*
Gustavus Adolphus College *T*
Hamline University *T*
Minnesota State University
    Mankato *B, M, T*
Saint Cloud State University *B, T*
St. John's University *T*
University of Minnesota
    Duluth *B*
    Morris *T*
    Twin Cities *M*
University of St. Thomas *B*

Missouri

Missouri Southern State
    University *B, T*
Missouri State University *B*
University of Central Missouri *B*
University of Missouri
    Columbia *M*
    Kansas City *B*
Washington University in St.
    Louis *B, M, T*

Montana

University of Montana *T*

Nebraska

Creighton University *T*
Hastings College *T*
Midland University *B, T*
Nebraska Wesleyan University *T*
University of Nebraska
    Kearney *B, T*
    Lincoln *B, T*

New Hampshire

University of New Hampshire *T*

New Jersey

County College of Morris *A*

New York

City University of New York
    Hunter College *B, T*
Dutchess Community College *A*
Fordham University *M, T*
Hofstra University *B, M*
Ithaca College *B, T*
New York University *B, M*
SUNY
    College at Oswego *B*
    University at Buffalo *M, T*
    University at Stony Brook *T*
St. Lawrence University *T*
University of Rochester *M*
Vassar College *T*
Wells College *T*

North Carolina

East Carolina University *B*
University of North Carolina
    Wilmington *B*
Wake Forest University *T*
Western Carolina University *B, T*

North Dakota

Minot State University *B*

Ohio

Baldwin Wallace University *T*
Bowling Green State University *M, T*
Hiram College *T*
Miami University
    Oxford *B, T*
Ohio Northern University *B, T*
Ohio University *B, T*
Ohio Wesleyan University *B*
University of Dayton *B*
University of Mount Union *T*
University of Toledo *B, M, T*

Oklahoma

Oklahoma Baptist University *B, T*
University of Central Oklahoma *B*
University of Tulsa *T*

Oregon

Linfield College *T*
Portland State University *T*
Western Oregon University *T*

Pennsylvania

Gettysburg College *T*
Juniata College *B, T*
La Salle University *B, T*
Lebanon Valley College *T*
Lycoming College *T*
Mansfield University of
    Pennsylvania *B, T*
Messiah College *B, T*
Moravian College *T*
Susquehanna University *T*
University of Scranton *B*
Villanova University *T*
Washington & Jefferson College *T*
Westminster College *T*

South Carolina

Furman University *T*

South Dakota

Augustana College *B, T*
University of South Dakota *B, M, T*

Tennessee

Belmont University *T*
Lipscomb University *B, T*
Tennessee Technological University *T*

Texas

University of Dallas *T*
University of Texas
    Arlington *T*
    San Antonio *T*

Utah

Brigham Young University *B*
Southern Utah University *B*
Utah State University *B*
Weber State University *B*

Virginia

Hollins University *T*
Longwood University *T*

Washington

Central Washington University *B, T*
Washington State University *B, M, T*
Western Washington University *B*
Whitworth University *T*

West Virginia

Bethany College *B*

Wisconsin

Carthage College *T*
Lawrence University *T*
St. Norbert College *T*
University of Wisconsin
    Green Bay *T*
    Platteville *B, T*
    River Falls *T*
    Whitewater *B*

Germanic languages

California

University of California
    Los Angeles *M, D*

Colorado

University of Colorado
    Boulder *B, M, D*

Illinois

University of Chicago *B, D*

Indiana

Indiana University
    Bloomington *B, M, D*

Kansas

University of Kansas *B, M, D*

Kentucky

Northern Kentucky University *B*

Michigan

Eastern Michigan University *B*
Lansing Community College *A*

Missouri

Washington University in St.
    Louis *B, M, D*

New York

Canisius College *B*
Columbia University *B*

North Carolina

Guilford College *B*

Ohio

Ohio Northern University *B*

Oklahoma

University of Oklahoma *B, M*

Texas

University of Texas
    Austin *M, D*

Utah

Brigham Young University *B*

Vermont

Bennington College *B*

Washington

University of Washington *B*

Wisconsin

University of Wisconsin
    Eau Claire *B*
    Madison *B, M, D*
    Milwaukee *B*

Gerontology

Alabama

Spring Hill College *C*

Arkansas

Arkansas State University *M*

California

American River College *A*
California State University
    Fullerton *M*
    Long Beach *M*
    Sacramento *B, M*
Chaffey College *A*
Cosumnes River College *A*
Folsom Lake College *A*
Loma Linda University *M*
MiraCosta College *A*
Mount St. Mary's College *B*
National University *M*
San Diego State University *B, M*
San Francisco State University *M*
University of La Verne *M*
University of Southern
    California *B, M, D*

Colorado

Aims Community College *C*

Connecticut

Naugatuck Valley Community
    College *C*
Norwalk Community College *C*
Quinnipiac University *B*
University of Saint Joseph *C, M*

Delaware

Wilmington University *M*

Florida

Bethune-Cookman University *B*
Nova Southeastern University *B*
University of South Florida *B, M, D*

Georgia

Georgia State University *M*

Illinois

Concordia University Chicago *M*
Eastern Illinois University *M*
McKendree University *B*
Northeastern Illinois University *M*

Indiana

Indiana University
    Purdue University Indianapolis *C*
Manchester University *A*
Martin University *B*
University of Indianapolis *B, M*
Valparaiso University *M*

Iowa

Ashford University *B*
University of Northern Iowa *B*

Kansas

Kansas State University *M*
University of Kansas *M, D*
Wichita State University *M*

Kentucky

Thomas More College *A*
University of Kentucky *D*

Louisiana

University of Louisiana at
Monroe *M, T*

Maryland

Anne Arundel Community College *A*
McDaniel College *M*
Sojourner-Douglass College *B*
Towson University *B, M*
University of Maryland
Baltimore *M, D*
Baltimore County *B, M, D*
University College *B*

Massachusetts

Bristol Community College *C*
University of Massachusetts
Boston *C, B, M, D*

Michigan

Central Michigan University *M*
Madonna University *C, A, B*
Siena Heights University *A*
Wayne State University *D*

Minnesota

Bethel University *M*
Capella University *M*
College of St. Scholastica *C*
Minnesota State University
Mankato *B, M*
Moorhead *B*
Saint Cloud State University *B, M*

Missouri

Lindenwood University *B, M*
Missouri State University *B*
University of Central Missouri *M*
University of Missouri
St. Louis *M*
Webster University *M*

Nebraska

Concordia University *B, M*
University of Nebraska
Omaha *B, M*

New Hampshire

Lakes Region Community
College *C, A*

New Jersey

College of St. Elizabeth *C*

New York

Alfred University *B*
City University of New York
Hostos Community College *A*
York College *B*
College of New Rochelle *M*
Dowling College *B*
Excelsior College *B*
Hofstra University *M*
Ithaca College *B*
Niagara University *B*
SUNY
College at Oneonta *B*
St. Joseph's College New York:
Suffolk Campus *C*
St. Joseph's College, New York *C*
St. Thomas Aquinas College *B*
Touro College *M*

North Carolina

Appalachian State University *M*
Barton College *B*

University of North Carolina
Charlotte *M*
Greensboro *M*
Winston-Salem State University *B*

North Dakota

North Dakota State University *D*

Ohio

Ashland University *C*
Bowling Green State University *B, M*
Case Western Reserve University *B*
College of Mount St. Joseph *C*
Miami University
Oxford *B, M*
Ohio Dominican University *C, A*
University of Akron *C*
University of Akron: Wayne
College *C*
Youngstown State University *B*

Oklahoma

University of Central Oklahoma *M*
University of Oklahoma *M*

Oregon

Clackamas Community College *C*
Marylhurst University *C*
Portland Community College *A*

Pennsylvania

California University of
Pennsylvania *B*
Cedar Crest College *C*
Gwynedd Mercy University *B*
Marywood University *M*
Widener University *M*

Puerto Rico

Inter American University of Puerto
Rico
Aguadilla Campus *C*
San German Campus *C*
Pontifical Catholic University of
Puerto Rico *B*
University of Puerto Rico
Medical Sciences *M*

Rhode Island

Rhode Island College *C*

Texas

McLennan Community College *A*
University of North Texas *B, M, D*
University of Texas
Health Science Center at
Houston *M*

Utah

University of Utah *M*
Utah State University *C*
Weber State University *B*

Virginia

New River Community College *A*
Northern Virginia Community
College *A*

West Virginia

Kanawha Valley Community and
Technical College *A*

Wisconsin

Northcentral Technical College *C*
University of Wisconsin
Milwaukee *C, B*

Geropsychology

Ohio

University of Akron *D*

Oregon

Western Oregon University *B*

Glazier

Indiana

Ivy Tech Community College
Central Indiana *C, A*

Global studies

Alabama

Samford University *B*
University of Alabama
Birmingham *B*

Alaska

University of Alaska
Anchorage *B*

Arizona

Arizona State University *B, M, D*
Paradise Valley Community College *C*
Phoenix College *C*
University of Arizona *B*

Arkansas

Arkansas Tech University *B*
Harding University *B*
John Brown University *B*
University of Central Arkansas *B*

California

California Baptist University *B*
California Maritime Academy *B*
Chapman University *M*
Concordia University Irvine *B, M*
Dominican University of California *B*
Humboldt State University *B*
La Sierra University *B*
National University *M*
Pepperdine University *B*
Pitzer College *B*
Point Loma Nazarene University *B*
Scripps College *B*
Skyline College *A*
Sonoma State University *B, M*
Stanford University *B*
University of California
Berkeley *M*
Irvine *B*
Los Angeles *B*
Riverside *B*
Santa Barbara *B, M*
University of San Francisco *M*
University of Southern California *B*
University of the Pacific *B*
Whittier College *B*

Colorado

Colorado Christian University *B*
Colorado State University *B*
University of Colorado
Boulder *B*
Denver *B*
University of Denver *B*
University of Northern Colorado *B*

Connecticut

Central Connecticut State
University *B, M*
Mitchell College *B*
University of New Haven *B*
University of Saint Joseph *B*

Delaware

Wesley College *B*

District of Columbia

American University *B, M*
Gallaudet University *B*

Georgetown University *M*
University of the Potomac *C*

Florida

Barry University *B*
Eckerd College *B*
Florida International University *M*
New College of Florida *B*
Schiller International University *B, M*
University of Central Florida *B*
University of Florida *B*
University of North Florida *B*

Georgia

Georgia Institute of Technology *B*
Georgia Southern University *C*
Mercer University *B*
Shorter University *B*
Spelman College *B*

Illinois

Benedictine University *B*
Greenville College *B*
Illinois College *B*
Knox College *B*
McKendree University *B*
Millikin University *B*
Monmouth College *B*
North Central College *B*
North Park University *B*
Northeastern Illinois University *B*
Northwestern University *D*
Principia College *B*
Southern Illinois University
Carbondale *B*
University of Illinois
Springfield *B*
Urbana-Champaign *B*

Indiana

Earlham College *B*
Hanover College *B*
Indiana Wesleyan University *B*
Manchester University *B*
Valparaiso University *B, M*

Iowa

Central College *B*
Graceland University *B*
Luther College *B*
Morningside College *B*
University of Iowa *B*

Kansas

Baker University *B*
University of Kansas *B, M*
Wichita State University *B*

Kentucky

Thomas More College *A, B*
University of Kentucky *C, B*

Louisiana

Louisiana State University and
Agricultural and Mechanical
College *B*
University of New Orleans *B*

Maine

Colby College *B*
College of the Atlantic *B, M*
University of Maine *M*
University of Maine
Farmington *B*
University of Southern Maine *B*

Maryland

Howard Community College *A*
Salisbury University *B*

Massachusetts

Assumption College *B*
Bard College at Simon's Rock *B*

Bentley University *B*
Brandeis University *B, M*
Cape Cod Community College *A*
Clark University *B*
Emmanuel College *B*
Endicott College *B*
Hampshire College *B*
Lesley University *B*
University of Massachusetts
   Lowell *D*
Western New England University *B*
Worcester Polytechnic Institute *B*

Michigan
Adrian College *B*
Albion College *B*
Aquinas College *B*
Hope College *B*
Michigan State University *B, M*
Oakland Community College *A*
Saginaw Valley State University *B*
Spring Arbor University *B*
University of Michigan *B*
Western Michigan University *B*

Minnesota
Bemidji State University *B*
Century College *C*
College of St. Scholastica *B*
Concordia College: Moorhead *B*
Crown College *M*
Hamline University *B*
Macalester College *B*
Minneapolis Community and
   Technical College *C*
Minnesota State University
   Moorhead *B*
Saint Cloud State University *B*
St. Mary's University of Minnesota *B*
University of Minnesota
   Duluth *B*
University of Northwestern - St.
   Paul *C, B*
University of St. Thomas *M*
Winona State University *B*

Mississippi
Belhaven University *B*
Mississippi College *B*

Missouri
Maryville University of Saint Louis *B*
Missouri State University *B, M*
Rockhurst University *B*
Southeast Missouri State University *B*
Washington University in St. Louis *B*
Webster University *C, B*

Nebraska
Doane College *B*
Nebraska Wesleyan University *B*
University of Nebraska
   Lincoln *B*
   Omaha *B*

Nevada
Sierra Nevada College *B*

New Jersey
Burlington County College *A*
College of St. Elizabeth *B*
Ramapo College of New Jersey *B*

New York
Adelphi University *B*
Bard College *B*
City University of New York
   City College *B, M*
College of New Rochelle *B*
D'Youville College *B*
Hofstra University *B*
Le Moyne College *B*
Manhattanville College *B*
Nazareth College *B*

Orange County Community
   College *A*
Rochester Institute of Technology *B*
SUNY
   College at Fredonia *B*
   College at Oswego *B*
   University at Albany *B*
Saint Bonaventure University *B*
St. Lawrence University *B*
Tompkins Cortland Community
   College *A*
Wells College *B*

North Carolina
Appalachian State University *B*
Meredith College *B*
North Carolina State University *B*
Roanoke-Chowan Community
   College *A*
University of North Carolina
   Chapel Hill *M*
   Charlotte *B*
Wake Technical Community
   College *A*
Warren Wilson College *B*

North Dakota
North Dakota State University *B*
University of North Dakota *B*

Ohio
Baldwin Wallace University *B*
Case Western Reserve University *B*
Cedarville University *B*
Lorain County Community College *A*
Ohio Northern University *B*
Ohio State University
   Columbus Campus *B*
University of Dayton *B*
Xavier University *B*

Oklahoma
Oklahoma State University *M*
University of Oklahoma *B, M*
University of Tulsa *B*

Oregon
George Fox University *B*
Oregon State University *B*
University of Oregon *B, M*
Willamette University *B*

Pennsylvania
Arcadia University *B*
Carnegie Mellon University *B*
Cedar Crest College *B*
Chestnut Hill College *C, B*
Gannon University *B*
Gettysburg College *B*
Juniata College *B*
Lebanon Valley College *B*
Lehigh University *B*
Mercyhurst University *B, M*
Penn State
   Abington *C*
   Altoona *C*
   Beaver *C*
   Berks *C*
   Brandywine *C*
   DuBois *C*
   Erie, The Behrend College *C*
   Fayette, The Eberly Campus *C*
   Greater Allegheny *C*
   Harrisburg *C*
   Hazleton *C*
   Lehigh Valley *C*
   Mont Alto *C*
   New Kensington *C*
   Schuylkill *C*
   Shenango *C*
   University Park *M*
   Wilkes-Barre *C*
   Worthington Scranton *C*
   York *C*

Point Park University *B*
Shippensburg University of
   Pennsylvania *B*
Susquehanna University *B*
University of Pennsylvania *B, M*
Villanova University *B*
Washington & Jefferson College *B*

Rhode Island
Bryant University *B*
Providence College *B*
Roger Williams University *B*
Salve Regina University *B*

South Carolina
College of Charleston *B*
Newberry College *B*
Presbyterian College *B*

South Dakota
Augustana College *B*
South Dakota State University *B*
University of South Dakota *B*

Tennessee
Sewanee: The University of the
   South *B*
Tennessee Wesleyan College *B*

Texas
Abilene Christian University *B*
Dallas Baptist University *M*
East Texas Baptist University *B*
Lubbock Christian University *B*
Midwestern State University *B*
St. Edward's University *B*
St. Philip's College *A*
San Antonio College *A*
Texas A&M University *B*
Texas State University *B, M*
Texas Tech University *B*
University of North Texas *B*
University of Texas
   Arlington *B*
   Austin *C, B*

Utah
Salt Lake Community College *A*
University of Utah *B, M*

Vermont
Bennington College *B*
Lyndon State College *B*
Marlboro College *B*
University of Vermont *B*

Virginia
George Mason University *M*
Randolph College *B*
Randolph-Macon College *B*
University of the Potomac *C*
Virginia Military Institute *B*
Virginia Wesleyan College *B*

Washington
Evergreen State College *B*
Pacific Lutheran University *B*
Seattle University *B*
University of Washington Bothell *B*

West Virginia
American Public University
   System *C, B, M*
Bethany College *B*
Concord University *B*
Wheeling Jesuit University *B*

Wisconsin
Carroll University *B*
Lawrence University *B*
Mount Mary University *B*
Ripon College *B*

University of Wisconsin
   Madison *B*
   Milwaukee *B*
   Platteville *B*
   River Falls *B*
   Whitewater *B*

Wyoming
Central Wyoming College *A*
University of Wyoming *B, M*

Golf management

Alabama
Virginia College
   Birmingham *B*

California
College of the Desert *C, A*

Florida
Florida Gateway College *C, A*
Golf Academy of America
   Orlando *A*

Indiana
Trine University *B*

Kansas
Cowley County Community
   College *A*

Maryland
Harford Community College *A*
University of Maryland
   Eastern Shore *B*

Minnesota
Anoka Technical College *C, A*
Century College *C*
Minnesota State Community and
   Technical College *C*
Rochester Community and Technical
   College *C*

New York
St. Thomas Aquinas College *B*

North Carolina
Methodist University *B, M*

Ohio
Owens Community College
   Toledo *A*

South Carolina
Golf Academy of America
   Myrtle Beach *A*
Horry-Georgetown Technical
   College *A*

Wisconsin
Lakeshore Technical College *A*
University of Wisconsin
   Stout *B*

Graphic communications

Arizona
Chandler-Gilbert Community
   College *C*

California
Allan Hancock College *A*
Art Center College of Design *B, M*
California Polytechnic State
   University: San Luis Obispo *B*
Cerritos College *A*
College of San Mateo *C, A*
College of the Siskiyous *C*
Ex'pression College *B*

Folsom Lake College *C*
Los Medanos College *C, A*
Moorpark College *C, A*
Platt College
   Ontario *C, A, B*
Santa Rosa Junior College *C*
Santiago Canyon College *A*
Westwood College
   South Bay *B*

Colorado

Aims Community College *C, A*
Colorado Mountain College *A*
Westwood College
   Denver South *A, B*

Connecticut

Mitchell College *A, B*
Northwestern Connecticut
   Community College *A*
Three Rivers Community College *C*

Florida

Miami Dade College *A*

Georgia

Art Institute of Atlanta *A, B*

Illinois

City Colleges of Chicago
   Kennedy-King College *C*
DePaul University *M*
Heartland Community College *C*
Illinois Institute of Art
   Schaumburg *C, A, B*
Illinois State University *B*
Prairie State College *A*
School of the Art Institute of
   Chicago *B, M*

Iowa

Briar Cliff University *B*
Clinton Community College *C, A*
Dordt College *B*
Grand View University *B*
Hawkeye Community College *A*
Kirkwood Community College *A*
Southeastern Community College *A*
University of Northern Iowa *B*

Kentucky

Murray State University *B*
Somerset Community College *C, A*
Sullivan College of Technology and
   Design *A, B*

Maryland

Anne Arundel Community
   College *C, A*
Montgomery College *C, A*
University of Maryland
   University College *B*

Massachusetts

Newbury College *A*

Michigan

Baker College
   Muskegon *A*
   Owosso *A, B*
Ferris State University *A*
Gogebic Community College *A*
International Academy of Design and
   Technology
   Detroit *B*

Minnesota

Art Institutes International
   Minnesota *A, B*
Brown College
   Mendota Heights *A, B*
Hennepin Technical College *C, A*
South Central College *C, A*

Mississippi

Meridian Community College *A*

Missouri

Ozarks Technical Community
   College *C, A*

Nevada

Western Nevada College *C, A*

New Hampshire

Manchester Community College *C, A*

New York

Rochester Institute of
   Technology *A, B, M*

North Carolina

Central Piedmont Community
   College *A*
Chowan University *B*

North Dakota

University of North Dakota *B*

Ohio

Notre Dame College *B*
University of Cincinnati
   Blue Ash College *C, A*

Oklahoma

Oklahoma City Community
   College *A*

Oregon

Linn-Benton Community College *C*

Pennsylvania

Philadelphia University *B*

Puerto Rico

Columbia Centro Universitario:
   Yauco *C*

Rhode Island

New England Institute of
   Technology *A*
Roger Williams University *B*

South Dakota

Mount Marty College *B*

Texas

North Lake College *C, A*

Virginia

Art Institute of Washington *A, B*
Bluefield College *B*
Westwood College
   Arlington Ballston *B*

Washington

Centralia College *A*
Clark College *A*
Eastern Washington University *B*
Seattle Central Community
   College *C, A*

West Virginia

Bethany College *B*

Wisconsin

Carroll University *B*
Carthage College *B*
Fox Valley Technical College *A*
Milwaukee Area Technical College *A*
Nicolet Area Technical College *A*
Waukesha County Technical
   College *A*

Wyoming

Northwest College *C*

Graphic design

Alabama

Herzing University
   Birmingham *B*
ITT Technical Institute
   Birmingham *A*
Samford University *B*
Spring Hill College *B*

Arizona

Arizona State University *B*
Art Institute of Phoenix *A, B*
Art Institute of Tucson *A, B*
Brown Mackie College
   Tucson *A*
Eastern Arizona College *C*
Glendale Community College *C, A*
Mesa Community College *C*
Phoenix College *C, A*
Sessions College for Professional
   Design *C, A*
Southwest University of Visual Arts *B*

Arkansas

Arkansas State University
   Mountain Home *C*
Harding University *B*
John Brown University *B*
National Park Community College *C*
Ouachita Baptist University *B*
University of Arkansas
   Fort Smith *B*

California

Academy of Art University *C, A, B, M*
Art Center College of Design *B*
Art Institute of California
   Hollywood *A, B*
   Inland Empire *A, B*
   Los Angeles *A, B*
   Orange County *A, B*
   Sacramento *A, B*
   San Diego *A, B*
   San Francisco *A, B*
   Silicon Valley *A, B*
Bakersfield College *C, A*
Brooks Institute *B*
California College of the Arts *B*
California State Polytechnic
   University: Pomona *B*
California State University
   Dominguez Hills *B*
   Fresno *B*
Chaffey College *C, A*
Chapman University *B*
City College of San Francisco *A*
College of San Mateo *C, A*
College of the Canyons *C, A*
College of the Desert *A*
College of the Siskiyous *C*
Concordia University Irvine *B*
Dominican University of California *B*
East Los Angeles College *C, A*
Ex'pression College *B*
Fashion Institute of Design and
   Merchandising
   Los Angeles *A*
   San Diego *A*
   San Francisco *A*
Hartnell College *C*
ITT Technical Institute
   Lathrop *A*
   National City *A*
   Oxnard *A*
   Rancho Cordova *A*
   San Bernardino *A*
   Sylmar *A*
   Torrance *A*
Institute of Technology: Clovis *C*
La Sierra University *B*
Monterey Peninsula College *C, A*
Mount St. Mary's College *A*
Mt. Sierra College *B*

Notre Dame de Namur University *B*
Ohlone College *C, A*
Otis College of Art and Design *B, M*
Pacific Union College *A, B*
Palomar College *C, A*
Platt College
   Ontario *A*
Point Loma Nazarene University *B*
San Diego State University *B*
San Joaquin Delta College *C, A*
San Jose State University *B*
Santa Barbara City College *C*
Santa Monica College *C, A*
Southwestern College *A*
University of the Pacific *B*
Westwood College
   Inland Empire *A*
   Los Angeles *A*
   South Bay *A*
Woodbury University *B*

Colorado

Aims Community College *C*
Arapahoe Community College *C, A*
Colorado Mesa University *B*
Colorado Mountain College *A*
Colorado State University *B*
Community College of Denver *C, A*
Rocky Mountain College of Art &
   Design *B*
University of Denver *B, M*
Westwood College
   Denver North *A, B*
   Denver South *A, B*

Connecticut

Gateway Community College *A*
Mitchell College *A, B*
Northwestern Connecticut
   Community College *C*
Norwalk Community College *A*
Paier College of Art *C, B*
Quinebaug Valley Community
   College *A*
Sacred Heart University *B*
University of Bridgeport *B*

Delaware

Delaware College of Art and
   Design *C, A*

District of Columbia

American University *B*
Corcoran College of Art and
   Design *C, A, B*

Florida

Art Institute of Fort Lauderdale *A, B*
College of Business and Technology
   Kendall *A*
Daytona State College *A*
Digital Media Arts College *B, M*
Florida Agricultural and Mechanical
   University *B*
Florida Gateway College *C, A*
Florida Southern College *B*
International Academy of Design and
   Technology: Tampa *A, B*
Jose Maria Vargas University *B*
Miami International University of Art
   and Design *A, B, M*
Palm Beach Atlantic University *B*
Pensacola State College *B*
Ringling College of Art and Design *B*
South Florida State College *A*
State College of Florida, Manatee-
   Sarasota *A*
University of Florida *B*
University of Miami *B*
University of South Florida *B*
University of Tampa *B*

Georgia

Art Institute of Atlanta *A, B*
Brenau University *B*
Darton College *C*
Georgia Southern University *B*
Savannah College of Art and
   Design *C, B, M*

Idaho

Northwest Nazarene University *B*
Stevens-Henager College
   Boise *A, B*

Illinois

Augustana College *B*
Benedictine University *B*
Bradley University *B*
Columbia College Chicago *B*
Elgin Community College *A*
Highland Community College *C, A*
Illinois Valley Community
   College *C, A*
John Wood Community College *A*
Judson University *B*
Lincoln Land Community College *A*
Moraine Valley Community College *A*
North Central College *B*
Prairie State College *C*
Quincy University *B*
Robert Morris University: Chicago *B*
School of the Art Institute of
   Chicago *B, M*
Trinity Christian College *B*
University of Illinois
   Chicago *B, M*
   Urbana-Champaign *B, M*
Waubonsee Community College *C, A*

Indiana

Bethel College *B*
Grace College *B*
Huntington University *B*
ITT Technical Institute
   Fort Wayne *A*
Indiana University
   Purdue University Fort Wayne *B*
International Business College *C, A*
International Business College:
   Indianapolis *C, A*
Oakland City University *B*
St. Mary-of-the-Woods College *B*

Iowa

Briar Cliff University *B*
Grand View University *B*
Iowa State University *B, M*
Morningside College *B*
Mount Mercy University *B*
St. Ambrose University *B*
Simpson College *B*

Kansas

Barton County Community College *A*
Bethany College *B*
Cloud County Community
   College *C, A*
Colby Community College *A*
Johnson County Community
   College *A*
Kansas Wesleyan University *B*
Pittsburg State University *B*
University of Kansas *B*
Wichita State University *B*

Kentucky

Brescia University *B*
Gateway Community and Technical
   College *C, A*
Sullivan College of Technology and
   Design *A, B*

Louisiana

Bossier Parish Community College *C*
Delgado Community College *A*

Herzing University
   Kenner *B*
Louisiana State University
   Shreveport *B*

Maine

College of the Atlantic *B, M*
Maine College of Art *B*

Maryland

Anne Arundel Community
   College *C, A*
Cecil College *C*
Harford Community College *A*
Howard Community College *A*
Maryland Institute College of
   Art *B, M*

Massachusetts

Anna Maria College *B*
Assumption College *B*
Becker College *B*
Boston University *B, M*
Bristol Community College *A*
Cape Cod Community College *A*
Curry College *B*
Emmanuel College *B*
Endicott College *B*
Fitchburg State University *B*
Lasell College *B*
Massachusetts College of Art and
   Design *C, B*
Massasoit Community College *A*
Montserrat College of Art *B*
Mount Ida College *B*
New England Institute of Art *B*
Newbury College *B*
North Shore Community
   College *C, A*
Northeastern University *B*
Stonehill College *B*
Suffolk University *M*

Michigan

Andrews University *B*
Art Institute of Michigan *A, B*
Baker College
   Muskegon *A*
   Port Huron *A*
Calvin College *B*
Central Michigan University *B*
College for Creative Studies *B*
Delta College *A*
Ferris State University *A, B*
Finlandia University *B*
International Academy of Design and
   Technology
   Detroit *A, B*
Jackson College *C, A*
Kirtland Community College *C, A*
Lake Michigan College *C, A*
Lansing Community College *C, A*
Lawrence Technological
   University *C, B*
Madonna University *A, B*
Mid Michigan Community College *A*
Mott Community College *C, A*
Northern Michigan University *B*
Oakland Community College *A*
Oakland University *B, T*
Saginaw Valley State University *B*
Southwestern Michigan College *A*
Spring Arbor University *B*
University of Michigan *B*
Western Michigan University *B*

Minnesota

Art Institutes International
   Minnesota *A, B*
Concordia University St. Paul *B*
Dakota County Technical
   College *C, A*
Dunwoody College of Technology *A*

Globe University
   Woodbury *A*
Herzing University
   Minneapolis *B*
ITT Technical Institute
   Eden Prairie *A*
Minneapolis College of Art and
   Design *B*
Minnesota School of Business
   Richfield *C, A*
   St. Cloud *C, A*
Minnesota State Community and
   Technical College *C, A*
Minnesota State University
   Moorhead *B*
North Hennepin Community
   College *A*
Rochester Community and Technical
   College *C, A*
St. Mary's University of Minnesota *B*
South Central College *C, A*
University of Minnesota
   Duluth *B*
   Twin Cities *B*
University of Northwestern - St.
   Paul *B*

Mississippi

Hinds Community College *C, A*
Mississippi College *B, M*

Missouri

Columbia College *B*
Culver-Stockton College *B*
Kansas City Art Institute *B*
Maryville University of Saint Louis *B*
Metropolitan Community College -
   Kansas City *C, A*
Missouri Western State University *B*
Park University *B*
Stephens College *B*
Washington University in St. Louis *B*
William Woods University *B*

Montana

Flathead Valley Community
   College *C, A*
Montana State University
   Great Falls College *A*
   Northern *A, B*

Nebraska

Bellevue University *B*
Concordia University *B*
Creative Center *A, B*
Creighton University *B*
Doane College *B*
Herzing University
   Omaha School of Massage Therapy
   and Healthcare *B*
Mid-Plains Community College *A*
Peru State College *B*
Union College *B*
University of Nebraska
   Omaha *B*
Vatterott College
   Spring Valley *A*
Wayne State College *B*

Nevada

Art Institute of Las Vegas *B*
International Academy of Design and
   Technology
   Henderson *A, B*

New Hampshire

Colby-Sawyer College *B*
Franklin Pierce University *B*
Mount Washington College *C, A*
New Hampshire Institute of Art *B*
Plymouth State University *B*
Southern New Hampshire
   University *B*

New Jersey

Berkeley College *B*
Brookdale Community College *A*
Burlington County College *A*
Caldwell College *B*
Cumberland County College *A*
Monmouth University *B*
Montclair State University *B*
Rider University *B*

New Mexico

Eastern New Mexico University:
   Roswell *C, A*
ITT Technical Institute
   Albuquerque *A*
New Mexico State University
   Alamogordo *C, A*
Santa Fe University of Art and
   Design *B*
Southwest University of Visual Arts *B*

New York

Art Institute of New York City *A*
Bryant & Stratton College
   Henrietta *A*
   Syracuse North *A*
City University of New York
   City College *B*
   Queens College *B*
Cooper Union for the Advancement
   of Science and Art *C, B*
Daemen College *B*
Dowling College *B*
Fashion Institute of Technology *B*
Marymount Manhattan College *B*
Nassau Community College *C, A*
Nazareth College *B*
Parsons The New School for
   Design *A*
Pratt Institute *A*
Rochester Institute of
   Technology *B, M*
SUNY
   College at New Paltz *B*
   College at Purchase *B*
   College of Agriculture and
      Technology at Cobleskill *A, B*
   College of Technology at Canton *B*
Sage Colleges *B*
St. John's University *B*
St. Thomas Aquinas College *B*
Syracuse University *M*
Villa Maria College of Buffalo *A, B*
Wood Tobe-Coburn School *A*

North Carolina

Appalachian State University *B*
Central Piedmont Community
   College *A*
Chowan University *B*
East Carolina University *B*
Elizabeth City State University *B*
Forsyth Technical Community
   College *A*
High Point University *B*
King's College *C, A*
Lenoir Community College *C, A*
Lenoir-Rhyne University *B*
Meredith College *B*
Methodist University *B*
North Carolina Agricultural and
   Technical State University *B*
North Carolina State University *B, M*
Stanly Community College *C, A*

North Dakota

University of North Dakota *B*

Ohio

Art Academy of Cincinnati *A*
Art Institute of Ohio: Cincinnati *A, B*
Ashland University *B*
Bradford School *C, A*
Cedarville University *B*

Cleveland Institute of Art *B*
College of Mount St. Joseph *A, B*
Davis College *C, A*
Defiance College *B*
Herzing University
  Toledo *A*
Mount Vernon Nazarene University *B*
Notre Dame College *B*
Ohio Dominican University *B*
Ohio University *B, M*
University of Akron *B*
University of Cincinnati
  Blue Ash College *C, A*
University of Dayton *B*
University of Rio Grande *B*
Ursuline College *B*
Wright State University: Lake
  Campus *A*
Xavier University *B*

Oklahoma

East Central University *B*
Oklahoma Christian University *B*
Oklahoma State University
  Institute of Technology:
    Okmulgee *A*
Oral Roberts University *B*
Southeastern Oklahoma State
  University *B*
Southern Nazarene University *B*
University of Central Oklahoma *B*

Oregon

Art Institute of Portland *A, B*
Chemeketa Community College *A*
ITT Technical Institute
  Portland *A*
Mt. Hood Community College *C, A*
Pacific Northwest College of Art *B*

Pennsylvania

Antonelli Institute of Art and
  Photography *A*
Arcadia University *B*
Art Institute of Philadelphia *A, B*
Art Institute of Pittsburgh *A, B*
Art Institute of York *A, B*
Bradford School: Pittsburgh *C, A*
Cabrini College *B*
California University of
  Pennsylvania *B*
Carnegie Mellon University *M*
Douglas Education Center *A*
Drexel University *B*
East Stroudsburg University of
  Pennsylvania *B*
Harrisburg Area Community
  College *C, A*
Holy Family University *B*
Immaculata University *C*
Lehigh Carbon Community College *A*
Luzerne County Community
  College *C, A*
Mansfield University of
  Pennsylvania *B*
Marywood University *B, M*
Mercyhurst University *B*
Montgomery County Community
  College *A*
Moore College of Art and Design *B*
Moravian College *B*
Northampton Community College *A*
Penn State
  Abington *B*
  Altoona *B*
  Beaver *B*
  Berks *B*
  Brandywine *B*
  DuBois *B*
  Erie, The Behrend College *B*
  Fayette, The Eberly Campus *B*
  Greater Allegheny *B*
  Harrisburg *B*
  Hazleton *B*

Lehigh Valley *B*
Mont Alto *B*
New Kensington *B*
Schuylkill *B*
Shenango *B*
University Park *B*
Wilkes-Barre *B*
Worthington Scranton *B*
York *B*
Pennsylvania College of Art and
  Design *B*
Philadelphia University *B*
St. Vincent College *B*
Shippensburg University of
  Pennsylvania *B*
South Hills School of Business &
  Technology *A*
Susquehanna University *B*
Temple University *B, M*
University of the Arts *B*
Westmoreland County Community
  College *C*

Puerto Rico

Atlantic University College *M*
Columbia Centro Universitario:
  Caguas *C*
Turabo University *C, B*
Universidad del Este *C*

Rhode Island

Johnson & Wales University
  Providence *B*
Rhode Island School of Design *B, M*
Roger Williams University *B*
Salve Regina University *B*

South Carolina

Bob Jones University *B*
Charleston Southern University *B*
Coastal Carolina University *B*
Coker College *B*
Limestone College *B*
Trident Technical College *C*
University of South Carolina
  Upstate *B*

South Dakota

South Dakota State University *B*

Tennessee

Memphis College of Art *B*
Nossi College of Art *B*
O'More College of Design *B*
Southern Adventist University *B*
Watkins College of Art, Design &
  Film *B*

Texas

Abilene Christian University *B*
Art Institute of Houston *B*
Brookhaven College *C, A*
Collin County Community College
  District *C, A*
Hardin-Simmons University *B*
ITT Technical Institute
  Arlington *A*
  Houston West *A*
  San Antonio *A*
International Academy of Design and
  Technology
  San Antonio *A*
St. Edward's University *B*
San Antonio College *A*
Schreiner University *B*
Texas A&M University
  Commerce *B*
Texas Christian University *B*
Texas State Technical College
  Waco *A*
University of Houston *B*
University of Texas
  El Paso *B, M*
University of the Incarnate Word *B*

Wayland Baptist University *B*
West Texas A&M University *B*

Utah

Brigham Young University *B*
Broadview University
  Broadview Entertainment Arts
    University *B*
Dixie State College *B*
Southern Utah University *B*
Utah State University *C, A*

Vermont

Burlington College *B*
Champlain College *B*
Community College of Vermont *A*
Lyndon State College *A, B*

Virginia

Art Institute of Washington *A, B*
Bluefield College *B*
Emory & Henry College *B*
George Mason University *M*
Germanna Community College *C*
Liberty University *B*
Marymount University *C, B*
Piedmont Virginia Community
  College *C*
Tidewater Community College *A*
Virginia Commonwealth University *B*
Virginia Intermont College *A*
Westwood College
  Annandale *A*
  Arlington Ballston *A*

Washington

Art Institute of Seattle *A, B*
Centralia College *A*
Cornish College of the Arts *B*
ITT Technical Institute
  Everett *A*
  Spokane *A*
International Academy of Design and
  Technology
  Seattle *B*
Western Washington University *B*

West Virginia

Concord University *B*
West Virginia Wesleyan College *B*

Wisconsin

Art Institute of Wisconsin *A, B*
Bryant & Stratton College
  Milwaukee *A*
Concordia University Wisconsin *B*
Edgewood College *B*
Gateway Technical College *A*
Globe University
  Green Bay *A*
  Madison East *A*
Herzing University
  Brookfield *A, B*
  Kenosha *B*
  Madison *A, B*
Marian University *B*
Milwaukee Area Technical College *A*
Milwaukee Institute of Art &
  Design *B*
Mount Mary University *B*
Nicolet Area Technical College *A*
St. Norbert College *B*
Viterbo University *B*
Waukesha County Technical
  College *A*
Western Technical College *A*
Wisconsin Lutheran College *B*

Wyoming

Casper College *A*
Central Wyoming College *A*
Northwest College *C*

Graphic/printing production

Alabama

Bishop State Community
  College *C, A*
Lawson State Community College *C*

Arkansas

Phillips Community College of the
  University of Arkansas *A*

California

Allan Hancock College *A*
American River College *A*
Antelope Valley College *C, A*
Butte College *A*
City College of San Francisco *A*
Fresno City College *C, A*
Fullerton College *A*
Laney College *C, A*
Long Beach City College *A*
Los Angeles Trade and Technical
  College *C, A*
Mission College *C, A*
Modesto Junior College *C, A*
Moorpark College *A*
Palomar College *C, A*
Rio Hondo College *A*
Riverside City College *C*
Sacramento City College *C, A*
Saddleback College *C*
Santa Barbara City College *C*

Colorado

Colorado Mountain College *A*
Westwood College
  Denver North *A, B*

Connecticut

Gateway Community College *C*

District of Columbia

University of the District of
  Columbia *A, B*

Florida

Florida State College at
  Jacksonville *A*
Indian River State College *A*
Miami Dade College *A*
Palm Beach State College *A*
Tallahassee Community College *C*

Georgia

Albany Technical College *C*
Art Institute of Atlanta *A, B*
Augusta Technical College *C*
Columbus Technical College *C*
Georgia Southern University *B*
West Georgia Technical College *C*
Wiregrass Georgia Technical
  College *C, A*

Hawaii

University of Hawaii
  Honolulu Community College *A*

Idaho

Lewis-Clark State College *A, B*

Illinois

College of DuPage *C, A*
Harper College *C*
Rock Valley College *C, A*
Western Illinois University *B*

Indiana

Vincennes University *A*

Iowa

Clinton Community College *A*
Iowa Western Community College *A*

Kansas
Coffeyville Community College *C*
Fort Scott Community College *C, A*

Kentucky
Eastern Kentucky University *A*

Maine
Central Maine Community
College *C, A*

Maryland
Montgomery College *A*

Massachusetts
Middlesex Community College *C, A*
Northern Essex Community
College *A*
Springfield Technical Community
College *C*

Michigan
Alpena Community College *C, A*
Baker College
Muskegon *A*
Delta College *C, A*
Ferris State University *B*
Macomb Community College *C, A*
Muskegon Community College *A*
Washtenaw Community College *A*

Minnesota
Hennepin Technical College *C, A*
Mesabi Range Community and
Technical College *C, A*

Mississippi
Hinds Community College *C*
Mississippi Delta Community
College *C*
Northwest Mississippi Community
College *C, A*

Missouri
Mineral Area College *C, A*
Moberly Area Community
College *C, A*
Ozarks Technical Community
College *C, A*
St. Louis Community College *A*
University of Central Missouri *B*

Nebraska
Metropolitan Community
College *C, A*

Nevada
College of Southern Nevada *C, A*
Truckee Meadows Community
College *C*

New Hampshire
Lakes Region Community
College *C, A*

New Jersey
Bergen Community College *C*
Cumberland County College *C*

New York
Erie Community College *A*
Fulton-Montgomery Community
College *A*
Rochester Institute of Technology *C*

North Carolina
Alamance Community College *C*
Central Piedmont Community
College *C, A*
Chowan University *A*
McDowell Technical Community
College *A*

Ohio
Columbus State Community
College *C, A*

Oregon
Chemeketa Community College *A*

Pennsylvania
Thaddeus Stevens College of
Technology *A*

Puerto Rico
University of Puerto Rico
Carolina Regional College *B*

South Carolina
Midlands Technical College *C, A*

South Dakota
Northern State University *A*
Southeast Technical Institute *A*

Texas
Central Texas College *C, A*
College of the Mainland *C*
Eastfield College *C, A*
Houston Community College
System *C, A*
Lee College *C, A*
Navarro College *A*
North Lake College *C*
South Plains College *A*
Tarrant County College *A*
Tyler Junior College *C, A*

Utah
Dixie State College *C, A*

Virginia
Dabney S. Lancaster Community
College *C, A*
Danville Community College *A*

Washington
Edmonds Community College *C*
Lake Washington Institute of
Technology *C*
Seattle Central Community
College *C, A*
Shoreline Community College *C, A*
Walla Walla University *A, B*
Yakima Valley Community College *A*

Wisconsin
Fox Valley Technical College *C, A*
Madison Area Technical College *C, A*
Milwaukee Area Technical College *A*
Moraine Park Technical College *C, A*
Northcentral Technical College *C, A*
Northeast Wisconsin Technical
College *C*
Waukesha County Technical
College *C*

Wyoming
Northwest College *C, A*

Greenhouse operations

California
Los Angeles Pierce College *C, A*
Southwestern College *C, A*
Yuba College *C*

Georgia
Albany Technical College *C*

Illinois
College of DuPage *C*
Joliet Junior College *C, A*
Kankakee Community College *C, A*

Kishwaukee College *C, A*
Southwestern Illinois College *A*

Indiana
Purdue University *B*

Minnesota
Century College *C, A*
Rochester Community and Technical
College *C*
University of Minnesota
Crookston *B*

Nebraska
Nebraska College of Technical
Agriculture *A*

North Carolina
Alamance Community College *C*
Pitt Community College *C*

North Dakota
Dakota College at Bottineau *C, A*

Ohio
Ohio State University
Agricultural Technical Institute *A*
Columbus Campus *A*

Pennsylvania
Community College of Allegheny
County *C*

South Dakota
Southeast Technical Institute *A*

Texas
Western Texas College *C, A*

Vermont
Vermont Technical College *A*

Washington
Spokane Community College *A*

Wisconsin
University of Wisconsin
River Falls *B*

Gunsmithing

Alabama
Jefferson Davis Community
College *C*

Arizona
Yavapai College *C, A*

California
Lassen Community College *C, A*

Colorado
Trinidad State Junior College *C, A*

Minnesota
Pine Technical College *C, A*

North Carolina
Lenoir Community College *C, A*
Montgomery Community
College *C, A*
Piedmont Community College *C*

South Carolina
Piedmont Technical College *C*

Hair styling

Alabama
Calhoun Community College *C*

California
San Jose City College *C, A*

Colorado
IBMC College
Fort Collins *C*
Pueblo Community College *C*
Red Rocks Community College *C*
Trinidad State Junior College *C*

North Carolina
Cape Fear Community College *C*

Pennsylvania
Laurel Business Institute *C*

Texas
Weatherford College *C*

Wisconsin
Chippewa Valley Technical College *C*
Gateway Technical College *C*
Mid-State Technical College *C*
Southwest Wisconsin Technical
College *C*
Waukesha County Technical
College *C*
Wisconsin Indianhead Technical
College *C*

Wyoming
Eastern Wyoming College *C*

Hazardous materials information systems

New Jersey
Burlington County College *C*

New Mexico
New Mexico State University
Carlsbad *C*

South Carolina
Spartanburg Community College *C*

Hazardous materials technology

Alabama
Central Alabama Community
College *C*
Faulkner State Community College *A*

Arizona
Cochise College *C*
GateWay Community College *C, A*
Paradise Valley Community
College *C, A*

California
Allan Hancock College *C*
Cabrillo College *C, A*
Hartnell College *C, A*
Oxnard College *C, A*

Connecticut
Three Rivers Community
College *C, A*

Florida
Pensacola State College *A*

Indiana
Vincennes University *C*

Kansas
Barton County Community
College *C, A*
Kansas City Kansas Community
College *A*

Massachusetts

Bristol Community College *C*

Mississippi

Jackson State University *M*

New Mexico

Central New Mexico Community
College *C*
New Mexico Junior College *C, A*

Ohio

Ohio University
Chillicothe Campus *C*
University of Findlay *C, A, B, M*

Washington

Green River Community College *C, A*

West Virginia

American Public University System *C*

Health aide

California

College of Alameda *C, A*

Colorado

Community College of Denver *C, A*

Georgia

Altamaha Technical College *C*

Illinois

McHenry County College *C*
Moraine Valley Community College *C*

Kansas

Barton County Community College *C*
Coffeyville Community College *C*
Garden City Community College *C*
Wichita Area Technical College *C*

Louisiana

Delgado Community College *C*
ITI Technical College *C*

Massachusetts

North Shore Community College *C*

Michigan

Delta College *C*

Minnesota

Minnesota West Community and
Technical College *C*
St. Cloud Technical and Community
College *C*

Ohio

Columbus State Community
College *C*

Pennsylvania

Community College of Beaver
County *A*

Texas

Howard College *C*

Virginia

Southwest Virginia Community
College *C*

West Virginia

Southern West Virginia Community
and Technical College *A*
West Virginia Northern Community
College *C*

Health and wellness, general

Alabama

Oakwood University *B*

California

Loma Linda University *D*
National University *C, B*
Point Loma Nazarene University *B*

District of Columbia

American University *C, B, M*
Trinity Washington University *B*

Georgia

Dalton State College *A*

Illinois

McKendree University *B*

Indiana

Indiana University
Kokomo *B*
Purdue University Indianapolis *C*
University of St. Francis *B*

Iowa

Ashford University *B*

Kentucky

Union College *B*

Maine

University of New England *B*

Massachusetts

Bay State College *A*

Missouri

Missouri Baptist University *B*

Montana

Blackfeet Community College *A*

Nebraska

Union College *B*

New Hampshire

Granite State College *B*
Keene State College *B*

New York

Canisius College *B*
Daemen College *B*
Genesee Community College *C, A*

Ohio

Muskingum University *B*

South Carolina

Furman University *B*

Tennessee

Trevecca Nazarene University *B*

Texas

Baylor University *D*
Howard Payne University *A*
Paul Quinn College *B*
St. Philip's College *A*
Texas A&M University *B*
Texas A&M University
Commerce *B*
University of Houston *B*
University of Texas
Pan American *B*
San Antonio *B*
Tyler *B*

West Virginia

Ohio Valley University *B*

Wisconsin

University of Wisconsin
La Crosse *B*
River Falls *B*
Stevens Point *B*
Superior *B*
Viterbo University *B*

Health care administration

Alabama

Auburn University *B*
Columbia Southern University *B*
Community College of the Air
Force *A*
Herzing University
Birmingham *B*
Oakwood University *B*
University of Alabama
Birmingham *M, D*
University of Phoenix
Birmingham *M*
Virginia College
Birmingham *A, B, M*
Mobile *A*

Alaska

Alaska Pacific University *B, M*
Charter College *B*
University of Alaska
Anchorage *M*
Fairbanks *C*
Southeast *A*

Arizona

Argosy University
Online *M*
Brookline College
Phoenix *A*
Brown Mackie College
Tucson *A*
Carrington College
Phoenix *C*
Central Arizona College *C, A*
GateWay Community College *C, A*
Grand Canyon University *B, M*
Northcentral University *B, M, D*
University of Phoenix
Phoenix-Hohokam *M*
Southern Arizona *M*

Arkansas

Arkansas State University *M*
Harding University *B*
University of Arkansas
Little Rock *M*
University of Central Arkansas *M*

California

California Baptist University *B*
California Coast University *A, B, M*
California College San Diego *B*
California State University
Bakersfield *M*
Chico *M*
Dominguez Hills *B*
East Bay *M*
Los Angeles *M*
Northridge *M*
California University of Management
and Sciences *A*
Carrington College California
Citrus Heights *C, A*
Pleasant Hill *C*
Sacramento *C*
Stockton *C, A*
Concorde Career College
San Diego *C*
Concordia University Irvine *B*
DeVry University
Pomona *B*
Loma Linda University *B, M, D*

Mount St. Mary's College *A, B*
National University *A, B, M*
St. Mary's College of California *B*
San Joaquin Valley College *A*
San Jose State University *B*
Santa Barbara Business College *B*
Santa Barbara Business College
Bakersfield *B*
Rancho Mirage *B*
Santa Maria *B*
Ventura *B*
Simpson University *B*
Trident University International *B*
University of California
Berkeley *D*
Irvine *M*
University of La Verne *B, M*
University of Phoenix
Bay Area *M*
Central Valley *C, M*
Sacramento Valley *M*
San Diego *M*
Southern California *C, M*
University of San Francisco *M*
University of Southern California *M*
West Coast University: Los Angeles *M*

Colorado

Adams State University *B*
CollegeAmerica
Colorado Springs *B*
Denver *B*
Colorado Christian University *C, A, B*
Community College of Denver *C*
Metropolitan State University of
Denver *B*
National American University
Denver *B*
Regis University *B*
University of Colorado
Denver *M*
University of Northern Colorado *B*
University of Phoenix
Denver *M*
Southern Colorado *M*

Connecticut

Charter Oak State College *C, B*
Quinnipiac University *B, M*
St. Vincent's College *C*
University of Connecticut *B, M*
University of New Haven *M*
Western Connecticut State
University *M*

District of Columbia

American University *M*
George Washington University *M*
Georgetown University *B, M*
University of Phoenix
Washington DC *M*

Florida

Barry University *C, B, M*
Broward College *A*
Florida Agricultural and Mechanical
University *B, M*
Florida Atlantic University *B, M*
Florida Institute of Technology *M*
Florida International University *B*
Florida Southern College *B*
Florida State University *M*
Hodges University *B*
Keiser University *B*
Northwest Florida State College *A*
Pensacola State College *A, B*
Rasmussen College
Fort Myers *B*
New Port Richey *B*
Ocala *B*
Pasco/Land O'Lakes *B*
Tampa/Brandon *B*
Saint Johns River State College *C, A*
Saint Leo University *B*

Saint Thomas University *B*
Santa Fe College *B*
Southwest Florida College *B*
University of Central Florida *B*
University of Florida *M, D*
University of Miami *B, M*
University of North Florida *B, M*
University of Phoenix
  Central Florida *M*
  North Florida *M*
  South Florida *M*
  West Florida *M*
University of South Florida *B, M*

Georgia

Armstrong Atlantic State
  University *M*
Brenau University *M*
Clayton State University *B, M*
Georgia Institute of Technology *M*
Georgia Southern University *M*
Georgia State University *M*
Southeastern Technical College *C*
University of Phoenix
  Atlanta *M*
  Augusta *M*
  Columbus *M*
  Savannah *M*

Hawaii

Hawaii Pacific University *B*
University of Hawaii
  Hawaii Community College *C*
  West Oahu *C*
University of Phoenix
  Hawaii *M*

Idaho

Broadview University
  Boise *B*
Idaho State University *B*
Stevens-Henager College
  Boise *B, M*
University of Phoenix
  Idaho *C, M*

Illinois

Benedictine University *B*
City Colleges of Chicago
  Wilbur Wright College *C*
DeVry University
  Online *B*
Governors State University *B, M*
Illinois Central College *C, A*
Illinois Institute of Technology *M*
Lewis University *B*
Lexington College *A, B*
Lincoln College *B*
Loyola University Chicago *B, M*
Monmouth College *B*
National-Louis University *B*
Northwestern University *M*
Rasmussen College
  Aurora *B*
  Mokena/Tinley Park *B*
  Rockford *B*
  Romeoville/Joliet *B*
Rush University *M, D*
Southern Illinois University
  Carbondale *B*
Spoon River College *A*
Triton College *C*
University of St. Francis *B, M*
Western Illinois University *B*

Indiana

Brown Mackie College
  Fort Wayne *A, B*
  Merrillville *B*
  Michigan City *A*
  South Bend *B*
Harrison College
  Indianapolis *B*

Indiana University
  Purdue University Fort Wayne *B*
  Purdue University
    Indianapolis *B, M*
University of Evansville *B, M*
University of Phoenix
  Indianapolis *M*
University of St. Francis *B, M*
University of Southern Indiana *B, M*
Valparaiso University *B, M*
Vincennes University *A*

Iowa

Ashford University *B, M*
Des Moines Area Community
  College *C, A*
Graceland University *M*
Iowa Central Community College *A*
Iowa Lakes Community College *A*
Mercy College of Health Sciences *B*
Mount Mercy University *B*
St. Ambrose University *M*
University of Iowa *M, D*
University of Phoenix
  Des Moines *M*
Upper Iowa University *B*

Kansas

Friends University *B, M*
Neosho County Community
  College *A*
University of St. Mary *B, M*
Wichita State University *B*
Wright Career College
  Overland Park *B*
  Wichita *B*

Kentucky

Brown Mackie College
  Louisville *B*
Daymar College
  Bowling Green *B*
  Louisville *B*
  Owensboro *B*
Eastern Kentucky University *B*
Midway College *B*
Thomas More College *B*
University of Kentucky *B, M*
Western Kentucky University *B, M*

Louisiana

Herzing University
  Kenner *B*
Our Lady of the Lake College *B*
Tulane University *M, D*
University of Louisiana at Lafayette *M*
University of Louisiana at Monroe *B*
University of New Orleans *M*
University of Phoenix
  Baton Rouge *M*
  Lafayette *M*
  Louisiana *M*
  Shreveport *M*

Maine

University of Southern Maine *M*

Maryland

Baltimore City Community
  College *C, A*
Howard Community College *A*
Mount St. Mary's University *M*
Salisbury University *B*
Sojourner-Douglass College *B*
Stevenson University *M*
Towson University *B*
University of Baltimore *B, M*
Washington Adventist University *B*

Massachusetts

Boston University *M*
Brandeis University *B, M*
Elms College *B*
Framingham State University *M*

Newbury College *B*
Simmons College *M*
Springfield College *B, M*
Stonehill College *B*
Suffolk University *M*
University of Massachusetts
  Dartmouth *B*
  Lowell *B*
University of Phoenix
  Boston *M*
Worcester State University *M*

Michigan

Alma College *B*
Baker College
  Clinton Township *B*
  Flint *B, M*
  Muskegon *B*
  Owosso *B*
  Port Huron *B*
Central Michigan University *B, M, D*
Davenport University *B*
Eastern Michigan University *B, M*
Ferris State University *B*
Madonna University *B*
Oakland Community College *C, A*
Robert B. Miller College *B*
Spring Arbor University *B*
University of Detroit Mercy *B, M*
University of Michigan *M*
University of Michigan
  Dearborn *B*
  Flint *B, M*
University of Phoenix
  Metro Detroit *C, M*
  West Michigan *M*

Minnesota

Capella University *B, M, D*
Century College *C*
Concordia University St. Paul *B, M*
Globe University
  Minneapolis *B*
  Moorhead *B*
  Woodbury *B*
Herzing University
  Minneapolis *B*
Minnesota School of Business
  Blaine *B*
  Brooklyn Center *B*
  Elk River *B*
  Lakeville *B*
  Plymouth *B*
  Richfield *B*
  Rochester *B*
  St. Cloud *B*
  Shakopee *B*
Minnesota State University
  Mankato *B, M*
  Moorhead *B*
National American University
  Bloomington *B*
  Roseville *B*
Rasmussen College
  Blaine *B*
  Bloomington *B*
  Brooklyn Park *B*
  Eagan *B*
  Lake Elmo/Woodbury *B*
  Mankato *B*
  Moorhead *B*
  St. Cloud *B*
Ridgewater College *C, A*
St. Mary's University of Minnesota *M*
University of Minnesota
  Crookston *B*
  Duluth *B*
  Twin Cities *M*
University of Phoenix
  Minneapolis-St. Paul *M*
Walden University *B, M*
Winona State University *B*

Mississippi

Belhaven University *B, M*
Jackson State University *B*
University of Mississippi *M*
University of Phoenix
  Jackson *M*

Missouri

Grantham University *M*
Harris-Stowe State University *B*
Lindenwood University *B, M*
Missouri Baptist University *B*
North Central Missouri College *A*
Saint Louis University *M*
University of Missouri
  Columbia *M*
  St. Louis *M*
University of Phoenix
  Kansas City *M*
  St. Louis *M*
Washington University in St. Louis *B*
Webster University *M*

Montana

Montana State University
  Billings *B, M*

Nebraska

Clarkson College *C, A, B, M*
Creighton University *B, M*
Hastings College *B*
Kaplan University
  Lincoln *M*
University of Nebraska
  Omaha *B*
University of Phoenix
  Omaha *M*
Wright Career College
  Omaha *B*

Nevada

University of Nevada
  Las Vegas *B*
University of Phoenix
  Las Vegas *M*
  Northern Nevada *M*

New Hampshire

Colby-Sawyer College *B*
Daniel Webster College *B*
Franklin Pierce University *M*
Granite State College *B*
New England College *B, M*
Rivier University *M*
Southern New Hampshire
  University *B, M*
University of New Hampshire *B, M*

New Jersey

Berkeley College *A, B*
College of St. Elizabeth *M*
Essex County College *A*
Rutgers, The State University of New
  Jersey
  New Brunswick/Piscataway
    Campus *M*
  Newark Campus *M*
Seton Hall University *M*

New Mexico

Carrington College
  Albuquerque *C, A*
National American University
  Albuquerque *B*
University of Phoenix
  New Mexico *M*

New York

ASA College *A*
Berkeley College *A, B*
Berkeley College of New York
  City *A, B*

Bryant & Stratton College
  Albany *B*
City University of New York
  Baruch College *M*
  Brooklyn College *M*
  CUNY Online *C*
College of Westchester *B*
Cornell University *M*
D'Youville College *B, M*
Dowling College *M*
Elmira College *M*
Excelsior College *B, M*
Globe Institute of
    Technology *C, A, B*
Hofstra University *M*
Long Island University
  LIU Brooklyn *M*
  LIU Post *B, M*
Pace University *M*
Plaza College *B*
Roberts Wesleyan College *B, M*
SUNY
  College at Brockport *B, M*
  College of Technology at Canton *B*
  Institute of Technology at Utica/
      Rome *M*
  University at Stony Brook *M*
St. Joseph's College New York:
    Suffolk Campus *C, B, M*
St. Joseph's College, New
    York *C, B, M*
Utica School of Commerce *A*

North Carolina

Appalachian State University *B*
Cabarrus College of Health
    Sciences *B*
Duke University *M*
Gardner-Webb University *B*
Methodist University *B*
Pfeiffer University *B, M*
Randolph Community College *C, A*
Rockingham Community College *C*
University of Mount Olive *B*
University of North Carolina
  Chapel Hill *B, M, D*
  Charlotte *M*
  Greensboro *M*
University of Phoenix
  Charlotte *M*
  Raleigh *M*
Western Carolina University *B, M*
Winston-Salem State University *B, M*

North Dakota

Minot State University *B*
Rasmussen College
  Bismarck *B*
  Fargo *B*
University of Mary *M*

Ohio

Akron Institute of Herzing
    University *B*
Baldwin Wallace University *B*
Bluffton University *B*
Bowling Green State University *B*
Brown Mackie College
  Cincinnati *A*
  Findlay *A*
  North Canton *A, B*
Columbus State Community
    College *C*
Fortis College
  Ravenna *A*
Franklin University *B, M*
Harrison College
  Grove City *B*
Heidelberg University *B*
Kent State University
  Trumbull *A*
Lourdes University *B*
Malone University *B*
Mercy College of Ohio *B*

Mount Vernon Nazarene
    University *M*
Muskingum University *B*
Ohio University *B, M*
Owens Community College
  Toledo *A*
Sinclair Community College *A*
Terra State Community College *A*
Tiffin University *B, M*
University of Akron *M*
University of Akron: Wayne
    College *A*
University of Findlay *B*
University of Northwestern Ohio *B*
University of Phoenix
  Cleveland *B*
University of Rio Grande *B*
University of Toledo *M*
Ursuline College *B*
Wilberforce University *B*
Wright State University *M, T*
Xavier University *M*
Youngstown State University *M*

Oklahoma

Langston University *B*
Mid-America Christian University *M*
Oklahoma State University
  Oklahoma City *A*
Southwestern Oklahoma State
    University *B*
University of Oklahoma *M*
University of Phoenix
  Oklahoma City *M*
  Tulsa *M*
Wright Career College
  Oklahoma City *B*

Oregon

Concordia University *B*
Oregon Health & Science
    University *M*
Oregon Institute of Technology *B*
Oregon State University *B*
Pioneer Pacific College *A, B*
Portland State University *M*

Pennsylvania

Arcadia University *C, B*
Butler County Community College *A*
Carlow University *B*
Carnegie Mellon University *D*
Cedar Crest College *C*
Chestnut Hill College *A, B*
Drexel University *B*
Harrisburg Area Community
    College *A*
Holy Family University *C*
Immaculata University *C, B*
King's College *B*
Lebanon Valley College *B*
Marywood University *B*
Misericordia University *B*
Moravian College *M*
Mount Aloysius College *M*
Peirce College *B*
Penn State
  Abington *C, B*
  Altoona *C, B*
  Beaver *C, B*
  Berks *C, B*
  Brandywine *C, B*
  DuBois *C, B*
  Fayette, The Eberly Campus *C, B*
  Greater Allegheny *C, B*
  Harrisburg *C, B, M*
  Hazleton *C, B*
  Lehigh Valley *C, B*
  Mont Alto *C, B*
  New Kensington *C, B*
  Schuylkill *C, B*
  Shenango *C, B*
  University Park *C, B, M, D*
  Wilkes-Barre *C, B*

Worthington Scranton *C, B*
York *C, B*
Pennsylvania College of Health
    Sciences *B*
Philadelphia University *C, B*
Saint Joseph's University *M*
Shippensburg University of
    Pennsylvania *B*
University of Pennsylvania *B, M, D*
University of Pittsburgh *M, D*
University of Scranton *C, A, B, M*

Puerto Rico

Columbia Centro Universitario:
    Caguas *M*
Universidad del Este *B*

Rhode Island

New England Institute of
    Technology *B*
Providence College *C, B*
Rhode Island College *B*
Roger Williams University *B*
Salve Regina University *M*
University of Rhode Island *B*

South Carolina

Coastal Carolina University *B*
Limestone College *B*
Medical University of South
    Carolina *M, D*
Tri-County Technical College *C*

South Dakota

Globe University
  Sioux Falls *B*
Presentation College *B*

Tennessee

Baptist College of Health Sciences *B*
Carson-Newman University *B*
Daymar Institute
  Clarksville *B*
  Murfreesboro *B*
Freed-Hardeman University *B*
Lee University *B*
Lipscomb University *M*
Southern Adventist University *B, M*
Tennessee State University *B*
Trevecca Nazarene University *C*
University of Phoenix
  Chattanooga *M*
  Knoxville *M*
  Memphis *M*
  Nashville *M*
Vanderbilt University *M*

Texas

Baylor University *M*
Concordia University Texas *B*
Dallas Baptist University *C, B, M*
DeVry University
  Houston *B*
Galveston College *A*
Houston Baptist University *M*
Howard Payne University *B*
LeTourneau University *M*
Midland College *C*
Midwestern State University *M*
National American University
  Austin *A, B*
Our Lady of the Lake University of
    San Antonio *M*
Tarrant County College *C*
Texas Southern University *B*
Texas State University *B, M*
Texas Tech University Health
    Sciences Center *B, M*
Texas Woman's University *M*
Trinity University *M*
University of Houston
  Clear Lake *B, M*

University of Phoenix
  Austin *M*
  Dallas Fort Worth *M*
  Houston Westside *M*
  San Antonio *M*
University of Texas
  Arlington *M*
  Dallas *M*
  Health Science Center at
      Houston *M, D*
University of the Incarnate Word *M*
West Texas A&M University *M*
Western Technical College: Diana
    Drive *C*

Utah

Broadview University
  Layton *B*
  Orem *B*
  West Jordan *B*
University of Phoenix
  Utah *C, M*
Weber State University *B*
Western Governors University *M*

Vermont

Champlain College *C, M*
Southern Vermont College *B*

Virginia

ECPI University *A, B*
George Mason University *M*
James Madison University *B*
Jefferson College of Health
    Sciences *B*
Mary Baldwin College *B*
Marymount University *M*
Norfolk State University *B*
Shenandoah University *B*
University of Management and
    Technology *C, B, M*
University of Phoenix
  Northern Virginia *C, M*
Virginia Commonwealth
    University *M, D*
Westwood College
  Arlington Ballston *B*

Washington

Eastern Washington University *C, B*
Heritage University *B*
Highline Community College *A*
University of Phoenix
  Western Washington *M*
University of Washington *M*
Washington State University *M*

West Virginia

American National University
  Parkersburg *A*
Fairmont State University *B*
Marshall University *M*
Wheeling Jesuit University *B*

Wisconsin

Concordia University Wisconsin *A*
Globe University
  Appleton *B*
  Eau Claire *B*
  La Crosse *B*
  Madison East *B*
  Middleton *B*
  Wausau *B*
Herzing University
  Brookfield *B*
  Madison *D*
Marian University *B*
Northeast Wisconsin Technical
    College *A*
Rasmussen College
  Appleton *B*
  Green Bay *B*
  Wausau *B*

University of Phoenix
Milwaukee *M*
University of Wisconsin
Eau Claire *B*

Health communications

Arkansas
Arkansas State University *M*

California
Chapman University *M*
Pacific Union College *B*
San Diego State University *B*

Illinois
DePaul University *M*

Indiana
Indiana University
Purdue University Indianapolis *D*

Massachusetts
Emerson College *M*
Fitchburg State University *M*

Michigan
Michigan State University *M*

Minnesota
Winona State University *B*

North Dakota
North Dakota State University *B*

Ohio
Ashland University *B*
Ohio University *M, D*
Ohio University
Southern Campus at Ironton *B*
Zanesville Campus *B*

Pennsylvania
Juniata College *B*

Rhode Island
Bryant University *M*

South Carolina
Clemson University *M*

South Dakota
South Dakota State University *C*

Texas
University of Houston *B, M*

Virginia
George Mason University *D*

Health information management

Alabama
Herzing University
Birmingham *B*
University of Alabama
Birmingham *B*
University of Phoenix
Birmingham *B*

Arizona
Central Arizona College *A*
University of Phoenix
Phoenix-Hohokam *B*
Southern Arizona *B*

Arkansas
Arkansas Tech University *B, M*
University of Phoenix
Little Rock *B*
Northwest Arkansas *B*

California
Allan Hancock College *C, A*
Chabot College *C, A*
Chaffey College *C*
City College of San Francisco *C, A*
Cypress College *C, A*
Heald College
Fresno *A*
Hayward *A*
Rancho Cordova *A*
Salinas *A*
San Francisco *A*
Stockton *C, A*
Lake Tahoe Community College *C, A*
Loma Linda University *B*
San Bernardino Valley College *C*
San Joaquin Valley College *A*
Santa Barbara Business College *A*
Santa Barbara Business College
Bakersfield *A*
Rancho Mirage *A*
Santa Rosa Junior College *C*
Southwestern College *C, A*
University of Phoenix
Bay Area *B*
Central Valley *B*
Sacramento Valley *B*
San Diego *B*
Southern California *M*

Colorado
Everest College
Colorado Springs *C*
Regis University *C, B*
University of Phoenix
Denver *B*
Southern Colorado *B*
Westwood College
Denver North *A*

Connecticut
Charter Oak State College *B*
Lincoln College of New England *B*

District of Columbia
University of Phoenix
Washington DC *B*

Florida
Broward College *A*
Florida Agricultural and Mechanical
University *B*
Indian River State College *A*
Keiser University *A, B*
Miami Dade College *A*
Pensacola State College *A*
Rasmussen College
Fort Myers *B*
New Port Richey *B*
Ocala *B*
Pasco/Land O'Lakes *B*
Tampa/Brandon *B*
St. Petersburg College *C, A*
University of Central Florida *B, M*
University of Phoenix
Central Florida *B*
North Florida *B*
South Florida *B*
West Florida *B*
Virginia College
Jacksonville *A*

Georgia
Atlanta Metropolitan College *A*
College of Coastal Georgia *B*
Darton College *A*
Georgia Regents University *B*
Gordon College *A*
University of Phoenix
Atlanta *B*
Augusta *B*
Columbus *B*
Savannah *B*

Hawaii
University of Phoenix
Hawaii *B*

Idaho
Boise State University *B*
University of Phoenix
Idaho *B*

Illinois
Chicago State University *B*
Illinois State University *B*
Kaskaskia College *C*
Rasmussen College
Aurora *B*
Mokena/Tinley Park *B*
Rockford *B*
Romeoville/Joliet *B*
Spoon River College *C*
University of Illinois
Chicago *B, M*

Indiana
Indiana University
Purdue University Indianapolis *B*
Southeast *B*
University of Phoenix
Indianapolis *B*

Iowa
Ashford University *B*

Kansas
Barton County Community College *A*
Hutchinson Community College *C*
Labette Community College *C*
Seward County Community
College *C*
University of Kansas Medical
Center *B*

Kentucky
Beckfield College *A*
Eastern Kentucky University *C, B*
Sullivan University *B*
University of Phoenix
Louisville *B*
Western Kentucky University *B*

Louisiana
Herzing University
Kenner *A*
ITI Technical College *A*
Louisiana Tech University *B*
Southern University
New Orleans *B*
University of Louisiana at Lafayette *B*
University of Phoenix
Baton Rouge *B*
Lafayette *B*
Louisiana *B*
Shreveport *B*

Maine
Kaplan University
South Portland *A*

Maryland
Baltimore City Community College *A*
Coppin State University *B*
Prince George's Community
College *C, A*

Massachusetts
Cape Cod Community College *C*
Northern Essex Community
College *C, A*

Michigan
Baker College
Auburn Hills *A*
Flint *B*
Jackson *A*

Bay de Noc Community College *A*
Davenport University *B*
Ferris State University *A, B*
University of Phoenix
Metro Detroit *B*
West Michigan *B*
Washtenaw Community College *A*

Minnesota
College of St. Scholastica *B, M*
Hennepin Technical College *C*
Rasmussen College
Blaine *B*
Bloomington *B*
Brooklyn Park *B*
Eagan *B*
Lake Elmo/Woodbury *B*
Mankato *B*
Moorhead *B*
St. Cloud *B*
St. Catherine University *A, B*
University of Phoenix
Minneapolis-St. Paul *B*

Mississippi
Coahoma Community College *A*
Hinds Community College *A*
Itawamba Community College *A*
Mississippi Delta Community
College *A*
Mississippi Gulf Coast Community
College *A*
Northeast Mississippi Community
College *A*
Southwest Mississippi Community
College *A*
University of Mississippi Medical
Center *B*

Missouri
Park University *A*
Saint Louis University *B*
Stephens College *B*
University of Phoenix
Kansas City *B*
St. Louis *B*

Montana
Montana State University
Great Falls College *A*

Nebraska
Herzing University
Omaha School of Massage Therapy
and Healthcare *A*

Nevada
University of Phoenix
Las Vegas *B*
Northern Nevada *B*

New Jersey
Cumberland County College *C, A*
Fairleigh Dickinson University
Metropolitan Campus *B*
Kean University *B*
Rutgers, The State University of New
Jersey
New Brunswick/Piscataway
Campus *B*
Newark Campus *B*
Thomas Edison State College *B*

New Mexico
Central New Mexico Community
College *A*

New York
ASA College *A*
City University of New York
CUNY Online *B*
Elmira Business Institute *C, A*
Globe Institute of Technology *C*

Long Island University
  LIU Post *B*
Medaille College *B*
Monroe College *A*
SUNY
  Institute of Technology at Utica/
    Rome *B*

North Carolina

Alamance Community College *A*
Durham Technical Community
  College *C, A*
East Carolina University *B*
Sandhills Community College *A*
Western Carolina University *B*

North Dakota

Rasmussen College
  Bismarck *B*
  Fargo *B*

Ohio

Akron Institute of Herzing
  University *A, B*
Bowling Green State University *B*
Columbus State Community
  College *C, A*
Cuyahoga Community College
  Metropolitan *C, A*
Herzing University
  Toledo *A*
National College
  Canton *B*
Ohio Business College
  Sandusky *A*
Ohio State University
  Columbus Campus *C, B*
Terra State Community College *A*
University of Akron: Wayne
  College *C*
University of Cincinnati *B*
University of Phoenix
  Cleveland *B*
University of Toledo *B*

Oklahoma

Southwestern Oklahoma State
  University *B*
University of Phoenix
  Tulsa *B*
Western Oklahoma State College *A*

Oregon

Mt. Hood Community College *A*
Oregon Institute of Technology *B*

Pennsylvania

Consolidated School of Business
  Lancaster *A*
Douglas Education Center *A*
Duquesne University *B, M*
Erie Business Center South *A*
Gwynedd Mercy University *B*
Peirce College *B*
Pennsylvania College of
  Technology *B*
Prism Career Institute *C*
Temple University *M*
University of Phoenix
  Harrisburg *B*
  Philadelphia *B*
  Pittsburgh *B*
University of Pittsburgh *B*

South Carolina

Forrest Junior College *C, A*
Midlands Technical College *C*
University of Phoenix
  Columbia *B*
Virginia College
  Charleston *A*
  Columbia *A*
  Greenville *A*
  Spartanburg *A*

South Dakota

Dakota State University *B, M*

Tennessee

Daymar Institute
  Nashville *C, A*
Fountainhead College of
  Technology *C, A*
National College of Business and
  Technology
  Knoxville *A*
Tennessee State University *B*
Trevecca Nazarene University *B*
University of Phoenix
  Chattanooga *B*
  Knoxville *B*
  Memphis *B*
University of Tennessee
  Knoxville *M*
Virginia College
  School of Business and Health in
    Chattanooga *A*

Texas

El Centro College *A*
Howard College *C, A*
Laredo Community College *C*
Texas Southern University *B*
Texas State University *B*
University of Phoenix
  Austin *B*
  Dallas Fort Worth *B*
  Houston Westside *B*
  San Antonio *B*

Utah

LDS Business College *A*
University of Phoenix
  Utah *B*
Weber State University *B*

Virginia

Marymount University *C, B*
Mountain Empire Community
  College *C*
Norfolk State University *B*
University of Phoenix
  Northern Virginia *B*
  Richmond *B*
Virginia College
  Richmond *A*
Westwood College
  Arlington Ballston *A*

Washington

Columbia Basin College *A*
Renton Technical College *C, A*
University of Phoenix
  Western Washington *B*

West Virginia

Bridgemont Community and
  Technical College *A*

Wisconsin

Herzing University
  Brookfield *A, B*
  Kenosha *A*
  Madison *A, B*
Madison Area Technical College *A*
Northeast Wisconsin Technical
  College *A*
Rasmussen College
  Appleton *B*
  Green Bay *B*
  Wausau *B*
University of Phoenix
  Milwaukee *B*
University of Wisconsin
  Green Bay *B*

Health information technology

Alabama

Bishop State Community College *A*
Central Alabama Community
  College *A*
Enterprise State Community
  College *A*
Gadsden State Community College *A*
Southern Union State Community
  College *A*
Virginia College
  Birmingham *A*
Wallace State Community College at
  Hanceville *A*

Alaska

Charter College *A*

Arizona

Brookline College
  Phoenix *A*
Penn Foster College *A*
Phoenix College *C, A*
Pima Community College *C, A*

Arkansas

Arkansas State University
  Beebe *C*
College of the Ouachitas *C*
National Park Community
  College *C, A*
North Arkansas College *C*
University of Arkansas
  Monticello *C*

California

Allan Hancock College *C, A*
Carrington College California
  Antioch *C, A*
  Sacramento *C, A*
  San Jose *A*
Cerritos College *A*
Chabot College *C, A*
Charles Drew University of Medicine
  and Science *A*
City College of San Francisco *C, A*
Cosumnes River College *A*
Cypress College *A*
DeVry University
  Pomona *A*
East Los Angeles College *C, A*
Fresno City College *C, A*
Heald College
  Concord *A*
  San Jose *A*
ITT Technical Institute
  Oxnard *A*
  San Bernardino *A*
  Sylmar *A*
Los Angeles City College *A*
Orange Coast College *C, A*
Santa Barbara Business College
  Santa Maria *A*
  Ventura *A*
Santa Barbara City College *C*
Santa Rosa Junior College *C*
Southwestern College *C, A*

Colorado

Aims Community College *C*
American Sentinel University *M*
Arapahoe Community College *C, A*
Community College of Aurora *C*
Front Range Community College *A*
Lamar Community College *C*
Red Rocks Community College *C, A*

Connecticut

Quinebaug Valley Community
  College *C*

Florida

College of Business and Technology
  Cutler Bay *A*
  Hialeah *A*
  Kendall *A*
College of Central Florida *C, A*
Daytona State College *C, A*
Eastern Florida State College *C, A*
Florida State College at
  Jacksonville *A*
Fortis College
  Winter Park *A*
Hillsborough Community College *C*
Hodges University *A*
ITT Technical Institute
  Ft. Lauderdale *A*
  Lake Mary *A*
  Miami *A*
  Tampa *A*
Indian River State College *A*
Lake-Sumter State College *A*
Miami Dade College *C*
Northwest Florida State College *C*
Polk State College *C, A*
Rasmussen College
  Fort Myers *A*
  New Port Richey *A*
  Ocala *A*
  Pasco/Land O'Lakes *A*
  Tampa/Brandon *A*
Saint Johns River State College *C, A*
Santa Fe College *C, A*
Seminole State College of
  Florida *C, A*
Southwest Florida College *A*
Tallahassee Community College *C*
Valencia College *C, A*
Virginia College
  Pensacola *A*

Georgia

Abraham Baldwin Agricultural
  College *A*
Atlanta Technical College *C, A*
Augusta Technical College *C*
Bainbridge College *C, A*
Darton College *A*
Gwinnett Technical College *A*
Southwest Georgia Technical
  College *C*
West Georgia Technical College *C, A*

Hawaii

Heald College
  Honolulu *A*

Idaho

Boise State University *A*
ITT Technical Institute
  Boise *A*
Idaho State University *C, A, B*

Illinois

Black Hawk College *A*
College of DuPage *A*
Danville Area Community College *A*
DeVry University
  Chicago *A*
  Online *A*
Highland Community College *A*
Illinois Central College *A*
Illinois Eastern Community Colleges
  Frontier Community College *C, A*
John A. Logan College *A*
Kaskaskia College *A*
Midstate College *A*
Moraine Valley Community College *A*
Morton College *A*
Northwestern College *A*
Oakton Community College *A*
Rasmussen College
  Aurora *A*
  Mokena/Tinley Park *A*

Rockford *A*
Romeoville/Joliet *A*
Rend Lake College *C, A*
Sauk Valley Community College *C*
Shawnee Community College *C, A*
South Suburban College of Cook
    County *C*
Southeastern Illinois College *A*
Southern Illinois University
    Edwardsville *M*
Southwestern Illinois College *A*
Spoon River College *C*
Triton College *C*
Waubonsee Community College *A*

Indiana

ITT Technical Institute
    Fort Wayne *A*
    Indianapolis *A*
Indiana University
    Kokomo *C*
    Northwest *A*
    Purdue University Indianapolis *C*
Ivy Tech Community College
    Bloomington *A*
    Central Indiana *A*
    Lafayette *A*
National College
    Indianapolis *A*
    South Bend *A*
National College: Fort Wayne *A*
Vincennes University *A*

Iowa

Des Moines Area Community
    College *A*
Kirkwood Community College *C, A*
Northeast Iowa Community
    College *C, A*
Northwest Iowa Community
    College *A*

Kansas

Cowley County Community
    College *C, A*
Dodge City Community College *A*
Hutchinson Community College *A*
Johnson County Community
    College *A*
Washburn University *C, A*

Kentucky

Daymar College
    Louisville *C, A*
Eastern Kentucky University *A, B*
Gateway Community and Technical
    College *C, A*
Henderson Community College *C*
Jefferson Community and Technical
    College *C, A*
National College
    Danville *C*
    Florence *C*
    Lexington *C*
    Louisville *C*
    Pikeville *C*
    Richmond *C*
Sullivan University *A*
Western Kentucky University *A*

Louisiana

Delgado Community College *C, A*
ITI Technical College *A*
Louisiana Tech University *A*
Southern University
    Shreveport *A*

Maine

Beal College *A*
Kaplan University
    South Portland *A*
Kennebec Valley Community
    College *C, A*

Northern Maine Community
    College *A*
Southern Maine Community
    College *A*
York County Community College *A*

Maryland

Anne Arundel Community College *A*
Baltimore City Community
    College *C, A*
Carroll Community College *C, A*
College of Southern Maryland *C*
Community College of Baltimore
    County *C*
Howard Community College *C, A*
Kaplan University
    Hagerstown *C, A*
Montgomery College *C, A*
Prince George's Community
    College *C, A*

Massachusetts

Benjamin Franklin Institute of
    Technology *B*
Bristol Community College *A*
Holyoke Community College *C*
Labource College *C, A*
Northern Essex Community
    College *C*

Michigan

Baker College
    Auburn Hills *A*
    Clinton Township *A*
    Flint *A*
    Jackson *A*
    Owosso *A*
    Port Huron *A*
Davenport University *A*
Delta College *C*
Ferris State University *A*
Gogebic Community College *C*
Henry Ford Community College *A*
Kirtland Community College *A*
Mid Michigan Community College *A*
Mott Community College *C, A*
Northern Michigan University *C, A*
St. Clair County Community
    College *A*
Schoolcraft College *C, A*
Southwestern Michigan College *A*

Minnesota

Academy College *C*
Anoka Technical College *A*
Brown College
    Mendota Heights *A*
Dakota County Technical College *C*
Duluth Business University *C, A*
Hennepin Technical College *C*
Minnesota State Community and
    Technical College *C, A*
National American University
    Bloomington *A*
    Roseville *A*
Rasmussen College
    Blaine *A*
    Bloomington *A*
    Brooklyn Park *A*
    Eagan *A*
    Lake Elmo/Woodbury *A*
    Mankato *A*
    Moorhead *A*
    St. Cloud *A*
Ridgewater College *C, A*
Riverland Community College *C*
Rochester Community and Technical
    College *A*
St. Catherine University *C, A*
St. Cloud Technical and Community
    College *A*
St. Paul College *A*

Mississippi

Hinds Community College *A*
Itawamba Community College *A*
Meridian Community College *A*
Southwest Mississippi Community
    College *A*

Missouri

East Central College *C, A*
Missouri Western State
    University *C, A*
North Central Missouri College *C*
Ozarks Technical Community
    College *A*
St. Charles Community College *A*
State Fair Community College *C, A*

Montana

Montana State University
    Great Falls College *C*

Nebraska

Central Community College *C, A*
Northeast Community College *A*
Western Nebraska Community
    College *C, A*

Nevada

Career College of Northern
    Nevada *C, A*
College of Southern Nevada *A*
Truckee Meadows Community
    College *C*

New Hampshire

Manchester Community College *C, A*

New Jersey

Berkeley College *A*
Brookdale Community College *C, A*
Burlington County College *C, A*
DeVry University
    North Brunswick *A*
Eastwick College *A*
Hudson County Community
    College *C, A*
Passaic County Community College *C*
Raritan Valley Community
    College *C, A*

New Mexico

Central New Mexico Community
    College *C*
Clovis Community College *C, A*
Eastern New Mexico University:
    Roswell *C*
ITT Technical Institute
    Albuquerque *A*
National American University
    Albuquerque *A*
San Juan College *A*

New York

Berkeley College of New York City *A*
Broome Community College *A*
City University of New York
    Borough of Manhattan Community
        College *A*
    Guttman Community College *A*
Elmira Business Institute *C, A*
Erie Community College *A*
Excelsior College *C*
Fulton-Montgomery Community
    College *C*
Globe Institute of Technology *C*
Jamestown Community College *C, A*
Molloy College *A*
Monroe Community College *A*
Onondaga Community College *A*
Plaza College *B*
SUNY
    College of Technology at Alfred *A*
St. John's University *B*

Suffolk County Community College *A*
Technical Career Institutes *A*
Touro College *C, B*
Trocaire College *A*
Utica School of Commerce *A*

North Carolina

Brunswick Community College *C, A*
Catawba Valley Community
    College *C, A*
Central Piedmont Community
    College *C, A*
Craven Community College *A*
Davidson County Community
    College *A*
Edgecombe Community College *A*
Fayetteville Technical Community
    College *C, A*
Pitt Community College *C, A*
Southwestern Community
    College *C, A*
Wake Technical Community
    College *C, A*

North Dakota

North Dakota State College of
    Science *C*
Rasmussen College
    Bismarck *A*
    Fargo *A*
Williston State College *A*

Ohio

Bowling Green State University:
    Firelands College *A*
Cincinnati State Technical and
    Community College *C, A*
Columbus State Community
    College *C*
Cuyahoga Community College
    Metropolitan *A*
DeVry University
    Columbus *A*
Franklin University *B*
Hocking College *A*
Mercy College of Ohio *A*
Miami-Jacobs Career College
    Columbus *C, A*
    Dayton *A*
    Sharonville *C, A*
National College
    Stow *A*
    Willoughby Hills *A*
    Youngstown *A*
Owens Community College
    Toledo *C, A*
Sinclair Community College *C, A*
Stark State College *A*
Terra State Community College *C, A*
Trumbull Business College *A*
University of Cincinnati
    Clermont College *C, A*

Oklahoma

Rose State College *C, A*

Oregon

Central Oregon Community
    College *C, A*
Chemeketa Community College *C*
Lane Community College *C*
Portland Community College *A*

Pennsylvania

Bidwell Training Center *C*
Community College of Allegheny
    County *C, A*
Community College of
    Philadelphia *A*
DeVry University
    Fort Washington *A*
Fortis Institute
    Erie *A*
Gwynedd Mercy University *A*

Laurel Technical Institute *A*
Lehigh Carbon Community College *A*
Mercyhurst University *B*
Peirce College *A*
Pennsylvania College of
Technology *A*
Sanford-Brown Institute
Pittsburgh *A*
South Hills School of Business &
Technology *A*
Yorktowne Business Institute *A*

Puerto Rico

Huertas College *A*
Humacao Community College *A*
Inter American University of Puerto
Rico
Barranquitas Campus *C*
Guayama Campus *C*
Universidad Adventista de las
Antillas *A*

Rhode Island

New England Institute of
Technology *A*

South Carolina

Aiken Technical College *C*
Florence-Darlington Technical
College *A*
Forrest Junior College *C, A*
Greenville Technical College *A*
Midlands Technical College *C, A*
Piedmont Technical College *C*
Spartanburg Community College *C*
University of South Carolina
Columbia *M*

South Dakota

Dakota State University *A*
National American University
Rapid City *A*
Presentation College *A*

Tennessee

Chattanooga College *C, A*
Chattanooga State Community
College *A*
Daymar Institute
Clarksville *A*
Dyersburg State Community
College *C, A*
Fountainhead College of
Technology *A*
Miller-Motte Technical College
Chattanooga *C, A*
National College of Business and
Technology
Bartlett *A*
Bristol *C*
Madison *A*
Memphis *A*
Nashville *C*
Roane State Community College *A*
Tennessee State University *A*
Volunteer State Community
College *C, A*
Walters State Community
College *C, A*

Texas

Amarillo College *A*
Austin Community College *A*
Brookhaven College *A*
Central Texas College *C*
Coastal Bend College *C, A*
Collin County Community College
District *C, A*
DeVry University
Houston *A*
Irving *A*
Del Mar College *C, A*
El Centro College *A*
El Paso Community College *C, A*

Galveston College *C, A*
Houston Community College
System *A*
Howard College *C, A*
Lamar Institute of Technology *A*
Lee College *C, A*
Lone Star College System *C, A*
McLennan Community College *A*
Midland College *C, A*
Panola College *C, A*
Paris Junior College *C*
Richland College *A*
St. Philip's College *C, A*
San Jacinto College *C, A*
South Plains College *A*
South Texas College *C, A*
Tarrant County College *A*
Texas State Technical College
Harlingen *A*
West Texas *C, A*
Tyler Junior College *A*
Wharton County Junior College *A*

Utah

LDS Business College *C*
Salt Lake Community College *C*
Weber State University *A*

Vermont

Community College of Vermont *C*

Virginia

American National University
Charlottesville *C*
Danville *C*
Harrisonburg *C*
Lynchburg *C*
Martinsville *C*
ECPI University *A*
J. Sargeant Reynolds Community
College *C*
Northern Virginia Community
College *A*
Piedmont Virginia Community
College *C*
Southwest Virginia Community
College *C*
Stratford University: Falls Church *A*
Tidewater Community College *A*
Virginia Western Community
College *C*
Wytheville Community College *C*

Washington

Centralia College *C*
Clark College *C*
Edmonds Community College *C, A*
Grays Harbor College *C*
North Seattle Community College *C*
Shoreline Community College *A*
Spokane Falls Community
College *C, A*
Tacoma Community College *C, A*
Yakima Valley Community College *C*

West Virginia

American National University
Princeton *C*
West Virginia Northern Community
College *A*

Wisconsin

Chippewa Valley Technical College *A*
Fox Valley Technical College *A*
Gateway Technical College *A*
Herzing University
Madison *C, B*
Moraine Park Technical College *C, A*
Rasmussen College
Appleton *A*
Green Bay *A*
Wausau *A*
Southwest Wisconsin Technical
College *A*

Waukesha County Technical
College *A*
Western Technical College *A*

Health management/
clinical assistant

Alaska

University of Alaska
Southeast *C, A*

Arizona

Central Arizona College *C*
Pima Community College *C*

California

California College San Diego *A*
Concorde Career College
San Diego *C*
Ohlone College *C*
Platt College
Ontario *A*

Colorado

Aims Community College *C, A*

Connecticut

Northwestern Connecticut
Community College *C*

Florida

Anthem College
Orlando *C*
Fortis College
Orange Park *C, A*
Remington College
Tampa *C*
Sanford-Brown Institute
Tampa *A*

Georgia

Georgia Northwestern Technical
College *C, A*
Southwest Georgia Technical
College *C*

Idaho

Lewis-Clark State College *C, A, B*

Iowa

Kirkwood Community College *A*

Kansas

Neosho County Community
College *C*

Maryland

Hagerstown Community College *C*

Michigan

Davenport University *C, B*
Henry Ford Community College *A*
Oakland Community College *C*

Missouri

Washington University in St. Louis *M*

Nevada

Career College of Northern Nevada *C*

New York

Globe Institute of Technology *C*

North Carolina

Pitt Community College *C*

Ohio

Owens Community College
Toledo *A*
Terra State Community College *A*

Oregon

Clackamas Community College *C*

Pennsylvania

Consolidated School of Business
Lancaster *A*
York *A*

Tennessee

Miller-Motte Technical College
Clarksville *C*

Texas

Sanford-Brown College
Houston *C*

Virginia

Everest College
McLean *C*

Washington

Centralia College *C*

Health/medical
psychology

Alabama

University of South Alabama *D*

Arizona

Northcentral University *M, D*

Colorado

University of Colorado
Denver *D*

Kansas

Kansas Wesleyan University *B*

Massachusetts

MCPHS University *B*

New York

SUNY
University at Stony Brook *D*

North Carolina

University of North Carolina
Charlotte *D*

Pennsylvania

University of the Sciences *B, M*

Texas

Texas State University *M*

Vermont

Goddard College *M*

Virginia

Jefferson College of Health
Sciences *B*
Virginia Commonwealth University *D*
Virginia State University *D*

Health occupations
teacher education

California

Crafton Hills College *A*

Florida

Palm Beach State College *A*

Illinois

North Park University *T*
University of Illinois
Chicago *M*
Urbana-Champaign *M*

Minnesota

Gustavus Adolphus College *T*
Minnesota State University
   Mankato *B*

New Mexico

Eastern New Mexico University:
   Roswell *A*

New York

SUNY
   College at Brockport *M, T*
   College at Buffalo *B, M*
   College at Oswego *B*

Oklahoma

University of Central Oklahoma *B*

Texas

Baylor University *B, T*
Kilgore College *A*
University of Houston *M*

Health/physical fitness

Alabama

Calhoun Community College *A*
Faulkner University *B, M, T*
Gadsden State Community College *A*
Oakwood University *B*
Samford University *B*
Stillman College *B*
University of Mobile *B, T*
University of Montevallo *B, T*

Arizona

Arizona Western College *A*
Brown Mackie College
   Tucson *C, A*
Cochise College *A*
Eastern Arizona College *A*

Arkansas

Arkansas State University *B*
Bryan University
   Rogers *C, A*
Southern Arkansas University *M*
University of Arkansas *B*
University of Arkansas
   Monticello *B, M*
University of the Ozarks *B*

California

Antelope Valley College *A*
Bakersfield College *A*
Biola University *B*
California Polytechnic State
   University: San Luis Obispo *B, M*
California State Polytechnic
   University: Pomona *B, M*
California State University
   Chico *B, M*
   Dominguez Hills *B*
   East Bay *B, M*
   Fresno *B, M*
   Fullerton *B, M*
   Long Beach *M*
   Monterey Bay *B*
   Sacramento *B, M*
   Stanislaus *B*
Chaffey College *C*
Citrus College *A*
College of the Canyons *A*
College of the Siskiyous *A*
Columbia College *A*
Concordia University Irvine *B*
Cypress College *C*
Diablo Valley College *C*
East Los Angeles College *A*
El Camino College *A*
Feather River College *C, A*
Foothill College *C*
Fremont College *C*

Fresno Pacific University *B*
Humboldt State University *B*
Imperial Valley College *A*
Irvine Valley College *C, A*
La Sierra University *B*
Lake Tahoe Community College *A*
Long Beach City College *A*
Master's College *B*
Merced College *A*
MiraCosta College *C*
Modesto Junior College *A*
Moreno Valley College *A*
Orange Coast College *A*
Pacific Union College *B, T*
Point Loma Nazarene University *B*
Saddleback College *A*
St. Mary's College of California *B, M*
San Deigo Miramar College
   San Diego Miramar College *A*
San Diego City College *C, A*
San Diego State University *B, M*
San Joaquin Delta College *A*
San Jose State University *B, M*
Santa Barbara City College *C, A*
Santa Monica College *A*
Shasta College *A*
Sierra College *A*
Skyline College *A*
Solano Community College *A*
Southwestern College *A*
Vanguard University of Southern
   California *B*
West Los Angeles College *C, A*

Colorado

Adams State University *B, M*
Arapahoe Community College *C, A*
Community College of Denver *A*

Delaware

Delaware State University *B*
University of Delaware *B, M*

District of Columbia

Gallaudet University *B*

Florida

Barry University *B*
Jacksonville University *B*
Palm Beach State College *A*
University of Tampa *B*
University of West Florida *B, M*

Georgia

Abraham Baldwin Agricultural
   College *A*
Albany State University *B*
Andrew College *A*
Atlanta Metropolitan College *A*
Darton College *A*
East Georgia State College *A*
Georgia State University *T*
Gordon College *A*
Middle Georgia State College *A*
South Georgia State College *A*
University of Georgia *B*
Valdosta State University *B*

Hawaii

Brigham Young University-Hawaii *B*

Idaho

Boise State University *B, M*
College of Southern Idaho *A*
North Idaho College *A*
Northwest Nazarene University *B*

Illinois

Blackburn College *B*
Chicago State University *B, M, T*
DePaul University *B*
Elgin Community College *A*
Elmhurst College *B*
Illinois Central College *C*

Illinois State University *M*
Illinois Valley Community College *A*
John Wood Community College *A*
Kishwaukee College *A*
Lincoln College *A*
McHenry County College *C*
McKendree University *B, T*
North Central College *B, T*
Northern Illinois University *B*
Prairie State College *C*
Quincy University *B*
Robert Morris University: Chicago *A*
Rock Valley College *C, A*
Sauk Valley Community College *A*
South Suburban College of Cook
   County *A*
Southern Illinois University
   Edwardsville *M, T*
Southwestern Illinois College *A*
Trinity International University *B*
University of Illinois
   Urbana-Champaign *M, D*
Waubonsee Community College *A*

Indiana

Bethel College *B*
Brown Mackie College
   Fort Wayne *A*
Goshen College *B*
Hanover College *B*
Huntington University *B*
Oakland City University *B*
Purdue University *B, M, D*
Saint Joseph's College *B*
Trine University *B*
Valparaiso University *B*
Vincennes University *A*

Iowa

Briar Cliff University *B*
Coe College *B*
Cornell College *B, T*
Dordt College *B*
Ellsworth Community College *A*
Graceland University *B, T*
Grand View University *B*
Iowa Wesleyan College *B, T*
Luther College *B*
Northwestern College *B, T*
St. Ambrose University *B*
University of Dubuque *B*
University of Northern Iowa *B, M*
Upper Iowa University *B*
William Penn University *B*

Kansas

Baker University *B, T*
Barton County Community College *A*
Bethel College *B*
Coffeyville Community College *A*
Colby Community College *A*
Dodge City Community College *A*
Friends University *B*
Garden City Community College *A*
Independence Community College *A*
Kansas Wesleyan University *B, T*
McPherson College *B, T*
Ottawa University *B*
Seward County Community
   College *A*
Sterling College *B, T*
Tabor College *B*
University of Kansas *B*
Washburn University *B*
Wichita State University *M*

Kentucky

Asbury University *B*
Berea College *B, T*
Campbellsville University *B*
Lindsey Wilson College *B*
University of Louisville *B*
University of the Cumberlands *B*

Louisiana

Centenary College of Louisiana *B, T*
Louisiana College *B, T*
Louisiana State University
   Shreveport *B*
Louisiana Tech University *B*
Northwestern State University *B, M*
University of New Orleans *B*

Maine

Husson University *B, T*

Maryland

Anne Arundel Community College *A*
College of Southern Maryland *C, A*
Frostburg State University *B*
Howard Community College *A*
Washington Adventist University *B*

Massachusetts

Becker College *B*
Berkshire Community College *C*
Bridgewater State University *M*
Dean College *A*
Eastern Nazarene College *B*
Holyoke Community College *C, A*
Regis College *B*
Roxbury Community College *C*
Salem State University *B*
Springfield College *B, M*
University of Massachusetts
   Boston *B*
Westfield State University *B, T*

Michigan

Alma College *B, T*
Aquinas College *B, T*
Bay Mills Community College *A*
Calvin College *B, T*
Central Michigan University *B*
Concordia University *B*
Delta College *C, A*
Eastern Michigan University *B, M*
Grand Valley State University *B*
Lake Michigan College *A*
Lake Superior State University *A*
Lansing Community College *A*
Northern Michigan University *B*
Olivet College *B, T*
Spring Arbor University *B*
University of Michigan *B*

Minnesota

Augsburg College *B*
Concordia College: Moorhead *B*
Concordia University St. Paul *B*
Dakota County Technical College *C*
Gustavus Adolphus College *B*
Minnesota State University
   Mankato *B, M, T*
   Moorhead *B*
Normandale Community College *C*
Rainy River Community College *C*
Ridgewater College *A*
Saint Cloud State University *B, M*
Southwest Minnesota State
   University *B*
University of Northwestern - St.
   Paul *B*

Mississippi

Mississippi University for
   Women *B, T*
William Carey University *B*

Missouri

College of the Ozarks *B*
Missouri Southern State
   University *B, T*
Missouri Western State
   University *B, T*
Southeast Missouri State University *B*
Southwest Baptist University *B, T*

Three Rivers Community College *A*
Truman State University *B*

Montana

Blackfeet Community College *A*
Miles Community College *A*
Montana State University
  Billings *B, T*
Rocky Mountain College *B*
University of Great Falls *B*
University of Montana *B, M*

Nebraska

Concordia University *B, T*
Hastings College *B*
Nebraska Wesleyan University *B*
Northeast Community College *A*
Union College *B*
University of Nebraska
  Omaha *M*
Vatterott College
  Spring Valley *C*
Wayne State College *B*

Nevada

University of Nevada
  Las Vegas *B*

New Hampshire

Colby-Sawyer College *C*
Keene State College *B*
Plymouth State University *B*

New Jersey

Camden County College *C*
County College of Morris *A*
Gloucester County College *A*
Middlesex County College *A*
Monmouth University *B*
Montclair State University *B*
Raritan Valley Community College *C*
Rowan University *B*
Salem Community College *A*

New Mexico

Clovis Community College *A*
Eastern New Mexico University *B*
New Mexico Highlands University *B*
San Juan College *A*
Santa Fe Community College *C, A*
University of the Southwest *B*

New York

Adelphi University *B*
City University of New York
  Brooklyn College *B, M*
Corning Community College *A*
Fulton-Montgomery Community
  College *A*
Ithaca College *B, M, T*
Monroe Community College *A*
Niagara County Community
  College *A*
SUNY
  College at Buffalo *B*
  College of Technology at Canton *B*

North Carolina

Barton College *B*
Campbell University *B, T*
Catawba College *B*
Chowan University *B, T*
Gardner-Webb University *B*
Greensboro College *C, B, T*
Mars Hill University *B*
Meredith College *B*
Methodist University *B*
North Carolina Agricultural and
  Technical State University *B, T*
North Carolina Central
  University *B, M*
St. Andrews University *B*
St. Augustine's University *B*
Sandhills Community College *A*

University of Mount Olive *B*
University of North Carolina
  Chapel Hill *B*
  Charlotte *B*
  Pembroke *B*
  Wilmington *B*

North Dakota

Dakota College at Bottineau *A*
Dickinson State University *B, T*
Mayville State University *B, T*
Valley City State University *B, T*

Ohio

Baldwin Wallace University *B*
Bluffton University *B*
Bowling Green State University *M*
Capital University *B*
Cedarville University *B*
Cincinnati State Technical and
  Community College *C*
Cleveland State University *M*
Defiance College *B, T*
Kent State University *M*
Miami University
  Oxford *B*
Mount Vernon Nazarene University *B*
Ohio State University
  Columbus Campus *B*
Ohio University *B, M*
Otterbein University *B, M*
Shawnee State University *B*
Sinclair Community College *C*
University of Cincinnati *C*
University of Findlay *B, T*
University of Rio Grande *A*
Walsh University *B*
Wright State University *B*
Youngstown State University *B*

Oklahoma

Cameron University *B*
Carl Albert State College *A*
Eastern Oklahoma State College *A*
Northeastern Oklahoma Agricultural
  and Mechanical College *A*
Northwestern Oklahoma State
  University *B*
Oklahoma Baptist University *B, T*
Oklahoma Christian University *B*
Oklahoma Panhandle State
  University *B*
Oklahoma State University *M, D*
Oral Roberts University *B*
Redlands Community College *A*
Rose State College *A*
Seminole State College *A*
University of Science and Arts of
  Oklahoma *B, T*
Western Oklahoma State College *A*

Oregon

Central Oregon Community
  College *A*
Concordia University *B*
Corban University *B*
Eastern Oregon University *B*
George Fox University *B*
Linfield College *B, T*
Oregon State University *B, M, D*
Portland Community College *C, A*
Southern Oregon University *B, T*
Warner Pacific College *B, T*

Pennsylvania

Baptist Bible College of
  Pennsylvania *B*
Cairn University *B*
Community College of Allegheny
  County *A*
Gettysburg College *B*
Indiana University of
  Pennsylvania *B, M*
Lincoln University *B*

Luzerne County Community
  College *A*
Marywood University *B*
Montgomery County Community
  College *A*
Slippery Rock University of
  Pennsylvania *B, T*
Ursinus College *B, T*
West Chester University of
  Pennsylvania *B, M, T*

Puerto Rico

Inter American University of Puerto
  Rico
  San German Campus *B*
Turabo University *A*
University of Puerto Rico
  Mayaguez *B*
University of the Sacred Heart *B*

South Carolina

Benedict College *B*
Bob Jones University *B*
Charleston Southern University *B*
Claflin University *B*
Coker College *B*
South Carolina State University *B*
Voorhees College *B*

South Dakota

Augustana College *B, T*
Black Hills State University *B*
Northern State University *B*
South Dakota State University *B, M*

Tennessee

Austin Peay State University *B, M*
Carson-Newman University *B, T*
Cumberland University *B*
East Tennessee State
  University *B, M, T*
Hiwassee College *A*
Jackson State Community College *A*
Lee University *B*
Lincoln Memorial University *B, T*
Martin Methodist College *B*
Maryville College *B, T*
Middle Tennessee State
  University *B, M, D*
Milligan College *B, T*
Tennessee Technological
  University *B*
Tennessee Wesleyan College *B*
Tusculum College *B*
University of Tennessee
  Martin *B*

Texas

Alvin Community College *A*
Amarillo College *A*
Angelo State University *B, M, T*
Austin Community College *C, A*
Baylor University *B*
Clarendon College *A*
Dallas Baptist University *B, M*
Del Mar College *A*
East Texas Baptist University *B*
El Paso Community College *A*
Hardin-Simmons University *B*
Hill College *A*
Houston Baptist University *B*
Houston Community College
  System *C, A*
Howard College *A*
Howard Payne University *B*
Kilgore College *A*
Lamar University *B, M*
Lee College *A*
Lubbock Christian University *B*
Midland College *A*
Northeast Texas Community
  College *A*
Northwest Vista College *A*
Palo Alto College *A*

Paris Junior College *A*
Prairie View A&M University *B*
St. Philip's College *A*
Sam Houston State University *B*
San Jacinto College *A*
South Plains College *A*
Southwestern Adventist
  University *A, B, T*
Sul Ross State University *B, T*
Tarleton State University *B, D*
Texas A&M International
  University *B, T*
Texas A&M University
  Corpus Christi *B*
Texas Christian University *B*
Texas College *B*
Texas Lutheran University *B, T*
Texas Southern University *B, M*
Texas Woman's University *B, M, D*
Trinity Valley Community College *A*
Tyler Junior College *A*
University of North Texas *B, M, T*
University of Texas
  Austin *B*
  Brownsville *B*
  El Paso *B, M*
Western Texas College *A*

Utah

Brigham Young University *B, M, D*
Snow College *A*
University of Utah *B*
Utah Valley University *A, B*
Weber State University *B*

Vermont

Castleton State College *B*
Johnson State College *B*
Lyndon State College *B*
Norwich University *B*

Virginia

Averett University *B*
Bluefield College *B*
Bridgewater College *B, T*
Emory & Henry College *B, T*
Ferrum College *B*
James Madison University *B, M, T*
Longwood University *B*
Lynchburg College *B*
Northern Virginia Community
  College *C*
Shenandoah University *C*
University of Virginia's College at
  Wise *T*
Virginia Intermont College *B, T*
Virginia Western Community
  College *C*

Washington

Centralia College *A*
Eastern Washington University *M*
Highline Community College *A*
Pacific Lutheran University *B*
Western Washington University *B, M*
Whitworth University *B, T*

West Virginia

Bethany College *B*
Concord University *B, T*
West Virginia University *B*
West Virginia Wesleyan College *B*

Wisconsin

Carroll University *B*
University of Wisconsin
  Platteville *B, T*
  Stevens Point *B, T*

Wyoming

Northwest College *C, A*
Sheridan College *A*

Health physics/ radiologic health

Arizona
University of Arizona *M*

California
California State University
Dominguez Hills *B*
San Diego State University *M*

Florida
Florida Atlantic University *M*
University of Miami *M*

Georgia
Georgia Institute of Technology *M*

Illinois
Illinois Institute of Technology *M*

Indiana
Indiana University
Bloomington *M*

Kentucky
West Kentucky Community and
Technical College *A*

Louisiana
Louisiana State University and
Agricultural and Mechanical
College *M*

Michigan
Delta College *A*
Wayne State University *M, D*

Nevada
University of Nevada
Las Vegas *B, M*

New York
Hofstra University *M*
Monroe Community College *A*

North Carolina
Cabarrus College of Health
Sciences *B*

Ohio
University of Cincinnati *D*

Oregon
Oregon Health & Science
University *M, D*
Oregon State University *B, M, D*

Pennsylvania
Bloomsburg University of
Pennsylvania *B*

Rhode Island
University of Rhode Island *M*

Tennessee
Belmont University *B*
Vanderbilt University *M*

Virginia
Central Virginia Community
College *A*

Wisconsin
University of Wisconsin
Madison *M, D*

Health policy analysis

California
Mount St. Mary's College *B*

Indiana
Indiana University
Purdue University
Indianapolis *C, D*

Missouri
Saint Louis University *M*

Pennsylvania
Franklin & Marshall College *B*
Mercyhurst University *B, M*

Virginia
George Mason University *M*

Health services

Alabama
Central Alabama Community
College *A*
Community College of the Air
Force *A*
Oakwood University *B*
University of Alabama
Birmingham *B*
Wallace State Community College at
Hanceville *A*

Alaska
Ilisagvik College *C, A*
University of Alaska
Anchorage *B*

Arizona
Anthem College
Bryman School *C*
Arizona Western College *C, A*

Arkansas
Arkansas State University
Beebe *A*
Mountain Home *C*
Central Baptist College *B*
East Arkansas Community College *C*
Hendrix College *B*
National Park Community College *C*
North Arkansas College *C*
Southeast Arkansas College *C*
Southern Arkansas University Tech *C*
University of Arkansas
Community College at Hope *C*
Little Rock *M*
Monticello *C*
University of Central Arkansas *B*

California
Allan Hancock College *C, A*
American River College *A*
California Baptist University *B*
California State University
Channel Islands *B*
Chico *C, B*
Dominguez Hills *B, M*
Fresno *B*
Fullerton *B*
Los Angeles *C*
Columbia College *A*
Contra Costa College *C, A*
Cypress College *A*
Diablo Valley College *A*
Dominican University of California *B*
Heald College
Roseville *A*
Kaplan College
Riverside *C*
Loma Linda University *B*
Los Angeles City College *A*
Los Angeles Trade and Technical
College *A*
Merced College *A*
Mission College *A*
Mount San Antonio College *C, A*
Napa Valley College *C, A*

National University *B*
Pacific Union College *A*
Platt College
Ontario *A*
Rio Hondo College *A*
San Diego State University *B*
San Jose State University *B*
Shasta College *A*
University of San Francisco *B*
University of Southern California *B*
West Hills College: Coalinga *A*
West Hills College: Lemoore *C, A*

Colorado
Adams State University *B*
CollegeAmerica
Denver *A*
Fort Collins *B*
Colorado Christian University *B*
Colorado Mountain College *C*
National American University
Denver *A, B*
Pikes Peak Community College *A*
University of Colorado
Colorado Springs *B*
Denver *M, D*
University of Northern Colorado *B*

Connecticut
Goodwin College *A, B*
Northwestern Connecticut
Community College *C, A*
Sacred Heart University *B*
University of Hartford *A, B*

District of Columbia
Trinity Washington University *B*

Florida
Adventist University of Health
Sciences *A, B*
Brown Mackie College
Miami *B*
City College
Altamonte Springs *A*
Florida Agricultural and Mechanical
University *B*
Florida College of Natural Health
Miami *C*
Florida Gulf Coast University *B, M*
Gulf Coast State College *A*
Keiser University *A*
Nova Southeastern
University *B, M, D*
Palm Beach State College *A*
Remington College
Tampa *C*
South Florida State College *A*
Southeastern College
Greenacres *C*
Stetson University *B*
Tallahassee Community College *C*
University of Central Florida *B, M*
University of Florida *B*
University of Miami *B, M*
University of North Florida *B*
University of West Florida *B*
Virginia College
Pensacola *B*

Georgia
Armstrong Atlantic State University *B*
Atlanta Technical College *C*
Brenau University *B*
Central Georgia Technical College *C*
Columbus State University *B*
Columbus Technical College *C, A*
Emory University *M, D*
Georgia Highlands College *A*
Georgia Military College *A*
Georgia State University *M*
Gwinnett Technical College *C*
South Georgia State College *A*

Idaho
College of Idaho *B*
Idaho State University *B*
North Idaho College *A*

Illinois
Benedictine University *B*
Benedictine University at
Springfield *B*
Bradley University *B*
DePaul University *B*
Hebrew Theological College *B*
Illinois Eastern Community Colleges
Frontier Community College *C*
Loyola University Chicago *C*
Methodist College *B*
National University of Health
Sciences *D*
Roosevelt University *B*
Rush University *D*
South Suburban College of Cook
County *C*
Spoon River College *A*
Wheaton College *B*

Indiana
Purdue University *B, M*

Iowa
Ashford University *B*
Dordt College *B*
Drake University *B*
Grand View University *B*
Marshalltown Community
College *C, A*
St. Luke's College *B*

Kansas
Bethel College *C*
Friends University *B*
Garden City Community College *A*
Washburn University *C, A, B*

Kentucky
Ashland Community and Technical
College *A*
Bellarmine University *M*
Brown Mackie College
North Kentucky *A*
Hopkinsville Community College *A*
Lindsey Wilson College *A*
Northern Kentucky University *B*
Spalding University *B*
Spencerian College: Lexington *C, A*
Western Kentucky University *B*

Louisiana
Nicholls State University *B*
Northwestern State University *B*
Our Lady of the Lake College *B*
Southern University
Shreveport *A*

Maine
Kennebec Valley Community
College *C*
University of New England *B*
York County Community College *A*

Maryland
Allegany College of Maryland *A*
Baltimore City Community
College *C, A*
Cecil College *A*
Towson University *B, M*

Massachusetts
Anna Maria College *B*
Bay Path College *B*
Curry College *B*
Dean College *A*
Lesley University *B*
MCPHS University *B*

Merrimack College *B*
Middlesex Community College *C, A*
Mount Wachusett Community
   College *C, A*
Northeastern University *B, M*
Quinsigamond Community College *A*
Roxbury Community College *C*
Western New England University *B*
Worcester State University *B*

Michigan

Baker College
   Allen Park *B*
Bay de Noc Community College *A*
Cornerstone University *A, B*
Kellogg Community College *A*
Lake Michigan College *A*
Macomb Community College *C, A*
Oakland University *B*
Saginaw Valley State University *B*
Schoolcraft College *A*
University of Michigan
   Flint *B*
Western Michigan University *D*

Minnesota

Anoka-Ramsey Community College *A*
Century College *A*
College of St. Scholastica *B*
Lake Superior College *A*
Minnesota West Community and
   Technical College *A*
Northland Community & Technical
   College *A*
Rainy River Community College *A*
Rochester Community and Technical
   College *A*
St. Cloud Technical and Community
   College *A*
St. Mary's University of Minnesota *B*
South Central College *A*
University of Minnesota
   Crookston *B*
   Rochester *B*
Walden University *B, D*

Mississippi

University of Southern Mississippi *B*
William Carey University *B*

Missouri

College of the Ozarks *B*
Drury University *B*
Mineral Area College *A*
State Fair Community College *A*
University of Missouri
   Kansas City *B*
Washington University in St. Louis *B*

Montana

Aaniiih Nakoda College *A*
Blackfeet Community College *A*
Carroll College *A*
Stone Child College *A*

Nebraska

College of Saint Mary *D*
Little Priest Tribal College *A*
Southeast Community College *A*
University of Nebraska
   Kearney *B*

New Hampshire

Colby-Sawyer College *B*
Franklin Pierce University *B*

New Jersey

Bergen Community College *A*
Berkeley College *A*
Burlington County College *A*
College of St. Elizabeth *B*
Cumberland County College *A*
Eastwick College *A*

Eastwick College
   Hackensack *A*
Essex County College *A*
Fairleigh Dickinson University
   College at Florham *B*
Felician College *B*
Monmouth University *B*
New Jersey City University *B, M*
Passaic County Community College *A*
Ramapo College of New Jersey *B*
Raritan Valley Community College *A*
Richard Stockton College of New
   Jersey *B*
Rutgers, The State University of New
   Jersey
   New Brunswick/Piscataway
     Campus *B, M, D*
   Newark Campus *B, M, D*
Salem Community College *A*
Seton Hall University *M, D*
Sussex County Community College *A*
Thomas Edison State College *B*
Warren County Community
   College *A*

New Mexico

Central New Mexico Community
   College *A*

New York

Albany College of Pharmacy and
   Health Sciences *B*
Canisius College *M*
Cayuga Community College *A*
City University of New York
   York College *B*
Dominican College of Blauvelt *B*
Excelsior College *B*
Hofstra University *B*
Ithaca College *B*
Long Island University
   LIU Brooklyn *B, M*
Mercy College *C, B*
Mohawk Valley Community
   College *C*
North Country Community
   College *C, A*
Orange County Community
   College *A*
SUNY
   College at Cortland *B*
   College of Technology at Canton *C*
   Farmingdale State College *C*
   University at Stony Brook *B*
Sage Colleges *B*
University of Rochester *D*
Utica College *B*

North Carolina

Brevard College *B*
Catawba Valley Community
   College *C, A*
East Carolina University *B, D*
Miller-Motte College
   Wilmington *B*
Pitt Community College *A*
Queens University of Charlotte *B*
University of Mount Olive *A*
Wilkes Community College *C, A*

North Dakota

Dakota College at Bottineau *A*

Ohio

Antioch University
   Midwest *B*
Belmont College *A*
Cuyahoga Community College
   Metropolitan *A*
Defiance College *B*
Mercy College of Ohio *B*
Muskingum University *B*
North Central State College *A*

Ohio State University
   Lima Campus *B*
Ohio University
   Chillicothe Campus *A*
   Southern Campus at Ironton *B*
University of Cincinnati
   Blue Ash College *A*
Urbana University *B*
Ursuline College *B*
Xavier University *B*
Youngstown State University *B*
Zane State College *A*

Oklahoma

Cameron University *A*
Oklahoma State University
   Institute of Technology:
     Okmulgee *A*
   Oklahoma City *A*
Redlands Community College *A*
University of Oklahoma *B, M, D*

Oregon

Oregon Institute of Technology *B*
Rogue Community College *C*
Warner Pacific College *A*

Pennsylvania

Alvernia University *B*
Carnegie Mellon University *D*
Clarion University of Pennsylvania *A*
Community College of
   Philadelphia *C*
Delaware County Community
   College *A*
Drexel University *M*
Gettysburg College *B*
Harcum College *A*
Immaculata University *A, B*
Keystone College *A*
King's College *B*
La Roche College *M*
Lebanon Valley College *B*
Manor College *A*
Marywood University *B*
Mercyhurst University *B*
Pennsylvania College of Health
   Sciences *B*
Pennsylvania College of
   Technology *A*
Reading Area Community College *A*
Saint Joseph's University *B*
University of the Sciences *B*
West Chester University of
   Pennsylvania *B*
Widener University *A, B*

Puerto Rico

Pontifical Catholic University of
   Puerto Rico *B, M*

Rhode Island

Rhode Island College *B*

South Carolina

Aiken Technical College *C*
Clemson University *B*
Horry-Georgetown Technical
   College *C*
Medical University of South
   Carolina *M*
Technical College of the
   Lowcountry *C*
York Technical College *C*

South Dakota

Southeast Technical Institute *A*

Tennessee

Dyersburg State Community
   College *C*
East Tennessee State University *B*
Lee University *B*

Victory University *A, B*
Walters State Community College *C*

Texas

Alvin Community College *A*
Clarendon College *A*
Houston Community College
   System *A*
Howard Payne University *A*
Northwest Vista College *A*
Paris Junior College *A*
Prairie View A&M University *B*
St. Philip's College *A*
Sam Houston State University *B*
South Plains College *A*
Stephen F. Austin State University *B*
Texas A&M University
   Corpus Christi *B*
Texas Christian University *M*
Texas Southern University *B*
Texas State Technical College
   Harlingen *A*
Texas Tech University Health
   Sciences Center *B*
Texas Woman's University *B*
University of North Texas *B, M*
University of Texas
   Brownsville *B*
   Dallas *B*
   El Paso *D*
   Pan American *B*
   Tyler *M*
Vernon College *C*
West Texas A&M University *B*

Utah

University of Utah *B, M*
Weber State University *A*

Vermont

Community College of Vermont *C*
Goddard College *B, M*
Lyndon State College *B*

Virginia

Blue Ridge Community College *A*
Everest College
   McLean *C*
Ferrum College *B*
Germanna Community College *C*
Randolph College *B*
Southside Virginia Community
   College *C*
Southwest Virginia Community
   College *C, A*
Stratford University: Falls
   Church *A, B, M*
Virginia Western Community
   College *A*

Washington

Clover Park Technical College *C, A*
Evergreen State College *B*
Spokane Falls Community College *A*

West Virginia

Fairmont State University *B*
Kanawha Valley Community and
   Technical College *A*
Mountain State College *A*

Wisconsin

College of Menominee Nation *A*
Concordia University Wisconsin *B*
Lac Courte Oreilles Ojibwa
   Community College *A*
Moraine Park Technical College *C, A*

Wyoming

Casper College *A*
Central Wyoming College *A*
Northwest College *A*
Sheridan College *A*

Health services administration

Arkansas

University of Arkansas
for Medical Sciences *M*

California

Chapman University *B*

Colorado

National American University
Denver *B*
Regis University *M*

Florida

Brown Mackie College
Miami *A*
Florida National University *A, B*
Keiser University *A, B*
Nova Southeastern University *M*
St. Petersburg College *B*
State College of Florida, Manatee-
Sarasota *B*

Georgia

Mercer University *M*
Middle Georgia State College *B*

Idaho

Carrington College
Boise *A*

Illinois

University of Illinois
Chicago *M*
Urbana-Champaign *B, M, D*

Indiana

Indiana University
Northwest *B*
Purdue University Fort Wayne *B*
Purdue University
Indianapolis *B, M*

Iowa

University of Iowa *M, D*

Kentucky

Sullivan University *B*

Louisiana

Our Lady of the Lake College *B*

Maine

Saint Joseph's College of Maine *M*

Maryland

University of Maryland
College Park *M, D*

Massachusetts

Elms College *B*
Quincy College *A*

Mississippi

Mississippi College *M*

Missouri

Saint Louis University *B, M*
University of Missouri
Columbia *B*
Washington University in St. Louis *M*

Nebraska

University of Nebraska
Medical Center *D*

New York

Ithaca College *B*
Monroe College *B*

SUNY
University at Albany *M*

Ohio

Ohio University *M*
Ohio University
Zanesville Campus *B*
Tiffin University *B, M*
University of Toledo *M*

Oklahoma

Northeastern State University *B*

Oregon

Northwest Christian University *B*
Oregon Health & Science
University *M*

Pennsylvania

Arcadia University *B*
Community College of
Philadelphia *A*
East Stroudsburg University of
Pennsylvania *B*
Harrisburg Area Community
College *A*
Indiana University of Pennsylvania *M*
Marywood University *M*
Robert Morris University *B*
Slippery Rock University of
Pennsylvania *B*
University of Pittsburgh *D*
University of the Sciences *M, D*

Puerto Rico

University of Puerto Rico
Medical Sciences *M*

Rhode Island

Roger Williams University *B*

South Dakota

University of South Dakota *B*

Tennessee

Vanderbilt University *M*

Texas

University of Texas
Health Science Center at
Houston *M, D*

Utah

Weber State University *M*

Virginia

George Mason University *B*

Washington

University of Washington Tacoma *M*

Health teacher education

Alabama

Auburn University *B*
Jacksonville State University *B, T*
Troy University *B*
University of Alabama
Birmingham *B, M, T*
University of Phoenix
Birmingham *M*
University of South Alabama *B, M, T*

Arizona

University of Phoenix
Phoenix-Hohokam *M*

Arkansas

Harding University *B, T*
Ouachita Baptist University *B, T*

California

Azusa Pacific University *T*
California State University
Chico *T*
Long Beach *T*
Northridge *B, T*
San Bernardino *M, T*
San Diego State University *T*
San Francisco State University *T*
University of Phoenix
Bay Area *M*
Central Valley *M*
Sacramento Valley *M*
San Diego *M*
Southern California *M*
University of San Diego *T*
Vanguard University of Southern
California *T*

Connecticut

Southern Connecticut State
University *M*
Western Connecticut State
University *B*

Delaware

Delaware State University *B*
University of Delaware *B, T*

District of Columbia

Howard University *B*
University of the District of
Columbia *B*

Florida

Palm Beach State College *A*
Tallahassee Community College *A*
University of Phoenix
Central Florida *M*
North Florida *M*
South Florida *M*
West Florida *M*

Georgia

Bainbridge College *A*
Georgia Military College *A*
Georgia Perimeter College *A*
Middle Georgia State College *A*
South Georgia State College *A*
University of Phoenix
Atlanta *M*
Augusta *M*
Columbus *M*
Savannah *M*

Hawaii

University of Phoenix
Hawaii *M*

Idaho

Idaho State University *B, M*
Northwest Nazarene University *B*
University of Idaho *T*

Illinois

Chicago State University *B*
DePaul University *B, M*
Eastern Illinois University *B, T*
Eureka College *B*
Illinois State University *B, T*
McKendree University *B*
North Park University *T*
Northern Illinois University *B, T*
Olivet Nazarene University *B, T*
Southern Illinois University
Carbondale *B, M, D*
Southern Illinois University
Edwardsville *B, T*
Western Illinois University *B, M*

Indiana

Ball State University *B, T*
Butler University *T*

Indiana State University *M, T*
Indiana University
Bloomington *B, M, T*
Indiana Wesleyan University *T*
Manchester University *B, T*
Oakland City University *B*
Purdue University *B, M, D*
Trine University *B, T*
University of Indianapolis *T*
University of St. Francis *B*
Vincennes University *A*

Iowa

Central College *T*
Dordt College *B*
Drake University *T*
Graceland University *T*
Grand View University *T*
Iowa State University *B, T*
Iowa Wesleyan College *B*
Northwestern College *T*
St. Ambrose University *B, T*
Simpson College *T*
University of Dubuque *B, T*
University of Northern Iowa *B, M*
Upper Iowa University *B, T*
Wartburg College *T*

Kansas

Bethany College *B*
Bethel College *T*
Colby Community College *A*
Emporia State University *B, T*
Garden City Community College *A*
Independence Community College *A*
McPherson College *T*
Tabor College *B*

Kentucky

Campbellsville University *B*
Hopkinsville Community College *A*
Kentucky Wesleyan College *T*
Morehead State University *B*
Murray State University *B, T*
Union College *B*
University of Kentucky *B*
University of the
Cumberlands *B, M, T*

Louisiana

Centenary College of Louisiana *T*
Louisiana College *B*
University of Phoenix
Baton Rouge *M*
Louisiana *M*
Shreveport *M*

Maine

University of Maine
Farmington *B, T*

Maryland

Allegany College of Maryland *A*
Morgan State University *B*
Prince George's Community
College *A*
Salisbury University *B*
University of Maryland
College Park *B, D*

Massachusetts

Boston University *M, T*
Bridgewater State University *B*
Cambridge College *M*
Springfield College *B, M, T*
Worcester State University *B, T*

Michigan

Adrian College *B, T*
Alma College *T*
Central Michigan University *B*
Eastern Michigan University *M, T*
Michigan State University *B*
Michigan Technological University *T*

Northern Michigan University *B, T*
Olivet College *B, T*
University of Phoenix
　Metro Detroit *M*
　West Michigan *M*
Wayne State University *B, M, T*
Western Michigan University *B*

Minnesota
Augsburg College *B, T*
Bemidji State University *B, T*
Bethel University *B*
Concordia College: Moorhead *B, T*
Concordia University St. Paul *B, T*
Gustavus Adolphus College *T*
Minnesota State University
　Mankato *B, M, T*
　Moorhead *B*
Ridgewater College *A*
Saint Cloud State University *B*
Southwest Minnesota State
　University *B, T*
University of Minnesota
　Duluth *B*
　Twin Cities *M*
University of Northwestern - St.
　Paul *B*
University of St. Thomas *B*
Winona State University *B, M, T*

Mississippi
Coahoma Community College *A*
Itawamba Community College *A*
Mississippi Delta Community
　College *A*
Mississippi University for Women *M*
Tougaloo College *B*

Missouri
Culver-Stockton College *T*
Missouri Baptist University *B, T*
Missouri Southern State
　University *B, T*
Northwest Missouri State
　University *T*
Southwest Baptist University *B, T*

Montana
Montana State University
　Billings *B, T*
University of Great Falls *B*
University of Montana *T*
University of Montana: Western *B, T*

Nebraska
Concordia University *B, T*
University of Nebraska
　Kearney *B, T*

Nevada
University of Nevada
　Las Vegas *B*

New Hampshire
Plymouth State University *B, M, T*

New Jersey
Caldwell College *T*
Montclair State University *B, M, T*
William Paterson University of New
　Jersey *B, T*

New Mexico
University of New Mexico *B, M*
Western New Mexico University *B*

New York
Adelphi University *B, M, T*
City University of New York
　Brooklyn College *M*
　Hunter College *B, T*
　Lehman College *B, M*
　York College *B, T*

Corning Community College *A*
Hofstra University *B, M*
Ithaca College *B, T*
Long Island University
　LIU Post *B, T*
Manhattan College *B, T*
Monroe Community College *A*
New York University *B, M, D*
SUNY
　College at Brockport *B, M, T*
　College at Cortland *B, M*
　College at Oswego *T*
Sage Colleges *M*

North Carolina
Appalachian State University *B, T*
East Carolina University *B, M*
Gardner-Webb University *B*
North Carolina Central
　University *B, T*

North Dakota
Mayville State University *B, T*
North Dakota State University *B, T*
Valley City State University *B, T*

Ohio
Baldwin Wallace University *T*
Bowling Green State University *B, M*
Capital University *T*
Defiance College *B, T*
Kent State University *B, M, D*
Malone University *B*
Mount Vernon Nazarene
　University *B, T*
Ohio Wesleyan University *B*
Otterbein University *B*
University of Akron *B*
University of Cincinnati *B, M, D, T*
University of Findlay *B, M, T*
University of Mount Union *B, T*
University of Rio Grande *B, T*
University of Toledo *B, M, D, T*
Wilmington College *B*
Youngstown State University *B, M*

Oklahoma
Bacone College *B*
East Central University *T*
Eastern Oklahoma State College *A*
Northwestern Oklahoma State
　University *B*
Oklahoma Baptist University *B, T*
Oral Roberts University *B, T*
Southwestern Oklahoma State
　University *B, M, T*

Oregon
Concordia University *B, M, T*
Eastern Oregon University *B*
Linfield College *T*
Portland State University *B, M, T*
Western Oregon University *B, T*

Pennsylvania
Arcadia University *M*
Baptist Bible College of
　Pennsylvania *B*
Chatham University *M*
East Stroudsburg University of
　Pennsylvania *B, M, T*
Penn State
　Harrisburg *M*
Saint Joseph's University *M*
Temple University *M*
West Chester University of
　Pennsylvania *M*

Puerto Rico
Inter American University of Puerto
　Rico
　Arecibo Campus *B*
　Metropolitan Campus *B*
　San German Campus *B*

National University College
　Arecibo *B*
Universidad del Este *B*

Rhode Island
Rhode Island College *B, M*

South Dakota
South Dakota State University *B*
University of Sioux Falls *B*
University of South Dakota *M, T*

Tennessee
Austin Peay State University *B*
Lee University *B*
Lincoln Memorial University *B, T*
Maryville College *B, T*
Middle Tennessee State University *B*
Tennessee Technological
　University *B, M, T*
Tusculum College *B, T*
Union University *T*
University of Phoenix
　Chattanooga *M*
Vanderbilt University *M*

Texas
Angelina College *A*
Austin Community College *A*
Brazosport College *A*
Del Mar College *A*
Kilgore College *A*
Lamar University *B, M, T*
Laredo Community College *A*
Prairie View A&M University *M*
Texas A&M University *M, D*
Texas A&M University
　Kingsville *B*
Texas Southern University *M*
Texas State University *M, T*
University of Houston *M*
University of Phoenix
　Austin *M*
　Dallas Fort Worth *M*
　Houston Westside *M*
University of Texas
　Austin *M, D*
　El Paso *M*
　San Antonio *T*

Utah
Brigham Young University *B*
Snow College *A*
Utah State University *B*
Utah Valley University *B*

Virginia
Averett University *B, M, T*
Bluefield College *B, T*
Eastern Mennonite University *T*
George Mason University *B*
Hampton University *B*
James Madison University *M, T*
Longwood University *T*
Radford University *T*
University of Phoenix
　Northern Virginia *M*
University of Virginia's College at
　Wise *T*
Virginia Commonwealth University *B*

Washington
Central Washington University *B, T*
Eastern Washington University *B*
Northwest University *T*
Washington State University *B, M, T*
Whitworth University *T*

West Virginia
Concord University *B*
Shepherd University *T*
University of Charleston *B*
West Liberty University *B*
West Virginia State University *B*

West Virginia University *T*
West Virginia Wesleyan College *B*

Wisconsin
Carroll University *B*
Carthage College *T*
Concordia University Wisconsin *B*
Ripon College *T*
University of Wisconsin
　La Crosse *B, M, T*
　Platteville *T*
　River Falls *T*
　Superior *T*

Health unit coordinator

Arizona
GateWay Community College *C*

California
City College of San Francisco *A*
Hartnell College *C*

Florida
Pasco-Hernando State College *C*
Pensacola State College *C*

Georgia
Southwest Georgia Technical
　College *C*

Illinois
Illinois Eastern Community Colleges
　Olney Central College *C*

Kansas
Highland Community College *A*

Kentucky
Jefferson Community and Technical
　College *C*

Michigan
Delta College *C*
Lansing Community College *C*

Minnesota
Hennepin Technical College *C, A*
Minnesota State College - Southeast
　Technical *C*
Rochester Community and Technical
　College *C*
St. Paul College *C*
South Central College *C*

Missouri
Cox College *C*

New Mexico
Central New Mexico Community
　College *C*

New York
Globe Institute of Technology *C*

North Carolina
Pitt Community College *C*
Roanoke-Chowan Community
　College *C*

Ohio
Cincinnati State Technical and
　Community College *C*

Pennsylvania
Career Training Academy:
　Monroeville *A*
Community College of Allegheny
　County *C*
Delaware County Community
　College *C*

South Carolina

Spartanburg Community College *C*

South Dakota

Southeast Technical Institute *C, A*
Western Dakota Technical Institute *C*

Utah

Salt Lake Community College *C*

Washington

Centralia College *C*
Clover Park Technical College *C*
Edmonds Community College *C*
Spokane Community College *C, A*
Whatcom Community College *C*

Wisconsin

Gateway Technical College *C*
Lakeshore Technical College *C*
Mid-State Technical College *C*
Milwaukee Area Technical College *C*
Waukesha County Technical
College *C*

Health unit manager

Illinois

Southern Illinois University
Carbondale *M*

Mississippi

University of Mississippi *M*

Pennsylvania

Delaware County Community
College *C, A*

Wisconsin

Herzing University
Madison *B*

Hearing instrument specialist

Washington

Bates Technical College *A*

Heating/air conditioning/ refrigeration maintenance

Alabama

Calhoun Community College *C, A*
Community College of the Air
Force *A*
Faulkner State Community College *A*
Gadsden State Community
College *C, A*
Jefferson Davis Community
College *C*
Lawson State Community College *C*
Southern Union State Community
College *C, A*
Wallace State Community College at
Hanceville *C, A*

Alaska

University of Alaska
Anchorage *C, A*

Arizona

Arizona Western College *C, A*
Cochise College *C*
Eastern Arizona College *C*
GateWay Community College *C, A*
Mohave Community College *C, A*
Northland Pioneer College *C, A*
Pima Community College *C*
Refrigeration School *C, A*

Arkansas

Arkansas Northeastern College *C*
Arkansas State University
Beebe *C*
Arkansas Tech University *C*
College of the Ouachitas *C*
National Park Community College *C*
North Arkansas College *C*
Pulaski Technical College *C, A*
Southeast Arkansas College *C*
University of Arkansas
Community College at Hope *C*
Community College at
Morrilton *C, A*

California

Cerro Coso Community College *C, A*
Citrus College *C, A*
College of the Desert *C, A*
Contra Costa College *C*
Cypress College *C, A*
El Camino College *C, A*
Foothill College *C*
Fresno City College *C, A*
Imperial Valley College *C, A*
Institute of Technology: Clovis *C*
Laney College *C, A*
Los Angeles Trade and Technical
College *C, A*
Los Medanos College *C*
Merced College *C, A*
Modesto Junior College *C, A*
Mount San Antonio College *C, A*
Orange Coast College *C, A*
Riverside City College *C, A*
Sacramento City College *C, A*
San Bernardino Valley College *C, A*
San Diego City College *C, A*
San Joaquin Valley College *A*
San Jose City College *C, A*
Santa Rosa Junior College *C*
Southwestern College *C*

Colorado

IntelliTec College *A*
Pikes Peak Community College *C, A*
Redstone College *C*
Westwood College
Denver North *A*

Delaware

Delaware Technical Community
College
Jack F. Owens Campus *C, A*

District of Columbia

University of the District of
Columbia *C*

Florida

College of Business and Technology
Flagler *C, A*
Hialeah *C, A*
College of Central Florida *C*
Daytona State College *C*
Eastern Florida State College *C*
Florida Gateway College *C*
Florida State College at
Jacksonville *C*
Hillsborough Community College *C*
Indian River State College *C, A*
Lincoln College of Technology
West Palm Beach *C, A*
Miami Dade College *C, A*
Palm Beach State College *C*
Santa Fe College *C*
Seminole State College of Florida *C*
South Florida State College *C*

Georgia

Albany Technical College *C*
Altamaha Technical College *C, A*
Athens Technical College *C*
Atlanta Technical College *C*

Augusta Technical College *C*
Central Georgia Technical College *C*
Chattahoochee Technical College *C*
Columbus Technical College *C*
Georgia Piedmont Technical
College *C, A*
Gwinnett Technical College *C, A*
Middle Georgia State College *A*
North Georgia Technical
College *C, A*
Savannah Technical College *C, A*
South Georgia State College *A*
Southeastern Technical College *C*
Southwest Georgia Technical
College *C*

Hawaii

University of Hawaii
Honolulu Community College *C, A*

Idaho

College of Southern Idaho *C, A*
Lewis-Clark State College *C, A, B*
North Idaho College *C, A*

Illinois

Black Hawk College *C, A*
City Colleges of Chicago
Kennedy-King College *C, A*
College of DuPage *C, A*
College of Lake County *C, A*
Danville Area Community College *C*
Elgin Community College *C, A*
Harper College *C, A*
Heartland Community College *C*
Illinois Central College *C, A*
Illinois Eastern Community Colleges
Lincoln Trail College *C, A*
Illinois Valley Community College *C*
John A. Logan College *C*
Joliet Junior College *C*
Kankakee Community College *C, A*
Kaskaskia College *C*
Lake Land College *C*
Lincoln Land Community College *C*
Moraine Valley Community
College *C, A*
Morton College *C, A*
Oakton Community College *C*
Prairie State College *C*
Rend Lake College *C*
Richland Community College *C, A*
Sauk Valley Community College *C, A*
Southwestern Illinois College *C, A*
Triton College *A*
Waubonsee Community College *C, A*

Indiana

Fortis College
Indianapolis *C*
Ivy Tech Community College
Bloomington *C, A*
Central Indiana *C, A*
Columbus *C, A*
East Central *C, A*
Kokomo *C, A*
Lafayette *C, A*
North Central *C, A*
Northeast *C, A*
Northwest *C, A*
Richmond *C, A*
South Central *C, A*
Southwest *C, A*
Wabash Valley *C, A*

Iowa

Des Moines Area Community
College *C, A*
Hawkeye Community College *C*
Kirkwood Community College *C*
Marshalltown Community College *A*
North Iowa Area Community
College *C, A*

Northeast Iowa Community
College *C*
Western Iowa Tech Community
College *C*

Kansas

Highland Community College *C*
Kansas City Kansas Community
College *C*
Manhattan Area Technical
College *C, A*
North Central Kansas Technical
College *C*
Wichita Area Technical College *C, A*

Kentucky

Big Sandy Community and Technical
College *C, A*
Bluegrass Community and Technical
College *C, A*
Elizabethtown Community and
Technical College *C*
Gateway Community and Technical
College *C, A*
Hopkinsville Community College *C*
Jefferson Community and Technical
College *C*
Madisonville Community College *C*
Owensboro Community and
Technical College *C*
Somerset Community College *C*
Sullivan College of Technology and
Design *A*
West Kentucky Community and
Technical College *C*

Louisiana

Delgado Community College *C, A*
ITI Technical College *C*
Nunez Community College *C, A*

Maine

Eastern Maine Community
College *C, A*
Northern Maine Community
College *A*
Southern Maine Community
College *C, A*
Washington County Community
College *C*

Massachusetts

Benjamin Franklin Institute of
Technology *C*
Massasoit Community College *C, A*
Quinsigamond Community College *C*
Springfield Technical Community
College *C*

Michigan

Baker College
Owosso *C*
Delta College *C, A*
Grand Rapids Community College *C*
Jackson College *C, A*
Kellogg Community College *C, A*
Kirtland Community College *C, A*
Lansing Community College *C, A*
Macomb Community College *C, A*
Mid Michigan Community
College *C, A*
Northern Michigan University *C, A*
Northwestern Michigan College *C, A*
Oakland Community College *C*
Washtenaw Community College *A*
Wayne County Community
College *C, A*

Minnesota

Century College *C, A*
Dunwoody College of
Technology *C, A*
Hennepin Technical College *C, A*
Hibbing Community College *C*

Minneapolis Community and
  Technical College *C, A*
Minnesota State College - Southeast
  Technical *C, A*
Minnesota State Community and
  Technical College *C*
Minnesota West Community and
  Technical College *A*
Northland Community & Technical
  College *C, A*
Rochester Community and Technical
  College *C*
St. Cloud Technical and Community
  College *C, A*
South Central College *C, A*

Mississippi

East Central Community College *C, A*
Hinds Community College *C, A*
Holmes Community College *A*
Itawamba Community College *C*
Mississippi Delta Community
  College *A*
Mississippi Gulf Coast Community
  College *C*
Northeast Mississippi Community
  College *C, A*
Northwest Mississippi Community
  College *C, A*
Pearl River Community College *C, A*
Southwest Mississippi Community
  College *C*

Missouri

East Central College *C, A*
Jefferson College *C, A*
Linn State Technical College *A*
Metropolitan Community College -
  Kansas City *C, A*
Mineral Area College *C, A*
Ranken Technical College *A*

Montana

Flathead Valley Community College *C*

Nebraska

Central Community College *C, A*
Metropolitan Community
  College *C, A*
Mid-Plains Community College *C, A*
Northeast Community College *A*
Southeast Community College *A*
Vatterott College
  Spring Valley *C*

Nevada

College of Southern Nevada *C, A*
Truckee Meadows Community
  College *C, A*

New Hampshire

Manchester Community College *C, A*

New Mexico

Central New Mexico Community
  College *C, A*
Dona Ana Community College of
  New Mexico State
  University *C, A*
Eastern New Mexico University:
  Roswell *C, A*
New Mexico State University
  Carlsbad *C*
Santa Fe Community College *C*

New York

Erie Community College *C*
Hudson Valley Community College *A*
Mohawk Valley Community
  College *C, A*
Monroe Community College *C, A*

SUNY
  College of Technology at Alfred *A*
  College of Technology at Canton *C*
  College of Technology at
    Delhi *C, A*

North Carolina

Alamance Community College *C, A*
Asheville-Buncombe Technical
  Community College *C, A*
Blue Ridge Community College *C*
Brunswick Community College *C*
Caldwell Community College and
  Technical Institute *C*
Cape Fear Community College *C*
Catawba Valley Community
  College *C*
Central Piedmont Community
  College *C*
Cleveland Community College *C*
Coastal Carolina Community
  College *C, A*
College of the Albemarle *C*
Davidson County Community
  College *C*
Fayetteville Technical Community
  College *C, A*
Forsyth Technical Community
  College *C*
Gaston College *C*
Guilford Technical Community
  College *C, A*
Johnston Community College *C, A*
Martin Community College *C, A*
McDowell Technical Community
  College *C*
Mitchell Community College *C*
Montgomery Community
  College *C, A*
Piedmont Community College *C*
Pitt Community College *C, A*
Roanoke-Chowan Community
  College *C*
Rockingham Community College *C*
Rowan-Cabarrus Community
  College *C*
South Piedmont Community
  College *C, A*
Southwestern Community College *C*
Stanly Community College *C*
Surry Community College *C, A*
Tri-County Community College *C*
Vance-Granville Community
  College *C*
Wake Technical Community
  College *C, A*
Wayne Community College *C*
Wilson Community College *C, A*

North Dakota

Bismarck State College *C, A*
North Dakota State College of
  Science *C, A*

Ohio

Belmont College *C, A*
ETI Technical College of Niles *C*
Fortis College
  Centerville *C*
Stark State College *A*
University of Northwestern
  Ohio *C, A*
Vatterott College
  Cleveland *C*
Washington State Community
  College *A*

Oklahoma

Oklahoma State University
  Institute of Technology:
  Okmulgee *A*
Tulsa Community College *A*

Oregon

Lane Community College *C, A*
Linn-Benton Community College *C*
Portland Community College *C, A*

Pennsylvania

Butler County Community College *A*
Community College of Allegheny
  County *C, A*
Dean Institute of Technology *A*
Delaware County Community
  College *C, A*
Fortis Institute
  Erie *A*
Harrisburg Area Community
  College *C, A*
Johnson College *A*
Kaplan Career Institute
  Franklin Mills *C*
Lehigh Carbon Community
  College *C, A*
Luzerne County Community
  College *A*
New Castle School of Trades *A*
Northampton Community
  College *C, A*
Orleans Technical Institute *C*
Pennco Tech *C*
Reading Area Community
  College *C, A*
Thaddeus Stevens College of
  Technology *A*
Triangle Tech
  Pittsburgh *A*
Westmoreland County Community
  College *C, A*

Puerto Rico

Huertas College *C, A*

Rhode Island

New England Institute of
  Technology *A*

South Carolina

Aiken Technical College *C*
Central Carolina Technical College *C*
Florence-Darlington Technical
  College *C, A*
Greenville Technical College *C*
Horry-Georgetown Technical
  College *C, A*
Midlands Technical College *C, A*
Piedmont Technical College *C, A*
Spartanburg Community College *C*
Technical College of the
  Lowcountry *C*
Tri-County Technical College *A*
Trident Technical College *C*
Williamsburg Technical College *C, A*
York Technical College *C, A*

South Dakota

Mitchell Technical Institute *A*
Oglala Lakota College *C*
Southeast Technical Institute *A*
Western Dakota Technical Institute *C*

Tennessee

Chattanooga State Community
  College *C*
Northeast State Community
  College *C*

Texas

Brazosport College *C, A*
Cedar Valley College *C, A*
Central Texas College *C, A*
Cisco College *C*
College of the Mainland *C, A*
Del Mar College *C, A*
Eastfield College *C, A*
El Paso Community College *C, A*

Everest College
  Arlington *C*
Frank Phillips College *C*
Galveston College *C, A*
Grayson College *C, A*
Houston Community College
  System *C*
Lamar State College at Port
  Arthur *C, A*
Laredo Community College *C*
Lee College *C, A*
Lincoln College of Technology
  Grand Prairie *C*
Lone Star College System *C, A*
Midland College *C, A*
Odessa College *C, A*
Panola College *C*
Paris Junior College *C, A*
St. Philip's College *C, A*
San Jacinto College *C, A*
South Plains College *C, A*
South Texas College *C, A*
Texarkana College *C*
Texas State Technical College
  Harlingen *C, A*
  West Texas *C*
Trinity Valley Community College *C*
Tyler Junior College *C, A*
Wharton County Junior College *C*

Utah

Salt Lake Community College *C, A*

Virginia

Advanced Technology Institute *C, A*
Central Virginia Community
  College *C*
Danville Community College *A*
John Tyler Community College *C*
Mountain Empire Community
  College *C*
New River Community College *C*
Northern Virginia Community
  College *C, A*
Patrick Henry Community College *C*
Southside Virginia Community
  College *C*
Southwest Virginia Community
  College *C*
Thomas Nelson Community
  College *C*
Tidewater Community College *C*
Virginia Highlands Community
  College *C*
Virginia Western Community
  College *C*

Washington

Bates Technical College *C, A*
Bellingham Technical College *A*
Clover Park Technical College *C, A*
North Seattle Community
  College *C, A*
Renton Technical College *C, A*
Spokane Community College *A*
Walla Walla Community College *C, A*
Wenatchee Valley College *C, A*
Yakima Valley Community College *A*

West Virginia

West Virginia Northern Community
  College *A*

Wisconsin

Blackhawk Technical College *A*
Chippewa Valley Technical College *C*
Milwaukee Area Technical College *C*
Moraine Park Technical College *C, A*
Northeast Wisconsin Technical
  College *A*
Waukesha County Technical
  College *C*
Western Technical College *C*

Wyoming

Laramie County Community
College *A*

Heating/ventilation/air conditioning/refrigeration technology

Alabama

Bevill State Community College *C, A*
Bishop State Community College *C*
Calhoun Community College *A*
Gadsden State Community
College *C, A*
George C. Wallace Community
College at Dothan *C, A*
Lawson State Community College *C*
Lurleen B. Wallace Community
College *C*
Northwest-Shoals Community
College *C, A*
Shelton State Community
College *C, A*

Alaska

Charter College *C*
University of Alaska
Anchorage *C*

Arizona

Refrigeration School *C*

California

Bakersfield College *C*
Citrus College *C*
City College of San Francisco *C*
College of the Desert *C, A*
Imperial Valley College *C, A*
Long Beach City College *C, A*
Orange Coast College *C, A*
Oxnard College *C, A*
San Joaquin Delta College *A*
San Jose City College *C, A*
WyoTech: Fremont *C*
WyoTech: Long Beach *C*
WyoTech: Sacramento *C*

Colorado

Community College of Denver *A*
Front Range Community College *C, A*

Delaware

Delaware Technical Community
College
Stanton/Wilmington Campus *A*

Florida

Florida Gateway College *C*
Palm Beach State College *C*

Georgia

Columbus Technical College *C*
Southeastern Technical College *C*

Idaho

University of Idaho *C*

Illinois

Oakton Community College *C*

Kansas

Johnson County Community
College *C, A*

Kentucky

Sullivan College of Technology and
Design *A*

Maryland

Community College of Baltimore
County *C, A*

Massachusetts

Springfield Technical Community
College *A*

Michigan

Delta College *C, A*
Ferris State University *A*
Grand Rapids Community College *A*
Henry Ford Community College *C*
Jackson College *C, A*
Mott Community College *C, A*
Northern Michigan University *A*
Oakland Community College *C, A*

Minnesota

Dunwoody College of Technology *A*
Hennepin Technical College *C, A*
Hibbing Community College *C*
Minnesota West Community and
Technical College *A*
South Central College *C, A*

Mississippi

Copiah-Lincoln Community
College *C, A*

Missouri

Metropolitan Community College -
Kansas City *C, A*
Ozarks Technical Community
College *C, A*

Nebraska

Northeast Community College *A*
Vatterott College
Spring Valley *A*

New Jersey

Mercer County Community
College *C, A*
Raritan Valley Community College *A*

New Mexico

Santa Fe Community College *C*

New York

City University of New York
New York City College of
Technology *C*
Dutchess Community College *C*
Monroe Community College *A*
SUNY
College of Technology at Alfred *A*
College of Technology at Canton *A*
Suffolk County Community College *A*
Technical Career Institutes *C, A*

North Carolina

College of the Albemarle *C, A*
Gaston College *C*
Roanoke-Chowan Community
College *C*
Robeson Community College *C*
Southeastern Community College *C*

North Dakota

North Dakota State College of
Science *A*

Ohio

Columbus State Community
College *C*
Fortis College
Centerville *C*
Ravenna *C, A*
North Central State College *C, A*
Northwest State Community
College *C*
Owens Community College
Toledo *C*
Sinclair Community College *C, A*
Terra State Community College *C, A*
University of Cincinnati *C*

Oklahoma

Western Oklahoma State College *A*

Pennsylvania

Community College of Beaver
County *A*
Dean Institute of Technology *A*
Delaware County Community
College *C*
Penn Commercial Business and
Technical School *A*
Pennsylvania College of
Technology *A*
Thaddeus Stevens College of
Technology *A*
Triangle Tech
Greensburg *A*

Puerto Rico

Humacao Community College *C, A*
Universal Technology College of
Puerto Rico *C*

Rhode Island

New England Institute of
Technology *A*

South Carolina

York Technical College *C, A*

South Dakota

Southeast Technical Institute *C, A*

Tennessee

Northeast State Community
College *C*
Vatterott College
Memphis *C, A*

Texas

Austin Community College *C, A*
Clarendon College *C*
Lamar Institute of Technology *C, A*
Midland College *C, A*
St. Philip's College *C, A*
Tarrant County College *C, A*
Texas State Technical College
Waco *C, A*
Weatherford College *C*
Western Technical College *C, A*

Virginia

Liberty University *A*
Lord Fairfax Community College *C*

Washington

Bates Technical College *C, A*

Wisconsin

Chippewa Valley Technical College *A*
Gateway Technical College *A*
Milwaukee Area Technical College *A*
Northeast Wisconsin Technical
College *A*
Western Technical College *A*
Wisconsin Indianhead Technical
College *C*

Heavy/earthmoving equipment operation

Alabama

Jefferson Davis Community
College *C*

Arizona

Mesa Community College *A*
Northland Pioneer College *C, A*

Arkansas

North Arkansas College *C*

California

Bakersfield College *C, A*

Colorado

Trinidad State Junior College *C, A*

Florida

Indian River State College *C*

Indiana

Ivy Tech Community College
Southwest *C, A*
Wabash Valley *C, A*

Iowa

Northwest Iowa Community
College *C*

Kansas

North Central Kansas Technical
College *C*

Maine

Southern Maine Community
College *C*
Washington County Community
College *C*

Michigan

Lansing Community College *C, A*

Minnesota

Central Lakes College *C*

Missouri

Linn State Technical College *C*

Montana

Flathead Valley Community College *C*
Fort Peck Community College *C*
Miles Community College *C*
Salish Kootenai College *C*

Pennsylvania

Pittsburgh Institute of Aeronautics *C*

South Dakota

Lake Area Technical Institute *A*

Utah

Utah State University *C*

Virginia

Southside Virginia Community
College *C*
Southwest Virginia Community
College *C*

Wisconsin

Mid-State Technical College *C*

Heavy equipment maintenance

Alaska

University of Alaska
Anchorage *C, A*

California

Rio Hondo College *C*
San Deigo Miramar College
San Diego Miramar College *C, A*
San Joaquin Delta College *C, A*
Shasta College *C*

Georgia

Albany Technical College *C*
Atlanta Technical College *C*
Gwinnett Technical College *C*
Southwest Georgia Technical
College *A*

Idaho
College of Western Idaho *C, A*

Illinois
Highland Community College *C, A*
Rend Lake College *C, A*

Kentucky
Bluegrass Community and Technical
College *C, A*

Michigan
Ferris State University *A, B*
Wayne County Community
College *C, A*

Minnesota
Central Lakes College *A*
Dakota County Technical
College *C, A*

Missouri
Linn State Technical College *A*

New York
SUNY
College of Technology at Alfred *A*

North Carolina
Asheville-Buncombe Technical
Community College *C*
Beaufort County Community
College *A*

Oregon
Linn-Benton Community College *A*

Pennsylvania
Pennsylvania College of
Technology *A*

Tennessee
Lincoln College of Technology
Nashville *C, A*

Washington
Clover Park Technical College *C, A*
Lower Columbia College *A*
South Seattle Community
College *C, A*

Wisconsin
Blackhawk Technical College *C*
Chippewa Valley Technical College *C*
Mid-State Technical College *C*
Western Technical College *C*

Wyoming
Western Wyoming Community
College *C, A*

Hebrew

California
University of California
Los Angeles *B*

District of Columbia
Catholic University of America *M, D*
George Washington University *B*

Illinois
Moody Bible Institute *B*
Trinity International University *M*
University of Illinois
Urbana-Champaign *B*

Massachusetts
Brandeis University *B*

Michigan
University of Michigan *B*

Minnesota
University of Minnesota
Twin Cities *B*

Missouri
Washington University in St.
Louis *B, M*

New Hampshire
Dartmouth College *B*

New York
Bard College *B*
City University of New York
Hunter College *B*
Queens College *B*
Hofstra University *B*
Jewish Theological Seminary of
America *M, D*
New York University *B, M, D*
SUNY
University at Binghamton *B*
Touro College *B*
Yeshiva University *A, B, M, D*

Ohio
Ohio State University
Columbus Campus *B*
University of Cincinnati *B*

Oregon
Multnomah University *B*

Texas
University of Texas
Austin *B, M, D*

Utah
University of Utah *B, M, D*

Washington
University of Washington *B*

Wisconsin
University of Wisconsin
Madison *B, M, D*

Hematology technology

Illinois
Elgin Community College *C*

New Mexico
Central New Mexico Community
College *C*

Oregon
Linn-Benton Community College *C*

Herbalism

Vermont
Goddard College *B, M*

Washington
Bastyr University *B*

High performance/ custom engine mechanic

Minnesota
Northwest Technical College *C, A*

Ohio
Ohio Technical College *A*

Rhode Island
New England Institute of
Technology *A*

Virginia
Advanced Technology Institute *C, A*

Higher education administration

Alabama
Auburn University *D*
University of Alabama *M, D*

Alaska
University of Alaska
Anchorage *T*

Arizona
Argosy University
Online *M*
Phoenix *M*
Arizona State University *M, D*
Grand Canyon University *D*
Northcentral University *M, D*
University of Arizona *M, D*

Arkansas
John Brown University *M*
University of Arkansas *M, D*
University of Arkansas
Little Rock *D*

California
Argosy University
Inland Empire *M*
Orange County *M*
San Diego *M*
San Francisco Bay Area *M*
Azusa Pacific University *M, D*
California Coast University *M*
California State University
Fullerton *M*
National University *M*
San Jose State University *M*
Stanford University *D*
University of San Diego *M*
University of Southern California *M*

Colorado
Argosy University
Denver *M*
Colorado State University *M*
University of Denver *M, D*
University of Northern Colorado *D*

Connecticut
University of Connecticut *M, T*

District of Columbia
George Washington University *M, D*

Florida
Barry University *M*
Florida International University *M, D*
Florida State University *M, T*
Nova Southeastern University *D*
University of Florida *D*
University of Miami *M, D*
University of South Florida *M*

Georgia
Georgia Southern University *M*
University of Georgia *M, D*

Illinois
Benedictine University *D*
Loyola University Chicago *M, D*
McKendree University *M*
Southern Illinois University
Carbondale *M*
University of Illinois
Urbana-Champaign *M, D*

Indiana
Indiana University
Bloomington *D*
Taylor University *M*

Iowa
Iowa State University *M, D*
University of Iowa *M, D*

Kansas
University of Kansas *M*

Kentucky
Northern Kentucky University *M*
University of Kentucky *M*
University of Louisville *M*

Maine
University of Maine *M, D*
University of Southern Maine *M*

Maryland
Morgan State University *M, D*

Massachusetts
Bay Path College *M*
Boston College *M, D*
Harvard College *M, D*
Merrimack College *M*
Salem State University *M*
Springfield College *D*

Michigan
Eastern Michigan University *M*
Grand Valley State University *M*
Michigan State University *M, D*
University of Michigan *M, D*
Western Michigan University *D, T*

Minnesota
Argosy University
Twin Cities *M*
Capella University *M, D*
Minnesota State University
Mankato *M*
Saint Cloud State University *M, D*
University of St. Thomas *M*
Walden University *M*

Mississippi
Jackson State University *D*
Mississippi College *M*
University of Mississippi *M, D*
University of Southern Mississippi *D*

Missouri
Maryville University of Saint Louis *D*
Missouri State University *M*
Northwest Missouri State
University *M*
Saint Louis University *M, D*
Southeast Missouri State University *M*
University of Central Missouri *M*
University of Missouri
Columbia *D*

New Hampshire
New England College *M, D*

New Jersey
Rowan University *M*
Seton Hall University *D*

New York
City University of New York
Baruch College *M*
Fordham University *M, D*
Hofstra University *T*
SUNY
College at Buffalo *M*
University at Albany *M, D*
University at Binghamton *M*

University at Buffalo *M, D*
University at Stony Brook *M, T*
Saint Bonaventure University *M*
Syracuse University *M, D*
University of Rochester *M, D*

North Carolina

Appalachian State University *M*
North Carolina State University *M, D*
University of North Carolina
Greensboro *M*

North Dakota

University of North Dakota *D*

Ohio

Baldwin Wallace University *M*
Bowling Green State University *D*
Kent State University *M, D*
Ohio University *M, D*
Union Institute & University *D*
University of Akron *M*
University of Dayton *M, D*
University of Findlay *M, T*
University of Toledo *M, D, T*
Youngstown State University *M*

Oklahoma

Northeastern State University *M*
Oklahoma State University *D*

Oregon

George Fox University *M*
Portland State University *D*

Pennsylvania

Drexel University *M, T*
Geneva College *M*
Marywood University *M*
Messiah College *M*
Penn State
University Park *M, D*
Slippery Rock University of
Pennsylvania *M*
University of Pennsylvania *M, D*
Villanova University *M*
Widener University *M, D*

Puerto Rico

Inter American University of Puerto
Rico
Metropolitan Campus *M*

South Carolina

University of South Carolina
Columbia *M*

South Dakota

Dakota Wesleyan University *M*
University of South Dakota *M, D*

Tennessee

Union University *D*
University of Memphis *D*
University of Tennessee
Knoxville *D*
Vanderbilt University *M, D*

Texas

Abilene Christian University *M*
Argosy University
Dallas *M*
Baylor University *M*
Dallas Baptist University *M, D*
Texas A&M University
Commerce *M, D*
Kingsville *M, D*
Texas State University *M*
University of Houston *M*
University of North Texas *M, D*
University of Texas
San Antonio *M*

Utah

Argosy University
Salt Lake City *M*

Vermont

University of Vermont *M*

Virginia

College of William and Mary *M, D*
Regent University *M*
University of Virginia *M, D*

Washington

City University of Seattle *M*
Seattle University *M*
University of Washington *M, D*
Washington State University *M, D*
Western Washington University *M*

Wisconsin

Concordia University Wisconsin *M*

Hispanic and Latin American languages

California

University of California
Merced *B*
University of Southern
California *M, D*

New York

Hamilton College *B*

Pennsylvania

University of Pittsburgh *M, D*

Texas

Stephen F. Austin State University *B*
University of Houston *D*
University of Texas
El Paso *M*

Histologic assistant

Alabama

Community College of the Air
Force *A*

Arizona

Pima Community College *A*

Connecticut

Goodwin College *C, A*

Georgia

Darton College *A*

Indiana

Indiana University
Purdue University
Indianapolis *C, A*

Michigan

Lansing Community College *C, A*
Mott Community College *A*
Northern Michigan University *B*
Oakland Community College *A*

New York

Broome Community College *C*
SUNY
College of Agriculture and
Technology at Cobleskill *A*

Ohio

Sinclair Community College *C*
University of Akron *A*
Youngstown State University *A*

Pennsylvania

Harcum College *A*

Rhode Island

Community College of Rhode
Island *A*

Texas

Houston Community College
System *A*
St. Philip's College *A*
Tarleton State University *A*

Washington

Clover Park Technical College *A*

Histologic technology

Arizona

Phoenix College *A*

Delaware

Delaware Technical Community
College
Stanton/Wilmington Campus *A*

Florida

Miami Dade College *A*

Georgia

Darton College *A*

Illinois

Southern Illinois University
Carbondale *C*

Massachusetts

Bristol Community College *C*

Michigan

Northern Michigan University *A*
Oakland Community College *A*
Oakland University *B*

Minnesota

North Hennepin Community
College *A*

Ohio

Lakeland Community College *A*

Pennsylvania

Drexel University *M*

Historic preservation

California

University of Southern California *M*

Colorado

Colorado Mountain College *A*
University of Colorado
Denver *M*

Delaware

Delaware State University *M*
University of Delaware *B, M*

District of Columbia

George Washington University *M*

Florida

University of Florida *M*

Georgia

Clayton State University *M*
Savannah College of Art and
Design *B, M*
University of Georgia *M*

Illinois

School of the Art Institute of
Chicago *M*

Indiana

Ball State University *M*

Kentucky

University of Kentucky *M*

Maryland

Goucher College *M*

Massachusetts

Boston University *M*

Michigan

Eastern Michigan University *M*

Missouri

Southeast Missouri State
University *C, B*

New York

Cornell University *M*

Ohio

Belmont College *A*
University of Cincinnati *C*
Ursuline College *B, M*

Oregon

Clatsop Community College *C, A*
University of Oregon *M*

Pennsylvania

Bucks County Community College *C*
University of Pennsylvania *M*

Rhode Island

Roger Williams University *D*
Salve Regina University *B*

South Carolina

Clemson University *M*
College of Charleston *B, M*

Texas

Texas Tech University *M*
University of Texas
Austin *M, D*

Vermont

University of Vermont *M*

Virginia

University of Mary Washington *B*

Wisconsin

University of Wisconsin
Milwaukee *C*

History

Alabama

Alabama State University *B*
Athens State University *B*
Auburn University *B, M, D*
Auburn University at Montgomery *B*
Birmingham-Southern College *B*
Calhoun Community College *A*
Community College of the Air
Force *A*
Faulkner University *B, T*
Huntingdon College *B*
Jacksonville State University *B, M*
Judson College *B*
Miles College *B*
Oakwood University *B*
Samford University *B*
Spring Hill College *B, T*
Stillman College *B*

Talladega College *B*
Troy University *B, M*
Tuskegee University *B*
University of Alabama *B, M, D*
University of Alabama
  Birmingham *B, M*
  Huntsville *B, M*
University of Mobile *B*
University of Montevallo *B, T*
University of North Alabama *B, M*
University of South Alabama *B, M*
University of West Alabama *B, T*

Alaska

University of Alaska
  Anchorage *B*
  Fairbanks *B*

Arizona

Arizona State University *B, M, D*
Arizona Western College *A*
Eastern Arizona College *A*
Grand Canyon University *B*
Northern Arizona University *B, M*
South Mountain Community
  College *A*
University of Arizona *B, M, D*

Arkansas

Arkansas State University *B, M*
Arkansas Tech University *B, M*
Harding University *B*
Henderson State University *B*
Hendrix College *B*
John Brown University *B*
Lyon College *B*
Ouachita Baptist University *B*
Southern Arkansas University *B*
University of Arkansas *B, M, D*
University of Arkansas
  Fort Smith *B*
  Little Rock *B, M*
  Monticello *B*
  Pine Bluff *B*
University of Central Arkansas *B, M*
University of the Ozarks *B*
Williams Baptist College *B*

California

Azusa Pacific University *B*
Bakersfield College *A*
Biola University *B*
Butte College *A*
Cabrillo College *A*
California Baptist University *B*
California Institute of Technology *B*
California Lutheran University *B*
California Polytechnic State
  University: San Luis Obispo *B, M*
California State Polytechnic
  University: Pomona *B, M*
California State University
  Bakersfield *B, M*
  Channel Islands *B*
  Chico *C, B, M*
  Dominguez Hills *B*
  East Bay *B, M*
  Fresno *B, M*
  Fullerton *B, M*
  Long Beach *B, M*
  Los Angeles *B, M*
  Northridge *B*
  Sacramento *B, M*
  San Bernardino *B, T*
  San Marcos *B, M*
  Stanislaus *B, M*
Canada College *A*
Cerritos College *A*
Chabot College *A*
Chaffey College *A*
Chapman University *B*
Claremont McKenna College *B*
College of Alameda *A*
College of Marin *A*

College of the Canyons *A*
College of the Desert *A*
College of the Siskiyous *A*
Concordia University Irvine *B*
Contra Costa College *A*
Copper Mountain College *A*
Crafton Hills College *A*
Cypress College *A*
De Anza College *A*
Dominican University of California *B*
El Camino College *A*
Feather River College *A*
Foothill College *A*
Fresno City College *A*
Fresno Pacific University *B*
Fullerton College *A*
Gavilan College *A*
Glendale Community College *A*
Golden West College *A*
Grossmont College *A*
Hartnell College *A*
Holy Names University *B*
Humboldt State University *B*
Imperial Valley College *A*
Irvine Valley College *A*
La Sierra University *B*
Lassen Community College *A*
Los Angeles Southwest College *A*
Los Angeles Valley College *A*
Loyola Marymount University *B*
Master's College *B*
Merced College *A*
Mills College *B*
MiraCosta College *A*
Monterey Peninsula College *A*
Moorpark College *A*
Mount St. Mary's College *B*
National University *B, M*
Notre Dame de Namur University *B*
Occidental College *B*
Orange Coast College *A*
Oxnard College *A*
Pacific Union College *B*
Palo Verde College *A*
Pepperdine University *B*
Pitzer College *B*
Point Loma Nazarene University *B*
Pomona College *B*
Providence Christian College *B*
Saddleback College *A*
St. Mary's College of California *B*
San Deigo Miramar College
  San Diego Miramar College *A*
San Diego Christian College *B*
San Diego City College *A*
San Diego State University *B, M*
San Francisco State University *B, M*
San Joaquin Delta College *A*
San Jose State University *B, M*
Santa Ana College *A*
Santa Barbara City College *A*
Santa Clara University *B*
Santa Rosa Junior College *A*
Santiago Canyon College *A*
Scripps College *B*
Sierra College *A*
Simpson University *B*
Solano Community College *A*
Sonoma State University *B, M*
Southwestern College *A*
Stanford University *B, M, D*
Taft College *A*
University of California
  Berkeley *B, M, D*
  Davis *B, M, D*
  Irvine *B, M, D*
  Los Angeles *B, M, D*
  Merced *B, M, D*
  Riverside *B, M, D*
  San Diego *B, M, D*
  Santa Barbara *B, M, D*
  Santa Cruz *B, M, D*
University of La Verne *B*
University of Redlands *B*
University of San Diego *B, M*

University of San Francisco *B*
University of Southern
  California *B, M, D*
University of the Pacific *B*
University of the West *B*
Vanguard University of Southern
  California *B*
West Los Angeles College *A*
West Valley College *A*
Westmont College *B*
Whittier College *B*
William Jessup University *B*
Woodland Community College *A*
Yuba College *A*

Colorado

Adams State University *B, M*
Colorado Christian University *B*
Colorado College *B*
Colorado Mesa University *B*
Colorado State University *B, M*
Colorado State University
  Pueblo *B*
Community College of Aurora *A*
Fort Lewis College *B*
Metropolitan State University of
  Denver *B, T*
Otero Junior College *A*
Regis University *B*
United States Air Force Academy *B*
University of Colorado
  Boulder *B, M, D*
  Colorado Springs *B, M*
  Denver *B, M*
University of Denver *B*
University of Northern
  Colorado *B, M, T*
Western State Colorado University *B*

Connecticut

Albertus Magnus College *B*
Central Connecticut State
  University *B, M, T*
Connecticut College *B*
Eastern Connecticut State
  University *B*
Fairfield University *B*
Quinnipiac University *B*
Sacred Heart University *B*
Southern Connecticut State
  University *B, M*
Trinity College *B, M*
University of Connecticut *B, M, D*
University of Hartford *B*
University of New Haven *B*
University of Saint Joseph *B*
Wesleyan University *B*
Western Connecticut State
  University *B, M*
Yale University *B, M, D*

Delaware

Delaware State University *B*
University of Delaware *B, M, D*
Wesley College *B*

District of Columbia

American University *B, M, D*
Catholic University of
  America *B, M, D*
Gallaudet University *B*
George Washington
  University *B, M, D*
Georgetown University *B, D*
Howard University *B, M, D*
Trinity Washington University *B*
University of the District of
  Columbia *B*

Florida

Ave Maria University *B*
Barry University *B*
Bethune-Cookman University *B*
Broward College *A*

Chipola College *A*
Clearwater Christian College *B*
Eckerd College *B*
Flagler College *B*
Florida Agricultural and Mechanical
  University *B* *
Florida Atlantic University *B, M*
Florida College *B*
Florida Gulf Coast University *B, M*
Florida International
  University *B, M, D*
Florida Southern College *B*
Florida State University *B, M, D*
Indian River State College *A*
Jacksonville University *B*
Miami Dade College *A*
New College of Florida *B*
Nova Southeastern University *B*
Palm Beach Atlantic University *B*
Palm Beach State College *A*
Pensacola State College *A*
Rollins College *B*
Saint Leo University *B*
Saint Thomas University *B*
Southeastern University *B*
Stetson University *B*
University of Central Florida *B, M*
University of Florida *B, M, D*
University of Miami *B, M, D*
University of North Florida *B, M*
University of South Florida *B, M, D*
University of South Florida
  Saint Petersburg
  Sarasota-Manatee *B*
University of Tampa *A, B*
University of West Florida *B, M*
Warner University *B*

Georgia

Abraham Baldwin Agricultural
  College *A*
Agnes Scott College *B*
Albany State University *B*
Andrew College *A*
Armstrong Atlantic State
  University *B, M, T*
Atlanta Metropolitan College *A*
Bainbridge College *A*
Berry College *B*
Brenau University *B*
Brewton-Parker College *B*
Clark Atlanta University *B, M, D*
Clayton State University *B*
College of Coastal Georgia *A*
Columbus State University *B*
Covenant College *B*
Dalton State College *B*
Darton College *A*
East Georgia State College *A*
Emmanuel College *B*
Emory University *B, D*
Georgia College and State
  University *B, M*
Georgia Gwinnett College *B*
Georgia Highlands College *A*
Georgia Military College *A*
Georgia Perimeter College *A*
Georgia Regents University *B*
Georgia Southern University *B, M*
Georgia Southwestern State
  University *B, T*
Georgia State University *B, M, D*
Gordon College *A, B, T*
Kennesaw State University *B*
LaGrange College *B*
Mercer University *B*
Middle Georgia State College *A, B*
Morehouse College *B*
Oglethorpe University *B*
Paine College *B*
Piedmont College *B*
Point University *B*
Reinhardt University *B*
Savannah State University *B*
Shorter University *B, T*

South Georgia State College *A*
Spelman College *B*
Thomas University *B*
Toccoa Falls College *B*
Truett-McConnell College *B*
University of Georgia *B, M, D*
University of North Georgia *A, B, M*
University of West Georgia *B, M*
Valdosta State University *B, M*
Wesleyan College *B*
Young Harris College *B*

Hawaii

Brigham Young University-Hawaii *B*
Chaminade University of Honolulu *B*
Hawaii Pacific University *B*
University of Hawaii
 Hilo *B*
 Manoa *B, M, D*
 West Oahu *B*

Idaho

Boise State University *B, M, T*
Brigham Young University-Idaho *B*
College of Idaho *B*
College of Southern Idaho *A*
College of Western Idaho *A*
Idaho State University *B, M*
North Idaho College *A*
Northwest Nazarene University *B*
University of Idaho *B, M, D*

Illinois

Augustana College *B*
Aurora University *B*
Benedictine University *B, T*
Blackburn College *B*
Bradley University *B, T*
Chicago State University *B, M*
Concordia University Chicago *B*
DePaul University *B, M*
Dominican University *B*
Eastern Illinois University *B, M, T*
Elmhurst College *B, T*
Eureka College *B, T*
Greenville College *B*
Illinois College *B, T*
Illinois State University *B, M, T*
Illinois Valley Community College *A*
Illinois Wesleyan University *B*
John Wood Community College *A*
Joliet Junior College *A*
Judson University *B*
Kankakee Community College *A*
Kishwaukee College *A*
Knox College *B*
Lake Forest College *B*
Lewis University *B*
Lincoln College *A*
Loyola University Chicago *B, M, D*
MacMurray College *B*
McKendree University *B*
Millikin University *B*
Monmouth College *B, T*
North Central College *B, T*
North Park University *B*
Northeastern Illinois University *B, M*
Northern Illinois University *B, M, D*
Northwestern University *B, M, D*
Olivet Nazarene University *B, T*
Principia College *B*
Quincy University *B, T*
Richland Community College *A*
Rockford University *B*
Roosevelt University *B, M*
Saint Xavier University *B*
Sauk Valley Community College *A*
South Suburban College of Cook
 County *A*
Southern Illinois University
 Carbondale *B, M, D*
Southern Illinois University
 Edwardsville *B, M, T*
Southwestern Illinois College *A*

Spoon River College *A*
Trinity Christian College *B*
Trinity International University *B*
University of Chicago *B, D*
University of Illinois
 Chicago *B, M, D*
 Springfield *B*
 Urbana-Champaign *B, M, D*
University of St. Francis *B*
Western Illinois University *B, M*
Wheaton College *B, T*

Indiana

Ancilla College *A*
Anderson University *B*
Ball State University *B, M, T*
Bethel College *B*
Butler University *B, M*
DePauw University *B*
Earlham College *B*
Franklin College *B*
Goshen College *B*
Grace College *B*
Hanover College *B*
Holy Cross College *B*
Huntington University *B*
Indiana State University *B, M*
Indiana University
 Bloomington *B, M, D*
 East *B*
 Northwest *B*
 Purdue University Fort Wayne *B*
 Purdue University
  Indianapolis *B, M*
 South Bend *B*
 Southeast *B*
Indiana Wesleyan University *A, B*
Manchester University *B, T*
Marian University *B, T*
Oakland City University *B*
Purdue University *B, M, D*
Purdue University
 Calumet *B, M*
 North Central *B*
Saint Joseph's College *B*
Saint Mary's College *B, T*
Taylor University *B*
University of Evansville *B*
University of Indianapolis *B, M*
University of Notre Dame *B, M, D*
University of St. Francis *B*
University of Southern Indiana *B*
Valparaiso University *B, M*
Vincennes University *A*
Wabash College *B*

Iowa

Ashford University *B*
Briar Cliff University *B*
Buena Vista University *B, T*
Central College *B*
Clarke University *A, B, T*
Coe College *B*
Cornell College *B, T*
Dordt College *B*
Drake University *B*
Ellsworth Community College *A*
Graceland University *B, T*
Grand View University *B*
Grinnell College *B*
Iowa State University *B, M*
Iowa Wesleyan College *B, T*
Loras College *B*
Luther College *B*
Morningside College *B, T*
Northwestern College *B, T*
St. Ambrose University *B, T*
Simpson College *B*
University of Iowa *B, M, D, T*
University of Northern Iowa *B, M*
Waldorf College *B*
Wartburg College *B, T*
William Penn University *B*

Kansas

Allen County Community College *A*
Baker University *B, T*
Barton County Community College *A*
Benedictine College *B, T*
Bethany College *B, T*
Bethel College *B*
Butler Community College *A*
Central Christian College of
 Kansas *A, B*
Coffeyville Community College *A*
Colby Community College *A*
Cowley County Community
 College *A*
Emporia State University *B, M, T*
Fort Hays State University *B, M*
Fort Scott Community College *A*
Friends University *B*
Independence Community College *A*
Kansas State University *B, M, D*
Kansas Wesleyan University *B, T*
Labette Community College *A*
McPherson College *B, T*
MidAmerica Nazarene University *B*
Newman University *B*
Ottawa University *B, T*
Pittsburg State University *B, M*
Pratt Community College *A*
Seward County Community
 College *A*
Southwestern College *B*
Sterling College *B, T*
Tabor College *B*
University of Kansas *B, M, D*
University of St. Mary *B*
Washburn University *B*
Wichita State University *B, M, T*

Kentucky

Alice Lloyd College *B*
Asbury University *B*
Bellarmine University *B*
Berea College *B, T*
Brescia University *B*
Campbellsville University *B*
Centre College *B*
Eastern Kentucky University *B, M*
Georgetown College *B, T*
Kentucky Christian University *B*
Kentucky Wesleyan College *B*
Lindsey Wilson College *A, B*
Morehead State University *B*
Murray State University *B, M, T*
Northern Kentucky University *B*
St. Catharine College *B*
Thomas More College *A, B*
Transylvania University *B*
Union College *B*
University of Kentucky *B, M, D*
University of Louisville *B, M*
University of Pikeville *B, T*
University of the Cumberlands *B*
Western Kentucky University *C, B, M*

Louisiana

Centenary College of Louisiana *B, T*
Dillard University *B*
Grambling State University *B*
Louisiana College *B, T*
Louisiana State University
 Alexandria *B*
 Shreveport *B*
Louisiana State University and
 Agricultural and Mechanical
 College *B, M, D*
Louisiana Tech University *B, M*
Loyola University New Orleans *B*
McNeese State University *B*
Nicholls State University *B*
Northwestern State University *B*
Our Lady of Holy Cross College *B*
Southeastern Louisiana
 University *B, M*

Southern University and Agricultural
 and Mechanical College *B*
Tulane University *B, M, D*
University of Louisiana at
 Lafayette *B, M*
University of Louisiana at
 Monroe *B, M*
University of New Orleans *B, M*
Xavier University of Louisiana *B*

Maine

Bates College *B*
Bowdoin College *B*
Colby College *B*
College of the Atlantic *B, M*
Saint Joseph's College of Maine *B*
University of Maine *B, M, D*
University of Maine
 Farmington *B*
 Machias *B, T*
 Presque Isle *B*
University of New England *B*
University of Southern Maine *B*

Maryland

Allegany College of Maryland *A*
Bowie State University *B*
Coppin State University *B*
Frederick Community College *A*
Frostburg State University *B*
Goucher College *B*
Harford Community College *A*
Hood College *B, T*
Howard Community College *A*
Johns Hopkins University *B, M, D*
Loyola University Maryland *B*
McDaniel College *B*
Morgan State University *B, M, D*
Mount St. Mary's University *B*
Notre Dame of Maryland
 University *B*
St. Mary's College of Maryland *B*
Salisbury University *B, M*
Towson University *B*
United States Naval Academy *B*
University of Baltimore *B*
University of Maryland
 Baltimore County *B, M*
 College Park *B, M, D*
 Eastern Shore *B*
 University College *B*
Washington Adventist University *B*
Washington College *B, M, T*

Massachusetts

American International College *B*
Amherst College *B*
Anna Maria College *B*
Assumption College *B*
Bard College at Simon's Rock *B*
Bentley University *B*
Boston College *B, M, D*
Boston University *B, M, D*
Brandeis University *B, M, D*
Bridgewater State University *B*
Bunker Hill Community College *A*
Cape Cod Community College *A*
Clark University *B, M, D*
College of the Holy Cross *B*
Dean College *A*
Eastern Nazarene College *B*
Elms College *B*
Emmanuel College *B*
Endicott College *B*
Fitchburg State University *B, M, T*
Framingham State University *B*
Gordon College *B*
Hampshire College *B*
Harvard College *B, M, D*
Lasell College *B*
Massachusetts College of Liberal
 Arts *B, T*
Massachusetts Institute of
 Technology *B*

Merrimack College *B*
Mount Holyoke College *B*
Nichols College *B, T*
Northeastern University *B, M, D*
Pine Manor College *B*
Regis College *B*
Salem State University *B, M*
Simmons College *B, M*
Smith College *B*
Springfield College *B*
Stonehill College *B*
Suffolk University *B*
Tufts University *B, M, D, T*
University of Massachusetts
  Amherst *B, M, D*
  Boston *B, M*
  Dartmouth *B*
  Lowell *B*
Wellesley College *B*
Western New England University *B*
Westfield State University *B, M, T*
Wheaton College *B*
Williams College *B*
Worcester State University *B, M, T*

Michigan

Adrian College *A, B, T*
Albion College *B, T*
Alma College *B, T*
Andrews University *B, M*
Aquinas College *B, T*
Calvin College *B, T*
Central Michigan University *B, M, D*
Cornerstone University *B, T*
Eastern Michigan University *B, M*
Ferris State University *B*
Gogebic Community College *A*
Grace Bible College *B*
Grand Valley State University *B*
Great Lakes Christian College *B*
Hillsdale College *B*
Hope College *B*
Kalamazoo College *B*
Lake Michigan College *A*
Lake Superior State University *B*
Lansing Community College *A*
Madonna University *B, M*
Marygrove College *B, T*
Michigan State University *B, M, D*
Michigan Technological University *B*
Northern Michigan University *B*
Oakland University *B, M, T*
Olivet College *B*
Rochester College *B*
Saginaw Valley State University *B, T*
Siena Heights University *B*
Spring Arbor University *B*
University of Detroit Mercy *B*
University of Michigan *B, M, D*
University of Michigan
  Dearborn *B*
  Flint *B, M, T*
Wayne State University *B, M, D*
Western Michigan University *B, M, D*

Minnesota

Augsburg College *B*
Bemidji State University *B*
Bethany Lutheran College *B*
Bethel University *B*
Carleton College *B*
College of St. Benedict *B*
College of St. Scholastica *B*
Concordia College: Moorhead *B*
Concordia University St. Paul *B*
Crown College *B*
Gustavus Adolphus College *B*
Hamline University *B*
Macalester College *B*
Metropolitan State University *B*
Minnesota State University
  Mankato *B, M*
  Moorhead *B*

Minnesota West Community and
  Technical College *A*
Ridgewater College *A*
St. Catherine University *B*
Saint Cloud State University *B, M*
St. John's University *B*
St. Mary's University of Minnesota *B*
St. Olaf College *B*
Southwest Minnesota State
  University *B*
University of Minnesota
  Duluth *B*
  Morris *B*
  Twin Cities *B, M, D*
University of Northwestern - St.
  Paul *B*
University of St. Thomas *B*
Vermilion Community College *A*
Winona State University *B*

Mississippi

Alcorn State University *B*
Belhaven University *B*
Blue Mountain College *B*
Delta State University *B*
East Mississippi Community
  College *A*
Hinds Community College *A*
Itawamba Community College *A*
Jackson State University *B, M*
Millsaps College *B*
Mississippi College *B, M*
Mississippi Delta Community
  College *A*
Mississippi State University *B, M, D*
Mississippi University for
  Women *B, T*
Mississippi Valley State University *B*
Northeast Mississippi Community
  College *A*
Tougaloo College *B*
University of Mississippi *B, M, D*
University of Southern
  Mississippi *B, M, D*
William Carey University *B*

Missouri

Avila University *B*
Calvary Bible College and Theological
  Seminary *B*
Central Methodist University *B*
College of the Ozarks *B*
Columbia College *B*
Crowder College *A*
Culver-Stockton College *B*
Drury University *B, T*
Evangel University *B*
Fontbonne University *B, T*
Hannibal-LaGrange University *B*
Lincoln University *B, M*
Lindenwood University *B*
Maryville University of Saint Louis *B*
Missouri Baptist University *B*
Missouri Southern State
  University *B, T*
Missouri State University *B, M*
Missouri University of Science and
  Technology *B, T*
Missouri Valley College *B*
Missouri Western State
  University *B, T*
Northwest Missouri State
  University *B, M*
Park University *C, B*
Rockhurst University *B*
St. Charles Community College *A*
Saint Louis University *B, M, D*
Southeast Missouri State
  University *B, M*
Southwest Baptist University *B*
Three Rivers Community College *A*
Truman State University *B*
University of Central Missouri *B, M*

University of Missouri
  Columbia *B, M, D*
  Kansas City *B, M, D*
  St. Louis *B, M*
Washington University in St.
  Louis *B, M, D*
Webster University *B*
Westminster College *B, T*
William Jewell College *B*
William Woods University *B*

Montana

Carroll College *B*
Montana State University *B, M*
Montana State University
  Billings *B, T*
Rocky Mountain College *B*
University of Great Falls *B*
University of Montana *B, M*
University of Montana: Western *B, T*

Nebraska

Bellevue University *B*
Chadron State College *B, M*
Concordia University *B, T*
Creighton University *B*
Doane College *B*
Grace University *B*
Hastings College *B*
Midland University *B, T*
Nebraska Wesleyan University *B*
Union College *B*
University of Nebraska
  Kearney *B, M, T*
  Lincoln *B, M, D*
  Omaha *B, M*
Wayne State College *B*
Western Nebraska Community
  College *A*
York College *B*

Nevada

Nevada State College *B*
University of Nevada
  Las Vegas *B, M, D*
  Reno *B, M, D*

New Hampshire

Colby-Sawyer College *B*
Dartmouth College *B*
Franklin Pierce University *B*
Granite State College *B*
Keene State College *B*
New England College *B*
Plymouth State University *B*
Rivier University *B*
Saint Anselm College *B, T*
Southern New Hampshire
  University *B*
University of New
  Hampshire *B, M, D*
University of New Hampshire at
  Manchester *B*

New Jersey

Bergen Community College *A*
Bloomfield College *B, T*
Caldwell College *B*
Centenary College *B*
College of New Jersey *B, T*
College of St. Elizabeth *B*
Cumberland County College *A*
Drew University *B, D*
Fairleigh Dickinson University
  College at Florham
  Metropolitan Campus *B, M*
Felician College *B*
Georgian Court University *B*
Gloucester County College *A*
Hudson County Community
  College *A*
Kean University *B, T*
Monmouth University *B, M*
Montclair State University *B, M*

New Jersey City University *B*
New Jersey Institute of
  Technology *B, M, D*
Princeton University *B, M, D*
Ramapo College of New Jersey *B*
Richard Stockton College of New
  Jersey *B*
Rider University *B*
Rowan University *B, M*
Rutgers, The State University of New
  Jersey
  Camden Campus *B, M*
  New Brunswick/Piscataway
    Campus *B, M, D*
  Newark Campus *B, M*
Saint Peter's University *B*
Salem Community College *A*
Seton Hall University *B, M, T*
Stevens Institute of Technology *B*
Thomas Edison State College *B*
William Paterson University of New
  Jersey *B*

New Mexico

Central New Mexico Community
  College *A*
Eastern New Mexico University *B*
New Mexico Highlands
  University *B, M*
New Mexico State University *B, M*
University of New Mexico *B, M, D*
University of the Southwest *B*
Western New Mexico University *B*

New York

Adelphi University *B*
Alfred University *B*
Bard College *B*
Barnard College *B*
Canisius College *B*
City University of New York
  Baruch College *B*
  Brooklyn College *B, M*
  City College *B, M*
  College of Staten Island *B, M*
  Hunter College *B, M*
  John Jay College of Criminal
    Justice *B*
  Lehman College *B, M*
  Queens College *B, M, T*
  Queensborough Community
    College *A*
  York College *B*
Clarkson University *B*
Colgate University *B*
College of Mount St. Vincent *A, B, T*
College of New Rochelle *B, T*
College of Saint Rose *B*
Columbia University *B*
Columbia University
  School of General Studies *B*
Concordia College *B, T*
Cornell University *B, M, D*
D'Youville College *B*
Daemen College *B*
Dominican College of Blauvelt *B*
Dowling College *B*
Elmira College *B, T*
Eugene Lang College The New
  School for Liberal Arts *B*
Excelsior College *B*
Fordham University *B, M, D*
Hamilton College *B*
Hartwick College *B, T*
Hobart and William Smith Colleges *B*
Hofstra University *B*
Houghton College *B*
Iona College *B, M*
Ithaca College *B*
Jewish Theological Seminary of
  America *M, D*
Keuka College *B*
Le Moyne College *B*

Long Island University
  LIU Brooklyn *B*
  LIU Post *B, M*
Manhattan College *B*
Manhattanville College *B*
Marist College *B*
Marymount Manhattan College *B*
Mercy College *B*
Molloy College *B*
Monroe Community College *A*
Mount Saint Mary College *B, T*
Nazareth College *B, T*
New York University *B, M, D*
Niagara University *B*
Nyack College *B*
Pace University *B*
Pace University: Pleasantville/
  Briarcliff *B*
Roberts Wesleyan College *B*
SUNY
  College at Brockport *B, M, T*
  College at Buffalo *B, M*
  College at Cortland *B, M*
  College at Fredonia *B*
  College at Geneseo *B, T*
  College at New Paltz *B*
  College at Oneonta *B*
  College at Oswego *B, M*
  College at Plattsburgh *B*
  College at Potsdam *B*
  College at Purchase *B*
  Empire State College *A, B*
  University at Albany *B, M, D*
  University at Binghamton *B, M, D*
  University at Buffalo *B, M, D*
  University at Stony Brook *B, M, D*
Sage Colleges *B*
Saint Bonaventure University *B*
St. Francis College *B*
St. John Fisher College *B*
St. John's University *B, M, D*
St. Joseph's College New York:
  Suffolk Campus *B*
St. Joseph's College, New York *B*
St. Lawrence University *B*
St. Thomas Aquinas College *B, T*
Siena College *B, T*
Skidmore College *B*
Suffolk County Community College *A*
Syracuse University *B, M, D*
Touro College *B*
Union College *B*
University of Rochester *B, M, D*
Utica College *B*
Vassar College *B*
Wagner College *B*
Wells College *B*
Yeshiva University *B*

North Carolina

Appalachian State University *B, M*
Barton College *B*
Belmont Abbey College *B*
Brevard College *B*
Campbell University *B*
Catawba College *B, T*
Chowan University *B*
Davidson College *B*
Duke University *B, D*
East Carolina University *B, M*
Elizabeth City State University *B*
Elon University *B, T*
Fayetteville State University *B*
Gardner-Webb University *B*
Greensboro College *C, B, T*
Guilford College *B, T*
High Point University *B, M*
Johnson C. Smith University *B*
Lenoir-Rhyne University *B, T*
Livingstone College *B*
Mars Hill University *B, T*
Meredith College *B*
Methodist University *A, B, T*
Montreat College *B*

North Carolina Agricultural and
  Technical State
  University *B, M, T*
North Carolina Central
  University *B, M*
North Carolina State University *B, M*
North Carolina Wesleyan College *B*
Pfeiffer University *B*
Queens University of Charlotte *B*
St. Andrews University *B*
St. Augustine's University *B*
Salem College *B*
Southeastern Baptist Theological
  Seminary *B*
Southeastern Community College *A*
University of Mount Olive *B*
University of North Carolina
  Asheville *B, T*
  Chapel Hill *B, M, D*
  Charlotte *B, M*
  Greensboro *B, M, D*
  Pembroke *B*
  Wilmington *B, M*
Wake Forest University *B*
Warren Wilson College *B*
Western Carolina University *B, M*
Western Piedmont Community
  College *A*
William Peace University *B*
Wingate University *B*
Winston-Salem State University *B*

North Dakota

Dakota College at Bottineau *A*
Dickinson State University *B*
Minot State University *B*
North Dakota State
  University *B, M, D, T*
University of Jamestown *B*
University of North Dakota *B, M, D*
Valley City State University *B*

Ohio

Ashland University *B*
Baldwin Wallace University *B*
Bluffton University *B*
Bowling Green State
  University *B, M, D*
Capital University *B*
Case Western Reserve
  University *B, M, D*
Cedarville University *B*
Central State University *B*
Cleveland State University *B, M, T*
College of Mount St. Joseph *B, T*
College of Wooster *B*
Defiance College *B, T*
Denison University *B*
Franciscan University of
  Steubenville *B*
Heidelberg University *B*
Hiram College *B, T*
John Carroll University *B, M*
Kent State University *B, M, D*
Kent State University
  Stark *B*
Kenyon College *B*
Lake Erie College *B*
Lourdes University *A, B*
Malone University *B*
Marietta College *B*
Miami University
  Middletown *A*
  Oxford *B, M, D*
Mount Vernon Nazarene University *B*
Muskingum University *B*
Northwest State Community
  College *A*
Notre Dame College *B, T*
Oberlin College *B*
Ohio Dominican University *B, T*
Ohio Northern University *B*

Ohio State University
  Columbus Campus *C, B, M, D*
  Lima Campus *B*
  Mansfield Campus *B*
  Marion Campus *B*
  Newark Campus *B*
Ohio University *B, M*
Ohio University
  Southern Campus at Ironton *B*
  Zanesville Campus *B*
Ohio Wesleyan University *B*
Otterbein University *B*
Pontifical College Josephinum *B*
Shawnee State University *B*
Sinclair Community College *A*
Terra State Community College *A*
Tiffin University *B*
University of Akron *B, M, D*
University of Cincinnati *B, M, D, T*
University of Dayton *B*
University of Findlay *B, T*
University of Mount Union *B*
University of Rio Grande *A, B*
University of Toledo *B, M, D*
Urbana University *B*
Ursuline College *B*
Walsh University *B*
Wilmington College *B*
Wittenberg University *B*
Wright State University *A, B, M*
Wright State University: Lake
  Campus *A*
Xavier University *A, B*
Youngstown State University *C, B, M*

Oklahoma

Cameron University *B*
Connors State College *A*
East Central University *B*
Eastern Oklahoma State College *A*
Murray State College *A*
Northeastern State University *B*
Northwestern Oklahoma State
  University *B*
Oklahoma Baptist University *B*
Oklahoma Christian University *B*
Oklahoma City Community
  College *A*
Oklahoma City University *B*
Oklahoma Panhandle State
  University *B*
Oklahoma State University *B, M, D*
Oklahoma Wesleyan University *B*
Oral Roberts University *B*
Rogers State University *A*
Rose State College *A*
St. Gregory's University *B*
Southeastern Oklahoma State
  University *B*
Southern Nazarene University *B*
Southwestern Christian University *B*
Southwestern Oklahoma State
  University *B*
Tulsa Community College *A*
University of Central Oklahoma *B, M*
University of Oklahoma *B, M, D*
University of Science and Arts of
  Oklahoma *B*
University of Tulsa *B, M*

Oregon

Central Oregon Community
  College *A*
Concordia University *B*
Corban University *B*
Eastern Oregon University *B*
George Fox University *B*
Lewis & Clark College *B*
Linfield College *B, T*
Mt. Hood Community College *A*
Multnomah University *B*
Northwest Christian University *B*
Oregon State University *B*
Pacific University *B*

Portland State University *B, M*
Reed College *B*
Southern Oregon University *B*
Treasure Valley Community
  College *A*
University of Oregon *B, M, D*
University of Portland *B*
Warner Pacific College *B*
Western Oregon University *B*
Willamette University *B*

Pennsylvania

Albright College *B, T*
Allegheny College *B*
Alvernia University *B*
Arcadia University *B*
Bloomsburg University of
  Pennsylvania *B*
Bryn Athyn College *B*
Bryn Mawr College *B*
Bucknell University *B*
Cabrini College *B*
California University of
  Pennsylvania *B*
Carlow University *B, T*
Carnegie Mellon University *B, M, D*
Cedar Crest College *B*
Chatham University *B*
Chestnut Hill College *B*
Clarion University of Pennsylvania *B*
Community College of Beaver
  County *A*
DeSales University *B, T*
Dickinson College *B*
Drexel University *B*
Duquesne University *B, M*
East Stroudsburg University of
  Pennsylvania *B, M*
Eastern University *B*
Edinboro University of
  Pennsylvania *B*
Elizabethtown College *B*
Franklin & Marshall College *B*
Gannon University *B*
Geneva College *B, T*
Gettysburg College *B*
Grove City College *B*
Gwynedd Mercy University *B*
Haverford College *B, T*
Holy Family University *B*
Immaculata University *B*
Indiana University of
  Pennsylvania *B, M*
Juniata College *B*
King's College *B*
Kutztown University of
  Pennsylvania *B*
La Roche College *B*
La Salle University *B, T*
Lafayette College *B*
Lebanon Valley College *B*
Lehigh University *B, M, D*
Lincoln University *B*
Lock Haven University of
  Pennsylvania *B*
Lycoming College *B*
Mansfield University of
  Pennsylvania *B, T*
Marywood University *B*
Mercyhurst University *B*
Messiah College *B*
Millersville University of
  Pennsylvania *B, M*
Misericordia University *B*
Moravian College *B, T*
Mount Aloysius College *B*
Muhlenberg College *C, B*
Penn State
  Abington *B*
  Altoona *B*
  Beaver *B*
  Berks *B*
  Brandywine *B*
  DuBois *B*
  Erie, The Behrend College *B*

Fayette, The Eberly Campus *B*
Greater Allegheny *B*
Harrisburg *B*
Hazleton *B*
Lehigh Valley *B*
Mont Alto *B*
New Kensington *B*
Schuylkill *B*
Shenango *B*
University Park *B, M, D*
Wilkes-Barre *B*
Worthington Scranton *B*
York *B*
Point Park University *B*
Rosemont College *B*
St. Francis University *B*
Saint Joseph's University *B*
St. Vincent College *B*
Seton Hill University *B, T*
Shippensburg University of
Pennsylvania *B, M, T*
Slippery Rock University of
Pennsylvania *B, T*
Susquehanna University *B*
Swarthmore College *B*
Temple University *B, M, D*
Thiel College *B*
University of Pennsylvania *B, M, D*
University of Pittsburgh *B, M, D*
University of Pittsburgh
Greensburg *B*
Johnstown *B*
University of Scranton *B*
Ursinus College *B, T*
Villanova University *B, M*
Washington & Jefferson College *B*
Waynesburg University *B*
West Chester University of
Pennsylvania *B, M, T*
Westminster College *B, M*
Widener University *B, T*
Wilkes University *B*
Wilson College *B*
York College of Pennsylvania *B*

Puerto Rico

Inter American University of Puerto
Rico
Metropolitan Campus *M, D*
Pontifical Catholic University of
Puerto Rico *B, M*
Universidad Adventista de las
Antillas *B*
University of Puerto Rico
Aguadilla *A*
Cayey University College *B*
Mayaguez *B*
Rio Piedras *M, D*

Rhode Island

Brown University *B, M, D*
Bryant University *B*
Providence College *B, M*
Rhode Island College *B, M*
Roger Williams University *B*
Salve Regina University *B*
University of Rhode Island *B, M*

South Carolina

Anderson University *B*
Benedict College *B*
Bob Jones University *B*
Charleston Southern University *B*
Citadel *B, M*
Claflin University *B*
Clemson University *B, M*
Coastal Carolina University *B*
Coker College *B*
College of Charleston *B, M, T*
Columbia College *B*
Converse College *B*
Erskine College *B*
Francis Marion University *B*
Furman University *B, T*

Lander University *B, T*
Limestone College *B*
Morris College *B*
Newberry College *B, T*
North Greenville University *B*
Presbyterian College *B, T*
South Carolina State University *B*
Southern Wesleyan University *B*
University of South Carolina
Aiken *B*
Beaufort *B*
Columbia *B, M, D*
Upstate *B*
Winthrop University *B, M*
Wofford College *B*

South Dakota

Augustana College *B, T*
Black Hills State University *B*
Dakota Wesleyan University *B*
Kilian Community College *A*
Mount Marty College *B*
Northern State University *B*
Oglala Lakota College *B*
South Dakota State University *B*
University of Sioux Falls *B*
University of South Dakota *B, M, D*

Tennessee

Aquinas College *B*
Austin Peay State University *B*
Belmont University *B, T*
Bethel University *B*
Bryan University
Dayton *B, T*
Carson-Newman University *B, T*
Christian Brothers University *B*
Cumberland University *B*
East Tennessee State
University *B, M, T*
Fisk University *B*
Freed-Hardeman University *B, T*
Hiwassee College *A*
Jackson State Community College *A*
King University *B, T*
Lane College *B*
LeMoyne-Owen College *B*
Lee University *B*
Lincoln Memorial University *B, T*
Lipscomb University *B*
Martin Methodist College *B*
Maryville College *B, T*
Middle Tennessee State
University *B, M, D*
Milligan College *B, T*
Rhodes College *B*
Sewanee: The University of the
South *B*
Southern Adventist University *B*
Tennessee State University *B, M*
Tennessee Technological
University *B, T*
Tennessee Temple University *B*
Tennessee Wesleyan College *B*
Trevecca Nazarene University *B*
Tusculum College *B*
Union University *B, T*
University of Memphis *B, M, D*
University of Tennessee
Chattanooga *B*
Knoxville *B, M, D*
Martin *B*
Vanderbilt University *B, M, D*
Victory University *B*
Welch College *B*

Texas

Abilene Christian University *B*
Angelo State University *B, T*
Austin College *B*
Austin Community College *A*
Baylor University *B, M, D*
Blinn College *A*
Brazosport College *A*

Clarendon College *A*
Coastal Bend College *A*
College of the Mainland *A*
Concordia University Texas *B*
Dallas Baptist University *B, M*
Del Mar College *A*
East Texas Baptist University *B*
El Paso Community College *A*
Frank Phillips College *A*
Galveston College *A*
Hardin-Simmons University *B, M*
Hill College *A*
Houston Baptist University *B*
Howard Payne University *B*
Huston-Tillotson University *B*
Jarvis Christian College *B, T*
Kilgore College *A*
Lamar University *B, M*
Laredo Community College *A*
LeTourneau University *B*
Lubbock Christian University *T*
McMurry University *B, T*
Midland College *A*
Midwestern State University *B, M*
Northeast Texas Community
College *A*
Northwest Vista College *A*
Our Lady of the Lake University of
San Antonio *B*
Palo Alto College *A*
Paris Junior College *A*
Prairie View A&M University *B*
Rice University *B, M, D*
St. Edward's University *B*
St. Mary's University *B, T*
St. Philip's College *A*
Sam Houston State University *B, M*
San Jacinto College *A*
Schreiner University *B*
South Plains College *A*
South Texas College *A*
Southern Methodist
University *B, M, D*
Southwestern Adventist
University *B, T*
Southwestern Assemblies of God
University *B*
Southwestern University *B, T*
Stephen F. Austin State
University *B, M, T*
Sul Ross State University *B, M, T*
Tarleton State University *B, M, T*
Texarkana College *A*
Texas A&M International
University *B, M, T*
Texas A&M University *B, M, D*
Texas A&M University
Commerce *B, M*
Corpus Christi *B, T*
Kingsville *B, M*
Texarkana *B, T*
Texas Christian University *B, M, D*
Texas College *B*
Texas Lutheran University *B, T*
Texas Southern University *B, M*
Texas State University *B, M, T*
Texas Tech University *B, M, D*
Texas Wesleyan University *B, T*
Texas Woman's University *B, M*
Trinity University *B*
Tyler Junior College *A*
University of Dallas *B*
University of Houston *B, M, D*
University of Houston
Clear Lake *B, M*
Downtown *B, T*
Victoria *B, T*
University of Mary Hardin-Baylor *B, T*
University of North Texas *B, M, D*
University of St. Thomas *B*
University of Texas
Arlington *B, M*
Austin *B, M, D*
Brownsville *B, M*
Dallas *B, M*

El Paso *B, M, D*
Pan American *B, M*
Permian Basin *B, M*
San Antonio *B, M*
Tyler *B, M*
University of the Incarnate Word *B*
Wayland Baptist University *B, M*
West Texas A&M University *B, M*
Western Texas College *A*
Wharton County Junior College *A*
Wiley College *B*

Utah

Brigham Young University *B, M*
Dixie State College *B*
Salt Lake Community College *A*
Snow College *A*
Southern Utah University *B*
University of Utah *B, M, D, T*
Utah State University *B, M*
Utah Valley University *A, B*
Weber State University *B*
Westminster College *B*

Vermont

Bennington College *B*
Castleton State College *B*
College of St. Joseph in Vermont *B*
Goddard College *B, M*
Green Mountain College *B*
Johnson State College *B*
Marlboro College *B*
Middlebury College *B*
Norwich University *B*
Saint Michael's College *B*
University of Vermont *B, M*

Virginia

Averett University *B*
Bluefield College *B*
Bridgewater College *B*
Christendom College *B*
Christopher Newport University *B*
College of William and Mary *B, M, D*
Eastern Mennonite University *B*
Emory & Henry College *B, T*
Ferrum College *B*
George Mason University *B, M, D*
Hampden-Sydney College *B*
Hampton University *B*
Hollins University *B*
James Madison University *B, M, T*
Liberty University *B, M, T*
Longwood University *B*
Lynchburg College *B, M*
Mary Baldwin College *B*
Marymount University *B, T*
Norfolk State University *B*
Old Dominion University *B, M*
Patrick Henry College *B*
Radford University *B*
Randolph College *B*
Randolph-Macon College *B*
Regent University *A, B*
Roanoke College *B, T*
Shenandoah University *C, B*
Southern Virginia University *B*
Sweet Briar College *B*
University of Mary Washington *B*
University of Richmond *B*
University of Virginia *B, M, D*
University of Virginia's College at
Wise *B, T*
Virginia Commonwealth
University *B, M*
Virginia Intermont College *B*
Virginia Military Institute *B*
Virginia Polytechnic Institute and
State University *B, M*
Virginia State University *B, M*
Virginia Union University *B*
Virginia Wesleyan College *B*
Washington and Lee University *B*

Washington

Central Washington University *B, M*
Centralia College *A*
Eastern Washington University *B, M*
Everett Community College *A*
Gonzaga University *B*
Highline Community College *A*
Northwest University *B*
Pacific Lutheran University *B*
Saint Martin's University *B*
Seattle Pacific University *B*
Seattle University *B*
University of Puget Sound *B, T*
University of Washington *B, M, D*
Walla Walla University *B*
Washington State University *B, M, D*
Western Washington University *B, M*
Whitman College *B*
Whitworth University *B, T*

West Virginia

Alderson-Broaddus University *B*
American Public University
    System *A, B, M*
Bethany College *B*
Concord University *B*
Davis and Elkins College *B*
Fairmont State University *B*
Glenville State College *B*
Marshall University *B, M*
Ohio Valley University *B*
Potomac State College of West
    Virginia University *A*
Shepherd University *B*
University of Charleston *B*
West Liberty University *B*
West Virginia State University *B*
West Virginia University *B, M, D*
West Virginia University Institute of
    Technology *B*
West Virginia Wesleyan College *B*
Wheeling Jesuit University *B*

Wisconsin

Alverno College *B*
Beloit College *B*
Cardinal Stritch University *B, T*
Carroll University *B*
Carthage College *B*
Concordia University Wisconsin *B, T*
Edgewood College *B*
Lakeland College *B*
Lawrence University *B*
Marian University *B*
Marquette University *B, M, D*
Mount Mary University *B, T*
Northland College *B*
Northland International University *B*
Ripon College *B, T*
St. Norbert College *B, T*
Silver Lake College of the Holy
    Family *B, T*
University of Wisconsin
    Eau Claire *B, M*
    Green Bay *B, T*
    La Crosse *B, T*
    Madison *B, M, D*
    Milwaukee *B, M, D*
    Oshkosh *B*
    Parkside *B, T*
    Platteville *B, T*
    River Falls *B*
    Stevens Point *B, M, T*
    Superior *B, T*
    Whitewater *B, T*
Wisconsin Lutheran College *B*

Wyoming

Casper College *A*
Laramie County Community
    College *A*
Northwest College *A*
Sheridan College *A*
University of Wyoming *B, M*

Western Wyoming Community
    College *A*

History of science/ technology

Arizona

Arizona State University *D*

California

California Institute of Technology *B*

Georgia

Georgia Institute of
    Technology *B, M, D*

Illinois

University of Chicago *B*

Indiana

Indiana University
    Bloomington *M, D*

Iowa

Iowa State University *M, D*

Maryland

Johns Hopkins University *B, M, D*

Massachusetts

Harvard College *B, M, D*

Minnesota

University of Minnesota
    Twin Cities *M, D*

New Jersey

Princeton University *M, D*

New York

Cornell University *M, D*

Ohio

Case Western Reserve University *B*

Oklahoma

University of Oklahoma *B, M, D*

Oregon

Oregon State University *M*

Pennsylvania

University of Pennsylvania *B, M, D*
University of Pittsburgh *B, M, D*

Wisconsin

University of Wisconsin
    Madison *B, M, D*

History teacher education

Alabama

Auburn University *M, T*
Birmingham-Southern College *T*
Faulkner University *B, M, T*
Huntingdon College *B, T*
Oakwood University *B*
Spring Hill College *B, M, T*
Talladega College *B*
University of Mobile *B, T*

Arizona

Cochise College *A*

Arkansas

Ouachita Baptist University *B, T*
University of Arkansas
    Fort Smith *B*

California

Azusa Pacific University *T*
California State University
    Chico *T*
    San Bernardino *M, T*
Master's College *T*
San Diego Christian College *B, T*
San Diego State University *T*
Stanford University *M, T*
Vanguard University of Southern
    California *T*

Colorado

Adams State University *B, M, T*
Colorado Christian University *B*
Colorado State University
    Pueblo *T*

Connecticut

Albertus Magnus College *B, T*
Quinnipiac University *B, M*
Sacred Heart University *T*
University of Saint Joseph *T*

Delaware

University of Delaware *B, T*

District of Columbia

Catholic University of America *B*

Florida

Baptist College of Florida *B*
Barry University *T*
University of Miami *B, M*

Georgia

Covenant College *B, T*
Emmanuel College *B*
Middle Georgia State College *B*
Paine College *B*
Piedmont College *B, M, T*
Shorter University *T*
Toccoa Falls College *B, T*
University of North Georgia *M*

Idaho

Boise State University *B, T*
Brigham Young University-Idaho *B, T*
Northwest Nazarene University *B*
University of Idaho *T*

Illinois

Augustana College *B, T*
Blackburn College *T*
Bradley University *B*
Chicago State University *B, T*
Concordia University Chicago *B, T*
DePaul University *M, T*
Dominican University *B, T*
Elmhurst College *B*
Eureka College *T*
Greenville College *B, T*
Illinois College *T*
Illinois Wesleyan University *B*
John A. Logan College *A*
Knox College *T*
MacMurray College *B, T*
McKendree University *B*
Monmouth College *T*
North Park University *T*
Olivet Nazarene University *B, T*
Rockford University *T*
Saint Xavier University *B*
Trinity Christian College *B, T*
Trinity International University *B, T*
University of Illinois
    Chicago *B, M*
    Urbana-Champaign *B, M, T*

Indiana

Butler University *T*
Franklin College *B*

Indiana University
    Purdue University Fort Wayne *B*
Manchester University *B, T*
Oakland City University *B*
University of Indianapolis *B, M, T*
Valparaiso University *B*

Iowa

Briar Cliff University *B*
Buena Vista University *B, T*
Central College *T*
Cornell College *B, T*
Dordt College *B*
Drake University *M, T*
Ellsworth Community College *A*
Graceland University *T*
Grand View University *T*
Iowa State University *T*
Iowa Wesleyan College *B*
Loras College *T*
Morningside College *B*
Mount Mercy University *T*
Northwestern College *T*
St. Ambrose University *B, T*
Simpson College *T*
University of Iowa *T*
Upper Iowa University *B, T*
Wartburg College *B, T*

Kansas

Benedictine College *B*
Bethany College *B*
Bethel College *T*
Central Christian College of Kansas *B*
Friends University *B*
Garden City Community College *A*
Independence Community College *A*
McPherson College *B, T*
Pittsburg State University *B*
Sterling College *T*
Tabor College *B, T*
University of Kansas *B, T*
University of St. Mary *T*
Washburn University *B, T*

Kentucky

Campbellsville University *B*

Louisiana

Centenary College of Louisiana *T*
Xavier University of Louisiana *B*

Maine

Saint Joseph's College of Maine *B*
University of Maine *B*
University of Maine
    Machias *T*
University of Southern Maine *T*

Maryland

Hood College *T*
Mount St. Mary's University *T*
Notre Dame of Maryland
    University *T*
Towson University *B*

Massachusetts

Anna Maria College *B*
Assumption College *T*
Bridgewater State University *M, T*
Eastern Nazarene College *B*
Elms College *M, T*
Fitchburg State University *B, M, T*
Framingham State University *M*
Lasell College *B, T*
Merrimack College *B, M*
Salem State University *M*
Tufts University *T*
University of Massachusetts
    Dartmouth *T*
Western New England
    University *B, T*
Westfield State University *M, T*

Michigan

Adrian College *B, T*
Alma College *T*
Andrews University *M*
Aquinas College *B, T*
Calvin College *B*
Central Michigan University *B*
Cornerstone University *B, T*
Eastern Michigan University *B, T*
Ferris State University *B*
Grand Valley State University *M, T*
Hope College *B, T*
Michigan State University *B, M*
Northern Michigan University *B, T*
Rochester College *B*
Spring Arbor University *B*
University of Detroit Mercy *B, M, T*
University of Michigan
  Flint *B, T*
Western Michigan University *B*

Minnesota

Concordia University St. Paul *B, T*
Minnesota State University
  Mankato *B, M, T*
Saint Cloud State University *B, M, T*
University of Minnesota
  Morris *T*

Mississippi

Itawamba Community College *A*
Millsaps College *T*

Missouri

College of the Ozarks *B, T*
Culver-Stockton College *T*
Lindenwood University *B*
Maryville University of Saint
  Louis *M, T*
Missouri Southern State
  University *B, T*
Missouri State University *B*
Northwest Missouri State
  University *M, T*
University of Missouri
  Kansas City *B*
Washington University in St.
  Louis *B, M, T*

Montana

Carroll College *B*
Montana State University
  Billings *B, T*
Rocky Mountain College *B*
University of Great Falls *B*
University of Montana *T*
University of Montana: Western *B, T*

Nebraska

Chadron State College *B*
Concordia University *B, T*
Creighton University *T*
Grace University *B*
Hastings College *B, M, T*
Midland University *B, T*
Nebraska Wesleyan University *T*
Union College *B*
University of Nebraska
  Kearney *B, T*
Wayne State College *B, T*
York College *B, T*

Nevada

Great Basin College *B*
Nevada State College *B*

New Hampshire

Franklin Pierce University *M, T*
Keene State College *B, T*
Rivier University *B, T*
Saint Anselm College *T*

New Jersey

College of New Jersey *B, T*
County College of Morris *A*
Saint Peter's University *T*

New York

Bard College *M*
City University of New York
  City College *B, M*
  College of Staten Island *B*
  Hunter College *B, T*
College of Mount St. Vincent *T*
D'Youville College *M, T*
Elmira College *B, T*
Fordham University *M, T*
Hobart and William Smith Colleges *T*
Houghton College *B, T*
Ithaca College *B, T*
Manhattan College *B, T*
Nazareth College *B, M, T*
Pace University *B, T*
Pace University: Pleasantville/
  Briarcliff *B, T*
Roberts Wesleyan College *B, M*
SUNY
  College at Brockport *B, M, T*
  College at Oswego *B, M*
  College at Plattsburgh *B*
St. John Fisher College *B, M, T*
St. Joseph's College New York:
  Suffolk Campus *B*
St. Joseph's College, New York *B*
St. Lawrence University *T*
St. Thomas Aquinas College *B, T*
Vassar College *T*
Wells College *T*

North Carolina

Appalachian State University *B, M, T*
Campbell University *B, T*
Chowan University *B*
East Carolina University *M*
Elizabeth City State University *B, T*
Elon University *T*
Gardner-Webb University *B*
Greensboro College *B, T*
Lenoir-Rhyne University *B*
Mars Hill University *T*
Meredith College *T*
North Carolina Agricultural and
  Technical State
  University *B, M, T*
North Carolina Central
  University *B, M, T*
North Carolina State University *M*
Sandhills Community College *A*
University of North Carolina
  Wilmington *B*
Wake Forest University *T*

North Dakota

Dickinson State University *B, T*
Mayville State University *B, T*
Minot State University *B*
North Dakota State University *B, T*
University of Jamestown *B*
University of Mary *B*
Valley City State University *B, T*

Ohio

Ashland University *B, M*
Bluffton University *B*
Bowling Green State
  University *B, M, T*
Case Western Reserve University *T*
Cedarville University *T*
Defiance College *B, T*
Hiram College *T*
John Carroll University *T*
Mount Vernon Nazarene
  University *B, T*
Ohio Northern University *B, T*
Otterbein University *B*
Tiffin University *B*

University of Findlay *B, M, T*
University of Mount Union *T*
University of Rio Grande *B, T*
University of Toledo *M, T*
Wilmington College *B*
Youngstown State University *B, M*

Oklahoma

East Central University *B, T*
Eastern Oklahoma State College *A*
Oklahoma Baptist University *B, T*
Oklahoma City University *B*
Southern Nazarene University *B*
Southwestern Oklahoma State
  University *B, M, T*
University of Central Oklahoma *B*
University of Tulsa *T*

Oregon

Concordia University *B, M, T*
Corban University *B*
Linfield College *T*
Warner Pacific College *T*
Western Oregon University *M, T*

Pennsylvania

Albright College *T*
Arcadia University *M*
Bucks County Community College *A*
Gettysburg College *T*
Grove City College *T*
Gwynedd Mercy University *B*
Holy Family University *B*
King's College *T*
La Salle University *B, T*
Lycoming College *T*
Mansfield University of
  Pennsylvania *B, T*
Moravian College *T*
Rosemont College *T*
St. Francis University *B, T*
Saint Joseph's University *M, T*
St. Vincent College *T*
Susquehanna University *T*
Thiel College *B*
University of Pittsburgh
  Greensburg *B, T*
University of Scranton *B*
Villanova University *T*
Waynesburg University *B, T*
Westminster College *T*
Widener University *T*
Wilkes University *M, T*

Puerto Rico

Inter American University of Puerto
  Rico
  Metropolitan Campus *B*
  San German Campus *B*
Pontifical Catholic University of
  Puerto Rico *B, T*
Turabo University *B*
University of Puerto Rico
  Cayey University College *B*

Rhode Island

Rhode Island College *B, M*

South Carolina

Anderson University *B, T*
Coker College *B, T*
Francis Marion University *B, T*
North Greenville University *M, T*

South Dakota

Augustana College *B, T*
Dakota Wesleyan University *B, T*
Mount Marty College *B*
Northern State University *B, T*
University of Sioux Falls *T*
University of South Dakota *B, T*

Tennessee

American Baptist College *B*
Aquinas College *B*
Belmont University *T*
Bethel University *B, T*
Bryan University
  Dayton *T*
Cumberland University *B, T*
Freed-Hardeman University *B, T*
King University *T*
Lee University *B*
Lincoln Memorial University *B, T*
Lipscomb University *B, T*
Martin Methodist College *B*
Maryville College *B*
Southern Adventist University *B*
Tennessee Technological University *T*
Tennessee Temple University *B*
Trevecca Nazarene University *B, T*
Tusculum College *B, T*
Union University *B, T*
Victory University *B, T*

Texas

Abilene Christian University *B, T*
Dallas Baptist University *B*
Dallas Christian College *B, T*
Del Mar College *A*
East Texas Baptist University *B*
Hardin-Simmons University *B, T*
Houston Baptist University *T*
Howard Payne University *B*
Jarvis Christian College *B, T*
Kilgore College *A*
Lamar University *T*
Laredo Community College *A*
LeTourneau University *B, T*
Lubbock Christian University *B*
McMurry University *B, T*
Our Lady of the Lake University of
  San Antonio *B*
St. Edward's University *B, T*
St. Mary's University *T*
Schreiner University *B*
Tarleton State University *T*
Texas A&M International
  University *B, T*
Texas A&M University
  Commerce *T*
  Kingsville *T*
Texas College *B, T*
Texas Lutheran University *B, T*
Texas State University *M, T*
Texas Wesleyan University *B, T*
University of Dallas *T*
University of Mary Hardin-Baylor *T*
University of Texas
  Arlington *T*
  San Antonio *T*
West Texas A&M University *T*

Utah

Brigham Young University *B*
Southern Utah University *B*
Utah Valley University *B*
Weber State University *B*

Vermont

Castleton State College *B, T*
College of St. Joseph in
  Vermont *B, M, T*
Goddard College *B, M*
Johnson State College *B*

Virginia

Averett University *M, T*
Bluefield College *B, T*
Bridgewater College *T*
Hampton University *M*
Hollins University *T*
Longwood University *T*
University of Virginia's College at
  Wise *T*
Virginia Intermont College *T*

Washington

Central Washington University *B, T*
Heritage University *B*
Northwest University *T*
Washington State University *B, M, T*
Western Washington University *B*
Whitworth University *B, T*

West Virginia

Bethany College *B*
West Virginia Wesleyan College *B*
Wheeling Jesuit University *B*

Wisconsin

Carroll University *B, T*
Carthage College *T*
Concordia University Wisconsin *B*
Lakeland College *T*
Lawrence University *T*
Maranatha Baptist Bible College *B*
Mount Mary University *B, T*
St. Norbert College *T*
University of Wisconsin
   Green Bay *T*
   Platteville *B*
   River Falls *T*
   Superior *B, T*
   Whitewater *B*

Holistic health

Arizona

Prescott College *B*

California

California Institute of Integral
   Studies *M*
National University *M*
Pacific College of Oriental Medicine:
   San Diego *A*

Colorado

Front Range Community College *C*
Red Rocks Community College *C, A*

Iowa

Ashford University *B*

Maine

College of the Atlantic *B, M*

Minnesota

Anoka-Ramsey Community
   College *C, A*

New Jersey

Georgian Court University *M*

Holocaust studies

New Hampshire

Keene State College *B*

New Jersey

Kean University *M*
Richard Stockton College of New
   Jersey *M*

Pennsylvania

Gratz College *M*

Home furnishings

California

Antelope Valley College *A*

Illinois

Harper College *C*
Triton College *C*

Home health attendant

Alabama

Jefferson Davis Community
   College *C*
Lawson State Community College *C*
Southern Union State Community
   College *C*

Arizona

Coconino County Community
   College *C*
Eastern Arizona College *C*
Pima Community College *C*

California

College of the Desert *C*
Contra Costa College *C*
Copper Mountain College *C*
MiraCosta College *C*
Palo Verde College *C*
Santa Barbara City College *C*

Florida

Fortis College
   Winter Park *C*
Seminole State College of Florida *C*

Georgia

Albany Technical College *C*
Columbus Technical College *C*
Gwinnett Technical College *C*
Savannah Technical College *C*

Illinois

City Colleges of Chicago
   Malcolm X College *C*

Kansas

Barton County Community College *C*
Cloud County Community College *C*
Coffeyville Community College *C*
Colby Community College *C*
Cowley County Community
   College *C*
Garden City Community College *C*
Highland Community College *C*
Hutchinson Community College *C*
Independence Community College *C*
Johnson County Community
   College *C*
Wichita Area Technical College *C*

Louisiana

ITI Technical College *C*

Maryland

Anne Arundel Community College *C*

Massachusetts

Bristol Community College *C*
Cape Cod Community College *C*

Michigan

Baker College
   Flint *C*

Minnesota

Itasca Community College *C*
Pine Technical College *C*
Ridgewater College *C*

New Mexico

Central New Mexico Community
   College *C*
Eastern New Mexico University:
   Roswell *C*

Pennsylvania

Drexel University *C*
Erie Business Center *C*

Virginia

Eastern Shore Community College *C*

Washington

Peninsula College *C, A*

Homeland security

Alabama

Herzing University
   Birmingham *B*

Arizona

Arizona Western College *A*
Chandler-Gilbert Community
   College *C*
Northcentral University *B, M, D*
Phoenix College *C*

Arkansas

Northwest Arkansas Community
   College *C, A*

California

National University *B, M*
Palomar College *A*
Trident University International *C*

Colorado

Pikes Peak Community College *C, A*
Regis University *C*

Connecticut

Goodwin College *A*
Mitchell College *B*
University of Connecticut *M*

Florida

Embry-Riddle Aeronautical
   University *B*
Herzing University
   Winter Park *B*
Keiser University *A, B*
Nova Southeastern University *M*
Saint Leo University *B*
State College of Florida, Manatee-
   Sarasota *B*

Georgia

Darton College *C*
Georgia Military College *A*
Georgia Perimeter College *A*
Savannah State University *B*

Hawaii

University of Hawaii
   Hawaii Community College *C*
   West Oahu *C*

Illinois

City Colleges of Chicago
   Olive-Harvey College *C*
   Wilbur Wright College *C*
College of DuPage *A*
Harper College *C, A*
Illinois Eastern Community Colleges
   Lincoln Trail College *C*
John Wood Community College *A*
MacMurray College *B*
Moraine Valley Community College *C*
Western Illinois University *B*

Indiana

Ivy Tech Community College
   Central Indiana *A*
Vincennes University *B*

Kansas

Kansas City Kansas Community
   College *C*

Kentucky

Midway College *B*

Louisiana

Baton Rouge Community College *C*
Herzing University
   Kenner *B*
Northwestern State University *M*
Tulane University *B, M*

Maryland

Frederick Community College *C, A*
Towson University *M*

Massachusetts

Endicott College *M*

Michigan

Lake Superior State University *B*
Wayne County Community College *C*

Minnesota

Capella University *B, M*

Mississippi

Mississippi College *M*

New Hampshire

Daniel Webster College *B*
Great Bay Community College *C*

New Jersey

Cumberland County College *C, A*
Fairleigh Dickinson University
   College at Florham *M*
   Metropolitan Campus *M*
Georgian Court University *M*
Ocean County College *A*
Passaic County Community College *A*
Salem Community College *C*
Union County College *C*

New York

Excelsior College *C, B*
Long Island Business Institute *A*
Medaille College *B*
Pace University *M*
SUNY
   College of Technology at Canton *B*
   Ulster County Community College *A*
Utica College *C*

North Carolina

Methodist University *B*

Ohio

Sinclair Community College *C*
Tiffin University *B*

Oregon

Concordia University *B*
Western Oregon University *A*

Pennsylvania

Butler County Community
   College *C, A*
Central Penn College *B*
Saint Joseph's University *M*

Rhode Island

Community College of Rhode
   Island *C*

South Carolina

Trident Technical College *A*

Texas

Central Texas College *C, A*
Cisco College *C*

Virginia

University of Management and
   Technology *A, B, M*

Virginia Commonwealth
  University *B, M*

West Virginia

American Public University
  System *C, B, M*
Blue Ridge Community and Technical
  College *C*

Wisconsin

Herzing University
  Madison *B*
Marian University *B*

Wyoming

Central Wyoming College *A*

Homeopathic medicine

Vermont

Goddard College *B, M*

Horse husbandry/ equine science

California

Feather River College *C, A*
Los Angeles Pierce College *C, A*
Santa Rosa Junior College *C, A*

Illinois

Black Hawk College *C, A*

Indiana

St. Mary-of-the-Woods College *B*

Iowa

Clinton Community College *C, A*
Kirkwood Community College *A*

Kansas

Cloud County Community
  College *C, A*
Colby Community College *A*

Kentucky

University of Kentucky *B*

Maryland

Cecil College *C, A*

Massachusetts

Becker College *B*

Michigan

Michigan State University *C*

Minnesota

Rochester Community and Technical
  College *A*
University of Minnesota
  Crookston *B*

Missouri

Stephens College *B*

New Mexico

Navajo Technical University *C*

New York

Cazenovia College *B*
SUNY
  College of Agriculture and
    Technology at Morrisville *B*

Ohio

Lake Erie College *B*
Ohio State University
  Agricultural Technical Institute *A*
Tiffin University *B*
Wilmington College *B*

Oklahoma

Oklahoma Panhandle State
  University *B*

Oregon

Linn-Benton Community College *A*
Treasure Valley Community
  College *A*

Rhode Island

Johnson & Wales University
  Providence *B*

Texas

Weatherford College *C, A*

Utah

Southern Utah University *A*

Vermont

Vermont Technical College *B*

Wisconsin

University of Wisconsin
  River Falls *B*

Horticultural science

Alabama

Auburn University *B, M, D*

Arizona

Eastern Arizona College *C*

Arkansas

University of Arkansas *M*

California

California State University
  Fresno *B*
Cosumnes River College *C, A*
Golden West College *C, A*
Los Angeles Pierce College *C, A*
Merritt College *C, A*
Reedley College *C*

Colorado

Colorado State University *B, M, D*

Connecticut

University of Connecticut *A, B*

Delaware

Delaware Technical Community
  College
  Jack F. Owens Campus *C*

Florida

Florida Gateway College *C*
South Florida State College *A*
University of Florida *B, M, D*

Georgia

Fort Valley State University *A, B*
Wiregrass Georgia Technical
  College *C, A*

Idaho

College of Southern Idaho *C, A*
University of Idaho *B*

Illinois

Kishwaukee College *A*
Lake Land College *C*
Richland Community College *A*
University of Illinois
  Urbana-Champaign *B, M, D*

Indiana

Purdue University *B, M, D*

Kansas

Kansas State University *B, M, D*

Kentucky

Maysville Community and Technical
  College *C*

Maine

University of Maine *B, M*

Maryland

Howard Community College *A*

Massachusetts

Cape Cod Community College *C*

Michigan

Michigan State University *C, B, M, D*

Minnesota

Century College *A*
University of Minnesota
  Crookston *B*
  Twin Cities *B, M, D*

Mississippi

Mississippi State University *B*

Missouri

College of the Ozarks *B*
Missouri State University *B*
Missouri State University: West
  Plains *C, A*
Northwest Missouri State
  University *B*
Southeast Missouri State University *B*
University of Missouri
  Columbia *M, D*

Montana

Montana State University *B*

Nebraska

Nebraska College of Technical
  Agriculture *A*
Northeast Community College *A*
University of Nebraska
  Lincoln *B, M, D*

New Hampshire

University of New Hampshire *B*

New Mexico

Eastern New Mexico University:
  Roswell *C*
New Mexico State University *B, M*

New York

City University of New York
  Bronx Community College *A*
Cornell University *M, D*
SUNY
  College of Agriculture and
    Technology at Morrisville *A, B*
  College of Technology at Delhi *A*

North Carolina

Alamance Community College *C, A*
Brunswick Community College *C, A*
Catawba Valley Community
  College *C, A*
North Carolina State
  University *B, M, D*
Rockingham Community College *C*

North Dakota

North Dakota State University *B, M*

Ohio

Ohio State University
  Agricultural Technical Institute *A*
  Columbus Campus *A, M, D*

Southern State Community College *C*
University of Cincinnati *C, B*

Oklahoma

Eastern Oklahoma State College *A*
Oklahoma State University *B, M*
Tulsa Community College *A*

Oregon

Chemeketa Community College *A*
Oregon State University *B*

Pennsylvania

Delaware Valley College *B*
Penn State
  Fayette, The Eberly Campus *C*
  University Park *M, D*
Temple University *A, B*

Puerto Rico

University of Puerto Rico
  Mayaguez *B, M*

South Carolina

Clemson University *B, M*
Trident Technical College *A*

Tennessee

Hiwassee College *A*
Tennessee Technological
  University *B*

Texas

Richland College *A*
Sam Houston State University *B*
Stephen F. Austin State University *B*

Utah

Utah State University *M*

Vermont

University of Vermont *B*
Vermont Technical College *A*

Virginia

Ferrum College *B*
Germanna Community College *C*
Northern Virginia Community
  College *A*
Virginia Polytechnic Institute and
  State University *B, M, D*

Washington

South Seattle Community
  College *C, A*
Washington State University *B, M, D*

West Virginia

Potomac State College of West
  Virginia University *A*
West Virginia University *B*

Wisconsin

Blackhawk Technical College *C*
University of Wisconsin
  Madison *B, M, D*
  River Falls *B*

Wyoming

Sheridan College *A*

Horticulture

Alabama

Calhoun Community College *C*
Faulkner State Community College *C*
Jefferson Davis Community
  College *C*

Arkansas

Arkansas Northeastern College *C, A*

California

Bakersfield College *C, A*
Butte College *C, A*
Diablo Valley College *C*
Fullerton College *A*
Los Angeles Pierce College *C, A*
Merced College *C, A*
Mount San Antonio College *C, A*
San Joaquin Delta College *C, A*
Santa Barbara City College *C, A*
Shasta College *C*

Colorado

Colorado State University *B*
Front Range Community College *C, A*
Northeastern Junior College *C, A*

Connecticut

Naugatuck Valley Community
College *C, A*

Delaware

Delaware Technical Community
College
Jack F. Owens Campus *A*

Florida

College of Central Florida *C, A*

Georgia

Albany Technical College *C*
Augusta Technical College *C*
Central Georgia Technical College *C*
Gwinnett Technical College *C, A*
University of Georgia *B, M, D*

Idaho

Brigham Young University-Idaho *B*
College of Western Idaho *C, A*

Illinois

Black Hawk College *C, A*
City Colleges of Chicago
Harold Washington College *C, A*
College of DuPage *C, A*
Illinois Central College *C, A*
Illinois Eastern Community Colleges
Lincoln Trail College *C, A*
Wabash Valley College *A*
Illinois Valley Community College *C*
John Wood Community College *C, A*
Joliet Junior College *C, A*
Kaskaskia College *C, A*
Kishwaukee College *C, A*
McHenry County College *C, A*
Rend Lake College *C, A*
Richland Community College *A*
Shawnee Community College *C, A*
Southwestern Illinois College *C, A*
Triton College *C*
University of Illinois
Urbana-Champaign *B, M, D*

Indiana

Purdue University *B, M, D*
Vincennes University *A*

Iowa

Hawkeye Community College *C, A*
Iowa State University *B, M, D*

Kansas

Coffeyville Community College *A*
Dodge City Community College *A*
Johnson County Community
College *C, A*

Kentucky

Bluegrass Community and Technical
College *C*
Jefferson Community and Technical
College *C, A*

Owensboro Community and
Technical College *C, A*

Louisiana

Delgado Community College *C, A*

Maine

Southern Maine Community
College *A*
University of Maine *B*

Maryland

Cecil College *C, A*
Community College of Baltimore
County *C, A*

Massachusetts

Cape Cod Community College *C*
University of Massachusetts
Amherst *A, B*

Michigan

Andrews University *B*
Lake Michigan College *A*
Michigan State University *C*

Minnesota

Central Lakes College *C, A*
Century College *C*
Rochester Community and Technical
College *A*

Mississippi

Mississippi Delta Community
College *A*
Northwest Mississippi Community
College *A*

Missouri

Mineral Area College *C, A*

Nebraska

Central Community College *C, A*
Metropolitan Community
College *C, A*
Nebraska College of Technical
Agriculture *A*
Nebraska Indian Community
College *C*
Northeast Community College *A*

New Hampshire

University of New Hampshire *A*

New Jersey

Bergen Community College *A*
Brookdale Community College *C*

New York

Paul Smith's College *A*
SUNY
College of Agriculture and
Technology at Cobleskill *A, B*
College of Technology at Delhi *A*
Farmingdale State College *B*

North Carolina

Alamance Community College *C, A*
Blue Ridge Community College *A*
Central Piedmont Community
College *C, A*
Fayetteville Technical Community
College *C, A*
Forsyth Technical Community
College *A*
Haywood Community College *C, A*
Johnston Community College *C*
Lenoir Community College *C, A*
Mayland Community College *C, A*
Sampson Community College *A*
Surry Community College *A*

Western Piedmont Community
College *C, A*
Wilkes Community College *C, A*

Ohio

Clark State Community College *A*
Cuyahoga Community College
Metropolitan *A*
Kent State University
Salem *A, B*
Ohio State University
Agricultural Technical Institute *A*

Oklahoma

Eastern Oklahoma State College *A*
Oklahoma State University
Oklahoma City *C, A*

Oregon

Chemeketa Community College *A*
Clackamas Community College *C, A*
Linn-Benton Community College *C, A*
Oregon State University *M, D*

Pennsylvania

Bidwell Training Center *C*
Community College of Allegheny
County *A*
Luzerne County Community
College *C*
Pennsylvania College of
Technology *A*
Temple University *C*
Westmoreland County Community
College *C, A*
Williamson Free School of
Mechanical Trades *A*

Puerto Rico

University of Puerto Rico
Mayaguez *M*
Utuado *A*

South Carolina

Clemson University *B*
Horry-Georgetown Technical
College *A*
Piedmont Technical College *A*
Spartanburg Community College *A*
Trident Technical College *C, A*

South Dakota

Mount Marty College *A*
South Dakota State University *B*
Southeast Technical Institute *A*

Tennessee

Southwest Tennessee Community
College *C, A*
Tennessee Technological
University *B*

Texas

Central Texas College *C, A*
Houston Community College
System *A*
Palo Alto College *C*
Richland College *C, A*
Tarrant County College *C, A*
Texas A&M University *B, M, D*
Texas State Technical College
Waco *C*
Texas Tech University *B, M*
Trinity Valley Community
College *C, A*
Western Texas College *C, A*

Vermont

Vermont Technical College *A*

Virginia

J. Sargeant Reynolds Community
College *A*

Tidewater Community College *A*
Virginia Western Community
College *C, A*

Washington

Clark College *A*
Edmonds Community College *C, A*
Heritage University *B*
Lake Washington Institute of
Technology *C, A*
Skagit Valley College *A*
South Puget Sound Community
College *C, A*
Spokane Community College *A*
Tacoma Community College *C*

Wisconsin

Fox Valley Technical College *C*
Gateway Technical College *A*
Lakeshore Technical College *C*
Madison Area Technical College *A*
Northeast Wisconsin Technical
College *C*
University of Wisconsin
River Falls *B*

Hospital/health care facilities administration

Alabama

University of Alabama *B*
University of Phoenix
Birmingham *B*

Arizona

Grand Canyon University *B*
University of Phoenix
Phoenix Hohokam *B*
Southern Arizona *B*

Arkansas

University of Phoenix
Little Rock *B*
Northwest Arkansas *B*

California

University of Phoenix
Bay Area *B*
Central Valley *B*
Sacramento Valley *B*
San Diego *B*
Southern California *B*

Colorado

National American University
Denver *B*
University of Phoenix
Denver *B*
Southern Colorado *B*

Connecticut

Quinnipiac University *M*

District of Columbia

Strayer University *M*
University of Phoenix
Washington DC *B*

Florida

Nova Southeastern University *M*
University of Miami *M*
University of Phoenix
Central Florida *B*
North Florida *B*
South Florida *B*
West Florida *B*

Georgia

Clayton State University *B*
University of Phoenix
Atlanta *B*
Augusta *B*

Columbus *B*
Savannah *B*

Hawaii
University of Phoenix
Hawaii *B*

Idaho
University of Phoenix
Idaho *B*

Illinois
University of Phoenix
Chicago *B*
University of St. Francis *B*

Indiana
University of Phoenix
Indianapolis *B*

Iowa
Upper Iowa University *B*

Kansas
University of Kansas Medical
Center *M, D*

Kentucky
University of Phoenix
Louisville *B*

Louisiana
Bossier Parish Community College *A*
Our Lady of the Lake College *B*
University of Phoenix
Baton Rouge *B*
Lafayette *B*
Louisiana *B*
Shreveport *B*

Maine
Husson University *M*

Maryland
University of Maryland
University College *M*

Massachusetts
Elms College *B*

Michigan
University of Phoenix
Metro Detroit *B*
West Michigan *B*

Minnesota
University of Minnesota
Twin Cities *M, D*
University of Phoenix
Minneapolis-St. Paul *B*

Missouri
Avila University *B*
Missouri State University *M*
Saint Louis University *M*
University of Phoenix
Kansas City *B*
St. Louis *B*
Washington University in St. Louis *M*

Nevada
University of Phoenix
Las Vegas *B*
Northern Nevada *B*

New Jersey
New Jersey Institute of
Technology *M*

Rutgers, The State University of New
Jersey
New Brunswick/Piscataway
Campus *M*
Newark Campus *M*
Thomas Edison State College *B*

New Mexico
University of Phoenix
New Mexico *B*

New York
City University of New York
Lehman College *B*
New York City College of
Technology *B*
Globe Institute of Technology *B*
Iona College *M*
Ithaca College *B*
Long Island University
LIU Brooklyn *M*
LIU Post *B, M*
Mercy College *M*
New York University *M*
Pace University: Pleasantville/
Briarcliff *M*
Rochester Institute of Technology *M*
Sage Colleges *M*
St. Joseph's College New York:
Suffolk Campus *B*
St. Joseph's College, New York *B*
University of Rochester *M*
Utica College *B*

North Carolina
Methodist University *B*

Ohio
Ohio State University
Columbus Campus *M, D*
University of Cincinnati *M*
University of Phoenix
Cleveland *B*
University of Rio Grande *B*
University of Toledo *B*
Ursuline College *B*
Youngstown State University *B, M*

Oklahoma
University of Phoenix
Oklahoma City *B*
Tulsa *B*
Wright Career College
Tulsa *B*

Oregon
University of Phoenix
Oregon *B*

Pennsylvania
Arcadia University *B*
Saint Joseph's University *B, M*
Temple University *M*
University of Phoenix
Harrisburg *B*
Philadelphia *B*
Pittsburgh *B*
Widener University *B, M*

South Carolina
University of Phoenix
Columbia *B*

South Dakota
National American University
Rapid City *B, M*

Tennessee
University of Memphis *M*
University of Phoenix
Chattanooga *B*
Knoxville *B*

Memphis *B*
Nashville *B*

Texas
St. Philip's College *A*
University of North Texas *M*
University of Phoenix
Austin *B*
Dallas Fort Worth *B*
Houston Westside *B*
San Antonio *B*

Utah
University of Phoenix
Utah *B*
University of Utah *M*

Vermont
Champlain College *B, M*

Virginia
University of Phoenix
Northern Virginia *B*
Richmond *B*

Washington
University of Phoenix
Western Washington *B*

West Virginia
Bridgemont Community and
Technical College *A*

Wisconsin
Herzing University
Madison *B*
University of Phoenix
Milwaukee *B*
University of Wisconsin
Milwaukee *B*

Hospitality administration/ management

Alabama
Columbia Southern University *C, B*
Faulkner State Community
College *C, A*
Jefferson State Community
College *C, A*
Tuskegee University *B*

Alaska
University of Alaska
Anchorage *B*

Arizona
Arizona Western College *A*
Coconino County Community
College *C, A*
Northern Arizona University *B*
Penn Foster College *A*
Pima Community College *C, A*
Scottsdale Community College *C, A*

Arkansas
Arkansas State University
Beebe *C, A*
Arkansas Tech University *B*
East Arkansas Community College *C*
National Park Community
College *C, A*
Northwest Arkansas Community
College *C*
Pulaski Technical College *A*
University of Arkansas
Monticello *C*

California
California State Polytechnic
University: Pomona *B, M*

Chaffey College *C*
College of the Canyons *A*
College of the Redwoods *C, A*
Columbia College *C, A*
Empire College *C*
Grossmont College *C, A*
Heald College
Fresno *A*
Rancho Cordova *C, A*
MiraCosta College *C, A*
Monterey Peninsula College *A*
National University *A*
Orange Coast College *C*
San Diego State University *B*
San Francisco State University *B*
San Jose State University *B*
Santa Rosa Junior College *C*
Skyline College *C, A*
University of San Francisco *B*
West Hills College: Lemoore *C*

Colorado
Arapahoe Community College *A*
Colorado Mesa University *A*
Colorado Mountain College *C, A*
Front Range Community College *C, A*
Johnson & Wales University
Denver *B, M*
Metropolitan State University of
Denver *B*
University of Denver *B*
Westwood College
Denver North *A*

Connecticut
Lincoln College of New England *C, A*
Mitchell College *B*
Northwestern Connecticut
Community College *A*
Norwalk Community College *A*
Three Rivers Community
College *C, A*
University of New Haven *B*

Delaware
Delaware State University *B*

District of Columbia
Howard University *B*

Florida
Beacon College *B*
Broward College *A*
Daytona State College *A*
Edison State College *A*
Everest University
Jacksonville *A, B*
Pompano Beach *A, B*
Florida Atlantic University *B*
Florida International University *B, M*
Florida National University *A*
Florida State College at
Jacksonville *A*
Florida State University *B*
Gulf Coast State College *A*
Hillsborough Community College *A*
Indian River State College *A*
Johnson & Wales University
North Miami *B*
Lynn University *B*
Palm Beach State College *A*
Saint Leo University *B*
St. Petersburg College *A*
Saint Thomas University *B*
State College of Florida, Manatee-
Sarasota *A*
University of Central Florida *B, M, D*
University of South Florida *B*
University of South Florida
Sarasota-Manatee *B, M*
University of West Florida *B*
Valencia College *A*
Webber International University *A, B*

Georgia

Abraham Baldwin Agricultural
  College *A*
Albany Technical College *C*
Atlanta Technical College *C, A*
Georgia State University *C, B, M*
Gwinnett Technical College *C, A*
Savannah Technical College *C*

Hawaii

Heald College
  Honolulu *A*
University of Hawaii
  Kauai Community College *C, A*

Idaho

Lewis-Clark State College *C, A, B*

Illinois

Bradley University *B*
DePaul University *B*
Elgin Community College *C*
Harper College *A*
Illinois Institute of Art
  Schaumburg *B*
Kendall College *C, B*
Lexington College *A, B*
Lincoln Land Community College *A*
Moraine Valley Community
  College *C, A*
Richland Community College *C, A*
Roosevelt University *B, M*
Southwestern Illinois College *C, A*
Triton College *C, A*
University of Illinois
  Urbana-Champaign *B*

Indiana

Indiana University
  Kokomo *B*
  Purdue University Fort Wayne *B*
Ivy Tech Community College
  Bloomington *C, A*
  Central Indiana *A*
  East Central *C, A*
  North Central *A*
  Northeast *C, A*
  Northwest *C, A*
  Southwest *C, A*
Oakland City University *A*
Purdue University *B, M, D*
Vincennes University *C, A*

Iowa

AIB College of Business *A*
Des Moines Area Community
  College *C, A*
Grand View University *B*
Iowa Central Community College *A*
Iowa State University *B*
Kirkwood Community College *C, A*
North Iowa Area Community
  College *A*

Kansas

Butler Community College *A*
Colby Community College *C*
Kansas State University *B, M*
Seward County Community
  College *C, A*

Kentucky

Sullivan University *C, A, B*
University of Kentucky *B*
Western Kentucky University *A, B*

Louisiana

Delgado Community College *C, A*
Northwestern State University *B*
Southern University
  Shreveport *C*
University of Louisiana at Lafayette *B*
University of New Orleans *B, M*

Maine

Central Maine Community College *A*
Husson University *B, M*
Kaplan University
  South Portland *A*
Thomas College *B*
University of Maine
  Machias *B*

Maryland

Allegany College of Maryland *A*
Baltimore City Community College *A*
College of Southern Maryland *A*
Frederick Community College *C, A*
Montgomery College *C, A*
Morgan State University *B*
Sojourner-Douglass College *B*
University of Maryland
  Eastern Shore *B*
Wor-Wic Community College *C, A*

Massachusetts

Bay State College *B*
Becker College *B*
Berkshire Community College *A*
Boston University *B*
Bunker Hill Community College *A*
Endicott College *B*
Fisher College *A, B*
Holyoke Community College *C, A*
Lasell College *B*
Marian Court College *A*
Massachusetts Bay Community
  College *C, A*
Massasoit Community College *A*
Middlesex Community College *C, A*
Mount Ida College *B*
Newbury College *B*
North Shore Community College *A*
Quinsigamond Community College *A*
Salem State University *B*
University of Massachusetts
  Amherst *B*

Michigan

Baker College
  Clinton Township *A*
Bay de Noc Community College *A*
Central Michigan University *B*
Eastern Michigan University *B, M*
Ferris State University *B*
Henry Ford Community College *A*
Lake Michigan College *C, A*
Madonna University *B*
Michigan State University *B, M*
Mid Michigan Community College *A*
Northern Michigan University *B*

Minnesota

Art Institutes International
  Minnesota *B*
Central Lakes College *C*
Concordia University St. Paul *B*
Metropolitan State University *B*
Minneapolis Business College *A*
National American University
  Bloomington *B*
Normandale Community College *A*
St. Paul College *C, A*
Southwest Minnesota State
  University *B*
University of Minnesota
  Crookston *B*

Mississippi

Delta State University *B*
East Mississippi Community
  College *A*
Hinds Community College *C, A*
Northeast Mississippi Community
  College *C, A*
University of Mississippi *B*

Missouri

College of the Ozarks *B*
Harris-Stowe State University *B*
Lindenwood University *B, M*
Missouri State University *B*
Saint Louis University *C, B, M*
Southeast Missouri State University *B*
Stevens Institute of Business &
  Arts *A*

Montana

Blackfeet Community College *C, A*

Nebraska

University of Nebraska
  Lincoln *B*

Nevada

College of Southern Nevada *A*
University of Nevada
  Las Vegas *B, M, D*

New Hampshire

Great Bay Community College *A*
NHTI-Concord's Community
  College *A*
Southern New Hampshire
  University *B, M*
University of New Hampshire *B*
White Mountains Community
  College *C*

New Jersey

Bergen Community College *C*
Burlington County College *A*
Essex County College *A*
Fairleigh Dickinson University
  College at Florham *B, M*
  Metropolitan Campus *B, M*
Georgian Court University *C*
Gloucester County College *C, A*
Hudson County Community
  College *C, A*
Passaic County Community College *A*
Richard Stockton College of New
  Jersey *B*
Rutgers, The State University of New
  Jersey
  Camden Campus *B*
Thomas Edison State College *B*
Union County College *A*

New Mexico

Central New Mexico Community
  College *C, A*
Dona Ana Community College of
  New Mexico State University *A*
New Mexico State University *B*

New York

Adirondack Community College *A*
City University of New York
  New York City College of
  Technology *A, B*
Excelsior College *B*
Globe Institute of
  Technology *C, A, B*
Long Island Business Institute *C, A*
Monroe College *A, B, M*
Niagara County Community
  College *C, A*
Niagara University *B*
Paul Smith's College *A, B*
Professional Business College *C*
Rochester Institute of
  Technology *C, A, B, M*
Rockland Community College *A*
SUNY
  College at Buffalo *B*
St. John's University *B*
St. Joseph's College New York:
  Suffolk Campus *B*
St. Joseph's College, New York *B*

North Carolina

Sullivan County Community
  College *A*

North Carolina

Appalachian State University *B*
Cape Fear Community College *A*
Central Piedmont Community
  College *C, A*
Methodist University *B, M*
North Carolina Central University *B*
University of North Carolina
  Greensboro *B*
Western Carolina University *B*

North Dakota

North Dakota State University *B*
University of Jamestown *B*

Ohio

Ashland University *C*
Bowling Green State University *B*
Cincinnati State Technical and
  Community College *A*
Columbus State Community
  College *C, A*
Cuyahoga Community College
  Metropolitan *A*
Kent State University *B, M*
Kent State University
  Ashtabula *B*
Lakeland Community College *C, A*
Ohio State University
  Lima Campus *B*
Stark State College *A*
Terra State Community College *A*
Tiffin University *B*
University of Akron *C, A*
University of Cincinnati *B*
University of Findlay *B*
Youngstown State University *A, B*

Oklahoma

Oklahoma State University *B, M*
Tulsa Community College *A*

Oregon

Chemeketa Community College *C, A*
Clackamas Community College *C*
Le Cordon Bleu College of Culinary
  Arts
  Portland *A*
Mt. Hood Community College *C, A*
Southern Oregon University *B*
Tillamook Bay Community College *A*

Pennsylvania

Art Institute of Pittsburgh *C*
Cheyney University of
  Pennsylvania *B*
East Stroudsburg University of
  Pennsylvania *B*
Harrisburg Area Community
  College *A*
Indiana University of Pennsylvania *B*
Marywood University *B*
Mercyhurst University *B*
Northampton Community College *C*
Robert Morris University *B*
Seton Hill University *B*
Temple University *B, M*
University of Pittsburgh
  Bradford *B*
Widener University *B, M, D*
York College of Pennsylvania *B*
Yorktowne Business Institute *A*

Rhode Island

Johnson & Wales University
  Providence *B, M*

South Carolina

College of Charleston *B*
Spartanburg Community College *A*
Trident Technical College *C*

University of South Carolina
Beaufort *B*
Columbia *B, M, D*

South Dakota
Sisseton Wahpeton College *A*
South Dakota State University *B*
University of Sioux Falls *B*

Tennessee
Hiwassee College *A*
National College of Business and
Technology
Madison *A*
University of Tennessee
Knoxville *D*

Texas
Austin Community College *C, A*
Central Texas College *C, A*
Collin County Community College
District *C, A*
Dallas Baptist University *B*
Galveston College *C*
Lone Star College System *C, A*
Stephen F. Austin State University *B*
Tarrant County College *C, A*
Texas Tech University *D*
University of Houston *M*
University of North Texas *B, M*

Utah
Southern Utah University *B*
Utah Valley University *A, B*

Vermont
Burlington College *B*
Champlain College *B*
Community College of Vermont *A*
Johnson State College *B*
New England Culinary Institute *A, B*

Virginia
J. Sargeant Reynolds Community
College *C*
James Madison University *B*
Norfolk State University *B*
Stratford University: Falls
Church *B, M*
Tidewater Community College *A*
Virginia Polytechnic Institute and
State University *B, M, D*
Virginia State University *B*

Washington
Edmonds Community College *C, A*
Northwest Indian College *C*
South Puget Sound Community
College *C, A*
South Seattle Community
College *A, B*
Washington State University *B, D*

West Virginia
American Public University System *B*
Bridgemont Community and
Technical College *A*
Concord University *B*
Davis and Elkins College *A, B*
New River Community and Technical
College *A*
Potomac State College of West
Virginia University *A*

Wisconsin
Fox Valley Technical College *A*
Madison Area Technical College *A*
University of Wisconsin
Stout *B*
Waukesha County Technical
College *A*

Wyoming
Casper College *C, A*
Sheridan College *C, A*

Hospitality/recreation marketing

Alaska
University of Alaska
Anchorage *B*

Arizona
Central Arizona College *A*
Northland Pioneer College *C*

California
American River College *A*
City College of San Francisco *A*
Cypress College *C, A*
Glendale Community College *A*
Los Angeles Trade and Technical
College *A*
Los Angeles Valley College *A*
Monterey Peninsula College *A*
Orange Coast College *C, A*
Pasadena City College *A*
Santa Barbara City College *C, A*

Colorado
Westwood College
Denver North *A*

Connecticut
Manchester Community College *C, A*

District of Columbia
Howard University *B*

Florida
City College
Fort Lauderdale *A*
Pensacola State College *A*

Hawaii
University of Hawaii
Kapiolani Community College *C, A*

Idaho
College of Southern Idaho *A*

Indiana
Purdue University *B, M*

Iowa
Des Moines Area Community
College *C*

Kansas
Butler Community College *C, A*

Maine
Husson University *B*
Kaplan University
South Portland *A*
University of Maine
Machias *B*

Maryland
Allegany College of Maryland *A*

Massachusetts
Bay State College *A, B*
Nichols College *B*
Roxbury Community College *A*

Michigan
Ferris State University *A, B*
Siena Heights University *A, B*

Minnesota
Art Institutes International
Minnesota *B*

University of Minnesota
Twin Cities *B*

Mississippi
Northwest Mississippi Community
College *A*

Nevada
College of Southern Nevada *A*

New Hampshire
Lakes Region Community
College *C, A*
NHTI-Concord's Community
College *C, A*

New Jersey
Cumberland County College *A*

New York
Finger Lakes Community College *A*
Paul Smith's College *B*
Rochester Institute of Technology *M*
SUNY
College at Buffalo *B*

North Carolina
Methodist University *B*
Wake Technical Community
College *A*

Ohio
University of Findlay *B*
Youngstown State University *A, B*

Oklahoma
Tulsa Community College *A*

Pennsylvania
McCann School of Business and
Technology
Hazleton *A*
Montgomery County Community
College *C, A*
Yorktowne Business Institute *A*

South Dakota
Sinte Gleska University *B*

Tennessee
Hiwassee College *A*

Texas
Central Texas College *C*
El Paso Community College *C, A*

Utah
Provo College *A*

Vermont
Green Mountain College *B*

Washington
Highline Community College *A*
Skagit Valley College *A*

West Virginia
Bridgemont Community and
Technical College *A*
Concord University *B*
Mountain State College *A*
Pierpont Community and Technical
College *C*

Wisconsin
Lac Courte Oreilles Ojibwa
Community College *C*
Madison Area Technical College *A*
Northeast Wisconsin Technical
College *A*

Hotel/motel administration

Arizona
Arizona Western College *C, A*
Estrella Mountain Community
College *C, A*

Arkansas
East Arkansas Community College *C*

California
College of the Canyons *A, T*
College of the Desert *A*
Long Beach City College *C, A*
Orange Coast College *C*
San Diego Mesa College *C, A*
Shasta College *A*
University of San Francisco *B*
West Hills College: Lemoore *C*

Colorado
Colorado Mountain College *A*
Johnson & Wales University
Denver *B*

Connecticut
Gateway Community College *A*
Lincoln College of New England *A*
Mitchell College *B*
University of New Haven *B*

Delaware
Delaware Technical Community
College
Stanton/Wilmington Campus *C, A*
Terry Campus *A*

Florida
Bethune-Cookman University *B*
Hillsborough Community College *C*
Johnson & Wales University
North Miami *B*
Northwood University
Florida *B*
St. Petersburg College *C*
Schiller International
University *A, B, M*
Valencia College *C*

Georgia
Atlanta Technical College *C*

Illinois
City Colleges of Chicago
Harold Washington College *C, A*
Elgin Community College *C, A*
Harper College *C*
Lexington College *A, B*
Lincoln Land Community College *C*
Parkland College *C, A*
Roosevelt University *B, M*
Triton College *C, A*

Indiana
Indiana University
Purdue University Fort Wayne *B*
International Business College *C, A*
International Business College:
Indianapolis *C, A*
Purdue University *B, M, D*
Purdue University
Calumet *B*
Vincennes University *A*

Iowa
Iowa Lakes Community College *C, A*

Louisiana
Grambling State University *B*

Maine

Husson University *B*
Southern Maine Community
College *A*

Maryland

Anne Arundel Community
College *C, A*
Community College of Baltimore
County *A*
Howard Community College *C, A*
Montgomery College *A*
University of Maryland
Eastern Shore *B*

Massachusetts

Bay State College *B*
Cape Cod Community College *C, A*
North Shore Community College *A*
Quinsigamond Community College *C*

Michigan

Central Michigan University *B*
Ferris State University *A, B*
Henry Ford Community College *C*
Lansing Community College *C, A*
Northwood University
Michigan *A, B*
Oakland Community College *A*

Minnesota

Art Institutes International
Minnesota *B*
Normandale Community College *C*

Mississippi

Coahoma Community College *A*
East Mississippi Community
College *A*
University of Southern Mississippi *B*

Missouri

University of Central Missouri *B*
University of Missouri
Columbia *B, M*

New Hampshire

NHTI-Concord's Community
College *C*

New Jersey

Atlantic Cape Community College *A*
Bergen Community College *A*
Mercer County Community
College *A*

New York

Broome Community College *A*
Bryant & Stratton College
Syracuse *A*
Cornell University *B, M, D*
Finger Lakes Community College *A*
Globe Institute of
Technology *C, A, B*
Mohawk Valley Community
College *A*
Monroe College *A*
New York University *B, M*
Niagara University *B*
Pace University *B*
Pace University: Pleasantville/
Briarcliff *B*
Paul Smith's College *A, B*
Rochester Institute of
Technology *A, B, M*
SUNY
College at Plattsburgh *B*
Tompkins Cortland Community
College *A*
Wood Tobe-Coburn School *C, A*

North Carolina

Cape Fear Community College *C, A*
Carteret Community College *C, A*
East Carolina University *B*
Johnson & Wales University
Charlotte *B*
King's College *C, A*
Nash Community College *A*
Sandhills Community College *A*
Southwestern Community College *C*

Ohio

Ashland University *B*
Bradford School *C, A*
Hocking College *C, A*
Lorain County Community College *A*
Ohio State University
Columbus Campus *B, M, D*
Sinclair Community College *A*
University of Akron *C, A*

Oregon

Central Oregon Community
College *A*
Chemeketa Community College *C*
Lane Community College *C, A*

Pennsylvania

Bradford School: Pittsburgh *C, A*
Delaware County Community
College *A*
Drexel University *M*
Erie Business Center *C*
Harrisburg Area Community
College *A*
Northampton Community College *A*
Restaurant School at Walnut Hill
College *A, B*
Westmoreland County Community
College *C, A*

Puerto Rico

ICPR Junior College *C, A*
Inter American University of Puerto
Rico
Aguadilla Campus *B*
Ponce Campus *B*
Universidad del Este *C, A, B*
University of Puerto Rico
Aguadilla *A*
Carolina Regional College *B*

Rhode Island

Johnson & Wales University
Providence *B*

South Carolina

Horry-Georgetown Technical
College *A*
Spartanburg Community College *A*

South Dakota

South Dakota State University *B*

Tennessee

Southwest Tennessee Community
College *A*
University of Memphis *B*
University of Tennessee
Knoxville *B*

Texas

Del Mar College *C, A*
Houston Community College
System *C, A*
St. Philip's College *C, A*
Texas Tech University *B, M*
University of Houston *B*

Virginia

J. Sargeant Reynolds Community
College *A*

Washington

Edmonds Community College *C*

West Virginia

Concord University *B*

Wisconsin

Gateway Technical College *A*
Lakeshore Technical College *A*
Milwaukee Area Technical College *A*

Wyoming

Central Wyoming College *C, A*

Hotel/motel/restaurant management

Arizona

Central Arizona College *C, A*

Georgia

Columbus Technical College *C, A*

Illinois

Roosevelt University *B, M*

Indiana

Harrison College
Indianapolis *B*
Purdue University
Calumet *C*

Iowa

Iowa Western Community College *A*

Maryland

Chesapeake College *C, A*

Massachusetts

Endicott College *B*

Michigan

Wayne County Community College *C*

Mississippi

Copiah-Lincoln Community
College *A*
Meridian Community College *A*
Tougaloo College *A*

New York

New York Institute of Technology *B*

North Carolina

Central Piedmont Community
College *A*
Fayetteville Technical Community
College *C, A*

Ohio

Davis College *A*

Housing and human environments

Arkansas

Harding University *B*

California

Allan Hancock College *C, A*
California State University
Northridge *B*

Georgia

University of Georgia *B, M, D*

Illinois

Olivet Nazarene University *B*

Iowa

Iowa State University *B*

Kentucky

Eastern Kentucky University *B*

Minnesota

Minnesota State University
Mankato *B, M, T*
University of Minnesota
Twin Cities *C, B*

Missouri

Missouri State University *B*
University of Missouri
Columbia *B, M*

Nebraska

University of Nebraska
Kearney *B*

New York

Cornell University *M, D*
Rochester Institute of Technology *M*

Ohio

Davis College *C*
Ohio University *B*
University of Akron *B*

Oklahoma

Oklahoma State University *B, M*

Oregon

Oregon State University *B*

Tennessee

Tennessee Technological
University *B*

Texas

Texas Tech University *M*

Human biology

California

Scripps College *B*
University of California
Irvine *B*
Los Angeles *B*
University of Southern California *B*

Indiana

Indiana University
Purdue University Indianapolis *B*

Kansas

University of Kansas *B*

Maine

College of the Atlantic *B, M*

Minnesota

Hamline University *B*

Missouri

Logan University *B*

Ohio

Ashland University *B*

Human computer interaction

Illinois

Loyola University Chicago *M*

Indiana

Indiana University
Bloomington *M*
Purdue University
Indianapolis *C, M*

Maine

College of the Atlantic *B, M*

Maryland

University of Maryland
  College Park *M*

Massachusetts

Bentley University *M*

Washington

DigiPen Institute of Technology *B*

Human development and family studies

Alabama

Auburn University *B, M, D*
Oakwood University *B*
Samford University *B*
University of Alabama *B*

Arizona

Central Arizona College *C, A*
University of Arizona *B*

Arkansas

University of Arkansas *B*

California

Azusa Pacific University *M*
California State University
  Northridge *B, M*
  San Bernardino *B*
  San Marcos *B*
City College of San Francisco *C*
College of the Siskiyous *C, A*
Folsom Lake College *C, A*
Fullerton College *A*
Hope International University *B*
Merced College *A*
MiraCosta College *A*
Moorpark College *A*
Pacific Oaks College *B, M*
San Deigo Miramar College
  San Diego Miramar College *A*
San Diego Christian College *B*
Shasta College *A*
Solano Community College *C*
Sonoma State University *B*
University of California
  Davis *B, M, D*
  San Diego *B*
University of La Verne *M*
Vanguard University of Southern
  California *B*

Colorado

Colorado State University *B, M, D*
Pikes Peak Community College *C*

Connecticut

Connecticut College *B*
Fairfield University *M*
Mitchell College *B, T*
Norwalk Community College *C*
Three Rivers Community
  College *C, A*
University of Connecticut *B, M*

Delaware

University of Delaware *B*

District of Columbia

University of the District of
  Columbia *B*

Florida

Florida State University *M, D*

Georgia

Fort Valley State University *B*
Georgia Southern University *B*
Middle Georgia State College *A*
University of Georgia *B, M, D*

Hawaii

Hawaii Pacific University *B*

Idaho

University of Idaho *B*

Illinois

City Colleges of Chicago
  Olive-Harvey College *A*
North Park University *B*
Northern Illinois University *B, M*
University of Illinois
  Urbana-Champaign *B, M, D*

Indiana

Indiana State University *B*
Purdue University *B, M, D*
Purdue University
  Calumet *B, M*

Iowa

Iowa State University *M, D*

Kansas

Kansas State University *B, M*

Kentucky

Eastern Kentucky University *B*
Kentucky State University *B*
University of Kentucky *M*

Louisiana

Louisiana Tech University *B*
Southern University
  New Orleans *B*
University of Louisiana at Lafayette *B*

Maine

University of Maine *B, M*

Massachusetts

Lesley University *B*
Merrimack College *B*
Springfield College *M*
Wheelock College *B*

Michigan

Andrews University *B*
Central Michigan University *M*
Concordia University *B*
Kalamazoo Valley Community
  College *C, A*
Kellogg Community College *C*
Michigan State University *M, D*
Spring Arbor University *B, M*

Minnesota

Concordia University St. Paul *C, B, M*
Minnesota State University
  Mankato *B, M, T*
Ridgewater College *A*
St. Mary's University of Minnesota *M*
University of Northwestern - St.
  Paul *B*
Walden University *B*

Mississippi

Mississippi State University *M, D*

Missouri

Missouri State University *B*
Northwest Missouri State
  University *B*
Stephens College *B*
University of Central Missouri *B*
University of Missouri
  Columbia *B, M*

Montana

Blackfeet Community College *C, A*

Nebraska

University of Nebraska
  Kearney *B*
  Lincoln *M*

Nevada

University of Nevada
  Reno *B, M*

New Hampshire

University of New
  Hampshire *B, M, D*

New Mexico

Central New Mexico Community
  College *A*
New Mexico State University *B*
University of New Mexico *B*

New York

Cornell University *B, M, D*
Mercy College *M*
SUNY
  College at Oneonta *B*
  College at Plattsburgh *B*
Sarah Lawrence College *M*
Syracuse University *B, M, D*

North Carolina

Campbell University *B*
North Carolina State University *M*
University of North Carolina
  Charlotte *B*
  Greensboro *B, M, D*

North Dakota

North Dakota State University *B, M*

Ohio

Bowling Green State University *B, M*
Kent State University *B, M*
Kent State University
  Salem *B*
  Stark *B*
Miami University
  Oxford *B, M*
Ohio State University
  Columbus Campus *B, M, D*
Ohio University *B, M*
University of Dayton *M*

Oklahoma

Langston University *B*
Oklahoma Christian University *B*
Oklahoma State University *B, M*
University of Central Oklahoma *M*

Oregon

Clackamas Community College *C*
Oregon State University *B, M, D*
Portland State University *B*
Southwestern Oregon Community
  College *A*
Warner Pacific College *B*

Pennsylvania

Bucks County Community College *A*
Indiana University of Pennsylvania *B*
Penn State
  Abington *B*
  Altoona *A, B*
  Beaver *B*
  Berks *B*
  Brandywine *C, A, B*
  DuBois *A, B*
  Fayette, The Eberly
    Campus *C, A, B*
  Greater Allegheny *B*
  Harrisburg *B*
  Hazleton *B*
  Lehigh Valley *B*
  Mont Alto *A, B*
  New Kensington *B*
  Schuylkill *A, B*
  Shenango *A, B*
  University Park *B, M, D*
  Wilkes-Barre *B*
  Worthington Scranton *A, B*
  York *C, A, B*
Waynesburg University *B*

Rhode Island

University of Rhode Island *B, M*

South Carolina

Benedict College *B*
Columbia College *B*
South Carolina State University *M*

South Dakota

South Dakota State University *B*

Tennessee

East Tennessee State University *B, T*
Freed-Hardeman University *B*
Northeast State Community
  College *C, A*
Tennessee State University *B*
University of Tennessee
  Knoxville *B, M, D*

Texas

Abilene Christian University *B*
Baylor University *B*
El Paso Community College *A*
Galveston College *A*
Howard Payne University *B*
Texas A&M University
  Kingsville *B*
Texas State University *B, M*
Texas Tech University *B, M, D*
Texas Woman's University *B, M, D*
University of Houston *B*
University of North Texas *B, M*
University of Texas
  Austin *B, M; D*
  Permian Basin *B*

Utah

Brigham Young University *B*
Salt Lake Community College *A*
University of Utah *B*
Utah State University *B, M, D*

Vermont

University of Vermont *B*

Virginia

Liberty University *B*
Virginia Polytechnic Institute and
  State University *B, M, D*

Washington

Washington State University *B, M*

Wisconsin

Moraine Park Technical College *C, A*
University of Wisconsin
  Madison *B*
  Stout *B*

Human/medical genetics

Alabama

University of Alabama
  Birmingham *D*

California

University of California
  Los Angeles *M, D*

Colorado

University of Colorado
Denver *D*

Connecticut

University of Connecticut *M*

Florida

University of Miami *M, D*

Illinois

University of Chicago *D*

Indiana

Indiana University
Purdue University
Indianapolis *M, D*

Iowa

University of Iowa *D*

Louisiana

Louisiana State University
Health Sciences Center *D*

Maryland

University of Maryland
Baltimore *D*

Michigan

University of Michigan *M, D*

Missouri

Washington University in St. Louis *D*

New York

SUNY
College at Oneonta *B*

North Carolina

University of North Carolina
Greensboro *M*

Ohio

Case Western Reserve University *D*
University of Cincinnati *M*

Pennsylvania

Arcadia University *M*
University of Pittsburgh *M*

South Carolina

Clemson University *D*
University of South Carolina
Columbia *M*

Tennessee

Vanderbilt University *D*

Utah

University of Utah *M, D*

Virginia

Virginia Commonwealth
University *M, D*

Wisconsin

University of Wisconsin
Madison *M*

Human nutrition

California

City College of San Francisco *A*
College of the Desert *A*
University of California
Davis *M*

Colorado

Colorado State University *B*

Connecticut

University of Bridgeport *M*

District of Columbia

Howard University *M, D*

Illinois

University of Illinois
Urbana-Champaign *B, M, D*

Iowa

Iowa State University *B, M, D*

Kansas

Kansas State University *B, M, D*

Michigan

Central Michigan University *M*
Michigan State University *M, D*

Missouri

University of Missouri
Columbia *B, M*

New Jersey

College of St. Elizabeth *M*

New York

Syracuse University *B*

North Carolina

Meredith College *M*

Ohio

Case Western Reserve
University *B, M, D*
Ohio State University
Columbus Campus *B, M, D*

Oklahoma

University of Central Oklahoma *B, M*

Pennsylvania

Mansfield University of
Pennsylvania *B*
Penn State
Abington *B*
Altoona *B*
Beaver *B*
Berks *B*
Brandywine *B*
DuBois *B*
Fayette, The Eberly Campus *B*
Greater Allegheny *B*
Harrisburg *B*
Hazleton *B*
Lehigh Valley *B*
Mont Alto *B*
New Kensington *B*
Schuylkill *B*
Shenango *B*
University Park *B, M, D*
Wilkes-Barre *B*
Worthington Scranton *B*
York *B*

South Carolina

Winthrop University *B, M*

South Dakota

South Dakota State University *M, D*

Texas

Baylor University *B, M*
Texas State University *M*
University of Houston *B, M*

Utah

Southern Utah University *B*

Washington

Bastyr University *M*
Washington State University *B*

Wisconsin

University of Wisconsin
Stout *M*

Wyoming

University of Wyoming *M*

Human resources development

Alabama

Auburn University *B, M*

Arizona

Northcentral University *M, D*

Arkansas

University of Arkansas *B*

California

University of San Francisco *M*

Colorado

Colorado Technical University *C*

Florida

Barry University *M*

Georgia

Mercer University *B*
Oglethorpe University *B*
West Georgia Technical College *C*

Illinois

Roosevelt University *M*
Trinity International University *B*
University of Illinois
Urbana-Champaign *M, D*
University of St. Francis *M*

Indiana

Oakland City University *B*
Purdue University *B*

Kansas

Pittsburg State University *M*

Kentucky

Northern Kentucky
University *C, A, B*

Maryland

Bowie State University *M*
McDaniel College *M*
Towson University *M*

Massachusetts

Dean College *C*
Fisher College *B*
Lasell College *M*
Nichols College *B*

Michigan

Andrews University *B*
Northern Michigan University *M*
Oakland University *B, M*
University of Michigan
Flint *B*
Western Michigan University *M*

Minnesota

Anoka Technical College *C*
Dakota County Technical College *C*
Rochester Community and Technical
College *C*
St. Cloud Technical and Community
College *C*

Missouri

Grantham University *M*
Webster University *M*

Montana

Montana State University
Billings *A*

Nebraska

Bellevue University *M, D*

New Jersey

Seton Hall University *M*

New Mexico

Eastern New Mexico University:
Roswell *C*

New York

College of New Rochelle *M*
Niagara University *B*
Rochester Institute of Technology *M*

North Carolina

Forsyth Technical Community
College *C*
Pitt Community College *C, A*

Ohio

Lake Erie College *B*
Xavier University *M*

Oregon

Clackamas Community College *C*

Pennsylvania

Drexel University *M*
La Salle University *M*

South Carolina

Converse College *B*
Limestone College *B*

South Dakota

Mount Marty College *C*

Tennessee

Vanderbilt University *M*

Texas

Concordia University Texas *B*
Midwestern State University *M*
Our Lady of the Lake University of
San Antonio *B*
Texas A&M University *B*
University of Dallas *M*
University of Houston *B, M*
University of Houston
Clear Lake *M*
University of North Texas *M, D*
University of Texas
Tyler *B, M, D*

Wisconsin

Blackhawk Technical College *A*
Northcentral Technical College *C*
University of Wisconsin
Milwaukee *B*
Stout *M*

Human resources management

Alabama

Athens State University *B*
Auburn University *B*
Auburn University at Montgomery *B*
Columbia Southern University *C, B*
Community College of the Air
Force *A*
Faulkner University *B, M*
Troy University *M*
Tuskegee University *M*
University of Phoenix
Birmingham *B, M*

Virginia College
Birmingham *A, B*

Alaska

University of Alaska
Fairbanks *A, B*

Arizona

DeVry University
Phoenix *M*
Northcentral University *M, D*
Pima Community College *C*
University of Arizona *B*
University of Phoenix
Phoenix-Hohokam *C, B, M*
Southern Arizona *C, B, M*
Western International University *B*

Arkansas

University of Phoenix
Northwest Arkansas *B*

California

Azusa Pacific University *M*
California National University for
Advanced Studies *M*
California State University
Dominguez Hills *M*
East Bay *B, M*
Fresno *B*
Long Beach *B*
Northridge *B, M*
Sacramento *B, M*
San Bernardino *B, M*
Cerritos College *A*
City College of San Francisco *A*
College of San Mateo *C*
DeVry University
Pomona *M*
Fresno Pacific University *B*
Golden Gate University *B, M*
Holy Names University *B*
Institute of Technology: Clovis *A*
La Sierra University *B, M*
Lincoln University *M*
Loyola Marymount University *B*
National University *C, M*
San Diego State University *B, M*
San Joaquin Valley College *A*
San Jose State University *B*
University of Phoenix
Bay Area *C, B, M*
Central Valley *C, B, M*
Sacramento Valley *C, B, M*
San Diego *C, B, M*
Southern California *C, B, M*
University of Redlands *C*
Yuba College *A*

Colorado

Colorado Christian University *B*
Colorado Technical University *B, M*
Community College of Aurora *C, A*
DeVry University
Westminster *M*
Regis University *C, B*
University of Denver *M*
University of Phoenix
Denver *B, M*
Southern Colorado *B, M*

Connecticut

Post University *C*
Quinnipiac University *B*
University of Bridgeport *M*
University of Connecticut *M*

Delaware

Delaware Technical Community
College
Terry Campus *A*
Wilmington University *B, M*

District of Columbia

Catholic University of America *B, M*
George Washington University *D*
Georgetown University *M*
Strayer University *M*
Trinity Washington University *M*
University of Phoenix
Washington DC *B, M*

Florida

DeVry University
Miramar *M*
Orlando *M*
Florida Institute of Technology *M*
Florida International University *B, M*
Florida State University *B*
Herzing University
Winter Park *B*
Nova Southeastern University *M*
Rasmussen College
Fort Myers *C, A, B*
New Port Richey *C, A, B*
Ocala *C, A, B*
Pasco/Land O'Lakes *C, A, B*
Tampa/Brandon *C, A, B*
Rollins College *M*
Saint Leo University *B*
Saint Thomas University *M*
University of Miami *B*
University of Phoenix
Central Florida *C, B, M*
North Florida *C, B, M*
South Florida *C, B, M*
West Florida *C, B, M*

Georgia

Atlanta Technical College *C*
Brenau University *B*
Columbus Technical College *A*
Georgia Piedmont Technical
College *C, A*
Georgia Southwestern State
University *B*
Georgia State University *M, D*
Gwinnett Technical College *C*
Middle Georgia State College *A*
University of Georgia *M*
University of Phoenix
Atlanta *B, M*
Augusta *B, M*
Columbus *B, M*
Savannah *B, M*

Hawaii

Hawaii Pacific University *B, M*
University of Hawaii
Manoa *B, M*
University of Phoenix
Hawaii *B, M*

Idaho

Boise State University *B*
Idaho State University *B, M*
University of Idaho *C, B*
University of Phoenix
Idaho *B, M*

Illinois

Bradley University *B*
City Colleges of Chicago
Wilbur Wright College *C*
Concordia University Chicago *C*
DePaul University *B, M*
DeVry University
Chicago *M*
Online *M*
Illinois Eastern Community Colleges
Olney Central College *A*
Illinois Institute of Technology *M*
Judson University *C, B*
Kishwaukee College *A*
Lake Land College *A*
Lewis University *B*
Loyola University Chicago *B, M*

McKendree University *B*
Moraine Valley Community
College *C, A*
National-Louis University *M*
North Central College *B*
Northwestern College *A*
Northwestern University *M*
Rasmussen College
Aurora *C, A, B*
Mokena/Tinley Park *C, A, B*
Rockford *C, A, B*
Romeoville/Joliet *C, A, B*
Roosevelt University *B, M*
Saint Xavier University *M*
Trinity International University *B, M*
Triton College *C, A*
University of Illinois
Urbana-Champaign *B*
University of Phoenix
Chicago *B*
University of St. Francis *B*
Waubonsee Community College *A*
Western Illinois University *B*

Indiana

Ball State University *B*
Harrison College
Indianapolis *A, B*
Huntington University *B*
Indiana State University *B, M*
Indiana University
Purdue University Indianapolis *C*
Southeast *C*
Martin University *B*
Oakland City University *B*
Purdue University *B, M, D*
Purdue University
Calumet *C*
North Central *C, A, B*
St. Mary-of-the-Woods College *B*
University of Phoenix
Indianapolis *B, M*

Iowa

Ashford University *B*
Briar Cliff University *B, M*
Buena Vista University *B*
Grand View University *B*
Hawkeye Community College *A*
Iowa Western Community College *A*
Northwestern College *B*
University of Iowa *B, D*
University of Phoenix
Des Moines *B, M*
Upper Iowa University *B, M*
Western Iowa Tech Community
College *A*

Kansas

Barton County Community College *A*
Emporia State University *B*
Friends University *B*
Kansas Wesleyan University *B*
MidAmerica Nazarene University *B*
University of St. Mary *M*
Wichita State University *B*

Kentucky

Mid-Continent University *M*
Midway College *B*
Sullivan University *C, B, M*
University of Phoenix
Louisville *B*

Louisiana

Herzing University
Kenner *B*
Louisiana Tech University *B*
University of Phoenix
Baton Rouge *C, B, M*
Lafayette *C, B, M*
Louisiana *B, M*
Shreveport *C, B, M*

Maine

Saint Joseph's College of Maine *B*
Thomas College *B*

Maryland

Cecil College *A*
Community College of Baltimore
County *C*
Harford Community College *C, A*
University of Baltimore *B*
University of Maryland
University College *B*

Massachusetts

Boston College *B*
Boston University *M*
Emerson College *M*
Emmanuel College *M*
Fisher College *B*
Fitchburg State University *M*
Framingham State University *M*
Holyoke Community College *A*
Nichols College *B*
Northeastern University *B*
Salem State University *B*
Springfield College *M*
University of Massachusetts
Dartmouth *B*
University of Phoenix
Boston *B, M*

Michigan

Albion College *B*
Aquinas College *B*
Baker College
Allen Park *B*
Cadillac *A, B*
Clinton Township *A, B*
Flint *M*
Muskegon *A, B*
Owosso *A, B*
Port Huron *A, B*
Central Michigan University *B, M*
Cleary University *B*
Davenport University *B, M*
Eastern Michigan University *M*
Ferris State University *B*
Grand Valley State University *B*
Lansing Community College *A*
Madonna University *B*
Marygrove College *M*
Michigan State University *B, M, D*
Northern Michigan University *M*
Oakland University *B*
University of Phoenix
Metro Detroit *B, M*
West Michigan *B, M*

Minnesota

Anoka-Ramsey Community College *A*
Capella University *B, M, D*
Concordia University St. Paul *B, M*
Inver Hills Community College *C*
Metropolitan State University *B*
Minnesota State Community and
Technical College *A*
Minnesota State University
Mankato *B*
National American University
Roseville *B*
Normandale Community College *C*
Rasmussen College
Blaine *C, A, B*
Bloomington *C, A, B*
Brooklyn Park *C, A, B*
Eagan *C, A, B*
Lake Elmo/Woodbury *C, A, B*
Mankato *B*
Moorhead *B*
St. Cloud *C, A, B*
Saint Cloud State University *B*
St. Mary's University of
Minnesota *B, M*
St. Paul College *C, A*

University of Minnesota
Duluth *B*
Twin Cities *B, M*
University of Northwestern - St.
Paul *B*
University of Phoenix
Minneapolis-St. Paul *B, M*
University of St. Thomas *B*
Winona State University *B*

Mississippi

University of Phoenix
Jackson *B, M*
University of Southern Mississippi *B*

Missouri

Avila University *B*
Columbia College *B*
DeVry University
Kansas City *B*
Fontbonne University *M*
Grantham University *B*
Lindenwood University *B, M*
University of Central Missouri *B*
University of Phoenix
Kansas City *B, M*
St. Louis *B, M*
Washington University in St.
Louis *B, M*
Webster University *M*

Montana

Montana State University
Billings *A*
University of Montana *A*

Nebraska

Bellevue University *B*
Doane College *B*
Hastings College *B*
University of Nebraska
Omaha *B*
University of Phoenix
Omaha *B, M*
York College *B*

Nevada

University of Nevada
Las Vegas *B*
University of Phoenix
Las Vegas *B, M*
Northern Nevada *B, M*

New Hampshire

Franklin Pierce University *M*
Granite State College *B*
New England College *B*
Southern New Hampshire
University *C*

New Jersey

Berkeley College *B*
College of St. Elizabeth *C*
Rider University *A, B*
Rowan University *B*
Rutgers, The State University of New
Jersey
New Brunswick/Piscataway
Campus *B, M*
Stevens Institute of Technology *M*
Thomas Edison State College *C, B, M*
University of Phoenix
Jersey City *B*

New Mexico

Central New Mexico Community
College *C, A*
Eastern New Mexico University *B*
National American University
Albuquerque *B*
University of Phoenix
New Mexico *B, M*

New York

Adelphi University *M*
Bryant & Stratton College
Albany *A*
Henrietta *A*
City University of New York
CUNY Online *C*
Daemen College *C*
Dominican College of Blauvelt *B*
Excelsior College *B, M*
Herkimer County Community
College *A*
Hofstra University *M*
Iona College *M*
Le Moyne College *B*
Long Island University
LIU Brooklyn *M*
Manhattanville College *M*
Mercy College *M*
Nazareth College *M*
New York Institute of Technology *B*
New York University *M*
Niagara University *B*
Pace University *B, M*
Pace University: Pleasantville/
Briarcliff *B*
Roberts Wesleyan College *B*
SUNY
College at Oswego *B*
College of Technology at Alfred *B*
University at Albany *B*
University at Stony Brook *M*
St. John Fisher College *B*
St. Joseph's College New York:
Suffolk Campus *C*
St. Joseph's College, New York *C*
Suffolk County Community College *A*

North Carolina

Barton College *B*
Central Piedmont Community
College *A*
Davidson County Community
College *A*
Fayetteville Technical Community
College *C, A*
Guilford Technical Community
College *A*
Pitt Community College *A*
Randolph Community College *A*
Stanly Community College *A*
University of Mount Olive *B*
University of North Carolina
Chapel Hill *B*
Western Carolina University *M*
William Peace University *B*

North Dakota

Rasmussen College
Bismarck *C, A, B*
Fargo *C, A, B*
University of North Dakota *B*
Valley City State University *B*

Ohio

Antioch University
Midwest *B*
Baldwin Wallace University *C, B, M*
Bowling Green State University *B*
Bryant & Stratton College
Eastlake *A*
Parma *A*
Cincinnati State Technical and
Community College *C*
Clark State Community College *A*
Davis College *A*
DeVry University
Columbus *M*
Edison State Community College *C, A*
Franklin University *B, M*
Harrison College
Grove City *A, B*
John Carroll University *B*
Lorain County Community College *A*

Lourdes University *B*
Marietta College *B*
Marion Technical College *A*
Notre Dame College *B*
Ohio Business College
Sandusky *A*
Ohio State University
Columbus Campus *B, M, D*
Ohio University *B*
Sinclair Community College *C*
Tiffin University *B*
University of Akron *B, M*
University of Cincinnati *M*
University of Findlay *B*
University of Phoenix
Cleveland *B, M*
University of Toledo *B, M*
Urbana University *B*
Ursuline College *B*
Wright State University *B*
Xavier University *B*
Youngstown State University *B*

Oklahoma

East Central University *B*
Langston University *B*
Southwestern Oklahoma State
University *B*
Tulsa Community College *A*
University of Central Oklahoma *B*
University of Phoenix
Oklahoma City *B, M*
Tulsa *B, M*

Oregon

Portland State University *B*

Pennsylvania

Alvernia University *B*
Arcadia University *B*
Butler County Community
College *C, A*
Cabrini College *B*
Cedar Crest College *C*
Chestnut Hill College *A, B*
Community College of Allegheny
County *A*
Community College of Beaver
County *A*
DeSales University *C, B*
DeVry University
Fort Washington *M*
Drexel University *M*
Gwynedd Mercy University *B*
Holy Family University *B, M*
Immaculata University *B*
Indiana University of Pennsylvania *B*
Juniata College *B*
King's College *A, B*
La Roche College *M*
La Salle University *B*
Lehigh Carbon Community
College *C, A*
Lincoln University *B*
Mansfield University of
Pennsylvania *B*
Mercyhurst University *B*
Muhlenberg College *B*
Peirce College *B*
Penn State
Beaver *C*
Brandywine *C*
DuBois *C*
Fayette, The Eberly Campus *C*
Greater Allegheny *C*
Hazleton *C*
Lehigh Valley *C*
Mont Alto *C*
New Kensington *C*
Schuylkill *C*
Shenango *C*
Wilkes-Barre *C*
Worthington Scranton *C*
York *C*

Point Park University *B*
Robert Morris University *M*
St. Francis University *M*
Saint Joseph's University *B, M*
Seton Hill University *B*
Temple University *B, M*
University of Pennsylvania *B, M*
University of Phoenix
Pittsburgh *B*
University of Scranton *C, A, B, M*
Villanova University *M*
Westmoreland County Community
College *A*
Widener University *B, M*
York College of Pennsylvania *M*

Puerto Rico

Bayamon Central University *B*
Caribbean University *B*
Columbia Centro Universitario:
Caguas *M*
Inter American University of Puerto
Rico
Aguadilla Campus *B, M*
Bayamon Campus *B, M*
Guayama Campus *B*
Metropolitan Campus *B, M, D*
Ponce Campus *B, M*
San German Campus *B, M, D*
Pontifical Catholic University of
Puerto Rico *B, M*
Turabo University *M*
Universidad Metropolitana *M*
Universidad del Este *B, M*
University of Phoenix
Puerto Rico *M*
University of Puerto Rico
Aguadilla *B*
Humacao *B*
Mayaguez *B, M*
Rio Piedras *B, M*
University of the Sacred Heart *M*

Rhode Island

Bryant University *B*

South Carolina

Anderson University *B*
Clemson University *M*
Forrest Junior College *A*
Limestone College *B*
University of Phoenix
Columbia *B*
University of South Carolina
Columbia *M*
York Technical College *A*

South Dakota

Black Hills State University *B*
National American University
Rapid City *B*
Southeast Technical Institute *A*

Tennessee

Daymar Institute
Nashville *C, A*
Freed-Hardeman University *B*
Lipscomb University *B*
Maryville College *B*
Southern Adventist University *B*
Tennessee Wesleyan College *B*
University of Phoenix
Chattanooga *B, M*
Knoxville *B, M*
Memphis *C, B, M*
Nashville *B, M*
University of Tennessee
Knoxville *B*

Texas

Amberton University *M*
Baylor University *B*
Dallas Baptist University *M*

DeVry University
  Irving *M*
Houston Baptist University *M*
Lamar University *B*
LeTourneau University *B*
Our Lady of the Lake University of
  San Antonio *B*
St. Mary's University *B*
Sam Houston State University *B*
Tarleton State University *B, M*
Texas A&M University
  Texarkana *B*
Texas State University *M*
University of Dallas *M*
University of Phoenix
  Austin *B, M*
  Dallas Fort Worth *B, M*
  Houston Westside *C, B, M*
  San Antonio *B, M*
University of Texas
  Arlington *M*
  San Antonio *B*
University of the Incarnate Word *B*
Vernon College *A*
Weatherford College *A*

Utah

University of Phoenix
  Utah *C, B, M*
University of Utah *M*
Utah State University *B, M*
Weber State University *B*
Western Governors University *B*
Westminster College *B*

Vermont

Champlain College *C*

Virginia

Bryant & Stratton College
  Richmond *A*
  Virginia Beach *A*
Lynchburg College *B*
Marymount University *M*
University of Management and
  Technology *C*
University of Phoenix
  Northern Virginia *B, M*
  Richmond *B*

Washington

Bellevue College *C*
Bellingham Technical College *A*
Clark College *A*
DeVry University
  Federal Way *M*
Eastern Washington University *B*
Edmonds Community College *C*
Gonzaga University *D*
Heritage University *B*
Lake Washington Institute of
  Technology *C*
Olympic College *C*
Pierce College *C*
Tacoma Community College *C*
University of Phoenix
  Western Washington *B, M*
University of Washington *B*
Walla Walla University *B*
Western Washington University *B*

West Virginia

Concord University *B*

Wisconsin

Carroll University *B*
Chippewa Valley Technical College *A*
Concordia University Wisconsin *A, M*
Fox Valley Technical College *A*
Herzing University
  Brookfield *B*
  Kenosha *B*
  Madison *B*
Lakeshore Technical College *A*

Madison Area Technical College *A*
Marian University *B*
Marquette University *B, M*
Mid-State Technical College *A*
Rasmussen College
  Appleton *C, A, B*
  Green Bay *C, A, B*
  Wausau *C, A, B*
St. Norbert College *B*
Silver Lake College of the Holy
  Family *B*
University of Phoenix
  Milwaukee *B, M*
University of Wisconsin
  Oshkosh *B*
  Parkside *B*
  Platteville *B*
  Whitewater *B, T*
Waukesha County Technical
  College *A*
Western Technical College *A*

Human sciences communication

Alabama

Faulkner University *B*

California

Antelope Valley College *A*

Georgia

University of Georgia *B*

Virginia

Virginia State University *B*

Wisconsin

University of Wisconsin
  Madison *M*

Human services

Alabama

Samford University *B*
Troy University *B*
University of Phoenix
  Birmingham *B*

Alaska

Alaska Pacific University *B*
University of Alaska
  Anchorage *C*

Arizona

Arizona Western College *C, A*
Northland Pioneer College *C*
University of Phoenix
  Phoenix-Hohokam *B*
  Southern Arizona *B*

Arkansas

Arkansas Baptist College *B*
Arkansas Tech University *A*

California

Allan Hancock College *C, A*
Bakersfield College *C, A*
Berkeley City College *C, A*
California State University
  Dominguez Hills *B*
  Fullerton *B*
  Monterey Bay *B*
Canada College *C, A*
City College of San Francisco *C*
College of the Sequoias *C, A*
College of the Siskiyous *A*
Columbia College *C*
Cypress College *C, A*
Folsom Lake College *A*
Gavilan College *C*
Holy Names University *B*

Hope International University *B*
Lassen Community College *C, A*
Long Beach City College *C, A*
Mendocino College *C, A*
Merced College *A*
Modesto Junior College *C, A*
Mount St. Mary's College *A*
Notre Dame de Namur University *B*
Oxnard College *A*
Riverside City College *C, A*
Saddleback College *C*
Santa Rosa Junior College *C*
Shasta College *C, A*
Solano Community College *C, A*
University of Phoenix
  Bay Area *B*
  Central Valley *B*
  Sacramento Valley *B*
  San Diego *B*
  Southern California *B*

Colorado

Community College of Denver *C, A*
Metropolitan State University of
  Denver *B*
University of Northern Colorado *B*
University of Phoenix
  Denver *B*
  Southern Colorado *B*

Connecticut

Albertus Magnus College *B*
Asnuntuck Community College *C, A*
Goodwin College *C, A, B*
Housatonic Community College *A*
Middlesex Community College *C, A*
Mitchell College *B*
Naugatuck Valley Community
  College *A*
Northwestern Connecticut
  Community College *C, A*
Post University *B*
Quinebaug Valley Community
  College *A*
St. Vincent's College *C*
Three Rivers Community
  College *C, A*
Tunxis Community College *C, A*

Delaware

Delaware Technical Community
  College
  Jack F. Owens Campus *C, A*
  Stanton/Wilmington Campus *C, A*
  Terry Campus *C, A*

District of Columbia

George Washington University *B, M*
University of Phoenix
  Washington DC *B*

Florida

Beacon College *A, B*
College of Central Florida *C, A*
Daytona State College *A*
Florida State College at
  Jacksonville *A*
Indian River State College *A*
Miami Dade College *A*
Palm Beach State College *A*
Pasco-Hernando State College *C, A*
Rasmussen College
  Fort Myers *C, A*
  New Port Richey *C, A*
  Ocala *C, A*
  Pasco/Land O'Lakes *C, A*
  Tampa/Brandon *C, A*
St. Petersburg College *C, A*
Saint Thomas University *B*
Southeastern University *B, M*
University of Phoenix
  Central Florida *B*
  North Florida *B*

South Florida *B*
West Florida *B*

Georgia

Abraham Baldwin Agricultural
  College *A*
Brewton-Parker College *B*
Darton College *A*
Fort Valley State University *B*
Georgia Highlands College *A*
Gordon College *B*
Kennesaw State University *C, B*
Mercer University *B*
Middle Georgia State College *B*
Spelman College *B*
University of North Georgia *B*
University of Phoenix
  Atlanta *B*
  Augusta *B*
  Columbus *B*
  Savannah *B*

Hawaii

Hawaii Pacific University *B*
University of Hawaii
  Honolulu Community College *A*
  Maui College *A*
University of Phoenix
  Hawaii *C, B*

Idaho

College of Southern Idaho *C, A*
North Idaho College *A*
University of Phoenix
  Idaho *B*

Illinois

Carl Sandburg College *C*
Concordia University Chicago *M*
DePaul University *M*
Harper College *C, A*
Judson University *B*
Lincoln Christian University *B*
Loyola University Chicago *B*
Millikin University *B*
National-Louis University *B, M*
North Park University *B*
Northern Illinois University *B*
Oakton Community College *C*
Quincy University *B*
Rock Valley College *C, A*
Roosevelt University *M*
South Suburban College of Cook
  County *A*
Southeastern Illinois College *A*
University of Illinois
  Springfield *M*
University of Phoenix
  Chicago *B*

Indiana

Bethel College *A, B*
Calumet College of St. Joseph *M*
Indiana Institute of Technology *B*
Indiana University
  Purdue University Indianapolis *C*
Oakland City University *A, B*
St. Mary-of-the-Woods College *B*
Vincennes University *C*

Iowa

Ellsworth Community College *C, A*
Grand View University *B*
Iowa Wesleyan College *B*
Iowa Western Community College *A*
Southeastern Community College *A*
University of Phoenix
  Des Moines *B*
Upper Iowa University *B*
William Penn University *B*

Kansas

Independence Community College *A*
Ottawa University *B*

Kentucky

Big Sandy Community and Technical
  College *A*
Brescia University *A*
Elizabethtown Community and
  Technical College *A*
Hazard Community and Technical
  College *A*
Kentucky Wesleyan College *B*
Northern Kentucky University *C*
University of Phoenix
  Louisville *A*
University of the Cumberlands *B*

Louisiana

Louisiana State University
  Shreveport *M*
Southern University
  Shreveport *A*
University of Phoenix
  Baton Rouge *B*
  Louisiana *B*
  Shreveport *B*

Maine

University of Maine
  Fort Kent *A*
  Machias *B*

Maryland

Anne Arundel Community
  College *C, A*
Coppin State University *M*
Frederick Community College *A*
Garrett College *C*
Howard Community College *C, A*
McDaniel College *M*
University of Baltimore *B, M*

Massachusetts

Anna Maria College *B*
Bristol Community College *C*
Bunker Hill Community College *C, A*
Cape Cod Community College *C, A*
Fitchburg State University *B*
Framingham State University *M*
Holyoke Community College *C*
Lasell College *B*
Massachusetts Bay Community
  College *C, A*
Massasoit Community College *A*
Merrimack College *B*
Middlesex Community College *A*
Mount Ida College *B*
Mount Wachusett Community
  College *C, A*
Northeastern University *B*
Quincy College *A*
Quinsigamond Community
  College *C, A*
Springfield College *B, M*
University of Massachusetts
  Boston *B, M*
Urban College of Boston *C, A*

Michigan

Baker College
  Allen Park *B*
  Auburn Hills *A*
  Cadillac *A, B*
  Clinton Township *A, B*
  Jackson *A*
  Muskegon *A, B*
  Owosso *A, B*
Bay de Noc Community College *A*
Delta College *A*
Finlandia University *B*
Grace Bible College *B*
Robert B. Miller College *B*
University of Phoenix
  Metro Detroit *B*
  West Michigan *B*

Minnesota

Alexandria Technical and Community
  College *C, A*
Capella University *M, D*
Century College *C, A*
Duluth Business University *A*
Fond du Lac Tribal and Community
  College *A*
Inver Hills Community College *C, A*
Itasca Community College *A*
Mesabi Range Community and
  Technical College *A*
Metropolitan State University *B*
Minneapolis Community and
  Technical College *C, A*
Minnesota State University
  Mankato *B, M*
Minnesota West Community and
  Technical College *A*
Pine Technical College *C, A*
Rasmussen College
  Blaine *C, A*
  Bloomington *C, A*
  Brooklyn Park *C, A*
  Eagan *C, A*
  Lake Elmo/Woodbury *C, A*
  Mankato *C, A*
  Moorhead *C, A*
  St. Cloud *C, A*
Riverland Community College *A*
Rochester Community and Technical
  College *C, A*
St. Mary's University of Minnesota *B*
South Central College *C, A*
University of Northwestern - St.
  Paul *M*
University of Phoenix
  Minneapolis-St. Paul *B*
Walden University *D*
White Earth Tribal and Community
  College *A*

Mississippi

University of Phoenix
  Jackson *B*

Missouri

Columbia College *A, B*
Drury University *B*
Fontbonne University *B*
Lindenwood University *B, M*
Missouri Baptist University *B*
St. Charles Community College *A*
Southwest Baptist University *B*
University of Phoenix
  Kansas City *B*
  St. Louis *B*

Montana

Aaniiih Nakoda College *A*
Flathead Valley Community
  College *A*
Fort Peck Community College *A*
Little Big Horn College *A*
Miles Community College *A*
Montana State University
  Billings *B*
Stone Child College *A*
University of Great Falls *M*

Nebraska

Bellevue University *B*
Hastings College *B*
Midland University *B*

Nevada

University of Phoenix
  Las Vegas *B*
  Northern Nevada *B*

New Hampshire

Lakes Region Community
  College *C, A*
Manchester Community College *C*

NHTI-Concord's Community
  College *C, A*
Nashua Community College *C, A*
River Valley Community College *A*
White Mountains Community
  College *C, A*

New Jersey

Atlantic Cape Community
  College *C, A*
Burlington County College *C, A*
College of St. Elizabeth *C*
Essex County College *A*
Mercer County Community
  College *A*
Ocean County College *A*
Passaic County Community
  College *C, A*
Thomas Edison State College *A, B*
Union County College *A*

New Mexico

New Mexico State University
  Alamogordo *A*
  Carlsbad *A*
  Grants *A*
Northern New Mexico College *A*
Santa Fe Community College *A*
University of Phoenix
  New Mexico *B*

New York

Boricua College *B, M*
Cazenovia College *A, B*
City University of New York
  Guttman Community College *A*
  New York City College of
    Technology *A, B*
Clinton Community College *A*
Corning Community College *A*
Dutchess Community College *A*
Elmira College *A, B*
Finger Lakes Community College *A*
Hilbert College *A, B*
Jamestown Community College *A*
Long Island Business Institute *C*
Mercy College *A*
Metropolitan College of New
  York *A, B*
Mohawk Valley Community
  College *A*
Monroe Community College *C, A*
Mount Saint Mary College *B*
Niagara County Community
  College *A*
Onondaga Community College *A*
Orange County Community
  College *A*
SUNY
  College at Oswego *M*
  College of Technology at Alfred *A*
Suffolk County Community College *A*
Sullivan County Community
  College *C, A*
Technical Career Institutes *A*
Touro College *A*
Westchester Community College *C*

North Carolina

Beaufort County Community
  College *C, A*
Central Carolina Community
  College *A*
Edgecombe Community College *A*
Elon University *B*
Halifax Community College *A*
Lenoir-Rhyne University *B*
Mitchell Community College *A*
Montreat College *B*
Pfeiffer University *B*
Queens University of Charlotte *B*
Sandhills Community College *A*
South Piedmont Community
  College *C, A*

Vance-Granville Community
  College *A*
Wake Technical Community
  College *C, A*
Wingate University *B*

North Dakota

Bismarck State College *C, A*
Fort Berthold Community College *A*
Rasmussen College
  Bismarck *C, A*
  Fargo *C, A*
Sitting Bull College *A*

Ohio

Antioch University
  Midwest *B*
Bowling Green State University:
  Firelands College *A*
Central Ohio Technical College *A*
Chatfield College *A*
Cincinnati State Technical and
  Community College *C*
Cleveland State University *M*
Lakeland Community College *C, A*
Marion Technical College *A*
Mount Vernon Nazarene University *A*
North Central State College *C, A*
Ohio University
  Southern Campus at Ironton *A*
Southern State Community College *A*
Stark State College *A*
Tiffin University *B*
University of Phoenix
  Cleveland *B*
Washington State Community
  College *A*

Oklahoma

East Central University *B, M*
University of Phoenix
  Oklahoma City *B*
  Tulsa *B*

Oregon

Chemeketa Community College *C, A*
Northwest Christian University *B*
Umpqua Community College *A*
University of Oregon *B, M*
University of Phoenix
  Oregon *B*

Pennsylvania

Chestnut Hill College *A, B, M*
Community College of
  Philadelphia *A*
Delaware County Community
  College *A*
Geneva College *B*
Gwynedd Mercy University *B*
Harcum College *A*
Harrisburg Area Community
  College *C, A*
Lackawanna College *A*
Lehigh Carbon Community
  College *C, A*
Lincoln University *B, M*
Luzerne County Community
  College *A*
Orleans Technical Institute *C*
Pennsylvania Highlands Community
  College *A*
Reading Area Community College *A*
Seton Hill University *B*
University of Scranton *A, B, M*
Valley Forge Christian College *A*
Villanova University *B*
Waynesburg University *B*
Westmoreland County Community
  College *A*

Puerto Rico

Caribbean University *A*

Rhode Island

Community College of Rhode
    Island *C*

South Carolina

Aiken Technical College *A*
Anderson University *B*
Denmark Technical College *A*
Midlands Technical College *A*
Southern Wesleyan University *B*
Trident Technical College *C, A*
Williamsburg Technical College *C*
York Technical College *C*

South Dakota

Dakota Wesleyan University *B*
Lake Area Technical Institute *A*
Oglala Lakota College *B*
Sinte Gleska University *B*

Tennessee

Bethel University *B*
Hiwassee College *A*
Martin Methodist College *B*
Milligan College *B*
Tennessee Wesleyan College *B*
University of Phoenix
    Knoxville *B*
    Memphis *B*

Texas

Angelina College *A*
Austin Community College *A*
Laredo Community College *C, A*
South Plains College *A*
University of Phoenix
    Dallas Fort Worth *B*
    San Antonio *B*
Wayland Baptist University *A, B*
Wharton County Junior College *C, A*

Utah

University of Phoenix
    Utah *B*

Vermont

Burlington College *B*
College of St. Joseph in Vermont *A*
Community College of Vermont *A*
Lyndon State College *B*

Virginia

Blue Ridge Community College *A*
Central Virginia Community
    College *C*
Liberty University *M*
New River Community College *C, A*
Northern Virginia Community
    College *A*
Shenandoah University *D*
Southside Virginia Community
    College *C, A*
Southwest Virginia Community
    College *C, A*
Thomas Nelson Community
    College *A*
University of Phoenix
    Northern Virginia *B*
    Richmond *B*
Virginia Wesleyan College *B*
Virginia Western Community
    College *A*

Washington

Central Washington University *B*
Highline Community College *A*
Seattle Central Community College *A*
Skagit Valley College *A*
University of Phoenix
    Western Washington *B*
Western Washington University *B*

Wisconsin

Gateway Technical College *A*
Lac Courte Oreilles Ojibwa
    Community College *A*
Milwaukee Area Technical College *A*
Northcentral Technical College *C, A*
Rasmussen College
    Appleton *C, A*
    Green Bay *C, A*
    Wausau *C, A*
St. Norbert College *B*
Southwest Wisconsin Technical
    College *A*
University of Phoenix
    Milwaukee *B*
University of Wisconsin
    Oshkosh *B*
    Superior *M*
Wisconsin Indianhead Technical
    College *A*
Wisconsin Lutheran College *B*

Wyoming

Central Wyoming College *A*
Laramie County Community
    College *A*

Humanities

Alabama

Faulkner University *B*
University of Mobile *B*

Arizona

Central Arizona College *A*
Cochise College *A*
Harrison Middleton
    University *A, B, M, D*
Paradise Valley Community College *C*
Prescott College *B*

Arkansas

Harding University *B*
University of Arkansas
    Little Rock *B*

California

Barstow Community College *A*
Berkeley City College *A*
California State University
    Chico *B*
    Dominguez Hills *M*
    Monterey Bay *B*
    Sacramento *B, M*
    San Bernardino *B*
Canada College *A*
College of the Canyons *A*
College of the Siskiyous *A*
Concordia University Irvine *B*
Contra Costa College *A*
Diablo Valley College *A*
Dominican University of
    California *B, M*
East Los Angeles College *A*
Feather River College *A*
Glendale Community College *A*
Holy Names University *B*
Imperial Valley College *A*
La Sierra University *B*
Lake Tahoe Community College *A*
Loyola Marymount University *B*
MiraCosta College *A*
Mount St. Mary's College *M*
Orange Coast College *A*
Oxnard College *C, A*
Palomar College *A*
Pepperdine University *B*
San Deigo Miramar College
    San Diego Miramar College *A*
San Diego State University *B*
San Francisco State University *B, M*
San Jose State University *B*
Santa Monica College *A*

Scripps College *B*
Shasta College *A*
Southwestern College *A*
Stanford University *B, M*
Taft College *A*
University of California
    Irvine *B*
    Riverside *B*
University of San Diego *B*
West Hills College: Lemoore *A*

Colorado

Adams State University *M*
Fort Lewis College *B*
United States Air Force Academy *B*
University of Colorado
    Boulder *B*
    Denver *M*

Connecticut

Fairfield University *M*
Holy Apostles College and
    Seminary *B*
Mitchell College *B*
University of Bridgeport *B*
Yale University *B*

District of Columbia

Georgetown University *B*

Florida

Clearwater Christian College *B*
Eckerd College *B*
Florida Institute of Technology *B*
Florida Southern College *B*
Florida State University *B*
Jacksonville University *B*
New College of Florida *B*
Nova Southeastern University *B*
Rollins College *B*
Stetson University *B*
University of Central Florida *B*
University of South Florida *B*
University of West Florida *B, M*

Georgia

Georgia Southwestern State
    University *M*
Point University *B*
Truett-McConnell College *B*

Illinois

Bradley University *B*
Elgin Community College *C*
Illinois Central College *A*
Prairie State College *C*
Principia College *B*
Quincy University *B*
Rockford University *B*
Shimer College *B*
Trinity International University *B*
Triton College *C*
University of Chicago *B, M*
University of Illinois
    Urbana-Champaign *B*

Indiana

Bethel College *B*
Indiana University
    East *B*
    Kokomo *B*
Martin University *B*
Oakland City University *B*
Purdue University *B*
Saint Mary's College *B*
St. Mary-of-the-Woods College *A, B*
Valparaiso University *A, B*

Iowa

Northwestern College *B*
University of Northern Iowa *B*
Waldorf College *B*

Kansas

Garden City Community College *A*
Kansas State University *B*
University of Kansas *B*
Washburn University *A*

Kentucky

Kentucky Christian University *B*
Lindsey Wilson College *B*
Spalding University *B*
Thomas More College *A, B*
University of Louisville *B, M, D*

Louisiana

Our Lady of the Lake College *B*

Maine

College of the Atlantic *B, M*
University of Southern Maine *B*

Maryland

Hood College *M*
St. Mary's College of Maryland *B*
Towson University *M*
Washington College *B*

Massachusetts

Anna Maria College *B*
Bristol Community College *A*
Lasell College *B*
Roxbury Community College *A*
Suffolk University *B*
University of Massachusetts
    Amherst *B*
Wheelock College *B*
Worcester Polytechnic Institute *B*

Michigan

Aquinas College *B*
Central Michigan University *M*
Kirtland Community College *A*
Lake Michigan College *A*
Lansing Community College *A*
Lawrence Technological University *B*
Madonna University *B*
Michigan State University *B*
Michigan Technological University *A*
University of Michigan *B*

Minnesota

Bemidji State University *B*
College of St. Benedict *B*
College of St. Scholastica *B*
Concordia College: Moorhead *B*
North Central University *A*
St. John's University *B*
University of Minnesota
    Morris *B*
    Twin Cities *B*
White Earth Tribal and Community
    College *A*

Mississippi

Belhaven University *B*

Missouri

Missouri State University *B*
Northwest Missouri State
    University *B*
Saint Louis University *B*
Washington University in St. Louis *B*
Webster University *C, B*

Montana

Flathead Valley Community
    College *A*

Nebraska

Grace University *B*

Nevada

Sierra Nevada College *B*

New Hampshire
Plymouth State University *B*
University of New Hampshire *B*
University of New Hampshire at
    Manchester *B*

New Jersey
Cumberland County College *A*
Fairleigh Dickinson University
    College at Florham *B*
    Metropolitan Campus *B*
Felician College *B*
Georgian Court University *B*
Montclair State University *B*
Passaic County Community College *A*
Ramapo College of New Jersey *B*
Salem Community College *A*
Seton Hall University *B*
Thomas Edison State College *B*

New Mexico
University of New Mexico *B*
University of the Southwest *B*

New York
Adelphi University *B*
Canisius College *A, B*
City University of New York
    Hunter College *B*
Clarkson University *B*
College of Saint Rose *B*
Corning Community College *A*
Dominican College of Blauvelt *B*
Dowling College *B*
Dutchess Community College *A*
Erie Community College *A*
Genesee Community College *A*
Herkimer County Community
    College *A*
Houghton College *A, B*
Jamestown Community College *A*
King's College *B*
Long Island University
    LIU Brooklyn *B*
Mohawk Valley Community
    College *A*
New York University *B, M, D, T*
Niagara County Community
    College *A*
Onondaga Community College *A*
Roberts Wesleyan College *B, T*
SUNY
    College at Buffalo *B*
    College at Old Westbury *B*
    College of Agriculture and
        Technology at Cobleskill *A*
    College of Agriculture and
        Technology at Morrisville *A*
    College of Technology at Alfred *A*
    University at Buffalo *M*
    University at Stony Brook *B*
Sage Colleges *B*
St. John's University *M*
St. Lawrence University *B*
Sullivan County Community
    College *A*
Tompkins Cortland Community
    College *A*
Ulster County Community College *A*
Union College *B*
United States Military Academy *B*
Villa Maria College of Buffalo *A*

Ohio
Antioch University
    Midwest *B*
Franciscan University of
    Steubenville *B*
John Carroll University *M*
Kent State University *B*
Miami University
    Middletown *A*
Muskingum University *B*

Ohio State University
    Columbus Campus *B, M, D*
Ohio University *A*
Ohio University
    Lancaster Campus *A*
Pontifical College Josephinum *B*
Terra State Community College *A*
Tiffin University *M*
University of Akron *B*
University of Rio Grande *B*
University of Toledo *B*
Ursuline College *B*
Wright State University *M*

Oklahoma
Oklahoma City University *B*
University of Central Oklahoma *B*
University of Oklahoma *B*

Oregon
Central Oregon Community
    College *A*
Corban University *B*
Northwest Christian University *B*
Pacific Northwest College of Art *M*
University of Oregon *B*
Western Oregon University *B*
Willamette University *B*

Pennsylvania
Arcadia University *M*
Bucknell University *B*
Bucks County Community College *A*
Community College of Allegheny
    County *A*
Community College of Beaver
    County *A*
Drexel University *B, M*
East Stroudsburg University of
    Pennsylvania *B*
Edinboro University of
    Pennsylvania *B*
Holy Family University *B*
Juniata College *B*
Lehigh Carbon Community College *A*
Luzerne County Community
    College *A*
Messiah College *B*
Montgomery County Community
    College *C, A*
Penn State
    Harrisburg *B, M*
Rosemont College *B*
University of Pennsylvania *B*
University of Pittsburgh *B*
University of Pittsburgh
    Bradford *B*
Villanova University *B*
Widener University *B*

Puerto Rico
Turabo University *B*
University of Puerto Rico
    Aguadilla *A*
    Cayey University College *B*
    Utuado *A*

Rhode Island
Providence College *B*
Roger Williams University *B*
Salve Regina University *M, D*
University of Rhode Island *B*

South Carolina
Bob Jones University *B*
Charleston Southern University *B*
Columbia International University *B*
Lander University *B*
Wofford College *B*

Tennessee
LeMoyne-Owen College *B*
Lee University *B*
Lincoln Memorial University *B*

Milligan College *B*
University of Tennessee
    Chattanooga *B*

Texas
Baylor University *B*
Brookhaven College *A*
Howard Payne University *B*
Lubbock Christian University *B*
Midwestern State University *B*
Palo Alto College *A*
St. Mary's University *B*
St. Philip's College *A*
Southwestern Baptist Theological
    Seminary *B*
Texarkana College *A*
University of Dallas *M*
University of Houston
    Clear Lake *B, M*
    Downtown *B*
University of Texas
    Austin *C, B*
    Permian Basin *B*
    San Antonio *B*

Utah
Brigham Young University *B*
Salt Lake Community College *A*
University of Utah *B, M*
Utah State University *M*
Utah Valley University *A*

Vermont
Bennington College *B*
Goddard College *B, M*

Virginia
Danville Community College *A*
George Mason University *D*
Hampden-Sydney College *B*
John Tyler Community College *A*
Old Dominion University *M*
University of Richmond *B*
Virginia Western Community
    College *A*

Washington
Eastern Washington University *B*
Evergreen State College *B*
Heritage University *A*
Seattle University *B*
University of Washington Bothell *B*
University of Washington Tacoma *B*
Washington State University *B*
Western Washington University *B*

West Virginia
American Public University System *M*
Bluefield State College *B*
Marshall University *B, M*
Ohio Valley University *B*

Wisconsin
Concordia University Wisconsin *B*
Maranatha Baptist Bible College *B*
Northland College *B*
St. Norbert College *B*
University of Wisconsin
    Green Bay *B*

Wyoming
Laramie County Community
    College *A*
University of Wyoming *B*

Hydraulics technology

Iowa
Des Moines Area Community
    College *C, A*

Maryland
Community College of Baltimore
    County *A*

Michigan
Lake Michigan College *C*

Minnesota
Hennepin Technical College *C, A*

Ohio
Ohio State University
    Agricultural Technical
        Institute *C, A*

Oklahoma
Western Oklahoma State College *A*

Pennsylvania
Community College of Allegheny
    County *C, A*

Washington
Spokane Community College *A*

Hydrology/water resources science

Arizona
University of Arizona *B, M, D*

California
California State University
    Chico *C*
    Fresno *M*
Santiago Canyon College *A*
University of California
    Davis *B, M, D*

Colorado
Colorado School of Mines *M, D*

Michigan
Western Michigan University *B*

Minnesota
Saint Cloud State University *B*
Vermilion Community College *A*

Montana
Salish Kootenai College *A, B*

New Hampshire
University of New Hampshire *B, M*

New Mexico
New Mexico Institute of Mining and
    Technology *M, D*
New Mexico State University *M, D*

New York
Rensselaer Polytechnic Institute *B, M*
SUNY
    College at Brockport *B*
    College at Oneonta *B*

Oregon
Oregon State University *M, D*

Pennsylvania
University of Pennsylvania *M*

Texas
Tarleton State University *B*
Texas A&M University *M, D*
Texas A&M University
    Galveston *B*
University of Texas
    Austin *B*

Utah

Brigham Young University *B, M*
Utah State University *M, D*

Wisconsin

Northland College *B*

Wyoming

University of Wyoming *D*

Illustration

Arizona

Southwest University of Visual Arts *B*

Arkansas

John Brown University *B*

California

Academy of Art University *C, A, B, M*
Art Center College of Design *B*
California College of the Arts *B*
Orange Coast College *C*
Otis College of Art and Design *B*

Colorado

Community College of Aurora *A*
Rocky Mountain College of Art &
   Design *B*

Connecticut

Lyme Academy College of Fine
   Arts *B*
Paier College of Art *B*
University of Bridgeport *B*

Delaware

Delaware College of Art and
   Design *A*

Florida

Art Institute of Fort Lauderdale *B*
Ringling College of Art and Design *B*

Georgia

Art Institute of Atlanta *B*
Savannah College of Art and
   Design *B, M*

Illinois

Columbia College Chicago *B*

Indiana

Grace College *B*

Kansas

University of Kansas *B*

Maine

College of the Atlantic *B, M*
Maine College of Art *B*

Maryland

Maryland Institute College of
   Art *B, M*

Massachusetts

Montserrat College of Art *B*
Northeastern University *B*
School of the Museum of Fine
   Arts *C, B, M*

Michigan

College for Creative Studies *B*
Ferris State University *B*
Finlandia University *B*
Henry Ford Community College *C*
Lawrence Technological University *B*
Northern Michigan University *B*
Oakland Community College *A*
University of Michigan *B*

Minnesota

Minneapolis College of Art and
   Design *B*

Missouri

Kansas City Art Institute *B*
Washington University in St. Louis *B*

Montana

University of Montana: Western *B*

New Hampshire

New Hampshire Institute of Art *B*

New Jersey

Montclair State University *B*

New Mexico

Southwest University of Visual Arts *B*

New York

Fashion Institute of
   Technology *A, B, M*
Parsons The New School for
   Design *B*
Pratt Institute *A*
Rochester Institute of Technology *M*
St. John's University *B*
Syracuse University *B, M*

North Carolina

East Carolina University *B*

Ohio

Art Academy of Cincinnati *B*
Cleveland Institute of Art *B*
Columbus College of Art and
   Design *B*
Virginia Marti College of Art and
   Design *A*

Oregon

Pacific Northwest College of Art *B*

Pennsylvania

Arcadia University *B*
Douglas Education Center *A*
Luzerne County Community
   College *C, A*
Marywood University *B, M*
Moore College of Art and Design *B*
Pennsylvania College of Art and
   Design *B*
University of the Arts *B*

Rhode Island

Rhode Island School of Design *B*

Tennessee

Memphis College of Art *B*

Texas

Collin County Community College
   District *C, A*
St. Philip's College *A*

Utah

Brigham Young University *B*
Broadview University
   Broadview Entertainment Arts
   University *B*

Vermont

Lyndon State College *B*

Virginia

Virginia Commonwealth University *B*

Washington

Cornish College of the Arts *B*

Wisconsin

Concordia University Wisconsin *B*
Milwaukee Institute of Art &
   Design *B*

Industrial and product design

Alabama

Auburn University *B, M*

Arizona

Arizona State University *B, M*
Yavapai College *C, A*

California

Academy of Art University *C, A, B, M*
Art Center College of Design *B, M*
Art Institute of California
   Hollywood *B*
   Orange County *B*
California College of the Arts *B*
California State University
   Long Beach *B, M*
Los Angeles Pierce College *C, A*
Otis College of Art and Design *B*
San Francisco State University *B, M*
San Jose State University *B*

Colorado

Metropolitan State University of
   Denver *B*

Connecticut

University of Bridgeport *B*

Florida

Art Institute of Fort Lauderdale *B*

Georgia

Georgia Institute of Technology *B, M*
Savannah College of Art and
   Design *B, M*

Illinois

Columbia College Chicago *B*
School of the Art Institute of
   Chicago *B, M*
University of Illinois
   Chicago *B, M*

Iowa

Iowa State University *M*

Kansas

University of Kansas *B*

Louisiana

University of Louisiana at Lafayette *B*

Massachusetts

Massachusetts College of Art and
   Design *C, B*
Wentworth Institute of Technology *B*

Michigan

College for Creative Studies *B*
Ferris State University *B*
Kirtland Community College *A*
Lawrence Technological University *B*
University of Michigan *B*

New Jersey

Kean University *B*
Montclair State University *B*
Salem Community College *C, A*

New York

City University of New York
   LaGuardia Community College *A*
Fashion Institute of Technology *B*

Parsons The New School for
   Design *B*
Pratt Institute *B, M*
Rochester Institute of
   Technology *B, M*
Syracuse University *B*

North Carolina

Appalachian State University *B*
North Carolina State University *B, M*

Ohio

Cedarville University *B*
Cleveland Institute of Art *B*
Columbus College of Art and
   Design *B*
Ohio State University
   Columbus Campus *B, M*
Owens Community College
   Toledo *A*
University of Cincinnati *B*

Oregon

Art Institute of Portland *B*

Pennsylvania

Art Institute of Philadelphia *B*
Art Institute of Pittsburgh *A, B*
Carnegie Mellon University *B*
Pennsylvania College of
   Technology *B*
Philadelphia University *B*
University of the Arts *B, M*

Puerto Rico

Escuela de Artes Plasticas de Puerto
   Rico *B*
Turabo University *B*

Rhode Island

Rhode Island School of Design *B, M*

South Carolina

Clemson University *B, M*

Texas

University of Houston *B, M*

Utah

Brigham Young University *B, M*
University of Utah *B*

Virginia

Lord Fairfax Community College *C*
Virginia Polytechnic Institute and
   State University *B*

Washington

Art Institute of Seattle *A, B*
University of Washington *B, M*
Western Washington University *B*

Wisconsin

Milwaukee Institute of Art &
   Design *B*

Industrial electronics technology

Alabama

Bevill State Community College *C, A*
Jefferson Davis Community
   College *C*
Lawson State Community College *C*
Lurleen B. Wallace Community
   College *A*
Northeast Alabama Community
   College *C, A*
Shelton State Community
   College *C, A*
Southern Union State Community
   College *C, A*

Wallace State Community College at
 Hanceville *C, A*

Arizona
Eastern Arizona College *C*
Mesa Community College *C*
Pima Community College *C, A*

Arkansas
Arkansas Northeastern College *C*
Arkansas State University
 Beebe *C*
East Arkansas Community College *C*
Southeast Arkansas College *C, A*
University of Arkansas
 Community College at Hope *C*
 Fort Smith *C*

California
Irvine Valley College *C*
Victor Valley College *A*

Georgia
Columbus Technical College *C*
Dalton State College *C, A*
Southeastern Technical College *C*

Idaho
Lewis-Clark State College *C, A, B*

Illinois
College of DuPage *C, A*
College of Lake County *C, A*
Danville Area Community College *A*
Harper College *C*
John Wood Community College *C*
Kankakee Community College *C, A*
Lincoln Land Community
 College *C, A*
Moraine Valley Community
 College *C, A*
Parkland College *C*
Sauk Valley Community College *C*
Spoon River College *C*

Indiana
Ivy Tech Community College
 Central Indiana *A*

Iowa
Des Moines Area Community
 College *A*
Iowa Central Community
 College *C, A*
Kirkwood Community College *A*
North Iowa Area Community
 College *A*
Northwest Iowa Community
 College *A*

Kansas
Hutchinson Community College *C*

Kentucky
Bluegrass Community and Technical
 College *C, A*
Jefferson Community and Technical
 College *C*
Owensboro Community and
 Technical College *C*
Somerset Community College *C, A*

Michigan
Ferris State University *A*
Wayne County Community College *A*

Minnesota
Central Lakes College *A*
Mesabi Range Community and
 Technical College *A*

Missouri
Crowder College *A*

North Carolina
Beaufort County Community
 College *A*
Lenoir Community College *C, A*
Surry Community College *A*

Ohio
Northwest State Community
 College *C, A*

Pennsylvania
Lackawanna College *A*
Lehigh Carbon Community
 College *C, A*
Luzerne County Community
 College *C, A*
Northampton Community
 College *C, A*
Pennsylvania College of
 Technology *A*

South Carolina
Aiken Technical College *C*
Horry-Georgetown Technical
 College *A*
Midlands Technical College *C*
Piedmont Technical College *C, A*
Spartanburg Community College *C, A*
Technical College of the
 Lowcountry *C, A*
Tri-County Technical College *C, A*
York Technical College *C*

Utah
Salt Lake Community College *C*

Virginia
Danville Community College *C*
J. Sargeant Reynolds Community
 College *C*
John Tyler Community College *C*

Washington
Bates Technical College *C, A*
Lower Columbia College *A*
North Seattle Community
 College *C, A*
Wenatchee Valley College *C, A*

Wisconsin
Gateway Technical College *C*
Herzing University
 Madison *A, B*
Milwaukee Area Technical College *C*
Waukesha County Technical
 College *C*
Western Technical College *C*

Wyoming
Western Wyoming Community
 College *C, A*

Industrial engineering

Alabama
University of Alabama
 Huntsville *B, D*

Alaska
University of Alaska
 Fairbanks *B*

Arizona
Arizona State University *B, M, D*
University of Arizona *B, M*

Arkansas
University of Arkansas *B, M*

California
California Polytechnic State
 University: San Luis Obispo *B, M*

California State Polytechnic
 University: Pomona *B*
San Jose State University *B, M*
Stanford University *M, D*
University of San Diego *B*
University of Southern
 California *B, M, D*

Colorado
Colorado State University
 Pueblo *B, M*

Connecticut
Fairfield University *M*
Quinnipiac University *B*
University of Connecticut *B*
University of New Haven *B, M*

Florida
Florida Agricultural and Mechanical
 University *B, M, D*
Florida State University *B, M, D*
University of Central Florida *B, M, D*
University of Miami *B, M, D*
University of South Florida *B, M, D*

Georgia
Georgia Institute of
 Technology *B, M, D*

Illinois
Bradley University *B, M*
Northern Illinois University *B, M*
Northwestern University *B, M, D*
Southern Illinois University
 Edwardsville *B, M*
University of Illinois
 Chicago *D, M, D*
 Urbana-Champaign *B, M, D*

Indiana
Indiana Institute of Technology *A, B*
Purdue University *B, M, D*

Iowa
Iowa State University *B, M, D*
St. Ambrose University *B*
University of Iowa *B, M, D*

Kansas
Kansas State University *B, M, D*
Wichita State University *B, M, D*

Kentucky
Maysville Community and Technical
 College *B*
University of Louisville *B, M, D*

Louisiana
Louisiana State University and
 Agricultural and Mechanical
 College *B, M*

Maryland
Morgan State University *B, M*

Massachusetts
Northeastern University *B, M, D*
University of Massachusetts
 Amherst *B, M, D*
Western New England University *B*
Worcester Polytechnic Institute *B*

Michigan
Andrews University *B*
Kettering University *B, M*
Lawrence Technological
 University *B, M*
Oakland University *B, M*
University of Michigan *B, M, D*
Wayne State University *B, M, D*
Western Michigan University *B, M, D*

Minnesota
University of Minnesota
 Duluth *B*
 Twin Cities *M, D*

Mississippi
Mississippi State University *B, M, D*

Missouri
Missouri Southern State University *B*
University of Missouri
 Columbia *B, M, D*

New Jersey
New Jersey Institute of
 Technology *B, M, D*
Rutgers, The State University of New
 Jersey
 New Brunswick/Piscataway
 Campus *B, M, D*

New Mexico
Eastern New Mexico University:
 Roswell *C, A*
Navajo Technical University *B*
New Mexico State University *B, M*

New York
Hofstra University *B*
Rochester Institute of
 Technology *B, M*
SUNY
 Maritime College *B*
 University at Binghamton *B, M, D*
 University at Buffalo *B, M, D*

North Carolina
North Carolina Agricultural and
 Technical State
 University *B, M, D*
North Carolina State
 University *B, M, D*

North Dakota
North Dakota State
 University *B, M, D*

Ohio
Cleveland State University *M*
Kent State University *B*
Lorain County Community College *A*
Ohio State University
 Columbus Campus *B, M, D*
Ohio University *B, M*
Sinclair Community College *A*
Wright State University *M*
Youngstown State University *B, M*

Oklahoma
Oklahoma State University *B, M, D*
University of Oklahoma *B, M, D*

Oregon
Clackamas Community College *A*
Oregon State University *B, M, D*

Pennsylvania
Drexel University *B*
Elizabethtown College *B*
Lehigh University *B, M, D*
Penn State
 Abington *B*
 Altoona *B*
 Beaver *B*
 Berks *B*
 Brandywine *B*
 DuBois *B*
 Erie, The Behrend College *B*
 Fayette, The Eberly Campus *B*
 Greater Allegheny *B*
 Harrisburg *B*
 Hazleton *B*
 Lehigh Valley *B*

Mont Alto *B*
New Kensington *B*
Schuylkill *B*
Shenango *B*
University Park *B, M, D*
Wilkes-Barre *B*
Worthington Scranton *B*
York *B*
Philadelphia University *B*
University of Pittsburgh *B, M, D*
University of Pittsburgh
  Bradford *B*

Puerto Rico

Caribbean University *B*
Inter American University of Puerto
  Rico
  Bayamon Campus *B*
Universidad Politecnica de Puerto
  Rico *B*
University of Puerto Rico
  Mayaguez *B, M*

Rhode Island

University of Rhode Island *B, M, D*

South Carolina

Clemson University *B, M, D*
Francis Marion University *T*

South Dakota

South Dakota School of Mines and
  Technology *B*

Tennessee

University of Tennessee
  Knoxville *B, M, D*

Texas

Lamar University *B, M*
Northeast Texas Community
  College *A*
St. Mary's University *B, M*
Texas A&M University *B, M, D*
Texas A&M University
  Commerce *B*
Texas State University *B*
Texas Tech University *B, M, D*
University of Houston *B, M, D*
University of Texas
  Arlington *B, M, D*
  Austin *M, D*
  El Paso *B, M*
  Pan American *B*

Vermont

University of Vermont *B*

Virginia

George Mason University *M*
Liberty University *B*
Tidewater Community College *A*
Virginia Polytechnic Institute and
  State University *B, M, D*

Washington

University of Washington *B*

West Virginia

West Virginia University *B, M, D*

Wisconsin

Milwaukee School of Engineering *B*
University of Wisconsin
  Madison *B, M, D*
  Milwaukee *B*
  Platteville *B*

Industrial equipment maintenance/repair

Alabama

Alabama Southern Community
  College *C, A*

Calhoun Community College *A*
Community College of the Air
  Force *A*
Faulkner State Community
  College *C, A*
Gadsden State Community
  College *C, A*
George C. Wallace Community
  College at Dothan *C, A*
George C. Wallace State Community
  College at Selma *C, A*
Lawson State Community College *C*
Northeast Alabama Community
  College *C, A*
Shelton State Community College *C*
Southern Union State Community
  College *C, A*
University of West Alabama *A*

Arizona

Central Arizona College *A*
Eastern Arizona College *C*
Northland Pioneer College *C, A*

Arkansas

Arkansas Northeastern College *C, A*
Black River Technical College *C*
College of the Ouachitas *C*
East Arkansas Community
  College *C, A*
Mid-South Community College *C*
Phillips Community College of the
  University of Arkansas *A*
Pulaski Technical College *C*
South Arkansas Community
  College *C, A*
Southeast Arkansas College *C, A*
Southern Arkansas University Tech *C*
University of Arkansas
  Community College at Batesville *A*
  Community College at Hope *C*
  Monticello *C, A*

California

Allan Hancock College *C*
Cabrillo College *C, A*
Fresno City College *C, A*
Merced College *C, A*
Taft College *A*

Florida

Hillsborough Community College *C*
Miami Dade College *A*

Georgia

Albany Technical College *C, A*
Altamaha Technical College *C, A*
Athens Technical College *C*
Augusta Technical College *C*
Bainbridge College *C, A*
Central Georgia Technical College *C*
Chattahoochee Technical College *C*
Columbus Technical College *C, A*
Gwinnett Technical College *C*
Middle Georgia State College *A*
Savannah Technical College *C, A*
South Georgia State College *A*
West Georgia Technical College *A*

Hawaii

University of Hawaii
  Hawaii Community College *C*

Idaho

North Idaho College *A*

Illinois

Black Hawk College *C*
City Colleges of Chicago
  Richard J. Daley College *C, A*
  Wilbur Wright College *C*
College of Lake County *C, A*
Danville Area Community
  College *C, A*

Elgin Community College *C, A*
Heartland Community College *C, A*
Highland Community College *C*
Illinois Central College *C*
Illinois Eastern Community Colleges
  Olney Central College *C, A*
  Wabash Valley College *C, A*
Illinois Valley Community College *C*
John A. Logan College *A*
John Wood Community College *C, A*
Kankakee Community College *C*
Kaskaskia College *C, A*
Lake Land College *C*
Moraine Valley Community College *C*
Prairie State College *C*
Rend Lake College *C, A*
Richland Community College *A*
Southwestern Illinois College *C, A*
Triton College *A*
Waubonsee Community College *C, A*

Iowa

Des Moines Area Community
  College *A*
Iowa Central Community College *C*
Marshalltown Community College *A*
Western Iowa Tech Community
  College *C, A*

Kansas

Haskell Indian Nations University *A*
Johnson County Community
  College *C, A*

Kentucky

Big Sandy Community and Technical
  College *C*
Gateway Community and Technical
  College *C, A*
Hopkinsville Community College *C*
Jefferson Community and Technical
  College *C*
Maysville Community and Technical
  College *C*
Owensboro Community and
  Technical College *C*
Somerset Community College *C, A*
West Kentucky Community and
  Technical College *C, A*

Louisiana

Bossier Parish Community College *C*

Maine

Northern Maine Community
  College *A*
Washington County Community
  College *C*

Michigan

Grand Rapids Community
  College *C, A*
Henry Ford Community College *C, A*
Kellogg Community College *C, A*
Lake Michigan College *A*
Lansing Community College *C*
Macomb Community College *C*
Muskegon Community College *C, A*
Northern Michigan University *A*
Southwestern Michigan College *A*

Minnesota

Alexandria Technical and Community
  College *C, A*
Central Lakes College *C*
Hennepin Technical College *C, A*
Mesabi Range Community and
  Technical College *C*
Minnesota State College - Southeast
  Technical *C, A*
Minnesota State Community and
  Technical College *C*
Rainy River Community College *C, A*

Riverland Community College *C*
St. Paul College *C, A*

Mississippi

Coahoma Community College *A*
East Mississippi Community
  College *C, A*
Hinds Community College *C*
Meridian Community College *C*
Mississippi Delta Community
  College *C*
Northeast Mississippi Community
  College *C, A*

Missouri

Jefferson College *A*
Mineral Area College *C, A*
Ranken Technical College *A*

Montana

University of Montana *C*

Nebraska

Central Community College *C, A*
Metropolitan Community College *A*

Nevada

Great Basin College *C, A*

New Hampshire

Nashua Community College *A*

New Mexico

San Juan College *C, A*

North Carolina

Alamance Community College *C, A*
Beaufort County Community
  College *C*
Bladen Community College *C*
Blue Ridge Community College *C*
Caldwell Community College and
  Technical Institute *A*
Central Carolina Community
  College *A*
Durham Technical Community
  College *C*
Halifax Community College *C, A*
McDowell Technical Community
  College *A*
Mitchell Community College *A*
Nash Community College *C*
Richmond Community College *C*
Roanoke-Chowan Community
  College *C*
Rockingham Community College *C*
Rowan-Cabarrus Community
  College *C, A*
Sampson Community College *C, A*
Surry Community College *A*
Vance-Granville Community
  College *C*

North Dakota

Bismarck State College *C, A*

Ohio

Eastern Gateway Community
  College *A*
Northwest State Community
  College *C, A*
Sinclair Community College *C*
Stark State College *A*

Oregon

Blue Mountain Community
  College *C, A*
Chemeketa Community College *A*
Lane Community College *C, A*
Linn-Benton Community College *A*
Mt. Hood Community College *C, A*
Portland Community College *C, A*
Rogue Community College *C*

Pennsylvania

Delaware County Community
College C, A
Johnson College A
Pennsylvania College of
Technology A
Reading Area Community College A
Westmoreland County Community
College A

South Carolina

Aiken Technical College C, A
Central Carolina Technical College C
Greenville Technical College C
Midlands Technical College C
Spartanburg Community College C
Technical College of the
Lowcountry C
Tri-County Technical College C, A
Trident Technical College C
York Technical College C, A

Tennessee

Dyersburg State Community
College C
Northeast State Community
College C, A
Walters State Community College C

Texas

Amarillo College C, A
Del Mar College C
Lamar Institute of Technology C, A
Texas State Technical College
Waco C

Virginia

Germanna Community College C
New River Community College C
Southside Virginia Community
College C
Southwest Virginia Community
College C
Thomas Nelson Community
College C
Tidewater Community College A
Virginia Highlands Community
College C

Washington

Bellingham Technical College A
Big Bend Community College C, A
Columbia Basin College C
Lake Washington Institute of
Technology C, A
Lower Columbia College A
Renton Technical College C, A
Spokane Community College A

West Virginia

Blue Ridge Community and Technical
College C
Eastern West Virginia Community and
Technical College C, A
West Virginia Northern Community
College C

Wisconsin

Blackhawk Technical College C
Chippewa Valley Technical College C
Gateway Technical College C, A
Lakeshore Technical College C
Madison Area Technical College C
Mid-State Technical College C, A
Milwaukee Area Technical College C
Moraine Park Technical College C
Northeast Wisconsin Technical
College C
Waukesha County Technical
College C
Western Technical College C
Wisconsin Indianhead Technical
College C

Wyoming

Casper College C, A
Western Wyoming Community
College C, A

Industrial/
organizational
psychology

Alabama

Auburn University D
Oakwood University B

Arizona

Grand Canyon University D
Northcentral University M, D

California

Alliant International University M, D
California State University
Long Beach M
San Bernardino M
Concordia University Irvine B
Golden Gate University M
John F. Kennedy University M
National University M
Point Loma Nazarene University B
St. Mary's College of California B
San Jose State University M
Touro University Worldwide M

Colorado

Colorado State University M
Fort Lewis College B

Connecticut

Fairfield University M
University of New Haven M

District of Columbia

George Washington University D

Florida

Carlos Albizu University M
Florida Institute of Technology M, D
University of Central Florida M, D

Georgia

Georgia Institute of
Technology B, M, D
University of Georgia M

Idaho

Northwest Nazarene University B

Illinois

Argosy University
Chicago M
DePaul University M, D
Roosevelt University M, D
Saint Xavier University B
University of Illinois
Urbana-Champaign M, D

Iowa

Coe College B
Morningside College B

Kentucky

Eastern Kentucky University M
Northern Kentucky University M

Louisiana

Louisiana Tech University M

Maryland

Notre Dame of Maryland
University B
University of Baltimore M

Massachusetts

Fitchburg State University B
Salem State University M
Springfield College M

Michigan

Central Michigan University M, D
University of Detroit Mercy B, M
Wayne State University M
Western Michigan University M

Minnesota

Capella University M, D
Minnesota State University
Mankato M
Saint Cloud State University M

Mississippi

William Carey University M

Missouri

Avila University M
Maryville University of Saint
Louis B, M
Northwest Missouri State
University B
Washington University in St. Louis B

Nebraska

University of Nebraska
Omaha M, D

New Jersey

Fairleigh Dickinson University
College at Florham M
Montclair State University M

New York

City University of New York
Baruch College M
Brooklyn College M
Hofstra University M, D
Ithaca College B
New York University M, D
SUNY
University at Albany M, D

North Carolina

Appalachian State University M
University of North Carolina
Charlotte M

Ohio

Baldwin Wallace University B
Franklin University M
Ohio University M, D
Tiffin University B
University of Akron M, D
Wright State University M, D
Xavier University M

Oklahoma

University of Tulsa M, D

Pennsylvania

Holy Family University B
Lincoln University B
Saint Joseph's University B

Puerto Rico

Inter American University of Puerto
Rico
Metropolitan Campus M, D
San German Campus M, D
University of Puerto Rico
Arecibo B
Rio Piedras M

South Carolina

Clemson University D

Tennessee

Southern Adventist University B
University of Tennessee
Knoxville D

Texas

Angelo State University M
Lamar University M
Rice University M, D
St. Mary's University M
Texas A&M University D
University of Houston D
University of Houston
Clear Lake M

Vermont

Goddard College M

Washington

Seattle Pacific University M, D

Wisconsin

University of Wisconsin
Oshkosh M

Industrial radiologic
technology

Alabama

Northwest-Shoals Community
College C

California

Moorpark College A

Kansas

Cowley County Community
College A
Wichita Area Technical College C, A

North Carolina

Central Piedmont Community
College C, A

Tennessee

Fountainhead College of
Technology C, A

Utah

Salt Lake Community College A

Industrial safety
technology

Alaska

University of Alaska
Anchorage C
Fairbanks C

Minnesota

Duluth Business University C, A
Northwest Technical College C, A

North Carolina

Nash Community College A

Ohio

James A. Rhodes State College C, A

Oklahoma

Northeastern State University B
Southeastern Oklahoma State
University M

Texas

University of Houston
Downtown B
University of Texas
Tyler B, M

Wisconsin

Fox Valley Technical College *A*

Industrial technology

Alabama

Alabama Agricultural and Mechanical
University *A, B*
Alabama Southern Community
College *C*
Gadsden State Community
College *C, A*

Alaska

Prince William Sound Community
College *C, A*

Arizona

Arizona Western College *A*
Penn Foster College *A*

Arkansas

Arkansas Tech University *A*
Pulaski Technical College *A*
Rich Mountain Community College *C*
Southern Arkansas University *A, B*
University of Arkansas
Pine Bluff *A, B*

California

California Polytechnic State
University: San Luis Obispo *B*
California State University
Fresno *B, M*
Los Angeles *B*
College of the Sequoias *C, A*
San Diego State University *B*
San Joaquin Valley College *C*

Colorado

Red Rocks Community College *C, A*

Connecticut

Asnuntuck Community College *A*
Central Connecticut State
University *B*
Northwestern Connecticut
Community College *A*

Delaware

Delaware State University *B*

Florida

St. Petersburg College *A*

Georgia

Columbus Technical College *A*
North Georgia Technical
College *C, A*

Idaho

University of Idaho *B, M*

Illinois

Eastern Illinois University *B, M*
Highland Community College *C, A*
Illinois Central College *A*
Illinois State University *B, M*
Northern Illinois University *B*
Parkland College *C, A*
Southern Illinois University
Carbondale *B*
Waubonsee Community College *C, A*

Indiana

Ball State University *B*
Indiana State University *B, M, D*
Indiana University
Purdue University Fort Wayne *A, B*
Ivy Tech Community College
Bloomington *C*
Central Indiana *C, A*

Columbus *C*
East Central *C*
Kokomo *C*
Lafayette *C*
North Central *C*
Northeast *C*
Northwest *C*
Richmond *C, A*
South Central *C*
Purdue University *A, B, M, D*
Vincennes University *B*

Iowa

University of Northern Iowa *B, M, D*
Upper Iowa University *B*
William Penn University *B*

Kansas

Manhattan Area Technical College *A*
Neosho County Community
College *C, A*
Pittsburg State University *A, B, M*

Kentucky

Bluegrass Community and Technical
College *C*
Maysville Community and Technical
College *C*
Murray State University *A*
Western Kentucky University *B*

Louisiana

Baton Rouge Community College *A*
Bossier Parish Community College *A*
Northwestern State University *B*
Nunez Community College *A*
South Louisiana Community
College *A*
Southeastern Louisiana
University *A, B*
University of Louisiana at Lafayette *B*

Maryland

Hagerstown Community College *C, A*

Massachusetts

Bristol Community College *C*
Fitchburg State University *B*
University of Massachusetts
Lowell *B*

Michigan

Delta College *A*
Eastern Michigan University *B*
Ferris State University *B*
Montcalm Community College *A*
Northern Michigan University *B*
Oakland Community College *C, A*
St. Clair County Community
College *C*

Minnesota

Bemidji State University *B*
Dunwoody College of
Technology *C, A*
Hennepin Technical College *C, A*
Northwest Technical College *A*

Mississippi

Jackson State University *B*
Mississippi State University *B*
Mississippi Valley State University *B*
University of Southern
Mississippi *B, M*

Missouri

Metropolitan Community College -
Kansas City *A*
St. Charles Community College *A*
Southeast Missouri State University *B*
University of Central Missouri *B, M*

Montana

Montana State University
Northern *B*

New Jersey

Salem Community College *A*

New Mexico

Eastern New Mexico University:
Roswell *C, A*
San Juan College *A*

New York

Broome Community College *C, A*
Clinton Community College *A*
Corning Community College *A*
Erie Community College *A*
SUNY
College at Buffalo *B*
College of Technology at
Alfred *A, B*
Farmingdale State College *B*
Ulster County Community College *A*

North Carolina

Appalachian State University *M*
Bladen Community College *C, A*
Central Carolina Community
College *C, A*
Davidson County Community
College *C*
East Carolina University *B, M*
Elizabeth City State University *B*
Gaston College *C, A*
Martin Community College *C, A*
North Carolina Agricultural and
Technical State University *B, M*
Roanoke-Chowan Community
College *A*
Rowan-Cabarrus Community
College *A*
Western Carolina University *B, M*
Wilkes Community College *C, A*

North Dakota

Bismarck State College *C, A*
University of North Dakota *B, M*

Ohio

Bowling Green State University *B*
Central State University *B*
Cincinnati State Technical and
Community College *C, A*
Clark State Community College *C, A*
Edison State Community College *A*
James A. Rhodes State College *C, A*
Kent State University
Trumbull *A*
Tuscarawas *A*
Ohio Northern University *B*
Ohio University *B*
Owens Community College
Toledo *C, A*
University of Dayton *B*
University of Rio Grande *C, B*

Oklahoma

Oklahoma Panhandle State
University *A, B*

Oregon

Central Oregon Community
College *C, A*
Clackamas Community College *C, A*
Lane Community College *C, A*
Umpqua Community College *A*

Pennsylvania

Bucks County Community College *A*
Lackawanna College *A*
Millersville University of
Pennsylvania *A, B*

South Hills School of Business &
Technology *A*

Puerto Rico

University of Puerto Rico
Arecibo *B*
Bayamon University College *A*

South Carolina

South Carolina State University *B*
Tri-County Technical College *C, A*

South Dakota

Black Hills State University *B*

Tennessee

Chattanooga State Community
College *A*
Cleveland State Community
College *C, A*
Jackson State Community College *A*
Middle Tennessee State
University *B, M*
Walters State Community
College *C, A*

Texas

Galveston College *C, A*
Lamar University *B*
Lone Star College System *C, A*
Northeast Texas Community
College *C, A*
Panola College *C, A*
Prairie View A&M University *B*
Sam Houston State University *B, M*
Tarleton State University *B*
Texas A&M University
Commerce *B, M*
Texas Southern University *B, M*
Texas State Technical College
Marshall *C, A*
Texas State University *B, M*
University of Texas
Brownsville *B*
Permian Basin *B*
Tyler *B*

Virginia

John Tyler Community College *C, A*
Piedmont Virginia Community
College *A*
Southwest Virginia Community
College *C, A*

Washington

Bates Technical College *C, A*
Central Washington University *B*
Olympic College *C, A*
Shoreline Community College *A*
Western Washington University *B*

West Virginia

West Virginia University Institute of
Technology *B*

Informatics

Alabama

University of Phoenix
Birmingham *M*

Arizona

Arizona State University *B*
University of Phoenix
Phoenix-Hohokam *M*

California

University of California
Irvine *B*
University of Phoenix
Bay Area *M*
Central Valley *M*

Sacramento Valley *M*
San Diego *M*

Florida
University of Phoenix
Central Florida *M*
North Florida *M*
South Florida *M*
West Florida *M*

Georgia
Mercer University *B*
University of Phoenix
Atlanta *M*
Augusta *M*
Columbus *M*
Savannah *M*

Indiana
Goshen College *B*
Indiana University
Bloomington *B, M, D*
East *B*
Kokomo *C, B*
Northwest *B*
Purdue University Indianapolis *B*
South Bend *C, B*
Southeast *B*
Trine University *B*

Kentucky
Bluegrass Community and Technical
College *A*

Louisiana
University of Phoenix
Baton Rouge *M*
Louisiana *M*
Shreveport *M*

Michigan
University of Michigan *B*
University of Phoenix
Metro Detroit *M*
West Michigan *M*

Missouri
Saint Louis University *M*

Nebraska
University of Nebraska
Omaha *M, D*

New York
Rochester Institute of
Technology *B, M*

North Carolina
Cape Fear Community College *A*

Ohio
College of Mount St. Joseph *B*

South Carolina
Clemson University *D*
University of South Carolina
Upstate *M*

Texas
University of Phoenix
Austin *M*
Dallas Fort Worth *M*
Houston Westside *M*

Virginia
University of Phoenix
Northern Virginia *M*

Information resources management

Alabama
Athens State University *B*

Alaska
Alaska Pacific University *M*

Arizona
Grand Canyon University *B*

Arkansas
Ozarka College *A*

California
California Lutheran University *M*
Coleman University *M*
Golden Gate University *B, M*
Santa Clara University *M*
University of California
Irvine *B*

Colorado
Colorado Technical University *B*

Delaware
Wilmington University *B*

District of Columbia
Georgetown University *B*
University of the Potomac *A*

Florida
Florida International University *M*
Rasmussen College
Fort Myers *B*
New Port Richey *B*
Ocala *B*
Pasco/Land O'Lakes *B*
Tampa/Brandon *B*

Georgia
Georgia College and State
University *M*
Georgia Southern University *T*

Illinois
DePaul University *M*
Lewis University *B*
Rasmussen College
Aurora *B*
Mokena/Tinley Park *B*
Rockford *B*
Romeoville/Joliet *B*

Iowa
Dordt College *B*

Maryland
Mount St. Mary's University *B*

Massachusetts
Bay Path College *M*

Michigan
Michigan State University *B, M, D*
Montcalm Community College *A*
Western Michigan University *B*

Minnesota
Capella University *M, D*
Rasmussen College
Blaine *B*
Bloomington *B*
Brooklyn Park *B*
Eagan *B*
Lake Elmo/Woodbury *B*
Mankato *B*
St. Cloud *B*

Missouri
Grantham University *B, M*

New Jersey
Seton Hall University *B*

North Carolina
Chowan University *B*
Coastal Carolina Community
College *A*

North Dakota
Rasmussen College
Bismarck *B*
Fargo *B*
University of Mary *B*

Oregon
Corban University *B*

Pennsylvania
Carnegie Mellon University *B*
Chestnut Hill College *B*
Juniata College *B*

Puerto Rico
Turabo University *D*

Rhode Island
Salve Regina University *B*

South Carolina
Southern Wesleyan University *B*
Williamsburg Technical College *A*

Texas
Abilene Christian University *B*
Houston Baptist University *B*
Lubbock Christian University *B*
St. Edward's University *M*
St. Mary's University *B*
University of Dallas *M*

Utah
Brigham Young University *B, M*
Westminster College *B*

Virginia
University of the Potomac *A*

Wisconsin
Rasmussen College
Appleton *B*
Green Bay *B*
Wausau *B*
University of Wisconsin
Eau Claire *B*

Information systems

Alabama
Faulkner University *B*
Gadsden State Community College *A*
Northwest-Shoals Community
College *A*
University of South Alabama *C, B*

Arizona
Cochise College *A*
Eastern Arizona College *C, A*
GateWay Community College *C, A*
Scottsdale Community College *C, A*
South Mountain Community
College *C, A*
Western International University *M*

Arkansas
Arkansas State University
Mountain Home *C, A*
Ozarka College *C*
Rich Mountain Community College *A*
University of Arkansas
Little Rock *B*

California
Antelope Valley College *C, A*
California Lutheran University *B*

California State University
East Bay *B, M*
Long Beach *B, M*
Los Angeles *M*
Sacramento *B, M*
Chabot College *A*
Cosumnes River College *A*
Cypress College *C, A*
Empire College *C, A*
Fresno City College *C, A*
La Sierra University *B*
Laney College *A*
Los Angeles Harbor College *A*
Merced College *A*
Mission College *C, A*
Moorpark College *C, A*
Ohlone College *C, A*
Orange Coast College *C, A*
Platt College
Ontario *A*
Reedley College *C, A*
San Diego City College *A*
San Jose State University *B*
Santa Rosa Junior College *C*
Santiago Canyon College *A*
Skyline College *C, A*
Southwestern College *A*
University of California
Berkeley *M, D*
Los Angeles *M, D*
San Diego *B*
University of Redlands *M*
University of San Francisco *B*
University of the Pacific *B*
West Hills College: Coalinga *C*

Colorado
American Sentinel University *M*
Colorado State University *B*
Colorado State University
Pueblo *B*
Colorado Technical
University *A, B, M*
National American University
Denver *A, B*
Pikes Peak Community College *A*
University of Colorado
Denver *M*
University of Denver *M*
Westwood College
Denver North *A, B*

Connecticut
Albertus Magnus College *C, A, B*
Central Connecticut State
University *M*
Gateway Community College *C, A*
Manchester Community College *C, A*
Middlesex Community College *C, A*
Norwalk Community College *C, A*
Three Rivers Community College *A*
University of Hartford *B*
University of New Haven *B*

District of Columbia
Gallaudet University *B*
George Washington University *B, M*
Howard University *B*
Strayer University *C, B, M*
University of the District of
Columbia *B*

Florida
Bethune-Cookman University *B*
Broward College *A*
Chipola College *A*
Everest University
Brandon *A, B*
Tampa *A, B*
Florida Institute of Technology *M*
Florida State College at
Jacksonville *A*
Florida State University *M, D*

Lincoln College of Technology
  West Palm Beach *A*
Miami Dade College *C, A*
Nova Southeastern University *D*
Palm Beach State College *A*
Pensacola State College *A*
Remington College
  Tampa *A*
Seminole State College of Florida *A*
University of Miami *C, B, M, D*
University of South Florida *B*

Georgia

Albany State University *B*
Armstrong Atlantic State University *B*
Clayton State University *C, A, B*
Darton College *A*
Fort Valley State University *B*
Georgia Institute of Technology *D*
Georgia Southern University *B*
Gordon College *A*
Kennesaw State University *B, M*
Mercer University *B*
Savannah State University *B*
Southern Crescent Technical
  College *A*
University of North Georgia *B*
Valdosta State University *B*

Hawaii

Brigham Young University-Hawaii *B*
Hawaii Pacific University *M*
University of Hawaii
  Hawaii Community College *C, A*
  Honolulu Community College *A*
  Maui College *B*

Idaho

Boise State University *B*
Idaho State University *B, M*

Illinois

Benedictine University *B*
Bradley University *B, M*
Chicago State University *B*
City Colleges of Chicago
  Harold Washington College *C*
  Harry S. Truman College *C*
  Kennedy-King College *C*
  Malcolm X College *C*
  Olive-Harvey College *C*
  Richard J. Daley College *C*
  Wilbur Wright College *C*
DePaul University *B, M*
Elmhurst College *B*
Harper College *C*
Illinois Eastern Community Colleges
  Frontier Community College *A*
Illinois Valley Community College *A*
John A. Logan College *C*
Joliet Junior College *A*
Kaskaskia College *A*
McKendree University *B*
Midstate College *B*
National-Louis University *C, B*
Northwestern University *B, M*
Olivet Nazarene University *B*
Quincy University *B*
Southeastern Illinois College *A*
Southern Illinois University
  Carbondale *B*
Southwestern Illinois College *A*
Triton College *C, A*
University of Illinois
  Chicago *B*

Indiana

Anderson University *B*
Butler University *B*
National College
  South Bend *A*
National College: Fort Wayne *A*
Purdue University *B*

Taylor University *A*
University of Indianapolis *A, B*

Iowa

Central College *B*
Dordt College *B*
Ellsworth Community College *C, A*
St. Ambrose University *B*
Simpson College *B*
Southwestern Community College *A*
University of Iowa *M, D*
Wartburg College *B*

Kansas

Barton County Community College *A*
Emporia State University *B*
Friends University *B*
Kansas State University *B*
Newman University *A, B*

Kentucky

Ashland Community and Technical
  College *A*
Daymar College
  Owensboro *A*
Murray State University *B, M*
Northern Kentucky University *B*
Sullivan College of Technology and
  Design *A*

Louisiana

Bossier Parish Community
  College *C, A*
Grambling State University *B*
ITI Technical College *A*
Louisiana State University and
  Agricultural and Mechanical
  College *M*
Northwestern State University *B*
Nunez Community College *C, A*
Remington College
  Baton Rouge *A*

Maine

Eastern Maine Community College *C*

Maryland

Allegany College of Maryland *A*
Baltimore City Community College *A*
Frederick Community College *A*
Frostburg State University *B*
Montgomery College *A*
Morgan State University *B*
Prince George's Community
  College *C*
Salisbury University *B*
Stevenson University *B, M*
TESST College of Technology
  Baltimore *C, A*
  Beltsville *C, A*
Towson University *B, M, D*
University of Maryland
  Baltimore County *B, M, D*
  College Park *B, M*
  University College *B, M*
Washington Adventist University *A, B*

Massachusetts

American International College *B*
Babson College *B*
Bentley University *B, M*
Boston College *B*
Boston University *M*
Bristol Community College *A*
Cape Cod Community College *A*
Massachusetts Bay Community
  College *C, A*
North Shore Community College *C*
Northeastern University *B, M, D*
Northern Essex Community
  College *A*
Simmons College *D*
Springfield College *B*
Suffolk University *B*

Tufts University *B*
University of Massachusetts
  Lowell *A, B*
Wentworth Institute of Technology *B*
Western New England University *B*
Westfield State University *B*

Michigan

Alpena Community College *C, A*
Andrews University *B*
Baker College
  Auburn Hills *A*
  Jackson *C*
  Muskegon *B*
  Owosso *A*
  Port Huron *A, B*
Davenport University *C*
Delta College *C, A*
Eastern Michigan University *M*
Grand Valley State University *B, M*
Lawrence Technological University *M*
Michigan State University *B*
Northwestern Michigan College *A*
University of Michigan *B, M, D*
University of Michigan
  Flint *B, M*
Washtenaw Community College *C, A*
Wayne State University *B*

Minnesota

Alexandria Technical and Community
  College *A*
Augsburg College *C*
Bemidji State University *B*
Brown College
  Mendota Heights *B*
Century College *A*
Hennepin Technical College *C, A*
Metropolitan State University *B*
Minnesota State University
  Moorhead *B*
Pine Technical College *A*
Rochester Community and Technical
  College *A*
St. Catherine University *B*
St. Mary's University of Minnesota *B*
University of St. Thomas *B*
Walden University *B, M*

Missouri

Lincoln University *B*
Missouri Southern State
  University *A, B*
Missouri University of Science and
  Technology *B, M*
Missouri Western State University *B*
National American University
  Kansas City *A, B*
Northwest Missouri State
  University *C*
University of Central Missouri *M*
Washington University in St.
  Louis *B, M*
Webster University *B*

Montana

Montana State University
  Northern *A, B*
Stone Child College *A*
University of Great Falls *M*

Nebraska

Chadron State College *B*
Doane College *B*
Southeast Community College *C, A*
University of Nebraska
  Kearney *B*
  Omaha *M*
Wayne State College *B*

Nevada

College of Southern Nevada *A*

New Hampshire

Great Bay Community College *C, A*
Nashua Community College *A*

New Jersey

Burlington County College *C, A*
Essex County College *C*
Fairleigh Dickinson University
  Metropolitan Campus *M*
New Jersey Institute of
  Technology *B, M, D*
Ramapo College of New Jersey *B*
Richard Stockton College of New
  Jersey *B*
Rutgers, The State University of New
  Jersey
  New Brunswick/Piscataway
    Campus *B, M*
  Newark Campus *B*
Saint Peter's University *C, A, B*

New Mexico

Central New Mexico Community
  College *C, A*

New York

Adelphi University *B*
Broome Community College *A*
Cayuga Community College *C*
City University of New York
  Baruch College *B*
  Brooklyn College *B, M*
  College of Staten Island *B*
  Lehman College *B*
  Medgar Evers College *B*
  New York City College of
    Technology *B*
  Queensborough Community
    College *A*
Columbia University *M, D*
Corning Community College *A*
Dutchess Community College *A*
Excelsior College *B*
Finger Lakes Community
  College *C, A*
Fulton-Montgomery Community
  College *A*
Genesee Community College *A*
Globe Institute of Technology *C*
Hartwick College *B*
Jefferson Community College *A*
Long Island University
  LIU Post *B, M, D*
Manhattan College *B*
Marist College *C*
Medaille College: Amherst *B*
Mercy College *B*
Molloy College *B*
Nazareth College *B*
New York University *B, M*
Niagara University *C, B*
Pace University *A, B, M*
Pace University: Pleasantville/
  Briarcliff *A, B, M*
Plaza College *A*
Rockland Community College *A*
SUNY
  College at Buffalo *B*
  College at Old Westbury *B*
  College at Oswego *B*
  College of Agriculture and
    Technology at Morrisville *A*
  College of Technology at Canton *A*
  Farmingdale State College *C, A*
  Institute of Technology at Utica/
    Rome *B, M*
  University at Albany *B, M, D*
  University at Buffalo *B, M*
  University at Stony Brook *B, M*
Sage Colleges *B*
St. John Fisher College *B*
Siena College *C*
Suffolk County Community
  College *C, A*

Syracuse University *B, M, D*
Tompkins Cortland Community
College *A*
United States Military Academy *B*
Westchester Community College *C, A*

North Carolina

Alamance Community College *A*
Beaufort County Community
College *A*
Blue Ridge Community College *A*
Brunswick Community College *A*
Campbell University *B*
Catawba Valley Community
College *C, A*
Central Carolina Community
College *C, A*
Central Piedmont Community
College *A*
Cleveland Community College *C, A*
Coastal Carolina Community
College *A*
College of the Albemarle *C, A*
Edgecombe Community College *A*
Elon University *B*
Fayetteville Technical Community
College *C, A*
Guilford College *B*
Guilford Technical Community
College *A*
Isothermal Community College *C, A*
Lees-McRae College *B*
Lenoir-Rhyne University *B*
Martin Community College *C, A*
Mitchell Community College *A*
Nash Community College *A*
North Carolina Central
University *B, M*
Pitt Community College *C, A*
Richmond Community College *C, A*
Roanoke-Chowan Community
College *A*
Rockingham Community
College *C, A*
Rowan-Cabarrus Community
College *C, A*
Sampson Community College *A*
Sandhills Community College *C, A*
Stanly Community College *C, A*
Surry Community College *C, A*
Tri-County Community College *A*
University of North Carolina
Chapel Hill *B, M*
Western Piedmont Community
College *C, A*
Wilkes Community College *C, A*
Winston-Salem State University *B*

North Dakota

University of Mary *B*

Ohio

Antonelli College
Cincinnati *A*
Case Western Reserve
University *M, D*
Clark State Community College *A*
Eastern Gateway Community
College *C*
Kent State University *M*
Lakeland Community College *C, A*
Marietta College *B*
Miami-Jacobs Career College
Dayton *C, A*
Muskingum University *B*
Ohio Dominican University *B*
Stark State College *A*
Tiffin University *B*
University of Cincinnati *M*
University of Toledo *A, B, M*
Urbana University *B*
Wilberforce University *B*
Wright State University: Lake
Campus *A*

Youngstown State University *A, B*
Zane State College *A*

Oklahoma

Oklahoma Baptist University *B*
Oklahoma Christian University *B*
Southeastern Oklahoma State
University *A*
Southwestern Oklahoma State
University *B*
University of Oklahoma *B*
Western Oklahoma State College *A*

Oregon

George Fox University *B*
Lane Community College *C*
Pioneer Pacific College *A*
Southwestern Oregon Community
College *A*
Umpqua Community College *A*

Pennsylvania

Albright College *B*
Bucks County Community College *A*
Carnegie Mellon University *M, D*
Clarion University of Pennsylvania *B*
DeSales University *M*
Delaware County Community
College *A*
Drexel University *B, M, D*
Elizabethtown College *B*
Fortis Institute
Erie *A*
Immaculata University *C, A, B*
La Salle University *A, B, M*
Mansfield University of
Pennsylvania *A, B*
Marywood University *B, M*
Montgomery County Community
College *C, A*
Penn State
Abington *A, B*
Altoona *A, B*
Beaver *A, B*
Berks *A, B*
Brandywine *C, A, B*
DuBois *C, A, B*
Erie, The Behrend College *A, B*
Fayette, The Eberly Campus *B*
Greater Allegheny *C, A, B*
Harrisburg *C, A, B*
Hazleton *C, A, B*
Lehigh Valley *A, B*
Mont Alto *A, B*
New Kensington *A, B*
Schuylkill *A, B*
Shenango *A, B*
University Park *A, B, M, D*
Wilkes-Barre *C, A, B*
Worthington Scranton *A, B*
York *A, B*
Robert Morris University *B, D*
St. Francis University *B*
Saint Joseph's University *A, B*
Slippery Rock University of
Pennsylvania *B*
Susquehanna University *B*
Thiel College *A, B*
University of Pittsburgh *B, M, D*
University of Pittsburgh
Bradford *A*
Greensburg *B*
University of Scranton *C, A, B*
Widener University *B*
Wilkes University *B*

Puerto Rico

EDP University of Puerto Rico: Hato
Rey *M*
Humacao Community College *A*
Inter American University of Puerto
Rico
Barranquitas Campus *B*
Metropolitan Campus *M*
Ponce Campus *B*

Universidad Adventista de las
Antillas *B*
University of the Sacred Heart *B*

Rhode Island

Johnson & Wales University
Providence *B*

South Carolina

Clemson University *B*
Coastal Carolina University *B*
College of Charleston *B*
Forrest Junior College *C, A*
Midlands Technical College *C, A*
Orangeburg-Calhoun Technical
College *C*
University of South Carolina
Columbia *B*
Upstate *B*

South Dakota

Dakota State University *C, B, M, D*
Southeast Technical Institute *C*

Tennessee

Dyersburg State Community
College *C, A*
Pellissippi State Community
College *A*

Texas

Amarillo College *C, A*
Baylor University *M, D*
Brookhaven College *A*
El Centro College *C, A*
El Paso Community College *C, A*
Frank Phillips College *C*
Galveston College *C, A*
Lamar University *M*
Laredo Community College *A*
LeTourneau University *B*
Lee College *C, A*
North Lake College *C, A*
Odessa College *A*
Palo Alto College *A*
Panola College *C*
Prairie View A&M University *M*
St. Philip's College *A*
Southwestern Adventist
University *B, T*
Tarleton State University *M*
Texas A&M University *M*
Texas A&M University
Commerce *B*
Texas Lutheran University *B*
Texas Tech University *B, M*
Tyler Junior College *C, A*
University of Houston *B*
University of Houston
Clear Lake *M*
Victoria *B, M*
University of Mary Hardin-
Baylor *B, M*
University of North Texas *B, M, D*
University of Texas
Arlington *B, M*
Brownsville *B*
Dallas *M*
El Paso *M*
Pan American *M*
Permian Basin *B*
San Antonio *M*
Victoria College *C, A*

Utah

Snow College *A*
Utah State University *B, M*
Utah Valley University *B*
Weber State University *B*

Vermont

Saint Michael's College *B*

Virginia

Averett University *B*
Blue Ridge Community College *A*
Central Virginia Community
College *A*
Christopher Newport University *B*
Danville Community College *C*
Ferrum College *B*
George Mason University *M*
James Madison University *B*
Marymount University *M*
Mountain Empire Community
College *A*
Radford University *C, B*
Thomas Nelson Community
College *C, A*
University of Management and
Technology *A, B, M*
Virginia Commonwealth
University *B, M*
Wytheville Community College *C, A*

Washington

Centralia College *A*
City University of Seattle *C*
Renton Technical College *C*
Seattle Central Community College *C*
Skagit Valley College *A*
South Puget Sound Community
College *C, A*
Spokane Community College *A*
University of Washington *B, M, D*
University of Washington Bothell *B*
Walla Walla Community College *A*
Walla Walla University *B*
Yakima Valley Community College *A*

West Virginia

American National University
Parkersburg *A*
Blue Ridge Community and Technical
College *C, A*
Eastern West Virginia Community and
Technical College *A*
Fairmont State University *B*
Kanawha Valley Community and
Technical College *A*
Marshall University *M*
West Liberty University *B*
West Virginia University at
Parkersburg *C, A*
West Virginia Wesleyan College *B*

Wisconsin

Bryant & Stratton College
Milwaukee *A*
Carroll University *B*
Carthage College *B*
Herzing University
Madison *A, B*
Silver Lake College of the Holy
Family *B*
University of Wisconsin
Green Bay *B*
Milwaukee *C, B, D*

Wyoming

Sheridan College *A*
Western Wyoming Community
College *A*

Information technology

Alabama

Columbia Southern University *B*
Gadsden State Community College *A*
Northwest-Shoals Community
College *A*
Oakwood University *B*
University of South Alabama *B*

Alaska

Charter College *B*
Ilisagvik College *C*

Arizona

Chandler-Gilbert Community
  College *A*
GateWay Community College *C*
University of Arizona *M*
University of Phoenix
  Phoenix-Hohokam *A*
Western International University *B*

Arkansas

Arkansas Tech University *A, B, M*
Harding University *B*
Phillips Community College of the
  University of Arkansas *A*

California

Allan Hancock College *C, A*
Bakersfield College *C, A*
Bethesda University of California *B*
California Baptist University *B*
California State University
  Chico *B*
  Dominguez Hills *B*
  Fresno *B*
  Fullerton *B, M*
Columbia College *C, A*
Diablo Valley College *C*
East Los Angeles College *C, A*
Foothill College *C, A*
Golden Gate University *C, B, M*
Hartnell College *C, A*
Kaplan College
  Riverside *A*
Mt. Sierra College *B*
Pacific States University *M*
Palomar College *C, A*
Platt College
  Ontario *A*
San Diego State University *B, M*
San Joaquin Delta College *C, A*
San Jose State University *B*
Sierra College *A*
Southern California Institute of
  Technology *C*
Southwestern College *C, A*
Stanbridge College *C, A, B, M*
Trident University International *B*
University of Phoenix
  San Diego *A*
University of San Francisco *B, M*
Vanguard University of Southern
  California *B*

Colorado

American Sentinel University *M*
Aspen University *M*
Colorado Mountain College *A*
Colorado State University *B*
Colorado Technical
  University *C, A, B, M*
University of Denver *C, B*
University of Phoenix
  Denver *A*

Connecticut

Central Connecticut State
  University *M*
Sacred Heart University *B, M*

District of Columbia

Strayer University *C, A, B, M*

Florida

Barry University *B*
Daytona State College *B*
Florida Agricultural and Mechanical
  University *B*
Florida Atlantic University *M*
Florida International University *B, M*
Florida State University *M*

Herzing University
  Winter Park *C, A, B*
Hodges University *A, B, M*
Indian River State College *A*
Keiser University *A, B*
Lake-Sumter State College *C, A*
Miami Dade College *C, A*
Pasco-Hernando State College *A*
Saint Johns River State College *C, A*
St. Petersburg College *C*
Santa Fe College *C*
Seminole State College of Florida *B*
University of Central Florida *B*
University of South Florida *B*
University of South Florida
  Sarasota-Manatee *B*
University of West Florida *B*
Valencia College *C*

Georgia

Abraham Baldwin Agricultural
  College *C, A*
Clayton State University *B*
Columbus State University *B*
Georgia Gwinnett College *B*
Georgia Military College *B*
Georgia Southwestern State
  University *B*
Gwinnett College *A*
Kennesaw State University *C*
Middle Georgia State College *C, A, B*
South Georgia State College *A*
Southern Polytechnic State
  University *B, M*

Hawaii

Brigham Young University-Hawaii *B*
University of Hawaii
  Maui College *B*

Idaho

Broadview University
  Boise *B*

Illinois

American InterContinental
  University *B, M*
City Colleges of Chicago
  Harold Washington College *A*
  Harry S. Truman College *A*
  Kennedy-King College *A*
  Malcolm X College *A*
  Olive-Harvey College *A*
  Richard J. Daley College *A*
  Wilbur Wright College *A*
DePaul University *B*
Heartland Community College *A*
Highland Community College *A*
Illinois Eastern Community Colleges
  Frontier Community College *C*
  Olney Central College *C, A*
Illinois Institute of Technology *B, M*
Illinois State University *B, M*
John A. Logan College *A*
Lewis and Clark Community
  College *A*
Loyola University Chicago *B, M*
McKendree University *B*
Morton College *A*
Prairie State College *A*
Robert Morris University: Chicago *B*
Rock Valley College *A*
Spoon River College *A*
University of St. Francis *B*

Indiana

Ancilla College *A*
Harrison College
  Indianapolis *C, B*
ITT Technical Institute
  Indianapolis *A*
Indiana State University *B*

Indiana University
  Purdue University Fort
    Wayne *A, B, M*
  Southeast *C*
Indiana Wesleyan University *B*
Ivy Tech Community College
  Bloomington *A*
  Central Indiana *A*
  Columbus *A*
  East Central *C, A*
  Kokomo *C, A*
  Lafayette *A*
  North Central *C, A*
  Northeast *C, A*
  Northwest *C, A*
  Richmond *C, A*
  South Central *C, A*
  Southeast *C, A*
  Southwest *A*
  Wabash Valley *A*
Valparaiso University *M*

Iowa

Des Moines Area Community
  College *C, A*
Drake University *B*
Grand View University *B*
Upper Iowa University *C, B*
William Penn University *B*

Kansas

Brown Mackie College
  Salina *A*
Colby Community College *C*
Cowley County Community
  College *A*
North Central Kansas Technical
  College *C, A*
Ottawa University *B*
Seward County Community
  College *C, A*
University of Kansas *B, M*
University of St. Mary *B*

Kentucky

Big Sandy Community and Technical
  College *A*
Bluegrass Community and Technical
  College *A*
Gateway Community and Technical
  College *A*
Kentucky State University *B*
Murray State University *B, M*
Northern Kentucky University *B*
Sullivan College of Technology and
  Design *A*
Sullivan University *M*
Western Kentucky University *B*

Louisiana

McNeese State University *A*

Maine

University of Maine *M*
University of Maine
  Fort Kent *B*

Maryland

College of Southern Maryland *C, A*
Frederick Community College *C, A*
Frostburg State University *B*
Howard Community College *A*
Prince George's Community
  College *A*
Towson University *B*
United States Naval Academy *B*

Massachusetts

Bay State College *A, B*
Bentley University *M*
Bristol Community College *C*
Bunker Hill Community College *C*
Cape Cod Community College *C, A*
Endicott College *M*

Merrimack College *B*
Mount Wachusett Community
  College *C*
Simmons College *B*
University of Massachusetts
  Boston *B, M*
  Lowell *M*

Michigan

Baker College
  Allen Park *B*
Bay Mills Community College *A*
Central Michigan University *B*
Cleary University *A*
Delta College *A*
Ferris State University *A, B, M*
Grace Bible College *B*
Lake Michigan College *C, A*
Lawrence Technological
  University *B, D*
Oakland University *B, M, D*
University of Phoenix
  Metro Detroit *A*
Walsh College of Accountancy and
  Business Administration *B, M*

Minnesota

Brown College
  Brooklyn Center *A*
  Mendota Heights *A, B*
Capella University *B, M, D*
Century College *C*
Globe University
  Minneapolis *B*
  Moorhead *B*
  Woodbury *B*
Minneapolis Community and
  Technical College *C*
Minnesota School of Business
  Blaine *B*
  Brooklyn Center *B*
  Elk River *B*
  Lakeville *B*
  Plymouth *B*
  Richfield *B*
  Rochester *B*
  St. Cloud *B*
  Shakopee *B*
Minnesota State Community and
  Technical College *C, A*
National American University
  Bloomington *B*
  Roseville *B*
South Central College *C, A*
Southwest Minnesota State
  University *B*
University of Minnesota
  Crookston *B*
University of St. Thomas *B, M*

Missouri

Calvary Bible College and Theological
  Seminary *A*
College of the Ozarks *B*
Grantham University *M*
Lindenwood University *B, M*
Missouri Baptist University *B*
Missouri State University: West
  Plains *A*
Missouri University of Science and
  Technology *B, M*
Saint Louis University *M*
University of Missouri
  Columbia *B*
  Kansas City *B*

Montana

Flathead Valley Community
  College *A*
Montana State University
  Great Falls *C, A*
Salish Kootenai College *A, B*
University of Montana: Western *C, A*

Nebraska

Bellevue University *B*
Creighton University *B, M*
Kaplan University
  Lincoln *A*
Mid-Plains Community College *C, A*
University of Nebraska
  Omaha *B, D*
Vatterott College
  Spring Valley *C*

New Hampshire

Franklin Pierce University *B*
Granite State College *B*
Mount Washington College *C*
NHTI-Concord's Community
  College *C, A*
Plymouth State University *B*
Southern New Hampshire
  University *B*
University of New Hampshire *B*

New Jersey

Bergen Community College *A*
Caldwell College *B*
Cumberland County College *A*
Fairleigh Dickinson University
  Metropolitan Campus *B*
Montclair State University *B*
New Jersey Institute of
  Technology *B, M*
Raritan Valley Community College *A*
Rutgers, The State University of New
  Jersey
  New Brunswick/Piscataway
    Campus *M*
  Newark Campus *M*
Union County College *A*

New Mexico

National American University
  Albuquerque *A, B*
Navajo Technical University *C, A, B*
New Mexico Institute of Mining and
  Technology *B*
New Mexico State University *B*
New Mexico State University
  Alamogordo *A*

New York

Adirondack Community College *C, A*
Berkeley College of New York
  City *A, B*
Briarcliffe College *B*
Bryant & Stratton College
  Henrietta *A*
  Rochester *A*
City University of New York
  Guttman Community College *A*
Clarkson University *M*
Columbia-Greene Community
  College *A*
Cornell University *B, D*
D'Youville College *B*
Erie Community College *A*
Excelsior College *B*
Globe Institute of
  Technology *C, A, B*
Hilbert College *B*
Long Island University
  LIU Post *B*
Marist College *C*
Mercy College *A*
Mildred Elley
  Albany *A*
Monroe College *A, B*
Monroe Community College *A*
Mount Saint Mary College *C, B*
New York Institute of Technology *B*
Pace University: Pleasantville/
  Briarcliff *M*
Rensselaer Polytechnic Institute *B, M*
Rochester Institute of
  Technology *A, B, M*

SUNY

College of Agriculture and
  Technology at Cobleskill *B*
College of Technology at Alfred *B*
College of Technology at Canton *B*
St. John Fisher College *B*
St. Joseph's College New York:
  Suffolk Campus *C, B*
St. Joseph's College, New York *C, B*
Suffolk County Community
  College *C, A*
United States Military Academy *B*

North Carolina

Blue Ridge Community College *A*
Cape Fear Community College *C, A*
Carteret Community College *C, A*
Catawba Valley Community
  College *A*
Central Carolina Community
  College *A*
Central Piedmont Community
  College *C, A*
Cleveland Community College *C, A*
Craven Community College *C, A*
Davidson County Community
  College *C, A*
Durham Technical Community
  College *C, A*
East Carolina University *B*
Fayetteville Technical Community
  College *C, A*
Forsyth Technical Community
  College *C, A*
Gaston College *A*
Guilford College *B*
Isothermal Community College *C, A*
James Sprunt Community
  College *C, A*
Johnson C. Smith University *B*
Lenoir Community College *C, A*
Montgomery Community
  College *C, A*
Robeson Community College *A*
Southeastern Community
  College *C, A*
Stanly Community College *C, A*
University of North Carolina
  Charlotte *M*
  Pembroke *B*
Vance-Granville Community
  College *A*
Wayne Community College *C, A*
Wilkes Community College *C, A*
Wilson Community College *C, A*
Winston-Salem State University *B*

North Dakota

Dakota College at Bottineau *A*
University of Jamestown *B*

Ohio

Akron Institute of Herzing
  University *B*
Bluffton University *B*
Bryant & Stratton College
  Cleveland *A*
Cincinnati Christian University *B*
ETI Technical College of Niles *A*
Franklin University *A, B*
Lorain County Community College *A*
Marion Technical College *C, A*
Miami University
  Oxford *B*
Miami-Jacobs Career College
  Dayton *A*
Ohio Valley College of Technology *A*
Owens Community College
  Toledo *A*
Stark State College *A*
Tiffin University *B*
University of Cincinnati *C, B, M*

University of Cincinnati
  Blue Ash College *C, A*
  Clermont College *C, A*
University of Toledo *B*
Vatterott College
  Cleveland *C*
Youngstown State University *A, B*

Oklahoma

Cameron University *A, B*
Oklahoma State University *B, M*
Oklahoma State University
  Institute of Technology:
    Okmulgee *A*
University of Central Oklahoma *B*
University of Tulsa *B*

Oregon

Mt. Hood Community College *C, A*
Oregon Institute of Technology *B*
Pioneer Pacific College *B*

Pennsylvania

Cabrini College *B*
Carnegie Mellon University *B, M, D*
DeSales University *C, B*
Harrisburg University of Science and
  Technology *B, M*
Juniata College *B*
Kaplan Career Institute
  Pittsburgh *A*
Keystone College *A, B*
La Roche College *B*
La Salle University *B*
Lincoln Technical Institute
  Northeast Philadelphia *C*
Lincoln University *B*
Misericordia University *B*
Montgomery County Community
  College *C, A*
Mount Aloysius College *B*
Peirce College *A, B*
Penn Commercial Business and
  Technical School *A*
Penn State
  DuBois *C*
  Schuylkill *C*
  University Park *C*
  Wilkes-Barre *C*
Pennsylvania Institute of Health and
  Technology *A*
Point Park University *A, B*
Slippery Rock University of
  Pennsylvania *B*
Temple University *B*
Washington & Jefferson College *B*
Waynesburg University *B*
West Chester University of
  Pennsylvania *M*

Puerto Rico

Inter American University of Puerto
  Rico
  Bayamon Campus *B*

Rhode Island

Bryant University *B*
New England Institute of
  Technology *A, B*

South Carolina

Bob Jones University *B*
Limestone College *A, B*
University of South Carolina
  Upstate *B*

South Dakota

Dakota State University *C*
Mount Marty College *B*
National American University
  Rapid City *A, B*
Northern State University *C*
Oglala Lakota College *C*

Tennessee

Fountainhead College of
  Technology *A, B*
King University *B*
LeMoyne-Owen College *B*
Lipscomb University *B*
Trevecca Nazarene University *C, A, B*
Vatterott College
  Memphis *C*

Texas

Abilene Christian University *B*
Baylor University *B*
Central Texas College *A*
Dallas Baptist University *C*
Hallmark College of Technology *A, B*
McMurry University *B*
National American University
  Austin *A, B*
North Lake College *C, A*
St. Mary's University *B*
Stephen F. Austin State University *B*
Texas Christian University *B*
Texas State Technical College
  Harlingen *A*
University of North Texas *B*

Utah

Brigham Young University *B, M*
Broadview University
  Layton *B*
  Orem *B*
  West Jordan *B*
Dixie State College *B*
Neumont University *B*
Southern Utah University *A*
Western Governors University *B*

Vermont

Champlain College *B*
Lyndon State College *B*
Vermont Technical College *A, B*

Virginia

Bluefield College *B*
Bryant & Stratton College
  Richmond *A*
Christopher Newport University *B*
George Mason University *B, M, D*
Germanna Community College *A*
John Tyler Community College *A*
Liberty University *B*
Marymount University *C, B, M*
Mountain Empire Community
  College *A*
New River Community College *A*
Regent University *A, B*
Stratford University: Falls Church *B*
University of Management and
  Technology *C, A, B, M*
Virginia Polytechnic Institute and
  State University *M*
Virginia State University *B*
Westwood College
  Arlington Ballston *B*

Washington

Central Washington University *B*
International Academy of Design and
  Technology
  Seattle *A, B*
Northwest Indian College *A*
Seattle Central Community
  College *C, A*
Shoreline Community College *C*
University of Washington *B, M, D*
University of Washington Tacoma *B*
Yakima Valley Community College *C*

West Virginia

American Public University System *B*
Blue Ridge Community and Technical
  College *C*

New River Community and Technical
College *A*
Ohio Valley University *B*
Potomac State College of West
Virginia University *A*
Southern West Virginia Community
and Technical College *C, A*
West Virginia Junior College
Bridgeport *A*

Wisconsin
Bryant & Stratton College
Milwaukee *A*
Concordia University Wisconsin *M*
Globe University
Eau Claire *B*
Green Bay *B*
La Crosse *B*
Madison East *B*
Middleton *B*
Wausau *B*
Herzing University
Madison *A, B*
Marian University *B*
Marquette University *B*
Nicolet Area Technical College *A*
University of Wisconsin
Stout *B, M*
Whitewater *B, M*

Information technology project management

Alabama
Shelton State Community College *C*

California
Diablo Valley College *C*
National University *C, B, M*

Colorado
Aspen University *M*

District of Columbia
Georgetown University *M*

Illinois
DePaul University *M*
Illinois Institute of Technology *M*

Maryland
Hood College *M*

Michigan
Davenport University *M*
Gogebic Community College *A*

Nevada
Morrison University *B*

New Hampshire
Rivier University *M*

New York
Elmira College *M*
Marist College *M*
Pace University *A, B*
Rochester Institute of Technology *M*

Ohio
Cincinnati State Technical and
Community College *A*
Owens Community College
Toledo *C*

Pennsylvania
Carnegie Mellon University *M*
DuBois Business College
Oil City *A*
Robert Morris University *M*

Tennessee
Fountainhead College of
Technology *C, A, B*

Virginia
University of Management and
Technology *M*

West Virginia
American Public University System *B*

Inorganic chemistry

Iowa
Iowa State University *M, D*

Massachusetts
Tufts University *M, D*

Minnesota
University of Minnesota
Twin Cities *M, D*

Montana
University of Montana *M, D*

New York
Fordham University *M*
SUNY
University at Albany *D*

Institutional food production

Alabama
Bishop State Community
College *C, A*
Jefferson Davis Community
College *C*
Shelton State Community College *C*

Arizona
Central Arizona College *C*
Mesa Community College *C, A*
Phoenix College *C, A*

California
American River College *A*
Bakersfield College *C, A*
Cerritos College *C*
Chaffey College *C*
College of the Redwoods *C*
College of the Sequoias *C*
Cypress College *C, A*
Fresno City College *C, A*
Long Beach City College *C, A*
Los Angeles Mission College *A*
Los Angeles Trade and Technical
College *C, A*
Modesto Junior College *C*
Monterey Peninsula College *A*
Ohlone College *C, A*
Orange Coast College *C, A*
Point Loma Nazarene University *B*
Santa Barbara City College *C, A*
Santa Rosa Junior College *C*
Shasta College *A*

Connecticut
Gateway Community College *C, A*
Manchester Community College *A*
Naugatuck Valley Community
College *A*

Delaware
Delaware Technical Community
College
Stanton/Wilmington Campus *C*

Florida
Eastern Florida State College *C*
Indian River State College *C*

Johnson & Wales University
North Miami *B*
Pensacola State College *A*

Georgia
Augusta Technical College *C*

Hawaii
University of Hawaii
Honolulu Community College *C, A*
Kapiolani Community College *C, A*

Illinois
City Colleges of Chicago
Harold Washington College *C*
Harry S. Truman College *C*
Kennedy-King College *C*
Malcolm X College *C*
Harper College *C, A*
Lexington College *A, B*

Iowa
Iowa State University *B*
Iowa Western Community College *A*

Kansas
Coffeyville Community College *A*
Johnson County Community
College *C, A*

Kentucky
Eastern Kentucky University *A*

Maine
Eastern Maine Community College *C*
Washington County Community
College *C*

Maryland
Anne Arundel Community College *C*
Montgomery College *C, A*

Massachusetts
Simmons College *B*

Michigan
Central Michigan University *B*
Mott Community College *A*
Northern Michigan University *A*
Wayne County Community
College *C, A*
Western Michigan University *B*

Mississippi
Mississippi Gulf Coast Community
College *C*

Missouri
Metropolitan Community College -
Kansas City *C*
Northwest Missouri State
University *B*
St. Louis Community College *A*

Nebraska
Metropolitan Community College *A*

Nevada
Truckee Meadows Community
College *C, A*

New Hampshire
University of New Hampshire *A*

New Mexico
Central New Mexico Community
College *C*

New York
Monroe Community College *C, A*
SUNY
College at Oneonta *B*
College of Agriculture and
Technology at Morrisville *A*
College of Technology at Delhi *A*

Sullivan County Community
College *C*
Westchester Community College *A*

North Carolina
Asheville-Buncombe Technical
Community College *A*
Cape Fear Community College *C, A*

Ohio
Ohio University *B*

Pennsylvania
Bucks County Community
College *C, A*
Butler County Community
College *C, A*
Community College of
Philadelphia *C, A*
Harrisburg Area Community
College *C, A*
Luzerne County Community
College *A*

Puerto Rico
Inter American University of Puerto
Rico
Aguadilla Campus *C, A*
Bayamon Campus *C*

Tennessee
Lipscomb University *B*
Southwest Tennessee Community
College *C*

Texas
El Paso Community College *A*
Sam Houston State University *B*
Texas Woman's University *M*

Virginia
Northern Virginia Community
College *A*

Washington
Central Washington University *B*

Wisconsin
Blackhawk Technical College *A*
Milwaukee Area Technical College *C*
Northeast Wisconsin Technical
College *C*
University of Wisconsin
Stout *B*
Wisconsin Indianhead Technical
College *C*

Institutional food service

California
Santa Barbara City College *C, A*
Shasta College *C*

Georgia
Atlanta Technical College *C*

Mississippi
Hinds Community College *C, A*

New Jersey
Atlantic Cape Community College *A*

New Mexico
Southwestern Indian Polytechnic
Institute *A*

North Carolina
Central Carolina Community
College *C*
James Sprunt Community College *C*

Pennsylvania

Immaculata University *A, B*
Montgomery County Community
    College *C*

South Carolina

Greenville Technical College *C*
Trident Technical College *C, A*

Texas

Lamar Institute of Technology *C, A*
San Jacinto College *C*
Texas State Technical College
    Harlingen *A*

Instrumentation technology

Alabama

Bishop State Community College *A*

Alaska

University of Alaska
    Anchorage *A*
    Fairbanks *C*

Arkansas

University of Arkansas
    Monticello *C*

Colorado

Colorado Northwestern Community
    College *C, A*

Georgia

Central Georgia Technical College *C*

Idaho

Idaho State University *C, A, B*

Illinois

Illinois Eastern Community Colleges
    Wabash Valley College *C*
Kaskaskia College *C*
Moraine Valley Community
    College *C, A*

Louisiana

ITI Technical College *C, A*

Maryland

Hagerstown Community College *A*

Michigan

Northern Michigan University *B*

Minnesota

Ridgewater College *C, A*
St. Cloud Technical and Community
    College *C, A*

Missouri

Ozarks Technical Community
    College *C, A*

New Mexico

San Juan College *C, A*
Southwestern Indian Polytechnic
    Institute *A*

New York

Excelsior College *A*
Finger Lakes Community College *A*
Monroe Community College *C, A*

North Carolina

Cape Fear Community College *A*

North Dakota

Bismarck State College *C, A*

Ohio

Cincinnati State Technical and
    Community College *C*
Sinclair Community College *C*

Oklahoma

Oklahoma State University
    Institute of Technology:
    Okmulgee *B*

Pennsylvania

Butler County Community College *A*

Puerto Rico

National University College
    Arecibo *A*
University College of San Juan *A*
University of Puerto Rico
    Bayamon University College *A*

Texas

Houston Community College
    System *C, A*
Lamar Institute of Technology *C, A*
St. Philip's College *A*
San Jacinto College *C, A*
Texas A&M University
    Corpus Christi *B*
Texas State Technical College
    Waco *A*
Victoria College *C, A*

Utah

Salt Lake Community College *A*

Virginia

New River Community College *A*

Washington

Bellingham Technical College *A*
Yakima Valley Community College *A*

Wisconsin

Mid-State Technical College *A*

Wyoming

Western Wyoming Community
    College *C, A*

Insurance

Arizona

Pima Community College *C*

Arkansas

University of Central Arkansas *B*

California

California State University
    Sacramento *B*
East Los Angeles College *C, A*
Fresno City College *C, A*
Los Angeles Southwest College *A*
Palomar College *C, A*
San Diego State University *B*
San Joaquin Delta College *C*
Santa Ana College *C, A*
Santa Monica College *C, A*
University of San Francisco *M*

Connecticut

University of Hartford *B*

District of Columbia

Howard University *B*

Florida

Florida State College at
    Jacksonville *C, A*
Florida State University *B, M, D*
Miami Dade College *C*

Georgia

Brenau University *M*
Central Georgia Technical College *C*
Columbus Technical College *C*
Georgia State University *B, M, D*
University of Georgia *B*

Idaho

Idaho State University *B*

Illinois

Bradley University *B*
Heartland Community College *C, A*
Illinois State University *B*
Illinois Wesleyan University *B*
University of Illinois
    Urbana-Champaign *B, M, D*

Indiana

Indiana State University *B*
Martin University *B*

Iowa

Ellsworth Community College *A*

Kentucky

Eastern Kentucky University *B*

Louisiana

University of Louisiana at Lafayette *B*
University of Louisiana at Monroe *B*

Massachusetts

Boston University *M*
Quinsigamond Community College *C*

Michigan

Delta College *C*
Ferris State University *B*
Mott Community College *C*
Olivet College *B, M*

Minnesota

Saint Cloud State University *B*
University of Minnesota
    Twin Cities *B*

Mississippi

Delta State University *B*
Hinds Community College *A*
Mississippi State University *B*
University of Mississippi *B*

Missouri

Missouri State University *B*

Nebraska

University of Nebraska
    Lincoln *B*

New York

Excelsior College *B*
Hudson Valley Community College *A*
Pace University *M*
St. John's University *B, M*

North Carolina

Appalachian State University *B*
Isothermal Community College *C*
Pitt Community College *C*

Ohio

Bowling Green State University *B*
Davis College *A*
Franklin University *B*
Kent State University
    Salem *B*
Ohio Northern University *B*
Ohio State University
    Columbus Campus *B*

Oklahoma

Oklahoma City Community College *C*
Tulsa Community College *C, A*
University of Central Oklahoma *B*

Pennsylvania

Gannon University *B*
La Salle University *B*
Saint Joseph's University *B*
Temple University *B, M*
University of Pennsylvania *B, M, D*

Puerto Rico

Inter American University of Puerto
    Rico
    Metropolitan Campus *C*
Universidad del Este *B*

South Carolina

University of South Carolina
    Columbia *B*

South Dakota

Southeast Technical Institute *A*

Texas

Baylor University *B*
Southern Methodist University *B*
University of Houston
    Downtown *B*
University of North Texas *B*

Washington

Bellevue College *C*
Renton Technical College *C*

Wisconsin

Madison Area Technical College *A*
Northcentral Technical College *A*
University of Wisconsin
    Madison *B, M*

Integrated circuit design

Arizona

Pima Community College *C*

Idaho

University of Idaho *C*

Texas

Collin County Community College
    District *C, A*

Intercultural/diversity studies

Alabama

University of Mobile *B*

California

Biola University *B*
College of San Mateo *A*
Foothill College *A*
Humboldt State University *B*
MiraCosta College *A*
Pitzer College *B*
Shasta College *A*
Stanford University *B*
University of California
    Berkeley *M*
Vanguard University of Southern
    California *B*

Colorado

Colorado Heights University *A, B*

Hawaii

Brigham Young University-Hawaii *B*

Idaho

University of Idaho *C*

Illinois

Judson University *B*
Trinity International University *D*

Indiana

Anderson University *M*
Indiana Wesleyan University *A, B*

Iowa

Divine Word College *A, B*

Kentucky

Midway College *B*
University of Louisville *C*

Maine

College of the Atlantic *B, M*

Maryland

Howard Community College *A*

Massachusetts

Bard College at Simon's Rock *B*
Lesley University *M*
University of Massachusetts
    Lowell *B*

Minnesota

Macalester College *B*
North Central University *B*
St. Catherine University *B*
University of Northwestern - St.
    Paul *B*

Missouri

Calvary Bible College and Theological
    Seminary *B*
Webster University *C*

Nebraska

Concordia University *B*

New Jersey

Montclair State University *B*

New York

Alfred University *B*
Columbia University *B*
Fordham University *B*
Ithaca College *B*

Ohio

Antioch University
    Midwest *M*

Oregon

Northwest Christian University *B*

Pennsylvania

Chestnut Hill College *C*
Villanova University *B*

Puerto Rico

University of Puerto Rico
    Rio Piedras *B*

South Carolina

Columbia International
    University *B, M*
Southern Wesleyan University *B*
Wofford College *B*

Tennessee

Tennessee Wesleyan College *B*
Trevecca Nazarene University *B*
Union University *B, M*

Texas

Dallas Christian College *B*
South Texas College *A*
University of Houston
    Clear Lake *M*
University of Texas
    Austin *C*
    San Antonio *M*
University of the Incarnate Word *B*

Washington

Evergreen State College *B*
University of Washington
    Tacoma *B, M*
Western Washington University *M*

Interior architecture

Alabama

Auburn University *B*

Arizona

Arizona State University *M*

California

California State Polytechnic
    University: Pomona *M*
California State University
    Long Beach *B*
    Sacramento *B, M*
City College of San Francisco *A*
Cosumnes River College *C, A*
Otis College of Art and Design *B*
Woodbury University *B, M*

Colorado

Westwood College
    Denver North *B*
    Denver South *B*

Connecticut

University of New Haven *B*

Florida

Florida International University *M*
Florida State College at
    Jacksonville *A*
Palm Beach State College *A*
Seminole State College of Florida *A*

Idaho

Brigham Young University-Idaho *B*

Illinois

Columbia College Chicago *B*
Illinois Central College *A*
School of the Art Institute of
    Chicago *B, M*

Indiana

Indiana State University *B*

Kansas

Kansas State University *M*

Kentucky

Sullivan College of Technology and
    Design *A*

Louisiana

Louisiana State University and
    Agricultural and Mechanical
    College *B*
Louisiana Tech University *B*
University of Louisiana at Lafayette *B*

Maryland

Anne Arundel Community
    College *C, A*

Massachusetts

Boston Architectural College *B, M*

Michigan

Central Michigan University *B*
Lawrence Technological University *B*

Mississippi

Mississippi State University *B*
University of Southern Mississippi *B*

Nebraska

Metropolitan Community College *A*
University of Nebraska
    Lincoln *B*

Nevada

University of Nevada
    Las Vegas *B*

New York

SUNY
    College of Technology at Alfred *A*
Suffolk County Community College *A*

North Carolina

Cape Fear Community College *A*

Ohio

Bowling Green State University *B*
Miami University
    Oxford *B*

Oklahoma

University of Oklahoma *M*

Oregon

University of Oregon *B, M*

Pennsylvania

Chatham University *B, M*
La Roche College *B*
Philadelphia University *B*

Rhode Island

Rhode Island School of Design *B, M*

Texas

Lamar University *B*
Sam Houston State University *B*
Stephen F. Austin State University *B*
Texas A&M University
    Kingsville *B, M*
Texas Tech University *B*
University of Houston *B*
University of North Texas *B*
University of Texas
    Arlington *B*
    San Antonio *B*

Wisconsin

University of Wisconsin
    Stevens Point *B*

Interior design

Alabama

Samford University *B*
University of Alabama *B*
Virginia College
    Birmingham *A, B*

Arizona

Arizona State University *B*
Art Institute of Phoenix *B*
Art Institute of Tucson *B*
Glendale Community College *C*
Mesa Community College *C, A*
Northern Arizona University *B*
Phoenix College *C, A*
Scottsdale Community College *C, A*
Southwest University of Visual Arts *B*

Arkansas

Harding University *B*
University of Arkansas *B*
University of Central Arkansas *B*

California

Academy of Art University *C, A, B, M*
Allan Hancock College *A*
American River College *A*
Antelope Valley College *C, A*
Art Center College of Design *B, M*
Art Institute of California
    Hollywood *B*
    Inland Empire *B*
    Los Angeles *B*
    Orange County *A, B*
    Sacramento *B*
    San Diego *B*
    San Francisco *B*
    Silicon Valley *B*
California College of the Arts *B*
California State University
    Fresno *B*
    Long Beach *B, M*
Canada College *C, A*
Cerritos College *A*
Chaffey College *C, A*
City College of San Francisco *A*
College of the Canyons *C, A*
Cosumnes River College *C, A*
Cuesta College *C, A*
Design Institute of San Diego *B*
Fashion Institute of Design and
    Merchandising
    Los Angeles *A*
    San Francisco *A*
Interior Designers
    Institute *C, A, B, M*
International Academy of Design and
    Technology
    Sacramento *C, A, B*
Long Beach City College *C, A*
Los Angeles Harbor College *A*
Los Angeles Mission College *C, A*
Modesto Junior College *C, A*
Monterey Peninsula College *C, A*
Mount San Antonio College *C, A*
Ohlone College *C, A*
Orange Coast College *C, A*
Otis College of Art and Design *B*
Palomar College *C, A*
Point Loma Nazarene University *B*
Saddleback College *C, A*
San Diego Mesa College *C, A*
San Diego State University *B*
San Francisco State University *B*
San Joaquin Delta College *C, A*
San Jose State University *B*
Santa Barbara City College *C, A*
Santa Monica College *C, A*
Santa Rosa Junior College *C*
Solano Community College *C, A*
West Valley College *C, A*
Westwood College
    Inland Empire *B*
    Los Angeles *B*
    South Bay *B*

Colorado

Arapahoe Community College *C, A*
Colorado State University *B, M*
Front Range Community College *C, A*
Pikes Peak Community College *C, A*
Red Rocks Community College *A*
Rocky Mountain College of Art &
    Design *B*
Westwood College
    Denver South *B*

Connecticut

Norwalk Community College *A*
Paier College of Art *C, B*
University of Bridgeport *B*

Delaware

Delaware College of Art and
   Design *C, A*
Delaware Technical Community
   College
   Terry Campus *A*

District of Columbia

Corcoran College of Art and
   Design *C, B, M*
George Washington University *B, M*
Howard University *B*

Florida

Art Institute of Fort
   Lauderdale *C, A, B*
Broward College *A*
Daytona State College *A*
Florida State College at
   Jacksonville *A*
Florida State University *B, M*
Indian River State College *A*
International Academy of Design and
   Technology
   Orlando *B*
International Academy of Design and
   Technology: Tampa *A, B*
Miami International University of Art
   and Design *B, M*
Palm Beach State College *A*
Ringling College of Art and Design *B*
Seminole State College of
   Florida *A, B*
Southwest Florida College *A, B*
University of Florida *B, M*

Georgia

Art Institute of Atlanta *B*
Athens Technical College *C, A*
Brenau University *B, M*
Georgia Southern University *B*
Gwinnett Technical College *C, A*
Savannah College of Art and
   Design *B, M*
Valdosta State University *B*

Hawaii

Chaminade University of
   Honolulu *A, B*

Idaho

Brigham Young University-Idaho *B*
University of Idaho *B*

Illinois

Black Hawk College *A*
Columbia College Chicago *B, M*
Illinois Institute of Art
   Chicago *A, B*
   Schaumburg *C, B*
Joliet Junior College *A*
Judson University *B*
Robert Morris University: Chicago *A*
School of the Art Institute of
   Chicago *B, M*
Southern Illinois University
   Carbondale *B*
Triton College *A*

Indiana

Indiana University
   Bloomington *B*
   Purdue University Fort Wayne *A, B*
   Purdue University
      Indianapolis *A, B*
Indiana Wesleyan University *B*
Ivy Tech Community College
   Columbus *A*
   North Central *A*
   Southwest *A*
Purdue University *B, M*

Iowa

Hawkeye Community College *A*
Iowa State University *B, M*
Kirkwood Community College *A*
University of Northern Iowa *B*
Western Iowa Tech Community
   College *C, A*

Kansas

Johnson County Community
   College *C, A*
Kansas State University *B*
University of Kansas *B*
Wichita Area Technical College *C, A*

Kentucky

Bluegrass Community and Technical
   College *A*
Eastern Kentucky University *B*
Sullivan College of Technology and
   Design *A, B*
University of Kentucky *B*
Western Kentucky University *C*

Louisiana

Delgado Community College *C, A*

Maryland

Anne Arundel Community
   College *C, A*
Harford Community College *C, A*
Maryland Institute College of Art *B*
Montgomery College *A*

Massachusetts

Bay Path College *C, B*
Becker College *B*
Endicott College *B, M*
Massachusetts Bay Community
   College *C*
Mount Ida College *B*
New England Institute of Art *B*
Newbury College *B*
Suffolk University *C, B, M*
University of Massachusetts
   Amherst *M*
Wentworth Institute of Technology *B*

Michigan

Adrian College *B*
Art Institute of Michigan *A, B*
Baker College
   Allen Park *A*
   Auburn Hills *A*
   Cadillac *A*
   Clinton Township *A*
   Flint *A, B*
   Muskegon *A*
   Owosso *A*
College for Creative Studies *B*
Delta College *A*
Eastern Michigan University *B, M*
Ferris State University *B*
Finlandia University *B*
Grand Rapids Community College *A*
Henry Ford Community College *A*
International Academy of Design and
   Technology
   Detroit *A, B*
Lawrence Technological University *M*
Michigan State University *B, M*
Oakland Community College *A*
Western Michigan University *B*

Minnesota

Alexandria Technical and Community
   College *C, A*
Art Institutes International
   Minnesota *A, B*
Century College *C, A*
Dakota County Technical
   College *C, A*
Dunwoody College of Technology *B*

University of Minnesota
   Twin Cities *B*

Mississippi

Mississippi College *B*
Mississippi Gulf Coast Community
   College *A*
Northeast Mississippi Community
   College *A*

Missouri

Maryville University of Saint Louis *B*
Park University *B*
Stephens College *B*
Stevens Institute of Business &
   Arts *C, A, B*
University of Central Missouri *B*

Montana

Montana State University *A*
Montana State University
   Great Falls College *A*

Nevada

Art Institute of Las Vegas *B*
International Academy of Design and
   Technology
   Henderson *B*

New Hampshire

Manchester Community College *C, A*
Mount Washington College *A*

New Jersey

Berkeley College *A, B*
Brookdale Community College *A*
Kean University *B*
New Jersey Institute of Technology *B*
Raritan Valley Community College *A*

New Mexico

Santa Fe Community College *C, A*
Southwest University of Visual Arts *B*

New York

Art Institute of New York City *A*
Cazenovia College *B*
Fashion Institute of Technology *A, B*
Marist College *B*
Monroe Community College *C, A*
Nassau Community College *C, A*
New York Institute of Technology *B*
New York School of Interior
   Design *C, A, B, M*
Onondaga Community College *A*
Parsons The New School for
   Design *C, A, B, M*
Pratt Institute *B, M*
Rochester Institute of
   Technology *B, M*
SUNY
   College at Buffalo *B*
   College of Technology at Alfred *A*
Sage Colleges *B*
School of Visual Arts *B*
Suffolk County Community College *A*
Villa Maria College of Buffalo *C, A, B*

North Carolina

Appalachian State University *B*
Cape Fear Community College *A*
Carteret Community College *C, A*
Central Piedmont Community
   College *C, A*
East Carolina University *B*
Forsyth Technical Community
   College *A*
High Point University *B*
Meredith College *B*
Queens University of Charlotte *B, M*
Randolph Community College *C, A*
Salem College *B*
University of North Carolina
   Greensboro *B, M*

Western Carolina University *B*
Western Piedmont Community
   College *C, A*

North Dakota

North Dakota State University *B*

Ohio

Antonelli College
   Cincinnati *A*
Art Institute of Ohio: Cincinnati *A, B*
Cleveland Institute of Art *B*
Columbus College of Art and
   Design *B*
Davis College *A*
Kent State University *B*
Ohio State University
   Columbus Campus *B*
Sinclair Community College *A*
University of Cincinnati *B, M*
Ursuline College *B*
Virginia Marti College of Art and
   Design *A*

Oklahoma

Oklahoma Christian University *B*
Tulsa Community College *C, A*
University of Central Oklahoma *B, M*
University of Oklahoma *M*

Oregon

Art Institute of Portland *A, B*
Marylhurst University *B*
Oregon State University *B*
Portland Community College *C, A*

Pennsylvania

Arcadia University *B*
Art Institute of Philadelphia *A, B*
Art Institute of Pittsburgh *A, B*
Art Institute of York *A, B*
Drexel University *B, M*
Harcum College *A*
Indiana University of Pennsylvania *B*
Lehigh Carbon Community College *A*
Marywood University *B, M*
Mercyhurst University *B*
Moore College of Art and
   Design *B, M*
Northampton Community
   College *C, A*
Philadelphia University *B*

Puerto Rico

EDP University of Puerto Rico: Hato
   Rey *A, B*
Turabo University *B*
Universal Technology College of
   Puerto Rico *C*
University of Puerto Rico
   Carolina Regional College *A*

Rhode Island

New England Institute of
   Technology *A, B*

South Carolina

Anderson University *B*
Converse College *B*
Winthrop University *B*

South Dakota

South Dakota State University *B*

Tennessee

Carson-Newman University *B*
Freed-Hardeman University *B*
Middle Tennessee State University *B*
O'More College of Design *B*
Pellissippi State Community
   College *A*
University of Memphis *B*

University of Tennessee
   Chattanooga *B*
   Knoxville *B*
Watkins College of Art, Design &
   Film *A, B*

Texas

Abilene Christian University *B*
Amarillo College *C, A*
Art Institute of Houston *B*
Baylor University *B*
Collin County Community College
   District *C, A*
El Centro College *C, A*
El Paso Community College *C, A*
Houston Community College
   System *C, A*
Lone Star College System *C, A*
San Jacinto College *C, A*
Texas A&M University
   Kingsville *B*
Texas Christian University *B*
Texas State University *B*
University of Texas
   Austin *B, M*
University of the Incarnate Word *B*

Utah

Dixie State College *B*
LDS Business College *C, A*
Salt Lake Community College *C*
Utah State University *B, M*
Weber State University *A*

Virginia

Art Institute of Washington *B*
Lord Fairfax Community College *C*
Marymount University *B, M*
Northern Virginia Community
   College *A*
Tidewater Community College *A*
Virginia Commonwealth University *B*
Virginia Polytechnic Institute and
   State University *B*
Virginia Western Community
   College *C*
Westwood College
   Annandale *B*
   Arlington Ballston *B*

Washington

Art Institute of Seattle *A, B*
Bellevue College *C, A, B*
Clover Park Technical College *C, A*
Cornish College of the Arts *B*
International Academy of Design and
   Technology
   Seattle *A, B*
Seattle Pacific University *B*
Spokane Falls Community
   College *C, A*
Washington State University *B, M*

West Virginia

University of Charleston *B*

Wisconsin

Art Institute of Wisconsin *B*
Concordia University Wisconsin *B*
Fox Valley Technical College *A*
Gateway Technical College *A*
Madison Area Technical College *A*
Milwaukee Area Technical College *A*
Milwaukee Institute of Art &
   Design *B*
Mount Mary University *B*
University of Wisconsin
   Madison *B*
   Stevens Point *B*
Waukesha County Technical
   College *A*
Western Technical College *A*

International agriculture

California

University of California
   Davis *B, M*

Illinois

University of Illinois
   Urbana-Champaign *B*

Indiana

Purdue University *B*

Iowa

Iowa State University *B*

Massachusetts

University of Massachusetts
   Amherst *C*

New York

Cornell University *B, M*

North Dakota

North Dakota State University *M*

Utah

Utah State University *B*

International business

Alabama

Auburn University *B*
Birmingham-Southern College *B*
Columbia Southern University *C*
Samford University *B*
Troy University *M*

Arizona

Dunlap-Stone University *A, B*
GateWay Community College *A*
Mesa Community College *C*
Northcentral University *B, M, D*
Paradise Valley Community College *A*
Rio Salado College *A*
Scottsdale Community College *A*
South Mountain Community
   College *A*
Western International University *M*

Arkansas

Arkansas State University *B*
Harding University *B*
John Brown University *B*
University of Arkansas *B*
University of Arkansas
   Little Rock *B*

California

Azusa Pacific University *M*
Biola University *B*
California Lutheran University *M*
California State University
   Dominguez Hills *B*
   East Bay *B*
   Fresno *B*
   Fullerton *B, M*
   Long Beach *B*
   Sacramento *B, M*
   San Bernardino *B*
Dominican University of California *M*
Foothill College *A*
Fresno Pacific University *B*
Fullerton College *A*
Golden Gate University *B, M*
Grossmont College *A*
Holy Names University *B*
Lincoln University *B, M*
Marymount California University *B*
Master's College *B*
Menlo College *B*
Monterey Peninsula College *A*

Mount St. Mary's College *B*
National University *M*
Orange Coast College *A*
Pacific States University *M, D*
Palomar College *C, A*
Pepperdine University *B, M*
Rio Hondo College *C, A*
St. Mary's College of California *B*
San Diego State University *B, M*
San Joaquin Delta College *C*
San Jose State University *B*
Santa Ana College *A*
Santa Barbara City College *A*
Santa Monica College *C*
Southwestern College *A*
University of La Verne *B*
University of San Diego *B, M*
University of San Francisco *B*
University of Southern California *M*
University of the West *B, M*
Vanguard University of Southern
   California *B*

Colorado

Adams State University *B*
Arapahoe Community College *A*
Colorado Heights University *A, B, M*
University of Colorado
   Denver *M*
University of Denver *B, M*

Connecticut

Albertus Magnus College *B*
Central Connecticut State
   University *B*
Post University *B*
Quinnipiac University *B*
University of Bridgeport *B, M*
Yale University *M*

Delaware

Goldey-Beacom College *B, M*

District of Columbia

Catholic University of America *B*
George Washington University *B, M*
Georgetown University *B, M*
Howard University *B*
Strayer University *B*
University of the Potomac *C, A, B*

Florida

Barry University *B*
Bethune-Cookman University *B*
Broward College *A*
Eckerd College *B*
Edison State College *A*
Everest University
   Largo *A, B*
   Pompano Beach *A, B*
Florida Atlantic University *B, M*
Florida Institute of Technology *B*
Florida International University *B, M*
Florida State University *B*
Jacksonville University *B*
Lynn University *B*
Northwood University
   Florida *B*
Nova Southeastern University *M*
Palm Beach Atlantic University *B*
Rollins College *A*
St. Petersburg College *B*
Saint Thomas University *B, M*
Schiller International
   University *A, B, M*
Southeastern University *B*
Stetson University *B*
University of Miami *B, M*
University of North Florida *B*
University of South Florida *B*
University of South Florida
   Saint Petersburg *B*
University of Tampa *B*
Webber International University *M*

Georgia

Georgia Southern University *B*
Georgia State University *C, M*
Kennesaw State University *B*
Mercer University *B, M*
University of Georgia *B*
Valdosta State University *B*
Wesleyan College *B*

Hawaii

Hawaii Pacific University *B*
Remington College
   Honolulu *B*
University of Hawaii
   Manoa *B, D*

Idaho

Boise State University *B*
Northwest Nazarene University *B*

Illinois

Augustana College *B*
Benedictine University *B*
Black Hawk College *C*
Bradley University *B*
Dominican University *B*
Elmhurst College *B*
Harper College *A*
Illinois Central College *A*
Illinois State University *B*
Illinois Wesleyan University *B*
Lewis University *B*
Loyola University Chicago *B*
Millikin University *B*
Monmouth College *B*
North Central College *B, M*
Northwestern University *M*
Oakton Community College *A*
Olivet Nazarene University *B*
Rasmussen College
   Aurora *A*
Roosevelt University *M*
Saint Xavier University *B, M*
University of St. Francis *B*

Indiana

Anderson University *B*
Butler University *B*
Grace College *B*
Indiana University
   Southeast *C*
Taylor University *B*
University of Evansville *B*
University of Indianapolis *B*
Valparaiso University *B, M*

Iowa

AIB College of Business *A*
Ashford University *B*
Buena Vista University *B*
Central College *B*
Coe College *B*
Drake University *B*
Iowa State University *B*
St. Ambrose University *B*
Simpson College *B*
Upper Iowa University *B, M*
Waldorf College *B*
Wartburg College *B*

Kansas

Baker University *B*
Benedictine College *B*
Friends University *B, M*
McPherson College *B*
Pittsburg State University *B*
Wichita State University *B*

Kentucky

Murray State University *B*
Northern Kentucky University *C*
Western Kentucky University *B*

Louisiana

Herzing University
    Kenner *B*
Louisiana State University and
    Agricultural and Mechanical
    College *B*
Loyola University New Orleans *B*

Maine

Husson University *B*
Maine Maritime Academy *B, M*
Saint Joseph's College of Maine *B*
Thomas College *B*

Maryland

Carroll Community College *A*
Frederick Community College *A*
Howard Community College *A*
Montgomery College *A*
Notre Dame of Maryland
    University *B*
University of Baltimore *B, M*
University of Maryland
    College Park *B*
    University College *B, M*

Massachusetts

American International College *B, M*
Assumption College *B*
Babson College *B, M*
Bentley University *M*
Boston University *B*
Brandeis University *M*
Bristol Community College *C*
Bunker Hill Community College *A*
Elms College *B*
Emerson College *M*
Endicott College *B*
Fitchburg State University *B*
Lasell College *B*
Massachusetts College of Liberal
    Arts *B*
Merrimack College *B*
Newbury College *B*
Nichols College *B*
Northeastern University *B, M*
Northern Essex Community
    College *A*
Salem State University *B*
Simmons College *B*
Stonehill College *B*
Suffolk University *B, M*
University of Massachusetts
    Boston *M*
    Dartmouth *C*
Western New England University *B*

Michigan

Adrian College *B*
Aquinas College *B*
Baker College
    Flint *M*
    Port Huron *B*
Central Michigan University *B, M*
Cornerstone University *B*
Davenport University *B*
Delta College *A*
Eastern Michigan University *B, M*
Finlandia University *B*
Grace Bible College *B*
Grand Valley State University *B*
Kuyper College *B*
Lansing Community College *A*
Madonna University *B, M*
Marygrove College *B*
Muskegon Community College *A*
Northwood University
    Michigan *B*
Oakland Community College *A*
Saginaw Valley State University *B*
University of Michigan
    Flint *B, M*
Wayne County Community College *C*
Wayne State University *B*

Minnesota

Augsburg College *B*
Concordia College: Moorhead *B*
Gustavus Adolphus College *B*
Hamline University *B*
Inver Hills Community College *A*
Metropolitan State University *B*
Minnesota State University
    Mankato *B*
    Moorhead *C*
National American University
    Bloomington *B*
St. Catherine University *B*
Saint Cloud State University *B*
St. Mary's University of
    Minnesota *B, M*
University of Minnesota
    Twin Cities *B*
University of Northwestern - St.
    Paul *B*
University of St. Thomas *B*

Mississippi

East Mississippi Community
    College *A*
University of Southern Mississippi *B*

Missouri

Avila University *B*
Central Methodist University *B*
College of the Ozarks *B*
Columbia College *B*
Lindenwood University *B, M*
Maryville University of Saint Louis *B*
Missouri Southern State University *B*
Northwest Missouri State
    University *B*
St. Louis Community College *A*
Saint Louis University *B, M, D*
Southeast Missouri State University *B*
Southwest Baptist University *B*
University of Missouri
    Columbia *B*
    St. Louis *B, M*
Washington University in St. Louis *B*
Webster University *M*
William Woods University *B*

Montana

University of Montana *B*

Nebraska

Creighton University *B*
Nebraska Wesleyan University *B*
Northeast Community College *A*
Union College *B*
University of Nebraska
    Lincoln *B*

Nevada

University of Nevada
    Reno *B*

New Hampshire

Southern New Hampshire
    University *B, M, D*

New Jersey

Berkeley College *A, B*
Caldwell College *B*
Felician College *B*
Kean University *B*
Monmouth University *B*
New Jersey Institute of
    Technology *B, M*
Passaic County Community College *A*
Ramapo College of New Jersey *B*
Rider University *B*
Saint Peter's University *A, B, M*
Seton Hall University *M*
Thomas Edison State College *B*

New Mexico

New Mexico Highlands University *B*
New Mexico State University *B*

New York

Berkeley College *A, B*
Berkeley College of New York
    City *A, B*
Canisius College *B*
City University of New York
    Baruch College *M*
    Queens College *B*
Concordia College *B*
D'Youville College *M*
Daemen College *M*
Dominican College of Blauvelt *B*
Elmira College *B*
Excelsior College *B*
Fashion Institute of Technology *M*
Fordham University *B, M*
Herkimer County Community
    College *A*
Hilbert College *A*
Hofstra University *C, B, M*
Hudson Valley Community College *A*
Iona College *B*
Long Island University
    LIU Post *B*
Manhattan College *B*
Manhattanville College *M*
Monroe Community College *A*
Nazareth College *B*
New York Institute of Technology *B*
New York University *C, B*
Niagara University *B*
Pace University *B, M*
Pace University: Pleasantville/
    Briarcliff *B, M*
Rochester Institute of Technology *M*
Rockland Community College *A*
SUNY
    College at Brockport *B*
    College at New Paltz *B, M*
    College at Plattsburgh *B*
    University at Binghamton *B*
    University at Buffalo *B, M*
Tompkins Cortland Community
    College *A*
Touro College *M*
Wagner College *B*
Westchester Community College *A*
Yeshiva University *B*

North Carolina

Appalachian State University *B*
Campbell University *B*
Central Piedmont Community
    College *C, A*
Elon University *B*
Forsyth Technical Community
    College *A*
Gardner-Webb University *B, M*
High Point University *B*
Lenoir-Rhyne University *B*
Mars Hill University *B*
Montreat College *B*
Pfeiffer University *B*
Piedmont Community College *A*
St. Andrews University *B*
Salem College *B*
University of North Carolina
    Charlotte *B*
    Greensboro *B*
Western Carolina University *B*

North Dakota

Minot State University *B*
University of Jamestown *B*

Ohio

Ashland University *B*
Baldwin Wallace University *C, B, M*
Bowling Green State University *B*
Cedarville University *B*
Cleveland State University *B*
Columbus State Community
    College *C, A*
John Carroll University *B*
Lake Erie College *B*
Marietta College *B*
Miami University
    Oxford *B*
Mount Vernon Nazarene University *B*
Muskingum University *B*
Northwest State Community
    College *A*
Notre Dame College *B*
Ohio Dominican University *B*
Ohio Northern University *B*
Ohio State University
    Columbus Campus *B*
Ohio University *B*
Ohio Wesleyan University *B*
Owens Community College
    Toledo *A*
Stark State College *A*
Tiffin University *B, M*
University of Akron *C, B, M*
University of Cincinnati *B*
University of Dayton *B*
University of Findlay *B*
University of Mount Union *B*
University of Toledo *B, M*
Walsh University *B*
Wright State University *B, M*
Xavier University *B*

Oklahoma

Mid-America Christian University *M*
Northeastern State University *B*
Oklahoma Baptist University *B*
Oklahoma Christian University *B, M*
Oklahoma State University *C, B*
Oral Roberts University *B*
University of Central Oklahoma *B*
University of Tulsa *B*

Oregon

Concordia University *B*
George Fox University *B*
Linfield College *B*
Portland State University *M*
University of Portland *B*
Warner Pacific College *B*

Pennsylvania

Albright College *B*
Arcadia University *B, M*
Bucknell University *B*
Carnegie Mellon University *B*
Chatham University *B*
Chestnut Hill College *B, M*
Clarion University of Pennsylvania *B*
DeSales University *B*
Dickinson College *B*
Duquesne University *B*
Eastern University *B*
Elizabethtown College *B*
Gannon University *B*
Gettysburg College *B*
Grove City College *B*
Holy Family University *B*
Indiana University of Pennsylvania *B*
Juniata College *B*
King's College *B*
La Roche College *B*
La Salle University *B*
Lehigh University *M*
Lycoming College *B*
Manor College *A*
Mansfield University of
    Pennsylvania *B*
Marywood University *B*
Mercyhurst University *B*
Messiah College *B*
Moravian College *B*
Neumann University *B*

Penn State
Erie, The Behrend College *B*
Harrisburg *B*
Philadelphia University *B*
Point Park University *M*
Saint Joseph's University *B, M*
St. Vincent College *B*
Seton Hill University *B*
Temple University *B*
Thiel College *B*
University of Pennsylvania *B, M*
University of Pittsburgh *B, M*
University of Scranton *B, M*
Villanova University *B*
Washington & Jefferson College *B*
Waynesburg University *B*
Westminster College *B*
Widener University *B*

Puerto Rico
Inter American University of Puerto
Rico
Barranquitas Campus *M*
Metropolitan Campus *M, D*
Ponce Campus *B, M*
San German Campus *D*
Pontifical Catholic University of
Puerto Rico *B, M*
Universidad Metropolitana *M*
University of Puerto Rico
Humacao *B*
Rio Piedras *M, D*

Rhode Island
Bryant University *B, M*
Johnson & Wales University
Providence *B*
Roger Williams University *B*
University of Rhode Island *B*

South Carolina
College of Charleston *B*
Converse College *B*
North Greenville University *B*
University of South Carolina
Columbia *M*

South Dakota
Northern State University *B*

Tennessee
Belmont University *B*
Chattanooga State Community
College *C*
Christian Brothers University *B, M*
Lipscomb University *B*
Maryville College *B*
Rhodes College *B*
Southern Adventist University *B*
Trevecca Nazarene University *B*
Union University *B*
University of Memphis *B, M*

Texas
Angelo State University *B*
Austin Community College *A*
Baylor University *B*
Dallas Baptist University *M*
El Paso Community College *A*
Houston Community College
System *C, A*
Howard Payne University *C*
Huston-Tillotson University *B*
LeTourneau University *B*
Our Lady of the Lake University of
San Antonio *B, M*
St. Edward's University *B*
St. Mary's University *B*
Sam Houston State University *B*
San Jacinto College *C, A*
Southwestern Adventist University *B*
Stephen F. Austin State University *B*
Sul Ross State University *M*
Tarleton State University *B*

Texas A&M International
University *M, D*
Texas A&M University
Galveston *B*
Kingsville *B*
Texarkana *B*
Texas Christian University *B*
Texas Tech University *B, M*
Texas Wesleyan University *B*
Trinity University *B*
University of Dallas *M*
University of Houston
Downtown *B*
University of Texas
Arlington *B*
Brownsville *B*
Dallas *B, M, D*
El Paso *D*
Pan American *B*
San Antonio *B, M*
University of the Incarnate Word *B*

Utah
Utah State University *B*
Westminster College *B*

Vermont
Champlain College *B*

Virginia
Eastern Mennonite University *B*
Emory & Henry College *B*
James Madison University *B*
Northern Virginia Community
College *A*
Regent University *B*
Stratford University: Falls Church *M*
University of Management and
Technology *B*
University of the Potomac *C, A, B*

Washington
City University of Seattle *B*
Edmonds Community College *A*
Gonzaga University *B*
Highline Community College *A*
Seattle University *B, M*
Shoreline Community College *A*
University of Washington *B*
Walla Walla University *B*
Washington State University *B*
Western Washington University *B*
Whitworth University *B, M*

West Virginia
Bethany College *B*
Davis and Elkins College *B*
Marshall University *B*
West Virginia Wesleyan College *B*
Wheeling Jesuit University *B*

Wisconsin
Alverno College *B*
Cardinal Stritch University *B*
Herzing University
Brookfield *B*
Kenosha *B*
Madison *B*
Lakeland College *B*
Milwaukee School of
Engineering *B, M*
St. Norbert College *B*
University of Wisconsin
Eau Claire *B*
La Crosse *B*
Madison *B*
Milwaukee *C*
Superior *B*
Whitewater *B*

International economics

California
San Diego State University *B*
University of California
Los Angeles *B*
Santa Cruz *D*
University of San Francisco *B*

Colorado
Colorado College *B*

Connecticut
University of Hartford *B*

District of Columbia
American University *M*
Catholic University of America *M*
Georgetown University *B*

Florida
Schiller International University *B*

Georgia
Georgia State University *B*
University of West Georgia *B*

Indiana
Valparaiso University *B, M*

Louisiana
Tulane University *B*

Maine
College of the Atlantic *B*

Maryland
Howard Community College *A*

Massachusetts
Brandeis University *M, D*
Fitchburg State University *B*
Hampshire College *B*
Suffolk University *M*

Michigan
Albion College *B*
Eastern Michigan University *M*

Minnesota
University of St. Thomas *B*

New York
Pace University *M*
Pace University: Pleasantville/
Briarcliff *M*

North Carolina
Elon University *B*

Ohio
Youngstown State University *B*

Pennsylvania
Carnegie Mellon University *B*
Eastern University *M*
La Salle University *B*
Lafayette College *B*

Rhode Island
Salve Regina University *B*

Tennessee
Belmont University *B*
Rhodes College *B*

Texas
Austin College *B*
Texas Tech University *B*

Utah
Weber State University *C, B*

Virginia
University of Richmond *B*

Washington
University of Puget Sound *B*

Wisconsin
Carthage College *B*

International finance

California
National University *M*

Colorado
University of Denver *M*

Connecticut
University of Bridgeport *M*

District of Columbia
Catholic University of America *B*

Hawaii
Hawaii Pacific University *B*

Illinois
University of Illinois
Urbana-Champaign *M, D*

Massachusetts
Babson College *B*
Bentley University *M*
Boston University *B, M*
Brandeis University *M*

Missouri
Washington University in St. Louis *B*

Nebraska
Union College *B*

New Jersey
William Paterson University of New
Jersey *B*

New York
Broome Community College *A*
Ithaca College *C*
Pace University *M*
Pace University: Pleasantville/
Briarcliff *M*

Ohio
University of Akron *M*

Oklahoma
Oklahoma Baptist University *B*

Pennsylvania
Lycoming College *B*
Westminster College *B*

Texas
Texas A&M University
Galveston *B*
Texas Christian University *B*

Virginia
Stratford University: Falls Church *M*

West Virginia
Bethany College *B*

Wisconsin
Concordia University Wisconsin *B*

International/intercultural communication

California
Pacific Union College *B*
University of Southern California *M*
University of the Pacific *M*

Florida
Florida Institute of Technology *M*

Illinois
DePaul University *M*

Michigan
Michigan Technological University *B*

New York
Professional Business College *C*

Oregon
Linfield College *B*

Pennsylvania
Valley Forge Christian College *B*

Tennessee
Southern Adventist University *B*

Utah
Utah State University *B*

Wisconsin
University of Wisconsin
  Milwaukee *C*

International marketing

California
Allan Hancock College *C, A*
Sacramento City College *C, A*

Connecticut
Quinnipiac University *B, M*

Florida
Broward College *A*
Schiller International University *B*

Maine
Husson University *B*

Massachusetts
Babson College *B*
Boston University *M*

Michigan
Hillsdale College *B*

Minnesota
St. Paul College *C, A*

Missouri
Saint Louis University *D*

Nevada
University of Nevada
  Las Vegas *B*

New York
Fashion Institute of Technology *B*
Pace University *C, B*
Pace University: Pleasantville/
  Briarcliff *C, B*
SUNY
  College at Brockport *B*
  Farmingdale State College *C*
St. Thomas Aquinas College *B*

Oklahoma
Oral Roberts University *B*

Pennsylvania
Community College of
  Philadelphia *A*
La Salle University *B*
Philadelphia University *M*
Saint Joseph's University *M*
Waynesburg University *B*

Texas
Texas Christian University *B*

West Virginia
Davis and Elkins College *B*

Wisconsin
Waukesha County Technical
  College *A*

International policy analysis

Connecticut
University of Connecticut *B*

Maine
College of the Atlantic *B, M*

International public health

California
California Baptist University *B*
Loma Linda University *M, D*
University of Southern
  California *B, M*

District of Columbia
Catholic University of America *A*
Georgetown University *B, M, D*

Michigan
Central Michigan University *M*
University of Michigan *M*

Pennsylvania
Allegheny College *B*

Tennessee
Vanderbilt University *M*

Texas
University of Texas
  Health Science Center at
  Houston *M, D*

International relations

Alabama
Oakwood University *B*
Samford University *B*
Spring Hill College *B*
Troy University *M*
University of Alabama *B*

Arizona
Embry-Riddle Aeronautical University
  Prescott Campus *B*
Northern Arizona University *B*

Arkansas
Hendrix College *B*
University of Arkansas *B*
University of Arkansas
  Little Rock *B*

California
Allan Hancock College *A*
American Jewish University *B*

Azusa Pacific University *B*
Bakersfield College *A*
California Lutheran University *B*
California State University
  Chico *B*
  Fresno *M*
  Monterey Bay *B*
  Sacramento *M*
Canada College *A*
Cerritos College *A*
Claremont McKenna College *B*
Holy Names University *B*
Mills College *B*
Occidental College *B*
Pitzer College *B*
Pomona College *B*
Saddleback College *A*
San Francisco State University *B, M*
San Jose State University *B*
Solano Community College *A*
Stanford University *B, M*
University of California
  Davis *B*
  San Diego *D*
University of La Verne *B*
University of Redlands *B*
University of San Diego *B, M*
University of San Francisco *B*
University of Southern
  California *B, M, D*
University of the Pacific *B*
Ventura College *C, A*
Whittier College *B*

Colorado
University of Denver *B, M, D*

Connecticut
Connecticut College *B*
Fairfield University *B*
Trinity College *B*
University of Bridgeport *B, M*
Yale University *B, M*

Delaware
University of Delaware *B, M*

District of Columbia
American University *C, B, M, D*
Catholic University of America *M*
George Washington University *B, M*
Georgetown University *B, M*
Trinity Washington University *B*

Florida
Bethune-Cookman University *B*
Eckerd College *B*
Florida International
  University *B, M, D*
Florida State University *B, M*
Miami Dade College *A*
New College of Florida *B*
Nova Southeastern University *B*
Palm Beach State College *A*
Rollins College *B*
Saint Leo University *B*
Schiller International University *B, M*
Stetson University *B*
University of Florida *M*
University of Miami *B, M, D*
University of South Florida *B*
University of West Florida *B*

Georgia
Agnes Scott College *B*
Berry College *B*
Emory University *B*
Georgia Institute of Technology *B, M*
Georgia Southern University *B*
Kennesaw State University *B, M*
Mercer University *B*
Morehouse College *B*
Oglethorpe University *B*

Southern Polytechnic State
  University *B*
University of Georgia *B, M*
University of North Georgia *B, M*
University of West Georgia *B*
Wesleyan College *B*

Hawaii
Chaminade University of Honolulu *B*
Hawaii Pacific University *B*
University of Hawaii
  Hilo *M*

Idaho
Brigham Young University-Idaho *B*
College of Idaho *B*
Idaho State University *B*
Northwest Nazarene University *B*
University of Idaho *B*

Illinois
Benedictine University *B*
Bradley University *B*
DePaul University *B, M*
Dominican University *B*
John A. Logan College *A*
Knox College *B*
Lake Forest College *B*
Lewis University *B*
Loyola University Chicago *C, B*
MacMurray College *B*
McKendree University *B*
Monmouth College *B*
Northwestern University *B*
Rockford University *B*
Roosevelt University *B*
Saint Xavier University *B*
University of Chicago *B, M*
Wheaton College *B*

Indiana
Butler University *B*
Indiana University
  Bloomington *B*
  Purdue University Indianapolis *B*
  Southeast *B*
Indiana Wesleyan University *B*
Saint Joseph's College *B*
Taylor University *B*
University of Evansville *B*
University of Indianapolis *B*
University of Southern Indiana *B*
Valparaiso University *B*

Iowa
Cornell College *B*
Drake University *B*
Iowa State University *B*
Loras College *B*
Morningside College *B*
Mount Mercy University *B*
Simpson College *B*
Wartburg College *B*

Kansas
Kansas State University *M, D*

Kentucky
Centre College *B*
Murray State University *B*
Northern Kentucky University *B*
University of Kentucky *M*
Western Kentucky University *B*

Maine
Colby College *B*
College of the Atlantic *B, M*
University of Maine *B*
University of Southern Maine *B*

Maryland
Frostburg State University *C, B*
Goucher College *B*
Harford Community College *A*

Johns Hopkins University *B, M, D*
Mount St. Mary's University *B*
Notre Dame of Maryland
  University *B*
Towson University *B*
Washington College *B*

Massachusetts

American International College *B*
Bard College at Simon's Rock *B*
Boston College *B, M, D*
Boston University *B, M*
Clark University *B, M*
Elms College *B*
Fitchburg State University *B*
Gordon College *B*
Hampshire College *B*
Mount Holyoke College *B*
Northeastern University *B*
Regis College *B*
Simmons College *B*
Tufts University *B, M, D*
University of Massachusetts
  Amherst *C*
Wellesley College *B*
Wheaton College *B*

Michigan

Aquinas College *B*
Calvin College *B*
Central Michigan University *B*
Grand Valley State University *B*
Lake Superior State University *C*
Lansing Community College *A*
Michigan State University *B*
Northern Michigan University *B*
Oakland University *B*
Saginaw Valley State University *B*

Minnesota

Augsburg College *B*
Bethel University *B*
Carleton College *B*
Minnesota State University
  Mankato *B*
St. Catherine University *B*
Saint Cloud State University *B*
University of Minnesota
  Duluth *B*
  Twin Cities *B, M*
University of St. Thomas *B*

Mississippi

University of Mississippi *B*
University of Southern Mississippi *B*

Missouri

Drury University *B*
Lindenwood University *B*
Missouri Southern State University *B*
Missouri State University *M*
Saint Louis University *B*
Washington University in St.
  Louis *B, M*
Webster University *B, M*
Westminster College *B*
William Jewell College *B*

Montana

Carroll College *B*
University of Montana *B*

Nebraska

Bellevue University *B*
Creighton University *B, M*
Doane College *B*
Hastings College *B*
University of Nebraska
  Kearney *B*
  Lincoln *B*

Nevada

University of Nevada
  Reno *B*

New Hampshire

Saint Anselm College *B*

New Jersey

College of New Jersey *B*
Fairleigh Dickinson University
  Metropolitan Campus *B, M*
Rider University *B*
Rutgers, The State University of New
  Jersey
  Newark Campus *M, D*
Seton Hall University *B, M*
Thomas Edison State College *B*
William Paterson University of New
  Jersey *M*

New York

Canisius College *B*
City University of New York
  City College *B, M*
  College of Staten Island *B*
  Hunter College *B*
Colgate University *B*
Elmira College *B*
Eugene Lang College The New
  School for Liberal Arts *B*
Hamilton College *B*
Hobart and William Smith Colleges *B*
Iona College *B*
Long Island University
  LIU Post *B, M*
Manhattan College *B*
Marymount Manhattan College *B*
New York University *B, M*
Rochester Institute of Technology *B*
SUNY
  College at Brockport *B*
  College at Cortland *B*
  College at Geneseo *B*
  College at New Paltz *B*
  College at Oneonta *B*
  University at Binghamton *B*
Sage Colleges *B*
St. John Fisher College *B, M*
Skidmore College *B*
Syracuse University *B, M*
United States Military Academy *B*
University of Rochester *B*
Utica College *B*
Vassar College *B*
Wells College *B*

North Carolina

Campbell University *B*
Duke University *M*
Elon University *B*
High Point University *B*
Lees-McRae College *B*
Lenoir-Rhyne University *B*
Mars Hill University *B*
Meredith College *B*
North Carolina State University *M*
Queens University of Charlotte *B*
Salem College *B*

Ohio

Ashland University *B*
Bowling Green State University *B*
Capital University *B*
Case Western Reserve University *B*
Cleveland State University *B, M*
College of Wooster *B*
Kent State University *B*
Kenyon College *B*
Miami University
  Oxford *B*
Muskingum University *B*
Ohio State University
  Columbus Campus *C, B*
Ohio University *B, M*
Ohio Wesleyan University *B*
Otterbein University *B*
Shawnee State University *B*
Tiffin University *B*

University of Akron *C*
University of Cincinnati *B*
University of Mount Union *B*
University of Toledo *B*
Walsh University *B*
Wittenberg University *B*
Wright State University *B, M*
Xavier University *B*

Oklahoma

Oral Roberts University *B*
University of Central Oklahoma *M*

Oregon

Lewis & Clark College *B*
Linfield College *B*
Pacific University *B*
Portland State University *B*
Reed College *B*
Western Oregon University *B*

Pennsylvania

Albright College *B*
Allegheny College *B*
Arcadia University *B*
Bucknell University *B*
Carnegie Mellon University *B*
Chatham University *B*
Dickinson College *B*
Duquesne University *B*
Gettysburg College *B*
Harrisburg Area Community
  College *A*
Immaculata University *C, A, B*
Indiana University of Pennsylvania *B*
Juniata College *B*
La Roche College *B*
La Salle University *B*
Lafayette College *B*
Lehigh University *B*
Lincoln University *B*
Lock Haven University of
  Pennsylvania *B*
Muhlenberg College *C, B*
Penn State
  Abington *B*
  Altoona *B*
  Beaver *B*
  Berks *B*
  Brandywine *B*
  DuBois *B*
  Erie, The Behrend College *B*
  Fayette, The Eberly Campus *B*
  Greater Allegheny *B*
  Harrisburg *B*
  Hazleton *B*
  Lehigh Valley *B*
  Mont Alto *B*
  New Kensington *B*
  Schuylkill *B*
  Shenango *B*
  University Park *B, M, D*
  Wilkes-Barre *B*
  Worthington Scranton *B*
  York *B*
Saint Joseph's University *B*
Seton Hill University *B*
Susquehanna University *B*
Temple University *B*
University of Pennsylvania *B*
University of Pittsburgh *M*
University of Scranton *B*
Ursinus College *B*
Westminster College *B*
Widener University *B*
Wilkes University *B*
Wilson College *B*
York College of Pennsylvania *B*

Rhode Island

Brown University *B*
Salve Regina University *M*

South Carolina

Bob Jones University *B*
Francis Marion University *B*
University of South Carolina
  Columbia *B, M*

Tennessee

Belmont University *B*
Maryville College *B*
Middle Tennessee State University *B*
Rhodes College *B*
University of Memphis *B*
University of Tennessee
  Martin *B*

Texas

Austin College *B*
Baylor University *B, M*
Howard Payne University *B*
St. Mary's University *B, M*
Southwestern Adventist University *B*
Southwestern University *B*
Texas A&M University *M*
Texas Christian University *B*
Texas State University *B*
University of St. Thomas *B*
University of Texas
  Austin *M*
University of the Incarnate Word *B*
Western Texas College *A*

Utah

Brigham Young University *B*

Vermont

Bennington College *B*
Burlington College *B*
Middlebury College *B*
Norwich University *B*

Virginia

Bridgewater College *B*
College of William and Mary *B*
Ferrum College *B*
George Mason University *B, M*
Hampden-Sydney College *B*
Hollins University *B*
James Madison University *B*
Liberty University *B*
Lynchburg College *B*
Mary Baldwin College *B*
Old Dominion University *B, M, D*
Regent University *M*
Roanoke College *B*
Sweet Briar College *B*
University of Mary Washington *B*
University of Richmond *B*
University of Virginia *B, M, D*
Virginia Military Institute *B*
Virginia Polytechnic Institute and
  State University *B*
Virginia Wesleyan College *B*

Washington

Eastern Washington University *B*
Gonzaga University *B*
University of Washington *B, M*
University of Washington Tacoma *B*
Whitworth University *B*

West Virginia

American Public University
  System *A, B, M*
Bethany College *B*
Marshall University *B*
West Virginia Wesleyan College *B*
Wheeling Jesuit University *B*

Wisconsin

Alverno College *B*
Beloit College *B*
Edgewood College *B*
Marquette University *M*

Mount Mary University *B*
St. Norbert College *B*
University of Wisconsin
Madison *M*

Wyoming

Casper College *A*
Northwest College *A*
Western Wyoming Community
College *A*

Investments/securities

California

Golden Gate University *M*
University of San Francisco *M*

Florida

Lynn University *B*

Illinois

Saint Xavier University *M*

Massachusetts

Babson College *B*

Missouri

Lindenwood University *M*

Nebraska

University of Nebraska
Lincoln *B*
Omaha *B*

New York

City University of New York
Baruch College *M*
Globe Institute of Technology *C*
Pace University *M*
Pace University: Pleasantville/
Briarcliff *M*
SUNY
University at Albany *M*

North Dakota

University of North Dakota *B*

Pennsylvania

Carnegie Mellon University *M*
Temple University *M*

Rhode Island

Johnson & Wales University
Providence *B*

Tennessee

Vanderbilt University *M*

Wisconsin

University of Wisconsin
Platteville *B*

Iranian languages

California

National University *B*

Maryland

University of Maryland
College Park *B*

Missouri

Washington University in St. Louis *B*

Texas

University of Texas
Austin *B*

Utah

University of Utah *B, M, D*

Irish studies

New York

Canisius College *B*
New York University *M*

Ironworking

California

Foothill College *C*

Indiana

Ivy Tech Community College
Central Indiana *C, A*
Lafayette *C, A*
North Central *C, A*
Northeast *C, A*
Northwest *C, A*
Southwest *C, A*
Wabash Valley *C, A*

Minnesota

Hennepin Technical College *C, A*
St. Paul College *C*

Missouri

Metropolitan Community College -
Kansas City *C, A*

Utah

Salt Lake Community College *A*

Wisconsin

Mid-State Technical College *C*

Islamic studies

California

University of California
Los Angeles *M, D*

District of Columbia

Georgetown University *D*

Illinois

DePaul University *B*

Missouri

Washington University in St.
Louis *B, M*

Ohio

Ohio State University
Columbus Campus *B*

Pennsylvania

Swarthmore College *B*
Villanova University *B*

South Carolina

Columbia International University *M*

Texas

University of Texas
Austin *B*

Italian

Arizona

Arizona State University *B*
University of Arizona *B*

California

Cabrillo College *A*
Chabot College *A*
Claremont McKenna College *B*
College of the Desert *A*
Los Angeles City College *A*
Los Angeles Pierce College *A*
Los Angeles Valley College *A*
Orange Coast College *A*

Pitzer College *B*
St. Mary's College of California *B*
San Diego City College *A*
San Francisco State University *B, M*
San Joaquin Delta College *A*
Santa Clara University *B*
Santiago Canyon College *A*
Scripps College *B*
Stanford University *B, M, D*
University of California
Berkeley *B, M, D*
Davis *B*
Los Angeles *B, M, D*
San Diego *B*
Santa Barbara *B*
University of Southern California *B*

Colorado

Colorado College *B*
University of Colorado
Boulder *B*
University of Denver *B*

Connecticut

Central Connecticut State
University *B*
Connecticut College *B*
Fairfield University *B*
Southern Connecticut State
University *B*
Trinity College *B*
University of Connecticut *B*
Wesleyan University *B*
Yale University *B, M, D*

Delaware

University of Delaware *B, M, T*

District of Columbia

George Washington University *B*
Georgetown University *B*

Florida

Florida State University *B*
University of South Florida *B*
University of Tampa *A*

Georgia

Emory University *B*
University of Georgia *B*

Illinois

DePaul University *B, M*
Dominican University *B*
Loyola University Chicago *B*
Northwestern University *B*
Triton College *A*
University of Illinois
Chicago *B*
Urbana-Champaign *B, M, D*

Indiana

Indiana University
Bloomington *B, M, D*
Purdue University *B*
Saint Mary's College *B*
University of Notre Dame *B, M*

Iowa

University of Iowa *B, T*

Kentucky

Bluegrass Community and Technical
College *A*

Louisiana

Tulane University *B*

Maryland

Johns Hopkins University *B, M, D*
University of Maryland
College Park *B*

Massachusetts

Assumption College *B*
Boston College *B, M*
Boston University *B*
College of the Holy Cross *B*
Mount Holyoke College *B*
Smith College *B, M*
Tufts University *B*
University of Massachusetts
Amherst *B, M*
Boston *B*
Wellesley College *B*

Michigan

University of Michigan *B, M, D*

Minnesota

University of Minnesota
Twin Cities *B, M, D*

Missouri

Saint Louis University *B*
Washington University in St. Louis *B*

New Hampshire

Dartmouth College *B*

New Jersey

Montclair State University *B, T*
Princeton University *B, M, D*
Rutgers, The State University of New
Jersey
New Brunswick/Piscataway
Campus *B, M, D, T*
Newark Campus *B*
Seton Hall University *B, T*

New York

Bard College *B*
Barnard College *B*
City University of New York
Brooklyn College *B*
College of Staten Island *B*
Hunter College *B, M*
Lehman College *B*
Queens College *B, M, T*
Columbia University *B*
Columbia University
School of General Studies *B*
Cornell University *B*
Fordham University *B*
Hofstra University *B*
Iona College *B, M*
Ithaca College *B*
Long Island University
LIU Post *B*
Marist College *B*
Nazareth College *B*
New York University *B, M, D*
SUNY
University at Binghamton *B, M*
University at Buffalo *B*
University at Stony Brook *B*
St. John's University *B*
Syracuse University *B*
Vassar College *B*

North Carolina

Duke University *B, M, D*

Ohio

Lake Erie College *B*
Ohio State University
Columbus Campus *B*
Youngstown State University *B*

Oklahoma

Tulsa Community College *A*
University of Oklahoma *B*

Oregon

University of Oregon *B, M*

Bryn Mawr College *B*
Dickinson College *B*
Gettysburg College *B*
Haverford College *B*
La Salle University *B, T*
Penn State
 Abington *B*
 Altoona *B*
 Beaver *B*
 Berks *B*
 Brandywine *B*
 DuBois *B*
 Erie, The Behrend College *B*
 Fayette, The Eberly Campus *B*
 Greater Allegheny *B*
 Harrisburg *B*
 Hazleton *B*
 Lehigh Valley *B*
 Mont Alto *B*
 New Kensington *B*
 Schuylkill *B*
 Shenango *B*
 University Park *B*
 Wilkes-Barre *B*
 Worthington Scranton *B*
 York *B*
Rosemont College *B*
Saint Joseph's University *B*
Susquehanna University *B*
Temple University *B*
University of Pennsylvania *B*
University of Pittsburgh *B, M*
University of Scranton *B*
Villanova University *B*

Rhode Island

Brown University *B, M, D*
Providence College *B*
University of Rhode Island *B*

South Carolina

University of South Carolina
 Columbia *B*

Tennessee

University of Tennessee
 Knoxville *B*

Texas

University of Houston *B*
University of Texas
 Austin *B*

Vermont

Bennington College *B*
Middlebury College *B, M, D*

Virginia

University of Virginia *B, M*

Washington

Gonzaga University *B*
University of Washington *B*

Wisconsin

University of Wisconsin
 Madison *B, M, D*
 Milwaukee *B*

Italian studies

California

Scripps College *B*
University of California
 San Diego
 Santa Cruz *B*
University of San Diego *B*

Colorado

Colorado College *B*

District of Columbia

Georgetown University *M*

Florida

Florida State University *M*

Georgia

Emory University *B, D*

Massachusetts

Boston University *B*
College of the Holy Cross *B*
Merrimack College *B*
Wheaton College *B*

New York

Bard College *B*
City University of New York
 College of Staten Island *B*
Columbia University *B*
Columbia University
 School of General Studies *B*

Ohio

Miami University
 Oxford *B*

Pennsylvania

Arcadia University *B*
Bucknell University *B*
Dickinson College *B*
University of Scranton *B*

Rhode Island

Brown University *B, M, D*

Texas

Southern Methodist University *B*
University of Texas
 Austin *M, D*

Vermont

University of Vermont *B*

Virginia

University of Richmond *B*

Washington

University of Washington *B, M*

Japanese

Alaska

University of Alaska
 Anchorage *B*
 Fairbanks *B*

California

Cabrillo College *A*
California State University
 Fullerton *B*
 Long Beach *B*
 Los Angeles *B*
 Monterey Bay *B*
Claremont McKenna College *B*
El Camino College *A*
Foothill College *A*
Grossmont College *A*
Los Angeles City College *A*
Orange Coast College *A*
Pitzer College *B*
Pomona College *B*
St. Mary's College of California *B*
San Diego State University *B*
San Francisco State University *B, M*
San Joaquin Delta College *A*
San Jose State University *B*
Scripps College *B*
Stanford University *B, M, D*
University of California
 Berkeley *B, M, D*
 Davis *B*

Irvine *B*
Los Angeles *B*
Riverside *B*
San Diego *B*
Santa Barbara *B*
University of San Francisco *B*

Colorado

University of Colorado
 Boulder *B*

Connecticut

Connecticut College *B*
Trinity College *B*
Wesleyan University *B*
Yale University *B*

District of Columbia

George Washington University *B*
Georgetown University *B*

Florida

Florida State University *B*

Georgia

Emory University *B*
Oglethorpe University *B*
University of Georgia *B*

Hawaii

University of Hawaii
 Manoa *B, M, D*

Illinois

DePaul University *M*
North Central College *B*

Indiana

Ball State University *B, T*
Indiana University
 Bloomington *M, D*
Purdue University *B*
University of Notre Dame *B*

Iowa

University of Iowa *B, M, T*

Kentucky

Murray State University *B, T*
University of Kentucky *B*

Maine

Bates College *B, T*

Maryland

University of Maryland
 College Park *B*

Massachusetts

Boston University *B*
Tufts University *B*
University of Massachusetts
 Amherst *B, M*
Wellesley College *B*
Williams College *B*

Michigan

Adrian College *B*
Calvin College *B*
Eastern Michigan University *B*
Lansing Community College *A*
Michigan State University *B*
Oakland University *B, T*
Western Michigan University *B*

Minnesota

Gustavus Adolphus College *B*
Macalester College *B*
University of Minnesota
 Twin Cities *B, M, D*

Missouri

Washington University in St.
 Louis *B, M, D*

Montana

University of Montana *B*

New Hampshire

Dartmouth College *B*

New York

Bard College *B*
Colgate University *B*
Columbia University *B*
Hobart and William Smith Colleges *B*
University of Rochester *B*
Vassar College *B*

North Carolina

University of North Carolina
 Charlotte *B*
Wake Forest University *B*

Ohio

Ohio State University
 Columbus Campus *B*
University of Findlay *B*
University of Mount Union *B, T*

Oklahoma

Tulsa Community College *A*

Oregon

Linfield College *B*
Pacific University *B*
Portland State University *B, T*
University of Oregon *B*

Pennsylvania

Carnegie Mellon University *B*
Elizabethtown College *B*
Gettysburg College *B*
Penn State
 Abington *B*
 Altoona *B*
 Beaver *B*
 Berks *B*
 Brandywine *B*
 DuBois *B*
 Erie, The Behrend College *B*
 Fayette, The Eberly Campus *B*
 Greater Allegheny *B*
 Harrisburg *B*
 Hazleton *B*
 Lehigh Valley *B*
 Mont Alto *B*
 New Kensington *B*
 Schuylkill *B*
 Shenango *B*
 University Park *B*
 Wilkes-Barre *B*
 Worthington Scranton *B*
 York *B*
Swarthmore College *B*
Temple University *B*
University of Pittsburgh *B*
Ursinus College *T*

Texas

Austin Community College *A*

Utah

Brigham Young University *B*
Snow College *A*
University of Utah *B*

Vermont

Bennington College *B*
Middlebury College *B*
University of Vermont *B*

Washington

Central Washington University *B*
University of Puget Sound *B*
University of Washington *B*
Western Washington University *B*

Wisconsin

Beloit College *B*
Carthage College *B*
Lawrence University *B*
University of Wisconsin
Madison *B, M, D*

Japanese studies

California

University of California
San Diego *B*

Georgia

Emory University *B*

Hawaii

University of Hawaii
Hilo *B*

Illinois

DePaul University *B*

Indiana

Earlham College *B*
Purdue University *B*

Michigan

Hope College *B*
Madonna University *C*

Minnesota

Gustavus Adolphus College *B*

New York

Columbia University *B*
SUNY
University at Albany *B*

Ohio

Case Western Reserve University *B*

Oregon

Linfield College *B*
Willamette University *B*

Pennsylvania

Gettysburg College *B*

Washington

University of Washington *B, M*

Wisconsin

Lawrence University *B*
University of Wisconsin
Whitewater *B*

Jazz studies

California

California State University
Long Beach *B, M*
Grossmont College *A*
University of Southern
California *B, M, D*
University of the Pacific *B*

Connecticut

University of Hartford *B*

District of Columbia

Howard University *B*

Florida

Florida State University *M*
Palm Beach State College *A*

University of Miami *B, M, D*
University of North Florida *B*

Illinois

Augustana College *B*
Columbia College Chicago *B*
DePaul University *B, M*
Lincoln College *A*
North Central College *B*
Northwestern University *B, M*
Roosevelt University *B*
University of Illinois
Urbana-Champaign *B*

Iowa

University of Iowa *B, M, D*
University of Northern Iowa *M*

Louisiana

Loyola University New Orleans *B, M*

Maine

University of Southern Maine *B, M*

Massachusetts

Berklee College of Music *B*
New England Conservatory of
Music *B, M, D*

Michigan

Aquinas College *B*
Hope College *B*
Michigan State University *B, M*
University of Michigan *B*
Western Michigan University *B*

Minnesota

Minnesota State University
Moorhead *B*
Saint Cloud State University *B*
University of Minnesota
Duluth *B*

Missouri

University of Missouri
Kansas City *B*
Webster University *B, M*

Nevada

University of Nevada
Las Vegas *B*

New Jersey

Rowan University *B, T*
Rutgers, The State University of New
Jersey
Newark Campus *M*
William Paterson University of New
Jersey *B*

New York

Bard College *B*
City University of New York
City College *B*
Columbia University *B*
Eastman School of Music of the
University of Rochester *B, M, D*
Five Towns College *A, B*
Hofstra University *B*
Ithaca College *B*
Juilliard School *B, M, D*
Long Island University
LIU Brooklyn *B*
University of Rochester *B, M, D*
Villa Maria College of Buffalo *A*

North Carolina

East Carolina University *B*
North Carolina Central University *B*
University of North Carolina
Greensboro *B*

Ohio

Capital University *B*
Central State University *B*
Oberlin College *B, M*
Ohio State University
Columbus Campus *B*
Terra State Community College *A*
University of Akron *B*
Youngstown State University *B, M*

Oregon

University of Oregon *B, M*

Pennsylvania

Carnegie Mellon University *B*
Temple University *B*
University of the Arts *M*

Puerto Rico

Conservatory of Music of Puerto
Rico *B*

Rhode Island

Community College of Rhode
Island *A*

South Carolina

Limestone College *B*
University of South Carolina
Columbia *M*

Texas

Texas State University *B*
University of North Texas *B, M*
University of Texas
Austin *B*

Utah

Brigham Young University *B*

Vermont

Bennington College *B*
Johnson State College *B*

Virginia

Shenandoah University *B*

Washington

Cornish College of the Arts *B*
Whitworth University *B*

Journalism

Alabama

Auburn University *B*
Faulkner State Community College *A*
Oakwood University *B*
Samford University *B*
Stillman College *B*
Troy University *B*
University of Alabama *B, M*

Alaska

University of Alaska
Anchorage *B*
Fairbanks *B*

Arizona

Central Arizona College *A*
Cochise College *A*
Glendale Community College *C*
Grand Canyon University *B*
Mesa Community College *A*
Northern Arizona University *B*
Paradise Valley Community College *C*
University of Arizona *B, M*

Arkansas

Arkansas State University *M*
Arkansas Tech University *B*
Central Baptist College *B*
Harding University *B*

Henderson State University *B*
John Brown University *A, B*
Southern Arkansas University *B*
University of Arkansas *B, M*
University of Arkansas
Little Rock *C, B, M*
Monticello *B*
Pine Bluff *B*
University of Central Arkansas *B*

California

Academy of Art University *A, B, M*
American River College *A*
Azusa Pacific University *B*
Bakersfield College *A*
Biola University *B*
Butte College *C, A*
Cabrillo College *A*
California Baptist University *B*
California Lutheran University *B*
California Polytechnic State
University: San Luis Obispo *B*
California State University
Chico *C, B*
Dominguez Hills *B*
East Bay *B*
Fullerton *B*
Long Beach *B*
Northridge *B, M*
Sacramento *B, M*
Cerritos College *A*
Chabot College *A*
Chaffey College *C*
City College of San Francisco *A*
College of San Mateo *A*
College of the Canyons *C, A*
College of the Desert *A*
College of the Redwoods *C, A*
College of the Sequoias *A*
Contra Costa College *C, A*
Cosumnes River College *A*
Cuesta College *C, A*
Cypress College *A*
East Los Angeles College *C, A*
El Camino College *C, A*
Fresno City College *A*
Fullerton College *A*
Gavilan College *A*
Glendale Community College *A*
Golden West College *C, A*
Grossmont College *C, A*
Humboldt State University *B*
Imperial Valley College *A*
Laney College *A*
Long Beach City College *C, A*
Los Angeles City College *A*
Los Angeles Pierce College *A*
Los Angeles Southwest College *A*
Los Angeles Trade and Technical
College *C, A*
Los Angeles Valley College *C, A*
Los Medanos College *A*
Merced College *A*
Modesto Junior College *C, A*
Moorpark College *A*
Mount San Antonio College *A*
Ohlone College *C, A*
Orange Coast College *A*
Palo Verde College *C*
Palomar College *C, A*
Pasadena City College *C, A*
Pepperdine University *B*
Point Loma Nazarene University *B*
Rio Hondo College *C, A*
Sacramento City College *C, A*
Saddleback College *C, A*
San Diego State University *B*
San Francisco State University *B*
San Jose State University *B*
Santa Ana College *C, A*
Santa Monica College *A*
Santa Rosa Junior College *C*
Shasta College *C, A*
Skyline College *C, A*
Solano Community College *A*

Southwestern College *A*
University of California
 Berkeley *M*
University of La Verne *B*
University of Southern
 California *B, M*
Yuba College *C, A*

Colorado

Adams State University *A*
Arapahoe Community College *A*
Colorado State University *B*
Metropolitan State University of
 Denver *B*
Trinidad State Junior College *A*
University of Colorado
 Boulder *B, M*
University of Denver *B*
University of Northern Colorado *B*

Connecticut

Central Connecticut State
 University *B*
Manchester Community College *A*
Mitchell College *A*
Norwalk Community College *A*
Quinnipiac University *B, M*
Southern Connecticut State
 University *B*
University of Bridgeport *B*
University of Connecticut *B*

Delaware

Delaware State University *B*
University of Delaware *B*

District of Columbia

American University *B, M*
George Washington University *B*
Georgetown University *M*
Howard University *B*

Florida

Broward College *A*
Chipola College *A*
Flagler College *B*
Florida Agricultural and Mechanical
 University *B*
Lynn University *B*
Miami Dade College *A*
Palm Beach Atlantic University *B*
Palm Beach State College *A*
Pensacola State College *A*
Southeastern University *B*
University of Central Florida *B*
University of Florida *B*
University of Miami *B, M*
University of South Florida
 Saint Petersburg *B, M*
University of Tampa *B*
Warner University *B*

Georgia

Abraham Baldwin Agricultural
 College *A*
Darton College *A*
Emory University *B*
Fort Valley State University *B*
Georgia College and State
 University *B*
Georgia Highlands College *A*
Georgia Perimeter College *A*
Georgia Southern University *B*
Georgia State University *B*
Mercer University *B*
Middle Georgia State College *A*
South Georgia State College *A*
University of Georgia *B*
University of North Georgia *A*
University of West Georgia *B*

Hawaii

Hawaii Pacific University *B*
University of Hawaii
 Manoa *B*

Idaho

Boise State University *B*
Brigham Young University-Idaho *B*
North Idaho College *A*
University of Idaho *B*

Illinois

Bradley University *B*
College of DuPage *C*
Columbia College Chicago *B, M*
Concordia University Chicago *B*
DePaul University *B, M*
Dominican University *B*
Eastern Illinois University *B*
Governors State University *B, M*
Harper College *C*
Illinois Central College *A*
Illinois Institute of Technology *B*
Illinois State University *B, T*
Illinois Valley Community College *A*
John A. Logan College *A*
Kishwaukee College *A*
Lake Land College *A*
Lewis University *B*
Lincoln College *A*
Loyola University Chicago *B*
MacMurray College *B*
North Central College *B*
Northern Illinois University *B*
Northwestern University *B, M*
Richland Community College *A*
Roosevelt University *B, M*
Southern Illinois University
 Carbondale *B*
University of Illinois
 Springfield *M*
 Urbana-Champaign *B, M*
Western Illinois University *B*

Indiana

Ball State University *B, M, T*
Butler University *B*
Franklin College *B*
Goshen College *B*
Grace College *B*
Huntington University *B*
Indiana University
 Bloomington *B, M*
 Purdue University
  Indianapolis *C, B*
 Southeast *B*
Indiana Wesleyan University *B*
Manchester University *B*
Purdue University *B*
St. Mary-of-the-Woods College *B*
University of Indianapolis *B*
University of Southern Indiana *B*
Vincennes University *A*

Iowa

Ashford University *B*
Dordt College *B*
Drake University *B*
Grand View University *B*
Iowa Lakes Community College *C, A*
Iowa State University *B, M*
Marshalltown Community College *A*
Mount Mercy University *B*
Northwestern College *B*
St. Ambrose University *B*
Southeastern Community College *A*
University of Iowa *B, M, T*
Wartburg College *B, T*

Kansas

Baker University *T*
Barton County Community College *A*
Benedictine College *B*
Butler Community College *A*

Cloud County Community
 College *C, A*
Coffeyville Community College *A*
Colby Community College *A*
Cowley County Community
 College *A*
Dodge City Community College *A*
Emporia State University *T*
Garden City Community College *A*
Haskell Indian Nations University *A*
Independence Community College *A*
Kansas State University *B, M*
Labette Community College *A*
Pratt Community College *A*
Seward County Community
 College *A*
Southwestern College *B*
Tabor College *B*
University of Kansas *B, M*

Kentucky

Asbury University *B*
Bluegrass Community and Technical
 College *A*
Campbellsville University *B*
Eastern Kentucky University *B*
Hopkinsville Community College *A*
Lindsey Wilson College *B*
Murray State University *B*
Northern Kentucky University *B*
University of Kentucky *B*
University of the Cumberlands *B*
Western Kentucky University *B*

Louisiana

Louisiana College *B*
Louisiana Tech University *B*

Maine

New England School of
 Communications *B*
Saint Joseph's College of Maine *B*
University of Maine *B*

Maryland

Howard Community College *A*
University of Maryland
 College Park *B, M, D*
Washington Adventist University *B*

Massachusetts

American International College *B*
Boston University *B, M*
Cape Cod Community College *A*
Eastern Nazarene College *B*
Emerson College *B, M*
Lasell College *B*
Massachusetts College of Liberal
 Arts *B*
Newbury College *B*
Northeastern University *B, M*
Northern Essex Community
 College *A*
Salem State University *B*
Springfield College *B*
Suffolk University *B*
University of Massachusetts
 Amherst *C, B*
Western New England University *B*

Michigan

Andrews University *B*
Aquinas College *B*
Bay de Noc Community College *A*
Central Michigan University *B*
Delta College *A*
Eastern Michigan University *B*
Grand Rapids Community College *A*
Grand Valley State University *B*
Hillsdale College *B*
Hope College *B*
Kuyper College *B*
Madonna University *A, B*
Michigan State University *B, M*

Oakland University *B*
Olivet College *B*
Wayne State University *B*
Western Michigan University *B*

Minnesota

Augsburg College *B*
Bethel University *B*
College of St. Scholastica *B*
Minnesota State University
 Mankato *B*
 Moorhead *B*
North Central University *B*
Ridgewater College *A*
Saint Cloud State University *B*
St. Mary's University of Minnesota *B*
University of Minnesota
 Twin Cities *B*
University of Northwestern - St.
 Paul *A, B*
Winona State University *B*

Mississippi

Coahoma Community College *A*
Delta State University *B*
East Mississippi Community
 College *A*
Hinds Community College *A*
Itawamba Community College *A*
Northeast Mississippi Community
 College *A*
Northwest Mississippi Community
 College *A*
Rust College *B*
University of Mississippi *B, M*
University of Southern Mississippi *B*
William Carey University *B*

Missouri

Calvary Bible College and Theological
 Seminary *B*
College of the Ozarks *B*
Crowder College *A*
Evangel University *A, B*
Lincoln University *B*
Lindenwood University *B*
Missouri Baptist University *B*
Missouri State University *B*
Moberly Area Community College *A*
Northwest Missouri State
 University *B*
Rockhurst University *C*
University of Central Missouri *B*
University of Missouri
 Columbia *B, M, D*
Washington University in St. Louis *B*
Webster University *B*
Westminster College *B*

Montana

Miles Community College *A*
University of Montana *B, M*

Nebraska

Concordia University *B*
Creighton University *B*
Doane College *B*
Hastings College *B, T*
Midland University *B, T*
Northeast Community College *A*
Union College *B*
University of Nebraska
 Kearney *B*
 Lincoln *M*
 Omaha *B*
Wayne State College *B*
Western Nebraska Community
 College *A*

Nevada

University of Nevada
 Reno *B, M*

New Hampshire

Keene State College *B*

New Jersey

Bergen Community College *A*
County College of Morris *A*
Cumberland County College *A*
Essex County College *A*
Felician College *B*
Gloucester County College *A*
Middlesex County College *A*
Passaic County Community College *A*
Rider University *B*
Rowan University *B*
Rutgers, The State University of New Jersey
  New Brunswick/Piscataway Campus *B*
  Newark Campus *B*
Salem Community College *A*
Seton Hall University *B*
Sussex County Community College *A*
Thomas Edison State College *B*

New Mexico

New Mexico State University *B*
University of New Mexico *B*

New York

Adelphi University *B*
Canisius College *B*
City University of New York
  Baruch College *B, M*
  Brooklyn College *B*
  City College *B*
  Kingsborough Community College *A*
  York College *B*
Five Towns College *B*
Fulton-Montgomery Community College *C, A*
Hofstra University *B, M*
Ithaca College *B*
Long Island University
  LIU Brooklyn *B*
  LIU Post *B*
Manhattan College *B*
New York University *B, M*
Rochester Institute of Technology *B*
SUNY
  College at Brockport *B*
  College at Buffalo *B*
  College at Fredonia *B*
  College at New Paltz *B*
  College at Oswego *B*
  College at Plattsburgh *B*
  College at Purchase *B*
  College of Agriculture and Technology at Morrisville *A*
  University at Albany *B*
  University at Buffalo *C*
  University at Stony Brook *B, M*
Saint Bonaventure University *B*
St. John's University *B*
St. Joseph's College New York: Suffolk Campus *B*
St. Joseph's College, New York *B*
St. Thomas Aquinas College *B*
Syracuse University *B, M*
Utica College *B*

North Carolina

Appalachian State University *B*
Bennett College for Women *B*
Campbell University *B*
Elon University *B*
Gardner-Webb University *B*
Lenoir-Rhyne University *B*
Methodist University *B*
Pfeiffer University *B*
Wingate University *B*

North Dakota

North Dakota State University *B*

Ohio

Ashland University *B*
Bowling Green State University *B*
Cedarville University *B*
Central State University *B*
Defiance College *B*
Kent State University *B, M*
Malone University *B*
Marietta College *B*
Miami University
  Oxford *B*
Mount Vernon Nazarene University *B*
Muskingum University *B*
Ohio Northern University *B*
Ohio State University
  Columbus Campus *B, M*
Ohio University *B, M, D*
Ohio Wesleyan University *B*
Otterbein University *B*
Tiffin University *B*
University of Cincinnati *C, B*
University of Cincinnati
  Blue Ash College *C*
University of Dayton *B*
University of Findlay *B*
University of Rio Grande *B*
University of Toledo *B*
Urbana University *B*
Wilberforce University *B*
Wilmington College *B*
Youngstown State University *B*

Oklahoma

Bacone College *A*
Carl Albert State College *A*
Connors State College *A*
East Central University *B*
Langston University *B*
Northeastern State University *B*
Northern Oklahoma College *A*
Oklahoma Baptist University *B*
Oklahoma Christian University *B*
Oklahoma City Community College *A*
Oklahoma State University *B*
Rose State College *A*
Southern Nazarene University *B*
Tulsa Community College *A*
University of Oklahoma *B, M*

Oregon

Corban University *B*
George Fox University *B*
Linn-Benton Community College *A*
Pacific University *B*
Southern Oregon University *B*
Umpqua Community College *C*
University of Oregon *B, M*

Pennsylvania

Albright College *B*
Allegheny College *B*
Bucks County Community College *A*
Chatham University *B*
Clarion University of Pennsylvania *B, M*
Community College of Allegheny County *A*
Delaware County Community College *A*
Duquesne University *B*
Edinboro University of Pennsylvania *B*
Gannon University *B*
Gettysburg College *B*
Indiana University of Pennsylvania *B*
La Salle University *B*
Lehigh University *B*
Lincoln University *B*
Luzerne County Community College *A*
Mansfield University of Pennsylvania *B*
Messiah College *B*

Northampton Community College *A*
Penn State
  Abington *B*
  Altoona *B*
  Beaver *B*
  Berks *B*
  Brandywine *B*
  DuBois *B*
  Fayette, The Eberly Campus *B*
  Greater Allegheny *B*
  Harrisburg *B*
  Hazleton *B*
  Lehigh Valley *B*
  Mont Alto *B*
  New Kensington *B*
  Schuylkill *B*
  Shenango *B*
  University Park *B*
  Wilkes-Barre *B*
  Worthington Scranton *B*
  York *B*
Point Park University *B, M*
Seton Hill University *B*
Shippensburg University of Pennsylvania *B*
Slippery Rock University of Pennsylvania *B*
Temple University *B, M*
University of Pittsburgh
  Greensburg *B*
  Johnstown *B*
Waynesburg University *B*

Puerto Rico

Bayamon Central University *B*
University of Puerto Rico
  Rio Piedras *B, M*
University of the Sacred Heart *B, M*

Rhode Island

Roger Williams University *B*
University of Rhode Island *B*

South Carolina

Columbia College *B*
North Greenville University *B*
University of South Carolina
  Columbia *B, M*
Winthrop University *B*

South Dakota

Augustana College *B*
Dakota Wesleyan University *B*
South Dakota State University *B*
University of Sioux Falls *B*
University of South Dakota *B, M*

Tennessee

Belmont University *B*
Carson-Newman University *B*
Freed-Hardeman University *B*
Lee University *B*
Lipscomb University *B*
Southern Adventist University *B*
Tennessee State University *B*
Tennessee Technological University *B*
Trevecca Nazarene University *B*
Tusculum College *B*
Union University *B*
University of Memphis *B, M*
University of Tennessee
  Knoxville *B*

Texas

Abilene Christian University *B*
Amarillo College *A*
Angelo State University *B, T*
Austin Community College *A*
Baylor University *B, M, T*
College of the Mainland *A*
Del Mar College *A*
El Paso Community College *A*
Howard College *A*

Kilgore College *A*
Lubbock Christian University *B*
Midland College *A*
North Lake College *C*
Northwest Vista College *A*
Our Lady of the Lake University of San Antonio *B*
Palo Alto College *A*
Paris Junior College *A*
St. Philip's College *A*
Sam Houston State University *B*
San Antonio College *A*
San Jacinto College *A*
South Plains College *A*
Southern Methodist University *B*
Southwestern Adventist University *B*
Texarkana College *A*
Texas A&M University
  Commerce *B*
Texas Christian University *B, M*
Texas Southern University *B*
Texas State University *B*
Texas Tech University *B*
Texas Wesleyan University *B*
Trinity Valley Community College *A*
Tyler Junior College *A*
University of Houston *B*
University of North Texas *B, M*
University of Texas
  Arlington *B*
  Austin *B, M, D*
  Pan American *B*
University of the Incarnate Word *B*
West Texas A&M University *B*
Western Texas College *A*
Wiley College *B*

Utah

Brigham Young University *B*
Snow College *A*
Utah State University *B*
Weber State University *B*

Vermont

Bennington College *B*
Castleton State College *B*
Johnson State College *B*
Lyndon State College *B*

Virginia

Averett University *B*
Bluefield College *B*
Hampton University *B*
Norfolk State University *B*
Patrick Henry College *B*
Radford University *B*
Regent University *M*
University of Richmond *B*
Virginia Union University *B*
Washington and Lee University *B*

Washington

Central Washington University *B*
Centralia College *A*
Eastern Washington University *B*
Gonzaga University *B*
Highline Community College *A*
Peninsula College *A*
Seattle University *B*
Walla Walla University *B*
Western Washington University *B*
Whitworth University *B*

West Virginia

Bethany College *B*
Concord University *B*
Marshall University *B, M*
Potomac State College of West Virginia University *A*
West Virginia University *B, M, T*
West Virginia University at Parkersburg *A*

Wisconsin

Carroll University *B*
Madison Area Technical College *C*
Marquette University *B*
University of Wisconsin
  Eau Claire *B*
  Madison *B, M*
  Oshkosh *B*
  River Falls *B, T*
  Superior *B*
  Whitewater *B*

Wyoming

Casper College *A*
Northwest College *C, A*
University of Wyoming *B*
Western Wyoming Community
  College *A*

Judaic studies

Arizona

Arizona State University *B*
University of Arizona *B*

California

American Jewish University *B*
San Diego State University *B*
San Francisco State University *B*
Scripps College *B*
Touro University Worldwide *B*
University of California
  Berkeley *D*
  Los Angeles *B*
  San Diego *B, M*
  Santa Cruz *B*
University of Southern California *B*

Colorado

University of Colorado
  Boulder *B*

Connecticut

Trinity College *B*
University of Connecticut *M*
University of Hartford *B*
Yale University *B*

District of Columbia

American University *B*
George Washington University *B*

Florida

Florida Atlantic University *B*
Talmudic University *B, M, D*
University of Florida *B*
University of Miami *B*
Yeshiva Gedolah Rabbinical
  College *B, M*

Georgia

Emory University *B, M*

Illinois

DePaul University *B*
Hebrew Theological College *B*
Moody Bible Institute *B*
University of Chicago *B*

Indiana

Indiana University
  Bloomington *B, M*

Louisiana

Tulane University *B*

Maryland

Towson University *M*
University of Maryland
  College Park *B, M*
Yeshiva College of the Nations
  Capital *B*

Massachusetts

Northeastern University *B*
University of Massachusetts
  Amherst *B*
Wellesley College *B*

Michigan

Michigan Jewish Institute *B*
University of Michigan *B, M*

Minnesota

University of Minnesota
  Twin Cities *B*

Missouri

Washington University in St.
  Louis *B, M*

New Jersey

Rabbinical College of America *B*
Rutgers, The State University of New
  Jersey
  New Brunswick/Piscataway
    Campus *B, M*
Seton Hall University *M*

New York

Bard College *B*
Beth Hamedrash Shaarei Yosher
  Institute *B, D*
Beth Hatalmud Rabbinical College *B*
Central Yeshiva Tomchei Tmimim-
  Lubavitch *B, M*
City University of New York
  Brooklyn College *B, M*
  City College *B*
  Hunter College *B*
  Queens College *B*
Eugene Lang College The New
  School for Liberal Arts *B*
Hofstra University *B*
Jewish Theological Seminary of
  America *B, M, D*
Kehilath Yakov Rabbinical
  Seminary *B*
Ohr Somayach Tanenbaum Education
  Center *B, M*
SUNY
  University at Binghamton *B*
  University at Buffalo *B*
Syracuse University *B*
Talmudical Institute of Upstate New
  York *B*
Touro College *B, M*
Vassar College *B*
Yeshivat Mikdash Melech *B, M*

Ohio

Oberlin College *B*
Ohio State University
  Columbus Campus *B*
University of Cincinnati *B*

Oklahoma

University of Oklahoma *B*

Oregon

University of Oregon *B*

Pennsylvania

Dickinson College *B*
Gratz College *B, M, D*
Muhlenberg College *C, B*
Penn State
  Abington *B*
  Altoona *B*
  Beaver *B*
  Berks *B*
  Brandywine *B*
  DuBois *B*
  Fayette, The Eberly Campus *B*
  Greater Allegheny *B*
  Harrisburg *B*
  Hazleton *B*
  Lehigh Valley *B*
  Mont Alto *B*
  New Kensington *B*
  Schuylkill *B*
  Shenango *B*
  University Park *B*
  Wilkes-Barre *B*
  Worthington Scranton *B*
  York *B*
Temple University *C, B*
University of Pennsylvania *B*
West Chester University of
  Pennsylvania *M*

Rhode Island

Brown University *B*

South Carolina

College of Charleston *B*

Tennessee

Vanderbilt University *B*

Texas

University of Texas
  Austin *B*

Vermont

Bennington College *B*

Washington

University of Washington *B*

Wisconsin

University of Wisconsin
  Madison *B*
  Milwaukee *C*

Junior high/middle school special education

California

Alliant International University *M, T*

Georgia

Brenau University *B*

Massachusetts

Merrimack College *B, M*

Nebraska

Concordia University *B, T*

New York

City University of New York
  Brooklyn College *M*
  College of Staten Island *M, T*
St. Joseph's College New York:
  Suffolk Campus *M*

Juvenile corrections

Arizona

Pima Community College *C*

California

Diablo Valley College *C*
National University *M*
Santa Rosa Junior College *C*

Connecticut

Mitchell College *B*

Illinois

Danville Area Community College *A*
Illinois Valley Community College *A*
Kaskaskia College *A*

Michigan

Lansing Community College *C, A*

Montana

University of Great Falls *B*

Nevada

Truckee Meadows Community
  College *A*

Oklahoma

University of Central Oklahoma *B*

Oregon

Central Oregon Community
  College *C*
Chemeketa Community College *C, A*
Clackamas Community College *C*
Linn-Benton Community College *C*
Rogue Community College *C*
Southwestern Oregon Community
  College *C*

Texas

Prairie View A&M University *M, D*

Keyboard instruments

Alabama

Birmingham-Southern College *B*
Oakwood University *B*
Samford University *B, M*

Arizona

Grand Canyon University *B*

Arkansas

Ouachita Baptist University *B*

California

Bethesda University of
  California *B, M*
California Baptist University *B*
California State University
  Chico *C*
  Long Beach *B, M*
Chapman University *B*
Fresno City College *A*
Master's College *B*
Ohlone College *C*
Point Loma Nazarene University *B*
San Francisco Conservatory of
  Music *B, M*
University of Southern
  California *B, M, D*
University of the Pacific *B*

Delaware

University of Delaware *B*

District of Columbia

Catholic University of
  America *B, M, D*
Howard University *B*

Florida

Florida State University *B, M, D*
Hobe Sound Bible College *B*
Palm Beach Atlantic University *B*
Southeastern University *B*
Stetson University *B*
University of Miami *B, M, D*

Georgia

Mercer University *M*
Shorter University *B*

Hawaii

Brigham Young University-Hawaii *B*

Idaho

Brigham Young University-Idaho *A*
Northwest Nazarene University *B*

Illinois

Augustana College *B*
Illinois Wesleyan University *B*
Lincoln College *A*
Millikin University *B*
Moody Bible Institute *B*
Northwestern University *B, M, D*
Olivet Nazarene University *B*
Roosevelt University *B, M*
Trinity International University *B*

Indiana

Ancilla College *C*
Butler University *B, M*
Huntington University *B*
Indiana University
    Bloomington *C*
    Purdue University Fort Wayne *B*
Valparaiso University *B*

Iowa

Dordt College *B*
University of Iowa *B, M, D*
University of Northern Iowa *M*

Kansas

Central Christian College of
    Kansas *A, B*
University of Kansas *B, M, D*

Kentucky

Campbellsville University *B, M*

Louisiana

Centenary College of Louisiana *B, T*
Louisiana College *B*
Xavier University of Louisiana *B*

Maine

University of Southern Maine *B, M*

Maryland

Johns Hopkins University: Peabody
    Conservatory of Music *B, M, D*

Massachusetts

Anna Maria College *B*
Berklee College of Music *B*
Boston Conservatory *B, M*
Boston University *B, M, D*
Eastern Nazarene College *B*
New England Conservatory of
    Music *B, M, D*

Michigan

Grand Rapids Community College *A*
Hope College *B*
Madonna University *B*
Northwestern Michigan College *A*
Oakland University *B, M*
University of Michigan *M*
Western Michigan University *B*

Minnesota

McNally Smith College of Music *B, M*
Saint Cloud State University *B*
University of Northwestern - St.
    Paul *B*

Mississippi

Mississippi College *B, M*

Missouri

University of Missouri
    Kansas City *B*

Nebraska

Concordia University *B, T*
Grace University *B*

Hastings College *B*
University of Nebraska
    Omaha *B*

New Jersey

Rider University *B, M*

New York

Bard College *B*
Eastman School of Music of the
    University of Rochester *B, M, D*
Five Towns College *A, B, M, D*
Houghton College *B, M*
Juilliard School *B, M, D*
Mannes College The New School for
    Music *B, M*
Nyack College *B*
Roberts Wesleyan College *B*
Syracuse University *B, M*
University of Rochester *M, D*

North Carolina

Campbell University *B*
East Carolina University *B*
Gardner-Webb University *B*
University of Mount Olive *B*

Ohio

Ashland University *B*
Baldwin Wallace University *B*
Bowling Green State University *B*
Capital University *B*
Oberlin College *B, M*
Ohio University *B*
University of Akron *C, B, M*
University of Cincinnati *B, M, D*
Youngstown State University *B, M*

Oklahoma

East Central University *B, T*
Oklahoma Baptist University *B*
Oklahoma Christian University *B*
Oklahoma City University *B*
Oral Roberts University *B*
Southwestern Oklahoma State
    University *B*
University of Central Oklahoma *B*
University of Tulsa *B*

Oregon

Corban University *B*
University of Oregon *M*
Willamette University *B*

Pennsylvania

Carnegie Mellon University *M*
Gettysburg College *B*
Mansfield University of
    Pennsylvania *B*
Penn State
    University Park *M*
Temple University *M*
Westminster College *B*

Puerto Rico

Conservatory of Music of Puerto
    Rico *B, M*

South Carolina

Bob Jones University *B, M*
Coker College *B*
Columbia College *B*
Converse College *B, M*
North Greenville University *B*
University of South Carolina
    Columbia *M, D*

Tennessee

Hiwassee College *A*
Lipscomb University *B*
Vanderbilt University *B*

Texas

Abilene Christian University *B*
Baylor University *M*
Concordia University Texas *B*
Dallas Baptist University *B*
East Texas Baptist University *B*
Hardin-Simmons University *B*
Howard Payne University *B*
Southern Methodist University *B, M*
Southwestern Assemblies of God
    University *B*
Texas Christian University *B, M, D*
University of Texas
    El Paso *B*

Utah

Brigham Young University *B*
Weber State University *B*

Vermont

Bennington College *B*
Johnson State College *B*

Virginia

Shenandoah University *B, M*

Washington

Central Washington University *B*
Cornish College of the Arts *B*
University of Washington *B, M, D*
Whitworth University *B*

Wisconsin

Concordia University Wisconsin *B*

Kindergarten/ preschool education

Alabama

Athens State University *B*
Concordia College *B*
Gadsden State Community College *A*

Arizona

Arizona Western College *C*
University of Arizona *B*

Arkansas

Ozarka College *C*
University of Arkansas *B*
University of Arkansas
    Monticello *B*
University of Central Arkansas *B*

California

California Polytechnic State
    University: San Luis Obispo *B*
California State University
    Los Angeles *B, M*
    Sacramento *B, M*
Contra Costa College *C, A*
Los Angeles Pierce College *C, A*
Orange Coast College *C, A*
Santa Barbara City College *C, A*
Southwestern College *C, A*

Connecticut

Central Connecticut State
    University *M*
Mitchell College *B*
Southern Connecticut State
    University *T*

Delaware

Delaware Technical Community
    College
    Jack F. Owens Campus *A*
    Stanton/Wilmington Campus *A*
    Terry Campus *A*

Florida

Nova Southeastern University *B*
Seminole State College of
    Florida *C, A*
University of Miami *M*

Georgia

Georgia Military College *A*
Georgia State University *B, M, D, T*
University of Georgia *B*
Valdosta State University *B*

Illinois

Columbia College Chicago *B*
DePaul University *T*
Eastern Illinois University *B, T*
Elmhurst College *B*
Illinois State University *B*
University of Illinois
    Urbana-Champaign *B, M, D, T*

Indiana

Ball State University *B, T*
Butler University *B*
Martin University *B*
Purdue University *B*
St. Mary-of-the-Woods College *B, T*

Iowa

Iowa State University *B*
University of Northern Iowa *B, M*
Upper Iowa University *B*

Kansas

Emporia State University *M*
Tabor College *B*

Kentucky

Berea College *B, T*
Northern Kentucky University *C, B*

Louisiana

South Louisiana Community
    College *A*

Maine

University of Maine
    Farmington *B, T*

Maryland

Bowie State University *B, M*
Hood College *T*
Stevenson University *B*
University of Maryland
    College Park *B*

Massachusetts

Anna Maria College *B*
Bristol Community College *A*
Cape Cod Community College *A*
Eastern Nazarene College *A, B, M, T*
Lesley University *B, M*
North Shore Community
    College *C, A*
Quinsigamond Community
    College *C, A*
Salem State University *M*
Westfield State University *B, M, T*
Wheelock College *M*

Michigan

Alma College *T*
Baker College
    Muskegon *B*
Delta College *A*
Kuyper College *A, B*
Michigan State University *B*

Minnesota

Bethel University *B*
Concordia University St. Paul *B, T*
Saint Cloud State University *B*

University of Minnesota
Crookston *B*
Duluth *B*
Twin Cities *B, M*
White Earth Tribal and Community
College *A*

Mississippi

Jackson State University *M, D*
Tougaloo College *A, B*

Missouri

University of Missouri
Kansas City *B*

Montana

University of Great Falls *A, B*

Nevada

College of Southern Nevada *A*

New Jersey

College of New Jersey *B, M, T*
Essex County College *A*
Kean University *B, M, T*
Raritan Valley Community
College *C, A*
William Paterson University of New
Jersey *B, T*

New Mexico

Santa Fe Community College *A*

New York

Adelphi University *M, T*
City University of New York
Brooklyn College *M, T*
Hunter College *M, T*
Lehman College *M*
College of Saint Rose *B, M, T*
Dutchess Community College *A*
Fulton-Montgomery Community
College *A*
Herkimer County Community
College *A*
Jamestown Community College *A*
Long Island University
LIU Post *B, M, T*
New York University *B, M*
SUNY
College at Buffalo *B*
College at Cortland *B*
College at Potsdam *B*
College of Agriculture and
Technology at Morrisville *A*
Tompkins Cortland Community
College *A*
Ulster County Community College *A*
University of Rochester *M*

North Carolina

Appalachian State University *B, M, T*
East Carolina University *B, M*
Elizabeth City State University *B, T*
Meredith College *T*
North Carolina Agricultural and
Technical State University *B, T*.
North Carolina Central
University *B, T*
University of North Carolina
Chapel Hill *M*
Charlotte *B, M*
Pembroke *B*
Wilmington *B*
Western Carolina University *B*
Winston-Salem State University *B*

Ohio

Bluffton University *B*
Bowling Green State University *B, T*
Clark State Community College *C, A*
Cleveland State University *B*
John Carroll University *T*

Miami University
Hamilton *A*
Oxford *A, T*
Northwest State Community
College *A*
Ohio Northern University *B, T*
Ohio Wesleyan University *B*
Shawnee State University *A*
Sinclair Community College *C, A*
Terra State Community College *C, A*
University of Cincinnati
Clermont College *A*
University of Findlay *B, M, T*
University of Toledo *B*
Youngstown State University *B*

Pennsylvania

Butler County Community College *A*
Cabrini College *B, T*
California University of
Pennsylvania *A, B*
Seton Hill University *T*

Puerto Rico

Inter American University of Puerto
Rico
Aguadilla Campus *B*
Guayama Campus *B, M*
San German Campus *B*
Universidad Metropolitana *B*
Universidad del Este *B*

Rhode Island

Community College of Rhode
Island *A*

South Dakota

Black Hills State University *B*
University of South Dakota *B*

Tennessee

Middle Tennessee State University *B*
Union University *B, T*

Texas

Arlington Baptist College *B, T*
Lone Star College System *A*
Mountain View College *A*
North Lake College *A*
Our Lady of the Lake University of
San Antonio *B*
San Jacinto College *A*
South Texas College *C*

Utah

Salt Lake Community College *A*
Utah Valley University *C*

Virginia

Norfolk State University *B, M*
Old Dominion University *M*
Virginia Intermont College *B, T*

Washington

University of Washington Tacoma *T*
Washington State University *B, M, T*
Yakima Valley Community College *C*

West Virginia

Glenville State College *B*
Marshall University *B*
West Virginia Wesleyan College *B*

Wisconsin

College of Menominee Nation *A, B*
Concordia University Wisconsin *B*
Lakeland College *B*
Northcentral Technical College *C*
University of Wisconsin
Superior *T*

Wyoming

Casper College *A*
Northwest College *C, A*

Kinesiotherapy

California

California State University
San Bernardino *B, M*
Humboldt State University *B, M*
Loyola Marymount University *B*

Connecticut

Sacred Heart University *B, M*

Massachusetts

Bridgewater State University *B, M*

North Carolina

University of North Carolina
Charlotte *M*

Knowledge management

California

National University *M*

Colorado

University of Denver *M*

District of Columbia

University of the Potomac *C*

Florida

University of Tampa *M*

Illinois

Dominican University *M*
Illinois Institute of Technology *M*

Massachusetts

Framingham State University *B*

Missouri

Grantham University *M*
Saint Louis University *B*

Ohio

Xavier University *M*

Oklahoma

University of Oklahoma *M*

Pennsylvania

Saint Joseph's University *B, M*

Texas

University of Texas
San Antonio *M*

Virginia

University of the Potomac *C*

Korean

California

University of California
Irvine *B*
Los Angeles *B*

Hawaii

University of Hawaii
Manoa *B, M, D*

Massachusetts

Boston University *B*

New York

Columbia University *B*

Ohio

Ohio State University
Columbus Campus *B*

Utah

Brigham Young University *B*

Washington

University of Washington *B*

Korean studies

New York

Columbia University *B*

Washington

University of Washington *B, M*

Labor/industrial relations

California

California State University
San Bernardino *M*
Los Angeles Trade and Technical
College *C, A*
Los Medanos College *C, A*
San Diego City College *A*

Connecticut

University of Bridgeport *B, M*
University of New Haven *M*

Florida

Nova Southeastern University *M*

Illinois

Kankakee Community College *C*
Northwestern University *M*
University of Illinois
Urbana-Champaign *M, D*

Indiana

Indiana University
Purdue University Fort
Wayne *C, A, B*

Iowa

University of Iowa *B*

Kentucky

Sullivan University *C*

Massachusetts

University of Massachusetts
Amherst *M*
Boston *C*
Dartmouth *C*

Michigan

Michigan State University *M*
Wayne State University *M*

Minnesota

University of Minnesota
Twin Cities *B, M, D*

New Jersey

Rutgers, The State University of New
Jersey
New Brunswick/Piscataway
Campus *B, M, D*
Seton Hall University *B*
Thomas Edison State College *C, B*

New York

City University of New York
Baruch College *B, M*
CUNY Online *C*
Cornell University *B, M, D*
Manhattan College *B*

New York Institute of Technology *M*
New York University *B*
SUNY
College at Old Westbury *B*
College at Potsdam *B*
Empire State College *A, B, M*
University at Stony Brook *M*

Ohio

Bowling Green State University *B*
Case Western Reserve University *M*
Cleveland State University *B, M, D*
Youngstown State University *A*

Pennsylvania

Clarion University of Pennsylvania *B*
Indiana University of Pennsylvania *M*
La Salle University *B*
Penn State
Abington *B*
Altoona *B*
Beaver *B*
Berks *B*
Brandywine *B*
DuBois *B*
Erie, The Behrend College *B*
Fayette, The Eberly Campus *B*
Greater Allegheny *B*
Harrisburg *B*
Hazleton *B*
Lehigh Valley *B*
Mont Alto *B*
New Kensington *B*
Schuylkill *B*
Shenango *B*
University Park *B, M*
Wilkes-Barre *B*
Worthington Scranton *B*
York *B*
St. Francis University *M*

Puerto Rico

Inter American University of Puerto
Rico
Metropolitan Campus *M*
San German Campus *M*
University of Puerto Rico
Rio Piedras *B*

Rhode Island

Providence College *C, A, B*
University of Rhode Island *M*

Tennessee

Tennessee Technological
University *B*

Texas

College of the Mainland *A*
University of North Texas *M*

West Virginia

Marshall University *M*
West Virginia University *M*

Labor studies

California

California State University
Dominguez Hills *B*
San Francisco State University *B*
San Jose City College *C, A*

Indiana

Indiana University
Northwest *A, B*
Purdue University
Indianapolis *C, A, B*
South Bend *C, B*
Purdue University *B*

Michigan

Eastern Michigan University *B*
Michigan State University *D*
Wayne State University *B*

New York

City University of New York
CUNY Online *C, M*
Queens College *B*
Hofstra University *B*

Pennsylvania

Penn State
Abington *C*
Altoona *C*
Berks *C*
Brandywine *C*
DuBois *C*
Lehigh Valley *C*
New Kensington *C*
Schuylkill *C*
Shenango *C*
University Park *C*

LAN/WAN
management

Alabama

Gadsden State Community College *A*
Virginia College
Birmingham *B*
Huntsville *A, B*

Alaska

University of Alaska
Anchorage *C*
Southeast *C, A*

Arizona

Arizona Western College *C*
Estrella Mountain Community
College *C, A*
GateWay Community College *C, A*
Glendale Community College *C*
ITT Technical Institute
Tempe *A*
Tucson *A*
Paradise Valley Community College *C*
University of Advancing
Technology *A, B*

Arkansas

Northwest Arkansas Community
College *A*
Phillips Community College of the
University of Arkansas *C, A*
University of Arkansas
Community College at Morrilton *C*

California

Allan Hancock College *C*
College of the Siskiyous *C*
DeVry University
Pomona *A*
Foothill College *C, A*
Grossmont College *C, A*
ITT Technical Institute
Lathrop *A*
National City *A*
Oxnard *A*
Rancho Cordova *A*
San Bernardino *A*
Sylmar *A*
Torrance *A*
Kaplan College
Riverside *A*
Vista *A*
Los Angeles Harbor College *C*
Monterey Peninsula College *C, A*
Ohlone College *C, A*
Orange Coast College *C*
Platt College
Ontario *A*

San Diego Mesa College *C*
Santa Barbara Business College
Bakersfield *C, A*
Santa Barbara City College *C*
Santa Rosa Junior College *C*
Shasta College *C*
Southwestern College *C*
Westwood College
Inland Empire *B*
South Bay *A, B*

Colorado

Arapahoe Community College *C, A*
Colorado Technical University *C*
Everest College
Colorado Springs *C, A*
Lamar Community College *C, A*
National American University
Denver *B*
Westwood College
Denver South *B*

District of Columbia

University of the Potomac *C, A, B*

Florida

College of Business and Technology
Kendall *A*
Herzing University
Winter Park *C, A*

Georgia

Georgia Piedmont Technical
College *C*
Southeastern Technical College *A*

Hawaii

University of Hawaii
West Oahu *B*

Idaho

College of Southern Idaho *C, A*
College of Western Idaho *C, A*
ITT Technical Institute
Boise *A*

Illinois

Harper College *C*
Lake Land College *A*
Lewis and Clark Community
College *A*
Moraine Valley Community
College *C, A*
Morrison Institute of Technology *A*
Oakton Community College *C*
Rend Lake College *C, A*
Sauk Valley Community College *C, A*
Southeastern Illinois College *A*

Indiana

Ivy Tech Community College
Bloomington *C*
Central Indiana *C*
Columbus *C*
East Central *C*
Kokomo *C*
Lafayette *C*
North Central *C*
Northeast *C*
Northwest *C*
Richmond *C*
South Central *C*
Purdue University *B*

Iowa

Dordt College *B*
Ellsworth Community College *C, A*
St. Ambrose University *B*

Kansas

Cloud County Community
College *C, A*

Colby Community College *C*
Labette Community College *C, A*

Kentucky

ITT Technical Institute
Louisville *A*
Northern Kentucky University *M*
Sullivan College of Technology and
Design *A*
Sullivan University *C, A*

Louisiana

Remington College
Baton Rouge *A*

Maine

Central Maine Community College *A*

Maryland

Howard Community College *C, A*
Kaplan University
Hagerstown *A, B*

Massachusetts

Bristol Community College *C*
Cape Cod Community College *A*
ITT Technical Institute
Norwood *A*
North Shore Community College *C*
University of Massachusetts
Lowell *C*

Michigan

Alpena Community College *C, A*
Baker College
Muskegon *C, A*
Grand Rapids Community College *A*
Lake Michigan College *C*
Northern Michigan University *B*
Oakland Community College *C*
Washtenaw Community College *C, A*
Wayne County Community College *A*

Minnesota

Capella University *B*
ITT Technical Institute
Eden Prairie *A*
National American University
Bloomington *B*
Roseville *B*
Riverland Community College *C, A*
South Central College *C, A*

Mississippi

Alcorn State University *B*
Meridian Community College *A*

Missouri

Ranken Technical College *A*

Montana

Montana State University
Billings *A*
Rocky Mountain College *B*
University of Great Falls *B*

Nebraska

ITT Technical Institute
Omaha *A*

Nevada

College of Southern Nevada *A*
Great Basin College *A, B*
Western Nevada College *C, A*

New Jersey

Cumberland County College *A*
Gloucester County College *C, A*

New Mexico

ITT Technical Institute
Albuquerque *A*

National American University
Albuquerque *B*
Southwestern Indian Polytechnic
Institute *C, A*

New York

College of Westchester *C, A*
Globe Institute of
Technology *C, A, B*
Rochester Institute of
Technology *B, M*
SUNY
College of Agriculture and
Technology at Morrisville *B*
College of Technology at Alfred *B*
Westchester Community College *C, A*

North Carolina

Carteret Community College *C, A*
Catawba Valley Community
College *C, A*
Central Piedmont Community
College *C, A*
Isothermal Community College *A*
Miller-Motte College
Wilmington *C, A*
Stanly Community College *C, A*
Surry Community College *C*
Wilkes Community College *C, A*

Ohio

Belmont College *A*
Cincinnati Christian University *B*
ITT Technical Institute
Dayton *A*
Strongsville *A*
Youngstown *A*
James A. Rhodes State College *A*
Lakeland Community College *A*
Lorain County Community College *C*
Marion Technical College *A*
Stautzenberger College *C, A*
University of Akron: Wayne
College *C*
Youngstown State University *C*

Oklahoma

Rose State College *A*

Oregon

Lane Community College *C*
Southwestern Oregon Community
College *C*

Pennsylvania

Consolidated School of Business
York *A*
Kaplan Career Institute
Harrisburg *A*
Pittsburgh *A*
McCann School of Business and
Technology
Hazleton *A*

Rhode Island

Community College of Rhode
Island *C*

South Carolina

York Technical College *C, A*

South Dakota

Dakota State University *A, B*
National American University
Rapid City *B*
Southeast Technical Institute *A*

Tennessee

ITT Technical Institute
Knoxville *A*
Memphis *A*
Nashville *A*

Northeast State Community
College *C*
Pellissippi State Community
College *C*
Remington College
Memphis *A*
South College *A*

Texas

Collin County Community College
District *C, A*
Hallmark College of Technology *B*
Houston Community College
System *A*
ITT Technical Institute
Arlington *A*
Houston West *A*
Richardson *A*
Webster *A*
Mountain View College *C, A*
North Lake College *C*
Paris Junior College *C, A*
St. Philip's College *C, A*
San Antonio College *C*
Temple College *C, A*
Texas A&M University *B*
Texas State Technical College
Marshall *C, A*
Waco *C, A*
Western Texas College *C, A*

Utah

LDS Business College *C, A*
Salt Lake Community College *C*

Virginia

Southwest Virginia Community
College *C, A*
University of Management and
Technology *A, B, M*
University of the Potomac *C, A, B*

Washington

Centralia College *C, A*
Green River Community College *C*
ITT Technical Institute
Everett *A*
Seattle *A*
Spokane *A*
South Seattle Community
College *C, A*
Yakima Valley Community College *C*

West Virginia

Blue Ridge Community and Technical
College *C*
New River Community and Technical
College *A*

Wisconsin

Blackhawk Technical College *A*
Herzing University
Madison *A, B*
ITT Technical Institute
Green Bay *A*
Greenfield *A*
Nicolet Area Technical College *A*

Land use planning

California

California State University
Bakersfield *B*

Colorado

Metropolitan State University of
Denver *B*

Louisiana

University of Louisiana at Lafayette *B*

Maine

University of Maine
Farmington *B*

Maryland

University of Maryland
College Park *M*

Michigan

Central Michigan University *B*

Minnesota

Vermilion Community College *A*

Montana

Montana State University *B, M, D*
Salish Kootenai College *A, B*

Texas

Texas State University *M*
Texas Tech University *D*

Utah

Brigham Young University *M*
Utah State University *M*

Wisconsin

University of Wisconsin
Madison *M, D*

Landscape architecture

Alabama

Auburn University *M*

Arizona

Arizona State University *B, M*
Southwest University of Visual Arts *B*
University of Arizona *M*

Arkansas

University of Arkansas *B*

California

Academy of Art University *A, B, M*
American River College *C, A*
California Polytechnic State
University: San Luis Obispo *B*
California State Polytechnic
University: Pomona *B, M*
Cosumnes River College *C, A*
Diablo Valley College *C*
East Los Angeles College *C*
Fullerton College *A*
MiraCosta College *C, A*
Modesto Junior College *A*
Otis College of Art and Design *B*
San Diego Mesa College *C, A*
Santa Rosa Junior College *C*
Southwestern College *C, A*
University of California
Berkeley *B, M*
Davis *B*
University of Southern
California *B, M*
West Valley College *A*

Colorado

Colorado State University *B, M*
University of Colorado
Denver *M*

Connecticut

Naugatuck Valley Community
College *C*
University of Connecticut *B*

Florida

Broward College *A*
University of Florida *B, M*

Georgia

University of Georgia *B, M*

Idaho

University of Idaho *B, M*

Illinois

Illinois Institute of Technology *M*
Kishwaukee College *A*
University of Illinois
Urbana-Champaign *B, D*

Indiana

Ball State University *B, M*
Purdue University *B*

Iowa

Iowa State University *B, M*

Kansas

Kansas State University *M*

Kentucky

Bluegrass Community and Technical
College *A*
University of Kentucky *B*

Louisiana

Louisiana State University and
Agricultural and Mechanical
College *B, M*

Maine

College of the Atlantic *B, M*

Maryland

Anne Arundel Community College *C*
Morgan State University *M*
University of Maryland
College Park *B, M*

Massachusetts

Boston Architectural College *B, M*
Harvard College *M*
Northeastern University *B*
University of Massachusetts
Amherst *B, M*

Michigan

Michigan State University *B*
University of Michigan *M, D*

Minnesota

University of Minnesota
Twin Cities *B, M*

Mississippi

Hinds Community College *A*
Mississippi State University *B*

Missouri

Washington University in St. Louis *M*

Nebraska

University of Nebraska
Lincoln *B*

Nevada

Truckee Meadows Community
College *A*
University of Nevada
Las Vegas *B*

New Hampshire

NHTI-Concord's Community
College *C, A*

New Jersey

Rutgers, The State University of New
Jersey
New Brunswick/Piscataway
Campus *B, M*

New Mexico

Southwest University of Visual Arts *B*
University of New Mexico *M*

New York

City University of New York
   City College *M*
Cornell University *B, M*
Monroe Community College *A*
SUNY
   College of Agriculture and
      Technology at Morrisville *A*
   College of Environmental Science
      and Forestry *B, M*
   College of Technology at Delhi *A*

North Carolina

Cape Fear Community College *A*
North Carolina Agricultural and
   Technical State University *B*
North Carolina State University *M*
Wake Technical Community
   College *C, A*

North Dakota

North Dakota State University *B*

Ohio

Ohio State University
   Columbus Campus *B, M*

Oklahoma

Oklahoma State University *B*
University of Oklahoma *M*

Oregon

Central Oregon Community
   College *A*
University of Oregon *B, M, D*

Pennsylvania

Chatham University *M*
Keystone College *A*
Penn State
   University Park *B, M*
Philadelphia University *B*
Temple University *C, B*
University of Pennsylvania *M*

Puerto Rico

Inter American University of Puerto
   Rico
   Barranquitas Campus *C*
Universidad Politecnica de Puerto
   Rico *M*

Rhode Island

Rhode Island School of Design *B, M*
University of Rhode Island *B*

South Carolina

Clemson University *B, M*

Tennessee

University of Tennessee
   Knoxville *M*

Texas

Howard College *C, A*
Texas A&M University *B, M*
Texas Tech University *B, M*
University of Texas
   Arlington *M*
   Austin *M*

Utah

Utah State University *B, M*

Virginia

University of Virginia *M*
Virginia Polytechnic Institute and
   State University *B, M*

Washington

University of Washington *B, M*
Washington State University *B, M*

West Virginia

West Virginia University *B, M*

Wisconsin

University of Wisconsin
   Madison *B, M*

Landscaping/ groundskeeping

Alabama

Faulkner State Community
   College *C, A*

Arizona

Mesa Community College *C*

Arkansas

University of Arkansas
   Little Rock *A*

California

Antelope Valley College *C, A*
City College of San Francisco *A*
College of Marin *C, A*
College of the Canyons *C, A*
College of the Redwoods *A*
College of the Sequoias *C, A*
Cosumnes River College *C*
Diablo Valley College *C*
Foothill College *C, A*
Los Angeles Pierce College *C, A*
Merritt College *C, A*
MiraCosta College *C, A*
Modesto Junior College *C, A*
Mount San Antonio College *C*
San Joaquin Delta College *C*
Santa Barbara City College *C, A*
Santa Rosa Junior College *C*
Shasta College *C*
Solano Community College *C, A*
Southwestern College *C, A*
Victor Valley College *C*
Yuba College *C, A*

Delaware

Delaware Technical Community
   College
   Jack F. Owens Campus *C*

Florida

College of Central Florida *C, A*
Florida Gateway College *C, A*
Florida Southern College *C*
Miami Dade College *A*
Pensacola State College *C, A*
South Florida State College *C, A*
Valencia College *C, A*

Georgia

Albany Technical College *C*
Gwinnett Technical College *C*
University of North Georgia *C*
West Georgia Technical College *C*

Idaho

Brigham Young University-Idaho *A*

Illinois

College of DuPage *C*
College of Lake County *C, A*
Danville Area Community College *C*
Illinois Central College *C*
Illinois Valley Community College *A*
Joliet Junior College *C, A*
Kishwaukee College *C, A*
Lincoln Land Community
   College *C, A*

McHenry County College *C*
Parkland College *A*
Southwestern Illinois College *A*
Triton College *C*

Indiana

Purdue University *B*

Iowa

Iowa Lakes Community College *A*

Kansas

Johnson County Community
   College *C*

Maryland

Harford Community College *A*
Wor-Wic Community College *C*

Massachusetts

Springfield Technical Community
   College *C, A*
University of Massachusetts
   Amherst *A*

Michigan

Grand Rapids Community College *A*
Lake Michigan College *A*
Michigan State University *C*
Northwestern Michigan College *A*
Oakland Community College *C, A*

Minnesota

Anoka Technical College *C, A*
Century College *C, A*
Dakota County Technical
   College *C, A*
Hennepin Technical College *C, A*
Northwest Technical College *A*
University of Minnesota
   Crookston *B*

Mississippi

East Mississippi Community
   College *A*
Hinds Community College *C, A*
Mississippi Gulf Coast Community
   College *C, A*
Mississippi State University *B*

Nebraska

Nebraska College of Technical
   Agriculture *A*
University of Nebraska
   Lincoln *B*

Nevada

College of Southern Nevada *A*

New Jersey

Bergen Community College *C*
Brookdale Community College *C*

New Mexico

Central New Mexico Community
   College *C*
Dona Ana Community College of
   New Mexico State University *A*
San Juan College *C, A*

New York

SUNY
   College of Agriculture and
      Technology at Cobleskill *A, B*
   College of Technology at Delhi *A*

North Carolina

Alamance Community College *C*
Blue Ridge Community College *C*
Cape Fear Community College *A*
Johnston Community College *C*
North Carolina State University *A*

Sampson Community College *C*
Sandhills Community College *A*

North Dakota

Dakota College at Bottineau *A*

Ohio

Cincinnati State Technical and
   Community College *C, A*
Hocking College *A*
Ohio State University
   Agricultural Technical Institute *A*
   Columbus Campus *B*
Owens Community College
   Toledo *A*

Oklahoma

Oklahoma State University *B*

Oregon

Clackamas Community College *C, A*
Portland Community College *C, A*
Rogue Community College *C*

Pennsylvania

Chatham University *M*
Community College of Allegheny
   County *C, A*
Community College of Beaver
   County *A*
Delaware Valley College *C*
Harrisburg Area Community
   College *C, A*
Luzerne County Community
   College *A*
Penn State
   Abington *B*
   Altoona *B*
   Beaver *B*
   Berks *B*
   Brandywine *B*
   DuBois *B*
   Erie, The Behrend College *B*
   Fayette, The Eberly Campus *B*
   Greater Allegheny *B*
   Harrisburg *B*
   Hazleton *B*
   Lehigh Valley *B*
   Mont Alto *B*
   New Kensington *B*
   Schuylkill *B*
   Shenango *B*
   University Park *B*
   Wilkes-Barre *B*
   Worthington Scranton *B*
   York *B*
Pennsylvania College of
   Technology *A*
Temple University *C*
Williamson Free School of
   Mechanical Trades *A*

South Carolina

Spartanburg Community College *C*
Trident Technical College *C*

South Dakota

Mount Marty College *C*
South Dakota State University *B*
Southeast Technical Institute *A*

Tennessee

Chattanooga State Community
   College *C*
Tennessee Technological
   University *B*

Texas

Houston Community College
   System *C*
Palo Alto College *C, A*
Western Texas College *C, A*

Utah
Brigham Young University *B*

Vermont
Vermont Technical College *A*

Virginia
Mountain Empire Community
College *C*

Washington
Clark College *C, A*
Edmonds Community College *C, A*
South Seattle Community
College *C, A*

Wisconsin
Lakeshore Technical College *A*
Milwaukee Area Technical College *A*
University of Wisconsin
River Falls *B*
Western Technical College *A*

Language interpretation/ translation

Arizona
Pima Community College *C, A*

California
Bethesda University of
California *B, M*
Santa Ana College *T*

Colorado
Community College of Aurora *C*

District of Columbia
American University *C*

Florida
Miami Dade College *A*

Georgia
East Georgia State College *A*

Illinois
Waubonsee Community College *C*

Indiana
Indiana University
Purdue University Indianapolis *C*

Iowa
Des Moines Area Community
College *C, A*
Northwestern College *B*

Kentucky
University of Louisville *C*

Massachusetts
Bristol Community College *C*
Salem State University *B*
University of Massachusetts
Amherst *C*

Minnesota
Century College *C, A*

Mississippi
Mississippi College *B*

Nebraska
University of Nebraska
Kearney *B*

Nevada
Great Basin College *C*

New Jersey
Union County College *A*

New York
Bard College *B*
SUNY
University at Binghamton *D*

North Carolina
Blue Ridge Community College *A*
Cape Fear Community College *C, A*
Cleveland Community College *A*
Johnston Community College *A*
Surry Community College *A*
Wilson Community College *A*

North Dakota
Lake Region State College *C, A*

Ohio
Kent State University *M, D*
Terra State Community College *A*

Oklahoma
Oklahoma City Community
College *A*

Pennsylvania
La Salle University *M*

Puerto Rico
University of Puerto Rico
Rio Piedras *M*

Texas
University of Texas
Brownsville *B*

Utah
Brigham Young University *B*

Vermont
Marlboro College *B*

Virginia
Shenandoah University *C*
Virginia Commonwealth University *C*

Washington
Pierce College *A*

Wisconsin
Milwaukee Area Technical College *C*
University of Wisconsin
Milwaukee *C*
Waukesha County Technical
College *C*

Laser/optical engineering

Delaware
Delaware State University *B*

Florida
University of Central Florida *B, M, D*

Michigan
University of Michigan *M*

New York
University of Rochester *B*

Laser/optical technology

California
San Jose City College *C, A*
Sierra College *C*
University of California
Davis *B*

Connecticut
Three Rivers Community
College *C, A*

Delaware
Delaware Technical Community
College
Stanton/Wilmington Campus *C*

Idaho
Idaho State University *C, A, B*

Indiana
Vincennes University *C*

Maryland
Howard Community College *C, A*

Massachusetts
Springfield Technical Community
College *C, A*

Michigan
Schoolcraft College *C*

New Mexico
Central New Mexico Community
College *C, A*

New York
Monroe Community College *C, A*

North Carolina
Central Carolina Community
College *A*

Texas
Texas State Technical College
Waco *A*

Latin

Alabama
Samford University *B*

California
Loyola Marymount University *B*
Santa Clara University *B*
University of California
Berkeley *B, M*
Los Angeles *B, M*

Connecticut
Yale University *B*

Delaware
University of Delaware *B, M, T*

District of Columbia
Catholic University of
America *B, M, D*
George Washington University *B*

Florida
Florida State University *B, M*
University of Florida *M*
University of Miami *B*

Georgia
Emory University *B*
Georgia State University *T*
Mercer University *B*
University of Georgia *B, M*

Illinois
Augustana College *B*
Knox College *B*
Loyola University Chicago *B*
Monmouth College *B, T*
Rockford University *B*

Indiana
Ball State University *B*
Butler University *B*
DePauw University *B*
Wabash College *B*

Iowa
Cornell College *T*
University of Iowa *M, D, T*

Kansas
Wichita State University *B*

Kentucky
Berea College *B, T*

Louisiana
Loyola University New Orleans *B*

Maine
University of Maine *B*

Maryland
Johns Hopkins University *B*
Loyola University Maryland *B*

Massachusetts
Amherst College *B*
Boston College *B, M*
Boston University *B*
Harvard College *B*
Mount Holyoke College *B*
Smith College *B*
Tufts University *B*
Wellesley College *B*
Wheaton College *B*

Michigan
Calvin College *B, T*
Grand Valley State University *B*
University of Michigan *B, M*
Western Michigan University *B*

Minnesota
Concordia College: Moorhead *B, T*
St. Olaf College *B*
University of Minnesota
Twin Cities *B, M, D*
University of St. Thomas *B*

Missouri
Missouri State University *B*
Washington University in St.
Louis *B, M*

Montana
University of Montana *B*

Nebraska
Creighton University *B*

New Hampshire
Saint Anselm College *T*
University of New Hampshire *B*

New Jersey
Montclair State University *B, T*
Seton Hall University *T*

New York
Bard College *B*
Barnard College *B*
Canisius College *B*
City University of New York
Hunter College *B*
Queens College *B, T*
Colgate University *B*
College of New Rochelle *B, T*
Columbia University *B*
Fordham University *B, M, D*
Hobart and William Smith Colleges *B*
Hofstra University *B*

SUNY
    University at Binghamton *B*
Saint Bonaventure University *B*

North Carolina

Duke University *B*
Lenoir-Rhyne University *B*
Wake Forest University *B*

Ohio

Bowling Green State University *B*
John Carroll University *B*
Kent State University *M*
Kenyon College *B*
Oberlin College *B*
Ohio State University
    Columbus Campus *D*
Ohio Wesleyan University *B*
University of Cincinnati *T*
Wright State University *B*

Pennsylvania

Bryn Mawr College *B, M, D*
Duquesne University *B*
Franklin & Marshall College *B*
Gettysburg College *B*
Haverford College *B, T*
La Salle University *B*
Saint Joseph's University *B*
Swarthmore College *B*
University of Scranton *B, T*
West Chester University of
    Pennsylvania *B, T*
Westminster College *B, T*

Rhode Island

Brown University *B*

South Carolina

Furman University *B, T*

Tennessee

Sewanee: The University of the
    South *B*

Texas

Austin College *B*
Austin Community College *A*
Baylor University *B*
Rice University *B*
Southwestern University *B, T*
University of Texas
    Austin *B*

Utah

Brigham Young University *B*

Vermont

Saint Michael's College *B*
University of Vermont *B*

Virginia

Hampden-Sydney College *B*
Randolph College *B*
Randolph-Macon College *B*
University of Richmond *B*

Washington

Seattle Pacific University *B*
University of Washington *B*

West Virginia

Marshall University *M*

Wisconsin

Lawrence University *B*
University of Wisconsin
    Madison *B, M*

Latin American/ Caribbean studies

Florida

Rollins College *B*

Georgia

University of Georgia *B*

Maine

College of the Atlantic *B, M*

Massachusetts

Mount Holyoke College *B*

Michigan

University of Michigan *B*

New York

City University of New York
    College of Staten Island *C*
Union College *B*

South Carolina

College of Charleston *B*

Vermont

Burlington College *B*
University of Vermont *B*

Wisconsin

University of Wisconsin
    Madison *B, M*
    Milwaukee *C, B*

Latin American studies

Alabama

Samford University *B*
University of Alabama *B, M*

Arizona

Prescott College *B*
University of Arizona *B, M*

California

California State University
    Chico *B*
    East Bay *B*
    Fresno *B*
    Fullerton *B*
    Los Angeles *B, M*
Claremont McKenna College *B*
Cypress College *A*
De Anza College *A*
Fullerton College *A*
Laney College *A*
Los Angeles Pierce College *A*
Mills College *B*
Occidental College *B*
Pepperdine University *B*
Pitzer College *B*
Pomona College *B*
St. Mary's College of California *B*
San Diego City College *A*
San Diego State University *B, M*
Santa Rosa Junior College *A*
Scripps College *B*
Stanford University *M*
University of California
    Berkeley *B, M, D*
    Los Angeles *B, M*
    Riverside *B*
    San Diego *B, M*
    Santa Barbara *B, M*
University of Redlands *B*
University of San Francisco *M*
Whittier College *B*

Connecticut

Connecticut College *B*
Trinity College *B*

University of Connecticut *B*
Wesleyan University *B*
Yale University *B*

Delaware

University of Delaware *B*

District of Columbia

American University *B, M*
George Washington University *B, M*
Georgetown University *M*

Florida

Flagler College *B*
Florida International University *M*
Miami Dade College *A*
New College of Florida *B*
University of Central Florida *B*
University of Florida *M*
University of Miami *B, M, D*
University of South Florida *M*

Georgia

Armstrong Atlantic State University *C*
Emory University *B*

Idaho

University of Idaho *B*

Illinois

Blackburn College *B*
DePaul University *B*
Illinois Wesleyan University *B*
Lake Forest College *B*
Northeastern Illinois University *M*
University of Chicago *B, M*
University of Illinois
    Chicago *B, M*
    Urbana-Champaign *B, M*

Indiana

Earlham College *D*
Indiana University
    Bloomington *M*

Iowa

Cornell College *B*
University of Iowa *B*
University of Northern Iowa *B*

Kansas

University of Kansas *B, M*

Kentucky

Bluegrass Community and Technical
    College *A*
Union College *B*
University of Kentucky *B*
University of Louisville *C*

Louisiana

Tulane University *B, M*

Maine

Bowdoin College *B*
Colby College *B*

Maryland

Hood College *B*
Johns Hopkins University *B, M*

Massachusetts

Assumption College *B*
Bard College at Simon's Rock *B*
Boston University *B*
Brandeis University *B*
Hampshire College *B*
Smith College *B*
Suffolk University *B*
Tufts University *B*
University of Massachusetts
    Amherst *C*
Wellesley College *B*

Michigan

Albion College *B*
Oakland University *B*

Minnesota

Carleton College *B*
Hamline University *B*
Macalester College *B*
Saint Cloud State University *B*
St. Olaf College *B*
University of Minnesota
    Duluth *B*
    Morris *B*
    Twin Cities *B*

Mississippi

Millsaps College *B*

Missouri

Saint Louis University *B*
University of Missouri
    Columbia *B*
Washington University in St. Louis *B*

Nebraska

University of Nebraska
    Lincoln *B*
    Omaha *B*

Nevada

University of Nevada
    Las Vegas *B*

New Hampshire

Dartmouth College *B*

New Jersey

Rutgers, The State University of New
    Jersey
    New Brunswick/Piscataway
        Campus *B*
Seton Hall University *B*
William Paterson University of New
    Jersey *B*

New Mexico

University of New Mexico *B, M, D*

New York

Adelphi University *B*
Bard College *B*
Barnard College *B*
Boricua College *B, M*
Canisius College *B*
City University of New York
    City College *B*
    Hunter College *B*
    Lehman College *B*
    Queens College *B, T*
Colgate University *B*
Columbia University *B*
Columbia University
    School of General Studies *B*
Fordham University *B*
Hobart and William Smith Colleges *B*
Hofstra University *B*
New York University *B*
Pace University *B*
SUNY
    College at New Paltz *B*
    College at Plattsburgh *B*
    University at Albany *B, M*
    University at Binghamton *B*
Syracuse University *B*
United States Military Academy *B*
University of Rochester *B*
Vassar College *B*

North Carolina

Davidson College *B*
University of North Carolina
    Chapel Hill *B*
    Charlotte *B, M*

Ohio

Bowling Green State University *B*
College of Wooster *B*
Denison University *B*
Miami University
  Oxford *B*
Oberlin College *B*
Ohio State University
  Columbus Campus *M*
Ohio University *B, M*
Pontifical College Josephinum *B*
University of Akron *C*
University of Cincinnati *C*
University of Toledo *B*

Oregon

Pacific University *B*
Portland State University *B*
University of Oregon *B*
Willamette University *B*

Pennsylvania

Albright College *B*
Bucknell University *B*
Dickinson College *B*
Gettysburg College *B*
Penn State
  Abington *B*
  Altoona *B*
  Beaver *B*
  Berks *B*
  Brandywine *B*
  DuBois *B*
  Erie, The Behrend College *B*
  Fayette, The Eberly Campus *B*
  Greater Allegheny *B*
  Harrisburg *B*
  Hazleton *B*
  Lehigh Valley *B*
  Mont Alto *B*
  New Kensington *B*
  Schuylkill *B*
  Shenango *B*
  University Park *B*
  Wilkes-Barre *B*
  Worthington Scranton *B*
  York *B*
Shippensburg University of
  Pennsylvania *C*
Swarthmore College *B*
Temple University *B*
University of Pennsylvania *M*
Villanova University *B*

Rhode Island

Brown University *B, M, D*
Rhode Island College *B*

South Carolina

University of South Carolina
  Columbia *B*
Wofford College *B*

Tennessee

Rhodes College *B*
Vanderbilt University *B, M*

Texas

Austin College *B*
Baylor University *B*
Rice University *B*
St. Edward's University *B*
Southern Methodist University *B*
Southwestern University *B*
Texas Tech University *B*
Trinity University *B*
University of Texas
  Austin *B, M, D*
  Dallas *M*
  El Paso *B, M*

Utah

Brigham Young University *B*
University of Utah *B, M*
Westminster College *B*

Vermont

Bennington College *B*
Goddard College *B, M*
Marlboro College *B*
Middlebury College *B*

Virginia

George Mason University *B*
University of Richmond *B*
University of Virginia *B*

Washington

Gonzaga University *B*
Seattle Pacific University *B*
University of Washington *B, M*
Whitman College *B*

Wisconsin

Ripon College *B*
University of Wisconsin
  Eau Claire *B*

Latin teacher education

Connecticut

Fairfield University *T*

Illinois

Augustana College *B, T*
DePaul University *T*
Knox College *T*
University of Illinois
  Urbana-Champaign *B, M, T*

Indiana

Indiana University
  Bloomington *B, T*

Iowa

Cornell College *T*
University of Iowa *T*

Maryland

Mount St. Mary's University *T*

Massachusetts

Assumption College *T*

Michigan

Western Michigan University *B*

Minnesota

Concordia College: Moorhead *B, T*

Mississippi

Millsaps College *T*

Missouri

Missouri State University *B*

Nebraska

Creighton University *B*

New York

City University of New York
  Hunter College *B, M, T*
Hobart and William Smith Colleges *T*
SUNY
  University at Buffalo *M, T*
University of Rochester *M*

Ohio

Case Western Reserve University *T*
Miami University
  Oxford *B, T*
Ohio Wesleyan University *B*

Pennsylvania

Albright College *T*
Duquesne University *B, M, T*
Gettysburg College *T*
Saint Joseph's University *M, T*
University of Scranton *B*

Tennessee

Belmont University *T*

Texas

University of Dallas *T*

Utah

Brigham Young University *B*

Vermont

Saint Michael's College *M, T*

Wisconsin

Lawrence University *T*

Law (J.D.)

Alabama

Samford University: Cumberland
  School of Law *P*
Thomas Goode Jones School of Law–
  Faulkner University *P*
University of Alabama: School of
  Law *P*

Arizona

Arizona State University: College of
  Law *P*
University of Arizona: College of
  Law *P*

Arkansas

University of Arkansas at Little Rock:
  School of Law *P*
University of Arkansas: School of
  Law *P*

California

California Western School of Law *P*
Golden Gate University: School of
  Law *P*
Humphreys College: School of Law *P*
John F. Kennedy University: School of
  Law *P*
Loyola Marymount University: School
  of Law *P*
McGeorge School of Law: University
  of the Pacific *P*
Pepperdine University: School of
  Law *P*
Santa Clara University: School of
  Law *P*
Southwestern University School of
  Law *P*
Stanford University: School of Law *P*
Thomas Jefferson School of Law *P*
University of California
  Hastings College of the Law *P*
University of California Berkeley:
  School of Law *P*
University of California Davis: School
  of Law *P*
University of California Los Angeles:
  School of Law *P*
University of La Verne College of Law
  at San Fernando Valley *P*
University of La Verne: School of
  Law *P*
University of San Diego: School of
  Law *P*
University of San Francisco: School of
  Law *P*
University of Southern California:
  Law School *P*
University of West Los Angeles:
  School of Law *P*

Western State University College of
  Law *P*
Whittier Law School *P*

Colorado

University of Colorado at Boulder:
  School of Law *P*
University of Denver: College of
  Law *P*

Connecticut

Quinnipiac College: School of Law *P*
University of Connecticut: School of
  Law *P*
Yale Law School *P*

Delaware

Widener University School of Law *P*

District of Columbia

American University: Washington
  College of Law *P*
Catholic University of America:
  School of Law *P*
George Washington University Law
  School *P*
Georgetown University: Law
  Center *P*
Howard University: School of Law *P*
University of the District of
  Columbia: School of Law *P*

Florida

Florida Coastal School of Law *P*
Florida State University: School of
  Law *P*
Nova Southeastern University:
  Shepard Broad Law Center *P*
St. Thomas University: School of
  Law *P*
Stetson University: College of Law *P*
University of Florida: College of
  Law *P*
University of Miami: School of Law *P*

Georgia

Emory University: School of Law *P*
Georgia State University: College of
  Law *P*
Mercer University: Walter F. George
  School of Law *P*
University of Georgia: School of
  Law *P*

Hawaii

University of Hawaii William S.
  Richardson: School of Law *P*

Idaho

University of Idaho: College of Law *P*

Illinois

Chicago-Kent College of Law, Illinois
  Institute of Technology *P*
De Paul University: College of Law *P*
Loyola University Chicago: School of
  Law *P*
Northern Illinois University: College
  of Law *P*
Northwestern University: School of
  Law *P*
Southern Illinois University at
  Carbondale: School of Law *P*
University of Chicago: School of
  Law *P*
University of Illinois
  Urbana-Champaign: College of
  Law *P*

Indiana

Indiana University Bloomington:
  School of Law *P*

Indiana University Indianapolis: School of Law *P*
University of Notre Dame: School of Law *P*
Valparaiso University: School of Law *P*

Iowa
Drake University Law School *P*
University of Iowa: College of Law *P*

Kansas
University of Kansas: School of Law *P*
Washburn University: School of Law *P*

Kentucky
Northern Kentucky University: Salmon P. Chase School of Law *P*
University of Kentucky: College of Law *P*
University of Louisville: School of Law *P*

Louisiana
Louisiana State University and Agricultural and Mechanical College: School of Law *P*
Loyola University: School of Law *P*
Southern University: Law Center *P*
Tulane University: School of Law *P*

Maine
University of Maine: School of Law *P*

Maryland
University of Baltimore: School of Law *P*
University of Maryland at Baltimore: School of Law *P*

Massachusetts
Boston College: Law School *P*
Boston University: School of Law *P*
Harvard University Law School *P*
New England Law *P*
Northeastern University: School of Law *P*
Suffolk University: Law School *P*
Western New England College: School of Law *P*

Michigan
Detroit College of Law *P*
Thomas M. Cooley Law School *P*
University of Detroit Mercy: School of Law *P*
University of Michigan: School of Law *P*
Wayne State University: School of Law *P*

Minnesota
Hamline University: School of Law *P*
University of Minnesota Twin Cities: School of Law *P*
William Mitchell College of Law: Law Professions *P*

Mississippi
Mississippi College: School of Law *P*
University of Mississippi: School of Law *P*

Missouri
St. Louis University: School of Law *P*
University of Missouri Columbia: School of Law *P*
University of Missouri Kansas City: School of Law *P*

Washington University: School of Law *P*

Montana
University of Montana: School of Law *P*

Nebraska
Creighton University: School of Law *P*
University of Nebraska Lincoln: College of Law *P*

New Hampshire
Franklin Pierce Law Center *P*

New Jersey
Seton Hall University: School of Law *P*

New Mexico
University of New Mexico: School of Law *P*

New York
Albany Law School of Union University *P*
Benjamin N. Cardozo School of Law *P*
Brooklyn Law School *P*
City University of New York School of Law at Queens College *P*
Columbia University School of Law *P*
Cornell University: School of Law *P*
Fordham University: School of Law *P*
Hofstra University: School of Law *P*
New York Law School *P*
New York University: School of Law *P*
Pace University Westchester: School of Law *P*
St. John's University: School of Law *P*
State University of New York at Buffalo: School of Law *P*
Syracuse University: College of Law *P*
Touro College: Jacob D. Fuchsberg Law Center *P*

North Carolina
Campbell University: Norman Adrian Wiggins School of Law *P*
Duke University: School of Law *P*
North Carolina Central University: School of Law *P*
University of North Carolina at Chapel Hill: School of Law *P*
Wake Forest University: School of Law *P*

North Dakota
University of North Dakota: School of Law *P*

Ohio
Capital University: School of Law *P*
Case Western Reserve University: School of Law *P*
Cleveland State University: College of Law *P*
Ohio Northern University: College of Law *P*
Ohio State University: College of Law *P*
University of Akron: School of Law *P*
University of Cincinnati: College of Law *P*
University of Dayton: School of Law *P*
University of Toledo: College of Law *P*

Oklahoma
Oklahoma City University: School of Law *P*
University of Oklahoma: College of Law *P*
University of Tulsa: College of Law *P*

Oregon
Lewis and Clark College: Northwestern School of Law *P*
University of Oregon: School of Law *P*
Willamette University: College of Law *P*

Pennsylvania
Dickinson School of Law *P*
Duquesne University: School of Law *P*
Temple University: School of Law *P*
University of Pennsylvania Law School *P*
University of Pittsburgh: School of Law *P*
Villanova University: School of Law *P*
Widener University School of Law *P*

Puerto Rico
Inter American University of Puerto Rico: School of Law *P*
Pontifical Catholic University of Puerto Rico: School of Law *P*
University of Puerto Rico Rio Piedras Campus: School of Law *P*

South Carolina
University of South Carolina: School of Law *P*

South Dakota
University of South Dakota: School of Law *P*

Tennessee
University of Memphis: School of Law *P*
University of Tennessee College of Law *P*
Vanderbilt University: School of Law *P*

Texas
Baylor University: School of Law *P*
St. Mary's University: School of Law *P*
South Texas College of Law *P*
Southern Methodist University: School of Law *P*
Texas Southern University: Thurgood Marshall School of Law *P*
Texas Tech University: School of Law *P*
University of Houston: Law Center *P*
University of Texas at Austin: School of Law *P*

Utah
Brigham Young University: School of Law *P*
University of Utah: College of Law *P*

Vermont
Vermont Law School *P*

Virginia
College of William and Mary: School of Law *P*
George Mason University: School of Law *P*
Regent University: School of Law *P*
University of Richmond: The T.C. Williams School of Law *P*

University of Virginia: School of Law *P*
Washington and Lee University: School of Law *P*

Washington
Gonzaga University: School of Law *P*
Seattle University: School of Law *P*
University of Washington: School of Law *P*

West Virginia
West Virginia University: College of Law *P*

Wisconsin
Marquette University: School of Law *P*
University of Wisconsin Madison: School of Law *P*

Wyoming
University of Wyoming: College of Law *P*

Law enforcement intelligence analysis

California
Diablo Valley College *C*

Minnesota
Century College *C*

Nebraska
Bellevue University *B*

Oklahoma
University of Central Oklahoma *M*

South Dakota
Lake Area Technical Institute *A*

Washington
Seattle University *T*

Law enforcement investigation and interviewing

Arizona
Arizona Western College *C*

Minnesota
Century College *C*

Nebraska
Western Nebraska Community College *C*

South Dakota
Lake Area Technical Institute *A*

Law enforcement records/evidence management

Arizona
Arizona Western College *C*

California
Woodland Community College *A*

South Dakota
Lake Area Technical Institute *A*

Lay ministry

Alabama
Oakwood University *B*
Southeastern Bible College *A, B*

Arizona
Arizona Christian University *B*

Illinois
Judson University *C, B*

Indiana
University of St. Francis *C, A, B*

Minnesota
Bethel University *B*
St. Mary's University of Minnesota *B*

Oklahoma
Mid-America Christian University *M*

Tennessee
Trevecca Nazarene University *B*

Texas
Abilene Christian University *B*
Howard Payne University *C, A*
Southwestern Adventist University *C*

Wisconsin
Maranatha Baptist Bible College *A*

Learning sciences

Arizona
University of Arizona *B*

Iowa
Ashford University *B*

Minnesota
Winona State University *B, T*

New Mexico
University of New Mexico *M, D, T*

Pennsylvania
Carnegie Mellon University *M*

Legal administrative assistance

Alabama
Faulkner State Community College *A*

Arizona
Brookline College
  Phoenix *C*
  Tempe *C*
  Tucson *C*
Coconino County Community
  College *C*
Yavapai College *C, A*

Arkansas
National Park Community College *C*
Pulaski Technical College *C*

California
Allan Hancock College *C, A*
Butte College *C, A*
Chabot College *A*
Chaffey College *C*
City College of San Francisco *C, A*
Coastline Community College *C*
College of the Redwoods *C, A*
Columbia College *C*
East Los Angeles College *C, A*
Empire College *C*
Fresno City College *C, A*

Fullerton College *A*
Glendale Community College *C, A*
Golden West College *C, A*
Heald College
  Fresno *A*
  San Jose *A*
Humphreys College *C, A, B*
Long Beach City College *C, A*
Los Angeles City College *C, A*
Los Angeles Harbor College *C, A*
MTI College *C*
Merced College *C, A*
Pasadena City College *A*
Platt College
  Ontario *C, A, B*
Porterville College *C*
Riverside City College *C*
Sacramento City College *C, A*
Saddleback College *A*
San Bernardino Valley College *C*
Santa Monica College *C, A*
Santa Rosa Junior College *C*
Shasta College *A*
Skyline College *C, A*
Solano Community College *C, A*
South Coast College *C*
Southwestern College *C, A*

Colorado
Everest College
  Colorado Springs *A*
Otero Junior College *A*

Connecticut
Gateway Community College *A*
Naugatuck Valley Community
  College *A*
Tunxis Community College *C, A*

Delaware
Delaware Technical Community
  College
  Jack F. Owens Campus *C, A*
  Terry Campus *C, A*

Florida
Broward College *C, A*
Eastern Florida State College *A*
Indian River State College *A*
Miami Dade College *C, A*
Seminole State College of Florida *A*

Georgia
Augusta Technical College *C*
Bainbridge College *C*
Central Georgia Technical College *C*
Georgia Piedmont Technical
  College *C*
Gwinnett College *C*

Hawaii
Heald College
  Honolulu *A*
University of Hawaii
  Kapiolani Community College *A*

Idaho
College of Western Idaho *A, B*
Lewis-Clark State College *C, A, B*
North Idaho College *A*

Illinois
Black Hawk College *C, A*
College of DuPage *C, A*
Elgin Community College *C, A*
Harper College *C, A*
John Wood Community College *A*
Joliet Junior College *A*
Kaskaskia College *C*
Kishwaukee College *C*
Lake Land College *A*
Lewis and Clark Community
  College *A*

Lincoln Land Community
  College *C, A*
McHenry County College *C*
Moraine Valley Community College *C*
Sauk Valley Community College *C, A*
Shawnee Community College *A*
Triton College *C*

Indiana
ITT Technical Institute
  Fort Wayne *A*
International Business College *A*
International Business College:
  Indianapolis *C, A*

Iowa
Ellsworth Community College *A*
Southeastern Community College *A*

Kansas
Colby Community College *A*
Dodge City Community College *C, A*
Highland Community College *A*
Independence Community
  College *C, A*
Labette Community College *A*
Pratt Community College *C, A*
Seward County Community
  College *C, A*
Washburn University *C, A*

Kentucky
Ashland Community and Technical
  College *A*
Daymar College
  Owensboro *A*
National College
  Lexington *A*
  Louisville *A*
  Pikeville *A*
Sullivan University *C, A*

Louisiana
Bossier Parish Community College *C*
Delgado Community College *C*

Maine
Beal College *A*
Kaplan University
  South Portland *A, B*
Northern Maine Community
  College *A*

Maryland
Allegany College of Maryland *C*
Baltimore City Community College *A*
Community College of Baltimore
  County *C*
Frederick Community College *C, A*
Howard Community College *C, A*
Kaplan University
  Hagerstown *C*
Prince George's Community
  College *C, A*

Massachusetts
Bristol Community College *C*
Cape Cod Community College *C, A*
Marian Court College *A, B*
North Shore Community
  College *C, A*
Roxbury Community College *A*

Michigan
Baker College
  Auburn Hills *A*
  Cadillac *A*
  Flint *A*
  Jackson *A*
  Owosso *A*
  Port Huron *A*
Bay de Noc Community College *A*
Delta College *A*
Henry Ford Community College *A*

Kalamazoo Valley Community
  College *C, A*
Kellogg Community College *A*
Kirtland Community College *A*
Lake Michigan College *C, A*
Mid Michigan Community College *A*
Monroe County Community
  College *C, A*
Muskegon Community College *A*

Minnesota
Alexandria Technical and Community
  College *C, A*
Anoka Technical College *C, A*
Dakota County Technical
  College *C, A*
Globe University
  Minneapolis *C*
  Moorhead *C*
  Woodbury *C*
Hibbing Community College *A*
Inver Hills Community College *C, A*
Lake Superior College *C, A*
Minneapolis Business College *C, A*
Minneapolis Community and
  Technical College *C*
Minnesota School of Business
  Blaine *C*
  Brooklyn Center *C*
  Elk River *C*
  Lakeville *C*
  Richfield *C*
  Rochester *C*
  St. Cloud *C*
  Shakopee *C*
Minnesota State College - Southeast
  Technical *C, A*
Ridgewater College *C, A*
Riverland Community College *C, A*
St. Cloud Technical and Community
  College *C, A*
South Central College *C, A*

Mississippi
Northwest Mississippi Community
  College *A*
Pearl River Community College *C, A*

Missouri
Jefferson College *A*
Metropolitan Community College -
  Kansas City *C*

Montana
Flathead Valley Community
  College *A*
Helena College University of
  Montana *C*
University of Montana *A*

Nebraska
Midland University *A*
Northeast Community College *A*

Nevada
Career College of Northern Nevada *C*
College of Southern Nevada *C, A*
Truckee Meadows Community
  College *A*

New Hampshire
Nashua Community College *C*

New Jersey
Gloucester County College *A*

New Mexico
Brookline College
  Albuquerque *C*
Clovis Community College *C, A*
Dona Ana Community College of
  New Mexico State University *A*
New Mexico Junior College *C, A*

New York

ASA College *C*
Briarcliffe College *A*
Bryant & Stratton College
  Rochester *A*
  Syracuse *A*
City University of New York
  Kingsborough Community
  College *A*
Elmira Business Institute *C, A*
Globe Institute of
  Technology *C, A, B*
Nassau Community College *C, A*
New York Career Institute *A*
Sanford-Brown Institute
  Melville *A*
Trocaire College *A*
Ulster County Community
  College *C, A*
Utica School of Commerce *C, A*

North Carolina

Alamance Community College *C, A*
Carteret Community College *A*
Central Carolina Community
  College *A*
Central Piedmont Community
  College *A*
Cleveland Community College *A*
Gaston College *A*
King's College *C, A*
Montgomery Community
  College *C, A*
Nash Community College *A*

North Dakota

Bismarck State College *C, A*

Ohio

Bradford School *C, A*
Clark State Community College *A*
ETI Technical College of Niles *A*
Eastern Gateway Community
  College *A*
Edison State Community College *A*
Miami-Jacobs Career College
  Columbus *C*
North Central State College *A*
Northwest State Community
  College *A*
Ohio Business College
  Sandusky *A*
Ohio University
  Chillicothe Campus *A*
  Southern Campus at Ironton *C*
Stark State College *A*
Trumbull Business College *A*
University of Akron: Wayne
  College *C, A*
University of Cincinnati
  Blue Ash College *A*
  Clermont College *C, A*
University of Northwestern Ohio *A*
University of Rio Grande *A*

Oklahoma

Eastern Oklahoma State College *A*
Oklahoma City Community
  College *C, A*
Tulsa Community College *C, A*

Oregon

Everest College
  Portland *C*
Lane Community College *C*
Linn-Benton Community College *A*
Southwestern Oregon Community
  College *C*
Treasure Valley Community
  College *A*
Umpqua Community College *A*

Pennsylvania

Bradford School: Pittsburgh *C, A*
Butler County Community College *A*
Cambria-Rowe Business College *A*
Consolidated School of Business
  York *A*
DuBois Business College *A*
DuBois Business College
  Huntingdon *C, A*
  Oil City *A*
Erie Business Center *C, A*
Erie Business Center South *A*
Kaplan Career Institute
  Pittsburgh *A*
McCann School of Business and
  Technology
  Hazleton *A*
Northampton Community
  College *C, A*
Pace Institute *C*
Penn Commercial Business and
  Technical School *A*
Prism Career Institute *C*
Reading Area Community
  College *C, A*
South Hills School of Business &
  Technology *A*
Yorktowne Business Institute *A*

Puerto Rico

Universidad del Este *C, A*

Rhode Island

Community College of Rhode
  Island *C, A*

South Carolina

Forrest Junior College *A*
York Technical College *C*

Tennessee

Nashville State Community College *A*
South College *C*

Texas

Blinn College *C*
El Centro College *C*
El Paso Community College *C*
Frank Phillips College *C, A*
Kilgore College *A*
Laredo Community College *C*
McLennan Community College *A*
North Central Texas College *A*
Northeast Texas Community
  College *C, A*
Odessa College *C, A*
St. Philip's College *A*
San Antonio College *C*
South Plains College *A*
South Texas College *C, A*
Trinity Valley Community
  College *C, A*
Tyler Junior College *A*

Utah

LDS Business College *A*
Salt Lake Community College *C*

Virginia

Blue Ridge Community College *C*
Danville Community College *C*
Mountain Empire Community
  College *A*
New River Community College *C, A*
Southwest Virginia Community
  College *C*
Virginia Highlands Community
  College *C, A*
Virginia Western Community
  College *A*

Washington

Bates Technical College *C, A*
Bellingham Technical College *C, A*

Centralia College *C, A*
Clark College *C, A*
Clover Park Technical College *C, A*
Edmonds Community College *A*
Everett Community College *C, A*
Green River Community College *A*
Lower Columbia College *C, A*
Olympic College *C*
Peninsula College *C*
Renton Technical College *C, A*
South Puget Sound Community
  College *A*
Spokane Community College *C, A*
Walla Walla Community College *C, A*
Wenatchee Valley College *C*
Yakima Valley Community College *C*

West Virginia

Kanawha Valley Community and
  Technical College *C*
Mountain State College *A*
New River Community and Technical
  College *C, A*
West Virginia Junior College
  Charleston *C, A*

Wisconsin

Blackhawk Technical College *A*
Bryant & Stratton College
  Milwaukee *A*
Globe University
  Appleton *C*
  Eau Claire *C*
  Green Bay *C*
  Madison East *C*
  Middleton *C*
  Wausau *C*
Madison Area Technical College *C*
Milwaukee Area Technical College *A*
Moraine Park Technical College *C, A*
Southwest Wisconsin Technical
  College *A*

Legal studies

Alabama

Faulkner University *A, B, D*

Alaska

University of Alaska
  Anchorage *B*

Arizona

Arizona State University *B, M, D*
National Paralegal College *C, A, B*
University of Arizona *M*
Western International University *B*

Arkansas

Harding University *B*

California

Claremont McKenna College *B*
Heald College
  Concord *A*
John F. Kennedy University *B*
Loyola Marymount University *M, D*
National University *C, B*
Palomar College *A*
Pepperdine University *M*
Santa Barbara City College *A*
Scripps College *B*
Southwestern College *A*
Stanford University *M, D*
Thomas Jefferson School of Law *D*
University of California
  Berkeley *B, M, D*
  Santa Barbara *B*
  Santa Cruz *B*
University of La Verne *B, D*
University of Southern
  California *M, D*
University of the Pacific *M, D*

Western State University College of
  Law *D*

Colorado

Everest College
  Aurora *A*
United States Air Force Academy *B*
University of Colorado
  Boulder *M, D*
University of Denver *B*

Connecticut

Mitchell College *A, B*
Post University *A, B*
Quinnipiac University *B*
University of Hartford *A, B*
University of New Haven *A, B*
University of Saint Joseph *C*
Yale University *M, D*

District of Columbia

American University *B, M, D*
Catholic University of America *M, D*
George Washington University *M, D*
Georgetown University *M*
Howard University *M*

Florida

Barry University *B, M, D*
City College
  Gainesville *A*
Florida National University *B*
Herzing University
  Winter Park *A*
Keiser University *B*
Nova Southeastern University *B, M*
Saint Thomas University *D*
Stetson University *D*
University of Miami *B*

Georgia

Brenau University *B*
Emory University *D*
Georgia State University *D*
Mercer University *D*
University of Georgia *M*

Idaho

University of Idaho *D*

Illinois

Dominican University *B*
Illinois Institute of Technology *D*
Illinois State University *B*
Illinois Valley Community College *A*
Loyola University Chicago *D*
Northern Illinois University *D*
Northwestern University *B, M*
Roosevelt University *B*
Southern Illinois University
  Carbondale *M*
University of Chicago *M, D*
University of Illinois
  Urbana-Champaign *M, D*

Indiana

University of St. Francis *B*

Iowa

Drake University *B*

Kansas

Colby Community College *A*

Kentucky

Kentucky Wesleyan College *B*

Louisiana

Herzing University
  Kenner *B*
Tulane University *A, B*

Maine

University of Southern Maine *M*

Maryland

Carroll Community College *A*
Harford Community College *A*
Hood College *B*
University of Baltimore *M*
University of Maryland
  Baltimore *D*
  University College *B*

Massachusetts

Amherst College *B*
Anna Maria College *B*
Bay Path College *B*
Becker College *B*
Boston College *M, D*
Boston University *M*
Elms College *B*
Hampshire College *B*
Lasell College *B*
Newbury College *B*
Northeastern University *M, D*
University of Massachusetts
  Amherst *M*
Western New England University *B*

Michigan

Central Michigan University *B*
Grand Valley State University *B*
University of Michigan *M, D*

Minnesota

Crown College *B*
Minnesota West Community and
  Technical College *A*

Missouri

Culver-Stockton College *B*
Park University *B*
Saint Louis University *B*
University of Missouri
  Columbia *M*
Webster University *B, M*
William Woods University *B*

Nebraska

Bellevue University *B*
Chadron State College *B*
Herzing University
  Omaha School of Massage Therapy
    and Healthcare *B*

Nevada

University of Nevada
  Las Vegas *D*

New Jersey

Berkeley College *A, B*
Montclair State University *M*
Ramapo College of New Jersey *B*
Seton Hall University *M, D*
Warren County Community
  College *A*

New York

Berkeley College of New York
  City *A, B*
Bryant & Stratton College
  Amherst *A*
City University of New York
  John Jay College of Criminal
    Justice *B*
College of New Rochelle *C*
College of Saint Rose *B*
Hofstra University *M, D*
Ithaca College *B*
Mercy College *B*
Nazareth College *B*
New York University *M, D*
Pace University: Pleasantville/
  Briarcliff *M*

SUNY
  College at Fredonia *B*
St. John Fisher College *B*
St. John's University *A, B*
Syracuse University *C*
Touro College *M*
United States Military Academy *B*

North Carolina

Duke University *D*
Elon University *D*
Livingstone College *B*
South College *B*
Wake Forest University *M, D*

Ohio

Capital University *M, D*
Fortis College
  Centerville *A*
Franciscan University of
  Steubenville *B*
Herzing University
  Toledo *A*
University of Dayton *M*
University of Toledo *M, D*

Oklahoma

University of Oklahoma *M*
University of Oklahoma: College of
  Law *D*
University of Tulsa *B, D*

Oregon

Everest College
  Portland *A*
Heald College
  Portland *A*
Lewis & Clark College *M, D*
University of Oregon *D*

Pennsylvania

Arcadia University *B*
California University of
  Pennsylvania *M*
Central Penn College *B*
DeSales University *B*
Dickinson College *B*
Elizabethtown College *B*
Penn State
  Abington *C*
  Altoona *C*
  Beaver *C*
  Berks *C*
  Brandywine *C*
  DuBois *C*
  Erie, The Behrend College *C*
  Fayette, The Eberly Campus *C*
  Greater Allegheny *C*
  Harrisburg *C*
  Hazleton *C*
  Lehigh Valley *C*
  Mont Alto *C*
  New Kensington *C*
  Schuylkill *C*
  Shenango *C*
  University Park *C*
  Wilkes-Barre *C*
  Worthington Scranton *C*
  York *C*
Point Park University *B*
Saint Joseph's University *B*
Sanford-Brown Institute
  Pittsburgh *C, A*
University of Pennsylvania *B, M, D*
University of Pittsburgh *B*
University of Pittsburgh: School of
  Law *D*
Villanova University *D*
Widener University *M, D*
Widener University School of Law *D*

Puerto Rico

Pontifical Catholic University of
  Puerto Rico *B, M*

University of Puerto Rico
  Rio Piedras *M*

Rhode Island

Roger Williams University *B*

South Dakota

University of South Dakota *D*

Tennessee

Daymar Institute
  Clarksville *A*
Lincoln Memorial University *D*
Lipscomb University *B*
South College *B*

Texas

Baylor University *D*
Brazosport College *A*
Paul Quinn College *B*
St. Mary's University *D*
Southern Methodist University *M, D*
Texas Southern University *D*

Vermont

Burlington College *B*
Champlain College *M*

Virginia

Bryant & Stratton College
  Virginia Beach *A*
College of William and Mary *M*
Hollins University *M*
Regent University *M*
Virginia Intermont College *B*

Washington

Gonzaga University *M, D*
Highline Community College *A*
Seattle University *D*
University of Washington *M, D*

West Virginia

American Public University
  System *B, M*
West Virginia University *M*

Wisconsin

Herzing University
  Brookfield *A*
  Kenosha *B*
  Madison *A, B*
University of Wisconsin
  Madison *B, M*
  Superior *B*

Wyoming

University of Wyoming *D*

Liberal arts and sciences

Alabama

Alabama Southern Community
  College *A*
Amridge University *A, B, M*
Athens State University *B*
Auburn University at
  Montgomery *B, M*
Bevill State Community College *A*
Bishop State Community College *A*
Calhoun Community College *A*
Central Alabama Community
  College *A*
Chattahoochee Valley Community
  College *A*
Concordia College *A*
Enterprise State Community
  College *A*
Faulkner State Community College *A*
Faulkner University *B, M*
Gadsden State Community College *A*

George C. Wallace Community
  College at Dothan *A*
George C. Wallace State Community
  College at Selma *A*
Jacksonville State University *B, M*
Jefferson Davis Community
  College *A*
Jefferson State Community College *A*
Lawson State Community College *A*
Lurleen B. Wallace Community
  College *A*
Marion Military Institute *A*
Northeast Alabama Community
  College *A*
Northwest-Shoals Community
  College *A*
Shelton State Community College *A*
Snead State Community College *A*
Southern Union State Community
  College *A*
Spring Hill College *M*
Troy University *A, B*
Wallace State Community College at
  Hanceville *A*

Alaska

Alaska Pacific University *B, M*
Prince William Sound Community
  College *A*
University of Alaska
  Anchorage *A, B*
  Fairbanks *A, B*
  Southeast *B*

Arizona

Argosy University
  Online *B*
  Phoenix *B*
Arizona Christian University *A*
Arizona State University *M*
Central Arizona College *A*
Dine College *A*
Eastern Arizona College *A*
Estrella Mountain Community
  College *A*
GateWay Community College *A*
Glendale Community College *A*
Harrison Middleton
  University *B, M, D*
Mesa Community College *C*
Mohave Community College *A*
Northern Arizona University *B*
Northland Pioneer College *A*
Paradise Valley Community College *A*
Phoenix College *A*
Pima Community College *C, A*
Scottsdale Community College *A*
South Mountain Community
  College *A*
Tohono O'odham Community
  College *A*
Western International University *A, B*
Yavapai College *A*

Arkansas

Arkansas Northeastern College *A*
Arkansas State University *A*
Arkansas State University
  Beebe *C, A*
  Mountain Home *A*
  Newport *A*
Arkansas Tech University *M*
Central Baptist College *B*
College of the Ouachitas *A*
Cossatot Community College of the
  University of Arkansas *A*
Crowley's Ridge College *A*
East Arkansas Community College *C*
Henderson State University *M*
Mid-South Community College *C, A*
National Park Community
  College *C, A*
North Arkansas College *C, A*

Northwest Arkansas Community
College *A*
Ozarka College *A*
Phillips Community College of the
University of Arkansas *A*
Pulaski Technical College *C, A*
Rich Mountain Community College *A*
South Arkansas Community
College *C, A*
Southeast Arkansas College *C, A*
Southern Arkansas University Tech *C*
University of Arkansas
Community College at Batesville *A*
Community College at Hope *A*
Community College at
Morrilton *C, A*
Fort Smith *A*
Little Rock *B, M*
University of Central Arkansas *B*

California

Allan Hancock College *A*
Alliant International University *B*
American Jewish University *B*
American River College *A*
Antelope Valley College *A*
Antioch University
Los Angeles *B*
Santa Barbara *B*
Argosy University
Inland Empire *B*
Los Angeles *B*
Orange County *B*
San Diego *B*
San Francisco Bay Area *B*
Azusa Pacific University *B*
Bakersfield College *A*
Berkeley City College *A*
Biola University *B*
Butte College *A*
Cabrillo College *A*
California Baptist University *B*
California Lutheran University *B*
California Polytechnic State
University: San Luis Obispo *B*
California State Polytechnic
University: Pomona *B*
California State University
Bakersfield *B*
Channel Islands *B*
Chico *C, B*
Dominguez Hills *B*
East Bay *B*
Fresno *B*
Fullerton *B*
Long Beach *B*
Los Angeles *B*
Monterey Bay *B*
Northridge *B*
Sacramento *B, M*
San Bernardino *B*
San Marcos *B*
Stanislaus *B*
Canada College *A*
Cerro Coso Community College *A*
Chabot College *A*
Chaffey College *A*
Chapman University *B*
Citrus College *A*
Coastline Community College *A*
College of Alameda *A*
College of Marin *A*
College of the Canyons *A*
College of the Desert *A*
College of the Redwoods *A*
College of the Sequoias *A*
College of the Siskiyous *A*
Columbia College *A*
Concordia University Irvine *A, B*
Contra Costa College *A*
Copper Mountain College *A*
Cosumnes River College *A*
Crafton Hills College *C, A*
Cuesta College *A*
Cuyamaca College *A*

Cypress College *A*
De Anza College *A*
Deep Springs College *A*
Diablo Valley College *A*
Dominican University of California *B*
East Los Angeles College *C, A*
Evergreen Valley College *A*
Feather River College *A*
Folsom Lake College *A*
Foothill College *A*
Fresno City College *A*
Fresno Pacific University *A, B*
Fullerton College *A*
Gavilan College *A*
Glendale Community College *A*
Golden West College *A*
Grossmont College *A*
Hartnell College *A*
Holy Names University *B*
Humboldt State University *B*
Humphreys College *A, B*
Imperial Valley College *A*
Irvine Valley College *A*
John F. Kennedy University *B*
La Sierra University *B*
Lake Tahoe Community College *A*
Laney College *A*
Lassen Community College *A*
Long Beach City College *A*
Los Angeles City College *A*
Los Angeles Harbor College *A*
Los Angeles Mission College *A*
Los Angeles Pierce College *A*
Los Angeles Southwest College *A*
Los Angeles Trade and Technical
College *A*
Los Angeles Valley College *A*
Los Medanos College *A*
Loyola Marymount University *B*
Marymount California University *A, B*
Master's College *B*
Mendocino College *A*
Merced College *A*
Merritt College *A*
MiraCosta College *A*
Mission College *A*
Monterey Peninsula College *A*
Moorpark College *A*
Mount St. Mary's College *A, B*
Mount San Antonio College *A*
Mount San Jacinto College *A*
Napa Valley College *A*
National University *B*
Notre Dame de Namur University *B*
Ohlone College *A*
Orange Coast College *A*
Oxnard College *C, A*
Palo Verde College *A*
Palomar College *C, A*
Pasadena City College *C, A*
Patten University *B*
Pepperdine University *B*
Point Loma Nazarene University *B*
Porterville College *A*
Providence Christian College *B*
Reedley College *A*
Rio Hondo College *A*
Sacramento City College *A*
Saddleback College *A*
St. Mary's College of California *B, M*
San Bernardino Valley College *A*
San Diego Christian College *A*
San Diego City College *A*
San Diego Mesa College *C, A*
San Diego State University *B, M*
San Francisco State University *B*
San Joaquin Delta College *A*
San Jose City College *A*
San Jose State University *B*
Santa Ana College *A*
Santa Barbara City College *A*
Santa Clara University *B*
Santa Monica College *C, A*
Santa Rosa Junior College *A*
Santiago Canyon College *A*

Sierra College *A*
Simpson University *B*
Skyline College *A*
Soka University of America *B*
Solano Community College *A*
Sonoma State University *B*
Southwestern College *A*
Stanford University *M*
Taft College *A*
Thomas Aquinas College *B*
University of California
Riverside *B*
University of La Verne *B*
University of Redlands *B*
University of San Diego *B*
University of San Francisco *B*
University of Southern California *M*
University of the Pacific *B*
Vanguard University of Southern
California *B*
Victor Valley College *A*
West Hills College: Coalinga *A*
West Hills College: Lemoore *A*
West Los Angeles College *C, A*
West Valley College *A*
Whittier College *B*
Yuba College *A*

Colorado

Adams State University *A, B*
Aims Community College *A*
Arapahoe Community College *A*
Argosy University
Denver *B*
Colorado Christian University *B*
Colorado College *B*
Colorado Mesa University *A, B*
Colorado Mountain College *A*
Colorado Northwestern Community
College *A*
Colorado State University *B*
Colorado State University
Pueblo *B*
Community College of Aurora *A*
Community College of Denver *A*
Fort Lewis College *B*
Front Range Community College *A*
Johnson & Wales University
Denver *B*
Lamar Community College *A*
Morgan Community College *A*
Northeastern Junior College *A*
Otero Junior College *A*
Pikes Peak Community College *A*
Pueblo Community College *A*
Red Rocks Community College *C, A*
Regis University *B*
Trinidad State Junior College *A*
University of Denver *B, M*

Connecticut

Albertus Magnus College *A, B, M*
Asnuntuck Community College *A*
Capital Community College *A*
Charter Oak State College *A, B*
Gateway Community College *A*
Housatonic Community College *A*
Manchester Community College *A*
Middlesex Community College *A*
Mitchell College *A, B*
Naugatuck Valley Community
College *A*
Northwestern Connecticut
Community College *A*
Norwalk Community College *A*
Quinebaug Valley Community
College *A*
Sacred Heart University *A, B*
Southern Connecticut State
University *B*
Three Rivers Community College *A*
Tunxis Community College *A*
University of Bridgeport *A, B*
University of Connecticut *B*

University of Hartford *A, B*
University of New Haven *B*
Wesleyan University *B, M*
Western Connecticut State
University *A, B*

Delaware

University of Delaware *A, B, M, D*
Wesley College *A, B*
Wilmington University *A, B*

District of Columbia

American University *A, B*
Catholic University of America *B*
George Washington University *B*
Georgetown University *B, M, D*
Strayer University *A*

Florida

Argosy University
Sarasota *B*
Tampa *B*
Ave Maria University *B*
Barry University *B, M*
Beacon College *A, B*
Broward College *A*
College of Central Florida *A*
Daytona State College *A*
Edison State College *A*
Flagler College *B*
Florida Agricultural and Mechanical
University *A*
Florida Atlantic University *A, B, M*
Florida College *A, B*
Florida Gateway College *A*
Florida Gulf Coast University *A, B*
Florida International University *B, M*
Gulf Coast State College *A*
Hillsborough Community College *A*
Indian River State College *A*
Jacksonville University *B*
Lake-Sumter State College *A*
Miami Dade College *A*
New College of Florida *B*
North Florida Community College *A*
Northwest Florida State College *A*
Nova Southeastern University *B*
Palm Beach State College *A*
Pasco-Hernando State College *A*
Pensacola State College *A*
Polk State College *A*
Rollins College *B, M*
Saint Johns River State College *A*
Saint Leo University *A, B*
St. Petersburg College *A*
Saint Thomas University *B*
Santa Fe College *A*
Schiller International University *A*
Seminole State College of
Florida *C, A*
South Florida State College *A*
Southeastern University *A*
State College of Florida, Manatee-
Sarasota *A*
Tallahassee Community College *A*
University of Miami *B, M*
University of North Florida *A*
University of South Florida *A, B, M*
University of South Florida
Saint Petersburg *B, M*
University of Tampa *B*
University of West Florida *A*
Valencia College *A*
Warner University *A*

Georgia

Abraham Baldwin Agricultural
College *A*
Andrew College *A*
Argosy University
Atlanta *B*
Armstrong Atlantic State
University *A, B*
Brenau University *A, B*

Clayton State University *A, B, M*
College of Coastal Georgia *A*
Columbus State University *A, B*
East Georgia State College *A*
Emmanuel College *A*
Emory University *A, D*
Fort Valley State University *A, B*
Georgia Regents University *A*
LaGrange College *B*
Mercer University *B*
Middle Georgia State College *A*
Oglethorpe University *B*
Oxford College of Emory
    University *A*
Reinhardt University *A, B*
Savannah State University *A*
Shorter University *B*
Southern Polytechnic State
    University *A*
Thomas University *A, B*
Toccoa Falls College *A*
University of Georgia *B*
University of North Georgia *A*
Valdosta State University *A*
Wesleyan College *B*
Young Harris College *A*

Hawaii

Argosy University
    Hawaii *B*
Brigham Young University-
    Hawaii *A, B*
Chaminade University of
    Honolulu *A, B*
Hawaii Pacific University *B*
Hawaii Tokai International College *A*
University of Hawaii
    Hawaii Community College *A*
    Hilo *B*
    Honolulu Community College *A*
    Kapiolani Community College *A*
    Kauai Community College *A*
    Leeward Community College *C, A*
    Manoa *B*
    Maui College *A*
    Windward Community College *A*

Idaho

Boise State University *B*
Brigham Young University-Idaho *A, B*
College of Southern Idaho *A*
College of Western Idaho *A*
Lewis-Clark State College *A*
New Saint Andrews College *A, B, M*
North Idaho College *A*
Northwest Nazarene University *B*

Illinois

Argosy University
    Schaumburg *B*
Aurora University *B*
Black Hawk College *A*
Bradley University *B, M*
City Colleges of Chicago
    Harold Washington College *A*
    Harry S. Truman College *A*
    Kennedy-King College *A*
    Malcolm X College *A*
    Olive-Harvey College *A*
    Richard J. Daley College *A*
    Wilbur Wright College *A*
College of DuPage *A*
College of Lake County *A*
Columbia College Chicago *B*
Concordia University Chicago *M*
Danville Area Community College *A*
DePaul University *B, M*
Dominican University *B*
East-West University *A, B*
Eastern Illinois University *B*
Elgin Community College *A*
Elmhurst College *B*
Eureka College *B*
Governors State University *B*

Greenville College *B*
Harper College *A*
Heartland Community College *A*
Hebrew Theological College *B*
Highland Community College *A*
Illinois Central College *A*
Illinois Eastern Community Colleges
    Frontier Community College *A*
    Lincoln Trail College *A*
    Olney Central College *A*
    Wabash Valley College *A*
Illinois Institute of Technology *B*
Illinois State University *B*
Illinois Valley Community College *A*
John A. Logan College *A*
John Wood Community College *A*
Joliet Junior College *A*
Kaskaskia College *A*
Kishwaukee College *A*
Lake Forest College *M*
Lake Land College *A*
Lewis University *B*
Lewis and Clark Community
    College *A*
Lincoln College *A, B*
Lincoln Land Community College *A*
McHenry County College *A*
Monmouth College *B*
Moraine Valley Community College *A*
Morton College *A*
National-Louis University *B*
North Central College *B, M*
Northeastern Illinois University *B*
Northern Illinois University *B*
Northwestern University *C, B, M*
Oakton Community College *A*
Olivet Nazarene University *B*
Parkland College *A*
Prairie State College *A*
Principia College *B*
Quincy University *A, B*
Rend Lake College *A*
Richland Community College *A*
Rock Valley College *A*
Roosevelt University *B*
St. Augustine College *A*
Saint Xavier University *B, M*
Sauk Valley Community College *A*
Shawnee Community College *A*
Shimer College *B*
South Suburban College of Cook
    County *A*
Southeastern Illinois College *A*
Southern Illinois University
    Carbondale *B*
Southern Illinois University
    Edwardsville *B*
Southwestern Illinois College *A*
Triton College *A*
University of Chicago *B, D*
University of Illinois
    Chicago *B*
    Springfield *B*
    Urbana-Champaign *B*
University of St. Francis *B*
Waubonsee Community College *A*
Western Illinois University *B, M*

Indiana

Ancilla College *A*
Ball State University *A, B*
Bethel College *A, B*
Butler University *B*
Calumet College of St. Joseph *A, B*
Holy Cross College *A, B*
Indiana State University *A, B*
Indiana University
    Bloomington *A*
    Kokomo *M*
    Northwest *A, M*
    Purdue University Fort Wayne *M*
    South Bend *M*
    Southeast *A, M*

Ivy Tech Community College
    Bloomington *A*
    Central Indiana *A*
    Columbus *A*
    East Central *A*
    Kokomo *A*
    Lafayette *A*
    North Central *A*
    Northeast *A*
    Northwest *A*
    Richmond *A*
    South Central *A*
    Southeast *A*
    Southwest *A*
    Wabash Valley *A*
Manchester University *B*
Marian University *A*
Martin University *B*
Purdue University *B, M, D*
Purdue University
    Calumet *A*
    North Central *B*
St. Mary-of-the-Woods College *A, B*
Taylor University *A*
University of Evansville *B*
University of Indianapolis *A*
University of Notre Dame *B*
University of St. Francis *A, B*
University of Southern Indiana *B, M*
Vincennes University *A*
Wabash College *B*

Iowa

Ashford University *B*
Briar Cliff University *A*
Clarke University *A*
Clinton Community College *C, A*
Des Moines Area Community
    College *C, A*
Dordt College *B*
Ellsworth Community College *A*
Graceland University *B*
Grand View University *B*
Hawkeye Community College *A*
Iowa Central Community College *A*
Iowa Lakes Community College *A*
Iowa State University *B*
Iowa Western Community College *A*
Kirkwood Community College *A*
Loras College *A, B*
Marshalltown Community College *A*
North Iowa Area Community
    College *A*
Northeast Iowa Community
    College *A*
Northwest Iowa Community
    College *A*
Northwestern College *B*
Simpson College *B, T*
Southeastern Community College *A*
Southwestern Community College *A*
University of Dubuque *B*
University of Iowa *B*
University of Northern Iowa *B*
Upper Iowa University *A, B*
Waldorf College *A*
Western Iowa Tech Community
    College *A*
William Penn University *A*

Kansas

Barton County Community College *A*
Benedictine College *B*
Bethany College *B*
Butler Community College *A*
Central Christian College of
    Kansas *A, B*
Cloud County Community College *A*
Coffeyville Community College *A*
Colby Community College *A*
Cowley County Community
    College *A*
Emporia State University *B*
Fort Scott Community College *A*

Friends University *B*
Garden City Community College *A*
Haskell Indian Nations University *A*
Hesston College *A*
Hutchinson Community College *A*
Independence Community College *A*
Johnson County Community
    College *A*
Kansas City Kansas Community
    College *A*
Kansas Wesleyan University *B*
Labette Community College *A*
McPherson College *B*
MidAmerica Nazarene University *A*
Neosho County Community
    College *A*
Newman University *A, B*
Pittsburg State University *B*
Pratt Community College *A*
Seward County Community
    College *A*
Southwestern College *B*
Tabor College *A*
University of Kansas *B*
University of St. Mary *A, B*
Washburn University *A, B, M*
Wichita State University *A, B, M*

Kentucky

Asbury University *A*
Ashland Community and Technical
    College *A*
Bellarmine University *B*
Big Sandy Community and Technical
    College *A*
Bluegrass Community and Technical
    College *A*
Brescia University *A*
Campbellsville University *A*
Eastern Kentucky University *B*
Elizabethtown Community and
    Technical College *A*
Hazard Community and Technical
    College *A*
Henderson Community College *A*
Hopkinsville Community College *A*
Jefferson Community and Technical
    College *A*
Kentucky State University *A, B*
Madisonville Community College *A*
Maysville Community and Technical
    College *A*
Midway College *B*
Murray State University *A, B*
Northern Kentucky
    University *A, B, M*
Owensboro Community and
    Technical College *A*
St. Catharine College *A, B*
Somerset Community College *A*
Southeast Kentucky Community and
    Technical College *A*
Spalding University *B*
Sullivan University *B*
Thomas More College *A, B*
Transylvania University *B*
University of Louisville *B*
West Kentucky Community and
    Technical College *A*

Louisiana

Baton Rouge Community College *A*
Centenary College of Louisiana *B*
Grambling State University *M*
Louisiana State University
    Alexandria *A, B*
    Eunice *A*
    Shreveport *B, M*
Louisiana State University and
    Agricultural and Mechanical
    College *B, M*
Louisiana Tech University *A, B*
McNeese State University *B*
Northwestern State University *B*

Our Lady of Holy Cross College *B*
River Parishes Community College *A*
St. Joseph Seminary College *B*
South Louisiana Community
  College *A*
Southeastern Louisiana University *B*
Southern University
  Shreveport *A*

Maine

Central Maine Community College *A*
College of the Atlantic *B, M*
Eastern Maine Community College *A*
Husson University *B*
Kennebec Valley Community
  College *A*
Thomas College *A*
Unity College *A*
University of Maine *B, M*
University of Maine
  Augusta *C, A*
  Fort Kent *A, B*
  Machias *A*
  Presque Isle *A, B*
University of New England *B*
University of Southern Maine *B*
Washington County Community
  College *A*

Maryland

Allegany College of Maryland *A*
Anne Arundel Community
  College *C, A*
Baltimore City Community College *A*
Carroll Community College *A*
Cecil College *A*
Chesapeake College *C, A*
College of Southern Maryland *C, A*
Community College of Baltimore
  County *A*
Coppin State University *B*
Frederick Community College *A*
Frostburg State University *B*
Garrett College *A*
Hagerstown Community College *A*
Harford Community College *A*
Howard Community College *A*
Johns Hopkins University *M*
Loyola University Maryland *M*
McDaniel College *M*
Montgomery College *A*
Mount St. Mary's University *M*
Notre Dame of Maryland
  University *B, M*
Prince George's Community
  College *A*
St. John's College *B, M*
Salisbury University *B*
University of Baltimore *B*
University of Maryland
  University College *A, B*
Washington Adventist University *B*
Washington College *B*
Wor-Wic Community College *A*

Massachusetts

American International College *A, B*
Anna Maria College *B*
Bard College at Simon's Rock *A, B*
Bay Path College *A, B*
Becker College *B*
Bentley University *B*
Berkshire Community College *A*
Bristol Community College *A*
Cambridge College *B*
Cape Cod Community College *A*
Clark University *B, M*
Curry College *B*
Dean College *A, B*
Eastern Nazarene College *B*
Elms College *B*
Emmanuel College *B*
Endicott College *B*
Fisher College *A*

Fitchburg State University *B*
Framingham State University *B*
Greenfield Community College *A*
Harvard College *B*
Hellenic College/Holy Cross *B*
Holyoke Community College *A*
Lesley University *A, B, M*
Marian Court College *A, B*
Massachusetts Bay Community
  College *C, A*
Massachusetts College of Liberal
  Arts *B*
Massachusetts Institute of
  Technology *B*
Massasoit Community College *A*
Merrimack College *C, B*
Middlesex Community College *A*
Mount Ida College *B*
Mount Wachusett Community
  College *A*
Newbury College *A*
North Shore Community College *A*
Northeastern University *B*
Northern Essex Community
  College *A*
Pine Manor College *A, B*
Quincy College *A*
Quinsigamond Community College *A*
Regis College *B*
Roxbury Community College *A*
Salem State University *B*
Simmons College *B, M*
Springfield College *B*
Springfield Technical Community
  College *A*
Suffolk University *A*
Tufts University *B*
University of Massachusetts
  Dartmouth *C, B*
  Lowell *B*
Urban College of Boston *C, A*
Western New England
  University *A, B*
Westfield State University *B*
Wheaton College *B*
Wheelock College *B*

Michigan

Albion College *B*
Alpena Community College *A*
Andrews University *B*
Aquinas College *A, B*
Bay de Noc Community College *A*
Central Michigan University *B*
Concordia University *A*
Delta College *A*
Finlandia University *A, B*
Glen Oaks Community College *A*
Gogebic Community College *A*
Grace Bible College *A, B*
Grand Rapids Community College *A*
Grand Valley State University *B*
Henry Ford Community College *A*
Hillsdale College *B*
Jackson College *A*
Kalamazoo Valley Community
  College *A*
Kellogg Community College *A*
Kirtland Community College *A*
Kuyper College *B*
Lake Michigan College *A*
Lake Superior State University *A, B*
Lansing Community College *A*
Macomb Community College *A*
Madonna University *M*
Marygrove College *A, T*
Michigan Technological University *B*
Mid Michigan Community College *A*
Monroe County Community
  College *A*
Montcalm Community College *A*
Mott Community College *A*
North Central Michigan College *A*
Northern Michigan
  University *C, A, B, M*

Northwestern Michigan College *A*
Oakland Community College *A*
Oakland University *B, M*
Olivet College *B*
Robert B. Miller College *B*
Rochester College *A*
Sacred Heart Major Seminary *B*
St. Clair County Community
  College *A*
Siena Heights University *A, B*
Southwestern Michigan College *C, A*
Spring Arbor University *A*
University of Detroit Mercy *B, M*
University of Michigan
  Dearborn *B*
  Flint *B, M*
Washtenaw Community College *A*
West Shore Community College *A*

Minnesota

Alexandria Technical and Community
  College *A*
Anoka-Ramsey Community College *A*
Argosy University
  Twin Cities *B*
Augsburg College *B*
Bemidji State University *A, B*
Bethany Lutheran College *B*
Bethel University *A*
Central Lakes College *A*
Century College *A*
College of St. Benedict *B*
Crossroads College *A*
Crown College *B*
Fond du Lac Tribal and Community
  College *A*
Hibbing Community College *A*
Inver Hills Community College *A*
Itasca Community College *A*
Lake Superior College *A*
Leech Lake Tribal College *A*
Mesabi Range Community and
  Technical College *A*
Metropolitan State University *B, M*
Minneapolis Community and
  Technical College *A*
Minnesota State Community and
  Technical College *A*
Minnesota State University
  Mankato *A*
  Moorhead *A*
Minnesota West Community and
  Technical College *A*
Normandale Community College *C, A*
North Hennepin Community
  College *A*
Northland Community & Technical
  College *A*
Oak Hills Christian College *A*
Rainy River Community College *A*
Ridgewater College *A*
Riverland Community College *A*
Rochester Community and Technical
  College *A*
St. Catherine University *A*
Saint Cloud State University *A, B*
St. Cloud Technical and Community
  College *A*
St. John's University *B*
St. Olaf College *B*
St. Paul College *A*
South Central College *A*
Southwest Minnesota State
  University *A, B*
University of Minnesota
  Duluth *M*
  Twin Cities *B*
University of Northwestern - St.
  Paul *A*
University of St. Thomas *B*
Vermilion Community College *A*
Winona State University *A*

Mississippi

Alcorn State University *B*
Copiah-Lincoln Community
  College *A*
Delta State University *M*
East Central Community College *A*
East Mississippi Community
  College *A*
Holmes Community College *A*
Itawamba Community College *A*
Jones County Junior College *A*
Mississippi Delta Community
  College *A*
Mississippi Gulf Coast Community
  College *A*
Mississippi State University *B*
Mississippi University for Women *B*
Northeast Mississippi Community
  College *A*
Northwest Mississippi Community
  College *A*
Pearl River Community College *A*
Southwest Mississippi Community
  College *A*
Tougaloo College *B*
University of Mississippi *B*

Missouri

Columbia College *A*
Cottey College *A*
Crowder College *A*
Culver-Stockton College *B*
Drury University *B*
Evangel University *A*
Fontbonne University *B*
Hannibal-LaGrange University *A, B*
Jefferson College *A*
Lincoln University *B*
Maryville University of Saint Louis *B*
Metropolitan Community College -
  Kansas City *A*
Mineral Area College *A*
Missouri Baptist University *B*
Missouri State University: West
  Plains *A*
Missouri Valley College *A, B*
Missouri Western State University *B*
Moberly Area Community College *A*
North Central Missouri College *A*
Ozarks Technical Community
  College *A*
Park University *A, B*
St. Charles Community College *C, A*
St. Louis Christian College *A*
St. Louis Community College *A*
State Fair Community College *C, A*
Stephens College *A, B*
Three Rivers Community College *A*
University of Missouri
  Kansas City *B, M*
  St. Louis *B*
Washington University in St.
  Louis *B, M*
Wentworth Military Junior College *A*
William Jewell College *B*

Montana

Aaniiih Nakoda College *A*
Blackfeet Community College *A*
Dawson Community College *A*
Flathead Valley Community
  College *A*
Helena College University of
  Montana *A*
Little Big Horn College *A*
Miles Community College *A*
Montana State University
  Billings *A, B*
Montana Tech of the University of
  Montana *B*
Rocky Mountain College *A*
Salish Kootenai College *A*
Stone Child College *A*

University of Montana *A, B*
University of Montana: Western *A, B*

Nebraska

Central Community College *A*
Chadron State College *B, M*
College of Saint Mary *A, B*
Creighton University *M*
Doane College *B*
Hastings College *B*
Little Priest Tribal College *A*
Metropolitan Community College *A*
Mid-Plains Community College *A*
Midland University *B*
Nebraska Christian College *A*
Nebraska Indian Community
   College *A*
Northeast Community College *A*
Peru State College *B*
Southeast Community College *A*
University of Nebraska
   Kearney *B*
   Lincoln *B*
Western Nebraska Community
   College *A*

Nevada

College of Southern Nevada *A*
Sierra Nevada College *B*
University of Nevada
   Las Vegas *B, M*
Western Nevada College *A*

New Hampshire

Colby-Sawyer College *A*
College of St. Mary Magdalen *A, B*
Dartmouth College *M*
Franklin Pierce University *B*
Granite State College *A, B*
Great Bay Community College *C, A*
Lakes Region Community College *A*
Manchester Community College *A*
Mount Washington College *A*
NHTI-Concord's Community
   College *A*
Nashua Community College *C, A*
New England College *A, B*
River Valley Community College *C, A*
Rivier University *A, B*
Saint Anselm College *B*
Thomas More College of Liberal
   Arts *B*
University of New Hampshire *M*
University of New Hampshire at
   Manchester *A, B*
White Mountains Community
   College *A*

New Jersey

Assumption College for Sisters *A*
Atlantic Cape Community College *A*
Bergen Community College *A*
Brookdale Community College *C, A*
Burlington County College *C, A*
Camden County College *A*
County College of Morris *A*
Cumberland County College *A*
Essex County College *A*
Fairleigh Dickinson University
   Metropolitan Campus *A*
Felician College *A*
Gloucester County College *A*
Hudson County Community
   College *A*
Kean University *M*
Mercer County Community
   College *A*
Montclair State University *B*
Ocean County College *A*
Passaic County Community
   College *C, A*
Ramapo College of New Jersey *B, M*
Raritan Valley Community
   College *C, A*

Richard Stockton College of New
   Jersey *B*
Rider University *B*
Rutgers, The State University of New
   Jersey
   Camden Campus *B, M*
   Newark Campus *M*
Salem Community College *A*
Seton Hall University *B*
Stevens Institute of Technology *B*
Sussex County Community College *A*
Thomas Edison State College *A, B, M*
Union County College *A*
Warren County Community
   College *A*
William Paterson University of New
   Jersey *B*

New Mexico

Central New Mexico Community
   College *C, A*
Clovis Community College *C, A*
Eastern New Mexico University *A, B*
Luna Community College *A*
Mesalands Community College *C, A*
New Mexico Junior College *A*
New Mexico Military Institute *A*
New Mexico State University *B*
Northern New Mexico College *A*
St. John's College *C, B, M*
San Juan College *C, A*
Santa Fe Community College *A*
Southwestern Indian Polytechnic
   Institute *A*
University of New Mexico *B*
University of the Southwest *B*
Western New Mexico
   University *C, A, B*

New York

Adelphi University *A, B*
Adirondack Community College *A*
Alfred University *B*
Bard College *B*
Boricua College *A, B*
Broome Community College *A*
Canisius College *B*
Cayuga Community College *A*
Cazenovia College *A, B*
City University of New York
   Baruch College *B*
   Borough of Manhattan Community
      College *A*
   Bronx Community College *A*
   Brooklyn College *B, M*
   College of Staten Island *A, B, M*
   Guttman Community College *A*
   Hostos Community College *A*
   Kingsborough Community
      College *A*
   LaGuardia Community College *A*
   Lehman College *B, M*
   Medgar Evers College *A, B*
   New York City College of
      Technology *A, B*
   Queens College *B, M*
   Queensborough Community
      College *A*
   York College *B*
Clarkson University *B*
Clinton Community College *A*
Colgate University *B*
College of Mount St. Vincent *A, B*
College of Saint Rose *B*
Columbia-Greene Community
   College *A*
Concordia College *A, B*
Cornell University *B*
Corning Community College *A*
Daemen College *B*
Dominican College of Blauvelt *A*
Dowling College *B, M*
Dutchess Community College *C, A*
Elmira College *A, B*

Erie Community College *A*
Eugene Lang College The New
   School for Liberal Arts *B*
Excelsior College *A, B, M*
Finger Lakes Community College *A*
Five Towns College *A*
Fulton-Montgomery Community
   College *A*
Genesee Community College *A*
Hartwick College *B*
Herkimer County Community
   College *A*
Hilbert College *B*
Hofstra University *B*
Hudson Valley Community College *C*
Iona College *B*
Ithaca College *B*
Jamestown Community College *C, A*
Jefferson Community College *A*
Keuka College *B*
Long Island University
   LIU Brooklyn *A, B*
   LIU Post *A, B, M*
Manhattanville College *B*
Maria College *A*
Marist College *B*
Medaille College *A, B*
Mercy College *C, A, B, T*
Mohawk Valley Community
   College *C, A*
Molloy College *A, B*
Monroe Community College *A*
Nassau Community College *A*
New York University *A, B, M*
Niagara County Community
   College *A*
Niagara University *A, B, T*
North Country Community College *A*
Nyack College *A*
Orange County Community
   College *A*
Pace University *A, B*
Pace University: Pleasantville/
   Briarcliff *A, B*
Paul Smith's College *A, B*
Roberts Wesleyan College *B*
Rockland Community College *A*
SUNY
   College at Brockport *M*
   College at New Paltz *B*
   College at Old Westbury *B*
   College at Plattsburgh *B, M*
   College at Purchase *B*
   College of Agriculture and
      Technology at Cobleskill *A*
   College of Agriculture and
      Technology at Morrisville *A*
   College of Technology at Alfred *A*
   College of Technology at Delhi *A*
   Empire State College *A, B, M*
   Farmingdale State College *A*
   Institute of Technology at Utica/
      Rome *A*
   University at Albany *M*
   University at Stony Brook *M*
Sage Colleges *B*
St. Francis College *A, B*
St. John Fisher College *B*
St. John's University *A, B, M*
St. Lawrence University *B*
St. Thomas Aquinas College *A, B*
Sarah Lawrence College *B*
Schenectady County Community
   College *C, A*
Skidmore College *B, M*
Suffolk County Community College *A*
Sullivan County Community
   College *A*
Syracuse University *A, B*
Tompkins Cortland Community
   College *A*
Touro College *A, B*
Trocaire College *A*
Ulster County Community College *A*
Union College *B*

University of Rochester *B, M*
Utica College *B, M*
Vassar College *B*
Villa Maria College of Buffalo *A*
Wagner College *B*
Westchester Community College *A*

North Carolina

Alamance Community College *A*
Appalachian State University *B*
Asheville-Buncombe Technical
   Community College *A*
Barton College *B*
Beaufort County Community
   College *A*
Belmont Abbey College *B*
Bladen Community College *A*
Blue Ridge Community College *A*
Brevard College *B*
Brunswick Community College *C, A*
Caldwell Community College and
   Technical Institute *A*
Campbell University *A*
Cape Fear Community College *A*
Carteret Community College *A*
Catawba Valley Community
   College *A*
Central Carolina Community
   College *A*
Central Piedmont Community
   College *A*
Chowan University *B*
Cleveland Community College *C, A*
Coastal Carolina Community
   College *A*
College of the Albemarle *A*
Craven Community College *C, A*
Davidson County Community
   College *A*
Duke University *M*
Durham Technical Community
   College *A*
East Carolina University *B*
Edgecombe Community College *A*
Fayetteville Technical Community
   College *C, A*
Forsyth Technical Community
   College *A*
Gaston College *A*
Greensboro College *C, B*
Guilford Technical Community
   College *C, A*
Halifax Community College *A*
Haywood Community College *A*
Isothermal Community College *A*
James Sprunt Community
   College *C, A*
Johnson C. Smith University *B*
Johnston Community College *A*
Lees-McRae College *B*
Lenoir Community College *C, A*
Lenoir-Rhyne University *B, M*
Louisburg College *A*
Mars Hill University *B*
Martin Community College *A*
Mayland Community College *C, A*
McDowell Technical Community
   College *A*
Methodist University *A, B*
Mitchell Community College *A*
Montgomery Community College *A*
Nash Community College *A*
North Carolina Agricultural and
   Technical State University *B*
North Carolina State University *B, M*
Pfeiffer University *B*
Piedmont Community College *A*
Pitt Community College *C, A*
Randolph Community College *A*
Richmond Community College *A*
Roanoke-Chowan Community
   College *A*
Rockingham Community College *A*
St. Andrews University *B*
St. Augustine's University *B*

Sandhills Community College *A*
Shaw University *B*
South Piedmont Community
 College *A*
Southeastern Community College *A*
Southwestern Community College *A*
Stanly Community College *C, A*
Surry Community College *A*
Tri-County Community College *C, A*
University of Mount Olive *B*
University of North Carolina
 Asheville *B, M*
 Chapel Hill *B*
 Charlotte *M*
 Greensboro *B, M*
 School of the Arts *B*
 Wilmington *M*
Vance-Granville Community
 College *A*
Wake Forest University *M*
Wake Technical Community
 College *C, A*
Wayne Community College *C, A*
Western Carolina University *B*
Western Piedmont Community
 College *A*
Wilkes Community College *A*
William Peace University *B*
Wilson Community College *C, A*
Wingate University *B*

North Dakota

Bismarck State College *A*
Cankdeska Cikana Community
 College *A*
Dakota College at Bottineau *A*
Dickinson State University *A, B*
Lake Region State College *A*
Minot State University *B*
North Dakota State College of
 Science *A*
University of Mary *B*
Valley City State University *B*
Williston State College *A*

Ohio

Antioch University
 Midwest *B, M*
Bowling Green State University *B*
Bowling Green State University:
 Firelands College *A, B*
Central Ohio Technical College *A*
Chatfield College *A*
Cincinnati State Technical and
 Community College *A*
Clark State Community College *A*
Cleveland State University *B*
College of Mount St. Joseph *B*
Columbus State Community
 College *A*
Cuyahoga Community College
 Metropolitan *A*
Defiance College *B*
Eastern Gateway Community
 College *A*
Edison State Community College *C, A*
Hocking College *A*
John Carroll University *B, M*
Lakeland Community College *A*
Lorain County Community College *A*
Lourdes University *A*
Malone University *B*
Marietta College *A, M*
Miami University
 Middletown *A*
 Oxford *B*
Northwest State Community
 College *A*
Ohio Dominican University *A, B, M*
Ohio Northern University *B*
Ohio State University
 Lima Campus *A*
 Mansfield Campus *A*

Marion Campus *A*
 Newark Campus *A*
Ohio University *A*
Ohio University
 Chillicothe Campus *A*
 Eastern Campus *A, B*
 Lancaster Campus *A*
 Zanesville Campus *A*
Ohio Wesleyan University *B*
Sinclair Community College *C, A*
Southern State Community College *A*
Stark State College *A*
Terra State Community College *A*
Tiffin University *B*
Union Institute & University *B, M*
University of Akron *A, B*
University of Akron: Wayne
 College *A*
University of Cincinnati *B*
University of Cincinnati
 Blue Ash College *A*
 Clermont College *A*
University of Rio Grande *A*
University of Toledo *B, M*
Urbana University *A, B*
Ursuline College *M*
Walsh University *A*
Washington State Community
 College *A*
Wilberforce University *B*
Wilmington College *B*
Wittenberg University *B*
Wright State University *B, M*
Wright State University: Lake
 Campus *A*
Xavier University *A, B*
Youngstown State University *A, B*

Oklahoma

Bacone College *A*
Connors State College *A*
Mid-America Christian University *A*
Murray State College *A*
Northern Oklahoma College *A*
Oklahoma Baptist University *B*
Oklahoma Christian University *B*
Oklahoma City Community
 College *A*
Oklahoma City University *B, M*
Oklahoma Panhandle State
 University *A*
Oklahoma State University *B*
Oral Roberts University *B*
Rogers State University *A, B*
Rose State College *A*
St. Gregory's University *A, B*
Seminole State College *A*
Southern Nazarene University *B*
Southwestern Christian
 University *A, B*
University of Central Oklahoma *B*
University of Oklahoma *B, M*
University of Tulsa *B*
Western Oklahoma State College *A*

Oregon

Blue Mountain Community College *A*
Central Oregon Community
 College *A*
Chemeketa Community College *A*
Clackamas Community College *A*
Clatsop Community College *A*
Corban University *B*
Eastern Oregon University *B*
Gutenberg College *B*
Klamath Community College *A*
Lane Community College *A*
Lewis & Clark College *B*
Linn-Benton Community College *A*
Marylhurst University *B*
Mount Angel Seminary *C, B, M*
Mt. Hood Community College *A*
Oregon State University *B*
Pacific University *B*

Portland Community College *A*
Portland State University *B*
Reed College *M*
Rogue Community College *A*
Southwestern Oregon Community
 College *A*
Tillamook Bay Community College *A*
Treasure Valley Community
 College *A*
Umpqua Community College *A*
Warner Pacific College *B*
Western Oregon University *A, B*

Pennsylvania

Alvernia University *A, B, M*
Arcadia University *B*
Baptist Bible College of
 Pennsylvania *A, B*
Bryn Athyn College *A*
Bucks County Community College *A*
Cabrini College *B*
California University of
 Pennsylvania *C, A, B*
Carlow University *B*
Carnegie Mellon University *B*
Chatham University *B*
Chestnut Hill College *A, B*
Clarion University of
 Pennsylvania *A, B*
Community College of Allegheny
 County *A*
Community College of Beaver
 County *A*
Community College of
 Philadelphia *A*
DeSales University *A*
Delaware County Community
 College *A*
Duquesne University *B, M*
East Stroudsburg University of
 Pennsylvania *B*
Eastern University *A*
Edinboro University of
 Pennsylvania *A, B*
Gannon University *A, B*
Gettysburg College *B*
Gwynedd Mercy University *A*
Haverford College *B*
Immaculata University *B*
Juniata College *B*
Keystone College *A*
La Roche College *B*
La Salle University *A, B*
Lackawanna College *A*
Lehigh Carbon Community College *A*
Lock Haven University of
 Pennsylvania *B*
Luzerne County Community
 College *A*
Manor College *A*
Mansfield University of
 Pennsylvania *A, B*
Mercyhurst University *B*
Misericordia University *B*
Montgomery County Community
 College *A*
Mount Aloysius College *A, B*
Neumann University *A, B*
Northampton Community College *A*
Penn State
 Abington *A, B*
 Altoona *A, B*
 Beaver *A, B*
 Berks *A, B*
 Brandywine *A, B*
 DuBois *A, B*
 Erie, The Behrend College *A, B*
 Fayette, The Eberly Campus *A, B*
 Greater Allegheny *C, A, B*
 Harrisburg *A, B*
 Hazleton *A, B*
 Lehigh Valley *A, B*
 Mont Alto *A, B*
 New Kensington *A, B*
 Schuylkill *A, B*

Shenango *A, B*
 University Park *A, B*
 Wilkes-Barre *A, B*
 Worthington Scranton *A, B*
 York *A, B*
Point Park University *B*
Reading Area Community College *A*
Rosemont College *B*
Saint Joseph's University *A, B*
St. Vincent College *B*
Susquehanna University *B*
Temple University *M*
Thiel College *A*
University of Pennsylvania *B, M*
University of Pittsburgh *B*
University of Pittsburgh
 Bradford *A*
 Greensburg *B*
 Johnstown *B*
 Titusville *A*
University of Scranton *B*
Valley Forge Military College *A*
Villanova University *A, B, M*
West Chester University of
 Pennsylvania *B*
Westmoreland County Community
 College *A*
Widener University *A, B, M*
Wilkes University *B*
Wilson College *A*

Puerto Rico

Pontifical Catholic University of
 Puerto Rico *B*
University of Puerto Rico
 Ponce *A*
 Rio Piedras *B*

Rhode Island

Community College of Rhode
 Island *A*
Johnson & Wales University
 Providence *B*
Providence College *A, B*
Rhode Island College *B*
Salve Regina University *B*

South Carolina

Aiken Technical College *A*
Anderson University *B*
Central Carolina Technical College *A*
Clinton Junior College *A*
Coastal Carolina University *B*
Columbia College *B*
Columbia International University *B*
Converse College *M*
Denmark Technical College *A*
Florence-Darlington Technical
 College *A*
Francis Marion University *B*
Greenville Technical College *C, A*
Horry-Georgetown Technical
 College *C, A*
Lander University *B*
Limestone College *A, B*
Midlands Technical College *C, A*
Morris College *B*
North Greenville University *B*
Northeastern Technical College *A*
Orangeburg-Calhoun Technical
 College *A*
Piedmont Technical College *C, A*
Spartanburg Community College *A*
Spartanburg Methodist College *A*
Technical College of the
 Lowcountry *C, A*
Tri-County Technical College *C, A*
Trident Technical College *A*
University of South Carolina
 Aiken *B*
 Beaufort *A, B*
 Columbia *B*
 Lancaster *A*
 Salkehatchie *A*

Sumter *A*
Union *A*
Upstate *B*
Williamsburg Technical College *A*
Winthrop University *M*
York Technical College *A*

South Dakota

Black Hills State University *B*
Dakota State University *B*
Dakota Wesleyan University *A, B*
Kilian Community College *A*
Northern State University *A*
Oglala Lakota College *A, B*
Sinte Gleska University *A*
Sisseton Wahpeton College *A*
South Dakota State University *B*
University of Sioux Falls *B*
University of South Dakota *A, B, M*

Tennessee

American Baptist College *B*
Aquinas College *A, B*
Argosy University
   Nashville *B*
Austin Peay State University *B*
Belmont University *B*
Bryan University
   Dayton *A, B*
Carson-Newman University *B*
Chattanooga State Community
   College *A*
Christian Brothers University *B*
Cleveland State Community
   College *C, A*
Columbia State Community
   College *A*
Cumberland University *B*
Dyersburg State Community
   College *A*
East Tennessee State University *B, M*
Freed-Hardeman University *B, T*
Hiwassee College *A*
Jackson State Community College *A*
Martin Methodist College *A*
Middle Tennessee State University *B*
Motlow State Community College *A*
Nashville State Community College *C*
Northeast State Community
   College *A*
Pellissippi State Community
   College *A*
Roane State Community College *A*
Southern Adventist University *A*
Southwest Tennessee Community
   College *C, A*
Tennessee State University *B*
Tennessee Temple University *A, B*
University of Memphis *B, M*
Vanderbilt University *M*
Victory University *B*
Volunteer State Community
   College *A*
Walters State Community College *A*
Welch College *A*

Texas

Abilene Christian University *M*
Alvin Community College *A*
Amarillo College *A*
Amberton University *B*
Angelina College *C*
Argosy University
   Dallas *B*
Blinn College *A*
Brazosport College *A*
Brookhaven College *A*
Central Texas College *A*
Cisco College *C*
Clarendon College *A*
Coastal Bend College *A*
College of Saints John Fisher &
   Thomas More *A, B*
College of the Mainland *A*

Collin County Community College
   District *A*
Concordia University Texas *B*
Dallas Baptist University *A, B, M*
Dallas Christian College *B*
Del Mar College *A*
Eastfield College *A*
El Centro College *A*
El Paso Community College *A*
Frank Phillips College *A*
Galveston College *A*
Grayson College *A*
Hill College *C, A*
Houston Baptist University *M*
Howard College *A*
Howard Payne University *B*
Huston-Tillotson University *B*
Jacksonville College *A*
Kilgore College *A*
Lamar State College at Orange *A*
Lamar University *B*
Laredo Community College *A*
Lee College *A*
Lone Star College System *A*
Lubbock Christian University *B*
Mountain View College *A*
Navarro College *A*
North Lake College *A*
Northeast Texas Community
   College *A*
Northwest Vista College *A*
Odessa College *A*
Our Lady of the Lake University of
   San Antonio *B*
Palo Alto College *A*
Panola College *C, A*
Paris Junior College *A*
Paul Quinn College *B*
Ranger College *A*
Richland College *A*
St. Edward's University *B*
St. Mary's University *B*
St. Philip's College *A*
San Antonio College *C*
Schreiner University *A, B*
South Plains College *A*
South Texas College *A*
Southwest Texas Junior College *A*
Stephen F. Austin State University *B*
Tarleton State University *B, M*
Temple College *A*
Texas A&M University
   Commerce *B*
   Galveston *B*
Texas Christian University *M*
Texas College *B*
Texas Tech University *B*
Texas Wesleyan University *B*
Trinity Valley Community College *A*
Tyler Junior College *A*
University of Houston *B*
University of Houston
   Downtown *B*
University of St. Thomas *B, M*
University of Texas
   Austin *B*
   Dallas *M, D*
University of the Incarnate
   Word *A, B*
Vernon College *A*
Victoria College *A*
Weatherford College *A*
Western Texas College *A*
Wharton County Junior College *A*

Utah

Argosy University
   Salt Lake City *B*
Utah State University *B*
Weber State University *B*

Vermont

Bennington College *B*
Champlain College *B*

College of St. Joseph in
   Vermont *B*
Community College of Vermont *A*
Goddard College *B, M*
Green Mountain College *B*
Johnson State College *A, B*
Landmark College *A, B*
Lyndon State College *A, B*
Marlboro College *B*
Middlebury College *B*
Southern Vermont College *A, B*
Sterling College *B*
University of Vermont *B*

Virginia

Argosy University
   Washington D.C. *B*
Averett University *A, B*
Blue Ridge Community College *A*
Bridgewater College *B*
Central Virginia Community
   College *A*
Christendom College *A*
Dabney S. Lancaster Community
   College *A*
Danville Community College *A*
Eastern Mennonite University *B*
Eastern Shore Community College *A*
Ferrum College *B*
George Mason University *B*
Germanna Community College *A*
Hampton University *B*
Hollins University *M*
J. Sargeant Reynolds Community
   College *A*
James Madison University *B*
John Tyler Community College *C, A*
Liberty University *B, T*
Longwood University *B*
Lord Fairfax Community College *A*
Marymount University *B*
Mountain Empire Community
   College *A*
New River Community College *A*
Northern Virginia Community
   College *A*
Patrick Henry College *B*
Patrick Henry Community College *A*
Piedmont Virginia Community
   College *A*
Rappahannock Community College *A*
Richard Bland College *A*
Shenandoah University *B*
Southern Virginia University *B*
Southside Virginia Community
   College *A*
Southwest Virginia Community
   College *C, A*
Sweet Briar College *B*
Thomas Nelson Community
   College *A*
Tidewater Community College *A*
University of Mary Washington *B*
University of Virginia *B*
University of Virginia's College at
   Wise *B, T*
Virginia Highlands Community
   College *A*
Virginia Polytechnic Institute and
   State University *B*
Virginia State University *B*
Virginia University of Lynchburg *A*
Virginia Western Community
   College *C, A*
Wytheville Community College *C, A*

Washington

Antioch University
   Seattle *B*
Argosy University
   Seattle *B*
Bellevue College *A*
Big Bend Community College *A*
Centralia College *A*

City University of Seattle *A, B*
Clark College *A*
Columbia Basin College *A*
Edmonds Community College *A*
Everett Community College *A*
Evergreen State College *B*
Gonzaga University *B*
Grays Harbor College *A*
Green River Community College *A*
Highline Community College *A*
Lower Columbia College *A*
Peninsula College *A*
Pierce College *A*
Seattle Central Community College *A*
Seattle Pacific University *B*
Seattle University *B*
Shoreline Community College *C, A*
Skagit Valley College *A*
South Puget Sound Community
   College *A*
South Seattle Community College *A*
Spokane Community College *A*
Spokane Falls Community College *A*
Tacoma Community College *A*
University of Washington *B*
University of Washington Tacoma *B*
Walla Walla Community College *A*
Walla Walla University *B*
Washington State University *B*
Wenatchee Valley College *A*
Whatcom Community College *A*
Whitworth University *B*
Yakima Valley Community College *A*

West Virginia

Blue Ridge Community and Technical
   College *C, A*
Bluefield State College *B*
Concord University *B*
Eastern West Virginia Community and
   Technical College *A*
Glenville State College *A*
Kanawha Valley Community and
   Technical College *A*
Ohio Valley University *A, B*
Pierpont Community and Technical
   College *A*
Potomac State College of West
   Virginia University *B*
Southern West Virginia Community
   and Technical College *A*
West Liberty University *B*
West Virginia Northern Community
   College *A*
West Virginia State University *B*
West Virginia University *B, M*
West Virginia University at
   Parkersburg *A*
Wheeling Jesuit University *B*

Wisconsin

Alverno College *A, B*
Beloit College *B*
Cardinal Stritch University *A*
Chippewa Valley Technical College *A*
College of Menominee Nation *A*
Concordia University Wisconsin *B*
Lac Courte Oreilles Ojibwa
   Community College *A*
Lakeland College *A*
Marian University *B*
Milwaukee Area Technical College *A*
Moraine Park Technical College *C*
Mount Mary University *B*
Nicolet Area Technical College *A*
St. Norbert College *M*
Silver Lake College of the Holy
   Family *A*
University of Wisconsin
   Baraboo/Sauk County *C, A*
   Barron County *A*
   Eau Claire *A, B*
   Fond du Lac *A*

Fox Valley *A*
Green Bay *A, B*
Manitowoc *A*
Marathon County *A*
Marinette *A*
Marshfield/Wood County *A*
Milwaukee *M*
Oshkosh *B*
Parkside *B*
Platteville *A, B*
Richland *A*
Rock County *A*
Sheboygan *A*
Stevens Point *A, B*
Superior *A, B*
Washington County *A*
Waukesha *A*
Whitewater *A, B*
Viterbo University *B*
Western Technical College *A*

Wyoming

Casper College *A*
Eastern Wyoming College *A*
Northwest College *A*

Library assistance

Arizona

Mesa Community College *C, A*
Northland Pioneer College *C, A*

California

Cabrillo College *A*
Chabot College *A*
Citrus College *C, A*
City College of San Francisco *A*
College of the Sequoias *C*
Cuesta College *C, A*
Foothill College *C, A*
Fresno City College *A*
Fullerton College *A*
Imperial Valley College *C*
Los Angeles Harbor College *A*
Palomar College *C, A*
Pasadena City College *C, A*
Rio Hondo College *A*
Sacramento City College *C, A*
San Bernardino Valley College *C, A*
Santa Ana College *A*
Santiago Canyon College *A*
Sierra College *C, A*

Colorado

Pueblo Community College *C, A*

Connecticut

Capital Community College *A*
Three Rivers Community
    College *C, A*

Florida

Indian River State College *A*

Georgia

Georgia Perimeter College *A*

Idaho

College of Southern Idaho *A*

Illinois

City Colleges of Chicago
    Wilbur Wright College *C, A*
College of DuPage *C, A*
College of Lake County *C, A*
Illinois Central College *A*
Waubonsee Community College *C, A*

Indiana

Indiana University
    Bloomington *M, D*
    Purdue University Indianapolis *M*

Ivy Tech Community College
    Bloomington *A*
    Central Indiana *A*
    Columbus *A*
    East Central *A*
    Kokomo *A*
    Lafayette *A*
    North Central *A*
    Northeast *A*
    Northwest *A*
    Richmond *A*
    South Central *A*
    Southeast *A*
    Southwest *A*
    Wabash Valley *A*

Kansas

Allen County Community College *A*
Seward County Community
    College *A*

Kentucky

Bluegrass Community and Technical
    College *C*

Maine

University of Maine
    Augusta *A*

Michigan

Bay de Noc Community College *C*
Grand Rapids Community College *A*
Oakland Community College *C, A*

Minnesota

Minneapolis Community and
    Technical College *C, A*

Mississippi

East Mississippi Community
    College *A*
Itawamba Community College *A*
Northeast Mississippi Community
    College *A*

Missouri

Three Rivers Community College *A*

Nebraska

Mid-Plains Community College *A*
Northeast Community College *A*

New Mexico

Dona Ana Community College of
    New Mexico State University *A*
Northern New Mexico College *C, A*

Ohio

Clark State Community College *A*

Oklahoma

Rose State College *A*
Tulsa Community College *A*

Oregon

Portland Community College *C*

Pennsylvania

Northampton Community College *C*
Westmoreland County Community
    College *C*

South Dakota

Western Dakota Technical
    Institute *C, A*

Texas

Brazosport College *A*
Tarrant County College *C, A*

Utah

Salt Lake Community College *C*

Washington

Highline Community College *A*
Spokane Falls Community
    College *C, A*

Library science

Alabama

University of Alabama *M*

Arizona

University of Arizona *M, D*

Arkansas

University of Central Arkansas *M*

California

Azusa Pacific University *M*
San Jose State University *M*

Colorado

University of Colorado
    Denver *M*
University of Denver *M*

Connecticut

Southern Connecticut State
    University *B, M*

District of Columbia

Catholic University of America *M*

Florida

University of South Florida *M*

Georgia

Valdosta State University *M*

Hawaii

University of Hawaii
    Manoa *M*

Illinois

Chicago State University *M*
Dominican University *M, D*
University of Illinois
    Urbana-Champaign *M, D*

Indiana

Ball State University *B*

Iowa

Ashford University *B*
University of Iowa *M*
University of Northern Iowa *M*

Kansas

Emporia State University *M, D*

Kentucky

University of Kentucky *M*
Western Kentucky University *M, T*

Louisiana

Louisiana State University and
    Agricultural and Mechanical
    College *M*

Maine

University of Maine
    Augusta *B*

Maryland

University of Maryland
    College Park *M, D*

Massachusetts

Simmons College *M, D*

Michigan

Wayne State University *M*

Minnesota

Minnesota State University
    Mankato *M*
St. Catherine University *M*
Saint Cloud State University *B, M*

Mississippi

University of Southern
    Mississippi *B, M*

Missouri

Lindenwood University *M*
University of Central Missouri *M*
University of Missouri
    Columbia *M*

Montana

University of Montana: Western *T*

Nebraska

Chadron State College *B*
University of Nebraska
    Omaha *B*

New Jersey

Rutgers, The State University of New
    Jersey
    New Brunswick/Piscataway
        Campus *M, D*

New York

City University of New York
    Queens College *M*
Long Island University
    LIU Post *M*
Pratt Institute *M*
SUNY
    University at Buffalo *M*
St. John's University *M*
Syracuse University *M*

North Carolina

Appalachian State University *M*
East Carolina University *M*
North Carolina Central University *M*
University of North Carolina
    Chapel Hill *M, D*
    Greensboro *M*

Ohio

Kent State University *M*

Oklahoma

East Central University *M*
Northeastern State University *M*
University of Oklahoma *M*

Pennsylvania

Arcadia University *M*
Clarion University of
    Pennsylvania *B, M, T*
Drexel University *M*
Kutztown University of
    Pennsylvania *B, M*
Mansfield University of
    Pennsylvania *M*
University of Pittsburgh *M, D*

Puerto Rico

Inter American University of Puerto
    Rico
    San German Campus *M*
Turabo University *M*
University of Puerto Rico
    Rio Piedras *M*

Rhode Island

University of Rhode Island *M*

South Carolina

University of South Carolina
    Columbia *M, D*

Tennessee

Tennessee Technological
University *M*
Trevecca Nazarene University *M*
Union University *T*
University of Tennessee
Knoxville *M*

Texas

Our Lady of the Lake University of
San Antonio *M*
Sam Houston State University *M*
Texas A&M University
Commerce *M*
Texas Woman's University *M, D*
University of Houston
Clear Lake *M*
University of North Texas *M*
University of Texas
Austin *M, D*

Virginia

University of Virginia's College at
Wise *T*

Washington

University of Washington *M*

West Virginia

Concord University *B, T*

Wisconsin

University of Wisconsin
Madison *M, D*
Milwaukee *M, D*

Licensed midwifery

Pennsylvania

Philadelphia University *M*

Washington

Bastyr University *B, M*

Wisconsin

Southwest Wisconsin Technical
College *A*

Licensed practical nursing

Alabama

Alabama Southern Community
College *C, A*
Bevill State Community College *C*
Bishop State Community College *C*
Calhoun Community College *C*
Chattahoochee Valley Community
College *C*
Gadsden State Community College *C*
George C. Wallace Community
College at Dothan *C*
George C. Wallace State Community
College at Selma *C*
Lurleen B. Wallace Community
College *C*
Northeast Alabama Community
College *C*
Northwest-Shoals Community
College *C*
Shelton State Community College *C*
Southern Union State Community
College *C*
Virginia College
Mobile *A*
Wallace State Community College at
Hanceville *C*

Arizona

Arizona Western College *C*
Brown Mackie College
Tucson *C*

Central Arizona College *C*
GateWay Community College *C*
Glendale Community College *C*
Mesa Community College *C*
Mohave Community College *C*
Northland Pioneer College *C*
Paradise Valley Community College *C*
Phoenix College *C*
Pima Community College *C*
Rio Salado College *C*
Scottsdale Community College *C*

Arkansas

Arkansas Northeastern College *C*
Arkansas State University
Beebe *C*
Mountain Home *C*
Newport *C*
Arkansas Tech University *C*
College of the Ouachitas *C*
Cossatot Community College of the
University of Arkansas *C*
National Park Community College *C*
North Arkansas College *C*
Ozarka College *C, A*
Phillips Community College of the
University of Arkansas *C*
Pulaski Technical College *C*
Rich Mountain Community College *C*
South Arkansas Community
College *C*
Southeast Arkansas College *C*
Southern Arkansas University Tech *C*
University of Arkansas
Community College at Hope *C*
Community College at Morrilton *C*
Fort Smith *C*
Monticello *C*

California

Allan Hancock College *C, A*
Antelope Valley College *C*
Bakersfield College *C*
Butte College *A*
Cabrillo College *A*
Carrington College California
Antioch *A*
Sacramento *A*
San Leandro *C, A*
Cerritos College *A*
Cerro Coso Community College *C, A*
Citrus College *C, A*
City College of San Francisco *C*
College of the Desert *C, A*
College of the Siskiyous *C, A*
Concorde Career College
North Hollywood *C*
San Bernardino *C*
San Diego *C*
Copper Mountain College *A*
El Camino College *A*
Feather River College *C, A*
Gavilan College *C*
Glendale Community College *A*
Hartnell College *C*
Imperial Valley College *C, A*
Lassen Community College *A*
Long Beach City College *C, A*
Los Angeles Trade and Technical
College *A*
Los Medanos College *C*
Merced College *C, A*
Merritt College *A*
MiraCosta College *C, A*
Mission College *A*
Modesto Junior College *C*
Mount San Jacinto College *C*
Napa Valley College *C, A*
National University *C, A, B*
Palo Verde College *C*
Pasadena City College *C, A*
Porterville College *C, A*
Rio Hondo College *C, A*
Riverside City College *C, A*

Sacramento City College *C, A*
San Joaquin Valley College *A*
Santa Barbara Business College
Rancho Mirage *C*
Santa Maria *C*
Santa Barbara City College *C, A*
Santa Rosa Junior College *C, A*
Shasta College *C*
Southwestern College *C, A*
Stanbridge College *C*

Colorado

Arapahoe Community College *C*
Colorado Mesa University *C*
Colorado Mountain College *C*
Community College of Denver *C*
Concorde Career College
Aurora *C*
Front Range Community College *C*
Morgan Community College *C*
Northeastern Junior College *C*
Otero Junior College *C*

Delaware

Delaware Technical Community
College
Jack F. Owens Campus *C*
Terry Campus *C*

Florida

College of Central Florida *C, A*
Daytona State College *C*
Eastern Florida State College *C*
Florida Gateway College *C*
Florida National University *C*
Florida State College at
Jacksonville *C*
Gulf Coast State College *C*
Indian River State College *C*
Miami Dade College *C*
Palm Beach State College *C*
Pasco-Hernando State College *C*
Pensacola State College *C*
Rasmussen College
Fort Myers *A*
Ocala *A*
Pasco/Land O'Lakes *A*
Tampa/Brandon *A*
Santa Fe College *C*
Seminole State College of Florida *C*
South Florida State College *C*
Virginia College
Pensacola *C*

Georgia

Albany Technical College *C*
Athens Technical College *C*
Atlanta Technical College *C*
Bainbridge College *C*
Central Georgia Technical College *C*
Chattahoochee Technical College *C*
Columbus Technical College *C, A*
Dalton State College *C*
Darton College *A*
Georgia Piedmont Technical
College *C*
Gwinnett Technical College *C, A*
Middle Georgia State College *A*
North Georgia Technical College *C*
Savannah Technical College *C*
Southeastern Technical College *C*
Southwest Georgia Technical
College *C*
West Georgia Technical College *C*

Hawaii

University of Hawaii
Hawaii Community College *C*
Kapiolani Community College *C, A*
Kauai Community College *C*

Idaho

Carrington College
Boise *C, A*

College of Southern Idaho *C*
Eastern Idaho Technical College *C*
Idaho State University *C*
Lewis-Clark State College *A*
North Idaho College *C*

Illinois

Black Hawk College *C*
Carl Sandburg College *C*
City Colleges of Chicago
Kennedy-King College *C*
Malcolm X College *C*
Olive-Harvey College *C*
Richard J. Daley College *C*
Wilbur Wright College *C*
College of DuPage *C*
Danville Area Community College *C*
Elgin Community College *C*
Harper College *C*
Heartland Community College *C*
Highland Community College *C*
Illinois Eastern Community Colleges
Olney Central College *C*
Illinois Valley Community College *C*
John A. Logan College *C*
John Wood Community College *C*
Joliet Junior College *C*
Kankakee Community College *C*
Kaskaskia College *C*
Kishwaukee College *C*
Lake Land College *C*
Lincoln Land Community College *C*
Moraine Valley Community College *C*
Morton College *C*
Parkland College *C*
Rend Lake College *C*
Richland Community College *C*
Rock Valley College *C*
Sauk Valley Community College *C*
South Suburban College of Cook
County *C*
Southeastern Illinois College *C*
Triton College *C*

Indiana

Brown Mackie College
Merrillville *C*
South Bend *C*
Ivy Tech Community College
Bloomington *C*
Central Indiana *C*
Columbus *C*
East Central *C*
Kokomo *C*
Lafayette *C*
North Central *C*
Northeast *C*
Northwest *C*
Richmond *C*
South Central *C*
Southeast *C*
Southwest *C*
Wabash Valley *C*
Vincennes University *C*

Iowa

Clinton Community College *C*
Des Moines Area Community
College *C*
Ellsworth Community College *C*
Hawkeye Community College *C*
Iowa Central Community College *C*
Iowa Lakes Community College *C*
Iowa Western Community College *C*
Kirkwood Community College *C*
Marshalltown Community College *C*
North Iowa Area Community
College *C*
Northeast Iowa Community
College *C*
Northwest Iowa Community
College *C*
Southeastern Community College *C*
Southwestern Community College *C*

Kansas

Barton County Community College *C*
Butler Community College *C, A*
Cloud County Community College *C*
Colby Community College *C*
Dodge City Community College *C, A*
Fort Scott Community College *A*
Garden City Community College *C*
Highland Community College *C*
Hutchinson Community College *C*
Johnson County Community
   College *C*
Kansas City Kansas Community
   College *C*
Labette Community College *C*
Manhattan Area Technical College *C*
Neosho County Community
   College *C, A*
Pratt Community College *A*
Seward County Community
   College *C*
Wichita Area Technical College *C, A*

Kentucky

Bluegrass Community and Technical
   College *C*
Elizabethtown Community and
   Technical College *C*
Gateway Community and Technical
   College *C*
Hopkinsville Community College *C*
Jefferson Community and Technical
   College *C*
Madisonville Community College *C*
Maysville Community and Technical
   College *C*
Owensboro Community and
   Technical College *C*
Somerset Community College *C, A*
Spencerian College *C*

Louisiana

Delgado Community College *C, A*
Delta College of Arts &
   Technology *A*
Louisiana State University
   Eunice *A*
Nunez Community College *C*
Our Lady of the Lake College *C, A*

Maine

Eastern Maine Community College *C*
Northern Maine Community
   College *C*

Maryland

Allegany College of Maryland *C*
Anne Arundel Community College *C*
Baltimore City Community College *A*
Carroll Community College *C*
Cecil College *C*
College of Southern Maryland *C, A*
Community College of Baltimore
   County *C*
Frederick Community College *C*
Hagerstown Community College *C*
Harford Community College *C*
Howard Community College *C, A*
Prince George's Community
   College *C*
Wor-Wic Community College *C*

Massachusetts

Bay State College *A, B*
Berkshire Community College *C*
Greenfield Community College *C*
Holyoke Community College *C*
Massachusetts Bay Community
   College *C*
Mount Wachusett Community
   College *C*
North Shore Community College *C*
Northern Essex Community
   College *C*

Quincy College *C*
Quinsigamond Community College *C*
Roxbury Community College *C*

Michigan

Alpena Community College *C*
Baker College
   Auburn Hills *A*
Bay de Noc Community College *C*
Davenport University *C*
Delta College *C, A*
Glen Oaks Community College *C*
Gogebic Community College *C*
Grand Rapids Community
   College *C, A*
Henry Ford Community College *A*
Jackson College *C*
Kalamazoo Valley Community
   College *A*
Kellogg Community College *C*
Kirtland Community College *C*
Lake Superior State University *C*
Lansing Community College *A*
Mid Michigan Community College *C*
Montcalm Community College *C*
Mott Community College *C*
Muskegon Community College *A*
Northwestern Michigan College *C*
Oakland Community College *C*
St. Clair County Community
   College *C*
Schoolcraft College *C, A*
Southwestern Michigan College *C*

Minnesota

Alexandria Technical and Community
   College *C*
Anoka Technical College *C, A*
Central Lakes College *C*
Dakota County Technical
   College *C, A*
Fond du Lac Tribal and Community
   College *C*
Hennepin Technical College *C, A*
Itasca Community College *C*
Lake Superior College *C*
Mesabi Range Community and
   Technical College *C*
Minneapolis Community and
   Technical College *C*
Minnesota State College - Southeast
   Technical *C*
Minnesota State Community and
   Technical College *C, A*
Minnesota West Community and
   Technical College *C*
Northland Community & Technical
   College *C, A*
Northwest Technical College *C, A*
Pine Technical College *C*
Rainy River Community College *C*
Rasmussen College
   Brooklyn Park *A*
   Eagan *A*
   Mankato *A*
   Moorhead *A*
   St. Cloud *A*
Ridgewater College *C*
Riverland Community College *C*
St. Cloud Technical and Community
   College *C, A*
St. Paul College *C, A*
South Central College *C, A*

Mississippi

Coahoma Community College *C*
Copiah-Lincoln Community
   College *C*
East Central Community College *C*
East Mississippi Community
   College *C*
Hinds Community College *C*
Itawamba Community College *C*
Meridian Community College *C*

Mississippi Gulf Coast Community
   College *C*
Northeast Mississippi Community
   College *C*
Pearl River Community College *C, A*
Southwest Mississippi Community
   College *C*

Missouri

Bolivar Technical College *C*
Jefferson College *C*
Metropolitan Community College -
   Kansas City *C*
Mineral Area College *C*
Moberly Area Community College *C*
North Central Missouri College *C*
Ozarks Technical Community
   College *C*
St. Charles Community College *C*
State Fair Community College *C*
Texas County Technical College *C*

Montana

Flathead Valley Community
   College *A*
Helena College University of
   Montana *A*
Montana State University
   Billings *A*
   Great Falls College *A*
University of Montana *A*

Nebraska

Central Community College *C, A*
Clarkson College *C*
College of Saint Mary *C*
Grace University *A*
Kaplan University
   Lincoln *C*
   Omaha *C*
Metropolitan Community College *C*
Mid-Plains Community College *C*
Northeast Community College *C*
Southeast Community College *C*
Western Nebraska Community
   College *C*

Nevada

College of Southern Nevada *C*
Kaplan College
   Las Vegas *C*

New Hampshire

NHTI-Concord's Community
   College *C*
River Valley Community College *C*

New Jersey

Berkeley College *C*
Cumberland County College *C*
Hudson County Community
   College *C*
Salem Community College *C*
Union County College *C*

New Mexico

Central New Mexico Community
   College *C, A*
Clovis Community College *C*
Luna Community College *C*
New Mexico Junior College *C*
New Mexico State University
   Alamogordo *A*
   Carlsbad *C*
Northern New Mexico College *C*

New York

City University of New York
   Bronx Community College *C*
   Hostos Community College *C*
   LaGuardia Community College *C*
   Medgar Evers College *C*
Maria College *C*

Mildred Elley
   New York City *C*
Niagara County Community
   College *C*
SUNY
   College of Technology at Canton *C*
   College of Technology at Delhi *C*
St. Joseph's College New York:
   Suffolk Campus *B, M*
St. Joseph's College, New York *B, M*
Suffolk County Community College *C*
Touro College *A*
Westchester Community College *C*

North Carolina

Alamance Community College *C*
Asheville-Buncombe Technical
   Community College *C*
Beaufort County Community
   College *C*
Bladen Community College *C*
Brunswick Community College *C*
Cape Fear Community College *C*
Carteret Community College *C*
Central Carolina Community
   College *A*
Cleveland Community College *C*
Coastal Carolina Community
   College *C*
College of the Albemarle *C*
Craven Community College *C*
Davidson County Community
   College *C*
Durham Technical Community
   College *C*
Edgecombe Community College *C*
Fayetteville Technical Community
   College *C*
Forsyth Technical Community
   College *A*
Isothermal Community College *C*
James Sprunt Community College *C*
Lenoir Community College *C*
Mayland Community College *C*
McDowell Technical Community
   College *C*
Montgomery Community College *C*
Nash Community College *A*
Robeson Community College *C*
Rockingham Community College *C*
Sampson Community College *A*
Sandhills Community College *C*
South Piedmont Community
   College *C*
Southeastern Community College *C*
Southwestern Community College *C*
Surry Community College *C*
Vance-Granville Community
   College *C*
Wayne Community College *C*
Wilson Community College *C*

North Dakota

Bismarck State College *C*
Dakota College at Bottineau *C*
Dickinson State University *A*
Lake Region State College *C*
North Dakota State College of
   Science *A*
Sitting Bull College *A*
United Tribes Technical College *C, A*
Williston State College *C*

Ohio

Belmont College *C*
Brown Mackie College
   Akron *C*
   Findlay *C*
   North Canton *C*
Central Ohio Technical College *C*
Cincinnati State Technical and
   Community College *C*
Clark State Community College *C*

Columbus State Community
College *C*
Eastern Gateway Community
College *C, A*
Hocking College *C*
Hondros College *C*
James A. Rhodes State College *C*
Lorain County Community College *C*
North Central State College *C*
Northwest State Community
College *C*
Owens Community College
Toledo *C*
Southern State Community College *C*
Washington State Community
College *C*

Oregon

Central Oregon Community
College *C, A*
Chemeketa Community College *C*
Clackamas Community College *C*
Clatsop Community College *C*
Klamath Community College *C*
Mt. Hood Community College *C*
Pioneer Pacific College *C*
Portland Community College *C*
Rogue Community College *C*
Southwestern Oregon Community
College *C, A*
Treasure Valley Community
College *C*
Umpqua Community College *C*

Pennsylvania

Community College of Allegheny
County *C*
Community College of Beaver
County *C*
Harrisburg Area Community
College *C*
Lehigh Carbon Community College *C*
Lincoln Technical Institute
Allentown *C*
Northampton Community College *C*
Pennsylvania College of
Technology *C*
Reading Area Community College *C*
Westmoreland County Community
College *C*
York College of Pennsylvania *B*

Puerto Rico

Centro de Estudios
Multidisciplinarios *C*
Inter American University of Puerto
Rico
Aguadilla Campus *A*
Bayamon Campus *A*
Metropolitan Campus *A*
Turabo University *C*
Universal Technology College of
Puerto Rico *C*
Universidad Metropolitana *C*

Rhode Island

Community College of Rhode
Island *C*

South Carolina

Aiken Technical College *C*
Central Carolina Technical College *C*
Denmark Technical College *C*
Florence-Darlington Technical
College *C*
Horry-Georgetown Technical
College *C*
Midlands Technical College *C*
Northeastern Technical College *C, A*
Orangeburg-Calhoun Technical
College *C*
Piedmont Technical College *C*
Spartanburg Community College *C*

Technical College of the
Lowcountry *C*
Tri-County Technical College *C*
Trident Technical College *C*
York Technical College *C*

South Dakota

Lake Area Technical Institute *C*
Mount Marty College *C*
Sisseton Wahpeton College *C*
Southeast Technical Institute *C*
Western Dakota Technical
Institute *C, A*

Tennessee

Chattanooga State Community
College *C*
Tennessee State University *A*

Texas

Alvin Community College *C*
Amarillo College *C*
Angelina College *C*
Austin Community College *C*
Brazosport College *C*
Central Texas College *C*
Cisco College *C*
Clarendon College *C*
Coastal Bend College *C*
College of the Mainland *A*
Del Mar College *C*
El Centro College *G*
El Paso Community College *C*
Frank Phillips College *C*
Galveston College *C*
Grayson College *C*
Hill College *C*
Houston Community College
System *C*
Howard College *C*
Kilgore College *C*
Lamar State College at Orange *C*
Lamar State College at Port Arthur *C*
Lone Star College System *C*
McLennan Community College *C*
Midland College *C*
Navarro College *C, A*
Northeast Texas Community
College *C*
Odessa College *C*
Panola College *C*
Paris Junior College *C*
Ranger College *C*
St. Philip's College *C*
San Jacinto College *C, A*
Schreiner University *C*
South Plains College *C*
South Texas College *C*
Southwest Texas Junior College *A*
Temple College *C*
Texarkana College *C*
Texas State Technical College
Harlingen *C*
West Texas *C, A*
Trinity Valley Community College *C*
Vernon College *C*
Victoria College *C*
Weatherford College *C, A*
Western Texas College *C*
Wharton County Junior College *C*

Utah

Snow College *C, A*

Vermont

Vermont Technical College *C*

Virginia

Danville Community College *C*
ECPI University *C*
Germanna Community College *C*
J. Sargeant Reynolds Community
College *C*
Lord Fairfax Community College *C*

Mountain Empire Community
College *C*
New River Community College *C*
Rappahannock Community College *C*
Skyline College: Roanoke *C*
Southside Virginia Community
College *C*
Southwest Virginia Community
College *C*
Thomas Nelson Community
College *A*
Virginia Western Community
College *C*
Wytheville Community College *C*

Washington

Bates Technical College *A*
Bellingham Technical College *C*
Big Bend Community College *C*
Centralia College *C*
Clover Park Technical College *C, A*
Columbia Basin College *A*
Edmonds Community College *C*
Everett Community College *C*
Grays Harbor College *C*
Green River Community College *C*
Heritage University *C, A*
Lake Washington Institute of
Technology *A*
Lower Columbia College *A*
North Seattle Community
College *C, A*
Olympic College *C*
Renton Technical College *C, A*
Skagit Valley College *C, A*
South Puget Sound Community
College *A*
South Seattle Community
College *C, A*
Spokane Community College *C*
Walla Walla Community College *C*
Wenatchee Valley College *C*
Yakima Valley Community
College *C, A*

West Virginia

Appalachian Bible College *A*
New River Community and Technical
College *C*

Wisconsin

Chippewa Valley Technical College *C*
Fox Valley Technical College *C*
Gateway Technical College *C*
Lakeshore Technical College *C*
Madison Area Technical College *C*
Mid-State Technical College *C*
Moraine Park Technical College *C*
Northeast Wisconsin Technical
College *C*
Southwest Wisconsin Technical
College *C*
Waukesha County Technical
College *C*
Western Technical College *C*

Wyoming

Casper College *C*
Laramie County Community
College *C*
Northwest College *C*
Sheridan College *C*
Western Wyoming Community
College *C, A*

Lineworker

Arizona

Cochise College *C*

California

Santa Rosa Junior College *C*

Colorado

Colorado Mesa University *C*
Trinidad State Junior College *C, A*

Florida

South Florida State College *C*

Georgia

Georgia Piedmont Technical
College *C*
North Georgia Technical College *C*
Southeastern Technical College *C*

Illinois

City Colleges of Chicago
Kennedy-King College *C*

Indiana

Ivy Tech Community College
Lafayette *C, A*

Iowa

Northwest Iowa Community
College *C, A*

Kentucky

Hopkinsville Community College *C*

Maine

Kennebec Valley Community
College *C*

Maryland

College of Southern Maryland *A*

Michigan

Alpena Community College *C*
Lansing Community College *C*
Northern Michigan University *C*

Minnesota

Dakota County Technical
College *C, A*
Minnesota State Community and
Technical College *C, A*
Minnesota West Community and
Technical College *A*

Mississippi

Mississippi Gulf Coast Community
College *A*

Missouri

Linn State Technical College *A*

Montana

Fort Peck Community College *C*

Nebraska

Northeast Community College *A*
Western Nebraska Community
College *C, A*

New Jersey

Brookdale Community College *A*
Raritan Valley Community College *A*

New Mexico

Dona Ana Community College of
New Mexico State University *A*

North Carolina

Nash Community College *A*

North Dakota

Bismarck State College *C, A*

Oregon

Clackamas Community College *C*
Linn-Benton Community College *C, A*

Pennsylvania

Harrisburg Area Community
College *A*

South Carolina

York Technical College *C*

South Dakota

Mitchell Technical Institute *A*

Texas

Lamar Institute of Technology *C*
Texas State Technical College
Waco *C*

Washington

Clover Park Technical College *C*

Wisconsin

Chippewa Valley Technical College *C*
Milwaukee Area Technical College *C*
Southwest Wisconsin Technical
College *C*

Linguistics

Alaska

University of Alaska
Fairbanks *B, M*

Arizona

Northern Arizona University *D*
University of Arizona *B, M, D*

Arkansas

University of Central Arkansas *B*

California

California State University
Dominguez Hills *B*
Fresno *B, M*
Fullerton *B, M*
Monterey Bay *B*
Northridge *B, M*
Foothill College *A*
Pitzer College *B*
Pomona College *B*
San Diego State University *B, M*
San Francisco State University *M*
San Jose State University *B, M*
Scripps College *B*
Stanford University *B, M, D*
University of California
Berkeley *B, M, D*
Davis *B, M, D*
Los Angeles *B, M, D*
Riverside *B*
San Diego *B, M, D*
Santa Barbara *B, M, D*
Santa Cruz *B, M, D*
University of Southern
California *B, M, D*

Colorado

Metropolitan State University of
Denver *B*
University of Colorado
Boulder *B, M, D*

Connecticut

University of Connecticut *B, M, D*
Yale University *B, M, D*

Delaware

University of Delaware *M, D*

District of Columbia

Gallaudet University *M, D*
Georgetown University *B, M, D*

Florida

Florida Atlantic University *B, M*
Florida International University *M*
University of Florida *B, M, D*
University of South Florida *M*

Georgia

Emory University *B*
Georgia State University *B*
University of Georgia *B, M, D*

Hawaii

University of Hawaii
Hilo *B*
Manoa *M, D*

Illinois

Benedictine University *M*
Moody Bible Institute *B*
Northeastern Illinois University *M*
Northwestern University *B, M, D*
Southern Illinois University
Carbondale *B, M*
University of Chicago *B, D*
University of Illinois
Chicago *M*
Urbana-Champaign *B, M, D*

Indiana

Ball State University *M*
Indiana University
Bloomington *B, M, D*
Purdue University *B, M, D*

Iowa

Central College *B*
Iowa State University *B*
University of Iowa *B, M, D*

Kansas

University of Kansas *B, M, D*

Kentucky

Bluegrass Community and Technical
College *A*
Hopkinsville Community College *A*
University of Kentucky *B*

Louisiana

Tulane University *B, M, D*

Maine

University of Southern Maine *B*

Maryland

University of Maryland
Baltimore County *B*
College Park *B, M, D*

Massachusetts

Bard College at Simon's Rock *B*
Boston College *B, M*
Boston University *B, M*
Brandeis University *B, M*
Gordon College *B*
Hampshire College *B*
Harvard College *B, M, D*
Massachusetts Institute of
Technology *B, M, D*
Northeastern University *B*
University of Massachusetts
Amherst *B, M, D*
Boston *M*
Wellesley College *B*

Michigan

Calvin College *B*
Eastern Michigan University *B, M*
Michigan State University *B, M, D*
Oakland University *B, M*
University of Michigan *B, M, D*

University of Michigan
Flint *B*
Wayne State University *B, M*

Minnesota

Bethel University *B*
Carleton College *B*
Crown College *B*
Macalester College *B*
Saint Cloud State University *B*
University of Minnesota
Duluth *B*
Twin Cities *B, M, D*

Mississippi

University of Mississippi *B*

Missouri

Truman State University *B*
University of Missouri
Columbia *B*
Washington University in St. Louis *B*

Montana

University of Montana *M*

New Hampshire

Dartmouth College *B*
University of New Hampshire *B*

New Jersey

Montclair State University *B, M*
Rutgers, The State University of New
Jersey
New Brunswick/Piscataway
Campus *B, M, D*

New Mexico

University of New Mexico *B, M, D*

New York

Barnard College *B*
City University of New York
Brooklyn College *B*
Lehman College *B*
Queens College *B, M*
Columbia University *B*
Cornell University *B, M, D*
Hofstra University *B*
New York University *B, M, D*
SUNY
College at Oswego *B*
University at Albany *B*
University at Binghamton *B*
University at Buffalo *B, M, D*
University at Stony Brook *B, M, D*
Syracuse University *B, M*
University of Rochester *B, M, D*

North Carolina

Appalachian State University *T*
University of North Carolina
Chapel Hill *B, M*

North Dakota

University of North Dakota *M*

Ohio

Cleveland State University *B*
Miami University
Oxford *B*
Ohio State University
Columbus Campus *B, M, D*
Ohio University *B, M*
University of Toledo *B*

Oklahoma

University of Oklahoma *B*

Oregon

Portland State University *B, M*
Reed College *B*
University of Oregon *B, M, D*

Pennsylvania

Bucknell University *B*
Carnegie Mellon University *B*
Penn State
University Park *D*
Swarthmore College *B*
Temple University *B, M*
University of Pennsylvania *B, M, D*
University of Pittsburgh *B, M, D*

Puerto Rico

University of Puerto Rico
Rio Piedras *M*

Rhode Island

Brown University *B*

South Carolina

University of South Carolina
Columbia *M, D*

Texas

Baylor University *B*
Navarro College *A*
Rice University *B, M, D*
University of Houston *B*
University of North Texas *M*
University of Texas
Arlington *B, M, D*
Austin *B, M, D*
El Paso *B, M*

Utah

Brigham Young University *B, M*
University of Utah *B, M, D*

Vermont

Marlboro College *B*
University of Vermont *B*

Virginia

College of William and Mary *B*
George Mason University *D*
University of Virginia *M*

Washington

Highline Community College *A*
University of Washington *B, M, D*
Washington State University *B*
Western Washington University *B*

Wisconsin

Lawrence University *B*
University of Wisconsin
Madison *B, M, D*
Milwaukee *B, M, D*

Livestock management

Colorado

Otero Junior College *A*

Indiana

Purdue University *B*

Kansas

Colby Community College *C*

Michigan

Michigan State University *C*

Montana

Dawson Community College *C*

Nebraska

Northeast Community College *A*

New Mexico

Navajo Technical University *C*

New York

SUNY
  College of Agriculture and
    Technology at Cobleskill *A*

Ohio

Ohio State University
  Columbus Campus *B*

Texas

Tarleton State University *B*

Locksmithing

Alabama

Jefferson Davis Community
  College *C*

Kentucky

Elizabethtown Community and
  Technical College *C, A*

Logic

California

University of California
  Berkeley *D*

Massachusetts

University of Massachusetts
  Amherst *C*

Pennsylvania

Carnegie Mellon University *B, M, D*
University of Pennsylvania *B*

Utah

University of Utah *B*

Logistics/materials/ supply chain management

Alabama

Alabama Agricultural and Mechanical
  University *B*
Athens State University *B*
Auburn University *B*

Alaska

University of Alaska
  Anchorage *C, A, B*

Arizona

Arizona Western College *C, A*
Central Arizona College *C*
Cochise College *C, A*
Pima Community College *C, A*
South Mountain Community
  College *C, A*

Arkansas

Arkansas State University *B*
Northwest Arkansas Community
  College *C*
Southern Arkansas University Tech *C*
University of Arkansas *B*

California

California Maritime Academy *B*
California State University
  Dominguez Hills *B, M*
  East Bay *M*
  Fresno *B*
Cerritos College *A*
Chabot College *A*
Golden Gate University *M*
National University *C*
San Joaquin Delta College *C, A*
San Jose State University *M*
Santa Monica College *C, A*

University of Redlands *C*
University of San Diego *M*
University of Southern California *M*

Colorado

Colorado Technical
  University *C, B, M*

Connecticut

Goodwin College *A*

Delaware

Wilmington University *M*

District of Columbia

University of the Potomac *C*

Florida

Florida Institute of Technology *M*
Miami Dade College *B*

Georgia

Albany State University *B*
Albany Technical College *C*
Athens Technical College *C*
Atlanta Technical College *C, A*
Central Georgia Technical
  College *C, A*
Clayton State University *B*
Georgia College and State
  University *M*
Georgia Institute of Technology *M*
Georgia Military College *A*
Georgia Southern University *B, D*
Middle Georgia State College *B*
Savannah Technical College *C*
West Georgia Technical College *C*

Illinois

City Colleges of Chicago
  Harold Washington College *C*
  Olive-Harvey College *C*
  Wilbur Wright College *C*
Elmhurst College *B, M*
Heartland Community College *C*
Illinois Central College *C*
Kishwaukee College *C*
Loyola University Chicago *M*
Moraine Valley Community College *C*
Sauk Valley Community College *C*
University of Illinois
  Urbana-Champaign *B*
University of St. Francis *B*
Western Illinois University *B*

Indiana

Ivy Tech Community College
  Central Indiana *A*
Vincennes University *A*

Iowa

Ashford University *B*
Iowa Central Community College *A*
Iowa State University *B*

Kansas

Johnson County Community
  College *A*
University of Kansas *B*

Kentucky

Murray State University *B*
Sullivan University *A, B*
University of Louisville *C*

Louisiana

Delgado Community College *C*
Southeastern Louisiana University *B*

Maine

Maine Maritime Academy *B, M*

Maryland

Cecil College *A*
Towson University *M*
University of Maryland
  College Park *B*

Massachusetts

Northeastern University *B*
Northern Essex Community
  College *C, A*

Michigan

Central Michigan University *B*
Eastern Michigan University *B, M*
Henry Ford Community College *C*
Lake Michigan College *C*
Michigan State University *B, M, D*
University of Michigan *M*
Wayne County Community College *C*
Western Michigan University *B*

Minnesota

Anoka Technical College *C*
Northland Community & Technical
  College *C*
St. Paul College *C, A*

Mississippi

University of Southern Mississippi *M*

Missouri

Fontbonne University *M*
Missouri State University *B*
Park University *A, B*
University of Missouri
  St. Louis *B, M, D*

Nebraska

Bellevue University *B*
University of Nebraska
  Lincoln *B*

New Jersey

Bloomfield College *C*
Rutgers, The State University of New
  Jersey
  New Brunswick/Piscataway
    Campus *B*
  Newark Campus *B*

New York

Clarkson University *B*
Globe Institute of Technology *C*
Hofstra University *B*
Niagara University *B*
Rochester Institute of Technology *C*
SUNY
  University at Binghamton *B*
  Syracuse University *B, M*

North Carolina

Forsyth Technical Community
  College *C, A*
Lenoir Community College *C, A*
Randolph Community College *C, A*

Ohio

Ashland University *B*
Bowling Green State University *B*
Clark State Community College *A*
Columbus State Community
  College *C, A*
Edison State Community College *C, A*
Harrison College
  Grove City *A*
John Carroll University *B*
Northwest State Community
  College *C, A*
Ohio State University
  Columbus Campus *B, M*
Sinclair Community College *C, A*
Stark State College *A*
Tiffin University *B*

University of Akron *M*
University of Toledo *A, B*
Wright State University *B, M*

Oklahoma

Northeastern State University *B*

Oregon

Portland State University *B*

Pennsylvania

Commonwealth Technical Institute *C*
Community College of
  Philadelphia *C, A*
Duquesne University *B*
Johnson College *A*
Lehigh University *B, M*
Penn State
  Beaver *C*
  Brandywine *C*
  DuBois *C*
  Fayette, The Eberly Campus *C*
  Hazleton *C*
  Lehigh Valley *C*
  Mont Alto *C*
  New Kensington *C*
  Schuylkill *C*
  Wilkes-Barre *C*
  Worthington Scranton *C*
Shippensburg University of
  Pennsylvania *B*
University of Pittsburgh *B*
York College of Pennsylvania *B, M*

Puerto Rico

Turabo University *M*
University of Puerto Rico
  Bayamon University College *B*

Rhode Island

Bryant University *B, M*
University of Rhode Island *B*

South Carolina

Trident Technical College *A*
York Technical College *C, A*

Tennessee

University of Memphis *B*
University of Tennessee
  Knoxville *B*
Volunteer State Community
  College *C*

Texas

Baylor University *B*
Del Mar College *C, A*
Houston Community College
  System *C, A*
Lone Star College System *C, A*
North Lake College *C*
Palo Alto College *C, A*
South Texas College *C, A*
Tarrant County College *C, A*
Texas A&M International
  University *M*
Texas A&M University *B, M*
Texas Christian University *B, M*
University of Dallas *M*
University of Houston *M*
University of North Texas *B*
University of Texas
  Arlington *M*
  Austin *B*
  Dallas *M*

Utah

Brigham Young University *B*
Weber State University *B*

Virginia

New River Community College *A*
University of the Potomac *C*

Washington
Shoreline Community College *C, A*
Tacoma Community College *C*

West Virginia
American Public University
System *B, M*

Wisconsin
Fox Valley Technical College *A*
Lac Courte Oreilles Ojibwa
Community College *A*
Lakeshore Technical College *A*
Milwaukee Area Technical College *A*
Northcentral Technical College *C*
Northeast Wisconsin Technical
College *A*
University of Wisconsin
Stout *B*

Long term care administration

Alabama
University of Phoenix
Birmingham *B*

Arizona
University of Phoenix
Phoenix-Hohokam *C, B*
Southern Arizona *B*

Arkansas
University of Phoenix
Little Rock *B*
Northwest Arkansas *B*

California
University of Phoenix
Bay Area *B*
Central Valley *C, B*
Sacramento Valley *B*
San Diego *B*
Southern California *C, B*
University of Southern California *M*

Colorado
University of Phoenix
Denver *B*
Southern Colorado *B*

District of Columbia
University of Phoenix
Washington DC *B*

Florida
University of Phoenix
Central Florida *B*
North Florida *B*
South Florida *B*
West Florida *B*

Georgia
University of Phoenix
Atlanta *B*
Augusta *B*
Columbus *B*
Savannah *B*

Hawaii
University of Phoenix
Hawaii *B*

Idaho
University of Phoenix
Idaho *B*

Illinois
College of DuPage *C*
University of Phoenix
Chicago *B*

Indiana
University of Phoenix
Indianapolis *B*

Kansas
Cowley County Community
College *C*

Kentucky
University of Phoenix
Louisville *B*

Louisiana
University of Phoenix
Lafayette *B*
Louisiana *B*
Shreveport *B*

Michigan
Central Michigan University *M*
University of Phoenix
Metro Detroit *C, B*
West Michigan *B*

Minnesota
University of Phoenix
Minneapolis-St. Paul *B*

Missouri
University of Phoenix
Kansas City *B*
St. Louis *B*

Nebraska
Bellevue University *B*

Nevada
University of Phoenix
Las Vegas *B*
Northern Nevada *B*

Ohio
Tiffin University *B, M*
University of Phoenix
Cleveland *B*

Oklahoma
University of Phoenix
Tulsa *B*

Pennsylvania
University of Phoenix
Harrisburg *B*
Philadelphia *B*
Pittsburgh *B*

South Carolina
University of Phoenix
Columbia *B*

Tennessee
University of Phoenix
Chattanooga *B*
Knoxville *B*
Memphis *B*

Texas
Midland College *C*
San Jacinto College *C*
University of Phoenix
Austin *B*
Dallas Fort Worth *B*
Houston Westside *B*
San Antonio *B*

Utah
University of Phoenix
Utah *C, B*
Weber State University *B*

Virginia
University of Phoenix
Northern Virginia *C, B*
Richmond *B*

Washington
University of Phoenix
Western Washington *B*

Wisconsin
University of Phoenix
Milwaukee *B*

Machine shop technology

Alabama
Southern Union State Community
College *C, A*

Arkansas
Mid-South Community College *C*
Rich Mountain Community College *C*

California
Long Beach City College *C, A*
Los Angeles Pierce College *C*
Los Angeles Valley College *C*

Colorado
Community College of Denver *C*
Pueblo Community College *C, A*
Red Rocks Community College *C, A*

Connecticut
Middlesex Community College *C*

Georgia
Athens Technical College *C*
Central Georgia Technical College *C*
Gwinnett Technical College *C*
Savannah Technical College *A*
Southwest Georgia Technical
College *C*

Illinois
College of Lake County *C, A*
Illinois Central College *C*
Illinois Eastern Community Colleges
Wabash Valley College *C*
John A. Logan College *A*
McHenry County College *C*
Triton College *C*

Indiana
Ivy Tech Community College
Central Indiana *A*

Iowa
North Iowa Area Community
College *C*
Northwest Iowa Community
College *C*

Kansas
Cowley County Community
College *C, A*

Kentucky
Bluegrass Community and Technical
College *C, A*
Elizabethtown Community and
Technical College *C, A*
Gateway Community and Technical
College *C, A*
Hopkinsville Community College *C*
Jefferson Community and Technical
College *C*
Madisonville Community
College *C, A*
Owensboro Community and
Technical College *C, A*

Somerset Community College *C, A*
West Kentucky Community and
Technical College *C*

Louisiana
Delgado Community College *C*

Michigan
Grand Rapids Community
College *C, A*
Mid Michigan Community College *C*
Montcalm Community College *C*
Northwestern Michigan College *C*

Minnesota
Central Lakes College *C*
Hennepin Technical College *C, A*
Minnesota State College - Southeast
Technical *C*
Northland Community & Technical
College *C*
Northwest Technical College *C*
Pine Technical College *C*
St. Paul College *C*

Missouri
Metropolitan Community College -
Kansas City *C, A*
Ranken Technical College *A*

New Mexico
San Juan College *C, A*

New York
Corning Community College *C, A*
Mohawk Valley Community
College *C*

North Carolina
Cape Fear Community College *C, A*
Catawba Valley Community
College *C*
Central Piedmont Community
College *C, A*
Cleveland Community College *C*
College of the Albemarle *A*
Craven Community College *C, A*
Fayetteville Technical Community
College *C, A*
Forsyth Technical Community
College *C*
Guilford Technical Community
College *C, A*
Isothermal Community College *C*
Lenoir Community College *C, A*
Mitchell Community College *C, A*
Pitt Community College *C, A*
Rockingham Community College *C*
Wayne Community College *A*

Oregon
Chemeketa Community College *C, A*
Clackamas Community College *A*
Mt. Hood Community College *C, A*
Portland Community College *C, A*

Pennsylvania
Butler County Community
College *C, A*
Community College of Allegheny
County *C*
New Castle School of Trades *A*
Thaddeus Stevens College of
Technology *A*
Westmoreland County Community
College *C, A*

South Carolina
Piedmont Technical College *C*

Texas
Houston Community College
System *C, A*
St. Philip's College *C*

Utah

Salt Lake Community College *C*
Utah State University *A*

Virginia

New River Community College *C, A*

Washington

Bellingham Technical College *C*
Everett Community College *C*
Renton Technical College *C, A*

West Virginia

West Virginia University at
  Parkersburg *C, A*

Wisconsin

Blackhawk Technical College *C*
Chippewa Valley Technical College *C*
Fox Valley Technical College *C*
Mid-State Technical College *C*
Milwaukee Area Technical College *C*
Waukesha County Technical
  College *C*
Western Technical College *C*
Wisconsin Indianhead Technical
  College *C*

Wyoming

Eastern Wyoming College *C*

Machine tool technology

Alabama

Calhoun Community College *C, A*
Northwest-Shoals Community
  College *C*

Arizona

Mesa Community College *C, A*
Pima Community College *C, A*

Arkansas

Arkansas State University
  Beebe *C*
Mid-South Community College *C*
Pulaski Technical College *C*

California

Long Beach City College *C, A*
Los Angeles Pierce College *C*
Orange Coast College *C, A*
San Joaquin Delta College *C*
San Jose City College *C, A*

Colorado

Colorado Mesa University *C, A*

Connecticut

Asnuntuck Community College *C, A*
Middlesex Community College *A*

Georgia

Altamaha Technical College *C, A*
Columbus Technical College *C*
West Georgia Technical College *C*

Idaho

College of Western Idaho *C, A*
Idaho State University *C, A, B*

Illinois

Black Hawk College *C*
City Colleges of Chicago
  Richard J. Daley College *C*
Danville Area Community College *C*
Elgin Community College *C, A*
Heartland Community College *C*
Illinois Eastern Community Colleges
  Olney Central College *C*
  Wabash Valley College *C, A*

Illinois Valley Community College *C*
John A. Logan College *C*
Kankakee Community College *C*
Prairie State College *C*
Sauk Valley Community College *C*
Spoon River College *C*
Triton College *C*

Indiana

Ivy Tech Community College
  Bloomington *C, A*
  Central Indiana *C, A*
  Columbus *C, A*
  East Central *C, A*
  Kokomo *C, A*
  Lafayette *C, A*
  North Central *C, A*
  Northeast *C, A*
  Northwest *C, A*
  Richmond *C, A*
  South Central *C, A*
  Southwest *C, A*
  Wabash Valley *C, A*

Iowa

Des Moines Area Community
  College *A*
Hawkeye Community College *C, A*
Iowa Central Community College *A*
Kirkwood Community College *C, A*
North Iowa Area Community
  College *A*
Northeast Iowa Community
  College *A*
Southeastern Community
  College *C, A*

Kansas

Hutchinson Community College *C, A*
Kansas City Kansas Community
  College *C*
Wichita Area Technical College *C, A*

Louisiana

Delgado Community College *C*

Maine

Central Maine Community
  College *C, A*
Eastern Maine Community
  College *C, A*
Kennebec Valley Community
  College *C, A*
Southern Maine Community
  College *A*
York County Community
  College *C, A*

Maryland

Community College of Baltimore
  County *C*

Michigan

Delta College *A*
Glen Oaks Community College *C*
Henry Ford Community College *C*
Lake Michigan College *C, A*
Lansing Community College *C, A*
Mid Michigan Community
  College *C, A*
Northern Michigan University *A*
Oakland Community College *C, A*
Southwestern Michigan College *C, A*
Wayne County Community
  College *C, A*

Minnesota

Alexandria Technical and Community
  College *C*
Anoka Technical College *C*
Central Lakes College *C*
Dunwoody College of Technology *A*
Hennepin Technical College *C, A*
Lake Superior College *C*

Minneapolis Community and
  Technical College *C*
Minnesota State College - Southeast
  Technical *C*
Minnesota West Community and
  Technical College *A*
Pine Technical College *C, A*
Ridgewater College *C, A*
St. Cloud Technical and Community
  College *C, A*
St. Paul College *C*
South Central College *C, A*

Mississippi

Copiah-Lincoln Community
  College *C, A*
East Mississippi Community
  College *C*
Hinds Community College *C*
Meridian Community College *C, A*
Northeast Mississippi Community
  College *C, A*

Missouri

East Central College *C, A*
Jefferson College *C, A*
Linn State Technical College *A*
Mineral Area College *C, A*
Ozarks Technical Community
  College *C, A*

Montana

Helena College University of
  Montana *C, A*

Nebraska

Central Community College *C, A*
Southeast Community College *A*

Nevada

Western Nevada College *C, A*

New Mexico

Central New Mexico Community
  College *C*

New York

SUNY
  College of Technology at
    Alfred *C, A*

North Carolina

Beaufort County Community
  College *C*
Randolph Community College *A*
Rowan-Cabarrus Community
  College *C*
Tri-County Community College *C*

North Dakota

North Dakota State College of
  Science *C, A*

Ohio

Northwest State Community
  College *C*
University of Cincinnati *C*

Oregon

Clackamas Community College *C*
Linn-Benton Community College *C, A*
Mt. Hood Community College *A*
Portland Community College *C, A*

Pennsylvania

Butler County Community College *C*
Community College of Beaver
  County *A*
Delaware County Community
  College *C, A*
Johnson College *A*
Luzerne County Community
  College *C*

Pennsylvania College of
  Technology *C, A*
Reading Area Community College *A*
Thaddeus Stevens College of
  Technology *A*
Westmoreland County Community
  College *C, A*
Williamson Free School of
  Mechanical Trades *A*

Rhode Island

Community College of Rhode
  Island *C*

South Carolina

Aiken Technical College *C, A*
Greenville Technical College *C, A*
Horry-Georgetown Technical
  College *A*
Midlands Technical College *C, A*
Piedmont Technical College *C, A*
Spartanburg Community College *C, A*
Tri-County Technical College *C, A*
Trident Technical College *C*
Williamsburg Technical College *C, A*
York Technical College *C, A*

Texas

Angelina College *C, A*
Del Mar College *C, A*
Kilgore College *C, A*
Lamar Institute of Technology *C, A*
Odessa College *C, A*
St. Philip's College *A*
Texas State Technical College
  Harlingen *C*
  West Texas *C, A*

Utah

Salt Lake Community College *A*
Snow College *C, A*
Utah State University *C*

Virginia

Danville Community College *C*

Washington

Bates Technical College *C, A*
Bellingham Technical College *C, A*
Clark College *C, A*
Clover Park Technical College *C, A*
Columbia Basin College *C, A*
Everett Community College *C, A*
Lake Washington Institute of
  Technology *C, A*
Shoreline Community College *C, A*

West Virginia

New River Community and Technical
  College *C*
Potomac State College of West
  Virginia University *A*

Wisconsin

Lakeshore Technical College *C*
Milwaukee Area Technical College *C*
Northcentral Technical College *C*
Southwest Wisconsin Technical
  College *C*
Waukesha County Technical
  College *C*
Western Technical College *C*
Wisconsin Indianhead Technical
  College *C*

Wyoming

Casper College *C, A*
Sheridan College *C, A*

Magnetic resonance imaging (MRI) technology

Maryland
Community College of Baltimore County *C*

Massachusetts
MCPHS University *B*

Michigan
Lake Michigan College *C, A*
Lansing Community College *C, A*

Missouri
Saint Louis University *B*

New Mexico
University of New Mexico *C*

Ohio
Owens Community College
 Toledo *A*
Xavier University *C*

Pennsylvania
Pennsylvania College of Technology *C*

South Carolina
Greenville Technical College *C*

Wyoming
Casper College *C*

Make-up artist

Colorado
IBMC College
 Fort Collins *C*

New Jersey
Montclair State University *C*

North Carolina
Carteret Community College *C*
Martin Community College *C*

Tennessee
West Tennessee Business College *C*

Mammography technology

Colorado
Aims Community College *C*

Illinois
Moraine Valley Community College *C*

Iowa
St. Luke's College *C*

North Carolina
Fayetteville Technical Community College *C*

Pennsylvania
Holy Family University *C*

Texas
Weatherford College *C*

Management information systems

Alabama
Auburn University *B, M*
Auburn University at Montgomery *B*
Central Alabama Community College *C, A*
Community College of the Air Force *A*
Enterprise State Community College *A*
Faulkner University *B*
Oakwood University *B*
University of Alabama *B*
University of Alabama
 Birmingham *B*
 Huntsville *B, M*
University of North Alabama *B*
University of West Alabama *B*
Virginia College
 Birmingham *B*

Alaska
Charter College *B*
Prince William Sound Community College *C, A*
University of Alaska
 Anchorage *B*
 Southeast *C, A*

Arizona
DeVry University
 Phoenix *M*
Mesa Community College *C*
Northcentral University *M, D*
Northern Arizona University *B*
Scottsdale Community College *C, A*
University of Arizona *B*
University of Phoenix
 Phoenix-Hohokam *M*
 Southern Arizona *M*
Western International University *B, M*

Arkansas
Arkansas Northeastern College *A*
Arkansas State University *A*
Arkansas State University
 Beebe *C, A*
 Newport *C, A*
Arkansas Tech University *C*
Black River Technical College *C, A*
Cossatot Community College of the University of Arkansas *A*
East Arkansas Community College *C, A*
Henderson State University *B*
John Brown University *B*
National Park Community College *A*
Pulaski Technical College *C, A*
Rich Mountain Community College *C, A*
Southeast Arkansas College *C, A*
University of Arkansas *B, M*
University of Arkansas
 Little Rock *B, M*
 Monticello *C, B*
University of Central Arkansas *B*

California
Allan Hancock College *A*
American River College *A*
Azusa Pacific University *B*
Biola University *B*
Butte College *C, A*
California Lutheran University *M*
California State University
 East Bay *B, M*
 Northridge *B*
 Sacramento *M*
 San Bernardino *B, M*
Chabot College *A*
Chaffey College *C*
Citrus College *A*
City College of San Francisco *A*
College of the Sequoias *C, A*
Columbia College *C*
Cypress College *C, A*

DeVry University
 Pomona *M*
Evergreen Valley College *A*
Folsom Lake College *C*
Fresno Pacific University *B*
Fullerton College *A*
Gavilan College *C*
Heald College
 Fresno *C, A*
Laney College *C, A*
Lincoln University *B, M*
Los Angeles City College *C, A*
Los Angeles Harbor College *C, A*
Los Angeles Southwest College *A*
Los Angeles Valley College *C, A*
Loyola Marymount University *B*
Master's College *B*
Menlo College *B*
Mission College *A*
Modesto Junior College *A*
National University *C, B, M*
Orange Coast College *C, A*
Pacific States University *B, M*
Pasadena City College *A*
Point Loma Nazarene University *B*
Porterville College *C*
Sacramento City College *C, A*
San Bernardino Valley College *C*
San Diego City College *C, A*
Santa Clara University *B*
Shasta College *A*
Skyline College *C, A*
University of La Verne *M*
University of Phoenix
 Bay Area *M*
 Central Valley *M*
 Sacramento Valley *M*
 San Diego *M*
 Southern California *M*
University of Redlands *B*
West Hills College: Coalinga *C, A*

Colorado
Adams State University *B*
Aims Community College *C, A*
Arapahoe Community College *A*
Colorado Christian University *B*
Colorado Mesa University *B*
Colorado Mountain College *A*
Colorado Northwestern Community College *A*
Colorado State University *B*
Colorado Technical University *B, M*
Community College of Denver *C, A*
DeVry University
 Westminster *M*
Metropolitan State University of Denver *B*
National American University
 Denver *B*
Northeastern Junior College *C, A*
Red Rocks Community College *C, A*
University of Colorado
 Boulder *B*
University of Denver *B*
University of Phoenix
 Denver *M*
Western State Colorado University *B*
Westwood College
 Denver North *B*

Connecticut
Albertus Magnus College *C, A, B*
Central Connecticut State University *B*
Eastern Connecticut State University *B*
Fairfield University *B*
Manchester Community College *C, A*
Post University *C, B*
Quinnipiac University *B, M*
University of Bridgeport *B, M*
University of Connecticut *B*
University of Hartford *B*

Western Connecticut State University *B*

Delaware
Delaware Technical Community College
 Jack F. Owens Campus *A*
 Stanton/Wilmington Campus *A*
 Terry Campus *A*
Goldey-Beacom College *B*
University of Delaware *B*
Wilmington University *M*

District of Columbia
American University *B, M*
Gallaudet University *B*
George Washington University *B, M*
Howard University *B*
University of Phoenix
 Washington DC *M*
University of the District of Columbia *A*
University of the Potomac *B*

Florida
Daytona State College *C, A*
DeVry University
 Miramar *M*
 Orlando *M*
Eastern Florida State College *A*
Everest University
 Pompano Beach *A, B*
Florida Atlantic University *B, M*
Florida Gulf Coast University *B, M*
Florida Institute of Technology *B, M*
Florida International University *B, M*
Florida Memorial University *B*
Florida State College at Jacksonville *A*
Florida State University *B, M, D*
Hillsborough Community College *C, A*
Indian River State College *A*
Keiser University *B*
Northwest Florida State College *C*
Northwood University
 Florida *B*
Nova Southeastern University *M*
Palm Beach State College *A*
Pensacola State College *A*
Rasmussen College
 Fort Myers *C, A*
 New Port Richey *C, A*
 Ocala *C, A*
 Pasco/Land O'Lakes *C, A*
 Tampa/Brandon *C, A*
Saint Johns River State College *C*
Santa Fe College *C*
Schiller International University *M*
Southeastern University *B*
Stetson University *B*
Tallahassee Community College *A*
University of Phoenix
 Central Florida *M*
 North Florida *M*
 South Florida *M*
 West Florida *M*
University of South Florida *B, M*
University of Tampa *A, B*
University of West Florida *B*
Valencia College *C*

Georgia
Albany State University *B*
Bainbridge College *C, A*
Columbus State University *B*
Dalton State College *B*
Emory University *B*
Georgia Regents University *B*
Georgia Southern University *B*
Life University *A, B*
Mercer University *B*
Thomas University *B*
University of Georgia *B*

University of Phoenix
  Atlanta *M*
  Augusta *M*
  Columbus *M*
  Savannah *M*
University of West Georgia *B*
West Georgia Technical College *C*

Hawaii

Hawaii Pacific University *B*
University of Hawaii
  Manoa *B*
University of Phoenix
  Hawaii *M*

Idaho

Boise State University *B, M*
University of Idaho *B*

Illinois

Augustana College *B*
Aurora University *B*
Benedictine University *M*
Bradley University *B*
Chicago State University *B*
DePaul University *B, M*
DeVry University
  Chicago *M*
  Online *M*
Eureka College *B*
Governors State University *B, M*
Greenville College *B*
Illinois College *B*
Illinois State University *B*
Joliet Junior College *C*
Kishwaukee College *A*
Lewis University *B*
Loyola University Chicago *C, B, M*
MacMurray College *B*
Millikin University *B*
Moraine Valley Community College *A*
North Central College *B, M*
Northern Illinois University *M*
Northwestern University *M*
Rasmussen College
  Aurora *C, A*
  Mokena/Tinley Park *C, A*
  Rockford *C, A*
  Romeoville/Joliet *C, A*
Richland Community College *A*
Robert Morris University: Chicago *M*
Saint Xavier University *M*
Sauk Valley Community College *C*
Southern Illinois University
  Edwardsville *B, M*
Southwestern Illinois College *C, A*
University of Illinois
  Chicago *M, D*
  Urbana-Champaign *B, M, D*
Western Illinois University *B*

Indiana

Ball State University *B*
Grace College *B*
Indiana State University *B*
Indiana University
  South Bend *M*
  Southeast *C*
Marian University *B*
Oakland City University *B*
Purdue University *B, M, D*
Saint Mary's College *B*
University of Evansville *B*
University of Indianapolis *B*
University of Notre Dame *B*

Iowa

Ashford University *B*
Briar Cliff University *B*
Buena Vista University *B*
Drake University *B*
Iowa State University *B, M*
Loras College *B*
Luther College *B*

Mount Mercy University *B*
University of Iowa *B, D*
University of Northern Iowa *B*
Upper Iowa University *B*

Kansas

Coffeyville Community College *A*
Dodge City Community College *C, A*
Fort Scott Community College *C, A*
Friends University *B, M*
Haskell Indian Nations University *A*
Newman University *B*
Southwestern College *B*
University of Kansas *B*
Wichita State University *B*

Kentucky

Ashland Community and Technical
  College *A*
Big Sandy Community and Technical
  College *A*
Brown Mackie College
  Hopkinsville *C, A*
Eastern Kentucky University *B*
Henderson Community College *A*
Madisonville Community College *A*
Morehead State University *A, B, M*
Northern Kentucky
  University *C, B, M*
Southeast Kentucky Community and
  Technical College *C, A*
University of Louisville *B*
University of the Cumberlands *B*
West Kentucky Community and
  Technical College *A*
Western Kentucky University *B*

Louisiana

Louisiana Tech University *B*
Nicholls State University *B*
Southern University
  New Orleans *B, M*
Tulane University *B*
University of Louisiana at Lafayette *B*
University of Louisiana at Monroe *B*
University of Phoenix
  Baton Rouge *M*
  Lafayette *M*
  Louisiana *M*
  Shreveport *M*

Maine

Husson University *B*
Kennebec Valley Community
  College *A*
Northern Maine Community
  College *A*
University of Maine
  Fort Kent *A, B*
University of Southern Maine *B*
York County Community College *A*

Maryland

Allegany College of Maryland *C, A*
Anne Arundel Community
  College *C, A*
Baltimore City Community College *A*
Bowie State University *M*
Capitol College *M*
Carroll Community College *A*
Cecil College *C, A*
Community College of Baltimore
  County *C, A*
Garrett College *C, A*
Hagerstown Community College *C, A*
Montgomery College *C, A*
Sojourner-Douglass College *B*
Stevenson University *B*
TESST College of Technology
  Towson *C, A*
University of Baltimore *B, M*
University of Maryland
  University College *M*

Massachusetts

Anna Maria College *B*
Babson College *B*
Bentley University *M*
Boston College *B*
Boston University *B, M*
Fisher College *B*
Greenfield Community College *C*
Massachusetts College of Liberal
  Arts *B*
New England College of Business and
  Finance *C*
Nichols College *B*
Northeastern University *B*
Roxbury Community College *A*
Salem State University *B, M*
Simmons College *B*
University of Massachusetts
  Boston *C*
  Dartmouth *B*
Western New England University *B*
Worcester Polytechnic Institute *B, M*

Michigan

Alpena Community College *A*
Aquinas College *B*
Baker College
  Flint *A, B*
  Muskegon *B*
  Owosso *B*
  Port Huron *B*
Calvin College *B*
Central Michigan University *B, M*
Cleary University *B*
Cornerstone University *B*
Eastern Michigan University *B, M*
Kalamazoo Valley Community
  College *A*
Kettering University *M*
Kirtland Community College *A*
Lake Superior State University *A*
Lansing Community College *A*
Madonna University *B*
Michigan State University *B, M, D*
Michigan Technological University *B*
Montcalm Community College *A*
Northern Michigan University *B*
Northwestern Michigan College *C, A*
Northwood University
  Michigan *A, B*
Oakland Community College *C, A*
Oakland University *B, M*
Rochester College *B*
Spring Arbor University *B*
University of Phoenix
  Metro Detroit *M*
  West Michigan *M*
Walsh College of Accountancy and
  Business Administration *M*
Wayne State University *B*
West Shore Community College *A*

Minnesota

Augsburg College *B*
Bemidji State University *B*
Dakota County Technical
  College *C, A*
Lake Superior College *A*
Metropolitan State University *B, M*
Minneapolis Business College *A*
Minnesota State Community and
  Technical College *A*
Minnesota State University
  Mankato *B*
National American University
  Bloomington *A, B*
Normandale Community College *A*
North Hennepin Community
  College *A*
Rasmussen College
  Blaine *C, A*
  Bloomington *C, A*
  Brooklyn Park *C, A*
  Eagan *C, A*

Lake Elmo/Woodbury *C, A*
  Mankato *C, A*
  St. Cloud *C, A*
Ridgewater College *A*
St. Catherine University *B*
Saint Cloud State University *B*
St. Paul College *C, A*
University of Minnesota
  Crookston *B*
  Duluth *B*
  Twin Cities *B*
University of Northwestern - St.
  Paul *B*
Walden University *M*
Winona State University *B*

Mississippi

Delta State University *B*
Itawamba Community College *A*
Mississippi Gulf Coast Community
  College *A*
Mississippi State University *B, M*
Northwest Mississippi Community
  College *A*
Pearl River Community College *A*
University of Mississippi *B*
University of Phoenix
  Jackson *M*
University of Southern Mississippi *B*

Missouri

Avila University *B, M*
Columbia College *B*
DeVry University
  Kansas City *B, M*
Drury University *B*
East Central College *A*
Grantham University *M*
Harris-Stowe State University *B*
Lindenwood University *B, M*
Linn State Technical College *C, A*
Maryville University of Saint Louis *B*
Missouri State University *B, M*
Missouri University of Science and
  Technology *B*
National American University
  Kansas City *A, B*
Northwest Missouri State
  University *B*
Park University *B*
Saint Louis University *B*
Three Rivers Community College *A*
University of Central Missouri *B*
University of Missouri
  St. Louis *B, M, D*
University of Phoenix
  Kansas City *M*
  St. Louis *M*
Webster University *B*
Westminster College *B*
William Woods University *B*

Montana

Little Big Horn College *C, A*
Stone Child College *A*
University of Montana *B*

Nebraska

Bellevue University *B, M*
Chadron State College *B*
Concordia University *B*
Metropolitan Community
  College *C, A*
Midland University *B*
Peru State College *B*

Nevada

College of Southern Nevada *C, A*
University of Nevada
  Las Vegas *B, M*
University of Phoenix
  Las Vegas *M*

New Hampshire

Daniel Webster College *B*
Franklin Pierce University *B*
Granite State College *B*
Nashua Community College *C*
New England College *B*
Rivier University *A, B, M*

New Jersey

Atlantic Cape Community College *A*
Bergen Community College *C*
Burlington County College *A*
Camden County College *A*
County College of Morris *A*
Cumberland County College *C, A*
Hudson County Community
  College *C, A*
Mercer County Community
  College *C, A*
Passaic County Community
  College *C, A*
Raritan Valley Community
  College *C, A*
Rowan University *B*
Rutgers, The State University of New
  Jersey
  New Brunswick/Piscataway
    Campus *B*
  Newark Campus *B*
Saint Peter's University *A, B, M*
Seton Hall University *B*
Stevens Institute of
  Technology *B, M, D*

New Mexico

Clovis Community College *C, A*
Eastern New Mexico University *B*
National American University
  Albuquerque *A, B*
New Mexico Highlands University *B*
Northern New Mexico College *A*
University of Phoenix
  New Mexico *M*
University of the Southwest *B*

New York

Berkeley College of New York
  City *A, B*
Bramson ORT College *A*
Canisius College *B*
City University of New York
  Baruch College *B, M*
  Bronx Community College *A*
  York College *B*
Clarkson University *B*
DeVry College of New York
  Midtown Campus *M*
Dominican College of Blauvelt *B*
Excelsior College *B*
Fordham University *B, M*
Globe Institute of
  Technology *C, A, B*
Hofstra University *C, B, M*
Iona College *B, M*
Le Moyne College *B*
Manhattan College *B*
Medaille College *B*
Medaille College: Amherst *B*
Medaille College: Rochester *B, M*
Nassau Community College *A*
Pace University: Pleasantville/
  Briarcliff *M*
Rochester Institute of Technology *B*
SUNY
  College at Fredonia *B*
  College at Plattsburgh *B*
  College of Agriculture and
    Technology at Morrisville *B*
  College of Technology at Delhi *A*
  University at Albany *M*
  University at Binghamton *B*
  University at Buffalo *M*
Saint Bonaventure University *B*
St. John's University *B*

Sullivan County Community
  College *A*
Touro College *B*
Utica School of Commerce *A*
Yeshiva University *B*

North Carolina

Appalachian State University *B*
Asheville-Buncombe Technical
  Community College *A*
Campbell University *A, B*
Catawba College *B*
Catawba Valley Community
  College *C, A*
Central Piedmont Community
  College *C, A*
East Carolina University *B*
Elon University *B*
Fayetteville State University *B*
Gardner-Webb University *B*
Guilford Technical Community
  College *C, A*
Lenoir-Rhyne University *B*
Martin Community College *C, A*
Methodist University *B*
Nash Community College *A*
Pfeiffer University *B*
Randolph Community College *A*
Richmond Community College *C, A*
Roanoke-Chowan Community
  College *A*
University of Mount Olive *B*
University of North Carolina
  Charlotte *B*
  Greensboro *D*
  Wilmington *B*
University of Phoenix
  Raleigh *M*
Western Carolina University *B*

North Dakota

Lake Region State College *A*
Minot State University *C, B*
North Dakota State University *B*
Rasmussen College
  Bismarck *C, A*
  Fargo *C, A*
University of Jamestown *B*
University of Mary *B*

Ohio

Ashland University *B*
Bowling Green State University *B*
Case Western Reserve
  University *M, D*
Cedarville University *B*
Cleveland State University *B, D*
Columbus State Community
  College *C*
Cuyahoga Community College
  Metropolitan *A*
DeVry University
  Columbus *M*
Defiance College *B*
Franklin University *B*
Lakeland Community College *A*
Marietta College *B*
Miami University
  Middletown *B*
  Oxford *B*
Mount Vernon Nazarene University *B*
Notre Dame College *B*
Ohio State University
  Columbus Campus *B*
Ohio University *B*
Ohio University
  Chillicothe Campus *A*
  Lancaster Campus *A*
Shawnee State University *A*
Stark State College *A*
University of Akron *B, M*
University of Akron: Wayne
  College *A*
University of Dayton *B*

Ursuline College *B*
Walsh University *B*
Wright State University *A, B, M*
Wright State University: Lake
  Campus *A*
Xavier University *C, B*
Youngstown State University *B*

Oklahoma

Eastern Oklahoma State College *A*
Northeastern State University *B*
Oklahoma Baptist University *B*
Oral Roberts University *B*
Southwestern Oklahoma State
  University *B*
Tulsa Community College *C, A*
University of Central Oklahoma *B*
University of Oklahoma *B, M*
University of Tulsa *B*

Oregon

Central Oregon Community
  College *A*
Corban University *B*
George Fox University *B*
Northwest Christian University *B*
Oregon Institute of Technology *B*
Oregon State University *B*
Portland Community College *C, A*
Portland State University *B*
Southwestern Oregon Community
  College *A*
Treasure Valley Community
  College *C, A*
Umpqua Community College *A*
University of Oregon *M, D*

Pennsylvania

Arcadia University *C, B*
Cambria-Rowe Business College:
  Indiana *A*
Carnegie Mellon University *M*
Community College of Allegheny
  County *C, A*
Community College of Beaver
  County *A*
DeSales University *B*
DeVry University
  Fort Washington *M*
Delaware County Community
  College *A*
Delaware Valley College *C, B*
Drexel University *B*
Duquesne University *B, M*
Gannon University *B*
Holy Family University *B, M*
Indiana University of Pennsylvania *B*
Lackawanna College *A*
Luzerne County Community
  College *A*
Marywood University *M*
Misericordia University *B*
Montgomery County Community
  College *C*
Muhlenberg College *C, B*
Penn State
  Abington *B*
  Altoona *B*
  Beaver *B*
  Berks *B*
  Brandywine *B*
  DuBois *B*
  Erie, The Behrend College *B*
  Fayette, The Eberly Campus *B*
  Greater Allegheny *B*
  Harrisburg *B, M*
  Hazleton *B*
  Lehigh Valley *B*
  Mont Alto *B*
  New Kensington *B*
  Schuylkill *B*
  Shenango *B*
  University Park *B*
  Wilkes-Barre *B*

Worthington Scranton *B*
York *B*
Philadelphia University *B*
Robert Morris University *B, M*
St. Francis University *A, B*
Saint Joseph's University *B, M*
Seton Hill University *B*
Thiel College *A, B*
University of Pennsylvania *B, M*
University of Pittsburgh *M*
University of Pittsburgh
  Greensburg *B*
  Titusville *A*
Villanova University *B*
Widener University *B, M*
Wilson College *A, B*
York College of Pennsylvania *B*

Puerto Rico

Bayamon Central University *A, B*
Columbia Centro Universitario:
  Caguas *C, A*
ICPR Junior College *A*
Inter American University of Puerto
  Rico
  Aguadilla Campus *B, M*
  Metropolitan Campus *B*
  Ponce Campus *B*
  San German Campus *B, M*
Pontifical Catholic University of
  Puerto Rico *B, M*
Turabo University *A, B, M*
Universidad Metropolitana *B, M*
Universidad del Este *B, M*
University of Puerto Rico
  Aguadilla *A*
  Rio Piedras *B*
University of the Sacred Heart *M*

Rhode Island

Rhode Island College *B*

South Carolina

Charleston Southern University *B, M*
Claflin University *B*
Francis Marion University *B*
Furman University *B*
Voorhees College *B*

South Dakota

National American University
  Rapid City *B, M*
Northern State University *B*
Oglala Lakota College *B*

Tennessee

Belmont University *B*
Bethel University *B, M*
Chattanooga State Community
  College *C, A*
Columbia State Community
  College *A*
Freed-Hardeman University *B*
Jackson State Community College *A*
King University *B, M*
Lee University *B*
Lipscomb University *B*
Middle Tennessee State University *B*
Southern Adventist University *B*
Southwest Tennessee Community
  College *A*
University of Memphis *B*
University of Tennessee
  Martin *B*
Vanderbilt University *M*
Walters State Community College *A*

Texas

Angelo State University *B*
Baylor University *B, M*
Cedar Valley College *C, A*
Dallas Baptist University *B, M*

DeVry University
  Houston *M*
  Irving *M*
Del Mar College *C, A*
Eastfield College *C*
El Centro College *C, A*
Hardin-Simmons University *B*
Houston Baptist University *B*
Howard Payne University *B*
Kilgore College *C, A*
Lamar University *B, M*
LeTourneau University *B*
McMurry University *B*
Midland College *C*
Midwestern State University *B*
Our Lady of the Lake University of
  San Antonio *M*
Prairie View A&M University *B*
Richland College *C, A*
St. Mary's University *B*
San Jacinto College *A*
Schreiner University *B*
Southwest Texas Junior College *A*
Southwestern Adventist University *B*
Tarleton State University *B*
Texas A&M International
  University *B, M*
Texas A&M University *B*
Texas A&M University
  Commerce *B*
  Corpus Christi *B*
  Kingsville *B*
  Texarkana *B*
Texas Southern University *B, M*
Texas State Technical College
  West Texas *C, A*
Texas State University *B*
Texas Wesleyan University *B*
University of Dallas *M*
University of Houston *B*
University of Houston
  Clear Lake *B*
  Downtown *B*
University of Mary Hardin-Baylor *B*
University of North Texas *B, M, D*
University of Phoenix
  Dallas Fort Worth *M*
  San Antonio *M*
University of Texas
  Arlington *B, M, D*
  Austin *B*
  Dallas *B*
  El Paso *B*
  Pan American *B*
  San Antonio *B, M, D*
University of the Incarnate Word *B*
West Texas A&M University *B, M*

Utah
Brigham Young University *B*
Dixie State College *B*
Neumont University *B*
University of Phoenix
  Utah *M*
University of Utah *B, M*
Weber State University *A, B, M*
Westminster College *B*

Vermont
Champlain College *B, M*

Virginia
Bridgewater College *B*
Central Virginia Community
  College *C, A*
DeVry University
  Arlington *M*
Ferrum College *B*
George Mason University *B*
Hampton University *B*
Liberty University *B*
Lord Fairfax Community College *A*
Northern Virginia Community
  College *A*

Old Dominion University *B*
Stratford University: Falls Church *M*
University of Management and
  Technology *M*
University of Mary Washington *M*
University of Phoenix
  Northern Virginia *M*
University of Virginia *M*
University of Virginia's College at
  Wise *B*
University of the Potomac *B*
Virginia Union University *B*
Virginia Western Community
  College *C, A*

Washington
City University of Seattle *C, B, M*
DeVry University
  Federal Way *M*
Eastern Washington University *B*
Everett Community College *A*
Gonzaga University *B*
Pacific Lutheran University *M*
Seattle Pacific University *M*
Seattle University *B*
Spokane Community College *A*
Spokane Falls Community
  College *C, A*
University of Phoenix
  Western Washington *M*
University of Puget Sound *B*
University of Washington *B*
Washington State University *B, D*
Western Washington University *B*

West Virginia
Davis and Elkins College *B*
Marshall University *B*
West Virginia University *B*
West Virginia University at
  Parkersburg *A*

Wisconsin
Cardinal Stritch University *C, B, M*
Carroll University *B*
Edgewood College *B*
Milwaukee School of Engineering *B*
Rasmussen College
  Appleton *C, A*
  Green Bay *C, A*
  Wausau *C, A*
St. Norbert College *B*
University of Wisconsin
  La Crosse *B*
  Madison *B, M*
  Milwaukee *B*
  Oshkosh *B, M*
  Parkside *B*
  Superior *B*
Viterbo University *B*

Management science

Alabama
Auburn University *B*
Faulkner University *B, M*
Tuskegee University *B*
University of Alabama *B, M, D*

Alaska
University of Alaska
  Anchorage *B, M*
  Southeast *B*

Arizona
Arizona State University *M*
Northcentral University *B, M, D*

California
Allan Hancock College *A*
California Lutheran University *B*
California State University
  East Bay *M*
  Fullerton *M*

Long Beach *B*
  Northridge *B, M*
Chabot College *A*
Coastline Community College *A*
Cypress College *A*
Folsom Lake College *A*
Grossmont College *A*
Los Angeles Mission College *A*
Los Angeles Pierce College *A*
MiraCosta College *A*
Mission College *A*
National University *B*
Notre Dame de Namur University *M*
Point Loma Nazarene University *B*
San Diego City College *A*
Santa Ana College *A*
University of California
  San Diego *B*

Colorado
Colorado Christian University *B*
National American University
  Denver *A, B*
University of Colorado
  Denver *M*

Connecticut
Quinnipiac University *B, M*
University of Connecticut *M*

Delaware
Delaware State University *B*
Delaware Technical Community
  College
  Stanton/Wilmington Campus *A*
Goldey-Beacom College *B, M*

District of Columbia
Catholic University of America *B, M*
University of the District of
  Columbia *A*

Florida
Broward College *A*
Eckerd College *B*
Everest University
  Pompano Beach *A, B*
Florida Institute of Technology *M*
Jacksonville University *B*
Miami Dade College *A*
Pensacola State College *A*
Saint Leo University *B*
University of Florida *B*
University of Miami *B, M, D*
University of South Florida
  Saint Petersburg *B*
University of Tampa *B*

Georgia
Emory University *B, D*
Southern Crescent Technical
  College *A*
West Georgia Technical College *A*

Illinois
Aurora University *B*
DePaul University *B*
Eastern Illinois University *B*
Illinois Institute of Technology *M, D*
Illinois State University *B*
Illinois Valley Community College *A*
Judson University *B*
Lewis University *M*
McKendree University *B*
Northern Illinois University *B*
Northwestern University *M*
Quincy University *B*
Roosevelt University *B*
Sauk Valley Community College *A*
Shawnee Community College *A*
Southern Illinois University
  Carbondale *B*
Southwestern Illinois College *A*
Trinity International University *B*

University of Illinois
  Chicago *B*
  Urbana-Champaign *B, M, D*
University of St. Francis *B, M*

Indiana
Oakland City University *B*
Valparaiso University *B*

Iowa
Drake University *B*
St. Ambrose University *B*
University of Iowa *B, D*

Kansas
Friends University *B*

Kentucky
Big Sandy Community and Technical
  College *A*
Hopkinsville Community College *A*
University of Kentucky *B*
Western Kentucky University *B*

Louisiana
Louisiana State University and
  Agricultural and Mechanical
  College *B, M*
Louisiana Tech University *B*
Southwest University *A, B, M*
Xavier University of Louisiana *B*

Maryland
Coppin State University *B*
Notre Dame of Maryland
  University *M*
University of Maryland
  College Park *B*

Massachusetts
American International College *B, M*
Babson College *B*
Bridgewater State University *B, M*
Cape Cod Community College *A*
Fisher College *B*
Fitchburg State University *B*
Lasell College *B, M*
Merrimack College *M*
Mount Ida College *M*
Worcester Polytechnic Institute *B, M*

Michigan
Baker College
  Auburn Hills *A, B*
  Clinton Township *A, B*
  Muskegon *A, B*
Cornerstone University *B*
Grand Valley State University *B*
Henry Ford Community College *A*
Lawrence Technological University *D*
University of Michigan
  Dearborn *B*

Minnesota
Minnesota State University
  Mankato *B*
Riverland Community College *A*
St. Mary's University of Minnesota *B*
University of Minnesota
  Morris *B*

Missouri
Central Methodist University *B*
Missouri Southern State University *B*
Southeast Missouri State University *M*

Montana
Rocky Mountain College *B*

Nebraska
Bellevue University *M*
Chadron State College *B*
Doane College *M*

Grace University *B*
Peru State College *B*

Nevada
Nevada State College *B*
Western Nevada College *A*

New Hampshire
Franklin Pierce University *B*
Great Bay Community College *A*
Manchester Community College *A*

New Jersey
Rider University *B*
Rowan University *B, M*
Rutgers, The State University of New Jersey
    Camden Campus *M*
    New Brunswick/Piscataway Campus *B*

New York
Canisius College *B*
LIM College *B*
Pace University: Pleasantville/ Briarcliff *B, M*
SUNY
    College at Fredonia *B*
    College at Oswego *B*
    University at Albany *M*
Saint Bonaventure University *B*
St. John's University *M*
Suffolk County Community College *A*

North Carolina
Alamance Community College *A*
Johnson & Wales University
    Charlotte *B*
Lenoir-Rhyne University *B*
St. Augustine's University *B*
Wake Forest University *B*

North Dakota
University of Mary *B*

Ohio
Brown Mackie College
    Cincinnati *A*
Case Western Reserve University *M*
Franklin University *B*
Heidelberg University *B*
Lourdes University *B*
Miami University
    Oxford *B, M*
Mount Vernon Nazarene University *M*
Ohio Northern University *B*
University of Cincinnati *M*
University of Dayton *M*
Wilmington College *B*

Oklahoma
Oklahoma Baptist University *B*
Oklahoma Christian University *B*
Oklahoma City University *B*
Oklahoma State University
    Oklahoma City *A*
Oral Roberts University *B, M*
Southeastern Oklahoma State University *B*

Pennsylvania
Arcadia University *B*
California University of Pennsylvania *M*
Carnegie Mellon University *M, D*
Drexel University *M*
Duquesne University *B*
Gettysburg College *B*
La Roche College *B*
La Salle University *B*
Lehigh University *B, M*
Penn State
    Harrisburg *M*

Rosemont College *B, M*
Shippensburg University of Pennsylvania *B, T*
Slippery Rock University of Pennsylvania *B*
Westminster College *B*
Widener University *M*

Puerto Rico
Bayamon Central University *B, M*
Inter American University of Puerto Rico
    Arecibo Campus *B*
    Ponce Campus *B, M*

Rhode Island
Bryant University *B*
Salve Regina University *B, M*

South Carolina
Central Carolina Technical College *A*
Southern Wesleyan University *M*
University of South Carolina
    Columbia *B*

Tennessee
Cumberland University *B*
Lincoln Memorial University *B*
Roane State Community College *A*
Southern Adventist University *B*
Tennessee Technological University *B*
University of Tennessee
    Knoxville *D*

Texas
Clarendon College *A*
El Paso Community College *A*
Hardin-Simmons University *B*
North Lake College *A*
Southwestern Adventist University *B*
Texas A&M University *B*
Texas A&M University
    Kingsville *B*
Texas Christian University *B*
Texas Wesleyan University *B*
Trinity University *B*
University of North Texas *M, D*
University of Texas
    San Antonio *B, M*

Utah
Westminster College *B*

Vermont
Castleton State College *B*

Virginia
Averett University *B*
Lynchburg College *B*
Miller-Motte Technical College
    Lynchburg *A*
Southside Virginia Community College *A*
Thomas Nelson Community College *A*
Virginia Polytechnic Institute and State University *B*
Virginia University of Lynchburg *B, M*

Washington
University of Washington Tacoma *B*
Walla Walla University *B*

West Virginia
Wheeling Jesuit University *B*

Wisconsin
University of Wisconsin
    Green Bay *M*

Wyoming
University of Wyoming *B*

Manicurist

Alabama
Gadsden State Community College *C*
Lawson State Community College *C*
Lurleen B. Wallace Community College *C*
Shelton State Community College *C*
Wallace State Community College at Hanceville *C*

Arizona
Eastern Arizona College *C*

Arkansas
Pulaski Technical College *C*

California
Cerritos College *C, A*

Colorado
IBMC College
    Fort Collins *C*
Pueblo Community College *C*
Red Rocks Community College *C, A*
Trinidad State Junior College *C*

Florida
College of Central Florida *C*
Indian River State College *C*
Palm Beach State College *C*
Pensacola State College *C*

Georgia
Altamaha Technical College *C*
Central Georgia Technical College *C*
Columbus Technical College *C*
Savannah Technical College *C*
Southeastern Technical College *C*
West Georgia Technical College *C*

Illinois
Highland Community College *C*
Kaskaskia College *C*

Kansas
Independence Community College *C*
Johnson County Community College *C*
Kansas City Kansas Community College *C*

Michigan
Mott Community College *C*

Minnesota
Century College *C*
Minnesota State College - Southeast Technical *C*
Minnesota State Community and Technical College *C*
Ridgewater College *C*
St. Paul College *C*

Mississippi
Meridian Community College *C*

New Mexico
Clovis Community College *C*

North Carolina
Brunswick Community College *C*
Carteret Community College *C*
Cleveland Community College *C*
Fayetteville Technical Community College *C*
Isothermal Community College *C*
Johnston Community College *C*
Martin Community College *C*

Miller-Motte College
    Wilmington *C*
Roanoke-Chowan Community College *C*
Southeastern Community College *C*
Southwestern Community College *C*
Vance-Granville Community College *C*

Pennsylvania
Laurel Business Institute *C*

Puerto Rico
Caribbean University *C*

Tennessee
Miller-Motte Technical College
    Chattanooga *C*
West Tennessee Business College *C*

Texas
Houston Community College System *C*
Howard College *C*
Lamar State College at Port Arthur *C*
Midland College *C*
Panola College *C*
Paris Junior College *C*
San Jacinto College *C*
Weatherford College *C*

Washington
Olympic College *C*

Wyoming
Eastern Wyoming College *C*

Manufacturing engineering

Alabama
Auburn University *B, M, D*

Arizona
Mesa Community College *A*

California
California Polytechnic State University: San Luis Obispo *B*
California State Polytechnic University: Pomona *B*
National University *B*
San Diego State University *M*
University of California
    Berkeley *B*
    Irvine *M, D*
    Los Angeles *M*
University of Southern California *M*

Connecticut
Fairfield University *B*

Florida
University of Miami *B*

Illinois
Bradley University *B, M*
Illinois Institute of Technology *M*
Northwestern University *B, M*
Southern Illinois University
    Edwardsville *B*
University of Illinois
    Urbana-Champaign *B, M, D*

Kansas
Wichita State University *B*

Kentucky
Maysville Community and Technical College *A*
University of Kentucky *M*

Massachusetts

Boston University *M*
Bristol Community College *A*
Worcester Polytechnic Institute *M, D*

Michigan

Central Michigan University *B*
Grand Valley State University *B, M*
Lawrence Technological
    University *M, D*
University of Detroit Mercy *B*
University of Michigan *M, D*
University of Michigan
    Dearborn *B*
Wayne State University *M*
Western Michigan University *B, M*

Minnesota

Saint Cloud State University *B*
University of St. Thomas *M*

Mississippi

Mississippi State University *C*

Missouri

Missouri University of Science and
    Technology *M*

Nebraska

University of Nebraska
    Lincoln *M*

New Jersey

New Jersey Institute of
    Technology *B, M*

New Mexico

University of New Mexico *M*

New York

Hofstra University *B*
Rochester Institute of Technology *M*

North Carolina

Edgecombe Community College *A*
North Carolina State University *M*

North Dakota

North Dakota State University *B, M*

Ohio

Central State University *B*
Miami University
    Oxford *B*

Oregon

Oregon State University *B*
Portland State University *M*

Pennsylvania

Lehigh University *M*
Penn State
    York *C*
Robert Morris University *B*

Puerto Rico

Universidad Politecnica de Puerto
    Rico *M*

Rhode Island

New England Institute of
    Technology *A, B*

Texas

Southern Methodist University *M*
Texas State University *B*
University of Texas
    El Paso *M*
    Pan American *B, M*
    San Antonio *M*

Utah

Brigham Young University *B, M*
Salt Lake Community College *A*

Virginia

Mountain Empire Community
    College *A*
Virginia State University *B*

Washington

Washington State University *B*

Wisconsin

University of Wisconsin
    Stout *B, M*

Manufacturing technologies

Alabama

Gadsden State Community
    College *C, A*
Jacksonville State University *B*
Lawson State Community
    College *C, A*
Southern Union State Community
    College *C*

Alaska

Charter College *C*

Arizona

GateWay Community College *C, A*
Mesa Community College *C, A*
Yavapai College *A*

Arkansas

East Arkansas Community
    College *C, A*
Mid-South Community College *C*
Phillips Community College of the
    University of Arkansas *C, A*
Pulaski Technical College *A*
Southern Arkansas University Tech *C*

California

Bakersfield College *C, A*
California State University
    Long Beach *B*
Cerritos College *C, A*
College of the Canyons *C, A*
College of the Sequoias *A*
Irvine Valley College *C, A*
Long Beach City College *C*
San Diego City College *C, A*

Colorado

Aims Community College *C, A*
Arapahoe Community College *C, A*
Colorado Mesa University *A*
Pueblo Community College *A*
Red Rocks Community College *C, A*
Trinidad State Junior College *C, A*

Connecticut

Asnuntuck Community College *C, A*
Central Connecticut State
    University *B*
Gateway Community College *A*
Goodwin College *C*
Manchester Community College *A*
Naugatuck Valley Community
    College *C, A*
Quinebaug Valley Community
    College *C*
Three Rivers Community College *A*
Tunxis Community College *A*

Delaware

Delaware State University *B*
Delaware Technical Community
    College
    Stanton/Wilmington Campus *A*

Florida

Florida Gateway College *C, A*
Northwest Florida State College *A*
Pensacola State College *A*
Tallahassee Community College *C*

Georgia

Atlanta Technical College *C*
Central Georgia Technical College *C*
Middle Georgia State College *A*

Idaho

Brigham Young University-Idaho *A*
Lewis-Clark State College *A, B*

Illinois

Black Hawk College *C, A*
Bradley University *B, M*
City Colleges of Chicago
    Olive-Harvey College *C, A*
    Richard J. Daley College *C*
Danville Area Community College *A*
Heartland Community College *C, A*
Highland Community College *C*
Illinois Eastern Community Colleges
    Wabash Valley College *C*
Illinois Valley Community College *C*
Kishwaukee College *C, A*
Moraine Valley Community College *A*
Morrison Institute of Technology *A*
Prairie State College *C, A*
Rend Lake College *A*
Rock Valley College *C, A*
Sauk Valley Community College *A*
Southern Illinois University
    Carbondale *M*
Western Illinois University *B, M*

Indiana

Harrison College
    Indianapolis *A*
ITT Technical Institute
    Fort Wayne *B*
    Indianapolis *B*
    Newburgh *B*
Indiana State University *B*
Ivy Tech Community College
    Bloomington *C*
    Central Indiana *C*
    Columbus *C*
    East Central *C*
    Kokomo *C*
    Lafayette *C*
    North Central *C*
    Northeast *C*
    Northwest *C*
    Richmond *C*
    South Central *C*
Purdue University *A, B*
University of Southern Indiana *B*
Vincennes University *A*

Iowa

Clinton Community College *A*
Hawkeye Community College *C, A*
Iowa Central Community College *A*
Northwest Iowa Community
    College *A*
University of Northern Iowa *B*

Kansas

Barton County Community College *C*
Garden City Community College *C*
Hutchinson Community College *C, A*
Pittsburg State University *B*

Kentucky

Berea College *B*
Bluegrass Community and Technical
    College *C*
Eastern Kentucky University *B, M*
Gateway Community and Technical
    College *C, A*
Hopkinsville Community College *C*

Morehead State University *A, B, M*
Murray State University *B*
Northern Kentucky
    University *C, A, B*
Western Kentucky University *A, B*

Louisiana

Bossier Parish Community College *C*

Maine

University of Southern Maine *B, M*

Maryland

College of Southern Maryland *C*

Massachusetts

Berkshire Community College *C*
Fitchburg State University *B*
Quinsigamond Community
    College *C, A*
University of Massachusetts
    Lowell *M*

Michigan

Alpena Community College *A*
Baker College
    Flint *A*
Central Michigan University *B*
Delta College *A*
Eastern Michigan University *B, M*
Ferris State University *B*
Henry Ford Community College *C, A*
Lake Michigan College *C, A*
Lake Superior State University *B*
Lawrence Technological University *A*
Macomb Community College *C, A*
Monroe County Community
    College *C, A*
Montcalm Community College *C, A*
Northern Michigan University *A, B*
Oakland Community College *C, A*
St. Clair County Community
    College *A*
Schoolcraft College *C, A*
Wayne County Community College *A*
Wayne State University *B*

Minnesota

Dakota County Technical
    College *C, A*
Hennepin Technical College *C, A*
Minnesota State College - Southeast
    Technical *A*
Minnesota State University
    Mankato *B, M*
Minnesota West Community and
    Technical College *A*
Normandale Community College *C, A*
Northland Community & Technical
    College *C, A*
Northwest Technical College *C, A*
Pine Technical College *C, A*
St. Paul College *A*

Mississippi

East Mississippi Community
    College *A*

Missouri

Linn State Technical College *C, A*
Mineral Area College *A*
Missouri Southern State
    University *C, A*
Missouri State University: West
    Plains *C, A*
Missouri Western State University *A*
Moberly Area Community
    College *C, A*
Ozarks Technical Community
    College *C, A*
State Fair Community College *C, A*

Montana

Flathead Valley Community College *C*

Nebraska

Southeast Community College *A*

New Hampshire

NHTI-Concord's Community
College *C, A*
Nashua Community College *A*
River Valley Community College *A*

New Jersey

Bergen Community College *C, A*
Essex County College *A*
Middlesex County College *A*
Raritan Valley Community
College *C, A*
Thomas Edison State College *A, B*

New Mexico

Central New Mexico Community
College *C, A*

New York

Corning Community College *A*
Erie Community College *C*
Excelsior College *A*
Monroe Community College *A*
Rochester Institute of
Technology *B, M*
SUNY
College of Technology at Alfred *B*
Farmingdale State College *C, B*

North Carolina

Central Carolina Community
College *A*
East Carolina University *B*
Edgecombe Community College *C, A*
Mitchell Community College *A*
Pitt Community College *C, A*
Randolph Community College *A*
Richmond Community College *A*
Wake Technical Community
College *A*

North Dakota

North Dakota State College of
Science *A*

Ohio

Bowling Green State University,
Firelands College *A*
Central Ohio Technical College *A*
Cincinnati State Technical and
Community College *C*
Eastern Gateway Community
College *C, A*
James A. Rhodes State College *C, A*
Lakeland Community College *C, A*
Lorain County Community College *A*
North Central State College *C*
Ohio Northern University *B*
Owens Community College
Toledo *A*
Sinclair Community College *C, A*
Stark State College *A*
Terra State Community College *C, A*
University of Akron *A, B*
University of Cincinnati *C*
University of Dayton *B*
University of Rio Grande *A, B*
Wright State University *A*
Wright State University: Lake
Campus *A*

Oklahoma

Oklahoma City Community
College *A*
Southwestern Oklahoma State
University *B*
Western Oklahoma State College *A*

Oregon

Central Oregon Community
College *C, A*
Chemeketa Community College *C*
Clackamas Community College *C, A*
ITT Technical Institute
Portland *B*
Lane Community College *A*
Mt. Hood Community College *C*
Oregon Institute of Technology *B, M*
Portland Community College *C, A*
Rogue Community College *C, A*

Pennsylvania

Butler County Community College *A*
Edinboro University of
Pennsylvania *A*
Erie Institute of Technology *C*
Lehigh Carbon Community
College *C, A*
Pennsylvania College of
Technology *A, B*
Westmoreland County Community
College *A*

Rhode Island

New England Institute of
Technology *A, B*
Roger Williams University *B*

South Carolina

Trident Technical College *C*

Tennessee

Middle Tennessee State University *M*
Tennessee Technological
University *B*

Texas

Frank Phillips College *C, A*
Houston Community College
System *C, A*
Richland College *A*
Sam Houston State University *B*
Tarleton State University *D*
Texas A&M University *B*
Texas State Technical College
Waco *C, A*
Texas State University *B*
University of North Texas *B*
University of Texas
Brownsville *B*

Utah

Salt Lake Community College *A*
Weber State University *A, B*

Virginia

Danville Community College *A*
Mountain Empire Community
College *A*
Thomas Nelson Community
College *C*

Washington

Bates Technical College *C, A*
Bellingham Technical College *A*
Clark College *A*
Highline Community College *A*
Lake Washington Institute of
Technology *C*
Olympic College *C*
Shoreline Community College *A*
Western Washington University *B*

West Virginia

Kanawha Valley Community and
Technical College *A*
West Virginia Northern Community
College *A*

Wisconsin

Fox Valley Technical College *A*
Gateway Technical College *A*
Northeast Wisconsin Technical
College *A*

Wyoming

Casper College *C, A*

Marine biology

Alabama

Auburn University *B*
Samford University *B*
Troy University *B*
University of Alabama *B, M*
University of Mobile *B*
University of North Alabama *B*
University of West Alabama *B*

Alaska

Alaska Pacific University *B*
University of Alaska
Fairbanks *M, D*
Southeast *B*

Arizona

Prescott College *B*

California

California State University
Fresno *M*
Monterey Bay *M*
Sacramento *M*
Stanislaus *M*
Mount San Antonio College *A*
Oxnard College *A*
San Francisco State University *M*
San Jose State University *B, M*
University of California
Los Angeles *B*
San Diego *D*
Santa Barbara *B*
Santa Cruz *B, M, D*
University of San Diego *B, M*
University of Southern
California *M, D*

Colorado

Colorado Northwestern Community
College *A*

Connecticut

University of Connecticut *B*
University of New Haven *B*

Delaware

University of Delaware *M, D*

Florida

Daytona State College *A*
Florida Institute of Technology *B, M*
Florida International University *B*
Florida Keys Community College *A*
Florida Southern College *B*
Florida State University *M, D*
Jacksonville University *B*
New College of Florida *B*
Nova Southeastern
University *B, M, D*
Rollins College *B*
University of Miami *B, M, D*
University of Tampa *B*
University of West Florida *B*

Georgia

Savannah State University *A, B, M*
University of Georgia *M, D*

Hawaii

Hawaii Pacific University *B, M*
University of Hawaii
Hilo *B*
Manoa *B*

Kansas

Southwestern College *B*

Louisiana

Nicholls State University *M*

Maine

College of the Atlantic *B, M*
Maine Maritime Academy *B, T*
Southern Maine Community
College *A*
Unity College *B*
University of Maine *B, M, D*
University of Maine
Machias *B*
University of New England *B, M*

Maryland

University of Maryland
Baltimore *M, D*
Baltimore County *M, D*
Eastern Shore *M, D*

Massachusetts

Boston University *B*
Massachusetts Bay Community
College *A*
Northeastern University *M*
Salem State University *B*
University of Massachusetts
Boston *M, D*
Lowell *M, D*

Minnesota

Saint Cloud State University *B*

Mississippi

University of Southern
Mississippi *B, M, D*

Missouri

Central Methodist University *B*
Missouri Southern State University *B*
Northwest Missouri State
University *B*

New Jersey

Fairleigh Dickinson University
Metropolitan Campus *B*
Richard Stockton College of New
Jersey *B*
Rutgers, The State University of New
Jersey
New Brunswick/Piscataway
Campus *B*

New York

SUNY
Maritime College *B*
University at Stony Brook *B*

North Carolina

Duke University *D*
University of North Carolina
Wilmington *B, M, D*

Oregon

Chemeketa Community College *A*
University of Oregon *B*

Pennsylvania

East Stroudsburg University of
Pennsylvania *B*
Mansfield University of
Pennsylvania *B*
St. Francis University *B*
Waynesburg University *B*

Puerto Rico
University of Puerto Rico
Humacao *B*
Mayaguez *B, M*

Rhode Island
Roger Williams University *B*
University of Rhode Island *B*

South Carolina
Coastal Carolina University *B, M*
College of Charleston *B, M*
University of South Carolina
Columbia *B, M, D*

Texas
Galveston College *A*
Lamar University *B*
Laredo Community College *A*
Texas A&M University *B, M, D*
Texas A&M University
Corpus Christi *M*
Galveston *B, D*

Virginia
College of William and Mary *M, D*
Hampton University *B*

Washington
University of Washington *B*
Western Washington University *B*

Marine engineering/ naval architecture

Alaska
University of Alaska
Anchorage *C*

California
Santa Barbara City College *A*

Connecticut
United States Coast Guard
Academy *B*

Louisiana
University of New Orleans *B*

Maine
Maine Maritime Academy *B*

Maryland
United States Naval Academy *B*

Michigan
University of Michigan *B, M, D*

Minnesota
University of Minnesota
Twin Cities *B*

New Jersey
Stevens Institute of Technology *M*

New York
SUNY
Maritime College *B*
United States Merchant Marine
Academy *B, M*
Webb Institute *B*

Texas
Texas A&M University *B*
Texas A&M University
Galveston *B*

Virginia
Virginia Polytechnic Institute and
State University *M*

Marine maintenance/ fitter/ship repair

Arkansas
National Park Community College *C*

Florida
Florida Keys Community
College *C, A*
Palm Beach State College *A*
WyoTech: Daytona *C, A*

Georgia
Central Georgia Technical College *C*

Hawaii
University of Hawaii
Honolulu Community College *A*

Iowa
Iowa Lakes Community College *C*

Maine
Landing School of Boatbuilding and
Design *A*

Massachusetts
Bristol Community College *C*

Minnesota
Alexandria Technical and Community
College *C*
Central Lakes College *C, A*
Hennepin Technical College *C, A*
Minnesota State Community and
Technical College *C, A*

Missouri
State Fair Community College *C, A*

New Hampshire
Lakes Region Community
College *C, A*

North Carolina
Cape Fear Community College *C*
Carteret Community College *C*

Rhode Island
New England Institute of
Technology *A*

Washington
Northwest School of Wooden
Boatbuilding *C, A*
Olympic College *A*

Wisconsin
Wisconsin Indianhead Technical
College *C*

Marine sciences

California
California State University
Fresno *M*
Monterey Bay *B*
San Francisco State University *M*
University of California
Santa Barbara *M, D*
University of Southern
California *M, D*

Florida
Florida Keys Community College *A*

Maine
College of the Atlantic *B, M*
Saint Joseph's College of Maine *B*
University of Maine *M*

Massachusetts
University of Massachusetts
Amherst *M, D*
Dartmouth *D*

Texas
Texas A&M University *B*
University of Texas
Austin *M, D*

Maritime studies

Maine
College of the Atlantic *B, M*

Texas
Texas A&M University *B*

Maritime technology/ Merchant Marine

Florida
Florida Keys Community College *A*

Maine
Maine Maritime Academy *A, B*

Massachusetts
Massachusetts Maritime Academy *B*

Michigan
Northwestern Michigan College *A*

New York
United States Merchant Marine
Academy *B*

Oregon
Clatsop Community College *C, A*

Puerto Rico
Pontifical Catholic University of
Puerto Rico *B*
Turabo University *C*

Texas
San Jacinto College *C, A*
Texas A&M University
Galveston *B*

Marketing

Alabama
Alabama Agricultural and Mechanical
University *B*
Auburn University *B*
Auburn University at Montgomery *B*
Birmingham-Southern College *B*
Columbia Southern University *C, B*
Faulkner University *B*
Jacksonville State University *B*
Oakwood University *B*
Samford University *B*
Talladega College *B*
University of Alabama *B, M, D*
University of Alabama
Birmingham *B*
Huntsville *B*
University of North Alabama *B*
University of Phoenix
Birmingham *B*
University of South Alabama *B*
University of West Alabama *B*

Alaska
University of Alaska
Anchorage *B*
Southeast *B*

Arizona
Arizona State University *B*
Arizona Western College *A*

Central Arizona College *A*
Coconino County Community
College *A*
Glendale Community College *C, A*
Grand Canyon University *B, M*
Mesa Community College *C, A*
Northcentral University *B, M, D*
Northern Arizona University *B*
Paradise Valley Community
College *C, A*
Penn Foster College *A*
Phoenix College *C, A*
Southwest University of Visual Arts *B*
University of Arizona *B*
University of Phoenix
Phoenix-Hohokam *B, M*
Southern Arizona *B, M*
Western International
University *B, M*

Arkansas
Arkansas State University *B*
Central Baptist College *B*
Harding University *B*
John Brown University *B*
University of Arkansas *B*
University of Arkansas
Little Rock *B*
University of Central Arkansas *B*
University of the Ozarks *B*

California
Azusa Pacific University *B*
Biola University *B*
Butte College *C, A*
California Baptist University *B*
California Lutheran University *B*
California State University
Dominguez Hills *B, M*
East Bay *B, M*
Fresno *B*
Fullerton *B, M*
Sacramento *B, M*
San Bernardino *B, M*
City College of San Francisco *A*
College of Alameda *C, A*
College of San Mateo *C, A*
Crafton Hills College *C, A*
De Anza College *C, A*
Diablo Valley College *C, A*
Fashion Institute of Design and
Merchandising
Los Angeles *A, B*
San Diego *A*
San Francisco *B*
Folsom Lake College *A*
Fresno Pacific University *B*
Golden Gate University *B, M*
Grossmont College *C, A*
Holy Names University *B, M*
Imperial Valley College *C, A*
La Sierra University *B, M*
Lake Tahoe Community College *C, A*
Los Angeles Pierce College *C, A*
Loyola Marymount University *B*
Master's College *B*
Menlo College *B*
MiraCosta College *C, A*
Modesto Junior College *A*
National University *C, B*
Norco College *C, A*
Ohlone College *C, A*
Pacific States University *B*
Pepperdine University *B*
Point Loma Nazarene University *B*
Riverside City College *C, A*
Saddleback College *C, A*
San Deigo Miramar College
San Diego Miramar College *A*
San Diego State University *B, M*
San Jose City College *C, A*
San Jose State University *B*
Santa Ana College *C, A*
Santa Barbara City College *C, A*

Santa Clara University *B*
Santiago Canyon College *A*
University of Phoenix
Bay Area *B, M*
Central Valley *B, M*
Sacramento Valley *B, M*
San Diego *B, M*
Southern California *B, M*
University of Redlands *C*
University of San Diego *B*
University of San Francisco *B*
Vanguard University of Southern
California *B*
Westwood College
Anaheim *B*
Inland Empire *B*
Woodbury University *B*
Yuba College *C*

Colorado

Adams State University *B*
Aims Community College *C, A*
Arapahoe Community College *C, A*
Colorado State University *B*
Community College of Aurora *C, A*
Community College of Denver *C*
Fort Lewis College *B*
Lamar Community College *A*
Metropolitan State University of
Denver *B*
Pikes Peak Community College *C, A*
Regis University *B*
University of Colorado
Boulder *B*
Denver *M*
University of Denver *B, M*
University of Phoenix
Denver *B, M*
Southern Colorado *B, M*
Westwood College
Denver North *B*

Connecticut

Asnuntuck Community College *C*
Central Connecticut State
University *B*
Fairfield University *B*
Middlesex Community College *A*
Northwestern Connecticut
Community College *A*
Norwalk Community College *A*
Post University *C, A, B*
Quinnipiac University *B, M*
Sacred Heart University *B*
University of Bridgeport *B, M*
University of Connecticut *B*
University of Hartford *B*
University of New Haven *B*
Western Connecticut State
University *B*

Delaware

Delaware State University *B*
Delaware Technical Community
College
Jack F. Owens Campus *C, A*
Stanton/Wilmington Campus *C, A*
Terry Campus *C, A*
Goldey-Beacom College *B, M*
Wilmington University *B*

District of Columbia

American University *M*
Georgetown University *B*
Strayer University *A*
University of Phoenix
Washington DC *B, M*

Florida

Barry University *B*
City College
Altamonte Springs *A*
Daytona State College *A*
Edison State College *C, A*

Everest University
Brandon *A, B*
Jacksonville *A, B*
Largo *A, B*
North Orlando *A, B*
Pompano Beach *A, B*
Tampa *A, B*
Florida Atlantic University *B*
Florida Gulf Coast University *B*
Florida Institute of Technology *B*
Florida International University *B*
Florida State University *B, M*
International Academy of Design and
Technology
Orlando *A, B*
Jacksonville University *B*
Johnson & Wales University
North Miami *B*
Lynn University *B*
Northwood University
Florida *B*
Nova Southeastern University *B*
Palm Beach Atlantic University *B*
Palm Beach State College *A*
Pasco-Hernando State College *C*
Rasmussen College
Fort Myers *C, A, B*
New Port Richey *C, A, B*
Ocala *C, A, B*
Pasco/Land O'Lakes *C, A, B*
Tampa/Brandon *C, A, B*
Saint Johns River State College *C, A*
Saint Leo University *B*
St. Petersburg College *C*
Schiller International University *B*
Seminole State College of
Florida *C, A*
Southeastern University *B*
Stetson University *B*
University of Central Florida *B*
University of Florida *B, M*
University of Miami *B, M, D*
University of North Florida *B*
University of Phoenix
Central Florida *B, M*
North Florida *B, M*
South Florida *B, M*
West Florida *B, M*
University of South Florida *B, M*
University of South Florida
Saint Petersburg *B*
Sarasota-Manatee *B*
University of Tampa *B, M*
University of West Florida *B*
Webber International University *A, B*

Georgia

Abraham Baldwin Agricultural
College *C*
Albany State University *B*
Altamaha Technical College *C, A*
Atlanta Technical College *C, A*
Bainbridge College *C, A*
Berry College *B*
Brenau University *B*
Chattahoochee Technical
College *C, A*
Clayton State University *B*
Columbus State University *B*
Dalton State College *B*
Emory University *B, D*
Fort Valley State University *B*
Georgia College and State
University *B*
Georgia Northwestern Technical
College *C, A*
Georgia Piedmont Technical
College *C, A*
Georgia Regents University *B*
Georgia Southern University *B*
Georgia Southwestern State
University *B*
Georgia State University *B, M, D*
Gwinnett Technical College *C, A*
Kennesaw State University *B*

Mercer University *B, M*
Middle Georgia State College *B*
Point University *B*
Savannah State University *B*
Southeastern Technical College *A*
Thomas University *B*
University of Georgia *B*
University of North Georgia *B*
University of Phoenix
Atlanta *B, M*
Augusta *B, M*
Columbus *B, M*
Savannah *B, M*
University of West Georgia *B*
Valdosta State University *B*

Hawaii

Chaminade University of Honolulu *B*
Hawaii Pacific University *B*
University of Hawaii
Hawaii Community College *C, A*
Manoa *B*
University of Phoenix
Hawaii *B, M*

Idaho

Boise State University *B*
Broadview University
Boise *A*
College of Western Idaho *C, A*
Eastern Idaho Technical College *C, A*
Idaho State University *B*
Northwest Nazarene University *B*
University of Idaho *B*
University of Phoenix
Idaho *B, M*

Illinois

Augustana College *B*
Aurora University *B*
Benedictine University *C, B*
Blackburn College *B*
Bradley University *B*
City Colleges of Chicago
Harold Washington College *C*
Harry S. Truman College *C*
Kennedy-King College *C*
Olive-Harvey College *C*
Richard J. Daley College *C*
Wilbur Wright College *C*
College of DuPage *C*
Columbia College Chicago *B, M*
Concordia University Chicago *B*
DePaul University *B, M*
Dominican University *B*
Eastern Illinois University *B*
Elgin Community College *C, A*
Elmhurst College *B*
Eureka College *B*
Greenville College *B*
Illinois Institute of Technology *M*
Illinois State University *B*
Judson University *B*
Lewis University *B*
Loyola University Chicago *C, B*
McKendree University *B*
Millikin University *B*
North Central College *B*
Northeastern Illinois University *B*
Northern Illinois University *B*
Northwestern University *M, D*
Olivet Nazarene University *B*
Parkland College *A*
Quincy University *B*
Rasmussen College
Aurora *C, A, B*
Mokena/Tinley Park *C, A, B*
Rockford *C, A, B*
Romeoville/Joliet *C, A, B*
Roosevelt University *B*
Saint Xavier University *M*
Sauk Valley Community College *C, A*
South Suburban College of Cook
County *C, A*

Southern Illinois University
Carbondale *B*
Trinity Christian College *B*
Trinity International University *B*
University of Illinois
Chicago *B*
Urbana-Champaign *B, D*
University of Phoenix
Chicago *B*
University of St. Francis *B*
Western Illinois University *B*

Indiana

Anderson University *B, D*
Ball State University *B*
Butler University *B*
Franklin College *B*
Grace College *B*
Huntington University *B*
Indiana State University *C, B*
Indiana University
Purdue University Fort Wayne *B*
Southeast *C*
Indiana Wesleyan University *B*
Manchester University *B*
Marian University *B*
Oakland City University *B*
Purdue University *B, M, D*
St. Mary-of-the-Woods College *B*
Taylor University *B*
University of Evansville *B*
University of Indianapolis *B*
University of Notre Dame *B*
University of Phoenix
Indianapolis *B, M*
University of Southern Indiana *B*
Valparaiso University *B*

Iowa

AIB College of Business *A*
Buena Vista University *B*
Des Moines Area Community
College *C, A*
Dordt College *B*
Drake University *B*
Grand View University *B*
Iowa State University *B*
Iowa Western Community College *A*
Kirkwood Community College *C, A*
Loras College *B*
Mount Mercy University *B*
Northwestern College *B*
St. Ambrose University *B*
Simpson College *B*
Southwestern Community College *A*
University of Iowa *B*
University of Northern Iowa *B*
University of Phoenix
Des Moines *B, M*
Wartburg College *B*

Kansas

Benedictine College *B*
Bethany College *B*
Emporia State University *B*
Fort Hays State University *B*
Friends University *B*
Kansas City Kansas Community
College *A*
Kansas State University *B*
Kansas Wesleyan University *B*
Pittsburg State University *B*
Southwestern College *B*
Tabor College *B*
University of Kansas *B*
Washburn University *B*
Wichita State University *B*

Kentucky

Berea College *B*
Campbellsville University *B, M*
Eastern Kentucky University *B*
Hazard Community and Technical
College *A*

Morehead State University *B*
Murray State University *C, B*
Northern Kentucky University *C, B*
Union College *B*
University of Kentucky *B*
University of Louisville *B*
University of Phoenix
  Louisville *B*
Western Kentucky University *B*

Louisiana

Grambling State University *B*
Herzing University
  Kenner *B*
Louisiana College *B*
Louisiana State University
  Shreveport *B*
Louisiana State University and
  Agricultural and Mechanical
  College *B*
Louisiana Tech University *B*
Loyola University New Orleans *B*
McNeese State University *B*
Nicholls State University *B*
Southeastern Louisiana University *B*
Southern University and Agricultural
  and Mechanical College *B*
Tulane University *B*
University of Louisiana at Lafayette *B*
University of Louisiana at Monroe *B*
University of New Orleans *B*
University of Phoenix
  Baton Rouge *B, M*
  Lafayette *B, M*
  Louisiana *B, M*
  Shreveport *B, M*
Xavier University of Louisiana *B*

Maine

Husson University *B*
Kennebec Valley Community
  College *A*
New England School of
  Communications *B*
Saint Joseph's College of Maine *B*
Thomas College *B*
University of Maine *B*
University of Maine
  Machias *B*
University of Southern Maine *B, M*

Maryland

Allegany College of Maryland *A*
Baltimore City Community College *A*
Cecil College *C, A*
Hagerstown Community College *C*
Harford Community College *C, A*
Montgomery College *C*
Morgan State University *B*
Prince George's Community
  College *C, A*
Salisbury University *B*
University of Baltimore *B, M*
University of Maryland
  College Park *B*
  University College *B*
Washington Adventist University *B*

Massachusetts

American International College *B, M*
Assumption College *B*
Babson College *B*
Bay Path College *B*
Becker College *B*
Bentley University *B, M*
Boston University *B*
Bristol Community College *A*
Cape Cod Community College *A*
Eastern Nazarene College *B*
Elms College *B*
Emerson College *C, B, M*
Endicott College *B*
Fisher College *B*
Fitchburg State University *B*

Greenfield Community College *C*
Lasell College *B, M*
Marian Court College *A*
Massachusetts College of Liberal
  Arts *B*
Massasoit Community College *A*
Merrimack College *B*
Newbury College *B*
Nichols College *B*
North Shore Community College *A*
Northeastern University *B*
Northern Essex Community
  College *A*
Salem State University *B, M*
Simmons College *B*
Springfield Technical Community
  College *A*
Stonehill College *B*
Suffolk University *B, M*
University of Massachusetts
  Amherst *B*
  Dartmouth *B*
University of Phoenix
  Boston *B, M*
Western New England University *B*
Worcester Polytechnic Institute *M*

Michigan

Adrian College *B*
Baker College
  Cadillac *A*
  Flint *A*
  Muskegon *A, B*
  Owosso *A, B*
  Port Huron *A, B*
Central Michigan University *B*
Cleary University *B*
Cornerstone University *B*
Davenport University *B*
Delta College *A*
Eastern Michigan University *B, M*
Ferris State University *C, A, B*
Finlandia University *B*
Glen Oaks Community College *C*
Grace Bible College *B*
Grand Valley State University *B*
Hillsdale College *B*
Kellogg Community College *C*
Lake Michigan College *C, A*
Lake Superior State University *B*
Macomb Community College *C, A*
Michigan State University *B, D*
Michigan Technological University *B*
Mid Michigan Community College *A*
Mott Community College *C, A*
Muskegon Community College *A*
Northern Michigan University *B*
Northwood University
  Michigan *A, B*
Oakland University *B*
Olivet College *B*
Rochester College *B*
Saginaw Valley State University *B*
St. Clair County Community
  College *C, A*
Schoolcraft College *A*
University of Michigan
  Flint *B, M*
University of Phoenix
  Metro Detroit *B, M*
  West Michigan *B, M*
Wayne State University *B*
West Shore Community College *A*
Western Michigan University *B*

Minnesota

Alexandria Technical and Community
  College *A*
Art Institutes International
  Minnesota *B*
Augsburg College *B*
Capella University *B, M*
Century College *B*
College of St. Scholastica *B*

Concordia University St. Paul *C, B*
Dakota County Technical
  College *C, A*
Globe University
  Minneapolis *A*
  Moorhead *A*
  Woodbury *A*
Hamline University *B*
Mesabi Range Community and
  Technical College *C, A*
Metropolitan State University *B*
Minnesota School of Business
  Blaine *A*
  Brooklyn Center *A*
  Elk River *A*
  Lakeville *A*
  Plymouth *A*
  Richfield *A*
  Rochester *A*
  St. Cloud *A*
  Shakopee *A*
Minnesota State Community and
  Technical College *A*
National American University
  Bloomington *B*
  Roseville *B*
Normandale Community College *C, A*
North Hennepin Community
  College *C, A*
Northwest Technical College *C*
Rasmussen College
  Blaine *C, A, B*
  Bloomington *C, A, B*
  Brooklyn Park *C, A, B*
  Eagan *C, A, B*
  Lake Elmo/Woodbury *C, A, B*
  Mankato *C, A, B*
  Moorhead *A*
  St. Cloud *C, A, B*
Ridgewater College *A*
Saint Cloud State University *B*
St. Mary's University of Minnesota *B*
South Central College *C*
Southwest Minnesota State
  University *A, B*
University of Minnesota
  Crookston *B*
  Duluth *B*
  Twin Cities *C, B*
University of Northwestern - St.
  Paul *A, B*
University of Phoenix
  Minneapolis-St. Paul *B, M*
University of St. Thomas *B*
Winona State University *B*

Mississippi

Copiah-Lincoln Community
  College *A*
Delta State University *B*
East Mississippi Community
  College *C, A*
Hinds Community College *C, A*
Jackson State University *B*
Meridian Community College *A*
Mississippi College *B*
Mississippi Gulf Coast Community
  College *A*
Mississippi State University *B*
Northeast Mississippi Community
  College *A*
Southwest Mississippi Community
  College *A*
University of Mississippi *B*
University of Phoenix
  Jackson *B, M*
University of Southern
  Mississippi *C, B*

Missouri

Calvary Bible College and Theological
  Seminary *B*
Central Methodist University *B*
College of the Ozarks *B*

Columbia College *B*
Drury University *B*
Evangel University *B*
Hannibal-LaGrange University *B*
Lincoln University *B*
Lindenwood University *B, M*
Maryville University of Saint Louis *B*
Missouri Baptist University *B*
Missouri Southern State
  University *B, T*
Missouri State University *B*
Missouri Western State University *B*
Moberly Area Community
  College *C, A*
National American University
  Kansas City *A, B*
Northwest Missouri State
  University *B*
Ozarks Technical Community
  College *C, A*
Park University *B*
St. Charles Community College *C, A*
Saint Louis University *B*
Southeast Missouri State University *B*
Southwest Baptist University *B*
Stephens College *B*
Three Rivers Community College *A*
University of Central Missouri *B*
University of Missouri
  Columbia *B*
  St. Louis *B, M*
University of Phoenix
  Kansas City *B, M*
  St. Louis *B, M*
Washington University in St.
  Louis *B, M*
Webster University *C, B, M*

Montana

University of Montana *A, B*

Nebraska

Concordia University *B*
Creighton University *B*
Hastings College *B*
Northeast Community College *C, A*
Peru State College *B*
Southeast Community College *A*
University of Nebraska
  Lincoln *B*
  Omaha *B*
University of Phoenix
  Omaha *B, M*
Western Nebraska Community
  College *C*

Nevada

Sierra Nevada College *B*
University of Nevada
  Las Vegas *B*
  Reno *B*
University of Phoenix
  Las Vegas *B, M*
  Northern Nevada *B, M*

New Hampshire

Daniel Webster College *B*
Franklin Pierce University *A, B*
Granite State College *B*
Great Bay Community College *C, A*
Manchester Community College *C, A*
NHTI-Concord's Community
  College *A*
New England College *B*
Plymouth State University *B*
Rivier University *B*
Southern New Hampshire
  University *A, B, M*

New Jersey

Bergen Community College *A*
Berkeley College *A, B*
Brookdale Community College *A*
Caldwell College *B*

Camden County College *A*
College of St. Elizabeth *C*
Cumberland County College *A*
Fairleigh Dickinson University
  College at Florham *B*
  Metropolitan Campus *B*
Felician College *B*
Gloucester County College *A*
Kean University *B*
Passaic County Community College *A*
Raritan Valley Community College *A*
Rider University *B*
Rowan University *B, M*
Rutgers, The State University of New
  Jersey
  Camden Campus *B*
  New Brunswick/Piscataway
    Campus *B*
  Newark Campus *B*
Seton Hall University *B*
Thomas Edison State College *C, B*
Union County College *A*
University of Phoenix
  Jersey City *B*

New Mexico

Dona Ana Community College of
  New Mexico State
  University *C, A*
Eastern New Mexico University *B*
New Mexico Highlands University *B*
New Mexico State University *B*
Southwest University of Visual Arts *B*
University of Phoenix
  New Mexico *B, M*
University of the Southwest *B*

New York

Adelphi University *B*
Alfred University *B*
Berkeley College *A, B*
Berkeley College of New York
  City *A, B*
Briarcliffe College *B*
Bryant & Stratton College
  Syracuse *A*
Canisius College *B*
City University of New York
  Baruch College *B, M*
  New York City College of
    Technology *A*
  York College *B*
Dominican College of Blauvelt *B*
Dowling College *B*
Elmira College *B*
Excelsior College *B*
Finger Lakes Community College *A*
Globe Institute of Technology *C*
Hofstra University *B, M*
Iona College *B, M*
Jamestown Business College *A*
Keuka College *B*
LIM College *B*
Le Moyne College *B*
Long Island University
  LIU Post *B*
Manhattanville College *B, M*
Monroe Community College *A*
Nazareth College *B*
New York Institute of Technology *B*
Niagara University *B*
Pace University *B, M*
Pace University: Pleasantville/
  Briarcliff *B, M*
Roberts Wesleyan College *B, M*
Rochester Institute of
  Technology *B, M*
Rockland Community College *A*
SUNY
  College at Fredonia *B*
  College at Old Westbury *B*
  College at Plattsburgh *B*
  College of Technology at Alfred *A*
  College of Technology at Delhi *A*

Farmingdale State College *C*
University at Albany *M*
University at Binghamton *B*
St. John Fisher College *B*
St. John's University *B*
St. Joseph's College New York:
  Suffolk Campus *B*
St. Joseph's College, New York *B*
St. Thomas Aquinas College *B, M*
Siena College *B, T*
Suffolk County Community
  College *C, A*
Syracuse University *B*
Touro College *B*
University of Rochester *B*
Wagner College *B*
Westchester Community College *A*
Yeshiva University *B*

North Carolina

Appalachian State University *B*
Central Piedmont Community
  College *A*
Chowan University *B*
Cleveland Community College *C, A*
East Carolina University *B*
Elon University *B*
Fayetteville Technical Community
  College *C, A*
Isothermal Community College *A*
Johnson & Wales University
  Charlotte *B*
Lenoir Community College *C, A*
Lenoir-Rhyne University *B*
Methodist University *B*
Montreat College *B*
North Carolina Agricultural and
  Technical State University *B*
North Carolina Wesleyan College *B*
Pitt Community College *C, A*
Southwestern Community College *A*
University of North Carolina
  Charlotte *B*
  Wilmington *B*
University of Phoenix
  Charlotte *B*
  Raleigh *B*
Wayne Community College *A*
Western Carolina University *B*
Wilkes Community College *C, A*
Wingate University *B*
Winston-Salem State University *B*

North Dakota

Lake Region State College *C, A*
Minot State University *B*
North Dakota State University *B*
Rasmussen College
  Bismarck *C, A, B*
  Fargo *C, A, B*
University of Jamestown *B*
University of Mary *D*
University of North Dakota *B*

Ohio

Ashland University *B*
Baldwin Wallace University *B*
Bluffton University *B*
Bowling Green State University:
  Firelands College *C*
Capital University *B*
Case Western Reserve
  University *B, M*
Cedarville University *B*
Cincinnati State Technical and
  Community College *A*
Clark State Community College *A*
Cleveland State University *B, M*
Columbus State Community
  College *A*
Davis College *A*
Edison State Community College *C, A*
Franklin University *B*
James A. Rhodes State College *C, A*

John Carroll University *B*
Kent State University *B*
Kent State University
  Stark *B*
Lake Erie College *B*
Lakeland Community College *C*
Lourdes University *B*
Malone University *B*
Marietta College *B*
Marion Technical College *A*
Miami University
  Hamilton *A*
  Oxford *A, B*
Mount Vernon Nazarene University *B*
Muskingum University *B*
North Central State College *C*
Northwest State Community
  College *A*
Notre Dame College *B*
Ohio Northern University *B*
Ohio State University
  Columbus Campus *B, M*
Ohio University *B*
Ohio University
  Southern Campus at Ironton *C*
Stark State College *A*
Terra State Community College *C, A*
Tiffin University *B*
University of Akron *C, A, B, M*
University of Akron: Wayne
  College *A*
University of Cincinnati *B, M*
University of Cincinnati
  Clermont College *A*
University of Dayton *B*
University of Findlay *B*
University of Northwestern Ohio *A*
University of Phoenix
  Cleveland *B, M*
University of Rio Grande *A, B*
University of Toledo *B, M*
Urbana University *B*
Ursuline College *B*
Walsh University *A, B*
Washington State Community
  College *A*
Wilmington College *B*
Wright State University *B, M*
Xavier University *B*
Youngstown State University *A, B, M*
Zane State College *A*

Oklahoma

Mid-America Christian University *B*
Northeastern Oklahoma Agricultural
  and Mechanical College *C, A*
Northeastern State University *B*
Oklahoma Baptist University *B*
Oklahoma Christian University *B*
Oklahoma City University *B, M*
Oklahoma State University *B*
Oral Roberts University *B*
Southeastern Oklahoma State
  University *B*
Southern Nazarene University *B*
University of Central Oklahoma *B*
University of Oklahoma *B*
University of Phoenix
  Oklahoma City *B, M*
  Tulsa *B, M*
University of Tulsa *B*

Oregon

Blue Mountain Community College *A*
Central Oregon Community
  College *C, A*
Clackamas Community College *C, A*
George Fox University *B*
Klamath Community College *C, A*
Linfield College *B*
Northwest Christian University *B*
Oregon Institute of Technology *B*
Oregon State University *B*
Pioneer Pacific College *A*

Portland Community College *C, A*
Portland State University *B*
Rogue Community College *A*
Southern Oregon University *B*
Umpqua Community College *A*
University of Oregon *M, D*
University of Phoenix
  Oregon *B*
University of Portland *B*

Pennsylvania

Albright College *B*
Alvernia University *B*
Arcadia University *B*
Bucknell University *B*
Cabrini College *B*
Carnegie Mellon University *B, M, D*
Cedar Crest College *B*
Central Penn College *A*
Chatham University *B*
Chestnut Hill College *A, B*
Clarion University of Pennsylvania *B*
Community College of Allegheny
  County *A*
Community College of Beaver
  County *A*
DeSales University *C, B*
Delaware Valley College *B*
Drexel University *B, M*
Duquesne University *B*
Erie Business Center *A*
Erie Business Center South *A*
Gannon University *B*
Gettysburg College *B*
Grove City College *B*
Holy Family University *B*
Immaculata University *B*
Indiana University of Pennsylvania *B*
Juniata College *B*
King's College *B*
La Roche College *B*
La Salle University *B*
Lansdale School of Business *A*
Lehigh University *B, M*
Lycoming College *B*
Manor College *A*
Mansfield University of
  Pennsylvania *B*
Marywood University *B*
McCann School of Business and
  Technology
  Hazleton *A*
Mercyhurst University *D*
Messiah College *B*
Misericordia University *B*
Neumann University *B*
Northampton Community College *A*
Penn State
  Abington *B*
  Altoona *C, B*
  Beaver *B*
  Berks *B*
  Brandywine *B*
  DuBois *B*
  Erie, The Behrend College *B*
  Fayette, The Eberly Campus *B*
  Greater Allegheny *B*
  Harrisburg *B*
  Hazleton *B*
  Lehigh Valley *C, B*
  Mont Alto *B*
  New Kensington *B*
  Schuylkill *B*
  Shenango *B*
  University Park *B*
  Wilkes-Barre *C, B*
  Worthington Scranton *C, B*
  York *B*
Philadelphia University *B*
Robert Morris University *B*
Rosemont College *B*
St. Francis University *B*
Saint Joseph's University *B, M*
St. Vincent College *B*
Seton Hill University *C, B*

Shippensburg University of
Pennsylvania *B*
Slippery Rock University of
Pennsylvania *B*
South Hills School of Business &
Technology *A*
Temple University *B, M*
University of Pennsylvania *B, M, D*
University of Phoenix
Harrisburg *B*
Philadelphia *B*
Pittsburgh *B*
University of Pittsburgh *B*
University of Pittsburgh
Johnstown *B*
University of Scranton *B*
University of the Sciences *B*
Villanova University *B*
Westmoreland County Community
College *C, A*
Wilkes University *B*
York College of Pennsylvania *B*

Puerto Rico

Bayamon Central University *B, M*
Caribbean University *B*
ICPR Junior College *C, A*
Inter American University of Puerto
Rico
Aguadilla Campus *B, M*
Bayamon Campus *B*
Guayama Campus *M*
Metropolitan Campus *B, M*
Ponce Campus *B, M*
San German Campus *B, M*
Pontifical Catholic University of
Puerto Rico *B, M*
Turabo University *B, M*
Universidad Metropolitana *A, B, M*
Universidad del Este *B*
University of Phoenix
Puerto Rico *B, M*
University of Puerto Rico
Aguadilla *B*
Arecibo *B*
Bayamon University College *B*
Mayaguez *B, M*
Ponce *B*
Rio Piedras *B, M*
University of the Sacred Heart *M*

Rhode Island

Bryant University *B*
Community College of Rhode
Island *C, A*
Johnson & Wales University
Providence *B, M*
Providence College *B*
Rhode Island College *B*
Roger Williams University *B*
Salve Regina University *B*
University of Rhode Island *B*

South Carolina

Anderson University *B*
Charleston Southern University *B*
Claflin University *B*
Clemson University *B, M*
Coastal Carolina University *B*
Converse College *B*
Forrest Junior College *A*
Francis Marion University *B*
Limestone College *B*
North Greenville University *B*
South Carolina State University *B*
Spartanburg Community College *A*
University of Phoenix
Columbia *B*
University of South Carolina
Columbia *B*

South Dakota

Dakota State University *B*
Globe University
Sioux Falls *A*

National American University
Rapid City *B*
Northern State University *B*
Southeast Technical Institute *A*

Tennessee

Belmont University *B*
Christian Brothers University *B*
East Tennessee State University *B*
Freed-Hardeman University *B*
Lipscomb University *B*
Maryville College *B*
Middle Tennessee State University *B*
Southern Adventist University *B, M*
Tennessee Wesleyan College *B*
Trevecca Nazarene University *B*
Union University *B*
University of Memphis *B*
University of Phoenix
Chattanooga *B, M*
Knoxville *B, M*
Memphis *B, M*
Nashville *B, M*
University of Tennessee
Knoxville *B*
Martin *B*
Vanderbilt University *M*

Texas

Abilene Christian University *B*
Angelo State University *B*
Austin Community College *C, A*
Baylor University *B*
Brookhaven College *C, A*
Cedar Valley College *C, A*
Clarendon College *A*
College of the Mainland *A*
Dallas Baptist University *C, B, M*
Del Mar College *A*
Galveston College *C, A*
Hardin-Simmons University *B*
Houston Baptist University *B*
Houston Community College
System *C, A*
Howard Payne University *B*
Huston-Tillotson University *B*
Lamar University *B*
Laredo Community College *A*
LeTourneau University *B*
Lubbock Christian University *B*
McMurry University *B*
Midwestern State University *B*
Northwood University
Texas *B*
Our Lady of the Lake University of
San Antonio *B*
St. Edward's University *B*
St. Mary's University *B*
Sam Houston State University *B*
Schreiner University *B*
South Texas College *C, A*
Southern Methodist University *B, M*
Southwestern Assemblies of God
University *B*
Stephen F. Austin State University *B*
Sul Ross State University *B*
Tarleton State University *B*
Texarkana College *C, A*
Texas A&M International
University *B*
Texas A&M University *B, M, D*
Texas A&M University
Commerce *B, M*
Corpus Christi *B*
Texarkana *B*
Texas Christian University *B*
Texas Southern University *B*
Texas State University *B*
Texas Tech University *B*
Texas Wesleyan University *B*
Texas Woman's University *B*
Trinity University *B*
Tyler Junior College *C, A*
University of Dallas *M*

University of Houston *B*
University of Houston
Clear Lake *B*
Downtown *B*
Victoria *B*
University of Mary Hardin-Baylor *B*
University of North Texas *B, D*
University of Phoenix
Austin *B, M*
Dallas Fort Worth *B, M*
Houston Westside *B, M*
San Antonio *B, M*
University of St. Thomas *B, M*
University of Texas
Arlington *B, D*
Austin *B, M, D*
Brownsville *B*
Dallas *B, M*
El Paso *B*
Pan American *B, M*
Permian Basin *B*
San Antonio *B, M, D*
Tyler *B*
University of the Incarnate Word *B*
Vernon College *A*
Weatherford College *C, A*
West Texas A&M University *B, M*

Utah

Brigham Young University *B*
Broadview University
Orem *A*
West Jordan *A*
Dixie State College *C, A, B*
Salt Lake Community College *C, A*
Southern Utah University *B*
University of Phoenix
Utah *B, M*
University of Utah *B, M*
Utah State University *B*
Utah Valley University *B*
Weber State University *B*
Western Governors University *B*
Westminster College *B*

Vermont

Castleton State College *B*
Champlain College *B*
Lyndon State College *B*

Virginia

Averett University *B*
Christopher Newport University *B*
Ferrum College *B*
George Mason University *B*
Hampton University *B*
James Madison University *B*
Lord Fairfax Community College *A*
Lynchburg College *B*
Old Dominion University *B*
Radford University *B*
University of Management and
Technology *B*
University of Phoenix
Northern Virginia *B, M*
Richmond *B*
Virginia Commonwealth University *B*
Virginia Intermont College *B*
Virginia Polytechnic Institute and
State University *B*
Virginia State University *B*

Washington

Bates Technical College *A*
Bellevue College *C, A*
Bellingham Technical College *C, A*
Centralia College *C, A*
City University of Seattle *C, B*
Clover Park Technical College *A*
Eastern Washington University *B*
Edmonds Community College *C*
Green River Community College *A*
Heritage University *B*
Peninsula College *C, A*

Pierce College *C*
Seattle University *B*
Shoreline Community College *C, A*
Spokane Community College *C, A*
Spokane Falls Community
College *C, A*
University of Phoenix
Western Washington *B, M*
University of Washington Tacoma *B*
Washington State University *B, D*
Western Washington University *B*
Whitworth University *B*
Yakima Valley Community College *A*

West Virginia

Alderson-Broaddus University *B*
American Public University System *B*
Concord University *B*
Davis and Elkins College *B*
Marshall University *B*
New River Community and Technical
College *A*
West Virginia University *B*
West Virginia Wesleyan College *B*
Wheeling Jesuit University *B*

Wisconsin

Blackhawk Technical College *A*
Carroll University *B*
Carthage College *B*
Chippewa Valley Technical College *A*
Concordia University Wisconsin *B*
Fox Valley Technical College *A*
Gateway Technical College *A*
Globe University
Eau Claire *A*
Green Bay *A*
La Crosse *A*
Middleton *A*
Wausau *A*
Herzing University
Kenosha *B*
Madison *B*
Lakeland College *B*
Lakeshore Technical College *A*
Maranatha Baptist Bible College *B*
Marian University *B*
Marquette University *B*
Mid-State Technical College *A*
Milwaukee Area Technical College *A*
Moraine Park Technical College *A*
Mount Mary University *B*
Northcentral Technical College *C, A*
Rasmussen College
Appleton *A, B*
Green Bay *C, A, B*
Wausau *C, A, B*
St. Norbert College *B*
Southwest Wisconsin Technical
College *A*
University of Phoenix
Milwaukee *B, M*
University of Wisconsin
Eau Claire *B*
La Crosse *B*
Madison *B, M*
Milwaukee *B*
River Falls *B*
Superior *B*
Whitewater *B*
Viterbo University *B*
Waukesha County Technical
College *A*
Western Technical College *A*

Wyoming

Casper College *C, A*
University of Wyoming *B*
Western Wyoming Community
College *A*

Marketing research

California

California State University
Northridge *M*

Los Angeles Mission College *A*
Southwestern College *C, A*

District of Columbia
Howard University *B*

Georgia
University of Georgia *M*

Hawaii
University of Hawaii
　Hawaii Community College *C, A*

Idaho
Boise State University *B*

Illinois
Benedictine University at
　Springfield *B*
Harper College *C*
Southern Illinois University
　Edwardsville *M*
University of Illinois
　Urbana-Champaign *B, D*

Kansas
Fort Hays State University *B*

Kentucky
Northern Kentucky University *C*

Maine
Husson University *B*

Massachusetts
Boston University *B*

Missouri
University of Missouri
　Kansas City *B*

Nebraska
University of Nebraska
　Lincoln *M, D*

New York
Fashion Institute of Technology *B*
Fordham University *B, M*
Hofstra University *M*
Rochester Institute of Technology *B*

Ohio
Bowling Green State University *B*
Stark State College *A*
University of Toledo *B*

Oklahoma
Oklahoma Christian University *B*

Pennsylvania
La Salle University *B*
Mercyhurst University *B*

Texas
University of Texas
　Arlington *M*

Virginia
University of Management and
　Technology *B*

Marriage/family therapy

Alabama
Auburn University *M*
Faulkner University *B*
University of Mobile *M*

Arizona
Arizona State University *D*
Grand Canyon University *M*

University of Phoenix
　Phoenix-Hohokam *M*
　Southern Arizona *M*

Arkansas
Harding University *M*
John Brown University *M*

California
Alliant International University *M, D*
Azusa Pacific University *M*
California State University
　Dominguez Hills *M*
　Fresno *M*
　Los Angeles *M*
Chapman University *M*
Loma Linda University *M, D*
Loyola Marymount University *M*
Mount St. Mary's College *M*
Notre Dame de Namur University *M*
Pacific Oaks College *M*
University of La Verne *M*
University of Phoenix
　Bay Area *M*
　Central Valley *M*
　Sacramento Valley *M*
　San Diego *M*
　Southern California *M*
University of San Diego *M*
University of Southern
　California *M, D*

Colorado
Argosy University
　Denver *D*
Colorado State University *M*
Regis University *M*
University of Phoenix
　Denver *M*
　Southern Colorado *M*

Connecticut
Central Connecticut State
　University *M*
Fairfield University *M, T*
Southern Connecticut State
　University *M*
University of Saint Joseph *M*

Florida
Argosy University
　Tampa *M*
Nova Southeastern University *M, D*
Saint Thomas University *M*
Stetson University *M*
University of Central Florida *M*
University of Florida *M, D*
University of Miami *M*

Georgia
Valdosta State University *M*

Hawaii
Argosy University
　Hawaii *M*

Idaho
Idaho State University *M*

Illinois
Northwestern University *M*
Wheaton College *M*

Indiana
Indiana Wesleyan University *M*

Iowa
Mount Mercy University *M*

Kansas
Friends University *M*

Louisiana
University of Louisiana at
　Monroe *M, D*

Maryland
University of Maryland
　College Park *M*

Massachusetts
Eastern Nazarene College *M*
University of Massachusetts
　Boston *M*

Michigan
Michigan State University *B, M*
Western Michigan University *M*

Minnesota
Argosy University
　Twin Cities *M, D*
Capella University *M*
Saint Cloud State University *M*
St. Mary's University of Minnesota *M*
Walden University *M*

Mississippi
Mississippi College *M*

Nevada
University of Phoenix
　Las Vegas *M*
　Northern Nevada *M*

New Hampshire
University of New Hampshire *M*

New Jersey
Kean University *M*
Seton Hall University *M, D*

New York
City University of New York
　Hunter College *M*
College of Saint Rose *M*
Hofstra University *M*
Iona College *M*
Medaille College: Amherst *M*
Mercy College *M*
New York Institute of Technology *M*
New York University *M, D*
Nyack College *M*
Syracuse University *M*
University of Rochester *M*

North Carolina
Appalachian State University *M*
East Carolina University *B, M, D*
Pfeiffer University *M*

Ohio
Ashland University *M*
University of Akron *M*
Wright State University *M*

Oregon
George Fox University *M*

Pennsylvania
Drexel University *M, D*
Duquesne University *M*
Eastern University *D*
Lancaster Bible College *M*
Seton Hill University *M*
Thomas Jefferson University *M*

Puerto Rico
University of Phoenix
　Puerto Rico *M*

South Carolina
Converse College *M*

Tennessee
Trevecca Nazarene University *M*
Vanderbilt University *D*

Texas
Abilene Christian University *M*
Del Mar College *A*
St. Mary's University *M, D*
Texas Tech University *M, D*
Texas Woman's University *M, D*
University of Houston
　Clear Lake *M*
University of Texas
　Tyler *M*

Utah
Argosy University
　Salt Lake City *D*
Brigham Young University *M, D*
Utah State University *M*

Vermont
Goddard College *M*

Washington
Pacific Lutheran University *M*
Seattle Pacific University *M*

Wisconsin
Edgewood College *M*
University of Wisconsin
　Stout *M*

Masonry

Alabama
Bishop State Community College *C*
Calhoun Community College *C*
Gadsden State Community College *C*
George C. Wallace Community
　College at Dothan *C*
George C. Wallace State Community
　College at Selma *C*
Jefferson Davis Community
　College *C*
Lawson State Community College *C*

Arizona
Arizona Western College *C*
Central Arizona College *C*
Eastern Arizona College *C*
GateWay Community College *C, A*

California
Palomar College *C, A*

Florida
North Florida Community College *C*
Palm Beach State College *C*

Georgia
Albany Technical College *C*
Savannah Technical College *C*

Illinois
City Colleges of Chicago
　Kennedy-King College *C*
Southwestern Illinois College *C, A*

Indiana
Ivy Tech Community College
　Central Indiana *C, A*
　Columbus *C, A*
　East Central *C, A*
　Lafayette *C, A*
　North Central *C, A*
　Northeast *C, A*
　Northwest *C, A*
　South Central *C, A*
　Southwest *C, A*
　Wabash Valley *C, A*

Iowa
Ellsworth Community College *C*
Kirkwood Community College *C*

Kansas
Fort Scott Community College *C*

Kentucky
Big Sandy Community and Technical
College *C*
Bluegrass Community and Technical
College *C*
Somerset Community College *C, A*

Michigan
Oakland Community College *C*

Minnesota
Dakota County Technical
College *C, A*
Riverland Community College *C*

Mississippi
Hinds Community College *C*
Mississippi Delta Community
College *C*
Pearl River Community College *C, A*

Nevada
Truckee Meadows Community
College *C, A*

New York
SUNY
College of Technology at Alfred *A*
College of Technology at
Delhi *C, A*

North Carolina
Blue Ridge Community College *C*
Piedmont Community College *C*
Pitt Community College *C*
Southeastern Community College *C*
Southwestern Community College *C*
Tri-County Community College *C*

Pennsylvania
Pennsylvania College of
Technology *A*
Thaddeus Stevens College of
Technology *A*
Williamson Free School of
Mechanical Trades *A*

South Carolina
Greenville Technical College *C*

Texas
Howard College *C*
Trinity Valley Community College *C*

Utah
Salt Lake Community College *C*

Virginia
Liberty University *A*
Southwest Virginia Community
College *C*

Wisconsin
Gateway Technical College *C*
Lakeshore Technical College *C*
Mid-State Technical College *C*
Milwaukee Area Technical College *C*
Southwest Wisconsin Technical
College *C*
Western Technical College *C*

Massage therapy

Alabama
Gadsden State Community College *C*
Southern Union State Community
College *C*

Virginia College
Birmingham *C, A*
Huntsville *C*
Montgomery *C, A*
Wallace State Community College at
Hanceville *C*

Alaska
Charter College *C*

Arizona
Arizona Western College *C, A*
Brookline College
Phoenix *C*
Tempe *C*
Tucson *C*
Carrington College
Mesa *C*
Phoenix *C*
Tucson *C*
Central Arizona College *C, A*
Chandler-Gilbert Community
College *C, A*
Phoenix College *C, A*
Pima Community College *C, A*

California
Bryan College: Sacramento *A*
Carrington College California
Antioch *C, A*
Citrus Heights *C, A*
Pleasant Hill *C, A*
Sacramento *C*
San Jose *C, A*
San Leandro *C*
Stockton *C, A*
Concorde Career College
North Hollywood *C*
San Bernardino *C*
San Diego *C*
Kaplan College
Palm Springs *C*
Vista *C*
MiraCosta College *C*
Pacific College of Oriental Medicine:
San Diego *C, A, B*
San Joaquin Valley College *A*
Santa Barbara City College *C*

Colorado
Anthem College
Aurora *C, A*
Colorado School of Healing Arts *C, A*
Community College of Denver *C*
Everest College
Colorado Springs *C*
IBMC College
Fort Collins *C, A*
IntelliTec College: Grand Junction *C*
Pueblo Community College *C*
Trinidad State Junior College *C, A*

Florida
Daytona State College *C*
Everest University
Brandon *C*
Lakeland *C*
Largo *C*
North Orlando *C*
Orange Park *C*
Tampa *C*
Florida Career College
Miami *C*
Florida College of Natural Health
Bradenton *C, A*
Maitland *C, A*
Miami *A*
Pompano Beach *C, A, B*
Herzing University
Winter Park *A*
Miami Dade College *C*
Palm Beach State College *A*
Pensacola State College *C*

Sanford-Brown Institute
Tampa *C*

Georgia
Gwinnett College *C*

Idaho
Broadview University
Boise *C, A*
Carrington College
Boise *C, A*
Idaho State University *C, A, B*

Illinois
Black Hawk College *C*
College of DuPage *C*
Elgin Community College *C*
Illinois Eastern Community Colleges
Olney Central College *C*
Illinois Valley Community
College *C, A*
Kaskaskia College *C*
Kishwaukee College *C*
Moraine Valley Community College *C*
Morton College *C*
National University of Health
Sciences *C, A*
Northwestern College *C, A*
Parkland College *C*
Rend Lake College *C*
Waubonsee Community College *C, A*

Indiana
Brown Mackie College
Michigan City *A*
Harrison College
Indianapolis *C, A*
Ivy Tech Community College
Northeast *C, A*
Kaplan College
Hammond *C, A*

Iowa
Clinton Community College *C*
Iowa Lakes Community College *C*
Northeast Iowa Community
College *C*

Kansas
Colby Community College *C*

Kentucky
Lincoln College of Technology
Florence *C*
Spencerian College *C, A*
Spencerian College: Lexington *C*

Louisiana
Blue Cliff College
Metairie *C, A*
Shreveport *C, A*
Delgado Community College *C*
Our Lady of the Lake College *C*

Maine
College of the Atlantic *B*
Kennebec Valley Community
College *C*

Maryland
Allegany College of Maryland *A*
College of Southern Maryland *A*
Community College of Baltimore
County *C, A*
Howard Community College *A*
TESST College of Technology
Towson *C*

Massachusetts
Berkshire Community College *C*
Bristol Community College *C*
Mount Wachusett Community
College *C*

Springfield Technical Community
College *C, A*

Michigan
Baker College
Allen Park *C*
Clinton Township *A*
Flint *C, A*
Jackson *C, A*
Muskegon *C*
Port Huron *C, A*
Lansing Community College *C*
Oakland Community College *C, A*
St. Clair County Community
College *A*
Schoolcraft College *C, A*

Minnesota
Duluth Business University *C, A*
Globe University
Moorhead *C, A*
Woodbury *C, A*
Lake Superior College *C*
Minnesota School of Business
Blaine *C, A*
Brooklyn Center *C, A*
Elk River *C, A*
Lakeville *C, A*
Plymouth *C, A*
Rochester *C, A*
St. Cloud *C, A*
Minnesota State College - Southeast
Technical *C, A*
Minnesota State Community and
Technical College *C, A*
Minnesota West Community and
Technical College *C*
Northland Community & Technical
College *C*
Northwestern Health Sciences
University *C, A*
Rasmussen College
Brooklyn Park *C, A*
Mankato *C, A*
Ridgewater College *C*
St. Paul College *C, A*

Mississippi
Hinds Community College *C*
Southwest Mississippi Community
College *C*

Nebraska
Herzing University
Omaha School of Massage Therapy
and Healthcare *C, A*
Myotherapy Institute *A*

New Hampshire
Great Bay Community College *A*
Mount Washington College *C*
Nashua Community College *C*
River Valley Community College *C*
White Mountains Community
College *C*

New Mexico
Carrington College
Albuquerque *C*

New York
ASA College *A*
Columbia-Greene Community
College *C, A*
Finger Lakes Community College *A*
Mildred Elley
Albany *C, A*
Niagara County Community
College *A*
North Country Community College *A*
SUNY
College of Agriculture and
Technology at Morrisville *A*

Swedish Institute *A*
Trocaire College *C, A*

North Carolina
Carteret Community College *C, A*
Forsyth Technical Community
   College *A*
Gaston College *C, A*
Johnston Community College *C*
Lenoir Community College *C, A*
Miller-Motte College
   Cary *A*
   Wilmington *C, A*
Sandhills Community College *C, A*
South Piedmont Community
   College *A*
Southeastern Community
   College *C, A*
Southwestern Community College *C*

North Dakota
Williston State College *C, A*

Ohio
Hocking College *C, A*
Lakeland Community College *C*
Lincoln College of Technology
   Dayton *C*
Miami-Jacobs Career College
   Columbus *C, A*
   Dayton *A*
   Sharonville *C, A*
Ohio Business College
   Hilliard *C, A*
Ohio College of Massotherapy *C, A*
Owens Community College
   Toledo *C*
Stark State College *C, A*
Stautzenberger College *C, A*
Stautzenberger College: Brecksville *A*

Oregon
Central Oregon Community
   College *C, A*
Pioneer Pacific College *C*
Rogue Community College *C*

Pennsylvania
Berks Technical Institute *C*
Butler County Community
   College *C, A*
Career Training Academy *A*
Career Training Academy:
   Monroeville *C*
Career Training Academy:
   Pittsburgh *A*
Everest Institute: Pittsburgh *C*
Keystone Technical Institute *C, A*
Lansdale School of Business *C*
Laurel Business Institute *A*
Lincoln Technical Institute
   Northeast Philadelphia *C*
Northampton Community College *C*
Penn Commercial Business and
   Technical School *C*
YTI Career Institute
   Capital Region *C*

Puerto Rico
Columbia Centro Universitario:
   Caguas *C*

Rhode Island
Community College of Rhode
   Island *C, A*

South Carolina
Horry-Georgetown Technical
   College *C*
Miller-Motte Technical College *C, A*
Miller-Motte Technical College
   Conway *A*

South Dakota
Globe University
   Sioux Falls *C, A*

Tennessee
Anthem Career College
   Memphis *C*
Daymar Institute
   Nashville *C*
Miller-Motte Technical College
   Chattanooga *C, A*
   Clarksville *C, A*
Roane State Community College *C*

Texas
Houston Community College
   System *C*
St. Philip's College *C*
San Jacinto College *C*
Western Technical College: Diana
   Drive *C*

Utah
Broadview University
   Layton *C, A*
   Orem *C, A*
   West Jordan *C, A*

Virginia
ECPI University *A*
Miller-Motte Technical College
   Lynchburg *A*

Washington
Carrington College
   Spokane *C*
Clover Park Technical College *A*
Lake Washington Institute of
   Technology *C, A*
Peninsula College *C*
Renton Technical College *C, A*
Whatcom Community College *A*

Wisconsin
Globe University
   Appleton *C, A*
   Eau Claire *C, A*
   Green Bay *C, A*
   La Crosse *C, A*
   Madison East *C, A*
   Middleton *C, A*
   Wausau *C, A*
Western Technical College *C*
Wisconsin Indianhead Technical
   College *C*

Wyoming
Sheridan College *C, A*

Materials chemistry

Arkansas
University of Arkansas *M, D*

Illinois
Illinois Institute of Technology *M*

Massachusetts
University of Massachusetts
   Dartmouth *M*

West Virginia
West Virginia Wesleyan College *B*

Materials engineering

Alabama
Auburn University *B, M, D*
Tuskegee University *D*
University of Alabama *D*
University of Alabama
   Birmingham *B, M, D*

Arizona
Arizona State University *B, M, D*

California
California Institute of
   Technology *M, D*
California Polytechnic State
   University: San Luis Obispo *B*
California State University
   Long Beach *B*
   Northridge *B, M*
San Jose State University *B, M*
Stanford University *B, M, D*
University of California
   Davis *B, M, D*
   Irvine *B, M, D*
   Los Angeles *B, M, D*
   Merced *B*
   Riverside *B, M, D*
   Santa Barbara *M, D*
University of Southern California *M*

Colorado
Colorado School of Mines *M, D*
University of Colorado
   Boulder *D*

Connecticut
University of Connecticut *B, M, D*

Delaware
University of Delaware *M, D*

District of Columbia
Catholic University of America *M*
George Washington University *M*
Howard University *M, D*

Florida
Florida International University *M, D*
University of Central Florida *M, D*
University of Florida *B, M, D*
University of South Florida *M*

Georgia
Georgia Institute of
   Technology *B, M, D*

Idaho
Boise State University *M, D*
University of Idaho *B, M, D*

Illinois
Illinois Institute of
   Technology *B, M, D*
Northwestern University *B, M, D*
University of Illinois
   Chicago *M, D*
   Urbana-Champaign *B, M, D*

Indiana
Purdue University *B, M, D*

Iowa
Iowa State University *B, M, D*

Kentucky
University of Kentucky *B, M, D*

Maine
Southern Maine Community
   College *B*

Maryland
Johns Hopkins University *B, M, D*
University of Maryland
   College Park *B, M, D*

Massachusetts
Boston University *M, D*
Massachusetts Institute of
   Technology *B, M, D*
Worcester Polytechnic Institute *M, D*

Michigan
Michigan State University *B, M, D*
Michigan Technological
   University *B, M, D*
University of Michigan *B, M, D*

Minnesota
University of Minnesota
   Twin Cities *B, M, D*
Winona State University *B*

Missouri
Washington University in St. Louis *M*

New Jersey
New Jersey Institute of
   Technology *M, D*
Stevens Institute of Technology *M, D*

New Mexico
New Mexico Institute of Mining and
   Technology *B, M, D*

New York
Alfred University *B, M, D*
Clarkson University *D*
Columbia University *B, M, D*
Cornell University *B, M, D*
Rensselaer Polytechnic
   Institute *B, M, D*
Rochester Institute of Technology *M*
SUNY
   University at Albany *B, M, D*
   University at Binghamton *M, D*
   University at Stony Brook *M, D*
University of Rochester *M, D*

North Carolina
North Carolina State
   University *B, M, D*

North Dakota
North Dakota State University *D*

Ohio
Case Western Reserve
   University *B, M, D*
Ohio State University
   Columbus Campus *B, M, D*
University of Cincinnati *M, D*
University of Dayton *M, D*
Wright State University *B, M*

Oklahoma
Oklahoma State University *M*

Pennsylvania
Carnegie Mellon University *B, M, D*
Community College of Beaver
   County *A*
Drexel University *B, M, D*
Lehigh University *B, M, D*
Penn State
   University Park *M, D*
University of Pennsylvania *B, M, D*
University of Pittsburgh *B, M, D*

Rhode Island
Brown University *B, M, D*

South Carolina
Clemson University *M, D*

South Dakota
South Dakota School of Mines and
   Technology *M, D*

Tennessee
University of Tennessee
   Knoxville *B, M, D*
Vanderbilt University *M, D*

Texas

Rice University *B, M, D*
Texas A&M University *M, D*
Texas State University *D*
University of Houston *M, D*
University of North Texas *B, M*
University of Texas
  Arlington *M, D*
  Austin *M, D*
  Dallas *M, D*
  El Paso *M, D*

Utah

Salt Lake Community College *A*
University of Utah *B, M, D*

Virginia

University of Virginia *M, D*
Virginia Polytechnic Institute and
  State University *B, M, D*

Washington

University of Washington *B, M, D*
Washington State University *B, M*

Wisconsin

University of Wisconsin
  Madison *B, M, D*
  Milwaukee *B*

Materials science

Alabama

Tuskegee University *D*
University of Alabama
  Birmingham *D*

Arizona

University of Arizona *B, M, D*

California

Stanford University *B, M, D*
University of California
  Berkeley *B, M, D*
  Los Angeles *B*
  Riverside *B*
  San Diego *M, D*
University of Southern
  California *M, D*

Colorado

Colorado School of Mines *M, D*
University of Denver *M, D*

Florida

Florida State University *M, D*

Idaho

Boise State University *B, M*

Illinois

Northwestern University *B*
University of Illinois
  Urbana-Champaign *B, M, D*

Iowa

Iowa State University *B, M, D*

Massachusetts

University of Massachusetts
  Amherst *C*
Worcester Polytechnic Institute *M, D*

Michigan

Central Michigan University *D*
Michigan State University *B, M, D*
Wayne State University *M, D*

Minnesota

University of Minnesota
  Twin Cities *B, M, D*

Missouri

Missouri State University *M*
Washington University in St.
  Louis *M, D*

New Hampshire

University of New
  Hampshire *B, M, D*

New Jersey

Stevens Institute of
  Technology *B, M, D*

New Mexico

University of New Mexico *M, D*

New York

Alfred University *B, M*
Columbia University *B, M, D*
Rochester Institute of Technology *M*
SUNY
  University at Albany *B, M, D*
  University at Binghamton *M, D*

North Carolina

University of North Carolina
  Chapel Hill *M, D*

Ohio

Case Western Reserve
  University *B, M, D*
Hocking College *A*
Youngstown State University *D*

Oregon

Oregon State University *M, D*

Pennsylvania

Carnegie Mellon University *B, M, D*
Penn State
  Abington *B*
  Altoona *B*
  Beaver *B*
  Berks *B*
  Brandywine *B*
  DuBois *B*
  Fayette, The Eberly Campus *B*
  Greater Allegheny *B*
  Harrisburg *B*
  Hazleton *B*
  Lehigh Valley *B*
  Mont Alto *B*
  New Kensington *B*
  Schuylkill *B*
  Shenango *B*
  University Park *B*
  Wilkes-Barre *B*
  Worthington Scranton *B*
  York *B*
University of Pennsylvania *B*

Tennessee

Vanderbilt University *M, D*

Texas

University of North Texas *B, M, D*

Vermont

University of Vermont *M, D*

Washington

University of Washington *B*
Washington State University *D*

Maternal/child health

California

Loma Linda University *M*

Maryland

University of Maryland
  College Park *D*

Massachusetts

Boston University *M, D*

Minnesota

University of Minnesota
  Twin Cities *M*

New York

Syracuse University *M*

North Carolina

University of North Carolina
  Chapel Hill *M, D*

Ohio

Union Institute & University *B*
University of Toledo *M*

Puerto Rico

Turabo University *A*
University of Puerto Rico
  Medical Sciences *M*

Maternal/child health nursing

Colorado

Regis University *M*

Louisiana

Louisiana State University
  Health Sciences Center *M*

Michigan

University of Michigan *M*
Wayne State University *M*

New York

City University of New York
  Hunter College *B, M*
SUNY
  University at Buffalo *M*
  University at Stony Brook *M, D*
University of Rochester *M*

Ohio

Case Western Reserve University *M*
University of Cincinnati *M*

Pennsylvania

University of Pennsylvania *M*

Puerto Rico

Caribbean University *M*

South Carolina

Medical University of South
  Carolina *M*

Tennessee

Vanderbilt University *M*

Texas

Baylor University *M*

Mathematical biology

Tennessee

Trevecca Nazarene University *B*

Texas

University of Houston *B*

Mathematical statistics/ probability

Alabama

University of Alabama *M, D*

Colorado

Colorado School of Mines *B*

Florida

University of Miami *B*

Indiana

Indiana University
  Bloomington *M*

New York

Rochester Institute of
  Technology *B, M*

North Carolina

University of North Carolina
  Chapel Hill *M, D*

Ohio

Bowling Green State University *M*

Pennsylvania

Carnegie Mellon University *B, D*

Texas

University of the Incarnate Word *M*

Virginia

George Mason University *D*

Mathematics

Alabama

Alabama Agricultural and Mechanical
  University *B*
Alabama State University *B, M*
Athens State University *B*
Auburn University *B, M, D, T*
Auburn University at Montgomery *B*
Birmingham-Southern College *B*
Calhoun Community College *A*
Faulkner State Community College *A*
Faulkner University *B, T*
Gadsden State Community College *A*
Huntingdon College *B*
Jacksonville State University *B, M*
Judson College *B*
Miles College *B*
Oakwood University *B*
Samford University *B*
Spring Hill College *B, T*
Stillman College *B*
Talladega College *B*
Troy University *B*
Tuskegee University *B, T*
University of Alabama *B, M, D*
University of Alabama
  Birmingham *B, M*
  Huntsville *B, M*
University of Mobile *B*
University of Montevallo *B, T*
University of North Alabama *B*
University of South Alabama *M*
University of West Alabama *B, T*

Alaska

University of Alaska
  Anchorage *B*
  Fairbanks *B, M*
  Southeast *B*

Arizona

Arizona State University *B, M, D*
Arizona Western College *A*
Central Arizona College *A*
Cochise College *A*
Eastern Arizona College *A*
Northern Arizona University *B, M*
South Mountain Community
  College *A*
University of Arizona *B, M, D*

Arkansas

Arkansas State University *B, M*
Arkansas Tech University *B*
Harding University *B*
Henderson State University *B*
Hendrix College *B*
John Brown University *B*
Lyon College *B*
Ouachita Baptist University *B*
Philander Smith College *B*
Phillips Community College of the University of Arkansas *A*
Southern Arkansas University *B*
University of Arkansas *B, M, D*
University of Arkansas
  Fort Smith *A*
  Little Rock *B*
  Monticello *B*
  Pine Bluff *B*
University of Central Arkansas *B, M*
University of the Ozarks *B*

California

Allan Hancock College *A*
Antelope Valley College *A*
Azusa Pacific University *B*
Bakersfield College *A*
Barstow Community College *A*
Berkeley City College *A*
Biola University *B*
Butte College *A*
Cabrillo College *A*
California Baptist University *B*
California Institute of Technology *B, M, D*
California Lutheran University *B*
California Polytechnic State University: San Luis Obispo *B, M*
California State Polytechnic University: Pomona *B, M*
California State University
  Bakersfield *B*
  Channel Islands *B*
  Chico *B*
  Dominguez Hills *B*
  East Bay *B, M*
  Fresno *B, M*
  Fullerton *B, M, T*
  Long Beach *B, M*
  Los Angeles *B, M*
  Monterey Bay *B*
  Northridge *B, M*
  Sacramento *B, M*
  San Bernardino *B, M*
  San Marcos *B, M*
  Stanislaus *B*
Canada College *A*
Cerritos College *A*
Chabot College *A*
Chaffey College *A*
Chapman University *B*
Citrus College *A*
Claremont McKenna College *B*
College of Alameda *A*
College of Marin *A*
College of San Mateo *A*
College of the Canyons *A*
College of the Desert *A*
College of the Sequoias *A*
College of the Siskiyous *A*
Columbia College *A*
Concordia University Irvine *B*
Contra Costa College *A*
Copper Mountain College *A*
Crafton Hills College *A*
Cuesta College *A*
Cypress College *A*
De Anza College *A*
Diablo Valley College *A*
East Los Angeles College *A*
El Camino College *A*
Feather River College *A*
Folsom Lake College *A*
Foothill College *A*

Fresno City College *A*
Fresno Pacific University *B*
Fullerton College *A*
Gavilan College *A*
Glendale Community College *A*
Golden West College *A*
Grossmont College *A*
Hartnell College *A*
Harvey Mudd College *B*
Humboldt State University *B*
Imperial Valley College *A*
Irvine Valley College *A*
La Sierra University *B*
Lake Tahoe Community College *A*
Laney College *A*
Lassen Community College *A*
Long Beach City College *A*
Los Angeles City College *A*
Los Angeles Mission College *A*
Los Angeles Southwest College *A*
Los Angeles Valley College *A*
Los Medanos College *A*
Loyola Marymount University *B, M*
Master's College *B*
Mendocino College *A*
Merritt College *A*
Mills College *B, M*
MiraCosta College *A*
Mission College *A*
Monterey Peninsula College *A*
Moorpark College *A*
Mount St. Mary's College *B*
Mount San Jacinto College *A*
National Hispanic University *A*
National University *B*
Occidental College *B*
Orange Coast College *A*
Oxnard College *A*
Pacific Union College *B, T*
Palomar College *A*
Pepperdine University *B*
Pitzer College *B*
Point Loma Nazarene University *B*
Pomona College *B*
Porterville College *A*
Reedley College *A*
Rio Hondo College *A*
Sacramento City College *A*
Saddleback College *A*
St. Mary's College of California *B*
San Bernardino Valley College *A*
San Diego Miramar College
  San Diego Miramar College *A*
San Diego City College *A*
San Diego Mesa College *A*
San Diego State University *B, M*
San Francisco State University *B, M*
San Joaquin Delta College *A*
San Jose State University *B, M*
Santa Ana College *A*
Santa Barbara City College *A*
Santa Clara University *B*
Santa Monica College *A*
Santa Rosa Junior College *A*
Santiago Canyon College *A*
Scripps College *B*
Shasta College *A*
Sierra College *A*
Simpson University *B*
Skyline College *A*
Solano Community College *A*
Sonoma State University *B*
Southwestern College *A*
Stanford University *B, M, D*
Taft College *A*
University of California
  Berkeley *B, M, D*
  Davis *B, M, D*
  Irvine *B, M, D*
  Los Angeles *B, M, D*
  Riverside *B, M, D*
  San Diego *B, M, D*
  Santa Barbara *B, M, D*
  Santa Cruz *B, M, D*
University of La Verne *B*

University of Redlands *B*
University of San Diego *B*
University of San Francisco *B*
University of Southern California *B, M, D*
University of the Pacific *B*
Vanguard University of Southern California *B*
Victor Valley College *A*
West Hills College: Lemoore *A*
West Valley College *A*
Westmont College *B*
Whittier College *B*
William Jessup University *B*
Woodland Community College *A*
Yuba College *A*

Colorado

Adams State University *B*
Colorado Christian University *B*
Colorado College *B*
Colorado Mesa University *B*
Colorado Mountain College *A*
Colorado State University *B, M, D*
Colorado State University Pueblo *B*
Community College of Aurora *A*
Fort Lewis College *B*
Metropolitan State University of Denver *B, T*
Otero Junior College *A*
Regis University *B*
United States Air Force Academy *B*
University of Colorado
  Boulder *B, M, D*
  Colorado Springs *B*
  Denver *B*
University of Denver *B, M, D*
University of Northern Colorado *B, M, T*
Western State Colorado University *B*

Connecticut

Albertus Magnus College *B*
Central Connecticut State University *B, T*
Connecticut College *B*
Eastern Connecticut State University *B*
Fairfield University *B, M*
Gateway Community College *A*
Mitchell College *B*
Quinnipiac University *B*
Sacred Heart University *B*
Southern Connecticut State University *B, M*
Trinity College *B*
University of Bridgeport *B*
University of Connecticut *B, M, D*
University of Hartford *B*
University of New Haven *B*
University of Saint Joseph *B*
Wesleyan University *B, M, D*
Western Connecticut State University *B, M*
Yale University *B, M, D*

Delaware

Delaware State University *B, M*
University of Delaware *B, M, D*
Wesley College *B*

District of Columbia

American University *B, M*
Catholic University of America *B*
Gallaudet University *B*
George Washington University *B, M, D*
Georgetown University *B*
Howard University *B, M, D*
Trinity Washington University *B*
University of the District of Columbia *B, M*

Florida

Ave Maria University *B*
Barry University *B*
Bethune-Cookman University *B*
Broward College *A*
Chipola College *A, B*
Clearwater Christian College *B*
Daytona State College *A*
Eckerd College *B*
Edward Waters College *B*
Florida Agricultural and Mechanical University *B*
Florida Atlantic University *B, M, D*
Florida Gulf Coast University *B*
Florida Institute of Technology *B*
Florida International University *B*
Florida Memorial University *B*
Florida Southern College *B*
Florida State University *B, M, D*
Indian River State College *A*
Jacksonville University *B, M*
Miami Dade College *A*
New College of Florida *B*
Palm Beach Atlantic University *B*
Palm Beach State College *A*
Pensacola State College *A*
Rollins College *B*
Saint Leo University *B*
South Florida State College *A*
Southeastern University *B*
Stetson University *B*
University of Central Florida *B*
University of Florida *B, M, D*
University of Miami *B, M, D*
University of North Florida *B*
University of South Florida *B, M, D*
University of Tampa *A, B*
University of West Florida *B, M*

Georgia

Abraham Baldwin Agricultural College *A*
Agnes Scott College *B*
Albany State University *B*
Andrew College *A*
Armstrong Atlantic State University *B, T*
Atlanta Metropolitan College *A*
Bainbridge College *A*
Berry College *B*
Brewton-Parker College *B*
Clark Atlanta University *B, M*
Clayton State University *B*
College of Coastal Georgia *A, B*
Columbus State University *B*
Covenant College *B*
Dalton State College *B*
Darton College *A*
East Georgia State College *A*
Emmanuel College *B*
Emory University *B, M, D*
Fort Valley State University *B*
Georgia College and State University *B*
Georgia Gwinnett College *B*
Georgia Highlands College *A*
Georgia Institute of Technology *M, D*
Georgia Perimeter College *A*
Georgia Regents University *B*
Georgia Southern University *B, M*
Georgia Southwestern State University *B, T*
Georgia State University *B, M*
Gordon College *A, B, T*
Kennesaw State University *B*
LaGrange College *B*
Mercer University *B*
Middle Georgia State College *A, B*
Morehouse College *B*
Oglethorpe University *B*
Paine College *B*
Piedmont College *B*
Reinhardt University *B*
Savannah State University *B*

Shorter University *B, T*
South Georgia State College *A*
Southern Polytechnic State
    University *B*
Spelman College *B*
University of Georgia *B, M, D*
University of North Georgia *A, B*
University of West Georgia *B*
Valdosta State University *B*
Wesleyan College *B, T*
Young Harris College *B*

Hawaii

Brigham Young University-Hawaii *B*
Hawaii Pacific University *B*
University of Hawaii
    Hilo *B*
    Manoa *B, M, D*

Idaho

Boise State University *B, M, T*
Brigham Young University-Idaho *B*
College of Idaho *B*
College of Southern Idaho *A*
Idaho State University *A, B, M, D*
Lewis-Clark State College *B*
North Idaho College *A*
Northwest Nazarene University *B*
University of Idaho *B, M, D*

Illinois

Augustana College *B*
Aurora University *B, M*
Benedictine University *B, T*
Blackburn College *B*
Bradley University *B, T*
Chicago State University *B, M, T*
City Colleges of Chicago
    Harold Washington College *A*
Concordia University Chicago *B, T*
DePaul University *B, M*
Dominican University *B*
East-West University *B*
Eastern Illinois University *B, M, T*
Elmhurst College *B, T*
Eureka College *B, T*
Governors State University *B*
Greenville College *B, T*
Harper College *A*
Illinois Central College *A*
Illinois College *B, T*
Illinois State University *B, M, T*
Illinois Valley Community College *A*
Illinois Wesleyan University *B*
John A. Logan College *A*
John Wood Community College *A*
Joliet Junior College *A*
Judson University *B*
Kankakee Community College *A*
Kishwaukee College *A*
Knox College *B*
Lake Forest College *B*
Lake Land College *A*
Lewis University *B*
Lincoln College *A*
Loyola University Chicago *B, M*
MacMurray College *B, T*
McKendree University *B, T*
Millikin University *B*
Monmouth College *B, T*
Moraine Valley Community College *A*
National-Louis University *B*
North Central College *B, T*
North Park University *B*
Northeastern Illinois University *B, M*
Northern Illinois
    University *B, M, D, T*
Northwestern University *B, M, D*
Olivet Nazarene University *B, T*
Principia College *B*
Quincy University *B, T*
Richland Community College *A*
Rockford University *B*
Roosevelt University *B, M*

Saint Xavier University *B*
Sauk Valley Community College *A*
South Suburban College of Cook
    County *A*
Southeastern Illinois College *A*
Southern Illinois University
    Carbondale *B, M, D*
Southern Illinois University
    Edwardsville *B, M*
Southwestern Illinois College *A*
Spoon River College *A*
Trinity Christian College *B, T*
Trinity International University *B*
University of Chicago *B, D*
University of Illinois
    Chicago *B, M, D*
    Springfield *B*
    Urbana-Champaign *B, M, D*
University of St. Francis *B*
Western Illinois University *B, M*
Wheaton College *B, T*

Indiana

Anderson University *B*
Ball State University *B, M, T*
Bethel College *B*
Butler University *B*
DePauw University *B*
Earlham College *B*
Franklin College *B*
Goshen College *B*
Grace College *B*
Hanover College *B*
Huntington University *B*
Indiana State University *B, M, T*
Indiana University
    Bloomington *B, M, D*
    East *B*
    Kokomo *B*
    Northwest *B*
    Purdue University Fort
        Wayne *B, M, T*
    Purdue University
        Indianapolis *B, M*
    South Bend *B*
    Southeast *B*
Indiana Wesleyan University *B*
Manchester University *B, T*
Marian University *B, T*
Martin University *B*
Purdue University *B, M, D*
Purdue University
    Calumet *B, M*
Rose-Hulman Institute of
    Technology *B*
Saint Joseph's College *B*
Saint Mary's College *B, T*
St. Mary-of-the-Woods College *B*
Taylor University *B*
Trine University *B*
University of Evansville *B*
University of Indianapolis *B*
University of Notre Dame *B, M, D*
University of St. Francis *B*
University of Southern Indiana *B, T*
Valparaiso University *B*
Vincennes University *A*
Wabash College *B*

Iowa

Briar Cliff University *B*
Buena Vista University *B, T*
Central College *B, T*
Clarke University *B, T*
Coe College *B*
Cornell College *B, T*
Dordt College *B*
Drake University *B*
Ellsworth Community College *A*
Graceland University *B, T*
Grinnell College *B*
Iowa State University *B, M, D*
Iowa Wesleyan College *T*
Iowa Western Community College *A*

Loras College *B*
Luther College *B*
Maharishi University of
    Management *B*
Marshalltown Community College *A*
Morningside College *B*
Mount Mercy University *B, T*
Northwestern College *B, T*
St. Ambrose University *B*
Simpson College *B*
University of Iowa *B, M, D, T*
University of Northern Iowa *B, M*
Upper Iowa University *B*
Wartburg College *B, T*
William Penn University *B*

Kansas

Allen County Community College *A*
Baker University *B, T*
Barton County Community College *A*
Benedictine College *B*
Bethany College *B, T*
Bethel College *B*
Butler Community College *A*
Central Christian College of
    Kansas *A, B*
Coffeyville Community College *A*
Colby Community College *A*
Cowley County Community
    College *A*
Dodge City Community College *A*
Donnelly College *A*
Emporia State University *B, M, T*
Fort Hays State University *B, M*
Friends University *B*
Garden City Community College *A*
Highland Community College *A*
Hutchinson Community College *A*
Independence Community College *A*
Kansas State University *B, M, D*
Kansas Wesleyan University *B, T*
McPherson College *B, T*
MidAmerica Nazarene University *B*
Neosho County Community
    College *A*
Newman University *B*
Ottawa University *B*
Pittsburg State University *B, M*
Pratt Community College *A*
Seward County Community
    College *A*
Southwestern College *B*
Sterling College *B, T*
Tabor College *B*
University of Kansas *B, M, D*
University of St. Mary *B*
Washburn University *B*
Wichita State University *B, M, D, T*

Kentucky

Asbury University *B, T*
Bellarmine University *B, T*
Berea College *B, T*
Bluegrass Community and Technical
    College *A*
Campbellsville University *B*
Centre College *B*
Eastern Kentucky University *B, M*
Georgetown College *B*
Hopkinsville Community College *A*
Kentucky State University *B*
Kentucky Wesleyan College *B, T*
Lindsey Wilson College *A, B, T*
Mid-Continent University *B*
Midway College *B*
Morehead State University *B*
Murray State University *B, M, T*
Northern Kentucky University *B*
Thomas More College *A, B*
Transylvania University *B*
Union College *B*
University of Kentucky *B, M, D*
University of Louisville *B, M*
University of Pikeville *B, T*

University of the Cumberlands *B, T*
Western Kentucky University *B, M, T*

Louisiana

Centenary College of Louisiana *B, T*
Dillard University *B*
Grambling State University *B*
Louisiana College *B, T*
Louisiana State University
    Alexandria *B*
    Shreveport *B*
Louisiana State University and
    Agricultural and Mechanical
    College *B, M, D*
Louisiana Tech University *B, M*
Loyola University New Orleans *B*
McNeese State University *B, M*
Nicholls State University *B*
Northwestern State University *B*
Southeastern Louisiana University *B*
Tulane University *B, M, D*
University of Louisiana at
    Lafayette *B, M, D*
University of Louisiana at Monroe *B*
University of New Orleans *B, M*
Xavier University of Louisiana *B*

Maine

Bates College *B, T*
Bowdoin College *B*
Colby College *B*
College of the Atlantic *B, M*
Saint Joseph's College of Maine *B*
University of Maine *B*
University of Maine
    Farmington *B*
    Presque Isle *B*
University of New England *B*
University of Southern Maine *B*

Maryland

Allegany College of Maryland *A*
Anne Arundel Community College *A*
Bowie State University *B*
Coppin State University *B*
Frederick Community College *A*
Frostburg State University *B*
Goucher College *B*
Harford Community College *A*
Hood College *B*
Howard Community College *A*
Johns Hopkins University *B, M, D*
McDaniel College *B*
Montgomery College *A*
Morgan State University *B, M*
Mount St. Mary's University *B, T*
Notre Dame of Maryland
    University *B*
St. Mary's College of Maryland *B*
Salisbury University *B*
Towson University *B*
United States Naval Academy *B*
University of Maryland
    Baltimore County *B*
    College Park *B, M, D*
    Eastern Shore *B*
Washington Adventist University *B*
Washington College *B, T*

Massachusetts

Amherst College *B*
Assumption College *B*
Bard College at Simon's Rock *B*
Bentley University *B*
Boston College *B, D*
Boston University *B, M, D*
Brandeis University *B, M, D*
Bridgewater State University *B*
Bunker Hill Community College *A*
Cape Cod Community College *A*
Clark University *B*
College of the Holy Cross *B*
Dean College *A*
Eastern Nazarene College *B*

Elms College *B*
Emmanuel College *B*
Endicott College *B*
Fitchburg State University *B*
Framingham State University *B*
Gordon College *B*
Hampshire College *B*
Harvard College *B, M, D*
Lesley University *B*
Massachusetts College of Liberal
    Arts *B, T*
Massachusetts Institute of
    Technology *B, D*
Merrimack College *B*
Mount Holyoke College *B*
Nichols College *B, T*
Northeastern University *B, M, D*
Roxbury Community College *A*
Salem State University *B, M*
Simmons College *B*
Smith College *B*
Springfield College *B*
Springfield Technical Community
    College *A*
Stonehill College *B*
Suffolk University *B*
Tufts University *B, M, D*
University of Massachusetts
    Amherst *B, M, D*
    Boston *B*
    Dartmouth *B*
    Lowell *B, M*
Wellesley College *B*
Western New England University *B*
Westfield State University *B, T*
Wheaton College *B*
Wheelock College *B*
Williams College *B*
Worcester Polytechnic
    Institute *B, M, D*
Worcester State University *B*

Michigan
Adrian College *B, T*
Albion College *B, T*
Alma College *B, T*
Andrews University *B*
Aquinas College *B, T*
Calvin College *B, T*
Central Michigan University *B, M, D*
Concordia University *B*
Cornerstone University *B, T*
Delta College *A*
Eastern Michigan University *B, M*
Ferris State University *B*
Gogebic Community College *A*
Grand Rapids Community College *A*
Grand Valley State University *B*
Hillsdale College *B*
Hope College *B*
Kalamazoo College *B*
Lake Michigan College *A*
Lake Superior State University *B, T*
Lansing Community College *A*
Lawrence Technological University *B*
Macomb Community College *A*
Madonna University *B*
Marygrove College *B, T*
Michigan State University *B, M, D*
Michigan Technological
    University *B, M, D*
Mid Michigan Community College *A*
Northern Michigan University *B*
Northwestern Michigan College *A*
Oakland University *B, M, T*
Olivet College *B, T*
Saginaw Valley State University *B*
Siena Heights University *A, B*
Spring Arbor University *B*
University of Detroit Mercy *B*
University of Michigan *B, M, D*
University of Michigan
    Dearborn *B, M*
    Flint *B, T*
Wayne State University *B, M, D*

West Shore Community College *A*
Western Michigan University *B, M, D*

Minnesota
Augsburg College *B*
Bemidji State University *B*
Bethany Lutheran College *B*
Bethel University *B*
Carleton College *B*
College of St. Benedict *B*
College of St. Scholastica *B*
Concordia College: Moorhead *B*
Concordia University St. Paul *B*
Gustavus Adolphus College *B*
Hamline University *B*
Macalester College *B*
Minneapolis Community and
    Technical College *A*
Minnesota State University
    Mankato *B, M, T*
    Moorhead *B*
Minnesota West Community and
    Technical College *A*
North Central University *B*
North Hennepin Community
    College *A*
Rainy River Community College *A*
Ridgewater College *A*
St. Catherine University *B*
Saint Cloud State University *B, M*
St. John's University *B*
St. Mary's University of Minnesota *B*
St. Olaf College *B*
Southwest Minnesota State
    University *B, T*
University of Minnesota
    Duluth *B*
    Morris *B*
    Twin Cities *B, M, D*
University of Northwestern - St.
    Paul *B*
University of St. Thomas *B*
Winona State University *B*

Mississippi
Alcorn State University *B*
Belhaven University *B, T*
Blue Mountain College *B*
Coahoma Community College *A*
Delta State University *B*
East Mississippi Community
    College *A*
Hinds Community College *A*
Holmes Community College *A*
Itawamba Community College *A*
Jackson State University *B, M*
Millsaps College *B*
Mississippi College *B, M*
Mississippi Gulf Coast Community
    College *A*
Mississippi State University *B, M, D*
Mississippi University for
    Women *B, T*
Mississippi Valley State University *B*
Northeast Mississippi Community
    College *A*
Rust College *B*
Tougaloo College *B*
University of Mississippi *B, M, D*
University of Southern
    Mississippi *B, M*
William Carey University *B*

Missouri
Avila University *B*
Calvary Bible College and Theological
    Seminary *B*
Central Methodist University *B*
College of the Ozarks *B*
Columbia College *B*
Crowder College *A*
Culver-Stockton College *B*
Drury University *B, T*
Evangel University *B, T*

Fontbonne University *B, T*
Hannibal-LaGrange University *B*
Harris-Stowe State University *B*
Lincoln University *B*
Lindenwood University *B*
Maryville University of Saint Louis *B*
Missouri Baptist University *B, T*
Missouri Southern State
    University *B, T*
Missouri State University *B, M*
Missouri University of Science and
    Technology *M*
Missouri Valley College *B*
Missouri Western State
    University *B, T*
Northwest Missouri State
    University *B*
Park University *B*
Rockhurst University *B*
St. Charles Community College *A*
St. Louis Community College *A*
Saint Louis University *B, M, D*
Southeast Missouri State University *B*
Southwest Baptist University *B, T*
Three Rivers Community College *A*
Truman State University *B*
University of Central Missouri *B, M*
University of Missouri
    Columbia *B, M, D*
    Kansas City *B, M, D*
    St. Louis *B, M*
Washington University in St.
    Louis *B, M, D*
Webster University *B*
Westminster College *B, T*
William Jewell College *B, T*
William Woods University *B, T*

Montana
Blackfeet Community College *A*
Carroll College *B*
Little Big Horn College *A*
Miles Community College *A*
Montana State University *B, M, D*
Montana State University
    Billings *B, T*
    Northern *B*
Montana Tech of the University of
    Montana *B*
Rocky Mountain College *B*
Stone Child College *A*
University of Great Falls *B*
University of Montana *B, M, D*
University of Montana: Western *B*

Nebraska
Chadron State College *B*
College of Saint Mary *B, T*
Concordia University *B, T*
Creighton University *A, B*
Doane College *B*
Hastings College *B*
Little Priest Tribal College *A*
Midland University *B, T*
Nebraska Wesleyan University *B*
Northeast Community College *A*
Peru State College *B*
Union College *B*
University of Nebraska
    Kearney *B, T*
    Lincoln *B, M, D*
    Omaha *B, M*
Wayne State College *B*
Western Nebraska Community
    College *A*
York College *B*

Nevada
Nevada State College *B*
University of Nevada
    Las Vegas *B, M, D*
    Reno *B, M*
Western Nevada College *A*

New Hampshire
Dartmouth College *B, M, D, T*
Franklin Pierce University *B*
Keene State College *B*
New England College *B*
Plymouth State University *B*
Rivier University *B, M, T*
Saint Anselm College *B, T*
Southern New Hampshire
    University *B*
University of New
    Hampshire *B, M, D*

New Jersey
Bergen Community College *A*
Caldwell College *B*
Centenary College *B*
College of New Jersey *B, T*
College of St. Elizabeth *B*
County College of Morris *A*
Cumberland County College *A*
Drew University *B*
Essex County College *A*
Fairleigh Dickinson University
    College at Florham *B, M*
    Metropolitan Campus *B, M*
Felician College *B*
Georgian Court University *B, M*
Gloucester County College *A*
Hudson County Community
    College *A*
Kean University *B, T*
Mercer County Community
    College *A*
Monmouth University *B, M*
Montclair State University *B, M, T*
New Jersey City University *B, M*
New Jersey Institute of
    Technology *B, D*
Passaic County Community College *A*
Princeton University *B, M, D*
Ramapo College of New Jersey *B*
Richard Stockton College of New
    Jersey *B*
Rider University *B*
Rowan University *B, M*
Rutgers, The State University of New
    Jersey
    Camden Campus *B, T*
    New Brunswick/Piscataway
        Campus *B, M, D, T*
    Newark Campus *B, T*
Saint Peter's University *B*
Salem Community College *A*
Seton Hall University *B, T*
Stevens Institute of Technology *M, D*
Sussex County Community College *A*
Thomas Edison State College *A, B*
Union County College *A*
William Paterson University of New
    Jersey *B, T*

New Mexico
Eastern New Mexico University *B, M*
Eastern New Mexico University:
    Roswell *A*
New Mexico Highlands University *B*
New Mexico Institute of Mining and
    Technology *B, M*
New Mexico Junior College *A*
New Mexico State University *B, M, D*
San Juan College *A*
University of New Mexico *B, M, D*
Western New Mexico University *B*

New York
Adelphi University *B*
Alfred University *B*
Bard College *B*
Barnard College *B*
Canisius College *B*
Cayuga Community College *A*

City University of New York
  Baruch College *B*
  Borough of Manhattan Community
    College *A*
  Brooklyn College *B, M*
  City College *B, M*
  College of Staten Island *B*
  Hostos Community College *A*
  Hunter College *B, M*
  Kingsborough Community
    College *A*
  Lehman College *B, M*
  Medgar Evers College *A, B*
  Queens College *B, M, T*
  York College *B*
Clarkson University *B, M, D*
Colgate University *B*
College of Mount St. Vincent *B, T*
College of New Rochelle *B, T*
College of Saint Rose *B*
Columbia University *B*
Columbia University
    School of General Studies *B*
Concordia College *A, B*
Cornell University *B, M, D*
Corning Community College *A*
D'Youville College *B*
Daemen College *B, T*
Dominican College of Blauvelt *B*
Dowling College *B*
Elmira College *B, T*
Excelsior College *B*
Finger Lakes Community College *A*
Fordham University *B, M, D*
Hamilton College *B*
Hartwick College *B, T*
Hobart and William Smith Colleges *B*
Hofstra University *B*
Houghton College *B*
Iona College *B*
Ithaca College *B, T*
Keuka College *B*
Le Moyne College *B*
Long Island University
  LIU Brooklyn *B*
  LIU Post *B, M*
Manhattan College *B, M*
Manhattanville College *B*
Marist College *B*
Medaille College *B*
Mercy College *B*
Molloy College *B*
Monroe Community College *A*
Mount Saint Mary College *B, T*
Nassau Community College *A*
Nazareth College *B*
New York University *B, M, D*
Niagara University *B*
Nyack College *B*
Orange County Community
    College *A*
Pace University *B*
Pace University: Pleasantville/
    Briarcliff *B*
Rensselaer Polytechnic
    Institute *B, M, D*
Roberts Wesleyan College *B*
SUNY
  College at Brockport *B, M, T*
  College at Buffalo *B*
  College at Cortland *B*
  College at Fredonia *B, T*
  College at Geneseo *B, T*
  College at New Paltz *B*
  College at Old Westbury *B, T*
  College at Oneonta *B, M*
  College at Oswego *B*
  College at Plattsburgh *B*
  College at Potsdam *B, M*
  College at Purchase *B*
  College of Agriculture and
      Technology at Cobleskill *A*
  College of Technology at Delhi *A*
  University at Albany *B, M, D*
  University at Binghamton *B, M, D*

University at Buffalo *B, M, D*
University at Stony
    Brook *B, M, D, T*
Sage Colleges *B*
Saint Bonaventure University *B*
St. Francis College *B*
St. John Fisher College *B*
St. John's University *B*
St. Joseph's College New York:
    Suffolk Campus *B*
St. Joseph's College, New York *B*
St. Lawrence University *B, T*
St. Thomas Aquinas College *B, T*
Siena College *B, T*
Skidmore College *B*
Suffolk County Community College *A*
Syracuse University *B, M, D*
Touro College *B*
Ulster County Community College *A*
Union College *B*
United States Military Academy *B*
University of Rochester *B, M, D*
Utica College *B*
Vassar College *B*
Wagner College *B, T*
Wells College *B*
Yeshiva University *B, T*

North Carolina

Appalachian State University *B, M*
Barton College *B*
Belmont Abbey College *B*
Bennett College for Women *B*
Brevard College *B*
Caldwell Community College and
    Technical Institute *A*
Campbell University *B*
Carteret Community College *A*
Catawba College *B, T*
Davidson College *B*
Duke University *B, M, D*
East Carolina University *B, M*
Elizabeth City State University *B, M*
Elon University *B, T*
Fayetteville State University *B, M*
Gardner-Webb University *B*
Greensboro College *B, T*
Guilford College *B*
High Point University *B*
Johnson C. Smith University *B*
Lees-McRae College *B*
Lenoir-Rhyne University *B, T*
Livingstone College *B*
Mars Hill University *B, T*
Meredith College *B*
Methodist University *B*
North Carolina Agricultural and
    Technical State
    University *B, M, T*
North Carolina Central
    University *B, M*
North Carolina State
    University *B, M, D*
North Carolina Wesleyan College *B*
Pfeiffer University *B*
Queens University of Charlotte *B*
St. Andrews University *B*
St. Augustine's University *B*
Salem College *B*
Sandhills Community College *A*
Shaw University *B*
Southeastern Community College *A*
University of Mount Olive *B*
University of North Carolina
  Asheville *B, T*
  Chapel Hill *B, M, D*
  Charlotte *B, M*
  Greensboro *B, M*
  Pembroke *B*
  Wilmington *B, M*
Wake Forest University *B, M*
Western Carolina University *B*
Western Piedmont Community
    College *A*

Wingate University *B*
Winston-Salem State University *B*

North Dakota

Dakota College at Bottineau *A*
Dickinson State University *B*
Mayville State University *B, T*
Minot State University *B*
North Dakota State
    University *B, M, D, T*
University of Jamestown *B*
University of Mary *B*
University of North Dakota *B, M*
Valley City State University *B*

Ohio

Antioch University
    Midwest *B*
Ashland University *B*
Baldwin Wallace University *B*
Bluffton University *B*
Bowling Green State
    University *B, M, D*
Capital University *B*
Case Western Reserve
    University *B, M, D*
Cedarville University *B*
Central State University *B*
Cleveland State University *B, M, T*
College of Mount St. Joseph *B, T*
College of Wooster *B*
Cuyahoga Community College
    Metropolitan *A*
Defiance College *B, T*
Denison University *B*
Franciscan University of
    Steubenville *B*
Heidelberg University *B*
Hiram College *B, T*
John Carroll University *B, M, T*
Kent State University *B, M, D*
Kent State University
    Stark *B*
Kenyon College *B*
Lake Erie College *B*
Lorain County Community College *A*
Malone University *B*
Marietta College *B*
Miami University
    Middletown *A*
    Oxford *B, M, T*
Mount Vernon Nazarene University *B*
Muskingum University *B*
Notre Dame College *B, T*
Oberlin College *B*
Ohio Dominican University *B*
Ohio Northern University *B*
Ohio State University
    Columbus Campus *B, M, D*
    Lima Campus *B*
Ohio University *B, M, D*
Ohio Wesleyan University *B*
Otterbein University *B*
Shawnee State University *A, B*
Sinclair Community College *A*
Stark State College *A*
Terra State Community College *A*
University of Akron *B, M*
University of Cincinnati *B, M, D, T*
University of Dayton *B*
University of Findlay *B, T*
University of Mount Union *B*
University of Rio Grande *A, B*
University of Toledo *B, M, D*
Urbana University *B*
Ursuline College *B*
Walsh University *B*
Washington State Community
    College *A*
Wilberforce University *B*
Wilmington College *B*
Wittenberg University *B*
Wright State University *B, M*

Xavier University *B*
Youngstown State University *B, M*

Oklahoma

Cameron University *B*
Carl Albert State College *A*
Connors State College *A*
East Central University *B, T*
Eastern Oklahoma State College *A*
Langston University *B*
Mid-America Christian University *B*
Murray State College *A*
Northeastern Oklahoma Agricultural
    and Mechanical College *A*
Northeastern State University *B*
Northern Oklahoma College *A*
Northwestern Oklahoma State
    University *B*
Oklahoma Baptist University *B, T*
Oklahoma Christian University *B, T*
Oklahoma City Community
    College *A*
Oklahoma City University *B*
Oklahoma Panhandle State
    University *B*
Oklahoma State University *B, M, D*
Oklahoma Wesleyan University *A, B*
Oral Roberts University *B*
Redlands Community College *A*
Rose State College *A*
St. Gregory's University *B*
Seminole State College *A*
Southeastern Oklahoma State
    University *B*
Southern Nazarene University *B*
Southwestern Oklahoma State
    University *B*
Tulsa Community College *A*
University of Central Oklahoma *B, M*
University of Oklahoma *B, M, D*
University of Science and Arts of
    Oklahoma *B, T*
University of Tulsa *B*
Western Oklahoma State College *A*

Oregon

Central Oregon Community
    College *A*
Corban University *B*
Eastern Oregon University *B*
George Fox University *B*
Lewis & Clark College *B*
Linfield College *B, T*
Linn-Benton Community College *A*
Mt. Hood Community College *A*
Northwest Christian University *B*
Oregon State University *B, M, D*
Pacific University *B*
Portland State University *B, D*
Reed College *B*
Southern Oregon University *B, T*
Southwestern Oregon Community
    College *A*
Treasure Valley Community
    College *A*
University of Oregon *B, M, D*
University of Portland *B, T*
Warner Pacific College *T*
Western Oregon University *B*
Willamette University *B*

Pennsylvania

Albright College *B, T*
Allegheny College *B*
Alvernia University *B*
Arcadia University *B*
Bloomsburg University of
    Pennsylvania *B, T*
Bryn Athyn College *B*
Bryn Mawr College *B, M, D*
Bucknell University *B, M*
Bucks County Community College *A*
Butler County Community College *A*
Cabrini College *B*

California University of
Pennsylvania *B, M*
Carlow University *B*
Carnegie Mellon University *B, M, D*
Cedar Crest College *B*
Chatham University *B*
Chestnut Hill College *B*
Cheyney University of
Pennsylvania *B, T*
Clarion University of Pennsylvania *B*
Community College of Allegheny
County *A*
Community College of
Philadelphia *A*
DeSales University *B, T*
Delaware Valley College *B*
Dickinson College *B*
Drexel University *B, M, D*
Duquesne University *B*
East Stroudsburg University of
Pennsylvania *B, T*
Eastern University *B*
Edinboro University of
Pennsylvania *B, T*
Elizabethtown College *B, T*
Franklin & Marshall College *B*
Gannon University *B*
Gettysburg College *B*
Grove City College *B*
Gwynedd Mercy University *B*
Harrisburg Area Community
College *A*
Haverford College *B, T*
Holy Family University *B, T*
Immaculata University *B*
Indiana University of
Pennsylvania *B, M*
Juniata College *B*
King's College *B, T*
Kutztown University of
Pennsylvania *B*
La Roche College *B*
La Salle University *B, T*
Lafayette College *B*
Lebanon Valley College *B, T*
Lehigh Carbon Community College *A*
Lehigh University *B, M, D*
Lincoln University *B, M*
Lock Haven University of
Pennsylvania *B*
Luzerne County Community
College *A*
Lycoming College *B*
Mansfield University of
Pennsylvania *B, T*
Marywood University *B*
Mercyhurst University *B, T*
Messiah College *B*
Millersville University of
Pennsylvania *B, M, T*
Misericordia University *B*
Montgomery County Community
College *A*
Moravian College *B, T*
Muhlenberg College *B*
Northampton Community College *A*
Penn State
Abington *B*
Altoona *B*
Beaver *B*
Berks *B*
Brandywine *B*
DuBois *B*
Erie, The Behrend College *B*
Fayette, The Eberly Campus *B*
Greater Allegheny *B*
Harrisburg *B*
Hazleton *B*
Lehigh Valley *B*
Mont Alto *B*
New Kensington *B*
Schuylkill *B*
Shenango *B*
University Park *B, M, D*
Wilkes-Barre *B*

Worthington Scranton *B*
York *B*
Rosemont College *B*
St. Francis University *B*
Saint Joseph's University *B*
St. Vincent College *B*
Seton Hill University *B, T*
Shippensburg University of
Pennsylvania *B, T*
Slippery Rock University of
Pennsylvania *B, T*
Susquehanna University *B, T*
Swarthmore College *B*
Temple University *B, M, D*
Thiel College *B*
University of Pennsylvania *B, M, D*
University of Pittsburgh *B, M, D*
University of Pittsburgh
Johnstown *B*
University of Scranton *B, T*
Ursinus College *B, T*
Villanova University *B, M*
Washington & Jefferson College *B*
Waynesburg University *B*
West Chester University of
Pennsylvania *B, M, T*
Westminster College *B*
Widener University *B, T*
Wilkes University *B, M*
Wilson College *B*
York College of Pennsylvania *B, T*

Puerto Rico

Inter American University of Puerto
Rico
Bayamon Campus *B*
Metropolitan Campus *B*
San German Campus *B*
Pontifical Catholic University of
Puerto Rico *B*
University of Puerto Rico
Cayey University College *B*
Mayaguez *B, M*
Ponce *B*
Rio Piedras *B, M, D*
University of the Sacred Heart *B*

Rhode Island

Brown University *B, M, D*
Providence College *B*
Rhode Island College *B, M*
Roger Williams University *B*
Salve Regina University *B*
University of Rhode Island *B, M, D*

South Carolina

Allen University *B*
Anderson University *B*
Benedict College *B*
Bob Jones University *B*
Charleston Southern University *B*
Citadel *B*
Claflin University *B*
Clemson University *B, M, D*
Coker College *B*
College of Charleston *B, M, T*
Columbia College *B, T*
Converse College *B*
Erskine College *B, T*
Francis Marion University *B*
Furman University *B, T*
Lander University *B, T*
Limestone College *B*
Morris College *B*
Newberry College *B, T*
North Greenville University *B*
Presbyterian College *B, T*
South Carolina State University *B*
Southern Wesleyan University *B, T*
University of South Carolina
Columbia *B, M, D*
Upstate *B*
Voorhees College *B*

Winthrop University *B, M*
Wofford College *B, T*

South Dakota

Augustana College *B, T*
Black Hills State University *B*
Dakota Wesleyan University *B*
Mount Marty College *B*
Northern State University *B*
South Dakota School of Mines and
Technology *B*
South Dakota State University *B, M*
University of Sioux Falls *B*
University of South Dakota *B, M*

Tennessee

Austin Peay State University *B*
Belmont University *B, T*
Bethel University *B*
Bryan University
Dayton *B, T*
Carson-Newman University *B, T*
Christian Brothers University *B*
Columbia State Community
College *A*
Cumberland University *B*
Dyersburg State Community
College *A*
East Tennessee State
University *B, M, T*
Fisk University *B*
Freed-Hardeman University *B, T*
Hiwassee College *A*
Jackson State Community College *A*
King University *B, T*
Lane College *B*
LeMoyne-Owen College *B*
Lee University *B*
Lincoln Memorial University *B, T*
Lipscomb University *B*
Maryville College *B, T*
Middle Tennessee State
University *B, M*
Milligan College *B, T*
Rhodes College *B*
Sewanee: The University of the
South *B*
Southern Adventist University *B*
Tennessee State University *B, M*
Tennessee Technological
University *B, M, T*
Tennessee Temple University *B*
Tennessee Wesleyan College *B*
Trevecca Nazarene University *B*
Tusculum College *B, T*
Union University *B, T*
University of Memphis *B, M, D*
University of Tennessee
Chattanooga *B, M, T*
Knoxville *B, M, D*
Martin *B*
Vanderbilt University *B, M, D*

Texas

Abilene Christian University *B*
Alvin Community College *A*
Amarillo College *A*
Angelina College *A*
Angelo State University *B, T*
Austin College *B*
Austin Community College *A*
Baylor University *B, M, D*
Blinn College *A*
Brazosport College *A*
Central Texas College *A*
Clarendon College *A*
Coastal Bend College *A*
College of the Mainland *A*
Concordia University Texas *B*
Dallas Baptist University *B*
Del Mar College *A*
East Texas Baptist University *B*
El Paso Community College *A*
Frank Phillips College *A*

Galveston College *A*
Grayson College *A*
Hardin-Simmons University *B*
Hill College *A*
Houston Baptist University *B*
Howard College *A*
Howard Payne University *B, T*
Huston-Tillotson University *B*
Jarvis Christian College *B, T*
Kilgore College *A*
Lamar University *B, M*
Laredo Community College *A*
LeTourneau University *B*
Lee College *A*
Lubbock Christian University *B*
McMurry University *B, T*
Midland College *A*
Midwestern State University *B*
Mountain View College *A*
Navarro College *A*
North Lake College *A*
Northeast Texas Community
College *A*
Northwest Vista College *A*
Odessa College *A*
Our Lady of the Lake University of
San Antonio *B*
Palo Alto College *A*
Paris Junior College *A*
Prairie View A&M University *B, M*
Rice University *B, M, D*
St. Edward's University *B*
St. Mary's University *B*
St. Philip's College *A*
Sam Houston State University *B, M*
San Antonio College *A*
San Jacinto College *A*
Schreiner University *B*
South Plains College *A*
South Texas College *A*
Southern Methodist University *B*
Southwestern Adventist
University *B, T*
Southwestern University *B, T*
Stephen F. Austin State
University *B, T*
Sul Ross State University *B, T*
Tarleton State University *B, M, T*
Temple College *A*
Texarkana College *A*
Texas A&M International
University *B, M, T*
Texas A&M University *B, M, D*
Texas A&M University
Commerce *B, M*
Corpus Christi *B, M, T*
Kingsville *B, M, T*
Texarkana *B, T*
Texas Christian University *B, M, D*
Texas College *B*
Texas Lutheran University *B, T*
Texas Southern University *B, M*
Texas State Technical College
Harlingen *A*
Texas State University *B, M, T*
Texas Tech University *B, M, D*
Texas Wesleyan University *B, T*
Texas Woman's University *B, M*
Trinity University *B*
Trinity Valley Community College *A*
Tyler Junior College *A*
University of Dallas *B*
University of Houston *B, M, D*
University of Houston
Clear Lake *B, M*
Downtown *B*
Victoria *B, T*
University of Mary Hardin-Baylor *B, T*
University of North Texas *B, M, D*
University of St. Thomas *B*
University of Texas
Arlington *B, M, D*
Austin *B, M, D*
Brownsville *B, M*
Dallas *B, M, D*

El Paso *B, M*
Pan American *B, M*
Permian Basin *B, M*
San Antonio *B, M*
Tyler *B, M*
University of the Incarnate
    Word *B, M*
Wayland Baptist University *B, T*
West Texas A&M University *B, M*
Western Texas College *A*
Wharton County Junior College *A*
Wiley College *B*

Utah

Brigham Young University *B, M, D*
Dixie State College *B*
Salt Lake Community College *A*
Snow College *A*
Southern Utah University *B*
University of Utah *B, M, D, T*
Utah State University *B, M*
Utah Valley University *A, B*
Weber State University *B*
Westminster College *B*

Vermont

Bennington College *B*
Castleton State College *B*
Johnson State College *B*
Lyndon State College *B*
Marlboro College *B*
Middlebury College *B*
Norwich University *B*
Saint Michael's College *B*
University of Vermont *B, M, D*

Virginia

Averett University *B*
Bluefield College *B*
Bridgewater College *B*
Christopher Newport University *B*
College of William and Mary *B*
Eastern Mennonite University *B*
Emory & Henry College *B, T*
Ferrum College *B*
George Mason University *B, M, D*
Hampden-Sydney College *B*
Hampton University *B, M*
Hollins University *B*
J. Sargeant Reynolds Community
    College *A*
James Madison University *B, T*
Liberty University *B, T*
Longwood University *B*
Lynchburg College *B*
Mary Baldwin College *B*
Marymount University *B, T*
Mountain Empire Community
    College *A*
Norfolk State University *B*
Northern Virginia Community
    College *A*
Old Dominion University *B*
Radford University *B*
Randolph College *B*
Randolph-Macon College *B*
Regent University *B*
Roanoke College *B, T*
Shenandoah University *B*
Sweet Briar College *B*
University of Mary Washington *B*
University of Richmond *B*
University of Virginia *B, M, D*
University of Virginia's College at
    Wise *B, T*
Virginia Commonwealth
    University *B, M*
Virginia Intermont College *B*
Virginia Military Institute *B*
Virginia Polytechnic Institute and
    State University *B, M, D*
Virginia State University *B, M*
Virginia Union University *B*
Virginia Wesleyan College *B*

Virginia Western Community
    College *A*
Washington and Lee University *B*

Washington

Central Washington University *B*
Centralia College *A*
Eastern Washington University *B*
Gonzaga University *B*
Heritage University *B*
Highline Community College *A*
Northwest University *B*
Pacific Lutheran University *B*
Saint Martin's University *B*
Seattle Pacific University *B*
Seattle University *B*
University of Puget Sound *B, T*
University of Washington *B, M, D*
Walla Walla University *B*
Washington State University *B*
Western Washington University *B, M*
Whitman College *B*
Whitworth University *B, T*

West Virginia

Bethany College *B*
Concord University *B*
Davis and Elkins College *B*
Fairmont State University *B*
Marshall University *B, M*
Ohio Valley University *B*
Potomac State College of West
    Virginia University *A*
Shepherd University *B, T*
West Liberty University *B*
West Virginia State University *B*
West Virginia University *B, M, D, T*
West Virginia University Institute of
    Technology *B*
West Virginia Wesleyan College *B*
Wheeling Jesuit University *B*

Wisconsin

Alverno College *B*
Beloit College *B*
Cardinal Stritch University *B, T*
Carroll University *B*
Carthage College *B*
College of Menominee Nation *A*
Concordia University Wisconsin *B, T*
Edgewood College *B*
Lakeland College *B*
Lawrence University *B*
Marian University *B*
Marquette University *B*
Mount Mary University *B, T*
Northland College *B*
Ripon College *B, T*
St. Norbert College *B, T*
Silver Lake College of the Holy
    Family *B, T*
University of Wisconsin
    Eau Claire *B*
    Green Bay *B*
    La Crosse *B, T*
    Madison *B, M, D*
    Milwaukee *B, M, D, T*
    Oshkosh *B*
    Parkside *B, T*
    Platteville *B, T*
    River Falls *B, T*
    Stevens Point *B, T*
    Superior *B, T*
    Whitewater *B, T*
Viterbo University *B, T*
Wisconsin Lutheran College *B*

Wyoming

Casper College *A*
Central Wyoming College *A*
Eastern Wyoming College *A*
Laramie County Community
    College *A*
Northwest College *A*

Sheridan College *A*
University of Wyoming *B, M, D*
Western Wyoming Community
    College *A*

Mathematics/computer science

Alabama

Birmingham-Southern College *B*
Oakwood University *B*

Arkansas

Philander Smith College *B*

California

California Lutheran University *B*
Claremont McKenna College *B*
Contra Costa College *A*
Harvey Mudd College *B*
Pepperdine University *B*
St. Mary's College of California *B*
San Diego State University *M, D*
Santa Clara University *B*
Stanford University *B*
University of California
    San Diego *B*

Colorado

Colorado College *B*
Colorado School of Mines *B, M, D*

Connecticut

Naugatuck Valley Community
    College *A*
Quinnipiac University *B*
Yale University *B*

Delaware

Delaware State University *B*

Florida

Florida Southern College *B*
University of Tampa *A, B*

Georgia

Emory University *B, M, D*
Piedmont College *B*

Illinois

DePaul University *B*
Dominican University *B*
Eastern Illinois University *B*
Eureka College *B*
Loyola University Chicago *B*
Monmouth College *B*
Southeastern Illinois College *A*
University of Illinois
    Urbana-Champaign *B*
University of St. Francis *B*

Indiana

Anderson University *B*
Indiana University
    Purdue University Fort Wayne *B*
    South Bend *M*
Manchester University *B*

Iowa

Central College *B, T*
Coe College *B*

Kansas

Seward County Community
    College *A*
Tabor College *B*

Kentucky

Brescia University *B*

Maine

Bowdoin College *B*
College of the Atlantic *B, M*
University of Maine
    Fort Kent *B*
University of Southern Maine *B*

Maryland

Washington College *B, T*

Massachusetts

Amherst College *B*
Boston University *B*
Clark University *B*
Massachusetts Institute of
    Technology *B*
Salem State University *B*
Tufts University *B, M, D*
Wheaton College *B*

Michigan

Alma College *B*
Central Michigan University *B*
Eastern Michigan University *M*
Hillsdale College *B*
Lake Superior State University *B*
Lawrence Technological University *B*

Minnesota

Minnesota State University
    Mankato *B, M*
Ridgewater College *A*
University of Minnesota
    Twin Cities *M, D*

Mississippi

Tougaloo College *B*

Missouri

Avila University *B*
Crowder College *A*
Evangel University *B*
Park University *B*
Washington University in St.
    Louis *B, M, D*

Montana

University of Montana *B*

New Hampshire

Saint Anselm College *B*

New Jersey

Cumberland County College *A*
Gloucester County College *A*
Stevens Institute of
    Technology *B, M, D*

New York

City University of New York
    Brooklyn College *B*
Colgate University *B*
Columbia University
    School of General Studies *B*
Hobart and William Smith Colleges *B*
Hofstra University *B*
Ithaca College *B*
Rochester Institute of Technology *B*
SUNY
    College at Purchase *B*
St. Lawrence University *B*
St. Thomas Aquinas College *B*
Schenectady County Community
    College *A*
Wells College *B*

North Carolina

Gardner-Webb University *B*
Warren Wilson College *B*

Ohio

Ashland University *B*
Defiance College *B, T*

Hiram College *B*
University of Akron *B*

Oklahoma

Connors State College *A*
Oklahoma Baptist University *B*
Oklahoma Christian University *B*
University of Central Oklahoma *M*

Oregon

Lewis & Clark College *B*
Southern Oregon University *B*
University of Oregon *B*
Western Oregon University *B*

Pennsylvania

Albright College *B*
Chestnut Hill College *B*
Duquesne University *M*
Gettysburg College *B*
Immaculata University *A, B*
La Salle University *B*
St. Francis University *B*
Temple University *B*
Westminster College *B*

Puerto Rico

University of Puerto Rico
  Mayaguez *B, M*

Rhode Island

Brown University *B*

South Carolina

Furman University *B*

Tennessee

Bryan University
  Dayton *B*
Christian Brothers University *B*
Sewanee: The University of the
  South *B*

Texas

Laredo Community College *A*
LeTourneau University *B*
University of Texas
  Austin *B*

Utah

Dixie State College *B*
University of Utah *M*

Vermont

Bennington College *B*
Castleton State College *B*
Marlboro College *B*

Virginia

George Mason University *M, D*
Hampden-Sydney College *B*
Virginia Wesleyan College *B*

Washington

Heritage University *A, B*
Whitman College *B*

West Virginia

Bethany College *B*

Wisconsin

Cardinal Stritch University *B, T*
Lawrence University *B*
Marquette University *M, D, T*
University of Wisconsin
  Parkside *B*

Mathematics/statistics

Alabama

University of South Alabama *B*

District of Columbia

Georgetown University *M*

Georgia

Georgia State University *D*

Iowa

Cornell College *B*
Dordt College *B*
Luther College *B*

Maine

Colby College *B*
University of Maine *M*

New York

Canisius College *B*
Columbia University
  School of General Studies *B*

South Dakota

Dakota State University *B*

Texas

Stephen F. Austin State University *M*

Washington

Evergreen State College *B*

West Virginia

West Virginia University *D*

Mathematics teacher education

Alabama

Auburn University *B, M, D*
Birmingham-Southern College *T*
Faulkner University *B, M, T*
Gadsden State Community College *A*
Huntingdon College *B, T*
Judson College *B*
Miles College *B*
Oakwood University *B*
Spring Hill College *B, T*
Talladega College *B*
Tuskegee University *B*
University of Mobile *B, T*

Arizona

Arizona Christian University *B*
Grand Canyon University *B*
Northern Arizona University *M*
University of Arizona *M*

Arkansas

Arkansas State University *B, M, T*
Arkansas Tech University *B*
Harding University *B, T*
John Brown University *B, T*
Ouachita Baptist University *B, T*
University of Arkansas *M*
University of Arkansas
  Fort Smith *B*
  Pine Bluff *B, M, T*
University of Central Arkansas *B*
University of the Ozarks *T*

California

Azusa Pacific University *T*
California Baptist University *B, T*
California Lutheran University *B, T*
California Polytechnic State
  University: San Luis Obispo *T*
California State University
  Chico *M, T*
  Dominguez Hills *M*
  East Bay *B, M*
  Long Beach *T*
  Northridge *B, T*
  Sacramento *B*
  San Bernardino *M, T*

Cuesta College *A*
Fresno Pacific University *B, M, T*
Humboldt State University *T*
Los Angeles Southwest College *A*
Master's College *T*
Mills College *T*
Mount St. Mary's College *T*
National University *B, M, T*
Saddleback College *A*
San Diego Christian College *B, T*
San Diego State University *M, T*
San Francisco State University *T*
Simpson University *B, T*
Sonoma State University *T*
Stanford University *M, T*
University of San Diego *T*
Vanguard University of Southern
  California *T*
Westmont College *T*

Colorado

Adams State University *B, M, T*
Colorado Christian University *B*
Colorado State University *B, T*
Colorado State University
  Pueblo *T*
Metropolitan State University of
  Denver *T*
University of Colorado
  Boulder *T*
  Denver *M*
Western State Colorado
  University *B, T*

Connecticut

Albertus Magnus College *B, T*
Central Connecticut State
  University *T*
Fairfield University *T*
Quinnipiac University *B, M*
Sacred Heart University *T*
Southern Connecticut State
  University *M*
University of Connecticut *T*
University of Saint Joseph *T*

Delaware

Delaware State University *B, M*
Delaware Technical Community
  College
  Jack F. Owens Campus *A*
  Stanton/Wilmington Campus *A*
  Terry Campus *A*
University of Delaware *B, T*

District of Columbia

Catholic University of America *M*
George Washington University *M, T*
Trinity Washington University *B, M*
University of the District of
  Columbia *M*

Florida

Barry University *T*
Broward College *A*
Chipola College *B*
Clearwater Christian College *B*
Daytona State College *B*
Florida Agricultural and Mechanical
  University *B, T*
Florida Atlantic University *B, M*
Florida Institute of
  Technology *B, M, D*
Hobe Sound Bible College *B, T*
Miami Dade College *A, B*
Northwest Florida State College *B*
Palm Beach Atlantic University *B, T*
St. Petersburg College *B*
Southeastern University *B, T*
Stetson University *B*
University of Central Florida *B*
University of Florida *B*
University of Miami *B, M*
University of North Florida *B*

University of South Florida *B, M*
University of West Florida *B, M*

Georgia

Albany State University *B, M*
Berry College *B*
Clayton State University *M*
Columbus State University *B, M*
Covenant College *B, T*
Darton College *A*
Emmanuel College *B*
Fort Valley State University *B, T*
Georgia Southwestern State
  University *M*
Georgia State University *M*
Kennesaw State University *B*
LaGrange College *B*
Middle Georgia State College *B*
Paine College *B*
Piedmont College *M, T*
Reinhardt University *B*
Shorter University *B, T*
Southern Polytechnic State
  University *B*
University of Georgia *B, M, D, T*
University of North Georgia *A, M*
Valdosta State University *M*

Hawaii

Brigham Young University-
  Hawaii *B, T*
Hawaii Pacific University *M*

Idaho

Boise State University *B, M, T*
Brigham Young University-Idaho *B, T*
Lewis-Clark State College *B, T*
Northwest Nazarene University *B*
University of Idaho *T*

Illinois

Augustana College *B, T*
Benedictine University *T*
Black Hawk College *A*
Blackburn College *B, T*
Bradley University *B*
Chicago State University *B*
City Colleges of Chicago
  Harry S. Truman College *A*
Concordia University Chicago *B*
DePaul University *M, T*
Dominican University *T*
Elmhurst College *B*
Eureka College *T*
Governors State University *B*
Greenville College *B, T*
Heartland Community College *A*
Highland Community College *A*
Illinois College *T*
Illinois Institute of Technology *M, D*
Illinois State University *D*
Illinois Wesleyan University *B*
John A. Logan College *A*
Kankakee Community College *A*
Kaskaskia College *A*
Knox College *T*
Lake Land College *A*
Loyola University Chicago *B, M*
MacMurray College *B, T*
Millikin University *B, T*
Moraine Valley Community College *A*
National-Louis University *M*
North Park University *T*
Northwestern University *B*
Olivet Nazarene University *B, T*
Prairie State College *A*
Rockford University *T*
Saint Xavier University *B, M, T*
Sauk Valley Community College *A*
Trinity Christian College *B, T*
Trinity International University *B, T*
Triton College *A*

University of Illinois
  Chicago *B, M*
  Urbana-Champaign *B, M, T*
University of St. Francis *B, M*

Indiana

Anderson University *B, T*
Bethel College *B*
Butler University *T*
Franklin College *B, T*
Goshen College *B, T*
Grace College *B*
Huntington University *B, M*
Indiana University
  Bloomington *B, T*
  East *M*
  Northwest *B*
  Purdue University Fort Wayne *B, T*
  South Bend *B, T*
  Southeast *T*
Indiana Wesleyan University *B, T*
Manchester University *B, T*
Oakland City University *B*
Purdue University *B, M, D*
Saint Mary's College *T*
Taylor University *B, T*
Trine University *B, T*
University of Evansville *B, T*
University of Indianapolis *B, T*
University of St. Francis *B*
Valparaiso University *B*
Vincennes University *A, B*

Iowa

Briar Cliff University *B*
Buena Vista University *B, T*
Central College *T*
Cornell College *B, T*
Dordt College *B*
Drake University *B, M, T*
Ellsworth Community College *A*
Graceland University *T*
Grand View University *T*
Iowa State University *M, T*
Iowa Wesleyan College *B, T*
Loras College *T*
Maharishi University of
  Management *T*
Morningside College *B*
Mount Mercy University *T*
Northwestern College *T*
St. Ambrose University *B, T*
Simpson College *T*
University of Dubuque *B, T*
University of Iowa *M, D, T*
Upper Iowa University *T*
Wartburg College *T*

Kansas

Allen County Community College *A*
Benedictine College *B*
Bethany College *B*
Bethel College *T*
Colby Community College *A*
Fort Hays State University *M*
Friends University *B*
Garden City Community College *A*
Independence Community College *A*
McPherson College *B, T*
MidAmerica Nazarene University *B, T*
Newman University *T*
Pittsburg State University *B*
Southwestern College *B*
Sterling College *B*
Tabor College *B*
University of Kansas *B, T*
University of St. Mary *T*
Washburn University *B, T*

Kentucky

Alice Lloyd College *B*
Campbellsville University *B*
Eastern Kentucky University *B*
Kentucky Christian University *B, T*

Kentucky Wesleyan College *B, T*
Lindsey Wilson College *B, T*
Midway College *M*

Louisiana

Centenary College of Louisiana *T*
Grambling State University *B*
Louisiana College *B, T*
Louisiana State University
  Shreveport *B*
McNeese State University *T*
Nicholls State University *B*
Northwestern State University *B*
Our Lady of Holy Cross College *B*
Southeastern Louisiana University *B*
University of Louisiana at Lafayette *B*
University of Louisiana at Monroe *B*
Xavier University of Louisiana *B*

Maine

Bowdoin College *B*
Saint Joseph's College of Maine *B*
University of Maine *B*
University of Maine
  Farmington *B, T*
University of Southern Maine *B, T*

Maryland

Anne Arundel Community College *A*
Carroll Community College *A*
Chesapeake College *A*
Community College of Baltimore
  County *A*
Coppin State University *B, T*
Frostburg State University *B, T*
Harford Community College *A*
Hood College *M, T*
Howard Community College *A*
Morgan State University *M, D*
Mount St. Mary's University *T*
Notre Dame of Maryland
  University *T*
Prince George's Community
  College *A*
Salisbury University *M, T*
Towson University *M*
Washington Adventist University *B*

Massachusetts

Assumption College *T*
Boston University *B, M, T*
Bridgewater State University *M, T*
Cambridge College *M*
Eastern Nazarene College *B*
Elms College *M, T*
Fitchburg State University *B, T*
Framingham State University *M*
Lasell College *B, T*
Lesley University *B, M*
Merrimack College *B, M*
Mount Holyoke College *M*
Regis College *B*
Salem State University *M*
Springfield College *T*
Tufts University *M, T*
University of Massachusetts
  Dartmouth *T*
Western New England
  University *B, M, T*
Westfield State University *M, T*
Worcester Polytechnic Institute *M*
Worcester State University *T*

Michigan

Adrian College *B, T*
Alma College *T*
Andrews University *B*
Calvin College *B*
Central Michigan University *B, M*
Concordia University *B, T*
Cornerstone University *B, T*
Eastern Michigan University *B, M*
Ferris State University *B*
Grand Valley State University *M, T*

Hope College *B, T*
Madonna University *B*
Michigan State University *B, M, D*
Michigan Technological University *T*
Northern Michigan
  University *B, M, T*
Olivet College *B, T*
Rochester College *B*
Spring Arbor University *B*
University of Detroit Mercy *B, M, T*
University of Michigan
  Dearborn *B*
  Flint *B, T*
Wayne State University *B, M, T*
Western Michigan
  University *B, M, D, T*

Minnesota

Augsburg College *T*
Bemidji State University *B, M, T*
Bethel University *B*
College of St. Benedict *T*
College of St. Scholastica *T*
Concordia College: Moorhead *B, T*
Concordia University St. Paul *B, T*
Gustavus Adolphus College *T*
Hamline University *T*
Martin Luther College *B*
Metropolitan State University *B*
Minnesota State University
  Mankato *B, M, T*
  Moorhead *B*
Ridgewater College *A*
St. Catherine University *B, T*
Saint Cloud State University *B, M, T*
St. John's University *T*
St. Mary's University of Minnesota *B*
Southwest Minnesota State
  University *B*
University of Minnesota
  Duluth *B*
  Morris *T*
  Twin Cities *M, T*
University of Northwestern - St.
  Paul *B*
University of St. Thomas *B*
Winona State University *B, T*

Mississippi

Blue Mountain College *B*
Coahoma Community College *A*
Delta State University *B*
Itawamba Community College *A*
Jackson State University *B*
Millsaps College *T*
Mississippi College *B, M*
Mississippi Gulf Coast Community
  College *A*
Northeast Mississippi Community
  College *A*
Northwest Mississippi Community
  College *A*
Rust College *B*
University of Mississippi *B, T*
William Carey University *B*

Missouri

Avila University *T*
College of the Ozarks *B, T*
Culver-Stockton College *T*
Evangel University *B, T*
Hannibal-LaGrange University *B*
Lincoln University *B*
Maryville University of Saint
  Louis *M, T*
Missouri Baptist University *T*
Missouri Southern State
  University *B, T*
Missouri State University *B*
Missouri Valley College *T*
Northwest Missouri State
  University *B, M, T*
Park University *T*
Southeast Missouri State University *B*

Southwest Baptist University *T*
Truman State University *M*
University of Central Missouri *B, M*
University of Missouri
  Columbia *B, M, D*
Washington University in St.
  Louis *B, M, T*
Webster University *M*
William Jewell College *B, T*
William Woods University *B, T*

Montana

Carroll College *B*
Montana State University
  Billings *B, T*
  Northern *B*
Rocky Mountain College *B*
University of Great Falls *B*
University of Montana *B, M, T*
University of Montana: Western *B, T*

Nebraska

Chadron State College *B, M*
College of Saint Mary *B, T*
Concordia University *B, T*
Creighton University *T*
Grace University *B*
Hastings College *B, M, T*
Midland University *B, T*
Nebraska Wesleyan University *T*
Union College *B*
University of Nebraska
  Kearney *B, T*
  Lincoln *B, M, T*
  Omaha *T*
Wayne State College *B, T*
York College *B, T*

Nevada

Great Basin College *B*
Nevada State College *B*

New Hampshire

Franklin Pierce University *M, T*
Granite State College *B*
Keene State College *B, T*
New England College *B, T*
Plymouth State University *B, M, T*
Rivier University *B, T*
Saint Anselm College *T*
Southern New Hampshire
  University *B*
University of New Hampshire *B, D, T*

New Jersey

Centenary College *T*
College of New Jersey *B, T*
Felician College *B*
Georgian Court University *T*
Kean University *M*
Montclair State University *M, T*
Richard Stockton College of New
  Jersey *M*
Rowan University *M, T*
Rutgers, The State University of New
  Jersey
  New Brunswick/Piscataway
    Campus *M, D, T*
Saint Peter's University *T*
William Paterson University of New
  Jersey *B, T*

New Mexico

New Mexico Highlands University *B*
New Mexico Institute of Mining and
  Technology *M*
University of the Southwest *B, T*
Western New Mexico University *B*

New York

Adelphi University *M, T*
Alfred University *B, T*
Bard College *M*

City University of New York
  Brooklyn College *B, M, T*
  City College *B, M, T*
  College of Staten Island *B, M*
  Hunter College *B, M, T*
  Lehman College *B, M*
  New York City College of
    Technology *B*
  Queens College *M, T*
Colgate University *M*
College of Saint Rose *B, T*
Cornell University *M, T*
D'Youville College *M, T*
Dominican College of Blauvelt *B, T*
Dowling College *B, M*
Dutchess Community College *A*
Elmira College *B, T*
Fordham University *T*
Hobart and William Smith Colleges *T*
Hofstra University *B, M, T*
Houghton College *B, T*
Iona College *B, M, T*
Ithaca College *B, M, T*
Keuka College *B, T*
Le Moyne College *T*
Long Island University
  LIU Brooklyn *B, M, T*
  LIU Post *B, M, T*
Manhattan College *B, T*
Manhattanville College *M, T*
Marist College *B*
Medaille College *B, M, T*
Medaille College: Amherst *M*
Molloy College *B, M*
Nazareth College *B, M, T*
New York Institute of
  Technology *M, T*
New York University *B, M*
Niagara University *B, M, T*
Nyack College *B*
Pace University *B, M, T*
Pace University: Pleasantville/
  Briarcliff *B, M, T*
Roberts Wesleyan College *B, M*
SUNY
  College at Brockport *B, M*
  College at Buffalo *B, M, T*
  College at Cortland *B, M*
  College at Fredonia *B, M, T*
  College at Geneseo *B, M, T*
  College at New Paltz *B, T*
  College at Old Westbury *B, M, T*
  College at Oneonta *B, M, T*
  College at Oswego *B, M*
  College at Plattsburgh *B, M*
  College at Potsdam *B, M*
  University at Albany *M, T*
  University at Binghamton *M*
  University at Buffalo *M, D, T*
  University at Stony Brook *T*
Saint Bonaventure University *M*
St. Francis College *B*
St. John Fisher College *B, M, T*
St. John's University *B, M, T*
St. Joseph's College New York:
  Suffolk Campus *B, M*
St. Joseph's College, New York *B, M*
St. Lawrence University *T*
St. Thomas Aquinas College *B, T*
Syracuse University *B, M, D, T*
Ulster County Community College *A*
University of Rochester *M*
Vassar College *T*
Wells College *T*

North Carolina

Appalachian State University *B, M, T*
Bennett College for Women *B*
Campbell University *B, T*
Catawba College *T*
Chowan University *T*
Davidson College *T*
East Carolina University *B, M*
Elizabeth City State University *B, T*
Elon University *T*

Gardner-Webb University *B*
Greensboro College *B, T*
Lenoir-Rhyne University *B, T*
Livingstone College *T*
Mars Hill University *T*
Meredith College *T*
Methodist University *A, B, T*
North Carolina Agricultural and
  Technical State
  University *B, M, T*
North Carolina Central
  University *B, M, T*
North Carolina State
  University *B, M, D, T*
University of Mount Olive *B*
University of North Carolina
  Charlotte *B, M*
  Greensboro *B*
  Pembroke *B, M*
  Wilmington *B*
Wake Forest University *T*
Western Carolina University *B, M, T*
Wingate University *B, T*
Winston-Salem State University *B*

North Dakota

Dickinson State University *B, T*
Mayville State University *B, T*
Minot State University *B, M*
North Dakota State University *B, T*
University of Jamestown *B*
University of Mary *B*
University of North Dakota *B*
Valley City State University *B, T*

Ohio

Antioch University
  Midwest *M*
Ashland University *B, T*
Baldwin Wallace University *T*
Bluffton University *B*
Bowling Green State
  University *B, M, T*
Capital University *T*
Case Western Reserve University *T*
Cedarville University *B, T*
Defiance College *B, T*
Hiram College *T*
John Carroll University *B, M*
Kent State University *B, M*
Malone University *T*
Miami University
  Oxford *B, M, T*
Mount Vernon Nazarene
  University *B, T*
Ohio Dominican University *B, T*
Ohio Northern University *B, T*
Ohio University *M, D, T*
Ohio Wesleyan University *B*
Otterbein University *B*
Shawnee State University *B, M*
Union Institute & University *B*
University of Akron *B, M*
University of Findlay *B, M, T*
University of Mount Union *T*
University of Rio Grande *B, T*
University of Toledo *B, M, T*
Urbana University *B*
Ursuline College *B, M, T*
Walsh University *B*
Wilmington College *B*
Wright State University *T*
Youngstown State University *B, M*

Oklahoma

Cameron University *B*
East Central University *B, T*
Eastern Oklahoma State College *A*
Langston University *B*
Mid-America Christian University *B*
Northeastern State University *B, M*
Northwestern Oklahoma State
  University *B*
Oklahoma Baptist University *B, T*

Oklahoma Christian University *B, T*
Oklahoma City University *B*
Oklahoma Wesleyan University *B*
Oral Roberts University *B*
Southeastern Oklahoma State
  University *B, M, T*
Southern Nazarene University *B*
Southwestern Oklahoma State
  University *B, M, T*
University of Central Oklahoma *B*
University of Oklahoma *B, T*
University of Tulsa *B, T*

Oregon

Concordia University *B, M, T*
Corban University *B*
Linfield College *T*
Oregon State University *M, D*
Portland State University *D, T*
Southern Oregon University *T*
Western Oregon University *M, T*

Pennsylvania

Albright College *T*
Alvernia University *B*
Arcadia University *B, M, T*
Baptist Bible College of
  Pennsylvania *B*
Bucks County Community College *A*
Cabrini College *T*
Cairn University *B, T*
Chatham University *M, T*
DeSales University *T*
Drexel University *M, T*
Duquesne University *B, M, T*
Geneva College *B, T*
Gettysburg College *T*
Grove City College *T*
Gwynedd Mercy University *B*
Holy Family University *B*
Immaculata University *B, M*
Juniata College *B, T*
Keystone College *B, T*
King's College *T*
La Salle University *B, T*
Lebanon Valley College *T*
Lycoming College *T*
Mansfield University of
  Pennsylvania *B, T*
Marywood University *B*
Mercyhurst University *B, T*
Messiah College *B, T*
Misericordia University *B, T*
Moravian College *T*
Point Park University *B*
Rosemont College *T*
St. Francis University *B, T*
Saint Joseph's University *M, T*
St. Vincent College *T*
Seton Hill University *B, T*
Susquehanna University *T*
Temple University *B*
Thiel College *B*
University of Pennsylvania *M, T*
University of Pittsburgh *T*
University of Pittsburgh
  Greensburg *B, T*
  Johnstown *B, T*
University of Scranton *B*
Villanova University *T*
Washington & Jefferson College *T*
Waynesburg University *B, T*
Westminster College *T*
Widener University *T*
Wilkes University *M, T*
Wilson College *T*
York College of Pennsylvania *B, T*

Puerto Rico

American University of Puerto
  Rico *B, T*
Bayamon Central University *B*

Inter American University of Puerto
  Rico
  Barranquitas Campus *B*
  Metropolitan Campus *B, M*
  San German Campus *B*
Pontifical Catholic University of
  Puerto Rico *B, T*
Turabo University *B*
University of Puerto Rico
  Cayey University College *B*
  Mayaguez *B*

Rhode Island

Bryant University *M*
Providence College *B, M*
Rhode Island College *B, M*

South Carolina

Anderson University *B, T*
Bob Jones University *B*
Charleston Southern University *B*
Citadel *M*
Claflin University *B*
Clemson University *B*
Coker College *B, T*
Francis Marion University *B, T*
Furman University *T*
Limestone College *B*
Morris College *B, T*
North Greenville University *B, M, T*
Southern Wesleyan University *B, T*
Wofford College *T*

South Dakota

Augustana College *B, T*
Black Hills State University *B, T*
Dakota State University *B, T*
Dakota Wesleyan University *B, T*
Mount Marty College *B*
Northern State University *B, T*
University of Sioux Falls *T*
University of South Dakota *B, M, T*

Tennessee

Belmont University *T*
Bryan University
  Dayton *T*
Cumberland University *B, T*
Freed-Hardeman University *B, T*
King University *T*
LeMoyne-Owen College *B*
Lee University *B*
Lincoln Memorial University *B, T*
Lipscomb University *B, M, T*
Maryville College *B, T*
Middle Tennessee State
  University *M, T*
Southern Adventist University *B*
Tennessee Technological University *T*
Tennessee Temple University *B*
Trevecca Nazarene University *B, T*
Tusculum College *B, T*
Union University *B, T*

Texas

Abilene Christian University *B, T*
Baylor University *B, T*
Del Mar College *A*
East Texas Baptist University *B*
Hardin-Simmons University *B, T*
Houston Baptist University *B, T*
Howard Payne University *B*
Jarvis Christian College *B, T*
Lamar University *B, M, T*
Laredo Community College *A*
LeTourneau University *B, T*
Lubbock Christian University *B*
McMurry University *B, T*
Midwestern State University *B*
Our Lady of the Lake University of
  San Antonio *B*
Prairie View A&M University *M*
St. Edward's University *B, T*
St. Mary's University *T*

Sam Houston State University *M, T*
Schreiner University *B*
Southern Methodist University *T*
Stephen F. Austin State University *M*
Tarleton State University *T*
Texas A&M International
University *B, T*
Texas A&M University
Kingsville *T*
Texas Christian University *B, M*
Texas College *B, T*
Texas Lutheran University *B, T*
Texas State University *M, D, T*
Texas Wesleyan University *B*
University of Dallas *T*
University of Houston
Victoria *M*
University of Mary Hardin-Baylor *B, T*
University of Texas
Arlington *T*
Austin *M, D*
Dallas *M, T*
Pan American *M*
San Antonio *M, T*
University of the Incarnate
Word *M, T*
West Texas A&M University *T*

Utah

Brigham Young University *B, M*
Dixie State College *B*
Southern Utah University *B*
Utah State University *B*
Utah Valley University *B*
Weber State University *B*
Western Governors
University *B, M, T*

Vermont

Castleton State College *B, T*
Johnson State College *B*
Saint Michael's College *M, T*
University of Vermont *B, T*

Virginia

Averett University *B, M, T*
Bluefield College *B, T*
Bridgewater College *T*
Eastern Mennonite University *T*
Emory & Henry College *B*
Hampton University *M*
Hollins University *T*
James Madison University *M, T*
Longwood University *T*
Radford University *T*
Regent University *M*
University of Virginia's College at
Wise *T*

Washington

Bellevue College *A*
Central Washington
University *B, M, T*
Eastern Washington University *B, M*
Heritage University *B, M*
Northwest University *T*
Seattle Pacific University *B, T*
Spokane Falls Community College *A*
Washington State
University *B, M, D, T*
Western Washington University *B*
Whitworth University *B, T*

West Virginia

Bethany College *B*
Concord University *B, M, T*
Davis and Elkins College *B*
Ohio Valley University *B*
Shepherd University *T*
West Liberty University *B*
West Virginia State University *B*
West Virginia University *T*
West Virginia Wesleyan College *B*
Wheeling Jesuit University *B*

Wisconsin

Carroll University *B, T*
Carthage College *T*
Concordia University Wisconsin *B*
Edgewood College *B*
Lakeland College *T*
Lawrence University *T*
Maranatha Baptist Bible College *B*
Marquette University *B*
Mount Mary University *B, T*
Northland International University *B*
St. Norbert College *T*
University of Wisconsin
Green Bay *T*
Oshkosh *M, T*
Platteville *B*
River Falls *T*
Superior *B, T*
Whitewater *B*
Viterbo University *B, T*

Wyoming

Eastern Wyoming College *A*

Meat cutting

Georgia

Art Institute of Atlanta *C*

Michigan

Bay de Noc Community College *C*

Mechanical drafting/CAD/CADD

Alabama

Gadsden State Community
College *C, A*
Lawson State Community
College *C, A*

Arizona

Mesa Community College *C*

California

City College of San Francisco *C*
Hartnell College *C*
Los Angeles Pierce College *C*
Ohlone College *C*
Orange Coast College *C, A*
San Joaquin Delta College *C, A*
Sierra College *C, A*

Colorado

IntelliTec College: Grand Junction *A*
Westwood College
Denver South *A*

Connecticut

Naugatuck Valley Community
College *C*

Delaware

Delaware Technical Community
College
Jack F. Owens Campus *A*

Florida

Lincoln College of Technology
West Palm Beach *A*
Palm Beach State College *C*

Georgia

Albany Technical College *C*
Southwest Georgia Technical
College *C*

Illinois

City Colleges of Chicago
Harry S. Truman College *C, A*
Wilbur Wright College *C*
John Wood Community College *A*

Kaskaskia College *C*
Moraine Valley Community College *C*
Morton College *C*
Parkland College *C*
Prairie State College *C*
Sauk Valley Community College *C*
Triton College *C, A*

Indiana

Indiana University
Purdue University Indianapolis *B*
Purdue University *A, B*
Purdue University
Calumet *C, B*
Vincennes University *A*

Iowa

Des Moines Area Community
College *C, A*
Iowa Central Community College *C*
Kirkwood Community College *C, A*
Western Iowa Tech Community
College *A*

Kansas

Hutchinson Community College *A*
Wichita Area Technical College *C, A*

Kentucky

Sullivan College of Technology and
Design *A*

Massachusetts

Benjamin Franklin Institute of
Technology *A*
Bristol Community College *C*
North Shore Community College *C*
Springfield Technical Community
College *C*

Michigan

Baker College
Muskegon *A*
Eastern Michigan University *B*
Grand Rapids Community
College *C, A*
Lansing Community College *C, A*
Mid Michigan Community
College *C, A*
Oakland Community College *C, A*
St. Clair County Community
College *C, A*

Minnesota

Alexandria Technical and Community
College *C, A*
Anoka Technical College *C, A*
Central Lakes College *C*
Globe University
Woodbury *A*
Minnesota State Community and
Technical College *C, A*
Rochester Community and Technical
College *C*
St. Cloud Technical and Community
College *C, A*

New Jersey

Bergen Community College *C, A*
Brookdale Community College *C*

New York

Cayuga Community College *C*
City University of New York
New York City College of
Technology *A*
SUNY
College of Technology at Alfred *A*

North Carolina

Central Carolina Community
College *C*

Central Piedmont Community
College *C*
Cleveland Community College *C, A*
Isothermal Community College *C, A*
Piedmont Community College *C*

Ohio

Edison State Community College *A*

Oklahoma

Western Oklahoma State College *A*

Oregon

Chemeketa Community College *A*
Portland Community College *A*

Pennsylvania

Butler County Community College *A*
Commonwealth Technical Institute *A*
Triangle Tech
DuBois *A*
Erie *A*
Greensburg *A*
Westmoreland County Community
College *A*

South Carolina

Aiken Technical College *A*
Greenville Technical College *C, A*
Midlands Technical College *C, A*
Piedmont Technical College *A*
Technical College of the
Lowcountry *C*
Tri-County Technical College *C, A*
York Technical College *C, A*

South Dakota

Southeast Technical Institute *A*

Tennessee

Northeast State Community
College *C, A*

Texas

Midland College *C, A*
North Lake College *C*

Washington

Bates Technical College *C*
Lake Washington Institute of
Technology *C*
Olympic College *C*

West Virginia

Bridgemont Community and
Technical College *A*

Wisconsin

Fox Valley Technical College *C, A*
Herzing University
Madison *A, B*
Lakeshore Technical College *C, A*
Milwaukee Area Technical
College *C, A*
Waukesha County Technical
College *A*
Western Technical College *A*

Wyoming

Casper College *C*

Mechanical engineering

Alabama

Alabama Agricultural and Mechanical
University *B*
Auburn University *B, M, D*
Tuskegee University *B, M*
University of Alabama *B, M, D*
University of Alabama
Birmingham *B, M, D*
Huntsville *B, D*
University of South Alabama *B, M*

Alaska
University of Alaska
Anchorage *M*
Fairbanks *B, M*

Arizona
Arizona State University *B, M, D*
Embry-Riddle Aeronautical University
Prescott Campus *B*
Northern Arizona University *B*
University of Arizona *B, M, D*

Arkansas
Arkansas State University *B*
Arkansas Tech University *B*
Harding University *B*
University of Arkansas *B, M*

California
California Baptist University *B*
California Institute of
Technology *B, M, D*
California Maritime Academy *B*
California Polytechnic State
University: San Luis Obispo *B, M*
California State Polytechnic
University: Pomona *B, M*
California State University
Chico *B*
Fresno *B, M*
Fullerton *B, M*
Long Beach *B, M*
Los Angeles *B, M*
Northridge *B, M*
Sacramento *B, M*
City College of San Francisco *A*
De Anza College *A*
Loyola Marymount University *B, M*
San Diego State University *B, M*
San Francisco State University *B*
San Jose State University *B, M*
Santa Clara University *B, M, D*
Stanford University *B, M, D*
University of California
Berkeley *B, M, D*
Davis *B, M, D*
Irvine *B, M, D*
Los Angeles *B, M, D*
Merced *B, M, D*
Riverside *B, M, D*
San Diego *B, M, D*
Santa Barbara *B, M, D*
University of San Diego *B*
University of Southern
California *B, M, D*
University of the Pacific *B*

Colorado
Colorado School of Mines *B, M, D*
Colorado State University *B, M, D*
United States Air Force Academy *B*
University of Colorado
Boulder *B, M, D*
Colorado Springs *B, M*
Denver *B, M*
University of Denver *B, M*

Connecticut
Central Connecticut State
University *B*
Fairfield University *B, M*
Quinnipiac University *B*
Trinity College *B*
United States Coast Guard
Academy *B*
University of Bridgeport *M*
University of Connecticut *B, M, D*
University of Hartford *B, M*
University of New Haven *B, M*
Yale University *B, M, D*

Delaware
University of Delaware *B, M, D*

District of Columbia
Catholic University of
America *B, M, D*
George Washington University *B, M*
Howard University *B, M, D*
University of the District of
Columbia *B*

Florida
Embry-Riddle Aeronautical
University *B, M*
Florida Agricultural and Mechanical
University *B, M, D*
Florida Atlantic University *B, M, D*
Florida Institute of
Technology *B, M, D*
Florida International
University *B, M, D*
Florida State University *B, M, D*
Jacksonville University *B*
University of Central Florida *B, M, D*
University of Florida *B, M, D*
University of Miami *B, M, D*
University of North Florida *B, M*
University of South Florida *B, M, D*

Georgia
Georgia Institute of
Technology *B, M, D*
Georgia Southern University *B*
Mercer University *B, M*
Southern Polytechnic State
University *B*
University of Georgia *B*

Hawaii
University of Hawaii
Manoa *B, M, D*

Idaho
Boise State University *B, M*
Brigham Young University-Idaho *B*
Idaho State University *B, M*
University of Idaho *B, M, D*

Illinois
Bradley University *B, M*
Illinois Institute of
Technology *B, M, D*
Northern Illinois University *B, M*
Northwestern University *B, M, D*
Southern Illinois University
Carbondale *B, M*
Southern Illinois University
Edwardsville *B, M*
University of Illinois
Chicago *B, M, D*
Urbana-Champaign *B, M, D*

Indiana
Anderson University *B*
Grace College *B*
Indiana Institute of Technology *B*
Indiana University
Purdue University Fort Wayne *B*
Purdue University
Indianapolis *B, D*
Purdue University *B, M, D*
Purdue University
Calumet *C, B*
North Central *B*
Rose-Hulman Institute of
Technology *B, M*
Trine University *B, M*
University of Evansville *B*
University of Notre Dame *B, M, D*
Valparaiso University *B*
Vincennes University *A*

Iowa
Dordt College *B*
Iowa State University *B, M, D*
University of Iowa *B, M, D*
William Penn University *B*

Kansas
Kansas State University *B, M, D*
University of Kansas *B, M, D*
Wichita State University *B, M, D*

Kentucky
University of Kentucky *B, M, D*
University of Louisville *B, M, D*
Western Kentucky University *B*

Louisiana
Louisiana State University and
Agricultural and Mechanical
College *B, M, D*
Louisiana Tech University *B*
Southern University and Agricultural
and Mechanical College *B*
University of Louisiana at
Lafayette *B, M*
University of New Orleans *B*

Maine
University of Maine *B, M, D*
University of Southern Maine *B*

Maryland
Johns Hopkins University *B, M, D*
United States Naval Academy *B*
University of Maryland
Baltimore County *B, M, D*
College Park *B, M, D*

Massachusetts
Boston University *B, M, D*
Bristol Community College *A*
Franklin W. Olin College of
Engineering *B*
Massachusetts Institute of
Technology *B, M, D*
Merrimack College *C, B*
Northeastern University *B, M, D*
Smith College *B*
Tufts University *B, M, D*
University of Massachusetts
Amherst *B, M, D*
Dartmouth *B, M*
Lowell *B, M, D*
Wentworth Institute of Technology *B*
Western New England
University *B, M*
Worcester Polytechnic
Institute *B, M, D*

Michigan
Andrews University *B*
Baker College
Flint *B*
Calvin College *B*
Central Michigan University *B*
Delta College *A*
Grand Valley State University *B, M*
Kettering University *B, M*
Lake Superior State University *B*
Lawrence Technological
University *B, M, D*
Michigan State University *B, M, D*
Michigan Technological
University *B, M, D*
Oakland University *B, M, D*
Saginaw Valley State University *B*
University of Detroit Mercy *B, M, D*
University of Michigan *B, M, D*
University of Michigan
Dearborn *B, M*
Flint *B*
Wayne State University *B, M, D*
Western Michigan University *B, M, D*

Minnesota
Minnesota State University
Mankato *B, M*
Saint Cloud State University *B, M*

University of Minnesota
Duluth *B*
Twin Cities *B, M, D*
University of St. Thomas *B*

Mississippi
Mississippi State University *B, M*
University of Mississippi *B*

Missouri
Missouri University of Science and
Technology *B, M, D*
St. Charles Community College *A*
Saint Louis University *B*
University of Missouri
Columbia *B, M, D*
Kansas City *B, M*
St. Louis *B*
Washington University in St.
Louis *B, M, D*

Montana
Montana State University *B, M*

Nebraska
University of Nebraska
Lincoln *B, M, D*

Nevada
University of Nevada
Las Vegas *B, M, D*
Reno *B, M, D*

New Hampshire
Daniel Webster College *B*
University of New
Hampshire *B, M, D*

New Jersey
College of New Jersey *B*
New Jersey Institute of
Technology *B, M, D*
Princeton University *B, M, D*
Rowan University *B, M*
Rutgers, The State University of New
Jersey
New Brunswick/Piscataway
Campus *B, M, D*
Stevens Institute of
Technology *B, M, D*

New Mexico
New Mexico Institute of Mining and
Technology *B, M*
New Mexico State University *B, M*
University of New Mexico *B, M*

New York
Alfred University *B, M*
City University of New York
City College *B, M, D*
LaGuardia Community College *A*
Clarkson University *B, M, D*
Columbia University *B, M, D*
Cooper Union for the Advancement
of Science and Art *B, M*
Cornell University *B, M, D*
Erie Community College *C*
Hofstra University *B*
Manhattan College *B, M*
New York Institute of Technology *B*
New York University *B*
Rensselaer Polytechnic
Institute *B, M, D*
Rochester Institute of
Technology *B, M*
SUNY
Maritime College *B*
University at Binghamton *B, M, D*
University at Buffalo *B, M, D*
University at Stony Brook *B, M, D*
Syracuse University *B, M, D*
Union College *B*

United States Military Academy *B*
University of Rochester *B, M, D*

North Carolina

Bennett College for Women *B*
Duke University *B, M, D*
North Carolina Agricultural and
Technical State
University *B, M, D*
North Carolina State
University *B, M, D*
University of North Carolina
Charlotte *B, M, D*

North Dakota

North Dakota State
University *B, M, D*
University of North Dakota *B, M*

Ohio

Case Western Reserve
University *B, M, D*
Cedarville University *B*
Cleveland State University *B, M, D*
Eastern Gateway Community
College *A*
Miami University
Oxford *B*
Ohio Northern University *B*
Ohio State University
Columbus Campus *B, M, D*
Ohio University *B, M*
University of Akron *C, B, M, D*
University of Cincinnati *B, M, D*
University of Dayton *B, M, D*
University of Mount Union *B*
University of Toledo *B, M*
Wilberforce University *B*
Wright State University *B, M*
Wright State University: Lake
Campus *B*
Youngstown State University *B, M*

Oklahoma

Oklahoma Christian University *B*
Oklahoma State University *B, M, D*
Oral Roberts University *B*
University of Central Oklahoma *B*
University of Oklahoma *B, M, D*
University of Tulsa *B, M, D*

Oregon

George Fox University *B*
Oregon Institute of Technology *B*
Oregon State University *B, M, D*
Portland State University *B, M, D*
University of Portland *B, M*

Pennsylvania

Bucknell University *B, M*
Carnegie Mellon University *B, M, D*
Drexel University *B, M, D*
Gannon University *B, M*
Grove City College *B*
Lafayette College *B*
Lehigh University *B, M, D*
Penn State
Abington *B*
Altoona *B*
Beaver *B*
Berks *B*
Brandywine *B*
DuBois *B*
Erie, The Behrend College *B*
Fayette, The Eberly Campus *B*
Greater Allegheny *B*
Harrisburg *B*
Hazleton *B*
Lehigh Valley *B*
Mont Alto *B*
New Kensington *B*
Schuylkill *B*
Shenango *B*
University Park *B, M, D*

Wilkes-Barre *B*
Worthington Scranton *B*
York *B*
Philadelphia University *B*
Temple University *B, M*
Thaddeus Stevens College of
Technology *A*
University of Pennsylvania *B, M, D*
University of Pittsburgh *B, M, D*
University of Pittsburgh
Bradford *B*
Villanova University *B, M*
Widener University *B, M*
Wilkes University *B, M*
York College of Pennsylvania *B*

Puerto Rico

Inter American University of Puerto
Rico
Bayamon Campus *B*
Turabo University *B, M*
Universidad Politecnica de Puerto
Rico *A, B, M*
University of Puerto Rico
Carolina Regional College *A*
Mayaguez *B, M*

Rhode Island

Brown University *B, M, D*
New England Institute of
Technology *A, B*
University of Rhode Island *B, M, D*

South Carolina

Citadel *B*
Clemson University *B, M, D*
University of South Carolina
Columbia *B, M, D*

South Dakota

South Dakota School of Mines and
Technology *B, M, D*
South Dakota State University *B, M*

Tennessee

Christian Brothers University *B*
Lipscomb University *B*
Tennessee Technological
University *B, M, D*
Union University *B*
University of Memphis *B, M*
University of Tennessee
Chattanooga *B*
Knoxville *B, M, D*
Vanderbilt University *B, M, D*

Texas

Baylor University *B, M*
Lamar University *B, M*
LeTourneau University *B*
Midwestern State University *B*
Northeast Texas Community
College *A*
Prairie View A&M University *B*
Rice University *B, M, D*
St. Mary's University *M*
St. Philip's College *A*
Southern Methodist
University *B, M, D*
Texas A&M University *B, M, D*
Texas A&M University
Corpus Christi *B*
Kingsville *B, M*
Texas Christian University *B*
Texas Tech University *B, M, D*
University of Houston *B, M, D*
University of North Texas *B, M*
University of Texas
Arlington *B, M, D*
Austin *B, M, D*
Dallas *B, M, D*
El Paso *B, M*
Pan American *B, M*
Permian Basin *B*

San Antonio *B, M*
Tyler *B, M*
West Texas A&M University *B*

Utah

Brigham Young University *B, M, D*
Salt Lake Community College *A*
University of Utah *B, M, D*
Utah State University *A, B, M, D*

Vermont

Norwich University *B*
University of Vermont *B, M, D*

Virginia

Lord Fairfax Community College *A*
Old Dominion University *B*
University of Virginia *B, M, D*
Virginia Commonwealth
University *B, M*
Virginia Military Institute *B*
Virginia Polytechnic Institute and
State University *B, M, D*

Washington

Bellevue College *A*
Eastern Washington University *B*
Edmonds Community College *A*
Gonzaga University *B*
Saint Martin's University *B, M*
Seattle University *B*
Shoreline Community College *A*
Spokane Falls Community College *A*
Tacoma Community College *A*
University of Washington *B, M, D*
Walla Walla University *B*
Washington State University *B, M, D*

West Virginia

Potomac State College of West
Virginia University *A*
West Virginia University *B, M, D*
West Virginia University Institute of
Technology *B*

Wisconsin

Marquette University *B, M, D*
Milwaukee School of Engineering *B*
University of Wisconsin
Madison *B, M, D*
Milwaukee *B*
Platteville *B*

Wyoming

University of Wyoming *B, M, D*

Mechanical engineering technology

Alabama

Gadsden State Community
College *C, A*

Arizona

Penn Foster College *A*

Arkansas

University of Arkansas
Little Rock *A, B*

California

California State University
Sacramento *B, M*
City College of San Francisco *A*
Diablo Valley College *C*
Hartnell College *C, A*
San Joaquin Delta College *C, A*

Colorado

Colorado Mesa University *A*
Metropolitan State University of
Denver *B*

Connecticut

Central Connecticut State
University *B*
Gateway Community College *A*
Naugatuck Valley Community
College *A*
University of Hartford *B, M*

Delaware

Delaware State University *B*
Delaware Technical Community
College
Stanton/Wilmington Campus *A*

Florida

Pensacola State College *C, A*

Georgia

Southern Polytechnic State
University *B*

Idaho

Idaho State University *A, B*

Illinois

College of Lake County *C, A*
Illinois Central College *A*
McHenry County College *C, A*
Moraine Valley Community
College *C, A*
Parkland College *C*
Prairie State College *A*
Sauk Valley Community College *A*
Triton College *C, A*

Indiana

Indiana University
Purdue University Fort Wayne *A, B*
Purdue University *A, B*
Purdue University
North Central *C, A, B*

Kansas

Pittsburg State University *B*
Wichita Area Technical College *C, A*

Maine

University of Maine *B*

Maryland

Hagerstown Community College *A*

Massachusetts

Benjamin Franklin Institute of
Technology *A*
Springfield Technical Community
College *C, A*

Michigan

Central Michigan University *B*
Eastern Michigan University *B*
Ferris State University *A, B*
Lawrence Technological University *A*
Michigan Technological University *B*
Mott Community College *C, A*
Northern Michigan University *B*
Wayne State University *B*

Minnesota

Globe University
Woodbury *B*
Hennepin Technical College *C, A*
Minnesota State University
Mankato *B, M*
Rochester Community and Technical
College *A*

Nevada

College of Southern Nevada *C, A*

New Hampshire

NHTI-Concord's Community
College *A*
University of New Hampshire *B*

New Jersey

Fairleigh Dickinson University
Metropolitan Campus *B*
Union County College *A*

New York

Broome Community College *A*
Cayuga Community College *A*
City University of New York
New York City College of
Technology *A, B*
Corning Community College *A*
Erie Community College *A*
Excelsior College *A*
Finger Lakes Community College *A*
Jamestown Community College *A*
Mohawk Valley Community
College *A*
Monroe Community College *A*
Niagara County Community
College *A*
Onondaga Community College *A*
Rochester Institute of Technology *B*
SUNY
College at Buffalo *B*
College of Agriculture and
Technology at Morrisville *A*
College of Technology at
Alfred *A, B*
College of Technology at Canton *A*
Farmingdale State College *A, B*
Institute of Technology at Utica/
Rome *B*
United States Military Academy *B*
Vaughn College of Aeronautics and
Technology *A, B*

North Carolina

Cape Fear Community College *C, A*
Catawba Valley Community
College *A*
Central Carolina Community
College *C, A*
Central Piedmont Community
College *A*
Craven Community College *C, A*
Edgecombe Community College *C*
Forsyth Technical Community
College *C, A*
Guilford Technical Community
College *C, A*
Isothermal Community College *A*
Lenoir Community College *C, A*
University of North Carolina
Charlotte *B*
Wayne Community College *C, A*
Wilson Community College *C, A*

Ohio

Bowling Green State University *B*
Central Ohio Technical College *A*
Cincinnati State Technical and
Community College *C, A*
Clark State Community College *A*
Columbus State Community
College *A*
Eastern Gateway Community
College *A*
Edison State Community College *C, A*
James A. Rhodes State College *C, A*
Kent State University
Trumbull *A*
Tuscarawas *A*
Lakeland Community College *C, A*
Lorain County Community College *C*
Marion Technical College *A*
Miami University
Hamilton *A, B*
Oxford *A*

North Central State College *A*
Sinclair Community College *A*
University of Akron *A, B*
University of Dayton *B*
University of Toledo *B*
Youngstown State University *A, B*

Oklahoma

Oklahoma State University *B*
Oklahoma State University
Institute of Technology:
Okmulgee *A*
Western Oklahoma State College *A*

Oregon

Mt. Hood Community College *C, A*
Oregon Institute of Technology *B*
Portland Community College *C, A*

Pennsylvania

Delaware County Community
College *C, A*
Harrisburg Area Community
College *C, A*
Lehigh Carbon Community College *A*
Montgomery County Community
College *A*
Penn State
DuBois *A*
Erie, The Behrend College *A, B*
York *A*
Pennsylvania College of
Technology *B*
Pennsylvania Institute of
Technology *A*
Point Park University *A, B*
Thaddeus Stevens College of
Technology *A*
University of Pittsburgh
Johnstown *B*
Westmoreland County Community
College *A*

Puerto Rico

Turabo University *A*

Rhode Island

New England Institute of
Technology *A, B*

South Carolina

Greenville Technical College *A*
Piedmont Technical College *C, A*
South Carolina State University *B*
Spartanburg Community College *A*
Trident Technical College *C*
York Technical College *A*

South Dakota

Southeast Technical Institute *A*

Tennessee

Chattanooga State Community
College *A*
Pellissippi State Community
College *A*
Southwest Tennessee Community
College *A*

Texas

LeTourneau University *B*
Texas A&M University
Corpus Christi *B*
Galveston *B*
Texas State Technical College
Waco *C, A*
Texas Tech University *B*
University of Houston *B*
University of North Texas *B*
University of Texas
Brownsville *B*

Utah

Salt Lake Community College *A*
Weber State University *A, B*

Virginia

Virginia State University *B*

Washington

Bates Technical College *C, A*
Bellingham Technical College *A*
Central Washington University *B*
Eastern Washington University *B*
Shoreline Community College *A*
South Seattle Community College *A*

West Virginia

Bluefield State College *A, B*
Bridgemont Community and
Technical College *A*
Fairmont State University *A, B*
West Virginia University Institute of
Technology *B*

Wisconsin

Gateway Technical College *A*
Milwaukee School of Engineering *B*
Wisconsin Indianhead Technical
College *A*

Mechanics/repairers, general

Alabama

Lawson State Community College *C*
Virginia College
Huntsville *C*

Arkansas

Pulaski Technical College *C*
University of Arkansas
Community College at
Batesville *C, A*

California

Allan Hancock College *C, A*
Cerritos College *A*
College of the Redwoods *C*
Columbia College *C*
Contra Costa College *C, A*
Fresno City College *C, A*
Imperial Valley College *C, A*
Long Beach City College *C, A*
Modesto Junior College *C, A*
Riverside City College *C, A*
San Jose City College *C*
Yuba College *C, A*

Colorado

Colorado Northwestern Community
College *C*
Colorado School of Trades *A*
Lincoln College of Technology
Denver *C, A*
Otero Junior College *C*
Westwood College
Denver North *A*

Connecticut

Gateway Community College *A*

Florida

Florida Career College
Miami *C, A*
Florida State College at
Jacksonville *C*
Seminole State College of Florida *C*

Georgia

Columbus Technical College *C*
Southwest Georgia Technical
College *C*
West Georgia Technical College *A*

Hawaii

University of Hawaii
Honolulu Community College *C, A*

Idaho

College of Western Idaho *A*
Idaho State University *A, B*
Lewis-Clark State College *C, A, B*
North Idaho College *C*

Illinois

Richland Community College *A*
Southwestern Illinois College *C, A*

Indiana

Ivy Tech Community College
Bloomington *C, A*
Central Indiana *C, A*
Northwest *C, A*
Richmond *C, A*

Iowa

Iowa Western Community College *A*
Southeastern Community College *A*

Kansas

Butler Community College *C, A*
Washburn University *A*

Kentucky

Maysville Community and Technical
College *C*

Louisiana

Baton Rouge School of Computers *A*
Nunez Community College *C*

Maine

Washington County Community
College *C, A*

Massachusetts

Benjamin Franklin Institute of
Technology *A*

Michigan

Glen Oaks Community College *C*
Lansing Community College *C*
Macomb Community College *C*
Muskegon Community College *C, A*
Northwestern Michigan College *C, A*

Minnesota

Hennepin Technical College *C, A*
Mesabi Range Community and
Technical College *A*

Mississippi

Northwest Mississippi Community
College *C*

Missouri

North Central Missouri College *A*
State Fair Community College *A*

Nebraska

Mid-Plains Community College *C, A*

New York

Sullivan County Community
College *A*

North Carolina

Alamance Community College *C*
Forsyth Technical Community
College *C*
Rockingham Community College *C*
Sandhills Community College *C*

Ohio

Ohio Technical College *C, A*
University of Cincinnati *C*

Oklahoma

Oklahoma City Community
College *A*

Oregon

Central Oregon Community
College *C*
Linn-Benton Community College *C*
Rogue Community College *A*
Treasure Valley Community
College *C*

Pennsylvania

Johnson College *A*
Lincoln Technical Institute
Philadelphia *C, A*
Penn Commercial Business and
Technical School *A*

South Carolina

Central Carolina Technical College *C*
Tri-County Technical College *C*
Williamsburg Technical College *C, A*
York Technical College *A*

South Dakota

Lake Area Technical Institute *A*
Southeast Technical Institute *A*

Tennessee

Chattanooga State Community
College *C*
Lincoln College of Technology
Nashville *C, A*
Northeast State Community
College *C, A*

Texas

Central Texas College *C, A*
Cisco College *C, A*
Laredo Community College *C*
Western Technical College *C, A*

Utah

Snow College *C, A*
Utah Valley University *A*

Virginia

Virginia Highlands Community
College *C*

Washington

Walla Walla Community College *C, A*

West Virginia

West Virginia University at
Parkersburg *A*

Wisconsin

Nicolet Area Technical College *C*

Wyoming

Laramie County Community
College *C*

Mechatronics/robotics/ automation engineering

Kansas

Cowley County Community
College *A*

Maryland

Johns Hopkins University *M*

Michigan

Lawrence Technological University *B*
Oakland Community College *C*
Oakland University *M*
University of Detroit Mercy *B*
University of Michigan *M*

New York

SUNY
University at Stony Brook *M*

North Carolina

Central Piedmont Community
College *A*

Pennsylvania

California University of
Pennsylvania *B*
Carnegie Mellon University *M, D*
Harrisburg Area Community
College *C, A*

Utah

Utah Valley University *A*

West Virginia

West Virginia Northern Community
College *A*

Media studies

Alabama

Auburn University *B, M*
Oakwood University *B*
Talladega College *B*
University of Alabama *D*
University of North Alabama *B*

Arizona

Arizona State University *M*

Arkansas

Ouachita Baptist University *B*
University of Arkansas
Little Rock *C*
University of the Ozarks *B*

California

Academy of Art University *B, M*
American Jewish University *B*
California State University
Fresno *B, M*
Claremont McKenna College *B*
College of Marin *A*
College of the Desert *A*
College of the Siskiyous *C, A*
Foothill College *C, A*
John Paul the Great Catholic
University *B*
Marymount California University *B*
Master's College *B*
Orange Coast College *A*
Point Loma Nazarene University *B*
Pomona College *B*
Rio Hondo College *C, A*
San Diego State University *B, M*
San Joaquin Delta College *A*
Scripps College *B*
University of California
Berkeley *B*
University of San Francisco *B*
Woodbury University *B*
Yuba College *C, A*

Colorado

Adams State University *B*
Colorado Mesa University *B*
Colorado State University
Pueblo *B*
Johnson & Wales University
Denver *B*
University of Denver *B, M*

Connecticut

Albertus Magnus College *B*
Mitchell College *B*
Sacred Heart University *B*
Southern Connecticut State
University *B*
University of Bridgeport *B*

Western Connecticut State
University *B*

Delaware

Delaware State University *B*

District of Columbia

American University *B, M, D*

Florida

Bethune-Cookman University *B*
Flagler College *B*
Florida Atlantic University *M*
Florida Gulf Coast University *B*
Florida International University *B, M*
Florida State University *D*
Johnson & Wales University
North Miami *B*
Lynn University *B, M*
Saint Thomas University *B*
University of Central Florida *M*
University of Florida *M, D*
University of Miami *B*
University of North Florida *B*
University of West Florida *B, M*

Georgia

Abraham Baldwin Agricultural
College *A*
Albany State University *B*
Brenau University *B*
Kennesaw State University *M*
Mercer University *B*
Middle Georgia State College *A*
Piedmont College *B*
Savannah State University *B*
University of Georgia *M, D*
Valdosta State University *B, M*

Hawaii

Chaminade University of Honolulu *B*
Hawaii Pacific University *M*

Idaho

Boise State University *B*
Idaho State University *B*
Northwest Nazarene University *B*

Illinois

DePaul University *B, M*
Eureka College *B*
Greenville College *B*
Illinois State University *B*
Lewis University *B*
Olivet Nazarene University *B*
Principia College *B*
Roosevelt University *B*
Sauk Valley Community College *A*
Southern Illinois University
Carbondale *M, D*
Southern Illinois University
Edwardsville *B, M*
University of Illinois
Urbana-Champaign *B, D*
University of St. Francis *B*

Indiana

Ancilla College *A*
Anderson University *B*
Calumet College of St. Joseph *C, A, B*
DePauw University *B*
Indiana University
Bloomington *D*
South Bend *B*
Indiana Wesleyan University *B*
Manchester University *B*
Saint Joseph's College *B*
Taylor University *B*
University of Southern Indiana *B*

Iowa

Briar Cliff University *B*
Buena Vista University *B*
Dordt College *B*

Drake University *B*
Grand View University *B*
Iowa Western Community College *A*
Loras College *B*
Maharishi University of
Management *B*
Morningside College *B*
St. Ambrose University *B*
University of Iowa *B, D*

Kansas

Baker University *B*
Benedictine College *B*
Bethel College *B*
Central Christian College of Kansas *B*
Colby Community College *A*
Cowley County Community
College *A*
MidAmerica Nazarene University *B*
Newman University *B*
University of Kansas *D*
Washburn University *B*

Kentucky

Berea College *B*
Georgetown College *B*
Spalding University *B*
Union College *B*
Western Kentucky University *B*

Louisiana

Centenary College of Louisiana *B*
Grambling State University *B, M*
Louisiana College *B*
Louisiana State University
Eunice *A*
Shreveport *B*
Louisiana State University and
Agricultural and Mechanical
College *B, M, D*
McNeese State University *B*
Nicholls State University *B*
Southern University and Agricultural
and Mechanical College *B*
Tulane University *A, B*
University of Louisiana at Lafayette *B*
University of Louisiana at Monroe *B*
Xavier University of Louisiana *B*

Maine

University of Maine *B*
University of Southern Maine *B*

Maryland

Goucher College *B*
Harford Community College *C, A*
Notre Dame of Maryland
University *B, M*
Towson University *B*
University of Maryland
Baltimore County *B*

Massachusetts

American International College *B*
Anna Maria College *B*
Bentley University *B*
Boston University *B, M*
Cape Cod Community College *A*
Emerson College *B*
Endicott College *B*
Fisher College *B*
Lasell College *B*
Massachusetts Institute of
Technology *B, M*
Massasoit Community College *A*
Newbury College *B*
Pine Manor College *B*
Salem State University *B*
Springfield College *B*
Suffolk University *B*
Tufts University *B*
Western New England University *B*
Wheelock College *B*
Worcester State University *B*

Michigan

Albion College *B*
Alma College *B*
Calvin College *B*
Cornerstone University *B*
Kuyper College *B*
Michigan State University *D*
Michigan Technological University *C*
Olivet College *B*
University of Michigan
   Flint *B*

Minnesota

Augsburg College *B*
Bemidji State University *B*
Bethel University *B*
Concordia University St. Paul *B*
Macalester College *B*
Minnesota State University
   Mankato *B*
Minnesota West Community and
   Technical College *A*
North Central University *A, B*
Ridgewater College *A*
Rochester Community and Technical
   College *A*
Saint Cloud State University *B, M*
University of Minnesota
   Twin Cities *M, D*
Winona State University *B*

Mississippi

Alcorn State University *B*
Jackson State University *B, M*
Mississippi College *B*
Tougaloo College *B*

Missouri

Culver-Stockton College *B*
Lindenwood University *B*
Maryville University of Saint Louis *B*
Missouri Southern State University *B*
Missouri State University *D*
Missouri Valley College *B*
University of Missouri
   St. Louis *B*
Webster University *B, M*
Westminster College *B*

Montana

Montana State University
   Billings *B*

Nebraska

Grace University *B*
Hastings College *B*
Wayne State College *B*

New Hampshire

Colby-Sawyer College *B*
Franklin Pierce University *B*
Saint Anselm College *B*

New Jersey

Essex County College *A*
Union County College *A*
William Paterson University of New
   Jersey *M*

New Mexico

New Mexico Highlands
   University *B, M*
University of New Mexico *B*

New York

Adelphi University *B*
City University of New York
   Brooklyn College *M*
   Hunter College *B, M*
   Queens College *B*
College of New Rochelle *B, M*
College of Saint Rose *B, M*
Dominican College of Blauvelt *B*

Five Towns College *B*
Hobart and William Smith Colleges *B*
Hofstra University *B*
Iona College *B*
Ithaca College *B*
Medaille College *B*
Mercy College *B*
Mount Saint Mary College *B*
Nassau Community College *A*
New York University *B, M, D*
Pace University *B, M*
Pace University: Pleasantville/
   Briarcliff *B*
SUNY
   College at Brockport *B, M*
   College at Buffalo *B*
   College at Fredonia *B*
   College at Oneonta *B*
   College at Plattsburgh *B*
   College at Purchase *B*
   Farmingdale State College *B*
   University at Buffalo *C*
Saint Bonaventure University *B, M*
Syracuse University *M, D*
University of Rochester *B*
Vassar College *B*

North Carolina

Barton College *B*
Johnson C. Smith University *B*
Lenoir-Rhyne University *B*
Meredith College *B*
Methodist University *A, B*
Montreat College *B*
North Carolina Agricultural and
   Technical State University *B*
North Carolina Central University *B*
St. Andrews University *B*
Shaw University *B*
University of North Carolina
   Asheville *B*
   Chapel Hill *B, M, D*
   Greensboro *B*
   Pembroke *B*
Winston-Salem State University *B*

North Dakota

North Dakota State University *M*
University of Mary *B*

Ohio

Baldwin Wallace University *B*
Bowling Green State University *M, D*
Cedarville University *B*
Lakeland Community College *C*
Miami University
   Middletown *B*
   Oxford *B*
Tiffin University *B*
University of Cincinnati
   Blue Ash College *C*
University of Dayton *B*
University of Mount Union *B*
University of Rio Grande *B*
University of Toledo *B*
Washington State Community
   College *A*
Wilmington College *B*
Wright State University *B*

Oklahoma

East Central University *B*
Eastern Oklahoma State College *A*
Northwestern Oklahoma State
   University *B*
Oklahoma Christian University *B*
Oklahoma City University *B, M*
Oklahoma State University *M*
University of Oklahoma *D*

Oregon

Eastern Oregon University *B*
Linfield College *B*
University of Portland *B, M*

Pennsylvania

Allegheny College *B*
Arcadia University *B*
Bloomsburg University of
   Pennsylvania *B*
Carlow University *B*
Cedar Crest College *B*
Chestnut Hill College *B*
Clarion University of
   Pennsylvania *C, B, M*
Drexel University *D*
Edinboro University of
   Pennsylvania *B*
Harrisburg Area Community
   College *A*
Holy Family University *B*
King's College *B*
La Roche College *B*
La Salle University *B*
Lock Haven University of
   Pennsylvania *B*
Penn State
   University Park *D*
Point Park University *B*
Temple University *D*
University of Pittsburgh *B*
Villanova University *B*
Wilson College *A, B*
York College of Pennsylvania *A, B*

Puerto Rico

University of Puerto Rico
   Rio Piedras *B, M*

Rhode Island

Bryant University *B*
Johnson & Wales University
   Providence *B*
Roger Williams University *B*

South Carolina

Aiken Technical College *C*
Benedict College *B*
Claflin University *B*
Columbia International University *B*
Francis Marion University *B*
Morris College *B*
North Greenville University *B*
South Carolina State University *B*
University of South Carolina
   Columbia *B, M, D*
Voorhees College *B*
Winthrop University *B*

South Dakota

Black Hills State University *B*
South Dakota State University *M*
University of South Dakota *B, M*

Tennessee

Austin Peay State University *B, M*
Belmont University *B*
East Tennessee State University *B*
Freed-Hardeman University *B*
Lipscomb University *B*
Middle Tennessee State
   University *B, M*
Southern Adventist University *B*
Trevecca Nazarene University *B*
University of Memphis *B, M, D*
University of Tennessee
   Knoxville *M, D*

Texas

Austin College *B*
East Texas Baptist University *B*
Hardin-Simmons University *B*
Houston Baptist University *B*
Howard Payne University *B*
Lubbock Christian University *B*
Midwestern State University *B*
Northwest Vista College *A*
Odessa College *A*
St. Edward's University *B*

St. Philip's College *A*
Sam Houston State University *B*
Stephen F. Austin State
   University *B, M*
Texas A&M University
   Texarkana *B*
Texas State University *B, M*
Texas Tech University *B, M, D*
University of Houston *B, M*
University of Texas
   Pan American *B*
   Tyler *B*
University of the Incarnate Word *B*
Wayland Baptist University *B*

Utah

Brigham Young University *M*
Dixie State College *B*
University of Utah *B*
Utah State University *M*

Vermont

Castleton State College *B*
Champlain College *B*
Community College of Vermont *A*
Green Mountain College *B*
Lyndon State College *B*
Norwich University *B*
Saint Michael's College *B*

Virginia

Bridgewater College *B*
Emory & Henry College *B, M*
Ferrum College *B*
Hampton University *B*
Norfolk State University *B, M*
Virginia Commonwealth
   University *B, M*
Virginia State University *B*
Virginia Union University *B*

Washington

Evergreen State College *B*
Northwest University *B*
Seattle University *B*
Trinity Lutheran College *B*
University of Washington Bothell *B*
Walla Walla University *B*
Washington State University *B, M*

West Virginia

University of Charleston *B*
West Virginia University *B, M, D*
Wheeling Jesuit University *B*

Wisconsin

Concordia University Wisconsin *B*
Marquette University *B*
St. Norbert College *B*
University of Wisconsin
   Eau Claire *B*
   Madison *B*
   Milwaukee *M*
   Superior *B*

Wyoming

Casper College *A*
Laramie County Community
   College *A*

Medical administrative assistant

Alabama

Faulkner State Community College *A*
Lawson State Community
   College *C, A*

Alaska

University of Alaska
   Fairbanks *C*

Arizona

Central Arizona College *C, A*
Coconino County Community
   College *A*
GateWay Community College *C*
Yavapai College *C, A*

Arkansas

Arkansas Tech University *C*
National Park Community College *A*

California

Antelope Valley College *C, A*
Butte College *C, A*
Carrington College California
   San Leandro *C, A*
Chaffey College *C*
City College of San Francisco *A*
College of the Redwoods *C*
Columbia College *C*
De Anza College *C*
East Los Angeles College *C, A*
Empire College *C, A*
Fresno City College *C, A*
Gavilan College *C*
Glendale Community College *C, A*
Heald College
   Concord *C, A*
Humphreys College *C, A, B*
Los Angeles City College *C, A*
Los Angeles Harbor College *C, A*
MTI College *C*
Merced College *C, A*
MiraCosta College *C, A*
Mount San Antonio College *C, A*
Palomar College *C, A*
Pasadena City College *C, A*
Sacramento City College *C, A*
San Joaquin Delta College *C*
San Joaquin Valley College *A*
Santa Monica College *C, A*
Santa Rosa Junior College *C*
Shasta College *C*
Skyline College *C, A*
Solano Community College *C, A*
Ventura College *C, A*

Colorado

Aims Community College *A*
Everest College
   Colorado Springs *C*
   Denver *C*
IBMC College
   Fort Collins *C, A*
National American University
   Denver *A*
Otero Junior College *A*

Connecticut

Gateway Community College *A*
Middlesex Community College *A*
Norwalk Community College *C*
Quinebaug Valley Community
   College *C*
Tunxis Community College *C, A*

Florida

Broward College *C*
Brown Mackie College
   Miami *A*
Everest University
   Lakeland *C*
   Largo *C*
   North Orlando *C*
Florida National University *C*
Florida State College at
   Jacksonville *C, A*
Florida Technical College
   Orlando *A*
Indian River State College *C*
Key College *A*
Miami Dade College *A*
Palm Beach State College *C*
Pasco-Hernando State College *C*

Rasmussen College
   Fort Myers *A*
   New Port Richey *A*
   Ocala *A*
   Pasco/Land O'Lakes *A*
   Tampa/Brandon *A*
Seminole State College of Florida *A*
South Florida State College *C*
Tallahassee Community College *C*

Georgia

Augusta Technical College *C*
Chattahoochee Technical College *C*
Gwinnett College *C, A*
Gwinnett Technical College *C*

Hawaii

Heald College
   Honolulu *A*

Idaho

Broadview University
   Boise *A*
North Idaho College *A*

Illinois

Black Hawk College *C*
City Colleges of Chicago
   Harry S. Truman College *C*
Danville Area Community College *A*
Harper College *C, A*
Illinois Central College *C*
Illinois Eastern Community Colleges
   Olney Central College *C, A*
John Wood Community College *A*
Joliet Junior College *A*
Kaskaskia College *C*
Lincoln Land Community College *C*
Moraine Valley Community College *C*
Rasmussen College
   Aurora *C, A*
   Mokena/Tinley Park *A*
   Rockford *A*
   Romeoville/Joliet *A*
Shawnee Community College *A*
Waubonsee Community College *C*

Indiana

Brown Mackie College
   Michigan City *C, A*
International Business College *C, A*

Iowa

Des Moines Area Community
   College *C, A*
Dordt College *A*
Ellsworth Community College *A*
Hawkeye Community College *C, A*
Iowa Lakes Community College *C*
Southeastern Community College *C*
Western Iowa Tech Community
   College *C, A*

Kansas

Bryan University
   Topeka *A*
Highland Community College *A*
Labette Community College *A*
Pratt Community College *C, A*
Seward County Community
   College *C, A*

Kentucky

Ashland Community and Technical
   College *A*
Bluegrass Community and Technical
   College *C, A*
Daymar College
   Bowling Green *C, A*
   Owensboro *C, A*
Elizabethtown Community and
   Technical College *C, A*
Gateway Community and Technical
   College *C, A*

Jefferson Community and Technical
   College *C*
Madisonville Community
   College *C, A*
Maysville Community and Technical
   College *C, A*
National College
   Danville *A*
   Florence *A*
   Lexington *A*
   Louisville *A*
   Pikeville *A*
   Richmond *A*
Owensboro Community and
   Technical College *C, A*
Somerset Community College *C, A*
Spencerian College *C, A*

Louisiana

ITI Technical College *A*

Maine

Beal College *A*
Kaplan University
   South Portland *A*
Northern Maine Community
   College *A*
Washington County Community
   College *C*

Maryland

Allegany College of Maryland *A*
Anne Arundel Community
   College *C, A*
Baltimore City Community College *A*
College of Southern Maryland *C*
Community College of Baltimore
   County *C, A*
Hagerstown Community College *A*
Kaplan University
   Hagerstown *C, A*
Prince George's Community
   College *C, A*

Massachusetts

Bristol Community College *A*
Bunker Hill Community College *C, A*
Cape Cod Community College *C, A*
Holyoke Community College *C*
Mount Wachusett Community
   College *C*
North Shore Community
   College *C, A*
Northern Essex Community
   College *A*
Quinsigamond Community
   College *C, A*
Roxbury Community College *A*
Springfield Technical Community
   College *A*

Michigan

Baker College
   Auburn Hills *C, A*
   Cadillac *A*
   Clinton Township *A*
   Flint *C, A*
   Jackson *C, A*
   Muskegon *C, A*
   Owosso *A*
   Port Huron *C, A*
Delta College *C, A*
Glen Oaks Community College *C*
Kalamazoo Valley Community
   College *C, A*
Kellogg Community College *C, A*
Kirtland Community College *C, A*
Macomb Community College *C, A*
Mid Michigan Community College *A*
Monroe County Community
   College *C, A*
Montcalm Community College *C, A*
Muskegon Community College *C, A*

St. Clair County Community
   College *A*

Minnesota

Alexandria Technical and Community
   College *A*
Anoka Technical College *A*
Central Lakes College *C, A*
Century College *A*
Dakota County Technical
   College *C, A*
Globe University
   Moorhead *C, A*
   Woodbury *C, A*
Hennepin Technical College *C, A*
Hibbing Community College *A*
Lake Superior College *A*
Minnesota School of Business
   Blaine *C, A*
   Brooklyn Center *C, A*
   Elk River *C, A*
   Lakeville *C*
   Plymouth *C, A*
   Richfield *C, A*
   Rochester *C, A*
   St. Cloud *C, A*
   Shakopee *A*
Minnesota State College - Southeast
   Technical *C, A*
Minnesota State Community and
   Technical College *C, A*
Minnesota West Community and
   Technical College *A*
National American University
   Bloomington *A*
Northland Community & Technical
   College *A*
Northwest Technical College *A*
Rasmussen College
   Blaine *A*
   Bloomington *A*
   Brooklyn Park *A*
   Eagan *A*
   Lake Elmo/Woodbury *A*
   Mankato *A*
   Moorhead *A*
   St. Cloud *A*
Ridgewater College *C, A*
Riverland Community College *C, A*
Rochester Community and Technical
   College *A*

Mississippi

Meridian Community College *A*
Mississippi Gulf Coast Community
   College *A*
Northwest Mississippi Community
   College *A*
Pearl River Community College *A*

Missouri

Bolivar Technical College *C, A*
Jefferson College *A*
Metropolitan Community College -
   Kansas City *C*
North Central Missouri College *C, A*
State Fair Community College *C*
Texas County Technical College *C, A*

Montana

Flathead Valley Community
   College *A*
Miles Community College *A*
Montana State University
   Billings *C*
   Great Falls College *C*
University of Montana *A*

Nebraska

Northeast Community College *C, A*
Vatterott College
   Spring Valley *C, A*

Nevada

Career College of Northern Nevada *A*
Truckee Meadows Community
College *A*

New Hampshire

Lakes Region Community College *C*
Manchester Community College *C*
River Valley Community College *C*

New Jersey

Bergen Community College *C*
Essex County College *A*
Gloucester County College *C, A*
Mercer County Community
College *C*

New Mexico

Dona Ana Community College of
New Mexico State University *A*
New Mexico State University
Carlsbad *C*
Western New Mexico University *C, A*

New York

Bryant & Stratton College
Henrietta *A*
Syracuse *A*
City University of New York
Hostos Community College *A*
Elmira Business Institute *C, A*
Fulton-Montgomery Community
College *C*
Genesee Community College *C, A*
Globe Institute of Technology *C*
Herkimer County Community
College *C*
Hudson Valley Community College *A*
Jamestown Business College *C, A*
Jefferson Community College *A*
Nassau Community College *C, A*
New York Career Institute *A*
SUNY
College of Agriculture and
Technology at Morrisville *A*
Sanford-Brown Institute
Melville *A*
Trocaire College *C*
Utica School of Commerce *C, A*

North Carolina

Alamance Community College *C, A*
Asheville-Buncombe Technical
Community College *C*
Beaufort County Community
College *A*
Blue Ridge Community College *C*
Caldwell Community College and
Technical Institute *C, A*
Central Carolina Community
College *A*
College of the Albemarle *A*
Durham Technical Community
College *A*
Gaston College *A*
Halifax Community College *C, A*
Martin Community College *C, A*
Mayland Community College *C, A*
Nash Community College *A*
Piedmont Community College *A*
Pitt Community College *C, A*
Rockingham Community College *A*
Wake Technical Community
College *C, A*

North Dakota

Bismarck State College *A*
Dakota College at Bottineau *A*
Fort Berthold Community College *A*
Rasmussen College
Bismarck *A*
Fargo *A*

Ohio

Bowling Green State University:
Firelands College *C*
Bryant & Stratton College
Parma *A*
Clark State Community College *A*
Davis College *A*
Daymar College
Chillicothe *A*
ETI Technical College of Niles *A*
Edison State Community College *C, A*
Gallipolis Career College *A*
Lincoln College of Technology
Dayton *A*
Lorain County Community College *A*
Miami-Jacobs Career College
Dayton *A*
Northwest State Community
College *A*
Ohio Business College
Sandusky *C, A*
Sheffield *C, A*
Ohio University
Chillicothe Campus *A*
Ohio Valley College of Technology *A*
Owens Community College
Toledo *C, A*
Sinclair Community College *C*
Stautzenberger College *C, A*
Terra State Community College *C, A*
University of Akron: Wayne
College *A*
University of Cincinnati
Blue Ash College *C, A*
University of Northwestern Ohio *A*
University of Rio Grande *A*

Oklahoma

Eastern Oklahoma State College *A*
Northeastern Oklahoma Agricultural
and Mechanical College *C, A*
Tulsa Community College *C, A*
Western Oklahoma State College *A*

Oregon

Blue Mountain Community
College *C, A*
Chemeketa Community College *A*
Clackamas Community College *C*
Everest College
Portland *C*
Heald College
Portland *C, A*
Lane Community College *C*
Linn-Benton Community College *A*
Mt. Hood Community College *C, A*
Portland Community College *C*
Southwestern Oregon Community
College *C*
Treasure Valley Community
College *A*
Umpqua Community College *A*

Pennsylvania

Berks Technical Institute *A*
Cambria-Rowe Business College *A*
Cambria-Rowe Business College:
Indiana *A*
Commonwealth Technical Institute *A*
Community College of Beaver
County *A*
Consolidated School of Business
Lancaster *A*
York *A*
Douglas Education Center *A*
DuBois Business College *A*
DuBois Business College
Huntingdon *A*
Erie Business Center *C, A*
Everest Institute: Pittsburgh *C, A*
Kaplan Career Institute
Pittsburgh *A*
Keystone Technical Institute *A*
Lackawanna College *A*

Lincoln Technical Institute
Northeast Philadelphia *C, A*
Luzerne County Community
College *C*
McCann School of Business and
Technology
Hazleton *A*
Northampton Community
College *C, A*
Pace Institute *C, A*
Penn Commercial Business and
Technical School *A*
Pennsylvania Institute of Health and
Technology *A*
Reading Area Community
College *C, A*
South Hills School of Business &
Technology *A*
Westmoreland County Community
College *A*
Yorktowne Business Institute *A*

Puerto Rico

Humacao Community College *C, A*
ICPR Junior College *C, A*
National University College
Arecibo *A*
Bayamon *A*
Rio Grande *A*
Turabo University *C*
Universal Technology College of
Puerto Rico *C*
Universidad del Este *A*

Rhode Island

Community College of Rhode
Island *A*

South Carolina

Aiken Technical College *C*
Florence-Darlington Technical
College *C*
Forrest Junior College *A*
Greenville Technical College *C*
Orangeburg-Calhoun Technical
College *C*
Spartanburg Community College *C*
Technical College of the
Lowcountry *C*
Tri-County Technical College *C*
Trident Technical College *C*
Williamsburg Technical College *C*
York Technical College *C*

South Dakota

Globe University
Sioux Falls *C, A*
Kilian Community College *A*
Lake Area Technical Institute *C*

Tennessee

Nashville State Community College *A*
National College of Business and
Technology
Nashville *A*
West Tennessee Business
College *C, A*

Texas

Blinn College *C*
Brookhaven College *C*
Central Texas College *C*
Coastal Bend College *C, A*
Del Mar College *C, A*
El Centro College *C*
El Paso Community College *C*
Everest College
Arlington *C*
Dallas *C*
Fort Worth *C*
Frank Phillips College *C, A*
Galveston College *C, A*
Grayson College *C*
Kilgore College *C*

Lamar State College at Orange *C, A*
Lamar State College at Port
Arthur *C, A*
Laredo Community College *A*
Lone Star College System *C, A*
McLennan Community College *C, A*
Northeast Texas Community
College *C, A*
Odessa College *C, A*
Remington College
Houston Southeast *C*
St. Philip's College *A*
San Jacinto College *C, A*
South Plains College *A*
Tyler Junior College *C, A*
Vernon College *C*

Utah

Broadview University
Layton *C, A*
Orem *C, A*
LDS Business College *A*
Provo College *A*
Salt Lake Community College *C*

Virginia

Bryant & Stratton College
Richmond *A*
Danville Community College *A*
Mountain Empire Community
College *A*
New River Community College *C, A*
Southwest Virginia Community
College *A*

Washington

Bates Technical College *C*
Bellingham Technical College *C*
Centralia College *C*
Clark College *A*
Columbia Basin College *C*
Edmonds Community College *C*
Everett Community College *C*
Green River Community College *A*
Lower Columbia College *A*
Peninsula College *C, A*
Pierce College *C, A*
Renton Technical College *C*
Shoreline Community College *C*
South Puget Sound Community
College *C, A*
Spokane Community College *C, A*
Tacoma Community College *C, A*
Walla Walla Community College *C, A*
Wenatchee Valley College *C*
Whatcom Community College *C*
Yakima Valley Community
College *C, A*

West Virginia

Bridgemont Community and
Technical College *A*
Valley College *C*
West Virginia Junior College
Bridgeport *A*
Charleston *C, A*

Wisconsin

Blackhawk Technical College *A*
Bryant & Stratton College
Milwaukee *A*
Globe University
Appleton *C, A*
Eau Claire *C, A*
Green Bay *C, A*
La Crosse *C, A*
Madison East *C, A*
Middleton *C, A*
Wausau *C, A*
Madison Area Technical College *A*
Milwaukee Area Technical College *A*
Moraine Park Technical College *C, A*
Northcentral Technical College *C*

Northeast Wisconsin Technical
College *A*
Rasmussen College
Appleton *A*
Green Bay *A*
Wausau *A*

Wyoming

Western Wyoming Community
College *A*

Medical anthropology

Florida

University of Miami *B*

Nebraska

Creighton University *B, M*

Medical claims examiner

Alabama

Virginia College
Huntsville *A*

Florida

Virginia College
Pensacola *A*

Pennsylvania

Career Training Academy:
Monroeville *C*

Puerto Rico

Inter American University of Puerto
Rico
Ponce Campus *C*
Universidad Metropolitana *C*

Medical/clinical assistant

Alabama

Central Alabama Community
College *A*
Chattahoochee Valley Community
College *C*
Community College of the Air
Force *A*
Enterprise State Community
College *A*
George C. Wallace Community
College at Dothan *C, A*
Northeast Alabama Community
College *C, A*
Northwest-Shoals Community
College *C, A*
Remington College
Mobile *C*
Virginia College
Birmingham *A*
Huntsville *C, A*
Mobile *C, A*
Montgomery *C*
Wallace State Community College at
Hanceville *A*

Alaska

Charter College *C*
University of Alaska
Anchorage *C*
Fairbanks *C, A*

Arizona

Brookline College
Phoenix *C*
Tempe *C*
Tucson *C*
Brown Mackie College
Tucson *A*

Carrington College
Mesa *C*
Phoenix *C*
Tucson *C*
Central Arizona College *C, A*
Cochise College *C*
Eastern Arizona College *C*
Northland Pioneer College *C, A*
Phoenix College *A*

Arkansas

Arkansas Tech University *A*
Bryan University
Rogers *C, A*
Cossatot Community College of the
University of Arkansas *A*
East Arkansas Community College *A*
National Park Community
College *C, A*
Remington College
Little Rock *C*

California

Allan Hancock College *C, A*
Antelope Valley College *C, A*
Butte College *A*
Cabrillo College *C, A*
Canada College *C, A*
Carrington College California
Antioch *C, A*
Citrus Heights *C, A*
Pleasant Hill *A*
Sacramento *C, A*
San Jose *A*
San Leandro *C*
Stockton *C, A*
Cerritos College *C, A*
Chabot College *C, A*
Citrus College *C, A*
City College of San Francisco *C, A*
College of Marin *C, A*
College of the Redwoods *C*
Concorde Career College
Garden Grove *C*
San Bernardino *C*
Cosumnes River College *C, A*
Cypress College *A*
De Anza College *C, A*
East Los Angeles College *C, A*
Empire College *C*
Fresno City College *C, A*
Glendale Community College *A*
Heald College
Concord *C, A*
Fresno *C, A*
Hayward *A*
Rancho Cordova *C, A*
Roseville *A*
Salinas *C, A*
San Francisco *C, A*
San Jose *A*
Stockton *C, A*
Imperial Valley College *C*
Institute of Technology: Clovis *C*
Kaplan College
Palm Springs *C*
Sacramento *C*
Salida *C*
La Sierra University *C*
Lake Tahoe Community College *C, A*
Long Beach City College *C, A*
MTI College *C*
Modesto Junior College *A*
Monterey Peninsula College *C, A*
Moreno Valley College *C, A*
Ohlone College *C, A*
Orange Coast College *C, A*
Pasadena City College *C, A*
Platt College
Ontario *A*
Saddleback College *C, A*
San Diego Mesa College *C, A*
San Joaquin Valley College *C, A*
Santa Ana College *C, A*

Santa Barbara Business College
Bakersfield *A*
Rancho Mirage *C, A*
Santa Maria *C, A*
Ventura *A*
Santa Monica College *C, A*
Santa Rosa Junior College *C*
Santiago Canyon College *A*
Shasta College *C*
Victor Valley College *C, A*
West Valley College *C, A*
Westwood College
Anaheim *C*
Inland Empire *C*
Los Angeles *C*
South Bay *C*
WyoTech: Long Beach *C*

Colorado

Anthem College
Aurora *C, A*
CollegeAmerica
Fort Collins *A*
Colorado Mesa University *C*
Concorde Career College
Aurora *A*
Everest College
Aurora *C*
Colorado Springs *C*
Denver *A*
IBMC College
Fort Collins *C, A*
IntelliTec College: Grand Junction *A*
Morgan Community College *C*
National American University
Denver *A*
Pueblo Community College *C*
Westwood College
Denver North *A*

Connecticut

Capital Community College *C, A*
Goodwin College *C, A*
Northwestern Connecticut
Community College *A*
Norwalk Community College *C*
Quinebaug Valley Community
College *A*
St. Vincent's College *C, A*

Delaware

Delaware Technical Community
College
Jack F. Owens Campus *C, A*
Stanton/Wilmington Campus *C, A*
Terry Campus *C, A*

Florida

Anthem College
Orlando *C*
Broward College *C*
City College
Gainesville *C*
College of Business and Technology
Cutler Bay *C, A*
Daytona State College *C*
Eastern Florida State College *C*
Everest University
Brandon *A*
Lakeland *C, A*
Largo *C, A*
Melbourne *A*
North Orlando *C*
Orange Park *A*
Tampa *C, A*
Florida Career College
Miami *C*
Florida Gateway College *C*
Florida National University *C, A*
Florida State College at
Jacksonville *C*
Florida Technical College
Orlando *C, A*

Fortis College
Winter Park *A*
Herzing University
Winter Park *C, A*
Hodges University *A*
Indian River State College *C*
Jones College *A, B*
Keiser University *A*
Lincoln College of Technology
West Palm Beach *C*
Miami Dade College *C, A*
Palm Beach State College *C*
Rasmussen College
Fort Myers *C, A*
New Port Richey *C, A*
Ocala *C, A*
Pasco/Land O'Lakes *C, A*
Tampa/Brandon *C, A*
Remington College
Tampa *C*
Sanford-Brown Institute
Jacksonville *C*
Tampa *C*
Seminole State College of Florida *C*
Southeastern College
Greenacres *A*
Southwest Florida College *C, A*
Virginia College
Pensacola *C, A*

Georgia

Albany Technical College *C*
Athens Technical College *C*
Atlanta Technical College *C*
Augusta Technical College *C*
Central Georgia Technical
College *C, A*
Columbus Technical College *C*
Fort Valley State University *A, B*
Gwinnett College *C, A*
Middle Georgia State College *A*
North Georgia Technical College *C*
Savannah Technical College *C*
Southwest Georgia Technical
College *C, A*
West Georgia Technical College *C*

Hawaii

Heald College
Honolulu *A*
Remington College
Honolulu *A*
University of Hawaii
Kapiolani Community College *C, A*

Idaho

Broadview University
Boise *A*
Carrington College
Boise *C, A*
College of Southern Idaho *C*
Eastern Idaho Technical College *C, A*
Idaho State University *A, B*
North Idaho College *A*

Illinois

Black Hawk College *C*
City Colleges of Chicago
Harry S. Truman College *C*
Olive-Harvey College *C*
Wilbur Wright College *C*
College of DuPage *C*
Harper College *C*
Highland Community College *A*
Illinois Central College *C*
Kankakee Community College *C, A*
Midstate College *C, A, B*
Moraine Valley Community College *C*
Northwestern College *A*
Parkland College *C*
Rasmussen College
Aurora *C, A*
Mokena/Tinley Park *C, A*

Rockford *C, A*
Romeoville/Joliet *C, A*
Robert Morris University: Chicago *A*
South Suburban College of Cook
   County *C*
Southwestern Illinois College *C, A*
Triton College *C, A*
Waubonsee Community College *C*

Indiana

Brown Mackie College
   Fort Wayne *C, A*
   Merrillville *C, A*
   Michigan City *A*
   South Bend *A*
Fortis College
   Indianapolis *C*
Harrison College
   Indianapolis *A*
International Business College *C, A*
International Business College:
   Indianapolis *C, A*
Ivy Tech Community College
   Central Indiana *C, A*
   Columbus *C, A*
   East Central *C, A*
   Kokomo *C, A*
   Lafayette *C, A*
   North Central *C, A*
   Northeast *C, A*
   Northwest *C, A*
   Richmond *C, A*
   South Central *C, A*
   Southeast *C, A*
   Southwest *C, A*
   Wabash Valley *C, A*
Kaplan College
   Hammond *A*
National College
   Indianapolis *C, A*
   South Bend *A*
National College: Fort Wayne *A*

Iowa

Des Moines Area Community
   College *C*
Hamilton Technical College *C*
Iowa Central Community
   College *C, A*
Iowa Lakes Community College *C*
Kirkwood Community College *C, A*
Marshalltown Community College *C*
Mercy College of Health
   Sciences *C, A*
North Iowa Area Community
   College *C*
Southeastern Community College *A*
Western Iowa Tech Community
   College *C*

Kansas

Barton County Community College *A*
Bryan University
   Topeka *C, A*
Highland Community College *C*
Kansas City Kansas Community
   College *C*
Wichita Area Technical College *C, A*
Wright Career College
   Overland Park *C*
   Wichita *C, A*

Kentucky

Beckfield College *C*
Bluegrass Community and Technical
   College *C, A*
Brown Mackie College
   Hopkinsville *C, A*
Daymar College
   Bowling Green *C, A*
   Owensboro *C*
Eastern Kentucky University *A, B*
Gateway Community and Technical
   College *C, A*

Jefferson Community and Technical
   College *C*
Lincoln College of Technology
   Florence *C, A*
National College
   Danville *A*
   Florence *A*
   Lexington *A*
   Louisville *A*
   Pikeville *A*
   Richmond *A*
Owensboro Community and
   Technical College *C*
Somerset Community College *C, A*
Spencerian College *C*
Spencerian College: Lexington *C*
Sullivan University *A*
West Kentucky Community and
   Technical College *C*

Louisiana

Blue Cliff College
   Metairie *C*
   Shreveport *C, A*
Bossier Parish Community
   College *C, A*
Delta School of Business &
   Technology *C, A*
Herzing University
   Kenner *C, A*
ITI Technical College *C*
Remington College
   Baton Rouge *C*
   Lafayette *C*
Virginia College
   Baton Rouge *C, A*
   Shreveport *A*

Maine

Beal College *A*
Central Maine Community College *A*
Kaplan University
   South Portland *A*
Kennebec Valley Community
   College *A*
Southern Maine Community
   College *A*
Washington County Community
   College *C, A*
York County Community College *A*

Maryland

Allegany College of Maryland *C, A*
Anne Arundel Community
   College *C, A*
College of Southern Maryland *C*
Harford Community College *C, A*
Kaplan University
   Hagerstown *C, A*
TESST College of Technology
   Towson *C*

Massachusetts

Bay State College *C, A*
Bristol Community College *C*
Bunker Hill Community College *C*
Cape Cod Community College *C*
Holyoke Community College *C*
Massasoit Community College *C*
Middlesex Community College *C, A*
Mount Wachusett Community
   College *A*
North Shore Community College *C*
Northern Essex Community
   College *C*
Quinsigamond Community College *C*
Springfield Technical Community
   College *C, A*

Michigan

Alpena Community College *A*
Baker College
   Auburn Hills *A*
   Cadillac *A*

Clinton Township *A*
Flint *A*
Jackson *A*
Muskegon *C, A*
Owosso *A*
Port Huron *A*
Bay de Noc Community College *C*
Davenport University *A*
Delta College *A*
Glen Oaks Community College *C*
Gogebic Community College *C*
Henry Ford Community College *C*
Jackson College *C, A*
Kalamazoo Valley Community
   College *C*
Kirtland Community College *C, A*
Lake Michigan College *C*
Macomb Community College *C, A*
Mid Michigan Community College *A*
Montcalm Community College *C*
North Central Michigan College *C*
Oakland Community College *C, A*
Southwestern Michigan College *C, A*

Minnesota

Academy College *C*
Anoka Technical College *C, A*
Brown College
   Brooklyn Center *A*
   Mendota Heights *A*
Century College *C*
Dakota County Technical
   College *C, A*
Duluth Business University *C, A*
Globe University
   Moorhead *C, A*
   Woodbury *C, A*
Herzing University
   Minneapolis *A*
Lake Superior College *C*
Minneapolis Business College *C, A*
Minnesota School of Business
   Blaine *C, A*
   Brooklyn Center *C, A*
   Elk River *C, A*
   Lakeville *C, A*
   Plymouth *C, A*
   Richfield *C, A*
   Rochester *A*
   St. Cloud *C, A*
   Shakopee *C, A*
Minnesota West Community and
   Technical College *A*
National American University
   Bloomington *A*
   Roseville *A*
Northland Community & Technical
   College *C, A*
Rasmussen College
   Blaine *C, A*
   Bloomington *C, A*
   Brooklyn Park *C, A*
   Eagan *C, A*
   Lake Elmo/Woodbury *C, A*
   Mankato *C, A*
   Moorhead *C, A*
   St. Cloud *C, A*
Ridgewater College *C, A*
South Central College *A*

Mississippi

Hinds Community College *A*
Northeast Mississippi Community
   College *A*

Missouri

East Central College *C, A*
National American University
   Kansas City *A*

Montana

Flathead Valley Community
   College *A*
Montana State University *C*

Montana State University
   Billings *A*
   Great Falls College *A*
Montana Tech of the University of
   Montana *A*
University of Montana *A*

Nebraska

Central Community College *C, A*
Herzing University
   Omaha School of Massage Therapy
      and Healthcare *C*
Kaplan University
   Lincoln *A*
   Omaha *A*
Nebraska Methodist College of
   Nursing and Allied Health *C*
Southeast Community College *C*
Vatterott College
   Spring Valley *C, A*
Wright Career College
   Omaha *C*

Nevada

Career College of Northern
   Nevada *C, A*
Carrington College
   Las Vegas *C*
   Reno *C*
Everest College
   Las Vegas *A*

New Hampshire

Manchester Community College *C, A*
Mount Washington College *C, A*
River Valley Community College *C*
White Mountains Community
   College *C, A*

New Jersey

Bergen Community College *A*
Berkeley College *A*
Eastern International College *A*
Hudson County Community
   College *C, A*
Raritan Valley Community
   College *C, A*

New Mexico

Brookline College
   Albuquerque *A*
Carrington College
   Albuquerque *C*
Eastern New Mexico University:
   Roswell *C, A*
National American University
   Albuquerque *A*
Santa Fe Community College *C*

New York

ASA College *C, A*
Broome Community College *A*
Bryant & Stratton College
   Albany *A*
   Buffalo *A*
   Henrietta *A*
   Syracuse *A*
City University of New York
   Bronx Community College *A*
   Queensborough Community
      College *C*
College of Westchester *C, A*
Elmira Business Institute *C, A*
Everest Institute
   Rochester *A*
Globe Institute of Technology *C*
Mildred Elley
   Albany *C, A*
   New York City *A*
Mohawk Valley Community
   College *C, A*
Niagara County Community
   College *A*
Plaza College *A*

Sullivan County Community
College *A*
Trocaire College *A*
Wood Tobe-Coburn School *A*

North Carolina
Cabarrus College of Health
Sciences *C, A*
Carteret Community College *C*
Central Carolina Community
College *A*
Central Piedmont Community
College *C, A*
College of the Albemarle *A*
Craven Community College *C, A*
Davidson County Community
College *C, A*
Durham Technical Community
College *C*
Edgecombe Community College *A*
Forsyth Technical Community
College *A*
Gaston College *A*
Guilford Technical Community
College *A*
Haywood Community College *C, A*
James Sprunt Community College *A*
Johnston Community College *C, A*
King's College *C, A*
Lenoir Community College *A*
Martin Community College *C, A*
Miller-Motte College
Cary *A*
Fayetteville *A*
Wilmington *C, A*
Montgomery Community College *A*
Pamlico Community College *C*
Piedmont Community College *A*
Pitt Community College *A*
Richmond Community College *A*
South College *A*
South Piedmont Community
College *C, A*
Stanly Community College *C, A*
Surry Community College *A*
Tri-County Community College *A*
Vance-Granville Community
College *A*
Wake Technical Community
College *C, A*
Wayne Community College *A*
Western Piedmont Community
College *C, A*
Wilkes Community College *C, A*

North Dakota
Cankdeska Cikana Community
College *A*
Dakota College at Bottineau *C, A*
Rasmussen College
Bismarck *C, A*
Fargo *C, A*

Ohio
Akron Institute of Herzing
University *C, A*
Belmont College *A*
Bradford School *C, A*
Brown Mackie College
Akron *C, A*
Cincinnati *C, A*
Findlay *C, A*
Bryant & Stratton College
Parma *A*
Cincinnati State Technical and
Community College *C*
Clark State Community College *A*
Columbus State Community
College *C, A*
Cuyahoga Community College
Metropolitan *C, A*
Davis College *A*
ETI Technical College of Niles *C, A*

Eastern Gateway Community
College *C, A*
Edison State Community College *C, A*
Fortis College
Centerville *C, A*
Cuyahoga *A*
Harrison College
Grove City *A*
Herzing University
Toledo *C*
Hocking College *C, A*
James A. Rhodes State College *C, A*
Kaplan College
Dayton *C*
Lakeland Community College *C*
Lincoln College of Technology
Dayton *C*
Lorain County Community
College *C, A*
Marion Technical College *C, A*
Miami-Jacobs Career College
Columbus *A*
Dayton *A*
Sharonville *A*
National College
Canton *A*
Stow *A*
Willoughby Hills *A*
Northwest State Community
College *A*
Ohio Business College
Hilliard *C, A*
Ohio University
Lancaster Campus *A*
Remington College
Cleveland *A*
Sinclair Community College *A*
Southern State Community College *A*
Stark State College *A*
Stautzenberger College *C, A*
Terra State Community College *C, A*
Trumbull Business College *A*
University of Akron *A*
University of Akron: Wayne
College *A*
University of Cincinnati
Clermont College *C, A*
University of Northwestern
Ohio *C, A*
Youngstown State University *C, A*
Zane State College *C, A*

Oklahoma
Tulsa Community College *A*
Wright Career College
Tulsa *C*

Oregon
Central Oregon Community
College *C*
Chemeketa Community College *C*
Clackamas Community College *C*
Clatsop Community College *C*
Everest College
Portland *C, A*
Heald College
Portland *C, A*
Linn-Benton Community College *A*
Mt. Hood Community College *A*
Pioneer Pacific College *C, A*
Portland Community College *C*
Southwestern Oregon Community
College *A*
Umpqua Community College *C*

Pennsylvania
Berks Technical Institute *A*
Bidwell Training Center *C*
Bradford School: Pittsburgh *C, A*
Bucks County Community
College *C, A*
Career Training Academy *A*
Career Training Academy:
Monroeville *C, A*

Career Training Academy:
Pittsburgh *A*
Central Penn College *A*
Community College of Allegheny
County *C, A*
Community College of
Philadelphia *A*
Delaware County Community
College *C, A*
Douglas Education Center *A*
DuBois Business College *A*
DuBois Business College
Huntingdon *A*
Oil City *A*
Erie Business Center *A*
Everest Institute: Pittsburgh *C*
Harrisburg Area Community
College *C, A*
Kaplan Career Institute
Broomall *A*
Franklin Mills *C*
Harrisburg *A*
Pittsburgh *A*
Keystone Technical Institute *C, A*
Lansdale School of Business *A*
Lehigh Carbon Community College *A*
Lincoln Technical Institute
Allentown *C, A*
Northeast Philadelphia *C, A*
Montgomery County Community
College *C*
Mount Aloysius College *A*
Northampton Community College *C*
Pennsylvania Institute of
Technology *C, A*
South Hills School of Business &
Technology *A*
Westmoreland County Community
College *C*
YTI Career Institute
Altoona *A*
Capital Region *A*
Lancaster *C, A*
York *A*
Yorktowne Business Institute *A*

Rhode Island
New England Institute of
Technology *A*

South Carolina
Aiken Technical College *C*
Central Carolina Technical College *C*
Forrest Junior College *C, A*
Horry-Georgetown Technical
College *C*
Midlands Technical College *C*
Miller-Motte Technical College *A*
Miller-Motte Technical College
Conway *C, A*
Piedmont Technical College *C*
Spartanburg Community College *C*
Tri-County Technical College *C*
Trident Technical College *C*
Virginia College
Florence *C, A*

South Dakota
Globe University
Sioux Falls *A*
Lake Area Technical Institute *C*
Mitchell Technical Institute *A*
Presentation College *A*
Western Dakota Technical
Institute *C, A*

Tennessee
Anthem Career College
Memphis *C, A*
Nashville *C, A*
Chattanooga College *C, A*

Daymar Institute
Clarksville *A*
Murfreesboro *C, A*
Nashville *C, A*
Miller-Motte Technical College
Chattanooga *C, A*
Clarksville *A*
National College of Business and
Technology
Bartlett *C, A*
Bristol *A*
Knoxville *A*
Madison *A*
Memphis *A*
Nashville *A*
Northeast State Community
College *A*
Remington College
Memphis *A*
Nashville *C*
South College *A*
Virginia College
School of Business and Health in
Chattanooga *C, A*
School of Business and Health in
Knoxville *A*
West Tennessee Business College *C*

Texas
Cisco College *C, A*
El Centro College *C*
El Paso Community College *C, A*
Everest College
Dallas *A*
Fort Worth *C, A*
Hallmark College of Technology *C, A*
Houston Community College
System *C*
Howard College *A*
Laredo Community College *A*
Lone Star College System *C*
National American University
Austin *A*
Northeast Texas Community
College *C, A*
Panola College *C, A*
Remington College
Dallas *A*
Houston *C*
North Houston *C, A*
St. Philip's College *A*
San Antonio College *C, A*
San Jacinto College *C*
Texas State Technical College
Harlingen *C, A*
Virginia College
Austin *C*
Western Technical College *C*
Western Technical College: Diana
Drive *C*

Utah
Broadview University
Layton *C, A*
Orem *C, A*
West Jordan *C, A*
LDS Business College *C*
Salt Lake Community College *C*
Utah State University *C*

Virginia
American National University
Charlottesville *A*
Danville *A*
Harrisonburg *A*
Lynchburg *A*
Salem *C*
Bryant & Stratton College
Richmond *A*
Virginia Beach *A*
ECPI University *A*
Miller-Motte Technical College
Lynchburg *A*
Skyline College: Roanoke *A*

Westwood College
Annandale *C*
Arlington Ballston *C*

Washington

Big Bend Community College *C, A*
Carrington College
  Spokane *C*
Centralia College *C*
Clark College *C, A*
Clover Park Technical College *C*
Everett Community College *C, A*
Highline Community College *A*
Lake Washington Institute of
  Technology *C, A*
Lower Columbia College *A*
North Seattle Community
  College *C, A*
Olympic College *C, A*
Peninsula College *C, A*
Renton Technical College *C, A*
Skagit Valley College *C*
South Puget Sound Community
  College *C, A*
Spokane Falls Community
  College *C, A*
Walla Walla Community College *C*
Wenatchee Valley College *C*
Whatcom Community College *C, A*
Yakima Valley Community
  College *C, A*

West Virginia

American National University
  Parkersburg *A*
  Princeton *A*
Blue Ridge Community and Technical
  College *C, A*
Bridgemont Community and
  Technical College *A*
Mountain State College *A*
New River Community and Technical
  College *A*
Valley College *C*
West Virginia Junior College
  Bridgeport *A*
West Virginia Northern Community
  College *A*

Wisconsin

Blackhawk Technical College *C*
Bryant & Stratton College
  Milwaukee *A*
Chippewa Valley Technical College *C*
Concordia University Wisconsin *C*
Fox Valley Technical College *C*
Gateway Technical College *C*
Globe University
  Appleton *C, A*
  Eau Claire *C, A*
  Green Bay *C, A*
  La Crosse *A*
  Madison East *C, A*
  Middleton *C, A*
  Wausau *C, A*
Herzing University
  Brookfield *C, A*
  Kenosha *C*
  Madison *C, A*
Lac Courte Oreilles Ojibwa
  Community College *A*
Lakeshore Technical College *C*
Madison Area Technical College *A*
Mid-State Technical College *C*
Milwaukee Area Technical College *C*
Nicolet Area Technical College *C*
Northcentral Technical College *C*
Northeast Wisconsin Technical
  College *C*
Rasmussen College
  Appleton *C, A*
  Green Bay *C, A*
  Wausau *C, A*

Southwest Wisconsin Technical
  College *C*
Western Technical College *C*
Wisconsin Indianhead Technical
  College *C*

Wyoming

Western Wyoming Community
  College *A*

Medical illustrating

California

California State University
  Long Beach *B*

Georgia

Georgia Regents University *M*

Illinois

University of Illinois
  Chicago *M*

Iowa

Iowa State University *B*

New Hampshire

Lebanon College *C*

New York

Rochester Institute of
  Technology *B, M*

Ohio

Cleveland Institute of Art *B*

Pennsylvania

Arcadia University *B*

Medical informatics

Arizona

Grand Canyon University *M*

California

National University *C, A, M*
University of California
  Davis *M*
University of San Diego *M*

Colorado

Regis University *M*

Florida

Nova Southeastern University *M*

Illinois

Northwestern University *M*

Indiana

Indiana University
  Purdue University
    Indianapolis *C, M*

Kansas

University of Kansas Medical
  Center *M*

Kentucky

Northern Kentucky University *C, M*

Maryland

Community College of Baltimore
  County *A*

Massachusetts

Brandeis University *M*
Massachusetts Bay Community
  College *A*
Northeastern University *M*
Simmons College *B*

Michigan

Michigan Technological University *M*
Mott Community College *A*
University of Michigan *M*
Western Michigan University *B*

Minnesota

Capella University *B*
Rochester Community and Technical
  College *C*
University of Minnesota
  Twin Cities *M, D*

Montana

Montana State University
  Great Falls College *C*
Montana Tech of the University of
  Montana *C, A, B*

New Hampshire

Southern New Hampshire
  University *B*

New Jersey

Rutgers, The State University of New
  Jersey
  New Brunswick/Piscataway
    Campus *M, D*
  Newark Campus *M, D*

New York

Le Moyne College *M*
Rochester Institute of
  Technology *B, M*
SUNY
  Downstate Medical Center *M*

North Carolina

University of North Carolina
  Charlotte *M*

Ohio

College of Mount St. Joseph *B*

Oregon

Mt. Hood Community College *A*

Pennsylvania

Carnegie Mellon University *D*
Drexel University *M*
Misericordia University *C*

Texas

Richland College *A*
Texas Tech University Health
  Sciences Center *M*

Utah

University of Utah *M, D*
Western Governors University *B*

Vermont

Champlain College *B*

Virginia

George Mason University *M*

West Virginia

Marshall University *M*

Wisconsin

Milwaukee School of Engineering *M*
University of Wisconsin
  Milwaukee *M, D*

Medical insurance coding specialist

Alabama

Herzing University
  Birmingham *C, A*

Remington College
  Mobile *C*
Southern Union State Community
  College *A*
Virginia College
  Birmingham *C, A*
  Huntsville *C*
  Mobile *C, A*
  Montgomery *C*

Alaska

Charter College *C, A*
Ilisagvik College *C*
University of Alaska
  Anchorage *C*
  Fairbanks *C*

Arizona

Anthem College
  Bryman School *A*
Carrington College
  Mesa *C*
  Tucson *C*
Phoenix College *C*

Arkansas

Arkansas State University
  Mountain Home *C*

California

Canada College *C*
City College of San Francisco *C*
Concorde Career College
  North Hollywood *C*
East Los Angeles College *C*
Empire College *C*
Heald College
  Concord *C*
  Fresno *C, A*
  Hayward *C, A*
  Rancho Cordova *C, A*
  Roseville *C*
  Salinas *C, A*
  San Francisco *C, A*
  San Jose *C, A*
  Stockton *C, A*
Kaplan College
  Vista *C*
Loma Linda University *C*
MiraCosta College *C*
National University *A*
San Joaquin Valley College *A*
Santa Barbara City College *C*
Santa Rosa Junior College *C*
Southwestern College *C, A*

Colorado

Aims Community College *C*
Concorde Career College
  Aurora *C*
Everest College
  Aurora *C*
  Colorado Springs *C*
  Denver *C*
IntelliTec College: Grand Junction *C*
National American University
  Denver *A*
Pueblo Community College *C, A*
Westwood College
  Denver North *A*

Connecticut

St. Vincent's College *C*

Delaware

Delaware Technical Community
  College
  Stanton/Wilmington Campus *C*

Florida

City College
  Gainesville *C*

College of Business and Technology
  Cutler Bay *C*
  Hialeah *C*
  Kendall *C*
College of Central Florida *C*
Everest University
  Lakeland *C, A*
  Largo *C, A*
  North Orlando *C*
  Orange Park *A*
  Pompano Beach *C*
Florida Career College
  Miami *C*
Florida Gateway College *C*
Florida Technical College
  Orlando *C*
Herzing University
  Winter Park *C, A*
Miami Dade College *C*
Palm Beach State College *C*
Pasco-Hernando State College *C*
Rasmussen College
  Fort Myers *C*
  New Port Richey *C*
  Ocala *C*
  Pasco/Land O'Lakes *C*
  Tampa/Brandon *C*
Remington College
  Tampa *C*
St. Petersburg College *C*
Southwest Florida College *C*
Virginia College
  Pensacola *C*

Georgia

Albany Technical College *C*
Altamaha Technical College *C*
Atlanta Technical College *C*
Central Georgia Technical College *C*
Columbus Technical College *C*
North Georgia Technical College *C*
Savannah Technical College *C*
Southwest Georgia Technical
  College *C*

Idaho

Carrington College
  Boise *C, A*

Illinois

Black Hawk College *C*
City Colleges of Chicago
  Harold Washington College *C*
  Harry S. Truman College *C*
  Kennedy-King College *C*
  Malcolm X College *C*
  Olive-Harvey College *C*
  Richard J. Daley College *C*
  Wilbur Wright College *C*
College of DuPage *C*
Danville Area Community College *C*
Harper College *C*
Highland Community College *C*
Illinois Eastern Community Colleges
  Frontier Community College *C*
Lincoln Land Community College *C*
Midstate College *C*
Moraine Valley Community College *C*
Rasmussen College
  Aurora *C*
  Mokena/Tinley Park *C*
  Rockford *C*
  Romeoville/Joliet *C*
Rock Valley College *C*
Spoon River College *C*
Waubonsee Community College *C*

Indiana

Brown Mackie College
  Michigan City *C*
Indiana University
  Southeast *C*

Iowa

Hamilton Technical College *C*

Kansas

Barton County Community College *C*
Hutchinson Community College *C*
Neosho County Community
  College *C*
Wichita Area Technical College *C*
Wright Career College
  Overland Park *A*
  Wichita *C, A*

Kentucky

Daymar College
  Bowling Green *C, A*
  Paducah *A*
Lincoln College of Technology
  Florence *C*
Midway College *A*
Spencerian College *C, A*
Spencerian College: Lexington *C*
Sullivan University *C*

Louisiana

ITI Technical College *C, A*
Nunez Community College *C*
Remington College
  Shreveport *C*
Virginia College
  Baton Rouge *C*

Maine

Beal College *C*
Central Maine Community
  College *C, A*

Maryland

Hagerstown Community College *C*

Massachusetts

Bunker Hill Community College *C*
Mount Wachusett Community
  College *C*
North Shore Community College *C*
Springfield Technical Community
  College *C, A*

Michigan

Baker College
  Clinton Township *A*
  Muskegon *C*
Davenport University *A*
Delta College *C*
Oakland Community College *C*

Minnesota

Academy College *C*
Alexandria Technical and Community
  College *C*
Anoka Technical College *C*
Herzing University
  Minneapolis *A*
Lake Superior College *C*
Minnesota State College - Southeast
  Technical *C*
Minnesota State Community and
  Technical College *C*
Minnesota West Community and
  Technical College *C*
Northland Community & Technical
  College *C*
Northwest Technical College *C, A*
Rasmussen College
  Blaine *C*
  Bloomington *C*
  Brooklyn Park *C*
  Eagan *C*
  Lake Elmo/Woodbury *C*
  Mankato *C*
  Moorhead *C*
  St. Cloud *C*

Rochester Community and Technical
  College *C*
St. Paul College *C*
South Central College *C*

Mississippi

Meridian Community College *A*

Missouri

Grantham University *A*
Ozarks Technical Community
  College *C*

Montana

Flathead Valley Community College *C*
Montana State University
  Billings *C*

Nebraska

Northeast Community College *C*
Wright Career College
  Omaha *A*

Nevada

Career College of Northern
  Nevada *C, A*
Great Basin College *C*
Kaplan College
  Las Vegas *C, A*

New Hampshire

Great Bay Community College *C*
Lebanon College *C*
NHTI-Concord's Community
  College *C*
River Valley Community College *C*
White Mountains Community
  College *C*

New Jersey

Salem Community College *C*

New Mexico

Carrington College
  Albuquerque *C*
National American University
  Albuquerque *C*
San Juan College *C*

New York

Elmira Business Institute *A*
Elmira Business Institute: Vestal *C, A*
Everest Institute
  Rochester *A*
Globe Institute of Technology *C*
Mildred Elley
  Albany *C*
SUNY
  College of Technology at Alfred *C*

North Carolina

Miller-Motte College
  Cary *A*
  Fayetteville *C*

North Dakota

Dakota College at Bottineau *C*
North Dakota State College of
  Science *A*
Rasmussen College
  Bismarck *C*
  Fargo *C*
Turtle Mountain Community
  College *A*
Williston State College *C*

Ohio

Akron Institute of Herzing
  University *C, A*
Brown Mackie College
  Akron *C*
Columbus State Community
  College *C*

Davis College *C, A*
ETI Technical College of Niles *A*
Fortis College
  Centerville *C*
  Cuyahoga *C*
Lakeland Community College *C*
Lincoln College of Technology
  Dayton *C*
Marion Technical College *C*
Mercy College of Ohio *C*
Ohio University
  Southern Campus at Ironton *C*
Remington College
  Cleveland *C*
Sinclair Community College *C*
Stark State College *C*
Stautzenberger College *C, A*
Terra State Community College *C, A*
University of Cincinnati
  Clermont College *C*

Oklahoma

Wright Career College
  Oklahoma City *A*
  Tulsa *A*

Oregon

Chemeketa Community College *C*
Everest College
  Portland *C*
Heald College
  Portland *C, A*
Lane Community College *C*
Mt. Hood Community College *C*
Umpqua Community College *C*

Pennsylvania

Bucks County Community
  College *C, A*
Butler County Community College *C*
Consolidated School of Business
  Lancaster *A*
  York *A*
Delaware County Community
  College *C*
Drexel University *C*
Erie Business Center *C*
Everest Institute: Pittsburgh *C*
Fortis Institute
  Erie *A*
Keystone Technical Institute *C*
Montgomery County Community
  College *C*
Northampton Community College *C*
Penn Commercial Business and
  Technical School *C*
Pennsylvania College of
  Technology *C*
Pennsylvania Highlands Community
  College *C*
Westmoreland County Community
  College *C*
YTI Career Institute
  Capital Region *C*

South Carolina

Virginia College
  Florence *C*

South Dakota

Dakota State University *C*
Kilian Community College *C*
National American University
  Rapid City *C*

Tennessee

Anthem Career College
  Memphis *A*
Daymar Institute
  Clarksville *B*
  Nashville *C, A, B*
Fountainhead College of
  Technology *C*

Remington College
  Nashville *C*
South College *C*
Virginia College
  School of Business and Health in
    Chattanooga *C, A*
  School of Business and Health in
    Knoxville *C*
Walters State Community College *C*
West Tennessee Business College *C*

Texas

Austin Community College *C*
Collin County Community College
  District *C, A*
Everest College
  Dallas *C*
  Fort Worth *C*
Hallmark College of Technology *C*
Houston Community College
  System *C*
Lamar State College at Port
  Arthur *C, A*
Midland College *C*
Panola College *C*
Paris Junior College *C*
Remington College
  Fort Worth *C*
  Houston Southeast *C*
  North Houston *C, A*
Richland College *A*
St. Philip's College *C*
San Jacinto College *C*
Sanford-Brown College
  Houston *C*
South Texas College *C*
Virginia College
  Austin *C*

Utah

LDS Business College *C*
Salt Lake Community College *C*
Utah State University *C*

Virginia

Lord Fairfax Community College *C*
Virginia Western Community
  College *C*

Washington

Bellingham Technical College *C, A*
Carrington College
  Spokane *C*
Centralia College *C*
Clark College *C*
Clover Park Technical College *C*
Everett Community College *C*
Grays Harbor College *C*
Lake Washington Institute of
  Technology *A*
Olympic College *C*
Renton Technical College *C, A*
Shoreline Community College *C*
Whatcom Community College *C*
Yakima Valley Community
  College *C, A*

West Virginia

Bridgemont Community and
  Technical College *C*
West Virginia Northern Community
  College *C*

Wisconsin

Blackhawk Technical College *C*
Fox Valley Technical College *C*
Herzing University
  Madison *C, A*
Lakeshore Technical College *C*
Milwaukee Area Technical College *C*
Northcentral Technical College *C*

Rasmussen College
  Appleton *C*
  Green Bay *C*
  Wausau *C*
Waukesha County Technical
  College *C*
Western Technical College *C*

Medical insurance specialist

Alabama

Virginia College
  Birmingham *A*
  Huntsville *C*

Alaska

University of Alaska
  Fairbanks *C*

Arizona

Anthem College
  Bryman School *A*
  Phoenix *A*
Brookline College
  Phoenix *C*
  Tempe *C*
  Tucson *C*
Carrington College
  Phoenix Westside *C*
  Tucson *C*

California

Carrington College California
  Antioch *C, A*
  Citrus Heights *C, A*
  Pleasant Hill *C*
  Sacramento *C*
  San Jose *C, A*
  San Leandro *C, A*
City College of San Francisco *C*
Long Beach City College *C*
MTI College *C*
Santa Barbara City College *C*

Colorado

Everest College
  Aurora *C*
  Colorado Springs *C*
National American University
  Denver *A*
Westwood College
  Denver North *A*

Connecticut

Goodwin College *C, A*

Florida

City College
  Gainesville *C*
Everest University
  Brandon *A*
  Orange Park *A*
Florida Gateway College *C*
Florida Technical College
  Orlando *C*
Fortis College
  Winter Park *A*
Herzing University
  Winter Park *C, A*
Lincoln College of Technology
  West Palm Beach *C*
Palm Beach State College *C*
Remington College
  Tampa *C*
Sanford-Brown Institute
  Tampa *C*
Virginia College
  Pensacola *C*

Georgia

Atlanta Technical College *C*
Gwinnett Technical College *C*
Savannah Technical College *C*

Idaho

Carrington College
  Boise *C, A*

Illinois

Black Hawk College *C*
College of Lake County *C*
Moraine Valley Community College *C*

Indiana

Harrison College
  Indianapolis *A*

Kansas

Brown Mackie College
  Salina *C*

Kentucky

Daymar College
  Paducah *A*
Lincoln College of Technology
  Florence *C*

Louisiana

Herzing University
  Kenner *C*
ITI Technical College *C, A*
Virginia College
  Baton Rouge *A*

Massachusetts

Holyoke Community College *C*
Massasoit Community College *C*

Michigan

Baker College
  Allen Park *C*
  Flint *C, A*
  Muskegon *C*
  Owosso *C, A*
  Port Huron *C, A*
Delta College *C*
Henry Ford Community College *C*
Kirtland Community College *C*
Lansing Community College *C*
Schoolcraft College *C*

Minnesota

Northwest Technical College *C*
Ridgewater College *C*

Mississippi

Meridian Community College *A*
Southwest Mississippi Community
  College *A*

Montana

Montana State University
  Great Falls College *C, A*

Nebraska

Herzing University
  Omaha School of Massage Therapy
    and Healthcare *C*

Nevada

Career College of Northern
  Nevada *C, A*
Carrington College
  Las Vegas *C*

New Jersey

Eastwick College
  Hackensack *C*

New Mexico

Brookline College
  Albuquerque *C*

New York

College of Westchester *C, A*
Elmira Business Institute *C*
Everest Institute
  Rochester *A*
Globe Institute of Technology *C*
Westchester Community College *C*

North Carolina

Miller-Motte College
  Fayetteville *C*

Ohio

Akron Institute of Herzing
  University *C, A*
Harrison College
  Grove City *A*
Herzing University
  Toledo *C*
Ohio University
  Southern Campus at Ironton *C*
Southern State Community College *C*
University of Cincinnati
  Blue Ash College *A*

Oregon

Mt. Hood Community College *C*
Pioneer Pacific College *C*

Pennsylvania

Career Training Academy:
  Monroeville *C*
Career Training Academy:
  Pittsburgh *A*
Consolidated School of Business
  Lancaster *A*
  York *A*
Delaware County Community
  College *A*
Kaplan Career Institute
  Franklin Mills *C*
Laurel Business Institute *A*
Lehigh Carbon Community College *C*
Lincoln Technical Institute
  Allentown *C*
Luzerne County Community
  College *C, A*
Prism Career Institute *C*
YTI Career Institute
  Altoona *C*
  Capital Region *C*

Puerto Rico

Centro de Estudios
  Multidisciplinarios *C*
Columbia Centro Universitario:
  Yauco *C*
Inter American University of Puerto
  Rico
  Aguadilla Campus *C*
  Barranquitas Campus *C*
  Metropolitan Campus *C*
  San German Campus *C*

Rhode Island

Community College of Rhode
  Island *C*

Tennessee

Anthem Career College
  Nashville *C*
National College of Business and
  Technology
  Knoxville *C*
Virginia College
  School of Business and Health in
    Knoxville *A*

Texas

Everest College
  Fort Worth *C*

Utah
Salt Lake Community College *C*

Vermont
Champlain College *C*

Virginia
American National University
   Salem *C*
Lord Fairfax Community College *C*

Washington
Carrington College
   Spokane *C*
Tacoma Community College *C*

West Virginia
American National University
   Parkersburg *C*
New River Community and Technical
   College *C*

Wisconsin
Herzing University
   Brookfield *C, A*
   Kenosha *C*
   Madison *C*
Northcentral Technical College *C*

Medical office administration

Alabama
Virginia College
   Huntsville *A*
   Montgomery *A*

Arizona
Brown Mackie College
   Tucson *A*
Carrington College
   Mesa *C, A*
   Phoenix *C, A*
   Tucson *C, A*
Mohave Community College *C*
Phoenix College *A*

Arkansas
College of the Ouachitas *C*
University of Arkansas
   Community College at Hope *C, A*

California
City College of San Francisco *A*
Concorde Career College
   San Bernardino *C*
Heald College
   Hayward *A*
   Roseville *C, A*
Institute of Technology: Clovis *C*
Merced College *C, A*
San Joaquin Valley College *C*
Santa Barbara Business College
   Bakersfield *C*

Colorado
Arapahoe Community College *C, A*
Community College of Denver *C*
Everest College
   Colorado Springs *C*
Pikes Peak Community College *C, A*
Pueblo Community College *C, A*
Red Rocks Community College *C, A*

Connecticut
Goodwin College *A*
Norwalk Community College *A*

Florida
Everest University
   Pompano Beach *C*

Florida Career College
   Miami *A*
Herzing University
   Winter Park *C*

Idaho
Carrington College
   Boise *C, A*

Illinois
College of Lake County *C, A*
East-West University *C*

Indiana
Brown Mackie College
   Merrillville *A*
   Michigan City *A*
Indiana University
   Purdue University Indianapolis *C*

Iowa
Western Iowa Tech Community
   College *A*

Kansas
Brown Mackie College
   Salina *A*

Kentucky
Sullivan University *C, A*

Louisiana
ITI Technical College *A*
Nunez Community College *A*
Virginia College
   Baton Rouge *A*

Massachusetts
Bristol Community College *C*
Marian Court College *A*
North Shore Community College *C*

Michigan
Baker College
   Clinton Township *B*
Henry Ford Community College *A*

Minnesota
Hennepin Technical College *C, A*
Herzing University
   Minneapolis *A*
Northwest Technical College *A*

Nevada
Career College of Northern Nevada *C*

New Hampshire
White Mountains Community
   College *A*

New Mexico
Carrington College
   Albuquerque *A*
Eastern New Mexico University:
   Roswell *C, A*

New York
Bryant & Stratton College
   Rochester *A*
Erie Community College *C, A*
Fulton-Montgomery Community
   College *C, A*
Globe Institute of
   Technology *C, A, B*
Monroe College *A*

North Carolina
Beaufort County Community
   College *A*
Carteret Community College *C, A*
Catawba Valley Community
   College *C, A*

Central Piedmont Community
   College *C*
Cleveland Community College *C, A*
College of the Albemarle *A*
Craven Community College *C, A*
Durham Technical Community
   College *C, A*
Fayetteville Technical Community
   College *C, A*
Forsyth Technical Community
   College *C, A*
Gaston College *C, A*
Isothermal Community College *C, A*
Johnston Community College *C, A*
Lenoir Community College *C, A*
Pitt Community College *C, A*
Randolph Community College *C, A*
Surry Community College *C, A*
Wayne Community College *C, A*
Western Piedmont Community
   College *A*
Wilson Community College *A*

North Dakota
Turtle Mountain Community
   College *C*

Ohio
Akron Institute of Herzing
   University *A*
Brown Mackie College
   Akron *A, B*
Eastern Gateway Community
   College *C*
Fortis College
   Cuyahoga *A*
University of Akron *C, A*
Youngstown State University *A*

Oregon
Chemeketa Community College *A*

Pennsylvania
Bidwell Training Center *C*
Consolidated School of Business
   Lancaster *A*
Douglas Education Center *A*
DuBois Business College
   Oil City *A*
Montgomery County Community
   College *A*
Pennsylvania Institute of
   Technology *C, A*

Tennessee
Chattanooga College *A*

Texas
Panola College *C, A*
Tyler Junior College *C, A*

Utah
LDS Business College *A*

Virginia
Westwood College
   Arlington Ballston *A*

Washington
Big Bend Community College *C, A*
Carrington College
   Spokane *A*
Lake Washington Institute of
   Technology *C*
North Seattle Community College *C*
Peninsula College *C*

West Virginia
Bridgemont Community and
   Technical College *A*

Wisconsin
Herzing University
   Madison *A, B*
Lac Courte Oreilles Ojibwa
   Community College *A*
Milwaukee Area Technical College *A*
Western Technical College *A*

Medical office assistant

Alabama
Virginia College
   Birmingham *A*
   Mobile *A*

Alaska
Charter College *A*

Arizona
Mohave Community College *C*
Phoenix College *C*

Arkansas
Bryan University
   Rogers *C*

California
Antelope Valley College *C, A*
City College of San Francisco *A*
Contra Costa College *C, A*
Heald College
   Concord *C, A*
   Fresno *C, A*
Kaplan College
   Palm Springs *C*
   Sacramento *C*
   Salida *C*
   Vista *C*
Ohlone College *C*
Platt College
   Ontario *A*
San Joaquin Valley College *A*
Santa Barbara Business College *C*
Santa Barbara Business College
   Bakersfield *C, A*
   Rancho Mirage *C*
   Santa Maria *C, A*
   Ventura *C, A*
Southwestern College *C*

Colorado
CollegeAmerica
   Colorado Springs *A*
Colorado Mountain College *C, A*
Front Range Community College *C, A*
National American University
   Denver *A*

Florida
Pasco-Hernando State College *C*
Rasmussen College
   Fort Myers *C*
   New Port Richey *C*
   Ocala *C*
   Pasco/Land O'Lakes *C*
   Tampa/Brandon *C*
Remington College
   Tampa *C*
Virginia College
   Pensacola *A*

Georgia
Altamaha Technical College *C*
Columbus Technical College *C*
Dalton State College *C, A*
Gwinnett Technical College *C*
Savannah Technical College *C*
Southeastern Technical College *C*

Hawaii
Heald College
   Honolulu *A*

Idaho

College of Western Idaho *C*
Lewis-Clark State College *C, A, B*
Stevens-Henager College
   Boise *A*

Illinois

College of DuPage *C*
Danville Area Community College *C*
Elgin Community College *C*
Illinois Eastern Community Colleges
   Frontier Community College *C*
Kankakee Community College *C, A*
Lincoln Land Community College *A*
Rasmussen College
   Aurora *C*
   Mokena/Tinley Park *C*
   Rockford *C*
   Romeoville/Joliet *C*
Southeastern Illinois College *A*

Indiana

Harrison College
   Indianapolis *C*
Vincennes University *C*

Kansas

Barton County Community College *A*
Colby Community College *C*
Cowley County Community
   College *C*
Fort Scott Community College *C*
Independence Community
   College *C, A*

Kentucky

Beckfield College *C*
Brown Mackie College
   Hopkinsville *C*
Daymar College
   Louisville *C, A*
Midway College *A*
Spencerian College: Lexington *C*

Louisiana

Bossier Parish Community College *C*
ITI Technical College *A*
Remington College
   Shreveport *C*
Virginia College
   Shreveport *A*

Maine

Beal College *A*

Maryland

Harford Community College *C*

Michigan

Baker College
   Clinton Township *A*
   Flint *A*
   Muskegon *A*
Bay Mills Community College *C*
Delta College *C, A*
Lake Michigan College *C, A*
Oakland Community College *C*
Schoolcraft College *C*
West Shore Community College *C*

Minnesota

Century College *C*
Dakota County Technical College *C*
Hennepin Technical College *C*
Lake Superior College *C*
Minneapolis Community and
   Technical College *C*
Northland Community & Technical
   College *C*
Northwest Technical College *C*
Rasmussen College
   Blaine *C*
   Bloomington *C*

Brooklyn Park *C*
Eagan *C*
Lake Elmo/Woodbury *C*
Mankato *C*
Moorhead *C*
St. Cloud *C*
St. Cloud Technical and Community
   College *C*
St. Paul College *A*

Missouri

Crowder College *A*
North Central Missouri College *C, A*

Montana

Flathead Valley Community
   College *A*
Helena College University of
   Montana *C, A*
Salish Kootenai College *C*

Nevada

Career College of Northern Nevada *C*
Kaplan College
   Las Vegas *C, A*

New Mexico

Central New Mexico Community
   College *C*

New York

Globe Institute of Technology *C*
Mildred Elley
   Albany *C*
   New York City *C*
Plaza College *C*

North Carolina

Miller-Motte College
   Fayetteville *C*
Pitt Community College *C*
South Piedmont Community
   College *C, A*

North Dakota

Rasmussen College
   Bismarck *C*
   Fargo *C*

Ohio

Brown Mackie College
   North Canton *C, A*
Bryant & Stratton College
   Eastlake *A*
Cincinnati State Technical and
   Community College *A*
Lakeland Community College *C*
Marion Technical College *C*
National College
   Canton *C*
   Columbus *C, A*
   Willoughby Hills *C*
   Youngstown *C*
Ohio Business College
   Sandusky *C*
Ohio Valley College of Technology *A*
Stark State College *A*
Stautzenberger College *C*
Terra State Community College *A*
University of Cincinnati
   Blue Ash College *A*
   Clermont College *C, A*

Oregon

Blue Mountain Community College *C*
Clackamas Community College *C*
Mt. Hood Community College *C, A*

Pennsylvania

Butler County Community
   College *C, A*
Consolidated School of Business
   Lancaster *A*

Fortis Institute
   Forty Fort *A*
Lansdale School of Business *C*
Laurel Business Institute *A*
Lincoln Technical Institute
   Northeast Philadelphia *A*
Penn Commercial Business and
   Technical School *A*
Pennsylvania Highlands Community
   College *A*
Pennsylvania Institute of Health and
   Technology *A*
Westmoreland County Community
   College *C*

South Carolina

Miller-Motte Technical College
   Conway *C*
Williamsburg Technical College *C*
York Technical College *C*

South Dakota

Mitchell Technical Institute *A*
Southeast Technical Institute *C*

Tennessee

Miller-Motte Technical College
   Chattanooga *C*
National College of Business and
   Technology
   Knoxville *C*
Virginia College
   School of Business and Health in
     Knoxville *A*

Texas

Remington College
   Fort Worth *C*
South Texas College *C, A*
Virginia College
   Austin *A*

Utah

LDS Business College *A*

Vermont

Community College of Vermont *A*

Virginia

Bryant & Stratton College
   Virginia Beach *A*
Danville Community College *A*
Miller-Motte Technical College
   Lynchburg *A*

Washington

Clover Park Technical College *C*
North Seattle Community
   College *C, A*
Yakima Valley Community College *C*

West Virginia

American National University
   Parkersburg *C, A*
Bridgemont Community and
   Technical College *A*
West Virginia Junior College
   Charleston *C, A*

Wisconsin

Herzing University
   Brookfield *A*
   Madison *A*
Mid-State Technical College *C*
Milwaukee Area Technical College *C*
Northcentral Technical College *C*
Rasmussen College
   Appleton *C*
   Green Bay *C*
   Wausau *C*

Wyoming

Central Wyoming College *C, A*

Medical office computer specialist

Arizona

Anthem College
   Phoenix *A*

California

Kaplan College
   Salida *C*

Colorado

Lamar Community College *C, A*

Kansas

Hutchinson Community College *C*

Louisiana

ITI Technical College *A*

Minnesota

Hennepin Technical College *C*
Normandale Community College *A*
Northland Community & Technical
   College *C*
St. Cloud Technical and Community
   College *A*

Missouri

Mineral Area College *C*

Nevada

Career College of Northern Nevada *C*

New Jersey

Burlington County College *C*

New York

Globe Institute of Technology *C*

Ohio

University of Rio Grande *C*

Oregon

Rogue Community College *C, A*

Pennsylvania

Consolidated School of Business
   Lancaster *A*
   York *A*

South Carolina

York Technical College *C*

Wisconsin

Fox Valley Technical College *C*
Herzing University
   Madison *C, A*
Northcentral Technical College *C*

Medical radiologic technology/radiation therapy

Alabama

Central Alabama Community
   College *A*
George C. Wallace Community
   College at Dothan *A*
Southern Union State Community
   College *A*
University of Alabama
   Birmingham *B*
Wallace State Community College at
   Hanceville *A*

Arizona

Carrington College
   Phoenix Westside *A*
GateWay Community College *A*
Scottsdale Community College *A*

Arkansas

Arkansas State University *A, B*
East Arkansas Community College *A*
National Park Community College *A*
North Arkansas College *A*
South Arkansas Community
    College *A*
Southeast Arkansas College *A*
University of Arkansas
    for Medical Sciences *A, B, M*
University of Central Arkansas *B*

California

Cabrillo College *A*
California State University
    Long Beach *B*
Chaffey College *A*
City College of San Francisco *A*
Crafton Hills College *A*
Cypress College *A*
El Camino College *A*
Foothill College *A*
Fresno City College *A*
Loma Linda University *A*
Long Beach City College *A*
Los Angeles City College *A*
Merced College *A*
Merritt College *A*
Moorpark College *A*
Mount San Antonio College *A*
National University *B*
Orange Coast College *A*
Pasadena City College *A*
San Diego Mesa College *A*
Santa Barbara City College *A*
Santa Rosa Junior College *A*
Yuba College *A*

Colorado

Concorde Career College
    Aurora *A*

Connecticut

Capital Community College *A*
Gateway Community College *A*
Middlesex Community College *A*
Naugatuck Valley Community
    College *A*
University of Hartford *B*

District of Columbia

Georgetown University *M*
Howard University *B*
University of the District of
    Columbia *A*

Florida

Broward College *A*
College of Central Florida *A*
Daytona State College *A*
Eastern Florida State College *A*
Edison State College *A*
Florida State College at
    Jacksonville *A*
Gulf Coast State College *A*
Hillsborough Community College *A*
Indian River State College *A*
Keiser University *A*
Miami Dade College *A*
Northwest Florida State College *A*
Palm Beach State College *A*
Pensacola State College *A*
Polk State College *A*
Saint Johns River State College *A*
Santa Fe College *A*
South Florida State College *A*
State College of Florida, Manatee-
    Sarasota *A*
Tallahassee Community College *A*
Valencia College *A*

Georgia

Armstrong Atlantic State University *B*
College of Coastal Georgia *A*

Darton College *A*
Georgia Regents University *B, M*
Middle Georgia State College *A*
South Georgia State College *A*
Southwest Georgia Technical
    College *A*

Hawaii

University of Hawaii
    Kapiolani Community College *A*

Idaho

Boise State University *A, B*
Idaho State University *A, B*

Illinois

College of DuPage *A*
College of Lake County *A*
Illinois Central College *A*
Illinois Eastern Community Colleges
    Olney Central College *A*
John Wood Community College *A*
Kishwaukee College *A*
National-Louis University *B*
North Central College *B*
Roosevelt University *B*
South Suburban College of Cook
    County *A*
Southern Illinois University
    Carbondale *A, B, M*
Southwestern Illinois College *A*
University of St. Francis *B*

Indiana

Ball State University *A, B*
Indiana University
    Kokomo *B*
    Purdue University Fort Wayne *A*
    Purdue University Indianapolis *B*
    South Bend *B*
Ivy Tech Community College
    Bloomington *A*
    Central Indiana *A*
    Columbus *A*
    East Central *A*
    North Central *A*
    Northwest *A*
    Richmond *A*
    South Central *A*
    Wabash Valley *A*
University of Southern Indiana *A, B*
Vincennes University *A*

Iowa

Briar Cliff University *B*
Iowa Central Community College *A*
Mercy College of Health Sciences *A*
Southeastern Community College *A*

Kansas

Fort Hays State University *A*
Hutchinson Community College *A*
Johnson County Community
    College *A*
Newman University *A*
Washburn University *A*

Kentucky

Bluegrass Community and Technical
    College *A*
Elizabethtown Community and
    Technical College *A*
Hazard Community and Technical
    College *A*
Madisonville Community College *A*
Morehead State University *A, B*
Northern Kentucky University *A, B*
Owensboro Community and
    Technical College *A*
St. Catharine College *B*
Southeast Kentucky Community and
    Technical College *A*
West Kentucky Community and
    Technical College *A*

Louisiana

Delgado Community College *A*
Louisiana State University
    Eunice *A*
Our Lady of Holy Cross College *B*
Southern University
    Shreveport *A*

Maine

Eastern Maine Community College *A*
Saint Joseph's College of Maine *B*
Southern Maine Community
    College *A*

Maryland

Allegany College of Maryland *A*
Anne Arundel Community College *A*
Chesapeake College *A*
Community College of Baltimore
    County *A*
Hagerstown Community College *A*
Montgomery College *A*
Notre Dame of Maryland
    University *B*
Prince George's Community
    College *A*
Wor-Wic Community College *A*

Massachusetts

Bunker Hill Community College *A*
Holyoke Community College *A*
MCPHS University *B*
Massachusetts Bay Community
    College *A*
Middlesex Community College *A*
Regis College *A*

Michigan

Baker College
    Muskegon *A*
    Owosso *A*
Delta College *A*
Ferris State University *A*
Grand Rapids Community College *A*
Grand Valley State University *B*
Kellogg Community College *A*
Mid Michigan Community College *A*
Mott Community College *A*
Oakland Community College *A*
Oakland University *B*
St. Clair County Community
    College *A*
University of Michigan
    Flint *B*
Washtenaw Community College *A*
Wayne State University *B*

Minnesota

Argosy University
    Twin Cities *A*
Dunwoody College of Technology *A*
Ridgewater College *A*
Riverland Community College *A*
Saint Cloud State University *B*

Mississippi

Copiah-Lincoln Community
    College *A*
Itawamba Community College *A*
Meridian Community College *A*
Mississippi Delta Community
    College *A*
Mississippi Gulf Coast Community
    College *A*

Missouri

Avila University *B*
Drury University *B*
East Central College *A*
Metropolitan Community College -
    Kansas City *A*
Missouri Southern State University *A*
North Central Missouri College *A*
St. Louis Community College *A*

Saint Louis University *B*
University of Missouri
    Columbia *B*

Montana

Flathead Valley Community
    College *A*

Nebraska

Clarkson College *A, B*
Northeast Community College *A*
Southeast Community College *A*
University of Nebraska
    Kearney *B*
    Medical Center *B*
Western Nebraska Community
    College *A*

Nevada

Truckee Meadows Community
    College *A*
University of Nevada
    Las Vegas *B*

New Jersey

Bergen Community College *A*
Brookdale Community College *A*
Burlington County College *A*
Cumberland County College *A*
Essex County College *A*
Fairleigh Dickinson University
    College at Florham *B*
Mercer County Community
    College *A*
Passaic County Community College *A*
Rutgers, The State University of New
    Jersey
    New Brunswick/Piscataway
        Campus *M*
    Newark Campus *M*
Thomas Edison State College *A, B*
Union County College *A*

New Mexico

Central New Mexico Community
    College *A*
Dona Ana Community College of
    New Mexico State University *A*
New Mexico Junior College *A*
Northern New Mexico College *A*
University of New Mexico *A, B*

New York

Broome Community College *A*
City University of New York
    Bronx Community College *A*
    Hostos Community College *A*
    LaGuardia Community College *A*
    New York City College of
        Technology *A, B*
Erie Community College *A*
Fulton-Montgomery Community
    College *A*
Hudson Valley Community College *A*
Long Island University
    LIU Post *B*
Manhattan College *B*
Mohawk Valley Community
    College *A*
Molloy College *A*
Nassau Community College *A*
Niagara County Community
    College *A*
North Country Community College *A*
Orange County Community
    College *A*
SUNY
    College at Oswego *B*
St. Francis College *B*
Trocaire College *A*
Westchester Community College *A*

North Carolina

Asheville-Buncombe Technical
   Community College *A*
Caldwell Community College and
   Technical Institute *A*
Cape Fear Community College *A*
Carolinas College of Health
   Sciences *A*
Carteret Community College *A*
Catawba Valley Community
   College *A*
Edgecombe Community College *A*
Forsyth Technical Community
   College *A*
Pitt Community College *A*
Sandhills Community College *A*
Southwestern Community College *A*
University of North Carolina
   Chapel Hill *B, M*
Vance-Granville Community
   College *A*
Wake Technical Community
   College *A*

North Dakota

Minot State University *B*

Ohio

Bowling Green State University:
   Firelands College *A*
Columbus State Community
   College *A*
Eastern Gateway Community
   College *A*
James A. Rhodes State College *A*
Kent State University
   Ashtabula *A*
   Salem *A, B*
Kettering College *A*
Lakeland Community College *A*
Lorain County Community College *A*
Marion Technical College *A*
North Central State College *A*
Ohio State University
   Columbus Campus *B*
Owens Community College
   Toledo *A*
Shawnee State University *A*
University of Akron *A*
University of Akron: Wayne
   College *A*
University of Cincinnati
   Blue Ash College *A, B*
Washington State Community
   College *A*
Zane State College *A*

Oklahoma

Bacone College *A, B*
Northern Oklahoma College *A*
Tulsa Community College *A*
University of Oklahoma *B, M, D*
Western Oklahoma State College *A*

Oregon

Oregon Health & Science
   University *B*
Portland Community College *A*

Pennsylvania

Bloomsburg University of
   Pennsylvania *B*
Clarion University of Pennsylvania *B*
Community College of Allegheny
   County *A*
Community College of
   Philadelphia *A*
Drexel University *A*
Gannon University *A*
Gwynedd Mercy University *B*
La Roche College *A, B*
Mansfield University of
   Pennsylvania *A*
Misericordia University *B*

Mount Aloysius College *A, B*
Penn State
   New Kensington *A*
   Schuylkill *A*
Pennsylvania College of
   Technology *A*

Puerto Rico

Inter American University of Puerto
   Rico
   Aguadilla Campus *A*
   Barranquitas Campus *A*
   Ponce Campus *A*
Universidad Central del Caribe *A*
Universidad del Este *B*
University of Puerto Rico
   Medical Sciences *A*

South Carolina

Aiken Technical College *A*
Florence-Darlington Technical
   College *A*
Greenville Technical College *A*
Horry-Georgetown Technical
   College *A*
Midlands Technical College *A*
Orangeburg-Calhoun Technical
   College *A*
Piedmont Technical College *A*
Southern Wesleyan University *B*
Spartanburg Community College *A*
Technical College of the
   Lowcountry *A*
Trident Technical College *A*
York Technical College *A*

South Dakota

Mitchell Technical Institute *A*
Presentation College *A, B*

Tennessee

Anthem Career College
   Nashville *A*
Austin Peay State University *B*
Baptist College of Health Sciences *B*
Chattanooga State Community
   College *A*
Columbia State Community
   College *A*
Jackson State Community College *A*
Roane State Community College *A*
Southwest Tennessee Community
   College *A*
Volunteer State Community
   College *A*

Texas

Amarillo College *A*
Blinn College *A*
El Centro College *A*
El Paso Community College *A*
Galveston College *A*
Kilgore College *A*
Lamar Institute of Technology *A*
Laredo Community College *A*
Lone Star College System *A*
McLennan Community College *A*
Odessa College *A*
South Plains College *A*
Texas State University *B*
Tyler Junior College *A*
Weatherford College *A*

Utah

Dixie State College *A*
Salt Lake Community College *A*
Weber State University *A, B, M*

Vermont

University of Vermont *B*

Virginia

Averett University *B*
Northern Virginia Community
   College *A*
Tidewater Community College *A*
Virginia Highlands Community
   College *A*

Washington

Bellevue College *A, B*
Bellingham Technical College *A*
Carrington College
   Spokane *A*
Edmonds Community College *A*
Tacoma Community College *A*
Yakima Valley Community College *A*

West Virginia

Alderson-Broaddus University *B*
Bluefield State College *A*
Southern West Virginia Community
   and Technical College *A*
University of Charleston *A, B*
West Virginia Northern Community
   College *A*

Wisconsin

Blackhawk Technical College *A*
Chippewa Valley Technical College *A*
Concordia University Wisconsin *B*
Gateway Technical College *A*
Lakeshore Technical College *A*
Madison Area Technical College *A*
Milwaukee Area Technical College *A*
Mount Mary University *B*
University of Wisconsin
   La Crosse *B, M*

Medical receptionist

Arizona

Mohave Community College *C*

California

City College of San Francisco *C*
Platt College
   Ontario *A*
Santa Rosa Junior College *C*

Colorado

Everest College
   Aurora *C*
Morgan Community College *C*
National American University
   Denver *A*

Georgia

Central Georgia Technical College *C*
Southeastern Technical College *C*

Illinois

Illinois Eastern Community Colleges
   Frontier Community College *C*

Iowa

Dordt College *A*
Iowa Western Community College *C*

Louisiana

ITI Technical College *A*

Michigan

Baker College
   Muskegon *C*
Delta College *C*
Henry Ford Community College *C*
Jackson College *C*

Minnesota

Anoka Technical College *C*
Dakota County Technical College *C*
Lake Superior College *C*
St. Paul College *C*

Montana

Flathead Valley Community
   College *A*
Montana Tech of the University of
   Montana *C*

Nevada

Career College of Northern Nevada *C*

New York

Globe Institute of Technology *C*
Utica School of Commerce *C*

Ohio

Sinclair Community College *C*
Stautzenberger College *C, A*

Oregon

Mt. Hood Community College *C*

Pennsylvania

Consolidated School of Business
   Lancaster *A*
   York *A*

South Carolina

York Technical College *C*

Washington

Clark College *C*
Edmonds Community College *C*
Everett Community College *C*
North Seattle Community College *C*
Olympic College *C*
Peninsula College *C*
Pierce College *C*
Renton Technical College *C*
Whatcom Community College *C*

West Virginia

Bridgemont Community and
   Technical College *A*

Wisconsin

Herzing University
   Madison *C, A*
Northcentral Technical College *C*

Medical scientist

Arizona

University of Arizona *M, D*

California

Loma Linda University *D*
University of California
   Irvine *M*
   Los Angeles *M*
University of Southern California *M*

Colorado

University of Colorado
   Denver *M, D*

Connecticut

University of Connecticut *M*
Yale University *D*

District of Columbia

Georgetown University *M*

Florida

University of Miami *M*

Georgia

Georgia Regents University *M*

Illinois

Northwestern University *M, D*
Rush University *M, D*

Indiana

Indiana University
Purdue University Indianapolis *M*

Iowa

University of Iowa *M, D*

Kentucky

University of Kentucky *M*

Maine

University of Southern Maine *M*

Michigan

Wayne State University *M, D*

Minnesota

University of Minnesota
Twin Cities *M, D*

Missouri

Washington University in St. Louis *M*

New Mexico

University of New Mexico *M, D*

New York

New York Institute of Technology *M*
SUNY
Upstate Medical University *D*
University of Rochester *M*

North Carolina

University of North Carolina
Chapel Hill *M*

Ohio

Case Western Reserve University *M*
University of Cincinnati *M*
Wright State University *M*

Oklahoma

University of Oklahoma *M*

Pennsylvania

University of Pennsylvania *M*
University of Pittsburgh *M, D*

South Carolina

Medical University of South
Carolina *M*

Tennessee

Vanderbilt University *M*

Texas

University of Texas
Medical Branch at Galveston *M, D*

West Virginia

West Virginia University *M*

Wisconsin

University of Wisconsin
Madison *M, D*

Medical staff services technology

Florida

Southwest Florida College *A*

Georgia

Thomas University *B*

Louisiana

ITI Technical College *C*

Maryland

Morgan State University *B*

Minnesota

National American University
Bloomington *A*

Missouri

Missouri Southern State University *A*

New Mexico

National American University
Albuquerque *A*

New York

Globe Institute of Technology *C*

Oregon

Umpqua Community College *A*

South Dakota

National American University
Rapid City *A*

Medical transcription

Alabama

Gadsden State Community College *C*
Snead State Community College *C*
Southern Union State Community
College *C*
Virginia College
Huntsville *C*
Wallace State Community College at
Hanceville *C*

Arizona

Central Arizona College *C, A*
Eastern Arizona College *C*
GateWay Community College *C, A*
Mohave Community College *C*
Northland Pioneer College *C, A*
Phoenix College *C, A*

Arkansas

Cossatot Community College of the
University of Arkansas *C*
Mid-South Community College *C*
National Park Community College *C*
North Arkansas College *C*
Ozarka College *A*
Pulaski Technical College *C*
South Arkansas Community
College *C*
Southern Arkansas University Tech *C*

California

Canada College *A*
Chabot College *C*
Chaffey College *C*
City College of San Francisco *C*
Columbia College *C*
Cosumnes River College *C*
De Anza College *C*
Fresno City College *C, A*
Modesto Junior College *C*
Ohlone College *C*
Orange Coast College *C*
Santa Rosa Junior College *C*
Shasta College *C*
Skyline College *C, A*
South Coast College *A*
Southwestern College *C, A*
Yuba College *C, A*

Colorado

Aims Community College *C*
National American University
Denver *A*
Westwood College
Denver North *A*

Delaware

Delaware Technical Community
College
Jack F. Owens Campus *C*
Stanton/Wilmington Campus *C*

Florida

Eastern Florida State College *C*
Florida Gateway College *C*
Florida State College at
Jacksonville *C*
Indian River State College *A*
Miami Dade College *C*
Palm Beach State College *C*
Pasco-Hernando State College *C*
Polk State College *C*
Seminole State College of Florida *C*

Georgia

Albany Technical College *C*
Atlanta Technical College *C*
Augusta Technical College *C*
Central Georgia Technical College *C*
Darton College *C*
Savannah Technical College *C*
Southeastern Technical College *C*
Southwest Georgia Technical
College *C*
West Georgia Technical College *C*

Idaho

North Idaho College *A*

Illinois

Black Hawk College *C*
City Colleges of Chicago
Malcolm X College *C*
Wilbur Wright College *C*
College of DuPage *C*
College of Lake County *C*
Harper College *C*
Heartland Community College *C*
Highland Community College *C*
Illinois Eastern Community Colleges
Olney Central College *C*
John A. Logan College *C*
Kaskaskia College *C*
Kishwaukee College *C*
Lincoln Land Community College *C*
MacCormac College *A*
McHenry County College *C*
Midstate College *C*
Moraine Valley Community College *C*
Oakton Community College *C*
Parkland College *C*
Rend Lake College *C*
Rock Valley College *C*
South Suburban College of Cook
County *C*
Southeastern Illinois College *C*
Spoon River College *C*
Triton College *C*

Indiana

College of Court Reporting *A*
Indiana University
Southeast *C*
Kaplan College
Hammond *C*

Iowa

Iowa Central Community College *C*
Kirkwood Community College *C*
Northeast Iowa Community
College *C*
Southwestern Community College *A*

Kansas

Barton County Community College *C*
Cowley County Community
College *C, A*
Hutchinson Community College *C*
Neosho County Community
College *C*

Kentucky

Daymar College
Louisville *C*
National College
Danville *C*
Florence *C*
Lexington *C*
Louisville *C*
Pikeville *C*
Richmond *C*

Louisiana

Bossier Parish Community College *C*
ITI Technical College *A*

Maine

Beal College *C*
Kaplan University
South Portland *A*

Maryland

Allegany College of Maryland *A*
Howard Community College *C*
Kaplan University
Hagerstown *C, A*
Prince George's Community
College *C*

Massachusetts

Bristol Community College *C*

Michigan

Baker College
Cadillac *A*
Clinton Township *A*
Flint *A*
Jackson *A*
Muskegon *A*
Port Huron *A*
Delta College *C*
Henry Ford Community College *C*
Jackson College *C, A*
Kirtland Community College *C, A*
Mid Michigan Community College *A*
Mott Community College *C*
North Central Michigan College *C*
Oakland Community College *C, A*
Schoolcraft College *C*

Minnesota

Alexandria Technical and Community
College *C*
Dakota County Technical College *C*
Hennepin Technical College *C*
Lake Superior College *C*
Minnesota State College - Southeast
Technical *C*
Minnesota State Community and
Technical College *C*
Northland Community & Technical
College *C*
Northwest Technical College *C*
Rochester Community and Technical
College *C*
St. Catherine University *C*
St. Paul College *C*
South Central College *C*

Mississippi

Itawamba Community College *C*

Missouri

Cox College *C*
Metropolitan Community College -
Kansas City *C*
North Central Missouri College *C*

Montana

Flathead Valley Community College *C*
Montana State University
Great Falls College *C, A*
University of Montana *A*

Nebraska

Metropolitan Community College *C*

Nevada

Great Basin College *C*

New Hampshire

Manchester Community College *C*

New Jersey

Gloucester County College *C*
Hudson County Community
  College *C*
Passaic County Community College *C*
Sussex County Community College *C*

New Mexico

Central New Mexico Community
  College *C*

New York

Broome Community College *C*
Elmira Business Institute *C, A*
Globe Institute of Technology *C*
Mildred Elley
  Albany *C*
Trocaire College *C*

North Carolina

Alamance Community College *C*
Carteret Community College *C*
Catawba Valley Community
  College *C*
Central Carolina Community
  College *C*
Cleveland Community College *C*
Durham Technical Community
  College *C*
Edgecombe Community College *C*
Forsyth Technical Community
  College *C*
Guilford Technical Community
  College *C*
Sandhills Community College *C*
South Piedmont Community
  College *C*
Wayne Community College *C*
Western Piedmont Community
  College *C*

North Dakota

Cankdeska Cikana Community
  College *C*
North Dakota State College of
  Science *C*

Ohio

Belmont College *C*
ETI Technical College of Niles *A*
Eastern Gateway Community
  College *C*
Mercy College of Ohio *C*
Miami-Jacobs Career College
  Dayton *C, A*
Owens Community College
  Toledo *C*
Southern State Community College *C*
Stark State College *C*
Stautzenberger College *C, A*
University of Akron *C*
University of Akron: Wayne
  College *C*
University of Cincinnati
  Blue Ash College *C, A*
Washington State Community
  College *A*

Oregon

Central Oregon Community
  College *C*
Chemeketa Community College *C, A*
Lane Community College *C*
Linn-Benton Community College *C*

Mt. Hood Community College *A*
Southwestern Oregon Community
  College *A*
Treasure Valley Community
  College *A*

Pennsylvania

Cambria-Rowe Business College *A*
Consolidated School of Business
  Lancaster *A*
  York *A*
Erie Business Center *A*
Erie Business Center South *A*
Fortis Institute
  Erie *A*
Luzerne County Community
  College *C, A*
Penn Commercial Business and
  Technical School *C*
Westmoreland County Community
  College *C*

Puerto Rico

Columbia Centro Universitario:
  Caguas *C*
Columbia Centro Universitario:
  Yauco *C*

Rhode Island

Community College of Rhode
  Island *C*

South Carolina

Aiken Technical College *C*
Florence-Darlington Technical
  College *C*
Forrest Junior College *C, A*
Tri-County Technical College *C*
York Technical College *C*

South Dakota

Presentation College *C*
Western Dakota Technical
  Institute *C, A*

Tennessee

Dyersburg State Community
  College *C*
National College of Business and
  Technology
  Bristol *C*
  Knoxville *C*
  Nashville *C*
Roane State Community College *C*
Walters State Community College *C*

Texas

Central Texas College *C*
El Centro College *C*
Galveston College *C*
Howard College *C*
Laredo Community College *C*
Lee College *C*
Lone Star College System *C*
North Central Texas College *C*
Paris Junior College *C*
St. Philip's College *C*
San Antonio College *C*
South Plains College *C*
South Texas College *C*
Texas State Technical College
  Harlingen *C*
  West Texas *C*
Tyler Junior College *C*

Virginia

American National University
  Charlottesville *C*
  Danville *C*
  Harrisonburg *C*
  Lynchburg *C*
  Martinsville *C*
  Salem *C*
Lord Fairfax Community College *C*

Mountain Empire Community
  College *A*
Northern Virginia Community
  College *C*
Tidewater Community College *C*
Virginia Western Community
  College *C*

Washington

Bates Technical College *C*
Bellingham Technical College *C*
Centralia College *C*
Clark College *C*
Clover Park Technical College *C*
Columbia Basin College *C, A*
Everett Community College *C*
Grays Harbor College *C*
Green River Community College *C*
Highline Community College *C, A*
North Seattle Community College *C*
Peninsula College *C*
Seattle Central Community College *C*
Shoreline Community College *C*
Skagit Valley College *C*
South Puget Sound Community
  College *C*
Spokane Community College *C*
Tacoma Community College *C*
Yakima Valley Community College *C*

West Virginia

American National University
  Princeton *C*
Mountain State College *A*

Wisconsin

Gateway Technical College *C*
Lac Courte Oreilles Ojibwa
  Community College *C*
Lakeshore Technical College *C*
Mid-State Technical College *C*
Moraine Park Technical College *C*
Northcentral Technical College *C*
Southwest Wisconsin Technical
  College *C*
Waukesha County Technical
  College *C*

Medication aide

Arizona

Cochise College *C*

Arkansas

Arkansas State University
  Mountain Home *C*
East Arkansas Community College *C*
National Park Community College *C*
Southeast Arkansas College *C*

Kansas

Barton County Community College *C*
Cloud County Community College *C*
Colby Community College *C*
Cowley County Community
  College *C*
Garden City Community College *C*
Highland Community College *C*
Hutchinson Community College *C*
Independence Community College *C*
Johnson County Community
  College *C*
Kansas City Kansas Community
  College *C*
Wichita Area Technical College *C*

Kentucky

Maysville Community and Technical
  College *C*
Somerset Community College *C*

Louisiana

Our Lady of the Lake College *C*

Texas

Tyler Junior College *C*

Wyoming

Central Wyoming College *C*

Medieval and Renaissance studies

California

University of California
  Davis *B*
  Santa Barbara *B*

Connecticut

University of Connecticut *M, D*
Wesleyan University *B*
Yale University *B, M, D*

District of Columbia

Catholic University of
  America *B, M, D*
Georgetown University *B*

Florida

New College of Florida *B*

Georgia

Emory University *B*

Illinois

University of Chicago *B*

Indiana

Hanover College *B*
University of Notre Dame *B, M, D*

Kentucky

University of Louisville *C*

Louisiana

Tulane University *B*

Massachusetts

Boston College *D*
College of the Holy Cross *B*
Mount Holyoke College *B*
Smith College *B*
University of Massachusetts
  Amherst *C*
Wellesley College *B*

Michigan

University of Michigan *B*
Western Michigan University *M*

Minnesota

Augsburg College *B*
St. Olaf College *B*

Nebraska

University of Nebraska
  Lincoln *B*

New Jersey

Rutgers, The State University of New
  Jersey
  New Brunswick/Piscataway
    Campus *B*

New York

Bard College *B*
Barnard College *B*
Columbia University *B*
Cornell University *M, D*
SUNY
  University at Albany *B*
  University at Binghamton *B*
Vassar College *B*

North Carolina

Duke University *B*

Ohio

Ohio State University
  Columbus Campus *C, B*
Ohio Wesleyan University *B*
University of Toledo *B*

Oregon

University of Oregon *B*

Pennsylvania

Dickinson College *B*
Gettysburg College *B*
Penn State
  Abington *B*
  Altoona *B*
  Beaver *B*
  Berks *B*
  Brandywine *B*
  DuBois *B*
  Erie, The Behrend College *B*
  Fayette, The Eberly Campus *B*
  Greater Allegheny *B*
  Harrisburg *B*
  Hazleton *B*
  Lehigh Valley *B*
  Mont Alto *B*
  New Kensington *B*
  Schuylkill *B*
  Shenango *B*
  University Park *B*
  Wilkes-Barre *B*
  Worthington Scranton *B*
  York *B*
Swarthmore College *B*

Rhode Island

Brown University *B*

Tennessee

Sewanee: The University of the
  South *B*

Texas

Rice University *B*
Southern Methodist University *B, M*

Virginia

College of William and Mary *B*
Washington and Lee University *B*

Medium/heavy vehicle technology

Arkansas

Mid-South Community College *C*
Pulaski Technical College *C*

California

Merced College *C*

Florida

Hillsborough Community College *C*

Georgia

Atlanta Technical College *C*

Maine

Washington County Community
  College *C*

Minnesota

Dakota County Technical
  College *C, A*
Hennepin Technical College *C, A*
St. Cloud Technical and Community
  College *C, A*
St. Paul College *C*

Missouri

Linn State Technical College *A*

Nebraska

Northeast Community College *A*

Ohio

Edison State Community College *C, A*
Ohio Technical College *A*

Texas

Houston Community College
  System *C*

Virginia

Advanced Technology Institute *C, A*

Meeting and event planning

Colorado

Johnson & Wales University
  Denver *B*

Florida

Johnson & Wales University
  North Miami *B*
Lynn University *B*
University of Central Florida *B*

Georgia

Atlanta Technical College *C*

Illinois

Lexington College *C, A, B*
Roosevelt University *B, M*

Indiana

Indiana University
  Purdue University Indianapolis *M*

Massachusetts

Lasell College *B*

Michigan

Cleary University *C, A*
Southwestern Michigan College *A*

Minnesota

Dakota County Technical
  College *C, A*

New York

Niagara County Community
  College *C*

North Carolina

Johnson & Wales University
  Charlotte *B*

Ohio

Cincinnati State Technical and
  Community College *C*
Sinclair Community College *A*

Oregon

Mt. Hood Community College *C*

Pennsylvania

Northampton Community College *A*

Puerto Rico

Universidad del Este *B*

Rhode Island

Johnson & Wales University
  Providence *B*

Vermont

Burlington College *C*
Champlain College *C*

West Virginia

American Public University System *C*

Wisconsin

Fox Valley Technical College *A*

Mental health counseling

Alabama

Auburn University *M*
Faulkner University *B*
University of Alabama *M*

Arizona

Argosy University
  Online *M*
  Phoenix *M*
University of Arizona *M*
University of Phoenix
  Phoenix-Hohokam *M*
  Southern Arizona *M*

Arkansas

Arkansas State University *M*
John Brown University *M*

California

Alliant International University *M*
Argosy University
  Inland Empire *M*
  Los Angeles *M*
  Orange County *M*
  San Diego *M*
  San Francisco Bay Area *M*
University of Phoenix
  Central Valley *M*
  Sacramento Valley *M*

Colorado

Argosy University
  Denver *M*
University of Phoenix
  Denver *M*
  Southern Colorado *M*

Florida

Barry University *M*
Nova Southeastern University *M*
Rollins College *M*
Stetson University *M*
University of Florida *M, D*
University of Miami *M*
University of North Florida *M*

Georgia

Fort Valley State University *M*

Hawaii

University of Phoenix
  Hawaii *M*

Idaho

Idaho State University *M*

Illinois

Lewis University *M*
Roosevelt University *M*

Indiana

University of St. Francis *M*

Kansas

Emporia State University *M*

Kentucky

Northern Kentucky University *B, M*

Louisiana

University of Louisiana at Monroe *M*
Xavier University of Louisiana *M*

Maryland

Bowie State University *M*
Chesapeake College *A*

Massachusetts

Bridgewater State University *M*
Fitchburg State University *M*
Lesley University *M*
Suffolk University *M*
University of Massachusetts
  Boston *M*

Michigan

University of Phoenix
  Metro Detroit *M*
  West Michigan *M*
Western Michigan University *M*

Minnesota

Capella University *M*
Saint Cloud State University *M*
University of Phoenix
  Minneapolis-St. Paul *M*
Walden University *M*

Mississippi

Mississippi College *M*

Nevada

University of Phoenix
  Las Vegas *M*
  Northern Nevada *M*

New Hampshire

Southern New Hampshire
  University *M*

New Jersey

Rider University *M*
Rowan University *M*

New Mexico

University of Phoenix
  New Mexico *M*

New York

Adelphi University *M*
Canisius College *M*
City University of New York
  Brooklyn College *M*
  College of Staten Island *M*
  John Jay College of Criminal
    Justice *M*
  Queens College *M*
College of New Rochelle *M*
Hofstra University *M*
Iona College *M*
Long Island University
  LIU Brooklyn *M*
  LIU Post *M*
Manhattan College *M*
Marist College *M*
Medaille College *M*
Medaille College: Amherst *M*
Medaille College: Rochester *M*
Nyack College *M*
Pace University *M*
Pace University: Pleasantville/
  Briarcliff *M*
SUNY
  College at New Paltz *M*
  University at Buffalo *M*
St. John Fisher College *M*
St. John's University *M*
Syracuse University *M*
Yeshiva University *M*

North Carolina

Gardner-Webb University *M*

North Dakota

University of Mary *M*

Ohio

Ashland University *M*
Malone University *M*
University of Toledo *M, D*

Walsh University *M*
Xavier University *M*

Oregon
Mt. Hood Community College *C, A*

Pennsylvania
Alvernia University *M*
Gannon University *M*
Lancaster Bible College *M*
Mount Aloysius College *M*

Puerto Rico
University of Phoenix
    Puerto Rico *M*

Rhode Island
Community College of Rhode
    Island *A*

Tennessee
Argosy University
    Nashville *M*
Lee University *M*

Texas
Argosy University
    Dallas *M*
St. Edward's University *M*
St. Mary's University *M*
San Jacinto College *C, A*
Southern Methodist University *M*
Stephen F. Austin State University *M*

Utah
Argosy University
    Salt Lake City *M*
University of Phoenix
    Utah *M*

Vermont
College of St. Joseph in Vermont *M*
Goddard College *M*

Virginia
Lynchburg College *M*

Wisconsin
Marquette University *M*
University of Wisconsin
    Stout *M*
Viterbo University *M*

Mental health services technology

Alabama
Columbia Southern University *B*

Alaska
University of Alaska
    Anchorage *A, B*

Arizona
Pima Community College *C*

California
Contra Costa College *C*
San Joaquin Delta College *A*
Santa Rosa Junior College *C, A*

Colorado
Pikes Peak Community College *C, A*
Pueblo Community College *C*

Connecticut
Asnuntuck Community College *C, A*
Capital Community College *A*
Housatonic Community College *C, A*
Middlesex Community College *A*

Naugatuck Valley Community
    College *C, A*
Norwalk Community College *C, A*

Florida
College of Central Florida *A*
Daytona State College *A*
Hillsborough Community College *A*

Georgia
Darton College *A*

Idaho
North Idaho College *A*

Illinois
City Colleges of Chicago
    Wilbur Wright College *C*
College of DuPage *C*
Elgin Community College *C*
Illinois Central College *C, A*
Illinois Valley Community College *C*

Indiana
Indiana University
    Purdue University Fort Wayne *B*
Ivy Tech Community College
    Bloomington *C, A*
    Central Indiana *A*
    Columbus *C, A*
    East Central *C, A*
    Kokomo *A*
    Lafayette *C, A*
    North Central *C, A*
    Northeast *C, A*
    Northwest *C, A*
    Richmond *A*
    South Central *C, A*
    Southeast *C, A*
    Southwest *A*
    Wabash Valley *A*

Louisiana
Southern University and Agricultural
    and Mechanical College *M*

Maine
University of Maine
    Machias *B*

Maryland
Allegany College of Maryland *A*
Anne Arundel Community
    College *C, A*
College of Southern Maryland *C*
Community College of Baltimore
    County *C, A*
Hagerstown Community College *A*
Howard Community College *C*

Massachusetts
Bunker Hill Community College *C*
Massasoit Community College *C*
Mount Wachusett Community
    College *C, A*
North Shore Community
    College *C, A*
Northern Essex Community
    College *C, A*

Michigan
Wayne County Community College *C*

Minnesota
Rochester Community and Technical
    College *C, A*

Missouri
Metropolitan Community College -
    Kansas City *A*

Nebraska
Vatterott College
    Spring Valley *C*

Nevada
Great Basin College *C, A*

New York
City University of New York
    Kingsborough Community
      College *A*
    LaGuardia Community College *A*

North Carolina
Central Piedmont Community
    College *C, A*
Guilford Technical Community
    College *A*
Pitt Community College *A*
Richmond Community College *A*
Roanoke-Chowan Community
    College *A*
Southwestern Community College *A*

North Dakota
Williston State College *C, A*

Ohio
Ashland University *M*
North Central State College *A*
Sinclair Community College *A*

Pennsylvania
Community College of Allegheny
    County *C, A*
Community College of
    Philadelphia *A*
Montgomery County Community
    College *C, A*
Pennsylvania College of
    Technology *A*

Texas
Alvin Community College *A*
Del Mar College *A*
El Paso Community College *A*
Houston Community College
    System *C, A*
Laredo Community College *A*
McLennan Community College *C, A*
San Jacinto College *C, A*
Tarrant County College *C, A*

Virginia
Rappahannock Community College *C*
Virginia Western Community
    College *C, A*

Washington
Edmonds Community College *C, A*
Pierce College *C, A*
Seattle Central Community College *A*

West Virginia
Kanawha Valley Community and
    Technical College *C, A*
Mountain State College *A*

Wisconsin
Madison Area Technical College *A*

Merchandising/buying operations

Arizona
Mesa Community College *C*

California
Fashion Institute of Design and
    Merchandising
    Los Angeles *A*
Merced College *C, A*

Connecticut
Naugatuck Valley Community
    College *C, A*

Florida
International Academy of Design and
    Technology: Tampa *B*

Georgia
Middle Georgia State College *A*

Michigan
Delta College *A*

Minnesota
Art Institutes International
    Minnesota *B*

Nebraska
Northeast Community College *A*

Nevada
International Academy of Design and
    Technology
    Henderson *A, B*

New York
Long Island Business Institute *C*
Westchester Community College *A*

Ohio
University of Akron *A*
Youngstown State University *A, B, M*

Oklahoma
Oklahoma Christian University *B*

Texas
International Academy of Design and
    Technology
    San Antonio *A*
University of North Texas *M*

Washington
International Academy of Design and
    Technology
    Seattle *A, B*

Metal building assembly

Wisconsin
Gateway Technical College *C*
Lakeshore Technical College *C*
Mid-State Technical College *C*
Milwaukee Area Technical College *C*
Western Technical College *C*

Metal fabricator

Kansas
Johnson County Community
    College *C, A*

Missouri
State Fair Community College *C, A*

Montana
Helena College University of
    Montana *A*

Wisconsin
Fox Valley Technical College *C*
Waukesha County Technical
    College *C*

Metal/jewelry arts

California
Academy of Art University *C, A, B, M*
Bethesda University of California *B*

California College of the Arts *B, M*
California State University
  Long Beach *B, M*
  Northridge *B, M*
El Camino College *C*
Fashion Institute of Design and
  Merchandising
  Los Angeles *A*
  San Francisco *A*
Monterey Peninsula College *C, A*
Orange Coast College *C*
Palomar College *A*
Santa Rosa Junior College *C*
Santiago Canyon College *A*

Colorado
Adams State University *B*

Connecticut
Middlesex Community College *A*

District of Columbia
Corcoran College of Art and
  Design *C*

Georgia
Savannah College of Art and
  Design *B, M*

Iowa
University of Iowa *B, M*

Kansas
University of Kansas *B, M*

Maine
Maine College of Art *B*

Massachusetts
Massachusetts College of Art and
  Design *B, M*
School of the Museum of Fine
  Arts *B, M*
University of Massachusetts
  Dartmouth *B, M*

Michigan
College for Creative Studies *B*
Ferris State University *B*
Grand Valley State University *B*
Northern Michigan University *B*
Siena Heights University *B*

Montana
Flathead Valley Community
  College *C, A*

New York
Fashion Institute of Technology *A*
Hofstra University *B*
Rochester Institute of
  Technology *B, M*
SUNY
  College at Buffalo *B*
  College at New Paltz *B, M*
Syracuse University *B, M*

North Carolina
East Carolina University *B*
Haywood Community College *A*
Montgomery Community College *C*

Ohio
Bowling Green State University *B*
Cleveland Institute of Art *B*
University of Akron *B*

Oregon
Oregon College of Art & Craft *C, B*
University of Oregon *B*

Pennsylvania
Arcadia University *B*
Seton Hill University *B*
Temple University *B, M*
University of the Arts *B*

Rhode Island
Rhode Island School of Design *B, M*

Tennessee
Memphis College of Art *B, M*

Texas
Paris Junior College *A*
University of Texas
  El Paso *B, M*
Western Texas College *A*

Washington
University of Washington *B, M*

Wisconsin
Northeast Wisconsin Technical
  College *C*

Metallurgical engineering

Alabama
University of Alabama *B, M*

Colorado
Colorado School of Mines *B, M, D*

Idaho
University of Idaho *M*

Illinois
University of Illinois
  Urbana-Champaign *B, M, D*

Minnesota
University of Minnesota
  Twin Cities *B, M*

Missouri
Missouri University of Science and
  Technology *B, M, D*

Montana
Montana Tech of the University of
  Montana *B, M*

Nevada
University of Nevada
  Reno *B, M, D*

New Mexico
New Mexico Institute of Mining and
  Technology *B*

New York
Columbia University *B, M, D*

Ohio
Cleveland State University *B, M*
Ohio State University
  Columbus Campus *B*
University of Cincinnati *M, D*

South Dakota
South Dakota School of Mines and
  Technology *B, M*

Texas
University of Texas
  El Paso *B*

Utah
University of Utah *B, M, D*

Washington
University of Washington *B*

Metallurgical technology

Arkansas
Arkansas Northeastern College *C, A*

California
City College of San Francisco *C*

Illinois
Black Hawk College *C*

Michigan
Mott Community College *C*
Schoolcraft College *C, A*

Minnesota
Ridgewater College *A*

Montana
Montana State University
  Northern *A*

Oregon
Linn-Benton Community College *C*

Pennsylvania
Penn State
  Altoona *A*
  Berks *A*
  DuBois *A*
  Erie, The Behrend College *A*
  Fayette, The Eberly Campus *A*
  Hazleton *A*
  New Kensington *A*
  Schuylkill *A*
  Shenango *A*
  Wilkes-Barre *A*
  York *A*

Texas
Kilgore College *C, A*

Meteorology

Florida
Daytona State College *A*
Florida Institute of Technology *B, M*
University of Miami *B*

Hawaii
University of Hawaii
  Manoa *B, M, D*

Illinois
Western Illinois University *B*

Indiana
Purdue University *B*

Iowa
Iowa State University *M, D*

Kansas
Hutchinson Community College *A*

Kentucky
Western Kentucky University *B*

Massachusetts
Massachusetts Institute of
  Technology *M, D*

Michigan
Central Michigan University *B*

Minnesota
Saint Cloud State University *B*

New Jersey
Rutgers, The State University of New
  Jersey
  New Brunswick/Piscataway
    Campus *B*

New York
SUNY
  College at Brockport *B*
  College at Oneonta *B*
  College at Oswego *B*
Suffolk County Community College *A*

North Carolina
University of North Carolina
  Charlotte *B*

Oklahoma
University of Oklahoma *B, M, D*

South Dakota
South Dakota School of Mines and
  Technology *C*

Texas
University of the Incarnate Word *B*

Utah
University of Utah *B, M, D*

Vermont
Lyndon State College *B*

Virginia
Virginia Polytechnic Institute and
  State University *B*

West Virginia
Kanawha Valley Community and
  Technical College *A*

Wisconsin
Northland College *B*
University of Wisconsin
  Milwaukee *B*

Microbiology

Alabama
University of Alabama *B*
University of Alabama
  Birmingham *D*

Arizona
Arizona State University *B, D*
Northern Arizona University *B*
University of Arizona *B, M, D*

California
California State University
  Chico *B*
  Dominguez Hills *B*
  Los Angeles *B*
Loma Linda University *M, D*
Pitzer College *B*
San Diego State University *B, M*
San Francisco State University *M*
San Jose State University *B, M*
University of California
  Berkeley *B, D*
  Davis *B, M, D*
  Riverside *M, D*

Colorado
Colorado State University *B, M, D*
University of Colorado
  Denver *D*

Connecticut
University of Connecticut *M, D*

District of Columbia
Howard University *M, D*

Florida
Daytona State College *A*

Georgia
University of Georgia *B, M, D*

Hawaii
University of Hawaii
Manoa *B, M, D*

Idaho
Idaho State University *B, M, D*
University of Idaho *B*

Illinois
Southern Illinois University
Carbondale *B*
University of Chicago *D*
University of Illinois
Urbana-Champaign *B, M, D*

Indiana
Indiana University
Bloomington *B, M, D*
Purdue University *B, M, D*

Iowa
Iowa State University *B, M, D*
Iowa Western Community College *A*
University of Iowa *B, M, D*
University of Northern Iowa *B*

Kansas
Kansas State University *B, D*
University of Kansas *B, M, D*

Louisiana
Louisiana State University and
Agricultural and Mechanical
College *B*
University of Louisiana at Lafayette *B*
Xavier University of Louisiana *B*

Maine
University of Maine *B, M, D*

Maryland
University of Maryland
Baltimore *D*
College Park *B*

Massachusetts
University of Massachusetts
Amherst *B, M, D*

Michigan
Michigan State University *B, M, D*
Northern Michigan University *B*
University of Michigan *B, D*

Minnesota
University of Minnesota
Twin Cities *M*

Missouri
Saint Louis University *D*
University of Missouri
Columbia *B*

Montana
Montana State University
Billings *B*

Nebraska
University of Nebraska
Lincoln *B*

New Hampshire
University of New Hampshire *M, D*

New Jersey
Rutgers, The State University of New
Jersey
New Brunswick/Piscataway
Campus *B, M, D*
Newark Campus *B, M, D*
Seton Hall University *M*

New York
Albany College of Pharmacy and
Health Sciences *B*
New York University *M*
SUNY
University at Stony Brook *D*
Upstate Medical University *M, D*
University of Rochester *B, M*

North Carolina
Methodist University *A, B*
North Carolina State
University *B, M, D*

North Dakota
North Dakota State University *B, M*

Ohio
Miami University
Oxford *B, M, D, T*
Ohio State University
Columbus Campus *B, M, D*
Ohio University *B, M, D*
Ohio Wesleyan University *B*

Oklahoma
Oklahoma State University *B, M, D*
University of Oklahoma *B, M, D*

Oregon
Oregon Health & Science
University *D*
Oregon State University *B, M*

Pennsylvania
University of Pittsburgh *B*
University of the Sciences *B*

Puerto Rico
Inter American University of Puerto
Rico
Aguadilla Campus *B*
Bayamon Campus *B*
Ponce Campus *B*
San German Campus *B*
Universidad del Este *B*
University of Puerto Rico
Humacao *B*
Mayaguez *B*
Medical Sciences *M, D*

Rhode Island
University of Rhode Island *B*

South Carolina
Clemson University *B, M, D*

South Dakota
South Dakota State University *B*

Tennessee
Vanderbilt University *M, D*

Texas
Texas A&M University *B, M, D*
Texas State University *B*
Texas Tech University *B, M*
University of Texas
Arlington *B*
Austin *M, D*
El Paso *B*
Health Science Center at
Houston *M, D*
San Antonio *B*

Utah
Brigham Young University *B, M, D*
Weber State University *B*

Vermont
University of Vermont *B*

Washington
University of Washington *B*
Washington State University *B, M, D*

West Virginia
West Virginia University *M, D*

Wisconsin
University of Wisconsin
La Crosse *B*
Madison *B, M, D*
Milwaukee *B*

Wyoming
University of Wyoming *B*

Microbiology and immunology

California
Stanford University *M, D*
University of California
Irvine *B*
University of Southern
California *M, D*

District of Columbia
Georgetown University *M, D*

Florida
University of Miami *B, M, D*

Illinois
University of Chicago *D*

Indiana
Indiana University
Purdue University
Indianapolis *M, D*

Maine
College of the Atlantic *B, M*

Michigan
University of Michigan *M, D*

Nebraska
Creighton University *M, D*

New York
Yeshiva University *M, D*

South Carolina
Medical University of South
Carolina *D*

Texas
University of Texas
Medical Branch at Galveston *M, D*

West Virginia
West Virginia University *B, D*

Middle Eastern and Semitic languages

Illinois
Trinity International University *M*

Indiana
Indiana University
Bloomington *B, M, D*

Michigan
University of Michigan *M, D*

Pennsylvania
University of Pennsylvania *B, M, D*

Texas
University of Texas
Austin *B, M, D*

Middle school education

Alabama
Birmingham-Southern College *T*

Alaska
Alaska Pacific University *A, B, M*

Arkansas
Arkansas Northeastern College *A*
Arkansas State University *B, T*
Arkansas State University
Newport *A*
Arkansas Tech University *B*
Cossatot Community College of the
University of Arkansas *A*
East Arkansas Community College *A*
Harding University *B, T*
Henderson State University *B*
John Brown University *B, T*
Mid-South Community College *A*
Northwest Arkansas Community
College *A*
Ouachita Baptist University *B, T*
Ozarka College *A*
Southern Arkansas University *B*
University of Arkansas
Fort Smith *B*
Little Rock *B, M*
Monticello *B*
Pine Bluff *B*
University of Central Arkansas *B*
University of the Ozarks *B*

California
Alliant International University *T*
Azusa Pacific University *B, T*
California Baptist University *T*
California Lutheran University *B, M*
California State University
East Bay *T*
Long Beach *T*
Northridge *M*
San Bernardino *M, T*
San Marcos *T*
Master's College *B, T*
Mills College *T*
Mount St. Mary's College *M*
St. Mary's College of California *T*
San Diego Christian College *B, T*
San Francisco State University *T*
Sonoma State University *M*
University of Redlands *B, T*
Whittier College *T*

Colorado
Adams State University *B, T*

Connecticut
Albertus Magnus College *B, T*
Eastern Connecticut State
University *B, T*
Quinnipiac University *B, M*
University of New Haven *M*

Delaware
Delaware State University *B*
Delaware Technical Community
College
Jack F. Owens Campus *A*
Stanton/Wilmington Campus *A*
Terry Campus *A*
University of Delaware *B, T*

Florida

Chipola College *B*
Florida Institute of Technology *B*
Saint Leo University *B*
University of Miami *B*
University of North Florida *B*
University of South Florida
    Saint Petersburg *M*
University of West Florida *B*

Georgia

Albany State University *B, M*
Armstrong Atlantic State
    University *M*
Bainbridge College *A*
Berry College *B, M*
Brenau University *B, M*
Brewton-Parker College *B*
Clayton State University *B*
College of Coastal Georgia *A, B*
Columbus State University *B, M*
Darton College *A*
Emmanuel College *B*
Fort Valley State University *B, M, T*
Georgia College and State
    University *B, M, T*
Georgia Regents University *B*
Georgia Southern University *B, M*
Georgia Southwestern State
    University *B*
Georgia State University *M*
Kennesaw State University *B, M, D*
Mercer University *B, M, T*
Middle Georgia State College *A, B*
Oglethorpe University *M*
Paine College *B*
Piedmont College *B, M, T*
Point University *B*
Reinhardt University *B*
Savannah State University *B*
Shorter University *B, T*
South Georgia State College *A*
Thomas University *B*
Toccoa Falls College *B, T*
Truett-McConnell College *B*
University of Georgia *B, M, D, T*
University of North Georgia *B, M*
Valdosta State University *B, M*
Young Harris College *B*

Idaho

Boise State University *T*

Illinois

Augustana College *T*
Dominican University *T*
Eastern Illinois University *B*
Eureka College *B*
Illinois State University *B, M, T*
McKendree University *T*
Monmouth College *T*
North Park University *B, M, T*
Southwestern Illinois College *A*

Indiana

Ball State University *M*
Bethel College *B*
Butler University *B, M*
Earlham College *M*
Huntington University *M*
Indiana Wesleyan University *B, T*
Manchester University *B, T*
Trine University *B, T*
University of Evansville *M*
University of Indianapolis *T*
Valparaiso University *B, M, T*

Iowa

Buena Vista University *T*
Central College *T*
Coe College *B*
Cornell College *B, T*
Dordt College *B, T*
Ellsworth Community College *A*

Faith Baptist Bible College and
    Theological Seminary *B, T*
Graceland University *T*
Grinnell College *T*
Iowa Wesleyan College *B*
Mount Mercy University *T*
Northwestern College *T*
Simpson College *T*
University of Northern Iowa *B, M*
Upper Iowa University *B, T*

Kansas

Baker University *B, T*
Bethel College *T*
Colby Community College *A*
Friends University *B, T*
Garden City Community College *A*
Independence Community College *A*
McPherson College *B, T*
MidAmerica Nazarene University *B, T*
Newman University *B, T*
Tabor College *B*
University of Kansas *B, T*

Kentucky

Alice Lloyd College *B*
Asbury University *B, T*
Bellarmine University *B, M, T*
Berea College *B, T*
Brescia University *B, T*
Campbellsville University *B*
Eastern Kentucky University *B, M*
Georgetown College *B, M*
Hopkinsville Community College *A*
Kentucky Christian University *B, T*
Kentucky Wesleyan College *B, T*
Lindsey Wilson College *B, T*
Midway College *B*
Morehead State University *B, M, T*
Murray State University *B, M, T*
Northern Kentucky University *B, M*
St. Catharine College *B*
Spalding University *B, M*
Thomas More College *B, M*
Transylvania University *B, T*
Union College *B, M*
University of Kentucky *B, M*
University of Pikeville *B*
University of the
    Cumberlands *B, M, T*
Western Kentucky University *B, M, T*

Louisiana

Centenary College of Louisiana *T*
Grambling State University *B*
Louisiana College *B*
Nicholls State University *B*
Northwestern State University *B, M*
Southeastern Louisiana University *B*
Southern University and Agricultural
    and Mechanical College *B*
University of Louisiana at Lafayette *B*
University of New Orleans *M*

Maine

University of Southern Maine *T*

Maryland

Hood College *T*
Morgan State University *M*
Stevenson University *B*
Towson University *B*
University of Maryland
    College Park *B*

Massachusetts

American International
    College *B, M, T*
Anna Maria College *T*
Assumption College *T*
Clark University *M*
Eastern Nazarene College *B, M, T*
Fitchburg State University *B, M, T*
Gordon College *B*

Lesley University *B, M*
Massachusetts College of Liberal
    Arts *T*
Merrimack College *B, M*
Salem State University *B, M*
Tufts University *M, T*
University of Massachusetts
    Dartmouth *M, T*
Wellesley College *T*
Westfield State University *M, T*
Worcester State University *M, T*

Michigan

Baker College
    Allen Park *B*
    Auburn Hills *B*
    Clinton Township *B*
    Flint *B*
    Jackson *B*
    Muskegon *B*
    Owosso *B*
Calvin College *B, T*
Central Michigan University *M*
Eastern Michigan University *M*
Grand Valley State University *T*
Michigan State University *B*
Rochester College *B*
University of Detroit Mercy *B, M, T*

Minnesota

Bethel University *B*
Concordia University St. Paul *B, T*
Hamline University *T*
Minnesota State University
    Mankato *B, T*
Ridgewater College *A*
St. Catherine University *B*
University of Minnesota
    Duluth *B*
University of St. Thomas *B*

Missouri

Avila University *B, T*
Central Methodist University *B*
College of the Ozarks *T*
Evangel University *B, T*
Fontbonne University *B, T*
Harris-Stowe State University *B*
Lincoln University *B, M*
Lindenwood University *B, M*
Maryville University of Saint
    Louis *B, M, T*
Missouri Baptist University *B, T*
Missouri Southern State
    University *B, T*
Missouri State University *B*
Missouri Valley College *T*
Missouri Western State University *B*
Northwest Missouri State
    University *B, M, T*
Ozark Christian College *A*
Saint Louis University *B, T*
Southeast Missouri State University *B*
Southwest Baptist University *B, T*
University of Central Missouri *B, T*
University of Missouri
    Columbia *B, M, D*
    Kansas City *B*
Washington University in St.
    Louis *B, M, T*
Webster University *B, M*
Westminster College *B, T*
William Jewell College *T*
William Woods University *B, T*

Montana

University of Great Falls *B, M*

Nebraska

Chadron State College *B*
College of Saint Mary *B, T*
Concordia University *B, T*
Grace University *B*
Midland University *B, T*

Nebraska Wesleyan University *B*
University of Nebraska
    Kearney *B, M, T*
Wayne State College *B, T*
York College *B, T*

Nevada

Sierra Nevada College *M*

New Hampshire

Granite State College *B, T*

New Jersey

Centenary College *T*
Rutgers, The State University of New
    Jersey
    Camden Campus *T*
    New Brunswick/Piscataway
        Campus *T*
    Newark Campus *T*

New Mexico

New Mexico Junior College *A*

New York

Alfred University *B, T*
Barnard College *T*
City University of New York
    Brooklyn College *M*
College of Mount St. Vincent *T*
D'Youville College *M*
Dowling College *B, M*
Dutchess Community College *A*
Elmira College *B, T*
Long Island University
    LIU Post *M, T*
Manhattan College *B, T*
Manhattanville College *M, T*
Medaille College *B*
Medaille College: Amherst *M*
Mercy College *M, T*
Mount Saint Mary College *M*
Nassau Community College *A*
Nazareth College *T*
SUNY
    College at Fredonia *T*
    College at Old Westbury *B, M, T*
Ulster County Community College *A*
University of Rochester *M*
Vassar College *T*
Wagner College *B, M, T*

North Carolina

Appalachian State University *B, M, T*
Barton College *B, T*
Campbell University *B, M, T*
Catawba College *B, M, T*
East Carolina University *B, M*
Elizabeth City State University *B, T*
Elon University *B, T*
Fayetteville State University *B, M, T*
Gardner-Webb University *B*
Greensboro College *B, T*
High Point University *B, T*
Lenoir-Rhyne University *B, M, T*
Mars Hill University *B, T*
Meredith College *T*
Methodist University *A, B, T*
North Carolina Central
    University *B, M, T*
North Carolina State
    University *B, M, T*
North Carolina Wesleyan College *B*
University of North Carolina
    Asheville *T*
    Chapel Hill *B*
    Charlotte *B*
    Greensboro *B*
    Pembroke *B, M*
    Wilmington *B, M*
Western Carolina University *B, T*
Wingate University *B, T*
Winston-Salem State University *B*

North Dakota

Dickinson State University B, T
University of North Dakota B

Ohio

Antioch University
    Midwest M
Ashland University B, T
Baldwin Wallace University B, T
Bluffton University B
Bowling Green State University B, T
Capital University B
Cedarville University B
Central State University B
Cincinnati Christian University B
Cleveland State University B
College of Mount St. Joseph B, T
College of Wooster T
Defiance College B, T
Hiram College T
Kent State University B
Kent State University
    Geauga B
    Stark B
Lourdes University B
Malone University B
Marietta College B
Miami University
    Oxford B, T
Mount Vernon Nazarene
    University B, T
Muskingum University B, M, T
Notre Dame College T
Ohio Dominican University B, T
Ohio Northern University B, T
Ohio State University
    Columbus Campus M
Ohio University M, D, T
Ohio University
    Chillicothe Campus B
    Southern Campus at Ironton M
    Zanesville Campus B
Ohio Wesleyan University B
Otterbein University B
University of Akron B
University of Cincinnati B
University of Cincinnati
    Blue Ash College A
    Clermont College A
University of Dayton B, M, T
University of Findlay B, M, T
University of Mount Union B, T
University of Rio Grande B, T
Urbana University B
Ursuline College B, M, T
Walsh University B
Wilmington College B
Wittenberg University B
Wright State University B, M, T
Wright State University: Lake
    Campus B
Xavier University B
Youngstown State University B, M

Oklahoma

Northwestern Oklahoma State
    University B
Oklahoma Christian University B, T
Southwestern Oklahoma State
    University M, T

Oregon

Concordia University B, M, T
Corban University B
George Fox University M, T
Lewis & Clark College M
Linfield College T
Portland State University T
University of Oregon M, T
University of Phoenix
    Oregon M
Warner Pacific College T
Western Oregon University B, M, T
Willamette University M

Pennsylvania

Alvernia University B
Bloomsburg University of
    Pennsylvania B, M, T
California University of
    Pennsylvania B
Carlow University B
Chestnut Hill College M, T
DeSales University T
Duquesne University B, T
Eastern University B
Edinboro University of
    Pennsylvania B, M
Elizabethtown College B, T
Gannon University B
Geneva College B, T
Gettysburg College T
Grove City College B, T
Indiana University of Pennsylvania B
Kutztown University of
    Pennsylvania B
La Salle University B, T
Lock Haven University of
    Pennsylvania B
Mansfield University of
    Pennsylvania B, T
Messiah College B, T
Millersville University of
    Pennsylvania B
Misericordia University B
Mount Aloysius College B
Northampton Community College A
Reading Area Community College A
St. Vincent College T
Shippensburg University of
    Pennsylvania B, T
Temple University B, M
University of Scranton B
Valley Forge Christian College D
Washington & Jefferson College T
West Chester University of
    Pennsylvania B, T
Westminster College B, T
Wilkes University B, T

Rhode Island

Roger Williams University T

South Carolina

Bob Jones University B
Claflin University D
Clemson University M
Coastal Carolina University B, T
College of Charleston B, T
Columbia College B, T
Newberry College B, T
Presbyterian College B, T
South Carolina State University B, T
University of South Carolina
    Aiken B, T
    Upstate B
Winthrop University B, M

Tennessee

Belmont University B, M, T
Carson-Newman University B, M
Christian Brothers University M, T
Cumberland University B, T
Freed-Hardeman University B, T
King University T
Lee University B
Lincoln Memorial University B, T
Martin Methodist College B
Milligan College M, T
Tennessee Technological University T
Tusculum College B, T
Union University B, T
University of Tennessee
    Chattanooga B, T
Victory University B, T

Texas

Alvin Community College A
Arlington Baptist College B, T

Austin College M
Austin Community College A
Collin County Community College
    District A
Dallas Christian College T
Del Mar College A
Houston Baptist University B, M
Howard Payne University B
Jarvis Christian College B, T
LeTourneau University B, T
Lone Star College System A
Lubbock Christian University B, T
McMurry University B
Mountain View College A
Our Lady of the Lake University of
    San Antonio M
St. Edward's University T
San Jacinto College A
Schreiner University B
South Texas College A
Tarrant County College A
Texas A&M University
    Kingsville M
Texas Christian University M
Texas College B, T
Texas Lutheran University B, T
Trinity Valley Community College A
University of Dallas T
University of Phoenix
    San Antonio M
Wayland Baptist University B, T
West Texas A&M University T

Vermont

Castleton State College B, M, T
Champlain College B
Goddard College B, M
Green Mountain College B, M
Johnson State College B, M
Saint Michael's College M, T
University of Vermont B, T

Virginia

Bluefield College B
Hollins University T
Longwood University T
Mary Baldwin College T
Radford University T
Virginia Wesleyan College B, T

Washington

Central Washington University B, T
City University of Seattle B, M, T
Heritage University B, M
Northwest University B
University of Puget Sound T
University of Washington M, T
Whitworth University B, M, T

West Virginia

Fairmont State University M
West Virginia State University B
Wheeling Jesuit University B

Wisconsin

Alverno College B, M, T
Beloit College T
Carroll University B, T
Concordia University Wisconsin B, T
Lakeland College B
Ripon College T
St. Norbert College T
University of Wisconsin
    Green Bay T
    Platteville T
    River Falls T
    Superior M, T

Military history

Missouri

Columbia College M

New York

United States Military Academy B

Oklahoma

Rogers State University B

Vermont

Norwich University M

West Virginia

American Public University
    System A, B, M

Military technologies

Alabama

Calhoun Community College A

Arizona

Cochise College A

Maryland

United States Naval Academy B

Minnesota

Northland Community & Technical
    College C, A

Ohio

Sinclair Community College C, A

Pennsylvania

Point Park University M

South Carolina

Coastal Carolina University B

West Virginia

American Public University
    System C, A

Mining and mineral engineering

Alaska

University of Alaska
    Fairbanks B, M

Arizona

University of Arizona B, M, D

Colorado

Colorado School of Mines B, M, D

Delaware

Delaware State University B

Illinois

Southern Illinois University
    Carbondale B, M

Kentucky

University of Kentucky B, M, D

Michigan

Michigan Technological
    University M, D

Minnesota

University of Minnesota
    Twin Cities B, M, D

Missouri

Missouri University of Science and
    Technology B, M, D

Montana

Montana Tech of the University of
    Montana B, M

Nevada

University of Nevada
Reno *B, M*

New Mexico

New Mexico Institute of Mining and
Technology *B, M*

New York

Columbia University *B, M, D*

Pennsylvania

Penn State
Abington *B*
Altoona *B*
Beaver *B*
Berks *B*
Brandywine *B*
DuBois *B*
Erie, The Behrend College *B*
Fayette, The Eberly Campus *B*
Greater Allegheny *B*
Harrisburg *B*
Hazleton *B*
Lehigh Valley *B*
Mont Alto *B*
New Kensington *B*
Schuylkill *B*
Shenango *B*
University Park *B*
Wilkes-Barre *B*
Worthington Scranton *B*
York *B*

South Dakota

South Dakota School of Mines and
Technology *B, M*

Utah

University of Utah *B, M, D*
Utah State University *A*

Virginia

Virginia Polytechnic Institute and
State University *B, M, D*

West Virginia

West Virginia University *B, M, D*

Mining technology

Alaska

University of Alaska
Fairbanks *C*

Arizona

Eastern Arizona College *A*

Colorado

Colorado Northwestern Community
College *C*

Illinois

Illinois Eastern Community Colleges
Wabash Valley College *C*

Indiana

Vincennes University *A*

Kentucky

Madisonville Community College *C*

Pennsylvania

Penn State
Fayette, The Eberly Campus *A*

Utah

Utah State University *A*

Virginia

Southwest Virginia Community
College *A*

West Virginia

Bluefield State College *B*

Wyoming

Casper College *C, A*
Sheridan College *A*
Western Wyoming Community
College *C, A*

Missionary studies

Alabama

Faulkner University *B, M*

Alaska

Alaska Bible College *B*

Arizona

International Baptist College *B*

Arkansas

Ecclesia College *B*
Harding University *B, M*
John Brown University *B*
Ouachita Baptist University *B*
Williams Baptist College *B*

California

Bethesda University of California *B*
Biola University *D*
California Baptist University *B*
Hope International
University *A, B, M*
Salvation Army College for Officer
Training at Crestmont *C, A*
San Diego Christian College *B*
Simpson University *B*
Vanguard University of Southern
California *B*
William Jessup University *C, B*

Florida

Hobe Sound Bible College *C, A, B*
Johnson University: Florida *B*
Palm Beach Atlantic University *B*
Southeastern University *B*
Trinity Baptist College *B*
Trinity College of Florida *B*

Georgia

Toccoa Falls College *B*
Truett-McConnell College *B*

Idaho

Boise Bible College *A, B*
Northwest Nazarene University *B*

Illinois

Lincoln Christian University *B, M*
Moody Bible Institute *B, M*
Olivet Nazarene University *B*
Trinity International University *M*
Wheaton College *M*

Indiana

Bethel College *B*
Grace College *B, M, D*
Huntington University *B*
Taylor University *C*

Iowa

Dordt College *B*
Emmaus Bible College *B*
Faith Baptist Bible College and
Theological Seminary *A, B*
University of Dubuque *M*

Kansas

Barclay College *B*
Central Christian College of Kansas *A*
Manhattan Christian College *A, B*

MidAmerica Nazarene University *B*
Sterling College *B*

Kentucky

Asbury University *B*
Kentucky Mountain Bible College *B*
Mid-Continent University *B*
Southern Baptist Theological
Seminary *B*

Louisiana

New Orleans Baptist Theological
Seminary *M, D*

Michigan

Andrews University *M, D*
Grace Bible College *B*
Kuyper College *B*
Spring Arbor University *B*

Minnesota

Bethel University *D*
Concordia University St. Paul *B, M*
Crossroads College *B*
Crown College *B*
North Central University *A, B*
Oak Hills Christian College *B*
University of Northwestern - St.
Paul *B*

Missouri

Baptist Bible College *B, M*
Evangel University *B*
Ozark Christian College *B*
St. Louis Christian College *A, B*
Southwest Baptist University *B*

Montana

Montana Bible College *B*

Nebraska

Grace University *B*
Nebraska Christian College *A, B*

New York

Nyack College *B, M*

North Carolina

Gardner-Webb University *B, M*
Mid-Atlantic Christian University *B*
Montreat College *B*
Piedmont International University *B*
Southeastern Baptist Theological
Seminary *C, B, M, D*

North Dakota

Trinity Bible College *B*

Ohio

Cedarville University *B*
Cincinnati Christian University *B*
God's Bible School and College *A, B*
Mount Vernon Nazarene University *B*
Ohio Christian University *B*

Oklahoma

Hillsdale Free Will Baptist
College *A, B*
Oklahoma Baptist University *B*
Oklahoma Christian University *B*
Oklahoma Wesleyan University *C, B*
Oral Roberts University *B, M*
Southern Nazarene University *B*
Southwestern Christian University *B*

Oregon

Corban University *B*
Multnomah University *B*
New Hope Christian College *B*
Northwest Christian University *B*

Pennsylvania

Baptist Bible College of
Pennsylvania *B*
Cairn University *B*
Eastern University *B*
Valley Forge Christian College *B*

Puerto Rico

Universidad Pentecostal Mizpa *A*

South Carolina

Bob Jones University *B*
Columbia International University *M*
North Greenville University *B*
W.L. Bonner Bible College *C, B*

Tennessee

Freed-Hardeman University *B*
Lee University *B*
Lipscomb University *B*
Southern Adventist University *B*
Tennessee Temple University *B*
Welch College *B*

Texas

Abilene Christian University *M*
Arlington Baptist College *B*
Criswell College *B, M*
Dallas Baptist University *M*
East Texas Baptist University *B*
Hardin-Simmons University *B*
Howard Payne University *B*
Lubbock Christian University *B*
Southwestern Assemblies of God
University *B, M*

Virginia

Liberty University *B, M*
Regent University *M*

Washington

Northwest University *B*
Trinity Lutheran College *B*

Wisconsin

Concordia University Wisconsin *B*
Maranatha Baptist Bible College *B, M*

Modern Greek

California

Loyola Marymount University *B*

District of Columbia

Howard University *B*

Florida

Ave Maria University *B*

Indiana

Butler University *B*

Louisiana

Tulane University *B*

Massachusetts

Boston University *B*
Wheaton College *B*

Michigan

Calvin College *B*
University of Michigan *B*

New York

Barnard College *B*
Colgate University *B*
Columbia University *B*
Fordham University *B*

Molecular biochemistry — Ohio

Ohio
Ohio State University
  Columbus Campus *B*
Wright State University *B*

Molecular biochemistry

Alabama
University of Alabama
  Birmingham *D*

Arkansas
University of Arkansas
  for Medical Sciences *M, D*

California
Mills College *C, B*
University of California
  Davis *B, M, D*
  Los Angeles *M, D*
  Santa Cruz *B*

Connecticut
Wesleyan University *B, D*

District of Columbia
Georgetown University *M, D*

Illinois
Southern Illinois University
  Carbondale *M, D*
University of Chicago *D*

Iowa
Cornell College *B*

New York
Clarkson University *B*

Ohio
Ohio State University
  Columbus Campus *M, D*

South Carolina
Bob Jones University *B*

Texas
University of Texas
  El Paso *B*
  Medical Branch at Galveston *M, D*

Molecular biology

Alabama
Auburn University *B*

Alaska
University of Alaska
  Fairbanks *M, D*

Arizona
Arizona State University *B*

California
California Lutheran University *B*
California State University
  Long Beach *B*
  Northridge *B*
  Sacramento *B, M*
Claremont McKenna College *B*
Dominican University of California *M*
Los Angeles Southwest College *A*
Pomona College *B*
San Diego State University *M*
San Jose State University *B*
Scripps College *B*
Stanford University *M, D*
University of California
  Los Angeles *D*
  Riverside *M, D*
  San Diego *B*
  Santa Barbara *B, M, D*

University of Southern
  California *M, D*

Colorado
University of Colorado
  Denver *D*
University of Denver *B*

Connecticut
Central Connecticut State
  University *B, M*
Quinnipiac University *B, M*
University of Connecticut *M, D*
Wesleyan University *B, D*
Yale University *B, M, D*

Florida
Florida Institute of Technology *B*
Rollins College *B*
Stetson University *B*

Georgia
Georgia Regents University *M, D*

Idaho
University of Idaho *B, M, D*

Illinois
Benedictine University *B*
Chicago State University *B*
Loyola University Chicago *M, D*
Millikin University *B*

Indiana
Goshen College *B*
Purdue University *B, M, D*

Iowa
Coe College *B*
Cornell College *B*
Iowa State University *M, D*
Iowa Western Community College *A*
University of Iowa *D*

Kansas
University of Kansas *B*
University of Kansas Medical
  Center *M*

Kentucky
Centre College *B*

Louisiana
Tulane University *B, M, D*

Maine
Colby College *B*
University of Maine *B, M, D*
University of Southern Maine *D*

Maryland
Johns Hopkins University *B, M, D*
University of Maryland
  Baltimore County *M*
  College Park *D*

Massachusetts
Assumption College *B*
Boston University *B, M, D*
Brandeis University *M, D*
Clark University *B*
Tufts University *M, D*

Michigan
Andrews University *B*
Eastern Michigan University *M*
Lawrence Technological University *B*
Michigan State University *B, M, D*
University of Michigan *B, M, D*
University of Michigan
  Flint *B*
Wayne State University *M, D*

Minnesota
University of Minnesota
  Twin Cities *D*

Mississippi
Mississippi State University *D*

Missouri
Saint Louis University *M, D*
Washington University in St. Louis *D*
William Jewell College *B*

Montana
Montana State University *M, D*

New Hampshire
Dartmouth College *B*

New Jersey
Montclair State University *B*
Princeton University *B, M, D*
Rutgers, The State University of New
  Jersey
  New Brunswick/Piscataway
    Campus *B*
Seton Hall University *D*

New Mexico
New Mexico State University *M, D*

New York
Colgate University *B*
Cornell University *M, D*
SUNY
  University at Albany *B, M, D*
  University at Stony Brook *D*
  Upstate Medical University *D*
Wells College *B*
Yeshiva University *B*

North Carolina
East Carolina University *M*
Meredith College *B*
Wake Forest University *M, D*

North Dakota
University of North Dakota *B*

Ohio
Case Western Reserve University *D*
Kenyon College *B*
Miami University
  Middletown *A*
Muskingum University *B*
Ohio Northern University *B*
Otterbein University *B*
University of Toledo *M, D*
Wittenberg University *B*

Oregon
Reed College *B*

Pennsylvania
Chestnut Hill College *B*
Clarion University of Pennsylvania *B*
DeSales University *B*
Drexel University *M*
Gettysburg College *B*
Lehigh University *B, M, D*
Lycoming College *B*
Mansfield University of
  Pennsylvania *B*
Messiah College *B*
University of Pittsburgh *B*
University of Scranton *B*
Westminster College *B*

Puerto Rico
Inter American University of Puerto
  Rico
  Bayamon Campus *M*
Universidad Metropolitana *B*

Rhode Island
Brown University *B, M, D*
University of Rhode Island *M, D*

Tennessee
Vanderbilt University *B, M, D*

Texas
Houston Baptist University *B*
Texas Lutheran University *B*
Texas Tech University Health
  Sciences Center *M, D*
Texas Woman's University *D*
University of North Texas *M, D*
University of Texas
  Dallas *B*
  Health Science Center at
    Houston *M, D*
Wayland Baptist University *B*

Utah
Brigham Young University *B, M, D*

Vermont
Johnson State College *B*
Marlboro College *B*
University of Vermont *B*

Virginia
Hampton University *B*

Washington
University of Washington *M, D*

Wisconsin
Alverno College *B*
Beloit College *B*
University of Wisconsin
  Eau Claire *B*
  Madison *B, M, D*
  Parkside *B, M*
  Superior *B*

Wyoming
University of Wyoming *B, M, D*

Molecular biophysics

Florida
Florida State University *D*

Missouri
Washington University in St. Louis *D*

Pennsylvania
University of Pittsburgh *M, D*

Molecular genetics

California
University of Southern California *D*

Georgia
Emory University *D*

Illinois
University of Chicago *D*
University of Illinois
  Chicago *D*

Michigan
Michigan State University *B*
Michigan Technological
  University *M, D*

Missouri
Washington University in St. Louis *D*

New Jersey
Rutgers, The State University of New Jersey
New Brunswick/Piscataway Campus *B, M, D*
Newark Campus *B, M, D*

New York
SUNY
College at Fredonia *B*
University of Rochester *B*
Yeshiva University *M, D*

North Carolina
Wake Forest University *D*

Ohio
Ohio State University
Columbus Campus *B, M, D*

Oregon
Oregon Health & Science University *D*

Pennsylvania
University of Pittsburgh *M, D*

South Dakota
Black Hills State University *M*

Texas
Texas A&M University *B, M, D*
University of Texas
Health Science Center at Houston *M, D*

Washington
Washington State University *B*

Molecular medicine

Arizona
University of Arizona *M, D*

California
University of Southern California *M, D*

Indiana
Indiana University
Purdue University Indianapolis *M, T*

Maryland
University of Maryland Baltimore *M, D*

New York
Hofstra University *D*

Ohio
Case Western Reserve University *D*
University of Cincinnati *M, D*

Molecular pharmacology

California
University of California
Los Angeles *M, D*
University of Southern California *M, D*

Indiana
Indiana University
Bloomington *M*

Kentucky
University of Kentucky *D*

New Jersey
Rutgers, The State University of New Jersey
New Brunswick/Piscataway Campus *D*
Newark Campus *D*

New York
SUNY
University at Stony Brook *D*
Yeshiva University *M, D*

Pennsylvania
University of Pittsburgh *M, D*
University of Scranton *B*

South Carolina
Medical University of South Carolina *D*

Molecular physiology

Alabama
University of Alabama
Birmingham *D*

California
University of California
Los Angeles *D*

Illinois
Southern Illinois University
Carbondale *M, D*
University of Chicago *D*

Michigan
University of Michigan *D*

Tennessee
Vanderbilt University *M, D*

Molecular toxicology

California
University of California
Los Angeles *D*

Pennsylvania
Penn State
University Park *M, D*

Montessori teacher education

California
Contra Costa College *A*
St. Mary's College of California *M*

Florida
Barry University *M*

Maryland
Loyola University Maryland *M*

Massachusetts
Endicott College *M*

Ohio
Xavier University *B, M*

Oklahoma
Oklahoma City University *M*

Pennsylvania
Chestnut Hill College *T*

South Carolina
Lander University *B, M*

Tennessee
Belmont University *M, T*

Texas
Dallas Baptist University *M*

Mortuary science/embalming

Florida
St. Petersburg College *C*

Georgia
Gupton Jones College of Funeral Service *A*

Illinois
City Colleges of Chicago
Malcolm X College *A*

Iowa
Marshalltown Community College *A*

Michigan
Wayne County Community College *A*

New York
Nassau Community College *A*

Motorcycle maintenance

California
WyoTech: Fremont *C*

Colorado
Red Rocks Community College *C, A*

Florida
WyoTech: Daytona *C, A*

Georgia
Georgia Piedmont Technical College *C*
North Georgia Technical College *C*

Iowa
Iowa Lakes Community College *C*
Western Iowa Tech Community College *A*

Kansas
Fort Scott Community College *A*

Minnesota
Hennepin Technical College *C, A*

Missouri
Linn State Technical College *A*

North Carolina
Central Carolina Community College *C*
Davidson County Community College *C*

Ohio
PowerSport Institute *C, A*

Texas
Austin Community College *C*
Cedar Valley College *C*

Virginia
Southside Virginia Community College *C*

Washington
Lake Washington Institute of Technology *C, A*

Movement therapy

California
Ohlone College *C*

Illinois
Columbia College Chicago *M*
Moraine Valley Community College *A*

Massachusetts
Eastern Nazarene College *B*

Missouri
Washington University in St. Louis *D*

New York
City University of New York
York College *B*

North Carolina
University of North Carolina
Chapel Hill *M, D*

Texas
Texas Christian University *B*

Vermont
Goddard College *B, M*

Multi/interdisciplinary studies, general

Alabama
Auburn University *B*
Bishop State Community College *A*
Northwest-Shoals Community College *A*
Oakwood University *B*
Southern Union State Community College *A*
University of Alabama *B, D*
University of North Alabama *B, M*
University of South Alabama *B*
University of West Alabama *B*

Alaska
University of Alaska
Fairbanks *A, B, M, D*

Arizona
Arizona State University *M*
Embry-Riddle Aeronautical University
Prescott Campus *B*
Grand Canyon University *B*
Northern Arizona University *B*
University of Arizona *B*

Arkansas
Arkansas Baptist College *A, B*
Harding University *B*
National Park Community College *A*
Rich Mountain Community College *A*
University of Arkansas
Little Rock *B*
University of the Ozarks *B*

California
California State University
Fresno *B*
Los Angeles *C*
Diablo Valley College *A*
Dominican University of California *B*
Moorpark College *A*
Mount St. Mary's College *B*
National University *B*
San Diego Christian College *B*
San Diego State University *B, M*
San Francisco State University *B*
University of California
Riverside *B*

Colorado

Regis University *B*
University of Northern
Colorado *B, M, T*

Connecticut

Southern Connecticut State
University *B*

Florida

Edward Waters College *B*
Florida Institute of Technology *B, M*
Florida Southern College *B*
Jacksonville University *B*
Jones College *B*
Keiser University *B*
Palm Beach Atlantic University *B*
University of Central Florida *B, M*
University of Miami *D*
University of North Florida *B*

Georgia

Georgia State University *B*
Middle Georgia State College *B*
Point University *A*
Truett-McConnell College *B*
Wesleyan College *B*

Idaho

Idaho State University *B, M*
University of Idaho *B, M*

Illinois

Blackburn College *B*
Eastern Illinois University *B*
Millikin University *B*
Wheaton College *B*

Indiana

Crossroads Bible College *B*
Indiana University
Bloomington *B, M*
East *C*
Kokomo *C*
Northwest *C*
Purdue University
Indianapolis *C, B, M*
South Bend *C*
Southeast *C, B*
Purdue University *B*
University of Evansville *B*
University of St. Francis *B*

Iowa

Buena Vista University *B*
Central College *B*
Mount Mercy University *B*
Simpson College *B*
University of Dubuque *B*
Waldorf College *B*

Kansas

Southwestern College *B*

Louisiana

Louisiana State University and
Agricultural and Mechanical
College *B*

Maine

Colby College *B*
College of the Atlantic *B, M*
University of Maine
Machias *A*
Presque Isle *B*

Maryland

Goucher College *B*
Hood College *B*
Howard Community College *A*
Mount St. Mary's University *B*
Stevenson University *B*
Towson University *B*

University of Maryland
University College *B*
Washington College *B*

Massachusetts

Bard College at Simon's Rock *B*
Bay Path College *B*
Boston University *B*
Hampshire College *B*
Lasell College *B*
Montserrat College of Art *B*
Simmons College *B*
Stonehill College *B*
University of Massachusetts
Dartmouth *B*
Western New England University *B*

Michigan

University of Michigan
Flint *B*

Minnesota

Hennepin Technical College *A*
Inver Hills Community College *A*
Minnesota State University
Moorhead *B*
Walden University *B*

Mississippi

University of Mississippi *M*

Missouri

Calvary Bible College and Theological
Seminary *B*
Grantham University *A, B*
Harris-Stowe State University *B*
Northwest Missouri State
University *A*
Truman State University *B*
University of Missouri
Kansas City *D*

Montana

Montana State University
Northern *B*

Nevada

Sierra Nevada College *B*

New Hampshire

Colby-Sawyer College *B*
Franklin Pierce University *C*
New Hampshire Institute of Art *B*
Plymouth State University *B*

New Jersey

Bloomfield College *B*
Fairleigh Dickinson University
Metropolitan Campus *B*
Monmouth University *B*
New Jersey Institute of
Technology *M*

New Mexico

Eastern New Mexico University *B*
University of New Mexico *B*

New York

Daemen College *B*
Hamilton College *B*
Houghton College *B*
Long Island University
LIU Post *M*
Manhattanville College *B*
Nyack College *B*
SUNY
College at Fredonia *B, M*
College at Potsdam *B*
Maritime College *B*
University at Binghamton *B*
University at Stony Brook *B*
Yeshiva University *B*

North Carolina

Brevard College *B*
Cabarrus College of Health
Sciences *B*
Campbell University *B*

North Dakota

North Dakota State College of
Science *C, A*
University of North Dakota *B*
Williston State College *C, A*

Ohio

Ashland University *B*
Lourdes University *B*
Ohio Christian University *A, B*
Ohio University
Lancaster Campus *A*
Tiffin University *B*
Union Institute & University *D*
University of Toledo *B*

Oklahoma

Mid-America Christian University *B*
Oklahoma State University
Institute of Technology:
Okmulgee *A*
University of Oklahoma *B, M, D*

Oregon

Concordia University *A, B*
Eastern Oregon University *B*
George Fox University *B*
Marylhurst University *B, M*
New Hope Christian College *B*

Pennsylvania

Clarion University of Pennsylvania *B*
Franklin & Marshall College *B*
Geneva College *B*
Grove City College *B*
La Roche College *B*
Millersville University of
Pennsylvania *B*
Pennsylvania College of
Technology *B*

Puerto Rico

Inter American University of Puerto
Rico
Arecibo Campus *B*

South Carolina

North Greenville University *B*
Trident Technical College *A*
University of South Carolina
Beaufort *A*

South Dakota

Mount Marty College *A, B*

Tennessee

Christian Brothers University *B*
Lee University *B*
Trevecca Nazarene University *B*
University of Tennessee
Chattanooga *B*

Texas

Austin College *B*
Del Mar College *A*
Howard Payne University *B*
Jarvis Christian College *B*
St. Mary's University *B*
Tarleton State University *B*
Texas Southern University *B*
Trinity University *B*
University of Houston
Clear Lake *B, M*
University of Texas
Tyler *B, M*

Vermont

Green Mountain College *B*

Virginia

George Mason University *M*
Liberty University *B*
Old Dominion University *B*
Sweet Briar College *B*
University of Mary Washington *B*
University of Richmond *B*
University of Virginia *B*
Virginia Commonwealth University *C*
Virginia State University *B, M*
Virginia Wesleyan College *B*

Washington

Central Washington University *B, M*
Northwest Indian College *A*
Saint Martin's University *B*

West Virginia

Ohio Valley University *B*
West Virginia University *B*
West Virginia University Institute of
Technology *B*
Wheeling Jesuit University *B*

Wisconsin

Fox Valley Technical College *A*
Maranatha Baptist Bible College *B*
Marian University *B*
Northland College *B*

Wyoming

University of Wyoming *M*

Multicultural education

California

Loyola Marymount University *M, T*
National University *M*
University of San Francisco *M, D*

Colorado

Fort Lewis College *B*

Illinois

Trinity International University *D*

Minnesota

University of Minnesota
Twin Cities *T*

Nevada

University of Nevada
Reno *M*

New York

College of New Rochelle *M, T*
SUNY
College at New Paltz *M, T*

Ohio

Bowling Green State University *M*
Ohio State University
Newark Campus *B*
University of Findlay *B*

Oklahoma

Langston University *M*
University of Central Oklahoma *M*

Pennsylvania

Carnegie Mellon University *B*

South Dakota

Augustana College *B*

Washington

University of Washington *M, D*

Multimedia

Arizona
Arizona Western College *C, A*
Sessions College for Professional
    Design *C*

California
Academy of Art University *C, A, B, M*
Antelope Valley College *C, A*
Art Institute of California
    Sacramento *A, B*
    San Diego *B*
Biola University *B*
Chaffey College *A*
College of San Mateo *C, A*
College of the Sequoias *A*
Fashion Institute of Design and
    Merchandising
    Los Angeles *A*
    San Francisco *A*
Long Beach City College *A*
Mills College *B*
Mt. Sierra College *B*
Ohlone College *C, A*
Otis College of Art and Design *B*
Pepperdine University *B*
Platt College
    Ontario *C*
Santa Barbara City College *A*

Connecticut
Naugatuck Valley Community
    College *C, A*

District of Columbia
American University *B*

Georgia
Art Institute of Atlanta *A, B*
Georgia Regents University *B*

Illinois
American Academy of Art *B*
Columbia College Chicago *B*
Illinois Institute of Art
    Schaumburg *C, B*
School of the Art Institute of
    Chicago *B, M*

Iowa
Luther College *B*
St. Ambrose University *B*
University of Iowa *M*

Louisiana
Tulane University *C, B*

Maine
College of the Atlantic *B, M*

Maryland
Howard Community College *A*
Maryland Institute College of Art *B*

Massachusetts
Bard College at Simon's Rock *B*
Bristol Community College *A*
Massachusetts College of Art and
    Design *B, M*
Northeastern University *B*
School of the Museum of Fine
    Arts *B, M*
University of Massachusetts
    Dartmouth *B, M*

Michigan
Andrews University *B*
College for Creative Studies *B*

Minnesota
Art Institutes International
    Minnesota *A, B*

Missouri
Lindenwood University *B*
Missouri State University *B*

Nevada
Art Institute of Las Vegas *B*

New Jersey
College of New Jersey *B*
Ramapo College of New Jersey *B*

New Mexico
Santa Fe University of Art and
    Design *B*

New York
Art Institute of New York City *A*
Bard College *B*
Long Island University
    LIU Post *M*
Marist College *B*
Medaille College *C*
Pratt Institute *A*
Rochester Institute of Technology *B*

Ohio
Art Institute of Ohio:
    Cincinnati *C, A, B*
Cleveland Institute of Art *B*
Sinclair Community College *C*
University of Rio Grande *B*

Oklahoma
Oklahoma State University
    Institute of Technology:
    Okmulgee *A*
Rose State College *A*

Oregon
Art Institute of Portland *A, B*
Pacific Northwest College of Art *B*
Pacific University *B*
University of Oregon *M*

Pennsylvania
California University of
    Pennsylvania *M*
Carnegie Mellon University *B*
Indiana University of
    Pennsylvania *B, M*
University of the Arts *B*

Puerto Rico
University of Puerto Rico
    Rio Piedras *B*

Rhode Island
Rhode Island College *M*
Rhode Island School of Design *M*

South Carolina
Benedict College *B*

Tennessee
Memphis College of Art *B, M*

Texas
Texas A&M University *M*

Utah
Weber State University *B*

Vermont
Bennington College *B*
Champlain College *B*

Virginia
Tidewater Community College *A*

Washington
Evergreen State College *B*
Highline Community College *A*
Western Washington University *B*

Museum studies

Arizona
Arizona State University *M*

California
California State University
    San Bernardino *B*
John F. Kennedy University *M*
San Francisco Art Institute *M*
San Francisco State University *M*

Colorado
University of Colorado
    Boulder *M*

District of Columbia
Corcoran College of Art and
    Design *M*
George Washington University *M*
Georgetown University *M*

Florida
University of Florida *M*

Illinois
Western Illinois University *M*

Indiana
Indiana University
    Purdue University
    Indianapolis *C, M*

Kansas
University of Kansas *M*

Maine
College of the Atlantic *B, M*

Maryland
Johns Hopkins University *M*

Massachusetts
Boston University *M*
Massasoit Community College *C*

Minnesota
University of Minnesota
    Twin Cities *M*

New Jersey
Seton Hall University *M*

New Mexico
Institute of American Indian
    Arts *C, A, B*

New York
City University of New York
    City College *M*
Fashion Institute of Technology *M*
Marist College *M*
Rochester Institute of Technology *B*
SUNY
    College at Oneonta *M*
St. John Fisher College *C*
Syracuse University *M*

Ohio
Walsh University *B*

Oklahoma
University of Tulsa *M*

Pennsylvania
Juniata College *B*
Moore College of Art and Design *B*
University of the Arts *M*

Tennessee
Tusculum College *B*

Texas
Baylor University *M*
Texas Tech University *M*

Virginia
Randolph College *B*

Washington
University of Washington *M*

Wisconsin
University of Wisconsin
    Milwaukee *C*

Wyoming
Casper College *A*

Music, general

Alabama
Alabama Agricultural and Mechanical
    University *B*
Alabama State University *B*
Auburn University *B*
Birmingham-Southern College *B*
Calhoun Community College *A*
Community College of the Air
    Force *A*
Faulkner State Community College *A*
Faulkner University *B*
Gadsden State Community College *A*
Jacksonville State University *B*
Judson College *B*
Miles College *B*
Oakwood University *B*
Samford University *B*
Stillman College *B*
Talladega College *B*
Troy University *B*
University of Alabama *B, M, D*
University of Alabama
    Birmingham *B*
    Huntsville *B*
University of Mobile *B*
University of Montevallo *B, T*
University of North Alabama *B*
University of South Alabama *B*
Wallace State Community College at
    Hanceville *A*

Alaska
University of Alaska
    Anchorage *B*
    Fairbanks *B, M*

Arizona
Arizona State University *B, M, D*
Arizona Western College *A*
Central Arizona College *A*
Cochise College *A*
Eastern Arizona College *A*
Northern Arizona University *B, M*
Scottsdale Community College *C, A*
South Mountain Community
    College *A*
University of Arizona *B, M, D*

Arkansas
Arkansas State University *B*
Arkansas State University
    Beebe *A*
Arkansas Tech University *B*
Central Baptist College *B*
Harding University *B*
Henderson State University *B*
Hendrix College *B*
John Brown University *B*
Lyon College *B*
Ouachita Baptist University *B*
Southern Arkansas University *B*
University of Arkansas
    Fort Smith *B*
    Little Rock *B*

Monticello *B*
Pine Bluff *B*
University of Central Arkansas *B*
University of the Ozarks *B*

California

Allan Hancock College *A*
Antelope Valley College *C, A*
Azusa Pacific University *B, M*
Bakersfield College *A*
Bethesda University of
    California *B, M*
Biola University *B*
Cabrillo College *A*
California Baptist University *B, M*
California Lutheran University *B*
California Polytechnic State
    University: San Luis Obispo *B*
California State Polytechnic
    University: Pomona *B*
California State University
    Bakersfield *B*
    Chico *B*
    Dominguez Hills *B*
    East Bay *B, M*
    Fresno *B, M*
    Fullerton *B, M*
    Long Beach *B, M*
    Los Angeles *B, M*
    Monterey Bay *B*
    Northridge *B, M*
    Sacramento *B, M*
    San Bernardino *B*
    Stanislaus *B*
Canada College *A*
Cerritos College *A*
Chabot College *A*
Chaffey College *A*
Chapman University *B*
Citrus College *A*
Claremont McKenna College *B*
College of Alameda *A*
College of Marin *A*
College of San Mateo *A*
College of the Canyons *A*
College of the Desert *C, A*
College of the Sequoias *A*
College of the Siskiyous *A*
Columbia College *A*
Concordia University Irvine *B*
Contra Costa College *A*
Cosumnes River College *A*
Crafton Hills College *A*
Cypress College *A*
De Anza College *A*
Diablo Valley College *A*
Dominican University of California *B*
East Los Angeles College *A*
El Camino College *A*
Foothill College *C, A*
Fresno City College *A*
Fresno Pacific University *B*
Fullerton College *A*
Gavilan College *A*
Golden West College *A*
Grossmont College *A*
Hartnell College *A*
Holy Names University *B, M*
Humboldt State University *B*
Imperial Valley College *A*
Irvine Valley College *A*
La Sierra University *B*
Lake Tahoe Community College *A*
Laney College *A*
Long Beach City College *A*
Los Angeles City College *A*
Los Angeles Pierce College *A*
Los Angeles Southwest College *A*
Los Angeles Valley College *A*
Los Medanos College *A*
Loyola Marymount University *B*
Master's College *B*
Mendocino College *A*
Merced College *C, A*
Mills College *B, M*

Modesto Junior College *A*
Monterey Peninsula College *C, A*
Moorpark College *A*
Mount St. Mary's College *B*
Mount San Jacinto College *A*
Notre Dame de Namur
    University *B, M*
Occidental College *B*
Orange Coast College *A*
Pacific Union College *A, B*
Palo Verde College *A*
Palomar College *A*
Pasadena City College *C, A*
Pepperdine University *B*
Point Loma Nazarene University *B*
Pomona College *B*
Porterville College *A*
Reedley College *A*
Rio Hondo College *A*
Sacramento City College *A*
Saddleback College *A*
St. Mary's College of California *B*
San Diego Christian College *B*
San Diego City College *A*
San Diego Mesa College *A*
San Diego State University *M*
San Francisco State University *B, M*
San Joaquin Delta College *A*
San Jose City College *A*
San Jose State University *B, M*
Santa Ana College *A*
Santa Barbara City College *A*
Santa Clara University *B*
Santa Monica College *A*
Santiago Canyon College *A*
Scripps College *B*
Shasta College *A*
Simpson University *B*
Skyline College *A*
Solano Community College *A*
Sonoma State University *B*
Southwestern College *A*
Stanford University *B, M, D*
Taft College *A*
University of California
    Berkeley *B, M, D*
    Davis *B, M, D*
    Irvine *B, M*
    Los Angeles *B, M, D*
    Riverside *B, M, D*
    San Diego *B, M, D*
    Santa Barbara *B, M, D*
    Santa Cruz *B, M, D*
University of La Verne *B*
University of Redlands *B, M*
University of San Diego *B*
University of Southern California *B*
University of the Pacific *B, M*
Vanguard University of Southern
    California *B*
Ventura College *C, A*
West Los Angeles College *C, A*
West Valley College *A*
Westmont College *B*
Whittier College *B*
William Jessup University *B*
World Mission University *B, M*
Yuba College *A*

Colorado

Adams State University *B*
Colorado Christian University *B*
Colorado College *B*
Colorado Mesa University *B*
Colorado State University *B, M*
Colorado State University
    Pueblo *B*
Fort Lewis College *B*
Metropolitan State University of
    Denver *B*
Naropa University *B*
Regis University *B*
University of Colorado
    Boulder *B*
    Denver *B*

University of Denver *B, M*
University of Northern
    Colorado *B, M, D, T*
Western State Colorado University *B*

Connecticut

Central Connecticut State
    University *B*
Connecticut College *B*
Fairfield University *B*
Manchester Community College *A*
Naugatuck Valley Community
    College *A*
Southern Connecticut State
    University *B*
Trinity College *B*
University of Bridgeport *B*
University of Connecticut *B, M, D*
University of Hartford *B*
University of New Haven *B*
Wesleyan University *B, M*
Western Connecticut State
    University *B*
Yale University *B, M, D*

Delaware

Delaware State University *B*
University of Delaware *B*
Wesley College *B*

District of Columbia

American University *B*
Catholic University of America *B*
George Washington University *B*
Georgetown University *B*
Howard University *M*
University of the District of
    Columbia *A, B*

Florida

Ave Maria University *B*
Baptist College of Florida *B*
Barry University *B*
Broward College *A*
Daytona State College *A*
Eckerd College *B*
Edward Waters College *B*
Florida Agricultural and Mechanical
    University *B*
Florida Atlantic University *B, M*
Florida College *B*
Florida International University *B, M*
Florida Memorial University *B*
Florida Southern College *B*
Florida State University *B, M*
Indian River State College *A*
Jacksonville University *B*
Miami Dade College *A*
New College of Florida *B*
Northwest Florida State College *A*
Nova Southeastern University *B*
Palm Beach Atlantic University *B*
Palm Beach State College *A*
Pensacola State College *A*
Rollins College *B*
St. Petersburg College *C, A*
Southeastern University *B*
Stetson University *B*
Trinity Baptist College *B*
University of Central Florida *M*
University of Florida *B, M, D*
University of Miami *B*
University of South Florida *D*
University of Tampa *A, B*

Georgia

Abraham Baldwin Agricultural
    College *A*
Agnes Scott College *B*
Albany State University *B*
Armstrong Atlantic State
    University *B, T*
Atlanta Metropolitan College *A*
Berry College *B*

Brenau University *B*
Clark Atlanta University *B*
Clayton State University *B*
Columbus State University *B, M*
Covenant College *B*
Darton College *A*
Emmanuel College *B*
Emory University *B, M*
Georgia College and State
    University *B*
Georgia Perimeter College *A*
Georgia Regents University *B*
Georgia Southern University *B, M*
Georgia Southwestern State
    University *B, T*
Gordon College *A*
Kennesaw State University *B*
LaGrange College *B*
Mercer University *B*
Middle Georgia State College *A*
Morehouse College *B*
Piedmont College *B, T*
Point University *B*
Reinhardt University *B, M*
Spelman College *B*
Toccoa Falls College *B*
Truett-McConnell College *B*
University of Georgia *B, M, D*
University of North Georgia *M*
Valdosta State University *B*
Wesleyan College *B*
Young Harris College *B*

Hawaii

University of Hawaii
    Hilo *B*
    Manoa *B, M, D*

Idaho

Brigham Young University-Idaho *B*
College of Idaho *B*
College of Southern Idaho *A*
Idaho State University *B*
Lewis-Clark State College *A*
North Idaho College *A*
Northwest Nazarene University *B*
University of Idaho *M*

Illinois

Augustana College *B*
Aurora University *B*
Benedictine University *B*
Blackburn College *B*
Bradley University *B*
Chicago State University *B*
City Colleges of Chicago
    Harold Washington College *C, A*
    Wilbur Wright College *A*
College of DuPage *C, A*
College of Lake County *A*
Columbia College Chicago *B*
Concordia University
    Chicago *B, M, T*
DePaul University *B*
Dominican University *B*
Eastern Illinois University *B, M, T*
Elgin Community College *C*
Elmhurst College *B, T*
Greenville College *B*
Harper College *A*
Illinois Central College *A*
Illinois College *B, T*
Illinois Eastern Community Colleges
    Wabash Valley College *A*
Illinois State University *B, M*
Illinois Valley Community College *A*
Illinois Wesleyan University *B*
John A. Logan College *A*
John Wood Community College *A*
Joliet Junior College *A*
Kaskaskia College *A*
Kishwaukee College *A*
Knox College *B*
Lake Forest College *B*

Lewis University *B*
Lewis and Clark Community
   College *A*
Lincoln College *A*
Lincoln Land Community College *A*
Loyola University Chicago *B*
MacMurray College *B*
McHenry County College *A*
McKendree University *B*
Millikin University *B*
Monmouth College *B, T*
Moraine Valley Community College *A*
North Central College *B*
North Park University *B*
Northeastern Illinois University *B, M*
Northern Illinois University *B, M*
Northwestern University *B, M, D*
Oakton Community College *A*
Olivet Nazarene University *B, T*
Parkland College *C, A*
Principia College *B*
Quincy University *B*
Richland Community College *A*
Rockford University *B*
Roosevelt University *B*
Saint Xavier University *B*
Sauk Valley Community College *A*
South Suburban College of Cook
   County *A*
Southern Illinois University
   Carbondale *B, M*
Southern Illinois University
   Edwardsville *B, M, T*
Southwestern Illinois College *A*
Trinity Christian College *B*
Trinity International University *B*
Triton College *A*
University of Chicago *B, D*
University of Illinois
   Chicago *B*
   Urbana-Champaign *B, M, D*
University of St. Francis *B*
Waubonsee Community College *A*
Western Illinois University *B, M*
Wheaton College *B*

Indiana

Anderson University *B*
Ball State University *B, M, D, T*
Bethel College *B*
Butler University *B*
DePauw University *B*
Earlham College *B*
Franklin College *B*
Goshen College *B*
Hanover College *B*
Huntington University *B*
Indiana State University *C, B, T*
Indiana University
   Bloomington *M, D*
   Purdue University Fort Wayne *B, T*
   South Bend *B*
   Southeast *B*
Indiana Wesleyan University *B*
Manchester University *B, T*
Marian University *A, B, T*
Oakland City University *B*
Purdue University *B*
Saint Mary's College *B*
St. Mary-of-the-Woods College *B*
Taylor University *B*
University of Evansville *B*
University of Indianapolis *B*
University of Notre Dame *B, M*
Valparaiso University *B*
Wabash College *B*

Iowa

Briar Cliff University *B*
Central College *B, T*
Clarke University *A, B, T*
Coe College *B*
Cornell College *B, T*
Dordt College *B*

Drake University *B*
Emmaus Bible College *B, T*
Grand View University *B*
Grinnell College *B*
Iowa State University *B*
Iowa Wesleyan College *B, T*
Iowa Western Community College *A*
Loras College *B*
Luther College *B*
Marshalltown Community College *A*
Morningside College *B*
Mount Mercy University *B*
Northwestern College *B, T*
St. Ambrose University *B*
Simpson College *B*
University of Iowa *B, M, D, T*
University of Northern Iowa *B, M*
Waldorf College *B*
Wartburg College *B, T*

Kansas

Allen County Community College *A*
Baker University *B, T*
Barton County Community College *A*
Benedictine College *B*
Bethany College *B, T*
Bethel College *B*
Butler Community College *A*
Central Christian College of
   Kansas *A, B*
Coffeyville Community College *A*
Cowley County Community
   College *A*
Dodge City Community College *A*
Emporia State University *B, M, T*
Fort Hays State University *B, M*
Friends University *B*
Garden City Community College *A*
Independence Community College *A*
Kansas State University *B, M*
Kansas Wesleyan University *B, T*
Labette Community College *A*
McPherson College *B*
MidAmerica Nazarene University *B*
Neosho County Community
   College *A*
Ottawa University *B, T*
Pratt Community College *A*
Seward County Community
   College *A*
Southwestern College *B*
Sterling College *B, T*
Tabor College *B*
University of Kansas *B, M, D*
Washburn University *B*
Wichita State University *B, M*

Kentucky

Asbury University *B*
Bellarmine University *B, T*
Berea College *B*
Bluegrass Community and Technical
   College *A*
Campbellsville University *B, M*
Centre College *B*
Eastern Kentucky University *B, M*
Georgetown College *B*
Hopkinsville Community College *A*
Kentucky State University *B*
Morehead State University *B, M*
Murray State University *B, T*
Northern Kentucky University *C, B*
Thomas More College *B*
University of Kentucky *D*
University of Louisville *B, M*
University of the Cumberlands *B*

Louisiana

Bossier Parish Community College *C*
Centenary College of Louisiana *B*
Delgado Community College *A*
Dillard University *B*
Louisiana College *B*

Louisiana State University and
   Agricultural and Mechanical
   College *B, D*
Louisiana Tech University *B*
Loyola University New Orleans *B*
Nicholls State University *B*
Tulane University *B, M*
University of New Orleans *B*
Xavier University of Louisiana *B*

Maine

Bates College *B*
Bowdoin College *B*
Colby College *B*
College of the Atlantic *B*
University of Maine *B*
University of Maine
   Augusta *A, B*
University of Southern Maine *B, M*

Maryland

Anne Arundel Community College *C*
Baltimore City Community College *A*
Carroll Community College *A*
Frostburg State University *B*
Goucher College *B*
Harford Community College *A*
Hood College *B*
Howard Community College *A*
Johns Hopkins University: Peabody
   Conservatory of Music *T*
McDaniel College *B*
Montgomery College *A*
Morgan State University *B, M*
Prince George's Community
   College *A*
St. Mary's College of Maryland *B*
Salisbury University *B*
Towson University *B*
University of Maryland
   Baltimore County *B*
   College Park *B, M, D*
Washington Adventist University *B*
Washington College *B, T*

Massachusetts

Amherst College *B*
Anna Maria College *B*
Assumption College *B*
Bard College at Simon's Rock *B*
Berklee College of Music *C, B*
Boston College *B*
Brandeis University *B, M*
Bridgewater State University *B*
Bunker Hill Community College *A*
Cape Cod Community College *A*
Clark University *B*
College of the Holy Cross *B*
Eastern Nazarene College *B*
Gordon College *B*
Hampshire College *B*
Harvard College *B, M, D*
Holyoke Community College *C, A*
Massachusetts College of Liberal
   Arts *B*
Massachusetts Institute of
   Technology *B*
Mount Holyoke College *B*
New England Conservatory of
   Music *B, M*
Northeastern University *B*
Roxbury Community College *A*
Salem State University *B*
Simmons College *B*
Tufts University *B, M*
University of Massachusetts
   Amherst *B*
   Boston *B*
   Dartmouth *B*
   Lowell *B, M*
Wellesley College *B*
Westfield State University *B, M, T*
Wheaton College *B*
Williams College *B*

Michigan

Adrian College *B, T*
Albion College *B, T*
Alma College *B, T*
Andrews University *B, M*
Aquinas College *B*
Calvin College *B, T*
Central Michigan University *B*
Concordia University *B*
Cornerstone University *B, T*
Delta College *A*
Eastern Michigan University *B, M*
Grand Rapids Community College *A*
Grand Valley State University *B*
Hillsdale College *B*
Hope College *B*
Kalamazoo College *B*
Kellogg Community College *C*
Lake Michigan College *A*
Lansing Community College *C, A*
Macomb Community College *C, A*
Madonna University *B*
Marygrove College *T*
Michigan State University *B*
Montcalm Community College *A*
Northern Michigan University *B*
Northwestern Michigan College *A*
Oakland Community College *C*
Oakland University *B*
Olivet College *B, T*
Rochester College *B*
Saginaw Valley State University *B*
Siena Heights University *B*
Spring Arbor University *B*
University of Michigan *B*
University of Michigan
   Dearborn *B*
   Flint *B, T*
Wayne State University *B, M, T*
Western Michigan University *B, M*

Minnesota

Anoka-Ramsey Community College *A*
Augsburg College *B*
Bemidji State University *B*
Bethany Lutheran College *B*
Bethel University *B*
Carleton College *B*
Century College *A*
College of St. Benedict *B*
Concordia College: Moorhead *B*
Concordia University St. Paul *B*
Crossroads College *B*
Crown College *A, B*
Gustavus Adolphus College *B*
Hamline University *B*
Macalester College *B*
Minnesota State Community and
   Technical College *A*
Minnesota State University
   Mankato *B, M, T*
   Moorhead *B*
Minnesota West Community and
   Technical College *A*
Normandale Community College *A*
North Central University *B*
Ridgewater College *A*
St. Catherine University *B*
Saint Cloud State University *B, M*
St. John's University *B*
St. Mary's University of Minnesota *B*
St. Olaf College *B*
Southwest Minnesota State
   University *B, T*
University of Minnesota
   Duluth *B, M*
   Morris *B*
   Twin Cities *B, M, D*
University of Northwestern - St.
   Paul *B*
University of St. Thomas *B*
Winona State University *B, T*

Mississippi

Belhaven University *B*
Blue Mountain College *B*
Delta State University *B*
East Mississippi Community
 College *A*
Hinds Community College *A*
Itawamba Community College *A*
Millsaps College *B*
Mississippi College *B*
Mississippi Delta Community
 College *A*
Mississippi Gulf Coast Community
 College *A*
Mississippi State University *B*
Mississippi University for
 Women *B, T*
Mississippi Valley State University *B*
Northeast Mississippi Community
 College *A*
Rust College *B*
Tougaloo College *B*
University of Mississippi *B, M, D*
University of Southern
 Mississippi *B, M*
William Carey University *B*

Missouri

Baptist Bible College *B*
Central Christian College of the
 Bible *B*
Central Methodist University *B*
College of the Ozarks *B*
Crowder College *A*
Culver-Stockton College *B*
Drury University *B, T*
Evangel University *A, B*
Lindenwood University *B*
Missouri Baptist University *B*
Missouri Southern State
 University *B, T*
Missouri State University *B, M*
Missouri Valley College *B*
Missouri Western State University *B*
Northwest Missouri State
 University *B*
Park University *C, B, M*
St. Louis Community College *A*
Saint Louis University *B*
Southeast Missouri State University *B*
Southwest Baptist University *B*
Three Rivers Community College *A*
Truman State University *B, M*
University of Central Missouri *B, M*
University of Missouri
 Columbia *B, M*
 Kansas City *B, M*
 St. Louis *B*
Washington University in St.
 Louis *B, M, D*
Webster University *B, M*
William Jewell College *B, T*

Montana

Montana State University *B*
Montana State University
 Billings *B*
Rocky Mountain College *B*
University of Montana *B, M*
University of Montana: Western *B, T*

Nebraska

Chadron State College *B*
Concordia University *B, T*
Creighton University *B*
Doane College *B*
Grace University *B*
Hastings College *B, T*
Midland University *B, T*
Nebraska Wesleyan University *B*
Northeast Community College *A*
Union College *B*

University of Nebraska
 Kearney *B, M, T*
 Lincoln *B, M, D*
 Omaha *B, M*
Wayne State College *B*

Nevada

Truckee Meadows Community
 College *C, A*
University of Nevada
 Las Vegas *B, M, D*
 Reno *B, M*
Western Nevada College *A*

New Hampshire

Dartmouth College *B*
Franklin Pierce University *B*
Plymouth State University *B*
University of New Hampshire *B, M*

New Jersey

Bergen Community College *C, A*
Burlington County College *A*
Caldwell College *B*
College of New Jersey *B, T*
College of St. Elizabeth *B*
Cumberland County College *A*
Drew University *B*
Essex County College *A*
Felician College *B*
Kean University *B*
Monmouth University *B*
Montclair State University *B, M*
New Jersey City University *B, T*
Passaic County Community College *A*
Princeton University *B, M, D*
Ramapo College of New Jersey *B*
Raritan Valley Community College *A*
Rider University *B*
Rowan University *B*
Rutgers, The State University of New
 Jersey
 Camden Campus *B, T*
 New Brunswick/Piscataway
  Campus *B, M, D*
 Newark Campus *B, T*
Seton Hall University *B, T*
Thomas Edison State College *B*
William Paterson University of New
 Jersey *B*

New Mexico

Eastern New Mexico University *B*
New Mexico Highlands University *B*
New Mexico Junior College *A*
Santa Fe University of Art and
 Design *B*

New York

Adelphi University *B*
Bard College *B, M*
Barnard College *B*
Canisius College *B*
City University of New York
 Baruch College *B*
 Brooklyn College *B*
 City College *B, M*
 College of Staten Island *B*
 Hunter College *B, M*
 York College *B*
Colgate University *B*
College of Saint Rose *B*
Columbia University *B*
Columbia University
 School of General Studies *B*
Concordia College *B*
Cornell University *B, M, D*
Dowling College *B*
Eastman School of Music of the
 University of Rochester *B*
Elmira College *B*
Excelsior College *B*
Finger Lakes Community College *A*
Five Towns College *A, B, M, D*

Fordham University *B*
Hamilton College *B*
Hartwick College *B*
Hobart and William Smith Colleges *B*
Hofstra University *B*
Houghton College *B, M*
Ithaca College *B, M, T*
Jamestown Community College *A*
Jewish Theological Seminary of
 America *M, D*
Long Island University
 LIU Brooklyn *B*
Manhattanville College *B*
Molloy College *B*
Nazareth College *B, T*
New York University *B, M, D*
Niagara County Community
 College *A*
Nyack College *A, B*
Onondaga Community College *A*
Roberts Wesleyan College *B*
Rockland Community College *A*
SUNY
 College at Buffalo *B, M*
 College at Cortland *B*
 College at Fredonia *B*
 College at New Paltz *B*
 College at Oneonta *B*
 College at Oswego *B*
 College at Plattsburgh *B*
 College at Potsdam *B*
 University at Albany *B*
 University at Binghamton *B*
 University at Buffalo *B*
 University at Stony Brook *B, M, D*
Saint Bonaventure University *B*
St. Lawrence University *B*
Schenectady County Community
 College *C, A*
Suffolk County Community College *A*
Syracuse University *B*
Ulster County Community College *A*
University of Rochester *B*
Vassar College *B*
Yeshiva University *B*

North Carolina

Alamance Community College *C, A*
Blue Ridge Community College *A*
Brevard College *B*
Caldwell Community College and
 Technical Institute *A*
Campbell University *B*
Catawba College *B, T*
College of the Albemarle *A*
Davidson College *B*
Duke University *B*
East Carolina University *B*
Elon University *B*
Fayetteville State University *B*
Gardner-Webb University *B*
Greensboro College *C, B, T*
Guilford College *B*
High Point University *B*
Johnson C. Smith University *B*
Lenoir-Rhyne University *B, T*
Livingstone College *B*
Mars Hill University *B, T*
Meredith College *B*
Methodist University *B*
North Carolina Agricultural and
 Technical State University *B, M*
North Carolina Central University *B*
Pfeiffer University *B*
Piedmont International University *B*
Queens University of Charlotte *B*
Salem College *B*
Sandhills Community College *A*
Shaw University *B*
University of North Carolina
 Asheville *B*
 Chapel Hill *B*
 Charlotte *B*
 Greensboro *B*

Pembroke *B*
Wilmington *B*
Western Carolina University *B*
Wingate University *B*
Winston-Salem State University *B*

North Dakota

Dickinson State University *B, T*
Minot State University *B*
North Dakota State
 University *B, M, D, T*
Trinity Bible College *A, B*
University of Jamestown *B*
University of North Dakota *B, M*
Valley City State University *B*

Ohio

Ashland University *B*
Baldwin Wallace University *B*
Bluffton University *B*
Bowling Green State
 University *B, M, D*
Capital University *B*
Case Western Reserve
 University *B, M, D*
Cedarville University *B*
Cleveland State University *B, T*
College of Mount St. Joseph *B, T*
College of Wooster *B*
Cuyahoga Community College
 Metropolitan *A*
Denison University *B*
Heidelberg University *B*
Hiram College *B, T*
Hocking College *C, A*
Kent State University *B*
Kenyon College *B*
Lake Erie College *B*
Malone University *B*
Marietta College *B*
Miami University
 Oxford *B*
Mount Vernon Nazarene
 University *A, B*
Muskingum University *B*
Oberlin College *B*
Ohio Northern University *B*
Ohio State University
 Columbus Campus *B, M, D*
Ohio Wesleyan University *B*
Otterbein University *B*
Terra State Community College *A*
Tiffin University *B*
University of Akron *B, M*
University of Cincinnati *B*
University of Dayton *B*
University of Mount Union *B*
University of Rio Grande *B*
University of Toledo *B*
Wilberforce University *B*
Wilmington College *B*
Wittenberg University *B*
Wright State University *B, M*
Xavier University *B*
Youngstown State University *B, M*

Oklahoma

Cameron University *B*
Carl Albert State College *A*
East Central University *B*
Eastern Oklahoma State College *A*
Hillsdale Free Will Baptist College *B*
Langston University *B*
Northeastern Oklahoma Agricultural
 and Mechanical College *A*
Northeastern State University *B*
Northwestern Oklahoma State
 University *B*
Oklahoma Baptist University *B, T*
Oklahoma Christian University *B*
Oklahoma City Community
 College *A*
Oklahoma City University *B*

Oklahoma Panhandle State
 University *B*
Oklahoma State University *B, M*
Oral Roberts University *B*
Southeastern Oklahoma State
 University *B*
Southern Nazarene University *B*
Southwestern Oklahoma State
 University *B, M*
Tulsa Community College *A*
University of Central Oklahoma *B*
University of Oklahoma *B, M*
University of Science and Arts of
 Oklahoma *B, T*
University of Tulsa *B*
Western Oklahoma State College *A*

Oregon

Concordia University *B*
Corban University *B*
Eastern Oregon University *B*
George Fox University *B, T*
Lewis & Clark College *B*
Linfield College *B*
Linn-Benton Community College *A*
Marylhurst University *B*
Northwest Christian University *B*
Oregon State University *B*
Pacific University *B*
Portland State University *B, M*
Reed College *B*
Southern Oregon University *B, T*
Treasure Valley Community
 College *A*
University of Oregon *B*
University of Portland *B, M, T*
Warner Pacific College *B, T*
Western Oregon University *B, M*

Pennsylvania

Allegheny College *B*
Baptist Bible College of
 Pennsylvania *B*
Bloomsburg University of
 Pennsylvania *B, T*
Bryn Mawr College *B*
Bucknell University *B*
Bucks County Community College *A*
Cairn University *B*
California University of
 Pennsylvania *A*
Carnegie Mellon University *M*
Cedar Crest College *B*
Chatham University *B*
Chestnut Hill College *B*
Cheyney University of
 Pennsylvania *B*
Clarion University of Pennsylvania *B*
Community College of Allegheny
 County *A*
Community College of
 Philadelphia *A*
Delaware County Community
 College *C*
Dickinson College *B*
Drexel University *B*
Eastern University *B*
Edinboro University of
 Pennsylvania *B, T*
Elizabethtown College *B, T*
Franklin & Marshall College *B*
Geneva College *B, T*
Gettysburg College *B*
Grove City College *B*
Haverford College *B*
Immaculata University *R*
Indiana University of
 Pennsylvania *B, M*
Kutztown University of
 Pennsylvania *B*
La Salle University *B*
Lafayette College *B*
Lehigh University *B*
Lincoln University *B*

Lock Haven University of
 Pennsylvania *B*
Lycoming College *B*
Mansfield University of
 Pennsylvania *B, M*
Mercyhurst University *B*
Messiah College *B*
Millersville University of
 Pennsylvania *B, T*
Moravian College *B, T*
Muhlenberg College *C, B*
Penn State
 Abington *B*
 Altoona *B*
 Beaver *B*
 Berks *B*
 Brandywine *B*
 DuBois *B*
 Erie, The Behrend College *B*
 Fayette, The Eberly Campus *B*
 Greater Allegheny *B*
 Harrisburg *B*
 Hazleton *B*
 Lehigh Valley *B*
 Mont Alto *B*
 New Kensington *B*
 Schuylkill *B*
 Shenango *B*
 University Park *B*
 Wilkes-Barre *B*
 Worthington Scranton *B*
 York *B*
Saint Joseph's University *B*
St. Vincent College *B*
Seton Hill University *B, T*
Slippery Rock University of
 Pennsylvania *B, T*
Susquehanna University *B, T*
Swarthmore College *B*
Temple University *B*
University of Pennsylvania *B, M, D*
University of Pittsburgh *B, M, D*
Washington & Jefferson College *B*
West Chester University of
 Pennsylvania *B, M, T*
Westminster College *B*
York College of Pennsylvania *A, B, T*

Puerto Rico

Inter American University of Puerto
 Rico
 San German Campus *B*
Pontifical Catholic University of
 Puerto Rico *B*
University of Puerto Rico
 Aguadilla *A*
 Rio Piedras *B*

Rhode Island

Brown University *B, M*
Community College of Rhode
 Island *A*
Providence College *B*
Rhode Island College *B*
Roger Williams University *B*
Salve Regina University *B*
University of Rhode Island *B, M*

South Carolina

Anderson University *B*
Charleston Southern University *B*
Claflin University *B*
Coastal Carolina University *B*
Coker College *B*
College of Charleston *B*
Columbia College *B*
Converse College *B, M*
Erskine College *B*
Francis Marion University *B*
Furman University *B, T*
Lander University *B, T*
Limestone College *B*
Newberry College *B*
North Greenville University *B*

Presbyterian College *B*
Southern Wesleyan University *B, T*
University of South Carolina
 Columbia *B*
Winthrop University *B, M*

South Dakota

Augustana College *B, T*
Black Hills State University *B*
Dakota Wesleyan University *B*
Mount Marty College *B*
Northern State University *B*
South Dakota State University *B*
University of Sioux Falls *B*
University of South Dakota *B*

Tennessee

Austin Peay State University *B, M*
Belmont University *B, M*
Bethel University *B*
Bryan University
 Dayton *B, T*
Carson-Newman University *B, T*
Cumberland University *B*
East Tennessee State University *B, T*
Fisk University *B*
Freed-Hardeman University *B, T*
Hiwassee College *A*
Lane College *B*
LeMoyne-Owen College *B*
Lee University *B, M*
Maryville College *B, T*
Middle Tennessee State
 University *B, M*
Milligan College *B, T*
Rhodes College *B*
Sewanee: The University of the
 South *B*
Southern Adventist University *B*
Tennessee State University *B*
Tennessee Wesleyan College *B*
Union University *B*
University of Memphis *B, M, D*
University of Tennessee
 Chattanooga *B, M*
 Knoxville *B, M*
 Martin *B*
Vanderbilt University *B*
Welch College *B*

Texas

Abilene Christian University *B*
Amarillo College *A*
Angelina College *A*
Angelo State University *B, T*
Arlington Baptist College *B*
Austin College *B*
Austin Community College *A*
Baylor University *B*
Blinn College *A*
Brazosport College *A*
Brookhaven College *A*
Central Texas College *A*
Clarendon College *A*
Coastal Bend College *A*
College of the Mainland *A*
Collin County Community College
 District *A*
Dallas Baptist University *A, B*
East Texas Baptist University *B*
El Paso Community College *A*
Frank Phillips College *A*
Galveston College *A*
Grayson College *A*
Hardin-Simmons University *B*
Hill College *A*
Houston Baptist University *B*
Howard College *A*
Huston-Tillotson University *B*
Jarvis Christian College *B*
Kilgore College *A*
Lamar State College at Port
 Arthur *C, A*
Lamar University *B*

Laredo Community College *A*
Lee College *A*
Lone Star College System *A*
Lubbock Christian University *B*
McMurry University *B, T*
Midland College *A*
Midwestern State University *B*
Mountain View College *A*
Navarro College *A*
Northeast Texas Community
 College *A*
Odessa College *A*
Our Lady of the Lake University of
 San Antonio *B*
Palo Alto College *A*
Paris Junior College *A*
Prairie View A&M University *B*
Rice University *B, M, D*
St. Mary's University *B, T*
St. Philip's College *A*
Sam Houston State University *B, M*
San Jacinto College *C, A*
Schreiner University *B*
South Plains College *A*
South Texas College *A*
Southern Methodist University *B*
Southwestern Adventist
 University *B, T*
Southwestern Assemblies of God
 University *A*
Southwestern University *B, T*
Stephen F. Austin State
 University *B, M, T*
Tarleton State University *B, T*
Temple College *A*
Texarkana College *A*
Texas A&M University *B*
Texas A&M University
 Commerce *B, M*
 Corpus Christi *B, T*
 Kingsville *B, M*
Texas Christian University *B*
Texas College *B*
Texas Lutheran University *B*
Texas Southern University *B, M*
Texas State University *B, M*
Texas Tech University *B, M, D*
Texas Wesleyan University *B, T*
Texas Woman's University *B, M*
Trinity University *B*
Trinity Valley Community College *A*
Tyler Junior College *A*
University of Houston *B, M, D*
University of Mary Hardin-Baylor *T*
University of North Texas *B, M*
University of St. Thomas *B*
University of Texas
 Arlington *B*
 Austin *B, M, D*
 Brownsville *B*
 El Paso *B*
 Pan American *B, M*
 Permian Basin *B*
 San Antonio *B*
 Tyler *B*
University of the Incarnate Word *B*
Wayland Baptist University *B*
West Texas A&M University *B, M*
Wharton County Junior College *A*
Wiley College *B*

Utah

Brigham Young University *B, M*
Dixie State College *B*
Salt Lake Community College *A*
Snow College *A, B*
Southern Utah University *B*
University of Utah *B, M, D, T*
Utah State University *B, M*
Utah Valley University *A, B*
Weber State University *B*
Westminster College *B*

Vermont

Bennington College *B, M*
Castleton State College *B*
Johnson State College *B*
Marlboro College *B*
Middlebury College *B*
Saint Michael's College *B*
University of Vermont *B*

Virginia

Averett University *B*
Bluefield College *B*
College of William and Mary *B*
Eastern Mennonite University *B*
Emory & Henry College *B, T*
George Mason University *M*
Hampton University *B*
Hollins University *B*
Liberty University *B*
Lynchburg College *B, M*
Mary Baldwin College *B*
Norfolk State University *B*
Northern Virginia Community
    College *A*
Radford University *B, M*
Randolph-Macon College *B*
Roanoke College *B, T*
Southern Virginia University *B*
Sweet Briar College *B*
University of Mary Washington *B*
University of Richmond *B*
University of Virginia *B, M, D*
Virginia Polytechnic Institute and
    State University *B*
Virginia Wesleyan College *B*
Washington and Lee University *B*

Washington

Central Washington University *B, M*
Centralia College *A*
Eastern Washington University *B, M*
Highline Community College *A*
North Seattle Community
    College *C, A*
Northwest University *B*
Pacific Lutheran University *B*
Saint Martin's University *B*
Seattle Pacific University *B*
Seattle University *B*
University of Puget Sound *B, T*
University of Washington *B, M, D*
Walla Walla University *B*
Washington State University *B, M*
Western Washington University *B, M*
Whitman College *B*
Whitworth University *B, T*

West Virginia

Alderson-Broaddus University *A, B*
Bethany College *B*
Concord University *B*
Fairmont State University *B*
Marshall University *M*
Shepherd University *B, T*
West Virginia State University *B*
West Virginia University *B, M, D, T*
West Virginia Wesleyan College *B*
Wheeling Jesuit University *B*

Wisconsin

Alverno College *B*
Beloit College *B*
Carroll University *B*
Carthage College *B*
Edgewood College *B*
Lakeland College *B*
Lawrence University *B, T*
Marian University *B*
Northland International University *B*
Ripon College *B, T*
St. Norbert College *B, T*
Silver Lake College of the Holy
    Family *B*

University of Wisconsin
    Eau Claire *B*
    Green Bay *B, T*
    La Crosse *B, T*
    Madison *B, M, D*
    Milwaukee *C, B, M*
    Oshkosh *B*
    Parkside *B, T*
    Platteville *B*
    River Falls *B*
    Stevens Point *B*
    Superior *B, T*
    Whitewater *B, T*
Viterbo University *B, T*
Wisconsin Lutheran College *B*

Wyoming

Casper College *A*
Central Wyoming College *A*
Eastern Wyoming College *A*
Laramie County Community
    College *A*
Northwest College *A*
Sheridan College *C, A*
University of Wyoming *B, M*
Western Wyoming Community
    College *A*

Music history/literature

Alabama

Birmingham-Southern College *B*
Chattahoochee Valley Community
    College *A*

Arkansas

Ouachita Baptist University *B*

California

California State University
    East Bay *M*
    Long Beach *B*
    Northridge *B, M*
    San Bernardino *B*
Foothill College *C*
Mills College *M*
Pepperdine University *B*
University of California
    Los Angeles *B*
University of Redlands *B*
University of Southern California *M*
University of the Pacific *B*
Vanguard University of Southern
    California *B*
Whittier College *B*

Colorado

University of Colorado
    Boulder *D*

Connecticut

University of Connecticut *M*
University of Hartford *B, M*
Yale University *M*

District of Columbia

American University *B*
Catholic University of
    America *B, M, D*
Howard University *B*

Florida

Broward College *A*
University of Miami *B*

Idaho

University of Idaho *B*

Illinois

Illinois Valley Community College *A*
Lincoln College *A*
Rockford University *B*

University of Illinois
    Urbana-Champaign *B, M*
Wheaton College *B*

Indiana

Butler University *M*
Saint Joseph's College *B*

Iowa

Cornell College *B*
University of Northern Iowa *M*

Kentucky

Bluegrass Community and Technical
    College *A*
University of Kentucky *B, M, D*

Maine

College of the Atlantic *B*

Maryland

Johns Hopkins University: Peabody
    Conservatory of Music *M*

Massachusetts

Boston University *B, M, D*
Eastern Nazarene College *B*
New England Conservatory of
    Music *B, M*
Tufts University *B, M*
Wellesley College *B*

Michigan

Calvin College *B*
Eastern Michigan University *M*
University of Michigan *B, M, D*

Minnesota

Saint Cloud State University *B*
University of Minnesota
    Twin Cities *B*

Missouri

St. Charles Community College *A*
University of Missouri
    Kansas City *M*
    St. Louis *B*
Washington University in St.
    Louis *B, M, D*

Nebraska

Hastings College *B*

New Hampshire

Keene State College *B*

New Jersey

Rider University *B*

New York

Bard College *B*
City University of New York
    Hunter College *M*
    Queensborough Community
        College *A*
Cornell University *M*
Eastman School of Music of the
    University of Rochester *B, M, D*
Hofstra University *B*
Long Island University
    LIU Post *M*
Nazareth College *B*
SUNY
    University at Buffalo *M*
Skidmore College *B*
Syracuse University *B*
University of Rochester *M*

North Carolina

Wake Forest University *B*

Ohio

Baldwin Wallace University *B*
Bowling Green State University *B, M*
Case Western Reserve University *M*
College of Wooster *B*
Kent State University *M*
Oberlin College *B, M*
Ohio State University
    Columbus Campus *B*
Ohio University *B, M*
Otterbein University *B*
University of Akron *B, M*
University of Cincinnati *B, M*
Wright State University *B*
Youngstown State University *B, M*

Pennsylvania

Bucknell University *B*
La Salle University *B*
Lafayette College *B*
Lehigh University *B*
Temple University *B, M*
West Chester University of
    Pennsylvania *M*

South Carolina

Converse College *B, M*
Furman University *B*
University of South Carolina
    Columbia *M*

South Dakota

University of South Dakota *M*

Texas

Baylor University *B, M*
Rice University *B, M*
Southern Methodist University *M*
Texas Lutheran University *B*
University of North Texas *B*

Utah

Brigham Young University *B*

Vermont

Bennington College *B*
Johnson State College *B*
Marlboro College *B*

Virginia

Bridgewater College *B*
Liberty University *B*
Randolph College *B*

Washington

University of Washington *B*
Western Washington University *B*
Whitman College *B*

Wisconsin

University of Wisconsin
    Stevens Point *B*

Music management

Arizona

Chandler-Gilbert Community
    College *C, A*
Glendale Community College *C, A*
Mesa Community College *C, A*
Paradise Valley Community
    College *C, A*
Phoenix College *C, A*

California

Bethesda University of
    California *B, M*
California State University
    Sacramento *B, M*
Fresno City College *A*
Los Medanos College *C*
Master's College *B*
MiraCosta College *C*

Orange Coast College *C, A*
Sacramento City College *C, A*
University of Southern California *B*
University of the Pacific *B*

Colorado
University of Northern Colorado *B*
Western State Colorado University *B*

Connecticut
University of Hartford *B*
University of New Haven *B*

District of Columbia
Howard University *B*

Florida
Florida Atlantic University *B, M*
Florida Southern College *B*
Jacksonville University *B*

Georgia
Berry College *B*
Georgia State University *B*
Kennesaw State University *C*

Idaho
Boise State University *B*
University of Idaho *B*

Illinois
Bradley University *B*
Columbia College Chicago *B, M*
DePaul University *B*
Elmhurst College *B*
Greenville College *B*
Judson University *B*
Lewis University *B*

Indiana
Anderson University *B*
Butler University *B*
DePauw University *B*
Huntington University *B*
Saint Joseph's College *B*
University of Evansville *B*

Iowa
Buena Vista University *B*
Drake University *B*
University of Iowa *B, M, D*

Kansas
Labette Community College *A*

Kentucky
Kentucky Christian University *B*
Kentucky Wesleyan College *B*
Murray State University *B*

Louisiana
Bossier Parish Community College *C*
Loyola University New Orleans *B*

Massachusetts
Bay State College *A, B*
Berklee College of Music *B*
Eastern Nazarene College *B*
University of Massachusetts
  Lowell *B*

Michigan
Aquinas College *B*
Ferris State University *A, B*
Grand Rapids Community College *A*

Minnesota
Augsburg College *B*
Concordia University St. Paul *B*
Globe University
  Woodbury *A*
Institute of Production and
  Recording *A*

McNally Smith College of
  Music *C, A, B*
Minnesota School of Business
  Brooklyn Center *A*
  Richfield *A*
  St. Cloud *A*
Minnesota State University
  Mankato *B, M, T*
  Moorhead *B*
North Central University *B*
Rochester Community and Technical
  College *A*
Southwest Minnesota State
  University *B*
Winona State University *B*

Mississippi
University of Southern Mississippi *B*

Missouri
Lindenwood University *B*
Missouri Baptist University *B*

Nebraska
Northeast Community College *A*

New Jersey
William Paterson University of New
  Jersey *B*

New York
City University of New York
  Baruch College *B*
Hofstra University *B*
Nazareth College *B*
SUNY
  College at Fredonia *B*
  College at Oneonta *B*
  College at Potsdam *B*
Syracuse University *B*
Villa Maria College of Buffalo *A, B*

North Carolina
Appalachian State University *B*
Elizabeth City State University *B*
Gardner-Webb University *B*
Guilford Technical Community
  College *A*
Montreat College *B*

Ohio
Capital University *B*
Heidelberg University *B*
Ohio Northern University *B*
Owens Community College
  Toledo *C*
Terra State Community College *A*
Tiffin University *B*
University of Rio Grande *B*

Oklahoma
Northern Oklahoma College *A*
Southwestern Oklahoma State
  University *B*
University of Central Oklahoma *A*

Oregon
Northwest Christian University *B*
Southern Oregon University *B*

Pennsylvania
Albright College *B*
California University of
  Pennsylvania *B*
Geneva College *B*
Grove City College *B*
Harrisburg Area Community
  College *A*
Lebanon Valley College *B*
Mansfield University of
  Pennsylvania *B*
University of the Arts *B*

Puerto Rico
Inter American University of Puerto
  Rico
  Metropolitan Campus *A*

South Carolina
South Carolina State University *B*

Tennessee
Belmont University *B*
Bethel University *B*
Middle Tennessee State University *B*
Trevecca Nazarene University *B*
Visible Music College *C, B*

Texas
Austin Community College *A*
Collin County Community College
  District *C, A*
Dallas Baptist University *B*
Hardin-Simmons University *B*
Houston Community College
  System *C, A*
Lubbock Christian University *B*
University of Texas
  Austin *B*
  El Paso *B*
  San Antonio *B*
University of the Incarnate Word *B*

Utah
Broadview University
  Broadview Entertainment Arts
    University *A*

Vermont
Lyndon State College *B*

Washington
Central Washington University *B*
Shoreline Community College *A*
University of Puget Sound *B*

Wisconsin
Globe University
  Madison East *A*
Marian University *B*

Music pedagogy

Alabama
Miles College *B*
Oakwood University *B*
Samford University *B*

Arizona
Mesa Community College *C*

California
Holy Names University *B, M, T*
University of Southern
  California *M, D*

Florida
University of Miami *M*

Illinois
Trinity International University *B*

Indiana
Butler University *B, M*

Kansas
Central Christian College of Kansas *A*

Louisiana
Louisiana College *B*

Massachusetts
Eastern Nazarene College *B*
New England Conservatory of
  Music *M*

Michigan
Central Michigan University *M*
Eastern Michigan University *M*
Madonna University *C*
Michigan State University *B, M, D*
Oakland University *M*
Spring Arbor University *A*
Western Michigan University *M, T*

Minnesota
St. Catherine University *T*
Saint Cloud State University *M*

Mississippi
Mississippi College *M*

Nebraska
Hastings College *B*
Union College *B*

New Jersey
Rider University *M*

New York
Ithaca College *M*

North Carolina
Meredith College *B*

Ohio
Cedarville University *B*

Oklahoma
University of Oklahoma *B*

Pennsylvania
Carnegie Mellon University *M*
Temple University *B, M*

South Carolina
Bob Jones University *B, M*
Converse College *B*

Tennessee
Belmont University *B, M*

Texas
Baylor University *B*

Utah
Weber State University *B*

Virginia
James Madison University *D*
Liberty University *B*

Wisconsin
Maranatha Baptist Bible College *B*
University of Wisconsin
  Parkside *C*
Viterbo University *B*

Music performance

Alabama
Huntingdon College *B*
Miles College *B*
Samford University *B*

Alaska
University of Alaska
  Anchorage *B*

Arizona
Arizona State University *B, M*
Northern Arizona University *B*
Phoenix College *C*
University of Arizona *B*

Arkansas
Arkansas State University *B, M*
Henderson State University *B*

John Brown University *B*
Ouachita Baptist University *B*
University of Arkansas *B, M*
University of Central Arkansas *B, M*

California

Antelope Valley College *C*
Azusa Pacific University *B*
Bethesda University of
California *B, M*
Biola University *B*
California Baptist University *B*
California Institute of the
Arts *C, B, M*
California State University
East Bay *M*
Fresno *B, M*
Fullerton *B, M*
Long Beach *B, M*
Los Angeles *B, M*
Northridge *B, M*
Sacramento *B, M*
San Bernardino *B*
Stanislaus *B*
Chabot College *A*
Chapman University *B*
College of the Siskiyous *A*
Cypress College *C, A*
Foothill College *C*
Fresno Pacific University *B*
Gavilan College *A*
Golden West College *C, A*
Holy Names University *B, M*
La Sierra University *C, B*
Los Angeles Harbor College *C*
Los Angeles Valley College *C*
Los Medanos College *C, A*
Mills College *M*
MiraCosta College *A*
Mount St. Mary's College *B*
Notre Dame de Namur
University *B, M*
Orange Coast College *C*
Pacific Union College *B*
Point Loma Nazarene University *B*
San Diego Christian College *B*
San Diego State University *B, M*
San Francisco Conservatory of
Music *B, M*
San Francisco State University *B, M*
San Jose State University *B*
Sierra College *A*
University of California
Irvine *B*
University of Redlands *B*
University of Southern
California *B, M, D*
University of the Pacific *B*
Vanguard University of Southern
California *B*

Colorado

Adams State University *B*
Colorado Christian University *B*
Colorado State University *B, M*
University of Colorado
Boulder *B, M, D*
University of Denver *C, B*

Connecticut

University of Connecticut *D*
University of Hartford *B, M, D*
Yale University *M, D*

Delaware

University of Delaware *B, M*

District of Columbia

American University *B*
Catholic University of
America *B, M, D*
George Washington University *M*

Florida

Baptist College of Florida *B*
Florida Gulf Coast University *B*
Florida Southern College *B*
Hobe Sound Bible College *B*
Jacksonville University *B*
Lynn University *B, M*
Palm Beach Atlantic University *B*
Seminole State College of Florida *C*
Southeastern University *B*
Stetson University *B*
University of Central Florida *B*
University of Miami *B, M, D*
University of North Florida *B*
University of South Florida *B, M*
University of Tampa *B*
University of West Florida *B*

Georgia

Brenau University *B*
Columbus State University *B, M*
Covenant College *B*
Georgia Regents University *B*
Georgia Southern University *B*
Georgia State University *B, M*
Kennesaw State University *B*
LaGrange College *B*
Mercer University *B, M*
Toccoa Falls College *B*
University of Georgia *B*
University of North Georgia *A, B*
University of West Georgia *B, M*
Valdosta State University *B, M*

Idaho

Boise State University *B, M*
Idaho State University *B*
North Idaho College *A*
Northwest Nazarene University *B*
University of Idaho *B*

Illinois

Augustana College *B*
Bradley University *B*
Columbia College Chicago *B*
DePaul University *B, M*
Eureka College *B, T*
Illinois State University *B*
Illinois Valley Community College *A*
Illinois Wesleyan University *B*
Judson University *B*
Lincoln College *A*
McKendree University *B*
Millikin University *B*
Moody Bible Institute *B*
North Park University *B*
Northern Illinois University *B, M*
Northwestern University *B, M, D*
Olivet Nazarene University *B*
Roosevelt University *B, M*
Trinity International University *B*
University of Illinois
Urbana-Champaign *B, M, D*
University of St. Francis *B*
Western Illinois University *B*
Wheaton College *B*

Indiana

Anderson University *B*
Bethel College *B*
Butler University *B, M*
DePauw University *B*
Huntington University *B*
Indiana State University *B, M*
Indiana University
Bloomington *B, M, D*
Purdue University Fort Wayne *B*
South Bend *B, M*
Manchester University *B*
Oakland City University *B*
University of Evansville *B*
University of Indianapolis *B*
Valparaiso University *B*
Vincennes University *A*

Iowa

Buena Vista University *B, T*
Coe College *B*
Cornell College *B*
Drake University *B*
Graceland University *B, T*
Morningside College *B*
Simpson College *B*
Southwestern Community College *A*
University of Iowa *B, M, D*
University of Northern Iowa *B, M*
Wartburg College *B*

Kansas

Bethany College *B*
Central Christian College of
Kansas *A, B*
Friends University *B*
Kansas State University *B*
Kansas Wesleyan University *B*
McPherson College *B*
MidAmerica Nazarene University *B*
Pittsburg State University *B, M*
Seward County Community
College *A*
Southwestern College *B*
University of Kansas *B, M, D*
Washburn University *B*
Wichita State University *B*

Kentucky

Berea College *B, T*
Bluegrass Community and Technical
College *A*
Campbellsville University *B, M*
Kentucky Christian University *B*
Kentucky Wesleyan College *B*
Morehead State University *M*
Transylvania University *B*
University of Kentucky *B, M*
Western Kentucky University *B, T*

Louisiana

Centenary College of Louisiana *B, T*
Grambling State University *B*
Louisiana College *B*
Louisiana State University and
Agricultural and Mechanical
College *B, M, D*
Louisiana Tech University *B*
Loyola University New Orleans *B, M*
McNeese State University *B*
Northwestern State University *B, M*
Southeastern Louisiana
University *B, M*
Southern University and Agricultural
and Mechanical College *B*
Tulane University *B*
University of Louisiana at
Lafayette *B, M*
University of Louisiana at Monroe *B*
University of New Orleans *M*
Xavier University of Louisiana *B*

Maine

University of Maine *B, M*
University of Southern Maine *B, M*

Maryland

Hood College *C*
Johns Hopkins University: Peabody
Conservatory of Music *B, M, D*
Towson University *M*
University of Maryland
College Park *B*
Washington Adventist University *B*

Massachusetts

Anna Maria College *B*
Berklee College of Music *B*
Boston Conservatory *B, M*
Boston University *B, M, D*
Eastern Nazarene College *B*
Gordon College *B*

Greenfield Community College *C*
New England Conservatory of
Music *B, M, D*
University of Massachusetts
Amherst *B, M, D*
Lowell *B, M*

Michigan

Adrian College *B*
Albion College *B*
Andrews University *B, M*
Aquinas College *A, B*
Calvin College *B*
Central Michigan University *M*
Cornerstone University *B, T*
Eastern Michigan University *B, M*
Grand Rapids Community College *A*
Hope College *B*
Lansing Community College *A*
Madonna University *B*
Marygrove College *B*
Michigan State University *B, M, D*
Oakland Community College *A*
Oakland University *B, M*
Rochester College *B*
Spring Arbor University *B*
University of Michigan *B, M, D, T*
University of Michigan
Flint *B*
Western Michigan University *B, M*

Minnesota

Augsburg College *B*
Bethel University *B*
College of St. Scholastica *B*
Concordia College: Moorhead *B*
Crown College *B*
Gustavus Adolphus College *B*
Hamline University *B*
Minnesota State University
Mankato *B, M, T*
Moorhead *B*
North Central University *B*
St. Catherine University *B*
Saint Cloud State University *B*
St. Mary's University of Minnesota *B*
St. Olaf College *B*
University of Minnesota
Duluth *B*
Morris *B*
University of Northwestern - St.
Paul *B*
University of St. Thomas *B*
Winona State University *B*

Mississippi

Alcorn State University *B*
Jackson State University *B*
Mississippi College *B*
Northeast Mississippi Community
College *A*
University of Southern Mississippi *D*
William Carey University *B*

Missouri

Avila University *B*
Calvary Bible College and Theological
Seminary *B*
Central Methodist University *B*
Evangel University *B*
Hannibal-LaGrange University *A, B*
Lindenwood University *B*
Missouri Baptist University *B*
Missouri State University *B*
Truman State University *B*
University of Missouri
Kansas City *B, M, D*
Webster University *B, M*
William Jewell College *B*

Montana

Montana State University
Billings *B*

Rocky Mountain College *B*
University of Montana *B, M*

Nebraska

Grace University *B*
Hastings College *B, T*
Nebraska Wesleyan University *B*
Northeast Community College *A*
Peru State College *B*
Union College *B*
University of Nebraska
  Kearney *B*
  Omaha *B*
Western Nebraska Community
  College *A*

Nevada

University of Nevada
  Reno *B*

New Hampshire

Keene State College *B*

New Jersey

Kean University *B*
Middlesex County College *A*
Montclair State University *B*
Rutgers, The State University of New
  Jersey
  New Brunswick/Piscataway
    Campus *B, M*
Seton Hall University *B*
William Paterson University of New
  Jersey *B*

New Mexico

New Mexico Highlands University *B*
New Mexico State University *B, M*
Santa Fe University of Art and
  Design *B*
University of New Mexico *B, M*

New York

Adirondack Community College *A*
Bard College *B, M*
Canisius College *B*
City University of New York
  Brooklyn College *B, M*
  City College *B, M*
  Hunter College *B, M*
  Lehman College *B*
  Queens College *B, M*
College of Saint Rose *B, M*
Dutchess Community College *C*
Eastman School of Music of the
  University of Rochester *B, M, D*
Five Towns College *A, B, M, D*
Hofstra University *B*
Houghton College *B, M*
Ithaca College *B, M, T*
Jewish Theological Seminary of
  America *B*
Juilliard School *B, M, D*
Long Island University
  LIU Post *B, M*
Manhattan School of Music *B, M, D*
Mannes College The New School for
  Music *B, M*
Molloy College *B*
Monroe Community College *A*
Nassau Community College *A*
Nazareth College *B*
New York University *B, M, D*
Nyack College *B*
SUNY
  College at Fredonia *B, M*
  College at Geneseo *B*
  College at Potsdam *B, M*
  College at Purchase *B, M*
  University at Albany *B*
  University at Binghamton *B, M*
  University at Buffalo *B, M*
  University at Stony Brook *M, D*
Syracuse University *B, M*

University of Rochester *B, M*
Villa Maria College of Buffalo *A, B*
Wagner College *B*
Westchester Community College *A*

North Carolina

Appalachian State University *B, M*
Brevard College *B*
Catawba College *B*
Chowan University *B*
Duke University *M*
East Carolina University *B, M*
Elon University *B*
Gardner-Webb University *B*
Greensboro College *C, B, T*
Lenoir-Rhyne University *B*
Mars Hill University *B*
Meredith College *B, M*
Methodist University *B*
Montreat College *B*
St. Augustine's University *B*
Salem College *B*
Southeastern Community College *A*
University of North Carolina
  Chapel Hill *B*
  Charlotte *B*
  Greensboro *B, M, D*
  Pembroke *B*
  School of the Arts *B, M*
  Wilmington *B*
Wake Forest University *B*
Western Carolina University *B, M*
William Peace University *B*
Wingate University *B*

North Dakota

Minot State University *B*
University of Jamestown *B*
University of Mary *B*
University of North Dakota *B*

Ohio

Ashland University *B*
Baldwin Wallace University *B*
Bowling Green State University *B, M*
Capital University *B*
Cedarville University *B*
Central State University *B*
Cleveland Institute of Music *B, M, D*
College of Wooster *B*
Heidelberg University *B*
Kent State University *M*
Miami University
  Oxford *B, M*
Mount Vernon Nazarene University *B*
Ohio Northern University *B*
Ohio State University
  Columbus Campus *B*
Ohio University *B, M*
Ohio Wesleyan University *B*
Otterbein University *B*
Terra State Community College *A*
University of Akron *B, M*
University of Cincinnati *B, M*
University of Dayton *B*
University of Mount Union *B*
University of Toledo *M*
Wright State University *B, M*
Youngstown State University *B, M*

Oklahoma

Langston University *B*
Mid-America Christian University *B*
Oklahoma Baptist University *B*
Oklahoma Christian University *B*
Oklahoma City University *B, M*
Oral Roberts University *B*
Southeastern Oklahoma State
  University *B*
Southwestern Christian University *B*
Southwestern Oklahoma State
  University *B*
University of Central Oklahoma *A, B*

University of Oklahoma *D*
University of Tulsa *B*

Oregon

Corban University *B*
Pacific University *B*
Portland Community College *C*
Portland State University *B, M*
University of Oregon *B, M, D*
Willamette University *B*

Pennsylvania

Allegheny College *B*
Bucknell University *B*
Cairn University *B*
Carnegie Mellon University *B, M*
Community College of
  Philadelphia *A*
Curtis Institute of Music *C, B*
Duquesne University *B, M*
Geneva College *B*
Gettysburg College *B*
Grove City College *B*
Immaculata University *B*
Indiana University of Pennsylvania *B*
Lebanon Valley College *B*
Mansfield University of
  Pennsylvania *B*
Marywood University *B*
Mercyhurst University *B*
Messiah College *B, M*
Penn State
  University Park *B, M*
St. Vincent College *B*
Seton Hill University *B*
Slippery Rock University of
  Pennsylvania *B*
Susquehanna University *B*
Temple University *C, B, M, D*
University of the Arts *B, M*
Valley Forge Christian College *B*
West Chester University of
  Pennsylvania *B, M*
Westminster College *B*

Puerto Rico

Conservatory of Music of Puerto
  Rico *B, M*
Inter American University of Puerto
  Rico
  Metropolitan Campus *A, B, M*

Rhode Island

Rhode Island College *B*
University of Rhode Island *B*

South Carolina

Anderson University *B*
Bob Jones University *B, M*
Charleston Southern University *B*
Columbia College *B*
Converse College *B, M*
Furman University *B*
Limestone College *B*
Newberry College *B*
North Greenville University *B*
South Carolina State University *B*
University of South Carolina
  Columbia *M, D*
  Upstate *B*

South Dakota

University of South Dakota *B, M*

Tennessee

Belmont University *B, M*
Carson-Newman University *B*
Dyersburg State Community
  College *A*
Fisk University *B*
Hiwassee College *A*
Lee University *B, M*
Lipscomb University *B*
Maryville College *B, T*

Southern Adventist University *B*
Tennessee Technological
  University *B*
Trevecca Nazarene University *B*
Union University *B*
Visible Music College *C, B*

Texas

Alvin Community College *A*
Baylor University *B, M*
Cedar Valley College *C, A*
Dallas Baptist University *B*
Del Mar College *A*
Hardin-Simmons University *B, M*
Houston Baptist University *B*
Houston Community College
  System *C, A*
Howard Payne University *B*
Lamar State College at Port
  Arthur *C, A*
Navarro College *A*
Prairie View A&M University *B*
Rice University *B, M, D*
Sam Houston State University *B*
Southern Methodist University *B, M*
Southwestern Assemblies of God
  University *B*
Texas Christian University *B, M, D*
Texas Lutheran University *B*
Texas State University *B*
Trinity University *B*
Tyler Junior College *A*
University of Houston *B*
University of Mary Hardin-Baylor *B*
University of North Texas *B, M, D*
University of Texas
  Arlington *B, M*
  Austin *C, B*
  El Paso *B, M*
  Pan American *B*
  San Antonio *B*
University of the Incarnate Word *B*
Wayland Baptist University *B*
West Texas A&M University *B, M*

Utah

Brigham Young University *B, M*
Utah Valley University *B*
Weber State University *B*

Vermont

Bennington College *B*
Johnson State College *B*
Lyndon State College *B*
University of Vermont *B*

Virginia

Bluefield College *B*
Christopher Newport University *B*
Emory & Henry College *B*
George Mason University *B*
Hampton University *B*
James Madison University *B, M, T*
Norfolk State University *M*
Old Dominion University *B*
Randolph College *B*
Shenandoah University *B, M, D*
Virginia Commonwealth
  University *B, M*
Virginia State University *B*

Washington

Central Washington University *B*
Cornish College of the Arts *B*
Gonzaga University *B*
Shoreline Community College *A*
University of Puget Sound *B, T*
University of Washington *B, M, D*
Walla Walla University *B*
Washington State University *B, M*
Western Washington University *B*
Whitman College *B*
Whitworth University *B, T*

West Virginia

Alderson-Broaddus University *B*
Glenville State College *B*

Wisconsin

Cardinal Stritch University *B, M, T*
Concordia University Wisconsin *B*
Lawrence University *B, T*
Maranatha Baptist Bible College *B*
University of Wisconsin
    Green Bay *B, T*
    Madison *B, M, D*
    Parkside *T*
    Stevens Point *B*
    Superior *B*
Viterbo University *B*

Wyoming

Casper College *A*
University of Wyoming *C, B*

Music teacher education

Alabama

Alabama Agricultural and Mechanical
    University *B*
Auburn University *B, M, D*
Birmingham-Southern College *B, T*
Huntingdon College *B, T*
Judson College *B*
Oakwood University *B*
Samford University *B, M*
Talladega College *B*
University of Alabama *B*
University of Alabama
    Birmingham *T*
University of Mobile *B, T*

Alaska

University of Alaska
    Anchorage *B*

Arizona

Arizona Christian University *B*
Arizona State University *B, M*
Grand Canyon University *B*
Northern Arizona University *B*
South Mountain Community
    College *A*
University of Arizona *B*

Arkansas

Arkansas State University *B, M, T*
Arkansas Tech University *B*
Harding University *B, T*
John Brown University *B, T*
Ouachita Baptist University *B, T*
Southern Arkansas University *B, T*
University of Arkansas
    Fort Smith *B*
    Monticello *B*
Williams Baptist College *B*

California

Azusa Pacific University *T*
Biola University *B, T*
California Baptist University *B, T*
California Lutheran University *B, T*
California State University
    Chico *T*
    East Bay *M*
    Fresno *B, M*
    Fullerton *B, M, T*
    Long Beach *M, T*
    Northridge *B, T*
    San Bernardino *T*
Chapman University *B*
Fresno Pacific University *B, T*
Holy Names University *M, T*
Hope International University *B*
Humboldt State University *T*
Los Angeles Southwest College *A*

Master's College *B, T*
Mount St. Mary's College *T*
Orange Coast College *A*
Pacific Union College *B*
Pepperdine University *B*
Point Loma Nazarene University *B*
Saddleback College *A*
San Diego Christian College *B, T*
San Diego State University *B, M, T*
San Francisco State University *T*
Simpson University *B, T*
Sonoma State University *T*
University of Redlands *B, T*
University of San Diego *T*
University of Southern California *M*
University of the Pacific *B, M, T*
Vanguard University of Southern
    California *B, T*
Westmont College *T*

Colorado

Adams State University *B, M, T*
Colorado Christian University *B*
Colorado State University *B, T*
Colorado State University
    Pueblo *T*
Metropolitan State University of
    Denver *B, T*
University of Colorado
    Boulder *B, M, T*
University of Northern Colorado *B, T*
Western State Colorado
    University *B, T*

Connecticut

Central Connecticut State
    University *B, M, T*
Fairfield University *B*
University of Connecticut *B*
University of Hartford *B, M, D, T*
University of New Haven *M*
Western Connecticut State
    University *B, M*

Delaware

Delaware State University *B*
University of Delaware *B, T*

District of Columbia

George Washington University *M, T*
Howard University *B, M*

Florida

Baptist College of Florida *B*
Bethune-Cookman University *B, T*
Broward College *A*
Clearwater Christian College *B*
Florida Agricultural and Mechanical
    University *B, T*
Florida Atlantic University *B*
Florida Gulf Coast University *B*
Florida International University *M*
Florida Southern College *B, T*
Florida State University *B, M, D*
Hobe Sound Bible College *B, T*
Jacksonville University *B, M, T*
Palm Beach Atlantic University *B, T*
Palm Beach State College *A*
Pensacola State College *A*
Southeastern University *B, T*
Stetson University *B*
University of Central Florida *B*
University of Florida *B, M, D*
University of Miami *B, M, D*
University of North Florida *B*
University of South Florida *B, M*
University of Tampa *B, T*
University of West Florida *B*
Warner University *B*

Georgia

Albany State University *B, M*
Armstrong Atlantic State University *B*
Berry College *B*

Brenau University *B*
Columbus State University *B, M*
Darton College *A*
Emmanuel College *B*
Fort Valley State University *B, T*
Georgia College and State
    University *B, M, T*
Georgia Regents University *B*
Georgia Southern University *B*
Georgia State University *M, T*
Kennesaw State University *B*
Mercer University *B*
Piedmont College *M, T*
Reinhardt University *B, M*
Shorter University *B, T*
Thomas University *B*
Toccoa Falls College *B, T*
Truett-McConnell College *B*
University of Georgia *B, M, D, T*
University of North Georgia *A, B*
University of West Georgia *B, M, T*
Valdosta State University *B, M*
Young Harris College *B*

Hawaii

Brigham Young University-
    Hawaii *B, T*

Idaho

Boise State University *B, M, T*
Brigham Young University-Idaho *B, T*
College of Idaho *B*
Idaho State University *B*
Northwest Nazarene University *B*
University of Idaho *B, T*

Illinois

Augustana College *B, T*
Bradley University *B, M, T*
Chicago State University *B*
City Colleges of Chicago
    Harold Washington College *A*
College of Lake County *A*
Concordia University
    Chicago *B, M, T*
DePaul University *B, M, T*
Elmhurst College *B*
Eureka College *T*
Greenville College *B, T*
Illinois College *T*
Illinois State University *B, M, T*
Illinois Wesleyan University *B*
Knox College *T*
MacMurray College *B, T*
McKendree University *B*
Millikin University *B, T*
Monmouth College *T*
North Central College *B, T*
North Park University *T*
Northern Illinois University *M*
Northwestern University *B, M, D*
Olivet Nazarene University *B, T*
Parkland College *A*
Quincy University *B, T*
Roosevelt University *B*
Saint Xavier University *B*
Trinity Christian College *B, T*
Trinity International University *B*
University of Illinois
    Urbana-Champaign *B, M, D, T*
University of St. Francis *B*
VanderCook College of Music *B, M, T*
Wheaton College *B, T*

Indiana

Anderson University *B, M, T*
Bethel College *B*
Butler University *B, M, T*
DePauw University *B*
Goshen College *B, T*
Grace College *B*
Huntington University *B*

Indiana University
    Bloomington *B, M, D, T*
    Purdue University Fort Wayne *B, T*
    South Bend *B*
Indiana Wesleyan University *B, T*
Manchester University *B, T*
Marian University *B*
Oakland City University *B*
Saint Mary's College *T*
Taylor University *B, T*
University of Evansville *B, T*
University of Indianapolis *B, T*
Valparaiso University *B*
Vincennes University *A*

Iowa

Briar Cliff University *B*
Buena Vista University *B, T*
Central College *B, T*
Clarke University *B, T*
Coe College *B*
Cornell College *B, T*
Dordt College *B*
Drake University *B*
Emmaus Bible College *B*
Faith Baptist Bible College and
    Theological Seminary *B, T*
Graceland University *T*
Grand View University *B, T*
Iowa State University *B, T*
Iowa Wesleyan College *B*
Loras College *T*
Morningside College *B*
Mount Mercy University *T*
Northwestern College *B, T*
St. Ambrose University *B, T*
Simpson College *B, T*
University of Iowa *M, D, T*
University of Northern Iowa *B, M*
Wartburg College *B, T*

Kansas

Allen County Community College *A*
Baker University *B, T*
Benedictine College *B*
Bethany College *B*
Bethel College *T*
Colby Community College *A*
Emporia State University *B, T*
Fort Hays State University *B*
Friends University *B*
Garden City Community College *A*
Independence Community College *A*
Kansas State University *B, M, T*
Labette Community College *A*
McPherson College *B, T*
MidAmerica Nazarene University *B, T*
Pittsburg State University *B*
Southwestern College *B*
Sterling College *B*
Tabor College *B*
University of Kansas *B, M, D, T*
Washburn University *B, T*
Wichita State University *B, M, T*

Kentucky

Asbury University *B, T*
Berea College *B, T*
Campbellsville University *B, M*
Eastern Kentucky University *B, M*
Georgetown College *B*
Kentucky Wesleyan College *T*
Lindsey Wilson College *B*
Murray State University *M, T*
Transylvania University *B*
University of Kentucky *B, M*
University of Louisville *M*
University of the
    Cumberlands *B, M, T*
Western Kentucky University *M*

Louisiana

Centenary College of Louisiana *T*
Grambling State University *B*

Louisiana College *B, T*
Louisiana State University and
    Agricultural and Mechanical
    College *B*
Louisiana Tech University *B*
Loyola University New Orleans *B*
McNeese State University *T*
Nicholls State University *B*
Northwestern State University *B, M*
Southeastern Louisiana University *B*
University of Louisiana at Lafayette *B*
Xavier University of Louisiana *B*

Maine

University of Maine *B, M*
University of Maine
    Fort Kent *B*
University of Southern Maine *B, T*

Maryland

Frostburg State University *B, T*
Johns Hopkins University: Peabody
    Conservatory of Music *B, M*
Mount St. Mary's University *M, T*
Notre Dame of Maryland
    University *T*
Towson University *B, M*
University of Maryland
    College Park *B*
    Eastern Shore *B*
Washington Adventist University *B*

Massachusetts

Anna Maria College *B*
Boston Conservatory *M*
Boston University *B, M, D*
Bridgewater State University *B, M, T*
Eastern Nazarene College *B, M, T*
Gordon College *B, M*
Smith College *M*
Tufts University *M*
University of Massachusetts
    Dartmouth *T*
    Lowell *M*

Michigan

Adrian College *B, T*
Alma College *T*
Andrews University *M*
Aquinas College *B, T*
Calvin College *B*
Central Michigan University *B, M*
Concordia University *B, T*
Cornerstone University *B, T*
Delta College *A*
Eastern Michigan University *B, M*
Grand Rapids Community College *A*
Grand Valley State University *B, T*
Hope College *B, T*
Madonna University *B*
Michigan State University *B*
Northern Michigan University *B, T*
Oakland University *B, M, D*
Olivet College *B, T*
Rochester College *B*
Spring Arbor University *B*
University of Michigan *B, M, D, T*
University of Michigan
    Flint *B, T*
Western Michigan University *B*

Minnesota

Augsburg College *B, T*
Bemidji State University *B, T*
Bethel University *B*
College of St. Benedict *T*
College of St. Scholastica *T*
Concordia College: Moorhead *B, T*
Concordia University St. Paul *B, T*
Crown College *B*
Gustavus Adolphus College *T*
Minnesota State University
    Mankato *B, M, T*
    Moorhead *B*

Ridgewater College *A*
Rochester Community and Technical
    College *A*
St. Catherine University *B, T*
Saint Cloud State University *B, T*
St. John's University *T*
St. Mary's University of Minnesota *B*
St. Olaf College *B*
Southwest Minnesota State
    University *B*
University of Minnesota
    Duluth *B*
    Morris *T*
    Twin Cities *B, M*
University of Northwestern - St.
    Paul *B*
University of St. Thomas *B, M*
Winona State University *B, T*

Mississippi

Blue Mountain College *B*
Coahoma Community College *A*
Delta State University *B*
Itawamba Community College *A*
Jackson State University *B, M*
Millsaps College *T*
Mississippi College *B, M*
Mississippi State University *B*
Mississippi University for
    Women *B, T*
Mississippi Valley State
    University *B, T*
Northeast Mississippi Community
    College *A*
Northwest Mississippi Community
    College *A*
University of Southern
    Mississippi *B, M, D*
William Carey University *B*

Missouri

Avila University *T*
Baptist Bible College *B*
Calvary Bible College and Theological
    Seminary *B*
Central Methodist University *B*
College of the Ozarks *B, T*
Culver-Stockton College *B, T*
Drury University *B, T*
Evangel University *B, T*
Hannibal-LaGrange University *B*
Lincoln University *B*
Missouri Baptist University *B, T*
Missouri Southern State
    University *B, T*
Missouri State University *B*
Missouri Western State University *B*
Northwest Missouri State
    University *B, M, T*
Southeast Missouri State University *B*
Southwest Baptist University *B, T*
Truman State University *M*
University of Central Missouri *B, M*
University of Missouri
    Columbia *B, M, D*
    Kansas City *B, M*
    St. Louis *B, M*
Washington University in St. Louis *M*
Webster University *B, M*
William Jewell College *B, T*

Montana

Montana State University *B*
Montana State University
    Billings *B, T*
Rocky Mountain College *B*
University of Montana *B, M, T*
University of Montana: Western *B, T*

Nebraska

Chadron State College *B*
Concordia University *B, T*
Grace University *B*
Hastings College *B, M, T*

Midland University *B, T*
Nebraska Wesleyan University *B*
Northeast Community College *A*
Union College *B*
University of Nebraska
    Kearney *B, M, T*
    Lincoln *B, T*
    Omaha *B, T*
Wayne State College *B, T*
Western Nebraska Community
    College *A*
York College *B, T*

Nevada

University of Nevada
    Reno *B, T*

New Hampshire

Keene State College *B, T*
Plymouth State University *B, M, T*
Southern New Hampshire
    University *B*

New Jersey

College of New Jersey *B, T*
Essex County College *A*
Georgian Court University *T*
Kean University *B, T*
New Jersey City University *M, T*
Rider University *B, M*
Rowan University *M*
Rutgers, The State University of New
    Jersey
    New Brunswick/Piscataway
        Campus *M*
William Paterson University of New
    Jersey *B, T*

New Mexico

Eastern New Mexico University *B*
New Mexico Highlands University *B*
New Mexico State University *B*
University of New Mexico *B*

New York

City University of New York
    Brooklyn College *B, M, T*
    City College *B, T*
    Hunter College *B, M, T*
    Lehman College *M*
    Queens College *B, M, T*
College of Saint Rose *B, M, T*
Dowling College *B*
Eastman School of Music of the
    University of
    Rochester *B, M, D, T*
Five Towns College *B, M, D*
Fordham University *T*
Hartwick College *B, T*
Hobart and William Smith Colleges *T*
Hofstra University *B, M*
Houghton College *B, T*
Ithaca College *B, M, T*
Long Island University
    LIU Brooklyn *B, T*
    LIU Post *B, M, T*
Manhattanville College *B, M, T*
Monroe Community College *A*
Nazareth College *B, M, T*
New York University *B, M, D, T*
Nyack College *B*
Roberts Wesleyan College *B, M*
SUNY
    College at Buffalo *B*
    College at Fredonia *B, M, T*
    College at Potsdam *B, M*
    University at Buffalo *M, T*
Syracuse University *B, M, T*
University of Rochester *M, D*
Wagner College *T*

North Carolina

Appalachian State University *B, M, T*
Brevard College *B*

Campbell University *B, T*
Catawba College *B, T*
Chowan University *B*
East Carolina University *B, M*
Elon University *T*
Fayetteville State University *B, T*
Gardner-Webb University *B*
Greensboro College *B, T*
Lenoir-Rhyne University *B, T*
Livingstone College *T*
Mars Hill University *B*
Meredith College *B, T*
Methodist University *A, B, T*
North Carolina Agricultural and
    Technical State University *B, T*
North Carolina Central
    University *B, T*
Pfeiffer University *B, T*
Piedmont International University *B*
Salem College *B*
University of Mount Olive *B*
University of North Carolina
    Charlotte *B*
    Greensboro *B, M, D*
    Pembroke *B, M*
    Wilmington *B*
Western Carolina University *B, T*
Wingate University *B, T*
Winston-Salem State University *B*

North Dakota

Dickinson State University *B, T*
Minot State University *B, M*
North Dakota State University *B, T*
University of Jamestown *B*
University of Mary *B*
University of North Dakota *B, D*
Valley City State University *B, T*

Ohio

Ashland University *B, T*
Baldwin Wallace University *B, T*
Bluffton University *B*
Bowling Green State
    University *B, M, T*
Capital University *B, M*
Case Western Reserve
    University *B, M, D*
Cedarville University *B*
College of Wooster *B*
God's Bible School and College *B*
Heidelberg University *B*
Hiram College *T*
Kent State University *B, M, D*
Malone University *B*
Marietta College *B*
Miami University
    Oxford *B, M, T*
Mount Vernon Nazarene
    University *B, T*
Oberlin College *M*
Ohio Christian University *B*
Ohio Northern University *B, T*
Ohio State University
    Columbus Campus *B*
Ohio Wesleyan University *B*
Otterbein University *B*
University of Akron *B, M*
University of Cincinnati *B, M, T*
University of Dayton *B, M*
University of Mount Union *B, T*
University of Rio Grande *B, T*
University of Toledo *B, M, T*
Wright State University *B, M, T*
Xavier University *B*
Youngstown State University *B, M*

Oklahoma

Cameron University *B*
East Central University *B*
Eastern Oklahoma State College *A*
Langston University *B*
Mid-America Christian University *B*
Northeastern State University *B*

Northwestern Oklahoma State
University *B*
Oklahoma Baptist University *B, T*
Oklahoma Christian University *B, T*
Oklahoma City University *B*
Oklahoma State University *B*
Oklahoma Wesleyan University *B*
Oral Roberts University *B, T*
Southeastern Oklahoma State
University *B, T*
Southern Nazarene University *B*
Southwestern Oklahoma State
University *B, M, T*
University of Central Oklahoma *B, M*
University of Oklahoma *B, M, D, T*
University of Tulsa *B, T*

Oregon

Corban University *B*
George Fox University *B, M, T*
Linfield College *B, T*
Oregon State University *M*
Portland State University *T*
Southern Oregon University *T*
University of Oregon *M, D, T*
University of Portland *B, M, T*
Warner Pacific College *B, T*
Willamette University *B, M*

Pennsylvania

Baptist Bible College of
Pennsylvania *A, B*
Bucknell University *B, T*
Cairn University *B, T*
Chestnut Hill College *B, T*
Duquesne University *B, M, T*
Geneva College *B, T*
Gettysburg College *B, T*
Grove City College *B, T*
Immaculata University *B*
Lebanon Valley College *B, M, T*
Lycoming College *T*
Mansfield University of
Pennsylvania *B, T*
Marywood University *B, M*
Mercyhurst University *B, T*
Messiah College *B, T*
Montgomery County Community
College *A*
Moravian College *B, T*
Penn State
University Park *B, M, D*
Seton Hill University *B, T*
Susquehanna University *B, T*
Temple University *B, M, D*
University of the Arts *M*
Valley Forge Christian College *B*
Westminster College *T*
York College of Pennsylvania *B, T*

Puerto Rico

Conservatory of Music of Puerto
Rico *B, M, T*
Inter American University of Puerto
Rico
San German Campus *B, M*
Pontifical Catholic University of
Puerto Rico *B, T*

Rhode Island

Providence College *B*
Rhode Island College *B, M*
Salve Regina University *B*

South Carolina

Anderson University *B, M, T*
Bob Jones University *B, M*
Charleston Southern University *B*
Claflin University *B*
Coker College *B, T*
Columbia College *B, T*
Converse College *T*
Furman University *B, T*
Limestone College *B*

Newberry College *B, T*
North Greenville University *B, T*
Presbyterian College *B, T*
South Carolina State University *B, T*
Southern Wesleyan University *B, T*
University of South Carolina
Aiken *B, T*
Columbia *M, D*
Winthrop University *B, M, T*

South Dakota

Augustana College *B, T*
Black Hills State University *B*
Dakota Wesleyan University *B, T*
Mount Marty College *B*
Northern State University *B, T*
South Dakota State University *B*
University of Sioux Falls *B*
University of South Dakota *B, M, T*

Tennessee

Belmont University *B, M, T*
Bethel University *B, T*
Bryan University
Dayton *T*
Carson-Newman University *B*
Cumberland University *B, T*
Fisk University *B*
Freed-Hardeman University *B, T*
Hiwassee College *A*
King University *B*
Lee University *B, M*
Lipscomb University *B, T*
Maryville College *B, T*
Milligan College *B, M, T*
Southern Adventist University *B*
Tennessee Technological
University *B, T*
Tennessee Temple University *B*
Trevecca Nazarene University *B, T*
Union University *B, T*
Vanderbilt University *B, M, T*
Welch College *B*

Texas

Abilene Christian University *B, T*
Amarillo College *A*
Arlington Baptist College *B, T*
Austin College *M*
Baylor University *B, M, T*
Dallas Baptist University *B*
Dallas Christian College *B, T*
Del Mar College *A*
East Texas Baptist University *B*
Hardin-Simmons University *B, M, T*
Houston Baptist University *B, M, T*
Howard Payne University *B*
Lamar University *B, M, T*
Laredo Community College *A*
Lubbock Christian University *B*
North Lake College *A*
Our Lady of the Lake University of
San Antonio *B*
Prairie View A&M University *M*
Sam Houston State University *M, T*
Schreiner University *B*
Southern Methodist
University *B, M, T*
Southwestern Assemblies of God
University *B*
Southwestern University *T*
Stephen F. Austin State University *M*
Tarleton State University *T*
Texas A&M University
Kingsville *B, M, T*
Texas Christian University *B, M*
Texas College *B, T*
Texas Lutheran University *B, T*
Texas State University *M, T*
Texas Tech University *M*
Texas Wesleyan University *B, T*
University of Mary Hardin-Baylor *B, T*
University of North Texas *M, D*
University of St. Thomas *B*

University of Texas
Arlington *M, T*
Austin *M, D*
Brownsville *M*
El Paso *M*
San Antonio *M, T*
University of the Incarnate
Word *B, T*
Wayland Baptist University *B, T*
West Texas A&M University *T*

Utah

Brigham Young University *B, M*
Dixie State College *B*
Southern Utah University *B*
Utah Valley University *B*
Weber State University *B*

Vermont

Castleton State College *B, T*
Johnson State College *B*
University of Vermont *B, T*

Virginia

Bluefield College *B, T*
Bridgewater College *T*
Eastern Mennonite University *T*
Emory & Henry College *B*
George Mason University *D*
Hampton University *M*
Hollins University *T*
James Madison University *T*
Longwood University *T*
Old Dominion University *M*
Radford University *T*
Shenandoah University *B, M*

Washington

Central Washington University *B, T*
Eastern Washington University *B*
Gonzaga University *B, T*
Northwest University *T*
Seattle Pacific University *B, T*
University of Puget Sound *B, T*
University of Washington *B, M, D*
Walla Walla University *B*
Washington State University *B, M, T*
Western Washington University *B*
Whitworth University *B, T*

West Virginia

Alderson-Broaddus University *B*
Concord University *B, T*
Shepherd University *M, T*
West Liberty University *B*
West Virginia State University *B*
West Virginia University *T*
West Virginia Wesleyan College *B*

Wisconsin

Alverno College *B, T*
Carroll University *B, T*
Carthage College *T*
Concordia University Wisconsin *B, T*
Edgewood College *B*
Lakeland College *T*
Lawrence University *B, T*
Maranatha Baptist Bible College *B*
Marian University *B, T*
Mount Mary University *B, T*
St. Norbert College *B, T*
Silver Lake College of the Holy
Family *B, M, T*
University of Wisconsin
Green Bay *B, T*
Madison *B, M*
Milwaukee *B, T*
Oshkosh *B, T*
River Falls *B, T*
Stevens Point *B, M, T*
Superior *B, T*
Whitewater *B*
Viterbo University *B, T*

Wyoming

Casper College *A*
Eastern Wyoming College *A*
University of Wyoming *B, M*

Music technology

Arizona

Mesa Community College *C*

California

Diablo Valley College *C*
La Sierra University *B*
MiraCosta College *C*

Colorado

Pikes Peak Community College *C*
University of Denver *B*

Connecticut

University of New Haven *B*

Florida

Bethune-Cookman University *B*
Stetson University *B*
University of Miami *M*
Valencia College *C*

Georgia

Georgia Institute of Technology *M*
LaGrange College *B*

Indiana

Indiana University
Purdue University
Indianapolis *B, M*
University of St. Francis *A, B*

Iowa

Buena Vista University *B*

Kentucky

Bellarmine University *B*
Transylvania University *B*

Michigan

Mott Community College *C, A*
University of Michigan *B*

Minnesota

McNally Smith College of
Music *C, A, B*
Rochester Community and Technical
College *C, A*

Montana

Dawson Community College *A*

New Hampshire

Keene State College *B*

New Jersey

Brookdale Community College *A*

New York

New York University *B, M, D*

North Carolina

Elon University *B*
University of North Carolina
Asheville *B*

Ohio

Owens Community College
Toledo *C, A*
Terra State Community College *A*

Oklahoma

University of Central Oklahoma *A*

Oregon

Northwest Christian University *B*

Pennsylvania

Carnegie Mellon University *M*
Valley Forge Christian College *M*

Texas

University of Texas
Austin *B*

Utah

Utah Valley University *B*

Virginia

Shenandoah University *B*

Wisconsin

Madison Media Institute *B*
Milwaukee Area Technical College *A*

Music theory and composition

Alabama

Birmingham-Southern College *B*
Oakwood University *B*
Samford University *B*

Arizona

Arizona State University *B, M*
Glendale Community College *C*
Mesa Community College *C*
Phoenix College *C*

Arkansas

Ouachita Baptist University *B*

California

Azusa Pacific University *B, M*
Bethesda University of
California *B, M*
Biola University *B*
California Baptist University *B*
California Institute of the
Arts *C, B, M, D*
California State University
Chico *B*
East Bay *M*
Long Beach *M*
Northridge *B, M*
Sacramento *B*
Chapman University *B*
Foothill College *C*
Fresno Pacific University *B*
Golden West College *C, A*
Los Angeles Harbor College *C*
Mills College *M*
Mount St. Mary's College *B*
Ohlone College *C*
Pepperdine University *B*
Point Loma Nazarene University *B*
Solano Community College *C*
University of California
Santa Cruz *D*
University of Redlands *B*
University of Southern
California *B, M, D*
University of the Pacific *B*

Colorado

Adams State University *B*
Colorado State University *B*

Connecticut

University of Hartford *B, M, D*
Western Connecticut State
University *B*
Yale University *M, D*

Delaware

University of Delaware *B*

District of Columbia

American University *B*
Catholic University of
America *B, M, D*
Howard University *B*

Florida

Florida Southern College *B*
Florida State University *B, M, D*
Jacksonville University *B*
Lynn University *B, M*
Palm Beach Atlantic University *B*
Stetson University *B*
University of Miami *B, M, D*

Georgia

Georgia Southern University *B*
University of Georgia *B*
University of West Georgia *B*

Idaho

Boise State University *B*
College of Idaho *B*
North Idaho College *A*
Northwest Nazarene University *B*
University of Idaho *B*

Illinois

Augustana College *B*
Bradley University *B*
DePaul University *B, M*
Illinois Wesleyan University *B*
Lincoln College *A*
Moody Bible Institute *B*
Northwestern University *B, M, D*
Roosevelt University *B, M*
Trinity International University *B*
University of Illinois
Urbana-Champaign *B, M, D*
Wheaton College *B*

Indiana

Butler University *B, M*
DePauw University *B*
Indiana Wesleyan University *B*
Manchester University *B*
Valparaiso University *B*

Iowa

Coe College *B*
Cornell College *B*
University of Iowa *B, M, D*
University of Northern Iowa *B, M*
Wartburg College *B*

Kansas

University of Kansas *B, M, D*
Wichita State University *B*

Kentucky

Bluegrass Community and Technical
College *A*
Campbellsville University *B*

Louisiana

Centenary College of Louisiana *B*
Loyola University New Orleans *B*
Tulane University *B*

Maryland

Johns Hopkins University: Peabody
Conservatory of Music *B, M, D*

Massachusetts

Berklee College of Music *B*
Boston Conservatory *B, M*
Boston University *B, M, D*
Brandeis University *M, D*
Eastern Nazarene College *B*
New England Conservatory of
Music *B, M, D*
Tufts University *B*

Michigan

Calvin College *B*
Central Michigan University *B, M*
Cornerstone University *B, T*
Hope College *B*
Madonna University *C, B*
Marygrove College *B*
Michigan State University *B, M, D*
Oakland Community College *A*
University of Michigan *B, M, D*
Western Michigan University *B, M*

Minnesota

Concordia College: Moorhead *B*
McNally Smith College of Music *B, M*
Minnesota State University
Moorhead *B*
Rochester Community and Technical
College *C, A*
St. Olaf College *B*
University of Minnesota
Duluth *B*
University of Northwestern - St.
Paul *B*

Mississippi

Mississippi College *B*

Missouri

Lindenwood University *B*
University of Missouri
Kansas City *B, M, D*
Washington University in St. Louis *B*
Webster University *B, M*
William Jewell College *B*

Montana

University of Montana *B, M*

Nebraska

Grace University *B*
University of Nebraska
Omaha *B*

New Hampshire

Keene State College *B*

New Jersey

Rider University *B, M*
Rowan University *M*

New Mexico

Santa Fe University of Art and
Design *B*

New York

Bard College *B, M*
City University of New York
Brooklyn College *B, M*
City College *B, M*
Hunter College *B, M*
Cornell University *M, D*
Eastman School of Music of the
University of Rochester *B, M, D*
Five Towns College *A, B, M, D*
Hofstra University *B*
Houghton College *B, M*
Ithaca College *B, M*
Jewish Theological Seminary of
America *B*
Juilliard School *B, M, D*
Manhattan School of Music *B, M, D*
Mannes College The New School for
Music *B, M*
Nazareth College *B*
New York University *M*
Nyack College *B*
SUNY
College at Fredonia *B, M*
College at Potsdam *B*
College at Purchase *B, M*
University at Albany *B*
University at Buffalo *M, D*

Syracuse University *B, M*
University of Rochester *B, M, D*

North Carolina

Duke University *M*
East Carolina University *B, M*
Gardner-Webb University *B*
University of North Carolina
Greensboro *B, M*

Ohio

Ashland University *B*
Baldwin Wallace University *B*
Bowling Green State University *B, M*
Capital University *B*
Cedarville University *B*
Cleveland Institute of Music *B, M, D*
College of Wooster *B*
Heidelberg University *B*
Kent State University *M, D*
Oberlin College *B*
Ohio Northern University *B*
Ohio State University
Columbus Campus *B*
Ohio University *B, M*
Otterbein University *B*
Sinclair Community College *A*
University of Akron *B, M*
University of Cincinnati *B, M, D*
University of Dayton *B*
Youngstown State University *B, M*

Oklahoma

Oklahoma Baptist University *B*
Oklahoma City University *B, M*
Oral Roberts University *B*
Southwestern Oklahoma State
University *B*
University of Tulsa *B*

Oregon

Lewis & Clark College *B*
University of Oregon *B, M, D*
Willamette University *B*

Pennsylvania

Bucknell University *B*
Cairn University *B*
Carnegie Mellon University *B, M*
Curtis Institute of Music *B*
Gettysburg College *B*
Penn State
University Park *M*
Susquehanna University *B*
Temple University *B, M*
University of the Arts *B*
Westminster College *B*

Puerto Rico

Conservatory of Music of Puerto
Rico *B*

South Carolina

Converse College *B, M*
Furman University *B*
Newberry College *B*
University of South Carolina
Columbia *M, D*

Tennessee

Belmont University *B*
Carson-Newman University *B*
Lipscomb University *B*
Maryville College *B*
Southern Adventist University *B*
Union University *B*
Vanderbilt University *B*

Texas

Baylor University *B, M*
Dallas Baptist University *B*
Del Mar College *A*
Hardin-Simmons University *B, M*
Houston Baptist University *B*

Houston Community College
    System *C, A*
Rice University *B, M, D*
Southern Methodist University *B, M*
Texas Christian University *B, M, D*
Trinity University *B*
University of Mary Hardin-Baylor *B*
University of North Texas *B, M, D*
University of Texas
    Austin *B*
    El Paso *B*
    San Antonio *B*
West Texas A&M University *B*

Utah

Brigham Young University *B, M*

Vermont

Bennington College *B, M*
Johnson State College *B*

Virginia

Bluefield College *B*
Liberty University *B*
Randolph College *B*
Shenandoah University *B, M*

Washington

Central Washington University *B*
Centralia College *A*
Cornish College of the Arts *B*
DigiPen Institute of Technology *B*
University of Washington *B, M*
Washington State University *B, M*
Western Washington University *B*
Whitman College *B*

Wisconsin

Lawrence University *B, T*
University of Wisconsin
    Whitewater *B, T*

Music therapy

Arizona

Arizona State University *B, M*

California

California State University
    Northridge *M*
University of the Pacific *B, M*

Colorado

Colorado State University *B, M*

District of Columbia

Howard University *B*

Florida

Florida State University *B, M*
University of Miami *B, M*

Georgia

Georgia College and State
    University *B, M*
University of Georgia *B*

Indiana

Indiana University
    Purdue University Fort Wayne *B*
    Purdue University
        Indianapolis *C, M*
St. Mary-of-the-Woods College *B, M*
University of Evansville *B*

Iowa

University of Iowa *B, M, D*
Wartburg College *B*

Kansas

University of Kansas *B, M*

Kentucky

University of Louisville *B*

Louisiana

Loyola University New Orleans *B, M*

Massachusetts

Anna Maria College *B*
Berklee College of Music *B*
Lesley University *M, D*

Michigan

Eastern Michigan University *B*
Western Michigan University *B, M*

Minnesota

Augsburg College *B*
University of Minnesota
    Twin Cities *B, M*

Mississippi

Mississippi University for Women *B*
William Carey University *B*

Missouri

Drury University *B*
Maryville University of Saint
    Louis *B, M*
University of Missouri
    Kansas City *B*

New Jersey

Montclair State University *B*

New York

Molloy College *B, M*
Nazareth College *D, M*
SUNY
    College at Fredonia *B, M*
    College at New Paltz *M*

North Carolina

Appalachian State University *B, M*
East Carolina University *B, M*
Queens University of Charlotte *B, M*

North Dakota

University of North Dakota *B*

Ohio

Baldwin Wallace University *B*
Cleveland State University *B*
College of Wooster *B*
Ohio University *M*
University of Dayton *B*

Oklahoma

Southwestern Oklahoma State
    University *B*

Pennsylvania

Duquesne University *B*
Elizabethtown College *B*
Immaculata University *B, M*
Mansfield University of
    Pennsylvania *B*
Marywood University *B, M*
Seton Hill University *B*
Slippery Rock University of
    Pennsylvania *B*
Temple University *B, M, D*

South Carolina

Charleston Southern University *B*
Converse College *B*

Texas

Lubbock Christian University *B*
Sam Houston State University *B*
Texas Woman's University *B*
University of the Incarnate Word *B*
West Texas A&M University *B*

Utah

Utah State University *B*

Virginia

Shenandoah University *B, M*

Wisconsin

Alverno College *B*

Musical instrument fabrication/repair

Indiana

Indiana University
    Bloomington *A*

Iowa

Western Iowa Tech Community
    College *A*

Minnesota

Minnesota State College - Southeast
    Technical *C*

Washington

Renton Technical College *C, A*

Musical theater

Alabama

University of Mobile *B*

Arizona

University of Arizona *B*

Arkansas

Ouachita Baptist University *B*

California

California State University
    Chico *B*
Grossmont College *C, A*
University of California
    Irvine *B*

Colorado

University of Northern Colorado *B*

District of Columbia

American University *B*

Florida

Florida Southern College *B*
Florida State University *B*
University of Tampa *B*

Georgia

Brenau University *B*
LaGrange College *B*
Young Harris College *B*

Idaho

University of Idaho *B*

Illinois

Blackburn College *B*
Illinois Wesleyan University *B*
Millikin University *B*
North Central College *B*
Rockford University *B*
Roosevelt University *B*
Western Illinois University *B*

Indiana

Indiana University
    Bloomington *B*

Kansas

Southwestern College *B*
Wichita State University *B*

Louisiana

Tulane University *B*

Maryland

Howard Community College *A*

Massachusetts

Boston Conservatory *M*

Michigan

Adrian College *B*
Central Michigan University *B*
Oakland University *B*
University of Michigan *B*
Western Michigan University *B*

Mississippi

Northeast Mississippi Community
    College *A*

Missouri

Culver-Stockton College *B*
Lindenwood University *B*
Missouri Baptist University *B*
Webster University *B*

Nebraska

Creighton University *B*

New Jersey

Rider University *B*

New Mexico

Santa Fe University of Art and
    Design *B*

New York

Genesee Community College *C*
Ithaca College *B*
Nazareth College *B*
New York University *M*
Pace University *B*
SUNY
    College at Fredonia *B*
Syracuse University *B*

North Carolina

Elon University *B*
Lees-McRae College *B*

North Dakota

University of North Dakota *B*

Ohio

Heidelberg University *B*

Oklahoma

Oklahoma City University *B, M*
University of Oklahoma *B*

Pennsylvania

Marywood University *B*
Messiah College *B*
University of the Arts *B*

South Carolina

Anderson University *B*
Coastal Carolina University *B*
Coker College *B*
Limestone College *B*
North Greenville University *B*

South Dakota

Northern State University *B*

Texas

Texas Christian University *B*
Texas State University *B*
University of Texas
    El Paso *B*
West Texas A&M University *B*

Utah
Brigham Young University *B*

Vermont
Johnson State College *B*

Virginia
Emory & Henry College *B*
Shenandoah University *B*

Wyoming
Casper College *A*

Musicology/ ethnomusicology

California
California State University
San Bernardino *B*
University of California
Los Angeles *B, M, D*
University of Southern California *D*

Colorado
University of Denver *B*

Connecticut
Wesleyan University *D*

Florida
Florida State University *M, D*
University of Miami *B, M, D*

Illinois
Northwestern University *B, M, D*
University of Illinois
Urbana-Champaign *D*

Indiana
Indiana University
Bloomington *M, D*

Kansas
University of Kansas *B, M*

Maryland
University of Maryland
Baltimore County *M, D*
College Park *M, D*

Massachusetts
Boston University *B, D*
Brandeis University *M, D*
New England Conservatory of
Music *B, M*
Tufts University *B*
University of Massachusetts
Amherst *C*

Michigan
Michigan State University *M*
University of Michigan *M*

Missouri
Washington University in St.
Louis *M, D*

New York
City University of New York
Brooklyn College *M*
Cornell University *M*
Eastman School of Music of the
University of Rochester *M, D*
SUNY
University at Buffalo *D*
University of Rochester *M, D*

North Carolina
Duke University *M, D*
University of North Carolina
Chapel Hill *M, D*

Ohio
Bowling Green State University *B, M*
Case Western Reserve University *D*
University of Cincinnati *D*

Oregon
University of Oregon *M, D*

Pennsylvania
Carnegie Mellon University *B*

Rhode Island
Brown University *B, M, D*

Texas
Rice University *M*
Texas Christian University *M*
University of North Texas *M, D*

Utah
Brigham Young University *M*
University of Utah *M*

Vermont
Bennington College *B*

Virginia
Liberty University *B*

Washington
University of Washington *B*

Mycology

Maine
College of the Atlantic *B, M*

Nanotechnology

Arizona
Arizona State University *M*

California
Foothill College *C, A*
University of California
San Diego *B, M, D*

Colorado
University of Denver *M*

Maryland
Allegany College of Maryland *A*

Michigan
Michigan Technological University *C*
Oakland Community College *C, A*

Minnesota
Normandale Community College *A*
University of Minnesota
Twin Cities *C*

New York
SUNY
University at Albany *B, M, D*

North Dakota
North Dakota State College of
Science *A*

Pennsylvania
Indiana University of Pennsylvania *M*
Lehigh Carbon Community College *A*

Virginia
Virginia Commonwealth University *D*

Washington
North Seattle Community
College *C, A*

Wisconsin
Chippewa Valley Technical College *A*

National security policy studies

California
San Diego State University *M*

Nebraska
Bellevue University *M*

Ohio
Baldwin Wallace University *B*

Pennsylvania
La Roche College *B*
University of Pittsburgh *M*

West Virginia
Fairmont State University *B*

Native American education

Alaska
Ilisagvik College *A*

Hawaii
University of Hawaii
Hilo *T*

Minnesota
College of St. Scholastica *B, T*
University of Minnesota
Duluth *B*

Oklahoma
Northeastern State University *B*

Washington
Northwest Indian College *A*

Native American languages

Alaska
University of Alaska
Fairbanks *A, B*

Arizona
Dine College *A*

Hawaii
University of Hawaii
Hilo *M, D*

Idaho
Idaho State University *A*

New Mexico
Navajo Technical University *A, B*

Native American studies

Alaska
Ilisagvik College *A*
University of Alaska
Fairbanks *B, D*

Arizona
Arizona State University *B, M*
Arizona Western College *A*
Dine College *A*
Northern Arizona University *B*
Phoenix College *C*
Pima Community College *A*
Scottsdale Community College *A*
University of Arizona *M, D*

California
California State University
East Bay *B*
De Anza College *A*
El Camino College *A*
Fresno City College *A*
Grossmont College *A*
Humboldt State University *B*
San Diego State University *B*
San Francisco State University *B*
Santa Barbara City College *A*
Solano Community College *A*
Stanford University *B*
University of California
Berkeley *B*
Davis *B, M, D*
Los Angeles *B, M*
Riverside *B*

Colorado
Fort Lewis College *B*

Hawaii
University of Hawaii
Hilo *B*
Honolulu Community College *C*
Manoa *B, M*

Idaho
North Idaho College *A*

Iowa
University of Iowa *B*

Kansas
Haskell Indian Nations University *B*
University of Kansas *M*

Massachusetts
Hampshire College *B*
University of Massachusetts
Amherst *C*

Michigan
Bay Mills Community College *A*
Michigan State University *B*
Saginaw Chippewa Tribal College *A*

Minnesota
Augsburg College *B*
Bemidji State University *B*
Itasca Community College *C, A*
Leech Lake Tribal College *A*
Minneapolis Community and
Technical College *C*
Rainy River Community College *A*
University of Minnesota
Duluth *B*
Morris *B*
Twin Cities *B*
White Earth Tribal and Community
College *A*

Montana
Aaniiih Nakoda College *A*
Blackfeet Community College *A*
Fort Peck Community College *A*
Little Big Horn College *C*
Montana State University *M*
Salish Kootenai College *C, A*
Stone Child College *A*
University of Montana *B*

Nebraska
Creighton University *B*
Little Priest Tribal College *A*
Nebraska Indian Community
College *A*
University of Nebraska
Omaha *B*

New Hampshire
Dartmouth College *B*

New Mexico

Institute of American Indian Arts *A*
San Juan College *A*
University of New Mexico *B*

New York

Colgate University *B*

North Carolina

University of North Carolina
  Pembroke *B*

North Dakota

Cankdeska Cikana Community
  College *A*
Fort Berthold Community
  College *A, B*
Sitting Bull College *A*
University of North Dakota *B*

Oklahoma

Bacone College *A, B*
College of the Muscogee Nation *A*
East Central University *B*
Northeastern Oklahoma Agricultural
  and Mechanical College *A*
Northeastern State University *B*
Northern Oklahoma College *A*
Rose State College *A*
University of Oklahoma *B, M*
University of Science and Arts of
  Oklahoma *B*

South Dakota

Black Hills State University *B*
Kilian Community College *A*
Oglala Lakota College *A, B, M*
Sisseton Wahpeton College *A*
South Dakota State University *B*
University of South Dakota *B*

Texas

University of Texas
  Austin *C*

Vermont

Goddard College *B, M*

Washington

Evergreen State College *B*
Northwest Indian College *C, A, B*
University of Washington *B*

Wisconsin

Lac Courte Oreilles Ojibwa
  Community College *A*
Northland College *B*
University of Wisconsin
  Eau Claire *B*
  Green Bay *B*

Wyoming

Central Wyoming College *C, A*
University of Wyoming *B*

Natural resource economics

California

California State University
  Stanislaus *M*

Michigan

Michigan State University *B*

New Hampshire

University of New Hampshire *B*

New Mexico

New Mexico State University *B*

New York

Cornell University *M*

Ohio

Baldwin Wallace University *C, B, M*
Malone University *B*

Pennsylvania

Juniata College *B*
Penn State
  University Park *M, D*

Puerto Rico

Universidad Metropolitana *M*

Rhode Island

University of Rhode Island *B*

Tennessee

University of Tennessee
  Knoxville *B*

West Virginia

West Virginia University *D*

Natural resource recreation and tourism

Colorado

Colorado State University *M*

Georgia

University of Georgia *B*

Idaho

University of Idaho *B*

Maine

Unity College *B*

Vermont

University of Vermont *B*

Natural resources and conservation

Alabama

Auburn University *B, M*
Tuskegee University *B, M*

Arizona

University of Arizona *B, M, D*

California

American River College *C, A*
California State University
  East Bay *B*
  Sacramento *B, M*
College of Marin *C*
College of the Desert *A*
Columbia College *A*
Feather River College *C, A*
Fresno City College *C, A*
Fullerton College *C, A*
Humboldt State University *M*
Irvine Valley College *C, A*
Mendocino College *A*
Modesto Junior College *C, A*
Mount San Antonio College *A*
Ohlone College *C*
Saddleback College *A*
Santa Rosa Junior College *C, A*
Shasta College *C*
Sonoma State University *B*
University of California
  Berkeley *B*
  Davis *B*
Ventura College *C, A*
Whittier College *B*

Colorado

Colorado Mountain College *A*
Colorado Northwestern Community
  College *A*
Colorado State University *B*
Metropolitan State University of
  Denver *B*
Pikes Peak Community College *A*
Trinidad State Junior College *A*

Connecticut

Gateway Community College *A*
University of Connecticut *B, M*

Delaware

University of Delaware *B*

District of Columbia

George Washington University *B*
University of the District of
  Columbia *B*

Georgia

Shorter University *B*
University of Georgia *M, D*

Hawaii

Hawaii Pacific University *B*

Idaho

College of Southern Idaho *A*
University of Idaho *B, M, D*

Illinois

Illinois Central College *A*
Lincoln College *A*
Principia College *B*
University of Illinois
  Urbana-Champaign *B, M, D*

Indiana

Ball State University *B, M*
Manchester University *B*
Purdue University *B, M*
Vincennes University *A*

Iowa

Dordt College *B*
Ellsworth Community College *A*
Kirkwood Community College *C, A*
Mount Mercy University *B*
Northwest Iowa Community
  College *A*
Upper Iowa University *B*

Kansas

Fort Scott Community College *C, A*
Haskell Indian Nations
  University *A, B*

Kentucky

Bluegrass Community and Technical
  College *A*
University of Kentucky *B*

Louisiana

Louisiana State University and
  Agricultural and Mechanical
  College *M, D*
Louisiana Tech University *B*

Maine

College of the Atlantic *B, M*
University of Maine *B, M, D*
University of Maine
  Machias *B, T*

Maryland

Frostburg State University *B, M*
University of Maryland
  College Park *B*
  University College *B*

Massachusetts

Cape Cod Community College *C, A*
Greenfield Community College *C, A*
Holyoke Community College *C*
Roxbury Community College *A*
Springfield College *B*
Suffolk University *A*
University of Massachusetts
  Amherst *B, M, D*

Michigan

Albion College *B*
Bay de Noc Community College *A*
Central Michigan University *B*
Delta College *A*
Gogebic Community College *A*
Grand Rapids Community College *A*
Lake Superior State University *A, B*
Lansing Community College *C*
Northern Michigan University *B*
University of Michigan *B, M*
University of Michigan
  Dearborn *B*

Minnesota

Central Lakes College *C, A*
Itasca Community College *A*
Minnesota State University
  Mankato *B*
University of Minnesota
  Crookston *B*
  Twin Cities *B*
Vermilion Community College *A*
White Earth Tribal and Community
  College *A*

Missouri

Missouri Southern State University *B*

Montana

Fort Peck Community College *A*
Little Big Horn College *A*
Miles Community College *A*
Montana State University *B, M*
Stone Child College *A*
University of Montana *B, M*
University of Montana: Western *B*

Nebraska

Little Priest Tribal College *A*
Midland University *B*
Nebraska Indian Community
  College *A*
University of Nebraska
  Lincoln *B, M, D*

Nevada

Great Basin College *B*
University of Nevada
  Las Vegas *B, M, D*
  Reno *B, M*
Western Nevada College *A*

New Hampshire

Dartmouth College *B*
New England College *B*
University of New Hampshire *B, M*

New Jersey

Montclair State University *M*
Rutgers, The State University of New
  Jersey
  New Brunswick/Piscataway
    Campus *B, M, D*
Warren County Community
  College *A*
William Paterson University of New
  Jersey *B*

New Mexico

Navajo Technical University *C*
New Mexico Institute of Mining and
  Technology *B*
Northern New Mexico College *C, A*

New York

Colgate University *B*
Columbia University *B*
Cornell University *B, M, D*
Finger Lakes Community
    College *C, A*
Paul Smith's College *A, B*
SUNY
    College at Brockport *B*
    College at Plattsburgh *B*
    College of Agriculture and
        Technology at Cobleskill *A, B*
    College of Agriculture and
        Technology at Morrisville *A, B*
    College of Environmental Science
        and Forestry *B, M, D*
Saint Bonaventure University *B*
Sullivan County Community
    College *A*

North Carolina

Blue Ridge Community College *C, A*
Cape Fear Community College *C, A*
Central Carolina Community
    College *C, A*
Duke University *B, M, D*
North Carolina State University *B, M*
Pamlico Community College *A*
Wake Technical Community
    College *A*
Western Piedmont Community
    College *C, A*

North Dakota

Dakota College at Bottineau *A*

Ohio

Defiance College *B*
Denison University *B*
Hocking College *A*
Kent State University *B*
Lake Erie College *B*
Ohio State University
    Agricultural Technical Institute *A*
    Columbus Campus *A, B, M, D*
Otterbein University *B*
University of Rio Grande *B*

Oklahoma

Eastern Oklahoma State College *A*
Murray State College *A*
Southeastern Oklahoma State
    University *B*
Southern Nazarene University *B*

Oregon

Central Oregon Community
    College *A*
Mt. Hood Community College *C, A*
Portland State University *B, D*
Treasure Valley Community
    College *A*

Pennsylvania

Arcadia University *M*
Gettysburg College *B*
La Salle University *B*
Mansfield University of
    Pennsylvania *B*
Penn State
    Abington *B*
    Altoona *B*
    Beaver *B*
    Berks *B*
    Brandywine *B*
    DuBois *B*
    Erie, The Behrend College *B*
    Fayette, The Eberly Campus *B*
    Greater Allegheny *B*
    Harrisburg *B*
    Hazleton *B*
    Lehigh Valley *B*
    Mont Alto *B*
    New Kensington *B*

Schuylkill *B*
Shenango *B*
University Park *B*
Wilkes-Barre *B*
Worthington Scranton *B*
York *B*
Slippery Rock University of
    Pennsylvania *M*
Thiel College *B*

Puerto Rico

Bayamon Central University *B*
Inter American University of Puerto
    Rico
    Ponce Campus *B*
Pontifical Catholic University of
    Puerto Rico *B*

Rhode Island

University of Rhode Island *M*

South Carolina

Clemson University *B*

South Dakota

Oglala Lakota College *A, B*
Sinte Gleska University *A*

Tennessee

Sewanee: The University of the
    South *B*
Tennessee Technological
    University *B, D*
Tusculum College *B*
University of Tennessee
    Knoxville *D*

Texas

Coastal Bend College *A*
Lamar University *B, M*
Lubbock Christian University *B*
Sul Ross State University *B*
Texas A&M International
    University *B*
Texas A&M University *B, M, D*
Texas A&M University
    Corpus Christi *B, M*
    Galveston *B, M*
Texas State University *D*
Texas Tech University *B*

Utah

Snow College *A*

Vermont

Green Mountain College *B*
Johnson State College *B*
Marlboro College *B*
Sterling College *B*
University of Vermont *B, M, D*

Virginia

Mountain Empire Community
    College *A*

Washington

Evergreen State College *B*
Heritage University *C, A, B*
Peninsula College *C*
University of Washington *B*
Washington State University *B, M*
Wenatchee Valley College *C, A*

West Virginia

Shepherd University *B*

Wisconsin

Carroll University *B*
College of Menominee Nation *A*
Fox Valley Technical College *A*
University of Wisconsin
    Madison *M*
    Platteville *B*

River Falls *B*
Stevens Point *B, T*

Wyoming

Western Wyoming Community
    College *A*

Natural resources law enforcement

Maine

Unity College *B*

Minnesota

University of Minnesota
    Crookston *B*
Vermilion Community College *C, A*

Puerto Rico

Universidad Metropolitana *B*

Texas

Texas Tech University *B*

Natural resources management/policy

Alaska

Alaska Pacific University *B*
University of Alaska
    Fairbanks *A*

Arizona

Northern Arizona University *M*
Phoenix College *C*

California

California State University
    Channel Islands *B*
Chapman University *B*
College of the Redwoods *C*
Los Angeles Pierce College *C, A*
University of Redlands *B*

Colorado

Adams State University *B*
Colorado State University *M*
Naropa University *M*
University of Denver *M*

Connecticut

University of Connecticut *D*
Yale University *M*

Delaware

Delaware State University *B, M*

Florida

Florida Gateway College *C*
Florida Institute of Technology *M*
Nova Southeastern University *M*
Pensacola State College *A*
University of Miami *B*

Hawaii

University of Hawaii
    Hawaii Community College *C, A*
    Manoa *B, M, D*

Illinois

College of Lake County *C, A*
Elmhurst College *B*
Southern Illinois University
    Carbondale *D*
Spoon River College *C, A*

Iowa

Drake University *B*
Hawkeye Community College *C, A*

Kansas

Garden City Community College *A*
Hutchinson Community College *A*
Kansas State University *B*
Wichita State University *M*

Kentucky

Eastern Kentucky University *B*

Louisiana

University of Louisiana at Lafayette *B*

Maine

University of Maine
    Fort Kent *B*

Michigan

Grand Valley State University *B*
Michigan State University *M, D*
University of Michigan *D*

Minnesota

University of Minnesota
    Twin Cities *M, D*

Missouri

Drury University *B*
Washington University in St. Louis *B*

Montana

Blackfeet Community College *A*
Flathead Valley Community
    College *C, A*
Rocky Mountain College *B*

Nevada

Sierra Nevada College *B*

New Jersey

Montclair State University *D*

New Mexico

New Mexico Highlands University *M*

New York

Bard College *M*

North Carolina

Western Carolina University *B*

North Dakota

Cankdeska Cikana Community
    College *A*
North Dakota State
    University *B, M, D*

Ohio

Bowling Green State University *B*
Heidelberg University *B*
Xavier University *B*
Zane State College *A*

Oregon

Oregon State University *B, M*
Portland State University *M*

Pennsylvania

Carnegie Mellon University *B*
Drexel University *M*
Keystone College *A, B*
Lehigh University *M*
Philadelphia University *M*
St. Vincent College *B*
University of Pennsylvania *M*

Puerto Rico

Universidad Metropolitana *M*

Rhode Island

University of Rhode Island *B*

South Carolina

Central Carolina Technical College *A*

South Dakota

South Dakota State University *B*

Tennessee

University of Tennessee
Martin *B*

Texas

Angelo State University *B*
Hardin-Simmons University *M*
Texas Christian University *M*
Texas Tech University *M*

Utah

Utah State University *C, M, D*

Virginia

Virginia Polytechnic Institute and
State University *M*

Washington

University of Washington *M, D*

West Virginia

Glenville State College *B*

Wisconsin

University of Wisconsin
Green Bay *M*

Wyoming

Northwest College *A*

Natural sciences

Alabama

Oakwood University *B*
University of Alabama
Birmingham *B*

Alaska

University of Alaska
Fairbanks *A*

Arizona

Arizona State University *M*
Glendale Community College *A*
Mesa Community College *C*
Paradise Valley Community College *C*
Phoenix College *C*
University of Arizona *B, M, D*

California

California State University
Chico *B*
Dominguez Hills *B*
Fullerton *M*
Los Angeles *B*
College of the Siskiyous *A*
Columbia College *A*
Lake Tahoe Community College *A*
Loma Linda University *M*
Loyola Marymount University *B*
Master's College *B*
National University *B*
Ohlone College *A*
Orange Coast College *A*
Pepperdine University *B*
Pitzer College *B*
Saddleback College *A*
San Jose State University *B, M*
Santa Rosa Junior College *A*
Shasta College *A*
University of California
Davis *B*
University of La Verne *B*

Colorado

Colorado Mountain College *A*
Colorado State University *B, M*
Colorado State University
Pueblo *M*
University of Colorado
Colorado Springs *D*

Florida

New College of Florida *B*
St. Petersburg College *A*

Georgia

Reinhardt University *A, B*

Hawaii

University of Hawaii
Hilo *B*

Idaho

College of Southern Idaho *A*
Lewis-Clark State College *B*

Illinois

Concordia University Chicago *B, T*
Dominican University *B*
Judson University *B*
Saint Xavier University *B*
Shimer College *B*
Southeastern Illinois College *A*

Indiana

Indiana University
East *B*
Taylor University *B*
Trine University *A*

Iowa

Central College *B, T*
Ellsworth Community College *A*
Northwestern College *T*
St. Ambrose University *B, T*

Kansas

Benedictine College *B*
Bethel College *B*
Central Christian College of Kansas *B*
Garden City Community College *A*
Kansas State University *B*
Neosho County Community
College *A*
Seward County Community
College *A*
Tabor College *B*
Washburn University *A*

Louisiana

Bossier Parish Community College *A*

Maine

College of the Atlantic *B, M*
University of Maine *B, M, D*
University of Southern Maine *B*

Maryland

Johns Hopkins University *B*

Massachusetts

Bard College at Simon's Rock *B*
Cape Cod Community College *A*
Elms College *B*
Lesley University *B*
Massasoit Community College *A*
University of Massachusetts
Amherst *C*

Michigan

Calvin College *B*
Madonna University *A, B*
Marygrove College *A, B, T*
Siena Heights University *A, B*

Minnesota

College of St. Benedict *B*
Concordia College: Moorhead *B*
Rochester Community and Technical
College *A*
Saint Cloud State University *B*
St. John's University *B*

Mississippi

Blue Mountain College *B*

Missouri

Lincoln University *M*
Missouri State University *M*
Missouri Western State University *B*
Park University *B*
Southeast Missouri State University *M*

Nebraska

Concordia University *B*
Doane College *B*
University of Nebraska
Omaha *B*

New Jersey

Felician College *B*
Georgian Court University *B*
Thomas Edison State College *B*
Warren County Community
College *A*

New Mexico

New Mexico State University
Carlsbad *A*

New York

Colgate University *B*
Daemen College *B*
Hofstra University *B*
Mount Saint Mary College *B*
Rensselaer Polytechnic Institute *M*
Roberts Wesleyan College *A*
SUNY
College at Plattsburgh *M*
University at Buffalo *M*

North Carolina

Western Piedmont Community
College *A*

North Dakota

Dickinson State University *B*

Ohio

Case Western Reserve University *B*
Cleveland State University *T*
College of Mount St. Joseph *B*
Defiance College *B*
Lourdes University *A*
Walsh University *B*
Washington State Community
College *A*
Xavier University *B*

Oklahoma

Northeastern State University *M*
Oklahoma State University *M*
St. Gregory's University *A, B*
University of Oklahoma *M*
University of Science and Arts of
Oklahoma *B, T*

Oregon

Oregon State University *B*
Western Oregon University *B*

Pennsylvania

Gettysburg College *B*
Harrisburg University of Science and
Technology *B*
Juniata College *B*
Muhlenberg College *C, B*
Temple University *B*

University of Pennsylvania *B*
University of Pittsburgh
Titusville *A*

Puerto Rico

Bayamon Central University *B*
Turabo University *B*
Universidad Metropolitana *A, B*
Universidad del Este *A*
University of Puerto Rico
Arecibo *A*
Cayey University College *B*
Ponce *A*
Rio Piedras *B*
Utuado *A*
University of the Sacred Heart *B*

Tennessee

Christian Brothers University *B*

Texas

Dallas Baptist University *B*
Lee College *A*
Mountain View College *A*
Our Lady of the Lake University of
San Antonio *B*
Tyler Junior College *A*
University of Texas
El Paso *M*

Utah

Snow College *A*

Vermont

Castleton State College *B*
Lyndon State College *B*

Virginia

Thomas Nelson Community
College *A*
Virginia Commonwealth University *D*
Virginia Union University *B*
Virginia Wesleyan College *B*
Virginia Western Community
College *A*

Washington

Evergreen State College *B*
Heritage University *B*
University of Puget Sound *B, T*

Wisconsin

Edgewood College *B*
Lawrence University *B*
Silver Lake College of the Holy
Family *T*
Viterbo University *B*

Wyoming

University of Wyoming *M*

Naturopathic medicine

Connecticut

University of Bridgeport *D*

Illinois

National University of Health
Sciences *D*

Puerto Rico

Turabo University *D*

Vermont

Goddard College *B, M*

Washington

Bastyr University *D*

Near and Middle Eastern studies

Arizona
University of Arizona *B, M, D*

California
Scripps College *B*
University of California
  Berkeley *B, M, D*
  Los Angeles *B*
University of Southern California *B*

Connecticut
Trinity College *B*
University of Connecticut *B*
Yale University *B*

District of Columbia
George Washington University *B*
Georgetown University *M*

Florida
Florida State University *B*

Georgia
Emory University *B*

Illinois
University of Chicago *B, M, D*

Kentucky
Western Kentucky University *C*

Maryland
Hood College *B*
Johns Hopkins University *B, D*
McDaniel College *B*

Massachusetts
Boston University *B*
Brandeis University *B, M, D*
Hampshire College *B*
Harvard College *B, M, D*
Mount Holyoke College *B*
Northeastern University *B*
Tufts University *B*
University of Massachusetts
  Amherst *C, B*
Wellesley College *B*

Michigan
University of Michigan *B, M*

Minnesota
University of Minnesota
  Twin Cities *B*

Missouri
Washington University in St.
  Louis *B, M*

New Hampshire
Dartmouth College *B*

New Jersey
Princeton University *B, M, D*
Rutgers, The State University of New
  Jersey
  New Brunswick/Piscataway
    Campus *B*

New York
Bard College *B*
Barnard College *B*
City University of New York
  Hunter College *B*
Columbia University *B*
Columbia University
  School of General Studies *B*
Cornell University *B, M, D*
Fordham University *B*

New York University *B, M*
Syracuse University *B*
United States Military Academy *B*

Ohio
College of Wooster *B*
University of Akron *C*
University of Cincinnati *C*
University of Toledo *B*

Oregon
Portland State University *B*

Pennsylvania
Dickinson College *B*
Swarthmore College *B*

Rhode Island
Brown University *B*

South Carolina
Columbia International University *B*

Texas
Texas State University *B*
University of Texas
  Austin *B, M*

Utah
University of Utah *B, M, D*

Vermont
Goddard College *B, M*
Marlboro College *B*
Middlebury College *B*

Virginia
Emory & Henry College *B*
George Mason University *M*
University of Virginia *M*

Washington
University of Washington *B, M, D*

Wisconsin
University of Wisconsin
  Milwaukee *C*

Network/system administration

Alabama
Remington College
  Mobile *A*
University of Phoenix
  Birmingham *B*
Virginia College
  Huntsville *A, B*

Alaska
University of Alaska
  Southeast *C, A*

Arizona
Arizona Western College *C*
Chandler-Gilbert Community
  College *A*
Cochise College *C*
Coconino County Community
  College *C, A*
Eastern Arizona College *A*
GateWay Community College *C, A*
Paradise Valley Community College *C*
South Mountain Community
  College *A*
Tohono O'odham Community
  College *A*
University of Phoenix
  Phoenix-Hohokam *A, B*
  Southern Arizona *B*

Arkansas
East Arkansas Community College *C*
University of Phoenix
  Little Rock *B*
  Northwest Arkansas *B*

California
Allan Hancock College *C*
Barstow Community College *C*
Diablo Valley College *A*
Foothill College *C*
Hartnell College *C, A*
Heald College
  Fresno *C, A*
  Hayward *C, A*
  Rancho Cordova *A*
  Roseville *A*
  San Francisco *C, A*
  Stockton *C, A*
ITT Technical Institute
  Lathrop *B*
  Rancho Cordova *B*
  San Bernardino *B*
  Sylmar *B*
  Torrance *B*
Kaplan College
  Riverside *A*
Long Beach City College *C*
MiraCosta College *C, A*
Ohlone College *A*
Platt College
  Ontario *A*
Sierra College *C, A*
Southern California Institute of
  Technology *C*
University of Phoenix
  Bay Area *B*
  Central Valley *B*
  Sacramento Valley *B*
  San Diego *A*
  Southern California *B*

Colorado
Colorado Technical University *B*
National American University
  Denver *B*
Regis University *B*
University of Phoenix
  Denver *A, B*
Westwood College
  Denver South *A, B*

Connecticut
University of Phoenix
  Fairfield County *B*

District of Columbia
University of Phoenix
  Washington DC *B*

Florida
College of Central Florida *A*
Florida National University *A*
Gulf Coast State College *C, A*
Lincoln College of Technology
  West Palm Beach *C, A*
Rasmussen College
  Fort Myers *B*
  New Port Richey *B*
  Ocala *B*
  Pasco/Land O'Lakes *B*
  Tampa/Brandon *B*
University of Phoenix
  Central Florida *B*
  North Florida *B*
  South Florida *B*
  West Florida *B*

Georgia
Atlanta Technical College *C, A*
Columbus Technical College *C, A*
Dalton State College *C, A*
Georgia Piedmont Technical
  College *C, A*

Gwinnett Technical College *C, A*
Southeastern Technical College *C*
University of Phoenix
  Atlanta *B*
  Augusta *B*
  Columbus *B*
  Savannah *B*

Hawaii
University of Phoenix
  Hawaii *B*

Idaho
College of Western Idaho *C, A*
University of Phoenix
  Idaho *B*

Illinois
Harper College *C*
Heartland Community College *C*
Illinois Valley Community College *A*
Kaskaskia College *C, A*
Lincoln Land Community College *C*
Moraine Valley Community
  College *C, A*
Morton College *C*
Prairie State College *C*
Rasmussen College
  Aurora *B*
  Mokena/Tinley Park *B*
  Rockford *B*
  Romeoville/Joliet *B*
Richland Community College *C*
Sauk Valley Community College *C, A*
Triton College *C*
University of Phoenix
  Chicago *B*

Indiana
ITT Technical Institute
  Fort Wayne *B*
  Indianapolis *A*
Ivy Tech Community College
  Bloomington *C*
  Central Indiana *C*
  Columbus *C*
  East Central *C*
  Kokomo *C*
  Lafayette *C*
  North Central *C*
  Northeast *C*
  Northwest *C*
  Richmond *C*
  South Central *C*
University of Phoenix
  Indianapolis *B*

Iowa
Dordt College *B*
Iowa Western Community College *A*
Kirkwood Community College *C, A*
North Iowa Area Community
  College *A*
Northwest Iowa Community
  College *A*

Kansas
Wright Career College
  Overland Park *C*

Kentucky
Daymar College
  Bowling Green *C, A*
Sullivan College of Technology and
  Design *A*
University of Phoenix
  Louisville *B*

Louisiana
University of Phoenix
  Baton Rouge *B*
  Louisiana *B*
  Shreveport *B*

Maryland

Frederick Community College *A*
ITT Technical Institute
  Owings Mills *B*
Kaplan University
  Hagerstown *A, B*
Prince George's Community
  College *C*
TESST College of Technology
  Beltsville *C*
University of Phoenix
  Maryland *B*

Massachusetts

Bunker Hill Community College *C, A*
Simmons College *B*
Springfield Technical Community
  College *C*
University of Phoenix
  Boston *B*

Michigan

Cleary University *A*
Lake Michigan College *C, A*
Michigan Technological University *B*
Mott Community College *C*
Oakland Community College *C*
University of Phoenix
  Metro Detroit *C, B*
  West Michigan *B*
Wayne County Community College *A*
West Shore Community College *C, A*

Minnesota

Academy College *C, A*
Anoka-Ramsey Community College *C*
Century College *C*
Crown College *A, B*
Dakota County Technical
  College *C, A*
Inver Hills Community College *C*
Lake Superior College *C, A*
Minneapolis Community and
  Technical College *C, A*
Rasmussen College
  Blaine *B*
  Bloomington *B*
  Brooklyn Park *B*
  Eagan *B*
  Lake Elmo/Woodbury *B*
  Mankato *B*
  Moorhead *B*
  St. Cloud *B*
St. Cloud Technical and Community
  College *C*
University of Phoenix
  Minneapolis-St. Paul *B*

Mississippi

University of Phoenix
  Jackson *B*

Missouri

Crowder College *A*
University of Phoenix
  Kansas City *B*
  St. Louis *B*

Montana

Montana State University
  Great Falls College *C*
University of Great Falls *B*

Nebraska

Bellevue University *B*
Vatterott College
  Spring Valley *A*
Wright Career College
  Omaha *A*

Nevada

Career College of Northern Nevada *A*
College of Southern Nevada *C*

University of Phoenix
  Las Vegas *B*

New Jersey

Bergen Community College *A*
Brookdale Community College *A*
Passaic County Community
  College *C, A*
University of Phoenix
  Jersey City *B*

New Mexico

Clovis Community College *C, A*
University of Phoenix
  New Mexico *B*

New York

Bryant & Stratton College
  Syracuse North *A*
Corning Community College *A*
Globe Institute of
  Technology *C, A, B*
Rochester Institute of
  Technology *B, M*
SUNY
  College of Technology at Alfred *B*
St. Francis College *B*
Ulster County Community
  College *C, A*

North Carolina

Brunswick Community College *C*
Central Carolina Community
  College *C, A*
College of the Albemarle *C*
North Carolina Agricultural and
  Technical State University *M*
University of Phoenix
  Charlotte *B*
  Raleigh *B*

North Dakota

Rasmussen College
  Bismarck *B*
  Fargo *B*
Williston State College *C, A*

Ohio

Belmont College *A*
Bryant & Stratton College
  Parma *A*
Cincinnati State Technical and
  Community College *A*
Daymar College
  Chillicothe *A*
Lorain County Community College *C*
National College
  Canton *A*
  Willoughby Hills *A*
Northwest State Community
  College *A*
University of Phoenix
  Cleveland *B*
Vatterott College
  Cleveland *A*

Oklahoma

University of Phoenix
  Oklahoma City *B*
Wright Career College
  Oklahoma City *A*

Oregon

Eastern Oregon University *C*
Heald College
  Portland *A*
ITT Technical Institute
  Portland *B*
Portland Community College *A*

Pennsylvania

Bucks County Community
  College *C, A*
Butler County Community College *A*

Carnegie Mellon University *M*
Community College of
  Philadelphia *A*
Lansdale School of Business *A*
Montgomery County Community
  College *C, A*
University of Phoenix
  Philadelphia *B*
  Pittsburgh *B*

Puerto Rico

Inter American University of Puerto
  Rico
  Ponce Campus *B*

South Carolina

University of Phoenix
  Columbia *B*
York Technical College *C*

South Dakota

Dakota State University *C*
Mitchell Technical Institute *C, A*
National American University
  Rapid City *B*

Tennessee

Fountainhead College of
  Technology *C, A, B*
ITT Technical Institute
  Knoxville *A*
  Nashville *B*
University of Phoenix
  Chattanooga *B*
  Memphis *B*
  Nashville *B*
Vatterott College
  Memphis *A*
Virginia College
  School of Business and Health in
    Knoxville *A*

Texas

Blinn College *A*
Central Texas College *C, A*
Collin County Community College
  District *C, A*
Houston Community College
  System *C, A*
St. Philip's College *C, A*
San Antonio College *C*
Temple College *C, A*
Texas State Technical College
  Waco *A*
Victoria College *C, A*

Utah

Salt Lake Community College *C*
University of Phoenix
  Utah *B*
Utah State University *C*
Western Governors University *B*

Vermont

Champlain College *C, B*
Community College of Vermont *A*

Virginia

ECPI University *A*
University of Phoenix
  Northern Virginia *B*
  Richmond *B*

Washington

Big Bend Community College *C*
Everett Community College *C*
Green River Community College *A*
Heritage University *C*
Pierce College *C*
South Seattle Community
  College *C, A*
University of Phoenix
  Western Washington *B*

West Virginia

American Public University System *C*

Wisconsin

Nicolet Area Technical College *C*
Rasmussen College
  Appleton *B*
  Green Bay *B*
  Wausau *B*

Wyoming

Laramie County Community
  College *C*

Neuroanatomy

Kentucky

Berea College *B*

New York

University of Rochester *M, D*

North Carolina

Wake Forest University *D*

Neurobiology/anatomy

Alabama

University of Alabama
  Birmingham *D*

California

University of California
  Davis *B*
  Irvine *B*
  Los Angeles *M, D*
University of Southern California *D*

Connecticut

Yale University *M, D*

District of Columbia

Georgetown University *B*

Florida

University of Miami *B*

Illinois

Northwestern University *M*
University of Chicago *D*

Iowa

University of Iowa *D*

Massachusetts

Boston University *M, D*
Harvard College *B, M, D*

Michigan

Wayne State University *M*

New Jersey

Rutgers, The State University of New
  Jersey
  New Brunswick/Piscataway
    Campus *D*
  Newark Campus *D*

New York

SUNY
  Upstate Medical University *D*

North Carolina

University of North Carolina
  Chapel Hill *M, D*

Pennsylvania

Carnegie Mellon University *M, D*
University of Pittsburgh *M, D*

Utah

University of Utah *M, D*

Virginia

George Mason University *D*

Neurobiology/behavior

California

University of California
Irvine *D*

Massachusetts

Fitchburg State University *B*

New Hampshire

University of New Hampshire *B*

Neuropharmacology

New Jersey

Fairleigh Dickinson University
Metropolitan Campus *M*

Texas

Texas Tech University Health
Sciences Center *M, D*

Neuroscience

Arizona

Arizona State University *D*
University of Arizona *B, M, D*

California

California Institute of
Technology *M, D*
Claremont McKenna College *B*
Pitzer College *B*
Pomona College *B*
Scripps College *B*
Stanford University *M, D*
University of California
Berkeley *D*
Davis *M, D*
Irvine *D*
Los Angeles *B, D*
Riverside *B, M, D*
San Diego *B, M, D*
Santa Cruz *B*
University of San Diego *B*
University of Southern
California *B, M, D*

Colorado

Colorado College *B*
Regis University *B*
University of Colorado
Boulder *D*
Denver *D*

Connecticut

Connecticut College *B*
Quinnipiac University *B*
Trinity College *B*
University of Hartford *M*
Wesleyan University *B, M*
Yale University *M, D*

Delaware

Delaware State University *M*
University of Delaware *D*

District of Columbia

George Washington University *D*
Georgetown University *M, D*

Florida

University of Miami *B, M, D*

Georgia

Agnes Scott College *B*
Emory University *B, D*
Georgia Regents University *M, D*
Georgia State University *B, D*
University of Georgia *D*

Idaho

Northwest Nazarene University *B*
University of Idaho *M, D*

Illinois

Augustana College *B*
Dominican University *B*
Knox College *B*
Lake Forest College *B*
Loyola University Chicago *M, D*
Northwestern University *B, D*
Rush University *D*
University of Chicago *D*
University of Illinois
Chicago *B, M, D*
Urbana-Champaign *D*

Indiana

Earlham College *B*
Indiana University
Bloomington *B, D*
Purdue University
Indianapolis *B, M, D*
University of Evansville *B*

Iowa

Drake University *B*
Iowa State University *M, D*
St. Ambrose University *B*
Wartburg College *B*

Kansas

University of Kansas *M, D*
University of Kansas Medical
Center *M, D*

Louisiana

Centenary College of Louisiana *B*
Louisiana State University
Health Sciences Center *D*
Tulane University *B, M, D*

Maine

Bates College *B*
Bowdoin College *B*
Colby College *B*
University of New England *B*

Maryland

Johns Hopkins University *B, M*
Notre Dame of Maryland
University *B*
University of Maryland
Baltimore *M, D*
Baltimore County *M, D*
College Park *M, D*

Massachusetts

Amherst College *B*
Bay Path College *M*
Boston University *B, M, D*
Brandeis University *B, M, D*
Emmanuel College *B*
Hampshire College *B*
Massachusetts Institute of
Technology *B, D*
Mount Holyoke College *B*
Northeastern University *D*
Smith College *B*
Stonehill College *B*
Tufts University *M, D*
University of Massachusetts
Amherst *M, D*
Wellesley College *B*
Western New England University *B*
Wheaton College *B*

Michigan

Andrews University *B*
Central Michigan University *B, M, T*
Michigan State University *M, D*
University of Michigan *B, M, D*
Wayne State University *D*

Minnesota

Macalester College *B*
University of Minnesota
Twin Cities *B, M, D*
University of St. Thomas *B*

Missouri

Saint Louis University *D*
University of Missouri
Columbia *M, D*
Washington University in St.
Louis *B, D*

Nebraska

University of Nebraska
Omaha *B*

Nevada

University of Nevada
Reno *B*

New Hampshire

Dartmouth College *B*

New Jersey

Drew University *B*
Princeton University *M*
Rutgers, The State University of New
Jersey
New Brunswick/Piscataway
Campus *D*
Newark Campus *D*

New York

Bard College *B*
Barnard College *B*
City University of New York
College of Staten Island *M*
Queens College *M*
Colgate University *B*
Columbia University *B*
Cornell University *M, D*
Hamilton College *B*
New York University *B, M, D*
SUNY
University at Buffalo *M, D*
University at Stony Brook *D*
St. Lawrence University *B*
Skidmore College *B*
Syracuse University *B*
Union College *B*
University of Rochester *B, M, D*
Vassar College *B*
Yeshiva University *M, D*

North Carolina

Duke University *B, M, D*
Wake Forest University *D*

Ohio

Baldwin Wallace University *B*
Bowling Green State University *B*
Case Western Reserve University *D*
College of Mount St. Joseph *B*
College of Wooster *B*
Kent State University *M, D*
Kenyon College *B*
Muskingum University *B*
Oberlin College *B*
Ohio State University
Columbus Campus *B, D*
Ohio University *B*
Ohio Wesleyan University *B*
University of Cincinnati *B, D*
University of Mount Union *B*
University of Toledo *M, D*

Oklahoma

University of Oklahoma *M, D*

Oregon

Oregon Health & Science
University *D*

Pennsylvania

Allegheny College *B*
Bucknell University *B*
Bucks County Community College *A*
Carnegie Mellon University *B*
Cedar Crest College *B*
Dickinson College *B*
Drexel University *M, D*
Franklin & Marshall College *B*
Gettysburg College *B*
King's College *B*
Lafayette College *B*
Lehigh University *B, D*
Moravian College *B*
Muhlenberg College *B*
Penn State
University Park *M, D*
Susquehanna University *B*
Temple University *B, D*
Thiel College *B*
University of Pennsylvania *B, M, D*
University of Pittsburgh *B, M, D*
University of Scranton *B*
Ursinus College *B*

Puerto Rico

Universidad Central del Caribe *D*

Rhode Island

Brown University *B, M, D*

South Carolina

Furman University *B*
Medical University of South
Carolina *D*

Tennessee

Belmont University *B*
King University *B*
Maryville College *B*
Rhodes College *B*
Vanderbilt University *B, M, D*

Texas

Baylor University *B, M*
Texas A&M University *M, D*
Texas Christian University *B*
University of Texas
Austin *B, M, D*
Dallas *B, D*
Health Science Center at
Houston *M, D*
Medical Branch at Galveston *D*
San Antonio *D*

Utah

Brigham Young University *B, M, D*
Westminster College *B*

Vermont

Middlebury College *B*
University of Vermont *B, D*

Virginia

Christopher Newport University *B*
College of William and Mary *D*
George Mason University *B, D*
University of Virginia *D*
Virginia Commonwealth University *D*
Washington and Lee University *B*

Washington

University of Washington *D*
Washington State University *B, M, D*

West Virginia

West Virginia University *D*

Wisconsin

Carthage College *B*
Lawrence University *B*
University of Wisconsin
Madison *M, D*

Wyoming

University of Wyoming *M, D*

Nonprofit/public organization management

Alabama

Oakwood University *B*

Arizona

Chandler-Gilbert Community
College *A*
DeVry University
Phoenix *M*
Grand Canyon University *D*
Northern Arizona University *M*

California

American Jewish University *M*
California State University
San Bernardino *M*
DeVry University
Pomona *M*
Fresno Pacific University *B*
Hope International University *M*
Mount St. Mary's College *M*
Point Loma Nazarene University *B*
University of San Francisco *M*
University of the West *M*

Colorado

DeVry University
Westminster *M*
Regis University *M*
University of Denver *M*

Connecticut

Goodwin College *A*
Quinnipiac University *B, M*
University of Connecticut *M*

Delaware

Delaware State University *B*

District of Columbia

Trinity Washington University *M*

Florida

DeVry University
Miramar *M*
Florida Atlantic University *M*
Florida Institute of Technology *M*
University of Central Florida *M*
University of West Florida *M*

Georgia

LaGrange College *B*
Toccoa Falls College *B*
University of Georgia *M*

Illinois

Concordia University Chicago *B*
DePaul University *M*
DeVry University
Online *M*
North Park University *B, M*
Northern Illinois University *B*
Northwestern University *M*
Trinity International University *B*

Indiana

Earlham College *B*
Grace College *B*
Huntington University *B*
St. Mary-of-the-Woods College *B, M*
University of Evansville *M*

Iowa

University of Northern Iowa *M*

Kansas

Donnelly College *B*
Friends University *B*

Maine

College of the Atlantic *B, M*

Maryland

Notre Dame of Maryland
University *B, M*

Massachusetts

American International College *M*
Bay Path College *M*
Boston University *M*
Lasell College *M*
Worcester State University *M*

Michigan

Andrews University *B, M*
Cleary University *M*
Eastern Michigan University *M*

Minnesota

Capella University *M, D*
Crossroads College *B*
Hamline University *M*
Metropolitan State University *B, M*
Saint Cloud State University *M*
Southwest Minnesota State
University *B*
University of Minnesota
Twin Cities *B*

Missouri

DeVry University
Kansas City *M*
Lindenwood University *B, M*
Rockhurst University *B*
Washington University in St. Louis *M*
Webster University *M*
William Jewell College *B*

Nebraska

Bellevue University *B*

Nevada

Sierra Nevada College *B*

New Hampshire

Southern New Hampshire
University *B*

New Jersey

Berkeley College *B*
Caldwell College *M*
Fairleigh Dickinson University
College at Florham *M*
Metropolitan Campus *B*
Thomas Edison State College *M*

New York

City University of New York
Baruch College *M*
Globe Institute of Technology *A, B*
Pace University *M*
Pace University: Pleasantville/
Briarcliff *B, M*
SUNY
College at Brockport *M*
Utica School of Commerce *A*

North Carolina

High Point University *B, M*
Salem College *B*

Ohio

Case Western Reserve University *M*
DeVry University
Columbus *M*
Franklin University *B*
John Carroll University *M*
Northwest State Community
College *A*
Tiffin University *B*

Oklahoma

Oral Roberts University *M*
Rogers State University *B*
University of Central Oklahoma *B*

Oregon

Corban University *M*

Pennsylvania

Alvernia University *M*
Cairn University *M*
Carnegie Mellon University *M, D*
DeVry University
Fort Washington *M*
Duquesne University *B*
Eastern University *M*
Gettysburg College *B*
La Salle University *B*
Moravian College *B*
Robert Morris University *M*
University of Pennsylvania *M*

Puerto Rico

University of the Sacred Heart *M*

Rhode Island

Bryant University *B*

South Carolina

Clemson University *M*
Columbia International University *B*
University of South Carolina
Columbia *B*
Upstate *B*

Tennessee

Austin Peay State University *B*
Belmont University *M*
East Tennessee State University *M*
Johnson University *B*
Lipscomb University *M*
Southern Adventist University *B, M*
Trevecca Nazarene University *B*
Williamson College *A, B*

Texas

Dallas Baptist University *M*
Hardin-Simmons University *B*
Our Lady of the Lake University of
San Antonio *M*
St. Mary's University *B*
Texas Christian University *M*
University of Dallas *M*
University of Phoenix
Dallas Fort Worth *M*

Virginia

DeVry University
Arlington *M*
University of Management and
Technology *M*

Washington

Seattle University *M*
Trinity Lutheran College *B*

West Virginia

Ohio Valley University *B*

Wisconsin

Lakeland College *B*
University of Wisconsin
Milwaukee *M*

Norwegian

Minnesota

St. Olaf College *B*

North Dakota

University of North Dakota *B*

Washington

Pacific Lutheran University *B*
University of Washington *B*

Nuclear engineering

California

University of California
Berkeley *B, M, D*

Colorado

Colorado School of Mines *M, D*

Florida

University of Florida *B, M, D*

Georgia

Georgia Institute of
Technology *B, M, D*

Idaho

Idaho State University *B, M, D*
University of Idaho *M, D*

Illinois

University of Illinois
Urbana-Champaign *B, M, D*

Indiana

Purdue University *B, M, D*

Kansas

Kansas State University *M, D*

Maryland

University of Maryland
College Park *M, D*

Massachusetts

Massachusetts Institute of
Technology *B, M, D*

Michigan

University of Michigan *B, M, D*

Missouri

Missouri University of Science and
Technology *B, M, D*
University of Missouri
Columbia *M, D*

New Mexico

University of New Mexico *B, M*

New York

Columbia University *M, D*
Cornell University *M, D*
Rensselaer Polytechnic
Institute *B, M, D*
United States Military Academy *B*

North Carolina

North Carolina State
University *B, M, D*

Ohio

Ohio State University
Columbus Campus *M, D*

Oregon

Oregon State University *B, M, D*

Pennsylvania

Penn State
  Abington *B*
  Altoona *B*
  Beaver *B*
  Berks *B*
  Brandywine *B*
  DuBois *B*
  Erie, The Behrend College *B*
  Fayette, The Eberly Campus *B*
  Greater Allegheny *B*
  Harrisburg *B*
  Hazleton *B*
  Lehigh Valley *B*
  Mont Alto *B*
  New Kensington *B, M*
  Schuylkill *B*
  Shenango *B*
  University Park *B, M, D*
  Wilkes-Barre *B*
  Worthington Scranton *B*
  York *B*
University of Pittsburgh *M*

South Carolina

South Carolina State University *B*
University of South Carolina
  Columbia *M, D*

Tennessee

University of Tennessee
  Knoxville *B, M, D*

Texas

Texas A&M University *B, M, D*

Utah

University of Utah *M, D*

Virginia

Virginia Commonwealth
  University *M*
Virginia Polytechnic Institute and
  State University *M, D*

Washington

University of Washington *M, D*

Wisconsin

University of Wisconsin
  Madison *B, M, D*

Nuclear engineering technology

Arkansas

Arkansas Tech University *A*

Connecticut

Three Rivers Community College *A*

Delaware

Delaware Technical Community
  College
  Jack F. Owens Campus *A*
  Stanton/Wilmington Campus *A*

Idaho

Idaho State University *A, B*

New Jersey

Salem Community College *A*
Thomas Edison State College *A, B*

New York

Excelsior College *B*
United States Military Academy *B*

North Dakota

Bismarck State College *C, A*

Ohio

Lakeland Community College *A*

Pennsylvania

Luzerne County Community
  College *A*

Texas

Wharton County Junior College *A*

Nuclear medical technology

Alabama

Community College of the Air
  Force *A*
University of Alabama
  Birmingham *B*

Arizona

GateWay Community College *A*

Arkansas

University of Arkansas
  for Medical Sciences *B*
University of Central Arkansas *B*

Connecticut

Gateway Community College *A*

Delaware

Delaware Technical Community
  College
  Stanton/Wilmington Campus *A*

Florida

Adventist University of Health
  Sciences *A*
Barry University *B*
Broward College *A*
College of Central Florida *A*
Hillsborough Community College *A*
Keiser University *A*
Santa Fe College *A*
University of Miami *B*

Georgia

Armstrong Atlantic State University *B*
Darton College *A*
Gordon College *A*

Illinois

Benedictine University *B*
Lewis University *B*
North Central College *B*
Roosevelt University *B*
Triton College *A*
University of St. Francis *B*

Indiana

Ball State University *A*
Indiana University
  Purdue University Indianapolis *B*
Vincennes University *A*

Iowa

Allen College *B*
Clinton Community College *A*
University of Iowa *B*

Kentucky

Bluegrass Community and Technical
  College *A*
Hopkinsville Community College *A*
Jefferson Community and Technical
  College *A*

Maine

Central Maine Medical Center College
  of Nursing and Health
  Professions *A*

Maryland

Carroll Community College *A*
Frederick Community College *A*
Prince George's Community
  College *A*

Massachusetts

Bunker Hill Community College *A*
MCPHS University *B*
Salem State University *B*

Michigan

Ferris State University *B*
Oakland Community College *A*
Oakland University *B*

Minnesota

Saint Cloud State University *B*
St. Mary's University of Minnesota *B*

Missouri

Saint Louis University *B*
University of Missouri
  Columbia *B*

Nebraska

University of Nebraska
  Medical Center *B*

Nevada

University of Nevada
  Las Vegas *B*

New Jersey

Felician College *B*
Gloucester County College *A*
Thomas Edison State College *A, B*
Union County College *A*

New York

City University of New York
  Bronx Community College *A*
Long Island University
  LIU Brooklyn *B*
Manhattan College *B*
SUNY
  University at Buffalo *B*

North Carolina

Caldwell Community College and
  Technical Institute *A*
Fayetteville Technical Community
  College *A*
Forsyth Technical Community
  College *A*
Johnston Community College *A*
Pitt Community College *A*

Ohio

Cincinnati State Technical and
  Community College *A*
Columbus State Community
  College *A*
Kettering College *A*
Lorain County Community College *A*
Owens Community College
  Toledo *A*
University of Cincinnati *B*
University of Cincinnati
  Blue Ash College *A*
University of Findlay *A, B*

Oklahoma

University of Oklahoma *B*

Oregon

Oregon Institute of Technology *B*

Pennsylvania

Cedar Crest College *B*
Community College of Allegheny
  County *A*
Edinboro University of
  Pennsylvania *B*
Harrisburg Area Community
  College *A*
Indiana University of Pennsylvania *B*
Pennsylvania College of Health
  Sciences *A*
Robert Morris University *B*
York College of Pennsylvania *B*

Puerto Rico

University of Puerto Rico
  Medical Sciences *B*

South Carolina

Midlands Technical College *A*

South Dakota

Southeast Technical Institute *A*

Tennessee

Baptist College of Health Sciences *B*
South College *B*

Texas

Amarillo College *A*
Del Mar College *A*
Galveston College *A*
Houston Community College
  System *A*
University of the Incarnate Word *B*

Utah

Weber State University *B*

Vermont

University of Vermont *B*

Virginia

Old Dominion University *B*

Washington

Bellevue College *A*

West Virginia

Kanawha Valley Community and
  Technical College *A*
Wheeling Jesuit University *B*

Wisconsin

University of Wisconsin
  La Crosse *B*

Nuclear physics

Arkansas

Arkansas Tech University *B*

Iowa

Iowa State University *M, D*

Nuclear power technology

Alabama

George C. Wallace Community
  College at Dothan *A*

California

MiraCosta College *A*

Connecticut

Three Rivers Community College *A*

Louisiana

ITI Technical College *A*

Minnesota

Dakota County Technical College *C*

Missouri

Linn State Technical College *A*

New Jersey

Cumberland County College *A*

New York

Excelsior College *A*

North Carolina

Cape Fear Community College *A*

Ohio

Lakeland Community College *A*
Terra State Community College *A*

South Carolina

Aiken Technical College *C, A*

Tennessee

Fountainhead College of
Technology *C, A*

Texas

Texas A&M University *M*
Texas State Technical College
Waco *A*
University of North Texas *B*
Wharton County Junior College *A*

Wisconsin

Lakeshore Technical College *A*
Mount Mary University *B*

Nurse anesthetist

Alabama

Samford University *M, T*
University of Alabama
Birmingham *M*

Arkansas

Arkansas State University *M*

California

California State University
Long Beach *M*
National University *M*
Samuel Merritt University *M*
University of Southern California *M*

Connecticut

Central Connecticut State
University *M*
Fairfield University *M*

Florida

Adventist University of Health
Sciences *M*
Florida International University *M*
University of Miami *M, D*

Georgia

Georgia Regents University *M*

Illinois

Bradley University *M*
DePaul University *M*
Rush University *M*
Southern Illinois University
Edwardsville *M*

Iowa

University of Iowa *M*

Kansas

Newman University *M*
University of Kansas Medical
Center *M*

Louisiana

Louisiana State University
Health Sciences Center *M*
Our Lady of the Lake College *M*

Maine

University of New England *M*

Massachusetts

Northeastern University *M*

Michigan

Oakland University *M*
University of Detroit Mercy *M*
University of Michigan
Flint *M, D*
Wayne State University *M*

Minnesota

St. Mary's University of Minnesota *M*

Missouri

Goldfarb School of Nursing at Barnes-
Jewish College *M*
Missouri State University *M*
Webster University *M*

Nebraska

BryanLGH College of Health
Sciences *M*

New York

SUNY
Downstate Medical Center *M*
University at Buffalo *M, D*

Ohio

Case Western Reserve University *M*
Lourdes University *M*
University of Cincinnati *M*
Youngstown State University *M*

Oregon

Oregon Health & Science
University *M*

Pennsylvania

Drexel University *M*
Gannon University *M*
Saint Joseph's University *M*
St. Vincent College *M*
University of Pennsylvania *M*
University of Pittsburgh *M, D*
University of Scranton *M*
Villanova University *M*

Puerto Rico

Inter American University of Puerto
Rico
Arecibo Campus *M*
University of Puerto Rico
Medical Sciences *M*

South Carolina

Medical University of South
Carolina *M*
University of South Carolina
Columbia *M*

South Dakota

Mount Marty College *M*

Tennessee

Union University *M*

Texas

Texas Christian University *M*
Texas Wesleyan University *M, D*
University of Texas
Health Science Center at
Houston *M*

Utah

Westminster College *M*

Virginia

Virginia Commonwealth
University *M, D*

Washington

Gonzaga University *M*

Nurse midwifery

Florida

University of Miami *M*

Georgia

Emory University *D*

Indiana

University of Indianapolis *M*

Minnesota

Bethel University *M*

New York

New York University *M, D*
SUNY
University at Stony Brook *M, D*

Ohio

Case Western Reserve University *M*
University of Cincinnati *M*

Oregon

Oregon Health & Science
University *M*

Pennsylvania

University of Pennsylvania *M*

Puerto Rico

University of Puerto Rico
Medical Sciences *M*

Tennessee

Vanderbilt University *M*

Texas

Baylor University *D*
Texas Tech University Health
Sciences Center *M*
University of Texas
El Paso *M*

Washington

Seattle University *M*

West Virginia

West Virginia Wesleyan College *M*

Nursery operations

California

City College of San Francisco *A*
College of Marin *C, A*
College of the Redwoods *C*
Cosumnes River College *C*
Diablo Valley College *C*
Foothill College *C, A*
Fullerton College *A*
Los Angeles Pierce College *C*
MiraCosta College *C, A*
Modesto Junior College *C*
San Joaquin Delta College *C*
Santa Rosa Junior College *C*
Southwestern College *C, A*

Colorado

Colorado State University *B*

Georgia

Albany Technical College *C*

Illinois

College of DuPage *C*
Joliet Junior College *C, A*
Kishwaukee College *C, A*
Southwestern Illinois College *A*

Indiana

Purdue University *B*

Kansas

Dodge City Community College *C*

Michigan

Michigan State University *C*
Northwestern Michigan College *A*

Minnesota

Hennepin Technical College *C, A*

Nebraska

Metropolitan Community
College *C, A*
Nebraska College of Technical
Agriculture *A*

New York

SUNY
College of Agriculture and
Technology at Cobleskill *A*

Ohio

Ohio State University
Agricultural Technical Institute *A*
Columbus Campus *A*

South Dakota

Southeast Technical Institute *A*

Tennessee

Tennessee Technological
University *B*

Texas

Western Texas College *C, A*

Washington

Clark College *C*
Edmonds Community College *C, A*
South Seattle Community College *C*
Spokane Community College *A*

Nursing (RN)

Alabama

Alabama Southern Community
College *A*
Auburn University *B, M*
Auburn University at
Montgomery *B, M*
Bevill State Community College *A*
Bishop State Community College *A*
Calhoun Community College *A*
Chattahoochee Valley Community
College *A*
Gadsden State Community College *A*
George C. Wallace Community
College at Dothan *A*
George C. Wallace State Community
College at Selma *A*
Herzing University
Birmingham *A*
Jacksonville State University *B, M*
Jefferson Davis Community
College *A*
Jefferson State Community College *A*
Judson College *A*
Lawson State Community College *A*
Lurleen B. Wallace Community
College *A*

Northeast Alabama Community
College *A*
Northwest-Shoals Community
College *A*
Oakwood University *B*
Samford University *B, M*
Shelton State Community College *A*
Snead State Community College *A*
Southern Union State Community
College *A*
Spring Hill College *B*
Stillman College *B*
Troy University *A, B, M*
University of Alabama *B, M*
University of Alabama
Birmingham *B, M*
Huntsville *B, M*
University of Mobile *A, B, M*
University of North Alabama *B, M*
University of South Alabama *B, M, D*
University of West Alabama *A*
Virginia College
Birmingham *A*
Montgomery *A*
Wallace State Community College at
Hanceville *A*

Alaska

University of Alaska
Anchorage *A, B, M*

Arizona

Arizona Western College *A*
Brookline College
Phoenix *B*
Carrington College
Phoenix Westside *A*
Central Arizona College *A*
Chamberlain College of Nursing
Phoenix *A, B*
Cochise College *A*
Eastern Arizona College *A*
Everest College
Phoenix *A*
GateWay Community College *A*
Glendale Community College *A*
Grand Canyon University *B, M*
Mesa Community College *A*
Mohave Community College *A*
Northern Arizona University *B, M*
Northland Pioneer College *A*
Paradise Valley Community College *A*
Phoenix College *A*
Pima Community College *A*
Scottsdale Community College *A*
University of Arizona *B, M, D*
University of Phoenix
Phoenix-Hohokam *B*
Southern Arizona *B*
Yavapai College *A*

Arkansas

Arkansas Northeastern College *A*
Arkansas State University *B, M*
Arkansas Tech University *A, B*
College of the Ouachitas *A*
Cossatot Community College of the
University of Arkansas *A*
East Arkansas Community College *A*
Harding University *B*
Henderson State University *B*
National Park Community College *A*
North Arkansas College *A*
Northwest Arkansas Community
College *A*
Phillips Community College of the
University of Arkansas *A*
Rich Mountain Community College *A*
South Arkansas Community
College *A*
Southeast Arkansas College *A*
Southern Arkansas University *A, B*
University of Arkansas *B, M*

University of Arkansas
Community College at Batesville *A*
Community College at Hope *A*
Community College at Morrilton *A*
Fort Smith *B*
Little Rock *A, B*
Monticello *A, B*
Pine Bluff *B*
for Medical Sciences *B, M*
University of Central Arkansas *B, M*

California

Allan Hancock College *A*
American River College *A*
Antelope Valley College *A*
Azusa Pacific University *B, M, D*
Bakersfield College *A*
Biola University *B*
Butte College *A*
Cabrillo College *A*
California Baptist University *B, M*
California State University
Bakersfield *B*
Chico *B*
Dominguez Hills *B, M*
Fresno *B, M*
Fullerton *B*
Long Beach *B*
Los Angeles *B, M*
Monterey Bay *B*
Northridge *B*
Sacramento *B, M*
San Bernardino *B, M*
Carrington College California
Sacramento *A*
Cerritos College *A*
Chabot College *A*
Chaffey College *A*
Citrus College *A*
City College of San Francisco *A*
College of Marin *A*
College of San Mateo *A*
College of the Canyons *A*
College of the Desert *A*
College of the Sequoias *A*
College of the Siskiyous *A*
Concordia University Irvine *B*
Contra Costa College *A*
Cuesta College *A*
Cypress College *A*
De Anza College *A*
Dominican University of
California *B, M*
East Los Angeles College *A*
El Camino College *A*
Evergreen Valley College *A*
Fresno City College *A*
Gavilan College *A*
Glendale Community College *A*
Golden West College *A*
Grossmont College *A*
Hartnell College *A*
Holy Names University *B*
Imperial Valley College *A*
Loma Linda University *B, M, D*
Long Beach City College *A*
Los Angeles County College of
Nursing and Allied Health *A*
Los Angeles Harbor College *A*
Los Angeles Pierce College *A*
Los Angeles Southwest College *A*
Los Angeles Valley College *A*
Los Medanos College *A*
Merced College *A*
Merritt College *A*
MiraCosta College *A*
Mission College *A*
Modesto Junior College *A*
Monterey Peninsula College *A*
Moorpark College *A*
Mount St. Mary's College *A, B, M*
Mount San Antonio College *A*
Mount San Jacinto College *A*
Napa Valley College *A*
National University *A, B, M*

Ohlone College *A*
Pacific Union College *A, B*
Palomar College *A*
Pasadena City College *A*
Point Loma Nazarene University *B, M*
Rio Hondo College *A*
Riverside City College *A*
Sacramento City College *A*
Saddleback College *A*
Samuel Merritt University *B*
San Diego City College *A*
San Diego State University *B, M*
San Francisco State University *B, M*
San Joaquin Delta College *A*
San Joaquin Valley College *A*
San Jose State University *B, M*
Santa Ana College *A*
Santa Barbara City College *A*
Santa Rosa Junior College *A*
Shasta College *A*
Sierra College *A*
Solano Community College *A*
Sonoma State University *B*
Southwestern College *A*
University of Phoenix
Bay Area *B*
Central Valley *B*
Sacramento Valley *B*
San Diego *B*
Southern California *B*
University of San Francisco *B, M, D*
Vanguard University of Southern
California *B*
Ventura College *A*
Victor Valley College *A*
West Coast University: Los
Angeles *A, B, M*
West Coast University: Ontario *A, B*
West Coast University: Orange
County *A*
West Hills College: Lemoore *A*
Yuba College *A*

Colorado

Adams State University *B*
Aims Community College *A*
American Sentinel University *B, M*
Arapahoe Community College *A*
Aspen University *M*
Colorado Christian University *A, B*
Colorado Mesa University *A, B*
Colorado Mountain College *A*
Colorado Northwestern Community
College *A*
Colorado State University
Pueblo *B, M*
Community College of Denver *A*
Concorde Career College
Aurora *A*
Denver School of Nursing *A, B*
Front Range Community College *A*
Lamar Community College *A*
Metropolitan State University of
Denver *B*
Morgan Community College *A*
Northeastern Junior College *A*
Otero Junior College *A*
Pikes Peak Community College *A*
Platt College
Aurora *B*
Pueblo Community College *A*
Regis University *B*
University of Colorado
Colorado Springs *B, M, D*
Denver *B, D*
University of Phoenix
Denver *B*

Connecticut

Capital Community College *A*
Central Connecticut State
University *B*
Fairfield University *B, M*
Gateway Community College *A*

Goodwin College *A, B*
Housatonic Community College *A*
Lincoln College of New England *B*
Naugatuck Valley Community
College *A*
Northwestern Connecticut
Community College *A*
Norwalk Community College *A*
Quinnipiac University *B, D*
Sacred Heart University *B, M*
St. Vincent's College *A, B*
Southern Connecticut State
University *B*
Three Rivers Community College *A*
University of Connecticut *B*
University of Hartford *B*
University of Saint Joseph *B, M*
Western Connecticut State
University *B*
Yale University *M, D*

Delaware

Delaware State University *B*
Delaware Technical Community
College
Jack F. Owens Campus *A*
Stanton/Wilmington Campus *A*
Terry Campus *A*
University of Delaware *B*
Wesley College *B, M*

District of Columbia

Catholic University of
America *B, M, D*
Georgetown University *B, M*
University of Phoenix
Washington DC *B*
University of the District of
Columbia *A, B*

Florida

Adventist University of Health
Sciences *A, B*
Barry University *B*
Bethune-Cookman University *B*
Broward College *A*
Chamberlain College of Nursing
Jacksonville *B*
Miramar *B*
Chipola College *A, B*
College of Central Florida *A*
Daytona State College *A, B*
Eastern Florida State College *A*
Edison State College *A*
Florida Agricultural and Mechanical
University *B, M*
Florida Atlantic University *B, M*
Florida Gateway College *A*
Florida Gulf Coast University *B, M*
Florida International University *B, M*
Florida Keys Community College *A*
Florida Southern College *B, M*
Florida State College at
Jacksonville *A*
Florida State University *B, M, D*
Gulf Coast State College *A, B*
Herzing University
Winter Park *A*
Hillsborough Community College *A*
Indian River State College *A, B*
Jacksonville University *B, M*
Keiser University *A, B, M*
Lake-Sumter State College *A*
Miami Dade College *A, B*
Northwest Florida State College *A, B*
Nova Southeastern University *B*
Palm Beach Atlantic University *B*
Palm Beach State College *A, B*
Pasco-Hernando State College *A*
Pensacola State College *A*
Polk State College *A, B*
Rasmussen College
Fort Myers *A, B*
New Port Richey *A, B*

Ocala *A, B*
Pasco/Land O'Lakes *B*
Tampa/Brandon *A, B*
Remington College
Nursing *B*
Saint Johns River State College *A*
St. Petersburg College *A, B*
Sanford-Brown Institute
Jacksonville *A*
Santa Fe College *A, B*
Seminole State College of Florida *A*
South Florida State College *A*
Southwest Florida College *A*
State College of Florida, Manatee-
Sarasota *A, B*
Tallahassee Community College *A*
University of Central Florida *B, M*
University of Florida *B, M*
University of Miami *B, M, D*
University of North Florida *B, M*
University of Phoenix
Central Florida *B*
North Florida *B*
South Florida *B*
West Florida *B*
University of South Florida *B, M*
University of Tampa *B*
University of West Florida *B, M*

Georgia

Albany State University *B, M*
Armstrong Atlantic State
University *B, M*
Athens Technical College *A*
Bainbridge College *A*
Berry College *B*
Chamberlain College of Nursing
Atlanta *B*
Clayton State University *B, M*
College of Coastal Georgia *A, B*
Columbus State University *B*
Columbus Technical College *A*
Dalton State College *A, B*
Darton College *A*
Emory University *B, M*
Georgia College and State
University *B*
Georgia Highlands College *A*
Georgia Perimeter College *A*
Georgia Regents University *B, M*
Georgia Southern University *B*
Georgia Southwestern State
University *B, M*
Georgia State University *B, M, D*
Gordon College *A, B*
Gwinnett Technical College *A*
Kennesaw State University *B*
LaGrange College *B*
Mercer University *B, D*
Middle Georgia State College *A, B*
Piedmont College *B*
South Georgia State College *A, B*
Southwest Georgia Technical
College *A*
Thomas University *B*
Truett-McConnell College *B*
University of North Georgia *A, B*
University of Phoenix
Atlanta *B*
Columbus *B*
Savannah *B*
University of West Georgia *B, M*
Valdosta State University *B, M*
Wesleyan College *B*

Hawaii

Chaminade University of Honolulu *B*
Hawaii Pacific University *B, M*
University of Hawaii
Hawaii Community College *A*
Hilo *B*
Kapiolani Community College *A*
Kauai Community College *A*
Manoa *B, M*

University of Phoenix
Hawaii *B*

Idaho

Boise State University *A, B, M*
Brigham Young University-Idaho *A, B*
College of Southern Idaho *A*
College of Western Idaho *A*
Eastern Idaho Technical College *A*
ITT Technical Institute
Boise *A*
Idaho State University *A, B, M, D*
Lewis-Clark State College *B*
North Idaho College *A*
Northwest Nazarene University *B*

Illinois

Aurora University *B, M*
Benedictine University *B, M*
Black Hawk College *A*
Blessing-Rieman College of
Nursing *B, M*
Bradley University *B*
Carl Sandburg College *A*
Chamberlain College of Nursing
Addison *B, M*
Chicago *A, B*
Chicago State University *B*
City Colleges of Chicago
Harry S. Truman College *A*
Kennedy-King College *A*
Malcolm X College *A*
Richard J. Daley College *A*
Wilbur Wright College *A*
College of DuPage *A*
College of Lake County *A*
Danville Area Community College *A*
DePaul University *B, M*
Dominican University *B*
Eastern Illinois University *B*
Elgin Community College *A*
Elmhurst College *B*
Governors State University *B*
Harper College *A*
Heartland Community College *A*
Highland Community College *A*
Illinois State University *B, M*
Illinois Valley Community College *A*
Illinois Wesleyan University *B*
John A. Logan College *A*
John Wood Community College *A*
Joliet Junior College *A*
Kankakee Community College *A*
Kaskaskia College *A*
Kishwaukee College *A*
Lake Land College *A*
Lakeview College of Nursing *B*
Lewis University *B*
Lewis and Clark Community
College *A*
Lincoln Land Community College *A*
Loyola University Chicago *B, M*
MacMurray College *B*
McHenry County College *A*
McKendree University *B, M*
Millikin University *B, M, D*
Moraine Valley Community College *A*
Morton College *A*
North Park University *B*
Northern Illinois University *B*
Oakton Community College *A*
Olivet Nazarene University *B*
Parkland College *A*
Prairie State College *A*
Quincy University *B*
Rend Lake College *A*
Resurrection University *B, M*
Richland Community College *A*
Robert Morris University: Chicago *A*
Rock Valley College *A*
Rockford University *B*
Rush University *M, D*
St. Francis Medical Center College of
Nursing *B, M*

St. John's College *B*
Saint Xavier University *B*
Sauk Valley Community College *A*
South Suburban College of Cook
County *A*
Southeastern Illinois College *A*
Southern Illinois University
Edwardsville *B*
Southwestern Illinois College *A*
Trinity Christian College *B*
Trinity College of Nursing & Health
Sciences *A, B, M*
Triton College *A*
University of Illinois
Chicago *B*
University of St. Francis *B, M*
Waubonsee Community College *A*
Western Illinois University *B*
Wheaton College *B*

Indiana

Ancilla College *A*
Anderson University *B*
Ball State University *B, M*
Bethel College *A, B*
Chamberlain College of Nursing
Indianapolis *B*
Fortis College
Indianapolis *A*
Goshen College *B*
Harrison College
Indianapolis *B*
ITT Technical Institute
Fort Wayne *A*
Indianapolis *A*
Newburgh *A*
Indiana State University *B, M*
Indiana University
Bloomington *B*
East *B, M*
Kokomo *B, M*
Northwest *B*
Purdue University Fort Wayne *B*
Purdue University
Indianapolis *B, M*
South Bend *B*
Southeast *B*
Indiana Wesleyan University *B*
Ivy Tech Community College
Bloomington *A*
Central Indiana *A*
Columbus *A*
East Central *A*
Kokomo *A*
Lafayette *A*
North Central *A*
Northeast *A*
Northwest *A*
Richmond *A*
South Central *A*
Southeast *A*
Southwest *A*
Wabash Valley *A*
Marian University *B*
Purdue University *B, M*
Purdue University
Calumet *B, M*
North Central *B*
Saint Joseph's College *B*
Saint Mary's College *B*
University of Evansville *B*
University of Indianapolis *A, B*
University of Phoenix
Indianapolis *B*
University of St. Francis *A, B*
University of Southern
Indiana *B, M, D*
Valparaiso University *B, M*
Vincennes University *A, B*

Iowa

Allen College *B, M, D*
Briar Cliff University *B, M*
Clarke University *B, M*

Clinton Community College *A*
Coe College *B*
Des Moines Area Community
College *A*
Dordt College *B*
Ellsworth Community College *A*
Graceland University *B*
Grand View University *B, M*
Hawkeye Community College *A*
Iowa Central Community College *A*
Iowa Lakes Community College *A*
Iowa Wesleyan College *B*
Iowa Western Community College *A*
Kirkwood Community College *A*
Luther College *B*
Marshalltown Community College *A*
Mercy College of Health
Sciences *A, B*
Morningside College *B*
Mount Mercy University *B*
North Iowa Area Community
College *A*
Northeast Iowa Community
College *A*
Northwest Iowa Community
College *A*
Northwestern College *B*
St. Ambrose University *B, M*
St. Luke's College *A, B*
Southeastern Community College *A*
Southwestern Community College *A*
University of Dubuque *B*
University of Iowa *B*

Kansas

Barton County Community College *A*
Bethel College *B*
Butler Community College *A*
Cloud County Community College *A*
Colby Community College *A*
Dodge City Community College *A*
Emporia State University *B*
Garden City Community College *A*
Hesston College *A*
Highland Community College *A*
Hutchinson Community College *A*
Johnson County Community
College *A*
Kansas City Kansas Community
College *A*
Kansas Wesleyan University *B*
Labette Community College *A*
Manhattan Area Technical College *A*
MidAmerica Nazarene
University *B, M*
Neosho County Community
College *A*
Newman University *B*
North Central Kansas Technical
College *A*
Pittsburg State University *B*
Pratt Community College *A*
Seward County Community
College *A*
University of Kansas Medical
Center *B*
University of St. Mary *B*
Washburn University *B, M, D*

Kentucky

Ashland Community and Technical
College *A*
Beckfield College *B*
Bellarmine University *B, M*
Berea College *B*
Big Sandy Community and Technical
College *A*
Bluegrass Community and Technical
College *A*
Campbellsville University *A, B*
Eastern Kentucky University *A, B*
Elizabethtown Community and
Technical College *A*

Gateway Community and Technical
College *A*
Hazard Community and Technical
College *A*
Hopkinsville Community College *A*
ITT Technical Institute
Louisville *A*
Jefferson Community and Technical
College *A*
Kentucky Christian University *B*
Kentucky State University *A, B*
Madisonville Community College *A*
Maysville Community and Technical
College *A*
Midway College *A, B*
Morehead State University *A, B*
Murray State University *B, M*
Northern Kentucky
University *A, B, M*
Owensboro Community and
Technical College *A*
St. Catharine College *A, B*
Somerset Community College *A*
Southeast Kentucky Community and
Technical College *A*
Spalding University *B, M*
Spencerian College *A*
Sullivan University *B*
Thomas More College *B*
Union College *B*
University of Kentucky *B, M*
University of Louisville *B, D*
University of Pikeville *A, B*
West Kentucky Community and
Technical College *A*
Western Kentucky University *A, B, M*

Louisiana

Baton Rouge Community College *A*
Bossier Parish Community College *A*
Delgado Community College *A*
Dillard University *B*
Grambling State University *B*
Louisiana College *B*
Louisiana State University
Alexandria *A, B*
Health Sciences Center *B*
Louisiana Tech University *A*
Loyola University New Orleans *B, M*
McNeese State University *B, M*
Nicholls State University *B*
Northwestern State
University *A, B, M*
Our Lady of the Lake College *A, B, M*
Southeastern Louisiana
University *B, M*
Southern University and Agricultural
and Mechanical College *B*
University of Louisiana at
Lafayette *B*
University of Louisiana at Monroe *B*
University of Phoenix
Baton Rouge *B*
Louisiana *B*

Maine

Central Maine Community College *A*
Central Maine Medical Center College
of Nursing and Health
Professions *A*
Eastern Maine Community College *A*
Husson University *B, M*
Kennebec Valley Community
College *A*
Northern Maine Community
College *A*
Saint Joseph's College of Maine *B*
Southern Maine Community
College *A*
University of Maine *B, M*
University of Maine
Augusta *A, B*
Fort Kent *B*

University of New England *A, B*
University of Southern Maine *B, M*

Maryland

Allegany College of Maryland *A*
Anne Arundel Community College *A*
Baltimore City Community College *A*
Bowie State University *B, M*
Carroll Community College *A*
Cecil College *A*
Chesapeake College *A*
College of Southern Maryland *A*
Community College of Baltimore
County *A*
Coppin State University *B, M, T*
Frederick Community College *A*
Frostburg State University *B*
Hagerstown Community College *A*
Harford Community College *A*
Howard Community College *A*
Montgomery College *A*
Prince George's Community
College *A*
Salisbury University *B, M, D*
Stevenson University *B, M*
Towson University *B, M*
University of Maryland
Baltimore *B*
University College *B*
Washington Adventist
University *B, M*
Wor-Wic Community College *A*

Massachusetts

American International College *B, M*
Anna Maria College *B*
Becker College *A, B*
Berkshire Community College *A*
Boston College *B, M*
Bristol Community College *A*
Bunker Hill Community College *A*
Cape Cod Community College *A*
Curry College *B*
Elms College *B*
Emmanuel College *M*
Endicott College *B*
Fitchburg State University *B*
Framingham State University *B, M*
Greenfield Community College *A*
Holyoke Community College *A*
Laboure College *A, B*
MCPHS University *B, M*
Massachusetts Bay Community
College *A*
Massasoit Community College *A*
Middlesex Community College *A*
Mount Wachusett Community
College *A*
North Shore Community College *A*
Northeastern University *B, M, D*
Northern Essex Community
College *A*
Quincy College *A*
Quinsigamond Community College *A*
Regis College *A, B, M*
Roxbury Community College *A*
Salem State University *B, M*
Simmons College *B, M*
Springfield Technical Community
College *A*
University of Massachusetts
Amherst *B*
Boston *B*
Dartmouth *B, M*
Lowell *B, M*
Westfield State University *B*
Worcester State University *B, M*

Michigan

Alpena Community College *A*
Andrews University *B*
Baker College
Clinton Township *B*
Flint *B*

Muskegon *A*
Owosso *A*
Bay de Noc Community College *A*
Calvin College *B*
Davenport University *B, M*
Delta College *A*
Eastern Michigan University *B, M*
Ferris State University *B*
Finlandia University *B*
Glen Oaks Community College *A*
Gogebic Community College *A*
Grand Rapids Community College *A*
Grand Valley State University *B, M*
Henry Ford Community College *A*
Hope College *B*
ITT Technical Institute
Canton *A*
Jackson College *A*
Kalamazoo Valley Community
College *A*
Kellogg Community College *A*
Kirtland Community College *A*
Lake Michigan College *A*
Lake Superior State University *B*
Lansing Community College *A*
Macomb Community College *A*
Madonna University *B, M, D*
Michigan State University *B, M*
Mid Michigan Community College *A*
Monroe County Community
College *A*
Montcalm Community College *A*
Mott Community College *A*
Muskegon Community College *A*
North Central Michigan College *A*
Northwestern Michigan College *A*
Oakland Community College *A*
Oakland University *B*
Robert B. Miller College *B*
Saginaw Valley State University *B, M*
St. Clair County Community
College *A*
Schoolcraft College *A*
Siena Heights University *B*
Southwestern Michigan College *A*
University of Detroit Mercy *B, M*
University of Michigan *B, D*
University of Michigan
Flint *B, M, D*
University of Phoenix
Metro Detroit *B*
West Michigan *B*
Washtenaw Community College *A*
Wayne County Community College *A*
West Shore Community College *A*
Western Michigan University *B, M*

Minnesota

Alexandria Technical and Community
College *A*
Anoka-Ramsey Community College *A*
Augsburg College *B*
Bemidji State University *B*
Bethel University *B*
Capella University *B*
Central Lakes College *A*
Century College *A*
College of St. Benedict *B*
College of St. Scholastica *B*
Concordia College: Moorhead *B*
Crown College *B*
Fond du Lac Tribal and Community
College *A*
Gustavus Adolphus College *B*
Hibbing Community College *A*
Inver Hills Community College *A*
Lake Superior College *A*
Metropolitan State University *B, M*
Minneapolis Community and
Technical College *A*
Minnesota School of Business
Richfield *B*
Minnesota State College - Southeast
Technical *A*

Minnesota State Community and
Technical College *A*
Minnesota State University
Mankato *B, M*
Moorhead *B, M*
Minnesota West Community and
Technical College *A*
National American University
Bloomington *B*
Normandale Community College *A*
North Hennepin Community
College *A*
Northland Community & Technical
College *A*
Northwest Technical College *A*
Rasmussen College
Blaine *A, B*
Bloomington *A, B*
Brooklyn Park *B*
Eagan *B*
Lake Elmo/Woodbury *B*
Mankato *A, B*
Moorhead *A, B*
St. Cloud *A, B*
Ridgewater College *A*
Riverland Community College *A*
Rochester Community and Technical
College *A*
St. Catherine University *A, B, M*
Saint Cloud State University *B, M*
St. Cloud Technical and Community
College *A*
St. John's University *B*
St. Mary's University of Minnesota *B*
St. Olaf College *B*
South Central College *A*
Southwest Minnesota State
University *B*
University of Minnesota
Twin Cities *M*
University of Phoenix
Minneapolis-St. Paul *B*
Walden University *B, M*
Winona State University *B*

Mississippi

Alcorn State University *A, B*
Coahoma Community College *A*
Copiah-Lincoln Community
College *A*
Delta State University *B, M, D*
East Central Community College *A*
East Mississippi Community
College *A*
Hinds Community College *A*
Itawamba Community College *A*
Meridian Community College *A*
Mississippi College *B*
Mississippi Gulf Coast Community
College *A*
Mississippi University for
Women *A, B, M*
Northeast Mississippi Community
College *A*
Southwest Mississippi Community
College *A*
University of Southern Mississippi *B*
William Carey University *B, M*

Missouri

Avila University *B*
Bolivar Technical College *A*
Central Methodist University *B*
Chamberlain College of Nursing
St. Louis *A, B*
College of the Ozarks *B*
Columbia College *A*
Cox College *A, B*
Crowder College *A*
Culver-Stockton College *B*
Drury University *B*
East Central College *A*
Goldfarb School of Nursing at Barnes-
Jewish College *B, M*

Grantham University *A*
Hannibal-LaGrange University *A, B*
Jefferson College *A*
Lincoln University *A, B*
Lindenwood University *B*
Maryville University of Saint
Louis *B, M*
Metropolitan Community College -
Kansas City *A*
Mineral Area College *A*
Missouri Southern State University *B*
Missouri State University *B*
Missouri State University: West
Plains *A*
Missouri Valley College *B*
Missouri Western State
University *B, M*
Moberly Area Community College *A*
National American University
Kansas City *A, B, M*
North Central Missouri College *A*
Northwest Missouri State
University *B*
Ozarks Technical Community
College *A*
Park University *A*
Research College of Nursing *B*
Rockhurst University *B*
St. Charles Community College *A*
Saint Louis University *B, M, D*
St. Luke's College *B, M*
Southeast Missouri Hospital College
of Nursing and Health
Sciences *A*
Southeast Missouri State
University *B, M*
Southwest Baptist University *A, B*
State Fair Community College *A*
Texas County Technical College *A*
Three Rivers Community College *A*
Truman State University *B*
University of Central Missouri *B, M*
University of Missouri
Columbia *B, M, D*
Kansas City *B, M, D*
St. Louis *B, M*
University of Phoenix
St. Louis *B*
Webster University *B, M*
William Jewell College *B*

Montana

Carroll College *B*
Flathead Valley Community
College *A*
Helena College University of
Montana *A*
Miles Community College *A*
Montana State University *B, M*
Montana State University
Great Falls College *A*
Northern *A, B*
Montana Tech of the University of
Montana *A, B*
Salish Kootenai College *A, B*

Nebraska

BryanLGH College of Health
Sciences *B*
Central Community College *A*
Clarkson College *B*
College of Saint Mary *A, B, M*
Creighton University *B*
Grace University *B*
ITT Technical Institute
Omaha *A*
Kaplan University
Lincoln *M*
Metropolitan Community College *A*
Mid-Plains Community College *A*
Nebraska Methodist College of
Nursing and Allied Health *B, M*
Nebraska Wesleyan University *B*
Northeast Community College *A*

Southeast Community College *A*
Union College *B*
University of Nebraska
Medical Center *B, M*
Western Nebraska Community
College *A*

Nevada

Carrington College
Reno *A*
College of Southern Nevada *A*
Great Basin College *A, B*
ITT Technical Institute
Henderson *A*
Nevada State College *B*
Roseman University of Health
Sciences *B*
Truckee Meadows Community
College *A*
University of Nevada
Las Vegas *B, M, D*
Reno *B*
Western Nevada College *A*

New Hampshire

Colby-Sawyer College *B*
Franklin Pierce University *B*
Granite State College *B*
Great Bay Community College *A*
Keene State College *B*
Manchester Community College *A*
NHTI-Concord's Community
College *A*
Nashua Community College *A*
Plymouth State University *B*
River Valley Community College *A*
Rivier University *A, B, M*
Saint Anselm College *B*
Southern New Hampshire
University *B*
University of New Hampshire *B, M*
White Mountains Community
College *A*

New Jersey

Atlantic Cape Community College *A*
Bergen Community College *A*
Bloomfield College *B*
Brookdale Community College *A*
Burlington County College *A*
Caldwell College *B*
Camden County College *A*
College of New Jersey *B, M*
College of St. Elizabeth *B*
County College of Morris *A*
Cumberland County College *A*
Eastern International College *A*
Eastwick College *A*
Essex County College *A*
Fairleigh Dickinson University
College at Florham *B*
Metropolitan Campus *B, M*
Felician College *A, B, M*
Georgian Court University *B*
Gloucester County College *A*
Hudson County Community
College *A*
Mercer County Community
College *A*
Middlesex County College *A*
Monmouth University *B*
New Jersey City University *B*
Ocean County College *A*
Passaic County Community College *A*
Raritan Valley Community College *A*
Richard Stockton College of New
Jersey *B, M*
Rutgers, The State University of New
Jersey
Camden Campus *B*
New Brunswick/Piscataway
Campus *B*
Newark Campus *B*
Saint Peter's University *B, M*

Salem Community College *A*
Seton Hall University *B*
Thomas Edison State College *B, M*
Union County College *A*
Warren County Community
College *A*
William Paterson University of New
Jersey *B*

New Mexico

Brookline College
Albuquerque *B*
Carrington College
Albuquerque *A*
Central New Mexico Community
College *A*
Clovis Community College *A*
Dona Ana Community College of
New Mexico State University *A*
Eastern New Mexico University *B*
Eastern New Mexico University:
Roswell *A*
ITT Technical Institute
Albuquerque *A*
Luna Community College *A*
National American University
Albuquerque *B*
Navajo Technical University *A*
New Mexico Highlands University *B*
New Mexico State University *B, M*
New Mexico State University
Carlsbad *A*
San Juan College *A*
Santa Fe Community College *A*
University of New Mexico *B, M, D*
University of Phoenix
New Mexico *B*
Western New Mexico University *A, B*

New York

Adelphi University *B, M, D*
Adirondack Community College *A*
Broome Community College *A*
Cayuga Community College *A*
City University of New York
Borough of Manhattan Community
College *A*
Bronx Community College *A*
College of Staten Island *A, B*
Hostos Community College *A*
Hunter College *B, M*
Kingsborough Community
College *A*
LaGuardia Community College *A*
Lehman College *B*
Medgar Evers College *A, B*
New York City College of
Technology *A, B*
Queensborough Community
College *A*
York College *B*
Clinton Community College *A*
Cochran School of Nursing *A*
College of Mount St. Vincent *B, M*
College of New Rochelle *B, M*
Columbia-Greene Community
College *A*
Concordia College *B*
Corning Community College *A*
D'Youville College *B, M*
Daemen College *B*
Dominican College of Blauvelt *B*
Dutchess Community College *A*
Elmira College *B*
Erie Community College *A*
Excelsior College *A, B, M*
Finger Lakes Community College *A*
Fulton-Montgomery Community
College *A*
Genesee Community College *A*
Hartwick College *B*
Helene Fuld College of Nursing *A*
Hudson Valley Community College *A*
Jamestown Community College *A*

Jefferson Community College *A*
Keuka College *B*
Le Moyne College *B, M*
Long Island University
LIU Brooklyn *B*
LIU Post *B, M*
Maria College *A*
Mercy College *M*
Mohawk Valley Community
College *A*
Molloy College *B*
Monroe College *A, B*
Monroe Community College *A*
Mount Saint Mary College *B*
Nassau Community College *A*
Nazareth College *B*
New York Institute of Technology *B*
New York University *B, M, D*
Niagara County Community
College *A*
Niagara University *B*
North Country Community College *A*
Nyack College *B*
Onondaga Community College *A*
Pace University *B*
Pace University: Pleasantville/
Briarcliff *B, M*
Phillips Beth Israel School of
Nursing *A*
Roberts Wesleyan College *B*
Rockland Community College *A*
SUNY
College at Brockport *B*
College at Plattsburgh *B*
College of Agriculture and
Technology at Morrisville *A*
College of Technology at Alfred *A*
College of Technology at
Canton *A, B*
College of Technology at
Delhi *A, B*
Downstate Medical Center *B, M*
Empire State College *B*
Farmingdale State College *B*
Institute of Technology at Utica/
Rome *B*
University at Binghamton *B, M*
University at Buffalo *B, D*
University at Stony Brook *B*
Upstate Medical University *B, M*
Sage Colleges *B*
St. Elizabeth College of Nursing *A*
St. Francis College *A, B*
St. John Fisher College *B*
St. Joseph's College of Nursing *A*
Suffolk County Community College *A*
Sullivan County Community
College *A*
Tompkins Cortland Community
College *A*
Touro College *B*
Trocaire College *A, B*
Ulster County Community College *A*
University of Rochester *B*
Utica College *B*
Wagner College *B, M*
Westchester Community College *A*

North Carolina

Alamance Community College *A*
Appalachian State University *B*
Asheville-Buncombe Technical
Community College *A*
Barton College *B*
Beaufort County Community
College *A*
Bladen Community College *A*
Blue Ridge Community College *A*
Brunswick Community College *A*
Cabarrus College of Health
Sciences *A, B*
Caldwell Community College and
Technical Institute *A*
Cape Fear Community College *A*

Carolinas College of Health
Sciences *A*
Catawba Valley Community
College *A*
Central Carolina Community
College *A*
Central Piedmont Community
College *A*
Cleveland Community College *A*
Coastal Carolina Community
College *A*
College of the Albemarle *A*
Craven Community College *A*
Davidson County Community
College *A*
Durham Technical Community
College *A*
East Carolina University *B, M*
Edgecombe Community College *A*
Fayetteville State University *B*
Fayetteville Technical Community
College *A*
Forsyth Technical Community
College *A*
Gardner-Webb University *A, B, M*
Gaston College *A*
Guilford Technical Community
College *A*
Halifax Community College *A*
Haywood Community College *A*
Isothermal Community College *A*
James Sprunt Community College *A*
Johnston Community College *A*
Lenoir Community College *A*
Lenoir-Rhyne University *B, M*
Mayland Community College *A*
McDowell Technical Community
College *A*
Methodist University *B*
Mitchell Community College *A*
Nash Community College *A*
North Carolina Central University *B*
Piedmont Community College *A*
Pitt Community College *A*
Queens University of Charlotte *A, B*
Randolph Community College *A*
Richmond Community College *A*
Roanoke-Chowan Community
College *A*
Robeson Community College *A*
Rockingham Community College *A*
Rowan-Cabarrus Community
College *A*
Sampson Community College *A*
Sandhills Community College *A*
South College *A*
South Piedmont Community
College *A*
Southwestern Community College *A*
Stanly Community College *A*
Surry Community College *A*
Tri-County Community College *A*
University of Mount Olive *B*
University of North Carolina
Chapel Hill *B, M*
Charlotte *B, M*
Greensboro *B, M*
Pembroke *B*
Wilmington *B*
Vance-Granville Community
College *A*
Wake Technical Community
College *A*
Wayne Community College *A*
Western Carolina University *B, M*
Western Piedmont Community
College *A*
Wilkes Community College *A*
Wilson Community College *A*
Winston-Salem State University *B*

North Dakota

Bismarck State College *A*
Dakota College at Bottineau *A*
Dickinson State University *B*

Lake Region State College *A*
Minot State University *B*
North Dakota State College of
Science *A*
North Dakota State University *B, M*
Sanford College of Nursing *B*
University of Jamestown *B*
University of Mary *B, M*
University of North Dakota *B, M, D*
Williston State College *A*

Ohio

ATS Institute of Technology *A*
Aultman College of Nursing and
Health Sciences *A, B*
Baldwin Wallace University *B*
Belmont College *A*
Bowling Green State University *B*
Bowling Green State University:
Firelands College *A*
Bryant & Stratton College
Eastlake *A*
Parma *A*
Capital University *B*
Case Western Reserve
University *B, M, D*
Cedarville University *B, M*
Central Ohio Technical College *A*
Chamberlain College Of Nursing
Chamberlain College of Nursing:
Cleveland *A, B*
Chamberlain College of Nursing
Columbus *A, B*
Cincinnati State Technical and
Community College *A*
Clark State Community College *A*
Cleveland State University *B, M*
College of Mount St. Joseph *B, M*
Columbus State Community
College *A*
Cuyahoga Community College
Metropolitan *A*
Edison State Community College *A*
Fortis College
Centerville *A*
Franciscan University of
Steubenville *B, M*
Good Samaritan College of Nursing
and Health Science *A, B*
Hocking College *A*
Hondros College *A, B*
James A. Rhodes State College *A*
Kent State University *B, M, D*
Kent State University
Ashtabula *A, B*
East Liverpool *A, B*
Geauga *A, B*
Salem *B*
Stark *B*
Trumbull *B*
Tuscarawas *A, B*
Kettering College *B*
Lakeland Community College *A*
Lorain County Community College *A*
Lourdes University *B, M*
Malone University *B, M*
Marion Technical College *A*
Mercy College of Ohio *A, B*
Miami University
Hamilton *A, B*
Middletown *A*
Oxford *B*
Mount Carmel College of
Nursing *B, M*
Mount Vernon Nazarene University *B*
Muskingum University *B*
North Central State College *A*
Northwest State Community
College *A*
Notre Dame College *A, B*
Ohio Northern University *B*
Ohio State University
Columbus Campus *B, M, D*
Ohio University *B, M*

Ohio University
Chillicothe Campus *A, B, M*
Southern Campus at Ironton *A, B*
Zanesville Campus *A, B*
Ohio Valley College of Technology *A*
Otterbein University *B*
Owens Community College
Toledo *A*
Shawnee State University *A, B*
Sinclair Community College *A*
Southern State Community College *A*
Stark State College *A*
Terra State Community College *A*
University of Akron *B, M, D*
University of Cincinnati *B, M*
University of Cincinnati
Blue Ash College *A*
University of Phoenix
Cleveland *B*
University of Rio Grande *A, B*
University of Toledo *A, B, M*
Ursuline College *B*
Walsh University *B*
Washington State Community
College *A*
Wright State University *B, M*
Wright State University: Lake
Campus *B*
Xavier University *B, M*
Youngstown State University *B*

Oklahoma

Bacone College *A, B*
Carl Albert State College *A*
Connors State College *A*
East Central University *B*
Eastern Oklahoma State College *A*
Northeastern Oklahoma Agricultural
and Mechanical College *A*
Northern Oklahoma College *A*
Northwestern Oklahoma State
University *B*
Oklahoma Baptist University *B, M*
Oklahoma Christian University *B*
Oklahoma City Community
College *A*
Oklahoma Panhandle State
University *B*
Oklahoma State University
Institute of Technology:
Okmulgee *A*
Oklahoma City *A*
Oklahoma Wesleyan University *A*
Oral Roberts University *B*
Redlands Community College *A*
Rogers State University *A, B*
Rose State College *A*
Seminole State College *A*
Southwestern Oklahoma State
University *A, B*
University of Central Oklahoma *B, M*
University of Oklahoma *B, M, D*
University of Phoenix
Oklahoma City *B*
University of Tulsa *B*
Western Oklahoma State College *A*

Oregon

Blue Mountain Community College *A*
Central Oregon Community
College *A*
Chemeketa Community College *A*
Clackamas Community College *A*
Clatsop Community College *A*
Concordia University *B*
George Fox University *B*
ITT Technical Institute
Portland *A*
Lane Community College *A*
Linfield College *B*
Linn-Benton Community College *A*
Mt. Hood Community College *A*
Oregon Health & Science
University *B, D*

Rogue Community College *A*
Southern Oregon University *B*
Treasure Valley Community
College *A*
Umpqua Community College *A*
University of Portland *B, M, D*
Western Oregon University *B*

Pennsylvania

Alvernia University *B*
Bloomsburg University of
Pennsylvania *B, M*
Bucks County Community College *A*
Butler County Community College *A*
California University of
Pennsylvania *A, B*
Carlow University *B*
Cedar Crest College *B, M*
Chatham University *B, M, D*
Clarion University of
Pennsylvania *A, B, M*
Community College of Allegheny
County *A*
Community College of Beaver
County *A*
Community College of
Philadelphia *A*
DeSales University *B*
Delaware County Community
College *A*
Drexel University *B, M*
Duquesne University *B*
East Stroudsburg University of
Pennsylvania *B*
Eastern University *B*
Edinboro University of
Pennsylvania *B, M*
Gannon University *B, M*
Gettysburg College *B*
Gwynedd Mercy University *A, B*
Harcum College *A*
Harrisburg Area Community
College *A*
Holy Family University *B, M*
Immaculata University *B*
Indiana University of
Pennsylvania *B, M*
La Roche College *A, B, M*
La Salle University *B*
Lehigh Carbon Community College *A*
Lock Haven University of
Pennsylvania *A, B*
Luzerne County Community
College *A*
Mercyhurst University *B*
Messiah College *B*
Misericordia University *B, M*
Montgomery County Community
College *A*
Moravian College *B*
Mount Aloysius College *A, B*
Neumann University *B*
Northampton Community College *A*
Penn State
Abington *A, B*
Altoona *A, B*
Beaver *A, B*
Berks *A, B*
Brandywine *A, B*
DuBois *A, B*
Erie, The Behrend College *A, B*
Fayette, The Eberly Campus *A, B*
Greater Allegheny *A, B*
Harrisburg *A, B*
Hazleton *A, B*
Lehigh Valley *A, B*
Mont Alto *A, B*
New Kensington *A, B*
Schuylkill *A, B*
Shenango *A, B*
University Park *A, B, M, D*
Wilkes-Barre *A, B*
Worthington Scranton *A, B*
York *A, B*

Pennsylvania College of Health
Sciences *A, B*
Pennsylvania College of
Technology *A*
Reading Area Community College *A*
Robert Morris University *B, M*
St. Francis University *B*
Slippery Rock University of
Pennsylvania *B*
Temple University *B, M*
Thomas Jefferson University *B, M*
University of Pennsylvania *B, M, D*
University of Pittsburgh *B, M, D*
University of Pittsburgh
Bradford *A, B*
Johnstown *B*
Titusville *A*
University of Scranton *B, M*
Villanova University *B*
Waynesburg University *B, M*
West Chester University of
Pennsylvania *B, M, D, T*
Westmoreland County Community
College *A*
Widener University *B, M*
Wilkes University *B, M*
York College of Pennsylvania *B*

Puerto Rico

Centro de Estudios
Multidisciplinarios *A, B*
Columbia Centro Universitario:
Caguas *A, B*
Columbia Centro Universitario:
Yauco *A, B*
ICPR Junior College *A*
Inter American University of Puerto
Rico
Aguadilla Campus *B*
Arecibo Campus *A, B*
Barranquitas Campus *A, B*
Bayamón Campus *A, B*
Guayama Campus *A, B*
Metropolitan Campus *A, B*
Ponce Campus *A, B*
San German Campus *B*
National University College
Bayamon *A, B*
Pontifical Catholic University of
Puerto Rico *B*
Turabo University *B*
Universal Technology College of
Puerto Rico *A*
Universidad Metropolitana *A, B, M*
Universidad del Este *A, B*
University College of San Juan *A, B*
University of Puerto Rico
Aguadilla *A*
Arecibo *A, B*
Humacao *B*
Mayaguez *B*
Medical Sciences *B, M, D*
University of the Sacred Heart *A, B*

Rhode Island

Community College of Rhode
Island *A*
New England Institute of
Technology *A*
Rhode Island College *B, M*
Salve Regina University *B*
University of Rhode Island *B*

South Carolina

Aiken Technical College *A*
Anderson University *B*
Bob Jones University *B*
Central Carolina Technical College *A*
Charleston Southern University *B*
Clemson University *B*
Coastal Carolina University *B*
Florence-Darlington Technical
College *A*
Francis Marion University *B*

Greenville Technical College *A*
Horry-Georgetown Technical
College *A*
Lander University *B*
Medical University of South
Carolina *B*
Midlands Technical College *A*
Northeastern Technical College *A*
Orangeburg-Calhoun Technical
College *A*
Piedmont Technical College *A*
South Carolina State University *B*
Spartanburg Community College *A*
Technical College of the
Lowcountry *A*
Tri-County Technical College *A*
Trident Technical College *A*
University of South Carolina
Aiken *B*
Beaufort *B*
Columbia *B*
Lancaster *A*
Upstate *B*
York Technical College *A*

South Dakota

Augustana College *B*
Dakota Wesleyan University *A, B*
Lake Area Technical Institute *A*
Mount Marty College *B*
Presentation College *A, B*
South Dakota State University *B, M*
Southeast Technical Institute *A*
University of Sioux Falls *B*
University of South Dakota *A, B*

Tennessee

Aquinas College *A, B*
Austin Peay State University *B*
Baptist College of Health Sciences *B*
Belmont University *B, M*
Bethel University *B*
Carson-Newman University *B*
Chattanooga State Community
College *A*
Cleveland State Community
College *A*
Columbia State Community
College *A*
Cumberland University *B*
Dyersburg State Community
College *A*
East Tennessee State University *B, M*
Fisk University *B*
Jackson State Community College *A*
King University *B, M*
Lincoln Memorial University *A, B*
Lipscomb University *B*
Martin Methodist College *B*
Maryville College *B*
Middle Tennessee State
University *B, M*
Milligan College *B*
Motlow State Community College *A*
Roane State Community College *A*
South College *B*
Southern Adventist University *A, B*
Southwest Tennessee Community
College *A*
Tennessee Technological
University *B*
Tennessee Wesleyan College *B*
Trevecca Nazarene University *B*
Union University *B*
University of Phoenix
Nashville *B*
University of Tennessee
Chattanooga *B, M*
Knoxville *B, M*
Martin *B*
Vanderbilt University *M*
Walters State Community College *A*

Texas

Abilene Christian University *B*
Alvin Community College *A*
Amarillo College *A*
Angelina College *A*
Angelo State University *B*
Austin Community College *A*
Baylor University *B*
Blinn College *A*
Brazosport College *A*
Brookhaven College *A*
Central Texas College *A*
Chamberlain College of Nursing
Houston *B*
Cisco College *A*
Clarendon College *A*
Coastal Bend College *A*
Collin County Community College
District *A*
Del Mar College *A*
East Texas Baptist University *B*
El Centro College *A*
El Paso Community College *A*
Galveston College *A*
Grayson College *A*
Hallmark College of Technology *A*
Hardin-Simmons University *B, M*
Hill College *A*
Houston Baptist University *B, M*
Houston Community College
System *A*
Howard College *A*
ITT Technical Institute
Richardson *A*
Kilgore College *A*
Lamar State College at Orange *A*
Lamar State College at Port Arthur *A*
Lamar University *A, B, M*
Laredo Community College *A*
Lone Star College System *A*
Lubbock Christian University *B*
McMurry University *B*
Midland College *A*
Midwestern State University *B, M*
Mountain View College *A*
North Central Texas College *A*
Northeast Texas Community
College *A*
Odessa College *A*
Panola College *A*
Paris Junior College *A*
Prairie View A&M University *B, M*
St. Philip's College *A*
San Antonio College *A*
San Jacinto College *A*
Schreiner University *B*
South Plains College *A*
Southwest Texas Junior College *A*
Southwestern Adventist University *B*
Stephen F. Austin State University *B*
Tarleton State University *B*
Tarrant County College *A*
Temple College *A*
Texarkana College *A*
Texas A&M International
University *B*
Texas A&M University
Commerce *B*
Corpus Christi *B*
Texarkana *B*
Texas Christian University *B*
Texas State University *B*
Texas Tech University Health
Sciences Center *B, M*
Texas Woman's University *B*
Trinity Valley Community College *A*
Tyler Junior College *A*
University of Houston
Victoria *B, M*
University of Mary Hardin-Baylor *B*
University of Phoenix
Austin *B*
Dallas Fort Worth *B*

Houston Westside *B*
San Antonio *B*
University of St. Thomas *B*
University of Texas
Arlington *B*
Austin *B*
Brownsville *B, M*
El Paso *B, M*
Health Science Center at
Houston *B*
Medical Branch at Galveston *B, M*
Pan American *B*
Permian Basin *B*
Tyler *B*
University of the Incarnate
Word *B, M*
Vernon College *A*
Victoria College *A*
Wayland Baptist University *B*
West Coast University: Dallas *B*
West Texas A&M University *B, M*
Wharton County Junior College *A*

Utah

Brigham Young University *B, M*
Dixie State College *A, B*
Salt Lake Community College *A*
Southern Utah University *B*
University of Phoenix
Utah *B*
University of Utah *B, M, D*
Utah Valley University *A, B, M*
Weber State University *A, B, M*
Western Governors University *B, M*
Westminster College *B*

Vermont

Castleton State College *A, B*
Norwich University *B*
Southern Vermont College *B*
University of Vermont *B*
Vermont Technical College *A*

Virginia

Averett University *B*
Blue Ridge Community College *A*
Bluefield College *D*
Chamberlain College of Nursing
Arlington *B*
ECPI University *A, B*
Eastern Mennonite University *B*
George Mason University *B, M, D*
Germanna Community College *A*
Hampton University *B*
ITT Technical Institute
Norfolk *A*
J. Sargeant Reynolds Community
College *A*
James Madison University *B*
Jefferson College of Health
Sciences *A, B*
John Tyler Community College *A*
Liberty University *B*
Lord Fairfax Community College *A*
Lynchburg College *B*
Marymount University *B*
Mountain Empire Community
College *A*
Norfolk State University *A, B*
Old Dominion University *B, M*
Paul D. Camp Community College *A*
Piedmont Virginia Community
College *A*
Radford University *B*
Rappahannock Community College *A*
Shenandoah University *B*
Southside Virginia Community
College *A*
Southwest Virginia Community
College *A*
Tidewater Community College *A*
University of Phoenix
Northern Virginia *B*
University of Virginia *B, M, D*

University of Virginia's College at
  Wise *B*
Virginia Commonwealth University *B*
Virginia Highlands Community
  College *A*
Virginia State University *A*
Virginia Western Community
  College *A*
Wytheville Community College *A*

Washington

Bellevue College *A*
Bellingham Technical College *A*
Big Bend Community College *A*
Centralia College *A*
Clark College *A*
Clover Park Technical College *A*
Columbia Basin College *A*
Eastern Washington University *B*
Edmonds Community College *A*
Everett Community College *A*
Grays Harbor College *A*
Highline Community College *A*
Lake Washington Institute of
  Technology *A*
Lower Columbia College *A*
North Seattle Community College *A*
Northwest University *B*
Olympic College *A, B*
Pacific Lutheran University *B, M*
Peninsula College *A*
Pierce College *A*
Saint Martin's University *B*
Seattle Pacific University *B*
Seattle University *B, M*
Shoreline Community College *A*
Skagit Valley College *A*
Spokane Falls Community College *A*
Tacoma Community College *A*
University of Washington *B*
University of Washington
  Bothell *B, M*
University of Washington
  Tacoma *B, M*
Walla Walla Community College *A*
Walla Walla University *B*
Washington State University *B, M, D*
Wenatchee Valley College *A*
Whatcom Community College *A*
Whitworth University *B*
Yakima Valley Community College *A*

West Virginia

Alderson-Broaddus University *B*
American Public University System *B*
Blue Ridge Community and Technical
  College *A*
Bluefield State College *A, B*
Davis and Elkins College *A*
Fairmont State University *A, B*
Kanawha Valley Community and
  Technical College *A*
Marshall University *A, B*
Shepherd University *B*
Southern West Virginia Community
  and Technical College *A*
University of Charleston *A, B*
West Virginia Northern Community
  College *A*
West Virginia University *B, M*
West Virginia University Institute of
  Technology *B*
West Virginia University at
  Parkersburg *A*
West Virginia Wesleyan College *B, M*
Wheeling Jesuit University *B, M*

Wisconsin

Bellin College *B, M*
Beloit College *B*
Blackhawk Technical College *A*
Bryant & Stratton College
  Milwaukee *A*
Cardinal Stritch University *B, M*

Carroll University *B*
Chippewa Valley Technical College *A*
College of Menominee Nation *A*
Columbia College of Nursing *B*
Concordia University Wisconsin *B, M*
Edgewood College *B, M*
Fox Valley Technical College *A*
Gateway Technical College *A*
Herzing University
  Kenosha *B*
  Madison *A*
Lac Courte Oreilles Ojibwa
  Community College *A*
Lakeshore Technical College *A*
Madison Area Technical College *A*
Maranatha Baptist Bible College *B*
Marian University *B, M*
Marquette University *B, M, D*
Mid-State Technical College *A*
Milwaukee School of Engineering *B*
Moraine Park Technical College *A*
Nicolet Area Technical College *A*
Northcentral Technical College *A*
Northeast Wisconsin Technical
  College *A*
Rasmussen College
  Appleton *B*
  Green Bay *A, B*
  Wausau *A, B*
Silver Lake College of the Holy
  Family *B*
Southwest Wisconsin Technical
  College *A*
University of Phoenix
  Milwaukee *B*
University of Wisconsin
  Eau Claire *B, M*
  Green Bay *B*
  Madison *B, M, D*
  Milwaukee *B, M, D*
  Oshkosh *B, M*
Viterbo University *B, M*
Waukesha County Technical
  College *A*
Western Technical College *A*
Wisconsin Indianhead Technical
  College *A*
Wisconsin Lutheran College *B*

Wyoming

Casper College *A*
Central Wyoming College *A*
Laramie County Community
  College *A*
Northwest College *A*
Sheridan College *A*
University of Wyoming *B, M*

Nursing administration

Alabama

Samford University *M*
Troy University *D*

Arizona

Arizona Western College *A*
Grand Canyon University *M*
University of Phoenix
  Phoenix-Hohokam *M*
  Southern Arizona *M*

Arkansas

Arkansas Tech University *M*

California

California College San Diego *B*
California State University
  San Bernardino *M*
Charles Drew University of Medicine
  and Science *M*
Holy Names University *M*
Mount St. Mary's College *M*
Samuel Merritt University *M*

University of Phoenix
  Bay Area *M*
  Central Valley *M*
  Sacramento Valley *M*
  San Diego *M*
  Southern California *M*
University of San Diego *M*
University of San Francisco *M, D*
West Coast University: Los Angeles *M*

Colorado

Regis University *M*
University of Colorado
  Denver *M, D*
University of Phoenix
  Denver *M*

Connecticut

Fairfield University *M*
Sacred Heart University *M*
University of Hartford *M*

District of Columbia

George Washington University *M*
University of Phoenix
  Washington DC *M*

Florida

Barry University *M, D*
Nova Southeastern University *M*
University of Miami *M*
University of Phoenix
  Central Florida *M*
  North Florida *M*
  South Florida *M*
  West Florida *M*

Georgia

Columbus State University *D*
Georgia College and State
  University *M*
Kennesaw State University *M*
University of Phoenix
  Atlanta *M*
  Augusta *M*
  Columbus *M*
  Savannah *M*

Hawaii

University of Phoenix
  Hawaii *M*

Illinois

Bradley University *M*
DePaul University *M*
Lewis University *M*
Loyola University Chicago *M*
North Park University *M*
Saint Xavier University *M*
Southern Illinois University
  Edwardsville *M*
University of St. Francis *M*

Indiana

Anderson University *M*
Ball State University *D*
Bethel College *M*
Indiana University
  Purdue University Fort Wayne *M*
  Purdue University Indianapolis *M*
Indiana Wesleyan University *M*
University of Indianapolis *M*
University of Phoenix
  Indianapolis *M*

Iowa

Allen College *M*
Clarke University *M*
University of Iowa *M, D*

Kansas

University of St. Mary *M*
Washburn University *M*

Kentucky

Kentucky Christian University *B*
Spalding University *M*
University of Louisville *M*

Louisiana

Louisiana State University
  Health Sciences Center *M*
Our Lady of the Lake College *M*
University of Phoenix
  Baton Rouge *M*
  Louisiana *M*

Maine

Husson University *M*
Saint Joseph's College of Maine *M*
University of Southern Maine *M*

Massachusetts

Elms College *M*
Endicott College *M*
Northeastern University *M*
Regis College *M*
Salem State University *M*
University of Massachusetts
  Boston *M, D*

Michigan

Andrews University *M*
Ferris State University *M*
Saginaw Valley State University *M*
Spring Arbor University *M*
University of Detroit Mercy *M*
University of Michigan *M*
University of Phoenix
  Metro Detroit *M*
  West Michigan *M*

Minnesota

Bethel University *M*
College of St. Scholastica *M*
Metropolitan State University *M*
Saint Cloud State University *M*
University of Minnesota
  Twin Cities *D*
University of Phoenix
  Minneapolis-St. Paul *M*

Mississippi

University of Southern Mississippi *M*

Missouri

Grantham University *B, M*
Missouri State University *B, M*
Research College of Nursing *M*
University of Phoenix
  St. Louis *M*

Nebraska

Clarkson College *M*
Nebraska Wesleyan University *M*

Nevada

University of Nevada
  Reno *M*
University of Phoenix
  Las Vegas *M*

New Hampshire

Franklin Pierce University *M*
Southern New Hampshire
  University *M*

New Jersey

Felician College *B, M*
Seton Hall University *M*

New York

Adelphi University *M*
City University of New York
  Hunter College *M*
College of Mount St. Vincent *M*
College of New Rochelle *M*

Le Moyne College *M*
Mercy College *B, M*
New York University *M*
Roberts Wesleyan College *M*
SUNY
University at Buffalo *M*
Sage Colleges *D*
Wagner College *M*

North Carolina
Queens University of Charlotte *M*

North Dakota
University of Mary *M*

Ohio
Ashland University *B*
Capital University *B, M*
Ohio University *M*
Otterbein University *M*
University of Cincinnati *M*
University of Phoenix
Cleveland *M*
Wright State University *M*
Xavier University *M*

Oklahoma
Oklahoma City University *B, M*
University of Phoenix
Oklahoma City *M*

Pennsylvania
California University of
Pennsylvania *M*
Carlow University *M*
DeSales University *M*
Holy Family University *M*
University of Pennsylvania *M*
Villanova University *M, D*
Widener University *M*
York College of Pennsylvania *M*

Puerto Rico
Universidad Metropolitana *M*

South Carolina
Medical University of South
Carolina *M*
University of South Carolina
Columbia *M*

Tennessee
Union University *M*
Vanderbilt University *M*

Texas
Baylor University *M*
Lubbock Christian University *M*
Paris Junior College *A*
Texas A&M University
Corpus Christi *M*
Texarkana *M*
Texas Christian University *D*
Texas Tech University Health
Sciences Center *M*
Texas Woman's University *M*
University of Phoenix
Austin *M*
Dallas Fort Worth *M*
Houston Westside *M*
San Antonio *M*
University of Texas
Arlington *M*
Brownsville *M*
El Paso *M*
Medical Branch at Galveston *M*
Tyler *M*
University of the Incarnate Word *M*

Utah
University of Phoenix
Utah *M*
Westminster College *M*

Vermont
Norwich University *M*

Virginia
Eastern Mennonite University *M*
Jefferson College of Health
Sciences *M*
University of Phoenix
Northern Virginia *M*

Washington
Gonzaga University *M*
Seattle Pacific University *M*
University of Washington Tacoma *B*

West Virginia
Marshall University *D*
West Virginia Wesleyan College *M*
Wheeling Jesuit University *M*

Wisconsin
University of Wisconsin
Oshkosh *M*
Viterbo University *M*

Nursing assistant

Alabama
Alabama Southern Community
College *C, A*
Bevill State Community College *C*
Bishop State Community College *C*
Gadsden State Community College *C*
George C. Wallace State Community
College at Selma *C*
Jefferson Davis Community
College *C*
Lawson State Community College *C*
Northwest-Shoals Community
College *C*
Shelton State Community College *C*

Alaska
Ilisagvik College *C*
University of Alaska
Fairbanks *C*

Arizona
Arizona Western College *C*
Brookline College
Phoenix *C*
Tucson *C*
Central Arizona College *A*
Chandler-Gilbert Community
College *C, A*
Cochise College *C*
Coconino County Community
College *C, A*
Eastern Arizona College *C*
GateWay Community College *C*
Mesa Community College *C*
Northland Pioneer College *C*
Paradise Valley Community College *C*
Phoenix College *C*
Rio Salado College *C, A*
Scottsdale Community College *C*

Arkansas
Arkansas State University
Beebe *C*
Mountain Home *C*
Arkansas Tech University *C*
Black River Technical College *C*
College of the Ouachitas *C*
National Park Community College *C*
North Arkansas College *C*
Northwest Arkansas Community
College *C*
Rich Mountain Community College *C*
South Arkansas Community
College *C*
Southeast Arkansas College *C*
Southern Arkansas University Tech *C*

University of Arkansas
Community College at Hope *C*
Community College at Morrilton *C*

California
Allan Hancock College *C*
Bakersfield College *C*
Chaffey College *C*
City College of San Francisco *C*
College of the Desert *C*
College of the Sequoias *C*
College of the Siskiyous *C*
Contra Costa College *C*
Copper Mountain College *C*
Gavilan College *C*
Kaplan College
Vista *C*
Lassen Community College *C*
Long Beach City College *C*
Los Angeles Harbor College *C*
Merritt College *C*
MiraCosta College *C*
Modesto Junior College *C*
Palo Verde College *C*
Rio Hondo College *C*
Santa Barbara City College *C*
Santa Rosa Junior College *C, A*
Shasta College *C*
Southwestern College *C*
Yuba College *C*

Colorado
Aims Community College *C*
Arapahoe Community College *C*
Colorado Mesa University *C*
Colorado Mountain College *C*
Community College of Denver *C*
Front Range Community College *C*
Lamar Community College *C*
Morgan Community College *C*
Northeastern Junior College *C*
Otero Junior College *C*
Pueblo Community College *C*
Red Rocks Community College *C*
Trinidad State Junior College *C*

Connecticut
Capital Community College *C*
Northwestern Connecticut
Community College *C*

Delaware
Delaware Technical Community
College
Jack F. Owens Campus *C*
Stanton/Wilmington Campus *C*
Terry Campus *C*

Florida
Chipola College *C*
Eastern Florida State College *C*
Florida Gateway College *C*
Florida National University *C*
Florida State College at
Jacksonville *C*
Florida Technical College
Orlando *C*
Fortis College
Orange Park *C*
Winter Park *C*
Gulf Coast State College *C*
Indian River State College *C*
North Florida Community
College *C, A*
Palm Beach State College *C*
Pasco-Hernando State College *C*
Pensacola State College *C*
Saint Johns River State College *C*
Santa Fe College *C*
Seminole State College of Florida *C*
South Florida State College *C*
Tallahassee Community College *C*

Georgia
Albany Technical College *C*
Athens Technical College *C*
Atlanta Technical College *C*
Bainbridge College *C*
Central Georgia Technical College *C*
Columbus Technical College *C*
Georgia Piedmont Technical
College *C*
Gwinnett Technical College *C*
Savannah Technical College *C*
Southeastern Technical College *C*
Southwest Georgia Technical
College *C*
West Georgia Technical College *C*

Hawaii
University of Hawaii
Hawaii Community College *C*
Kapiolani Community College *A*
Kauai Community College *C*

Illinois
Black Hawk College *C*
City Colleges of Chicago
Harold Washington College *C*
Harry S. Truman College *C*
Kennedy-King College *C*
Malcolm X College *C*
Olive-Harvey College *C*
Richard J. Daley College *C*
Wilbur Wright College *C*
College of DuPage *C*
College of Lake County *C*
Danville Area Community College *C*
East-West University *C*
Elgin Community College *C*
Harper College *C*
Heartland Community College *C*
Highland Community College *C*
Illinois Eastern Community Colleges
Frontier Community College *C*
Lincoln Trail College *C*
Olney Central College *C*
Wabash Valley College *C*
Illinois Valley Community College *C*
John A. Logan College *C*
John Wood Community College *C*
Kankakee Community College *C*
Kaskaskia College *C*
Kishwaukee College *C*
Lewis and Clark Community
College *C*
Lincoln Land Community College *C*
McHenry County College *C*
Morton College *C*
Parkland College *C*
Prairie State College *C*
Rend Lake College *C*
Richland Community College *C*
Rock Valley College *C*
Sauk Valley Community College *C*
South Suburban College of Cook
County *C*
Southeastern Illinois College *C*
Southwestern Illinois College *C*
Spoon River College *C*
Triton College *C*
Waubonsee Community College *C*

Iowa
Des Moines Area Community
College *C*
Iowa Central Community College *C*
Iowa Lakes Community College *C*
Mercy College of Health Sciences *C*
North Iowa Area Community
College *C*

Kansas
Allen County Community College *A*
Barton County Community College *C*
Brown Mackie College
Salina *C*

Cloud County Community College *C*
Coffeyville Community College *A*
Colby Community College *C*
Cowley County Community
College *C, A*
Dodge City Community College *A*
Highland Community College *C*
Hutchinson Community College *C*
Independence Community College *C*
Johnson County Community
College *C*
Kansas City Kansas Community
College *C*
Neosho County Community
College *C*
Wichita Area Technical College *C*

Kentucky
Owensboro Community and
Technical College *C*
Spencerian College *C*

Maryland
Allegany College of Maryland *C*
College of Southern Maryland *C*

Massachusetts
Bunker Hill Community College *C*
Cape Cod Community College *C*
Middlesex Community College *C*

Michigan
Baker College
Flint *C*
Delta College *C*
Gogebic Community College *C*
Henry Ford Community College *C*
Kellogg Community College *C*
Lansing Community College *C*
Montcalm Community College *C*
Schoolcraft College *C*
West Shore Community College *A*

Minnesota
Alexandria Technical and Community
College *C*
Anoka Technical College *C*
Century College *C*
Dakota County Technical College *C*
Fond du Lac Tribal and Community
College *C*
Inver Hills Community College *C*
Itasca Community College *C*
Lake Superior College *C*
Mesabi Range Community and
Technical College *C*
Minneapolis Community and
Technical College *C*
Minnesota State College - Southeast
Technical *C*
Normandale Community College *C*
Northland Community & Technical
College *C*
Northwest Technical College *C*
Ridgewater College *C*
Rochester Community and Technical
College *C*
St. Cloud Technical and Community
College *C*
St. Paul College *C*
South Central College *C*

Mississippi
East Mississippi Community
College *C*
Hinds Community College *C*
Itawamba Community College *C*
Meridian Community College *C*
Mississippi Gulf Coast Community
College *C*
Northwest Mississippi Community
College *C*
Southwest Mississippi Community
College *C*

Missouri
Bolivar Technical College *C*
Moberly Area Community College *C*
State Fair Community College *C*

Montana
Montana Tech of the University of
Montana *C*

Nebraska
BryanLGH College of Health
Sciences *C*
Nebraska Methodist College of
Nursing and Allied Health *C*

New Jersey
Berkeley College *C*

New Mexico
Central New Mexico Community
College *C*
Dona Ana Community College of
New Mexico State University *C*
Eastern New Mexico University:
Roswell *C*
Navajo Technical University *C, A*
Northern New Mexico College *C*
Western New Mexico University *C*

New York
Mildred Elley
New York City *C*
Monroe College *C, A*
Westchester Community College *C, A*

North Carolina
Beaufort County Community
College *C*
Bladen Community College *C*
Brunswick Community College *C*
Cabarrus College of Health
Sciences *C*
Carolinas College of Health
Sciences *C*
Carteret Community College *C*
Central Carolina Community
College *C*
Central Piedmont Community
College *C*
Cleveland Community College *C*
Coastal Carolina Community
College *C*
College of the Albemarle *C*
Edgecombe Community College *C*
Fayetteville Technical Community
College *C*
Gaston College *C*
Halifax Community College *C*
Haywood Community College *C*
McDowell Technical Community
College *C*
Mitchell Community College *C*
Nash Community College *C*
Randolph Community College *C*
Richmond Community College *C*
Robeson Community College *C*
Sampson Community College *C*
Sandhills Community College *C*
Southeastern Community
College *C, A*
Stanly Community College *C*
Tri-County Community College *C*
Vance-Granville Community
College *C*

North Dakota
Fort Berthold Community College *A*

Ohio
Central Ohio Technical College *C*
Cincinnati State Technical and
Community College *C*

Columbus State Community
College *C*
Sinclair Community College *C*

Oregon
Southwestern Oregon Community
College *C*
Umpqua Community College *C*

Pennsylvania
Commonwealth Technical Institute *C*
Community College of Allegheny
County *C*
Delaware County Community
College *C*
Erie Business Center *C*
Everest Institute: Pittsburgh *C*
Pennsylvania Institute of
Technology *C*

Puerto Rico
Universidad Metropolitana *A, B, M*
Universidad del Este *C*

South Carolina
Forrest Junior College *C*
Trident Technical College *C*
Williamsburg Technical College *C*
York Technical College *C*

South Dakota
Oglala Lakota College *A*

Tennessee
Miller-Motte Technical College
Chattanooga *C*

Texas
Cedar Valley College *C*
El Centro College *C*
El Paso Community College *C*
Galveston College *C*
Howard College *C*
Lamar State College at Port Arthur *C*
Paris Junior College *C*
South Plains College *C*
South Texas College *A*
Texas State Technical College
Harlingen *C*

Utah
Dixie State College *C*
Salt Lake Community College *C*

Virginia
Germanna Community College *C*
Mountain Empire Community
College *C*
Rappahannock Community College *C*
Southside Virginia Community
College *C*
Virginia Western Community
College *C*

Washington
Bellingham Technical College *C*
Big Bend Community College *C*
Centralia College *C*
Clark College *C*
Clover Park Technical College *C*
Columbia Basin College *C*
Everett Community College *C*
Grays Harbor College *C*
Lower Columbia College *C, A*
North Seattle Community College *C*
Olympic College *C*
Pierce College *C*
Renton Technical College *C*
South Puget Sound Community
College *C, A*
South Seattle Community College *C*
Tacoma Community College *C*
Wenatchee Valley College *C*

West Virginia
West Virginia Northern Community
College *C*

Wisconsin
Blackhawk Technical College *C*
Chippewa Valley Technical College *C*
College of Menominee Nation *C*
Fox Valley Technical College *C*
Gateway Technical College *C*
Lakeshore Technical College *C*
Madison Area Technical College *C*
Mid-State Technical College *C*
Milwaukee Area Technical College *C*
Moraine Park Technical College *C*
Nicolet Area Technical College *C*
Northcentral Technical College *C*
Northeast Wisconsin Technical
College *C*
Southwest Wisconsin Technical
College *C*
Waukesha County Technical
College *C*
Western Technical College *C*
Wisconsin Indianhead Technical
College *C*

Wyoming
Central Wyoming College *C*
Northwest College *C*

Nursing education

Alabama
University of South Alabama *C*

Alaska
University of Alaska
Anchorage *M*

Arizona
University of Phoenix
Phoenix-Hohokam *M*
Southern Arizona *M*

California
Mount St. Mary's College *M*
University of Phoenix
Bay Area *M*
Central Valley *M*
Sacramento Valley *M*
San Diego *M*
Southern California *M*

Colorado
Regis University *C*
University of Phoenix
Denver *M*

Connecticut
Sacred Heart University *M*
Southern Connecticut State
University *M, D*

District of Columbia
University of Phoenix
Washington DC *M*
University of the District of
Columbia *B*

Florida
Florida Southern College *M*
South Florida State College *A*
University of Phoenix
Central Florida *M*
North Florida *M*
South Florida *M*

Georgia
Georgia Southern University *T*
Mercer University *M*
University of North Georgia *M*

University of Phoenix
Augusta *M*
University of West Georgia *D*

Hawaii
University of Phoenix
Hawaii *M*

Illinois
Methodist College *B*
Northwestern College *A*
Southern Illinois University
Edwardsville *M*

Indiana
Indiana University
Purdue University Indianapolis *C*
University of Indianapolis *M*
Valparaiso University *M*

Iowa
Allen College *M*
Mount Mercy University *M*

Kansas
University of St. Mary *M*

Kentucky
Spalding University *M*
Western Kentucky University *C*

Louisiana
Louisiana State University
Health Sciences Center *M*

Massachusetts
University of Massachusetts
Lowell *C*

Michigan
Northern Michigan University *D*
Oakland University *M*
University of Phoenix
Metro Detroit *M*
West Michigan *M*

Minnesota
Bethel University *T*
Metropolitan State University *M*
University of Phoenix
Minneapolis-St. Paul *M*
Winona State University *M*

Missouri
Missouri State University *M*

Nebraska
Kaplan University
Lincoln *M*

Nevada
University of Phoenix
Las Vegas *M*

New Jersey
Passaic County Community College *A*

New Mexico
University of Phoenix
New Mexico *M*

New York
Adelphi University *M*
Daemen College *M*
Le Moyne College *M*
Long Island University
LIU Brooklyn *M*
LIU Post *M*
Molloy College *M*
New York University *M*
Pace University *M*
Roberts Wesleyan College *M*

SUNY
Institute of Technology at Utica/
Rome *M*
St. Joseph's College New York:
Suffolk Campus *M*
St. Joseph's College, New York *M*

North Carolina
Western Piedmont Community
College *A*

North Dakota
University of Mary *M*

Ohio
Cleveland State University *M*
Lourdes University *M*
Walsh University *M*

Oklahoma
Northeastern State University *M*
Oklahoma City University *M*

Oregon
Oregon Health & Science
University *M*

Pennsylvania
Alvernia University *M*
Carlow University *M*
DeSales University *M*
Gwynedd Mercy University *M*
Holy Family University *M*
Messiah College *M*
Millersville University of
Pennsylvania *T*
Neumann University *M*
Widener University *M, D*

South Dakota
National American University
Rapid City *M*
South Dakota State University *C*

Tennessee
Aquinas College *M*

Texas
McMurry University *M*
Midwestern State University *M*
Texas Christian University *M*
Texas Tech University Health
Sciences Center *M*
University of Phoenix
Austin *M*
Dallas Fort Worth *M*
University of Texas
Arlington *M*
Medical Branch at Galveston *M*
Tyler *M*
Wayland Baptist University *M*

Utah
University of Phoenix
Utah *M*
Western Governors University *M*

Virginia
Jefferson College of Health
Sciences *M*
Lynchburg College *M*
University of Phoenix
Northern Virginia *M*

Washington
Gonzaga University *M*

West Virginia
West Virginia Wesleyan College *M*
Wheeling Jesuit University *M*

Wisconsin
Bellin College *M*

Nursing practice

Alabama
Samford University *D*
University of Alabama *D*
University of Alabama
Huntsville *D*
University of South Alabama *C*
Virginia College
Birmingham *A*

Arizona
Glendale Community College *C*
Northern Arizona University *D*
University of Arizona *D*

Arkansas
Arkansas State University *D*
University of Arkansas *D*
University of Central Arkansas *D*

California
California State University
Fresno *D*
Fullerton *D*
Charles Drew University of Medicine
and Science *M*
Everest College
Ontario Metro *A*
La Sierra University *C*
National University *M*
San Jose State University *D*
Simpson University *B*
University of San Diego *D*

Colorado
American Sentinel University *D*
Colorado Mesa University *D*
Regis University *D*

Connecticut
Fairfield University *D*
Sacred Heart University *D*
University of Connecticut *M, D*
Yale University *D*

Florida
Florida Atlantic University *D*
Florida International University *D*
Florida Southern College *M*
Florida State University *D*
University of Central Florida *D*
University of Miami *D*
University of North Florida *D*

Georgia
Altamaha Technical College *C*
Brenau University *B*
Columbus Technical College *C*

Hawaii
University of Hawaii
Hilo *D*

Illinois
DePaul University *M*
Lewis University *D*
Loyola University Chicago *D*
St. Francis Medical Center College of
Nursing *D*
Southern Illinois University
Edwardsville *D*
University of St. Francis *D*

Indiana
Huntington University *B*
Valparaiso University *D*

Iowa
Graceland University *D*
Iowa Wesleyan College *B*

Kansas
Benedictine College *B*
University of Kansas Medical
Center *D*
Wright Career College
Wichita *A*

Kentucky
Murray State University *D*
Northern Kentucky University *D*
Union College *B*
University of Kentucky *D*
Western Kentucky University *D*

Louisiana
Northwestern State University *D*
Southeastern Louisiana University *D*
Southern University and Agricultural
and Mechanical College *D*

Maryland
Salisbury University *D*
University of Maryland
Baltimore *D*

Massachusetts
University of Massachusetts
Amherst *D*
Lowell *D*

Michigan
Madonna University *D*
Oakland University *M, D*
University of Michigan
Flint *M, D*

Minnesota
Rasmussen College
Blaine *A*
Walden University *D*

Mississippi
Hinds Community College *A*
University of Southern Mississippi *M*

Missouri
University of Missouri
Kansas City *D*
St. Louis *D*

Nebraska
University of Nebraska
Medical Center *D*

Nevada
University of Nevada
Reno *D*

New Hampshire
Franklin Pierce University *M*

New Jersey
Rutgers, The State University of New
Jersey
Camden Campus *D*
Newark Campus *D*
Saint Peter's University *D*
Seton Hall University *D*

New Mexico
New Mexico State University *D*

New York
ASA College *A*
City University of New York
CUNY Online *B*
Daemen College *D*
New York University *B*
SUNY
University at Stony Brook *D*

North Carolina
University of North Carolina
　Chapel Hill *D*
　Charlotte *D*

North Dakota
University of North Dakota *D*

Ohio
Case Western Reserve
　University *M, D*
College of Mount St. Joseph *D*
University of Akron *C*
University of Cincinnati *D*
Ursuline College *D*
Walsh University *D*

Oklahoma
Oklahoma City University *D*

Oregon
Oregon Health & Science
　University *D*

Pennsylvania
Carlow University *D*
DeSales University *D*
Duquesne University *D*
Eastern University *B*
Gannon University *D*
Gwynedd Mercy University *D*
Misericordia University *B*
Widener University *D*
Wilkes University *D*
York College of Pennsylvania *D*

South Carolina
Newberry College *B*

Tennessee
Christian Brothers University *B*
Vanderbilt University *D*

Texas
Baylor University *D*
Texas Christian University *D*
Texas Tech University Health
　Sciences Center *D*
University of Texas
　Arlington *D*
　Medical Branch at Galveston *D*
University of the Incarnate Word *D*

Virginia
George Mason University *D*
Marymount University *D*
Shenandoah University *M, D*

Washington
Gonzaga University *M, D*
Seattle University *D*

West Virginia
West Virginia University *D*
Wheeling Jesuit University *M*

Wisconsin
Marquette University *D*
University of Wisconsin
　Eau Claire *D*
　Madison *D*
　Milwaukee *D*

Wyoming
University of Wyoming *D*

Nursing science

Alabama
University of Alabama
　Birmingham *D*

Arkansas
University of Arkansas
　for Medical Sciences *B, M, D*

California
California State University
　Stanislaus *B, M*
University of California
　Irvine *B, M, D*
University of San Diego *D*
West Coast University: Orange
　County *B*

Colorado
University of Northern Colorado *D*

Connecticut
University of Connecticut *D*
Yale University *D*

Florida
Brown Mackie College
　Miami *A*
Florida Atlantic University *D*
Florida International University *D*
Pensacola State College *B*
University of Central Florida *D*
University of Florida *D*
University of Miami *D*
University of South Florida *D*
Valencia College *A*

Georgia
Emory University *M, D*
Georgia College and State
　University *D*
Georgia Regents University *D*
Georgia Southern University *D*
Kennesaw State University *D*
Mercer University *D*
North Georgia Technical College *A*

Hawaii
University of Hawaii
　Manoa *D*

Illinois
Benedictine University at
　Springfield *B*
DePaul University *M*
Governors State University *M, D*
Illinois State University *D*
Loyola University Chicago *D*
Northern Illinois University *M*
University of Illinois
　Chicago *M, D*

Indiana
Indiana University
　Purdue University Indianapolis *D*

Iowa
University of Iowa *M, D*
William Penn University *B*

Kansas
Pittsburg State University *M*
University of Kansas Medical
　Center *M, D*
Wichita State University *B, M, D*

Kentucky
Lindsey Wilson College *B*
Union College *B*
University of Kentucky *D*
University of Louisville *M*

Louisiana
Louisiana State University
　Health Sciences Center *D*
Our Lady of the Lake College *M*
Southern University and Agricultural
　and Mechanical College *D*

Maryland
Notre Dame of Maryland
　University *B, M*
University of Maryland
　Baltimore *M, D*

Massachusetts
Elms College *M*
Regis College *D*
Salem State University *M*
Simmons College *B, M, D*
University of Massachusetts
　Amherst *M, D*
　Boston *M*
　Dartmouth *D*
　Lowell *M, D*

Michigan
Michigan State University *D*
Northern Michigan University *B, M*
Spring Arbor University *B*
Wayne State University *B, D*

Minnesota
College of St. Scholastica *D*
Metropolitan State University *M, D*
Minnesota State University
　Mankato *D*
Saint Cloud State University *M*
Winona State University *D*

Missouri
University of Missouri
　St. Louis *D*

Nebraska
Bellevue University *B*
Clarkson College *M*
Creighton University *M, D*
University of Nebraska
　Medical Center *D*

New Jersey
College of St. Elizabeth *M*
Fairleigh Dickinson University
　Metropolitan Campus *D*
Kean University *B, M, D, T*
Monmouth University *M, D*
Ramapo College of New Jersey *B, M*
Rowan University *B, M*
Rutgers, The State University of New
　Jersey
　New Brunswick/Piscataway
　　Campus *B, M, D*
　Newark Campus *B, M, D*
Seton Hall University *M, D*
William Paterson University of New
　Jersey *B, M, D*

New Mexico
New Mexico State University *D*
University of New Mexico *D*

New York
Adelphi University *D*
New York University *D*
SUNY
　University at Binghamton *D*
University of Rochester *D*

North Carolina
Duke University *B, D*
East Carolina University *D*
University of North Carolina
　Chapel Hill *D*
　Greensboro *D, T*
Wingate University *B*

Ohio
Ashland University *B*
Case Western Reserve
　University *M, D*
Cleveland State University *M*

University of Toledo *D*
Wright State University *D*

Oklahoma
Oklahoma City University *B, M, D*

Pennsylvania
DeSales University *M*
Drexel University *D*
Duquesne University *D*
Fortis Institute
　Erie *A*
Immaculata University *M*
Indiana University of Pennsylvania *D*
Millersville University of
　Pennsylvania *B*
Moravian College *M*
Widener University *D*

Puerto Rico
Columbia Centro Universitario:
　Caguas *M*
Inter American University of Puerto
　Rico
　San German Campus *A, B*
National University College
　Arecibo *A, B*
　Bayamon *A, B*
　Ponce *A, B*
　Rio Grande *A, B*

Rhode Island
University of Rhode Island *M, D*

South Carolina
Clemson University *M*
Medical University of South
　Carolina *D*
University of South Carolina
　Columbia *M, D*

South Dakota
Mount Marty College *M*
South Dakota State University *D*

Tennessee
East Tennessee State University *D*
University of Tennessee
　Knoxville *D*
Vanderbilt University *M, D*

Texas
Our Lady of the Lake University of
　San Antonio *B, M*
Texas Woman's University *D*
University of Texas
　Arlington *D*
　Austin *D*
　Medical Branch at Galveston *D*
　Tyler *D*

Vermont
University of Vermont *M*

Virginia
Hampton University *M, D*
Virginia Commonwealth
　University *M, D*

West Virginia
West Virginia University *D*

Nutrition sciences

Alabama
Auburn University *B, M, D*
Community College of the Air
　Force *A*
University of Alabama
　Birmingham *D*

Arizona
University of Arizona *B, M, D*

Arkansas

University of Arkansas
for Medical Sciences *M*

California

Chapman University *M*
Pepperdine University *B*
University of California
Berkeley *B, M, D*
Davis *B, M, D*

Colorado

Metropolitan State University of
Denver *B*
University of Northern Colorado *B*

Connecticut

University of Connecticut *B, M, D*
University of Saint Joseph *M*

Delaware

University of Delaware *B, M*

District of Columbia

Howard University *B, M, D*

Florida

University of Florida *D*

Georgia

Life University *A, B*
University of Georgia *B*

Hawaii

University of Hawaii
Manoa *B, M*

Illinois

Rush University *M*
Southern Illinois University
Carbondale *B*
University of Chicago *M*
University of Illinois
Urbana-Champaign *M, D*

Indiana

Purdue University *B, M, D*
University of Southern Indiana *B*

Iowa

University of Iowa *M, D*

Kansas

University of Kansas Medical
Center *M, D*

Kentucky

University of Kentucky *M, D*

Louisiana

Louisiana State University and
Agricultural and Mechanical
College *B*
McNeese State University *B*

Massachusetts

Boston University *B, M, D*
Tufts University *M, D*
University of Massachusetts
Amherst *B, M*
Lowell *C, B*

Michigan

Michigan State University *B*
University of Michigan *M, D*

Minnesota

College of St. Benedict *B*
Concordia College: Moorhead *B*
St. John's University *B*
University of Minnesota
Twin Cities *B, M, D*

Missouri

Southeast Missouri State University *M*
University of Missouri
Columbia *B, M, D*

Nebraska

University of Nebraska
Lincoln *M, D*

Nevada

University of Nevada
Las Vegas *B*
Reno *B*

New Hampshire

University of New Hampshire *B, M*

New Jersey

Rutgers, The State University of New
Jersey
New Brunswick/Piscataway
Campus *B, M, D*

New York

Canisius College *M*
City University of New York
Brooklyn College *M*
Cornell University *B, M, D*
Long Island University
LIU Post *B, M*
New York Institute of Technology *M*
SUNY
University at Buffalo *M*
Sage Colleges *B, M*
Syracuse University *B, M*

North Carolina

North Carolina State University *M, D*
University of North Carolina
Chapel Hill *M, D*
Greensboro *B, M, D*

Ohio

Ashland University *B*
Case Western Reserve
University *B, M, D*
Ohio State University
Columbus Campus *B*
University of Cincinnati *C, B, M*
University of Cincinnati
Blue Ash College *A*

Oklahoma

Tulsa Community College *A*
University of Central Oklahoma *M*
University of Oklahoma *B, M*

Pennsylvania

Drexel University *B, M*
La Salle University *B*
Messiah College *B*

Puerto Rico

University of Puerto Rico
Medical Sciences *M*

Rhode Island

Johnson & Wales University
Providence *B*

Texas

Baylor University *M*
St. Philip's College *A*
Texas A&M University *M, D*
Texas Woman's University *B, M, D*
University of Texas
Austin *M, D*
University of the Incarnate
Word *B, M*

Utah

Brigham Young University *B, M*
University of Utah *M*

Vermont

University of Vermont *B, M*

Washington

Bastyr University *B, M*
University of Washington *M, D*

Wisconsin

University of Wisconsin
Madison *B, M, D*
Milwaukee *C, B*

Wyoming

Casper College *A*

Occupational/ environmental health nursing

Ohio

University of Cincinnati *M*

Pennsylvania

University of Pennsylvania *M*

Occupational health/ industrial hygiene

Arkansas

University of Arkansas
for Medical Sciences *M*

Hawaii

University of Hawaii
Honolulu Community College *A*

Illinois

Illinois State University *B*

Indiana

Purdue University *B, M*

Massachusetts

Harvard College *M, D*
University of Massachusetts
Lowell *M, D, T*

Michigan

Grand Valley State University *B*
Oakland University *B, M*

Mississippi

Itawamba Community College *A*

Missouri

University of Central Missouri *M*

Montana

Montana Tech of the University of
Montana *B, M*

North Carolina

Durham Technical Community
College *A*
East Carolina University *M*
North Carolina Agricultural and
Technical State University *B*
St. Augustine's University *B*

Ohio

Ohio University *B*
University of Cincinnati *M, D*
University of Findlay *B*
University of Toledo *M*

Oklahoma

University of Central Oklahoma *B*

Pennsylvania

University of Pittsburgh *M*

Puerto Rico

Bayamon Central University *B*
University of Puerto Rico
Medical Sciences *M*
University of the Sacred Heart *M*

Texas

Laredo Community College *A*
North Central Texas College *A*

Utah

University of Utah *M*

Occupational safety/ health technology

Alabama

Columbia Southern
University *C, A, B, M*
Jacksonville State University *B*

Alaska

University of Alaska
Anchorage *A*

Arizona

GateWay Community College *C, A*

California

DeVry University
Pomona *B*
Southwestern College *C, A*

Colorado

Trinidad State Junior College *C, A*

Connecticut

University of Connecticut *M*

Florida

Embry-Riddle Aeronautical
University *B*

Georgia

Georgia Southern University *T*

Hawaii

University of Hawaii
Honolulu Community College *C, A*

Indiana

Indiana State University *B*
Indiana University
Bloomington *A*
Ivy Tech Community College
Central Indiana *A*
East Central *C, A*
Kokomo *C, A*
North Central *C, A*
Northeast *A*
Northwest *A*
Southwest *C, A*
Wabash Valley *C, A*

Iowa

Clinton Community College *A*

Kentucky

Murray State University *B, M*

Louisiana

Southeastern Louisiana University *B*

Maryland

Anne Arundel Community
College *C, A*
Community College of Baltimore
County *C, A*

Massachusetts

Anna Maria College *M*

Michigan

Grand Valley State University *B*
Madonna University *C*

Minnesota

South Central College *C, A*
University of Minnesota
   Duluth *M*

Missouri

Mineral Area College *A*

New Hampshire

Keene State College *B*

New Jersey

New Jersey Institute of
   Technology *M*
Rider University *C*

New Mexico

Central New Mexico Community
   College *C*
San Juan College *C, A*

New York

Rochester Institute of
   Technology *C, B*

North Carolina

Central Piedmont Community
   College *A*
Methodist University *B*
North Carolina Agricultural and
   Technical State University *B*

North Dakota

University of North Dakota *B*

Ohio

Cincinnati State Technical and
   Community College *C, A*
Columbus State Community
   College *C*
James A. Rhodes State College *C*
Ohio University
   Chillicothe Campus *C*

Oklahoma

Southeastern Oklahoma State
   University *B*

Pennsylvania

Indiana University of
   Pennsylvania *B, M*
Millersville University of
   Pennsylvania *B*
Slippery Rock University of
   Pennsylvania *B*

Texas

Del Mar College *A*
Kilgore College *C, A*
Lamar Institute of Technology *A*
Odessa College *C, A*
St. Philip's College *C, A*
San Antonio College *C, A*
San Jacinto College *C, A*
Tarrant County College *C, A*
Texas State Technical College
   Waco *A*
University of Houston
   Downtown *B*

Virginia

Tidewater Community College *A*

Washington

Edmonds Community College *C, A*
Pierce College *A*

West Virginia

Blue Ridge Community and Technical
   College *A*
Fairmont State University *A, B*
Marshall University *B, M*

Wisconsin

University of Wisconsin
   Stout *M*
   Whitewater *B, M*

Wyoming

Central Wyoming College *C, A*

Occupational therapy

Alabama

Oakwood University *A*
University of Alabama
   Birmingham *M*
University of South Alabama *M*

Arkansas

University of Central Arkansas *M*

California

California State University
   Dominguez Hills *M*
Dominican University of California *M*
Loma Linda University *M, D*
Samuel Merritt University *M*
San Jose State University *M*
University of Southern
   California *B, M, D*

Colorado

Colorado State University *M, D*

Connecticut

Quinnipiac University *M*
Sacred Heart University *M*

District of Columbia

Trinity Washington University *B*

Florida

Barry University *M*
Florida Agricultural and Mechanical
   University *M*
Florida Gulf Coast University *M*
Florida International University *M*
Nova Southeastern University *M, D*
University of Florida *M*

Georgia

Brenau University *M*
Georgia Regents University *M*

Idaho

Idaho State University *M*

Illinois

Dominican University *B*
Governors State University *M, D*
Rush University *M*
University of Illinois
   Chicago *M, D*

Indiana

Purdue University *B*
University of Indianapolis *M, D*
University of Southern Indiana *M*

Iowa

St. Ambrose University *M*

Kansas

University of Kansas Medical
   Center *M, D*

Kentucky

Eastern Kentucky University *M*
Spalding University *M*

Louisiana

Louisiana State University
   Health Sciences Center *M*

Maine

Husson University *M*
University of New England *M*
University of Southern Maine *M*

Maryland

Community College of Baltimore
   County *A*
Towson University *B, M, D*

Massachusetts

American International College *M*
Bay Path College *M*
Boston University *M, D*
Quinsigamond Community College *A*
Salem State University *M*
Springfield College *M*
University of Massachusetts
   Lowell *M*
Worcester State University *M*

Michigan

Baker College
   Flint *D*
   Port Huron *M*
Calvin College *M*
Eastern Michigan University *M*
Grand Rapids Community College *A*
Grand Valley State University *M*
Saginaw Valley State University *M*
Wayne State University *M*
Western Michigan University *B, M*

Minnesota

College of St. Scholastica *M*
St. Catherine University *M*
University of Minnesota
   Twin Cities *M*

Mississippi

Hinds Community College *A*

Missouri

Maryville University of Saint Louis *M*
Rockhurst University *M*
Saint Louis University *B, M*
University of Missouri
   Columbia *M*
Washington University in St.
   Louis *M, D*

Nebraska

College of Saint Mary *M*
Creighton University *D*

New Hampshire

University of New Hampshire *M*

New Jersey

Kean University *M*
Richard Stockton College of New
   Jersey *M*
Seton Hall University *M*

New Mexico

University of New Mexico *M*
Western New Mexico University *A*

New York

City University of New York
   York College *M*
D'Youville College *M*
Dominican College of Blauvelt *M*
Ithaca College *B, M*
Keuka College *B, M*

Long Island University

LIU Brooklyn *B, M*
Mercy College *M*
Nazareth College *M*
New York Institute of Technology *M*
New York University *M, D*
SUNY
   Downstate Medical Center *M*
   University at Buffalo *B, M*
   University at Stony Brook *M*
Sage Colleges *M*
Touro College *M*
Utica College *M*

North Carolina

East Carolina University *M*
Lenoir-Rhyne University *M*
University of North Carolina
   Chapel Hill *M, D*
Winston-Salem State University *M*

North Dakota

University of Mary *M*
University of North Dakota *M*

Ohio

Cleveland State University *M*
Ohio State University
   Columbus Campus *B, M*
Shawnee State University *M*
University of Findlay *M*
University of Toledo *D*
Xavier University *M*

Oklahoma

Northeastern State University *M*
University of Oklahoma *M*

Oregon

Pacific University *M*

Pennsylvania

Alvernia University *M*
Chatham University *M, D*
Duquesne University *M*
Elizabethtown College *B, M*
Gannon University *B, M*
Misericordia University *M, D*
Philadelphia University *M*
St. Francis University *M*
Temple University *M*
Thomas Jefferson University *M, D*
University of Pittsburgh *B, M*
University of Scranton *M*
University of the Sciences *M*

Puerto Rico

University of Puerto Rico
   Medical Sciences *M*

Rhode Island

New England Institute of
   Technology *M*

South Dakota

University of South Dakota *M*

Tennessee

Belmont University *D*
Milligan College *M*
University of Tennessee
   Chattanooga *D*
   Knoxville *M*

Texas

Baylor University *D*
Texas Tech University Health
   Sciences Center *M*
Texas Woman's University *M, D*
University of Texas
   El Paso *M*
   Medical Branch at Galveston *M*
   Pan American *M*

Utah

University of Utah *B, M, D*

Virginia

James Madison University *M*
Jefferson College of Health
  Sciences *M*
Radford University *M*
Shenandoah University *M*
Virginia Commonwealth
  University *M, D*

Washington

Eastern Washington University *M*
University of Puget Sound *M*

West Virginia

West Virginia University *M*

Wisconsin

Concordia University Wisconsin *M*
Milwaukee Area Technical College *A*
Mount Mary University *M*
University of Wisconsin
  La Crosse *M*
  Madison *M*
  Milwaukee *B, M, D*

Occupational therapy assistant

Alabama

Central Alabama Community
  College *A*
Wallace State Community College at
  Hanceville *A*

Arizona

Brown Mackie College
  Tucson *A*

Arkansas

Arkansas Tech University *A*
East Arkansas Community College *A*
Pulaski Technical College *A*
South Arkansas Community
  College *A*

California

Grossmont College *A*
La Sierra University *C*
Sacramento City College *C, A*
Santa Ana College *A*

Colorado

Arapahoe Community College *A*
Morgan Community College *A*
Pueblo Community College *A*

Connecticut

Goodwin College *A*
Manchester Community College *A*

Delaware

Delaware Technical Community
  College
  Jack F. Owens Campus *A*
  Stanton/Wilmington Campus *A*

Florida

Adventist University of Health
  Sciences *A*
Daytona State College *A*
Keiser University *A*
Palm Beach State College *A*
Polk State College *A*
State College of Florida, Manatee-
  Sarasota *A*
Tallahassee Community College *C*

Georgia

Atlanta Technical College *A*
Darton College *A*
Middle Georgia State College *A*

Hawaii

University of Hawaii
  Kapiolani Community College *A*

Illinois

City Colleges of Chicago
  Wilbur Wright College *A*
College of DuPage *A*
Illinois Central College *A*
John A. Logan College *A*
Kaskaskia College *A*
Lewis and Clark Community
  College *A*
Lincoln Land Community College *A*
Parkland College *A*
Rend Lake College *A*
Sauk Valley Community College *A*
South Suburban College of Cook
  County *A*
Southeastern Illinois College *A*

Indiana

Brown Mackie College
  Fort Wayne *A*
  Merrillville *A*
  South Bend *A*
University of Southern Indiana *A*

Iowa

Hawkeye Community College *A*
Iowa Central Community College *A*
Iowa Lakes Community College *C*
Kirkwood Community College *A*

Kansas

Johnson County Community
  College *A*
Newman University *A*
Washburn University *A*

Kentucky

Jefferson Community and Technical
  College *A*
Madisonville Community College *A*

Louisiana

Bossier Parish Community College *A*
Delgado Community College *A*
University of Louisiana at Monroe *A*

Maine

Kennebec Valley Community
  College *A*

Maryland

Allegany College of Maryland *A*
Wor-Wic Community College *A*

Massachusetts

Bristol Community College *A*
Greenfield Community College *A*
North Shore Community College *A*
Springfield Technical Community
  College *A*

Michigan

Baker College
  Cadillac *A*
  Muskegon *A*
Grand Rapids Community College *A*
Macomb Community College *A*
Mott Community College *A*
Oakland Community College *A*
Schoolcraft College *A*

Minnesota

Anoka Technical College *A*
Herzing University
  Minneapolis *A*
Northland Community & Technical
  College *A*
St. Catherine University *A*

Missouri

East Central College *A*
Metropolitan Community College -
  Kansas City *A*
Ozarks Technical Community
  College *A*
St. Charles Community College *A*
State Fair Community College *A*

New Hampshire

River Valley Community College *A*

New Jersey

Ocean County College *A*
Passaic County Community College *A*
Rutgers, The State University of New
  Jersey
  New Brunswick/Piscataway
    Campus *A*
  Newark Campus *A*

New Mexico

Eastern New Mexico University:
  Roswell *A*

New York

City University of New York
  LaGuardia Community College *A*
Erie Community College *A*
Jamestown Community College *A*
Maria College *A*
Mercy College *A*
Orange County Community
  College *A*
Rockland Community College *A*
Suffolk County Community College *A*
Touro College *A*

North Carolina

Cabarrus College of Health
  Sciences *A*
Cape Fear Community College *A*
Durham Technical Community
  College *A*
Pitt Community College *A*
Southwestern Community College *A*

North Dakota

North Dakota State College of
  Science *A*

Ohio

Brown Mackie College
  Akron *A*
Cincinnati State Technical and
  Community College *A*
Cuyahoga Community College
  Metropolitan *A*
James A. Rhodes State College *A*
Kent State University
  Ashtabula *A*
  East Liverpool *A*
Marion Technical College *A*
North Central State College *A*
Owens Community College
  Toledo *A*
Shawnee State University *A*
Sinclair Community College *A*
Stark State College *A*
Zane State College *A*

Oklahoma

Oklahoma City Community
  College *A*

Southwestern Oklahoma State
  University *A*
Tulsa Community College *A*

Oregon

Linn-Benton Community College *A*

Pennsylvania

Central Penn College *A*
Community College of Allegheny
  County *A*
Harcum College *A*
Kaplan Career Institute
  Pittsburgh *A*
Lehigh Carbon Community College *A*
Penn State
  Berks *A*
  DuBois *A*
  Mont Alto *A*
  Shenango *A*
Pennsylvania College of
  Technology *A*

Puerto Rico

Inter American University of Puerto
  Rico
  Ponce Campus *A*
University of Puerto Rico
  Humacao *A*

Rhode Island

Community College of Rhode
  Island *A*
New England Institute of
  Technology *A*

South Carolina

Central Carolina Technical College *C*
Greenville Technical College *A*
Midlands Technical College *C*
Piedmont Technical College *C*
Tri-County Technical College *C*
Trident Technical College *A*

South Dakota

Lake Area Technical Institute *A*

Tennessee

Roane State Community College *A*

Texas

Amarillo College *A*
Austin Community College *A*
Del Mar College *A*
Houston Community College
  System *C, A*
Laredo Community College *A*
Lone Star College System *A*
North Central Texas College *A*
Panola College *A*
St. Philip's College *A*
South Texas College *A*
Weatherford College *C, A*

Utah

Salt Lake Community College *A*

Virginia

Jefferson College of Health
  Sciences *A*
Southwest Virginia Community
  College *A*
Tidewater Community College *A*

Washington

Bates Technical College *A*
Green River Community College *A*
Lake Washington Institute of
  Technology *A*
Spokane Falls Community College *A*

West Virginia

University of Charleston *A*

Wisconsin

Fox Valley Technical College *A*
Madison Area Technical College *A*
Milwaukee Area Technical College *A*
Western Technical College *A*
Wisconsin Indianhead Technical
   College *A*

Wyoming

Casper College *A*

Ocean engineering

California

University of California
   San Diego *M, D*

Florida

Florida Atlantic University *B, M, D*
Florida Institute of
   Technology *B, M, D*
University of Florida *M, D*
University of Miami *M, D*

Hawaii

University of Hawaii
   Manoa *M, D*

Louisiana

Louisiana State University and
   Agricultural and Mechanical
   College *M*

Maryland

United States Naval Academy *B*

New Hampshire

University of New Hampshire *M, D*

New Jersey

Stevens Institute of Technology *M, D*

Rhode Island

University of Rhode Island *B, M, D*

Texas

Texas A&M University *B, M, D*
Texas A&M University
   Galveston *B*

Oceanography

Alaska

University of Alaska
   Fairbanks *M, D*

California

Humboldt State University *B*
Shasta College *A*
University of California
   Berkeley *B*
   San Diego *D*
   Santa Cruz *M, D*

Connecticut

United States Coast Guard
   Academy *B*
University of Connecticut *M, D*

Delaware

University of Delaware *M, D*

Florida

Florida Institute of
   Technology *B, M, D*
Nova Southeastern University *D*
University of Miami *B, M, D*
University of South Florida *M, D*
University of West Florida *B*

Hawaii

Hawaii Pacific University *B*
University of Hawaii
   Manoa *M, D*

Illinois

Illinois Valley Community College *A*

Louisiana

Louisiana State University and
   Agricultural and Mechanical
   College *B, M, D*

Maine

Maine Maritime Academy *B*
University of Maine *M, D*

Maryland

United States Naval Academy *B*

Massachusetts

Massachusetts Institute of
   Technology *M, D*
University of Massachusetts
   Amherst *C*

Michigan

Central Michigan University *B*
Grand Rapids Community College *A*
University of Michigan *B, M, D*

Mississippi

University of Southern
   Mississippi *B, M, D*

New Hampshire

University of New Hampshire *M*

New Jersey

Rider University *B*
Rutgers, The State University of New
   Jersey
   New Brunswick/Piscataway
   Campus *M, D*

New York

Columbia University
   School of General Studies *B*
SUNY
   University at Stony Brook *D*

North Carolina

Cape Fear Community College *A*
Elizabeth City State University *B*
North Carolina State University *B*
University of North Carolina
   Chapel Hill *M, D*
   Wilmington *M*

Oregon

Oregon State University *M, D*

Pennsylvania

Kutztown University of
   Pennsylvania *B*
Millersville University of
   Pennsylvania *B*

Rhode Island

University of Rhode Island *B, M, D*

Texas

Texas A&M University *M, D*
Texas A&M University
   Galveston *B*

Virginia

Old Dominion University *M, D*

Washington

Shoreline Community College *A*
University of Washington *B, M, D*

Wisconsin

University of Wisconsin
   Madison *M, D*

Office/clerical services

Alabama

Faulkner State Community College *C*
Gadsden State Community College *C*
Lawson State Community College *C*

Alaska

University of Alaska
   Anchorage *C, A*
   Southeast *A*

Arizona

Arizona Western College *C*
Cochise College *C*
Coconino County Community
   College *C*
Dine College *C, A*
Eastern Arizona College *C*
Paradise Valley Community
   College *C, A*

Arkansas

Arkansas State University
   Beebe *C*
   Newport *C*
College of the Ouachitas *C*
East Arkansas Community College *C*
Mid-South Community College *C*
National Park Community College *C*
Pulaski Technical College *C*
University of Arkansas
   Community College at Hope *C*

California

Allan Hancock College *A*
American River College *A*
Barstow Community College *C, A*
Berkeley City College *C, A*
Cerritos College *A*
Cerro Coso Community College *C, A*
Chabot College *A*
Chaffey College *C*
Citrus College *C, A*
City College of San Francisco *A*
Coastline Community College *C*
College of Alameda *A*
College of Marin *C*
College of San Mateo *C, A*
College of the Redwoods *C*
College of the Sequoias *C, A*
College of the Siskiyous *C*
Columbia College *C*
Contra Costa College *C, A*
Crafton Hills College *C, A*
Cypress College *C, A*
Empire College *C*
Evergreen Valley College *A*
Fresno City College *C, A*
Gavilan College *C*
Golden West College *C, A*
Heald College
   Fresno *C, A*
Humphreys College *C, A, B*
Imperial Valley College *C, A*
Kaplan College
   Riverside *C*
Laney College *C, A*
Long Beach City College *C, A*
Los Angeles City College *C, A*
Los Angeles Harbor College *A*
Los Angeles Mission College *C, A*
Los Angeles Southwest College *A*
Los Angeles Trade and Technical
   College *C, A*
Los Angeles Valley College *A*
MTI College *C*
Mission College *A*
Modesto Junior College *C*

Monterey Peninsula College *C, A*
Mount St. Mary's College *A*
Mount San Antonio College *C, A*
Mount San Jacinto College *C*
Ohlone College *C, A*
Orange Coast College *C, A*
Palo Verde College *C, A*
Pasadena City College *C, A*
Porterville College *A*
Reedley College *C*
Sacramento City College *C, A*
Saddleback College *C*
San Bernardino Valley College *C*
San Deigo Miramar College
   San Diego Miramar College *A*
San Diego City College *C, A*
San Jose City College *C, A*
Santa Barbara City College *C*
Santa Rosa Junior College *C*
Shasta College *A*
Skyline College *C, A*
Southwestern College *C, A*
Ventura College *C, A*
West Hills College: Coalinga *C, A*
West Valley College *A*
Yuba College *C*

Colorado

Trinidad State Junior College *C*

Connecticut

Gateway Community College *C, A*
Quinebaug Valley Community
   College *C*
Tunxis Community College *A*

Florida

Broward College *A*
College of Central Florida *C*
Eastern Florida State College *C*
Florida Gateway College *C, A*
Herzing University
   Winter Park *C*
Miami Dade College *C, A*
Pensacola State College *C*
Seminole State College of Florida *C*

Georgia

Abraham Baldwin Agricultural
   College *A*
Atlanta Technical College *C*
Augusta Technical College *C*
Central Georgia Technical College *C*
Chattahoochee Technical College *C*
Clayton State University *C*
Gwinnett Technical College *C*
Southeastern Technical College *C*
Southwest Georgia Technical
   College *C, A*

Hawaii

University of Hawaii
   Kauai Community College *C, A*
   Leeward Community College *C, A*

Illinois

East-West University *C*
Elgin Community College *C*
Highland Community College *C*
Illinois Central College *C*
Illinois Valley Community College *C*
John A. Logan College *C*
Joliet Junior College *A*
Kankakee Community College *C*
Kaskaskia College *C*
Kishwaukee College *C, A*
Lake Land College *C*
Lewis and Clark Community
   College *C*
Lincoln Land Community College *C*
Midstate College *C*
Morton College *C*
Sauk Valley Community College *C*
Southeastern Illinois College *C*

Southwestern Illinois College *C, A*
Spoon River College *C*

Indiana

Vincennes University *C*

Iowa

Des Moines Area Community
College *C*
Dordt College *A*
Ellsworth Community College *C, A*
Iowa Lakes Community College *C*
Marshalltown Community College *C*
Southeastern Community
College *C, A*

Kansas

Allen County Community College *C*
Butler Community College *C, A*
Coffeyville Community College *A*
Cowley County Community
College *C, A*
Donnelly College *A*
Kansas City Kansas Community
College *C*
Labette Community College *A*
Neosho County Community
College *C*
Pratt Community College *C, A*
Seward County Community
College *C, A*
Washburn University *C, A*
Wichita Area Technical College *A*

Kentucky

Ashland Community and Technical
College *A*
Daymar College
Owensboro *C, A*
National College
Lexington *A*

Maine

Kaplan University
South Portland *A*
Northern Maine Community
College *A*
University of Maine
Machias *B*

Maryland

Kaplan University
Hagerstown *C*

Massachusetts

Bristol Community College *C*
Bunker Hill Community College *A*
Cape Cod Community College *C, A*
Massasoit Community College *C*
Northern Essex Community
College *C*
Quinsigamond Community College *C*
Springfield Technical Community
College *C*

Michigan

Baker College
Auburn Hills *C*
Cadillac *C*
Clinton Township *C*
Flint *C*
Jackson *C*
Muskegon *C*
Owosso *C, A*
Port Huron *C*
Glen Oaks Community College *C*
Henry Ford Community College *A*
Kellogg Community College *C*
Kirtland Community College *C*
Lansing Community College *C*
Mid Michigan Community College *C*
Monroe County Community
College *C, A*
North Central Michigan College *C, A*

Northern Michigan University *C*
Oakland Community College *C*
St. Clair County Community
College *C*
West Shore Community College *C, A*

Minnesota

Central Lakes College *C*
Century College *C*
Hennepin Technical College *C, A*
Hibbing Community College *C, A*
Lake Superior College *C*
Minnesota State College - Southeast
Technical *C*
Ridgewater College *C*
Rochester Community and Technical
College *C*

Mississippi

Itawamba Community College *C, A*
Southwest Mississippi Community
College *A*

Missouri

Crowder College *C, A*
Jefferson College *C, A*
Metropolitan Community College -
Kansas City *C*
Moberly Area Community
College *C, A*
North Central Missouri College *C, A*
Three Rivers Community College *C*

Montana

Miles Community College *C, A*
Stone Child College *C, A*

Nebraska

Kaplan University
Lincoln *C*
Northeast Community College *C, A*
Southeast Community College *A*
University of Nebraska
Kearney *B*
Western Nebraska Community
College *C, A*

New Hampshire

River Valley Community College *C*
White Mountains Community
College *A*

New Jersey

Berkeley College *C*
Essex County College *C*
Gloucester County College *C, A*

New Mexico

Central New Mexico Community
College *C, A*
Clovis Community College *A*
Dona Ana Community College of
New Mexico State University *C*
Eastern New Mexico University:
Roswell *C*
New Mexico State University
Alamogordo *A*
Carlsbad *C, A*

New York

Berkeley College of New York City *C*
Erie Community College *C*
Fulton-Montgomery Community
College *C*
Globe Institute of Technology *C*
North Country Community
College *C, A*
Plaza College *C*
Professional Business College *C*
Schenectady County Community
College *C*
Trocaire College *C*
Ulster County Community College *A*

Utica School of Commerce *C*
Westchester Community College *C, A*

North Carolina

Asheville-Buncombe Technical
Community College *C, A*
Bladen Community College *C, A*
Carteret Community College *A*
Central Carolina Community
College *A*
College of the Albemarle *A*
Forsyth Technical Community
College *C, A*
Gaston College *C*
Halifax Community College *C, A*
McDowell Technical Community
College *A*
Pamlico Community College *A*
Rockingham Community
College *C, A*
Sampson Community College *A*
Surry Community College *C, A*
Western Piedmont Community
College *C, A*

North Dakota

Dakota College at Bottineau *C, A*
United Tribes Technical College *C, A*

Ohio

Ashland University *C*
Belmont College *C, A*
Bowling Green State University:
Firelands College *C*
Columbus State Community
College *C*
Lorain County Community College *C*
Miami University
Hamilton *C*
Middletown *C, A*
Miami-Jacobs Career College
Dayton *C, A*
Northwest State Community
College *C*
Southern State Community College *C*
Stark State College *C*
University of Cincinnati
Blue Ash College *C, A*
University of Northwestern Ohio *C*

Oklahoma

Carl Albert State College *C*
Eastern Oklahoma State College *A*
Northeastern Oklahoma Agricultural
and Mechanical College *C*
Oklahoma City Community
College *A*
Oklahoma State University
Institute of Technology:
Okmulgee *A*
Seminole State College *A*
Tulsa Community College *C*
Western Oklahoma State College *A*

Oregon

Central Oregon Community
College *C*
Chemeketa Community College *C*
Clackamas Community College *C*
Clatsop Community College *C*
Lane Community College *A*
Linn-Benton Community College *C*
Mt. Hood Community College *C*
Portland Community College *C*
Southwestern Oregon Community
College *C*
Umpqua Community College *C*

Pennsylvania

Bucks County Community College *C*
Butler County Community College *C*
Commonwealth Technical Institute *C*
Community College of
Philadelphia *C, A*

McCann School of Business and
Technology
Hazleton *A*
Northampton Community College *C*
Pennsylvania Highlands Community
College *C*
Reading Area Community
College *C, A*
South Hills School of Business &
Technology *C*

Puerto Rico

American University of Puerto
Rico *B*
Humacao Community College *C*
Inter American University of Puerto
Rico
Metropolitan Campus *A, B*
Pontifical Catholic University of
Puerto Rico *A*
Universidad Adventista de las
Antillas *A*
University of Puerto Rico
Cayey University College *B*

Rhode Island

Community College of Rhode
Island *C*

South Carolina

Aiken Technical College *C*
Bob Jones University *A*
Florence-Darlington Technical
College *C*
Forrest Junior College *A*
Horry-Georgetown Technical
College *C*
Northeastern Technical College *C, A*
Orangeburg-Calhoun Technical
College *C*
Piedmont Technical College *C*
Spartanburg Community College *C*
Technical College of the
Lowcountry *C*
Tri-County Technical College *C*
Trident Technical College *C*
Williamsburg Technical College *C*
York Technical College *C*

South Dakota

Northern State University *A, B*
Sinte Gleska University *A*

Tennessee

Chattanooga State Community
College *A*
Lincoln Memorial University *B*
West Tennessee Business College *C*

Texas

Alvin Community College *C*
Amarillo College *A*
Blinn College *A*
Central Texas College *C*
Cisco College *C*
Coastal Bend College *C, A*
College of the Mainland *A*
Del Mar College *C*
El Centro College *C*
El Paso Community College *C, A*
Galveston College *C, A*
Grayson College *C, A*
Howard College *C, A*
Kilgore College *C*
Laredo Community College *C, A*
Lee College *C, A*
McLennan Community College *C*
Midland College *C, A*
North Central Texas College *A*
Palo Alto College *C*
Panola College *C*
St. Philip's College *C, A*
South Plains College *C*
Texarkana College *C*

Tyler Junior College *C*
Vernon College *C*
Victoria College *C*
Weatherford College *C, A*

Utah

LDS Business College *C*
Salt Lake Community College *C*

Virginia

Central Virginia Community
College *C*
Dabney S. Lancaster Community
College *C, A*
Eastern Shore Community
College *C, A*
Lord Fairfax Community College *C*
Mountain Empire Community
College *A*
Patrick Henry Community College *C*
Paul D. Camp Community College *C*
Southside Virginia Community
College *C*
Tidewater Community College *C*
Wytheville Community College *C*

Washington

Bellevue College *C*
Bellingham Technical College *C*
Big Bend Community College *C*
Centralia College *C, A*
Clark College *C*
Edmonds Community College *C, A*
Everett Community College *C, A*
Grays Harbor College *C*
Green River Community College *C, A*
Highline Community College *C, A*
Lake Washington Institute of
Technology *C*
Lower Columbia College *A*
North Seattle Community
College *C, A*
Northwest Indian College *C*
Peninsula College *C*
Pierce College *C, A*
Renton Technical College *C*
Shoreline Community College *C*
Skagit Valley College *C*
South Puget Sound Community
College *C, A*
Spokane Community College *C, A*
Spokane Falls Community
College *C, A*
Tacoma Community College *C*
Walla Walla Community College *C*
Wenatchee Valley College *C*
Yakima Valley Community College *C*

West Virginia

Concord University *A*
New River Community and Technical
College *C*

Wisconsin

College of Menominee Nation *A*
Fox Valley Technical College *C*
Gateway Technical College *C*
Herzing University
Madison *A, B*
Lakeshore Technical College *C*
Madison Area Technical College *C*
Moraine Park Technical College *C*
Nicolet Area Technical College *C*
Southwest Wisconsin Technical
College *C*
Waukesha County Technical
College *C*

Wyoming

Central Wyoming College *C*
Eastern Wyoming College *C*

Office management

Alabama

Community College of the Air
Force *A*
Enterprise State Community
College *C, A*
Jefferson State Community
College *C, A*
Lawson State Community College *A*
Wallace State Community College at
Hanceville *A*

Alaska

Ilisagvik College *C, A*

Arizona

Arizona Western College *C, A*
Everest College
Phoenix *A*
GateWay Community College *A*
Glendale Community College *C*
Mohave Community College *C*
Rio Salado College *C, A*
South Mountain Community
College *C*
Yavapai College *C, A*

Arkansas

Arkansas State University
Mountain Home *C*
East Arkansas Community College *C*
National Park Community College *C*
Southern Arkansas University Tech *A*

California

Barstow Community College *C, A*
Cerritos College *A*
Cerro Coso Community College *C, A*
Chabot College *A*
Chaffey College *A*
Citrus College *C, A*
Coastline Community College *C*
College of the Desert *C, A*
College of the Siskiyous *C, A*
De Anza College *A*
Diablo Valley College *C, A*
El Camino College *C, A*
Foothill College *C*
Glendale Community College *A*
Golden West College *C, A*
Irvine Valley College *C, A*
Kaplan College
Riverside *A*
Los Angeles Harbor College *C, A*
Los Angeles Mission College *C, A*
Los Medanos College *C, A*
MTI College *A*
MiraCosta College *C, A*
Mission College *A*
Modesto Junior College *C*
Napa Valley College *C*
Ohlone College *C, A*
Porterville College *C*
Saddleback College *C, A*
San Joaquin Delta College *C, A*
San Jose City College *C*
Santa Barbara City College *C, A*
Santa Monica College *C*
Santa Rosa Junior College *C*
Shasta College *C, A*
Skyline College *C*
Solano Community College *C, A*
Southwestern College *C, A*
Ventura College *C, A*
West Valley College *A*
Yuba College *C*

Colorado

Arapahoe Community College *C, A*
Colorado Mesa University *C, A*
Colorado Northwestern Community
College *C, A*

Community College of Aurora *C, A*
Pikes Peak Community College *C, A*

Connecticut

Goodwin College *A*
Quinnipiac University *B*

Delaware

Delaware Technical Community
College
Jack F. Owens Campus *C, A*
Stanton/Wilmington Campus *C, A*
Terry Campus *C, A*

District of Columbia

University of the District of
Columbia *B*
University of the Potomac *C*

Florida

Eastern Florida State College *C, A*
Florida Gateway College *C, A*
Florida State College at
Jacksonville *C, A, B*
Herzing University
Winter Park *C*
Indian River State College *A*
Miami Dade College *C, A*
Pensacola State College *C, A*
Polk State College *A*
Saint Johns River State College *C, A*
Santa Fe College *C, A*
Seminole State College of
Florida *C, A*
South Florida State College *C, A*
Trinity Baptist College *A*
Virginia College
Pensacola *A*

Georgia

Atlanta Metropolitan College *C, A*
Chattahoochee Technical
College *C, A*
Clayton State University *B*
Dalton State College *C, A*
Darton College *A*
Fort Valley State University *B*
Georgia Highlands College *A*
Southeastern Technical College *C*

Idaho

Northwest Nazarene University *B*

Illinois

Black Hawk College *C*
College of DuPage *C, A*
Danville Area Community College *C*
Elgin Community College *C*
Illinois Central College *C*
John A. Logan College *C, A*
Joliet Junior College *C, A*
Kaskaskia College *C*
Kishwaukee College *C*
Loyola University Chicago *C, B*
MacCormac College *A*
Oakton Community College *C, A*
Sauk Valley Community College *C*
South Suburban College of Cook
County *C, A*
Spoon River College *C*

Indiana

Ball State University *B*
Brown Mackie College
Fort Wayne *A*
Indiana State University *B*
Oakland City University *A*
University of Southern Indiana *B*

Iowa

Des Moines Area Community
College *C, A*
Iowa Lakes Community College *A*

Iowa Western Community College *A*
Southeastern Community College *A*

Kansas

Allen County Community College *A*
Coffeyville Community College *A*
Cowley County Community
College *C*
Dodge City Community College *C, A*
Fort Hays State University *B*
Haskell Indian Nations University *A*
Neosho County Community
College *A*
Pratt Community College *C, A*
Seward County Community
College *C, A*
Tabor College *B*
Washburn University *C, A*

Kentucky

Campbellsville University *A, B*
Daymar College
Owensboro *A*
Paducah *C*
Eastern Kentucky University *B*
Hopkinsville Community College *A*
Maysville Community and Technical
College *C, A*
National College
Lexington *A*
Spencerian College *C, A*
Sullivan University *C, A*

Louisiana

ITI Technical College *A*
Virginia College
Baton Rouge *A*

Maine

Beal College *A*
Eastern Maine Community College *A*
Kaplan University
South Portland *A*
Northern Maine Community
College *A*
University of Maine
Machias *A, B*

Maryland

Baltimore City Community College *A*
Cecil College *C*
Howard Community College *A*
Prince George's Community
College *C, A*

Massachusetts

Babson College *B*
Bristol Community College *C*
Cape Cod Community College *C, A*
Fitchburg State University *C*
Massasoit Community College *A*
Middlesex Community College *A*
Northern Essex Community
College *A*
Roxbury Community College *A*

Michigan

Baker College
Auburn Hills *A*
Cadillac *A, B*
Clinton Township *B*
Flint *B*
Jackson *C, A*
Muskegon *B*
Owosso *A, B*
Port Huron *A, B*
Delta College *A*
Eastern Michigan University *B*
Ferris State University *C*
Gogebic Community College *A*
Henry Ford Community College *C*
Lake Superior State University *A*
Lansing Community College *C*
Oakland Community College *A*

St. Clair County Community
College *A*
Wayne County Community
College *C, A*

Minnesota

Alexandria Technical and Community
College *A*
Anoka Technical College *C, A*
Dakota County Technical
College *C, A*
Inver Hills Community College *C*
Lake Superior College *A*
Minneapolis Business College *A*
Minnesota West Community and
Technical College *C, A*
Northland Community & Technical
College *C*
Northwest Technical College *C, A*
Rochester Community and Technical
College *A*
St. Paul College *A*
South Central College *A*

Mississippi

East Mississippi Community
College *A*
Mississippi Valley State University *B*

Missouri

Evangel University *A*
Metropolitan Community College -
Kansas City *A*
St. Charles Community College *C, A*
Southwest Baptist University *B*
University of Central Missouri *B*

Montana

Blackfeet Community College *A*
Chief Dull Knife College *A*
Miles Community College *A*
Salish Kootenai College *A*
University of Montana *A*
University of Montana: Western *B*

Nebraska

Chadron State College *B*
Mid-Plains Community College *C, A*
Midland University *A, B*
Northeast Community College *C*
Union College *A*
University of Nebraska
Kearney *B*

Nevada

College of Southern Nevada *C, A*
Great Basin College *A*
Truckee Meadows Community
College *A*

New Hampshire

Lakes Region Community College *C*
Manchester Community College *C, A*
White Mountains Community
College *A*

New Jersey

Cumberland County College *C, A*
Gloucester County College *C, A*
Middlesex County College *A*
Rider University *B*

New Mexico

Clovis Community College *C, A*
Dona Ana Community College of
New Mexico State
University *C, A*
New Mexico Junior College *C, A*
New Mexico State University
Grants *A*

New York

Bryant & Stratton College
Syracuse *A*

City University of New York
Kingsborough Community
College *A*
Queensborough Community
College *A*
Erie Community College *A*
Globe Institute of
Technology *C, A, B*
Jamestown Business College *C*
Professional Business College *C*
SUNY
College at Buffalo *B, M*
College of Agriculture and
Technology at Morrisville *A*
Farmingdale State College *C*
St. Joseph's College New York:
Suffolk Campus *C*
St. Joseph's College, New York *C*
Sanford-Brown Institute
Melville *A*
Suffolk County Community College *A*
Trocaire College *A*

North Carolina

Alamance Community College *A*
Catawba Valley Community
College *C, A*
Central Piedmont Community
College *A*
Cleveland Community College *C, A*
Fayetteville Technical Community
College *C, A*
Halifax Community College *C, A*
Isothermal Community College *C, A*
James Sprunt Community
College *C, A*
Johnston Community College *C, A*
Lenoir Community College *C, A*
Montgomery Community
College *C, A*
Pitt Community College *C, A*
Southeastern Community
College *C, A*
Wayne Community College *C, A*
Wilkes Community College *C, A*
Wilson Community College *C, A*

North Dakota

Lake Region State College *A*
University of Mary *M*
Valley City State University *B*

Ohio

Ashland University *C*
Bowling Green State University *B*
Brown Mackie College
Akron *A*
Eastern Gateway Community
College *C, A*
Miami University
Hamilton *C, A*
Middletown *C, A*
Oxford *A*
Miami-Jacobs Career College
Dayton *C, A*
Northwest State Community
College *A*
Ohio University
Chillicothe Campus *A*
Owens Community College
Toledo *A*
Shawnee State University *A*
Stark State College *A*
University of Akron *C, A*
University of Akron: Wayne
College *A*
University of Cincinnati
Clermont College *A*
University of Toledo *B*
Youngstown State University *A*

Oklahoma

Eastern Oklahoma State College *C*
Northern Oklahoma College *A*
Seminole State College *A*

Oregon

Clackamas Community College *C, A*
Eastern Oregon University *C*
Everest College
Portland *A*
Lane Community College *A*
Linn-Benton Community College *C, A*
Portland Community College *C, A*
Southwestern Oregon Community
College *C, A*
Treasure Valley Community
College *A*
Umpqua Community College *C*

Pennsylvania

Community College of Beaver
County *C*
Delaware County Community
College *A*
Indiana University of Pennsylvania *B*
Reading Area Community College *A*

Puerto Rico

Inter American University of Puerto
Rico
Aguadilla Campus *A, B*
Bayamon Campus *A, B*
Guayama Campus *A, B*
Metropolitan Campus *A, B*
San German Campus *A, B*
Turabo University *A, B*
Universidad Metropolitana *A, B*
University of Puerto Rico
Mayaguez *B*

South Carolina

Forrest Junior College *A*
Northeastern Technical College *C*
University of South Carolina
Columbia *B*
Williamsburg Technical College *A*

South Dakota

Oglala Lakota College *A*
Southeast Technical Institute *C*

Tennessee

Middle Tennessee State University *B*
National College of Business and
Technology
Bristol *A*
Pellissippi State Community
College *C*
Tennessee Temple University *B*

Texas

Brookhaven College *A*
Cedar Valley College *C, A*
Central Texas College *C, A*
College of the Mainland *A*
Eastfield College *C, A*
Grayson College *C, A*
Lamar State College at Orange *C*
Lamar University *B*
Laredo Community College *C, A*
North Lake College *A*
Panola College *A*
Paris Junior College *A*
South Plains College *C, A*
South Texas College *A*
Sul Ross State University *C, B*
Tarleton State University *B*
Temple College *C, A*
Tyler Junior College *A*
Virginia College
Austin *A*

Utah

LDS Business College *A*

Vermont

Community College of Vermont *A*

Virginia

American National University
Harrisonburg *A*
Blue Ridge Community College *C*
Central Virginia Community
College *C*
Dabney S. Lancaster Community
College *C, A*
Germanna Community College *C*
Lord Fairfax Community College *C, A*
Mountain Empire Community
College *A*
Northern Virginia Community
College *A*
Paul D. Camp Community College *A*
Thomas Nelson Community
College *A*
University of the Potomac *C*
Virginia Highlands Community
College *C, A*

Washington

Bellevue College *C, A*
Big Bend Community College *C, A*
Clover Park Technical College *A*
Columbia Basin College *C, A*
Edmonds Community College *C, A*
Grays Harbor College *C, A*
North Seattle Community
College *C, A*
Peninsula College *C, A*
Pierce College *A*
Renton Technical College *C, A*
South Seattle Community
College *C, A*
Spokane Community College *A*
Spokane Falls Community College *A*
Walla Walla Community College *C, A*
Wenatchee Valley College *A*
Whatcom Community College *C*
Yakima Valley Community College *A*

West Virginia

American National University
Princeton *A*
Bridgemont Community and
Technical College *A*
Concord University *A*

Wisconsin

Blackhawk Technical College *A*
Fox Valley Technical College *A*
Herzing University
Madison *A, B*
Lac Courte Oreilles Ojibwa
Community College *A*
Madison Area Technical College *A*
Maranatha Baptist Bible College *A, B*
Moraine Park Technical College *C, A*
Northeast Wisconsin Technical
College *C*
Southwest Wisconsin Technical
College *A*
University of Wisconsin
Whitewater *B*

Wyoming

Eastern Wyoming College *A*

Office technology/data entry

Alabama

Faulkner State Community
College *C, A*
Lawson State Community College *A*

Alaska

Charter College *A*
University of Alaska
Anchorage *A*

Arizona

Brookline College
  Tempe *C*
  Tucson *C*
Brown Mackie College
  Tucson *C*
Central Arizona College *A*
Chandler-Gilbert Community
  College *C*
Coconino County Community
  College *C*
Eastern Arizona College *C, A*
GateWay Community College *C*
Glendale Community College *C*
Paradise Valley Community
  College *C, A*
Phoenix College *C*
Scottsdale Community College *C*
South Mountain Community
  College *C, A*
Yavapai College *C, A*

Arkansas

Mid-South Community College *A*
Phillips Community College of the
  University of Arkansas *A*
Rich Mountain Community College *C*
Southern Arkansas University Tech *C*

California

Allan Hancock College *C, A*
Barstow Community College *C*
Butte College *C, A*
Cabrillo College *C, A*
Cerro Coso Community College *A*
Chabot College *C, A*
Chaffey College *C*
City College of San Francisco *C, A*
Coastline Community College *A*
College of the Redwoods *C, A*
College of the Sequoias *C*
Columbia College *C*
Cypress College *C, A*
Diablo Valley College *C*
Evergreen Valley College *A*
Foothill College *C, A*
Fresno City College *C*
Gavilan College *C*
Golden West College *C, A*
Heald College
  Rancho Cordova *C, A*
  Stockton *C, A*
Humphreys College *C, A, B*
Imperial Valley College *C, A*
Irvine Valley College *C, A*
Kaplan College
  Riverside *C*
  Vista *C*
Laney College *C, A*
Long Beach City College *C, A*
Los Angeles City College *C, A*
Los Angeles Harbor College *C, A*
Los Angeles Southwest College *A*
Los Angeles Valley College *C, A*
Ohlone College *C, A*
Orange Coast College *C, A*
Reedley College *C*
Saddleback College *C*
San Diego City College *C, A*
San Jose City College *A*
Santa Barbara City College *C*
Santa Rosa Junior College *C*
Shasta College *C, A*
West Hills College: Coalinga *C, A*
West Hills College: Lemoore *C*
West Valley College *C, A*

Colorado

Aims Community College *C, A*
Colorado Mesa University *C, A*
Community College of Denver *C*
IntelliTec College: Grand Junction *C*
Lamar Community College *C, A*

Morgan Community College *C*
Pueblo Community College *C, A*

Connecticut

Asnuntuck Community College *C, A*
Gateway Community College *C*
Middlesex Community College *C*
Quinebaug Valley Community
  College *C, A*
Three Rivers Community College *A*
Tunxis Community College *C*

Delaware

Delaware Technical Community
  College
  Jack F. Owens Campus *C, A*
  Stanton/Wilmington Campus *A*

District of Columbia

University of the District of
  Columbia *C, A*
University of the Potomac *C*

Florida

College of Central Florida *C*
Florida State College at
  Jacksonville *C, A*
Indian River State College *C*
Pasco-Hernando State College *C*
Saint Johns River State College *C*
Santa Fe College *C*
Seminole State College of Florida *C*
Tallahassee Community College *C*

Georgia

Abraham Baldwin Agricultural
  College *C, A*
Georgia Highlands College *A*
Middle Georgia State College *A*
North Georgia Technical
  College *C, A*
Savannah Technical College *C, A*
Southwest Georgia Technical
  College *C*
West Georgia Technical College *C*

Hawaii

University of Hawaii
  Kapiolani Community College *C, A*

Illinois

Black Hawk College *C, A*
City Colleges of Chicago
  Wilbur Wright College *C*
College of Lake County *C, A*
Danville Area Community
  College *C, A*
Elgin Community College *C*
Heartland Community College *C*
Illinois Central College *C*
Illinois Eastern Community Colleges
  Frontier Community College *C, A*
  Lincoln Trail College *C, A*
  Olney Central College *C, A*
  Wabash Valley College *C, A*
Illinois Valley Community
  College *C, A*
John Wood Community College *C*
Joliet Junior College *C, A*
Kaskaskia College *C, A*
Kishwaukee College *C*
Lake Land College *C*
Lincoln Land Community
  College *C, A*
McHenry County College *C*
Moraine Valley Community College *C*
Morton College *C*
National-Louis University *C*
Parkland College *C*
Prairie State College *C*
Rend Lake College *C*
Rock Valley College *C, A*
Sauk Valley Community College *C*
Shawnee Community College *C*

Southeastern Illinois College *A*
Spoon River College *C*
Waubonsee Community College *C, A*

Indiana

College of Court Reporting *A*
Ivy Tech Community College
  Columbus *C*
  Kokomo *C*
  Lafayette *C*
  North Central *C*
  Northeast *C*
  Northwest *C*
  Richmond *C*
Oakland City University *A*

Iowa

Ellsworth Community College *C, A*
Northeast Iowa Community
  College *C, A*
Southeastern Community College *A*
Western Iowa Tech Community
  College *C, A*

Kansas

Allen County Community College *C*
North Central Kansas Technical
  College *C*
Pratt Community College *C, A*
Seward County Community
  College *C, A*
Washburn University *A*

Kentucky

Brown Mackie College
  Hopkinsville *C*
Daymar College
  Owensboro *C, A*
West Kentucky Community and
  Technical College *A*

Louisiana

Baton Rouge Community
  College *C, A*
ITI Technical College *A*

Maine

Central Maine Community
  College *C, A*
Kaplan University
  South Portland *A*
Northern Maine Community
  College *A*

Maryland

Baltimore City Community
  College *C, A*
Garrett College *C, A*
Kaplan University
  Hagerstown *C, A, B*
Montgomery College *C*
Prince George's Community
  College *C, A*
TESST College of Technology
  Towson *C*

Massachusetts

Berkshire Community College *A*
Bristol Community College *C*
Middlesex Community College *C*
North Shore Community College *C*
Northern Essex Community
  College *A*
Roxbury Community College *A*

Michigan

Baker College
  Auburn Hills *A*
  Flint *A*
  Muskegon *A*
  Port Huron *A*
Delta College *A*
Glen Oaks Community College *C*
Gogebic Community College *A*

Lake Michigan College *C*
Lake Superior State University *A*
Macomb Community College *C, A*
Monroe County Community
  College *C, A*
Montcalm Community College *C, A*
North Central Michigan College *A*
Northern Michigan University *A*
Northwestern Michigan College *A*
Oakland Community College *C, A*
Schoolcraft College *C, A*
West Shore Community College *A*

Minnesota

Anoka-Ramsey Community College *C*
Century College *C*
Dakota County Technical College *C*
Hennepin Technical College *C, A*
Inver Hills Community College *C*
Lake Superior College *C, A*
Mesabi Range Community and
  Technical College *C, A*
Minneapolis Community and
  Technical College *A*
Minnesota State Community and
  Technical College *C, A*
North Hennepin Community
  College *C*
Northwest Technical College *C*
Pine Technical College *C*
Riverland Community College *C*
Rochester Community and Technical
  College *C*
St. Cloud Technical and Community
  College *C*
South Central College *A*
University of Northwestern - St.
  Paul *A*

Mississippi

Coahoma Community College *A*
Copiah-Lincoln Community
  College *C, A*
East Mississippi Community
  College *A*
Hinds Community College *A*
Itawamba Community College *C*
Mississippi Gulf Coast Community
  College *A*
Northeast Mississippi Community
  College *A*
Northwest Mississippi Community
  College *A*
Pearl River Community College *A*

Missouri

Baptist Bible College *A*
Metropolitan Community College -
  Kansas City *C, A*
North Central Missouri College *C, A*
St. Louis Community College *C*

Montana

Aaniiih Nakoda College *A*
Helena College University of
  Montana *C*
Salish Kootenai College *C*

Nevada

Everest College
  Las Vegas *C*
Great Basin College *C, A*
Truckee Meadows Community
  College *A*
Western Nevada College *A*

New Hampshire

Mount Washington College *A*
Nashua Community College *C*
River Valley Community College *A*
White Mountains Community
  College *C, A*

New Jersey

Berkeley College *C*
Camden County College *C*
Essex County College *A*
Gloucester County College *A*

New Mexico

New Mexico Junior College *C, A*

New York

Berkeley College of New York City *C*
Bryant & Stratton College
   Rochester *A*
Business Informatics Center *A*
City University of New York
   Borough of Manhattan Community
      College *C*
   Bronx Community College *A*
   Hostos Community College *C, A*
   Queensborough Community
      College *C*
Everest Institute
   Rochester *A*
Globe Institute of Technology *C*
Hudson Valley Community
   College *C, A*
Long Island Business Institute *C, A*
Mercy College *A*
Mildred Elley
   Albany *A*
Orange County Community
   College *C, A*
Plaza College *C*
Professional Business College *C, A*
Rockland Community College *C, A*
Suffolk County Community
   College *C, A*
Sullivan County Community
   College *C, A*
Trocaire College *C*

North Carolina

Asheville-Buncombe Technical
   Community College *A*
Bladen Community College *A*
Central Piedmont Community
   College *C*
East Carolina University *B*
Piedmont Community College *A*
Rockingham Community
   College *C, A*
Rowan-Cabarrus Community
   College *C, A*
Vance-Granville Community
   College *A*
Western Piedmont Community
   College *C, A*

North Dakota

Bismarck State College *C, A*
Cankdeska Cikana Community
   College *C, A*
Fort Berthold Community College *A*
Minot State University *C*
Sitting Bull College *A*

Ohio

Bowling Green State University:
   Firelands College *C*
Brown Mackie College
   Akron *A*
   Findlay *A*
Cincinnati State Technical and
   Community College *C*
Miami University
   Middletown *C*
Miami-Jacobs Career College
   Dayton *A*
Ohio Business College
   Sheffield *C, A*
Ohio University
   Chillicothe Campus *A*
   Southern Campus at Ironton *A*
Sinclair Community College *C, A*

Southern State Community College *C*
Stark State College *A*
Stautzenberger College *C, A*
Trumbull Business College *C, A*
University of Akron *M*
University of Akron: Wayne
   College *C, A*
University of Cincinnati
   Blue Ash College *C*
   Clermont College *C, A*
University of Northwestern
   Ohio *C, A*
University of Rio Grande *C, A, B*

Oklahoma

Oklahoma State University
   Oklahoma City *A*
Tulsa Community College *A*

Oregon

Chemeketa Community College *C, A*
Mt. Hood Community College *C*
Portland Community College *C*
Rogue Community College *C*
Treasure Valley Community
   College *C*

Pennsylvania

Community College of Allegheny
   County *A*
Consolidated School of Business
   Lancaster *A*
   York *A*
Douglas Education Center *A*
Lansdale School of Business *C, A*
Pace Institute *C*
Penn Commercial Business and
   Technical School *C*
Reading Area Community
   College *C, A*

Puerto Rico

American University of Puerto
   Rico *B*
Columbia Centro Universitario:
   Yauco *A*
Huertas College *C*
ICPR Junior College *C, A*
Inter American University of Puerto
   Rico
   Ponce Campus *A, B*
National University College
   Bayamon *A*
   Rio Grande *A*

South Carolina

Aiken Technical College *C*
Central Carolina Technical College *C*
Denmark Technical College *C*
Florence-Darlington Technical
   College *C*
Forrest Junior College *A*
Northeastern Technical College *C, A*
Orangeburg-Calhoun Technical
   College *C*
Technical College of the
   Lowcountry *C*
Trident Technical College *C*
York Technical College *C*

South Dakota

Mitchell Technical Institute *C, A*

Tennessee

Chattanooga State Community
   College *C*
Remington College
   Memphis *A*

Texas

Amarillo College *C*
Angelina College *C*
Cedar Valley College *A*
Central Texas College *C*

Clarendon College *C, A*
Coastal Bend College *C, A*
College of the Mainland *C, A*
Eastfield College *A*
El Centro College *C*
El Paso Community College *C*
Galveston College *C*
Grayson College *C, A*
Hallmark College of
   Technology *C, A, B*
Houston Community College
   System *C, A*
Laredo Community College *C, A*
Lone Star College System *C*
McLennan Community College *C, A*
Navarro College *A*
North Central Texas College *A*
North Lake College *A*
Northeast Texas Community
   College *C, A*
Panola College *C*
Paris Junior College *C, A*
St. Philip's College *C, A*
San Antonio College *C*
San Jacinto College *C, A*
Southwest Texas Junior College *A*
Tarrant County College *C*
Trinity Valley Community
   College *C, A*
Vernon College *C, A*
Weatherford College *C*

Utah

Salt Lake Community College *C*
Utah Valley University *A*

Virginia

Blue Ridge Community College *C*
Dabney S. Lancaster Community
   College *C*
Mountain Empire Community
   College *C*
New River Community College *A*
Northern Virginia Community
   College *C*
Paul D. Camp Community College *C*
University of the Potomac *C*
Virginia Western Community
   College *C, A*

Washington

Centralia College *C, A*
Clark College *C, A*
Green River Community College *C, A*
Lower Columbia College *C, A*
North Seattle Community College *A*
Peninsula College *C*
Renton Technical College *A*
Seattle Central Community College *C*
South Seattle Community
   College *C, A*
Spokane Community College *C, A*
Walla Walla Community College *C*

West Virginia

Blue Ridge Community and Technical
   College *C, A*
New River Community and Technical
   College *C*
Pierpont Community and Technical
   College *A*
Potomac State College of West
   Virginia University *A*

Wisconsin

Herzing University
   Madison *A, B*
Madison Area Technical College *C*
Mid-State Technical College *C*
Moraine Park Technical College *C, A*
Southwest Wisconsin Technical
   College *C*
Western Technical College *C*

Wyoming

Casper College *C, A*
Central Wyoming College *C*
Western Wyoming Community
   College *C, A*

Oncology

Arizona

University of Arizona *M, D*

California

Stanford University *M, D*

Colorado

University of Colorado
   Denver *D*

District of Columbia

George Washington University *D*
Georgetown University *M, D*

Florida

University of Miami *D*
University of South Florida *D*

Illinois

University of Chicago *D*

Michigan

University of Michigan *D*
Wayne State University *M, D*

Nebraska

University of Nebraska
   Medical Center *M, D*

North Carolina

Wake Forest University *D*

Ohio

University of Toledo *M, D*

Oregon

Oregon Health & Science
   University *D*

Tennessee

Vanderbilt University *M, D*

Texas

University of Texas
   Health Science Center at
      Houston *M, D*

Utah

University of Utah *M, D*

West Virginia

West Virginia University *D*

Wisconsin

University of Wisconsin
   Madison *M, D*

Operations management

Alabama

Community College of the Air
   Force *A*
Lawson State Community College *A*
Remington College
   Mobile *B*
University of Phoenix
   Birmingham *B*

Alaska

University of Alaska
   Fairbanks *C*

Arizona

Arizona Western College *C, A*
Eastern Arizona College *C*
University of Arizona *B*
University of Phoenix
  Phoenix-Hohokam *B*
  Southern Arizona *B*

Arkansas

East Arkansas Community College *C*

California

California State University
  Dominguez Hills *B*
  East Bay *M*
  Long Beach *B*
  Sacramento *B, M*
  San Bernardino *B, M*
Citrus College *C*
City College of San Francisco *C, A*
Diablo Valley College *C, A*
Fashion Institute of Design and
  Merchandising
  Los Angeles *A*
Golden Gate University *C, B, M*
Laney College *C, A*
San Diego City College *C, A*
San Diego State University *B, M*
University of Phoenix
  Bay Area *B*
  Central Valley *B*
  Sacramento Valley *B*
  Southern California *B*

Colorado

Fort Lewis College *B*
University of Phoenix
  Denver *B*

Connecticut

Central Connecticut State
  University *M*
Goodwin College *B*
University of Bridgeport *M*

Delaware

University of Delaware *B*

District of Columbia

George Washington University *M*
University of the Potomac *C, A*

Florida

Daytona State College *A*
Florida State College at
  Jacksonville *C*
Hillsborough Community College *A*
Northwest Florida State College *A*
Pasco-Hernando State College *C*
Polk State College *A*
Saint Johns River State College *A, B*
University of Phoenix
  Central Florida *B*
  North Florida *B*
  South Florida *B*
  West Florida *B*
Valencia College *A*

Georgia

Albany Technical College *C*
Central Georgia Technical
  College *C, A*
Dalton State College *B*
Georgia Piedmont Technical
  College *C*
Georgia State University *D*
Gwinnett Technical College *C*
Middle Georgia State College *B*
Savannah Technical College *C, A*
Southwest Georgia Technical
  College *C, A*
University of Phoenix
  Atlanta *B*
  Augusta *B*

  Columbus *B*
  Savannah *B*

Hawaii

University of Hawaii
  Hawaii Community College *C, A*
University of Phoenix
  Hawaii *B*

Idaho

Boise State University *B*
University of Phoenix
  Idaho *B*

Illinois

Aurora University *B*
Carl Sandburg College *A*
Illinois Eastern Community Colleges
  Wabash Valley College *C*
Illinois Institute of Technology *B, M*
Kishwaukee College *A*
Loyola University Chicago *C, B*
McHenry County College *C, A*
Northern Illinois University *B*
Northwestern University *M*
University of Illinois
  Urbana-Champaign *B, D*
University of Phoenix
  Chicago *B*

Indiana

Ball State University *B*
Indiana University
  Purdue University Fort
    Wayne *C, A, B, M*
  Purdue University
    Indianapolis *C, B*
  Southeast *C*
Purdue University *A, B*
Purdue University
  Calumet *C, B*
  North Central *C, A, B*
Trine University *B*
University of Phoenix
  Indianapolis *B*
University of Southern Indiana *B, M*

Iowa

Ashford University *B*
Iowa Central Community College *A*
Iowa State University *B*

Kansas

Barton County Community College *A*
Friends University *M*
Johnson County Community
  College *C*
Wichita Area Technical College *C*

Kentucky

Daymar College
  Owensboro *A*
Northern Kentucky University *A*
University of Phoenix
  Louisville *B*

Louisiana

University of Phoenix
  Baton Rouge *B*
  Louisiana *B*
  Shreveport *B*

Maine

Northern Maine Community
  College *A*

Maryland

University of Maryland
  University College *M*

Massachusetts

Babson College *B*
Bentley University *M*

Boston College *B*
Boston University *B*
Bunker Hill Community College *A*
University of Massachusetts
  Amherst *B*
  Dartmouth *B*
  Lowell *C*
University of Phoenix
  Boston *B*
Wentworth Institute of
  Technology *B, M*
Worcester Polytechnic Institute *B, M*

Michigan

Baker College
  Flint *A, B*
Central Michigan University *B*
Ferris State University *C, B*
Kettering University *M*
Lawrence Technological University *M*
Macomb Community College *C, A*
Michigan State University *D*
Oakland University *B*
Saginaw Valley State University *B*
Spring Arbor University *B, M*
University of Michigan
  Flint *B*
University of Phoenix
  Metro Detroit *B*
  West Michigan *B*

Minnesota

Alexandria Technical and Community
  College *C*
Crown College *B*
Dakota County Technical College *C*
Metropolitan State University *B*
Minnesota State University
  Mankato *B*
  Moorhead *B*
Northland Community & Technical
  College *C*
University of Minnesota
  Crookston *B*
  Twin Cities *B*
University of Phoenix
  Minneapolis-St. Paul *B*
University of St. Thomas *B*

Mississippi

University of Phoenix
  Jackson *B*

Missouri

Missouri Southern State University *B*
University of Missouri
  St. Louis *B, M*
University of Phoenix
  Kansas City *B*
  St. Louis *B*

Nebraska

University of Nebraska
  Kearney *B*
University of Phoenix
  Omaha *B*

Nevada

Truckee Meadows Community
  College *C*
University of Phoenix
  Las Vegas *B*

New Hampshire

Granite State College *B*
Nashua Community College *C*
Southern New Hampshire
  University *B, M*

New Jersey

Cumberland County College *A*
Thomas Edison State College *C, B*
University of Phoenix
  Jersey City *B*

New Mexico

University of Phoenix
  New Mexico *B*
Western New Mexico University *B*

New York

City University of New York
  Baruch College *B*
Excelsior College *B*
Globe Institute of
  Technology *C, A, B*
Le Moyne College *B*
Pace University *M*

North Carolina

Asheville-Buncombe Technical
  Community College *A*
Catawba Valley Community
  College *A*
Central Piedmont Community
  College *C*
Cleveland Community College *C, A*
Craven Community College *C, A*
Durham Technical Community
  College *C, A*
Fayetteville Technical Community
  College *C, A*
Isothermal Community College *C, A*
Lenoir Community College *C, A*
Mitchell Community College *A*
Pitt Community College *C, A*
University of North Carolina
  Asheville *B*
  Charlotte *B*
Wayne Community College *C, A*
Western Piedmont Community
  College *C, A*

North Dakota

Bismarck State College *B*
University of Mary *M*
University of North Dakota *B*

Ohio

Bowling Green State University *B*
Bowling Green State University:
  Firelands College *C, A*
Case Western Reserve University *M*
Franklin University *B*
Lakeland Community College *C*
Miami University
  Oxford *B*
North Central State College *C, A*
Ohio State University
  Columbus Campus *B*
Owens Community College
  Toledo *A*
Stark State College *A*
Terra State Community College *C, A*
Tiffin University *B*
University of Akron *B, M*
University of Cincinnati *B*
University of Dayton *B*
University of Phoenix
  Cleveland *B*
University of Toledo *B, M, D*
Wright State University *M*
Youngstown State University *B*

Oklahoma

Northeastern State University *B*
University of Central Oklahoma *B*

Oregon

Clackamas Community College *C, A*
Oregon Institute of Technology *B*
Oregon State University *B*

Pennsylvania

Carnegie Mellon University *B, M, D*
Community College of
  Philadelphia *A*
Drexel University *B*
La Salle University *B*

Reading Area Community College *A*
University of Pennsylvania *B, M, D*
University of Phoenix
Pittsburgh *B*
University of Scranton *B, M*
Widener University *B*

Puerto Rico

Inter American University of Puerto Rico
Bayamon Campus *B*
Ponce Campus *B*
University of Puerto Rico
Rio Piedras *B, M*

Rhode Island

Roger Williams University *B*

South Carolina

Clemson University *M, D*
Morris College *B*
University of Phoenix
Columbia *B*

South Dakota

South Dakota State University *B, M*

Tennessee

Chattanooga State Community College *C*
Tennessee Technological University *B*
University of Phoenix
Chattanooga *B*
Memphis *B*
Nashville *B*
Vanderbilt University *M*

Texas

El Paso Community College *A*
Kilgore College *C, A*
Lamar University *M*
LeTourneau University *B*
Odessa College *C*
Sam Houston State University *B*
San Antonio College *C*
Tarrant County College *C, A*
Texas A&M University *M*
Texas Southern University *B*
University of Dallas *M*
University of Houston *B, M*
University of North Texas *B*
University of Phoenix
Austin *B*
Dallas Fort Worth *B*
Houston Westside *B*
San Antonio *B*
University of Texas
Austin *C*
El Paso *B*
San Antonio *M*
Weatherford College *C, A*
Wiley College *B*

Utah

Dixie State College *A, B*
University of Phoenix
Utah *B*
University of Utah *B*
Utah State University *B*
Utah Valley University *B*

Vermont

College of St. Joseph in Vermont *B*

Virginia

University of Phoenix
Northern Virginia *B*
University of the Potomac *C, A*

Washington

City University of Seattle *M*
Seattle Central Community College *C*

University of Phoenix
Western Washington *B*
Washington State University *B*
Western Washington University *B*

West Virginia

Blue Ridge Community and Technical College *C*

Wisconsin

Blackhawk Technical College *A*
Gateway Technical College *A*
Lakeshore Technical College *A*
Marian University *B*
Mid-State Technical College *A*
Milwaukee Area Technical College *A*
Northcentral Technical College *C*
Southwest Wisconsin Technical College *A*
University of Phoenix
Milwaukee *B*
University of Wisconsin
Madison *B, M*
Milwaukee *B*
Oshkosh *B*
Stout *B*
Whitewater *B*
Waukesha County Technical College *A*
Western Technical College *A*
Wisconsin Indianhead Technical College *A*

Operations research

California

California State University
Fullerton *B, M*
San Diego State University *B, M*
University of California
Berkeley *B, M, D*
University of Southern California *M*

Colorado

United States Air Force Academy *B*

Delaware

Delaware Technical Community College
Stanton/Wilmington Campus *A*
University of Delaware *B, M, D*

District of Columbia

George Washington University *M, D*

Florida

Florida Institute of Technology *M, D*

Georgia

Georgia Institute of Technology *M*
Georgia State University *M, D*

Illinois

University of Illinois
Urbana-Champaign *B, M, D*

Iowa

Iowa State University *M*

Kansas

Kansas State University *M*

Maryland

United States Naval Academy *B*

Massachusetts

Massachusetts Institute of Technology *M, D*
Northeastern University *M*

Minnesota

University of Minnesota
Twin Cities *M, D*

New Jersey

Princeton University *B, M, D*
Rutgers, The State University of New Jersey
New Brunswick/Piscataway Campus *M, D*

New York

City University of New York
Baruch College *B, M*
Columbia University *B, M, D*
Cornell University *B, M, D*
New York University *B, M, D*
United States Military Academy *B*

North Carolina

North Carolina State University *M, D*

Ohio

Bowling Green State University *B*
Case Western Reserve University *M*

Pennsylvania

Carnegie Mellon University *B, D*
University of Pennsylvania *D*

Texas

Southern Methodist University *B, M, D*

Utah

Utah State University *M*

Wisconsin

Milwaukee School of Engineering *B*

Ophthalmic laboratory technology

Alabama

Community College of the Air Force *A*

Connecticut

Middlesex Community College *A*

Florida

Broward College *A*

Georgia

Georgia Piedmont Technical College *A*

Minnesota

St. Catherine University *A*

Ohio

Lakeland Community College *A*

Puerto Rico

Inter American University of Puerto Rico
Ponce Campus *A*
University of Puerto Rico
Medical Sciences *A*

Texas

Tyler Junior College *A*

Ophthalmic technology

Arkansas

University of Arkansas
for Medical Sciences *M*

Illinois

City Colleges of Chicago
Olive-Harvey College *A*
Triton College *A*

Indiana

Ivy Tech Community College
Columbus *A*

Massachusetts

Benjamin Franklin Institute of Technology *A*

Oregon

Portland Community College *A*

Tennessee

Volunteer State Community College *A*

Washington

Renton Technical College *C, A*

Opticianry/ophthalmic dispensing

Connecticut

Goodwin College *A*
Middlesex Community College *A*

Florida

Hillsborough Community College *A*
Miami Dade College *A*

Massachusetts

Benjamin Franklin Institute of Technology *A*
Holyoke Community College *A*

Michigan

Baker College
Jackson *A*

Mississippi

East Mississippi Community College *A*
Mississippi Gulf Coast Community College *A*

Nevada

College of Southern Nevada *A*

New Jersey

Camden County College *A*
Essex County College *A*
Raritan Valley Community College *A*

New Mexico

Southwestern Indian Polytechnic Institute *A*

New York

City University of New York
New York City College of Technology *A*
Erie Community College *A*

North Carolina

Durham Technical Community College *A*

Ohio

Brown Mackie College
Cincinnati *A*
Cuyahoga Community College
Metropolitan *A*
Hocking College *A*
Lakeland Community College *A*

Pennsylvania

Sanford-Brown Institute
Pittsburgh *A*

Rhode Island

Community College of Rhode Island *A*

Tennessee
Roane State Community College *A*

Texas
El Paso Community College *A*

Virginia
J. Sargeant Reynolds Community
College *A*

Washington
Spokane Community College *A*

Optics

Arizona
University of Arizona *B, M, D*

California
Yuba College *C*

Delaware
Delaware State University *M, D*

Massachusetts
Tufts University *M, D*

Michigan
Saginaw Valley State University *B*

New Mexico
University of New Mexico *M, D*

New York
Excelsior College *A, B*
Monroe Community College *A*
University of Rochester *B, M, D*

North Carolina
University of North Carolina
Charlotte *M, D*

Ohio
Ohio State University
Columbus Campus *B*
University of Dayton *M, D*

Oklahoma
Oklahoma State University *D*

Pennsylvania
Albright College *B*
Indiana University of Pennsylvania *A*

Puerto Rico
EDIC College *A*

South Carolina
Clemson University *M, D*

Virginia
Norfolk State University *B*

Optometric assistant

Florida
Hillsborough Community College *A*

Indiana
Indiana University
Bloomington *C, A*

Michigan
Delta College *A*
Oakland Community College *C*

New Jersey
Raritan Valley Community College *C*

New Mexico
Southwestern Indian Polytechnic
Institute *C*

New York
Technical Career Institutes *A*

Ohio
Mercy College of Ohio *C*

Texas
San Jacinto College *C, A*

Organic chemistry

California
Pitzer College *B*

Iowa
Iowa State University *M, D*

Massachusetts
Tufts University *M, D*

Minnesota
University of Minnesota
Twin Cities *B, M, D*

Montana
University of Montana *M, D*

New York
Fordham University *M*
SUNY
University at Albany *D*

Vermont
Marlboro College *B*

Wisconsin
University of Wisconsin
River Falls *B*

Organizational behavior studies

Arizona
Argosy University
Online *M*
Estrella Mountain Community
College *C, A*
Mesa Community College *A*
Paradise Valley Community
College *C, A*
Western International University *M*

Arkansas
Central Baptist College *B*
John Brown University *M*

California
Argosy University
Inland Empire *M*
California Institute of Integral
Studies *M, D*
California Lutheran University *M*
California State University
San Bernardino *B*
Fresno Pacific University *B*
National University *B*
Pepperdine University *M*
Pitzer College *B*
St. Mary's College of California *M*
Santa Clara University *B*
Scripps College *B*
Simpson University *B*
University of La Verne *M*
University of San Francisco *B*
University of the Pacific *B*
Woodbury University *B, M*

Colorado
Argosy University
Denver *M*
Colorado Christian University *C, B*
Colorado Technical University *C*
Regis University *B*
University of Colorado
Denver *M*
University of Denver *B*

Connecticut
Central Connecticut State
University *B*
Eastern Connecticut State
University *M*
Goodwin College *B*
University of Hartford *M*

Delaware
Wilmington University *M*

District of Columbia
George Washington University *M*

Florida
Bethune-Cookman University *M*
Gulf Coast State College *B*
Nova Southeastern University *M*
Palm Beach Atlantic University *M*
Rollins College *B*
Saint Thomas University *B*

Georgia
Emory University *B*
Oglethorpe University *B*

Illinois
Benedictine University *B, M, D*
DePaul University *B*
Greenville College *B*
Lewis University *B, M*
Loyola University Chicago *M*
North Park University *B*
Northwestern University *B, M, D*
Roosevelt University *B*
Trinity International University *B, M*
University of Illinois
Urbana-Champaign *B, D*
University of St. Francis *B*

Indiana
Anderson University *B*
Calumet College of St. Joseph *B*
Indiana Wesleyan University *B, M, D*
Oakland City University *B*
Purdue University, *B*

Iowa
St. Ambrose University *B*
Waldorf College *B*

Kansas
Central Christian College of Kansas *B*
Cowley County Community
College *C, A*

Kentucky
Mid-Continent University *B*
Midway College *B*
Northern Kentucky
University *C, B, M*

Maine
University of Southern Maine *B*

Maryland
Towson University *T*
Washington Adventist University *B*

Massachusetts
Boston College *D*
Boston University *B*
Emerson College *M*

Fitchburg State University *C*
Harvard College *M, D*

Michigan
Central Michigan University *M*
Concordia University *M*
Michigan State University *D*
University of Michigan *B*
Wayne State University *B*

Minnesota
Argosy University
Twin Cities *M*
Bethel University *B, M*
Capella University *M*
College of St. Scholastica *B*
University of Northwestern - St.
Paul *B, M*

Missouri
Fontbonne University *B*
Hannibal-LaGrange University *B*
St. Louis Community College *C, A*
Saint Louis University *B*
University of Missouri
St. Louis *B*
Washington University in St. Louis *M*

Nebraska
Union College *B*
University of Nebraska
Omaha *B*

New Jersey
Rider University *B*

New York
City University of New York
Baruch College *M*
CUNY Online *C*
United States Military Academy *B*

North Carolina
High Point University *B*

Ohio
Bluffton University *B, M*
Bowling Green State University *B, M*
Case Western Reserve
University *M, D*
College of Mount St. Joseph *B, M*
Denison University *B*
Lourdes University *M*
Owens Community College
Toledo *C*
Terra State Community College *C*
Tiffin University *B, M*
University of Cincinnati *C, B*
University of Toledo *B*
Urbana University *B*

Oklahoma
Oral Roberts University *B*
University of Oklahoma *B, M*
University of Tulsa *B*

Pennsylvania
Alvernia University *D*
Cabrini College *M*
Carnegie Mellon University *M, D*
Keystone College *B*
La Salle University *B*
Penn State
Abington *B*
Altoona *B*
Beaver *B*
Berks *B*
Brandywine *B*
DuBois *B*
Erie, The Behrend College *B*
Fayette, The Eberly Campus *B*
Greater Allegheny *B*
Harrisburg *B, M*

Hazleton *B*
Lehigh Valley *B*
Mont Alto *B*
New Kensington *B*
Schuylkill *B*
Shenango *B*
University Park *B*
Wilkes-Barre *B*
Worthington Scranton *B*
York *B*
Robert Morris University *B, M*
Rosemont College *B, M*
Saint Joseph's University *B*
Shippensburg University of
Pennsylvania *M*
University of Pennsylvania *M*
Westminster College *B*

Puerto Rico

University of Puerto Rico
Mayaguez *B, M*

Rhode Island

Providence College *B*

South Carolina

Anderson University *B*
Claflin University *B*
Voorhees College *B*

South Dakota

Black Hills State University *M*
University of Sioux Falls *B*

Tennessee

Vanderbilt University *M*

Texas

Argosy University
Dallas *M*
University of Dallas *M*
University of North Texas *B*
University of Texas
San Antonio *D*
University of the Incarnate Word *B*

Utah

Brigham Young University *B*

Virginia

Eastern Mennonite University *B*
George Mason University *M*
Regent University *B, M, D*

Washington

Antioch University
Seattle *M*
University of Washington *B, M*

West Virginia

American Public University System *C*

Wisconsin

Carroll University *B*
Edgewood College *B, M*
University of Wisconsin
Platteville *B*

Organizational communication

California

College of the Desert *A*
Folsom Lake College *A*
Ohlone College *C*
Pepperdine University *B*

Connecticut

Mitchell College *B*
Three Rivers Community College *C*

Florida

Barry University *M*
Florida College *B*
Rollins College *B*
University of Miami *B*

Idaho

Idaho State University *M*
University of Idaho *C, B*

Illinois

Bradley University *B*
Judson University *C, B*
Lewis University *B*
McKendree University *B*
North Central College *B*
Roosevelt University *B*
Saint Xavier University *B*
University of Illinois
Urbana-Champaign *B*

Indiana

Purdue University *B*

Iowa

Buena Vista University *B*
Coe College *B*
Graceland University *B*
University of Northern Iowa *B*

Kansas

Central Christian College of Kansas *B*
Tabor College *B*

Kentucky

Murray State University *B, M*
Western Kentucky University *B*

Louisiana

Southeastern Louisiana University *M*

Maryland

Bowie State University *M*
Howard Community College *A*

Massachusetts

Assumption College *B*
Fitchburg State University *M*
Regis College *M*
Suffolk University *B, M*

Michigan

Calvin College *B*
Central Michigan University *B, M*
Western Michigan University *B*

Minnesota

Augsburg College *B*
Concordia University St. Paul *M*

Missouri

Lindenwood University *B, M*
Missouri State University *B*
Northwest Missouri State
University *B*
Rockhurst University *C*
Saint Louis University *M*
Southeast Missouri State University *B*

Nebraska

Bellevue University *B*
Creighton University *A*
Doane College *B*

New Hampshire

Southern New Hampshire
University *M*

New Jersey

Fairleigh Dickinson University
Metropolitan Campus *B*
Montclair State University *B*

New York

Canisius College *M*
Ithaca College *B*
SUNY
College at Cortland *B*
College at Plattsburgh *B*

North Carolina

Methodist University *B*
North Carolina State University *M*
Pfeiffer University *B*
University of North Carolina
Charlotte *B, M*

Ohio

Ashland University *B*
Capital University *B*
Cedarville University *B*
Franklin University *B*
Marietta College *B*
Ohio Northern University *B*
Ohio University *M, D*
Ohio University
Chillicothe Campus *B*
Southern Campus at Ironton *B*
Zanesville Campus *B*
Otterbein University *B*
University of Akron *C, B*

Oregon

George Fox University *B*
Marylhurst University *B*
University of Portland *B, M*

Pennsylvania

Butler County Community College *A*
Penn State
Lehigh Valley *C*
University Park *C*
Temple University *C, B, M*

Rhode Island

Bryant University *M*

South Carolina

College of Charleston *M*

Tennessee

Lipscomb University *B*
Trevecca Nazarene University *B*

Texas

Howard Payne University *B*
Lubbock Christian University *B*
University of Texas
El Paso *B*

Utah

Dixie State College *B*
Weber State University *B*

Washington

Northwest University *B*

Wisconsin

Carroll University *B*
Marian University *B*
Viterbo University *B*

Organizational leadership

Alabama

Auburn University at Montgomery *B*
Columbia Southern University *B, M*
Samford University *B*
Spring Hill College *C, B*

Arizona

Western International University *M*

Arkansas

University of Arkansas
Fort Smith *C*

California

Alliant International University *D*
California Baptist University *B, M*
Dominican University of California *M*
Holy Names University *M*
National University *B, M*
University of Redlands *C*

Colorado

Regis University *M*

District of Columbia

Strayer University *M*

Florida

St. Petersburg College *C*
Southeastern University *B*

Georgia

Brenau University *B, M*
Columbus State University *M*
Kennesaw State University *C*
LaGrange College *B, M*
Point University *A, B*
Toccoa Falls College *B*
Valdosta State University *B*

Idaho

University of Idaho *C*

Illinois

Benedictine University at
Springfield *B*
Blackburn College *B*
Judson University *M*
Lincoln Christian University *B, M*
Millikin University *B*
Roosevelt University *B*

Indiana

Grace College *A*
Harrison College
Indianapolis *A*
Huntington University *A*
Indiana Institute of
Technology *B, M, D*
Indiana University
Purdue University Indianapolis *C*
University of Evansville *B*
University of St. Francis *M*

Iowa

AIB College of Business *A*
Ashford University *B*
Buena Vista University *B*
Upper Iowa University *M*

Kansas

Kansas Wesleyan University *B*

Kentucky

St. Catharine College *M*
Sullivan University *C*
Western Kentucky University *C, B, M*

Louisiana

McNeese State University *B*
Northwestern State University *B*
University of New Orleans *B*

Maryland

University of Maryland
Eastern Shore *D*

Massachusetts

Wheelock College *M*

Michigan

Central Michigan University *M*
Cleary University *M*

Minnesota

Capella University *M*
Concordia University St. Paul *M*
Lake Superior College *C*
St. Mary's University of Minnesota *M*
Walden University *M*

Missouri

Calvary Bible College and Theological
    Seminary *B*
Truman State University *M*

New Hampshire

Franklin Pierce University *C, T*
Granite State College *M*

New Jersey

Thomas Edison State College *B*

New Mexico

National American University
    Albuquerque *B*

New York

City University of New York
    CUNY Online *C*
Daemen College *M*
Hilbert College *B*
Manhattanville College *M*
Nyack College *M*
Rochester Institute of Technology *M*
St. John Fisher College *D*
St. Joseph's College New York:
    Suffolk Campus *C*
St. Joseph's College, New York *C*
Syracuse University *C*

North Carolina

Mid-Atlantic Christian University *B*
North Carolina Wesleyan College *B*
Pfeiffer University *M*
Queens University of Charlotte *M*

North Dakota

University of Mary *M*

Ohio

Ashland University *D*
Malone University *M*
Union Institute & University *B, M*
Xavier University *M*

Oklahoma

Oral Roberts University *B*
Southeastern Oklahoma State
    University *B*
University of Central Oklahoma *B*

Pennsylvania

Central Penn College *B, M*
Drexel University *M*
Eastern University *B, M, D*
Gannon University *B, D*
Keystone College *B*
Neumann University *M*
Peirce College *M*
Valley Forge Christian College *M*

Rhode Island

Roger Williams University *M*

South Carolina

Charleston Southern University *M*

Tennessee

Trevecca Nazarene University *M*

Texas

Dallas Baptist University *C, M, D*
Hardin-Simmons University *D*
Lubbock Christian University *B*
National American University
    Austin *B*
Our Lady of the Lake University of
    San Antonio *B, M, D*
University of Houston *B*

Vermont

Champlain College *C*

Virginia

Lynchburg College *D*

Washington

Faith Evangelical College &
    Seminary *B*
Olympic College *C, A*

West Virginia

Wheeling Jesuit University *B, M*

Wisconsin

Marquette University *B, M*
University of Wisconsin
    Eau Claire *B*

Ornamental horticulture

Arkansas

University of Arkansas *B*

California

Antelope Valley College *C, A*
Butte College *C, A*
Cabrillo College *C, A*
Cerritos College *A*
City College of San Francisco *A*
College of the Desert *C, A*
College of the Sequoias *C, A*
Cuyamaca College *A*
El Camino College *C, A*
Foothill College *C, A*
Long Beach City College *C, A*
Los Angeles Pierce College *C, A*
Merced College *C, A*
Modesto Junior College *A*
Monterey Peninsula College *C, A*
Mount San Antonio College *C*
Orange Coast College *C, A*
Saddleback College *C, A*
Santa Barbara City College *C, A*
Santa Rosa Junior College *C*
Shasta College *C, A*
Solano Community College *C, A*
Southwestern College *C, A*
Victor Valley College *C, A*
Yuba College *C, A*

Delaware

University of Delaware *B, M*

Florida

Palm Beach State College *A*
University of Florida *B*

Georgia

Abraham Baldwin Agricultural
    College *A*
Fort Valley State University *A*

Illinois

College of DuPage *C*
College of Lake County *C, A*
Joliet Junior College *C, A*
Kishwaukee College *C, A*
McHenry County College *C*
Triton College *C, A*
University of Illinois
    Urbana-Champaign *B*

Indiana

Purdue University *B*

Kentucky

Eastern Kentucky University *B*

Maryland

Prince George's Community
    College *C*

Mississippi

Mississippi Gulf Coast Community
    College *C, A*

Nebraska

Nebraska College of Technical
    Agriculture *A*

Nevada

College of Southern Nevada *C, A*

New Jersey

Brookdale Community College *C*
Cumberland County College *C, A*
Mercer County Community
    College *C, A*

New York

Cornell University *M, D*
Finger Lakes Community
    College *C*
Niagara County Community
    College *C*
SUNY
    College of Agriculture and
        Technology at Cobleskill *A*
    College of Agriculture and
        Technology at Morrisville *B*
    College of Technology at Delhi *A*
    Farmingdale State College *C, A*

North Carolina

Blue Ridge Community College *C*
Sampson Community College *A*

Ohio

Ohio State University
    Agricultural Technical Institute *A*
    Columbus Campus *A, B*

Oklahoma

Eastern Oklahoma State College *A*

Oregon

Clackamas Community College *C, A*

Pennsylvania

Community College of Allegheny
    County *C*
Delaware Valley College *B*

Puerto Rico

Inter American University of Puerto
    Rico
    Barranquitas Campus *C, A*

Tennessee

Walters State Community
    College *C, A*

Texas

Houston Community College
    System *C*
Tarleton State University *B*
Texas A&M University *B*

Utah

Utah State University *C, A*

Vermont

Vermont Technical College *A*

Washington

South Puget Sound Community
    College *C, A*
Spokane Community College *C*

Wisconsin

Blackhawk Technical College *C*
University of Wisconsin
    Platteville *B*

Orthotics/prosthetics

California

Loma Linda University *M*

Connecticut

University of Hartford *M*

Florida

St. Petersburg College *B*

Georgia

Georgia Institute of Technology *M*

Illinois

Northwestern University *C*

Massachusetts

Boston University *M, D*

Michigan

Baker College
    Flint *A*
Eastern Michigan University *M*

Minnesota

Century College *C, A*
Concordia University St. Paul *B*

Mississippi

Mississippi Gulf Coast Community
    College *A*

Nevada

College of Southern Nevada *A*

Oklahoma

Oklahoma State University
    Institute of Technology:
    Okmulgee *A*

Pennsylvania

University of Pittsburgh *M*

Washington

Centralia College *C*
Spokane Falls Community College *A*
University of Washington *B*

Outdoor education

Alaska

Prince William Sound Community
    College *A*
University of Alaska
    Anchorage *C*

Colorado

Colorado Northwestern Community
    College *C, A*

Georgia

Toccoa Falls College *B*

Indiana

Huntington University *B*

Kentucky

Murray State University *B*

Maine

College of the Atlantic *B, M*
Unity College *B*

Minnesota

Vermilion Community College *C*

Nevada

Sierra Nevada College *B*

Oregon

Mt. Hood Community College *A*

South Dakota

Black Hills State University *B*

Texas

Lubbock Christian University *B*

Utah

Snow College *A*

Virginia

Shenandoah University *B*

Wisconsin

Northland College *B*

Pacific area/rim studies

California

Claremont McKenna College *B*
University of California
San Diego *M*

Hawaii

Brigham Young University-Hawaii *B*
University of Hawaii
Manoa *M*
West Oahu *B*

Washington

Central Washington University *B*

Packaging science

Michigan

Michigan State University *B, M, D*

New York

Rochester Institute of
Technology *B, M*

South Carolina

Clemson University *B, M*

Wisconsin

University of Wisconsin
Stout *B*

Painting

Alabama

Birmingham-Southern College *B*

Arkansas

Harding University *B*

California

Academy of Art University *C, A, B, M*
Art Center College of Design *B, M*
Biola University *B*
California College of the Arts *B, M*
California State University
East Bay *B*
Long Beach *B, M*
Northridge *B, M*
Chabot College *A*
College of the Desert *A*
De Anza College *C, A*
Grossmont College *A*

Laguna College of Art and
Design *B, M*
Monterey Peninsula College *C, A*
Ohlone College *C*
Otis College of Art and Design *B, M*
Palomar College *A*
Pasadena City College *A*
San Francisco Art Institute *B, M*
Santa Rosa Junior College *C*
Solano Community College *A*

Colorado

Adams State University *B*
Rocky Mountain College of Art &
Design *B*

Connecticut

Lyme Academy College of Fine
Arts *C, B*
University of Hartford *B*

District of Columbia

American University *M*
George Washington University *M*

Florida

Ringling College of Art and Design *B*
University of Miami *B*

Georgia

Savannah College of Art and
Design *B, M*

Illinois

American Academy of Art *B*
Bradley University *B*
Lewis University *B*
Lincoln College *A*
Richland Community College *A*
School of the Art Institute of
Chicago *B, M*
University of Illinois
Urbana-Champaign *B, M*

Indiana

Indiana University
Purdue University Fort Wayne *B*
Indiana Wesleyan University *B*

Iowa

Coe College *B*
Drake University *B*
University of Iowa *B, M*

Kansas

Allen County Community College *A*
Central Christian College of Kansas *A*
Kansas Wesleyan University *B*
Pratt Community College *A*
Seward County Community
College *A*
University of Kansas *B, M*

Kentucky

Eastern Kentucky University *B*

Louisiana

Centenary College of Louisiana *B*

Maine

College of the Atlantic *B, M*
Maine College of Art *B*
University of Southern Maine *B*

Maryland

Maryland Institute College of
Art *B, M*

Massachusetts

Boston University *B, M*
Massachusetts College of Art and
Design *B, M*
Montserrat College of Art *B*

Salem State University *B*
School of the Museum of Fine
Arts *B, M*
University of Massachusetts
Dartmouth *B, M*

Michigan

Andrews University *B*
Aquinas College *B*
College for Creative Studies *B*
Ferris State University *B*
Finlandia University *B*
Grand Valley State University *B*
Northern Michigan University *B*
Oakland University *B, T*
Siena Heights University *B*
University of Michigan
Dearborn *B*

Minnesota

Minneapolis College of Art and
Design *B*
Minnesota State University
Mankato *B, M*
Saint Cloud State University *B*

Missouri

Columbia College *B*
Kansas City Art Institute *B*
Washington University in St.
Louis *B, M*

Nevada

Sierra Nevada College *B*

New Hampshire

New Hampshire Institute of Art *B*
Plymouth State University *B*
University of New Hampshire *M*

New Mexico

Santa Fe University of Art and
Design *B*

New York

Hofstra University *B*
Pratt Institute *A*
Rochester Institute of
Technology *B, M*
SUNY
College at Buffalo *B*
College at Fredonia *B*
College at New Paltz *B, M*
College at Oneonta *B*
College at Purchase *B, M*
Syracuse University *B, M*

North Carolina

East Carolina University *B*
Elon University *B*
Gardner-Webb University *B*
Methodist University *B*

Ohio

Art Academy of Cincinnati *B*
Bowling Green State University *B*
Cleveland Institute of Art *B*
Kent State University *B, M*
Ohio University *M*
Youngstown State University *B*

Oregon

Mt. Hood Community College *A*
Oregon College of Art & Craft *C, B*
Pacific Northwest College of Art *B*
Portland State University *B, M*
University of Oregon *B*

Pennsylvania

Arcadia University *B*
Lycoming College *B*
Marywood University *B, M*

Pennsylvania Academy of the Fine
Arts *C, B, M*
Pennsylvania College of Art and
Design *B*
Seton Hill University *B*
Temple University *B, M*
University of the Arts *B*

Puerto Rico

Escuela de Artes Plasticas de Puerto
Rico *B*
Inter American University of Puerto
Rico
San German Campus *M*
University of Puerto Rico
Rio Piedras *B*

Rhode Island

Providence College *B*
Rhode Island School of Design *B, M*
Salve Regina University *B*

South Carolina

Technical College of the
Lowcountry *C*

South Dakota

South Dakota State University *C*

Tennessee

Carson-Newman University *B*
Memphis College of Art *B, M*
Tennessee Technological
University *B*

Texas

Texas Christian University *B*
University of Dallas *B, M*
University of Houston *B*
University of Texas
El Paso *B, M*
Western Texas College *A*

Utah

Dixie State College *B*

Vermont

Bennington College *B*
Marlboro College *B*

Virginia

Virginia Commonwealth University *B*

Washington

Cornish College of the Arts *B*
North Seattle Community College *C*
University of Washington *B, M*
Western Washington University *B*

West Virginia

Davis and Elkins College *B*
West Virginia State University *B*
West Virginia Wesleyan College *B*

Wisconsin

Milwaukee Institute of Art &
Design *B*

Painting/wall covering

Arizona

Tohono O'odham Community
College *C, A*

California

Allan Hancock College *C*

Illinois

City Colleges of Chicago
Kennedy-King College *C*
Parkland College *C*

Indiana

Ivy Tech Community College
  Central Indiana *C, A*
  East Central *C, A*
  Lafayette *C, A*
  North Central *C, A*
  Northeast *C, A*
  Northwest *C, A*
  Southwest *C, A*
  Wabash Valley *C, A*

Kentucky

Big Sandy Community and Technical
  College *C*

Louisiana

Delgado Community College *C*

Pennsylvania

Community College of Allegheny
  County *A*

Wisconsin

Gateway Technical College *C*
Milwaukee Area Technical College *C*

Paleontology

New Mexico

Mesalands Community College *A*

Ohio

Bowling Green State University *B*

South Dakota

South Dakota School of Mines and
  Technology *M*

Palliative care nursing

Michigan

Madonna University *C, A, B, M*

New York

Le Moyne College *M*
New York University *M*

Ohio

Case Western Reserve University *M*

Paper science and engineering

Georgia

Georgia Institute of Technology *M, D*

Michigan

Western Michigan University *B, M, D*

Ohio

Miami University
  Oxford *C*

Paralegal studies

Alabama

Bevill State Community College *C, A*
Calhoun Community College *A*
Community College of the Air
  Force *A*
Enterprise State Community
  College *C, A*
Faulkner State Community College *A*
Gadsden State Community College *A*
ITT Technical Institute
  Birmingham *A*
Samford University *C, B*
Shelton State Community College *C*

Virginia College
  Birmingham *A, B*
  Huntsville *A*
  Mobile *C, A*
Wallace State Community College at
  Hanceville *A*

Alaska

Charter College *C, A*
University of Alaska
  Anchorage *C, A*
  Fairbanks *A*

Arizona

Arizona Western College *C*
Brookline College
  Phoenix *A*
  Tempe *A*
  Tucson *A*
Brown Mackie College
  Tucson *A*
Coconino County Community
  College *A*
Everest College
  Phoenix *A*
ITT Technical Institute
  Tempe *A*
  Tucson *A*
Mohave Community College *C, A*
Penn Foster College *A*
Phoenix College *C, A*
Pima Community College *C, A*
Yavapai College *C, A*

Arkansas

ITT Technical Institute
  Little Rock *A*
National Park Community College *C*
Northwest Arkansas Community
  College *A*
Pulaski Technical College *A*
Southeast Arkansas College *A*
University of Arkansas
  Fort Smith *A*

California

American River College *A*
Butte College *C, A*
California State University
  East Bay *C*
  San Bernardino *C*
California University of Management
  and Sciences *A*
Canada College *C, A*
Cerritos College *A*
City College of San Francisco *C, A*
Coastline Community College *C*
College of the Canyons *A*
College of the Redwoods *C, A*
College of the Sequoias *A*
De Anza College *C, A*
El Camino College *C, A*
Empire College *C, A*
Everest College
  Ontario Metro *A*
Fremont College *A*
Fresno City College *C, A*
Fullerton College *A*
Glendale Community College *A*
Heald College
  Concord *A*
  Fresno *A*
  Hayward *C, A*
  Rancho Cordova *A*
  Roseville *A*
  Salinas *A*
  San Francisco *A*
  San Jose *A*
  Stockton *A*
Humphreys College *C, B*
ITT Technical Institute
  Lathrop *A*
  National City *A*
  Oxnard *A*

  Rancho Cordova *A*
  San Bernardino *A*
  Sylmar *A*
  Torrance *A*
Imperial Valley College *C, A*
John F. Kennedy University *C, B*
Kaplan College
  Sacramento *A*
  Vista *A*
Los Angeles City College *A*
Los Angeles Mission College *C, A*
Los Angeles Southwest College *A*
Los Medanos College *C*
MTI College *A*
Merritt College *C, A*
Mount San Antonio College *A*
Napa Valley College *C, A*
National University *C, A, B*
Oxnard College *C, A*
Pasadena City College *C, A*
Platt College
  Ontario *C, A, B*
Saddleback College *C, A*
Sage College *C, A*
San Deigo Miramar College
  San Diego Miramar College *C, A*
San Diego City College *A*
Santa Ana College *C, A*
Santa Barbara Business College *A*
Santa Barbara Business College
  Bakersfield *A*
  Rancho Mirage *C, A*
  Santa Maria *C, A*
  Ventura *C, A*
Santiago Canyon College *A*
Shasta College *A*
Skyline College *C, A*
South Coast College *A*
Southwestern College *C, A*
University of La Verne *C*
West Los Angeles College *C, A*
West Valley College *A*

Colorado

Arapahoe Community College *C, A*
Colorado Mountain College *C, A*
Colorado Northwestern Community
  College *A*
Community College of Aurora *C, A*
Community College of Denver *C, A*
Ecotech Institute *A*
Everest College
  Aurora *A*
  Colorado Springs *A*
  Denver *A*
Front Range Community College *C, A*
IBMC College
  Fort Collins *A*
ITT Technical Institute
  Westminster *A*
Pikes Peak Community College *C, A*

Connecticut

Charter Oak State College *C*
Manchester Community College *C, A*
Naugatuck Valley Community
  College *A*
Norwalk Community College *C, A*
Post University *C*
Quinnipiac University *B*
University of Hartford *C, A, B*
University of New Haven *C*

Delaware

Wesley College *C, A, B*

District of Columbia

George Washington University *C*
University of the District of
  Columbia *A*

Florida

Broward College *A*
Brown Mackie College
  Miami *C, A*

City College
  Fort Lauderdale *A*
College of Central Florida *A*
Daytona State College *A*
Eastern Florida State College *A*
Edison State College *A*
Everest University
  Brandon *A, B*
  Lakeland *A*
  North Orlando *A*
  Pompano Beach *A*
  Tampa *A*
Florida Gulf Coast University *B*
Florida National University *A*
Florida State College at
  Jacksonville *A*
Gulf Coast State College *A*
Herzing University
  Winter Park *A*
Hillsborough Community
  College *C, A*
Hodges University *A, B*
ITT Technical Institute
  Ft. Lauderdale *A*
  Jacksonville *A*
  Lake Mary *A*
Indian River State College *A*
Jones College *A, B*
Keiser University *A*
Key College *A*
Lincoln College of Technology
  West Palm Beach *A*
Miami Dade College *C, A*
Northwest Florida State College *A*
Nova Southeastern University *B*
Palm Beach State College *A*
Pasco-Hernando State College *A*
Pensacola State College *A*
Rasmussen College
  Fort Myers *C, A*
  New Port Richey *C, A*
  Ocala *C, A*
  Pasco/Land O'Lakes *C, A*
  Tampa/Brandon *C, A*
St. Petersburg College *A, B*
Santa Fe College *A*
Seminole State College of Florida *A*
State College of Florida, Manatee-
  Sarasota *A*
Tallahassee Community College *A*
University of Central Florida *B*
University of West Florida *B*
Valencia College *A*
Virginia College
  Pensacola *A*

Georgia

Athens Technical College *A*
Atlanta Technical College *C, A*
Clayton State University *C, A, B*
Columbus Technical College *A*
Darton College *C, A*
Georgia Military College *A*
Georgia Piedmont Technical
  College *A*
Gwinnett College *C, A*
Savannah Technical College *A*
Thomas University *A*
University of North Georgia *C, A*
Valdosta State University *B*

Hawaii

Heald College
  Honolulu *A*
University of Hawaii
  Kapiolani Community College *C, A*

Idaho

Broadview University
  Boise *A, B*
Eastern Idaho Technical College *C, A*
ITT Technical Institute
  Boise *A*

Idaho State University *A, B*
Lewis-Clark State College *C, A, B*

Illinois

City Colleges of Chicago
  Harry S. Truman College *C*
  Wilbur Wright College *A*
College of Lake County *C, A*
Elgin Community College *C, A*
Harper College *C, A*
Illinois Central College *C, A*
Illinois Eastern Community Colleges
  Wabash Valley College *A*
Kankakee Community College *A*
Lewis University *B*
MacCormac College *A*
Midstate College *A*
Northwestern College *C, A*
Rasmussen College
  Aurora *A*
  Mokena/Tinley Park *A*
  Rockford *A*
  Romeoville/Joliet *A*
Robert Morris University: Chicago *A*
Roosevelt University *C*
South Suburban College of Cook
  County *C, A*
Southern Illinois University
  Carbondale *B*
Southwestern Illinois College *C, A*

Indiana

Brown Mackie College
  Fort Wayne *C, A*
  Merrillville *C, A, B*
  Michigan City *C, A, B*
  South Bend *A*
Calumet College of St. Joseph *C, A, B*
Harrison College
  Indianapolis *A*
ITT Technical Institute
  Indianapolis *A*
  Newburgh *A*
Indiana University
  Purdue University Indianapolis *C*
  South Bend *C*
International Business College *C, A*
International Business College:
  Indianapolis *A*
Ivy Tech Community College
  Bloomington *A*
  Central Indiana *A*
  Columbus *A*
  East Central *A*
  Kokomo *A*
  Lafayette *A*
  North Central *A*
  Northeast *A*
  Northwest *A*
  Richmond *A*
  South Central *A*
  Southeast *A*
  Southwest *A*
  Wabash Valley *A*
St. Mary-of-the-Woods College *A, B*
University of Evansville *B*
Vincennes University *A*

Iowa

Des Moines Area Community
  College *C, A*
Grand View University *B*
Iowa Lakes Community College *A*
Iowa Western Community College *A*
Western Iowa Tech Community
  College *C, A*

Kansas

Brown Mackie College
  Salina *A*
Cloud County Community
  College *C, A*
Hutchinson Community College *C, A*
Independence Community College *A*

Johnson County Community
  College *C, A*
Kansas City Kansas Community
  College *A*
Newman University *A*
Washburn University *C, A, B*

Kentucky

Beckfield College *C, A, B*
Brown Mackie College
  Hopkinsville *C*
Daymar College
  Bowling Green *A*
  Louisville *A*
  Owensboro *A*
Eastern Kentucky University *A, B*
Morehead State University *B*
Sullivan University *A, B*
University of Louisville *A*
Western Kentucky University *A*

Louisiana

Grambling State University *B*
Herzing University
  Kenner *A*
ITT Technical Institute
  St. Rose *A*
McNeese State University *A*
Nunez Community College *C, A*
Tulane University *C, A, B*

Maine

Beal College *C, A*
Husson University *C, A, B*
Kaplan University
  South Portland *A, B*
University of Maine
  Augusta *A*

Maryland

Anne Arundel Community
  College *C, A*
Baltimore City Community
  College *C, A*
Chesapeake College *C, A*
College of Southern Maryland *A*
Community College of Baltimore
  County *C, A*
Frederick Community College *C, A*
Hagerstown Community College *C*
Harford Community College *C, A*
Kaplan University
  Hagerstown *A*
Montgomery College *C, A*
Prince George's Community
  College *C, A*
Stevenson University *B*

Massachusetts

Anna Maria College *C, B*
Bay Path College *C, A, B*
Bristol Community College *A*
Bunker Hill Community College *C*
Cape Cod Community College *C*
Eastern Nazarene College *C*
Elms College *C, A, B*
Fisher College *A*
Marian Court College *C, A, B*
Massachusetts Bay Community
  College *C, A*
Middlesex Community College *C, A*
Mount Wachusett Community
  College *C, A*
North Shore Community
  College *C, A*
Northern Essex Community
  College *C, A*
Quincy College *C, A*
Roxbury Community College *A*
Suffolk University *A, B*

Michigan

Baker College
  Auburn Hills *A*

Davenport University *C, A, B*
Delta College *C, A*
Eastern Michigan University *B*
Ferris State University *A*
Grand Valley State University *B*
Henry Ford Community College *A*
ITT Technical Institute
  Canton *A*
  Troy *A*
Kellogg Community College *C, A*
Lansing Community College *C, A*
Macomb Community College *A*
Madonna University *A, B*
North Central Michigan College *A*
Oakland Community College *C, A*
University of Detroit Mercy *C, B*
Wayne County Community College *A*

Minnesota

Academy College *C*
Alexandria Technical and Community
  College *A*
Duluth Business University *A*
Globe University
  Minneapolis *A, B*
  Moorhead *A, B*
  Woodbury *C, A, B*
Hamline University *B*
ITT Technical Institute
  Eden Prairie *A*
Inver Hills Community College *C, A*
Lake Superior College *C, A*
Minnesota School of Business
  Blaine *A, B*
  Brooklyn Center *C, A, B*
  Elk River *A, B*
  Lakeville *A, B*
  Plymouth *A, B*
  Richfield *C, A, B*
  Rochester *A, B*
  St. Cloud *A, B*
  Shakopee *A, B*
Minnesota State Community and
  Technical College *A*
Minnesota State University
  Moorhead *B*
National American University
  Bloomington *A, B*
  Roseville *A, B*
North Hennepin Community
  College *C, A*
Rasmussen College
  Blaine *C, A*
  Bloomington *C, A*
  Brooklyn Park *C, A*
  Eagan *C, A*
  Lake Elmo/Woodbury *C, A*
  Mankato *C, A*
  Moorhead *C, A*
  St. Cloud *C, A*
St. Cloud Technical and Community
  College *A*
University of Minnesota
  Twin Cities *C*
Winona State University *B*

Mississippi

East Mississippi Community
  College *A*
Hinds Community College *C, A*
Itawamba Community College *A*
Mississippi College *B*
Mississippi Gulf Coast Community
  College *A*
Mississippi University for Women *B*
Northeast Mississippi Community
  College *A*
Northwest Mississippi Community
  College *A*
University of Mississippi *B*
University of Southern Mississippi *B*

Missouri

Avila University *B*
Drury University *B*
Maryville University of Saint Louis *B*
Metropolitan Community College -
  Kansas City *C, A*
Missouri Southern State University *C*
Missouri Western State
  University *C, A*
National American University
  Kansas City *A, B*
Rockhurst University *C*
Stevens Institute of Business &
  Arts *A, B*
Webster University *C*
William Woods University *B*

Montana

Chief Dull Knife College *A*
University of Great Falls *A, B*
University of Montana *A*

Nebraska

Central Community College *C, A*
College of Saint Mary *A, B*
Doane College *B*
Kaplan University
  Lincoln *A*
  Omaha *A*
Metropolitan Community College *A*
Midland University *B*
Northeast Community College *C, A*

Nevada

Career College of Northern Nevada *A*
College of Southern Nevada *C, A*
Everest College
  Las Vegas *A*
Truckee Meadows Community
  College *A*
Western Nevada College *A*

New Hampshire

Mount Washington College *A*
NHTI-Concord's Community
  College *A*
Nashua Community College *C, A*
River Valley Community College *C*

New Jersey

Atlantic Cape Community College *A*
Bergen Community College *A*
Berkeley College *A*
Brookdale Community College *A*
Burlington County College *A*
Cumberland County College *A*
Essex County College *A*
Gloucester County College *C, A*
Hudson County Community
  College *A*
Mercer County Community
  College *C, A*
Middlesex County College *A*
Montclair State University *C*
Ocean County College *C*
Raritan Valley Community
  College *C, A*
Rider University *C*
Sussex County Community
  College *C, A*
Union County College *C, A*
Warren County Community
  College *C, A*

New Mexico

Brookline College
  Albuquerque *A*
Central New Mexico Community
  College *C, A*
Dona Ana Community College of
  New Mexico State University *A*
ITT Technical Institute
  Albuquerque *A*
Navajo Technical University *C*

New Mexico Junior College *C, A*
New Mexico State University
  Alamogordo *C, A*
  Carlsbad *C*
  Grants *A*
San Juan College *A*
Santa Fe Community College *C, A*

New York

Bramson ORT College *A*
Broome Community College *C, A*
Bryant & Stratton College
  Albany *A*
  Henrietta *A*
  Rochester *A*
  Syracuse North *A*
City University of New York
  Bronx Community College *C, A*
  Hostos Community College *A*
  LaGuardia Community College *A*
  New York City College of
    Technology *A, B*
Daemen College *C, B*
Dutchess Community College *C, A*
Elmira Business Institute *C, A*
Erie Community College *A*
Everest Institute
  Rochester *A*
Finger Lakes Community
  College *C, A*
Genesee Community College *A*
Globe Institute of
  Technology *C, A, B*
Herkimer County Community
  College *A*
Hilbert College *A, B*
Jefferson Community College *A*
Maria College *C, A*
Marist College *C*
Mildred Elley
  Albany *C, A*
Monroe Community College *C, A*
Nassau Community College *C, A*
New York Career Institute *A*
Rockland Community College *C, A*
SUNY
  College of Technology at Canton *B*
Suffolk County Community
  College *C, A*
Technical Career Institutes *A*
Tompkins Cortland Community
  College *C, A*
Westchester Community College *C, A*

North Carolina

Caldwell Community College and
  Technical Institute *A*
Cape Fear Community College *C, A*
Carteret Community College *A*
Central Carolina Community
  College *C, A*
Central Piedmont Community
  College *C, A*
Coastal Carolina Community
  College *A*
Davidson County Community
  College *C, A*
Durham Technical Community
  College *A*
Fayetteville Technical Community
  College *C, A*
Forsyth Technical Community
  College *A*
Gaston College *A*
Guilford Technical Community
  College *A*
Halifax Community College *C, A*
Isothermal Community College *A*
Johnston Community College *A*
King's College *A*
Miller-Motte College
  Fayetteville *A*
  Wilmington *A*
Pitt Community College *A*

Rowan-Cabarrus Community
  College *A*
South College *A*
South Piedmont Community
  College *A*
Southwestern Community College *A*
Surry Community College *A*
Western Piedmont Community
  College *A*
Wilson Community College *A*

North Dakota

Rasmussen College
  Bismarck *C, A*
  Fargo *C, A*
Turtle Mountain Community
  College *C*

Ohio

Akron Institute of Herzing
  University *A*
Bradford School *A*
Brown Mackie College
  Akron *C, A*
  Findlay *A*
  North Canton *C, A*
Bryant & Stratton College
  Parma *A*
Cincinnati State Technical and
  Community College *C*
College of Mount St. Joseph *C, A, B*
Columbus State Community
  College *C, A*
Cuyahoga Community College
  Metropolitan *C, A*
ETI Technical College of Niles *A*
Edison State Community College *C, A*
Fortis College
  Centerville *A*
  Ravenna *A*
ITT Technical Institute
  Dayton *A*
  Hilliard *A*
  Norwood *A*
  Strongsville *A*
  Youngstown *A*
James A. Rhodes State College *C, A*
Kent State University *B*
Kent State University
  East Liverpool *A*
  Trumbull *A*
Lake Erie College *B*
Lakeland Community College *C, A*
Miami-Jacobs Career College
  Columbus *A*
  Sharonville *A*
North Central State College *A*
Northwest State Community
  College *A*
Shawnee State University *A*
Sinclair Community College *A*
Stautzenberger College *A*
Stautzenberger College: Brecksville *A*
Tiffin University *B*
University of Akron *C, A*
University of Cincinnati *C, B*
University of Cincinnati
  Clermont College *C, A*
University of Northwestern
  Ohio *C, A*
University of Toledo *C, A, B*
Ursuline College *C, B*
Zane State College *A*

Oklahoma

East Central University *B*
Oklahoma Wesleyan University *A*
Rose State College *A*
Tulsa Community College *A*

Oregon

Everest College
  Portland *A*

Heald College
  Portland *A*
ITT Technical Institute
  Portland *A*
Pioneer Pacific College *A*
Portland Community College *C, A*
Umpqua Community College *C, A*

Pennsylvania

Berks Technical Institute *A*
Bradford School: Pittsburgh *A*
Central Penn College *A*
Clarion University of Pennsylvania *A*
Community College of
  Philadelphia *A*
Consolidated School of Business
  Lancaster *A*
  York *A*
Delaware County Community
  College *C, A*
Erie Business Center *A*
Everest Institute: Pittsburgh *A*
Fortis Institute
  Erie *A*
  Forty Fort *C*
Gannon University *C, A, B*
Harrisburg Area Community
  College *C, A*
Immaculata University *C*
Keystone Technical Institute *C, A*
Lackawanna College *A*
Lansdale School of Business *A*
Lehigh Carbon Community
  College *C, A*
Luzerne County Community
  College *A*
Manor College *C, A*
McCann School of Business and
  Technology
  Hazleton *A*
Mount Aloysius College *A*
Northampton Community College *A*
Pace Institute *A*
Peirce College *C, A, B*
Pennsylvania College of
  Technology *C, A, B*
Prism Career Institute *C, A*
Sanford-Brown Institute
  Pittsburgh *A*
Westmoreland County Community
  College *C, A*
Widener University *C, A*
Yorktowne Business Institute *A*

Puerto Rico

Turabo University *C*
Universidad Metropolitana *C*
Universidad del Este *A, B*

Rhode Island

Community College of Rhode
  Island *A*
Roger Williams University *C, B*

South Carolina

Central Carolina Technical College *A*
Florence-Darlington Technical
  College *A*
Forrest Junior College *C, A*
Greenville Technical College *A*
Horry-Georgetown Technical
  College *A*
ITT Technical Institute
  Greenville *A*
Midlands Technical College *C, A*
Miller-Motte Technical College *A*
Orangeburg-Calhoun Technical
  College *A*
Technical College of the
  Lowcountry *C, A*
Trident Technical College *C, A*
York Technical College *C, A*

South Dakota

Globe University
  Sioux Falls *A, B*
National American University
  Rapid City *A, B*
Western Dakota Technical Institute *A*

Tennessee

Anthem Career College
  Memphis *A*
Chattanooga College *A*
Chattanooga State Community
  College *A*
Daymar Institute
  Clarksville *A, B*
  Murfreesboro *A*
  Nashville *A, B*
ITT Technical Institute
  Knoxville *A*
  Memphis *A*
  Nashville *A*
Miller-Motte Technical College
  Clarksville *A*
Pellissippi State Community
  College *A*
Roane State Community College *A*
South College *A*
Southwest Tennessee Community
  College *A*
University of Tennessee
  Chattanooga *B*
Volunteer State Community
  College *A*

Texas

Alvin Community College *C, A*
Angelina College *A*
Austin Community College *C, A*
Blinn College *C, A*
Brazosport College *A*
Central Texas College *A*
Collin County Community College
  District *C, A*
Del Mar College *A*
El Centro College *A*
El Paso Community College *C, A*
Everest College
  Dallas *A*
  Fort Worth *A*
Houston Community College
  System *C, A*
Howard College *A*
ITT Technical Institute
  Arlington *A*
  Houston West *A*
  Richardson *A*
  San Antonio *A*
  Webster *A*
Kilgore College *C, A*
Lamar State College at Port Arthur *A*
Lee College *A*
Lone Star College System *C, A*
McLennan Community College *A*
Midland College *C, A*
Navarro College *C, A*
North Central Texas College *A*
Odessa College *C, A*
St. Philip's College *A*
San Antonio College *A*
San Jacinto College *A*
South Plains College *A*
South Texas College *A*
Stephen F. Austin State University *B*
Tarrant County College *C, A*
Texas A&M University
  Commerce *B*
Texas State University *M*
Texas Wesleyan University *B*
Texas Woman's University *B*
Trinity Valley Community
  College *C, A*
Tyler Junior College *A*
University of Houston
  Clear Lake *B*

Vernon College *A*
Victoria College *C, A*
Virginia College
  Austin *A*
Wharton County Junior College *C, A*

Utah

Broadview University
  Layton *A, B*
  Orem *A, B*
  West Jordan *A, B*
LDS Business College *A*
Salt Lake Community College *A*
Southern Utah University *A*
Utah Valley University *C, A, B*

Vermont

Burlington College *C*
Champlain College *A, B*

Virginia

American National University
  Salem *A*
Blue Ridge Community College *C*
Bryant & Stratton College
  Richmond *A*
Central Virginia Community
  College *C*
Germanna Community College *C*
Hampton University *C, B*
ITT Technical Institute
  Chantilly *A*
  Norfolk *A*
  Richmond *A*
J. Sargeant Reynolds Community
  College *C*
John Tyler Community College *C*
Mountain Empire Community
  College *A*
New River Community College *C, A*
Northern Virginia Community
  College *A*
Patrick Henry Community College *A*
Thomas Nelson Community
  College *C*
Tidewater Community College *C, A*
Virginia Highlands Community
  College *C*
Virginia Western Community
  College *A*

Washington

Centralia College *A*
Clark College *C, A*
Columbia Basin College *A*
Edmonds Community College *C, A*
Highline Community College *A*
ITT Technical Institute
  Everett *A*
  Seattle *A*
  Spokane *A*
Lower Columbia College *C, A*
Pierce College *A*
South Puget Sound Community
  College *C, A*
Spokane Community College *C, A*
Tacoma Community College *C, A*
Whatcom Community College *C, A*

West Virginia

American National University
  Parkersburg *A*
American Public University
  System *C, A*
Blue Ridge Community and Technical
  College *C, A*
Fairmont State University *A*
Mountain State College *A*
West Virginia Northern Community
  College *C, A*

Wisconsin

Bryant & Stratton College
  Milwaukee *A*

Chippewa Valley Technical College *A*
Fox Valley Technical College *A*
Globe University
  Appleton *A, B*
  Eau Claire *A, B*
  Green Bay *A, B*
  La Crosse *A, B*
  Madison East *C, A, B*
  Middleton *A, B*
  Wausau *A, B*
Herzing University
  Madison *A*
ITT Technical Institute
  Green Bay *A*
  Greenfield *A*
Lakeshore Technical College *A*
Milwaukee Area Technical College *A*
Northeast Wisconsin Technical
  College *A*
Rasmussen College
  Appleton *C, A*
  Green Bay *C, A*
  Wausau *C, A*
University of Wisconsin
  Superior *C*
Western Technical College *A*

Wyoming

Casper College *C, A*
Laramie County Community
  College *C, A*

Parasitology

Louisiana

Tulane University *M, D*

New York

New York University *D*

Ohio

Bowling Green State University *B*

Pennsylvania

University of Pennsylvania *D*

Parks, recreation, and leisure studies

Alabama

Community College of the Air
  Force *A*
Jacksonville State University *B*
University of South Alabama *B*

Alaska

University of Alaska
  Southeast *C, B*

Arizona

Mesa Community College *C, A*
Northern Arizona University *B*
Northland Pioneer College *C, A*
Scottsdale Community College *A*

Arkansas

National Park Community College *A*
University of Arkansas *B*
University of Arkansas
  Pine Bluff *B*

California

Allan Hancock College *A*
American River College *A*
California Polytechnic State
  University: San Luis Obispo *B*
California State University
  Chico *B, M*
  East Bay *B*
  Fresno *B*
  Northridge *B, M*

Sacramento *B, M*
Stanislaus *M*
Cerritos College *A*
Chabot College *A*
College of the Canyons *A*
College of the Desert *A*
Feather River College *A*
Fresno City College *A*
Fullerton College *A*
Glendale Community College *C, A*
Los Angeles Southwest College *A*
Los Angeles Valley College *A*
Merritt College *A*
Modesto Junior College *A*
Mount San Antonio College *A*
Palomar College *C, A*
Pasadena City College *A*
San Diego State University *B*
San Joaquin Delta College *C*
San Jose State University *B*
Santa Barbara City College *A*
Santa Rosa Junior College *C, A*
Sierra College *A*
Simpson University *B*
Southwestern College *A*

Colorado

Colorado Mountain College *A*
Community College of Denver *C, A*
Fort Lewis College *B*
Metropolitan State University of
  Denver *B*
Red Rocks Community College *C*

Connecticut

Norwalk Community College *C, A*
Southern Connecticut State
  University *B, M*

District of Columbia

Gallaudet University *B, M*
Howard University *B*

Florida

Bethune-Cookman University *B*
Broward College *A*
Chipola College *A*
Palm Beach State College *A*
Pensacola State College *A*
St. Petersburg College *A*

Georgia

College of Coastal Georgia *A*
Darton College *A*
East Georgia State College *A*
Georgia College and State
  University *B*
Georgia Southern University *B*
Gwinnett Technical College *C*
South Georgia State College *A*

Idaho

Brigham Young University-Idaho *B*
Northwest Nazarene University *B*

Illinois

Aurora University *B*
Greenville College *B*
Southern Illinois University
  Carbondale *B, M*
Triton College *C*
University of Illinois
  Urbana-Champaign *B, M, D*

Indiana

Huntington University *B*
Indiana University
  Bloomington *B, M*

Iowa

Dordt College *B*
Graceland University *M, D*
University of Iowa *B, M*
University of Northern Iowa *B, M, D*

Kansas

Emporia State University *B*
Ottawa University *B*
Pittsburg State University *B*
Seward County Community
  College *A*
Tabor College *B*

Kentucky

Campbellsville University *B*
Eastern Kentucky University *B*

Louisiana

Grambling State University *B*

Maine

University of Maine
  Machias *A, B*
  Presque Isle *A, B*
University of Southern Maine *B*

Maryland

Community College of Baltimore
  County *C, A*
Frostburg State University *B, M*
Salisbury University *B*

Massachusetts

American International College *B*
Gordon College *B*
Salem State University *B*

Michigan

Aquinas College *B*
Calvin College *B*
Central Michigan University *B*
Grand Valley State University *B*
Michigan State University *B*
Northern Michigan University *B*
Northwood University
  Michigan *A, B*
Spring Arbor University *B*
Western Michigan University *B*

Minnesota

Minnesota State University
  Mankato *B*
Ridgewater College *A*
Saint Cloud State University *B*
University of Minnesota
  Duluth *B*
  Twin Cities *B, M*

Mississippi

Alcorn State University *B*
East Mississippi Community
  College *A*
University of Southern
  Mississippi *B, M*

Missouri

Evangel University *B*
Lindenwood University *B*
Missouri State University *B*
Southeast Missouri State University *B*
Southwest Baptist University *B*
University of Central Missouri *B*
University of Missouri
  Columbia *B, M*
William Jewell College *B*

Nebraska

Chadron State College *B*
University of Nebraska
  Omaha *B*

Nevada

University of Nevada
  Las Vegas *B*

New Hampshire

New England College *B*
River Valley Community College *A*

New Mexico

San Juan College *A*

New York

City University of New York
  Kingsborough Community
    College *A*
Houghton College *B*
Ithaca College *B*
Niagara County Community
    College *A*
Onondaga Community College *A*
Paul Smith's College *A, B*
SUNY
  College at Brockport *B, M*
  College at Cortland *B, M*
  College at Plattsburgh *B*
Sullivan County Community
    College *A*
Tompkins Cortland Community
    College *A*
Ulster County Community College *A*

North Carolina

Catawba College *B*
Montreat College *C, B*
Shaw University *B*
Southwestern Community College *A*
University of Mount Olive *B*
University of North Carolina
  Greensboro *B*
Vance-Granville Community
    College *A*

North Dakota

Dakota College at Bottineau *A*
University of Jamestown *B*

Ohio

Bowling Green State University *B, M*
Central State University *B*
Ohio University *B*
University of Toledo *B, M*
Urbana University *B*

Oklahoma

East Central University *B*
Oklahoma State University *B, M*
Southeastern Oklahoma State
    University *B*
Southwestern Oklahoma State
    University *B*
University of Central Oklahoma *B*

Oregon

Central Oregon Community
    College *A*
Oregon State University *B*

Pennsylvania

Butler County Community College *A*
Kutztown University of
    Pennsylvania *B*
Messiah College *B*
Temple University *B, M*
University of Pittsburgh
    Bradford *B*
York College of Pennsylvania *B*

South Carolina

Clemson University *M*
Newberry College *B*
North Greenville University *B*
Southern Wesleyan University *B*

South Dakota

Presentation College *B*
University of South Dakota *B, M*

Tennessee

Carson-Newman University *B*
Maryville College *B*

Texas

Clarendon College *A*
Midwestern State University *B*
Texas A&M University *B, M, D*
Texas A&M University
  Galveston *B*
Texas State University *M*

Utah

Brigham Young University *B*
Snow College *A*
Southern Utah University *B*
University of Utah *B, M, D*
Utah State University *B*

Vermont

Green Mountain College *B*
Johnson State College *B*
Sterling College *B*

Virginia

Ferrum College *B*
Hampton University *B*
Radford University *B*
Tidewater Community College *A*
Virginia Commonwealth University *B*
Virginia Wesleyan College *B*

Washington

Central Washington University *B*
Eastern Washington University *B*
Pacific Lutheran University *B*
Western Washington University *B*

West Virginia

Concord University *B*
Davis and Elkins College *B*
Shepherd University *B*

Wisconsin

University of Wisconsin
  Parkside *C*

Wyoming

Central Wyoming College *A*
Northwest College *C, A*

Parks/recreational/leisure facilities management

Alabama

Alabama State University *B*
Faulkner State Community
    College *C, A*

Alaska

Alaska Pacific University *B, M*

Arizona

Golf Academy of America
  Phoenix *A*

Arkansas

Arkansas Tech University *B*
Henderson State University *B*
University of Arkansas *M, D*

California

Butte College *C, A*
California State University
  East Bay *B*
  Long Beach *B, M*
Cerro Coso Community College *C, A*
College of the Desert *A*
College of the Sequoias *A*
Fresno City College *A*
Golf Academy of America
  San Diego *A*
Mount San Antonio College *A*
Professional Golfers Career College *A*
San Francisco State University *B, M*

Santa Rosa Junior College *C*
West Valley College *C, A*

Colorado

Colorado Mountain College *A*
Colorado State University *B, M, D*
University of Northern Colorado *B*

Delaware

University of Delaware *B*

Florida

Edison State College *A*
Florida International University *B, M*
Tallahassee Community College *A*
University of Florida *B, M*
Webber International
    University *A, B, M*

Georgia

Abraham Baldwin Agricultural
    College *A*
Gwinnett Technical College *C, A*
University of West Georgia *B*

Idaho

University of Idaho *B, M*

Illinois

Aurora University *M*
Eastern Illinois University *B*
Illinois State University *B*
Moraine Valley Community College *A*
Triton College *A*
University of St. Francis *B*
Western Illinois University *B, M*

Indiana

Indiana Institute of Technology *A, B*
Indiana State University *B*
Indiana Wesleyan University *B*
Purdue University *B, M, D*

Iowa

Iowa Lakes Community College *A*
University of Iowa *B, M*
University of Northern Iowa *M*
Upper Iowa University *B*

Kansas

Bethany College *B*
Kansas State University *B*

Kentucky

Asbury University *B*
Eastern Kentucky University *B, M*
Union College *B*
Western Kentucky University *B, M*

Maine

Husson University *B*
University of Maine *B, M*
University of Maine
  Machias *B*

Maryland

Allegany College of Maryland *A*

Massachusetts

Greenfield Community College *C*
Springfield College *B, M*

Michigan

Central Michigan University *B, M*
Eastern Michigan University *B*
Ferris State University *B*
Gogebic Community College *A*
Lake Superior State University *B*

Minnesota

Minnesota State University
  Mankato *B*

University of Minnesota
  Crookston *B*
  Twin Cities *B*
Vermilion Community College *A*
Winona State University *B*

Mississippi

East Mississippi Community
    College *A*
University of Mississippi *B, M*

Missouri

Central Methodist University *B*
College of the Ozarks *B*
Hannibal-LaGrange University *B*
Missouri Valley College *B*
Missouri Western State University *B*
Northwest Missouri State
    University *B*
University of Central Missouri *B*

Montana

University of Montana *B, M*

Nebraska

Hastings College *B*
University of Nebraska
  Kearney *B*

Nevada *

Truckee Meadows Community
    College *A*

New Hampshire

Franklin Pierce University *B*
New England College *B*
University of New Hampshire *B, M*

New Jersey

Kean University *B*

New York

Dutchess Community College *A*
Herkimer County Community
    College *A*
Mohawk Valley Community
    College *A*
New York University *B, M, D, T*
North Country Community College *A*
Orange County Community
    College *A*
Paul Smith's College *A, B*
SUNY
  College at Brockport *B, M*
  College at Cortland *B*
  College of Technology at Delhi *A*
St. Joseph's College New York:
  Suffolk Campus *A*
St. Joseph's College, New York *B*
St. Thomas Aquinas College *B*
Sullivan County Community
    College *A*
Tompkins Cortland Community
    College *A*

North Carolina

Appalachian State University *B*
Belmont Abbey College *B*
Brevard College *B*
Central Piedmont Community
    College *A*
East Carolina University *B, M*
Mars Hill University *B*
Methodist University *B*
North Carolina Agricultural and
  Technical State University *B*
North Carolina Central
    University *B, M*
North Carolina State
    University *B, M, D*
University of North Carolina
  Greensboro *M*
  Wilmington *B*
Western Carolina University *B*

Wingate University *B*
Winston-Salem State University *B*

North Dakota
Dakota College at Bottineau *A*
University of North Dakota *B*

Ohio
Bluffton University *B*
Kent State University *B*
University of Dayton *B*

Oklahoma
Bacone College *B*
Eastern Oklahoma State College *A*
Oklahoma Baptist University *B*
Oral Roberts University *B*
Southwestern Oklahoma State
   University *B*

Pennsylvania
Bucks County Community College *C*
California University of
   Pennsylvania *B*
Cheyney University of
   Pennsylvania *B*
East Stroudsburg University of
   Pennsylvania *B*
Lock Haven University of
   Pennsylvania *B*
Penn State
   Abington *B*
   Altoona *B*
   Beaver *B*
   Berks *B*
   Brandywine *B*
   DuBois *B*
   Fayette, The Eberly Campus *B*
   Greater Allegheny *B*
   Harrisburg *B*
   Hazleton *B*
   Lehigh Valley *B*
   Mont Alto *B*
   New Kensington *B*
   Schuylkill *B*
   Shenango *B*
   University Park *B, M, D*
   Wilkes-Barre *B*
   Worthington Scranton *B*
   York *B*
Slippery Rock University of
   Pennsylvania *B, M*
Temple University *C*

Puerto Rico
Universidad Metropolitana *M*
Universidad del Este *C*
University of Puerto Rico
   Mayaguez *B*

South Carolina
Clemson University *B, M, D*
Morris College *B*

South Dakota
Mount Marty College *B*
South Dakota State University *B*

Tennessee
Middle Tennessee State University *B*

Texas
Golf Academy of America
   Dallas *A*
Stephen F. Austin State University *M*
Texas A&M University *B*
Texas State University *B, M*
University of North Texas *B, M*
Wayland Baptist University *B*
Western Texas College *A*

Vermont
Lyndon State College *B*

Virginia
Bluefield College *B*
Hampton University *B*
John Tyler Community College *C*
Northern Virginia Community
   College *A*
Old Dominion University *B*
Tidewater Community College *A*

Washington
Bellevue College *C*
Central Washington University *B*
Eastern Washington University *C, B*
Skagit Valley College *C*
Spokane Community College *A*
Walla Walla Community College *C, A*

West Virginia
Concord University *B*
Marshall University *B*
Potomac State College of West
   Virginia *A*
West Virginia State University *B*
West Virginia University *B, M*

Wisconsin
Carroll University *B*
University of Wisconsin
   La Crosse *B, M*

Wyoming
Central Wyoming College *A*

Particle physics

Massachusetts
Tufts University *M, D*

Parts/warehousing operations

Arkansas
Pulaski Technical College *C*

Colorado
Red Rocks Community College *C, A*

Georgia
Columbus Technical College *C*

Michigan
Northwestern Michigan College *C*

Pastoral counseling

Alabama
Amridge University *M, D*
Oakwood University *M*

Arizona
Grand Canyon University *B*
International Baptist College *B*

Arkansas
Ecclesia College *B*
Harding University *M*
Ouachita Baptist University *B*

California
Biola University *M, D*
California Baptist University *M*
Holy Names University *M*
Life Pacific College *B*
Loyola Marymount University *M*
Master's College *B, M, D*
Shasta Bible College and Graduate
   School *M*
Simpson University *B*
Vanguard University of Southern
   California *B*
William Jessup University *C, A, B*

Colorado
Nazarene Bible College *C, B*

Florida
Baptist College of Florida *B*
Barry University *M*
Johnson University: Florida *B*
Trinity Baptist College *B*
Trinity College of Florida *B*

Georgia
Emmanuel College *B*
Emory University *D*
Toccoa Falls College *B*

Hawaii
Chaminade University of Honolulu *M*

Idaho
Boise Bible College *B*
Northwest Nazarene University *B, M*

Illinois
Dominican University *C, B*
Greenville College *B*
Lincoln Christian University *B, M*
Loyola University Chicago *B, M*
Moody Bible Institute *B, M*
North Park University *B*
Olivet Nazarene University *B, M*
Saint Xavier University *C, B, M*
Trinity International University *B, M*

Indiana
Crossroads Bible College *B*
Huntington University *M*
Indiana Wesleyan University *A, B, M*
Marian University *C, A, B*
Saint Joseph's College *B*

Iowa
St. Ambrose University *M*
Wartburg College *B*

Kansas
Barclay College *B*
Central Christian College of
   Kansas *A, B*
Manhattan Christian College *B*
Newman University *B*
University of St. Mary *B*

Kentucky
Brescia University *B*
Kentucky Christian University *B*
Southern Baptist Theological
   Seminary *B*

Louisiana
New Orleans Baptist Theological
   Seminary *M, D*

Maryland
Loyola University Maryland *M, D*

Massachusetts
Anna Maria College *M*
Boston College *M*
Eastern Nazarene College *B*
Elms College *M*

Michigan
Andrews University *M, D*
Grace Bible College *B*
Griggs University *C*
Madonna University *B, M*
Marygrove College *M*
Spring Arbor University *B*

Minnesota
Bethel University *M*
Crown College *B*

North Central University *B*
University of St. Thomas *M*

Missouri
Baptist Bible College *B, M*
Calvary Bible College and Theological
   Seminary *B, M*
Central Christian College of the
   Bible *B*
Lindenwood University *B*

Montana
Montana Bible College *B*

Nebraska
Grace University *M*
Union College *B*

New Jersey
College of St. Elizabeth *C*
Seton Hall University *M*

New Mexico
University of the Southwest *B*

North Carolina
Gardner-Webb University *M*
Laurel University *B*
Mid-Atlantic Christian University *B*
Pfeiffer University *M*
Shepherds Theological Seminary *M*
Southeastern Baptist Theological
   Seminary *M, D*

Ohio
Ashland University *M*
Cedarville University *B*
God's Bible School and College *B*
Mount Vernon Nazarene University *B*
Ohio Christian University *A, B, M*
University of Dayton *M*

Oklahoma
Mid-America Christian University *B*
Oral Roberts University *B, M*
St. Gregory's University *B*
Southwestern Christian University *B*

Oregon
Corban University *B, M*
Multnomah University *B*
New Hope Christian College *B*
Northwest Christian University *B*

Pennsylvania
Cairn University *B*
Duquesne University *M*
Eastern University *D*
La Salle University *M*
Moravian College *M*
Neumann University *M*
Valley Forge Christian College *B*

Puerto Rico
Bayamon Central University *M*
Inter American University of Puerto
   Rico
   Metropolitan Campus *D*
Universidad Pentecostal
   Mizpa *A, B, M*

South Carolina
Columbia International University *M*
Erskine College *M*
W.L. Bonner Bible College *B*

Tennessee
American Baptist College *B, M*
Hiwassee College *B*
Lee University *B*
Southern Adventist University *B*

Texas

Arlington Baptist College *B*
Criswell College *B, M*
Dallas Baptist University *M*
East Texas Baptist University *B*
Hardin-Simmons University *M*
Houston Baptist University *B*
St. Mary's University *M*
Southwestern Assemblies of God
   University *B*
University of Dallas *M*
University of Mary Hardin-Baylor *B*
University of St. Thomas *B, M*

Virginia

Eastern Mennonite University *M*
Liberty University *B*

Washington

Northwest University *B*
Seattle University *M, T*
University of Puget Sound *M*

Wisconsin

Cardinal Stritch University *B*
Concordia University Wisconsin *B*
Maranatha Baptist Bible College *B, M*

Pathology assistant

Connecticut

Quinnipiac University *M*

Maryland

University of Maryland
   Baltimore *M*

Massachusetts

Boston University *M, D*

Michigan

Wayne State University *B*

Pennsylvania

Drexel University *M*

West Virginia

West Virginia University *M*

Pathology, human/ animal

Alabama

Auburn University *M*
University of Alabama
   Birmingham *D*

Arkansas

University of Arkansas
   for Medical Sciences *M*

California

University of California
   Davis *M, D*
   Irvine *D*
   Los Angeles *M, D*
University of Southern
   California *M, D*

Colorado

Colorado State University *D*

Connecticut

University of Connecticut *B, M, D*
Yale University *M, D*

Illinois

University of Chicago *D*
University of Illinois
   Chicago *M, D*

Indiana

Indiana University
   Bloomington *M, D*
   Purdue University
      Indianapolis *M, D*

Kansas

Kansas State University *M, D*
University of Kansas Medical
   Center *M, D*

Maine

University of Maine *B, M*

Massachusetts

Boston University *D*
Harvard College *D*
Tufts University *M, D*

Michigan

Michigan State University *M, D*
University of Michigan *D*
Wayne State University *D*

Minnesota

University of Minnesota
   Twin Cities *M, D*

Mississippi

University of Mississippi Medical
   Center *M, D*

Missouri

Saint Louis University *D*
University of Missouri
   Columbia *M, D*

Nebraska

University of Nebraska
   Medical Center *M, D*

New York

New York University *M, D*
SUNY
   University at Buffalo *M, D*
   University at Stony Brook *D*
University of Rochester *M, D*
Yeshiva University *M, D*

North Carolina

Duke University *M, D*
University of North Carolina
   Chapel Hill *B, M, D*

North Dakota

North Dakota State University *D*

Ohio

Case Western Reserve University *D*
Ohio State University
   Columbus Campus *M*

Oklahoma

University of Oklahoma *M, D*

Pennsylvania

Drexel University *M, D*
Penn State
   University Park *M, D*
University of Pennsylvania *D*
University of Pittsburgh *M, D*

South Carolina

Medical University of South
   Carolina *D*

Tennessee

Vanderbilt University *M, D*

Texas

University of Texas
   El Paso *D*
   Health Science Center at
      Houston *M, D*
   Medical Branch at Galveston *M, D*

Utah

University of Utah *M, D*

Vermont

University of Vermont *M*

Virginia

University of Virginia *D*
Virginia Commonwealth University *D*

Washington

University of Washington *M, D*

Wisconsin

University of Wisconsin
   Madison *M, D*

Peace and conflict studies

California

California State University
   Dominguez Hills *B, M*
   San Bernardino *M*
Chapman University *B*
University of California
   Berkeley *B*
University of San Diego *M*

Colorado

Naropa University *B*
Regis University *B*
University of Denver *M*

District of Columbia

American University *M*
Georgetown University *B, M*

Florida

Nova Southeastern University *M, D*

Georgia

Kennesaw State University *M, D*

Illinois

DePaul University *B*

Indiana

DePauw University *B*
Earlham College *B*
Goshen College *B*
Manchester University *B*
University of Notre Dame *M*

Kentucky

University of Louisville *C*

Maine

College of the Atlantic *B, M*

Maryland

Goucher College *B*
Howard Community College *A*
Salisbury University *B, M*
University of Baltimore *M*

Massachusetts

Brandeis University *M*
Hampshire College *B*
Tufts University *B*
University of Massachusetts
   Boston *M*
   Lowell *C, B, M*
Wellesley College *B*

Minnesota

Bethel University *B*
College of St. Benedict *B*
Hamline University *B*
St. John's University *B*
University of St. Thomas *B*

Missouri

Missouri State University *M*
University of Missouri
   Columbia *B*

Nebraska

Creighton University *B*

New Jersey

Montclair State University *B*

New York

Colgate University *B*
Hilbert College *B*
Manhattan College *B*
Nazareth College *B*

North Carolina

Guilford College *B*
University of North Carolina
   Chapel Hill *B*

Ohio

Antioch University
   Midwest *M*
John Carroll University *B*
Kent State University *B*
University of Akron *C*

Oregon

University of Oregon *M*

Pennsylvania

Arcadia University *M*
Gettysburg College *B*
Juniata College *B*
La Salle University *B*
Messiah College *B*
Swarthmore College *B*
University of Pennsylvania *D*

Puerto Rico

Turabo University *M*

Tennessee

Lipscomb University *B, M*

Texas

Abilene Christian University *M*
University of Texas
   Austin *C*

Utah

University of Utah *B*

Vermont

Bennington College *B*
Marlboro College *B*
Norwich University *B*

Virginia

Eastern Mennonite University *B, M*
George Mason University *B, M, D*

Washington

University of Washington *B*
Whitworth University *B*

Wisconsin

Marquette University *B*
University of Wisconsin
   Milwaukee *C*

Pediatric nursing

Florida
Florida International University *M*

Georgia
Emory University *D*
Georgia Regents University *M*

Illinois
DePaul University *M*

Indiana
Indiana University
   Purdue University Indianapolis *M*

Iowa
University of Iowa *M*

Kentucky
Spalding University *M*

Maine
University of Southern Maine *B, M*

Massachusetts
Elms College *B*

Michigan
University of Michigan *M*

New Jersey
Caldwell College *T*
Seton Hall University *M*

New York
City University of New York
   Hunter College *B, M*
Molloy College *M*
New York University *M, D*
SUNY
   University at Buffalo *M*
University of Rochester *M*

Ohio
Case Western Reserve University *M*
University of Cincinnati *M*
University of Toledo *M*
Wright State University *M, T*
Youngstown State University *M*

Pennsylvania
Gwynedd Mercy University *M*
University of Pennsylvania *M*

Tennessee
Vanderbilt University *M*

Percussion instruments

California
University of Southern
   California *B, M, D*

Kansas
University of Kansas *B, M*

Massachusetts
New England Conservatory of
   Music *B, M, D*

Minnesota
McNally Smith College of
   Music *C, A, B, M*

New York
Houghton College *B, M*
Ithaca College *B*
Syracuse University *B, M*

Ohio
Ashland University *B*

Puerto Rico
Conservatory of Music of Puerto
   Rico *B, M*

Tennessee
Vanderbilt University *B*

Washington
Central Washington University *B*

Perfusion technology

Illinois
Rush University *B, M*

Nebraska
University of Nebraska
   Medical Center *M*

New York
Long Island University
   LIU Post *M*
SUNY
   College at Oswego *B*
   Upstate Medical University *B*

Ohio
Ohio State University
   Columbus Campus *B*

Pennsylvania
Carlow University *C*

Wisconsin
Milwaukee School of Engineering *M*

Personal/culinary services

Arkansas
Northwest Arkansas Community
   College *C*

California
Art Institute of California
   Los Angeles *B*
   Sacramento *A*
Cerritos College *C, A*
Chabot College *A*
Diablo Valley College *A*

Colorado
Colorado Mountain College *A*

Connecticut
Naugatuck Valley Community
   College *C, A*

Florida
Broward College *A*
Florida College of Natural Health
   Miami *C*
   Pompano Beach *C, B*
Florida State College at
   Jacksonville *C*
Le Cordon Bleu College of Culinary
   Arts
   Orlando *A*
Palm Beach State College *C*

Georgia
Atlanta Technical College *A*

Maryland
Allegany College of Maryland *A*

Michigan
Baker College
   Muskegon *A, B*

Minnesota
Le Cordon Bleu College of Culinary
   Arts
   Minneapolis-St. Paul *C, A*

New Mexico
Northern New Mexico College *C*

New York
Monroe Community College *A*

North Carolina
Cape Fear Community College *C, A*
College of the Albemarle *C*
Piedmont Community College *C*

Pennsylvania
Career Training Academy:
   Monroeville *C*
Thiel College *B*

Puerto Rico
Inter American University of Puerto
   Rico
   Ponce Campus *C*

South Carolina
Denmark Technical College *C*
Forrest Junior College *A*

Texas
Art Institute of Houston *A*
South Texas College *A*

Washington
Pierce College *C*
Renton Technical College *C*
Seattle Central Community
   College *C, A*

Personal/financial services marketing

Alabama
Jefferson Davis Community
   College *C*

Missouri
Lindenwood University *B*

New York
Mohawk Valley Community
   College *C*

North Carolina
Blue Ridge Community College *A*

Pennsylvania
DeSales University *B*

South Dakota
National American University
   Rapid City *B*

Personality psychology

Connecticut
University of Connecticut *M, D*

Massachusetts
Clark University *M, D*

New York
Pace University *B*
SUNY
   University at Albany *D*

Vermont
Goddard College *M*

Petroleum engineering

Alaska
University of Alaska
   Fairbanks *B, M*

California
Stanford University *B, M, D*
University of Southern
   California *M, D*

Colorado
Colorado School of Mines *B, M, D*

Kansas
University of Kansas *B, M*

Louisiana
Louisiana State University and
   Agricultural and Mechanical
   College *B, M, D*
University of Louisiana at
   Lafayette *B, M*

Missouri
Missouri University of Science and
   Technology *B, M, D*

Montana
Montana Tech of the University of
   Montana *B, M*

New Mexico
New Mexico Institute of Mining and
   Technology *B, M, D*

North Dakota
University of North Dakota *B*

Ohio
Marietta College *B*

Oklahoma
University of Oklahoma *B, M, D*
University of Tulsa *B, M, D*

Pennsylvania
Penn State
   Abington *B*
   Altoona *B*
   Beaver *B*
   Berks *B*
   Brandywine *B*
   DuBois *B*
   Erie, The Behrend College *B*
   Fayette, The Eberly Campus *B*
   Greater Allegheny *B*
   Harrisburg *B*
   Hazleton *B*
   Lehigh Valley *B*
   Mont Alto *B*
   New Kensington *B*
   Schuylkill *B*
   Shenango *B*
   University Park *B, M, D*
   Wilkes-Barre *B*
   Worthington Scranton *B*
   York *B*
University of Pittsburgh *M*

Texas
Laredo Community College *A*
Midland College *A*
Texas A&M University *B, M, D*
Texas A&M University
   Kingsville *B, M*
Texas Tech University *B, M, D*
University of Houston *B, M*
University of Texas
   Austin *B, M, D*
   Permian Basin *B*

West Virginia
West Virginia University B, M, D

Wyoming
University of Wyoming B, M, D

Petroleum technology

Alaska
University of Alaska
Anchorage C

Arkansas
Arkansas State University
Beebe C
University of Arkansas
Community College at
Morrilton C, A

California
Los Medanos College A
Taft College C, A

Colorado
Colorado Northwestern Community
College C, A

Louisiana
Bossier Parish Community College A
Nicholls State University A, B

Mississippi
Southwest Mississippi Community
College A

Montana
Montana State University
Billings A

North Dakota
Bismarck State College C, A

Oklahoma
Oklahoma State University
Institute of Technology:
Okmulgee A

Pennsylvania
Lackawanna College A
University of Pittsburgh
Bradford B

Texas
Houston Community College
System C, A
Odessa College C, A
Panola College C, A

Pharmaceutical marketing and management

Ohio
Ohio Northern University B

Pennsylvania
DeSales University B

Pharmaceutical sciences

Alabama
Auburn University M, D

Arizona
University of Arizona M, D

California
University of California
Irvine B
University of Southern
California M, D

Colorado
Regis University D

Connecticut
University of Connecticut M, D

Florida
Florida Agricultural and Mechanical
University B, M, D

Georgia
Columbus Technical College A
Mercer University D
University of Georgia B, M

Hawaii
Heald College
Honolulu A
University of Hawaii
Hilo D

Indiana
Butler University B, M
Huntington University B

Iowa
Drake University B

Kentucky
Midway College B

Louisiana
University of Louisiana at
Monroe M, D

Maryland
University of Maryland
Baltimore M, D

Massachusetts
MCPHS University B, M, D
Northeastern University B, M, D

Michigan
University of Michigan B, M, D
Wayne State University D

Mississippi
East Mississippi Community
College A
University of Mississippi B, M, D

Missouri
University of Missouri
Kansas City B, M, D

Nebraska
Creighton University M

New York
Albany College of Pharmacy and
Health Sciences B, M
Long Island University
LIU Brooklyn M, D
SUNY
University at Buffalo B, M, D
St. John's University M, D

North Carolina
University of North Carolina
Chapel Hill B, M, D

North Dakota
North Dakota State
University B, M, D

Ohio
University of Findlay D
University of Toledo B, D

Oregon
Oregon State University M, D

Pennsylvania
Duquesne University B
Temple University M, D
University of Pittsburgh M, D

South Carolina
Francis Marion University B
University of South Carolina
Columbia M, D

South Dakota
South Dakota State University B, D

Tennessee
Belmont University B, D

Texas
Texas Southern University M, D
Texas Tech University Health
Sciences Center M, D
University of Houston B
University of Texas
Austin M, D

Utah
University of Utah B

Virginia
Virginia Commonwealth
University M, D

West Virginia
University of Charleston D
West Virginia University D

Pharmacology

Alabama
Auburn University M

Arizona
University of Arizona M, D

Arkansas
University of Arkansas
for Medical Sciences M, D

California
Loma Linda University D
University of California
Irvine D
Santa Barbara B

Colorado
University of Colorado
Denver D

Connecticut
Yale University M, D

District of Columbia
George Washington
University B, M, D
Georgetown University M, D
Howard University M, D

Florida
University of Miami M, D

Georgia
Emory University D
Georgia Regents University M, D

Illinois
Loyola University Chicago M, D
Rush University M, D
Southern Illinois University
Carbondale M, D
University of Illinois
Chicago M, D

Indiana
Indiana University
Bloomington D
Purdue University
Indianapolis M, D

Iowa
Drake University B, M
University of Iowa M, D

Kansas
University of Kansas Medical
Center M, D

Kentucky
University of Kentucky D

Louisiana
Louisiana State University
Health Sciences Center D
Tulane University M, D

Massachusetts
Boston University M, D
MCPHS University M, D
Northeastern University M, D
Tufts University M

Michigan
University of Michigan M, D

Minnesota
University of Minnesota
Duluth M, D
Twin Cities M, D

Mississippi
University of Mississippi Medical
Center M, D

Missouri
Saint Louis University M, D
University of Missouri
Columbia M, D

Montana
University of Montana D

Nebraska
Creighton University M, D
University of Nebraska
Medical Center M, D

Nevada
University of Nevada
Reno D

New Hampshire
Dartmouth College D

New Jersey
Rutgers, The State University of New
Jersey
New Brunswick/Piscataway
Campus M, D
Newark Campus M, D

New York
City University of New York
Hunter College B, M
York College B
Cornell University M, D
Long Island University
LIU Brooklyn M
New York University M, D
SUNY
Downstate Medical Center D
University at Buffalo M, D
University at Stony Brook B
Upstate Medical University D
University of Rochester M, D

North Carolina

University of North Carolina
 Chapel Hill *M, D*
Wake Forest University *D*

North Dakota

University of North Dakota *M, D*

Ohio

Case Western Reserve University *D*
Kent State University *M, D*
Ohio State University
 Columbus Campus *M*
University of Cincinnati *M, D*

Oregon

Chemeketa Community College *A*
Oregon Health & Science
 University *D*

Pennsylvania

Drexel University *M, D*
University of Pennsylvania *M, D*

Puerto Rico

Turabo University *A*
University of Puerto Rico
 Medical Sciences *M, D*

South Carolina

Medical University of South
 Carolina *D*

Tennessee

Maryville College *B*
University of Tennessee
 Knoxville *M*
Vanderbilt University *D*

Texas

University of Texas
 Health Science Center at
 Houston *M, D*

Vermont

University of Vermont *M*

Virginia

University of Virginia *D*
Virginia Commonwealth
 University *M, D*

Washington

University of Washington *M, D*
Washington State University *M, D*

Wisconsin

University of Wisconsin
 Madison *M, D*

Pharmacology/
toxicology

Alabama

University of Alabama
 Birmingham *D*

Arizona

University of Arizona *M, D*

California

University of California
 Davis *M, D*
 Irvine *M, D*

Kansas

University of Kansas *M, D*

Kentucky

University of Louisville *M, D*

Massachusetts

MCPHS University *B*

Michigan

Michigan State University *M, D*

New York

SUNY
 University at Buffalo *B, M*

Ohio

University of Toledo *M*
Wright State University *M*

Pennsylvania

Duquesne University *M, D*
University of the Sciences *B, M, D*

Texas

University of Texas
 Health Science Center at
 Houston *M, D*
 Medical Branch at Galveston *M, D*

Wisconsin

University of Wisconsin
 Madison *B*

Pharmacy assistant

Alabama

Community College of the Air
 Force *A*
Lawson State Community College *C*
Remington College
 Mobile *C*
Virginia College
 Birmingham *C*
 Huntsville *C*
 Mobile *C*
 Montgomery *C*

Alaska

Charter College *C, A*
University of Alaska
 Anchorage *C*

Arizona

Brookline College
 Phoenix *C*
 Tempe *C*
 Tucson *C*
Carrington College
 Mesa *C*
 Phoenix *C*
 Tucson *C*
Central Arizona College *A*
Eastern Arizona College *C, A*
Mohave Community College *C, A*
Pima Community College *C, A*

Arkansas

Arkansas State University
 Beebe *C, A*
National Park Community
 College *C, A*
Remington College
 Little Rock *C*

California

Carrington College California
 Antioch *A*
 Citrus Heights *A*
 Pleasant Hill *A*
 Sacramento *A*
 San Jose *A*
 San Leandro *A*
 Stockton *A*
City College of San Francisco *C*
Foothill College *C, A*
Heald College
 Concord *A*
 Fresno *A*

Hayward *A*
Rancho Cordova *A*
Roseville *A*
Salinas *A*
San Francisco *A*
San Jose *A*
Institute of Technology: Clovis *C*
Kaplan College
 Vista *C*
La Sierra University *C*
Palo Verde College *C*
San Joaquin Valley College *A*
Santa Ana College *C, A*
Santa Barbara Business College *C, A*
Santa Barbara Business College
 Bakersfield *C, A*
 Santa Maria *C, A*
Santa Rosa Junior College *C, A*

Colorado

Arapahoe Community College *C*
Everest College
 Aurora *C*
 Denver *C*
Front Range Community College *C*
IBMC College
 Fort Collins *A*
Otero Junior College *A*
Pikes Peak Community College *C, A*
Pueblo Community College *C*

Connecticut

Manchester Community College *A*
St. Vincent's College *C*

Florida

Everest University
 Brandon *A*
 Lakeland *C*
 Largo *C*
 North Orlando *C*
Gulf Coast State College *C*
Rasmussen College
 Fort Myers *C, A*
 New Port Richey *C, A*
 Ocala *C, A*
 Pasco/Land O'Lakes *C, A*
 Tampa/Brandon *C, A*
Sanford-Brown Institute
 Jacksonville *C*
 Tampa *C*
Seminole State College of
 Florida *C, A*
Virginia College
 Pensacola *C, A*

Georgia

Albany Technical College *C, A*
Atlanta Technical College *C, A*
Augusta Technical College *C, A*
Central Georgia Technical College *C*
Columbus Technical College *C, A*
Middle Georgia State College *A*
North Georgia Technical
 College *C, A*
Southeastern Technical College *C*
Southwest Georgia Technical
 College *C, A*
West Georgia Technical College *C, A*

Idaho

Carrington College
 Boise *C, A*
College of Southern Idaho *A*
North Idaho College *A*

Illinois

City Colleges of Chicago
 Harold Washington College *C*
 Harry S. Truman College *C*
 Kennedy-King College *C*
 Malcolm X College *C*
 Olive-Harvey College *C*

Richard J. Daley College *C*
 Wilbur Wright College *C*
College of DuPage *C*
Rasmussen College
 Aurora *C, A*
 Mokena/Tinley Park *C, A*
 Rockford *C, A*
 Romeoville/Joliet *C, A*
Richland Community College *C*
Robert Morris University: Chicago *A*
South Suburban College of Cook
 County *C, A*

Indiana

National College
 Indianapolis *A*
 South Bend *A*
National College: Fort Wayne *A*
Vincennes University *C, A*

Iowa

Clinton Community College *C*
Kirkwood Community College *C*
Northwest Iowa Community
 College *C*
Western Iowa Tech Community
 College *C*

Kansas

Barton County Community College *C*
Hutchinson Community College *C*
Labette Community College *C*

Kentucky

Daymar College
 Bowling Green *C, A*
 Louisville *A*
 Owensboro *A*
 Paducah *A*
Gateway Community and Technical
 College *C*
Hopkinsville Community College *A*
National College
 Florence *C*
 Richmond *C*
Owensboro Community and
 Technical College *C*
St. Catharine College *C, A*
Sullivan University *C, A*
West Kentucky Community and
 Technical College *C*

Louisiana

Bossier Parish Community
 College *C, A*
Delgado Community College *C*
Louisiana State University
 Alexandria *C*
Virginia College
 Baton Rouge *C*

Maryland

Allegany College of Maryland *C*
Anne Arundel Community College *C*
College of Southern Maryland *C*
Hagerstown Community College *C*

Massachusetts

Benjamin Franklin Institute of
 Technology *C*
Bristol Community College *C*

Michigan

Baker College
 Flint *C, A*
 Jackson *C, A*
 Muskegon *C, A*
Delta College *A*
Henry Ford Community College *C*
Kirtland Community College *C*
Lansing Community College *C*
Mid Michigan Community College *C*
Oakland Community College *C, A*
Southwestern Michigan College *C*

Washtenaw Community College *C*
Wayne County Community
  College *C, A*

Minnesota

Anoka-Ramsey Community College *C*
Brown College
  Brooklyn Center *A*
  Mendota Heights *A*
Minnesota State Community and
  Technical College *C, A*
National American University
  Bloomington *A*
Northland Community & Technical
  College *C, A*
Rasmussen College
  Blaine *C, A*
  Bloomington *C, A*
  Brooklyn Park *C, A*
  Eagan *C, A*
  Lake Elmo/Woodbury *C, A*
  Mankato *C, A*
  St. Cloud *C, A*
South Central College *A*

Missouri

Mineral Area College *C*
North Central Missouri College *A*
State Fair Community College *C*

Montana

Flathead Valley Community College *C*
Montana State University
  Great Falls College *C*
University of Montana *C*

Nebraska

Southeast Community College *C*
Vatterott College
  Spring Valley *C, A*

Nevada

Career College of Northern Nevada *C*
Kaplan College
  Las Vegas *C, A*

New Jersey

Middlesex County College *A*

New Mexico

Brookline College
  Albuquerque *C*
Carrington College
  Albuquerque *C*
Central New Mexico Community
  College *C*
Eastern New Mexico University:
  Roswell *C*

New York

ASA College *A*

North Carolina

Cabarrus College of Health
  Sciences *A*
Cape Fear Community College *C, A*
Craven Community College *C*
Davidson County Community
  College *C*
Durham Technical Community
  College *C*
Fayetteville Technical Community
  College *C, A*
Johnston Community College *A*
Southeastern Community College *C*
Wayne Community College *C*

North Dakota

North Dakota State College of
  Science *C, A*

Ohio

Brown Mackie College
  Akron *A*
  Cincinnati *A*
  Findlay *A*
Cuyahoga Community College
  Metropolitan *C, A*
Kaplan College
  Dayton *C*
Marion Technical College *A*
Mercy College of Ohio *C*
National College
  Canton *A*
  Cincinnati *A*
  Stow *A*
  Willoughby Hills *A*
Ohio Valley College of Technology *A*
Remington College
  Cleveland *C*
Sinclair Community College *C*
Southern State Community College *C*
University of Northwestern
  Ohio *C, A*

Oregon

Central Oregon Community
  College *C*
Chemeketa Community College *C, A*
Everest College
  Portland *C, A*
Heald College
  Portland *A*
Linn-Benton Community College *C*
Pioneer Pacific College *C*

Pennsylvania

Bidwell Training Center *C*
Community College of Allegheny
  County *C, A*
Everest Institute: Pittsburgh *C*
Kaplan Career Institute
  Franklin Mills *C*
Lansdale School of Business *C*
Laurel Business Institute *C*
Laurel Technical Institute *C*
Lincoln Technical Institute
  Allentown *C*
  Northeast Philadelphia *C*
Pennco Tech *C*
Pennsylvania Highlands Community
  College *C*
Pennsylvania Institute of
  Technology *C, A*
YTI Career Institute
  Altoona *C*
  Capital Region *C*

Puerto Rico

Centro de Estudios
  Multidisciplinarios *A*
Columbia Centro Universitario:
  Caguas *C*
EDP University of Puerto Rico: Hato
  Rey *C*
Huertas College *A*
Humacao Community College *A*
Inter American University of Puerto
  Rico
  Aguadilla Campus *A*
  Barranquitas Campus *A*
  Guayama Campus *A*
  Metropolitan Campus *C*
  Ponce Campus *C*
  San German Campus *C*
National University College
  Arecibo *A*
  Bayamon *A*
  Ponce *A*
  Rio Grande *A*
Turabo University *C*
Universidad Metropolitana *C*
Universidad del Este *A*

South Carolina

Aiken Technical College *C*
Central Carolina Technical College *C*
Greenville Technical College *C*
Horry-Georgetown Technical
  College *A*
Midlands Technical College *C, A*
Piedmont Technical College *C*
Spartanburg Community College *C*
Tri-County Technical College *C*
Trident Technical College *C*
Virginia College
  Florence *C*
York Technical College *C*

South Dakota

Southeast Technical Institute *C*
Western Dakota Technical
  Institute *C, A*

Tennessee

Anthem Career College
  Memphis *C*
Chattanooga State Community
  College *C*
Daymar Institute
  Clarksville *B*
  Murfreesboro *A*
  Nashville *C, A*
National College of Business and
  Technology
  Bartlett *A*
  Knoxville *C, A*
  Madison *A*
  Memphis *A*
  Nashville *C*
Remington College
  Memphis *C*
Roane State Community College *C*
South College *D*
Southwest Tennessee Community
  College *C*
Virginia College
  School of Business and Health in
    Chattanooga *C*
  School of Business and Health in
    Knoxville *A*
Walters State Community College *C*

Texas

Alvin Community College *C*
Amarillo College *C*
Angelina College *C*
Austin Community College *C*
Cisco College *C*
Del Mar College *C, A*
El Paso Community College *C*
Everest College
  Arlington *C*
  Fort Worth *C*
Houston Community College
  System *C*
Lamar Institute of Technology *C*
Lamar State College at Orange *C*
Lone Star College System *C, A*
Northwest Vista College *C*
Remington College
  Fort Worth *C*
  North Houston *C, A*
San Jacinto College *C*
Sanford-Brown College
  Houston *C*
South Texas College *C, A*
Texas State Technical College
  Waco *C*
Virginia College
  Austin *C*
Weatherford College *C, A*

Utah

Salt Lake Community College *C*
Snow College *A*

Virginia

American National University
  Salem *C*
J. Sargeant Reynolds Community
  College *C*
Miller-Motte Technical College
  Lynchburg *A*
Southwest Virginia Community
  College *C*
Wytheville Community College *C*

Washington

Carrington College
  Spokane *C*
Centralia College *C*
Clark College *C*
Clover Park Technical College *C, A*
Edmonds Community College *C*
Grays Harbor College *C*
North Seattle Community
  College *C, A*
Renton Technical College *A*
Spokane Community College *C, A*
Spokane Falls Community College *C*
Yakima Valley Community
  College *C, A*

West Virginia

American National University
  Parkersburg *C*

Wisconsin

Blackhawk Technical College *C*
Chippewa Valley Technical College *C*
Fox Valley Technical College *C*
Gateway Technical College *C*
Lakeshore Technical College *C, A*
Madison Area Technical College *C*
Mid-State Technical College *C*
Milwaukee Area Technical College *C*
Rasmussen College
  Appleton *C, A*
  Green Bay *C, A*
  Wausau *C, A*
Waukesha County Technical
  College *C*

Wyoming

Casper College *C, A*

Philosophy

Alabama

Auburn University *B*
Birmingham-Southern College *B*
Faulkner University *D*
Samford University *B*
Spring Hill College *B*
University of Alabama *B*
University of Alabama
  Birmingham *B*
  Huntsville *B*
University of South Alabama *B*

Alaska

University of Alaska
  Anchorage *C, B*
  Fairbanks *B*

Arizona

Arizona State University *B, M, D*
Arizona Western College *A*
Cochise College *A*
Harrison Middleton
  University *B, M, D*
Northern Arizona University *B*
University of Arizona *B, M, D*

Arkansas

Arkansas State University *B*
Hendrix College *B*
Lyon College *B*
Ouachita Baptist University *B*

Philander Smith College *B*
University of Arkansas *B, M, D*
University of Arkansas
  Little Rock *B*
University of Central Arkansas *B*
University of the Ozarks *B*

California

Azusa Pacific University *B*
Bakersfield College *A*
Berkeley City College *A*
Biola University *B, M, D*
California Baptist University *B*
California Institute of Technology *B*
California Lutheran University *B*
California Polytechnic State
  University: San Luis Obispo *B*
California State Polytechnic
  University: Pomona *B*
California State University
  Bakersfield *B*
  Chico *C, B*
  Dominguez Hills *B*
  East Bay *B*
  Fresno *B*
  Fullerton *B*
  Long Beach *B, M*
  Los Angeles *B, M*
  Northridge *B*
  Sacramento *B, M*
  San Bernardino *B*
  Stanislaus *B*
Canada College *A*
Cerritos College *A*
Chabot College *A*
Chaffey College *A*
Chapman University *B*
Claremont McKenna College *B*
College of Alameda *A*
College of the Canyons *A*
College of the Desert *A*
College of the Siskiyous *A*
Copper Mountain College *A*
Cypress College *A*
De Anza College *A*
El Camino College *A*
Foothill College *A*
Fresno Pacific University *B*
Fullerton College *A*
Gavilan College *A*
Glendale Community College *A*
Golden West College *A*
Grossmont College *A*
Holy Names University *B*
Humboldt State University *B*
Irvine Valley College *A*
John Paul the Great Catholic
  University *C*
Loma Linda University *M*
Los Angeles Mission College *A*
Los Angeles Southwest College *A*
Los Angeles Valley College *A*
Loyola Marymount University *B, M*
Merced College *A*
Mills College *B*
Monterey Peninsula College *A*
Mount St. Mary's College *B*
Notre Dame de Namur University *B*
Occidental College *B*
Orange Coast College *A*
Oxnard College *C, A*
Pepperdine University *B*
Pitzer College *B*
Point Loma Nazarene University *B*
Pomona College *B*
Rio Hondo College *A*
Saddleback College *A*
St. Mary's College of California *B*
San Diego City College *A*
San Diego Mesa College *A*
San Diego State University *B, M*
San Francisco State University *B, M*
San Jose State University *B, M*
Santa Ana College *A*
Santa Barbara City College *A*

Santa Clara University *B*
Santa Rosa Junior College *A*
Santiago Canyon College *A*
Scripps College *B*
Sierra College *A*
Sonoma State University *B*
Southwestern College *A*
Stanford University *B, M, D*
University of California
  Berkeley *B, D*
  Davis *B, M, D*
  Irvine *B, M, D*
  Los Angeles *B, M, D*
  Riverside *B, M, D*
  San Diego *B, M, D*
  Santa Barbara *B, M, D*
  Santa Cruz *B, M, D*
University of La Verne *B*
University of Redlands *B*
University of San Diego *B*
University of San Francisco *B*
University of Southern
  California *B, M, D*
University of the Pacific *B*
West Los Angeles College *A*
Westmont College *B*
Whittier College *B*

Colorado

Colorado College *B*
Colorado State University *B, M*
Community College of Aurora *A*
Fort Lewis College *B*
Metropolitan State University of
  Denver *B*
Regis University *B*
University of Colorado
  Boulder *B, M, D*
  Colorado Springs *B*
  Denver *B*
University of Denver *B, M*
University of Northern Colorado *B*

Connecticut

Albertus Magnus College *B*
Central Connecticut State
  University *B*
Connecticut College *B*
Fairfield University *B*
Holy Apostles College and
  Seminary *B, M*
Sacred Heart University *B*
Southern Connecticut State
  University *B*
Trinity College *B*
University of Connecticut *B, M, D*
University of Hartford *B*
University of Saint Joseph *B*
Wesleyan University *B*
Yale University *B, M, D*

Delaware

Delaware State University *B*
University of Delaware *B*

District of Columbia

American University *B, M*
Catholic University of
  America *B, M, D*
Gallaudet University *B*
George Washington University *B*
Georgetown University *B, M, D*
Howard University *B, M*
Trinity Washington University *B*
University of the District of
  Columbia *A, B*

Florida

Ave Maria University *B*
Barry University *B*
Daytona State College *A*
Eckerd College *B*
Flagler College *B*
Florida Atlantic University *B*

Florida Gulf Coast University *B*
Florida International University *B*
Florida Southern College *B*
Florida State University *B, M, D*
Indian River State College *A*
Jacksonville University *B*
Miami Dade College *A*
New College of Florida *B*
Nova Southeastern University *B*
Palm Beach Atlantic University *B*
Palm Beach State College *A*
Pensacola State College *A*
Rollins College *B*
St. John Vianney College Seminary *B*
Stetson University *B*
University of Central Florida *B*
University of Florida *B, M, D*
University of Miami *B, M, D*
University of North Florida *B*
University of South Florida *B, M, D*
University of Tampa *A, B*
University of West Florida *B*

Georgia

Agnes Scott College *B*
Clark Atlanta University *B*
Clayton State University *B*
Covenant College *B*
Darton College *A*
Emory University *B, D*
Georgia College and State
  University *B*
Georgia Highlands College *A*
Georgia Perimeter College *A*
Georgia Southern University *B*
Georgia State University *B, M*
Kennesaw State University *B*
Mercer University *B*
Morehouse College *B*
Oglethorpe University *B*
Paine College *B*
Piedmont College *B*
South Georgia State College *A*
Spelman College *B*
Toccoa Falls College *B*
University of Georgia *B, M, D*
University of West Georgia *B*
Valdosta State University *B*
Wesleyan College *B*

Hawaii

University of Hawaii
  Hilo *B*
  Manoa *B, M, D*
  West Oahu *B*

Idaho

Boise State University *B*
College of Idaho *B*
Idaho State University *B*
North Idaho College *A*
Northwest Nazarene University *B*
University of Idaho *B, M*

Illinois

Augustana College *B*
Benedictine University *B*
Bradley University *B*
Concordia University Chicago *B*
DePaul University *B, M, D*
Dominican University *B*
Eastern Illinois University *B*
Elmhurst College *B*
Eureka College *B*
Greenville College *B*
Harper College *A*
Illinois College *B*
Illinois State University *B*
Illinois Wesleyan University *B*
Knox College *B*
Lake Forest College *B*
Lewis University *B*
Lincoln Christian University *B*
Lincoln College *A*

Loyola University Chicago *B, M, D*
MacMurray College *B*
McKendree University *B*
Millikin University *B*
Monmouth College *B*
North Central College *B*
North Park University *B*
Northeastern Illinois University *B*
Northern Illinois University *B, M*
Northwestern University *B, M, D*
Principia College *B*
Richland Community College *A*
Rockford University *B*
Roosevelt University *B*
Saint Xavier University *B*
South Suburban College of Cook
  County *A*
Southern Illinois University
  Carbondale *B, M, D*
Southern Illinois University
  Edwardsville *B*
Southwestern Illinois College *A*
Trinity Christian College *B*
Trinity International University *B, M*
University of Chicago *B, D*
University of Illinois
  Chicago *B, M, D*
  Springfield *B*
  Urbana-Champaign *B, M, D*
Western Illinois University *B*
Wheaton College *B*

Indiana

Anderson University *B*
Ball State University *B*
Bethel College *B*
Butler University *B*
DePauw University *B*
Earlham College *B*
Franklin College *B*
Hanover College *B*
Huntington University *B*
Indiana State University *B*
Indiana University
  Bloomington *B, M, D*
  Northwest *B*
  Purdue University Fort Wayne *B*
  Purdue University
    Indianapolis *B, M*
  South Bend *B*
  Southeast *B*
Manchester University *B*
Marian University *B*
Purdue University *B, M, D*
Purdue University
  Calumet *B*
Saint Joseph's College *B*
Saint Mary's College *B*
Taylor University *B*
University of Evansville *B*
University of Indianapolis *B*
University of Notre Dame *B, M, D*
University of St. Francis *B*
University of Southern Indiana *B*
Valparaiso University *B*
Vincennes University *A*
Wabash College *B*

Iowa

Buena Vista University *B*
Central College *B*
Clarke University *A, B*
Coe College *B*
Cornell College *B*
Divine Word College *B*
Dordt College *B*
Drake University *B*
Grinnell College *B*
Iowa State University *B*
Iowa Wesleyan College *B*
Loras College *B*
Luther College *B*
Morningside College *B*
Mount Mercy University *B*

Northwestern College *B*
St. Ambrose University *B*
Simpson College *B*
University of Dubuque *B*
University of Iowa *B, M, D*
University of Northern Iowa *B*
Wartburg College *B*

Kansas

Baker University *B*
Barton County Community College *A*
Benedictine College *B*
Colby Community College *A*
Cowley County Community College *A*
Fort Hays State University *B*
Kansas State University *B*
Kansas Wesleyan University *B*
Newman University *B*
University of Kansas *B, M, D*
Washburn University *B*
Wichita State University *B*

Kentucky

Asbury University *B*
Bellarmine University *B*
Berea College *B*
Bluegrass Community and Technical College *A*
Centre College *B*
Eastern Kentucky University *B*
Georgetown College *B*
Hopkinsville Community College *A*
Morehead State University *B*
Murray State University *B*
Northern Kentucky University *B*
Thomas More College *A, B*
Transylvania University *B*
University of Kentucky *B, M, D*
University of Louisville *B*

Louisiana

Centenary College of Louisiana *B*
Dillard University *B*
Louisiana State University and Agricultural and Mechanical College *B, M*
Loyola University New Orleans *B*
Tulane University *B, M, D*
University of New Orleans *B*
Xavier University of Louisiana *B*

Maine

Bates College *B*
Bowdoin College *B*
Colby College *B*
Saint Joseph's College of Maine *B*
University of Maine *B*
University of Southern Maine *B*

Maryland

Frederick Community College *A*
Frostburg State University *B*
Goucher College *B*
Harford Community College *A*
Hood College *B*
Johns Hopkins University *B, M, D*
Loyola University Maryland *B*
McDaniel College *B*
Mount St. Mary's University *B, M*
Notre Dame of Maryland University *B*
St. Mary's College of Maryland *B*
Salisbury University *B*
Towson University *B*
University of Maryland
   Baltimore County *B*
   College Park *B, M, D*
Washington College *B*

Massachusetts

Amherst College *B*
Anna Maria College *B*
Assumption College *B*

Bard College at Simon's Rock *B*
Bentley University *B*
Boston College *B, M, D*
Boston University *B, M, D*
Brandeis University *B, M*
Bridgewater State University *B*
Cape Cod Community College *A*
Clark University *B*
College of the Holy Cross *B*
Curry College *B*
Emmanuel College *B*
Gordon College *B*
Hampshire College *B*
Harvard College *B, M, D*
Massachusetts College of Liberal Arts *B, T*
Massachusetts Institute of Technology *B, D*
Merrimack College *B*
Mount Holyoke College *B*
Northeastern University *B*
Simmons College *B*
Smith College *B, D*
Stonehill College *B*
Suffolk University *B*
Tufts University *B, M*
University of Massachusetts
   Amherst *B, M, D*
   Boston *B*
   Dartmouth *B*
   Lowell *B*
Wellesley College *B*
Western New England University *B*
Wheaton College *B*
Williams College *B*

Michigan

Adrian College *B*
Albion College *B*
Alma College *B*
Aquinas College *B*
Calvin College *B*
Central Michigan University *B*
Eastern Michigan University *B*
Grand Valley State University *B*
Hillsdale College *B*
Hope College *B*
Kalamazoo College *B*
Lake Michigan College *A*
Lansing Community College *A*
Madonna University *B*
Michigan State University *B, M, D*
Northern Michigan University *B*
Oakland University *B*
Sacred Heart Major Seminary *B*
Siena Heights University *B*
Spring Arbor University *B*
University of Detroit Mercy *B*
University of Michigan *B, M, D*
University of Michigan
   Dearborn *B*
   Flint *B*
Wayne State University *B, M, D*
Western Michigan University *B, M*

Minnesota

Augsburg College *B*
Bethel University *B*
Carleton College *B*
College of St. Benedict *B*
Concordia College: Moorhead *B*
Gustavus Adolphus College *B*
Hamline University *B*
Macalester College *B*
Metropolitan State University *B*
Minneapolis Community and Technical College *A*
Minnesota State University
   Mankato *B*
   Moorhead *C, B*
Minnesota West Community and Technical College *A*
St. Catherine University *B*
Saint Cloud State University *B*

St. John's University *B*
St. Mary's University of Minnesota *B*
St. Olaf College *B*
Southwest Minnesota State University *B*
University of Minnesota
   Duluth *B*
   Morris *B*
   Twin Cities *B, M, D*
University of St. Thomas *B*

Mississippi

Belhaven University *B*
Itawamba Community College *A*
Millsaps College *B*
Mississippi State University *B*
University of Mississippi *B, M*
University of Southern Mississippi *B, M*

Missouri

Central Methodist University *B*
Columbia College *B*
Conception Seminary College *B*
Drury University *B*
Lindenwood University *B*
Maryville University of Saint Louis *B*
Missouri State University *B*
Missouri University of Science and Technology *B*
Missouri Valley College *B*
Northwest Missouri State University *B*
Rockhurst University *B*
St. Charles Community College *A*
Saint Louis University *B, M, D*
Southeast Missouri State University *B*
Three Rivers Community College *A*
University of Missouri
   Columbia *B, M, D*
   Kansas City *B*
   St. Louis *B, M*
Washington University in St. Louis *B, M, D*
Webster University *B*
Westminster College *B*
William Jewell College *B*

Montana

Carroll College *A, B*
Montana State University *B*
University of Montana *B, M*

Nebraska

Bellevue University *B*
Creighton University *B*
Doane College *B*
Hastings College *B*
Nebraska Wesleyan University *B*
University of Nebraska
   Kearney *B*
   Lincoln *B, M, D*
   Omaha *B*

Nevada

University of Nevada
   Las Vegas *B*
   Reno *B, M*

New Hampshire

Colby-Sawyer College *B*
Dartmouth College *B*
New England College *B*
Plymouth State University *B*
Saint Anselm College *B*
University of New Hampshire *B*

New Jersey

Bergen Community College *A*
Bloomfield College *B, T*
College of New Jersey *B*
College of St. Elizabeth *B*
Drew University *B*

Fairleigh Dickinson University
   College at Florham *B*
   Metropolitan Campus *B*
Felician College *B*
Montclair State University *B*
New Jersey City University *B*
Princeton University *B, M, D*
Rider University *B*
Rutgers, The State University of New Jersey
   Camden Campus *B*
   New Brunswick/Piscataway Campus *B, M, D*
   Newark Campus *B*
Saint Peter's University *B*
Seton Hall University *B*
Stevens Institute of Technology *B*
Thomas Edison State College *B*
William Paterson University of New Jersey *B*

New Mexico

New Mexico State University *B*
University of New Mexico *B, M, D*

New York

Adelphi University *B*
Alfred University *B*
Bard College *B*
Barnard College *B*
Canisius College *B*
City University of New York
   Baruch College *B*
   Brooklyn College *B*
   City College *B*
   College of Staten Island *B*
   Hunter College *B*
   LaGuardia Community College *A*
   Lehman College *B*
   Queens College *B, M*
   York College *B*
Colgate University *B*
College of Mount St. Vincent *B*
College of New Rochelle *B*
College of Saint Rose *B*
Columbia University *B*
Columbia University
   School of General Studies *B*
Cornell University *B, M, D*
D'Youville College *B*
Dowling College *B*
Eugene Lang College The New School for Liberal Arts *B*
Excelsior College *B*
Fordham University *B, M, D*
Hamilton College *B*
Hartwick College *B*
Hobart and William Smith Colleges *B*
Hofstra University *B*
Houghton College *B*
Iona College *B*
Ithaca College *B*
Le Moyne College *B*
Long Island University
   LIU Brooklyn *B*
   LIU Post *B*
Manhattan College *B*
Manhattanville College *B*
Marist College *B*
Marymount Manhattan College *B*
Molloy College *B*
Nazareth College *B*
New York University *B, M, D*
Niagara University *B*
Nyack College *B*
Pace University: Pleasantville/Briarcliff *B*
Rensselaer Polytechnic Institute *B*
Rochester Institute of Technology *B*
SUNY
   College at Brockport *B*
   College at Buffalo *B*
   College at Cortland *B*
   College at Fredonia *B*

College at Geneseo *B*
College at New Paltz *B*
College at Old Westbury *B*
College at Oneonta *B*
College at Oswego *B*
College at Plattsburgh *B*
College at Potsdam *B*
College at Purchase *B*
University at Albany *B, M, D*
University at Binghamton *B, M, D*
University at Buffalo *B, M, D*
University at Stony Brook *B, M, D*
Saint Bonaventure University *B*
St. Francis College *B*
St. John Fisher College *B*
St. John's University *B*
St. Lawrence University *B*
St. Thomas Aquinas College *B*
Siena College *B*
Skidmore College *B*
Syracuse University *B, M, D*
Touro College *B*
Union College *B*
Union Theological Seminary:
    Theological Professions *D*
University of Rochester *B, M, D*
Utica College *B*
Vassar College *B*
Wagner College *B*
Wells College *B*
Yeshiva University *B*

North Carolina

Appalachian State University *B*
Davidson College *B*
Duke University *B, M, D*
East Carolina University *B*
Elon University *B*
Gardner-Webb University *B*
Guilford College *B*
High Point University *B*
Lenoir-Rhyne University *B*
Methodist University *A, B*
North Carolina State University *B*
Queens University of Charlotte *B*
St. Andrews University *B*
Salem College *B*
Southeastern Baptist Theological
    Seminary *M, D*
University of North Carolina
    Asheville *B*
    Chapel Hill *B, M, D*
    Charlotte *B*
    Greensboro *B*
    Wilmington *B*
Wake Forest University *B*
Warren Wilson College *B*
Western Carolina University *B*

North Dakota

North Dakota State University *B*
University of North Dakota *B*

Ohio

Ashland University *B*
Baldwin Wallace University *B*
Bowling Green State University *B, M*
Capital University *B*
Case Western Reserve University *B*
Cedarville University *B*
Cleveland State University *B, M*
College of Wooster *B*
Denison University *B*
Franciscan University of
    Steubenville *B, M*
Hiram College *B*
John Carroll University *B*
Kent State University *B, M*
Kenyon College *B*
Malone University *B*
Miami University
    Middletown *A*
    Oxford *B, M*
Mount Vernon Nazarene University *B*

Muskingum University *B*
Oberlin College *B*
Ohio Dominican University *B*
Ohio Northern University *B*
Ohio State University
    Columbus Campus *B, M, D*
Ohio University *B, M*
Ohio Wesleyan University *B*
Otterbein University *B*
Pontifical College Josephinum *B*
Sinclair Community College *A*
University of Akron *B*
University of Cincinnati *C, B, M, D*
University of Dayton *B*
University of Findlay *B*
University of Mount Union *B*
University of Toledo *B, M*
Urbana University *B*
Ursuline College *B*
Walsh University *B*
Wittenberg University *B*
Wright State University *B*
Xavier University *B*
Youngstown State University *B*

Oklahoma

Oklahoma Baptist University *B*
Oklahoma City University *B*
Oklahoma State University *B, M*
St. Gregory's University *B*
Southern Nazarene University *B*
Tulsa Community College *A*
University of Central Oklahoma *B*
University of Oklahoma *B, M, D*
University of Tulsa *B*

Oregon

George Fox University *B*
Lewis & Clark College *B*
Linfield College *B*
Mount Angel Seminary *B, M*
Mt. Hood Community College *A*
Oregon State University *B*
Pacific University *B*
Portland State University *B*
Reed College *B*
University of Oregon *B, M, D*
University of Portland *B*
Western Oregon University *B*
Willamette University *B*

Pennsylvania

Albright College *B*
Allegheny College *B*
Alvernia University *B*
Arcadia University *B*
Bloomsburg University of
    Pennsylvania *B*
Bryn Mawr College *B*
Bucknell University *B*
Cabrini College *B*
California University of
    Pennsylvania *B*
Carlow University *B*
Carnegie Mellon University *B, M*
Clarion University of Pennsylvania *B*
DeSales University *C, B*
Dickinson College *B*
Drexel University *B*
Duquesne University *B, M, D*
East Stroudsburg University of
    Pennsylvania *B*
Eastern University *B*
Edinboro University of
    Pennsylvania *B*
Elizabethtown College *B*
Franklin & Marshall College *B*
Gannon University *B*
Geneva College *B*
Gettysburg College *B*
Grove City College *B*
Gwynedd Mercy University *B*
Harrisburg Area Community
    College *A*

Haverford College *B*
Indiana University of Pennsylvania *B*
Juniata College *B*
King's College *B*
Kutztown University of
    Pennsylvania *B*
La Salle University *B*
Lafayette College *B*
Lancaster Bible College *D*
Lebanon Valley College *B*
Lehigh University *B*
Lincoln University *B*
Lock Haven University of
    Pennsylvania *B*
Lycoming College *B*
Mansfield University of
    Pennsylvania *B*
Marywood University *B*
Mercyhurst University *B*
Messiah College *B*
Millersville University of
    Pennsylvania *B*
Misericordia University *B*
Moravian College *B*
Muhlenberg College *C, B*
Penn State
    Abington *B*
    Altoona *B*
    Beaver *B*
    Berks *B*
    Brandywine *B*
    DuBois *B*
    Fayette, The Eberly Campus *B*
    Greater Allegheny *B*
    Harrisburg *B*
    Hazleton *B*
    Lehigh Valley *B*
    Mont Alto *B*
    New Kensington *B*
    Schuylkill *B*
    Shenango *B*
    University Park *B, M, D*
    Wilkes-Barre *B*
    Worthington Scranton *B*
    York *B*
Rosemont College *B*
St. Charles Borromeo Seminary -
    Overbrook *B*
St. Francis University *B*
Saint Joseph's University *B*
St. Vincent College *B*
Slippery Rock University of
    Pennsylvania *B*
Susquehanna University *B*
Swarthmore College *B*
Temple University *B, M, D*
Thiel College *B*
University of Pennsylvania *B, M, D*
University of Pittsburgh *B, M, D*
University of Scranton *B*
Ursinus College *B*
Villanova University *B, M, D*
Washington & Jefferson College *B*
West Chester University of
    Pennsylvania *B, M*
Westminster College *B*
Wilkes University *B*
Wilson College *B*
York College of Pennsylvania *B*

Puerto Rico

Bayamon Central University *B*
Pontifical Catholic University of
    Puerto Rico *B*
Universidad Metropolitana *D*
University of Puerto Rico
    Aguadilla *A*
    Mayaguez *B*
    Rio Piedras *B, M*

Rhode Island

Brown University *B, M, D*
Providence College *B*
Rhode Island College *B*

Roger Williams University *B*
Salve Regina University *B*
University of Rhode Island *B*

South Carolina

Claflin University *B*
Clemson University *B*
Coastal Carolina University *B*
College of Charleston *B*
Converse College *B*
Erskine College *B*
Furman University *B*
Newberry College *B*
University of South Carolina
    Columbia *B, M, D*
Winthrop University *B*
Wofford College *B*

South Dakota

Augustana College *B*
University of South Dakota *B*

Tennessee

Aquinas College *B*
Austin Peay State University *B*
Belmont University *B*
Carson-Newman University *B*
East Tennessee State University *B, T*
Freed-Hardeman University *B*
Jackson State Community College *A*
Lee University *B*
Lipscomb University *B*
Maryville College *B*
Middle Tennessee State University *B*
Rhodes College *B*
Sewanee: The University of the
    South *B*
Union University *B*
University of Memphis *B, M, D*
University of Tennessee
    Knoxville *B, M, D*
    Martin *B*
Vanderbilt University *B, M, D*

Texas

Austin College *B*
Austin Community College *A*
Baylor University *B, M, D*
Blinn College *A*
Criswell College *A, B, M*
Dallas Baptist University *B*
Frank Phillips College *A*
Hardin-Simmons University *B*
Houston Baptist University *B*
Howard Payne University *B*
Laredo Community College *A*
Our Lady of the Lake University of
    San Antonio *B*
Rice University *B, M, D*
St. Edward's University *B*
St. Mary's University *B*
St. Philip's College *A*
Sam Houston State University *B*
San Jacinto College *A*
South Texas College *A*
Southern Methodist University *B*
Southwestern Baptist Theological
    Seminary: Theological
    Professions *B*
Southwestern University *B*
Stephen F. Austin State University *B*
Texas A&M University *B, M, D*
Texas Christian University *B*
Texas Lutheran University *B*
Texas State University *B, M*
Texas Tech University *B, M*
Trinity University *B*
University of Dallas *B, M, D*
University of Houston *B, M*
University of Houston
    Downtown *B*
University of North Texas *B, M, D*
University of St. Thomas *B, M, D*

University of Texas
Arlington *B*
Austin *B, M, D*
El Paso *B, M*
Pan American *B*
San Antonio *B*
University of the Incarnate Word *B*
Western Texas College *A*

Utah

Brigham Young University *B*
Snow College *A*
Southern Utah University *B*
University of Utah *B, M, D, T*
Utah State University *B*
Utah Valley University *A, B*
Weber State University *B*
Westminster College *B*

Vermont

Bennington College *B*
Castleton State College *B*
Green Mountain College *B*
Lyndon State College *B*
Marlboro College *B*
Middlebury College *B*
Saint Michael's College *B*
University of Vermont *B*

Virginia

Christendom College *B*
Christopher Newport University *B*
College of William and Mary *B*
Emory & Henry College *B*
Ferrum College *B*
George Mason University *B, M*
Hampden-Sydney College *B*
Hollins University *B*
Liberty University *B*
Lord Fairfax Community College *A*
Lynchburg College *B*
Mary Baldwin College *B*
Marymount University *B*
Old Dominion University *B*
Randolph College *B*
Randolph-Macon College *B*
Roanoke College *B*
Southern Virginia University *B*
Sweet Briar College *B*
University of Richmond *B*
University of Virginia *B, M, D*
Virginia Commonwealth University *B*
Virginia Polytechnic Institute and
State University *B, M*
Virginia Wesleyan College *B*
Washington and Lee University *B*

Washington

Central Washington University *B*
Eastern Washington University *B*
Everett Community College *A*
Evergreen State College *B*
Gonzaga University *B, M*
Northwest University *B*
Pacific Lutheran University *B*
Saint Martin's University *B*
Seattle Pacific University *B*
Seattle University *B*
University of Puget Sound *B*
University of Washington *B, M, D*
Washington State University *B, M*
Western Washington University *B*
Whitman College *B*
Whitworth University *B*

West Virginia

American Public University System *B*
West Virginia University *B*
West Virginia Wesleyan College *B*
Wheeling Jesuit University *B*

Wisconsin

Alverno College *B*
Beloit College *B*

Carthage College *B*
Lawrence University *B*
Marquette University *B, M, D, T*
Mount Mary University *B*
Ripon College *B*
St. Norbert College *B*
University of Wisconsin
Eau Claire *B*
Green Bay *B*
La Crosse *B*
Madison *B, M, D*
Milwaukee *B, M*
Oshkosh *B*
Parkside *B*
Platteville *B*
Stevens Point *B, T*
Viterbo University *B*
Wisconsin Lutheran College *B*

Wyoming

University of Wyoming *B, M*

Philosophy and religious studies, general

Delaware

Wesley College *B*

Florida

Bethune-Cookman University *B*
Florida Agricultural and Mechanical
University *B*

Georgia

Berry College *B*
Covenant College *B*
LaGrange College *B*

Indiana

Bethel College *B*
Indiana Wesleyan University *A, B*

Iowa

Iowa Wesleyan College *B*

Kansas

Central Christian College of
Kansas *A, B*
Friends University *B*
Southwestern College *B*
Sterling College *B*

Maine

College of the Atlantic *B, M*

Maryland

Howard Community College *A*

Missouri

College of the Ozarks *B*
Truman State University *B*

New Hampshire

Colby-Sawyer College *B*

New Jersey

Richard Stockton College of New
Jersey *B*
Rowan University *B*

New York

Elmira College *B*
Ithaca College *B*
Pace University *B*
Roberts Wesleyan College *B*
St. Joseph's College New York:
Suffolk Campus *B*
St. Joseph's College, New York *B*

North Carolina

Montreat College *B*
Southeastern Baptist Theological
Seminary *C, A, B, M, D*

Ohio

Shawnee State University *B*

Oklahoma

Oklahoma City University *B*

Pennsylvania

Baptist Bible College of
Pennsylvania *C, A, B, M*

South Carolina

Benedict College *B*

Tennessee

Christian Brothers University *B*
Lincoln Memorial University *B*

Virginia

Radford University *B*

Phlebotomy technician

Alabama

Bevill State Community College *C*

Alaska

University of Alaska
Anchorage *C*

Arizona

Brookline College
Phoenix *C*
Tempe *C*
Tucson *C*
Phoenix College *C*
Pima Community College *C*

Arkansas

Arkansas State University
Mountain Home *C*
National Park Community College *C*
North Arkansas College *C*
Phillips Community College of the
University of Arkansas *A*
South Arkansas Community
College *C*
Southeast Arkansas College *C*

California

Heald College
Concord *C*
MTI College *C*
Palo Verde College *C*

Colorado

Aims Community College *C*
Front Range Community College *C*
Pikes Peak Community College *C*
Pueblo Community College *C*
Red Rocks Community College *C*

Connecticut

Goodwin College *C*

Florida

City College
Gainesville *C*
Florida Gateway College *C*
Pasco-Hernando State College *C*
Saint Johns River State College *C*
South Florida State College *C*

Georgia

Atlanta Technical College *C*
Columbus Technical College *C*
Dalton State College *C*
Darton College *C*

Georgia Piedmont Technical
College *C*
Southeastern Technical College *C*

Illinois

City Colleges of Chicago
Harry S. Truman College *C*
Kennedy-King College *C*
Malcolm X College *C*
Olive-Harvey College *C*
Richard J. Daley College *C*
Wilbur Wright College *C*
Harper College *C*
Illinois Eastern Community Colleges
Frontier Community College *C*
Illinois Valley Community College *C*
Kankakee Community College *C*
Kaskaskia College *C*
Moraine Valley Community College *C*
Waubonsee Community College *C*

Iowa

Des Moines Area Community
College *C*
St. Luke's College *C*

Kansas

Colby Community College *C*
Hutchinson Community College *C*
Wichita Area Technical College *C*

Kentucky

Bluegrass Community and Technical
College *C*
Lincoln College of Technology
Florence *C*
Somerset Community College *C*
Spencerian College *C*
Spencerian College: Lexington *C*
West Kentucky Community and
Technical College *C*

Louisiana

Bossier Parish Community College *C*
ITI Technical College *C*

Maryland

Hagerstown Community College *C*

Massachusetts

Bunker Hill Community College *C*
Massasoit Community College *C*
Mount Wachusett Community
College *C*
Quincy College *C*

Michigan

Davenport University *C*
Lansing Community College *C*
Oakland Community College *C*
Schoolcraft College *C*
Wayne County Community College *C*

Minnesota

Alexandria Technical and Community
College *C*
Duluth Business University *C, A*
Lake Superior College *C*
Minneapolis Community and
Technical College *C*
Minnesota State Community and
Technical College *C*
Minnesota West Community and
Technical College *C*
Northland Community & Technical
College *C*
St. Catherine University *C*
South Central College *C*

Mississippi

University of Southern Mississippi *C*

New Hampshire
Manchester Community College *C*

New Mexico
Central New Mexico Community
College *C*
Santa Fe Community College *C*

New York
Broome Community College *C*
Dutchess Community College *C*
Niagara County Community
College *C*

North Carolina
Brunswick Community College *C*
College of the Albemarle *C*
Halifax Community College *C*
Rockingham Community College *C*
Southeastern Community College *C*
Wayne Community College *C*

North Dakota
Bismarck State College *C*

Ohio
Columbus State Community
College *C*
Eastern Gateway Community
College *C*
Edison State Community College *C*
Lincoln College of Technology
Dayton *C*
Lorain County Community College *C*
Mercy College of Ohio *C*
Miami-Jacobs Career College
Columbus *C*
North Central State College *C*
Northwest State Community
College *C*
Sinclair Community College *C*
Southern State Community College *C*
Stautzenberger College *C*

Pennsylvania
Bucks County Community College *C*
Harrisburg Area Community
College *C*
Montgomery County Community
College *C*
Penn Commercial Business and
Technical School *C*
Westmoreland County Community
College *C*

Rhode Island
Community College of Rhode
Island *C*

South Carolina
York Technical College *C*

South Dakota
Southeast Technical Institute *C*
Western Dakota Technical Institute *C*

Tennessee
Jackson State Community College *C*
Miller-Motte Technical College
Chattanooga *C*
Clarksville *A*
West Tennessee Business College *C*

Texas
Howard College *C*
Weatherford College *C*

Utah
Dixie State College *C*

Virginia
Southwest Virginia Community
College *C*
Wytheville Community College *C*

Washington
Centralia College *C*
Clark College *C*
Renton Technical College *C*
Yakima Valley Community College *C*

West Virginia
American National University
Parkersburg *C*
Bridgemont Community and
Technical College *C*
New River Community and Technical
College *C*

Wisconsin
Blackhawk Technical College *C*
Mid-State Technical College *C*
Northcentral Technical College *C*
Waukesha County Technical
College *C*

Wyoming
Casper College *C*

Photographic/film/ video technology

Alabama
Calhoun Community College *A*
Lawson State Community College *C*

California
Allan Hancock College *C, A*
College of the Canyons *C*
Cypress College *C*
East Los Angeles College *C, A*
Ex'pression College *B*
Palomar College *C, A*
Santiago Canyon College *A*

Colorado
Aims Community College *C, A*
Colorado Mountain College *A*

Florida
Daytona State College *C, A*
Pensacola State College *A*

Georgia
Art Institute of Atlanta *A, B*

Illinois
Illinois Institute of Art
Schaumburg *B*
School of the Art Institute of
Chicago *B, M*

Louisiana
Bossier Parish Community College *C*

Maine
New England School of
Communications *B*

Maryland
Anne Arundel Community
College *C, A*
Frederick Community College *C*

Michigan
Lawrence Technological University *C*
Oakland Community College *A*

Minnesota
Art Institutes International
Minnesota *B*

Central Lakes College *C, A*
Hennepin Technical College *C, A*

Mississippi
Hinds Community College *C, A*

New Jersey
Burlington County College *A*

New Mexico
New Mexico State University
Alamogordo *C, A*

New York
Cayuga Community College *A*
Herkimer County Community
College *A*
Mohawk Valley Community
College *C*
Rochester Institute of Technology *B*
Rockland Community College *A*
St. John's University *A, B*
Tompkins Cortland Community
College *A*

North Carolina
Carteret Community College *C, A*
Catawba Valley Community
College *A*
Randolph Community College *A*

Ohio
Sinclair Community College *C*

Oklahoma
Oklahoma City Community
College *C, A*

Pennsylvania
Westmoreland County Community
College *C, A*

Tennessee
Columbia State Community
College *C*

Texas
Austin Community College *C*
Del Mar College *A*
North Lake College *C, A*

Utah
LDS Business College *C*
Salt Lake Community College *A*

Washington
Bellevue College *A*
Seattle Central Community
College *C, A*

Wisconsin
Madison Media Institute *A*

Photography

Alabama
Birmingham-Southern College *B*
Calhoun Community College *A*

Arizona
Art Institute of Phoenix *C*
Art Institute of Tucson *B*
Northern Arizona University *B*
Southwest University of Visual Arts *B*

Arkansas
John Brown University *B*
National Park Community College *C*

California
Academy of Art University *C, A, B, M*
Allan Hancock College *A*

Antelope Valley College *C, A*
Art Center College of Design *B*
Art Institute of California
Hollywood *A, B*
Biola University *B*
Brooks Institute *C, B, M*
Butte College *A*
California Baptist University *B*
California College of the Arts *B, M*
California Institute of the
Arts *C, B, M*
California State University
East Bay *B*
Long Beach *B*
Sacramento *B, M*
Cerritos College *A*
Chabot College *A*
Chaffey College *C, A*
Citrus College *C, A*
City College of San Francisco *A*
College of San Mateo *A*
College of the Canyons *C, A*
College of the Desert *A*
Columbia College *A*
Cosumnes River College *C, A*
Cypress College *C*
De Anza College *A*
East Los Angeles College *A*
El Camino College *C, A*
Foothill College *C, A*
Fresno City College *C, A*
Glendale Community College *C*
Golden West College *A*
Grossmont College *A*
Hartnell College *C, A*
Irvine Valley College *A*
Los Angeles City College *A*
Los Angeles Southwest College *A*
Los Angeles Trade and Technical
College *C, A*
Merced College *C, A*
Modesto Junior College *A*
Monterey Peninsula College *C, A*
Moorpark College *A*
Mount San Antonio College *C, A*
Mount San Jacinto College *A*
Ohlone College *C*
Orange Coast College *C, A*
Otis College of Art and Design *B, M*
Pacific Union College *A, B*
Rio Hondo College *A*
Riverside City College *C, A*
Saddleback College *A*
San Diego City College *C, A*
San Francisco Art Institute *B, M*
San Joaquin Delta College *A*
Santa Ana College *C, A*
Santa Monica College *A*
Santa Rosa Junior College *C*
Sierra College *C, A*
Southwestern College *A*
University of La Verne *B*
Ventura College *C, A*
Yuba College *C, A*

Colorado
Adams State University *B*
Colorado Mountain College *C, A*
Pikes Peak Community College *A*
Red Rocks Community College *C, A*
Rocky Mountain College of Art &
Design *B*

Connecticut
Paier College of Art *A, B*
Quinebaug Valley Community
College *C, A*
University of Hartford *B*

Delaware
Delaware College of Art and
Design *A*

Delaware Technical Community
College
Terry Campus *A*

District of Columbia
Corcoran College of Art and
Design *A, B*
George Washington University *M*

Florida
Barry University *C, B, M*
Daytona State College *A*
International Academy of Design and
Technology: Tampa *A, B*
Palm Beach State College *A*
Ringling College of Art and Design *B*
St. Petersburg College *A*
University of Central Florida *B*
University of Miami *B*

Georgia
Art Institute of Atlanta *A, B*
Savannah College of Art and
Design *B, M*

Idaho
Brigham Young University-Idaho *B*
College of Southern Idaho *A*

Illinois
Bradley University *B*
Columbia College Chicago *B, M*
Dominican University *B*
Lincoln College *A*
School of the Art Institute of
Chicago *B, M*
Southwestern Illinois College *A*
University of Illinois
Chicago *B, M*
Urbana-Champaign *B, M*

Indiana
Indiana University
Purdue University Fort Wayne *B*
Indiana Wesleyan University *B*
Purdue University *B*

Iowa
Coe College *B*
Iowa Lakes Community College *A*
Morningside College *B*
University of Iowa *B, M*

Kansas
Kansas Wesleyan University *B*

Louisiana
Louisiana Tech University *B*

Maine
College of the Atlantic *B*
Maine College of Art *B*
University of Maine
Augusta *A*

Maryland
Cecil College *A*
Harford Community College *C, A*
Howard Community College *A*
Maryland Institute College of
Art *B, M*
Montgomery College *A*
Notre Dame of Maryland
University *B*

Massachusetts
Bard College at Simon's Rock *B*
Endicott College *B*
Fitchburg State University *B*
Massachusetts College of Art and
Design *B, M*
Montserrat College of Art *B*
New England Institute of Art *C, A, B*

Salem State University *B*
School of the Museum of Fine
Arts *B, M*
University of Massachusetts
Dartmouth *B, M*

Michigan
Andrews University *B*
Aquinas College *B*
Art Institute of Michigan *C*
College for Creative Studies *B*
Delta College *A*
Ferris State University *B*
Grand Rapids Community College *A*
Grand Valley State University *B*
Lansing Community College *C, A*
Mott Community College *A*
Northern Michigan University *B*
Oakland Community College *C, A*
Oakland University *B*
Siena Heights University *B*
Washtenaw Community College *A*

Minnesota
Art Institutes International
Minnesota *B*
Dakota County Technical
College *C, A*
Minneapolis College of Art and
Design *B*
Ridgewater College *C, A*

Mississippi
Northeast Mississippi Community
College *A*

Missouri
Calvary Bible College and Theological
Seminary *B*
Columbia College *B*
Kansas City Art Institute *B*
St. Louis Community College *C, A*
University of Central Missouri *B*
Washington University in St.
Louis *B, M*
Webster University *B*

Montana
Miles Community College *A*

Nevada
Art Institute of Las Vegas *B*

New Hampshire
New England College *B*
New Hampshire Institute of Art *B*
Rivier University *B*

New Jersey
Burlington County College *C, A*
Camden County College *A*
Thomas Edison State College *A, B*

New Mexico
Santa Fe University of Art and
Design *B*
Southwest University of Visual Arts *B*

New York
Bard College *B, M*
Briarcliffe College *A*
Cazenovia College *B*
City University of New York
College of Staten Island *B*
Queensborough Community
College *C, A*
Fordham University *B*
Hofstra University *B*
Ithaca College *B*
Long Island University
LIU Post *B*
Marymount Manhattan College *B*
Monroe Community College *A*

Nassau Community College *C, A*
New York University *B*
Onondaga Community College *A*
Parsons The New School for
Design *B, M*
Pratt Institute *B*
Rochester Institute of
Technology *B, M*
Rockland Community College *A*
SUNY
College at Buffalo *B*
College at Fredonia *B*
College at New Paltz *B*
College at Oneonta *B*
College at Purchase *B*
St. John's University *B*
School of Visual Arts *B, M*
Syracuse University *B, M*
Tompkins Cortland Community
College *A*
Villa Maria College of Buffalo *A, B*

North Carolina
Carteret Community College *C, A*
East Carolina University *B*
Elon University *B*
Gardner-Webb University *B*
Randolph Community College *A*

North Dakota
Dakota College at Bottineau *C, A*

Ohio
Antonelli College
Cincinnati *A*
Art Academy of Cincinnati *B*
Bowling Green State University *B*
Clark State Community College *C*
Cleveland Institute of Art *B*
Columbus College of Art and
Design *B*
Columbus State Community
College *C*
Cuyahoga Community College
Metropolitan *A*
Kaplan College
Dayton *A*
Ohio University *B, M*
University of Akron *B*
University of Dayton *B*
Virginia Marti College of Art and
Design *A*
Youngstown State University *B*

Oklahoma
Oklahoma City University *B*
Oklahoma State University
Institute of Technology:
Okmulgee *A*

Oregon
Oregon College of Art & Craft *C, B*
Pacific Northwest College of Art *B*
University of Oregon *B*

Pennsylvania
Antonelli Institute of Art and
Photography *A*
Arcadia University *B*
Art Institute of Pittsburgh *C*
Butler County Community College *A*
Chatham University *B*
Delaware County Community
College *C*
Drexel University *B*
Harrisburg Area Community
College *C, A*
Luzerne County Community
College *A*
Lycoming College *B*
Marywood University *B, M*
Moore College of Art and Design *B*
Pennsylvania College of Art and
Design *B*

Point Park University *B*
Temple University *B, M*
University of the Arts *B*

Puerto Rico
Inter American University of Puerto
Rico
Bayamon Campus *A*
San German Campus *M*
University of Puerto Rico
Rio Piedras *B*
University of the Sacred Heart *A, B*

Rhode Island
Providence College *B*
Rhode Island School of Design *B, M*
Salve Regina University *B*

South Carolina
Coker College *B*
Trident Technical College *C*

Tennessee
Carson-Newman University *B*
King University *B*
Memphis College of Art *B, M*
Nashville State Community
College *C, A*
Pellissippi State Community
College *C*
Southern Adventist University *B*
Watkins College of Art, Design &
Film *B*

Texas
Amarillo College *A*
El Paso Community College *A*
St. Edward's University *B*
Sam Houston State University *B*
Texas Christian University *B*
Texas State University *B*
Tyler Junior College *C*
University of Houston *B*
Western Texas College *A*

Utah
Brigham Young University *B*
Dixie State College *B*
LDS Business College *C, A*
Salt Lake Community College *A*
Weber State University *B*

Vermont
Bennington College *B*
Burlington College *B*
Marlboro College *B*

Virginia
Central Virginia Community
College *C*
Eastern Mennonite University *B*
Lord Fairfax Community College *C*
Northern Virginia Community
College *A*
Southwest Virginia Community
College *C*
Thomas Nelson Community
College *A*
Tidewater Community College *C, A*
Virginia Commonwealth University *B*
Virginia Intermont College *B*

Washington
Cornish College of the Arts *B*
Seattle University *B*
Shoreline Community College *A*
University of Washington *B, M*
Western Washington University *B*

West Virginia
West Virginia State University *B*
West Virginia Wesleyan College *B*

Wisconsin
Cardinal Stritch University *B*
Carroll University *B*
Concordia University Wisconsin *B*
Milwaukee Institute of Art &
Design *B*

Wyoming
Casper College *A*

Photojournalism

Alabama
Oakwood University *B*

Arkansas
Rich Mountain Community College *C*

California
Brooks Institute *B, M*
Long Beach City College *C*
Los Angeles Pierce College *C, A*

Colorado
Colorado Mountain College *A*

District of Columbia
Corcoran College of Art and
Design *B, M*

Florida
University of Miami *B*

Illinois
Bradley University *B*

Indiana
Vincennes University *A*

Kentucky
Western Kentucky University *B*

Massachusetts
Boston University *B*

Michigan
Central Michigan University *B*

Minnesota
Art Institutes International
Minnesota *B*
Minnesota State University
Moorhead *B*
Winona State University *B*

Missouri
University of Missouri
Columbia *B*
Webster University *C*

Nevada
Sierra Nevada College *B*

New York
Rochester Institute of Technology *B*
St. John's University *B*
Syracuse University *B, M*

North Carolina
Carteret Community College *A*

Ohio
Ashland University *B*
Kent State University *B*
Ohio University *B*

Oklahoma
Rose State College *A*
University of Central Oklahoma *B*

Pennsylvania
Point Park University *B*

Texas
North Lake College *C*

Vermont
Lyndon State College *B*

Physical/biological anthropology

California
Merced College *A*

New York
SUNY
University at Binghamton *M*

Pennsylvania
Mercyhurst University *M*

Physical chemistry

Iowa
Iowa State University *M, D*

Minnesota
University of Minnesota
Twin Cities *M, D*

Montana
University of Montana *M, D*

New York
Fordham University *M*
SUNY
University at Albany *D*

Puerto Rico
University of Puerto Rico
Rio Piedras *D*

Texas
LeTourneau University *B*
Rice University *B, M, D*

Physical education

Alabama
Alabama Agricultural and Mechanical
University *B, M*
Athens State University *B*
Auburn University *B, M, D*
Faulkner State Community College *A*
Faulkner University *B, M, T*
Huntingdon College *B, T*
Jacksonville State University *B, M, T*
Oakwood University *B*
Tuskegee University *B*
United States Sports Academy *B, M*
University of Alabama *B, M*
University of Alabama
Birmingham *B, M, T*
University of Mobile *B, T*
University of South Alabama *B, M, T*
University of West Alabama *B, M*

Arizona
Grand Canyon University *B*
South Mountain Community
College *A*

Arkansas
Arkansas State University *B, M, T*
Arkansas Tech University *B, M*
Harding University *T*
Henderson State University *B*
Ouachita Baptist University *B, T*
Southern Arkansas University *B, T*
University of Arkansas *M*
University of Arkansas
Monticello *B*
Pine Bluff *B, M, T*

University of Central Arkansas *B*
University of the Ozarks *B, T*
Williams Baptist College *B*

California
Allan Hancock College *A*
Azusa Pacific University *B, M, T*
Biola University *B, T*
Butte College *A*
California Baptist University *T*
California Lutheran University *B, T*
California State University
Chico *T*
East Bay *B, M, T*
Long Beach *B, M, T*
Los Angeles *B, M*
Northridge *B, T*
San Bernardino *B, M, T*
Chaffey College *A*
College of the Sequoias *A*
Cuesta College *A*
Cypress College *A*
Diablo Valley College *A*
Fresno Pacific University *B, T*
Golden West College *A*
Humboldt State University *B, M, T*
Irvine Valley College *A*
Lassen Community College *A*
Master's College *B, T*
Mount San Jacinto College *A*
National University *B*
Pacific Union College *B*
Pepperdine University *B*
Reedley College *A*
Saddleback College *A*
San Diego Christian College *B, T*
San Diego Mesa College *A*
San Diego State University *T*
San Francisco State University *T*
Santa Barbara City College *A*
Sonoma State University *M, T*
Southwestern College *A*
University of La Verne *B*
University of San Diego *T*
Vanguard University of Southern
California *B, T*
Westmont College *T*
Yuba College *A*

Colorado
Adams State University *B, M, T*
Colorado State University
Pueblo *T*
Metropolitan State University of
Denver *T*
University of Northern
Colorado *M, D, T*
Western State Colorado
University *B, T*

Connecticut
Central Connecticut State
University *M, T*
Eastern Connecticut State
University *B, M, T*
Southern Connecticut State
University *B*
University of Connecticut *B*

Delaware
Delaware State University *B*
University of Delaware *B, M, T*
Wesley College *B*

District of Columbia
Gallaudet University *B, T*
George Washington
University *A, B, M*
Howard University *B, M, T*
University of the District of
Columbia *B*

Florida
Barry University *B*
Bethune-Cookman University *B, T*
Clearwater Christian College *B*
Edward Waters College *B*
Florida Agricultural and Mechanical
University *B, T*
Florida International University *B, M*
Florida Memorial University *B, T*
Jacksonville University *B, T*
Miami Dade College *A*
Palm Beach Atlantic University *B, T*
Palm Beach State College *A*
Pensacola State College *A*
University of Central Florida *B, M*
University of Miami *B, M*
University of North Florida *B*
University of South Florida *B, M*
University of Tampa *B*
Warner University *B*

Georgia
Albany State University *B, M*
Bainbridge College *A*
Berry College *B*
Columbus State University *B, M*
Fort Valley State University *B, T*
Georgia College and State
University *M, T*
Georgia Perimeter College *A*
Georgia Regents University *B*
Georgia Southern University *B*
Georgia Southwestern State
University *B*
Georgia State University *B, M*
Kennesaw State University *B*
Reinhardt University *B*
South Georgia State College *A*
University of North Georgia *A, B, M*
University of West Georgia *B, T*
Valdosta State University *B, M*

Hawaii
Brigham Young University-
Hawaii *B, T*

Idaho
Boise State University *B, M, T*
College of Idaho *B*
College of Southern Idaho *A*
College of Western Idaho *A*
Idaho State University *B, M*
Lewis-Clark State College *T*
Northwest Nazarene University *B*
University of Idaho *B, M, T*

Illinois
Augustana College *B, T*
Aurora University *B*
Blackburn College *B, T*
Chicago State University *B, M*
Concordia University Chicago *B, T*
DePaul University *B, T*
Elmhurst College *B*
Eureka College *T*
Greenville College *B, T*
Illinois Central College *A*
Illinois College *B, T*
Illinois State University *B, T*
John A. Logan College *A*
Judson University *B*
Kishwaukee College *A*
MacMurray College *B, T*
McKendree University *B*
Millikin University *B, T*
Monmouth College *B, T*
North Central College *B, T*
North Park University *T*
Northeastern Illinois University *B*
Northern Illinois University *B, M, T*
Olivet Nazarene University *B, T*
Quincy University *B, T*
Rockford University *B, M, T*
Sauk Valley Community College *A*

Southern Illinois University
   Carbondale *B*
Trinity Christian College *B, T*
Trinity International University *B*
University of Illinois
   Urbana-Champaign *B, M, T*

Indiana

Anderson University *B, T*
Ball State University *B, M, T*
Bethel College *B*
Butler University *T*
Franklin College *T*
Goshen College *B, T*
Huntington University *B*
Indiana Institute of Technology *B*
Indiana State University *B, M, T*
Indiana Wesleyan University *B, T*
Manchester University *B, T*
Marian University *B, T*
Oakland City University *B*
Purdue University *B, M, D*
Taylor University *B, T*
Trine University *B, T*
University of Indianapolis *B, T*
University of Southern Indiana *B*
Valparaiso University *B*
Vincennes University *A*

Iowa

Ashford University *B*
Briar Cliff University *B*
Buena Vista University *B, T*
Central College *T*
Clarke University *B, T*
Coe College *B*
Cornell College *B, T*
Dordt College *B*
Ellsworth Community College *A*
Graceland University *T*
Grand View University *B, T*
Iowa State University *T*
Iowa Wesleyan College *B*
Loras College *B*
Marshalltown Community College *A*
North Iowa Area Community
   College *A*
Northwestern College *B, T*
St. Ambrose University *B, T*
Simpson College *B, T*
University of Dubuque *B, T*
University of Iowa *M*
University of Northern Iowa *B, M*
Upper Iowa University *B, T*
Wartburg College *B, T*

Kansas

Benedictine College *B*
Bethany College *B, T*
Bethel College *T*
Butler Community College *A*
Central Christian College of Kansas *B*
Coffeyville Community College *A*
Colby Community College *A*
Emporia State University *M, T*
Fort Hays State University *B, M, T*
Friends University *B*
Garden City Community College *A*
Independence Community College *A*
McPherson College *B, T*
MidAmerica Nazarene University *B, T*
Pittsburg State University *B, M*
Southwestern College *B*
Sterling College *T*
Tabor College *B*
University of Kansas *B, M, D, T*
Washburn University *B, T*
Wichita State University *B, M, T*

Kentucky

Alice Lloyd College *B*
Asbury University *B, T*
Campbellsville University *B*
Eastern Kentucky University *B, M*

Hopkinsville Community College *A*
Kentucky State University *B*
Kentucky Wesleyan College *B, T*
Lindsey Wilson College *B, T*
Morehead State University *B, M*
Northern Kentucky University *B*
Transylvania University *B, T*
Union College *B*
University of Kentucky *B*
University of Louisville *M*
University of the
   Cumberlands *B, M, T*
Western Kentucky University *B, M*

Louisiana

Centenary College of Louisiana *T*
Grambling State University *B*
Louisiana College *B, T*
Louisiana State University and
   Agricultural and Mechanical
   College *B, M, D*
Louisiana Tech University *B, M*
McNeese State University *B, T*
Nicholls State University *B*
Northwestern State University *B*
Southeastern Louisiana
   University *B, M*
University of Louisiana at Lafayette *B*
Xavier University of Louisiana *B*

Maine

Husson University *B, T*
Saint Joseph's College of Maine *B*
University of Maine *B, M*
University of Maine
   Presque Isle *B*

Maryland

Allegany College of Maryland *A*
Frederick Community College *A*
Frostburg State University *B, M, T*
McDaniel College *M*
Morgan State University *B, M*
Prince George's Community
   College *A*
Salisbury University *B*
Towson University *B*
University of Maryland
   College Park *B*
Washington Adventist University *B, T*

Massachusetts

Boston University *M, T*
Bridgewater State University *B, T*
Dean College *A*
Eastern Nazarene College *B, M, T*
Endicott College *B*
Salem State University *B, M*
Springfield College *B, M, D, T*
Westfield State University *M, T*

Michigan

Adrian College *B, T*
Alma College *T*
Aquinas College *B, T*
Calvin College *B, T*
Central Michigan University *B, M*
Concordia University *B, T*
Cornerstone University *B, T*
Delta College *A*
Eastern Michigan University *B, M, T*
Grand Rapids Community College *A*
Grand Valley State University *B, T*
Hillsdale College *B*
Hope College *B, T*
Madonna University *B*
Michigan State University *B*
Michigan Technological University *T*
Northern Michigan University *B, T*
Saginaw Valley State University *B*
Spring Arbor University *B*
University of Michigan *B, T*
Wayne State University *B, M, T*
Western Michigan University *B, M, T*

Minnesota

Augsburg College *B, T*
Bemidji State University *B, T*
Bethel University *B*
Concordia College: Moorhead *B, T*
Concordia University St. Paul *B, T*
Crown College *B*
Gustavus Adolphus College *T*
Hamline University *T*
Inver Hills Community College *A*
Minnesota State University
   Mankato *B, M, T*
   Moorhead *B*
Minnesota West Community and
   Technical College *A*
North Hennepin Community
   College *A*
Ridgewater College *A*
St. Catherine University *B, T*
Saint Cloud State University *B, M, T*
Southwest Minnesota State
   University *B, T*
University of Minnesota
   Duluth *B*
   Twin Cities *B, M, D, T*
University of Northwestern - St.
   Paul *B*
University of St. Thomas *B*
Winona State University *B, T*

Mississippi

Blue Mountain College *B*
Coahoma Community College *A*
Delta State University *B, M*
East Mississippi Community
   College *A*
Hinds Community College *A*
Itawamba Community College *A*
Jackson State University *B, M*
Mississippi College *B*
Mississippi Delta Community
   College *A*
Mississippi State University *B, M*
Mississippi Valley State
   University *B, T*
Northeast Mississippi Community
   College *A*
Northwest Mississippi Community
   College *A*
University of Southern
   Mississippi *B, M, D*
William Carey University *B*

Missouri

Central Methodist University *B*
College of the Ozarks *B, T*
Crowder College *A*
Culver-Stockton College *B, T*
Drury University *B, T*
Evangel University *B, T*
Hannibal-LaGrange University *B*
Lincoln University *B*
Lindenwood University *B*
Missouri Baptist University *B, T*
Missouri Southern State
   University *B, T*
Missouri State University *B*
Missouri Valley College *B*
Northwest Missouri State
   University *B, M, T*
Southeast Missouri State University *B*
Southwest Baptist University *B, T*
Truman State University *M*
University of Central Missouri *B, M*
University of Missouri
   St. Louis *B*
Westminster College *B, T*
William Jewell College *B, T*
William Woods University *B, T*

Montana

Carroll College *B*
Montana State University
   Billings *B, T*
   Northern *B*

Rocky Mountain College *B*
University of Great Falls *B*
University of Montana *B, M, T*
University of Montana: Western *B, T*

Nebraska

Bellevue University *B*
Chadron State College *B, M*
Concordia University *B, T*
Doane College *B*
Grace University *B*
Hastings College *B, M, T*
Midland University *B, T*
Nebraska Wesleyan University *B*
Union College *B*
University of Nebraska
   Kearney *B, M, T*
   Lincoln *B, T*
   Omaha *T*
Wayne State College *B, T*
Western Nebraska Community
   College *A*
York College *B, T*

Nevada

University of Nevada
   Las Vegas *B*

New Hampshire

Keene State College *B, T*
New England College *B, T*

New Jersey

College of New Jersey *B, M, T*
Essex County College *A*
Gloucester County College *A*
Kean University *B, T*
Montclair State University *B, M, T*
William Paterson University of New
   Jersey *B, T*

New Mexico

Eastern New Mexico University *B, M*
New Mexico Junior College *A*
New Mexico State University *B*
University of New Mexico *B, M, D*
University of the Southwest *B, T*
Western New Mexico University *B*

New York

Adelphi University *B, M, T*
Canisius College *B, M, T*
City University of New York
   Brooklyn College *B, M, T*
   Hunter College *B, T*
   Lehman College *B, M*
   Queens College *B, M, T*
   York College *B, T*
College of Mount St. Vincent *T*
Columbia-Greene Community
   College *A*
Corning Community College *A*
Dowling College *B*
Dutchess Community College *A*
Erie Community College *A*
Finger Lakes Community College *A*
Genesee Community College *A*
Hofstra University *B, M*
Houghton College *B, T*
Hudson Valley Community College *A*
Ithaca College *B, M, T*
Jamestown Community College *A*
Long Island University
   LIU Brooklyn *B, T*
   LIU Post *B, T*
Manhattan College *B, T*
Monroe Community College *A*
New York University *M, D*
Roberts Wesleyan College *B*
Rockland Community College *A*
SUNY
   College at Brockport *B, M, T*
   College at Buffalo *B*
   College at Cortland *B, M*

College of Technology at Delhi *A*
University at Stony Brook *T*
Sage Colleges *B*
Saint Bonaventure University *B*
St. Francis College *B*
Syracuse University *B, T*

North Carolina

Appalachian State University *B, T*
Barton College *B, T*
Campbell University *B, T*
Catawba College *B, T*
Chowan University *B, T*
East Carolina University *B, M*
Elizabeth City State University *B, T*
Elon University *T*
Fayetteville State University *B, T*
Gardner-Webb University *B, M*
Greensboro College *B, T*
Guilford College *B, T*
High Point University *B, T*
Lees-McRae College *B, T*
Lenoir-Rhyne University *B, T*
Livingstone College *T*
Mars Hill University *B, T*
Meredith College *B, T*
Methodist University *A, B, T*
North Carolina Agricultural and
    Technical State University *M, T*
North Carolina Central
    University *B, M, T*
Pfeiffer University *B*
Piedmont International University *B*
St. Andrews University *B*
University of Mount Olive *B*
University of North Carolina
    Greensboro *B*
    Pembroke *B, M*
    Wilmington *B*
Western Carolina University *B, M, T*
Wingate University *B, T*
Winston-Salem State University *B*

North Dakota

Dickinson State University *B, T*
Mayville State University *B, T*
Minot State University *B*
North Dakota State University *B, T*
University of Jamestown *B*
University of Mary *B*
University of North Dakota *B*
Valley City State University *B, T*

Ohio

Ashland University *M, T*
Baldwin Wallace University *T*
Bowling Green State University *B, T*
Capital University *B*
Cedarville University *B*
Cleveland State University *B, M, T*
Defiance College *B, T*
Denison University *B*
Heidelberg University *B*
John Carroll University *B*
Kent State University *B*
Malone University *B*
Mount Vernon Nazarene
    University *B, T*
Ohio State University
    Columbus Campus *B*
Ohio University *B, T*
Ohio Wesleyan University *B*
Otterbein University *B*
Sinclair Community College *A*
University of Akron *B, M*
University of Dayton *B, M*
University of Findlay *B, M, T*
University of Mount Union *B, T*
University of Rio Grande *A, B, T*
University of Toledo *B, M, T*
Walsh University *B*
Wilmington College *B*
Wright State University *B, M, T*

Xavier University *M*
Youngstown State University *B, M*

Oklahoma

Bacone College *B*
Cameron University *B*
Connors State College *A*
East Central University *B, T*
Eastern Oklahoma State College *A*
Langston University *B*
Northeastern State University *B*
Northern Oklahoma College *A*
Northwestern Oklahoma State
    University *B*
Oklahoma Baptist University *B, T*
Oklahoma Christian University *B, T*
Oklahoma State University *B*
Oklahoma Wesleyan University *B*
Oral Roberts University *B, T*
Southeastern Oklahoma State
    University *B, T*
Southern Nazarene University *B*
Southwestern Oklahoma State
    University *B, M, T*
Tulsa Community College *A*
University of Central Oklahoma *B*
Western Oklahoma State College *A*

Oregon

Concordia University *B, M, T*
Corban University *B*
Linfield College *T*
Linn-Benton Community College *A*
Treasure Valley Community
    College *A*
Warner Pacific College *B, T*
Western Oregon University *B, M, T*

Pennsylvania

Baptist Bible College of
    Pennsylvania *B*
Bucks County Community College *A*
Cairn University *B, T*
East Stroudsburg University of
    Pennsylvania *B, M, T*
Lancaster Bible College *B*
Messiah College *B, T*
Montgomery County Community
    College *A*
University of Pittsburgh *B, M, D, T*
University of Pittsburgh
    Bradford *B*

Puerto Rico

American University of Puerto
    Rico *B, T*
Bayamon Central University *B*
Caribbean University *B*
Inter American University of Puerto
    Rico
    Aguadilla Campus *B*
    Guayama Campus *B*
    Metropolitan Campus *B, M*
    San German Campus *B, M*
Pontifical Catholic University of
    Puerto Rico *B, T*
Turabo University *B, M, D*
Universidad Metropolitana *B*
Universidad del Este *B*
University of Puerto Rico
    Arecibo *B*
    Cayey University College *B*
    Mayaguez *B*

Rhode Island

Rhode Island College *B, T*

South Carolina

Anderson University *B, T*
Charleston Southern University *B*
Citadel *B, M, T*
Coastal Carolina University *B, T*
Coker College *B, T*
College of Charleston *B, T*

Erskine College *B, T*
Furman University *T*
Lander University *B*
Limestone College *B*
Newberry College *B, T*
South Carolina State University *B, T*
Southern Wesleyan University *B, T*
University of South Carolina
    Columbia *B, M, D*
    Upstate *B, T*
Winthrop University *B, M, T*

South Dakota

Augustana College *B, T*
Dakota State University *B, T*
Dakota Wesleyan University *B, T*
Mount Marty College *B*
Northern State University *B, T*
University of Sioux Falls *T*
University of South Dakota *B, M, T*

Tennessee

Belmont University *B, T*
Bethel University *B, T*
Bryan University
    Dayton *T*
Carson-Newman University *B*
Cumberland University *B, T*
Freed-Hardeman University *B, T*
Hiwassee College *A*
King University *B*
Lane College *B*
Lee University *B*
Lincoln Memorial University *B, T*
Lipscomb University *B, T*
Martin Methodist College *B*
Maryville College *B, T*
Southern Adventist University *B*
Tennessee State University *B*
Tennessee Technological
    University *B, M, T*
Trevecca Nazarene University *B, T*
Tusculum College *B, T*
Union University *B, T*
University of Memphis *B*
Welch College *B*

Texas

Alvin Community College *A*
Amarillo College *A*
Austin College *M*
Baylor University *B, M, T*
Dallas Baptist University *B, M, T*
East Texas Baptist University *B*
El Paso Community College *A*
Galveston College *A*
Hardin-Simmons University *B, T*
Houston Baptist University *B, M*
Howard Payne University *B*
Huston-Tillotson University *B*
Jarvis Christian College *B, T*
Kilgore College *A*
Lamar University *B, M, T*
Laredo Community College *A*
LeTourneau University *B, T*
Lubbock Christian University *B*
McMurry University *B, T*
Midland College *A*
Navarro College *A*
Prairie View A&M University *M*
St. Edward's University *B, T*
Sam Houston State University *M, T*
Schreiner University *B*
Southwestern Adventist
    University *B, T*
Southwestern University *T*
Sul Ross State University *M*
Tarleton State University *M, T*
Texas A&M International University *T*
Texas A&M University
    Kingsville *B, M*
Texas Christian University *B*
Texas College *B, T*
Texas Lutheran University *B, T*

Texas Southern University *M*
Texas State University *M, T*
University of Houston *M*
University of Mary Hardin-
    Baylor *B, M, T*
University of Texas
    Arlington *T*
    Austin *M*
    San Antonio *T*
    Tyler *M*
University of the Incarnate
    Word *B, T*
Wayland Baptist University *B, T*
West Texas A&M University *T*
Wiley College *B*

Utah

Brigham Young University *B, M*
Snow College *A*
Southern Utah University *B*
Utah State University *B, M*
Utah Valley University *B*
Weber State University *B*

Vermont

Castleton State College *B, T*
Johnson State College *B*
Lyndon State College *B*
Norwich University *B, T*
University of Vermont *B, T*

Virginia

Bluefield College *B, T*
Bridgewater College *T*
Eastern Mennonite University *B, T*
Emory & Henry College *B*
George Mason University *B, M*
Hampton University *B*
Longwood University *T*
Old Dominion University *B, M*
Radford University *B, T*
Randolph College *T*
Roanoke College *B, T*
Shenandoah University *B*
University of Virginia's College at
    Wise *T*
Virginia Commonwealth
    University *M*
Virginia Intermont College *T*
Virginia State University *B*

Washington

Central Washington
    University *B, M, T*
Gonzaga University *B, M, T*
Northwest University *T*
Walla Walla University *B*
Washington State University *B, M, T*
Western Washington University *B*
Whitworth University *B, T*

West Virginia

Alderson-Broaddus University *B*
Bethany College *B*
Concord University *B, T*
Davis and Elkins College *B*
Marshall University *B, M*
Ohio Valley University *B*
Potomac State College of West
    Virginia University *A*
Shepherd University *T*
University of Charleston *B*
West Liberty University *B*
West Virginia State University *B*
West Virginia University *B, M, D, T*
West Virginia University Institute of
    Technology *B*
West Virginia Wesleyan College *B*

Wisconsin

Carroll University *B, T*
Carthage College *B, T*
Concordia University Wisconsin *B, T*
Maranatha Baptist Bible College *B*

Ripon College *T*
University of Wisconsin
Oshkosh *B, T*
River Falls *B, T*
Stevens Point *B, T*
Superior *B, T*
Whitewater *B, M, T*

Wyoming

Casper College *A*
Eastern Wyoming College *A*
Laramie County Community
College *A*
University of Wyoming *B*

Physical fitness technician

Arizona

Arizona Western College *C*
Paradise Valley Community College *C*
Pima Community College *C*

California

Canada College *C, A*
Cerritos College *C*
Contra Costa College *C*
Palomar College *C*
San Joaquin Delta College *C*

Colorado

Community College of Aurora *C*

Indiana

Indiana University
Purdue University Indianapolis *C*

Iowa

Western Iowa Tech Community
College *C*

Kentucky

Spencerian College *C, A*

Maryland

Cecil College *C*

Michigan

Lansing Community College *C, A*

Minnesota

Alexandria Technical and Community
College *C, A*
Anoka-Ramsey Community College *C*
Dakota County Technical
College *C, A*
Fond du Lac Tribal and Community
College *A*
Globe University
Woodbury *C, A, B*
Minnesota School of Business
Plymouth *A, B*
Richfield *A, B*
Rochester *B*
St. Cloud *A, B*
Shakopee *A*
Northland Community & Technical
College *C*
Rochester Community and Technical
College *C*

Nebraska

Wayne State College *B*

New Mexico

Central New Mexico Community
College *C*
Clovis Community College *C*

North Dakota

Lake Region State College *A*

Oklahoma

Wright Career College
Oklahoma City *A*
Tulsa *B*

Oregon

Rogue Community College *C*

Pennsylvania

Keystone Technical Institute *C*

South Carolina

Trident Technical College *C*

Tennessee

Trevecca Nazarene University *B*

Utah

Broadview University
West Jordan *A, B*

Washington

Bellevue College *C*
Skagit Valley College *C*

Wisconsin

Globe University
Middleton *A, B*

Wyoming

Sheridan College *C*

Physical sciences

Alabama

Auburn University at Montgomery *B*

Arizona

Arizona State University *B*
Glendale Community College *A*
Mesa Community College *A*
Paradise Valley Community College *A*
Phoenix College *A*
Scottsdale Community College *A*
South Mountain Community
College *A*

Arkansas

Arkansas Tech University *B*
University of Arkansas
Little Rock *M, D*

California

Azusa Pacific University *B*
California State University
Fresno *B*
Sacramento *B*
Stanislaus *B*
Cerro Coso Community College *C, A*
College of Marin *A*
College of the Siskiyous *A*
Cuyamaca College *A*
Feather River College *A*
Imperial Valley College *A*
La Sierra University *B*
Lassen Community College *A*
Long Beach City College *A*
Master's College *B*
Merced College *A*
San Diego State University *B*
Shasta College *A*
Taft College *A*
University of California
Riverside *B*
University of Southern California *B*

Colorado

Colorado Mesa University *B*
Colorado Mountain College *C*
University of Denver *B*

Connecticut

Mitchell College *A*
Naugatuck Valley Community
College *A*
Three Rivers Community College *A*

District of Columbia

University of the District of
Columbia *A, B*

Florida

Daytona State College *A*
Florida Institute of Technology *B*

Georgia

Andrew College *A*
Covenant College *B*
Georgia Southern University *M*

Illinois

City Colleges of Chicago
Harold Washington College *C*
Concordia University Chicago *B*
Harper College *A*
John Wood Community College *A*
Spoon River College *A*
University of Chicago *M*

Indiana

Anderson University *B*
Bethel College *B*
Grace College *B*
Purdue University
Calumet *B*

Iowa

Coe College *B*
Dordt College *B*
Loras College *B*

Kansas

Barton County Community College *A*
Colby Community College *A*
Cowley County Community
College *A*
Donnelly College *A*
Emporia State University *B, M, T*
Garden City Community College *A*
Hutchinson Community College *A*
Independence Community College *A*
Kansas State University *B*

Kentucky

Bluegrass Community and Technical
College *A*
Hopkinsville Community College *A*
Western Kentucky University *B*

Louisiana

Louisiana State University
Eunice *A*
Northwestern State University *B*

Maine

Bates College *T*

Maryland

Howard Community College *A*
Salisbury University *B*
United States Naval Academy *B*
University of Maryland
College Park *B*

Massachusetts

Cape Cod Community College *A*
Dean College *A*
Middlesex Community College *A*
Roxbury Community College *A*
Westfield State University *B, T*
Worcester State University *B*

Michigan

Delta College *C, A*
Gogebic Community College *A*
Kalamazoo Valley Community
College *A*
Lake Michigan College *A*
Michigan State University *B, M*
Northwestern Michigan College *A*

Minnesota

Bethany Lutheran College *B*
Saint Cloud State University *B*
University of Minnesota
Twin Cities *B, M*

Mississippi

Hinds Community College *A*
Mississippi University for
Women *B, T*

Missouri

Crowder College *A*
William Woods University *B*

Montana

Miles Community College *A*
Montana Tech of the University of
Montana *B*

Nebraska

Concordia University *B, T*

New Hampshire

Keene State College *B*
Southern New Hampshire
University *B*

New Jersey

Bergen Community College *A*
Burlington County College *A*
Gloucester County College *C, A*
Rowan University *B, T*

New Mexico

Northern New Mexico College *A*
San Juan College *A*
Santa Fe Community College *A*
Western New Mexico University *B*

New York

City University of New York
Borough of Manhattan Community
College *A*
LaGuardia Community College *A*
New York City College of
Technology *A*
Corning Community College *A*
Roberts Wesleyan College *A*
Rochester Institute of
Technology *B, M*
SUNY
College of Agriculture and
Technology at Cobleskill *A*
College of Agriculture and
Technology at Morrisville *B*
St. John's University *B*
Schenectady County Community
College *A*
United States Military Academy *B*
Villa Maria College of Buffalo *A*
Westchester Community College *A*
Yeshiva University *B*

North Carolina

Chowan University *B*
Western Piedmont Community
College *A*

North Dakota

Dakota College at Bottineau *A*
Minot State University *B*
University of North Dakota *B*

Ohio

Bowling Green State University *M*
Mount Vernon Nazarene University *B*
University of Dayton *B*
Wright State University *M, T*
Youngstown State University *B, M*

Oklahoma

Northeastern Oklahoma Agricultural
and Mechanical College *A*
Redlands Community College *A*

Oregon

Central Oregon Community
College *A*
Linfield College *B*
Warner Pacific College *B*

Pennsylvania

Butler County Community College *A*
California University of
Pennsylvania *B*
Carnegie Mellon University *B*
Community College of
Philadelphia *A*
East Stroudsburg University of
Pennsylvania *B*
Harrisburg Area Community
College *A*
Harrisburg University of Science and
Technology *B*
Juniata College *B*
Lehigh Carbon Community College *A*
Lincoln University *B*
Millersville University of
Pennsylvania *T*
Montgomery County Community
College *A*
Muhlenberg College *C, B*
University of Pittsburgh *B*
University of Pittsburgh
Bradford *B*
Valley Forge Military College *A*
Villanova University *B*

Puerto Rico

Universidad Metropolitana *B*
University of Puerto Rico
Mayaguez *B*

Rhode Island

Roger Williams University *A*

South Carolina

Aiken Technical College *C*
Clinton Junior College *A*
Florence-Darlington Technical
College *A*
Midlands Technical College *C*
University of South Carolina
Columbia *M*

South Dakota

Black Hills State University *B*
Dakota State University *B*

Tennessee

Freed-Hardeman University *B*
Jackson State Community College *A*
Tennessee Temple University *B*
Union University *B*

Texas

Alvin Community College *A*
Amarillo College *A*
Angelo State University *T*
Austin Community College *A*
Brazosport College *C, A*
Lee College *A*
McMurry University *T*
Paris Junior College *A*
St. Philip's College *A*
San Jacinto College *A*

Southwestern University *B, T*
Texas A&M University
Galveston *B*
University of Houston
Clear Lake *B*
University of Texas
Pan American *B*

Utah

University of Utah *B*
Utah Valley University *A*

Vermont

Bennington College *B*

Washington

Bellevue College *A*
Big Bend Community College *A*
Centralia College *A*
Columbia Basin College *A*
Edmonds Community College *A*
Everett Community College *A*
Evergreen State College *B*
Grays Harbor College *A*
Heritage University *B*
Northwest Indian College *A*
Pierce College *A*
Seattle University *B*
Shoreline Community College *A*
Spokane Falls Community College *A*
Tacoma Community College *A*
Washington State University *B*
Yakima Valley Community College *A*

West Virginia

Marshall University *M*

Wisconsin

St. Norbert College *T*

Wyoming

Central Wyoming College *A*
University of Wyoming *B*

Physical therapy

Alabama

Alabama State University *D*
University of Alabama
Birmingham *D*
University of South Alabama *D*

Arizona

Northern Arizona University *D*

Arkansas

Arkansas State University *D*
Harding University *D*
University of Central Arkansas *D*

California

Azusa Pacific University *D*
California State University
Fresno *D*
Long Beach *M*
Sacramento *D*
Chapman University *D*
Loma Linda University *M, D*
Mount St. Mary's College *D*
Samuel Merritt University *D*
San Diego State University *D*
San Francisco State University *M, D*
University of Southern
California *M, D*
University of the Pacific *M, D*

Colorado

Regis University *D*
University of Colorado
Denver *M, D*

Connecticut

Quinnipiac University *D*
Sacred Heart University *D*
University of Connecticut *D*
University of Hartford *M, D*

Delaware

University of Delaware *D*

District of Columbia

George Washington University *D*
Howard University *M*

Florida

Florida Agricultural and Mechanical
University *D*
Florida Gulf Coast University *D*
Florida International University *D*
Nova Southeastern University *D*
University of Central Florida *D*
University of Miami *B, M, D*
University of North Florida *D*
University of South Florida *M, D*

Georgia

Armstrong Atlantic State
University *B, D*
Emory University *D*
Georgia Regents University *D*
Georgia State University *D*
Mercer University *D*
University of North Georgia *D*

Idaho

Idaho State University *D*

Illinois

Bradley University *D*
Dominican University *B*
Governors State University *D*
Northern Illinois University *B, M, D*
Northwestern University *M, D*
University of Illinois
Chicago *M, D*

Indiana

Indiana University
Purdue University Indianapolis *D*
University of Evansville *D*
University of Indianapolis *M, D*

Iowa

Clarke University *D*
St. Ambrose University *D*
University of Iowa *D*

Kansas

University of Kansas Medical
Center *D*
Wichita State University *D*

Kentucky

Bellarmine University *D*
Hopkinsville Community College *A*
University of Kentucky *M*
Western Kentucky University *D*

Louisiana

Louisiana State University
Health Sciences Center *D*

Maine

Husson University *D*
University of New England *M, D*

Maryland

University of Maryland
Baltimore *M, D*
Eastern Shore *D*

Massachusetts

American International College *D*
Boston University *M, D*

MCPHS University *D*
Northeastern University *D*
Simmons College *B, D*
Springfield College *D*
University of Massachusetts
Lowell *B, M, D*

Michigan

Andrews University *M, D*
Baker College
Flint *M*
Central Michigan University *M, D*
Grand Rapids Community College *A*
Grand Valley State University *D*
Oakland University *M, D*
University of Michigan
Flint *D*
Wayne State University *D*

Minnesota

College of St. Scholastica *D*
St. Catherine University *D*
University of Minnesota
Twin Cities *M, D*

Mississippi

Hinds Community College *A*

Missouri

Maryville University of Saint Louis *D*
Missouri State University *D*
Rockhurst University *D*
Saint Louis University *M, D*
Southwest Baptist University *D*
University of Missouri
Columbia *M*
Washington University in St.
Louis *M, D*

Montana

University of Montana *M, D*

Nebraska

Creighton University *D*
University of Nebraska
Medical Center *D*

Nevada

University of Nevada
Las Vegas *M, D*

New Hampshire

Franklin Pierce University *D*

New Jersey

Richard Stockton College of New
Jersey *D*
Rutgers, The State University of New
Jersey
Camden Campus *D*
New Brunswick/Piscataway
Campus *M, D*
Newark Campus *M, D*
Seton Hall University *D*

New Mexico

University of New Mexico *D*

New York

City University of New York
College of Staten Island *D*
Hunter College *M, D*
Clarkson University *D*
D'Youville College *M, D*
Daemen College *D*
Dominican College of Blauvelt *M, D*
Ithaca College *B, D*
Long Island University
LIU Brooklyn *D*
Mercy College *M, D*
Nazareth College *D*
New York Institute of Technology *D*
New York University *M, D*

SUNY
  Downstate Medical Center *D*
  University at Buffalo *D*
  University at Stony Brook *M, D*
  Upstate Medical University *D*
Sage Colleges *D*
Touro College *M, D*
Utica College *D*

North Carolina
Blue Ridge Community College *A*
Duke University *M*
East Carolina University *D*
Elon University *D*
University of North Carolina
  Chapel Hill *M, D*
Western Carolina University *M, D*
Wingate University *D*
Winston-Salem State University *M, D*

North Dakota
University of Mary *D*
University of North Dakota *B, M, D*

Ohio
Bowling Green State University *B*
Cleveland State University *D*
College of Mount St. Joseph *D*
Ohio State University
  Columbus Campus *M, D*
Ohio University *D*
University of Akron *B*
University of Cincinnati *D*
University of Dayton *D*
University of Findlay *D*
University of Toledo *D*
Walsh University *D*
Youngstown State University *D*

Oklahoma
Langston University *D*
University of Oklahoma *D*

Oregon
Central Oregon Community
  College *A*
George Fox University *D*
Pacific University *D*
Treasure Valley Community
  College *A*

Pennsylvania
Arcadia University *D*
Chatham University *D*
DeSales University *D*
Drexel University *M, D*
Duquesne University *D*
Gannon University *D*
Harcum College *A*
Lebanon Valley College *D*
Misericordia University *M, D*
Neumann University *T*
St. Francis University *D*
Slippery Rock University of
  Pennsylvania *D*
Temple University *M, D*
Thomas Jefferson University *D*
University of Pittsburgh *D*
University of Scranton *D*
University of the Sciences *M, D*
Widener University *D*

Puerto Rico
University of Puerto Rico
  Medical Sciences *M*

Rhode Island
University of Rhode Island *D*

South Carolina
Medical University of South
  Carolina *D*
University of South Carolina
  Columbia *D*

South Dakota
University of South Dakota *D*

Tennessee
Belmont University *D*
Carson-Newman University *T*
East Tennessee State University *D*
University of Tennessee
  Chattanooga *D*
  Knoxville *M, D*

Texas
Angelo State University *M, D*
Baylor University *D*
Hardin-Simmons University *D*
Texas State University *D*
Texas Tech University Health
  Sciences Center *D, T*
Texas Woman's University *M, D*
University of Texas
  El Paso *M*
  Medical Branch at Galveston *M, D*
University of the Incarnate Word *D*

Utah
University of Utah *D*

Vermont
University of Vermont *D*

Virginia
Lynchburg College *D*
Marymount University *D*
Old Dominion University *M, D*
Radford University *D*
Shenandoah University *D*
Virginia Commonwealth University *D*

Washington
Eastern Washington University *D*
University of Puget Sound *D*
University of Washington *M*

West Virginia
Marshall University *D*
Wheeling Jesuit University *D*

Wisconsin
Carroll University *M, D*
Concordia University Wisconsin *M*
Marquette University *D*
University of Wisconsin
  La Crosse *D*
  Madison *M*
  Milwaukee *D*

Physical therapy assistant

Alabama
Bishop State Community College *A*
Central Alabama Community
  College *A*
Community College of the Air
  Force *A*
George C. Wallace Community
  College at Dothan *A*
Jefferson State Community College *A*
Wallace State Community College at
  Hanceville *A*

Alaska
University of Alaska
  Anchorage *A*

Arizona
Carrington College
  Mesa *C, A*
  Phoenix Westside *C*
  Tucson *C*
GateWay Community College *C, A*
Mohave Community College *A*

Arkansas
Arkansas State University *A*
Arkansas Tech University *A*
Northwest Arkansas Community
  College *A*
South Arkansas Community
  College *A*

California
Allan Hancock College *A*
Carrington College California
  Pleasant Hill *A*
Cerritos College *A*
De Anza College *C*
Loma Linda University *A*
Ohlone College *A*
Sacramento City College *C, A*
San Diego Mesa College *A*

Colorado
Arapahoe Community College *A*
Morgan Community College *A*
Pueblo Community College *A*

Connecticut
Capital Community College *A*
Housatonic Community College *A*
Manchester Community College *A*
Naugatuck Valley Community
  College *A*
Northwestern Connecticut
  Community College *A*
Norwalk Community College *A*

Delaware
Delaware Technical Community
  College
  Jack F. Owens Campus *A*
  Stanton/Wilmington Campus *A*

Florida
Broward College *C, A*
College of Central Florida *A*
Daytona State College *A*
Florida Gateway College *A*
Florida State College at
  Jacksonville *A*
Gulf Coast State College *C, A*
Indian River State College *A*
Keiser University *A*
Pensacola State College *A*
Polk State College *A*
St. Petersburg College *A*
Seminole State College of Florida *A*
State College of Florida, Manatee-
  Sarasota *A*

Georgia
Athens Technical College *A*
Atlanta Technical College *C*
Columbus Technical College *C*
Darton College *A*
Middle Georgia State College *A*

Hawaii
University of Hawaii
  Kapiolani Community College *A*

Idaho
Carrington College
  Boise *A*
Idaho State University *A, B*
North Idaho College *A*

Illinois
Black Hawk College *A*
College of DuPage *A*
Elgin Community College *A*
Illinois Central College *A*
Kankakee Community College *A*
Kaskaskia College *A*
Lake Land College *A*
Morton College *A*

Oakton Community College *A*
Southern Illinois University
  Carbondale *A*
Southwestern Illinois College *A*

Indiana
Brown Mackie College
  South Bend *A*
Ivy Tech Community College
  East Central *A*
  Northwest *A*
University of Evansville *A*
University of Indianapolis *A*
University of St. Francis *A*
Vincennes University *A*

Iowa
Clinton Community College *A*
Hawkeye Community College *A*
Iowa Central Community College *A*
Iowa Lakes Community College *C*
Kirkwood Community College *A*
Mercy College of Health Sciences *A*
North Iowa Area Community
  College *A*
Upper Iowa University *B*
Western Iowa Tech Community
  College *A*

Kansas
Colby Community College *A*
Fort Hays State University *B*
Hutchinson Community College *A*
Johnson County Community
  College *A*
Kansas City Kansas Community
  College *A*
Washburn University *A*

Kentucky
Ashland Community and Technical
  College *A*
Hazard Community and Technical
  College *A*
Jefferson Community and Technical
  College *A*
Madisonville Community College *A*
Somerset Community College *A*
Southeast Kentucky Community and
  Technical College *A*
West Kentucky Community and
  Technical College *A*

Louisiana
Bossier Parish Community College *A*
Delgado Community College *C, A*
Louisiana College *A, B*
Our Lady of the Lake College *A*

Maine
Kennebec Valley Community
  College *A*

Maryland
Allegany College of Maryland *A*
Anne Arundel Community College *A*
Baltimore City Community College *A*
Carroll Community College *A*
Chesapeake College *A*
College of Southern Maryland *A*
Howard Community College *A*
Montgomery College *A*

Massachusetts
Bay State College *A*
Berkshire Community College *A*
Massachusetts Bay Community
  College *A*
Mount Wachusett Community
  College *A*
North Shore Community College *A*
Springfield Technical Community
  College *A*

Michigan

Baker College
  Allen Park *A*
  Cadillac *A*
  Flint *A*
  Muskegon *A*
Delta College *A*
Finlandia University *A*
Henry Ford Community College *A*
Kellogg Community College *A*
Macomb Community College *A*
Mid Michigan Community College *A*
Mott Community College *A*
Oakland Community College *A*

Minnesota

Anoka-Ramsey Community College *A*
Lake Superior College *A*
Northland Community & Technical
  College *A*
St. Catherine University *A*

Mississippi

Hinds Community College *A*
Itawamba Community College *A*
Meridian Community College *A*

Missouri

Linn State Technical College *A*
Metropolitan Community College -
  Kansas City *A*
Missouri Western State University *A*
North Central Missouri College *A*
Ozarks Technical Community
  College *A*
State Fair Community College *A*

Montana

Flathead Valley Community
  College *A*
Montana State University
  Great Falls College *A*

Nebraska

Clarkson College *A*
Nebraska Methodist College of
  Nursing and Allied Health *A, B*
Northeast Community College *A*

Nevada

Carrington College
  Las Vegas *A*
College of Southern Nevada *A*

New Hampshire

Mount Washington College *A*
River Valley Community College *A*

New Jersey

Bergen Community College *A*
Essex County College *A*
Mercer County Community
  College *A*
Ocean County College *C*
Union County College *A*

New Mexico

Carrington College
  Albuquerque *A*
Clovis Community College *A*
San Juan College *A*

New York

Broome Community College *A*
City University of New York
  Kingsborough Community
    College *A*
  LaGuardia Community College *A*
Genesee Community College *A*
Herkimer County Community
  College *A*
Nassau Community College *A*

Niagara County Community
  College *A*
Onondaga Community College *A*
Orange County Community
  College *A*
SUNY
  College of Technology at Canton *A*
Suffolk County Community College *A*
Touro College *A*
Villa Maria College of Buffalo *A*

North Carolina

Caldwell Community College and
  Technical Institute *A*
Central Carolina Community
  College *A*
Central Piedmont Community
  College *A*
Craven Community College *A*
Fayetteville Technical Community
  College *A*
Guilford Technical Community
  College *A*
Martin Community College *A*
South College *A*
Southwestern Community College *A*
Surry Community College *A*

Ohio

Bradford School *A*
Clark State Community College *A*
Columbus State Community
  College *C*
Cuyahoga Community College
  Metropolitan *A*
Edison State Community College *A*
Hocking College *A*
James A. Rhodes State College *C, A*
Kent State University
  Ashtabula *A*
  East Liverpool *A*
Lorain County Community College *A*
Marion Technical College *A*
National College
  Youngstown *A*
North Central State College *A*
Owens Community College
  Toledo *A*
Remington College
  Cleveland West *A*
Shawnee State University *A*
Sinclair Community College *A*
Stark State College *A*
University of Cincinnati
  Clermont College *A*
Washington State Community
  College *A*
Zane State College *A*

Oklahoma

Carl Albert State College *A*
Northeastern Oklahoma Agricultural
  and Mechanical College *A*
Oklahoma City Community
  College *A*
Southwestern Oklahoma State
  University *A*
Tulsa Community College *A*

Oregon

Lane Community College *A*
Mt. Hood Community College *A*

Pennsylvania

Butler County Community College *A*
California University of
  Pennsylvania *A*
Central Penn College *A*
Community College of Allegheny
  County *A*
Community College of
  Philadelphia *A*
Erie Business Center *C*
Harcum College *A*

Lehigh Carbon Community College *A*
Mount Aloysius College *A*
Penn State
  DuBois *A*
  Fayette, The Eberly Campus *A*
  Hazleton *A*
  Mont Alto *A*
  Shenango *A*
Pennsylvania Institute of
  Technology *A*
University of Pittsburgh
  Titusville *A*

Puerto Rico

Inter American University of Puerto
  Rico
  Ponce Campus *A*
National University College
  Arecibo *A*
  Ponce *A*
  Rio Grande *A*
University of Puerto Rico
  Humacao *A*
  Ponce *A*

Rhode Island

Community College of Rhode
  Island *A*
New England Institute of
  Technology *A*

South Carolina

Aiken Technical College *C*
Florence-Darlington Technical
  College *C, A*
Greenville Technical College *C, A*
Horry-Georgetown Technical
  College *C*
Midlands Technical College *C, A*
Orangeburg-Calhoun Technical
  College *C*
Piedmont Technical College *C*
Spartanburg Community College *C*
Technical College of the
  Lowcountry *C, A*
Trident Technical College *C, A*
York Technical College *C*

South Dakota

Lake Area Technical Institute *A*

Tennessee

Chattanooga State Community
  College *A*
Jackson State Community College *A*
Roane State Community College *A*
South College *A*
Southwest Tennessee Community
  College *A*
Volunteer State Community
  College *A*
Walters State Community College *A*

Texas

Amarillo College *A*
Austin Community College *A*
Del Mar College *A*
El Paso Community College *A*
Houston Community College
  System *C*
Howard College *A*
Kilgore College *A*
Laredo Community College *A*
Lee College *A*
Lone Star College System *A*
Northeast Texas Community
  College *A*
Odessa College *A*
St. Philip's College *A*
San Jacinto College *A*
South Texas College *A*
Tarrant County College *A*

Western Technical College: Diana
  Drive *A*
Wharton County Junior College *A*

Utah

Dixie State College *A*
Provo College *A*
Salt Lake Community College *A*

Vermont

Lyndon State College *B*

Virginia

ECPI University *A*
Jefferson College of Health
  Sciences *A*
Northern Virginia Community
  College *A*
Tidewater Community College *A*
Virginia Highlands Community
  College *A*
Wytheville Community College *A*

Washington

Green River Community College *A*
Lake Washington Institute of
  Technology *A*
Olympic College *A*
Spokane Falls Community College *A*
Whatcom Community College *A*

West Virginia

Blue Ridge Community and Technical
  College *A*

Wisconsin

Blackhawk Technical College *A*
Chippewa Valley Technical College *A*
Gateway Technical College *A*
Milwaukee Area Technical College *A*
Northeast Wisconsin Technical
  College *A*
Southwest Wisconsin Technical
  College *A*
Western Technical College *A*

Wyoming

Laramie County Community
  College *A*

Physician assistant

Alabama

Oakwood University *A*
University of Alabama
  Birmingham *M*
University of South Alabama *M*

Arizona

Northern Arizona University *M*

California

City College of San Francisco *A*
Foothill College *A*
Hartnell College *A*
Loma Linda University *M*
Moreno Valley College *A*
Samuel Merritt University *M*
San Joaquin Valley College *A*
University of Southern California *M*

Colorado

University of Colorado
  Denver *M*

Connecticut

Quinnipiac University *M*
University of Bridgeport *M*
Yale University *M*

District of Columbia

George Washington University *B, M*
Howard University *B*

Florida

Barry University *M*
Keiser University *M*
Miami Dade College *A, B*
Nova Southeastern University *M*
University of Florida *M*

Georgia

Brenau University *B*
Georgia Highlands College *A*
Georgia Regents University *B, M*
Gordon College *A*
Mercer University *D*

Hawaii

University of Hawaii
 Kapiolani Community College *A*

Idaho

Idaho State University *M*
Northwest Nazarene University *B*

Illinois

City Colleges of Chicago
 Malcolm X College *A*
Southern Illinois University
 Carbondale *B, M*
University of St. Francis *M*

Indiana

Butler University *B, M*
University of St. Francis *M*

Iowa

University of Iowa *M*

Kansas

Wichita State University *M*

Kentucky

National College
 Danville *A*
 Lexington *A*
University of Kentucky *B, M*
University of the Cumberlands *M*

Louisiana

Our Lady of the Lake College *M*

Maine

University of New England *M*

Maryland

Towson University *M*
University of Maryland
 Eastern Shore *B*

Massachusetts

Bay Path College *M*
MCPHS University *M*
Northeastern University *M*
Springfield College *M*

Michigan

Central Michigan University *M*
Grand Valley State University *M*
University of Detroit Mercy *M*
Wayne County Community College *A*
Wayne State University *M*
Western Michigan University *M*

Minnesota

Augsburg College *M*
Bethel University *M*

Mississippi

Mississippi College *M*

Missouri

Missouri State University *M*
Saint Louis University *M*

Montana

Rocky Mountain College *M*

Nebraska

College of Saint Mary *M*
Union College *M*
University of Nebraska
 Medical Center *M*

New Jersey

Rutgers, The State University of New
 Jersey
 New Brunswick/Piscataway
 Campus *M*
 Newark Campus *M*
Seton Hall University *M*

New Mexico

University of New Mexico *M*

New York

City University of New York
 City College *B*
 York College *B*
Clarkson University *M*
D'Youville College *B, M*
Daemen College *M*
Hofstra University *M*
Hudson Valley Community College *A*
Le Moyne College *M*
Long Island University
 LIU Brooklyn *M*
Mercy College *M*
New York Institute of Technology *M*
Pace University *M*
Pace University: Pleasantville/
 Briarcliff *B*
Rochester Institute of
 Technology *B, M*
SUNY
 Downstate Medical Center *B*
 University at Stony Brook *M*
 Upstate Medical University *M*
St. Francis College *B*
St. John's University *B*
Touro College *B*
Wagner College *B, M*

North Carolina

Duke University *M*
East Carolina University *M*
Elon University *M*
Gardner-Webb University *M*
Mars Hill University *B*
Methodist University *B, M*
Wake Forest University *M*
Wingate University *M*

North Dakota

University of North Dakota *M*

Ohio

Baldwin Wallace University *M*
Cleveland State University *B*
Kettering College *M*
Marietta College *M*
University of Findlay *M*
University of Mount Union *M*
University of Toledo *M*

Oklahoma

University of Oklahoma *M*

Oregon

Oregon Health & Science
 University *M*
Pacific University *M*

Pennsylvania

Arcadia University *M*
Chatham University *M*
DeSales University *M*
Drexel University *B, M*

Duquesne University *M*
Gannon University *B, M*
King's College *M*
Lock Haven University of
 Pennsylvania *M*
Marywood University *M*
Mercyhurst University *M*
Pennsylvania College of
 Technology *B*
Philadelphia University *M*
St. Francis University *B, M*
Seton Hill University *B, M*
University of Pittsburgh *M*
University of the Sciences *B, M*

Rhode Island

Johnson & Wales University
 Providence *M*

South Carolina

Medical University of South
 Carolina *M*

South Dakota

University of South Dakota *M*

Tennessee

Bethel University *M*
Carson-Newman University *T*
Christian Brothers University *M*
South College *M*
Trevecca Nazarene University *M*

Texas

Baylor University *D*
Texas Tech University Health
 Sciences Center *M*
University of Texas
 Medical Branch at Galveston *M*
 Pan American *M*

Utah

University of Utah *M*
Weber State University *B*

Vermont

Lyndon State College *B*

Virginia

James Madison University *M*
Jefferson College of Health
 Sciences *M*
Shenandoah University *M*

Washington

University of Washington *B*

West Virginia

Alderson-Broaddus University *M*
University of Charleston *M*

Wisconsin

Marquette University *M*
University of Wisconsin
 La Crosse *M*
 Madison *M*

Physics

Alabama

Alabama Agricultural and Mechanical
 University *B, M, D*
Auburn University *B, M, D*
Birmingham-Southern College *B*
Jacksonville State University *B*
Samford University *B*
Troy University *B*
Tuskegee University *B*
University of Alabama *B, M, D*
University of Alabama
 Birmingham *B, M, D*
 Huntsville *B, M, D*

University of North Alabama *B*
University of South Alabama *B*

Alaska

University of Alaska
 Fairbanks *B, M, D*

Arizona

Arizona State University *B, M, D*
Arizona Western College *A*
Cochise College *A*
Eastern Arizona College *A*
Northern Arizona University *B, M*
South Mountain Community
 College *A*
University of Arizona *B, M, D*

Arkansas

Arkansas State University *B*
Arkansas Tech University *B*
Harding University *B*
Henderson State University *B*
Hendrix College *B*
Ouachita Baptist University *B*
Phillips Community College of the
 University of Arkansas *A*
Southern Arkansas University *B*
University of Arkansas *B, M, D*
University of Arkansas
 Little Rock *B*
 Pine Bluff *B*
University of Central Arkansas *B*

California

Allan Hancock College *A*
Azusa Pacific University *B*
Bakersfield College *A*
Biola University *B*
Cabrillo College *A*
California Institute of
 Technology *B, M, D*
California Lutheran University *B*
California Polytechnic State
 University: San Luis Obispo *B*
California State Polytechnic
 University: Pomona *B*
California State University
 Bakersfield *B*
 Channel Islands *B*
 Chico *B*
 Dominguez Hills *B*
 East Bay *B*
 Fresno *B, M*
 Fullerton *B, M*
 Long Beach *B, M*
 Los Angeles *B, M*
 Northridge *B, M*
 Sacramento *B, M*
 San Bernardino *B*
 San Marcos *B*
 Stanislaus *B*
Canada College *A*
Cerritos College *A*
Chabot College *A*
Chaffey College *A*
Citrus College *A*
Claremont McKenna College *B*
College of Marin *A*
College of San Mateo *A*
College of the Canyons *A*
College of the Desert *A*
College of the Siskiyous *A*
Columbia College *A*
Concordia University Irvine *B*
Contra Costa College *A*
Crafton Hills College *A*
Cuesta College *A*
Cypress College *A*
De Anza College *A*
El Camino College *A*
Foothill College *A*
Fullerton College *A*
Glendale Community College *A*
Grossmont College *A*

Hartnell College *A*
Harvey Mudd College *B*
Humboldt State University *B*
Los Angeles City College *A*
Los Angeles Southwest College *A*
Los Angeles Valley College *A*
Loyola Marymount University *B*
Merced College *A*
Mission College *A*
Monterey Peninsula College *A*
Moorpark College *A*
Occidental College *B*
Orange Coast College *A*
Pacific Union College *B*
Pepperdine University *B*
Pitzer College *B*
Point Loma Nazarene University *B*
Pomona College *B*
Saddleback College *A*
St. Mary's College of California *B*
San Bernardino Valley College *A*
San Deigo Miramar College
   San Diego Miramar College *A*
San Diego City College *A*
San Diego Mesa College *A*
San Diego State University *B, M*
San Francisco State University *B, M*
San Joaquin Delta College *A*
San Jose State University *B, M*
Santa Ana College *A*
Santa Barbara City College *A*
Santa Clara University *B*
Santa Rosa Junior College *A*
Santiago Canyon College *A*
Scripps College *B*
Sierra College *A*
Skyline College *A*
Solano Community College *A*
Sonoma State University *B*
Southwestern College *A*
Stanford University *B, M, D*
University of California
   Berkeley *B, D*
   Davis *B, M, D*
   Irvine *B, D*
   Los Angeles *B, M, D*
   Merced *B, M, D*
   Riverside *B, M, D*
   San Diego *B, M, D*
   Santa Barbara *B, M, D*
   Santa Cruz *B, M, D*
University of La Verne *B*
University of Redlands *B*
University of San Diego *B*
University of San Francisco *B*
University of Southern
   California *B, M, D*
University of the Pacific *B, M*
West Los Angeles College *A*
West Valley College *A*
Westmont College *B*
Whittier College *B*

Colorado

Adams State University *B*
Colorado College *B*
Colorado School of Mines *B, M, D*
Colorado State University *B, M, D*
Colorado State University
   Pueblo *B*
Community College of Aurora *A*
Fort Lewis College *B*
Metropolitan State University of
   Denver *B*
Regis University *B*
United States Air Force Academy *B*
University of Colorado
   Boulder *B, M, D*
   Colorado Springs *B*
   Denver *B*
University of Denver *B, M, D*
University of Northern Colorado *B, T*

Connecticut

Central Connecticut State
   University *B*
Connecticut College *B*
Fairfield University *B*
Southern Connecticut State
   University *B*
Trinity College *B*
University of Connecticut *B, M, D*
University of Hartford *B*
Wesleyan University *B, M, D*
Yale University *B, M, D*

Delaware

Delaware State University *B, M, D*
University of Delaware *B, M, D*

District of Columbia

American University *B*
Catholic University of
   America *B, M, D*
Gallaudet University *B*
George Washington
   University *B, M, D*
Georgetown University *B, M, D*
Howard University *B, M, D*
University of the District of
   Columbia *B*

Florida

Ave Maria University *B*
Broward College *A*
Eckerd College *B*
Embry-Riddle Aeronautical
   University *B*
Florida Agricultural and Mechanical
   University *B, M, D*
Florida Atlantic University *B, M, D*
Florida Institute of
   Technology *B, M, D*
Florida International
   University *B, M, D*
Florida State University *B, M, D*
Indian River State College *A*
Jacksonville University *B*
Miami Dade College *A*
New College of Florida *B*
Palm Beach State College *A*
Pensacola State College *A*
Rollins College *B*
South Florida State College *A*
Stetson University *B*
University of Central Florida *B, M, D*
University of Florida *B, M, D*
University of Miami *B, M, D*
University of North Florida *B*
University of South Florida *B, M, D*
University of West Florida *B*

Georgia

Abraham Baldwin Agricultural
   College *A*
Agnes Scott College *B*
Armstrong Atlantic State University *B*
Atlanta Metropolitan College *A*
Berry College *B*
Clark Atlanta University *B, M*
College of Coastal Georgia *A*
Covenant College *B*
Dalton State College *B*
Darton College *A*
Emory University *B, M, D*
Georgia College and State
   University *B*
Georgia Highlands College *A*
Georgia Institute of
   Technology *B, M, D*
Georgia Perimeter College *A*
Georgia Regents University *B*
Georgia Southern University *B*
Georgia State University *B, M, D*
Gordon College *A*
Mercer University *B*
Middle Georgia State College *A*

Morehouse College *B*
Oglethorpe University *B*
Paine College *B*
South Georgia State College *A*
Southern Polytechnic State
   University *B*
Spelman College *B*
University of Georgia *B, M, D*
University of North Georgia *A, B*
University of West Georgia *B*
Valdosta State University *B*
Wesleyan College *B*

Hawaii

University of Hawaii
   Hilo *B*
   Manoa *B, M, D*

Idaho

Boise State University *B, T*
Brigham Young University-Idaho *B*
College of Southern Idaho *A*
Idaho State University *A, B, M, D*
North Idaho College *A*
Northwest Nazarene University *B*
University of Idaho *B, M, D*

Illinois

Augustana College *B*
Benedictine University *B, T*
Bradley University *B, T*
Chicago State University *B*
DePaul University *B, M*
Eastern Illinois University *B, T*
Elmhurst College *B, T*
Greenville College *B, T*
Illinois Central College *A*
Illinois College *B*
Illinois Institute of
   Technology *B, M, D*
Illinois State University *B, T*
Illinois Valley Community College *A*
Illinois Wesleyan University *B*
John A. Logan College *A*
John Wood Community College *A*
Kankakee Community College *A*
Kishwaukee College *A*
Knox College *B*
Lake Forest College *B*
Lewis University *B*
Lincoln College *A*
Loyola University Chicago *B*
MacMurray College *B*
Millikin University *B*
Monmouth College *B, T*
North Central College *B, T*
North Park University *B*
Northeastern Illinois University *B*
Northern Illinois
   University *B, M, D, T*
Northwestern University *B*
Principia College *B*
Sauk Valley Community College *A*
South Suburban College of Cook
   County *A*
Southern Illinois University
   Carbondale *B, M, D*
Southern Illinois University
   Edwardsville *B*
Southwestern Illinois College *A*
University of Chicago *B, D*
University of Illinois
   Chicago *B, M, D*
   Urbana-Champaign *B, M, D*
Western Illinois University *B, M*
Wheaton College *B, T*

Indiana

Anderson University *B*
Ball State University *B, M, T*
Butler University *B*
DePauw University *B*
Earlham College *B*
Goshen College *B*

Hanover College *B*
Indiana University
   Bloomington *B, M, D*
   Purdue University Fort Wayne *B, T*
   Purdue University
      Indianapolis *B, M*
   South Bend *B*
Manchester University *B, T*
Marian University *T*
Purdue University *B, M, D*
Purdue University
   Calumet *B*
Rose-Hulman Institute of
   Technology *B*
Taylor University *B*
University of Evansville *B*
University of Indianapolis *B*
University of Notre Dame *B, M, D*
University of Southern Indiana *T*
Valparaiso University *B*
Vincennes University *A*
Wabash College *B*

Iowa

Buena Vista University *B, T*
Central College *B, T*
Coe College *B*
Cornell College *B, T*
Dordt College *B*
Drake University *B*
Ellsworth Community College *A*
Grinnell College *B*
Iowa State University *B, M, D*
Luther College *B*
Morningside College *B*
Northwestern College *T*
St. Ambrose University *B*
Simpson College *B*
University of Iowa *B, M, D, T*
University of Northern Iowa *B, M, T*
Wartburg College *B, T*

Kansas

Allen County Community College *A*
Baker University *B, T*
Barton County Community College *A*
Benedictine College *B*
Bethany College *B*
Butler Community College *A*
Central Christian College of Kansas *A*
Coffeyville Community College *A*
Colby Community College *A*
Emporia State University *B, T*
Fort Hays State University *B*
Kansas State University *B, M, D*
Kansas Wesleyan University *B, T*
MidAmerica Nazarene University *B*
Pittsburg State University *B, M*
Seward County Community
   College *A*
University of Kansas *B, M, D*
Washburn University *B*
Wichita State University *B, M, T*

Kentucky

Bellarmine University *B*
Berea College *B, T*
Bluegrass Community and Technical
   College *A*
Campbellsville University *B*
Centre College *B*
Eastern Kentucky University *B*
Georgetown College *B, T*
Hopkinsville Community College *A*
Kentucky Wesleyan College *B*
Morehead State University *B*
Murray State University *B, T*
Northern Kentucky University *B*
Thomas More College *A, B*
Transylvania University *B*
University of Kentucky *B, M, D*
University of Louisville *B, M, D*
University of the Cumberlands *B, T*
Western Kentucky University *B*

Louisiana

Centenary College of Louisiana *B*
Dillard University *B*
Grambling State University *B*
Louisiana State University
   Shreveport *B*
Louisiana State University and
   Agricultural and Mechanical
   College *B, M, D*
Louisiana Tech University *B, M*
Loyola University New Orleans *B*
Southeastern Louisiana University *B*
Southern University
   New Orleans *B*
Tulane University *B, M, D*
University of Louisiana at
   Lafayette *B, M*
University of New Orleans *B, M*
Xavier University of Louisiana *B*

Maine

Bates College *B*
Bowdoin College *B*
Colby College *B*
University of Maine *B, M, D*
University of Southern Maine *B*

Maryland

Allegany College of Maryland *A*
Frostburg State University *B, T*
Goucher College *B*
Harford Community College *A*
Johns Hopkins University *B, M, D*
Loyola University Maryland *B*
McDaniel College *B*
Montgomery College *A*
Morgan State University *B*
Notre Dame of Maryland
   University *B*
St. Mary's College of Maryland *B*
Salisbury University *B*
Towson University *B*
United States Naval Academy *B*
University of Maryland
   Baltimore County *B, M, D*
   College Park *B, M, D*
Washington College *B, T*

Massachusetts

Amherst College *B*
Bard College at Simon's Rock *B*
Boston College *B, M, D*
Boston University *B, M, D*
Brandeis University *B, M, D*
Bridgewater State University *B*
Bunker Hill Community College *A*
Clark University *B, M, D*
College of the Holy Cross *B*
Eastern Nazarene College *B*
Gordon College *B*
Hampshire College *B*
Harvard College *B, M, D*
Massachusetts College of Liberal
   Arts *B, T*
Massachusetts Institute of
   Technology *B, M, D*
Merrimack College *B*
Mount Holyoke College *B*
Northeastern University *B, M, D*
Simmons College *B*
Smith College *B*
Springfield Technical Community
   College *A*
Stonehill College *B*
Suffolk University *B*
Tufts University *B, M, D*
University of Massachusetts
   Amherst *B, M, D*
   Boston *B, M*
   Dartmouth *B, M*
   Lowell *B, M, D*
Wellesley College *B*
Wheaton College *B*
Williams College *B*

Worcester Polytechnic
   Institute *B, M, D*

Michigan

Adrian College *A, B, T*
Albion College *B, T*
Alma College *B, T*
Andrews University *B*
Calvin College *B, T*
Central Michigan University *B, M*
Eastern Michigan University *B, M*
Gogebic Community College *A*
Grand Rapids Community College *A*
Grand Valley State University *B*
Hillsdale College *B*
Hope College *B*
Kalamazoo College *B*
Kettering University *B*
Lake Michigan College *A*
Lawrence Technological University *B*
Madonna University *B*
Michigan State University *B, M, D*
Michigan Technological
   University *B, M, D*
Northern Michigan University *B*
Oakland University *B, M, T*
Saginaw Valley State University *B*
University of Michigan *B, M, D*
University of Michigan
   Dearborn *B*
   Flint *B*
Wayne State University *B, M, D*
Western Michigan University *B, M, D*

Minnesota

Augsburg College *B*
Bethel University *B*
Carleton College *B*
College of St. Benedict *B*
Concordia College: Moorhead *B*
Gustavus Adolphus College *B*
Hamline University *B*
Macalester College *B*
Minnesota State University
   Mankato *B, M, T*
   Moorhead *B*
Minnesota West Community and
   Technical College *A*
St. Catherine University *B*
Saint Cloud State University *B*
St. John's University *B*
St. Mary's University of Minnesota *B*
St. Olaf College *B*
University of Minnesota
   Duluth *B, M*
   Morris *B*
   Twin Cities *B, M, D*
University of St. Thomas *B*
Winona State University *B*

Mississippi

East Mississippi Community
   College *A*
Itawamba Community College *A*
Jackson State University *B*
Millsaps College *B*
Mississippi College *B*
Mississippi State University *B, M*
Northeast Mississippi Community
   College *A*
Tougaloo College *B*
University of Mississippi *B, M, D*
University of Southern
   Mississippi *B, M*

Missouri

Central Methodist University *B*
Crowder College *A*
Drury University *B*
Lincoln University *B*
Missouri Southern State
   University *B, T*
Missouri State University *B*

Missouri University of Science and
   Technology *B, M, D, T*
Northwest Missouri State
   University *B*
Rockhurst University *B*
St. Louis Community College *A*
Saint Louis University *B*
Southeast Missouri State University *B*
Truman State University *B*
University of Central Missouri *B*
University of Missouri
   Columbia *B, M, D*
   Kansas City *B, M, D*
   St. Louis *B, M, D*
Washington University in St.
   Louis *B, M, D*
Westminster College *B, T*
William Jewell College *B, T*

Montana

Montana State University *B, M, D*
Montana State University
   Billings *T*
University of Montana *B, M*

Nebraska

Creighton University *B, M*
Doane College *B*
Hastings College *B*
Nebraska Wesleyan University *B*
Northeast Community College *A*
Union College *B*
University of Nebraska
   Kearney *B, T*
   Lincoln *B, M, D*
   Omaha *B*
Western Nebraska Community
   College *A*

Nevada

University of Nevada
   Las Vegas *B, M, D*
   Reno *B, M, D*
Western Nevada College *A*

New Hampshire

Dartmouth College *B, M, D, T*
Saint Anselm College *B*
University of New
   Hampshire *B, M, D*

New Jersey

Bergen Community College *A*
College of New Jersey *B, T*
Drew University *B*
Fairleigh Dickinson University
   Metropolitan Campus *B, M*
Middlesex County College *A*
Montclair State University *B*
New Jersey City University *B*
New Jersey Institute of
   Technology *B, M, D*
Princeton University *B, M, D*
Ramapo College of New Jersey *B*
Richard Stockton College of New
   Jersey *B*
Rider University *B*
Rowan University *B*
Rutgers, The State University of New
   Jersey
   Camden Campus *B, T*
   New Brunswick/Piscataway
     Campus *B, M, D*
   Newark Campus *B, M, D*
Saint Peter's University *B*
Salem Community College *A*
Seton Hall University *B, T*
Stevens Institute of
   Technology *B, M, D*

New Mexico

Central New Mexico Community
   College *A*

New Mexico Institute of Mining and
   Technology *B, M, D*
New Mexico Junior College *A*
New Mexico State University *B, M, D*
San Juan College *A*
University of New Mexico *B, M, D*

New York

Adelphi University *B*
Alfred University *B*
Bard College *B*
Barnard College *B*
Canisius College *B*
City University of New York
   Brooklyn College *B, M*
   City College *B, M*
   College of Staten Island *B, D*
   Hunter College *B, M*
   Kingsborough Community
     College *A*
   Lehman College *B*
   Queens College *B, M, T*
   York College *B*
Clarkson University *B, M, D*
Colgate University *B*
Columbia University *B*
Columbia University
   School of General Studies *B*
Cornell University *B, M, D*
Excelsior College *B*
Fordham University *B, M, D*
Hamilton College *B*
Hartwick College *B, T*
Hobart and William Smith Colleges *B*
Hofstra University *B*
Houghton College *B*
Iona College *B*
Ithaca College *B, T*
Le Moyne College *B*
Long Island University
   LIU Post *B*
Manhattan College *B*
Monroe Community College *A*
New York University *B, M, D*
Pace University: Pleasantville/
   Briarcliff *B*
Rensselaer Polytechnic
   Institute *B, M, D*
Roberts Wesleyan College *B*
Rochester Institute of
   Technology *B, M*
SUNY
   College at Brockport *B, T*
   College at Buffalo *B*
   College at Cortland *B*
   College at Fredonia *B, T*
   College at Geneseo *B, T*
   College at New Paltz *B*
   College at Oneonta *B*
   College at Oswego *B*
   College at Plattsburgh *B*
   College at Potsdam *B*
   University at Albany *B, M, D*
   University at Binghamton *B, M, D*
   University at Buffalo *B, M, D*
   University at Stony Brook *B, M, D*
Saint Bonaventure University *B*
St. John Fisher College *B*
St. John's University *B*
St. Lawrence University *B, T*
St. Thomas Aquinas College *B, T*
Siena College *B, T*
Skidmore College *B*
Suffolk County Community College *A*
Syracuse University *B, M, D*
Union College *B*
United States Military Academy *B*
University of Rochester *B, M, D*
Utica College *B*
Vassar College *B*
Wagner College *B, T*
Yeshiva University *B*

North Carolina

Appalachian State University *B, M*
Davidson College *B*
Duke University *B, M, D*
East Carolina University *B, M*
Elizabeth City State University *B*
Elon University *B*
Guilford College *B*
High Point University *B*
Lenoir-Rhyne University *B*
North Carolina Agricultural and
 Technical State
 University *B, M, T*
North Carolina Central University *B*
North Carolina State
 University *B, M, D*
University of North Carolina
 Asheville *B, T*
 Chapel Hill *B, M, D*
 Charlotte *B, M*
 Greensboro *B*
 Pembroke *B*
 Wilmington *B*
Wake Forest University *B, M, D*

North Dakota

Minot State University *B*
North Dakota State
 University *B, M, D, T*
University of North Dakota *B, M, D*

Ohio

Ashland University *B*
Baldwin Wallace University *B*
Bluffton University *B*
Bowling Green State University *B, M*
Case Western Reserve
 University *B, M, D*
Cedarville University *B*
Cleveland State University *B, M, T*
College of Wooster *B*
Denison University *B*
Heidelberg University *B*
Hiram College *B*
John Carroll University *B*
Kent State University *B, M, D*
Kenyon College *B*
Marietta College *B*
Miami University
 Middletown *A*
 Oxford *B, M*
Mount Vernon Nazarene University *B*
Muskingum University *B*
Oberlin College *B*
Ohio Northern University *B*
Ohio State University
 Columbus Campus *B, M, D*
Ohio University *B, M, D*
Ohio Wesleyan University *B*
Otterbein University *B*
Sinclair Community College *A*
Terra State Community College *A*
University of Akron *B, M*
University of Cincinnati *B, M, D, T*
University of Dayton *B*
University of Mount Union *B*
University of Toledo *B, M, D*
Wittenberg University *B*
Wright State University *B, M, T*
Xavier University *B*
Youngstown State University *B*

Oklahoma

Cameron University *B*
Connors State College *A*
East Central University *B, T*
Eastern Oklahoma State College *A*
Mid-America Christian University *B*
Northern Oklahoma College *A*
Oklahoma Baptist University *B, T*
Oklahoma Christian University *B*
Oklahoma City Community
 College *A*
Oklahoma City University *B*

Oklahoma State University *B, M, D*
Oral Roberts University *B*
Rogers State University *A*
Rose State College *A*
Southern Nazarene University *B*
Southwestern Oklahoma State
 University *B*
Tulsa Community College *A*
University of Central Oklahoma *B, M*
University of Oklahoma *B, M, D*
University of Science and Arts of
 Oklahoma *B*
University of Tulsa *B, M, D*

Oregon

Lewis & Clark College *B*
Linfield College *B, T*
Linn-Benton Community College *A*
Mt. Hood Community College *A*
Oregon State University *B, M, D*
Pacific University *B*
Portland State University *B, M*
Reed College *B*
Southern Oregon University *B*
Treasure Valley Community
 College *A*
University of Oregon *B, M, D*
University of Portland *B*
Willamette University *B*

Pennsylvania

Albright College *B, T*
Allegheny College *B*
Arcadia University *B*
Bloomsburg University of
 Pennsylvania *B, T*
Bryn Mawr College *B, M, D*
Bucknell University *B*
California University of
 Pennsylvania *B, M*
Carnegie Mellon University *B, M, D*
Chatham University *B*
Clarion University of Pennsylvania *B*
Community College of Allegheny
 County *A*
Dickinson College *B*
Drexel University *B, M, D*
Duquesne University *B*
East Stroudsburg University of
 Pennsylvania *B, T*
Edinboro University of
 Pennsylvania *B, T*
Elizabethtown College *B, T*
Franklin & Marshall College *B*
Geneva College *B, T*
Gettysburg College *B*
Grove City College *B*
Haverford College *B, T*
Indiana University of Pennsylvania *B*
Juniata College *B*
King's College *B*
Kutztown University of
 Pennsylvania *B*
Lafayette College *B*
Lebanon Valley College *B, T*
Lehigh University *B, M, D*
Lincoln University *B*
Lock Haven University of
 Pennsylvania *B*
Lycoming College *B*
Mansfield University of
 Pennsylvania *B, T*
Messiah College *B*
Millersville University of
 Pennsylvania *B, T*
Moravian College *B, T*
Muhlenberg College *C, B*
Northampton Community College *A*
Penn State
 Abington *B*
 Altoona *B*
 Beaver *B*
 Berks *B*
 Brandywine *B*

DuBois *B*
Erie, The Behrend College *B*
Fayette, The Eberly Campus *B*
Greater Allegheny *B*
Harrisburg *B*
Hazleton *B*
Lehigh Valley *B*
Mont Alto *B*
New Kensington *B*
Schuylkill *B*
Shenango *B*
University Park *B, M, D*
Wilkes-Barre *B*
Worthington Scranton *B*
York *B*
Saint Joseph's University *B*
St. Vincent College *B*
Shippensburg University of
 Pennsylvania *B, T*
Slippery Rock University of
 Pennsylvania *B*
Susquehanna University *B, T*
Swarthmore College *B*
Temple University *B, M, D*
Thiel College *B*
University of Pennsylvania *B, M, D*
University of Pittsburgh *B, M, D*
University of Scranton *B, T*
University of the Sciences *B*
Ursinus College *B, T*
Villanova University *B*
Washington & Jefferson College *B*
West Chester University of
 Pennsylvania *B, T*
Westminster College *B*
Widener University *B*
Wilkes University *B*
York College of Pennsylvania *A*

Puerto Rico

Pontifical Catholic University of
 Puerto Rico *B*
University of Puerto Rico
 Humacao *B*
 Mayaguez *B, M*
 Ponce *A*
 Rio Piedras *B, M*

Rhode Island

Brown University *B, M, D*
Rhode Island College *B*
University of Rhode Island *B, M, D*

South Carolina

Benedict College *B*
Bob Jones University *B*
Citadel *B*
Clemson University *B, M, D*
Coastal Carolina University *B*
College of Charleston *B, T*
Erskine College *B*
Francis Marion University *B*
Furman University *B, T*
Presbyterian College *B*
South Carolina State University *B*
University of South Carolina
 Columbia *B, M, D*
Wofford College *B*

South Dakota

Augustana College *B, T*
South Dakota School of Mines and
 Technology *B, M*
South Dakota State University *B*
University of South Dakota *B, M*

Tennessee

Austin Peay State University *B*
Belmont University *B, T*
Carson-Newman University *B*
Christian Brothers University *B*
East Tennessee State University *B, T*
Fisk University *B, M*
Hiwassee College *A*

King University *B, T*
Lane College *B*
Lipscomb University *B*
Middle Tennessee State University *B*
Rhodes College *B*
Sewanee: The University of the
 South *B*
Southern Adventist University *B*
Tennessee State University *B*
Tennessee Technological
 University *B, T*
Trevecca Nazarene University *B, T*
Union University *B, T*
University of Memphis *B, M*
University of Tennessee
 Chattanooga *B*
 Knoxville *B, M, D*
Vanderbilt University *B, M, D*

Texas

Abilene Christian University *B*
Amarillo College *A*
Angelina College *A*
Angelo State University *B*
Austin College *B*
Austin Community College *A*
Baylor University *B, M, D*
Blinn College *A*
Brazosport College *A*
Central Texas College *A*
Clarendon College *A*
Coastal Bend College *A*
Del Mar College *A*
El Paso Community College *A*
Frank Phillips College *A*
Galveston College *A*
Grayson College *A*
Hardin-Simmons University *B*
Houston Baptist University *B*
Howard College *A*
Kilgore College *A*
Lamar University *B*
Laredo Community College *A*
McMurry University *B*
Midland College *A*
Navarro College *A*
Northeast Texas Community
 College *A*
Paris Junior College *A*
Prairie View A&M University *B*
Rice University *B, M, D*
St. Mary's University *B*
St. Philip's College *A*
Sam Houston State University *B*
San Jacinto College *A*
South Plains College *A*
South Texas College *A*
Southern Methodist
 University *B, M, D*
Southwestern University *B, T*
Stephen F. Austin State
 University *B, T*
Tarleton State University *B*
Texarkana College *A*
Texas A&M University *B, M, D*
Texas A&M University
 Commerce *B, M*
 Kingsville *B, M*
Texas Christian University *B, M, D*
Texas Lutheran University *B*
Texas Southern University *B*
Texas State Technical College
 Harlingen *A*
Texas State University *B, M, T*
Texas Tech University *B, M, D*
Trinity University *B*
Trinity Valley Community College *A*
Tyler Junior College *A*
University of Dallas *B*
University of Houston *B, M, D*
University of Houston
 Clear Lake *B, M*
University of North Texas *B, M, D*

University of Texas
Arlington *B, M, D*
Austin *B, M, D*
Brownsville *B, M*
Dallas *B, M, D*
El Paso *B, M*
Pan American *B*
San Antonio *B, M, D*
West Texas A&M University *B*
Western Texas College *A*
Wharton County Junior College *A*

Utah

Brigham Young University *B, M, D*
Salt Lake Community College *A*
Snow College *A*
University of Utah *B, M, D, T*
Utah State University *B, M, D*
Utah Valley University *B*
Weber State University *B*
Westminster College *B*

Vermont

Bennington College *B*
Marlboro College *B*
Middlebury College *B*
Norwich University *B*
Saint Michael's College *B*
University of Vermont *B, M*

Virginia

Bridgewater College *B*
College of William and Mary *B, M, D*
Emory & Henry College *B, T*
George Mason University *B, M, D*
Hampden-Sydney College *B*
Hampton University *B, M, D*
Hollins University *B*
James Madison University *B, T*
Longwood University *B*
Lynchburg College *B*
Mary Baldwin College *B*
Norfolk State University *B*
Old Dominion University *B, M, D*
Radford University *B*
Randolph College *B*
Randolph-Macon College *B*
Roanoke College *B, T*
Sweet Briar College *B*
University of Mary Washington *B*
University of Richmond *B*
University of Virginia *B, M, D*
Virginia Commonwealth
    University *B, M*
Virginia Military Institute *B*
Virginia Polytechnic Institute and
    State University *B, M, D*
Virginia State University *B, M*
Washington and Lee University *B*

Washington

Cascadia Community College *A*
Central Washington University *B*
Centralia College *A*
Eastern Washington University *B*
Gonzaga University *B*
Pacific Lutheran University *B*
Seattle Pacific University *B*
Seattle University *B*
University of Puget Sound *B, T*
University of Washington *B, M, D*
Walla Walla University *B*
Washington State University *B, M, D*
Western Washington University *B*
Whitman College *B*
Whitworth University *B, T*

West Virginia

Marshall University *B*
Potomac State College of West
    Virginia University *A*
West Virginia State University *B*
West Virginia University *B, M, D, T*

West Virginia Wesleyan College *B*
Wheeling Jesuit University *B*

Wisconsin

Beloit College *B*
Carthage College *B*
Lawrence University *B, T*
Marquette University *B*
Ripon College *B*
St. Norbert College *B, T*
University of Wisconsin
    Eau Claire *B*
    Green Bay *B*
    La Crosse *B, T*
    Madison *B, M, D*
    Milwaukee *B, M, D*
    Oshkosh *B, M*
    Parkside *B, T*
    Platteville *B*
    River Falls *B*
    Stevens Point *B, T*
    Whitewater *B, T*

Wyoming

Casper College *A*
Northwest College *A*
University of Wyoming *B, M, D*

Physics teacher education

Alabama

Auburn University *M, T*
Birmingham-Southern College *T*

Arkansas

Arkansas State University *B, T*
Ouachita Baptist University *B, T*

California

Azusa Pacific University *T*
California Polytechnic State
    University: San Luis Obispo *T*
California State University
    Chico *T*
    San Bernardino *T*
San Diego State University *T*
San Francisco State University *T*
Stanford University *M, T*
University of San Diego *T*
Vanguard University of Southern
    California *T*

Colorado

Colorado State University *B, T*
Colorado State University
    Pueblo *T*

Connecticut

Fairfield University *T*
University of Connecticut *T*

Delaware

Delaware State University *B, M*
University of Delaware *B, T*

Florida

Florida Institute of Technology *B*
Florida State University *M*
University of Miami *M*

Georgia

Southern Polytechnic State
    University *B*
University of West Georgia *B, T*

Hawaii

Brigham Young University-
    Hawaii *B, T*

Idaho

Boise State University *B, T*
Brigham Young University-Idaho *B, T*

Northwest Nazarene University *B*
University of Idaho *T*

Illinois

Augustana College *B, T*
Benedictine University *T*
Bradley University *B*
DePaul University *M, T*
Elmhurst College *B*
Greenville College *B, T*
Illinois Institute of Technology *B*
Illinois Wesleyan University *B*
Knox College *T*
North Park University *T*
University of Illinois
    Chicago *B*
    Urbana-Champaign *B, M, T*

Indiana

Anderson University *B, T*
Bethel College *B*
Butler University *T*
Goshen College *B, T*
Indiana University
    Bloomington *B, T*
    Purdue University Fort Wayne *B, T*
    South Bend *B, T*
Manchester University *B, T*
Purdue University *B, M, D*
University of Evansville *B, T*
University of Indianapolis *B, T*
Valparaiso University *B*

Iowa

Buena Vista University *B, T*
Central College *T*
Cornell College *B, T*
Dordt College *B*
Drake University *T*
Ellsworth Community College *A*
Graceland University *T*
Iowa State University *T*
Iowa Wesleyan College *B*
Loras College *T*
Maharishi University of
    Management *T*
Morningside College *B*
Northwestern College *T*
St. Ambrose University *B, T*
Simpson College *T*
University of Iowa *T*
Wartburg College *T*

Kansas

Benedictine College *B*
Bethel College *T*
Garden City Community College *A*
Pittsburg State University *B*
Washburn University *T*

Kentucky

Campbellsville University *B*

Louisiana

Grambling State University *B*
Louisiana State University
    Shreveport *B*
Southeastern Louisiana University *B*
University of Louisiana at Lafayette *B*

Maine

University of Maine
    Farmington *B, T*
University of Southern Maine *T*

Maryland

Anne Arundel Community College *A*
Chesapeake College *A*
Community College of Baltimore
    County *A*
Harford Community College *A*
Howard Community College *A*
University of Maryland
    Baltimore County *B*

Massachusetts

Bridgewater State University *M, T*
Eastern Nazarene College *B*
Merrimack College *B*
Tufts University *T*
University of Massachusetts
    Dartmouth *T*
Worcester State University *T*

Michigan

Alma College *T*
Calvin College *B*
Central Michigan University *B*
Eastern Michigan University *B, M*
Grand Valley State University *M, T*
Hope College *B, T*
Madonna University *B*
Michigan State University *B*
Michigan Technological University *T*
Northern Michigan University *B, T*
Western Michigan University *B, D*

Minnesota

Augsburg College *T*
Bethel University *B*
Concordia College: Moorhead *B, T*
Gustavus Adolphus College *T*
Hamline University *T*
Minnesota State University
    Mankato *B, M, T*
    Moorhead *B*
St. Catherine University *T*
Saint Cloud State University *B, T*
St. Mary's University of Minnesota *B*
University of Minnesota
    Duluth *B*
    Morris *T*
    Twin Cities *M*
University of St. Thomas *B*
Winona State University *B, T*

Mississippi

Itawamba Community College *A*
Millsaps College *T*

Missouri

Central Methodist University *B*
Lincoln University *B*
Missouri Southern State
    University *B, T*
Missouri State University *B*
Northwest Missouri State
    University *B, T*
University of Central Missouri *B*
University of Missouri
    Columbia *B*
    Kansas City *B*
Washington University in St.
    Louis *B, M, T*
William Jewell College *B, T*

Montana

Montana State University
    Billings *B, T*
University of Montana *T*

Nebraska

Chadron State College *B*
Concordia University *B, T*
Creighton University *T*
Hastings College *B, M, T*
Nebraska Wesleyan University *T*
Union College *B*
University of Nebraska
    Kearney *B, T*
    Lincoln *B, T*

New Hampshire

University of New Hampshire *T*

New Jersey

College of New Jersey *B, T*
County College of Morris *A*
Saint Peter's University *T*

New Mexico

New Mexico Institute of Mining and
    Technology *M*

New York

Adelphi University *M, T*
Alfred University *B, T*
Bard College *M*
City University of New York
    Brooklyn College *B, M*
    City College *B, M*
    Hunter College *B, D, T*
    Queens College *M, T*
Colgate University *M*
Cornell University *M, T*
D'Youville College *M, T*
Fordham University *M, T*
Hobart and William Smith Colleges *T*
Hofstra University *B, M*
Houghton College *B, T*
Ithaca College *B, M, T*
Le Moyne College *T*
Manhattan College *B, T*
New York University *B, M*
Pace University: Pleasantville/
    Briarcliff *B, T*
Roberts Wesleyan College *B, M*
SUNY
    College at Brockport *B, M, T*
    College at Buffalo *B*
    College at Cortland *B, M*
    College at Fredonia *B, T*
    College at Geneseo *B, T*
    College at New Paltz *B, T*
    College at Oneonta *B, T*
    College at Oswego *B, M*
    College at Plattsburgh *B*
    College at Potsdam *B, M*
    University at Albany *M, T*
    University at Binghamton *M*
    University at Buffalo *M, T*
    University at Stony Brook *T*
St. John Fisher College *B, M, T*
St. John's University *B, T*
St. Lawrence University *T*
St. Thomas Aquinas College *B, T*
Syracuse University *B, T*
University of Rochester *M*
Vassar College *T*
Wagner College *T*
Wells College *T*

North Carolina

North Carolina Agricultural and
    Technical State University *B, T*
North Carolina Central
    University *B, T*
Wake Forest University *T*

North Dakota

Minot State University *B*
North Dakota State University *B, T*

Ohio

Bluffton University *B*
Bowling Green State
    University *B, M, T*
Case Western Reserve University *T*
Cedarville University *B*
Hiram College *T*
John Carroll University *T*
Mount Vernon Nazarene
    University *B, T*
Ohio Dominican University *B, T*
Ohio Northern University *B, T*
Ohio Wesleyan University *B*
Otterbein University *B*
University of Mount Union *T*
University of Rio Grande *B, T*
University of Toledo *M, T*
Xavier University *B*
Youngstown State University *B, M*

Oklahoma

East Central University *B, T*
Eastern Oklahoma State College *A*
Oklahoma Baptist University *B, T*
University of Central Oklahoma *B*
University of Tulsa *T*

Oregon

Linfield College *T*
Portland State University *T*

Pennsylvania

Albright College *T*
Chatham University *M, T*
Duquesne University *M, T*
Geneva College *T*
Gettysburg College *T*
Grove City College *B, T*
Juniata College *B, T*
Lebanon Valley College *T*
Lycoming College *T*
Mansfield University of
    Pennsylvania *B, T*
Messiah College *B, T*
Moravian College *T*
Saint Joseph's University *M, T*
St. Vincent College *B, T*
Susquehanna University *T*
Thiel College *B*
University of Scranton *B*
Villanova University *T*
Washington & Jefferson College *T*
Westminster College *T*
Widener University *T*

Rhode Island

Rhode Island College *B*

South Carolina

Furman University *T*

South Dakota

Augustana College *B, T*
University of South Dakota *B, M, T*

Tennessee

Belmont University *T*
King University *T*
Lipscomb University *B, T*
Southern Adventist University *B*
Tennessee Technological University *T*
Trevecca Nazarene University *B, T*

Texas

Abilene Christian University *B, T*
Houston Baptist University *T*
Lamar University *T*
Laredo Community College *A*
McMurry University *T*
St. Mary's University *T*
Tarleton State University *T*
Texas A&M University
    Commerce *T*
    Kingsville *T*
University of Dallas *T*
University of Texas
    Arlington *T*
    San Antonio *T*
West Texas A&M University *T*

Utah

Brigham Young University *B*
Utah State University *B*
Weber State University *B*
Western Governors
    University *B, M, T*

Vermont

Castleton State College *B, T*

Virginia

Averett University *M*
Bridgewater College *T*

Hampton University *M*
Hollins University *T*
Longwood University *T*

Washington

Central Washington University *B, T*
Eastern Washington University *B*
Spokane Falls Community College *A*
Washington State University *B, M, T*
Whitworth University *B, T*

West Virginia

Wheeling Jesuit University *B*

Wisconsin

Carthage College *T*
Lawrence University *T*
St. Norbert College *T*
University of Wisconsin
    Green Bay *T*
    River Falls *T*

Physiological
psychology/
psychobiology

California

Holy Names University *B*
La Sierra University *B*
University of California
    Los Angeles *B*

Colorado

Colorado Christian University *B*
University of Colorado
    Denver *B*

Connecticut

University of Connecticut *M, D*

Florida

Florida Atlantic University *B, D*

Georgia

Emory University *D*

Maine

University of New England *B*

Massachusetts

Simmons College *B*
Wheaton College *B*

Michigan

University of Michigan *B*

Missouri

Northwest Missouri State
    University *B*

Nebraska

University of Nebraska
    Omaha *M, D*

New York

Pace University *B*
SUNY
    University at Albany *D*
    University at Binghamton *B, D*
    University at Buffalo *D*
    University at Stony Brook *D*

Oklahoma

University of Oklahoma *M, D*

Pennsylvania

Albright College *B*
Arcadia University *M*
Carnegie Mellon University *B*
Holy Family University *B*
Lebanon Valley College *B*

Lincoln University *B*
Wilson College *B*

Tennessee

Southern Adventist University *B*

Physiology

Arizona

University of Arizona *B, M, D*

California

Loma Linda University *M, D*
San Diego State University *M*
San Francisco State University *M*
San Jose State University *B, M*
Santa Rosa Junior College *A*
University of California
    Irvine *D*
    Los Angeles *B, M*
University of Southern
    California *M, D*

Colorado

University of Colorado
    Boulder *B, M, D*
    Denver *D*

Connecticut

University of Connecticut *M, D*
Yale University *M, D*

District of Columbia

Georgetown University *M, D*
Howard University *M, D*

Florida

University of Miami *M, D*

Georgia

Georgia Regents University *M, D*

Hawaii

University of Hawaii
    Manoa *M, D*

Illinois

Loyola University Chicago *M, D*
University of Illinois
    Chicago *M, D*
    Urbana-Champaign *B, M, D*

Indiana

Ball State University *M*
Indiana University
    Bloomington *M, D*

Iowa

Iowa State University *M, D*
University of Iowa *M, D*

Kansas

University of Kansas Medical
    Center *M, D*

Kentucky

University of Kentucky *D*
University of Louisville *M, D*

Louisiana

Louisiana State University
    Health Sciences Center *D*

Massachusetts

Boston University *B, M, D*

Michigan

Eastern Michigan University *M*
Michigan State University *B, M, D*
Northern Michigan University *B*
University of Michigan *M*
Wayne State University *M, D*

Minnesota
University of Minnesota
Twin Cities *B*

Missouri
University of Missouri
Columbia *M, D*

Nebraska
University of Nebraska
Medical Center *M, D*

New Jersey
Rutgers, The State University of New
Jersey
New Brunswick/Piscataway
Campus *M, D*
Newark Campus *M, D*

New York
New York University *M, D*
SUNY
University at Buffalo *M, D*
University at Stony Brook *D*
Upstate Medical University *M, D*
University of Rochester *M, D*

North Carolina
East Carolina University *D*
North Carolina State University *M, D*
University of North Carolina
Chapel Hill *M, D*

Ohio
Case Western Reserve
University *M, D*
Kent State University *M, D*
Ohio State University
Columbus Campus *M, D*
University of Cincinnati *M*
Wright State University *M*

Oklahoma
Oklahoma State University *B*
University of Oklahoma *M, D*

Oregon
University of Oregon *B, M, D*

Texas
Texas Tech University Health
Sciences Center *M, D*
University of Texas
Health Science Center at
Houston *M, D*

Utah
Brigham Young University *B, M, D*
Snow College *A*
University of Utah *M, D*

Virginia
University of Virginia *D*
Virginia Commonwealth
University *M, D*

Wisconsin
Marquette University *B*
University of Wisconsin
Madison *M, D*

Wyoming
University of Wyoming *B*

Pipefitting

Alabama
Lawson State Community College *C*

Alaska
Ilisagvik College *C*

Arizona
Central Arizona College *C*
GateWay Community College *C, A*

California
Allan Hancock College *C*
College of San Mateo *C, A*
Foothill College *C*
Fresno City College *A*
Los Angeles Trade and Technical
College *C, A*
Modesto Junior College *C, A*
Orange Coast College *C, A*
San Diego City College *C, A*
Santa Rosa Junior College *C*

Florida
Florida State College at
Jacksonville *C*
Hillsborough Community College *C*
Palm Beach State College *C*
Seminole State College of Florida *C*
Tallahassee Community College *C*

Illinois
Black Hawk College *C, A*
City Colleges of Chicago
Kennedy-King College *C*

Indiana
Ivy Tech Community College
Central Indiana *C, A*
East Central *C, A*
North Central *C, A*
Northeast *C, A*
Northwest *C, A*
South Central *C, A*
Southwest *C, A*
Wabash Valley *C, A*

Kentucky
Somerset Community College *C, A*

Louisiana
Delgado Community College *C*

Maine
Eastern Maine Community
College *C, A*
Northern Maine Community
College *C, A*

Michigan
Delta College *A*
Kellogg Community College *C, A*
Macomb Community College *C*
Oakland Community College *C, A*

Minnesota
Dunwoody College of Technology *C*
St. Paul College *C*

Mississippi
Mississippi Gulf Coast Community
College *C, A*

Missouri
Ranken Technical College *C*
St. Louis Community College *A*

Nevada
Truckee Meadows Community
College *C, A*

New Mexico
Central New Mexico Community
College *C*
New Mexico State University
Grants *C*
Northern New Mexico College *C, A*

North Carolina
Blue Ridge Community College *C*
Tri-County Community College *C*
Wake Technical Community
College *C*

Ohio
Sinclair Community College *C*

Oklahoma
Tulsa Welding School *C*

Pennsylvania
Community College of Allegheny
County *C*

South Carolina
Denmark Technical College *C*

Texas
Brazosport College *C, A*
Frank Phillips College *C, A*
Howard College *C*
Lee College *A*
North Lake College *C*
St. Philip's College *C*

Utah
Salt Lake Community College *A*

Virginia
Central Virginia Community
College *C*

Wisconsin
Blackhawk Technical College *C*
Chippewa Valley Technical College *C*
Gateway Technical College *C*
Mid-State Technical College *C*
Milwaukee Area Technical College *C*
Western Technical College *C*

Planetary sciences

Arizona
University of Arizona *M, D*

Arkansas
University of Arkansas *M, D*

California
California Institute of
Technology *B, M, D*
California State University
Northridge *B*
Cerritos College *A*
Chaffey College *A*
College of the Redwoods *A*
Columbia College *A*
Los Angeles Valley College *A*
University of California
San Diego *B, D*

Connecticut
Wesleyan University *B, M*

Delaware
University of Delaware *B, T*

Florida
Florida Institute of Technology *B*

Illinois
Illinois Central College *A*
Illinois Valley Community College *A*
Richland Community College *A*

Iowa
Iowa State University *B, M, D*

Massachusetts
Boston University *B*
Massachusetts Institute of
Technology *M, D*
Tufts University *T*

Minnesota
Saint Cloud State University *B*

Missouri
University of Central Missouri *B*
Washington University in St.
Louis *B, M, D*

Montana
Montana State University *M*

Nebraska
Midland University *T*

New Jersey
Rutgers, The State University of New
Jersey
Newark Campus *T*
William Paterson University of New
Jersey *T*

New York
City University of New York
City College *B*
Columbia University *B*
SUNY
College at Brockport *B*
College at Buffalo *B*
University at Stony Brook *B*
Suffolk County Community College *A*

Ohio
Muskingum University *B*
Wilmington College *B*
Youngstown State University *B*

Oregon
Western Oregon University *B*

Pennsylvania
Edinboro University of
Pennsylvania *B, T*
La Salle University *B*
Mansfield University of
Pennsylvania *T*

Texas
Brazosport College *A*
College of the Mainland *A*
Lamar University *B*
Stephen F. Austin State University *T*
Texas A&M University
Corpus Christi *T*

Washington
Centralia College *A*
University of Washington *B*

Wisconsin
University of Wisconsin
River Falls *B, T*

Plant breeding

Georgia
University of Georgia *M, D*

Indiana
Purdue University *B*

Iowa
Iowa State University *M, D*

Minnesota
University of Minnesota
Twin Cities *M, D*

Texas
Texas A&M University *M, D*

Plant genetics

California
University of California
Riverside *D*

Indiana
Purdue University *B, M, D*

Michigan
Michigan State University *M, D*

Wisconsin
University of Wisconsin
Madison *M, D*

Plant molecular biology

Florida
University of Florida *M, D*

Illinois
University of Illinois
Urbana-Champaign *B, M, D*

Washington
Washington State University *M, D*

Plant pathology

Alabama
Auburn University *M, D*

Arizona
University of Arizona *M, D*

Arkansas
University of Arkansas *M*

California
University of California
Davis *M, D*
Riverside *M, D*

Colorado
Colorado State University *M, D*

Delaware
University of Delaware *B*

Florida
University of Florida *M, D*

Georgia
University of Georgia *M, D*

Hawaii
University of Hawaii
Manoa *M, D*

Illinois
University of Illinois
Urbana-Champaign *M, D*

Iowa
Iowa State University *M, D*

Kansas
Kansas State University *M, D*

Kentucky
University of Kentucky *M, D*

Louisiana
Louisiana State University and
Agricultural and Mechanical
College *M, D*

Michigan
Michigan State University *B, M, D*

Minnesota
University of Minnesota
Twin Cities *B, M, D*

Missouri
University of Missouri
Columbia *M, D*

Montana
Montana State University *M*

New Mexico
New Mexico State University *B, M*

New York
Cornell University *M, D*

North Carolina
North Carolina State University *M, D*

North Dakota
North Dakota State University *M, D*

Ohio
Ohio State University
Columbus Campus *B, M, D*

Oklahoma
Oklahoma State University *D*

Pennsylvania
Penn State
University Park *M, D*

Texas
Texas A&M University *M, D*

Virginia
Virginia Polytechnic Institute and
State University *D*

Washington
Washington State University *M, D*

Wisconsin
University of Wisconsin
Madison *B, M, D*

Plant physiology

Iowa
Iowa State University *M, D*

Kentucky
University of Kentucky *D*

Minnesota
University of Minnesota
Twin Cities *M, D*

Missouri
Washington University in St. Louis *D*

Texas
Texas A&M University *M, D*

Vermont
Marlboro College *B*

Washington
Washington State University *M, D*

Plant protection/pest management

California
California State Polytechnic
University: Pomona *B*

California State University
Fresno *M*
College of the Sequoias *C*
University of California
Davis *M*
Riverside *M*

Colorado
Colorado State University *M, D*

Georgia
University of Georgia *M*

Hawaii
University of Hawaii
Manoa *B*

Indiana
Purdue University *B*

Iowa
Iowa State University *B*

Kansas
Barton County Community
College *C, A*

Michigan
Michigan State University *M*

Minnesota
South Central College *C*
University of Minnesota
Twin Cities *B*

New York
SUNY
College of Environmental Science
and Forestry *B, M, D*

North Carolina
North Carolina State University *A*

Ohio
Ohio State University
Columbus Campus *M*

Puerto Rico
University of Puerto Rico
Mayaguez *B, M*
Utuado *A*

Tennessee
University of Tennessee
Knoxville *M*

Texas
Texas A&M University *M*

Washington
Washington State University *B*

Plant sciences

Alabama
Auburn University *B, M, D*
Tuskegee University *B, M*

Arizona
Arizona Western College *A*
University of Arizona *B, M, D*

Arkansas
Arkansas State University *B*

California
College of the Desert *A*
College of the Redwoods *C, A*
College of the Sequoias *C*
Cosumnes River College *A*
Mendocino College *C, A*
Modesto Junior College *A*

Reedley College *A*
Santa Rosa Junior College *C*
University of California
Santa Cruz *B*
Ventura College *C, A*
Yuba College *C*

Connecticut
University of Connecticut *M, D*

Delaware
Delaware State University *B, M*
University of Delaware *B, M, D*

Florida
University of Florida *B*

Georgia
Abraham Baldwin Agricultural
College *A*
Fort Valley State University *B*

Idaho
University of Idaho *M, D*

Illinois
Southern Illinois University
Carbondale *B, M*

Indiana
Purdue University *B*

Iowa
Dordt College *B*
Iowa State University *B*

Louisiana
Louisiana State University and
Agricultural and Mechanical
College *B*

Maine
University of Maine *B, M, D*

Massachusetts
University of Massachusetts
Amherst *B, M*

Minnesota
Minnesota State University
Mankato *B, M, T*
Minnesota West Community and
Technical College *A*
University of Minnesota
Crookston *B*
Twin Cities *B, M, D*

Mississippi
Northwest Mississippi Community
College *A*

Missouri
Missouri State University *M*
Southeast Missouri State University *B*
University of Missouri
Columbia *B*

Montana
Montana State University *B, M, D*

New Jersey
Mercer County Community
College *A*
Rutgers, The State University of New
Jersey
New Brunswick/Piscataway
Campus *B*

New York
Cornell University *B, M, D*
SUNY
College of Agriculture and
Technology at Cobleskill *B*
College of Environmental Science
and Forestry *M, D*

North Carolina

North Carolina Agricultural and
    Technical State University *B*

Ohio

Ohio State University
    Agricultural Technical Institute *A*
    Columbus Campus *B, M*

Oregon

Oregon State University *M, D*

Pennsylvania

Penn State
    Abington *B*
    Altoona *B*
    Beaver *B*
    Berks *B*
    Brandywine *B*
    DuBois *B*
    Erie, The Behrend College *B*
    Fayette, The Eberly Campus *B*
    Greater Allegheny *B*
    Harrisburg *B*
    Hazleton *B*
    Lehigh Valley *B*
    Mont Alto *B*
    New Kensington *B*
    Schuylkill *B*
    Shenango *B*
    University Park *B*
    Wilkes-Barre *B*
    Worthington Scranton *B*
    York *B*

Rhode Island

University of Rhode Island *B*

South Carolina

Clemson University *B, M, D*

South Dakota

South Dakota State University *M*

Tennessee

Hiwassee College *A*
Middle Tennessee State University *B*
University of Tennessee
    Knoxville *B, M*

Texas

Texas A&M University
    Kingsville *B, M*

Utah

Utah State University *B, M, D*

Vermont

University of Vermont *M, D*
Vermont Technical College *A*

Virginia

Virginia State University *M*

Washington

Washington State University *B*

West Virginia

West Virginia University *B, M*

Plasma/high-temperature physics

Texas

Rice University *M, D*

Plastics/polymer engineering technology

California

Cerritos College *C, A*

Connecticut

Naugatuck Valley Community
    College *C*
Quinebaug Valley Community
    College *C, A*

Illinois

Black Hawk College *C*
College of DuPage *C, A*
Elgin Community College *C*

Kansas

Pittsburg State University *B*

Kentucky

Maysville Community and Technical
    College *C*

Massachusetts

Fitchburg State University *C*
Mount Wachusett Community
    College *A*
University of Massachusetts
    Lowell *C*

Michigan

Eastern Michigan University *B, M*
Ferris State University *A, B*
Grand Rapids Community
    College *C, A*

Minnesota

Hennepin Technical College *C, A*
Northland Community & Technical
    College *C*

North Carolina

Edgecombe Community College *C, A*
Guilford Technical Community
    College *A*
Isothermal Community College *C, A*

Ohio

Cincinnati State Technical and
    Community College *A*
Northwest State Community
    College *C, A*
Shawnee State University *C, A, B*
Terra State Community College *C, A*

Pennsylvania

Penn State
    Abington *C*
    Altoona *C*
    Beaver *C*
    Berks *C*
    Brandywine *C*
    DuBois *C*
    Erie, The Behrend College *C, A*
    Fayette, The Eberly Campus *C*
    Greater Allegheny *C*
    Harrisburg *C*
    Hazleton *C*
    Lehigh Valley *C*
    Mont Alto *C*
    New Kensington *C*
    Schuylkill *C*
    Shenango *C*
    University Park *C*
    Wilkes-Barre *C*
    Worthington Scranton *C*
    York *C*
Pennsylvania College of
    Technology *A, B*

Washington

Everett Community College *C, A*
Olympic College *C*
Peninsula College *C*
Western Washington University *B*

Wisconsin

Milwaukee Area Technical College *A*

Platemaker/imager

Illinois

City Colleges of Chicago
    Kennedy-King College *C, A*

Ohio

Cincinnati State Technical and
    Community College *C*

Playwriting/screenwriting

Alaska

Prince William Sound Community
    College *A*

Arizona

Scottsdale Community College *C*

California

California State University
    Fullerton *M*
Chapman University *B, M*
Loyola Marymount University *B, M*
National University *M*
Otis College of Art and Design *M*
Pacific Union College *A*
University of Southern
    California *B, M*

Connecticut

Yale University *M*

Florida

Florida State University *B*
University of South Florida *M*

Georgia

Savannah College of Art and
    Design *B, M*

Illinois

Columbia College Chicago *B*
DePaul University *B*
Judson University *B*
Northwestern University *M*

Iowa

University of Iowa *M*

Maine

College of the Atlantic *B*

Massachusetts

Bard College at Simon's Rock *B*
Boston University *M*
Emerson College *B, M*
Smith College *M*

Minnesota

Metropolitan State University *B*
Minneapolis Community and
    Technical College *A*

New Mexico

Santa Fe University of Art and
    Design *B*
University of New Mexico *M*

New York

Bard College *B*
City University of New York
    Hunter College *M*
SUNY
    College at Purchase *B*

Ohio

Ashland University *B*
Ohio University *B, M*

Pennsylvania

Carnegie Mellon University *M*
Drexel University *B*
Point Park University *B*
University of the Arts *B*

Vermont

Bennington College *B*
Burlington College *C*
Marlboro College *B*

Virginia

Hollins University *M*
Regent University *M*

Washington

Cornish College of the Arts *B*

Wyoming

Northwest College *A*

Plumbing

Alabama

Bishop State Community College *C*
George C. Wallace Community
    College at Dothan *C*
Lawson State Community College *C*

Alaska

Ilisagvik College *C*

Arizona

Arizona Western College *C, A*
Northland Pioneer College *C, A*
Tohono O'odham Community
    College *C, A*

California

Bakersfield College *C, A*
City College of San Francisco *C*
Diablo Valley College *C, A*
Foothill College *C*
WyoTech: Fremont *C*
WyoTech: Long Beach *C*

Florida

Daytona State College *C*
Hillsborough Community College *C*
Indian River State College *C*
Santa Fe College *C*
South Florida State College *C*

Georgia

Athens Technical College *C*
Atlanta Technical College *C*
Savannah Technical College *C*

Indiana

Ivy Tech Community College
    Bloomington *C, A*
    Central Indiana *C, A*
    North Central *C, A*
    Richmond *C, A*

Iowa

Kirkwood Community College *C*
Northeast Iowa Community
    College *A*

Kentucky

Elizabethtown Community and
    Technical College *C*
Jefferson Community and Technical
    College *C*
Somerset Community College *C, A*

Maine

Southern Maine Community
    College *C*
Washington County Community
    College *C*

Michigan

Delta College *A*
Northwestern Michigan College *C, A*

Minnesota

Anoka Technical College *C*
Minnesota State Community and
Technical College *C, A*
Minnesota West Community and
Technical College *A*
Northland Community & Technical
College *C*
Northwest Technical College *C*
St. Cloud Technical and Community
College *C, A*
St. Paul College *C*

Mississippi

Hinds Community College *C, A*

Montana

Montana State University
Northern *A*

New Mexico

Central New Mexico Community
College *A*
Dona Ana Community College of
New Mexico State University *C*

New York

SUNY
College of Technology at Alfred *A*

North Carolina

Cleveland Community College *C*
Fayetteville Technical Community
College *C*
Forsyth Technical Community
College *C*
Southeastern Community College *C*
Southwestern Community College *C*

North Dakota

North Dakota State College of
Science *C*

Pennsylvania

Community College of Allegheny
County *C*
Delaware County Community
College *C*
Harrisburg Area Community
College *C*
Luzerne County Community
College *C*
Orleans Technical Institute *C*
Pennco Tech *C*
Pennsylvania College of
Technology *C*
Thaddeus Stevens College of
Technology *A*

Rhode Island

New England Institute of
Technology *A*

South Carolina

York Technical College *C*

South Dakota

Western Dakota Technical Institute *C*

Texas

Paris Junior College *C*
Texas State Technical College
Waco *C*

Utah

Salt Lake Community College *A*

Virginia

Liberty University *A*
Southwest Virginia Community
College *C*

Wisconsin

Blackhawk Technical College *C*
Chippewa Valley Technical College *C*
Gateway Technical College *C*
Mid-State Technical College *C*
Southwest Wisconsin Technical
College *C*
Waukesha County Technical
College *C*
Western Technical College *C*
Wisconsin Indianhead Technical
College *C*

Polarity therapy

Vermont

Goddard College *B, M*

Washington

Centralia College *A*

Police science

Alabama

Calhoun Community College *C*
Chattahoochee Valley Community
College *C, A*
Columbia Southern University *A, B*
Enterprise State Community
College *C*
George C. Wallace Community
College at Dothan *A*
George C. Wallace State Community
College at Selma *C*
Jefferson State Community
College *C, A*
Lawson State Community College *A*
Northeast Alabama Community
College *C, A*
Northwest-Shoals Community
College *A*
Wallace State Community College at
Hanceville *A*

Alaska

University of Alaska
Fairbanks *C*

Arizona

Anthem College
Phoenix *A, B*
Arizona Western College *A*
Central Arizona College *C, A*
Cochise College *C, A*
Eastern Arizona College *C, A*
Glendale Community College *C*
Mesa Community College *C, A*
Mohave Community College *C, A*
Penn Foster College *A, B*
Pima Community College *C, A*
Scottsdale Community College *C*

Arkansas

Arkansas Northeastern College *C, A*
Arkansas State University *A*
Arkansas State University
Beebe *C, A*
Black River Technical College *C, A*
East Arkansas Community
College *C, A*
National Park Community College *A*
Northwest Arkansas Community
College *C*
South Arkansas Community
College *C, A*
Southern Arkansas University Tech *C*

University of Arkansas
Community College at Hope *A*
Little Rock *A*

California

Allan Hancock College *C*
American River College *A*
Argosy University
Inland Empire *B*
Los Angeles *B*
Orange County *B*
San Diego *B*
San Francisco Bay Area *B*
Bakersfield College *A*
Barstow Community College *C, A*
Butte College *C, A*
Cabrillo College *C, A*
California Lutheran University *B*
Carrington College California
Stockton *A*
Cerritos College *A*
Cerro Coso Community College *C, A*
Chabot College *A*
Citrus College *A*
City College of San Francisco *C, A*
College of the Canyons *C, A*
College of the Redwoods *C*
College of the Siskiyous *A*
East Los Angeles College *C, A*
El Camino College *A*
Evergreen Valley College *A*
Feather River College *C, A*
Fresno City College *C, A*
Fullerton College *A*
Glendale Community College *A*
Grossmont College *C, A*
Irvine Valley College *C, A*
Lassen Community College *C, A*
Los Angeles City College *C, A*
Los Angeles Harbor College *C, A*
Los Angeles Valley College *C, A*
Merced College *C, A*
MiraCosta College *C, A*
Moorpark College *C, A*
Mount San Antonio College *C, A*
Mount San Jacinto College *C, A*
Napa Valley College *C, A*
Palomar College *C, A*
Pasadena City College *C, A*
Porterville College *C, A*
Rio Hondo College *A*
Sacramento City College *C, A*
San Bernardino Valley College *C*
San Joaquin Delta College *C, A*
Santa Ana College *C, A*
Santa Rosa Junior College *C, A*
Shasta College *A*
Sierra College *A*
Solano Community College *C, A*
Southwestern College *C*
West Hills College: Coalinga *A*
Westwood College
Inland Empire *B*
Yuba College *A*

Colorado

Aims Community College *C*
Arapahoe Community College *C*
Colorado Mesa University *C*
Colorado Mountain College *C*
Pikes Peak Community College *C*
Red Rocks Community College *C, A*
Trinidad State Junior College *A*
Western State Colorado University *B*

Connecticut

Asnuntuck Community College *A*
Housatonic Community College *C, A*
Middlesex Community College *A*
Naugatuck Valley Community
College *C, A*
Three Rivers Community College *A*
University of Hartford *B*
University of New Haven *C, A*

Western Connecticut State
University *B*

Delaware

Delaware Technical Community
College
Jack F. Owens Campus *A*
Stanton/Wilmington Campus *A*
Terry Campus *A*

District of Columbia

George Washington University *A, B*
Strayer University *A*

Florida

Argosy University
Sarasota *B*
Tampa *B*
College of Central Florida *C*
Daytona State College *C*
Eastern Florida State College *C, A*
Everest University
Orange Park *A*
Florida Gateway College *C*
Florida State College at
Jacksonville *C*
Fortis College
Winter Park *A*
Gulf Coast State College *C*
Hillsborough Community College *C*
Indian River State College *C*
Miami Dade College *C*
Northwest Florida State College *C*
Palm Beach State College *C*
Polk State College *C, A*
Remington College
Tampa *A*
Saint Johns River State College *C*
Santa Fe College *C*
Seminole State College of Florida *C*
South Florida State College *C*
Tallahassee Community College *C*
Valencia College *C*

Georgia

Abraham Baldwin Agricultural
College *A*
Altamaha Technical College *C, A*
Argosy University
Atlanta *B*
Armstrong Atlantic State
University *A, B, M*
Bainbridge College *C, A*
Dalton State College *B*
Georgia Gwinnett College *B*
Georgia Highlands College *A*
Middle Georgia State College *C, A*
Reinhardt University *A, B*
South Georgia State College *A*
Southwest Georgia Technical
College *C, A*

Hawaii

Argosy University
Hawaii *B*
University of Hawaii
Honolulu Community College *A*

Idaho

Idaho State University *C, A, B*
North Idaho College *A*

Illinois

Argosy University
Schaumburg *B*
Black Hawk College *C, A*
City Colleges of Chicago
Harold Washington College *C*
College of DuPage *C, A*
College of Lake County *C, A*
Danville Area Community College *A*
Elgin Community College *A*
Harper College *A*
Illinois Central College *C, A*

Illinois Eastern Community Colleges
  Frontier Community College *C*
Illinois Valley Community College *A*
John Wood Community College *A*
Kankakee Community College *C, A*
Kishwaukee College *C, A*
Lake Land College *A*
Lincoln College *C, A*
Lincoln Land Community
  College *C, A*
McHenry County College *A*
Moraine Valley Community College *A*
Morton College *A*
Oakton Community College *C, A*
Parkland College *A*
Prairie State College *C, A*
Rend Lake College *C, A*
Richland Community College *A*
Rock Valley College *A*
Sauk Valley Community College *A*
Southeastern Illinois College *C, A*
Southwestern Illinois College *C, A*
Triton College *A*
Waubonsee Community College *A*

Indiana

Calumet College of St. Joseph *A, B*
Indiana Wesleyan University *A*
Vincennes University *A*

Iowa

Clinton Community College *C, A*
Des Moines Area Community
  College *C, A*
Dordt College *B*
Hawkeye Community College *A*
Iowa Central Community
  College *C, A*
Iowa Lakes Community College *A*
Marshalltown Community College *A*
North Iowa Area Community
  College *A*
Western Iowa Tech Community
  College *C, A*

Kansas

Allen County Community College *A*
Barton County Community
  College *C, A*
Bethany College *B*
Butler Community College *C, A*
Cloud County Community
  College *C, A*
Colby Community College *A*
Cowley County Community
  College *A*
Garden City Community College *A*
Highland Community College *A*
Hutchinson Community College *C, A*
Johnson County Community
  College *C, A*
Kansas City Kansas Community
  College *C, A*
Seward County Community
  College *C, A*
Washburn University *B*

Kentucky

Ashland Community and Technical
  College *A*
Big Sandy Community and Technical
  College *A*
Eastern Kentucky University *B, M*
Northern Kentucky University *A*
Somerset Community College *C, A*
Southeast Kentucky Community and
  Technical College *A*

Louisiana

Baton Rouge Community College *A*
Delgado Community College *A*
Grambling State University *A*

Maine

Beal College *A*
Kaplan University
  South Portland *A, B, M*
Southern Maine Community
  College *A*

Maryland

Allegany College of Maryland *C, A*
Anne Arundel Community
  College *C, A*
Baltimore City Community College *A*
Carroll Community College *A*
Cecil College *C, A*
Chesapeake College *C*
Community College of Baltimore
  County *A*
Frederick Community College *A*
Frostburg State University *B*
Hagerstown Community College *C, A*
Harford Community College *A*
Howard Community College *A*
University of Maryland
  Eastern Shore *B*
Wor-Wic Community College *C, A*

Massachusetts

American International College *B*
Becker College *B*
Eastern Nazarene College *B*
Greenfield Community College *A*
Massasoit Community College *A*
Quinsigamond Community
  College *C, A*
Springfield Technical Community
  College *C, A*

Michigan

Delta College *C, A*
Ferris State University *A, B*
Grand Rapids Community College *A*
Kalamazoo Valley Community
  College *C, A*
Kellogg Community College *A*
Kirtland Community College *C, A*
Lake Michigan College *A*
Lansing Community College *C, A*
Macomb Community College *C, A*
Mid Michigan Community College *A*
Mott Community College *C, A*
North Central Michigan College *C*
Northwestern Michigan College *A*
Oakland Community College *C, A*
Schoolcraft College *A*
University of Detroit Mercy *B, M*
Washtenaw Community College *A*

Minnesota

Alexandria Technical and Community
  College *C, A*
Argosy University
  Twin Cities *B*
Brown College
  Brooklyn Center *A, B*
Central Lakes College *A*
Century College *A*
Fond du Lac Tribal and Community
  College *C, A*
Hennepin Technical College *C*
Hibbing Community College *A*
Inver Hills Community College *A*
Leech Lake Tribal College *A*
Metropolitan State University *B*
Minneapolis Community and
  Technical College *A*
Minnesota State University
  Mankato *B*
Minnesota West Community and
  Technical College *A*
Normandale Community College *A*
North Hennepin Community
  College *A*
Northland Community & Technical
  College *C, A*

Rasmussen College
  Blaine *C*
  Bloomington *C*
  Brooklyn Park *C*
  Eagan *C*
  Lake Elmo/Woodbury *C, A*
  Mankato *C*
  Moorhead *C*
  St. Cloud *C, A*
Ridgewater College *A*
Riverland Community College *C, A*
Rochester Community and Technical
  College *C, A*
St. Mary's University of Minnesota *B*
University of Minnesota
  Twin Cities *C*
Vermilion Community College *A*

Mississippi

East Mississippi Community
  College *A*

Missouri

College of the Ozarks *B*
Drury University *M*
Jefferson College *C, A*
Mineral Area College *C, A*
Missouri Southern State University *C*
Missouri State University: West
  Plains *C*
Missouri Western State University *A*
Moberly Area Community College *C*
St. Charles Community College *C, A*
State Fair Community College *A*
Three Rivers Community College *A*
University of Missouri
  Kansas City *B*

Montana

Dawson Community College *C, A*
University of Great Falls *B*

Nebraska

Bellevue University *B*
Metropolitan Community College *A*
Mid-Plains Community College *A*
Nebraska Indian Community
  College *A*
Northeast Community College *C*
University of Nebraska
  Kearney *B*
Western Nebraska Community
  College *C, A*

Nevada

College of Southern Nevada *C, A*
Great Basin College *A*
Truckee Meadows Community
  College *A*
Western Nevada College *C, A*

New Jersey

Atlantic Cape Community College *A*
Bergen Community College *A*
Berkeley College *A*
Brookdale Community College *A*
Burlington County College *C, A*
Camden County College *A*
County College of Morris *A*
Cumberland County College *C, A*
Essex County College *A*
Gloucester County College *A*
Mercer County Community
  College *A*
Ocean County College *C, A*
Passaic County Community
  College *C, A*
Raritan Valley Community College *A*

New Mexico

Brookline College
  Albuquerque *B*
Clovis Community College *C, A*

Eastern New Mexico University:
  Roswell *A*
New Mexico Junior College *A*
Santa Fe Community College *A*

New York

Adirondack Community College *A*
Berkeley College *A*
Berkeley College of New York City *A*
Broome Community College *A*
Bryant & Stratton College
  Syracuse *C*
Cayuga Community College *A*
City University of New York
  Borough of Manhattan Community
    College *A*
  John Jay College of Criminal
    Justice *B*
Corning Community College *C*
Dutchess Community College *A*
Erie Community College *C, A*
Everest Institute
  Rochester *A*
Excelsior College *B*
Jamestown Community College *C, A*
Medaille College *B*
Mercy College *C*
Mohawk Valley Community
  College *C*
Monroe College *A*
Monroe Community College *A*
Onondaga Community College *A*
Orange County Community
  College *A*
Rockland Community College *A*
SUNY
  College at Brockport *B*
  College of Technology at Canton *B*
  Farmingdale State College *A*
St. Joseph's College New York:
  Suffolk Campus *C*
St. Joseph's College, New York *C*
Sullivan County Community
  College *A*
Tompkins Cortland Community
  College *A*
Ulster County Community College *C*
Westchester Community College *A*

North Carolina

Asheville-Buncombe Technical
  Community College *C, A*
Bladen Community College *C*
Blue Ridge Community College *A*
Brunswick Community College *C*
Cape Fear Community College *C, A*
Carteret Community College *A*
Catawba Valley Community
  College *C*
Central Piedmont Community
  College *C*
Cleveland Community College *C*
Coastal Carolina Community
  College *C, A*
College of the Albemarle *C*
Craven Community College *C*
Davidson County Community
  College *C*
Durham Technical Community
  College *C*
Fayetteville Technical Community
  College *C*
Gaston College *C*
Halifax Community College *A*
Isothermal Community College *C*
James Sprunt Community College *C*
Johnston Community College *C*
Lenoir Community College *C*
Mayland Community College *C, A*
Mitchell Community College *C, A*
Montgomery Community College *C*
Nash Community College *A*
Pfeiffer University *B*
Pitt Community College *C, A*

Randolph Community College *C, A*
Rockingham Community College *C*
Sampson Community College *C*
Sandhills Community College *C*
Southwestern Community College *C*
Stanly Community College *C*
Vance-Granville Community
    College *C*
Wake Technical Community
    College *A*
Wayne Community College *C*
Western Piedmont Community
    College *C*
Wilkes Community College *C*
Wilson Community College *C*

North Dakota

Lake Region State College *C, A*
Rasmussen College
    Bismarck *C*
    Fargo *C*

Ohio

Akron Institute of Herzing
    University *A*
Bowling Green State University *B*
Central Ohio Technical College *C, A*
Columbus State Community
    College *A*
Cuyahoga Community College
    Metropolitan *A*
Eastern Gateway Community
    College *A*
Edison State Community College *C, A*
Hocking College *C, A*
James A. Rhodes State College *C, A*
Lakeland Community College *C, A*
Lorain County Community
    College *C, A*
Muskingum University *B*
North Central State College *C, A*
Northwest State Community
    College *A*
Ohio University
    Chillicothe Campus *A*
    Lancaster Campus *A*
    Zanesville Campus *B*
Owens Community College
    Toledo *A*
Remington College
    Cleveland West *A*
Sinclair Community College *C, A*
Southern State Community College *A*
Terra State Community College *C, A*
University of Akron *C, A*
Youngstown State University *C, A*

Oklahoma

Connors State College *A*
East Central University *B, M*
Langston University *B*
Northwestern Oklahoma State
    University *B*
Oklahoma Panhandle State
    University *A*
Oklahoma State University
    Oklahoma City *A*
Redlands Community College *A*
Rogers State University *A*
Rose State College *A*
Tulsa Community College *A*
University of Central Oklahoma *B*
Western Oklahoma State College *A*

Oregon

Clackamas Community College *A*
Everest College
    Portland *A*
Rogue Community College *A*
Southern Oregon University *B*
Southwestern Oregon Community
    College *A*
Treasure Valley Community
    College *C, A*

Umpqua Community College *C, A*
Western Oregon University *M*

Pennsylvania

Butler County Community College *A*
Community College of Allegheny
    County *A*
Community College of Beaver
    County *C, A*
Community College of
    Philadelphia *C, A*
Delaware County Community
    College *C, A*
Gwynedd Mercy University *B*
Harrisburg Area Community
    College *C, A*
Kaplan Career Institute
    Pittsburgh *A*
Lackawanna College *C, A*
Montgomery County Community
    College *A*
Reading Area Community College *A*

Puerto Rico

Caribbean University *A, B, M*
Turabo University *A*
Universidad Metropolitana *A*
Universidad del Este *A*
University College of San Juan *A, B*

Rhode Island

Community College of Rhode
    Island *A*

South Carolina

Williamsburg Technical College *C*
York Technical College *C, A*

South Dakota

Lake Area Technical Institute *A*
National American University
    Rapid City *A, B*
University of Sioux Falls *B*
Western Dakota Technical Institute *A*

Tennessee

Argosy University
    Nashville *B*
Cleveland State Community
    College *C*
Columbia State Community
    College *A*
Dyersburg State Community
    College *A*
Jackson State Community College *A*
LeMoyne-Owen College *B*
Nashville State Community College *A*
Northeast State Community
    College *A*
Roane State Community College *A*
Southwest Tennessee Community
    College *A*
Volunteer State Community
    College *C, A*
Walters State Community
    College *C, A*

Texas

Alvin Community College *C, A*
Amarillo College *C, A*
Angelina College *C*
Austin Community College *C, A*
Brazosport College *C, A*
Central Texas College *C, A*
Coastal Bend College *A*
College of the Mainland *A*
Del Mar College *C, A*
El Centro College *C*
Grayson College *A*
Houston Community College
    System *C, A*
Kilgore College *C, A*
Lamar Institute of Technology *C*
Lee College *A*

Midland College *A*
Navarro College *A*
North Central Texas College *A*
Northeast Texas Community
    College *C, A*
Odessa College *C, A*
St. Philip's College *A*
San Antonio College *C, A*
San Jacinto College *C, A*
Stephen F. Austin State University *B*
Tarrant County College *C*
Texas State University *B*
Tyler Junior College *C, A*
Vernon College *C*
Weatherford College *C, A*
Wharton County Junior College *C, A*

Utah

Southern Utah University *A, B*
Weber State University *B*

Vermont

Southern Vermont College *B*

Virginia

Argosy University
    Washington D.C. *B*
Bluefield College *B*
Dabney S. Lancaster Community
    College *C, A*
George Mason University *B*
Germanna Community College *C, A*
Lord Fairfax Community College *C*
Mountain Empire Community
    College *C*
Paul D. Camp Community College *A*
Piedmont Virginia Community
    College *C, A*
Southside Virginia Community
    College *C, A*
Southwest Virginia Community
    College *C, A*
Virginia Highlands Community
    College *A*
Virginia Western Community
    College *A*
Westwood College
    Arlington Ballston *B*
Wytheville Community College *C, A*

Washington

Argosy University
    Seattle *B*
Centralia College *A*
Columbia Basin College *A*
Everett Community College *A*
Grays Harbor College *C, A*
Green River Community College *A*
Spokane Community College *A*
University of Washington Tacoma *B*
Wenatchee Valley College *C, A*
Whatcom Community College *A*

West Virginia

Kanawha Valley Community and
    Technical College *A*
Pierpont Community and Technical
    College *A*
West Virginia Northern Community
    College *A*
West Virginia State University *B*

Wisconsin

Blackhawk Technical College *C, A*
Carthage College *B*
Chippewa Valley Technical College *A*
Fox Valley Technical College *C, A*
Gateway Technical College *A*
Lakeshore Technical College *C, A*
Madison Area Technical College *A*
Marian University *B*
Mid-State Technical College *C, A*
Milwaukee Area Technical College *A*
Moraine Park Technical College *A*

Nicolet Area Technical College *A*
Northcentral Technical College *A*
Northeast Wisconsin Technical
    College *A*
Southwest Wisconsin Technical
    College *C, A*
University of Wisconsin
    Superior *B*
Waukesha County Technical
    College *C, A*
Western Technical College *C, A*
Wisconsin Indianhead Technical
    College *C*

Wyoming

Eastern Wyoming College *A*

Polish

Illinois

University of Illinois
    Chicago *B*

Michigan

University of Michigan *B*

Pennsylvania

University of Pittsburgh *B*

Wisconsin

University of Wisconsin
    Madison *B*

Polish studies

New York

Columbia University *B*

Political communications

District of Columbia

George Washington University *B*

Florida

Florida Southern College *B*

Massachusetts

Emerson College *B, M*
Suffolk University *B*

Missouri

Missouri State University *B*

Nebraska

Nebraska Wesleyan University *B*

Ohio

Ashland University *B*
Cedarville University *B*
Ohio University
    Southern Campus at Ironton *B*

Utah

Weber State University *B*

Political economy

California

La Sierra University *B*
University of Southern
    California *M, D*

Colorado

Colorado School of Mines *M*

District of Columbia

Georgetown University *B*

Florida

Ave Maria University *B*

Maine

College of the Atlantic *B*

Massachusetts

Williams College *B*

Michigan

Spring Arbor University *B*

Tennessee

Rhodes College *B*

Washington

Evergreen State College *B*
University of Puget Sound *B*

Political science

Alabama

Alabama Agricultural and Mechanical
University *B*
Alabama State University *B*
Athens State University *B*
Auburn University *B*
Auburn University at
Montgomery *B, M*
Birmingham-Southern College *B*
Huntingdon College *B*
Jacksonville State University *B*
Miles College *B*
Oakwood University *B*
Samford University *B*
Spring Hill College *B*
Troy University *B*
Tuskegee University *B*
University of Alabama *B, M, D*
University of Alabama
Birmingham *B*
Huntsville *B*
University of Mobile *B*
University of Montevallo *B, T*
University of North Alabama *B*
University of South Alabama *B*

Alaska

University of Alaska
Anchorage *B*
Fairbanks *B*
Southeast *B*

Arizona

Arizona State University *B, M, D*
Arizona Western College *A*
Eastern Arizona College *A*
Northern Arizona University *B, M, D*
Pima Community College *A*
South Mountain Community
College *A*
University of Arizona *B*

Arkansas

Arkansas State University *B, M*
Arkansas Tech University *B*
Harding University *B*
Henderson State University *B*
Hendrix College *B*
John Brown University *B*
Lyon College *B*
Ouachita Baptist University *B*
Philander Smith College *B*
Southern Arkansas University *B*
University of Arkansas *B, M*
University of Arkansas
Little Rock *B*
Monticello *B*
Pine Bluff *B*
University of Central Arkansas *B*
University of the Ozarks *B*

California

American Jewish University *B*
Azusa Pacific University *B*
Bakersfield College *A*

Berkeley City College *A*
Cabrillo College *A*
California Baptist University *B*
California Institute of Technology *B*
California Lutheran University *B*
California Polytechnic State
University: San Luis Obispo *B*
California State Polytechnic
University: Pomona *B*
California State University
Bakersfield *B*
Channel Islands *B*
Chico *B, M*
Dominguez Hills *B*
East Bay *B*
Fresno *B*
Fullerton *B, M*
Los Angeles *B, M*
Northridge *B*
Sacramento *B, M*
San Bernardino *B, T*
San Marcos *B*
Stanislaus *B*
Canada College *A*
Cerritos College *A*
Chabot College *A*
Chaffey College *A*
Chapman University *B*
Claremont McKenna College *B*
College of Alameda *A*
College of the Canyons *A*
College of the Desert *A*
Concordia University Irvine *B*
Copper Mountain College *A*
Crafton Hills College *A*
Cypress College *A*
De Anza College *A*
Diablo Valley College *A*
Dominican University of California *B*
El Camino College *A*
Foothill College *A*
Fresno Pacific University *B*
Fullerton College *A*
Gavilan College *A*
Golden West College *A*
Grossmont College *A*
Humboldt State University *B*
Irvine Valley College *A*
Los Angeles Southwest College *A*
Los Angeles Valley College *A*
Loyola Marymount University *B*
Master's College *B*
Mills College *B*
Monterey Peninsula College *A*
Mount St. Mary's College *B*
National University *B*
Notre Dame de Namur University *B*
Occidental College *B*
Orange Coast College *A*
Oxnard College *A*
Pacific Union College *B*
Pepperdine University *B*
Pitzer College *B*
Point Loma Nazarene University *B*
Pomona College *B*
Saddleback College *A*
St. Mary's College of California *B*
San Diego City College *A*
San Diego State University *B, M*
San Francisco State University *B, M*
San Jose State University *B*
Santa Ana College *A*
Santa Barbara City College *A*
Santa Clara University *B*
Santa Rosa Junior College *A*
Santiago Canyon College *A*
Scripps College *B*
Solano Community College *A*
Sonoma State University *B*
Southwestern College *A*
Stanford University *B, M, D*
University of California
Berkeley *B, D*
Davis *B, M, D*
Irvine *B, D*

Los Angeles *B, M, D*
Merced *B*
Riverside *B, M, D*
San Diego *B, M, D*
Santa Barbara *B, M, D*
Santa Cruz *B, D*
University of La Verne *B*
University of Redlands *B*
University of San Diego *B*
University of San Francisco *B*
University of Southern California *B*
University of the Pacific *B*
Vanguard University of Southern
California *B*
West Los Angeles College *A*
Westmont College *B*
Whittier College *B*

Colorado

Colorado College *B*
Colorado Mesa University *B*
Colorado State University *B, M, D*
Colorado State University
Pueblo *B*
Community College of Aurora *A*
Fort Lewis College *B*
Metropolitan State University of
Denver *B, T*
Otero Junior College *A*
Regis University *B*
United States Air Force Academy *B*
University of Colorado
Boulder *B, M, D*
Colorado Springs *B*
Denver *B, M*
University of Denver *B*
University of Northern Colorado *B*
Western State Colorado University *B*

Connecticut

Albertus Magnus College *B*
Central Connecticut State
University *B*
Connecticut College *B*
Eastern Connecticut State
University *B*
Fairfield University *B*
Quinnipiac University *B*
Sacred Heart University *B*
Southern Connecticut State
University *B, M*
Trinity College *B*
United States Coast Guard
Academy *B*
University of Bridgeport *B*
University of Connecticut *B, M, D*
University of Hartford *B*
University of New Haven *B*
Wesleyan University *B*
Western Connecticut State
University *B*
Yale University *B, M, D*

Delaware

Delaware State University *B*
University of Delaware *B, M, D*
Wesley College *B*

District of Columbia

American University *C, B, M, D*
Catholic University of
America *B, M, D*
Gallaudet University *B*
George Washington
University *B, M, D*
Georgetown University *B, M, D*
Howard University *B, M, D*
Trinity Washington University *B*
University of the District of
Columbia *B*

Florida

Ave Maria University *B*
Barry University *B*

Bethune-Cookman University *B*
Broward College *A*
Daytona State College *A*
Eckerd College *B*
Flagler College *B*
Florida Agricultural and Mechanical
University *B*
Florida Atlantic University *B, M*
Florida Gulf Coast University *B*
Florida International
University *B, M, D*
Florida Southern College *B*
Florida State University *B, D*
Indian River State College *A*
Jacksonville University *B*
Lynn University *B*
Miami Dade College *A*
New College of Florida *B*
Palm Beach Atlantic University *B*
Palm Beach State College *A*
Rollins College *B*
Saint Leo University *B*
Saint Thomas University *B*
Stetson University *B*
University of Central Florida *B, M, D*
University of Florida *B, M, D*
University of Miami *B, M*
University of North Florida *B*
University of South Florida *B, M*
University of South Florida
Saint Petersburg *B*
University of Tampa *A, B*
University of West Florida *B, M*

Georgia

Agnes Scott College *B*
Albany State University *B*
Armstrong Atlantic State
University *B, T*
Atlanta Metropolitan College *A*
Bainbridge College *A*
Berry College *B*
Brenau University *B*
Brewton-Parker College *B*
Clark Atlanta University *B, M, D*
Clayton State University *B*
Columbus State University *B*
Dalton State College *A*
Darton College *A*
East Georgia State College *A*
Emory University *B, D*
Fort Valley State University *B*
Georgia College and State
University *B*
Georgia Gwinnett College *B*
Georgia Highlands College *A*
Georgia Perimeter College *A*
Georgia Regents University *B*
Georgia Southern University *B*
Georgia Southwestern State
University *B*
Georgia State University *B, M, D*
Gordon College *A*
Kennesaw State University *B*
LaGrange College *B*
Mercer University *B*
Middle Georgia State College *A*
Morehouse College *B*
Oglethorpe University *B*
Piedmont College *B*
Reinhardt University *B*
Savannah State University *B*
South Georgia State College *A*
Southern Polytechnic State
University *B*
Spelman College *B*
University of Georgia *B, M, D*
University of North Georgia *A, B*
University of West Georgia *B*
Valdosta State University *B*

Hawaii

Brigham Young University-Hawaii *B*
Chaminade University of Honolulu *B*

Hawaii Pacific University *B*
University of Hawaii
  Hilo *B*
  Manoa *B, M, D*
  West Oahu *B*

Idaho

Boise State University *B, T*
Brigham Young University-Idaho *B*
College of Idaho *B*
College of Southern Idaho *A*
College of Western Idaho *A*
Idaho State University *B, M, D*
North Idaho College *A*
Northwest Nazarene University *B*
University of Idaho *B, M, D*

Illinois

Augustana College *B*
Aurora University *B*
Benedictine University *B*
Blackburn College *B*
Bradley University *B*
Chicago State University *B*
Concordia University Chicago *B*
DePaul University *B*
Dominican University *B*
Eastern Illinois University *B, M, T*
Elmhurst College *B, T*
Eureka College *B*
Governors State University *M*
Illinois College *B*
Illinois Institute of Technology *B*
Illinois State University *B, M*
Illinois Valley Community College *A*
Illinois Wesleyan University *B*
John A. Logan College *A*
Joliet Junior College *A*
Kankakee Community College *A*
Kishwaukee College *A*
Knox College *B*
Lake Forest College *B*
Lewis University *B*
Loyola University Chicago *B, M, D*
MacMurray College *B*
McKendree University *B*
Millikin University *B*
Monmouth College *B, T*
North Central College *B*
North Park University *B*
Northeastern Illinois University *B, M*
Northern Illinois University *B, M, D*
Northwestern University *B, M, D*
Olivet Nazarene University *B*
Principia College *B*
Quincy University *B*
Richland Community College *A*
Rockford University *B*
Roosevelt University *B*
Saint Xavier University *B*
Sauk Valley Community College *A*
South Suburban College of Cook
  County *A*
Southern Illinois University
  Carbondale *B, M, D*
Southern Illinois University
  Edwardsville *B*
Southwestern Illinois College *A*
Trinity Christian College *B*
University of Chicago *B, D*
University of Illinois
  Chicago *B, M, D*
  Springfield *B, M*
  Urbana-Champaign *B, M, D*
University of St. Francis *B*
Western Illinois University *B, M*
Wheaton College *B*

Indiana

Anderson University *B*
Ball State University *B, M, T*
Butler University *B*
DePauw University *B*
Earlham College *B*

Franklin College *B*
Grace College *B*
Hanover College *B*
Huntington University *B*
Indiana State University *B, M, T*
Indiana University
  Bloomington *B, M, D*
  East *B*
  Northwest *B*
  Purdue University Fort Wayne *B*
  Purdue University
    Indianapolis *B, M*
  South Bend *B*
  Southeast *B*
Indiana Wesleyan University *A, B*
Manchester University *B*
Marian University *B, T*
Purdue University *B, M, D*
Purdue University
  Calumet *B*
Saint Joseph's College *B*
Saint Mary's College *B*
Taylor University *B*
University of Evansville *B*
University of Indianapolis *B*
University of Notre Dame *B, M, D*
University of Southern Indiana *B*
Valparaiso University *B*
Vincennes University *A*
Wabash College *B*

Iowa

Ashford University *B*
Briar Cliff University *B*
Buena Vista University *B, T*
Central College *B, T*
Coe College *B*
Cornell College *B, T*
Dordt College *B*
Drake University *B*
Grand View University *B*
Grinnell College *B*
Iowa State University *B, M*
Iowa Western Community College *A*
Loras College *B*
Luther College *B*
Morningside College *B*
Mount Mercy University *B*
North Iowa Area Community
  College *A*
Northwestern College *B*
St. Ambrose University *B, T*
Simpson College *B*
University of Iowa *B, M, D, T*
University of Northern Iowa *B*
Wartburg College *B, T*

Kansas

Barton County Community College *A*
Benedictine College *B*
Butler Community College *A*
Central Christian College of Kansas *A*
Coffeyville Community College *A*
Emporia State University *B, T*
Fort Hays State University *B, M*
Friends University *B*
Independence Community College *A*
Kansas State University *B, M*
Labette Community College *A*
Pittsburg State University *B*
Pratt Community College *A*
University of Kansas *B, M, D*
University of St. Mary *B*
Washburn University *B*
Wichita State University *B*

Kentucky

Asbury University *B*
Bellarmine University *B*
Berea College *B*
Brescia University *B*
Campbellsville University *B*
Centre College *B*
Eastern Kentucky University *B, M*

Georgetown College *B, T*
Hopkinsville Community College *A*
Kentucky State University *B*
Kentucky Wesleyan College *B, T*
Morehead State University *B*
Murray State University *B, T*
Northern Kentucky University *B*
Thomas More College *A, B*
Transylvania University *B*
University of Kentucky *B, M, D*
University of Louisville *B, M*
University of the Cumberlands *B*
Western Kentucky University *B*

Louisiana

Centenary College of Louisiana *B*
Dillard University *B*
Grambling State University *B*
Louisiana College *B*
Louisiana State University and
  Agricultural and Mechanical
  College *B, M, D*
Louisiana Tech University *B*
Loyola University New Orleans *B*
McNeese State University *B*
Nicholls State University *B*
Southeastern Louisiana University *B*
Southern University and Agricultural
  and Mechanical College *B*
Tulane University *B, M*
University of Louisiana at Lafayette *B*
University of Louisiana at Monroe *B*
University of New Orleans *B, M, D*
Xavier University of Louisiana *B*

Maine

Bates College *B*
Bowdoin College *B*
Colby College *B*
College of the Atlantic *B, M*
Saint Joseph's College of Maine *B*
University of Maine *B*
University of Maine
  Farmington *B*
  Presque Isle *B*
University of New England *B*
University of Southern Maine *B*

Maryland

Allegany College of Maryland *A*
Coppin State University *B*
Frederick Community College *A*
Frostburg State University *B*
Goucher College *B*
Harford Community College *A*
Hood College *B*
Howard Community College *A*
Johns Hopkins University *B, M, D*
Loyola University Maryland *B*
McDaniel College *B*
Morgan State University *B*
Mount St. Mary's University *B*
Notre Dame of Maryland
  University *B*
St. Mary's College of Maryland *B*
Salisbury University *B*
Towson University *B*
United States Naval Academy *B*
University of Baltimore *B*
University of Maryland
  Baltimore County *B*
  College Park *B, M, D*
  University College *B*
Washington Adventist University *B*
Washington College *B*

Massachusetts

American International College *B*
Amherst College *B*
Anna Maria College *B*
Assumption College *B*
Bard College at Simon's Rock *B*
Boston College *B, M, D*
Boston University *B, M, D*

Brandeis University *B, M, D*
Bridgewater State University *B*
Clark University *B*
College of the Holy Cross *B*
Emmanuel College *B*
Endicott College *B*
Fitchburg State University *B*
Framingham State University *B*
Gordon College *B*
Hampshire College *B*
Harvard College *B, M, D*
Massachusetts College of Liberal
  Arts *B*
Massachusetts Institute of
  Technology *B, M, D*
Merrimack College *B*
Mount Holyoke College *B*
Northeastern University *B, M, D*
Pine Manor College *B*
Regis College *B*
Salem State University *B*
Simmons College *B, M*
Smith College *B*
Suffolk University *B, M*
Tufts University *B*
University of Massachusetts
  Amherst *B, M, D*
  Boston *B*
  Dartmouth *B*
  Lowell *B*
Wellesley College *B*
Western New England University *B*
Westfield State University *B*
Wheaton College *B*
Williams College *B*

Michigan

Adrian College *A, B, T*
Albion College *B, T*
Alma College *B, T*
Andrews University *B*
Aquinas College *B, T*
Calvin College *B, T*
Central Michigan University *B, M*
Eastern Michigan University *B*
Ferris State University *B*
Grand Rapids Community College *A*
Grand Valley State University *B*
Hillsdale College *B*
Hope College *B*
Kalamazoo College *B*
Lake Michigan College *A*
Lake Superior State University *B*
Lansing Community College *A*
Madonna University *B*
Marygrove College *B, T*
Michigan State University *B, M, D*
Northern Michigan University *B*
Oakland University *B*
Saginaw Valley State University *B*
University of Detroit Mercy *B*
University of Michigan *B, M, D*
University of Michigan
  Dearborn *B*
  Flint *B, M*
Wayne State University *B, M, D*
Western Michigan University *B, M, D*

Minnesota

Augsburg College *B*
Bemidji State University *B*
Bethel University *B*
Carleton College *B*
College of St. Benedict *B*
Concordia College: Moorhead *B*
Gustavus Adolphus College *B*
Hamline University *B*
Macalester College *B*
Minnesota State University
  Mankato *B, M*
  Moorhead *B*
Minnesota West Community and
  Technical College *A*
Ridgewater College *A*

St. Catherine University *B*
Saint Cloud State University *B*
St. John's University *B*
St. Mary's University of Minnesota *B*
St. Olaf College *B*
Southwest Minnesota State
    University *B*
University of Minnesota
    Duluth *B*
    Morris *B*
    Twin Cities *B, M, D*
University of St. Thomas *B*
Winona State University *B*

Mississippi

Alcorn State University *B*
Belhaven University *B*
Delta State University *B*
East Mississippi Community
    College *A*
Hinds Community College *A*
Jackson State University *B, M*
Millsaps College *B*
Mississippi College *B, M*
Mississippi State University *B, M*
Mississippi University for Women *B*
Mississippi Valley State University *B*
Northeast Mississippi Community
    College *A*
Rust College *B*
Tougaloo College *B*
University of Mississippi *B, M, D*
University of Southern
    Mississippi *B, M*

Missouri

Avila University *B*
Calvary Bible College and Theological
    Seminary *B*
Central Methodist University *B*
Columbia College *B*
Culver-Stockton College *B*
Drury University *B, T*
Evangel University *B*
Lincoln University *B*
Lindenwood University *B*
Missouri Southern State
    University *B, T*
Missouri State University *B*
Missouri Valley College *B*
Missouri Western State
    University *B, T*
Northwest Missouri State
    University *B*
Park University *B*
Rockhurst University *B*
St. Charles Community College *A*
Saint Louis University *B, M, D*
Southeast Missouri State University *B*
Southwest Baptist University *B*
Three Rivers Community College *A*
Truman State University *B*
University of Central Missouri *B*
University of Missouri
    Columbia *B, M, D*
    Kansas City *B, M*
    St. Louis *B, M, D*
Washington University in St.
    Louis *B, M, D*
Webster University *B*
Westminster College *B*
William Jewell College *B*
William Woods University *B*

Montana

Carroll College *B*
Miles Community College *A*
Montana State University *B*
Montana State University
    Billings *B, T*
University of Great Falls *B*
University of Montana *B, M*
University of Montana: Western *B*

Nebraska

Creighton University *B*
Doane College *B*
Hastings College *B*
Nebraska Wesleyan University *B*
University of Nebraska
    Kearney *B, T*
    Lincoln *B, M, D*
    Omaha *B, M*
Wayne State College *B*
Western Nebraska Community
    College *A*

Nevada

University of Nevada
    Las Vegas *B, M*
    Reno *B, M, D*

New Hampshire

Dartmouth College *B*
Franklin Pierce University *B*
Keene State College *B*
New England College *B, M*
Plymouth State University *B*
Rivier University *B*
Saint Anselm College *B, T*
Southern New Hampshire
    University *B*
University of New Hampshire *B, M*
University of New Hampshire at
    Manchester *B*

New Jersey

Bloomfield College *B, T*
Caldwell College *B*
Centenary College *B*
College of New Jersey *B*
Drew University *B*
Fairleigh Dickinson University
    College at Florham *B*
    Metropolitan Campus *B, M*
Felician College *B*
Gloucester County College *A*
Kean University *B, M, T*
Middlesex County College *A*
Monmouth University *B*
Montclair State University *B*
New Jersey City University *B*
Princeton University *B, M, D*
Ramapo College of New Jersey *B*
Richard Stockton College of New
    Jersey *B*
Rider University *B*
Rowan University *B*
Rutgers, The State University of New
    Jersey
    Camden Campus *B*
    New Brunswick/Piscataway
        Campus *B, M, D*
    Newark Campus *B, M*
Saint Peter's University *B*
Salem Community College *A*
Seton Hall University *B*
Thomas Edison State College *B*
William Paterson University of New
    Jersey *B*

New Mexico

Central New Mexico Community
    College *A*
Eastern New Mexico University *B*
New Mexico Highlands
    University *B, M*
New Mexico State University *B, M*
University of New Mexico *B, M, D*

New York

Adelphi University *B*
Alfred University *B*
Bard College *B*
Barnard College *B*
Canisius College *B*

City University of New York
    Baruch College *B*
    Brooklyn College *B, M*
    City College *B*
    College of Staten Island *B*
    Hunter College *B*
    John Jay College of Criminal
        Justice *B*
    Lehman College *B*
    Queens College *B, T*
    Queensborough Community
        College *A*
    York College *B*
Clarkson University *B*
Colgate University *B*
College of New Rochelle *B*
College of Saint Rose *B, M*
Columbia University *B*
Columbia University
    School of General Studies *B*
Cornell University *B, M, D*
Daemen College *B*
Dowling College *B*
Elmira College *B*
Eugene Lang College The New
    School for Liberal Arts *B*
Excelsior College *B*
Fordham University *B, M, D*
Hamilton College *B*
Hartwick College *B*
Hilbert College *B*
Hobart and William Smith Colleges *B*
Hofstra University *B*
Houghton College *B*
Iona College *B*
Ithaca College *B*
Le Moyne College *B*
Long Island University
    LIU Brooklyn *B, M*
    LIU Post *B, M*
Manhattan College *B*
Manhattanville College *B*
Marist College *B*
Marymount Manhattan College *B*
Mercy College *B*
Molloy College *B*
Monroe Community College *A*
Nazareth College *B*
New York Institute of Technology *B*
New York University *B, M, D*
Niagara University *B*
Pace University *B, M*
Pace University: Pleasantville/
    Briarcliff *B, M*
SUNY
    College at Brockport *B*
    College at Buffalo *B, M*
    College at Cortland *B*
    College at Fredonia *B*
    College at Geneseo *B*
    College at New Paltz *B*
    College at Oneonta *B*
    College at Oswego *B*
    College at Plattsburgh *B*
    College at Potsdam *B*
    College at Purchase *B*
    University at Albany *B, M, D*
    University at Binghamton *B, M, D*
    University at Buffalo *B, M, D*
    University at Stony Brook *B, M, D*
Sage Colleges *B*
Saint Bonaventure University *B*
St. Francis College *B*
St. John Fisher College *B*
St. John's University *B, M*
St. Joseph's College New York:
    Suffolk Campus *B*
St. Joseph's College, New York *B*
St. Lawrence University *B*
Siena College *B, T*
Skidmore College *B*
Suffolk County Community College *A*
Syracuse University *B, M, D*
Touro College *B*
Union College *B*

United States Military Academy *B*
University of Rochester *B, M, D*
Utica College *B*
Vassar College *B*
Wagner College *B*
Wells College *B*
Yeshiva University *B*

North Carolina

Appalachian State University *B, M*
Barton College *B*
Bennett College for Women *B*
Campbell University *B*
Catawba College *B*
Davidson College *B*
Duke University *B, M, D*
East Carolina University *B*
Elizabeth City State University *B*
Elon University *B*
Fayetteville State University *B*
Gardner-Webb University *B*
Greensboro College *B*
Guilford College *B*
High Point University *B*
Johnson C. Smith University *B*
Lenoir-Rhyne University *B, T*
Livingstone College *B*
Mars Hill University *B*
Meredith College *B*
Methodist University *A, B*
North Carolina Agricultural and
    Technical State University *B*
North Carolina Central University *B*
North Carolina State University *B*
North Carolina Wesleyan College *B*
Pfeiffer University *B*
Queens University of Charlotte *B*
St. Andrews University *B*
St. Augustine's University *B*
Shaw University *B*
University of North Carolina
    Asheville *B, T*
    Chapel Hill *B, M, D*
    Charlotte *B*
    Greensboro *B, M*
    Pembroke *B*
    Wilmington *B*
Wake Forest University *B*
Western Carolina University *B*
Western Piedmont Community
    College *A*
William Peace University *B*
Wingate University *B*
Winston-Salem State University *B*

North Dakota

Dickinson State University *B*
North Dakota State University *B*
University of Jamestown *B*
University of North Dakota *B*

Ohio

Ashland University *B*
Baldwin Wallace University *B*
Bowling Green State University *B, M*
Capital University *B*
Case Western Reserve
    University *B, M, D*
Cedarville University *B*
Central State University *B*
Cleveland State University *B*
College of Wooster *B*
Denison University *B*
Franciscan University of
    Steubenville *B*
Heidelberg University *B*
Hiram College *B*
John Carroll University *B*
Kent State University *B, M, D*
Kenyon College *B*
Malone University *B*
Marietta College *B*

Miami University
  Middletown *A*
  Oxford *B, M*
Mount Vernon Nazarene University *B*
Muskingum University *B*
Notre Dame College *B, T*
Oberlin College *B*
Ohio Dominican University *B*
Ohio Northern University *B*
Ohio State University
  Columbus Campus *C, B, M, D*
Ohio University *B, M*
Ohio Wesleyan University *B*
Otterbein University *B*
Sinclair Community College *A*
University of Akron *B, M*
University of Cincinnati *C, B, M, D*
University of Dayton *B*
University of Findlay *B*
University of Mount Union *B*
University of Toledo *B, M*
Urbana University *B*
Walsh University *B*
Wilberforce University *B*
Wilmington College *B*
Wittenberg University *B*
Wright State University *B*
Xavier University *A, B*
Youngstown State University *B*

Oklahoma

Cameron University *B*
East Central University *B*
Northeastern State University *B*
Northwestern Oklahoma State
  University *B*
Oklahoma Baptist University *B*
Oklahoma Christian University *B*
Oklahoma City University *B*
Oklahoma State University *B, M*
Oklahoma Wesleyan University *B*
Oral Roberts University *B*
Rose State College *A*
St. Gregory's University *B*
Southeastern Oklahoma State
  University *B*
Southern Nazarene University *B*
Southwestern Oklahoma State
  University *B*
Tulsa Community College *A*
University of Central Oklahoma *B, M*
University of Oklahoma *B, M, D*
University of Science and Arts of
  Oklahoma *B*
University of Tulsa *B*

Oregon

George Fox University *B*
Lewis & Clark College *B*
Linfield College *B, T*
Linn-Benton Community College *A*
Mt. Hood Community College *A*
Oregon State University *B*
Pacific University *B*
Portland State University *B, M*
Reed College *B*
Southern Oregon University *B*
Treasure Valley Community
  College *A*
University of Oregon *B, M, D*
University of Portland *B*
Western Oregon University *B*
Willamette University *B*

Pennsylvania

Albright College *B*
Allegheny College *B*
Alvernia University *B*
Arcadia University *B*
Bloomsburg University of
  Pennsylvania *B*
Bryn Mawr College *B*
Bucknell University *B*
Cabrini College *B*

California University of
  Pennsylvania *B, M*
Carlow University *B*
Carnegie Mellon University *B, D*
Cedar Crest College *B*
Chatham University *B*
Chestnut Hill College *B*
Cheyney University of
  Pennsylvania *B*
Clarion University of Pennsylvania *B*
DeSales University *B, T*
Dickinson College *B*
Drexel University *B*
Duquesne University *B*
East Stroudsburg University of
  Pennsylvania *B, M*
Eastern University *B*
Edinboro University of
  Pennsylvania *B*
Elizabethtown College *B*
Franklin & Marshall College *B*
Gannon University *B*
Geneva College *B, T*
Gettysburg College *B*
Grove City College *B*
Haverford College *B, T*
Holy Family University *B*
Immaculata University *C, A, B*
Indiana University of Pennsylvania *B*
Juniata College *B*
King's College *B*
Kutztown University of
  Pennsylvania *B*
La Roche College *B*
La Salle University *B*
Lafayette College *B*
Lebanon Valley College *B*
Lehigh University *B, M*
Lincoln University *B*
Lock Haven University of
  Pennsylvania *B*
Lycoming College *B*
Mansfield University of
  Pennsylvania *B, T*
Mercyhurst University *B*
Messiah College *B*
Millersville University of
  Pennsylvania *B*
Moravian College *B*
Muhlenberg College *C, B*
Neumann University *B, T*
Penn State
  Abington *B*
  Altoona *B*
  Beaver *B*
  Berks *B*
  Brandywine *B*
  DuBois *B*
  Erie, The Behrend College *B*
  Fayette, The Eberly Campus *B*
  Greater Allegheny *B*
  Harrisburg *B*
  Hazleton *B*
  Lehigh Valley *B*
  Mont Alto *B*
  New Kensington *B*
  Schuylkill *B*
  Shenango *B*
  University Park *B, M, D*
  Wilkes-Barre *B*
  Worthington Scranton *B*
  York *B*
Point Park University *B*
Rosemont College *B*
St. Francis University *B*
Saint Joseph's University *B*
St. Vincent College *B*
Seton Hill University *B*
Shippensburg University of
  Pennsylvania *B*
Slippery Rock University of
  Pennsylvania *B*
Susquehanna University *B*
Swarthmore College *B*
Temple University *B, M, D*

Thiel College *B*
University of Pennsylvania *B, M, D*
University of Pittsburgh *B, M, D*
University of Pittsburgh
  Bradford *B*
  Greensburg *B*
  Johnstown *B*
University of Scranton *B*
Ursinus College *B, T*
Villanova University *B, M*
Washington & Jefferson College *B*
Waynesburg University *B*
West Chester University of
  Pennsylvania *B, T*
Westminster College *B, T*
Widener University *B*
Wilkes University *B*
York College of Pennsylvania *B*

Puerto Rico

Inter American University of Puerto
  Rico
  Metropolitan Campus *B*
  San German Campus *B*
Pontifical Catholic University of
  Puerto Rico *B*
University of Puerto Rico
  Aguadilla *A*
  Mayaguez *B*
  Rio Piedras *B*

Rhode Island

Brown University *B, M, D*
Bryant University *B*
Providence College *B*
Rhode Island College *B*
Roger Williams University *B*
Salve Regina University *B*
University of Rhode Island *B, M*

South Carolina

Benedict College *B*
Charleston Southern University *B*
Citadel *B*
Claflin University *B*
Clemson University *B*
Coastal Carolina University *B*
Coker College *B*
College of Charleston *B, T*
Columbia College *B*
Converse College *B*
Erskine College *B*
Francis Marion University *B*
Furman University *B*
Lander University *B*
Morris College *B*
Newberry College *B*
Presbyterian College *B*
South Carolina State University *B*
University of South Carolina
  Aiken *B*
  Columbia *B, M, D*
  Upstate *B*
Winthrop University *B*
Wofford College *B*

South Dakota

Augustana College *B, T*
Black Hills State University *B*
Northern State University *B*
South Dakota State University *B*
University of Sioux Falls *B*
University of South Dakota *B, M*

Tennessee

Austin Peay State University *B*
Belmont University *B*
Bryan University
  Dayton *B*
Carson-Newman University *B, T*
Cumberland University *B*
East Tennessee State University *B, T*
Fisk University *B*
Jackson State Community College *A*

King University *B, T*
LeMoyne-Owen College *B*
Lee University *B*
Lipscomb University *B*
Maryville College *B, T*
Middle Tennessee State University *B*
Milligan College *B*
Rhodes College *B*
Sewanee: The University of the
  South *B*
Tennessee State University *B*
Tennessee Technological
  University *B*
Tennessee Temple University *B*
Tusculum College *B*
Union University *B, T*
University of Memphis *B, M*
University of Tennessee
  Chattanooga *B*
  Knoxville *B, M, D*
  Martin *B*
Vanderbilt University *B, M, D*

Texas

Abilene Christian University *B*
Angelo State University *B, T*
Austin College *B*
Austin Community College *A*
Baylor University *B, M, D*
Brazosport College *A*
Clarendon College *A*
Coastal Bend College *A*
College of the Mainland *A*
Dallas Baptist University *B, M*
Del Mar College *A*
East Texas Baptist University *B*
El Paso Community College *A*
Frank Phillips College *A*
Galveston College *A*
Hardin-Simmons University *B*
Houston Baptist University *B*
Howard Payne University *B*
Huston-Tillotson University *B*
Lamar University *B, M*
Laredo Community College *A*
LeTourneau University *B*
McMurry University *B*
Midland College *A*
Midwestern State University *B, M*
Northeast Texas Community
  College *A*
Northwest Vista College *A*
Our Lady of the Lake University of
  San Antonio *B*
Palo Alto College *A*
Paris Junior College *A*
Prairie View A&M University *B*
Rice University *B, M, D*
St. Edward's University *B*
St. Mary's University *B, M, T*
St. Philip's College *A*
Sam Houston State University *B, M*
San Jacinto College *A*
Schreiner University *B*
South Plains College *A*
South Texas College *A*
Southern Methodist University *B*
Southwestern University *B, T*
Stephen F. Austin State
  University *B, T*
Sul Ross State University *B, M*
Tarleton State University *B, M, T*
Texarkana College *A*
Texas A&M International
  University *B, M, T*
Texas A&M University *B, M, D*
Texas A&M University
  Commerce *B, M*
  Corpus Christi *B, T*
  Kingsville *B, M, T*
  Texarkana *B*
Texas Christian University *B*
Texas College *B*
Texas Lutheran University *B*
Texas Southern University *B*

Texas State University *B, M, T*
Texas Tech University *B, M, D*
Texas Wesleyan University *B, T*
Texas Woman's University *B, M*
Trinity University *B*
University of Dallas *B, M, D*
University of Houston *B, M, D*
University of Houston
  Clear Lake *B*
  Downtown *B*
University of Mary Hardin-Baylor *B*
University of North Texas *B, M, D*
University of St. Thomas *B*
University of Texas
  Arlington *B, M*
  Austin *B, M, D*
  Brownsville *B*
  Dallas *B, M, D*
  El Paso *B, M*
  Pan American *B*
  Permian Basin *B*
  San Antonio *B, M*
  Tyler *B, M*
University of the Incarnate Word *B*
West Texas A&M University *B, M*
Western Texas College *A*

Utah
Brigham Young University *B*
Salt Lake Community College *A*
Snow College *A*
Southern Utah University *B*
University of Utah *B, M, D, T*
Utah State University *B, M*
Utah Valley University *B*
Weber State University *B*
Westminster College *B*

Vermont
Bennington College *B*
Johnson State College *B*
Marlboro College *B*
Middlebury College *B*
Norwich University *B*
Saint Michael's College *B*
University of Vermont *B*

Virginia
Averett University *B*
Bridgewater College *B*
Christendom College *B*
Christopher Newport University *B*
College of William and Mary *B*
Emory & Henry College *B*
Ferrum College *B*
George Mason University *M, D*
Hampden-Sydney College *B*
Hampton University *B*
Hollins University *B*
James Madison University *B, M*
Liberty University *B*
Longwood University *B*
Lynchburg College *B*
Mary Baldwin College *B*
Marymount University *B*
Norfolk State University *B*
Old Dominion University *B*
Patrick Henry College *B*
Radford University *B*
Randolph College *B*
Randolph-Macon College *B*
Regent University *B, M*
Roanoke College *B, T*
Sweet Briar College *B*
University of Mary Washington *B*
University of Richmond *B*
University of Virginia *B, M, D*
University of Virginia's College at
  Wise *B, T*
Virginia Commonwealth University *B*
Virginia Intermont College *B*
Virginia Military Institute *B*
Virginia Polytechnic Institute and
  State University *B, M*

Virginia State University *B*
Virginia Union University *B*
Virginia Wesleyan College *B*
Washington and Lee University *B*

Washington
Centralia College *A*
Eastern Washington University *B*
Evergreen State College *B*
Gonzaga University *B*
Northwest University *B*
Pacific Lutheran University *B*
Saint Martin's University *B*
Seattle Pacific University *B*
Seattle University *B*
University of Puget Sound *B, T*
University of Washington *B, M, D*
University of Washington Tacoma *B*
Washington State University *B, M, D*
Western Washington University *B, M*
Whitman College *B*
Whitworth University *B*

West Virginia
Alderson-Broaddus University *B*
American Public University
  System *B, M*
Bethany College *B*
Concord University *B*
Davis and Elkins College *B*
Fairmont State University *B*
Marshall University *B, M*
Potomac State College of West
  Virginia University *A*
Shepherd University *B*
University of Charleston *B*
West Liberty University *B*
West Virginia State University *B*
West Virginia University *B, M, D*
West Virginia Wesleyan College *B*
Wheeling Jesuit University *B*

Wisconsin
Alverno College *B*
Beloit College *B*
Cardinal Stritch University *B*
Carroll University *B*
Carthage College *B*
Edgewood College *B*
Lawrence University *B*
Marquette University *B, M*
Ripon College *B*
St. Norbert College *B, T*
University of Wisconsin
  Eau Claire *B*
  Green Bay *B, T*
  La Crosse *B, T*
  Madison *B, M, D*
  Milwaukee *M, D*
  Oshkosh *B*
  Parkside *B, T*
  Platteville *B, T*
  River Falls *B, T*
  Stevens Point *B*
  Superior *B*
  Whitewater *B*

Wyoming
Casper College *A*
Laramie County Community
  College *A*
Northwest College *A*
University of Wyoming *B, M*
Western Wyoming Community
  College *A*

Polymer chemistry

California
California Polytechnic State
  University: San Luis Obispo *M*

Connecticut
University of Connecticut *M, D*

Massachusetts
University of Massachusetts
  Lowell *M, D*

Michigan
University of Michigan *M, D*

Mississippi
East Mississippi Community
  College *A*

North Dakota
North Dakota State University *M, D*

Ohio
University of Akron *B, M, D*

Pennsylvania
Carnegie Mellon University *M*

Wisconsin
University of Wisconsin
  River Falls *B*

Polymer/plastics engineering

Alabama
Auburn University *B, M, D*

Connecticut
Quinebaug Valley Community
  College *A*

Hawaii
University of Hawaii
  Honolulu Community College *A*

Illinois
University of Illinois
  Urbana-Champaign *B, M, D*

Massachusetts
University of Massachusetts
  Amherst *M, D*
  Lowell *B, M, D*

Michigan
University of Michigan *M*

Mississippi
University of Southern
  Mississippi *M, D*

New Jersey
Stevens Institute of Technology *M*

New York
Rochester Institute of Technology *B*

Ohio
Case Western Reserve
  University *B, M, D*
University of Akron *C, B, M, D*

Pennsylvania
Lehigh University *M, D*
Penn State
  Erie, The Behrend College *B*

Tennessee
University of Tennessee
  Knoxville *M, D*

Texas
Trinity Valley Community College *A*

Virginia
Virginia Polytechnic Institute and
  State University *M, D*

Wisconsin
University of Wisconsin
  Stout *B*

Polysomnography

Alabama
Wallace State Community College at
  Hanceville *C*

Arizona
GateWay Community College *C, A*

California
Loma Linda University *C*

Colorado
Pueblo Community College *C*

Florida
Santa Fe College *C*

Georgia
Darton College *A*

Iowa
Mercy College of Health Sciences *A*

Minnesota
Minneapolis Community and
  Technical College *A*

New Jersey
Thomas Edison State College *C, A*

New York
Genesee Community College *C, A*

North Carolina
Lenoir Community College *A*

Pennsylvania
Gannon University *C*

Tennessee
Roane State Community College *C*

Population biology

California
University of California
  Davis *M, D*
  Riverside *D*

Missouri
Washington University in St. Louis *D*

Texas
Texas State University *M*

Portuguese

California
Chabot College *A*
University of California
  Los Angeles *B, M*
  Santa Barbara *B, M*

Connecticut
Yale University *B, M, D*

District of Columbia
George Washington University *B*
Georgetown University *B*

Florida
Florida International University *B*
University of Florida *B*

Illinois

University of Illinois
  Urbana-Champaign *B, M, D*

Indiana

Indiana University
  Bloomington *B, M, D*

Iowa

University of Iowa *B, T*

Louisiana

Tulane University *B, M*

Massachusetts

Smith College *B*
University of Massachusetts
  Amherst *B*
  Dartmouth *B, M, D*

Minnesota

University of Minnesota
  Twin Cities *M*

New Jersey

Princeton University *B, M, D*
Rutgers, The State University of New
  Jersey
  New Brunswick/Piscataway
    Campus *B*
  Newark Campus *B*

New Mexico

University of New Mexico *B, M*

New York

Columbia University
  School of General Studies *B*
United States Military Academy *B*

Ohio

Ohio State University
  Columbus Campus *B*

Rhode Island

Brown University *B, M, D*
Rhode Island College *B*

Texas

University of Texas
  Austin *B, M, D*

Utah

Brigham Young University *B, M*

Wisconsin

University of Wisconsin
  Madison *B, M, D*

Poultry science

Alabama

Auburn University *B, M, D*
Tuskegee University *B, M*
Wallace State Community College at
  Hanceville *C*

Arkansas

National Park Community College *A*
University of Arkansas *B, M, D*

California

Modesto Junior College *A*

Delaware

Delaware State University *B, M*
Delaware Technical Community
  College
  Jack F. Owens Campus *C, A*

Georgia

Abraham Baldwin Agricultural
  College *A*
University of Georgia *B, M, D*

Minnesota

Ridgewater College *C*

Mississippi

East Mississippi Community
  College *A*
Mississippi State University *B*
Northwest Mississippi Community
  College *A*

Missouri

Crowder College *A*

North Carolina

North Carolina State University *B, M*
Wayne Community College *A*

Puerto Rico

Inter American University of Puerto
  Rico
  Barranquitas Campus *C*

South Carolina

Clemson University *M*

Texas

Stephen F. Austin State University *B*
Texas A&M University *B, M, D*

Wisconsin

University of Wisconsin
  Madison *B*

Power/electrical transmission

Alabama

Alabama Southern Community
  College *C*
Lawson State Community College *C*

Arizona

Coconino County Community
  College *C*
GateWay Community College *C, A*

Arkansas

Phillips Community College of the
  University of Arkansas *C*

California

Chabot College *A*
Coastline Community College *C*
College of the Redwoods *C*
Foothill College *C*
Fresno City College *C, A*
Los Angeles Trade and Technical
  College *A*
Orange Coast College *C, A*
San Diego City College *C, A*
San Jose City College *A*

Colorado

Colorado Northwestern Community
  College *C, A*
Ecotech Institute *A*

Florida

Florida State College at
  Jacksonville *C*
Palm Beach State College *C*

Georgia

Augusta Technical College *C*
Chattahoochee Technical College *C*
Savannah Technical College *C, A*

Hawaii

University of Hawaii
  Hawaii Community College *C, A*

Illinois

Illinois Eastern Community Colleges
  Lincoln Trail College *C, A*
Kishwaukee College *C*
Southwestern Illinois College *C, A*

Kansas

Allen County Community College *C*
Highland Community College *C*
Johnson County Community
  College *C, A*
Manhattan Area Technical
  College *C, A*

Louisiana

Delgado Community College *C*
ITI Technical College *C*

Maine

Eastern Maine Community College *A*
Northern Maine Community
  College *A*

Michigan

Lansing Community College *C, A*
Macomb Community College *C*

Minnesota

Fond du Lac Tribal and Community
  College *C, A*
Minnesota West Community and
  Technical College *A*

Mississippi

East Mississippi Community
  College *C*
Mississippi Delta Community
  College *C*
Mississippi Gulf Coast Community
  College *C, A*
Pearl River Community College *A*

Missouri

State Fair Community College *C, A*

Montana

Miles Community College *A*

Nebraska

Metropolitan Community
  College *C, A*

Nevada

Truckee Meadows Community
  College *C, A*

New York

Mohawk Valley Community
  College *C*
SUNY
  College of Technology at Canton *C*

North Carolina

Durham Technical Community
  College *C*
Mayland Community College *C*
Randolph Community College *C*
Richmond Community College *C*
Robeson Community College *C*
Wake Technical Community
  College *C, A*

Ohio

Eastern Gateway Community
  College *A*
Ohio State University
  Agricultural Technical Institute *A*

Oregon

Chemeketa Community College *A*
Clackamas Community College *A*
Linn-Benton Community College *C, A*
Mt. Hood Community College *C, A*
Portland Community College *C, A*
Rogue Community College *C, A*

Pennsylvania

Community College of Allegheny
  County *A*
Delaware County Community
  College *A*
Fortis Institute
  Erie *A*
Thaddeus Stevens College of
  Technology *A*
Triangle Tech
  Pittsburgh *A*

South Carolina

Aiken Technical College *C*

Tennessee

Northeast State Community
  College *A*

Texas

Amarillo College *C, A*
Frank Phillips College *C, A*
Houston Community College
  System *C*
Laredo Community College *A*
Lone Star College System *C, A*
North Lake College *A*
San Jacinto College *C, A*
South Plains College *C, A*
Texas State Technical College
  Waco *C*
Western Texas College *C, A*

Virginia

Tidewater Community College *C*

Washington

Clark College *C*
Clover Park Technical College *C*
Spokane Community College *A*

Wisconsin

College of Menominee Nation *C*
Northeast Wisconsin Technical
  College *C*

Pre-engineering

Alabama

Spring Hill College *B*

Arizona

Dine College *A*
Pima Community College *C*

California

Bakersfield College *A*
College of the Canyons *A*
La Sierra University *C*
Palomar College *A*
San Joaquin Delta College *C, A*

Florida

Palm Beach Atlantic University *A*

Georgia

Darton College *A*
Middle Georgia State College *A*

Indiana

Indiana Wesleyan University *B*

Iowa

Coe College *B*
Simpson College *B*

Kansas

Cowley County Community
  College *A*
Kansas Wesleyan University *B*

Kentucky

Asbury University *B*

Massachusetts

Bard College at Simon's Rock *B*

Michigan

Bay de Noc Community College *A*
Lake Michigan College *A*
Madonna University *B*
Wayne County Community College *A*
West Shore Community College *A*

Minnesota

Alexandria Technical and Community
  College *A*
Anoka-Ramsey Community College *A*
Century College *A*
Inver Hills Community College *A*
Normandale Community College *A*
South Central College *A*

Missouri

Columbia College *A*
St. Charles Community College *A*

Nebraska

Peru State College *B*

New Mexico

Central New Mexico Community
  College *A*

New York

Canisius College *B*
Genesee Community College *A*
Le Moyne College *B*
Yeshiva University *B*

North Carolina

Central Piedmont Community
  College *A*
Cleveland Community College *A*
Craven Community College *A*
Lenoir Community College *A*
Lenoir-Rhyne University *B*

North Dakota

Cankdeska Cikana Community
  College *A*

Ohio

Baldwin Wallace University *B*
Ohio Wesleyan University *B*

Pennsylvania

University of Scranton *B*

Puerto Rico

Inter American University of Puerto
  Rico
  San German Campus *B*

South Carolina

Trident Technical College *C*

Tennessee

Chattanooga State Community
  College *A*

Texas

University of Mary Hardin-Baylor *B*

Utah

Dixie State College *A*
Southern Utah University *A*
Utah Valley University *A*
Weber State University *A*

West Virginia

West Virginia Wesleyan College *B*
Wheeling Jesuit University *B*

Wisconsin

Ripon College *B*

Prechiropractic studies

California

La Sierra University *C*
Pacific Union College *B*

Illinois

McKendree University *B*
Millikin University *B*

Indiana

Bethel College *B*

Iowa

Cornell College *B*

Massachusetts

MCPHS University *B*

Michigan

Hillsdale College *B*
Lake Michigan College *A*

Missouri

Drury University *B*

Nebraska

Concordia University *B*

Ohio

Ashland University *B*

Oregon

Mt. Hood Community College *A*
Treasure Valley Community
  College *A*

Pennsylvania

Keystone College *B*
Luzerne County Community
  College *A*
Mercyhurst University *B*

Utah

Weber State University *B*

Precision production trades, general

Alabama

Shelton State Community
  College *C, A*

Arkansas

College of the Ouachitas *A*

California

Yuba College *C, A*

Connecticut

Naugatuck Valley Community
  College *C*

Illinois

Sauk Valley Community College *A*

Iowa

Southeastern Community
  College *C, A*

Michigan

Grand Rapids Community College *A*
West Shore Community College *C, A*

Minnesota

Anoka Technical College *C*
Ridgewater College *C, A*

Missouri

Metropolitan Community College -
  Kansas City *C, A*
Mineral Area College *A*
Ozarks Technical Community
  College *A*

Nebraska

Central Community College *C, A*

Pennsylvania

Bucks County Community College *A*
Butler County Community College *C*

Texas

South Texas College *C, A*

Predental

Alabama

Auburn University *B*
Calhoun Community College *A*
Faulkner State Community College *A*
Faulkner University *B*
Gadsden State Community College *A*

Arkansas

Ouachita Baptist University *B*
University of the Ozarks *B*

California

Azusa Pacific University *B*
Bakersfield College *A*
California Lutheran University *B*
Chabot College *A*
Chapman University *B*
College of the Siskiyous *A*
Cypress College *A*
El Camino College *A*
Foothill College *A*
Golden West College *A*
Monterey Peninsula College *A*
Mount St. Mary's College *B*
Pacific Union College *B*
Westmont College *B*
Whittier College *B*

Colorado

Adams State University *B*
Otero Junior College *A*

Connecticut

Quinnipiac University *B*
Sacred Heart University *B*

Delaware

University of Delaware *B*

Florida

Barry University *B*
Broward College *A*
Florida Southern College *B*
Florida State University *B*
Indian River State College *A*
Jacksonville University *B*
Miami Dade College *A*
Pensacola State College *A*
University of Central Florida *B*

Georgia

Abraham Baldwin Agricultural
  College *A*
Andrew College *A*
Darton College *A*
Georgia Perimeter College *A*
Mercer University *B*
Middle Georgia State College *A*
Oglethorpe University *B*
Young Harris College *B*

Idaho

Boise State University *B*
Brigham Young University-Idaho *B*
College of Southern Idaho *A*
North Idaho College *A*
Northwest Nazarene University *B*

Illinois

Elmhurst College *B*
Eureka College *B*
Greenville College *B*
Illinois Central College *A*
Kishwaukee College *A*
Lewis and Clark Community
  College *A*
MacMurray College *B*
McKendree University *B*
Millikin University *B*
University of Illinois
  Chicago *B*
University of St. Francis *B*

Indiana

Ball State University *B*
Bethel College *B*
Indiana University
  Purdue University Fort Wayne *B*
Indiana Wesleyan University *B*
Manchester University *B*
Purdue University *B*
Saint Joseph's College *B*
University of Evansville *B*
Vincennes University *A*

Iowa

Clarke University *B*
Coe College *B*
Cornell College *B*
Dordt College *B*
Ellsworth Community College *A*
Iowa Wesleyan College *B*
Marshalltown Community College *A*
Simpson College *B*
University of Iowa *B*
Upper Iowa University *B*

Kansas

Barton County Community College *A*
Coffeyville Community College *A*
McPherson College *B*
Pratt Community College *A*
Seward County Community
  College *A*
Tabor College *B*
Washburn University *B*

Kentucky

Campbellsville University *B*
Eastern Kentucky University *B*
Georgetown College *B*
Midway College *B*

Louisiana

Centenary College of Louisiana *B*
Louisiana College *B*
Loyola University New Orleans *B*

Maine

University of Southern Maine *B*

Maryland

Frostburg State University *B*
Howard Community College *A*
Montgomery College *A*
University of Maryland
 College Park *B*
Washington Adventist University *B*

Massachusetts

American International College *B*
Cape Cod Community College *A*
Eastern Nazarene College *B*
Elms College *B*
MCPHS University *B*
Springfield College *B*
University of Massachusetts
 Amherst *B*
Worcester Polytechnic Institute *B*

Michigan

Adrian College *B*
Calvin College *B*
Cornerstone University *B*
Delta College *A*
Eastern Michigan University *B*
Gogebic Community College *A*
Grand Rapids Community College *A*
Grand Valley State University *B*
Hillsdale College *B*
Kalamazoo College *B*
Lake Michigan College *A*
Madonna University *B*
Northern Michigan University *B*
Siena Heights University *A, B*
University of Detroit Mercy *B*
University of Michigan
 Flint *B*

Minnesota

Gustavus Adolphus College *B*
Hamline University *B*
Minnesota State University
 Mankato *B*
Minnesota West Community and
 Technical College *A*
St. Catherine University *B*
Saint Cloud State University *B*
University of Minnesota
 Twin Cities *B*
University of St. Thomas *B*

Mississippi

Coahoma Community College *A*
Hinds Community College *A*
Holmes Community College *A*
Itawamba Community College *A*
Mississippi Delta Community
 College *A*

Missouri

Drury University *B*
Evangel University *B*
Maryville University of Saint Louis *B*
Missouri Southern State University *B*
Missouri State University *B*
Missouri University of Science and
 Technology *B*
University of Missouri
 Kansas City *B*
Washington University in St. Louis *B*

Montana

University of Great Falls *B*

Nebraska

College of Saint Mary *B*
Concordia University *B*
Hastings College *B*
Midland University *B*
Northeast Community College *A*
Peru State College *B*
University of Nebraska
 Lincoln *B*

Western Nebraska Community
 College *A*
York College *A*

New Hampshire

Rivier University *B*
Saint Anselm College *B*

New Jersey

Rutgers, The State University of New
 Jersey
 Camden Campus *B*
 New Brunswick/Piscataway
 Campus *B*
 Newark Campus *B*
Sussex County Community College *A*

New Mexico

New Mexico Junior College *A*

New York

Alfred University *B*
Colgate University *B*
D'Youville College *B*
Elmira College *B*
Fordham University *B*
Hobart and William Smith Colleges *B*
Hofstra University *B*
Houghton College *B*
Ithaca College *B*
Le Moyne College *B*
Manhattan College *B*
Niagara University *B*
Paul Smith's College *B*
Rochester Institute of Technology *B*
SUNY
 College at Brockport *B*
 University at Albany *B*
 University at Binghamton *B*
St. Thomas Aquinas College *B*
Syracuse University *B*
Touro College *B*
Wagner College *B*
Wells College *B*

North Carolina

Brevard College *B*
Campbell University *B*
Carteret Community College *A*
Chowan University *B*
Elon University *B*
Gardner-Webb University *B*
Lees-McRae College *B*
Livingstone College *B*
Mars Hill University *B*
Methodist University *B*
Mitchell Community College *A*
Sandhills Community College *A*
Wingate University *B*

North Dakota

Dickinson State University *B*
Mayville State University *B*
Valley City State University *B*

Ohio

Ashland University *B*
Baldwin Wallace University *B*
Bowling Green State University *B*
Cedarville University *B*
Defiance College *B*
Heidelberg University *B*
John Carroll University *B*
Kent State University *B*
Kettering College *B*
Muskingum University *B*
Oberlin College *B*
Ohio Northern University *B*
Ohio Wesleyan University *B*
Otterbein University *B*
University of Cincinnati
 Blue Ash College *A*
 Clermont College *A*
University of Dayton *B*

Urbana University *B*
Walsh University *B*
Youngstown State University *B*

Oklahoma

Eastern Oklahoma State College *A*
Northeastern Oklahoma Agricultural
 and Mechanical College *A*
Oklahoma Christian University *B*
Oklahoma City University *B*
Rose State College *A*

Oregon

Corban University *B*
Southern Oregon University *B*
Treasure Valley Community
 College *A*

Pennsylvania

Albright College *B*
Allegheny College *B*
Gettysburg College *B*
Keystone College *B*
King's College *B*
La Salle University *B*
Mansfield University of
 Pennsylvania *B*
Mercyhurst University *B*
Reading Area Community College *A*
St. Vincent College *B*
University of Pittsburgh
 Greensburg *B*
 Johnstown *B*
Villanova University *B*
Waynesburg University *B*
Westminster College *B*
Widener University *B*

Rhode Island

Rhode Island College *B*

South Carolina

Clemson University *B*
Furman University *B*
Limestone College *B*
North Greenville University *B*
Southern Wesleyan University *B*
Spartanburg Community College *A*
Voorhees College *B*

South Dakota

Augustana College *B*

Tennessee

Carson-Newman University *B*
Cumberland University *B*
Hiwassee College *A*
Lincoln Memorial University *B*
Lipscomb University *B*
Maryville College *B*
Tennessee Technological
 University *B*
Tennessee Wesleyan College *B*

Texas

Abilene Christian University *B*
Amarillo College *A*
Angelina College *A*
Austin Community College *A*
Clarendon College *A*
Coastal Bend College *A*
El Paso Community College *A*
Galveston College *A*
Howard College *A*
Laredo Community College *A*
LeTourneau University *B*
Lubbock Christian University *B*
Midwestern State University *B*
Navarro College *A*
Paris Junior College *A*
St. Philip's College *A*
South Plains College *A*
Texas Wesleyan University *B*
Trinity Valley Community College *A*

Tyler Junior College *A*
Weatherford College *A*
Western Texas College *A*

Utah

Snow College *A*
University of Utah *B*
Weber State University *B*

Virginia

Bluefield College *B*
Virginia Wesleyan College *B*

Washington

Everett Community College *A*

West Virginia

Concord University *B*
Potomac State College of West
 Virginia University *A*
University of Charleston *B*
West Virginia Wesleyan College *B*

Wisconsin

Carroll University *B*
Mount Mary University *B*
Ripon College *B*
St. Norbert College *B*
University of Wisconsin
 Oshkosh *B*
 Parkside *B*

Wyoming

Casper College *A*
Eastern Wyoming College *A*
Northwest College *A*
Western Wyoming Community
 College *A*

Prelaw

Alabama

Calhoun Community College *A*
Faulkner University *B*
Gadsden State Community College *A*

Arizona

Eastern Arizona College *A*
Northern Arizona University *B*

Arkansas

Phillips Community College of the
 University of Arkansas *A*
University of the Ozarks *B*

California

Biola University *B*
Butte College *A*
California Lutheran University *B*
California State University
 Dominguez Hills *B*
Chabot College *A*
Claremont McKenna College *B*
College of the Siskiyous *A*
Foothill College *A*
Golden West College *A*
Master's College *B*
Mount St. Mary's College *B*
National University *B*
Notre Dame de Namur University *B*
Pacific Union College *B*
San Diego City College *A*
Vanguard University of Southern
 California *B*
Westmont College *B*
Whittier College *B*

Colorado

Adams State University *B*
Colorado Mountain College *A*
Otero Junior College *A*
Western State Colorado University *B*

Connecticut

Albertus Magnus College *B*
Mitchell College *B*
Post University *B*
Quinnipiac University *B*
Trinity College *B*

Delaware

University of Delaware *B*
Wilmington University *B*

Florida

Barry University *B*
Broward College *A*
Chipola College *A*
Clearwater Christian College *B*
Florida Institute of Technology *B*
Florida Southern College *B*
Florida State University *B*
Indian River State College *A*
Jacksonville University *B*
Miami Dade College *A*
Nova Southeastern University *B*
Palm Beach Atlantic University *B*
Saint Thomas University *B*
University of Miami *B*
Webber International University *B*

Georgia

Abraham Baldwin Agricultural
    College *A*
Andrew College *A*
College of Coastal Georgia *A*
Darton College *A*
Emmanuel College *B*
Middle Georgia State College *A*
Oglethorpe University *B*
Young Harris College *B*

Idaho

College of Southern Idaho *A*
North Idaho College *A*
Northwest Nazarene University *B*

Illinois

Aurora University *B*
Blackburn College *B*
Dominican University *B*
Elmhurst College *B*
Eureka College *B*
Illinois Central College *A*
John Wood Community College *A*
Kishwaukee College *A*
Lake Land College *A*
Lewis and Clark Community
    College *A*
Millikin University *B*
Richland Community College *A*
Saint Xavier University *B*
Southeastern Illinois College *A*
Southwestern Illinois College *A*
Spoon River College *A*
Trinity International University *B*
University of Illinois
    Urbana-Champaign *B*

Indiana

Anderson University *B*
Bethel College *B*
Huntington University *B*
Indiana Institute of Technology *B*
Indiana Wesleyan University *B*
Manchester University *B*
Saint Joseph's College *B*
St. Mary-of-the-Woods College *B*

Iowa

Coe College *B*
Dordt College *B*
Ellsworth Community College *A*
Grand View University *B*
Iowa Central Community College *A*
Iowa Wesleyan College *B*
Iowa Western Community College *A*

Marshalltown Community College *A*
Simpson College *B*
University of Iowa *B*
Upper Iowa University *B*
William Penn University *B*

Kansas

Barton County Community College *A*
Butler Community College *A*
Central Christian College of
    Kansas *A, B*
Coffeyville Community College *A*
Colby Community College *A*
Dodge City Community College *A*
Garden City Community College *A*
Independence Community College *A*
Labette Community College *A*
McPherson College *B*
Pratt Community College *A*
Seward County Community
    College *A*
Tabor College *B*
Washburn University *B*
Wichita State University *B*

Kentucky

Lindsey Wilson College *A, B*
Thomas More College *A*
Union College *B*

Louisiana

Grambling State University *B*
Louisiana College *B*
Xavier University of Louisiana *B*

Maine

College of the Atlantic *B*
University of Southern Maine *B*

Maryland

Anne Arundel Community College *A*
Notre Dame of Maryland
    University *B*
University of Baltimore *B*
University of Maryland
    College Park *B*
Washington Adventist University *B*

Massachusetts

American International College *B*
Babson College *B*
Becker College *B*
Boston College *B*
Eastern Nazarene College *B*
Elms College *B*
Fitchburg State University *B*
Lasell College *B*
Massachusetts College of Liberal
    Arts *B*
Springfield College *B*
Worcester Polytechnic Institute *B*

Michigan

Adrian College *B*
Concordia University *B*
Delta College *A*
Eastern Michigan University *B*
Ferris State University *A*
Gogebic Community College *A*
Grand Rapids Community College *A*
Hillsdale College *B*
Kalamazoo College *B*
Madonna University *B*
Michigan State University *B*
Northern Michigan University *B*
Siena Heights University *B*
University of Detroit Mercy *B*

Minnesota

Gustavus Adolphus College *B*
Minnesota State University
    Mankato *B*
Ridgewater College *A*
St. Catherine University *B*

Saint Cloud State University *B*
University of St. Thomas *B*

Mississippi

Coahoma Community College *A*
Hinds Community College *A*
Itawamba Community College *A*
Mississippi Delta Community
    College *A*
Mississippi Gulf Coast Community
    College *A*

Missouri

Evangel University *B*
Fontbonne University *B*
Missouri University of Science and
    Technology *B*
Three Rivers Community College *A*
University of Missouri
    Kansas City *B*

Montana

University of Montana: Western *B*

Nebraska

Chadron State College *B*
Concordia University *B*
Creighton University *B*
Hastings College *B*
Midland University *B*
Northeast Community College *A*
Peru State College *B*
Union College *A*
Western Nebraska Community
    College *A*

New Hampshire

New England College *B*
Rivier University *B*
Saint Anselm College *B*

New Jersey

Rutgers, The State University of New
    Jersey
    Camden Campus *B*
    New Brunswick/Piscataway
        Campus *B*
    Newark Campus *B*
Warren County Community
    College *A*

New Mexico

Navajo Technical University *A*
New Mexico Junior College *A*

New York

Bard College *B*
City University of New York
    City College *B*
College of New Rochelle *B*
College of Saint Rose *B*
Concordia College *B*
D'Youville College *B*
Dominican College of Blauvelt *B*
Elmira College *B*
Hofstra University *B*
Ithaca College *B*
Keuka College *B*
Le Moyne College *B*
Manhattan College *B*
Niagara University *B*
Rensselaer Polytechnic Institute *B*
Rochester Institute of Technology *B*
SUNY
    College at Oswego *B*
    University at Binghamton *B*
St. Thomas Aquinas College *B*
Syracuse University *B*
Wells College *B*

North Carolina

Campbell University *B*
Catawba College *B*
Chowan University *B*

Elon University *B*
Gardner-Webb University *B*
Lenoir-Rhyne University *B*
Mars Hill University *B*
Methodist University *B*
Mitchell Community College *A*
Pfeiffer University *B*
St. Andrews University *B*
St. Augustine's University *B*
Sandhills Community College *A*
Wingate University *B*

North Dakota

Mayville State University *B*
North Dakota State University *B*
Valley City State University *B*

Ohio

Ashland University *B*
Bowling Green State University *B*
Cedarville University *B*
Defiance College *B*
Heidelberg University *B*
Hiram College *B*
John Carroll University *B*
Lake Erie College *B*
Muskingum University *B*
Oberlin College *B*
Ohio Wesleyan University *B*
Otterbein University *B*
University of Cincinnati
    Blue Ash College *A*
    Clermont College *A*
University of Dayton *B*
University of Findlay *B*
Urbana University *B*
Wilmington College *B*
Youngstown State University *B*

Oklahoma

Carl Albert State College *A*
Connors State College *A*
Eastern Oklahoma State College *A*
Langston University *B*
Northern Oklahoma College *A*
Northwestern Oklahoma State
    University *B*
Oklahoma Christian University *B*
Oklahoma City Community
    College *A*
Oklahoma City University *B*
Southern Nazarene University *B*
University of Tulsa *B*

Oregon

Corban University *B*
Mt. Hood Community College *A*
Southern Oregon University *B*

Pennsylvania

Albright College *B*
Allegheny College *B*
Chatham University *B*
Dickinson College *B*
Gettysburg College *B*
Immaculata University *A*
La Salle University *B*
Mansfield University of
    Pennsylvania *B*
Philadelphia University *B*
Reading Area Community College *A*
Seton Hill University *B*
University of Pittsburgh
    Johnstown *B*
Waynesburg University *B*
Westminster College *B*
Widener University *B*

Puerto Rico

Pontifical Catholic University of
    Puerto Rico *B*
University of Puerto Rico
    Rio Piedras *B*

Rhode Island

Bryant University *B*
Rhode Island College *B*

South Carolina

Furman University *B*
Limestone College *B*
North Greenville University *B*

South Dakota

Dakota Wesleyan University *B*
National American University
   Rapid City *B*

Tennessee

Cumberland University *B*
Hiwassee College *A*
Jackson State Community College *A*
Lincoln Memorial University *B*
Lipscomb University *B*
Tennessee Temple University *B*
Tennessee Wesleyan College *B*
Tusculum College *B*
Victory University *B*

Texas

Abilene Christian University *B*
Amarillo College *A*
Clarendon College *A*
Coastal Bend College *A*
Concordia University Texas *B*
Del Mar College *A*
Galveston College *A*
Howard Payne University *B*
Kilgore College *A*
LeTourneau University *B*
Lubbock Christian University *B*
Midwestern State University *B*
Northwest Vista College *A*
Paris Junior College *A*
St. Philip's College *A*
Texas Wesleyan University *B*
Trinity Valley Community College *A*
University of Texas
   Pan American *B*
Wayland Baptist University *B*
West Texas A&M University *B*
Western Texas College *A*

Utah

Snow College *A*
University of Utah *B*
Utah State University *B*
Weber State University *B*

Vermont

Bennington College *B*
Marlboro College *B*

Virginia

Averett University *B*
Bluefield College *B*
Emory & Henry College *B*
Hampton University *B*
Mountain Empire Community
   College *A*

Washington

Everett Community College *A*
Highline Community College *A*
Seattle Pacific University *B*
Spokane Community College *A*

West Virginia

Concord University *B*
Potomac State College of West
   Virginia University *A*
West Virginia Wesleyan College *B*

Wisconsin

Cardinal Stritch University *B*
Concordia University Wisconsin *B*
Mount Mary University *B*

Ripon College *B*
St. Norbert College *B*
University of Wisconsin
   Oshkosh *B*
   Parkside *B*
   Superior *B*
   Whitewater *B*

Wyoming

Casper College *A*
Central Wyoming College *A*
Laramie County Community
   College *A*
Western Wyoming Community
   College *A*

Premedicine

Alabama

Auburn University *B*
Calhoun Community College *A*
Faulkner State Community College *A*
Faulkner University *B*
Gadsden State Community College *A*
Samford University *B*

Arizona

Eastern Arizona College *A*
Phoenix College *A*

Arkansas

Ouachita Baptist University *B*
University of Arkansas *B*
University of the Ozarks *B*

California

Azusa Pacific University *B*
Bakersfield College *A*
California Lutheran University *B*
California State University
   San Bernardino *B*
Chabot College *A*
Chapman University *B*
Claremont McKenna College *B*
College of the Siskiyous *A*
Cypress College *A*
El Camino College *A*
Foothill College *A*
Fresno Pacific University *B*
Golden West College *A*
Master's College *B*
Monterey Peninsula College *A*
Mount St. Mary's College *B*
Notre Dame de Namur University *B*
Pacific Union College *B*
Vanguard University of Southern
   California *B*
Westmont College *B*
Whittier College *B*

Colorado

Adams State University *B*
Otero Junior College *A*

Connecticut

Albertus Magnus College *B*
Quinnipiac University *B*
Sacred Heart University *B*
Trinity College *B*

Delaware

University of Delaware *B*

Florida

Barry University *B*
Broward College *A*
Clearwater Christian College *B*
Florida Southern College *B*
Florida State University *B*
Indian River State College *A*
Jacksonville University *B*
Miami Dade College *A*
Nova Southeastern University *B*

Palm Beach State College *A*
Pensacola State College *A*
Saint Thomas University *B*
Southeastern University *B*
University of Central Florida *B*
University of Miami *B*

Georgia

Abraham Baldwin Agricultural
   College *A*
Andrew College *A*
Darton College *A*
Emmanuel College *B*
Georgia Highlands College *A*
Georgia Perimeter College *A*
Mercer University *B*
Middle Georgia State College *A*
Oglethorpe University *B*
Young Harris College *B*

Hawaii

Hawaii Pacific University *B*

Idaho

Boise State University *B*
Brigham Young University-Idaho *B*
College of Southern Idaho *A*
North Idaho College *A*
Northwest Nazarene University *B*

Illinois

Augustana College *B*
Dominican University *B*
Elmhurst College *B*
Eureka College *B*
Greenville College *B*
Illinois Central College *A*
Kishwaukee College *A*
Lake Land College *A*
Lewis and Clark Community
   College *A*
MacMurray College *B*
McKendree University *B*
Millikin University *B*
Northwestern University *B*
Saint Xavier University *B*
Sauk Valley Community College *A*
Southwestern Illinois College *A*
Trinity International University *B*
University of St. Francis *B*

Indiana

Ball State University *B*
Bethel College *B*
Earlham College *B*
Huntington University *B*
Indiana University
   Purdue University Fort Wayne *B*
Indiana Wesleyan University *B*
Manchester University *B*
Purdue University *B*
Saint Joseph's College *B*
Trine University *B*
University of Evansville *B*
University of Notre Dame *B*
Vincennes University *A*

Iowa

Clarke University *B*
Coe College *B*
Cornell College *B*
Dordt College *B*
Ellsworth Community College *A*
Grand View University *B*
Iowa Central Community College *A*
Iowa State University *B*
Iowa Wesleyan College *B*
Iowa Western Community College *A*
Maharishi University of
   Management *B*
Marshalltown Community College *A*
Mercy College of Health Sciences *B*
Simpson College *B*

University of Iowa *B*
Upper Iowa University *B*

Kansas

Barton County Community College *A*
Butler Community College *A*
Coffeyville Community College *A*
Cowley County Community
   College *A*
Dodge City Community College *A*
Garden City Community College *A*
McPherson College *B*
Pratt Community College *A*
Seward County Community
   College *A*
Tabor College *B*
Washburn University *B*

Kentucky

Campbellsville University *B*
Eastern Kentucky University *B*
Midway College *B*

Louisiana

Centenary College of Louisiana *B*
Louisiana College *B*
Loyola University New Orleans *B*
Our Lady of the Lake College *B*
Xavier University of Louisiana *B*

Maine

University of Southern Maine *B*

Maryland

Frostburg State University *B*
Howard Community College *A*
Montgomery College *A*
Prince George's Community
   College *A*
Washington Adventist University *B*

Massachusetts

American International College *B*
Bard College at Simon's Rock *B*
Eastern Nazarene College *B*
Elms College *B*
MCPHS University *B*
Massachusetts College of Liberal
   Arts *B*
Springfield Technical Community
   College *A*
University of Massachusetts
   Amherst *B*
Worcester Polytechnic Institute *B*

Michigan

Adrian College *B*
Calvin College *B*
Concordia University *B*
Cornerstone University *B*
Delta College *A*
Eastern Michigan University *B*
Gogebic Community College *A*
Grand Rapids Community College *A*
Grand Valley State University *B*
Hillsdale College *B*
Kalamazoo College *B*
Lake Michigan College *A*
Lansing Community College *A*
Madonna University *B*
Michigan State University *B*
Northern Michigan University *B*
Siena Heights University *B*
University of Detroit Mercy *B*
University of Michigan
   Flint *B*
Washtenaw Community College *A*

Minnesota

Gustavus Adolphus College *B*
Hamline University *B*
Minnesota State University
   Mankato *B*

Minnesota West Community and
    Technical College *A*
St. Catherine University *B*
Saint Cloud State University *B*
University of Minnesota
    Twin Cities *B*

Mississippi

Coahoma Community College *A*
Hinds Community College *A*
Holmes Community College *A*
Itawamba Community College *A*
Northeast Mississippi Community
    College *A*

Missouri

Avila University *B*
Drury University *B*
Evangel University *B*
Missouri Southern State University *B*
Missouri State University *B*
Missouri University of Science and
    Technology *B*
Three Rivers Community College *A*
University of Missouri
    Columbia *B*
    Kansas City *B*
Washington University in St. Louis *B*

Montana

Little Big Horn College *A*
University of Great Falls *B*

Nebraska

College of Saint Mary *B*
Concordia University *B*
Hastings College *B*
Midland University *B*
Northeast Community College *A*
Peru State College *B*
University of Nebraska
    Lincoln *B*
Western Nebraska Community
    College *A*
York College *A*

Nevada

Sierra Nevada College *B*

New Hampshire

New England College *B*
Rivier University *B*
Saint Anselm College *B*

New Jersey

Essex County College *A*
Rutgers, The State University of New
    Jersey
    Camden Campus *B*
    New Brunswick/Piscataway
        Campus *B*
    Newark Campus *B*
Sussex County Community College *A*

New Mexico

New Mexico Junior College *A*
San Juan College *A*

New York

Alfred University *B*
Bard College *B*
City University of New York
    City College *B*
Colgate University *B*
Columbia University
    School of General Studies *B*
Concordia College *B*
D'Youville College *B*
Elmira College *B*
Fordham University *B*
Hobart and William Smith Colleges *B*
Hofstra University *B*
Houghton College *B*
Ithaca College *B*

Le Moyne College *B*
Manhattan College *B*
Niagara College *B*
Paul Smith's College *B*
Rensselaer Polytechnic Institute *B*
Rochester Institute of Technology *B*
SUNY
    College at Brockport *B*
    University at Albany *B*
    University at Binghamton *B*
St. Thomas Aquinas College *B*
Syracuse University *B*
Touro College *B*
Wagner College *B*
Wells College *B*

North Carolina

Brevard College *B*
Campbell University *B*
Carteret Community College *A*
Chowan University *B*
Elon University *B*
Gardner-Webb University *B*
Lees-McRae College *B*
Lenoir-Rhyne University *B*
Mars Hill University *B*
Methodist University *B*
Mitchell Community College *A*
Pfeiffer University *B*
St. Andrews University *B*
St. Augustine's University *B*
Sandhills Community College *A*
Wingate University *B*

North Dakota

Dakota College at Bottineau *A*
Dickinson State University *B*
Mayville State University *B*
Valley City State University *B*

Ohio

Ashland University *B*
Baldwin Wallace University *B*
Bluffton University *B*
Bowling Green State University *B*
Cedarville University *B*
Defiance College *B*
Heidelberg University *B*
John Carroll University *B*
Kent State University *B*
Kettering College *B*
Miami University
    Oxford *B*
Muskingum University *B*
Oberlin College *B*
Ohio Northern University *B*
Ohio Wesleyan University *B*
Otterbein University *B*
University of Akron *B*
University of Cincinnati
    Blue Ash College *A*
    Clermont College *A*
University of Dayton *B*
Urbana University *B*
Walsh University *B*
Youngstown State University *B*

Oklahoma

Carl Albert State College *A*
Connors State College *A*
Eastern Oklahoma State College *A*
Northeastern Oklahoma Agricultural
    and Mechanical College *A*
Northern Oklahoma College *A*
Oklahoma Christian University *B*
Oklahoma City University *B*
Rose State College *A*

Oregon

Central Oregon Community
    College *A*
Concordia University *B*
Corban University *B*
Southern Oregon University *B*

Treasure Valley Community
    College *A*

Pennsylvania

Albright College *B*
Allegheny College *B*
Gettysburg College *B*
Immaculata University *B*
Keystone College *B*
King's College *B*
La Salle University *B*
Mansfield University of
    Pennsylvania *B*
Mercyhurst University *B*
Penn State
    Abington *C, B*
    Altoona *C, B*
    Beaver *C, B*
    Berks *C, B*
    Brandywine *C, B*
    DuBois *C, B*
    Fayette, The Eberly Campus *C, B*
    Greater Allegheny *C, B*
    Harrisburg *C, B*
    Hazleton *C, B*
    Lehigh Valley *C, B*
    Mont Alto *C, B*
    New Kensington *C, B*
    Schuylkill *C, B*
    Shenango *C, B*
    University Park *C, B*
    Wilkes-Barre *C, B*
    Worthington Scranton *C, B*
    York *C, B*
Philadelphia University *B*
Reading Area Community College *A*
St. Vincent College *B*
University of Pittsburgh
    Greensburg *B*
    Johnstown *B*
Villanova University *B*
Waynesburg University *B*
West Chester University of
    Pennsylvania *B*
Westminster College *B*
Widener University *B*

Puerto Rico

Caribbean University *B*
Pontifical Catholic University of
    Puerto Rico *B*
University of Puerto Rico
    Mayaguez *B*
    Ponce *A*

Rhode Island

Rhode Island College *B*

South Carolina

Bob Jones University *B*
Clemson University *B*
Furman University *B*
Limestone College *B*
North Greenville University *B*
Southern Wesleyan University *B*
Voorhees College *B*

South Dakota

Augustana College *B*

Tennessee

Bethel University *B*
Carson-Newman University *B*
Cumberland University *B*
Hiwassee College *A*
Jackson State Community College *A*
Lincoln Memorial University *B*
Lipscomb University *B*
Maryville College *B*
Tennessee Technological
    University *B*
Tennessee Temple University *B*
Tennessee Wesleyan College *B*
Tusculum College *B*

Texas

Abilene Christian University *B*
Amarillo College *A*
Angelina College *A*
Austin Community College *A*
Central Texas College *A*
Clarendon College *A*
Coastal Bend College *A*
El Paso Community College *A*
Galveston College *A*
Hill College *A*
Howard College *A*
Laredo Community College *A*
LeTourneau University *B*
Lubbock Christian University *B*
Midland College *A*
Midwestern State University *B*
Navarro College *A*
Paris Junior College *A*
St. Philip's College *A*
South Plains College *A*
Trinity Valley Community College *A*
Tyler Junior College *A*
Weatherford College *A*
Western Texas College *A*

Utah

Snow College *A*
University of Utah *B*
Weber State University *B*

Vermont

Bennington College *B*
Johnson State College *B*

Virginia

Averett University *B*
Bluefield College *B*
Jefferson College of Health
    Sciences *B*
Virginia Intermont College *B*
Virginia Wesleyan College *B*

Washington

Everett Community College *A*
Northwest University *B*
South Seattle Community College *A*
Washington State University *B*

West Virginia

Concord University *B*
Potomac State College of West
    Virginia University *A*
University of Charleston *B*
West Virginia Wesleyan College *B*

Wisconsin

Carroll University *B*
Mount Mary University *B*
Ripon College *B*
St. Norbert College *B*
University of Wisconsin
    Madison *B*
    Milwaukee *B*
    Oshkosh *B*
    Parkside *B*

Wyoming

Casper College *A*
Eastern Wyoming College *A*
Northwest College *A*
Western Wyoming Community
    College *A*

Preministerial studies

Arkansas

Ecclesia College *B*

California

Epic Bible College *C, A, B*
Point Loma Nazarene University *B*

Florida

Southeastern University *B*
Trinity College of Florida *B*

Georgia

Wesleyan College *B*

Illinois

Elmhurst College *B*
Trinity International University *B*

Indiana

Bethel College *B*
Manchester University *B*

Iowa

Simpson College *B*

Massachusetts

Eastern Nazarene College *B*

Michigan

Adrian College *B*
Concordia University *B*
Hillsdale College *B*
Kuyper College *B*

Minnesota

Martin Luther College *C, B*
St. John's University *B*
University of Northwestern - St.
   Paul *B*
University of St. Thomas *B, D*

Nebraska

Concordia University *B*

New York

Houghton College *B*
Nyack College *B*
Roberts Wesleyan College *B*

North Carolina

Mid-Atlantic Christian University *B*
Southeastern Baptist Theological
   Seminary *C, A, B, M*

Ohio

Ohio Wesleyan University *B*

Oklahoma

Oral Roberts University *B*

Oregon

Corban University *B*
Warner Pacific College *B*

Pennsylvania

Baptist Bible College of
   Pennsylvania *B*
Gettysburg College *B*

South Carolina

Columbia International University *B*

Tennessee

Hiwassee College *A*
Lee University *B*
Martin Methodist College *B*
Tennessee Wesleyan College *B*
Victory University *C, A, B*

Texas

College of Biblical Studies-Houston *B*
Hardin-Simmons University *B*
Texas Lutheran University *B*
University of Dallas *B*

Virginia

Bluefield College *B*
Eastern Mennonite University *C, A, B*
Shenandoah University *C*

Wisconsin

Concordia University Wisconsin *B*

Prenursing

Alabama

Auburn University *B*
Calhoun Community College *A*
Faulkner State Community College *A*
Faulkner University *B*
Gadsden State Community College *A*

Alaska

University of Alaska
   Fairbanks *C*

Arkansas

Ouachita Baptist University *B*

California

California State University
   Channel Islands *B*
   East Bay *B*
   Fresno *B*
   Fullerton *B*
   Sacramento *B, M*
College of the Siskiyous *A*
Fullerton College *A*
National University *A, B*
Notre Dame de Namur University *B*
Southwestern College *A*
Westmont College *B*

Colorado

Adams State University *B*
Colorado Mountain College *A*

Delaware

Delaware State University *B*

Florida

Broward College *A*
Jacksonville University *B*
Pensacola State College *A*

Georgia

Andrew College *A*
Berry College *B*
East Georgia State College *A*
Emmanuel College *A*
Georgia Highlands College *A*
Georgia Military College *A*
Mercer University *B*
Middle Georgia State College *A*
Reinhardt University *A*
Young Harris College *B*

Idaho

College of Idaho *B*

Illinois

Eureka College *B*
Greenville College *B*
Kishwaukee College *A*
Lewis and Clark Community
   College *A*
Lincoln Christian University *A*
Trinity International University *A*

Indiana

Ancilla College *A*

Iowa

Cornell College *B*
Marshalltown Community College *A*
Simpson College *B*
University of Iowa *B*

Kansas

Barton County Community College *A*
Coffeyville Community College *A*

Cowley County Community
   College *A*
Donnelly College *A*
Garden City Community College *A*
Seward County Community
   College *A*
Tabor College *A*

Kentucky

Georgetown College *B*

Maryland

Carroll Community College *A*
Frederick Community College *A*
Frostburg State University *B*

Massachusetts

Anna Maria College *B*
Cape Cod Community College *A*
Eastern Nazarene College *B*
Roxbury Community College *A*

Michigan

Delta College *A*
Gogebic Community College *A*
Hillsdale College *B*
Kuyper College *B*
Madonna University *B*
Siena Heights University *B*
Southwestern Michigan College *A*
University of Michigan
   Flint *B*

Minnesota

Itasca Community College *A*
Minnesota West Community and
   Technical College *A*
University of Northwestern - St.
   Paul *B*

Mississippi

Coahoma Community College *A*
East Mississippi Community
   College *A*

Missouri

Drury University *B*
Missouri Baptist University *A*
University of Missouri
   Kansas City *B*

Montana

Blackfeet Community College *A*
Little Big Horn College *A*
Miles Community College *A*

Nebraska

Concordia University *B*
Northeast Community College *A*
Peru State College *B*
Western Nebraska Community
   College *A*

Nevada

Sierra Nevada College *B*

New Hampshire

Manchester Community College *A*

New Jersey

Passaic County Community College *A*

New Mexico

New Mexico State University
   Carlsbad *A*

New York

City University of New York
   Kingsborough Community
   College *A*
Houghton College *B*
St. Thomas Aquinas College *B*

North Carolina

Brevard College *B*
Carteret Community College *A*
Chowan University *B*
Cleveland Community College *A*
Lenoir Community College *A*
Methodist University *B*
Sandhills Community College *A*
Southeastern Community College *A*
Wingate University *B*

North Dakota

Cankdeska Cikana Community
   College *A*
Dakota College at Bottineau *A*
Mayville State University *B*
Valley City State University *B*

Ohio

Edison State Community College *A*
Heidelberg University *B*
Notre Dame College *B*
University of Cincinnati
   Clermont College *A*
University of Findlay *B*
University of Rio Grande *B*
Ursuline College *B*
Wright State University *B*

Oklahoma

Eastern Oklahoma State College *A*
Northeastern Oklahoma Agricultural
   and Mechanical College *A*
Oklahoma Christian University *B*
Rose State College *A*

Oregon

Chemeketa Community College *A*
Corban University *B*

Pennsylvania

Allegheny College *B*
Keystone College *A*
Manor College *A*
Widener University *B*

South Carolina

Furman University *B*
Limestone College *B*
Voorhees College *B*

Tennessee

Hiwassee College *A*
Jackson State Community College *A*
Lee University *B*
Lipscomb University *B*
Maryville College *B*
Tennessee Wesleyan College *B*

Texas

Baylor University *B*
Del Mar College *A*
Hardin-Simmons University *B*
Lubbock Christian University *A, B*
Palo Alto College *A*
Paris Junior College *A*
St. Philip's College *A*
South Plains College *A*
Texas State Technical College
   Harlingen *A*
Trinity Valley Community College *A*
Tyler Junior College *A*
Weatherford College *A*
Western Texas College *A*

Utah

Snow College *A*
University of Utah *B*

Vermont

Lyndon State College *B*

Virginia
Stratford University: Falls Church *A*

Washington
Lake Washington Institute of
Technology *A*
Skagit Valley College *A*
South Seattle Community College *A*
Spokane Falls Community College *A*

West Virginia
Potomac State College of West
Virginia University *A*
West Virginia University *B*

Wisconsin
College of Menominee Nation *A*
Ripon College *B*
St. Norbert College *B*

Wyoming
Eastern Wyoming College *A*
Western Wyoming Community
College *A*

Preoccupational therapy studies

California
Pacific Union College *C*

Connecticut
Sacred Heart University *B*

Illinois
McKendree University *B*
Millikin University *B*

Indiana
Bethel College *B*

Iowa
Iowa Western Community College *A*

Massachusetts
MCPHS University *B*

Michigan
Hillsdale College *B*

Missouri
Drury University *B*

Nebraska
College of Saint Mary *B*
Concordia University *B*

New York
Pace University *B*

Ohio
Ashland University *B*

Pennsylvania
Keystone College *A*
Mercyhurst University *B*

Tennessee
Trevecca Nazarene University *B*

Texas
Lubbock Christian University *B*

West Virginia
Potomac State College of West
Virginia University *A*

Wyoming
Casper College *A*
Northwest College *A*

Preoperative/surgical nursing

California
Sonoma State University *M*

Connecticut
Sacred Heart University *B*

Delaware
Wilmington University *B*

Georgia
Georgia Regents University *B, M*

Illinois
Saint Xavier University *M*
Southern Illinois University
Edwardsville *M*

Kentucky
Eastern Kentucky University *B, M*

Maine
Eastern Maine Community College *A*
Husson University *M*
University of Maine *M*
University of Southern Maine *B*

Massachusetts
Elms College *B*

Michigan
University of Michigan *M*

Minnesota
Minnesota State University
Mankato *B, M*
Winona State University *M*

Nebraska
Clarkson College *B*
Midland University *B*

New Hampshire
Rivier University *B, M*

New York
College of Mount St. Vincent *B*
D'Youville College *B, M*
Roberts Wesleyan College *B*

Ohio
Case Western Reserve University *M*
Miami University
Middletown *B*
Ursuline College *B*

Oregon
Southern Oregon University *B*

Pennsylvania
La Salle University *M*
Mansfield University of
Pennsylvania *B*
Thomas Jefferson University *B, M*
University of Pennsylvania *M*

Puerto Rico
Pontifical Catholic University of
Puerto Rico *M*

Texas
South Plains College *A*
Texas A&M International
University *B*
University of Texas
Health Science Center at
Houston *M, D*

Washington
Gonzaga University *B, M*
Seattle Central Community College *A*

Preoptometry studies

California
Pacific Union College *B*

Illinois
McKendree University *B*
Millikin University *B*

Indiana
Bethel College *B*
University of Evansville *B*

Iowa
Cornell College *B*
Simpson College *B*

Kentucky
Midway College *B*

Maryland
Howard Community College *A*

Massachusetts
MCPHS University *B*

Michigan
Lake Michigan College *A*

Nebraska
Concordia University *B*
Peru State College *B*

New York
Houghton College *B*
Le Moyne College *B*
Pace University *B*
SUNY
University at Binghamton *B*
Wagner College *B*

Ohio
Ashland University *B*
Walsh University *B*

Pennsylvania
Luzerne County Community
College *A*

Texas
Abilene Christian University *B*

Wyoming
Casper College *A*
Northwest College *A*

Prepharmacy

Alabama
Auburn University *B*
Calhoun Community College *A*
Faulkner State Community College *A*
Faulkner University *B*
Gadsden State Community College *A*

Arizona
Eastern Arizona College *A*

Arkansas
Harding University *B*
Ouachita Baptist University *B*
University of the Ozarks *B*

California
Bakersfield College *A*
California Lutheran University *B*
Chabot College *A*

College of the Siskiyous *A*
Cypress College *A*
El Camino College *A*
Foothill College *A*
Golden West College *A*
Monterey Peninsula College *A*
Pacific Union College *B*
University of the Pacific *D*
Westmont College *B*
Whittier College *B*

Colorado
Adams State University *B*
Otero Junior College *A*

Connecticut
Sacred Heart University *B*

Delaware
University of Delaware *B*

Florida
Barry University *B*
Broward College *A*
Florida State University *B*
Indian River State College *A*
Miami Dade College *A*
Pensacola State College *A*
South Florida State College *A*
University of Central Florida *B*
University of Miami *B*

Georgia
Abraham Baldwin Agricultural
College *A*
Andrew College *A*
Darton College *A*
Emmanuel College *A, B*
Georgia Highlands College *A*
Georgia Perimeter College *A*
Gordon College *A*
Mercer University *B*
Middle Georgia State College *A*
Oglethorpe University *B*
Young Harris College *B*

Idaho
Brigham Young University-Idaho *B*
College of Idaho *B*
College of Southern Idaho *A*
College of Western Idaho *A*
North Idaho College *A*
Northwest Nazarene University *B*

Illinois
Dominican University *B*
Elmhurst College *B*
Illinois Central College *A*
Illinois Institute of Technology *B*
John A. Logan College *A*
Kishwaukee College *A*
Lake Land College *A*
Lewis and Clark Community
College *A*
McKendree University *B*
Millikin University *B*
Saint Xavier University *B*
Southwestern Illinois College *A*
University of St. Francis *B*

Indiana
Indiana University
Purdue University Indianapolis *B*
Indiana Wesleyan University *B*
Manchester University *B*
University of Evansville *B*
University of St. Francis *B*
Vincennes University *A*

Iowa
Clarke University *B*
Cornell College *B*
Dordt College *B*
Ellsworth Community College *A*

Grand View University *B*
Iowa Central Community College *A*
Iowa Wesleyan College *B*
Iowa Western Community College *A*
Marshalltown Community College *A*
Simpson College *B*
University of Iowa *B*
Upper Iowa University *B*

Kansas

Barton County Community College *A*
Coffeyville Community College *A*
Cowley County Community
  College *A*
Dodge City Community College *A*
Garden City Community College *A*
McPherson College *B*
Pratt Community College *A*
Seward County Community
  College *A*
Tabor College *B*
Washburn University *B*

Kentucky

Campbellsville University *B*
Eastern Kentucky University *B*
Georgetown College *B*
Midway College *B*

Louisiana

Centenary College of Louisiana *B*
Louisiana College *B*
Xavier University of Louisiana *B*

Maine

Husson University *B*

Maryland

Allegany College of Maryland *A*
Frederick Community College *A*
Frostburg State University *B*
Howard Community College *A*
Montgomery College *A*
Prince George's Community
  College *A*
Washington Adventist University *B*

Massachusetts

Eastern Nazarene College *B*
Quinsigamond Community College *A*

Michigan

Adrian College *B*
Calvin College *B*
Concordia University *B*
Delta College *A*
Eastern Michigan University *B*
Ferris State University *A*
Gogebic Community College *A*
Grand Rapids Community College *A*
Grand Valley State University *B*
Henry Ford Community College *A*
Hillsdale College *B*
Lake Michigan College *A*
Madonna University *A*
Northern Michigan University *B*
Siena Heights University *A*, *B*
University of Michigan
  Flint *B*

Minnesota

Hamline University *B*
Minnesota State University
  Mankato *B*
Minnesota West Community and
  Technical College *A*
St. Catherine University *B*
Saint Cloud State University *B*

Mississippi

Coahoma Community College *A*
Hinds Community College *A*
Holmes Community College *A*
Itawamba Community College *A*

Mississippi Delta Community
  College *A*
Mississippi Gulf Coast Community
  College *A*
Northeast Mississippi Community
  College *A*

Missouri

Drury University *B*
Missouri Southern State University *B*
Missouri State University *B*
Three Rivers Community College *A*
University of Missouri
  Columbia *B*
  Kansas City *B*
Washington University in St. Louis *B*

Nebraska

College of Saint Mary *B*
Concordia University *B*
Midland University *B*
Northeast Community College *A*
Peru State College *B*
University of Nebraska
  Lincoln *B*
Western Nebraska Community
  College *A*

Nevada

Sierra Nevada College *B*

New Jersey

Sussex County Community College *A*

New Mexico

New Mexico Junior College *A*

New York

City University of New York
  City College *B*
D'Youville College *B*
Fordham University *B*
Houghton College *B*
Le Moyne College *B*
Long Island University
  LIU Post *B*
Rochester Institute of Technology *B*
SUNY
  University at Albany *B*
St. Thomas Aquinas College *B*
Touro College *B*

North Carolina

Campbell University *B*
Carteret Community College *A*
Chowan University *B*
Gardner-Webb University *B*
Livingstone College *B*
Mars Hill University *B*
Methodist University *B*
Mitchell Community College *A*
Sandhills Community College *A*
Wingate University *B*

North Dakota

Dakota College at Bottineau *A*
Dickinson State University *B*
Mayville State University *B*
Valley City State University *B*

Ohio

Ashland University *B*
Baldwin Wallace University *B*
Cedarville University *B*
John Carroll University *B*
Kent State University *B*
Muskingum University *B*
Otterbein University *B*
University of Cincinnati
  Blue Ash College *A*
  Clermont College *A*
Walsh University *B*
Youngstown State University *B*

Oklahoma

Carl Albert State College *A*
Eastern Oklahoma State College *A*
Northeastern Oklahoma Agricultural
  and Mechanical College *A*
Northern Oklahoma College *A*
Oklahoma Christian University *B*
Oklahoma City University *B*
Rose State College *A*

Oregon

Central Oregon Community
  College *A*
Corban University *B*
Mt. Hood Community College *A*
Southern Oregon University *B*
Treasure Valley Community
  College *A*

Pennsylvania

Allegheny College *B*
Edinboro University of
  Pennsylvania *B*
Gettysburg College *B*
Keystone College *B*
King's College *B*
Luzerne County Community
  College *A*
Mansfield University of
  Pennsylvania *B*
Mercyhurst University *B*
Reading Area Community College *A*
St. Vincent College *B*
University of Pittsburgh
  Greensburg *B*
Westminster College *B*

South Carolina

Clemson University *B*
Furman University *B*
Limestone College *B*
North Greenville University *B*

South Dakota

Augustana College *B*

Tennessee

Bethel University *B*
Carson-Newman University *B*
Cumberland University *B*
Hiwassee College *A*
Lincoln Memorial University *B*
Lipscomb University *B*
Maryville College *B*
Tennessee Technological
  University *B*
Tennessee Wesleyan College *B*
Tusculum College *B*

Texas

Abilene Christian University *B*
Amarillo College *A*
Angelina College *A*
Austin Community College *A*
Clarendon College *A*
Coastal Bend College *A*
Del Mar College *A*
El Paso Community College *A*
Laredo Community College *A*
LeTourneau University *B*
Lubbock Christian University *B*
Midland College *A*
Midwestern State University *B*
Navarro College *A*
Paris Junior College *A*
St. Philip's College *A*
South Plains College *A*
Texas Southern University *B*
Trinity Valley Community College *A*
Tyler Junior College *A*
University of the Incarnate Word *B*
Weatherford College *A*
Western Texas College *A*

Utah

Snow College *A*
University of Utah *B*
Weber State University *B*

Vermont

Saint Michael's College *B*

Virginia

Bluefield College *B*
Emory & Henry College *B*
Virginia Wesleyan College *B*

Washington

Everett Community College *A*
South Seattle Community College *A*

West Virginia

Concord University *B*
Potomac State College of West
  Virginia University *A*
University of Charleston *B*
West Virginia University *B*
West Virginia Wesleyan College *B*

Wisconsin

Carroll University *B*
Ripon College *B*
St. Norbert College *B*
University of Wisconsin
  Oshkosh *B*

Wyoming

Casper College *A*
Eastern Wyoming College *A*
Laramie County Community
  College *A*
Northwest College *A*
Western Wyoming Community
  College *A*

Prephysical therapy studies

Alabama

Oakwood University *B*

Arkansas

Ouachita Baptist University *B*

California

California Baptist University *B*
La Sierra University *C*
Pacific Union College *C*

Connecticut

Sacred Heart University *B*

Georgia

Darton College *A*
Gordon College *A*
Mercer University *B*

Illinois

McKendree University *B*
Millikin University *B*
University of St. Francis *B*

Indiana

Bethel College *B*

Iowa

Coe College *B*
Cornell College *B*
Iowa Wesleyan College *B*
Iowa Western Community College *A*
Simpson College *B*

Kentucky

University of Kentucky *B*

Massachusetts

MCPHS University *B*
Massachusetts College of Liberal
    Arts *B*
Merrimack College *B*

Michigan

Calvin College *B*
Concordia University *B*
Hillsdale College *B*
Lake Michigan College *A*
Northern Michigan University *B*
University of Michigan
    Flint *B*

Minnesota

St. Mary's University of Minnesota *B*
University of St. Thomas *B*

Missouri

Drury University *B*

Nebraska

Concordia University *B*
Peru State College *B*

New York

Houghton College *B*
Pace University *B*

North Carolina

Gardner-Webb University *B*

Ohio

Ashland University *B*
Muskingum University *B*

Pennsylvania

Keystone College *A, B*
Mercyhurst University *B*

South Dakota

Augustana College *B*

Tennessee

Tennessee Wesleyan College *B*
Trevecca Nazarene University *B*

Texas

Lubbock Christian University *B*

Utah

Weber State University *B*

Virginia

Bluefield College *B*

West Virginia

Pierpont Community and Technical
    College *A*
Potomac State College of West
    Virginia University *A*

Wyoming

Casper College *A*
Northwest College *A*

Preveterinary

Alabama

Auburn University *B*
Calhoun Community College *A*
Faulkner State Community College *A*
Faulkner University *B*
Gadsden State Community College *A*

Arizona

Central Arizona College *A*
University of Arizona *B*

Arkansas

Ouachita Baptist University *B*
University of the Ozarks *B*

California

Bakersfield College *A*
California Lutheran University *B*
Chabot College *A*
Chapman University *B*
College of the Siskiyous *A*
Cypress College *A*
Foothill College *A*
Golden West College *A*
Los Angeles Pierce College *A*
Monterey Peninsula College *A*
Mount St. Mary's College *B*
Pacific Union College *B*
Westmont College *B*
Whittier College *B*

Colorado

Adams State University *B*
Otero Junior College *A*

Connecticut

Quinnipiac University *B*
Sacred Heart University *B*

Delaware

Delaware State University *B*
University of Delaware *B*

Florida

Barry University *B*
Broward College *A*
Florida Southern College *B*
Florida State University *B*
Indian River State College *A*
Jacksonville University *B*
Miami Dade College *A*
Pensacola State College *A*
Saint Thomas University *B*
University of Central Florida *B*

Georgia

Andrew College *A*
Darton College *A*
Georgia Highlands College *A*
Middle Georgia State College *A*
Oglethorpe University *B*
Young Harris College *B*

Idaho

Boise State University *B*
Brigham Young University-Idaho *B*
College of Southern Idaho *A*
North Idaho College *A*
Northwest Nazarene University *B*

Illinois

Elmhurst College *B*
Eureka College *B*
Greenville College *B*
Illinois Central College *A*
Kishwaukee College *A*
Lake Land College *A*
MacMurray College *B*
McKendree University *B*
Millikin University *B*
Southwestern Illinois College *A*
University of Illinois
    Urbana-Champaign *B*
University of St. Francis *B*

Indiana

Bethel College *B*
Indiana University
    Purdue University Fort Wayne *B*
    Purdue University Indianapolis *B*
Indiana Wesleyan University *B*
Manchester University *B*
Saint Joseph's College *B*

University of Evansville *B*
Vincennes University *A*

Iowa

Clarke University *B*
Coe College *B*
Cornell College *B*
Dordt College *B*
Ellsworth Community College *A*
Iowa Central Community College *A*
Iowa State University *B*
Iowa Wesleyan College *B*
Marshalltown Community College *A*
Simpson College *B*
University of Iowa *B*
Upper Iowa University *B*

Kansas

Barton County Community College *A*
Coffeyville Community College *A*
Cowley County Community
    College *A*
Dodge City Community College *A*
Garden City Community College *A*
Kansas State University *B*
McPherson College *B*
Pratt Community College *A*
Seward County Community
    College *A*
Tabor College *B*
Washburn University *B*

Kentucky

Campbellsville University *B*
Georgetown College *B*

Louisiana

Centenary College of Louisiana *B*
Louisiana College *B*
Loyola University New Orleans *B*

Maine

University of Southern Maine *B*

Maryland

Frostburg State University *B*
Howard Community College *A*
University of Maryland
    College Park *B*
Washington Adventist University *B*

Massachusetts

American International College *B*
Becker College *B*
Eastern Nazarene College *B*
Elms College *B*
MCPHS University *B*
University of Massachusetts
    Amherst *B*
Worcester Polytechnic Institute *B*

Michigan

Adrian College *B*
Calvin College *B*
Cornerstone University *B*
Delta College *A*
Eastern Michigan University *B*
Gogebic Community College *A*
Grand Rapids Community College *A*
Grand Valley State University *B*
Hillsdale College *B*
Kalamazoo College *B*
Lake Michigan College *A*
Madonna University *B*
Northern Michigan University *B*
Siena Heights University *A*
University of Michigan
    Flint *B*

Minnesota

Gustavus Adolphus College *B*
Hamline University *B*
Minnesota State University
    Mankato *B*

Minnesota West Community and
    Technical College *A*
St. Catherine University *B*
Saint Cloud State University *B*
University of Minnesota
    Crookston *B*
University of St. Thomas *B*

Mississippi

Coahoma Community College *A*
Hinds Community College *A*
Holmes Community College *A*
Itawamba Community College *A*
Mississippi Delta Community
    College *A*
Northeast Mississippi Community
    College *A*

Missouri

Drury University *B*
Evangel University *B*
Missouri Southern State University *B*
Missouri State University *B*
Northwest Missouri State
    University *B*
Three Rivers Community College *A*
University of Missouri
    Columbia *B*
Washington University in St. Louis *B*

Montana

University of Great Falls *B*

Nebraska

College of Saint Mary *B*
Concordia University *B*
Hastings College *B*
Midland University *B*
Northeast Community College *A*
Peru State College *B*
University of Nebraska
    Lincoln *B*
Western Nebraska Community
    College *A*
York College *A*

Nevada

University of Nevada
    Reno *B*

New Hampshire

Rivier University *B*

New York

Alfred University *B*
City University of New York
    City College *B*
Colgate University *B*
D'Youville College *B*
Elmira College *B*
Fordham University *B*
Hobart and William Smith Colleges *B*
Hofstra University *B*
Houghton College *B*
Ithaca College *B*
Le Moyne College *B*
Manhattan College *B*
Niagara University *B*
Paul Smith's College *B*
Rochester Institute of Technology *B*
SUNY
    College at Brockport *B*
    College of Technology at Canton *B*
    University at Albany *B*
    University at Binghamton *B*
St. Thomas Aquinas College *B*
Syracuse University *B*
Touro College *B*
Wagner College *B*
Wells College *B*

North Carolina

Brevard College *B*
Campbell University *B*

Carteret Community College *A*
Chowan University *B*
Gardner-Webb University *B*
Lees-McRae College *B*
Mars Hill University *B*
Methodist University *B*
Mitchell Community College *A*
St. Andrews University *B*
Sandhills Community College *A*
Wingate University *B*

North Dakota
Dakota College at Bottineau *A*
Dickinson State University *B*
Mayville State University *B*
Valley City State University *B*

Ohio
Ashland University *B*
Baldwin Wallace University *B*
Cedarville University *B*
Defiance College *B*
Heidelberg University *B*
John Carroll University *B*
Kent State University *B*
Muskingum University *B*
Oberlin College *B*
Ohio Northern University *B*
Ohio Wesleyan University *B*
Otterbein University *B*
University of Cincinnati
  Blue Ash College *A*
  Clermont College *A*
University of Findlay *B*
University of Rio Grande *A*
Walsh University *B*
Youngstown State University *B*

Oklahoma
Carl Albert State College *A*
Connors State College *A*
Eastern Oklahoma State College *A*
Murray State College *A*
Northeastern Oklahoma Agricultural
  and Mechanical College *A*
Oklahoma Christian University *B*
Oklahoma City University *B*

Oregon
Corban University *B*
Mt. Hood Community College *A*
Southern Oregon University *B*
Treasure Valley Community
  College *A*

Pennsylvania
Albright College *B*
Allegheny College *B*
Gettysburg College *B*
Keystone College *B*
King's College *B*
La Salle University *B*
Manor College *A*
Mansfield University of
  Pennsylvania *B*
Mercyhurst University *B*
Penn State
  Abington *B*
  Altoona *B*
  Beaver *B*
  Berks *B*
  Brandywine *B*
  DuBois *B*
  Fayette, The Eberly Campus *B*
  Greater Allegheny *B*
  Harrisburg *B*
  Hazleton *B*
  Lehigh Valley *B*
  Mont Alto *B*
  New Kensington *B*
  Schuylkill *B*
  Shenango *B*
  University Park *B*
  Wilkes-Barre *B*

Worthington Scranton *B*
York *B*
St. Vincent College *B*
University of Pittsburgh
  Greensburg *B*
  Johnstown *B*
Waynesburg University *B*
Westminster College *B*
Widener University *B*

Rhode Island
Rhode Island College *B*

South Carolina
Clemson University *B*
Furman University *B*
Limestone College *B*

South Dakota
Augustana College *B*

Tennessee
Cumberland University *B*
Hiwassee College *A*
Lincoln Memorial University *B*
Lipscomb University *B*
Maryville College *B*
Tennessee Technological
  University *B*
Tennessee Wesleyan College *B*

Texas
Abilene Christian University *B*
Amarillo College *A*
Angelina College *A*
Austin Community College *A*
Clarendon College *A*
Coastal Bend College *A*
El Paso Community College *A*
Galveston College *A*
Laredo Community College *A*
LeTourneau University *B*
Lubbock Christian University *B*
Midwestern State University *B*
Navarro College *A*
Paris Junior College *A*
South Plains College *A*
Texas A&M University *B*
Trinity Valley Community College *A*
Tyler Junior College *A*
Western Texas College *A*

Utah
Snow College *A*
Weber State University *B*

Virginia
Bluefield College *B*
Emory & Henry College *B*
Virginia Intermont College *B*
Virginia Wesleyan College *B*

Washington
Everett Community College *A*

West Virginia
Concord University *B*
Pierpont Community and Technical
  College *A*
Potomac State College of West
  Virginia University *A*
University of Charleston *B*
West Virginia Wesleyan College *B*

Wisconsin
Carroll University *B*
Mount Mary University *B*
Ripon College *B*
St. Norbert College *B*
University of Wisconsin
  Oshkosh *B*
  Parkside *B*

Wyoming
Casper College *A*
Eastern Wyoming College *A*
Northwest College *A*
Western Wyoming Community
  College *A*

Printing management

Kansas
Pittsburg State University *B*

Kentucky
Somerset Community College *C, A*

Maryland
Montgomery College *C*

Michigan
Ferris State University *B*

Minnesota
University of Minnesota
  Duluth *B*

Missouri
College of the Ozarks *B*

New York
Rochester Institute of
  Technology *B, M*

Washington
Seattle Central Community
  College *C, A*

Wisconsin
Carroll University *B*

Printing press operator

California
City College of San Francisco *C*

Georgia
Albany Technical College *C*

Minnesota
Dunwoody College of
  Technology *C, A*
Hennepin Technical College *A*

Pennsylvania
Commonwealth Technical Institute *C*

West Virginia
Fairmont State University *B*

Wisconsin
Fox Valley Technical College *C*

Printmaking

Arkansas
Phillips Community College of the
  University of Arkansas *C, A*

California
Academy of Art University *C, A, B, M*
California College of the Arts *B, M*
California State University
  East Bay
  Long Beach *B, M*
  Northridge *B, M*
City College of San Francisco *C, A*
College of the Desert *A*
De Anza College *C, A*
Fresno City College *C, A*
Long Beach City College *A*
Monterey Peninsula College *C, A*
Ohlone College *C*

Pasadena City College *C, A*
San Francisco Art Institute *B, M*
Santa Rosa Junior College *C*

Colorado
Adams State University *B*

Connecticut
Capital Community College *C*
University of Hartford *B*

District of Columbia
American University *M*
Corcoran College of Art and
  Design *C*
George Washington University *M*

Florida
Ringling College of Art and Design *B*
University of Miami *B*

Georgia
Savannah College of Art and
  Design *B, M*

Illinois
Bradley University *B*
School of the Art Institute of
  Chicago *B, M*

Indiana
Indiana University
  Purdue University Fort Wayne *B*
Indiana Wesleyan University *B*

Iowa
Drake University *B*
University of Iowa *B, M*

Kansas
University of Kansas *B, M*

Kentucky
Eastern Kentucky University *B*

Maine
College of the Atlantic *B*
Maine College of Art *B*

Maryland
Maryland Institute College of Art *B*

Massachusetts
Massachusetts College of Art and
  Design *B, M*
Montserrat College of Art *B*
Salem State University *B*
School of the Museum of Fine
  Arts *B, M*
University of Massachusetts
  Dartmouth *M*

Michigan
Andrews University *B*
Aquinas College *B*
College for Creative Studies *B*
Ferris State University *B*
Grand Valley State University *B*
Northern Michigan University *B*
University of Michigan *B*

Minnesota
Minneapolis College of Art and
  Design *B*
Saint Cloud State University *B*

Missouri
Columbia College *B*
Kansas City Art Institute *B*
Washington University in St.
  Louis *B, M*

Nevada
Sierra Nevada College *B*

New Hampshire
Plymouth State University *B*

New York
Rochester Institute of
Technology *B, M*
SUNY
College at Buffalo *B*
College at New Paltz *B, M*
College at Purchase *B, M*
Syracuse University *B, M*

North Carolina
East Carolina University *B*
Gardner-Webb University *B*
Methodist University *B*

Ohio
Art Academy of Cincinnati *B*
Bowling Green State University *B*
Cleveland Institute of Art *B*
Ohio University *B, M*
Sinclair Community College *C*
University of Akron *B*
Youngstown State University *B*

Oregon
Mt. Hood Community College *A*
Pacific Northwest College of Art *B*
Portland State University *B*
University of Oregon *B*

Pennsylvania
Arcadia University *B*
Lycoming College *B*
Marywood University *M*
Pennsylvania Academy of the Fine
Arts *C, B, M*
Pennsylvania College of Art and
Design *B*
Seton Hill University *B*
Temple University *B, M*
University of the Arts *B, M*

Puerto Rico
Escuela de Artes Plasticas de Puerto
Rico *B*
Inter American University of Puerto
Rico
San German Campus *M*

Rhode Island
Providence College *B*
Rhode Island School of Design *B, M*

South Dakota
South Dakota State University *C*

Tennessee
Memphis College of Art *B, M*

Texas
Texas Christian University *B*
University of Dallas *B, M*
University of Texas
El Paso *B, M*

Vermont
Bennington College *B*

Washington
Cornish College of the Arts *B*
University of Washington *B, M*
Western Washington University *B*

West Virginia
West Virginia State University *B*

Wisconsin
Milwaukee Institute of Art &
Design *B*

Project management

Alabama
Columbia Southern University *C*

Arizona
University of Phoenix
Phoenix-Hohokam *C*
Southern Arizona *C*

California
College of San Mateo *C*
Golden Gate University *M*
ITT Technical Institute
Lathrop *B*
National City *B*
Oxnard *B*
Rancho Cordova *B*
San Bernardino *B*
Sylmar *B*
Torrance *B*
National University *C*
University of Phoenix
Bay Area *C*
Central Valley *C*
Sacramento Valley *C*
Southern California *C*
University of Redlands *C*
University of San Francisco *M*

Colorado
Aspen University *M*
Regis University *C*
University of Phoenix
Southern Colorado *C*

Connecticut
Charter Oak State College *C*

District of Columbia
University of the Potomac *C*

Florida
Florida Institute of Technology *M*
University of Phoenix
Central Florida *C*
North Florida *C*
South Florida *C*
West Florida *C*

Georgia
Brenau University *M*

Illinois
DeVry University
Chicago *M*
Online *M*
Lewis University *M*
Saint Xavier University *M*

Iowa
Ashford University *B*

Kansas
University of Kansas *M*

Kentucky
Sullivan University *C*

Louisiana
University of Phoenix
Baton Rouge *C*
Lafayette *C*
Louisiana *C*

Maine
Thomas College *M*

Massachusetts
Brandeis University *M*
Lasell College *M*
Wentworth Institute of Technology *B*

Michigan
Wayne County Community College *C*

Minnesota
ITT Technical Institute
Eden Prairie *B*
Inver Hills Community College *C*
Minneapolis College of Art and
Design *B*
Minnesota State University
Moorhead *B*
St. Mary's University of Minnesota *M*
Walden University *M*

Missouri
DeVry University
Kansas City *M*
University of Phoenix
St. Louis *C*

Nebraska
Bellevue University *B, M*

Nevada
University of Phoenix
Las Vegas *C*

New Hampshire
Granite State College *M*

New Jersey
Stevens Institute of Technology *M*

New Mexico
Central New Mexico Community
College *C*
University of Phoenix
New Mexico *C*

New York
City University of New York
CUNY Online *C*
Professional Business College *C*

Ohio
Malone University *B*

Oklahoma
University of Phoenix
Oklahoma City *C*
Tulsa *C*

Pennsylvania
Drexel University *M*
Harrisburg University of Science and
Technology *M*
Lehigh University *M*

Puerto Rico
Turabo University *M*
Universidad del Este *M*

Tennessee
University of Phoenix
Memphis *C*

Texas
Dallas Baptist University *M*
ITT Technical Institute
Arlington *B*
Houston West *B*
Richardson *B*
San Antonio *B*
St. Edward's University *M*
University of Phoenix
Houston Westside *C*

Utah
University of Phoenix
Utah *C*

Vermont
Champlain College *C*

Virginia
DeVry University
Arlington *M*
George Mason University *M*
University of Management and
Technology *M*
University of Phoenix
Northern Virginia *C*
University of the Potomac *C*

Washington
Columbia Basin College *C*
Edmonds Community College *C*
ITT Technical Institute
Everett *B*
Seattle *B*
Spokane *B*
Olympic College *C*
Pierce College *C*

Wisconsin
University of Phoenix
Milwaukee *C*
University of Wisconsin
Platteville *M*

Protective services operations

Florida
Nova Southeastern University *M*

Pennsylvania
Indiana University of Pennsylvania *M*

Psychiatric nursing

Alaska
University of Alaska
Anchorage *M*

California
University of San Diego *M, D*

Florida
Florida International University *M*

Illinois
Southern Illinois University
Edwardsville *M*

Indiana
Indiana University
Purdue University Indianapolis *M*

Iowa
Allen College *M*
University of Iowa *M*

Maine
Husson University *M*
University of Southern Maine *B, M*

Massachusetts
Northeastern University *M*

Michigan
University of Michigan *M*
University of Michigan
Flint *M, D*
Wayne State University *M*

Minnesota
College of St. Scholastica *M*

New Hampshire

Rivier University *M*

New York

City University of New York
 Hunter College *B, M*
Molloy College *M*
New York University *D*
SUNY
 University at Binghamton *D*
 University at Buffalo *M, D*
 University at Stony Brook *M, D*
 Upstate Medical University *M*
Sage Colleges *M*
University of Rochester *M*

Ohio

Case Western Reserve University *M*
University of Toledo *M*

Oregon

Oregon Health & Science
 University *M*

Pennsylvania

University of Pennsylvania *M*
Widener University *M*

Puerto Rico

Pontifical Catholic University of
 Puerto Rico *M*

Tennessee

Vanderbilt University *M*

West Virginia

West Virginia Wesleyan College *M*

Wisconsin

Alverno College *M*

Psychoanalysis

Vermont

Goddard College *M*

Psychology

Alabama

Alabama Agricultural and Mechanical
 University *B*
Alabama State University *B*
Athens State University *B*
Auburn University *B, M, D*
Auburn University at
 Montgomery *B, M*
Birmingham-Southern College *B*
Faulkner University *B*
Gadsden State Community College *A*
Huntingdon College *B*
Jacksonville State University *B, M*
Judson College *B*
Oakwood University *B*
Samford University *B*
Spring Hill College *B*
Talladega College *B*
Troy University *B*
Tuskegee University *B*
University of Alabama *B, M, D*
University of Alabama
 Birmingham *B, M, D*
 Huntsville *B, M*
University of Mobile *B*
University of Montevallo *B*
University of North Alabama *B*
University of South Alabama *B, M*
University of West Alabama *B*

Alaska

Alaska Pacific University *B, D*
University of Alaska
 Anchorage *B, D*
 Fairbanks *B, D*

Arizona

Argosy University
 Online *B*
 Phoenix *B*
Arizona State University *B, D*
Arizona Western College *A*
Central Arizona College *A*
Cochise College *A*
Coconino County Community
 College *A*
Dine College *A*
Eastern Arizona College *A*
Estrella Mountain Community
 College *A*
Grand Canyon University *M*
Northcentral University *B, M, D*
Northern Arizona University *B, M*
Prescott College *B*
South Mountain Community
 College *A*
University of Arizona *B, M, D*

Arkansas

Arkansas State University *B*
Arkansas Tech University *B, M*
Central Baptist College *B*
Harding University *B*
Henderson State University *B*
Hendrix College *B*
John Brown University *B*
Lyon College *B*
Ouachita Baptist University *B*
Philander Smith College *B*
Phillips Community College of the
 University of Arkansas *A*
Southern Arkansas University *B*
University of Arkansas *B, M, D*
University of Arkansas
 Fort Smith *B*
 Little Rock *B*
 Monticello *B*
 Pine Bluff *B*
University of Central Arkansas *B*
University of the Ozarks *B*
Williams Baptist College *B*

California

Allan Hancock College *A*
Alliant International
 University *B, M, D*
American Jewish University *B*
Antioch University
 Los Angeles *M*
 Santa Barbara *M*
Argosy University
 Inland Empire *B*
 Los Angeles *B*
 Orange County *B*
 San Diego *B*
 San Francisco Bay Area *B, M*
Azusa Pacific University *B*
Bakersfield College *A*
Barstow Community College *A*
Berkeley City College *C, A*
Biola University *B, M, D*
Cabrillo College *A*
California Baptist University *B*
California Coast University *A, B, M*
California Lutheran University *B*
California Polytechnic State
 University: San Luis Obispo *B, M*
California State Polytechnic
 University: Pomona *B, M*
California State University
 Bakersfield *B, M*
 Channel Islands *B*
 Chico *B, M*
 Dominguez Hills *B, M*
 East Bay *B*
 Fresno *B, M, D*
 Fullerton *B, M*
 Long Beach *B, M*
 Los Angeles *B, M*
 Monterey Bay *B*

 Northridge *B*
 Sacramento *B, M*
 San Bernardino *B, M*
 San Marcos *B, M*
 Stanislaus *B, M*
Canada College *A*
Cerritos College *A*
Chabot College *A*
Chaffey College *A*
Chapman University *B*
Citrus College *A*
Claremont McKenna College *B*
College of Alameda *A*
College of Marin *A*
College of San Mateo *A*
College of the Canyons *A*
College of the Desert *A*
College of the Siskiyous *A*
Concordia University Irvine *B*
Contra Costa College *A*
Copper Mountain College *A*
Crafton Hills College *C, A*
Cypress College *A*
De Anza College *A*
Diablo Valley College *A*
Dominican University of California *B*
El Camino College *A*
Folsom Lake College *A*
Foothill College *A*
Fresno City College *A*
Fresno Pacific University *B*
Fullerton College *A*
Gavilan College *A*
Glendale Community College *A*
Golden West College *A*
Hartnell College *A*
Holy Names University *B*
Hope International University *B*
Humboldt State University *B, M*
Imperial Valley College *A*
Irvine Valley College *A*
John F. Kennedy University *B, D*
La Sierra University *B*
Lake Tahoe Community College *A*
Lassen Community College *A*
Loma Linda University *D*
Los Angeles City College *A*
Los Angeles Harbor College *A*
Los Angeles Mission College *A*
Los Angeles Southwest College *A*
Los Angeles Valley College *A*
Los Medanos College *A*
Loyola Marymount University *B*
Marymount California University *B*
Mendocino College *A*
Menlo College *B*
Merced College *A*
Mills College *B*
Monterey Peninsula College *A*
Moorpark College *A*
Mount St. Mary's College *B*
National Hispanic University *B*
National University *B, M*
Notre Dame de Namur University *B*
Occidental College *B*
Orange Coast College *A*
Oxnard College *A*
Pacific Union College *B*
Palomar College *C, A*
Pasadena City College *A*
Patten University *B*
Pepperdine University *B, M, D*
Pitzer College *B*
Point Loma Nazarene University *B*
Pomona College *B*
Rio Hondo College *A*
Saddleback College *A*
St. Mary's College of California *B*
San Bernardino Valley College *A*
San Deigo Miramar College
 San Diego Miramar College *A*
San Diego Christian College *B*
San Diego City College *A*
San Diego Mesa College *A*
San Diego State University *B, M*

San Francisco State University *B, M*
San Joaquin Delta College *A*
San Jose City College *A*
San Jose State University *B, M*
Santa Ana College *A*
Santa Barbara City College *A*
Santa Clara University *B*
Santa Rosa Junior College *A*
Santiago Canyon College *A*
Scripps College *B*
Sierra College *A*
Simpson University *B, M*
Skyline College *A*
Solano Community College *A*
Sonoma State University *B, M*
Southwestern College *A*
Stanford University *B, M, D*
Taft College *A*
Touro University Worldwide *B*
University of California
 Berkeley *B, D*
 Davis *B, D*
 Irvine *B, D*
 Los Angeles *B, M, D*
 Merced *B, M, D*
 Riverside *B, M, D*
 San Diego *B, M, D*
 Santa Barbara *B, M, D*
 Santa Cruz *B, D*
University of La Verne *B*
University of Redlands *B*
University of San Diego *B*
University of San Francisco *B*
University of Southern
 California *B, M, D*
University of the Pacific *B, M*
University of the West *B, M*
Vanguard University of Southern
 California *B*
West Hills College: Coalinga *A*
West Hills College: Lemoore *A*
West Los Angeles College *A*
West Valley College *A*
Westmont College *B*
Whittier College *B*
William Jessup University *B*
Woodbury University *B*
Woodland Community College *A*
Yuba College *A*

Colorado

Adams State University *B*
Argosy University
 Denver *B*
Colorado Christian University *B*
Colorado College *B*
Colorado Mesa University *B*
Colorado Mountain College *C*
Colorado State University *B, M, D*
Colorado State University
 Pueblo *B*
Community College of Aurora *A*
Fort Lewis College *B*
Metropolitan State University of
 Denver *B*
Naropa University *B, M*
Otero Junior College *A*
Regis University *B*
University of Colorado
 Boulder *B, M, D*
 Colorado Springs *B, M, D*
 Denver *B, M*
University of Denver *B, M, D*
University of Northern
 Colorado *B, M*
Western State Colorado University *B*

Connecticut

Albertus Magnus College *B*
Central Connecticut State
 University *B, M*
Connecticut College *B, M*
Eastern Connecticut State
 University *B*

Fairfield University *B, M*
Mitchell College *B*
Naugatuck Valley Community
   College *A*
Post University *B*
Quinnipiac University *B*
Sacred Heart University *B*
Southern Connecticut State
   University *B, M*
Trinity College *B*
University of Bridgeport *B*
University of Connecticut *B, M, D*
University of Hartford *B, M*
University of New Haven *B*
University of Saint Joseph *B*
Wesleyan University *B, M*
Western Connecticut State
   University *B*
Yale University *B, M, D*

Delaware

Delaware State University *B*
Goldey-Beacom College *B*
University of Delaware *B, M, D*
Wesley College *B*
Wilmington University *B*

District of Columbia

American University *B, M*
Catholic University of America *B, M*
Gallaudet University *B*
George Washington
   University *B, M, D*
Georgetown University *B, M, D*
Howard University *B, M, D*
Trinity Washington University *B*
University of the District of
   Columbia *B*

Florida

Argosy University
   Sarasota *B*
   Tampa *B*
Ave Maria University *B*
Barry University *B, M*
Beacon College *A, B*
Bethune-Cookman University *B*
Broward College *A*
Carlos Albizu University *B, M, D*
Clearwater Christian College *B*
Daytona State College *A*
Eckerd College *B*
Edward Waters College *B*
Flagler College *B*
Florida Agricultural and Mechanical
   University *B*
Florida Atlantic University *B, M*
Florida Gulf Coast University *B*
Florida Institute of Technology *B*
Florida International
   University *B, M, D*
Florida Memorial University *B*
Florida Southern College *B*
Florida State University *B, M*
Indian River State College *A*
Jacksonville University *B*
Lynn University *B*
Miami Dade College *A*
New College of Florida *B*
Nova Southeastern University *B*
Palm Beach Atlantic University *B*
Palm Beach State College *A*
Pensacola State College *A*
Rollins College *B*
Saint Leo University *B*
Saint Thomas University *B*
South Florida State College *A*
Southeastern University *B*
Stetson University *B*
University of Central Florida *B, M, D*
University of Florida *B, M, D*
University of Miami *B, M, D*
University of North Florida *B, M*
University of South Florida *B, M, D*

University of South Florida
   Saint Petersburg *B, M*
   Sarasota-Manatee *B*
University of Tampa *A, B*
University of West Florida *B, M*
Warner University *A, B*

Georgia

Abraham Baldwin Agricultural
   College *A*
Agnes Scott College *B*
Albany State University *B*
Andrew College *A*
Argosy University
   Atlanta *B*
Armstrong Atlantic State University *B*
Atlanta Metropolitan College *A*
Bainbridge College *A*
Berry College *B*
Brenau University *B, M*
Brewton-Parker College *B*
Clark Atlanta University *B*
College of Coastal Georgia *A, B*
Columbus State University *B*
Covenant College *B*
Dalton State College *A*
Darton College *A*
East Georgia State College *A*
Emmanuel College *B*
Emory University *B, D*
Fort Valley State University *B*
Georgia College and State
   University *B*
Georgia Gwinnett College *B*
Georgia Highlands College *A*
Georgia Military College *A*
Georgia Perimeter College *A*
Georgia Regents University *B, M*
Georgia Southern University *B, M*
Georgia Southwestern State
   University *B*
Georgia State University *B, M, D*
Gordon College *A*
Kennesaw State University *B*
LaGrange College *B*
Life University *C, A*
Mercer University *B*
Middle Georgia State College *A, B*
Morehouse College *B*
Oglethorpe University *B*
Paine College *B*
Piedmont College *B*
Point University *B*
Reinhardt University *B*
Shorter University *B*
South Georgia State College *A*
Southern Polytechnic State
   University *B*
Spelman College *B*
Thomas University *B*
Truett-McConnell College *B*
University of Georgia *B, M, D*
University of North Georgia *A, B*
University of West Georgia *B, M*
Valdosta State University *B, M*
Wesleyan College *B*
Young Harris College *B*

Hawaii

Argosy University
   Hawaii *B*
Brigham Young University-Hawaii *B*
Chaminade University of Honolulu *B*
Hawaii Pacific University *B*
University of Hawaii
   Hilo *B*
   Manoa *B, M, D*
   West Oahu *B*

Idaho

Boise State University *B, T*
Brigham Young University-Idaho *B*
College of Idaho *B*
College of Southern Idaho *A*

College of Western Idaho *A*
Idaho State University *B, M, D*
Lewis-Clark State College *B*
North Idaho College *A*
Northwest Nazarene University *B*
University of Idaho *B, M*

Illinois

Argosy University
   Chicago *B*
   Schaumburg *B*
Augustana College *B*
Aurora University *B*
Benedictine University *B*
Benedictine University at
   Springfield *B*
Blackburn College *B*
Bradley University *B, T*
Chicago State University *B*
Concordia University Chicago *B, M*
DePaul University *B, M*
Dominican University *B*
Eastern Illinois University *B, T*
Elmhurst College *B, T*
Eureka College *B*
Governors State University *B, M*
Greenville College *B*
Hebrew Theological College *B*
Illinois College *B*
Illinois Institute of
   Technology *B, M, D*
Illinois State University *B, M*
Illinois Valley Community College *A*
Illinois Wesleyan University *B*
John A. Logan College *A*
John Wood Community College *A*
Joliet Junior College *A*
Judson University *B*
Kankakee Community College *A*
Kishwaukee College *A*
Knox College *B*
Lake Forest College *B*
Lake Land College *A*
Lewis University *B*
Lincoln Christian University *B*
Lincoln College *A*
Loyola University Chicago *B*
MacMurray College *B*
McKendree University *B*
Millikin University *B*
Monmouth College *B*
National-Louis University *B, M*
North Central College *B*
North Park University *B*
Northeastern Illinois University *B*
Northern Illinois University *B, M, D*
Northwestern University *B, M, D*
Olivet Nazarene University *B, M*
Quincy University *B*
Richland Community College *A*
Rockford University *B*
Roosevelt University *B*
Saint Xavier University *B*
Sauk Valley Community College *A*
South Suburban College of Cook
   County *A*
Southern Illinois University
   Carbondale *B, M, D*
Southern Illinois University
   Edwardsville *B, M*
Southwestern Illinois College *A*
Spoon River College *A*
Trinity Christian College *B*
Trinity International University *B, M*
University of Chicago *B, D*
University of Illinois
   Chicago *B, M, D*
   Springfield *B*
   Urbana-Champaign *B, M, D*
University of St. Francis *B*
Western Illinois University *B, M*
Wheaton College *B, M*

Indiana

Anderson University *B*
Ball State University *B, M, T*
Bethel College *B*
Butler University *B*
Calumet College of St. Joseph *A, B*
DePauw University *B*
Earlham College *B*
Franklin College *B*
Goshen College *B*
Grace College *B*
Hanover College *B*
Holy Cross College *B*
Huntington University *B*
Indiana Institute of Technology *B*
Indiana State University *B, M*
Indiana University
   Bloomington *B, M, D*
   East *B*
   Kokomo *B*
   Northwest *B*
   Purdue University Fort Wayne *A, B*
   Purdue University
     Indianapolis *B, M*
   South Bend *B*
   Southeast *B*
Indiana Wesleyan University *B, T*
Manchester University *B*
Marian University *B, T*
Martin University *B*
Oakland City University *B*
Purdue University *B, M, D*
Purdue University
   Calumet *B*
   North Central *B*
Saint Joseph's College *B*
Saint Mary's College *B*
St. Mary-of-the-Woods College *B*
Taylor University *B*
Trine University *B*
University of Evansville *B*
University of Indianapolis *B*
University of Notre Dame *B, M, D*
University of Southern Indiana *B*
Valparaiso University *B, M*
Vincennes University *A*
Wabash College *B*

Iowa

Ashford University *B*
Briar Cliff University *B*
Buena Vista University *B*
Central College *B*
Clarke University *B, T*
Coe College *B*
Cornell College *B, T*
Dordt College *B*
Drake University *B*
Ellsworth Community College *A*
Graceland University *B*
Grand View University *B*
Grinnell College *B*
Iowa State University *B, M, D*
Iowa Wesleyan College *B*
Iowa Western Community College *A*
Loras College *B, M*
Luther College *B*
Marshalltown Community College *A*
Morningside College *B*
Mount Mercy University *B*
Northwestern College *B, T*
St. Ambrose University *B, T*
Simpson College *B*
University of Dubuque *B*
University of Iowa *B, D, T*
University of Northern Iowa *B, M*
Upper Iowa University *B*
Waldorf College *B*
Wartburg College *B, T*
William Penn University *B*

Kansas

Baker University *B, T*
Barclay College *B*

Barton County Community College *A*
Benedictine College *B*
Bethany College *B, T*
Bethel College *B*
Butler Community College *A*
Central Christian College of
    Kansas *A, B*
Coffeyville Community College *A*
Colby Community College *A*
Cowley County Community
    College *A*
Donnelly College *A*
Emporia State University *B, M, T*
Fort Hays State University *B, M*
Friends University *B*
Garden City Community College *A*
Hutchinson Community College *A*
Independence Community College *A*
Kansas State University *B, M, D*
Kansas Wesleyan University *B*
Labette Community College *A*
McPherson College *B, T*
MidAmerica Nazarene University *B*
Neosho County Community
    College *A*
Newman University *B*
Ottawa University *B*
Pittsburg State University *B, M*
Pratt Community College *A*
Seward County Community
    College *A*
Southwestern College *B*
Sterling College *B*
Tabor College *B*
University of Kansas *B, M, D*
University of St. Mary *B, M*
Washburn University *B, M*
Wichita State University *B, M, D*

Kentucky

Asbury University *B, T*
Bellarmine University *B*
Berea College *B*
Bluegrass Community and Technical
    College *A*
Brescia University *B*
Campbellsville University *B*
Centre College *B*
Eastern Kentucky University *B, M*
Georgetown College *B*
Hopkinsville Community College *A*
Kentucky State University *B*
Kentucky Wesleyan College *B*
Lindsey Wilson College *B*
Mid-Continent University *B*
Midway College *B*
Morehead State University *B, M*
Murray State University *B, M*
Northern Kentucky University *B*
St. Catharine College *B*
Spalding University *B*
Thomas More College *A, B*
Transylvania University *B*
Union College *B, M*
University of Kentucky *B*
University of Louisville *B*
University of Pikeville *B*
University of the Cumberlands *B*
Western Kentucky University *B, M*

Louisiana

Centenary College of Louisiana *B*
Dillard University *B*
Grambling State University *B*
Louisiana College *B*
Louisiana State University
    Alexandria *B*
    Shreveport *B*
Louisiana State University and
    Agricultural and Mechanical
    College *B, M, D*
Louisiana Tech University *B*
Loyola University New Orleans *B*
McNeese State University *B, M*

Nicholls State University *B*
Northwestern State University *B*
Our Lady of the Lake College *B*
Southeastern Louisiana
    University *B, M*
Southern University
    New Orleans *B*
Southern University and Agricultural
    and Mechanical College *B*
Tulane University *B, M, D*
University of Louisiana at
    Lafayette *B, M*
University of Louisiana at
    Monroe *B, M*
University of New Orleans *B, M*
Xavier University of Louisiana *B*

Maine

Bates College *B*
Bowdoin College *B*
Colby College *B*
College of the Atlantic *B, M*
Husson University *B*
Saint Joseph's College of Maine *B*
Thomas College *B*
University of Maine *B, M, D*
University of Maine
    Farmington *B*
    Fort Kent *B*
    Machias *B*
    Presque Isle *B*
University of New England *B*
University of Southern Maine *B*

Maryland

Allegany College of Maryland *A*
Bowie State University *B*
Carroll Community College *A*
Coppin State University *B*
Frederick Community College *A*
Frostburg State University *B*
Goucher College *B*
Harford Community College *A*
Hood College *B*
Howard Community College *A*
Johns Hopkins University *B, M, D*
Loyola University Maryland *B, M*
McDaniel College *B*
Morgan State University *B*
Mount St. Mary's University *B*
Notre Dame of Maryland
    University *B*
Prince George's Community
    College *A*
St. Mary's College of Maryland *B*
Salisbury University *B*
Stevenson University *B*
Towson University *B, M*
University of Baltimore *B, M, D*
University of Maryland
    Baltimore County *B, M*
    College Park *B, M, D*
    Eastern Shore *B*
    University College *B*
Washington Adventist University *B*
Washington College *B, M, T*

Massachusetts

American International College *B*
Amherst College *B*
Anna Maria College *B*
Assumption College *B*
Bard College at Simon's Rock *B*
Bay Path College *B*
Becker College *B*
Boston College *B, M, D*
Boston University *B, M, D*
Brandeis University *B, M, D*
Bridgewater State University *B, M*
Bunker Hill Community College *A*
Cambridge College *B*
Cape Cod Community College *A*
Clark University *B, M, D*
College of the Holy Cross

Curry College *B*
Dean College *A*
Eastern Nazarene College *B*
Elms College *B*
Emmanuel College *B*
Endicott College *B*
Fisher College *A*
Fitchburg State University *B*
Framingham State University *B*
Gordon College *B*
Hampshire College *B*
Harvard College *B, M, D*
Hellenic College/Holy Cross *B*
Lasell College *B*
Massachusetts College of Liberal
    Arts *B*
Merrimack College *B*
Middlesex Community College *A*
Mount Holyoke College *B, M*
Mount Ida College *B*
Newbury College *B*
Nichols College *B, T*
Northeastern University *B, M, D*
Northern Essex Community
    College *A*
Pine Manor College *B*
Regis College *B*
Salem State University *B*
Simmons College *B*
Smith College *B*
Springfield College *B*
Stonehill College *B*
Suffolk University *B*
Tufts University *B, M, D*
University of Massachusetts
    Amherst *B, M, D*
    Boston *B*
    Dartmouth *B, M*
    Lowell *B*
Wellesley College *B*
Western New England University *B*
Westfield State University *B, M*
Wheaton College *B*
Williams College *B*
Worcester Polytechnic Institute *B*
Worcester State University *B*

Michigan

Adrian College *A, B, T*
Albion College *B, T*
Alma College *B, T*
Andrews University *B, M, D*
Aquinas College *B*
Calvin College *B, T*
Central Michigan University *B, M*
Concordia University *B*
Cornerstone University *B*
Delta College *A*
Eastern Michigan University *B, M*
Ferris State University *A, B*
Finlandia University *B*
Gogebic Community College *A*
Grand Rapids Community College *A*
Grand Valley State University *B, T*
Hillsdale College *B*
Hope College *B*
Kalamazoo College *B*
Lake Michigan College *A*
Lake Superior State University *B*
Lansing Community College *A*
Lawrence Technological University *B*
Madonna University *C, B*
Marygrove College *B*
Michigan State University *B, M, D*
Michigan Technological University *B*
Mid Michigan Community College *A*
Northern Michigan University *B*
Oakland University *B, M, D*
Olivet College *B*
Rochester College *B*
Saginaw Valley State University *B*
Siena Heights University *A, B*
Spring Arbor University *B*
University of Detroit Mercy *B*
University of Michigan *M*

University of Michigan
    Dearborn *B*
    Flint *B, T*
Wayne State University *B, M, D*
Western Michigan
    University *B, M, D, T*

Minnesota

Argosy University
    Twin Cities *B*
Augsburg College *B*
Bemidji State University *B*
Bethany Lutheran College *B*
Bethel University *B*
Capella University *B, M, D*
Carleton College *B*
College of St. Benedict *B*
College of St. Scholastica *B*
Concordia College: Moorhead *B*
Concordia University St. Paul *B*
Crown College *A, B*
Gustavus Adolphus College *B*
Hamline University *B*
Itasca Community College *A*
Macalester College *B*
Metropolitan State University *B, M*
Minnesota State University
    Mankato *B, M*
    Moorhead *B*
Minnesota West Community and
    Technical College *A*
North Central University *A, B*
Oak Hills Christian College *B*
Ridgewater College *A*
St. Catherine University *B*
Saint Cloud State University *B*
St. John's University *B*
St. Mary's University of Minnesota *B*
St. Olaf College *B*
Southwest Minnesota State
    University *B*
University of Minnesota
    Duluth *B*
    Morris *B*
    Twin Cities *B, M, D*
University of Northwestern - St.
    Paul *B*
University of St. Thomas *B*
Walden University *B, M, D*
Winona State University *B*

Mississippi

Alcorn State University *B*
Belhaven University *B*
Blue Mountain College *B*
Delta State University *B*
East Mississippi Community
    College *A*
Hinds Community College *A*
Itawamba Community College *A*
Jackson State University *B*
Millsaps College *B*
Mississippi College *B*
Mississippi Delta Community
    College *A*
Mississippi Gulf Coast Community
    College *A*
Mississippi State University *B, M*
Mississippi University for Women *B*
Northeast Mississippi Community
    College *A*
Tougaloo College *B*
University of Mississippi *B, M, D*
University of Southern
    Mississippi *B, M, D*
William Carey University *B*

Missouri

Avila University *B, M*
Central Methodist University *B*
College of the Ozarks *B*
Columbia College *B*
Crowder College *A*
Culver-Stockton College *B*

Drury University *B*
Evangel University *B, M*
Fontbonne University *B*
Hannibal-LaGrange University *B*
Lincoln University *B*
Lindenwood University *B*
Maryville University of Saint Louis *B*
Missouri Baptist University *B*
Missouri Southern State University *B*
Missouri State University *B, M*
Missouri University of Science and Technology *B, T*
Missouri Valley College *B*
Missouri Western State University *B*
Northwest Missouri State University *B*
Park University *B*
Rockhurst University *B*
St. Charles Community College *A*
St. Louis Community College *A*
Saint Louis University *B, M, D*
Southeast Missouri State University *B*
Southwest Baptist University *B*
Stephens College *B*
Three Rivers Community College *A*
Truman State University *B*
University of Central Missouri *B, M*
University of Missouri
    Columbia *B, M, D*
    Kansas City *B, M, D*
    St. Louis *B, M, D*
Washington University in St. Louis *B, M, D*
Webster University *B*
Westminster College *B*
William Jewell College *B*
William Woods University *B*

Montana
Carroll College *B*
Miles Community College *A*
Montana State University *B, M*
Montana State University Billings *A, B, M, T*
Rocky Mountain College *B*
Salish Kootenai College *A, B*
University of Great Falls *B*
University of Montana *B, M, D*
University of Montana: Western *B*

Nebraska
Bellevue University *B*
Chadron State College *B*
College of Saint Mary *B*
Concordia University *B*
Creighton University *C, B*
Doane College *B*
Grace University *B*
Hastings College *B, T*
Midland University *B*
Nebraska Wesleyan University *B*
Northeast Community College *A*
Peru State College *B*
Union College *B*
University of Nebraska
    Kearney *B, T*
    Lincoln *B, M, D*
    Omaha *B, M, D*
Wayne State College *B*
Western Nebraska Community College *A*
York College *B*

Nevada
College of Southern Nevada *A*
Nevada State College *B*
Sierra Nevada College *B*
University of Nevada
    Las Vegas *B, M, D*
    Reno *B, M, D*

New Hampshire
Colby-Sawyer College *B*
Daniel Webster College *B*

Dartmouth College *B, M, D*
Franklin Pierce University *B*
Granite State College *B*
Keene State College *B*
Mount Washington College *A*
New England College *B*
Plymouth State University *B*
Rivier University *B*
Saint Anselm College *B*
Southern New Hampshire University *B*
University of New Hampshire *B, M, D*
University of New Hampshire at Manchester *B*

New Jersey
Bergen Community College *A*
Bloomfield College *B, T*
Caldwell College *B*
Centenary College *B*
College of New Jersey *B*
College of St. Elizabeth *B*
Drew University *B*
Fairleigh Dickinson University
    College at Florham *B*
    Metropolitan Campus *B, M*
Felician College *B*
Georgian Court University *B*
Gloucester County College *A*
Hudson County Community College *A*
Kean University *B, M*
Monmouth University *B*
Montclair State University *B, M, T*
New Jersey City University *B, M*
Passaic County Community College *A*
Princeton University *B, M, D*
Ramapo College of New Jersey *B*
Richard Stockton College of New Jersey *B*
Rider University *B*
Rowan University *B*
Rutgers, The State University of New Jersey
    Camden Campus *B, M*
    New Brunswick/Piscataway Campus *B, D*
    Newark Campus *B, D*
Saint Peter's University *B*
Salem Community College *A*
Seton Hall University *B, M*
Sussex County Community College *A*
Thomas Edison State College *B*
William Paterson University of New Jersey *B*

New Mexico
Central New Mexico Community College *A*
Clovis Community College *A*
Eastern New Mexico University *A, B*
New Mexico Highlands University *B, M*
New Mexico Institute of Mining and Technology *B*
New Mexico Junior College *A*
New Mexico State University *B, M, D*
San Juan College *A*
Santa Fe Community College *A*
University of New Mexico *B, M, D*
University of the Southwest *B*
Western New Mexico University *B*

New York
Adelphi University *B, M*
Alfred University *B*
Bard College *B*
Barnard College *B*
Canisius College *B*
Cazenovia College *B*
City University of New York
    Baruch College *B*
    Brooklyn College *B*

CUNY Online *B*
City College *B, M*
College of Staten Island *B*
Hunter College *B, M*
LaGuardia Community College *A*
Lehman College *B*
Medgar Evers College *B*
Queens College *B, M*
Queensborough Community College *A*
York College *B*
Clarkson University *B*
Colgate University *B*
College of Mount St. Vincent *A, B*
College of New Rochelle *B*
College of Saint Rose *B*
Columbia University *B*
Columbia University School of General Studies *B*
Concordia College *B*
Cornell University *B, M, D*
D'Youville College *B*
Daemen College *B*
Dominican College of Blauvelt *B*
Dowling College *B*
Elmira College *B*
Eugene Lang College The New School for Liberal Arts *B*
Excelsior College *B*
Fordham University *B, M, D*
Hamilton College *B*
Hartwick College *B*
Hilbert College *B*
Hobart and William Smith Colleges *B*
Hofstra University *B*
Houghton College *B*
Iona College *B, M*
Ithaca College *B*
Keuka College *B*
Le Moyne College *B*
Long Island University
    LIU Brooklyn *B, M*
    LIU Post *B, M*
Manhattan College *B*
Manhattanville College *B*
Marist College *B, M*
Marymount Manhattan College *B*
Medaille College *B, M, D*
Medaille College: Amherst *M, D*
Mercy College *B, M*
Molloy College *B*
Mount Saint Mary College *B, T*
Nazareth College *B*
New York Institute of Technology *B*
New York University *B, M*
Niagara University *B*
Nyack College *B*
Pace University *B, M*
Pace University: Pleasantville/ Briarcliff *B, M*
Rensselaer Polytechnic Institute *B*
Roberts Wesleyan College *B*
Rochester Institute of Technology *B*
SUNY
    College at Brockport *B, M*
    College at Buffalo *B*
    College at Cortland *B*
    College at Fredonia *B*
    College at Geneseo *B, T*
    College at New Paltz *B, M*
    College at Old Westbury *B*
    College at Oneonta *B*
    College at Oswego *B*
    College at Plattsburgh *B*
    College at Potsdam *B*
    College at Purchase *B*
    Empire State College *A, B*
    Institute of Technology at Utica/ Rome *B*
    University at Albany *B, D*
    University at Binghamton *B, M*
    University at Buffalo *B, M*
    University at Stony Brook *B, M*
Sage Colleges *B*
Saint Bonaventure University *B*

St. Francis College *B, M*
St. John Fisher College *B*
St. John's University *B*
St. Joseph's College New York: Suffolk Campus *B*
St. Joseph's College, New York *B*
St. Lawrence University *B*
St. Thomas Aquinas College *B*
Siena College *B*
Skidmore College *B*
Suffolk County Community College *A*
Sullivan County Community College *A*
Syracuse University *B*
Touro College *B*
Union College *B*
United States Military Academy *B*
University of Rochester *B, M*
Utica College *B*
Vassar College *B*
Wagner College *B*
Wells College *B*
Yeshiva University *B, M*

North Carolina
Appalachian State University *B, M*
Barton College *B*
Belmont Abbey College *B*
Bennett College for Women *B*
Brevard College *B*
Campbell University *B*
Carteret Community College *A*
Catawba College *B*
Chowan University *B*
Davidson College *B*
Duke University *B*
East Carolina University *B, M*
Elizabeth City State University *B*
Elon University *B*
Fayetteville State University *B, M*
Gardner-Webb University *B*
Greensboro College *B*
Guilford College *B*
High Point University *B*
Johnson C. Smith University *B*
Lees-McRae College *B*
Lenoir-Rhyne University *B*
Livingstone College *B*
Mars Hill University *B*
Meredith College *B*
Methodist University *A, B*
Montreat College *B*
North Carolina Agricultural and Technical State University *B*
North Carolina Central University *B, M*
North Carolina State University *B, M, D*
North Carolina Wesleyan College *B*
Pfeiffer University *B*
Queens University of Charlotte *B*
St. Andrews University *B*
St. Augustine's University *B*
Salem College *B*
Sandhills Community College *A*
Shaw University *B*
Southeastern Community College *A*
University of Mount Olive *B*
University of North Carolina
    Asheville *B*
    Chapel Hill *B, M, D*
    Charlotte *B*
    Greensboro *B, M, D*
    Pembroke *B*
    Wilmington *B, M*
Wake Forest University *B, M*
Warren Wilson College *B*
Western Carolina University *B, M*
Western Piedmont Community College *A*
William Peace University *B*
Wingate University *B*
Winston-Salem State University *B*

North Dakota

Dakota College at Bottineau *A*
Dickinson State University *B*
Mayville State University *B*
Minot State University *B, T*
North Dakota State
    University *B, M, D*
University of Jamestown *B*
University of Mary *B*
University of North Dakota *B, M, D*
Valley City State University *B*

Ohio

Antioch University
    Midwest *M*
Ashland University *B*
Baldwin Wallace University *B*
Bluffton University *B*
Bowling Green State
    University *B, M, D*
Capital University *B*
Case Western Reserve
    University *B, M, D*
Cedarville University *B*
Central State University *B*
Cincinnati Christian University *A, B*
Cleveland State University *B, M*
College of Mount St. Joseph *B*
College of Wooster *B*
Defiance College *B*
Denison University *B*
Franciscan University of
    Steubenville *B*
Heidelberg University *B, M*
Hiram College *B, T*
John Carroll University *B*
Kent State University *B*
Kent State University
    Ashtabula *B*
    East Liverpool *B*
    Geauga *B*
    Salem *B*
    Stark *B*
    Trumbull *B*
    Tuscarawas *B*
Kenyon College *B*
Lake Erie College *B*
Lourdes University *B*
Malone University *B*
Marietta College *B, M*
Miami University
    Middletown *A*
    Oxford *B, M, D*
Mount Vernon Nazarene University *B*
Muskingum University *B*
Notre Dame College *B*
Oberlin College *B*
Ohio Christian University *B*
Ohio Dominican University *B*
Ohio Northern University *B*
Ohio State University
    Columbus Campus *B, M, D*
    Lima Campus *B*
    Mansfield Campus *B*
    Marion Campus *B*
    Newark Campus *B*
Ohio University *B*
Ohio University
    Chillicothe Campus *B*
    Southern Campus at Ironton *B*
    Zanesville Campus *B*
Ohio Wesleyan University *B*
Otterbein University *B*
Shawnee State University *B*
Sinclair Community College *A*
Terra State Community College *A*
Tiffin University *B*
University of Akron *B, M*
University of Cincinnati *C, B, M, D*
University of Cincinnati
    Clermont College *A*
University of Dayton *B, M*
University of Findlay *B*
University of Mount Union *B*

University of Rio Grande *A, B*
University of Toledo *B, M, D*
Urbana University *B*
Ursuline College *B*
Walsh University *B*
Wilberforce University *B*
Wilmington College *B*
Wittenberg University *B*
Wright State University *A, B*
Wright State University: Lake
    Campus *A*
Xavier University *A, B, M*
Youngstown State University *B*

Oklahoma

Cameron University *B*
Carl Albert State College *A*
Connors State College *A*
East Central University *B*
Eastern Oklahoma State College *A*
Hillsdale Free Will Baptist College *B*
Langston University *B*
Mid-America Christian University *B*
Northeastern Oklahoma Agricultural
    and Mechanical College *A*
Northeastern State University *B*
Northwestern Oklahoma State
    University *B*
Oklahoma Baptist University *B*
Oklahoma Christian University *B*
Oklahoma City Community
    College *A*
Oklahoma City University *B*
Oklahoma Panhandle State
    University *B*
Oklahoma State University *B, M, D*
Oklahoma Wesleyan University *B*
Oral Roberts University *B*
Redlands Community College *A*
Rose State College *A*
St. Gregory's University *B*
Southeastern Oklahoma State
    University *B*
Southern Nazarene University *B*
Southwestern Christian University *B*
Southwestern Oklahoma State
    University *B, M*
Tulsa Community College *A*
University of Central Oklahoma *B, M*
University of Oklahoma *B, M, D*
University of Phoenix
    Oklahoma City *M*
University of Science and Arts of
    Oklahoma *B*
University of Tulsa *B*

Oregon

Concordia University *B*
Corban University *B*
Eastern Oregon University *B*
George Fox University *B*
Lewis & Clark College *B*
Linfield College *B, T*
Linn-Benton Community College *A*
Marylhurst University *B*
Mt. Hood Community College *A*
Multnomah University *B*
Northwest Christian University *B*
Oregon Institute of Technology *B*
Oregon State University *B*
Pacific University *B, M, D*
Portland State University *B, M, D*
Reed College *B*
Southern Oregon University *B, M*
Treasure Valley Community
    College *A*
University of Oregon *B, M, D*
University of Portland *B*
Warner Pacific College *A, B*
Western Oregon University *B*
Willamette University *B*

Pennsylvania

Albright College *B*
Allegheny College *B*
Alvernia University *B*
Arcadia University *B*
Bloomsburg University of
    Pennsylvania *B*
Bryn Athyn College *B*
Bryn Mawr College *B*
Bucknell University *B, M*
Bucks County Community College *A*
Butler County Community College *A*
Cabrini College *B*
California University of
    Pennsylvania *B*
Carlow University *B*
Carnegie Mellon University *B, M, D*
Cedar Crest College *B*
Chatham University *B*
Chestnut Hill College *B*
Cheyney University of
    Pennsylvania *B*
Clarion University of Pennsylvania *B*
Community College of Allegheny
    County *A*
Community College of Beaver
    County *A*
DeSales University *B, T*
Delaware County Community
    College *A*
Dickinson College *B*
Drexel University *B, M*
Duquesne University *B*
East Stroudsburg University of
    Pennsylvania *B*
Eastern University *B*
Edinboro University of
    Pennsylvania *B*
Elizabethtown College *B*
Franklin & Marshall College *B*
Gannon University *B*
Geneva College *B*
Gettysburg College *B*
Grove City College *B*
Gwynedd Mercy University *B*
Harcum College *A*
Harrisburg Area Community
    College *A*
Haverford College *B*
Holy Family University *B*
Immaculata University *B*
Indiana University of Pennsylvania *B*
Juniata College *B*
Keystone College *B*
King's College *B*
Kutztown University of
    Pennsylvania *B*
La Roche College *B*
La Salle University *B, M, D*
Lafayette College *B*
Lebanon Valley College *B*
Lehigh Carbon Community College *A*
Lehigh University *B, M, D*
Lincoln University *B*
Lock Haven University of
    Pennsylvania *B*
Lycoming College *B*
Manor College *A*
Mansfield University of
    Pennsylvania *B*
Marywood University *B, M*
Mercyhurst University *B*
Messiah College *B*
Millersville University of
    Pennsylvania *B, M*
Misericordia University *B*
Montgomery County Community
    College *A*
Moravian College *B, D*
Mount Aloysius College *B, M*
Muhlenberg College *C, A, B*
Neumann University *B*

Penn State

Abington *B*
Altoona *B*
Beaver *B*
Berks *B*
Brandywine *B*
DuBois *B*
Erie, The Behrend College *B*
Fayette, The Eberly Campus *B*
Greater Allegheny *B*
Harrisburg *B, M*
Hazleton *B*
Lehigh Valley *B*
Mont Alto *B*
New Kensington *B*
Schuylkill *B*
Shenango *B*
University Park *B, M, D*
Wilkes-Barre *B*
Worthington Scranton *B*
York *B*
Philadelphia University *B*
Point Park University *B*
Reading Area Community College *A*
Robert Morris University *B*
Rosemont College *B*
St. Francis University *B*
Saint Joseph's University *B, M*
St. Vincent College *B*
Seton Hill University *B*
Shippensburg University of
    Pennsylvania *B, M*
Slippery Rock University of
    Pennsylvania *B*
Susquehanna University *A, B*
Swarthmore College *B*
Temple University *B, M, D*
Thiel College *B*
University of Pennsylvania *A, B, M, D*
University of Pittsburgh *B, M, D*
University of Pittsburgh
    Bradford *B*
    Greensburg *B*
    Johnstown *B*
University of Scranton *B*
University of the Sciences *D*
Ursinus College *B*
Valley Forge Christian College *B*
Villanova University *B, M*
Washington & Jefferson College *B*
Waynesburg University *B*
West Chester University of
    Pennsylvania *B, M*
Westminster College *B*
Widener University *B*
Wilkes University *B*
Wilson College *B*
York College of Pennsylvania *B*

Puerto Rico

Bayamon Central University *B, M*
Inter American University of Puerto
    Rico
    Aguadilla Campus *B*
    Arecibo Campus *B*
    Metropolitan Campus *B, M*
    Ponce Campus *B*
    San German Campus *B*
Pontifical Catholic University of
    Puerto Rico *B*
Turabo University *B*
Universidad Adventista de las
    Antillas *B*
Universidad Metropolitana *B*
Universidad del Este *B*
University of Puerto Rico
    Aguadilla *B*
    Cayey University College *B*
    Mayaguez *B*
    Ponce *B*
    Rio Piedras *B, M, D*
University of the Sacred Heart *B*

Rhode Island

Brown University *B, M, D*
Bryant University *B*
Providence College *B*
Rhode Island College *B, M*
Roger Williams University *B*
Salve Regina University *B, M*
University of Rhode Island *B*

South Carolina

Anderson University *B*
Charleston Southern University *B*
Citadel *B, M*
Claflin University *B*
Clemson University *B*
Coastal Carolina University *B*
Coker College *B*
College of Charleston *B*
Columbia College *B*
Columbia International University *B*
Converse College *B*
Erskine College *B*
Francis Marion University *B*
Furman University *B*
Lander University *B*
Limestone College *B*
Newberry College *B*
North Greenville University *B*
Presbyterian College *B*
South Carolina State University *B*
Southern Wesleyan University *B*
University of South Carolina
   Aiken *B*
   Beaufort *B*
   Upstate *B*
Winthrop University *B*
Wofford College *B, T*

South Dakota

Augustana College *B*
Black Hills State University *B*
Dakota Wesleyan University *B*
Kilian Community College *A*
Mount Marty College *B*
Northern State University *B*
South Dakota State University *B*
University of Sioux Falls *B*
University of South Dakota *B, M, D*

Tennessee

Argosy University
   Nashville *B*
Austin Peay State University *B, M*
Belmont University *B, T*
Bethel University *B*
Bryan University
   Dayton *B, T*
Carson-Newman University *B*
Christian Brothers University *B*
Cumberland University *B*
Dyersburg State Community
   College *A*
East Tennessee State
   University *B, M, D, T*
Fisk University *B, M*
Freed-Hardeman University *B*
Hiwassee College *A*
Jackson State Community College *A*
King University *B*
Lee University *B*
Lincoln Memorial University *B*
Lipscomb University *B*
Martin Methodist College *B*
Maryville College *B*
Middle Tennessee State
   University *B, M*
Milligan College *B, T*
Rhodes College *B*
Sewanee: The University of the
   South *B*
Southern Adventist University *B*
Tennessee State University *B, M*
Tennessee Technological
   University *B*

Tennessee Temple University *B*
Tennessee Wesleyan College *B*
Trevecca Nazarene University *B*
Tusculum College *B*
Union University *B*
University of Memphis *B, M, D*
University of Tennessee
   Chattanooga *B, M*
   Knoxville *B, M, D*
   Martin *B*
Vanderbilt University *B, M, D*
Victory University *B*
Welch College *B*

Texas

Abilene Christian University *B, M*
Alvin Community College *A*
Amarillo College *A*
Angelo State University *B, M*
Argosy University
   Dallas *B*
Austin College *B*
Austin Community College *A*
Baylor University *B, D*
Blinn College *A*
Brazosport College *A*
Clarendon College *A*
Coastal Bend College *A*
College of the Mainland *A*
Dallas Baptist University *B*
Dallas Christian College *B*
Del Mar College *A*
East Texas Baptist University *B*
El Paso Community College *A*
Frank Phillips College *A*
Galveston College *A*
Grayson College *A*
Hardin-Simmons University *B*
Houston Baptist University *B*
Howard College *A*
Howard Payne University *B*
Huston-Tillotson University *B*
Kilgore College *A*
Lamar University *B, M*
Laredo Community College *A*
LeTourneau University *B*
Lubbock Christian University *B*
McMurry University *B*
Midland College *A*
Midwestern State University *B, M*
Navarro College *A*
North Lake College *C, A*
Northeast Texas Community
   College *A*
Northwest Vista College *A*
Odessa College *A*
Our Lady of the Lake University of
   San Antonio *B, M, D*
Palo Alto College *A*
Paris Junior College *A*
Prairie View A&M University *B*
Rice University *B, M, D*
St. Edward's University *B*
St. Mary's University *B*
St. Philip's College *A*
Sam Houston State University *B, M*
San Antonio College *A*
San Jacinto College *A*
Schreiner University *B*
South Plains College *A*
South Texas College *A*
Southern Methodist University *B, M*
Southwestern Adventist
   University *B, T*
Southwestern Assemblies of God
   University *A*
Southwestern University *B, T*
Stephen F. Austin State
   University *B, M, T*
Sul Ross State University *B*
Tarleton State University *B*
Texas A&M International
   University *B, M, T*
Texas A&M University *B, M, D*

Texas A&M University
   Commerce *B, M*
   Corpus Christi *B, M*
   Kingsville *B, M*
   Texarkana *B*
Texas Christian University *B, M, D*
Texas Lutheran University *B*
Texas Southern University *B, M*
Texas State University *B*
Texas Tech University *B, M*
Texas Wesleyan University *B, T*
Texas Woman's University *B*
Trinity University *B*
Trinity Valley Community College *A*
Tyler Junior College *A*
University of Dallas *B, M*
University of Houston *B, M*
University of Houston
   Clear Lake *B, M*
   Downtown *B*
   Victoria *B*
University of Mary Hardin-
   Baylor *B, M*
University of North Texas *B, M*
University of St. Thomas *B*
University of Texas
   Arlington *B, M*
   Austin *B, M, D*
   Brownsville *B*
   Dallas *B*
   El Paso *B, M, D*
   Pan American *B*
   Permian Basin *B, M*
   San Antonio *B, M, D*
   Tyler *B*
University of the Incarnate Word *B*
Wayland Baptist University *B*
West Texas A&M University *B, M*
Western Texas College *A*
Wharton County Junior College *A*

Utah

Argosy University
   Salt Lake City *B*
Brigham Young University *B, M, D*
Dixie State College *B*
Salt Lake Community College *A*
Snow College *A*
Southern Utah University *B*
University of Utah *B, M, D, T*
Utah State University *B, M, D*
Utah Valley University *A, B*
Weber State University *B*
Westminster College *B*

Vermont

Bennington College *B*
Castleton State College *B*
Champlain College *B*
College of St. Joseph in Vermont *B*
Goddard College *B, M*
Green Mountain College *B*
Johnson State College *B*
Lyndon State College *B*
Marlboro College *B*
Middlebury College *B*
Norwich University *B*
Saint Michael's College *B*
Southern Vermont College *B*
University of Vermont *B, M, D*

Virginia

Argosy University
   Washington D.C. *B*
Averett University *B*
Bluefield College *B*
Bridgewater College *B*
Christopher Newport University *B*
College of William and Mary *B, M*
Eastern Mennonite University *B*
Emory & Henry College *B*
Ferrum College *B*
George Mason University *B, M, D*
Germanna Community College *A*

Hampden-Sydney College *B*
Hampton University *B*
Hollins University *B*
James Madison University *B, M, D*
Liberty University *B*
Longwood University *B*
Lynchburg College *B*
Mary Baldwin College *B*
Marymount University *B*
Norfolk State University *B*
Northern Virginia Community
   College *A*
Old Dominion University *B, M, D*
Radford University *B, M*
Randolph College *B*
Randolph-Macon College *B*
Regent University *A, B*
Roanoke College *B, T*
Shenandoah University *B*
Sweet Briar College *B*
University of Mary Washington *B*
University of Richmond *B*
University of Virginia *B, M, D*
University of Virginia's College at
   Wise *B, T*
Virginia Commonwealth
   University *B, M, D*
Virginia Intermont College *B*
Virginia Military Institute *B*
Virginia Polytechnic Institute and
   State University *B, M, D*
Virginia State University *B, M*
Virginia Union University *B*
Virginia Wesleyan College *B*
Washington and Lee University *B*

Washington

Antioch University
   Seattle *M, D*
Argosy University
   Seattle *B*
Bastyr University *B*
Central Washington University *B*
Centralia College *A*
City University of Seattle *B*
Eastern Washington University *B, M*
Everett Community College *A*
Evergreen State College *B*
Gonzaga University *B*
Heritage University *A, B*
Highline Community College *A*
Northwest University *B, D*
Pacific Lutheran University *B*
Saint Martin's University *B*
Seattle Pacific University *B*
Seattle University *B, M*
Trinity Lutheran College *B*
University of Puget Sound *B*
University of Washington *B, M, D*
University of Washington Tacoma *B*
Walla Walla University *B*
Washington State University *B, M, D*
Western Washington University *B*
Whitman College *B*
Whitworth University *B*

West Virginia

Alderson-Broaddus University *B*
American Public University
   System *B, M*
Bethany College *B*
Concord University *B*
Davis and Elkins College *B*
Fairmont State University *B*
Marshall University *B, M*
Ohio Valley University *B*
Potomac State College of West
   Virginia University *A*
Shepherd University *B*
University of Charleston *B*
West Liberty University *B*
West Virginia State University *B*
West Virginia University *B, M, D*

West Virginia University Institute of
Technology *B*
West Virginia Wesleyan College *B*
Wheeling Jesuit University *B*

Wisconsin

Alverno College *B*
Beloit College *B*
Cardinal Stritch University *B, M*
Carroll University *B*
Carthage College *B*
Concordia University Wisconsin *B*
Edgewood College *B*
Lakeland College *B*
Lawrence University *B*
Marian University *B*
Marquette University *B*
Mount Mary University *B*
Northcentral Technical College *C*
Ripon College *B*
St. Norbert College *B, T*
Silver Lake College of the Holy
Family *B, T*
University of Wisconsin
Eau Claire *B*
Green Bay *B*
La Crosse *B, T*
Madison *B, M, D*
Milwaukee *B, M, D*
Oshkosh *B, M*
Parkside *B*
Platteville *B, T*
River Falls *B, T*
Stevens Point *B, T*
Stout *B, M*
Superior *B*
Whitewater *B, T*
Viterbo University *B*
Wisconsin Lutheran College *B*

Wyoming

Casper College *A*
Central Wyoming College *A*
Laramie County Community
College *A*
Northwest College *A*
Sheridan College *A*
University of Wyoming *B, M, D*
Western Wyoming Community
College *A*

Psychology teacher education

Delaware

University of Delaware *B, T*

Idaho

Northwest Nazarene University *B*

Illinois

Bradley University *B*

Indiana

Valparaiso University *B*

Iowa

Buena Vista University *B, T*
St. Ambrose University *B*
Simpson College *T*

Kansas

Pittsburg State University *B*

Louisiana

Centenary College of Louisiana *T*

Massachusetts

Western New England
University *B, T*

Michigan

University of Michigan
Flint *B, T*

Minnesota

Saint Cloud State University *B*
University of Minnesota
Morris *T*

Mississippi

Millsaps College *T*

Montana

Rocky Mountain College *B*
University of Great Falls *B*

Nebraska

Wayne State College *B, T*

New Jersey

Rowan University *M, D*

North Carolina

Lenoir-Rhyne University *B*

Ohio

University of Findlay *B, M, T*

Pennsylvania

Arcadia University *M*
St. Francis University *B, T*
St. Vincent College *B*
University of Pittsburgh *T*
Widener University *T*

South Carolina

Wofford College *T*

South Dakota

Augustana College *B, T*

Tennessee

Belmont University *T*
Bryan University
Dayton *T*
King University *T*
Lee University *B*
Tusculum College *B, T*
Victory University *B, T*

Utah

Utah State University *B*

West Virginia

Wheeling Jesuit University *B*

Wisconsin

Carroll University *B, T*
Carthage College *T*
Lawrence University *T*
St. Norbert College *T*

Psychometrics/ quantitative psychology

Connecticut

University of Connecticut *M, D*

Minnesota

Capella University *M*

North Dakota

North Dakota State University *B*

Utah

University of Utah *M*

Virginia

James Madison University *D*

Psychopharmacology

California

Alliant International University *M*

Florida

Nova Southeastern University *M*

Hawaii

University of Hawaii
Hilo *M*

Ohio

University of Akron *M*

Public administration

Alabama

Auburn University *B, M, D*
Auburn University at
Montgomery *M, D*
Columbia Southern University *M*
Jacksonville State University *M*
Samford University *B*
Talladega College *B*
Troy University *M*
University of Alabama *M*
University of Alabama
Birmingham *M*
Huntsville *M*
University of Phoenix
Birmingham *B, M*
University of South Alabama *M*

Alaska

University of Alaska
Anchorage *M*
Southeast *M*

Arizona

Brookline College
Phoenix *B*
Central Arizona College *A*
DeVry University
Phoenix *M*
Grand Canyon University *M*
Northcentral University *B, M, D*
Northern Arizona University *B, M*
Rio Salado College *C, A*
Scottsdale Community College *C*
University of Arizona *B, M*
University of Phoenix
Phoenix-Hohokam *B, M*
Southern Arizona *B, M*
Western International University *M*

Arkansas

Arkansas Baptist College *A, B*
Arkansas State University *M*
Harding University *B*
Henderson State University *B*
Southern Arkansas University *M*
University of Arkansas *M*
University of Arkansas
Little Rock *M*
University of Central Arkansas *B*
University of Phoenix
Northwest Arkansas *B*
University of the Ozarks *B*

California

California Baptist University *M*
California Lutheran University *M*
California Miramar University *B*
California Polytechnic State
University: San Luis Obispo *M*
California State Polytechnic
University: Pomona *M*
California State University
Bakersfield *B, M*
Chico *B, M*
Dominguez Hills *B, M*
East Bay *B, M*

Fresno *B, M*
Fullerton *B, M*
Long Beach *M*
Los Angeles *M*
Monterey Bay *M*
Northridge *M*
Sacramento *M*
San Bernardino *B, M*
Stanislaus *M*
Fresno City College *C, A*
Golden Gate University *M*
Loma Linda University *D*
Long Beach City College *C, A*
National University *B, M*
Notre Dame de Namur University *M*
Palomar College *C, A*
San Diego State University *B, M*
San Francisco State University *M*
San Joaquin Delta College *A*
San Jose State University *M*
Santa Barbara City College *A*
Sonoma State University *M*
University of California
Los Angeles *M*
University of La Verne *B, M, D*
University of Phoenix
Bay Area *B, M*
Central Valley *B, M*
Sacramento Valley *B, M*
San Diego *B, M*
Southern California *B, M*
University of San Francisco *B, M*
University of Southern
California *B, M, D*

Colorado

Colorado Mesa University *B*
DeVry University
Westminster *M*
Regis University *B*
University of Colorado
Colorado Springs *M*
Denver *M, D*
University of Denver *M*
University of Phoenix
Denver *B, M*
Southern Colorado *B*

Connecticut

Fairfield University *M*
University of Connecticut *M*
University of Hartford *M*
University of New Haven *B, M*

Delaware

University of Delaware *M*
Wilmington University *M*

District of Columbia

American University *M, D*
Howard University *M*
Strayer University *M*
University of Phoenix
Washington DC *B*
University of the District of
Columbia *M*

Florida

Barry University *C, B*
Flagler College *B*
Florida Atlantic University *B, M, D*
Florida Gulf Coast University *M*
Florida International
University *B, M, D*
Florida Memorial University *B*
Florida National University *A*
Florida State University *M, D*
Hodges University *M*
Lynn University *M*
Miami Dade College *A*
Northwest Florida State College *C, A*
Nova Southeastern University *M, D*
St. Petersburg College *B*
Tallahassee Community College *A*

University of Central Florida *B, M, D*
University of Miami *M, D*
University of North Florida *M*
University of Phoenix
   Central Florida *B, M*
   North Florida *B, M*
   South Florida *B, M*
   West Florida *B, M*
University of South Florida *M*
University of West Florida *M*

Georgia

Albany State University *M*
Clark Atlanta University *M*
Georgia College and State
   University *M*
Georgia Regents University *M*
Georgia Southern University *M, T*
Georgia State University *M*
Kennesaw State University *M*
Middle Georgia State College *A*
Savannah State University *M*
University of Georgia *M, D*
University of North Georgia *M*
University of Phoenix
   Atlanta *B, M*
   Augusta *B, M*
   Columbus *B, M*
   Savannah *B, M*
University of West Georgia *M*
Valdosta State University *M, D*

Hawaii

Hawaii Pacific University *B*
University of Hawaii
   Hilo *B*
   Manoa *M*
   West Oahu *B*
University of Phoenix
   Hawaii *B*

Idaho

Boise State University *M, D*
Idaho State University *M*
University of Idaho *M*
University of Phoenix
   Idaho *B, M*

Illinois

Blackburn College *B*
DePaul University *M*
Governors State University *B, M*
Illinois Institute of Technology *M*
Lewis University *B*
Northern Illinois University *M*
Northwestern University *M*
Roosevelt University *M*
Southern Illinois University
   Carbondale *M*
Southern Illinois University
   Edwardsville *M*
University of Illinois
   Chicago *M, D*
   Springfield *M, D*
   Urbana-Champaign *M*
University of Phoenix
   Chicago *B*

Indiana

Ball State University *M*
Indiana State University *M*
Indiana University
   Bloomington *A, B, M, D*
   East *B*
   Kokomo *C, B, M*
   Northwest *B, M*
   Purdue University Fort
      Wayne *C, B, M*
   Purdue University
      Indianapolis *C, B, M*
   South Bend *B, M*
University of Notre Dame *M*
University of Phoenix
   Indianapolis *B*

University of Southern Indiana *M*
Vincennes University *A*

Iowa

Ashford University *B, M*
Buena Vista University *B*
Dordt College *B*
Drake University *M*
Iowa State University *M*
St. Ambrose University *B*
University of Northern Iowa *B*
University of Phoenix
   Des Moines *B*

Kansas

Barton County Community College *A*
Kansas State University *M*
MidAmerica Nazarene University *B*
University of Kansas *B, M, D*
Washburn University *C, B*
Wichita State University *M*

Kentucky

Eastern Kentucky University *M*
Kentucky State University *B, M*
Morehead State University *M*
Murray State University *B, M*
Northern Kentucky University *B, M*
Sullivan University *M*
University of Kentucky *M, D*
University of Louisville *M*
University of Phoenix
   Louisville *B*
Western Kentucky University *M*

Louisiana

Grambling State University *M*
Louisiana College *B*
Louisiana State University and
   Agricultural and Mechanical
   College *M*
Southern University
   New Orleans *B*
Southern University and Agricultural
   and Mechanical College *M*
University of New Orleans *M*
University of Phoenix
   Baton Rouge *B, M*
   Louisiana *B, M*
   Shreveport *B, M*

Maine

University of Maine *B, M*
University of Maine
   Augusta *A, B*
University of Southern Maine *M, D*

Maryland

Bowie State University *M*
Johns Hopkins University *B*
University of Baltimore *M, D*
University of Maryland
   University College *B*

Massachusetts

American International College *M*
Anna Maria College *M*
Bridgewater State University *M*
Clark University *B, M*
Framingham State University *M*
Harvard College *M, D*
Northeastern University *M*
Regis College *M*
Stonehill College *B*
Suffolk University *M*
University of Massachusetts
   Boston *B, M*
University of Phoenix
   Boston *B*
Westfield State University *M*

Michigan

Calvin College *B*
Central Michigan University *M*

Eastern Michigan University *B, M*
Grand Valley State University *B, M*
Michigan State University *B*
Northern Michigan University *B, M*
Oakland University *B, M*
Saginaw Valley State University *B, M*
University of Michigan *M*
University of Michigan
   Dearborn *B, M*
   Flint *B, M*
University of Phoenix
   Metro Detroit *B, M*
   West Michigan *B, M*
Wayne State University *B, M*
Western Michigan University *M, D*

Minnesota

Argosy University
   Twin Cities *M*
Capella University *B, M, D*
Hamline University *M, D*
Minnesota State University
   Mankato *B, M*
Saint Cloud State University *B*
Southwest Minnesota State
   University *B*
University of Minnesota
   Twin Cities *C, M*
University of Phoenix
   Minneapolis-St. Paul *B, M*
Walden University *B, M, D*
Winona State University *B*

Mississippi

Belhaven University *M*
Jackson State University *M, D*
Millsaps College *B*
Mississippi State University *M, D*
Mississippi Valley State University *B*
University of Phoenix
   Jackson *B*

Missouri

Columbia College *B*
Lincoln University *B*
Lindenwood University *B, M*
Missouri State University *B, M*
Missouri Valley College *B*
Northwest Missouri State
   University *B*
Park University *B, M*
Saint Louis University *M*
Southeast Missouri State University *M*
University of Missouri
   Columbia *M*
   Kansas City *M*
   St. Louis *B, M*
University of Phoenix
   Kansas City *B, M*
   St. Louis *B, M*
Webster University *M*

Montana

Carroll College *B*
Miles Community College *A*
Montana State University *M*
Montana State University
   Billings *M*
University of Montana *M*

Nebraska

Bellevue University *B, M*
Doane College *B*
Hastings College *B*
University of Nebraska
   Omaha *B, M, D*
University of Phoenix
   Omaha *B*

Nevada

University of Nevada
   Las Vegas *M*
   Reno *M*

University of Phoenix
   Las Vegas *B*
   Northern Nevada *B, M*

New Hampshire

Plymouth State University *B*
Southern New Hampshire
   University *B*
University of New Hampshire *M*
University of New Hampshire at
   Manchester *M*

New Jersey

County College of Morris *A*
Cumberland County College *A*
Fairleigh Dickinson University
   College at Florham *M*
   Metropolitan Campus *M*
Kean University *B, M*
Princeton University *B, M, D*
Rider University *C*
Rutgers, The State University of New
   Jersey
   Camden Campus *M*
   Newark Campus *M, D*
Seton Hall University *M*
Thomas Edison State College *C, B*
University of Phoenix
   Jersey City *B*
William Paterson University of New
   Jersey *M*

New Mexico

Navajo Technical University *A*
New Mexico State University *M*
University of New Mexico *M*
University of Phoenix
   New Mexico *B, M*
Western New Mexico University *B*

New York

City University of New York
   Baruch College *B, M*
   CUNY Online *C*
   City College *M*
   Hostos Community College *A*
   John Jay College of Criminal
      Justice *B, M*
   Medgar Evers College *A, B*
College of New Rochelle *M*
Cornell University *M*
Dowling College *M*
Elmira College *B*
Hilbert College *M*
Long Island University
   LIU Brooklyn *M*
   LIU Post *B, M*
Marist College *M*
New York University *M, D*
Pace University *M*
Pace University: Pleasantville/
   Briarcliff *M*
SUNY
   College at Brockport *M*
   University at Albany *M, D*
   University at Binghamton *M*
   University at Stony Brook *M*
St. John's University *B*
Syracuse University *B, M, D*

North Carolina

Appalachian State University *M*
Campbell University *B*
Catawba College *B*
East Carolina University *M*
Elon University *B*
Fayetteville Technical Community
   College *C, A*
Lenoir Community College *C, A*
North Carolina Central University *M*
North Carolina State University *M, D*
Shaw University *B*

University of North Carolina
Chapel Hill *M*
Charlotte *M*
Greensboro *M*
Pembroke *M*
Wilmington *M*
Western Carolina University *B, M*

North Dakota

Cankdeska Cikana Community
College *A*
Fort Berthold Community College *A*
University of North Dakota *B, M*

Ohio

Ashland University *B*
Bowling Green State University *B, M*
Capital University *B*
Cedarville University *B*
Cleveland State University *M*
Franklin University *B, M*
Heidelberg University *B*
Kent State University *M*
Lorain County Community
College *C, A*
Miami University
Oxford *B*
Ohio State University
Columbus Campus *B, M, D*
Ohio University *M*
University of Akron *C, M, D*
University of Dayton *M*
University of Phoenix
Cleveland *B*
University of Rio Grande *B*
University of Toledo *M*
Wright State University *M*
Youngstown State University *B*

Oklahoma

Mid-America Christian University *M*
Rogers State University *B*
University of Oklahoma *B, M*
University of Phoenix
Oklahoma City *B*
Tulsa *B*

Oregon

Eastern Oregon University *B*
Portland Community College *C, A*
Portland State University *M, D*
University of Oregon *B, M*
University of Phoenix
Oregon *B*
Western Oregon University *B*

Pennsylvania

Carnegie Mellon University *M*
Cheyney University of
Pennsylvania *M*
Gannon University *M*
Indiana University of Pennsylvania *M*
Kutztown University of
Pennsylvania *B, M*
La Salle University *B*
Lehigh Carbon Community College *A*
Lincoln University *B*
Marywood University *M*
Penn State
Harrisburg *M, D*
Point Park University *A, B*
St. Francis University *B*
Saint Joseph's University *B*
Shippensburg University of
Pennsylvania *B, M, T*
University of Pennsylvania *M*
University of Phoenix
Pittsburgh *B*
University of Pittsburgh *B, M*
Villanova University *M*
Widener University *M*

Puerto Rico

Bayamon Central University *B*
Pontifical Catholic University of
Puerto Rico *B*
Turabo University *A, B*
University of Puerto Rico
Rio Piedras *M*

Rhode Island

Rhode Island College *B, M*
Roger Williams University *B, M*
University of Rhode Island *M*

South Carolina

Clemson University *M*
College of Charleston *M*
University of Phoenix
Columbia *B*
University of South Carolina
Columbia *M*

South Dakota

Oglala Lakota College *M*
University of South Dakota *M*

Tennessee

Cleveland State Community
College *A*
Cumberland University *B*
Jackson State Community College *A*
Lipscomb University *B*
Tennessee State University *M, D*
University of Memphis *M*
University of Phoenix
Chattanooga *B*
Knoxville *B*
Memphis *B*
Nashville *B*
University of Tennessee
Chattanooga *M*
Knoxville *B*

Texas

Angelo State University *M*
Baylor University *B, M*
Brazosport College *A*
College of the Mainland *A*
Houston Community College
System *C, A*
Lamar Institute of Technology *C, A*
Lamar University *M*
Midwestern State University *M*
St. Mary's University *M*
Sam Houston State University *M*
San Antonio College *C, A*
Stephen F. Austin State
University *B, M*
Sul Ross State University *M*
Tarrant County College *C, A*
Texas A&M International
University *M*
Texas A&M University *M*
Texas A&M University
Corpus Christi *M*
Texas Southern University *B, M*
Texas State University *B, M*
Texas Tech University *M*
Tyler Junior College *A*
University of Houston *M*
University of Houston
Clear Lake *B*
University of North Texas *B, M, D*
University of Phoenix
Austin *B, M*
Dallas Fort Worth *B, M*
Houston Westside *B*
San Antonio *B, M*
University of Texas
Arlington *B, M*
Brownsville *B, M*
Dallas *B, M, D*
El Paso *M*
Pan American *M*
Permian Basin *M*

San Antonio *B, M*
Tyler *M*
Wayland Baptist University *M*
West Texas A&M University *B*

Utah

Brigham Young University *M*
Southern Utah University *M*
University of Phoenix
Utah *B, M*
University of Utah *M*

Vermont

Norwich University *M*
University of Vermont *M*

Virginia

George Mason University *B, M*
James Madison University *B, M*
Old Dominion University *M, D*
Regent University *M*
Thomas Nelson Community
College *A*
Tidewater Community College *A*
University of Management and
Technology *M*
University of Phoenix
Northern Virginia *B, M*
Richmond *B, M*
University of Virginia's College at
Wise *B*
Virginia Commonwealth
University *M, D*
Virginia Polytechnic Institute and
State University *M, D*
Virginia State University *B*
Virginia Union University *B*

Washington

Eastern Washington University *C, M*
Evergreen State College *M*
Seattle University *B, M*
University of Phoenix
Western Washington *B*
University of Washington *M*

West Virginia

American Public University System *M*
Concord University *B*
West Virginia University *M*

Wisconsin

College of Menominee Nation *A, B*
University of Phoenix
Milwaukee *B*
University of Wisconsin
Green Bay *B*
Milwaukee *M*
Oshkosh *M*
Stevens Point *B*
Superior *B*
Whitewater *B, M*

Wyoming

Laramie County Community
College *C, A*
University of Wyoming *M*

Public finance

Maine

Husson University *B*

Massachusetts

Boston University *M*

New Jersey

Thomas Edison State College *M*

New York

City University of New York
Baruch College *M*

Ohio

Youngstown State University *B*

Rhode Island

Johnson & Wales University
Providence *B*

Public health

Alabama

University of Alabama
Birmingham *B, M, D*

Alaska

University of Alaska
Anchorage *M*
Fairbanks *A*

Arizona

Argosy University
Phoenix *M*
Grand Canyon University *M*
Northern Arizona University *B*
University of Arizona *B, M, D*

Arkansas

University of Arkansas
Little Rock *B*
for Medical Sciences *M, D, T*

California

Argosy University
Inland Empire *M*
Los Angeles *M*
Orange County *M*
San Diego *M*
San Francisco Bay Area *M*
California State University
Fresno *M*
Fullerton *M*
Long Beach *M*
Northridge *M*
Charles Drew University of Medicine
and Science *M*
Loma Linda University *M*
National University *B, M*
San Diego State University *M, D*
San Francisco State University *M*
San Jose State University *M*
Santa Clara University *B*
University of California
Berkeley *M, D*
Davis *M*
Irvine *M, D*
Los Angeles *M, D*
University of Southern
California *B, M, D*

Colorado

Argosy University
Denver *M*
Colorado State University *M*
University of Colorado
Denver *B, M, D*

Connecticut

Southern Connecticut State
University *B, M*
University of Connecticut *M, D*
University of Saint Joseph *B*
Yale University *M, D*

Delaware

Delaware State University *B*

District of Columbia

American University *B*
George Washington University *M, D*

Florida

Barry University *M*
Florida Agricultural and Mechanical
University *M, D*

Florida International University *M, D*
Florida State University *M*
Nova Southeastern University *M*
Palm Beach State College *A*
University of Florida *M, D*
University of Miami *M*
University of South Florida *M, D*
University of Tampa *B*
University of West Florida *M*

Georgia
Agnes Scott College *B*
Armstrong Atlantic State
　University *M*
Emory University *M*
Fort Valley State University *M*
Georgia Southern University *D*
Georgia State University *M, D*
LaGrange College *B*
Mercer University *M*
University of Georgia *M, D*

Hawaii
University of Hawaii
　Manoa *M, D*

Idaho
Boise State University *M*
Idaho State University *M*

Illinois
Benedictine University *M*
DePaul University *M*
Loyola University Chicago *M*
Northern Illinois University *B, M*
Northwestern University *M*
University of Illinois
　Chicago *M, D*
　Springfield *M*
　Urbana-Champaign *M, D*

Indiana
Indiana University
　Purdue University
　　Indianapolis *B, M*
University of Evansville *B*

Iowa
Allen College *B*
University of Iowa *M, D*

Kansas
Kansas State University *M*
University of Kansas Medical
　Center *M*

Kentucky
University of Kentucky *M*
University of Louisville *B, M*
Western Kentucky University *M*

Louisiana
Louisiana State University
　Health Sciences Center *M*
Tulane University *M, D*

Maine
University of New England *M*
University of Southern Maine *M*

Maryland
Howard Community College *A*
Johns Hopkins University *B, M*
Morgan State University *M, D*
University of Maryland
　Baltimore *M*
　College Park *B, M*

Massachusetts
Boston University *M, D*
Harvard College *M, D*
MCPHS University *B*
Northeastern University *M*

Springfield College *B, M*
University of Massachusetts
　Amherst *B, M, D*

Michigan
Calvin College *B*
Michigan State University *M*
Wayne State University *B, M*

Minnesota
Minnesota State University
　Mankato *M*
University of Minnesota
　Twin Cities *M*
Walden University *B, M, D*

Mississippi
Jackson State University *M, D*
University of Southern
　Mississippi *B, M*

Missouri
Maryville University of Saint Louis *B*
Missouri State University *M*
Saint Louis University *B, M, D*
University of Missouri
　Columbia *M*
Washington University in St. Louis *M*

Nebraska
University of Nebraska
　Medical Center *M*
　Omaha *B*

Nevada
University of Nevada
　Reno *M, D*

New Hampshire
Colby-Sawyer College *B*
University of New Hampshire *M*

New Jersey
Montclair State University *M*
New Jersey Institute of
　Technology *M*
Richard Stockton College of New
　Jersey *B*
Rutgers, The State University of New
　Jersey
　Camden Campus *M*
　New Brunswick/Piscataway
　　Campus *B, M, D*
　Newark Campus *M, D*

New Mexico
University of New Mexico *M*

New York
City University of New York
　Brooklyn College *M*
　Lehman College *M*
Hilbert College *M*
Hofstra University *M*
Ithaca College *B*
Long Island University
　LIU Brooklyn *M*
Monroe College *B, M*
New York University *B, M, D*
SUNY
　Downstate Medical Center *M, D*
　University at Albany *B, M, D*
　University at Buffalo *M*
　University at Stony Brook *M*
　Upstate Medical University *M*
St. John's University *M*
Syracuse University *B, M*
University of Rochester *M*
Yeshiva University *M*

North Carolina
East Carolina University *M*
Meredith College *B*

University of North Carolina
　Chapel Hill *M*
　Charlotte *D*

North Dakota
North Dakota State University *M*
University of North Dakota *M*

Ohio
Bluffton University *B*
Case Western Reserve University *M*
Cleveland State University *M*
Kent State University *B, M, D*
Ohio State University
　Columbus Campus *B, M, D*
University of Akron *M*
University of Toledo *M*
Wright State University *M*
Youngstown State University *M*

Oklahoma
Southwestern Oklahoma State
　University *B*
University of Central Oklahoma *M*
University of Oklahoma *M, D*

Oregon
Oregon Health & Science
　University *M*
Oregon State University *B, M, D*
Portland State University *B, M*

Pennsylvania
Arcadia University *M*
Drexel University *M, D*
East Stroudsburg University of
　Pennsylvania *M*
Keystone College *B*
La Salle University *M*
Mercyhurst University *B*
Slippery Rock University of
　Pennsylvania *B*
Temple University *M*
University of the Sciences *M*
West Chester University of
　Pennsylvania *B, M*

Puerto Rico
University of Puerto Rico
　Medical Sciences *M, D*

South Carolina
Benedict College *B*
University of South Carolina
　Columbia *B, M, D*

Tennessee
East Tennessee State University *B, M*
University of Memphis *M, D*
University of Tennessee
　Knoxville *M*
Vanderbilt University *M*

Texas
Argosy University
　Dallas *M*
University of Texas
　Austin *B*
　El Paso *M*
　Health Science Center at
　　Houston *M, D*
　Medical Branch at Galveston *M*
　San Antonio *B*

Utah
Argosy University
　Salt Lake City *M*
Snow College *A*
University of Utah *M, D*
Westminster College *M*

Virginia
George Mason University *M*
Liberty University *M*
Mary Baldwin College *B*
Old Dominion University *M*
Shenandoah University *B*
University of Virginia *M*
Virginia Commonwealth
　University *M*
Virginia Polytechnic Institute and
　State University *M*

Washington
Central Washington University *B*
Highline Community College *A*
University of Washington *B, M*

West Virginia
American Public University
　System *A, B, M*
Marshall University *B*
West Virginia University *M, D*

Wisconsin
University of Wisconsin
　Madison *M*
　Milwaukee *M, D*

Public health education

Arizona
Dine College *A*

Arkansas
University of Arkansas *B, M, D*

California
California Baptist University *B*
California State University
　Chico *T*
　Long Beach *B, M*
Loma Linda University *M, D*
San Francisco State University *B*

Colorado
University of Northern
　Colorado *B, M*

Georgia
Georgia Southern University *B, M*
University of Georgia *B, M, D*

Indiana
University of Indianapolis *B*

Iowa
University of Iowa *M, D*
University of Northern Iowa *D*

Kansas
Emporia State University *B*

Louisiana
Dillard University *B*
Southeastern Louisiana University *B*

Maryland
University of Maryland
　Baltimore *M, D*

Massachusetts
Boston University *M*
Hampshire College *B*
Simmons College *B*
Springfield College *B, M*

Michigan
Central Michigan University *B, M*
Eastern Michigan University *M*
University of Michigan *M, D*
University of Michigan
　Flint *B, M*

Minnesota

Minnesota State University
 Mankato *B, M*
Saint Cloud State University *B*
University of Minnesota
 Twin Cities *M*
University of St. Thomas *B*
Winona State University *B*

Nebraska

Nebraska Methodist College of
 Nursing and Allied Health *B, M*

New Hampshire

Colby-Sawyer College *B*
Plymouth State University *B, M*
Southern New Hampshire
 University *B*

New Jersey

Felician College *D*
Thomas Edison State College *B*

New Mexico

New Mexico State University *B, M*

New York

City University of New York
 Hunter College *M*
 York College *B*
SUNY
 College at Oswego *B*
 College at Potsdam *B*
 University at Buffalo *M*
Sarah Lawrence College *M*

North Carolina

Appalachian State University *B*
East Carolina University *B, M*
Elon University *B*
North Carolina Central University *B*
University of North Carolina
 Asheville *B*
 Chapel Hill *M, D*
 Charlotte *B, M*
 Greensboro *B, M, D*
 Wilmington *B*

North Dakota

University of North Dakota *B*

Ohio

Baldwin Wallace University *B*
Malone University *B*
University of Cincinnati *M*
University of Toledo *B, M*
Youngstown State University *B*

Oklahoma

Oklahoma State University *B*
University of Central Oklahoma *B, M*
University of Oklahoma *M, D*

Oregon

Oregon State University *B*
Portland State University *B, M*

Pennsylvania

Arcadia University *M*
Temple University *B, M, D*
University of Scranton *B*

Puerto Rico

Turabo University *D*
University of Puerto Rico
 Medical Sciences *B, M*

South Carolina

Coastal Carolina University *B*
University of South Carolina
 Columbia *M*

Texas

Baylor University *M*
Texas State University *B*
University of Texas
 Austin *B, M, D*
 El Paso *B, M*

Utah

University of Utah *B, M, D, T*

Vermont

Goddard College *B, M*

Virginia

Liberty University *B*
Lynchburg College *B*
Marymount University *B, M*
Virginia Commonwealth University *D*

Wisconsin

Carroll University *B*

Public health nursing

Alaska

University of Alaska
 Anchorage *M*

Arizona

Grand Canyon University *M*

California

California State University
 San Bernardino *M*

Connecticut

University of Hartford *M*

Florida

University of Miami *B*

Illinois

Northern Illinois University *B*
Southern Illinois University
 Edwardsville *M*

Indiana

Indiana University
 Purdue University Indianapolis *M*

Iowa

Allen College *M*
University of Iowa *M*

Louisiana

Louisiana State University
 Health Sciences Center *M*

Maryland

Coppin State University *M*

Massachusetts

Elms College *B*

Michigan

University of Michigan *M*
Wayne State University *M*

Minnesota

Augsburg College *B, M, D*
Metropolitan State University *M*

Missouri

University of Central Missouri *B*

Nebraska

Creighton University *M*
Kaplan University
 Lincoln *M*

New Jersey

William Paterson University of New
 Jersey *B, M*

New York

City University of New York
 Hunter College *B, M, D*
College of New Rochelle *M*
SUNY
 University at Binghamton *M*
Sage Colleges *M*

Ohio

Capital University *M*
Case Western Reserve University *M*
University of Cincinnati *M*
Wright State University *B, M, T*

Pennsylvania

Holy Family University *M*
St. Francis University *B*
Widener University *M*

South Carolina

University of South Carolina
 Columbia *M*

Texas

University of Texas
 Brownsville *M*
 El Paso *M*

Washington

Seattle University *M*

Public policy analysis

Arkansas

University of Arkansas *D*
University of Arkansas
 Little Rock *C*

California

California State University
 East Bay *B*
Loma Linda University *D*
Mills College *B, M*
Pepperdine University *M*
Pomona College *B*
Scripps College *B*
Stanford University *B*
University of California
 Berkeley *M, D*
 Irvine *M*
 Los Angeles *B*
 Riverside *B*
 San Diego *B*
University of Redlands *B*
University of Southern
 California *M, D*

Colorado

University of Denver *B, M*

Connecticut

Trinity College *B, M*
University of Saint Joseph *B*

District of Columbia

American University *M*
George Washington
 University *B, M, D*
Georgetown University *M*

Florida

Jacksonville University *M*
New College of Florida *B*
Southeastern University *B*
University of Miami *B*

Georgia

Georgia Institute of
 Technology *B, M, D*
Georgia State University *B, D*

Illinois

DePaul University *B, M*
Loyola University Chicago *M*
Northwestern University *B, M*
Olivet Nazarene University *B*
University of Chicago *B, M, D*
University of Illinois
 Chicago *D*

Indiana

Indiana University
 Bloomington *D*
 Purdue University Fort Wayne *B*
Indiana Wesleyan University *B*

Iowa

University of Northern Iowa *M*

Louisiana

Southern University and Agricultural
 and Mechanical College *D*

Maine

College of the Atlantic *B, M*
University of Southern Maine *M, D*

Maryland

Johns Hopkins University *B, M*
St. Mary's College of Maryland *B*
University of Maryland
 Baltimore County *M, D*
 College Park *M, D*

Massachusetts

Anna Maria College *B*
Bentley University *B*
Brandeis University *M, D*
Bristol Community College *C*
Hampshire College *B*
Harvard College *M, D*
Massachusetts College of Liberal
 Arts *B*
Northeastern University *M, D*
Simmons College *B*
University of Massachusetts
 Amherst *M*
 Boston *M, D*
 Dartmouth *M*

Michigan

Albion College *B*
Michigan State University *B, M*
Michigan Technological
 University *M, D*
University of Michigan *B, M, D*

Minnesota

University of Minnesota
 Twin Cities *M*
University of St. Thomas *M*
Walden University *M*

Mississippi

University of Mississippi *B*

Missouri

Saint Louis University *M, D*

New Hampshire

New England College *M*

New Jersey

Monmouth University *M*
New Jersey Institute of
 Technology *M*

Rutgers, The State University of New
Jersey
Camden Campus *D*
New Brunswick/Piscataway
Campus *M, D*
Saint Peter's University *A, B*
William Paterson University of New
Jersey *M*

New York

City University of New York
CUNY Online *C*
Cornell University *B*
Hamilton College *B*
Hobart and William Smith Colleges *B*
Niagara University *D*
Rochester Institute of
Technology *B, M*
SUNY
University at Albany *B, M*
University at Stony Brook *M*
Sage Colleges *B*
Wagner College *B*

North Carolina

Duke University *B, M, D*
Elon University *B*
University of North Carolina
Chapel Hill *B, M, D*
Charlotte *D*

Ohio

University of Akron *C*

Oregon

Oregon State University *M, D*

Pennsylvania

Carnegie Mellon University *B, M, D*
Chatham University *B*
Dickinson College *B*
Drexel University *M*
Duquesne University *M*
Immaculata University *A, B*
Lafayette College *B*
Penn State
Harrisburg *B*
St. Vincent College *B*
University of Pennsylvania *B, M, D*
University of Pittsburgh *M*

Rhode Island

Brown University *B*
Bryant University *B*
University of Rhode Island *B, M, D*

South Carolina

Clemson University *D*

Tennessee

Trevecca Nazarene University *B*
University of Tennessee
Knoxville *M*
Vanderbilt University *B*

Texas

Houston Baptist University *B*
Howard Payne University *B*
Rice University *B*
Southern Methodist University *B*
University of Texas
Austin *M, D*
Dallas *B, M, D*

Utah

Brigham Young University *M*
University of Utah *M*

Vermont

Bennington College *B*

Virginia

College of William and Mary *B, M*
George Mason University *M, D*
Regent University *B, M*
University of Virginia *M*
Virginia Polytechnic Institute and
State University *B*

Washington

University of Washington *M*
University of Washington Bothell *M*
Washington State University *B, M*

West Virginia

Marshall University *M*

Wisconsin

University of Wisconsin
Madison *M*
Superior *B*
Whitewater *B, T*

Public relations

Alabama

Auburn University *B*
Community College of the Air
Force *A*
Oakwood University *B*
University of Alabama *B*

Arizona

Glendale Community College *A*
Grand Canyon University *M*
Mesa Community College *A*
Scottsdale Community College *C, A*

Arkansas

Harding University *B*
John Brown University *A, B*

California

Biola University *B*
California Lutheran University *B*
California State University
Dominguez Hills *B*
East Bay *B*
Fullerton *B, M*
Long Beach *B*
Chapman University *B*
Cosumnes River College *A*
Fullerton College *C*
Golden Gate University *M*
Golden West College *C, A*
Long Beach City College *C, A*
Los Angeles City College *A*
Master's College *B*
Pepperdine University *B*
San Diego State University *B, M*
San Jose State University *B*
University of San Francisco *M*
University of Southern
California *B, M*

Colorado

University of Denver *M*

Connecticut

Manchester Community College *C*
Mitchell College *B*
Quinnipiac University *B*
Three Rivers Community College *A*
University of Bridgeport *B*

District of Columbia

Georgetown University *M*

Florida

Barry University *B, M*
Florida Agricultural and Mechanical
University *B*
Florida State University *B*
Indian River State College *A*

Palm Beach Atlantic University *B*
South Florida State College *A*
University of Florida *B*
University of Miami *B, M*

Georgia

Fort Valley State University *B*
Georgia Southern University *B*
Shorter University *B*
University of Georgia *B*

Hawaii

Chaminade University of Honolulu *B*
Hawaii Pacific University *B*

Idaho

Brigham Young University-Idaho *B*
North Idaho College *A*
University of Idaho *B*

Illinois

Bradley University *B*
Columbia College Chicago *B*
Dominican University *B*
Eureka College *B*
Greenville College *B*
Illinois State University *B*
Lewis University *B*
Loyola University Chicago *C*
McKendree University *B*
Monmouth College *B*
University of St. Francis *B*

Indiana

Ball State University *M*
Goshen College *B*
Grace College *B*
Huntington University *B*
Indiana University
Purdue University Indianapolis *M*
Indiana Wesleyan University *B*
Purdue University *B, M, D*
Taylor University *B*
Vincennes University *A*

Iowa

Coe College *B*
Dordt College *B*
Drake University *B*
Grand View University *B*
Loras College *B*
Mount Mercy University *B*
Northwestern College *B*
St. Ambrose University *B*
University of Northern Iowa *B*
Wartburg College *B*
William Penn University *B*

Kansas

Fort Scott Community College *A*
Kansas Wesleyan University *B*
Tabor College *B*

Kentucky

Campbellsville University *B*
Eastern Kentucky University *B*
Murray State University *B*
Northern Kentucky University *B*
Western Kentucky University *B*

Louisiana

University of Louisiana at Lafayette *B*

Maine

New England School of
Communications *B*
Saint Joseph's College of Maine *B*

Maryland

Cecil College *C*
Hood College *B*
Towson University *M*
University of Baltimore *B*

Massachusetts

American International College *B*
Boston University *B, M*
Cape Cod Community College *A*
Emerson College *B, M*
Lasell College *B, M*
Salem State University *B*
Simmons College *B*
Suffolk University *B, M*
Western New England University *B*

Michigan

Andrews University *B*
Central Michigan University *B*
Eastern Michigan University *B*
Ferris State University *B*
Grand Valley State University *B*
Kuyper College *B*
Macomb Community College *C, A*
Michigan State University *B, M*
Northern Michigan University *B*
Spring Arbor University *B*
Wayne State University *B*

Minnesota

Minneapolis College of Art and
Design *B*
Minnesota State University
Mankato *B*
Moorhead *B*
Saint Cloud State University *B*
Southwest Minnesota State
University *B*
University of Northwestern - St.
Paul *B*

Mississippi

Itawamba Community College *A*
Mississippi College *M*
Northwest Mississippi Community
College *A*
University of Southern Mississippi *M*

Missouri

Avila University *B*
College of the Ozarks *B*
Crowder College *A*
Drury University *B*
Missouri Baptist University *B*
Missouri State University *B*
Northwest Missouri State
University *B*
Stephens College *B*
University of Central Missouri *B*
University of Missouri
Columbia *M*
Webster University *B, M*

Montana

Carroll College *B*
Montana State University
Billings *B, M*

Nebraska

Hastings College *B*
Midland University *B*
Union College *B*
University of Nebraska
Kearney *B*

New Hampshire

Mount Washington College *A*
New England College *B*

New Jersey

Kean University *M*
Monmouth University *M*
Rider University *B*
Rowan University *B, M*
Seton Hall University *B*

New York

City University of New York
  City College *B*
Hofstra University *B, M*
Iona College *M*
Long Island University
  LIU Post *B*
Monroe Community College *A*
Mount Saint Mary College *B*
Rochester Institute of
    Technology *C, B*
SUNY
  College at Fredonia *B*
  College at New Paltz *B*
  College at Oswego *B*
St. Francis College *B*
St. Joseph's College New York:
  Suffolk Campus *C*
St. Joseph's College, New York *C*
Syracuse University *B, M*
Utica College *B*

North Carolina

Appalachian State University *B*
Campbell University *B*
Gardner-Webb University *B*
Wingate University *B*

North Dakota

Bismarck State College *A*
North Dakota State University *B*

Ohio

Ashland University *B*
Baldwin Wallace University *B*
Bowling Green State University *B*
Capital University *B*
Cleveland State University *B*
Defiance College *B*
Franklin University *A, B*
Heidelberg University *B*
Kent State University *B*
Malone University *B*
Marietta College *B*
Miami University
  Oxford *B*
Mount Vernon Nazarene University *B*
Notre Dame College *B*
Ohio Dominican University *B*
Otterbein University *B*
Tiffin University *B*
University of Akron *B*
University of Cincinnati *C*
University of Dayton *B*
University of Findlay *B*
University of Rio Grande *A, B*
Ursuline College *B*
Wilmington College *B*
Xavier University *B*
Youngstown State University *B*

Oklahoma

Northern Oklahoma College *A*
Oklahoma Baptist University *B*
Oklahoma Christian University *B*
Oklahoma City University *B*

Oregon

Marylhurst University *C*
Southern Oregon University *B*
University of Oregon *B*

Pennsylvania

Chatham University *B*
La Salle University *B*
Mansfield University of
  Pennsylvania *B*
Penn State
  Abington *C*
  Altoona *C*
  Beaver *C*
  Berks *C*
  Brandywine *C*
  DuBois *C*

Erie, The Behrend College *C*
Fayette, The Eberly Campus *C*
Greater Allegheny *C*
Harrisburg *C*
Hazleton *C*
Lehigh Valley *C*
Mont Alto *C*
New Kensington *C*
Schuylkill *C*
Shenango *C*
University Park *C*
Wilkes-Barre *C*
Worthington Scranton *C*
York *C*
St. Francis University *B*
Slippery Rock University of
  Pennsylvania *B*
Temple University *B, M*
University of Pittsburgh
  Bradford *B*
  Greensburg *B*
Waynesburg University *B*
Westminster College *B*
York College of Pennsylvania *B*

Puerto Rico

Inter American University of Puerto
  Rico
  Ponce Campus *B*
University of Puerto Rico
  Rio Piedras *B*
University of the Sacred Heart *M*

Rhode Island

University of Rhode Island *B*

South Carolina

University of South Carolina
  Columbia *B*
Winthrop University *B*

Tennessee

Belmont University *B*
Freed-Hardeman University *B*
Lee University *B*
Lipscomb University *B*
Southern Adventist University *B*
Union University *B*
University of Tennessee
  Knoxville *B*

Texas

Hardin-Simmons University *B*
North Lake College *C*
Our Lady of the Lake University of
  San Antonio *B*
Sam Houston State University *B*
Southern Methodist University *B*
Texas State University *B*
Texas Tech University *B*
Texas Wesleyan University *B*
University of Houston *B, M*
University of Texas
  Arlington *B*
  Austin *B*
  San Antonio *B*

Utah

Brigham Young University *B*
Weber State University *B*

Vermont

Champlain College *B*
University of Vermont *B*

Virginia

Hampton University *B*

Washington

Central Washington University *B*
Gonzaga University *B*
Seattle University *B*

West Virginia

Bethany College *B*
Concord University *B*
West Virginia University *B*
West Virginia Wesleyan College *B*
Wheeling Jesuit University *B*

Wisconsin

Carroll University *B*
Carthage College *B*
Marquette University *B*
Mount Mary University *B*

Public relations/advertising/applied communication

Arkansas

University of Central Arkansas *B*

California

California Baptist University *B, M*
California State University
  Dominguez Hills *B*
La Sierra University *B*

Florida

Flagler College *B*
Florida Southern College *B*
Lynn University *B*
University of Tampa *B*

Illinois

Quincy University *M*

Indiana

Butler University *B*
Franklin College *B*
Indiana University
  Purdue University Indianapolis *C*
Indiana Wesleyan University *B*
Purdue University *B*
Taylor University *B*

Kansas

Central Christian College of Kansas *B*
Colby Community College *A*

Kentucky

Northern Kentucky University *C*
University of Kentucky *B*

Maine

New England School of
  Communications *B*
Thomas College *B*

Maryland

Howard Community College *A*

Massachusetts

Endicott College *B*
Massachusetts College of Liberal
  Arts *B*

Michigan

Western Michigan University *B*

Minnesota

Augsburg College *B*
Crown College *B*
Minnesota State University
  Moorhead *B*
St. Mary's University of Minnesota *B*
Winona State University *B*

Missouri

Columbia College *B*

Nebraska

University of Nebraska
  Lincoln *B*

New York

Ithaca College *B*
Marist College *M*
SUNY
  College at Fredonia *B*

North Dakota

North Dakota State University *B*

Ohio

Ashland University *B*
Bluffton University *B*
Ohio Northern University *B*

Oklahoma

Mid-America Christian University *B*
University of Central Oklahoma *B*

Pennsylvania

Albright College *B*
Messiah College *B*
Point Park University *B*

Puerto Rico

Universidad Metropolitana *B*

Tennessee

Belmont University *B*

Texas

Howard Payne University *B*
Texas Christian University *B, M*

Utah

Weber State University *B*

West Virginia

Wheeling Jesuit University *B*

Publishing

California

Foothill College *C*
Long Beach City College *C, A*

Illinois

Benedictine University *B*

Massachusetts

Emerson College *B, M*

Michigan

Grand Rapids Community College *C*

Minnesota

Hennepin Technical College *C, A*
Minnesota State University
  Moorhead *C*
Ridgewater College *C, A*

New York

New York University *M*
Pace University *M*

Oregon

Clackamas Community College *C*

Texas

North Lake College *C*

Purchasing/procurement/contracts

Alabama

Athens State University *B*
Community College of the Air
  Force *A*
Miles College *B*

Arizona

Arizona State University *B*

Arkansas

Southern Arkansas University Tech *C*

California

California State University
   East Bay *C, B*
Coastline Community College *C*
De Anza College *C, A*
Folsom Lake College *C*
Fresno City College *C, A*
Fullerton College *A*
San Diego City College *C, A*
University of Redlands *C*

District of Columbia

Strayer University *C, A*
University of the District of
   Columbia *B*
University of the Potomac *B*

Florida

Florida Institute of Technology *M*
Northwest Florida State College *B*

Georgia

Atlanta Technical College *C*

Illinois

Harper College *C*
University of Illinois
   Urbana-Champaign *B, D*

Iowa

St. Ambrose University *C*

Maryland

Cecil College *C, A*

Massachusetts

Northern Essex Community
   College *C*

Michigan

Central Michigan University *B, M*

Minnesota

Capella University *M*

Missouri

Webster University *M*

New York

Cazenovia College *C*
Globe Institute of Technology *C*

Ohio

Columbus State Community
   College *C, A*
North Central State College *C*

Pennsylvania

Saint Joseph's University *B*

Puerto Rico

American University of Puerto
   Rico *B*

South Carolina

Greenville Technical College *A*

Tennessee

Middle Tennessee State University *B*

Texas

Brazosport College *A*
University of Houston
   Downtown *B*

Utah

Weber State University *M*

Virginia

Central Virginia Community
   College *C*
Northern Virginia Community
   College *C, A*
University of Management and
   Technology *M*
University of the Potomac *B*

Washington

Columbia Basin College *A*

Wisconsin

Northeast Wisconsin Technical
   College *C*

Quality control technology

Arkansas

East Arkansas Community College *C*

California

California State University
   Dominguez Hills *B, M*
San Jose State University *B, M*

Connecticut

Goodwin College *A*
Naugatuck Valley Community
   College *C, A*

Florida

College of Central Florida *A*
Tallahassee Community College *C*

Georgia

Southern Polytechnic State
   University *M*

Illinois

Heartland Community College *C*
Sauk Valley Community College *C*
Triton College *C*

Indiana

Indiana University
   Purdue University Fort Wayne *C*

Kentucky

Elizabethtown Community and
   Technical College *A*
Hopkinsville Community College *C*
Western Kentucky University *C*

Maryland

Community College of Baltimore
   County *C*

Michigan

Baker College
   Muskegon *C, A*
Eastern Michigan University *M*
Ferris State University *B*
Grand Rapids Community
   College *C, A*
Schoolcraft College *C, A*

Minnesota

Lake Superior College *C*
St. Cloud Technical and Community
   College *C*
St. Paul College *C*

Missouri

Metropolitan Community College -
   Kansas City *C, A*
Missouri Southern State University *C*

Nebraska

Central Community College *C, A*
Southeast Community College *A*

New Jersey

Burlington County College *C, A*

New Mexico

Eastern New Mexico University:
   Roswell *C, A*

New York

Broome Community College *C, A*

Ohio

Bowling Green State University *B*
Columbus State Community
   College *A*
James A. Rhodes State College *C, A*
Lorain County Community College *C*
Northwest State Community
   College *C, A*
Owens Community College
   Toledo *C, A*
Sinclair Community College *C, A*
University of Akron *C*

Oklahoma

Spartan College of Aeronautics and
   Technology *A, B*

Oregon

Clackamas Community College *C*

Pennsylvania

Northampton Community College *A*

Puerto Rico

Turabo University *A*

South Carolina

Tri-County Technical College *C*
Trident Technical College *C*

Tennessee

Southwest Tennessee Community
   College *C*

Texas

Tarleton State University *M*
Tarrant County College *C, A*

Utah

Weber State University *A*

Virginia

Tidewater Community College *A*

Wisconsin

Gateway Technical College *A*
Lakeshore Technical College *A*

Rabbinical studies (M.H.L., Rav.)

California

Hebrew Union College-Jewish
   Institute of Religion *P*

Colorado

Yeshiva Toras Chaim Talmudical
   Seminary *P*

Connecticut

Beth Benjamin Academy of
   Connecticut *P*

Illinois

Brisk Rabbinical College *P*
Hebrew Theological College: First
   Professional *P*

Maryland

Ner Israel Rabbinical College *P*

New York

Jewish Theological Seminary of
   America: First Professional *P*
Kehilath Yakov Rabbinical
   Seminary *P*
Kol Yaakov Torah Center *P*
Mesivta Eastern Parkway Rabbinical
   Seminary *P*
Mesivta Tifereth Jerusalem of
   America *P*
Mirrer Yeshiva Central Institute *P*
Ohr Hameir Theological Seminary *P*
Ohr Somayach Institutions: School of
   Theology *P*
Rabbi Isaac Elchanan Theological
   Seminary *P*
Rabbinical College Bobover Yeshiva
   B'nei Zion *P*
Rabbinical Seminary M'Kor Chaim *P*
Sh'or Yoshuv Rabbinical College *P*
Yeshiva Karlin Stolin Beth Aron
   Y'Israel Rabbinical Institute *P*
Yeshiva of Nitra Rabbinical College *P*
Yeshivat Mikdash Melech *P*

Ohio

Hebrew Union College-Jewish
   Institute of Religion *P*

Radiation biology

District of Columbia

George Washington University *D*

Iowa

University of Iowa *M, D*

Massachusetts

Suffolk University *B*

Ohio

University of Toledo *M*

Radiation protection/ health physics technology

Illinois

Lewis University *B*

Indiana

Indiana University
   Purdue University Indianapolis *B*

Kentucky

University of Kentucky *M*

New Jersey

Thomas Edison State College *A, B*

Ohio

University of Cincinnati
   Blue Ash College *A*

Tennessee

Fountainhead College of
   Technology *A*

Radio and television

Alabama

Auburn University *B*
Jacksonville State University *B*
Lawson State Community College *C*
Troy University *B*
University of Alabama *B, M*
University of Montevallo *B*

Arizona

Arizona Western College *A*
Northern Arizona University *B*

Arkansas

Arkansas State University *M*
John Brown University *B*

California

Biola University *B*
California State University
  Fullerton *B, M*
  Los Angeles *B, M*
  Monterey Bay *B*
  San Bernardino *B*
College of San Mateo *C, A*
College of the Canyons *C, A*
College of the Siskiyous *C, A*
Foothill College *C, A*
Master's College *B*
Moorpark College *C, A*
Oxnard College *A*
Palomar College *C, A*
Pepperdine University *B*
Rio Hondo College *C*
San Diego State University *B, M*
San Francisco State University *B, M*
San Joaquin Delta College *C, A*
San Jose State University *B*
Santa Monica College *C, A*
University of La Verne *B*

Colorado

Aims Community College *C, A*

Connecticut

Mitchell College *B*
Norwalk Community College *A*

Delaware

Delaware State University *B*

District of Columbia

Howard University *B*

Florida

Barry University *B, M*
Southeastern University *B*
University of Central Florida *B*
University of Florida *B*
University of Miami *B, M*

Georgia

Savannah College of Art and
  Design *B*

Illinois

Bradley University *B*
City Colleges of Chicago
  Kennedy-King College *A*
Columbia College Chicago *B*
DePaul University *M*
Lewis University *B*
Lewis and Clark Community
  College *A*
North Central College *B*
Northwestern University *B, M, D*
Parkland College *A*
Rock Valley College *C*
Southern Illinois University
  Carbondale *B*
University of St. Francis *B*
Western Illinois University *B*

Indiana

Ball State University *B, M*
Butler University *B*
Huntington University *B*
Indiana University
  Purdue University Indianapolis *M*
University of Southern Indiana *B, T*

Iowa

Drake University *B*
Grand View University *B*
Iowa Western Community College *A*
St. Ambrose University *B*

Kansas

Colby Community College *C, A*
Southwestern College *B*

Kentucky

Bluegrass Community and Technical
  College *A*
Murray State University *B*
Northern Kentucky University *B*
Owensboro Community and
  Technical College *C*
University of Kentucky *B*
Western Kentucky University *B*

Maine

New England School of
  Communications *B*

Massachusetts

American International College *B*
Boston University *M*
Lasell College *B*
Springfield College *B*

Michigan

Lawrence Technological University *A*
Michigan State University *B, M*
Wayne State University *B*

Minnesota

Northland Community & Technical
  College *C*
Saint Cloud State University *B*
Southwest Minnesota State
  University *B*
University of Northwestern - St.
  Paul *A, B*

Mississippi

Hinds Community College *A*
University of Southern Mississippi *B*

Missouri

Missouri Baptist University *B*
Missouri State University *B*
Northwest Missouri State
  University *B*
University of Missouri
  Columbia *B*

Nebraska

Hastings College *B*

New Jersey

Cumberland County College *A*
Montclair State University *B*
Rider University *B*
Rowan University *B*
Seton Hall University *B*

New York

Cayuga Community College *A*
City University of New York
  Brooklyn College *B, M*
Five Towns College *B*
Hofstra University *B*
Ithaca College *B*
New York Institute of Technology *B*
New York University *B*
Onondaga Community College *A*
SUNY
  College at Fredonia *B*
  College at Plattsburgh *B*
St. Francis College *B*
Syracuse University *B, M*

North Carolina

Appalachian State University *B*
Campbell University *B*
Elon University *B*

North Dakota

Minot State University *B*

Ohio

Ashland University *B*
Bowling Green State University *B, M*
Capital University *B*
Cedarville University *B*
International College of
  Broadcasting *C, A*
Kent State University *B*
Malone University *B*
Marietta College *B*
Ohio Northern University *B*
Ohio University *B, M, D*
Ohio University
  Southern Campus at Ironton *A*
University of Akron *B*
University of Cincinnati *B*
Xavier University *A, B*
Youngstown State University *B*

Oklahoma

Northeastern Oklahoma Agricultural
  and Mechanical College *A*

Oregon

Mt. Hood Community College *A*

Pennsylvania

Arcadia University *B*
Drexel University *M*
La Salle University *B*
Messiah College *B*
Point Park University *B*
Temple University *B, M*
University of Pittsburgh
  Bradford *B*

Puerto Rico

Colegio de Cinematografía, Artes y
  Televisión *A*
University of Puerto Rico
  Arecibo *B*

Texas

Alvin Community College *C, A*
Austin Community College *A*
Central Texas College *C, A*
Del Mar College *A*
Howard Payne University *B*
Lamar State College at Port Arthur *A*
North Lake College *C*
Palo Alto College *A*
Sam Houston State University *B*
San Antonio College *C, A*
Texas A&M University
  Commerce *B*
Texas Southern University *B*
Texas State University *B*
Texas Tech University *B*
Texas Wesleyan University *B*
University of Houston *B*
University of North Texas *B, M*
University of Texas
  Arlington *B*
  Austin *B, M, D*
University of the Incarnate Word *B*

Utah

Weber State University *B*

Vermont

Lyndon State College *B*

Virginia

Shenandoah University *C*

Washington

Centralia College *A*

West Virginia

Bethany College *B*

Wisconsin

Fox Valley Technical College *A*

Wyoming

Central Wyoming College *A*
Northwest College *C, A*

Radio/television broadcasting

Alabama

Alabama Agricultural and Mechanical
  University *B*

Arizona

Arizona Western College *A*
Scottsdale Community College *C, A*

Arkansas

Cossatot Community College of the
  University of Arkansas *C, A*
Mid-South Community College *C*
Southern Arkansas University Tech *C*

California

Cerritos College *A*
Chabot College *C, A*
City College of San Francisco *C*
College of San Mateo *C, A*
Diablo Valley College *C, A*
San Bernardino Valley College *C*
Southwestern College *C, A*

Colorado

Aims Community College *C, A*
Pikes Peak Community College *C, A*
Pueblo Community College *C*

Connecticut

Asnuntuck Community College *C, A*
Middlesex Community College *C, A*

Florida

Art Institute of Fort Lauderdale *A*
Miami Dade College *A*

Georgia

Savannah Technical College *C*

Hawaii

University of Hawaii
  Leeward Community College *C, A*

Illinois

Parkland College *A*
Waubonsee Community College *C, A*

Indiana

Vincennes University *A*

Iowa

Iowa Central Community College *A*

Kansas

Cloud County Community
  College *C, A*
Hutchinson Community College *A*

Louisiana

Bossier Parish Community College *C*

Maine

New England School of
  Communications *B*

Maryland

Bowie State University *B*
Montgomery College *C*
Towson University *B*

Massachusetts

Mount Wachusett Community
  College *A*
Newbury College *A*
Roxbury Community College *A*

Springfield Technical Community
College *A*
Suffolk University *B*
Worcester State University *B*

Michigan
Eastern Michigan University *B*
Ferris State University *B*
Oakland Community College *A*
Schoolcraft College *A*

Minnesota
Lake Superior College *C*

Mississippi
Hinds Community College *A*
Meridian Community College *A*

Missouri
College of the Ozarks *B*

Nebraska
Northeast Community College *A*
Southeast Community College *A*

New Hampshire
Mount Washington College *A*

New Jersey
Bergen Community College *A*
Brookdale Community College *A*
Mercer County Community
College *A*

New York
Adirondack Community College *C, A*
College of Saint Rose *B, M*
Long Island University
LIU Post *B*
Mercy College *C*
Monroe Community College *A*
New York Institute of
Technology *A, B, M*
New York University *C, B*
Tompkins Cortland Community
College *A*

North Carolina
Central Carolina Community
College *C, A*
Cleveland Community College *C, A*
Isothermal Community College *C, A*
Southeastern Community College *A*
Wilkes Community College *C, A*

Ohio
Hocking College *A*
North Central State College *A*

Oregon
Mt. Hood Community College *A*

Pennsylvania
Gannon University *B*
La Salle University *B*
Lehigh Carbon Community College *A*
Northampton Community College *A*
Thiel College *B*
Westmoreland County Community
College *C*

Puerto Rico
University of Puerto Rico
Aguadilla *B*
Arecibo *A, B*

Rhode Island
New England Institute of
Technology *A*

South Carolina
Technical College of the
Lowcountry *C*

Tri-County Technical College *C, A*
Trident Technical College *C, A*
York Technical College *C*

Tennessee
Trevecca Nazarene University *B*

Texas
Austin Community College *C*
Houston Community College
System *C, A*
San Jacinto College *C, A*
Tarrant County College *C, A*
Western Texas College *C, A*

Utah
Salt Lake Community College *A*

Virginia
Southwest Virginia Community
College *C*

Washington
Bates Technical College *C, A*
Centralia College *A*
Yakima Valley Community College *C*

Wisconsin
Gateway Technical College *A*
Milwaukee Area Technical College *A*

Radiologic technology/ medical imaging

Alabama
Community College of the Air
Force *A*
Gadsden State Community College *A*
George C. Wallace Community
College at Dothan *A*
Jefferson State Community College *A*
Southern Union State Community
College *A*
University of South Alabama *B*
Virginia College
Birmingham *A*
Wallace State Community College at
Hanceville *A*

Alaska
University of Alaska
Anchorage *A*

Arizona
Arizona Western College *A*
Central Arizona College *A*
GateWay Community College *A*
Pima Community College *A*

Arkansas
Henderson State University *B*
South Arkansas Community
College *A*
University of Arkansas
Fort Smith *A, B*

California
Bakersfield College *A*
Canada College *A*
Charles Drew University of Medicine
and Science *A*
Foothill College *A*
Fresno City College *A*
Loma Linda University *B, M*
Orange Coast College *A*
San Joaquin Delta College *A*

Colorado
Aims Community College *A*
Anthem College
Aurora *A*
Colorado Mesa University *A, B*
Colorado State University *M, D*

Community College of Denver *A*
Pikes Peak Community College *A*
Pueblo Community College *A*
Red Rocks Community College *A*

Connecticut
Gateway Community College *A*
Quinnipiac University *B, M*
St. Vincent's College *A*

Delaware
Delaware Technical Community
College
Jack F. Owens Campus *A*
Stanton/Wilmington Campus *A*

Florida
Adventist University of Health
Sciences *A, B*
Florida National University *A*
Herzing University
Winter Park *A*
Pasco-Hernando State College *A*
St. Petersburg College *A*
Valencia College *A, B*

Georgia
Athens Technical College *A*
Atlanta Technical College *A*
Columbus Technical College *A*
Georgia Highlands College *A*
Gordon College *A*
Gwinnett Technical College *A*
Southeastern Technical College *A*
Southern Crescent Technical
College *A*
Southwest Georgia Technical
College *A*
Wiregrass Georgia Technical
College *A*

Idaho
Lewis-Clark State College *A*

Illinois
Black Hawk College *A*
City Colleges of Chicago
Malcolm X College *A*
Wilbur Wright College *A*
Danville Area Community College *A*
Harper College *A*
Heartland Community College *A*
Kankakee Community College *A*
Kaskaskia College *A*
Lewis University *B*
Lincoln Land Community College *A*
Moraine Valley Community College *A*
Northwestern College *A*
Parkland College *A*
Richland Community College *A*
Sauk Valley Community College *A*
Trinity College of Nursing & Health
Sciences *A*
Triton College *A*
University of St. Francis *B*

Indiana
Indiana University
Kokomo *A*
Northwest *A, B*
Purdue University Indianapolis *A*
South Bend *A*
University of St. Francis *A*

Iowa
Allen College *A*
Clinton Community College *A*
Iowa Central Community College *A*
Northeast Iowa Community
College *A*
Northwest Iowa Community
College *A*
St. Luke's College *A*
University of Iowa *B*

Kansas
Friends University *B*
Labette Community College *A*
Washburn University *A*

Kentucky
St. Catharine College *B*
Spencerian College *A*

Louisiana
Delgado Community College *A*
Louisiana State University
Alexandria
Health Sciences Center *M*
McNeese State University *B*
Northwestern State University *B, M*
Our Lady of Holy Cross College *A*
Our Lady of the Lake College *A*
Southeastern Louisiana University *B*
University of Louisiana at Monroe *B*

Maine
Central Maine Medical Center College
of Nursing and Health
Professions *A*
Kennebec Valley Community
College *A*
Southern Maine Community
College *A*

Maryland
Carroll Community College *A*
Howard Community College *A*

Massachusetts
Boston University *M*
MCPHS University *B*
Massasoit Community College *A*
North Shore Community College *A*
Quinsigamond Community College *A*
Springfield Technical Community
College *A*

Michigan
Baker College
Clinton Township *A*
Muskegon *A*
Henry Ford Community College *A*
Jackson College *A*
Lake Michigan College *A*
Lansing Community College *A*
Northern Michigan University *A, B*
Oakland University *B*
Wayne State University *M*

Minnesota
Century College *A*
Lake Superior College *A*
Minnesota State College - Southeast
Technical *A*
Minnesota State Community and
Technical College *A*
Minnesota West Community and
Technical College *A*
Normandale Community College *A*
Northland Community & Technical
College *A*
Rochester Community and Technical
College *A*
St. Catherine University *A*
St. Mary's University of Minnesota *B*

Mississippi
Hinds Community College *A*
Meridian Community College *A*
Northeast Mississippi Community
College *A*

Missouri
Missouri State University *B*
Southeast Missouri Hospital College
of Nursing and Health
Sciences *A*

State Fair Community College *A*
University of Missouri
Columbia *B*

Montana
Montana State University
Billings *A*
Great Falls College *A*
Montana Tech of the University of
Montana *A*

Nebraska
Clarkson College *B*
Nebraska Methodist College of
Nursing and Allied Health *A, B*
University of Nebraska
Kearney *B*
Medical Center *B*

Nevada
Great Basin College *A*
Truckee Meadows Community
College *A*

New Hampshire
Lebanon College *A*
NHTI-Concord's Community
College *A*

New Jersey
Fairleigh Dickinson University
Metropolitan Campus *A, B*
Union County College *A*

New Mexico
Central New Mexico Community
College *A*
Eastern New Mexico University:
Roswell *A*

New York
Adirondack Community College *A*
St. John's University *B*
Trocaire College *B*

North Carolina
Carteret Community College *A*
Cleveland Community College *A*
Fayetteville Technical Community
College *A*
Forsyth Technical Community
College *A*
Johnston Community College *A*
Lenoir Community College *A*
Robeson Community College *A*
Rowan-Cabarrus Community
College *A*
South College *A, B*
Stanly Community College *A*

North Dakota
North Dakota State University *B*
University of Jamestown *B*
University of Mary *B*

Ohio
Aultman College of Nursing and
Health Sciences *A*
Central Ohio Technical College *A*
Kettering College *A*
Mercy College of Ohio *A*
North Central State College *A*
Sinclair Community College *A*
University of Cincinnati
Blue Ash College *A*
University of Rio Grande *A*
Xavier University *A*

Oklahoma
Oklahoma State University
Oklahoma City *A*
Rose State College *A*

Southwestern Oklahoma State
University *A*

Oregon
Central Oregon Community
College *A*
Linn-Benton Community College *A*
Oregon Institute of Technology *B*

Pennsylvania
Butler County Community College *A*
Gwynedd Mercy University *B*
Harcum College *A*
Harrisburg Area Community
College *A*
Holy Family University *A, B*
Johnson College *A*
Montgomery County Community
College *A*
Northampton Community College *A*
Pennsylvania College of Health
Sciences *A*
Pennsylvania Highlands Community
College *A*
University of Pittsburgh
Bradford *B*
Westmoreland County Community
College *A*
Widener University *A*
York College of Pennsylvania *B*

Puerto Rico
EDIC College *A*
Inter American University of Puerto
Rico
Aguadilla Campus *B*
Barranquitas Campus *A, B*
San German Campus *A, B*
Universidad Central del Caribe *B*
Universidad del Este *A*

Rhode Island
Community College of Rhode
Island *A*
Rhode Island College *B*

South Carolina
York Technical College *A*

South Dakota
Mitchell Technical Institute *A*
Mount Marty College *B*

Tennessee
Anthem Career College
Memphis *A*
Baptist College of Health Sciences *B*
South College *A, B*

Texas
Angelina College *A*
Austin Community College *A*
Brookhaven College *A*
Del Mar College *A*
Houston Community College
System *A*
Midwestern State University *A, B, M*
Paris Junior College *A*
St. Philip's College *A*
San Jacinto College *A*
South Texas College *A*
Tarrant County College *A*
Tyler Junior College *A*
Weatherford College *A*
Wharton County Junior College *A*

Utah
Dixie State College *A*

Vermont
Champlain College *A*
College of St. Joseph in
Vermont *A, B*
Southern Vermont College *B*

Virginia
ECPI University *A*
Germanna Community College *A*
Piedmont Virginia Community
College *A*
Southwest Virginia Community
College *A*
Virginia Commonwealth University *B*
Virginia Western Community
College *A*
Wytheville Community College *A*

Washington
Bellingham Technical College *A*
Clark College *A*
Wenatchee Valley College *A*

West Virginia
Bluefield State College *B*
Marshall University *B*
Pierpont Community and Technical
College *A*

Wisconsin
Carroll University *B*
Herzing University
Madison *A*
Lakeshore Technical College *A*
Marian University *B*
Nicolet Area Technical College *A*
Northcentral Technical College *A*
Western Technical College *A*

Wyoming
Casper College *A*
Laramie County Community
College *A*

Radiologist assistant

Arkansas
South Arkansas Community
College *A*

California
La Sierra University *C*
Loma Linda University *M*

Georgia
Dalton State College *A*

Massachusetts
MCPHS University *M*

New Mexico
Clovis Community College *A*

Texas
Midwestern State University *M*
Weatherford College *A*

Wisconsin
Bellin College *B*
Waukesha County Technical
College *A*

Railroad/railway transportation

Kansas
Johnson County Community
College *C, A*

Montana
Montana State University
Northern *A*

Range science

California
College of the Redwoods *C*
Humboldt State University *B, M*

University of California
Berkeley *M*
Davis *B*

Colorado
Colorado State University *B, M, D*

Idaho
College of Southern Idaho *A*
University of Idaho *B*

Indiana
Purdue University *B*

Kansas
Pratt Community College *A*

Montana
Montana State University *M, D*

Nebraska
Chadron State College *B*
University of Nebraska
Lincoln *B*

New Mexico
Navajo Technical University *C*
New Mexico State University *B, M, D*

North Dakota
North Dakota State
University *B, M, D*

Oregon
Oregon State University *B, M, D*
Treasure Valley Community
College *C, A*

South Dakota
Sinte Gleska University *A*
South Dakota State University *C, B*

Texas
Frank Phillips College *A*
Sul Ross State University *B, M*
Texas A&M University *B, M, D*
Texas A&M University
Kingsville *B, M, D*
Texas Tech University *B, M, D*

Utah
Utah State University *B, M, D*

Wyoming
Casper College *A*
Central Wyoming College *A*
Eastern Wyoming College *A*
Northwest College *A*
Sheridan College *A*
University of Wyoming *B, M, D*

Reading teacher education

Alabama
Auburn University *M, T*
Jacksonville State University *M, T*

Alaska
University of Alaska
Fairbanks *T*

Arizona
University of Arizona *M, D*

Arkansas
Arkansas State University *M, T*
Harding University *M, T*
University of Arkansas
Little Rock *M, D*
University of Central Arkansas *M*

California

Azusa Pacific University *M, T*
California Baptist University *T*
California Lutheran University *B, T*
California State University
  Chico *T*
  Dominguez Hills *M*
  East Bay *M, T*
  Fresno *M*
  Fullerton *M, T*
  Long Beach *T*
  Sacramento *M*
  San Bernardino *M, T*
Fresno Pacific University *M, T*
Loyola Marymount University *M, T*
National University *T*
St. Mary's College of California *M*
San Diego State University *M, T*
Sonoma State University *M, T*
University of La Verne *M*
University of San Francisco *M*

Colorado

Adams State University *M*
Regis University *M*
University of Northern
  Colorado *M, T*

Connecticut

Central Connecticut State
  University *M*
Eastern Connecticut State
  University *M*
Southern Connecticut State
  University *M*

District of Columbia

Howard University *M*

Florida

Barry University *M*
Florida Atlantic University *M*
Florida Gulf Coast University *M*
Florida International University *M*
Florida Memorial University *M*
Florida State University *D*
Saint Leo University *M*
Stetson University *M*
University of Central Florida *M*
University of Florida *M*
University of Miami *M*
University of South Florida *M*
University of South Florida
  Saint Petersburg *M*
  Sarasota-Manatee *M*
University of West Florida *M*

Georgia

Armstrong Atlantic State
  University *M*
Berry College *M*
Georgia College and State
  University *M*
Georgia Southern University *M*
Georgia State University *M*
Kennesaw State University *M*
Mercer University *M*
University of Georgia *M, D, T*
University of West Georgia *M*
Valdosta State University *M*

Idaho

Boise State University *M*
Northwest Nazarene University *M*

Illinois

Aurora University *M*
Benedictine University *M*
Chicago State University *M, T*
Concordia University Chicago *M*
DePaul University *M, T*
Dominican University *M*
Governors State University *M*
Greenville College *M, T*

Illinois State University *M*
Judson University *M, D*
Lewis University *M*
Loyola University Chicago *M*
National-Louis University *M, D*
North Central College *T*
North Park University *T*
Northeastern Illinois University *M*
Northern Illinois University *M, D*
Rockford University *M*
Roosevelt University *M*
Saint Xavier University *M*
Southern Illinois University
  Edwardsville *M*
University of St. Francis *M*
Western Illinois University *M*

Indiana

Butler University *M, T*
Huntington University *M*
Oakland City University *B*
Saint Mary's College *T*
University of Indianapolis *T*

Iowa

Briar Cliff University *B*
Buena Vista University *B, T*
Central College *T*
Dordt College *B*
Drake University *M, T*
Graceland University *T*
Grand View University *T*
Iowa State University *T*
Iowa Wesleyan College *T*
Mount Mercy University *M, T*
Northwestern College *T*
St. Ambrose University *T*
Simpson College *T*
University of Iowa *M*
University of Northern Iowa *B, M*
Upper Iowa University *B, M, T*
Wartburg College *T*

Kansas

Garden City Community College *A*
Washburn University *M, T*

Kentucky

Campbellsville University *B*
Georgetown College *M*
Murray State University *M, T*
Union College *M*
University of Louisville *M*
University of the Cumberlands *M, T*
Western Kentucky University *M*

Louisiana

Centenary College of Louisiana *T*
Nicholls State University *M*

Maine

University of Maine *M, D*
University of Southern Maine *M, T*

Maryland

Bowie State University *M*
Coppin State University *M*
Frostburg State University *M, T*
Hood College *M*
Loyola University Maryland *M*
McDaniel College *M*
Mount St. Mary's University *T*
Salisbury University *M*
Towson University *M*

Massachusetts

Boston College *M*
Boston University *M, T*
Bridgewater State University *M, T*
Eastern Nazarene College *M, T*
Elms College *M*
Endicott College *M*
Fitchburg State University *M, T*
Framingham State University *M*

Lesley University *M*
Salem State University *M*
Tufts University *M*
University of Massachusetts
  Lowell *M, D*
Westfield State University *M, T*
Wheelock College *M*
Worcester State University *M, T*

Michigan

Andrews University *M*
Aquinas College *B, T*
Calvin College *B, M, T*
Central Michigan University *M*
Eastern Michigan University *B, M*
Marygrove College *M*
Michigan State University *B, M*
Northern Michigan University *M*
Oakland University *M, D*
Saginaw Valley State University *M, T*
University of Detroit Mercy *B, M, T*
Wayne State University *M, D*
Western Michigan University *M, T*

Minnesota

Capella University *M*
Hamline University *M, T*
Saint Cloud State University *B, T*
St. Mary's University of Minnesota *M*
University of St. Thomas *M*

Mississippi

Jackson State University *M*
Millsaps College *T*
Mississippi University for Women *M*
University of Mississippi *M*

Missouri

Avila University *T*
Evangel University *M*
Maryville University of Saint
  Louis *M, T*
Missouri Baptist University *T*
Missouri Southern State
  University *B, T*
Missouri State University *M*
Northwest Missouri State
  University *M, T*
University of Central Missouri *M*
University of Missouri
  Columbia *M, D*
  Kansas City *M*
Webster University *M*

Montana

Montana State University
  Billings *M, T*
University of Great Falls *B*
University of Montana: Western *T*

Nebraska

Chadron State College *M*
College of Saint Mary *T*
Concordia University *M*
Hastings College *M*
University of Nebraska
  Kearney *M, T*
  Omaha *M*
York College *B, T*

New Hampshire

Granite State College *T*
Plymouth State University *M, T*
Rivier University *M*
Southern New Hampshire
  University *M*
University of New Hampshire *M*

New Jersey

Caldwell College *M, T*
College of New Jersey *M, T*
Georgian Court University *T*
Kean University *M, T*
Monmouth University *M*

Montclair State University *M, T*
New Jersey City University *B*
Richard Stockton College of New
  Jersey *M*
Rider University *M*
Rowan University *M, T*
Rutgers, The State University of New
  Jersey
  New Brunswick/Piscataway
    Campus *M*
Saint Peter's University *M, T*
William Paterson University of New
  Jersey *T*

New Mexico

Western New Mexico University *M*

New York

Adelphi University *M, T*
Canisius College *M, T*
City University of New York
  Lehman College *M*
  Queens College *M, T*
College of New Rochelle *M, T*
College of Saint Rose *M*
Dowling College *M, T*
Hofstra University *M, D, T*
Iona College *M, T*
Le Moyne College *M*
Long Island University
  LIU Brooklyn *M, T*
  LIU Post *B, M, T*
Manhattanville College *M, T*
Medaille College *M, T*
Medaille College: Amherst *M*
Mercy College *M*
Nazareth College *M*
New York University *M*
Pace University *M, T*
Pace University: Pleasantville/
  Briarcliff *M, T*
Roberts Wesleyan College *M*
SUNY
  College at Brockport *M*
  College at Buffalo *B, M, T*
  College at Cortland *M*
  College at Fredonia *M, T*
  College at Geneseo *M, T*
  College at New Paltz *M, T*
  College at Oneonta *M*
  College at Oswego *M*
  College at Plattsburgh *M*
  College at Potsdam *M*
  University at Albany *M, D*
  University at Binghamton *M*
  University at Buffalo *M, D*
Sage Colleges *M*
Saint Bonaventure University *M*
St. John's University *M, D, T*
St. Joseph's College New York:
  Suffolk Campus *M*
St. Joseph's College, New York *M*
St. Thomas Aquinas College *M*
Syracuse University *M, D*
University of Rochester *M*

North Carolina

Appalachian State University *M, T*
Catawba College *T*
East Carolina University *M*
Mars Hill University *T*
Meredith College *M*
North Carolina Agricultural and
  Technical State University *M, T*
North Carolina State University *M, T*
Queens University of Charlotte *M*
University of North Carolina
  Asheville *T*
  Charlotte *M*
  Pembroke *M*
  Wilmington *M*
Wingate University *B, T*

North Dakota

Dickinson State University *B, T*
University of Mary *B*
University of North Dakota *M*

Ohio

Ashland University *M, T*
Baldwin Wallace University *M*
Bowling Green State University *M, T*
Hiram College *T*
John Carroll University *M, T*
Kent State University *M*
Lake Erie College *B, M*
Malone University *M*
Miami University
    Oxford *M*
Notre Dame College *M, T*
Ohio Northern University *B, T*
Ohio University *M*
Otterbein University *M*
Union Institute & University *B*
University of Akron *M*
University of Cincinnati *M, D*
University of Dayton *M, T*
University of Findlay *B, M, T*
University of Rio Grande *B, T*
Ursuline College *T*
Walsh University *B*
Wilmington College *M, T*
Wright State University *M*
Xavier University *M*

Oklahoma

Cameron University *M*
East Central University *M*
Northeastern State University *M, T*
Northwestern Oklahoma State
    University *M*
Southeastern Oklahoma State
    University *M, T*
Southern Nazarene University *B*
University of Central Oklahoma *B, M*

Oregon

George Fox University *M, T*
Portland State University *T*
Warner Pacific College *T*
Western Oregon University *B, M, T*

Pennsylvania

Arcadia University *M*
Bloomsburg University of
    Pennsylvania *M, T*
Bucknell University *M*
Cabrini College *T*
California University of
    Pennsylvania *M*
Chestnut Hill College *M, T*
Clarion University of
    Pennsylvania *M, T*
Duquesne University *M, T*
East Stroudsburg University of
    Pennsylvania *M, T*
Edinboro University of
    Pennsylvania *M*
Gannon University *M*
Geneva College *M*
Gwynedd Mercy University *M, T*
Holy Family University *M, T*
Indiana University of
    Pennsylvania *M, T*
King's College *M*
Kutztown University of
    Pennsylvania *M*
Lincoln University *M, T*
Marywood University *M*
Millersville University of
    Pennsylvania *M, T*
Penn State
    Harrisburg *M*
Saint Joseph's University *M, T*
Shippensburg University of
    Pennsylvania *M, T*
University of Pennsylvania *M, D*

University of Scranton *M*
West Chester University of
    Pennsylvania *M, T*
Westminster College *M*
Widener University *M, D*
York College of Pennsylvania *M, T*

Rhode Island

Providence College *M*
Rhode Island College *M*
Roger Williams University *M*

South Carolina

Citadel *M*
Clemson University *M*
University of South Carolina
    Columbia *M, D*
Winthrop University *M, T*

South Dakota

Black Hills State University *M*
University of Sioux Falls *M*

Tennessee

Austin Peay State University *M*
Christian Brothers University *M, T*
East Tennessee State University *M, T*
Middle Tennessee State University *M*
Tennessee Technological
    University *M, D, T*
Trevecca Nazarene University *M, T*
Vanderbilt University *M, T*

Texas

Angelo State University *M*
Dallas Baptist University *B, M, T*
Hardin-Simmons University *M, T*
Houston Baptist University *M*
Jarvis Christian College *B*
Laredo Community College *A*
Midwestern State University *M*
Prairie View A&M University *M*
St. Mary's University *M, T*
Sam Houston State
    University *M, D, T*
Southern Methodist University *T*
Southwestern Assemblies of God
    University *B*
Southwestern University *T*
Stephen F. Austin State University *T*
Sul Ross State University *M*
Texas A&M International
    University *B, M, T*
Texas A&M University
    Commerce *M, T*
    Corpus Christi *M, D, T*
    Kingsville *M, T*
Texas Lutheran University *B, T*
Texas State University *M, T*
Texas Tech University *M*
Texas Wesleyan University *M*
Texas Woman's University *M, D*
University of Dallas *T*
University of Houston
    Clear Lake *M, T*
    Victoria *M*
University of Mary Hardin-
    Baylor *M, T*
University of North Texas *M, D*
University of St. Thomas *M*
University of Texas
    Brownsville *M*
    El Paso *M*
    Pan American *M*
    Permian Basin *M*
    San Antonio *M, T*
    Tyler *M*
West Texas A&M University *T*

Vermont

College of St. Joseph in
    Vermont *M, T*
Johnson State College *M*
Saint Michael's College *M, T*

Virginia

Averett University *M*
Bluefield College *B*
College of William and Mary *M*
James Madison University *T*
Lynchburg College *M*
Old Dominion University *M*
Radford University *M*
Virginia Commonwealth
    University *M*

Washington

Central Washington
    University *B, M, T*
City University of Seattle *M*
Eastern Washington University *B, M*
Heritage University *B*
Northwest University *T*
Pacific Lutheran University *M*
Seattle Pacific University *M*
Walla Walla University *M*
Washington State
    University *B, M, D, T*
Western Washington University *M*
Whitworth University *T*

West Virginia

Marshall University *M*
West Virginia University *M, T*
West Virginia Wesleyan College *M*

Wisconsin

Alverno College *M, T*
Cardinal Stritch University *M*
Carroll University *T*
Carthage College *M, T*
Concordia University Wisconsin *M, T*
Mount Mary University *T*
Silver Lake College of the Holy
    Family *T*
University of Wisconsin
    Oshkosh *M*
    Platteville *T*
    River Falls *M, T*
    Superior *M, T*
    Whitewater *M*

Real estate

Alabama

Calhoun Community College *A*
Jefferson Davis Community
    College *C*

Arizona

Coconino County Community
    College *C*
Mesa Community College *C, A*
Paradise Valley Community College *C*
Phoenix College *C*
Yavapai College *C*

California

American River College *C, A*
Antelope Valley College *C, A*
Bakersfield College *C, A*
Butte College *C, A*
Cabrillo College *C, A*
California State University
    Dominguez Hills *B*
    East Bay *B*
    Fresno *B*
    Long Beach *B*
    Northridge *B*
    Sacramento *B, M*
    San Bernardino *B*
Cerritos College *C, A*
Chabot College *A*
Citrus College *C*
City College of San Francisco *C, A*
Coastline Community College *C, A*
College of Marin *C, A*
College of San Mateo *C, A*

College of the Canyons *C, A*
College of the Redwoods *A*
College of the Sequoias *C, A*
Contra Costa College *A*
Cosumnes River College *C, A*
Cuesta College *C, A*
Cuyamaca College *A*
De Anza College *C, A*
Diablo Valley College *C, A*
East Los Angeles College *C, A*
El Camino College *C, A*
Folsom Lake College *C, A*
Foothill College *C, A*
Fresno City College *C, A*
Fullerton College *C, A*
Glendale Community College *C, A*
Golden West College *C, A*
Hartnell College *C, A*
Irvine Valley College *C, A*
Long Beach City College *C, A*
Los Angeles City College *C, A*
Los Angeles Harbor College *C, A*
Los Angeles Mission College *C, A*
Los Angeles Southwest College *C, A*
Los Angeles Trade and Technical
    College *C, A*
Los Medanos College *C, A*
Menlo College *B*
Merced College *C, A*
Merritt College *C, A*
MiraCosta College *C, A*
Mission College *A*
Modesto Junior College *A*
Monterey Peninsula College *C, A*
Moreno Valley College *C, A*
Mount San Antonio College *C, A*
Mount San Jacinto College *C, A*
Napa Valley College *C, A*
National University *A*
Norco College *C, A*
Ohlone College *C, A*
Orange Coast College *C, A*
Pacific States University *M*
Palomar College *C, A*
Pasadena City College *C, A*
Porterville College *C, A*
Riverside City College *C, A*
Sacramento City College *C, A*
Saddleback College *C, A*
San Bernardino Valley College *C, A*
San Diego City College *C, A*
San Diego Mesa College *C, A*
San Diego State University *B, M*
San Joaquin Delta College *C, A*
San Jose City College *C, A*
Santa Barbara City College *C, A*
Santa Rosa Junior College *C*
Shasta College *A*
Sierra College *C, A*
Solano Community College *C, A*
Southwestern College *C, A*
University of San Diego *B, M*
Victor Valley College *C, A*
West Los Angeles College *C, A*
West Valley College *C, A*

Colorado

Arapahoe Community College *C*
Colorado Mesa University *C*
Colorado Mountain College *C, A*
Colorado State University *B*
Community College of Aurora *C*
Red Rocks Community College *C, A*
University of Denver *B*

Connecticut

Manchester Community College *C*
University of Connecticut *B*

District of Columbia

American University *M*
George Washington University *M*
Georgetown University *M*

Florida

Florida Atlantic University *B*
Florida International University *B, M*
Florida State College at
    Jacksonville *C*
Florida State University *B*
Miami Dade College *C, A*
Nova Southeastern University *M*
Seminole State College of Florida *C*
University of Central Florida *B, M*
University of Florida *B, M*
University of Miami *B*
University of South Florida *M*

Georgia

Georgia State University *B, M, D*
University of Georgia *B*
University of West Georgia *B*

Idaho

College of Southern Idaho *A*

Illinois

City Colleges of Chicago
    Harry S. Truman College *C*
    Richard J. Daley College *C*
College of DuPage *C, A*
DePaul University *B, M*
Harper College *C*
Illinois Central College *C, A*
Joliet Junior College *C*
Kishwaukee College *C*
Lewis and Clark Community
    College *C*
Lincoln Land Community College *C*
McHenry County College *C, A*
Northwestern University *M*
Roosevelt University *M*
Southwestern Illinois College *C*
University of Illinois
    Chicago *M*
    Urbana-Champaign *B, M, D*
Waubonsee Community College *C*

Iowa

Ashford University *B*
Grand View University *C, B*
University of Northern Iowa *B*

Kentucky

Ashland Community and Technical
    College *A*
Big Sandy Community and Technical
    College *A*
Elizabethtown Community and
    Technical College *A*
Jefferson Community and Technical
    College *C, A*
Madisonville Community College *A*
Morehead State University *B*
Northern Kentucky University *A*
University of Louisville *C*
West Kentucky Community and
    Technical College *A*
Western Kentucky University *C*

Maryland

University of Baltimore *B*

Massachusetts

Bristol Community College *A*
Greenfield Community College *C*

Michigan

Central Michigan University *B*
Delta College *C*
Henry Ford Community College *A*
Lansing Community College *C, A*

Minnesota

Dakota County Technical
    College *C, A*
Saint Cloud State University *B*

University of Minnesota
    Twin Cities *B*
University of St. Thomas *B, M*

Mississippi

Hinds Community College *A*
Mississippi State University *B*
University of Mississippi *B*

Missouri

State Fair Community College *C*
University of Missouri
    Columbia *B*

Nebraska

Northeast Community College *A*
University of Nebraska
    Omaha *B*

Nevada

College of Southern Nevada *C, A*
Truckee Meadows Community
    College *A*
University of Nevada
    Las Vegas *B*
Western Nevada College *A*

New Hampshire

Lakes Region Community College *C*

New Jersey

Burlington County College *C, A*
Camden County College *C*
Gloucester County College *C*
Thomas Edison State College *B*

New Mexico

New Mexico Junior College *A*

New York

City University of New York
    Baruch College *B*
Cornell University *M*
Hudson Valley Community College *A*
New York University *B, M*
Syracuse University *B*
Utica School of Commerce *C*

North Carolina

Asheville-Buncombe Technical
    Community College *C*
Blue Ridge Community College *C*
Cape Fear Community College *C*
Catawba Valley Community
    College *A*
Central Piedmont Community
    College *C, A*
Forsyth Technical Community
    College *C*
Isothermal Community College *C*
Pitt Community College *C*
St. Augustine's University *B*
Sampson Community College *C*
Southwestern Community College *C*
Surry Community College *C, A*
Tri-County Community College *C*
University of North Carolina
    Charlotte *M*

Ohio

Bowling Green State University *B*
Cincinnati State Technical and
    Community College *A*
Columbus State Community
    College *C, A*
Cuyahoga Community College
    Metropolitan *A*
Eastern Gateway Community
    College *C*
Edison State Community College *C, A*
Hocking College *C*
Hondros College *A*
Lakeland Community College *C*

Miami University
    Hamilton *A*
Northwest State Community
    College *C*
Ohio Business College
    Sandusky *C*
Ohio State University
    Columbus Campus *B*
Ohio University
    Southern Campus at Ironton *C*
Sinclair Community College *C, A*
Southern State Community College *A*
Terra State Community College *A*
University of Akron *B*
University of Cincinnati *B*
University of Cincinnati
    Blue Ash College *C, A*

Oklahoma

Oklahoma City Community
    College *A*
Tulsa Community College *A*

Oregon

Marylhurst University *B, M*

Pennsylvania

Clarion University of Pennsylvania *B*
Community College of
    Philadelphia *A*
Drexel University *B*
Harrisburg Area Community
    College *C, A*
La Roche College *B*
Luzerne County Community
    College *A*
Montgomery County Community
    College *C, A*
Northampton Community College *C*
St. Francis University *A*
Temple University *B*
University of Pennsylvania *B, M, D*
Villanova University *B*
Westmoreland County Community
    College *C, A*

South Carolina

Clemson University *M*
University of South Carolina
    Columbia *B*

Texas

Amarillo College *C, A*
Angelina College *C*
Angelo State University *B*
Austin Community College *C, A*
Baylor University *B*
Blinn College *C*
Cedar Valley College *C, A*
Central Texas College *C, A*
Cisco College *C*
College of the Mainland *A*
Collin County Community College
    District *C, A*
Del Mar College *C*
El Paso Community College *C, A*
Houston Community College
    System *C, A*
Lamar Institute of Technology *C, A*
Laredo Community College *C, A*
Lee College *C*
McLennan Community College *C, A*
North Lake College *A*
Richland College *C, A*
San Antonio College *C*
San Jacinto College *C, A*
South Plains College *C, A*
Southern Methodist University *B, M*
Tarrant County College *C, A*
Texarkana College *C*
Texas A&M University *M*
Texas Christian University *B*
Trinity Valley Community College *C*
University of North Texas *B, M*

University of Texas
    Arlington *B, M*
    Austin *C*
    San Antonio *B*

Utah

University of Utah *M*

Virginia

Eastern Shore Community College *C*
George Mason University *M*
J. Sargeant Reynolds Community
    College *C*
John Tyler Community College *C*
Lord Fairfax Community College *C*
Northern Virginia Community
    College *C, A*
Tidewater Community College *A*
Virginia Commonwealth University *B*
Virginia Polytechnic Institute and
    State University *B*

Washington

Bellevue College *C, A*
Green River Community College *C, A*
North Seattle Community
    College *C, A*
Washington State University *B*

West Virginia

American Public University
    System *C, A*
Davis and Elkins College *A*

Wisconsin

Madison Area Technical College *A*
Marquette University *B*
Milwaukee Area Technical College *A*
University of Wisconsin
    Madison *B, M*
    Milwaukee *C, B*
    Stout *B*
Waukesha County Technical
    College *A*

Real estate development

Alabama

Auburn University *M*

Arizona

Arizona State University *M*

California

University of Southern California *M*

District of Columbia

Catholic University of America *M*

Massachusetts

Massachusetts Institute of
    Technology *M*

Receptionist

Arizona

Cochise College *C*

California

Empire College *C*
Kaplan College
    Riverside *C*
Ohlone College *A*

Illinois

Illinois Eastern Community Colleges
    Frontier Community College *C*
    Wabash Valley College *C*

Iowa

Southeastern Community College *A*

Massachusetts

Bristol Community College *A*
Bunker Hill Community College *C*
Holyoke Community College *C*

Michigan

Baker College
  Muskegon *C*

Minnesota

Alexandria Technical and Community
  College *C*
Anoka Technical College *C*
Dakota County Technical College *C*
Minnesota State College - Southeast
  Technical *C*
Minnesota State Community and
  Technical College *C*
Minnesota West Community and
  Technical College *C*
South Central College *C*

New York

Globe Institute of Technology *C*

North Dakota

Dakota College at Bottineau *A*

Oregon

Clackamas Community College *C*

Texas

Brookhaven College *C*
Eastfield College *C*

Utah

Salt Lake Community College *C*

Virginia

Danville Community College *A*

Washington

Bellingham Technical College *C*
Centralia College *C, A*
Clark College *C*
Columbia Basin College *C*
Peninsula College *C*

West Virginia

New River Community and Technical
  College *C*

Recording arts

Arizona

Glendale Community College *C, A*
Mesa Community College *C, A*
Paradise Valley Community
  College *C, A*
Phoenix College *C, A*

California

Art Institute of California
  Inland Empire *B*
City College of San Francisco *C*
Los Medanos College *C, A*
Loyola Marymount University *B*
Southwestern College *C, A*

Colorado

Aims Community College *C, A*

Florida

Full Sail University *A*
Miami International University of Art
  and Design *B*

Georgia

Art Institute of Atlanta *B*
Savannah College of Art and
  Design *B, M*

Illinois

Columbia College Chicago *B*
School of the Art Institute of
  Chicago *B, M*
Waubonsee Community College *C*

Indiana

Butler University *B*
Indiana University
  Bloomington *A, B*
Vincennes University *C, A*

Iowa

Western Iowa Tech Community
  College *C, A*

Kansas

Kansas City Kansas Community
  College *A*

Louisiana

Bossier Parish Community College *C*

Maine

New England School of
  Communications *B*

Maryland

Johns Hopkins University: Peabody
  Conservatory of Music *B, M*
Montgomery College *C*

Massachusetts

Springfield Technical Community
  College *A*

Michigan

Art Institute of Michigan *B*
Michigan Technological University *B*
Schoolcraft College *C, A*

Minnesota

Art Institutes International
  Minnesota *B*
Hennepin Technical College *C, A*
Institute of Production and
  Recording *A*
Minneapolis Community and
  Technical College *C, A*
North Central University *B*

Nebraska

Northeast Community College *C, A*

Nevada

Art Institute of Las Vegas *B*
International Academy of Design and
  Technology
  Henderson *B*

New Jersey

Bergen Community College *A*
Union County College *C, A*

New York

Cayuga Community College *A*
City University of New York
  LaGuardia Community College *A*
  Queensborough Community
    College *A*
Finger Lakes Community College *A*
Five Towns College *A, B, M*
Ithaca College *B*
Jamestown Community College *C*
SUNY
  College at Fredonia *B*

North Carolina

Elon University *B*
Guilford Technical Community
  College *A*

Ohio

Cleveland Institute of Music *B*
Malone University *B*

Oregon

Clackamas Community College *C*

Pennsylvania

Art Institute of Philadelphia *B*
Community College of
  Philadelphia *A*
Harrisburg Area Community
  College *A*
Lebanon Valley College *B*
Lehigh Carbon Community College *A*
Luzerne County Community
  College *A*
Montgomery County Community
  College *A*
York College of Pennsylvania *B*

Puerto Rico

Colegio de Cinematografía, Artes y
  Televisión *C, A*
Columbia Centro Universitario:
  Caguas *C*

Rhode Island

New England Institute of
  Technology *A, B*

Tennessee

Belmont University *B*

Texas

Angelina College *A*
Cedar Valley College *C, A*
Del Mar College *A*
Texas Southern University *B*
Texas State University *B*

Utah

Brigham Young University *B*
Broadview University
  Broadview Entertainment Arts
    University *A*

Virginia

Art Institute of Washington *A, B*

Washington

Art Institute of Seattle *A, B*
Bates Technical College *C*
Spokane Falls Community
  College *C, A*

Wisconsin

Madison Media Institute *A*

Wyoming

Northwest College *C*

Recreational therapy

California

California State University
  Chico *B*
  East Bay *B*
Santa Barbara City College *A*

Connecticut

Northwestern Connecticut
  Community College *A*

District of Columbia

Gallaudet University *B*
Howard University *B*

Florida

Broward College *A*
University of Miami *B*

Illinois

University of St. Francis *B*

Indiana

Indiana Institute of Technology *B*

Iowa

University of Iowa *B*

Louisiana

Southern University and Agricultural
  and Mechanical College *B, M*

Maine

Unity College *B*
University of Southern Maine *B*

Massachusetts

Springfield College *B, M*

Michigan

Calvin College *B*
Central Michigan University *B, M*
Eastern Michigan University *B*
Lake Superior State University *B*

Minnesota

Minnesota State University
  Mankato *B*
Saint Cloud State University *B*
University of Minnesota
  Twin Cities *M*

Missouri

Northwest Missouri State
  University *M*

New Hampshire

University of New Hampshire *B*

New York

Genesee Community College *A*
Ithaca College *B*
SUNY
  College at Cortland *B*
Utica College *B*

North Carolina

Carteret Community College *A*
Catawba College *B*
East Carolina University *B, M*
North Carolina Central University *M*
St. Andrews University *B*
Shaw University *B*
University of North Carolina
  Wilmington *B*
Vance-Granville Community
  College *A*
Western Carolina University *B*
Western Piedmont Community
  College *A*
Winston-Salem State University *B*

Ohio

University of Toledo *B*

Pennsylvania

Lincoln University *B*
Slippery Rock University of
  Pennsylvania *B*
Temple University *B, M*

Texas

Austin Community College *A*
Texas State University *M*

Utah

Brigham Young University *B*

Virginia

Longwood University *B*

Washington
Eastern Washington University *B*
Spokane Community College *A*

West Virginia
Alderson-Broaddus University *B*
West Virginia State University *B*

Wisconsin
University of Wisconsin
La Crosse *B*
Milwaukee *B*

Regional studies

Alaska
University of Alaska
Fairbanks *M*

Arizona
Phoenix College *C*
Prescott College *B*

Arkansas
Arkansas Tech University *A*

California
Claremont McKenna College *B*

Colorado
Colorado College *B*

Georgia
Mercer University *B*

Maine
University of Southern Maine *M*

Mississippi
University of Mississippi *B, M*

New Mexico
Northern New Mexico College *A*
Santa Fe Community College *A*

New York
Columbia University *B*
Houghton College *B*
United States Military Academy *B*

Pennsylvania
La Salle University *B*

Rehabilitation aide

Kansas
Cloud County Community College *C*
Colby Community College *C*
Garden City Community College *C*

Rehabilitation engineering/assistive technology

Maryland
University of Maryland
Baltimore *D*

Rehabilitation science

Alabama
Auburn University *M*

Arkansas
Arkansas Tech University *B*

California
Contra Costa College *C*
Loma Linda University *D*

Colorado
University of Colorado
Denver *D*

Florida
University of Florida *D*

Indiana
Indiana University
Purdue University
Indianapolis *C, D*

Kansas
University of Kansas Medical
Center *D*

Kentucky
University of Kentucky *D*

Maine
University of Maine
Farmington *B*

New Mexico
Western New Mexico University *B*

North Dakota
University of North Dakota *B*

Pennsylvania
Clarion University of
Pennsylvania *A, B, M*
Duquesne University *M, D*
University of Pittsburgh *B, M, D*

Texas
Stephen F. Austin State University *B*
Texas Tech University Health
Sciences Center *D*
University of Texas
Medical Branch at Galveston *D*
Pan American *B*
University of the Incarnate Word *B*

Wisconsin
Marquette University *M, D*

Reiki

Vermont
Goddard College *B, M*

Religious education

Alabama
Huntingdon College *B*
Oakwood University *B*

Arizona
International Baptist
College *A, B, M, D*

Arkansas
Arkansas Baptist College *B*
Ecclesia College *B*
Harding University *B*
Williams Baptist College *B*

California
Azusa Pacific University *B, M, D*
Bethesda University of California *B*
Biola University *B, M, D*
California Lutheran University *B*
Concordia University Irvine *B*
Master's College *B*
Mount St. Mary's College *M*
Patten University *B*
Vanguard University of Southern
California *B*
Yeshiva Ohr Elchonon Chabad/West
Coast Talmudical Seminary *B*

Colorado
Nazarene Bible College *C, A, B*

Connecticut
Holy Apostles College and
Seminary *M*

District of Columbia
Catholic University of America *M, D*

Florida
Baptist College of Florida *A, B*
Florida College *B*
Saint Thomas University *B*
Talmudic University *B, M, D*
Yeshiva Gedolah Rabbinical
College *B, M*

Georgia
Toccoa Falls College *B*

Idaho
Boise Bible College *A, B*
Northwest Nazarene University *B*

Illinois
Concordia University
Chicago *B, M, T*
Lincoln Christian University *M*
Loyola University Chicago *B, M*
Moody Bible Institute *B, T*
North Park University *M*
Olivet Nazarene University *B*
Trinity International University *B, M*
Wheaton College *B, M*

Indiana
Crossroads Bible College *C, A, B*
Earlham College *M*
Huntington University *B, M*
Indiana Wesleyan University *A, B*
Marian University *A, B*
Taylor University *B*
University of St. Francis *C*

Iowa
Faith Baptist Bible College and
Theological Seminary *B*
Northwestern College *B*
Wartburg College *B, T*

Kansas
Central Christian College of Kansas *A*
Manhattan Christian College *A, B*
MidAmerica Nazarene
University *A, B*
Sterling College *B*

Kentucky
Asbury University *B*
Campbellsville University *B*
Kentucky Mountain Bible College *B*
Mid-Continent University *C, B*
Union College *B*
University of the Cumberlands *B*

Louisiana
Louisiana College *B*
Loyola University New Orleans *M*
New Orleans Baptist Theological
Seminary *A, B, M, D*

Maryland
Washington Adventist University *B*

Massachusetts
Boston College *M, D*

Michigan
Andrews University *B, M, D*
Grace Bible College *B*
Great Lakes Christian College *B*

Griggs University *B*
Kuyper College *B*

Minnesota
Bethel University *M*
Concordia University St. Paul *B*
Crossroads College *B*
Crown College *B*
North Central University *B*
St. Mary's University of Minnesota *B*
University of St. Thomas *M*

Missouri
Baptist Bible College *B*
Calvary Bible College and Theological
Seminary *A, B*
Central Christian College of the
Bible *B*
Hannibal-LaGrange University *B*
Ozark Christian College *B*
St. Louis Christian College *B*
Saint Louis University *M*
Southwest Baptist University *B*

Nebraska
Concordia University *B, T*
Grace University *B*
Nebraska Christian College *A, B*
Union College *B, T*
York College *B, T*

New Jersey
College of St. Elizabeth *C*
Felician College *M*
Georgian Court University *C*
Seton Hall University *B, T*

New York
Concordia College *B*
Davis College *B*
Jewish Theological Seminary of
America *M*

North Carolina
Apex School of Theology *A, M, D*
Campbell University *B, M, D*
Duke University *M*
Gardner-Webb University *B, M*
Laurel University *B, M*
Methodist University *A, B, T*
Mid-Atlantic Christian University *B*
Montreat College *B*
Pfeiffer University *B*
Shaw University *M*
Southeastern Baptist Theological
Seminary *M, D*

North Dakota
Trinity Bible College *B*

Ohio
Cedarville University *B*
Cincinnati Christian University *B, M*
College of Mount St. Joseph *B*
Defiance College *B, T*
Franciscan University of
Steubenville *B*
God's Bible School and College *B*
Lourdes University *C*
Mount Vernon Nazarene University *B*
Muskingum University *B*
Notre Dame College *C*
Ohio Christian University *A, B*
Ohio Mid-Western College *B*

Oklahoma
Hillsdale Free Will Baptist College *A*
Oklahoma Baptist University *B*
Oklahoma Christian University *B*
Oklahoma City University *B, M*
Oral Roberts University *B, M*
Southern Nazarene University *B*

Oregon

Concordia University *B*
Corban University *B*
Multnomah University *B*
New Hope Christian College *B*
Warner Pacific College *A*

Pennsylvania

Cairn University *B, T*
Duquesne University *M*
Gratz College *M, T*
Immaculata University *C*
La Salle University *B, M, D*
Mercyhurst University *B*
Messiah College *B*
St. Vincent College *B*
Thiel College *B*
Valley Forge Christian College *B*
Westminster College *B, T*

Puerto Rico

Inter American University of Puerto
  Rico
  Metropolitan Campus *B, D*
Pontifical Catholic University of
  Puerto Rico *M*
Universidad Pentecostal
  Mizpa *C, A, B*

South Carolina

Columbia College *B*
Columbia International
  University *B, M*
Erskine College *B, M*
Morris College *B*
Presbyterian College *B*
W.L. Bonner Bible College *A*

Tennessee

American Baptist College *B*
Bryan University
  Dayton *B*
Lee University *B*
Martin Methodist College *B*
Southern Adventist University *B*
Tennessee Temple University *B, M*
Welch College *B*

Texas

Arlington Baptist College *D*
Concordia University Texas *B, T*
Dallas Baptist University *A, B, M, D*
Dallas Christian College *B*
Howard Payne University *B*
Southwestern Assemblies of God
  University *B*
University of Dallas *M*
Wayland Baptist University *B*

Utah

Brigham Young University *M*

Virginia

Catholic Distance
  University *C, A, B, M*
Liberty University *M*

Washington

Seattle Pacific University *B*
Seattle University *M, T*

West Virginia

Davis and Elkins College *B*
West Virginia Wesleyan College *B*

Wisconsin

Cardinal Stritch University *T*
Concordia University Wisconsin *B*
Edgewood College *B, M*
Mount Mary University *B, T*
St. Norbert College *B*

Religious studies

Alabama

Athens State University *B*
Auburn University *B*
Birmingham-Southern College *B*
Faulkner University *B*
Gadsden State Community College *A*
Huntingdon College *B*
Judson College *B*
Oakwood University *B*
Samford University *B*
Selma University *A, B, M*
Spring Hill College *C, B, M*
Stillman College *B*
University of Alabama *B*
University of Mobile *B, M*

Arizona

Arizona State University *B, M, D*
Harrison Middleton
  University *B, M, D*
University of Arizona *B*

Arkansas

Arkansas Baptist College *A, B*
Crowley's Ridge College *A, B*
Hendrix College *B*
Lyon College *B*
Philander Smith College *B*
University of Central Arkansas *B*
University of the Ozarks *B*

California

Azusa Pacific University *B, M*
Bethesda University of
  California *B, M*
Biola University *B*
California Lutheran University *B*
California State University
  Bakersfield *B*
  Chico *B*
  East Bay *B*
  Fresno *B*
  Fullerton *B*
  Long Beach *B, M*
  Northridge *B*
  Sacramento *B, M*
Chaffey College *A*
Chapman University *B*
Claremont McKenna College *B*
Concordia University Irvine *B*
Crafton Hills College *C*
Dominican University of California *B*
Holy Names University *B*
Hope International University *M*
Humboldt State University *B*
La Sierra University *B, M*
Master's College *B*
Mount St. Mary's College *B, M*
Notre Dame de Namur University *B*
Occidental College *B*
Orange Coast College *A*
Pacific Union College *B, T*
Patten University *A, B*
Pepperdine University *B, M*
Pitzer College *B*
Point Loma Nazarene University *M*
Pomona College *B*
St. Mary's College of California *B*
San Diego State University *B*
San Jose State University *B*
Santa Clara University *B*
Scripps College *B*
Simpson University *B*
Stanford University *B, M, D*
University of California
  Berkeley *B*
  Davis *B*
  Irvine *B*
  Los Angeles *B*
  Riverside *B, M, D*
  San Diego *B*
  Santa Barbara *B, M, D*

University of La Verne *B*
University of Redlands *B*
University of San Diego *B*
University of Southern
  California *B, M, D*
University of the Pacific *B*
University of the West *B, M, D*
Vanguard University of Southern
  California *B, M*
Westmont College *B*
Whittier College *B*

Colorado

Colorado College *B*
Naropa University *B, M*
Nazarene Bible College *A*
Regis University *B*
University of Colorado
  Boulder *B, M*
University of Denver *B, M, D*

Connecticut

Albertus Magnus College *B*
Connecticut College *B*
Fairfield University *B*
Holy Apostles College and
  Seminary *A, B, M*
Sacred Heart University *B, M*
Trinity College *B*
University of Bridgeport *B*
University of Saint Joseph *B*
Wesleyan University *B*
Yale University *B, M, D*

District of Columbia

American University *B*
Catholic University of
  America *B, M, D*
George Washington University *B, M*
Georgetown University *B*
Howard University *M, D*

Florida

Baptist College of Florida *B*
Broward College *A*
Eckerd College *B*
Florida International University *B, M*
Florida Southern College *B*
Florida State University *B, M, D*
Hobe Sound Bible College *B*
Johnson University: Florida *C, A, B*
Miami Dade College *A*
New College of Florida *B*
Pensacola State College *A*
Rollins College *B*
Saint Leo University *B*
Saint Thomas University *B*
Stetson University *B*
University of Central Florida *B*
University of Florida *B, M, D*
University of Miami *B*
University of North Florida *B*
University of South Florida *B, M*
University of West Florida *B*

Georgia

Agnes Scott College *B*
Clark Atlanta University *B*
Emory University *B, D*
Georgia State University *B, M*
LaGrange College *B*
Morehouse College *B*
Paine College *B*
Piedmont College *B*
Reinhardt University *B*
Shorter University *B*
Spelman College *B*
Thomas University *C*
University of Georgia *B, M*
Wesleyan College *B*
Young Harris College *B*

Hawaii

Chaminade University of Honolulu *B*
University of Hawaii
  Manoa *B, M*

Idaho

College of Idaho *B*
Northwest Nazarene University *B*

Illinois

Augustana College *B*
Aurora University *B*
Bradley University *B*
Concordia University Chicago *B*
DePaul University *B*
Eureka College *B*
Greenville College *B*
Illinois College *B*
Illinois Wesleyan University *B*
Lake Forest College *B*
Lewis University *B*
Lincoln College *A*
MacMurray College *B*
McKendree University *B*
Monmouth College *B*
North Central College *B*
Northwestern University *B, M, D*
Olivet Nazarene University *B, M*
Principia College *B*
Saint Xavier University *B*
Trinity International University *M*
University of Chicago *B, M, D*
University of Illinois
  Urbana-Champaign *B*
Western Illinois University *B*

Indiana

Anderson University *B*
Ball State University *B*
Bethel College *B*
Butler University *B*
Calumet College of St. Joseph *C, A, B*
DePauw University *B*
Earlham College *B*
Franklin College *B*
Huntington University *B*
Indiana University
  Bloomington *B, M, D*
  Purdue University Indianapolis *B*
Manchester University *B*
Martin University *B*
Oakland City University *C, A, B*
Purdue University *B*
Saint Mary's College *B*
University of Indianapolis *B*
Vincennes University *C*
Wabash College *B*

Iowa

Central College *B*
Clarke University *A, B*
Coe College *B*
Cornell College *B*
Divine Word College *B*
Dordt College *B*
Drake University *B*
Faith Baptist Bible College and
  Theological Seminary *M*
Graceland University *B, M*
Grand View University *B*
Grinnell College *B*
Iowa State University *B*
Iowa Wesleyan College *B*
Loras College *B*
Luther College *B*
Morningside College *B*
Mount Mercy University *B*
Northwestern College *B*
Simpson College *B*
University of Dubuque *B, M*
University of Iowa *B, M, D*
University of Northern Iowa *B*
Wartburg College *B*

Kansas

Baker University *B*
Barclay College *B*
Bethel College *B*
Cowley County Community
  College *A*
Friends University *B*
Kansas Wesleyan University *B*
Manhattan Christian College *B*
MidAmerica Nazarene University *B*
Ottawa University *B*
Seward County Community
  College *A*
Tabor College *B*
University of Kansas *B, M*
Washburn University *B*

Kentucky

Berea College *B*
Bluegrass Community and Technical
  College *A*
Brescia University *A, B*
Centre College *B*
Georgetown College *B*
Hopkinsville Community College *A*
Kentucky Mountain Bible College *A*
Kentucky Wesleyan College *B*
Lindsey Wilson College *A*
Thomas More College *C, A, B*
Transylvania University *B*
Union College *B*
University of Pikeville *B*
Western Kentucky University *B, M*

Louisiana

Centenary College of Louisiana *B*
Dillard University *B*
Louisiana College *B, M*
Loyola University New Orleans *B, M*

Maine

Bates College *B*
Bowdoin College *B*
Colby College *B*

Maryland

Goucher College *B*
Hood College *B*
Loyola University Maryland *B*
McDaniel College *B*
Notre Dame of Maryland
  University *B*
St. Mary's College of Maryland *B*
Towson University *B*
Washington Adventist
  University *B, M*

Massachusetts

Amherst College *B*
Boston University *B, M, D*
College of the Holy Cross *B*
Eastern Nazarene College *B*
Elms College *B, M*
Emmanuel College *B*
Hampshire College *B*
Harvard College *B, M, D*
Merrimack College *B*
Mount Holyoke College *B*
Northeastern University *B*
Smith College *B*
Stonehill College *B*
Tufts University *B*
University of Massachusetts
  Amherst *C*
Wellesley College *B*
Wheaton College *B*
Williams College *B*

Michigan

Adrian College *B, T*
Albion College *B*
Alma College *B*
Andrews University *B, M*
Aquinas College *B*

Calvin College *B, T*
Central Michigan University *B*
Concordia University *B*
Griggs University *B*
Henry Ford Community College *A*
Hillsdale College *B*
Hope College *B*
Kalamazoo College *B*
Lansing Community College *A*
Madonna University *A, B*
Marygrove College *B*
Michigan State University *B*
Rochester College *B*
Siena Heights University *B*
Spring Arbor University *C, B, M*
University of Detroit Mercy *B, M*
University of Michigan *B*
Western Michigan University *B, M*

Minnesota

Augsburg College *B*
Bethany Lutheran College *B*
Bethel University *M*
Carleton College *B*
College of St. Scholastica *B*
Concordia College: Moorhead *B*
Gustavus Adolphus College *B*
Hamline University *B*
Macalester College *B*
North Central University *A, B*
St. Olaf College *B*
University of Minnesota
  Twin Cities *B, M*
University of St. Thomas *B, M*

Mississippi

Millsaps College *B*
Southeastern Baptist College *A, B*
Tougaloo College *A*
University of Mississippi *B*
University of Southern Mississippi *B*

Missouri

Avila University *B*
Baptist Bible College *B*
Calvary Bible College and Theological
  Seminary *M*
Central Christian College of the
  Bible *B*
Central Methodist University *B*
Culver-Stockton College *B*
Drury University *B*
Lindenwood University *B*
Missouri State University *B, M*
Missouri Valley College *B*
Rockhurst University *B*
Southwest Baptist University *B*
University of Missouri
  Columbia *B, M*
Washington University in St.
  Louis *B, M*
Webster University *B*
Westminster College *B*
William Jewell College *B*

Montana

University of Great Falls *B*

Nebraska

Doane College *B*
Hastings College *B*
Midland University *B*
Nebraska Wesleyan University *B*
Union College *B*
University of Nebraska
  Omaha *B*
York College *B, T*

New Hampshire

Dartmouth College *B*

New Jersey

Bergen Community College *A*
Bloomfield College *B, T*

Drew University *B*
Felician College *B*
Georgian Court University *B*
Montclair State University *B*
Princeton University *B, M, D*
Rabbinical College of America *B*
Rutgers, The State University of New
  Jersey
    New Brunswick/Piscataway
    Campus *B, M*
Saint Peter's University *B*
Seton Hall University *B*
Thomas Edison State College *B*

New Mexico

Eastern New Mexico University *B*
University of New Mexico *B*

New York

Bard College *B*
Barnard College *B*
Canisius College *B*
City University of New York
  Baruch College *B*
  Brooklyn College *B*
  Hunter College *B*
  Queens College *B*
Colgate University *B*
College of Mount St. Vincent *B*
College of New Rochelle *B*
College of Saint Rose *B*
Columbia University *B*
Columbia University
  School of General Studies *B*
Concordia College *A, B*
Cornell University *B*
Daemen College *B*
Eugene Lang College The New
  School for Liberal Arts *B*
Fordham University *B, M, D*
Hamilton College *B*
Hartwick College *B*
Hobart and William Smith Colleges *B*
Hofstra University *B*
Houghton College *B*
Iona College *B*
Le Moyne College *B*
Manhattan College *B*
Manhattanville College *B*
Marymount Manhattan College *B*
Molloy College *B*
Nazareth College *B*
New York University *B, M, D*
Niagara University *B*
Nyack College *B*
Pace University: Pleasantville/
  Briarcliff *B*
SUNY
  University at Albany *B*
  University at Stony Brook *B*
St. Francis College *B*
St. John Fisher College *B*
St. Lawrence University *B*
St. Thomas Aquinas College *B*
Siena College *B*
Skidmore College *B*
Syracuse University *B, M, D*
Union College *B*
University of Rochester *B*
Vassar College *B*

North Carolina

Appalachian State University *B*
Barton College *B*
Brevard College *B*
Campbell University *B, M, D*
Catawba College *B*
Chowan University *B*
Davidson College *B*
Duke University *B, M, D*
Elon University *B*
Gardner-Webb University *B*
Greensboro College *C, B*
Guilford College *B*

High Point University *B*
Lees-McRae College *B*
Lenoir-Rhyne University *B*
Mars Hill University *B*
Meredith College *B*
Methodist University *A, B, T*
North Carolina State University *B*
North Carolina Wesleyan College *B*
Pfeiffer University *B*
Queens University of Charlotte *B*
St. Andrews University *B*
St. Augustine's University *B*
Salem College *B*
Shaw University *A, B*
Southeastern Baptist Theological
  Seminary *C, A, B, M, D*
University of Mount Olive *B*
University of North Carolina
  Asheville *B*
  Chapel Hill *B, M, D*
  Charlotte *B, M*
  Greensboro *B*
  Wilmington *B*
Wake Forest University *B, M*
Warren Wilson College *B*
Wingate University *B*

North Dakota

Trinity Bible College *A, B*
University of Jamestown *B*
University of Mary *B*
University of North Dakota *B*

Ohio

Ashland University *B, M*
Baldwin Wallace University *B*
Capital University *B*
Case Western Reserve
  University *B, M*
Cleveland State University *B*
College of Mount St. Joseph *B, M*
College of Wooster *B*
Defiance College *B*
Denison University *B*
Heidelberg University *B*
Hiram College *B*
John Carroll University *B, M, T*
Kenyon College *B*
Lourdes University *A, B*
Miami University
  Oxford *B, M*
Mount Vernon Nazarene
  University *B, M*
Muskingum University *B*
Oberlin College *B*
Ohio Christian University *A, B, M*
Ohio Northern University *B*
Ohio State University
  Columbus Campus *B*
Ohio University *B*
Ohio Wesleyan University *B*
Otterbein University *B*
Pontifical College Josephinum *B*
University of Cincinnati *C*
University of Dayton *B*
University of Findlay *A, B*
University of Mount Union *B*
University of Toledo *B*
Urbana University *B*
Wittenberg University *B*
Wright State University *B*
Xavier University *A, B, M*
Youngstown State University *B*

Oklahoma

Mid-America Christian University *B*
Oklahoma Baptist University *B*
Oklahoma Christian University *B*
Oklahoma City University *B, M*
Southern Nazarene University *B*
Southwestern Christian
  University *A, B*
University of Oklahoma *B*

University of Tulsa *B*
Western Oklahoma State College *A*

Oregon

Concordia University *B*
Corban University *A, B*
Lewis & Clark College *B*
Linfield College *B*
Marylhurst University *B*
New Hope Christian College *B*
Reed College *B*
University of Oregon *B*
Warner Pacific College *A, B, M*
Willamette University *B*

Pennsylvania

Albright College *B*
Allegheny College *B*
Alvernia University *B*
Arcadia University *B*
Bryn Athyn College *B, M*
Bryn Mawr College *B*
Bucknell University *B*
Cabrini College *B*
Chestnut Hill College *C*
Dickinson College *B*
Elizabethtown College *B*
Franklin & Marshall College *B*
Gettysburg College *B*
Gratz College *B, M*
Grove City College *B*
Haverford College *B*
Holy Family University *B*
Indiana University of Pennsylvania *B*
Juniata College *B*
La Roche College *B*
La Salle University *B, M*
Lafayette College *B*
Lebanon Valley College *B*
Lehigh University *B*
Lincoln University *B*
Lycoming College *B*
Marywood University *B*
Mercyhurst University *B*
Moravian College *B*
Muhlenberg College *C, B*
Rosemont College *B*
St. Francis University *B*
Saint Joseph's University *B, M*
Seton Hill University *C, B*
Susquehanna University *B*
Swarthmore College *B*
Temple University *B, M, D*
Thiel College *B*
University of Pennsylvania *B, M, D*
University of Pittsburgh *B, M, D*
University of Scranton *B, M*
Villanova University *B, M*
Waynesburg University *B*
Westminster College *B*
Wilson College *B*

Puerto Rico

Bayamon Central University *B*
Inter American University of Puerto Rico
   Fajardo Campus *B*
   Metropolitan Campus *C*
Universidad Adventista de las Antillas *M*

Rhode Island

Brown University *B, M, D*
Salve Regina University *B*

South Carolina

Allen University *B*
Bob Jones University *D*
Charleston Southern University *B*
Claflin University *B*
College of Charleston *B*
Columbia College *B*
Converse College *B*
Erskine College *B*

Furman University *B*
Newberry College *B*
Presbyterian College *B*
Southern Wesleyan University *B, M*
University of South Carolina
   Columbia *B, M*
Winthrop University *B*
Wofford College *B*

South Dakota

Augustana College *B*
Dakota Wesleyan University *B*
Mount Marty College *B*
Presentation College *A*
University of Sioux Falls *B*

Tennessee

Belmont University *B*
Carson-Newman University *B*
Christian Brothers University *M*
Hiwassee College *A*
King University *B*
Lane College *B*
Martin Methodist College *B*
Maryville College *B*
Rhodes College *B*
Sewanee: The University of the South *B*
Southern Adventist University *B, M*
Trevecca Nazarene University *B*
Union University *B*
University of Tennessee
   Knoxville *B*
Vanderbilt University *B, M, D*
Williamson College *B*

Texas

Abilene Christian University *M*
Amarillo College *A*
Arlington Baptist College *B*
Austin College *B*
Baptist Missionary Association
   Theological Seminary *A, B, M*
Baylor University *B, M, D*
Clarendon College *A*
Criswell College *A, B, M*
East Texas Baptist University *C, B, M*
Jarvis Christian College *B*
Our Lady of the Lake University of
   San Antonio *B*
Paul Quinn College *B*
Rice University *B, D*
Schreiner University *B*
Southern Methodist
   University *B, M, D*
Southwestern Adventist University *B*
Southwestern University *B*
Texas Christian University *B*
Texas College *B*
Texas Wesleyan University *B*
Trinity University *B*
University of Texas
   Austin *B, M, D*
   Tyler *B*
University of the Incarnate
   Word *B, M*

Utah

Utah State University *B*

Vermont

Bennington College *B*
Marlboro College *B*
Middlebury College *B*
Saint Michael's College *B*
University of Vermont *B*

Virginia

Averett University *B*
Christendom College *M*
College of William and Mary *B*
Emory & Henry College *B*
Ferrum College *B*
George Mason University *B*

Hampden-Sydney College *B*
Hollins University *B*
Liberty University *A, B, M*
Lord Fairfax Community College *A*
Lynchburg College *B*
Mary Baldwin College *B*
Marymount University *B*
Randolph College *B*
Randolph-Macon College *B*
Regent University *B, M, D*
Roanoke College *B*
Shenandoah University *B*
Sweet Briar College *B*
University of Richmond *B*
University of Virginia *B, M, D*
Virginia Commonwealth University *B*
Virginia Intermont College *B*
Virginia Union University *B*
Virginia University of Lynchburg *B*
Virginia Wesleyan College *B*
Washington and Lee University *B*

Washington

Central Washington University *B*
Evergreen State College *B*
Faith Evangelical College &
   Seminary *B*
Gonzaga University *B, M*
Pacific Lutheran University *B*
Saint Martin's University *B*
Seattle University *B*
Trinity Lutheran College *A, B*
University of Puget Sound *B*
University of Washington *B, M*
Walla Walla University *B*
Washington State University *B*
Whitman College *B*
Whitworth University *B*

West Virginia

American Public University System *B*
Bethany College *B*
Davis and Elkins College *B*
Ohio Valley University *B*
West Virginia Wesleyan College *B*

Wisconsin

Alverno College *B*
Beloit College *B*
Cardinal Stritch University *B, M*
Carroll University *B*
Carthage College *B*
Concordia University Wisconsin *B*
Edgewood College *B*
Lakeland College *B*
Lawrence University *B*
Marian University *B*
Marquette University *D*
Mount Mary University *B*
Northland College *B*
Ripon College *B*
St. Norbert College *B, T*
University of Wisconsin
   Eau Claire *B*
   Madison *B*
   Milwaukee *B*
   Oshkosh *B*
Viterbo University *B, T*

Wyoming

Laramie County Community
   College *A*
University of Wyoming *B*

Renal/dialysis technology

Georgia

Atlanta Technical College *C*

Illinois

City Colleges of Chicago
   Harry S. Truman College *C*
   Malcolm X College *A*

Minnesota

Lake Superior College *C*

Pennsylvania

Drexel University *M*

Rhode Island

Community College of Rhode
   Island *C*

Wisconsin

Chippewa Valley Technical College *C*

Reproductive biology

Kentucky

University of Kentucky *M, D*

Texas

University of Texas
   Health Science Center at
   Houston *M, D*

West Virginia

West Virginia University *M, D*

Research and development management

Kansas

University of Kansas *M*

New York

Rochester Institute of Technology *M*

Texas

Texas Christian University *M*

Vermont

Champlain College *M*

Research methodology

Illinois

DePaul University *C*

Indiana

Indiana University
   Purdue University Indianapolis *C*

Maine

College of the Atlantic *B*

New York

New York University *M*

Resort management

California

Orange Coast College *C*

Colorado

Colorado Mountain College *C, A*
Western State Colorado University *B*

Florida

Florida Gulf Coast University *B*

Massachusetts

Bristol Community College *C*

Minnesota

Art Institutes International
   Minnesota *B*
Central Lakes College *C*
Dakota County Technical
   College *C, A*

Nevada

Sierra Nevada College *B*

New York

Globe Institute of
Technology *C, A, B*
Paul Smith's College *B*
Rochester Institute of
Technology *A, B, M*
SUNY
College of Agriculture and
Technology at Morrisville *B*

North Carolina

Methodist University *B, M*

Oregon

Mt. Hood Community College *C, A*

Pennsylvania

Lehigh Carbon Community College *A*
Northampton Community College *C*

South Carolina

Coastal Carolina University *B*

Vermont

Green Mountain College *C, B*
Lyndon State College *B*

Washington

Wenatchee Valley College *C*

West Virginia

Concord University *B*

Wisconsin

Lakeland College *B*

Respiratory therapy

Alabama

Central Alabama Community
College *A*
George C. Wallace Community
College at Dothan *A*
Shelton State Community College *A*
University of Alabama
Birmingham *B*
University of South Alabama *B*
Wallace State Community College at
Hanceville *A*

Arizona

Carrington College
Mesa *A*
Phoenix Westside *A*
Cochise College *A*
GateWay Community College *A*
Grand Canyon University *B*
Pima Community College *A*

Arkansas

Arkansas State University
Mountain Home *A*
National Park Community College *A*
Northwest Arkansas Community
College *A*
Pulaski Technical College *A*
Southeast Arkansas College *A*
University of Arkansas
Community College at Hope *A*
for Medical Sciences *A*

California

American River College *A*
Butte College *A*
California College San Diego *A, B*
Concorde Career College
Garden Grove *A*
North Hollywood *A*
San Bernardino *A*

Crafton Hills College *A*
East Los Angeles College *A*
El Camino College *A*
Foothill College *A*
Fresno City College *A*
Grossmont College *A*
Loma Linda University *B*
Los Angeles Southwest College *A*
Los Angeles Valley College *A*
Modesto Junior College *A*
Mount San Antonio College *A*
Napa Valley College *A*
Ohlone College *A*
Orange Coast College *A*
San Joaquin Valley College *A*
Santa Monica College *A*
Skyline College *A*
Victor Valley College *A*

Colorado

Community College of Aurora *A*
Concorde Career College
Aurora *A*
Pueblo Community College *A*

Connecticut

Goodwin College *A*
Manchester Community College *A*
Naugatuck Valley Community
College *A*
Norwalk Community College *A*
University of Hartford *B*

District of Columbia

University of the District of
Columbia *A, B*

Florida

Broward College *A*
Daytona State College *A*
Edison State College *A*
Florida Agricultural and Mechanical
University *B*
Florida National University *A*
Florida State College at
Jacksonville *A*
Gulf Coast State College *A*
Hillsborough Community College *A*
Indian River State College *A*
Miami Dade College *A*
Nova Southeastern University *B*
Palm Beach State College *A*
Polk State College *A*
Saint Johns River State College *A*
St. Petersburg College *A*
Santa Fe College *A*
Seminole State College of Florida *A*
Tallahassee Community College *A*
Valencia College *A*

Georgia

Armstrong Atlantic State University *B*
Athens Technical College *A*
Augusta Technical College *A*
Columbus Technical College *A*
Darton College *A*
Georgia Highlands College *A*
Georgia Regents University *B*
Georgia State University *B*
Gwinnett Technical College *A*
Middle Georgia State College *A, B*
Southwest Georgia Technical
College *A*

Hawaii

University of Hawaii
Kapiolani Community College *A*

Idaho

Boise State University *A, B*
College of Southern Idaho *A*
Idaho State University *A*

Illinois

City Colleges of Chicago
Malcolm X College *A*
Olive-Harvey College *A*
College of DuPage *A*
Illinois Central College *A*
Kankakee Community College *A*
Kaskaskia College *A*
Moraine Valley Community College *A*
National-Louis University *B*
Parkland College *A*
Rock Valley College *A*
Rush University *B, M*
St. Augustine College *A*
Southwestern Illinois College *A*
Trinity College of Nursing & Health
Sciences *A*
Triton College *A*

Indiana

Ball State University *B*
Indiana University
Purdue University Indianapolis *B*
Ivy Tech Community College
Bloomington *A*
Central Indiana *A*
East Central *A*
Lafayette *A*
North Central *A*
Northeast *A*
Northwest *A*
Richmond *A*
South Central *A*
Wabash Valley *A*
University of Indianapolis *B*
University of Southern Indiana *A*

Iowa

Des Moines Area Community
College *A*
Hawkeye Community College *A*
Kirkwood Community College *A*
Northeast Iowa Community
College *A*
St. Luke's College *A*

Kansas

Johnson County Community
College *A*
Kansas City Kansas Community
College *A*
Labette Community College *A*
Newman University *A*
Seward County Community
College *A*
University of Kansas Medical
Center *B*
Washburn University *A*

Kentucky

Ashland Community and Technical
College *A*
Bellarmine University *B*
Bluegrass Community and Technical
College *A*
Jefferson Community and Technical
College *A*
Madisonville Community College *A*
Morehead State University *A*
Northern Kentucky University *A*
Southeast Kentucky Community and
Technical College *A*
Spencerian College *A*
West Kentucky Community and
Technical College *A*

Louisiana

Bossier Parish Community College *A*
Delgado Community College *A*
Louisiana State University
Eunice *A*
Our Lady of the Lake College *A*
Southern University
Shreveport *A*

Maine

Kennebec Valley Community
College *A*
Southern Maine Community
College *A*

Maryland

Allegany College of Maryland *A*
Baltimore City Community College *A*
Carroll Community College *A*
Community College of Baltimore
County *A*
Frederick Community College *A*
Howard Community College *A*
Prince George's Community
College *A*
Salisbury University *B*
Washington Adventist University *A*

Massachusetts

Berkshire Community College *A*
Bunker Hill Community College *A*
Massachusetts Bay Community
College *A*
Massasoit Community College *A*
North Shore Community College *A*
Northern Essex Community
College *A*
Quinsigamond Community College *A*
Springfield Technical Community
College *A*

Michigan

Delta College *A*
Ferris State University *A*
Henry Ford Community College *A*
Kalamazoo Valley Community
College *A*
Macomb Community College *A*
Monroe County Community
College *A*
Mott Community College *A*
Muskegon Community College *A*
Northern Michigan University *B*
Oakland Community College *A*
Washtenaw Community College *A*

Minnesota

Concordia University St. Paul *B*
Lake Superior College *A*
Northland Community & Technical
College *A*
St. Catherine University *B*
St. Paul College *A*
University of Minnesota
Twin Cities *B*

Mississippi

Coahoma Community College *A*
Copiah-Lincoln Community
College *A*
Hinds Community College *A*
Itawamba Community College *A*
Meridian Community College *A*
Mississippi Gulf Coast Community
College *A*
Northeast Mississippi Community
College *A*
Northwest Mississippi Community
College *A*
Pearl River Community College *A*

Missouri

East Central College *A*
Hannibal-LaGrange University *A*
Metropolitan Community College -
Kansas City *A*
Mineral Area College *A*
Missouri Southern State University *A*
Missouri State University *B*
Missouri State University: West
Plains *A*
Ozarks Technical Community
College *A*

St. Louis Community College *A*
University of Missouri
Columbia *B*

Montana

Montana State University
Great Falls College *A*
University of Montana *A*

Nebraska

Metropolitan Community College *A*
Midland University *A, B*
Nebraska Methodist College of
Nursing and Allied Health *A, B*
Southeast Community College *A*
University of Nebraska
Kearney *B*

Nevada

Carrington College
Las Vegas *A*

New Hampshire

River Valley Community College *A*

New Jersey

Atlantic Cape Community College *A*
Bergen Community College *A*
Brookdale Community College *A*
Burlington County College *A*
Camden County College *A*
County College of Morris *A*
Essex County College *A*
Fairleigh Dickinson University
College at Florham *B*
Felician College *B*
Gloucester County College *A*
Hudson County Community
College *A*
Mercer County Community
College *A*
Middlesex County College *A*
Raritan Valley Community College *A*
Rutgers, The State University of New
Jersey
New Brunswick/Piscataway
Campus *A*
Newark Campus *A*
Sussex County Community College *A*
Thomas Edison State College *A, B*
Union County College *A*

New Mexico

Central New Mexico Community
College *A*
Dona Ana Community College of
New Mexico State University *A*
Eastern New Mexico University:
Roswell *A*
San Juan College *A*
Santa Fe Community College *A*

New York

Canisius College *M*
Erie Community College *A*
Genesee Community College *A*
Hudson Valley Community College *A*
Mohawk Valley Community
College *A*
Molloy College *A*
Nassau Community College *A*
Onondaga Community College *A*
SUNY
University at Stony Brook *B*
Upstate Medical University *B*
Sullivan County Community
College *A*
Westchester Community College *A*

North Carolina

Carteret Community College *A*
Catawba Valley Community
College *A*

Central Piedmont Community
College *A*
Durham Technical Community
College *A*
Edgecombe Community College *A*
Fayetteville Technical Community
College *A*
Forsyth Technical Community
College *A*
Pitt Community College *A*
Robeson Community College *A*
Rockingham Community College *A*
Sandhills Community College *A*
Southwestern Community College *A*
Stanly Community College *A*
University of North Carolina
Charlotte *B*

North Dakota

North Dakota State University *B*
University of Mary *B, M*

Ohio

Bowling Green State University:
Firelands College *A*
Columbus State Community
College *A*
Eastern Gateway Community
College *A*
James A. Rhodes State College *A*
Kent State University
Ashtabula *A*
Kettering College *A*
Lakeland Community College *A*
Miami-Jacobs Career College
Dayton *A*
North Central State College *A*
Ohio State University
Columbus Campus *B*
Shawnee State University *A*
Sinclair Community College *A*
Southern State Community College *A*
Stark State College *A*
University of Akron *B*
University of Akron: Wayne
College *A*
University of Cincinnati *B*
University of Cincinnati
Clermont College *A*
University of Toledo *A, B*
Washington State Community
College *A*
Youngstown State University *B, M*

Oklahoma

Northern Oklahoma College *A*
Rose State College *A*
Tulsa Community College *A*

Oregon

Lane Community College *A*
Mt. Hood Community College *A*
Oregon Institute of Technology *A, B*

Pennsylvania

Community College of Allegheny
County *A*
Community College of
Philadelphia *A*
Delaware County Community
College *A*
Gannon University *A, B*
Gwynedd Mercy University *A, B*
Harrisburg Area Community
College *A*
Indiana University of Pennsylvania *B*
Laurel Business Institute *A*
Luzerne County Community
College *A*
Mansfield University of
Pennsylvania *A*
Millersville University of
Pennsylvania *T*

Pennsylvania College of Health
Sciences *A*
Reading Area Community College *A*
Sanford-Brown Institute
Pittsburgh *A*
University of Pittsburgh
Johnstown *A*
York College of Pennsylvania *A, B*

Puerto Rico

Centro de Estudios
Multidisciplinarios *A*
Huertas College *A*
Inter American University of Puerto
Rico
Guayama Campus *A, B*
Universidad Adventista de las
Antillas *A, B*
Universidad Metropolitana *A, B*

Rhode Island

Community College of Rhode
Island *A*
New England Institute of
Technology *A*

South Carolina

Florence-Darlington Technical
College *A*
Greenville Technical College *A*
Midlands Technical College *A*
Piedmont Technical College *A*
Spartanburg Community College *A*
Trident Technical College *A*

South Dakota

Dakota State University *A, B*

Tennessee

Baptist College of Health Sciences *B*
Chattanooga State Community
College *A*
Columbia State Community
College *A*
Jackson State Community College *A*
Roane State Community College *A*
Southern Adventist University *A*
Volunteer State Community
College *A*
Walters State Community College *A*

Texas

Alvin Community College *A*
Amarillo College *A*
Angelina College *A*
Collin County Community College
District *A*
Del Mar College *A*
El Centro College *A*
El Paso Community College *A*
Houston Community College
System *A*
Howard College *A*
Lamar Institute of Technology *A*
Lone Star College System *A*
McLennan Community College *A*
Midland College *A*
Midwestern State University *B*
Odessa College *A*
St. Philip's College *A*
San Jacinto College *A*
South Plains College *A*
Tarrant County College *A*
Temple College *A*
Texas Southern University *B*
Texas State University *B*
Tyler Junior College *A*
University of Texas
Medical Branch at Galveston *B*
Victoria College *A*
Virginia College
Austin *A*
Weatherford College *A*

Utah

Dixie State College *A*
Weber State University *A, B*

Virginia

J. Sargeant Reynolds Community
College *A*
Jefferson College of Health
Sciences *B*
Mountain Empire Community
College *A*
Northern Virginia Community
College *A*
Shenandoah University *B*
Southside Virginia Community
College *A*
Tidewater Community College *A*
Wytheville Community College *A*

Washington

Highline Community College *A*
Seattle Central Community College *A*
Spokane Community College *A*

West Virginia

Bridgemont Community and
Technical College *A*
Marshall University *B*
Southern West Virginia Community
and Technical College *A*
West Virginia Northern Community
College *A*
Wheeling Jesuit University *B*

Wisconsin

Chippewa Valley Technical College *A*
Madison Area Technical College *A*
Mid-State Technical College *A*
Milwaukee Area Technical College *A*
Northeast Wisconsin Technical
College *A*
Western Technical College *A*

Wyoming

Casper College *A*

Respiratory therapy assistant

Alabama

George C. Wallace Community
College at Dothan *A*
Virginia College
Birmingham *A*

Arizona

Carrington College
Phoenix *B*

Arkansas

South Arkansas Community
College *A*

California

Carrington College California
Pleasant Hill *A*
Concorde Career College
Garden Grove *C*
San Diego *A*
Diablo Valley College *A*
Foothill College *C, A*
Kaplan College
Salida *A*
La Sierra University *C*
Santa Rosa Junior College *C*

Delaware

Delaware Technical Community
College
Jack F. Owens Campus *A*
Stanton/Wilmington Campus *A*

Florida
Keiser University *A*

Georgia
Dalton State College *A*
Darton College *A*
Gordon College *A*

Hawaii
University of Hawaii
West Oahu *C*

Illinois
College of DuPage *C*

Kansas
Hutchinson Community College *A*
Kansas City Kansas Community
College *A*

Louisiana
Our Lady of the Lake College *A*

Michigan
Baker College
Auburn Hills *A*
Delta College *A*
Northern Michigan University *B*
Northwestern Michigan College *A*

Mississippi
Meridian Community College *A*

Montana
Montana State University
Great Falls College *A*

Nevada
Carrington College
Las Vegas *A*

New Jersey
Cumberland County College *A*

New York
City University of New York
Borough of Manhattan Community
College *A*
Long Island University
LIU Brooklyn *B*

North Carolina
Durham Technical Community
College *A*
Pitt Community College *A*
Southwestern Community College *A*

Ohio
Stark State College *A*
University of Rio Grande *A*

Oklahoma
Rose State College *A*

Pennsylvania
Clarion University of Pennsylvania *A*
Kaplan Career Institute
Franklin Mills *A*
Laurel Technical Institute *A*
YTI Career Institute
Capital Region *C, A*

Puerto Rico
Columbia Centro Universitario:
Yauco *C*
Universal Technology College of
Puerto Rico *C*

Rhode Island
Rhode Island College *B*

South Carolina
Midlands Technical College *C, A*

Texas
Cisco College *A*
Weatherford College *A*

Virginia
Danville Community College *A*

Washington
Tacoma Community College *A*

West Virginia
Bridgemont Community and
Technical College *A*
Pierpont Community and Technical
College *A*

Wisconsin
Milwaukee Area Technical College *A*

Restaurant/catering management

Arizona
Arizona Western College *C, A*
Pima Community College *C, A*

Arkansas
Arkansas Tech University *A*

California
American River College *C, A*
Art Institute of California
Inland Empire *B*
Los Angeles *B*
Orange County *A, B*
Sacramento *B*
San Diego *A, B*
San Francisco *A, B*
Silicon Valley *B*
Bakersfield College *A*
City College of San Francisco *A*
College of the Canyons *A*
College of the Desert *C, A*
Diablo Valley College *C, A*
Grossmont College *C, A*
Le Cordon Bleu College of Culinary
Arts
San Francisco *A*
Long Beach City College *C, A*
Mendocino College *C*
Orange Coast College *C, A*
Oxnard College *C, A*
Shasta College *C, A*
West Hills College: Lemoore *C, A*

Colorado
Colorado Mountain College *A*
Johnson & Wales University
Denver *B*

Connecticut
Gateway Community College *A*
Naugatuck Valley Community
College *C, A*
Three Rivers Community
College *C, A*

Delaware
Delaware Technical Community
College
Stanton/Wilmington Campus *A*

Florida
Art Institute of Fort Lauderdale *B*
College of Central Florida *A*
Daytona State College *A*
Gulf Coast State College *A*
Hillsborough Community College *A*
Indian River State College *A*

Johnson & Wales University
North Miami *B*
Le Cordon Bleu College of Culinary
Arts
Miami *C, A*
Orlando *A*
Lincoln College of Technology
West Palm Beach *C, A, B*
Miami Dade College *C, A*
Miami International University of Art
and Design *A, B*
Pensacola State College *A*
St. Petersburg College *C, A*
Valencia College *C, A*

Georgia
Art Institute of Atlanta *B*
College of Coastal Georgia *A*

Hawaii
University of Hawaii
Hawaii Community College *C, A*
West Oahu *B*

Illinois
Black Hawk College *A*
College of DuPage *C, A*
College of Lake County *C, A*
Elgin Community College *C, A*
John Wood Community College *A*
Kaskaskia College *C*
Lexington College *A, B*
Lincoln Land Community College *C*
Moraine Valley Community
College *C, A*
Parkland College *C, A*
Richland Community College *C*

Indiana
Harrison College
Indianapolis *B*
Indiana University
Purdue University Indianapolis *C*
Vincennes University *A*

Iowa
Clinton Community College *C, A*
Kirkwood Community College *A*

Kansas
Johnson County Community
College *C*

Kentucky
Sullivan University *A*

Louisiana
Delgado Community College *A*

Maryland
Anne Arundel Community
College *C, A*

Massachusetts
Massasoit Community College *C*
Newbury College *A, B*

Michigan
Art Institute of Michigan *B*
Baker College
Muskegon *B*
Ferris State University *A*
Grand Rapids Community College *A*
Henry Ford Community College *A*
Schoolcraft College *C*
Washtenaw Community College *C*

Minnesota
Art Institutes International
Minnesota *B*
Hennepin Technical College *C, A*

Minneapolis Community and
Technical College *C*
Normandale Community College *C*

Missouri
College of the Ozarks *B*
Jefferson College *C, A*
Ozarks Technical Community
College *A*

Nebraska
Bellevue University *B*
Central Community College *C, A*
Southeast Community College *A*

Nevada
Art Institute of Las Vegas *B*

New Hampshire
White Mountains Community
College *C, A*

New Jersey
Bergen Community College *C, A*
County College of Morris *A*
Hudson County Community
College *C*
Raritan Valley Community College *A*
Warren County Community
College *A*

New York
Erie Community College *A*
Mohawk Valley Community
College *A*
Monroe College *A*
Nassau Community College *A*
Niagara County Community
College *A*
Paul Smith's College *A, B*
Rochester Institute of
Technology *A, B, M*
SUNY
College of Agriculture and
Technology at Cobleskill *A*
College of Agriculture and
Technology at Morrisville *A*
College of Technology at Delhi *A*
Schenectady County Community
College *A*
Suffolk County Community
College *C, A*
Sullivan County Community
College *A*
Westchester Community College *A*

North Carolina
Cape Fear Community College *C, A*
Carteret Community College *C, A*
Johnson & Wales University
Charlotte *B*

Ohio
Art Institute of Ohio: Cincinnati *B*
Bowling Green State University *B*
Cincinnati State Technical and
Community College *A*
Lakeland Community College *A*
Ohio State University
Agricultural Technical Institute *A*

Oregon
Lane Community College *C, A*
Linn-Benton Community College *A*
Mt. Hood Community College *C, A*

Pennsylvania
Art Institute of Philadelphia *B*
Art Institute of Pittsburgh *B*
Community College of Allegheny
County *C, A*
Community College of
Philadelphia *A*

Harrisburg Area Community
College *C*
JNA Institute of Culinary Arts *A*
Luzerne County Community
College *C*
Pennsylvania College of
Technology *B*
Restaurant School at Walnut Hill
College *A, B*
Westmoreland County Community
College *A*
YTI Career Institute
Lancaster *A*

Puerto Rico

Universidad del Este *B*

Rhode Island

Johnson & Wales University
Providence *B*

Texas

Central Texas College *C, A*
Del Mar College *A*
St. Philip's College *C, A*
San Jacinto College *C, A*

Vermont

New England Culinary Institute *A, B*

Virginia

Art Institute of Washington *B*
Stratford University: Falls
Church *A, B*

Washington

Art Institute of Seattle *B*
South Seattle Community
College *C, A*

West Virginia

Blue Ridge Community and Technical
College *C, A*

Wisconsin

Art Institute of Wisconsin *A*
Chippewa Valley Technical College *A*
Gateway Technical College *A*
Lakeshore Technical College *C, A*
Milwaukee Area Technical College *A*
Northeast Wisconsin Technical
College *A*
Southwest Wisconsin Technical
College *A*
Waukesha County Technical
College *A*
Western Technical College *A*

Restaurant/food services management

Alabama

University of Alabama *B*

Alaska

University of Alaska
Anchorage *B*

Arizona

South Mountain Community
College *C*

California

College of the Desert *C, A*
Diablo Valley College *C, A*
Long Beach City College *C, A*
MiraCosta College *C, A*
Shasta College *A*
University of San Francisco *B*
West Hills College: Lemoore *C*

Colorado

Aspen University *B*
Colorado State University *B*

Connecticut

Gateway Community College *A*
Mitchell College *B*
Three Rivers Community
College *C, A*

Florida

College of Central Florida *C, A*
Hillsborough Community
College *C, A*
St. Petersburg College *C*
University of Central Florida *B*
Valencia College *C*

Georgia

Atlanta Technical College *C*
Gwinnett Technical College *C*
Kennesaw State University *B*

Illinois

Lexington College *A, B*
Roosevelt University *B, M*
Triton College *C, A*

Indiana

Vincennes University *C*

Iowa

Iowa Lakes Community College *C, A*

Maryland

Howard Community College *C, A*

Massachusetts

Holyoke Community College *A*
Quinsigamond Community
College *C, A*

Michigan

Baker College
Muskegon *A, B*
Lake Michigan College *A*
Michigan State University *M*
Oakland Community College *A*

Minnesota

Art Institutes International
Minnesota *B*
Minneapolis Community and
Technical College *A*
South Central College *C, A*
Southwest Minnesota State
University *B*

Missouri

College of the Ozarks *B*
University of Missouri
Columbia *B, M*

New Hampshire

White Mountains Community
College *C, A*

New Jersey

Burlington County College *C, A*
Mercer County Community
College *A*

New Mexico

Santa Fe Community College *C*

New York

City University of New York
LaGuardia Community College *A*
Culinary Institute of America *B*
Globe Institute of
Technology *C, A, B*
Niagara University *B*
Paul Smith's College *B*

Rochester Institute of
Technology *A, B, M*
SUNY
College at Plattsburgh *B*
College of Agriculture and
Technology at Morrisville *A*

North Carolina

Cape Fear Community College *C, A*
Johnson & Wales University
Charlotte *B*
Sandhills Community College *A*
Southwestern Community College *C*

Ohio

Ohio State University
Agricultural Technical Institute *A*
Owens Community College
Toledo *C, A*
Sinclair Community College *C*
University of Akron *C, A*

Oregon

Lane Community College *C*

Pennsylvania

Messiah College *B*
Northampton Community College *A*
Pennsylvania College of
Technology *A*
Restaurant School at Walnut Hill
College *A, B*

South Carolina

Spartanburg Community College *A*

Texas

Houston Community College
System *C, A*

Utah

Salt Lake Community College *A*

Vermont

New England Culinary Institute *A, B*

Virginia

ECPI University *B*
J. Sargeant Reynolds Community
College *A*
Stratford University: Falls
Church *A, B*

Washington

South Seattle Community
College *C, A*

West Virginia

American Public University System *A*
Concord University *B*
Pierpont Community and Technical
College *A*

Retail management

Arizona

Arizona Western College *C*
Penn Foster College *A*
University of Arizona *B*

Arkansas

University of Arkansas *B*

California

Bakersfield College *C*
Canada College *C*
College of San Mateo *C, A*
College of the Canyons *C*
MiraCosta College *C, A*
Palomar College *C*
San Joaquin Delta College *C, A*

Massachusetts

New England Institute of Art *B*

Michigan

Central Michigan University *B*
Oakland Community College *A*

Minnesota

Anoka-Ramsey Community College *C*

Nevada

Great Basin College *C*

Oregon

Tillamook Bay Community College *A*

Texas

Collin County Community College
District *C, A*

Washington

Bellevue College *C*
Clover Park Technical College *C*
Edmonds Community College *C*
Olympic College *C*
Spokane Falls Community College *C*
Tacoma Community College *C*

Retailing

Arizona

Arizona Western College *C*
Chandler-Gilbert Community
College *C*
Eastern Arizona College *C*
Pima Community College *C*
Scottsdale Community College *C, A*

Arkansas

Northwest Arkansas Community
College *C*

California

Fashion Institute of Design and
Merchandising
Los Angeles *A*
Los Angeles Pierce College *C*
MiraCosta College *C*
Orange Coast College *C*
Shasta College *C*
West Hills College: Lemoore *C*

Illinois

Black Hawk College *C, A*
Elgin Community College *C, A*
Harper College *C*
Highland Community College *C*
Kaskaskia College *C*
McHenry County College *C*
Moraine Valley Community College *A*
Spoon River College *C*
Waubonsee Community College *A*

Indiana

International Business College *C, A*
Purdue University *B, M, D*

Iowa

Des Moines Area Community
College *C*
Northeast Iowa Community
College *C*
Western Iowa Tech Community
College *C*

Kansas

Coffeyville Community College *A*
Colby Community College *C*
Garden City Community College *A*
Hutchinson Community College *C*

Maryland
Anne Arundel Community College *C*

Massachusetts
Bay State College *A*
Holyoke Community College *C, A*

Minnesota
Art Institutes International
    Minnesota *B*
Capella University *B*
Minnesota State College - Southeast
    Technical *C, A*
North Hennepin Community
    College *C*
Ridgewater College *A*
Rochester Community and Technical
    College *C, A*
University of Minnesota
    Twin Cities *B*

Missouri
Lindenwood University *B*
Stevens Institute of Business &
    Arts *A, B*

Nebraska
Bellevue University *B*

New Hampshire
Southern New Hampshire
    University *B*

New Jersey
Mercer County Community
    College *C*

New Mexico
Eastern New Mexico University:
    Roswell *C*

New York
Genesee Community College *A*
Niagara County Community
    College *A*
Utica School of Commerce *A*

North Carolina
Central Piedmont Community
    College *C, A*

Ohio
Ashland University *C*
Bowling Green State University *B*
University of Akron *C*
University of Rio Grande *B*
Youngstown State University *B*

Oregon
Chemeketa Community College *C*
Clackamas Community College *C*
Clatsop Community College *C*
Lane Community College *C, A*
Linn-Benton Community College *C*
Mt. Hood Community College *C*
Portland Community College *C, A*
Rogue Community College *C*

Pennsylvania
Bradford School: Pittsburgh *C, A*
Bucks County Community College *A*
Commonwealth Technical Institute *C*
Montgomery County Community
    College *C*
South Hills School of Business &
    Technology *C*
York College of Pennsylvania *M*

South Carolina
Anderson University *B*
University of South Carolina
    Columbia *B, M*

Utah
Weber State University *A*

Washington
Bates Technical College *C*
Clark College *C*
Pierce College *C*
Tacoma Community College *C*
Walla Walla Community College *C, A*

West Virginia
American Public University
    System *C, A, B*
New River Community and Technical
    College *C*

Wisconsin
Northcentral Technical College *C*
University of Wisconsin
    Madison *B*

Wyoming
Casper College *C, A*

Rhetoric/composition

Alabama
Faulkner University *B*
University of Montevallo *B, T*

Arizona
University of Arizona *M, D*

Arkansas
Phillips Community College of the
    University of Arkansas *A*

California
Cabrillo College *A*
California Lutheran University *B*
California State University
    Chico *B*
    East Bay *B, M*
    Long Beach *B, M*
    Northridge *B, M*
Cerritos College *A*
Chabot College *A*
College of Marin *A*
College of the Desert *A*
College of the Sequoias *A*
Columbia College *A*
Cypress College *A*
El Camino College *A*
Foothill College *C, A*
Fresno City College *A*
Fullerton College *A*
Golden West College *A*
Grossmont College *A*
Irvine Valley College *A*
Long Beach City College *A*
Master's College *B*
Mendocino College *A*
Modesto Junior College *C, A*
National University *M*
Ohlone College *C*
Orange Coast College *A*
Pasadena City College *C, A*
Saddleback College *A*
San Deigo Miramar College
    San Diego Miramar College *A*
San Diego City College *A*
San Diego State University *B*
San Francisco State University *B, M*
San Jose State University *B*
Santa Barbara City College *A*
Santa Rosa Junior College *C*
Santiago Canyon College *A*
Sierra College *A*
Skyline College *A*
University of California
    Berkeley *B, D*
West Los Angeles College *C, A*
West Valley College *A*

Colorado
Colorado Mountain College *A*
Colorado State University *M*
Metropolitan State University of
    Denver *B*

District of Columbia
Catholic University of America *M, D*

Florida
Miami Dade College *A*
University of South Florida *B, M, D*

Georgia
Albany State University *B*
Atlanta Metropolitan College *A*
Clark Atlanta University *B*
Columbus State University *B*
Georgia College and State
    University *B*
Georgia Southern University *B*
Oglethorpe University *B*
Valdosta State University *B*

Illinois
Chicago State University *B*
DePaul University *B, M*
Greenville College *B*
Illinois Central College *A*
Illinois College *B*
Illinois Valley Community College *A*
Lake Land College *A*
Lincoln College *A*
McKendree University *B*
Monmouth College *B*
Richland Community College *A*
Southern Illinois University
    Carbondale *B, M, D*
Southern Illinois University
    Edwardsville *B, M*
Southwestern Illinois College *A*
University of Illinois
    Urbana-Champaign *B, M, D*

Indiana
Ball State University *B, M*
Indiana University
    Purdue University Indianapolis *C*
    South Bend *B*
Wabash College *B*

Iowa
Coe College *B*
Dordt College *B*
Drake University *B*
Iowa State University *B, M, D*
Mount Mercy University *B, T*
St. Ambrose University *B, T*
University of Iowa *B, M, D*
University of Northern Iowa *B*
Wartburg College *B, T*

Kansas
Bethany College *B*
Butler Community College *A*
Central Christian College of
    Kansas *A, B*
Coffeyville Community College *A*
Donnelly College *A*
Pratt Community College *A*

Kentucky
Bluegrass Community and Technical
    College *A*
Eastern Kentucky University *B*
Northern Kentucky University *B*
University of Louisville *D*

Louisiana
Louisiana State University
    Shreveport *B*
Louisiana Tech University *B, M*

Maine
Bates College *B*
University of Maine *B, M*

Maryland
Frederick Community College *A*
Frostburg State University *B, T*
Morgan State University *B*

Massachusetts
Emerson College *B, M*

Michigan
Calvin College *B*
Cornerstone University *B, T*
Eastern Michigan University *B, M*
Ferris State University *A, B*
Grand Rapids Community College *A*
Hillsdale College *B*
Madonna University *B*
Michigan State University *D*
Spring Arbor University *B*
University of Detroit Mercy *B*
University of Michigan *D*
University of Michigan
    Flint *B, M*

Minnesota
College of St. Benedict *B*
Minnesota State University
    Mankato *B, M*
Ridgewater College *A*
St. Catherine University *B*
Saint Cloud State University *B*
St. John's University *B*
Southwest Minnesota State
    University *B*
University of Minnesota
    Twin Cities *B, M, D*

Mississippi
Jackson State University *B*
Mississippi Valley State University *B*

Missouri
Evangel University *B*
Missouri Western State
    University *B, T*
St. Charles Community College *A*
Three Rivers Community College *A*
University of Central Missouri *B*

Montana
Miles Community College *A*
University of Montana *B, M*

Nebraska
Chadron State College *B*
Concordia University *B*
Hastings College *B, T*
Northeast Community College *A*
University of Nebraska
    Kearney *B, T*

New Jersey
Rider University *B*
Rutgers, The State University of New
    Jersey
    Camden Campus *T*

New Mexico
New Mexico State University *D*
University of New Mexico *B, M, D*

New York
City University of New York
    Brooklyn College *B*
    Lehman College *B*
Ithaca College *B*
Long Island University
    LIU Brooklyn *M*
New York University *B, M, T*

Pace University: Pleasantville/
  Briarcliff *B*
SUNY
  College at Plattsburgh *B*
  College at Potsdam *B*
  University at Albany *B, M*
St. John's University *B*
St. Joseph's College New York:
  Suffolk Campus *B*
St. Joseph's College, New York *B*
Syracuse University *D*
Touro College *B*

North Carolina

Elon University *B*
Methodist University *A, B*
North Carolina Agricultural and
  Technical State University *B*

North Dakota

Minot State University *B*
North Dakota State University *D*

Ohio

Bowling Green State
  University *B, M, D*
Defiance College *B, T*
Miami University
  Oxford *B*
University of Cincinnati *B*
Youngstown State University *B*

Oklahoma

Carl Albert State College *A*
Connors State College *A*
East Central University *B*
Oklahoma Baptist University *B, T*
Redlands Community College *A*
Southern Nazarene University *B*
Tulsa Community College *A*
University of Central Oklahoma *B, M*

Oregon

Linn-Benton Community College *A*
Portland State University *B, M*
Southern Oregon University *B, T*
Western Oregon University *B*
Willamette University *B*

Pennsylvania

Carnegie Mellon University *B, M, D*
Community College of
  Philadelphia *A*
Duquesne University *B, D*
Kutztown University of
  Pennsylvania *B*
La Salle University *B*
Mansfield University of
  Pennsylvania *B*
Shippensburg University of
  Pennsylvania *B*
University of Pittsburgh *B, M, D*
University of Pittsburgh
  Bradford *B*
West Chester University of
  Pennsylvania *B, M*

Rhode Island

University of Rhode Island *B*

South Carolina

Clemson University *B*
Spartanburg Community College *C*
Tri-County Technical College *C*

South Dakota

Augustana College *T*
Black Hills State University *B*
Northern State University *B*
University of Sioux Falls *B*
University of South Dakota *B, M, D*

Tennessee

Carson-Newman University *B*
East Tennessee State University *B, T*
Lipscomb University *B*
Tennessee Temple University *B*
Union University *B, T*

Texas

Amarillo College *A*
Angelina College *A*
Austin Community College *A*
Blinn College *A*
Brazosport College *A*
Clarendon College *A*
Coastal Bend College *A*
Del Mar College *A*
East Texas Baptist University *B*
El Paso Community College *A*
Galveston College *A*
Grayson College *A*
Hardin-Simmons University *B*
Hill College *A*
Lamar State College at Orange *A*
Lamar University *B, M*
Midland College *A*
Navarro College *A*
North Lake College *C*
Northwest Vista College *A*
St. Mary's University *B*
St. Philip's College *A*
Sam Houston State University *B*
San Jacinto College *A*
Stephen F. Austin State University *B*
Sul Ross State University *B*
Texas A&M University
  Commerce *B*
Texas Christian University *D*
Texas Southern University *B*
Texas State University *M, T*
Texas Tech University *B, M*
Texas Woman's University *D*
Trinity University *B*
Trinity Valley Community College *A*
Tyler Junior College *A*
University of Houston *M*
University of Houston
  Victoria *B, T*
University of North Texas *B, M*
University of Texas
  Arlington *B*
  Austin *M, D*
  El Paso *D*
  Tyler *B*

Utah

University of Utah *B*
Utah State University *B*

Virginia

George Mason University *B, D*
Hampton University *B*
Old Dominion University *B*
University of Richmond *B*
Virginia Polytechnic Institute and
  State University *D*

Washington

Gonzaga University *B*
University of Puget Sound *B*
University of Washington *B, M, D*

West Virginia

Marshall University *B, M*

Wisconsin

University of Wisconsin
  River Falls *B*
  Superior *B, M*

Robotics technology

Arizona

University of Advancing
  Technology *A, B*

California

Allan Hancock College *C, A*
American River College *C*
Cerritos College *A*
Long Beach City College *C*
Orange Coast College *C*
University of California
  San Diego *M, D*

Connecticut

Central Connecticut State
  University *B*

Idaho

Idaho State University *C, A, B*

Illinois

College of DuPage *C, A*
Illinois Central College *C, A*
Kaskaskia College *A*
Oakton Community College *A*
Triton College *C*

Indiana

Indiana State University *B*
Indiana University
  Purdue University Fort Wayne *C*
  Purdue University Indianapolis *B*
Purdue University *A, B*
Purdue University
  Calumet *C*

Iowa

Southeastern Community College *A*

Kentucky

Sullivan College of Technology and
  Design *A, B*

Massachusetts

Bristol Community College *C*
Springfield Technical Community
  College *C*

Michigan

Kirtland Community College *A*
Mott Community College *C*
Oakland Community College *C, A*
St. Clair County Community
  College *A*

Minnesota

Central Lakes College *C, A*
Dunwoody College of
  Technology *C, A*
Mesabi Range Community and
  Technical College *C, A*
Minnesota West Community and
  Technical College *A*

Mississippi

Alcorn State University *B*

New Hampshire

NHTI-Concord's Community
  College *A*
Nashua Community College *A*

New York

SUNY
  College of Technology at Alfred *A*

Ohio

James A. Rhodes State College *C, A*
Terra State Community College *C, A*
University of Rio Grande *A*

Pennsylvania

Butler County Community College *A*
Community College of Allegheny
  County *A*
Delaware County Community
  College *C, A*

Luzerne County Community
  College *A*
Pennsylvania College of
  Technology *A*

Puerto Rico

University of Puerto Rico
  Carolina Regional College *A*

Rhode Island

Johnson & Wales University
  Providence *B*

South Carolina

Trident Technical College *A*
York Technical College *C*

Texas

Tarrant County College *C, A*
Texas State Technical College
  Waco *A*
  West Texas *A*

Utah

Utah Valley University *A*

Washington

Bates Technical College *C, A*
Spokane Community College *A*

Wisconsin

Blackhawk Technical College *A*
Chippewa Valley Technical College *A*
Gateway Technical College *A*

Wyoming

Casper College *C, A*

Romance languages

Alabama

University of Alabama *M, D*

California

Point Loma Nazarene University *B*
Pomona College *B*
University of California
  Berkeley *D*

Connecticut

Southern Connecticut State
  University *M*
Wesleyan University *B*

District of Columbia

George Washington University *B*

Georgia

University of Georgia *B, M, D*

Illinois

Rockford University *B*
University of Chicago *B, D*

Indiana

DePauw University *B*
University of Notre Dame *B, M*

Louisiana

University of New Orleans *M*

Maine

Bowdoin College *B*

Maryland

Johns Hopkins University *B, M, D*
University of Maryland
  College Park *B*

Massachusetts

Boston College *M*
Harvard College *B, M, D*

Merrimack College *B*
Mount Holyoke College *B*

Michigan
Michigan State University *D*
University of Michigan *B, D*

Minnesota
Carleton College *B*

Missouri
Truman State University *B*
University of Missouri
Columbia *D*
Washington University in St. Louis *B*

New York
City University of New York
Hunter College *B*
Cornell University *M, D*
SUNY
University at Stony Brook *M*

North Carolina
Duke University *D*
University of North Carolina
Chapel Hill *B, M, D*

Oregon
University of Oregon *B, M, D*

Pennsylvania
Carnegie Mellon University *B*

Tennessee
University of Memphis *M*
Vanderbilt University *B, M, D*

Texas
Texas Tech University *M*

Virginia
Washington and Lee University *B*

Romanian

Georgia
Clark Atlanta University *D*

Roofing

Indiana
Ivy Tech Community College
North Central *A*

Washington
Clover Park Technical College *C*

Wisconsin
Milwaukee Area Technical College *C*

Rural sociology

Alabama
Auburn University *M*

Wisconsin
University of Wisconsin
Madison *B, M*

Russian

Alaska
University of Alaska
Anchorage *B*

Arizona
Arizona State University *B*
University of Arizona *B, M*

California
Claremont McKenna College *B*
Grossmont College *A*
Pitzer College *B*
Pomona College *B*
San Diego State University *B, M*
Scripps College *B*
Stanford University *M*
University of California
Davis *B*
Los Angeles *B*
Riverside *B*
San Diego *B*
Santa Barbara *B*
University of Southern California *B*

Colorado
Colorado College *B*
University of Denver *B*

Connecticut
Trinity College *B*
Wesleyan University *B*
Yale University *B*

Delaware
University of Delaware *B, T*

District of Columbia
American University *B*
George Washington University *B*
Georgetown University *B*
Howard University *B*

Florida
Florida State University *B*
New College of Florida *B*
University of Florida *B*
University of South Florida *B*

Georgia
Emory University *B*
University of Georgia *B*

Hawaii
University of Hawaii
Manoa *B*

Idaho
Idaho State University *A*

Illinois
Northern Illinois University *B*
University of Illinois
Chicago *B*
Urbana-Champaign *B, T*

Indiana
Purdue University *B*
University of Notre Dame *B*

Iowa
Cornell College *B, T*
Grinnell College *B*
University of Iowa *B, T*

Kentucky
Bluegrass Community and Technical
College *A*
University of Kentucky *B*

Louisiana
Tulane University *B*

Maine
Bates College *B*
Bowdoin College *B*
Colby College *B*

Maryland
Goucher College *B*
University of Maryland
College Park *B*

Massachusetts
Amherst College *B*
Boston College *B, M*
Boston University *B*
College of the Holy Cross *B*
Smith College *B*
Tufts University *B*
Wellesley College *B*
Wheaton College *B*
Williams College *B*

Michigan
Michigan State University *B*
University of Michigan *B*

Minnesota
Carleton College *B*
Gustavus Adolphus College *B*
Macalester College *B*
St. Olaf College *B*
University of Minnesota
Twin Cities *B, M*

Missouri
Saint Louis University *B*
Truman State University *B*
University of Missouri
Columbia *B, M*

Montana
University of Montana *B*

Nebraska
University of Nebraska
Lincoln *B*

New Hampshire
Dartmouth College *B*
University of New Hampshire *B*

New Jersey
Montclair State University *T*
Rider University *B*
Rutgers, The State University of New
Jersey
New Brunswick/Piscataway
Campus *B, T*

New York
Bard College *B*
Barnard College *B*
City University of New York
Brooklyn College *B*
Hunter College *B*
Queens College *B*
Colgate University *B*
Columbia University *B*
Columbia University
School of General Studies *B*
Fordham University *B, M*
Hobart and William Smith Colleges *B*
Hofstra University *B*
New York University *B, M*
SUNY
University at Stony Brook *B*
Syracuse University *B*
United States Military Academy *B*
University of Rochester *B*
Vassar College *B*

North Carolina
Duke University *B, M*
Wake Forest University *B*

Ohio
Bowling Green State University *B*
College of Wooster *B*
Kent State University *B*
Oberlin College *B*
Ohio State University
Columbus Campus *B*
Ohio University *B*

Oklahoma
Oklahoma State University *B*
Tulsa Community College *A*
University of Oklahoma *B*

Oregon
Portland State University *B, T*
Reed College *B*

Pennsylvania
Bryn Mawr College *B, M*
Bucknell University *B*
California University of
Pennsylvania *B*
Carnegie Mellon University *B*
Dickinson College *B*
Haverford College *B, T*
Juniata College *B*
Penn State
Abington *B*
Altoona *B*
Beaver *B*
Berks *B*
Brandywine *B*
DuBois *B*
Erie, The Behrend College *B*
Fayette, The Eberly Campus *B*
Greater Allegheny *B*
Harrisburg *B*
Hazleton *B*
Lehigh Valley *B*
Mont Alto *B*
New Kensington *B*
Schuylkill *B*
Shenango *B*
University Park *B, M*
Wilkes-Barre *B*
Worthington Scranton *B*
York *B*
Swarthmore College *B*
University of Pennsylvania *B, D*
University of Pittsburgh *B*
West Chester University of
Pennsylvania *B, T*

South Carolina
University of South Carolina
Columbia *B*

Tennessee
Sewanee: The University of the
South *B*
University of Tennessee
Knoxville *B*
Vanderbilt University *B*

Texas
Austin Community College *A*
Baylor University *B*
Texas A&M University *B*
Trinity University *B*
University of Texas
Arlington *B*
Austin *B*

Utah
Brigham Young University *B*
University of Utah *B*

Vermont
Middlebury College *B, M, D*
University of Vermont *B*

Virginia
Ferrum College *B*

Washington
Central Washington University *B*
Seattle Pacific University *B*
University of Washington *B, M, D*

West Virginia
West Virginia University *T*

Wisconsin

Beloit College *B, T*
Lawrence University *B*
University of Wisconsin
  Madison *B*
  Milwaukee *B*

Wyoming

University of Wyoming *B*

Russian/Central and Eastern European/ Eurasian studies

California

Pomona College *B*
San Diego State University *B*
Scripps College *B*
Stanford University *M*

Connecticut

Wesleyan University *B*

District of Columbia

Georgetown University *M*

Florida

Florida State University *B, M*

Illinois

Illinois Wesleyan University *B*

Maine

Bowdoin College *B*

Massachusetts

Amherst College *B*
Tufts University *R*
Wellesley College *B*

Michigan

Michigan State University *B*
Wayne State University *B*

Minnesota

Augsburg College *B*

New Jersey

Rutgers, The State University of New
  Jersey
  Newark Campus *B*

New York

Columbia University *B*
Columbia University
  School of General Studies *B*

Ohio

Wittenberg University *B*

Oregon

Portland State University *B*

Pennsylvania

Carnegie Mellon University *B*
La Salle University *B, M*

Utah

Brigham Young University *B*

Vermont

Marlboro College *B*

Washington

University of Washington *B, M*

Wisconsin

University of Wisconsin
  Madison *M*

Russian/Slavic studies

Alaska

University of Alaska
  Fairbanks *B*

California

Stanford University *M*
University of California
  Los Angeles *B*
  Riverside *B*
  San Diego *B*

Colorado

Colorado College *B*
University of Colorado
  Boulder *B*

Connecticut

Trinity College *B*
Wesleyan University *B*
Yale University *B, M*

District of Columbia

American University *B*
Georgetown University *M, D*

Florida

Florida State University *B, M*
Stetson University *B*

Georgia

Emory University *B*

Illinois

University of Chicago *B, D*
University of Illinois
  Urbana-Champaign *B, M*

Indiana

Indiana University
  Bloomington *M*

Iowa

Cornell College *B*
Luther College *B*
University of Iowa *B*

Kansas

University of Kansas *B, M*

Kentucky

Bluegrass Community and Technical
  College *A*

Louisiana

Tulane University *B*

Maine

University of Southern Maine *B*

Maryland

University of Maryland
  College Park *B*

Massachusetts

Bard College at Simon's Rock *B*
Boston College *M*
Boston University *B*
Brandeis University *B*
College of the Holy Cross *B*
Mount Holyoke College *B*
Tufts University *B*
University of Massachusetts
  Amherst *C, B*
Wellesley College *B*
Wheaton College *B*

Michigan

Grand Valley State University *B*
Michigan State University *B*
University of Michigan *B, M*

Minnesota

Gustavus Adolphus College *B*
St. Olaf College *B*
University of Minnesota
  Twin Cities *B, M*

New Hampshire

Dartmouth College *B*

New Mexico

University of New Mexico *B*

New York

Bard College *B*
Barnard College *B*
City University of New York
  Hunter College *M*
Colgate University *B*
Columbia University *B*
Columbia University
  School of General Studies *B*
Cornell University *M, D*
Fordham University *B*
Hamilton College *B*
Hobart and William Smith Colleges *B*
New York University *M, D*
Syracuse University *B*
United States Military Academy *B*
University of Rochester *B*

Ohio

Bowling Green State University *B*
College of Wooster *B*
Oberlin College *B*
University of Akron *C*
Wittenberg University *B*

Oklahoma

University of Tulsa *B*

Oregon

University of Oregon *B, M*

Pennsylvania

Carnegie Mellon University *B*
La Salle University *B*
Lafayette College *B*
Mercyhurst University *B*
Muhlenberg College *C, B*

Tennessee

Rhodes College *B*

Texas

Texas Tech University *B*
University of Texas
  Austin *B, M*

Vermont

Marlboro College *B*
Middlebury College *B*
University of Vermont *B*

Virginia

George Mason University *B*
University of Richmond *B*
Washington and Lee University *B*

Washington

University of Washington *B, M*

Wisconsin

Lawrence University *B*

Sacred music

Alabama

Birmingham-Southern College *B*
Samford University *B, M*
University of Mobile *B*

Arizona

Arizona Christian University *B*
International Baptist College *B*

Arkansas

Central Baptist College *B*
Ecclesia College *B*
John Brown University *B*
Ouachita Baptist University *B*
Williams Baptist College *B*

California

Azusa Pacific University *B*
Bethesda University of California *B*
Hope International University *B, M*
Master's College *B*
Mount St. Mary's College *B*
Patten University *B*
Point Loma Nazarene University *B*

Colorado

Colorado Christian University *B*
Nazarene Bible College *A, B*

Connecticut

University of Hartford *B*

District of Columbia

Catholic University of America *M, D*

Florida

Ave Maria University *B*
Baptist College of Florida *A, B*
Hobe Sound Bible College *C, B*
Jacksonville University *B*
Johnson University: Florida *B*
Southeastern University *B*
Warner University *B*

Georgia

Brewton-Parker College *B*
Darton College *C*
Emmanuel College *B*
Emory University *M*
Mercer University *M*
Shorter University *B*

Idaho

Boise Bible College *A, B*
Northwest Nazarene University *B*

Illinois

Concordia University Chicago *B, M*
Judson University *B*
Moody Bible Institute *B*
Northwestern University *M, D*
Olivet Nazarene University *B*
Quincy University *B*
Trinity International University *B*

Indiana

Anderson University *R*
Bethel College *B*
Indiana Wesleyan University *A, B*
Saint Joseph's College *M*

Iowa

Dordt College *B*
Faith Baptist Bible College and
  Theological Seminary *B*
Northwestern College *B*
Wartburg College *B*

Kansas

Barclay College *B*
Central Christian College of
  Kansas *A, B*
Manhattan Christian College *A*
MidAmerica Nazarene University *B*

Kentucky

Asbury University *B*
Campbellsville University *B, M*

Kentucky Christian University *B*
Kentucky Mountain Bible College *B*
University of the Cumberlands *B*

Louisiana

Centenary College of Louisiana *B*
Louisiana College *B*
New Orleans Baptist Theological
 Seminary *A, B, M, D*

Massachusetts

Boston University *M, D*
Eastern Nazarene College *B*

Michigan

Andrews University *B*
Aquinas College *B*
Calvin College *B*
Grace Bible College *B*
Great Lakes Christian College *B*
Kuyper College *B*
Madonna University *B*
Marygrove College *C*
Spring Arbor University *B*

Minnesota

Concordia University St. Paul *B*
Crossroads College *B*
Gustavus Adolphus College *B*
North Central University *C, B*
Oak Hills Christian College *B*
St. Catherine University *C*
St. John's University *M*
St. Olaf College *B*

Mississippi

Blue Mountain College *B*
Mississippi College *B*
William Carey University *B*

Missouri

Baptist Bible College *B*
Central Christian College of the
 Bible *B*
College of the Ozarks *B*
Evangel University *B*
Hannibal-LaGrange University *B*
Lincoln University *B*
Missouri Baptist University *B*
Ozark Christian College *A, B*
St. Louis Christian College *B*
Southwest Baptist University *B*
Webster University *M*
William Jewell College *B*

Nebraska

Concordia University *B*
Grace University *B*
Nebraska Christian College *A, B*

New Jersey

Rider University *B, M*

New York

Concordia College *B*
Holy Trinity Orthodox Seminary *C*
Jewish Theological Seminary of
 America *B, M, D*
Nyack College *B*

North Carolina

Gardner-Webb University *B*
Lenoir-Rhyne University *B*
Southeastern Baptist Theological
 Seminary *C, B*
University of Mount Olive *B*

North Dakota

University of Mary *B*

Ohio

Bowling Green State University *B*
Cedarville University *B*

Cincinnati Christian University *B*
Franciscan University of
 Steubenville *B*
God's Bible School and College *A, B*
Malone University *B*
Mount Vernon Nazarene
 University *A, B*
Ohio Christian University *B*

Oklahoma

East Central University *B*
Mid-America Christian University *B*
Oklahoma Baptist University *B*
Oklahoma City University *B*
Oklahoma Wesleyan University *B*
Oral Roberts University *B, M*
Southern Nazarene University *B*
Southwestern Christian University *B*
Southwestern Oklahoma State
 University *B*

Oregon

Corban University *B*
Multnomah University *B*
New Hope Christian College *B*
Northwest Christian University *B*

Pennsylvania

Baptist Bible College of
 Pennsylvania *B*
Cairn University *B*
Duquesne University *M*
Gratz College *M, T*
Immaculata University *C, A*
St. Charles Borromeo Seminary -
 Overbrook *C*
Seton Hill University *C, B*
Valley Forge Christian College *B, M*

South Carolina

Bob Jones University *B, M*
Charleston Southern University *B*
Columbia International University *B*
Erskine College *M*
Furman University *B*
Newberry College *B*
North Greenville University *B*

South Dakota

Augustana College *B*

Tennessee

Carson-Newman University *B*
Johnson University *B*
Lee University *B, M*
Martin Methodist College *B*
Tennessee Temple University *B*
Trevecca Nazarene University *C, B*
Union University *B*

Texas

Arlington Baptist College *B*
Baylor University *B, M*
Concordia University Texas *B*
Dallas Baptist University *B, M*
Dallas Christian College *B*
East Texas Baptist University *B*
Hardin-Simmons University *B, M*
Houston Baptist University *B*
Howard Payne University *B*
Southern Methodist University *M*
Southwestern Assemblies of God
 University *A, B*
Southwestern Baptist Theological
 Seminary *B, M, D*
Southwestern Baptist Theological
 Seminary: Theological
 Professions *M*
Texas Christian University *B*
University of Mary Hardin-Baylor *B*
Wayland Baptist University *B*

Virginia

Bluefield College *B*
Liberty University *B, M*
Shenandoah University *C, B, M*

Washington

Northwest University *B*
Trinity Lutheran College *B*

Wisconsin

Concordia University Wisconsin *B*
Maranatha Baptist Bible College *B*

Sales/distribution

Alabama

Gadsden State Community College *A*
University of Alabama
 Birmingham *B*

Arizona

Cochise College *C*
Mesa Community College *C*

Arkansas

Harding University *B*
Rich Mountain Community College *A*

California

Bakersfield College *C, A*
Chabot College *A*
Chaffey College *C, A*
Citrus College *C*
College of the Canyons *C, A*
College of the Sequoias *C, A*
Columbia College *C*
East Los Angeles College *C, A*
El Camino College *C, A*
Fashion Institute of Design and
 Merchandising
 Los Angeles *A*
Golden West College *C, A*
Grossmont College *C, A*
Laney College *C, A*
Long Beach City College *C, A*
Orange Coast College *C, A*
Pasadena City College *A*
Rio Hondo College *C, A*
San Joaquin Delta College *C*
Santa Barbara City College *C, A*
Santa Monica College *C*
Shasta College *A*
Sierra College *C, A*
Skyline College *C*

Colorado

Community College of Denver *C*

Connecticut

Gateway Community College *A*
Middlesex Community College *C*
University of Saint Joseph *C*

Florida

Florida State College at
 Jacksonville *A*
Indian River State College *A*
Palm Beach State College *A*
Tallahassee Community College *A*

Georgia

Albany Technical College *C, A*
Athens Technical College *C, A*
Atlanta Technical College *C, A*
Augusta Technical College *C, A*
Clayton State University *A*
Georgia State University *C*
Gwinnett Technical College *C, A*
Kennesaw State University *B*
Middle Georgia State College *A*
Savannah Technical College *C, A*

Hawaii

Heald College
 Honolulu *A*
University of Hawaii
 Kapiolani Community College *C, A*

Illinois

City Colleges of Chicago
 Richard J. Daley College *A*
 Wilbur Wright College *C, A*
College of DuPage *C, A*
Harper College *C, A*
Illinois Eastern Community Colleges
 Wabash Valley College *C*
John Wood Community College *C, A*
Joliet Junior College *C*
Kishwaukee College *C*
Southwestern Illinois College *A*
Spoon River College *C*
University of Illinois
 Urbana-Champaign *B*
Waubonsee Community College *C*

Indiana

Vincennes University *C*

Iowa

AIB College of Business *A*
Des Moines Area Community
 College *A*
Hawkeye Community College *A*
Iowa Lakes Community College *C, A*
Iowa Western Community College *A*
Northeast Iowa Community
 College *C, A*
Western Iowa Tech Community
 College *C, A*

Kansas

Allen County Community College *A*
Bethany College *B*
Hutchinson Community College *C*
Johnson County Community
 College *A*
Seward County Community
 College *C, A*

Kentucky

Henderson Community College *C*
Madisonville Community College *A*
Sullivan University *C*

Maine

Beal College *A*
Husson University *B*

Massachusetts

Babson College *B*
Simmons College *B*

Michigan

Cleary University *B*
Grand Rapids Community
 College *C, A*
Lansing Community College *C, A*

Minnesota

Alexandria Technical and Community
 College *A*
Anoka-Ramsey Community College *A*
Concordia University St. Paul *B*
Dakota County Technical College *A*
Inver Hills Community College *C*
Metropolitan State University *B*
Minnesota State College - Southeast
 Technical *A*
Minnesota State Community and
 Technical College *C, A*
Northland Community & Technical
 College *A*
Northwest Technical College *C, A*
Rasmussen College
 Blaine *A*

Ridgewater College *C, A*
St. Catherine University *B*
St. Cloud Technical and Community
College *C, A*
St. Mary's University of Minnesota *B*
University of Minnesota
Twin Cities *B*

Missouri

Avila University *B*
Metropolitan Community College -
Kansas City *A*

Montana

Flathead Valley Community College *C*
University of Montana *C*

Nevada

College of Southern Nevada *A*

New Jersey

Bergen Community College *A*
Burlington County College *C, A*
Camden County College *A*
Cumberland County College *C*
Gloucester County College *C, A*
Passaic County Community College *A*

New York

Bryant & Stratton College
Syracuse *A*
Finger Lakes Community
College *C, A*
Long Island University
LIU Brooklyn *B*
Mercy College *M*
Monroe Community College *C, A*
Nassau Community College *A*
New York University *B, M, D*
Orange County Community
College *A*
Rochester Institute of Technology *B*
Suffolk County Community College *A*
Trocaire College *A*
Utica School of Commerce *A*
Westchester Community College *A*

North Carolina

Alamance Community College *C, A*
Asheville-Buncombe Technical
Community College *A*
Blue Ridge Community College *A*
Pitt Community College *C, A*
Wake Technical Community
College *C*
Western Piedmont Community
College *C, A*

North Dakota

United Tribes Technical College *C, A*

Ohio

Bowling Green State University *B*
Cincinnati State Technical and
Community College *C*
Edison State Community College *A*
Owens Community College
Toledo *C, A*
Stark State College *A*
University of Akron *B*
University of Cincinnati
Blue Ash College *C, A*
University of Northwestern Ohio *C*
Wilmington College *B*
Youngstown State University *A, B, M*
Zane State College *A*

Oregon

Clackamas Community College *C, A*
Southwestern Oregon Community
College *C, A*
Umpqua Community College *C*

Pennsylvania

Community College of
Philadelphia *C, A*
Harcum College *A*
Harrisburg Area Community
College *A*
Montgomery County Community
College *C, A*
Seton Hill University *B*
University of Pennsylvania *B, M*
West Chester University of
Pennsylvania *B*

Puerto Rico

Inter American University of Puerto
Rico
Aguadilla Campus *A*
San German Campus *A*
Universidad Metropolitana *A, B*
University of Puerto Rico
Mayaguez *B*

South Carolina

Aiken Technical College *C, A*
Florence-Darlington Technical
College *C, A*
Greenville Technical College *C, A*
Midlands Technical College *C*
Tri-County Technical College *C*
Trident Technical College *C*

Tennessee

Middle Tennessee State University *B*

Texas

Baylor University *B*
Brookhaven College *C*
Del Mar College *C*
Lamar University *B*
Laredo Community College *A*
Texas A&M University *B*
University of Houston *B*
University of North Texas *B*
University of the Incarnate Word *B*
Wade College *A, B*

Utah

Weber State University *C*

Virginia

Lord Fairfax Community College *C*
Tidewater Community College *C, A*
Virginia Union University *B*

Washington

Centralia College *C, A*
Highline Community College *A*
Lake Washington Institute of
Technology *C*
Shoreline Community College *A*

West Virginia

Kanawha Valley Community and
Technical College *A*

Wisconsin

Lac Courte Oreilles Ojibwa
Community College *A*
Moraine Park Technical College *C, A*
Northeast Wisconsin Technical
College *A*
University of Wisconsin
Madison *M*
Stout *B*

Sales/marketing education

California

San Diego Mesa College *A*

Colorado

Colorado State University *B, M, T*

Florida

Palm Beach State College *A*

Kansas

Colby Community College *A*
Independence Community College *A*

Michigan

Eastern Michigan University *B*
Western Michigan University *B*

Minnesota

University of Minnesota
Twin Cities *B, M, T*

Mississippi

Northwest Mississippi Community
College *A*

New Jersey

Rider University *B*

New Mexico

Eastern New Mexico University *B*

New York

College of Saint Rose *M, T*
Nazareth College *T*
SUNY
College at Buffalo *B, M, T*

North Carolina

East Carolina University *B*
North Carolina State University *B*

Ohio

Bowling Green State
University *B, M, T*
Wright State University *B*

South Carolina

Forrest Junior College *A*

Tennessee

Middle Tennessee State University *B*

Wisconsin

University of Wisconsin
Stout *B, T*
Whitewater *B, T*

Salon management

Alabama

Northeast Alabama Community
College *C, A*
Virginia College
Birmingham *A*
Huntsville *A*

Michigan

Mott Community College *A*
Oakland Community College *A*
Schoolcraft College *C*

North Carolina

Cape Fear Community College *C*

Texas

Houston Community College
System *C*

Sanskrit/classical Indian languages

Iowa

University of Iowa *B*

Massachusetts

Harvard College *B, D*

New York

Bard College *B*

Scandinavian languages

California

University of California
Berkeley *B, M, D*
Los Angeles *B, M*

Illinois

Augustana College *B*
North Park University *B*

Iowa

Luther College *B*

Minnesota

Augsburg College *B*
Gustavus Adolphus College *B*
University of Minnesota
Twin Cities *B, M, D*

Texas

University of Texas
Austin *B*

Washington

University of Washington *B, M, D*

Scandinavian studies

California

University of California
Los Angeles *B*

Illinois

North Park University *B*

Minnesota

Augsburg College *B*
Concordia College: Moorhead *B*
Gustavus Adolphus College *B*
Minnesota State University
Mankato *B*
University of Minnesota
Twin Cities *M, D*

Washington

Pacific Lutheran University *B*
University of Washington *B, M*

Wisconsin

University of Wisconsin
Madison *B, M, D*
Milwaukee *C*

School librarian education

Alabama

Auburn University *M, T*

Georgia

Columbus State University *M*
Georgia State University *M, T*

Illinois

University of Illinois
Urbana-Champaign *M, T*

Kentucky

Eastern Kentucky University *M*
Murray State University *M*

Maryland

McDaniel College *M*

Massachusetts

Fitchburg State University *M*

Michigan

Central Michigan University *M*

Minnesota

College of St. Scholastica *B, M, T*
Minnesota State University
   Mankato *M*

Missouri

Lindenwood University *M*
Missouri Baptist University *T*
University of Missouri
   Columbia *M*

Montana

University of Montana: Western *B, T*

New Jersey

Rowan University *M*
Seton Hall University *M*

New York

City University of New York
   Queens College *M*
Syracuse University *M*

Oklahoma

East Central University *M*

Oregon

George Fox University *M, T*

Pennsylvania

Arcadia University *M*
Drexel University *T*
St. Vincent College *M*

Puerto Rico

Turabo University *M*

Wisconsin

University of Wisconsin
   Superior *M, T*

School psychology

Alabama

University of Alabama *D*

Arizona

Argosy University
   Phoenix *M, D*
Northern Arizona University *M*
University of Arizona *M, D*

Arkansas

University of Central Arkansas *M, D*

California

Alliant International University *M*
Azusa Pacific University *M*
California State University
   East Bay *T*
   Long Beach *M*
Chapman University *M, D, T*
Loyola Marymount University *M*
National University *M*
Stanford University *D*
University of the Pacific *T*

Colorado

University of Colorado
   Denver *T*
University of Denver *M, D*
University of Northern Colorado *D, T*

Connecticut

Fairfield University *M, T*
Southern Connecticut State
   University *M*

District of Columbia

Gallaudet University *M*
Howard University *M, D*

Florida

Barry University *M*
Carlos Albizu University *M*
Nova Southeastern University *M*
University of Central Florida *M*
University of Florida *M, D*
University of South Florida *M, D*

Georgia

Georgia Southern University *M*
Georgia State University *M, D*
University of Georgia *D, T*

Illinois

Eastern Illinois University *M*
Governors State University *M*
Illinois State University *D*
Loyola University Chicago *M, D*
National-Louis University *M, D*
Western Illinois University *M*

Indiana

Ball State University *M, T*
Indiana State University *M, T*
Indiana University
   Bloomington *M, D*
Valparaiso University *M*

Iowa

University of Iowa *D*
University of Northern Iowa *M*

Kansas

University of Kansas *M, D*
Wichita State University *M*

Kentucky

Eastern Kentucky University *M*

Louisiana

Louisiana State University
   Shreveport *M*

Maine

University of Southern Maine *M*

Maryland

Bowie State University *M*
Towson University *T*

Massachusetts

Northeastern University *M, D*
University of Massachusetts
   Amherst *D*
   Boston *M*
Worcester State University *M*

Michigan

Andrews University *M*
Central Michigan University *M, D*
Michigan State University *M, D*
University of Detroit Mercy *M*
Wayne State University *M*

Minnesota

Capella University *M*
Minnesota State University
   Mankato *M*
   Moorhead *M*
Saint Cloud State University *M*

Missouri

Lindenwood University *M*
University of Missouri
   Columbia *M, D*

Montana

University of Great Falls *M*
University of Montana *M*

Nebraska

University of Nebraska
   Kearney *M*
   Omaha *M*

Nevada

University of Nevada
   Las Vegas *M*

New Hampshire

Rivier University *M, D*

New Jersey

Caldwell College *T*
Fairleigh Dickinson University
   Metropolitan Campus *M, D*
Georgian Court University *M*
Kean University *M, D*
New Jersey City University *M*
Rider University *M*
Rutgers, The State University of New
   Jersey
   New Brunswick/Piscataway
     Campus *D*
Seton Hall University *M*

New Mexico

New Mexico State University *D*

New York

Adelphi University *M*
Alfred University *M, D*
City University of New York
   Brooklyn College *M, T*
   Queens College *M, T*
College of New Rochelle *M*
College of Saint Rose *M*
Hofstra University *M, D*
Iona College *M*
Long Island University
   LIU Brooklyn *M*
Marist College *M*
Roberts Wesleyan College *M*
Rochester Institute of Technology *M*
SUNY
   College at Oswego *M*
   College at Plattsburgh *M, T*
   University at Buffalo *M*
St. John's University *M, D*
Syracuse University *D*
Yeshiva University *M, D*

North Carolina

Appalachian State University *M*
East Carolina University *M*
University of North Carolina
   Chapel Hill *M, D*
Western Carolina University *M*

North Dakota

Minot State University *M*

Ohio

John Carroll University *M*
Kent State University *M, D*
Miami University
   Oxford *M*
University of Cincinnati *M, D*
University of Dayton *M*
University of Toledo *M*
Youngstown State University *M*

Oklahoma

University of Central Oklahoma *M*

Oregon

George Fox University *M*
Lewis & Clark College *M*
University of Oregon *M, D*

Pennsylvania

Bucknell University *M*
California University of
   Pennsylvania *M*
Duquesne University *D*
Eastern University *M*
Edinboro University of
   Pennsylvania *M*
Immaculata University *D*
Indiana University of Pennsylvania *D*
Lehigh University *D*
Millersville University of
   Pennsylvania *T*
Penn State
   University Park *M, D*
Temple University *M, D*

Puerto Rico

Inter American University of Puerto
   Rico
   Metropolitan Campus *M, D*
   San German Campus *M, D*
Turabo University *M*
University of Puerto Rico
   Rio Piedras *M*

Rhode Island

Rhode Island College *M*
University of Rhode Island *D*

South Carolina

Citadel *M*
Francis Marion University *M*
University of South Carolina
   Columbia *M, D*
Winthrop University *M, T*

Tennessee

Southern Adventist University *M*
University of Tennessee
   Knoxville *D*

Texas

Abilene Christian University *M*
Baylor University *M*
Sam Houston State University *M*
Stephen F. Austin State
   University *M, D*
Tarleton State University *M*
Texas A&M University *D*
Texas A&M University
   Commerce *M*
   Texarkana *M*
Texas State University *M*
Texas Wesleyan University *M*
Texas Woman's University *M, D*
Trinity University *M*
University of Houston *D*
University of Houston
   Clear Lake *M*
University of North Texas *M*
University of Texas
   Pan American *M*
   San Antonio *M*
   Tyler *M*
West Texas A&M University *M*

Utah

Brigham Young University *D*

Virginia

College of William and Mary *M*
James Madison University *M, T*

Washington

Central Washington University *M, T*
Eastern Washington University *M*
Seattle University *M*

West Virginia

Marshall University *T*

Wisconsin

University of Wisconsin
La Crosse *M*
Milwaukee *T*
River Falls *M*
Stout *M*
Whitewater *M*

Science teacher education

Alabama

Auburn University *B, M, D, T*
Birmingham-Southern College *T*
Faulkner University *B, M, T*
Judson College *B*
Miles College *B*
Oakwood University *B*
Tuskegee University *B*

Arizona

Arizona Christian University *B*
Northern Arizona University *M*
University of Arizona *B, M*

Arkansas

Arkansas Tech University *B*
Harding University *B, T*
Ouachita Baptist University *B, T*
University of Arkansas
Pine Bluff *B, M, T*
University of Central Arkansas *B*
University of the Ozarks *B, T*

California

Azusa Pacific University *T*
California Lutheran University *B, T*
California State University
Chico *T*
Long Beach *B, T*
San Bernardino *M*
Fresno Pacific University *B, M, T*
Humboldt State University *T*
Master's College *B, T*
Mills College *T*
Mount St. Mary's College *T*
San Diego State University *D*
San Francisco State University *T*
Shasta College *A*
Sonoma State University *T*
Stanford University *M, T*
University of San Diego *T*
Vanguard University of Southern
California *T*

Colorado

Adams State University *B, M, T*
Colorado Christian University *B*
Colorado State University *B, T*
Colorado State University
Pueblo *T*
Metropolitan State University of
Denver *T*
University of Colorado
Boulder *T*
Western State Colorado
University *B, T*

Connecticut

Albertus Magnus College *B, T*
Central Connecticut State
University *T*
Eastern Connecticut State
University *M*
Fairfield University *T*
Quinnipiac University *B, M*
Sacred Heart University *T*
Southern Connecticut State
University *M*
University of Connecticut *B, T*
University of Saint Joseph *T*

Delaware

Delaware State University *B, M*
University of Delaware *B, T*

District of Columbia

George Washington University *M, T*
Trinity Washington University *B, M*

Florida

Broward College *A, B*
Chipola College *B*
Florida Agricultural and Mechanical
University *B, T*
Florida Atlantic University *B*
Florida Institute of
Technology *B, M, D*
Miami Dade College *A, B*
Northwest Florida State College *B*
Palm Beach State College *A*
St. Petersburg College *B*
South Florida State College *A*
University of Central Florida *B*
University of Florida *M*
University of Miami *M*
University of North Florida *B*
University of South Florida *B, M*
University of West Florida *B, M*
Warner University *B*

Georgia

Albany State University *B*
Columbus State University *B, M*
Covenant College *B, T*
Darton College *A*
Georgia State University *M, T*
Piedmont College *M, T*
Shorter University *T*
Toccoa Falls College *B, T*
University of Georgia *B, M, D, T*
University of North Georgia *A, M*
Valdosta State University *M*

Hawaii

Brigham Young University-
Hawaii *B, T*
Hawaii Pacific University *M*

Idaho

Boise State University *B, M, T*
Brigham Young University-Idaho *B, T*
Lewis-Clark State College *B, T*
University of Idaho *T*

Illinois

Augustana College *B, T*
Benedictine University *M*
Bradley University *B, M*
Chicago State University *T*
Concordia University Chicago *B, T*
DePaul University *M*
Eastern Illinois University *B, M, T*
Eureka College *T*
Illinois Institute of Technology *M, D*
Loyola University Chicago *B, M*
McKendree University *B*
Monmouth College *T*
Moraine Valley Community College *A*
National-Louis University *M*
North Park University *T*
Olivet Nazarene University *B, T*
Southern Illinois University
Edwardsville *B, T*
University of Illinois
Urbana-Champaign *B, M, T*
University of St. Francis *B, M*

Indiana

Ball State University *B, D, T*
Bethel College *B*
Butler University *T*
Calumet College of St. Joseph *T*
Goshen College *B, T*
Grace College *B*
Huntington University *B, M*

Indiana State University *B, M, T*
Indiana University
Purdue University Fort Wayne *B, T*
South Bend *B, T*
Indiana Wesleyan University *B, T*
Manchester University *B, T*
Oakland City University *B*
Saint Mary's College *T*
Taylor University *B, T*
Trine University *B, T*
University of Indianapolis *B, T*
University of Notre Dame *B*
Valparaiso University *B*
Vincennes University *B*

Iowa

Briar Cliff University *B*
Buena Vista University *B, T*
Central College *T*
Coe College *B*
Cornell College *B, T*
Dordt College *B*
Drake University *M, T*
Ellsworth Community College *A*
Graceland University *T*
Grand View University *B*
Iowa State University *T*
Loras College *T*
Morningside College *B*
Mount Mercy University *T*
Northwestern College *T*
St. Ambrose University *B, T*
Simpson College *T*
University of Dubuque *B, T*
University of Iowa *B, M, D, T*
University of Northern Iowa *B*
Upper Iowa University *B*
Wartburg College *T*

Kansas

Bethany College *T*
Friends University *B*
Garden City Community College *A*
Independence Community College *A*
Kansas Wesleyan University *T*
McPherson College *B, T*
Pittsburg State University *B*
Tabor College *B*
University of Kansas *B, T*

Kentucky

Campbellsville University *B*
Eastern Kentucky University *B*
Kentucky Wesleyan College *T*
Northern Kentucky University *B*
Union College *B*
University of Kentucky *B*

Louisiana

Centenary College of Louisiana *T*
Louisiana College *B, T*
Louisiana State University
Shreveport *B*
Nicholls State University *B*
Our Lady of Holy Cross College *T*
University of Louisiana at Lafayette *B*
Xavier University of Louisiana *B*

Maine

University of Maine *B, M*
University of Maine
Fort Kent *B*
Machias *T*
University of Southern Maine *T*

Maryland

Bowie State University *B*
Montgomery College *A*
Morgan State University *B, M, D*
Notre Dame of Maryland
University *T*
Prince George's Community
College *A*
Washington Adventist University *B*

Massachusetts

Assumption College *T*
Boston University *B, M, T*
Bridgewater State University *M*
Cambridge College *M*
Eastern Nazarene College *B*
Fitchburg State University *M, T*
Lesley University *B, M*
Merrimack College *B, M*
Salem State University *M*
Smith College *M*
Tufts University *M, T*
Westfield State University *M, T*
Worcester State University *T*

Michigan

Adrian College *B, T*
Andrews University *M*
Aquinas College *B, T*
Calvin College *B, T*
Central Michigan University *B*
Concordia University *B, T*
Cornerstone University *B, T*
Eastern Michigan University *B*
Grand Valley State University *B, T*
Hope College *B, T*
Lawrence Technological University *M*
Madonna University *B*
Michigan State University *B, M*
Michigan Technological
University *M, T*
Northern Michigan
University *B, M, T*
Olivet College *B*
Rochester College *B*
Saginaw Valley State University *B, T*
University of Detroit Mercy *B, M, T*
University of Michigan
Dearborn *B*
Wayne State University *B, M, T*
Western Michigan University *M, D, T*

Minnesota

Augsburg College *T*
Bemidji State University *B, M, T*
College of St. Benedict *T*
College of St. Scholastica *T*
Concordia University St. Paul *B, T*
Crown College *B*
Gustavus Adolphus College *T*
Hamline University *M, T*
Martin Luther College *B*
Minnesota State University
Mankato *B, M, T*
Rainy River Community College *A*
Ridgewater College *A*
St. Catherine University *T*
Saint Cloud State University *B, T*
St. John's University *T*
Southwest Minnesota State
University *B, T*
University of Minnesota
Duluth *B*
Morris *T*
Twin Cities *B, M*
University of St. Thomas *B*
Winona State University *B, T*

Mississippi

Coahoma Community College *A*
Itawamba Community College *A*
Millsaps College *T*
Mississippi Gulf Coast Community
College *A*
Northeast Mississippi Community
College *A*
Northwest Mississippi Community
College *A*
University of Mississippi *B*
University of Southern
Mississippi *M, D*

Missouri

Central Methodist University *B*
College of the Ozarks *B, T*
Culver-Stockton College *T*
Evangel University *B*
Hannibal-LaGrange University *B*
Lindenwood University *B*
Maryville University of Saint
  Louis *B, T*
Missouri Baptist University *B, T*
Missouri Southern State
  University *B, T*
Missouri State University *B*
Missouri Valley College *T*
Northwest Missouri State
  University *B, M, T*
Saint Louis University *T*
Southeast Missouri State University *B*
Southwest Baptist University *B, T*
Truman State University *M*
University of Central Missouri *B, T*
University of Missouri
  Columbia *B, M, D*
  Kansas City *B*
Washington University in St.
  Louis *B, M, T*
Webster University *B*
William Woods University *B*

Montana

Fort Peck Community College *A*
Montana State University *M*
Montana State University
  Billings *B, T*
  Northern *B*
Rocky Mountain College *B*
University of Great Falls *B*
University of Montana *T*
University of Montana: Western *B, T*

Nebraska

Chadron State College *B, M*
College of Saint Mary *B, T*
Concordia University *B, T*
Hastings College *B, M, T*
Midland University *B, T*
Nebraska Wesleyan University *B*
Union College *B*
University of Nebraska
  Kearney *B, M, T*
  Lincoln *B, T*
Wayne State College *T*

Nevada

Great Basin College *B*

New Hampshire

Franklin Pierce University *M, T*
Keene State College *B, T*
New England College *B, T*
Plymouth State University *M, T*
Rivier University *B, T*
Saint Anselm College *T*
Southern New Hampshire
  University *M*
University of New Hampshire *T*

New Jersey

Centenary College *T*
College of New Jersey *M, T*
Ramapo College of New Jersey *M*
Richard Stockton College of New
  Jersey *M*
Rider University *B*
Rowan University *M, T*
Rutgers, The State University of New
  Jersey
  New Brunswick/Piscataway
    Campus *M, D, T*
  Newark Campus *T*
Saint Peter's University *T*
William Paterson University of New
  Jersey *T*

New Mexico

New Mexico Highlands University *B*
New Mexico Institute of Mining and
  Technology *M*
University of the Southwest *B, T*
Western New Mexico University *B*

New York

Adelphi University *M, T*
Bard College *M*
City University of New York
  Brooklyn College *M, T*
  City College *B, M, T*
  Lehman College *M, T*
  Queens College *M, T*
  York College *T*
College of Mount St. Vincent *T*
Cornell University *T*
D'Youville College *M, T*
Dowling College *B, M*
Dutchess Community College *A*
Elmira College *B, T*
Fordham University *M, T*
Hofstra University *B, M*
Ithaca College *B, T*
Le Moyne College *T*
Manhattan College *B, T*
Manhattanville College *M, T*
Nazareth College *T*
New York University *B, D*
Pace University: Pleasantville/
  Briarcliff *B, M, T*
Roberts Wesleyan College *B, M*
SUNY
  College at Brockport *B, M, T*
  College at Buffalo *B, M*
  College at Cortland *B, M*
  College at Fredonia *M, T*
  College at Geneseo *B, T*
  College at New Paltz *B, T*
  College at Old Westbury *B, M, T*
  College at Oswego *B, M*
  College at Plattsburgh *B, M*
  College at Potsdam *B, M*
  College of Environmental Science
    and Forestry *B, T*
  University at Albany *M, T*
  University at Binghamton *M*
  University at Buffalo *M, D, T*
  University at Stony Brook *D, T*
Saint Bonaventure University *M*
St. Lawrence University *T*
St. Thomas Aquinas College *B, M, T*
Syracuse University *D*
Ulster County Community College *A*
University of Rochester *M*
Vassar College *T*
Wagner College *T*
Wells College *T*

North Carolina

Catawba College *T*
East Carolina University *B, M*
Elon University *T*
Forsyth Technical Community
  College *A*
Gardner-Webb University *B*
Lenoir-Rhyne University *B, T*
Livingstone College *T*
Mars Hill University *T*
Meredith College *T*
North Carolina Agricultural and
  Technical State
  University *B, M, T*
North Carolina State
  University *B, M, D, T*
Pfeiffer University *B*
Sandhills Community College *A*
University of Mount Olive *B*
University of North Carolina
  Pembroke *B, M*
Wake Forest University *T*
Western Carolina University *B*

North Dakota

Dickinson State University *B, T*
Minot State University *B, M*
North Dakota State University *B, T*
University of North Dakota *B*
Valley City State University *B, T*

Ohio

Antioch University
  Midwest *M*
Ashland University *B, T*
Baldwin Wallace University *T*
Bluffton University *B*
Bowling Green State
  University *B, M, T*
Capital University *T*
Cedarville University *B*
Defiance College *B, T*
Hiram College *T*
Kent State University *B*
Malone University *B*
Miami University
  Oxford *B, M, T*
Mount Vernon Nazarene
  University *B, T*
Ohio Dominican University *B, T*
Ohio Northern University *B, T*
Ohio University *D, T*
Ohio Wesleyan University *B*
Otterbein University *B*
Shawnee State University *B*
Tiffin University *B*
University of Akron *B, M*
University of Findlay *B, M, T*
University of Mount Union *T*
University of Rio Grande *B, T*
University of Toledo *B, T*
Urbana University *B*
Ursuline College *B, M, T*
Walsh University *B*
Wilmington College *B*
Wright State University *B, M*
Xavier University *B*
Youngstown State University *B, M*

Oklahoma

Cameron University *B*
East Central University *B*
Eastern Oklahoma State College *A*
Northeastern State University *B, M*
Northwestern Oklahoma State
  University *B*
Oklahoma Baptist University *B, T*
Oklahoma Christian University *B, T*
Oklahoma City University *B*
Oklahoma Wesleyan University *B*
Oral Roberts University *B, T*
Southeastern Oklahoma State
  University *B, T*
Southern Nazarene University *B*
Southwestern Oklahoma State
  University *B, M, T*
University of Central Oklahoma *B*
University of Oklahoma *B, T*
University of Tulsa *B*

Oregon

Concordia University *B, M, T*
Corban University *B*
Linfield College *T*
Oregon State University *M, D*
Western Oregon University *B, M, T*

Pennsylvania

Albright College *T*
Alvernia University *B*
Arcadia University *B, M, T*
Baptist Bible College of
  Pennsylvania *B*
Elizabethtown College *B, T*
Gettysburg College *T*
Grove City College *B, T*
Holy Family University *T*
Juniata College *B, T*

La Salle University *B, T*
Lebanon Valley College *M*
Lycoming College *T*
Marywood University *B*
Mercyhurst University *B, T*
Moravian College *B*
St. Francis University *T*
Saint Joseph's University *M, T*
St. Vincent College *T*
Shippensburg University of
  Pennsylvania *M*
Susquehanna University *T*
Temple University *B*
Thiel College *B*
University of Pennsylvania *M, T*
University of Pittsburgh
  Greensburg *B, T*
  Johnstown *B, T*
University of Scranton *T*
University of the Sciences *T*
Villanova University *T*
Waynesburg University *B, T*
Widener University *B, T*
Wilkes University *M, T*
York College of Pennsylvania *B, T*

Puerto Rico

Bayamon Central University *B*
Inter American University of Puerto
  Rico
  Metropolitan Campus *B, M*
  San German Campus *B, M*
Pontifical Catholic University of
  Puerto Rico *B, T*
Turabo University *B*
Universidad del Este *B*
University of Puerto Rico
  Cayey University College *B*

Rhode Island

Bryant University *M*
Rhode Island College *B*

South Carolina

Bob Jones University *B*
Charleston Southern University *B*
Clemson University *B*
Converse College *B, T*
Furman University *T*
North Greenville University *M, T*

South Dakota

Black Hills State University *B, T*
Dakota Wesleyan University *T*
Northern State University *B, T*
University of South Dakota *B, M, T*

Tennessee

Bethel University *B, T*
Freed-Hardeman University *B, T*
King University *T*
LeMoyne-Owen College *B*
Lincoln Memorial University *B, T*
Tennessee Technological University *T*
Tennessee Temple University *B*
Union University *B, T*
Vanderbilt University *M*

Texas

Abilene Christian University *B, T*
Arlington Baptist College *B, T*
Baylor University *B, T*
Dallas Baptist University *B, T*
Hardin-Simmons University *B, T*
Houston Baptist University *B, T*
Lamar University *B, M, T*
LeTourneau University *B, T*
McMurry University *T*
Midwestern State University *B*
Our Lady of the Lake University of
  San Antonio *B*
Prairie View A&M University *M*
Sam Houston State University *M, T*
San Jacinto College *A*

Southern Methodist University *T*
Southwestern University *T*
Stephen F. Austin State University *T*
Tarleton State University *T*
Texas A&M University
 Commerce *T*
 Kingsville *T*
Texas Christian University *B, M, D*
Texas Tech University *M*
Texas Wesleyan University *M*
Texas Woman's University *M*
University of Dallas *T*
University of Mary Hardin-Baylor *B, T*
University of Texas
 Arlington *T*
 Austin *M, D*
 San Antonio *T*
Wayland Baptist University *B, T*
West Texas A&M University *T*

Utah

Brigham Young University *B*
Dixie State College *B*
Southern Utah University *B*
Utah State University *B*
Utah Valley University *B*
Weber State University *B*
Western Governors
 University *B, M, T*

Vermont

Castleton State College *B, T*
Johnson State College *B*
Lyndon State College *B*
Saint Michael's College *M, T*
University of Vermont *B, T*

Virginia

Eastern Shore Community College *A*
Longwood University *T*
Lynchburg College *M*
University of Virginia's College at
 Wise *T*

Washington

Central Washington University *B, T*
Eastern Washington University *B*
Heritage University *B, M*
Seattle Pacific University *B, T*
University of Washington *M*
University of Washington Tacoma *T*
Washington State University *B, M, T*
Western Washington University *B, M*
Whitworth University *T*

West Virginia

Concord University *B, T*
Ohio Valley University *B*
Shepherd University *T*
University of Charleston *B*
West Liberty University *B*
West Virginia State University *B*
West Virginia University *T*
West Virginia Wesleyan College *B*
Wheeling Jesuit University *B*

Wisconsin

Alverno College *B, M, T*
Beloit College *B*
Carroll University *B, T*
Carthage College *M, T*
Concordia University Wisconsin *B, T*
Edgewood College *B*
Lakeland College *T*
Lawrence University *T*
Maranatha Baptist Bible College *B*
Marian University *B, T*
Mount Mary University *B, T*
Northland College *B, T*
St. Norbert College *T*
University of Wisconsin
 Eau Claire *B*
 Green Bay *T*
 La Crosse *B, T*

Oshkosh *B*
Platteville *B, T*
River Falls *T*
Stout *B*
Superior *B, T*
Whitewater *B, T*
Viterbo University *B, T*

Science technologies, general

Indiana

Calumet College of St. Joseph *B*

Kansas

Washburn University *A*

Maryland

Harford Community College *A*

Massachusetts

Northern Essex Community
 College *A*

Minnesota

Leech Lake Tribal College *A*

Ohio

Tiffin University *B*

Science, technology, and society

Alabama

University of Alabama
 Huntsville *M*

Arizona

Arizona State University *M, D*

California

California State Polytechnic
 University: Pomona *B*
Chaffey College *A*
College of San Mateo *A*
Pitzer College *B*
Pomona College *B*
Scripps College *B*
Stanford University *B*
University of California
 Davis *B*

Colorado

Colorado Mountain College *A*
University of Colorado
 Boulder *D*
University of Denver *B*

Connecticut

Wesleyan University *B*

District of Columbia

George Washington University *M*
Georgetown University *B, M*

Georgia

Georgia Institute of Technology *B*

Illinois

Northwestern University *B*
University of Illinois
 Urbana-Champaign *B*

Indiana

Butler University *B*

Louisiana

Southeastern Louisiana University *M*

Maine

Colby College *B*
College of the Atlantic *B, M*

Massachusetts

Clark University *B*
Massachusetts Institute of
 Technology *B, D*
Wellesley College *B*
Worcester Polytechnic Institute *B*

Michigan

Eastern Michigan University *B, M*
Michigan State University *B*

Minnesota

Saint Cloud State University *M*
University of Minnesota
 Twin Cities *M*

Missouri

Washington University in St.
 Louis *B, M, D*

New Jersey

New Jersey Institute of Technology *B*
Rutgers, The State University of New
 Jersey
 Newark Campus *B*

New York

Cornell University *B, M, D*
Rensselaer Polytechnic
 Institute *B, M, D*
SUNY
 College of Agriculture and
 Technology at Morrisville *B*
 Farmingdale State College *B*
Vassar College *B*

North Carolina

North Carolina State University *B*

Pennsylvania

Carnegie Mellon University *B, M, D*
Drexel University *M*
Lehigh University *B*
Penn State
 Abington *B*
 Altoona *B*
 Beaver *B*
 Berks *B*
 Brandywine *B*
 DuBois *C, B*
 Erie, The Behrend College *B*
 Fayette, The Eberly Campus *B*
 Greater Allegheny *B*
 Harrisburg *B*
 Hazleton *B*
 Lehigh Valley *B*
 Mont Alto *B*
 New Kensington *B*
 Schuylkill *B*
 Shenango *B*
 University Park *B*
 Wilkes-Barre *B*
 Worthington Scranton *B*
 York *B*
Slippery Rock University of
 Pennsylvania *B*

South Dakota

South Dakota School of Mines and
 Technology *B*

Tennessee

Vanderbilt University *B*

Texas

Angelina College *A*
Texas Tech University *B*

Virginia

Danville Community College *A*
George Mason University *D*
James Madison University *B, M*

Virginia Polytechnic Institute and
 State University *B, M, D*

Washington

University of Puget Sound *B*
University of Washington Bothell *B*

West Virginia

Kanawha Valley Community and
 Technical College *A*
West Virginia University *D*

Wisconsin

Beloit College *B*

Sculpture

Alabama

Birmingham-Southern College *B*

California

Academy of Art University *C, A, B, M*
Art Center College of Design *B, M*
Biola University *B*
California College of the Arts *B, M*
California State University
 East Bay *B*
 Long Beach *B, M*
 Northridge *B, M*
Chabot College *A*
De Anza College *C, A*
Grossmont College *A*
Hartnell College *C*
Long Beach City College *A*
Monterey Peninsula College *C, A*
Ohlone College *C*
Otis College of Art and Design *B, M*
Oxnard College *A*
Palomar College *A*
Pasadena City College *A*
San Francisco Art Institute *B, M*
Santa Rosa Junior College *C*
Solano Community College *A*

Colorado

Adams State University *B*
Rocky Mountain College of Art &
 Design *B*

Connecticut

Lyme Academy College of Fine
 Arts *C, B*
University of Hartford *B*

District of Columbia

American University *M*
George Washington University *M*

Florida

Ringling College of Art and Design *B*
University of Miami *B*

Georgia

Savannah College of Art and
 Design *B, M*

Illinois

Bradley University *B*
Dominican University *B*
Lincoln College *A*
Richland Community College *A*
School of the Art Institute of
 Chicago *B, M*
University of Illinois
 Urbana-Champaign *B, M*

Indiana

Indiana University
 Purdue University Fort Wayne *B*

Iowa

Drake University *B*
University of Iowa *B, M*

Kansas
University of Kansas *B, M*

Kentucky
Eastern Kentucky University *B*

Louisiana
Centenary College of Louisiana *B*

Maine
College of the Atlantic *B*
Maine College of Art *B*
University of Southern Maine *B*

Maryland
Maryland Institute College of Art *B, M*

Massachusetts
Bard College at Simon's Rock *B*
Boston University *B, M*
Massachusetts College of Art and Design *B, M*
Montserrat College of Art *B*
Salem State University *B*
School of the Museum of Fine Arts *B, M*
University of Massachusetts Dartmouth *B, M*

Michigan
Aquinas College *B*
College for Creative Studies *B*
Ferris State University *B*
Grand Valley State University *B*
Northern Michigan University *B*
Siena Heights University *B*
University of Michigan *B*

Minnesota
Minneapolis College of Art and Design *B*
Minnesota State University Mankato *B, M*
Saint Cloud State University *B*

Mississippi
Mississippi Gulf Coast Community College *A*

Missouri
Kansas City Art Institute *B*
Washington University in St. Louis *B, M*

Nevada
Sierra Nevada College *B*

New Hampshire
Plymouth State University *B*

New Mexico
Santa Fe University of Art and Design *B*

New York
Alfred University *M*
Rochester Institute of Technology *B, M*
SUNY
  College at Buffalo *B*
  College at Fredonia *B*
  College at New Paltz *B, M*
  College at Oneonta *B*
  College at Purchase *B, M*
Syracuse University *B, M*

North Carolina
East Carolina University *B*
Gardner-Webb University *B*
Methodist University *B*

Ohio
Art Academy of Cincinnati *B*
Bowling Green State University *B*
Cleveland Institute of Art *B*
Ohio University *B, M*
University of Akron *B*

Oregon
Mt. Hood Community College *A*
Pacific Northwest College of Art *B*
Portland State University *B, M*
University of Oregon *B*

Pennsylvania
Lycoming College *B*
Marywood University *B, M*
Pennsylvania Academy of the Fine Arts *C, B, M*
Pennsylvania College of Art and Design *B*
Seton Hill University *B*
Temple University *B, M*
University of the Arts *B*

Puerto Rico
Escuela de Artes Plasticas de Puerto Rico *B*
Inter American University of Puerto Rico
  San German Campus *M*
University of Puerto Rico
  Rio Piedras *B*

Rhode Island
Providence College *B*
Rhode Island School of Design *B, M*

South Dakota
South Dakota State University *C*

Tennessee
Memphis College of Art *B, M*
Tennessee Technological University *B*

Texas
Texas Christian University *B*
University of Dallas *B, M*
University of Houston *B*
University of Texas
  El Paso *B, M*
Western Texas College *A*

Utah
Brigham Young University *M*
Dixie State College *B*

Vermont
Bennington College *B*
Marlboro College *B*

Virginia
Virginia Commonwealth University *B*

Washington
Cornish College of the Arts *B*
University of Washington *B, M*
Western Washington University *B*

West Virginia
West Virginia State University *B*

Wisconsin
Milwaukee Institute of Art & Design *B*

Secondary education

Alabama
Alabama Agricultural and Mechanical University *B, M*
Alabama State University *B, M*
Auburn University at Montgomery *B, M*
Birmingham-Southern College *B, T*
Calhoun Community College *A*
Faulkner University *B, M, T*
Jacksonville State University *B, M, T*
Miles College *B*
Samford University *M, T*
Troy University *B, M, T*
University of Alabama *B, M, D*
University of Alabama Birmingham *B, M*
University of Montevallo *M, T*
University of North Alabama *B, M*
University of South Alabama *B, M, T*
University of West Alabama *M*

Alaska
University of Alaska
  Fairbanks *T*
  Southeast *M, T*

Arizona
Arizona Christian University *B*
Arizona State University *B, M*
Arizona Western College *A*
Eastern Arizona College *A*
Estrella Mountain Community College *A*
Grand Canyon University *B, M*
Northern Arizona University *M*
Prescott College *B, M, T*
University of Arizona *M*
University of Phoenix
  Phoenix-Hohokam *M*
  Southern Arizona *M*

Arkansas
Harding University *M, T*
Ouachita Baptist University *B, T*
South Arkansas Community College *A*
Southern Arkansas University *M, T*
University of Arkansas *M*
University of Arkansas
  Little Rock *M*
  Monticello *M*
Williams Baptist College *B*

California
Alliant International University *T*
Azusa Pacific University *B, T*
Biola University *B, T*
California Baptist University *T*
California Lutheran University *B, M*
California State University
  Channel Islands *T*
  East Bay *T*
  Fullerton *M, T*
  Long Beach *M, T*
  Los Angeles *M*
  Northridge *M*
  San Bernardino *M, T*
  San Marcos *T*
Chapman University *M, T*
Concordia University Irvine *M, T*
Cypress College *A*
Dominican University of California *M*
Holy Names University *T*
Humboldt State University *T*
La Sierra University *T*
Loyola Marymount University *M, T*
Master's College *B, T*
Mills College *T*
Mount St. Mary's College *M*
National University *B, M*
Notre Dame de Namur University *T*
Pacific Union College *M, T*
St. Mary's College of California *M*
San Diego Christian College *B, T*
San Diego State University *M*
San Francisco State University *T*
San Jose State University *M*
Sonoma State University *M*
Stanford University *M, T*
University of California
  Santa Barbara *T*
University of La Verne *B, M, T*
University of Phoenix
  Bay Area *M*
  Central Valley *M*
  Sacramento Valley *M*
  San Diego *M*
  Southern California *M*
University of Redlands *B, T*
University of San Diego *M*
University of San Francisco *T*
Vanguard University of Southern California *T*
Westmont College *T*
Whittier College *T*

Colorado
Adams State University *B, M, T*
Colorado Christian University *B*
Colorado College *M*
Colorado State University
  Pueblo *T*
Metropolitan State University of Denver *T*
Otero Junior College *A*
University of Colorado
  Boulder *T*
University of Phoenix
  Denver *M*
  Southern Colorado *M*

Connecticut
Albertus Magnus College *B, T*
Central Connecticut State University *B, T*
Eastern Connecticut State University *B, M, T*
Quinnipiac University *B, M*
Sacred Heart University *M, T*
Southern Connecticut State University *T*
University of Bridgeport *M, T*
University of Connecticut *T*
University of Hartford *B, M, T*
University of New Haven *M*
University of Saint Joseph *T*
Western Connecticut State University *B, M*

Delaware
University of Delaware *B, M, T*
Wesley College *B, M*

District of Columbia
American University *B, M, T*
Catholic University of America *B, M*
Gallaudet University *B, T*
George Washington University *M, T*
Howard University *M*

Florida
Chipola College *B*
Daytona State College *B*
Florida Gulf Coast University *B*
Florida Institute of Technology *T*
Indian River State College *A*
Jacksonville University *B, M, T*
Miami Dade College *A, B*
Nova Southeastern University *B*
Palm Beach State College *A*
Saint Thomas University *B, T*
Stetson University *B*
Trinity Baptist College *B*
University of Miami *B, M*
University of North Florida *B, M*
University of Phoenix
  Central Florida *M*
  North Florida *M*
  South Florida *M*
  West Florida *M*
University of Tampa *B, T*

Georgia

Bainbridge College *A*
Berry College *M*
Brenau University *B, M*
Clark Atlanta University *M*
College of Coastal Georgia *A*
Columbus State University *B, M*
Fort Valley State University *B, T*
Georgia College and State
  University *M, T*
Georgia Military College *A*
Georgia Southern University *M*
Kennesaw State University *M, D*
Mercer University *M*
Middle Georgia State College *A*
Piedmont College *B, M, T*
South Georgia State College *A*
Thomas University *M*
University of North Georgia *A*
University of West Georgia *B, M, T*
Valdosta State University *M*

Hawaii

Brigham Young University-
  Hawaii *B, T*
Chaminade University of
  Honolulu *B, M, T*
Hawaii Pacific University *M*
University of Hawaii
  Hilo *T*
  Manoa *B, T*
University of Phoenix
  Hawaii *M*

Idaho

Boise State University *T*
College of Southern Idaho *A*
Idaho State University *B*
Lewis-Clark State College *T*
North Idaho College *A*
Northwest Nazarene University *B*
University of Idaho *B, T*
University of Phoenix
  Idaho *M*

Illinois

Augustana College *B, T*
Aurora University *B*
Benedictine University *M, T*
Bradley University *T*
Chicago State University *B, M, T*
Columbia College Chicago *M*
Concordia University
  Chicago *B, M, T*
DePaul University *B, M, T*
Dominican University *B, T*
Elmhurst College *B*
Eureka College *B*
Greenville College *M, T*
Illinois Central College *A*
John A. Logan College *A*
Joliet Junior College *A*
Judson University *B*
Kankakee Community College *A*
Kishwaukee College *A*
Knox College *B, T*
Lake Forest College *T*
Lewis University *B, M*
Loyola University Chicago *B, M, T*
MacMurray College *B, T*
McKendree University *B*
Monmouth College *T*
National-Louis University *M, T*
North Central College *T*
North Park University *B, M, T*
Northwestern University *B*
Olivet Nazarene University *B, M, T*
Rockford University *M, T*
Roosevelt University *B, M*
Saint Xavier University *B*
Sauk Valley Community College *A*
Southwestern Illinois College *A*
Spoon River College *A*

Trinity International
  University *B, M, T*
University of Illinois
  Urbana-Champaign *B, M, D, T*
University of St. Francis *M*
Western Illinois University *M*
Wheaton College *B, M, T*

Indiana

Ancilla College *A*
Anderson University *T*
Ball State University *M, T*
Bethel College *B, M*
Butler University *B, M*
Calumet College of St. Joseph *T*
Earlham College *M*
Goshen College *B, T*
Huntington University *B*
Indiana University
  Bloomington *B, M, T*
  East *B*
  Kokomo *B*
  Northwest *B, M, T*
  Purdue University Fort
    Wayne *B, M, T*
  Purdue University
    Indianapolis *M, T*
  South Bend *B, M, T*
  Southeast *B, M*
Indiana Wesleyan University *B, T*
Manchester University *B, T*
Marian University *T*
Purdue University *B*
Saint Mary's College *T*
Taylor University *T*
University of Evansville *T*
University of Indianapolis *A, B, T*
University of Phoenix
  Indianapolis *M*
University of Southern Indiana *M*
Valparaiso University *B, M, T*
Vincennes University *A*
Wabash College *T*

Iowa

Briar Cliff University *B*
Buena Vista University *T*
Central College *T*
Coe College *B*
Cornell College *B, T*
Dordt College *B, T*
Drake University *B, M*
Ellsworth Community College *A*
Faith Baptist Bible College and
  Theological Seminary *B*
Graceland University *T*
Grand View University *B, T*
Grinnell College *T*
Iowa State University *T*
Iowa Wesleyan College *B*
Loras College *B*
Maharishi University of
  Management *B, M*
Marshalltown Community College *A*
Mount Mercy University *B, T*
North Iowa Area Community
  College *A*
Northwestern College *T*
St. Ambrose University *B, T*
Simpson College *T*
University of Iowa *M, D, T*
Upper Iowa University *B, T*
Waldorf College *B*
Wartburg College *T*
William Penn University *B*

Kansas

Allen County Community College *A*
Baker University *B, T*
Benedictine College *B*
Bethany College *B, T*
Bethel College *T*
Butler Community College *A*
Central Christian College of Kansas *B*

Coffeyville Community College *A*
Colby Community College *A*
Cowley County Community
  College *A*
Dodge City Community College *A*
Emporia State University *B, M, T*
Fort Hays State University *M*
Friends University *B, T*
Garden City Community College *A*
Kansas State University *B, T*
Kansas Wesleyan University *B, T*
Labette Community College *A*
MidAmerica Nazarene University *B, T*
Neosho County Community
  College *A*
Newman University *B, T*
Pratt Community College *A*
Southwestern College *M*
Tabor College *B*
University of Kansas *B, T*
Washburn University *B, T*
Wichita State University *B, T*

Kentucky

Bellarmine University *B, M, T*
Berea College *B, T*
Brescia University *B, T*
Campbellsville University *B*
Centre College *T*
Eastern Kentucky University *M*
Georgetown College *B, M*
Kentucky Wesleyan College *T*
Lindsey Wilson College *B, T*
Midway College *B*
Morehead State University *M*
Murray State University *M, T*
Northern Kentucky University *B*
Spalding University *B, M*
Thomas More College *B, M*
Union College *B, M*
University of Kentucky *M*
University of the
  Cumberlands *B, M, T*
Western Kentucky University *M, T*

Louisiana

Centenary College of Louisiana *M, T*
Dillard University *B, T*
Louisiana College *B, T*
Louisiana State University and
  Agricultural and Mechanical
  College *M*
Louisiana Tech University *B*
McNeese State University *B, M, T*
Nicholls State University *M*
Northwestern State University *M*
Our Lady of Holy Cross College *B*
Southeastern Louisiana University *M*
Southern University and Agricultural
  and Mechanical College *B, M*
University of Louisiana at Lafayette *B*
University of Louisiana at
  Monroe *B, M*
University of New Orleans *B, M*
Xavier University of Louisiana *M*

Maine

Bowdoin College *T*
Husson University *B*
Unity College *B, T*
University of Maine *B, M*
University of Maine
  Farmington *B, T*
  Fort Kent *B*
  Machias *B, T*
  Presque Isle *B*
University of Southern Maine *T*

Maryland

Allegany College of Maryland *A*
Anne Arundel Community College *A*
Bowie State University *M*
Carroll Community College *A*
Chesapeake College *A*

Coppin State University *B, T*
Frostburg State University *M, T*
Goucher College *M*
Harford Community College *A*
Hood College *T*
McDaniel College *M, T*
Mount St. Mary's University *M, T*
Notre Dame of Maryland
  University *B, M*
Prince George's Community
  College *A*
Salisbury University *M*
Stevenson University *M*
University of Maryland
  College Park *B*
  Eastern Shore *M*
  University College *M*
Washington Adventist University *B, T*

Massachusetts

American International
  College *B, M, T*
Amherst College *T*
Anna Maria College *B*
Assumption College *T*
Boston College *B, M, T*
Clark University *M*
Eastern Nazarene College *M, T*
Elms College *B, M, T*
Emmanuel College *B, M*
Endicott College *B*
Fitchburg State University *B, M, T*
Framingham State University *M*
Gordon College *B*
Lasell College *B, T*
Lesley University *B, M*
Massachusetts College of Liberal
  Arts *T*
Merrimack College *B*
Nichols College *B*
Salem State University *B, M*
Simmons College *B, M*
Smith College *M*
Springfield College *B, T*
Springfield Technical Community
  College *A*
Tufts University *M, T*
University of Massachusetts
  Dartmouth *B, T*
Wellesley College *T*
Western New England
  University *B, T*
Westfield State University *M, T*
Wheaton College *T*
Worcester State University *M, T*

Michigan

Albion College *T*
Alma College *B, T*
Andrews University *B, M*
Aquinas College *B, T*
Baker College
  Allen Park *B*
  Auburn Hills *B*
  Clinton Township *B*
  Flint *B*
  Jackson *B*
  Muskegon *B*
  Owosso *B*
Calvin College *B, T*
Central Michigan University *M*
Concordia University *B, T*
Cornerstone University *B*
Delta College *A*
Eastern Michigan University *B, M, T*
Ferris State University *A*
Gogebic Community College *A*
Grace Bible College *B*
Grand Valley State University *M, T*
Henry Ford Community College *A*
Hillsdale College *B*
Kuyper College *B*
Lake Michigan College *A*
Lake Superior State University *B, T*

Madonna University *T*
Marygrove College *T*
Michigan State University *B*
Michigan Technological University *T*
Mid Michigan Community College *A*
Northern Michigan
   University *B, M, T*
Oakland University *M*
Rochester College *B*
Saginaw Valley State University *B, T*
Siena Heights University *B, M, T*
Spring Arbor University *B*
University of Detroit Mercy *B, M, T*
University of Michigan *B, T*
University of Michigan
   Dearborn *B, T*
   Flint *B, T*
Washtenaw Community College *A*
Wayne State University *M, T*
Western Michigan University *M*

Minnesota

Augsburg College *B, T*
Bethel University *B*
College of St. Benedict *T*
Concordia University St. Paul *B, T*
Crown College *B*
Gustavus Adolphus College *B*
Hamline University *B, T*
Minnesota State University
   Mankato *B, M, T*
Minnesota West Community and
   Technical College *A*
North Central University *B*
Ridgewater College *A*
St. Catherine University *B, T*
Saint Cloud State University *B, T*
St. John's University *T*
University of Minnesota
   Morris *T*
   Twin Cities *M, T*
University of St. Thomas *M*

Mississippi

Alcorn State University *M*
Belhaven University *T*
Delta State University *M*
East Mississippi Community
   College *A*
Hinds Community College *A*
Holmes Community College *A*
Itawamba Community College *A*
Jackson State University *M*
Millsaps College *T*
Mississippi College *M*
Mississippi Delta Community
   College *A*
Mississippi Gulf Coast Community
   College *A*
Mississippi State University *B, M, D*
Mississippi University for Women *M*
Northwest Mississippi Community
   College *A*
Tougaloo College *B, T*
University of Southern Mississippi *M*
William Carey University *M*

Missouri

Calvary Bible College and Theological
   Seminary *B*
Central Methodist University *B*
College of the Ozarks *B, T*
Crowder College *A*
Drury University *B, T*
Evangel University *B, M, T*
Hannibal-LaGrange University *B*
Harris-Stowe State University *B*
Jefferson College *A*
Lincoln University *M*
Missouri Baptist University *B, T*
Missouri Southern State
   University *B, T*
Missouri State University *M*

Missouri University of Science and
   Technology *T*
Missouri Valley College *B, T*
Northwest Missouri State
   University *M, T*
Ozark Christian College *A*
Park University *T*
Rockhurst University *B*
Southeast Missouri State University *M*
University of Central Missouri *B, M*
University of Missouri
   Columbia *B, M, D*
   Kansas City *B*
   St. Louis *B, M*
University of Phoenix
   Kansas City *M*
   St. Louis *M*
Washington University in St.
   Louis *B, M, T*
Webster University *B, M*
Westminster College *B, T*
William Jewell College *B, T*
William Woods University *B, T*

Montana

Montana State University *B*
Montana State University
   Billings *B, M, T*
   Northern *B*
University of Great Falls *B, M*
University of Montana *B, M*
University of Montana: Western *B, T*

Nebraska

Chadron State College *B, M*
College of Saint Mary *B, T*
Concordia University *B, T*
Creighton University *B*
Grace University *B*
Hastings College *B, M, T*
Midland University *B, T*
Nebraska Wesleyan University *T*
Northeast Community College *A*
Union College *B*
University of Nebraska
   Kearney *B, M, T*
   Omaha *B, M, T*
Western Nebraska Community
   College *A*
York College *B, T*

Nevada

Great Basin College *A, B*
Sierra Nevada College *M*
Truckee Meadows Community
   College *A*
University of Nevada
   Las Vegas *B, T*
   Reno *B, M, T*
University of Phoenix
   Las Vegas *M*
   Northern Nevada *M*

New Hampshire

Dartmouth College *T*
Franklin Pierce University *B, M, T*
Granite State College *B, T*
Keene State College *B, T*
New England College *B, T*
Plymouth State University *M, T*
Rivier University *B, M, T*
Saint Anselm College *T*
Southern New Hampshire
   University *M*
University of New Hampshire *M*
University of New Hampshire at
   Manchester *T*

New Jersey

Caldwell College *B, T*
Centenary College *T*
College of New Jersey *M, T*
Drew University *M*
Essex County College *A*

Felician College *B*
Monmouth University *M*
Rider University *B*
Rowan University *M*
Rutgers, The State University of New
   Jersey
   Camden Campus *T*
   New Brunswick/Piscataway
     Campus *T*
   Newark Campus *T*
Saint Peter's University *T*
Seton Hall University *B, M*
Sussex County Community College *A*

New Mexico

Central New Mexico Community
   College *A*
New Mexico Highlands University *B*
New Mexico Junior College *A*
New Mexico State University *B*
San Juan College *A, T*
Santa Fe Community College *T*
University of New Mexico *B, M*
University of Phoenix
   New Mexico *M*
University of the Southwest *B, T*
Western New Mexico
   University *B, M, T*

New York

Alfred University *T*
Bard College *M*
Barnard College *T*
Canisius College *B, M, T*
City University of New York
   City College *B, M, T*
   Hunter College *B, M, T*
   York College *T*
Colgate University *M, T*
College of Mount St. Vincent *T*
College of Saint Rose *M, T*
Columbia University
   School of General Studies *T*
Cornell University *M*
D'Youville College *M, T*
Dominican College of Blauvelt *B, T*
Dowling College *M, T*
Dutchess Community College *A*
Elmira College *B, M, T*
Fordham University *M, T*
Fulton-Montgomery Community
   College *A*
Hobart and William Smith Colleges *T*
Hofstra University *B, M, T*
Houghton College *B, T*
Iona College *B, M, T*
Ithaca College *B, M, T*
Keuka College *B, T*
Le Moyne College *M, T*
Long Island University
   LIU Brooklyn *B, M, T*
   LIU Post *B, M, T*
Manhattan College *B, T*
Manhattanville College *M, T*
Medaille College *B, T*
Medaille College: Amherst *M*
Mercy College *M, T*
Molloy College *B, M*
Mount Saint Mary College *B, M*
Nassau Community College *A*
Nazareth College *B, M, T*
New York University *M*
Niagara University *B, M, T*
Pace University *M, T*
Pace University: Pleasantville/
   Briarcliff *M, T*
SUNY
   College at Brockport *B, M, T*
   College at Buffalo *B, M, T*
   College at Fredonia *B, M, T*
   College at Old Westbury *B, M, T*
   College at Oswego *B, M, T*
   College at Plattsburgh *M*

College of Technology at Delhi *A*
   University at Albany *M, T*
Sage Colleges *M*
Saint Bonaventure University *M*
St. John Fisher College *B, M, T*
St. John's University *M, T*
St. Joseph's College New York:
   Suffolk Campus *T*
St. Joseph's College, New York *T*
St. Thomas Aquinas College *B, M, T*
Suffolk County Community College *A*
Syracuse University *M, T*
Tompkins Cortland Community
   College *A*
University of Rochester *M*
Utica College *B, M*
Vassar College *T*
Wagner College *B, M*
Wells College *T*
Yeshiva University *M*

North Carolina

Campbell University *B, M*
Catawba College *T*
Chowan University *B*
Davidson College *T*
Duke University *M*
Elon University *B, T*
Gardner-Webb University *B, M*
Greensboro College *T*
Guilford College *B, T*
High Point University *B*
Mars Hill University *B, T*
Martin Community College *A*
Meredith College *T*
Methodist University *A, B, T*
North Carolina Agricultural and
   Technical State
   University *B, M, T*
Pfeiffer University *B, T*
Salem College *B, T*
Sandhills Community College *A*
Southeastern Community College *A*
University of Mount Olive *B*
University of North Carolina
   Asheville *T*
   Wilmington *M*
Wake Forest University *M, T*

North Dakota

Dickinson State University *B, T*
University of Jamestown *B*
University of North Dakota *B*
Valley City State University *B, T*

Ohio

Bowling Green State University *M, T*
Central State University *B*
Cincinnati Christian University *B*
College of Wooster *T*
Defiance College *B, T*
Heidelberg University *T*
Hiram College *T*
John Carroll University *M, T*
Kent State University *M*
Lake Erie College *B, M*
Lourdes University *B*
Malone University *T*
Marietta College *B*
Miami University
   Oxford *M, T*
Muskingum University *B, M, T*
Notre Dame College *B, T*
Ohio Christian University *B*
Ohio Dominican University *B, T*
Ohio State University
   Columbus Campus *M*
Ohio University *B, M, D, T*
Ohio Wesleyan University *B*
Otterbein University *B*
Union Institute & University *B*
University of Akron *M, D*
University of Cincinnati *B, M, T*

University of Cincinnati
  Blue Ash College *A*
  Clermont College *A*
University of Dayton *B, M, T*
University of Findlay *B, M, T*
University of Mount Union *T*
University of Rio Grande *B, T*
University of Toledo *B, M, T*
Urbana University *B*
Walsh University *B*
Washington State Community
  College *A*
Wilmington College *B*
Wright State University *M*
Xavier University *M*
Youngstown State University *B, M*

Oklahoma

Carl Albert State College *A*
East Central University *M, T*
Eastern Oklahoma State College *A*
Langston University *B*
Mid-America Christian University *B*
Northern Oklahoma College *A*
Northwestern Oklahoma State
  University *B*
Oklahoma Baptist University *B, T*
Oklahoma Christian University *B, T*
Oklahoma City Community
  College *A*
Oklahoma State University *B*
Rogers State University *A*
St. Gregory's University *B*
Southern Nazarene University *B*
Southwestern Oklahoma State
  University *M, T*

Oregon

Concordia University *B, M, T*
Corban University *B, M*
George Fox University *M, T*
Lewis & Clark College *M*
Linfield College *T*
Linn-Benton Community College *A*
Northwest Christian University *B, M*
Oregon State University *M*
Portland State University *T*
Southern Oregon University *M, T*
Treasure Valley Community
  College *A*
University of Portland *B, M, T*
Warner Pacific College *B, T*
Western Oregon University *B, M, T*
Willamette University *M*

Pennsylvania

Albright College *B, M, T*
Alvernia University *B*
Arcadia University *B, M, T*
Baptist Bible College of
  Pennsylvania *B*
Bryn Mawr College *T*
Bucknell University *B, T*
California University of
  Pennsylvania *M*
Carlow University *M, T*
Cedar Crest College *B, T*
Chatham University *M, T*
Chestnut Hill College *M, T*
Community College of
  Philadelphia *A*
DeSales University *T*
Delaware Valley College *B*
Drexel University *B, M, T*
East Stroudsburg University of
  Pennsylvania *M, T*
Eastern University *B, T*
Gannon University *B*
Gettysburg College *T*
Grove City College *B, T*
Gwynedd Mercy University *M, T*
Harrisburg Area Community
  College *A*
Holy Family University *M, T*

King's College *T*
Kutztown University of
  Pennsylvania *B, M, T*
La Salle University *B, M, T*
Lebanon Valley College *T*
Lehigh University *M*
Lycoming College *T*
Mansfield University of
  Pennsylvania *B, T*
Marywood University *M*
Mercyhurst University *B, M*
Montgomery County Community
  College *A*
Mount Aloysius College *B*
Muhlenberg College *T*
Northampton Community College *A*
Penn State
  Abington *B*
  Altoona *B*
  Beaver *B*
  Berks *B*
  Brandywine *B*
  DuBois *B*
  Erie, The Behrend College *B*
  Fayette, The Eberly Campus *B*
  Greater Allegheny *B*
  Harrisburg *B*
  Hazleton *B*
  Lehigh Valley *B*
  Mont Alto *B*
  New Kensington *B*
  Schuylkill *B*
  Shenango *B*
  University Park *B*
  Wilkes-Barre *B*
  Worthington Scranton *B*
  York *B*
Point Park University *M*
Reading Area Community College *A*
Robert Morris University *T*
Rosemont College *B, T*
St. Francis University *B, T*
Saint Joseph's University *M, T*
St. Vincent College *T*
Slippery Rock University of
  Pennsylvania *B, M, T*
Susquehanna University *T*
Temple University *M*
University of Pennsylvania *M, T*
University of Pittsburgh *T*
University of Pittsburgh
  Bradford *B*
  Greensburg *B, T*
  Johnstown *B, T*
University of Scranton *B, M*
Valley Forge Christian College *B*
Villanova University *B, M*
Washington & Jefferson College *T*
Waynesburg University *B, T*
West Chester University of
  Pennsylvania *M, T*
Westminster College *B, T*
Widener University *M*
Wilson College *T*

Puerto Rico

American University of Puerto
  Rico *B, T*
Bayamon Central University *B*
Caribbean University *B, T*
Inter American University of Puerto
  Rico
  Arecibo Campus *B*
  Barranquitas Campus *B*
  Fajardo Campus *B, T*
  Ponce Campus *B, M*
  San German Campus *B*
Pontifical Catholic University of
  Puerto Rico *B*
Universidad Adventista de las
  Antillas *B*
Universidad Metropolitana *B*
University of Puerto Rico
  Rio Piedras *B*
University of the Sacred Heart *B*

Rhode Island

Bryant University *M*
Providence College *B, M, T*
Rhode Island College *B, M, T*
Roger Williams University *B*
Salve Regina University *B*
University of Rhode Island *B*

South Carolina

Charleston Southern University *M*
Citadel *B, M, T*
Clemson University *B, M*
Coastal Carolina University *M, T*
College of Charleston *B, T*
Converse College *B, M, T*
Erskine College *B, T*
Francis Marion University *B, M, T*
Furman University *T*
Lander University *B, M, T*
Presbyterian College *T*
South Carolina State University *M, T*
University of South Carolina
  Aiken *B, T*
  Columbia *M*
  Upstate *B, T*
Winthrop University *M, T*
Wofford College *T*

South Dakota

Augustana College *B, T*
Black Hills State University *M*
Mount Marty College *B*
University of Sioux Falls *T*
University of South Dakota *M, T*

Tennessee

Aquinas College *M*
Belmont University *B, M, T*
Bethel University *B, M, T*
Carson-Newman University *B*
Christian Brothers University *M, T*
Cumberland University *B, T*
East Tennessee State University *M, T*
Fisk University *T*
Freed-Hardeman University *B, T*
Hiwassee College *A*
King University *T*
Lee University *M*
Lincoln Memorial University *B, T*
Martin Methodist College *B*
Motlow State Community College *A*
Rhodes College *T*
Tennessee State University *B, M, T*
Tennessee Technological
  University *B, M, T*
Tennessee Temple University *B, M, T*
Tennessee Wesleyan College *B, T*
Trevecca Nazarene University *B, M, T*
Tusculum College *B, T*
Union University *B, T*
University of Phoenix
  Chattanooga *M*
  Memphis *M*
  Nashville *M*
University of Tennessee
  Chattanooga *B, M, T*
  Martin *B*
Vanderbilt University *B, M, T*
Welch College *B*

Texas

Abilene Christian University *B, T*
Alvin Community College *A*
Arlington Baptist College *B, T*
Austin College *M*
Austin Community College *A*
Baylor University *T*
Brazosport College *A*
Brookhaven College *A*
Clarendon College *A*
Coastal Bend College *A*
College of the Mainland *A*
Collin County Community College
  District *A*

Concordia University Texas *B*
Dallas Baptist University *B, M*
Dallas Christian College *B, T*
Del Mar College *A*
El Paso Community College *A*
Frank Phillips College *A*
Grayson College *A*
Houston Baptist University *B, M*
Howard Payne University *B*
Huston-Tillotson University *T*
Jarvis Christian College *B, T*
Lamar University *B, M, T*
LeTourneau University *B, T*
Lubbock Christian University *B, M, T*
McMurry University *B*
Midland College *A*
Navarro College *A*
Our Lady of the Lake University of
  San Antonio *M*
Paris Junior College *A*
Paul Quinn College *B*
Rice University *M, T*
St. Edward's University *T*
St. Philip's College *A*
San Jacinto College *A*
South Texas College *A*
Southwestern Assemblies of God
  University *B*
Southwestern University *T*
Stephen F. Austin State University *M*
Sul Ross State University *M*
Tarrant County College *A*
Texas A&M International
  University *M, T*
Texas A&M University
  Commerce *M, T*
  Corpus Christi *M, T*
  Kingsville *B, M*
  Texarkana *T*
Texas Christian University *M*
Texas Lutheran University *T*
Texas State University *M, T*
Texas Tech University *M*
Trinity University *M*
University of Dallas *T*
University of Houston
  Victoria *M*
University of Mary Hardin-Baylor *T*
University of North Texas *M*
University of Phoenix
  San Antonio *M*
University of St. Thomas *B, M*
University of Texas
  Pan American *M*
University of the Incarnate
  Word *M, T*
Wayland Baptist University *M*
West Texas A&M University *T*
Wiley College *B*

Utah

Dixie State College *T*
Snow College *A*
University of Phoenix
  Utah *M*
Utah State University *B, M*
Weber State University *T*
Westminster College *B, T*

Vermont

Castleton State College *B, M*
Champlain College *B*
College of St. Joseph in
  Vermont *B, M, T*
Goddard College *B, M*
Green Mountain College *B, T*
Johnson State College *B, M*
Middlebury College *T*
Norwich University *T*
Saint Michael's College *B, M, T*
University of Vermont *B, T*

Virginia

Bluefield College *B, T*
College of William and Mary *M, T*
Eastern Mennonite University *T*
Hampton University *M*
Hollins University *T*
James Madison University *T*
Longwood University *T*
Lynchburg College *B*
Mary Baldwin College *T*
Marymount University *M*
Old Dominion University *M*
Radford University *T*
Randolph College *T*
Randolph-Macon College *T*
University of Virginia's College at
    Wise *T*
Virginia Baptist College *A, B*
Virginia Wesleyan College *B, T*

Washington

Central Washington University *M*
Gonzaga University *T*
Heritage University *B, M*
Northwest University *B*
Pacific Lutheran University *B*
Saint Martin's University *T*
Seattle Pacific University *M, T*
University of Washington *M, T*
University of Washington
    Bothell *M, T*
Walla Walla University *M, T*
Washington State University *B, M, T*
Western Washington University *M*
Whitworth University *B, M, T*

West Virginia

Alderson-Broaddus University *B*
Bethany College *B*
Glenville State College *B*
Marshall University *B, M*
Ohio Valley University *B*
Potomac State College of West
    Virginia University *A*
Shepherd University *B, T*
University of Charleston *B*
West Liberty University *B*
West Virginia State University *B*
West Virginia University *M*
West Virginia Wesleyan College *B*
Wheeling Jesuit University *B*

Wisconsin

Beloit College *T*
Carthage College *T*
Concordia University Wisconsin *B, T*
Lakeland College *B*
Lawrence University *T*
Marian University *B, T*
Marquette University *B*
Mount Mary University *B, T*
Northland College *B, T*
Ripon College *T*
St. Norbert College *T*
University of Wisconsin
    Green Bay *T*
    Oshkosh *B, T*
    Platteville *M, T*
    River Falls *T*
    Stevens Point *B, T*
    Superior *M, T*
    Whitewater *B, T*
Viterbo University *B, M, T*
Wisconsin Lutheran College *B*

Wyoming

Central Wyoming College *A*
Eastern Wyoming College *A*
Northwest College *A*
Sheridan College *A*
University of Wyoming *B*
Western Wyoming Community
    College *A*

Secondary school administration

Alabama

University of Alabama *D*

Alaska

University of Alaska
    Anchorage *M*

Illinois

Concordia University Chicago *M*
McKendree University *M*
University of Illinois
    Urbana-Champaign *M, D, T*

Kentucky

Murray State University *M, T*

Louisiana

Xavier University of Louisiana *M*

Massachusetts

Lesley University *M*
Westfield State University *M*

Michigan

Eastern Michigan University *M*
Michigan State University *M, D*

Minnesota

Capella University *M, D*
Hamline University *T*

Missouri

Lincoln University *M*
Lindenwood University *M*
Missouri Baptist University *M, T*
Northwest Missouri State
    University *M*
Southeast Missouri State University *M*
Southwest Baptist University *M*

Montana

University of Great Falls *M*

Nebraska

Concordia University *M, T*
Creighton University *M*
Wayne State College *M*

New Hampshire

New England College *M, D*

New Jersey

Rutgers, The State University of New
    Jersey
    New Brunswick/Piscataway
        Campus *M*
William Paterson University of New
    Jersey *M*

New York

Le Moyne College *M*
Saint Bonaventure University *M*
St. John Fisher College *M, T*
University of Rochester *M, D*

North Carolina

Appalachian State University *M, T*
North Carolina Agricultural and
    Technical State University *M*
North Carolina Central University *M*
University of North Carolina
    Chapel Hill *M*
    Pembroke *M*
Western Carolina University *M*
Wingate University *M, T*

North Dakota

University of Mary *M*

Ohio

Antioch University
    Midwest *M*
Kent State University *M, D*
University of Findlay *M, T*
Youngstown State University *M*

Pennsylvania

East Stroudsburg University of
    Pennsylvania *T*
Widener University *M, T*

Puerto Rico

Inter American University of Puerto
    Rico
    Barranquitas Campus *M*

South Carolina

Charleston Southern University *M*

South Dakota

University of South Dakota *M, D*

Texas

Wayland Baptist University *M*

Vermont

Saint Michael's College *M, T*

Washington

City University of Seattle *M, T*
Seattle University *M*
University of Washington *M, D, T*
Washington State University *M, T*
Western Washington University *M*
Whitworth University *M*

West Virginia

Wheeling Jesuit University *M*

Wisconsin

Concordia University Wisconsin *M*
University of Wisconsin
    Superior *M*

Secondary special education

Georgia

Brenau University *B*

Iowa

Upper Iowa University *M*

New York

Canisius College *B, M*
City University of New York
    Brooklyn College *M*
Hofstra University *T*
St. John's University *M, T*
St. Joseph's College New York:
    Suffolk Campus *M*
Syracuse University *M*

Pennsylvania

Carlow University *M*

Security/loss prevention

Arkansas

Bryan University
    Rogers *C*

California

De Anza College *C, A*
Diablo Valley College *C*
East Los Angeles College *C*
Grossmont College *C, A*
Sierra College *A*

Colorado

Community College of Denver *C, A*

Connecticut

Three Rivers Community College *C*
University of New Haven *C, B, M*

Florida

Broward College *A*
Gulf Coast State College *C*
Hillsborough Community College *C*
Miami Dade College *C*
Tallahassee Community College *C*

Georgia

Albany Technical College *C*

Illinois

Black Hawk College *C*
City Colleges of Chicago
    Richard J. Daley College *C*
Lewis University *B*
Lincoln Land Community College *C*
Moraine Valley Community College *C*
Southwestern Illinois College *C, A*
Triton College *C*
Waubonsee Community College *C*

Indiana

Vincennes University *A*

Kansas

Highland Community College *C, A*
Washburn University *B*

Kentucky

Eastern Kentucky University *B, M*
Midway College *B*

Michigan

Baker College
    Muskegon *C*
Grand Valley State University *B*
Lake Superior State University *B*
Macomb Community College *C*
Northern Michigan University *B*
Schoolcraft College *A*

Missouri

St. Louis Community College *C*
Saint Louis University *B*
University of Central Missouri *M*

Nevada

College of Southern Nevada *A*

New Jersey

Cumberland County College *C*
Essex County College *C*
New Jersey City University *B*

New York

SUNY
    College of Technology at Canton *C*
    Farmingdale State College *B*
Schenectady County Community
    College *A*

Ohio

Eastern Gateway Community
    College *A*
Lakeland Community College *C, A*
University of Cincinnati
    Clermont College *A*
Youngstown State University *B*

Oregon

Chemeketa Community College *C*

Pennsylvania

Kaplan Career Institute
    Pittsburgh *A*

Texas
Tarrant County College *C*

Virginia
Northern Virginia Community
College *C, A*

Washington
Spokane Community College *A*

Security services management

Alabama
University of Phoenix
Birmingham *B*

Arizona
University of Phoenix
Phoenix-Hohokam *B*
Southern Arizona *B*

California
Diablo Valley College *C*
Everest College
Ontario Metro *A, B*
University of Phoenix
Bay Area *B*
Central Valley *B*
Sacramento Valley *B*
San Diego *B*
Southern California *B*

Colorado
University of Denver *M*
University of Phoenix
Denver *B*
Southern Colorado *B*

District of Columbia
University of Phoenix
Washington DC *B*

Florida
City College
Altamonte Springs *A*
Everest University
Orange Park *A, B*
University of Phoenix
Central Florida *B*
North Florida *B*
South Florida *B*
West Florida *B*
Webber International University *B, M*

Georgia
University of Phoenix
Atlanta *B*
Augusta *B*
Columbus *B*
Savannah *B*

Hawaii
University of Phoenix
Hawaii *B*

Illinois
University of Chicago *M*

Indiana
University of Phoenix
Indianapolis *B*
Vincennes University *A, B*

Iowa
Western Iowa Tech Community
College *C, A*

Kansas
Barton County Community
College *C, A*

Kentucky
Bluegrass Community and Technical
College *C*

Louisiana
University of Phoenix
Baton Rouge *B*
Louisiana *B*
Shreveport *B*

Maryland
Washington Adventist University *C*

Massachusetts
Anna Maria College *M*
Bunker Hill Community College *A*
Massachusetts Maritime Academy *B*
Quincy College *C*

Michigan
Henry Ford Community College *A*
University of Phoenix
Metro Detroit *B*
West Michigan *B*

Minnesota
Century College *C*
University of Phoenix
Minneapolis-St. Paul *B*

Missouri
University of Phoenix
Kansas City *B*
St. Louis *B*

Nebraska
Bellevue University *M*

Nevada
University of Phoenix
Las Vegas *B*

New York
Rockland Community College *A*
SUNY
College at Brockport *B*
Farmingdale State College *B*
St. John's University *B*
Technical Career Institutes *A*

Pennsylvania
Everest Institute: Pittsburgh *A*
Montgomery County Community
College *C, A*

Puerto Rico
Inter American University of Puerto
Rico
Metropolitan Campus *C*

Rhode Island
Johnson & Wales University
Providence *B*
Roger Williams University *B*

Tennessee
University of Phoenix
Chattanooga *B*
Knoxville *B*

Texas
Sam Houston State University *M*
San Antonio College *C, A*
University of Houston
Downtown *M*
University of Phoenix
Austin *B*
Dallas Fort Worth *B*
Houston Westside *B*
San Antonio *B*

Utah
University of Phoenix
Utah *B*

Virginia
University of Phoenix
Northern Virginia *B*
Richmond *B*

West Virginia
American Public University
System *C, B, M*

Wisconsin
University of Phoenix
Milwaukee *B*

Security system installation/repair/ inspection

Florida
Valencia College *C*

Selling/sales operations

California
Orange Coast College *A*
Santa Barbara City College *C, A*
Santa Monica College *C, A*
Santiago Canyon College *A*

Colorado
Arapahoe Community College *C, A*

Georgia
Georgia Piedmont Technical
College *C*
Gwinnett Technical College *C*

Illinois
Bradley University *B*
Danville Area Community College *A*
Harper College *C, A*
Illinois Central College *A*
Illinois Valley Community
College *C, A*
McHenry County College *C, A*
Parkland College *A*
Rock Valley College *C*

Indiana
Purdue University *B, M, D*

Iowa
AIB College of Business *A*
Des Moines Area Community
College *C*

Kansas
Brown Mackie College
Salina *A*

Kentucky
Sullivan University *C*

Michigan
Lansing Community College *C, A*

Minnesota
Alexandria Technical and Community
College *C*
Art Institutes International
Minnesota *B*
Dakota County Technical College *C*
Lake Superior College *C*
Minnesota State College - Southeast
Technical *C, A*
North Hennepin Community
College *C*
Northwest Technical College *C*

Nebraska
Bellevue University *B*

New Jersey
Passaic County Community College *A*

New York
Genesee Community College *C*

Ohio
University of Akron *C, A*
University of Toledo *A*
Youngstown State University *A, B, M*

Oklahoma
University of Central Oklahoma *B*

Pennsylvania
Butler County Community College *A*

Tennessee
University of Memphis *B*

Texas
Dallas Baptist University *M*

Utah
LDS Business College *C, A*
Weber State University *B*

Washington
Olympic College *C*
Pierce College *C*
Spokane Community College *A*

West Virginia
Kanawha Valley Community and
Technical College *C*

Wyoming
Central Wyoming College *C*

Semiconductor manufacturing technology

Minnesota
Normandale Community College *C*

New York
Mohawk Valley Community
College *A*

Sheet metal technology

California
Bakersfield College *C, A*
Foothill College *C*
Palomar College *C, A*
Yuba College *C, A*

Florida
Hillsborough Community College *C*

Illinois
Black Hawk College *C*
Elgin Community College *C*
Rock Valley College *C*

Indiana
Ivy Tech Community College
Bloomington *C, A*
Central Indiana *C, A*
Lafayette *C, A*
North Central *C, A*
Northeast *C, A*
Northwest *C, A*
Richmond *C, A*
South Central *C, A*
Southwest *C, A*
Wabash Valley *C, A*

Kansas

Wichita Area Technical College *C*

Minnesota

Hennepin Technical College *C, A*
Lake Superior College *C, A*
St. Paul College *C*

Montana

Montana State University
　Billings *C*

Ohio

Columbus State Community
　College *A*
Terra State Community College *A*

Oregon

Lane Community College *A*
Mt. Hood Community College *C, A*

Pennsylvania

Community College of Allegheny
　County *C*
Thaddeus Stevens College of
　Technology *A*

Washington

Bates Technical College *C, A*

Wisconsin

Chippewa Valley Technical College *C*

Shoe/leather repair

Alabama

Jefferson Davis Community
　College *C*

Sign language interpretation

Alabama

Troy University *B*

Arizona

Phoenix College *C, A*
Pima Community College *A*

Arkansas

University of Arkansas
　Little Rock *A, B*

California

Berkeley City College *C, A*
College of the Canyons *A*
College of the Sequoias *C*
Golden West College *C, A*
Los Angeles Pierce College *A*
Los Medanos College *C*
Mount San Antonio College *C, A*
Palomar College *C, A*
Riverside City College *C, A*
Saddleback College *C, A*
San Diego City College *C*

Colorado

Front Range Community College *A*
Pikes Peak Community College *C, A*
University of Northern
　Colorado *B, M*

Connecticut

Northwestern Connecticut
　Community College *C, A*

District of Columbia

Gallaudet University *M*

Florida

Florida State College at
　Jacksonville *A*

Miami Dade College *C, A*
University of North Florida *B, M*

Georgia

Georgia Perimeter College *C, A*
Valdosta State University *B*

Idaho

College of Southern Idaho *A*
Idaho State University *B*

Illinois

Black Hawk College *A*
Columbia College Chicago *B*
Harper College *C*
Illinois Central College *C, A*
MacMurray College *A, B*
Moraine Valley Community College *C*
Quincy University *B*
Waubonsee Community College *C, A*

Indiana

Bethel College *A, B*
Goshen College *B*
Indiana University
　Purdue University Indianapolis *B*

Iowa

Iowa Western Community College *A*
University of Iowa *B*

Kansas

Cowley County Community
　College *A*
Johnson County Community
　College *A*

Kentucky

Eastern Kentucky University *A, B*
University of Louisville *B*

Louisiana

Delgado Community College *C, A*

Maryland

Community College of Baltimore
　County *C, A*
Frederick Community College *C*

Massachusetts

Bristol Community College *C*
Northern Essex Community
　College *C, A*

Michigan

Lansing Community College *C, A*
Madonna University *B*
Mott Community College *A*
Oakland Community College *A*

Minnesota

Minnesota State Community and
　Technical College *A*
North Central University *A, B*
St. Catherine University *B*
St. Paul College *C, A*

Mississippi

Hinds Community College *C, A*
Itawamba Community College *A*

Missouri

Metropolitan Community College -
　Kansas City *A*

Nebraska

Metropolitan Community
　College *C, A*

New Hampshire

Nashua Community College *C*
University of New Hampshire at
　Manchester *B*

New Jersey

Burlington County College *C, A*
Camden County College *A*
Ocean County College *A*
Union County College *C, A*

New Mexico

Santa Fe Community College *C, A*
University of New Mexico *B*

New York

Dutchess Community College *A*
Keuka College *B*
Mohawk Valley Community
　College *A*
New York University *M*
Rochester Institute of
　Technology *A, B*
Suffolk County Community College *A*
Ulster County Community College *C*

North Carolina

Blue Ridge Community College *A*
Central Piedmont Community
　College *C, A*
Gardner-Webb University *B*
Wilson Community College *C, A*

Ohio

Cincinnati State Technical and
　Community College *A*
Columbus State Community
　College *C, A*
Cuyahoga Community College
　Metropolitan *A*
Kent State University *B*
Shawnee State University *C*
Sinclair Community College *C, A*
University of Akron *C*
University of Cincinnati *B*
Wright State University *B*

Oklahoma

Oklahoma State University
　Oklahoma City *C, A*
Tulsa Community College *C, A*

Oregon

Portland Community College *C, A*
Western Oregon University *B*

Pennsylvania

Bloomsburg University of
　Pennsylvania *B*
Community College of
　Philadelphia *C, A*
Mount Aloysius College *B*

Puerto Rico

Turabo University *B, M*

South Dakota

Augustana College *B*

Tennessee

Chattanooga State Community
　College *A*
Maryville College *B*
Nashville State Community College *A*

Texas

Austin Community College *C, A*
Blinn College *A*
Collin County Community College
　District *C, A*
Del Mar College *C, A*
El Paso Community College *C, A*
Houston Community College
　System *C, A*
Howard College *C, A*
Lone Star College System *C, A*
McLennan Community College *C, A*
San Antonio College *C, A*

South Texas College *A*
Tarrant County College *C, A*
Tyler Junior College *C, A*

Utah

Salt Lake Community College *A*

Virginia

J. Sargeant Reynolds Community
　College *C, A*
New River Community College *C*

Washington

Seattle Central Community College *A*
Spokane Falls Community
　College *C, A*

Wisconsin

Milwaukee Area Technical College *A*
Northcentral Technical College *C, A*

Sign language linguistics

Oklahoma

Oklahoma State University
　Oklahoma City *A*

Slavic languages

California

Stanford University *B, D*
University of California
　Berkeley *B, M, D*
　Los Angeles *B, M, D*
　Santa Barbara *B*

Connecticut

Connecticut College *B*
Yale University *M, D*

Florida

Florida State University *M*

Illinois

Northwestern University *B, M, D*
University of Chicago *B, D*
University of Illinois
　Urbana-Champaign *M, D*

Indiana

Indiana University
　Bloomington *B, M, D*

Kansas

University of Kansas *B, M, D*

Massachusetts

Harvard College *B, M, D*

Michigan

University of Michigan *M, D*
Wayne State University *B*

New Jersey

Princeton University *B, M, D*

New York

Columbia University *B*

North Carolina

Duke University *B, M*

Ohio

Ohio State University
　Columbus Campus *M, D*

Pennsylvania

University of Pittsburgh *B, M, D*

Rhode Island

Brown University *B, M, D*

Texas

Rice University *B*
University of Texas
Austin *M, D*

Virginia

University of Virginia *B, M, D*

Wisconsin

University of Wisconsin
Madison *M, D*

Slavic studies

California

Stanford University *D*

Illinois

University of Chicago *B, D*

New York

Barnard College *B*
Columbia University *B*

Rhode Island

Brown University *B, M, D*

Texas

Baylor University *B*
Rice University *B*

Washington

University of Washington *B, M*

Slovak

New York

SUNY
University at Stony Brook *M*

Small business administration/ management

Alaska

University of Alaska
Anchorage *A*
Southeast *C*

Arizona

Mesa Community College *C*
Paradise Valley Community College *C*

Arkansas

Rich Mountain Community College *C*

California

Berkeley City College *C, A*
California Lutheran University *M*
Canada College *C, A*
College of the Canyons *C, A*
Diablo Valley College *C, A*
Folsom Lake College *C, A*
Foothill College *C*
Ohlone College *C, A*
Santa Barbara City College *C, A*
Santa Monica College *C*
Sierra College *C, A*
Woodland Community College *C, A*

Colorado

Adams State University *B*
Colorado Technical University *C*
Lamar Community College *C*
Northeastern Junior College *C*
Pueblo Community College *C*

Connecticut

Mitchell College *B*
University of Bridgeport *M*

Florida

College of Central Florida *C*
Santa Fe College *C, A*

Georgia

Athens Technical College *C*
Atlanta Technical College *C*
Georgia Piedmont Technical
College *C*
Gwinnett Technical College *C*
Southeastern Technical College *C*

Idaho

Lewis-Clark State College *C, A, B*

Illinois

Black Hawk College *C, A*
Bradley University *B*
Elgin Community College *C*
Harper College *C, A*
Illinois Central College *C*
Moraine Valley Community College *A*
North Central College *B*
University of Illinois
Urbana-Champaign *T*
Waubonsee Community College *C, A*

Indiana

Huntington University *B*

Iowa

Des Moines Area Community
College *C*

Kansas

Central Christian College of
Kansas *A, B*
Hutchinson Community College *A*
Independence Community
College *C, A*

Maine

Husson University *B*
Washington County Community
College *A*

Massachusetts

Babson College *B*
Quinsigamond Community College *C*
Springfield Technical Community
College *A*

Michigan

Baker College
Clinton Township *A*
Muskegon *C, A*
Bay de Noc Community College *A*
Delta College *C, A*
Henry Ford Community College *C*
Northern Michigan University *B*
Oakland Community College *C*
Schoolcraft College *A*

Minnesota

Central Lakes College *C*
Inver Hills Community College *C*
Normandale Community College *C*
South Central College *C*

Montana

Blackfeet Community College *A*
Flathead Valley Community
College *A*
Helena College University of
Montana *A*
Rocky Mountain College *B*
University of Montana: Western *B*

Nebraska

University of Nebraska
Omaha *B*

New Jersey

Raritan Valley Community College *C*

New Mexico

Luna Community College *C*

New York

City University of New York
Borough of Manhattan Community
College *A*
Columbia-Greene Community
College *C*
Globe Institute of
Technology *C, A, B*
Mohawk Valley Community
College *C*
Westchester Community College *C*

North Carolina

Brunswick Community College *C, A*
Chowan University *B*
Stanly Community College *C*

Ohio

Baldwin Wallace University *M*
Lakeland Community College *C, A*
Miami University
Hamilton *C*
Tiffin University *C*
University of Akron *C, A*

Oregon

Oregon Institute of Technology *B*

Pennsylvania

Harrisburg Area Community
College *C, A*
Saint Joseph's University *B*

Puerto Rico

Inter American University of Puerto
Rico
Metropolitan Campus *C*

Tennessee

Carson-Newman University *B*

Texas

Blinn College *C, A*
Odessa College *C*

Vermont

Champlain College *C*
Lyndon State College *B*

Virginia

Germanna Community College *C*
J. Sargeant Reynolds Community
College *A*

Washington

Olympic College *C*
Pierce College *C*
Shoreline Community College *C, A*

Wisconsin

Carroll University *B*
Lac Courte Oreilles Ojibwa
Community College *A*
Milwaukee Area Technical College *C*
Northcentral Technical College *C, A*

Small engine mechanics

Alabama

Jefferson Davis Community
College *C*

Arkansas

Arkansas State University
Beebe *C*
Cossatot Community College of the
University of Arkansas *C*
Pulaski Technical College *C*

California

College of the Desert *C*
Los Medanos College *C*
Merced College *C*
Southwestern College *C, A*

Georgia

Central Georgia Technical College *C*
Southwest Georgia Technical
College *C*

Idaho

College of Western Idaho *C, A*

Illinois

Triton College *C*

Kentucky

Bluegrass Community and Technical
College *C*

Minnesota

Hennepin Technical College *C, A*
Minnesota State College - Southeast
Technical *C*
Minnesota State Community and
Technical College *C*

Nebraska

Southeast Community College *C*

North Carolina

Haywood Community College *C*

North Dakota

North Dakota State College of
Science *C, A*

Pennsylvania

Commonwealth Technical Institute *C*

South Dakota

Mitchell Technical Institute *C, A*

Texas

Austin Community College *C*
Cedar Valley College *C*
Tarrant County College *C*
Texarkana College *C*

Washington

Bates Technical College *C, A*

Wisconsin

Chippewa Valley Technical College *C*
Fox Valley Technical College *C*
Wisconsin Indianhead Technical
College *C*

Social/philosophical foundations of education

Arizona

Arizona State University *M*

Arkansas

University of Arkansas *D*

California

California State University
Long Beach *M*
Northridge *M*
Hope International University *M*

National University *B*
Stanford University *M, D*

Colorado

University of Colorado
  Boulder *M, D*

Connecticut

Central Connecticut State
  University *M*

Florida

Florida Atlantic University *M*
Florida State University *M, D*

Georgia

Georgia State University *M*

Hawaii

University of Hawaii
  Manoa *M*

Illinois

DePaul University *M*
Loyola University Chicago *M, D*
Northern Illinois University *M*
Northwestern University *M*
University of Illinois
  Urbana-Champaign *M, D*
Western Illinois University *M*

Indiana

Indiana University
  Bloomington *M, D*

Iowa

Ashford University *B*
Iowa State University *M*
Iowa Wesleyan College *B*
University of Iowa *M, D*
University of Northern Iowa *M*

Kansas

University of Kansas *M*

Kentucky

Transylvania University *B*
University of Kentucky *M*

Massachusetts

Tufts University *M*

Michigan

Eastern Michigan University *M*
Western Michigan University *M, T*

Minnesota

University of Minnesota
  Twin Cities *M*

Missouri

University of Missouri
  Columbia *M, D*

New Jersey

Rutgers, The State University of New
  Jersey
  New Brunswick/Piscataway
    Campus *M, D, T*

New Mexico

University of New Mexico *M, D*

New York

Eugene Lang College The New
    School for Liberal Arts *B*
Fordham University *M*
Hofstra University *M, T*
New York University *M, D*
SUNY
  University at Buffalo *D*
Syracuse University *M, D*

Ohio

Ohio University *M, D*
University of Akron *M*
University of Cincinnati *M, D*
University of Findlay *B, M*
University of Toledo *M, D*

Oklahoma

University of Oklahoma *M, D*

Pennsylvania

Penn State
  University Park *M, D*
University of Pennsylvania *M, D*

South Carolina

University of South Carolina
  Columbia *D*

Texas

University of Texas
  San Antonio *M*

Utah

University of Utah *M, D*

Vermont

Goddard College *B, M*

Washington

Eastern Washington University *M*
University of Washington *M, D*

Wisconsin

University of Wisconsin
  Madison *M, D*
  Milwaukee *M*
  Whitewater *M*

Social psychology

California

St. Mary's College of California *B*
University of California
  Irvine *B, D*

Connecticut

University of Connecticut *M, D*

District of Columbia

George Washington University *D*

Florida

Florida State University *D*

Illinois

Loyola University Chicago *M, D*
University of Illinois
  Urbana-Champaign *M, D*

Indiana

Ball State University *M*

Iowa

University of Iowa *D*

Maine

University of New England *B*

Massachusetts

Clark University *M, D*
Eastern Nazarene College *B*
Harvard College *M, D*
Tufts University *M, D*
University of Massachusetts
  Lowell *M*

Michigan

Grand Valley State University *B*
Western Michigan University *B*

Missouri

Maryville University of Saint Louis *B*
Northwest Missouri State
  University *B*
University of Missouri
  Columbia *M, D*

Nebraska

University of Nebraska
  Omaha *M*

Nevada

University of Nevada
  Reno *D*

New Hampshire

Keene State College *B*

New York

City University of New York
  Queens College *M*
Fordham University *M, D*
New York University *D*
SUNY
  University at Albany *D*
  University at Buffalo *D*
  University at Stony Brook *D*
Syracuse University *D*
University of Rochester *D*

North Carolina

Duke University *M, D*

Pennsylvania

Clarion University of Pennsylvania *B*
Penn State
  Abington *B*

Texas

University of Houston *D*

Vermont

Bennington College *B*
Goddard College *M*

Social science teacher education

Alabama

Auburn University *B, M, D, T*
Birmingham-Southern College *T*
Faulkner University *B, T*
Judson College *B*
Miles College *B*
Oakwood University *B*
University of Mobile *B, T*

Arkansas

Arkansas State University *B, M, T*
Henderson State University *B*
University of Arkansas
  Pine Bluff *B, T*

California

Azusa Pacific University *T*
California Baptist University *T*
California Lutheran University *B, T*
California Polytechnic State
  University: San Luis Obispo *T*
California State University
  Chico *T*
  Long Beach *B, T*
  Northridge *B, T*
  San Bernardino *T*
Fresno Pacific University *B, T*
Hope International University *B*
Humboldt State University *T*
Master's College *T*
Mills College *T*
Mount St. Mary's College *T*
Pacific Union College *B*
Saddleback College *A*

San Diego Christian College *B, T*
San Francisco State University *T*
Simpson University *B, T*
Sonoma State University *T*
Stanford University *M, T*
University of Redlands *T*
University of San Diego *T*
Vanguard University of Southern
  California *T*
Westmont College *T*

Colorado

Adams State University *B, T*
Colorado State University
  Pueblo *T*
Metropolitan State University of
  Denver *T*
Western State Colorado
  University *B, T*

Delaware

Delaware State University *B*
University of Delaware *B, T*

District of Columbia

George Washington University *T*

Florida

Flagler College *B*
Florida Agricultural and Mechanical
  University *B, T*
Florida Atlantic University *B*
Florida State University *B, M, D, T*
Palm Beach State College *A*
Southeastern University *B, T*
Stetson University *B*
University of Central Florida *B*
University of Miami *B*
University of South Florida *B, M*
University of West Florida *B, M*
Warner University *B*

Georgia

Albany State University *B*
Columbus State University *B, M*
Darton College *A*
Shorter University *T*
University of North Georgia *A, M*

Hawaii

Brigham Young University-
  Hawaii *B, T*

Idaho

Boise State University *B, T*
Lewis-Clark State College *B, T*
Northwest Nazarene University *B*

Illinois

Augustana College *B, T*
Benedictine University *T*
Blackburn College *B, T*
Bradley University *B*
Concordia University Chicago *B, T*
DePaul University *M, T*
Dominican University *T*
Eastern Illinois University *B, T*
Knox College *B*
Lake Land College *A*
McKendree University *B*
Millikin University *B, T*
North Park University *T*
Olivet Nazarene University *B, T*
Saint Xavier University *B*
University of Illinois
  Urbana-Champaign *B, M, T*

Indiana

Butler University *T*
Manchester University *B, T*
Oakland City University *B*
Valparaiso University *B*

Iowa

Briar Cliff University *B*
Buena Vista University *B, T*
Central College *T*
Cornell College *B, T*
Dordt College *B*
Drake University *M, T*
Ellsworth Community College *A*
Iowa State University *T*
Iowa Wesleyan College *T*
Loras College *T*
Mount Mercy University *T*
Northwestern College *T*
St. Ambrose University *B, T*
Simpson College *T*
University of Northern Iowa *B*
Upper Iowa University *B, M, T*
Wartburg College *T*

Kansas

Bethany College *B*
Emporia State University *M, T*
Friends University *B*
Garden City Community College *A*
Independence Community College *A*
Newman University *T*
Tabor College *B*

Kentucky

Campbellsville University *B*
Lindsey Wilson College *B, T*

Louisiana

Grambling State University *M*

Maine

University of Maine
  Farmington *B, T*
University of Southern Maine *T*

Maryland

Frostburg State University *B, T*
Mount St. Mary's University *B, T*

Massachusetts

Worcester State University *T*

Michigan

Andrews University *B, M*
Calvin College *B*
Cornerstone University *B, T*
Eastern Michigan University *B*
Grand Valley State University *T*
Michigan State University *B*
Michigan Technological University *T*
Northern Michigan University *B, T*
Spring Arbor University *B*
University of Detroit Mercy *B, M, T*
Western Michigan University *B*

Minnesota

College of St. Scholastica *B, T*
Gustavus Adolphus College *T*
Minnesota State University
  Mankato *B, M, T*
Saint Cloud State University *B, M, T*
St. Mary's University of Minnesota *B*
University of Minnesota
  Morris *T*
Winona State University *B, T*

Mississippi

Blue Mountain College *B*
Coahoma Community College *A*
Delta State University *B*
Jackson State University *B*
Millsaps College *T*
Mississippi College *M*
Northeast Mississippi Community
  College *A*
Northwest Mississippi Community
  College *A*

Rust College *B*
William Carey University *B, M*

Missouri

Central Methodist University *B*
Evangel University *T*
Lincoln University *B*
Missouri Baptist University *T*
Missouri Southern State
  University *B, T*
Northwest Missouri State
  University *B, T*
Saint Louis University *T*
Southwest Baptist University *B, T*
University of Missouri
  Kansas City *B*
Washington University in St.
  Louis *B, M, T*
Webster University *M*
William Woods University *B, T*

Montana

Carroll College *B*
Montana State University
  Billings *B, T*
  Northern *B*
University of Great Falls *B*
University of Montana *T*

Nebraska

Chadron State College *B*
College of Saint Mary *B, T*
Creighton University *T*
Grace University *B*
Hastings College *B, M, T*
Midland University *B, T*
Nebraska Wesleyan University *B*
Union College *B*
University of Nebraska
  Kearney *B, M, T*
  Lincoln *B, T*
Wayne State College *B, T*
York College *B, T*

Nevada

Great Basin College *B*

New Hampshire

Franklin Pierce University *M, T*
Great Bay Community College *A*
New England College *B, T*
Rivier University *B, T*
Saint Anselm College *T*

New Jersey

Georgian Court University *T*
Saint Peter's University *T*

New Mexico

University of the Southwest *B, T*

New York

Dominican College of Blauvelt *B, T*
Dowling College *B, M*
Fordham University *M, T*
Manhattan College *B, T*
Manhattanville College *M, T*
Pace University: Pleasantville/
  Briarcliff *T*
Roberts Wesleyan College *B, M*
SUNY
  College at Plattsburgh *B*
Vassar College *T*
Wells College *T*

North Carolina

Gardner-Webb University *B*
Lenoir-Rhyne University *B*
Mars Hill University *T*
North Carolina Agricultural and
  Technical State
  University *B, M, T*
Sandhills Community College *A*

University of North Carolina
  Greensboro *B*

North Dakota

Dickinson State University *B, T*
Mayville State University *B, T*
Minot State University *B*
University of Mary *B*
University of North Dakota *B*
Valley City State University *B, T*

Ohio

Bowling Green State
  University *B, M, T*
Defiance College *B, T*
Hiram College *T*
Ohio Wesleyan University *B*
Shawnee State University *B*
University of Findlay *B, M, T*
University of Rio Grande *B, T*
University of Toledo *M*
Walsh University *B*
Wilmington College *B*
Youngstown State University *B, M*

Oklahoma

Eastern Oklahoma State College *A*
Mid-America Christian University *B*
Northwestern Oklahoma State
  University *B*
Oklahoma Baptist University *B, T*
Oklahoma City University *B*
Southwestern Oklahoma State
  University *B, M, T*
University of Tulsa *T*

Oregon

Corban University *B*
Linfield College *T*

Pennsylvania

Arcadia University *B, M, T*
Grove City College *T*
Holy Family University *B*
La Salle University *B, T*
Marywood University *B*
Mercyhurst University *B, T*
Moravian College *B*
St. Francis University *B, T*
St. Vincent College *T*
Susquehanna University *T*
University of Pittsburgh
  Bradford *B*
  Greensburg *B, T*
  Johnstown *B, T*
Washington & Jefferson College *T*
Wilson College *T*

Puerto Rico

Turabo University *B*
University of Puerto Rico
  Cayey University College *B*

Rhode Island

Rhode Island College *B*

South Carolina

Converse College *B, T*
Wofford College *T*

South Dakota

Mount Marty College *B*
Northern State University *B, T*
University of Sioux Falls *T*
University of South Dakota *B, M, T*

Tennessee

American Baptist College *B*
Belmont University *T*
Cumberland University *B, T*
Lincoln Memorial University *B, T*
Maryville College *B, T*

Texas

Kilgore College *A*
Lubbock Christian University *B*
Stephen F. Austin State University *T*
Texas A&M University
  Commerce *T*
University of Mary Hardin-Baylor *T*
University of Texas
  San Antonio *T*
West Texas A&M University *T*

Utah

Brigham Young University *B*
Southern Utah University *B*
University of Utah *B*
Weber State University *B*
Western Governors University *M, T*

Vermont

Castleton State College *B, T*
Johnson State College *B*
Lyndon State College *B*

Virginia

Bridgewater College *T*
Eastern Mennonite University *T*
Longwood University *T*
Radford University *T*
University of Virginia's College at
  Wise *T*
Virginia Western Community
  College *A*

Washington

Central Washington University *B, T*
Seattle Pacific University *B*
Western Washington University *B*
Whitworth University *T*

West Virginia

West Liberty University *B*
Wheeling Jesuit University *B*

Wisconsin

Carroll University *B, T*
Carthage College *M, T*
Concordia University Wisconsin *B*
Lawrence University *T*
St. Norbert College *T*
University of Wisconsin
  Green Bay *T*
  Oshkosh *B, T*
  Platteville *B, T*
  River Falls *T*
  Superior *B, T*
  Whitewater *B, T*

Social sciences

Alabama

Calhoun Community College *A*
Faulkner State Community College *A*
Faulkner University *B*
Troy University *B*
University of Mobile *B*
University of Montevallo *B, T*
University of North Alabama *B*

Alaska

University of Alaska
  Fairbanks *C*
  Southeast *B*

Arizona

Arizona Western College *A*
Central Arizona College *A*
Cochise College *A*
Dine College *A*
Harrison Middleton
  University *B, M, D*
Tohono O'odham Community
  College *A*

Arkansas

Harding University *B*
Phillips Community College of the
    University of Arkansas *A*
Southern Arkansas University *B*
University of Arkansas
    Fort Smith *B*
    Monticello *B*

California

Allan Hancock College *A*
Azusa Pacific University *B, M*
Barstow Community College *A*
Berkeley City College *A*
Biola University *B*
Butte College *A*
Cabrillo College *A*
California Institute of
    Technology *B, M, D*
California State University
    Chico *B, M*
    Los Angeles *M*
    Monterey Bay *B*
    Sacramento *B, M*
    San Bernardino *C, B, M*
    San Marcos *B*
    Stanislaus *B*
Canada College *A*
Cerro Coso Community College *A*
Chabot College *A*
Chaffey College *A*
Citrus College *A*
College of Alameda *A*
College of Marin *A*
College of San Mateo *A*
College of the Canyons *A*
College of the Desert *A*
College of the Sequoias *A*
College of the Siskiyous *A*
Columbia College *A*
Contra Costa College *A*
Copper Mountain College *A*
Crafton Hills College *A*
East Los Angeles College *A*
Feather River College *A*
Foothill College *A*
Fresno City College *A*
Fresno Pacific University *B*
Gavilan College *A*
Glendale Community College *A*
Golden West College *A*
Hartnell College *A*
Hope International University *B*
Humboldt State University *B, M*
Humphreys College *B*
Imperial Valley College *A*
Lake Tahoe Community College *A*
Laney College *A*
Lassen Community College *A*
Long Beach City College *A*
Mendocino College *A*
Merced College *A*
Merritt College *A*
Mills College *B*
MiraCosta College *A*
Mission College *A*
Modesto Junior College *A*
Moorpark College *A*
Mount St. Mary's College *B*
Mount San Jacinto College *A*
Napa Valley College *A*
National University *B*
Ohlone College *A*
Orange Coast College *A*
Palomar College *A*
Pasadena City College *A*
Pitzer College *B*
Point Loma Nazarene University *B*
Porterville College *A*
Reedley College *A*
Sacramento City College *C, A*
Saddleback College *A*
San Deigo Miramar College
    San Diego Miramar College *A*
San Diego City College *A*
San Diego Mesa College *A*
San Diego State University *B*
San Francisco State University *M*
San Joaquin Delta College *A*
San Jose City College *A*
San Jose State University *B, M*
Santa Ana College *A*
Santiago Canyon College *A*
Shasta College *A*
Sierra College *A*
Simpson University *B*
Solano Community College *A*
University of California
    Irvine *B*
    Merced *B*
University of La Verne *B*
University of Southern California *B*
University of the Pacific *B, T*
Vanguard University of Southern
    California *B*
West Hills College: Coalinga *A*
West Hills College: Lemoore *A*
West Valley College *A*
Westmont College *B*
Whittier College *B*
Woodland Community College *A*
Yuba College *A*

Colorado

Colorado Christian University *B*
Colorado Mesa University *B*
Colorado Mountain College *A*
Regis University *B*
United States Air Force Academy *B*
University of Colorado
    Denver *M*
University of Denver *B*
University of Northern
    Colorado *B, M, T*

Connecticut

Albertus Magnus College *B*
Central Connecticut State
    University *B, M*
Holy Apostles College and
    Seminary *B*
Quinnipiac University *B*
Trinity College *B*
University of Bridgeport *B*
Western Connecticut State
    University *B*

Florida

Florida Agricultural and Mechanical
    University *M*
Florida Atlantic University *B*
Florida Southern College *B*
Florida State University *B*
Jacksonville University *B*
New College of Florida *B*
Palm Beach State College *A*
Stetson University *B*
Tallahassee Community College *A*
University of Central Florida *B*
University of Miami *B*
University of South Florida *B*
University of South Florida
    Sarasota-Manatee *B*
University of West Florida *B*
Warner University *B*

Georgia

Abraham Baldwin Agricultural
    College *A*
Andrew College *A*
Berry College *B*
Columbus State University *M*
Covenant College *B*
Piedmont College *B*
Shorter University *B, T*
Thomas University *B*
University of North Georgia *B*
Wesleyan College *B*

Hawaii

Chaminade University of Honolulu *B*
Hawaii Pacific University *B*
University of Hawaii
    West Oahu *B*

Idaho

Boise State University *A, B, T*
Lewis-Clark State College *B*
North Idaho College *A*
Northwest Nazarene University *B*

Illinois

Benedictine University *B, T*
DePaul University *B*
Governors State University *B*
Illinois College *T*
Illinois Institute of Technology *B*
Illinois Valley Community College *A*
Kishwaukee College *A*
Lake Land College *A*
Lincoln College *A*
McKendree University *B*
National-Louis University *B*
North Central College *B, T*
Northern Illinois University *T*
Olivet Nazarene University *B, T*
Principia College *B*
Richland Community College *A*
Rockford University *B*
Saint Xavier University *B*
Shimer College *B*
Southern Illinois University
    Carbondale *B*
Trinity International University *B*
University of Chicago *M, D*

Indiana

Ancilla College *A*
Ball State University *B, M, T*
Bethel College *A, B*
Calumet College of St. Joseph *B*
Indiana University
    Bloomington *M*
Indiana Wesleyan University *B*
Manchester University *B, T*
Martin University *B*
Oakland City University *B*
Purdue University *B, M*
St. Mary-of-the-Woods College *B*
Trine University *A, B*
University of Southern
    Indiana *A, B, T*
Valparaiso University *A, B, M*
Vincennes University *A*

Iowa

Ashford University *B*
Buena Vista University *B, T*
Central College *B, T*
Dordt College *B*
Drake University *B*
Ellsworth Community College *A*
Grand View University *B*
Iowa Western Community College *A*
Marshalltown Community College *A*
Mount Mercy University *T*
North Iowa Area Community
    College *A*
Northwestern College *T*
University of Iowa *M*
Upper Iowa University *B*
Wartburg College *T*

Kansas

Benedictine College *B*
Bethany College *B, T*
Central Christian College of
    Kansas *A, B*
Coffeyville Community College *A*
Colby Community College *A*
Cowley County Community
    College *A*
Dodge City Community College *A*
Donnelly College *A*
Emporia State University *B, T*
Garden City Community College *A*
Hutchinson Community College *A*
Independence Community College *A*
Kansas State University *B*
Labette Community College *A*
McPherson College *T*
MidAmerica Nazarene University *B*
Neosho County Community
    College *A*
Pratt Community College *A*
Seward County Community
    College *A*

Kentucky

Asbury University *B, T*
Campbellsville University *A, B, M*
Hopkinsville Community College *A*
Kentucky State University *B*
Lindsey Wilson College *A, B, T*
Mid-Continent University *B*
Morehead State University *B*
Northern Kentucky University *B*
Spalding University *B*
Western Kentucky University *B, T*

Louisiana

Louisiana College *B*
Louisiana State University
    Eunice *A*
Loyola University New Orleans *B*
Our Lady of Holy Cross College *B, T*
Southern University
    Shreveport *A*
Southern University and Agricultural
    and Mechanical College *M*

Maine

Bates College *T*
College of the Atlantic *B, M*
Saint Joseph's College of Maine *B*
University of Maine
    Augusta *B*
    Fort Kent *B*
University of Southern Maine *B*
Washington County Community
    College *A*

Maryland

Allegany College of Maryland *A*
Coppin State University *B, M*
Frostburg State University *B, T*
Howard Community College *A*
Johns Hopkins University *B, M*
Salisbury University *B*
Sojourner-Douglass College *B, M*
Towson University *B, M*
University of Maryland
    University College *B*

Massachusetts

Berkshire Community College *C, A*
Boston University *M*
Bristol Community College *A*
Cape Cod Community College *A*
Harvard College *B*
Lasell College *B*
Lesley University *B*
Massachusetts Bay Community
    College *A*
Middlesex Community College *A*
Roxbury Community College *A*
University of Massachusetts
    Boston *B*
Worcester Polytechnic Institute *B*

Michigan

Andrews University *B*
Aquinas College *B, T*
Calvin College *B*
Central Michigan University *B*
Concordia University *B*
Cornerstone University *B*

Eastern Michigan University *B, M*
Finlandia University *B*
Grand Valley State University *B*
Lake Superior State University *B, T*
Lansing Community College *A*
Marygrove College *B*
Michigan State University *B*
Michigan Technological University *B*
Northwestern Michigan College *A*
Olivet College *B*
Siena Heights University *B*
Spring Arbor University *B*
University of Michigan *B*
University of Michigan
   Flint *B, M*
Washtenaw Community College *A*
Wayne County Community College *A*

Minnesota

Augsburg College *B*
Bemidji State University *B*
Bethany Lutheran College *B*
Bethel University *B*
College of St. Benedict *B*
College of St. Scholastica *B*
Concordia College: Moorhead *B*
Metropolitan State University *B*
Ridgewater College *A*
St. Catherine University *B*
Saint Cloud State University *B*
St. John's University *B*
St. Mary's University of Minnesota *B*
University of Northwestern - St.
   Paul *B*
University of St. Thomas *B*

Mississippi

Belhaven University *B*
Coahoma Community College *A*
Delta State University *B*
East Mississippi Community
   College *A*
Hinds Community College *A*
Mississippi Delta Community
   College *A*
Mississippi University for
   Women *B, T*
Rust College *B*
William Carey University *B*

Missouri

Crowder College *A*
Evangel University *A, B*
Mineral Area College *A*
Missouri Baptist University *B, T*
Missouri Southern State
   University *B, T*
Rockhurst University *B*
St. Louis Community College *A*
Southeast Missouri State University *B*
Washington University in St. Louis *B*

Montana

Miles Community College *A*
University of Great Falls *B*
University of Montana: Western *A, B*

Nebraska

Bellevue University *B, M*
Chadron State College *B*
College of Saint Mary *T*
Doane College *B*
Midland University *B, T*
Northeast Community College *A*
Peru State College *B*
Union College *B*
University of Nebraska
   Kearney *B, M, T*
Wayne State College *B*

Nevada

College of Southern Nevada *A*
Great Basin College *B*

New Hampshire

Dartmouth College *T*
Granite State College *B*
Keene State College *B*
Plymouth State University *B*
Rivier University *B, T*
Southern New Hampshire
   University *B*

New Jersey

Brookdale Community College *A*
Caldwell College *B*
County College of Morris *A*
Cumberland County College *A*
Essex County College *A*
Felician College *B*
Montclair State University *M*
Saint Peter's University *A, B*
Salem Community College *A*
Sussex County Community College *A*
Thomas Edison State College *B*
Warren County Community
   College *A*

New Mexico

Eastern New Mexico University *B*
New Mexico Junior College *A*
University of the Southwest *B*
Western New Mexico University *B*

New York

Adelphi University *B*
Bard College *B*
Canisius College *B*
Cazenovia College *B*
City University of New York
   Queens College *B, M, T*
   York College *B*
Clarkson University *B*
Colgate University *B*
Concordia College *B, T*
Corning Community College *A*
Daemen College *B, T*
Dominican College of Blauvelt *B*
Dowling College *B*
Elmira College *B, T*
Eugene Lang College The New
   School for Liberal Arts *B*
Finger Lakes Community College *A*
Hudson Valley Community College *A*
Ithaca College *B, T*
Keuka College *B*
Long Island University
   LIU Brooklyn *A, B, M*
Marymount Manhattan College *A*
Mercy College *B*
Metropolitan College of New
   York *A, B*
Monroe Community College *A*
Mount Saint Mary College *B, T*
Nazareth College *B*
New York University *B, M, D*
Niagara University *B*
Pace University *B*
Pace University. Pleasantville/
   Briarcliff *B*
Roberts Wesleyan College *B*
SUNY
   College at Old Westbury *B*
   College of Agriculture and
      Technology at Cobleskill *A*
   Empire State College *A, B*
   University at Binghamton *B*
   University at Buffalo *B, M*
Sage Colleges *B*
Saint Bonaventure University *B*
St. John's University *B*
St. Joseph's College New York:
   Suffolk Campus *B*
St. Joseph's College, New York *B*
St. Thomas Aquinas College *B, T*
Sarah Lawrence College *B*
Schenectady County Community
   College *A*

Siena College *T*
Suffolk County Community College *A*
Syracuse University *M, D*
Touro College *B*
Ulster County Community College *A*
Union College *B*
Westchester Community College *A*

North Carolina

Chowan University *B*
Gardner-Webb University *B*
Livingstone College *B*
North Carolina Agricultural and
   Technical State
   University *B, M, T*
Sandhills Community College *A*
Southeastern Community College *A*
Western Carolina University *B*

North Dakota

Dakota College at Bottineau *A*
Dickinson State University *B*
Mayville State University *B, T*
Minot State University *B*
North Dakota State
   University *B, M, T*
University of Mary *B*
University of North Dakota *B*
Valley City State University *B*

Ohio

Bluffton University *B*
Bowling Green State University *B*
Bowling Green State University:
   Firelands College *A*
Cedarville University *B*
Cleveland State University *B*
Defiance College *B, T*
Heidelberg University *B*
Hiram College *B*
Lake Erie College *B*
Lorain County Community College *A*
Notre Dame College *T*
Ohio State University
   Columbus Campus *A*
Ohio University *M*
Ohio University
   Chillicothe Campus *M*
   Southern Campus at Ironton *A*
Shawnee State University *A, B*
Stark State College *A*
University of Akron *C, B*
University of Findlay *A, B*
University of Rio Grande *A, B, T*
Urbana University *B*
Wilmington College *B*
Wright State University *T*
Youngstown State University *B, M*

Oklahoma

Carl Albert State College *A*
Connors State College *A*
Eastern Oklahoma State College *A*
Langston University *B*
Mid-America Christian University *B*
Northeastern Oklahoma Agricultural
   and Mechanical College *A*
Northern Oklahoma College *A*
Northwestern Oklahoma State
   University *B*
Oklahoma Baptist University *B, T*
Oklahoma Panhandle State
   University *B*
Oklahoma Wesleyan University *A, B*
Redlands Community College *A*
Rogers State University *B*
Rose State College *A*
St. Gregory's University *A, B*
Seminole State College *A*
Southern Nazarene University *B*
Tulsa Community College *A*
Western Oklahoma State College *A*

Oregon

Central Oregon Community
   College *A*
Concordia University *B*
Corban University *B*
Linn-Benton Community College *A*
Marylhurst University *B*
Mt. Hood Community College *A*
Portland State University *B, M*
Southern Oregon University *B, T*
Treasure Valley Community
   College *A*
University of Oregon *B*
Warner Pacific College *A, B*
Western Oregon University *B*

Pennsylvania

California University of
   Pennsylvania *B, M*
Cheyney University of
   Pennsylvania *B, T*
Community College of Allegheny
   County *A*
Community College of Beaver
   County *A*
East Stroudsburg University of
   Pennsylvania *B, T*
Edinboro University of
   Pennsylvania *B, M, T*
Elizabethtown College *B, T*
Harrisburg Area Community
   College *A*
Juniata College *B*
Keystone College *B*
Kutztown University of
   Pennsylvania *B*
La Salle University *B, T*
Lackawanna College *A*
Lock Haven University of
   Pennsylvania *B*
Luzerne County Community
   College *A*
Mansfield University of
   Pennsylvania *B*
Marywood University *B*
Misericordia University *B*
Montgomery County Community
   College *A*
Reading Area Community College *A*
Robert Morris University *B*
Rosemont College *B*
University of Pennsylvania *A, B, D*
University of Pittsburgh *B*
University of Pittsburgh
   Bradford *B*
   Greensburg *B*
   Johnstown *B*
Waynesburg University *B*
Wilson College *B*

Puerto Rico

Inter American University of Puerto
   Rico
   Metropolitan Campus *B*
Turabo University *A, B*
University of Puerto Rico
   Aguadilla *A*
   Cayey University College *B*
   Humacao *B*
   Mayaguez *B*
   Ponce *A*
   Rio Piedras *B*
   Utuado *A*
University of the Sacred Heart *B*

Rhode Island

Providence College *B*
Rhode Island College *B*
Roger Williams University *B*

South Carolina

Allen University *B*
Charleston Southern University *B*
Citadel *M*

South Carolina State University *B*
Southern Wesleyan University *B*
University of South Carolina
  Beaufort *B*
  Columbia *M*
Wofford College *T*

South Dakota

Augustana College *T*
Black Hills State University *B*
Mount Marty College *B*
Sinte Gleska University *A, B*
University of Sioux Falls *A, B*

Tennessee

American Baptist College *A, B*
Cumberland University *B*
Dyersburg State Community
  College *A*
Freed-Hardeman University *B, T*
Hiwassee College *A*
LeMoyne-Owen College *B*
Lincoln Memorial University *B, T*
Northeast State Community
  College *A*
Tennessee State University *B*
Vanderbilt University *B, M*

Texas

Amarillo College *A*
Blinn College *A*
Central Texas College *A*
College of the Mainland *A*
Concordia University Texas *A, B*
El Paso Community College *A*
Frank Phillips College *A*
Howard College *A*
Howard Payne University *B*
Huston-Tillotson University *B*
Laredo Community College *A*
Midland College *A*
Navarro College *A*
Northwest Vista College *A*
Odessa College *A*
Paris Junior College *A*
Rice University *B*
St. Mary's University *B*
San Jacinto College *A*
South Texas College *A*
Southwestern Adventist
  University *B, T*
Southwestern Assemblies of God
  University *A*
Sul Ross State University *B, M, T*
Texarkana College *A*
Texas A&M International
  Beaufort *B*
Trinity Valley Community College *A*
University of Houston
  Downtown *B*
University of North Texas *B*
University of Texas
  Pan American *B*
  Tyler *B*
West Texas A&M University *B*
Western Texas College *A*

Utah

Snow College *A*
University of Utah *B*
Westminster College *B*

Vermont

Bennington College *B*
Castleton State College *B*
Goddard College *B, M*
Johnson State College *B*
Lyndon State College *B*
Marlboro College *B*

Virginia

Eastern Mennonite University *B*
Ferrum College *B*
Hollins University *M*

J. Sargeant Reynolds Community
  College *A*
James Madison University *B*
Liberty University *A, B, T*
Radford University *B*
Thomas Nelson Community
  College *A*
Tidewater Community College *A*
University of Virginia's College at
  Wise *T*
Virginia Wesleyan College *B*
Virginia Western Community
  College *A*

Washington

Central Washington University *B*
Centralia College *C, A*
Evergreen State College *B*
Highline Community College *A*
University of Puget Sound *T*
University of Washington *B*
Washington State University *B*
Whitworth University *B, T*

West Virginia

Bluefield State College *B*
Glenville State College *B*
West Liberty University *B*

Wisconsin

Alverno College *B*
Cardinal Stritch University *B, T*
Carthage College *B*
College of Menominee Nation *A*
Edgewood College *B*
Mount Mary University *B*
St. Norbert College *T*
Silver Lake College of the Holy
  Family *T*
University of Wisconsin
  Platteville *B*
  River Falls *B*
  Stevens Point *B, T*
  Stout *B*
  Superior *B, T*
  Whitewater *B*
Viterbo University *B*
Wisconsin Lutheran College *B*

Wyoming

Central Wyoming College *A*
Eastern Wyoming College *A*
Laramie County Community
  College *A*
Northwest College *A*
Sheridan College *A*
University of Wyoming *B*
Western Wyoming Community
  College *A*

Social studies teacher education

Alabama

Birmingham-Southern College *T*
Faulkner University *B, T*
Miles College *B*
Spring Hill College *B, M, T*

Arizona

Arizona Christian University *B*

Arkansas

Arkansas Tech University *B*
Harding University *B, T*
John Brown University *B, T*
Ouachita Baptist University *B, T*
University of Arkansas
  Pine Bluff *M, T*
University of Central Arkansas *B*
University of the Ozarks *T*
Williams Baptist College *B*

California

Azusa Pacific University *T*
California Lutheran University *B, T*
California State University
  Northridge *B, T*
Master's College *T*
Mills College *T*
Mount St. Mary's College *T*
San Diego State University *T*
Stanford University *M, T*
University of San Francisco *T*
Vanguard University of Southern
  California *T*

Colorado

Adams State University *B, M, T*
Colorado State University *B, T*
Colorado State University
  Pueblo *T*
Metropolitan State University of
  Denver *T*
University of Colorado
  Boulder *T*
Western State Colorado
  University *B, T*

Connecticut

Albertus Magnus College *B, T*
Central Connecticut State
  University *T*
Fairfield University *T*
Quinnipiac University *B, M*
Sacred Heart University *T*
University of Connecticut *T*
University of Saint Joseph *T*

Delaware

University of Delaware *T*

District of Columbia

Catholic University of America *M*
George Washington University *M, T*
Trinity Washington University *B, M*

Florida

Barry University *T*
Bethune-Cookman University *B, T*
Clearwater Christian College *B*
Saint Thomas University *B, T*
University of Florida *M*
University of Miami *B, M*

Georgia

Columbus State University *B*
Georgia State University *M*
Kennesaw State University *B*
LaGrange College *B*
University of Georgia *B, M, D, T*

Hawaii

Hawaii Pacific University *M*

Idaho

Boise State University *B, T*
Brigham Young University-Idaho *B, T*

Illinois

Bradley University *B*
Chicago State University *T*
Eureka College *T*
Illinois College *T*
John A. Logan College *A*
Knox College *T*
Monmouth College *T*
North Park University *T*
Olivet Nazarene University *B, T*
University of Illinois
  Urbana-Champaign *B, M*
University of St. Francis *B, M*
Wheaton College *B, T*

Indiana

Anderson University *B, T*
Bethel College *B*
Butler University *B*
Franklin College *B, T*
Goshen College *B, T*
Grace College *B*
Huntington University *B, M*
Indiana State University *B, M, T*
Indiana University
  Bloomington *B, M, T*
  Northwest *T*
  Purdue University Fort Wayne *B, T*
  Purdue University
    Indianapolis *B, T*
  South Bend *B, T*
  Southeast *B*
Indiana Wesleyan University *B, T*
Manchester University *B, T*
Oakland City University *B*
Purdue University *B, M, D*
Saint Mary's College *T*
St. Mary-of-the-Woods College *B, T*
Taylor University *B, T*
Trine University *B, T*
University of Evansville *B, T*
University of Indianapolis *B, T*
University of St. Francis *B*

Iowa

Cornell College *B, T*
Dordt College *B*
Drake University *M, T*
Ellsworth Community College *A*
Graceland University *T*
Grand View University *T*
Iowa Wesleyan College *B*
Mount Mercy University *T*
Northwestern College *T*
St. Ambrose University *T*
Simpson College *T*
University of Iowa *M, D*
Upper Iowa University *B, T*
Wartburg College *T*

Kansas

Central Christian College of Kansas *B*
Garden City Community College *A*
Independence Community College *A*
Kansas Wesleyan University *T*
McPherson College *B, T*
MidAmerica Nazarene University *B, T*
Tabor College *B*
University of Kansas *B, T*
University of St. Mary *T*

Kentucky

Alice Lloyd College *B*
Brescia University *B, T*
Campbellsville University *B*
Kentucky Christian University *B, T*
Kentucky Wesleyan College *B, T*
Union College *B*
University of Kentucky *B*
University of the
  Cumberlands *B, M, T*

Louisiana

Centenary College of Louisiana *T*
Grambling State University *B*
Louisiana College *B, T*
Louisiana State University
  Shreveport *B*
McNeese State University *T*
Nicholls State University *B*
Our Lady of Holy Cross College *B, T*
Southeastern Louisiana University *B*
University of Louisiana at Lafayette *B*
University of Louisiana at Monroe *B*
Xavier University of Louisiana *B*

Maine

Bowdoin College *T*
College of the Atlantic *T*

University of Maine *B, M*
University of Maine
    Fort Kent *B*
University of Southern Maine *T*

Maryland

Notre Dame of Maryland
    University *T*

Massachusetts

Boston University *B, M, T*
Eastern Nazarene College *B*
Elms College *T*
Lesley University *B, M*
Merrimack College *B*
Springfield College *T*
Tufts University *M, T*
University of Massachusetts
    Dartmouth *T*
Worcester State University *T*

Michigan

Adrian College *B, T*
Albion College *T*
Alma College *T* ·
Andrews University *B*
Aquinas College *B, T*
Calvin College *B*
Central Michigan University *B*
Concordia University *B, T*
Cornerstone University *B, T*
Eastern Michigan University *B*
Ferris State University *B*
Grand Valley State University *T*
Hope College *B, T*
Madonna University *B*
Michigan State University *B*
Michigan Technological University *T*
Northern Michigan University *D, T*
Spring Arbor University *B*
University of Detroit Mercy *B, M, T*
University of Michigan
    Dearborn *B*
    Flint *B, T*
Wayne State University *B, M, T*
Western Michigan University *B*

Minnesota

Augsburg College *T*
Bemidji State University *B, T*
Bethel University *B*
College of St. Benedict *T*
Concordia College: Moorhead *B, T*
Concordia University St. Paul *B, T*
Crown College *B*
Gustavus Adolphus College *T*
Hamline University *T*
Metropolitan State University *B*
Minnesota State University
    Mankato *B, M, T*
    Moorhead *B*
St. Catherine University *T*
Saint Cloud State University *B, T*
St. John's University *T*
St. Olaf College *B*
Southwest Minnesota State
    University *T*
University of Minnesota
    Duluth *B*
    Morris *T*
    Twin Cities *B, M*
University of Northwestern - St.
    Paul *B*
University of St. Thomas *B*
Winona State University *B, T*

Mississippi

Itawamba Community College *A*
Millsaps College *T*
Mississippi College *B*
Northwest Mississippi Community
    College *A*
University of Mississippi *B, T*

Missouri

Avila University *T*
College of the Ozarks *B, T*
Evangel University *B, T*
Hannibal-LaGrange University *B*
Lindenwood University *B*
Missouri Baptist University *T*
Missouri Valley College *B, T*
Park University *T*
Southeast Missouri State University *B*
Truman State University *M*
University of Central Missouri *B*
University of Missouri
    Columbia *B, M, D*
    Kansas City *B*
Washington University in St.
    Louis *B, M, T*
William Jewell College *B, T*

Montana

Carroll College *B*
Montana State University
    Billings *B, T*
Rocky Mountain College *B*
University of Great Falls *B*
University of Montana *B*
University of Montana: Western *B, T*

Nebraska

Concordia University *B, T*
Creighton University *T*
Grace University *B*
Hastings College *B, M, T*
Midland University *B, T*

New Hampshire

Franklin Pierce University *M, T*
Granite State College *B*
Keene State College *B, T*
New England College *B, T*
Plymouth State University *B, M, T*
Rivier University *B, T*
Southern New Hampshire
    University *D*
University of New Hampshire *T*
University of New Hampshire at
    Manchester *M*

New Jersey

Centenary College *T*
College of New Jersey *B, T*
Georgian Court University *T*
Rutgers, The State University of New
    Jersey
    Camden Campus *T*
    New Brunswick/Piscataway
        Campus *M, D, T*
    Newark Campus *T*
Saint Peter's University *T*
William Paterson University of New
    Jersey *T*

New Mexico

Western New Mexico University *B*

New York

Adelphi University *M, T*
Alfred University *B, T*
Bard College *M*
City University of New York
    Brooklyn College *B, M, T*
    City College *B, T*
    College of Staten Island *M*
    Hunter College *B, M, T*
    Lehman College *M, T*
    Queens College *B, M, T*
Colgate University *M*
College of Mount St. Vincent *T*
College of Saint Rose *B, T*
D'Youville College *M, T*
Dowling College *B, M*
Dutchess Community College *A*
Elmira College *B, T*
Fordham University *T*

Hobart and William Smith Colleges *T*
Hofstra University *B, M*
Houghton College *B, T*
Iona College *B, M, T*
Ithaca College *B, M, T*
Keuka College *B, T*
Le Moyne College *T*
Long Island University
    LIU Brooklyn *B, M, T*
    LIU Post *B, M, T*
Manhattan College *B, T*
Manhattanville College *M, T*
Marist College *B*
Medaille College *B, T*
Medaille College: Amherst *M*
Molloy College *B, M*
Nazareth College *T*
New York University *B, M, D*
Niagara University *B, M, T*
Nyack College *B*
Pace University *B, M, T*
Pace University: Pleasantville/
    Briarcliff *B, M, T*
Roberts Wesleyan College *B, M*
SUNY
    College at Brockport *B, M, T*
    College at Buffalo *B, M, T*
    College at Cortland *B, M*
    College at Fredonia *B, T*
    College at Geneseo *B, M, T*
    College at New Paltz *B, M, T*
    College at Old Westbury *B, M, T*
    College at Oneonta *T*
    College at Oswego *B, M*
    College at Plattsburgh *B, M*
    College at Potsdam *B, M*
    University at Albany *M, T*
    University at Binghamton *M*
    University at Buffalo *M, T*
    University at Stony Brook *T*
Saint Bonaventure University *M*
St. Francis College *B*
St. John Fisher College *B, M, T*
St. John's University *B, M, T*
St. Joseph's College New York:
    Suffolk Campus *B*
St. Joseph's College, New York *B*
St. Lawrence University *T*
St. Thomas Aquinas College *B, T*
Syracuse University *B, M, T*
Ulster County Community College *A*
University of Rochester *M*
Wagner College *T*
Wells College *T*

North Carolina

Barton College *B, T*
Campbell University *B, T*
Catawba College *T*
Davidson College *T*
East Carolina University *B*
Greensboro College *B, T*
Lenoir-Rhyne University *B, T*
Livingstone College *T*
Mars Hill University *T*
Meredith College *T*
Methodist University *A, B, T*
North Carolina State
    University *B, M, T*
Pfeiffer University *B*
Sandhills Community College *A*
University of Mount Olive *B*
University of North Carolina
    Greensboro *B*
    Pembroke *B, M*
Wake Forest University *B, T*
Western Carolina University *B, T*
Wingate University *B, T*

North Dakota

North Dakota State University *B, T*

Ohio

Antioch University
    Midwest *M*
Ashland University *B, T*
Baldwin Wallace University *T*
Bluffton University *B*
Bowling Green State University *B, T*
Capital University *T*
Cedarville University *B*
Defiance College *B, T*
Hiram College *T*
John Carroll University *T*
Kent State University *B*
Malone University *B*
Miami University
    Oxford *B, M, T*
Mount Vernon Nazarene
    University *B*
Ohio Dominican University *B, T*
Ohio Northern University *B, T*
Ohio University *D, T*
Ohio Wesleyan University *B*
Otterbein University *B*
Union Institute & University *B*
University of Akron *B, M*
University of Findlay *B, M, T*
University of Mount Union *T*
University of Toledo *B, T*
Urbana University *B*
Ursuline College *B, M, T*
Walsh University *B*
Wilmington College *B*
Youngstown State University *B, M*

Oklahoma

Cameron University *B*
East Central University *B, T*
Eastern Oklahoma State College *A*
Langston University *B*
Mid-America Christian University *B*
Northeastern State University *B*
Oklahoma Baptist University *B, T*
Oklahoma Christian University *B, T*
Oklahoma City University *B*
Oklahoma Wesleyan University *B*
Oral Roberts University *B, T*
Southeastern Oklahoma State
    University *B, T*
University of Central Oklahoma *B*
University of Oklahoma *B, T*
University of Tulsa *T*

Oregon

Concordia University *B, M, T*
Corban University *B*
Portland State University *T*
Southern Oregon University *T*
Warner Pacific College *T*
Western Oregon University *B, M, T*

Pennsylvania

Albright College *T*
Alvernia University *B*
Arcadia University *B, M, T*
Baptist Bible College of
    Pennsylvania *B*
Cabrini College *T*
Cairn University *B, T*
Cedar Crest College *T*
Chatham University *M, T*
Duquesne University *B, M, T*
Gannon University *B, T*
Geneva College *T*
Gettysburg College *T*
Holy Family University *B*
Juniata College *B, T*
Keystone College *B, T*
King's College *T*
La Salle University *B, T*
Lebanon Valley College *T*
Lycoming College *T*
Mansfield University of
    Pennsylvania *B, T*
Messiah College *B, T*

Misericordia University *B, T*
Penn State
Harrisburg *B*
Rosemont College *T*
St. Francis University *B, T*
St. Vincent College *T*
Seton Hill University *B*
Susquehanna University *T*
Temple University *B*
Thiel College *B*
University of Pennsylvania *M, T*
University of Pittsburgh
Greensburg *B, T*
Johnstown *B, T*
University of Scranton *B*
Villanova University *T*
Washington & Jefferson College *T*
Waynesburg University *B, T*
West Chester University of
Pennsylvania *T*
Westminster College *B, T*
Widener University *M, T*
York College of Pennsylvania *B, T*

Puerto Rico

Inter American University of Puerto
Rico
Barranquitas Campus *B, T*
Fajardo Campus *B, T*
San German Campus *B*
Pontifical Catholic University of
Puerto Rico *B, T*
University of Puerto Rico
Cayey University College *B*

Rhode Island

Bryant University *M*
Rhode Island College *B, M*

South Carolina

Bob Jones University *B*
Charleston Southern University *B*
Converse College *B, T*
Erskine College *T*
Francis Marion University *B, T*
Furman University *T*
Morris College *B, T*
North Greenville University *B, M, T*
Presbyterian College *T*

South Dakota

Augustana College *B, T*

Tennessee

Belmont University *T*
King University *T*
LeMoyne-Owen College *B*
Lincoln Memorial University *B, T*
Maryville College *B, T*
Tennessee Technological University *T*

Texas

Abilene Christian University *B, T*
Arlington Baptist College *B, T*
Baylor University *B, T*
Dallas Baptist University *T*
Del Mar College *A*
East Texas Baptist University *B*
Hardin-Simmons University *B, T*
Houston Baptist University *B*
Howard Payne University *B*
Lamar University *B, M, T*
LeTourneau University *B, T*
Lubbock Christian University *B*
McMurry University *T*
Midwestern State University *B*
Our Lady of the Lake University of
San Antonio *B*
St. Edward's University *B, T*
St. Mary's University *T*
Sam Houston State University *M, T*
Southwestern Assemblies of God
University *B*
Southwestern University *T*

Texas A&M International
University *B, T*
Texas A&M University
Commerce *T*
Kingsville *T*
Texas Christian University *B*
Texas Lutheran University *B, T*
University of Dallas *T*
University of Mary Hardin-Baylor *B, T*
University of Texas
Arlington *T*
San Antonio *T*
Wayland Baptist University *B, T*
West Texas A&M University *T*

Utah

Utah State University *B*
Weber State University *B*

Vermont

Castleton State College *B, T*
College of St. Joseph in
Vermont *B, M, T*
Goddard College *B, M*
Green Mountain College *B, T*
Johnson State College *B*
Saint Michael's College *M, T*
University of Vermont *B, T*

Virginia

Averett University *B, M, T*
Bluefield College *B, T*
Hollins University *T*
Longwood University *T*
University of Virginia's College at
Wise *T*
Virginia Intermont College *T*

Washington

Eastern Washington University *B*
Northwest University *T*
Washington State University *B, M, T*
Western Washington University *B*
Whitworth University *T*

West Virginia

American Public University System *M*
Bethany College *B*
Concord University *B, M, T*
Ohio Valley University *B*
Shepherd University *T*
University of Charleston *B*
West Virginia State University *B*
West Virginia University *T*
West Virginia Wesleyan College *B*
Wheeling Jesuit University *B*

Wisconsin

Alverno College *B, T*
Carroll University *B, T*
Concordia University Wisconsin *B, T*
Maranatha Baptist Bible College *B*
Marian University *B, T*
Mount Mary University *B, T*
Northland College *B, T*
St. Norbert College *T*
University of Wisconsin
Eau Claire *B*
Green Bay *T*
La Crosse *B, T*
Platteville *B, T*
River Falls *T*
Superior *B, T*
Whitewater *T*
Viterbo University *B, T*

Wyoming

Casper College *A*

Social work

Alabama

Alabama Agricultural and Mechanical
University *B, M*

Auburn University *B*
Community College of the Air
Force *A*
Jacksonville State University *B*
Judson College *B*
Lawson State Community College *A*
Miles College *B*
Oakwood University *B*
Talladega College *B*
Troy University *B, M*
Tuskegee University *B*
University of Alabama *B, M, D*
University of Alabama
Birmingham *B*
University of Montevallo *B*
University of North Alabama *B*
University of South Alabama *B*

Alaska

University of Alaska
Anchorage *C, B, M*
Fairbanks *B*

Arizona

Central Arizona College *A*
Cochise College *C, A*
Coconino County Community
College *A*
Estrella Mountain Community
College *A*
Northern Arizona University *B*

Arkansas

Arkansas State University *B, M*
Central Baptist College *B*
Harding University *B*
Henderson State University *B, M*
Philander Smith College *B*
Southern Arkansas University *B*
University of Arkansas *B, M*
University of Arkansas
Little Rock *B, M*
Monticello *B*
Pine Bluff *B*

California

Azusa Pacific University *B*
Berkeley City College *C, A*
California State University
Chico *C, B, M*
Dominguez Hills *M*
East Bay *B*
Fresno *B, M*
Fullerton *M*
Long Beach *B, M*
Los Angeles *B, M*
Monterey Bay *M*
Sacramento *B, M*
San Bernardino *B, M*
Stanislaus *M*
Chapman University *B*
Fresno City College *A*
Fresno Pacific University *B*
Humboldt State University *B, M*
La Sierra University *B*
Loma Linda University *M*
Merced College *A*
Mount St. Mary's College *B*
Pacific Union College *B*
Point Loma Nazarene University *B*
San Bernardino Valley College *A*
San Diego State University *B, M*
San Francisco State University *B, M*
San Jose State University *B, M*
Southwestern College *A*
University of California
Berkeley *B, M, D*
Los Angeles *M, D*
University of Southern
California *M, D*
Whittier College *B*

Colorado

Adams State University *B*
Colorado State University *B, M, D*
Colorado State University
Pueblo *B*
Metropolitan State University of
Denver *B, M*
University of Denver *M, D*

Connecticut

Central Connecticut State
University *B*
Eastern Connecticut State
University *B*
Naugatuck Valley Community
College *A*
Quinnipiac University *M*
Sacred Heart University *B*
Southern Connecticut State
University *B, M*
University of Connecticut *M, D*
University of Saint Joseph *B, M*
Western Connecticut State
University *B*

Delaware

Delaware State University *B, M*

District of Columbia

Catholic University of
America *B, M, D*
Gallaudet University *B, M*
Howard University *M, D*
University of the District of
Columbia *B*

Florida

Barry University *B, M, D*
Broward College *A*
Daytona State College *A*
Florida Agricultural and Mechanical
University *B, M*
Florida Atlantic University *B, M*
Florida Gulf Coast University *B, M*
Florida International
University *B, M, D*
Florida State University *B, M, D*
Miami Dade College *A*
Palm Beach State College *A*
Saint Leo University *B*
South Florida State College *A*
Southeastern University *B*
University of Central Florida *B, M*
University of South Florida *B, M, D*
University of West Florida *B, M*
Warner University *B*

Georgia

Albany State University *B, M*
Athens Technical College *C, A*
Atlanta Metropolitan College *A*
Clark Atlanta University *B, M, D*
Dalton State College *B*
Darton College *A*
Fort Valley State University *B*
Georgia Military College *A*
Georgia Regents University *B*
Georgia State University *B, M*
Gordon College *A*
Kennesaw State University *M*
Middle Georgia State College *A*
Oglethorpe University *B*
Savannah State University *B, M*
Thomas University *B*
University of Georgia *B, M, D*
University of North Georgia *A*
Valdosta State University *M*

Hawaii

Brigham Young University-Hawaii *B*
Hawaii Pacific University *B, M*
University of Hawaii
Honolulu Community College *A*
Manoa *B, M, D*

Idaho

Boise State University *B, M*
Idaho State University *B*
Lewis-Clark State College *B*
Northwest Nazarene University *B, M*

Illinois

Aurora University *B, M*
Bradley University *B*
City Colleges of Chicago
   Harold Washington College *A*
   Kennedy-King College *A*
   Wilbur Wright College *C, A*
College of DuPage *A*
College of Lake County *A*
Concordia University Chicago *B*
DePaul University *M*
Dominican University *M*
Elgin Community College *C, A*
Governors State University *B, M*
Greenville College *B*
Illinois Eastern Community Colleges
   Wabash Valley College *A*
Illinois State University *B, M*
Illinois Valley Community College *A*
John A. Logan College *A*
Kishwaukee College *A*
Lewis University *B*
Loyola University Chicago *B, M, D*
MacMurray College *B*
McKendree University *B*
Monmouth College *B*
Northeastern Illinois University *B*
Olivet Nazarene University *B*
Parkland College *A*
St. Augustine College *B*
Sauk Valley Community College *A*
Southern Illinois University
   Carbondale *B, M*
Southern Illinois University
   Edwardsville *B, M*
Southwestern Illinois College *A*
Trinity Christian College *B*
University of Chicago *M, D*
University of Illinois
   Chicago *M, D*
   Springfield *B*
   Urbana-Champaign *M, D, T*
University of St. Francis *B, M*
Waubonsee Community College *A*
Western Illinois University *B*

Indiana

Anderson University *B*
Ball State University *B*
Goshen College *B*
Huntington University *B*
Indiana State University *B*
Indiana University
   Bloomington *B*
   East *B, M*
   Northwest *B*
   Purdue University
      Indianapolis *B, M, D*
   South Bend *M*
Indiana Wesleyan University *B*
Manchester University *B*
Purdue University *B, M, D*
Purdue University
   North Central *B*
Saint Mary's College *B*
Taylor University *B*
University of Indianapolis *B*
University of St. Francis *A, B*
University of Southern Indiana *B*
Valparaiso University *B*
Vincennes University *A*

Iowa

Briar Cliff University *B*
Buena Vista University *B*
Clarke University *B*
Dordt College *B*
Ellsworth Community College *A*

Graceland University *B*
Iowa Central Community College *A*
Iowa Western Community College *A*
Loras College *B*
Luther College *B*
Mount Mercy University *B*
Northeast Iowa Community
   College *C, A*
Northwestern College *B*
St. Ambrose University *M*
University of Iowa *B, M, D*
University of Northern Iowa *B, M*
Wartburg College *B*

Kansas

Barton County Community College *A*
Bethel College *B*
Butler Community College *A*
Central Christian College of Kansas *A*
Coffeyville Community College *A*
Colby Community College *A*
Cowley County Community
   College *A*
Fort Hays State University *B*
Garden City Community College *A*
Haskell Indian Nations University *A*
Independence Community College *A*
Kansas State University *B*
Neosho County Community
   College *A*
Newman University *M*
Pittsburg State University *B*
Seward County Community
   College *A*
University of Kansas *B, M, D*
Washburn University *B, M*
Wichita State University *B, M*

Kentucky

Asbury University *B, M*
Bluegrass Community and Technical
   College *A*
Brescia University *B*
Campbellsville University *B, M*
Eastern Kentucky University *B*
Elizabethtown Community and
   Technical College *A*
Gateway Community and Technical
   College *A*
Henderson Community College *A*
Hopkinsville Community
   College *C, A*
Jefferson Community and Technical
   College *C, A*
Kentucky Christian University *B*
Kentucky State University *B*
Morehead State University *B*
Murray State University *B*
Northern Kentucky
   University *C, B, M*
Owensboro Community and
   Technical College *C, A*
Spalding University *B, M*
Union College *B*
University of Kentucky *B, M, D*
University of Louisville *B, M, D*
University of Pikeville *B*
Western Kentucky University *B, M*

Louisiana

Grambling State University *B, M*
Louisiana College *B*
Louisiana State University and
   Agricultural and Mechanical
   College *M, D*
Northwestern State University *B*
Southeastern Louisiana University *B*
Southern University
   New Orleans *B, M*
Southern University and Agricultural
   and Mechanical College *B*
Tulane University *M, D*
University of Louisiana at Monroe *B*

Maine

University of Maine *B, M*
University of Maine
   Fort Kent *A, B*
   Presque Isle *B*
University of New England *M*
University of Southern Maine *B, M*
York County Community College *A*

Maryland

Allegany College of Maryland *A*
Baltimore City Community College *A*
Bowie State University *B*
Coppin State University *B*
Frostburg State University *B*
Harford Community College *A*
Hood College *B*
Howard Community College *A*
McDaniel College *B*
Salisbury University *B, M*
Sojourner-Douglass College *B*
University of Maryland
   Baltimore *M, D*
   Baltimore County *B*

Massachusetts

Anna Maria College *B*
Boston College *M, D*
Boston University *M, D*
Bridgewater State University *B, M*
Bristol Community College *A*
Eastern Nazarene College *B*
Elms College *B*
Gordon College *B*
Holyoke Community College *C, A*
Northern Essex Community
   College *A*
Regis College *B*
Salem State University *B, M*
Simmons College *B, M, D*
Smith College *M, D*
Springfield College *M*
Western New England University *B*
Westfield State University *B, M*
Wheelock College *B, M*

Michigan

Adrian College *B*
Andrews University *B, M*
Calvin College *B*
Central Michigan University *B*
Cornerstone University *B*
Delta College *A*
Eastern Michigan University *B, M*
Ferris State University *A, B*
Gogebic Community College *A*
Grand Rapids Community College *A*
Grand Valley State University *B, M*
Hope College *B*
Kellogg Community College *A*
Kuyper College *B*
Madonna University *B*
Marygrove College *B*
Michigan State University *B, M, D*
Northern Michigan University *B*
Oakland University *B*
Rochester College *B*
Saginaw Valley State University *B*
Siena Heights University *A, B*
Southwestern Michigan College *A*
Spring Arbor University *B*
University of Detroit Mercy *B*
University of Michigan *M*
University of Michigan
   Flint *B*
Wayne County Community College *A*
Wayne State University *B, M, D*
Western Michigan University *B, M*

Minnesota

Augsburg College *B, M*
Bemidji State University *B*
Bethel University *B*
Capella University *D*

College of St. Scholastica *B*
Concordia College: Moorhead *B*
Itasca Community College *A*
Metropolitan State University *B*
Minnesota State University
   Mankato *B*
   Moorhead *B*
North Central University *B*
Ridgewater College *A*
St. Catherine University *B, M*
Saint Cloud State University *B, M*
St. Olaf College *B*
Southwest Minnesota State
   University *B*
University of Minnesota
   Duluth *M*
   Morris *B*
   Twin Cities *B, M, D*
University of St. Thomas *B, M*
Walden University *M, D*
Winona State University *B*

Mississippi

Alcorn State University *B*
Coahoma Community College *A*
Delta State University *B*
East Mississippi Community
   College *A*
Itawamba Community College *A*
Jackson State University *B, M, D*
Mississippi College *B*
Mississippi Delta Community
   College *A*
Mississippi Gulf Coast Community
   College *A*
Mississippi State University *B*
Mississippi Valley State
   University *B, M*
Northeast Mississippi Community
   College *A*
Rust College *B*
University of Mississippi *B, M*
University of Southern
   Mississippi *B, M*

Missouri

Avila University *B*
College of the Ozarks *B*
Evangel University *A, B*
Fontbonne University *B*
Hannibal-LaGrange University *B*
Lincoln University *B*
Lindenwood University *B*
Missouri State University *B, M*
Missouri Western State University *B*
Park University *B*
St. Charles Community College *A*
Saint Louis University *B, M*
Southeast Missouri State University *B*
University of Central Missouri *B*
University of Missouri
   Columbia *B, M, D*
   Kansas City *M*
   St. Louis *B, M*
Washington University in St.
   Louis *M, D*
William Woods University *B*

Montana

Blackfeet Community College *A*
Miles Community College *A*
Salish Kootenai College *B*
University of Montana *B, M*

Nebraska

Chadron State College *B*
Creighton University *B*
Grace University *B*
Metropolitan Community College *A*
Nebraska Indian Community
   College *A*
Nebraska Wesleyan University *B*
Union College *B*

University of Nebraska
Kearney *B*
Omaha *B, M*
Western Nebraska Community
College *A*

Nevada

Great Basin College *A*
University of Nevada
Las Vegas *B, M*
Reno *B, M*

New Hampshire

Franklin Pierce University *B*
Lakes Region Community
College *C, A*
Plymouth State University *B*
University of New Hampshire *B, M*
University of New Hampshire at
Manchester *M*

New Jersey

Brookdale Community College *A*
Camden County College *A*
Cumberland County College *A*
Essex County College *A*
Georgian Court University *B*
Kean University *M*
Monmouth University *B*
Montclair State University *M, T*
Ramapo College of New Jersey *B*
Richard Stockton College of New
Jersey *B, M*
Rutgers, The State University of New
Jersey
Camden Campus *B, M*
New Brunswick/Piscataway
Campus *B, M, D*
Newark Campus *B, M*
Salem Community College *C*
Seton Hall University *B*
Sussex County Community College *A*

New Mexico

Eastern New Mexico University:
Roswell *A*
New Mexico Highlands
University *B, M*
New Mexico State University *B, M*
Northern New Mexico College *A*
San Juan College *A*
Santa Fe Community College *A*
Western New Mexico
University *B, M*

New York

Adelphi University *B, M, D*
City University of New York
College of Staten Island *B*
Hunter College *M*
Lehman College *B, M*
York College *B*
College of New Rochelle *B*
College of Saint Rose *B*
Columbia-Greene Community
College *A*
Concordia College *B, D*
Daemen College *B*
Dominican College of Blauvelt *B*
Fordham University *B, M, D*
Hudson Valley Community College *A*
Iona College *B*
Keuka College *B*
Long Island University
LIU Brooklyn *B, M*
LIU Post *B, M*
Marist College *B*
Mercy College *B*
Metropolitan College of New
York *A, B*
Molloy College *B*
Nazareth College *B, M*
New York University *B, M, D*

Niagara County Community
College *C*
Niagara University *B*
Nyack College *B*
Roberts Wesleyan College *B, M*
SUNY
College at Brockport *B, M*
College at Buffalo *B*
College at Fredonia *B*
College at Plattsburgh *B*
College of Agriculture and
Technology at Cobleskill *A*
University at Albany *B, M, D*
University at Binghamton *M*
University at Buffalo *M, D*
University at Stony Brook *B, M*
Siena College *B*
Skidmore College *B*
Syracuse University *B, M*
Ulster County Community College *C*
Westchester Community College *C, A*
Yeshiva University *M, D*

North Carolina

Appalachian State University *B, M*
Asheville-Buncombe Technical
Community College *A*
Barton College *B*
Bennett College for Women *B*
Campbell University *B*
East Carolina University *B, M*
Elizabeth City State University *B*
Fayetteville State University *M*
Gaston College *A*
Johnson C. Smith University *B*
Livingstone College *B*
Mars Hill University *B*
Meredith College *B, T*
Methodist University *A, B*
North Carolina Agricultural and
Technical State University *B, M*
North Carolina Central University *B*
North Carolina State University *B, M*
Piedmont Community College *A*
Richmond Community College *A*
Sandhills Community College *A*
Shaw University *B*
University of North Carolina
Chapel Hill *M, D*
Charlotte *B, M*
Greensboro *B, M*
Pembroke *B, M*
Wilmington *B, M*
Warren Wilson College *B*
Western Carolina University *B, M*
Winston-Salem State University *B*

North Dakota

Minot State University *B*
University of Mary *B*
University of North Dakota *B, M*

Ohio

Ashland University *B*
Bluffton University *B*
Bowling Green State University *B*
Bowling Green State University:
Firelands College *B*
Capital University *B*
Case Western Reserve
University *M, D*
Cedarville University *B*
Central State University *B*
Clark State Community College *C, A*
Cleveland State University *B, M*
College of Mount St. Joseph *B*
Defiance College *B*
Edison State Community College *A*
Franciscan University of
Steubenville *B*
James A. Rhodes State College *C, A*
Lorain County Community College *A*
Lourdes University *B*
Malone University *B*

Miami University
Oxford *B, M*
Mount Vernon Nazarene University *B*
Northwest State Community
College *A*
Ohio Dominican University *B*
Ohio State University
Columbus Campus *B, M, D*
Lima Campus *M*
Ohio University *B, M*
Ohio University
Chillicothe Campus *A*
Zanesville Campus *B*
Sinclair Community College *C, A*
Terra State Community College *C, A*
Union Institute & University *B*
University of Akron *B, M*
University of Akron: Wayne
College *A*
University of Cincinnati *B, M*
University of Cincinnati
Blue Ash College *A*
Clermont College *A*
University of Findlay *B*
University of Rio Grande *A, B*
University of Toledo *B, M*
Ursuline College *B*
Wilmington College *B*
Wright State University *A, B*
Wright State University: Lake
Campus *A*
Xavier University *B*
Youngstown State University *A, B, M*
Zane State College *A*

Oklahoma

Connors State College *A*
East Central University *B*
Northeastern State University *B*
Northwestern Oklahoma State
University *B*
Oklahoma Baptist University *B*
Oral Roberts University *B*
Rose State College *A*
Southwestern Oklahoma State
University *B*
Tulsa Community College *C, A*
University of Oklahoma *B, M*

Oregon

Chemeketa Community College *A*
Clackamas Community College *C, A*
Concordia University *B*
George Fox University *B*
Linn-Benton Community College *A*
Pacific University *B*
Portland State University *B, M, D*
Rogue Community College *A*
Southwestern Oregon Community
College *A*
Treasure Valley Community
College *A*
University of Portland *B*
Warner Pacific College *B*

Pennsylvania

Alvernia University *B*
Bloomsburg University of
Pennsylvania *B*
Bryn Mawr College *M, D*
Cabrini College *B*
Cairn University *B*
California University of
Pennsylvania *B, M*
Carlow University *B*
Cedar Crest College *B*
Chatham University *B*
Community College of Allegheny
County *A*
Eastern University *B*
Edinboro University of
Pennsylvania *A, B, M*
Elizabethtown College *B*
Gannon University *B*

Harrisburg Area Community
College *A*
Juniata College *B*
Kutztown University of
Pennsylvania *B, M*
La Salle University *B*
Lehigh Carbon Community College *A*
Lock Haven University of
Pennsylvania *B*
Mansfield University of
Pennsylvania *B*
Marywood University *B, M*
Mercyhurst University *B*
Messiah College *B*
Millersville University of
Pennsylvania *B, M*
Misericordia University *B*
Northampton Community College *A*
Reading Area Community College *A*
St. Francis University *B*
Seton Hill University *B*
Shippensburg University of
Pennsylvania *B, M*
Slippery Rock University of
Pennsylvania *B*
Temple University *B, M*
University of Pennsylvania *M, D*
University of Pittsburgh *B, M, D*
Valley Forge Christian College *B*
West Chester University of
Pennsylvania *B, M*
Westminster College *B*
Widener University *B, M, D*

Puerto Rico

Bayamon Central University *B*
Caribbean University *B*
Inter American University of Puerto
Rico
Aguadilla Campus *B*
Arecibo Campus *B*
Metropolitan Campus *B, M*
Pontifical Catholic University of
Puerto Rico *B*
Turabo University *B*
Universidad Metropolitana *B*
Universidad del Este *B, M*
University of Puerto Rico
Humacao *B*
Rio Piedras *B, M, D*
University of the Sacred Heart *B*

Rhode Island

Community College of Rhode
Island *A*
Providence College *B*
Rhode Island College *B, M*
Salve Regina University *B*

South Carolina

Aiken Technical College *A*
Benedict College *B*
Coker College *B*
Columbia College *B*
Florence-Darlington Technical
College *A*
Greenville Technical College *C*
Horry-Georgetown Technical
College *A*
Limestone College *B*
Piedmont Technical College *A*
South Carolina State University *B*
University of South Carolina
Columbia *B, M, D*
Winthrop University *B, M*

South Dakota

Kilian Community College *A*
Northern State University *B*
Oglala Lakota College *B*
Presentation College *B*
University of Sioux Falls *B*
University of South Dakota *B, M*

Tennessee

Austin Peay State University *B, M*
Belmont University *B, T*
East Tennessee State University *B, M*
Freed-Hardeman University *B*
Jackson State Community College *A*
LeMoyne-Owen College *B*
Lincoln Memorial University *B*
Lipscomb University *B*
Middle Tennessee State University *B*
Southern Adventist University *B, M*
Tennessee State University *B*
Trevecca Nazarene University *B*
Union University *B, M, T*
University of Memphis *B*
University of Tennessee
  Chattanooga *B*
  Knoxville *B, M, D*
  Martin *B*

Texas

Abilene Christian University *B, M*
Amarillo College *A*
Austin Community College *A*
Baylor University *B, M, D*
Central Texas College *A*
Clarendon College *A*
College of the Mainland *A*
Del Mar College *A*
Eastfield College *C, A*
Galveston College *A*
Hardin-Simmons University *B*
Howard Payne University *B*
Lamar University *B*
Laredo Community College *A*
Lubbock Christian University *B*
Midwestern State University *B*
Northeast Texas Community
  College *A*
Northwest Vista College *A*
Our Lady of the Lake University of
  San Antonio *B, M*
Palo Alto College *A*
Paris Junior College *A*
Prairie View A&M University *B*
St. Edward's University *B*
St. Philip's College *A*
Stephen F. Austin State
  University *B, M*
Tarleton State University *B*
Temple College *A*
Texas A&M University
  Commerce *B, M*
Texas Christian University *B, M*
Texas College *B*
Texas Southern University *B*
Texas State University *B, M*
Texas Tech University *B*
Texas Woman's University *B*
Tyler Junior College *A*
University of Houston *M, D*
University of Houston
  Clear Lake *B*
  Downtown *B*
University of Mary Hardin-Baylor *B*
University of North Texas *B*
University of Texas
  Arlington *B, M, D*
  Austin *B, M, D*
  El Paso *B, M*
  Pan American *B, M*
  Permian Basin *B*
  San Antonio *M*
West Texas A&M University *B, M*

Utah

Brigham Young University *M*
Salt Lake Community College *A*
Snow College *A*
University of Utah *B, M, D*
Utah State University *B, M*
Utah Valley University *B*
Weber State University *B*

Vermont

Castleton State College *B*
Champlain College *B*
University of Vermont *B, M*

Virginia

Christopher Newport University *B*
Eastern Mennonite University *B*
Ferrum College *B*
George Mason University *B, M*
James Madison University *B*
Longwood University *B*
Mountain Empire Community
  College *A*
Norfolk State University *B, M, D*
Radford University *B, M*
Thomas Nelson Community
  College *A*
Virginia Commonwealth
  University *B, M, D*
Virginia Highlands Community
  College *A*
Virginia Intermont College *B*
Virginia State University *B*
Virginia Union University *B*

Washington

Eastern Washington University *B, M*
Heritage University *B*
Pacific Lutheran University *B*
Saint Martin's University *B*
Seattle University *B*
University of Washington *B, M, D*
University of Washington
  Tacoma *B, M*
Walla Walla University *B, M*

West Virginia

Bethany College *B*
Concord University *B*
Marshall University *B*
Potomac State College of West
  Virginia University *A*
Shepherd University *B*
University of Charleston *B*
West Virginia Northern Community
  College *A*
West Virginia State University *B*
West Virginia University *B, M*

Wisconsin

Cardinal Stritch University *C*
Carthage College *B*
Concordia University Wisconsin *B*
Lac Courte Oreilles Ojibwa
  Community College *A*
Marian University *B*
Mount Mary University *B*
University of Wisconsin
  Eau Claire *B*
  Green Bay *B, M*
  Madison *B, M, D*
  Milwaukee *B, M, D*
  Oshkosh *B, M*
  River Falls *B*
  Stevens Point *B*
  Superior *B*
  Whitewater *B, T*
Viterbo University *B*

Wyoming

Casper College *A*
University of Wyoming *B, M*
Western Wyoming Community
  College *A*

Sociology

Alabama

Alabama Agricultural and Mechanical
  University *B*
Athens State University *B*
Auburn University *B, M*
Auburn University at Montgomery *B*
Birmingham-Southern College *B*
Gadsden State Community College *A*
Jacksonville State University *B*
Samford University *B*
Spring Hill College *B*
Talladega College *B*
Troy University *B*
Tuskegee University *B*
University of Alabama *B*
University of Alabama
  Birmingham *B, M, D*
  Huntsville *B*
University of Mobile *B*
University of Montevallo *B, T*
University of North Alabama *B*
University of South Alabama *B, M*
University of West Alabama *B*

Alaska

University of Alaska
  Anchorage *B*
  Fairbanks *B*

Arizona

Arizona State University *B, D*
Arizona Western College *A*
Coconino County Community
  College *A*
Eastern Arizona College *A*
GateWay Community College *A*
Grand Canyon University *B*
Mesa Community College *C*
Northern Arizona University *B, M*
Pima Community College *A*
South Mountain Community
  College *A*
University of Arizona *B, M, D*

Arkansas

Arkansas State University *B, M*
Arkansas Tech University *B*
Henderson State University *B*
Hendrix College *B*
Ouachita Baptist University *B*
Philander Smith College *B*
Southern Arkansas University *B*
University of Arkansas *B, M*
University of Arkansas
  Little Rock *B*
  Pine Bluff *B*
University of Central Arkansas *B*
University of the Ozarks *B*

California

Azusa Pacific University *B*
Bakersfield College *A*
Barstow Community College *A*
Berkeley City College *C, A*
Biola University *B*
Cabrillo College *A*
California Baptist University *B*
California Lutheran University *B*
California Polytechnic State
  University: San Luis Obispo *B*
California State Polytechnic
  University: Pomona *B*
California State University
  Bakersfield *B*
  Channel Islands *B*
  Chico *B*
  Dominguez Hills *B, M*
  East Bay *B, M*
  Fresno *B*
  Fullerton *B, M*
  Long Beach *B*
  Los Angeles *B, M*
  Northridge *B*
  Sacramento *B, M*
  San Bernardino *B*
  San Marcos *B, M*
  Stanislaus *B*
Canada College *A*
Cerritos College *A*
Chabot College *A*
Chaffey College *A*
Chapman University *B*
College of Alameda *A*
College of the Canyons *A*
College of the Desert *A*
Contra Costa College *A*
Cosumnes River College *A*
Crafton Hills College *A*
Cypress College *A*
De Anza College *A*
Diablo Valley College *A*
El Camino College *A*
Foothill College *A*
Fresno City College *A*
Fresno Pacific University *B*
Fullerton College *A*
Gavilan College *A*
Glendale Community College *A*
Golden West College *A*
Holy Names University *B*
Humboldt State University *B, M*
Irvine Valley College *A*
La Sierra University *B*
Lake Tahoe Community College *A*
Los Angeles Southwest College *A*
Los Angeles Valley College *A*
Los Medanos College *A*
Loyola Marymount University *B*
Mills College *B*
MiraCosta College *A*
Monterey Peninsula College *A*
Mount St. Mary's College *B*
National University *B*
Notre Dame de Namur University *B*
Occidental College *B*
Ohlone College *C*
Orange Coast College *A*
Oxnard College *A*
Palomar College *A*
Pepperdine University *B*
Pitzer College *B*
Point Loma Nazarene University *B*
Pomona College *B*
Rio Hondo College *A*
Saddleback College *A*
St. Mary's College of California *B*
San Diego Mesa College *A*
San Diego State University *B, M*
San Francisco State University *B*
San Jose State University *B, M*
Santa Ana College *A*
Santa Barbara City College *A*
Santa Clara University *B*
Santa Rosa Junior College *A*
Santiago Canyon College *A*
Scripps College *B*
Sonoma State University *B*
Southwestern College *A*
Stanford University *B, M, D*
Taft College *A*
University of California
  Berkeley *B, D*
  Davis *B, M, D*
  Irvine *B, D*
  Los Angeles *B, M, D*
  Merced *B*
  Riverside *B, M, D*
  San Diego *B, M, D*
  Santa Barbara *B, M, D*
  Santa Cruz *B, D*
University of La Verne *B*
University of Redlands *B*
University of San Diego *B*
University of San Francisco *B*
University of Southern
  California *B, M, D*
University of the Pacific *B*
Vanguard University of Southern
  California *B*
West Los Angeles College *A*
West Valley College *A*
Westmont College *B*
Whittier College *B*
Woodland Community College *A*

Colorado

Adams State University *B*
Colorado College *B*
Colorado Mesa University *B*
Colorado State University *B, M, D*
Colorado State University
    Pueblo *B*
Community College of Aurora *A*
Fort Lewis College *B*
Metropolitan State University of
    Denver *B, T*
Regis University *B*
University of Colorado
    Boulder *B, D*
    Colorado Springs *B, M*
    Denver *B, M*
University of Denver *B*
University of Northern
    Colorado *B, M*
Western State Colorado University *B*

Connecticut

Albertus Magnus College *B*
Central Connecticut State
    University *B*
Connecticut College *B*
Eastern Connecticut State
    University *B*
Post University *B*
Quinnipiac University *B*
Sacred Heart University *B*
Southern Connecticut State
    University *B, M*
Trinity College *B*
University of Bridgeport *B*
University of Connecticut *B, M, D*
University of Hartford *C, B*
Wesleyan University *B*
Western Connecticut State
    University *B*
Yale University *B, M, D*

Delaware

Delaware State University *B*
University of Delaware *B, M, D*

District of Columbia

American University *B, M*
Catholic University of America *B, M*
Gallaudet University *B*
George Washington University *B, M*
Georgetown University *B*
Howard University *B, M, D*
Trinity Washington University *B*
University of the District of
    Columbia *B*

Florida

Barry University *B*
Bethune-Cookman University *B*
Broward College *A*
Daytona State College *A*
Eckerd College *B*
Flagler College *B*
Florida Agricultural and Mechanical
    University *B*
Florida Atlantic University *B, M*
Florida Gulf Coast University *B*
Florida International
    University *B, M, D*
Florida Memorial University *B*
Florida State University *B, M, D*
Indian River State College *A*
Jacksonville University *B*
Miami Dade College *A*
New College of Florida *B*
Nova Southeastern University *B*
Palm Beach State College *A*
Pensacola State College *A*
Rollins College *B*
Saint Leo University *B*
Stetson University *B*
University of Central Florida *B, M, D*
University of Florida *B, M, D*

University of Miami *B, M, D*
University of North Florida *B*
University of South Florida *B, M*
University of Tampa *A, B*
University of West Florida *B*

Georgia

Abraham Baldwin Agricultural
    College *A*
Albany State University *B*
Andrew College *A*
Brewton-Parker College *B*
Clark Atlanta University *B, M*
Clayton State University *B*
College of Coastal Georgia *A*
Columbus State University *B*
Covenant College *B*
Darton College *A*
East Georgia State College *A*
Emory University *B, D*
Fort Valley State University *B*
Georgia College and State
    University *B*
Georgia Highlands College *A*
Georgia Military College *A*
Georgia Perimeter College *A*
Georgia Regents University *B*
Georgia Southern University *B, M*
Georgia Southwestern State
    University *B*
Georgia State University *B, M, D*
Gordon College *A*
Kennesaw State University *B*
LaGrange College *B*
Mercer University *B*
Middle Georgia State College *A*
Morehouse College *B*
Oglethorpe University *B*
Paine College *B*
Piedmont College *B*
Point University *B*
Reinhardt University *B*
Savannah State University *B*
Shorter University *B*
South Georgia State College *A*
Spelman College *B*
University of Georgia *B, M, D*
University of North Georgia *A, B*
University of West Georgia *B, M*
Valdosta State University *B, M*

Hawaii

Hawaii Pacific University *B*
University of Hawaii
    Hilo *B*
    Manoa *B, M, D*
    West Oahu *B*

Idaho

Boise State University *A, B, T*
Brigham Young University-Idaho *B*
College of Southern Idaho *A*
College of Western Idaho *A*
Idaho State University *B, M*
North Idaho College *A*
University of Idaho *B*

Illinois

Augustana College *B*
Aurora University *B*
Benedictine University *B*
Benedictine University at
    Springfield *B*
Bradley University *B*
Chicago State University *B*
Concordia University Chicago *B*
DePaul University *B, M*
Dominican University *B*
Eastern Illinois University *B, T*
Elmhurst College *B, T*
Greenville College *B*
Illinois College *B*
Illinois Institute of Technology *B*
Illinois State University *B, M*

Illinois Valley Community College *A*
Illinois Wesleyan University *B*
John A. Logan College *A*
John Wood Community College *A*
Joliet Junior College *A*
Judson University *B*
Kankakee Community College *A*
Kishwaukee College *A*
Knox College *B*
Lewis University *B*
Lincoln College *A*
Loyola University Chicago *B, M, D*
McKendree University *B*
Millikin University *B*
Monmouth College *B*
North Central College *B*
North Park University *B*
Northeastern Illinois University *B*
Northern Illinois University *B, M*
Northwestern University *B, M, D*
Olivet Nazarene University *B*
Principia College *B*
Richland Community College *A*
Roosevelt University *B, M*
Saint Xavier University *B*
Sauk Valley Community College *A*
South Suburban College of Cook
    County *A*
Southern Illinois University
    Carbondale *B, M, D*
Southern Illinois University
    Edwardsville *B, M*
Southwestern Illinois College *A*
Spoon River College *A*
Trinity Christian College *B*
University of Chicago *B, D*
University of Illinois
    Chicago *B, M, D*
    Urbana-Champaign *B, M, D*
Western Illinois University *B, M*
Wheaton College *B*

Indiana

Anderson University *B*
Ball State University *B, M, T*
Bethel College *B*
Butler University *B*
DePauw University *B*
Earlham College *B*
Franklin College *B*
Goshen College *B*
Grace College *B*
Hanover College *B*
Huntington University *B*
Indiana University
    Bloomington *B, M, D*
    East *B*
    Kokomo *B*
    Northwest *B*
    Purdue University Fort
      Wayne *B, M*
    Purdue University
      Indianapolis *B, M*
    South Bend *B*
    Southeast *B*
Indiana Wesleyan University *B*
Manchester University *B*
Marian University *B, T*
Martin University *B*
Oakland City University *B*
Purdue University *B, M, D*
Purdue University
    Calumet *B*
Saint Joseph's College *B*
Saint Mary's College *B*
Taylor University *B*
University of Evansville *B*
University of Indianapolis *B, M*
University of Notre Dame *B, M, D*
University of St. Francis *B*
University of Southern Indiana *B*
Valparaiso University *B*
Vincennes University *A*

Iowa

Ashford University *B*
Briar Cliff University *B*
Buena Vista University *B*
Central College *B, T*
Coe College *B*
Cornell College *B, T*
Drake University *B*
Ellsworth Community College *A*
Grinnell College *B*
Iowa State University *B, M, D*
Iowa Wesleyan College *B*
Iowa Western Community College *A*
Loras College *B*
Luther College *B*
Mount Mercy University *B*
North Iowa Area Community
    College *A*
Northwestern College *B, T*
St. Ambrose University *B, T*
Simpson College *B*
University of Dubuque *B*
University of Iowa *B, M, D, T*
University of Northern Iowa *B*
Upper Iowa University *B*
Wartburg College *B, T*
William Penn University *B*

Kansas

Allen County Community College *A*
Baker University *B*
Barton County Community College *A*
Benedictine College *B*
Bethany College *B*
Central Christian College of Kansas *A*
Coffeyville Community College *A*
Colby Community College *A*
Cowley County Community
    College *A*
Dodge City Community College *A*
Emporia State University *B, T*
Fort Hays State University *B*
Friends University *B*
Independence Community College *A*
Kansas State University *B, M, D*
Kansas Wesleyan University *B*
McPherson College *B, T*
MidAmerica Nazarene University *B*
Newman University *B*
Ottawa University *B*
Pittsburg State University *B*
Pratt Community College *A*
Seward County Community
    College *A*
University of Kansas *B, M, D*
Washburn University *B*
Wichita State University *B, M*

Kentucky

Alice Lloyd College *B*
Asbury University *B*
Bellarmine University *B*
Berea College *B*
Campbellsville University *B*
Centre College *B*
Eastern Kentucky University *B*
Georgetown College *B*
Hopkinsville Community College *A*
Morehead State University *B, M*
Murray State University *B*
Northern Kentucky University *B*
Thomas More College *A, B*
Transylvania University *B*
Union College *B*
University of Kentucky *B, M, D*
University of Louisville *B, M, D*
University of Pikeville *B*
Western Kentucky University *B, M*

Louisiana

Centenary College of Louisiana *B*
Dillard University *B*
Grambling State University *B*
Louisiana College *B*

Louisiana State University
    Shreveport *B*
Louisiana State University and
    Agricultural and Mechanical
    College *B, M, D*
Louisiana Tech University *B*
Loyola University New Orleans *B*
McNeese State University *B*
Nicholls State University *B*
Southeastern Louisiana
    University *B, M*
Southern University
    New Orleans *B*
    Shreveport *A*
Southern University and Agricultural
    and Mechanical College *B*
Tulane University *B, M, D*
University of Louisiana at Lafayette *B*
University of Louisiana at Monroe *B*
University of New Orleans *B, M*
Xavier University of Louisiana *B*

Maine

Bates College *B*
Bowdoin College *B*
Colby College *B*
Saint Joseph's College of Maine *B*
University of Maine *B*
University of Maine
    Presque Isle *B*
University of New England *B*
University of Southern Maine *B*

Maryland

Allegany College of Maryland *A*
Bowie State University *B*
Coppin State University *B*
Frederick Community College *A*
Frostburg State University *B*
Goucher College *B*
Harford Community College *A*
Hood College *B*
Howard Community College *A*
Johns Hopkins University *B, M, D*
Loyola University Maryland *B*
McDaniel College *B*
Morgan State University *B, M*
Mount St. Mary's University *B*
St. Mary's College of Maryland *B*
Salisbury University *B*
University of Maryland
    Baltimore County *B, M*
    College Park *B, M, D*
    Eastern Shore *B*
Washington College *B, T*

Massachusetts

American International College *B*
Amherst College *B*
Anna Maria College *B*
Assumption College *B*
Boston College *B, M, D*
Boston University *B, M, D*
Brandeis University *B, M, D*
Bridgewater State University *B*
Bunker Hill Community College *A*
Cape Cod Community College *A*
Clark University *B*
College of the Holy Cross *B*
Curry College *B*
Elms College *B*
Emmanuel College *B*
Fitchburg State University *B*
Framingham State University *B*
Gordon College *B*
Hampshire College *B*
Harvard College *B, M, D*
Lasell College *B*
Massachusetts College of Liberal
    Arts *B*
Merrimack College *B*
Mount Holyoke College *B*
Northeastern University *B, M, D*
Regis College *B*

Salem State University *B*
Simmons College *B, M*
Smith College *B*
Springfield College *B*
Stonehill College *B*
Suffolk University *B*
Tufts University *B*
University of Massachusetts
    Amherst *B, M, D*
    Boston *B, M*
    Dartmouth *B*
    Lowell *B*
Wellesley College *B*
Western New England University *B*
Westfield State University *B*
Wheaton College *B*
Williams College *B*
Worcester State University *B*

Michigan

Adrian College *A, B, T*
Albion College *B*
Andrews University *B*
Aquinas College *B, T*
Calvin College *B*
Central Michigan University *B, M*
Delta College *A*
Eastern Michigan University *B, M*
Ferris State University *B*
Gogebic Community College *A*
Grand Rapids Community College *A*
Grand Valley State University *B*
Hillsdale College *B*
Hope College *B*
Kalamazoo College *B*
Lake Michigan College *A*
Lake Superior State University *B*
Lansing Community College *A*
Madonna University *B*
Michigan State University *B, M, D*
Mid Michigan Community College *A*
Northern Michigan University *B*
Oakland University *B*
Olivet College *B*
Saginaw Valley State University *B*
Spring Arbor University *B*
University of Detroit Mercy *B*
University of Michigan *B, M, D*
University of Michigan
    Dearborn *B*
    Flint *B*
Wayne State University *B, M, D*
Western Michigan University *B, M, D*

Minnesota

Augsburg College *B*
Bemidji State University *B*
Bethany Lutheran College *B*
Carleton College *B*
College of St. Benedict *B*
Concordia College: Moorhead *B*
Concordia University St. Paul *B*
Gustavus Adolphus College *B*
Hamline University *B*
Macalester College *B*
Minnesota State University
    Mankato *B, M*
    Moorhead *B*
Minnesota West Community and
    Technical College *A*
Ridgewater College *A*
St. Catherine University *B*
Saint Cloud State University *B*
St. John's University *B*
St. Mary's University of Minnesota *B*
Southwest Minnesota State
    University *B*
University of Minnesota
    Duluth *B*
    Morris *B*
    Twin Cities *B, M, D*
University of St. Thomas *B*
Winona State University *B*

Mississippi

Alcorn State University *B*
East Mississippi Community
    College *A*
Hinds Community College *A*
Itawamba Community College *A*
Jackson State University *B, M*
Mississippi College *B*
Mississippi Delta Community
    College *A*
Mississippi State University *B, M, D*
Mississippi Valley State University *B*
Northeast Mississippi Community
    College *A*
Rust College *B*
Tougaloo College *B*
University of Mississippi *B, M*
University of Southern Mississippi *B*

Missouri

Avila University *B*
Central Methodist University *B*
College of the Ozarks *B*
Columbia College *B*
Drury University *B*
Evangel University *B*
Fontbonne University *B*
Hannibal-LaGrange University *B*
Lincoln University *B, M*
Lindenwood University *B*
Maryville University of Saint Louis *B*
Missouri Southern State
    University *B, T*
Missouri State University *B*
Missouri Valley College *B*
Northwest Missouri State
    University *B*
Park University *B*
St. Charles Community College *A*
Saint Louis University *B, M*
Southwest Baptist University *B*
Three Rivers Community College *A*
Truman State University *B*
University of Central Missouri *B, M*
University of Missouri
    Columbia *B, M, D*
    Kansas City *B, M*
    St. Louis *B*
Webster University *B*
Westminster College *B*

Montana

Carroll College *B*
Montana State University *B*
Montana State University
    Billings *B, T*
Rocky Mountain College *B*
University of Great Falls *B*
University of Montana *B, M*
University of Montana: Western *B*

Nebraska

Bellevue University *B*
Chadron State College *B*
Creighton University *B*
Doane College *B*
Hastings College *B*
Midland University *B*
Nebraska Wesleyan University *B*
University of Nebraska
    Kearney *B*
    Lincoln *B, M, D*
    Omaha *B, M*
Wayne State College *B*
Western Nebraska Community
    College *A*

Nevada

University of Nevada
    Las Vegas *B, M, D*
    Reno *B, M*

New Hampshire

Colby-Sawyer College *B*
Dartmouth College *B*
Keene State College *B*
New England College *B*
Plymouth State University *B*
Rivier University *B*
Saint Anselm College *B*
University of New
    Hampshire *B, M, D*

New Jersey

Bergen Community College *A*
Bloomfield College *B, T*
Caldwell College *B*
Centenary College *B*
College of New Jersey *B*
College of St. Elizabeth *B*
Drew University *B*
Fairleigh Dickinson University
    College at Florham *B*
    Metropolitan Campus *B*
Felician College *B*
Gloucester County College *A*
Hudson County Community
    College *A*
Kean University *B, M*
Middlesex County College *A*
Monmouth University *B*
Montclair State University *B, M*
New Jersey City University *B*
Passaic County Community College *A*
Princeton University *B, M, D*
Ramapo College of New Jersey *B*
Richard Stockton College of New
    Jersey *B*
Rider University *B*
Rowan University *B*
Rutgers, The State University of New
    Jersey
    Camden Campus *B*
    New Brunswick/Piscataway
        Campus *B, M, D*
    Newark Campus *B*
Saint Peter's University *B*
Salem Community College *A*
Seton Hall University *B*
Thomas Edison State College *B*
William Paterson University of New
    Jersey *B, M*

New Mexico

Central New Mexico Community
    College *A*
Eastern New Mexico University *B*
New Mexico Highlands University *B*
New Mexico State University *B, M*
University of New Mexico *B, M, D*
Western New Mexico University *B*

New York

Adelphi University *B*
Alfred University *B*
Bard College *B*
Barnard College *B*
Canisius College *B*
City University of New York
    Baruch College *B*
    Brooklyn College *B, M*
    CUNY Online *B*
    City College *B, M*
    Hunter College *B, M*
    Lehman College *B*
    Queens College *B, M, T*
    Queensborough Community
        College *A*
    York College *B*
Clarkson University *B*
Colgate University *B*
College of Mount St. Vincent *B*
College of New Rochelle *B*
College of Saint Rose *B*
Columbia University *B*

Columbia University
  School of General Studies *B*
Cornell University *B, M, D*
D'Youville College *B*
Dowling College *B*
Excelsior College *B*
Fordham University *B, M, D*
Hamilton College *B*
Hartwick College *B*
Hobart and William Smith Colleges *B*
Hofstra University *B, M*
Houghton College *B*
Iona College *B*
Ithaca College *B*
Keuka College *B*
Le Moyne College *B*
Long Island University
  LIU Brooklyn *B*
  LIU Post *B*
Manhattan College *B*
Manhattanville College *B*
Marymount Manhattan College *B*
Mercy College *B*
Metropolitan College of New
  York *A, B*
Molloy College *B*
Mount Saint Mary College *B, T*
Nazareth College *B*
New York Institute of Technology *B*
New York University *B, M, D*
Niagara University *B*
Nyack College *B*
Roberts Wesleyan College *B*
SUNY
  College at Brockport *B*
  College at Buffalo *B*
  College at Cortland *B*
  College at Fredonia *B*
  College at Geneseo *B*
  College at New Paltz *B*
  College at Old Westbury *B*
  College at Oneonta *B*
  College at Oswego *B*
  College at Plattsburgh *B*
  College at Potsdam *B*
  College at Purchase *B*
  Institute of Technology at Utica/
    Rome *B*
  University at Albany *B, M, D*
  University at Binghamton *B, M, D*
  University at Buffalo *B, M, D*
  University at Stony Brook *B, M, D*
Sage Colleges *B*
Saint Bonaventure University *B*
St. Francis College *B*
St. John Fisher College *B*
St. John's University *B, M*
St. Joseph's College New York:
  Suffolk Campus *B*
St. Joseph's College, New York *B*
St. Lawrence University *B*
Siena College *B, T*
Skidmore College *B*
Syracuse University *B, D*
Touro College *B*
Union College *B*
United States Military Academy *B*
Utica College *B*
Vassar College *B*
Wagner College *B*
Wells College *B*
Yeshiva University *B*

North Carolina

Appalachian State University *B*
Catawba College *B*
Davidson College *B*
Duke University *B, M, D*
East Carolina University *B, M*
Elizabeth City State University *B*
Elon University *B*
Fayetteville State University *B, M*
Gardner-Webb University *B*
Greensboro College *C, B*
Guilford College *B*

High Point University *B*
Lees-McRae College *B*
Lenoir-Rhyne University *B*
Livingstone College *B*
Mars Hill University *B, T*
Meredith College *B*
Methodist University *A, B*
North Carolina Agricultural and
  Technical State University *B*
North Carolina Central
  University *B, M*
North Carolina State
  University *B, M, D*
North Carolina Wesleyan College *B*
Queens University of Charlotte *B*
St. Augustine's University *B*
Salem College *B*
Shaw University *B*
University of North Carolina
  Asheville *B, T*
  Chapel Hill *B, M, D*
  Charlotte *B, M*
  Greensboro *B, M*
  Pembroke *B*
  Wilmington *B, M*
Wake Forest University *B*
Warren Wilson College *B*
Western Carolina University *B*
Western Piedmont Community
  College *A*
Wingate University *B*
Winston-Salem State University *B*

North Dakota

Minot State University *B*
North Dakota State University *B, M*
University of North Dakota *B, M*

Ohio

Baldwin Wallace University *B*
Bowling Green State
  University *B, M, D*
Capital University *B*
Case Western Reserve
  University *B, M, D*
Cedarville University *B*
Central State University *B*
Cleveland State University *B, M*
College of Mount St. Joseph *B*
College of Wooster *B*
Denison University *B*
Franciscan University of
  Steubenville *B*
Hiram College *B*
John Carroll University *B*
Kent State University *B, M, D*
Kent State University
  Ashtabula *B*
  Stark *B*
Kenyon College *B*
Lake Erie College *B*
Lourdes University *A, B*
Miami University
  Middletown *A*
  Oxford *B*
Mount Vernon Nazarene University *B*
Muskingum University *B*
Oberlin College *B*
Ohio Dominican University *B*
Ohio Northern University *B*
Ohio State University
  Columbus Campus *B, M, D*
Ohio University *B, M*
Ohio Wesleyan University *B*
Otterbein University *B*
Shawnee State University *B*
Sinclair Community College *A*
University of Akron *C, B, M, D*
University of Cincinnati *B, M, D*
University of Dayton *B*
University of Findlay *B*
University of Mount Union *B*
University of Rio Grande *A*
University of Toledo *B, M*

Urbana University *B*
Ursuline College *B*
Walsh University *B*
Wilberforce University *B*
Wilmington College *B*
Wittenberg University *B*
Wright State University *A, B*
Wright State University: Lake
  Campus *A*
Xavier University *A, B*
Youngstown State University *B*

Oklahoma

Cameron University *B*
Carl Albert State College *A*
Connors State College *A*
East Central University *B*
Eastern Oklahoma State College *A*
Langston University *B*
Northeastern State University *B*
Northwestern Oklahoma State
  University *B*
Oklahoma Baptist University *B*
Oklahoma City Community
  College *A*
Oklahoma City University *B*
Oklahoma State University *B, M, D*
Rose State College *A*
Southeastern Oklahoma State
  University *B*
Southern Nazarene University *B*
Southwestern Oklahoma State
  University *B*
Tulsa Community College *A*
University of Central Oklahoma *B*
University of Oklahoma *B, M, D*
University of Science and Arts of
  Oklahoma *B*
University of Tulsa *B*

Oregon

George Fox University *B*
Lewis & Clark College *B*
Linfield College *B, T*
Linn-Benton Community College *A*
Mt. Hood Community College *A*
Oregon State University *B*
Pacific University *B*
Portland State University *B, M, D*
Reed College *B*
Southern Oregon University *B*
University of Oregon *B, M, D*
University of Portland *B*
Western Oregon University *B*
Willamette University *B*

Pennsylvania

Albright College *B*
Arcadia University *B*
Bloomsburg University of
  Pennsylvania *B*
Bryn Mawr College *B*
Bucknell University *B*
Cabrini College *B*
Carlow University *B*
Carnegie Mellon University *B, D*
Chestnut Hill College *B*
Cheyney University of
  Pennsylvania *B*
Clarion University of Pennsylvania *B*
Community College of Allegheny
  County *A*
Delaware County Community
  College *A*
Dickinson College *B*
Drexel University *B*
Duquesne University *B*
East Stroudsburg University of
  Pennsylvania *B*
Eastern University *B*
Edinboro University of
  Pennsylvania *B*
Elizabethtown College *B*
Franklin & Marshall College *B*

Geneva College *B*
Gettysburg College *B*
Grove City College *B*
Haverford College *B, T*
Holy Family University *B*
Immaculata University *B*
Indiana University of
  Pennsylvania *B, M*
Juniata College *B*
King's College *B*
Kutztown University of
  Pennsylvania *B*
La Roche College *B*
La Salle University *B*
Lafayette College *B*
Lebanon Valley College *B*
Lehigh University *B, M*
Lincoln University *B*
Lock Haven University of
  Pennsylvania *B*
Lycoming College *B*
Mansfield University of
  Pennsylvania *B*
Mercyhurst University *B, T*
Messiah College *B*
Millersville University of
  Pennsylvania *B*
Moravian College *B*
Muhlenberg College *C, B*
Penn State
  Abington *B*
  Altoona *B*
  Beaver *B*
  Berks *B*
  Brandywine *B*
  DuBois *B*
  Erie, The Behrend College *B*
  Fayette, The Eberly Campus *B*
  Greater Allegheny *B*
  Harrisburg *B*
  Hazleton *B*
  Lehigh Valley *B*
  Mont Alto *B*
  New Kensington *B*
  Schuylkill *B*
  Shenango *B*
  University Park *B, M, D*
  Wilkes-Barre *B*
  Worthington Scranton *B*
  York *B*
Rosemont College *B*
St. Francis University *B*
Saint Joseph's University *B*
St. Vincent College *B*
Seton Hill University *B*
Shippensburg University of
  Pennsylvania *B*
Susquehanna University *B*
Temple University *B, M, D*
Thiel College *B*
University of Pennsylvania *A, B, M, D*
University of Pittsburgh *B, M, D*
University of Pittsburgh
  Bradford *B*
  Johnstown *B*
University of Scranton *A, B*
Ursinus College *B*
Villanova University *B*
Washington & Jefferson College *B*
Waynesburg University *B*
West Chester University of
  Pennsylvania *B*
Westminster College *B, T*
Widener University *B*
Wilkes University *B*
Wilson College *B*
York College of Pennsylvania *B*

Puerto Rico

Inter American University of Puerto
  Rico
  Metropolitan Campus *B*
  San German Campus *B*
Pontifical Catholic University of
  Puerto Rico *B*

Turabo University *B*
University of Puerto Rico
  Aguadilla *A*
  Cayey University College *B*
  Mayaguez *B*
  Rio Piedras *B, M*

Rhode Island

Brown University *B, M, D*
Bryant University *B*
Providence College *B*
Rhode Island College *B*
Roger Williams University *B*
Salve Regina University *B*
University of Rhode Island *B*

South Carolina

Charleston Southern University *B*
Claflin University *B*
Clemson University *B*
Coastal Carolina University *B*
Coker College *B*
College of Charleston *B, T*
Francis Marion University *B*
Furman University *B*
Lander University *B*
Morris College *B*
Newberry College *B*
Presbyterian College *B*
South Carolina State University *B*
University of South Carolina
  Aiken *B*
  Beaufort *B*
  Columbia *B, M, D*
  Upstate *B*
Voorhees College *B*
Winthrop University *B*
Wofford College *B*

South Dakota

Augustana College *B, T*
Black Hills State University *B*
Kilian Community College *A*
Northern State University *B*
Oglala Lakota College *B*
South Dakota State
  University *B, M, D*
University of Sioux Falls *B*
University of South Dakota *B*

Tennessee

Austin Peay State University *B*
Belmont University *B*
Bethel University *B*
Carson-Newman University *B*
Cumberland University *B*
East Tennessee State
  University *B, M, T*
Fisk University *B*
Hiwassee College *A*
Jackson State Community College *A*
Lane College *B*
LeMoyne-Owen College *B*
Lee University *B*
Maryville College *B*
Middle Tennessee State
  University *B, M*
Milligan College *B, T*
Tennessee State University *B*
Tennessee Technological
  University *B*
Tennessee Wesleyan College *B*
Trevecca Nazarene University *B*
Union University *B, T*
University of Memphis *B, M*
University of Tennessee
  Knoxville *B, M, D*
  Martin *B*
Vanderbilt University *B, M, D*

Texas

Abilene Christian University *B*
Alvin Community College *A*
Angelo State University *B*

Austin College *B*
Austin Community College *A*
Baylor University *B, M, D*
Brazosport College *A*
Clarendon College *A*
Coastal Bend College *A*
College of the Mainland *A*
Dallas Baptist University *B*
Del Mar College *A*
East Texas Baptist University *B*
El Paso Community College *A*
Frank Phillips College *A*
Galveston College *A*
Grayson College *A*
Hardin-Simmons University *B*
Hill College *A*
Houston Baptist University *B*
Howard Payne University *B*
Huston-Tillotson University *B*
Jarvis Christian College *B*
Kilgore College *A*
Lamar State College at Orange *A*
Lamar University *B*
Laredo Community College *A*
McMurry University *B*
Midland College *A*
Midwestern State University *B*
Northeast Texas Community
  College *A*
Northwest Vista College *A*
Odessa College *A*
Our Lady of the Lake University of
  San Antonio *B*
Palo Alto College *A*
Paris Junior College *A*
Prairie View A&M University *B, M*
Rice University *B*
St. Edward's University *B*
St. Mary's University *B, T*
St. Philip's College *A*
Sam Houston State University *B, M*
San Jacinto College *A*
South Plains College *A*
Southern Methodist University *B*
Southwestern University *B*
Stephen F. Austin State
  University *B, T*
Tarleton State University *B*
Texas A&M International
  University *B, M*
Texas A&M University *B, M, D*
Texas A&M University
  Commerce *B, M*
  Corpus Christi *B*
  Kingsville *B, M*
Texas Christian University *B*
Texas College *B*
Texas Lutheran University *B*
Texas Southern University *B, M*
Texas State University *B, M, T*
Texas Tech University *B, M*
Texas Wesleyan University *B*
Texas Woman's University *B, M, D*
Trinity University *B*
Trinity Valley Community College *A*
Tyler Junior College *A*
University of Houston *B, M*
University of Houston
  Clear Lake *B, M*
  Downtown *B*
University of Mary Hardin-Baylor *B*
University of North Texas *B, M, D*
University of Texas
  Arlington *B, M*
  Austin *B, M, D*
  Brownsville *B*
  Dallas *B, M*
  El Paso *B, M*
  Pan American *B, M*
  Permian Basin *B*
  San Antonio *B, M*
University of the Incarnate Word *B*
Wayland Baptist University *B*
Weatherford College *A*
West Texas A&M University *B*

Western Texas College *A*
Wharton County Junior College *A*
Wiley College *B*

Utah

Brigham Young University *B, M, D*
Salt Lake Community College *A*
Snow College *A*
Southern Utah University *B*
University of Utah *B, M, D, T*
Utah State University *B, M, D*
Weber State University *B*
Westminster College *B*

Vermont

Castleton State College *B*
Green Mountain College *B*
Johnson State College *B*
Marlboro College *B*
Middlebury College *B*
Saint Michael's College *B*
University of Vermont *B*

Virginia

Averett University *B*
Bridgewater College *B*
Christopher Newport University *B*
College of William and Mary *B*
Emory & Henry College *B*
George Mason University *B, M, D*
Hampton University *B*
Hollins University *B*
James Madison University *B*
Longwood University *B, M*
Lynchburg College *B*
Mary Baldwin College *B*
Marymount University *B*
Norfolk State University *B, M*
Old Dominion University *B, M*
Radford University *B*
Randolph College *B*
Randolph-Macon College *B*
Roanoke College *B, T*
Shenandoah University *B*
Sweet Briar College *B*
University of Mary Washington *B*
University of Richmond *B*
University of Virginia *B, M, D*
University of Virginia's College at
  Wise *B, T*
Virginia Commonwealth
  University *B, M*
Virginia Polytechnic Institute and
  State University *B, M, D*
Virginia State University *B*
Virginia University of Lynchburg *B*
Virginia Wesleyan College *B*
Washington and Lee University *B*

Washington

Central Washington University *B*
Centralia College *A*
Eastern Washington University *B*
Evergreen State College *B*
Gonzaga University *B*
Highline Community College *A*
Pacific Lutheran University *B*
Seattle Pacific University *B*
Seattle University *B*
University of Puget Sound *B*
University of Washington *B, M, D*
Walla Walla University *B*
Washington State University *B, M, D*
Western Washington University *B, M*
Whitman College *B*
Whitworth University *B*

West Virginia

American Public University System *B*
Concord University *B*
Davis and Elkins College *B*
Fairmont State University *B*
Marshall University *B, M*
Ohio Valley University *B*

Potomac State College of West
  Virginia University *A*
Shepherd University *B*
West Liberty University *B*
West Virginia State University *B*
West Virginia University *B, M*
West Virginia Wesleyan College *B*

Wisconsin

Alverno College *B*
Beloit College *B*
Cardinal Stritch University *B*
Carroll University *B*
Carthage College *B, T*
Edgewood College *B*
Lakeland College *B*
Marquette University *B*
Northland College *B*
Ripon College *B*
St. Norbert College *B, T*
University of Wisconsin
  Eau Claire *B*
  Green Bay *B*
  La Crosse *B, T*
  Madison *B, M, D*
  Milwaukee *B, M, D*
  Oshkosh *B*
  Parkside *B, T*
  Platteville *B*
  River Falls *B, T*
  Stevens Point *B, T*
  Superior *B*
  Whitewater *B, T*
Viterbo University *B*

Wyoming

Casper College *A*
Laramie County Community
  College *A*
Northwest College *A*
University of Wyoming *B, M*
Western Wyoming Community
  College *A*

Sociology and anthropology

Connecticut

Fairfield University *B*

Georgia

Spelman College *B*

Idaho

College of Idaho *B*

Illinois

Augustana College *B*
Lake Forest College *B*
North Central College *B*
University of Illinois
  Springfield *B*

Kentucky

Transylvania University *B*

Maine

University of Maine
  Farmington *B*

Maryland

Goucher College *B*
Towson University *B*

Massachusetts

University of Massachusetts
  Dartmouth *B*

Michigan

Albion College *B*
Alma College *B, T*
Oakland University *B*

Minnesota

St. Olaf College *B*

Mississippi

Millsaps College *B*

New Hampshire

Keene State College *B*

New York

City University of New York
    College of Staten Island *B*
Columbia University
    School of General Studies *B*
Elmira College *B*
Pace University *B*

Pennsylvania

Lycoming College *B*
Swarthmore College *B*

Texas

Midland College *A*

Software engineering

Alabama

Auburn University *B, M*

Arizona

DeVry University
    Phoenix *B*
Embry-Riddle Aeronautical University
    Prescott Campus *B*
University of Advancing
    Technology *A, B, M*

California

California Baptist University *B*
California State University
    East Bay *B*
    Fullerton *M*
Chapman University *B*
DeVry University
    Pomona *B*
Foothill College *A*
Los Angeles City College *A*
National University *B, M*
Northwestern Polytechnic
    University *B, M*
San Jose State University *B, M*
Santa Clara University *M*
University of California
    Irvine *B, M, D*

Colorado

Colorado Technical
    University *B, M, D*
DeVry University
    Westminster *B*
University of Denver *M*
University of Northern Colorado *B*

Connecticut

Fairfield University *B, M*
Quinnipiac University *B*

District of Columbia

George Washington University *M*

Florida

Broward College *A*
DeVry University
    Orlando *B*
Embry-Riddle Aeronautical
    University *B, M*
Florida Institute of Technology *B, M*
Florida State University *B*
Rasmussen College
    Fort Myers *C, A*
    New Port Richey *C, A*
    Ocala *C, A*

Pasco/Land O'Lakes *C, A*
    Tampa/Brandon *C, A*
Seminole State College of Florida *A*
Tallahassee Community College *A*
University of Miami *B*

Georgia

Mercer University *B, M*
Southern Polytechnic State
    University *C, B, M*

Idaho

Boise State University *D*

Illinois

DeVry University
    Online *B*
Rasmussen College
    Aurora *C, A*
    Mokena/Tinley Park *C, A*
    Rockford *C, A*
    Romeoville/Joliet *C, A*
University of Illinois
    Urbana-Champaign *B, M, D*

Indiana

Indiana Institute of Technology *B*
Indiana University
    Purdue University Indianapolis *C*
Indiana Wesleyan University *B*
Rose-Hulman Institute of
    Technology *B, M*

Iowa

Iowa State University *B*
William Penn University *B*

Maryland

Capitol College *B, M*

Massachusetts

Northeastern University *M*

Michigan

Andrews University *M*
Baker College
    Flint *M*
Michigan Technological University *B*
University of Detroit Mercy *B, M*
University of Michigan
    Dearborn *M*

Minnesota

Rasmussen College
    Blaine *C, A*
    Bloomington *C, A*
    Brooklyn Park *C, A*
    Eagan *C, A*
    Lake Elmo/Woodbury *C, A*
    Mankato *C, A*
    Moorhead *C, A*
    St. Cloud *C, A*
Riverland Community College *A*
University of Minnesota
    Crookston *B*

Mississippi

East Mississippi Community
    College *A*

Montana

Montana Tech of the University of
    Montana *B*

Nevada

College of Southern Nevada *A*
University of Nevada
    Las Vegas *B*

New Jersey

Monmouth University *B, M*
New Jersey Institute of
    Technology *M*

New York

Clarkson University *B*
Pace University *M*
Pace University: Pleasantville/
    Briarcliff *M*
Rochester Institute of
    Technology *B, M*
SUNY
    College at Oswego *B*

North Carolina

East Carolina University *M*

North Dakota

North Dakota State University *M, D*
Rasmussen College
    Bismarck *C, A*
    Fargo *C, A*
Valley City State University *B*

Ohio

Baldwin Wallace University *B*
Cleveland State University *M*
Miami University
    Oxford *B*
Miami-Jacobs Career College
    Dayton *A*
Ohio Business College
    Sandusky *A*
Stark State College *A*
University of Cincinnati *C*

Oregon

Portland State University *M*

Pennsylvania

Allegheny College *B*
Carnegie Mellon University *M, D*
DeVry University
    Fort Washington *B*
Drexel University *B, M*
Montgomery County Community
    College *C, A*
Penn State
    Erie, The Behrend College *B*
Robert Morris University *B*
Shippensburg University of
    Pennsylvania *B*
University of Scranton *M*
Widener University *M*

Rhode Island

New England Institute of
    Technology *A, B*

South Carolina

Claflin University *B*
University of South Carolina
    Columbia *B*

Texas

DeVry University
    Irving *B*
Remington College
    Houston *A*
St. Mary's University *B, M*
Southern Methodist University *M, D*
Texas State University *M*
Texas Tech University *M*
University of Houston
    Clear Lake *M*
University of Texas
    Arlington *B, M*
    Dallas *B, M, D*

Utah

Utah Valley University *B*

Vermont

Champlain College *B*

Virginia

DeVry University
    Arlington *B*
George Mason University *M*
Liberty University *B*
University of Management and
    Technology *B, M*

Washington

DeVry University
    Federal Way *B*
Seattle University *M*
South Seattle Community College *A*

West Virginia

West Virginia University *M*

Wisconsin

Carroll University *B, M*
Herzing University
    Madison *A, B*
Milwaukee School of Engineering *B*
Rasmussen College
    Appleton *C, A*
    Green Bay *C, A*
    Wausau *C, A*
University of Wisconsin
    La Crosse *M*
    Platteville *B*

Soil chemistry/physics

Indiana

Purdue University *B*

Tennessee

University of Tennessee
    Knoxville *B, M*

Soil science

Alabama

Auburn University *B, M, D*
Tuskegee University *B, M*

Arizona

University of Arizona *M, D*

California

California Polytechnic State
    University: San Luis Obispo *B*
Merced College *A*
Modesto Junior College *A*
University of California
    Davis *B*

Colorado

Colorado Mountain College *A*
Colorado State University *B, M, D*
Otero Junior College *A*

Delaware

Delaware State University *B*
University of Delaware *B, M, D*

Florida

University of Florida *B, M, D*

Georgia

University of Georgia *B*

Idaho

University of Idaho *M, D*

Illinois

Southern Illinois University
    Carbondale *B*

Indiana

Purdue University *B*

Iowa

Iowa State University *M, D*

Kentucky

University of Kentucky *D*

Maine

University of Maine *B, M*

Michigan

Michigan State University *B, M, D*

Minnesota

Southwest Minnesota State
University *B*
University of Minnesota
Twin Cities *B, M, D*

Missouri

University of Missouri
Columbia *B, M, D*

Nebraska

University of Nebraska
Lincoln *B*

New Hampshire

University of New Hampshire *M*

New Mexico

New Mexico State University *B*

New York

Cornell University *M, D*
SUNY
College of Environmental Science
and Forestry *M, D*

North Carolina

North Carolina State University *M, D*

North Dakota

North Dakota State
University *B, M, D*

Ohio

Ohio State University
Agricultural Technical Institute *A*
Columbus Campus *D*

Oklahoma

Eastern Oklahoma State College *A*
Oklahoma State University *B, M, D*

Oregon

Oregon State University *M, D*
Treasure Valley Community
College *A*

Pennsylvania

Penn State
University Park *M, D*

Puerto Rico

University of Puerto Rico
Mayaguez *B, M*

Tennessee

Hiwassee College *A*
Middle Tennessee State University *B*
Tennessee Technological
University *B*

Texas

Prairie View A&M University *M*
Texas A&M University *M, D*
Texas A&M University
Kingsville *M*
Texas Tech University *M*

Utah

Utah State University *M, D*

Virginia

Mountain Empire Community
College *A*

Washington

Spokane Community College *A*
Washington State University *B, M, D*

West Virginia

West Virginia University *B*

Wisconsin

University of Wisconsin
Madison *B, M, D*
River Falls *B*
Stevens Point *B*

Wyoming

University of Wyoming *M, D*

Solar energy technology

Arizona

Arizona State University *M*
Arizona Western College *C, A*
Coconino County Community
College *A*

California

Cabrillo College *A*
Sierra College *C*

Colorado

Ecotech Institute *A*
Pueblo Community College *C, A*

Georgia

Gwinnett Technical College *C*

Idaho

Idaho State University *C, B*

Illinois

Sauk Valley Community College *C*
Waubonsee Community College *C*

Massachusetts

Bristol Community College *C*

Michigan

Henry Ford Community College *C*
Lansing Community College *C*

Minnesota

Century College *C*
Northwest Technical College *C*

Missouri

Crowder College *A*

Nevada

Truckee Meadows Community
College *C, A*

New Jersey

Mercer County Community
College *C*

New Mexico

Central New Mexico Community
College *C*
Clovis Community College *C, A*
Eastern New Mexico University:
Roswell *A*
San Juan College *C, A*
Santa Fe Community College *C*

North Carolina

Appalachian State University *B*

Ohio

Marion Technical College *A*

Oregon

Treasure Valley Community
College *A*

Pennsylvania

Harrisburg Area Community
College *C*
Pennsylvania College of
Technology *A*

Texas

Texas State Technical College
Waco *C, A*

Wisconsin

Northeast Wisconsin Technical
College *A*

Somatic bodywork

Texas

Hill College *C*

Vermont

Goddard College *B, M*

South Asian languages

Illinois

University of Chicago *B, D*

Minnesota

University of Minnesota
Twin Cities *B, M, D*

Missouri

University of Missouri
Columbia *B*

New Hampshire

Dartmouth College *B*

Washington

University of Washington *B*

South Asian studies

California

Claremont McKenna College *B*

Georgia

Emory University *B*

Illinois

University of Chicago *B, D*

Indiana

Indiana University
Bloomington *B*

Massachusetts

Hampshire College *B*
Mount Holyoke College *B*
Wellesley College *B*

Michigan

University of Michigan *M*

Minnesota

University of Minnesota
Twin Cities *B*

Missouri

University of Missouri
Columbia *B*

New York

Columbia University
School of General Studies *B*
SUNY
University at Binghamton *B*

Ohio

College of Wooster *B*

Pennsylvania

University of Pennsylvania *B, M, D*

Rhode Island

Brown University *B*

Vermont

Marlboro College *B*
Middlebury College *B*

Virginia

University of Virginia *M*

Washington

University of Washington *B, M*

Wisconsin

University of Wisconsin
Madison *B, M, D*

Southeast Asian languages

Washington

University of Washington *B*

Southeast Asian studies

California

Claremont McKenna College *B*
University of California
Berkeley *B*
Riverside *D*

Michigan

University of Michigan *M*

Ohio

Ohio University *M*

Vermont

Marlboro College *B*

Washington

University of Washington *B, M*

Wisconsin

University of Wisconsin
Madison *M*
Milwaukee *C*

Spanish

Alabama

Auburn University *B, M*
Birmingham-Southern College *B*
Judson College *B*
Oakwood University *B*
Samford University *B*
Spring Hill College *B, T*
Troy University *B*
University of Alabama *B*

Alaska

University of Alaska
Anchorage *B*

Arizona

Arizona State University *B, M, D*
Arizona Western College *A*
Northern Arizona University *B*
University of Arizona *B, M, D*

Arkansas

Arkansas Tech University *M*
Harding University *B*
Henderson State University *B*
Hendrix College *B*
John Brown University *B*
Lyon College *B*
Ouachita Baptist University *B*
Southern Arkansas University *B*
University of Arkansas *B, M*
University of Arkansas
    Fort Smith *B*
    Little Rock *B*
University of Central Arkansas *B, M*
University of the Ozarks *B*

California

Allan Hancock College *A*
Azusa Pacific University *B*
Bakersfield College *A*
Berkeley City College *C, A*
Biola University *B*
Cabrillo College *A*
California Baptist University *B*
California Lutheran University *B*
California State Polytechnic
    University: Pomona *B*
California State University
    Bakersfield *B*
    Channel Islands *B*
    Chico *B*
    Dominguez Hills *B*
    East Bay *B*
    Fresno *B, M*
    Fullerton *B, M*
    Long Beach *B, M*
    Los Angeles *B, M*
    Monterey Bay *B*
    Northridge *B, M*
    Sacramento *B, M*
    San Bernardino *B, M, T*
    San Marcos *B, M*
    Stanislaus *B*
Canada College *A*
Cerritos College *A*
Chabot College *A*
Chaffey College *A*
Chapman University *B*
Claremont McKenna College *B*
College of Alameda *A*
College of Marin *A*
College of San Mateo *C, A*
College of the Canyons *A*
College of the Desert *A*
College of the Siskiyous *A*
Contra Costa College *A*
Copper Mountain College *A*
Crafton Hills College *A*
Cuyamaca College *A*
Cypress College *A*
De Anza College *A*
Diablo Valley College *C*
El Camino College *A*
Foothill College *A*
Fresno City College *A*
Fresno Pacific University *B*
Gavilan College *A*
Glendale Community College *A*
Golden West College *A*
Grossmont College *A*
Holy Names University *B*
Humboldt State University *B*
Imperial Valley College *A*
Irvine Valley College *A*
La Sierra University *B*
Lake Tahoe Community College *C, A*
Long Beach City College *A*
Los Angeles City College *A*
Los Angeles Mission College *A*
Los Angeles Pierce College *A*
Los Angeles Southwest College *A*
Los Angeles Valley College *A*
Los Medanos College *C*
Loyola Marymount University *B*

Mendocino College *A*
Merced College *A*
Merritt College *A*
Mills College *B*
Modesto Junior College *A*
Moorpark College *A*
Mount St. Mary's College *B*
National University *B*
Occidental College *B*
Orange Coast College *A*
Oxnard College *A*
Pacific Union College *B, T*
Pepperdine University *B*
Pitzer College *B*
Point Loma Nazarene University *B*
Pomona College *B*
St. Mary's College of California *B*
San Diego City College *A*
San Diego Mesa College *A*
San Diego State University *B, M*
San Francisco State University *B, M*
San Joaquin Delta College *A*
San Jose State University *B, M*
Santa Barbara City College *A*
Santa Clara University *B*
Santa Rosa Junior College *A*
Santiago Canyon College *A*
Scripps College *B*
Skyline College *A*
Solano Community College *A*
Sonoma State University *B*
Southwestern College *A*
Stanford University *B, M, D*
University of California
    Berkeley *B, M, D*
    Davis *B, M, D*
    Irvine *B, D*
    Los Angeles *B, M*
    Riverside *B, M, D*
    San Diego *B, M*
    Santa Barbara *B, M, D*
University of La Verne *B*
University of Redlands *B*
University of San Diego *B*
University of San Francisco *B*
University of Southern California *B*
University of the Pacific *B*
West Los Angeles College *A*
Westmont College *B*
Whittier College *B*

Colorado

Adams State University *B, M*
Colorado College *B*
Colorado Mesa University *B*
Colorado State University *B, M*
Fort Lewis College *B*
Regis University *B*
University of Colorado
    Boulder *B, M, D*
    Colorado Springs *B*
    Denver *B, M*
University of Denver *B*
University of Northern Colorado *B, T*
Western State Colorado University *B*

Connecticut

Albertus Magnus College *B*
Central Connecticut State
    University *B, M*
Eastern Connecticut State
    University *B*
Fairfield University *B*
Quinnipiac University *B*
Sacred Heart University *B*
Southern Connecticut State
    University *B*
Trinity College *B*
University of Connecticut *B*
University of Saint Joseph *B*
Wesleyan University *B*
Western Connecticut State
    University *B*
Yale University *B, M, D*

Delaware

Delaware State University *B, M*
University of Delaware *B, M, T*

District of Columbia

American University *B, M*
Catholic University of
    America *B, M, D*
Gallaudet University *B*
George Washington University *B*
Georgetown University *B, M, D*
Howard University *B, M, D*
University of the District of
    Columbia *B*

Florida

Barry University *B*
Eckerd College *B*
Flagler College *B*
Florida Atlantic University *B, M*
Florida Gulf Coast University *B*
Florida International
    University *B, M, D*
Florida Southern College *B*
Florida State University *B, M, D*
Jacksonville University *B*
New College of Florida *B*
Rollins College *B*
Stetson University *B*
University of Central Florida *B, M*
University of Florida *B, M*
University of Miami *B, M, D*
University of North Florida *B*
University of South Florida *B, M*
University of Tampa *A, B*
University of West Florida *B*

Georgia

Agnes Scott College *B*
Albany State University *B*
Armstrong Atlantic State
    University *B, T*
Berry College *B*
Brewton-Parker College *B*
Clark Atlanta University *B, M*
Covenant College *B*
Emory University *B, D*
Georgia College and State
    University *B*
Georgia State University *B, M, T*
LaGrange College *B*
Mercer University *B*
Morehouse College *B*
Oglethorpe University *B*
Piedmont College *B*
Shorter University *B*
Southern Polytechnic State
    University *C*
Spelman College *B*
University of Georgia *B, M*
University of North Georgia *B*
Valdosta State University *B*
Wesleyan College *B*

Hawaii

University of Hawaii
    Manoa *B, M*

Idaho

Boise State University *B, T*
College of Idaho *B*
Idaho State University *B*
Northwest Nazarene University *B*
University of Idaho *B*

Illinois

Augustana College *B*
Aurora University *B*
Benedictine University *B, T*
Blackburn College *B*
Bradley University *B, T*
Chicago State University *B*
Concordia University Chicago *B*
DePaul University *B, M*

Dominican University *B*
Elmhurst College *B, T*
Greenville College *B*
Illinois College *B, T*
Illinois State University *B, T*
Illinois Wesleyan University *B*
John Wood Community College *A*
Kishwaukee College *A*
Knox College *B*
Lake Forest College *B*
Loyola University Chicago *B, M*
MacMurray College *B, T*
McKendree University *B*
Millikin University *B*
Monmouth College *B, T*
North Central College *B, T*
North Park University *B*
Northeastern Illinois University *B*
Northern Illinois University *B, M, T*
Northwestern University *B*
Olivet Nazarene University *B, T*
Principia College *B*
Richland Community College *A*
Rockford University *B*
Saint Xavier University *B*
South Suburban College of Cook
    County *A*
Southern Illinois University
    Carbondale *B*
Trinity Christian College *B*
Triton College *A*
University of Illinois
    Chicago *B, M, D*
    Urbana-Champaign *B, M, D*
Western Illinois University *B*
Wheaton College *B, T*

Indiana

Anderson University *B*
Ball State University *B, T*
Bethel College *B*
Butler University *B*
DePauw University *B*
Earlham College *B*
Franklin College *B*
Goshen College *B*
Grace College *B*
Hanover College *B*
Indiana University
    Bloomington *B, M, D*
    Northwest *B*
    Purdue University Fort Wayne *B, T*
    Purdue University
        Indianapolis *B, M*
    South Bend *B*
    Southeast *B*
Indiana Wesleyan University *B*
Manchester University *B, T*
Marian University *B, T*
Purdue University *B, M, D*
Saint Mary's College *B*
St. Mary-of-the-Woods College *B*
Taylor University *B*
University of Evansville *B*
University of Indianapolis *B*
University of Notre Dame *B, M*
University of Southern Indiana *B, T*
Valparaiso University *C, B*
Wabash College *B*

Iowa

Briar Cliff University *B*
Buena Vista University *B, T*
Central College *B, T*
Clarke University *B, T*
Coe College *B*
Cornell College *B, T*
Dordt College *B*
Graceland University *B, T*
Grand View University *B*
Grinnell College *B*
Loras College *B*
Luther College *B*
Marshalltown Community College *A*

Morningside College *B*
Northwestern College *B, T*
St. Ambrose University *B, T*
Simpson College *B*
University of Iowa *B, M, D, T*
University of Northern Iowa *B, M*
Wartburg College *B, T*

Kansas

Baker University *B, T*
Benedictine College *B*
Butler Community College *A*
Coffeyville Community College *A*
Friends University *B*
Independence Community College *A*
McPherson College *B, T*
MidAmerica Nazarene University *B*
Pittsburg State University *B*
University of Kansas *B, M, D*
Washburn University *B*
Wichita State University *B, M, T*

Kentucky

Asbury University *B, T*
Bellarmine University *B*
Berea College *B, T*
Bluegrass Community and Technical
   College *A*
Brescia University *B*
Campbellsville University *B*
Centre College *B*
Eastern Kentucky University *B*
Georgetown College *B*
Kentucky State University *B*
Kentucky Wesleyan College *B*
Morehead State University *B*
Murray State University *B, T*
Northern Kentucky University *B*
Thomas More College *A, B*
Transylvania University *B, T*
University of Kentucky *B, M, D*
University of Louisville *B, M*
University of Pikeville *B*
University of the Cumberlands *B*
Western Kentucky University *B, T*

Louisiana

Grambling State University *B*
Louisiana College *T*
Louisiana State University and
   Agricultural and Mechanical
   College *B, M*
Louisiana Tech University *B*
Loyola University New Orleans *B*
Southeastern Louisiana University *B*
Tulane University *B, M, D*
Xavier University of Louisiana *B*

Maine

Bates College *B, T*
Bowdoin College *B*
Colby College *B*
University of Maine *B*

Maryland

Allegany College of Maryland *A*
Frostburg State University *T*
Goucher College *B*
Hood College *B, T*
Howard Community College *A*
Johns Hopkins University *B, M, D*
Loyola University Maryland *B*
McDaniel College *B*
Mount St. Mary's University *B, T*
Notre Dame of Maryland
   University *B*
Salisbury University *B*
University of Maryland
   College Park *B, M, D*
Washington College *B, T*

Massachusetts

Amherst College *B*
Assumption College *B*

Bard College at Simon's Rock *B*
Bentley University *B*
Boston College *B, M, D*
Boston University *B, M, D*
Bridgewater State University *B*
Clark University *B*
College of the Holy Cross *B*
Elms College *B, M, T*
Emmanuel College *B*
Gordon College *B*
Merrimack College *B*
Mount Holyoke College *B*
Northeastern University *B*
Regis College *B*
Salem State University *B, M*
Simmons College *B, M*
Smith College *B*
Stonehill College *B*
Suffolk University *B*
Tufts University *B*
University of Massachusetts
   Amherst *B, M, D*
   Boston *B*
   Dartmouth *B*
Wellesley College *B*
Westfield State University *B*
Williams College *B*
Worcester State University *B, M, T*

Michigan

Adrian College *A, B, T*
Albion College *B, T*
Alma College *B, T*
Andrews University *B*
Aquinas College *B, T*
Calvin College *B, T*
Central Michigan University *B, M*
Cornerstone University *B*
Eastern Michigan University *B, M*
Grand Valley State University *B*
Hillsdale College *B*
Hope College *B*
Kalamazoo College *B*
Lake Superior State University *B*
Lansing Community College *A*
Madonna University *C, B*
Michigan State University *B, M, D*
Michigan Technological University *T*
Northern Michigan University *B*
Oakland University *B, T*
Saginaw Valley State University *B, T*
Siena Heights University *B*
Spring Arbor University *B*
University of Detroit Mercy *C*
University of Michigan *B, M, D*
University of Michigan
   Dearborn *B*
   Flint *B, T*
Western Michigan University *B, M, D*

Minnesota

Augsburg College *B*
Bemidji State University *B*
Bethel University *B*
Carleton College *B*
College of St. Benedict *B*
College of St. Scholastica *B*
Concordia College: Moorhead *B, T*
Gustavus Adolphus College *B*
Hamline University *B*
Macalester College *B*
Minnesota State University
   Mankato *B, M, T*
   Moorhead *B*
St. Catherine University *B*
Saint Cloud State University *B*
St. John's University *B*
St. Mary's University of Minnesota *B*
St. Olaf College *B*
Southwest Minnesota State
   University *B*

University of Minnesota
   Duluth *B*
   Morris *B*
   Twin Cities *B, M, D*
University of Northwestern - St.
   Paul *B*
University of St. Thomas *B*
Winona State University *B*

Mississippi

Blue Mountain College *B*
East Mississippi Community
   College *A*
Itawamba Community College *A*
Millsaps College *B*
Mississippi College *B*
Mississippi University for
   Women *B, T*
University of Mississippi *B*

Missouri

Central Methodist University *B*
College of the Ozarks *B*
Crowder College *A*
Drury University *B, T*
Evangel University *B, T*
Lincoln University *B*
Lindenwood University *B*
Missouri Southern State University *B*
Missouri State University *B*
Missouri Western State
   University *B, T*
Northwest Missouri State
   University *B*
Park University *B*
Rockhurst University *B*
St. Charles Community College *A*
Saint Louis University *B, M*
Southwest Baptist University *B*
Truman State University *B*
University of Central Missouri *B*
University of Missouri
   Columbia *B, M*
   Kansas City *B*
   St. Louis *B*
Washington University in St.
   Louis *B, M, D*
Webster University *B*
Westminster College *B*
William Jewell College *B*
William Woods University *B*

Montana

Carroll College *B*
Montana State University
   Billings *B, T*
University of Montana *B, M*

Nebraska

Chadron State College *B*
College of Saint Mary *T*
Concordia University *B, T*
Creighton University *B*
Doane College *B*
Hastings College *B*
Midland University *B*
Nebraska Wesleyan University *B*
University of Nebraska
   Kearney *B, M, T*
   Lincoln *B*
Wayne State College *B*
Western Nebraska Community
   College *A*

Nevada

University of Nevada
   Las Vegas *B, M*
   Reno *B*

New Hampshire

Dartmouth College *B, T*
Keene State College *B*
Plymouth State University *B*
Rivier University *B, M, T*

Saint Anselm College *B, T*
University of New Hampshire *B, M*

New Jersey

Caldwell College *B*
College of New Jersey *B, T*
College of St. Elizabeth *B*
Drew University *B*
Fairleigh Dickinson University
   College at Florham *B*
   Metropolitan Campus *B*
Georgian Court University *B*
Kean University *B, T*
Montclair State University *B, M, T*
New Jersey City University *B*
Princeton University *B, M, D*
Ramapo College of New Jersey *B*
Rider University *B, T*
Rowan University *B, T*
Rutgers, The State University of New
   Jersey
   Camden Campus *B, T*
   New Brunswick/Piscataway
      Campus *B, M, D, T*
   Newark Campus *B, T*
Saint Peter's University *B*
Seton Hall University *B, T*
William Paterson University of New
   Jersey *B*

New Mexico

Eastern New Mexico University *B*
New Mexico Highlands University *B*
New Mexico Junior College *A*
New Mexico State University *M*
Santa Fe Community College *A*
University of New Mexico *B, M, D*
Western New Mexico University *B*

New York

Adelphi University *B*
Alfred University *B*
Bard College *B*
Barnard College *B*
Canisius College *B*
City University of New York
   Baruch College *B*
   Brooklyn College *B, M*
   City College *B, M*
   College of Staten Island *B*
   Hunter College *B, M*
   LaGuardia Community College *A*
   Lehman College *B, M*
   Queens College *B, M, T*
   York College *B*
Colgate University *B*
College of Mount St. Vincent *B, T*
College of New Rochelle *B, T*
College of Saint Rose *B*
Columbia University *B*
Columbia University
   School of General Studies *B*
Cornell University *B, D*
Daemen College *B, T*
Dominican College of Blauvelt *B*
Elmira College *T*
Fordham University *B, M*
Hartwick College *B, T*
Hobart and William Smith Colleges *B*
Hofstra University *B*
Houghton College *B*
Iona College *B, M*
Ithaca College *B, T*
Le Moyne College *B*
Long Island University
   LIU Post *B, M*
Manhattan College *B*
Manhattanville College *B*
Marist College *B*
Mercy College *B*
Molloy College *B*
Mount Saint Mary College *B*
Nazareth College *B*
New York University *B, M, D*

Niagara University *B*
Orange County Community
  College *A*
Pace University *B*
Pace University: Pleasantville/
  Briarcliff *B*
Roberts Wesleyan College *B*
SUNY
  College at Brockport *B, T*
  College at Buffalo *B*
  College at Cortland *B*
  College at Fredonia *B, T*
  College at Geneseo *B, T*
  College at New Paltz *B*
  College at Old Westbury *B, T*
  College at Oneonta *B*
  College at Oswego *B*
  College at Plattsburgh *B*
  College at Potsdam *B*
  University at Albany *B, M, D*
  University at Binghamton *B, M*
  University at Buffalo *B, M, D*
  University at Stony Brook *B, M, D*
Saint Bonaventure University *B*
St. Francis College *B*
St. John Fisher College *B*
St. John's University *B, M*
St. Joseph's College New York:
  Suffolk Campus *B*
St. Joseph's College, New York *B*
St. Lawrence University *B, T*
St. Thomas Aquinas College *B*
Siena College *B, T*
Skidmore College *B*
Syracuse University *B, M*
Union College *B*
United States Military Academy *B*
University of Rochester *B, M*
Vassar College *B*
Wagner College *B*
Wells College *B*

North Carolina

Barton College *B, T*
Campbell University *B*
Catawba College *B*
Davidson College *B*
Duke University *B, M, D*
East Carolina University *B*
Elon University *B*
Fayetteville State University *B*
Gardner-Webb University *B*
Greensboro College *B, T*
Guilford College *B, T*
High Point University *B*
Johnson C. Smith University *B*
Lenoir-Rhyne University *B*
Mars Hill University *B*
Meredith College *B*
Methodist University *A, B, T*
North Carolina Central University *B*
North Carolina State University *B, M*
Queens University of Charlotte *B*
Salem College *B*
University of North Carolina
  Asheville *B, T*
  Charlotte *B, M*
  Greensboro *B*
  Pembroke *B*
  Wilmington *B, M*
Wake Forest University *B*
Warren Wilson College *B*
Western Carolina University *B*
William Peace University *B*
Winston-Salem State University *B*

North Dakota

Dickinson State University *B*
Minot State University *B*
North Dakota State University *B, T*
University of Jamestown *B*
University of North Dakota *B*
Valley City State University *B*

Ohio

Ashland University *B*
Baldwin Wallace University *B*
Bluffton University *B*
Bowling Green State University *B, M*
Capital University *B*
Case Western Reserve University *B*
Cedarville University *B*
Cleveland State University *B, M*
College of Wooster *B*
Denison University *B*
Franciscan University of
  Steubenville *B*
Heidelberg University *B*
Hiram College *B, T*
John Carroll University *B*
Kent State University *B, M*
Kenyon College *B*
Lake Erie College *B*
Malone University *B*
Marietta College *B*
Miami University
  Middletown *A*
  Oxford *B, M*
Mount Vernon Nazarene University *B*
Muskingum University *B*
Notre Dame College *T*
Oberlin College *B*
Ohio Northern University *B*
Ohio State University
  Columbus Campus *B*
Ohio University *B, M*
Ohio Wesleyan University *B*
Otterbein University *B*
University of Akron *B, M*
University of Cincinnati *C, B, M, T*
University of Dayton *B*
University of Findlay *B, T*
University of Mount Union *B*
University of Rio Grande *A, B*
University of Toledo *B, M*
Walsh University *B*
Wilmington College *B*
Wittenberg University *B*
Wright State University *B, M, D, T*
Xavier University *A, B*
Youngstown State University *B*

Oklahoma

Northeastern State University *B*
Northwestern Oklahoma State
  University *B*
Oklahoma Baptist University *B, T*
Oklahoma Christian University *B*
Oklahoma City Community
  College *A*
Oklahoma City University *B*
Oklahoma State University *B*
Oral Roberts University *B*
Southeastern Oklahoma State
  University *B*
Southern Nazarene University *B*
Tulsa Community College *A*
University of Central Oklahoma *B*
University of Oklahoma *B, M, D*
University of Tulsa *B*

Oregon

George Fox University *B*
Linfield College *B, T*
Oregon State University *B*
Pacific University *B*
Portland State University *B, M*
Reed College *B*
Southern Oregon University *B*
University of Oregon *B, M*
University of Portland *B, T*
Western Oregon University *B, T*
Willamette University *B*

Pennsylvania

Albright College *B, T*
Allegheny College *B*
Arcadia University *B*
Bloomsburg University of
  Pennsylvania *T*
Bryn Mawr College *B*
Bucknell University *B*
Cabrini College *B*
California University of
  Pennsylvania *C, B*
Carnegie Mellon University *B*
Cedar Crest College *B*
Chatham University *B*
Chestnut Hill College *B*
Cheyney University of
  Pennsylvania *B, T*
Clarion University of Pennsylvania *B*
DeSales University *B, T*
Dickinson College *B*
Duquesne University *B*
East Stroudsburg University of
  Pennsylvania *B, T*
Eastern University *B*
Edinboro University of
  Pennsylvania *B, T*
Elizabethtown College *B, T*
Franklin & Marshall College *B*
Gettysburg College *B*
Grove City College *B, T*
Haverford College *B, T*
Immaculata University *A, B, T*
Indiana University of
  Pennsylvania *B, M*
Juniata College *B*
King's College *B, T*
Kutztown University of
  Pennsylvania *B*
La Salle University *B, T*
Lafayette College *B*
Lebanon Valley College *B*
Lehigh University *B*
Lincoln University *B*
Lycoming College *B*
Marywood University *B*
Mercyhurst University *B*
Messiah College *B*
Millersville University of
  Pennsylvania *B, M, T*
Moravian College *B, T*
Muhlenberg College *C, B*
Penn State
  Abington *B*
  Altoona *B*
  Beaver *B*
  Berks *B*
  Brandywine *B*
  DuBois *B*
  Erie, The Behrend College *B*
  Fayette, The Eberly Campus *B*
  Greater Allegheny *B*
  Harrisburg *B*
  Hazleton *B*
  Lehigh Valley *B*
  Mont Alto *B*
  New Kensington *B*
  Schuylkill *B*
  Shenango *B*
  University Park *B, M, D*
  Wilkes-Barre *B*
  Worthington Scranton *B*
  York *B*
Rosemont College *B*
St. Francis University *B*
Saint Joseph's University *B*
St. Vincent College *B*
Seton Hill University *B, T*
Shippensburg University of
  Pennsylvania *C, B, T*
Slippery Rock University of
  Pennsylvania *B, T*
Susquehanna University *B, T*
Swarthmore College *B*
Temple University *B, M, D*
University of Pennsylvania *B*
University of Pittsburgh *B*
University of Pittsburgh
  Greensburg *B*
University of Scranton *B, T*

Ursinus College *B, T*
Villanova University *B, M*
Washington & Jefferson College *B*
West Chester University of
  Pennsylvania *B, M, T*
Westminster College *B*
Widener University *B, T*
Wilkes University *B*
Wilson College *B*
York College of Pennsylvania *B*

Puerto Rico

Bayamon Central University *B*
Inter American University of Puerto
  Rico
  Metropolitan Campus *B, M*
Pontifical Catholic University of
  Puerto Rico *B, M*
University of Puerto Rico
  Cayey University College *B*
  Mayaguez *B, M*
  Rio Piedras *B, M, D*

Rhode Island

Brown University *B, M, D*
Bryant University *B*
Providence College *B*
Rhode Island College *B*
Salve Regina University *B*
University of Rhode Island *B, M*

South Carolina

Anderson University *B*
Bob Jones University *B*
Charleston Southern University *B*
Clemson University *B*
Coastal Carolina University *B*
Coker College *B*
College of Charleston *B, T*
Columbia College *B*
Converse College *B*
Erskine College *B*
Francis Marion University *B*
Furman University *B, T*
Lander University *B, T*
Newberry College *B*
North Greenville University *B*
Presbyterian College *B*
Spartanburg Community College *C*
University of South Carolina
  Beaufort *B*
  Columbia *B, M, D*
  Upstate *B*
Winthrop University *M*
Wofford College *B, T*

South Dakota

Augustana College *B, T*
Black Hills State University *B*
Northern State University *B*
South Dakota State University *B*
University of Sioux Falls *B*
University of South Dakota *B*

Tennessee

Belmont University *B*
Bryan University
  Dayton *B*
Carson-Newman University *B, T*
Fisk University *B*
Hiwassee College *A*
King University *B, T*
Lee University *B*
Lipscomb University *B*
Maryville College *B, T*
Milligan College *T*
Rhodes College *B*
Sewanee: The University of the
  South *B*
Southern Adventist University *B*
Tennessee State University *B*
Tennessee Technological
  University *B, T*
Union University *B, T*

University of Tennessee
  Knoxville B, M
  Martin B
Vanderbilt University B, M, D

Texas

Abilene Christian University B
Angelo State University B, T
Austin College B
Austin Community College A
Baptist University of the Americas B
Baylor University B, M, T
Blinn College A
Coastal Bend College A
East Texas Baptist University B
Galveston College A
Hardin-Simmons University B
Houston Baptist University B
Howard Payne University B
Kilgore College A
Lamar University B
Laredo Community College A
McMurry University B, T
Midwestern State University B
Northeast Texas Community
  College A
Our Lady of the Lake University of
  San Antonio B
Palo Alto College A
Paris Junior College A
Prairie View A&M University B
Rice University B, M
St. Edward's University B
St. Mary's University B
St. Philip's College A
Sam Houston State University B
South Plains College A
South Texas College A
Southern Methodist University B
Southwestern University B, T
Stephen F. Austin State University T
Sul Ross State University B
Tarleton State University B, T
Texas A&M International
  University B, M, T
Texas A&M University B, M
Texas A&M University
  Commerce B, M
  Corpus Christi B, T
  Kingsville B, M
Texas Christian University B
Texas Lutheran University B
Texas Southern University B
Texas State University B, M, T
Texas Tech University B, D
Texas Wesleyan University B, T
Trinity University B
Trinity Valley Community College A
University of Dallas B
University of Houston B, M, D
University of Houston
  Downtown B
University of Mary Hardin-Baylor B, T
University of North Texas B, M
University of St. Thomas B
University of Texas
  Arlington B
  Austin B, M, D
  Brownsville B, M
  El Paso B, M
  Pan American B, M
  Permian Basin B, M
  San Antonio B, M
  Tyler B
University of the Incarnate Word B
Wayland Baptist University B, T
West Texas A&M University B

Utah

Brigham Young University B, M
Dixie State College B
Snow College A
Southern Utah University B
University of Utah B

Utah State University B
Utah Valley University B
Weber State University B

Vermont

Bennington College B
Castleton State College B
Marlboro College B
Middlebury College B, M, D
Norwich University B
Saint Michael's College B
University of Vermont B

Virginia

Bridgewater College B
Christopher Newport University B
College of William and Mary B
Eastern Mennonite University B
Emory & Henry College B, T
Ferrum College B
Hampden-Sydney College B
Hampton University B
Hollins University B
Liberty University B, T
Lynchburg College B
Mary Baldwin College B
Randolph College B
Randolph-Macon College B
Roanoke College B, T
Shenandoah University B
Southern Virginia University B
Sweet Briar College B
University of Richmond B
University of Virginia B, M, D
University of Virginia's College at
  Wise B, T
Virginia Wesleyan College B
Washington and Lee University B

Washington

Central Washington University B
Centralia College A
Eastern Washington University B
Gonzaga University B
Pacific Lutheran University B
Seattle Pacific University B
Seattle University B
University of Puget Sound B
University of Washington B
Walla Walla University B
Washington State University B, M
Western Washington University D
Whitman College B
Whitworth University B, T

West Virginia

Bethany College B
Fairmont State University B
Marshall University M
Shepherd University B, T
West Virginia University T
Wheeling Jesuit University B

Wisconsin

Beloit College B
Cardinal Stritch University B
Carroll University B
Carthage College B
Concordia University Wisconsin B
Edgewood College B
Lakeland College B
Lawrence University B, T
Marian University B
Marquette University B
Mount Mary University B, T
Ripon College B, T
St. Norbert College B, T
Silver Lake College of the Holy
  Family T
University of Wisconsin
  Eau Claire B
  Green Bay B, T
  La Crosse B, T
  Madison B, M, D

Milwaukee B, M
Oshkosh B
Parkside B, T
Platteville B, T
River Falls B
Stevens Point B, T
Whitewater B, T
Viterbo University B, T
Wisconsin Lutheran College B

Wyoming

Laramie County Community
  College A
Northwest College A
University of Wyoming B, M
Western Wyoming Community
  College A

Spanish/Iberian studies

California

Claremont McKenna College B
Scripps College B
Stanford University B, M, D

Florida

New College of Florida B

Iowa

Coe College B
Iowa Western Community College A

Massachusetts

Bard College at Simon's Rock B
Brandeis University B
Elms College B

New Hampshire

Dartmouth College B

New York

Bard College B
Barnard College B
Columbia University B
New York University B

Pennsylvania

Arcadia University B

Virginia

Emory & Henry College B

Spanish teacher education

Alabama

Auburn University B, M, T
Birmingham-Southern College T
Spring Hill College B, T

Arizona

Northern Arizona University M

Arkansas

Harding University B, T
Ouachita Baptist University B, T
University of Arkansas
  Fort Smith B

California

Azusa Pacific University T
California State University
  Long Beach T
  San Bernardino M, T
Humboldt State University T
San Francisco State University T
Stanford University M, T
University of San Diego T
Vanguard University of Southern
  California T

Colorado

Adams State University B, M, T
Colorado State University B, T
Colorado State University
  Pueblo T
Metropolitan State University of
  Denver T

Connecticut

Albertus Magnus College B, T
Fairfield University T
Quinnipiac University B, M
Sacred Heart University T
University of Connecticut T
University of Saint Joseph T

Delaware

Delaware State University B
University of Delaware B, T

District of Columbia

Catholic University of America B

Florida

Barry University T
Stetson University B
University of Miami B

Georgia

Georgia Southern University M
Piedmont College B, T
Valdosta State University B

Idaho

Boise State University B, T
Brigham Young University-Idaho B, T
Northwest Nazarene University B
University of Idaho T

Illinois

Augustana College B, T
Benedictine University T
Bradley University B
DePaul University M, T
Dominican University T
Elmhurst College B
Greenville College B, T
Illinois College T
Illinois Wesleyan University B
Knox College T
MacMurray College B, T
North Park University T
Olivet Nazarene University B, T
Rockford University T
Saint Xavier University B
Trinity Christian College B, T
University of Illinois
  Chicago B
  Urbana-Champaign B, M, T

Indiana

Anderson University B, T
Butler University T
Franklin College B, T
Goshen College B, T
Grace College B
Indiana University
  Bloomington B, T
  Northwest B
  Purdue University Fort Wayne B, T
  Purdue University Indianapolis B
  South Bend B, T
Indiana Wesleyan University T
Manchester University B, T
Purdue University B, M, D
Saint Mary's College B
Taylor University B, T
University of Evansville B, T
University of Indianapolis B, T
Valparaiso University B

Iowa

Buena Vista University *B, T*
Central College *T*
Cornell College *B, T*
Dordt College *B*
Graceland University *T*
Grand View University *T*
Iowa State University *T*
Loras College *T*
Morningside College *B*
Northwestern College *T*
St. Ambrose University *B, T*
Simpson College *T*
University of Iowa *T*
Wartburg College *T*

Kansas

Benedictine College *B*
Bethel College *T*
Friends University *B*
McPherson College *B, T*
MidAmerica Nazarene University *B, T*
Pittsburg State University *B*
University of St. Mary *T*
Washburn University *B, T*

Kentucky

Brescia University *B, T*
Eastern Kentucky University *B*
Kentucky Wesleyan College *B, T*
Thomas More College *B*
University of the Cumberlands *B, T*

Louisiana

Centenary College of Louisiana *T*
Louisiana College *B, T*
Southeastern Louisiana University *B*
University of Louisiana at Lafayette *B*
Xavier University of Louisiana *B*

Maine

University of Maine *B, M*

Maryland

Anne Arundel Community College *A*
Carroll Community College *A*
Community College of Baltimore
　County *A*
Frederick Community College *A*
Harford Community College *A*
Hood College *T*
Howard Community College *A*
Mount St. Mary's University *T*
Notre Dame of Maryland
　University *T*

Massachusetts

Assumption College *T*
Elms College *T*
Framingham State University *M*
Merrimack College *B*
Salem State University *B, M*
Tufts University *T*
University of Massachusetts
　Dartmouth *T*

Michigan

Adrian College *B, T*
Alma College *T*
Aquinas College *B, T*
Calvin College *B*
Central Michigan University *B*
Eastern Michigan University *B*
Grand Valley State University *T*
Hope College *B, T*
Michigan State University *B*
Northern Michigan University *B, T*
Spring Arbor University *B*
University of Michigan
　Flint *B, T*
Western Michigan University *B*

Minnesota

Augsburg College *T*
Bemidji State University *B, T*
Bethel University *B*
College of St. Benedict *T*
Concordia College: Moorhead *B, T*
Gustavus Adolphus College *T*
Hamline University *T*
Minnesota State University
　Mankato *B, M, T*
　Moorhead *B*
St. Catherine University *T*
Saint Cloud State University *B, T*
St. John's University *T*
St. Mary's University of Minnesota *B*
University of Minnesota
　Duluth *B*
　Morris *T*
　Twin Cities *M*
University of Northwestern - St.
　Paul *B*
University of St. Thomas *B*
Winona State University *B, T*

Mississippi

Blue Mountain College *B*
Itawamba Community College *A*
Millsaps College *T*

Missouri

Lindenwood University *B*
Missouri Southern State
　University *B, T*
Missouri State University *B*
Missouri Western State University *B*
Northwest Missouri State
　University *B, T*
Park University *T*
University of Central Missouri *B, M*
University of Missouri
　Columbia *B*
　Kansas City *B*
Washington University in St.
　Louis *B, M, T*
William Jewell College *B, T*

Montana

Carroll College *B*
Montana State University
　Billings *B, T*
University of Montana *T*

Nebraska

Chadron State College *B*
College of Saint Mary *B, T*
Concordia University *B, T*
Creighton University *T*
Hastings College *T*
Midland University *B, T*
Nebraska Wesleyan University *T*
University of Nebraska
　Kearney *B, T*
　Lincoln *B, T*

New Hampshire

Keene State College *B, T*
Rivier University *B, M, T*
Saint Anselm College *T*
University of New Hampshire *T*

New Jersey

College of New Jersey *B, T*
County College of Morris *A*
Georgian Court University *T*
Saint Peter's University *T*
William Paterson University of New
　Jersey *T*

New Mexico

Western New Mexico University *B*

New York

Adelphi University *M, T*
Alfred University *B, T*

City University of New York
　Brooklyn College *B, M, T*
　City College *B, M*
　College of Staten Island *B*
　Hunter College *B, M, T*
　Lehman College *M*
　Queens College *M, T*
College of Mount St. Vincent *T*
College of Saint Rose *B, T*
D'Youville College *M, T*
Dowling College *B, M*
Dutchess Community College *A*
Elmira College *B, T*
Fordham University *M, T*
Hobart and William Smith Colleges *T*
Hofstra University *B, M*
Houghton College *B, T*
Iona College *B, M, T*
Ithaca College *B, M, T*
Le Moyne College *T*
Long Island University
　LIU Brooklyn *B, T*
　LIU Post *B, M, T*
Manhattan College *B, T*
Marist College *B*
Molloy College *B, M*
New York University *B, M*
Niagara University *B, M, T*
Pace University *B, M, T*
Pace University: Pleasantville/
　Briarcliff *B, M, T*
Roberts Wesleyan College *B*
SUNY
　College at Brockport *B, M, T*
　College at Buffalo *B*
　College at Cortland *B*
　College at Fredonia *B*
　College at Geneseo *B, M, T*
　College at New Paltz *B, M, T*
　College at Old Westbury *B, M, T*
　College at Oneonta *B, T*
　College at Oswego *B, M*
　College at Plattsburgh *B*
　College at Potsdam *B*
　University at Albany *M, T*
　University at Binghamton *M*
　University at Buffalo *M, T*
　University at Stony Brook *T*
Saint Bonaventure University *M*
St. John Fisher College *B, M, T*
St. John's University *B, M, T*
St. Joseph's College New York:
　Suffolk Campus *B*
St. Joseph's College, New York *B*
St. Lawrence University *T*
St. Thomas Aquinas College *B, T*
Syracuse University *B*
Ulster County Community College *A*
University of Rochester *M*
Vassar College *T*
Wells College *T*

North Carolina

Campbell University *B, T*
Davidson College *T*
East Carolina University *B*
Elon University *T*
Gardner-Webb University *B*
Greensboro College *B, T*
Meredith College *T*
North Carolina Agricultural and
　Technical State University *B, T*
North Carolina Central
　University *B, T*
North Carolina State University *B, T*
Salem College *T*
University of North Carolina
　Greensboro *B*
　Wilmington *B*
Wake Forest University *T*
Western Carolina University *B, T*

North Dakota

Dickinson State University *B, T*
Minot State University *B*

North Dakota State University *B, T*
Valley City State University *B, T*

Ohio

Ashland University *B, T*
Baldwin Wallace University *T*
Bowling Green State University *M, T*
Case Western Reserve University *T*
Cedarville University *B*
Hiram College *T*
Malone University *B*
Miami University
　Oxford *B, T*
Mount Vernon Nazarene
　University *B, T*
Ohio Northern University *B, T*
Ohio University *B, T*
Ohio Wesleyan University *B*
Otterbein University *B*
University of Akron *B, M*
University of Dayton *T*
University of Findlay *B, M, T*
University of Mount Union *T*
University of Toledo *B, M, T*
Youngstown State University *B, M*

Oklahoma

Northeastern State University *B*
Oklahoma Baptist University *B, T*
Oklahoma City University *B*
Oral Roberts University *B, T*
Southeastern Oklahoma State
　University *B, T*
Southern Nazarene University *B*
University of Central Oklahoma *B*
University of Tulsa *T*

Oregon

Linfield College *T*
Portland State University *T*
Western Oregon University *B, T*

Pennsylvania

Albright College *T*
Cabrini College *T*
Duquesne University *B, M, T*
Gettysburg College *T*
Grove City College *T*
Holy Family University *B*
Juniata College *B, T*
King's College *T*
La Salle University *B, T*
Lebanon Valley College *T*
Lycoming College *T*
Mansfield University of
　Pennsylvania *B, T*
Marywood University *B*
Messiah College *B, T*
Moravian College *T*
Rosemont College *T*
St. Francis University *B, T*
Saint Joseph's University *M, T*
St. Vincent College *T*
Seton Hill University *B, T*
Susquehanna University *T*
University of Scranton *B*
Villanova University *T*
Washington & Jefferson College *T*
Westminster College *T*
Widener University *T*
Wilson College *T*
York College of Pennsylvania *B*

Puerto Rico

American University of Puerto
　Rico *B, T*
Bayamon Central University *B*
Inter American University of Puerto
　Rico
　Aguadilla Campus *B*
　Arecibo Campus *B*
　Barranquitas Campus *B, T*
　Fajardo Campus *B, T*

Metropolitan Campus *B*
San German Campus *B*
Pontifical Catholic University of
Puerto Rico *B, T*
Turabo University *B*
University of Puerto Rico
Cayey University College *B*

Rhode Island

Rhode Island College *B, M*

South Carolina

Bob Jones University *B*
Charleston Southern University *B*
Furman University *T*
Wofford College *T*

South Dakota

Augustana College *B, T*
University of South Dakota *B, M, T*

Tennessee

Belmont University *T*
Bryan University
Dayton *T*
King University *T*
Lee University *B*
Lipscomb University *B, T*
Maryville College *B, T*
Southern Adventist University *B*
Union University *B, T*

Texas

Abilene Christian University *B, T*
Baylor University *T*
East Texas Baptist University *B*
Hardin-Simmons University *B, T*
Houston Baptist University *T*
Howard Payne University *B*
Lamar University *T*
Laredo Community College *A*
Lubbock Christian University *B*
McMurry University *B, T*
Our Lady of the Lake University of
San Antonio *B*
St. Edward's University *B, T*
St. Mary's University *T*
Sam Houston State University *M, T*
Texas A&M International
University *B, T*
Texas A&M University
Commerce *T*
Kingsville *T*
Texas Wesleyan University *B, T*
University of Dallas *T*
University of Mary Hardin-Baylor *T*
University of Texas
Arlington *T*
San Antonio *T*
West Texas A&M University *T*

Utah

Brigham Young University *B, M*
Southern Utah University *B*
Utah State University *B*
Utah Valley University *B*
Weber State University *B*

Vermont

Bennington College *M*
Castleton State College *B, T*
Saint Michael's College *M, T*

Virginia

Bridgewater College *T*
Eastern Mennonite University *T*
Emory & Henry College *B*
Hollins University *T*
Longwood University *T*
University of Virginia's College at
Wise *T*

Washington

Central Washington University *B, T*
Eastern Washington University *B*
Heritage University *B*
Washington State University *B, M, T*
Western Washington University *B*
Whitworth University *B, T*

West Virginia

Bethany College *B*
Shepherd University *T*
Wheeling Jesuit University *B*

Wisconsin

Carroll University *B, T*
Carthage College *T*
Concordia University Wisconsin *B*
Edgewood College *B*
Lawrence University *T*
Marian University *B, T*
Mount Mary University *B, T*
St. Norbert College *T*
University of Wisconsin
Green Bay *T*
Platteville *B, T*
River Falls *T*
Whitewater *B*
Viterbo University *B, T*

Special education

Alabama

Alabama Agricultural and Mechanical
University *B, M*
Alabama State University *B, M*
Athens State University *B*
Auburn University *B, M, D, T*
Birmingham-Southern College *B*
Jacksonville State University *B, M, T*
Samford University *M*
University of Alabama *B, M, D*
University of Alabama
Birmingham *B, M*
University of North Alabama *M*
University of South Alabama *B, M, T*
University of West Alabama *B, M, T*

Alaska

Prince William Sound Community
College *A*
University of Alaska
Anchorage *M*
Fairbanks *M, T*

Arizona

Arizona State University *B, M*
Central Arizona College *A*
Grand Canyon University *B, M*
Northcentral University *B, M, D*
Northern Arizona University *B, M*
University of Arizona *B, M, D*
University of Phoenix
Phoenix-Hohokam *M*
Southern Arizona *M*

Arkansas

Arkansas State University *M, T*
Harding University *B, M, T*
Henderson State University *M*
University of Arkansas *M*
University of Arkansas
Little Rock *M*
Pine Bluff *M*
University of Central Arkansas *M*
University of the Ozarks *B*

California

Alliant International University *M, T*
Azusa Pacific University *M, D*
California Baptist University *T*
California Lutheran University *B, M*

California State University
Chico *T*
Dominguez Hills *M*
East Bay *M, T*
Fresno *M*
Fullerton *M, T*
Long Beach *M, T*
Los Angeles *M*
Northridge *M*
Sacramento *M*
San Bernardino *M*
San Marcos *T*
Cerritos College *A*
Chapman University *M, D, T*
Concordia University Irvine *M, T*
Cuesta College *A*
Diablo Valley College *A*
Dominican University of California *M*
Fresno Pacific University *M, T*
Holy Names University *M*
La Sierra University *M*
Loyola Marymount University *M, T*
Mills College *M, T*
Mount St. Mary's College *M*
National University *M*
Notre Dame de Namur
University *M, T*
Point Loma Nazarene University *M*
Sacramento City College *A*
St. Mary's College of California *M*
San Diego State University *M, T*
San Francisco State
University *M, D, T*
San Jose State University *M*
University of California
Berkeley *D, T*
Los Angeles *D*
University of La Verne *M, T*
University of San Diego *M, T*
University of San Francisco *M*
University of the Pacific *D, T*

Colorado

Adams State University *B, M, T*
Metropolitan State University of
Denver *B, T*
University of Colorado
Colorado Springs *M*
Denver *M*
University of Denver *M, D*
University of Northern
Colorado *B, M, D, T*
University of Phoenix
Denver *M*
Southern Colorado *M*
Western State Colorado
University *M, T*

Connecticut

Central Connecticut State
University *M*
Fairfield University *M, T*
Gateway Community College *A*
Southern Connecticut State
University *B, M, T*
Three Rivers Community College *A*
University of Connecticut *B, M, D, T*
University of Hartford *B, M*
University of Saint Joseph *B, M, T*
Western Connecticut State
University *M*

Delaware

Delaware State University *B*
University of Delaware *B, M, T*
Wilmington University *M*

District of Columbia

Catholic University of America *A, M*
George Washington University *M*
Howard University *M*
Trinity Washington University *M*
University of the District of
Columbia *M*

Florida

Barry University *B, M*
Broward College *A, B*
Chipola College *B*
Flagler College *B*
Florida Atlantic University *B, M, D*
Florida Gulf Coast University *B, M*
Florida International
University *B, M, D*
Florida State University *M, D, T*
Lynn University *M*
Miami Dade College *A, B*
Nova Southeastern University *B*
Pensacola State College *A*
Saint Leo University *M*
St. Petersburg College *B*
Saint Thomas University *M*
Southeastern University *B, M*
Trinity Baptist College *B*
University of Central Florida *M*
University of Florida *B, M, D*
University of Miami *B, M*
University of North Florida *B, M*
University of South Florida *B, M*
University of South Florida
Saint Petersburg *B, M*
University of West Florida *B, M, T*
Warner University *B*

Georgia

Albany State University *B, M*
Armstrong Atlantic State
University *B, M*
Brenau University *B*
Clark Atlanta University *M*
College of Coastal Georgia *A, B*
Columbus State University *B, M*
Georgia College and State
University *B, M, T*
Georgia Regents University *B, M*
Georgia Southern University *B*
Georgia Southwestern State
University *B*
Georgia State University *D*
Kennesaw State University *M*
Middle Georgia State College *A*
Piedmont College *B, M, T*
University of Georgia *B, M, D, T*
University of North Georgia *B, M*
University of West Georgia *B, M, T*
Valdosta State University *D, M*

Hawaii

Brigham Young University-
Hawaii *B, T*
Chaminade University of Honolulu *M*
University of Hawaii
Manoa *M, T*
University of Phoenix
Hawaii *M*

Idaho

Boise State University *B, M, T*
Brigham Young University-Idaho *A*
Idaho State University *B, M, D*
University of Idaho *M, T*

Illinois

Aurora University *B, M*
Benedictine University *B, M, T*
Black Hawk College *A*
Concordia University Chicago *B*
DePaul University *B, M*
Dominican University *M*
Eastern Illinois University *B, M, T*
Elmhurst College *B*
Eureka College *B*
Governors State University *M, T*
Greenville College *B, M, T*
Hebrew Theological College *B*
Illinois Central College *A*
Illinois State University *B, M, D, T*
John A. Logan College *A*
Joliet Junior College *A*

Kankakee Community College *A*
Kishwaukee College *A*
Lewis University *B, M*
Loyola University Chicago *B, M*
MacMurray College *B, T*
McKendree University *M*
Moraine Valley Community College *A*
National-Louis University *M*
Northeastern Illinois University *B, M*
Northern Illinois University *B, M*
Quincy University *B, T*
Rockford University *B, M, T*
Roosevelt University *B, M*
Sauk Valley Community College *A*
South Suburban College of Cook
   County *A*
Southern Illinois University
   Carbondale *B, M*
Southern Illinois University
   Edwardsville *B, M, T*
Trinity Christian College *B, M, T*
University of Illinois
   Chicago *M, D*
   Urbana-Champaign *B, M, D, T*
University of St. Francis *B, M*
Western Illinois University *B, M*

Indiana

Ball State University *M, D, T*
Butler University *M*
Goshen College *B, T*
Grace College *B*
Huntington University *B*
Indiana State University *B, M, T*
Indiana University
   Bloomington *B, M, D, T*
   Purdue University Fort Wayne *M*
   Purdue University Indianapolis *M*
   South Bend *B, M*
   Southeast *B*
Indiana Wesleyan University *A*
Manchester University *B, T*
Marian University *T*
Oakland City University *B*
St. Mary-of-the-Woods College *B, T*
University of Evansville *B, T*
University of St. Francis *B, M*
Vincennes University *A, B*

Iowa

Central College *T*
Dordt College *B*
Drake University *M*
Grand View University *T*
Iowa State University *M, T*
Iowa Wesleyan College *T*
Loras College *B*
Morningside College *B, M*
Mount Mercy University *M, T*
St. Ambrose University *M, T*
Simpson College *T*
University of Iowa *M, D*
University of Northern Iowa *M*
Upper Iowa University *B, T*
Wartburg College *T*

Kansas

Benedictine College *B*
Bethel College *T*
Emporia State University *M, T*
Fort Hays State University *M*
Kansas State University *M, D*
Kansas Wesleyan University *T*
McPherson College *B, T*
Pittsburg State University *M*
Southwestern College *M*
Tabor College *B*
University of Kansas *M, D*
University of St. Mary *M*
Washburn University *M, T*
Wichita State University *M*

Kentucky

Asbury University *M, T*
Bellarmine University *B, M, T*
Brescia University *B, T*
Campbellsville University *B, M*
Eastern Kentucky University *B, M*
Georgetown College *M*
Hopkinsville Community College *A*
Kentucky State University *M*
Midway College *B*
Morehead State University *B, M*
Murray State University *B, M, T*
Northern Kentucky University *B*
Spalding University *B, M*
Union College *B, M*
University of Kentucky *B, M, D*
University of Louisville *M*
University of the
   Cumberlands *B, M, T*
Western Kentucky University *B, M, T*

Louisiana

Dillard University *B*
Grambling State University *B, M*
Louisiana State University and
   Agricultural and Mechanical
   College *M*
Louisiana Tech University *B*
McNeese State University *T*
Northwestern State University *M*
Our Lady of Holy Cross College *B, T*
Southeastern Louisiana
   University *B, M*
Southern University and Agricultural
   and Mechanical College *M*
University of Louisiana at Lafayette *B*
University of New Orleans *M, D*
Xavier University of Louisiana *B, M*

Maine

University of Maine *M*
University of Maine
   Farmington *B, T*
University of Southern Maine *M*

Maryland

Bowie State University *M*
Coppin State University *B, M, T*
Goucher College *B, M*
Hood College *B, T*
Loyola University Maryland *M*
McDaniel College *M*
Mount St. Mary's University *M, T*
Notre Dame of Maryland
   University *B*
Towson University *B, M*
University of Maryland
   College Park *B, M, D*
   Eastern Shore *B, M, T*

Massachusetts

American International
   College *B, M, T*
Assumption College *M*
Bay Path College *M*
Boston University *B, M, D, T*
Bridgewater State University *B, M, T*
Curry College *B*
Eastern Nazarene College *B, M, T*
Elms College *B, M, T*
Endicott College *M*
Fitchburg State University *B, M, T*
Framingham State University *M*
Gordon College *B*
Lesley University *B, M*
Merrimack College *B, M*
Regis College *M*
Salem State University *M*
Simmons College *B, M, D*
Springfield College *B*
University of Massachusetts
   Boston *M*
Westfield State University *B, M, T*
Wheelock College *B, M*

Michigan

Andrews University *M*
Aquinas College *B, T*
Calvin College *B, T*
Central Michigan University *M*
Delta College *A*
Eastern Michigan University *B, M*
Gogebic Community College *A*
Grand Valley State University *B, M, T*
Henry Ford Community College *A*
Marygrove College *B, M, T*
Michigan State University *B, M, D*
Northern Michigan University *B, T*
Oakland University *M*
Saginaw Valley State
   University *B, M, T*
Spring Arbor University *B, M*
University of Detroit Mercy *B, M*
University of Michigan
   Flint *M*
Wayne State University *B, M, D, T*
Western Michigan University *M, D, T*

Minnesota

Bemidji State University *M*
Bethel University *M*
Capella University *M*
Minnesota State University
   Mankato *M*
   Moorhead *B, M*
Minnesota West Community and
   Technical College *A*
Normandale Community College *A*
Ridgewater College *A*
Saint Cloud State University *B, M, T*
St. Mary's University of Minnesota *M*
Southwest Minnesota State
   University *B, M*
University of Minnesota
   Duluth *M*
   Twin Cities *M, T*
University of St. Thomas *M*
Winona State University *B, M, T*

Mississippi

Delta State University *M*
East Mississippi Community
   College *A*
Itawamba Community College *A*
Jackson State University *B, M*
Millsaps College *T*
Mississippi College *B*
Mississippi Delta Community
   College *A*
Mississippi State University *B, M*
Mississippi Valley State University *M*
Northeast Mississippi Community
   College *A*
Northwest Mississippi Community
   College *A*
Tougaloo College *B, T*
University of Mississippi *B, T*
University of Southern
   Mississippi *B, M*

Missouri

Avila University *T*
Central Methodist University *B*
Evangel University *B, T*
Fontbonne University *B, T*
Lincoln University *B*
Missouri Southern State
   University *B, T*
Missouri State University *B, M*
Missouri Valley College *B*
Northwest Missouri State
   University *T*
Saint Louis University *B, T*
Southeast Missouri State
   University *B, M*
Truman State University *M*
University of Central
   Missouri *B, M, T*

University of Missouri
   Columbia *M, D*
   Kansas City *M*
   St. Louis *B, M*
Webster University *B, M*
William Woods University *B*

Montana

Montana State University
   Billings *A, B, M, T*
University of Great Falls *B*
University of Montana: Western *T*

Nebraska

College of Saint Mary *B, T*
Doane College *B*
Hastings College *B, M, T*
Nebraska Wesleyan University *B*
University of Nebraska
   Kearney *B, M, T*
   Omaha *B, M*
Wayne State College *B, M, T*
York College *B, T*

Nevada

University of Nevada
   Las Vegas *B, M, D, T*
   Reno *M*
University of Phoenix
   Las Vegas *B*
   Northern Nevada *M*

New Hampshire

Franklin Pierce University *M, T*
Keene State College *M, T*
NHTI-Concord's Community
   College *A*
New England College *B, M, T*
Rivier University *T*
University of New Hampshire *M*

New Jersey

Caldwell College *M, T*
Centenary College *M*
College of New Jersey *B, M, T*
Georgian Court University *M, T*
Gloucester County College *A*
Kean University *B, M, T*
Monmouth University *B, M*
Montclair State University *M*
New Jersey City University *B, M*
Richard Stockton College of New
   Jersey *M*
Rider University *M*
Rowan University *M*
Rutgers, The State University of New
   Jersey
   New Brunswick/Piscataway
     Campus *M, D, T*
Seton Hall University *B, M, T*
William Paterson University of New
   Jersey *B, M, T*

New Mexico

Eastern New Mexico University *B, M*
New Mexico Highlands
   University *B, M*
New Mexico State University *B, D*
San Juan College *A*
University of New Mexico *B, M, D, T*
University of Phoenix
   New Mexico *M*
University of the Southwest *B, M*
Western New Mexico
   University *B, M, T*

New York

Adelphi University *M, T*
Canisius College *M, T*
Cazenovia College *B*
City University of New York
   Brooklyn College *M, T*
   College of Staten Island *M*
   Hunter College *M, T*

Lehman College *M, T*
Medgar Evers College *B*
Queens College *M, T*
College of Mount St. Vincent *T*
College of New Rochelle *B, M, T*
College of Saint Rose *B, M, T*
D'Youville College *M*
Daemen College *B, M, T*
Dominican College of Blauvelt *B*
Dowling College *B, M*
Fordham University *M*
Hobart and William Smith Colleges *T*
Hofstra University *M, T*
Iona College *M*
Keuka College *B, T*
Le Moyne College *M, T*
Long Island University
  LIU Brooklyn *M, T*
  LIU Post *M, T*
Manhattan College *B, M, T*
Manhattanville College *M, T*
Medaille College *M, T*
Molloy College *B, T*
Mount Saint Mary College *M*
Nazareth College *B, M, T*
New York University *B, M, T*
Niagara University *B, M, T*
Pace University *B, M, T*
Pace University: Pleasantville/
  Briarcliff *M, T*
Roberts Wesleyan College *B, M*
SUNY
  College at Brockport *B, M, T*
  College at Buffalo *M*
  College at Cortland *B*
  College at Fredonia *T*
  College at Geneseo *T*
  College at New Paltz *M, T*
  College at Old Westbury *B, M, T*
  College at Oneonta *M*
  College at Oswego *M*
  College at Plattsburgh *B, M*
  College at Potsdam *M*
  University at Albany *M*
  University at Binghamton *M*
  University at Buffalo *D*
Sage Colleges *M*
Saint Bonaventure University *B, M*
St. John Fisher College *B, M, T*
St. John's University *B, M, T*
St. Joseph's College New York:
  Suffolk Campus *B, M*
St. Joseph's College, New York *B, M*
St. Thomas Aquinas College *B, M, T*
Syracuse University *D*
Touro College *B, M*
University of Rochester *M*
Utica College *B, M*

North Carolina

Appalachian State University *M*
East Carolina University *B*
Elizabeth City State University *B, T*
Elon University *B, M, T*
Fayetteville State University *M*
Forsyth Technical Community
  College *A*
Greensboro College *B, M, T*
High Point University *B*
Meredith College *M*
Methodist University *A, B, T*
North Carolina Agricultural and
  Technical State University *B*
North Carolina Central University *M*
North Carolina State University *M, T*
North Carolina Wesleyan College *B*
Pfeiffer University *B*
Stanly Community College *A*
University of North Carolina
  Charlotte *B, M, D*
  Greensboro *B, M, D*
  Pembroke *B*
  Wilmington *B*
Western Carolina University *B*

Western Piedmont Community
  College *A*
Winston-Salem State University *B*

North Dakota

Minot State University *M*
University of Jamestown *B*
University of Mary *M*
University of North Dakota *M*

Ohio

Antioch University
  Midwest *M*
Ashland University *B*
Bluffton University *B*
Bowling Green State
  University *B, M, T*
Capital University *B, T*
Cedarville University *B*
Central State University *B*
Cincinnati Christian University *B*
Cleveland State University *B, T*
College of Mount St. Joseph *B, T*
Kent State University *B, M, D*
Miami University
  Middletown *B*
  Oxford *B, M, T*
Mount Vernon Nazarene
  University *B, M, T*
Muskingum University *B, T*
Ohio Dominican University *B, M, T*
Ohio State University
  Columbus Campus *B*
Ohio University *B, M, D, T*
Otterbein University *B*
Shawnee State University *B*
Union Institute & University *B*
University of Akron *B, M*
University of Cincinnati *B, M, D*
University of Dayton *B, M, T*
University of Findlay *B, M, T*
University of Mount Union *B, T*
University of Rio Grande *B, T*
University of Toledo *M, T*
Urbana University *B*
Ursuline College *B, M, T*
Wilmington College *M*
Xavier University *B, M*
Youngstown State University *B, M*

Oklahoma

East Central University *B, M, T*
Langston University *B*
Northwestern Oklahoma State
  University *B*
Oklahoma Baptist University *B, T*
Oral Roberts University *B, T*
Southeastern Oklahoma State
  University *B*
Southwestern Oklahoma State
  University *B, M, T*
University of Central Oklahoma *B, M*
University of Oklahoma *B, M, D, T*

Oregon

Portland State University *M, D, T*
Southern Oregon University *T*
University of Oregon *M, D, T*
Western Oregon University *M, T*

Pennsylvania

Albright College *M, T*
Alvernia University *B*
Arcadia University *B, M, D, T*
Bloomsburg University of
  Pennsylvania *B, M, T*
Cabrini College *B, T*
California University of
  Pennsylvania *B, M*
Cedar Crest College *T*
Chatham University *M, T*
Chestnut Hill College *M, T*
Cheyney University of
  Pennsylvania *B, M, T*

Clarion University of
  Pennsylvania *B, M, T*
DeSales University *B, M, T*
Drexel University *B, M, D, T*
Duquesne University *M, T*
East Stroudsburg University of
  Pennsylvania *B, M, T*
Edinboro University of
  Pennsylvania *A, B, M*
Elizabethtown College *M*
Geneva College *B, M, T*
Grove City College *B, T*
Gwynedd Mercy University *M, T*
Holy Family University *B, M, T*
Indiana University of
  Pennsylvania *B, M, T*
King's College *B, T*
Kutztown University of
  Pennsylvania *B*
La Salle University *B, T*
Lebanon Valley College *B, T*
Lehigh Carbon Community College *A*
Lehigh University *M, D*
Lycoming College *T*
Mansfield University of
  Pennsylvania *B, M, T*
Marywood University *B, M*
Mercyhurst University *B, M, T*
Millersville University of
  Pennsylvania *B, M, T*
Misericordia University *B, T*
Neumann University *T*
Penn State
  Abington *B*
  Altoona *B*
  Beaver *B*
  Berks *B*
  Brandywine *B*
  DuBois *B*
  Erie, The Behrend College *B*
  Fayette, The Eberly Campus *B*
  Greater Allegheny *B*
  Harrisburg *B*
  Hazleton *B*
  Lehigh Valley *B*
  Mont Alto *B*
  New Kensington *B*
  Schuylkill *B*
  Shenango *B*
  University Park *B, M, D*
  Wilkes-Barre *B*
  Worthington Scranton *B*
  York *B*
Point Park University *M*
Robert Morris University *M*
Rosemont College *T*
St. Francis University *M*
Saint Joseph's University *M, T*
St. Vincent College *M*
Seton Hill University *M, T*
Shippensburg University of
  Pennsylvania *M, T*
Slippery Rock University of
  Pennsylvania *B, M, T*
Temple University *M*
University of Scranton *M*
Washington & Jefferson College *T*
Waynesburg University *B*
West Chester University of
  Pennsylvania *B, M, T*
Widener University *B, M, T*
Wilkes University *B, M, T*

Puerto Rico

American University of Puerto
  Rico *B, T*
Bayamon Central University *B, M*
Caribbean University *B, M*
Inter American University of Puerto
  Rico
  Arecibo Campus *B, M*
  Metropolitan Campus *B, M*
  Ponce Campus *B, T*
  San German Campus *B, M*

Pontifical Catholic University of
  Puerto Rico *B*
Turabo University *B, M*
Universidad Metropolitana *M*
Universidad del Este *B, M*
University of Puerto Rico
  Cayey University College *B*
  Rio Piedras *M*

Rhode Island

Community College of Rhode
  Island *A*
Providence College *B, M*
Rhode Island College *B, M*
Salve Regina University *B*
University of Rhode Island *M*

South Carolina

Anderson University *B, T*
Bob Jones University *B*
Clemson University *B, M*
Coastal Carolina University *B, T*
College of Charleston *B, M, T*
Columbia College *B, T*
Converse College *B, M, T*
Erskine College *B, T*
Francis Marion University *M*
Furman University *M, T*
Lander University *B, T*
South Carolina State
  University *B, M, T*
Southern Wesleyan University *B, T*
University of South Carolina
  Aiken *B, T*
  Columbia *M, D*
  Upstate *B, T*
Winthrop University *B, M, T*

South Dakota

Augustana College *B, T*
Black Hills State University *B*
Dakota Wesleyan University *B, T*
Mount Marty College *B*
Northern State University *B, T*
Sinte Gleska University *A, B*
University of South Dakota *B, M*

Tennessee

Austin Peay State University *B*
Bethel University *B, M, T*
Carson-Newman University *B, T*
Christian Brothers University *B*
Cumberland University *B*
East Tennessee State
  University *B, M, T*
Fisk University *B*
Freed-Hardeman University *B, M, T*
LeMoyne-Owen College *B*
Lee University *B*
Middle Tennessee State
  University *B, M, T*
Southern Adventist University *M*
Tennessee State University *B, M, T*
Tennessee Technological
  University *B, M, T*
Tennessee Wesleyan College *B, T*
Trevecca Nazarene University *B, T*
Tusculum College *B, T*
Union University *B, T*
University of Memphis *B*
University of Tennessee
  Chattanooga *B, M, T*
  Knoxville *B*
  Martin *B*
Vanderbilt University *B, M, D, T*

Texas

Abilene Christian University *T*
Angelo State University *M*
Baylor University *B, T*
Dallas Baptist University *M*
Del Mar College *A*
El Paso Community College *A*
Houston Baptist University *M*

Jarvis Christian College *B, T*
Lamar University *B, M, T*
Laredo Community College *A*
Lubbock Christian University *B, M, T*
Midwestern State University *M*
Our Lady of the Lake University of
San Antonio *B, M*
Prairie View A&M University *M*
St. Edward's University *B, T*
Sam Houston State University *M, T*
Southwestern University *T*
Stephen F. Austin State
University *M, T*
Sul Ross State University *M*
Texas A&M International
University *B, M, T*
Texas A&M University *M*
Texas A&M University
Commerce *M, T*
Corpus Christi *M, T*
Kingsville *M*
Texarkana *M, T*
Texas Christian University *M*
Texas State University *M, T*
Texas Tech University *M, D*
Texas Woman's University *M, D, T*
Tyler Junior College *A*
University of Houston *M*
University of Houston
Victoria *M*
University of Mary Hardin-Baylor *B*
University of North Texas *M, D*
University of Phoenix
San Antonio *M*
University of St. Thomas *M*
University of Texas
Austin *M, D*
Brownsville *M*
El Paso *M*
Pan American *M*
Permian Basin *M*
San Antonio *M, T*
Tyler *M*
West Texas A&M University *M, T*

Utah

Brigham Young University *B, M*
Snow College *A*
University of Phoenix
Utah *M*
University of Utah *B, M, D*
Utah State University *B, M, D*
Weber State University *B*
Western Governors
University *B, M, T*
Westminster College *B, T*

Vermont

Castleton State College *M, T*
College of St. Joseph in
Vermont *M, T*
Johnson State College *M*
Lyndon State College *B, M*
Saint Michael's College *M, T*
University of Vermont *M, T*

Virginia

Averett University *M*
College of William and Mary *M*
Eastern Mennonite University *T*
George Mason University *M*
Hampton University *B, M*
James Madison University *M, T*
Longwood University *T*
Lynchburg College *M*
Marymount University *B, M*
Norfolk State University *B*
Old Dominion University *M*
Radford University *M*
Randolph-Macon College *T*
Regent University *M*
University of Virginia *M, D*
University of Virginia's College at
Wise *T*

Virginia Commonwealth
University *M*
Virginia Intermont College *T*

Washington

Central Washington
University *B, M, T*
City University of Seattle *B, M, T*
Eastern Washington University *B*
Gonzaga University *B, M, T*
Heritage University *B, M*
Pacific Lutheran University *M*
Saint Martin's University *B, T*
Seattle Pacific University *B*
Seattle University *M*
Shoreline Community College *A*
University of Washington *M, D*
Walla Walla University *B, M*
Washington State
University *B, M, D, T*
Western Washington University *B, M*
Whitworth University *B, M, T*

West Virginia

Bethany College *B*
Glenville State College *B*
Marshall University *M*
University of Charleston *B*
West Liberty University *B*
West Virginia State University *B*
West Virginia University *M, D*
West Virginia Wesleyan College *B, M*
Wheeling Jesuit University *B*

Wisconsin

Cardinal Stritch University *B, M*
Carthage College *B, T*
Concordia University Wisconsin *M*
Silver Lake College of the Holy
Family *M*
University of Wisconsin
Eau Claire *B, M*
La Crosse *M*
Madison *B, M, D*
Milwaukee *B, M, T*
Oshkosh *B, M, T*
Stout *B*
Superior *M*
Whitewater *B, M, T*

Wyoming

University of Wyoming *B*

Special education administration

Alaska

University of Alaska
Anchorage *M*

Arizona

Northcentral University *M, D*

California

California Coast University *M*

District of Columbia

Gallaudet University *D*

Georgia

Georgia Southern University *M*
Kennesaw State University *M, D*

Illinois

University of Illinois
Urbana-Champaign *M, D, T*

Massachusetts

Cambridge College *T*
Simmons College *M, D*
Westfield State University *M*

Michigan

Northern Michigan University *M*
Western Michigan University *M, T*

Minnesota

Capella University *D*
Hamline University *T*
Walden University *M*

Missouri

Missouri Baptist University *T*
University of Missouri
Columbia *M, D*

New York

Hofstra University *T*
Le Moyne College *M*

Pennsylvania

Drexel University *M, T*
Marywood University *M*

Texas

Our Lady of the Lake University of
San Antonio *M*
St. Mary's University *M*
University of St. Thomas *M*

Virginia

College of William and Mary *D*
Regent University *M*

Special products marketing

Illinois

Illinois Institute of Art
Schaumburg *B*

Iowa

Northeast Iowa Community
College *C*

Minnesota

Century College *C*
Northland Community & Technical
College *C, A*
Rochester Community and Technical
College *C, A*

Missouri

State Fair Community College *A*

New Jersey

Bergen Community College *A*

New York

Fashion Institute of Technology *B*
Rochester Institute of Technology *B*

Oklahoma

Oklahoma State University
Oklahoma City *C*

Pennsylvania

Saint Joseph's University *B, M*

Texas

Stephen F. Austin State University *B*
University of North Texas *B*

Washington

Central Washington University *B*

Speech-language pathology assistant

Arizona

Estrella Mountain Community
College *C, A*

California

Grossmont College *A*
La Sierra University *C*
Orange Coast College *A*
Pasadena City College *A*

Illinois

College of DuPage *A*
Trinity Christian College *B*

Massachusetts

Elms College *A, B*

Minnesota

Alexandria Technical and Community
College *A*

North Carolina

Caldwell Community College and
Technical Institute *A*
Fayetteville Technical Community
College *A*

North Dakota

Williston State College *A*

Oregon

Chemeketa Community College *C, A*

Puerto Rico

Caribbean University *B*

South Dakota

Mitchell Technical Institute *A*

Speech pathology

Alabama

Alabama Agricultural and Mechanical
University *M*
University of Alabama *M*
University of Montevallo *B, M, T*
University of South Alabama *M*

Arizona

Northern Arizona University *M*

Arkansas

Arkansas State University *M*
Harding University *B, T*

California

California State University
Chico *M*
Northridge *B*
Loma Linda University *B, M*
Stanford University *D*
University of the Pacific *B, M*

Colorado

University of Northern
Colorado *B, M*

District of Columbia

University of the District of
Columbia *B, M*

Florida

Nova Southeastern University *M, D*

Georgia

University of West Georgia *B, M*
Valdosta State University *B, M*

Idaho

Idaho State University *M*

Illinois

Elmhurst College *B, T*
Governors State University *B, M*
Northwestern University *M, D*

Rush University *M*
Saint Xavier University *B, M*

Indiana

Ball State University *M*
Purdue University *B, M, D*

Iowa

St. Ambrose University *M*
University of Northern Iowa *B, M*

Kansas

University of Kansas *M, D*
University of Kansas Medical
    Center *M, D*

Louisiana

Centenary College of Louisiana *B*
Southeastern Louisiana University *M*
Xavier University of Louisiana *B*

Maryland

Loyola University Maryland *B*
Towson University *B, M*
University of Maryland
    College Park *M*

Massachusetts

Boston University *M, D*
Elms College *B*
Emerson College *B, M*
Worcester State University *M*

Michigan

Calvin College *B, M*
Central Michigan University *M*
Eastern Michigan University *B*
Michigan State University *M, D*
Northern Michigan University *B*
Western Michigan University *M*

Minnesota

Minnesota State University
    Mankato *M*
    Moorhead *M*

Mississippi

Jackson State University *B*
Mississippi University for
    Women *B, M*

Missouri

Fontbonne University *B, M*
Rockhurst University *B, M*
University of Central Missouri *B*

Nebraska

University of Nebraska
    Kearney *B, M, T*
    Lincoln *B*

Nevada

Nevada State College *B*
University of Nevada
    Reno *B, D*

New Jersey

Montclair State University *T*
Richard Stockton College of New
    Jersey *M*
Seton Hall University *M*
William Paterson University of New
    Jersey *T*

New Mexico

University of New Mexico *M*

New York

City University of New York
    Brooklyn College *M*
    Hunter College *B, M*
    Queens College *M, T*
College of New Rochelle *M*

Elmira College *B*
Hofstra University *M*
Ithaca College *B, M, T*
Long Island University
    LIU Brooklyn *B, M*
Nazareth College *B, M, T*
Pace University: Pleasantville/
    Briarcliff *B*
SUNY
    College at Buffalo *B, M*
    College at Fredonia *M*
    College at Plattsburgh *M*
Touro College *M*

North Carolina

Appalachian State University *M*

Ohio

Case Western Reserve
    University *M, D*
Muskingum University *B*
Ohio University *M*

Oklahoma

Northeastern State University *M*
Oklahoma State University *B, M*
University of Central Oklahoma *B, M*
University of Oklahoma *M, D*
University of Science and Arts of
    Oklahoma *B*

Oregon

Portland State University *M*

Pennsylvania

Bloomsburg University of
    Pennsylvania *M, T*
Clarion University of
    Pennsylvania *B, M*
Duquesne University *M*
Edinboro University of
    Pennsylvania *M*
Geneva College *B*
La Salle University *B, M*
Misericordia University *M*
University of Pittsburgh *D*

Puerto Rico

Inter American University of Puerto
    Rico
    Ponce Campus *B*
Turabo University *B, M*
Universidad Metropolitana *B*
University of Puerto Rico
    Medical Sciences *M*

Rhode Island

University of Rhode Island *M*

South Carolina

Columbia College *B, T*
University of South Carolina
    Columbia *M*

Tennessee

University of Tennessee
    Knoxville *M*
Vanderbilt University *M*

Texas

Abilene Christian University *B, M*
Lamar University *M*
Our Lady of the Lake University of
    San Antonio *B*
Stephen F. Austin State
    University *M, T*
Texas A&M University
    Kingsville *B, M*
Texas Christian University *B, M*
Texas Woman's University *M*
University of North Texas *M*

Utah

Brigham Young University *M*
University of Utah *M*

Virginia

James Madison University *B, M, D, T*

Washington

Eastern Washington University *B, M*
University of Washington *M*
Western Washington University *M*

West Virginia

Marshall University *B*
West Virginia University *M*

Wisconsin

Marquette University *M*
University of Wisconsin
    Whitewater *B, T*

Speech teacher education

Arkansas

Arkansas Tech University *B*
Harding University *B, T*
Ouachita Baptist University *B, T*

California

California State University
    East Bay *B, M, T*
Pepperdine University *B*
San Diego Mesa College *A*
San Francisco State University *T*

Colorado

Adams State University *B, T*
Colorado State University *B, T*
Metropolitan State University of
    Denver *T*

Georgia

Darton College *A*

Idaho

Boise State University *B, T*

Illinois

Augustana College *B, T*
Bradley University *B*
North Park University *T*
University of Illinois
    Urbana-Champaign *M*

Indiana

Indiana University
    Bloomington *M, D, T*
Purdue University Fort Wayne *B, T*
Purdue University
    Indianapolis *M, T*
University of Indianapolis *B, T*
Vincennes University *A*

Iowa

Buena Vista University *B, T*
Central College *T*
Dordt College *B*
Graceland University *T*
Loras College *T*
Northwestern College *T*
Simpson College *T*
University of Iowa *T*
University of Northern Iowa *B*
Upper Iowa University *T*
Wartburg College *T*

Kansas

Bethel College *T*
Coffeyville Community College *A*
Emporia State University *B, T*
Friends University *B*

McPherson College *B, T*
Southwestern College *B*

Louisiana

McNeese State University *T*
Southeastern Louisiana University *B*
University of Louisiana at Lafayette *B*

Massachusetts

Emerson College *B, M*

Michigan

Central Michigan University *B*
University of Michigan
    Flint *B, T*

Minnesota

Augsburg College *T*
Minnesota State University
    Mankato *B, M*
Saint Cloud State University *B, T*
Southwest Minnesota State
    University *B, T*
University of Minnesota
    Morris *T*

Mississippi

Itawamba Community College *A*
Mississippi Delta Community
    College *A*
William Carey University *B*

Missouri

Avila University *T*
Culver-Stockton College *B, T*
Missouri Baptist University *T*
Missouri Southern State
    University *B, T*
Southwest Baptist University *T*
University of Central Missouri *B, M*
William Jewell College *B, T*
William Woods University *T*

Montana

Carroll College *B*
Montana State University
    Billings *T*

Nebraska

Concordia University *B, T*
Creighton University *T*
Hastings College *B, T*
Midland University *B, T*
Nebraska Wesleyan University *T*
University of Nebraska
    Kearney *B, M, T*
Wayne State College *B, T*
York College *B, T*

New York

Elmira College *B, T*
Nazareth College *B, M, T*
SUNY
    College at Fredonia *M, T*

North Carolina

North Carolina Agricultural and
    Technical State University *B, T*

North Dakota

Dickinson State University *B, T*

Ohio

Bowling Green State University *B, M*
Capital University *T*
Defiance College *B, T*
Hiram College *T*
University of Findlay *B, M, T*
University of Rio Grande *B, T*
Youngstown State University *B, M*

Oklahoma

East Central University *B, T*
Eastern Oklahoma State College *A*
Oklahoma Baptist University *B, T*
Oklahoma Christian University *B, T*
Southern Nazarene University *B*
Southwestern Oklahoma State
    University *T*

Oregon

Portland State University *T*
Southern Oregon University *T*

Pennsylvania

St. Francis University *B, T*

South Dakota

Augustana College *B, T*
Northern State University *B, T*
University of Sioux Falls *T*
University of South Dakota *B, M, T*

Tennessee

Belmont University *T*
Tennessee Technological University *T*
Tennessee Temple University *B*
Trevecca Nazarene University *B, T*

Texas

Austin College *M*
East Texas Baptist University *B*
Hardin-Simmons University *B, T*
Howard Payne University *B*
Lamar University *T*
Laredo Community College *A*
Lubbock Christian University *B*
Sam Houston State University *M, T*
Texas A&M University
    Commerce *T*
    Kingsville *T*
University of Mary Hardin-Baylor *B, T*
University of Texas
    Arlington *T*
West Texas A&M University *T*

Utah

Southern Utah University *B*

Vermont

Johnson State College *M*

Virginia

University of Virginia's College at
    Wise *T*

Washington

Western Washington University *B*
Whitworth University *B, T*

West Virginia

Concord University *B, T*

Wisconsin

Northland International University *B*
University of Wisconsin
    Green Bay *T*
    Platteville *B, T*
    River Falls *T*
    Whitewater *B, T*

Sports and fitness administration

Alabama

Athens State University *B*
Columbia Southern University *C*
Faulkner University *B*
Huntingdon College *B*
Samford University *B*
Shelton State Community College *C*
Troy University *B, M*

United States Sports
    Academy *B, M, D*

Arizona

Arizona Western College *C*
Grand Canyon University *B*

Arkansas

Arkansas State University *B, M*
Ecclesia College *B*
Harding University *B*
Henderson State University *M*
John Brown University *B*

California

California University of Management
    and Sciences *A, B, M*
Concordia University Irvine *M*
Feather River College *C*
Fresno Pacific University *B*
Holy Names University *B*
Mendocino College *A*
National University *C, A*
Orange Coast College *C, A*
Pepperdine University *B*
St. Mary's College of California *B*
Solano Community College *A*
Southwestern College *C*
University of San Francisco *M*

Colorado

Colorado Mesa University *B*
Johnson & Wales University
    Denver *B*

Connecticut

Albertus Magnus College *B*
Eastern Connecticut State
    University *B*
Gateway Community College *C, A*
Mitchell College *B*
Post University *B*
Sacred Heart University *B*
University of Connecticut *B*
University of New Haven *M*

Delaware

Delaware State University *B, M*
University of Delaware *B*
Wesley College *B*

District of Columbia

Georgetown University *M*

Florida

Barry University *B, M*
Clearwater Christian College *B*
Flagler College *B*
Florida Agricultural and Mechanical
    University *M*
Florida Institute of Technology *B*
Florida State University *B, M, D*
Jacksonville University *B*
Johnson & Wales University
    North Miami *B*
Lynn University *B*
Northwood University
    Florida *B*
Nova Southeastern University *B*
Saint Leo University *B*
Saint Thomas University *B, M*
Southeastern University *B*
Stetson University *B*
University of Central Florida *M*
University of Florida *B, M*
University of Miami *B, M*
University of North Florida *B*
University of Tampa *B*
Warner University *A, B*

Georgia

Brewton-Parker College *B*
Clayton State University *B*
Darton College *A*

Emmanuel College *B*
Georgia Southern University *B, M*
Georgia State University *M*
Kennesaw State University *B*
Reinhardt University *B*
Shorter University *B*
Toccoa Falls College *B*
University of Georgia *B*

Idaho

College of Western Idaho *A*
Northwest Nazarene University *B*

Illinois

Concordia University
    Chicago *B, M, D*
Elmhurst College *B*
Greenville College *B*
Illinois Valley Community College *A*
Judson University *C, B*
Lewis University *B*
Lincoln College *B*
MacMurray College *B*
McKendree University *B*
Millikin University *B*
North Central College *B*
Northern Illinois University *M*
Northwestern University *M*
Olivet Nazarene University *B*
Quincy University *B*
South Suburban College of Cook
    County *C, A*
Southern Illinois University
    Carbondale *B*
University of Illinois
    Urbana-Champaign *B, M, D*
University of St. Francis *C*
Western Illinois University *M*

Indiana

Bethel College *B*
Grace College *B*
Huntington University *B*
Indiana Institute of Technology *B*
Indiana State University *M*
Indiana Wesleyan University *B*
Manchester University *B*
Marian University *B*
Saint Joseph's College *B*
Taylor University *B*
Trine University *B*
University of Evansville *B*
University of Indianapolis *B*
University of Southern Indiana *B*
Valparaiso University *B, M*
Vincennes University *A*

Iowa

AIB College of Business *A, B*
Ashford University *B*
Briar Cliff University *B*
Buena Vista University *B*
Clarke University *B*
Des Moines Area Community
    College *A*
Dordt College *B*
Graceland University *B*
Grand View University *B*
North Iowa Area Community
    College *A*
Northwestern College *B*
St. Ambrose University *B*
Simpson College *B*
University of Iowa *B, M, D*
Waldorf College *B*
Wartburg College *B*
William Penn University *B*

Kansas

Baker University *B*
Barton County Community College *A*
Bethany College *B*
Central Christian College of
    Kansas *A, B*

Cowley County Community
    College *A*
Friends University *B*
Hutchinson Community College *A*
Kansas Wesleyan University *B*
MidAmerica Nazarene University *B*
Southwestern College *B*
Sterling College *B*
Tabor College *B*
University of Kansas *B*
University of St. Mary *B*
Washburn University *B*
Wichita State University *B, M*
Wright Career College
    Overland Park *A*

Kentucky

Alice Lloyd College *B*
Asbury University *B*
Kentucky Wesleyan College *B*
Midway College *B*
Northern Kentucky University *C, B*
St. Catharine College *B*
Thomas More College *B*
Union College *B*
University of Louisville *B, M*
University of Pikeville *M*
University of the Cumberlands *B*

Louisiana

Grambling State University *M*
Louisiana State University and
    Agricultural and Mechanical
    College *B*
Southeastern Louisiana University *B*

Maine

Husson University *B*
Saint Joseph's College of Maine *B*
Thomas College *B*
University of New England *B*

Maryland

Cecil College *C*
Coppin State University *B*
Frostburg State University *B*
Garrett College *C, A*
Howard Community College *A*
Mount St. Mary's University *B*
Towson University *B*
Washington Adventist University *B*

Massachusetts

American International College *B*
Becker College *B*
Dean College *A*
Eastern Nazarene College *B*
Elms College *B*
Endicott College *B*
Fitchburg State University *B*
Holyoke Community College *C, A*
Lasell College *B, M*
Merrimack College *B*
Mount Ida College *B*
Nichols College *B*
Northern Essex Community
    College *A*
Roxbury Community College *C*
Salem State University *B*
Springfield College *B, M*
Springfield Technical Community
    College *A*
University of Massachusetts
    Amherst *C, B, M*
Western New England University *B*

Michigan

Aquinas College *B*
Central Michigan University *B, M*
Cornerstone University *B*
Davenport University *B*
Eastern Michigan University *M*
Madonna University *B*
Michigan Technological University *B*

Northern Michigan University *B*
Olivet College *B*
Siena Heights University *B*
University of Michigan *B*
Wayne State University *M*
Western Michigan University *M*

Minnesota

Bemidji State University *B*
Century College *C*
Concordia University St. Paul *B, M*
Crown College *B*
Dakota County Technical College *C*
Hamline University *B*
Minnesota State University
   Mankato *B, M, T*
North Central University *B*
Rochester Community and Technical
   College *A*
Saint Cloud State University *M*
University of Minnesota
   Crookston *B*
   Twin Cities *C, B, M*
Vermilion Community College *A*

Mississippi

Alcorn State University *B*
Belhaven University *B, M*
Coahoma Community College *A*
Jackson State University *M*
Mississippi College *B, M*
University of Southern
   Mississippi *B, M*

Missouri

Columbia College *B*
Culver-Stockton College *B*
Fontbonne University *B*
Lindenwood University *B, M*
Maryville University of Saint Louis *B*
Missouri Baptist University *B, M*
Southeast Missouri State University *B*
Southwest Baptist University *B*
Westminster College *B*
William Woods University *B*

Montana

Carroll College *B*
Montana State University *B*
Montana State University
   Billings *B, M*
Rocky Mountain College *B*

Nebraska

Concordia University *B*
Hastings College *B*
Nebraska Wesleyan University *B*
Union College *B*
University of Nebraska
   Kearney *B*
Wayne State College *B, M*

Nevada

University of Nevada
   Las Vegas *M*

New Hampshire

Colby-Sawyer College *B*
Daniel Webster College *B*
Franklin Pierce University *M*
Mount Washington College *A*
NHTI-Concord's Community
   College *A*
New England College *B*
Plymouth State University *B*
Southern New Hampshire
   University *B, M*

New Jersey

Fairleigh Dickinson University
   Metropolitan Campus *M*
Ocean County College *C*
Rowan University *B*

Seton Hall University *B*
Union County College *C, A*

New Mexico

New Mexico Highlands
   University *B, M*
University of the Southwest *B, M*

New York

Adelphi University *B, M*
Canisius College *B, M*
Cazenovia College *B*
Dowling College *B, M*
Finger Lakes Community College *A*
Hilbert College *B*
Ithaca College *B*
Medaille College *B*
Niagara County Community
   College *A*
SUNY
   College at Brockport *B*
   College at Cortland *B, M*
   College at Fredonia *B*
   College of Agriculture and
     Technology at Morrisville *A*
   College of Technology at Alfred *A*
   Farmingdale State College *A*
Saint Bonaventure University *B*
St. John Fisher College *B*
St. John's University *B, M*
Syracuse University *B*
Tompkins Cortland Community
   College *A*

North Carolina

Barton College *B*
Belmont Abbey College *B*
Campbell University *B*
Catawba College *B*
Chowan University *B*
East Carolina University *B*
Elon University *B*
Gardner-Webb University *B*
Greensboro College *C, B*
Guilford College *B*
Johnson & Wales University
   Charlotte *B*
Johnson C. Smith University *B*
Lenoir-Rhyne University *B*
Livingstone College *B*
Methodist University *B*
North Carolina Agricultural and
   Technical State University *B*
North Carolina State University *B*
Pfeiffer University *B*
Queens University of Charlotte *B*
St. Augustine's University *B*
University of Mount Olive *B*
Western Carolina University *B, M*
Wingate University *B*
Winston-Salem State University *B*

North Dakota

Mayville State University *B*
Minot State University *B*
North Dakota State University *B*
University of Jamestown *B*
University of Mary *B*

Ohio

Ashland University *B*
Baldwin Wallace University *B*
Bluffton University *B*
Bowling Green State University *B*
Cedarville University *B*
Cleveland State University *M*
College of Mount St. Joseph *B*
Columbus State Community
   College *C, A*
Defiance College *B*
Heidelberg University *B*
Hocking College *A*
Kent State University *B*
Lorain County Community College *A*

Malone University *B*
Marietta College *B*
Miami University
   Oxford *B, M*
Mount Vernon Nazarene
   University *A, B*
Ohio Dominican University *B*
Ohio Northern University *B*
Ohio State University
   Columbus Campus *B*
Ohio University *M*
Otterbein University *B, M*
Shawnee State University *B*
Tiffin University *B, M*
University of Akron *C, B, M*
University of Cincinnati *C, B*
University of Dayton *B*
University of Findlay *B*
University of Mount Union *B*
University of Rio Grande *B*
Urbana University *B*
Wilmington College *B*
Xavier University *B, M*
Youngstown State University *B*

Oklahoma

Bacone College *B*
Northeastern Oklahoma Agricultural
   and Mechanical College *A*
Oklahoma Baptist University *B*
Rogers State University *B*
Southeastern Oklahoma State
   University *M*
Southwestern Christian University *B*
Tulsa Community College *A*

Oregon

Concordia University *B*
Corban University *B*
Lane Community College *C, A*
Southern Oregon University *B*
Warner Pacific College *B*

Pennsylvania

Alvernia University *B*
Bucks County Community College *A*
Butler County Community College *A*
California University of
   Pennsylvania *B, M*
DeSales University *B*
Drexel University *B, M*
Gannon University *B*
Geneva College *B*
Gettysburg College *B*
Harcum College *A*
Holy Family University *B*
Keystone College *A, B*
Lehigh Carbon Community College *A*
Lock Haven University of
   Pennsylvania *B*
Messiah College *B*
Millersville University of
   Pennsylvania *M*
Misericordia University *B*
Neumann University *B, M*
Northampton Community College *A*
Robert Morris University *B*
Seton Hill University *B*
Slippery Rock University of
   Pennsylvania *B*
Temple University *B, M*
University of Pittsburgh
   Bradford *B*
University of the Sciences *B*
Valley Forge Christian College *B*
Waynesburg University *B*
Wilson College *B*
York College of Pennsylvania *B*

Puerto Rico

Turabo University *B*
Universidad Metropolitana *M*

Rhode Island

Johnson & Wales University
   Providence *B*

South Carolina

Claflin University *B*
Coastal Carolina University *B*
Coker College *B, M*
Erskine College *B*
Limestone College *B*
Newberry College *B*
North Greenville University *B*
Southern Wesleyan University *B*
University of South Carolina
   Columbia *B*
Winthrop University *B, M*

South Dakota

Augustana College *B, M*
Black Hills State University *B*
Dakota Wesleyan University *B*
Northern State University *B*

Tennessee

Belmont University *M*
Cumberland University *B*
East Tennessee State University *B*
Martin Methodist College *B*
Southern Adventist University *B*
Tennessee Wesleyan College *B*
Trevecca Nazarene University *B*
Tusculum College *B*
Union University *B*
University of Memphis *B*
University of Tennessee
   Knoxville *B, M*

Texas

Abilene Christian University *B*
Hardin-Simmons University *M*
Howard Payne University *B*
LeTourneau University *B*
Lubbock Christian University *B*
Midwestern State University *M*
Rice University *B*
Schreiner University *B*
Texas A&M University *B, M*
Texas A&M University
   Commerce *B*
Texas Lutheran University *B*
Texas Southern University *B*
Texas State University *B*
Texas Wesleyan University *B*
University of Houston *B, M*
University of Mary Hardin-Baylor *B*
University of Texas
   Austin *B*
University of the Incarnate
   Word *B, M*
Wayland Baptist University *B*

Utah

Salt Lake Community College *A*

Vermont

Castleton State College *B*
College of St. Joseph in Vermont *B*
Johnson State College *B*
Lyndon State College *B*
Norwich University *B*
Southern Vermont College *B*

Virginia

Averett University *B*
Bluefield College *B*
Eastern Mennonite University *B*
Emory & Henry College *B*
Ferrum College *B*
George Mason University *M*
Hampton University *B*
Liberty University *B, M*
Lynchburg College *B*
Roanoke College *B*
Shenandoah University *B*

Virginia Commonwealth
University *M*
Virginia Intermont College *B*
Virginia State University *M*

Washington

Bellevue College *C*
Bellingham Technical College *C*
Clark College *A*
Gonzaga University *B, M*
Lake Washington Institute of
Technology *C, A*
Pierce College *C, A*
Seattle University *M*
Spokane Falls Community College *A*
Washington State University *B, M*

West Virginia

Alderson-Broaddus University *B*
American Public University System *M*
Bethany College *B*
Concord University *B*
Davis and Elkins College *B*
Potomac State College of West
Virginia University *A*
University of Charleston *B*

Wisconsin

Cardinal Stritch University *B*
Maranatha Baptist Bible College *B*
Marian University *B*
University of Wisconsin
Parkside *B*
Viterbo University *B*

Sports communications

Arizona

Central Arizona College *A*

Connecticut

Albertus Magnus College *B*

Illinois

Bradley University *B*
University of St. Francis *C*

Indiana

Indiana University
Purdue University Indianapolis *M*
University of Evansville *B*
Valparaiso University *M*

Iowa

Iowa Western Community College *A*

Kansas

Newman University *B*

Massachusetts

Lasell College *B*
Springfield College *B*

Michigan

Ferris State University *C*

Nebraska

University of Nebraska
Kearney *B*

New York

Ithaca College *B*

Ohio

Ashland University *B*
Bluffton University *B*

Oklahoma

Oklahoma State University *B*

South Carolina

Clemson University *B*

Sports studies

California

California State University
Fresno *B*
National University *B, M*

Indiana

Bethel College *B*
Huntington University *B*
Purdue University *B, M, D*

Kansas

Southwestern College *B*

Kentucky

Western Kentucky University *B*

Michigan

Central Michigan University *B*

Minnesota

Concordia University St. Paul *B*

Nebraska

Concordia University *B*

New Mexico

Luna Community College *A*

New York

Ithaca College *B*
Manhattanville College *B*

Rhode Island

Bryant University *B*

Tennessee

Trevecca Nazarene University *B*

Texas

Lubbock Christian University *B*
Texas Christian University *B*

Statistics

Alabama

Auburn University *M*

Arizona

Arizona State University *M, D*
Northern Arizona University *M*
University of Arizona *M, D*

Arkansas

University of Arkansas *M*

California

California Baptist University *B*
California Polytechnic State
University: San Luis Obispo *B*
California State University
East Bay *B, M*
Fullerton *B*
Long Beach *B*
Northridge *B*
San Diego State University *B, M*
San Francisco State University *B*
Stanford University *D*
University of California
Berkeley *B, M, D*
Davis *B, M, D*
Irvine *M, D*
Los Angeles *B, M, D*
Riverside *B, M, D*
San Diego *M*
Santa Barbara *B, M, D*
University of Southern California *M*

Colorado

Colorado School of Mines *B*
Colorado State University *M, D*

Connecticut

University of Connecticut *B, M, D*
Yale University *B, M, D*

Delaware

University of Delaware *B, M, D*

District of Columbia

American University *B, M*
George Washington
University *B, M, D*

Florida

Daytona State College *A*
Florida International University *B, M*
Florida State University *B, M, D*
University of Central Florida *B, M*
University of Florida *B, M, D*
University of Miami *M,*
University of North Florida *B*
University of South Florida *B, M*

Georgia

Georgia Institute of Technology *M*
Kennesaw State University *M*
University of Georgia *B, M, D*

Idaho

Idaho State University *B*
University of Idaho *M*

Illinois

DePaul University *M*
Loyola University Chicago *B, M*
Northern Illinois University *M*
Northwestern University *B, M, D*
University of Chicago *B, M, D*
University of Illinois
Chicago *B*
Urbana-Champaign *B, M, D*

Indiana

Ball State University *M*
Indiana University
Bloomington *B, M, D*
Purdue University Fort Wayne *B*
Purdue University *B, M, D*
Saint Mary's College *B*

Iowa

Cornell College *B*
Iowa State University *B, M, D*
University of Iowa *B, M, D*

Kansas

Independence Community College *A*
Kansas State University *B, M, D*

Kentucky

Bluegrass Community and Technical
College *B*
Eastern Kentucky University *B*
Northern Kentucky University *B*
University of Kentucky *M, D*

Louisiana

Louisiana State University and
Agricultural and Mechanical
College *M*
Tulane University *M*
Xavier University of Louisiana *B*

Maine

University of Southern Maine *M*

Maryland

Johns Hopkins University *B*
University of Maryland
Baltimore County *B, M, D*
College Park *M, D*

Massachusetts

Harvard College *B, M, D*
Mount Holyoke College *B*
Williams College *B*
Worcester Polytechnic Institute *M*

Michigan

Central Michigan University *B*
Eastern Michigan University *B, M*
Grand Valley State University *B*
Michigan State University *B, M, D*
Oakland University *B, M*
University of Michigan *B, M, D*
Wayne State University *M*
Western Michigan University *B, M, D*

Minnesota

Carleton College *B*
Minnesota State University
Mankato *M*
Saint Cloud State University *B, M*
University of Minnesota
Duluth *B*
Morris *B*
Twin Cities *B, M, D*
University of St. Thomas *B*
Winona State University *B*

Mississippi

Mississippi State University *M*

Missouri

Missouri University of Science and
Technology *D*
Northwest Missouri State
University *B*
University of Missouri
Columbia *M, D*
Kansas City *B, M, D*
Washington University in St.
Louis *B, M*

Montana

Montana State University *M, D*
Montana Tech of the University of
Montana *B*

Nebraska

University of Nebraska
Lincoln *M, D*

New Jersey

Montclair State University *M*
New Jersey Institute of
Technology *M*
Rutgers, The State University of New
Jersey
New Brunswick/Piscataway
Campus *B, M, D*
Stevens Institute of Technology *M*

New Mexico

New Mexico State University *M*
University of New Mexico *B, M, D*

New York

Barnard College *B*
City University of New York
Baruch College *B, M*
Hunter College *B, M*
Columbia University *B*
Columbia University
School of General Studies *B*
Cornell University *B, M, D*
New York University *M*
Rochester Institute of
Technology *B, M*
SUNY
College at Oneonta *B*
St. John Fisher College *B*
Syracuse University *M*
University of Rochester *B, M, D*

North Carolina

Duke University *B*
Elon University *B*
North Carolina State
 University *B, M, D*
University of North Carolina
 Wilmington *B*

North Dakota

North Dakota State
 University *B, M, D*

Ohio

Bowling Green State
 University *B, M, D*
Case Western Reserve
 University *B, M*
Miami University
 Oxford *B, M*
Ohio Northern University *B*
Ohio State University
 Columbus Campus *M, D*
Ohio Wesleyan University *B*
University of Akron *B, M*
University of Cincinnati *M, D*
Wright State University *B, M*

Oklahoma

Oklahoma State University *B, M, D*
University of Central Oklahoma *B*

Oregon

Oregon State University *M, D*
Portland State University *M*

Pennsylvania

Carnegie Mellon University *B, M, D*
La Salle University *B*
Lehigh University *B, M*
Penn State
 Abington *B*
 Altoona *B*
 Beaver *B*
 Berks *B*
 Brandywine *B*
 DuBois *B*
 Fayette, The Eberly Campus *B*
 Greater Allegheny *B*
 Harrisburg *B*
 Hazleton *B*
 Lehigh Valley *B*
 Mont Alto *B*
 New Kensington *B*
 Schuylkill *B*
 Shenango *B*
 University Park *B, M, D*
 Wilkes-Barre *B*
 Worthington Scranton *B*
 York *B*
Slippery Rock University of
 Pennsylvania *B*
Temple University *M, D*
University of Pennsylvania *B, M, D*
University of Pittsburgh *B, M, D*
West Chester University of
 Pennsylvania *M*

Puerto Rico

University of Puerto Rico
 Mayaguez *M*

Rhode Island

Brown University *B*
Bryant University *B*
University of Rhode Island *M*

South Carolina

University of South Carolina
 Columbia *B, M, D*

South Dakota

South Dakota State University *M*

Tennessee

University of Tennessee
 Knoxville *B, M*

Texas

Baylor University *B, M, D*
North Lake College *A*
Rice University *B, M, D*
St. Philip's College *A*
Sam Houston State University *M*
Southern Methodist
 University *B, M, D*
Texas A&M University *M, D*
Texas Tech University *M*
University of Houston
 Clear Lake *M*
University of Texas
 Austin *M, D*
 El Paso *M*
 San Antonio *B, M*

Utah

Brigham Young University *B, M*
Snow College *A*
University of Utah *M*
Utah State University *B, M*

Vermont

Castleton State College *B*
University of Vermont *B, M*

Virginia

George Mason University *M*
University of Virginia *M, D*
Virginia Polytechnic Institute and
 State University *B, M, D*

Washington

University of Washington *M, D*
Washington State University *M*

West Virginia

West Virginia University *M*

Wisconsin

University of Wisconsin
 La Crosse *B*
 Madison *B, M, D*

Wyoming

Eastern Wyoming College *A*
University of Wyoming *B, M, D*

Sterile processing technology

Georgia

Columbus Technical College *C*

Minnesota

Minneapolis Community and
 Technical College *C*

New Jersey

Berkeley College *C*

North Carolina

Wilson Community College *C*

South Carolina

Greenville Technical College *C*

Wisconsin

Waukesha County Technical
 College *C*
Western Technical College *C*

Stringed instruments

California

Bethesda University of
 California *B, M*

Orange Coast College *C*
San Francisco Conservatory of
 Music *B, M*
University of Southern
 California *B, M, D*

Florida

Florida State University *B, M, D*
Stetson University *B*

Illinois

Illinois Wesleyan University *B*
Northwestern University *B, M, D*
Roosevelt University *B, M*

Indiana

Butler University *B, M*
Indiana University
 Bloomington *C*

Iowa

Cornell College *B*
Dordt College *B*
University of Iowa *B, M, D*

Kansas

University of Kansas *B, M, D*

Louisiana

Xavier University of Louisiana *B*

Maine

University of Southern Maine *B, M*

Massachusetts

Eastern Nazarene College *B*
New England Conservatory of
 Music *B, M, D*

Michigan

Hope College *B*
University of Michigan *M*

Minnesota

McNally Smith College of
 Music *A, B, M*
Saint Cloud State University *B*
University of Northwestern - St.
 Paul *B*

Missouri

University of Missouri
 Kansas City *B*

Nebraska

Hastings College *B*
University of Nebraska
 Omaha *B*

New York

Bard College *B*
Five Towns College *A, B, M, D*
Houghton College *B, M*
Juilliard School *B, M, D*
Mannes College The New School for
 Music *B, M*
Syracuse University *B, M*

North Carolina

East Carolina University *B*
Gardner-Webb University *B*
University of Mount Olive *B*

Ohio

Oberlin College *B, M*
University of Akron *B, M*
Youngstown State University *B, M*

Oklahoma

Oklahoma City University *B*
University of Central Oklahoma *B*

Oregon

Willamette University *B*

Pennsylvania

Carnegie Mellon University *M*

Puerto Rico

Conservatory of Music of Puerto
 Rico *B, M*

South Carolina

Converse College *B, M*
North Greenville University *B*

Tennessee

Vanderbilt University *B*

Texas

Hardin-Simmons University *B*
Texas Christian University *B, M, D*

Utah

Brigham Young University *B*

Vermont

Bennington College *B*

Washington

Central Washington University *B*
Cornish College of the Arts *B*
Seattle University *B*
University of Washington *B, M, D*

Structural biology

California

Stanford University *D*

New York

SUNY
 University at Buffalo *M, D*
 University at Stony Brook *D*
Yeshiva University *M, D*

Structural engineering

California

San Diego State University *D*
University of California
 San Diego *B, M, D*
University of Southern
 California *B, M*

Florida

University of Central Florida *B*

Illinois

Illinois Institute of Technology *M*
University of Illinois
 Urbana-Champaign *B, M, D*

Massachusetts

Bristol Community College *A*

Michigan

University of Michigan *M*
Western Michigan University *B*

Missouri

Washington University in St.
 Louis *M, D*

New Jersey

Stevens Institute of Technology *M*

New York

SUNY
 University at Buffalo *B*

Ohio

University of Akron *C*

Pennsylvania

Carnegie Mellon University *D*
Lehigh University *M, D*
Penn State
  Harrisburg *B*

Wisconsin

Milwaukee School of Engineering *M*

Substance abuse counseling

Alabama

Gadsden State Community College *A*
Wallace State Community College at
  Hanceville *C, A*

Alaska

University of Alaska
  Anchorage *A*

Arizona

Grand Canyon University *B, M*
Rio Salado College *C, A*
Tohono O'odham Community
  College *C*

Arkansas

Arkansas State University *M*
University of Arkansas
  Pine Bluff *M*
University of Central Arkansas *B*

California

Allan Hancock College *C*
Butte College *C, A*
California State University
  East Bay *C*
City College of San Francisco *C*
College of San Mateo *C, A*
College of the Redwoods *C*
College of the Siskiyous *C, A*
Cypress College *C*
Diablo Valley College *C*
East Los Angeles College *C*
Fresno City College *C, A*
Glendale Community College *C*
Hartnell College *C, A*
Imperial Valley College *C, A*
Lake Tahoe Community College *C, A*
Los Angeles Pierce College *C, A*
Mendocino College *C, A*
Merced College *C, A*
Modesto Junior College *C*
Mount San Jacinto College *C, A*
National University *C, A*
Oxnard College *C, A*
Palo Verde College *C*
Palomar College *C, A*
Saddleback College *C*
San Diego City College *C, A*
San Joaquin Delta College *C*
San Jose City College *C, A*
Santa Barbara City College *C, A*
Yuba College *C, A*

Connecticut

Gateway Community College *C, A*
Housatonic Community College *A*
Manchester Community College *A*
Middlesex Community College *A*
Naugatuck Valley Community
  College *C, A*
Tunxis Community College *A*

Delaware

Delaware Technical Community
  College
    Stanton/Wilmington Campus *C, A*
    Terry Campus *C, A*

Florida

Florida Keys Community College *C*
Florida State College at
  Jacksonville *A*
St. Petersburg College *C, A*

Georgia

Darton College *C*

Illinois

City Colleges of Chicago
  Harold Washington College *C, A*
  Kennedy-King College *C, A*
  Wilbur Wright College *C*
College of DuPage *C, A*
College of Lake County *C, A*
Danville Area Community College *C*
Elgin Community College *C*
Governors State University *M*
Illinois Central College *A*
Illinois Valley Community College *C*
Kaskaskia College *C*
Moraine Valley Community
  College *C, A*
National-Louis University *C, B, M*
Oakton Community College *C*
Rock Valley College *C*
Triton College *C, A*
University of St. Francis *B*
Waubonsee Community College *C*

Indiana

Indiana University
  Northwest *M*
  Purdue University Fort Wayne *B*
  South Bend *C*
Indiana Wesleyan University *A, B*
Martin University *B*
Vincennes University *C*

Iowa

Iowa Western Community College *A*
Southeastern Community College *A*
University of Iowa *M*

Kansas

Colby Community College *A*
Dodge City Community College *A*
Garden City Community College *A*
Kansas City Kansas Community
  College *C, A*
Neosho County Community
  College *C*
Washburn University *C*

Kentucky

Brescia University *A, B*

Louisiana

Northwestern State University *B*
Our Lady of Holy Cross College *A*
Southern University
  New Orleans *A, B*

Maine

Beal College *C*
University of Southern Maine *M*

Maryland

Anne Arundel Community
  College *C, A*
Chesapeake College *A*
Community College of Baltimore
  County *C, A*
Coppin State University *M*
Howard Community College *C, A*
Washington Adventist University *C*
Wor-Wic Community College *C, A*

Massachusetts

Holyoke Community College *C*
Middlesex Community College *C*

North Shore Community
  College *C, A*
Northern Essex Community
  College *C, A*
Springfield College *M*
University of Massachusetts
  Boston *C*

Michigan

Grand Rapids Community College *C*
Lake Superior State University *A*
Madonna University *C*
University of Detroit Mercy *B, M*
Washtenaw Community College *A*
Wayne County Community College *C*

Minnesota

Bemidji State University *C*
Capella University *M*
Century College *C, A*
Fond du Lac Tribal and Community
  College *C*
Mesabi Range Community and
  Technical College *C, A*
Metropolitan State University *B*
Minneapolis Community and
  Technical College *C, A*
North Central University *B*
Ridgewater College *A*
Rochester Community and Technical
  College *C*
Saint Cloud State University *B, M*
University of Minnesota
  Twin Cities *C*
Walden University *M*

Missouri

Missouri Valley College *B*

Montana

Blackfeet Community College *A*
Dawson Community College *A*
Flathead Valley Community
  College *A*
Fort Peck Community College *A*
Stone Child College *A*
University of Great Falls *A, B*

Nebraska

Bellevue University *M*
Little Priest Tribal College *A*
Vatterott College
  Spring Valley *A*

Nevada

Truckee Meadows Community
  College *C, A*

New Hampshire

Keene State College *B*
NHTI-Concord's Community
  College *A*

New Jersey

Burlington County College *C*
Georgian Court University *C*
Ocean County College *C*

New Mexico

Eastern New Mexico University:
  Roswell *C*
Northern New Mexico College *A*
Santa Fe Community College *C*
Western New Mexico University *B*

New York

Adirondack Community College *A*
Broome Community College *A*
City University of New York
  Kingsborough Community
    College *C*
  New York City College of
    Technology *C*

Corning Community College *A*
Dutchess Community College *C*
Erie Community College *A*
Finger Lakes Community College *A*
Genesee Community College *A*
Hudson Valley Community College *A*
Iona College *C*
Mercy College *M*
Metropolitan College of New York *C*
Mohawk Valley Community
  College *A*
Niagara County Community
  College *C*
Pace University *M*
Pace University: Pleasantville/
  Briarcliff *M*
St. Joseph's College, New York *C*
Suffolk County Community College *A*
Tompkins Cortland Community
  College *C, A*
Ulster County Community College *A*
Westchester Community College *C, A*

North Carolina

Central Piedmont Community
  College *C, A*
East Carolina University *M*
Guilford Technical Community
  College *C, A*
Roanoke-Chowan Community
  College *A*
Sandhills Community College *A*
South Piedmont Community
  College *C*
Southwestern Community
  College *C, A*
Wayne Community College *A*

North Dakota

Minot State University *B*
University of Mary *B, M*

Ohio

Ashland University *M*
Cincinnati State Technical and
  Community College *C*
Columbus State Community
  College *C, A*
North Central State College *C*
Sinclair Community College *C, A*
Southern State Community College *A*
Tiffin University *C, B*
University of Akron *C, A*
University of Cincinnati *C, B*
Wright State University *M*

Oklahoma

Northeastern State University *M*
Oklahoma State University
  Oklahoma City *A*
University of Central Oklahoma *B*

Oregon

Central Oregon Community
  College *C, A*
Chemeketa Community College *C, A*
Portland Community College *C, A*
Rogue Community College *C*
Southwestern Oregon Community
  College *A*

Pennsylvania

Alvernia University *B*
Carlow University *C, M*
Community College of Allegheny
  County *C*
Community College of
  Philadelphia *C*
Drexel University *B*
Misericordia University *C*
Montgomery County Community
  College *C, A*

Penn State
  Altoona *C*
  DuBois *C*
  Greater Allegheny *C*
St. Vincent College *C*
Seton Hill University *C*
Slippery Rock University of
  Pennsylvania *M*

Rhode Island

Community College of Rhode
  Island *A*
Rhode Island College *B*

South Dakota

Kilian Community College *C, A*
Oglala Lakota College *A*
Sisseton Wahpeton College *A*
University of South Dakota *B, M, D*

Tennessee

Southwest Tennessee Community
  College *C*

Texas

Alvin Community College *C*
Amarillo College *C, A*
Angelina College *C, A*
Austin Community College *C, A*
Central Texas College *C, A*
Del Mar College *A*
Eastfield College *C, A*
El Paso Community College *A*
Grayson College *C, A*
Houston Community College
  System *C*
Howard College *C, A*
Lamar State College at Port Arthur *A*
Lee College *C, A*
Lone Star College System *C, A*
McLennan Community College *C, A*
Midland College *C, A*
Odessa College *A*
St. Mary's University *M*
San Antonio College *C, A*
Tarrant County College *C*
Texarkana College *C, A*
Texas State Technical College
  West Texas *A*
Tyler Junior College *A*
Weatherford College *C*

Utah

Utah Valley University *C*

Vermont

College of St. Joseph in
  Vermont *B, M*
Community College of Vermont *C*

Virginia

J. Sargeant Reynolds Community
  College *C*
Northern Virginia Community
  College *C, A*
Virginia Commonwealth
  University *M*

Washington

Bellevue College *C*
Clark College *C, A*
Edmonds Community College *C, A*
Lower Columbia College *C, A*
Northwest Indian College *A*
Olympic College *A*
Peninsula College *C, A*
Pierce College *C, A*
Spokane Falls Community
  College *C, A*
Tacoma Community College *C*
Wenatchee Valley College *C, A*
Yakima Valley Community
  College *C, A*

West Virginia

Mountain State College *A*

Wisconsin

Chippewa Valley Technical College *A*
College of Menominee Nation *A*
Fox Valley Technical College *A*
Gateway Technical College *C*
Lac Courte Oreilles Ojibwa
  Community College *A*
Moraine Park Technical College *A*
Northcentral Technical College *C, A*

Wyoming

Casper College *C, A*

Surgical technology

Alabama

Bevill State Community College *C*
Calhoun Community College *C*
Community College of the Air
  Force *A*
Gadsden State Community College *C*
Southern Union State Community
  College *C*
Virginia College
  Birmingham *A*
  Mobile *C, A*
  Montgomery *A*

Arizona

Brookline College
  Tempe *C*
Brown Mackie College
  Tucson *A*
GateWay Community College *A*
Mohave Community College *C, A*

Arkansas

North Arkansas College *C, A*
South Arkansas Community
  College *A*
Southeast Arkansas College *C, A*
University of Arkansas
  Fort Smith *A*
  for Medical Sciences *C, A*

California

Carrington College California
  Citrus Heights *C, A*
  San Jose *C, A*
Concorde Career College
  North Hollywood *C*
  San Bernardino *C*
  San Diego *C*
Kaplan College
  Salida *A*
MiraCosta College *C, A*
Saddleback College *C, A*
San Joaquin Valley College *A*
Skyline College *C, A*
Southwestern College *C, A*

Colorado

Aims Community College *A*
Anthem College
  Aurora *A*
Concorde Career College
  Aurora *C*
Everest College
  Denver *A*

Connecticut

Manchester Community College *A*

Florida

Anthem College
  Orlando *C, A*
College of Central Florida *C*
Daytona State College *C*
Eastern Florida State College *C*

Everest University
  Brandon *A*
Florida State College at
  Jacksonville *A*
Gulf Coast State College *C, A*
Herzing University
  Winter Park *A*
Indian River State College *C*
Palm Beach State College *C*
Sanford-Brown Institute
  Jacksonville *C*
Santa Fe College *C*
Southwest Florida College *A*
Tallahassee Community College *A*
Virginia College
  Jacksonville *A*
  Pensacola *A*

Georgia

Albany Technical College *C*
Athens Technical College *C*
Atlanta Technical College *C, A*
Augusta Technical College *C*
Central Georgia Technical College *C*
Chattahoochee Technical College *C*
Columbus Technical College *C, A*
Georgia Piedmont Technical
  College *C*
Gwinnett Technical College *C*
Middle Georgia State College *A*
Savannah Technical College *C, A*
South Georgia State College *A*
Southwest Georgia Technical
  College *C, A*

Idaho

College of Southern Idaho *C*
College of Western Idaho *C, A*
Eastern Idaho Technical College *A*

Illinois

City Colleges of Chicago
  Malcolm X College *C, A*
College of DuPage *C, A*
College of Lake County *C, A*
Elgin Community College *C*
Illinois Central College *C, A*
John A. Logan College *C*
John Wood Community College *C*
Kaskaskia College *C*
Parkland College *C, A*
Prairie State College *C*
Rend Lake College *C*
Richland Community College *C, A*
Robert Morris University: Chicago *A*
Rock Valley College *C*
Southeastern Illinois College *C*
Triton College *C*
Waubonsee Community College *C*

Indiana

Brown Mackie College
  Michigan City *A*
Harrison College
  Indianapolis *A*
Ivy Tech Community College
  Central Indiana *A*
  Columbus *A*
  East Central *A*
  Kokomo *A*
  Lafayette *A*
  Northwest *A*
  Southwest *A*
  Wabash Valley *A*
National College
  Indianapolis *A*
University of St. Francis *A*
Vincennes University *C, A*

Iowa

Iowa Lakes Community College *C*
Iowa Western Community College *A*
Kirkwood Community College *C, A*
Marshalltown Community College *A*

Mercy College of Health
  Sciences *C, A*
Western Iowa Tech Community
  College *C, A*

Kansas

Hutchinson Community College *C, A*
Johnson County Community
  College *A*
Seward County Community
  College *C*
Washburn University *A*
Wichita Area Technical College *C, A*
Wright Career College
  Wichita *A*

Kentucky

Bluegrass Community and Technical
  College *C, A*
Jefferson Community and Technical
  College *C*
Madisonville Community College *C*
Maysville Community and Technical
  College *C*
Owensboro Community and
  Technical College *C, A*
St. Catharine College *A*
Somerset Community College *C*
Spencerian College *A*
West Kentucky Community and
  Technical College *C*

Louisiana

Bossier Parish Community College *C*
Delgado Community College *C*
Herzing University
  Kenner *A*
Our Lady of the Lake College *A*
Southern University
  Shreveport *A*
Virginia College
  Baton Rouge *A*

Maine

Southern Maine Community
  College *A*

Maryland

Anne Arundel Community College *A*
Baltimore City Community College *C*
Carroll Community College *A*
Chesapeake College *C*
Frederick Community College *C, A*
Howard Community College *C, A*
Montgomery College *A*

Massachusetts

Bristol Community College *C*
Bunker Hill Community College *C*
Massachusetts Bay Community
  College *C*
North Shore Community College *C*
Quincy College *C*
Quinsigamond Community College *C*
Springfield Technical Community
  College *A*

Michigan

Baker College
  Allen Park *A*
  Cadillac *A*
  Clinton Township *A*
  Flint *A*
  Jackson *A*
  Muskegon *A*
  Port Huron *A*
Delta College *C, A*
Grand Rapids Community College *A*
Henry Ford Community College *A*
Kalamazoo Valley Community
  College *C*
Kirtland Community College *C, A*
Lansing Community College *A*
Macomb Community College *C, A*

Northern Michigan University *A, B*
Oakland Community College *C, A*
Washtenaw Community College *C*
Wayne County Community College *A*

Minnesota

Anoka Technical College *C, A*
Herzing University
 Minneapolis *A*
Lake Superior College *C, A*
Minnesota West Community and
 Technical College *C*
Northland Community & Technical
 College *A*
Rasmussen College
 Brooklyn Park *A*
 Lake Elmo/Woodbury *A*
 Moorhead *A*
 St. Cloud *A*
Rochester Community and Technical
 College *A*
St. Cloud Technical and Community
 College *C, A*
St. Mary's University of Minnesota *C*

Mississippi

East Central Community College *C, A*
Hinds Community College *C, A*
Itawamba Community College *C, A*
Meridian Community College *C*

Missouri

Lincoln University *A*
Metropolitan Community College -
 Kansas City *C*
North Central Missouri College *A*
Ozarks Technical Community
 College *C, A*
St. Louis Community College *A*
Southeast Missouri Hospital College
 of Nursing and Health
 Sciences *C*
Three Rivers Community College *C*

Montana

Flathead Valley Community
 College *A*
Montana State University
 Billings *A*
 Great Falls College *A*
University of Montana *A*

Nebraska

Nebraska Methodist College of
 Nursing and Allied Health *A, B*
Northeast Community College *A*
Southeast Community College *C, A*

New Hampshire

Great Bay Community College *A*

New Jersey

Bergen Community College *C*
Berkeley College *A*

New Mexico

Central New Mexico Community
 College *C*
San Juan College *A*

New York

City University of New York
 Kingsborough Community
 College *A*
Mohawk Valley Community
 College *C*
Nassau Community College *A*
Niagara County Community
 College *A*
Onondaga Community College *C*
Trocaire College *A*

North Carolina

Blue Ridge Community College *C, A*
Cabarrus College of Health
 Sciences *C, A*
Carolinas College of Health
 Sciences *C*
Catawba Valley Community
 College *C*
Cleveland Community College *C*
Coastal Carolina Community
 College *C*
College of the Albemarle *C*
Durham Technical Community
 College *C*
Edgecombe Community College *C*
Fayetteville Technical Community
 College *A*
Guilford Technical Community
 College *C, A*
Isothermal Community College *C*
Lenoir Community College *C*
Miller-Motte College
 Cary *A*
 Wilmington *C, A*
Robeson Community College *A*
Rockingham Community College *C*
Sandhills Community College *C, A*
South College *C*
South Piedmont Community
 College *C*
Wake Technical Community
 College *C*
Wayne Community College *C*
Wilson Community College *C, A*

North Dakota

Bismarck State College *A*

Ohio

Brown Mackie College
 Akron *A*
 Cincinnati *A*
 Findlay *A*
 North Canton *A*
Central Ohio Technical College *C, A*
Cincinnati State Technical and
 Community College *C, A*
Columbus State Community
 College *C, A*
Cuyahoga Community College
 Metropolitan *A*
Lakeland Community College *A*
Lorain County Community
 College *C, A*
Miami-Jacobs Career College
 Columbus *A*
 Dayton *A*
 Sharonville *A*
National College
 Cincinnati *A*
Owens Community College
 Toledo *C, A*
Sinclair Community College *A*
University of Akron *C, A*
University of Akron: Wayne
 College *A*
University of Cincinnati
 Clermont College *C, A*

Oklahoma

Northern Oklahoma College *A*

Oregon

Mt. Hood Community College *A*

Pennsylvania

Community College of Allegheny
 County *C, A*
Delaware County Community
 College *C, A*
Harrisburg Area Community
 College *C, A*
Lackawanna College *A*

Luzerne County Community
 College *A*
Montgomery County Community
 College *C, A*
Mount Aloysius College *A*
Pennsylvania College of Health
 Sciences *A*
Pennsylvania College of
 Technology *A*
Sanford-Brown Institute
 Pittsburgh *A*
University of Pittsburgh
 Johnstown *A*

Rhode Island

New England Institute of
 Technology *A*

South Carolina

Aiken Technical College *C*
Central Carolina Technical College *A*
Florence-Darlington Technical
 College *C*
Greenville Technical College *C*
Horry-Georgetown Technical
 College *C*
Midlands Technical College *C*
Miller-Motte Technical College *A*
Piedmont Technical College *C*
Spartanburg Community College *C*
Technical College of the
 Lowcountry *C*
Tri-County Technical College *C*
Virginia College
 Charleston *A*
 Columbia *A*
 Greenville *A*
 Spartanburg *A*
York Technical College *C*

South Dakota

Presentation College *A*
Southeast Technical Institute *C*
Western Dakota Technical Institute *C*

Tennessee

Anthem Career College
 Nashville *C, A*
Miller-Motte Technical College
 Chattanooga *A*
 Clarksville *A*
Nashville State Community College *C*
National College of Business and
 Technology
 Knoxville *A*
 Memphis *A*
Northeast State Community
 College *C*
Virginia College
 School of Business and Health in
 Chattanooga *A*
 School of Business and Health in
 Knoxville *A*

Texas

Amarillo College *C, A*
Angelina College *C*
Austin Community College *C, A*
Cisco College *C*
Del Mar College *C, A*
El Centro College *C*
El Paso Community College *A*
Galveston College *C*
Houston Community College
 System *C*
Kilgore College *C, A*
Lamar State College at Port
 Arthur *C, A*
Odessa College *A*
Paris Junior College *C*
St. Philip's College *C*
San Jacinto College *C, A*
Sanford-Brown College
 Houston *C*

South Plains College *C*
Tarrant County College *C*
Temple College *C*
Texas State Technical College
 Harlingen *A*
Trinity Valley Community College *C*
Tyler Junior College *C, A*
Virginia College
 Austin *A*
Wharton County Junior College *C*

Utah

Dixie State College *C*
Salt Lake Community College *C*

Virginia

ECPI University *A*
John Tyler Community College *C*
Lord Fairfax Community College *C*
Miller-Motte Technical College
 Lynchburg *A*
Piedmont Virginia Community
 College *C*
Virginia College
 Richmond *A*

Washington

Bellingham Technical College *C, A*
Centralia College *C*
Clover Park Technical College *A*
Columbia Basin College *C, A*
Renton Technical College *C, A*
Seattle Central Community College *C*
Spokane Community College *A*
Yakima Valley Community
 College *C, A*

West Virginia

American National University
 Parkersburg *A*
Blue Ridge Community and Technical
 College *A*
Southern West Virginia Community
 and Technical College *A*
West Virginia Northern Community
 College *A*
West Virginia University at
 Parkersburg *C*

Wisconsin

Chippewa Valley Technical College *C*
Gateway Technical College *A*
Herzing University
 Madison *A*
Madison Area Technical College *C*
Mid-State Technical College *C*
Milwaukee Area Technical College *A*
Nicolet Area Technical College *A*
Northcentral Technical College *C*
Northeast Wisconsin Technical
 College *C*
Waukesha County Technical
 College *A*
Western Technical College *A*

Wyoming

Laramie County Community
 College *A*

Surveying engineering

California

Cuyamaca College *A*

Florida

Florida Atlantic University *B*

Indiana

Purdue University *B*
Vincennes University *A*

Iowa
Des Moines Area Community
  College *A*
Kirkwood Community College *C, A*

Maine
University of Maine *B, M, D*

Massachusetts
Bristol Community College *C*

Michigan
Baker College
  Flint *A*
Ferris State University *B*
Michigan Technological University *B*

Nevada
Great Basin College *B*

New Mexico
Central New Mexico Community
  College *C, A*

New York
Paul Smith's College *A*

North Carolina
North Carolina Agricultural and
  Technical State University *B*
Southwestern Community College *A*

North Dakota
Dakota College at Bottineau *A*

Pennsylvania
Penn State
  Wilkes-Barre *B*

Rhode Island
Community College of Rhode
  Island *A*

Texas
Texas A&M University
  Corpus Christi *M*
University of Houston *M*

Virginia
John Tyler Community College *C*
Virginia Western Community
  College *C, A*

Wyoming
Northwest College *C*

Surveying technology

Alabama
Troy University *B*

Alaska
University of Alaska
  Anchorage *A, B*

Arizona
Phoenix College *C, A*
Pima Community College *C*

Arkansas
University of Arkansas
  Community College at
    Morrilton *C, A*
    Monticello *A, B*

California
California State University
  Fresno *B*
Chabot College *A*
City College of San Francisco *C*
Coastline Community College *C*
College of the Canyons *C, A*
Cuyamaca College *A*
Diablo Valley College *C*
Santiago Canyon College *C*
Shasta College *C*

Colorado
Metropolitan State University of
  Denver *B*
Westwood College
  Denver North *A*

Delaware
Delaware Technical Community
  College
  Jack F. Owens Campus *A*
  Stanton/Wilmington Campus *A*

Florida
Palm Beach State College *A*
University of Florida *B*

Georgia
Albany Technical College *C*
Middle Georgia State College *A*
Southern Polytechnic State
  University *C, B*

Idaho
Idaho State University *B*

Illinois
Kaskaskia College *C*
Morrison Institute of Technology *A*
Parkland College *A*
Rend Lake College *A*
Rock Valley College *C*
Triton College *A*
Waubonsee Community College *C, A*

Indiana
Vincennes University *A*

Louisiana
Nicholls State University *B*

Maine
University of Maine *B*

Maryland
College of Southern Maryland *C*
Community College of Baltimore
  County *C, A*

Massachusetts
Bristol Community College *C*
Wentworth Institute of Technology *C*

Michigan
Ferris State University *A*
Lansing Community College *C, A*
Macomb Community College *C, A*
Montcalm Community College *A*

Minnesota
Dunwoody College of Technology *C*
Saint Cloud State University *B*
Vermilion Community College *C*

Missouri
Metropolitan Community College -
  Kansas City *A*

Montana
Flathead Valley Community
  College *A*

Nevada
College of Southern Nevada *A*

New Hampshire
White Mountains Community
  College *C, A*

New Jersey
Essex County College *A*
Gloucester County College *A*
Middlesex County College *A*

New Mexico
Central New Mexico Community
  College *C, A*
New Mexico State University *B*

New York
Mohawk Valley Community
  College *A*
Monroe Community College *C*
Orange County Community
  College *C*
Paul Smith's College *A*
SUNY
  College of Environmental Science
    and Forestry *A*
  College of Technology at
    Alfred *A, B*
  Sullivan County Community
    College *A*

North Carolina
Asheville-Buncombe Technical
  Community College *A*
Central Piedmont Community
  College *C, A*
Fayetteville Technical Community
  College *A*
Guilford Technical Community
  College *C, A*
Sandhills Community College *A*
Tri-County Community College *A*
Wake Technical Community
  College *A*

North Dakota
Bismarck State College *C, A*

Ohio
Cincinnati State Technical and
  Community College *C*
Columbus State Community
  College *C, A*
James A. Rhodes State College *C*
Lakeland Community College *C*
Ohio State University
  Columbus Campus *B, M, D*
Sinclair Community College *C*
Stark State College *A*
University of Akron *C, A, B*

Oregon
Chemeketa Community College *C, A*
Clackamas Community College *C*
Oregon Institute of Technology *B*

Pennsylvania
Penn State
  Wilkes-Barre *A*
Pennsylvania College of
  Technology *A*

Puerto Rico
Universidad Politecnica de Puerto
  Rico *A, B, M*
University of Puerto Rico
  Mayaguez *A*

South Carolina
Piedmont Technical College *A*
Technical College of the
  Lowcountry *C*
Trident Technical College *C*

South Dakota
Southeast Technical Institute *A*

Tennessee
East Tennessee State University *B*

Texas
Austin Community College *C, A*
Lone Star College System *C, A*
Texas A&M University
  Corpus Christi *B*
Texas State Technical College
  Waco *C, A*
Tyler Junior College *C, A*

Utah
Salt Lake Community College *A*
Utah Valley University *A, B*

Virginia
J. Sargeant Reynolds Community
  College *C*
Virginia Western Community
  College *C*

Washington
Bates Technical College *C, A*
Bellingham Technical College *A*
Centralia College *A*
Clark College *C, A*
Peninsula College *A*
Renton Technical College *C, A*
Walla Walla Community College *C*

West Virginia
Glenville State College *A*
Southern West Virginia Community
  and Technical College *C, A*

Wisconsin
Nicolet Area Technical College *A*

Wyoming
Sheridan College *A*
University of Wyoming *C*

Sustainability studies

California
California Baptist University *B*
Dominican University of California *M*
Mendocino College *C*
National University *M*

Colorado
Colorado Mountain College *B*

Connecticut
University of New Haven *B*

Florida
Jacksonville University *B*
University of Florida *B*
University of South Florida *M*

Georgia
Savannah College of Art and
  Design *M*

Illinois
Illinois Institute of Technology *M*
Roosevelt University *B*

Iowa
Ashford University *B*

Maine
College of the Atlantic *B, M*

Maryland
Notre Dame of Maryland
  University *B*

Massachusetts
Bentley University *B*
Hampshire College *B*

University of Massachusetts
  Amherst *M*
  Dartmouth *C*

Michigan

Albion College *B*
Aquinas College *B, M*
Michigan Technological University *C*
Wayne County Community College *C*

Missouri

Saint Louis University *M*

Nebraska

Creighton University *B*

Nevada

Sierra Nevada College *B*

New Hampshire

Southern New Hampshire
  University *C*

New Jersey

Burlington County College *A*
Kean University *B*
Richard Stockton College of New
  Jersey *B*

New York

Columbia University
  School of General Studies *B*
Hofstra University *B*
Long Island University
  LIU Post *M*
Rochester Institute of Technology *D*
SUNY
  University at Stony Brook *B*

Ohio

Miami University
  Oxford *B*

Oregon

Oregon State University *B*

Pennsylvania

Messiah College *B*
Temple University *C*

South Dakota

Black Hills State University *M*

Texas

Stephen F. Austin State University *B*

Utah

Weber State University *M*

Vermont

Goddard College *B, M*

Virginia

Ferrum College *B*
George Mason University *B*

Washington

Evergreen State College *B*

West Virginia

Wheeling Jesuit University *B*

Wisconsin

Milwaukee Area Technical College *A*
University of Wisconsin
  Green Bay *M*
  Stout *B*
Viterbo University *B*

Swedish

Washington

University of Washington *B*

Systems engineering

Alabama

University of South Alabama *D*

Arizona

Arizona State University *D*
University of Arizona *B, M, D*

Arkansas

University of Arkansas
  Little Rock *B, M*

California

California Institute of
  Technology *M, D*
California State University
  Fullerton *M*
  Northridge *M*
Loyola Marymount University *M*
National University *M*
Northwestern Polytechnic
  University *B, M, D*
University of California
  San Diego *B, M, D*
University of Southern California *M*

Colorado

Colorado School of Mines *M, D*
Colorado State University *M, D*
United States Air Force Academy *B*

District of Columbia

Howard University *B, M*

Florida

Embry-Riddle Aeronautical University
  Worldwide Campus *M*
Florida Institute of Technology *M, D*
University of Florida *B, M, D*

Georgia

Georgia Institute of Technology *M*
Southern Polytechnic State
  University *B, M*

Illinois

University of Illinois
  Urbana-Champaign *M, D*

Indiana

Rose-Hulman Institute of
  Technology *M*
Taylor University *B*

Iowa

Iowa State University *M*

Louisiana

Louisiana Tech University *M*

Maine

Maine Maritime Academy *B*

Maryland

Johns Hopkins University *M*
United States Naval Academy *B*
University of Maryland
  Baltimore County *M*
  College Park *M*

Massachusetts

Boston University *M, D*
Massachusetts Institute of
  Technology *M, D*
Northeastern University *M*
Worcester Polytechnic Institute *B, M*

Michigan

Ferris State University *B*
Lawrence Technological University *M*
Oakland University *M, D*
University of Michigan *M*
Wayne State University *C*

Minnesota

University of Minnesota
  Twin Cities *M*
University of St. Thomas *M*

Missouri

Missouri University of Science and
  Technology *M, D*
Washington University in St.
  Louis *B, M, D*

New Hampshire

University of New Hampshire *D*

New Jersey

New Jersey Institute of
  Technology *M*
Stevens Institute of Technology *M, D*

New York

Cornell University *M*
Rensselaer Polytechnic Institute *M*
Rochester Institute of
  Technology *B, M*
SUNY
  University at Binghamton *M*
  University at Stony Brook *M*
Syracuse University *M*
United States Merchant Marine
  Academy *M*
United States Military Academy *B*

North Carolina

University of North Carolina
  Charlotte *B*

Ohio

Case Western Reserve
  University *B, M, D*
Ohio State University
  Columbus Campus *B*

Oregon

Portland State University *M*

Pennsylvania

University of Pennsylvania *B, M, D*

Puerto Rico

University of Puerto Rico
  Mayaguez *M*

Rhode Island

Johnson & Wales University
  Providence *B*
Providence College *B*

South Carolina

Clemson University *M, D*

Tennessee

Belmont University *B*
University of Tennessee
  Chattanooga *D*

Texas

St. Mary's University *M*
Southern Methodist University *M, D*
Texas A&M International
  University *D*
Texas A&M University
  Galveston *M*
Texas Tech University *M, D*
University of Houston *M*
University of Houston
  Clear Lake *M*

University of Texas

  Arlington *M*
  Dallas *M*
  El Paso *M*

Virginia

George Mason University *B, M, D*
University of Virginia *B, M, D*
Virginia Polytechnic Institute and
  State University *M*

Wisconsin

University of Wisconsin
  Madison *M*

Wyoming

University of Wyoming *B*

Systems science/theory

California

Stanford University *B*

Florida

University of Central Florida *M, D*
University of Miami *M*

Idaho

Idaho State University *M*

Illinois

Eastern Illinois University *M*
Northwestern University *D*
Southern Illinois University
  Carbondale *M*

Indiana

St. Mary-of-the-Woods College *M*

Maine

College of the Atlantic *B, M*

Massachusetts

Boston University *B, M*
Worcester Polytechnic Institute *M*

Mississippi

Mississippi State University *D*

Missouri

Saint Louis University *D*
Washington University in St.
  Louis *B, M, D*

New York

SUNY
  University at Binghamton *M, D*
United States Military Academy *B*

North Carolina

North Carolina State University *M*

Ohio

Kent State University *M*
Wright State University *M*

Oregon

Portland State University *D*

Pennsylvania

Carnegie Mellon University *B*
La Salle University *B*
West Chester University of
  Pennsylvania *M*

Tennessee

University of Tennessee
  Knoxville *M*

Virginia

James Madison University *B*

Washington

Antioch University
Seattle *M, T*

West Virginia

Marshall University *B*

Talmudic studies

California

Yeshiva Ohr Elchonon Chabad/West
Coast Talmudical Seminary *B*

Florida

Yeshiva Gedolah Rabbinical
College *B, M*

Illinois

Telshe Yeshiva-Chicago *B, M*

Maryland

Ner Israel Rabbinical College *B, M, D*
Yeshiva College of the Nations
Capital *B*

Michigan

Yeshiva Beth Yehuda-Yeshiva Gedolah
of Greater Detroit *B, M, D*

New Jersey

Beth Medrash Govoha *B, M*
Rabbi Jacob Joseph School *B*
Talmudical Academy of New Jersey *B*

New York

Beis Medrash Heichal Dovid *B, D*
Central Yeshiva Tomchei Tmimim-
Lubavitch *B, M*
Kehilath Yakov Rabbinical
Seminary *B*
Machzikei Hadath Rabbinical
College *B*
Mesivta Torah Vodaath Seminary *B*
Mirrer Yeshiva Central
Institute *B, M, D*
Ohr Somayach Tanenbaum Education
Center *B, M*
Rabbinical Academy Mesivta Rabbi
Chaim Berlin *B, M, D*
Rabbinical College Beth Shraga *B*
Rabbinical College Bobover Yeshiva
B'nei Zion *B, M*
Rabbinical College Ch'san Sofer of
New York *B, M*
Rabbinical College of Long Island *B*
Rabbinical College of Ohr Shimon
Yisroel *B*
Rabbinical Seminary of
America *B, M, D*
Shor Yoshuv Rabbinical College *B, M*
Talmudical Institute of Upstate New
York *B, D*
Talmudical Seminary Oholei Torah *D*
Torah Temimah Talmudical
Seminary *B, D*
U.T.A. Mesivta-Kiryas Joel *B*
United Talmudical Seminary *B, M*
Yeshiva D'Monsey Rabbinical
College *B, D*
Yeshiva Derech Chaim *B, D*
Yeshiva Gedolah Imrei Yosef
D'Spinka *B*
Yeshiva Gedolah Zichron Moshe *B, D*
Yeshiva Karlin Stolin *B*
Yeshiva Shaar Hatorah *B, M*
Yeshiva Shaarei Torah of Rockland *B*
Yeshiva University *M*
Yeshiva and Kolel Bais Medrash
Elyon *B, D*
Yeshiva and Kollel Harbotzas
Torah *B, D*
Yeshiva of Nitra *B, M*
Yeshiva of the Telshe Alumni *B*

Yeshivas Novominsk *B*
Yeshivat Mikdash Melech *B, M*
Yeshivath Viznitz *B, D*

Pennsylvania

Talmudical Yeshiva of Philadelphia *B*
Yeshivath Beth Moshe *B*

Taxation

Alabama

Troy University *M*
University of Alabama *M*

Arizona

Arizona State University *M*

Arkansas

Northwest Arkansas Community
College *C*
University of Arkansas
Little Rock *M*

California

California State University
East Bay *M*
Fullerton *M*
Northridge *M*
San Bernardino *M*
De Anza College *C, A*
Golden Gate University *M*
Los Angeles Pierce College *C*
MiraCosta College *C*
National University *M*
San Diego State University *M*
San Joaquin Delta College *C*
San Jose State University *M*
Santa Rosa Junior College *C*
University of San Diego *M*
University of Southern California *M*
Yuba College *A*

Colorado

Colorado Technical University *C*
University of Colorado
Boulder *M*
University of Denver *M*

Connecticut

Fairfield University *M*
Manchester Community College *C*
University of New Haven *M*

Delaware

Goldey-Beacom College *M*

District of Columbia

American University *M*

Florida

Florida Atlantic University *M*
Florida International University *M*
Florida State University *M*
Nova Southeastern University *M*
University of Central Florida *M*
University of Miami *M*

Georgia

Georgia State University *M*

Illinois

DePaul University *M*
Northern Illinois University *M*
University of Illinois
Urbana-Champaign *M*

Indiana

Indiana University
Purdue University Indianapolis *M*

Kentucky

Bellarmine University *M*

Maryland

University of Baltimore *M*

Massachusetts

American International College *M*
Bentley University *M*
Boston University *M*
Northeastern University *M*
Suffolk University *M*

Michigan

Grand Valley State University *M*
Walsh College of Accountancy and
Business Administration *M*
Washtenaw Community College *C*
Wayne State University *M*

Minnesota

University of Minnesota
Twin Cities *M*

Mississippi

Mississippi State University *M*
University of Mississippi *M*

Missouri

Fontbonne University *M*

New Jersey

Fairleigh Dickinson University
College at Florham *M*
Metropolitan Campus *M*
Rutgers, The State University of New
Jersey
New Brunswick/Piscataway
Campus *M*
Newark Campus *M*
Seton Hall University *M*

New York

City University of New York
Baruch College *M*
Hofstra University *M*
Long Island University
LIU Brooklyn *M*
LIU Post *M*
Pace University *M*
Pace University: Pleasantville/
Briarcliff *M*
SUNY
College at Old Westbury *M*
University at Albany *M*
St. John's University *M*

Ohio

Capital University *M*
Columbus State Community
College *C*
Ohio University
Southern Campus at Ironton *C*
Stark State College *A*
University of Akron *M*
University of Cincinnati *M*
University of Toledo *M*

Oregon

Chemeketa Community College *C*

Pennsylvania

Philadelphia University *M*
Robert Morris University *M*
Villanova University *M*
Widener University *M*

Puerto Rico

Turabo University *M*
University of the Sacred Heart *M*

Rhode Island

Bryant University *M*

South Carolina

York Technical College *C*

Texas

Baylor University *M*
Southern Methodist University *M*
University of North Texas *M*
University of Texas
Arlington *M*
San Antonio *M*

Utah

Weber State University *M*

Virginia

Old Dominion University *M*
Virginia Commonwealth
University *M*

Washington

Olympic College *C*

Wisconsin

University of Wisconsin
Milwaukee *C*

Taxidermy

Minnesota

Vermilion Community College *C*

New York

Finger Lakes Community College *C*

North Carolina

Montgomery Community College *C*

Teacher assistance

Alaska

University of Alaska
Fairbanks *C, A*

Arizona

Arizona Western College *C*
Estrella Mountain Community
College *A*

Arkansas

Northwest Arkansas Community
College *C*

California

American River College *A*
Antelope Valley College *A*
Cerritos College *A*
Chabot College *A*
City College of San Francisco *A*
College of Alameda *A*
Hartnell College *C, A*
Long Beach City College *A*
Los Angeles Mission College *A*
Los Angeles Southwest College *A*
Moorpark College *A*
Mount St. Mary's College *A*
National University *A*
West Hills College: Lemoore *C*

Colorado

Aims Community College *C, A*
Community College of Denver *A*
Otero Junior College *A*
Red Rocks Community College *C*

Connecticut

Manchester Community College *A*

Florida

Rasmussen College
Fort Myers *C, A*
New Port Richey *C, A*
Ocala *C, A*
Tampa/Brandon *C, A*

Georgia

Atlanta Technical College *C*
Gwinnett Technical College *C*

Illinois

City Colleges of Chicago
    Harold Washington College *C, A*
College of Lake County *C*
Danville Area Community College *A*
Harper College *C*
Heartland Community College *A*
Highland Community College *C*
Illinois Central College *A*
Illinois Eastern Community Colleges
    Lincoln Trail College *A*
Illinois Valley Community
    College *C, A*
John A. Logan College *A*
Joliet Junior College *A*
Kankakee Community College *C, A*
Kaskaskia College *A*
Lewis and Clark Community
    College *A*
Lincoln Land Community College *A*
Moraine Valley Community
    College *C, A*
Prairie State College *C, A*
Rasmussen College
    Aurora *C, A*
    Mokena/Tinley Park *C, A*
    Rockford *C, A*
    Romeoville/Joliet *C, A*
Rock Valley College *A*
Sauk Valley Community College *A*
South Suburban College of Cook
    County *A*
Triton College *C, A*
Waubonsee Community College *C, A*

Indiana

St. Mary-of-the-Woods College *A*
Valparaiso University *A*
Vincennes University *A*

Iowa

Dordt College *A*
Ellsworth Community College *A*
Western Iowa Tech Community
    College *C*

Kansas

Butler Community College *A*
Central Christian College of Kansas *A*
Cloud County Community College *A*
Seward County Community
    College *A*

Kentucky

Bluegrass Community and Technical
    College *C, A*
Elizabethtown Community and
    Technical College *A*
Hopkinsville Community
    College *C, A*
Jefferson Community and Technical
    College *A*
Owensboro Community and
    Technical College *C, A*
Somerset Community College *A*

Maine

Kaplan University
    South Portland *A*
Kennebec Valley Community
    College *A*

Massachusetts

Bristol Community College *C*
North Shore Community
    College *C, A*

Michigan

Baker College
    Cadillac *A*
    Flint *A*
    Port Huron *A*
Gogebic Community College *A*
Grand Rapids Community College *A*
Henry Ford Community College *C*
Kirtland Community College *A*
Lansing Community College *C, A*
Montcalm Community College *A*
Southwestern Michigan College *A*

Minnesota

Central Lakes College *A*
Century College *C, A*
Lake Superior College *C*
Mesabi Range Community and
    Technical College *A*
Minneapolis Community and
    Technical College *C*
Minnesota State Community and
    Technical College *A*
Northland Community & Technical
    College *A*
Rasmussen College
    Blaine *C, A*
    Bloomington *C, A*
    Brooklyn Park *C, A*
    Eagan *C, A*
    Lake Elmo/Woodbury *C, A*
    Mankato *C, A*
    Moorhead *C, A*
    St. Cloud *C, A*
Ridgewater College *A*
St. Cloud Technical and Community
    College *A*

Missouri

St. Charles Community College *A*
St. Louis Community College *A*
State Fair Community College *A*

Montana

University of Montana: Western *A*

New Hampshire

Lebanon College *C, A*

New Jersey

Brookdale Community College *A*
Middlesex County College *A*
Ocean County College *C*

New Mexico

Central New Mexico Community
    College *C*
Clovis Community College *A*
New Mexico State University
    Carlsbad *A*

New York

Adirondack Community College *C*
City University of New York
    Borough of Manhattan Community
        College *A*
    Bronx Community College *C, A*
    Kingsborough Community
        College *A*
    LaGuardia Community College *A*
    Medgar Evers College *A*
Columbia-Greene Community
    College *C*
Dutchess Community College *C*
Erie Community College *C*
Finger Lakes Community College *C*
Genesee Community College *C, A*
Herkimer County Community
    College *C*
Jefferson Community College *C*
Maria College *A*
Mercy College *C*
Monroe Community College *C*
Nassau Community College *C*

New York University *A*
Westchester Community College *C*

North Carolina

Carteret Community College *C, A*
Durham Technical Community
    College *A*
Edgecombe Community College *A*
Johnston Community College *A*
Mitchell Community College *A*
Nash Community College *A*
Roanoke-Chowan Community
    College *A*
Sandhills Community College *A*
Vance-Granville Community
    College *A*

North Dakota

Dakota College at Bottineau *A*
Mayville State University *B*
Rasmussen College
    Fargo *C*

Ohio

Hocking College *A*
North Central State College *A*
Northwest State Community
    College *A*
Southern State Community College *A*

Oregon

Blue Mountain Community
    College *C, A*
Chemeketa Community College *C*
Clackamas Community College *C*
Klamath Community College *C, A*
Linn-Benton Community College *C, A*
Portland Community College *C, A*
Southwestern Oregon Community
    College *A*
Treasure Valley Community
    College *A*
Umpqua Community College *C*

Pennsylvania

Community College of Allegheny
    County *A*
Community College of Beaver
    County *A*
Delaware County Community
    College *A*
Lehigh Carbon Community
    College *C, A*
Luzerne County Community
    College *A*
McCann School of Business and
    Technology
    Hazleton *A*
Montgomery County Community
    College *A*
Northampton Community
    College *C, A*
Pennsylvania Highlands Community
    College *A*

Puerto Rico

Turabo University *C*
Universidad Metropolitana *C*
Universidad del Este *C*

South Carolina

Forrest Junior College *A*
Williamsburg Technical College *A*

South Dakota

Mount Marty College *A*
Oglala Lakota College *A*
Sinte Gleska University *A*
University of Sioux Falls *A*

Tennessee

Johnson University *A*

Texas

El Centro College *A*
Midland College *A*
North Lake College *A*
Odessa College *A*
Richland College *A*
San Antonio College *A*
Temple College *A*
Texas State Technical College
    Harlingen *A*

Virginia

Eastern Mennonite University *A*
Lord Fairfax Community College *C*
Tidewater Community College *A*

Washington

Bellingham Technical College *C*
Centralia College *A*
Everett Community College *A*
Green River Community College *C, A*
Highline Community College *A*
Lower Columbia College *A*
Pierce College *A*
Renton Technical College *C, A*
Shoreline Community College *A*
Spokane Falls Community
    College *C, A*
Tacoma Community College *C, A*
Walla Walla Community College *C, A*
Whatcom Community College *A*
Yakima Valley Community College *C*

West Virginia

New River Community and Technical
    College *A*
West Virginia University at
    Parkersburg *C, A*

Wisconsin

Alverno College *A*
Gateway Technical College *A*
Rasmussen College
    Appleton *C, A*
    Green Bay *C, A*
    Wausau *C, A*
Waukesha County Technical
    College *A*
Western Technical College *C, A*

Wyoming

Central Wyoming College *A*
Sheridan College *A*

Teacher education, multiple levels

Alabama

Auburn University *M, D, T*
Faulkner University *B, M, T*
Samford University *B*
Troy University *B, M, T*
University of North Alabama *B, M*
University of West Alabama *B*

Arizona

Northcentral University *B, M, D*

Arkansas

Arkansas State University
    Beebe *A*
    Mountain Home *A*
East Arkansas Community College *A*
Harding University *B, M, T*
National Park Community College *A*
North Arkansas College *A*
Rich Mountain Community College *A*
Southeast Arkansas College *A*
Southern Arkansas University *M*
Southern Arkansas University Tech *A*

University of Arkansas
  Community College at Hope *A*
  Community College at Morrilton *A*
  Monticello *M*
University of Central Arkansas *M*

California

Alliant International University *T*
Azusa Pacific University *B, T*
Dominican University of California *M*
Fresno City College *A*
Glendale Community College *A*
Hope International University *M*
Pepperdine University *T*
Simpson University *T*
University of California
  Irvine *M*
University of San Francisco *M*
Vanguard University of Southern
  California *T*
Whittier College *T*

Colorado

Adams State University *B, M, T*
Colorado College *B, M*
University of Colorado
  Colorado Springs *T*

Connecticut

Quinnipiac University *B, M*
Western Connecticut State
  University *M*

Delaware

Delaware Technical Community
  College
  Jack F. Owens Campus *A*
  Stanton/Wilmington Campus *A*
  Terry Campus *A*

District of Columbia

George Washington University *M*
Howard University *M*

Florida

Edward Waters College *B*
Florida Atlantic University *M*
Florida Institute of Technology *M*
Saint Thomas University *M*
Southeastern University *M, T*
University of Miami *M*
University of South Florida *B*
University of Tampa *M*

Georgia

Atlanta Metropolitan College *A*
Darton College *A*
East Georgia State College *A*
Georgia Highlands College *A*
Georgia Southern University *M*
Gordon College *A*
LaGrange College *M*
University of West Georgia *M, T*

Hawaii

Chaminade University of
  Honolulu *M, T*
University of Hawaii
  Leeward Community College *A*
  Manoa *M, T*

Idaho

Boise State University *T*
College of Idaho *B, M*

Illinois

Chicago State University *B*
Concordia University
  Chicago *B, M, T*
DePaul University *B, M*
Dominican University *B, M*
Eureka College *B*
Lincoln College *A*

North Park University *B, M, T*
Quincy University *B, T*
Southern Illinois University
  Carbondale *M, T*
Southern Illinois University
  Edwardsville *M*
University of Illinois
  Urbana-Champaign *B, M, D, T*

Indiana

Earlham College *M*
Indiana University
  Bloomington *B, T*
Manchester University *B, T*
Marian University *M, T*
Purdue University *B, M, D*
St. Mary-of-the-Woods College *B, T*
University of Indianapolis *T*
University of Notre Dame *M*

Iowa

Ashford University *M*
Buena Vista University *T*
Cornell College *B, T*
Ellsworth Community College *A*
Loras College *B*

Kansas

Bethany College *T*
Bethel College *T*
Central Christian College of Kansas *B*
Coffeyville Community College *A*
Colby Community College *A*
Friends University *M, T*
Tabor College *B*

Kentucky

Asbury University *M, T*
Eastern Kentucky University *M*
Midway College *B*
Murray State University *M*
Spalding University *B, M*
Thomas More College *M*
Union College *M*
University of Louisville *B, M*
Western Kentucky University *B*

Louisiana

Centenary College of Louisiana *T*
Nicholls State University *M*
University of Louisiana at Monroe *M*
Xavier University of Louisiana *B*

Maine

University of Maine
  Fort Kent *B*
University of New England *M*
University of Southern Maine *T*

Maryland

Baltimore City Community College *A*
Coppin State University *M*
Frederick Community College *A*
Frostburg State University *B, T*
Goucher College *M*
Hood College *T*
McDaniel College *M*

Massachusetts

Brandeis University *M*
Bridgewater State University *M*
Eastern Nazarene College *M*
Framingham State University *M*
Lesley University *M*
Merrimack College *B*
Smith College *M*
University of Massachusetts
  Dartmouth *M*

Michigan

Aquinas College *B, T*
Baker College
  Auburn Hills *B*
  Clinton Township *B*

Flint *B*
Jackson *B*
Muskegon *B*
Owosso *B*
Concordia University *B, T*
Grand Rapids Community College *A*
Hillsdale College *B*
Lake Superior State
  University *B, M, T*
Western Michigan University *M, T*

Minnesota

Capella University *M, D*
College of St. Scholastica *B, M*
Hamline University *B, M, T*
Martin Luther College *B*
Minnesota State University
  Mankato *B*
Ridgewater College *A*
Saint Cloud State University *B*
University of Minnesota
  Duluth *B*
University of St. Thomas *B, M*

Mississippi

Alcorn State University *M*
Delta State University *M*
Jackson State University *M*
Millsaps College *T*
Mississippi Gulf Coast Community
  College *A*
Pearl River Community College *A*

Missouri

Maryville University of Saint
  Louis *M, T*
Missouri Baptist University *T*
Missouri Southern State
  University *B, T*
Missouri State University *M*
Saint Louis University *M, D*
Washington University in St. Louis *T*
William Jewell College *T*
William Woods University *T*

Montana

Montana State University
  Northern *M*
University of Montana: Western *B, T*

Nebraska

Concordia University *B, T*
Hastings College *T*
Midland University *B*
University of Nebraska
  Lincoln *B, T*
York College *B, T*

Nevada

Sierra Nevada College *M*

New Hampshire

Plymouth State University *M, T*
White Mountains Community
  College *A*

New Jersey

College of St. Elizabeth *B, T*
Cumberland County College *A*
Fairleigh Dickinson University
  College at Florham *M*
  Metropolitan Campus *M*
Felician College *B*
Gloucester County College *A*
Passaic County Community College *A*
Richard Stockton College of New
  Jersey *B, M*
Saint Peter's University *M*

New Mexico

Central New Mexico Community
  College *A*
Luna Community College *A*

New Mexico Institute of Mining and
  Technology *T*
University of the Southwest *B*

New York

Canisius College *M*
Columbia-Greene Community
  College *A*
D'Youville College *M, T*
Dowling College *B, M*
Elmira College *B, M, T*
Hofstra University *B, M*
Ithaca College *B, M, T*
Jewish Theological Seminary of
  America *M, D*
Marist College *M*
Mount Saint Mary College *B, T*
Nyack College *B*
Onondaga Community College *A*
Pace University: Pleasantville/
  Briarcliff *M*
SUNY
  College at Oneonta *B*
  College at Plattsburgh *B*
  University at Buffalo *M*
Saint Bonaventure University *M*
St. Thomas Aquinas College *B, M, T*
Schenectady County Community
  College *A*

North Carolina

Gardner-Webb University *B*
Halifax Community College *A*
University of North Carolina
  Asheville *T*
  Charlotte *M*
William Peace University *B*

North Dakota

North Dakota State University *M*
Sitting Bull College *A*

Ohio

Bowling Green State University *B, T*
Central State University *B*
Defiance College *B*
John Carroll University *M, T*
Lorain County Community College *A*
Marietta College *B*
Ohio Northern University *B, T*
Ohio Wesleyan University *B*
Otterbein University *B*
Shawnee State University *B*
Union Institute & University *B*
University of Dayton *B, M, T*
University of Findlay *B, M, T*
University of Mount Union *T*
University of Rio Grande *B, T*
University of Toledo *B*
Washington State Community
  College *A*
Wilmington College *B*
Wright State University *M*
Youngstown State University *B, M*

Oklahoma

Family of Faith College *B*
Hillsdale Free Will Baptist College *B*
Oklahoma City Community
  College *A*
Oklahoma State University
  Institute of Technology:
    Okmulgee *A*
Oral Roberts University *M*
Rose State College *A*
Southwestern Oklahoma State
  University *M*
University of Tulsa *M*

Oregon

Concordia University *B, M, T*
Corban University *B*
Eastern Oregon University *M*
George Fox University *M, T*

Lewis & Clark College *M*
Linfield College *T*
Multnomah University *M*
Northwest Christian University *B, M*
University of Oregon *M, T*
University of Phoenix
Oregon *M*
Warner Pacific College *T*
Western Oregon University *B, M, T*

Pennsylvania

Arcadia University *B, M, T*
Baptist Bible College of
Pennsylvania *B, M*
Cedar Crest College *M, T*
Delaware County Community
College *A*
Delaware Valley College *M*
Duquesne University *M, T*
Edinboro University of
Pennsylvania *M*
Gannon University *B*
Geneva College *B, T*
Gettysburg College *T*
Gwynedd Mercy University *B, M, T*
La Salle University *B, T*
Mansfield University of
Pennsylvania *B, T*
Moravian College *T*
St. Francis University *B, M, T*
University of Pittsburgh
Greensburg *B, T*
Washington & Jefferson College *T*
Westminster College *B, T*

Puerto Rico

Universidad Metropolitana *B*
University of Puerto Rico
Bayamon University College *B*

Rhode Island

Rhode Island College *B*

South Carolina

Charleston Southern University *B*
Columbia International University *M*
Furman University *T*
Winthrop University *T*

South Dakota

Northern State University *B, M, T*
University of Sioux Falls *B*

Tennessee

Christian Brothers University *M, T*
Cumberland University *B, M*
Freed-Hardeman University *B, T*
LeMoyne-Owen College *T*
Southern Adventist University *M*
Tennessee Wesleyan College *B, T*
University of Memphis *B*
University of Tennessee
Martin *M*

Texas

Arlington Baptist College *B, T*
Blinn College *A*
Brookhaven College *A*
Dallas Christian College *B, T*
Lamar State College at Port Arthur *A*
LeTourneau University *B, T*
Midland College *A*
Northeast Texas Community
College *A*
Our Lady of the Lake University of
San Antonio *B*
Palo Alto College *A*
Paris Junior College *A*
St. Edward's University *B, T*
St. Mary's University *T*
St. Philip's College *A*
San Jacinto College *A*
Tarleton State University *M, T*
Texas Lutheran University *B, T*

University of Mary Hardin-Baylor *T*
University of Texas
Permian Basin *M*
University of the Incarnate
Word *M, T*
Wayland Baptist University *B, T*
West Texas A&M University *T*

Utah

Brigham Young University *M*

Vermont

College of St. Joseph in
Vermont *B, M*
Goddard College *B, M*
Johnson State College *B, M*

Virginia

Averett University *B, T*
Bluefield College *B, T*
Longwood University *T*
Virginia Union University *B*

Washington

Antioch University
Seattle *T*
Eastern Washington University *M, T*
Evergreen State College *M*
Seattle University *M*
University of Puget Sound *M*
University of Washington *M*
Washington State
University *B, M, D, T*
Whitworth University *B, M, T*

West Virginia

Bethany College *B*
Ohio Valley University *B*
Wheeling Jesuit University *B*

Wisconsin

Beloit College *T*
Carroll University *T*
Concordia University Wisconsin *B*
Northland College *B, T*
University of Wisconsin
Green Bay *T*
Superior *B, M, T*

Wyoming

Western Wyoming Community
College *A*

Technical and business writing

Alabama

Auburn University *M*
Oakwood University *B*

Arizona

Pima Community College *C*

Arkansas

University of Arkansas
Fort Smith *B*
Little Rock *B, M*

California

De Anza College *C, A*
Orange Coast College *A*
San Francisco State University *C, B*

Colorado

University of Colorado
Denver *M*

Connecticut

Three Rivers Community College *C*
University of Hartford *B*

Florida

University of Central Florida *D*
University of South Florida
Sarasota-Manatee *B*

Georgia

Athens Technical College *C*
Atlanta Technical College *C*
Georgia Piedmont Technical
College *C*
Gwinnett Technical College *C*
Kennesaw State University *C*
Savannah College of Art and
Design *B, M*
Savannah Technical College *C*

Idaho

Boise State University *M*
University of Idaho *B*

Illinois

Black Hawk College *A*
Chicago State University *B*
College of Lake County *C, A*
Illinois Institute of Technology *D*
McKendree University *B*

Indiana

Bethel College *A*
Indiana University
East *C*
Purdue University Fort Wayne *B*
Purdue University *B*
St. Mary-of-the-Woods College *B*
Taylor University *B*
Valparaiso University *B*

Iowa

Iowa State University *B*

Kentucky

Northern Kentucky University *C*

Maine

University of Maine *M*

Maryland

Montgomery College *C*
Towson University *M*

Massachusetts

Fitchburg State University *B, M*
Massachusetts College of Liberal
Arts *B*
Northeastern University *M*
Salem State University *B*
University of Massachusetts
Boston *C*
Dartmouth *M*
Worcester Polytechnic Institute *B*

Michigan

Albion College *B*
Eastern Michigan University *B*
Ferris State University *A, B*
Grand Valley State University *B*
Madonna University *B*
Michigan State University *B, M*
Saginaw Valley State University *B*
Southwestern Michigan College *A*
Washtenaw Community College *A*

Minnesota

Bemidji State University *C*
Concordia University St. Paul *B*
Inver Hills Community College *C*
Metropolitan State University *B, M*
Minnesota State University
Mankato *B, M*
Moorhead *C*
University of Northwestern - St.
Paul *B*

Missouri

Missouri Southern State University *B*
Missouri State University *B*
Missouri University of Science and
Technology *B, M*

Montana

Montana Tech of the University of
Montana *B, M*
University of Montana *M*

New Hampshire

New England College *M*

New Jersey

New Jersey Institute of
Technology *B, M*

New Mexico

Eastern New Mexico University:
Roswell *C*
New Mexico Institute of Mining and
Technology *B*

New York

D'Youville College *B*
SUNY
Farmingdale State College *B*
Yeshiva University *B*

North Carolina

East Carolina University *D*
Gardner-Webb University *B*
North Carolina State University *M*
University of Mount Olive *C*

Ohio

Bowling Green State University *B, M*
Cedarville University *B*
Cincinnati State Technical and
Community College *C*
John Carroll University *B*
Miami University
Oxford *B*
Ohio Northern University *B*
University of Akron *C*
University of Findlay *C*
Youngstown State University *B*

Oregon

Portland Community College *C*
Portland State University *M*

Pennsylvania

Carnegie Mellon University *B, M, D*
Chatham University *M*
Elizabethtown College *B*
Juniata College *B*
La Salle University *B*
Penn State
Berks *B*
Lehigh Valley *B*
Slippery Rock University of
Pennsylvania *B*
York College of Pennsylvania *B*

South Carolina

Clemson University *M*
Coker College *B*
Trident Technical College *C*
Winthrop University *B*

South Dakota

Dakota State University *C, B*

Tennessee

Chattanooga State Community
College *A*
Maryville College *B*
Tennessee Technological
University *B*

Texas

Austin Community College *C, A*
Baylor University *B*
Lee College *A*
Lubbock Christian University *B*
Texas State University *M, T*
Texas Tech University *B, M, D*
University of Houston
Downtown *B, M*
University of North Texas *M*
University of Texas
El Paso *M*
San Antonio *B*

Utah

Dixie State College *B*
Utah State University *D*
Utah Valley University *C*
Weber State University *B*

Virginia

James Madison University *B, M*
Northern Virginia Community
College *C*
Thomas Nelson Community
College *C*

Washington

Eastern Washington University *B*
University of Washington *B*
Washington State University *C*

West Virginia

West Virginia State University *B*
West Virginia University *M*

Wisconsin

Fox Valley Technical College *A*
Gateway Technical College *A*
Mount Mary University *B, M, T*
University of Wisconsin
Stout *B, M*

Technical/scientific communication

Georgia

Southern Polytechnic State
University *B*

Illinois

Illinois Institute of Technology *B, M*

Indiana

Indiana University
Purdue University
Indianapolis *C, B*

Michigan

Michigan Technological
University *B, M, D*

New York

New York University *B*

Pennsylvania

Lehigh University *B*

Texas

Texas A&M University *M*

Technology/industrial arts education

Alabama

Community College of the Air
Force *A*

Alaska

University of Alaska
Southeast *M*

Arizona

Eastern Arizona College *A*

California

Azusa Pacific University *M*
California Baptist University *T*
California State University
Los Angeles *B, M*
Cypress College *A*
Pepperdine University *M*
San Diego State University *B, M*
San Francisco State University *T*

Colorado

Colorado State University *B, T*

Connecticut

Central Connecticut State
University *B, M, T*
University of Hartford *M*

Delaware

Wilmington University *M*

Florida

Miami Dade College *A*
St. Petersburg College *B*

Georgia

Valdosta State University *M*

Hawaii

University of Hawaii
Honolulu Community College *A*

Idaho

University of Idaho *M, T*

Illinois

Chicago State University *B*
Concordia University Chicago *M*
Illinois State University *B, T*
Loyola University Chicago *M*

Indiana

Ball State University *B, M, T*
Indiana State University *M*
Purdue University *B, M, D*
Vincennes University *A*

Iowa

Iowa State University *B, M, D, T*
Iowa Wesleyan College *B*
University of Northern Iowa *B*

Kansas

Fort Hays State University *B*
Independence Community College *A*
McPherson College *B, T*
Pittsburg State University *B, M*

Kentucky

Berea College *B, T*
Eastern Kentucky University *B, M*

Louisiana

University of Louisiana at Lafayette *B*

Maine

University of Southern Maine *B, T*

Maryland

Loyola University Maryland *M*
University of Maryland
Eastern Shore *B, M*

Massachusetts

Fitchburg State University *B, M, T*
Westfield State University *B, M, T*

Michigan

Central Michigan University *B, M*
Delta College *A*
Eastern Michigan University *B, T*
Michigan Technological University *T*
Northern Michigan University *B, T*
Western Michigan University *B*

Minnesota

Minnesota State University
Mankato *B, M, T*
Saint Cloud State University *B*
University of Minnesota
Crookston *B*
Twin Cities *B, M, D*

Mississippi

Hinds Community College *A*
Jackson State University *M*

Missouri

Drury University *B, T*
Lindenwood University *B*
Missouri Southern State
University *B, M, T*
Missouri State University *B*
Southeast Missouri State University *B*
University of Central Missouri *B, M*

Montana

Montana State University *B*
Montana State University
Northern *B*
University of Montana: Western *B, T*

Nebraska

Chadron State College *B, M*
Union College *B*
University of Nebraska
Kearney *B, M*
Wayne State College *B, T*

New Hampshire

Keene State College *B*

New Jersey

College of New Jersey *B, M, T*
Montclair State University *B, M, T*

New Mexico

Central New Mexico Community
College *A*
University of New Mexico *B*
Western New Mexico University *B*

New York

City University of New York
New York City College of
Technology *B*
College of Saint Rose *M, T*
Dowling College *T*
Hofstra University *T*
Pace University *M, T*
Pace University: Pleasantville/
Briarcliff *M, T*
SUNY
College at Buffalo *B, M, T*
College at Oswego *B, M, T*

North Carolina

Appalachian State University *B, T*
North Carolina Agricultural and
Technical State
University *B, M, T*
North Carolina State
University *B, M, D, T*

North Dakota

University of North Dakota *M*
Valley City State University *B, T*

Ohio

Bowling Green State University *B, M*
Ohio Northern University *B, T*
Ohio State University
Columbus Campus *B*
University of Rio Grande *T*
University of Toledo *M*
Youngstown State University *M*

Oklahoma

Langston University *B*
Southwestern Oklahoma State
University *B, M, T*
University of Central Oklahoma *B*

Pennsylvania

Arcadia University *M*

Rhode Island

Rhode Island College *B, M*

South Carolina

South Carolina State University *B, T*

Tennessee

Middle Tennessee State University *B*

Texas

El Paso Community College *A*
Our Lady of the Lake University of
San Antonio *B*
Prairie View A&M University *M*
Sam Houston State University *M, T*
Sul Ross State University *M*
Texas A&M University
Kingsville *M*
Texas Southern University *M*
Wayland Baptist University *B, T*

Utah

Southern Utah University *B*
Utah State University *B, M*

Washington

Central Washington University *B, T*
Western Washington University *B*

Wisconsin

University of Wisconsin
Platteville *B, T*
Stout *B, M, T*
Viterbo University *B, T*

Wyoming

Casper College *A*
University of Wyoming *B*

Telecommunications engineering

California

National University *M*
University of Southern California *M*

Colorado

University of Colorado
Boulder *M, D*

Florida

Florida International University *M*

Maryland

University of Maryland
College Park *M*

Oklahoma

University of Oklahoma *M*

Texas

University of Texas
Dallas *B, M, D*

Telecommunications management

California
National University *M*

Indiana
Purdue University *B*

New Jersey
Stevens Institute of Technology *M*

West Virginia
American Public University System *C*
Blue Ridge Community and Technical
College *C*

Telecommunications technology

Alabama
Gadsden State Community
College *C, A*
Herzing University
Birmingham *A*

California
City College of San Francisco *C*
Southwestern College *C, A*

Colorado
University of Denver *M*

Connecticut
Gateway Community College *C*

Florida
Palm Beach State College *C*

Georgia
Southern Polytechnic State
University *B*

Idaho
Idaho State University *B*

Indiana
Ivy Tech Community College
Central Indiana *C, A*
North Central *C, A*
Northeast *C, A*
Northwest *C, A*
South Central *C, A*
Southwest *C, A*

Iowa
Kirkwood Community College *C, A*
Western Iowa Tech Community
College *A*

Maryland
Capitol College *A, B*
Howard Community College *C, A*
TESST College of Technology
Baltimore *C, A*

Massachusetts
Massasoit Community College *A*
North Shore Community College *A*
Quinsigamond Community College *A*
Springfield Technical Community
College *A*

Michigan
Ferris State University *B*
Lawrence Technological University *B*
Wayne County Community College *A*

Mississippi
Hinds Community College *C, A*

Nebraska
University of Nebraska
Lincoln *M*

New Jersey
Mercer County Community
College *A*

New Mexico
Eastern New Mexico University:
Roswell *C*

New York
Canisius College *M*
Cayuga Community College *A*
City University of New York
New York City College of
Technology *A, B*
Erie Community College *A*
Pace University *C, B, M*
Rochester Institute of
Technology *B, M*
SUNY
Farmingdale State College *B*
Institute of Technology at Utica/
Rome *M*
St. John's University *A, B*
Schenectady County Community
College *A*

North Carolina
Central Carolina Community
College *C*

Ohio
Marion Technical College *C, A*

Puerto Rico
Turabo University *M*

South Carolina
York Technical College *C*

South Dakota
Mitchell Technical Institute *A*

Texas
Collin County Community College
District *C, A*
Eastfield College *C, A*
St. Philip's College *C, A*
San Antonio College *A*
Southern Methodist University *M*
Texas State Technical College
Harlingen *C, A*
Marshall *C, A*
Waco *C, A*

Utah
Salt Lake Community College *C, A*

Washington
Clark College *C, A*

West Virginia
Bridgemont Community and
Technical College *C*

Wisconsin
Herzing University
Madison *A, B*

Terrorism/ counterterrorism

Minnesota
Itasca Community College *A*

Ohio
Tiffin University *B*

West Virginia
American Public University System *A*

Textile science

Alabama
Auburn University *M*

California
Fashion Institute of Design and
Merchandising
Los Angeles *A*
San Diego *A*
San Francisco *A*

Georgia
University of Georgia *D*

Michigan
Michigan State University *B, M*

Nebraska
University of Nebraska
Lincoln *B*

Pennsylvania
Philadelphia University *C, B, M*

Textile sciences/ engineering

Georgia
Georgia Institute of
Technology *B, M, D*

Massachusetts
University of Massachusetts
Dartmouth *B, M*

North Carolina
North Carolina State
University *B, M, D*

Pennsylvania
Philadelphia University *B, M, D*

Theater arts management

Alabama
Calhoun Community College *A*
Faulkner University *B*

Alaska
University of Alaska
Anchorage *B*

California
Biola University *B*
Ohlone College *C*

Colorado
Colorado Mountain College *C*

Connecticut
Yale University *M*

District of Columbia
American University *B*
Howard University *B*

Florida
Florida State University *M*
Nova Southeastern University *B*
University of Miami *B*

Georgia
Berry College *B*
Young Harris College *B*

Illinois
DePaul University *M*
Lake Forest College *B*
McKendree University *B*

Indiana
Bethel College *B*
Indiana Wesleyan University *B*
Purdue University *B*
University of Evansville *B*

Iowa
Buena Vista University *B*
Iowa Western Community College *A*
St. Ambrose University *B*

Kansas
Benedictine College *B*

Kentucky
Lindsey Wilson College *B*

Maine
University of Southern Maine *B*

Massachusetts
Eastern Nazarene College *B*
Emerson College *B*
Massachusetts College of Liberal
Arts *B*

Michigan
Aquinas College *B*
Eastern Michigan University *M*
Michigan State University *B, M*
University of Michigan
Flint *M*
Western Michigan University *B*

Missouri
Crowder College *A*
Lindenwood University *B, M*

Nebraska
Metropolitan Community
College *C, A*

New Hampshire
Franklin Pierce University *B, M*

New Jersey
Bergen Community College *A*
Passaic County Community College *A*
Rider University *B*

New Mexico
Santa Fe University of Art and
Design *B*

New York
Ithaca College *B*
Pace University *B*
SUNY
College at Buffalo *B*
University of Rochester *B*

North Carolina
Guilford College *B*
William Peace University *B*

Ohio
Lake Erie College *B*
Ohio University *B*
University of Akron *M*

Oklahoma
Oklahoma City University *B*
Rose State College *A*

Oregon
University of Portland *B*
Western Oregon University *B*

Pennsylvania

Albright College *B*
Carnegie Mellon University *M*
Drexel University *B*
Gettysburg College *B*
Lafayette College *B*
Messiah College *B*
Seton Hill University *B*
Slippery Rock University of
    Pennsylvania *B*

South Carolina

Converse College *B*

Texas

Texas Wesleyan University *B*
University of Texas
    El Paso *B*

Virginia

Regent University *B*
University of Richmond *B*

Washington

Pacific Lutheran University *B*

West Virginia

West Virginia Wesleyan College *B*

Wisconsin

University of Wisconsin
    Whitewater *B*

Theater design and technology

Alabama

Faulkner University *B*

Alaska

University of Alaska
    Anchorage *B*
    Fairbanks *B*

Arizona

Phoenix College *C*
University of Arizona *B*

California

Allan Hancock College *C*
California Institute of the
    Arts *C, B, M*
California State University
    East Bay *R*
    Long Beach *B, M*
    San Bernardino *B*
College of the Sequoias *A*
Cypress College *C, A*
Diablo Valley College *C, A*
Fashion Institute of Design and
    Merchandising
    Los Angeles *A*
    San Francisco *A*
Foothill College *C, A*
Fresno City College *C, A*
Gavilan College *A*
Glendale Community College *A*
Grossmont College *C, A*
Irvine Valley College *A*
Long Beach City College *A*
Los Angeles Pierce College *C, A*
Moorpark College *C, A*
Ohlone College *C, A*
Palomar College *C*
Pepperdine University *B*
San Francisco State University *M*
San Joaquin Delta College *A*
Santa Barbara City College *A*
Santa Rosa Junior College *C*
University of Southern
    California *B, M*
Vanguard University of Southern
    California *B*

Colorado

Community College of Denver *C*
Red Rocks Community College *C, A*

Connecticut

University of Connecticut *B*
Yale University *M*

Delaware

University of Delaware *B*

District of Columbia

Howard University *B*

Florida

Florida Southern College *B*
Florida State College at
    Jacksonville *A*
Florida State University *B*
Saint Johns River State College *C, A*
University of Miami *B*

Georgia

Brenau University *B*
Savannah College of Art and
    Design *B, M*

Illinois

City Colleges of Chicago
    Kennedy-King College *C*
Columbia College Chicago *B*
DePaul University *B, M*
Illinois Wesleyan University *B*
Lincoln College *A*
Millikin University *B*

Indiana

Huntington University *B*
Vincennes University *A*

Iowa

Coe College *B*
Cornell College *B*
Drake University *B*
University of Iowa *M*
University of Northern Iowa *B*

Kansas

Southwestern College *B*
University of Kansas *B, M*

Louisiana

Centenary College of Louisiana *R*
Delgado Community College *C*

Maine

New England School of
    Communications *B*

Maryland

Carroll Community College *A*
Harford Community College *A*
Montgomery College *A*
University of Maryland
    College Park *M*

Massachusetts

Bard College at Simon's Rock *B*
Boston University *B, M*
Emerson College *B*
Fitchburg State University *B*
Salem State University *B*
University of Massachusetts
    Amherst *C*

Michigan

Aquinas College *B*
Central Michigan University *B*
Lansing Community College *C*
Lawrence Technological University *C*
Michigan Technological University *B*
Oakland University *B*
University of Michigan *B*

University of Michigan
    Flint *B*
Western Michigan University *B*

Minnesota

Minnesota State University
    Mankato *B*
Normandale Community College *A*

Missouri

College of the Ozarks *B*
Lindenwood University *B*
Northwest Missouri State
    University *B*
University of Missouri
    Kansas City *M*

Montana

Rocky Mountain College *B*

New Hampshire

Franklin Pierce University *B*
Keene State College *B*

New Jersey

Essex County College *A*
Kean University *B*

New Mexico

San Juan College *A*
Santa Fe University of Art and
    Design *B*
University of New Mexico *B*

New York

City University of New York
    New York City College of
        Technology *C, B*
Fordham University *B*
Genesee Community College *A*
Ithaca College *B*
SUNY
    College at Fredonia *R*
    College at Purchase *B, M*
    University at Binghamton *B*
Suffolk County Community College *A*
Syracuse University *R*
Wagner College *B*

North Carolina

Elon University *B*
Greensboro College *C, B*
Lees-McRae College *B*
University of North Carolina
    School of the Arts *C, B, M*

Ohio

Baldwin Wallace University *B*
Ohio University *M*
Otterbein University *B*
Sinclair Community College *A*
University of Cincinnati *B, M*
University of Findlay *B*
University of Rio Grande *A*
Wright State University *B*
Youngstown State University *B*

Oklahoma

Oklahoma City Community
    College *A*
Oklahoma City University *M*
Oral Roberts University *B*
University of Central Oklahoma *B*

Pennsylvania

Carnegie Mellon University *M*
Penn State
    Abington *B*
    Altoona *B*
    Beaver *B*
    Berks *B*
    Brandywine *B*
    DuBois *B*

Erie, The Behrend College *B*
Fayette, The Eberly Campus *B*
Greater Allegheny *B*
Harrisburg *B*
Hazleton *B*
Lehigh Valley *B*
Mont Alto *B*
New Kensington *B*
Schuylkill *B*
Shenango *B*
University Park *B*
Wilkes-Barre *B*
Worthington Scranton *B*
York *B*
Seton Hill University *B*
Slippery Rock University of
    Pennsylvania *B*
Temple University *M*
University of the Arts *B*

South Carolina

Coker College *B*

Tennessee

Belmont University *B*
Freed-Hardeman University *B*

Texas

Baylor University *B*
Texas Christian University *B*
Trinity University *B*

Utah

Broadview University
    Broadview Entertainment Arts
        University *B*
Dixie State College *B*
Salt Lake Community College *A*
Utah Valley University *A*

Vermont

Bennington College *B*
Johnson State College *A, B*
Marlboro College *B*

Virginia

Shenandoah University *B*

Washington

Cornish College of the Arts *B*
North Seattle Community College *C*
Shoreline Community College *A*

West Virginia

Davis and Elkins College *B*

Wisconsin

Carthage College *B*

Wyoming

Casper College *A*
Central Wyoming College *A*
Western Wyoming Community
    College *C, A*

Theater history/ criticism

California

California State University
    San Bernardino *B*
College of the Desert *A*
Whittier College *B*

Connecticut

Yale University *M*

Delaware

University of Delaware *B*

District of Columbia
American University *B*
George Washington University *B*
Howard University *B*

Georgia
Clark Atlanta University *B*
Oglethorpe University *B*

Illinois
DePaul University *B*
Northwestern University *B*
University of Illinois
   Urbana-Champaign *B*

Iowa
Buena Vista University *B, T*

Louisiana
Tulane University *B, M*

Maine
Bowdoin College *B*

Maryland
University of Maryland
   College Park *M, D*

Massachusetts
Boston University *B*
Emerson College *M*
Salem State University *B*
Suffolk University *B*
Tufts University *B, M, D*

Michigan
Michigan State University *M*
Western Michigan University *B*

Minnesota
Augsburg College *B*

Missouri
Washington University in St.
   Louis *B, M*

New Hampshire
Keene State College *B*

New York
Bard College *B*
Columbia University *B*
SUNY
   College at Purchase *B*

Ohio
Ohio University *M*

Pennsylvania
Arcadia University *B*
Washington & Jefferson College *B*

Utah
Brigham Young University *B*

Vermont
Bennington College *B*
Marlboro College *B*

Virginia
Averett University *B*
Virginia Wesleyan College *B*

West Virginia
West Virginia University *B*

Wisconsin
University of Wisconsin
   Whitewater *B, T*

Theological studies

Alabama
Amridge University *M, D*
Faulkner University *B, M*
Huntsville Bible College *B*
Oakwood University *B, M*
Samford University *M*

Alaska
Alaska Bible College *B*

Arizona
American Indian College of the
   Assemblies of God *A, B*

Arkansas
Ecclesia College *B*
Harding University *B, M, D*
John Brown University *B*
Ouachita Baptist University *B*
Williams Baptist College *A, B*

California
Azusa Pacific University *B, D*
Bethesda University of California *B*
Biola University *B, M, D*
California Christian College *B*
California Lutheran University *B*
Concordia University Irvine *B, M*
Hope International
   University *C, A, B, M*
La Sierra University *M*
Loyola Marymount University *B, M*
Master's College *B, D*
Pacific Union College *B, T*
Pepperdine University *M*
Providence Christian College *B*
Santa Clara University *M, D*
Shasta Bible College and Graduate
   School *B*
Simpson University *B, M*
Southern California Seminary *M*
University of San Francisco *B, M*
Vanguard University of Southern
   California *B, M*
William Jessup University *B*
World Mission University *M*

Colorado
Colorado Christian University *B*

Connecticut
Holy Apostles College and
   Seminary *B, M*
Yale University *M*

District of Columbia
Catholic University of America *M, D*

Florida
Ave Maria University *B, M, D*
Baptist College of Florida *A, B*
Barry University *C, B, M*
Hobe Sound Bible College *B*
Johnson University: Florida *B*
Palm Beach Atlantic University *B, M*
Saint Leo University *M*
Saint Thomas University *M, D*
Warner University *C, A, B*

Georgia
Emory University *M, D*
Mercer University *M, D*
Shorter University *B*

Hawaii
Chaminade University of Honolulu *M*

Idaho
Boise Bible College *A, B*
New Saint Andrews College *M*

Illinois
Benedictine University *B*
Benedictine University at
   Springfield *B*
Concordia University Chicago *B*
Dominican University *B*
Elmhurst College *B*
Judson University *B*
Lincoln Christian University *M*
Loyola University Chicago *B, M, D*
Moody Bible Institute *B, M*
North Park University *B, M, D*
Olivet Nazarene University *B, M*
Trinity Christian College *B*
Trinity International University *B, M*
University of Chicago *B, M, D*
University of St. Francis *B*
Wheaton College *M, D*

Indiana
Anderson University *B, M*
Bethel College *B, M*
Hanover College *B*
Holy Cross College *B*
Huntington University *M*
Indiana Wesleyan University *A, B*
Marian University *B*
Martin University *B*
Oakland City University *M, D*
University of Evansville *B*
University of Notre Dame *B, M, D*
University of St. Francis *C, B, M*
Valparaiso University *B, M*

Iowa
Briar Cliff University *A, B*
Dordt College *B*
Emmaus Bible College *B*
Faith Baptist Bible College and
   Theological Seminary *B, M*
Loras College *M*
St. Ambrose University *M*
University of Dubuque *M, D*

Kansas
Barclay College *B*
Benedictine College *B*
Central Christian College of Kansas *A*
Hesston College *A*
Manhattan Christian College *A, B*
Newman University *B, M*
Sterling College *B*
Tabor College *B*
University of St. Mary *B*

Kentucky
Bellarmine University *B, M*
Brescia University *B*
Campbellsville University *M*
Kentucky Christian University *M*
Kentucky Mountain Bible College *B*

Louisiana
New Orleans Baptist Theological
   Seminary *M, D*
Xavier University of Louisiana *B, M*

Maine
Saint Joseph's College of Maine *B*

Maryland
Mount St. Mary's University *B, M*
Washington Adventist University *B*

Massachusetts
Anna Maria College *B, M*
Assumption College *B*
Boston College *D*
Boston University *M, D*
Eastern Nazarene College *B, M*
Elms College *M*
Harvard College *M*
Hellenic College/Holy Cross *B, M*

Michigan
Andrews University *B, M, D*
Aquinas College *B*
Grace Bible College *B*
Rochester College *B*
Sacred Heart Major Seminary *A, M*
Spring Arbor University *B*

Minnesota
Bethel University *M*
College of St. Benedict *B*
Concordia University St. Paul *B*
Crossroads College *B*
Crown College *B*
North Central University *B*
St. Catherine University *M*
St. John's University *B, M*
St. Mary's University of Minnesota *B*
University of Northwestern - St.
   Paul *M*

Mississippi
Northeast Mississippi Community
   College *A*
Southeastern Baptist College *B*

Missouri
Baptist Bible College *B*
Calvary Bible College and Theological
   Seminary *M*
Central Christian College of the
   Bible *B*
Missouri Baptist University *A*
Ozark Christian College *B*
St. Louis Christian College *A, B*
Saint Louis University *B, M, D*
Southwest Baptist University *B*

Montana
Carroll College *B*

Nebraska
College of Saint Mary *B, T*
Concordia University *B*
Creighton University *C, A, B, M*
Grace University *B*
Nebraska Christian College *A, B*
Union College *B*

New Hampshire
Saint Anselm College *B*

New Jersey
Assumption College for Sisters *C, A*
Caldwell College *B*
College of St. Elizabeth *C, B, M*
Drew University *M, D*
Georgian Court University *M*
Seton Hall University *B, M*

New York
Holy Trinity Orthodox Seminary *C, B*
Jewish Theological Seminary of
   America *D*
Saint Bonaventure University *B*
St. John's University *B, M*

North Carolina
Apex School of Theology *B*
Belmont Abbey College *B*
Campbell University *B, M*
Duke University *M, D*
Laurel University *C, A, B, M, D*
Lenoir-Rhyne University *B*
Livingstone College *B*
Mid-Atlantic Christian University *B*
Shaw University *M*
Shepherds Theological Seminary *M*
Southeastern Baptist Theological
   Seminary *C, A, B, M, D*

Southeastern Baptist Theological
Seminary: Theological
Professions *D*
Wake Forest University *M*

North Dakota

Trinity Bible College *B*
University of Mary *B*

Ohio

Allegheny Wesleyan College *A, B*
Ashland University *M, D*
Cedarville University *B*
Cincinnati Christian University *M*
Franciscan University of
Steubenville *A, B, M*
God's Bible School and College *B*
Lourdes University *M*
Malone University *B, M*
Mount Vernon Nazarene
University *B, M*
Notre Dame College *A, B*
Ohio Christian University *B*
Ohio Dominican University *A, B, M*
Pontifical College Josephinum *M*
Rabbinical College of Telshe *B, M, D*
University of Dayton *M, D*
University of Findlay *B*
Walsh University *B, M*

Oklahoma

Family of Faith College *C, B*
Hillsdale Free Will Baptist College *B*
Mid-America Christian University *B*
Oklahoma Baptist University *C, A, B*
Oklahoma Christian University *B, M*
Oklahoma Wesleyan University *B*
Oral Roberts University *B, M, D*
St. Gregory's University *B*
Southern Nazarene University *B*
Southwestern Christian
University *B, M*

Oregon

Concordia University *B*
Corban University *B, M*
George Fox University *M*
Mount Angel Seminary *C, B*
Multnomah University *B, M*
New Hope Christian College *B*
Northwest Christian University *B*
University of Portland *B, M*
Warner Pacific College *M*

Pennsylvania

Baptist Bible College of
Pennsylvania *M*
Bryn Athyn College *B, M*
Cairn University *B*
Carlow University *B*
DeSales University *C, B, T*
Duquesne University *B, M, D*
Eastern University *B, M*
Gannon University *B*
Immaculata University *B*
King's College *B*
Moravian College *M*
St. Charles Borromeo Seminary -
Overbrook *M*
St. Vincent College *B*
Valley Forge Christian College *B, M*
Villanova University *M*
Waynesburg University *B*
Yeshivath Beth Moshe *M*

Puerto Rico

Bayamon Central University *M*
Pontifical Catholic University of
Puerto Rico *M*
Universidad Adventista de las
Antillas *B*

Rhode Island

Providence College *B, M*

South Carolina

Bob Jones University *M, D*
Columbia International
University *M, D*
Erskine College *M, D*
Morris College *B*

South Dakota

University of Sioux Falls *B*

Tennessee

American Baptist College *C, A, B*
Aquinas College *B*
Carson-Newman University *A, B*
Freed-Hardeman University *B, M*
Lee University *B, M*
Lipscomb University *M*
Sewanee: The University of the
South *M, D*
Southern Adventist University *B, M*
Tennessee Temple University *B*
Trevecca Nazarene University *M*
Union University *B*
Vanderbilt University *M*
Visible Music College *B*
Welch College *B*

Texas

Abilene Christian University *M*
Austin Graduate School of
Theology *B, M*
Baptist Missionary Association
Theological Seminary *A, B, M*
Baptist University of the
Americas *C, A, B*
Baylor University *M, D*
Brazosport College *A*
Criswell College *B, M*
Dallas Baptist University *M*
Dallas Christian College *D*
Hardin-Simmons University *B, M, D*
Houston Baptist University *M*
Howard Payne University *B*
Lubbock Christian University *B, M*
St. Edward's University *B*
St. Mary's University *B, M*
Southern Methodist University *M, D*
Southwestern Adventist University *B*
Southwestern Assemblies of God
University *A*
Southwestern Baptist Theological
Seminary *D*
Southwestern Baptist Theological
Seminary: Theological
Professions *M, D*
University of Dallas *B, M*
University of Mary Hardin-Baylor *B*
University of St. Thomas *B, M*

Virginia

Bluefield College *B*
Catholic Distance
University *C, A, B, M*
Eastern Mennonite University *M*
Hampton University *B*
Liberty University *M, D*
Regent University *B, M, D*
Virginia Union University *M, D*

Washington

Faith Evangelical College &
Seminary *B, M, D*
Northwest University *B, M*
Seattle University *M, T*
Trinity Lutheran College *A, B*
Walla Walla University *B*
Whitworth University *M*

West Virginia

Wheeling Jesuit University *B*

Wisconsin

Concordia University Wisconsin *B*
Maranatha Baptist Bible College *M*

Marquette University *B, M*
St. Norbert College *M*
Silver Lake College of the Holy
Family *B*
Wisconsin Lutheran College *B*

Theoretical/ mathematical physics

California

Chapman University *B*

Indiana

Indiana University
Bloomington *D*

Kansas

Washburn University *B*

Michigan

Spring Arbor University *B*

New York

SUNY
College at Fredonia *B*
University at Buffalo *B*

Pennsylvania

Carnegie Mellon University *B*

Texas

Rice University *M, D*
Southwestern Adventist
University *B, T*

Vermont

Marlboro College *B*

Virginia

Sweet Briar College *B*

Wisconsin

Viterbo University *B*

Tool and die technology

Alabama

Alabama Southern Community
College *C*
Bevill State Community College *C, A*
Bishop State Community College *C*
Calhoun Community College *C, A*
Gadsden State Community
College *C, A*
George C. Wallace Community
College at Dothan *C, A*
Lawson State Community College *C*
Northeast Alabama Community
College *C*
Shelton State Community
College *C, A*
Wallace State Community College at
Hanceville *C, A*

Arkansas

Rich Mountain Community College *C*

Georgia

North Georgia Technical College *C*

Illinois

Black Hawk College *C*
College of DuPage *C*
College of Lake County *C*
Illinois Valley Community College *C*
John A. Logan College *C, A*
Prairie State College *C, A*
Rock Valley College *C*

Indiana

Ivy Tech Community College
Bloomington *C, A*
Central Indiana *C, A*
Columbus *C, A*
East Central *C, A*
Kokomo *C, A*
Lafayette *C, A*
North Central *C, A*
Northeast *C, A*
Northwest *C, A*
Richmond *C, A*
South Central *C, A*
Southwest *C, A*
Wabash Valley *C, A*
Vincennes University *A*

Iowa

Des Moines Area Community
College *C, A*
Marshalltown Community College *C*
North Iowa Area Community
College *A*
Northwest Iowa Community
College *C, A*
Southeastern Community
College *C, A*

Michigan

Ferris State University *A*
Montcalm Community College *C*
Oakland Community College *C*

Minnesota

Hennepin Technical College *C, A*
Minnesota State College - Southeast
Technical *C*
Ridgewater College *C, A*
St. Paul College *C*

Mississippi

Itawamba Community College *A*
Northeast Mississippi Community
College *C, A*

North Carolina

Asheville-Buncombe Technical
Community College *C*

Ohio

Lakeland Community College *C, A*
North Central State College *C, A*
Owens Community College
Toledo *C, A*
Sinclair Community College *C*
Zane State College *A*

Pennsylvania

Lehigh Carbon Community College *C*
Thaddeus Stevens College of
Technology *A*

South Carolina

York Technical College *A*

South Dakota

Lake Area Technical Institute *A*

Texas

Texas State Technical College
Harlingen *C*

Washington

Edmonds Community College *C*

Wisconsin

Lakeshore Technical College *C*
Milwaukee Area Technical College *C*
Northcentral Technical College *C*
Waukesha County Technical
College *C*
Western Technical College *C*

Tourism promotion

California

Butte College *C, A*
City College of San Francisco *A*
Coastline Community College *C*
Cypress College *C, A*
Foothill College *C, A*
Fullerton College *C, A*
Grossmont College *C, A*
Long Beach City College *C, A*
Los Angeles City College *C, A*
Los Medanos College *C, A*
Pasadena City College *C, A*
Saddleback College *C*
San Diego City College *C, A*
Southwestern College *C, A*

District of Columbia

George Washington University *B, M*

Florida

Florida National University *A*
Miami Dade College *C, A*

Idaho

College of Southern Idaho *A*

Illinois

College of DuPage *C, A*
Lincoln College *A*

Maine

Beal College *A*
Kaplan University
  South Portland *A*
University of Maine
  Machias *B*

Maryland

Allegany College of Maryland *C*

Massachusetts

Northern Essex Community
  College *A*

Michigan

Grand Valley State University *B*

Minnesota

Central Lakes College *C*

Missouri

University of Central Missouri *B*

Nebraska

Midland University *A*

New Hampshire

NHTI-Concord's Community
  College *C, A*

New York

Bryant & Stratton College
  Syracuse *A*
City University of New York
  Kingsborough Community
    College *A*
Finger Lakes Community College *A*
Genesee Community College *C*
Jefferson Community College *C, A*
Monroe Community College *A*
Paul Smith's College *B*
Rochester Institute of
  Technology *B, M*
Rockland Community College *A*
SUNY
  College of Technology at Delhi *A*
Schenectady County Community
  College *C, A*
Wood Tobe-Coburn School *C*

North Carolina

Blue Ridge Community College *A*

Ohio

Bowling Green State University *B*
Fortis College
  Centerville *C*
Lakeland Community College *C, A*
Youngstown State University *A, B*

Oklahoma

Oklahoma City Community
  College *A*

Pennsylvania

Mansfield University of
  Pennsylvania *A, B*
Yorktowne Business Institute *A*

Puerto Rico

University of Puerto Rico
  Carolina Regional College *B*
University of the Sacred Heart *B*

Rhode Island

Community College of Rhode
  Island *C*
Johnson & Wales University
  Providence *B*

Texas

Amarillo College *A*
Central Texas College *C*
El Paso Community College *C, A*

West Virginia

Concord University *B*
Mountain State College *A*
West Liberty University *B*

Wisconsin

Lac Courte Oreilles Ojibwa
  Community College *C*

Tourism/travel management

California

Chabot College *A*
City College of San Francisco *A*
Coastline Community College *C*
College of the Redwoods *C*
Empire College *C*
Grossmont College *C, A*
Long Beach City College *C, A*
Los Angeles City College *C, A*
Saddleback College *C, A*
San Diego Mesa College *C, A*
Santiago Canyon College *C, A*
Southwestern College *C, A*

Colorado

Colorado Mountain College *C, A*

Connecticut

Mitchell College *B*
Three Rivers Community
  College *C, A*

Florida

Broward College *A*
Edison State College *A*
Florida National University *A*
Florida State College at
  Jacksonville *C, A*
Johnson & Wales University
  North Miami *B*
Miami Dade College *C, A*
Rasmussen College
  New Port Richey *A*
Saint Thomas University *B*

Schiller International
  University *A, B, M*

Georgia

Atlanta Technical College *C*
Gwinnett Technical College *C*

Hawaii

Hawaii Pacific University *B*
Heald College
  Honolulu *A*
University of Hawaii
  Manoa *B, M*
  Maui College *A*

Illinois

Illinois Central College *C*
Lexington College *A, B*
Lincoln College *A, B*
Moraine Valley Community
  College *C, A*
Roosevelt University *B, M*

Indiana

Indiana University
  Purdue University
    Indianapolis *C, B*
Purdue University *B, M, D*
University of Indianapolis *A, B*

Iowa

AIB College of Business *A*

Kentucky

Sullivan University *C, A*

Louisiana

Delta School of Business &
  Technology *C*

Maine

Kaplan University
  South Portland *A*
University of Maine
  Machias *B*

Maryland

Allegany College of Maryland *C*

Massachusetts

Becker College *B*
Bristol Community College *C*
Bunker Hill Community College *C, A*
Middlesex Community College *C*
Northern Essex Community
  College *A*
Salem State University *B*

Michigan

Baker College
  Clinton Township *A*
  Flint *A*
Central Michigan University *M*
Grand Valley State University *B*

Minnesota

Central Lakes College *A*
Dakota County Technical
  College *C, A*
Minneapolis Business College *C, A*
Saint Cloud State University *B*

Mississippi

Hinds Community College *C, A*
University of Southern Mississippi *B*

Missouri

St. Louis Community College *A*
Stevens Institute of Business &
  Arts *A*

Montana

University of Montana: Western *A, B*

Nebraska

Kaplan University
  Lincoln *C*
University of Nebraska
  Kearney *B*

New Hampshire

NHTI-Concord's Community
  College *C, A*
Plymouth State University *B*

New Jersey

Cumberland County College *C, A*
Essex County College *A*
Mercer County Community
  College *C*

New York

Bryant & Stratton College
  Syracuse *A*
City University of New York
  Kingsborough Community
    College *A*
  LaGuardia Community College *A*
Genesee Community College *A*
Globe Institute of
  Technology *C, A, B*
Mildred Elley
  Albany *C, A*
Monroe Community College *A*
New York University *M*
Niagara County Community
  College *C, A*
Niagara University *B*
Paul Smith's College *A, B*
Rochester Institute of
  Technology *A, B, M*
Rockland Community College *A*
SUNY
  College at Plattsburgh *B*
  College of Technology at
    Delhi *A, B*
Sanford-Brown Institute
  Melville *A*
Sullivan County Community
  College *A*

North Carolina

Central Piedmont Community
  College *C, A*
Methodist University *B*

North Dakota

University of Jamestown *B*

Ohio

Columbus State Community
  College *A*
Fortis College
  Centerville *C*
Lakeland Community College *C, A*
Lorain County Community College *A*
Sinclair Community College *A*
University of Northwestern
  Ohio *C, A*
Youngstown State University *A, B*

Oklahoma

Northeastern State University *B*
Oklahoma City Community
  College *A*
Tulsa Community College *C, A*

Oregon

Blue Mountain Community College *C*
Chemeketa Community College *C, A*
Everest College
  Portland *A*
Mt. Hood Community College *C, A*

Pennsylvania

Bucks County Community
  College *C, A*

California University of
Pennsylvania *M*
Erie Business Center *A*
Erie Business Center South *A*
Harrisburg Area Community
College *C, A*
Mansfield University of
Pennsylvania *B*
Pace Institute *A*
Westmoreland County Community
College *A*

Puerto Rico

ICPR Junior College *C, A*
Inter American University of Puerto
Rico
Fajardo Campus *A*
National University College
Rio Grande *A*
Pontifical Catholic University of
Puerto Rico *A, B*

Rhode Island

Johnson & Wales University
Providence *B*

South Carolina

University of South Carolina
Columbia *B*

South Dakota

Black Hills State University *A*
National American University
Rapid City *B*

Tennessee

Chattanooga College *A*
National College of Business and
Technology
Madison *A*

Texas

Amarillo College *C*
Austin Community College *C*
Central Texas College *C*
El Paso Community College *C, A*
Houston Community College
System *C, A*
Richland College *A*
St. Philip's College *C, A*
Tarrant County College *C, A*
Texas A&M University *B*
Texas A&M University
Galveston *B*
University of Texas
San Antonio *B*

Vermont

Community College of Vermont *A*
Johnson State College *B*

Virginia

George Mason University *B*
Northern Virginia Community
College *C, A*
Virginia Highlands Community
College *C*

Washington

Edmonds Community College *C*
Highline Community College *C, A*

West Virginia

Concord University *B*
Mountain State College *A*
New River Community and Technical
College *A*
West Liberty University *B*

Wisconsin

Madison Area Technical College *A*
Milwaukee Area Technical
College *C, A*

Tourism/travel services

California

Los Medanos College *C, A*
Orange Coast College *C, A*

Connecticut

Central Connecticut State
University *B*

Georgia

Athens Technical College *C, A*

Michigan

Western Michigan University *B*

Minnesota

Dakota County Technical
College *C, A*
Normandale Community College *C*

Missouri

Stevens Institute of Business &
Arts *A*
University of Missouri
Columbia *B, M*

New York

Herkimer County Community
College *A*
Rochester Institute of
Technology *B, M*
SUNY
College of Agriculture and
Technology at Morrisville *A*
Schenectady County Community
College *A*

Pennsylvania

Montgomery County Community
College *A*
Westmoreland County Community
College *C*

Puerto Rico

Inter American University of Puerto
Rico
Metropolitan Campus *C, A*

Washington

Edmonds Community College *C, A*

Toxicology

Arkansas

University of Arkansas
for Medical Sciences *M, D*

California

University of California
Berkeley *B, M, D*

Colorado

Colorado State University *M, D*
University of Colorado
Denver *D*

District of Columbia

George Washington University *M, D*

Florida

University of Miami *B*

Georgia

University of Georgia *M, D*

Indiana

Indiana University
Purdue University
Indianapolis *M, D*

Iowa

Iowa State University *M, D*

Kansas

University of Kansas Medical
Center *M, D*

Kentucky

University of Kentucky *M, D*

Louisiana

University of Louisiana at Monroe *B*

Maryland

University of Maryland
Baltimore *M, D*
Baltimore County *M, D*
College Park *M, D*
Eastern Shore *M, D*

Massachusetts

Northeastern University *B*

Michigan

Eastern Michigan University *B*
University of Michigan *M, D*

Minnesota

Minnesota State University
Mankato *B, T*
University of Minnesota
Twin Cities *M, D*

Mississippi

Mississippi State University *D*

New Hampshire

Dartmouth College *D*

New Jersey

Felician College *B*
Montclair State University *B*
Rutgers, The State University of New
Jersey
New Brunswick/Piscataway
Campus *M, D*
Newark Campus *M, D*
Saint Peter's University *B*

New York

Nazareth College *B*
SUNY
University at Albany *M, D*
St. John's University *B, M*
University of Rochester *M, D*

North Carolina

North Carolina State University *M, D*
University of North Carolina
Chapel Hill *M, D*

Ohio

Ashland University *B*
University of Cincinnati *M, D*
University of Toledo *M*

Oregon

Oregon State University *M, D*

Pennsylvania

Penn State
Abington *B*
Altoona *B*
Beaver *B*
Berks *B*
Brandywine *B*
DuBois *B*
Erie, The Behrend College *B*
Fayette, The Eberly Campus *B*
Greater Allegheny *B*
Harrisburg *B*
Hazleton *B*
Lehigh Valley *B*

Mont Alto *B*
New Kensington *B*
Schuylkill *B*
Shenango *B*
University Park *B*
Wilkes-Barre *B*
Worthington Scranton *B*
York *B*

South Carolina

Clemson University *M, D*

Texas

Prairie View A&M University *M*
Texas A&M University *M, D*
Texas Southern University *M, D*
Texas Tech University *M, D*
University of Texas
Health Science Center at
Houston *M, D*

Utah

Utah State University *M, D*

Trade/industrial education

Arkansas

University of Arkansas
Pine Bluff *B, T*

California

California State University
Los Angeles *B*
San Bernardino *B, M*
Fullerton College *A*
Humboldt State University *T*
San Diego State University *B*
Vanguard University of Southern
California *T*

Colorado

Colorado School of Trades *A*
Colorado State University *B, T*

Delaware

Delaware State University *B*

Florida

Florida Agricultural and Mechanical
University *B, M, T*
University of Central Florida *B, M*
University of South Florida *B, M*
University of West Florida *B*

Georgia

Valdosta State University *B, M*

Idaho

University of Idaho *T*

Illinois

Chicago State University *M, D*
Southern Illinois University
Carbondale *B, M, D*

Indiana

Indiana State University *B, M, T*
Purdue University *A*

Iowa

Iowa State University *B, T*

Kansas

Fort Hays State University *B, T*

Kentucky

Eastern Kentucky University *B, M*
Murray State University *A, B*
Northern Kentucky University *B*
University of Louisville *B, M*
Western Kentucky University *B, T*

Massachusetts

Fitchburg State University *B, M, T*

Michigan

Western Michigan University *B*

Minnesota

Saint Cloud State University *T*
University of Minnesota
   Twin Cities *B, M, D, T*

Mississippi

Mississippi Gulf Coast Community
   College *A*

Missouri

Lindenwood University *B*

Nebraska

Chadron State College *B*
University of Nebraska
   Kearney *B*
   Lincoln *B, T*

Nevada

Great Basin College *B*

New Mexico

Eastern New Mexico University *B*

New York

New York University *B, M, D, T*
SUNY
   College at Buffalo *B, M, T*
   College at Oswego *B, M, T*

North Carolina

Isothermal Community College *A*
Lenoir Community College *A*
North Carolina Agricultural and
   Technical State University *B, T*
Southwestern Community College *A*

North Dakota

Valley City State University *B, T*

Ohio

Bowling Green State University *B*
Kent State University *B, M*
University of Toledo *B, M*

Pennsylvania

Indiana University of
   Pennsylvania *B, T*

Puerto Rico

Turabo University *B*

Texas

Sam Houston State University *M, T*
Texas A&M University
   Corpus Christi *M, T*
Texas State University *M, T*
Wayland Baptist University *B, T*

Virginia

Norfolk State University *B*
Virginia Polytechnic Institute and
   State University *M, D*
Virginia State University *B, M*

Washington

Central Washington University *B, T*
Western Washington University *M*

West Virginia

Marshall University *M*

Wisconsin

University of Wisconsin
   Stout *M*

Wyoming

University of Wyoming *B*

Traditional Chinese medicine/herbology

Connecticut

University of Bridgeport *M*

Minnesota

Northwestern Health Sciences
   University *M*

Washington

Bastyr University *B, M, D*

Transportation

Alabama

Community College of the Air
   Force *A*

California

Fresno City College *C, A*

Delaware

Wilmington University *M*

Florida

Florida Gateway College *C, A*
Florida State College at
   Jacksonville *C*

Illinois

Richland Community College *C*

Maryland

Cecil College *C, A*
Morgan State University *M*

Michigan

Baker College
   Muskegon *C*
Henry Ford Community College *A*

Nevada

University of Nevada
   Las Vegas *M*

New York

Nassau Community College *A*
Niagara University *B*
United States Merchant Marine
   Academy *B*

Ohio

Ohio Technical College *C, A*

South Carolina

Trident Technical College *C*
York Technical College *A*

Texas

Lee College *A*
Texas A&M University
   Galveston *B*
Texas Southern University *M*

Virginia

Central Virginia Community
   College *C*

Washington

Green River Community College *C, A*
Highline Community College *A*

Wisconsin

Milwaukee Area Technical College *A*
Northeast Wisconsin Technical
   College *A*

University of Wisconsin
   Superior *B*

Transportation/ highway engineering

California

California Polytechnic State
   University: San Luis Obispo *M*
University of Southern California *M*

Illinois

Illinois Institute of Technology *M*
University of Illinois
   Urbana-Champaign *B, M, D*

Massachusetts

Massachusetts Institute of
   Technology *M, D*

Missouri

Washington University in St.
   Louis *M, D*

New Jersey

New Jersey Institute of
   Technology *M, D*

New York

Rensselaer Polytechnic Institute *M, D*

Ohio

University of Akron *C*

Pennsylvania

Penn State
   Altoona *B*
Villanova University *M*

Wisconsin

Mid-State Technical College *A*

Transportation management

Arizona

Coconino County Community
   College *C*

California

University of California
   Davis *M, D*

Colorado

University of Denver *M*

Delaware

Wilmington University *M*

Florida

Embry-Riddle Aeronautical University
   Worldwide Campus *M*
Florida Institute of Technology *M*
Gulf Coast State College *C*
Polk State College *A*
University of North Florida *B*

Illinois

Kankakee Community College *C*
Northwestern University *M*

Iowa

Iowa State University *M*

Maryland

Anne Arundel Community College *C*
Cecil College *C, A*
Hagerstown Community College *C, A*

Massachusetts

Massachusetts Maritime Academy *B*
University of Massachusetts
   Amherst *C*

Michigan

College for Creative Studies *B*
Mott Community College *C*

New York

City University of New York
   CUNY Online *C*
SUNY
   Maritime College *B, M*

North Carolina

North Carolina Agricultural and
   Technical State University *B*

North Dakota

Bismarck State College *A*
North Dakota State University *M, D*

Ohio

North Central State College *C*
Ohio State University
   Columbus Campus *B, M, D*
Ohio Technical College *C*

Pennsylvania

University of Pennsylvania *B*

Puerto Rico

Pontifical Catholic University of
   Puerto Rico *B*

South Carolina

South Carolina State University *M*

Tennessee

Southwest Tennessee Community
   College *C*

Texas

Texas A&M University *B, M*
Texas A&M University
   Galveston *B*
Texas Southern University *M*

Truck/bus/commercial vehicle operation

Alabama

Bevill State Community College *C*
Bishop State Community College *C*

Arizona

Glendale Community College *C*
Pima Community College *C*

Arkansas

College of the Ouachitas *C*
North Arkansas College *C*
Pulaski Technical College *C*

Delaware

Delaware Technical Community
   College
   Jack F. Owens Campus *C*

Florida

College of Central Florida *C*
Florida Gateway College *C*
Indian River State College *C*
South Florida State College *C*

Georgia

Albany Technical College *C*
Athens Technical College *C*
Atlanta Technical College *C*
Bainbridge College *C*

Georgia Piedmont Technical
College *C*
Savannah Technical College *C*
Southeastern Technical College *C*

Idaho

College of Western Idaho *C*
Eastern Idaho Technical College *C*

Illinois

Black Hawk College *C*
City Colleges of Chicago
Harold Washington College *C*
Olive-Harvey College *C*
Danville Area Community College *C*
Elgin Community College *C*
Illinois Central College *C*
Illinois Valley Community College *C*
John Wood Community College *C*
Kaskaskia College *C*
Lincoln Land Community College *C*
Sauk Valley Community College *C*
Spoon River College *C*

Iowa

Hawkeye Community College *C*

Kansas

Fort Scott Community College *C*

Kentucky

Big Sandy Community and Technical
College *C*

Maryland

College of Southern Maryland *C*
Hagerstown Community College *C*

Michigan

Baker College
Cadillac *C, A*
Flint *C, A*
Glen Oaks Community College *C*

Minnesota

Alexandria Technical and Community
College *C*
Dakota County Technical College *C*
Lake Superior College *C*
Minnesota State College - Southeast
Technical *C*
Northland Community & Technical
College *C*

Mississippi

Copiah-Lincoln Community
College *C*
East Mississippi Community
College *C*
Hinds Community College *C*
Itawamba Community College *C*
Meridian Community College *C*
Mississippi Gulf Coast Community
College *C*

Missouri

Crowder College *C*

Montana

Blackfeet Community College *C*
Fort Peck Community College *C*

Nebraska

Central Community College *C*
Northeast Community College *C*
Southeast Community College *C*

New Mexico

Central New Mexico Community
College *C*
Eastern New Mexico University:
Roswell *C*
San Juan College *C*

North Carolina

Beaufort County Community
College *C*
Cape Fear Community College *C*
Davidson County Community
College *C*
Johnston Community College *C*

Oregon

Clatsop Community College *C*
Rogue Community College *C*

Pennsylvania

Pittsburgh Institute of Aeronautics *C*

South Carolina

Greenville Technical College *C*

South Dakota

Southeast Technical Institute *C*

Texas

Houston Community College
System *C*
San Jacinto College *C*
Weatherford College *C*

Utah

Salt Lake Community College *C*

Virginia

Advanced Technology Institute *C*
Dabney S. Lancaster Community
College *C*
Southside Virginia Community
College *C*
Southwest Virginia Community
College *C*
Tidewater Community College *C, A*
Wytheville Community College *C*

Washington

Bates Technical College *C*
Big Bend Community College *C*
Grays Harbor College *C*
Walla Walla Community College *C*

Wisconsin

Chippewa Valley Technical College *C*
Fox Valley Technical College *C*
Waukesha County Technical
College *C*

Turf management

Arizona

Northland Pioneer College *C, A*

California

Butte College *C*
College of the Desert *C, A*
Los Angeles Pierce College *C*
Monterey Peninsula College *C*
Mount San Antonio College *C*
Mount San Jacinto College *C, A*
San Joaquin Delta College *C*
Shasta College *C*
Southwestern College *C, A*

Delaware

Delaware Technical Community
College
Jack F. Owens Campus *C, A*
Stanton/Wilmington Campus *C*
Terry Campus *C*

Florida

Edison State College *C*
Florida Gateway College *C*
Florida Southern College *B*
Indian River State College *A*

Georgia

Abraham Baldwin Agricultural
College *A, B*
North Georgia Technical
College *C, A*
University of Georgia *B*

Illinois

College of DuPage *C*
College of Lake County *A*
Danville Area Community College *A*
Illinois Central College *C*
Illinois Eastern Community Colleges
Wabash Valley College *C*
Joliet Junior College *C, A*
Kishwaukee College *C*
McHenry County College *C*
Southwestern Illinois College *A*

Indiana

Purdue University *B*

Iowa

Iowa Central Community College *A*
Kirkwood Community College *C, A*

Kentucky

Eastern Kentucky University *B*

Maryland

Harford Community College *A*

Massachusetts

University of Massachusetts
Amherst *A, B*

Michigan

Michigan State University *C*
Northwestern Michigan College *A*

Minnesota

University of Minnesota
Crookston *B*

Mississippi

Mississippi Gulf Coast Community
College *C, A*

Missouri

Linn State Technical College *C, A*
Metropolitan Community College -
Kansas City *C, A*
Ozarks Technical Community
College *C, A*

Nebraska

Nebraska College of Technical
Agriculture *A*
University of Nebraska
Lincoln *B*

New Mexico

New Mexico State University *B*

New York

SUNY
College of Agriculture and
Technology at Cobleskill *B*
College of Technology at Delhi *A*

North Carolina

Blue Ridge Community College *C*
Brunswick Community College *C, A*
Catawba Valley Community
College *A*
Central Piedmont Community
College *C, A*
Guilford Technical Community
College *C, A*
North Carolina State University *A*
Sandhills Community College *A*
Wayne Community College *C, A*

North Dakota

Dakota College at Bottineau *A*
North Dakota State University *B*

Ohio

Cincinnati State Technical and
Community College *A*
Ohio State University
Agricultural Technical Institute *A*
Columbus Campus *C, A, B*

Oklahoma

Oklahoma State University
Oklahoma City *A*

Oregon

Southwestern Oregon Community
College *C, A*

Pennsylvania

Community College of Allegheny
County *C, A*
Delaware Valley College *B*
Penn State
Abington *B*
Altoona *B*
Beaver *B*
Berks *B*
Brandywine *B*
DuBois *B*
Erie, The Behrend College *B*
Fayette, The Eberly Campus *B*
Greater Allegheny *B*
Harrisburg *B*
Hazleton *B*
Lehigh Valley *B*
Mont Alto *B*
New Kensington *B*
Schuylkill *B*
Shenango *B*
University Park *B*
Wilkes-Barre *B*
Worthington Scranton *B*
York *B*
Westmoreland County Community
College *A*
Williamson Free School of
Mechanical Trades *A*

South Carolina

Horry-Georgetown Technical
College *C, A*
Trident Technical College *C*

South Dakota

Southeast Technical Institute *A*

Tennessee

Chattanooga State Community
College *C*

Texas

Houston Community College
System *C, A*
Palo Alto College *C, A*
Texas A&M University *B*
Texas State Technical College
Waco *C, A*

Virginia

Northern Virginia Community
College *C*

Washington

Edmonds Community College *C*
Spokane Community College *A*
Walla Walla Community College *C, A*

Wyoming

Sheridan College *A*

Turkish

Texas
University of Texas
 Austin *B*

Utah
University of Utah *B, M, D*

Washington
University of Washington *B*

Ukrainian

Washington
University of Washington *B*

Underwater diving

California
National University *C*
Santa Barbara City College *C, A*

Florida
Florida Keys Community College *A*

New Mexico
Navajo Technical University *C*

Upholstery

Alabama
Calhoun Community College *C*
Jefferson Davis Community
 College *C*
Southern Union State Community
 College *C*

Arkansas
Arkansas State University
 Beebe *C*

North Carolina
Catawba Valley Community
 College *C*

Washington
Spokane Falls Community College *C*

Urban, community, and regional planning

Alabama
Alabama Agricultural and Mechanical
 University *B, M*
Auburn University *M*

Arizona
Arizona State University *B, M, D*
University of Arizona *B, M*

California
California Polytechnic State
 University: San Luis Obispo *B, M*
California State Polytechnic
 University: Pomona *B, M*
Modesto Junior College *A*
San Diego State University *M*
San Jose State University *M*
University of California
 Berkeley *M, D*
 Davis *B, M*
 Irvine *M, D*
 Los Angeles *M, D*
 San Diego *B*
University of Southern
 California *B, M, D*

Colorado
University of Colorado
 Denver *M*

District of Columbia
Catholic University of America *M*
Georgetown University *M*
University of the District of
 Columbia *A, B, M*

Florida
Florida Atlantic University *B, M*
Florida State University *M, D*
University of Central Florida *M*
University of Florida *M*
University of Miami *B, M*

Georgia
Georgia Institute of Technology *M, D*
Savannah College of Art and
 Design *M*
Southern Polytechnic State
 University *C*
University of Georgia *M*

Hawaii
University of Hawaii
 Manoa *M, D*

Idaho
University of Idaho *M*

Illinois
University of Illinois
 Chicago *M, D*
 Urbana-Champaign *B, M, D*

Indiana
Ball State University *B, M*
Indiana University
 Northwest *C*

Iowa
Iowa State University *B, M*
University of Iowa *M*

Kansas
Kansas State University *M*
University of Kansas *M*

Kentucky
University of Louisville *M*

Louisiana
University of New Orleans *M*

Maine
University of Southern Maine *M*

Maryland
Frostburg State University *B*
University of Maryland
 College Park *D*

Massachusetts
Harvard College *M*
Massachusetts Institute of
 Technology *B, M, D*
Tufts University *M*
University of Massachusetts
 Amherst *M, D*
Westfield State University *B*

Michigan
Eastern Michigan University *B, M*
Grand Valley State University *B*
Lawrence Technological University *M*
Michigan State University *B, M*
University of Michigan *M, D*
Wayne State University *M*
Western Michigan University *B*

Minnesota
Minnesota State University
 Mankato *B, M*
University of Minnesota
 Twin Cities *M*

Mississippi
Jackson State University *M, D*

Missouri
Missouri State University *B, M*
Saint Louis University *M*
University of Missouri
 Kansas City *B*
Washington University in St. Louis *M*

Montana
University of Montana *B, M*

Nebraska
University of Nebraska
 Lincoln *M*

Nevada
University of Nevada
 Las Vegas *B*

New Hampshire
Plymouth State University *B*
University of New Hampshire *B*

New Jersey
New Jersey Institute of
 Technology *M*
Rutgers, The State University of New
 Jersey
 New Brunswick/Piscataway
 Campus *B, M, D*

New Mexico
University of New Mexico *M*

New York
City University of New York
 City College *M*
Cornell University *B, M, D*
New York Institute of Technology *M*
New York University *B, M*
Pratt Institute *M*
SUNY
 College at Buffalo *B*
 University at Albany *B, M*
 University at Buffalo *M, D*

North Carolina
Appalachian State University *B*
Cape Fear Community College *A*
East Carolina University *B*
University of North Carolina
 Chapel Hill *M, D*
 Charlotte *M*

Ohio
Kent State University *M*
Miami University
 Oxford *B*
Ohio State University
 Columbus Campus *B, M, D*
Stark State College *A*
University of Akron *C, B, M*
University of Cincinnati *A, B, M, D*
University of Cincinnati
 Clermont College *A*

Oklahoma
University of Oklahoma *M*

Oregon
Portland State University *B, M, D*
University of Oregon *M*

Pennsylvania
Bryn Mawr College *B*
Carnegie Mellon University *M*
Haverford College *B*
Indiana University of Pennsylvania *B*
Mansfield University of
 Pennsylvania *B*

Temple University *B, M*
University of Pennsylvania *M, D*

Puerto Rico
University of Puerto Rico
 Rio Piedras *M*

South Carolina
Clemson University *M*

Tennessee
University of Memphis *M*

Texas
Prairie View A&M University *M*
Rice University *M*
Texas A&M University *B, M, D*
Texas Southern University *M, D*
Texas State University *B*
University of Texas
 Arlington *B, M*
 Austin *M, D*
 San Antonio *M*

Virginia
University of Virginia *B, M*
Virginia Polytechnic Institute and
 State University *M*

Washington
Eastern Washington University *B, M*
University of Washington *B, M, D*

Wisconsin
University of Wisconsin
 Madison *M, D*
 Milwaukee *M*

Wyoming
University of Wyoming *M*

Urban education

California
Holy Names University *M*
Loyola Marymount University *M*
University of Southern California *D*

Colorado
University of Colorado
 Denver *D*

Florida
Florida International University *M*
Nova Southeastern University *M*

Illinois
Columbia College Chicago *M*
University of Illinois
 Chicago *D*
 Urbana-Champaign *M, D*

Indiana
Indiana University
 Purdue University Indianapolis *D*

Louisiana
Southern University
 New Orleans *M*

Maryland
Morgan State University *M, D*

Massachusetts
Harvard College *M, D*
Simmons College *M*

Minnesota
Capella University *M, D*

New Jersey
College of New Jersey *M, T*
Kean University *D*
Saint Peter's University *M*

New York
Le Moyne College *M*
Mercy College *M*

Oklahoma
Langston University *M*

Pennsylvania
Alvernia University *M*

Tennessee
Vanderbilt University *M*

Virginia
Norfolk State University *M*

Wisconsin
University of Wisconsin
Milwaukee *T*

Urban forestry

California
University of California
Davis *B*

Illinois
University of Illinois
Urbana-Champaign *B, M, D*

Louisiana
Southern University and Agricultural
and Mechanical College *B, M, D*

Maryland
University of Maryland
Eastern Shore *B*

Minnesota
University of Minnesota
Crookston *B*

New York
Paul Smith's College *A*
SUNY
College of Technology at Alfred *A*

North Dakota
Dakota College at Bottineau *C*

Ohio
Kent State University
Trumbull *A*
Ohio State University
Columbus Campus *B*

Wisconsin
Mid-State Technical College *A*

Urban ministry

Indiana
Crossroads Bible College *B*

Kansas
Sterling College *B*

New York
Nyack College *M*

Pennsylvania
Valley Forge Christian College *B*

Urban studies

California
California State University
Dominguez Hills *B*
Northridge *B*
San Bernardino *M*
Loyola Marymount University *B*
San Diego State University *B*
San Francisco Art Institute *B, M*
San Francisco State University *B*
Stanford University *B*
University of California
Berkeley *B*
Irvine *B*
San Diego *B*
University of Southern California *D*
Whittier College *B*

Connecticut
Connecticut College *B*
Trinity College *B*
University of Connecticut *B*

Delaware
Delaware State University *B*
University of Delaware *M, D*

District of Columbia
University of the District of
Columbia *A, B*

Florida
New College of Florida *B*

Georgia
Georgia State University *M*
Morehouse College *B*
Savannah State University *M*
University of West Georgia *M*

Illinois
DePaul University *B, M*
Elmhurst College *B*
Loyola University Chicago *M*
Northwestern University *B*
University of Illinois
Chicago *B, D*
Wheaton College *B*

Indiana
Ball State University *B*
Butler University *B*

Kansas
MidAmerica Nazarene University *B*

Kentucky
University of Louisville *D*

Louisiana
Dillard University *B*
Tulane University *B*
University of New Orleans *B, M, D*

Maryland
Towson University *B*
University of Maryland
College Park *M*

Massachusetts
Boston University *B, M*
Hampshire College *B*
Tufts University *M*
Worcester State University *B*

Michigan
Spring Arbor University *B*
Wayne County Community College *C*
Wayne State University *B*

Minnesota
Augsburg College *B*
Crown College *B*
Minnesota State University
Mankato *B, M*
North Central University *B*
Ridgewater College *A*
Saint Cloud State University *B*
University of Minnesota
Duluth *B*
Twin Cities *B*

Mississippi
Jackson State University *B*

Missouri
Calvary Bible College and Theological
Seminary *B*
Harris-Stowe State University *B*
Saint Louis University *B, M*
University of Missouri
Kansas City *B*
Washington University in St. Louis *B*

Nebraska
University of Nebraska
Omaha *B, M*

Nevada
University of Nevada
Reno *M*

New Jersey
New Jersey Institute of
Technology *D*
Rutgers, The State University of New
Jersey
Camden Campus *B*
New Brunswick/Piscataway
Campus *B, M*
Saint Peter's University *A, B*

New York
Barnard College *B*
Canisius College *B*
City University of New York
Guttman Community College *A*
Hunter College *B, M*
Queens College *B, M, T*
Columbia University *B*
Columbia University
School of General Studies *B*
Eugene Lang College The New
School for Liberal Arts *B*
Fordham University *B*
Hobart and William Smith Colleges *B*
Long Island University
LIU Brooklyn *M*
Manhattan College *B*
Metropolitan College of New
York *A, B*
New York University *B*
Rochester Institute of Technology *B*
SUNY
University at Albany *B*
Vassar College *B*

Ohio
Cleveland State University *B, M, D*
College of Wooster *B*
Ohio State University
Columbus Campus *B*
Ohio University *B*
Ohio Wesleyan University *B*
University of Akron *M, D*
University of Cincinnati *B*
University of Cincinnati
Blue Ash College *A*
University of Toledo *B*
Wright State University *B*

Oklahoma
Langston University *B*
University of Central Oklahoma *B, M*

Oregon
Portland State University *B, M, D*
Warner Pacific College *B*

Pennsylvania
Bryn Mawr College *B*
Eastern University *M*
Haverford College *B*
Temple University *D*
University of Pennsylvania *B*
University of Pittsburgh *B*

Rhode Island
Brown University *B*

South Carolina
College of Charleston *B*
Furman University *B*

Tennessee
Lipscomb University *B*
Rhodes College *B*
Tennessee State University *B*

Texas
St. Philip's College *A*
Texas A&M International
University *B*
Trinity University *B*
University of Texas
Arlington *M*
Austin *B*

Utah
University of Utah *B, M, D*

Virginia
Norfolk State University *M*
Old Dominion University *M*
Virginia Commonwealth
University *B, M*
Virginia Polytechnic Institute and
State University *M, D*

Washington
University of Washington Tacoma *B*

Wisconsin
University of Wisconsin
Green Bay *B*
Milwaukee *C, M, D*
Oshkosh *B*

Vehicle emissions inspection/maintenance

California
College of the Desert *C*
Los Medanos College *C*
Southwestern College *C*

Vehicle maintenance and repair technologies, general

Alabama
Faulkner State Community College *C*

California
Los Medanos College *C*
MiraCosta College *C, A*

Colorado
Red Rocks Community College *C, A*

Georgia
Columbus Technical College *C*

Michigan
Northwestern Michigan College *C, A*

Ohio

Ohio Technical College *A*

Texas

Hill College *C, A*

Washington

Clover Park Technical College *C, A*
Everett Community College *C, A*

Vehicle parts/ accessories marketing

Florida

Northwood University
  Florida *B*

Iowa

Iowa Lakes Community College *C*

Michigan

Northwood University
  Michigan *A, B*

Mississippi

Hinds Community College *C*

Nebraska

Central Community College *C, A*
Southeast Community College *A*

Pennsylvania

Pennsylvania College of
  Technology *A*

Washington

Bates Technical College *C*
Spokane Community College *C, A*

Vendor/product certification

Arizona

Chandler-Gilbert Community
  College *C, A*
Estrella Mountain Community
  College *C, A*
Glendale Community College *C*
Paradise Valley Community College *C*

Arkansas

Cossatot Community College of the
  University of Arkansas *C*

California

City College of San Francisco *C*
College of Marin *C*
Diablo Valley College *C*
Foothill College *C*
Heald College
  Roseville *C*
Kaplan College
  Vista *C*
Long Beach City College *C*
San Jose City College *C*
Santa Rosa Junior College *C*
Shasta College *C*
Southwestern College *C*

Colorado

Colorado Technical University *C*

Florida

Florida Gateway College *C*
Herzing University
  Winter Park *C*
Polk State College *A*
Saint Johns River State College *C*
Santa Fe College *C*

Hawaii

Heald College
  Honolulu *C, A*

Illinois

Illinois Eastern Community Colleges
  Lincoln Trail College *C*
Morton College *C*
Richland Community College *C*

Indiana

Ivy Tech Community College
  Bloomington *C*
  Central Indiana *C*
  Columbus *C*
  East Central *C*
  Kokomo *C*
  Lafayette *C*
  North Central *C*
  Northeast *C*
  Northwest *C*
  Richmond *C*
  South Central *C*

Kansas

Neosho County Community
  College *C*

Kentucky

Ashland Community and Technical
  College *A*
Sullivan College of Technology and
  Design *A*

Maryland

Cecil College *C*
Hagerstown Community College *C*

Massachusetts

Bristol Community College *C*

Michigan

Baker College
  Port Huron *C, A*

Minnesota

Pine Technical College *C*
St. Paul College *C*

Missouri

Moberly Area Community College *C*

Montana

Dawson Community College *A*

New Jersey

Cumberland County College *A*
Raritan Valley Community College *C*

New Mexico

Clovis Community College *C*

New York

Globe Institute of
  Technology *C, A, B*

North Carolina

Beaufort County Community
  College *A*
Pitt Community College *C, A*

Ohio

James A. Rhodes State College *C*
Marion Technical College *A*
University of Cincinnati
  Clermont College *A*

Pennsylvania

Peirce College *C*

Tennessee

Fountainhead College of
  Technology *C, A*

Texas

Blinn College *C*

Washington

Bellevue College *C*
Big Bend Community College *A*
Edmonds Community College *C*
Peninsula College *A*

Wyoming

Laramie County Community
  College *C*

Veterinary technology

Alabama

Jefferson State Community College *A*

Alaska

University of Alaska
  Fairbanks *C*

Arizona

Carrington College
  Mesa *C*
  Phoenix *C*
  Tucson *C*
Mesa Community College *A*
Pima Community College *A*

Arkansas

Arkansas State University
  Beebe *A*

California

Bakersfield College *C*
California University of Management
  and Sciences *A*
Carrington College California
  Citrus Heights *A*
  Pleasant Hill *A*
  Sacramento *A*
  San Jose *A*
  San Leandro *A*
  Stockton *A*
Foothill College *A*
Hartnell College *A*
La Sierra University *C*
Los Angeles Pierce College *A*
San Joaquin Valley College *A*
Yuba College *A*

Colorado

Bel-Rea Institute of Animal
  Technology *A*
Colorado Mountain College *A*
Community College of Denver *A*
Front Range Community College *C, A*
Otero Junior College *A*

Connecticut

Middlesex Community College *A*
Northwestern Connecticut
  Community College *A*
Norwalk Community College *A*

Delaware

Delaware Technical Community
  College
  Jack F. Owens Campus *A*

Florida

Daytona State College *A*
Florida Gateway College *A*
Hillsborough Community College *A*
Miami Dade College *A*
St. Petersburg College *A, B*
Sanford-Brown Institute
  Tampa *A*

Georgia

Athens Technical College *A*
Fort Valley State University *A, B*
Gwinnett Technical College *C, A*

Idaho

Broadview University
  Boise *A*
College of Southern Idaho *A*

Illinois

Joliet Junior College *A*
Kaskaskia College *A*
Parkland College *A*

Indiana

Brown Mackie College
  Michigan City *A*
  South Bend *A*
Harrison College
  Indianapolis *C, A*
International Business College *A*
International Business College:
  Indianapolis *A*
Purdue University *A, B*

Iowa

Des Moines Area Community
  College *A*
Iowa Western Community College *A*
Kirkwood Community College *A*
Western Iowa Tech Community
  College *C*

Kansas

Colby Community College *A*
Independence Community College *A*
Johnson County Community
  College *A*

Kentucky

Morehead State University *A*
Murray State University *B*
Owensboro Community and
  Technical College *A*

Louisiana

Baton Rouge Community College *C*
Delgado Community College *A*
Northwestern State University *A*

Maine

University of Maine
  Augusta *A*

Maryland

Community College of Baltimore
  County *A*

Massachusetts

Becker College *A, B*
Berkshire Community College *C*
Holyoke Community College *A*
Mount Ida College *A, B*
North Shore Community College *A*

Michigan

Baker College
  Cadillac *A*
  Flint *A*
  Muskegon *A*
  Port Huron *A*
Lansing Community College *A*
Macomb Community College *A*
Michigan State University *C, B*
Oakland Community College *A*
Wayne County Community College *A*

Minnesota

Argosy University
  Twin Cities *A*
Duluth Business University *A*

Globe University
　Moorhead *A*
　Woodbury *A, B*
Minnesota School of Business
　Blaine *A*
　Elk River *A*
　Lakeville *A*
　Plymouth *A, B*
　Rochester *A*
　St. Cloud *A*
　Shakopee *A*
Ridgewater College *A*
Rochester Community and Technical
　College *A*

Mississippi

Hinds Community College *A*
Mississippi Gulf Coast Community
　College *A*

Missouri

Jefferson College *A*
Metropolitan Community College -
　Kansas City *A*

Nebraska

Nebraska College of Technical
　Agriculture *A*
Northeast Community College *A*
University of Nebraska
　Lincoln *B*
Vatterott College
　Spring Valley *A*

New Hampshire

Great Bay Community College *A*
University of New Hampshire *A*

New Jersey

Bergen Community College *A*
Camden County College *A*
Thomas Edison State College *A, B*

New Mexico

Central New Mexico Community
　College *A*
Eastern New Mexico University:
　Roswell *C*
Navajo Technical University *A*
San Juan College *C, A*

New York

City University of New York
　LaGuardia Community College *A*
Genesee Community College *A*
Medaille College *A, B*
SUNY
　College of Technology at Alfred *A*
　College of Technology at
　　Canton *A, B*
　College of Technology at Delhi *A*
Suffolk County Community College *A*
Ulster County Community College *A*

North Carolina

Central Carolina Community
　College *A*
Gaston College *A*

North Dakota

North Dakota State University *B*

Ohio

Bradford School *A*
Brown Mackie College
　Akron *C, A, B*
Columbus State Community
　College *A*
Kent State University
　Tuscarawas *A*
Stautzenberger College *A*
Stautzenberger College: Brecksville *A*

University of Cincinnati
　Blue Ash College *A*

Oklahoma

Oklahoma State University
　Oklahoma City *A*
Redlands Community College *A*

Oregon

Central Oregon Community
　College *A*
Linn-Benton Community College *C*
Portland Community College *A*

Pennsylvania

Harcum College *A*
Johnson College *A*
Lehigh Carbon Community College *A*
Manor College *A*
Northampton Community College *A*
Vet Tech Institute *A*
Wilson College *A, B*
YTI Career Institute
　York *A*

Puerto Rico

Turabo University *C, A*
University of Puerto Rico
　Medical Sciences *B*

Rhode Island

New England Institute of
　Technology *A*

South Carolina

Greenville Technical College *C*
Piedmont Technical College *A*
Tri-County Technical College *A*
Trident Technical College *C*

South Dakota

Globe University
　Sioux Falls *A*
National American University
　Rapid City *C, A*

Tennessee

Chattanooga State Community
　College *A*
Columbia State Community
　College *A*
Lincoln Memorial University *A, B*
Volunteer State Community
　College *C, A*

Texas

Cedar Valley College *C, A*
Collin County Community College
　District *C*
Houston Community College
　System *C*
Lone Star College System *C, A*
Palo Alto College *C, A*
Vet Tech Institute of Houston *A*
Weatherford College *C, A*

Utah

Broadview University
　Layton *A*
　Orem *A*
　West Jordan *A*
Snow College *A*

Vermont

Vermont Technical College *A*

Virginia

Blue Ridge Community College *C, A*
Northern Virginia Community
　College *A*

Washington

Bellingham Technical College *C, A*
Centralia College *C*
Pierce College *A*
Renton Technical College *C*
Yakima Valley Community
　College *C, A*

West Virginia

Bridgemont Community and
　Technical College *A*

Wisconsin

Globe University
　Appleton *A*
　Eau Claire *A*
　Green Bay *A*
　La Crosse *A*
　Madison East *A, B*
　Middleton *A*
　Wausau *A*
Madison Area Technical College *A*
Northcentral Technical College *C*

Wyoming

Eastern Wyoming College *A*
Northwest College *A*

Virology

Massachusetts

Harvard College *D*

Ohio

Case Western Reserve University *D*

Texas

University of Texas
　Health Science Center at
　　Houston *M, D*

Vision science

Alabama

University of Alabama
　Birmingham *M, D*

California

University of California
　Berkeley *M, D*

Florida

Nova Southeastern University *M*
University of Miami *M*

Indiana

Indiana University
　Bloomington *B, M, D*

Missouri

University of Missouri
　St. Louis *M, D*

Ohio

Ohio State University
　Columbus Campus *M, D*

Texas

University of Houston *M, D*
University of the Incarnate Word *B*

Visual/performing arts

Alabama

Birmingham-Southern College *B*
Faulkner State Community College *A*
Virginia College
　Huntsville *A*

Arizona

Arizona State University *B*
Central Arizona College *A*

Glendale Community College *A*
Paradise Valley Community College *A*
Phoenix College *A*
Pima Community College *A*
Prescott College *B*
Scottsdale Community College *A*

Arkansas

Arkansas Baptist College *A*

California

Antelope Valley College *C, A*
Cabrillo College *A*
California Baptist University *B*
California Lutheran University *B*
California State University
　Bakersfield *B*
　Channel Islands *B*
　San Marcos *B*
Canada College *A*
College of Alameda *A*
College of the Siskiyous *C, A*
Contra Costa College *A*
Cypress College *C, A*
Feather River College *A*
Fresno City College *C, A*
Fullerton College *A*
Glendale Community College *A*
Irvine Valley College *A*
Los Angeles City College *C*
Merced College *A*
MiraCosta College *A*
Modesto Junior College *C, A*
Moorpark College *A*
Platt College
　Los Angeles *C, A*
　Ontario *C, A, B*
　San Diego *C, A, B*
Point Loma Nazarene University *B*
Porterville College *A*
Rio Hondo College *A*
Sacramento City College *A*
St. Mary's College of California *B*
San Diego City College *A*
San Jose State University *B*
Santa Ana College *C, A*
Skyline College *A*
Sonoma State University *B*
University of California
　Irvine *B, M*
　Riverside *M*
　San Diego *M*
　Santa Barbara *B, M*
University of San Francisco *B*
University of Southern California *B*

Colorado

Colorado Mountain College *A*
Metropolitan State University of
　Denver *B*
Naropa University *B*
Rocky Mountain College of Art &
　Design *C*
University of Colorado
　Colorado Springs *B*

Connecticut

Albertus Magnus College *B*
Eastern Connecticut State
　University *B*
Trinity College *B*
Tunxis Community College *C, A*
University of Hartford *B*

Delaware

Delaware State University *B*
University of Delaware *M*

District of Columbia

American University *B*
Catholic University of America *M, D*
Corcoran College of Art and
　Design *A, B*
Gallaudet University *B*

George Washington University *B, M*
Howard University *B*

Florida

Daytona State College *A*
Flagler College *B*
Florida State College at
   Jacksonville *A*
Northwest Florida State College *A*
Palm Beach Atlantic University *B*
Palm Beach State College *A*
Tallahassee Community College *A*
University of Miami *B, M*

Georgia

Abraham Baldwin Agricultural
   College *A*
Andrew College *A*
Brewton-Parker College *B*
LaGrange College *B*
Savannah State University *B*
Southern Polytechnic State
   University *B*
Valdosta State University *B*

Illinois

American Academy of Art *B*
Columbia College Chicago *B*
Concordia University Chicago *B*
Illinois Institute of Art
   Schaumburg *B*
Illinois Valley Community College *A*
Kankakee Community College *A*
Kishwaukee College *A*
Lincoln College *A*
Moraine Valley Community College *A*
Northwestern University *B, M*
Richland Community College *A*
School of the Art Institute of
   Chicago *B, M*
University of Chicago *B*
University of St. Francis *B*

Indiana

Bethel College *B*
Indiana University
   Purdue University
      Indianapolis *C, M*
Purdue University *B, M, D*

Iowa

Ashford University *B*
Iowa State University *B, M*
Marshalltown Community College *A*

Kansas

Coffeyville Community College *A*
Colby Community College *A*
Cowley County Community
   College *A*
Garden City Community College *A*
Hutchinson Community College *A*
Kansas Wesleyan University *B*
MidAmerica Nazarene University *B, T*
Pratt Community College *A*
Seward County Community
   College *A*
Washburn University *B*
Wichita State University *B*

Kentucky

Bluegrass Community and Technical
   College *A*
St. Catharine College *B*
Union College *B*

Louisiana

Centenary College of Louisiana *B*
Delta College of Arts &
   Technology *C, A*
Louisiana State University
   Shreveport *B*
Loyola University New Orleans *B*
University of Louisiana at Lafayette *B*

Maine

College of the Atlantic *B, M*
University of Maine
   Farmington *B*
   Machias *B*
University of Southern Maine *B*

Maryland

Community College of Baltimore
   County *A*
Frostburg State University *C, B*
Harford Community College *A*
Montgomery College *A*
Mount St. Mary's University *B, T*
University of Maryland
   Baltimore County *B*

Massachusetts

Bard College at Simon's Rock *B*
Berkshire Community College *A*
Boston University *B, M*
Cape Cod Community College *A*
Clark University *B*
Emerson College *B, M*
Harvard College *B*
Massachusetts College of Liberal
   Arts *B, T*
Middlesex Community College *A*
Pine Manor College *B*
Roxbury Community College *A*
Stonehill College *B*
Suffolk University *B*
Tufts University *M*
University of Massachusetts
   Dartmouth *B, M*
Wheelock College *B*
Worcester State University *B*

Michigan

Andrews University *B*
Calvin College *B*
Michigan Technological University *B*
Mid Michigan Community College *A*
Mott Community College *A*
University of Michigan
   Flint *B*
Wayne County Community College *A*

Minnesota

Minnesota State University
   Mankato *B*
Minnesota West Community and
   Technical College *A*

Mississippi

Blue Mountain College *B*
Coahoma Community College *A*
Delta State University *B*
East Mississippi Community
   College *A*
Jackson State University *B*
Mississippi State University *B*
Mississippi University for Women *B*
University of Mississippi *B, M*
University of Southern Mississippi *B*

Missouri

Lindenwood University *B*
Missouri State University *B*
Southeast Missouri State University *B*
Washington University in St.
   Louis *B, M*

Montana

Carroll College *A, B*
University of Montana *B, M*
University of Montana, Western *B*

Nebraska

Concordia University *B*
Union College *B*
University of Nebraska
   Kearney *B, M, T*

Nevada

Art Institute of Las Vegas *B*
Sierra Nevada College *B*

New Hampshire

Franklin Pierce University *B*

New Jersey

Bergen Community College *A*
Bloomfield College *C, B, T*
College of New Jersey *B*
County College of Morris *A*
Fairleigh Dickinson University
   College at Florham
      Metropolitan Campus *B*
Mercer County Community
   College *C, A*
Ramapo College of New Jersey *B*
Richard Stockton College of New
   Jersey *B*
Seton Hall University *B, T*
William Paterson University of New
   Jersey *M*

New Mexico

New Mexico State University *B*
Northern New Mexico College *A*
Santa Fe University of Art and
   Design *B*

New York

Bard College *B, M*
Barnard College *B*
Briarcliffe College *B*
Bryant & Stratton College
   Amherst *A*
City University of New York
   Borough of Manhattan Community
      College *A*
   Brooklyn College *M*
   City College *B, M*
   Kingsborough Community
      College *A*
   Queensborough Community
      College *A*
College of Saint Rose *C*
Columbia University *B*
Cornell University *M*
Dowling College *B*
Dutchess Community College *A*
Eugene Lang College The New
   School for Liberal Arts *B*
Herkimer County Community
   College *A*
Ithaca College *B, M*
Long Island University
   LIU Brooklyn *B*
Medaille College *B*
SUNY
   College at Brockport *B, M*
   College at Buffalo *B*
   College at New Paltz *B*
   College at Old Westbury *B*
   College at Plattsburgh *B*
   College at Potsdam *B*
Saint Bonaventure University *B*
Siena College *B*
Sullivan County Community
   College *A*
Ulster County Community College *A*
Union College *B*
Wells College *B*
Westchester Community College *A*

North Carolina

Bennett College for Women *B*
Carteret Community College *A*
Fayetteville State University *B*
Johnson C. Smith University *B*
Lees-McRae College *B*
Methodist University *B*
North Carolina Agricultural and
   Technical State University *B*
St. Andrews University *B*

St. Augustine's University *B*
Warren Wilson College *B*

Ohio

Antioch University
   Midwest *M*
Baldwin Wallace University *T*
Columbus College of Art and
   Design *M, T*
Columbus State Community
   College *C*
International College of
   Broadcasting *C, A*
Kent State University *B*
Kent State University
   Stark *B*
Lake Erie College *B*
Notre Dame College *B, T*
Ohio Northern University *B*
Ohio University *D*
Otterbein University *B*
University of Mount Union *T*
University of Rio Grande *B*
Wittenberg University *B*
Wright State University *M, T*
Youngstown State University *B, M*

Oklahoma

Murray State College *A*
Oklahoma City University *B, M*
Rogers State University *B*
St. Gregory's University *B*
Southern Nazarene University *B*

Oregon

Oregon State University *B*
Pacific University *B*
Rogue Community College *C, A*
Western Oregon University *B*

Pennsylvania

Arcadia University *B*
Bucknell University *B*
Bucks County Community College *A*
Cedar Crest College *B*
East Stroudsburg University of
   Pennsylvania *B*
Gannon University *B*
Gettysburg College *B*
Harrisburg Area Community
   College *A*
Indiana University of Pennsylvania *B*
Lycoming College *B*
Penn State
   Abington *B*
   Altoona *B*
   Beaver *B*
   Berks *B*
   Brandywine *B*
   DuBois *B*
   Erie, The Behrend College *B*
   Fayette, The Eberly Campus *B*
   Greater Allegheny *B*
   Harrisburg *B*
   Hazleton *B*
   Lehigh Valley *B*
   Mont Alto *B*
   New Kensington *B*
   Schuylkill *B*
   Shenango *B*
   University Park *B*
   Wilkes-Barre *B*
   Worthington Scranton *B*
   York *B*
Pennsylvania College of Art and
   Design *B*
Saint Joseph's University *B*
University of Pennsylvania *B*
University of Pittsburgh
   Bradford *B*
   Greensburg *B*

Puerto Rico

Escuela de Artes Plasticas de Puerto
Rico *B*
Inter American University of Puerto
Rico
San German Campus *B, M*
University of Puerto Rico
Rio Piedras *B*
University of the Sacred Heart *B*

Rhode Island

Brown University *B*
Providence College *B*

South Carolina

College of Charleston *M*
Spartanburg Methodist College *A*

South Dakota

South Dakota State University *C, B*

Tennessee

Carson-Newman University *B*
King University *B*
Lincoln Memorial University *B, T*
Milligan College *B*
Nossi College of Art *A*
Tennessee Wesleyan College *B*
Tusculum College *B*
University of Tennessee
Martin *B*

Texas

Art Institute of Dallas *A*
Art Institute of Houston *A*
Coastal Bend College *A*
College of the Mainland *A*
Dallas Baptist University *M*
Howard College *A*
Rice University *B, M*
South Texas College *A*
Texas A&M University *M*
Texas A&M University
Corpus Christi *B*
Texas Lutheran University *B*
Texas Southern University *B, M*
Texas Tech University *D*
Trinity Valley Community College *A*
Tyler Junior College *A*
University of Houston
Downtown *B*
University of Texas
Austin *B*
Dallas *B*

Utah

Provo College *A*
Snow College *A*
University of Utah *B*

Vermont

Bennington College *B*
Castleton State College *B*
Champlain College *B*
Community College of Vermont *A*
Johnson State College *B*
Lyndon State College *B*
Marlboro College *B*

Virginia

Ferrum College *B*
George Mason University *B, M*
Hampden-Sydney College *B*
Longwood University *B*
Mary Baldwin College *B*
Norfolk State University *M*
Old Dominion University *M*
Piedmont Virginia Community
College *A*
Regent University *M*
Shenandoah University *B*
University of Mary Washington *B*
Virginia State University *B*

Virginia Western Community
College *C*

Washington

Centralia College *A*
Cornish College of the Arts *B*
Evergreen State College *B*
Green River Community College *C, A*
Highline Community College *A*
ITT Technical Institute
Seattle *A*
North Seattle Community
College *C, A*
Seattle Pacific University *B, T*
Seattle University *B*
Western Washington University *B*
Whitworth University *B, T*

West Virginia

Bethany College *B*
West Virginia University *M*

Wisconsin

University of Wisconsin
Green Bay *B*
Milwaukee *M*
River Falls *B*
Stevens Point *B*
Superior *B, M, T*
Viterbo University *B*

Wyoming

Western Wyoming Community
College *A*

Viticulture/enology

Arkansas

Arkansas Tech University *C*

California

California Polytechnic State
University: San Luis Obispo *B*
California State University
Fresno *B, M*
MiraCosta College *C*

Kansas

Highland Community College *C*

Michigan

Lake Michigan College *A*
Northwestern Michigan College *A*

Missouri

Missouri State University: West
Plains *C, A*

New York

Cornell University *B*
Finger Lakes Community College *A*

North Carolina

James Sprunt Community
College *C, A*

Ohio

Kent State University
Ashtabula *A*

Pennsylvania

Harrisburg Area Community
College *C, A*

Texas

Texas State Technical College
Waco *C, A*

Washington

Lake Washington Institute of
Technology *C*

Yakima Valley Community
College *C, A*

Vocational rehabilitation counseling

Alabama

University of Alabama *M*

Arizona

University of Arizona *D*

Arkansas

Arkansas State University *M*
University of Arkansas *M, D*
University of Arkansas
Little Rock *M*

California

California State University
Fresno *M*
San Bernardino *M*
San Diego State University *M*

Colorado

University of Northern
Colorado *B, M*

Florida

Florida State University *M*
University of South Florida *M*

Georgia

Fort Valley State University *M*
Georgia State University *M*
University of Georgia *M*

Illinois

Illinois Institute of Technology *M*
Southern Illinois University
Carbondale *M*
University of Illinois
Urbana-Champaign *B, M, D*

Indiana

University of St. Francis *B, M*

Kansas

Emporia State University *B, M*

Kentucky

University of Kentucky *M*

Louisiana

Louisiana State University
Health Sciences Center *M*
Southern University and Agricultural
and Mechanical College *B, M*

Massachusetts

Boston University *M, D*
Springfield College *M*

Michigan

Michigan State University *M, D*
Wayne State University *M*

Minnesota

Saint Cloud State University *M*

Mississippi

Jackson State University *M*

Missouri

Maryville University of Saint
Louis *B, M*

Montana

Montana State University
Billings *B, M*

New Jersey

Seton Hall University *M*

New York

Hofstra University *M*
SUNY
University at Buffalo *M*

North Carolina

East Carolina University *B, M, D*
University of North Carolina
Chapel Hill *M*
Winston-Salem State University *B, M*

Ohio

Bowling Green State University *B, M*
University of Cincinnati
Blue Ash College *A*
Wilberforce University *M*
Wright State University *B*

Oklahoma

East Central University *B, M*

Oregon

Western Oregon University *M*

Pennsylvania

Edinboro University of
Pennsylvania *M*
University of Scranton *M*

Puerto Rico

University of Puerto Rico
Rio Piedras *M*

Rhode Island

Salve Regina University *M*

South Dakota

South Dakota State University *M*

Texas

Stephen F. Austin State University *M*
Texas Tech University Health
Sciences Center *M*
University of North Texas *B, M*
University of Texas
El Paso *M*
Pan American *M, D*

Utah

Utah State University *M*

Virginia

Virginia Commonwealth
University *M*

Washington

Edmonds Community College *A*
Spokane Falls Community College *A*
Western Washington University *M*

West Virginia

West Virginia University *M*

Wisconsin

University of Wisconsin
Madison *B, M, D*
Stout *B, M*

Vocational/technical education

Alabama

Athens State University *B*
Auburn University *B, M, D, T*
Tuskegee University *B*

Arkansas

University of Arkansas *B*

Delaware

Wilmington University *M*

Florida

Palm Beach State College *A*
University of Miami *M*

Georgia

University of Georgia *M, D, T*

Hawaii

University of Hawaii
  Honolulu Community College *A*

Idaho

University of Idaho *B, M, T*

Illinois

Eastern Illinois University *B, T*
University of Illinois
  Urbana-Champaign *M, D*

Indiana

Ball State University *M*
Oakland City University *B*

Kansas

Independence Community College *A*

Kentucky

Eastern Kentucky University *A*
Northern Kentucky University *A*
University of Kentucky *B*
Western Kentucky University *A*

Maine

University of Southern Maine *B, T*

Michigan

Cornerstone University *B, T*
Ferris State University *B, M*
Wayne State University *B, M, T*
Western Michigan University *B, M, T*

Minnesota

Minnesota State University
  Mankato *B, M, T*
Ridgewater College *A*
Saint Cloud State University *B*
University of Minnesota
  Twin Cities *B*

Mississippi

Mississippi State University *B*

Missouri

East Central College *A*
Mineral Area College *A*
Moberly Area Community College *A*
Ozarks Technical Community
  College *A*
University of Missouri
  Columbia *B, M, D*

Nebraska

Chadron State College *M*

New Jersey

Rutgers, The State University of New
  Jersey
  New Brunswick/Piscataway
  Campus *M, D, T*

New Mexico

Western New Mexico University *B*

New York

SUNY
  College at Buffalo *B, M, T*
  College at Oswego *B*

North Carolina

East Carolina University *M*

North Dakota

University of North Dakota *M*
Valley City State University *B*

Ohio

Bowling Green State University *B, M*
Ohio State University
  Columbus Campus *B*
University of Akron *B, M*
Wright State University *B, M, T*

Oklahoma

Oklahoma State University *B*

Pennsylvania

Temple University *B, M*

Rhode Island

Rhode Island College *B*

South Carolina

Aiken Technical College *A*
Florence-Darlington Technical
  College *A*
Horry-Georgetown Technical
  College *A*
Piedmont Technical College *A*
Spartanburg Community College *A*

Tennessee

Middle Tennessee State University *M*

Texas

Southern Methodist University *T*
Texas A&M University
  Commerce *T*

Washington

Bellingham Technical College *A*
Renton Technical College *A*
Walla Walla University *B*

Wisconsin

University of Wisconsin
  Platteville *B, T*
  Stout *B*

Voice/opera

Alabama

Birmingham-Southern College *B*
Oakwood University *B*
Samford University *B*
University of Mobile *B*

Arizona

Arizona Christian University *B*
Grand Canyon University *B*

Arkansas

Ouachita Baptist University *B*

California

Bethesda University of
  California *B, M*
California Baptist University *B*
California State University
  Chico *C*
  Long Beach *B*
  Sacramento *B, M*
Chapman University *B*
College of the Siskiyous *A*
Fresno City College *A*
Master's College *B*
Notre Dame de Namur
  University *B, M*
Ohlone College *C*
Point Loma Nazarene University *B*

San Francisco Conservatory of
  Music *B, M*
Solano Community College *C*
University of Southern
  California *B, M, D*
University of the Pacific *B*

Colorado

Adams State University *B*

Delaware

University of Delaware *B*

District of Columbia

Catholic University of
  America *B, M, D*
Howard University *B*

Florida

Florida State University *B, M, D*
Jacksonville University *B*
Palm Beach Atlantic University *B*
Southeastern University *B*
Stetson University *B*
University of Miami *B, M, D*

Georgia

Shorter University *B*

Hawaii

Brigham Young University-Hawaii *B*

Idaho

Northwest Nazarene University *B*
University of Idaho *B*

Illinois

Augustana College *B*
Columbia College Chicago *B*
Illinois Wesleyan University *B*
Lincoln College *A*
Millikin University *B*
Moody Bible Institute *B*
North Park University *M*
Northwestern University *B, M, D*
Olivet Nazarene University *B*
Roosevelt University *B, M*
Saint Xavier University *B*
Trinity International University *B*
University of Illinois
  Urbana-Champaign *B, M, D*

Indiana

Anderson University *B*
Butler University *B, M*
Huntington University *B*
Indiana University
  Purdue University Fort Wayne *B, T*
Valparaiso University *B*

Iowa

Cornell College *B*
Dordt College *B*
University of Iowa *B, M, D*

Kansas

Allen County Community College *A*
Central Christian College of Kansas *A*
MidAmerica Nazarene University *B, T*
Seward County Community
  College *A*
University of Kansas *B, M, D*
Wichita State University *B*

Kentucky

Berea College *B*
Campbellsville University *B*

Louisiana

Centenary College of Louisiana *B, T*
Louisiana College *B*
Xavier University of Louisiana *B*

Maine

University of Southern Maine *B, M*

Maryland

Johns Hopkins University: Peabody
  Conservatory of Music *B, M, D*

Massachusetts

Anna Maria College *B*
Berklee College of Music *B*
Boston Conservatory *B, M*
Boston University *B, M, D*
Eastern Nazarene College *B*
New England Conservatory of
  Music *B, M, D*

Michigan

Eastern Michigan University *M*
Grand Rapids Community College *A*
Hope College *B*
Madonna University *B*
Northwestern Michigan College *A*
Oakland Community College *A*
Oakland University *B, M*
Western Michigan University *B*

Minnesota

McNally Smith College of
  Music *A, B, M*
Saint Cloud State University *B*
University of Northwestern - St.
  Paul *B*

Mississippi

Mississippi College *B*

Missouri

University of Missouri
  Kansas City *B*
Washington University in St.
  Louis *B, M*

Nebraska

Concordia University *B, T*
Grace University *B*
Hastings College *B*
University of Nebraska
  Omaha *B*
York College *B*

New Jersey

Rider University *B, M*

New York

Bard College *B, M*
Eastman School of Music of the
  University of Rochester *B, M, D*
Five Towns College *A, B, M, D*
Houghton College *B, M*
Mannes College The New School for
  Music *B, M*
Nyack College *B*
Roberts Wesleyan College *B*
Syracuse University *B, M*
University of Rochester *M*

North Carolina

Campbell University *B*
East Carolina University *B*
Gardner-Webb University *B*
University of Mount Olive *B*
University of North Carolina
  School of the Arts *M*

Ohio

Ashland University *B*
Baldwin Wallace University *B*
Bowling Green State University *B*
Capital University *D*
Cleveland Institute of Music *B, M, D*
Oberlin College *B*
Ohio University *B*
University of Akron *B, M*

University of Cincinnati *B, M, D*
Youngstown State University *B, M*

Oklahoma
East Central University *B, T*
Oklahoma Baptist University *B*
Oklahoma Christian University *B*
Oklahoma City University *B, M*
Oral Roberts University *B*
Southwestern Oklahoma State
   University *B*
University of Central Oklahoma *B*
University of Tulsa *B*

Oregon
Corban University *B*
Willamette University *B*

Pennsylvania
Carnegie Mellon University *B, M*
Curtis Institute of Music *M*
Gettysburg College *B*
Mansfield University of
   Pennsylvania *B*
Temple University *M*
Westminster College *B*

Puerto Rico
Conservatory of Music of Puerto
   Rico *B, M*

South Carolina
Bob Jones University *B*
Charleston Southern University *B*
Coker College *B*
Columbia College *B*
Converse College *B, M*
North Greenville University *B*
University of South Carolina
   Columbia *M*

Tennessee
Belmont University *M*
Hiwassee College *A*
Lipscomb University *B*
Vanderbilt University *B*

Texas
Abilene Christian University *B*
Dallas Baptist University *B*
East Texas Baptist University *B*
Hardin-Simmons University *B*
Howard Payne University *B*
Lamar University *B, M*
Navarro College *A*
Southern Methodist University *B, M*
Southwestern Assemblies of God
   University *B*
Texas Christian University *B, M, D*
Trinity University *B*
University of Texas
   El Paso *B*

Utah
Brigham Young University *B*
Weber State University *B*

Vermont
Bennington College *B, M*
Johnson State College *B*

Washington
Central Washington University *B*
Cornish College of the Arts *B*
University of Washington *B, M, D*
Whitworth University *B*

Wisconsin
University of Wisconsin
   Milwaukee *C*
   Parkside *T*

Warehousing/ inventory management

Arizona
Arizona Western College *C*

Illinois
Black Hawk College *C*
City Colleges of Chicago
   Harold Washington College *C*
   Kennedy-King College *C*
   Olive-Harvey College *C*
   Richard J. Daley College *C*
Illinois Valley Community College *C*
Lincoln Land Community College *C*

Iowa
Iowa Lakes Community College *C*

Massachusetts
Bristol Community College *C*

Missouri
Saint Louis University *M*

Washington
Bates Technical College *C*

Watch/jewelrymaking

Minnesota
Minnesota State College - Southeast
   Technical *C*
St. Paul College *C*

Montana
Flathead Valley Community
   College *C, A*

Pennsylvania
Commonwealth Technical Institute *C*

Texas
Austin Community College *C, A*
Paris Junior College *C, A*

Washington
North Seattle Community
   College *C, A*

Water quality/ treatment/recycling technology

Alabama
Gadsden State Community College *C*
Northwest-Shoals Community
   College *C*

Arizona
Arizona Western College *C, A*
GateWay Community College *C, A*
Rio Salado College *C, A*

California
Citrus College *C*
College of the Canyons *C, A*
Hartnell College *C, A*
Imperial Valley College *A*
Palomar College *C, A*
San Diego Mesa College *C, A*
Santa Barbara City College *C*
Shasta College *C*
Solano Community College *C, A*
Ventura College *C, A*
Yuba College *C, A*

Colorado
Colorado Mesa University *A*
Pikes Peak Community College *C, A*
Red Rocks Community College *C, A*

Connecticut
Gateway Community College *C*
Three Rivers Community
   College *C, A*

Delaware
Delaware Technical Community
   College
   Jack F. Owens Campus *A*

Florida
Florida Gateway College *C, A*
Hillsborough Community College *C*

Iowa
Kirkwood Community College *C, A*

Kentucky
Eastern Kentucky University *B*
Western Kentucky University *C, A*

Massachusetts
Bristol Community College *A*
Cape Cod Community College *C*

Michigan
Bay de Noc Community College *C, A*
Grand Rapids Community College *A*

Minnesota
St. Cloud Technical and Community
   College *C, A*
Vermilion Community College *C, A*

Montana
Aaniiih Nakoda College *C*
Montana State University
   Northern *A, B*

Nevada
College of Southern Nevada *C, A*

New Mexico
Central New Mexico Community
   College *C*
Santa Fe Community College *C, A*

North Dakota
Bismarck State College *C, A*

Ohio
Columbus State Community
   College *C*
Eastern Gateway Community
   College *A*

Oregon
Clackamas Community College *C, A*
Linn-Benton Community College *C, A*

South Carolina
York Technical College *C*

Utah
Utah Valley University *C*

Wisconsin
Milwaukee Area Technical College *A*

Wyoming
Casper College *C, A*

Water resource engineering

California
California State University
   Fresno *M*
University of Southern California *M*

Idaho
University of Idaho *M, D*

Illinois
Illinois Institute of Technology *M*
University of Illinois
   Urbana-Champaign *B, M, D*

Massachusetts
Bristol Community College *A*

Minnesota
University of Minnesota
   Twin Cities *D*

Montana
Helena College University of
   Montana *A*

Nevada
University of Nevada
   Reno *B, M, D*

New Jersey
Stevens Institute of Technology *M*

New Mexico
University of New Mexico *M*

Ohio
Central State University *B*

Oregon
Oregon State University *M, D*

Pennsylvania
Villanova University *M*

Water, wetlands, and marine management

California
California State University
   Monterey Bay *M*
Santa Rosa Junior College *C*

Colorado
Colorado State University *B, M*

Florida
Florida Gulf Coast University *B*
University of Miami *M*

Idaho
College of Southern Idaho *C, A*

Maine
University of Maine *B, M, D*

Michigan
Delta College *C, A*

Minnesota
University of Minnesota
   Crookston *B*

Montana
Salish Kootenai College *A, B*

New Hampshire
University of New Hampshire *M*

New York
SUNY
   University at Stony Brook *B*

Oregon
Lane Community College *A*
Oregon State University *M*

Pennsylvania

Gettysburg College *B*

Rhode Island

University of Rhode Island *B*

Texas

Texas A&M University *B, M*
Texas State University *B*

Vermont

Sterling College *B*

Washington

Green River Community College *A*
Spokane Community College *A*

Wisconsin

University of Wisconsin
　Madison *M*
　Milwaukee *M, D*
　Stevens Point *B*

Wyoming

Western Wyoming Community
　College *A*

Web/multimedia management

Alabama

Gadsden State Community College *C*
ITT Technical Institute
　Birmingham *A*
Shelton State Community College *C*
University of Phoenix
　Birmingham *B*

Arizona

Art Institute of Phoenix *B*
Cochise College *C*
Eastern Arizona College *C*
ITT Technical Institute
　Tempe *A*
　Tucson *A*
Paradise Valley Community College *C*
University of Advancing
　Technology *A, B*
University of Phoenix
　Phoenix-Hohokam *B*
　Southern Arizona *B*

Arkansas

Mid-South Community College *C*
Northwest Arkansas Community
　College *A*
University of Phoenix
　Little Rock *B*
　Northwest Arkansas *B*

California

Allan Hancock College *C*
Art Institute of California
　Orange County *A, B*
　San Diego *B*
Barstow Community College *C*
City College of San Francisco *C*
College of the Siskiyous *C*
Diablo Valley College *C*
Fashion Institute of Design and
　Merchandising
　San Francisco *A*
Foothill College *C*
Grossmont College *C, A*
Los Angeles Pierce College *C*
Orange Coast College *C*
Santa Rosa Junior College *C*
Shasta College *C*
Sierra College *C, A*
Skyline College *C, A*
Southwestern College *C, A*

University of Phoenix

University of Phoenix
　Bay Area *B*
　Central Valley *B*
　Sacramento Valley *B*
　Southern California *B*
University of San Francisco *M*
Westwood College
　Anaheim *B*

Colorado

Colorado Technical University *C*
Morgan Community College *C, A*
Red Rocks Community College *C, A*
University of Phoenix
　Denver *B*
　Southern Colorado *B*
Westwood College
　Denver North *B*
　Denver South *B*

Connecticut

Northwestern Connecticut
　Community College *C*
University of Phoenix
　Fairfield County *B*

District of Columbia

University of Phoenix
　Washington DC *B*

Florida

Florida Career College
　Miami *A*
International Academy of Design and
　Technology
　Orlando *B*
St. Petersburg College *C, A*
University of Phoenix
　Central Florida *B*
　North Florida *B*
　South Florida *B*
　West Florida *B*

Georgia

Art Institute of Atlanta *A, B*
Georgia College and State
　University *B*
University of Phoenix
　Atlanta *B*
　Augusta *B*
　Columbus *B*
　Savannah *B*

Hawaii

University of Phoenix
　Hawaii *B*

Idaho

Lewis-Clark State College *A, B*
University of Phoenix
　Idaho *B*

Illinois

Illinois Central College *A*
Illinois Institute of Art
　Schaumburg *C, A, B*
Judson University *C*
Kaskaskia College *A*
Lewis and Clark Community
　College *A*
Moraine Valley Community College *A*
Oakton Community College *C*
Prairie State College *C*
Quincy University *B*
Rend Lake College *C*
Sauk Valley Community College *C*
University of Phoenix
　Chicago *B*
University of St. Francis *B*

Indiana

Indiana Institute of Technology *A, B*
Ivy Tech Community College
　Bloomington *C*
　Central Indiana *C*

(Indiana continued)

Columbus *C*
East Central *C*
Kokomo *C*
Lafayette *C*
North Central *C*
Northeast *C*
Northwest *C*
Richmond *C*
South Central *C*
University of Phoenix
　Indianapolis *B*
Vincennes University *A*

Iowa

Des Moines Area Community
　College *C, A*
Iowa Central Community
　College *C, A*
Southwestern Community College *A*

Kansas

Johnson County Community
　College *C*

Kentucky

Big Sandy Community and Technical
　College *C, A*
Daymar College
　Bowling Green *C, A*
Elizabethtown Community and
　Technical College *C*
University of Phoenix
　Louisville *B*

Louisiana

Bossier Parish Community College *C*
Louisiana College *B*
University of Phoenix
　Baton Rouge *B*
　Lafayette *B*
　Louisiana *B*
　Shreveport *B*

Maryland

Kaplan University
　Hagerstown *A, B*
Montgomery College *C*
University of Phoenix
　Maryland *B*

Massachusetts

Cape Cod Community College *A*
ITT Technical Institute
　Norwood *A*
Massachusetts Bay Community
　College *C*
University of Phoenix
　Boston *B*

Michigan

Delta College *C, A*
Gogebic Community College *C*
Grand Rapids Community
　College *C, A*
Kirtland Community College *C, A*
Northern Michigan University *B*
Northwestern Michigan College *C*
Oakland Community College *C*
St. Clair County Community
　College *A*
University of Phoenix
　Metro Detroit *B*
　West Michigan *B*
Wayne County Community
　College *C, A*

Minnesota

Art Institutes International
　Minnesota *A, B*
Century College *C*
Dakota County Technical College *A*
Ridgewater College *C, A*
South Central College *C*

(Minnesota continued)

University of Phoenix
　Minneapolis-St. Paul *B*

Mississippi

University of Phoenix
　Jackson *B*

Missouri

Missouri Southern State University *A*
Ranken Technical College *A*
University of Phoenix
　Kansas City *B*
　St. Louis *B*

Montana

Montana Tech of the University of
　Montana *A*

Nebraska

Bellevue University *B*

Nevada

College of Southern Nevada *A*
University of Phoenix
　Las Vegas *B*
　Northern Nevada *B*
Western Nevada College *A*

New Hampshire

Manchester Community College *C*
Nashua Community College *C, A*

New Jersey

Fairleigh Dickinson University
　Metropolitan Campus *M*
University of Phoenix
　Jersey City *B*

New Mexico

New Mexico State University
　Alamogordo *C, A*
University of Phoenix
　New Mexico *B*

New York

Bryant & Stratton College
　Rochester *A*
College of Saint Rose *C*
Dutchess Community College *C*
Erie Community College *C*
Genesee Community College *A*
Globe Institute of
　Technology *C, A, B*
Mohawk Valley Community
　College *A*
Onondaga Community College *C*
Pace University *C*
Rochester Institute of
　Technology *B, M*
SUNY
　College of Technology at Alfred *B*
　Farmingdale State College *C*
Suffolk County Community College *A*
Tompkins Cortland Community
　College *A*
Westchester Community College *C*

North Carolina

Carteret Community College *C, A*
Central Carolina Community
　College *C*
Central Piedmont Community
　College *C, A*
College of the Albemarle *C*
Durham Technical Community
　College *C*
Sandhills Community College *C, A*
University of Phoenix
　Charlotte *B*
　Raleigh *B*

North Dakota

Dakota College at Bottineau *A*

Ohio

Davis College *A*
ITT Technical Institute
   Dayton *A*
   Norwood *A*
   Strongsville *A*
   Youngstown *A*
James A. Rhodes State College *C*
Marion Technical College *A*
Sinclair Community College *C*
Stark State College *A*
University of Cincinnati
   Blue Ash College *C, A*
University of Phoenix
   Cleveland *B*
Youngstown State University *C*

Oklahoma

University of Phoenix
   Oklahoma City *B*
   Tulsa *B*

Oregon

Clackamas Community College *A*
ITT Technical Institute
   Portland *A*
Pioneer Pacific College *A*
Southwestern Oregon Community
   College *C, A*

Pennsylvania

Community College of
   Philadelphia *A*
Consolidated School of Business
   Lancaster *A*
   York *A*
Delaware County Community
   College *C, A*
DuBois Business College *A*
DuBois Business College
   Huntingdon *A*
Kaplan Career Institute
   Harrisburg *A*
   Pittsburgh *A*
Lansdale School of Business *A*
Montgomery County Community
   College *C, A*
Reading Area Community
   College *C, A*
University of Phoenix
   Philadelphia *B*
   Pittsburgh *B*

Puerto Rico

Inter American University of Puerto
   Rico
   Bayamon Campus *C*

Rhode Island

Community College of Rhode
   Island *C, A*
Johnson & Wales University
   Providence *B*

South Carolina

ITT Technical Institute
   Greenville *A*
Limestone College *A, B*
University of Phoenix
   Columbia *B*
York Technical College *C*

South Dakota

National American University
   Rapid City *B*

Tennessee

ITT Technical Institute
   Knoxville *A*
   Memphis *A*
   Nashville *A*
Northeast State Community
   College *A*

Trevecca Nazarene University *B*
University of Phoenix
   Chattanooga *B*
   Knoxville *B*
   Memphis *B*
   Nashville *B*

Texas

Central Texas College *C*
Mountain View College *C*
North Lake College *C*
St. Philip's College *C, A*
South Texas College *A*
Temple College *C, A*
Texas State Technical College
   Waco *A*
University of Phoenix
   Dallas Fort Worth *B*
   San Antonio *B*
Victoria College *C, A*

Utah

Neumont University *B*
University of Phoenix
   Utah *B*

Vermont

Champlain College *B*

Virginia

ECPI University *A, B*
Lord Fairfax Community College *C, A*
University of Management and
   Technology *A, B, M*
University of Phoenix
   Northern Virginia *B*
   Richmond *B*

Washington

Bates Technical College *C, A*
Cascadia Community College *C*
Clark College *C, A*
Columbia Basin College *A*
Edmonds Community College *C, A*
Heritage University *C*
Peninsula College *C*
University of Phoenix
   Western Washington *B*
Walla Walla Community College *C, A*
Yakima Valley Community College *C*

West Virginia

American Public University
   System *C, A, B*

Wisconsin

Fox Valley Technical College *A*
Gateway Technical College *A*
ITT Technical Institute
   Green Bay *A*
   Greenfield *A*
Milwaukee Area Technical College *A*
Nicolet Area Technical College *A*
Northcentral Technical College *C, A*
University of Phoenix
   Milwaukee *B*

Wyoming

Casper College *A*
Sheridan College *A*
Western Wyoming Community
   College *C*

Web page/multimedia design

Alabama

Gadsden State Community College *C*
ITT Technical Institute
   Birmingham *A*
University of Phoenix
   Birmingham *B*

Alaska

University of Alaska
   Southeast *C, A*

Arizona

Anthem College
   Phoenix *A*
Art Institute of Phoenix *B*
Art Institute of Tucson *B*
DeVry University
   Phoenix *A, B*
Estrella Mountain Community
   College *C*
GateWay Community College *C*
Glendale Community College *C, A*
ITT Technical Institute
   Tempe *A*
   Tucson *A*
Mesa Community College *C, A*
Paradise Valley Community College *C*
Phoenix College *C, A*
Pima Community College *C*
Sessions College for Professional
   Design *C, A*
University of Advancing
   Technology *A, B*
University of Arizona *B*
University of Phoenix
   Phoenix-Hohokam *B*
   Southern Arizona *B*

Arkansas

East Arkansas Community
   College *C, A*
Harding University *B*
ITT Technical Institute
   Little Rock *A*
National Park Community College *C*
Southern Arkansas University Tech *C*
University of Phoenix
   Little Rock *B*
   Northwest Arkansas *B*

California

Academy of Art University *C, A, B*
Art Institute of California
   Hollywood *C, A, B*
   Inland Empire *B*
   Los Angeles *A, B*
   Orange County *A, B*
   San Diego *B*
   San Francisco *A, B*
   Silicon Valley *A, B*
Bakersfield College *C, A*
California State University
   East Bay *M*
Canada College *C*
City College of San Francisco *C*
Coleman University *A, B*
Coleman University: San Marcos *A*
College of Marin *A*
College of San Mateo *C, A*
College of the Siskiyous *C*
DeVry University
   Pomona *A, B*
Ex'pression College *B*
Foothill College *C*
Hartnell College *C, A*
ITT Technical Institute
   Lathrop *A*
   National City *A*
   Rancho Cordova *A*
   Sylmar *A*
   Torrance *A*
Imperial Valley College *C, A*
Los Angeles Harbor College *C*
Los Angeles Pierce College *C*
Los Medanos College *C*
MiraCosta College *C, A*
Monterey Peninsula College *A*
Mt. Sierra College *B*
Ohlone College *C*
Orange Coast College *C*
Palomar College *C, A*

Platt College
   Ontario *C, B*
San Diego Mesa College *C, A*
San Jose City College *C*
Santa Clara University *B*
Santiago Canyon College *A*
Sierra College *C, A*
Southwestern Community College *C, A*
University of California
   Santa Cruz *B*
University of Phoenix
   Bay Area *C, B*
   Central Valley *C, B*
   Sacramento Valley *C, B*
   Southern California *C, B*
University of San Francisco *M*
Westwood College
   Anaheim *B*
   Inland Empire *B*
   Los Angeles *B*

Colorado

Aims Community College *C*
Arapahoe Community College *C, A*
Colorado Mountain College *C*
Colorado Technical University *C*
Community College of Aurora *C, A*
DeVry University
   Westminster *A, B*
ITT Technical Institute
   Westminster *A*
Pueblo Community College *C, A*
Red Rocks Community College *C, A*
University of Phoenix
   Denver *B*
   Southern Colorado *B*
Westwood College
   Denver North *B*
   Denver South *B*

Connecticut

Asnuntuck Community College *C*
Gateway Community College *C*
Naugatuck Valley Community
   College *A*
University of Phoenix
   Fairfield County *B*

Delaware

Wilmington University *B, M*

District of Columbia

University of Phoenix
   Washington DC *B*

Florida

Art Institute of Fort Lauderdale *A, B*
DeVry University
   Miramar *A, B*
   Orlando *A, B*
Florida Career College
   Miami *C*
Florida Gateway College *C*
Florida National University *A*
Florida Technical College
   Orlando *A*
Full Sail University *A, B, M, T*
ITT Technical Institute
   Ft. Lauderdale *A*
   Lake Mary *A*
   Miami *A*
Indian River State College *A*
International Academy of Design and
   Technology: Tampa *A, B*
Lincoln College of Technology
   West Palm Beach *A*
Miami Dade College *C, A*
Miami International University of Art
   and Design *A*
Pasco-Hernando State College *C*
Polk State College *A*
Rasmussen College
   Fort Myers *C, A, B*
   New Port Richey *C, A, B*

Ocala *C, A, B*
Pasco/Land O'Lakes *C, A, B*
Tampa/Brandon *C, A, B*
Saint Johns River State College *C, A*
St. Petersburg College *C, A*
Santa Fe College *A*
University of Phoenix
Central Florida *B*
North Florida *B*
South Florida *B*
West Florida *B*

Georgia

Abraham Baldwin Agricultural
College *A*
Albany Technical College *C*
Art Institute of Atlanta *C, A, B*
Central Georgia Technical
College *C, A*
Gwinnett Technical College *C, A*
Savannah Technical College *C*
Southeastern Technical College *C*
Southwest Georgia Technical
College *C*
University of Georgia *M*
University of Phoenix
Atlanta *B*
Augusta *B*
Columbus *B*
Savannah *B*
West Georgia Technical College *C, A*

Hawaii

Heald College
Honolulu *C, A*
University of Phoenix
Hawaii *B*

Idaho

College of Western Idaho *C, A*
Eastern Idaho Technical College *A*
ITT Technical Institute
Boise *A*
Idaho State University *C, A, B*
University of Phoenix
Idaho *B*

Illinois

Black Hawk College *C*
City Colleges of Chicago
Harry S. Truman College *C*
Kennedy-King College *C*
College of Lake County *C, A*
Columbia College Chicago *B*
Danville Area Community College *C*
DePaul University *B, M*
DeVry University
Chicago *A, B*
Online *A, B*
Elgin Community College *C*
Harper College *C, A*
Heartland Community College *C*
Highland Community College *C*
Illinois Institute of Technology *B, M*
John Wood Community College *C*
Kaskaskia College *C*
Lake Land College *C*
Lewis and Clark Community
College *A*
Lincoln Land Community College *C*
Moraine Valley Community College *C*
Morton College *C*
North Central College *M*
Oakton Community College *C*
Prairie State College *C*
Rasmussen College
Aurora *C, A, B*
Mokena/Tinley Park *C, A*
Rockford *C, A, B*
Romeoville/Joliet *C, A, B*
Spoon River College *C, A*
Triton College *C*

University of Phoenix
Chicago *B*
Waubonsee Community College *C, A*

Indiana

Grace College *B*
ITT Technical Institute
Fort Wayne *A*
Indianapolis *A*
Newburgh *A*
Indiana Wesleyan University *B*
University of Phoenix
Indianapolis *B*
Valparaiso University *C*
Vincennes University *C*

Iowa

Graceland University *B*
Hawkeye Community College *A*
Iowa Central Community
College *C, A*
Iowa Western Community College *A*
Kirkwood Community College *C, A*
Southeastern Community College *A*
Western Iowa Tech Community
College *A*

Kansas

Cloud County Community
College *C, A*
Cowley County Community
College *A*
Hutchinson Community College *A*
Independence Community
College *C, A*
Kansas City Kansas Community
College *C*

Kentucky

ITT Technical Institute
Louisville *A*
Sullivan College of Technology and
Design *A*
Thomas More College *A*
University of Phoenix
Louisville *B*

Louisiana

Delgado Community College *C*
ITT Technical Institute
St. Rose *A*
University of Phoenix
Baton Rouge *B*
Lafayette *B*
Louisiana *B*
Shreveport *B*

Maine

New England School of
Communications *B*

Maryland

Cecil College *C, A*
Chesapeake College *C, A*
Garrett College *C*
Hagerstown Community College *C, A*
Howard Community College *C, A*
ITT Technical Institute
Owings Mills *A*
Montgomery College *C*
University of Phoenix
Maryland *B*

Massachusetts

Bristol Community College *C*
Bunker Hill Community College *C, A*
Cape Cod Community College *A*
Fitchburg State University *C*
ITT Technical Institute
Norwood *A*
Wilmington *A*
Massachusetts Bay Community
College *C*

Mount Wachusett Community
College *C, A*
New England Institute of Art *C, B*
North Shore Community College *C*
Quinsigamond Community
College *C, A*
University of Phoenix
Boston *B*
Worcester Polytechnic Institute *B*

Michigan

Art Institute of Michigan *C, A, B*
Baker College
Allen Park *C*
Jackson *C*
Muskegon *A*
Port Huron *C, A*
Delta College *C, A*
Henry Ford Community College *C*
ITT Technical Institute
Canton *A*
Troy *A*
Jackson College *C, A*
Lake Michigan College *C, A*
Macomb Community College *C, A*
Mott Community College *C, A*
Oakland Community College *C*
Schoolcraft College *C, A*
University of Phoenix
Metro Detroit *B*
West Michigan *B*
Washtenaw Community College *C, A*

Minnesota

Academy College *A*
Art Institutes International
Minnesota *A, B*
Capella University *B*
Dakota County Technical
College *C, A*
Dunwoody College of Technology *A*
Hennepin Technical College *C, A*
ITT Technical Institute
Eden Prairie *A*
Lake Superior College *C, A*
Minneapolis Community and
Technical College *C, A*
Minnesota State College - Southeast
Technical *C, A*
Minnesota State Community and
Technical College *C, A*
North Hennepin Community
College *C*
Rasmussen College
Blaine *C, A, B*
Bloomington *C, A, B*
Brooklyn Park *C, A, B*
Eagan *C, A, B*
Lake Elmo/Woodbury *C, A, B*
Mankato *C, A, B*
Moorhead *C, A, B*
St. Cloud *C, A, B*
Ridgewater College *C, A*
Rochester Community and Technical
College *A*
St. Paul College *C*
South Central College *C*
University of Phoenix
Minneapolis-St. Paul *B*

Mississippi

Northeast Mississippi Community
College *A*
University of Phoenix
Jackson *B*

Missouri

DeVry University
Kansas City *A, B*
Fontbonne University *C*
Lindenwood University *B*
Northwest Missouri State
University *B*

University of Phoenix
Kansas City *B*
St. Louis *B*
Webster University *C*

Montana

Flathead Valley Community
College *A*
Montana State University
Great Falls College *A*
Salish Kootenai College *A*

Nebraska

Creighton University *B*
ITT Technical Institute
Omaha *A*

Nevada

Art Institute of Las Vegas *C*
College of Southern Nevada *C*
Great Basin College *A*
ITT Technical Institute
Henderson *A*
University of Phoenix
Las Vegas *B*
Northern Nevada *B*

New Hampshire

Great Bay Community College *A*
Nashua Community College *C*

New Jersey

DeVry University
North Brunswick *A, B*
Gloucester County College *C, A*
Passaic County Community
College *C, A*
Raritan Valley Community College *C*
Rider University *B*
Salem Community College *C*
University of Phoenix
Jersey City *B*

New Mexico

Clovis Community College *C, A*
ITT Technical Institute
Albuquerque *A*
University of Phoenix
New Mexico *B*

New York

Cayuga Community College *A*
City University of New York
Borough of Manhattan Community
College *A*
Brooklyn College *B*
New York City College of
Technology *B*
College of Westchester *C, A*
Erie Community College *C*
Genesee Community College *C*
Globe Institute of
Technology *C, A, B*
ITT Technical Institute
Albany *A*
Getzville *A*
Liverpool *A*
Iona College *B*
Jamestown Community College *C*
Mildred Elley
Albany *C, A*
Mohawk Valley Community
College *A*
New York University *M*
Parsons The New School for
Design *C*
Rochester Institute of
Technology *B, M*
Rockland Community College *C*
SUNY
College of Agriculture and
Technology at Morrisville *B*

North Carolina

Carteret Community College *A*
College of the Albemarle *C*
Durham Technical Community
    College *C*
Methodist University *B*
Southeastern Community
    College *C, A*
University of North Carolina
    Asheville *B*
University of Phoenix
    Charlotte *B*
    Raleigh *B*
Vance-Granville Community
    College *A*

North Dakota

Bismarck State College *C, A*
Dakota College at Bottineau *C*
North Dakota State College of
    Science *C*
Rasmussen College
    Bismarck *C, A, B*
    Fargo *C, A, B*

Ohio

Belmont College *A*
Central Ohio Technical College *A*
Cincinnati State Technical and
    Community College *C*
College of Mount St. Joseph *C*
DeVry University
    Columbus *A, B*
ETI Technical College of Niles *A*
Edison State Community College *C, A*
Franklin University *B*
ITT Technical Institute
    Dayton *A*
    Hilliard *A*
    Norwood *A*
    Strongsville *A*
    Youngstown *A*
James A. Rhodes State College *C, A*
Lakeland Community College *C, A*
Lorain County Community College *A*
Marion Technical College *A*
Northwest State Community
    College *A*
Ohio Business College
    Sandusky *A*
Sinclair Community College *C, A*
Stark State College *A*
Stautzenberger College *C, A*
Terra State Community College *A*
University of Akron *C*
University of Cincinnati *C*
University of Cincinnati
    Blue Ash College *C, A*
University of Mount Union *B*
University of Phoenix
    Cleveland *B*
University of Rio Grande *A*
Youngstown State University *C*

Oklahoma

Northern Oklahoma College *A*
Oklahoma City Community
    College *A*
Rose State College *A*
University of Phoenix
    Oklahoma City *B*
    Tulsa *B*

Oregon

Art Institute of Portland *A, B*
Chemeketa Community College *A*
Clackamas Community College *C, A*
Eastern Oregon University *C*
Mt. Hood Community College *C, A*
Portland Community College *C, A*

Pennsylvania

Albright College *B*
Art Institute of Philadelphia *C, A, B*
Art Institute of Pittsburgh *C, A, B*
Art Institute of York *B*
Bucks County Community
    College *C, A*
Butler County Community College *A*
Consolidated School of Business
    Lancaster *A*
    York *A*
DeVry University
    Fort Washington *A, B*
Delaware County Community
    College *C, A*
Drexel University *B, M*
Duquesne University *B, M*
Gwynedd Mercy University *B*
Harrisburg Area Community
    College *C, A*
ITT Technical Institute
    Pittsburgh *A*
    Plymouth Meeting *A*
Juniata College *B*
Kaplan Career Institute
    Harrisburg *A*
La Salle University *B*
Lansdale School of Business *C, A*
Lehigh Carbon Community College *A*
Luzerne County Community
    College *C, A*
Montgomery County Community
    College *A*
Northampton Community
    College *C, A*
Penn State
    Abington *C*
    Altoona *C*
    Beaver *C*
    Berks *C*
    Brandywine *C*
    DuBois *C*
    Erie, The Behrend College *C*
    Fayette, The Eberly Campus *C*
    Greater Allegheny *C*
    Harrisburg *C*
    Hazleton *C*
    Lehigh Valley *C*
    Mont Alto *C*
    New Kensington *C*
    Schuylkill *C*
    Shenango *C*
    University Park *C*
    Wilkes-Barre *C*
    Worthington Scranton *C*
    York *C*
Pennsylvania College of
    Technology *B*
Reading Area Community
    College *C, A*
University of Phoenix
    Philadelphia *B*
    Pittsburgh *B*
University of the Arts *B*
Westmoreland County Community
    College *C, A*

Puerto Rico

EDP University of Puerto Rico: Hato
    Rey *B*
Inter American University of Puerto
    Rico
    Ponce Campus *C*
Turabo University *A*

Rhode Island

Johnson & Wales University
    Providence *A*
New England Institute of
    Technology *A*

South Carolina

ITT Technical Institute
    Greenville *A*
University of Phoenix
    Columbia *B*
York Technical College *C*

South Dakota

Dakota State University *C*
Dakota Wesleyan University *B*
National American University
    Rapid City *B*

Tennessee

Belmont University *B*
Chattanooga State Community
    College *C, A*
Columbia State Community
    College *C, A*
Daymar Institute
    Nashville *A*
ITT Technical Institute
    Knoxville *A*
    Memphis *A*
    Nashville *A*
Pellissippi State Community
    College *C, A*
Roane State Community College *C, A*
Southwest Tennessee Community
    College *C, A*
Tennessee Technological
    University *B*
Trevecca Nazarene University *B*
Union University *B*
University of Phoenix
    Chattanooga *B*
    Knoxville *B*
    Memphis *B*
    Nashville *B*
University of Tennessee
    Chattanooga *C*
Volunteer State Community
    College *C, A*
Walters State Community
    College *C, A*

Texas

Blinn College *C*
Brookhaven College *C*
Collin County Community College
    District *C, A*
DeVry University
    Houston *A*
    Irving *A, B*
Eastfield College *C*
ITT Technical Institute
    Arlington *A*
    Austin *A*
    San Antonio *A*
Lamar Institute of Technology *A*
Lamar State College at Port
    Arthur *C, A*
Mountain View College *C, A*
North Lake College *C, A*
Panola College *C*
St. Philip's College *C, A*
San Antonio College *C*
South Texas College *C, A*
Tarrant County College *C*
Texas State Technical College
    Waco *C, A*
    West Texas *A*
Tyler Junior College *A*
University of Phoenix
    Dallas Fort Worth *B*
    San Antonio *B*
Victoria College *C, A*
Wharton County Junior College *A*

Utah

Neumont University *B*
University of Phoenix
    Utah *B*
Utah State University *A*
Utah Valley University *A, B*

Vermont

Champlain College *C, B*
Community College of Vermont *C*

Virginia

Art Institute of Washington *A, B*
DeVry University
    Arlington *A, B*
ITT Technical Institute
    Chantilly *A*
    Norfolk *A*
    Richmond *A*
    Springfield *A*
J. Sargeant Reynolds Community
    College *A*
John Tyler Community College *C*
Mountain Empire Community
    College *C*
Rappahannock Community College *C*
Southwest Virginia Community
    College *C*
University of Management and
    Technology *A, B, M*
University of Phoenix
    Northern Virginia *B*
    Richmond *B*
Virginia Western Community
    College *C*

Washington

Art Institute of Seattle *A, B*
Bates Technical College *A*
Bellevue College *C, A*
Cascadia Community College *C*
Clark College *C*
Clover Park Technical College *C, A*
DeVry University
    Federal Way *A, B*
Edmonds Community College *C, A*
Everett Community College *C, A*
Heritage University *C*
ITT Technical Institute
    Everett *A*
    Seattle *A*
    Spokane *A*
International Academy of Design and
    Technology
    Seattle *A, B*
Lake Washington Institute of
    Technology *C*
Northwest Indian College *C*
Peninsula College *C, A*
Shoreline Community College *C, A*
Spokane Falls Community
    College *C, A*
Tacoma Community College *C*
University of Phoenix
    Western Washington *B*
Walla Walla Community College *A*
Yakima Valley Community
    College *C, A*

West Virginia

American Public University
    System *C, A*

Wisconsin

Blackhawk Technical College *A*
ITT Technical Institute
    Green Bay *A*
    Greenfield *A*
Lakeshore Technical College *A*
Milwaukee Area Technical College *C*
Nicolet Area Technical College *A*
Northcentral Technical College *C, A*
Rasmussen College
    Appleton *C, A, B*
    Green Bay *C, A, B*
    Wausau *C, A, B*
Southwest Wisconsin Technical
    College *A*
University of Phoenix
    Milwaukee *B*
University of Wisconsin
    Milwaukee *C*
    Parkside *C*
    Stevens Point *B*
    Whitewater *B*

College A
Western Technical College A

Wyoming

Casper College C, A
Laramie County Community College C
Western Wyoming Community College C

Welding

Alabama

Alabama Southern Community College C
Bevill State Community College C
Bishop State Community College C
Calhoun Community College C
Gadsden State Community College C
George C. Wallace Community College at Dothan C
George C. Wallace State Community College at Selma C
Jefferson Davis Community College C
Lawson State Community College C
Lurleen B. Wallace Community College C
Northeast Alabama Community College C
Northwest-Shoals Community College C, A
Shelton State Community College C
Southern Union State Community College C, A
Wallace State Community College at Hanceville C

Alaska

Charter College C
University of Alaska
Anchorage C, A
Fairbanks C

Arizona

Arizona Western College C, A
Cochise College C, A
Eastern Arizona College C
Mesa Community College C, A
Northland Pioneer College C, A
Pima Community College C, A

Arkansas

Arkansas Northeastern College C
Arkansas State University
Beebe C, A
Mountain Home C, A
Arkansas Tech University C
College of the Ouachitas C
Cossatot Community College of the University of Arkansas C
Mid-South Community College C
National Park Community College C
North Arkansas College C
Pulaski Technical College C
Rich Mountain Community College C
South Arkansas Community College C
Southeast Arkansas College C
Southern Arkansas University Tech C
University of Arkansas
Community College at Hope C
Community College at Morrilton C
Fort Smith C
Monticello C

California

Antelope Valley College C, A
Bakersfield College C, A
Barstow Community College C
Butte College A
Chabot College A
City College of San Francisco C

College of the Canyons C, A
College of the Siskiyous C, A
Imperial Valley College C, A
Long Beach City College C, A
Los Angeles Pierce College C
Los Medanos College A
Merced College C, A
Orange Coast College C
Palo Verde College C
Palomar College C, A
San Joaquin Delta College C
Santa Ana College C, A
Shasta College C, A
Solano Community College C, A
Ventura College C, A
Victor Valley College C, A

Colorado

Aims Community College C, A
Colorado Mountain College C
Community College of Denver C, A
Front Range Community College C, A
Morgan Community College C
Pikes Peak Community College C, A
Pueblo Community College C, A
Red Rocks Community College C, A
Trinidad State Junior College C, A

Connecticut

Asnuntuck Community College C, A

Florida

College of Central Florida C
Daytona State College C
Florida Gateway College C
Hillsborough Community College C
Palm Beach State College C
Santa Fe College C
Tallahassee Community College C

Georgia

Albany Technical College C
Athens Technical College C
Atlanta Technical College C
Central Georgia Technical College C
Columbus Technical College C
Georgia Piedmont Technical College C
Gwinnett Technical College C
North Georgia Technical College C
Savannah Technical College A
Southeastern Technical College C
Southwest Georgia Technical College C
West Georgia Technical College C

Idaho

Brigham Young University-Idaho A, B
College of Southern Idaho C, A
College of Western Idaho C, A
Eastern Idaho Technical College C, A
Idaho State University C, A, B
Lewis-Clark State College C, A, B

Illinois

Black Hawk College C
City Colleges of Chicago
Kennedy-King College C
Richard J. Daley College C
College of DuPage C
College of Lake County C
Danville Area Community College C
Harper College C
Heartland Community College C, A
Highland Community College C
Illinois Central College C
Illinois Eastern Community Colleges
Lincoln Trail College C
Illinois Valley Community College C
John A. Logan College C, A
Kankakee Community College C, A
Kaskaskia College C, A
Lincoln Land Community College C
Moraine Valley Community College C

Prairie State College C
Rend Lake College C
Rock Valley College C
Sauk Valley Community College C
Southwestern Illinois College C, A
Spoon River College C
Waubonsee Community College C, A

Indiana

Vincennes University C, A

Iowa

Des Moines Area Community College C
Hawkeye Community College C
Iowa Central Community College C
Iowa Lakes Community College C
Kirkwood Community College C, A
North Iowa Area Community College C
Northeast Iowa Community College C
Northwest Iowa Community College C
Southeastern Community College C
Western Iowa Tech Community College C

Kansas

Barton County Community College C
Coffeyville Community College C
Cowley County Community College C, A
Highland Community College C
Hutchinson Community College C, A
Johnson County Community College C
Kansas City Kansas Community College C
Manhattan Area Technical College C, A
Neosho County Community College C
North Central Kansas Technical College C
Wichita Area Technical College C, A

Kentucky

Bluegrass Community and Technical College C, A
Elizabethtown Community and Technical College C, A
Gateway Community and Technical College C, A
Hopkinsville Community College C
Jefferson Community and Technical College C, A
Madisonville Community College C
Owensboro Community and Technical College C, A
Somerset Community College C, A
West Kentucky Community and Technical College C

Louisiana

Delgado Community College C
Nunez Community College C

Maine

Eastern Maine Community College C, A
Southern Maine Community College C, A

Michigan

Bay de Noc Community College C
Delta College C, A
Ferris State University A
Grand Rapids Community College C, A
Kirtland Community College C, A
Lansing Community College C, A
Mid Michigan Community College C
Montcalm Community College C

Mott Community College C
Oakland Community College C
St. Clair County Community College C, A
Schoolcraft College C
Southwestern Michigan College C
Wayne County Community College C, A
West Shore Community College C, A

Minnesota

Alexandria Technical and Community College C
Anoka Technical College C, A
Central Lakes College C, A
Dakota County Technical College C
Dunwoody College of Technology C, A
Hennepin Technical College C, A
Lake Superior College C
Minneapolis Community and Technical College C
Minnesota State College - Southeast Technical C
Northland Community & Technical College C, A
Northwest Technical College C
Ridgewater College C, A
St. Cloud Technical and Community College C
St. Paul College C, A

Mississippi

Copiah-Lincoln Community College C
East Mississippi Community College C, A
Hinds Community College C
Itawamba Community College C
Meridian Community College C
Southwest Mississippi Community College C

Missouri

East Central College C, A
Jefferson College C, A
Linn State Technical College C, A
Metropolitan Community College - Kansas City C, A
Mineral Area College C, A
Moberly Area Community College C, A
Ozarks Technical Community College C, A

Montana

Aaniiih Nakoda College A
Dawson Community College C, A
Flathead Valley Community College C
Helena College University of Montana C, A
Montana State University C
Montana State University
Great Falls College C
Northern C

Nebraska

Central Community College C, A
Mid-Plains Community College C, A
Northeast Community College C
Southeast Community College C, A
Western Nebraska Community College C

Nevada

College of Southern Nevada C, A
Great Basin College C, A
Western Nevada College C, A

New Hampshire

Manchester Community College C, A

New Mexico

Central New Mexico Community
College *C, A*
Clovis Community College *C, A*
Eastern New Mexico University:
Roswell *C, A*
Luna Community College *C*
New Mexico State University
Carlsbad *C, A*
Grants *C*
Northern New Mexico College *C, A*
San Juan College *C, A*

New York

Excelsior College *A*
Jamestown Community College *C, A*
Mohawk Valley Community
College *C, A*
SUNY
College of Technology at
Alfred *C, A*

North Carolina

Asheville-Buncombe Technical
Community College *C*
Beaufort County Community
College *A*
Bladen Community College *C, A*
Brunswick Community College *C*
Cape Fear Community College *C, A*
Catawba Valley Community
College *C*
Central Piedmont Community
College *C, A*
Cleveland Community College *C*
Coastal Carolina Community
College *C*
Craven Community College *C*
Davidson County Community
College *C*
Fayetteville Technical Community
College *C*
Forsyth Technical Community
College *C*
Guilford Technical Community
College *C*
Halifax Community College *C*
Haywood Community College *C*
Isothermal Community College *C, A*
James Sprunt Community College *C*
Johnston Community College *C*
Lenoir Community College *C, A*
Pitt Community College *C, A*
Randolph Community College *C*
Robeson Community College *C*
Rowan-Cabarrus Community
College *C*
Southwestern Community College *C*
Surry Community College *C*
Tri-County Community College *C*
Vance-Granville Community
College *C*
Wayne Community College *C*
Wilkes Community College *C*
Wilson Community College *C*

North Dakota

Bismarck State College *C, A*
Fort Berthold Community College *C*
Lake Region State College *C*
North Dakota State College of
Science *C, A*
Turtle Mountain Community
College *C*
Williston State College *C, A*

Ohio

Columbus State Community
College *C*
Eastern Gateway Community
College *A*
Lorain County Community
College *C, A*
North Central State College *C*

Ohio Technical College *C*
Owens Community College
Toledo *C, A*
Terra State Community College *C, A*
University of Cincinnati *C*

Oklahoma

Tulsa Welding School *C, A*

Oregon

Chemeketa Community College *C, A*
Clackamas Community College *C, A*
Clatsop Community College *C*
Klamath Community College *C*
Lane Community College *C, A*
Linn-Benton Community College *C, A*
Mt. Hood Community College *C, A*
Portland Community College *C, A*
Rogue Community College *C, A*
Southwestern Oregon Community
College *C, A*
Treasure Valley Community
College *C, A*
Umpqua Community College *C*

Pennsylvania

Community College of Allegheny
County *C, A*
Community College of Beaver
County *A*
Dean Institute of Technology *C*
Delaware County Community
College *C*
Harrisburg Area Community
College *C*
Laurel Technical Institute *C*
Northampton Community College *C*
Pennsylvania College of
Technology *C, A*
Pennsylvania Highlands Community
College *A*
Thaddeus Stevens College of
Technology *A*
Triangle Tech
Bethlehem *A*
DuBois *A*
Pittsburgh *A*
Sunbury *A*
Westmoreland County Community
College *C, A*

Puerto Rico

Turabo University *C*

South Carolina

Aiken Technical College *C*
Greenville Technical College *C*
Horry-Georgetown Technical
College *C*
Midlands Technical College *C*
Piedmont Technical College *C, A*
Spartanburg Community College *C*
Tri-County Technical College *C, A*
Trident Technical College *C*
Williamsburg Technical College *C*
York Technical College *C, A*

South Dakota

Lake Area Technical Institute *A*

Texas

Alvin Community College *C*
Angelina College *C, A*
Austin Community College *C, A*
Central Texas College *C, A*
Cisco College *C*
Clarendon College *C*
Del Mar College *C, A*
Frank Phillips College *C*
Galveston College *C, A*
Houston Community College
System *C*
Kilgore College *C*
Lamar Institute of Technology *C, A*

Lincoln College of Technology
Grand Prairie *C*
Lone Star College System *C, A*
Midland College *C, A*
Mountain View College *C, A*
Northeast Texas Community
College *C, A*
Odessa College *C, A*
Panola College *C*
Paris Junior College *C, A*
Ranger College *C, A*
St. Philip's College *C, A*
San Jacinto College *C, A*
Tarrant County College *C, A*
Texarkana College *C*
Texas State Technical College
Harlingen *C, A*
Waco *C, A*
West Texas *C*
Tyler Junior College *C, A*
Victoria College *C*
Western Technical College *C*
Western Texas College *C, A*

Utah

Salt Lake Community College *C, A*
Snow College *C, A*
Utah State University *C, A*
Weber State University *B*

Virginia

Advanced Technology Institute *C, A*
Eastern Shore Community College *C*
J. Sargeant Reynolds Community
College *C*
John Tyler Community College *C*
Liberty University *A*
Mountain Empire Community
College *C, A*
New River Community College *C*
Rappahannock Community College *C*
Southwest Virginia Community
College *C*
Tidewater Community College *C, A*
Virginia Western Community
College *C*

Washington

Bates Technical College *C, A*
Bellingham Technical College *C, A*
Big Bend Community College *C, A*
Centralia College *C, A*
Clark College *C, A*
Clover Park Technical College *C, A*
Columbia Basin College *C, A*
Everett Community College *C, A*
Grays Harbor College *C, A*
Lower Columbia College *C, A*
Olympic College *C, A*
Peninsula College *C, A*
Pierce College *C*
Renton Technical College *C, A*
South Puget Sound Community
College *C, A*
South Seattle Community
College *C, A*
Walla Walla Community College *C, A*

West Virginia

Bridgemont Community and
Technical College *A*
New River Community and Technical
College *C*
West Virginia University at
Parkersburg *C, A*

Wisconsin

Blackhawk Technical College *C*
Chippewa Valley Technical College *C*
Fox Valley Technical College *C, A*
Gateway Technical College *C*
Lakeshore Technical College *C*
Mid-State Technical College *C*

Milwaukee Area Technical
College *C, A*
Nicolet Area Technical College *C*
Northcentral Technical College *C*
Southwest Wisconsin Technical
College *C*
Western Technical College *C*
Wisconsin Indianhead Technical
College *C*

Wyoming

Casper College *C, A*
Central Wyoming College *C, A*
Eastern Wyoming College *C, A*
Northwest College *C, A*
Sheridan College *C, A*
Western Wyoming Community
College *C, A*

Welding engineering technology

Florida

Pasco-Hernando State College *C*

Maine

Washington County Community
College *C*

Maryland

Chesapeake College *C*

North Carolina

Central Carolina Community
College *C*
Western Piedmont Community
College *C, A*

Ohio

Eastern Gateway Community
College *C, A*

Washington

Bates Technical College *C, A*

Well drilling

Mississippi

Southwest Mississippi Community
College *C*

Western European studies

California

Claremont McKenna College *B*

District of Columbia

Georgetown University *M*

Illinois

Illinois Wesleyan University *B*

Indiana

Indiana University
Bloomington *M*

Massachusetts

Amherst College *B*
Tufts University *B*

Nebraska

University of Nebraska
Lincoln *B*

New York

New York University *M, D*

Ohio

College of Wooster *B*
Denison University *B*

Oregon

Pacific University *B*

Tennessee

Vanderbilt University *B*

Vermont

Marlboro College *B*

Wildland/forest firefighting

California

Bakersfield College *A*

Colorado

Aims Community College *C, A*
Colorado Mesa University *A*
Northeastern Junior College *C, A*
Pikes Peak Community College *A*

Idaho

College of Western Idaho *A*

New Mexico

San Juan College *C*

Oregon

Central Oregon Community
    College *C, A*

Washington

Skagit Valley College *C*

Wisconsin

Fox Valley Technical College *C, A*

Wildlife biology

Arizona

Eastern Arizona College *A*

Colorado

Adams State University *B*
Colorado State University *B, M, D*

Kansas

Barton County Community College *A*
Colby Community College *A*
Friends University *B*
Garden City Community College *A*
Kansas State University *B*

Maine

College of the Atlantic *B, M*
Unity College *B*
University of Maine *M*

Michigan

University of Michigan
    Flint *B*

Montana

University of Montana: Western *B*

New York

SUNY
    College of Environmental Science
    and Forestry *B*

North Dakota

Dakota College at Bottineau *A*

Ohio

Ohio University *B*

Pennsylvania

Keystone College *A, B*

Texas

Texas State University *B*
West Texas A&M University *B*

Utah

Brigham Young University *B*
Utah State University *B, M, D*

Vermont

Sterling College *B*
University of Vermont *B*

Wyoming

University of Wyoming *B*
Western Wyoming Community
    College *A*

Wildlife, fish and wilderness management

Alabama

Auburn University *B, M, D*

Alaska

University of Alaska
    Fairbanks *B, M, D*

Arkansas

Arkansas State University *B*
Arkansas Tech University *B, M*
University of Arkansas
    Monticello *B*

California

Cerritos College *A*
Feather River College *C, A*
Humboldt State University *B, M*
Modesto Junior College *C, A*
Napa Valley College *C, A*

Colorado

Colorado State University *B, M*
Front Range Community College *C, A*

Delaware

Delaware State University *B*
University of Delaware *B*

District of Columbia

University of the District of
    Columbia *A*

Florida

University of Florida *B, M, D*
University of Miami *B*

Georgia

Abraham Baldwin Agricultural
    College *A*
Southeastern Technical College *C, A*
University of Georgia *B*

Idaho

Brigham Young University-Idaho *B*
College of Southern Idaho *A*
North Idaho College *A*
University of Idaho *B*

Illinois

Lake Land College *A*
Shawnee Community College *A*
Southeastern Illinois College *A*
University of Illinois
    Urbana-Champaign *B, M, D*

Indiana

Purdue University *B, M, D*

Iowa

Ellsworth Community College *A*
Iowa State University *M, D*

Kansas

Colby Community College *A*
Garden City Community College *A*
Pratt Community College *A*
Seward County Community
    College *A*

Kentucky

Bluegrass Community and Technical
    College *A*
Eastern Kentucky University *B*
Murray State University *B*

Louisiana

McNeese State University *B*

Maine

Unity College *B*
University of Maine *B, M, D*

Maryland

Frostburg State University *B, M*
Garrett College *A*

Michigan

Lake Superior State University *B*
Michigan State University *B, M, D*
Michigan Technological University *B*

Minnesota

Bemidji State University *B*
University of Minnesota
    Twin Cities *B, M, D*
Vermilion Community College *C, A*

Mississippi

East Mississippi Community
    College *A*
Mississippi State University *B, M*

Missouri

College of the Ozarks *B*
Missouri State University *B*
Northwest Missouri State
    University *B*
University of Missouri
    Columbia *B, M, D*

Montana

Miles Community College *A*
Montana State University *M, D*
University of Montana *B, M, D*
University of Montana: Western *B*

Nevada

University of Nevada
    Reno *B*

New Hampshire

University of New Hampshire *B, M*

New Mexico

Eastern New Mexico University *B*
New Mexico State University *B, M*
Western New Mexico University *B*

New York

Finger Lakes Community College *A*
Paul Smith's College *B*
SUNY
    College of Agriculture and
        Technology at Cobleskill *B*
    College of Environmental Science
        and Forestry *B, M, D*

North Carolina

Haywood Community College *A*

North Dakota

Dakota College at Bottineau *A*
Sitting Bull College *A*
Valley City State University *B*

Ohio

Hocking College *C, A*
Otterbein University *B*
University of Rio Grande *B*

Oklahoma

Eastern Oklahoma State College *A*

Oregon

Oregon State University *B, M, D*
Treasure Valley Community
    College *A*

Pennsylvania

Delaware Valley College *B*
Juniata College *B*
Penn State
    DuBois *A*

Puerto Rico

University of Puerto Rico
    Humacao *B*

Rhode Island

University of Rhode Island *B*

South Dakota

Dakota Wesleyan University *B*
South Dakota State
    University *B, M, D*

Tennessee

Lincoln Memorial University *B*
Tennessee Technological
    University *B*
University of Tennessee
    Knoxville *B, M*

Texas

Stephen F. Austin State University *B*
Sul Ross State University *B, M*
Tarleton State University *B*
Texas A&M University *B, M*
Texas A&M University
    Commerce *B*
    Kingsville *B, M, D*
Texas Tech University *B, M, D*

Utah

Brigham Young University *M, D*
Snow College *A*
Utah State University *B, M, D*

Vermont

Sterling College *B*

Washington

Centralia College *A*
Spokane Community College *A*
University of Washington *B*
Washington State University *B*

West Virginia

Potomac State College of West
    Virginia University *A*
West Virginia University *B, M*

Wisconsin

University of Wisconsin
    Madison *B, M, D*
    Stevens Point *B*

Wyoming

Casper College *A*
Eastern Wyoming College *A*
Laramie County Community
    College *A*
Western Wyoming Community
    College *A*

Wine steward/sommelier

Minnesota
St. Paul College *C*

Women's health nurse/nursing

Illinois
Loyola University Chicago *M*

Indiana
Indiana University
  Purdue University Indianapolis *M*

New York
SUNY
  University at Buffalo *D*

Ohio
Case Western Reserve University *M*
University of Cincinnati *M*

Wisconsin
Northcentral Technical College *C*

Women's studies

Alabama
University of Alabama *M*

Arizona
Arizona State University *B*
Northern Arizona University *B*
Prescott College *B*
University of Arizona *D, M, D*

California
California State University
  Fresno *B*
  Fullerton *B*
  Long Beach *B*
  San Marcos *B*
Cerritos College *A*
Claremont McKenna College *B*
Cosumnes River College *A*
Dominican University of California *B*
Folsom Lake College *A*
Foothill College *A*
Fresno City College *A*
Humboldt State University *B*
Irvine Valley College *A*
Loyola Marymount University *B*
Mills College *B*
Monterey Peninsula College *A*
Palomar College *A*
Pitzer College *B*
Pomona College *B*
Sacramento City College *A*
Saddleback College *A*
St. Mary's College of California *B*
San Diego State University *B, M*
San Francisco State University *B, M*
Santa Ana College *A*
Santa Clara University *B*
Santa Monica College *A*
Scripps College *B*
Sierra College *A*
Sonoma State University *B*
Southwestern College *A*
Stanford University *B*
University of California
  Berkeley *B*
  Davis *B*
  Irvine *B*
  Riverside *B*
  San Diego *B*
  Santa Barbara *B, M, D*
  Santa Cruz *B*
University of Redlands *B*
West Valley College *A*

Colorado
Colorado College *B*
Fort Lewis College *B*
Metropolitan State University of
  Denver *B*
Regis University *B*
University of Colorado
  Boulder *B*
  Colorado Springs *B*
University of Denver *B*

Connecticut
Connecticut College *B*
Manchester Community College *A*
Southern Connecticut State
  University *M*
Trinity College *B*
University of Connecticut *B*
University of Hartford *B*
University of Saint Joseph *B*
Yale University *B*

Delaware
University of Delaware *B*

District of Columbia
American University *C, B*
George Washington University *M*
Georgetown University *B*
Trinity Washington University *B*

Florida
Eckerd College *B*
Florida Atlantic University *M*
Florida International University *B*
University of Florida *B, M*
University of Miami *B*
University of South Florida *B, M*

Georgia
Agnes Scott College *B*
Armstrong Atlantic State
  University *C, B*
Emory University *B, D*
Georgia State University *B, M*
Mercer University *B*
Spelman College *B*
University of Georgia *B*

Illinois
Augustana College *B*
Concordia University Chicago *B*
DePaul University *B, M*
Dominican University *B*
Illinois Wesleyan University *B*
Knox College *B*
Loyola University Chicago *C, B, M*
Northeastern Illinois University *B*
Northwestern University *B*
Roosevelt University *B, M*
University of Chicago *B*
University of Illinois
  Urbana-Champaign *B*
Western Illinois University *B*

Indiana
Ball State University *B*
DePauw University *B*
Earlham College *B*
Indiana University
  Purdue University Fort
    Wayne *C, A, B*
Manchester University *B*
Purdue University *B*

Iowa
Cornell College *B*
Grinnell College *B*
Iowa State University *B*
Luther College *B*
University of Iowa *C, B*
University of Northern Iowa *M*

Kansas
Kansas State University *B*
University of Kansas *B, M, D*
Wichita State University *B*

Kentucky
Berea College *B*
Northern Kentucky University *B*
University of Louisville *B, M*
Western Kentucky University *C*

Louisiana
Tulane University *B*

Maine
Bates College *B*
Bowdoin College *B*
Colby College *B*
College of the Atlantic *B, M*
University of Maine *B*
University of Southern Maine *B*

Maryland
Goucher College *B*
Howard Community College *A*
Prince George's Community
  College *A*
Towson University *B, M*
University of Maryland
  College Park *B, M, D*

Massachusetts
Amherst College *B*
Brandeis University *B, M*
Clark University *B*
Hampshire College *B*
Harvard College *B*
Merrimack College *B*
Simmons College *B*
Smith College *B*
Tufts University *B*
University of Massachusetts
  Amherst *B*
  Boston *B*
  Dartmouth *B*
Wellesley College *B*
Wheaton College *B*
Williams College *B*

Michigan
Albion College *B*
Central Michigan University *B*
Eastern Michigan University *B, M*
Hope College *B*
Kalamazoo College *B*
Michigan State University *B*
Oakland University *B*
University of Detroit Mercy *C*
University of Michigan *B, D*
University of Michigan
  Flint *M*
Western Michigan University *B*

Minnesota
Augsburg College *B*
Carleton College *B*
Century College *C*
College of St. Benedict *B*
College of St. Scholastica *C*
Gustavus Adolphus College *B*
Hamline University *B*
Macalester College *B*
Metropolitan State University *B*
Minneapolis Community and
  Technical College *C*
Minnesota State University
  Mankato *B*
  Moorhead *C, B*
St. Catherine University *B*
Saint Cloud State University *B*
St. John's University *B*
St. Olaf College *B*

University of Minnesota
  Duluth *B*
  Morris *B*
  Twin Cities *B*
University of St. Thomas *B*
Winona State University *B*

Mississippi
Mississippi University for Women *B*

Missouri
Saint Louis University *B*
University of Missouri
  Columbia *B*
Washington University in St. Louis *B*
Webster University *C*

Montana
University of Montana *B*

Nebraska
University of Nebraska
  Lincoln *B*

Nevada
University of Nevada
  Las Vegas *B*
  Reno *B*

New Hampshire
Dartmouth College *B*
Keene State College *B*
University of New Hampshire *B*

New Jersey
Bergen Community College *A*
College of New Jersey *B*
College of St. Elizabeth *B*
Drew University *B, M, D*
Montclair State University *B*
New Jersey City University *B*
Rutgers, The State University of New
  Jersey
  New Brunswick/Piscataway
    Campus *B, M, D*
  Newark Campus *B*
William Paterson University of New
  Jersey *B*

New Mexico
New Mexico State University *B*
University of New Mexico *B*

New York
Barnard College *B*
Canisius College *T*
City University of New York
  Brooklyn College *B*
  College of Staten Island *B*
  Hunter College *B*
  Queens College *B*
Colgate University *B*
College of New Rochelle *B*
College of Saint Rose *B*
Columbia University *B*
Columbia University
  School of General Studies *B*
Fordham University *B*
Hamilton College *B*
Hobart and William Smith Colleges *B*
Hofstra University *B*
Pace University *B, M*
Pace University: Pleasantville/
  Briarcliff *B*
SUNY
  College at Brockport *B*
  College at Fredonia *B*
  College at New Paltz *B*
  College at Oswego *B*
  College at Plattsburgh *B*
  College at Potsdam *B*
  College at Purchase *B*
  University at Albany *B, M*
  University at Stony Brook *B*

Saint Bonaventure University *B*
Sarah Lawrence College *M*
Suffolk County Community College *A*
Syracuse University *B*
University of Rochester *B*
Vassar College *B*
Wells College *B*

North Carolina

Appalachian State University *B*
Duke University *B*
East Carolina University *B*
Guilford College *B*
North Carolina State University *B*
Southeastern Baptist Theological
   Seminary *M*
University of North Carolina
   Asheville *B*
   Chapel Hill *B*
   Charlotte *B*
   Greensboro *B, M*
Wake Forest University *B*
Warren Wilson College *B*

North Dakota

North Dakota State University *B*

Ohio

Bowling Green State University *B*
Case Western Reserve University *B*
Cleveland State University *B*
College of Wooster *B*
Denison University *B*
John Carroll University *B*
Kenyon College *B*
Miami University
   Oxford *B*
Oberlin College *B*
Ohio State University
   Columbus Campus *B, M, D*
Ohio University *B*
Ohio Wesleyan University *B*
University of Akron *C*
University of Cincinnati *C, B, M*
University of Toledo *B*
Wright State University *B*

Oklahoma

University of Oklahoma *B*
University of Tulsa *B*

Oregon

Oregon State University *B*
Pacific University *B*
Portland State University *B*
University of Oregon *B*
Willamette University *B*

Pennsylvania

Albright College *B*
Allegheny College *B*
Bucknell University *B*
Bucks County Community
   College *C, A*
Chatham University *B*
Community College of
   Philadelphia *A*
Dickinson College *B*
Duquesne University *B*
Gettysburg College *B*
Lehigh University *B*
Penn State
   Abington *B*
   Altoona *B*
   Beaver *B*
   Berks *B*
   Brandywine *B*
   DuBois *B*
   Erie, The Behrend College *B*
   Fayette, The Eberly Campus *B*
   Greater Allegheny *B*
   Harrisburg *B*
   Hazleton *B*
   Lehigh Valley *B*

Mont Alto *B*
New Kensington *B*
Schuylkill *B*
Shenango *B*
University Park *B*
Wilkes-Barre *B*
Worthington Scranton *B*
York *B*
Rosemont College *B*
Swarthmore College· *B*
Temple University *C, B*
University of Pennsylvania *A, B*
University of Scranton *B*
Villanova University *B*
West Chester University of
   Pennsylvania *B*
Widener University *B*

Puerto Rico

Inter American University of Puerto
   Rico
   Metropolitan Campus *M*

Rhode Island

Brown University *B*
Bryant University *B*
Providence College *B*
Rhode Island College *B*
University of Rhode Island *B*

South Carolina

Clemson University *B*
College of Charleston *B*
University of South Carolina
   Columbia *B*

Tennessee

Vanderbilt University *B*

Texas

El Paso Community College *A*
Rice University *B*
Southwestern University *B*
Texas A&M University *B*
Texas Woman's University *M*
University of Houston
   Clear Lake *B*
University of Texas
   Austin *B, M*
   San Antonio *B*

Utah

University of Utah *B*

Vermont

Bennington College *B*
Goddard College *B, M*
Middlebury College *B*
University of Vermont *B*

Virginia

College of William and Mary *B*
Hollins University *B*
Old Dominion University *B*
Randolph-Macon College *B*
University of Richmond *B*
Virginia Commonwealth
   University *C, B*
Virginia Wesleyan College *B*

Washington

Eastern Washington University *C, B*
Gonzaga University *B*
Pacific Lutheran University *B*
Seattle University *B*
University of Washington *B, M, D*
Washington State University *B*

Wisconsin

Alverno College *B*
Beloit College *B*
Northland College *B*
Ripon College *B*

University of Wisconsin
   Eau Claire *B*
   Green Bay *B*
   Madison *B, M*
   Marinette *A*
   Milwaukee *B, M*
   Whitewater *B*

Wyoming

Casper College *A*
University of Wyoming *B*

Wood science/pulp/ paper technology

Idaho

University of Idaho *B*

Maine

University of Maine *B*

Minnesota

University of Minnesota
   Twin Cities *C, B, M*

Mississippi

Mississippi State University *M*

New York

SUNY
   College of Agriculture and
      Technology at Morrisville *A*
   College of Environmental Science
      and Forestry *B*

North Carolina

Haywood Community College *A*
North Carolina State
   University *B, M, D*

Ohio

Miami University
   Oxford *M*

Oregon

Oregon State University *B, M, D*

West Virginia

Potomac State College of West
   Virginia University *A*
West Virginia University *B*

Wisconsin

University of Wisconsin
   Stevens Point *B*

Woodwind instruments

California

University of Southern
   California *B, M, D*

Kansas

University of Kansas *B, M*

Massachusetts

New England Conservatory of
   Music *B, M, D*

Michigan

University of Michigan *B, M*

New York

Houghton College *B, M*
Ithaca College *B*
Mannes College The New School for
   Music *B, M*

Ohio

Ashland University *B*

Puerto Rico

Conservatory of Music of Puerto
   Rico *B, M*

Tennessee

Vanderbilt University *B*

Woodworking

Arkansas

Phillips Community College of the
   University of Arkansas *C*

California

College of the Redwoods *C*
Laney College *C, A*
Sierra College *C, A*

Colorado

Red Rocks Community College *A*

Idaho

College of Southern Idaho *C, A*

Illinois

Illinois Eastern Community Colleges
   Olney Central College *A*

Kansas

Allen County Community College *A*

Maine

Northern Maine Community
   College *A*

Minnesota

Dakota County Technical College *C*
Hennepin Technical College *C, A*

Mississippi

East Central Community College *C, A*
Northwest Mississippi Community
   College *C*

New Mexico

Central New Mexico Community
   College *C*
Northern New Mexico College *C, A*
Santa Fe Community College *C*

New York

Rochester Institute of
   Technology *A, B, M*

North Carolina

Haywood Community College *C, A*
Mayland Community College *C*
Tri-County Community College *C*

Ohio

University of Cincinnati *C*
University of Rio Grande *C, A*

Oregon

Oregon College of Art & Craft *C, B*

Pennsylvania

Thaddeus Stevens College of
   Technology *A*

Vermont

Burlington College *C, A, B*

Washington

Peninsula College *C*
Seattle Central Community College *A*

Wisconsin

Madison Area Technical College *C*
Northeast Wisconsin Technical
   College *C*

Word processing

Alabama
Gadsden State Community College *C*

Arizona
GateWay Community College *C*
Paradise Valley Community
  College *C, A*
Pima Community College *C*

California
Foothill College *C*
Kaplan College
  Riverside *C*
Long Beach City College *C, A*
Monterey Peninsula College *C, A*
Ohlone College *C*

Colorado
Trinidad State Junior College *C, A*

Connecticut
Gateway Community College *C, A*

Georgia
Columbus Technical College *C*
Southeastern Technical College *C*

Illinois
Elgin Community College *C*
Lincoln Land Community College *C*
Sauk Valley Community College *C*
Southeastern Illinois College *C*

Kansas
Independence Community
  College *C, A*

Maryland
Frederick Community College *C*
Kaplan University
  Hagerstown *C*

Massachusetts
Bristol Community College *C*
Bunker Hill Community College *C, A*

Minnesota
Ridgewater College *C*

New Mexico
Central New Mexico Community
  College *C*

New York
Globe Institute of Technology *C*
SUNY
  College of Agriculture and
    Technology at Morrisville *A*
Utica School of Commerce *C, A*

North Carolina
Beaufort County Community
  College *C*
Carteret Community College *C, A*
Central Carolina Community
  College *C*
Durham Technical Community
  College *C*
Rockingham Community College *C*

Ohio
James A. Rhodes State College *C*
Stark State College *A*
University of Cincinnati
  Blue Ash College *C*

Oregon
Portland Community College *C*

Pennsylvania
Consolidated School of Business
  Lancaster *A*
  York *A*

South Carolina
Williamsburg Technical College *C*
York Technical College *C*

Texas
North Lake College *C*

Virginia
Mountain Empire Community
  College *A*

Washington
Lower Columbia College *C*
Spokane Falls Community College *A*
Yakima Valley Community College *C*

West Virginia
American Public University System *C*

Wisconsin
Nicolet Area Technical College *C*

Wyoming
Western Wyoming Community
  College *C*

Work/family studies

Arizona
Estrella Mountain Community
  College *C*

California
California State University
  Los Angeles *C*

Michigan
Cornerstone University *B*
Michigan State University *M*

Ohio
Youngstown State University *B*

South Dakota
South Dakota State University *M*

Texas
Hill College *C, A*

Writing, general

Alabama
Spring Hill College *B*

Arizona
Central Arizona College *A*
Mesa Community College *C*

Arkansas
University of Central Arkansas *B*

California
California State University
  Fresno *M*
  Long Beach *B*
  San Bernardino *M*
College of the Desert *A*
College of the Siskiyous *A*
Glendale Community College *A*
Humboldt State University *B*
Irvine Valley College *A*
La Sierra University *B*
Point Loma Nazarene University *B*
San Diego State University *M*
Stanford University *B, M, D*
University of California
  San Diego *B*

Colorado
University of Colorado
  Denver *B*

Connecticut
Quinnipiac University *B*
Western Connecticut State
  University *B*

Florida
Nova Southeastern University *M*
University of Tampa *A, B*

Georgia
Georgia Southern University *B*

Idaho
Brigham Young University-Idaho *B*

Illinois
Eureka College *B*
Illinois State University *M*
Illinois Valley Community College *A*
Lincoln College *A*
National-Louis University *M*
Northwestern University *C*
Quincy University *M*
Richland Community College *A*
University of Illinois
  Urbana-Champaign *B*

Indiana
DePauw University *B*
Goshen College *B*
Huntington University *B*
Indiana University
  East *C*
  Purdue University Fort Wayne *B*
  Purdue University Indianapolis *C*
Indiana Wesleyan University *B*
University of Evansville *B*

Iowa
Briar Cliff University *B*
Dordt College *B*
Drake University *B*
Wartburg College *B*

Kansas
Butler Community College *A*
Kansas Wesleyan University *B, T*

Kentucky
Northern Kentucky University *C*

Maine
College of the Atlantic *B, M*
University of Southern Maine *B*

Massachusetts
Emerson College *M*
Massachusetts College of Liberal
  Arts *B*
Northeastern University *M*
Salem State University *B*

Michigan
Calvin College *B*
Central Michigan University *M*
Eastern Michigan University *B, M*
Ferris State University *B*
Michigan Technological University *C*
Oakland University *B*
University of Michigan
  Flint *B, M*
Western Michigan University *B*

Minnesota
Saint Cloud State University *B*

Mississippi
Mississippi College *B*
Northeast Mississippi Community
  College *A*

Missouri
Drury University *B*
Washington University in St.
  Louis *C, M*
William Woods University *B*

Montana
Carroll College *A, B*

New Jersey
College of St. Elizabeth *C*
Kean University *M*
Rowan University *B, M*

New Mexico
New Mexico Highlands University *M*

New York
Houghton College *B*
Ithaca College *B*
Manhattan College *B*
SUNY
  College at Potsdam *B*

North Carolina
Gardner-Webb University *B*
Salem College *B*

North Dakota
University of Jamestown *B*

Ohio
Bluffton University *B*
John Carroll University *B*
Ohio State University
  Columbus Campus *B*
Ohio Wesleyan University *B*
Otterbein University *B*
University of Akron *M*

Oklahoma
Oklahoma Christian University *B*
Oral Roberts University *B*
University of Central Oklahoma *B, M*

Pennsylvania
Geneva College *B*
La Roche College *B*
La Salle University *B*
Thiel College *B*
University of Pittsburgh
  Greensburg *B*

South Carolina
Limestone College *B*

Texas
Austin Community College *A*
Huston-Tillotson University *B*
St. Edward's University *B*
University of Texas
  Austin *B*

Utah
Snow College *A*

Vermont
Bennington College *B*
Champlain College *B*
Marlboro College *B*

Virginia
Bluefield College *B*

West Virginia
Concord University *B*

Wisconsin

Lakeland College *B*
Marian University *B*
Marquette University *B*
University of Wisconsin
  Superior *B*

Yoga teacher/therapy

Arizona

Scottsdale Community College *C*

Massachusetts

Mount Wachusett Community
  College *A*

Minnesota

St. Paul College *C*

Youth ministry

Alabama

Faulkner University *B, M*
Huntingdon College *B*

Arizona

Grand Canyon University *B*

Arkansas

Ecclesia College *B*
Harding University *B*
John Brown University *B*
Williams Baptist College *B*

California

Azusa Pacific University *M*
California Lutheran University *B*
Hope International University *B*
Point Loma Nazarene University *B*
San Diego Christian College *B*
Simpson University *B*
Vanguard University of Southern
  California *B*
William Jessup University *B*

Colorado

Colorado Christian University *B*

Florida

Florida Southern College *B*
Trinity College of Florida *B*

Georgia

Toccoa Falls College *B*
Truett-McConnell College *B*

Idaho

Boise Bible College *B*
Northwest Nazarene University *B*

Illinois

Greenville College *B*
Judson University *B*
Lincoln Christian University *B*
North Park University *B, M*
Olivet Nazarene University *B, M*
Trinity International University *B*

Indiana

Anderson University *B*
Bethel College *B*
Goshen College *B*
Grace College *B*
Huntington University *B, M*
Indiana Wesleyan University *A, B*

Iowa

Dordt College *B*
Emmaus Bible College *B*

Kansas

Barclay College *B*
Benedictine College *B*
Central Christian College of Kansas *A*
Friends University *B*
MidAmerica Nazarene University *B*
Sterling College *B*
Tabor College *B*

Kentucky

Asbury University *B*
Southern Baptist Theological
  Seminary *B*

Massachusetts

Eastern Nazarene College *B*
Gordon College *B*

Michigan

Andrews University *B, M*
Cornerstone University *B*
Grace Bible College *B*
Kuyper College *B*
Spring Arbor University *B*

Minnesota

Augsburg College *B*
Bethel University *B, M*
Crossroads College *B*
Crown College *B*
North Central University *B*
Oak Hills Christian College *B*
University of Northwestern - St.
  Paul *B*

Missouri

Calvary Bible College and Theological
  Seminary *B*
Lindenwood University *B*

Nebraska

Concordia University *B*
Grace University *B*

New Jersey

College of St. Elizabeth *C*
Seton Hall University *M*

New York

Nyack College *B*

North Carolina

Gardner-Webb University *B*
Lenoir-Rhyne University *B*
Mid-Atlantic Christian University *B*
Montreat College *B*
Pfeiffer University *B*
Piedmont International University *B*

Ohio

Bluffton University *B*
Cedarville University *B*
God's Bible School and College *B*
Malone University *B*
Mount Vernon Nazarene University *B*
Ohio Christian University *B*
Ohio Northern University *B*

Oklahoma

Oklahoma Christian University *B*
Oklahoma City University *B*
Southwestern Christian University *B*

Oregon

Corban University *B*
Multnomah University *B*
New Hope Christian College *B*
Northwest Christian University *B*
Warner Pacific College *A*

Pennsylvania

Baptist Bible College of
  Pennsylvania *B*

Eastern University *B*
Geneva College *B*
Messiah College *M*
Valley Forge Christian College *B*

South Carolina

Charleston Southern University *B*
Columbia International University *B*
North Greenville University *B*
W.L. Bonner Bible College *C, B*

Tennessee

King University *B*
Lee University *B, M*
Lipscomb University *B*
Trevecca Nazarene University *B*
Union University *B*

Texas

Arlington Baptist College *B*
Dallas Baptist University *M*
East Texas Baptist University *B*
Hardin-Simmons University *B*
Howard Payne University *B, M*
Lubbock Christian University *B, M*
Southwestern Assemblies of God
  University *B*
Texas Lutheran University *B*

Virginia

Bluefield College *B*

Washington

Northwest University *B*
Trinity Lutheran College *B*

Wisconsin

Cardinal Stritch University *B*
Concordia University Wisconsin *B*
Maranatha Baptist Bible College *B*

Youth services

Alabama

Samford University *B*

Alaska

University of Alaska
  Anchorage *C*

California

San Francisco State University *C*

Kentucky

Murray State University *B, M*

Massachusetts

Brandeis University *M*
Wheelock College *B*

New York

City University of New York
  York College *B*

Oregon

Mt. Hood Community College *C*

Pennsylvania

Cedar Crest College *C*

Rhode Island

Rhode Island College *C, B*

South Carolina

Trident Technical College *C*

South Dakota

Lake Area Technical Institute *A*

Wisconsin

University of Wisconsin
  Milwaukee *C*

Zoology

Alabama

Auburn University *B, M, D*

California

Cerritos College *A*
Citrus College *A*
El Camino College *A*
Fullerton College *A*
Humboldt State University *B*
San Diego State University *B, M*
University of California
  Davis *B, M, D*
  Santa Barbara *B*

Colorado

Colorado State University *B, M, D*

District of Columbia

George Washington University *M, D*

Florida

Daytona State College *A*
Palm Beach State College *A*
Pensacola State College *A*
University of Florida *B, M, D*

Hawaii

University of Hawaii
  Manoa *B, M, D*

Idaho

Brigham Young University-Idaho *B*
Idaho State University *B*
North Idaho College *A*

Illinois

Olivet Nazarene University *B*
Southern Illinois University
  Carbondale *B, M, D*

Indiana

Indiana University
  Bloomington *M, D*
Purdue University *B*

Iowa

Iowa State University *M, D*

Kansas

Hutchinson Community College *A*
Independence Community College *A*

Kentucky

Kentucky Wesleyan College *B*

Maine

College of the Atlantic *B, M*
University of Maine *B, M, D*

Michigan

Andrews University *B*
Michigan State University *B, M, D*
Northern Michigan University *B*

Minnesota

Minnesota State University
  Mankato *B, T*
University of Minnesota
  Twin Cities *B, M, D*

Montana

University of Montana *B, M, D*

New Hampshire

University of New
  Hampshire *B, M, D*

New Jersey

Rutgers, The State University of New
  Jersey
  Newark Campus *B*

New Mexico

Western New Mexico University *B*

New York

Canisius College *B*
Cornell University *M, D*
SUNY
  College at Oswego *B*

North Carolina

Davidson County Community
    College *A*
Duke University *D*
Mars Hill University *B*
Methodist University *A, B*
North Carolina State
    University *B, M, D*

North Dakota

Dakota College at Bottineau *A*
North Dakota State
    University *B, M, D*

Ohio

Kent State University *B*
Malone University *B*
Miami University
  Middletown *A*
  Oxford *B, M, D*
Ohio State University
  Columbus Campus *B, M, D*
Ohio University *B, M, D*
Ohio Wesleyan University *B*

Oklahoma

Carl Albert State College *A*
Langston University *B*
Northern Oklahoma College *A*
Oklahoma State University *B, M, D*
University of Oklahoma *B, M, D*

Oregon

Oregon State University *B, M, D*

Pennsylvania

Delaware Valley College *B*

Rhode Island

University of Rhode Island *B*

Tennessee

Union University *B*

Texas

Tarleton State University *B, T*
Texas A&M University *B, M, D*
Texas A&M University
  Galveston *B*
Texas Tech University *B, M, D*
Texas Woman's University *B*

Utah

Snow College *A*
Weber State University *B*

Vermont

Bennington College *B*
University of Vermont *B*

Virginia

Liberty University *B*

Washington

Evergreen State College *B*
University of Washington *B, M, D*
Washington State University *B, M, D*
Western Washington University *B*

Wisconsin

University of Wisconsin
  Madison *B, M, D*

Wyoming

University of Wyoming *B, M, D*

Special academic programs

Combined bachelor's/graduate programs

Combined bachelor's/graduate program in accounting

Alabama

Alabama State University
Jacksonville State University
Samford University
Tuskegee University
University of Alabama
Birmingham
Huntsville
University of Mobile
University of Montevallo

Arizona

Arizona State University

Arkansas

University of Arkansas
University of Arkansas
Monticello
University of Central Arkansas

California

California College San Diego
California State University
Fresno
Los Angeles
National University
Pacific States University
Southern California Institute of
Technology
University of Southern California
Vanguard University of Southern
California

Colorado

CollegeAmerica
Colorado Springs
Regis University
University of Colorado
Boulder
University of Denver

Connecticut

Quinnipiac University
Sacred Heart University
University of Bridgeport
University of Hartford

Delaware

Goldey-Beacom College

District of Columbia

American University
Catholic University of America

Florida

Barry University
Florida Atlantic University
Florida Memorial University
Nova Southeastern University
University of Miami
Warner University
Webber International University

Georgia

Clark Atlanta University
Georgia Southern University
Mercer University
Shorter University
Southeastern Technical College
University of Georgia

Hawaii

University of Hawaii
Hawaii Community College
Hilo

Idaho

Lewis-Clark State College

Illinois

Benedictine University
Bradley University
DePaul University
Dominican University
Illinois State University
Loyola University Chicago
Southern Illinois University
Carbondale
University of Illinois
Chicago
Urbana-Champaign
Western Illinois University

Indiana

Purdue University
University of Indianapolis
Wabash College

Iowa

University of Dubuque
University of Northern Iowa

Kansas

Fort Hays State University

Kentucky

Kentucky Christian University

Louisiana

Herzing University
Kenner

Maine

Husson University
Thomas College
University of Southern Maine

Maryland

Bowie State University
Towson University
University of Baltimore

Massachusetts

American International College
Babson College
Bentley University
Elms College
Nichols College
Suffolk University
Western New England University

Michigan

Baker College
Allen Park
Clinton Township

Flint
Muskegon
Port Huron
Cleary University
Davenport University
Eastern Michigan University
Grace Bible College
Grand Valley State University
Kuyper College
Rochester College

Minnesota

Capella University
Minnesota State University
Mankato

Mississippi

Millsaps College
Mississippi State University
University of Mississippi
University of Southern Mississippi

Missouri

Avila University
Missouri Southern State University
Missouri State University
Saint Louis University
Truman State University
University of Central Missouri
University of Missouri
Columbia
Washington University in St. Louis
Webster University

Montana

Rocky Mountain College
Salish Kootenai College

Nebraska

Grace University
Hastings College
University of Nebraska
Kearney
Omaha

Nevada

Morrison University

New Hampshire

New England College
University of New Hampshire

New Jersey

Caldwell College
Fairleigh Dickinson University
College at Florham
Metropolitan Campus
Seton Hall University
William Paterson University of New
Jersey

New Mexico

National American University
Albuquerque
University of the Southwest

New York

Canisius College
Cazenovia College
City University of New York
Baruch College
Clinton Community College
College of Saint Rose

Concordia College
Daemen College
Excelsior College
Fordham University
Globe Institute of Technology
Hilbert College
Hofstra University
Iona College
Ithaca College
Le Moyne College
Long Island University
LIU Brooklyn
LIU Post
Manhattan College
Medaille College
Mercy College
Molloy College
Mount Saint Mary College
Nazareth College
New York Institute of Technology
New York University
Pace University
Pace University: Pleasantville/
Briarcliff
Rochester Institute of Technology
SUNY
College at Old Westbury
College at Oswego
University at Binghamton
University at Buffalo
St. Francis College
St. John's University
St. Joseph's College New York:
Suffolk Campus
St. Joseph's College, New York
Siena College
Wagner College
Yeshiva University

North Carolina

East Carolina University
Gardner-Webb University
Guilford College
North Carolina State University
Wake Forest University

Ohio

Ashland University
Baldwin Wallace University
Case Western Reserve University
Defiance College
Hiram College
John Carroll University
Mount Vernon Nazarene University
Ohio State University
Columbus Campus
Ohio University
Lancaster Campus
University of Akron
University of Dayton
Urbana University
Xavier University
Zane State College

Oklahoma

Oklahoma City University
Oklahoma State University
Southeastern Oklahoma State
University
University of Oklahoma
University of Tulsa

Oregon

Corban University
Oregon Institute of Technology

Pennsylvania

Chatham University
DeSales University
La Salle University
Mount Aloysius College
Penn State
  University Park
Philadelphia University
Temple University
University of Pennsylvania
University of Pittsburgh
  Greensburg
University of Scranton
Widener University
York College of Pennsylvania

Puerto Rico

Atlantic University College
Pontifical Catholic University of
  Puerto Rico
Universidad Adventista de las Antillas
Universidad Metropolitana
University of Puerto Rico
  Aguadilla

Rhode Island

University of Rhode Island

South Carolina

Coastal Carolina University
College of Charleston
Converse College
Voorhees College
Winthrop University

South Dakota

National American University
  Rapid City
University of South Dakota

Tennessee

Freed-Hardeman University
Lipscomb University

Texas

Abilene Christian University
Angelo State University
Baylor University
Houston Baptist University
Paul Quinn College
Prairie View A&M University
Stephen F. Austin State University
Texas A&M University
Texas A&M University
  Commerce
  Corpus Christi
  Kingsville
  Texarkana
Texas Lutheran University
Texas State University
Texas Tech University
Trinity University
University of Houston
University of Houston
  Clear Lake
University of North Texas
University of Texas
  Arlington
  Austin
  El Paso
  Pan American
  Permian Basin
University of the Incarnate Word
West Texas A&M University

Utah

Southern Utah University

Vermont

Castleton State College
Lyndon State College

Virginia

George Mason University
Randolph-Macon College

Washington

Northwest University
University of Washington Bothell

West Virginia

Wheeling Jesuit University

Wisconsin

Herzing University
  Madison
Marquette University
University of Wisconsin
  Madison
  Oshkosh
  Whitewater

Combined bachelor's/graduate program in architecture

Alabama

Tuskegee University

California

Academy of Art University
California Baptist University
California College of the Arts
California State University
  Fresno

Connecticut

Yale University

District of Columbia

Catholic University of America
University of the District of Columbia

Florida

Florida Atlantic University
University of Miami

Georgia

Georgia Institute of Technology
Savannah College of Art and Design

Hawaii

University of Hawaii
  Hawaii Community College

Idaho

University of Idaho

Illinois

Illinois Institute of Technology
Monmouth College
Southern Illinois University
  Carbondale
University of Illinois
  Chicago

Indiana

Ball State University
Purdue University
  Calumet

Iowa

Cornell College

Kansas

University of Kansas

Louisiana

Tulane University

Maine

University of Maine
  Augusta

Massachusetts

Boston Architectural College
Northeastern University
Tufts University
University of Massachusetts
  Amherst
Wentworth Institute of Technology

Michigan

Adrian College
Andrews University
Lawrence Technological University
University of Detroit Mercy
University of Michigan

Mississippi

Mississippi State University

Missouri

Drury University
Washington University in St. Louis

Montana

Montana State University

Nebraska

Nebraska Wesleyan University
University of Nebraska
  Kearney

New Jersey

New Jersey Institute of Technology

New York

City University of New York
  City College
Colgate University
Cooper Union for the Advancement
  of Science and Art
Hobart and William Smith Colleges
New York Institute of Technology
Rensselaer Polytechnic Institute

North Carolina

North Carolina State University

North Dakota

North Dakota State University

Ohio

College of Wooster
Kent State University

Oregon

Eastern Oregon University

Pennsylvania

Chatham University
Marywood University
Penn State
  University Park
Temple University
University of Pennsylvania

Rhode Island

Roger Williams University

Texas

Prairie View A&M University
Texas Tech University

Vermont

Norwich University

Washington

University of Washington
Washington State University

Combined bachelor's/graduate program in business administration

Alabama

Alabama State University
Jacksonville State University
Troy University
University of Alabama
University of Alabama
  Huntsville
University of Mobile

Alaska

University of Alaska
  Anchorage

Arkansas

Southern Arkansas University
University of Arkansas
University of Arkansas
  Monticello
University of Central Arkansas

California

Alliant International University
American Jewish University
California College of the Arts
California State University
  Fresno
  Los Angeles
Chapman University
Claremont McKenna College
Coleman University
Dominican University of California
Harvey Mudd College
Holy Names University
Hope International University
John F. Kennedy University
La Sierra University
Mills College
National University
Pacific States University
Pepperdine University
Pitzer College
Scripps College
Sonoma State University
University of the West
Vanguard University of Southern
  California

Colorado

CollegeAmerica
  Fort Collins
Colorado Heights University
Colorado Mesa University
Colorado State University
  Pueblo
Jones International University
Regis University
University of Colorado
  Colorado Springs
  Denver
University of Denver
Western State Colorado University

Connecticut

Quinnipiac University
Sacred Heart University
University of Bridgeport
University of Hartford

Delaware

Goldey-Beacom College

District of Columbia

American University
Georgetown University
University of the District of Columbia

Florida

Barry University
Embry-Riddle Aeronautical University

Everest University
  Melbourne
Florida Agricultural and Mechanical
  University
Florida Institute of Technology
Florida International University
Florida Memorial University
Jacksonville University
Northwood University
  Florida
Nova Southeastern University
Rollins College
Stetson University
University of Miami
University of South Florida
University of Tampa
Warner University
Webber International University

Georgia

Mercer University
Savannah State University
University of Georgia

Hawaii

Hawaii Pacific University
University of Hawaii
  Hawaii Community College

Idaho

Northwest Nazarene University

Illinois

Benedictine University
Benedictine University at Springfield
Bradley University
Concordia University Chicago
Dominican University
Illinois Institute of Technology
Loyola University Chicago
National-Louis University
North Central College
North Park University
Robert Morris University: Chicago
Southern Illinois University
  Carbondale
University of Illinois
  Urbana-Champaign
University of St. Francis
Western Illinois University

Indiana

Grace College
Indiana Institute of Technology
Indiana University
  Bloomington
Purdue University
Taylor University
University of Indianapolis

Iowa

Ashford University
Drake University
Iowa State University
University of Dubuque
University of Northern Iowa

Kansas

Fort Hays State University
Kansas Wesleyan University
Tabor College

Kentucky

Bellarmine University
Kentucky Christian University
Murray State University
University of Kentucky

Louisiana

Centenary College of Louisiana
Louisiana State University
  Shreveport
Louisiana Tech University
Loyola University New Orleans

Tulane University
University of Louisiana at Monroe
Xavier University of Louisiana

Maine

Husson University
Thomas College
University of Maine
University of Southern Maine

Maryland

Bowie State University
Capitol College
Frostburg State University
Salisbury University
University of Baltimore

Massachusetts

American International College
Anna Maria College
Assumption College
Babson College
Bay Path College
Bentley University
Clark University
Elms College
Endicott College
Franklin W. Olin College of
  Engineering
Massachusetts Maritime Academy
Nichols College
Simmons College
Springfield College
Suffolk University
University of Massachusetts
  Boston
  Lowell
Western New England University
Wheaton College
Worcester Polytechnic Institute

Michigan

Baker College
  Allen Park
  Auburn Hills
  Cadillac
  Clinton Township
  Flint
  Jackson
  Muskegon
  Owosso
  Port Huron
Cleary University
Davenport University
Ferris State University
Northern Michigan University
Northwood University
  Michigan
Saginaw Valley State University
Schoolcraft College
University of Detroit Mercy
University of Michigan
  Flint
Walsh College of Accountancy and
  Business Administration
Wayne State University

Minnesota

Capella University
Globe University
  Woodbury
Minnesota School of Business
  Richfield
Minnesota State University
  Mankato
Southwest Minnesota State University

Mississippi

Millsaps College
Mississippi State University
University of Mississippi
University of Southern Mississippi

Missouri

Avila University
Maryville University of Saint Louis
Missouri Southern State University
Missouri State University
Missouri University of Science and
  Technology
Missouri Valley College
Rockhurst University
University of Central Missouri
University of Missouri
  Kansas City
Washington University in St. Louis
Webster University
William Woods University

Montana

Salish Kootenai College

Nebraska

Hastings College
University of Nebraska
  Kearney

Nevada

Morrison University

New Hampshire

Daniel Webster College
Franklin Pierce University
New England College
Southern New Hampshire University
University of New Hampshire

New Jersey

Caldwell College
College of St. Elizabeth
Fairleigh Dickinson University
  College at Florham
Georgian Court University
Monmouth University
New Jersey Institute of Technology
Richard Stockton College of New
  Jersey
Rutgers, The State University of New
  Jersey
  New Brunswick/Piscataway
    Campus
  Newark Campus
Saint Peter's University
Seton Hall University
William Paterson University of New
  Jersey

New Mexico

New Mexico Highlands University
University of New Mexico
University of the Southwest

New York

Adelphi University
Albany College of Pharmacy and
  Health Sciences
Alfred University
Bard College
Canisius College
Clarkson University
College of Saint Rose
Dowling College
Elmira College
Excelsior College
Fordham University
Hartwick College
Hilbert College
Hobart and William Smith Colleges
Hofstra University
Houghton College
Iona College
Ithaca College
LIM College
Long Island University
  LIU Post
Manhattan College
Medaille College

Medaille College: Amherst
Medaille College: Rochester
Molloy College
Mount Saint Mary College
New York Institute of Technology
Niagara University
Pace University
Pace University: Pleasantville/
  Briarcliff
Paul Smith's College
Rensselaer Polytechnic Institute
Rochester Institute of Technology
SUNY
  College at Brockport
  College at Cortland
  College at Fredonia
  College at Geneseo
  College at Oneonta
  College at Oswego
  College at Plattsburgh
  College at Potsdam
  College of Agriculture and
    Technology at Morrisville
  Empire State College
  University at Albany
  University at Binghamton
  University at Buffalo
  University at Stony Brook
Sage Colleges
Saint Bonaventure University
St. John's University
St. Joseph's College New York:
  Suffolk Campus
St. Joseph's College, New York
St. Lawrence University
St. Thomas Aquinas College
Siena College
Skidmore College
Syracuse University
Touro College
Union College
University of Rochester
Wells College

North Carolina

Campbell University
Elon University
Fayetteville State University
Gardner-Webb University
Lenoir-Rhyne University
North Carolina State University
Pfeiffer University
University of North Carolina
  Greensboro
  Pembroke

North Dakota

University of North Dakota

Ohio

Ashland University
Baldwin Wallace University
College of Mount St. Joseph
Defiance College
Franciscan University of Steubenville
Franklin University
Heidelberg University
John Carroll University
Kent State University
Lake Erie College
Mount Vernon Nazarene University
Ohio State University
  Columbus Campus
Otterbein University
University of Dayton
University of Toledo
Urbana University
Ursuline College

Oklahoma

Mid-America Christian University
Oklahoma Baptist University
Oklahoma Christian University
Oklahoma City University

Oral Roberts University
Southeastern Oklahoma State
University
Southern Nazarene University

Oregon

Corban University
Portland State University
Southern Oregon University
Willamette University

Pennsylvania

Cairn University
California University of Pennsylvania
Carnegie Mellon University
Chatham University
DeSales University
Drexel University
Duquesne University
Gannon University
Gwynedd Mercy University
La Salle University
Lehigh University
Marywood University
Mercyhurst University
Moravian College
Mount Aloysius College
Penn State
Erie, The Behrend College
University Park
Philadelphia University
Robert Morris University
Rosemont College
St. Francis University
St. Vincent College
Temple University
University of Pennsylvania
University of Pittsburgh
Greensburg
University of Scranton
University of the Sciences
Waynesburg University
Widener University
Wilkes University
York College of Pennsylvania

Puerto Rico

Pontifical Catholic University of
Puerto Rico
Universidad Metropolitana
University of Puerto Rico
Rio Piedras
University of the Sacred Heart

Rhode Island

Providence College
Salve Regina University
University of Rhode Island

South Carolina

Coastal Carolina University
Winthrop University

South Dakota

National American University
Rapid City
University of South Dakota

Tennessee

Bethel University
Cumberland University
Fisk University
Freed-Hardeman University
King University
Tennessee State University
Union University
Vanderbilt University

Texas

Angelo State University
Baylor University
Dallas Baptist University
Midwestern State University
Prairie View A&M University

St. Mary's University
Sul Ross State University
Texas Wesleyan University
University of Dallas
University of Mary Hardin-Baylor
University of St. Thomas
University of Texas
Arlington
Dallas
El Paso
University of the Incarnate Word

Utah

Brigham Young University
Southern Utah University

Vermont

Castleton State College
Norwich University
Saint Michael's College
Southern Vermont College
University of Vermont

Virginia

Hampton University
Longwood University
Marymount University
Old Dominion University
Randolph-Macon College
Regent University
Shenandoah University
University of Management and
Technology
University of Mary Washington

Washington

Northwest University
University of Washington Bothell
Washington State University
Whitman College

West Virginia

University of Charleston
West Virginia Wesleyan College
Wheeling Jesuit University

Wisconsin

Carroll University
Herzing University
Madison
Lakeland College
Marquette University
Milwaukee School of Engineering
University of Wisconsin
Oshkosh
River Falls
Whitewater
Viterbo University

Combined bachelor's/ graduate program in chemistry

Alabama

Alabama State University
Jacksonville State University
Tuskegee University
University of Alabama
University of Alabama
Huntsville

Arkansas

University of Arkansas
Monticello
University of Central Arkansas

California

California State University
Fresno
Los Angeles
Stanford University

Vanguard University of Southern
California

Colorado

Colorado School of Mines
Colorado State University
Pueblo
University of Colorado
Colorado Springs

Connecticut

Sacred Heart University
University of Saint Joseph
Wesleyan University
Yale University

District of Columbia

American University

Florida

Florida Institute of Technology
Florida International University
University of Tampa

Georgia

Clark Atlanta University
Emory University
Georgia Institute of Technology
University of Georgia

Hawaii

University of Hawaii
Hilo

Idaho

Idaho State University
Lewis-Clark State College

Illinois

Bradley University
DePaul University
Illinois Institute of Technology
Northwestern University
Southern Illinois University
Carbondale
University of Chicago
University of Illinois
Urbana-Champaign
Western Illinois University

Indiana

Purdue University
Purdue University
Calumet

Iowa

Iowa Wesleyan College
University of Northern Iowa

Kentucky

Murray State University

Maine

University of Maine

Maryland

University of Maryland
Baltimore County

Massachusetts

Brandeis University
Clark University
MCPHS University
Tufts University
University of Massachusetts
Dartmouth
Worcester Polytechnic Institute

Michigan

University of Detroit Mercy
University of Michigan
University of Michigan
Flint

Minnesota

Minnesota State University
Mankato

Mississippi

Mississippi State University
Rust College
University of Mississippi
University of Southern Mississippi

Missouri

Missouri Southern State University
Missouri State University
Missouri University of Science and
Technology
University of Central Missouri

Montana

Montana Tech of the University of
Montana

Nebraska

Hastings College
University of Nebraska
Kearney

New Hampshire

University of New Hampshire

New Jersey

Fairleigh Dickinson University
College at Florham
Metropolitan Campus
Rutgers, The State University of New
Jersey
Camden Campus
Stevens Institute of Technology

New Mexico

Eastern New Mexico University
New Mexico Highlands University

New York

City University of New York
Hunter College
Queens College
Clinton Community College
Iona College
Rensselaer Polytechnic Institute
Rochester Institute of Technology
SUNY
College at Oswego
College at Potsdam
University at Binghamton
University at Stony Brook
St. John's University
University of Rochester
Vassar College

North Carolina

Guilford College
Western Carolina University

North Dakota

University of North Dakota

Ohio

Case Western Reserve University
Mount Vernon Nazarene University
Urbana University
Youngstown State University

Oklahoma

Southeastern Oklahoma State
University
University of Tulsa

Oregon

Southern Oregon University

Pennsylvania

Bryn Mawr College
Bucknell University

Duquesne University
Marywood University
Temple University
University of Pennsylvania
University of Pittsburgh
Greensburg
University of Scranton

Rhode Island

University of Rhode Island

South Carolina

Converse College
Winthrop University

South Dakota

University of South Dakota

Tennessee

Tennessee State University

Texas

Prairie View A&M University
University of North Texas
University of Texas
Arlington

Virginia

George Mason University

Wisconsin

University of Wisconsin
Oshkosh
Parkside

Combined bachelor's/ graduate program in dentistry

California

California State University
Fresno
La Sierra University
University of the Pacific

Colorado

Western State Colorado University

Connecticut

University of Connecticut

District of Columbia

Howard University

Florida

Nova Southeastern University
Saint Leo University
University of North Florida

Georgia

Georgia Regents University
Mercer University

Idaho

Idaho State University

Illinois

Southern Illinois University
Edwardsville
University of Illinois
Chicago

Indiana

Purdue University
Purdue University
Calumet

Iowa

Buena Vista University
Iowa Wesleyan College
University of Iowa

Kansas

Fort Hays State University

Kentucky

Kentucky Christian University
Murray State University
Union College

Maryland

Coppin State University
University of Maryland
College Park

Massachusetts

Boston University
Springfield College
Tufts University

Michigan

Adrian College
University of Detroit Mercy

Minnesota

College of St. Benedict
St. John's University
University of Minnesota
Twin Cities

Mississippi

Mississippi College

Nebraska

Chadron State College
Hastings College
University of Nebraska
Kearney
Lincoln

Nevada

University of Nevada
Las Vegas

New Jersey

Caldwell College
Fairleigh Dickinson University
College at Florham
Metropolitan Campus
Montclair State University
New Jersey Institute of Technology
Ramapo College of New Jersey
Richard Stockton College of New
Jersey
Rutgers, The State University of New
Jersey
Camden Campus
New Brunswick/Piscataway
Campus
Newark Campus
Saint Peter's University
Stevens Institute of Technology
William Paterson University of New
Jersey

New York

Adelphi University
Alfred University
Canisius College
Le Moyne College
Manhattanville College
New York University
SUNY
College at Fredonia
College at Geneseo
University at Albany
University at Binghamton
University at Buffalo
University at Stony Brook
Saint Bonaventure University
Siena College
Utica College
Wagner College

North Dakota

Valley City State University

Ohio

Case Western Reserve University
College of Wooster
Ohio State University
Columbus Campus

Oregon

Eastern Oregon University
Portland State University

Pennsylvania

Cabrini College
East Stroudsburg University of
Pennsylvania
Edinboro University of Pennsylvania
Elizabethtown College
Grove City College
Indiana University of Pennsylvania
Juniata College
La Roche College
Lehigh University
Moravian College
Mount Aloysius College
Muhlenberg College
Penn State
Erie, The Behrend College
Rosemont College
St. Francis University
Shippensburg University of
Pennsylvania
Slippery Rock University of
Pennsylvania
Susquehanna University
Temple University
Thiel College
University of Pennsylvania
University of Pittsburgh
University of Pittsburgh
Bradford
Greensburg
Villanova University
Widener University
Wilkes University

Puerto Rico

Universidad Adventista de las Antillas
University of Puerto Rico
Medical Sciences

South Carolina

Furman University

Tennessee

Fisk University
Union University
University of Tennessee
Knoxville

Texas

McMurry University
Texas A&M University
Baylor College of Dentistry
Texas State University
University of Texas
Arlington
Health Science Center at Houston

Virginia

Old Dominion University

Washington

Washington State University

Wisconsin

Marquette University
University of Wisconsin
Green Bay

Combined bachelor's/ graduate program in education

Alabama

Alabama State University
Jacksonville State University
Tuskegee University
University of Montevallo

Alaska

University of Alaska
Anchorage

Arizona

Harrison Middleton University

Arkansas

Southern Arkansas University
University of Arkansas
Monticello
University of Central Arkansas

California

Academy of Art University
American Jewish University
Antioch University
Los Angeles
Bethesda University of California
California State University
Fresno
Los Angeles
Chapman University
Hope International University
John F. Kennedy University
Mills College
Pitzer College
Pomona College
Simpson University
Stanford University
University of California
Santa Cruz
University of San Francisco
Vanguard University of Southern
California

Colorado

Colorado Christian University
University of Denver

Connecticut

Fairfield University
Quinnipiac University
Sacred Heart University
University of Bridgeport
University of Connecticut
University of New Haven
University of Saint Joseph

District of Columbia

American University
Catholic University of America
Corcoran College of Art and Design
Gallaudet University
University of the District of Columbia

Florida

Florida Memorial University
Florida State University
Jacksonville University
Nova Southeastern University
University of Miami
Warner University

Georgia

Albany State University
Bainbridge College
Emory University
Georgia State University
LaGrange College
University of Georgia

Hawaii

Hawaii Pacific University
University of Hawaii
    Hawaii Community College
    Hilo

Idaho

Lewis-Clark State College
Northwest Nazarene University

Illinois

Benedictine University
DePaul University
Dominican University
Kendall College
Lake Forest College
Loyola University Chicago
National-Louis University
Southern Illinois University
    Carbondale
University of Chicago
University of Illinois
    Chicago

Indiana

Earlham College
Oakland City University
Purdue University
Purdue University
    Calumet
Taylor University
Valparaiso University

Iowa

Emmaus Bible College
Graceland University
Iowa Wesleyan College
St. Ambrose University
Waldorf College

Kansas

Fort Hays State University
Independence Community College

Kentucky

Bellarmine University
Kentucky Christian University
Murray State University
St. Catharine College

Louisiana

Centenary College of Louisiana

Maine

Thomas College
University of Maine
University of Maine
    Presque Isle
University of Southern Maine

Maryland

Bowie State University
Goucher College
Loyola University Maryland
Maryland Institute College of Art
Notre Dame of Maryland University
Salisbury University
University of Maryland
    Baltimore County

Massachusetts

American International College
Anna Maria College
Assumption College
Boston College
Bridgewater State University
Clark University
Endicott College
Lesley University
Merrimack College
School of the Museum of Fine Arts
Simmons College
Tufts University

University of Massachusetts
    Dartmouth
    Lowell
Wheelock College

Michigan

Baker College
    Cadillac
    Flint
    Port Huron
College for Creative Studies
Ferris State University
Grace Bible College
Great Lakes Christian College
Kuyper College
Lake Superior State University
Northern Michigan University
Rochester College
University of Michigan

Minnesota

Bemidji State University
Minnesota State University
    Mankato
Southwest Minnesota State University
University of Minnesota
    Twin Cities

Mississippi

Mississippi State University
University of Mississippi
University of Southern Mississippi

Missouri

Avila University
Columbia College
Lindenwood University
Maryville University of Saint Louis
Missouri Southern State University
Missouri University of Science and
    Technology
Missouri Valley College
Truman State University
University of Central Missouri
Washington University in St. Louis
Webster University

Montana

Montana State University
    Northern
Salish Kootenai College

Nebraska

Grace University
Hastings College
Nebraska Christian College
University of Nebraska
    Kearney

Nevada

Sierra Nevada College

New Hampshire

Franklin Pierce University
Keene State College
New England College
University of New Hampshire
University of New Hampshire at
    Manchester

New Jersey

Caldwell College
Centenary College
College of New Jersey
Fairleigh Dickinson University
    College at Florham
    Metropolitan Campus
Kean University
Monmouth University
Richard Stockton College of New
    Jersey

Rutgers, The State University of New
    Jersey
    New Brunswick/Piscataway
        Campus
William Paterson University of New
    Jersey

New Mexico

New Mexico Highlands University
University of the Southwest

New York

Adelphi University
Cazenovia College
City University of New York
    Hunter College
Clinton Community College
Colgate University
College of Mount St. Vincent
College of New Rochelle
College of Saint Rose
Concordia College
D'Youville College
Fordham University
Hilbert College
Hobart and William Smith Colleges
Hofstra University
Iona College
Le Moyne College
Long Island University
    LIU Brooklyn
    LIU Post
Manhattan College
Manhattanville College
Marist College
Medaille College: Amherst
Mercy College
Molloy College
Mount Saint Mary College
Nazareth College
Nyack College
Pace University
Pace University: Pleasantville/
    Briarcliff
SUNY
    College at Old Westbury
    College at Oswego
    College at Plattsburgh
    College at Potsdam
    University at Albany
    University at Binghamton
    University at Stony Brook
Sage Colleges
St. John's University
St. Joseph's College New York:
    Suffolk Campus
St. Joseph's College, New York
Sarah Lawrence College
Union College
University of Rochester
Wells College

North Carolina

Campbell University
Elon University
Fayetteville Technical Community
    College
Gardner-Webb University
Guilford College
High Point University
Pfeiffer University
University of North Carolina
    Pembroke
Western Piedmont Community
    College

Ohio

Antioch University
    Midwest
Defiance College
Heidelberg University
Kenyon College
Mount Vernon Nazarene University
Oberlin College

Ohio Christian University
Ohio State University
    Columbus Campus
Ohio University
    Lancaster Campus
Otterbein University
University of Mount Union
Urbana University
Zane State College

Oklahoma

Mid-America Christian University
Southeastern Oklahoma State
    University
Southern Nazarene University

Oregon

Corban University
Lewis & Clark College
Pacific University
Portland State University
Southern Oregon University
Willamette University

Pennsylvania

Albright College
Arcadia University
Baptist Bible College of Pennsylvania
Cairn University
California University of Pennsylvania
Cedar Crest College
Chatham University
Chestnut Hill College
Drexel University
Duquesne University
Immaculata University
Lehigh University
Marywood University
Penn State
    Altoona
    University Park
St. Francis University
Saint Joseph's University
Temple University
University of Pennsylvania
University of Pittsburgh
    Greensburg
University of Scranton
Waynesburg University
Widener University
Wilkes University

Puerto Rico

Atlantic University College
Universidad Adventista de las Antillas
Universidad Metropolitana
University of Puerto Rico
    Aguadilla
    Carolina Regional College
    Utuado
University of the Sacred Heart

Rhode Island

Brown University
Roger Williams University
University of Rhode Island

South Carolina

Coastal Carolina University
College of Charleston
Columbia International University
Converse College
University of South Carolina
    Columbia
Winthrop University

South Dakota

University of South Dakota

Tennessee

Christian Brothers University
Cumberland University
Johnson University
King University

Memphis College of Art
Rhodes College
Tennessee State University
Trevecca Nazarene University

Texas

Austin College
Dallas Baptist University
Paul Quinn College
Prairie View A&M University
Sul Ross State University
Texas Christian University
Texas Wesleyan University
Trinity University

Vermont

Lyndon State College
Marlboro College
University of Vermont

Virginia

Averett University
College of William and Mary
Emory & Henry College
George Mason University
Hampton University
Hollins University
Longwood University
Mary Baldwin College
Old Dominion University
Randolph College
Regent University
University of Mary Washington
University of Virginia

Washington

Northwest University
Trinity Lutheran College
University of Washington Bothell
Walla Walla University
Washington State University

West Virginia

Appalachian Bible College
West Virginia University
West Virginia University Institute of
    Technology
West Virginia Wesleyan College
Wheeling Jesuit University

Wisconsin

Carroll University
Lakeland College
Marian University
University of Wisconsin
    Oshkosh
    Parkside
    River Falls
    Superior
    Whitewater
Viterbo University

Combined bachelor's/ graduate program in engineering

Alabama

Birmingham-Southern College
Huntingdon College
Stillman College
Tuskegee University
University of Alabama
University of Alabama
    Birmingham
    Huntsville

Alaska

University of Alaska
    Anchorage
    Fairbanks

Arizona

Arizona State University

Arkansas

Hendrix College
Lyon College

California

Biola University
California State University
    Fresno
    Los Angeles
Claremont McKenna College
La Sierra University
Loyola Marymount University
Mills College
National University
Occidental College
Pepperdine University
St. Mary's College of California
Santa Clara University
Scripps College
Southern California Institute of
    Technology
Stanford University
University of California
    Riverside
    Santa Cruz
University of San Francisco
University of Southern California
Whittier College

Colorado

Colorado College
Colorado School of Mines
Colorado State University
University of Colorado
    Boulder
    Colorado Springs
    Denver
University of Denver
Western State Colorado University

Connecticut

Fairfield University
Trinity College
University of Bridgeport
Yale University

District of Columbia

Catholic University of America
Howard University
University of the District of Columbia

Florida

Eckerd College
Embry-Riddle Aeronautical University
Florida Atlantic University
Florida Institute of Technology
Florida International University
Florida Memorial University
Florida State University
Palm Beach Atlantic University
Remington College
    Tampa
Rollins College
University of Miami
Valencia College

Georgia

Agnes Scott College
Albany State University
Berry College
Columbus State University
Georgia Institute of Technology
LaGrange College
Mercer University
Morehouse College
Paine College
University of Georgia
University of North Georgia
Wesleyan College

Hawaii

Hawaii Pacific University
University of Hawaii
    Hilo

Idaho

University of Idaho

Illinois

Augustana College
Dominican University
Illinois College
Illinois Institute of Technology
Illinois Wesleyan University
Knox College
Lake Forest College
MacMurray College
Monmouth College
North Park University
Northwestern University
Southern Illinois University
    Carbondale
Southern Illinois University
    Edwardsville
University of Illinois
    Chicago
    Urbana-Champaign
Wheaton College

Indiana

Anderson University
Ball State University
Butler University
DePauw University
Earlham College
Franklin College
Goshen College
Purdue University
Purdue University
    Calumet
Saint Mary's College
Taylor University
Trine University
Wabash College

Iowa

Buena Vista University
Central College
Cornell College
Iowa State University
Iowa Wesleyan College
Luther College
Simpson College
University of Iowa
University of Northern Iowa

Kansas

Baker University
Bethany College
Kansas State University

Kentucky

Berea College
Brescia University
Kentucky Wesleyan College
Murray State University
Transylvania University
University of Kentucky
University of Louisville
University of Pikeville

Louisiana

Dillard University
Xavier University of Louisiana

Maine

Bates College
Bowdoin College
Colby College
Saint Joseph's College of Maine
University of Maine

Maryland

Capitol College
Goucher College
Hood College
Johns Hopkins University
University of Maryland
    Baltimore County
Washington College

Massachusetts

Assumption College
Bard College at Simon's Rock
Clark University
Gordon College
Massachusetts Institute of Technology
Massachusetts Maritime Academy
Mount Holyoke College
Northeastern University
Tufts University
University of Massachusetts
    Amherst
    Boston
    Dartmouth
    Lowell
Western New England University
Wheaton College
Williams College
Worcester Polytechnic Institute

Michigan

Adrian College
Albion College
Alma College
Grand Valley State University
Kalamazoo College
Kettering University
Lawrence Technological University
Michigan State University
Schoolcraft College
Spring Arbor University
University of Detroit Mercy
University of Michigan
Wayne State University
Western Michigan University

Minnesota

Augsburg College
Bethany Lutheran College
Bethel University
Carleton College
College of St. Benedict
Hamline University
Minnesota State University
    Mankato
St. John's University
University of Minnesota
    Morris
University of Northwestern - St. Paul

Mississippi

Belhaven University
Millsaps College
Mississippi College
Mississippi State University
University of Mississippi

Missouri

Central Methodist University
College of the Ozarks
Drury University
Fontbonne University
Maryville University of Saint Louis
Missouri Southern State University
Missouri University of Science and
    Technology
Rockhurst University
University of Central Missouri
Washington University in St. Louis
Webster University
Westminster College

Montana

Montana Tech of the University of
    Montana

Salish Kootenai College
University of Great Falls

Nebraska

Doane College
Hastings College
Nebraska Wesleyan University
University of Nebraska
 Kearney

New Hampshire

Dartmouth College
New England College

New Jersey

Drew University
Fairleigh Dickinson University
 College at Florham
 Metropolitan Campus
Kean University
Monmouth University
New Jersey Institute of Technology
Richard Stockton College of New
 Jersey
Rutgers, The State University of New
 Jersey
 Newark Campus
Saint Peter's University
Stevens Institute of Technology
William Paterson University of New
 Jersey

New York

Adelphi University
Alfred University
Bard College
Barnard College
Canisius College
City University of New York
 City College
Clarkson University
Colgate University
Columbia University
Columbia University
 School of General Studies
Cooper Union for the Advancement
 of Science and Art
Fordham University
Hamilton College
Hartwick College
Houghton College
Ithaca College
Le Moyne College
Manhattan College
New York Institute of Technology
New York University
Pace University
Rensselaer Polytechnic Institute
Roberts Wesleyan College
Rochester Institute of Technology
SUNY
 College at Geneseo
 College at New Paltz
 College at Oneonta
 College at Oswego
 College at Potsdam
 University at Albany
 University at Binghamton
 University at Buffalo
 University at Stony Brook
St. John's University
St. Lawrence University
St. Thomas Aquinas College
Sarah Lawrence College
Siena College
Skidmore College
Union College
University of Rochester
Vassar College
Wells College
Yeshiva University

North Carolina

Duke University
Elon University
North Carolina State University

North Dakota

Dickinson State University
University of Jamestown
University of North Dakota
Valley City State University

Ohio

Baldwin Wallace University
Capital University
Case Western Reserve University
Cleveland State University
College of Wooster
Heidelberg University
Hiram College
John Carroll University
Kenyon College
Ohio State University
 Columbus Campus
Ohio Wesleyan University
University of Cincinnati
University of Dayton
Wittenberg University
Zane State College

Oklahoma

Oklahoma Baptist University
Oklahoma Christian University
University of Oklahoma
University of Tulsa

Oregon

Lewis & Clark College
Oregon Institute of Technology
Pacific University
Portland State University
Southern Oregon University
Willamette University

Pennsylvania

Allegheny College
Arcadia University
Bryn Mawr College
Bucknell University
Carnegie Mellon University
Chatham University
Dickinson College
Drexel University
Edinboro University of Pennsylvania
Franklin & Marshall College
Gettysburg College
Haverford College
Indiana University of Pennsylvania
Juniata College
Kutztown University of Pennsylvania
La Roche College
Lehigh University
Lycoming College
Millersville University of Pennsylvania
Moravian College
Muhlenberg College
Penn State
 Altoona
 University Park
Robert Morris University
St. Francis University
St. Vincent College
Slippery Rock University of
 Pennsylvania
Temple University
Thiel College
University of Pennsylvania
University of Pittsburgh
 Bradford
 Greensburg
Ursinus College
Villanova University
Washington & Jefferson College
Waynesburg University

Widener University
Wilkes University

Puerto Rico

Inter American University of Puerto
 Rico
 Barranquitas Campus
Pontifical Catholic University of
 Puerto Rico
Universidad Adventista de las Antillas

Rhode Island

University of Rhode Island

South Carolina

Charleston Southern University
Clemson University
Converse College
Furman University
Lander University
North Greenville University
Presbyterian College
University of South Carolina
 Columbia
Wofford College

Tennessee

Bethel University
King University
Maryville College
Rhodes College
Tennessee State University
University of Tennessee
 Knoxville

Texas

Angelo State University
Baylor University
Our Lady of the Lake University of
 San Antonio
Prairie View A&M University
St. Mary's University
Southern Methodist University
Southwestern University
Texas Lutheran University
Texas State University
Texas Tech University
University of Dallas
University of Houston
University of Texas
 Arlington
 Dallas

Utah

University of Utah
Westminster College

Vermont

Norwich University
University of Vermont

Virginia

College of William and Mary
George Mason University
Hampden-Sydney College
Hampton University
Longwood University
Lynchburg College
Norfolk State University
Old Dominion University
Randolph College
Randolph-Macon College
Roanoke College
Sweet Briar College
University of Management and
 Technology
University of Virginia
Virginia Polytechnic Institute and
 State University
Virginia Wesleyan College

Washington

DigiPen Institute of Technology
Pacific Lutheran University

Saint Martin's University
University of Washington Bothell
Whitman College

West Virginia

Bethany College
West Virginia University Institute of
 Technology
West Virginia Wesleyan College
Wheeling Jesuit University

Wisconsin

Beloit College
Carroll University
Carthage College
Lawrence University
Marquette University
Milwaukee School of Engineering
Ripon College
University of Wisconsin
 Milwaukee
 Oshkosh
 Platteville
 River Falls

Combined bachelor's/graduate program in environmental studies

Alabama

Birmingham-Southern College
Tuskegee University
University of Alabama

Alaska

University of Alaska
 Anchorage

Arkansas

University of Central Arkansas

California

California State University
 Fresno
 Los Angeles
Stanford University
University of Southern California

Colorado

Colorado School of Mines
Western State Colorado University

Connecticut

Sacred Heart University
University of New Haven
Wesleyan University
Yale University

District of Columbia

American University

Florida

Bethune-Cookman University
Florida International University

Georgia

Georgia Institute of Technology
University of Georgia

Hawaii

University of Hawaii
 Hilo

Illinois

Augustana College
DePaul University
Illinois Institute of Technology
Loyola University Chicago
Southern Illinois University
 Carbondale

Indiana

Purdue University
Taylor University

Iowa

Cornell College
University of Northern Iowa

Kentucky

Murray State University
St. Catharine College

Louisiana

Southern University and Agricultural
and Mechanical College

Maine

University of Maine

Maryland

University of Baltimore
University of Maryland
Baltimore County

Massachusetts

Anna Maria College
Assumption College
Bard College at Simon's Rock
Clark University
Lesley University
Tufts University

Michigan

Albion College

Minnesota

Bemidji State University
Minnesota State University
Mankato

Mississippi

University of Southern Mississippi

Missouri

Missouri Southern State University
University of Central Missouri
William Jewell College

Montana

Salish Kootenai College

Nebraska

Doane College

New Hampshire

Franklin Pierce University

New Jersey

Richard Stockton College of New
Jersey
William Paterson University of New
Jersey

New York

Adelphi University
Bard College
Cazenovia College
Clinton Community College
New York Institute of Technology
Pace University
Pace University: Pleasantville/
Briarcliff
Rochester Institute of Technology
SUNY
College at Cortland
College at Fredonia
Siena College
University of Rochester

North Carolina

Guilford College
University of North Carolina
Chapel Hill
Wake Forest University

Ohio

Cleveland State University
College of Wooster
Defiance College
Kenyon College
Miami University
Oxford
Ohio State University
Columbus Campus
Wittenberg University
Xavier University
Zane State College

Oklahoma

Southeastern Oklahoma State
University

Oregon

Pacific University
Portland State University
Reed College
Southern Oregon University

Pennsylvania

Arcadia University
Duquesne University
Elizabethtown College
Franklin & Marshall College
Gettysburg College
Lycoming College
Marywood University
Muhlenberg College
Penn State
Altoona
St. Francis University
Susquehanna University
Temple University
University of Pennsylvania
University of Pittsburgh
Greensburg

Puerto Rico

University of Puerto Rico
Aguadilla
Medical Sciences

Rhode Island

University of Rhode Island

South Carolina

College of Charleston
Furman University
Presbyterian College
Winthrop University

Texas

Texas A&M University
Galveston

Vermont

Lyndon State College

Washington

Northwest University
University of Washington Bothell
Western Washington University
Whitman College

Wisconsin

University of Wisconsin
Green Bay
Oshkosh
Parkside

Combined bachelor's/ graduate program in fine arts

Alabama

Jacksonville State University

Alaska

University of Alaska
Anchorage

California

Academy of Art University
Art Institute of California
San Francisco
Brooks Institute
California College of the Arts
California State University
Fresno
Los Angeles
John F. Kennedy University
University of California
Santa Cruz

Colorado

Western State Colorado University

Florida

Digital Media Arts College
Full Sail University

Hawaii

University of Hawaii
Hawaii Community College

Idaho

University of Idaho

Illinois

Bradley University
University of Illinois
Chicago

Kentucky

Murray State University

Maine

Maine College of Art
University of Maine
University of Southern Maine

Maryland

University of Baltimore

Massachusetts

Endicott College
Lesley University
School of the Museum of Fine Arts
Simmons College
Tufts University

Michigan

Ferris State University
Northern Michigan University

Minnesota

Bemidji State University
Minneapolis College of Art and
Design
Minnesota State University
Mankato

Mississippi

Mississippi State University
University of Mississippi
University of Southern Mississippi

Missouri

Missouri Southern State University
University of Central Missouri
Webster University

Nebraska

University of Nebraska
Kearney

Nevada

Sierra Nevada College

New Hampshire

New England College

New Jersey

Fairleigh Dickinson University
College at Florham
William Paterson University of New
Jersey

New York

New York Institute of Technology
Pace University
Rensselaer Polytechnic Institute
St. Joseph's College, New York

North Carolina

North Carolina State University

Oregon

Pacific University
Portland State University

Pennsylvania

California University of Pennsylvania
Chatham University
Marywood University
Temple University
Wilkes University

Rhode Island

Roger Williams University

South Carolina

Converse College
Winthrop University

South Dakota

University of South Dakota

Tennessee

Cumberland University
Memphis College of Art

Texas

Sul Ross State University
University of Texas
Dallas

Vermont

Champlain College
Lyndon State College

Virginia

Mary Baldwin College
Regent University

Combined bachelor's/ graduate program in forestry

Alabama

Tuskegee University

Arkansas

University of Arkansas
Monticello

California

California State University
Fresno

Colorado

Western State Colorado University

Connecticut

Yale University

Florida

Rollins College

Georgia

Southeastern Technical College

Hawaii

University of Hawaii
    Hawaii Community College

Illinois

Augustana College
Illinois Wesleyan University
Knox College
Southern Illinois University
    Carbondale

Indiana

Purdue University

Iowa

Cornell College
Iowa Wesleyan College

Maine

University of Maine

Massachusetts

Assumption College

Michigan

Albion College

Mississippi

Mississippi State University

Missouri

William Jewell College

Montana

Salish Kootenai College

Nebraska

Doane College

New Jersey

Drew University

New York

Alfred University
Bard College
Clinton Community College
Paul Smith's College
SUNY
    College at Cortland

North Carolina

Guilford College
North Carolina State University

Ohio

College of Wooster
Miami University
    Oxford
Xavier University
Zane State College

Oregon

Portland State University
Reed College
Willamette University

Pennsylvania

Elizabethtown College
Franklin & Marshall College
Gettysburg College
Lycoming College
Moravian College
Muhlenberg College

St. Francis University
Susquehanna University
Thiel College

South Carolina

Furman University
Presbyterian College

Virginia

James Madison University
Randolph-Macon College

Washington

Whitman College

West Virginia

Marshall University

Wisconsin

Beloit College
Lawrence University
Ripon College

Combined bachelor's/ graduate program in law

Arkansas

University of Arkansas

California

California State University
    Fresno
Claremont McKenna College
Humphreys College
John F. Kennedy University
La Sierra University
Occidental College
University of San Francisco
Whittier College

Colorado

University of Colorado
    Denver
University of Denver
Western State Colorado University

Connecticut

Quinnipiac University

Florida

Nova Southeastern University
Saint Thomas University
Stetson University
University of Miami

Georgia

Georgia State University
University of Georgia

Idaho

College of Idaho

Illinois

Illinois Institute of Technology
Lake Forest College
Roosevelt University
Shimer College
University of Illinois
    Chicago

Indiana

Valparaiso University

Iowa

Drake University
Iowa Wesleyan College
Simpson College
University of Iowa
Wartburg College

Kentucky

Kentucky Christian University
Union College

Louisiana

Loyola University New Orleans
Southern University and Agricultural
    and Mechanical College

Maine

Bowdoin College
University of Southern Maine

Maryland

Towson University
University of Baltimore
University of Maryland
    College Park

Massachusetts

Assumption College
Springfield College
Suffolk University
Western New England University

Michigan

Adrian College
Grand Valley State University
Siena Heights University
University of Detroit Mercy

Minnesota

Carleton College
Hamline University

Mississippi

Mississippi College
Mississippi State University

Missouri

College of the Ozarks
Columbia College
University of Missouri
    Kansas City
Washington University in St. Louis

Nebraska

Creighton University
Hastings College
University of Nebraska
    Kearney
    Lincoln

New Hampshire

New England College

New Jersey

Rutgers, The State University of New
    Jersey
    Camden Campus
    New Brunswick/Piscataway
        Campus
    Newark Campus
Saint Peter's University
Stevens Institute of Technology

New York

Adelphi University
Albany College of Pharmacy and
    Health Sciences
College of Saint Rose
Columbia University
Fordham University
Hamilton College
Hartwick College
Hofstra University
Long Island University
    LIU Post
Pace University
Pace University: Pleasantville/
    Briarcliff
Rensselaer Polytechnic Institute

SUNY

University at Albany
Sage Colleges
St. John's University
St. Thomas Aquinas College
Siena College
Union College

North Carolina

Campbell University
Johnson C. Smith University

North Dakota

Valley City State University

Ohio

College of Wooster
Ohio Northern University
Ohio State University
    Columbus Campus
University of Toledo

Oklahoma

Oklahoma City University
University of Tulsa

Oregon

Portland State University
Willamette University

Pennsylvania

Dickinson College
Drexel University
Duquesne University
East Stroudsburg University of
    Pennsylvania
Edinboro University of Pennsylvania
Gannon University
Juniata College
Mercyhurst University
St. Francis University
St. Vincent College
Seton Hill University
Temple University
Thomas Jefferson University
University of Pennsylvania
University of Pittsburgh
University of Pittsburgh
    Greensburg
Washington & Jefferson College
Widener University

Puerto Rico

Pontifical Catholic University of
    Puerto Rico

Rhode Island

Roger Williams University

Tennessee

Belmont University
University of Tennessee
    Knoxville
Vanderbilt University

Utah

Brigham Young University

Vermont

Green Mountain College
University of Vermont

Virginia

Regent University

Washington

Western Washington University
Whitman College

West Virginia

Bethany College
Wheeling Jesuit University

Wisconsin

Marquette University
University of Wisconsin
 Green Bay

Combined bachelor's/ graduate program in mathematics

Alabama

Alabama State University
Jacksonville State University
Tuskegee University
University of Alabama
University of Alabama
 Birmingham
 Huntsville
University of Montevallo

Arizona

Arizona State University

Arkansas

University of Arkansas
 Monticello
University of Central Arkansas

California

California State University
 Fresno
 Los Angeles
Mills College
Pitzer College
Stanford University
University of Southern California
Vanguard University of Southern
 California

Colorado

Colorado School of Mines
University of Colorado
 Boulder

Connecticut

Wesleyan University
Yale University

District of Columbia

American University
University of the District of Columbia

Florida

Florida Atlantic University
Florida International University
Florida State University

Georgia

Clark Atlanta University
Emory University

Hawaii

University of Hawaii
 Hilo

Idaho

Lewis-Clark State College

Illinois

Loyola University Chicago
National-Louis University
Roosevelt University
Southern Illinois University
 Carbondale
University of Chicago

Indiana

Purdue University
Purdue University
 Calumet

Kansas

Fort Hays State University

Kentucky

Kentucky Christian University
Murray State University

Maine

University of Maine

Maryland

Bowie State University
Hood College
Johns Hopkins University
University of Maryland
 Baltimore County

Massachusetts

Brandeis University
Tufts University
University of Massachusetts
 Dartmouth
Worcester Polytechnic Institute

Michigan

Central Michigan University
Northern Michigan University
University of Michigan
Wayne State University

Minnesota

Bemidji State University
Minnesota State University
 Mankato

Mississippi

Mississippi State University
University of Mississippi
University of Southern Mississippi

Missouri

Missouri Southern State University
Missouri State University
Missouri University of Science and
 Technology
University of Central Missouri

Montana

Montana State University
 Northern
Salish Kootenai College

Nebraska

University of Nebraska
 Kearney

New Jersey

Kean University
New Jersey Institute of Technology
Rowan University
Rutgers, The State University of New
 Jersey
 Camden Campus
Stevens Institute of Technology
William Paterson University of New
 Jersey

New Mexico

Eastern New Mexico University

New York

City University of New York
 City College
 Hunter College
Clinton Community College
Hofstra University
Long Island University
 LIU Post
Manhattan College
Rensselaer Polytechnic Institute
Rochester Institute of Technology

SUNY
 College at Oswego
 College at Potsdam
 University at Buffalo
 University at Stony Brook
St. Joseph's College New York:
 Suffolk Campus
University of Rochester

North Carolina

Guilford College
University of North Carolina
 Chapel Hill
Western Carolina University

Ohio

Case Western Reserve University
Defiance College
Mount Vernon Nazarene University
University of Akron
Urbana University

Oklahoma

Southeastern Oklahoma State
 University
University of Oklahoma
University of Tulsa

Oregon

Corban University
Southern Oregon University

Pennsylvania

Baptist Bible College of Pennsylvania
Bryn Mawr College
Bucknell University
Duquesne University
La Salle University
Marywood University
Mount Aloysius College
Penn State
 Altoona
 University Park
Temple University
University of Pennsylvania
University of Pittsburgh
University of Pittsburgh
 Greensburg
Villanova University
Wilkes University

Rhode Island

University of Rhode Island

South Carolina

College of Charleston
Voorhees College
Winthrop University

Tennessee

King University
Tennessee State University

Texas

Prairie View A&M University
Sul Ross State University
Texas Tech University
University of Texas
 Brownsville

Utah

University of Utah

Vermont

Lyndon State College
University of Vermont

Virginia

George Mason University

Washington

Northwest University
Western Washington University

Wisconsin

University of Wisconsin
 Oshkosh
 Parkside

Combined bachelor's/ graduate program in medicine

Alaska

University of Alaska
 Anchorage

Arkansas

University of Arkansas
 for Medical Sciences

California

California Institute of Technology
California State University
 Fresno
University of California
 San Diego
University of Southern California

Colorado

Western State Colorado University

Connecticut

Quinnipiac University
University of Connecticut

District of Columbia

Howard University

Florida

University of Central Florida
University of Miami
University of South Florida

Georgia

Georgia Regents University

Illinois

Illinois Institute of Technology
Northwestern University
Southern Illinois University
 Carbondale
University of Chicago
University of Illinois
 Chicago

Indiana

Purdue University
 Calumet

Iowa

Iowa Wesleyan College

Kentucky

Murray State University
Union College

Louisiana

Louisiana State University
 Shreveport

Maryland

University of Maryland
 College Park

Massachusetts

Boston College
Boston University
MCPHS University
Springfield College
Tufts University

Michigan

Northern Michigan University
Wayne State University

Minnesota

University of Minnesota
 Duluth

Mississippi

Mississippi College
Mississippi State University
Rust College

Missouri

University of Missouri
 Kansas City

Nebraska

Chadron State College
Hastings College
University of Nebraska
 Kearney
 Lincoln
 Medical Center

Nevada

University of Nevada
 Reno

New Jersey

Caldwell College
College of New Jersey
Drew University
Fairleigh Dickinson University
 College at Florham
 Metropolitan Campus
Kean University
Monmouth University
Montclair State University
New Jersey Institute of Technology
Richard Stockton College of New
 Jersey
Rutgers, The State University of New
 Jersey
 Camden Campus
 New Brunswick/Piscataway
 Campus
 Newark Campus
Saint Peter's University
Stevens Institute of Technology

New Mexico

University of New Mexico

New York

Albany College of Pharmacy and
 Health Sciences
Canisius College
City University of New York
 Brooklyn College
 City College
 York College
Colgate University
Cooper Union for the Advancement
 of Science and Art
Hobart and William Smith Colleges
Hofstra University
Rensselaer Polytechnic Institute
SUNY
 College at Fredonia
 College of Environmental Science
 and Forestry
 University at Binghamton
 Upstate Medical University
Sage Colleges
Saint Bonaventure University
Siena College
Union College
University of Rochester
Utica College

North Dakota

Valley City State University

Ohio

College of Wooster
Kent State University

Ohio State University
 Columbus Campus
University of Akron
University of Dayton

Oregon

Portland State University

Pennsylvania

Delaware Valley College
Drexel University
Duquesne University
Gannon University
Indiana University of Pennsylvania
Juniata College
Lehigh University
Moravian College
Muhlenberg College
Penn State
 Erie, The Behrend College
 University Park
Rosemont College
St. Francis University
Temple University
Thomas Jefferson University
University of Pittsburgh
 Bradford
 Greensburg
Ursinus College
Villanova University
Washington & Jefferson College
Widener University
Wilkes University

Puerto Rico

Pontifical Catholic University of
 Puerto Rico
Universidad Adventista de las Antillas
University of Puerto Rico
 Medical Sciences
University of the Sacred Heart

Rhode Island

Brown University

South Carolina

Furman University

Tennessee

East Tennessee State University
Fisk University
Union University
University of Tennessee
 Knoxville

Texas

McMurry University
Rice University
Texas State University
Texas Tech University Health
 Sciences Center
University of Texas
 Arlington
 Health Science Center at Houston

Virginia

Old Dominion University
Randolph-Macon College

Washington

Washington State University

Wisconsin

University of Wisconsin
 Green Bay

Combined bachelor's/ graduate program in nursing

Alabama

Birmingham-Southern College
Jacksonville State University

Stillman College
Talladega College
Troy University
Tuskegee University
University of Alabama
 Huntsville

Alaska

University of Alaska
 Anchorage

Arizona

Glendale Community College
Grand Canyon University

Arkansas

University of Arkansas
 Monticello
 for Medical Sciences
University of Central Arkansas

California

California State University
 Fresno
 Los Angeles
La Sierra University
St. Mary's College of California
Samuel Merritt University
Vanguard University of Southern
 California

Colorado

American Sentinel University
Colorado Christian University
University of Colorado
 Colorado Springs

Connecticut

Quinnipiac University
Sacred Heart University
University of Saint Joseph

District of Columbia

Catholic University of America

Florida

Barry University
Florida Atlantic University
Florida Gulf Coast University
Florida Memorial University
Florida State University
Nova Southeastern University
Polk State College
University of Central Florida
University of Tampa

Georgia

Agnes Scott College
Berry College
Emory University
Georgia Highlands College
Georgia Southern University
South Georgia State College
Southeastern Technical College
Thomas University

Hawaii

Hawaii Pacific University
University of Hawaii
 Hawaii Community College
 Hilo

Idaho

College of Idaho
Lewis-Clark State College

Illinois

Augustana College
Benedictine University
Blessing-Rieman College of Nursing
Dominican University
Lake Forest College
McKendree University

Monmouth College
St. Francis Medical Center College of
 Nursing
St. John's College
Southern Illinois University
 Carbondale
Trinity College of Nursing & Health
 Sciences
University of Illinois
 Chicago
Wheaton College

Indiana

Purdue University
University of Southern Indiana
Valparaiso University

Iowa

Allen College
Central College
Dordt College
Emmaus Bible College
Graceland University
Iowa Wesleyan College
Loras College
St. Luke's College
Simpson College
Wartburg College

Kansas

Fort Hays State University
Manhattan Christian College
University of Kansas Medical Center

Kentucky

Beckfield College
Bellarmine University
Brescia University
Kentucky Christian University
Kentucky Wesleyan College
Murray State University
St. Catharine College

Louisiana

Loyola University New Orleans
Our Lady of the Lake College
Southern University and Agricultural
 and Mechanical College

Maine

Saint Joseph's College of Maine
University of Maine
University of Southern Maine

Maryland

Bowie State University
Salisbury University
University of Baltimore
University of Maryland
 Baltimore
Washington College

Massachusetts

Assumption College
Boston College
Endicott College
MCPHS University
Northeastern University
Regis College
Simmons College
University of Massachusetts
 Boston
 Dartmouth

Michigan

Albion College
Ferris State University
Kuyper College
Northern Michigan University
Schoolcraft College
University of Michigan

Minnesota

Minnesota State University
  Mankato
Walden University

Mississippi

Blue Mountain College
Millsaps College
Mississippi State University
University of Mississippi
University of Mississippi Medical
  Center
University of Southern Mississippi

Missouri

Avila University
Culver-Stockton College
Grantham University
Lindenwood University
Missouri Southern State University
Missouri State University
Missouri University of Science and
  Technology
Rockhurst University
St. Luke's College
University of Central Missouri
Webster University
Westminster College

Montana

Montana State University
  Northern
Salish Kootenai College
University of Great Falls

Nebraska

BryanLGH College of Health Sciences
Chadron State College
Clarkson College
Grace University
Hastings College
Nebraska Methodist College of
  Nursing and Allied Health
University of Nebraska
  Kearney

New Hampshire

Franklin Pierce University

New Jersey

College of St. Elizabeth
Felician College
Ramapo College of New Jersey
Richard Stockton College of New
  Jersey
Saint Peter's University
Thomas Edison State College
William Paterson University of New
  Jersey

New Mexico

San Juan College

New York

Adelphi University
Clinton Community College
Cochran School of Nursing
Concordia College
D'Youville College
Daemen College
Excelsior College
Hobart and William Smith Colleges
Long Island University
  LIU Brooklyn
Mercy College
Molloy College
New York University
Pace University
Pace University: Pleasantville/
  Briarcliff
SUNY
  College at Geneseo
  Institute of Technology at Utica/
    Rome

University at Stony Brook
  Upstate Medical University
Sage Colleges
St. Lawrence University
Skidmore College
University of Rochester

North Carolina

Carolinas College of Health Sciences
Gardner-Webb University
University of North Carolina
  Greensboro

North Dakota

Valley City State University

Ohio

Bowling Green State University
College of Wooster
Defiance College
Franciscan University of Steubenville
Good Samaritan College of Nursing
  and Health Science
Hondros College
Kent State University
Mercy College of Ohio
Mount Vernon Nazarene University
Ohio Christian University
Ohio State University
  Columbus Campus
Otterbein University
University of Akron
University of Findlay
Wittenberg University

Oklahoma

Southeastern Oklahoma State
  University
Southern Nazarene University

Oregon

Eastern Oregon University
Oregon Health & Science University
Oregon Institute of Technology
Portland State University
Southern Oregon University
Western Oregon University

Pennsylvania

Allegheny College
Arcadia University
Carlow University
Cedar Crest College
Chatham University
Clarion University of Pennsylvania
Dickinson College
Drexel University
Gannon University
Gettysburg College
Juniata College
Kutztown University of Pennsylvania
Marywood University
Mount Aloysius College
Penn State
  Altoona
  Worthington Scranton
Rosemont College
St. Francis University
Susquehanna University
Temple University
Thomas Jefferson University
University of Pennsylvania
University of Pittsburgh
University of Scranton
Widener University
Wilkes University

Puerto Rico

Universidad Adventista de las Antillas
University of Puerto Rico
  Aguadilla
  Carolina Regional College
  Medical Sciences
  Utuado

Rhode Island

University of Rhode Island

South Carolina

Converse College
Furman University

South Dakota

National American University
  Rapid City

Tennessee

Bryan University
  Dayton
Fisk University
King University
Maryville College
Southern Adventist University
Tennessee State University
Union University
Vanderbilt University

Texas

Baylor University
Prairie View A&M University
Texas Tech University Health
  Sciences Center
Texas Woman's University
University of Dallas
University of Texas
  Health Science Center at Houston
University of the Incarnate Word
West Texas A&M University

Vermont

Lyndon State College
Norwich University
University of Vermont

Virginia

Bridgewater College
Hampton University
Mary Baldwin College
Old Dominion University
Randolph College
Randolph-Macon College
Shenandoah University

Washington

Gonzaga University
Northwest University
University of Washington Bothell

West Virginia

Appalachian Bible College
Glenville State College
West Virginia Wesleyan College
Wheeling Jesuit University

Wisconsin

Herzing University
  Madison
Marian University
Marquette University
Ripon College
University of Wisconsin
  Milwaukee
  Oshkosh
  Parkside
Viterbo University

Combined bachelor's/ graduate program in occupational therapy

Alabama

Alabama State University
Tuskegee University
University of South Alabama

Alaska

University of Alaska
  Anchorage

Arkansas

University of Central Arkansas

California

California State University
  Fresno
Dominican University of California
La Sierra University
Loma Linda University

Connecticut

Quinnipiac University
Sacred Heart University

District of Columbia

Howard University

Florida

Florida Agricultural and Mechanical
  University
Nova Southeastern University
Saint Leo University

Georgia

Brenau University

Illinois

Augustana College
Hebrew Theological College
Illinois College
Knox College
McKendree University
Monmouth College
University of Illinois
  Chicago

Indiana

University of Southern Indiana

Iowa

St. Ambrose University

Kansas

Newman University
University of Kansas Medical Center

Kentucky

Spalding University

Maine

Husson University
University of Southern Maine

Maryland

Mount St. Mary's University
Towson University

Massachusetts

American International College
Bay Path College
Boston University
Salem State University
Springfield College
Tufts University
Worcester State University

Michigan

Alma College
Baker College
  Allen Park
  Flint
Calvin College
Eastern Michigan University
Grand Valley State University

Minnesota

College of St. Scholastica
St. Catherine University

Mississippi

Mississippi State University

Missouri

Avila University
Culver-Stockton College
Fontbonne University
Maryville University of Saint Louis
Missouri Southern State University
Saint Louis University
University of Missouri
   Columbia
Washington University in St. Louis
Webster University
William Jewell College

Nebraska

Chadron State College
College of Saint Mary
Hastings College
University of Nebraska
   Kearney

Nevada

University of Nevada
   Las Vegas

New Hampshire

University of New Hampshire

New Jersey

Caldwell College
Kean University
Richard Stockton College of New
   Jersey
Saint Peter's University
Seton Hall University

New York

City University of New York
   York College
College of Saint Rose
D'Youville College
Dominican College of Blauvelt
Hartwick College
Ithaca College
Keuka College
Long Island University
   LIU Brooklyn
Nazareth College
New York Institute of Technology
Pace University
Pace University: Pleasantville/
   Briarcliff
SUNY
   University at Buffalo
   University at Stony Brook
Sage Colleges
Siena College
Skidmore College
Touro College
Utica College

North Dakota

University of Mary
Valley City State University

Ohio

Capital University
Mount Vernon Nazarene University
Shawnee State University
University of Findlay
Wittenberg University
Xavier University
Zane State College

Oregon

Pacific University
Portland State University

Pennsylvania

Allegheny College
Alvernia University

Bloomsburg University of
   Pennsylvania
Chatham University
Duquesne University
Elizabethtown College
Gannon University
La Roche College
La Salle University
Messiah College
Misericordia University
Moravian College
Mount Aloysius College
Muhlenberg College
St. Francis University
St. Vincent College
Shippensburg University of
   Pennsylvania
Susquehanna University
Temple University
Thiel College
Thomas Jefferson University
University of Pittsburgh
   Greensburg
University of Scranton
University of the Sciences
Villanova University

Puerto Rico

University of Puerto Rico
   Medical Sciences

Rhode Island

New England Institute of Technology

Tennessee

Belmont University
Tennessee State University

Texas

Texas Tech University Health
   Sciences Center

Vermont

Castleton State College
Lyndon State College
Southern Vermont College

Virginia

Shenandoah University

Washington

Eastern Washington University

West Virginia

West Virginia University

Wisconsin

Carroll University
Carthage College
Concordia University Wisconsin
Lawrence University
Mount Mary University
University of Wisconsin
   Green Bay
   La Crosse
   Milwaukee

Combined bachelor's/graduate program in optometry

California

California State University
   Fresno

Colorado

Western State Colorado University

Florida

Nova Southeastern University

Illinois

Augustana College
Illinois Institute of Technology
Knox College

Indiana

Indiana University
   Bloomington
Purdue University
   Calumet

Iowa

Iowa Wesleyan College

Kentucky

Murray State University

Maine

Saint Joseph's College of Maine
University of Maine

Massachusetts

Assumption College
MCPHS University
Wheaton College

Michigan

Adrian College
Ferris State University

Mississippi

Mississippi State University

Missouri

Maryville University of Saint Louis

New Jersey

Caldwell College
College of New Jersey
Fairleigh Dickinson University
   Metropolitan Campus
Felician College
Ramapo College of New Jersey
William Paterson University of New
   Jersey

New York

Adelphi University
Canisius College
City University of New York
   City College
Ithaca College
Le Moyne College
Mount Saint Mary College
Pace University
SUNY
   College at Fredonia
   College at Geneseo
   College at New Paltz
   College at Oneonta
   College at Oswego
   College at Plattsburgh
   College at Potsdam
   University at Albany
   University at Binghamton
St. John's University
Siena College
Utica College
Wagner College

North Dakota

Valley City State University

Ohio

Ohio State University
   Columbus Campus

Oregon

Pacific University
Portland State University
Southern Oregon University

Pennsylvania

Arcadia University
Gannon University
Gettysburg College
Grove City College
Indiana University of Pennsylvania
Juniata College
Lehigh University
Lycoming College
Millersville University of Pennsylvania
Muhlenberg College
St. Francis University
Shippensburg University of
   Pennsylvania
University of Pittsburgh
   Bradford
   Greensburg
   Johnstown
Villanova University
Washington & Jefferson College
Wilkes University

Puerto Rico

Universidad Adventista de las Antillas

Rhode Island

Providence College

Tennessee

Christian Brothers University
Union University

Virginia

Old Dominion University

Wisconsin

University of Wisconsin
   Green Bay

Combined bachelor's/graduate program in osteopathic medicine

California

California State University
   Fresno
La Sierra University
Pitzer College

Florida

Nova Southeastern University
Saint Leo University

Illinois

Illinois Institute of Technology

Indiana

University of St. Francis

Kentucky

Murray State University
University of Pikeville

Maine

University of Maine
University of New England

Massachusetts

Assumption College
MCPHS University
Springfield College

Missouri

Avila University
Central Methodist University
Culver-Stockton College
Missouri Western State University
Rockhurst University
William Jewell College

Nevada

University of Nevada
  Las Vegas

New Jersey

Caldwell College
Fairleigh Dickinson University
  Metropolitan Campus
Ramapo College of New Jersey
Richard Stockton College of New Jersey
Rutgers, The State University of New Jersey
  Camden Campus

New York

New York Institute of Technology
Pace University
Pace University: Pleasantville/Briarcliff
SUNY
  College at Fredonia
  College at Geneseo
  College at New Paltz
  College at Old Westbury
Saint Bonaventure University
Siena College
Touro College
Utica College

North Carolina

Campbell University

Ohio

Heidelberg University
Kent State University
Ohio University

Oregon

Portland State University

Pennsylvania

Allegheny College
Edinboro University of Pennsylvania
Elizabethtown College
Gannon University
Grove City College
Indiana University of Pennsylvania
Juniata College
La Roche College
Mercyhurst University
Mount Aloysius College
Penn State
  Erie, The Behrend College
St. Francis University
St. Vincent College
Seton Hill University
Shippensburg University of Pennsylvania
Slippery Rock University of Pennsylvania
Thiel College
University of Pittsburgh
  Bradford
  Greensburg
Widener University
Wilkes University

South Carolina

Converse College

Texas

University of Texas
  Dallas

Virginia

Bluefield College

West Virginia

Wheeling Jesuit University

Combined bachelor's/graduate program in pharmacy

Alaska

University of Alaska
  Anchorage

Arizona

University of Arizona

Arkansas

Harding University
University of Arkansas
  for Medical Sciences

California

California State University
  Fresno
Chapman University
La Sierra University
University of California
  San Diego
University of Southern California
University of the Pacific

Colorado

Regis University

Connecticut

University of Connecticut
University of Saint Joseph

Florida

Nova Southeastern University

Georgia

Mercer University
University of Georgia

Hawaii

Hawaii Pacific University
University of Hawaii
  Hilo

Idaho

College of Idaho
Idaho State University

Illinois

Benedictine University at Springfield
Dominican University
Elmhurst College
Hebrew Theological College
Illinois Institute of Technology
Lake Forest College
Millikin University
University of Illinois
  Chicago

Indiana

Butler University
Huntington University
Manchester University
Purdue University
Purdue University
  Calumet
University of St. Francis

Iowa

Drake University
Iowa Wesleyan College
Loras College
University of Iowa

Kansas

University of Kansas

Kentucky

Kentucky Christian University
Murray State University

Sullivan University
University of Pikeville

Louisiana

University of Louisiana at Monroe

Maine

Husson University
Saint Joseph's College of Maine

Maryland

Coppin State University
Notre Dame of Maryland University
University of Baltimore
Washington College

Massachusetts

Assumption College
Eastern Nazarene College
MCPHS University
Northeastern University
Simmons College
Worcester State University

Michigan

Adrian College
Ferris State University

Minnesota

University of Minnesota
  Duluth
  Twin Cities

Mississippi

Mississippi State University
Rust College
University of Mississippi

Missouri

Missouri Southern State University

Montana

University of Montana

Nebraska

Chadron State College
Hastings College
University of Nebraska
  Kearney
  Lincoln

Nevada

Nevada State College

New Hampshire

New England College
University of New Hampshire at Manchester

New Jersey

Fairleigh Dickinson University
  Metropolitan Campus
New Jersey Institute of Technology
Richard Stockton College of New Jersey
Rutgers, The State University of New Jersey
  Camden Campus
  New Brunswick/Piscataway Campus
Saint Peter's University
William Paterson University of New Jersey

New Mexico

New Mexico State University
University of New Mexico

New York

Albany College of Pharmacy and Health Sciences
Canisius College
Houghton College

Long Island University
  LIU Brooklyn
  LIU Post
Roberts Wesleyan College
SUNY
  College at Fredonia
Saint Bonaventure University
St. John's University
St. Thomas Aquinas College
Touro College

North Carolina

Campbell University
Elizabeth City State University
High Point University
University of North Carolina
  Chapel Hill
Wingate University

North Dakota

North Dakota State University
Valley City State University

Ohio

Cedarville University
Kent State University
Ohio Northern University
Ohio State University
  Columbus Campus
University of Findlay
University of Toledo
Ursuline College

Oklahoma

Southwestern Oklahoma State University

Oregon

Pacific University
Portland State University

Pennsylvania

East Stroudsburg University of Pennsylvania
Edinboro University of Pennsylvania
Gannon University
Grove City College
Indiana University of Pennsylvania
Juniata College
Keystone College
La Roche College
Mercyhurst University
Messiah College
Mount Aloysius College
Penn State
  Erie, The Behrend College
St. Francis University
St. Vincent College
Seton Hill University
Shippensburg University of Pennsylvania
Slippery Rock University of Pennsylvania
Temple University
Thiel College
Thomas Jefferson University
University of Pittsburgh
  Bradford
  Greensburg
  Johnstown
Wilkes University

Puerto Rico

Pontifical Catholic University of Puerto Rico
University of Puerto Rico
  Medical Sciences

Rhode Island

Roger Williams University
University of Rhode Island

South Carolina

Clemson University
Furman University
Presbyterian College

South Dakota

South Dakota State University

Tennessee

Belmont University
Bethel University
East Tennessee State University
Fisk University
King University
Lipscomb University
Maryville College
Milligan College
Tusculum College
Union University
University of Tennessee
 Knoxville

Texas

Texas Tech University Health
 Sciences Center
University of Texas
 El Paso

Vermont

Saint Michael's College

Virginia

Bluefield College
Hampton University
Old Dominion University
Shenandoah University

Washington

University of Washington
Washington State University

West Virginia

University of Charleston
West Virginia University
West Virginia Wesleyan College
Wheeling Jesuit University

Wisconsin

Carroll University
University of Wisconsin
 Green Bay
 Madison

Combined bachelor's/ graduate program in physical therapy

Alabama

Alabama State University
University of South Alabama

Arkansas

University of Central Arkansas

California

California State University
 Fresno
La Sierra University
Loma Linda University

Colorado

Regis University
Western State Colorado University

Connecticut

Quinnipiac University
Sacred Heart University
University of Connecticut
University of Hartford

Florida

Nova Southeastern University
Saint Leo University
University of Miami

Georgia

Mercer University

Illinois

Bradley University
Monmouth College
University of Illinois
 Chicago

Indiana

Purdue University
 Calumet

Iowa

Iowa Wesleyan College
St. Ambrose University

Kentucky

Bellarmine University
University of Kentucky

Maine

Husson University

Maryland

Coppin State University
Mount St. Mary's University
University of Maryland
 College Park

Massachusetts

American International College
Assumption College
Boston University
MCPHS University
Northeastern University
Simmons College
Springfield College
University of Massachusetts
 Lowell

Michigan

Andrews University
Grand Valley State University

Minnesota

St. Catherine University

Mississippi

Mississippi State University

Missouri

Avila University
Central Methodist University
Maryville University of Saint Louis
Missouri Southern State University
Saint Louis University
University of Missouri
 Columbia
Washington University in St. Louis

Nebraska

Chadron State College
Hastings College
University of Nebraska
 Kearney
 Medical Center

New Hampshire

Franklin Pierce University
New England College

New Jersey

Caldwell College
Fairleigh Dickinson University
 Metropolitan Campus
Kean University
Ramapo College of New Jersey

Richard Stockton College of New
 Jersey
Saint Peter's University
Seton Hall University
William Paterson University of New
 Jersey

New York

Adelphi University
College of Saint Rose
Daemen College
Dominican College of Blauvelt
Hartwick College
Ithaca College
Le Moyne College
Manhattanville College
Mount Saint Mary College
Nazareth College
New York Institute of Technology
Pace University
Pace University: Pleasantville/
 Briarcliff
SUNY
 College at Brockport
 College at Geneseo
 College at Oswego
 College of Environmental Science
 and Forestry
 Downstate Medical Center
 Upstate Medical University
Sage Colleges
Saint Bonaventure University
St. Lawrence University
St. Thomas Aquinas College
Siena College
Skidmore College
Touro College
Utica College

North Carolina

Campbell University

North Dakota

University of Mary
University of North Dakota
Valley City State University

Ohio

Bowling Green State University
Mount Vernon Nazarene University
Ohio University
University of Findlay
Walsh University
Zane State College

Oregon

Pacific University
Portland State University

Pennsylvania

Allegheny College
Alvernia University
Arcadia University
Bloomsburg University of
 Pennsylvania
Cabrini College
Chatham University
DeSales University
Drexel University
Duquesne University
Elizabethtown College
Gannon University
Gettysburg College
Indiana University of Pennsylvania
Juniata College
Keystone College
La Roche College
Lebanon Valley College
Moravian College
Mount Aloysius College
Muhlenberg College
Penn State
 Brandywine
St. Francis University

St. Vincent College
Shippensburg University of
 Pennsylvania
Slippery Rock University of
 Pennsylvania
Temple University
Thiel College
University of Pittsburgh
University of Pittsburgh
 Greensburg
University of Scranton
University of the Sciences
Villanova University
Washington & Jefferson College
Widener University
Wilkes University

Puerto Rico

Universidad Adventista de las Antillas
University of Puerto Rico
 Medical Sciences

Rhode Island

University of Rhode Island

South Carolina

Furman University

Tennessee

Belmont University
King University
Tennessee State University

Texas

Texas Tech University Health
 Sciences Center
University of Texas
 El Paso

Vermont

Castleton State College
Lyndon State College
Southern Vermont College

Virginia

Bridgewater College
Hampton University
Shenandoah University

West Virginia

West Virginia University
Wheeling Jesuit University

Wisconsin

Carroll University
Concordia University Wisconsin
Marquette University
University of Wisconsin
 Green Bay
 La Crosse

Combined bachelor's/ graduate program in podiatry

California

California State University
 Fresno
La Sierra University

District of Columbia

Howard University

Florida

Barry University

Massachusetts

Assumption College
MCPHS University
Massachusetts College of Liberal Arts

Michigan

Adrian College

Mississippi

Mississippi State University

New Jersey

Bloomfield College
Caldwell College
Fairleigh Dickinson University
   Metropolitan Campus
Felician College
Kean University
Ramapo College of New Jersey
Richard Stockton College of New
   Jersey

New York

Canisius College
Le Moyne College
Mount Saint Mary College
Pace University
Pace University: Pleasantville/
   Briarcliff
St. Francis College
St. John's University
St. Joseph's College New York:
   Suffolk Campus
St. Joseph's College, New York
St. Thomas Aquinas College
Siena College
Utica College

Oregon

Portland State University

Pennsylvania

Cabrini College
Gannon University
Indiana University of Pennsylvania
Juniata College
Lycoming College
Millersville University of Pennsylvania
St. Francis University
St. Vincent College
Shippensburg University of
   Pennsylvania
Temple University
Washington & Jefferson College
Widener University

Tennessee

Union University

Wisconsin

University of Wisconsin
   Oshkosh

Combined bachelor's/ graduate program in psychology

Alabama

Alabama State University
Jacksonville State University
Tuskegee University
University of Montevallo

Alaska

University of Alaska
   Anchorage

Arkansas

University of Arkansas
   Monticello
University of Central Arkansas

California

California State University
   Fresno
   Los Angeles
Claremont McKenna College

Hope International University
Humboldt State University
John F. Kennedy University
Menlo College
Mills College
Pitzer College
Simpson University
Stanford University
University of Southern California
University of the West
Vanguard University of Southern
   California

Colorado

Colorado Christian University

Connecticut

Fairfield University
Sacred Heart University
Wesleyan University
Yale University

District of Columbia

American University
Catholic University of America
University of the District of Columbia

Florida

Florida Institute of Technology
Nova Southeastern University
Warner University

Hawaii

Hawaii Pacific University
University of Hawaii
   Hilo

Idaho

Lewis-Clark State College

Illinois

Benedictine University
DePaul University
Illinois Institute of Technology
National-Louis University
Roosevelt University
Southern Illinois University
   Carbondale

Indiana

Purdue University
Valparaiso University

Iowa

Iowa State University
Iowa Wesleyan College
University of Iowa
Waldorf College

Kansas

Fort Hays State University

Kentucky

Kentucky Christian University
Mid-Continent University
Murray State University
St. Catharine College
Union College

Louisiana

Centenary College of Louisiana

Maine

University of Maine

Maryland

Bowie State University
University of Baltimore
University of Maryland
   Baltimore County

Massachusetts

American International College
Anna Maria College
Lesley University
Tufts University
University of Massachusetts
   Dartmouth
   Lowell

Michigan

Central Michigan University
Northern Michigan University
Rochester College
Schoolcraft College
University of Michigan
Wayne State University

Minnesota

Bemidji State University
Capella University
Minnesota State University
   Mankato
Oak Hills Christian College
Walden University

Mississippi

Mississippi State University
University of Mississippi
University of Southern Mississippi

Missouri

Avila University
Missouri Southern State University
Missouri University of Science and
   Technology
University of Central Missouri

Montana

Salish Kootenai College
University of Great Falls

Nebraska

Grace University
Nebraska Christian College
University of Nebraska
   Kearney

New Hampshire

Colby-Sawyer College
New England College

New Jersey

Caldwell College
College of St. Elizabeth
Fairleigh Dickinson University
   College at Florham
   Metropolitan Campus
Monmouth University
Seton Hall University
William Paterson University of New
   Jersey

New Mexico

New Mexico Highlands University

New York

Adelphi University
Cazenovia College
City University of New York
   City College
   John Jay College of Criminal Justice
Clinton Community College
College of New Rochelle
Hofstra University
Iona College
Marist College
Medaille College: Amherst
Pace University
SUNY
   College at Old Westbury
   College at Oswego
   University at Albany
Sage Colleges

St. John's University
St. Thomas Aquinas College
Sarah Lawrence College
Touro College
University of Rochester

North Carolina

Guilford College

Ohio

Case Western Reserve University
Defiance College
Heidelberg University
Marietta College
Mount Vernon Nazarene University
Ohio Christian University
Ohio University
   Lancaster Campus
Walsh University

Oklahoma

Mid-America Christian University
Southeastern Oklahoma State
   University
Southern Nazarene University
Southwestern Christian University

Oregon

Corban University
Oregon Institute of Technology
Southern Oregon University

Pennsylvania

Baptist Bible College of Pennsylvania
Bryn Mawr College
California University of Pennsylvania
Carlow University
Chatham University
Chestnut Hill College
Drexel University
Duquesne University
Marywood University
Mount Aloysius College
Penn State
   Altoona
Rosemont College
Saint Joseph's University
Shippensburg University of
   Pennsylvania
Temple University
University of Pittsburgh
   Greensburg
University of the Sciences
Widener University

Puerto Rico

Carlos Albizu University: San Juan
Universidad Adventista de las Antillas
University of Puerto Rico
   Aguadilla
   Utuado

Rhode Island

Roger Williams University
Salve Regina University
University of Rhode Island

South Carolina

Converse College
Winthrop University

South Dakota

University of South Dakota

Tennessee

Bryan University
   Dayton
Tennessee State University
Union University

Texas

Prairie View A&M University
Sul Ross State University

Texas Tech University
University of Dallas

Vermont

Goddard College
Lyndon State College
Southern Vermont College

Virginia

George Mason University
Regent University

Washington

Northwest University
Trinity Lutheran College
Walla Walla University

Wisconsin

University of Wisconsin
Oshkosh
Parkside
Whitewater

Combined bachelor's/ graduate program in social work

Alabama

Alabama State University
Jacksonville State University
Tuskegee University
University of Montevallo

Alaska

University of Alaska
Anchorage

Arkansas

University of Arkansas
Monticello

California

California State University
Fresno
Los Angeles

Colorado

University of Denver

Connecticut

Quinnipiac University
Sacred Heart University

Florida

Barry University
Warner University

Georgia

Albany State University
Savannah State University
University of Georgia

Hawaii

Hawaii Pacific University
University of Hawaii
Hawaii Community College

Idaho

Lewis-Clark State College
Northwest Nazarene University

Illinois

Dominican University
Loyola University Chicago
Roosevelt University
Southern Illinois University
Carbondale
University of Chicago

Kansas

Manhattan Christian College

Kentucky

Brescia University
Kentucky Christian University

Louisiana

Southern University
New Orleans

Maine

University of Maine
University of Maine
Presque Isle
University of Southern Maine

Maryland

Bowie State University
University of Maryland
Baltimore County
Washington Adventist University

Massachusetts

Boston College
Lesley University
Regis College
Simmons College
Springfield College
Wheelock College

Michigan

Andrews University
Davenport University
Kuyper College
Lake Superior State University
Northern Michigan University
Western Michigan University

Minnesota

Minnesota State University
Mankato

Mississippi

Mississippi State University
University of Mississippi
University of Southern Mississippi

Missouri

Avila University
Fontbonne University
Maryville University of Saint Louis
Missouri Southern State University
Saint Louis University
University of Central Missouri
Washington University in St. Louis

Montana

Salish Kootenai College

Nebraska

Chadron State College
Nebraska Christian College
University of Nebraska
Kearney

New Hampshire

University of New Hampshire

New Jersey

Caldwell College
Fairleigh Dickinson University
College at Florham
Metropolitan Campus
Monmouth University
Richard Stockton College of New
Jersey
William Paterson University of New
Jersey

New Mexico

New Mexico Highlands University

New York

Adelphi University
Bard College

Clinton Community College
Concordia College
Fordham University
Molloy College
Mount Saint Mary College
Nazareth College
Roberts Wesleyan College
SUNY
College at Oswego
College at Potsdam
University at Albany
University at Buffalo
St. Thomas Aquinas College
Siena College
Touro College
Yeshiva University

North Carolina

North Carolina State University
University of North Carolina
Pembroke
Western Piedmont Community
College

North Dakota

Dickinson State University
Valley City State University

Ohio

Baldwin Wallace University
College of Wooster
Defiance College
Mount Vernon Nazarene University
Ohio Christian University
Ohio State University
Columbus Campus
Ohio University
Lancaster Campus

Oklahoma

Northwestern Oklahoma State
University

Oregon

Portland State University
Southern Oregon University

Pennsylvania

Bryn Mawr College
California University of Pennsylvania
Cedar Crest College
Kutztown University of Pennsylvania
Marywood University
Millersville University of Pennsylvania
Shippensburg University of
Pennsylvania
Temple University
University of Pittsburgh
Bradford
Greensburg
Widener University

Rhode Island

Rhode Island College

South Carolina

Winthrop University

South Dakota

University of South Dakota

Tennessee

Tennessee State University
Union University

Texas

University of Texas
Health Science Center at Houston

Vermont

Lyndon State College

Washington

Walla Walla University

Wisconsin

University of Wisconsin
Oshkosh
River Falls
Superior

Combined bachelor's/ graduate program in veterinary medicine

Alabama

Tuskegee University

California

California State University
Fresno
La Sierra University

Colorado

University of Colorado
Denver
Western State Colorado University

Georgia

University of Georgia

Illinois

Augustana College

Indiana

Purdue University

Iowa

Iowa Wesleyan College

Kentucky

Kentucky Christian University
Murray State University

Maryland

University of Maryland
College Park

Massachusetts

MCPHS University
Tufts University
Worcester Polytechnic Institute

Mississippi

Mississippi College
Mississippi State University

Nebraska

University of Nebraska
Kearney

New Jersey

Caldwell College
Fairleigh Dickinson University
Metropolitan Campus
William Paterson University of New
Jersey

New York

SUNY
College at Fredonia

North Carolina

North Carolina State University

North Dakota

Valley City State University

Ohio

College of Wooster
Ohio State University
Columbus Campus
University of Findlay

Pennsylvania
Delaware Valley College
Edinboro University of Pennsylvania
Gannon University
St. Francis University
Widener University

Puerto Rico
Pontifical Catholic University of
   Puerto Rico

Tennessee
Union University
University of Tennessee
   Knoxville

Vermont
University of Vermont

Virginia
Old Dominion University

Washington
Washington State University

Wisconsin
University of Wisconsin
   Madison
Viterbo University

Double major

Alabama

Alabama Agricultural and Mechanical
  University
Alabama State University
Amridge University
Athens State University
Auburn University
Auburn University at Montgomery
Birmingham-Southern College
Faulkner State Community College
Faulkner University
George C. Wallace State Community
  College at Selma
Huntingdon College
Jacksonville State University
Judson College
Lawson State Community College
Miles College
Northwest-Shoals Community College
Oakwood University
Samford University
Shelton State Community College
Southeastern Bible College
Spring Hill College
Stillman College
Talladega College
Troy University
Tuskegee University
University of Alabama
University of Alabama
  Birmingham
  Huntsville
University of Mobile
University of Montevallo
University of North Alabama
University of South Alabama
University of West Alabama
Wallace State Community College at
  Hanceville

Alaska

Alaska Bible College
Alaska Pacific University
Charter College
Ilisagvik College
Prince William Sound Community
  College
University of Alaska
  Anchorage
  Fairbanks
  Southeast

Arizona

American Indian College of the
  Assemblies of God
Arizona Christian University
Arizona State University
Dine College
Eastern Arizona College
Embry-Riddle Aeronautical University
  Prescott Campus
GateWay Community College
Grand Canyon University
Northern Arizona University
Prescott College
Rio Salado College
Southwest University of Visual Arts
University of Advancing Technology
University of Arizona

Arkansas

Arkansas Baptist College
Arkansas Northeastern College
Arkansas State University
Arkansas State University
  Beebe
Arkansas Tech University
Cossatot Community College of the
  University of Arkansas
Ecclesia College
Harding University

Hendrix College
John Brown University
Lyon College
National Park Community College
Northwest Arkansas Community
  College
Ouachita Baptist University
Philander Smith College
Pulaski Technical College
Southern Arkansas University
Southern Arkansas University Tech
University of Arkansas
University of Arkansas
  Community College at Batesville
  Community College at Hope
  Fort Smith
  Little Rock
  Monticello
  Pine Bluff
  for Medical Sciences
University of Central Arkansas
University of the Ozarks
Williams Baptist College

California

Academy of Couture Art
Allan Hancock College
American Jewish University
Antioch University
  Los Angeles
Azusa Pacific University
Bakersfield College
Barstow Community College
Biola University
Brooks Institute
Butte College
California Baptist University
California College of the Arts
California Institute of Technology
California Lutheran University
California Maritime Academy
California Polytechnic State
  University: San Luis Obispo
California State Polytechnic
  University: Pomona
California State University
  Bakersfield
  Channel Islands
  Chico
  Dominguez Hills
  East Bay
  Fresno
  Fullerton
  Long Beach
  Los Angeles
  Monterey Bay
  Northridge
  Sacramento
  San Bernardino
  San Marcos
  Stanislaus
Canada College
Cerro Coso Community College
Chabot College
Chapman University
Citrus College
Claremont McKenna College
Cogswell Polytechnical College
Coleman University
Coleman University: San Marcos
College of San Mateo
College of the Canyons
College of the Desert
College of the Redwoods
Columbia College
Concordia University Irvine
Contra Costa College
Cosumnes River College
Crafton Hills College
Cuesta College
Cuyamaca College
Dominican University of California
East Los Angeles College
El Camino College
Empire College

Evergreen Valley College
Feather River College
Fresno City College
Fresno Pacific University
Fullerton College
Golden West College
Grossmont College
Harvey Mudd College
Holy Names University
Hope International University
Humboldt State University
Humphreys College
Imperial Valley College
Irvine Valley College
La Sierra University
Laguna College of Art and Design
Lake Tahoe Community College
Lincoln University
Loma Linda University
Los Angeles Harbor College
Los Angeles Southwest College
Los Angeles Trade and Technical
  College
Los Medanos College
Loyola Marymount University
Marymount California University
Master's College
Mendocino College
Menlo College
Mills College
MiraCosta College
Modesto Junior College
Monterey Peninsula College
Mount St. Mary's College
Mount San Jacinto College
Napa Valley College
National University
Notre Dame de Namur University
Occidental College
Ohlone College
Pacific States University
Pacific Union College
Patten University
Pepperdine University
Pitzer College
Point Loma Nazarene University
Pomona College
Porterville College
Reedley College
Rio Hondo College
Sacramento City College
Saddleback College
St. Mary's College of California
San Bernardino Valley College
San Diego Christian College
San Diego City College
San Diego Mesa College
San Diego State University
San Francisco Art Institute
San Francisco State University
San Jose State University
Santa Ana College
Santa Barbara City College
Santa Clara University
Santa Rosa Junior College
Santiago Canyon College
Scripps College
Shasta College
Sierra College
Simpson University
Skyline College
Solano Community College
Sonoma State University
Southern California Institute of
  Technology
Southwestern College
Stanford University
Taft College
Trident University International
University of California
  Berkeley
  Davis
  Irvine
  Los Angeles
  Merced

  Riverside
  San Diego
  Santa Barbara
  Santa Cruz
University of La Verne
University of Redlands
University of San Diego
University of San Francisco
University of Southern California
University of the Pacific
University of the West
Vanguard University of Southern
  California
Victor Valley College
West Hills College: Coalinga
West Valley College
Westmont College
Whittier College
William Jessup University
Woodbury University

Colorado

Adams State University
Aims Community College
Arapahoe Community College
Colorado Christian University
Colorado College
Colorado Heights University
Colorado Mesa University
Colorado School of Mines
Colorado State University
Colorado State University
  Pueblo
Colorado Technical University
Community College of Denver
Everest College
  Aurora
  Colorado Springs
Fort Lewis College
Front Range Community College
Metropolitan State University of
  Denver
Morgan Community College
Naropa University
National American University
  Denver
Nazarene Bible College
Northeastern Junior College
Pikes Peak Community College
Pueblo Community College
Regis University
Rocky Mountain College of Art &
  Design
Trinidad State Junior College
United States Air Force Academy
University of Colorado
  Boulder
  Colorado Springs
  Denver
University of Denver
University of Northern Colorado
Western State Colorado University

Connecticut

Albertus Magnus College
Asnuntuck Community College
Capital Community College
Central Connecticut State University
Connecticut College
Eastern Connecticut State University
Fairfield University
Goodwin College
Housatonic Community College
Manchester Community College
Naugatuck Valley Community College
Northwestern Connecticut
  Community College
Norwalk Community College
Post University
Quinebaug Valley Community College
Quinnipiac University
Sacred Heart University
Southern Connecticut State
  University

Three Rivers Community College
Trinity College
Tunxis Community College
United States Coast Guard Academy
University of Bridgeport
University of Connecticut
University of Hartford
University of New Haven
University of Saint Joseph
Wesleyan University
Yale University

Delaware

Delaware State University
Goldey-Beacom College
University of Delaware
Wesley College
Wilmington University

District of Columbia

American University
Catholic University of America
Gallaudet University
George Washington University
Georgetown University
Howard University
Trinity Washington University
University of the District of Columbia

Florida

Ave Maria University
Baptist College of Florida
Barry University
Beacon College
Bethune-Cookman University
Brown Mackie College
　Miami
Carlos Albizu University
Clearwater Christian College
Eastern Florida State College
Eckerd College
Edison State College
Edward Waters College
Embry-Riddle Aeronautical University
Embry-Riddle Aeronautical University
　Worldwide Campus
Everest University
　Largo
　Pompano Beach
　Tampa
Flagler College
Florida Agricultural and Mechanical
　University
Florida Atlantic University
Florida College
Florida Gulf Coast University
Florida Institute of Technology
Florida International University
Florida Keys Community College
Florida Memorial University
Florida Southern College
Florida State College at Jacksonville
Florida State University
Hillsborough Community College
Hobe Sound Bible College
Hodges University
Jacksonville University
Jones College
Jose Maria Vargas University
Lincoln College of Technology
　West Palm Beach
Lynn University
New College of Florida
Northwood University
　Florida
Nova Southeastern University
Palm Beach Atlantic University
Palm Beach State College
Pasco-Hernando State College
Pensacola State College
Polk State College
Rasmussen College
　New Port Richey
　Ocala

Rollins College
Saint Leo University
Saint Thomas University
Schiller International University
South Florida State College
Southeastern University
Stetson University
Tallahassee Community College
Trinity College of Florida
University of Central Florida
University of Florida
University of Miami
University of North Florida
University of South Florida
University of South Florida
　Sarasota-Manatee
University of Tampa
University of West Florida
Valencia College
Warner University
Webber International University

Georgia

Agnes Scott College
Albany State University
Andrew College
Armstrong Atlantic State University
Bainbridge College
Berry College
Beulah Heights University
Brenau University
Brewton-Parker College
Clark Atlanta University
Clayton State University
Columbus State University
Covenant College
Dalton State College
Darton College
East Georgia State College
Emory University
Fort Valley State University
Georgia College and State University
Georgia Gwinnett College
Georgia Highlands College
Georgia Institute of Technology
Georgia Military College
Georgia Perimeter College
Georgia Regents University
Georgia Southern University
Georgia Southwestern State
　University
Georgia State University
Gwinnett College
Gwinnett Technical College
Kennesaw State University
LaGrange College
Life University
Mercer University
Middle Georgia State College
Morehouse College
Oglethorpe University
Oxford College of Emory University
Piedmont College
Point University
Reinhardt University
Savannah College of Art and Design
Savannah State University
Shorter University
Southern Polytechnic State University
Spelman College
Toccoa Falls College
Truett-McConnell College
University of Georgia
University of North Georgia
University of West Georgia
Valdosta State University
Wesleyan College
Wiregrass Georgia Technical College

Hawaii

Brigham Young University-Hawaii
Chaminade University of Honolulu
Hawaii Pacific University

University of Hawaii
　Hilo
　Kapiolani Community College
　Manoa
　Maui College
　West Oahu
　Windward Community College

Idaho

Boise Bible College
Boise State University
Brigham Young University-Idaho
College of Idaho
College of Western Idaho
Idaho State University
Lewis-Clark State College
Northwest Nazarene University
University of Idaho

Illinois

Augustana College
Aurora University
Benedictine University
Benedictine University at Springfield
Blackburn College
Bradley University
Chicago State University
College of DuPage
Columbia College Chicago
Concordia University Chicago
Danville Area Community College
DePaul University
Dominican University
East-West University
Eastern Illinois University
Elgin Community College
Elmhurst College
Eureka College
Governors State University
Greenville College
Heartland Community College
Hebrew Theological College
Illinois College
Illinois Eastern Community Colleges
　Frontier Community College
　Lincoln Trail College
　Olney Central College
　Wabash Valley College
Illinois Institute of Technology
Illinois State University
Illinois Wesleyan University
John A. Logan College
Judson University
Kaskaskia College
Kishwaukee College
Knox College
Lake Forest College
Lewis University
Lewis and Clark Community College
Lincoln Christian University
Lincoln Land Community College
Loyola University Chicago
MacCormac College
MacMurray College
McKendree University
Millikin University
Monmouth College
Moody Bible Institute
Moraine Valley Community College
Morrison Institute of Technology
Morton College
National-Louis University
North Central College
North Park University
Northeastern Illinois University
Northern Illinois University
Northwestern College
Northwestern University
Olivet Nazarene University
Parkland College
Principia College
Quincy University
Richland Community College
Robert Morris University: Chicago

Rockford University
Roosevelt University
St. Augustine College
Saint Xavier University
School of the Art Institute of Chicago
Shimer College
South Suburban College of Cook
　County
Southeastern Illinois College
Southern Illinois University
　Carbondale
Southern Illinois University
　Edwardsville
Southwestern Illinois College
Trinity Christian College
Trinity International University
University of Chicago
University of Illinois
　Chicago
　Urbana-Champaign
University of St. Francis
Western Illinois University
Wheaton College

Indiana

Ancilla College
Anderson University
Ball State University
Bethel College
Brown Mackie College
　South Bend
Butler University
Calumet College of St. Joseph
DePauw University
Earlham College
Franklin College
Goshen College
Grace College
Hanover College
Harrison College
　Indianapolis
Holy Cross College
Huntington University
Indiana Institute of Technology
Indiana State University
Indiana University
　Bloomington
　East
　Kokomo
　Northwest
　Purdue University Fort Wayne
　Purdue University Indianapolis
　South Bend
　Southeast
Indiana Wesleyan University
Manchester University
Marian University
Martin University
Oakland City University
Purdue University
Purdue University
　Calumet
　North Central
Rose-Hulman Institute of Technology
Saint Joseph's College
Saint Mary's College
St. Mary-of-the-Woods College
Taylor University
Trine University
University of Evansville
University of Indianapolis
University of Notre Dame
University of St. Francis
University of Southern Indiana
Valparaiso University
Vincennes University
Wabash College

Iowa

AIB College of Business
Ashford University
Briar Cliff University
Buena Vista University
Central College

Clarke University
Clinton Community College
Coe College
Cornell College
Divine Word College
Dordt College
Drake University
Ellsworth Community College
Emmaus Bible College
Faith Baptist Bible College and
    Theological Seminary
Graceland University
Grand View University
Grinnell College
Iowa State University
Iowa Wesleyan College
Loras College
Luther College
Morningside College
Mount Mercy University
Northeast Iowa Community College
Northwestern College
St. Ambrose University
Simpson College
Southwestern Community College
University of Dubuque
University of Iowa
University of Northern Iowa
Upper Iowa University
Waldorf College
Wartburg College
Western Iowa Tech Community
    College
William Penn University

Kansas

Allen County Community College
Baker University
Barclay College
Benedictine College
Bethany College
Bethel College
Central Christian College of Kansas
Cowley County Community College
Dodge City Community College
Donnelly College
Emporia State University
Fort Hays State University
Friends University
Highland Community College
Hutchinson Community College
Independence Community College
Johnson County Community College
Kansas State University
Kansas Wesleyan University
Manhattan Christian College
McPherson College
MidAmerica Nazarene University
Newman University
Ottawa University
Pittsburg State University
Seward County Community College
Southwestern College
Sterling College
Tabor College
University of Kansas
University of St. Mary
Washburn University
Wichita State University

Kentucky

Alice Lloyd College
Asbury University
Bellarmine University
Berea College
Bluegrass Community and Technical
    College
Brescia University
Campbellsville University
Centre College
Clear Creek Baptist Bible College
Daymar College
    Bowling Green
    Owensboro

Eastern Kentucky University
Georgetown College
Henderson Community College
Kentucky Christian University
Kentucky State University
Kentucky Wesleyan College
Lindsey Wilson College
Madisonville Community College
Maysville Community and Technical
    College
Mid-Continent University
Midway College
Morehead State University
Murray State University
National College
    Danville
    Florence
    Lexington
    Pikeville
    Richmond
Northern Kentucky University
Spalding University
Spencerian College: Lexington
Sullivan College of Technology and
    Design
Sullivan University
Thomas More College
Transylvania University
Union College
University of Kentucky
University of Louisville
University of Pikeville
University of the Cumberlands
Western Kentucky University

Louisiana

Baton Rouge Community College
Centenary College of Louisiana
Delgado Community College
Delta School of Business &
    Technology
Dillard University
Grambling State University
Louisiana College
Louisiana State University
    Health Sciences Center
    Shreveport
Louisiana State University and
    Agricultural and Mechanical
    College
Louisiana Tech University
Loyola University New Orleans
McNeese State University
Nicholls State University
Northwestern State University
Nunez Community College
South Louisiana Community College
Southeastern Louisiana University
Southern University
    New Orleans
Southern University and Agricultural
    and Mechanical College
Southwest University
Tulane University
University of Louisiana at Lafayette
University of Louisiana at Monroe
University of New Orleans
Xavier University of Louisiana

Maine

Bates College
Beal College
Bowdoin College
Colby College
Husson University
Maine College of Art
Maine Maritime Academy
New England School of
    Communications
Northern Maine Community College
Saint Joseph's College of Maine
Southern Maine Community College
Thomas College
Unity College

University of Maine
University of Maine
    Augusta
    Farmington
    Fort Kent
    Machias
    Presque Isle
University of New England
University of Southern Maine
Washington County Community
    College

Maryland

Allegany College of Maryland
Baltimore City Community College
Bowie State University
Capitol College
Cecil College
Coppin State University
Frostburg State University
Garrett College
Goucher College
Hagerstown Community College
Harford Community College
Hood College
Johns Hopkins University
Johns Hopkins University: Peabody
    Conservatory of Music
Kaplan University
    Hagerstown
Loyola University Maryland
Maryland Institute College of Art
McDaniel College
Montgomery College
Morgan State University
Mount St. Mary's University
Notre Dame of Maryland University
Prince George's Community College
St. Mary's College of Maryland
Salisbury University
Towson University
United States Naval Academy
University of Maryland
    Baltimore
    Baltimore County
    College Park
    Eastern Shore
    University College
Washington Adventist University
Washington College
Wor-Wic Community College

Massachusetts

American International College
Amherst College
Anna Maria College
Assumption College
Bard College at Simon's Rock
Bay Path College
Bay State College
Becker College
Bentley University
Berklee College of Music
Berkshire Community College
Boston College
Boston Conservatory
Boston University
Brandeis University
Bridgewater State University
Bunker Hill Community College
Cambridge College
Clark University
College of the Holy Cross
Curry College
Dean College
Eastern Nazarene College
Elms College
Emerson College
Emmanuel College
Fitchburg State University
Framingham State University
Gordon College
Greenfield Community College
Harvard College

Holyoke Community College
Lasell College
Lesley University
MCPHS University
Marian Court College
Massachusetts College of Art and
    Design
Massachusetts College of Liberal Arts
Massachusetts Institute of Technology
Massachusetts Maritime Academy
Merrimack College
Montserrat College of Art
Mount Holyoke College
Mount Ida College
Mount Wachusett Community
    College
Newbury College
Nichols College
North Shore Community College
Northeastern University
Northern Essex Community College
Northpoint Bible College
Pine Manor College
Quinsigamond Community College
Regis College
Roxbury Community College
Salem State University
School of the Museum of Fine Arts
Simmons College
Smith College
Springfield College
Stonehill College
Suffolk University
Tufts University
University of Massachusetts
    Amherst
    Boston
    Dartmouth
    Lowell
Wellesley College
Western New England University
Westfield State University
Wheaton College
Wheelock College
Williams College
Worcester Polytechnic Institute
Worcester State University

Michigan

Adrian College
Albion College
Alma College
Alpena Community College
Andrews University
Aquinas College
Baker College
    Allen Park
    Auburn Hills
    Cadillac
    Clinton Township
    Flint
    Jackson
    Muskegon
    Owosso
    Port Huron
Bay Mills Community College
Calvin College
Central Michigan University
Cleary University
College for Creative Studies
Concordia University
Cornerstone University
Delta College
Eastern Michigan University
Ferris State University
Finlandia University
Glen Oaks Community College
Gogebic Community College
Grace Bible College
Grand Valley State University
Great Lakes Christian College
Henry Ford Community College
Hillsdale College
Hope College
Kalamazoo College

Kellogg Community College
Kettering University
Kuyper College
Lake Michigan College
Lake Superior State University
Lansing Community College
Lawrence Technological University
Madonna University
Marygrove College
Michigan Jewish Institute
Michigan State University
Michigan Technological University
Mid Michigan Community College
Montcalm Community College
Mott Community College
Muskegon Community College
Northern Michigan University
Northwood University
  Michigan
Oakland University
Olivet College
Sacred Heart Major Seminary
Saginaw Valley State University
St. Clair County Community College
Schoolcraft College
Siena Heights University
Southwestern Michigan College
Spring Arbor University
University of Detroit Mercy
University of Michigan
University of Michigan
  Dearborn
  Flint
Walsh College of Accountancy and
  Business Administration
Wayne County Community College
Wayne State University
Western Michigan University

Minnesota

Alexandria Technical and Community
  College
Anoka-Ramsey Community College
Augsburg College
Bemidji State University
Bethany Lutheran College
Bethel University
Capella University
Carleton College
College of St. Benedict
College of St. Scholastica
Concordia College: Moorhead
Concordia University St. Paul
Crossroads College
Crown College
Dakota County Technical College
Dunwoody College of Technology
Gustavus Adolphus College
Hamline University
Inver Hills Community College
Lake Superior College
Leech Lake Tribal College
Macalester College
Martin Luther College
Metropolitan State University
Minnesota State College - Southeast
  Technical
Minnesota State Community and
  Technical College
Minnesota State University
  Mankato
  Moorhead
Minnesota West Community and
  Technical College
National American University
  Bloomington
Normandale Community College
North Central University
North Hennepin Community College
Northland Community & Technical
  College
Northwest Technical College
Oak Hills Christian College
Pine Technical College

Rasmussen College
  Bloomington
  Brooklyn Park
  Eagan
  Mankato
  St. Cloud
Riverland Community College
St. Catherine University
Saint Cloud State University
St. Cloud Technical and Community
  College
St. John's University
St. Mary's University of Minnesota
St. Olaf College
Southwest Minnesota State University
University of Minnesota
  Crookston
  Duluth
  Morris
  Twin Cities
University of Northwestern - St. Paul
University of St. Thomas
Winona State University

Mississippi

Alcorn State University
Belhaven University
Blue Mountain College
Delta State University
East Mississippi Community College
Itawamba Community College
Jackson State University
Jones County Junior College
Millsaps College
Mississippi College
Mississippi State University
Mississippi University for Women
Mississippi Valley State University
Rust College
Southeastern Baptist College
Tougaloo College
University of Mississippi
University of Southern Mississippi
William Carey University

Missouri

Avila University
Calvary Bible College and Theological
  Seminary
Central Methodist University
College of the Ozarks
Columbia College
Culver-Stockton College
Drury University
Evangel University
Fontbonne University
Hannibal-LaGrange University
Kansas City Art Institute
Lincoln University
Lindenwood University
Linn State Technical College
Maryville University of Saint Louis
Missouri Baptist University
Missouri Southern State University
Missouri State University
Missouri University of Science and
  Technology
Missouri Valley College
Missouri Western State University
National American University
  Kansas City
Northwest Missouri State University
Ozark Christian College
Park University
Ranken Technical College
Research College of Nursing
Rockhurst University
St. Charles Community College
St. Louis Community College
Saint Louis University
Southeast Missouri State University
Southwest Baptist University
Stephens College
Truman State University

University of Central Missouri
University of Missouri
  Columbia
  Kansas City
  St. Louis
Washington University in St. Louis
Webster University
Westminster College
William Jewell College
William Woods University

Montana

Blackfeet Community College
Carroll College
Chief Dull Knife College
Dawson Community College
Montana State University
Montana State University
  Billings
  Northern
Montana Tech of the University of
  Montana
Rocky Mountain College
Salish Kootenai College
Stone Child College
University of Great Falls
University of Montana
University of Montana: Western

Nebraska

Bellevue University
Central Community College
Chadron State College
Clarkson College
College of Saint Mary
Concordia University
Creighton University
Doane College
Grace University
Hastings College
Metropolitan Community College
Midland University
Nebraska Christian College
Nebraska College of Technical
  Agriculture
Nebraska Indian Community College
Nebraska Wesleyan University
Peru State College
Union College
University of Nebraska
  Kearney
  Lincoln
  Omaha
Wayne State College
Western Nebraska Community
  College
York College

Nevada

College of Southern Nevada
Nevada State College
Sierra Nevada College
University of Nevada
  Las Vegas
  Reno
Western Nevada College

New Hampshire

Colby-Sawyer College
Daniel Webster College
Dartmouth College
Franklin Pierce University
Granite State College
Great Bay Community College
Keene State College
Lakes Region Community College
Manchester Community College
NHTI-Concord's Community College
Nashua Community College
New England College
Plymouth State University
River Valley Community College
Rivier University
Saint Anselm College

Southern New Hampshire University
University of New Hampshire
University of New Hampshire at
  Manchester
White Mountains Community College

New Jersey

Atlantic Cape Community College
Bloomfield College
Burlington County College
Caldwell College
Camden County College
Centenary College
College of New Jersey
College of St. Elizabeth
County College of Morris
Cumberland County College
Drew University
Essex County College
Fairleigh Dickinson University
  College at Florham
Felician College
Georgian Court University
Kean University
Mercer County Community College
Middlesex County College
Monmouth University
Montclair State University
New Jersey City University
New Jersey Institute of Technology
Passaic County Community College
Ramapo College of New Jersey
Raritan Valley Community College
Rider University
Rowan University
Rutgers, The State University of New
  Jersey
  Camden Campus
  New Brunswick/Piscataway
    Campus
  Newark Campus
Saint Peter's University
Salem Community College
Seton Hall University
Stevens Institute of Technology
Sussex County Community College
Warren County Community College
William Paterson University of New
  Jersey

New Mexico

Central New Mexico Community
  College
Clovis Community College
Dona Ana Community College of
  New Mexico State University
Eastern New Mexico University
Institute of American Indian Arts
Luna Community College
Navajo Technical University
New Mexico Highlands University
New Mexico Institute of Mining and
  Technology
New Mexico State University
New Mexico State University
  Alamogordo
  Carlsbad
  Grants
Northern New Mexico College
San Juan College
Santa Fe Community College
Santa Fe University of Art and Design
Southwest University of Visual Arts
Southwestern Indian Polytechnic
  Institute
University of New Mexico
University of the Southwest
Western New Mexico University

New York

Adelphi University
Adirondack Community College
Alfred University
Bard College

Barnard College
Bramson ORT College
Bryant & Stratton College
  Albany
  Rochester
  Southtowns
Canisius College
Cayuga Community College
Cazenovia College
City University of New York
  Baruch College
  Bronx Community College
  Brooklyn College
  City College
  College of Staten Island
  Hunter College
  Lehman College
  Queens College
  York College
Clarkson University
Colgate University
College of New Rochelle
College of Saint Rose
College of Westchester
Columbia University
Columbia University
  School of General Studies
Concordia College
Cornell University
Corning Community College
D'Youville College
Daemen College
Dowling College
Eastman School of Music of the
  University of Rochester
Elmira College
Erie Community College
Eugene Lang College The New
  School for Liberal Arts
Finger Lakes Community College
Fordham University
Fulton-Montgomery Community
  College
Genesee Community College
Hamilton College
Hartwick College
Hobart and William Smith Colleges
Hofstra University
Houghton College
Hudson Valley Community College
Institute of Design and Construction
Iona College
Ithaca College
Jefferson Community College
Jewish Theological Seminary of
  America
Juilliard School
Keuka College
Le Moyne College
Long Island University
  LIU Brooklyn
  LIU Post
Manhattan College
Manhattanville College
Mannes College The New School for
  Music
Marist College
Marymount Manhattan College
Medaille College
Mercy College
Mohawk Valley Community College
Molloy College
Mount Saint Mary College
Nazareth College
New York Institute of Technology
New York University
Niagara County Community College
Niagara University
North Country Community College
Nyack College
Onondaga Community College
Pace University
Pace University: Pleasantville/
  Briarcliff
Paul Smith's College

Rensselaer Polytechnic Institute
Roberts Wesleyan College
Rochester Institute of Technology
Rockland Community College
SUNY
  College at Brockport
  College at Buffalo
  College at Cortland
  College at Fredonia
  College at Geneseo
  College at New Paltz
  College at Old Westbury
  College at Oneonta
  College at Oswego
  College at Plattsburgh
  College at Potsdam
  College at Purchase
  College of Agriculture and
    Technology at Morrisville
  College of Environmental Science
    and Forestry
  College of Technology at Delhi
  Empire State College
  Farmingdale State College
  Institute of Technology at Utica/
    Rome
  Maritime College
  University at Albany
  University at Binghamton
  University at Buffalo
  University at Stony Brook
Sage Colleges
Saint Bonaventure University
St. Francis College
St. John Fisher College
St. John's University
St. Joseph's College New York:
  Suffolk Campus
St. Joseph's College, New York
St. Lawrence University
St. Thomas Aquinas College
Sarah Lawrence College
Schenectady County Community
  College
Siena College
Skidmore College
Syracuse University
Ulster County Community College
Union College
United States Military Academy
University of Rochester
Utica College
Vassar College
Villa Maria College of Buffalo
Wagner College
Webb Institute
Wells College
Westchester Community College
Yeshiva Shaar Hatorah
Yeshiva University

North Carolina

Alamance Community College
Appalachian State University
Asheville-Buncombe Technical
  Community College
Barton College
Belmont Abbey College
Bennett College for Women
Bladen Community College
Blue Ridge Community College
Brevard College
Brunswick Community College
Campbell University
Carolinas College of Health Sciences
Carteret Community College
Catawba College
Catawba Valley Community College
Central Carolina Community College
Central Piedmont Community College
Chef's Academy
Chowan University
Cleveland Community College
College of the Albemarle
Davidson College

Duke University
East Carolina University
Edgecombe Community College
Elizabeth City State University
Elon University
Fayetteville State University
Fayetteville Technical Community
  College
Forsyth Technical Community
  College
Gardner-Webb University
Gaston College
Greensboro College
Guilford College
Guilford Technical Community
  College
High Point University
James Sprunt Community College
Johnson C. Smith University
Johnston Community College
Laurel University
Lees-McRae College
Lenoir Community College
Lenoir-Rhyne University
Livingstone College
Mars Hill University
Martin Community College
Mayland Community College
McDowell Technical Community
  College
Meredith College
Methodist University
Mid-Atlantic Christian University
Miller-Motte College
  Wilmington
Montreat College
North Carolina Agricultural and
  Technical State University
North Carolina Central University
North Carolina State University
North Carolina Wesleyan College
Pfeiffer University
Piedmont Community College
Piedmont International University
Pitt Community College
Queens University of Charlotte
Randolph Community College
Richmond Community College
Robeson Community College
St. Andrews University
St. Augustine's University
Salem College
Sandhills Community College
Shaw University
Southeastern Baptist Theological
  Seminary
Southwestern Community College
Surry Community College
Tri-County Community College
University of Mount Olive
University of North Carolina
  Asheville
  Chapel Hill
  Charlotte
  Greensboro
  Pembroke
  Wilmington
Vance-Granville Community College
Wake Forest University
Wake Technical Community College
Warren Wilson College
Wayne Community College
Western Carolina University
Western Piedmont Community
  College
Wilkes Community College
William Peace University
Wilson Community College
Wingate University
Winston-Salem State University

North Dakota

Dakota College at Bottineau
Dickinson State University
Fort Berthold Community College

Lake Region State College
Mayville State University
Minot State University
North Dakota State University
Rasmussen College
  Bismarck
  Fargo
Trinity Bible College
University of Jamestown
University of Mary
University of North Dakota
Valley City State University
Williston State College

Ohio

Allegheny Wesleyan College
Antioch University
  Midwest
Art Academy of Cincinnati
Ashland University
Baldwin Wallace University
Belmont College
Bluffton University
Bowling Green State University
Bryant & Stratton College
  Cleveland
  Eastlake
Capital University
Case Western Reserve University
Cedarville University
Central Ohio Technical College
Central State University
Cincinnati Christian University
Cincinnati State Technical and
  Community College
Clark State Community College
Cleveland Institute of Art
Cleveland Institute of Music
Cleveland State University
College of Mount St. Joseph
College of Wooster
Columbus College of Art and Design
Columbus State Community College
Defiance College
Denison University
Edison State Community College
Franciscan University of Steubenville
Franklin University
Gallipolis Career College
God's Bible School and College
Harrison College
  Grove City
Heidelberg University
Hiram College
Hocking College
James A. Rhodes State College
John Carroll University
Kaplan College
  Dayton
Kent State University
Kent State University
  Ashtabula
  East Liverpool
  Geauga
  Salem
  Stark
  Trumbull
  Tuscarawas
Kenyon College
Kettering College
Lake Erie College
Lourdes University
Malone University
Marietta College
Marion Technical College
Mercy College of Ohio
Miami University
  Hamilton
  Middletown
  Oxford
Miami-Jacobs Career College
  Dayton
Mount Vernon Nazarene University
Muskingum University
Notre Dame College

Oberlin College
Ohio Business College
  Sandusky
  Sheffield
Ohio Christian University
Ohio Dominican University
Ohio Northern University
Ohio State University
  Agricultural Technical Institute
  Columbus Campus
  Lima Campus
  Mansfield Campus
  Marion Campus
  Newark Campus
Ohio University
Ohio University
  Chillicothe Campus
  Eastern Campus
  Lancaster Campus
  Southern Campus at Ironton
  Zanesville Campus
Ohio Wesleyan University
Otterbein University
Owens Community College
  Toledo
Pontifical College Josephinum
Rosedale Bible College
Shawnee State University
Stark State College
Stautzenberger College
Terra State Community College
Tiffin University
Union Institute & University
University of Akron
University of Cincinnati
University of Cincinnati
  Blue Ash College
  Clermont College
University of Dayton
University of Findlay
University of Mount Union
University of Northwestern Ohio
University of Rio Grande
University of Toledo
Urbana University
Ursuline College
Walsh University
Washington State Community College
Wilmington College
Wittenberg University
Wright State University
Wright State University: Lake Campus
Xavier University
Youngstown State University
Zane State College

Oklahoma

Bacone College
Cameron University
East Central University
Hillsdale Free Will Baptist College
Langston University
Mid-America Christian University
Northeastern Oklahoma Agricultural
  and Mechanical College
Northeastern State University
Northwestern Oklahoma State
  University
Oklahoma Baptist University
Oklahoma Christian University
Oklahoma City Community College
Oklahoma City University
Oklahoma Panhandle State University
Oklahoma State University
Oklahoma State University
  Institute of Technology: Okmulgee
  Oklahoma City
Oklahoma Wesleyan University
Oral Roberts University
Redlands Community College
Rogers State University
Rose State College
St. Gregory's University
Southeastern Oklahoma State
  University

Southern Nazarene University
Southwestern Christian University
Southwestern Oklahoma State
  University
University of Central Oklahoma
University of Oklahoma
University of Science and Arts of
  Oklahoma
University of Tulsa

Oregon

Central Oregon Community College
Chemeketa Community College
Clackamas Community College
Clatsop Community College
Concordia University
Corban University
Eastern Oregon University
George Fox University
Lane Community College
Lewis & Clark College
Linfield College
Marylhurst University
Mount Angel Seminary
Multnomah University
New Hope Christian College
Northwest Christian University
Oregon Institute of Technology
Oregon State University
Pacific University
Portland Community College
Portland State University
Reed College
Rogue Community College
Southern Oregon University
Southwestern Oregon Community
  College
University of Oregon
University of Portland
Warner Pacific College
Western Oregon University
Willamette University

Pennsylvania

Albright College
Allegheny College
Alvernia University
Arcadia University
Baptist Bible College of Pennsylvania
Bloomsburg University of
  Pennsylvania
Bryn Mawr College
Bucknell University
Cabrini College
Cairn University
California University of Pennsylvania
Carlow University
Carnegie Mellon University
Cedar Crest College
Central Penn College
Chatham University
Chestnut Hill College
Cheyney University of Pennsylvania
Clarion University of Pennsylvania
Community College of Beaver County
Curtis Institute of Music
DeSales University
Delaware County Community College
Delaware Valley College
Dickinson College
Drexel University
DuBois Business College
Duquesne University
East Stroudsburg University of
  Pennsylvania
Eastern University
Edinboro University of Pennsylvania
Elizabethtown College
Franklin & Marshall College
Gannon University
Geneva College
Gettysburg College
Gratz College
Grove City College

Gwynedd Mercy University
Harcum College
Harrisburg Area Community College
Harrisburg University of Science and
  Technology
Haverford College
Immaculata University
Indiana University of Pennsylvania
Juniata College
Kaplan Career Institute
  Pittsburgh
Keystone College
King's College
Kutztown University of Pennsylvania
La Roche College
La Salle University
Lackawanna College
Lafayette College
Lancaster Bible College
Lansdale School of Business
Laurel Business Institute
Lebanon Valley College
Lehigh University
Lock Haven University of
  Pennsylvania
Lycoming College
Manor College
Mansfield University of Pennsylvania
Marywood University
Mercyhurst University
Messiah College
Millersville University of Pennsylvania
Misericordia University
Moore College of Art and Design
Moravian College
Mount Aloysius College
Muhlenberg College
Neumann University
Penn State
  Abington
  Altoona
  Beaver
  Brandywine
  DuBois
  Erie, The Behrend College
  Fayette, The Eberly Campus
  Greater Allegheny
  Harrisburg
  Hazleton
  Mont Alto
  New Kensington
  Schuylkill
  Shenango
  University Park
  Wilkes-Barre
  Worthington Scranton
  York
Pennsylvania Institute of Technology
Philadelphia University
Point Park University
Prism Career Institute
Robert Morris University
Rosemont College
St. Francis University
Saint Joseph's University
St. Vincent College
Seton Hill University
Shippensburg University of
  Pennsylvania
Slippery Rock University of
  Pennsylvania
South Hills School of Business &
  Technology
Susquehanna University
Swarthmore College
Temple University
Thiel College
University of Pennsylvania
University of Pittsburgh
University of Pittsburgh
  Bradford
  Greensburg
  Johnstown
  Titusville
University of Scranton

University of the Arts
University of the Sciences
Ursinus College
Valley Forge Christian College
Villanova University
Washington & Jefferson College
Waynesburg University
West Chester University of
  Pennsylvania
Westminster College
Westmoreland County Community
  College
Widener University
Wilkes University
Wilson College
York College of Pennsylvania
Yorktowne Business Institute

Puerto Rico

Bayamon Central University
Inter American University of Puerto
  Rico
  Aguadilla Campus
  Fajardo Campus
  San German Campus
Pontifical Catholic University of
  Puerto Rico
Universidad Adventista de las Antillas
Universidad del Este
University College of San Juan
University of Puerto Rico
  Arecibo
  Bayamon University College
  Cayey University College
  Mayaguez
  Rio Piedras
University of the Sacred Heart

Rhode Island

Brown University
Bryant University
Community College of Rhode Island
New England Institute of Technology
Providence College
Rhode Island College
Rhode Island School of Design
Roger Williams University
Salve Regina University
University of Rhode Island

South Carolina

Aiken Technical College
Anderson University
Benedict College
Charleston Southern University
Citadel
Claflin University
Clemson University
Coastal Carolina University
Coker College
College of Charleston
Columbia College
Columbia International University
Converse College
Erskine College
Florence-Darlington Technical College
Forrest Junior College
Francis Marion University
Furman University
Horry-Georgetown Technical College
Lander University
Limestone College
Morris College
Newberry College
North Greenville University
Orangeburg-Calhoun Technical
  College
Piedmont Technical College
Presbyterian College
South Carolina State University
Southern Wesleyan University
Spartanburg Community College
Technical College of the Lowcountry
Trident Technical College

University of South Carolina
  Aiken
  Columbia
  Upstate
Williamsburg Technical College
Winthrop University
Wofford College

South Dakota

Augustana College
Black Hills State University
Dakota State University
Dakota Wesleyan University
Kilian Community College
Mitchell Technical Institute
Mount Marty College
Northern State University
Oglala Lakota College
Presentation College
Sinte Gleska University
Sisseton Wahpeton College
South Dakota State University
Southeast Technical Institute
University of Sioux Falls
University of South Dakota

Tennessee

American Baptist College
Aquinas College
Austin Peay State University
Belmont University
Bethel University
Bryan University
  Dayton
Carson-Newman University
Chattanooga State Community
  College
Christian Brothers University
Cleveland State Community College
Cumberland University
East Tennessee State University
Fisk University
Freed-Hardeman University
Jackson State Community College
Johnson University
King University
LeMoyne-Owen College
Lee University
Lincoln Memorial University
Lipscomb University
Martin Methodist College
Maryville College
Memphis College of Art
Middle Tennessee State University
Milligan College
Motlow State Community College
Nashville State Community College
National College of Business and
  Technology
  Bristol
Northeast State Community College
O'More College of Design
Pellissippi State Community College
Rhodes College
Roane State Community College
Sewanee: The University of the South
South College
Southern Adventist University
Southwest Tennessee Community
  College
Tennessee State University
Tennessee Technological University
Tennessee Temple University
Tennessee Wesleyan College
Trevecca Nazarene University
Tusculum College
Union University
University of Memphis
University of Tennessee
  Chattanooga
  Knoxville
  Martin
Vanderbilt University
Victory University

Volunteer State Community College
Welch College

Texas

Abilene Christian University
Angelo State University
Arlington Baptist College
Austin College
Baylor University
College of the Mainland
Concordia University Texas
Criswell College
Dallas Baptist University
Dallas Christian College
Del Mar College
East Texas Baptist University
El Centro College
El Paso Community College
Hardin-Simmons University
Houston Baptist University
Howard Payne University
Huston-Tillotson University
Jarvis Christian College
Lamar State College at Port Arthur
Lamar University
LeTourneau University
Lubbock Christian University
McMurry University
Midwestern State University
North Lake College
Northwood University
  Texas
Our Lady of the Lake University of
  San Antonio
Prairie View A&M University
Rice University
St. Edward's University
St. Mary's University
St. Philip's College
Sam Houston State University
San Jacinto College
Schreiner University
South Texas College
Southern Methodist University
Southwestern Adventist University
Southwestern Assemblies of God
  University
Southwestern University
Stephen F. Austin State University
Sul Ross State University
Tarleton State University
Tarrant County College
Texas A&M International University
Texas A&M University
Texas A&M University
  Commerce
  Corpus Christi
  Galveston
  Kingsville
Texas Christian University
Texas College
Texas Lutheran University
Texas Southern University
Texas State Technical College
  Waco
Texas State University
Texas Tech University
Texas Wesleyan University
Texas Woman's University
Trinity University
University of Dallas
University of Houston
University of Houston
  Clear Lake
  Downtown
  Victoria
University of Mary Hardin-Baylor
University of North Texas
University of St. Thomas
University of Texas
  Arlington
  Austin
  Brownsville
  Dallas
  El Paso

Pan American
Permian Basin
San Antonio
Tyler
University of the Incarnate Word
Wade College
Wayland Baptist University
West Texas A&M University
Wiley College

Utah

Brigham Young University
Dixie State College
Southern Utah University
University of Utah
Utah State University
Utah Valley University
Weber State University
Westminster College

Vermont

Burlington College
Castleton State College
Champlain College
College of St. Joseph in Vermont
Community College of Vermont
Green Mountain College
Johnson State College
Lyndon State College
Middlebury College
Norwich University
Saint Michael's College
Southern Vermont College
Sterling College
University of Vermont
Vermont Technical College

Virginia

American National University
  Charlottesville
  Danville
  Harrisonburg
  Lynchburg
  Martinsville
  Salem
Averett University
Blue Ridge Community College
Bluefield College
Bridgewater College
Bryant & Stratton College
  Richmond
  Virginia Beach
Christendom College
Christopher Newport University
College of William and Mary
Dabney S. Lancaster Community
  College
Danville Community College
Eastern Mennonite University
Emory & Henry College
Ferrum College
George Mason University
Germanna Community College
Hampden-Sydney College
Hampton University
Hollins University
J. Sargeant Reynolds Community
  College
James Madison University
Jefferson College of Health Sciences
Liberty University
Longwood University
Lord Fairfax Community College
Lynchburg College
Mary Baldwin College
Marymount University
Mountain Empire Community College
Norfolk State University
Northern Virginia Community
  College
Old Dominion University
Patrick Henry Community College
Radford University
Randolph College

Randolph-Macon College
Rappahannock Community College
Regent University
Roanoke College
Shenandoah University
Southern Virginia University
Southwest Virginia Community
  College
Sweet Briar College
Tidewater Community College
University of Mary Washington
University of Richmond
University of Virginia
University of Virginia's College at
  Wise
Virginia Commonwealth University
Virginia Highlands Community
  College
Virginia Intermont College
Virginia Military Institute
Virginia Polytechnic Institute and
  State University
Virginia State University
Virginia Union University
Virginia Wesleyan College
Virginia Western Community College
Washington and Lee University

Washington

Bastyr University
Central Washington University
Centralia College
City University of Seattle
Eastern Washington University
Evergreen State College
Gonzaga University
Grays Harbor College
Heritage University
Highline Community College
Lake Washington Institute of
  Technology
Northwest College of Art & Design
Northwest University
Pacific Lutheran University
Peninsula College
Pierce College
Saint Martin's University
Seattle Pacific University
Seattle University
Trinity Lutheran College
University of Puget Sound
University of Washington
University of Washington Bothell
University of Washington Tacoma
Walla Walla University
Washington State University
Wenatchee Valley College
Western Washington University
Whitman College
Whitworth University

West Virginia

Alderson-Broaddus University
American National University
  Princeton
Appalachian Bible College
Bethany College
Bluefield State College
Concord University
Davis and Elkins College
Eastern West Virginia Community and
  Technical College
Fairmont State University
Glenville State College
Kanawha Valley Community and
  Technical College
Marshall University
Mountain State College
New River Community and Technical
  College
Ohio Valley University
Potomac State College of West
  Virginia University
Shepherd University

University of Charleston
West Liberty University
West Virginia State University
West Virginia University
West Virginia University Institute of
    Technology
West Virginia Wesleyan College
Wheeling Jesuit University

Wisconsin

Alverno College
Beloit College
Bryant & Stratton College
    Milwaukee
Carroll University
Carthage College
Chippewa Valley Technical College
College of Menominee Nation
Concordia University Wisconsin
Edgewood College
Fox Valley Technical College
Lac Courte Oreilles Ojibwa
    Community College
Lakeland College
Lakeshore Technical College
Lawrence University
Maranatha Baptist Bible College
Marian University
Marquette University
Mid-State Technical College
Milwaukee Area Technical College
Milwaukee Institute of Art & Design
Milwaukee School of Engineering
Moraine Park Technical College
Mount Mary University
Nicolet Area Technical College
Northcentral Technical College
Northeast Wisconsin Technical
    College
Northland College
Northland International University
Ripon College
St. Norbert College
Silver Lake College of the Holy
    Family
Southwest Wisconsin Technical
    College
University of Wisconsin
    Eau Claire
    Green Bay
    La Crosse
    Madison
    Milwaukee
    Oshkosh
    Parkside
    Platteville
    River Falls
    Stevens Point
    Stout
    Superior
    Whitewater
Viterbo University
Waukesha County Technical College
Western Technical College
Wisconsin Indianhead Technical
    College
Wisconsin Lutheran College

Wyoming

Central Wyoming College
Laramie County Community College
Northwest College
Sheridan College
University of Wyoming
WyoTech: Laramie

External Degree

Alabama
Auburn University at Montgomery
Judson College
Troy University
University of Alabama
Wallace State Community College at
  Hanceville

Alaska
Prince William Sound Community
  College
University of Alaska
  Fairbanks

Arizona
GateWay Community College
Penn Foster College
Prescott College
University of Arizona

Arkansas
Arkansas State University
  Beebe
Pulaski Technical College
Rich Mountain Community College
University of Arkansas
  Fort Smith

California
Bethesda University of California
California Coast University
California State Polytechnic
  University: Pomona
California State University
  Bakersfield
  Chico
  Dominguez Hills
  Stanislaus
King's University
Life Pacific College
Pacific Union College
San Diego State University
Sonoma State University
University of San Francisco

Colorado
Adams State University
Aims Community College
Colorado State University
  Pueblo
Community College of Denver
National American University
  Denver
Pikes Peak Community College
University of Northern Colorado

Connecticut
Charter Oak State College
Eastern Connecticut State University
Southern Connecticut State
  University
University of Connecticut

Florida
Flagler College
Florida Southern College
Florida State College at Jacksonville
Hobe Sound Bible College
Northwood University
  Florida
Pasco-Hernando State College
South Florida State College
University of Florida
Webber International University

Georgia
Atlanta Metropolitan College
Brewton-Parker College
Georgia College and State University
Georgia Military College

Luther Rice University
Reinhardt University
University of Georgia
University of North Georgia
University of West Georgia
Valdosta State University

Hawaii
University of Hawaii
  Kapiolani Community College

Idaho
Stevens-Henager College
  Boise

Illinois
Greenville College
Loyola University Chicago
McKendree University
Moody Bible Institute
Saint Xavier University
Triton College

Indiana
Ball State University
Indiana Institute of Technology
Indiana University
  Bloomington
  East
  Kokomo
  Northwest
  Purdue University Indianapolis
  South Bend
  Southeast
St. Mary-of-the-Woods College
University of Evansville
Vincennes University

Iowa
Allen College
Ashford University
Briar Cliff University
Buena Vista University
Hawkeye Community College
Iowa Central Community College
Iowa State University
Kirkwood Community College
Northeast Iowa Community College
University of Iowa
University of Northern Iowa
Upper Iowa University
Western Iowa Tech Community
  College

Kansas
Fort Hays State University
Kansas City Kansas Community
  College
Seward County Community College

Kentucky
Murray State University
Somerset Community College

Maine
Eastern Maine Community College

Maryland
Coppin State University
Howard Community College
University of Maryland
  College Park
  University College
Washington Adventist University

Massachusetts
Bard College at Simon's Rock
Bunker Hill Community College

Michigan
Baker College
  Cadillac
  Clinton Township

  Flint
  Jackson
  Muskegon
  Owosso
  Port Huron
Eastern Michigan University
Ferris State University
Griggs University
Northwood University
  Michigan
Schoolcraft College
University of Michigan

Minnesota
College of St. Scholastica
Metropolitan State University
Minnesota State University
  Mankato
  Moorhead
Northland Community & Technical
  College
Southwest Minnesota State University
University of Minnesota
  Twin Cities
Winona State University

Missouri
Lindenwood University
Missouri Valley College
Stephens College
University of Missouri
  Columbia

Montana
Helena College University of Montana
Montana State University
  Billings
Montana Tech of the University of
  Montana
University of Montana

Nebraska
Clarkson College

New Hampshire
Manchester Community College
New England College
Plymouth State University
University of New Hampshire at
  Manchester

New Jersey
Caldwell College
County College of Morris
Fairleigh Dickinson University
  College at Florham
Mercer County Community College
Ramapo College of New Jersey
Raritan Valley Community College
Thomas Edison State College

New Mexico
San Juan College

New York
City University of New York
  Bronx Community College
Fulton-Montgomery Community
  College
Hofstra University
Iona College
Manhattanville College
Rockland Community College
SUNY
  College at Oswego
  Empire State College

North Carolina
Forsyth Technical Community
  College
University of North Carolina
  Pembroke

North Dakota
Minot State University
University of North Dakota

Ohio
Capital University
Marion Technical College
Ohio University
Ohio University
  Chillicothe Campus
  Eastern Campus
Tiffin University
University of Akron
University of Findlay
Walsh University

Oklahoma
Mid-America Christian University
Oklahoma City University
Oral Roberts University
Redlands Community College
Southern Nazarene University
University of Oklahoma

Oregon
Eastern Oregon University
Linfield College
Mt. Hood Community College
Oregon Institute of Technology

Pennsylvania
Bucks County Community College
DeSales University
Duquesne University
Elizabethtown College
Indiana University of Pennsylvania
Lehigh Carbon Community College
Lehigh University
Penn State
  Abington
  Altoona
  New Kensington
  University Park
Seton Hill University
Temple University
University of Pittsburgh
University of Pittsburgh
  Bradford
Wilkes University

Puerto Rico
Inter American University of Puerto
  Rico
  Guayama Campus
Universidad Pentecostal Mizpa
University of Puerto Rico
  Rio Piedras
University of the Sacred Heart

Rhode Island
Roger Williams University

South Carolina
Benedict College
Clemson University
University of South Carolina
  Columbia

South Dakota
Presentation College
University of South Dakota

Tennessee
East Tennessee State University
Lee University
Tennessee Temple University
University of Memphis
University of Tennessee
  Knoxville

Texas
Arlington Baptist College
El Centro College

Huston-Tillotson University
LeTourneau University
Lone Star College System
Northwood University
    Texas
Southwestern Adventist University
Southwestern Assemblies of God
    University
Texas Tech University
Texas Woman's University
Wayland Baptist University

Utah

Brigham Young University
Weber State University

Vermont

Burlington College
Community College of Vermont
Goddard College
Johnson State College

Virginia

Emory & Henry College
Liberty University
Mary Baldwin College
Virginia University of Lynchburg
Virginia Western Community College

Washington

Olympic College
Renton Technical College
Seattle Pacific University
Skagit Valley College
Walla Walla Community College
Washington State University

West Virginia

Davis and Elkins College
Eastern West Virginia Community and
    Technical College
West Liberty University
West Virginia University
West Virginia University Institute of
    Technology
West Virginia University at
    Parkersburg

Wisconsin

Chippewa Valley Technical College
Madison Area Technical College
University of Wisconsin
    Baraboo/Sauk County
    Eau Claire
    Green Bay
    Milwaukee
    Platteville
    River Falls
    Stout
    Superior
    Whitewater
Wisconsin Indianhead Technical
    College

Wyoming

Central Wyoming College
University of Wyoming
Western Wyoming Community
    College

Semester at sea

Alabama
Birmingham-Southern College
University of Alabama
  Birmingham

Alaska
University of Alaska
  Anchorage
  Fairbanks
  Southeast

Arizona
Arizona State University
University of Arizona

Arkansas
University of Arkansas

California
California Lutheran University
California Maritime Academy
California Polytechnic State
    University: San Luis Obispo
California State University
  Monterey Bay
Chapman University
Loyola Marymount University
Point Loma Nazarene University
San Diego State University
Sonoma State University
Stanford University
University of California
  Irvine
  San Diego
University of La Verne
University of San Diego
Victor Valley College
Westmont College
Whittier College

Colorado
Colorado Christian University
Colorado College
Colorado State University
Colorado State University
  Pueblo
Fort Lewis College
University of Colorado
  Boulder
University of Denver
University of Northern Colorado
Western State Colorado University

Connecticut
Manchester Community College
Quinnipiac University
Trinity College
University of Bridgeport
University of Connecticut
Wesleyan University

Delaware
Delaware State University

Florida
Eckerd College
Jacksonville University
New College of Florida
University of Florida
University of Tampa

Georgia
Agnes Scott College
Morehouse College

Hawaii
Chaminade University of Honolulu
University of Hawaii
  Hilo
  Manoa

Illinois
Greenville College
Monmouth College
Rockford University
Saint Xavier University
University of Illinois
  Urbana-Champaign
University of St. Francis

Indiana
Franklin College
Huntington University
Indiana State University
Indiana University
  Bloomington
Indiana Wesleyan University
Taylor University
University of Evansville
Wabash College

Iowa
Cornell College
Drake University
Graceland University
University of Iowa

Kentucky
Bellarmine University
Northern Kentucky University
University of Louisville
Western Kentucky University

Maine
Bates College
Colby College
College of the Atlantic
Maine Maritime Academy
Saint Joseph's College of Maine
Unity College
University of Maine
University of Southern Maine

Maryland
Garrett College
McDaniel College
St. Mary's College of Maryland
University of Maryland
  Baltimore County
  College Park

Massachusetts
Assumption College
Bard College at Simon's Rock
Becker College
Bentley University
Boston University
Brandeis University
College of the Holy Cross
Curry College
Eastern Nazarene College
Emmanuel College
Endicott College
Massachusetts College of Liberal Arts
Massachusetts Institute of Technology
Massachusetts Maritime Academy
Mount Ida College
Nichols College
Northeastern University
Pine Manor College
Salem State University
Simmons College
Smith College
Tufts University
University of Massachusetts
  Dartmouth
Wellesley College
Westfield State University
Wheaton College

Michigan
Adrian College
Albion College
Central Michigan University

Michigan Technological University
Northern Michigan University

Minnesota
Bethel University
Macalester College
Minnesota State University
  Mankato
University of Minnesota
  Morris

Mississippi
Millsaps College
Mississippi State University

Missouri
Culver-Stockton College
Fontbonne University
Maryville University of Saint Louis
Rockhurst University
Stephens College
Truman State University
University of Missouri
  St. Louis
Westminster College
William Jewell College

Nebraska
Creighton University
Nebraska Wesleyan University
University of Nebraska
  Lincoln

New Hampshire
Colby-Sawyer College
Dartmouth College
Keene State College
New England College
Plymouth State University
Saint Anselm College
Southern New Hampshire University
University of New Hampshire

New Jersey
College of New Jersey
Kean University
Richard Stockton College of New
  Jersey

New Mexico
University of New Mexico

New York
Alfred University
Clarkson University
Colgate University
Cornell University
Hartwick College
Ithaca College
Le Moyne College
Pace University
Pace University: Pleasantville/
  Briarcliff
SUNY
  College at Brockport
  College of Environmental Science
    and Forestry
United States Merchant Marine
  Academy
University of Rochester
Vassar College
Wagner College

North Carolina
Appalachian State University
Bennett College for Women
Duke University
Elon University
St. Augustine's University
University of North Carolina
  Asheville

North Dakota
University of Mary
University of North Dakota

Ohio
Baldwin Wallace University
Denison University
Kenyon College
Miami University
  Oxford
Ohio Northern University
Ohio State University
  Columbus Campus
  Lima Campus
University of Dayton
University of Findlay
University of Toledo
Wright State University
Xavier University
Youngstown State University

Oklahoma
Oklahoma State University
University of Oklahoma

Oregon
Concordia University
Eastern Oregon University
Linfield College
University of Oregon
Western Oregon University

Pennsylvania
Albright College
Bucknell University
Cabrini College
Chatham University
Drexel University
Duquesne University
Gannon University
Gettysburg College
Immaculata University
Indiana University of Pennsylvania
Keystone College
Lafayette College
Marywood University
Mercyhurst University
Penn State
  University Park
Philadelphia University
St. Francis University
Seton Hill University
Shippensburg University of
  Pennsylvania
Susquehanna University
Thiel College
University of Pittsburgh
  Bradford
University of Scranton
Ursinus College
Waynesburg University
Westminster College

Puerto Rico
University of Puerto Rico
  Rio Piedras
University of the Sacred Heart

Rhode Island
Providence College
Roger Williams University
University of Rhode Island

South Carolina
College of Charleston
Presbyterian College

Texas
Texas A&M University
  Galveston
Trinity University

Utah

Westminster College

Vermont

Saint Michael's College

Virginia

George Mason University
Hampden-Sydney College
Mary Baldwin College
University of Mary Washington
University of Virginia
Virginia Polytechnic Institute and
    State University

Washington

Evergreen State College
Gonzaga University
University of Washington Tacoma
Washington State University

West Virginia

West Virginia University
Wheeling Jesuit University

Wisconsin

Alverno College
Carroll University
Lawrence University
Milwaukee Institute of Art & Design

Student-designed major

Alabama

Birmingham-Southern College
Huntingdon College
Judson College
Lawson State Community College
Snead State Community College
Spring Hill College
United States Sports Academy
University of Alabama
University of Alabama
 Birmingham
 Huntsville
University of North Alabama
University of South Alabama

Alaska

Alaska Pacific University
University of Alaska
 Anchorage
 Fairbanks
 Southeast

Arizona

Arizona State University
Harrison Middleton University
Mesa Community College
Mohave Community College
Pima Community College
Prescott College
University of Arizona

Arkansas

Cossatot Community College of the
 University of Arkansas
Harding University
Hendrix College
John Brown University
Lyon College
National Park Community College
North Arkansas College
University of Arkansas
University of Arkansas
 Fort Smith

California

American Jewish University
Antioch University
 Los Angeles
California College of the Arts
California Institute of Technology
California Institute of the Arts
California Lutheran University
California State University
 Bakersfield
 Chico
 Dominguez Hills
 East Bay
 Fresno
 Long Beach
 Los Angeles
 Monterey Bay
 Northridge
 Sacramento
 San Bernardino
 San Marcos
 Stanislaus
Chabot College
Chapman University
Claremont McKenna College
Cogswell Polytechnical College
College of the Sequoias
Concordia University Irvine
Cuesta College
Dominican University of California
Fresno Pacific University
Grossmont College
Harvey Mudd College
Holy Names University
La Sierra University

Las Positas College
Los Angeles Pierce College
Loyola Marymount University
Mendocino College
Menlo College
Mills College
Mount St. Mary's College
Notre Dame de Namur University
Occidental College
Orange Coast College
Pepperdine University
Pitzer College
Pomona College
Saddleback College
St. Mary's College of California
San Diego City College
San Diego Mesa College
San Francisco State University
San Jose State University
Santa Clara University
Scripps College
Simpson University
Sonoma State University
Stanford University
University of California
 Berkeley
 Davis
 Los Angeles
 San Diego
 Santa Barbara
 Santa Cruz
University of La Verne
University of Redlands
University of Southern California
University of the Pacific
West Los Angeles College
Westmont College
Whittier College
Woodbury University

Colorado

Adams State University
Aims Community College
Colorado Christian University
Colorado College
Fort Lewis College
Lamar Community College
Metropolitan State University of
 Denver
Naropa University
Regis University
University of Colorado
 Boulder
 Denver
University of Denver
University of Northern Colorado

Connecticut

Albertus Magnus College
Central Connecticut State University
Charter Oak State College
Connecticut College
Eastern Connecticut State University
Fairfield University
Manchester Community College
Middlesex Community College
Mitchell College
Post University
Quinnipiac University
Sacred Heart University
Southern Connecticut State
 University
Trinity College
University of Bridgeport
University of Connecticut
University of Hartford
University of Saint Joseph
Wesleyan University
Western Connecticut State University
Yale University

Delaware

University of Delaware

District of Columbia

American University
Gallaudet University
George Washington University
Georgetown University
Howard University
Trinity Washington University

Florida

Clearwater Christian College
Eckerd College
Embry-Riddle Aeronautical University
Everest University
 Pompano Beach
Florida Atlantic University
Florida Gulf Coast University
Florida Institute of Technology
Florida Southern College
Jacksonville University
Johnson University: Florida
New College of Florida
Northwest Florida State College
Palm Beach Atlantic University
Rollins College
Stetson University
Talmudic University
University of Florida
University of Miami
University of North Florida
Valencia College

Georgia

Agnes Scott College
Berry College
Brenau University
Clayton State University
Covenant College
Emory University
Georgia College and State University
Georgia Institute of Technology
Georgia Southern University
LaGrange College
Mercer University
Oglethorpe University
Piedmont College
Shorter University
Spelman College
University of Georgia
Wesleyan College

Hawaii

Brigham Young University-Hawaii
Hawaii Pacific University
University of Hawaii
 Hilo
 Honolulu Community College
 Manoa
 Windward Community College

Idaho

Boise State University
Brigham Young University-Idaho
Idaho State University
Northwest Nazarene University

Illinois

Augustana College
Aurora University
Blackburn College
Bradley University
Carl Sandburg College
Chicago State University
College of DuPage
College of Lake County
Columbia College Chicago
DePaul University
Eureka College
Governors State University
Greenville College
Highland Community College
Illinois College
Illinois Eastern Community Colleges
 Frontier Community College
 Lincoln Trail College

Olney Central College
 Wabash Valley College
Illinois State University
Illinois Wesleyan University
John Wood Community College
Judson University
Kaskaskia College
Knox College
Lake Forest College
Lewis University
Lewis and Clark Community College
Lexington College
MacMurray College
McKendree University
Millikin University
Monmouth College
Moody Bible Institute
North Central College
North Park University
Northeastern Illinois University
Northern Illinois University
Northwestern University
Olivet Nazarene University
Parkland College
Principia College
Quincy University
Roosevelt University
Saint Xavier University
School of the Art Institute of Chicago
Southeastern Illinois College
Southern Illinois University
 Carbondale
Southern Illinois University
 Edwardsville
Trinity International University
University of Chicago
University of Illinois
 Chicago
 Urbana-Champaign
University of St. Francis
Western Illinois University
Wheaton College

Indiana

Anderson University
Ball State University
Bethel College
Butler University
Calumet College of St. Joseph
DePauw University
Earlham College
Goshen College
Hanover College
Indiana Institute of Technology
Indiana University
 Bloomington
 Northwest
 Purdue University Fort Wayne
 Purdue University Indianapolis
 Southeast
Manchester University
Martin University
Saint Joseph's College
Saint Mary's College
St. Mary-of-the-Woods College
Taylor University
University of Evansville
University of Indianapolis
University of Notre Dame
Valparaiso University
Vincennes University

Iowa

AIB College of Business
Briar Cliff University
Buena Vista University
Central College
Clarke University
Coe College
Cornell College
Dordt College
Drake University
Graceland University
Grand View University

Grinnell College
Iowa State University
Iowa Wesleyan College
Iowa Western Community College
Kirkwood Community College
Loras College
Luther College
Maharishi University of Management
Morningside College
North Iowa Area Community College
Northwestern College
St. Ambrose University
Simpson College
Southeastern Community College
University of Dubuque
University of Iowa
University of Northern Iowa
Upper Iowa University
Waldorf College
Wartburg College

Kansas

Allen County Community College
Baker University
Benedictine College
Bethany College
Bethel College
Central Christian College of Kansas
Emporia State University
Fort Hays State University
Friends University
Garden City Community College
Kansas Wesleyan University
McPherson College
MidAmerica Nazarene University
Newman University
Ottawa University
Pittsburg State University
Southwestern College
Sterling College
Tabor College
University of St. Mary
Washburn University

Kentucky

Alice Lloyd College
Bellarmine University
Berea College
Brescia University
Centre College
Eastern Kentucky University
Georgetown College
Kentucky State University
Kentucky Wesleyan College
Lindsey Wilson College
Morehead State University
Murray State University
Northern Kentucky University
St. Catharine College
Thomas More College
Transylvania University
Union College
University of Louisville
University of Pikeville
University of the Cumberlands
Western Kentucky University

Louisiana

Centenary College of Louisiana
Delgado Community College
Louisiana College
Louisiana State University and
    Agricultural and Mechanical
    College
Loyola University New Orleans
Nunez Community College
Tulane University
University of Louisiana at Lafayette

Maine

Bates College
Bowdoin College
Colby College
College of the Atlantic

Eastern Maine Community College
Husson University
Maine Maritime Academy
Saint Joseph's College of Maine
University of Maine
    Augusta
    Farmington
    Fort Kent
    Machias
University of New England
University of Southern Maine

Maryland

Chesapeake College
Goucher College
Hood College
Johns Hopkins University
Maryland Institute College of Art
McDaniel College
Mount St. Mary's University
St. Mary's College of Maryland
Salisbury University
Stevenson University
Towson University
University of Baltimore
University of Maryland
    Baltimore County
    College Park
Washington Adventist University
Washington College

Massachusetts

Amherst College
Anna Maria College
Assumption College
Babson College
Bard College at Simon's Rock
Bay Path College
Bentley University
Berklee College of Music
Berkshire Community College
Boston College
Boston University
Brandeis University
Bristol Community College
Cambridge College
Clark University
College of the Holy Cross
Curry College
Dean College
Emerson College
Emmanuel College
Endicott College
Fitchburg State University
Framingham State University
Franklin W. Olin College of
    Engineering
Gordon College
Hampshire College
Harvard College
Holyoke Community College
Lasell College
Lesley University
Massachusetts College of Art and
    Design
Massachusetts College of Liberal Arts
Merrimack College
Montserrat College of Art
Mount Holyoke College
Newbury College
North Shore Community College
Northeastern University
Pine Manor College
Regis College
Salem State University
School of the Museum of Fine Arts
Simmons College
Smith College
Stonehill College
Tufts University
University of Massachusetts
    Amherst
    Boston
Wellesley College

Western New England University
Westfield State University
Wheaton College
Williams College
Worcester Polytechnic Institute

Michigan

Adrian College
Albion College
Alma College
Andrews University
Aquinas College
Calvin College
Central Michigan University
Concordia University
Delta College
Eastern Michigan University
Ferris State University
Finlandia University
Gogebic Community College
Grand Valley State University
Griggs University
Hope College
Kalamazoo College
Lake Superior State University
Madonna University
Marygrove College
Michigan State University
Northern Michigan University
Oakland University
Olivet College
Saginaw Valley State University
Siena Heights University
Spring Arbor University
University of Michigan
University of Michigan
    Dearborn
    Flint
Western Michigan University

Minnesota

Alexandria Technical and Community
    College
Augsburg College
Bethany Lutheran College
Bethel University
Carleton College
Century College
College of St. Benedict
College of St. Scholastica
Concordia College: Moorhead
Concordia University St. Paul
Crossroads College
Dakota County Technical College
Gustavus Adolphus College
Hamline University
Hennepin Technical College
Inver Hills Community College
Macalester College
Metropolitan State University
Minnesota State University
    Mankato
    Moorhead
Minnesota West Community and
    Technical College
North Central University
North Hennepin Community College
Northwest Technical College
Pine Technical College
Ridgewater College
St. Catherine University
Saint Cloud State University
St. John's University
St. Mary's University of Minnesota
St. Olaf College
Southwest Minnesota State University
University of Minnesota
    Crookston
    Duluth
    Morris
    Twin Cities
University of Northwestern - St. Paul
University of St. Thomas

Walden University
Winona State University

Mississippi

Belhaven University
Delta State University
Millsaps College
Mississippi State University
Tougaloo College

Missouri

Calvary Bible College and Theological
    Seminary
Central Methodist University
College of the Ozarks
Columbia College
Culver-Stockton College
Drury University
Fontbonne University
Hannibal-LaGrange University
Harris-Stowe State University
Lindenwood University
Maryville University of Saint Louis
Missouri Baptist University
Missouri State University
Missouri State University: West Plains
Missouri Valley College
Park University
Saint Louis University
Southeast Missouri State University
Stephens College
Truman State University
University of Central Missouri
University of Missouri
    Columbia
    Kansas City
    St. Louis
Washington University in St. Louis
Webster University
Westminster College
William Jewell College

Montana

Carroll College
Montana State University
Rocky Mountain College

Nebraska

Chadron State College
Doane College
Grace University
Hastings College
Midland University
Union College
University of Nebraska
    Lincoln
    Omaha
Wayne State College
Western Nebraska Community
    College
York College

Nevada

College of Southern Nevada
Nevada State College
Sierra Nevada College

New Hampshire

Dartmouth College
Franklin Pierce University
Granite State College
Keene State College
Manchester Community College
Nashua Community College
New England College
Plymouth State University
River Valley Community College
Southern New Hampshire University
University of New Hampshire
University of New Hampshire at
    Manchester
White Mountains Community College

New Jersey

Bloomfield College
Caldwell College
Centenary College
College of New Jersey
College of St. Elizabeth
Drew University
Fairleigh Dickinson University
  College at Florham
  Metropolitan Campus
Felician College
Monmouth University
Princeton University
Ramapo College of New Jersey
Richard Stockton College of New
  Jersey
Rutgers, The State University of New
  Jersey
  Camden Campus
  New Brunswick/Piscataway
    Campus
  Newark Campus
Saint Peter's University
Thomas Edison State College

New Mexico

Eastern New Mexico University
New Mexico Institute of Mining and
  Technology
New Mexico State University
New Mexico State University
  Carlsbad
  Grants
Santa Fe University of Art and Design
University of New Mexico
Western New Mexico University

New York

Adelphi University
Alfred University
Bard College
Barnard College
Broome Community College
Canisius College
City University of New York
  Baruch College
  Bronx Community College
  Brooklyn College
  Hostos Community College
  Hunter College
  John Jay College of Criminal Justice
  Kingsborough Community College
  LaGuardia Community College
  Lehman College
  Medgar Evers College
  New York City College of
    Technology
  Queens College
  Queensborough Community
    College
Clarkson University
Clinton Community College
Colgate University
College of Saint Rose
Columbia University
Columbia University
  School of General Studies
Columbia-Greene Community College
Concordia College
Cooper Union for the Advancement
  of Science and Art
Cornell University
Corning Community College
Daemen College
Davis College
Dowling College
Eastman School of Music of the
  University of Rochester
Elmira College
Erie Community College
Eugene Lang College The New
  School for Liberal Arts
Excelsior College
Fordham University

Fulton-Montgomery Community
  College
Genesee Community College
Hamilton College
Hartwick College
Hobart and William Smith Colleges
Hofstra University
Houghton College
Hudson Valley Community College
Iona College
Ithaca College
Jefferson Community College
Jewish Theological Seminary of
  America
Keuka College
Long Island University
  LIU Brooklyn
  LIU Post
Manhattanville College
Medaille College
Mohawk Valley Community College
Molloy College
Mount Saint Mary College
New York University
North Country Community College
Parsons The New School for Design
Rensselaer Polytechnic Institute
Roberts Wesleyan College
Rochester Institute of Technology
SUNY
  College at Brockport
  College at Cortland
  College at Fredonia
  College at New Paltz
  College at Plattsburgh
  College at Potsdam
  College at Purchase
  College of Agriculture and
    Technology at Morrisville
  College of Technology at Alfred
  College of Technology at Canton
  Empire State College
  University at Albany
  University at Binghamton
  University at Buffalo
  University at Stony Brook
Sage Colleges
Saint Bonaventure University
St. Francis College
St. John Fisher College
St. Lawrence University
Sarah Lawrence College
Skidmore College
Syracuse University
Touro College
Ulster County Community College
Union College
University of Rochester
Vassar College
Wells College
Westchester Community College
Yeshiva University

North Carolina

Appalachian State University
Bennett College for Women
Brevard College
Catawba College
Catawba Valley Community College
Davidson College
Duke University
Durham Technical Community
  College
East Carolina University
Elon University
Fayetteville Technical Community
  College
Forsyth Technical Community
  College
Greensboro College
Guilford College
High Point University
Johnson C. Smith University
Laurel University
Lenoir-Rhyne University

Mars Hill University
Meredith College
Methodist University
Montreat College
North Carolina State University
Richmond Community College
St. Augustine's University
Salem College
Shaw University
University of North Carolina
  Asheville
  Chapel Hill
  Greensboro
Warren Wilson College
Western Carolina University

North Dakota

Dickinson State University
Mayville State University
Minot State University
North Dakota State University
University of Jamestown
University of Mary
University of North Dakota
Valley City State University
Williston State College

Ohio

Antioch University
  Midwest
Art Academy of Cincinnati
Ashland University
Baldwin Wallace University
Belmont College
Bluffton University
Bowling Green State University
Bowling Green State University:
  Firelands College
Capital University
Case Western Reserve University
Cedarville University
Cincinnati State Technical and
  Community College
Cleveland State University
College of Wooster
Columbus State Community College
Defiance College
Denison University
Edison State Community College
Heidelberg University
Hiram College
Hocking College
James A. Rhodes State College
John Carroll University
Kent State University
Kent State University
  Ashtabula
  East Liverpool
  Geauga
  Salem
  Stark
  Trumbull
  Tuscarawas
Kenyon College
Lake Erie College
Lourdes University
Malone University
Marietta College
Marion Technical College
Miami University
  Hamilton
  Middletown
  Oxford
Muskingum University
North Central State College
Northwest State Community College
Notre Dame College
Oberlin College
Ohio Christian University
Ohio State University
  Agricultural Technical Institute
  Columbus Campus
  Lima Campus
  Mansfield Campus

Marion Campus
Newark Campus
Ohio University
Ohio University
  Chillicothe Campus
  Eastern Campus
  Lancaster Campus
  Zanesville Campus
Ohio Wesleyan University
Otterbein University
Shawnee State University
Sinclair Community College
Southern State Community College
Stark State College
Terra State Community College
Union Institute & University
University of Akron
University of Akron: Wayne College
University of Cincinnati
  Blue Ash College
  Clermont College
University of Findlay
University of Mount Union
University of Rio Grande
University of Toledo
Urbana University
Washington State Community College
Wilmington College
Wittenberg University
Wright State University
Wright State University: Lake Campus
Youngstown State University
Zane State College

Oklahoma

Bacone College
Cameron University
Northeastern State University
Oklahoma Baptist University
Oklahoma Christian University
Oklahoma City Community College
Oklahoma City University
Oklahoma State University
Oklahoma Wesleyan University
Oral Roberts University
Southern Nazarene University
Southwestern Oklahoma State
  University
University of Oklahoma
University of Science and Arts of
  Oklahoma
University of Tulsa

Oregon

Central Oregon Community College
Clatsop Community College
Concordia University
Corban University
Eastern Oregon University
George Fox University
Lewis & Clark College
Linfield College
Marylhurst University
Oregon State University
Pacific Northwest College of Art
Pacific University
Reed College
Southern Oregon University
Umpqua Community College
University of Oregon
Warner Pacific College
Western Oregon University
Willamette University

Pennsylvania

Albright College
Allegheny College
Alvernia University
Arcadia University
Bloomsburg University of
  Pennsylvania
Bryn Athyn College
Bryn Mawr College
Bucknell University

Bucks County Community College
Cabrini College
Carnegie Mellon University
Cedar Crest College
Chatham University
Chestnut Hill College
Clarion University of Pennsylvania
Delaware County Community College
Delaware Valley College
Dickinson College
Drexel University
Duquesne University
East Stroudsburg University of
    Pennsylvania
Eastern University
Edinboro University of Pennsylvania
Franklin & Marshall College
Geneva College
Gettysburg College
Harrisburg University of Science and
    Technology
Haverford College
Indiana University of Pennsylvania
Juniata College
King's College
Kutztown University of Pennsylvania
La Roche College
Lafayette College
Lebanon Valley College
Lock Haven University of
    Pennsylvania
Lycoming College
Mansfield University of Pennsylvania
Marywood University
Mercyhurst University
Messiah College
Millersville University of Pennsylvania
Misericordia University
Montgomery County Community
    College
Moravian College
Mount Aloysius College
Muhlenberg College
Northampton Community College
Penn State
    Abington
    Altoona
    DuBois
    Fayette, The Eberly Campus
    Greater Allegheny
    Harrisburg
    Hazleton
    Mont Alto
    Shenango
    University Park
    Wilkes-Barre
    York
Pennsylvania College of Technology
Point Park University
Reading Area Community College
Rosemont College
St. Francis University
Saint Joseph's University
St. Vincent College
Seton Hill University
Slippery Rock University of
    Pennsylvania
Susquehanna University
Swarthmore College
Thiel College
University of Pennsylvania
University of Pittsburgh
University of Pittsburgh
    Greensburg
    Johnstown
University of Scranton
Ursinus College
Washington & Jefferson College
Waynesburg University
West Chester University of
    Pennsylvania
Westminster College
Westmoreland County Community
    College
Widener University

Wilkes University
Wilson College
York College of Pennsylvania

Puerto Rico

Atlantic University College
University of Puerto Rico
    Rio Piedras

Rhode Island

Brown University
New England Institute of Technology
Providence College
Rhode Island College
Roger Williams University

South Carolina

Anderson University
Coastal Carolina University
Coker College
Columbia College
Columbia International University
Converse College
Furman University
Limestone College
Newberry College
North Greenville University
South Carolina State University
Southern Wesleyan University
University of South Carolina
    Aiken
    Beaufort
    Columbia
    Salkehatchie
    Sumter
    Union
    Upstate
Williamsburg Technical College
Wofford College

South Dakota

Augustana College
Dakota Wesleyan University
Mount Marty College
Northern State University
University of Sioux Falls
University of South Dakota

Tennessee

Belmont University
Bethel University
Carson-Newman University
Chattanooga State Community
    College
Christian Brothers University
East Tennessee State University
Fisk University
Freed-Hardeman University
King University
Maryville College
Middle Tennessee State University
Nashville State Community College
Rhodes College
Sewanee: The University of the South
Southern Adventist University
Southwest Tennessee Community
    College
Tusculum College
University of Memphis
University of Tennessee
    Chattanooga
    Knoxville
    Martin
Vanderbilt University
Victory University

Texas

Abilene Christian University
Austin College
Baylor University
Cedar Valley College
Clarendon College
Concordia University Texas
East Texas Baptist University

Jarvis Christian College
McMurry University
Prairie View A&M University
Rice University
Schreiner University
Southern Methodist University
Southwestern Adventist University
Southwestern University
Stephen F. Austin State University
Texas A&M University
    Texarkana
Texas Tech University
Trinity University
University of Dallas
University of Houston
University of Houston
    Clear Lake
University of North Texas
University of St. Thomas
University of Texas
    Arlington
    Austin
    Brownsville
    Dallas
    El Paso
    San Antonio
    Tyler
University of the Incarnate Word

Utah

Dixie State College
Southern Utah University
University of Utah
Utah State University
Utah Valley University
Weber State University
Westminster College

Vermont

Bennington College
Burlington College
Castleton State College
Community College of Vermont
Goddard College
Green Mountain College
Landmark College
Lyndon State College
Marlboro College
Middlebury College
Saint Michael's College
Southern Vermont College
Sterling College
University of Vermont

Virginia

Christopher Newport University
College of William and Mary
Emory & Henry College
Ferrum College
George Mason University
Hollins University
Liberty University
Mary Baldwin College
Marymount University
Mountain Empire Community College
Northern Virginia Community
    College
Old Dominion University
Radford University
Randolph College
Shenandoah University
Sweet Briar College
University of Mary Washington
University of Richmond
University of Virginia
University of Virginia's College at
    Wise
Virginia Commonwealth University
Virginia Wesleyan College
Washington and Lee University

Washington

Antioch University
    Seattle

Central Washington University
Centralia College
Eastern Washington University
Evergreen State College
Heritage University
Highline Community College
Lower Columbia College
Northwest Indian College
Northwest University
Olympic College
Pacific Lutheran University
Pierce College
Renton Technical College
Seattle Pacific University
Seattle University
Spokane Community College
Trinity Lutheran College
University of Puget Sound
University of Washington
University of Washington Bothell
University of Washington Tacoma
Washington State University
Wenatchee Valley College
Western Washington University
Whatcom Community College
Whitman College
Whitworth University

West Virginia

Bethany College
Concord University
Davis and Elkins College
Eastern West Virginia Community and
    Technical College
Glenville State College
Ohio Valley University
University of Charleston
West Liberty University
West Virginia University
West Virginia Wesleyan College
Wheeling Jesuit University

Wisconsin

Alverno College
Beloit College
Blackhawk Technical College
Carroll University
Carthage College
Chippewa Valley Technical College
Concordia University Wisconsin
Edgewood College
Fox Valley Technical College
Gateway Technical College
Lakeshore Technical College
Lawrence University
Marian University
Marquette University
Mid-State Technical College
Moraine Park Technical College
Mount Mary University
Nicolet Area Technical College
Northcentral Technical College
Northland College
Northland International University
Ripon College
St. Norbert College
Silver Lake College of the Holy
    Family
Southwest Wisconsin Technical
    College
University of Wisconsin
    Eau Claire
    Green Bay
    Madison
    Milwaukee
    Oshkosh
    Stevens Point
    Superior
    Whitewater
Viterbo University
Waukesha County Technical College
Western Technical College

Wisconsin Indianhead Technical
    College
Wisconsin Lutheran College

Wyoming
Central Wyoming College
University of Wyoming

Alabama

Alabama Agricultural and Mechanical
  University
Alabama State University
Athens State University
Auburn University
Auburn University at Montgomery
Birmingham-Southern College
Faulkner University
Huntingdon College
Jacksonville State University
Judson College
Miles College
Oakwood University
Samford University
Spring Hill College
Stillman College
Talladega College
Troy University
Tuskegee University
University of Alabama
University of Alabama
  Birmingham
  Huntsville
University of Mobile
University of Montevallo
University of North Alabama
University of South Alabama
University of West Alabama

Alaska

Alaska Pacific University
University of Alaska
  Anchorage
  Fairbanks
  Southeast

Arizona

American Indian College of the
  Assemblies of God
Arizona Christian University
Arizona State University
Arizona Western College
Central Arizona College
Chandler-Gilbert Community College
Estrella Mountain Community College
Grand Canyon University
Mesa Community College
Northcentral University
Northern Arizona University
Paradise Valley Community College
Pima Community College
Prescott College
Rio Salado College
Scottsdale Community College
University of Arizona
Yavapai College

Arkansas

Arkansas State University
Arkansas State University
  Newport
Arkansas Tech University
Harding University
Henderson State University
Hendrix College
John Brown University
Lyon College
Northwest Arkansas Community
  College
Ouachita Baptist University
Philander Smith College
Southern Arkansas University
University of Arkansas
University of Arkansas
  Fort Smith
  Little Rock
  Monticello
  Pine Bluff
University of Central Arkansas
University of the Ozarks

California

Academy of Art University
Antelope Valley College
Antioch University
  Los Angeles
  Santa Barbara
Azusa Pacific University
Bethesda University of California
California Baptist University
California Lutheran University
California Polytechnic State
    University: San Luis Obispo
California State Polytechnic
    University: Pomona
California State University
  Bakersfield
  Channel Islands
  Chico
  Dominguez Hills
  East Bay
  Fresno
  Fullerton
  Long Beach
  Los Angeles
  Monterey Bay
  Northridge
  Sacramento
  San Bernardino
  San Marcos
  Stanislaus
Chapman University
College of the Redwoods
Concordia University Irvine
Dominican University of California
Fresno Pacific University
Holy Names University
Hope International University
Humboldt State University
John F. Kennedy University
La Sierra University
Loyola Marymount University
Master's College
Mills College
MiraCosta College
Mount St. Mary's College
Mount San Antonio College
National Hispanic University
National University
Notre Dame de Namur University
Otis College of Art and Design
Pacific Oaks College
Pacific Union College
Patten University
Pepperdine University
Point Loma Nazarene University
St. Mary's College of California
San Diego Christian College
San Diego City College
San Diego Mesa College
San Diego State University
San Francisco State University
San Jose State University
Santa Clara University
Shasta Bible College and Graduate
  School
Simpson University
Sonoma State University
University of California
  Davis
  Irvine
  Riverside
  San Diego
  Santa Barbara
  Santa Cruz
University of La Verne
University of Redlands
University of San Diego
University of San Francisco
University of the Pacific
Vanguard University of Southern
  California
West Valley College
Westmont College
Whittier College
William Jessup University

Colorado

Adams State University
Colorado Christian University
Colorado College
Colorado Mesa University
Colorado State University
Colorado State University
  Pueblo
Fort Lewis College
Front Range Community College
Jones International University
Metropolitan State University of
  Denver
Northeastern Junior College
Red Rocks Community College
Regis University
Rocky Mountain College of Art &
  Design
University of Colorado
  Boulder
  Colorado Springs
  Denver
University of Denver
University of Northern Colorado
Western State Colorado University

Connecticut

Albertus Magnus College
Central Connecticut State University
Connecticut College
Eastern Connecticut State University
Fairfield University
Mitchell College
Post University
Quinnipiac University
Sacred Heart University
Southern Connecticut State
  University
Trinity College
University of Bridgeport
University of Connecticut
University of Hartford
University of New Haven
University of Saint Joseph
Western Connecticut State University
Yale University

Delaware

Delaware State University
University of Delaware
Wesley College
Wilmington University

District of Columbia

American University
Catholic University of America
Corcoran College of Art and Design
Gallaudet University
Howard University
Trinity Washington University
University of the District of Columbia

Florida

Baptist College of Florida
Barry University
Bethune-Cookman University
Broward College
Carlos Albizu University
Chipola College
Clearwater Christian College
College of Central Florida
Daytona State College
Edward Waters College
Flagler College
Florida Agricultural and Mechanical
  University
Florida Atlantic University
Florida College
Florida Gateway College
Florida Gulf Coast University
Florida Institute of Technology
Florida International University
Florida Memorial University
Florida Southern College
Florida State College at Jacksonville
Florida State University
Gulf Coast State College
Hillsborough Community College
Hobe Sound Bible College
Indian River State College
Jacksonville University
Johnson University: Florida
Lake-Sumter State College
Lynn University
Miami Dade College
North Florida Community College
Northwest Florida State College
Nova Southeastern University
Palm Beach Atlantic University
Pasco-Hernando State College
Pensacola State College
Rollins College
Saint Johns River State College
Saint Leo University
St. Petersburg College
Saint Thomas University
Santa Fe College
Seminole State College of Florida
South Florida State College
Southeastern University
Southwest Florida College
State College of Florida, Manatee-
  Sarasota
Stetson University
University of Central Florida
University of Florida
University of Miami
University of North Florida
University of South Florida
University of South Florida
  Sarasota-Manatee
University of Tampa
University of West Florida
Warner University

Georgia

Albany State University
Armstrong Atlantic State University
Berry College
Brenau University
Brewton-Parker College
Clark Atlanta University
Clayton State University
College of Coastal Georgia
Columbus State University
Covenant College
Dalton State College
Emmanuel College
Emory University
Fort Valley State University
Georgia College and State University
Georgia Institute of Technology
Georgia Regents University
Georgia Southern University
Georgia Southwestern State
  University
Georgia State University
Kennesaw State University
LaGrange College
Mercer University
Paine College
Piedmont College
Point University
Reinhardt University
Shorter University
Southern Polytechnic State University
Spelman College
Thomas University
Toccoa Falls College
Truett-McConnell College
University of Georgia
University of North Georgia
University of West Georgia
Valdosta State University
Wesleyan College
Young Harris College

Hawaii

Brigham Young University-Hawaii
Chaminade University of Honolulu
Hawaii Pacific University
University of Hawaii
    Hawaii Community College
    Hilo
    Kapiolani Community College
    Leeward Community College
    Manoa
    West Oahu

Idaho

Boise State University
Brigham Young University-Idaho
College of Idaho
Idaho State University
Lewis-Clark State College
Northwest Nazarene University
University of Idaho

Illinois

Augustana College
Aurora University
Benedictine University
Benedictine University at Springfield
Blackburn College
Bradley University
Carl Sandburg College
Chicago State University
Columbia College Chicago
Concordia University Chicago
DePaul University
Dominican University
Eastern Illinois University
Elmhurst College
Eureka College
Governors State University
Greenville College
Hebrew Theological College
Illinois College
Illinois Eastern Community Colleges
    Frontier Community College
Illinois Institute of Technology
Illinois State University
Illinois Wesleyan University
Judson University
Kankakee Community College
Kendall College
Knox College
Lake Forest College
Lewis University
Loyola University Chicago
MacMurray College
McKendree University
Millikin University
Monmouth College
National-Louis University
North Central College
North Park University
Northeastern Illinois University
Northern Illinois University
Northwestern University
Oakton Community College
Olivet Nazarene University
Principia College
Quincy University
Rend Lake College
Richland Community College
Rockford University
Roosevelt University
Saint Xavier University
School of the Art Institute of Chicago
Southern Illinois University
    Carbondale
Southern Illinois University
    Edwardsville
Trinity Christian College
Trinity International University
Triton College
University of Illinois
    Chicago
    Springfield
    Urbana-Champaign

University of St. Francis
VanderCook College of Music
Western Illinois University
Wheaton College

Indiana

Anderson University
Ball State University
Bethel College
Butler University
Calumet College of St. Joseph
DePauw University
Franklin College
Goshen College
Grace College
Hanover College
Holy Cross College
Huntington University
Indiana State University
Indiana University
    Bloomington
    East
    Kokomo
    Northwest
    Purdue University Fort Wayne
    Purdue University Indianapolis
    South Bend
    Southeast
Indiana Wesleyan University
Ivy Tech Community College
    Bloomington
    Central Indiana
    Columbus
    East Central
    Kokomo
    Lafayette
    North Central
    Northeast
    Northwest
    Richmond
    South Central
    Southeast
    Southwest
    Wabash Valley
Manchester University
Marian University
Oakland City University
Purdue University
Purdue University
    Calumet
    North Central
Saint Joseph's College
Saint Mary's College
St. Mary of the Woods College
Taylor University
Trine University
University of Evansville
University of Indianapolis
University of Notre Dame
University of St. Francis
University of Southern Indiana
Valparaiso University
Wabash College

Iowa

Ashford University
Briar Cliff University
Buena Vista University
Central College
Clarke University
Coe College
Cornell College
Dordt College
Drake University
Emmaus Bible College
Faith Baptist Bible College and
    Theological Seminary
Graceland University
Grand View University
Grinnell College
Iowa State University
Iowa Wesleyan College
Loras College
Luther College

Maharishi University of Management
Morningside College
Mount Mercy University
Northwestern College
St. Ambrose University
Simpson College
University of Dubuque
University of Iowa
University of Northern Iowa
Upper Iowa University
Waldorf College
Wartburg College
William Penn University

Kansas

Baker University
Barclay College
Benedictine College
Bethany College
Bethel College
Central Christian College of Kansas
Cowley County Community College
Emporia State University
Fort Hays State University
Friends University
Kansas State University
Kansas Wesleyan University
McPherson College
MidAmerica Nazarene University
Newman University
Ottawa University
Pittsburg State University
Southwestern College
Sterling College
Tabor College
University of Kansas
University of St. Mary
Washburn University
Wichita State University

Kentucky

Alice Lloyd College
Asbury University
Bellarmine University
Berea College
Brescia University
Campbellsville University
Eastern Kentucky University
Elizabethtown Community and
    Technical College
Georgetown College
Jefferson Community and Technical
    College
Kentucky Christian University
Kentucky Mountain Bible College
Kentucky State University
Kentucky Wesleyan College
Lindsey Wilson College
Mid-Continent University
Midway College
Morehead State University
Murray State University
Northern Kentucky University
St. Catharine College
Spalding University
Thomas More College
Transylvania University
Union College
University of Kentucky
University of Louisville
University of Pikeville
University of the Cumberlands
Western Kentucky University

Louisiana

Baton Rouge Community College
Dillard University
Grambling State University
Louisiana College
Louisiana State University
    Shreveport
Louisiana State University and
    Agricultural and Mechanical
    College

Louisiana Tech University
Loyola University New Orleans
McNeese State University
Nicholls State University
Northwestern State University
Our Lady of Holy Cross College
Southeastern Louisiana University
Southern University
    New Orleans
Southern University and Agricultural
    and Mechanical College
Tulane University
University of Louisiana at Lafayette
University of Louisiana at Monroe
University of New Orleans
Xavier University of Louisiana

Maine

Bates College
Bowdoin College
Colby College
College of the Atlantic
Husson University
Maine College of Art
Maine Maritime Academy
Saint Joseph's College of Maine
Thomas College
Unity College
University of Maine
University of Maine
    Augusta
    Farmington
    Fort Kent
    Machias
    Presque Isle
University of New England
University of Southern Maine

Maryland

Anne Arundel Community College
Baltimore City Community College
Bowie State University
Cecil College
Community College of Baltimore
    County
Coppin State University
Frederick Community College
Frostburg State University
Goucher College
Harford Community College
Hood College
Howard Community College
Johns Hopkins University: Peabody
    Conservatory of Music
Loyola University Maryland
Maryland Institute College of Art
McDaniel College
Montgomery College
Morgan State University
Mount St. Mary's University
Notre Dame of Maryland University
Prince George's Community College
Salisbury University
Stevenson University
Towson University
University of Maryland
    Baltimore County
    College Park
    Eastern Shore
    University College
Washington Adventist University
Washington College

Massachusetts

American International College
Amherst College
Anna Maria College
Assumption College
Bay Path College
Becker College
Berklee College of Music
Boston College
Boston Conservatory
Boston University

Brandeis University
Bridgewater State University
Clark University
College of the Holy Cross
Curry College
Dean College
Eastern Nazarene College
Elms College
Emerson College
Emmanuel College
Endicott College
Fitchburg State University
Framingham State University
Gordon College
Hampshire College
Harvard College
Holyoke Community College
Lasell College
Lesley University
Massachusetts College of Liberal Arts
Massachusetts Institute of Technology
Merrimack College
Montserrat College of Art
Mount Holyoke College
Mount Ida College
Nichols College
Northeastern University
Pine Manor College
Regis College
Salem State University
School of the Museum of Fine Arts
Simmons College
Smith College
Springfield College
Stonehill College
Tufts University
University of Massachusetts
    Amherst
    Boston
    Dartmouth
    Lowell
Wellesley College
Western New England University
Westfield State University
Wheaton College
Wheelock College
Worcester Polytechnic Institute
Worcester State University

Michigan

Adrian College
Albion College
Alma College
Andrews University
Aquinas College
Baker College
    Allen Park
    Auburn Hills
    Clinton Township
    Muskegon
Calvin College
Central Michigan University
College for Creative Studies
Concordia University
Cornerstone University
Eastern Michigan University
Ferris State University
Finlandia University
Grand Valley State University
Hillsdale College
Hope College
Kuyper College
Lake Superior State University
Lansing Community College
Madonna University
Marygrove College
Michigan State University
Michigan Technological University
Northern Michigan University
Oakland University
Olivet College
Robert B. Miller College
Rochester College
Saginaw Valley State University
Siena Heights University

Spring Arbor University
University of Detroit Mercy
University of Michigan
University of Michigan
    Dearborn
    Flint
Wayne State University
Western Michigan University

Minnesota

Augsburg College
Bemidji State University
Bethany Lutheran College
Bethel University
Carleton College
College of St. Benedict
College of St. Scholastica
Concordia College: Moorhead
Concordia University St. Paul
Crown College
Gustavus Adolphus College
Hamline University
Leech Lake Tribal College
Martin Luther College
Metropolitan State University
Minneapolis Community and
    Technical College
Minnesota State University
    Mankato
    Moorhead
Normandale Community College
North Central University
St. Catherine University
Saint Cloud State University
St. John's University
St. Mary's University of Minnesota
St. Olaf College
Southwest Minnesota State University
University of Minnesota
    Crookston
    Duluth
    Morris
    Twin Cities
University of Northwestern - St. Paul
University of St. Thomas
Walden University
Winona State University

Mississippi

Alcorn State University
Belhaven University
Blue Mountain College
Delta State University
Jackson State University
Millsaps College
Mississippi College
Mississippi State University
Mississippi University for Women
Mississippi Valley State University
Rust College
Tougaloo College
University of Mississippi
University of Southern Mississippi
William Carey University

Missouri

Avila University
Calvary Bible College and Theological
    Seminary
Central Methodist University
College of the Ozarks
Columbia College
Culver-Stockton College
Drury University
Evangel University
Fontbonne University
Hannibal-LaGrange University
Harris-Stowe State University
Jefferson College
Lincoln University
Lindenwood University
Maryville University of Saint Louis
Missouri Baptist University
Missouri Southern State University

Missouri State University
Missouri University of Science and
    Technology
Missouri Valley College
Missouri Western State University
Moberly Area Community College
Northwest Missouri State University
Park University
Rockhurst University
St. Charles Community College
Saint Louis University
Southeast Missouri State University
Southwest Baptist University
Stephens College
Truman State University
University of Central Missouri
University of Missouri
    Columbia
    Kansas City
    St. Louis
Washington University in St. Louis
Webster University
Westminster College
William Jewell College
William Woods University

Montana

Carroll College
Montana State University
Montana State University
    Billings
    Northern
Montana Tech of the University of
    Montana
Rocky Mountain College
University of Great Falls
University of Montana
University of Montana: Western

Nebraska

Chadron State College
College of Saint Mary
Creighton University
Doane College
Grace University
Hastings College
Midland University
Nebraska Christian College
Nebraska Wesleyan University
Peru State College
Union College
University of Nebraska
    Kearney
    Lincoln
    Omaha
Wayne State College
York College

Nevada

Great Basin College
Nevada State College
Sierra Nevada College
University of Nevada
    Las Vegas
    Reno

New Hampshire

Colby-Sawyer College
Dartmouth College
Franklin Pierce University
Granite State College
Keene State College
NHTI-Concord's Community College
New England College
Plymouth State University
Rivier University
Saint Anselm College
Southern New Hampshire University
University of New Hampshire
University of New Hampshire at
    Manchester

New Jersey

Bloomfield College
Caldwell College
Centenary College
College of New Jersey
College of St. Elizabeth
County College of Morris
Drew University
Essex County College
Fairleigh Dickinson University
    College at Florham
    Metropolitan Campus
Felician College
Georgian Court University
Hudson County Community College
Kean University
Monmouth University
Montclair State University
New Jersey City University
New Jersey Institute of Technology
Ocean County College
Princeton University
Ramapo College of New Jersey
Richard Stockton College of New
    Jersey
Rider University
Rowan University
Rutgers, The State University of New
    Jersey
    Camden Campus
    New Brunswick/Piscataway
        Campus
    Newark Campus
Saint Peter's University
Seton Hall University
Sussex County Community College
William Paterson University of New
    Jersey

New Mexico

Central New Mexico Community
    College
Clovis Community College
Eastern New Mexico University
Navajo Technical University
New Mexico Highlands University
New Mexico Institute of Mining and
    Technology
New Mexico State University
Northern New Mexico College
San Juan College
Santa Fe Community College
University of New Mexico
University of the Southwest
Western New Mexico University

New York

Adelphi University
Alfred University
Barnard College
Boricua College
Canisius College
Cazenovia College
City University of New York
    Brooklyn College
    City College
    College of Staten Island
    Hunter College
    Lehman College
    Medgar Evers College
    New York City College of
        Technology
    Queens College
    York College
Colgate University
College of Mount St. Vincent
College of New Rochelle
College of Saint Rose
Columbia University
Columbia University
    School of General Studies
Concordia College
Cornell University
D'Youville College

Daemen College
Dominican College of Blauvelt
Dowling College
Eastman School of Music of the
    University of Rochester
Elmira College
Erie Community College
Five Towns College
Fordham University
Hartwick College
Hobart and William Smith Colleges
Hofstra University
Houghton College
Iona College
Ithaca College
Jefferson Community College
Keuka College
Le Moyne College
Long Island University
    LIU Brooklyn
    LIU Post
Manhattan College
Manhattanville College
Marist College
Medaille College
Medaille College: Amherst
Mercy College
Metropolitan College of New York
Molloy College
Monroe College
Mount Saint Mary College
Nazareth College
New York Institute of Technology
New York University
Niagara University
Nyack College
Ohr Somayach Tanenbaum Education
    Center
Pace University
Pace University: Pleasantville/
    Briarcliff
Pratt Institute
Roberts Wesleyan College
Rochester Institute of Technology
SUNY
    College at Brockport
    College at Buffalo
    College at Cortland
    College at Fredonia
    College at Geneseo
    College at New Paltz
    College at Old Westbury
    College at Oneonta
    College at Oswego
    College at Plattsburgh
    College at Potsdam
    College of Environmental Science
        and Forestry
    Empire State College
    University at Binghamton
    University at Buffalo
    University at Stony Brook
Sage Colleges
Saint Bonaventure University
St. Francis College
St. John Fisher College
St. John's University
St. Joseph's College New York:
    Suffolk Campus
St. Joseph's College, New York
St. Lawrence University
St. Thomas Aquinas College
Sarah Lawrence College
Schenectady County Community
    College
Siena College
Skidmore College
Syracuse University
Touro College
Union College
University of Rochester
Utica College
Vassar College
Wagner College

Wells College
Yeshiva University

North Carolina
Appalachian State University
Barton College
Belmont Abbey College
Bennett College for Women
Blue Ridge Community College
Brevard College
Campbell University
Catawba College
Catawba Valley Community College
Chowan University
Craven Community College
Davidson College
Duke University
East Carolina University
Elizabeth City State University
Elon University
Fayetteville State University
Gardner-Webb University
Greensboro College
Guilford College
Guilford Technical Community
    College
High Point University
Johnson C. Smith University
Lees-McRae College
Lenoir-Rhyne University
Livingstone College
Mars Hill University
Martin Community College
Meredith College
Methodist University
Mid-Atlantic Christian University
Montreat College
North Carolina Agricultural and
    Technical State University
North Carolina Central University
North Carolina State University
North Carolina Wesleyan College
Pfeiffer University
Piedmont International University
Queens University of Charlotte
Richmond Community College
Rowan-Cabarrus Community College
St. Andrews University
St. Augustine's University
Salem College
Sandhills Community College
Shaw University
University of Mount Olive
University of North Carolina
    Asheville
    Chapel Hill
    Charlotte
    Greensboro
    Pembroke
    Wilmington
Wake Forest University
Wayne Community College
Western Carolina University
William Peace University
Wingate University
Winston-Salem State University

North Dakota
Dickinson State University
Mayville State University
Minot State University
North Dakota State University
Trinity Bible College
University of Jamestown
University of Mary
University of North Dakota
Valley City State University

Ohio
Antioch University
    Midwest
Ashland University
Baldwin Wallace University
Bluffton University

Bowling Green State University
Bowling Green State University:
    Firelands College
Capital University
Case Western Reserve University
Cedarville University
Central State University
Cincinnati Christian University
Cleveland State University
College of Mount St. Joseph
College of Wooster
Defiance College
Denison University
Franciscan University of Steubenville
Heidelberg University
Hiram College
John Carroll University
Kent State University
Kent State University
    Geauga
    Salem
    Stark
Lake Erie College
Lorain County Community College
Lourdes University
Malone University
Marietta College
Miami University
    Hamilton
    Middletown
    Oxford
Mount Vernon Nazarene University
Muskingum University
Notre Dame College
Oberlin College
Ohio Christian University
Ohio Dominican University
Ohio Northern University
Ohio State University
    Columbus Campus
    Lima Campus
    Mansfield Campus
    Marion Campus
    Newark Campus
Ohio University
Ohio University
    Chillicothe Campus
    Eastern Campus
    Southern Campus at Ironton
    Zanesville Campus
Ohio Wesleyan University
Otterbein University
Shawnee State University
Tiffin University
Union Institute & University
University of Akron
University of Cincinnati
University of Cincinnati
    Blue Ash College
University of Dayton
University of Findlay
University of Mount Union
University of Rio Grande
University of Toledo
Urbana University
Ursuline College
Walsh University
Wilmington College
Wittenberg University
Wright State University
Xavier University
Youngstown State University

Oklahoma
Bacone College
Cameron University
East Central University
Mid-America Christian University
Northeastern State University
Northwestern Oklahoma State
    University
Oklahoma Baptist University
Oklahoma Christian University
Oklahoma City University
Oklahoma Panhandle State University

Oklahoma State University
Oklahoma Wesleyan University
Oral Roberts University
Southeastern Oklahoma State
    University
Southern Nazarene University
Southwestern Oklahoma State
    University
University of Central Oklahoma
University of Oklahoma
University of Science and Arts of
    Oklahoma
University of Tulsa

Oregon
Chemeketa Community College
Concordia University
Corban University
Eastern Oregon University
George Fox University
Linfield College
Marylhurst University
Multnomah University
Northwest Christian University
Oregon State University
Pacific University
Portland State University
Southern Oregon University
University of Oregon
University of Portland
Warner Pacific College
Western Oregon University
Willamette University

Pennsylvania
Albright College
Alvernia University
Arcadia University
Baptist Bible College of Pennsylvania
Bloomsburg University of
    Pennsylvania
Bryn Athyn College
Bryn Mawr College
Bucknell University
Cabrini College
Cairn University
California University of Pennsylvania
Carlow University
Carnegie Mellon University
Cedar Crest College
Chatham University
Chestnut Hill College
Cheyney University of Pennsylvania
Clarion University of Pennsylvania
DeSales University
Delaware Valley College
Dickinson College
Drexel University
Duquesne University
East Stroudsburg University of
    Pennsylvania
Eastern University
Edinboro University of Pennsylvania
Elizabethtown College
Franklin & Marshall College
Gannon University
Geneva College
Gettysburg College
Gratz College
Grove City College
Gwynedd Mercy University
Haverford College
Holy Family University
Immaculata University
Indiana University of Pennsylvania
Juniata College
Keystone College
King's College
Kutztown University of Pennsylvania
La Roche College
La Salle University
Lancaster Bible College
Lebanon Valley College

Lock Haven University of
    Pennsylvania
Lycoming College
Mansfield University of Pennsylvania
Marywood University
Mercyhurst University
Messiah College
Millersville University of Pennsylvania
Misericordia University
Montgomery County Community
    College
Moore College of Art and Design
Moravian College
Mount Aloysius College
Muhlenberg College
Neumann University
Northampton Community College
Penn State
    Abington
    Altoona
    Berks
    Brandywine
    Erie, The Behrend College
    Harrisburg
    Lehigh Valley
    University Park
Point Park University
Robert Morris University
Rosemont College
St. Francis University
Saint Joseph's University
Seton Hill University
Shippensburg University of
    Pennsylvania
Slippery Rock University of
    Pennsylvania
Susquehanna University
Swarthmore College
Temple University
Thiel College
University of Pennsylvania
University of Pittsburgh
University of Pittsburgh
    Bradford
    Johnstown
University of Scranton
University of the Arts
Ursinus College
Valley Forge Christian College
Villanova University
Washington & Jefferson College
Waynesburg University
West Chester University of
    Pennsylvania
Westminster College
Widener University
Wilkes University
Wilson College
York College of Pennsylvania

Puerto Rico

Bayamon Central University
Caribbean University
Conservatory of Music of Puerto Rico
Escuela de Artes Plasticas de Puerto
    Rico
Inter American University of Puerto
    Rico
    Aguadilla Campus
    Arecibo Campus
    Barranquitas Campus
    Fajardo Campus
    Guayama Campus
    Ponce Campus
    San German Campus
Pontifical Catholic University of
    Puerto Rico
Universidad Adventista de las Antillas
Universidad Metropolitana
Universidad del Este
University of Puerto Rico
    Aguadilla
    Cayey University College
    Humacao
    Mayaguez

Rio Piedras
Utuado
University of the Sacred Heart

Rhode Island

Brown University
Bryant University
Providence College
Rhode Island College
Roger Williams University
Salve Regina University
University of Rhode Island

South Carolina

Allen University
Anderson University
Benedict College
Bob Jones University
Charleston Southern University
Citadel
Claflin University
Clemson University
Coastal Carolina University
Coker College
College of Charleston
Columbia College
Columbia International University
Converse College
Erskine College
Francis Marion University
Furman University
Greenville Technical College
Lander University
Limestone College
Morris College
Newberry College
North Greenville University
Presbyterian College
South Carolina State University
Southern Wesleyan University
University of South Carolina
    Aiken
    Beaufort
    Columbia
    Sumter
    Upstate
Winthrop University
Wofford College

South Dakota

Augustana College
Black Hills State University
Dakota State University
Dakota Wesleyan University
Mount Marty College
Northern State University
Oglala Lakota College
South Dakota State University
University of Sioux Falls
University of South Dakota

Tennessee

Aquinas College
Austin Peay State University
Belmont University
Bethel University
Bryan University
    Dayton
Carson-Newman University
Chattanooga State Community
    College
Christian Brothers University
Cumberland University
Dyersburg State Community College
East Tennessee State University
Fisk University
Freed-Hardeman University
Johnson University
King University
Lane College
LeMoyne-Owen College
Lee University
Lincoln Memorial University
Lipscomb University

Martin Methodist College
Maryville College
Memphis College of Art
Middle Tennessee State University
Milligan College
Roane State Community College
South College
Southern Adventist University
Tennessee State University
Tennessee Technological University
Tennessee Temple University
Tennessee Wesleyan College
Trevecca Nazarene University
Tusculum College
Union University
University of Memphis
University of Tennessee
    Chattanooga
    Knoxville
    Martin
Vanderbilt University
Victory University
Welch College

Texas

Abilene Christian University
Angelo State University
Arlington Baptist College
Austin College
Austin Community College
Baylor University
Blinn College
College of the Mainland
Concordia University Texas
Dallas Baptist University
Dallas Christian College
Del Mar College
East Texas Baptist University
El Centro College
El Paso Community College
Hardin-Simmons University
Houston Baptist University
Houston Community College System
Howard Payne University
Huston-Tillotson University
Jarvis Christian College
Lamar University
Laredo Community College
LeTourneau University
Lone Star College System
Lubbock Christian University
McLennan Community College
McMurry University
Midwestern State University
Mountain View College
North Lake College
Northwest Vista College
Our Lady of the Lake University of
    San Antonio
Paul Quinn College
Prairie View A&M University
Rice University
Richland College
St. Edward's University
St. Mary's University
Sam Houston State University
San Antonio College
San Jacinto College
Schreiner University
Southern Methodist University
Southwestern Adventist University
Southwestern Assemblies of God
    University
Southwestern University
Stephen F. Austin State University
Sul Ross State University
Tarleton State University
Texas A&M International University
Texas A&M University
Texas A&M University
    Commerce
    Corpus Christi
    Galveston
    Kingsville
    Texarkana

Texas Christian University
Texas College
Texas Lutheran University
Texas Southern University
Texas State Technical College
    Harlingen
Texas State University
Texas Tech University
Texas Wesleyan University
Texas Woman's University
Trinity University
Tyler Junior College
University of Dallas
University of Houston
University of Houston
    Clear Lake
    Downtown
    Victoria
University of Mary Hardin-Baylor
University of North Texas
University of St. Thomas
University of Texas
    Arlington
    Austin
    Brownsville
    Dallas
    El Paso
    Pan American
    Permian Basin
    San Antonio
    Tyler
University of the Incarnate Word
Wayland Baptist University
Weatherford College
West Texas A&M University
Wharton County Junior College
Wiley College

Utah

Brigham Young University
Dixie State College
Southern Utah University
University of Utah
Utah State University
Utah Valley University
Weber State University
Western Governors University
Westminster College

Vermont

Castleton State College
Champlain College
College of St. Joseph in Vermont
Goddard College
Green Mountain College
Johnson State College
Lyndon State College
Middlebury College
Norwich University
Saint Michael's College
University of Vermont

Virginia

Averett University
Blue Ridge Community College
Bluefield College
Bridgewater College
Christopher Newport University
College of William and Mary
Eastern Mennonite University
Emory & Henry College
Ferrum College
George Mason University
Hampton University
Hollins University
James Madison University
Liberty University
Longwood University
Lynchburg College
Mary Baldwin College
Marymount University
New River Community College
Norfolk State University
Old Dominion University

Patrick Henry Community College
Radford University
Randolph College
Randolph-Macon College
Regent University
Roanoke College
Shenandoah University
Sweet Briar College
University of Mary Washington
University of Richmond
University of Virginia
University of Virginia's College at
    Wise
Virginia Commonwealth University
Virginia Intermont College
Virginia Military Institute
Virginia Polytechnic Institute and
    State University
Virginia State University
Virginia Union University
Virginia Wesleyan College
Washington and Lee University

Washington

Antioch University
    Seattle
Bates Technical College
Central Washington University
Centralia College
City University of Seattle
Eastern Washington University
Evergreen State College
Gonzaga University
Heritage University
Lower Columbia College
Northwest University
Pacific Lutheran University
Saint Martin's University
Seattle Pacific University
Seattle University
University of Puget Sound
University of Washington
University of Washington Bothell
University of Washington Tacoma
Walla Walla University
Washington State University
Western Washington University
Whitworth University

West Virginia

Alderson-Broaddus University
American Public University System
Appalachian Bible College
Bethany College
Bluefield State College
Concord University
Davis and Elkins College
Fairmont State University
Glenville State College
Marshall University
Ohio Valley University
Shepherd University
Southern West Virginia Community
    and Technical College
University of Charleston
West Liberty University
West Virginia State University
West Virginia University
West Virginia University at
    Parkersburg
West Virginia Wesleyan College
Wheeling Jesuit University

Wisconsin

Alverno College
Beloit College
Cardinal Stritch University
Carroll University
Carthage College
College of Menominee Nation
Concordia University Wisconsin
Edgewood College
Lakeland College
Lawrence University

Maranatha Baptist Bible College
Marian University
Marquette University
Mount Mary University
Northland College
Ripon College
St. Norbert College
Silver Lake College of the Holy
    Family
University of Wisconsin
    Eau Claire
    Green Bay
    La Crosse
    Madison
    Milwaukee
    Oshkosh
    Parkside
    Platteville
    River Falls
    Stevens Point
    Stout
    Superior
    Whitewater
Viterbo University
Wisconsin Lutheran College

Wyoming

Central Wyoming College

United Nations semester

Arkansas
University of Arkansas

California
Mount St. Mary's College
Occidental College
Point Loma Nazarene University
Scripps College
Sonoma State University
University of Redlands
University of the Pacific
Whittier College

Connecticut
Sacred Heart University
Trinity College
University of Bridgeport

Florida
Florida Southern College

Illinois
Illinois Wesleyan University
Lincoln Land Community College
Millikin University
North Central College
Rockford University

Indiana
Franklin College
Indiana University
    Bloomington
Indiana Wesleyan University
Valparaiso University
Wabash College

Iowa
Morningside College

Kansas
Fort Hays State University

Maryland
McDaniel College

Massachusetts
Bentley University

Minnesota
University of Minnesota
    Morris

Nebraska
Nebraska Wesleyan University
University of Nebraska
    Lincoln

New Hampshire
Southern New Hampshire University
University of New Hampshire

New Jersey
Drew University

New York
Alfred University
College of New Rochelle
Marist College
Pace University
Pace University: Pleasantville/
    Briarcliff
SUNY
    College at New Paltz
Utica College
Wagner College

North Carolina
Meredith College

Ohio
College of Wooster
Muskingum University
Ohio Wesleyan University

Pennsylvania
Gettysburg College
Lycoming College
Seton Hill University
Susquehanna University
Thiel College
University of Scranton
Ursinus College

South Carolina
Furman University
Winthrop University

Texas
Trinity University

Virginia
Randolph-Macon College

West Virginia
Wheeling Jesuit University

Wisconsin
Carroll University

Urban semester

Arkansas
University of Arkansas

California
Azusa Pacific University
Biola University
Hope International University
Marymount California University
Pitzer College
Scripps College
Sonoma State University
University of California
  Los Angeles
University of Redlands
Westmont College
William Jessup University

Colorado
Colorado Christian University
Colorado College
University of Northern Colorado

Connecticut
Trinity College
University of Bridgeport
University of Connecticut
Wesleyan University

District of Columbia
Corcoran College of Art and Design

Florida
Florida Southern College
Ringling College of Art and Design

Georgia
Savannah College of Art and Design
Spelman College
Wesleyan College

Idaho
Brigham Young University-Idaho

Illinois
Greenville College
Illinois State University
Illinois Wesleyan University
Judson University
Knox College
Lake Forest College
Millikin University
Monmouth College
North Central College
School of the Art Institute of Chicago
Trinity Christian College
Trinity International University
Wheaton College

Indiana
Anderson University
Bethel College
Earlham College
Goshen College
Huntington University
Indiana Wesleyan University
Manchester University
Purdue University
Taylor University
Valparaiso University
Wabash College

Iowa
Briar Cliff University
Central College
Coe College
Cornell College
Dordt College
Grinnell College
Loras College
Northwestern College
University of Dubuque
University of Iowa
Wartburg College

Kansas
Bethany College
Bethel College
Central Christian College of Kansas
McPherson College
Southwestern College
Sterling College

Kentucky
Asbury University

Maine
Bates College

Maryland
Maryland Institute College of Art
McDaniel College
University of Maryland
  Eastern Shore

Massachusetts
Assumption College
Bentley University
Curry College
Dean College
Eastern Nazarene College
Gordon College
Lesley University
Montserrat College of Art
Nichols College
School of the Museum of Fine Arts
Stonehill College

Michigan
Albion College
Alma College
Aquinas College
Calvin College
College for Creative Studies
Cornerstone University
Hope College
Kalamazoo College

Minnesota
Augsburg College
Bethel University
Concordia College: Moorhead
Crown College
Hamline University
Macalester College
Minneapolis College of Art and
  Design
St. Catherine University
St. Mary's University of Minnesota
St. Olaf College
University of Minnesota
  Morris

Mississippi
Tougaloo College

Missouri
Kansas City Art Institute
Missouri Baptist University
Rockhurst University
University of Missouri
  Columbia
Westminster College

Nebraska
Grace University
Hastings College
Nebraska Wesleyan University
University of Nebraska
  Lincoln

New Hampshire
University of New Hampshire

New Jersey
Berkeley College
Drew University

New Mexico
Santa Fe University of Art and Design

New York
Alfred University
Bard College
Berkeley College
Colgate University
Cornell University
Eugene Lang College The New
  School for Liberal Arts
Hamilton College
Hartwick College
Hofstra University
Houghton College
Ithaca College
Jewish Theological Seminary of
  America
Marist College
Niagara University
Onondaga Community College
Pace University
Pace University: Pleasantville/
  Briarcliff
SUNY
  College at Brockport
  College at Buffalo
  College at Fredonia
  College at New Paltz
  College at Oneonta
  University at Stony Brook
St. Joseph's College New York:
  Suffolk Campus
St. Lawrence University
Syracuse University
University of Rochester
Vassar College
Wagner College

North Carolina
Bennett College for Women
Duke University
Elon University
Meredith College

Ohio
Art Academy of Cincinnati
Ashland University
Cleveland Institute of Art
College of Wooster
Columbus College of Art and Design
Denison University
Kent State University
Kent State University
  Ashtabula
  East Liverpool
  Geauga
  Salem
  Stark
  Trumbull
  Tuscarawas
Mount Vernon Nazarene University
Oberlin College
Ohio Wesleyan University
Ursuline College
Wittenberg University
Xavier University
Youngstown State University

Oklahoma
Southern Nazarene University

Oregon
George Fox University
Lewis & Clark College
Pacific Northwest College of Art
Willamette University

Pennsylvania
California University of Pennsylvania
Franklin & Marshall College
Indiana University of Pennsylvania
Juniata College
Lafayette College
Lebanon Valley College
Lehigh University
Lycoming College
Mercyhurst University
Messiah College
Seton Hill University
Susquehanna University

South Dakota
Augustana College

Tennessee
Memphis College of Art

Texas
Southwestern University
Trinity University

Virginia
Washington and Lee University

Washington
Trinity Lutheran College
Whitman College

West Virginia
Bethany College
West Virginia Wesleyan College

Wisconsin
Beloit College
Lawrence University
Milwaukee Institute of Art & Design
Ripon College
Viterbo University

Washington semester

Alabama

Alabama Agricultural and Mechanical
    University
Auburn University
Huntingdon College
Judson College
Spring Hill College
University of Alabama

Alaska

University of Alaska
    Anchorage

Arizona

Arizona State University

Arkansas

Hendrix College
John Brown University
Lyon College
University of Arkansas

California

Azusa Pacific University
Biola University
California Baptist University
California Lutheran University
California State University
    Long Beach
Chapman University
Claremont McKenna College
Fresno Pacific University
Hope International University
Loyola Marymount University
Master's College
Mills College
Mount St. Mary's College
Occidental College
Pepperdine University
Point Loma Nazarene University
Pomona College
San Francisco State University
Santa Clara University
Scripps College
Simpson University
Sonoma State University
Stanford University
University of California
    Davis
    Irvine
    Los Angeles
    Merced
    Riverside
    San Diego
    Santa Barbara
    Santa Cruz
University of Redlands
University of San Diego
University of San Francisco
University of Southern California
University of the Pacific
Vanguard University of Southern
    California
Westmont College
Whittier College
William Jessup University

Colorado

Colorado Christian University
Colorado College
Metropolitan State University of
    Denver
University of Denver

Connecticut

Connecticut College
Fairfield University
Quinnipiac University
Sacred Heart University

Trinity College
University of Bridgeport
University of Connecticut
University of Hartford
Wesleyan University

Delaware

University of Delaware

District of Columbia

American University
Catholic University of America
Georgetown University

Florida

Florida Gulf Coast University
Florida Southern College
Jacksonville University
New College of Florida
Palm Beach Atlantic University
Rollins College
Stetson University
University of Florida
University of Miami
University of South Florida
University of Tampa
Warner University

Georgia

Agnes Scott College
Clark Atlanta University
Covenant College
Emory University
Georgia College and State University
Georgia Southern University
LaGrange College
Piedmont College
Spelman College
University of Georgia

Idaho

College of Idaho

Illinois

Blackburn College
Bradley University
Dominican University
Elmhurst College
Eureka College
Greenville College
Illinois College
Illinois State University
Illinois Wesleyan University
Judson University
Knox College
Lake Forest College
Loyola University Chicago
Millikin University
Monmouth College
North Central College
North Park University
Olivet Nazarene University
Quincy University
Rockford University
Trinity International University
University of Illinois
    Urbana-Champaign
University of St. Francis
Wheaton College

Indiana

Bethel College
Butler University
Franklin College
Goshen College
Hanover College
Huntington University
Indiana University
    Bloomington
    Northwest
    Purdue University Fort Wayne
Indiana Wesleyan University
Saint Joseph's College
Saint Mary's College

Taylor University
University of Indianapolis
University of Notre Dame
Valparaiso University
Wabash College

Iowa

Buena Vista University
Central College
Coe College
Cornell College
Dordt College
Drake University
Grand View University
Grinnell College
Iowa State University
Iowa Wesleyan College
Loras College
Luther College
Morningside College
Northwestern College
Simpson College
University of Iowa
University of Northern Iowa
Wartburg College

Kansas

Bethany College
Bethel College
Central Christian College of Kansas
MidAmerica Nazarene University
Southwestern College
Sterling College
Tabor College
University of Kansas
Wichita State University

Kentucky

Alice Lloyd College
Asbury University
Bellarmine University
Campbellsville University
Centre College
Kentucky Wesleyan College
Lindsey Wilson College
Morehead State University
Transylvania University
University of Pikeville

Louisiana

Centenary College of Louisiana
Louisiana State University
    Shreveport
Loyola University New Orleans
Tulane University
University of New Orleans

Maine

Bates College
Bowdoin College
Colby College
Saint Joseph's College of Maine
Thomas College
Unity College
University of Southern Maine

Maryland

Hood College
Johns Hopkins University
McDaniel College
Mount St. Mary's University
St. Mary's College of Maryland
Salisbury University
Stevenson University
Washington Adventist University
Washington College

Massachusetts

American International College
Anna Maria College
Assumption College
Bard College at Simon's Rock
Bay Path College
Bentley University

Boston College
Boston University
Brandeis University
Bridgewater State University
Clark University
College of the Holy Cross
Dean College
Eastern Nazarene College
Elms College
Emerson College
Emmanuel College
Framingham State University
Gordon College
Lasell College
Lesley University
Massachusetts College of Liberal Arts
Merrimack College
Mount Holyoke College
Nichols College
Northeastern University
Pine Manor College
Regis College
Salem State University
Simmons College
Smith College
Stonehill College
Suffolk University
Tufts University
University of Massachusetts
    Dartmouth
Wellesley College
Western New England University
Westfield State University
Wheaton College
Worcester State University

Michigan

Adrian College
Albion College
Alma College
Calvin College
Central Michigan University
Cornerstone University
Eastern Michigan University
Grand Valley State University
Hillsdale College
Hope College
Northern Michigan University
Spring Arbor University
University of Detroit Mercy
University of Michigan
University of Michigan
    Dearborn
Western Michigan University

Minnesota

Bethel University
College of St. Scholastica
Concordia College: Moorhead
Gustavus Adolphus College
Hamline University
Macalester College
St. Catherine University
St. Mary's University of Minnesota
St. Olaf College
University of Minnesota
    Morris
University of Northwestern - St. Paul

Mississippi

Millsaps College
Tougaloo College

Missouri

Avila University
Culver-Stockton College
Drury University
Evangel University
Maryville University of Saint Louis
Missouri Baptist University
Northwest Missouri State University
Park University
Rockhurst University

University of Missouri
   Columbia
Washington University in St. Louis
Westminster College
William Jewell College

Nebraska

Creighton University
Nebraska Wesleyan University
University of Nebraska
   Lincoln

New Hampshire

Colby-Sawyer College
Dartmouth College
Franklin Pierce University
New England College
Saint Anselm College
Southern New Hampshire University
University of New Hampshire

New Jersey

Caldwell College
College of New Jersey
Drew University
Fairleigh Dickinson University
   College at Florham
   Metropolitan Campus
Kean University
Monmouth University
Montclair State University
New Jersey City University
Richard Stockton College of New
   Jersey
Rider University
Rutgers, The State University of New
   Jersey
   New Brunswick/Piscataway
      Campus
   Newark Campus
Saint Peter's University
Seton Hall University
William Paterson University of New
   Jersey

New Mexico

University of New Mexico

New York

Adelphi University
Alfred University
Bard College
Cazenovia College
City University of New York
   Brooklyn College
   College of Staten Island
Clarkson University
Colgate University
College of New Rochelle
Cornell University
Daemen College
Hamilton College
Hartwick College
Hilbert College
Hobart and William Smith Colleges
Hofstra University
Houghton College
Le Moyne College
Manhattan College
Marist College
Nazareth College
New York University
Niagara University
Pace University
Pace University: Pleasantville/
   Briarcliff
Roberts Wesleyan College
SUNY
   College at Brockport
   College at Buffalo
   College at Cortland
   College at Fredonia
   College at Geneseo
   College at Old Westbury

College at Oneonta
College at Oswego
College at Plattsburgh
University at Albany
University at Binghamton
University at Buffalo
University at Stony Brook
Saint Bonaventure University
St. John Fisher College
St. Lawrence University
St. Thomas Aquinas College
Siena College
Skidmore College
Syracuse University
University of Rochester
Utica College
Vassar College
Wagner College
Wells College

North Carolina

Appalachian State University
Barton College
Bennett College for Women
Campbell University
Davidson College
Duke University
East Carolina University
Elon University
Guilford College
Lenoir-Rhyne University
Meredith College
Methodist University
Montreat College
Pfeiffer University
Queens University of Charlotte
Salem College
University of North Carolina
   Chapel Hill
   Charlotte
   Greensboro
   Pembroke
Wake Forest University
Winston-Salem State University

Ohio

Ashland University
Bluffton University
Bowling Green State University
Capital University
Case Western Reserve University
Cedarville University
College of Wooster
Denison University
Heidelberg University
Hiram College
John Carroll University
Kent State University
Kent State University
   Ashtabula
   East Liverpool
   Geauga
   Salem
   Stark
   Trumbull
   Tuscarawas
Kenyon College
Malone University
Marietta College
Miami University
   Oxford
Mount Vernon Nazarene University
Muskingum University
Ohio Dominican University
Ohio Northern University
Ohio State University
   Columbus Campus
   Lima Campus
Ohio Wesleyan University
Otterbein University
Tiffin University
University of Cincinnati
University of Dayton
University of Findlay

University of Mount Union
Walsh University
Wittenberg University
Xavier University
Youngstown State University

Oklahoma

Oklahoma City University
Oklahoma State University
Oklahoma Wesleyan University
Oral Roberts University
Rogers State University
Southern Nazarene University
University of Oklahoma
University of Tulsa

Oregon

Corban University
George Fox University
Lewis & Clark College
Linfield College
Pacific University
Portland State University
University of Portland
Warner Pacific College
Willamette University

Pennsylvania

Albright College
Allegheny College
Alvernia University
Arcadia University
Bucknell University
Cabrini College
California University of Pennsylvania
Carnegie Mellon University
Chatham University
Dickinson College
Duquesne University
Eastern University
Elizabethtown College
Franklin & Marshall College
Gannon University
Geneva College
Gettysburg College
Grove City College
Immaculata University
Indiana University of Pennsylvania
Juniata College
King's College
Lafayette College
Lebanon Valley College
Lehigh University
Lycoming College
Mansfield University of Pennsylvania
Mercyhurst University
Messiah College
Moravian College
Muhlenberg College
Rosemont College
St. Francis University
Saint Joseph's University
Seton Hill University
Shippensburg University of
   Pennsylvania
Susquehanna University
Thiel College
University of Pennsylvania
University of Scranton
Ursinus College
Villanova University
Washington & Jefferson College
West Chester University of
   Pennsylvania
Westminster College
Wilson College

Puerto Rico

Inter American University of Puerto
   Rico
   Barranquitas Campus
   Fajardo Campus
Universidad Metropolitana

University of Puerto Rico
   Arecibo
   Rio Piedras

Rhode Island

Bryant University
Providence College
Roger Williams University
Salve Regina University

South Carolina

Anderson University
Clemson University
Columbia College
Francis Marion University
Furman University
Lander University
Presbyterian College
South Carolina State University
Southern Wesleyan University
University of South Carolina
   Upstate
Wofford College

South Dakota

Augustana College
University of Sioux Falls

Tennessee

Belmont University
Bryan University
   Dayton
Carson-Newman University
Lee University
Maryville College
Milligan College
Rhodes College
Sewanee: The University of the South
Tennessee Temple University
Union University
Vanderbilt University

Texas

Austin College
Dallas Baptist University
East Texas Baptist University
Midland College
St. Mary's University
Southern Methodist University
Southwestern University
Texas Christian University
Texas Lutheran University
Texas State University
Trinity University
University of Texas
   Austin
   Dallas
West Texas A&M University

Utah

Brigham Young University
University of Utah

Vermont

Middlebury College
Saint Michael's College
University of Vermont

Virginia

Bridgewater College
College of William and Mary
Eastern Mennonite University
Hampden-Sydney College
Hollins University
James Madison University
Liberty University
Randolph College
Randolph-Macon College
Regent University
Roanoke College
Sweet Briar College
University of Mary Washington
University of Richmond

Virginia Polytechnic Institute and
    State University
Washington and Lee University

Washington

Gonzaga University
Northwest University
Saint Martin's University
Seattle Pacific University
University of Washington
Whitman College
Whitworth University

West Virginia

Bethany College
Fairmont State University
Glenville State College
Marshall University
Ohio Valley University
Shepherd University
West Liberty University
West Virginia University
West Virginia Wesleyan College
Wheeling Jesuit University

Wisconsin

Alverno College
Beloit College
Carroll University
Carthage College
Lawrence University
Marquette University
Ripon College
St. Norbert College
Viterbo University

Wyoming

University of Wyoming

Alphabetical index of majors

Applying to College?

Remove the anxiety with these newly revised guides.

Campus Visits & College Interviews, 3rd Edition

By Zola Dincin Schneider & Norman G. Schneider

176 pages, paperback
ISBN: 978-0-87447-988-1

Price: $14.99

The College Application Essay, 5th Edition

By Sarah Myers McGinty

176 pages, paperback
ISBN: 978-0-87447-987-4

Price: $15.99

◇ CollegeBoard

14b-9204a

More College Planning Resources
from the College Board

College Handbook 2015

The only guide listing all accredited universities, two-year and four-year colleges, and technical schools in the United States — more than 3,900 in total.

2,400 pages, paperback
ISBN: 978-1-4573-0316-6
$31.99

The Official SAT Study Guide™: Second Edition

The Official SAT Study Guide™ is the only book that features 10 official practice tests created by the test maker. The No. 1 best-selling guide is packed with valuable test-taking approaches and focused sets of practice questions — just like those on the actual SAT® — to help students get ready for the test.

998 pages, trade paper
ISBN: 978-0-87447-852-5
$21.99

Book of Majors 2015

Explore in-depth descriptions of 200 majors, and see where over 1,100 majors are offered at colleges nationwide.

1,350 pages, paperback
ISBN: 978-1-4573-0317-3
$28.99

Get It Together for College, 2nd Edition

Take advantage of expert tips that help students stay on top of the college admission process.

240 pages, paperback
ISBN: 978-0-87447-974-4
$15.99

PAYING FOR COLLEGE

Getting Financial Aid 2015

A must-have book in today's economy, this is the perfect resource for families managing the high cost of college. This easy step-by-step guide shows why, when and how to apply for financial aid.

1,050 pages, paperback
978-1-4573-0318-0
$23.99

Scholarship Handbook 2015

The most complete and comprehensive guide to help families tap into the more than 1.7 million scholarships, internships and loans available to students each year.

624 pages, paperback
ISBN: 978-1-4573-0319-7
$31.99

CollegeBoard